Texas Business and Commerce Code

2008 Edition

WITH TABLES
AND INDEX

As Amended through the
2007 Regular Session
of the 80th Legislature

THOMSON
WEST

Mat #40519028

ISBN 978–0–31497–206–4

PREFACE

This pamphlet contains the text of the Business and Commerce Code, as amended through the 2007 Regular Session of the 80th Legislature. Included in this pamphlet are Uniform Commercial Code Comments and Reasons for Changes prepared by the American Law Institute and the National Conference of Commissioners on Uniform State Laws.

The Business and Commerce Code constitutes a unit of the Texas Legislative Council's statutory revision program. The Code was originally enacted by Acts 1967, 60th Leg., ch. 785. Title 1 of the Business and Commerce Code is the Uniform Commercial Code.

Disposition Tables are included preceding the Code, thus providing a means of tracing repealed subject matter into the Code.

A detailed descriptive word Index at the end of the Code is furnished to facilitate the search for specific textual provisions. A Table of Sections Affected indicates sections of the Business and Commerce Code affected through the 2007 Regular Session of the 80th Legislature.

Comprehensive coverage of the judicial constructions and interpretations of the Code, together with cross references, references to law review commentaries discussing particular provisions, and other editorial features are provided in the volumes of Vernon's Texas Statutes and Codes Annotated.

WEST

November, 2007

*

RELATED PRODUCTS FROM WEST

TEXAS PRACTICE SERIES

Guide to the Texas Rules of Evidence
Steven Goode, Olin Guy Wellborn III, and M. Michael Sharlot

Courtroom Handbook on Texas Evidence
Steven Goode, Olin Guy Wellborn III, and M. Michael Sharlot

Texas Land Titles and Title Examination
Fred A. Lange and Aloysius A. Leopold

Texas Criminal Law
Michael B. Charlton

Texas Criminal Forms and Trial Manual
Michael J. McCormick, Thomas D. Blackwell and Betty Blackwell

Texas Law of Wills
Gerry W. Beyer

Texas Methods of Practice
Frank W. Elliott, John E. Krahmer, Hal M. Bateman and Nancy Saint-Paul

Texas Foreclosure: Law and Practice
Mike Baggett

Texas Probate and Decedents' Estates
M. K. Woodward and Ernest E. Smith III

Texas Business Organizations
Robert W. Hamilton

Texas Property Taxes
Jay D. Howell, Jr.

Texas Municipal Law and Practice
David B. Brooks

Texas Consumer Rights and Remedies
Stephen G. Cochran

Texas Consumer Law Handbook
Stephen G. Cochran

Texas Juvenile Law and Practice
Thomas S. Morgan and Harold C. Gaither, Jr.

Handbook of Texas Family Law
Don Koons

RELATED PRODUCTS

The Jury Charge in Texas Civil Litigation
T. Ray Guy

Texas County and Special District Law
David B. Brooks

Texas Workers' Compensation Law and Practice
Karen A. Lerner

Texas Marital Property and Homesteads
Aloysius A. Leopold

Texas Criminal Practice and Procedure
George E. Dix and Robert O. Dawson

Texas Medical Malpractice
Michael P. Penick

Texas Environmental Law
Jeff Civins, Jimmy Alan Hall and Mark K. Sahs

Handbook on Texas Discovery Practice
Alex Wilson Albright, Charles Herring, Jr. and Robert H. Pemberton

Handbook of Texas Lawyer and Judicial Ethics
Robert P. Schuwerk and Lillian B. Hardwick

WEST'S TEXAS FORMS

Texas Creditors' Remedies and Debtors' Rights
Allen E. Smith

Texas Administrative Practice
Steven L. Martin

Texas Business Litigation—Forms and Commentary
Glidden Partners

Texas Minerals, Oil and Gas
John S. Lowe

Texas Business Entities
Ben Bateman and Nancy Saint–Paul

Texas Civil Trial and Appellate Practice
Frank W. Elliott

Texas Estate Planning
Donald J. Malouf and Henry J. Lischer

Administration of Decedents' Estates and Guardianships
Aloysius A. Leopold and Gerry W. Beyer

RELATED PRODUCTS

Texas Real Property
Gerry W. Beyer

Texas Family Law
John F. Elder

STATUTES, CODES AND RULES

Vernon's Texas Codes Annotated

Vernon's Texas Rules Annotated—Civil Procedure, Evidence and Appellate Procedure

Texas Administrative Code

Texas Rules of Court—State, Federal and Local

Texas Business and Commerce Code

Texas Civil Practice and Remedies Code

Texas Corporation and Partnership Laws

Texas Criminal and Motor Vehicle Code

Texas Criminal Procedure—Code and Rules

Texas Environmental Laws

Texas Family Code

Texas Finance Code

Texas Insurance Code

Texas Local Government Code

Texas Penal Code

Texas Probate Code

Texas Property Code

TEXAS ANNOTATED CODE SERIES

Anderson, Bartlett & East's Texas Uniform Commercial Code Annotated

Carlson's Texas Employment Laws Annotated

Cooper, Hensley & Marshall's Texas Rules of Civil Procedure Annotated

Elliott & Morris' Texas Tax Code Annotated

Gaba's Texas Environmental Laws Annotated

Hanby's Texas Rules of Appellate Procedure Annotated

Johanson's Texas Probate Code Annotated

RELATED PRODUCTS

Kinkeade & McColloch's Texas Penal Code Annotated

McGehee's Texas Civil Practice and Remedies Code Annotated

Roach's Texas Rules of Evidence Annotated

Sampson & Tindall's Texas Family Code Annotated

Texas Business Statutes Annotated

Texas Civil Practice Statutes and Rules Annotated

CASES

Texas Cases: Covering Southwestern 1st

Texas Cases: Covering Southwestern 2d

Texas Cases: Covering Southwestern 3d

FORMS

Vernon's Texas Code Forms Annotated–UCC Forms

Texas Forms: Legal and Business

Texas Jurisprudence Pleading and Practice Forms 2d

West's Texas Forms

Texas Legal Practice Forms 2d

DIGESTS & ENCYCLOPEDIAS

Texas Jurisprudence 3d

West's Texas Digest (1840–1934)

West's Texas Digest 2d (1935–date)

Texas Encyclopedia of Criminal Law

OTHER RESEARCH TOOLS FOR TEXAS

Texas Practice Guide

Texas Family Law Service

West's Complete Texas Family Law (CD–ROM)

Texas Lawdesk Library (CD–ROM)

Texas Litigation Library (CD–ROM)

Texas Practice Series

McDonald & Carlson Texas Civil Practice 2d

Westlaw & KeyCite

RELATED PRODUCTS

Texas Digest

Texas Law Finder

Westlaw®

Westcheck.com™

West CD–ROM Libraries™

Many of these products are also available on CD–ROM and online via Westlaw.

To order any of these Texas practice tools,
call your West Representative or
1–800–328–9352.

NEED RESEARCH HELP?

You can get quality research results with free help—call
the West Reference Attorneys when you have questions
concerning Westlaw or West Publications at
1–800–733–2889.

INTERNET ACCESS

Contact the West Editorial Department directly
with your questions and suggestions by e-mail at
west.editor@thomson.com.
Visit West's home page at
west.thomson.com

*

TABLE OF CONTENTS

BUSINESS AND COMMERCE CODE

Section Analysis, see beginning of each Chapter.

TITLE 1. UNIFORM COMMERCIAL CODE

TABLE OF CONTENTS

TABLE OF CONTENTS

TABLE OF CONTENTS

TITLE 4. MISCELLANEOUS COMMERCIAL PROVISIONS

TABLE OF CONTENTS

TABLE OF CONTENTS

TABLE OF CONTENTS

TABLE OF CONTENTS

TABLE OF CONTENTS

TITLE 12. RIGHTS AND DUTIES OF CONSUMERS AND MERCHANTS

TITLE 13. CONTESTS AND OTHER PROMOTIONS

TITLE 14. RECORDINGS

TITLE 15. CURRENCY AND TRADE
SUBTITLE A. CURRENCY

TABLE OF CONTENTS

SUBTITLE B. PORT OF ENTRY AUTHORITIES

SUBTITLE C. TRADE ZONES

TITLE 99. MISCELLANEOUS COMMERCIAL PROVISIONS

INDEX

*

EFFECTIVE DATES

The following table shows the date of adjournment and the effective date of ninety day bills enacted at sessions of the legislature beginning with the year 1945:

Year	Leg.	Session	Adjournment Date	Effective Date
1945	49	Regular	June 5, 1945	September 4, 1945
1947	50	Regular	June 6, 1947	September 5, 1947
1949	51	Regular	June 6, 1949	September 5, 1949
1951	52	Regular	June 8, 1951	September 7, 1951
1953	53	Regular	May 27, 1953	August 26, 1953
1954	53	1st C.S.	May 13, 1954	August 12, 1954
1955	54	Regular	June 7, 1955	September 6, 1955
1957	55	Regular	May 23, 1957	August 22, 1957
1957	55	1st C.S.	November 12, 1957	February 11, 1958
1957	55	2nd C.S.	December 3, 1957	March 4, 1958
1959	56	Regular	May 12, 1959	August 11, 1959
1959	56	1st C.S.	June 16, 1959	September 15, 1959
1959	56	2nd C.S.	July 16, 1959	October 15, 1959
1959	56	3rd C.S.	August 6, 1959	November 5, 1959
1961	57	Regular	May 29, 1961	August 28, 1961
1961	57	1st C.S.	August 8, 1961	November 7, 1961
1961	57	2nd C.S.	August 14, 1961	November 13, 1961
1962	57	3rd C.S.	February 1, 1962	May 3, 1962
1963	58	Regular	May 24, 1963	August 23, 1963
1965	59	Regular	May 31, 1965	August 30, 1965
1966	59	1st C.S.	February 23, 1966	*
1967	60	Regular	May 29, 1967	August 28, 1967
1968	60	1st C.S.	July 3, 1968	*
1969	61	Regular	June 2, 1969	September 1, 1969
1969	61	1st C.S.	August 26, 1969	*
1969	61	2nd C.S.	September 9, 1969	December 9, 1969
1971	62	Regular	May 31, 1971	August 30, 1971
1971	62	1st C.S.	June 4, 1971	September 3, 1971
1972	62	2nd C.S.	March 30, 1972	June 29, 1972
1972	62	3rd C.S.	July 7, 1972	*
1972	62	4th C.S.	October 17, 1972	January 16, 1973
1973	63	Regular	May 28, 1973	August 27, 1973
1973	63	1st C.S.	December 20, 1973	*
1975	64	Regular	June 2, 1975	September 1, 1975
1977	65	Regular	May 30, 1977	August 29, 1977
1977	65	1st C.S.	July 21, 1977	*
1978	65	2nd C.S.	August 8, 1978	November 7, 1978
1979	66	Regular	May 28, 1979	August 27, 1979

EFFECTIVE DATES

Year	Leg.	Session	Adjournment Date	Effective Date
1981	67	Regular	June 1, 1981	August 31, 1981
1981	67	1st C.S.	August 11, 1981	November 10, 1981
1982	67	2nd C.S.	May 28, 1982	*
1982	67	3rd C.S.	September 9, 1982	*
1983	68	Regular	May 30, 1983	August 29, 1983
1983	68	1st C.S.	June 25, 1983	September 23, 1983
1984	68	2nd C.S.	July 3, 1984	October 2, 1984
1985	69	Regular	May 27, 1985	August 26, 1985
1985	69	1st C.S.	May 30, 1985	August 29, 1985
1986	69	2nd C.S.	September 4, 1986	December 4, 1986
1986	69	3rd C.S.	September 30, 1986	December 30, 1986
1987	70	Regular	June 1, 1987	August 31, 1987
1987	70	1st C.S.	June 3, 1987	September 2, 1987
1987	70	2nd C.S.	July 21, 1987	October 20, 1987
1989	71	Regular	May 29, 1989	August 28, 1989
1989	71	1st C.S.	July 19, 1989	October 18, 1989
1989	71	2nd C.S.	December 12, 1989	*
1990	71	3rd C.S.	March 28, 1990	*
1990	71	4th C.S.	May 1, 1990	*
1990	71	5th C.S.	May 30, 1990	*
1990	71	6th C.S.	June 7, 1990	September 6, 1990
1991	72	Regular	May 27, 1991	August 26, 1991
1991	72	1st C.S.	August 13, 1991	November 12, 1991
1991	72	2nd C.S.	August 25, 1991	November 24, 1991
1992	72	3rd C.S.	January 8, 1992	April 8, 1992
1992	72	4th C.S.	December 3, 1992	*
1993	73	Regular	May 31, 1993	August 30, 1993
1995	74	Regular	May 29, 1995	August 28, 1995
1997	75	Regular	June 2, 1997	September 1, 1997
1999	76	Regular	May 31, 1999	August 30, 1999
2001	77	Regular	May 28, 2001	September 1, 2001
2003	78	Regular	June 2, 2003	September 1, 2003
2003	78	1st C.S.	July 28, 2003	*
2003	78	2nd C.S.	August 26, 2003	*
2003	78	3rd C.S.	October 12, 2003	January 10, 2004
2004	78	4th C.S.	May 17, 2004	*
2005	79	Regular	May 30, 2005	August 29, 2005
2005	79	1st C.S.	July 20, 2005	October 19, 2005
2005	79	2nd C.S.	August 19, 2005	November 18, 2005
2006	79	3rd C.S.	May 16, 2006	August 15, 2006
2007	80	Regular	May 28, 2007	August 27, 2007

* No legislation for which the ninety day effective date is applicable.

ACKNOWLEDGMENT
UNIFORM COMMERCIAL CODE COMMENTS

Acknowledgment is gratefully made to The American Law Institute and to the National Conference of Commissioners on Uniform State Laws for permission to reproduce the official Comments on the Uniform Commercial Code in the Texas Business and Commerce Code under the chapters and sections of the Uniform Commercial Code.

Section 1.102 of the Texas Code provides that the code "shall be liberally construed and applied to promote its underlying purposes and policies" which include "to make uniform the law among the various jurisdictions".

It follows, therefore, that the official comments are indispensable to an understanding of the objectives and purposes of the Uniform Commercial Code and the substantive changes effected in the law. These comments are important to the legal profession in the interpretation and application of the Code to specific legal problems which arise in commercial transactions governed by the Code.

WEST

*

DISPOSITION TABLE 1

Former Texas Statutes and Uniform Laws to Business and Commerce Code

(Title 1)

Disposition Table No. 1 shows where the subject matter of articles and sections repealed by the Uniform Commercial Code in 1965 is covered in Title 1, Uniform Commercial Code, of the Business and Commerce Code, as originally enacted. Table No. 2 shows where the subject matter of other repealed articles and sections is covered in the remaining Titles of the Business and Commerce Code, as originally enacted.

Where there are no relevant sections in the Texas Business and Commerce Code, that fact is noted by the use of the abbreviation "N" for "None."

The letter "S" before a section of the Business and Commerce Code means "Sec.". The abbreviation "Cf." before a section means "Compare."

ACCOUNTS RECEIVABLE

Vernon's Civ.Stats. Article	Prior Uniform Act Sec.	Texas Bus. & C. Sec.
260–1, § 1	N.	1.201(11)
		9.105(1)(d)
		9.106
		9.306(5)
§ 2	N.	9.204
		9.302
		S. 9.405
§ 3	N.	9.203
		9.302
		9.402
§ 4	N.	9.303
		9.401
		9.403
		9.407
260–1, § 5	N.	9.403
		9.404
§ 6	N.	9.201
		9.302
		9.306
		9.318
§ 7	N.	9.306
		9.318
§ 8	N.	9.205
		9.306

COLLECTIONS

Vernon's Civ.Stats. Article	Prior Uniform Act Sec.	Texas Bus. & C. Sec.
342–701	N.	1.201(4)
		4.104
		4.105
342–702	N.	4.201
342–703	N.	4.103
		4.201
		4.202
342–704	N.	4.301
342–705	N.	4.213
342–706	N.	4.214
342–711	N.	4.406
342–712	N.	4.303

DISPOSITION TABLE 1

Vernon's Civ.Stats. Article	Prior Uniform Act Sec.	Texas Bus. & C. Sec.
		4.403

BILLS AND NOTES

Vernon's Civ.Stats. Article	Prior Uniform Act Sec.	Texas Bus. & C. Sec.
567	N.	3.413
568	N.	3.122
		3.201
		3.302
		3.305
		3.409
569	N.	1.103
		3.409
570	N.	3.122
		3.304
		3.409
571	N.	S. 3.122
		S. 3.202
		S. 3.306
575	N.	3.501
		3.502
		3.509
576	N.	3.509
		3.510

BILLS OF LADING

Vernon's Civ.Stats. Article	Prior Uniform Act Sec.	Texas Bus. & C. Sec.
890	N.	S. 7.102
		S. 7.301
891	N.	7.104
		7.309
892	N.	1.201(6)
		7.104
		7.304
		7.402
893	N.	S. 7.104
894	N.	N.
895	N.	7.304
		7.403
896	N.	7.403
897	N.	7.601
898	N.	7.308
		7.403

STOCK TRANSFERS

Vernon's Civ.Stats. Article	U.S.T.A.[1] Sec.	Texas Bus. & C. Sec.
1302–6.02	1	8.309
1302–6.03	2	N.
1302–6.04	3	8.207
1302–6.05	4	N.
1302–6.06	5	N.
1302–6.07	6	N.
1302–6.08	7	8.301
		8.315
1302–6.09	8	S. 8.308(5)
1302–6.10	9	8.307
1302–6.11	10	8.309
1302–6.12	11	8.306
1302–6.13	12	8.306
1302–6.14	13	8.317
1302–6.15	14	8.317
1302–6.16	15	8.103
		8.204
1302–6.17	16	8.206
1302–6.18	17	8.405
1302–6.19	18	1.103
1302–6.20	19	1.102(1)
1302–6.21	20	8.308
1302–6.22	21	N.
1302–6.23	N.	N.
1302–6.24	22	1.201(19)
		1.201(28)
		1.201(30)
		1.201(32)

DISPOSITION TABLE 1

Vernon's Civ.Stats. Article	U.S.T.A.[1] Sec.	Texas Bus. & C. Sec.
		1.201(33)
		1.201(44)
		8.313
1302–6.01	26	S. 8.101

[1] Uniform Stock Transfer Act.

FRAUDULENT CONVEYANCES

Vernon's Civ.Stats. Article	Prior Uniform Act Sec.	Texas Bus. & C. Sec.
4000	N.	9.201
		9.202
4001	N.	6.102
		6.103
		6.104
4001	N.	6.105
		6.106
4002	N.	6.104
		6.106
4003	N.	6.103

CHATTEL MORTGAGES

Vernon's Civ.Stats. Article	Prior Uniform Act Sec.	Texas Bus. & C. Sec.
5489	N.	9.204
5490	N.	9.201
		9.301
		9.302
		9.401
		9.403
5492	N.	9.403(4)
5493	N.	N.
5494	N.	9.403(4)
5495	N.	9.404
5496	N.	N.
5497	N.	9.401
5497a	N.	S. 9.301
		S. 9.312
5498	N.	S. 9.401
		S. 9.403
5499	N.	N.
5499a	N.	N.

TRUST RECEIPTS

Vernon's Civ.Stats. Article	U.T.R.A.[1] Sec.	Texas Bus. & C. Sec.
5499a–51, § 1	1	1.201(9)
		1.201(15)
		1.201(28)
		1.201(30)
		1.201(32)
		1.201(33)
		1.201(37)
		1.201(44)
		S. 2.403
		9.105
		9.301(3)
§ 2	2	9.110
		9.203
§ 3	3	9.201
		9.304
§ 4	4	9.401
§ 5	5	9.201
§ 6	6	9.207(2)(a)
		9.501
		9.503
		9.504
		9.505
§ 7	7	9.302(1)
		9.304
		9.501
5499a–51, § 8	8	9.301(1)
		9.302
		9.311
§ 8(1)	8(1)	9.304
§ 8(2)	8(2)	9.301
§ 9	9	2.403

DISPOSITION TABLE 1

Vernon's Civ.Stats. Article	U.T.R.A.[1] Sec.	Texas Bus. & C. Sec.
§ 9(1)(a)	9(1)(a)	9.308
		9.309
§ 9(2)	9(2)	2.403
		9.307
§ 9(2)(b)	9(2)(b)	9.301
§ 9(3)	9(3)	9.318
§ 10	10	9.306
		9.308
§ 11	11	9.310
§ 12	12	9.317
§ 13	13	9.401
		9.402
§ 13(3)	13(3)	9.402
		9.403
§ 13(4)	13(4)	9.402
		9.403
§§ 14 to 22 (incl.)	14 to 22 (incl.)	N.

LIENS

Vernon's Civ.Stats. Article	Prior Uniform Act Sec.	Texas Bus. & C. Sec.
5506c, § 1	N.	9.109
§ 2	N.	9.110
		9.201
		9.203
		9.207(2)(a)
		9.301
		9.302
		9.303
		9.401
§ 3	N.	9.401
		9.403
§ 4	N.	9.303
		9.307(1)
5506c, § 4	N.	9.310
		9.317
§ 5	N.	9.403
		9.404
§ 6	N.	9.205
		9.306
§ 7	N.	9.302
§ 8	N.	S. 9.302
		9.401
§ 9	N.	N.
§ 10	N.	9.307
		9.310

WAREHOUSE RECEIPTS

Vernon's Civ.Stats. Article	U.W.R.A.[1] Sec.	Texas Bus. & C. Sec.
5575	N.	S. 7.202
		S. 7.204
5576	N.	7.104
		S. 7.205
		7.501
		7.502
5604	N.	7.209
5605	N.	7.210
5606	N.	S. 7.209
5607	N.	7.206
		7.403
5609	N.	7.104
		7.501
		7.502
5612	1	1.201(45)
		7.201
		7.401
5613	2	7.104
		7.202
		7.209(2)
5614	3	7.104
		7.204
5615	4	7.104
5616	5	7.104
5617	6	7.402
5618	7	7.104
5619	8	7.403
5620	9	S. 2.705
		7.403
5621	10	7.403
		7.404
5622	11	2.705
		7.403
5623	12	7.403
5624	13	7.208
5625	14	7.601
5626	15	N.
5627	16	7.403
		7.603
5628	17	7.603

DISPOSITION TABLE 1

Vernon's Civ.Stats. Article	U.W.R.A.[1] Sec.	Texas Bus. & C. Sec.
5629	18	7.603
5630	19	7.403
5631	20	7.203
		7.401
5632	21	7.204
5633	22	7.207
5634	23	7.207
5635	24	7.207(2)
5636	25	7.602
5637	26	N.
5638	27	7.209
		7.307
5639	28	7.209
		7.307
5640	29	7.209
		7.307
5641	30	7.209
		7.307
5642	31	7.209
		7.307
5643	32	7.209
		7.210(7)
		7.307
5644	33	7.206
		7.210
		7.308
5645	34	7.206
5646	35	7.210(7)
5647	36	7.403(1)(c)
5648	37	7.501
5649	38	7.501
5650	39	7.501
5651	40	7.501
5652	41	7.502
		7.503
		7.504
5653	42	7.504
5654	43	7.506
5655	44	7.507
5656	45	7.505
5657	46	2.506(2)
		7.508
5658	47	7.501
		7.502
5659	48	7.502
5660	49	S. 2.705
		7.502
5661	N.	N.
5662	N.	N.
5663	56	1.103
	57	1.102(1)
5664	58	S. 1.201(1)
		1.201(14)
		S. 1.201(17)
		S. 1.201(19)
		S. 1.201(20)
		1.201(28)
		1.201(30)
		1.201(32)
		1.201(33)
		1.201(44)
		7.102
5665	62	S. 7.101

1. Uniform Warehouse Receipts Act.

NEGOTIABLE INSTRUMENTS

Vernon's Civ.Stats. Article	U.N.I.L.[1] Sec.	Texas Bus. & C. Sec.
5932, § 1	1	3.104
	1(5)	3.102
5932, § 2	2	3.106
5932, § 3	3	3.105
5932, § 4	4	3.109
5932, § 5	5	3.104
		3.112
5932, § 6	6	3.112
	6(1)	3.114
	6(4)	3.113
	6(5)	1.201(24)
		3.106
		3.107
5932, § 7	7	3.108
		3.502
5932, § 8	8	3.110
5932, § 9	9	3.111
	9(3)	3.405
	9(5)	3.204
5932, § 10	10	3.104
5932, § 11	11	3.114
5932, § 12	12	3.114
5932, § 13	13	3.115
5932, § 14	14	3.115
		3.407
		8.206
5932, § 15	15	3.115
		3.305
		3.407
		8.206
5932, § 16	16	3.305
		3.306
		8.202
5932, § 17	17	3.118
	17(3)	3.109
		3.114
	17(6)	3.402
5932, § 18	18	3.401
5932, § 19	19	3.403
5932, § 20	20	3.403
5932, § 21	21	3.403
5932, § 22	22	3.207

DISPOSITION TABLE 1

Vernon's Civ.Stats. Article	U.N.I.L.[1] Sec.	Texas Bus. & C. Sec.
5932, § 23	23	3.404
		8.202
		8.205
		8.311
5933, § 24	24	3.408
5933, § 25	25	1.201(44)
		3.303
		3.408
5933, § 26	26	1.201(44)
		3.303
5933, § 27	27	1.201(44)
		3.201
		3.303
		4.209
5933, § 28	28	3.306
		3.408
		3.415
		8.202
5933, § 29	29	3.415
		8.201
5934, § 30	30	3.102
		3.202
		8.309
5934, § 31	31	3.202
		8.308
5934, § 32	32	3.202
		8.308
5934, § 33	33	3.204
		8.308
5934, § 34	34	3.204
		8.308
5934, § 35	35	3.204
		8.308
5934, § 36	36	3.204
		3.205
		3.206
		8.308
5934, § 37	37	3.205
		3.206
		8.304
		8.308
5934, § 38	38	3.414
5934, § 39	39	3.205
		3.206
5934, § 40	40	3.204
		8.310
5934, § 41	41	3.116
5934, § 42	42	3.117
5934, § 43	43	3.203
5934, § 44	44	3.414
5934, § 45	45	3.304
5934, § 46	46	N.
5934, § 47	47	3.206
5934, § 48	48	3.208
		3.605
5934, § 49	49	3.201
		8.307
5934, § 50	50	3.208
5935, § 51	51	3.301
		3.603
5935, § 52	52	3.302
		3.304
		8.301
		8.302
5935, § 52(2)	52(2)	3.302(1)(c)
		8.203
		8.305
5935, § 53	53	3.304
		8.203
		8.305
5935, § 54	54	3.303
5935, § 55	55	3.304
5935, § 56	56	1.201(25)
		3.304
		8.202
		8.304
5935, § 57	57	3.305
		8.202
		8.301
5935, § 58	58	3.201
		3.207
		3.306
		8.301
5935, § 59	59	3.207
		3.306
		3.307
		8.105
		8.301
5936, § 60	60	3.413
		8.201
		8.202
5936, § 61	61	3.413
		8.201
		8.202
5936, § 62	62	3.413
		3.418
		8.201
		8.202
5936, § 63	63	3.402
5936, § 64	64	3.415
		8.308
5936, § 65	65	3.417
		4.207(2)
		8.306
		8.308
5936, § 66	66	3.414
		4.207(2)
		8.306
		8.308
5936, § 67	67	3.414
		8.306
		8.308
5936, § 68	68	3.118
		3.414
		8.308
5936, § 69	69	3.417
		8.306
		8.308
5937, § 70	70	3.501
		3.502
		3.604
5937, § 71	71	3.503
5937, § 72	72	3.503
		3.504
5937, § 73	73	3.504
5937, § 74	74	3.505

DISPOSITION TABLE 1

Vernon's Civ.Stats. Article	U.N.I.L.[1] Sec.	Texas Bus. & C. Sec.
5937, § 75	75	3.503
5937, § 76	76	S. 3.504
5937, § 77	77	3.504
5937, § 78	78	3.504
5937, § 79	79	3.511
5937, § 80	80	3.511
5937, § 81	81	3.511
5937, § 82	82	3.511
5937, § 83	83	3.507
5937, § 84	84	3.507(2)
5937, § 85	85	3.503
5937, § 86	86	3.503
5937, § 87	87	3.121
5937, § 88	88	3.603
5938, § 89	89	3.501
		3.502
5938, § 90	90	3.508
5938, § 91	91	3.508
5938, § 92	92	3.508
5938, § 93	93	3.508
5938, § 94	94	3.508
5938, § 95	95	3.508
5938, § 96	96	3.508
5938, § 97	97	3.508
5938, § 98	98	3.508
5938, § 99	99	3.508
5938, § 100	100	3.508
5938, § 101	101	3.508
5938, § 102	102	3.508
5938, § 103	103	3.508
5938, § 104	104	3.508
5938, § 105	105	3.508
5938, § 106	106	3.508
5938, § 107	107	3.508
5938, § 108	108	3.508
5938, § 109	109	3.511
5938, § 110	110	3.511(6)
5938, § 111	111	3.511
5938, § 112	112	3.511
5938, § 113	113	3.511
5938, § 114	114	3.511
5938, § 115	115	3.511
5938, § 116	116	3.511
5938, § 117	117	N.
5938, § 118	118	3.501
5939, § 119	119	3.601
		3.603
5939, § 119(3)	119(3)	Cf. 1.107
		3.605
5939, § 120	120	3.208
		3.601
		3.604
		3.606
5939, § 120(2)	120(2)	Cf. 1.107
		3.605
5939, § 121	121	3.208
		3.601
		3.603
5939, § 122	122	Cf. 1.107
		3.605
5939, § 123	123	3.605
5939, § 124	124	3.407
		8.206
5939, § 125	125	3.407
5940, § 126	126	3.104
5940, § 127	127	3.409
5940, § 128	128	3.102
5940, § 129	129	3.501
5940, § 130	130	3.118
		3.511
5940, § 131	131	4.503
5941, § 132	132	3.410
5941, § 133	133	3.410
5941, § 134	134	3.410
5941, § 135	135	3.410
5941, § 136	136	3.410
		3.506
		5.112
5941, § 137	137	3.410
		3.419
5941, § 138	138	3.410
5941, § 139	139	3.412
5941, § 140	140	3.412
5941, § 141	141	3.412
5941, § 142	142	3.412
5942, § 143	143	3.501
5942, § 144	144	3.501
		3.502
		3.503
5942, § 145	145	3.503
		3.504
5942, § 146	146	3.503
5942, § 147	147	3.511
5942, § 148	148	3.511
5942, § 149	149	3.507
5942, § 150	150	3.501
		3.502
		3.511
5942, § 151	151	3.501
		3.507(2)
		3.511
5943, § 152	152	3.501
		3.502
5943, § 153	153	3.509
5943, § 154	154	3.509
5943, § 155	155	3.509
5943, § 156	156	3.509
5943, § 157	157	3.501
5943, § 158	158	3.501
		3.509
5943, § 159	159	3.511
5943, § 160	160	3.509
5944, § 161	161	3.410
5944, § 162	162	3.410
5944, § 163	163	3.410
5944, § 164	164	3.410
5944, § 165	165	3.410
5944, § 166	166	3.410
5944, § 167	167	3.410
5944, § 168	168	3.410
5944, § 169	169	3.410
5944, § 170	170	3.410
5945, § 171	171	3.603
5945, § 172	172	3.603
5945, § 173	173	3.603
5945, § 174	174	3.603
5945, § 175	175	3.603

DISPOSITION TABLE 1

Vernon's Civ.Stats. Article	U.N.I.L.[1] Sec.	Texas Bus. & C. Sec.
5945, § 176	176	3.603
5945, § 177	177	3.603
5946, § 178	178	3.801
5946, § 179	179	3.801
5946, § 180	180	3.801
5946, § 181	181	3.801
5946, § 182	182	3.801
5946, § 183	183	3.801
5947, § 184	184	3.104
5947, § 185	185	3.104
5947, § 186	186	3.501
		3.502
		3.503
5947, § 187	187	3.411
5947, § 188	188	3.411
5947, § 189	189	3.409
5948, § 190	190	N.
5948, § 191	191	S. 1.201(1)
		S. 1.201(4)
		S. 1.201(5)
		1.201(14)
		S. 1.201(20)
		1.201(28)
		1.201(30)
		1.201(44)
		1.201(46)
		3.102
		3.410
		8.313
5948, § 192	192	N.
5948, § 193	193	3.503
5948, § 194	194	N.
5948, § 195	195	N.
5948, § 196	196	1.103

1. Uniform Negotiable Instruments Law.

DISPOSITION TABLE 2

Former Articles to Business and Commerce Code

(Titles 2, 3 and 4)

Disposition Table No. 1 shows where the subject matter of articles and sections repealed by the Uniform Commercial Code in 1965 is covered in Title 1, Uniform Commercial Code, of the Business and Commerce Code, as originally enacted. Table No. 2 shows where the subject matter of other repealed articles and sections is covered in the remaining Titles of the Business and Commerce Code, as originally enacted.

CIVIL STATUTES

Vernon's Civil Statutes Article		Business and Commerce Code Section
261		23.02(b), (c)
262		23.08
263		23.10
264		23.17
265	sent. 1	23.30 subsec. (a)
	sent. 2	23.30 subsec. (d)
	sent. 3, 4	23.30 subsecs. (b), (c)
266	sent. 1, 2, 3	23.16
	sent. 4, 5	23.18
267		23.09 subsec. (a)
268		23.09 subsecs. (b), (c)
269	sent. 1, 2	23.31
	sent. 3	23.32 subsec. (b)
	sent. 4	23.32 subsec. (a)
270		23.19
		23.21
271		23.33
272		23.22
273		23.20
274	sent. 1, 2	23.23
	sent. 3	23.23
		23.24
577		35.39
578		35.40 subsecs. (a), (b)
582–1	§ 1	33.01
	§ 2	33.02
	§ 3	33.03
	§ 3a	33.04
	§ 4	33.05
	§ 5	33.06
582–1	§ 6	33.07
	§ 7	33.08
	§ 8	33.09
	§ 9	33.10

Vernon's Civil Statutes Article		Business and Commerce Code Section
843	sent. 1	17.29 subsec. (d)
	sent. 2	17.29 subsec. (b)
851–C	§ 1 (part)	16.01 subsec. (a) (part)
	§ 1(a)	16.01 subsec. (a)(2)(4)(5)
	§ 1(b)	——
	§ 1(c)	16.01 subsec. (a)(1)
	§ 1(d)	16.01 subsec. (a)(3)
	§ 1(e)	16.02
	§ 1(f)	16.01 subsec. (a)(6)
851–C	§ 2(a)–(d), (e) sent. (part)	116.08 subsec. (a)(1)–(5)
	§ 2(e) sent. 1 (part), 2	16.08 subsec. (b)
	§ 2(f)	16.08 subsec. (a)(6)
	§ 3 sent. 1	16.10 subsecs. (a), (b)
	§ 3 sent. 2	16.10 subsec. (d)
	§ 3 sent. 3, 4	16.10 subsec. (c)(2)
	§ 4 sent. 1	16.10 subsec. (c)(1)
	§ 4	16.11
		16.15 subsec. (c)
	§ 5	16.15 subsec. (b)
	§ 6	16.24
	§ 7 sent. 1 (part)	16.12 subsec. (a)
	§ 7 sent. 1 (part), 2, 3, 4	16.14 subsecs. (a), (b)
	§ 7 sent. 5	16.12 subsec. (b)
		16.14 subsec. (c)
	§ 7 sent. 6, 7	16.13
	§ 8 sent. 1, 2 (part)	16.17
	§ 8 sent. 2 (part), 4, 5	16.18 subsecs. (a), (b)
	§ 8 sent. 3	16.18 subsec. (c)
	§ 9	16.15 subsec. (a)
	§ 10	16.16 subsec. (a)
	§ 11 sent. 1, 2 (part)	16.25 subsec. (a)
	§ 11 sent. 2 (part)	16.25 subsec. (c)
	§ 11 sent. 3	16.25 subsec. (b)

DISPOSITION TABLE 2

Vernon's Civil Statutes Article		Business and Commerce Code Section
	§ 11 sent. 4	16.25 subsec. (d)
	§ 11 sent. 5	16.16 subsec. (b)
	§ 12 (part)	16.09 subsecs. (b), (c)
	§ 12 sent. 1	16.09 subsec. (d)
	§ 12 sent. 2, 3	16.09 subsec. (a)
	§ 12 sent. 4	16.09 subsec. (d)
	§ 13	16.28
	§ 14 sent. 1, 2 (part)	16.27 subsec. (a)
	§ 14 sent. 2 (part)	16.01 subsec. (b)
	§ 15 sent. 1	16.26 subsec. (a)
	§ 15 sent. 2	16.27 subsec. (b)
	§ 16	16.26 subsecs. (b), (c), (d)
899		35.15
1438a	§ 1	35.01 subsec. (a)
	§ 2 sent. 1	35.02
	§ 2 sent. 2	35.07
	§ 3	35.03
	§ 4	35.06
	§ 5 sent. 1	35.04
	§ 5 sent. 2, 3, 4	35.05 subsecs. (a), (b)
	§ 5 sent. 5, 6	35.08
	§ 6	35.08
3995		26.01 subsecs. (a), (b)(1)–(6)
3995a		26.01 subsec. (b)(7)
3996 (part)		24.01
3996 (part)		24.02
3997		24.03
3998		24.04
3999		24.05
4004	sent. 1, 3, 4	27.01
6244		34.02 subsec. (a)
6245		34.02 subsec. (b)
6247		34.03
6248		34.04 subsec. (a)
		34.04 subsec. (b)(1)
		34.04 subsec. (c)
6249		34.04 subsec. (b)(2)
6250		34.05
6252		34.01
7426		15.02
7427		15.01
7428	subd. 1, 2	15.03 subsec. (a)(1), (2)
	subd. 3 (part)	15.03 subsec. (b)(1)
	subd. 3 (part)	15.03 subsec. (a)(3)
7428a		15.05
7428–1		15.03 subsec. (a)(4)
7428–2		15.03 subsec. (b)(2)
7429		15.04 subsec. (a)
7430		15.29 subsec. (c)
7431		15.29 subsec. (a)
7432		15.29 subsec. (d)
7433		15.30 subsecs. (a), (b)
7434		15.29 subsec. (b)
7435	sent. 1	15.31 subsec. (a)
		15.31 subsec. (c)(1)
	sent. 2	15.31 subsec. (c)(2), (3)
	sent. 3	15.31 subsec. (a)
	sent. 4	15.31 subsec. (g)
	sent. 5	15.31 subsec. (b)
		15.31 subsec. (c)(1)
		15.31 subsec. (e)
	sent. 6	15.31 subsec. (b)
	sent. 7	15.31 subsec. (a)
	sent. 8	15.31 subsec. (b)
	sent. 9	15.31 subsec. (f)
	sent. 10, 11	15.31 subsec. (d)
7436	sent. 1	15.32 subsec. (a)
	sent. 2	15.32 subsec. (b)
	sent. 3	15.32 subsec. (a)
	sent. 4	15.32 subsec. (c)
		15.32 subsec. (d)
	sent. 6, 7	15.32 subsec. (e)
	sent. 8	15.32 subsec. (c)
7436a		15.12
7437		15.04 subsec. (b)
7438		15.21 subsec. (a)
7439		15.14
7439a	sent. 1, 2	15.15 subsec. (a)
	sent. 3	15.15 subsec. (b)
		15.22 subsec. (a)
	sent. 4	15.22 subsec. (a)
7440		15.16 subsec. (b)
7441	sent. 1	15.16 subsec. (c)
	sent. 2	15.16 subsec. (d)
	sent. 3	15.16 subsec. (f)
7442		15.16 subsec. (e)(2)
7443	sent. 1	15.16 subsec. (e)(1)
	sent. 2	15.17 subsec. (a)
	sent. 3	15.17 subsecs. (a), (b), (c)
	sent. 4	15.19 subsec. (e)
	sent. 5, 6	15.22 subsec. (b)
7444	sent. 1	15.19 subsec. (a)
	sent. 2	15.19 subsec. (b)
	sent. 3	15.19 subsecs. (a), (c)
	sent. 4, 5	15.19 subsec. (c)
	sent. 6	15.19 subsec. (d)
	sent. 7	15.19 subsec. (f)
7445	sent. 1	15.18 subsec. (a)
	sent. 2	15.16 subsec. (f)
	sent. 3–5	15.18 subsec. (b)
7446		15.20
7447		15.21 subsec. (b)

PENAL CODE (1925)

Vernon's Penal Code Article		Business and Commerce Code Section
150	sent. 1	17.07 subsec. (a)
	sent. 2	17.07 subsec. (d)

DISPOSITION TABLE 2

Vernon's Penal Code Article		Business and Commerce Code Section
	sent. 3	17.07 subsec. (c)
151	sent. 1	17.07 subsec. (b)
	sent. 2	17.07 subsec. (e)
	sent. 3	17.07 subsec. (f)
157a	sent. 1	17.08 subsec. (a)
	sent. 2	17.08 subsecs. (c), (d)
	sent. 3	17.08 subsec. (b)
527a		15.06
1018		35.30
1019		35.28
1020		35.31 subsecs. (a), (b)(1), (c)
1021		35.31 subsec. (b)(2)
1022		35.29
1023		35.32 subsecs. (a), (c)
1024		35.32 subsec. (b)
1025		35.33
1058	sent. 1	17.29 subsec. (d)
	sent. 2	17.29 subsec. (b)
1059		17.29 subsec. (c)
1060		17.29 subsec. (e)
1063		17.30 subsecs. (a), (b)
1064		17.30 subsecs. (c), (e)
1065		17.30 subsec. (d)
1066a		17.10
1113		17.28
1114		17.09 subsec. (a)(1), (2), (b)
1115		17.09 subsecs. (a)(3), (c)
1130		35.40 subsecs. (c), (d)
1137*l*		17.19
1137*l*–1		17.20
1137*l*–2		17.21
1137*l*–3	par. (a)	17.18 subsec. (a)(1)
		17.18 subsec. (b)(1)
	par. (b)	17.18 subsec. (a)(2)
	par. (c) sent. 1	17.18 subsec. (a)(3)
	par. (c) sent. 2	17.18 subsec. (b)(2)
1137*l*–4		17.22
1137*l*–5		17.18 subsec. (c)
1554	sent. 1	17.12 subsecs. (a), (c)
	sent. 2	17.12 subsec. (b)
1554a	§ 1 sent. 1	17.11 subsec. (b)
	§ 1 sent. 2	17.11 subsec. (a)
	§ 1a	17.11 subsec. (c)
	§ 2	17.11 subsec. (d)
1557		25.01
		25.03 subsec. (a)
1558	sent. 1	25.02 subsec. (a)
		25.03 subsec. (b)
	sent. 2	25.01 subsec. (b)
1632		15.02
1633		15.01
1634	subd. 1, 2	15.03 subsec. (a)(1), (2)
	subd. 3	15.03 subsecs. (a)(3), (b)(1)
1635		15.33 subsec. (d)
1636		15.14
1637		15.33 subsec. (a)
1638		15.33 subsec. (b)
1639		15.33 subsecs. (c), (d)
1640		15.33 subsec. (d)
1641		15.33 subsec. (e)
1642		15.34
1643		——
1644		——
1674 to 1677		See 7.301 et seq.
1678		35.16
1679		35.17
1680		35.19
1681		35.18
1682		35.21
1683		35.20

*

BUSINESS AND COMMERCE CODE TABLE OF SECTIONS AFFECTED BY THE 80th LEGISLATURE

Sec.	Effect	Acts 2007 Ch.	Acts 2007 Sec.
1.301(c)	Amended	885	2.02
2A.104(a)	Amended	885	2.03
3.103(a)(2)	Amended	427	1
3.103(b)	Amended	427	2
3.104(k)	Repealed	427	4
3.507	Added	976	4
3.605(g)	Amended	427	3
7.103(d)	Amended	885	2.04
9.311(a)	Amended	885	2.05
9.503(a)	Amended	565	1
9.516(b)	Amended	565	2
9.517	Amended	565	3
9.518(a)	Amended	565	4
9.518(d)	Added	565	4
9.705(c)	Amended	565	5
9.705(g)	Added	565	5
17.08(a)(5)	Amended	921	2A.001
17.45(8)	Amended	411	1
17.46(b)	Amended	1230	26
17.46 note	—	1230	32
17.61(b)	Amended	411	2
17.61(f)	Amended	411	2
17.901	Added	595	1
17.902	Added	595	1
17.903	Added	595	1
17.904	Added	595	1
19.01 note	—	885	2.47(a)(1)
19.02 note	—	885	2.47(a)(1)
19.03 note	—	885	2.47(a)(1)
19.04 note	—	885	2.47(a)(1)
19.05 note	—	885	2.47(a)(1)
19.21 note	—	885	2.47(a)(1)
19.22 note	—	885	2.47(a)(1)
19.23 note	—	885	2.47(a)(1)
19.24 note	—	885	2.47(a)(1)
19.25 note	—	885	2.47(a)(1)
19.26 note	—	885	2.47(a)(1)
19.27 note	—	885	2.47(a)(1)
19.28 note	—	885	2.47(a)(1)
19.41 note	—	885	2.47(a)(1)
19.42 note	—	885	2.47(a)(1)
19.43 note	—	885	2.47(a)(1)
19.44 note	—	885	2.47(a)(1)
19.45 note	—	885	2.47(a)(1)
19.47 note	—	885	2.47(a)(1)
20.034(a)	Amended	1143	1
20.034 note	—	1143	5
20.037(e)	Repealed	1143	4
20.0385	Amended	1143	2
20.04	Amended	1143	3
34.01 note	—	885	2.47(a)(1)
34.02 note	—	885	2.47(a)(1)
34.03 note	—	885	2.47(a)(1)
34.04 note	—	885	2.47(a)(1)
34.05 note	—	885	2.47(a)(1)

Sec.	Effect	Acts 2007 Ch.	Acts 2007 Sec.
35.01 note	—	885	2.47(a)(1)
35.01A note	—	885	2.47(a)(1)
35.015 note	—	885	2.47(a)(1)
35.02 note	—	885	2.47(a)(1)
35.03 note	—	885	2.47(a)(1)
35.04 note	—	885	2.47(a)(1)
35.05 note	—	885	2.47(a)(1)
35.06 note	—	885	2.47(a)(1)
35.07 note	—	885	2.47(a)(1)
35.08 note	—	885	2.47(a)(1)
35.09 note	—	885	2.47(a)(1)
35.101 note	—	885	2.47(a)(1)
35.102(c)	Amended	937	2.01
35.102 note	—	885	2.47(a)(1)
35.103 note	—	885	2.47(a)(1)
35.111 note	—	885	2.47(a)(1)
35.112 note	—	885	2.47(a)(1)
35.113 note	—	885	2.47(a)(1)
35.114 note	—	885	2.47(a)(1)
35.121 note	—	885	2.47(a)(1)
35.122 note	—	885	2.47(a)(1)
35.123 note	—	885	2.47(a)(1)
35.124 note	—	885	2.47(a)(1)
35.125 note	—	885	2.47(a)(1)
35.131	Added	130	1
35.132	Added	130	1
35.133	Added	130	1
35.134	Added	130	1
35.135	Added	130	1
35.136	Added	130	1
35.137	Added	130	1
35.14 note	—	885	2.47(a)(1)
35.15 note	—	885	2.47(a)(1)
35.151	Added	822	1
35.152	Added	822	1
35.153	Added	822	1
35.154	Added	822	1
35.155	Added	822	1
35.156	Added	822	1
35.157	Added	822	1
35.16 note	—	885	2.47(a)(1)
35.17 note	—	885	2.47(a)(1)
35.18 note	—	885	2.47(a)(1)
35.20 note	—	885	2.47(a)(1)
35.21 note	—	885	2.47(a)(1)
35.27 note	—	885	2.47(a)(1)
35.28 note	—	885	2.47(a)(1)
35.29 note	—	885	2.47(a)(1)
35.30 note	—	885	2.47(a)(1)
35.31 note	—	885	2.47(a)(1)
35.32 note	—	885	2.47(a)(1)
35.33 note	—	885	2.47(a)(1)
35.39 note	—	885	2.47(a)(1)
35.395 note	—	885	2.47(a)(1)
35.40 note	—	885	2.47(a)(1)
35.41 note	—	885	2.47(a)(1)
35.42 note	—	885	2.47(a)(1)
35.43	Added	123	1
35.44 note	—	885	2.47(a)(1)
35.45 note	—	885	2.47(a)(1)
35.455 note	—	885	2.47(a)(1)

Sec.	Effect	Acts 2007 Ch.	Sec.
35.46 note	—	885	2.47(a)(1)
35.47 note	—	885	2.47(a)(1)
35.48 note	—	885	2.47(a)(1)
35.49 note	—	885	2.47(a)(1)
35.50 note	—	885	2.47(a)(1)
35.51 note	—	885	2.47(a)(1)
35.52 note	—	885	2.47(a)(1)
35.521	Added	498	1
35.521 note	—	498	2
35.53 note	—	885	2.47(a)(1)
35.531 note	—	885	2.47(a)(1)
35.54 note	—	885	2.47(a)(1)
35.55 note	—	885	2.47(a)(1)
35.56 note	—	885	2.47(a)(1)
35.57 note	—	885	2.47(a)(1)
35.58	Redes. as 35.60	921	17.001(6)
35.58 note	—	885	2.47(a)(1)
35.581(c)	Amended	93	1
35.581 note	—	885	2.47(a)(1)
35.585 note	—	885	2.47(a)(1)
35.59 note	—	885	2.47(a)(1)
35.591 note	—	885	2.47(a)(1)
35.595	Added	1044	1
35.595 note	—	1044	3
35.60	Redes. as 35.63	921	17.001(7)
	Redes. from 35.58	921	17.001(6)
35.60 note	—	885	2.47(a)(1)
35.61 note	—	885	2.47(a)(1)
35.62 note	—	885	2.47(a)(1)
35.63	Added	307	1
	Redes. from 35.60	921	17.001(7)
35.64	Added	182	1
		916	1
35.71 note	—	885	2.47(a)(1)
35.72 note	—	885	2.47(a)(1)
35.721 note	—	885	2.47(a)(1)
35.722 note	—	885	2.47(a)(1)
35.73 note	—	885	2.47(a)(1)
35.74 note	—	885	2.47(a)(1)
35.81 note	—	885	2.47(a)(1)
35.82 note	—	885	2.47(a)(1)
35.83 note	—	885	2.47(a)(1)
35.84 note	—	885	2.47(a)(1)
35.85 note	—	885	2.47(a)(1)
35.86 note	—	885	2.47(a)(1)
35.91 note	—	885	2.47(a)(1)
35.92 note	—	885	2.47(a)(1)
35.93 note	—	885	2.47(a)(1)
35.935 note	—	885	2.47(a)(1)
35.94 note	—	885	2.47(a)(1)
35.95 note	—	885	2.47(a)(1)
35.96 note	—	885	2.47(a)(1)
36.01 note	—	885	2.47(a)(1)
36.02 note	—	885	2.47(a)(1)
36.03 note	—	885	2.47(a)(1)
36.10 note	—	885	2.47(a)(1)
36.11 note	—	885	2.47(a)(1)
36.12 note	—	885	2.47(a)(1)
36.13 note	—	885	2.47(a)(1)
36.14 note	—	885	2.47(a)(1)
36.15 note	—	885	2.47(a)(1)

TABLE OF SECTIONS AFFECTED

Sec.	Effect	Acts 2007 Ch.	Sec.
36.16 note	—	885	2.47(a)(1)
36.17 note	—	885	2.47(a)(1)
36.18 note	—	885	2.47(a)(1)
36.25 note	—	885	2.47(a)(1)
36.26 note	—	885	2.47(a)(1)
36.27 note	—	885	2.47(a)(1)
37.01 note	—	885	2.47(a)(1)
37.02 note	—	885	2.47(a)(1)
37.03 note	—	885	2.47(a)(1)
37.04 note	—	885	2.47(a)(1)
37.05 note	—	885	2.47(a)(1)
38.001 note	—	885	2.47(a)(1)
38.002 note	—	885	2.47(a)(1)
38.003 note	—	885	2.47(a)(1)
38.051 note	—	885	2.47(a)(1)
38.052 note	—	885	2.47(a)(1)
38.053 note	—	885	2.47(a)(1)
38.054 note	—	885	2.47(a)(1)
38.055 note	—	885	2.47(a)(1)
38.056 note	—	885	2.47(a)(1)
38.057 note	—	885	2.47(a)(1)
38.058 note	—	885	2.47(a)(1)
38.059 note	—	885	2.47(a)(1)
38.060 note	—	885	2.47(a)(1)
38.061 note	—	885	2.47(a)(1)
38.101 note	—	885	2.47(a)(1)
38.102 note	—	885	2.47(a)(1)
38.103 note	—	885	2.47(a)(1)
38.104 note	—	885	2.47(a)(1)
38.105 note	—	885	2.47(a)(1)
38.106 note	—	885	2.47(a)(1)
38.107 note	—	885	2.47(a)(1)
38.108 note	—	885	2.47(a)(1)
38.151 note	—	885	2.47(a)(1)
38.152 note	—	885	2.47(a)(1)
38.153 note	—	885	2.47(a)(1)
38.201 note	—	885	2.47(a)(1)
38.202 note	—	885	2.47(a)(1)
38.203 note	—	885	2.47(a)(1)
38.251 note	—	885	2.47(a)(1)
38.252 note	—	885	2.47(a)(1)
38.253 note	—	885	2.47(a)(1)
38.301 note	—	885	2.47(a)(1)
38.302 note	—	885	2.47(a)(1)
38.303 note	—	885	2.47(a)(1)
38.304 note	—	885	2.47(a)(1)
38.305 note	—	885	2.47(a)(1)
39.001 note	—	885	2.47(a)(1)
39.002 note	—	885	2.47(a)(1)
39.003 note	—	885	2.47(a)(1)
39.004 note	—	885	2.47(a)(1)
39.005 note	—	885	2.47(a)(1)
39.006 note	—	885	2.47(a)(1)
39.007 note	—	885	2.47(a)(1)
39.008 note	—	885	2.47(a)(1)
39.009 note	—	885	2.47(a)(1)
40.001 note	—	885	2.47(a)(1)
40.002 note	—	885	2.47(a)(1)
40.003 note	—	885	2.47(a)(1)
40.004 note	—	885	2.47(a)(1)
40.005 note	—	885	2.47(a)(1)

Sec.	Effect	Acts 2007 Ch.	Sec.
40.006 note	—	885	2.47(a)(1)
40.007 note	—	885	2.47(a)(1)
40.031 note	—	885	2.47(a)(1)
40.032 note	—	885	2.47(a)(1)
40.033 note	—	885	2.47(a)(1)
40.034 note	—	885	2.47(a)(1)
40.035 note	—	885	2.47(a)(1)
40.036 note	—	885	2.47(a)(1)
40.061 note	—	885	2.47(a)(1)
40.062 note	—	885	2.47(a)(1)
40.063 note	—	885	2.47(a)(1)
40.064 note	—	885	2.47(a)(1)
40.065 note	—	885	2.47(a)(1)
40.066 note	—	885	2.47(a)(1)
40.067 note	—	885	2.47(a)(1)
40.091 note	—	885	2.47(a)(1)
40.092 note	—	885	2.47(a)(1)
40.093 note	—	885	2.47(a)(1)
40.094 note	—	885	2.47(a)(1)
40.095 note	—	885	2.47(a)(1)
40.121 note	—	885	2.47(a)(1)
40.122 note	—	885	2.47(a)(1)
41.001 note	—	885	2.47(a)(1)
41.002 note	—	885	2.47(a)(1)
41.003 note	—	885	2.47(a)(1)
41.004 note	—	885	2.47(a)(1)
41.005 note	—	885	2.47(a)(1)
41.006 note	—	885	2.47(a)(1)
41.007 note	—	885	2.47(a)(1)
41.008 note	—	885	2.47(a)(1)
41.009 note	—	885	2.47(a)(1)
41.051 note	—	885	2.47(a)(1)
41.052 note	—	885	2.47(a)(1)
41.053 note	—	885	2.47(a)(1)
41.054 note	—	885	2.47(a)(1)
41.101 note	—	885	2.47(a)(1)
41.102 note	—	885	2.47(a)(1)
41.151 note	—	885	2.47(a)(1)
41.152 note	—	885	2.47(a)(1)
41.153 note	—	885	2.47(a)(1)
41.154 note	—	885	2.47(a)(1)
41.155 note	—	885	2.47(a)(1)
41.156 note	—	885	2.47(a)(1)
41.157 note	—	885	2.47(a)(1)
41.158 note	—	885	2.47(a)(1)
41.159 note	—	885	2.47(a)(1)
41.160 note	—	885	2.47(a)(1)
41.161 note	—	885	2.47(a)(1)
41.162 note	—	885	2.47(a)(1)
41.163 note	—	885	2.47(a)(1)
41.201 note	—	885	2.47(a)(1)
41.202 note	—	885	2.47(a)(1)
41.203 note		885	2.47(a)(1)
41.251 note	—	885	2.47(a)(1)
41.252 note	—	885	2.47(a)(1)
41.301 note	—	885	2.47(a)(1)
41.302 note	—	885	2.47(a)(1)
41.303 note	—	885	2.47(a)(1)
42.001 note	—	885	2.47(a)(1)
42.002 note	—	885	2.47(a)(1)
42.003 note	—	885	2.47(a)(1)

Sec.	Effect	Acts 2007 Ch.	Sec.
42.004 note	—	885	2.47(a)(1)
42.005 note	—	885	2.47(a)(1)
43.001 note	—	885	2.47(a)(1)
43.002 note	—	885	2.47(a)(1)
43.003 note	—	885	2.47(a)(1)
43.004 note	—	885	2.47(a)(1)
43.005 note	—	885	2.47(a)(1)
43.006 note	—	885	2.47(a)(1)
43.007 note	—	885	2.47(a)(1)
43.008 note	—	885	2.47(a)(1)
43.009 note	—	885	2.47(a)(1)
43.010 note	—	885	2.47(a)(1)
43.011 note	—	885	2.47(a)(1)
43.012 note	—	885	2.47(a)(1)
43.013 note	—	885	2.47(a)(1)
43.014 note	—	885	2.47(a)(1)
43.015 note	—	885	2.47(a)(1)
43.016 note	—	885	2.47(a)(1)
43.017 note	—	885	2.47(a)(1)
43.018 note	—	885	2.47(a)(1)
43.019 note	—	885	2.47(a)(1)
43.020 note	—	885	2.47(a)(1)
43.021 note	—	885	2.47(a)(1)
44.001 note	—	885	2.47(a)(1)
44.002(9)	Amended	206	1
44.002 note	—	885	2.47(a)(1)
44.003 note	—	885	2.47(a)(1)
44.004 note	—	885	2.47(a)(1)
44.005 note	—	885	2.47(a)(1)
44.006 note	—	885	2.47(a)(1)
44.051 note	—	885	2.47(a)(1)
44.052 note	—	885	2.47(a)(1)
44.101 note	—	885	2.47(a)(1)
44.102 note	—	885	2.47(a)(1)
44.103(c)	Added	206	2
44.103 note	—	885	2.47(a)(1)
44.104 note	—	885	2.47(a)(1)
44.151 note	—	885	2.47(a)(1)
44.152 note	—	885	2.47(a)(1)
44.153 note	—	885	2.47(a)(1)
44.201 note	—	885	2.47(a)(1)
44.202 note	—	885	2.47(a)(1)
44.251 note	—	885	2.47(a)(1)
44.252 note	—	885	2.47(a)(1)
44.253 note	—	885	2.47(a)(1)
45.001 note	—	885	2.47(a)(1)
45.002 note	—	885	2.47(a)(1)
45.003 note	—	885	2.47(a)(1)
45.004 note	—	885	2.47(a)(1)
46.001 note	—	885	2.47(a)(1)
46.002 note	—	885	2.47(a)(1)
46.003 note	—	885	2.47(a)(1)
46.004 note	—	885	2.47(a)(1)
46.005 note	—	885	2.47(a)(1)
46.006 note	—	885	2.47(a)(1)
46.007 note	—	885	2.47(a)(1)
46.008 note	—	885	2.47(a)(1)
46.009 note	—	885	2.47(a)(1)
46.010 note	—	885	2.47(a)(1)
46.011 note	—	885	2.47(a)(1)

Sec.	Effect	Acts 2007 Ch.	Sec.
Ch. 47, Subch. A heading	Added	1206	1
47.001	Amended	1206	2
47.001 note	—	885	2.47(a)(1)
47.002 note	—	885	2.47(a)(1)
47.003 note	—	885	2.47(a)(1)
47.004 note	—	885	2.47(a)(1)
47.051	Added	1206	3
47.052	Added	1206	3
47.052 note	—	1206	8
47.053	Added	1206	3
47.054	Added	1206	3
47.055	Added	1206	3
47.0551	Added	1206	3
47.056	Added	1206	3
48.001 note	—	885	2.47(a)(2) 2.47(a)(3) 2.47(a)(4)
48.002 note	—	885	2.47(a)(2) 2.47(a)(3) 2.47(a)(4)
48.003 note	—	885	2.47(a)(3) 2.47(a)(4)
48.004 note	—	885	2.47(a)(4)
48.005 note	—	885	2.47(a)(4)
48.006 note	—	885	2.47(a)(4)
48.051 note	—	885	2.47(a)(3)
48.052 note	—	885	2.47(a)(3)
48.053 note	—	885	2.47(a)(3)
48.054 note	—	885	2.47(a)(3)
48.055 note	—	885	2.47(a)(3)
48.056 note	—	885	2.47(a)(3)
48.101 note	—	885	2.47(a)(2) 2.47(a)(3)
48.102 note	—	885	2.47(a)(2) 2.47(a)(3)
48.103 note	—	885	2.47(a)(2)
48.201 note	—	885	2.47(a)(2)
48.202 note	—	885	2.47(a)(2)
48.203 note	—	885	2.47(a)(2)
51.001	Added	885	2.01
51.002	Added	885	2.01
51.003	Added	885	2.01
51.004	Added	885	2.01
51.005	Added	885	2.01
51.006	Added	885	2.01
51.007	Added	885	2.01
51.008	Added	885	2.01
51.009	Added	885	2.01
51.051	Added	885	2.01
51.052	Added	885	2.01
51.053	Added	885	2.01
51.054	Added	885	2.01
51.101	Added	885	2.01
51.102	Added	885	2.01
51.151	Added	885	2.01
51.152	Added	885	2.01
51.153	Added	885	2.01
51.154	Added	885	2.01
51.155	Added	885	2.01
51.156	Added	885	2.01

TABLE OF SECTIONS AFFECTED

Sec.	Effect	Acts 2007 Ch.	Sec.
51.157	Added	885	2.01
51.158	Added	885	2.01
51.159	Added	885	2.01
51.160	Added	885	2.01
51.161	Added	885	2.01
51.162	Added	885	2.01
51.163	Added	885	2.01
51.164	Added	885	2.01
51.201	Added	885	2.01
51.202	Added	885	2.01
51.203	Added	885	2.01
51.251	Added	885	2.01
51.252	Added	885	2.01
51.301	Added	885	2.01
51.302	Added	885	2.01
51.303	Added	885	2.01
52.001	Added	885	2.01
52.002	Added	885	2.01
52.003	Added	885	2.01
52.004	Added	885	2.01
52.051	Added	885	2.01
52.052	Added	885	2.01
52.053	Added	885	2.01
52.101	Added	885	2.01
52.102	Added	885	2.01
52.103	Added	885	2.01
52.104	Added	885	2.01
52.105	Added	885	2.01
52.106	Added	885	2.01
52.151	Added	885	2.01
52.152	Added	885	2.01
52.153	Added	885	2.01
52.154	Added	885	2.01
52.155	Added	885	2.01
52.156	Added	885	2.01
52.157	Added	885	2.01
53.001	Added	885	2.01
54.001	Added	885	2.01
54.002	Added	885	2.01
54.003	Added	885	2.01
54.004	Added	885	2.01
54.005	Added	885	2.01
54.006	Added	885	2.01
55.001	Added	885	2.01
55.002	Added	885	2.01
55.003	Added	885	2.01
55.051	Added	885	2.01
55.052	Added	885	2.01
55.053	Added	885	2.01
55.054	Added	885	2.01
55.055	Added	885	2.01
55.056	Added	885	2.01
55.057	Added	885	2.01
55.101	Added	885	2.01
55.102	Added	885	2.01
55.103	Added	885	2.01
55.104	Added	885	2.01
55.151	Added	885	2.01
55.152	Added	885	2.01
55.153	Added	885	2.01
55.154	Added	885	2.01

Sec.	Effect	Acts 2007 Ch.	Sec.
55.155	Added	885	2.01
55.156	Added	885	2.01
55.157	Added	885	2.01
55.158	Added	885	2.01
55.201	Added	885	2.01
71.001	Added	885	2.01
71.002	Added	885	2.01
71.003	Added	885	2.01
71.051	Added	885	2.01
71.052	Added	885	2.01
71.053	Added	885	2.01
71.054	Added	885	2.01
71.101	Added	885	2.01
71.102	Added	885	2.01
71.103	Added	885	2.01
71.104	Added	885	2.01
71.151	Added	885	2.01
71.152	Added	885	2.01
71.153	Added	885	2.01
71.154	Added	885	2.01
71.155	Added	885	2.01
71.156	Added	885	2.01
71.157	Added	885	2.01
71.158	Added	885	2.01
71.201	Added	885	2.01
71.202	Added	885	2.01
71.203	Added	885	2.01
72.001	Added	885	2.01
72.002	Added	885	2.01
72.003	Added	885	2.01
72.004	Added	885	2.01
72.051	Added	885	2.01
91.001	Added	885	2.01
91.051	Added	885	2.01
91.052	Added	885	2.01
91.053	Added	885	2.01
91.054	Added	885	2.01
91.055	Added	885	2.01
91.056	Added	885	2.01
91.101	Added	885	2.01
91.102	Added	885	2.01
91.103	Added	885	2.01
92.001	Added	885	2.01
92.002	Added	885	2.01
92.051	Added	885	2.01
92.052	Added	885	2.01
92.053	Added	885	2.01
92.054	Added	885	2.01
92.055	Added	885	2.01
92.101	Added	885	2.01
92.102	Added	885	2.01
92.103	Added	885	2.01
92.104	Added	885	2.01
92.151	Added	885	2.01
92.152	Added	885	2.01
92.153	Added	885	2.01
92.154	Added	885	2.01
92.155	Added	885	2.01
92.156	Added	885	2.01
92.157	Added	885	2.01
92.158	Added	885	2.01

TABLE OF SECTIONS AFFECTED

Sec.	Effect	Acts 2007 Ch.	Sec.
92.159	Added	885	2.01
92.160	Added	885	2.01
92.201	Added	885	2.01
92.202	Added	885	2.01
101.001	Added	885	2.01
101.002	Added	885	2.01
101.003	Added	885	2.01
101.004	Added	885	2.01
101.005	Added	885	2.01
102.001	Added	885	2.01
102.002	Added	885	2.01
102.003	Added	885	2.01
102.004	Added	885	2.01
102.005	Added	885	2.01
103.001	Added	885	2.01
103.002	Added	885	2.01
104.001	Added	885	2.01
104.002	Added	885	2.01
104.003	Added	885	2.01
105.001	Added	885	2.01
105.002	Added	885	2.01
105.003	Added	885	2.01
105.004	Added	885	2.01
105.005	Added	885	2.01
105.006	Added	885	2.01
201.001	Added	885	2.01
201.002	Added	885	2.01
201.003	Added	885	2.01
201.004	Added	885	2.01
201.005	Added	885	2.01
201.006	Added	885	2.01
202.001	Added	885	2.01
203.001	Added	885	2.01
251.001	Added	885	2.01
251.002	Added	885	2.01
251.003	Added	885	2.01
251.004	Added	885	2.01
251.005	Added	885	2.01
251.006	Added	885	2.01
251.007	Added	885	2.01
251.008	Added	885	2.01
252.001	Added	885	2.01
252.002	Added	885	2.01
252.003	Added	885	2.01
252.004	Added	885	2.01
252.005	Added	885	2.01
252.006	Added	885	2.01
252.007	Added	885	2.01
253.001	Added	885	2.01
254.001	Added	885	2.01
254.002	Added	885	2.01
261.001	Added	885	2.01
261.002	Added	885	2.01
261.003	Added	885	2.01
261.004	Added	885	2.01
261.005	Added	885	2.01
261.006	Added	885	2.01
261.007	Added	885	2.01
261.008	Added	885	2.01
261.009	Added	885	2.01
261.010	Added	885	2.01

Sec.	Effect	Acts 2007 Ch.	Sec.
261.011	Added	885	2.01
271.001	Added	885	2.01
271.002	Added	885	2.01
271.003	Added	885	2.01
271.004	Added	885	2.01
271.005	Added	885	2.01
271.006	Added	885	2.01
271.007	Added	885	2.01
271.008	Added	885	2.01
271.009	Added	885	2.01
271.010	Added	885	2.01
271.011	Added	885	2.01
272.001	Added	885	2.01
272.002	Added	885	2.01
273.001	Added	885	2.01
273.002	Added	885	2.01
273.003	Added	885	2.01
274.001	Added	885	2.01
274.002	Added	885	2.01
274.003	Added	885	2.01
274.004	Added	885	2.01
301.001	Added	885	2.01
301.051	Added	885	2.01
301.052	Added	885	2.01
301.101	Added	885	2.01
301.102	Added	885	2.01
301.103	Added	885	2.01
301.104	Added	885	2.01
301.105	Added	885	2.01
302.001	Added	885	2.01
302.002	Added	885	2.01
302.003	Added	885	2.01
302.004	Added	885	2.01
302.051	Added	885	2.01
302.052	Added	885	2.01
302.053	Added	885	2.01
302.054	Added	885	2.01
302.055	Added	885	2.01
302.056	Added	885	2.01
302.057	Added	885	2.01
302.058	Added	885	2.01
302.059	Added	885	2.01
302.060	Added	885	2.01
302.061	Added	885	2.01
302.101	Added	885	2.01
302.102	Added	885	2.01
302.103	Added	885	2.01
302.104	Added	885	2.01
302.105	Added	885	2.01
302.106	Added	885	2.01
302.107	Added	885	2.01
302.108	Added	885	2.01
302.151	Added	885	2.01
302.152	Added	885	2.01
302.153	Added	885	2.01
302.201	Added	885	2.01
302.202	Added	885	2.01
302.203	Added	885	2.01
302.251	Added	885	2.01
302.252	Added	885	2.01
302.253	Added	885	2.01

TABLE OF SECTIONS AFFECTED

Sec.	Effect	Acts 2007 Ch.	Sec.
302.301	Added	885	2.01
302.302	Added	885	2.01
302.303	Added	885	2.01
302.304	Added	885	2.01
303.001	Added	885	2.01
303.002	Added	885	2.01
303.003	Added	885	2.01
303.004	Added	885	2.01
303.051	Added	885	2.01
303.052	Added	885	2.01
303.053	Added	885	2.01
303.054	Added	885	2.01
303.055	Added	885	2.01
303.056	Added	885	2.01
303.057	Added	885	2.01
303.058	Added	885	2.01
303.059	Added	885	2.01
303.101	Added	885	2.01
303.102	Added	885	2.01
303.103	Added	885	2.01
303.104	Added	885	2.01
303.151	Added	885	2.01
303.152	Added	885	2.01
303.153	Added	885	2.01
303.154	Added	885	2.01
304.001	Added	885	2.01
304.002	Added	885	2.01
304.003	Added	885	2.01
304.004	Added	885	2.01
304.005	Added	885	2.01
304.006	Added	885	2.01
304.051	Added	885	2.01
304.052	Added	885	2.01
304.053	Added	885	2.01
304.054	Added	885	2.01
304.055	Added	885	2.01
304.056	Added	885	2.01
304.057	Added	885	2.01
304.058	Added	885	2.01
304.059	Added	885	2.01
304.060	Added	885	2.01
304.061	Added	885	2.01
304.062	Added	885	2.01
304.101	Added	885	2.01
304.102	Added	885	2.01
304.151	Added	885	2.01
304.152	Added	885	2.01
304.201	Added	885	2.01
304.202	Added	885	2.01
304.251	Added	885	2.01
304.252	Added	885	2.01
304.253	Added	885	2.01
304.254	Added	885	2.01
304.255	Added	885	2.01
304.256	Added	885	2.01
304.257	Added	885	2.01
304.258	Added	885	2.01
304.259	Added	885	2.01
305.001	Added	885	2.01
305.002	Added	885	2.01
305.003	Added	885	2.01

Sec.	Effect	Acts 2007 Ch.	Sec.
305.051	Added	885	2.01
305.052	Added	885	2.01
305.053	Added	885	2.01
321.001	Added	885	2.01
321.051	Added	885	2.01
321.052	Added	885	2.01
321.053	Added	885	2.01
321.101	Added	885	2.01
321.102	Added	885	2.01
321.103	Added	885	2.01
321.104	Added	885	2.01
321.105	Added	885	2.01
321.106	Added	885	2.01
321.107	Added	885	2.01
321.108	Added	885	2.01
321.109	Added	885	2.01
321.110	Added	885	2.01
321.111	Added	885	2.01
321.112	Added	885	2.01
321.113	Added	885	2.01
321.114	Added	885	2.01
322.001	Added	885	2.01
322.002	Added	885	2.01
322.003	Added	885	2.01
322.004	Added	885	2.01
322.005	Added	885	2.01
322.006	Added	885	2.01
322.007	Added	885	2.01
322.008	Added	885	2.01
322.009	Added	885	2.01
322.010	Added	885	2.01
322.011	Added	885	2.01
322.012	Added	885	2.01
322.013	Added	885	2.01
322.014	Added	885	2.01
322.015	Added	885	2.01
322.016	Added	885	2.01
322.017	Added	885	2.01
322.018	Added	885	2.01
322.019	Added	885	2.01
322.020	Added	885	2.01
322.021	Added	885	2.01
323.001	Added	885	2.01
323.002	Added	885	2.01
323.003	Added	885	2.01
324.001	Added	885	2.01
324.002	Added	885	2.01
324.003	Added	885	2.01
324.004	Added	885	2.01
324.005	Added	885	2.01
324.006	Added	885	2.01
324.051	Added	885	2.01
324.052	Added	885	2.01
324.053	Added	885	2.01
324.054	Added	885	2.01
324.101	Added	885	2.01
324.102	Added	885	2.01
325.001	Added	885	2.01
325.002	Added	885	2.01
325.003	Added	885	2.01
325.004	Added	885	2.01

Sec.	Effect	Acts 2007 Ch.	Sec.
325.005	Added	885	2.01
325.006	Added	885	2.01
501.001	Added	885	2.01
501.002	Added	885	2.01
501.051	Added	885	2.01
501.052	Added	885	2.01
501.053	Added	885	2.01
501.101	Added	885	2.01
501.102	Added	885	2.01
502.001	Added	885	2.01
502.002	Added	885	2.01
502.003	Added	885	2.01
503.001	Added	885	2.01
504.001	Added	885	2.01
504.002	Added	885	2.01
521.001	Added	885	2.01
521.002	Added	885	2.01
521.051	Added	885	2.01
521.052	Added	885	2.01
521.053	Added	885	2.01
521.101	Added	885	2.01
521.102	Added	885	2.01
521.103	Added	885	2.01
521.104	Added	885	2.01
521.105	Added	885	2.01
521.151	Added	885	2.01
521.152	Added	885	2.01
522.001	Added	885	2.01
522.002	Added	885	2.01
523.001	Added	885	2.01
523.002	Added	885	2.01
523.003	Added	885	2.01
601.001	Added	885	2.01
601.002	Added	885	2.01
601.051	Added	885	2.01
601.052	Added	885	2.01
601.053	Added	885	2.01
601.054	Added	885	2.01
601.055	Added	885	2.01
601.101	Added	885	2.01
601.102	Added	885	2.01
601.103	Added	885	2.01
601.151	Added	885	2.01
601.152	Added	885	2.01
601.153	Added	885	2.01
601.154	Added	885	2.01
601.201	Added	885	2.01
601.202	Added	885	2.01
601.203	Added	885	2.01
601.204	Added	885	2.01
601.205	Added	885	2.01
602.001	Added	885	2.01
602.002	Added	885	2.01
602.003	Added	885	2.01
602.004	Added	885	2.01
603.001	Added	885	2.01
603.002	Added	885	2.01
603.051	Added	885	2.01
603.052	Added	885	2.01
603.053	Added	885	2.01
603.101	Added	885	2.01

Sec.	Effect	Acts 2007 Ch.	Sec.
604.001	Added	885	2.01
604.002	Added	885	2.01
604.003	Added	885	2.01
604.051	Added	885	2.01
604.052	Added	885	2.01
604.101	Added	885	2.01
604.102	Added	885	2.01
604.103	Added	885	2.01
621.001	Added	885	2.01
621.002	Added	885	2.01
621.003	Added	885	2.01
621.004	Added	885	2.01
621.005	Added	885	2.01
621.006	Added	885	2.01
621.051	Added	885	2.01
621.052	Added	885	2.01
621.053	Added	885	2.01
621.054	Added	885	2.01
621.055	Added	885	2.01
621.101	Added	885	2.01
621.102	Added	885	2.01
621.103	Added	885	2.01
621.104	Added	885	2.01
621.105	Added	885	2.01
621.106	Added	885	2.01
621.107	Added	885	2.01
621.108	Added	885	2.01
621.109	Added	885	2.01
621.151	Added	885	2.01
621.152	Added	885	2.01
621.153	Added	885	2.01
621.154	Added	885	2.01
621.201	Added	885	2.01
621.202	Added	885	2.01
621.203	Added	885	2.01
621.204	Added	885	2.01
621.205	Added	885	2.01
621.251	Added	885	2.01
621.252	Added	885	2.01
622.001	Added	885	2.01
622.002	Added	885	2.01
622.051	Added	885	2.01
622.052	Added	885	2.01
622.053	Added	885	2.01
622.054	Added	885	2.01
622.055	Added	885	2.01
622.056	Added	885	2.01
622.057	Added	885	2.01
622.058	Added	885	2.01
622.059	Added	885	2.01
622.060	Added	885	2.01
622.061	Added	885	2.01
622.101	Added	885	2.01
622.102	Added	885	2.01
622.103	Added	885	2.01
622.104	Added	885	2.01
622.105	Added	885	2.01
622.106	Added	885	2.01
622.107	Added	885	2.01
622.108	Added	885	2.01
622.109	Added	885	2.01

TABLE OF SECTIONS AFFECTED

Sec.	Effect	Acts 2007 Ch.	Sec.
622.110	Added	885	2.01
622.151	Added	885	2.01
622.152	Added	885	2.01
622.201	Added	885	2.01
622.202	Added	885	2.01
622.203	Added	885	2.01
622.204	Added	885	2.01
622.205	Added	885	2.01
622.206	Added	885	2.01
641.001	Added	885	2.01
641.051	Added	885	2.01
641.052	Added	885	2.01
641.053	Added	885	2.01
641.054	Added	885	2.01
641.055	Added	885	2.01
641.056	Added	885	2.01
641.057	Added	885	2.01
661.001	Added	885	2.01
661.002	Added	885	2.01
661.003	Added	885	2.01
661.004	Added	885	2.01
661.005	Added	885	2.01
661.006	Added	885	2.01
671.001	Added	885	2.01
671.002	Added	885	2.01
671.003	Added	885	2.01
671.051	Added	885	2.01
671.052	Added	885	2.01
671.053	Added	885	2.01
671.054	Added	885	2.01
671.055	Added	885	2.01
671.101	Added	885	2.01
671.102	Added	885	2.01
671.103	Added	885	2.01
671.104	Added	885	2.01
671.105	Added	885	2.01
671.106	Added	885	2.01
681.001	Added	885	2.01
681.002	Added	885	2.01
681.051	Added	885	2.01
681.052	Added	885	2.01
681.101	Added	885	2.01
681.102	Added	885	2.01
681.151	Added	885	2.01
681.152	Added	885	2.01
681.153	Added	885	2.01
681.154	Added	885	2.01
681.155	Added	885	2.01
681.156	Added	885	2.01
681.157	Added	885	2.01
681.158	Added	885	2.01
681.159	Added	885	2.01
681.160	Added	885	2.01
681.161	Added	885	2.01
681.162	Added	885	2.01
681.163	Added	885	2.01
681.164	Added	885	2.01
681.165	Added	885	2.01
681.166	Added	885	2.01
681.167	Added	885	2.01
681.168	Added	885	2.01

Sec.	Effect	Acts 2007 Ch.	Sec.
681.169	Added	885	2.01
681.170	Added	885	2.01
681.171	Added	885	2.01
681.172	Added	885	2.01
681.173	Added	885	2.01
681.174	Added	885	2.01
681.175	Added	885	2.01
681.176	Added	885	2.01
681.177	Added	885	2.01
681.178	Added	885	2.01
2001.001	Added	885	2.01
2001.002	Added	885	2.01
2001.003	Added	885	2.01
2001.004	Added	885	2.01
2001.005	Added	885	2.01
2001.006	Added	885	2.01
2002.001	Added	885	2.01
2002.002	Added	885	2.01
2002.003	Added	885	2.01
2002.004	Added	885	2.01
2002.005	Added	885	2.01

*

BUSINESS AND COMMERCE CODE

TITLE 1. UNIFORM COMMERCIAL CODE

TITLE 2. COMPETITION AND TRADE PRACTICES

TITLE 3. INSOLVENCY, FRAUDULENT TRANSFERS, AND FRAUD

TITLE 4. MISCELLANEOUS COMMERCIAL PROVISIONS

TITLE 5. REGULATION OF BUSINESSES AND SERVICES

SUBTITLE A. GENERAL PRACTICES

SUBTITLE B. RENTAL PRACTICES

SUBTITLE C. BUSINESS OPERATIONS

TITLE 6. SALE OR TRANSFER OF GOODS

TITLE 7. RECEIPTS, DOCUMENTS OF TITLE, AND OTHER INSTRUMENTS

TITLE 8. SECURITY INSTRUMENTS

TITLE 1. UNIFORM COMMERCIAL CODE

Enactment

The Uniform Commercial Code was first enacted in Texas in 1965 (Acts 1965, chapter 721) to become effective at midnight June 30, 1966. Section 10–102 of the Code as then enacted repealed numerous existing provisions of the Texas Statutes relating to commercial transactions, but provided that transactions validly entered into before the effective date and the rights, duties and interests flowing from them should remain valid thereafter and could be terminated, completed, consummated or enforced as required or permitted by any statute or other law amended or repealed by the Act as though such repeal or amendment had not occurred.

Acts 1967, chapter 785, reenacted the Uniform Commercial Code as a part of the Business and Commerce Code and repealed Acts 1965, chapter 721. However, section 5 of the 1967 Act provided in part that the repeal of a statute by the Act did not affect the prior operation of the statute or any prior action taken under it.

Section Numbers

The text of the Texas Uniform Commercial Code as set out herein is identified by section rather than article numbers. The section numbers correspond to the section numbers of the Uniform Commercial Code, except that as enacted in 1967 a period has been substituted for a dash so that section 1–101 in the official text is section 1.101 in the Texas Code, and so on. Additionally, most lettered subsections and numbered subdivisions of the Texas Code have been substituted for the numbered subsections and lettered subdivisions of the official text so that subdivision (a) of subsection (2) of section 1–102 in the official text is subdivision (1) of subsection (b) of section 1.102 in the Texas Code, and so on.

Effective Date

Section 3 of Acts 1967, ch. 785 provided that "This Act takes effect on September 1, 1967."

CHAPTER 1. GENERAL PROVISIONS

SUBCHAPTER A. GENERAL PROVISIONS

SUBCHAPTER B. GENERAL DEFINITIONS AND PRINCIPLES OF INTERPRETATION

SUBCHAPTER C. TERRITORIAL APPLICABILITY AND GENERAL RULES

Acts 2003, 78th Leg., ch. 542, § 1 amended Chapter 1 extensively, effective September 1, 2003. The former Chapter 1, consisting of §§ 1.101 to 1.208, was amended to consist of §§ 1.101 to 1.310.

DISPOSITION TABLE

Showing where the subject matter of provisions contained in former Chapter 1, General Provisions, may be found in Chapter 1, General Provisions, as amended by Acts 2003, 78th Leg., ch. 542, § 1.

Former Section	Amended Section
1.101	1.101
1.102	1.103
1.103	1.103
1.104	1.104
1.105	—
1.106	—
1.107	—
1.108	1.105
1.109	1.107
1.201	1.201
1.202	—
1.203	—
1.204	1.205
1.205	1.303
1.206	—
1.207	1.308
1.208	1.309

SUBCHAPTER A. GENERAL PROVISIONS

Acts 2003, 78th Leg., ch. 542, § 1 amended the subchapter heading by substituting "General Provisions" for "Short Title, Construction, Application and Subject Matter of the Title".

§ 1.101. Short Titles

(a) This title may be cited as the Uniform Commercial Code.

(b) This chapter may be cited as Uniform Commercial Code—General Provisions.

Amended by Acts 2003, 78th Leg., ch. 542, § 1, eff. Sept. 1, 2003.

Uniform Commercial Code Comment

Source: Former Section 1–101.

Changes from former law: Subsection (b) is new. It is added in order to make the structure of Article 1 parallel with that of the other articles of the Uniform Commercial Code.

1. Each other article of the Uniform Commercial Code (except Articles 10 and 11) may also be cited by its own short title. See Sections 2–101, 2A–101, 3–101, 4–101, 4A–101, 5–101, 6–101, 7–101, 8–101, and 9–101.

§ 1.102. Scope of Chapter

This chapter applies to a transaction to the extent that it is governed by another chapter of this title.

Amended by Acts 2003, 78th Leg., ch. 542, § 1, eff. Sept. 1, 2003.

Uniform Commercial Code Comment

Source: New.

1. This section is intended to resolve confusion that has occasionally arisen as to the applicability of the substantive rules in this article. This section makes clear what has always been the case–the rules in Article 1 apply to transactions to the extent that those transactions are governed by one of the other articles of the Uniform Commercial Code. See also Comment 1 to Section 1–301.

§ 1.103. Construction of Title to Promote Its Purposes and Policies; Applicability of Supplemental Principles of Law

(a) This title must be liberally construed and applied to promote its underlying purposes and policies, which are:

(1) to simplify, clarify and modernize the law governing commercial transactions;

(2) to permit the continued expansion of commercial practices through custom, usage and agreement of the parties; and

(3) to make uniform the law among the various jurisdictions.

(b) Unless displaced by the particular provisions of this title, the principles of law and equity, including the law merchant and the law relative to capacity to contract, principal and agent, estoppel, fraud, misrepresentation, duress, coercion, mistake, bankruptcy, or other validating or invalidating cause shall supplement its provisions.

Amended by Acts 2003, 78th Leg., ch. 542, § 1, eff. Sept. 1, 2003.

Uniform Commercial Code Comment

Source: Former Section 1–102 (1)-(2); Former Section 1–103.

Changes from former law: This section is derived from subsections (1) and (2) of former Section 1–102 and from former Section 1–103. Subsection (a) of this section combines subsections (1) and (2) of former Section 1–102. Except for changing the form of reference to the Uniform Commercial Code and minor stylistic changes, its language is the same as subsections (1) and (2) of former Section 1–102. Except for changing the form of reference to the Uniform Commercial Code and minor stylistic changes, subsection (b) of this section is identical to former Section 1–103. The provisions have been combined in this section to reflect the interrelationship between them.

1. The Uniform Commercial Code is drawn to provide flexibility so that, since it is intended to be a semi-permanent and infrequently-amended piece of legislation, it will provide its own machinery for expansion of commercial practices. It is intended to make it possible for the law embodied in the Uniform Commercial Code to be applied by the courts in the light of unforeseen and new circumstances and practices. The proper construction of the Uniform Commercial Code requires, of course, that its interpretation and application be limited to its reason.

Even prior to the enactment of the Uniform Commercial Code, courts were careful to keep broad acts from being hampered in their effects by later acts of limited scope. See *Pacific Wool Growers v. Draper & Co.*, 158 Or. 1, 73 P.2d 1391 (1937), and compare Section 1–104. The courts have often recognized that the policies embodied in an act are applicable in reason to subject-matter that was not expressly included in the language of the act, *Commercial Nat. Bank of New Orleans v. Canal–Louisiana Bank & Trust Co.*, 239 U.S. 520, 36 S.Ct. 194, 60 L.Ed. 417 (1916) (bona fide purchase policy of Uniform Warehouse Receipts Act extended to case not covered but of equivalent nature), and did the same where reason and policy so required, even where the subject-matter had been intentionally excluded from the act in general. *Agar v. Orda*, 264 N.Y. 248, 190 N.E. 479 (1934) (Uniform Sales Act change in seller's remedies applied to contract for sale of choses in action even though the general coverage of that Act was intentionally limited to goods "other than things in action.") They implemented a statutory policy with liberal and useful remedies not provided in the statutory text. They disregarded a statutory limitation of remedy where the reason of the limitation did not apply. *Fiterman v. J. N. Johnson & Co.*, 156 Minn. 201, 194 N.W. 399 (1923) (requirement of return of the goods as a condition to rescission for breach of warranty; also, partial rescission allowed). Nothing in the Uniform Commercial Code stands in the way of the continuance of such action by the courts.

The Uniform Commercial Code should be construed in accordance with its underlying purposes and policies. The text of each section should be read in the light of the purpose and policy of the rule or principle in question, as also of the Uniform Commercial Code as a whole, and the application of the language should be construed narrowly or broadly, as the case may be, in conformity with the purposes and policies involved.

2. **Applicability of supplemental principles of law.** Subsection (b) states the basic relationship of the Uniform Commercial Code to supplemental bodies of law. The Uniform Commercial Code was drafted against the backdrop of existing bodies of law, including the common law and equity, and relies on those bodies of law to supplement it provisions in many important ways. At the same time, the Uniform

Commercial Code is the primary source of commercial law rules in areas that it governs, and its rules represent choices made by its drafters and the enacting legislatures about the appropriate policies to be furthered in the transactions it covers. Therefore, while principles of common law and equity may *supplement* provisions of the Uniform Commercial Code, they may not be used to *supplant* its provisions, or the purposes and policies those provisions reflect, unless a specific provision of the Uniform Commercial Code provides otherwise. In the absence of such a provision, the Uniform Commercial Code preempts principles of common law and equity that are inconsistent with either its provisions or its purposes and policies.

The language of subsection (b) is intended to reflect both the concept of supplementation and the concept of preemption. Some courts, however, had difficulty in applying the identical language of former Section 1–103 to determine when other law appropriately may be applied to supplement the Uniform Commercial Code, and when that law has been displaced by the Code. Some decisions applied other law in situations in which that application, while not inconsistent with the text of any particular provision of the Uniform Commercial Code, clearly was inconsistent with the underlying purposes and policies reflected in the relevant provisions of the Code. *See, e.g., Sheerbonnet, Ltd. v. American Express Bank, Ltd.*, 951 F. Supp. 403 (S.D.N.Y. 1995). In part, this difficulty arose from Comment 1 to former Section 1–103, which stated that "this section indicates the continued applicability to commercial contracts of all supplemental bodies of law except insofar as they are explicitly displaced by this Act." The "explicitly displaced" language of that Comment did not accurately reflect the proper scope of Uniform Commercial Code preemption, which extends to displacement of other law that is inconsistent with the purposes and policies of the Uniform Commercial Code, as well as with its text.

3. **Application of subsection (b) to statutes.** The primary focus of Section 1–103 is on the relationship between the Uniform Commercial Code and principles of common law and equity as developed by the courts. State law, however, increasingly is statutory. Not only are there a growing number of state statutes addressing specific issues that come within the scope of the Uniform Commercial Code, but in some States many general principles of common law and equity have been codified. When the other law relating to a matter within the scope of the Uniform Commercial Code is a statute, the principles of subsection (b) remain relevant to the court's analysis of the relationship between that statute and the Uniform Commercial Code, but other principles of statutory interpretation that specifically address the interrelationship between statutes will be relevant as well. In some situations, the principles of subsection (b) still will be determinative. For example, the mere fact that an equitable principle is stated in statutory form rather than in judicial decisions should not change the court's analysis of whether the principle can be used to supplement the Uniform Commercial Code–under subsection (b), equitable principles may supplement provisions of the Uniform Commercial Code only if they are consistent with the purposes and policies of the Uniform Commercial Code as well as its text. In other situations, however, other interpretive principles addressing the interrelationship between statutes may lead the court to conclude that the other statute is controlling, even though it conflicts with the Uniform Commercial Code. This, for example, would be the result in a situation where the other statute was specifically intended to provide additional protection to a class of individuals engaging in transactions covered by the Uniform Commercial Code.

4. **Listing not exclusive.** The list of sources of supplemental law in subsection (b) is intended to be merely illustrative of the other law that may supplement the Uniform Commercial Code, and is not exclusive. No listing could be exhaustive. Further, the fact that a particular section of the Uniform Commercial Code makes express reference to other law is not intended to suggest the negation of the general application of the principles of subsection (b). Note also that the word "bankruptcy" in subsection (b), continuing the use of that word from former Section 1–103, should be understood not as a specific reference to federal bankruptcy law but, rather as a reference to general principles of insolvency, whether under federal or state law.

§ 1.104. Construction Against Implied Repeal

This title being a general act intended as a unified coverage of its subject matter, no part of it shall be deemed to be impliedly repealed by subsequent legislation if such construction can reasonably be avoided.

Amended by Acts 2003, 78th Leg., ch. 542, § 1, eff. Sept. 1, 2003.

Uniform Commercial Code Comment

Source: Former Section 1–104.

Changes from former law: Except for changing the form of reference to the Uniform Commercial Code, this section is identical to former Section 1–104.

1. This section embodies the policy that an act that bears evidence of carefully considered permanent regulative intention should not lightly be regarded as impliedly repealed by subsequent legislation. The Uniform Commercial Code, carefully integrated and intended as a uniform codification of permanent character covering an entire "field" of law, is to be regarded as particularly resistant to implied repeal.

§ 1.105. Severability

If any provision or clause of this title or its application to any person or circumstance is held invalid, the invalidity does not affect other provisions or applications of this title which can be given effect without the invalid provision or application, and to this end the provisions of this title are severable.

Amended by Acts 2003, 78th Leg., ch. 542, § 1, eff. Sept. 1, 2003.

Uniform Commercial Code Comment

Source: Former Section 1–108.

Changes from former law: Except for changing the form of reference to the Uniform Commercial Code, this section is identical to former Section 1–108.

1. This is the model severability section recommended by the National Conference of Commissioners on Uniform State Laws for inclusion in all acts of extensive scope.

§ 1.106. Use of Singular and Plural; Gender

In this title, unless the statutory context otherwise requires:

(1) words in the singular number include the plural, and those in the plural include the singular; and

(2) words of any gender also refer to any other gender.

Amended by Acts 2003, 78th Leg., ch. 542, § 1, eff. Sept. 1, 2003.

Uniform Commercial Code Comment

Source: Former Section 1–102(5). See also 1 U.S.C. Section 1.

Changes from former law: Other than minor stylistic changes, this section is identical to former Section 1–102(5).

1. This section makes it clear that the use of singular or plural in the text of the Uniform Commercial Code is generally only a matter of drafting style–singular words may be applied in the plural, and plural words may be applied in the singular. Only when it is clear from the statutory context that the use of the singular or plural does not include the other is this rule inapplicable. *See, e.g.*, Section 9–322.

§ 1.107. Section Captions

Section captions are parts of this title.

Amended by Acts 2003, 78th Leg., ch. 542, § 1, eff. Sept. 1, 2003.

Uniform Commercial Code Comment

Source: Former Section 1–109.

Changes from former law: None.

1. Section captions are a part of the text of the Uniform Commercial Code, and not mere surplusage. This is not the case, however, with respect to subsection headings appearing in Article 9. See Comment 3 to Section 9–101 ("subsection headings are not a part of the official text itself and have not been approved by the sponsors.").

§ 1.108. Relation to Electronic Signatures in Global and National Commerce Act

This title modifies, limits, and supersedes the federal Electronic Signatures in Global and National Commerce Act (15 U.S.C. Section 7001 et seq.) but does not modify, limit, or supersede Section 101(c) of that Act (15 U.S.C. Section 7001(c)) or authorize electronic delivery of any of the notices described in Section 103(b) of that Act (15 U.S.C. Section 7003(b)).

Amended by Acts 2003, 78th Leg., ch. 542, § 1, eff. Sept. 1, 2003.

Uniform Commercial Code Comment

Source: New

1. The federal Electronic Signatures in Global and National Commerce Act, 15 U.S.C. Section 7001 *et seq.* became effective in 2000. Section 102(a) of that Act provides that a State statute may modify, limit, or supersede the provisions of section 101 of that Act with respect to state law if such statute, *inter alia*, specifies the alternative procedures or requirements for the use or acceptance (or both) of electronic records or electronic signatures to establish the legal effect, validity, or enforceability of contracts or other records, and (i) such alternative procedures or requirements are consistent with Titles I and II of that Act, (ii) such alternative procedures or requirements do not require, or accord greater legal status or effect to, the implementation or application of a specific technology or technical specification for performing the functions of creating, storing, generating, receiving, communicating, or authenticating electronic records or electronic signatures; and (iii) if enacted or adopted after the date of the enactment of that Act, makes specific reference to that Act. Article 1 fulfills the first two of those three criteria; this Section fulfills the third criterion listed above.

2. As stated in this section, however, Article 1 does not modify, limit, or supersede Section 101(c) of the Electronic Signatures in Global and National Commerce Act (requiring affirmative consent from a consumer to electronic delivery of transactional disclosures that are required by state law to be in writing); nor does it authorize electronic delivery of any of the notices described in Section 103(b) of that Act.

§ 1.109. Deleted by Acts 2003, 78th Leg., ch. 542, § 1, eff. Sept. 1, 2003

SUBCHAPTER B. GENERAL DEFINITIONS AND PRINCIPLES OF INTERPRETATION

§ 1.201. General Definitions

(a) Unless the context otherwise requires, words or phrases defined in this section, or in the additional definitions contained in other chapters of this title that apply to particular chapters or parts thereof, have the meanings stated.

(b) Subject to definitions contained in other chapters of this title that apply to particular chapters or parts thereof:

(1) "Action," in the sense of a judicial proceeding, includes recoupment, counterclaim, set-off, suit in equity, and any other proceeding in which rights are determined.

(2) "Aggrieved party" means a party entitled to pursue a remedy.

(3) "Agreement," as distinguished from "contract," means the bargain of the parties in fact, as found in their language or inferred from other circumstances, including course of performance, course of dealing, or usage of trade as provided in Section 1.303.

(4) "Bank" means a person engaged in the business of banking and includes a savings bank, savings and loan association, credit union, and trust company.

(5) "Bearer" means a person in control of a negotiable electronic document of title or a person in possession of a negotiable instrument, a negotiable tangible document of title, or a certificated security that is payable to bearer or indorsed in blank.

(6) "Bill of lading" means a document of title evidencing the receipt of goods for shipment issued by a person engaged in the business of directly or indirectly transporting or forwarding goods. The term does not include a warehouse receipt.

(7) "Branch" includes a separately incorporated foreign branch of a bank.

(8) "Burden of establishing" a fact means the burden of persuading the trier of fact that the existence of the fact is more probable than its nonexistence.

(9) "Buyer in ordinary course of business" means a person that buys goods in good faith, without knowledge that the sale violates the rights of another person in the goods, and in the ordinary course from a person, other than a pawnbroker, in the business of selling goods of that kind. A person buys goods in the ordinary course if the sale to the person comports with the usual or customary practices in the kind of business in which the seller is engaged or with the seller's own usual or customary practices. A person that sells oil, gas, or other minerals at the wellhead or minehead is a person in the business of selling goods of that kind. A buyer in ordinary course of business may buy for cash, by exchange of other property, or on secured or unsecured credit, and may acquire goods or documents of title under a preexisting contract for sale. Only a buyer that takes possession of the goods or has a right to recover the goods from the seller under Chapter 2 may be a buyer in ordinary course of business. "Buyer in ordinary course of business" does not include a person that acquires goods in a transfer in bulk or as security for or in total or partial satisfaction of a money debt.

(10) "Conspicuous," with reference to a term, means so written, displayed, or presented that a reasonable person against which it is to operate ought to have noticed it. Whether a term is "conspicuous" or not is a decision for the court. Conspicuous terms include the following:

(A) a heading in capitals equal to or greater in size than the surrounding text, or in contrasting type, font, or color to the surrounding text of the same or lesser size; and

(B) language in the body of a record or display in larger type than the surrounding text, or in contrasting type, font, or color to the surrounding text of the same size, or set off from surrounding text of the same size by symbols or other marks that call attention to the language.

(11) "Consumer" means an individual who enters into a transaction primarily for personal, family, or household purposes.

(12) "Contract," as distinguished from "agreement," means the total legal obligation that results from the parties' agreement as determined by this title as supplemented by any other applicable laws.

(13) "Creditor" includes a general creditor, a secured creditor, a lien creditor and any representative of creditors, including an assignee for the benefit of creditors, a trustee in bankruptcy, a receiver in equity and an executor or administrator of an insolvent debtor's or assignor's estate.

(14) "Defendant" includes a person in the position of defendant in a counterclaim, cross-claim, or third-party claim.

(15) "Delivery," with respect to an electronic document of title, means voluntary transfer of control, and with respect to an instrument, a tangible document of title, or chattel paper, means voluntary transfer of possession.

(16) "Document of title" means a record that in the regular course of business or financing is treated as adequately evidencing that the person in possession or control of the record is entitled to receive, control, hold, and dispose of the record and the goods the record covers, and purports to be issued by or addressed to a bailee and to cover goods in the bailee's possession which are either identified or are fungible portions of an identified mass. The term includes a bill of lading, transport document, dock warrant, dock receipt, warehouse

receipt, and order for delivery of goods. An electronic document of title is evidenced by a record consisting of information stored in an electronic medium. A tangible document of title is evidenced by a record consisting of information that is inscribed on a tangible medium.

(17) "Fault" means a default, breach, or wrongful act or omission.

(18) "Fungible goods" means:

(A) goods of which any unit, by nature or usage of trade, is the equivalent of any other like unit; or

(B) goods that by agreement are treated as equivalent.

(19) "Genuine" means free of forgery or counterfeiting.

(20) "Good faith," except as otherwise provided in Chapter 5, means honesty in fact and the observance of reasonable commercial standards of fair dealing.

(21) "Holder" means:

(A) the person in possession of a negotiable instrument that is payable either to bearer or to an identified person that is the person in possession;

(B) the person in possession of a negotiable tangible document of title if the goods are deliverable either to bearer or to the order of the person in possession; or

(C) a person in control of a negotiable electronic document of title.

(22) "Insolvency proceeding " includes an assignment for the benefit of creditors or other proceeding intended to liquidate or rehabilitate the estate of the person involved.

(23) "Insolvent" means:

(A) having generally ceased to pay debts in the ordinary course of business other than as a result of a bona fide dispute;

(B) being unable to pay debts as they become due; or

(C) being insolvent within the meaning of the federal bankruptcy law.

(24) "Money" means a medium of exchange currently authorized or adopted by a domestic or foreign government. The term includes a monetary unit of account established by an intergovernmental organization or by agreement between two or more countries.

(25) "Organization" means a person other than an individual.

(26) "Party," as distinguished from "third party," means a person that has engaged in a transaction or made an agreement subject to this title.

(27) "Person" means an individual, corporation, business trust, estate, trust, partnership, limited liability company, association, joint venture, government, governmental subdivision, agency, or instrumentality, public corporation, or any other legal or commercial entity.

(28) "Present value" means the amount as of a date certain of one or more sums payable in the future, discounted to the date certain by use of either an interest rate specified by the parties if that rate is not manifestly unreasonable at the time the transaction is entered into or, if an interest rate is not so specified, a commercially reasonable rate that takes into account the facts and circumstances at the time the transaction is entered into.

(29) "Purchase" means taking by sale, lease, discount, negotiation, mortgage, pledge, lien, security interest, issue or reissue, gift, or any other voluntary transaction creating an interest in property.

(30) "Purchaser" means a person that takes by purchase.

(31) "Record" means information that is inscribed on a tangible medium or that is stored in an electronic or other medium and is retrievable in perceivable form.

(32) "Remedy" means any remedial right to which an aggrieved party is entitled with or without resort to a tribunal.

(33) "Representative" means a person empowered to act for another, including an agent, an officer of a corporation or association, and a trustee, executor, or administrator of an estate.

(34) "Right" includes remedy.

(35) "Security interest" means an interest in personal property or fixtures which secures payment or performance of an obligation. "Security interest" includes any interest of a consignor and a buyer of accounts, chattel paper, a payment intangible, or a promissory note in a transaction that is subject to Chapter 9. "Security interest" does not include the special property interest of a buyer of goods on identification of those goods to a contract for sale under Section 2.401, but a buyer may also acquire a "security interest" by complying with Chapter 9. Except as otherwise provided in Section 2.505, the

right of a seller or lessor of goods under Chapter 2 or 2A to retain or acquire possession of the goods is not a "security interest," but a seller or lessor may also acquire a "security interest" by complying with Chapter 9. The retention or reservation of title by a seller of goods notwithstanding shipment or delivery to the buyer under Section 2.401 is limited in effect to a reservation of a "security interest." Whether a transaction in the form of a lease creates a security interest is determined pursuant to Section 1.203.

(36) "Send" in connection with a writing, record, or notice means:

(A) to deposit in the mail or deliver for transmission by any other usual means of communication with postage or cost of transmission provided for and properly addressed and, in the case of an instrument, to an address specified thereon or otherwise agreed, or if there be none to any address reasonable under the circumstances; or

(B) in any other way cause to be received any record or notice within the time at which it would have arrived if properly sent.

(37) "Signed" includes using any symbol executed or adopted with present intention to adopt or accept a writing.

(38) "State" means a State of the United States, the District of Columbia, Puerto Rico, the United States Virgin Islands, or any territory or insular possession subject to the jurisdiction of the United States.

(39) "Surety" includes a guarantor or other secondary obligor.

(40) "Term" means a portion of an agreement that relates to a particular matter.

(41) "Unauthorized signature" means a signature made without actual, implied, or apparent authority. The term includes a forgery.

(42) "Warehouse receipt" means a document of title issued by a person engaged in the business of storing goods for hire.

(43) "Writing" includes printing, typewriting, or any other intentional reduction to tangible form. "Written" has a corresponding meaning.

Amended by Acts 2003, 78th Leg., ch. 542, § 1, eff. Sept. 1, 2003; Acts 2005, 79th Leg., ch. 122, § 2, eff. Sept. 1, 2005.

Uniform Commercial Code Comment

Source: Former Section 1–201.

Changes from former law: In order to make it clear that all definitions in the Uniform Commercial Code (not just those appearing in Article 1, as stated in former Section 1–201, but also those appearing in other Articles) do not apply if the context otherwise requires, a new subsection (a) to that effect has been added, and the definitions now appear in subsection (b). The reference in subsection (a) to the "context" is intended to refer to the context in which the defined term is used in the Uniform Commercial Code. In other words, the definition applies whenever the defined term is used unless the context in which the defined term is used in the statute indicates that the term was not used in its defined sense. Consider, for example, Sections 3–103(a)(9) (defining "promise," in relevant part, as "a written undertaking to pay money signed by the person undertaking to pay") and 3–303(a)(1) (indicating that an instrument is issued or transferred for value if "the instrument is issued or transferred for a promise of performance, to the extent that the promise has been performed.") It is clear from the statutory context of the use of the word "promise" in Section 3–303(a)(1) that the term was not used in the sense of its definition in Section 3–103(a)(9). Thus, the Section 3–103(a)(9) definition should not be used to give meaning to the word "promise" in Section 3–303(a).

Some definitions in former Section 1–201 have been reformulated as substantive provisions and have been moved to other sections. See Sections 1–202 (explicating concepts of notice and knowledge formerly addressed in Sections 1–201(25)-(27)), 1–204 (determining when a person gives value for rights, replacing the definition of "value" in former Section 1–201(44)), and 1–206 (addressing the meaning of presumptions, replacing the definitions of "presumption" and "presumed" in former Section 1–201(31)). Similarly, the portion of the definition of "security interest" in former Section 1–201(37) which explained the difference between a security interest and a lease has been relocated to Section 1–203.

Two definitions in former Section 1–201 have been deleted. The definition of "honor" in former Section 1–201(21) has been moved to Section 2–103(1)(b), inasmuch as the definition only applies to the use of the word in Article 2. The definition of "telegram" in former Section 1–201(41) has been deleted because that word no longer appears in the definition of "conspicuous."

Other than minor stylistic changes and renumbering, the remaining definitions in this section are as in former Article 1 except as noted below.

1. "Action". Unchanged from former Section 1–201, which was derived from similar definitions in Section 191, Uniform Negotiable Instruments Law; Section 76, Uniform Sales Act; Section 58, Uniform Warehouse Receipts Act; Section 53, Uniform Bills of Lading Act.

2. "Aggrieved party". Unchanged from former Section 1–201.

3. "Agreement". Derived from former Section 1–201. As used in the Uniform Commercial Code the word is intended to include full recognition of usage of trade, course of dealing, course of performance and the surrounding circumstances as effective parts thereof, and of any agreement permitted under the provisions of the Uniform Commercial Code to displace a stated rule of law. Whether an agree-

ment has legal consequences is determined by applicable provisions of the Uniform Commercial Code and, to the extent provided in Section 1–103, by the law of contracts.

4. "Bank". Derived from Section 4A–104.

5. "Bearer". Unchanged, except in one respect, from former section 1–201, which was derived from Section 191, Uniform Negotiable Instruments Law. The term bearer applies to negotiable documents of title and has been broadened to include a person in control of an electronic negotiable document of title. Control of an electronic document of title is defined in Article 7 (Section 7–106).

6. "Bill of Lading". Derived from former Section 1–201. The reference to, and definition of, an "airbill" has been deleted as no longer necessary. A bill of lading is one type of document of title as defined in subsection (16). This definition should be read in conjunction with the definition of carrier in Article 7 (Section 7–102).

7. "Branch". Unchanged from former Section 1–201.

8. "Burden of establishing a fact". Unchanged from former Section 1–201.

9. "Buyer in ordinary course of business". Except for minor stylistic changes, identical to former Section 1–201 (as amended in conjunction with the 1999 revisions to Article 9). The major significance of the phrase lies in Section 2–403 and in the Article on Secured Transactions (Article 9).

The first sentence of paragraph (9) makes clear that a buyer from a pawnbroker cannot be a buyer in ordinary course of business. The second sentence explains what it means to buy "in the ordinary course." The penultimate sentence prevents a buyer that does not have the right to possession as against the seller from being a buyer in ordinary course of business. Concerning when a buyer obtains possessory rights, see Sections 2–502 and 2–716. However, the penultimate sentence is not intended to affect a buyer's status as a buyer in ordinary course of business in cases (such as a "drop shipment") involving delivery by the seller to a person buying from the buyer or a donee from the buyer. The requirement relates to whether *as against the seller* the buyer or one taking through the buyer has possessory rights.

10. "Conspicuous". Derived from former Section 1–201(10). This definition states the general standard that to be conspicuous a term ought to be noticed by a reasonable person. Whether a term is conspicuous is an issue for the court. Subparagraphs (A) and (B) set out several methods for making a term conspicuous. Requiring that a term be conspicuous blends a notice function (the term ought to be noticed) and a planning function (giving guidance to the party relying on the term regarding how that result can be achieved). Although these paragraphs indicate some of the methods for making a term attention-calling, the test is whether attention can reasonably be expected to be called to it. The statutory language should not be construed to permit a result that is inconsistent with that test.

11. "Consumer". Derived from Section 9–102(a)(25).

12. "Contract". Except for minor stylistic changes, identical to former Section 1–201.

13. "Creditor". Unchanged from former Section 1–201.

14. "Defendant". Except for minor stylistic changes, identical to former Section 1–201, which was derived from Section 76, Uniform Sales Act.

15. "Delivery". Derived from former Section 1–201. The reference to certificated securities has been deleted in light of the more specific treatment of the matter in Section 8–301. The definition has been revised to accommodate electronic documents of title. Control of an electronic document of title is defined in Article 7 (Section 7–106).

16. "Document of title". Derived from former Section 1–201, which was derived from Section 76, Uniform Sales Act. This definition makes explicit that the obligation or designation of a third party as "bailee" is essential to a document of title and clearly rejects any such result as obtained in Hixson v. Ward, 254 Ill.App. 505 (1929), which treated a conditional sales contract as a document of title. Also the definition is left open so that new types of documents may be included, including documents which gain commercial recognition in the international arena. See UNCITRAL Draft Instrument on the Carriage of Goods By Sea. It is unforeseeable what documents may one day serve the essential purpose now filled by warehouse receipts and bills of lading. The definition is stated in terms of the function of the documents with the intention that any document which gains commercial recognition as accomplishing the desired result shall be included within its scope. Fungible goods are adequately identified within the language of the definition by identification of the mass of which they are a part.

Dock warrants were within the Sales Act definition of document of title apparently for the purpose of recognizing a valid tender by means of such paper. In current commercial practice a dock warrant or receipt is a kind of interim certificate issued by shipping companies upon delivery of the goods at the dock, entitling a designated person to be issued a bill of lading. The receipt itself is invariably nonnegotiable in form although it may indicate that a negotiable bill is to be forthcoming. Such a document is not within the general compass of the definition, although trade usage may in some cases entitle such paper to be treated as a document of title. If the dock receipt actually represents a storage obligation undertaken by the shipping company, then it is a warehouse receipt within this Section regardless of the name given to the instrument.

The goods must be "described", but the description may be by marks or labels and may be qualified in such a way as to disclaim personal knowledge of the issuer regarding contents or condition. However, baggage and parcel checks and similar "tokens" of storage which identify stored goods only as those received in exchange for the token are not covered by this Article. The definition is broad enough to include an airway bill.

A document of title may be either tangible or electronic. Tangible documents of title should be construed to mean traditional paper documents. Electronic documents of title are documents that are stored in an electronic medium instead of in tangible form. The concept of an electronic medium should be construed liberally to include electronic, digital, magnetic, optical, electromagnetic, or any other current or similar emerging technologies. As to reissuing a document of title in an alternative medium, see Article 7,

Section 7–105. Control for electronic documents of title is defined in Article 7 (Section 7–106).

17. "Fault". Derived from former Section 1–201. "Default" has been added to the list of events constituting fault.

18. "Fungible goods". Derived from former Section 1–201. References to securities have been deleted because Article 8 no longer uses the term "fungible" to describe securities. Accordingly, this provision now defines the concept only in the context of goods.

19. "Genuine". Unchanged from former Section 1–201.

20. "Good faith". Former Section 1–201(19) defined "good faith" simply as honesty in fact; the definition contained no element of commercial reasonableness. Initially, that definition applied throughout the Code with only one exception. Former Section 2–103(1)(b) provided that in that Article, " 'good faith' in the case of a merchant means honesty in fact and the observance of reasonable commercial standards of fair dealing in the trade." This alternative definition was limited in applicability, though because it applied only to transactions within the scope of Article 2 and it applied only to merchants.

Over time, however, amendments to the Uniform Commercial Code brought the Article 2 merchant concept of good faith (subjective honesty and objective commercial reasonableness) into other Articles. First, Article 2A explicitly incorporated the Article 2 standard. See Section 2A–103(7). Then, other Articles broadened the applicability of that standard by adopting it for all parties rather than just for merchants. *See, e.g.*, Sections 3–103(a)(4), 4A–105(a)(6), 8–102(a)(10), and 9–102(a)(43). Finally, Articles 2 and 2A were amended so as to apply the standard to non-merchants as well as merchants. See Sections 2–103(1)(j), 2A–103(1)(m). All of these definitions are comprised of two elements–honesty in fact *and* the observance of reasonable commercial standards of fair dealing. Only revised Article 5 defines "good faith" solely in terms of subjective honesty, and only Article 6 (in the few states that have not chosen to delete the Article) is without a definition of good faith. (It should be noted that, while revised Article 6 did not define good faith, Comment 2 to revised Section 6–102 states that "this Article adopts the definition of 'good faith' in Article 1 in all cases, even when the buyer is a merchant.")

Thus, the definition of "good faith" in this section merely confirms what has been the case for a number of years as Articles of the UCC have been amended or revised–the obligation of "good faith," applicable in each Article, is to be interpreted in the context of all Articles except for Article 5 as including both the subjective element of honesty in fact and the objective element of the observance of reasonable commercial standards of fair dealing. As a result, both the subjective and objective elements are part of the standards of "good faith," whether that obligation is specifically referenced in another Article of the Code (other than Article 5) or is provided by this Article.

Of course, as noted in the statutory text, the definition of "good faith" in this section does not apply when the narrower definition of "good faith" in revised Article 5 is applicable.

As noted above, the definition of "good faith" in this section requires not only honesty in fact but also "observance of reasonable commercial standards of fair dealing." Although "fair dealing" is a broad term that must be defined in context, it is clear that it is concerned with the fairness of conduct rather than the care with which an act is performed. This is an entirely different concept than whether a party exercised ordinary care in conducting a transaction. Both concepts are to be determined in the light of reasonable commercial standards, but those standards in each case are directed to different aspects of commercial conduct. See e.g., Sections 3–103(a)(9) and 4–104(c) and Comment 4 to Section 3–103.

21. "Holder". Derived from former Section 1–201. The definition has been reorganized for clarity and amended to provide for electronic negotiable documents of title.

22. "Insolvency proceedings". Unchanged from former Section 1–201.

23. "Insolvent". Derived from former Section 1–201. The three tests of insolvency–"generally ceased to pay debts in the ordinary course of business other than as a result of a bona fide dispute as to them," "unable to pay debts as they become due," and "insolvent within the meaning of the federal bankruptcy law" are expressly set up as alternative tests and must be approached from a commercial standpoint.

24. "Money". Substantively identical to former Section 1–201. The test is that of sanction of government, whether by authorization before issue or adoption afterward, which recognizes the circulating medium as a part of the official currency of that government. The narrow view that money is limited to legal tender is rejected.

25. "Organization". The former definition of this word has been replaced with the standard definition used in acts prepared by the National Conference of Commissioners on Uniform State Laws.

26. "Party". Substantively identical to former Section 1–201. Mention of a party includes, of course, a person acting through an agent. However, where an agent comes into opposition or contrast to the principal, particular account is taken of that situation.

27. "Person". The former definition of this word has been replaced with the standard definition used in acts prepared by the National Conference of Commissioners on Uniform State Laws.

28. "Present value". This definition was formerly contained within the definition of "security interest" in former Section 1–201(37).

29. "Purchase". Derived from former Section 1–201. The form of definition has been changed from "includes" to "means."

30. "Purchaser". Unchanged from former Section 1–201.

31. "Record". Derived from Section 9–102(a)(69).

32. "Remedy". Unchanged from former Section 1–201. The purpose is to make it clear that both remedy and right (as defined) include those remedial rights of "self help" which are among the most important bodies of rights under the Uniform Commercial Code, remedial rights being those to which an aggrieved party may resort on its own.

33. "Representative". Derived from former Section 1–201. Reorganized, and form changed from "includes" to "means."

34. "Right". Except for minor stylistic changes, identical to former Section 1–201.

35. "Security Interest". The definition is the first paragraph of the definition of "security interest" in former Section 1–201, with minor stylistic changes. The remaining portion of that definition has been moved to Section 1–203. Note that, because of the scope of Article 9, the term includes the interest of certain outright buyers of certain kinds of property.

36. "Send". Derived from former Section 1–201. Compare "notifies".

37. "Signed". Derived from former Section 1–201. Former Section 1–201 referred to "intention to authenticate"; because other articles now use the term "authenticate," the language has been changed to "intention to adopt or accept." The latter formulation is derived from the definition of "authenticate" in Section 9–102(a)(7). This provision refers only to writings, because the term "signed," as used in some articles, refers only to writings. This provision also makes it clear that, as the term "signed" is used in the Uniform Commercial Code, a complete signature is not necessary. The symbol may be printed, stamped or written; it may be by initials or by thumbprint. It may be on any part of the document and in appropriate cases may be found in a billhead or letterhead. No catalog of possible situations can be complete and the court must use common sense and commercial experience in passing upon these matters. The question always is whether the symbol was executed or adopted by the party with present intention to adopt or accept the writing.

38. "State". This is the standard definition of the term used in acts prepared by the National Conference of Commissioners on Uniform State Laws.

39. "Surety". This definition makes it clear that "surety" includes all secondary obligors,not just those whose obligation refers to the person obligated as a surety. As to the nature of secondary obligations generally, see Restatement (Third), Suretyship and Guaranty Section 1 (1996).

40. "Term". Unchanged from former Section 1–201.

41. "Unauthorized signature". Unchanged from former Section 1–201.

42. "Warehouse receipt". Derived from former Section 1–201, which was derived from Section 76(1), Uniform Sales Act; Section 1, Uniform Warehouse Receipts Act. Receipts issued by a field warehouse are included, provided the warehouseman and the depositor of the goods are different persons. The definition makes clear that the receipt must qualify as a document of title under subsection (16).

43. "Written" or "writing". Unchanged from former Section 1–201.

Sections 31 and 32 of Acts 2005, 79th Leg., ch. 122 provide:

"Sec. 31. This Act applies to a document of title that is issued or a bailment that arises on or after the effective date of this Act. This Act does not apply to a document of title that is issued or a bailment that arises before the effective date of this Act even if the document of title or bailment would be subject to this Act if the document of title had been issued or bailment had arisen after the effective date of this Act. This Act does not apply to a right of action that has accrued before the effective date of this Act.

"Sec. 32. A document of title issued or a bailment that arises before the effective date of this Act and the rights, obligations, and interests flowing from that document or bailment are governed by any statute or other rule amended or repealed by this Act as if amendment or repeal had not occurred and may be terminated, completed, consummated, or enforced under that statute or other rule."

§ 1.202. Notice; Knowledge

(a) Subject to Subsection (f), a person has "notice" of a fact if the person:

(1) has actual knowledge of it;

(2) has received a notice or notification of it; or

(3) from all the facts and circumstances known to the person at the time in question, has reason to know that it exists.

(b) "Knowledge" means actual knowledge. "Knows" has a corresponding meaning.

(c) "Discover," "learn," or words of similar import refer to knowledge rather than to reason to know.

(d) A person "notifies" or "gives" a notice or notification to another person by taking such steps as may be reasonably required to inform the other person in ordinary course, whether or not the other person actually comes to know of it.

(e) Subject to Subsection (f), a person "receives" a notice or notification when:

(1) it comes to that person's attention; or

(2) it is duly delivered in a form reasonable under the circumstances at the place of business through which the contract was made or at another location held out by that person as the place for receipt of such communications.

(f) Notice, knowledge, or a notice or notification received by an organization is effective for a particular transaction from the time it is brought to the attention of the individual conducting that transaction and, in any event, from the time it would have been brought to the individual's attention if the organization had exercised due diligence. An organization exercises due diligence if it maintains reasonable routines for communicating significant information to the person conducting the transaction and there is reasonable compliance with the routines. Due diligence does not require an individual acting for the organization to communicate information unless the communication is part of the individual's regular duties or the individual has reason to know of the transaction and that the transaction would be materially affected by the information.

Amended by Acts 2003, 78th Leg., ch. 542, § 1, eff. Sept. 1, 2003.

Uniform Commercial Code Comment

Source: Derived from former Section 1–201(25)-(27).

Changes from former law: These provisions are substantive rather than purely definitional. Accordingly, they have been relocated from Section 1–201 to this section. The reference to the "forgotten notice" doctrine has been deleted.

1. Under subsection (a), a person has notice of a fact when, *inter alia*, the person has received a notification of the fact in question.

2. As provided in subsection (d), the word "notifies" is used when the essential fact is the proper dispatch of the notice, not its receipt. Compare "Send." When the essential fact is the other party's receipt of the notice, that is stated. Subsection (e) states when a notification is received.

3. Subsection (f) makes clear that notice, knowledge, or a notification, although "received," for instance, by a clerk in Department A of an organization, is effective for a transaction conducted in Department B only from the time when it was or should have been communicated to the individual conducting that transaction.

§ 1.203. Lease Distinguished From Security Interest

(a) Whether a transaction in the form of a lease creates a lease or security interest is determined by the facts of each case.

(b) A transaction in the form of a lease creates a security interest if the consideration that the lessee is to pay the lessor for the right to possession and use of the goods is an obligation for the term of the lease and is not subject to termination by the lessee, and:

(1) the original term of the lease is equal to or greater than the remaining economic life of the goods;

(2) the lessee is bound to renew the lease for the remaining economic life of the goods or is bound to become the owner of the goods;

(3) the lessee has an option to renew the lease for the remaining economic life of the goods for no additional consideration or for nominal additional consideration upon compliance with the lease agreement; or

(4) the lessee has an option to become the owner of the goods for no additional consideration or for nominal additional consideration upon compliance with the lease agreement.

(c) A transaction in the form of a lease does not create a security interest merely because:

(1) the present value of the consideration the lessee is obligated to pay the lessor for the right to possession and use of the goods is substantially equal to or is greater than the fair market value of the goods at the time the lease is entered into;

(2) the lessee assumes risk of loss of the goods;

(3) the lessee agrees to pay, with respect to the goods, taxes, insurance, filing, recording, or registration fees, or service or maintenance costs;

(4) the lessee has an option to renew the lease or to become the owner of the goods;

(5) the lessee has an option to renew the lease for a fixed rent that is equal to or greater than the reasonably predictable fair market rent for the use of the goods for the term of the renewal at the time the option is to be performed; or

(6) the lessee has an option to become the owner of the goods for a fixed price that is equal to or greater than the reasonably predictable fair market value of the goods at the time the option is to be performed.

(d) Additional consideration is nominal if it is less than the lessee's reasonably predictable cost of performing under the lease agreement if the option is not exercised. Additional consideration is not nominal if:

(1) when the option to renew the lease is granted to the lessee, the rent is stated to be the fair market rent for the use of the goods for the term of the renewal determined at the time the option is to be performed; or

(2) when the option to become the owner of the goods is granted to the lessee, the price is stated to be the fair market value of the goods determined at the time the option is to be performed.

(e) The "remaining economic life of the goods" and "reasonably predictable" fair market rent, fair market value, or cost of performing under the lease agreement must be determined with reference to the facts and circumstances at the time the transaction is entered into.

Amended by Acts 2003, 78th Leg., ch. 542, § 1, eff. Sept. 1, 2003.

Uniform Commercial Code Comment

Source: Former Section 1–201(37).

Changes from former law: This section is substantively identical to those portions of former Section 1–201(37) that distinguished "true" leases from security interests, except that the definition of "present value" formerly embedded in Section 1–201(37) has been placed in Section 1–201(28).

1. An interest in personal property or fixtures which secures payment or performance of an obligation is a "security interest." See Section 1–201(37). Security interests are sometimes created by transactions in the form of leases. Because it can be difficult to distinguish leases that create security interests from those that do not, this section provides rules that govern the determination of whether a transaction in the form of a lease creates a security interest.

2. One of the reasons it was decided to codify the law with respect to leases was to resolve an issue that created considerable confusion in the courts: what is a lease? The confusion existed, in part, due to the last two sentences of the definition of security interest in the 1978 Official Text of the Act, Section 1–201(37). The confusion was compounded by the rather considerable change in the federal, state and local tax laws and accounting rules as they relate to leases of goods. The answer is important because the definition of lease determines not only the rights and remedies of the parties to the lease but also those of third parties. If a transaction creates a lease and not a security interest, the lessee's interest in the goods is limited to its leasehold estate; the residual interest in the goods belongs to the lessor. This has significant implications to the lessee's creditors. "On common law theory, the lessor, since he has not parted with title, is entitled to full protection against the lessee's creditors and trustee in bankruptcy . . . . " 1 G. Gilmore, *Security Interests in Personal Property* Section 3.6, at 76 (1965).

Under pre-UCC chattel security law there was generally no requirement that the lessor file the lease, a financing statement, or the like, to enforce the lease agreement against the lessee or any third party; the Article on Secured Transactions (Article 9) did not change the common law in that respect. Coogan, Leasing and the Uniform Commercial Code, in *Equipment Leasing—Leveraged Leasing* 681, 700 n.25, 729 n.80 (2d ed.1980). The Article on Leases (Article 2A) did not change the law in that respect, except for leases of fixtures. Section 2A–309. An examination of the common law will not provide an adequate answer to the question of what is a lease. The definition of security interest in Section 1–201(37) of the 1978 Official Text of the Act provided that the Article on Secured Transactions (Article 9) governs security interests disguised as leases, *i.e.*, leases intended as security; however, the definition became vague and outmoded.

Lease is defined in Article 2A as a transfer of the right to possession and use of goods for a term, in return for consideration. Section 2A–103(1)(j). The definition continues by stating that the retention or creation of a security interest is not a lease. Thus, the task of sharpening the line between true leases and security interests disguised as leases continues to be a function of this Article.

This section begins where Section 1–201(35) leaves off. It draws a sharper line between leases and security interests disguised as leases to create greater certainty in commercial transactions.

Prior to enactment of the rules now codified in this section, the 1978 Official Text of Section 1–201(37) provided that whether a lease was intended as security (*i.e.*, a security interest disguised as a lease) was to be determined from the facts of each case; however, (a) the inclusion of an option to purchase did not itself make the lease one intended for security, and (b) an agreement that upon compliance with the terms of the lease the lessee would become, or had the option to become, the owner of the property for no additional consideration, or for a nominal consideration, did make the lease one intended for security.

Reference to the intent of the parties to create a lease or security interest led to unfortunate results. In discovering intent, courts relied upon factors that were thought to be more consistent with sales or loans than leases. Most of these criteria, however, were as applicable to true leases as to security interests. Examples include the typical net lease provisions, a purported lessor's lack of storage facilities or its character as a financing party rather than a dealer in goods. Accordingly, this section contains no reference to the parties' intent.

Subsections (a) and (b) were originally taken from Section 1(2) of the Uniform Conditional Sales Act (act withdrawn 1943), modified to reflect current leasing practice. Thus, reference to the case law prior to the incorporation of those concepts in this article will provide a useful source of precedent. Gilmore, *Security Law, Formalism and Article 9*, 47 Neb.L.Rev. 659, 671 (1968). Whether a transaction creates a lease or a security interest continues to be determined by the facts of each case. Subsection (b) further provides that a transaction creates a security interest if the lessee has an obligation to continue paying consideration for the term of the lease, if the obligation is not terminable by the lessee (thus correcting early statutory gloss, *e.g.*, *In re Royer's Bakery, Inc.*, 1 U.C.C. Rep.Serv. (Callaghan) 342 (Bankr. E.D.Pa.1963)) and if one of four additional tests is met. The first of these four tests, subparagraph (1), is that the original lease term is equal to or greater than the remaining economic life of the goods. The second of these tests, subparagraph (2), is that the lessee is either bound to renew the lease for the remaining economic life of the goods or to become the owner of the goods. *In re Gehrke Enters.*, 1 Bankr. 647, 651–52 (Bankr.W.D.Wis.1979). The third of these tests, subparagraph (3), is whether the lessee has an option to renew the lease for the remaining economic life of the goods for no additional consideration or for nominal additional consideration, which is defined later in this section. *In re Celeryvale Transp.*, 44 Bankr. 1007, 1014–15 (Bankr.E.D.Tenn.1984). The fourth of these tests, subparagraph (4), is whether the lessee has an option to become the owner of the goods for no additional consideration or for nominal additional consideration. All of these tests focus on economics, not the intent of the parties. *In re Berge*, 32 Bankr. 370, 371–73 (Bankr. W.D.Wis.1983).

The focus on economics is reinforced by subsection (c). It states that a transaction does not create a security interest merely because the transaction has certain characteristics listed therein. Subparagraph (1) has no statutory derivative; it states that a full payout lease does not *per se* create a security interest. *Rushton v. Shea*, 419 F.Supp. 1349, 1365 (D.Del.1976). Subparagraphs (2) and (3) provide the same regarding the provisions of the typical net lease. *Compare All–States Leasing Co. v. Ochs*, 42 Or.App. 319, 600 P.2d 899(Ct.App.1979), *with In re Tillery*, 571 F.2d 1361 (5th Cir.1978). Subparagraph (4) restates and expands the provisions of the 1978 Official Text of Section 1–201(37) to make clear that the option can be to buy or renew. Subparagraphs (5) and (6) treat fixed price options and provide that fair market value must be determined at the time the transaction is entered into. *Compare Arnold Mach. Co. v. Balls*, 624 P.2d 678 (Utah 1981), *with Aoki v. Shepherd Mach. Co.*, 665 F.2d 941 (9th Cir.1982).

The relationship of subsection (b) to subsection (c) deserves to be explored. The fixed price purchase option provides a useful example. A fixed price purchase option in a lease does not of itself create a security interest. This is particularly true if the fixed price is equal to or greater than the reasonably predictable fair market value of the goods at the time the option is to be performed. A security interest is created only if the option price is nominal and the conditions stated in the introduction to the second paragraph of this subsection are met. There is a set of purchase options whose fixed price is less than fair market value but greater than nominal that must be determined on the facts of each case to ascertain whether the transaction in which the option is included creates a lease or a security interest.

It was possible to provide for various other permutations and combinations with respect to options to purchase and renew. For example, this section could have stated a rule to govern the facts of *In re Marhoefer Packing Co.*, 674 F.2d 1139 (7th Cir.1982). This was not done because it would unnecessarily complicate the definition. Further development of this rule is left to the courts.

Subsections (d) and (e) provide definitions and rules of construction.

§ 1.204. Value

Except as otherwise provided in Chapters 3, 4, and 5, a person gives value for rights if the person acquires them:

(1) in return for a binding commitment to extend credit or for the extension of immediately available credit, whether or not drawn upon and whether or not a charge-back is provided for in the event of difficulties in collection;

(2) as security for, or in total or partial satisfaction of, a preexisting claim;

(3) by accepting delivery under a preexisting contract for purchase; or

(4) in return for any consideration sufficient to support a simple contract.

Amended by Acts 2003, 78th Leg., ch. 542, § 1, eff. Sept. 1, 2003.

Official Comments

Source: Former Section 1–201(44).

Changes from former law: Unchanged from former Section 1–201, which was derived from Sections 25, 26, 27, 191, Uniform Negotiable Instruments Law; Section 76, Uniform Sales Act; Section 53, Uniform Bills of Lading Act; Section 58, Uniform Warehouse Receipts Act; Section 22(1), Uniform Stock Transfer Act; Section 1, Uniform Trust Receipts Act. These provisions are substantive rather than purely definitional. Accordingly, they have been relocated from former Section 1–201 to this section.

1. All the Uniform Acts in the commercial law field (except the Uniform Conditional Sales Act) have carried definitions of "value." All those definitions provided that value was any consideration sufficient to support a simple contract, including the taking of property in satisfaction of or as security for a pre-existing claim. Subsections (1), (2), and (4) in substance continue the definitions of "value" in the earlier acts. Subsection (3) makes explicit that "value" is also given in a third situation: where a buyer by taking delivery under a pre-existing contract converts a contingent into a fixed obligation.

This definition is not applicable to Articles 3 and 4, but the express inclusion of immediately available credit as value follows the separate definitions in those Articles. See Sections 4–208, 4–209, 3–303. A bank or other financing agency which in good faith makes advances against property held as collateral becomes a bona fide purchaser of that property even though provision may be made for charge-back in case of trouble. Checking credit is "immediately available" within the meaning of this section if the bank would be subject to an action for slander of credit in case checks drawn against the credit were dishonored, and when a charge-back is not discretionary with the bank, but may only be made when difficulties in collection arise in connection with the specific transaction involved.

§ 1.205. Reasonable Time; Seasonableness

(a) Whether a time for taking an action required by this title is reasonable depends on the nature, purpose, and circumstances of the action.

(b) An action is taken seasonably if it is taken at or within the time agreed or, if no time is agreed, at or within a reasonable time.

Amended by Acts 2003, 78th Leg., ch. 542, § 1, eff. Sept. 1, 2003.

Uniform Commercial Code Comment

Source: Former Section 1–204(2)-(3).

Changes from former law: This section is derived from subsections (2) and (3) of former Section 1–204. Subsection (1) of that section is now incorporated in Section 1–302(b).

1. Subsection (a) makes it clear that requirements that actions be taken within a "reasonable" time are to be applied in the transactional context of the particular action.

2. Under subsection (b), the agreement that fixes the time need not be part of the main agreement, but may occur separately. Notice also that under the definition of "agreement" (Section 1–201) the circumstances of the transaction, including course of dealing or usages of trade or course of performance may be material. On the question what is a reasonable time these matters will often be important.

§ 1.206. Presumptions

Whenever this title creates a "presumption" with respect to a fact, or provides that a fact is "presumed," the trier of fact must find the existence of the fact unless and until evidence is introduced that supports a finding of its nonexistence.

Amended by Acts 2003, 78th Leg., ch. 542, § 1, eff. Sept. 1, 2003.

Uniform Commercial Code Comment

Source: Former Section 1–201(31).

Changes from former law. None, other than stylistic changes.

1. Several sections of the Uniform Commercial Code state that there is a "presumption" as to a certain fact, or that the fact is "presumed." This section, derived from the definition appearing in former Section 1–201(31), indicates the effect of those provisions on the proof process.

§§ 1.207, 1.208. Deleted by Acts 2003, 78th Leg., ch. 542, § 1, eff. Sept. 1, 2003

SUBCHAPTER C. TERRITORIAL APPLICABILITY AND GENERAL RULES

§ 1.301. Territorial Application of the Title; Parties' Power to Choose Applicable Law

(a) Except as provided hereafter in this section, when a transaction bears a reasonable relation to this state and also to another state or nation the parties may agree that the law either of this state or of such other state or nation shall govern their rights and duties. Failing such agreement this title applies to transactions bearing an appropriate relation to this state.

(b) Where one of the following provisions of this title specifies the applicable law, that provision governs and a contrary agreement is effective only to the extent permitted by the law (including the conflict of laws rules) so specified:

Rights of creditors against sold goods. Section 2.402.

Applicability of the chapter on Leases. Sections 2A.105 and 2A.106.

Applicability of the chapter on Bank Deposits and Collections. Section 4.102.

Governing law in the chapter on Funds Transfers. Section 4A.507.

Letters of Credit. Section 5.116.

Applicability of the chapter on Investment Securities. Section 8.110.

Law governing perfection, the effect of perfection or nonperfection, and the priority of security interests and agricultural liens. Sections 9.301–9.307.

Text of subsec. (c) effective until April 1, 2009

(c) If a transaction that is subject to this title is a "qualified transaction," as defined in Section 35.51 of this code, then except as provided in Subsection (b) of this section, Section 35.51 governs the effect of an agreement by the parties that the law of a particular jurisdiction governs an issue relating to the transaction or that the law of a particular jurisdiction governs the interpretation or construction of an agreement relating to the transaction or a provision of the agreement.

Text of subsec. (c) effective April 1, 2009

(c) If a transaction that is subject to this title is a "qualified transaction," as defined in Section 271.001, then except as provided in Subsection (b) of this section, Chapter 271 governs the effect of an agreement by the parties that the law of a particular jurisdiction governs an issue relating to the transaction or that the law of a particular jurisdiction governs the interpretation or construction of an agreement relating to the transaction or a provision of the agreement.

Added by Acts 2003, 78th Leg., ch. 542, § 1, eff. Sept. 1, 2003. Amended by Acts 2007, 80th Leg., ch. 885, § 2.02, eff. April 1, 2009.

Uniform Commercial Code Comment

Prior Uniform Statutory Provision:

None.

Purposes:

1. Subsection (1) states affirmatively the right of the parties to a multi-state transaction or a transaction involving foreign trade to choose their own law. That right is subject to the firm rules stated in the five sections listed in subsection (2), and is limited to jurisdictions to which the transaction bears a "reasonable relation." In general, the test of "reasonable relation" is similar to that laid down by the Supreme Court in Seeman v. Philadelphia Warehouse Co., 274 U.S. 403, 47 S.Ct. 626, 71 L.Ed. 1123 (1927). Ordinarily the law chosen must be that of a jurisdiction where a significant enough portion of the making or performance of the contract is to occur or occurs. But an agreement as to choice of law may sometimes take effect as a shorthand expression of the intent of the parties as to matters governed by their agreement, even though the transaction has no significant contact with the jurisdiction chosen.

2. Where there is no agreement as to the governing law, the Act is applicable to any transaction having an "appropriate" relation to any state which enacts it. Of course, the Act applies to any transaction which takes place in its entirety in a state which has enacted the Act. But the mere fact that suit is brought in a state does not make it appropriate to apply the substantive law of that state. Cases where a relation to the enacting state is not "appropriate" include, for example, those where the parties have clearly contracted on the basis of some other law, as where the law of the place of contracting and the law of the place of contemplated performance are the same and are contrary to the law under the Code.

3. Where a transaction has significant contacts with a state which has enacted the Act and also with other jurisdictions, the question what relation is "appropriate" is left to judicial decision. In deciding that question, the court is not strictly bound by precedents established in other contexts. Thus a conflict-of-laws decision refusing to apply a purely local statute or rule of law to a particular multi-state transaction may not be valid precedent for refusal to apply the Code in an analogous situation. Application of the Code in such circumstances may be justified by its comprehensiveness, by the policy of uniformity, and by the fact that it is in large part a reformulation and restatement of the law merchant and of the understanding of a business community which transcends state and even national boundaries. Compare Global Commerce Corp. v. Clark-Babbitt Industries, Inc., 239 F.2d 716, 719 (2d Cir. 1956). In particular, where a transaction is governed in large part by the Code, application of another law to some detail of performance because of an accident of geography may violate the commercial understanding of the parties.

4. The Act does not attempt to prescribe choice-of-law rules for states which do not enact it, but this section does not prevent application of the Act in a court of such a state. Common-law choice of law often rests on policies of giving effect to agreements and of uniformity of result regardless of where suit is brought. To the extent that such policies prevail, the relevant considerations are similar in such a court to those outlined above.

5. Subsection (2) spells out essential limitations on the parties' right to choose the applicable law. Especially in Article 9 parties taking a security interest or asked to extend credit which may be subject to a security interest must have sure ways to find out whether and where to file and where to look for possible existing filings.

6. Sections 9–301 through 9–307 should be consulted as to the rules for perfection of security interests and agricultural liens, the effect of perfection and nonperfection, and priority.

§ 1.302. Variation by Agreement

(a) Except as otherwise provided in Subsection (b) or elsewhere in this title, the effect of provisions of this title may be varied by agreement.

(b) The obligations of good faith, diligence, reasonableness, and care prescribed by this title may not be disclaimed by agreement. The parties, by agreement, may determine the standards by which the performance of those obligations is to be measured if those standards are not manifestly unreasonable. Whenever this title requires an action to be taken within a reasonable time, a time that is not manifestly unreasonable may be fixed by agreement.

(c) The presence in certain provisions of this title of the phrase "unless otherwise agreed," or words of similar import, does not imply that the effect of other provisions may not be varied by agreement under this section.

Added by Acts 2003, 78th Leg., ch. 542, § 1, eff. Sept. 1, 2003.

Uniform Commercial Code Comment

Source: Former Sections 1–102(3)-(4) and 1–204(1).

Changes: This section combines the rules from subsections (3) and (4) of former Section 1–102 and subsection (1) of former Section 1–204. No substantive changes are made.

1. Subsection (a) states affirmatively at the outset that freedom of contract is a principle of the Uniform Commercial Code: "the effect" of its provisions may be varied by "agreement." The meaning of the statute itself must be found in its text, including its definitions, and in appropriate extrinsic aids; it cannot be varied by agreement. But the Uniform Commercial Code seeks to avoid the type of interference with evolutionary growth found in pre-Code cases such as *Manhattan Co. v. Morgan*, 242 N.Y. 38, 150 N.E. 594 (1926). Thus, private parties cannot make an instrument negotiable within the meaning of Article 3 except as provided in Section 3–104; nor can they change the meaning of such terms as "bona fide purchaser," "holder in due course," or "due negotiation," as used in the Uniform Commercial Code. But an agreement can change the legal consequences that would otherwise flow from the provisions of the Uniform Commercial Code. "Agreement" here includes the effect given to course of dealing, usage of trade and course of performance by Sections 1–201 and 1–303; the effect of an agreement on the rights of third parties is left to specific provisions of the Uniform Commercial Code and to supplementary principles applicable under Section 1–103. The rights of third parties under Section 9–317 when a security interest is unperfected, for example, cannot be destroyed by a clause in the security agreement.

This principle of freedom of contract is subject to specific exceptions found elsewhere in the Uniform Commercial Code and to the general exception stated here. The specific exceptions vary in explicitness: the statute of frauds found in Section 2–201, for example, does not explicitly preclude oral waiver of the requirement of a writing, but a fair reading denies enforcement to such a waiver as part of the "contract" made unenforceable; Section 9–602, on the other hand, is a quite explicit limitation on freedom of contract. Under the exception for "the obligations of good faith, diligence, reasonableness and care prescribed by [the Uniform Commercial Code]," provisions of the Uniform Commercial Code prescribing such obligations are not to be disclaimed. However, the section also recognizes the prevailing practice of having agreements set forth standards by which due diligence is measured and explicitly provides that, in the absence of a showing that the standards manifestly are unreasonable, the agreement controls. In this connection, Section 1–303 incorporating into the agreement prior course of dealing and usages of trade is of particular importance.

Subsection (b) also recognizes that nothing is stronger evidence of a reasonable time than the fixing of such time by a fair agreement between the parties. However, provision is made for disregarding a clause which whether by inadvertence or overreaching fixes a time so unreasonable that it amounts to eliminating all remedy under the contract. The parties are not required to fix the most reasonable time but may fix any time which is not obviously unfair as judged by the time of contracting.

2. An agreement that varies the effect of provisions of the Uniform Commercial Code may do so by stating the rules that will govern in lieu of the provisions varied. Alternatively, the parties may vary the effect of such provisions by stating that their relationship will be governed by recognized bodies of rules or principles applicable to commercial transactions. Such bodies of rules or principles may include, for example, those that are promulgated by intergovernmental authorities such as UNCITRAL or Unidroit (*see, e.g.*, Unidroit Principles of International Commercial Contracts), or non-legal codes such as trade codes.

3. Subsection (c) is intended to make it clear that, as a matter of drafting, phrases such as "unless otherwise agreed" have been used to avoid controversy as to whether the subject matter of a particular section does or does not fall within the exceptions to subsection (b), but absence of such words contains no negative implication since under subsection (b) the general and residual rule is that the effect of all provisions of the Uniform Commercial Code may be varied by agreement.

§ 1.303. Course of Performance, Course of Dealing, and Usage of Trade

(a) A "course of performance" is a sequence of conduct between the parties to a particular transaction that exists if:

(1) the agreement of the parties with respect to the transaction involves repeated occasions for performance by a party; and

(2) the other party, with knowledge of the nature of the performance and opportunity for objection to it, accepts the performance or acquiesces in it without objection.

(b) A course of dealing is a sequence of conduct concerning previous transactions between the parties to a particular transaction that is fairly to be regarded as establishing a common basis of understanding for interpreting their expressions and other conduct.

(c) A "usage of trade" is any practice or method of dealing having such regularity of observance in a place, vocation, or trade as to justify an expectation that it will be observed with respect to the transaction in question. The existence and scope of such a usage must be proved as facts. If it is established that such a usage is embodied in a trade code or similar record, the interpretation of the record is a question of law.

(d) A course of performance or course of dealing between the parties or usage of trade in the vocation or trade in which they are engaged or of which they are or should be aware is relevant in ascertaining the meaning of the parties' agreement, may give particular meaning to specific terms of the agreement, and may supplement or qualify the terms of the agreement. A usage of trade applicable in the place in which part of the performance under the agreement is to occur may be so utilized as to that part of the performance.

(e) Except as otherwise provided in Subsection (f), the express terms of an agreement and any applicable course of performance, course of dealing, or usage of trade must be construed whenever reasonable as consistent with each other. If such a construction is unreasonable:

(1) express terms prevail over course of performance, course of dealing, and usage of trade;

(2) course of performance prevails over course of dealing and usage of trade; and

(3) course of dealing prevails over usage of trade.

(f) Subject to Section 2.209, a course of performance is relevant to show a waiver or modification of any term inconsistent with the course of performance.

(g) Evidence of a relevant usage of trade offered by one party is not admissible unless that party has given the other party notice that the court finds sufficient to prevent unfair surprise to the other party.

Added by Acts 2003, 78th Leg., ch. 542, § 1, eff. Sept. 1, 2003.

Uniform Commercial Code Comment

Source: Former Sections 1–205, 2–208, and Section 2A–207.

Changes from former law: This section integrates the "course of performance" concept from Articles 2 and 2A into the principles of former Section 1–205, which deals with course of dealing and usage of trade. In so doing, the section slightly modifies the articulation of the course of performance rules to fit more comfortably with the approach and structure of former Section 1–205. There are also slight modifications to be more consistent with the definition of "agreement" in former Section 1–201(3). It should be noted that a course of performance that might otherwise establish a defense to the obligation of a party to a negotiable instrument is not available as a defense against a holder in due course who took the instrument without notice of that course of performance.

1. The Uniform Commercial Code rejects both the "lay-dictionary" and the "conveyancer's" reading of a commercial agreement. Instead the meaning of the agreement of the parties is to be determined by the language used by them and by their action, read and interpreted in the light of commercial practices and other surrounding circumstances. The measure and background for interpretation are set by the commercial context, which may explain and supplement even the language of a formal or final writing.

2. "Course of dealing," as defined in subsection (b), is restricted, literally, to a sequence of conduct between the parties previous to the agreement. A sequence of conduct after or under the agreement, however, is a "course of performance." "Course of dealing" may enter the agreement either by explicit provisions of the agreement or by tacit recognition.

3. The Uniform Commercial Code deals with "usage of trade" as a factor in reaching the commercial meaning of the agreement that the parties have made. The language used is to be interpreted as meaning what it may fairly be expected to mean to parties involved in the particular commercial transaction in a given locality or in a given vocation or trade. By adopting in this context the term "usage of trade," the Uniform Commercial Code expresses its intent to reject those cases which see evidence of "custom" as representing an effort to displace or negate "established rules of law." A distinction is to be drawn between mandatory rules of law such as the Statute of Frauds provisions of Article 2 on Sales whose very office is to control and restrict the actions of the parties, and which cannot be abrogated by agreement, or by a usage of trade, and those rules of law (such as those in Part 3 of Article 2 on Sales) which fill in points which the parties have not considered and in fact agreed upon. The latter rules hold "unless otherwise agreed" but yield to the contrary agreement of the parties. Part of the agreement of the parties to which such rules yield is to be sought for in the usages of trade which furnish the background and give particular meaning to the language used, and are the framework of common understanding controlling any general rules of law which hold only when there is no such understanding.

4. A usage of trade under subsection (c) must have the "regularity of observance" specified. The ancient English tests for "custom" are abandoned in this connection. Therefore, it is not required that a usage of trade be "ancient or immemorial," "universal," or the like. Under the requirement of subsection (c) full recognition is thus available for new usages and for usages currently observed by the great majority of decent dealers, even though dissidents ready to cut corners do not agree. There is room also for proper recognition of usage agreed upon by merchants in trade codes.

5. The policies of the Uniform Commercial Code controlling explicit unconscionable contracts and clauses (Sections 1–304, 2–302) apply to implicit clauses that rest on usage of trade and carry forward the policy underlying the ancient requirement that a custom or usage must be "reasonable." However, the emphasis is shifted. The very fact of commercial acceptance makes out a *prima facie* case that the usage is reasonable, and the burden is no longer on the usage to establish itself as being reasonable. But the anciently established policing of usage by the courts is continued to the extent necessary to cope with the situation arising if an unconscionable or dishonest practice should become standard.

6. Subsection (d), giving the prescribed effect to usages of which the parties "are or should be aware," reinforces the provision of subsection (c) requiring not universality but only the described "regularity of observance" of the practice or method. This subsection also reinforces the point of subsection (c) that such usages may be either general to trade or particular to a special branch of trade.

7. Although the definition of "agreement" in Section 1–201 includes the elements of course of performance, course of dealing, and usage of trade, the fact that express reference is made in some sections to those elements is not to be construed as carrying a contrary intent or implication elsewhere. Compare Section 1–302(c).

8. In cases of a well established line of usage varying from the general rules of the Uniform Commercial Code where the precise amount of the variation has not been worked out into a single standard, the party relying on the usage is entitled, in any event, to the minimum variation demonstrated. The whole is not to be disregarded because no particular line of detail has been established. In case a dominant pattern has been fairly evidenced, the party relying on the usage is entitled under this section to go to the trier of fact on the question of whether such dominant pattern has been incorporated into the agreement.

9. Subsection (g) is intended to insure that this Act's liberal recognition of the needs of commerce in regard to usage of trade shall not be made into an instrument of abuse.

§ 1.304. Obligation of Good Faith

Every contract or duty within this title imposes an obligation of good faith in its performance and enforcement.

Added by Acts 2003, 78th Leg., ch. 542, § 1, eff. Sept. 1, 2003.

Uniform Commercial Code Comment

Source: Former Section 1–203.

Changes from former law: Except for changing the form of reference to the Uniform Commercial Code, this section is identical to former Section 1–203.

1. This section sets forth a basic principle running throughout the Uniform Commercial Code. The principle is that in commercial transactions good faith is required in the performance and enforcement of all agreements or duties. While this duty is explicitly stated in some provisions of the Uniform Commercial Code, the applicability of the duty is broader than merely these situations and applies generally, as stated in this section, to the performance or enforcement of every contract or duty within this Act. It is further implemented by Section 1–303 on course of dealing, course of performance, and usage of trade. This section does not support an independent cause of action for failure to perform or enforce in good faith. Rather, this section means that a

failure to perform or enforce, in good faith, a specific duty or obligation under the contract, constitutes a breach of that contract or makes unavailable, under the particular circumstances, are medial right or power. This distinction makes it clear that the doctrine of good faith merely directs a court towards interpreting contracts within the commercial context in which they are created, performed, and enforced, and does not create a separate duty of fairness and reasonableness which can be independently breached.

2. "Performance and enforcement" of contracts and duties within the Uniform Commercial Code include the exercise of rights created by the Uniform Commercial Code.

3. "Consequential" or "special" damages and "penal" damages are not defined in the Uniform Commercial Code; rather, these terms are used in the sense in which they are used outside the Uniform Commercial Code.

§ 1.305. Remedies to be Liberally Administered

(a) The remedies provided by this title must be liberally administered to the end that the aggrieved party may be put in as good a position as if the other party had fully performed but neither consequential or special damages nor penal damages may be had except as specifically provided in this title or by other rule of law.

(b) Any right or obligation declared by this title is enforceable by action unless the provision declaring it specifies a different and limited effect.

Added by Acts 2003, 78th Leg., ch. 542, § 1, eff. Sept. 1, 2003.

Uniform Commercial Code Comment

Source: Former Section 1–106.

Changes from former law: Other than changes in the form of reference to the Uniform Commercial Code, this section is identical to former Section 1–106.

1. Subsection (a) is intended to effect three propositions. The first is to negate the possibility of unduly narrow or technical interpretation of remedial provisions by providing that the remedies in the Uniform Commercial Code are to be liberally administered to the end stated in this section. The second is to make it clear that compensatory damages are limited to compensation. They do not include consequential or special damages, or penal damages; and the Uniform Commercial Code elsewhere makes it clear that damages must be minimized. Cf. Sections 1–304, 2–706(1), and 2–712(2). The third purpose of subsection (a) is to reject any doctrine that damages must be calculable with mathematical accuracy. Compensatory damages are often at best approximate: they have to be proved with whatever definiteness and accuracy the facts permit, but no more. Cf. Section 2–204(3).

2. Under subsection (b), any right or obligation described in the Uniform Commercial Code is enforceable by action, even though no remedy may be expressly provided, unless a particular provision specifies a different and limited effect. Whether specific performance or other equitable relief is available is determined not by this section but by specific provisions and by supplementary principles. Cf. Sections 1–103, 2–716.

§ 1.306. Waiver of Renunciation of Claim or Right After Breach

A claim or right arising out of an alleged breach may be discharged in whole or in part without consideration by agreement of the aggrieved party in an authenticated record.

Added by Acts 2003, 78th Leg., ch. 542, § 1, eff. Sept. 1, 2003.

Uniform Commercial Code Comment

Source: Former Section 1–107.

Changes from former law: This section changes former law in two respects. First, former Section 1–107, requiring the "delivery" of a "written waiver or renunciation" merges the separate concepts of the aggrieved party's agreement to forego rights and the manifestation of that agreement. This section separates those concepts, and explicitly requires *agreement* of the aggrieved party. Second, the revised section reflects developments in electronic commerce by providing for memorialization in an authenticated record. In this context, a party may "authenticate" a record by (i) signing a record that is a writing or (ii) attaching to or logically associating with a record that is not a writing an electronic sound, symbol or process with the present intent to adopt or accept the record. See Sections 1–201(b)(37) and 9–102(a)(7).

1. This section makes consideration unnecessary to the effective renunciation or waiver of rights or claims arising out of an alleged breach of a commercial contract where the agreement effecting such renunciation is memorialized in a record authenticated by the aggrieved party. Its provisions, however, must be read in conjunction with the section imposing an obligation of good faith. (Section 1–304).

§ 1.307. Prima Facie Evidence by Third–Party Documents

A document in due form purporting to be a bill of lading, policy or certificate of insurance, official weigher's or inspector's certificate, consular invoice, or any other document authorized or required by the contract to be issued by a third party is prima facie evidence of its own authenticity and genuineness and of the facts stated in the document by the third party.

Added by Acts 2003, 78th Leg., ch. 542, § 1, eff. Sept. 1, 2003.

Uniform Commercial Code Comment

Source: Former Section 1–202.

Changes from former law: Except for minor stylistic changes, this Section is identical to former Section 1–202.

1. This section supplies judicial recognition for documents that are relied upon as trustworthy by commercial parties.

2. This section is concerned only with documents that have been given a preferred status by the parties themselves who have required their procurement in the agreement, and for this reason the applicability of the section is limited to actions arising out of the contract that authorized or required the document. The list of documents is intended to be illustrative and not exclusive.

3. The provisions of this section go no further than establishing the documents in question as prima facie evidence and leave to the court the ultimate determination of the facts where the accuracy or authenticity of the documents is questioned. In this connection the section calls for a commercially reasonable interpretation.

4. Documents governed by this section need not be writings if records in another medium are generally relied upon in the context.

§ 1.308. Performance or Acceptance Under Reservation of Rights

(a) A party that with explicit reservation of rights performs or promises performance or assents to performance in a manner demanded or offered by the other party does not thereby prejudice the rights reserved. Such words as "without prejudice," "under protest," or the like are sufficient.

(b) Subsection (a) does not apply to an accord and satisfaction.

Added by Acts 2003, 78th Leg., ch. 542, § 1, eff. Sept. 1, 2003.

Uniform Commercial Code Comment

Source: Former Section 1–207.

Changes from former law: This section is identical to former Section 1–207.

1. This section provides machinery for the continuation of performance along the lines contemplated by the contract despite a pending dispute, by adopting the mercantile device of going ahead with delivery, acceptance, or payment "without prejudice," "under protest," "under reserve," "with reservation of all our rights," and the like. All of these phrases completely reserve all rights within the meaning of this section. The section therefore contemplates that limited as well as general reservations and acceptance by a party may be made "subject to satisfaction of our purchaser," "subject to acceptance by our customers," or the like.

2. This section does not add any new requirement of language of reservation where not already required by law, but merely provides a specific measure on which a party can rely as that party makes or concurs in any interim adjustment in the course of performance. It does not affect or impair the provisions of this Act such as those under which the buyer's remedies for defect survive acceptance without being expressly claimed if notice of the defects is given within a reasonable time. Nor does it disturb the policy of those cases which restrict the effect of a waiver of a defect to reasonable limits under the circumstances, even though no such reservation is expressed.

The section is not addressed to the creation or loss of remedies in the ordinary course of performance but rather to a method of procedure where one party is claiming as of right something which the other believes to be unwarranted.

3. Subsection (b) states that this section does not apply to an accord and satisfaction. Section 3–311 governs if an accord and satisfaction is attempted by tender of a negotiable instrument as stated in that section. If Section 3–311 does not apply, the issue of whether an accord and satisfaction has been effected is determined by the law of contract. Whether or not Section 3–311 applies, this section has no application to an accord and satisfaction.

§ 1.309. Option to Accelerate at Will

A term providing that one party or that party's successor in interest may accelerate payment or performance or require collateral or additional collateral "at will" or when the party "deems itself insecure," or words of similar import, means that the party has power to do so only if that party in good faith believes that the prospect of payment or performance is impaired. The burden of establishing lack of good faith is on the party against which the power has been exercised.

Added by Acts 2003, 78th Leg., ch. 542, § 1, eff. Sept. 1, 2003.

Uniform Commercial Code Comment

Source: Former Section 1–208.

Changes from former law: Except for minor stylistic changes, this section is identical to former Section 1–208.

1. The common use of acceleration clauses in many transactions governed by the Uniform Commercial Code, including sales of goods on credit, notes payable at a definite time, and secured transactions, raises an issue as to the effect to be given to a clause that seemingly grants the power to accelerate at the whim and caprice of one party. This section is intended to make clear that despite language that might be so construed and which further might be held to make the agreement void as against public policy or to make the contract illusory or too indefinite for enforcement, the option is to be exercised only in the good faith belief that the prospect of payment or performance is impaired.

Obviously this section has no application to demand instruments or obligations whose very nature permits call at any time with or without reason. This section applies only to an obligation of payment or performance which in the first instance is due at a future date.

§ 1.310. Subordinated Obligations

An obligation may be issued as subordinated to performance of another obligation of the person obligated, or a creditor may subordinate its right to performance of an obligation by agreement with either the person obligated or another creditor of the person obligated. Subordination does not create a security interest as against either the common debtor or a subordinated creditor.

Added by Acts 2003, 78th Leg., ch. 542, § 1, eff. Sept. 1, 2003.

Uniform Commercial Code Comment

Source: Former Section 1–209.

Changes from former law: This section is substantively identical to former Section 1–209. The language in that section stating that it "shall be construed as declaring the law as it existed prior to the enactment of this section and not as modifying it" has been deleted.

1. Billions of dollars of subordinated debt are held by the public and by institutional investors. Commonly, the subordinated debt is subordinated on issue or acquisition and is evidenced by an investment security or by a negotiable or non-negotiable note. Debt is also sometimes subordinated after it arises, either by agreement between the subordinating creditor and the debtor, by agreement between two creditors of the same debtor, or by agreement of all three parties. The subordinated creditor may be a stockholder or other "insider" interested in the common debtor; the subordinated debt may consist of accounts or other rights to payment not evidenced by any instrument. All such cases are included in the terms "subordinated obligation," "subordination," and "subordinated creditor."

2. Subordination agreements are enforceable between the parties as contracts; and in the bankruptcy of the common debtor dividends otherwise payable to the subordinated creditor are turned over to the superior creditor. This "turnover" practice has on occasion been explained in terms of "equitable lien," "equitable assignment," or "constructive trust," but whatever the label the practice is essentially an equitable remedy and does not mean that there is a transaction "that creates a security interest in personal property . . . by contract" or a "sale of accounts, chattel paper, payment intangibles, or promissory notes" within the meaning of Section 9–109. On the other hand, nothing in this section prevents one creditor from assigning his rights to another creditor of the same debtor in such a way as to create a security interest within Article 9, where the parties so intend.

3. The enforcement of subordination agreements is largely left to supplementary principles under Section 1–103. If the subordinated debt is evidenced by a certificated security, Section 8–202(a) authorizes enforcement against purchasers on terms stated or referred to on the security certificate. If the fact of subordination is noted on a negotiable instrument, a holder under Sections 3–302 and 3–306 is subject to the term because notice precludes him from taking free of the subordination. Sections 3–302(3)(a), 3–306, and 8–317 severely limit the rights of levying creditors of a subordinated creditor in such cases.

CHAPTER 2. SALES

SUBCHAPTER A. SHORT TITLE, GENERAL CONSTRUCTION AND SUBJECT MATTER

Section

SUBCHAPTER B. FORM, FORMATION AND READJUSTMENT OF CONTRACT

SUBCHAPTER C. GENERAL OBLIGATION AND CONSTRUCTION OF CONTRACT

SUBCHAPTER A. SHORT TITLE, GENERAL CONSTRUCTION AND SUBJECT MATTER

§ 2.101. Short Title

This chapter may be cited as Uniform Commercial Code—Sales.

Acts 1967, 60th Leg., p. 2343, ch. 785, § 1, eff. Sept. 1, 1967.

Uniform Commercial Code Comment

This Article is a complete revision and modernization of the Uniform Sales Act which was promulgated by the National Conference of Commissioners on Uniform State Laws in 1906 and has been adopted in 34 states and Alaska, the District of Columbia and Hawaii.

The coverage of the present Article is much more extensive than that of the old Sales Act and extends to the various bodies of case law which have been developed both outside of and under the latter.

The arrangement of the present Article is in terms of contract for sale and the various steps of its performance. The legal consequences are stated as following directly from the contract and action taken under it without resorting to the idea of when property or title passed or was to pass as being the determining factor. The purpose is to avoid making practical issues between practical men turn upon the location of an intangible something, the passing of which no man can prove by evidence and to substitute for such abstractions proof of words and actions of a tangible character.

§ 2.102. Scope; Certain Security and Other Transactions Excluded From This Chapter

Unless the context otherwise requires, this chapter applies to transactions in goods; it does not apply to any transaction which although in the form of an unconditional contract to sell or present sale is intended to operate only as a security transaction nor does this chapter impair or repeal any statute regulating sales to consumers, farmers or other specified classes of buyers.

Acts 1967, 60th Leg., p. 2343, ch. 785, § 1, eff. Sept. 1, 1967.

Uniform Commercial Code Comment

Prior Uniform Statutory Provision:

Section 75, Uniform Sales Act.

Changes: Section 75 has been rephrased.

Purposes of Changes and New Matter: To make it clear that:

The Article leaves substantially unaffected the law relating to purchase money security such as conditional sale or chattel mortgage though it regulates the general sales aspects of such transactions. "Security transaction" is used in the same sense as in the Article on Secured Transactions (Article 9).

Cross Reference:

Article 9.

Definitional Cross References:

"Contract". Section 1–201.

"Contract for sale". Section 2–106.

"Present sale". Section 2–106.

"Sale". Section 2–106.

§ 2.103. Definitions and Index of Definitions

(a) In this chapter unless the context otherwise requires

(1) "Buyer" means a person who buys or contracts to buy goods.

(2) Reserved.

(3) "Receipt" of goods means taking physical possession of them.

(4) "Seller" means a person who sells or contracts to sell goods.

(b) Other definitions applying to this chapter or to specified subchapters thereof, and the sections in which they appear are:

"Acceptance". Section 2.606.

"Banker's credit". Section 2.325.

"Between merchants". Section 2.104.

"Cancellation". Section 2.106(d).

"Commercial unit". Section 2.105.

"Confirmed credit". Section 2.325.

"Conforming to contract". Section 2.106.

"Contract for sale". Section 2.106.

"Cover". Section 2.712.

"Entrusting". Section 2.403.

"Financing agency". Section 2.104.

"Future goods". Section 2.105.

"Goods". Section 2.105.

"Identification". Section 2.501.

"Installment contract". Section 2.612.

"Letter of credit". Section 2.325.

"Lot". Section 2.105.

"Merchant". Section 2.104.

"Overseas". Section 2.323.

"Person in position of seller". Section 2.707.

"Present sale". Section 2.106.

"Sale". Section 2.106.

"Sale on approval". Section 2.326.

"Sale or return". Section 2.326.

"Termination". Section 2.106.

(c) The following definitions in other chapters apply to this chapter:

"Check". Section 3.104.

"Consignee". Section 7.102.

"Consignor". Section 7.102.

"Consumer goods". Section 9.102.

"Control". Section 7.106.

"Dishonor". Section 3.502.

"Draft". Section 3.104.

(d) In addition Chapter 1 contains general definitions and principles of construction and interpretation applicable throughout this chapter.

Acts 1967, 60th Leg., p. 2343, ch. 785, § 1, eff. Sept. 1, 1967. Amended by Acts 1999, 76th Leg., ch. 414, § 2.14, eff. July 1, 2001; Acts 2003, 78th Leg., ch. 542, § 2, eff. Sept. 1, 2003; Acts 2005, 79th Leg., ch. 122, § 3, eff. Sept. 1, 2005.

Uniform Commercial Code Comment

Prior Uniform Statutory Provision:

Subsection (1): Section 76, Uniform Sales Act.

Changes:

The definitions of "buyer" and "seller" have been slightly rephrased, the reference in Section 76 of the prior Act to "any legal successor in interest of such person" being omitted. The definition of "receipt" is new.

Purposes of Changes and New Matter:

1. The phrase "any legal successor in interest of such person" has been eliminated since Section 2–210 of this Article, which limits some types of delegation of performance on assignment of a sales contract, makes it clear that not every such successor can be safely included in the definition. In every ordinary case, however, such successors are as of course included.

2. "Receipt" must be distinguished from delivery particularly in regard to the problems arising out of shipment of goods, whether or not the contract calls for making delivery by way of documents of title, since the seller may frequently fulfill his obligations to "deliver" even though the buyer may never "receive" the goods. Delivery with respect to documents of title is defined in Article 1 and requires transfer of physical delivery of a tangible document of title and transfer of control of an electronic document of title. Otherwise the many divergent incidents of delivery are handled incident by incident.

Cross References:

Point 1: See Section 2–210 and Comment thereon.

Point 2: Section 1–201.

Definitional Cross Reference:

"Person". Section 1–201.

Sections 31 and 32 of Acts 2005, 79th Leg., ch. 122 provide:

"Sec. 31. This Act applies to a document of title that is issued or a bailment that arises on or after the effective date of this Act. This Act does not apply to a document of title that is issued or a bailment that arises before the effective date of this Act even if the document of title or bailment would be subject to this Act if the document of title had been issued or bailment had arisen after the effective date of this Act. This Act does not apply to a right of action that has accrued before the effective date of this Act.

"Sec. 32. A document of title issued or a bailment that arises before the effective date of this Act and the rights, obligations, and interests flowing from that document or bailment are governed by any statute or other rule amended or repealed by this Act as if amendment or repeal had not occurred and may be terminated, completed, consummated, or enforced under that statute or other rule."

§ 2.104. Definitions: "Merchant"; "Between Merchants"; "Financing Agency"

(a) "Merchant" means a person who deals in goods of the kind or otherwise by his occupation holds himself out as having knowledge or skill peculiar to the practices or goods involved in the transaction or to whom such knowledge or skill may be attributed by his employment of an agent or broker or other intermediary who by his occupation holds himself out as having such knowledge or skill.

(b) "Financing agency" means a bank, finance company or other person who in the ordinary course of business makes advances against goods or documents of title or who by arrangement with either the seller or the buyer intervenes in ordinary course to make or collect payment due or claimed under the contract for sale, as by purchasing or paying the seller's draft or making advances against it or by merely taking it for collection whether or not documents of title accompany or are associated with the draft. "Financing agency" includes also a bank or other person who similarly intervenes between persons who are in the position of seller and buyer in respect to the goods (Section 2.707).

(c) "Between merchants" means in any transaction with respect to which both parties are chargeable with the knowledge or skill of merchants.

Acts 1967, 60th Leg., p. 2343, ch. 785, § 1, eff. Sept. 1, 1967. Amended by Acts 2005, 79th Leg., ch. 122, § 4, eff. Sept. 1, 2005.

Uniform Commercial Code Comment

Prior Uniform Statutory Provision:

None. But see Sections 15(2), (5), 16(c), 45(2) and 71, Uniform Sales Act, and Sections 35 and 37, Uniform Bills of Lading Act for examples of the policy expressly provided for in this Article.

Purposes:

1. This Article assumes that transactions between professionals in a given field require special and clear rules which may not apply to a casual or inexperienced seller or buyer. It thus adopts a policy of expressly stating rules applicable "between merchants" and "as against a merchant" wherever they are needed instead of making them depend upon the circumstances of each case as in the statutes cited above. This section lays the foundation of this policy by defining those who are to be regarded as professionals or "merchants" and by stating when a transaction is deemed to be "between merchants".

2. The term "merchant" as defined here roots in the "law merchant" concept of a professional in business. The professional status under the definition may be based upon specialized knowledge as to the goods, specialized knowledge as to business practices, or specialized knowledge as to both and which kind of specialized knowledge may be sufficient to establish the merchant status is indicated by the nature of the provisions.

The special provisions as to merchants appear only in this Article and they are of three kinds. Sections 2–201(2), 2–205, 2–207 and 2–209 dealing with the statute of frauds, firm offers, confirmatory memoranda and modification rest on normal business practices which are or ought to be typical of and familiar to any person in business. For purposes of these sections almost every person in business would, therefore, be deemed to be a "merchant" under the language "who . . . . by his occupation holds himself out as having knowledge or skill peculiar to the practices . . . involved in the transaction . . ." since the practices involved in the transaction are non-specialized business practices such as answering mail. In this type of provision, banks or even universities, for example, well may be "merchants." But even these sections only apply to a merchant in his mercantile capacity; a lawyer or bank president buying fishing tackle for his own use is not a merchant.

On the other hand, in Section 2–314 on the warranty of merchantability, such warranty is implied only "if the seller is a merchant with respect to goods of that kind." Obviously this qualification restricts the implied warranty to a much smaller group than everyone who is engaged in business and requires a professional status as to particular kinds of goods. The exception in Section 2–402(2) for retention of possession by a merchant-seller falls in the same class; as does Section 2–403(2) on entrusting of possession to a merchant "who deals in goods of that kind".

A third group of sections includes 2–103(1)(b), which provides that in the case of a merchant "good faith" includes observance of reasonable commercial standards of fair dealing in the trade; 2–327(1)(c), 2–603 and 2–605, dealing with responsibilities of merchant buyers to follow seller's instructions, etc.; 2–509 on risk of loss, and 2–609 on adequate assurance of performance. This group of sections applies to persons who are merchants under either the "practices" or the "goods" aspect of the definition of merchant.

3. The "or to whom such knowledge or skill may be attributed by his employment of an agent or broker . . ." clause of the definition of merchant means that even persons such as universities, for example, can come within the definition of merchant if they have regular purchasing departments or business personnel who are familiar with business practices and who are equipped to take any action required.

Cross References:

Point 1: See Sections 1–102 and 1–203.

Point 2: See Sections 2–314, 2–315 and 2–320 to 2–325, of this Article, and Article 9.

Definitional Cross References:

"Bank". Section 1–201.

"Buyer". Section 2–103.

"Contract for sale". Section 2–106.

"Document of title". Section 1–201.

"Draft". Section 3–104.

"Goods". Section 2–105.

"Person". Section 1–201.

"Purchase". Section 1–201.

"Seller". Section 2–103.

Sections 31 and 32 of Acts 2005, 79th Leg., ch. 122 provide:

"Sec. 31. This Act applies to a document of title that is issued or a bailment that arises on or after the effective date of this Act. This Act does not apply to a document of title that is issued or a bailment that arises before the effective date of this Act even if the document of title or bailment would be subject to this Act if the document of title had been issued or bailment had arisen after the effective date of this Act. This Act does not apply to a right of action that has accrued before the effective date of this Act.

"Sec. 32. A document of title issued or a bailment that arises before the effective date of this Act and the rights, obligations, and interests flowing from that document or bailment are governed by any statute or other rule amended or repealed by this Act as if amendment or repeal had not occurred and may be terminated, completed, consummated, or enforced under that statute or other rule."

§ 2.105. Definitions: Transferability; "Goods"; "Future" Goods; "Lot"; "Commercial Unit"

(a) "Goods" means all things (including specially manufactured goods) which are movable at the time of identification to the contract for sale other than the money in which the price is to be paid, investment securities (Chapter 8) and things in action. "Goods" also includes the unborn young of animals and growing crops and other identified things attached to realty as described in the section on goods to be severed from realty (Section 2.107).

(b) Goods must be both existing and identified before any interest in them can pass. Goods which are not both existing and identified are "future" goods. A purported present sale of future goods or of any interest therein operates as a contract to sell.

(c) There may be a sale of a part interest in existing identified goods.

(d) An undivided share in an identified bulk of fungible goods is sufficiently identified to be sold although the quantity of the bulk is not determined. Any agreed proportion of such a bulk or any quantity thereof agreed upon by number, weight or other measure may to the extent of the seller's interest in the bulk be sold to the buyer who then becomes an owner in common.

(e) "Lot" means a parcel or a single article which is the subject matter of a separate sale or delivery, whether or not it is sufficient to perform the contract.

(f) "Commercial unit" means such a unit of goods as by commercial usage is a single whole for purposes of sale and division of which materially impairs its character or value on the market or in use. A commercial unit may be a single article (as a machine) or a set of articles (as a suite of furniture or an assortment of sizes) or a quantity (as a bale, gross, or carload) or any other unit treated in use or in the relevant market as a single whole.

Acts 1967, 60th Leg., p. 2343, ch. 785, § 1, eff. Sept. 1, 1967.

Uniform Commercial Code Comment

Prior Uniform Statutory Provision:

Subsections (1), (2), (3) and (4)—Sections 5, 6 and 76, Uniform Sales Act; Subsections (5) and (6)—none.

Changes: Rewritten.

Purposes of Changes and New Matter:

1. Subsection (1) on "goods": The phraseology of the prior uniform statutory provision has been changed so that:

The definition of goods is based on the concept of movability and the term "chattels personal" is not used. It is not intended to deal with things which are not fairly identifiable as movables before the contract is performed.

Growing crops are included within the definition of goods since they are frequently intended for sale. The concept of "industrial" growing crops has been abandoned, for under modern practices fruit, perennial hay, nursery stock and the like must be brought within the scope of this Article. The young of animals are also included expressly in this definition since they, too, are frequently intended for sale and may be contracted for before birth. The period of gestation of domestic animals is such that the provisions of the section on identification can apply as in the case of crops to be planted. The reason of this definition also leads to the inclusion of a wool crop or the like as "goods" subject to identification under this Article.

The exclusion of "money in which the price is to be paid" from the definition of goods does not mean that foreign currency which is included in the definition of money may not be the subject matter of a sales transaction. Goods is intended to cover the sale of money when money is being treated as a commodity but not to include it when money is the medium of payment.

As to contracts to sell timber, minerals, or structures to be removed from the land Section 2–107(1) (Goods to be severed from Realty: recording) controls.

The use of the word "fixtures" is avoided in view of the diversity of definitions of that term. This Article in including within its scope "things attached to realty" adds the further test that they must be capable of severance without material harm thereto. As between the parties any identified things which falls within that definition becomes "goods" upon the making of the contract for sale.

"Investment securities" are expressly excluded from the coverage of this Article. It is not intended by this exclusion, however, to prevent the application of a particular section of this Article by analogy to securities (as was done with the Original Sales Act in *Agar v. Orda*, 264 N.Y. 248, 190 N.E. 479, 99 A.L.R. 269 (1934)) when the reason of that section makes such application sensible and the situation involved is not covered by the Article of this Act dealing specifically with such securities (Article 8).

2. References to the fact that a contract for sale can extend to future or contingent goods and that ownership in common follows the sale of a part interest have been omitted here as obvious without need for expression; hence no inference to negate these principles should be drawn from their omission.

3. Subsection (4) does not touch the question of how far an appropriation of a bulk of fungible goods may or may not satisfy the contract for sale.

4. Subsections (5) and (6) on "lot" and "commercial unit" are introduced to aid in the phrasing of later sections.

5. The question of when an identification of goods takes place is determined by the provisions of Section 2–501 and all that this section says is what kinds of goods may be the subject of a sale.

Cross References:

Point 1: Sections 2–107, 2–201, 2–501 and Article 8.

Point 5: Section 2–501.

See also Section 1–201.

Definitional Cross References:

"Buyer". Section 2–103.

"Contract". Section 1–201.

"Contract for sale". Section 2–106.

"Fungible". Section 1–201.

"Money". Section 1–201.

"Present sale". Section 2–106.

"Sale". Section 2–106.

"Seller". Section 2–103.

§ 2.106. Definitions: "Contract"; "Agreement"; "Contract for Sale"; "Sale"; "Present Sale"; "Conforming" to Contract; "Termination"; "Cancellation"

(a) In this chapter unless the context otherwise requires "contract" and "agreement" are limited to those relating to the present or future sale of goods. "Contract for sale" includes both a present sale of goods and a contract to sell goods at a future time. A "sale" consists in the passing of title from the seller to the buyer for a price (Section 2.401). A "present sale" means a sale which is accomplished by the making of the contract.

(b) Goods or conduct including any part of a performance are "conforming" or conform to the contract when they are in accordance with the obligations under the contract.

(c) "Termination" occurs when either party pursuant to a power created by agreement or law puts an end to the contract otherwise than for its breach. On "termination" all obligations which are still executory on both sides are discharged but any right based on prior breach or performance survives.

(d) "Cancellation" occurs when either party puts an end to the contract for breach by the other and its effect is the same as that of "termination" except that the cancelling party also retains any remedy for breach of the whole contract or any unperformed balance.

Acts 1967, 60th Leg., p. 2343, ch. 785, § 1, eff. Sept. 1, 1967.

Uniform Commercial Code Comment

Prior Uniform Statutory Provision:

Subsection (1)—Section 1(1) and (2), Uniform Sales Act; Subsection (2)—none, but subsection generally continues policy of Sections 11, 44 and 69, Uniform Sales Act; Subsections (3) and (4)—none.

Changes: Completely rewritten.

Purposes of Changes and New Matter:

1. Subsection (1): "Contract for sale" is used as a general concept throughout this Article, but the rights of the parties do not vary according to whether the transaction is a present sale or a contract to sell unless the Article expressly so provides.

2. Subsection (2): It is in general intended to continue the policy of requiring exact performance by the seller of his obligations as a condition to his right to require acceptance. However, the seller is in part safeguarded against surprise as a result of sudden technicality on the buyer's part by the provisions of Section 2–508 on seller's cure of improper tender or delivery. Moreover usage of trade frequently permits commercial leeways in performance and the language of the agreement itself must be read in the light of such custom or usage and also, prior course of dealing, and in a long term contract, the course of performance.

3. Subsections (3) and (4): These subsections are intended to make clear the distinction carried forward throughout this Article between termination and cancellation.

Cross References:

Point 2: Sections 1–203, 1–205, 2–208 and 2–508.

Definitional Cross References:

"Agreement". Section 1–201.

"Buyer". Section 2–103.

"Contract". Section 1–201.

"Goods". Section 2–105.

"Party". Section 1–201.

"Remedy". Section 1–201.

"Rights". Section 1–201.

"Seller". Section 2–103.

§ 2.107. Goods to be Severed From Realty: Recording

(a) A contract for the sale of minerals or the like (including oil and gas) or a structure or its materials to be removed from realty is a contract for the sale of goods within this chapter if they are to be severed by the seller but until severance a purported present sale thereof which is not effective as a transfer of an interest in land is effective only as a contract to sell.

(b) A contract for the sale apart from the land of growing crops or other things attached to realty and capable of severance without material harm thereto but not described in Subsection (a) or of timber to be cut is a contract for the sale of goods within this chapter whether the subject matter is to be severed by the buyer or by the seller even though it forms part of the realty at the time of contracting, and the parties can by identification effect a present sale before severance.

(c) The provisions of this section are subject to any third party rights provided by the law relating to realty records, and the contract for sale may be executed and recorded as a document transferring an interest in land and shall then constitute notice to third parties of the buyer's rights under the contract for sale.

Acts 1967, 60th Leg., p. 2343, ch. 785, § 1, eff. Sept. 1, 1967. Amended by Acts 1973, 63rd Leg., p. 998, ch. 400, § 3, eff. Jan. 1, 1974.

Uniform Commercial Code Comment

Prior Uniform Statutory Provision:

See Section 76, Uniform Sales Act on prior policy; Section 7, Uniform Conditional Sales Act.

Purposes:

1. Subsection (1). Notice that this subsection applies only if the minerals or structures "are to be severed by the seller". If the buyer is to sever, such transactions are considered contracts affecting land and all problems of the Statute of Frauds and of the recording of land rights apply to them. Therefore, the Statute of Frauds section of this Article does not apply to such contracts though they must conform to the Statute of Frauds affecting the transfer of interests in land.

2. Subsection (2). "Things attached" to the realty which can be severed without material harm are goods within this Article regardless of who is to effect the severance. The word "fixtures" has been avoided because of the diverse definitions of this term, the test of "severance without material harm" being substituted.

The provision in subsection (3) for recording such contracts is within the purview of this Article since it is a means of preserving the buyer's rights under the contract of sale.

3. The security phases of things attached to or to become attached to realty are dealt with in the Article on Secured Transactions (Article 9) and it is to be noted that the definition of goods in that Article differs from the definition of goods in this Article.

However, both Articles treat as goods growing crops and also timber to be cut under a contract of severance.

Cross References:

Point 1: Section 2–201.

Point 2: Section 2–105.

Point 3: Articles 9 and 9–105.

Definitional Cross References:

"Buyer". Section 2–103.

"Contract". Section 1–201.

"Contract for sale". Section 2–106.

"Goods". Section 2–105.

"Party". Section 1–201.

"Present sale". Section 2–106.

"Rights". Section 1–201.

"Seller". Section 2–103.

§ 2.108. Repealed by Acts 2001, 77th Leg., ch. 702, § 5, eff. Jan. 1, 2002

SUBCHAPTER B. FORM, FORMATION AND READJUSTMENT OF CONTRACT

§ 2.201. Formal Requirements; Statute of Frauds

(a) Except as otherwise provided in this section a contract for the sale of goods for the price of $500 or more is not enforceable by way of action or defense unless there is some writing sufficient to indicate that a contract for sale has been made between the parties and signed by the party against whom enforcement is sought or by his authorized agent or broker. A writing is not insufficient because it omits or incorrectly states a term agreed upon but the contract is not enforceable under this paragraph beyond the quantity of goods shown in such writing.

(b) Between merchants if within a reasonable time a writing in confirmation of the contract and sufficient against the sender is received and the party receiving it has reason to know its contents, it satisfies the requirements of Subsection (a) against such party unless written notice of objection to its contents is given within ten days after it is received.

(c) A contract which does not satisfy the requirements of Subsection (a) but which is valid in other respects is enforceable

(1) if the goods are to be specially manufactured for the buyer and are not suitable for sale to others in the ordinary course of the seller's business and the seller, before notice of repudiation is received and under circumstances which reasonably indicate that the goods are for the buyer, has made either a substantial beginning of their manufacture or commitments for their procurement; or

(2) if the party against whom enforcement is sought admits in his pleading, testimony or otherwise in court that a contract for sale was made, but the contract is not enforceable under this provision beyond the quantity of goods admitted; or

(3) with respect to goods for which payment has been made and accepted or which have been received and accepted (Section 2.606).

Acts 1967, 60th Leg., p. 2343, ch. 785, § 1, eff. Sept. 1, 1967.

Uniform Commercial Code Comment

Prior Uniform Statutory Provision:

Section 4, Uniform Sales Act (which was based on Section 17 of the Statute of 29 Charles II).

Changes: Completely rephrased; restricted to sale of goods. See also Sections 1–206, 8–319 and 9–203.

Purposes of Changes: The changed phraseology of this section is intended to make it clear that:

1. The required writing need not contain all the material terms of the contract and such material terms as are stated need not be precisely stated. All that is required is that the writing afford a basis for believing that the offered oral evidence rests on a real transaction. It may be written in lead pencil on a scratch pad. It need not indicate which party is the buyer and which the seller. The only term which must appear is the quantity term which need not be accurately stated but recovery is limited to the amount stated. The price, time and place of payment or delivery, the general quality of the goods, or any particular warranties may all be omitted.

Special emphasis must be placed on the permissibility of omitting the price term in view of the insistence of some courts on the express inclusion of this term even where the parties have contracted on the basis of a published price list. In many valid contracts for sale the parties do not mention the price in express terms, the buyer being bound to pay and the seller to accept a reasonable price which the trier of the fact may well be trusted to determine. Again, frequently the price is not mentioned since the parties have based their agreement on a price list or catalogue known to both of them and this list serves as an efficient safeguard against perjury. Finally, "market" prices and valuations that are current in the vicinity constitute a similar check. Thus if the price is not stated in the memorandum it can normally be supplied without danger of fraud. Of course if the "price" consists of goods rather than money the quantity of goods must be stated.

Only three definite and invariable requirements as to the memorandum are made by this subsection. First, it must evidence a contract for the sale of goods; second, it must be "signed", a word which includes any authentication which identifies the party to be charged; and third, it must specify a quantity.

2. "Partial performance" as a substitute for the required memorandum can validate the contract only for the goods which have been accepted or for which payment has been made and accepted.

Receipt and acceptance either of goods or of the price constitutes an unambiguous overt admission by both parties that a contract actually exists. If the court can make a just apportionment, therefore, the agreed price of any goods actually delivered can be recovered without a writing or, if the price has been paid, the seller can be forced to deliver an apportionable part of the goods. The overt actions of the parties make admissible evidence of the other terms of the contract necessary to a just apportionment. This is true even though the actions of the parties are not in themselves inconsistent with a different transaction such as a consignment for resale or a mere loan of money.

Part performance by the buyer requires the delivery of something by him that is accepted by the seller as such performance. Thus, part payment may be made by money or check, accepted by the seller. If the agreed price consists of goods or services, then they must also have been delivered and accepted.

3. Between merchants, failure to answer a written confirmation of a contract within ten days of receipt is tantamount to a writing under subsection (2) and is sufficient against both parties under subsection (1). The only effect, however, is to take away from the party who fails to answer the defense of the Statute of Frauds; the burden of persuading the trier of fact that a contract was in fact made orally prior to the written confirmation is unaffected. Compare the effect of a failure to reply under Section 2–207.

4. Failure to satisfy the requirements of this section does not render the contract void for all purposes, but merely prevents it from being judicially enforced in favor of a party to the contract. For example, a buyer who takes possession of goods as provided in an oral contract which the seller has not meanwhile repudiated, is not a trespasser. Nor would the Statute of Frauds provisions of this section be a defense to a third person who wrongfully induces a party to refuse to perform an oral contract, even though the injured party cannot maintain an action for damages against the party so refusing to perform.

5. The requirement of "signing" is discussed in the comment to Section 1–201.

6. It is not necessary that the writing be delivered to anybody. It need not be signed or authenticated by both parties but it is, of course, not sufficient against one who has not signed it. Prior to a dispute no one can determine which party's signing of the memorandum may be necessary but from the time of contracting each party should be aware that to him it is signing by the other which is important.

7. If the making of a contract is admitted in court, either in a written pleading, by stipulation or by oral statement before the court, no additional writing is necessary for protection against fraud. Under this section it is no longer possible to admit the contract in court and still treat the Statute as a defense. However, the contract is not thus conclusively established. The admission so made by a party is itself evidential against him of the truth of the facts so admitted and of nothing more; as against the other party, it is not evidential at all.

Cross References:

See Sections 1–201, 2–202, 2–207, 2–209 and 2–304.

Definitional Cross References:

"Action". Section 1–201.

"Between merchants". Section 2–104.

"Buyer". Section 2–103.

"Contract". Section 1–201.

"Contract for sale". Section 2–106.

"Goods". Section 2–105.

"Notice". Section 1–201.

"Party". Section 1–201.

"Reasonable time". Section 1–204.

"Sale". Section 2–106.

"Seller". Section 2–103.

§ 2.202. Final Written Expression: Parol or Extrinsic Evidence

Terms with respect to which the confirmatory memoranda of the parties agree or which are otherwise set forth in a writing intended by the parties as a final expression of their agreement with respect to such terms as are included therein may not be contradicted by evidence of any prior agreement or of a contemporaneous oral agreement but may be explained or supplemented

(1) by course of performance, course of dealing, or usage of trade (Section 1.303); and

(2) by evidence of consistent additional terms unless the court finds the writing to have been intended also as a complete and exclusive statement of the terms of the agreement.

Acts 1967, 60th Leg., p. 2343, ch. 785, § 1, eff. Sept. 1, 1967. Amended by Acts 2003, 78th Leg., ch. 542, § 3, eff. Sept. 1, 2003.

Uniform Commercial Code Comment

Prior Uniform Statutory Provision:

None.

Purposes:

1. This section definitely rejects:

(a) Any assumption that because a writing has been worked out which is final on some matters, it is to be taken as including all the matters agreed upon;

(b) The premise that the language used has the meaning attributable to such language by rules of construction existing in the law rather than the meaning which arises out of the commercial context in which it was used; and

(c) The requirement that a condition precedent to the admissibility of the type of evidence specified in paragraph (a) is an original determination by the court that the language used is ambiguous.

2. Paragraph (a) makes admissible evidence of course of dealing, usage of trade and course of performance to explain or supplement the terms of any writing stating the agreement of the parties in order that the true understanding of the parties as to the agreement may be reached. Such writings are to be read on the assumption that the course of prior dealings between the parties and the usages of trade were taken for granted when the document was phrased. Unless carefully negated they have become an element of the meaning of the words used. Similarly, the course of actual performance by the parties is considered the best indication of what they intended the writing to mean.

3. Under paragraph (b) consistent additional terms, not reduced to writing, may be proved unless the court finds that the writing was intended by both parties as a complete and exclusive statement of all the terms. If the additional terms are such that, if agreed upon, they would certainly have been included in the document in the view of the court, then evidence of their alleged making must be kept from the trier of fact.

Cross References:

Point 3: Sections 1–205, 2–207, 2–302 and 2–316.

Definitional Cross References:

"Agreed" and "agreement". Section 1–201.

"Course of dealing". Section 1–205.

"Parties". Section 1–201.

"Term". Section 1–201.

"Usage of trade". Section 1–205.

"Written" and "writing". Section 1–201.

§ 2.203. Seals Inoperative

The affixing of a seal to a writing evidencing a contract for sale or an offer to buy or sell goods does not constitute the writing a sealed instrument and the law with respect to sealed instruments does not apply to such a contract or offer.

Acts 1967, 60th Leg., p. 2343, ch. 785, § 1, eff. Sept. 1, 1967.

Uniform Commercial Code Comment

Prior Uniform Statutory Provision:

Section 3, Uniform Sales Act.

Changes: Portion pertaining to "seals" rewritten.

Purposes of Changes:

1. This section makes it clear that every effect of the seal which relates to "sealed instruments" as such is wiped out insofar as contracts for sale are concerned. However, the substantial effects of a seal, except extension of the period of limitations, may be had by appropriate drafting as in the case of firm offers (see Section 2–205).

2. This section leaves untouched any aspects of a seal which relate merely to signatures or to authentication of execution and the like. Thus, a statute providing that a purported signature gives prima facie evidence of its own authenticity or that a signature gives prima facie evidence of consideration is still applicable to sales transactions even though a seal may be held to be a signature within the meaning of such a statute. Similarly, the authorized affixing of a corporate seal bearing the corporate name to a contractual writing purporting to be made by the corporation may have effect as a signature without any reference to the law of sealed instruments.

Cross Reference:

Point 1: Section 2–205.

Definitional Cross References:

"Contract for sale". Section 2–106.

"Goods". Section 2–105.

"Writing". Section 1–201.

§ 2.204. Formation in General

(a) A contract for sale of goods may be made in any manner sufficient to show agreement, including conduct by both parties which recognizes the existence of such a contract.

(b) An agreement sufficient to constitute a contract for sale may be found even though the moment of its making is undetermined.

(c) Even though one or more terms are left open a contract for sale does not fail for indefiniteness if the parties have intended to make a contract and there is a reasonably certain basis for giving an appropriate remedy.

Acts 1967, 60th Leg., p. 2343, ch. 785, § 1, eff. Sept. 1, 1967.

Uniform Commercial Code Comment

Prior Uniform Statutory Provision:

Sections 1 and 3, Uniform Sales Act.

Changes: Completely rewritten by this and other sections of this Article.

Purposes of Changes:

Subsection (1) continues without change the basic policy of recognizing any manner of expression of agreement, oral, written or otherwise. The legal effect of such an agreement is, of course, qualified by other provisions of this Article.

Under subsection (1) appropriate conduct by the parties may be sufficient to establish an agreement. Subsection (2) is directed primarily to the situation where the interchanged correspondence does not disclose the exact point at which the deal was closed, but the actions of the parties indicate that a binding obligation has been undertaken.

Subsection (3) states the principle as to "open terms" underlying later sections of the Article. If the parties intend to enter into a binding agreement, this subsection recognizes that agreement as valid in law, despite missing terms, if there is any reasonably certain basis for granting a remedy. The test is not certainty as to what the parties were to do nor as to the exact amount of damages due the plaintiff. Nor is the fact that one or more terms are left to be agreed upon enough of itself to defeat an otherwise adequate agreement. Rather, commercial standards on the point of "indefiniteness" are intended to be applied, this Act making provision elsewhere for missing terms needed for performance, open price, remedies and the like.

The more terms the parties leave open, the less likely it is that they have intended to conclude a binding agreement, but their actions may be frequently conclusive on the matter despite the omissions.

Cross References:

Subsection (1): Sections 1–103, 2–201 and 2–302.

Subsection (2): Sections 2–205 through 2–209.

Subsection (3): See Part 3.

Definitional Cross References:

"Agreement". Section 1–201.

"Contract". Section 1–201.

"Contract for sale". Section 2–106.

"Goods". Section 2–105.

"Party". Section 1–201.

"Remedy". Section 1–201.

"Term". Section 1–201.

§ 2.205. Firm Offers

An offer by a merchant to buy or sell goods in a signed writing which by its terms gives assurance that it will be held open is not revocable, for lack of consideration, during the time stated or if no time is stated for a reasonable time, but in no event may such period of irrevocability exceed three months; but any such term of assurance on a form supplied by the offeree must be separately signed by the offeror.

Acts 1967, 60th Leg., p. 2343, ch. 785, § 1, eff. Sept. 1, 1967.

Uniform Commercial Code Comment

Prior Uniform Statutory Provision:

Sections 1 and 3, Uniform Sales Act.

Changes: Completely rewritten by this and other sections of this Article.

Purposes of Changes:

1. This section is intended to modify the former rule which required that "firm offers" be sustained by consideration in order to bind, and to require instead that they must merely be characterized as such and expressed in signed writings.

2. The primary purpose of this section is to give effect to the deliberate intention of a merchant to make a current firm offer binding. The deliberation is shown in the case of an individualized document by the merchant's signature to the offer, and in the case of an offer included on a form supplied by the other party to the transaction by the separate signing of the particular clause which contains the offer. "Signed" here also includes authentication but the reasonableness of the authentication herein allowed must be determined in the light of the purpose of the section. The circumstances surrounding the signing may justify something less than a formal signature or initialing but typically the kind of authentication involved here would consist of a minimum of initialing of the clause involved. A handwritten memorandum on the writer's letterhead purporting in its terms to "confirm" a firm offer already made would be enough to satisfy this section, although not subscribed, since under the circumstances it could not be considered a memorandum of mere negotiation and it would adequately show its own authenticity. Similarly, an authorized telegram will suffice, and this is true even though the original draft contained only a typewritten signature. However, despite settled courses of dealing or usages of the trade whereby firm offers are made by oral communication and relied upon without more evidence, such offers remain revocable under this Article since authentication by a writing is the essence of this section.

3. This section is intended to apply to current "firm" offers and not to long term options, and an outside time limit of three months during which such offers remain irrevocable has been set. The three month period during which firm offers remain irrevocable under this section need not be stated by days or by date. If the offer states that it is "guaranteed" or "firm" until the happening of a contingency which will occur within the three month period, it will remain irrevocable until that event. A promise made for a longer period will operate under this section to bind the offeror only for the first three months of the period but may of course be renewed. If supported by consideration it may continue for as long as the parties specify. This section deals only with the offer which is not supported by consideration.

4. Protection is afforded against the inadvertent signing of a firm offer when contained in a form prepared by the offeree by requiring that such a clause be separately authenticated. If the offer clause is called to the offeror's attention and he separately authenticates it, he will be bound; Section 2–302 may operate, however, to prevent an unconscionable result which otherwise would flow from other terms appearing in the form.

5. Safeguards are provided to offer relief in the case of material mistake by virtue of the requirement of good faith and the general law of mistake.

Cross References:

Point 1: Section 1–102.

Point 2: Section 1–102.

Point 3: Section 2–201.

Point 5: Section 2–302.

Definitional Cross References:

"Goods". Section 2–105.

"Merchant". Section 2–104.

"Signed". Section 1–201.

"Writing". Section 1–201.

§ 2.206. Offer and Acceptance in Formation of Contract

(a) Unless otherwise unambiguously indicated by the language or circumstances

(1) an offer to make a contract shall be construed as inviting acceptance in any manner and by any medium reasonable in the circumstances;

(2) an order or other offer to buy goods for prompt or current shipment shall be construed as inviting acceptance either by a prompt promise to ship or by the prompt or current shipment of conforming or non-conforming goods, but such a shipment of non-conforming goods does not constitute an acceptance if the seller seasonably notifies the buyer that the shipment is offered only as an accommodation to the buyer.

(b) Where the beginning of a requested performance is a reasonable mode of acceptance an offeror who is not notified of acceptance within a reasonable time may treat the offer as having lapsed before acceptance.

Acts 1967, 60th Leg., p. 2343, ch. 785, § 1, eff. Sept. 1, 1967.

Uniform Commercial Code Comment

Prior Uniform Statutory Provision:

Sections 1 and 3, Uniform Sales Act.

Changes: Completely rewritten in this and other sections of this Article.

Purposes of Changes: To make it clear that:

1. Any reasonable manner of acceptance is intended to be regarded as available unless the offeror has made quite clear that it will not be acceptable. Former technical rules as to acceptance, such as requiring that telegraphic offers be accepted by telegraphed acceptance, etc., are rejected and a criterion that the acceptance be "in any manner and by any medium reasonable under the circumstances," is substituted. This section is intended to remain flexible and its applicability to be enlarged as new media of communication develop or as the more time-saving present day media come into general use.

2. Either shipment or a prompt promise to ship is made a proper means of acceptance of an offer looking to current shipment. In accordance with ordinary commercial understanding the section interprets an order looking to current shipment as allowing acceptance either by actual shipment or by a prompt promise to ship and rejects the artificial theory that only a single mode of acceptance is normally envisaged by an offer. This is true even though the language of the offer happens to be "ship at once" or the like. "Shipment" is here used in the same sense as in Section 2–504; it does not include the beginning of delivery by the seller's own truck or by messenger. But loading on the seller's own truck might be a beginning of performance under subsection (2).

3. The beginning of performance by an offeree can be effective as acceptance so as to bind the offeror only if followed within a reasonable time by notice to the offeror. Such a beginning of performance must unambiguously express the offeree's intention to engage himself. For the protection of both parties it is essential that notice follow in due course to constitute acceptance. Nothing in this section however bars the possibility that under the common law performance begun may have an intermediate effect of temporarily barring revocation of the offer, or at the offeror's option, final effect in constituting acceptance.

4. Subsection (1)(b) deals with the situation where a shipment made following an order is shown by a notification of shipment to be referable to that order but has a defect. Such a non-conforming shipment is normally to be understood as intended to close the bargain, even though it proves to have been at the same time a breach. However, the seller by stating that the shipment is non-conforming and is offered only as an accommodation to the buyer keeps the shipment or notification from operating as an acceptance.

Definitional Cross References:

"Buyer". Section 2–103.

"Conforming". Section 2–106.

"Contract". Section 1–201.

"Goods". Section 2–105.

"Notifies". Section 1–201.

"Reasonable time". Section 1–204.

§ 2.207. Additional Terms in Acceptance or Confirmation

(a) A definite and seasonable expression of acceptance or a written confirmation which is sent within a reasonable time operates as an acceptance even though it states terms additional to or different from those offered or agreed upon, unless acceptance is expressly made conditional on assent to the additional or different terms.

(b) The additional terms are to be construed as proposals for addition to the contract. Between merchants such terms become part of the contract unless:

(1) the offer expressly limits acceptance to the terms of the offer;

(2) they materially alter it; or

(3) notification of objection to them has already been given or is given within a reasonable time after notice of them is received.

(c) Conduct by both parties which recognizes the existence of a contract is sufficient to establish a contract for sale although the writings of the parties do not otherwise establish a contract. In such case the terms of the particular contract consist of those terms on which the writings of the parties agree, together with any supplementary terms incorporated under any other provisions of this title.

Acts 1967, 60th Leg., p. 2343, ch. 785, § 1, eff. Sept. 1, 1967.

Uniform Commercial Code Comment

Prior Uniform Statutory Provision:

Sections 1 and 3, Uniform Sales Act.

Changes: Completely rewritten by this and other sections of this Article.

Purposes of Changes:

1. This section is intended to deal with two typical situations. The one is the written confirmation, where an agreement has been reached either orally or by informal correspondence between the parties and is followed by one or both of the parties sending formal memoranda embodying the terms so far as agreed upon and adding terms not discussed. The other situation is offer and acceptance, in which a wire or letter expressed and intended as an acceptance or the closing of an agreement adds further minor suggestions or proposals such as "ship by Tuesday," "rush," "ship draft against bill of lading inspection allowed," or the like. A frequent example of the second situation is the exchange of printed purchase order and acceptance (sometimes called "acknowledgment") forms. Because the forms are oriented to the thinking of the respective drafting parties, the terms contained in them often do not correspond. Often the seller's form contains terms different from or additional to those set forth in the buyer's form. Nevertheless, the parties proceed with the transaction.

2. Under this Article a proposed deal which in commercial understanding has in fact been closed is recognized as a contract. Therefore, any additional matter contained in the confirmation or in the acceptance falls within subsection (2) and must be regarded as a proposal for an added term unless the acceptance is made conditional on the acceptance of the additional or different terms.

3. Whether or not additional or different terms will become part of the agreement depends upon the provisions of subsection (2). If they are such as materially to alter the original bargain, they will not be included unless expressly agreed to by the other party. If, however, they are terms which would not so change the bargain they will be incorporated unless notice of objection to them has already been given or is given within a reasonable time.

4. Examples of typical clauses which would normally "materially alter" the contract and so result in surprise or hardship if incorporated without express awareness by the other party are: a clause negating such standard warranties as that of merchantability or fitness for a particular purpose in circumstances in which either warranty normally attaches; a clause requiring a guaranty of 90% or 100% deliveries in a case such as a contract by cannery, where the usage of the trade allows greater quantity leeways; a clause reserving to the seller the power to cancel upon the buyer's failure to meet any invoice when due; a clause requiring that complaints be made in a time materially shorter than customary or reasonable.

5. Examples of clauses which involve no element of unreasonable surprise and which therefore are to be incorporated in the contract unless notice of objection is seasonably given are: a clause setting forth and perhaps enlarging slightly upon the seller's exemption due to supervening causes beyond his control, similar to those covered by the provision of this Article on merchant's excuse by failure of presupposed conditions or a clause fixing in advance any reasonable formula of proration under such circumstances; a clause fixing a reasonable time for complaints within customary limits, or in the case of a purchase for sub-sale, providing for inspection by the sub-purchaser; a clause providing for interest on overdue invoices or fixing the seller's standard credit terms where they are within the range of trade practice and do not limit any credit bargained for; a clause limiting the right of rejection for defects which fall within the customary trade tolerances for acceptance "with adjustment" or otherwise limiting remedy in a reasonable manner (see Sections 2–718 and 2–719).

6. If no answer is received within a reasonable time after additional terms are proposed, it is both fair and commercially sound to assume that their inclusion has been assented to. Where clauses on confirming forms sent by both parties conflict each party must be assumed to object to a clause of the other conflicting with one on the confirmation sent by himself. As a result the requirement that there be notice of objection which is found in subsection (2) is satisfied and the conflicting terms do not become a part of the contract. The contract then consists of the terms originally expressly agreed to, terms on which the confirmations agree, and terms supplied by this Act, including subsection (2). The written confirmation is also subject to Section 2–201. Under that section a failure to respond permits enforcement of a prior oral agreement; under this section a failure to respond permits additional terms to become part of the agreement.

7. In many cases, as where goods are shipped, accepted and paid for before any dispute arises, there is no question whether a contract has been made. In such cases, where the writings of the parties do not establish a contract, it is not necessary to determine which act or document constituted the offer and which the acceptance. See Section 2–204. The only question is what terms are included in the contract, and subsection (3) furnishes the governing rule.

Cross References:

See generally Section 2–302.

Point 5: Sections 2–513, 2–602, 2–607, 2–609, 2–612, 2–614, 2–615, 2–616, 2–718 and 2–719.

Point 6: Sections 1–102 and 2–104.

Definitional Cross References:

"Between merchants". Section 2–104.

"Contract". Section 1–201.

"Notification". Section 1–201.

"Reasonable time". Section 1–204.

"Seasonably". Section 1–204.

"Send". Section 1–201.

"Term". Section 1–201.

"Written". Section 1–201.

§ 2.208. Repealed by Acts 2003, 78th Leg., ch. 542, § 20, eff. Sept. 1, 2003.

§ 2.209. Modification, Rescission and Waiver

(a) An agreement modifying a contract within this chapter needs no consideration to be binding.

(b) A signed agreement which excludes modification or rescission except by a signed writing cannot be otherwise modified or rescinded, but except as between merchants such a requirement on a form supplied by the merchant must be separately signed by the other party.

(c) The requirements of the statute of frauds section of this chapter (Section 2.201) must be satisfied if the contract as modified is within its provisions.

(d) Although an attempt at modification or rescission does not satisfy the requirements of Subsection (b) or (c) it can operate as a waiver.

(e) A party who has made a waiver affecting an executory portion of the contract may retract the waiver by reasonable notification received by the other party that strict performance will be required of any term waived, unless the retraction would be unjust in view of a material change of position in reliance on the waiver.

Acts 1967, 60th Leg., p. 2343, ch. 785, § 1, eff. Sept. 1, 1967.

Uniform Commercial Code Comment

Prior Uniform Statutory Provision:

Subsection (1)—Compare Section 1,

Uniform Written Obligations Act; Subsections (2) to (5)—none.

Purposes of Changes and New Matter:

1. This section seeks to protect and make effective all necessary and desirable modifications of sales contracts without regard to the technicalities which at present hamper such adjustments.

2. Subsection (1) provides that an agreement modifying a sales contract needs no consideration to be binding.

However, modifications made thereunder must meet the test of good faith imposed by this Act. The effective use of bad faith to escape performance on the original contract terms is barred, and the extortion of a "modification" without legitimate commercial reason is ineffective as a violation of the duty of good faith. Nor can a mere technical consideration support a modification made in bad faith.

The test of "good faith" between merchants or as against merchants includes "observance of reasonable commercial standards of fair dealing in the trade" (Section 2–103), and may in some situations require an objectively demonstrable reason for seeking a modification. But such matters as a market shift which makes performance come to involve a loss may provide such a reason even though there is no such unforeseen difficulty as would make out a legal excuse from performance under Sections 2–615 and 2–616.

3. Subsections (2) and (3) are intended to protect against false allegations of oral modifications. "Modification or rescission" includes abandonment or other change by mutual consent, contrary to the decision in Green v. Doniger, 300 N.Y. 238, 90 N.E.2d 56 (1949); it does not include unilateral "termination" or "cancellation" as defined in Section 2–106.

The Statute of Frauds provisions of this Article are expressly applied to modifications by subsection (3). Under those provisions the "delivery and acceptance" test is limited to the goods which have been accepted, that is, to the past. "Modification" for the future cannot therefore be conjured up by oral testimony if the price involved is $500.00 or more since such modification must be shown at least by an authenticated memo. And since a memo is limited in its effect to the quantity of goods set forth in it there is safeguard against oral evidence.

Subsection (2) permits the parties in effect to make their own Statute of Frauds as regards any future modification of the contract by giving effect to a clause in a signed agreement which expressly requires any modification to be by signed writing. But note that if a consumer is to be held to such a clause on a form supplied by a merchant it must be separately signed.

4. Subsection (4) is intended, despite the provisions of subsections (2) and (3), to prevent contractual provisions excluding modification except by a signed writing from limiting in other respects the legal effect of the parties' actual later conduct. The effect of such conduct as a waiver is further regulated in subsection (5).

Cross References:

Point 1: Section 1–203.

Point 2: Sections 1–201, 1–203, 2–615 and 2–616.

Point 3: Sections 2–106, 2–201 and 2–202.

Point 4: Sections 2–202 and 2–208.

Definitional Cross References:

"Agreement". Section 1–201.

"Between merchants". Section 2–104.

"Contract". Section 1–201.

"Notification". Section 1–201.

"Signed". Section 1–201.

"Term". Section 1–201.

"Writing". Section 1–201.

§ 2.210. Delegation of Performance; Assignment of Rights

(a) A party may perform his duty through a delegate unless otherwise agreed or unless the other party has a substantial interest in having his original promisor perform or control the acts required by the contract. No delegation of performance relieves the party delegating of any duty to perform or any liability for breach.

(b) Unless otherwise agreed all rights of either seller or buyer can be assigned except where the assignment would materially change the duty of the other party, or increase materially the burden or risk imposed on him by his contract, or impair materially his chance of obtaining return performance. A right to damages for breach of the whole contract or a right arising out of the assignor's due performance of his entire obligation can be assigned despite agreement otherwise.

(c) The creation, attachment, perfection, or enforcement of a security interest in the seller's interest under a contract is not a transfer that materially changes the duty of or increases materially the burden or risk imposed on the buyer or impairs materially the buyer's chance of obtaining return performance within the purview of Subsection (b) unless, and then only to the extent that, enforcement actually results in a delegation of material performance of the seller. Even in that event, the creation, attachment, perfection, and enforcement of the security interest remain effective, but (i) the seller is liable to the buyer for damages caused by the delegation to the extent that the damages could not reasonably be prevented by the buyer, and (ii) a court having jurisdiction may grant other appropriate relief, including cancellation of the contract for sale or an injunction against enforcement of the security interest or consummation of the enforcement.

(d) Unless the circumstances indicate the contrary a prohibition of assignment of "the contract" is to be construed as barring only the delegation to the assignee of the assignor's performance.

(e) An assignment of "the contract" or of "all my rights under the contract" or an assignment in similar general terms is an assignment of rights and unless the language or the circumstances (as in an assignment for security) indicate the contrary, it is a delegation of performance of the duties of the assignor and its acceptance by the assignee constitutes a promise by him to perform those duties. This promise is enforceable by either the assignor or the other party to the original contract.

(f) The other party may treat any assignment which delegates performance as creating reasonable grounds for insecurity and may without prejudice to his rights against the assignor demand assurances from the assignee (Section 2.609).

Acts 1967, 60th Leg., p. 2343, ch. 785, § 1, eff. Sept. 1, 1967. Amended by Acts 1999, 76th Leg., ch. 414, § 2.15, eff. July 1, 2001.

Uniform Commercial Code Comment

Prior Uniform Statutory Provision:

None.

Purposes:

1. Generally, this section recognizes both delegation of performance and assignability as normal and permissible incidents of a contract for the sale of goods.

2. Delegation of performance, either in conjunction with an assignment or otherwise, is provided for by subsection (1) where no substantial reason can be shown as to why the delegated performance will not be as satisfactory as personal performance.

3. Under subsection (2) rights which are no longer executory such as a right to damages for breach may be assigned although the agreement prohibits assignment. In such cases no question of delegation of any performance is involved. Subsection (2) is subject to Section 9–406, which makes rights to payment for goods sold ("accounts"), whether or not earned, freely alienable notwithstanding a contrary agreement or rule of law.

4. The nature of the contract or the circumstances of the case, however, may bar assignment of the contract even where delegation of performance is not involved. This Article and this section are intended to clarify this problem, particularly in cases dealing with output requirement and exclusive dealing contracts. In the first place the section on requirements and exclusive dealing removes from the construction of the original contract most of the "personal discretion" element by substituting the reasonably objective standard of good faith operation of the plant or business to be supplied. Secondly, the section on insecurity and assurances, which is specifically referred to in subsection (5) of this section, frees the other party from the doubts and uncertainty which may afflict him under an assignment of the character in question by permitting him to demand adequate assurance of due performance without which he may suspend his own performance. Subsection (5) is not in any way intended to limit the effect of the section on insecurity and assurances and the word "performance" includes the giving of orders under a requirements contract. Of course, in any case where a material personal discretion is sought to be transferred, effective assignment is barred by subsection (2).

5. Subsection (4) lays down a general rule of construction distinguishing between a normal commercial assignment, which substitutes the assignee for the assignor both as to rights and duties, and a financing assignment in which only the assignor's rights are transferred.

This Article takes no position on the possibility of extending some recognition or power to the original parties to work out normal commercial readjustments of the contract in the case of financing assignments even after the original obligor has been notified of the assignment. This question is dealt with in the Article on Secured Transactions (Article 9).

6. Subsection (5) recognizes that the non-assigning original party has a stake in the reliability of the person with whom he has closed the original contract, and is, therefore, entitled to due assurance that any delegated performance will be properly forthcoming.

7. This section is not intended as a complete statement of the law of delegation and assignment but is limited to clarifying a few points doubtful under the case law. Particularly, neither this section nor this Article touches directly on such questions as the need or effect of notice of the assignment, the rights of successive assignees, or any question of the form of an assignment, either as between the parties or as against any third parties. Some of these questions are dealt with in Article 9.

Cross References:

Point 3: Articles 5 and 9.

Point 4: Sections 2–306 and 2–609.

Point 5: Article 9, Sections 9–317 and 9–318.

Point 7: Article 9.

Definitional Cross References:

"Agreement". Section 1–201.

"Buyer". Section 2–103.

"Contract". Section 1–201.

"Party". Section 1–201.

"Rights". Section 1–201.

"Seller". Section 2–103.

"Term". Section 1–201.

SUBCHAPTER C. GENERAL OBLIGATION AND CONSTRUCTION OF CONTRACT

§ 2.301. General Obligations of Parties

The obligation of the seller is to transfer and deliver and that of the buyer is to accept and pay in accordance with the contract.

Acts 1967, 60th Leg., p. 2343, ch. 785, § 1, eff. Sept. 1, 1967.

Uniform Commercial Code Comment

Prior Uniform Statutory Provision:

Sections 11 and 41, Uniform Sales Act.

Changes: Rewritten.

Purposes of Changes:

This section uses the term "obligation" in contrast to the term "duty" in order to provide for the "condition" aspects of delivery and payment insofar as they are not modified by other sections of this Article such as those on cure of tender. It thus replaces not only the general provisions of the Uniform Sales Act on the parties' duties, but also the general provisions of that Act on the effect of conditions. In order to determine what is "in accordance with the contract" under this Article usage of trade, course of dealing and performance, and the general background of circumstances must be given due consideration in conjunction with the lay meaning of the words used to define the scope of the conditions and duties.

Cross References:

Section 1–106. See also Sections 1–205, 2–208, 2–209, 2–508 and 2–612.

Definitional Cross References:

"Buyer". Section 2–103.

"Contract". Section 1–201.

"Party". Section 1–201.

"Seller". Section 2–103.

§ 2.302. Unconscionable Contract or Clause

(a) If the court as a matter of law finds the contract or any clause of the contract to have been unconscionable at the time it was made the court may refuse to enforce the contract, or it may enforce the remainder of the contract without the unconscionable clause, or it may so limit the application of any unconscionable clause as to avoid any unconscionable result.

(b) When it is claimed or appears to the court that the contract or any clause thereof may be unconscionable the parties shall be afforded a reasonable opportunity to present evidence as to its commercial setting, purpose and effect to aid the court in making the determination.

Acts 1967, 60th Leg., p. 2343, ch. 785, § 1, eff. Sept. 1, 1967.

Uniform Commercial Code Comment

Prior Uniform Statutory Provision:

None.

Purposes:

1. This section is intended to make it possible for the courts to police explicitly against the contracts or clauses which they find to be unconscionable. In the past such policing has been accomplished by adverse construction of language, by manipulation of the rules of offer and acceptance or by determinations that the clause is contrary to public policy or to the dominant purpose of the contract. This section is intended to allow the court to pass directly on the unconscionability of the contract or particular clause therein and to make a conclusion of law as to its unconscionability. The basic test is whether, in the light of the general commercial background and the commercial needs of the particular trade or case, the clauses involved are so one-sided as to be unconscionable under the circumstances existing at the time of the making of the contract. Subsection (2) makes it clear that it is proper for the court to hear evidence upon these questions. The principle is one of the prevention of oppression and unfair surprise (Cf. *Campbell Soup Co. v. Wentz,* 172 F.2d 80, 3d Cir. 1948) and not of disturbance of allocation of risks because of superior bargaining power.

The underlying basis of this section is illustrated by the results in cases such as the following:

Kansas City Wholesale Grocery Co. v. Weber Packing Corporation, 3 Utah 414, 73 P.2d 1272 (1937), where a clause limiting time for complaints was held inapplicable to latent defects in a shipment of catsup which could be discovered only by microscopic analysis; *Hardy v. General Motors Acceptance Corporation*, 38 Ga.App. 463, 144 S.E. 327 (1928), holding that a disclaimer of warranty clause applied only to express warranties, thus letting in a fair implied warranty; *Andrews Bros. v. Singer & Co.* (1934 CA) 1 K.B. 17, holding that where a car with substantial mileage was delivered instead of a "new" car, a disclaimer of warranties, including those "implied," left unaffected an "express obligation" on the description, even though the Sale of Goods Act called such an implied warranty; *New Prague Flouring Mill Co. v. G. A. Spears*, 194 Iowa 417, 189 N.W. 815 (1922), holding that a clause permitting the seller, upon the buyer's failure to supply shipping instructions, to cancel, ship, or allow delivery date to be indefinitely postponed 30 days at a time by the inaction, does not indefinitely postpone the date of measuring damages for the buyer's breach, to the seller's advantage; and *Kansas Flour Mills Co. v. Dirks*, 100 Kan. 376, 164 P. 273 (1917), where under a similar clause in a rising market the court permitted the buyer to measure his damages for non-delivery at the end of only one 30 day postponement; *Green v. Arcos, Ltd.* 1931 CA) 47 T.L.R. 336, where a blanket clause prohibiting rejection of shipments by the buyer was restricted to apply to shipments where discrepancies represented merely mercantile variations; *Meyer v. Packard Cleveland Motor Co.*, 106 Ohio St. 328, 140 N.E. 118 (1922), in which the court held that a "waiver" of all agreements not specified did not preclude implied warranty of fitness of a rebuilt dump truck for ordinary use as a dump truck; *Austin Co. v. J. H. Tillman Co.*, 104 Or. 541, 209 P. 131 (1922), where a clause limiting the buyer's remedy to return was held to be applicable only if the seller had delivered a machine needed for a construction job which reasonably met the contract description; *Bekkevold v. Potts*, 173 Minn. 87, 216 N.W. 790, 59 A.L.R. 1164 (1927), refusing to allow warranty of fitness for purpose imposed by law to be negated by clause excluding all warranties "made" by the seller; *Robert A. Munroe & Co. v. Meyer* (1930) 2 K.B. 312, holding that the warranty of description overrides a clause reading "with all faults and defects" where adulterated meat not up to the contract description was delivered.

2. Under this section the court, in its discretion, may refuse to enforce the contract as a whole if it is permeated by the unconscionability, or it may strike any single clause or group of clauses which are so tainted or which are contrary to the essential purpose of the agreement, or it may simply limit unconscionable clauses so as to avoid unconscionable results.

3. The present section is addressed to the court, and the decision is to be made by it. The commercial evidence referred to in subsection (2) is for the court's consideration, not the jury's. Only the agreement which results from the court's action on these matters is to be submitted to the general triers of the facts.

Definitional Cross Reference:

"Contract". Section 1–201.

§ 2.303. Allocation or Division of Risks

Where this chapter allocates a risk or a burden as between the parties "unless otherwise agreed", the agreement may not only shift the allocation but may also divide the risk or burden.

Acts 1967, 60th Leg., p. 2343, ch. 785, § 1, eff. Sept. 1, 1967.

Uniform Commercial Code Comment

Prior Uniform Statutory Provision:

None.

Purposes:

1. This section is intended to make it clear that the parties may modify or allocate "unless otherwise agreed" risks or burdens imposed by this Article as they desire, always subject, of course, to the provisions on unconscionability.

Compare Section 1–102(4).

2. The risk or burden may be divided by the express terms of the agreement or by the attending circumstances, since under the definition of "agreement" in this Act the circumstances surrounding the transaction as well as the express language used by the parties enter into the meaning and substance of the agreement.

Cross References:

Point 1: Sections 1–102, 2–302.

Point 2: Section 1–201.

Definitional Cross References:

"Agreement". Section 1–201.

"Party". Section 1–201.

§ 2.304. Price Payable in Money, Goods, Realty, or Otherwise

(a) The price can be made payable in money or otherwise. If it is payable in whole or in part in goods each party is a seller of the goods which he is to transfer.

(b) Even though all or part of the price is payable in an interest in realty the transfer of the goods and the seller's obligations with reference to them are subject to this chapter, but not the transfer of the interest in realty or the transferor's obligations in connection therewith.

Acts 1967, 60th Leg., p. 2343, ch. 785, § 1, eff. Sept. 1, 1967.

Uniform Commercial Code Comment

Prior Uniform Statutory Provision:

Subsections (2) and (3) of Section 9, Uniform Sales Act.

Changes: Rewritten.

Purposes of Changes:

1. This section corrects the phrasing of the Uniform Sales Act so as to avoid misconstruction and produce greater accuracy in commercial result. While it continues the essential intent and purpose of the Uniform Sales Act it rejects any purely verbalistic construction in disregard of the underlying reason of the provisions.

2. Under subsection (1) the provisions of this Article are applicable to transactions where the "price" of goods is payable in something other than money. This does not mean, however, that this whole Article applies automatically and in its entirety simply because an agreed transfer of title to goods is not a gift. The basic purposes and reasons of the Article must always be considered in determining the applicability of any of its provisions.

3. Subsection (2) lays down the general principle that when goods are to be exchanged for realty, the provisions of this Article apply only to those aspects of the transaction which concern the transfer of title to goods but do not affect the transfer of the realty since the detailed regulation of various particular contracts which fall outside the scope of this Article is left to the courts and other legislation. However, the complexities of these situations may be such that each must be analyzed in the light of the underlying reasons in order to determine the applicable principles. Local statutes dealing with realty are not to be lightly disregarded or altered by language of this Article. In contrast, this Article declares definite policies in regard to certain matters legitimately within its scope though concerned with real property situations, and in those instances the provisions of this Article control.

Cross References:

Point 1: Section 1–102.

Point 3: Sections 1–102, 1–103, 1–104 and 2–107.

Definitional Cross References:

"Goods". Section 2–105.

"Money". Section 1–201.

"Party". Section 1–201.

"Seller". Section 2–103.

§ 2.305. Open Price Term

(a) The parties if they so intend can conclude a contract for sale even though the price is not settled. In such a case the price is a reasonable price at the time for delivery if

(1) nothing is said as to price; or

(2) the price is left to be agreed by the parties and they fail to agree; or

(3) the price is to be fixed in terms of some agreed market or other standard as set or recorded by a third person or agency and it is not so set or recorded.

(b) A price to be fixed by the seller or by the buyer means a price for him to fix in good faith.

(c) When a price left to be fixed otherwise than by agreement of the parties fails to be fixed through fault of one party the other may at his option treat the contract as cancelled or himself fix a reasonable price.

(d) Where, however, the parties intend not to be bound unless the price be fixed or agreed and it is not fixed or agreed there is no contract. In such a case the buyer must return any goods already received or if unable so to do must pay their reasonable value at the time of delivery and the seller must return any portion of the price paid on account.

Acts 1967, 60th Leg., p. 2343, ch. 785, § 1, eff. Sept. 1, 1967.

Uniform Commercial Code Comment

Prior Uniform Statutory Provision:

Sections 9 and 10, Uniform Sales Act.

Changes: Completely rewritten.

Purposes of Changes:

1. This section applies when the price term is left open on the making of an agreement which is nevertheless intended by the parties to be a binding agreement. This Article rejects in these instances the formula that "an agreement to agree is unenforceable" if the case falls within subsection (1) of this section, and rejects also defeating such agreements on the ground of "indefiniteness". Instead this Article recognizes the dominant intention of the parties to have the deal continue to be binding upon both. As to future performance, since this Article recognizes remedies such as cover (Section 2–712), resale (Section 2–706) and specific performance (Section 2–716) which go beyond any mere arithmetic as between contract price and market price, there is usually a "reasonably certain basis for granting an appropriate remedy for breach" so that the contract need not fail for indefiniteness.

2. Under some circumstances the postponement of agreement on price will mean that no deal has really been concluded, and this is made express in the preamble of subsection (1) ("The parties *if they so intend*") and in subsection (4). Whether or not this is so is, in most cases, a question to be determined by the trier of fact.

3. Subsection (2), dealing with the situation where the price is to be fixed by one party rejects the uncommercial idea that an agreement that the seller may fix the price means that he may fix any price he may wish by the express qualification that the price so fixed must be fixed in good faith. Good faith includes observance of reasonable commercial standards of fair dealing in the trade if the party is a merchant. (Section 2–103). But in the normal case a "posted price" or a future seller's or buyer's "given price," "price in effect," "market price," or the like satisfies the good faith requirement.

4. The section recognizes that there may be cases in which a particular person's judgment is not chosen merely as a barometer or index of a fair price but is an essential condition to the parties' intent to make any contract at all. For example, the case where a known and trusted expert is to "value" a particular painting for which there is no market

standard differs sharply from the situation where a named expert is to determine the grade of cotton, and the difference would support a finding that in the one the parties did not intend to make a binding agreement if that expert were unavailable whereas in the other they did so intend. Other circumstances would of course affect the validity of such a finding.

5. Under subsection (3), wrongful interference by one party with any agreed machinery for price fixing in the contract may be treated by the other party as a repudiation justifying cancellation, or merely as a failure to take cooperative action thus shifting to the aggrieved party the reasonable leeway in fixing the price.

6. Throughout the entire section, the purpose is to give effect to the agreement which has been made. That effect, however, is always conditioned by the requirement of good faith action which is made an inherent part of all contracts within this Act. (Section 1–203).

Cross References:

Point 1: Sections 2–204(3), 2–706, 2–712 and 2–716.

Point 3: Section 2–103.

Point 5: Sections 2–311 and 2–610.

Point 6: Section 1–203.

Definitional Cross References:

"Agreement". Section 1–201.

"Burden of establishing". Section 1–201.

"Buyer". Section 2–103.

"Cancellation". Section 2–106.

"Contract". Section 1–201.

"Contract for sale". Section 2–106.

"Fault". Section 1–201.

"Goods". Section 2–105.

"Party". Section 1–201.

"Receipt of goods". Section 2–103.

"Seller". Section 2–103.

"Term". Section 1–201.

§ 2.306. Output, Requirements and Exclusive Dealings

(a) A term which measures the quantity by the output of the seller or the requirements of the buyer means such actual output or requirements as may occur in good faith, except that no quantity unreasonably disproportionate to any stated estimate or in the absence of a stated estimate to any normal or otherwise comparable prior output or requirements may be tendered or demanded.

(b) A lawful agreement by either the seller or the buyer for exclusive dealing in the kind of goods concerned imposes unless otherwise agreed an obligation by the seller to use best efforts to supply the goods and by the buyer to use best efforts to promote their sale.

Acts 1967, 60th Leg., p. 2343, ch. 785, § 1, eff. Sept. 1, 1967.

Uniform Commercial Code Comment

Prior Uniform Statutory Provision:

None.

Purposes:

1. Subsection (1) of this section, in regard to output and requirements, applies to this specific problem the general approach of this Act which requires the reading of commercial background and intent into the language of any agreement and demands good faith in the performance of that agreement. It applies to such contracts of nonproducing establishments such as dealers or distributors as well as to manufacturing concerns.

2. Under this Article, a contract for output or requirements is not too indefinite since it is held to mean the actual good faith output or requirements of the particular party. Nor does such a contract lack mutuality of obligation since, under this section, the party who will determine quantity is required to operate his plant or conduct his business in good faith and according to commercial standards of fair dealing in the trade so that his output or requirements will approximate a reasonably foreseeable figure. Reasonable elasticity in the requirements is expressly envisaged by this section and good faith variations from prior requirements are permitted even when the variation may be such as to result in discontinuance. A shut-down by a requirements buyer for lack of orders might be permissible when a shut-down merely to curtail losses would not. The essential test is whether the party is acting in good faith. Similarly, a sudden expansion of the plant by which requirements are to be measured would not be included within the scope of the contract as made but normal expansion undertaken in good faith would be within the scope of this section. One of the factors in an expansion situation would be whether the market price had risen greatly in a case in which the requirements contract contained a fixed price. Reasonable variation of an extreme sort is exemplified in *Southwest Natural Gas Co. v. Oklahoma Portland Cement Co.,* 102 F.2d 630 (C.C.A.10,1939). This Article takes no position as to whether a requirements contract is a provable claim in bankruptcy.

3. If an estimate of output or requirements is included in the agreement, no quantity unreasonably disproportionate to it may be tendered or demanded. Any minimum or maximum set by the agreement shows a clear limit on the intended elasticity. In similar fashion, the agreed estimate is to be regarded as a center around which the parties intend the variation to occur.

4. When an enterprise is sold, the question may arise whether the buyer is bound by an existing output or requirements contract. That question is outside the scope of this Article, and is to be determined on other principles of law. Assuming that the contract continues, the output or requirements in the hands of the new owner continue to be measured by the actual good faith output or requirements under the normal operation of the enterprise prior to sale. The sale itself is not grounds for sudden expansion or decrease.

5. Subsection (2), on exclusive dealing, makes explicit the commercial rule embodied in this Act under which the parties to such contracts are held to have impliedly, even when not expressly, bound themselves to use reasonable diligence as well as good faith in their performance of the contract. Under such contracts the exclusive agent is required, although no express commitment has been made, to use reasonable effort and due diligence in the expansion of the market or the promotion of the product, as the case may be. The principal is expected under such a contract to refrain from supplying any other dealer or agent within the exclusive territory. An exclusive dealing agreement brings into play all of the good faith aspects of the output and requirement problems of subsection (1). It also raises questions of insecurity and right to adequate assurance under this Article.

Cross References:

Point 4: Section 2–210.

Point 5: Sections 1–203 and 2–609.

Definitional Cross References:

"Agreement". Section 1–201.

"Buyer". Section 2–103.

"Contract for sale". Section 2–106.

"Good faith". Section 1–201.

"Goods". Section 2–105.

"Party". Section 1–201.

"Seller". Section 2–103.

"Term". Section 1–201.

§ 2.307. Delivery in Single Lot or Several Lots

Unless otherwise agreed all goods called for by a contract for sale must be tendered in a single delivery and payment is due only on such tender but where the circumstances give either party the right to make or demand delivery in lots the price if it can be apportioned may be demanded for each lot.

Acts 1967, 60th Leg., p. 2343, ch. 785, § 1, eff. Sept. 1, 1967.

Uniform Commercial Code Comment

Prior Uniform Statutory Provision:

Section 45(1), Uniform Sales Act.

Changes: Rewritten and expanded.

Purposes of Changes:

1. This section applies where the parties have not specifically agreed whether delivery and payment are to be by lots and generally continues the essential intent of original Act, Section 45(1) by assuming that the parties intended delivery to be in a single lot.

2. Where the actual agreement or the circumstances do not indicate otherwise, delivery in lots is not permitted under this section and the buyer is properly entitled to reject for a deficiency in the tender, subject to any privilege in the seller to cure the tender.

3. The "but" clause of this section goes to the case in which it is not commercially feasible to deliver or to receive the goods in a single lot as for example, where a contract calls for the shipment of ten carloads of coal and only three cars are available at a given time. Similarly, in a contract involving brick necessary to build a building the buyer's storage space may be limited so that it would be impossible to receive the entire amount of brick at once, or it may be necessary to assemble the goods as in the case of cattle on the range, or to mine them.

In such cases, a partial delivery is not subject to rejection for the defect in quantity alone, if the circumstances do not indicate a repudiation or default by the seller as to the expected balance or do not give the buyer ground for suspending his performance because of insecurity under the provisions of Section 2–609. However, in such cases the undelivered balance of goods under the contract must be forthcoming within a reasonable time and in a reasonable manner according to the policy of Section 2–503 on manner of tender of delivery. This is reinforced by the express provisions of Section 2–608 that if a lot has been accepted on the reasonable assumption that its nonconformity will be cured, the acceptance may be revoked if the cure does not seasonably occur. The section rejects the rule of *Kelly Construction Co. v. Hackensack Brick Co.*, 91 N.J.L. 585, 103 A. 417 (1918) and approves the result in *Lynn M. Ranger, Inc. v. Gildersleeve*, 106 Conn. 372, 138 A. 142 (1927) in which a contract was made for six carloads of coal then rolling from the mines and consigned to the seller but the seller agreed to divert the carloads to the buyer as soon as the car numbers became known to him. He arranged a diversion of two cars and then notified the buyer who then repudiated the contract. The seller was held to be entitled to his full remedy for the two cars diverted because simultaneous delivery of all of the cars was not contemplated by either party.

4. Where the circumstances indicate that a party has a right to delivery in lots, the price may be demanded for each lot if it is apportionable.

Cross References:

Point 1: Section 1–201.

Point 2: Sections 2–508 and 2–601.

Point 3: Sections 2–503, 2–608 and 2–609.

Definitional Cross References:

"Contract for sale". Section 2–106.

"Goods". Section 2–105.

"Lot". Section 2–105.

"Party". Section 1–201.

"Rights". Section 1–201.

§ 2.308. Absence of Specified Place for Delivery

Unless otherwise agreed

(1) the place for delivery of goods is the seller's place of business or if he has none his residence; but

(2) in a contract for sale of identified goods which to the knowledge of the parties at the time of

contracting are in some other place, that place is the place for their delivery; and

(3) documents of title may be delivered through customary banking channels.

Acts 1967, 60th Leg., p. 2343, ch. 785, § 1, eff. Sept. 1, 1967.

Uniform Commercial Code Comment

Prior Uniform Statutory Provision:

Paragraphs (a) and (b)—Section 43(1), Uniform Sales Act; Paragraph (c)—none.

Changes: Slight modification in language.

Purposes of Changes and New Matter:

1. Paragraphs (a) and (b) provide for those noncommercial sales and for those occasional commercial sales where no place or means of delivery has been agreed upon by the parties. Where delivery by carrier is "required or authorized by the agreement", the seller's duties as to delivery of the goods are governed not by this section but by Section 2–504.

2. Under paragraph (b) when the identified goods contracted for are known to both parties to be in some location other than the seller's place of business or residence, the parties are presumed to have intended that place to be the place of delivery. This paragraph also applies (unless, as would be normal, the circumstances show that delivery by way of documents is intended) to a bulk of goods in the possession of a bailee. In such a case, however, the seller has the additional obligation to procure the acknowledgment by the bailee of the buyer's right to possession.

3. Where "customary banking channels" call only for due notification by the banker that the documents are available, leaving the buyer himself to see to the physical receipt of the goods, tender at the buyer's address is not required under paragraph (c). But that paragraph merely eliminates the possibility of a default by the seller if "customary banking channels" have been properly used in giving notice to the buyer. Where the bank has purchased a draft accompanied by or associated with documents or has undertaken its collection on behalf of the seller, Part 5 of Article 4 spells out its duties and relations to its customer. Where the documents move forward under a letter of credit the Article on Letters of Credit spells out the duties and relations between the bank, the seller and the buyer. Delivery in relationship to either tangible or electronic documents of title is defined in Article 1, Section 1–201.

4. The rules of this section apply only "unless otherwise agreed." The surrounding circumstances, usage of trade, course of dealing and course of performance, as well as the express language of the parties, may constitute an "otherwise agreement".

Cross References:

Point 1: Sections 2–504 and 2–505.

Point 2: Section 2–503.

Point 3: Section 2–512, Articles 4, Part 5, and 5.

Definitional Cross References:

"Contract for sale". Section 2–106.

"Delivery". Section 1–201.

"Document of title". Section 1–201.

"Goods". Section 2–105.

"Party". Section 1–201.

"Seller". Section 2–103.

§ 2.309. Absence of Specific Time Provisions; Notice of Termination

(a) The time for shipment or delivery or any other action under a contract if not provided in this chapter or agreed upon shall be a reasonable time.

(b) Where the contract provides for successive performances but is indefinite in duration it is valid for a reasonable time but unless otherwise agreed may be terminated at any time by either party.

(c) Termination of a contract by one party except on the happening of an agreed event requires that reasonable notification be received by the other party and an agreement dispensing with notification is invalid if its operation would be unconscionable.

Acts 1967, 60th Leg., p. 2343, ch. 785, § 1, eff. Sept. 1, 1967.

Uniform Commercial Code Comment

Prior Uniform Statutory Provision:

Subsection (1)—see Sections 43(2), 45(2), 47(1) and 48, Uniform Sales Act, for policy continued under this Article; Subsection (2)—none; Subsection (3)—none.

Changes: Completely different in scope.

Purposes of Changes and New Matter:

1. Subsection (1) requires that all actions taken under a sales contract must be taken within a reasonable time where no time has been agreed upon. The reasonable time under this provision turns on the criteria as to "reasonable time" and on good faith and commercial standards set forth in Sections 1–203, 1–204 and 2–103. It thus depends upon what constitutes acceptable commercial conduct in view of the nature, purpose and circumstances of the action to be taken. Agreement as to a definite time, however, may be found in a term implied from the contractual circumstances, usage of trade or course of dealing or performance as well as in an express term. Such cases fall outside of this subsection since in them the time for action is "agreed" by usage.

2. The time for payment, where not agreed upon, is related to the time for delivery; the particular problems which arise in connection with determining the appropriate time of payment and the time for any inspection before payment which is both allowed by law and demanded by the buyer are covered in Section 2–513.

3. The facts in regard to shipment and delivery differ so widely as to make detailed provision for them in the text of this Article impracticable. The applicable principles, however, make it clear that surprise is to be avoided, good faith

judgment is to be protected, and notice or negotiation to reduce the uncertainty to certainty is to be favored.

4. When the time for delivery is left open, unreasonably early offers of or demands for delivery are intended to be read under this Article as expressions of desire or intention, requesting the assent or acquiescence of the other party, not as final positions which may amount without more to breach or to create breach by the other side. See Sections 2–207 and 2–609.

5. The obligation of good faith under this Act requires reasonable notification before a contract may be treated as breached because a reasonable time for delivery or demand has expired. This operates both in the case of a contract originally indefinite as to time and of one subsequently made indefinite by waiver.

When both parties let an originally reasonable time go by in silence, the course of conduct under the contract may be viewed as enlarging the reasonable time for tender or demand of performance. The contract may be terminated by abandonment.

6. Parties to a contract are not required in giving reasonable notification to fix, at peril of breach, a time which is in fact reasonable in the unforeseeable judgment of a later trier of fact. Effective communication of a proposed time limit calls for a response, so that failure to reply will make out acquiescence. Where objection is made, however, or if the demand is merely for information as to when goods will be delivered or will be ordered out, demand for assurances on the ground of insecurity may be made under this Article pending further negotiations. Only when a party insists on undue delay or on rejection of the other party's reasonable proposal is there a question of flat breach under the present section.

7. Subsection (2) applies a commercially reasonable view to resolve the conflict which has arisen in the cases as to contracts of indefinite duration. The "reasonable time" of duration appropriate to a given arrangement is limited by the circumstances. When the arrangement has been carried on by the parties over the years, the "reasonable time" can continue indefinitely and the contract will not terminate until notice.

8. Subsection (3) recognizes that the application of principles of good faith and sound commercial practice normally call for such notification of the termination of a going contract relationship as will give the other party reasonable time to seek a substitute arrangement. An agreement dispensing with notification or limiting the time for the seeking of a substitute arrangement is, of course, valid under this subsection unless the results of putting it into operation would be the creation of an unconscionable state of affairs.

9. Justifiable cancellation for breach is a remedy for breach and is not the kind of termination covered by the present subsection.

10. The requirement of notification is dispensed with where the contract provides for termination on the happening of an "agreed event." "Event" is a term chosen here to contrast with "option" or the like.

Cross References:

Point 1: Sections 1–203, 1–204 and 2–103.

Point 2: Sections 2–320, 2–321, 2–504 and 2–511 through 2–514.

Point 5: Section 1–203.

Point 6: Section 2–609.

Point 7: Section 2–204.

Point 9: Sections 2–106, 2–318, 2–610 and 2–703.

Definitional Cross References:

"Agreement". Section 1–201.

"Contract". Section 1–201.

"Notification". Section 1–201.

"Party". Section 1–201.

"Reasonable time". Section 1–204.

"Termination". Section 2–106.

§ 2.310. Open Time for Payment or Running of Credit; Authority to Ship Under Reservation

Unless otherwise agreed

(1) payment is due at the time and place at which the buyer is to receive the goods even though the place of shipment is the place of delivery; and

(2) if the seller is authorized to send the goods he may ship them under reservation, and may tender the documents of title, but the buyer may inspect the goods after their arrival before payment is due unless such inspection is inconsistent with the terms of the contract (Section 2.513); and

(3) if delivery is authorized and made by way of documents of title otherwise than by Subdivision (2) then payment is due regardless of where the goods are to be received:

(A) at the time and place at which the buyer is to receive delivery of the tangible documents; or

(B) at the time the buyer is to receive delivery of the electronic documents and at the seller's place of business or if none, the seller's residence; and

(4) where the seller is required or authorized to ship the goods on credit the credit period runs from the time of shipment but post-dating the invoice or delaying its dispatch will correspondingly delay the starting of the credit period.

Acts 1967, 60th Leg., p. 2343, ch. 785, § 1, eff. Sept. 1, 1967. Amended by Acts 2005, 79th Leg., ch. 122, § 5, eff. Sept. 1, 2005.

Uniform Commercial Code Comment

Prior Uniform Statutory Provision:

Sections 42 and 47(2), Uniform Sales Act.

Changes: Completely rewritten in this and other sections.

Purposes of Changes: This section is drawn to reflect modern business methods of dealing at a distance rather than face to face. Thus:

1. Paragraph (a) provides that payment is due at the time and place "the buyer is to receive the goods" rather than at the point of delivery except in documentary shipment cases (paragraph (c)). This grants an opportunity for the exercise by the buyer of his preliminary right to inspection before paying even though under the delivery term the risk of loss may have previously passed to him or the running of the credit period has already started.

2. Paragraph (b) while providing for inspection by the buyer before he pays, protects the seller. He is not required to give up possession of the goods until he has received payment, where no credit has been contemplated by the parties. The seller may collect through a bank by a sight draft against an order bill of lading "hold until arrival; inspection allowed." The obligations of the bank under such a provision are set forth in Part 5 of Article 4. Under subsection (c), in the absence of a credit term, the seller is permitted to ship under reservation and if he does payment is then due where and when the buyer is to receive delivery of the tangible documents of title. In the case of an electronic document of title, payment is due when the buyer is to receive delivery of the electronic document and at the seller's place of business, or if none, the seller's residence. Delivery as to documents of title is stated in Article 1, Section 1–201.

3. Unless otherwise agreed, the place for the delivery of the documents and payment is the buyer's city but the time for payment is only after arrival of the goods, since under paragraph (b), and Sections 2–512 and 2–513 the buyer is under no duty to pay prior to inspection. Tender of a document of title requires that the seller be ready, willing and able to transfer possession of a tangible document of title or control of an electronic document of title to the buyer.

4. Where the mode of shipment is such that goods must be unloaded immediately upon arrival, too rapidly to permit adequate inspection before receipt, the seller must be guided by the provisions of this Article on inspection which provide that if the seller wishes to demand payment before inspection, he must put an appropriate term into the contract. Even requiring payment against documents will not of itself have this desired result if the documents are to be held until the arrival of the goods. But under (b) and (c) if the terms are C.I.F., C.O.D., or cash against documents payment may be due before inspection.

5. Paragraph (d) states the common commercial understanding that an agreed credit period runs from the time of shipment or from that dating of the invoice which is commonly recognized as a representation of the time of shipment. The provision concerning any delay in sending forth the invoice is included because such conduct results in depriving the buyer of his full notice and warning as to when he must be prepared to pay.

Cross References:

Generally: Part 5.

Point 1: Section 2–509.

Point 2: Sections 2–505, 2–511, 2–512, 2–513 and Article 4.

Point 3: Sections 2–308(b), 2–512 and 2–513.

Point 4: Section 2–513(3)(b).

Definitional Cross References:

"Buyer". Section 2–103.

"Delivery". Section 1–201.

"Document of title". Section 1–201.

"Goods". Section 2–105.

"Receipt of goods". Section 2–103.

"Seller". Section 2–103.

"Send". Section 1–201.

"Term". Section 1–201.

Sections 31 and 32 of Acts 2005, 79th Leg., ch. 122 provide:

"Sec. 31. This Act applies to a document of title that is issued or a bailment that arises on or after the effective date of this Act. This Act does not apply to a document of title that is issued or a bailment that arises before the effective date of this Act even if the document of title or bailment would be subject to this Act if the document of title had been issued or bailment had arisen after the effective date of this Act. This Act does not apply to a right of action that has accrued before the effective date of this Act.

"Sec. 32. A document of title issued or a bailment that arises before the effective date of this Act and the rights, obligations, and interests flowing from that document or bailment are governed by any statute or other rule amended or repealed by this Act as if amendment or repeal had not occurred and may be terminated, completed, consummated, or enforced under that statute or other rule."

§ 2.311. Options and Cooperation Respecting Performance

(a) An agreement for sale which is otherwise sufficiently definite (Subsection (c) of Section 2.204) to be a contract is not made invalid by the fact that it leaves particulars of performance to be specified by one of the parties. Any such specification must be made in good faith and within limits set by commercial reasonableness.

(b) Unless otherwise agreed specifications relating to assortment of the goods are at the buyer's option and except as otherwise provided in Subsections (a)(3) and (c) of Section 2.319 specifications or arrangements relating to shipment are at the seller's option.

(c) Where such specification would materially affect the other party's performance but is not seasonably made or where one party's cooperation is necessary to the agreed performance of the other but is not seasonably forthcoming, the other party in addition to all other remedies

(1) is excused for any resulting delay in his own performance; and

(2) may also either proceed to perform in any reasonable manner or after the time for a material part of his own performance treat the failure to

specify or to cooperate as a breach by failure to deliver or accept the goods.

Acts 1967, 60th Leg., p. 2343, ch. 785, § 1, eff. Sept. 1, 1967.

Uniform Commercial Code Comment

Prior Uniform Statutory Provision:

None.

Purposes:

1. Subsection (1) permits the parties to leave certain detailed particulars of performance to be filled in by either of them without running the risk of having the contract invalidated for indefiniteness. The party to whom the agreement gives power to specify the missing details is required to exercise good faith and to act in accordance with commercial standards so that there is no surprise and the range of permissible variation is limited by what is commercially reasonable. The "agreement" which permits one party so to specify may be found as well in a course of dealing, usage of trade, or implication from circumstances as in explicit language used by the parties.

2. Options as to assortment of goods or shipping arrangements are specifically reserved to the buyer and seller respectively under subsection (2) where no other arrangement has been made. This section rejects the test which mechanically and without regard to usage or the purpose of the option gave the option to the party "first under a duty to move" and applies instead a standard commercial interpretation to these circumstances. The "unless otherwise agreed" provision of this subsection covers not only express terms but the background and circumstances which enter into the agreement.

3. Subsection (3) applies when the exercise of an option or cooperation by one party is necessary to or materially affects the other party's performance, but it is not seasonably forthcoming; the subsection relieves the other party from the necessity for performance or excuses his delay in performance as the case may be. The contract-keeping party may at his option under this subsection proceed to perform in any commercially reasonable manner rather than wait. In addition to the special remedies provided, this subsection also reserves "all other remedies". The remedy of particular importance in this connection is that provided for insecurity. Request may also be made pursuant to the obligation of good faith for a reasonable indication of the time and manner of performance for which a party is to hold himself ready.

4. The remedy provided in subsection (3) is one which does not operate in the situation which falls within the scope of Section 2–614 on substituted performance. Where the failure to cooperate results from circumstances set forth in that Section, the other party is under a duty to proffer or demand (as the case may be) substitute performance as a condition to claiming rights against the noncooperating party.

Cross References:

Point 1: Sections 1–201, 1–203 and 2–204.

Point 3: Sections 1–203 and 2–609.

Point 4: Section 2–614.

Definitional Cross References:

"Agreement". Section 1–201.

"Buyer". Section 2–103.

"Contract for sale". Section 2–106.

"Goods". Section 2–105.

"Party". Section 1–201.

"Remedy". Section 1–201.

"Seasonably". Section 1–204.

"Seller". Section 2–103.

§ 2.312. Warranty of Title and Against Infringement; Buyer's Obligation Against Infringement

(a) Subject to Subsection (b) there is in a contract for sale a warranty by the seller that

(1) the title conveyed shall be good, and its transfer rightful; and

(2) the goods shall be delivered free from any security interest or other lien or encumbrance of which the buyer at the time of contracting has no knowledge.

(b) A warranty under Subsection (a) will be excluded or modified only by specific language or by circumstances which give the buyer reason to know that the person selling does not claim title in himself or that he is purporting to sell only such right or title as he or a third person may have.

(c) Unless otherwise agreed a seller who is a merchant regularly dealing in goods of the kind warrants that the goods shall be delivered free of the rightful claim of any third person by way of infringement or the like but a buyer who furnishes specifications to the seller must hold the seller harmless against any such claim which arises out of compliance with the specifications.

Acts 1967, 60th Leg., p. 2343, ch. 785, § 1, eff. Sept. 1, 1967.

Uniform Commercial Code Comment

Prior Uniform Statutory Provision:

Section 13, Uniform Sales Act.

Changes: Completely rewritten, the provisions concerning infringement being new.

Purposes of Changes:

1. Subsection (1) makes provision for a buyer's basic needs in respect to a title which he in good faith expects to acquire by his purchase, namely, that he receive a good, clean title transferred to him also in a rightful manner so that he will not be exposed to a lawsuit in order to protect it.

The warranty extends to a buyer whether or not the seller was in possession of the goods at the time the sale or contract to sell was made.

The warranty of quiet possession is abolished. Disturbance of quiet possession, although not mentioned specifically, is one way, among many, in which the breach of the warranty of title may be established.

The "knowledge" referred to in subsection 1(b) is actual knowledge as distinct from notice.

2. The provisions of this Article requiring notification to the seller within a reasonable time after the buyer's discovery of a breach apply to notice of a breach of the warranty of title, where the seller's breach was innocent. However, if the seller's breach was in bad faith he cannot be permitted to claim that he has been misled or prejudiced by the delay in giving notice. In such case the "reasonable" time for notice should receive a very liberal interpretation. Whether the breach by the seller is in good or bad faith Section 2–725 provides that the cause of action accrues when the breach occurs. Under the provisions of that section the breach of the warranty of good title occurs when tender of delivery is made since the warranty is not one which extends to "future performance of the goods."

3. When the goods are part of the seller's normal stock and are sold in his normal course of business, it is his duty to see that no claim of infringement of a patent or trademark by a third party will mar the buyer's title. A sale by a person other than a dealer, however, raises no implication in its circumstances of such a warranty. Nor is there such an implication when the buyer orders goods to be assembled, prepared or manufactured on his own specifications. If, in such a case, the resulting product infringes a patent or trademark, the liability will run from buyer to seller. There is, under such circumstances, a tacit representation on the part of the buyer that the seller will be safe in manufacturing according to the specifications, and the buyer is under an obligation in good faith to indemnify him for any loss suffered.

4. This section rejects the cases which recognize the principle that infringements violate the warranty of title but deny the buyer a remedy unless he has been expressly prevented from using the goods. Under this Article "eviction" is not a necessary condition to the buyer's remedy since the buyer's remedy arises immediately upon receipt of notice of infringement; it is merely one way of establishing the fact of breach.

5. Subsection (2) recognizes that sales by sheriffs, executors, foreclosing lienors and persons similarly situated are so out of the ordinary commercial course that their peculiar character is immediately apparent to the buyer and therefore no personal obligation is imposed upon the seller who is purporting to sell only an unknown or limited right. This subsection does not touch upon and leaves open all questions of restitution arising in such cases, when a unique article so sold is reclaimed by a third party as the rightful owner.

Foreclosure sales under Article 9 are another matter. Section 9–610 provides that a disposition of collateral under that section includes warranties such as those imposed by this section on a voluntary disposition of property of the kind involved. Consequently, unless properly excluded under subsection (2) or under the special provisions for exclusion in Section 9–610, a disposition under Section 9–610 of collateral consisting of goods includes the warranties imposed by subsection (1) and, if applicable, subsection (3).

6. The warranty of subsection (1) is not designated as an "implied" warranty, and hence is not subject to Section 2–316(3). Disclaimer of the warranty of title is governed instead by subsection (2), which requires either specific language or the described circumstances.

Cross References:

Point 1: Section 2–403.

Point 2: Sections 2–607 and 2–725.

Point 3: Section 1–203.

Point 4: Sections 2–609 and 2–725.

Point 6: Section 2–316.

Definitional Cross References:

"Buyer". Section 2–103.

"Contract for sale". Section 2–106.

"Goods". Section 2–105.

"Person". Section 1–201.

"Right". Section 1–201.

"Seller". Section 2–103.

§ 2.313. Express Warranties by Affirmation, Promise, Description, Sample

(a) Express warranties by the seller are created as follows:

(1) Any affirmation of fact or promise made by the seller to the buyer which relates to the goods and becomes part of the basis of the bargain creates an express warranty that the goods shall conform to the affirmation or promise.

(2) Any description of the goods which is made part of the basis of the bargain creates an express warranty that the goods shall conform to the description.

(3) Any sample or model which is made part of the basis of the bargain creates an express warranty that the whole of the goods shall conform to the sample or model.

(b) It is not necessary to the creation of an express warranty that the seller use formal words such as "warrant" or "guarantee" or that he have a specific intention to make a warranty, but an affirmation merely of the value of the goods or a statement purporting to be merely the seller's opinion or commendation of the goods does not create a warranty.

Acts 1967, 60th Leg., p. 2343, ch. 785, § 1, eff. Sept. 1, 1967.

Uniform Commercial Code Comment

Prior Uniform Statutory Provision:

Sections 12, 14 and 16, Uniform Sales Act.

Changes: Rewritten.

Purposes of Changes: To consolidate and systematize basic principles with the result that:

1. "Express" warranties rest on "dickered" aspects of the individual bargain, and go so clearly to the essence of that bargain that words of disclaimer in a form are repugnant to the basic dickered terms. "Implied" warranties rest so clearly on a common factual situation or set of conditions that no particular language or action is necessary to evidence them and they will arise in such a situation unless unmistakably negated.

This section reverts to the older case law insofar as the warranties of description and sample are designated "express" rather than "implied".

2. Although this section is limited in its scope and direct purpose to warranties made by the seller to the buyer as part of a contract for sale, the warranty sections of this Article are not designed in any way to disturb those lines of case law growth which have recognized that warranties need not be confined either to sales contracts or to the direct parties to such a contract. They may arise in other appropriate circumstances such as in the case of bailments for hire, whether such bailment is itself the main contract or is merely a supplying of containers under a contract for the sale of their contents. The provisions of Section 2–318 on third party beneficiaries expressly recognize this case law development within one particular area. Beyond that, the matter is left to the case law with the intention that the policies of this Act may offer useful guidance in dealing with further cases as they arise.

3. The present section deals with affirmations of fact by the seller, descriptions of the goods or exhibitions of samples, exactly as any other part of a negotiation which ends in a contract is dealt with. No specific intention to make a warranty is necessary if any of these factors is made part of the basis of the bargain. In actual practice affirmations of fact made by the seller about the goods during a bargain are regarded as part of the description of those goods; hence no particular reliance on such statements need be shown in order to weave them into the fabric of the agreement. Rather, any fact which is to take such affirmations, once made, out of the agreement requires clear affirmative proof. The issue normally is one of fact.

4. In view of the principle that the whole purpose of the law of warranty is to determine what it is that the seller has in essence agreed to sell, the policy is adopted of those cases which refuse except in unusual circumstances to recognize a material deletion of the seller's obligation. Thus, a contract is normally a contract for a sale of something describable and described. A clause generally disclaiming "all warranties, express or implied" cannot reduce the seller's obligation with respect to such description and therefore cannot be given literal effect under Section 2–316.

This is not intended to mean that the parties, if they consciously desire, cannot make their own bargain as they wish. But in determining what they have agreed upon good faith is a factor and consideration should be given to the fact that the probability is small that a real price is intended to be exchanged for a pseudo-obligation.

5. Paragraph (1)(b) makes specific some of the principles set forth above when a description of the goods is given by the seller.

A description need not be by words. Technical specifications, blueprints and the like can afford more exact description than mere language and if made part of the basis of the bargain goods must conform with them. Past deliveries may set the description of quality, either expressly or impliedly by course of dealing. Of course, all descriptions by merchants must be read against the applicable trade usages with the general rules as to merchantability resolving any doubts.

6. The basic situation as to statements affecting the true essence of the bargain is no different when a sample or model is involved in the transaction. This section includes both a "sample" actually drawn from the bulk of goods which is the subject matter of the sale, and a "model" which is offered for inspection when the subject matter is not at hand and which has not been drawn from the bulk of the goods.

Although the underlying principles are unchanged, the facts are often ambiguous when something is shown as illustrative, rather than as a straight sample. In general, the presumption is that any sample or model just as any affirmation of fact is intended to become a basis of the bargain. But there is no escape from the question of fact. When the seller exhibits a sample purporting to be drawn from an existing bulk, good faith of course requires that the sample be fairly drawn. But in mercantile experience the mere exhibition of a "sample" does not of itself show whether it is merely intended to "suggest" or to "be" the character of the subject-matter of the contract. The question is whether the seller has so acted with reference to the sample as to make him responsible that the whole shall have at least the values shown by it. The circumstances aid in answering this question. If the sample has been drawn from an existing bulk, it must be regarded as describing values of the goods contracted for unless it is accompanied by an unmistakable denial of such responsibility. If, on the other hand, a model of merchandise not on hand is offered, the mercantile presumption that it has become a literal description of the subject matter is not so strong, and particularly so if modification on the buyer's initiative impairs any feature of the model.

7. The precise time when words of description or affirmation are made or samples are shown is not material. The sole question is whether the language or samples or models are fairly to be regarded as part of the contract. If language is used after the closing of the deal (as when the buyer when taking delivery asks and receives an additional assurance), the warranty becomes a modification, and need not be supported by consideration if it is otherwise reasonable and in order (Section 2–209).

8. Concerning affirmations of value or a seller's opinion or commendation under subsection (2), the basic question remains the same: What statements of the seller have in the circumstances and in objective judgment become part of the basis of the bargain? As indicated above, all of the statements of the seller do so unless good reason is shown to the contrary. The provisions of subsection (2) are included, however, since common experience discloses that some state-

ments or predictions cannot fairly be viewed as entering into the bargain. Even as to false statements of value, however, the possibility is left open that a remedy may be provided by the law relating to fraud or misrepresentation.

Cross References:

Point 1: Section 2–316.

Point 2: Sections 1–102(3) and 2–318.

Point 3: Section 2–316(2)(b).

Point 4: Section 2–316.

Point 5: Sections 1–205(4) and 2–314.

Point 6: Section 2–316.

Point 7: Section 2–209.

Point 8: Section 1–103.

Definitional Cross References:

"Buyer". Section 2–103.

"Conforming". Section 2–106.

"Goods". Section 2–105.

"Seller". Section 2–103.

§ 2.314. Implied Warranty: Merchantability; Usage of Trade

(a) Unless excluded or modified (Section 2.316), a warranty that the goods shall be merchantable is implied in a contract for their sale if the seller is a merchant with respect to goods of that kind. Under this section the serving for value of food or drink to be consumed either on the premises or elsewhere is a sale.

(b) Goods to be merchantable must be at least such as

(1) pass without objection in the trade under the contract description; and

(2) in the case of fungible goods, are of fair average quality within the description; and

(3) are fit for the ordinary purposes for which such goods are used; and

(4) run, within the variations permitted by the agreement, of even kind, quality and quantity within each unit and among all units involved; and

(5) are adequately contained, packaged, and labeled as the agreement may require; and

(6) conform to the promises or affirmations of fact made on the container or label if any.

(c) Unless excluded or modified (Section 2.316) other implied warranties may arise from course of dealing or usage of trade.

Acts 1967, 60th Leg., p. 2343, ch. 785, § 1, eff. Sept. 1, 1967.

Uniform Commercial Code Comment

Prior Uniform Statutory Provision:

Section 15(2), Uniform Sales Act.

Changes: Completely rewritten.

Purposes of Changes: This section, drawn in view of the steadily developing case law on the subject, is intended to make it clear that:

1. The seller's obligation applies to present sales as well as to contracts to sell subject to the effects of any examination of specific goods. (Subsection (2) of Section 2–316). Also, the warranty of merchantability applies to sales for use as well as to sales for resale.

2. The question when the warranty is imposed turns basically on the meaning of the terms of the agreement as recognized in the trade. Goods delivered under an agreement made by a merchant in a given line of trade must be of a quality comparable to that generally acceptable in that line of trade under the description or other designation of the goods used in the agreement. The responsibility imposed rests on any merchant-seller, and the absence of the words "grower or manufacturer or not" which appeared in Section 15(2) of the Uniform Sales Act does not restrict the applicability of this section.

3. A specific designation of goods by the buyer does not exclude the seller's obligation that they be fit for the general purposes appropriate to such goods. A contract for the sale of second-hand goods, however, involves only such obligation as is appropriate to such goods for that is their contract description. A person making an isolated sale of goods is not a "merchant" within the meaning of the full scope of this section and, thus, no warranty of merchantability would apply. His knowledge of any defects not apparent on inspection would, however, without need for express agreement and in keeping with the underlying reason of the present section and the provisions on good faith, impose an obligation that known material but hidden defects be fully disclosed.

4. Although a seller may not be a "merchant" as to the goods in question, if he states generally that they are "guaranteed" the provisions of this section may furnish a guide to the content of the resulting express warranty. This has particular significance in the case of second-hand sales, and has further significance in limiting the effect of fine-print disclaimer clauses where their effect would be inconsistent with large-print assertions of "guarantee".

5. The second sentence of subsection (1) covers the warranty with respect to food and drink. Serving food or drink for value is a sale, whether to be consumed on the premises or elsewhere. Cases to the contrary are rejected. The principal warranty is that stated in subsections (1) and (2)(c) of this section.

6. Subsection (2) does not purport to exhaust the meaning of "merchantable" nor to negate any of its attributes not specifically mentioned in the text of the statute, but arising by usage of trade or through case law. The language used is "must be at least such as . . .," and the intention is to leave open other possible attributes of merchantability.

7. Paragraphs (a) and (b) of subsection (2) are to be read together. Both refer, as indicated above, to the standards of

that line of the trade which fits the transaction and the seller's business. "Fair average" is a term directly appropriate to agricultural bulk products and means goods centering around the middle belt of quality, not the least or the worst that can be understood in the particular trade by the designation, but such as can pass "without objection." Of course a fair percentage of the least is permissible but the goods are not "fair average" if they are all of the least or worst quality possible under the description. In cases of doubt as to what quality is intended, the price at which a merchant closes a contract is an excellent index of the nature and scope of his obligation under the present section.

8. Fitness for the ordinary purposes for which goods of the type are used is a fundamental concept of the present section and is covered in paragraph (c). As stated above, merchantability is also a part of the obligation owing to the purchaser for use. Correspondingly, protection, under this aspect of the warranty, of the person buying for resale to the ultimate consumer is equally necessary, and merchantable goods must therefore be "honestly" resalable in the normal course of business because they are what they purport to be.

9. Paragraph (d) on evenness of kind, quality and quantity follows case law. But precautionary language has been added as a reminder of the frequent usages of trade which permit substantial variations both with and without an allowance or an obligation to replace the varying units.

10. Paragraph (e) applies only where the nature of the goods and of the transaction require a certain type of container, package or label. Paragraph (f) applies, on the other hand, wherever there is a label or container on which representations are made, even though the original contract, either by express terms or usage of trade, may not have required either the labelling or the representation. This follows from the general obligation of good faith which requires that a buyer should not be placed in the position of reselling or using goods delivered under false representations appearing on the package or container. No problem of extra consideration arises in this connection since, under this Article, an obligation is imposed by the original contract not to deliver mislabeled articles, and the obligation is imposed where mercantile good faith so requires and without reference to the doctrine of consideration.

11. Exclusion or modification of the warranty of merchantability, or of any part of it, is dealt with in the section to which the text of the present section makes explicit precautionary references. That section must be read with particular reference to its subsection (4) on limitation of remedies. The warranty of merchantability, wherever it is normal, is so commonly taken for granted that its exclusion from the contract is a matter threatening surprise and therefore requiring special precaution.

12. Subsection (3) is to make explicit that usage of trade and course of dealing can create warranties and that they are implied rather than express warranties and thus subject to exclusion or modification under Section 2–316. A typical instance would be the obligation to provide pedigree papers to evidence conformity of the animal to the contract in the case of a pedigreed dog or blooded bull.

13. In an action based on breach of warranty, it is of course necessary to show not only the existence of the warranty but the fact that the warranty was broken and that the breach of the warranty was the proximate cause of the loss sustained. In such an action an affirmative showing by the seller that the loss resulted from some action or event following his own delivery of the goods can operate as a defense. Equally, evidence indicating that the seller exercised care in the manufacture, processing or selection of the goods is relevant to the issue of whether the warranty was in fact broken. Action by the buyer following an examination of the goods which ought to have indicated the defect complained of can be shown as matter bearing on whether the breach itself was the cause of the injury.

Cross References:

Point 1: Section 2–316.

Point 3: Sections 1–203 and 2–104.

Point 5: Section 2–315.

Point 11: Section 2–316.

Point 12: Sections 1–201, 1–205 and 2–316.

Definitional Cross References:

"Agreement". Section 1–201.

"Contract". Section 1–201.

"Contract for sale". Section 2–106.

"Goods". Section 2–105.

"Merchant". Section 2–104.

"Seller". Section 2–103.

§ 2.315. Implied Warranty: Fitness for Particular Purpose

Where the seller at the time of contracting has reason to know any particular purpose for which the goods are required and that the buyer is relying on the seller's skill or judgment to select or furnish suitable goods, there is unless excluded or modified under the next section an implied warranty that the goods shall be fit for such purpose.

Acts 1967, 60th Leg., p. 2343, ch. 785, § 1, eff. Sept. 1, 1967.

Uniform Commercial Code Comment

Prior Uniform Statutory Provision:

Section 15(1), (4), (5), Uniform Sales Act.

Changes: Rewritten.

Purposes of Changes:

1. Whether or not this warranty arises in any individual case is basically a question of fact to be determined by the circumstances of the contracting. Under this section the buyer need not bring home to the seller actual knowledge of the particular purpose for which the goods are intended or of his reliance on the seller's skill and judgment, if the circumstances are such that the seller has reason to realize the purpose intended or that the reliance exists. The buyer, of course, must actually be relying on the seller.

2. A "particular purpose" differs from the ordinary purpose for which the goods are used in that it envisages a specific use by the buyer which is peculiar to the nature of

his business whereas the ordinary purposes for which goods are used are those envisaged in the concept of merchantability and go to uses which are customarily made of the goods in question. For example, shoes are generally used for the purpose of walking upon ordinary ground, but a seller may know that a particular pair was selected to be used for climbing mountains.

A contract may of course include both a warranty of merchantability and one of fitness for a particular purpose.

The provisions of this Article on the cumulation and conflict of express and implied warranties must be considered on the question of inconsistency between or among warranties. In such a case any question of fact as to which warranty was intended by the parties to apply must be resolved in favor of the warranty of fitness for particular purpose as against all other warranties except where the buyer has taken upon himself the responsibility of furnishing the technical specifications.

3. In connection with the warranty of fitness for a particular purpose the provisions of this Article on the allocation or division of risks are particularly applicable in any transaction in which the purpose for which the goods are to be used combines requirements both as to the quality of the goods themselves and compliance with certain laws or regulations. How the risks are divided is a question of fact to be determined, where not expressly contained in the agreement, from the circumstances of contracting, usage of trade, course of performance and the like, matters which may constitute the "otherwise agreement" of the parties by which they may divide the risk or burden.

4. The absence from this section of the language used in the Uniform Sales Act in referring to the seller, "whether he be the grower or manufacturer or not," is not intended to impose any requirement that the seller be a grower or manufacturer. Although normally the warranty will arise only where the seller is a merchant with the appropriate "skill or judgment," it can arise as to nonmerchants where this is justified by the particular circumstances.

5. The elimination of the "patent or other trade name" exception constitutes the major extension of the warranty of fitness which has been made by the cases and continued in this Article. Under the present section the existence of a patent or other trade name and the designation of the article by that name, or indeed in any other definite manner, is only one of the facts to be considered on the question of whether the buyer actually relied on the seller, but it is not of itself decisive of the issue. If the buyer himself is insisting on a particular brand he is not relying on the seller's skill and judgment and so no warranty results. But the mere fact that the article purchased has a particular patent or trade name is not sufficient to indicate nonreliance if the article has been recommended by the seller as adequate for the buyer's purposes.

6. The specific reference forward in the present section to the following section on exclusion or modification of warranties is to call attention to the possibility of eliminating the warranty in any given case. However it must be noted that under the following section the warranty of fitness for a particular purpose must be excluded or modified by a conspicuous writing.

Cross References:

Point 2: Sections 2–314 and 2–317.

Point 3: Section 2–303.

Point 6: Section 2–316.

Definitional Cross References:

"Buyer". Section 2–103.

"Goods". Section 2–105.

"Seller". Section 2–103.

§ 2.316. Exclusion or Modification of Warranties

(a) Words or conduct relevant to the creation of an express warranty and words or conduct tending to negate or limit warranty shall be construed wherever reasonable as consistent with each other; but subject to the provisions of this chapter on parol or extrinsic evidence (Section 2.202) negation or limitation is inoperative to the extent that such construction is unreasonable.

(b) Subject to Subsection (c), to exclude or modify the implied warranty of merchantability or any part of it the language must mention merchantability and in case of a writing must be conspicuous, and to exclude or modify any implied warranty of fitness the exclusion must be by a writing and conspicuous. Language to exclude all implied warranties of fitness is sufficient if it states, for example, that "There are no warranties which extend beyond the description on the face hereof."

(c) Notwithstanding Subsection (b)

(1) unless the circumstances indicate otherwise, all implied warranties are excluded by expressions like "as is", "with all faults" or other language which in common understanding calls the buyer's attention to the exclusion of warranties and makes plain that there is no implied warranty; and

(2) when the buyer before entering into the contract has examined the goods or the sample or model as fully as he desired or has refused to examine the goods there is no implied warranty with regard to defects which an examination ought in the circumstances to have revealed to him; and

(3) an implied warranty can also be excluded or modified by course of dealing or course of performance or usage of trade.

(d) Remedies for breach of warranty can be limited in accordance with the provisions of this chapter on liquidation or limitation of damages and on contractual modification of remedy (Sections 2.718 and 2.719).

(e) The implied warranties of merchantability and fitness shall not be applicable to the furnishing of human blood, blood plasma, or other human tissue or organs from a blood bank or reservoir of such other tissues or organs. Such blood, blood plasma or tissue or organs shall not for the purpose of this Title be considered commodities subject to sale or barter, but shall be considered as medical services.

(f) The implied warranties of merchantability and fitness do not apply to the sale or barter of livestock or its unborn young.

Acts 1967, 60th Leg., p. 2343, ch. 785, § 1, eff. Sept. 1, 1967. Amended by Acts 1979, 66th Leg., p. 190, ch. 99, § 1, eff. May 2, 1979.

Uniform Commercial Code Comment

Prior Uniform Statutory Provision:

None. See sections 15 and 71, Uniform Sales Act.

Purposes:

1. This section is designed principally to deal with those frequent clauses in sales contracts which seek to exclude "all warranties, express or implied." It seeks to protect a buyer from unexpected and unbargained language of disclaimer by denying effect to such language when inconsistent with language of express warranty and permitting the exclusion of implied warranties only by conspicuous language or other circumstances which protect the buyer from surprise.

2. The seller is protected under this Article against false allegations of oral warranties by its provisions on parol and extrinsic evidence and against unauthorized representations by the customary "lack of authority" clauses. This Article treats the limitation or avoidance of consequential damages as a matter of limiting remedies for breach, separate from the matter of creation of liability under a warranty. If no warranty exists, there is of course no problem of limiting remedies for breach of warranty. Under subsection (4) the question of limitation of remedy is governed by the sections referred to rather than by this section.

3. Disclaimer of the implied warranty of merchantability is permitted under subsection (2), but with the safeguard that such disclaimers must mention merchantability and in case of a writing must be conspicuous.

4. Unlike the implied warranty of merchantability, implied warranties of fitness for a particular purpose may be excluded by general language, but only if it is in writing and conspicuous.

5. Subsection (2) presupposes that the implied warranty in question exists unless excluded or modified. Whether or not language of disclaimer satisfies the requirements of this section, such language may be relevant under other sections to the question whether the warranty was ever in fact created. Thus, unless the provisions of this Article on parol and extrinsic evidence prevent, oral language of disclaimer may raise issues of fact as to whether reliance by the buyer occurred and whether the seller had "reason to know" under the section on implied warranty of fitness for a particular purpose.

6. The exceptions to the general rule set forth in paragraphs (a), (b) and (c) of subsection (3) are common factual situations in which the circumstances surrounding the transaction are in themselves sufficient to call the buyer's attention to the fact that no implied warranties are made or that a certain implied warranty is being excluded.

7. Paragraph (a) of subsection (3) deals with general terms such as "as is," "as they stand," "with all faults," and the like. Such terms in ordinary commercial usage are understood to mean that the buyer takes the entire risk as to the quality of the goods involved. The terms covered by paragraph (a) are in fact merely a particularization of paragraph (c) which provides for exclusion or modification of implied warranties by usage of trade.

8. Under paragraph (b) of subsection (3) warranties may be excluded or modified by the circumstances where the buyer examines the goods or a sample or model of them before entering into the contract. "Examination" as used in this paragraph is not synonymous with inspection before acceptance or at any other time after the contract has been made. It goes rather to the nature of the responsibility assumed by the seller at the time of the making of the contract. Of course if the buyer discovers the defect and uses the goods anyway, or if he unreasonably fails to examine the goods before he uses them, resulting injuries may be found to result from his own action rather than proximately from a breach of warranty. See Sections 2–314 and 2–715 and comments thereto.

In order to bring the transaction within the scope of "refused to examine" in paragraph (b), it is not sufficient that the goods are available for inspection. There must in addition be a demand by the seller that the buyer examine the goods fully. The seller by the demand puts the buyer on notice that he is assuming the risk of defects which the examination ought to reveal. The language "refused to examine" in this paragraph is intended to make clear the necessity for such demand.

Application of the doctrine of "caveat emptor" in all cases where the buyer examines the goods regardless of statements made by the seller is, however, rejected by this Article. Thus, if the offer of examination is accompanied by words as to their merchantability or specific attributes and the buyer indicates clearly that he is relying on those words rather than on his examination, they give rise to an "express" warranty. In such cases the question is one of fact as to whether a warranty of merchantability has been expressly incorporated in the agreement. Disclaimer of such an express warranty is governed by subsection (1) of the present section.

The particular buyer's skill and the normal method of examining goods in the circumstances determine what defects are excluded by the examination. A failure to notice defects which are obvious cannot excuse the buyer. However, an examination under circumstances which do not permit chemical or other testing of the goods would not exclude defects which could be ascertained only by such testing. Nor can latent defects be excluded by a simple examination. A professional buyer examining a product in his field will be held to have assumed the risk as to all defects which a professional in the field ought to observe, while a nonprofessional buyer will be held to have assumed the risk only for such defects as a layman might be expected to observe.

9. The situation in which the buyer gives precise and complete specifications to the seller is not explicitly covered in this section, but this is a frequent circumstance by which the implied warranties may be excluded. The warranty of fitness for a particular purpose would not normally arise since in such a situation there is usually no reliance on the seller by the buyer. The warranty of merchantability in such a transaction, however, must be considered in connection with the next section on the cumulation and conflict of warranties. Under paragraph (c) of that section in case of such an inconsistency the implied warranty of merchantability is displaced by the express warranty that the goods will comply with the specifications. Thus, where the buyer gives detailed specifications as to the goods, neither of the implied warranties as to quality will normally apply to the transaction unless consistent with the specifications.

Cross References:

Point 2: Sections 2–202, 2–718 and 2–719.

Point 7: Sections 1–205 and 2–208.

Definitional Cross References:

"Agreement". Section 1–201.

"Buyer". Section 2–103.

"Contract". Section 1–201.

"Course of dealing". Section 1–205.

"Goods". Section 2–105.

"Remedy". Section 1–201.

"Seller". Section 2–103.

"Usage of trade". Section 1–205.

§ 2.317. Cumulation and Conflict of Warranties Express or Implied

Warranties whether express or implied shall be construed as consistent with each other and as cumulative, but if such construction is unreasonable the intention of the parties shall determine which warranty is dominant. In ascertaining that intention the following rules apply:

(1) Exact or technical specifications displace an inconsistent sample or model or general language of description.

(2) A sample from an existing bulk displaces inconsistent general language of description.

(3) Express warranties displace inconsistent implied warranties other than an implied warranty of fitness for a particular purpose.

Acts 1967, 60th Leg., p. 2343, ch. 785, § 1, eff. Sept. 1, 1967.

Uniform Commercial Code Comment

Prior Uniform Statutory Provision:

On cumulation of warranties see Sections 14, 15, and 16, Uniform Sales Act.

Changes: Completely rewritten into one section.

Purposes of Changes:

1. The present section rests on the basic policy of this Article that no warranty is created except by some conduct (either affirmative action or failure to disclose) on the part of the seller. Therefore, all warranties are made cumulative unless this construction of the contract is impossible or unreasonable.

This Article thus follows the general policy of the Uniform Sales Act except that in case of the sale of an article by its patent or trade name the elimination of the warranty of fitness depends solely on whether the buyer has relied on the seller's skill and judgment; the use of the patent or trade name is but one factor in making this determination.

2. The rules of this section are designed to aid in determining the intention of the parties as to which of inconsistent warranties which have arisen from the circumstances of their transaction shall prevail. These rules of intention are to be applied only where factors making for an equitable estoppel of the seller do not exist and where he has in perfect good faith made warranties which later turn out to be inconsistent. To the extent that the seller has led the buyer to believe that all of the warranties can be performed, he is estopped from setting up any essential inconsistency as a defense.

3. The rules in subsections (a), (b) and (c) are designed to ascertain the intention of the parties by reference to the factor which probably claimed the attention of the parties in the first instance. These rules are not absolute but may be changed by evidence showing that the conditions which existed at the time of contracting make the construction called for by the section inconsistent or unreasonable.

Cross Reference:

Point 1: Section 2–315.

Definitional Cross Reference:

"Party". Section 1–201.

§ 2.318. Chapter Neutral on Question of Third Party Beneficiaries of Warranties of Quality and on Need for Privity of Contract

This chapter does not provide whether anyone other than a buyer may take advantage of an express or implied warranty of quality made to the buyer or whether the buyer or anyone entitled to take advantage of a warranty made to the buyer may sue a third party other than the immediate seller for deficiencies in the quality of the goods. These matters are left to the courts for their determination.

Acts 1967, 60th Leg., p. 2343, ch. 785, § 1, eff. Sept. 1, 1967.

§ 2.319. F.O.B. and F.A.S. Terms

(a) Unless otherwise agreed the term F.O.B. (which means "free on board") at a named place, even though used only in connection with the stated price, is a delivery term under which

(1) when the term is F.O.B. the place of shipment, the seller must at that place ship the goods in the manner provided in this chapter (Section 2.504) and bear the expense and risk of putting them into the possession of the carrier; or

(2) when the term is F.O.B. the place of destination, the seller must at his own expense and risk transport the goods to that place and there tender delivery of them in the manner provided in this chapter (Section 2.503);

(3) when under either Subdivision (1) or (2) the term is also F.O.B. vessel, car or other vehicle, the seller must in addition at his own expense and risk load the goods on board. If the term is F.O.B. vessel the buyer must name the vessel and in an appropriate case the seller must comply with the provisions of this chapter on the form of bill of lading (Section 2.323).

(b) Unless otherwise agreed the term F.A.S. vessel (which means "free alongside") at a named port, even though used only in connection with the stated price, is a delivery term under which the seller must

(1) at his own expense and risk deliver the goods alongside the vessel in the manner usual in that port or on a dock designated and provided by the buyer; and

(2) obtain and tender a receipt for the goods in exchange for which the carrier is under a duty to issue a bill of lading.

(c) Unless otherwise agreed in any case falling within Subsection (a)(1) or (3) or Subsection (b) the buyer must seasonably give any needed instructions for making delivery, including when the term is F.A.S. or F.O.B. the loading berth of the vessel and in an appropriate case its name and sailing date. The seller may treat the failure of needed instructions as a failure of cooperation under this chapter (Section 2.311). He may also at his option move the goods in any reasonable manner preparatory to delivery or shipment.

(d) Under the term F.O.B. vessel or F.A.S. unless otherwise agreed the buyer must make payment against tender of the required documents and the seller may not tender nor the buyer demand delivery of the goods in substitution for the documents.

Acts 1967, 60th Leg., p. 2343, ch. 785, § 1, eff. Sept. 1, 1967.

Uniform Commercial Code Comment

Prior Uniform Statutory Provision:

None.

Purposes:

1. This section is intended to negate the uncommercial line of decision which treats an "F.O.B." term as "merely a price term." The distinctions taken in subsection (1) handle most of the issues which have on occasion led to the unfortunate judicial language just referred to. Other matters which have led to sound results being based on unhappy language in regard to F.O.B. clauses are dealt with in this Act by Section 2–311(2) (seller's option re arrangements relating to shipment) and Sections 2–614 and 615 (substituted performance and seller's excuse).

2. Subsection (1)(c) not only specifies the duties of a seller who engages to deliver "F.O.B. vessel," or the like, but ought to make clear that no agreement is soundly drawn when it looks to reshipment from San Francisco or New York, but speaks merely of "F.O.B." the place.

3. The buyer's obligations stated in subsection (1)(c) and subsection (3) are, as shown in the text, obligations of cooperation. The last sentence of subsection (3) expressly, though perhaps unnecessarily, authorizes the seller, pending instructions, to go ahead with such preparatory moves as shipment from the interior to the named point of delivery. The sentence presupposes the usual case in which instructions "fail"; a prior repudiation by the buyer, giving notice that breach was intended, would remove the reason for the sentence, and would normally bring into play, instead, the second sentence of Section 2–704, which duly calls for lessening damages.

4. The treatment of "F.O.B. vessel" in conjunction with F.A.S. fits, in regard to the need for payment against documents, with standard practice and caselaw; but "F.O.B. vessel" is a term which by its very language makes express the need for an "on board" document. In this respect, that term is stricter than the ordinary overseas "shipment" contract (C.I.F., etc., Section 2–320).

Cross References:

Sections 2–311(3), 2–323, 2–503 and 2–504.

Definitional Cross References:

"Agreed". Section 1–201.

"Bill of lading". Section 1–201.

"Buyer". Section 2–103.

"Goods". Section 2–105.

"Seasonably". Section 1–204.

"Seller". Section 2–103.

"Term". Section 1–201.

§ 2.320. C.I.F. and C. & F. Terms

(a) The term C.I.F. means that the price includes in a lump sum the cost of the goods and the insurance and freight to the named destination. The term C. & F. or C.F. means that the price so includes cost and freight to the named destination.

(b) Unless otherwise agreed and even though used only in connection with the stated price and destination, the term C.I.F. destination or its equivalent requires the seller at his own expense and risk to

(1) put the goods into the possession of a carrier at the port for shipment and obtain a negotiable bill or bills of lading covering the entire transportation to the named destination; and

(2) load the goods and obtain a receipt from the carrier (which may be contained in the bill of lading) showing that the freight has been paid or provided for; and

(3) obtain a policy or certificate of insurance, including any war risk insurance, of a kind and on terms then current at the port of shipment in the usual amount, in the currency of the contract, shown to cover the same goods covered by the bill of lading and providing for payment of loss to the order of the buyer or for the account of whom it may concern; but the seller may add to the price the amount of the premium for any such war risk insurance; and

(4) prepare an invoice of the goods and procure any other documents required to effect shipment or to comply with the contract; and

(5) forward and tender with commercial promptness all the documents in due form and with any indorsement necessary to perfect the buyer's rights.

(c) Unless otherwise agreed the term C. & F. or its equivalent has the same effect and imposes upon the seller the same obligations and risks as a C.I.F. term except the obligation as to insurance.

(d) Under the term C.I.F. or C. & F. unless otherwise agreed the buyer must make payment against tender of the required documents and the seller may not tender nor the buyer demand delivery of the goods in substitution for the documents.

Acts 1967, 60th Leg., p. 2343, ch. 785, § 1, eff. Sept. 1, 1967.

Uniform Commercial Code Comment

Prior Uniform Statutory Provision:

None.

Purposes: To make it clear that:

1. The C.I.F. contract is not a destination but a shipment contract with risk of subsequent loss or damage to the goods passing to the buyer upon shipment if the seller has properly performed all his obligations with respect to the goods. Delivery to the carrier is delivery to the buyer for purposes of risk and "title". Delivery of possession of the goods is accomplished by delivery of the bill of lading, and upon tender of the required documents the buyer must pay the agreed price without awaiting the arrival of the goods and if they have been lost or damaged after proper shipment he must seek his remedy against the carrier or insurer. The buyer has no right of inspection prior to payment or acceptance of the documents.

2. The seller's obligations remain the same even though the C.I.F. term is "used only in connection with the stated price and destination".

3. The insurance stipulated by the C.I.F. term is for the buyer's benefit, to protect him against the risk of loss or damage to the goods in transit. A clause in a C.I.F. contract "insurance—for the account of sellers" should be viewed in its ordinary mercantile meaning that the sellers must pay for the insurance and not that it is intended to run to the seller's benefit.

4. A bill of lading covering the entire transportation from the port of shipment is explicitly required but the provision on this point must be read in the light of its reason to assure the buyer of as full protection as the conditions of shipment reasonably permit, remembering always that this type of contract is designed to move the goods in the channels commercially available. To enable the buyer to deal with the goods while they are afloat the bill of lading must be one that covers only the quantity of goods called for by the contract. The buyer is not required to accept his part of the goods without a bill of lading because the latter covers a larger quantity, nor is he required to accept a bill of lading for the whole quantity under a stipulation to hold the excess for the owner. Although the buyer is not compelled to accept either goods or documents under such circumstances he may of course claim his rights in any goods which have been identified to his contract.

5. The seller is given the option of paying or providing for the payment of freight. He has no option to ship "freight collect" unless the agreement so provides. The rule of the common law that the buyer need not pay the freight if the goods do not arrive is preserved.

Unless the shipment has been sent "freight collect" the buyer is entitled to receive documentary evidence that he is not obligated to pay the freight; the seller is therefore required to obtain a receipt "showing that the freight has been paid or provided for." The usual notation on the bill of lading that the freight has been prepaid is a sufficient receipt, as at common law. The phrase "provided for" is intended to cover the frequent situation in which the carrier extends credit to a shipper for the freight on successive shipments and receives periodical payments of the accrued freight charges from him.

6. The requirement that unless otherwise agreed the seller must procure insurance "of a kind and on terms then current at the port for shipment in the usual amount, in the currency of the contract, sufficiently shown to cover the same goods covered by the bill of lading", applies to both marine and war risk insurance. As applied to marine insurance, it means such insurance as is usual or customary at the port for shipment with reference to the particular kind of goods involved, the character and equipment of the vessel, the route of the voyage, the port of destination and any other considerations that affect the risk. It is the substantial equivalent of the ordinary insurance in the particular trade

and on the particular voyage and is subject to agreed specifications of type or extent of coverage. The language does not mean that the insurance must be adequate to cover all risks to which the goods may be subject in transit. There are some types of loss or damage that are not covered by the usual marine insurance and are excepted in bills of lading or in applicable statutes from the causes of loss or damage for which the carrier or the vessel is liable. Such risks must be borne by the buyer under this Article.

Insurance secured in compliance with a C.I.F. term must cover the entire transportation of the goods to the named destination.

7. An additional obligation is imposed upon the seller in requiring him to procure customary war risk insurance at the buyer's expense. This changes the common law on the point. The seller is not required to assume the risk of including in the C.I.F. price the cost of such insurance, since it often fluctuates rapidly, but is required to treat it simply as a necessary for the buyer's account. What war risk insurance is "current" or usual turns on the standard forms of policy or rider in common use.

8. The C.I.F. contract calls for insurance covering the value of the goods at the time and place of shipment and does not include any increase in market value during transit or any anticipated profit to the buyer on a sale by him.

The contract contemplates that before the goods arrive at their destination they may be sold again and again on C.I.F. terms and that the original policy of insurance and bill of lading will run with the interest in the goods by being transferred to each successive buyer. A buyer who becomes the seller in such an intermediate contract for sale does not thereby, if his sub-buyer knows the circumstances, undertake to insure the goods again at an increased price fixed in the new contract or to cover the increase in price by additional insurance, and his buyer may not reject the documents on the ground that the original policy does not cover such higher price. If such a sub-buyer desires additional insurance he must procure it for himself.

Where the seller exercises an option to ship "freight collect" and to credit the buyer with the freight against the C.I.F. price, the insurance need not cover the freight since the freight is not at the buyer's risk. On the other hand, where the seller prepays the freight upon shipping under a bill of lading requiring prepayment and providing that the freight shall be deemed earned and shall be retained by the carrier "ship and/or cargo lost or not lost," or using words of similar import, he must procure insurance that will cover the freight, because notwithstanding that the goods are lost in transit the buyer is bound to pay the freight as part of the C.I.F. price and will be unable to recover it back from the carrier.

9. Insurance "for the account of whom it may concern" is usual and sufficient. However, for a valid tender the policy of insurance must be one which can be disposed of together with the bill of lading and so must be "sufficiently shown to cover the same goods covered by the bill of lading". It must cover separately the quantity of goods called for by the buyer's contract and not merely insure his goods as part of a larger quantity in which others are interested, a case provided for in American mercantile practice by the use of negotiable certificates of insurance which are expressly authorized by this section. By usage these certificates are treated as the equivalent of separate policies and are good tender under C.I.F. contracts. The term "certificate of insurance", however, does not of itself include certificates or "cover notes" issued by the insurance broker and stating that the goods are covered by a policy. Their sufficiency as substitutes for policies will depend upon proof of an established usage or course of dealing. The present section rejects the English rule that not only brokers' certificates and "cover notes" but also certain forms of American insurance certificates are not the equivalent of policies and are not good tender under a C.I.F. contract.

The seller's failure to tender a proper insurance document is waived if the buyer refuses to make payment on other and untenable grounds at a time when proper insurance could have been obtained and tendered by the seller if timely objection had been made. Even a failure to insure on shipment may be cured by seasonable tender of a policy retroactive in effect; e. g., one insuring the goods "lost or not lost." The provisions of this Article on cure of improper tender and on waiver of buyer's objections by silence are applicable to insurance tenders under a C.I.F. term. Where there is no waiver by the buyer as described above, however, the fact that the goods arrive safely does not cure the seller's breach of his obligations to insure them and tender to the buyer a proper insurance document.

10. The seller's invoice of the goods shipped under a C.I.F. contract is regarded as a usual and necessary document upon which reliance may properly be placed. It is the document which evidences points of description, quality and the like which do not readily appear in other documents. This Article rejects those statements to the effect that the invoice is a usual but not a necessary document under a C.I.F. term.

11. The buyer needs all of the documents required under a C.I.F. contract, in due form and, if a tangible document of title, with necessary endorsements, so that before the goods arrive he may deal with them by negotiating the documents or may obtain prompt possession of the goods after their arrival. If the goods are lost or damaged in transit the documents are necessary to enable him promptly to assert his remedy against the carrier or insurer. The seller is therefore obligated to do what is mercantilely reasonable in the circumstances and should make every reasonable exertion to send forward the documents as soon as possible after the shipment. The requirement that the documents be forwarded with "commercial promptness" expresses a more urgent need for action than that suggested by the phrase "reasonable time".

12. Under a C.I.F. contract the buyer, as under the common law, must pay the price upon tender of the required documents without first inspecting the goods, but his payment in these circumstances does not constitute an acceptance of the goods nor does it impair his right of subsequent inspection or his options and remedies in the case of improper delivery. All remedies and rights for the seller's breach are reserved to him. The buyer must pay before inspection and assert his remedy against the seller afterward unless the nonconformity of the goods amounts to a real failure of consideration, since the purpose of choosing this form of contract is to give the seller protection against the buyer's

unjustifiable rejection of the goods at a distant port of destination which would necessitate taking possession of the goods and suing the buyer there.

13. A valid C.I.F. contract may be made which requires part of the transportation to be made on land and part on the sea, as where the goods are to be brought by rail from an inland point to a seaport and thence transported by vessel to the named destination under a "through" or combination bill of lading issued by the railroad company. In such a case shipment by rail from the inland point within the contract period is a timely shipment notwithstanding that the loading of the goods on the vessel is delayed by causes beyond the seller's control.

14. Although subsection (2) stating the legal effects of the C.I.F. term is an "unless otherwise agreed" provision, the express language used in an agreement is frequently a precautionary, fuller statement of the normal C.I.F. terms and hence not intended as a departure or variation from them. Moreover, the dominant outlines of the C.I.F. term are so well understood commercially that any variation should, whenever reasonably possible, be read as falling within those dominant outlines rather than as destroying the whole meaning of a term which essentially indicates a contract for proper shipment rather than one for delivery at destination. Particularly careful consideration is necessary before a printed form or clause is construed to mean agreement otherwise and where a C.I.F. contract is prepared on a printed form designed for some other type of contract, the C.I.F. terms must prevail over printed clauses repugnant to them.

15. Under subsection (4) the fact that the seller knows at the time of the tender of the documents that the goods have been lost in transit does not affect his rights if he has performed his contractual obligations. Similarly, the seller cannot perform under a C.I.F. term by purchasing and tendering landed goods.

16. Under the C. & F. term, as under the C.I.F. term, title and risk of loss are intended to pass to the buyer on shipment. A stipulation in a C. & F. contract that the seller shall effect insurance on the goods and charge the buyer with the premium (in effect that he shall act as the buyer's agent for that purpose) is entirely in keeping with the pattern. On the other hand, it often happens that the buyer is in a more advantageous position than the seller to effect insurance on the goods or that he has in force an "open" or "floating" policy covering all shipments made by him or to him, in either of which events the C. & F. term is adequate without mention of insurance.

17. It is to be remembered that in a French contract the term "C.A.F." does not mean "Cost and Freight" but has exactly the same meaning as the term "C.I.F." since it is merely the French equivalent of that term. The "A" does not stand for "and" but for "assurance" which means insurance.

Cross References:

Point 4: Section 2–323.

Point 6: Section 2–509(1)(a).

Point 9: Sections 2–508 and 2–605(1)(a).

Point 12: Sections 2–321(3), 2–512 and 2–513(3) and Article 5.

Definitional Cross References:

"Bill of lading". Section 1–201.

"Buyer". Section 2–103.

"Contract". Section 1–201.

"Goods". Section 2–105.

"Rights". Section 1–201.

"Seller". Section 2–103.

"Term". Section 1–201.

§ 2.321. C.I.F. or C. & F.: "Net Landed Weights"; "Payment on Arrival"; Warranty of Condition on Arrival

Under a contract containing a term C.I.F. or C. & F.

(a) Where the price is based on or is to be adjusted according to "net landed weights", "delivered weights", "out turn" quantity or quality or the like, unless otherwise agreed the seller must reasonably estimate the price. The payment due on tender of the documents called for by the contract is the amount so estimated, but after final adjustment of the price a settlement must be made with commercial promptness.

(b) An agreement described in Subsection (a) or any warranty of quality or condition of the goods on arrival places upon the seller the risk of ordinary deterioration, shrinkage and the like in transportation but has no effect on the place or time of identification to the contract for sale or delivery or on the passing of the risk of loss.

(c) Unless otherwise agreed where the contract provides for payment on or after arrival of the goods the seller must before payment allow such preliminary inspection as is feasible; but if the goods are lost delivery of the documents and payment are due when the goods should have arrived.

Acts 1967, 60th Leg., p. 2343, ch. 785, § 1, eff. Sept. 1, 1967.

Uniform Commercial Code Comment

Prior Uniform Statutory Provision:

None.

Purposes:

This section deals with two variations of the C.I.F. contract which have evolved in mercantile practice but are entirely consistent with the basic C.I.F. pattern. Subsections (1) and (2), which provide for a shift to the seller of the risk of quality and weight deterioration during shipment, are designed to conform the law to the best mercantile practice and usage without changing the legal consequences of the C.I.F. or C. & F. term as to the passing of marine risks to the buyer at the point of shipment. Subsection (3) provides that where under the contract documents are to be presented for payment after arrival of the goods, this amounts merely to a postponement of the payment under the C.I.F. contract and is not to be confused with the "no arrival, no sale" contract. If the goods are lost, delivery of the documents and payment against them are due when the goods should have arrived. The clause for payment on or after arrival is not to be construed as such a condition precedent to payment that if the goods are lost in transit the buyer need never pay and the seller must bear the loss.

Cross Reference:

Section 2–324.

Definitional Cross References:

"Agreement". Section 1–201.

"Contract". Section 1–201.

"Delivery". Section 1–201.

"Goods". Section 2–105.

"Seller". Section 2–103.

"Term". Section 1–201.

§ 2.322. Delivery "Ex-Ship"

(a) Unless otherwise agreed a term for delivery of goods "ex-ship" (which means from the carrying vessel) or in equivalent language is not restricted to a particular ship and requires delivery from a ship which has reached a place at the named port of destination where goods of the kind are usually discharged.

(b) Under such a term unless otherwise agreed

(1) the seller must discharge all liens arising out of the carriage and furnish the buyer with a direction which puts the carrier under a duty to deliver the goods; and

(2) the risk of loss does not pass to the buyer until the goods leave the ship's tackle or are otherwise properly unloaded.

Acts 1967, 60th Leg., p. 2343, ch. 785, § 1, eff. Sept. 1, 1967.

Uniform Commercial Code Comment

Prior Uniform Statutory Provision:

None.

Purposes:

1. The delivery term, "ex ship", as between seller and buyer, is the reverse of the f.a.s. term covered.

2. Delivery need not be made from any particular vessel under a clause calling for delivery "ex ship", even though a vessel on which shipment is to be made originally is named in the contract, unless the agreement by appropriate language, restricts the clause to delivery from a named vessel.

3. The appropriate place and manner of unloading at the port of destination depend upon the nature of the goods and the facilities and usages of the port.

4. A contract fixing a price "ex ship" with payment "cash against documents" calls only for such documents as are appropriate to the contract. Tender of a delivery order and of a receipt for the freight after the arrival of the carrying vessel is adequate. The seller is not required to tender a bill of lading as a document of title nor is he required to insure the goods for the buyer's benefit, as the goods are not at the buyer's risk during the voyage.

Cross Reference:

Point 1: Section 2–319(2).

Definitional Cross References:

"Buyer". Section 2–103.

"Goods". Section 2–105.

"Seller". Section 2–103.

"Term". Section 1–201.

§ 2.323. Form of Bill of Lading Required in Overseas Shipment; "Overseas"

(a) Where the contract contemplates overseas shipment and contains a term C.I.F. or C. & F. or F.O.B. vessel, the seller unless otherwise agreed must obtain a negotiable bill of lading stating that the goods have been loaded on board or, in the case of a term C.I.F. or C. & F., received for shipment.

(b) Where in a case within Subsection (a) a bill of lading has been issued in a set of parts, unless otherwise agreed if the documents are not to be sent from abroad the buyer may demand tender of the full set; otherwise only one part of the bill of lading need be tendered. Even if the agreement expressly requires a full set

(1) due tender of a single part is acceptable within the provisions of this chapter on cure of improper delivery (Subsection (a) of Section 2.508); and

(2) even though the full set is demanded, if the documents are sent from abroad the person tendering an incomplete set may nevertheless require payment upon furnishing an indemnity which the buyer in good faith deems adequate.

(c) A shipment by water or by air or a contract contemplating such shipment is "overseas" insofar as by usage of trade or agreement it is subject to the commercial, financing or shipping practices characteristic of international deep water commerce.

Acts 1967, 60th Leg., p. 2343, ch. 785, § 1, eff. Sept. 1, 1967.

Uniform Commercial Code Comment

Prior Uniform Statutory Provision:

None.

Purposes:

1. Subsection (1) follows the "American" rule that a regular bill of lading indicating delivery of the goods at the dock for shipment is sufficient, except under a term "F.O.B. vessel." See Section 2–319 and comment thereto.

2. Subsection (2) deals with the problem of bills of lading covering deep water shipments, issued not as a single bill of lading but in a set of parts, each part referring to the other parts and the entire set constituting in commercial practice and at law a single bill of lading. Commercial practice in international commerce is to accept and pay against presentation of the first part of a set if the part is sent from overseas even though the contract of the buyer requires presentation of a full set of bills of lading provided adequate indemnity for the missing parts is forthcoming. In accord with the amendment to Section 7–304, bills of lading in a set are limited to tangible bills.

This subsection codifies that practice as between buyer and seller. Article 5 (Section 5–113) authorizes banks presenting drafts under letters of credit to give indemnities against the missing parts, and this subsection means that the buyer must accept and act on such indemnities if he in good faith deems them adequate. But neither this subsection nor Article 5 decides whether a bank which has issued a letter of credit is similarly bound. The issuing bank's obligation under a letter of credit is independent and depends on its own terms. See Article 5.

Cross References:

Sections 2–508(2), 5–113.

Definitional Cross References:

"Bill of lading". Section 1–201.

"Buyer". Section 2–103.

"Contract". Section 1–201.

"Delivery". Section 1–201.

"Financing agency". Section 2–104.

"Person". Section 1–201.

"Seller". Section 2–103.

"Send". Section 1–201.

"Term". Section 1–201.

§ 2.324. "No Arrival, No Sale" Term

Under a term "no arrival, no sale" or terms of like meaning, unless otherwise agreed,

(1) the seller must properly ship conforming goods and if they arrive by any means he must tender them on arrival but he assumes no obligation that the goods will arrive unless he has caused the non-arrival; and

(2) where without fault of the seller the goods are in part lost or have so deteriorated as no longer to conform to the contract or arrive after the contract time, the buyer may proceed as if there had been casualty to identified goods (Section 2.613).

Acts 1967, 60th Leg., p. 2343, ch. 785, § 1, eff. Sept. 1, 1967.

Uniform Commercial Code Comment

Prior Uniform Statutory Provision:

None.

Purposes:

1. The "no arrival, no sale" term in a "destination" overseas contract leaves risk of loss on the seller but gives him an exemption from liability for nondelivery. Both the nature of the case and the duty of good faith require that the seller must not interfere with the arrival of the goods in any way. If the circumstances impose upon him the responsibility for making or arranging the shipment, he must have a shipment made despite the exemption clause. Further, the shipment made must be a conforming one, for the exemption under a "no arrival, no sale" term applies only to the hazards of transportation and the goods must be proper in all other respects.

The reason of this section is that where the seller is reselling goods bought by him as shipped by another and this fact is known to the buyer, so that the seller is not under any obligation to make the shipment himself, the seller is entitled under the "no arrival, no sale" clause to exemption from payment of damages for non-delivery if the goods do not arrive or if the goods which actually arrive are non-conforming. This does not extend to sellers who arrange shipment by their own agents, in which case the clause is limited to casualty due to marine hazards. But sellers who make known that they are contracting only with respect to what will be delivered to them by parties over whom they assume no control are entitled to the full quantum of the exemption.

2. The provisions of this Article on identification must be read together with the present section in order to bring the exemption into application. Until there is some designation of the goods in a particular shipment or on a particular ship as being those to which the contract refers there can be no application of an exemption for their non-arrival.

3. The seller's duty to tender the agreed or declared goods if they do arrive is not impaired because of their delay in arrival or by their arrival after trans-shipment.

4. The phrase "to arrive" is often employed in the same sense as "no arrival, no sale" and may then be given the same effect. But a "to arrive" term, added to a C.I.F. or C. & F. contract, does not have the full meaning given by this section to "no arrival, no sale". Such a "to arrive" term is usually intended to operate only to the extent that the risks are not covered by the agreed insurance and the loss or casualty is due to such uncovered hazards. In some instances the "to arrive" term may be regarded as a time of payment term, or, in the case of the reselling seller discussed in point 1 above, as negating responsibility for conformity of the goods, if they arrive, to any description which was based on his good faith belief of the quality. Whether this is the intention of the parties is a question of fact based on all the circumstances surrounding the resale and in case of ambiguity the rules of Sections 2–316 and 2–317 apply to preclude dishonor.

5. Paragraph (b) applies where goods arrive impaired by damage or partial loss during transportation and makes the policy of this Article on casualty to identified goods applicable to such a situation. For the term cannot be regarded as intending to give the seller an unforeseen profit through casualty; it is intended only to protect him from loss due to causes beyond his control.

Cross References:

Point 1: Section 1–203.

Point 2: Section 2–501(a) and (c).

Point 5: Section 2–613.

Definitional Cross References:

"Buyer". Section 2–103.

"Conforming". Section 2–106.

"Contract". Section 1–201.

"Fault". Section 1–201.

"Goods". Section 2–105.

"Sale". Section 2–106.

"Seller". Section 2–103.

"Term". Section 1–201.

§ 2.325. "Letter of Credit" Term; "Confirmed Credit"

(a) Failure of the buyer seasonably to furnish an agreed letter of credit is a breach of the contract for sale.

(b) The delivery to seller of a proper letter of credit suspends the buyer's obligation to pay. If the letter of credit is dishonored, the seller may on seasonable notification to the buyer require payment directly from him.

(c) Unless otherwise agreed the term "letter of credit" or "banker's credit" in a contract for sale means an irrevocable credit issued by a financing agency of good repute and, where the shipment is overseas, of good international repute. The term "confirmed credit" means that the credit must also carry the direct obligation of such an agency which does business in the seller's financial market.

Acts 1967, 60th Leg., p. 2343, ch. 785, § 1, eff. Sept. 1, 1967.

Uniform Commercial Code Comment

Prior Uniform Statutory Provision:

None.

Purposes: To express the established commercial and banking understanding as to the meaning and effects of terms calling for "letters of credit" or "confirmed credit":

1. Subsection (2) follows the general policy of this Article and Article 3 (Section 3–802) on conditional payment, under which payment by check or other short-term instrument is not ordinarily final as between the parties if the recipient duly presents the instrument and honor is refused. Thus the furnishing of a letter of credit does not substitute the financing agency's obligation for the buyer's, but the seller must first give the buyer reasonable notice of his intention to demand direct payment from him.

2. Subsection (3) requires that the credit be irrevocable and be a prime credit as determined by the standing of the issuer. It is not necessary, unless otherwise agreed, that the credit be a negotiation credit; the seller can finance himself by an assignment of the proceeds under Section 5–116(2).

3. The definition of "confirmed credit" is drawn on the supposition that the credit is issued by a bank which is not doing direct business in the seller's financial market; there is no intention to require the obligation of two banks both local to the seller.

Cross References:

Sections 2–403, 2–511(3) and 3–802 and Article 5.

Definitional Cross References:

"Buyer". Section 2–103.

"Contract for sale". Section 2–106.

"Draft". Section 3–104.

"Financing agency". Section 2–104.

"Notifies". Section 1–201.

"Overseas". Section 2–323.

"Purchaser". Section 1–201.

"Seasonably". Section 1–204.

"Seller". Section 2–103.

"Term". Section 1–201.

§ 2.326. Sale on Approval and Sale or Return; Rights of Creditors

(a) Unless otherwise agreed, if delivered goods may be returned by the buyer even though they conform to the contract, the transaction is

(1) a "sale on approval" if the goods are delivered primarily for use, and

(2) a "sale or return" if the goods are delivered primarily for resale.

(b) Goods held on approval are not subject to the claims of the buyer's creditors until acceptance; goods held on sale or return are subject to such claims while in the buyer's possession.

(c) Any "or return" term of a contract for sale is to be treated as a separate contract for sale within the statute of frauds section of this chapter (Section 2.201) and as contradicting the sale aspect of the contract within the provisions of this chapter on parol or extrinsic evidence (Section 2.202).

Acts 1967, 60th Leg., p. 2343, ch. 785, § 1, eff. Sept. 1, 1967. Amended by Acts 1977, 65th Leg., p. 1530, ch. 623, § 4, eff. Aug. 29, 1977; Acts 1999, 76th Leg., ch. 414, § 2.16, eff. July 1, 2001.

Uniform Commercial Code Comment

1999 Amendment (effective July 1, 2001)

Prior Uniform Statutory Provision:

Section 19(3), Uniform Sales Act.

Changes: Completely rewritten in this and the succeeding section.

Purposes of Changes: To make it clear that:

1. Both a "sale on approval" and a "sale or return" should be distinguished from other types of transactions with which they frequently have been confused. A "sale on approval," sometimes also called a sale "on trial" or "on satisfaction," deals with a contract under which the seller undertakes a risk in order to satisfy its prospective buyer with the appearance or performance of the goods that are sold. The goods are delivered to the proposed purchaser but they remain the property of the seller until the buyer accepts them. The price has already been agreed. The buyer's willingness to receive and test the goods is the consideration for the seller's engagement to deliver and sell. A "sale or return," on the other hand, typically is a sale to a merchant whose unwillingness to buy is overcome by the seller's engagement to take back the goods (or any commercial unit of goods) in lieu of payment if they fail to be resold. A sale or return is a present sale of goods which may be undone at the buyer's option. Accordingly, subsection (2) provides that goods delivered on approval are not subject to the prospective buyer's creditors until acceptance, and goods delivered in a sale or return are subject to the buyer's creditors while in the buyer's possession.

These two transactions are so strongly delineated in practice and in general understanding that every presumption runs against a delivery to a consumer being a "sale or return" and against a delivery to a merchant for resale being a "sale on approval."

2. The right to return goods for failure to conform to the contract of sale does not make the transaction a "sale on approval" or "sale or return" and has nothing to do with this section or Section 2–327. This section is not concerned with remedies for breach of contract. It deals instead with a power given by the contract to turn back the goods even though they are wholly as warranted. This section nevertheless presupposes that a contract for sale is contemplated by the parties, although that contract may be of the particular character that this section addresses (i.e., a sale on approval or a sale or return).

If a buyer's obligation as a buyer is conditioned not on its personal approval but on the article's passing a described objective test, the risk of loss by casualty pending the test is properly the seller's and proper return is at its expense. On the point of "satisfaction" as meaning "reasonable satisfaction" when an industrial machine is involved, this Article takes no position.

3. Subsection (3) resolves a conflict in the pre-UCC case law recognizing that an "or return" provision is so definitely at odds with any ordinary contract for sale of goods that if a written agreement is involved the "or return" term must be contained in a written memorandum. The "or return" aspect of a sales contract must be treated as a separate contract under the Statute of Frauds section and as contradicting the sale insofar as questions of parol or extrinsic evidence are concerned.

4. Certain true consignment transactions were dealt with in former Sections 2–326(3) and 9–114. These provisions have been deleted and have been replaced by new provisions in Article 9. See, e.g., Sections 9–109(a)(4); 9–103(b); 9–319.

Cross References:

Point 2: Article 9.

Point 3: Sections 2–201 and 2–202.

Definitional Cross References:

"Between merchants". Section 2–104.

"Buyer". Section 2–103.

"Conform". Section 2–106.

"Contract for sale". Section 2–106.

"Creditor". Section 1–201.

"Goods". Section 2–105.

"Sale". Section 2–106.

"Seller". Section 2–103

§ 2.327. Special Incidents of Sale on Approval and Sale or Return

(a) Under a sale on approval unless otherwise agreed

(1) although the goods are identified to the contract the risk of loss and the title do not pass to the buyer until acceptance; and

(2) use of the goods consistent with the purpose of trial is not acceptance but failure seasonably to notify the seller of election to return the goods is acceptance, and if the goods conform to the contract acceptance of any part is acceptance of the whole; and

(3) after due notification of election to return, the return is at the seller's risk and expense but a merchant buyer must follow any reasonable instructions.

(b) Under a sale or return unless otherwise agreed

(1) the option to return extends to the whole or any commercial unit of the goods while in substantially their original condition, but must be exercised seasonably; and

(2) the return is at the buyer's risk and expense.

Acts 1967, 60th Leg., p. 2343, ch. 785, § 1, eff. Sept. 1, 1967.

Uniform Commercial Code Comment

Prior Uniform Statutory Provision:

Section 19(3), Uniform Sales Act.

Changes: Completely rewritten in preceding and this section.

Purposes of Changes: To make it clear that:

1. In the case of a sale on approval:

If all of the goods involved conform to the contract, the buyer's acceptance of part of the goods constitutes acceptance of the whole. Acceptance of part falls outside the normal intent of the parties in the "on approval" situation and the policy of this Article allowing partial acceptance of a defective delivery has no application here. A case where a buyer takes home two dresses to select one commonly involves two distinct contracts; if not, it is covered by the words "unless otherwise agreed".

2. In the case of a sale or return, the return of any unsold unit merely because it is unsold is the normal intent of the "sale or return" provision, and therefore the right to return for this reason alone is independent of any other action under the contract which would turn on wholly different considerations. On the other hand, where the return of goods is for breach, including return of items resold by the buyer and returned by the ultimate purchasers because of defects, the return procedure is governed not by the present section but by the provisions on the effects and revocation of acceptance.

3. In the case of a sale on approval the risk rests on the seller until acceptance of the goods by the buyer, while in a sale or return the risk remains throughout on the buyer.

4. Notice of election to return given by the buyer in a sale on approval is sufficient to relieve him of any further liability. Actual return by the buyer to the seller is required in the case of a sale or return contract. What constitutes due "giving" of notice, as required in "on approval" sales, is governed by the provisions on good faith and notice. "Seasonable" is used here as defined in Section 1–204. Nevertheless, the provisions of both this Article and of the contract on this point must be read with commercial reason and with full attention to good faith.

Cross References:

Point 1: Sections 2–501, 2–601 and 2–603.

Point 2: Sections 2–607 and 2–608.

Point 4: Sections 1–201 and 1–204.

Definitional Cross References:

"Agreed". Section 1–201.

"Buyer". Section 2 103.

"Commercial unit". Section 2–105.

"Conform". Section 2–106.

"Contract". Section 1–201.

"Goods". Section 2–105.

"Merchant". Section 2–104.

"Notification". Section 1–201.

"Notifies". Section 1–201.

"Sale on approval". Section 2–326.

"Sale or return". Section 2–326.

"Seasonably". Section 1–204.

"Seller". Section 2–103.

§ 2.328. Sale by Auction

(a) In a sale by auction if goods are put up in lots each lot is the subject of a separate sale.

(b) A sale by auction is complete when the auctioneer so announces by the fall of the hammer or in other customary manner. Where a bid is made while the hammer is falling in acceptance of a prior bid the auctioneer may in his discretion reopen the bidding or declare the goods sold under the bid on which the hammer was falling.

(c) Such a sale is with reserve unless the goods are in explicit terms put up without reserve. In an auction with reserve the auctioneer may withdraw the goods at any time until he announces completion of the sale. In an auction without reserve, after the auctioneer calls for bids on an article or lot, that article or lot cannot be withdrawn unless no bid is made within a reasonable time. In either case a bidder may retract his bid until the auctioneer's announcement of completion of the sale, but a bidder's retraction does not revive any previous bid.

(d) If the auctioneer knowingly receives a bid on the seller's behalf or the seller makes or procures such a bid, and notice has not been given that liberty for such bidding is reserved, the buyer may at his option avoid the sale or take the goods at the price of the last good faith bid prior to the completion of the sale. This subsection shall not apply to any bid at a forced sale.

Acts 1967, 60th Leg., p. 2343, ch. 785, § 1, eff. Sept. 1, 1967.

Uniform Commercial Code Comment

Prior Uniform Statutory Provision:

Section 21, Uniform Sales Act.

Changes: Completely rewritten.

Purposes of Changes: To make it clear that:

1. The auctioneer may in his discretion either reopen the bidding or close the sale on the bid on which the hammer was falling when a bid is made at that moment. The recognition of a bid of this kind by the auctioneer in his discretion does not mean a closing in favor of such a bidder, but only that the bid has been accepted as a continuation of

the bidding. If recognized, such a bid discharges the bid on which the hammer was falling when it was made.

2. An auction "with reserve" is the normal procedure. The crucial point, however, for determining the nature of an auction is the "putting up" of the goods. This Article accepts the view that the goods may be withdrawn before they are actually "put up," regardless of whether the auction is advertised as one without reserve, without liability on the part of the auction announcer to persons who are present. This is subject to any peculiar facts which might bring the case within the "firm offer" principle of this Article, but an offer to persons generally would require unmistakable language in order to fall within that section. The prior announcement of the nature of the auction either as with reserve or without reserve will, however, enter as an "explicit term" in the "putting up" of the goods and conduct thereafter must be governed accordingly. The present section continues the prior rule permitting withdrawal of bids in auctions both with and without reserve; and the rule is made explicit that the retraction of a bid does not revive a prior bid.

Cross Reference:

Point 2: Section 2–205.

Definitional Cross References:

"Buyer". Section 2–103.

"Good faith". Section 1–201.

"Goods". Section 2–105.

"Lot". Section 2–105.

"Notice". Section 1–201.

"Sale". Section 2–106.

"Seller". Section 2–103.

SUBCHAPTER D. TITLE, CREDITORS AND GOOD FAITH PURCHASERS

§ 2.401. Passing of Title; Reservation for Security; Limited Application of This Section

Each provision of this chapter with regard to the rights, obligations and remedies of the seller, the buyer, purchasers or other third parties applies irrespective of title to the goods except where the provision refers to such title. Insofar as situations are not covered by the other provisions of this chapter and matters concerning title become material the following rules apply:

(a) Title to goods cannot pass under a contract for sale prior to their identification to the contract (Section 2.501), and unless otherwise explicitly agreed the buyer acquires by their identification a special property as limited by this title. Any retention or reservation by the seller of the title (property) in goods shipped or delivered to the buyer is limited in effect to a reservation of a security interest. Subject to these provisions and to the provisions of the chapter on Secured Transactions (Chapter 9), title to goods passes from the seller to the buyer in any manner and on any conditions explicitly agreed on by the parties.

(b) Unless otherwise explicitly agreed title passes to the buyer at the time and place at which the seller completes his performance with reference to the physical delivery of the goods, despite any reservation of a security interest and even though a document of title is to be delivered at a different time or place; and in particular and despite any reservation of a security interest by the bill of lading

(1) if the contract requires or authorizes the seller to send the goods to the buyer but does not require him to deliver them at destination, title passes to the buyer at the time and place of shipment; but

(2) if the contract requires delivery at destination, title passes on tender there.

(c) Unless otherwise explicitly agreed where delivery is to be made without moving the goods,

(1) if the seller is to deliver a tangible document of title, title passes at the time when and the place where he delivers such documents and if the seller is to deliver an electronic document of title, title passes when the seller delivers the document; or

(2) if the goods are at the time of contracting already identified and no documents are to be delivered, title passes at the time and place of contracting.

(d) A rejection or other refusal by the buyer to receive or retain the goods, whether or not justified, or a justified revocation of acceptance revests title to the goods in the seller. Such revesting occurs by operation of law and is not a "sale".

Acts 1967, 60th Leg., p. 2343, ch. 785, § 1, eff. Sept. 1, 1967. Amended by Acts 2005, 79th Leg., ch. 122, § 6, eff. Sept. 1, 2005.

Uniform Commercial Code Comment

Prior Uniform Statutory Provision:

See generally, Sections 17, 18, 19 and 20, Uniform Sales Act.

Purposes: To make it clear that:

1. This Article deals with the issues between seller and buyer in terms of step by step performance or non-performance under the contract for sale and not in terms of whether or not "title" to the goods has passed. That the rules of this section in no way alter the rights of either the buyer, seller or third parties declared elsewhere in the Article is made clear by the preamble of this section. This section, however, in no way intends to indicate which line of interpretation

should be followed in cases where the applicability of "public" regulation depends upon a "sale" or upon location of "title" without further definition. The basic policy of this Article that known purpose and reason should govern interpretation cannot extend beyond the scope of its own provisions. It is therefore necessary to state what a "sale" is and when title passes under this Article in case the courts deem any public regulation to incorporate the defined term of the "private" law.

2. "Future" goods cannot be the subject of a present sale. Before title can pass the goods must be identified in the manner set forth in Section 2–501. The parties, however, have full liberty to arrange by specific terms for the passing of title to goods which are existing.

3. The "special property" of the buyer in goods identified to the contract is excluded from the definition of "security interest"; its incidents are defined in provisions of this Article such as those on the rights of the seller's creditors, on good faith purchase, on the buyer's right to goods on the seller's insolvency, and on the buyer's right to specific performance or replevin.

4. The factual situations in subsections (2) and (3) upon which passage of title turn actually base the test upon the time when the seller has finally committed himself in regard to specific goods. Thus in a "shipment" contract he commits himself by the act of making the shipment. If shipment is not contemplated subsection (3) turns on the seller's final commitment, i.e. the delivery of documents or the making of the contract. As to delivery of an electronic document of title, see definition of delivery in Article 1, Section 1–201. This Article does not state a rule as to the place of title passage as to goods covered by an electronic document of title.

Cross References:

Point 2: Sections 2–102, 2–501 and 2–502.

Point 3: Sections 1–201, 2–402, 2–403, 2–502 and 2–716.

Definitional Cross References:

"Agreement". Section 1–201.

"Bill of lading". Section 1–201.

"Buyer". Section 2–103.

"Contract". Section 1–201.

"Contract for sale". Section 2–106.

"Delivery". Section 1–201.

"Document of title". Section 1–201.

"Good faith". Section 2–103.

"Goods". Section 2–105.

"Party". Section 1–201.

"Purchaser". Section 1–201.

"Receipt" of goods. Section 2–103.

"Remedy". Section 1–201.

"Rights". Section 1–201.

"Sale". Section 2–106.

"Security interest". Section 1–201.

"Seller". Section 2–103.

"Send". Section 1–201.

Sections 31 and 32 of Acts 2005, 79th Leg., ch. 122 provide:

"Sec. 31. This Act applies to a document of title that is issued or a bailment that arises on or after the effective date of this Act. This Act does not apply to a document of title that is issued or a bailment that arises before the effective date of this Act even if the document of title or bailment would be subject to this Act if the document of title had been issued or bailment had arisen after the effective date of this Act. This Act does not apply to a right of action that has accrued before the effective date of this Act.

"Sec. 32. A document of title issued or a bailment that arises before the effective date of this Act and the rights, obligations, and interests flowing from that document or bailment are governed by any statute or other rule amended or repealed by this Act as if amendment or repeal had not occurred and may be terminated, completed, consummated, or enforced under that statute or other rule."

§ 2.402. Rights of Seller's Creditors Against Sold Goods

(a) Except as provided in Subsections (b) and (c), rights of unsecured creditors of the seller with respect to goods which have been identified to a contract for sale are subject to the buyer's rights to recover the goods under this chapter (Sections 2.502 and 2.716).

(b) A creditor of the seller may treat a sale or an identification of goods to a contract for sale as void if as against him a retention of possession by the seller is fraudulent under any rule of law of the state where the goods are situated, except that retention of possession in good faith and current course of trade by a merchant-seller for a commercially reasonable time after a sale or identification is not fraudulent.

(c) Nothing in this chapter shall be deemed to impair the rights of creditors of the seller

(1) under the provisions of the chapter on Secured Transactions (Chapter 9); or

(2) where identification to the contract or delivery is made not in current course of trade but in satisfaction of or as security for a pre-existing claim for money, security or the like and is made under circumstances which under any rule of law of the state where the goods are situated would apart from this chapter constitute the transaction a fraudulent transfer or voidable preference.

Acts 1967, 60th Leg., p. 2343, ch. 785, § 1, eff. Sept. 1, 1967.

Uniform Commercial Code Comment

Prior Uniform Statutory Provision:

Subsection (2)—Section 26, Uniform Sales Act; Subsections (1) and (3)—none.

Changes: Rephrased.

Purposes of Changes and New Matter: To avoid confusion on ordinary issues between current sellers and buyers and issues in the field of preference and hindrance by making it clear that:

1. Local law on questions of hindrance of creditors by the seller's retention of possession of the goods are outside the scope of this Article, but retention of possession in the current course of trade is legitimate. Transactions which fall within the law's policy against improper preferences are reserved from the protection of this Article.

2. The retention of possession of the goods by a merchant seller for a commercially reasonable time after a sale or identification in current course is exempted from attack as fraudulent. Similarly, the provisions of subsection (3) have no application to identification or delivery made in the current course of trade, as measured against general commercial understanding of what a "current" transaction is.

Definitional Cross References:

"Contract for sale". Section 2–106.

"Creditor". Section 1–201.

"Good faith". Section 2–103.

"Goods". Section 2–105.

"Merchant". Section 2–104.

"Money". Section 1–201.

"Reasonable time". Section 1–204.

"Rights". Section 1–201.

"Sale". Section 2–106.

"Seller". Section 2–103.

§ 2.403. Power to Transfer; Good Faith Purchase of Goods; "Entrusting"

(a) A purchaser of goods acquires all title which his transferor had or had power to transfer except that a purchaser of a limited interest acquires rights only to the extent of the interest purchased. A person with voidable title has power to transfer a good title to a good faith purchaser for value. When goods have been delivered under a transaction of purchase the purchaser has such power even though

(1) the transferor was deceived as to the identity of the purchaser, or

(2) the delivery was in exchange for a check which is later dishonored, or

(3) it was agreed that the transaction was to be a "cash sale", or

(4) the delivery was procured through fraud punishable as larcenous under the criminal law.

(b) Any entrusting of possession of goods to a merchant who deals in goods of that kind gives him power to transfer all rights of the entruster to a buyer in ordinary course of business.

(c) "Entrusting" includes any delivery and any acquiescence in retention of possession regardless of any condition expressed between the parties to the delivery or acquiescence and regardless of whether the procurement of the entrusting or the possessor's disposition of the goods have been such as to be larcenous under the criminal law.

(d) The rights of other purchasers of goods and of lien creditors are governed by the chapters on Secured Transactions (Chapter 9) and Documents of Title (Chapter 7).

Acts 1967, 60th Leg., p. 2343, ch. 785, § 1, eff. Sept. 1, 1967. Amended by Acts 1993, 73rd Leg., ch. 570, § 3, eff. Sept. 1, 1993.

Uniform Commercial Code Comment

Prior Uniform Statutory Provision:

Sections 20(4), 23, 24, 25, Uniform Sales Act; Section 9, especially 9(2), Uniform Trust Receipts Act; Section 9, Uniform Conditional Sales Act.

Changes: Consolidated and rewritten.

Purposes of Changes: To gather together a series of prior uniform statutory provisions and the case-law thereunder and to state a unified and simplified policy on good faith purchase of goods.

1. The basic policy of our law allowing transfer of such title as the transferor has is generally continued and expanded under subsection (1). In this respect the provisions of the section are applicable to a person taking by any form of "purchase" as defined by this Act. Moreover the policy of this Act expressly providing for the application of supplementary general principles of law to sales transactions wherever appropriate joins with the present section to continue unimpaired all rights acquired under the law of agency or of apparent agency or ownership or other estoppel, whether based on statutory provisions or on case law principles. The section also leaves unimpaired the powers given to selling factors under the earlier Factors Acts. In addition subsection (1) provides specifically for the protection of the good faith purchaser for value in a number of specific situations which have been troublesome under prior law.

On the other hand, the contract of purchase is of course limited by its own terms as in a case of pledge for a limited amount or of sale of a fractional interest in goods.

2. The many particular situations in which a buyer in ordinary course of business from a dealer has been protected against reservation of property or other hidden interest are gathered by subsections (2)–(4) into a single principle protecting persons who buy in ordinary course out of inventory. Consignors have no reason to complain, nor have lenders who hold a security interest in the inventory, since the very purpose of goods in inventory is to be turned into cash by sale.

The principle is extended in subsection (3) to fit with the abolition of the old law of "cash sale" by subsection (1)(c). It is also freed from any technicalities depending on the extended law of larceny; such extension of the concept of theft to include trick, particular types of fraud, and the like is for the purpose of helping conviction of the offender; it has no proper application to the long-standing policy of civil protection of buyers from persons guilty of such trick or fraud. Finally, the policy is extended, in the interest of simplicity and sense, to any entrusting by a bailor; this is in consonance with the explicit provisions of Section 7–205 on the powers of a warehouse who is also in the business of buying and selling fungible goods of the kind he stores. As to entrusting by a secured party, subsection (2) is limited by the more specific provisions of Section 9–320, which deny protection to a person buying farm products from a person engaged in farming operations.

3. The definition of "buyer in ordinary course of business" (Section 1–201) is effective here and preserves the essence of the healthy limitations engrafted by the case-law on the older statutes. The older loose concept of good faith and wide definition of value combined to create apparent good faith purchasers in many situations in which the result outraged common sense; the court's solution was to protect the original title especially by use of "cash sale" or of overtechnical construction of the enabling clauses of the statutes. But such rulings then turned into limitations on the proper protection of buyers in the ordinary market. Section 1–201(9) cuts down the category of buyer in ordinary course in such fashion as to take care of the results of the cases, but with no price either in confusion or in injustice to proper dealings in the normal market.

4. Except as provided in subsection (1), the rights of purchasers other than buyers in ordinary course are left to the Articles on Secured Transactions, Documents of Title, and Bulk Sales.

Cross References:

Point 1: Sections 1–103 and 1–201.

Point 2: Sections 1–201, 2–402, 7–205 and 9–307(1).

Points 3 and 4: Sections 1–102, 1–201, 2–104, 2–707 and Articles 6, 7 and 9.

Definitional Cross References:

"Buyer in ordinary course of business". Section 1–201.

"Good faith". Sections 1–201 and 2–103.

"Goods". Section 2–105.

"Person". Section 1–201.

"Purchaser". Section 1–201.

"Signed". Section 1–201.

"Term". Section 1–201.

"Value". Section 1–201.

SUBCHAPTER E. PERFORMANCE

§ 2.501. Insurable Interest in Goods; Manner of Identification of Goods

(a) The buyer obtains a special property and an insurable interest in goods by identification of existing goods as goods to which the contract refers even though the goods so identified are non-conforming and he has an option to return or reject them. Such identification can be made at any time and in any manner explicitly agreed to by the parties. In the absence of explicit agreement identification occurs

(1) when the contract is made if it is for the sale of goods already existing and identified;

(2) if the contract is for the sale of future goods other than those described in Subdivision (3), when goods are shipped, marked or otherwise designated by the seller as goods to which the contract refers;

(3) when the crops are planted or otherwise become growing crops or the young are conceived if the contract is for the sale of unborn young to be born within twelve months after contracting or for the sale of crops to be harvested within twelve months or the next normal harvest season after contracting whichever is longer.

(b) The seller retains an insurable interest in goods so long as title to or any security interest in the goods remains in him and where the identification is by the seller alone he may until default or insolvency or notification to the buyer that the identification is final substitute other goods for those identified.

(c) Nothing in this section impairs any insurable interest recognized under any other statute or rule of law.

Acts 1967, 60th Leg., p. 2343, ch. 785, § 1, eff. Sept. 1, 1967.

Uniform Commercial Code Comment

Prior Uniform Statutory Provision:

See Sections 17 and 19, Uniform Sales Act.

Purposes:

1. The present section deals with the manner of identifying goods to the contract so that an insurable interest in the buyer and the rights set forth in the next section will accrue. Generally speaking, identification may be made in any manner "explicitly agreed to" by the parties. The rules of paragraphs (a), (b) and (c) apply only in the absence of such "explicit agreement".

2. In the ordinary case identification of particular existing goods as goods to which the contract refers is unambiguous and may occur in one of many ways. It is possible, however, for the identification to be tentative or contingent. In view of the limited effect given to identification by this Article, the general policy is to resolve all doubts in favor of identification.

3. The provision of this section as to "explicit agreement" clarifies the present confusion in the law of sales which has arisen from the fact that under prior uniform legislation all rules of presumption with reference to the passing of title or to appropriation (which in turn depended upon identification) were regarded as subject to the contrary intention of the parties or of the party appropriating. Such uncertainty is reduced to a minimum under this section by requiring "explicit agreement" of the parties before the rules of para-

graphs (a), (b) and (c) are displaced—as they would be by a term giving the buyer power to select the goods. An "explicit" agreement, however, need not necessarily be found in the terms used in the particular transaction. Thus, where a usage of the trade has previously been made explicit by reduction to a standard set of "rules and regulations" currently incorporated by reference into the contracts of the parties, a relevant provision of those "rules and regulations" is "explicit" within the meaning of this section.

4. In view of the limited function of identification there is no requirement in this section that the goods be in deliverable state or that all of the seller's duties with respect to the processing of the goods be completed in order that identification occur. For example, despite identification the risk of loss remains on the seller under the risk of loss provisions until completion of his duties as to the goods and all of his remedies remain dependent upon his not defaulting under the contract.

5. Undivided shares in an identified fungible bulk, such as grain in an elevator or oil in a storage tank, can be sold. The mere making of the contract with reference to an undivided share in an identified fungible bulk is enough under subsection (a) to effect an identification if there is no explicit agreement otherwise. The seller's duty, however, to segregate and deliver according to the contract is not affected by such an identification but is controlled by other provisions of this Article.

6. Identification of crops under paragraph (c) is made upon planting only if they are to be harvested within the year or within the next normal harvest season. The phrase "next normal harvest season" fairly includes nursery stock raised for normally quick "harvest," but plainly excludes a "timber" crop to which the concept of a harvest "season" is inapplicable.

Paragraph (c) is also applicable to a crop of wool or the young of animals to be born within twelve months after contracting. The product of a lumbering, mining or fishing operation, though seasonal, is not within the concept of "growing". Identification under a contract for all or part of the output of such an operation can be effected early in the operation.

Cross References:

Point 1: Section 2–502.

Point 4: Sections 2–509, 2–510 and 2–703.

Point 5: Sections 2–105, 2–308, 2–503 and 2–509.

Point 6: Sections 2–105(1), 2–107(1) and 2–402.

Definitional Cross References:

"Agreement". Section 1–201.

"Contract". Section 1–201.

"Contract for sale". Section 2–106.

"Future goods". Section 2–105.

"Goods". Section 2–105.

"Notification". Section 1–201.

"Party". Section 1–201.

"Sale". Section 2–106.

"Security interest". Section 1–201.

"Seller". Section 2–103.

§ 2.502. Buyer's Right to Goods on Seller's Repudiation, Failure to Deliver, Or Insolvency

(a) Subject to Subsections (b) and (c) and even though the goods have not been shipped a buyer who has paid a part or all of the price of goods in which he has a special property under the provisions of the immediately preceding section may on making and keeping good a tender of any unpaid portion of their price recover them from the seller if:

(1) in the case of goods bought for personal, family, or household purposes, the seller repudiates or fails to deliver as required by the contract; or

(2) in all cases, the seller becomes insolvent within ten days after receipt of the first installment on their price.

(b) The buyer's right to recover the goods under Subsection (a)(1) vests upon acquisition of a special property, even if the seller had not then repudiated or failed to deliver.

(c) If the identification creating his special property has been made by the buyer he acquires the right to recover the goods only if they conform to the contract for sale.

Acts 1967, 60th Leg., p. 2343, ch. 785, § 1, eff. Sept. 1, 1967. Amended by Acts 1999, 76th Leg., ch. 414, § 2.17, eff. July 1, 2001.

Uniform Commercial Code Comment

1999 Amendment (effective July 1, 2001)

Prior Uniform Statutory Provision:

Compare Sections 17, 18 and 19, Uniform Sales Act.

Purposes:

1. This section gives an additional right to the buyer as a result of identification of the goods to the contract in the manner provided in Section 2–501. The buyer is given a right to recover the goods, conditioned upon making and keeping good a tender of any unpaid portion of the price, in two limited circumstances. First, the buyer may recover goods bought for personal, family, or household purposes if the seller repudiates the contract or fails to deliver the goods. Second, in any case, the buyer may recover the goods if the seller becomes insolvent within 10 days after the seller receives the first installment on their price. The buyer's right to recover the goods under this section is an exception to the usual rule, under which the disappointed buyer must resort to an action to recover damages.

2. The question of whether the buyer also acquires a security interest in identified goods and has rights to the goods when insolvency takes place after the ten-day period

provided in this section depends upon compliance with the provisions of the Article on Secured Transactions (Article 9).

3. Under subsection (2), the buyer's right to recover consumer goods under subsection (1)(a) vests upon acquisition of a special property, which occurs upon identification of the goods to the contract. See Section 2–501. Inasmuch as a secured party normally acquires no greater rights in its collateral that its debtor had or had power to convey, see Section 2–403(1) (first sentence), a buyer who acquires a right to recover under this section will take free of a security interest created by the seller if it attaches to the goods after the goods have been identified to the contract. The buyer will take free, even if the buyer does not buy in ordinary course and even if the security interest is perfected. Of course, to the extent that the buyer pays the price after the security interest attaches, the payments will constitute proceeds of the security interest.

4. Subsection (3) is included to preclude the possibility of unjust enrichment, which would exist if the buyer were permitted to recover goods even though they were greatly superior in quality or quantity to that called for by the contract for sale.

Cross References:

Point 1: Sections 1–201 and 2–702.

Point 2: Article 9.

Definitional Cross References:

"Buyer". Section 2–103.

"Conform". Section 2–106.

"Contract for sale". Section 2–106.

"Goods". Section 2–105.

"Insolvent". Section 1–201.

"Right". Section 1–201.

"Seller". Section 2–103.

§ 2.503. Manner of Seller's Tender of Delivery

(a) Tender of delivery requires that the seller put and hold conforming goods at the buyer's disposition and give the buyer any notification reasonably necessary to enable him to take delivery. The manner, time and place for tender are determined by the agreement and this chapter, and in particular

(1) tender must be at a reasonable hour, and if it is of goods they must be kept available for the period reasonably necessary to enable the buyer to take possession; but

(2) unless otherwise agreed the buyer must furnish facilities reasonably suited to the receipt of the goods.

(b) Where the case is within the next section respecting shipment tender requires that the seller comply with its provisions.

(c) Where the seller is required to deliver at a particular destination tender requires that he comply with Subsection (a) and also in any appropriate case tender documents as described in Subsections (d) and (e) of this section.

(d) Where goods are in the possession of a bailee and are to be delivered without being moved

(1) tender requires that the seller either tender a negotiable document of title covering such goods or procure acknowledgment by the bailee of the buyer's right to possession of the goods; but

(2) tender to the buyer of a non-negotiable document of title or of a written direction to the bailee to deliver is sufficient tender unless the buyer seasonably objects, and receipt by the bailee of notification of the buyer's rights fixes those rights as against the bailee and all third persons; but risk of loss of the goods and of any failure by the bailee to honor the non-negotiable document of title or to obey the direction remains on the seller until the buyer has had a reasonable time to present the document or direction, and a refusal by the bailee to honor the document or to obey the direction defeats the tender.

(e) Where the contract requires the seller to deliver documents

(1) he must tender all such documents in correct form, except as provided in this chapter with respect to bills of lading in a set (Subsection (b) of Section 2.323); and

(2) tender through customary banking channels is sufficient and dishonor of a draft accompanying or associated with the documents constitutes non-acceptance or rejection.

Acts 1967, 60th Leg., p. 2343, ch. 785, § 1, eff. Sept. 1, 1967. Amended by Acts 1983, 68th Leg., p. 1530, ch. 290, § 1, eff. Aug. 29, 1983; Acts 2005, 79th Leg., ch. 122, § 7, eff. Sept. 1, 2005.

Uniform Commercial Code Comment

Prior Uniform Statutory Provision:

See Sections 11, 19, 20, 43(3) and (4), 46 and 51, Uniform Sales Act.

Changes: The general policy of the above sections is continued and supplemented but subsection (3) changes the rule of prior section 19(5) as to what constitutes a "destination" contract and subsection (4) incorporates a minor correction as to tender of delivery of goods in the possession of a bailee.

Purposes of Changes:

1. The major general rules governing the manner of proper or due tender of delivery are gathered in this section.

The term "tender" is used in this Article in two different senses. In one sense it refers to "due tender" which contemplates an offer coupled with a present ability to fulfill all the conditions resting on the tendering party and must be followed by actual performance if the other party shows himself ready to proceed. Unless the context unmistakably indicates otherwise this is the meaning of "tender" in this Article and the occasional addition of the word "due" is only for clarity and emphasis. At other times it is used to refer to an offer of goods or documents under a contract as if in fulfillment of its conditions even though there is a defect when measured against the contract obligation. Used in either sense, however, "tender" connotes such performance by the tendering party as puts the other party in default if he fails to proceed in some manner. These concepts of tender would apply to tender of either tangible or electronic documents of title.

2. The seller's general duty to tender and deliver is laid down in Section 2–301 and more particularly in Section 2–507. The seller's right to a receipt if he demands one and receipts are customary is governed by Section 1–205. Subsection (1) of the present section proceeds to set forth two primary requirements of tender: first, that the seller "put and hold conforming goods at the buyer's disposition" and, second, that he "give the buyer any notice reasonably necessary to enable him to take delivery."

In cases in which payment is due and demanded upon delivery the "buyer's disposition" is qualified by the seller's right to retain control of the goods until payment by the provision of this Article on delivery on condition. However, where the seller is demanding payment on delivery he must first allow the buyer to inspect the goods in order to avoid impairing his tender unless the contract for sale is on C.I.F., C.O.D., cash against documents or similar terms negating the privilege of inspection before payment.

In the case of contracts involving documents the seller can "put and hold conforming goods at the buyer's disposition" under subsection (1) by tendering documents which give the buyer complete control of the goods under the provisions of Article 7 on due negotiation.

3. Under paragraph (a) of subsection (1) usage of the trade and the circumstances of the particular case determine what is a reasonable hour for tender and what constitutes a reasonable period of holding the goods available.

4. The buyer must furnish reasonable facilities for the receipt of the goods tendered by the seller under subsection (1), paragraph (b). This obligation of the buyer is no part of the seller's tender.

5. For the purposes of subsections (2) and (3) there is omitted from this Article the rule under prior uniform legislation that a term requiring the seller to pay the freight or cost of transportation to the buyer is equivalent to an agreement by the seller to deliver to the buyer or at an agreed destination. This omission is with the specific intention of negating the rule, for under this Article the "shipment" contract is regarded as the normal one and the "destination" contract as the variant type. The seller is not obligated to deliver at a named destination and bear the concurrent risk of loss until arrival, unless he has specifically agreed so to deliver or the commercial understanding of the terms used by the parties contemplates such delivery.

6. Paragraph (a) of subsection (4) continues the rule of the prior uniform legislation as to acknowledgment by the bailee. Paragraph (b) of subsection (4) adopts the rule that between the buyer and the seller the risk of loss remains on the seller during a period reasonable for securing acknowledgment of the transfer from the bailee, while as against all other parties the buyer's rights are fixed as of the time the bailee receives notice of the transfer.

7. Under subsection (5) documents are never "required" except where there is an express contract term or it is plainly implicit in the peculiar circumstances of the case or in a usage of trade. Documents may, of course, be "authorized" although not required, but such cases are not within the scope of this subsection. When documents are required, there are three main requirements of this subsection: (1) "All": each required document is essential to a proper tender; (2) "Such": the documents must be the ones actually required by the contract in terms of source and substance; (3) "Correct form": All documents must be in correct form. These requirements apply to both tangible and electronic documents of title. When tender is made through customary banking channels, a draft may accompany or be associated with a document of title. The language has been broadened to allow for drafts to be associated with an electronic document of title. Compare Section 2–104(2) definition of financing agency.

When a prescribed document cannot be procured, a question of fact arises under the provision of this Article on substituted performance as to whether the agreed manner of delivery is actually commercially impracticable and whether the substitute is commercially reasonable.

Cross References:

Point 2: Sections 1–205, 2–301, 2–310, 2–507 and 2–513 and Article 7.

Point 5: Sections 2–308, 2–310 and 2–509.

Point 7: Section 2–614(1).

Specific matters involving tender are covered in many additional sections of this Article. See Sections 1–205, 2–301, 2–306 to 2–319, 2–321(3), 2–504, 2–507(2), 2–511(1), 2–513, 2–612 and 2–614.

Definitional Cross References:

"Agreement". Section 1–201.

"Bill of lading". Section 1–201.

"Buyer". Section 2–103.

"Conforming". Section 2–106.

"Contract". Section 1–201.

"Delivery". Section 1–201.

"Dishonor". Section 3–508.

"Document of title". Section 1–201.

"Draft". Section 3–104.

"Goods". Section 2–105.

"Notification". Section 1–201.

"Reasonable time". Section 1–204.

"Receipt" of goods. Section 2–103.

"Rights". Section 1–201.

"Seasonably". Section 1–204.

"Seller". Section 2–103.

"Written". Section 1–201.

Sections 31 and 32 of Acts 2005, 79th Leg., ch. 122 provide:

"Sec. 31. This Act applies to a document of title that is issued or a bailment that arises on or after the effective date of this Act. This Act does not apply to a document of title that is issued or a bailment that arises before the effective date of this Act even if the document of title or bailment would be subject to this Act if the document of title had been issued or bailment had arisen after the effective date of this Act. This Act does not apply to a right of action that has accrued before the effective date of this Act.

"Sec. 32. A document of title issued or a bailment that arises before the effective date of this Act and the rights, obligations, and interests flowing from that document or bailment are governed by any statute or other rule amended or repealed by this Act as if amendment or repeal had not occurred and may be terminated, completed, consummated, or enforced under that statute or other rule."

§ 2.504. Shipment by Seller

Where the seller is required or authorized to send the goods to the buyer and the contract does not require him to deliver them at a particular destination, then unless otherwise agreed he must

(1) put the goods in the possession of such a carrier and make such a contract for their transportation as may be reasonable having regard to the nature of the goods and other circumstances of the case; and

(2) obtain and promptly deliver or tender in due form any document necessary to enable the buyer to obtain possession of the goods or otherwise required by the agreement or by usage of trade; and

(3) promptly notify the buyer of the shipment.

Failure to notify the buyer under Subdivision (3) or to make a proper contract under Subdivision (1) is a ground for rejection only if material delay or loss ensues.

Acts 1967, 60th Leg., p. 2343, ch. 785, § 1, eff. Sept. 1, 1967.

Uniform Commercial Code Comment

Prior Uniform Statutory Provision:

Section 46, Uniform Sales Act.

Changes: Rewritten.

Purpose of Changes: To continue the general policy of the prior uniform statutory provision while incorporating certain modifications with respect to the requirement that the contract with the carrier be made expressly on behalf of the buyer and as to the necessity of giving notice of the shipment to the buyer, so that:

1. The section is limited to "shipment" contracts as contrasted with "destination" contracts or contracts for delivery at the place where the goods are located. The general principles embodied in this section cover the special cases of F.O.B. point of shipment contracts and C.I.F. and C. & F. contracts. Under the preceding section on manner of tender of delivery, due tender by the seller requires that he comply with the requirements of this section in appropriate cases.

2. The contract to be made with the carrier under paragraph (a) must conform to all express terms of the agreement, subject to any substitution necessary because of failure of agreed facilities as provided in the later provision on substituted performance. However, under the policies of this Article on good faith and commercial standards and on buyer's rights on improper delivery, the requirements of explicit provisions must be read in terms of their commercial and not their literal meaning. This policy is made express with respect to bills of lading in a set in the provision of this Article on form of bills of lading required in overseas shipment.

3. In the absence of agreement, the provision of this Article on options and cooperation respecting performance gives the seller the choice of any reasonable carrier, routing and other arrangements. Whether or not the shipment is at the buyer's expense the seller must see to any arrangements, reasonable in the circumstances, such as refrigeration, watering of live stock, protection against cold, the sending along of any necessary help, selection of specialized cars and the like for paragraph (a) is intended to cover all necessary arrangements whether made by contract with the carrier or otherwise. There is, however, a proper relaxation of such requirements if the buyer is himself in a position to make the appropriate arrangements and the seller gives him reasonable notice of the need to do so. It is an improper contract under paragraph (a) for the seller to agree with the carrier to a limited valuation below the true value and thus cut off the buyer's opportunity to recover from the carrier in the event of loss, when the risk of shipment is placed on the buyer by his contract with the seller.

4. Both the language of paragraph (b) and the nature of the situation it concerns indicate that the requirement that the seller must obtain and deliver promptly to the buyer in due form any document necessary to enable him to obtain possession of the goods is intended to cumulate with the other duties of the seller such as those covered in paragraph (a).

In this connection, in the case of pool car shipments a delivery order furnished by the seller on the pool car consignee, or on the carrier for delivery out of a larger quantity, satisfies the requirements of paragraph (b) unless the contract requires some other form of document.

5. This Article, unlike the prior uniform statutory provision, makes it the seller's duty to notify the buyer of shipment in all cases. The consequences of his failure to do so, however, are limited in that the buyer may reject on this ground only where material delay or loss ensues.

A standard and acceptable manner of notification in open credit shipments is the sending of an invoice and in the case of documentary contracts is the prompt forwarding of the documents as under paragraph (b) of this section. It is also usual to send on a straight bill of lading but this is not necessary to the required notification. However, should such a document prove necessary or convenient to the buyer, as in the case of loss and claim against the carrier, good faith would require the seller to send it on request.

Frequently the agreement expressly requires prompt notification as by wire or cable. Such a term may be of the essence and the final clause of paragraph (c) does not prevent the parties from making this a particular ground for rejection. To have this vital and irreparable effect upon the seller's duties, such a term should be part of the "dickered" terms written in any "form," or should otherwise be called seasonably and sharply to the seller's attention.

6. Generally, under the final sentence of the section, rejection by the buyer is justified only when the seller's dereliction as to any of the requirements of this section in fact is followed by material delay or damage. It rests on the seller, so far as concerns matters not within the peculiar knowledge of the buyer, to establish that his error has not been followed by events which justify rejection.

Cross References:

Point 1: Sections 2–319, 2–320 and 2–503(2).

Point 2: Sections 1–203, 2–323(2), 2–601 and 2–614(1).

Point 3: Section 2–311(2).

Point 5: Section 1–203.

Definitional Cross References:

"Agreement". Section 1–201.

"Buyer". Section 2–103.

"Contract". Section 1–201.

"Delivery". Section 1–201.

"Goods". Section 2–105.

"Notifies". Section 1–201.

"Seller". Section 2–103.

"Send". Section 1–201.

"Usage of trade". Section 1–205.

§ 2.505. Seller's Shipment Under Reservation

(a) Where the seller has identified goods to the contract by or before shipment:

(1) his procurement of a negotiable bill of lading to his own order or otherwise reserves in him a security interest in the goods. His procurement of the bill to the order of a financing agency or of the buyer indicates in addition only the seller's expectation of transferring that interest to the person named.

(2) a non-negotiable bill of lading to himself or his nominee reserves possession of the goods as security but except in a case of conditional delivery (Subsection (b) of Section 2.507) a non-negotiable bill of lading naming the buyer as consignee reserves no security interest even though the seller retains possession or control of the bill of lading.

(b) When shipment by the seller with reservation of a security interest is in violation of the contract for sale it constitutes an improper contract for transportation within the preceding section but impairs neither the rights given to the buyer by shipment and identification of the goods to the contract nor the seller's powers as a holder of a negotiable document of title.

Acts 1967, 60th Leg., p. 2343, ch. 785, § 1, eff. Sept. 1, 1967. Amended by Acts 2005, 79th Leg., ch. 122, § 8, eff. Sept. 1, 2005.

Uniform Commercial Code Comment

Prior Uniform Statutory Provision:

Section 20(2), (3), (4), Uniform Sales Act.

Changes: Completely rephrased, the "powers" of the parties in cases of reservation being emphasized primarily rather than the "rightfulness" of reservation.

Purposes of Changes: To continue in general the policy of the prior uniform statutory provision with certain modifications of emphasis and language, so that:

1. The security interest reserved to the seller under subsection (1) is restricted to securing payment or performance by the buyer and the seller is strictly limited in his disposition and control of the goods as against the buyer and third parties. Under this Article, the provision as to the passing of interest expressly applies "despite any reservation of security title" and also provides that the "rights, obligations and remedies" of the parties are not altered by the incidence of title generally. The security interest, therefore, must be regarded as a means given to the seller to enforce his rights against the buyer which is unaffected by and in turn does not affect the location of title generally. The rules set forth in subsection (1) are not to be altered by any apparent "contrary intent" of the parties as to passing of title, since the rights and remedies of the parties to the contract of sale, as defined in this Article, rest on the contract and its performance or breach and not on stereotyped presumptions as to the location of title.

This Article does not attempt to regulate local procedure in regard to the effective maintenance of the seller's security interest when the action is in replevin by the buyer against the carrier.

2. Every shipment of identified goods under a negotiable bill of lading reserves a security interest in the seller under subsection (1) paragraph (a).

It is frequently convenient for the seller to make the bill of lading to the order of a nominee such as his agent at destination, the financing agency to which he expects to negotiate the document or the bank issuing a credit to him. In many instances, also, the buyer is made the order party. This Article does not deal directly with the question as to whether a bill of lading made out by the seller to the order of a nominee gives the carrier notice of any rights which the nominee may have so as to limit its freedom or obligation to honor the bill of lading in the hands of the seller as the original shipper if the expected negotiation fails. This is dealt with in the Article on Documents of Title (Article 7).

3. A non-negotiable bill of lading taken to a party other than the buyer under subsection (1) paragraph (b) reserves possession of the goods as security in the seller but if he

seeks to withhold the goods improperly the buyer can tender payment and recover them.

4. In the case of a shipment by non-negotiable bill of lading taken to a buyer, the seller, under subsection (1) retains no security interest or possession as against the buyer and by the shipment he *de facto* loses control as against the carrier except where he rightfully and effectively stops delivery in transit. In cases in which the contract gives the seller the right to payment against delivery, the seller, by making an immediate demand for payment, can show that his delivery is conditional, but this does not prevent the buyer's power to transfer full title to a sub-buyer in ordinary course or other purchaser under Section 2–403.

5. Under subsection (2) an improper reservation by the seller which would constitute a breach in no way impairs such of the buyer's rights as result from identification of the goods. The security title reserved by the seller under subsection (1) does not protect his retaining possession or control of the document or the goods for the purpose of exacting more than is due him under the contract.

Cross References:

Point 1: Section 1–201.

Point 2: Article 7.

Point 3: Sections 2–501(2) and 2–504.

Point 4: Sections 2–403, 2–507(2) and 2–705.

Point 5: Sections 2–310, 2–319(4), 2–320(4), 2–501 and 2–502 and Article 7.

Definitional Cross References:

"Bill of lading". Section 1–201.

"Buyer". Section 2–103.

"Consignee". Section 7–102.

"Contract". Section 1–201.

"Contract for sale". Section 2–106.

"Delivery". Section 1–201.

"Financing agency". Section 2–104.

"Goods". Section 2–105.

"Holder". Section 1–201.

"Person". Section 1–201.

"Security interest". Section 1–201.

"Seller". Section 2–103.

Sections 31 and 32 of Acts 2005, 79th Leg., ch. 122 provide:

"Sec. 31. This Act applies to a document of title that is issued or a bailment that arises on or after the effective date of this Act. This Act does not apply to a document of title that is issued or a bailment that arises before the effective date of this Act even if the document of title or bailment would be subject to this Act if the document of title had been issued or bailment had arisen after the effective date of this Act. This Act does not apply to a right of action that has accrued before the effective date of this Act.

"Sec. 32. A document of title issued or a bailment that arises before the effective date of this Act and the rights, obligations, and interests flowing from that document or bailment are governed by any statute or other rule amended or repealed by this Act as if amendment or repeal had not occurred and may be terminated, completed, consummated, or enforced under that statute or other rule."

§ 2.506. Rights of Financing Agency

(a) A financing agency by paying or purchasing for value a draft which relates to a shipment of goods acquires to the extent of the payment or purchase and in addition to its own rights under the draft and any document of title securing it any rights of the shipper in the goods including the right to stop delivery and the shipper's right to have the draft honored by the buyer.

(b) The right to reimbursement of a financing agency which has in good faith honored or purchased the draft under commitment to or authority from the buyer is not impaired by subsequent discovery of defects with reference to any relevant document which was apparently regular.

Acts 1967, 60th Leg., p. 2343, ch. 785, § 1, eff. Sept. 1, 1967. Amended by Acts 2005, 79th Leg., ch. 122, § 9, eff. Sept. 1, 2005.

Uniform Commercial Code Comment

Prior Uniform Statutory Provision:

None.

Purposes:

1. "Financing agency" is broadly defined in this Article to cover every normal instance in which a party aids or intervenes in the financing of a sales transaction. The term as used in subsection (1) is not in any sense intended as a limitation and covers any other appropriate situation which may arise outside the scope of the definition.

2. "Paying" as used in subsection (1) is typified by the letter of credit, or "authority to pay" situation in which a banker, by arrangement with the buyer or other consignee, pays on his behalf a draft for the price of the goods. It is immaterial whether the draft is formally drawn on the party paying or his principal, whether it is a sight draft paid in cash or a time draft "paid" in the first instance by acceptance, or whether the payment is viewed as absolute or conditional. All of these cases constitute "payment" under this subsection. Similarly, "purchasing for value" is used to indicate the whole area of financing by the seller's banker, and the principle of subsection (1) is applicable without any niceties of distinction between "purchase," "discount," "advance against collection" or the like. But it is important to notice that the only right to have the draft honored that is acquired is that *against the buyer;* if any right against any one else is claimed it will have to be under some separate obligation of that other person. A letter of credit does not necessarily protect *purchasers* of drafts. See Article 5. And for the relations of the parties to documentary drafts see Part 5 of Article 4.

3. Subsection (1) is made applicable to payments or advances against a draft which "relates to" a shipment of goods and this has been chosen as a term of maximum breadth. In particular the term is intended to cover the case of a draft against an invoice or against a delivery order. Further, it is unnecessary that there be an explicit assignment of the

invoice attached to the draft to bring the transaction within the reason of this subsection.

4. After shipment, "the rights of the shipper in the goods" are merely security rights and are subject to the buyer's right to force delivery upon tender of the price. The rights acquired by the financing agency are similarly limited and, moreover, if the agency fails to procure any outstanding negotiable document of title, it may find its exercise of these rights hampered or even defeated by the seller's disposition of the document to a third party. This section does not attempt to create any new rights in the financing agency against the carrier which would force the latter to honor a stop order from the agency, a stranger to the shipment, or any new rights against a holder to whom a document of title has been duly negotiated under Article 7.

5. The deletion of the language "on its face" from subsection (2) is designed to accommodate electronic documents of title without changing the requirement of regularity of the document.

Cross References:

Point 1: Section 2–104(2) and Article 4.

Point 2: Part 5 of Article 4, and Article 5.

Point 4: Sections 2–501 and 2–502(1) and Article 7.

Definitional Cross References:

"Buyer". Section 2–103.

"Document of title". Section 1–201.

"Draft". Section 3–104.

"Financing agency". Section 2–104.

"Good faith". Section 2–103.

"Goods". Section 2–105.

"Honor". Section 1–201.

"Purchase". Section 1–201.

"Rights". Section 1–201.

"Value". Section 1–201.

Sections 31 and 32 of Acts 2005, 79th Leg., ch. 122 provide:

"Sec. 31. This Act applies to a document of title that is issued or a bailment that arises on or after the effective date of this Act. This Act does not apply to a document of title that is issued or a bailment that arises before the effective date of this Act even if the document of title or bailment would be subject to this Act if the document of title had been issued or bailment had arisen after the effective date of this Act. This Act does not apply to a right of action that has accrued before the effective date of this Act.

"Sec. 32. A document of title issued or a bailment that arises before the effective date of this Act and the rights, obligations, and interests flowing from that document or bailment are governed by any statute or other rule amended or repealed by this Act as if amendment or repeal had not occurred and may be terminated, completed, consummated, or enforced under that statute or other rule."

§ 2.507. Effect of Seller's Tender; Delivery on Condition

(a) Tender of delivery is a condition to the buyer's duty to accept the goods and, unless otherwise agreed, to his duty to pay for them. Tender entitles the seller to acceptance of the goods and to payment according to the contract.

(b) Where payment is due and demanded on the delivery to the buyer of goods or documents of title, his right as against the seller to retain or dispose of them is conditional upon his making the payment due.

Acts 1967, 60th Leg., p. 2343, ch. 785, § 1, eff. Sept. 1, 1967.

Uniform Commercial Code Comment

Prior Uniform Statutory Provision:

See Sections 11, 41, 42 and 69, Uniform Sales Act.

Purposes:

1. Subsection (1) continues the policies of the prior uniform statutory provisions with respect to tender and delivery by the seller. Under this Article the same rules in these matters are applied to present sales and to contracts for sale. But the provisions of this subsection must be read within the framework of the other sections of this Article which bear upon the question of delivery and payment.

2. The "unless otherwise agreed" provision of subsection (1) is directed primarily to cases in which payment in advance has been promised or a letter of credit term has been included. Payment "according to the contract" contemplates immediate payment, payment at the end of an agreed credit term, payment by a time acceptance or the like. Under this Act, "contract" means the total obligation in law which results from the parties' agreement including the effect of this Article. In this context, therefore, there must be considered the effect in law of such provisions as those on means and manner of payment and on failure of agreed means and manner of payment.

3. Subsection (2) deals with the effect of a conditional delivery by the seller and in such a situation makes the buyer's "right as against the seller" conditional upon payment. These words are used as words of limitation to conform with the policy set forth in the bona fide purchase sections of this Article. Should the seller after making such a conditional delivery fail to follow up his rights, the condition is waived. This subsection (2) codifies the cash seller's right of reclamation which is in the nature of a lien. There is no specific time limit for a cash seller to exercise the right of reclamation. However, the right will be defeated by delay causing prejudice to the buyer, waiver, estoppel, or ratification of the buyer's right to retain possession. Common law rules and precedents governing such principles are applicable (Section 1–103). If third parties are involved, Section 2–403(1) protects good faith purchasers. See PEB Commentary No. 1, dated March 10, 1990.

Cross References:

Point 1: Sections 2–310, 2–503, 2–511, 2–601 and 2–711 to 2–713.

Point 2: Sections 1–201, 2–511 and 2–614.

Point 3: Sections 2–401, 2–403, and 2–702(1)(b).

Definitional Cross References:

"Buyer". Section 2–103.

"Contract". Section 1–201.

"Delivery". Section 1–201.

"Document of title". Section 1–201.

"Goods". Section 2–105.

"Rights". Section 1–201.

"Seller". Section 2–103.

§ 2.508. Cure by Seller of Improper Tender or Delivery; Replacement

(a) Where any tender or delivery by the seller is rejected because non-conforming and the time for performance has not yet expired, the seller may seasonably notify the buyer of his intention to cure and may then within the contract time make a conforming delivery.

(b) Where the buyer rejects a non-conforming tender which the seller had reasonable grounds to believe would be acceptable with or without money allowance the seller may if he seasonably notifies the buyer have a further reasonable time to substitute a conforming tender.

Acts 1967, 60th Leg., p. 2343, ch. 785, § 1, eff. Sept. 1, 1967.

Uniform Commercial Code Comment

Prior Uniform Statutory Provision:

None.

Purposes:

1. Subsection (1) permits a seller who has made a non-conforming tender in any case to make a conforming delivery within the contract time upon seasonable notification to the buyer. It applies even where the seller has taken back the non-conforming goods and refunded the purchase price. He may still make a good tender within the contract period. The closer, however, it is to the contract date, the greater is the necessity for extreme promptness on the seller's part in notifying of his intention to cure, if such notification is to be "seasonable" under this subsection.

The rule of this subsection, moreover, is qualified by its underlying reasons. Thus if, after contracting for June delivery, a buyer later makes known to the seller his need for shipment early in the month and the seller ships accordingly, the "contract time" has been cut down by the supervening modification and the time for cure of tender must be referred to this modified time term.

2. Subsection (2) seeks to avoid injustice to the seller by reason of a surprise rejection by the buyer. However, the seller is not protected unless he had "reasonable grounds to believe" that the tender would be acceptable. Such reasonable grounds can lie in prior course of dealing, course of performance or usage of trade as well as in the particular circumstances surrounding the making of the contract. The seller is charged with commercial knowledge of any factors in a particular sales situation which require him to comply strictly with his obligations under the contract as, for example, strict conformity of documents in an overseas shipment or the sale of precision parts or chemicals for use in manufacture. Further, if the buyer gives notice either implicitly, as by a prior course of dealing involving rigorous inspections, or expressly, as by the deliberate inclusion of a "no replacement" clause in the contract, the seller is to be held to rigid compliance. If the clause appears in a "form" contract evidence that it is out of line with trade usage or the prior course of dealing and was not called to the seller's attention may be sufficient to show that the seller had reasonable grounds to believe that the tender would be acceptable.

3. The words "a further reasonable time to substitute a conforming tender" are intended as words of limitation to protect the buyer. What is a "reasonable time" depends upon the attending circumstances. Compare Section 2–511 on the comparable case of a seller's surprise demand for legal tender.

4. Existing trade usages permitting variations without rejection but with price allowance enter into the agreement itself as contractual limitations of remedy and are not covered by this section.

Cross References:

Point 2: Section 2–302.

Point 3: Section 2–511.

Point 4: Sections 1–205 and 2–721.

Definitional Cross References:

"Buyer". Section 2–103.

"Conforming". Section 2–106.

"Contract". Section 1–201.

"Money". Section 1–201.

"Notifies". Section 1–201.

"Reasonable time". Section 1–204.

"Seasonably". Section 1–204.

"Seller". Section 2–103.

§ 2.509. Risk of Loss in the Absence of Breach

(a) Where the contract requires or authorizes the seller to ship the goods by carrier

(1) if it does not require him to deliver them at a particular destination, the risk of loss passes to the buyer when the goods are duly delivered to the carrier even though the shipment is under reservation (Section 2.505); but

(2) if it does require him to deliver them at a particular destination and the goods are there duly tendered while in the possession of the carrier, the risk of loss passes to the buyer when the goods are there duly so tendered as to enable the buyer to take delivery.

(b) Where the goods are held by a bailee to be delivered without being moved, the risk of loss passes to the buyer

(1) on the buyer's receipt of possession or control of a negotiable document of title covering the goods; or

(2) on acknowledgment by the bailee of the buyer's right to possession of the goods; or

(3) after the buyer's receipt of possession or control of a non-negotiable document of title or other written direction to deliver, as provided in Subsection (d)(2) of Section 2.503.

(c) In any case not within Subsection (a) or (b), the risk of loss passes to the buyer on his receipt of the goods if the seller is a merchant; otherwise the risk passes to the buyer on tender of delivery.

(d) The provisions of this section are subject to contrary agreement of the parties and to the provisions of this chapter on sale on approval (Section 2.327) and on effect of breach on risk of loss (Section 2.510).

Acts 1967, 60th Leg., p. 2343, ch. 785, § 1, eff. Sept. 1, 1967. Amended by Acts 1983, 68th Leg., p. 1531, ch. 290, § 2, eff. Aug. 29, 1983; Acts 2005, 79th Leg., ch. 122, § 10, eff. Sept. 1, 2005.

Uniform Commercial Code Comment

Prior Uniform Statutory Provision:

Section 22, Uniform Sales Act.

Changes: Rewritten, subsection (3) of this section modifying prior law.

Purposes of Changes: To make it clear that:

1. The underlying theory of these sections on risk of loss is the adoption of the contractual approach rather than an arbitrary shifting of the risk with the "property" in the goods. The scope of the present section, therefore, is limited strictly to those cases where there has been no breach by the seller. Where for any reason his delivery or tender fails to conform to the contract, the present section does not apply and the situation is governed by the provisions on effect of breach on risk of loss.

2. The provisions of subsection (1) apply where the contract "requires or authorizes" shipment of the goods. This language is intended to be construed parallel to comparable language in the section on shipment by seller. In order that the goods be "duly delivered to the carrier" under paragraph (a) a contract must be entered into with the carrier which will satisfy the requirements of the section on shipment by the seller and the delivery must be made under circumstances which will enable the seller to take any further steps necessary to a due tender. The underlying reason of this subsection does not require that the shipment be made after contracting, but where, for example, the seller buys the goods afloat and later diverts the shipment to the buyer, he must identify the goods to the contract before the risk of loss can pass. To transfer the risk it is enough that a proper shipment and a proper identification come to apply to the same goods although, aside from special agreement, the risk will not pass retroactively to the time of shipment in such a case.

3. Whether the contract involves delivery at the seller's place of business or at the situs of the goods, a merchant seller cannot transfer risk of loss and it remains upon him until actual receipt by the buyer, even though full payment has been made and the buyer has been notified that the goods are at his disposal. Protection is afforded him, in the event of breach by the buyer, under the next section.

The underlying theory of this rule is that a merchant who is to make physical delivery at his own place continues meanwhile to control the goods and can be expected to insure his interest in them. The buyer, on the other hand, has no control of the goods and it is extremely unlikely that he will carry insurance on goods not yet in his possession.

4. Where the agreement provides for delivery of the goods as between the buyer and seller without removal from the physical possession of a bailee, the provisions on manner of tender of delivery apply on the point of transfer of risk. Due delivery of a negotiable document of title covering the goods or acknowledgment by the bailee that he holds for the buyer completes the "delivery" and passes the risk. See definition of delivery in Article 1, Section 1–201 and the definition of control in Article 7, Section 7–106.

5. The provisions of this section are made subject by subsection (4) to the "contrary agreement" of the parties. This language is intended as the equivalent of the phrase "unless otherwise agreed" used more frequently throughout this Act. "Contrary" is in no way used as a word of limitation and the buyer and seller are left free to readjust their rights and risks as declared by this section in any manner agreeable to them. Contrary agreement can also be found in the circumstances of the case, a trade usage or practice, or a course of dealing or performance.

Cross References:

Point 1: Section 2–510(1).

Point 2: Sections 2–503 and 2–504.

Point 3: Sections 2–104, 2–503 and 2–510.

Point 4: Section 2–503(4).

Point 5: Section 1–201.

Definitional Cross References:

"Agreement". Section 1–201.

"Buyer". Section 2–103.

"Contract". Section 1–201.

"Delivery". Section 1–201.

"Document of title". Section 1–201.

"Goods". Section 2–105.

"Merchant". Section 2–104.

"Party". Section 1–201.

"Receipt" of goods. Section 2–103.

"Sale on approval". Section 2–326.

"Seller". Section 2–103.

Sections 31 and 32 of Acts 2005, 79th Leg., ch. 122 provide:

"Sec. 31. This Act applies to a document of title that is issued or a bailment that arises on or after the effective date of this Act. This

Act does not apply to a document of title that is issued or a bailment that arises before the effective date of this Act even if the document of title or bailment would be subject to this Act if the document of title had been issued or bailment had arisen after the effective date of this Act. This Act does not apply to a right of action that has accrued before the effective date of this Act.

"Sec. 32. A document of title issued or a bailment that arises before the effective date of this Act and the rights, obligations, and interests flowing from that document or bailment are governed by any statute or other rule amended or repealed by this Act as if amendment or repeal had not occurred and may be terminated, completed, consummated, or enforced under that statute or other rule."

§ 2.510. Effect of Breach on Risk of Loss

(a) Where a tender or delivery of goods so fails to conform to the contract as to give a right of rejection the risk of their loss remains on the seller until cure or acceptance.

(b) Where the buyer rightfully revokes acceptance he may to the extent of any deficiency in his effective insurance coverage treat the risk of loss as having rested on the seller from the beginning.

(c) Where the buyer as to conforming goods already identified to the contract for sale repudiates or is otherwise in breach before risk of their loss has passed to him, the seller may to the extent of any deficiency in his effective insurance coverage treat the risk of loss as resting on the buyer for a commercially reasonable time.

Acts 1967, 60th Leg., p. 2343, ch. 785, § 1, eff. Sept. 1, 1967.

Uniform Commercial Code Comment

Prior Uniform Statutory Provision:

None.

Purposes: To make clear that:

1. Under subsection (1) the seller by his individual action cannot shift the risk of loss to the buyer unless his action conforms with all the conditions resting on him under the contract.

2. The "cure" of defective tenders contemplated by subsection (1) applies only to those situations in which the seller makes changes in goods already tendered, such as repair, partial substitution, sorting out from an improper mixture and the like since "cure" by repossession and new tender has no effect on the risk of loss of the goods originally tendered. The seller's privilege of cure does not shift the risk, however, until the cure is completed.

Where defective documents are involved a cure of the defect by the seller or a waiver of the defects by the buyer will operate to shift the risk under this section. However, if the goods have been destroyed prior to the cure or the buyer is unaware of their destruction at the time he waives the defect in the documents, the risk of the loss must still be borne by the seller, for the risk shifts only at the time of cure, waiver of documentary defects or acceptance of the goods.

3. In cases where there has been a breach of the contract, if the one in control of the goods is the aggrieved party, whatever loss or damage may prove to be uncovered by his insurance falls upon the contract breaker under subsections (2) and (3) rather than upon him. The word "effective" as applied to insurance coverage in those subsections is used to meet the case of supervening insolvency of the insurer. The "deficiency" referred to in the text means such deficiency in the insurance coverage as exists without subrogation. This section merely distributes the risk of loss as stated and is not intended to be disturbed by any subrogation of an insurer.

Cross Reference:

Section 2–509.

Definitional Cross References:

"Buyer". Section 2–103.

"Conform". Section 2–106.

"Contract for sale". Section 2–106.

"Goods". Section 2–105.

"Seller". Section 2–103.

§ 2.511. Tender of Payment by Buyer; Payment by Check

(a) Unless otherwise agreed tender of payment is a condition to the seller's duty to tender and complete any delivery.

(b) Tender of payment is sufficient when made by any means or in any manner current in the ordinary course of business unless the seller demands payment in legal tender and gives any extension of time reasonably necessary to procure it.

(c) Subject to the provisions of this title on the effect of an instrument on an obligation (Section 3.802), payment by check is conditional and is defeated as between the parties by dishonor of the check on due presentment.

Acts 1967, 60th Leg., p. 2343, ch. 785, § 1, eff. Sept. 1, 1967.

Uniform Commercial Code Comment

Prior Uniform Statutory Provision:

Section 42, Uniform Sales Act.

Changes: Rewritten by this section and Section 2–507.

Purposes of Changes:

1. The requirement of payment against delivery in subsection (1) is applicable to noncommercial sales generally and to ordinary sales at retail although it has no application to the great body of commercial contracts which carry credit terms. Subsection (1) applies also to documentary contracts in general and to contracts which look to shipment by the seller but contain no term on time and manner of payment,

in which situations the payment may, in proper case, be demanded against delivery of appropriate documents.

In the case of specific transactions such as C.O.D. sales or agreements providing for payment against documents, the provisions of this subsection must be considered in conjunction with the special sections of the Article dealing with such terms. The provision that tender of payment is a condition to the seller's duty to tender and complete "any delivery" integrates this section with the language and policy of the section on delivery in several lots which call for separate payment. Finally, attention should be directed to the provision on right to adequate assurance of performance which recognizes, even before the time for tender, an obligation on the buyer not to impair the seller's expectation of receiving payment in due course.

2. Unless there is agreement otherwise the concurrence of the conditions as to tender of payment and tender of delivery requires their performance at a single place or time. This Article determines that place and time by determining in various other sections the place and time for tender of delivery under various circumstances and in particular types of transactions. The sections dealing with time and place of delivery together with the section on right to inspection of goods answer the subsidiary question as to when payment may be demanded before inspection by the buyer.

3. The essence of the principle involved in subsection (2) is avoidance of commercial surprise at the time of performance. The section on substituted performance covers the peculiar case in which legal tender is not available to the commercial community.

4. Subsection (3) is concerned with the rights and obligations as between the parties to a sales transaction when payment is made by check. This Article recognizes that the taking of a seemingly solvent party's check is commercially normal and proper and, if due diligence is exercised in collection, is not to be penalized in any way. The conditional character of the payment under this section refers only to the effect of the transaction "as between the parties" thereto and does not purport to cut into the law of "absolute" and "conditional" payment as applied to such other problems as the discharge of sureties or the responsibilities of a drawee bank which is at the same time an agent for collection.

The phrase "by check" includes not only the buyer's own but any check which does not effect a discharge under Article 3 (Section 3–802). Similarly the reason of this subsection should apply and the same result should be reached where the buyer "pays" by sight draft on a commercial firm which is financing him.

5. Under subsection (3) payment by check is defeated if it is not honored upon due presentment. This corresponds to the provisions of article on Commercial Paper. (Section 3–802). But if the seller procures certification of the check instead of cashing it, the buyer is discharged. (Section 3–411).

6. Where the instrument offered by the buyer is not a payment but a credit instrument such as a note or a check post-dated by even one day, the seller's acceptance of the instrument insofar as third parties are concerned, amounts to a delivery on credit and his remedies are set forth in the section on buyer's insolvency. As between the buyer and the seller, however, the matter turns on the present subsection and the section on conditional delivery and subsequent dishonor of the instrument gives the seller rights on it as well as for breach of the contract for sale.

Cross References:

Point 1: Sections 2–307, 2–310, 2–320, 2–325, 2–503, 2–513 and 2–609.

Point 2: Sections 2–307, 2–310, 2–319, 2–322, 2–503, 2–504 and 2–513.

Point 3: Section 2–614.

Point 5: Article 3, esp. Sections 3–802 and 3–411.

Point 6: Sections 2–507, 2–702, and Article 3.

Definitional Cross References:

"Buyer". Section 2–103.

"Check". Section 3–104.

"Dishonor". Section 3–508.

"Party". Section 1–201.

"Reasonable time". Section 1–204.

"Seller". Section 2–103.

§ 2.512. Payment by Buyer Before Inspection

(a) Where the contract requires payment before inspection non-conformity of the goods does not excuse the buyer from so making payment unless

(1) the non-conformity appears without inspection; or

(2) despite tender of the required documents circumstances would justify injunction against honor under this title (Section 5.109(b)).

(b) Payment pursuant to Subsection (a) does not constitute an acceptance of goods or impair the buyer's right to inspect or any of his remedies.

Acts 1967, 60th Leg., p. 2343, ch. 785, § 1, eff. Sept. 1, 1967. Amended by Acts 1999, 76th Leg., ch. 4, § 3, eff. Sept. 1, 1999.

Uniform Commercial Code Comment

Prior Uniform Statutory Provision:

None, but see Sections 47 and 49, Uniform Sales Act.

Purposes:

1. Subsection (1) of the present section recognizes that the essence of a contract providing for payment before inspection is the intention of the parties to shift to the buyer the risks which would usually rest upon the seller. The basic nature of the transaction is thus preserved and the buyer is in most cases required to pay first and litigate as to any defects later.

2. "Inspection" under this section is an inspection in a manner reasonable for detecting defects in goods whose surface appearance is satisfactory.

3. Clause (a) of this subsection states an exception to the general rule based on common sense and normal commercial practice. The apparent non-conformity referred to is one which is evident in the mere process of taking delivery.

4. Clause (b) is concerned with contracts for payment against documents and incorporates the general clarification and modification of the case law contained in the section on excuse of a financing agency. Section 5–114.

5. Subsection (2) makes explicit the general policy of the Uniform Sales Act that the payment required before inspection in no way impairs the buyer's remedies or rights in the event of a default by the seller. The remedies preserved to the buyer are all of his remedies, which include as a matter of reason the remedy for total non-delivery after payment in advance.

The provision on performance or acceptance under reservation of rights does not apply to the situations contemplated here in which payment is made in due course under the contract and the buyer need not pay "under protest" or the like in order to preserve his rights as to defects discovered upon inspection.

6. This section applies to cases in which the contract requires payment before inspection either by the express agreement of the parties or by reason of the effect in law of that contract. The present section must therefore be considered in conjunction with the provision on right to inspection of goods which sets forth the instances in which the buyer is not entitled to inspection before payment.

Cross References:

Point 4: Article 5.

Point 5: Section 1–207.

Point 6: Section 2–513(3).

Definitional Cross References:

"Buyer". Section 2–103.

"Conform". Section 2–106.

"Contract". Section 1–201.

"Financing agency". Section 2–104.

"Goods". Section 2–105.

"Remedy". Section 1–201.

"Rights". Section 1–201.

§ 2.513. Buyer's Right to Inspection of Goods

(a) Unless otherwise agreed and subject to Subsection (c), where goods are tendered or delivered or identified to the contract for sale, the buyer has a right before payment or acceptance to inspect them at any reasonable place and time and in any reasonable manner. When the seller is required or authorized to send the goods to the buyer, the inspection may be after their arrival.

(b) Expenses of inspection must be borne by the buyer but may be recovered from the seller if the goods do not conform and are rejected.

(c) Unless otherwise agreed and subject to the provisions of this chapter on C.I.F. contracts (Subsection (c) of Section 2.321), the buyer is not entitled to inspect the goods before payment of the price when the contract provides

(1) for delivery "C.O.D." or on other like terms; or

(2) for payment against documents of title, except where such payment is due only after the goods are to become available for inspection.

(d) A place or method of inspection fixed by the parties is presumed to be exclusive but unless otherwise expressly agreed it does not postpone identification or shift the place for delivery or for passing the risk of loss. If compliance becomes impossible, inspection shall be as provided in this section unless the place or method fixed was clearly intended as an indispensable condition failure of which avoids the contract.

Acts 1967, 60th Leg., p. 2343, ch. 785, § 1, eff. Sept. 1, 1967.

Uniform Commercial Code Comment

Prior Uniform Statutory Provision:

Section 47(2), (3), Uniform Sales Act.

Changes: Rewritten, Subsections (2) and (3) being new.

Purposes of Changes and New Matter: To correspond in substance with the prior uniform statutory provision and to incorporate in addition some of the results of the better case law so that:

1. The buyer is entitled to inspect goods as provided in subsection (1) unless it has been otherwise agreed by the parties. The phrase "unless otherwise agreed" is intended principally to cover such situations as those outlined in subsections (3) and (4) and those in which the agreement of the parties negates inspection before tender of delivery. However, no agreement by the parties can displace the entire right of inspection except where the contract is simply for the sale of "this thing." Even in a sale of boxed goods "as is" inspection is a right of the buyer, since if the boxes prove to contain some other merchandise altogether the price can be recovered back; nor do the limitations of the provision on effect of acceptance apply in such a case.

2. The buyer's right of inspection is available to him upon tender, delivery or appropriation of the goods with notice to him. Since inspection is available to him on tender, where payment is due against delivery he may, unless otherwise agreed, make his inspection before payment of the price. It is also available to him after receipt of the goods and so may be postponed after receipt for a reasonable time. Failure to inspect before payment does not impair the right to inspect after receipt of the goods unless the case falls within subsection (4) on agreed and exclusive inspection provisions. The right to inspect goods which have been appropriated with notice to the buyer holds whether or not the sale was by sample.

3. The buyer may exercise his right of inspection at any reasonable time or place and in any reasonable manner. It is not necessary that he select the most appropriate time, place or manner to inspect or that his selection be the customary one in the trade or locality. Any reasonable time, place or manner is available to him and the reasonableness will be determined by trade usages, past practices between the parties and the other circumstances of the case.

The last sentence of subsection (1) makes it clear that the place of arrival of shipped goods is a reasonable place for their inspection.

4. Expenses of an inspection made to satisfy the buyer of the seller's performance must be assumed by the buyer in the first instance. Since the rule provides merely for an allocation of expense there is no policy to prevent the parties from providing otherwise in the agreement. Where the buyer would normally bear the expenses of the inspection but the goods are rightly rejected because of what the inspection reveals, demonstrable and reasonable costs of the inspection are part of his incidental damage caused by the seller's breach.

5. In the case of payment against documents, subsection (3) requires payment before inspection, since shipping documents against which payment is to be made will commonly arrive and be tendered while the goods are still in transit. This Article recognizes no exception in any peculiar case in which the goods happen to arrive before the documents are tendered. However, where by the agreement payment is to await the arrival of the goods, inspection before payment becomes proper since the goods are then "available for inspection."

Where by the agreement the documents are to be tendered after arrival of the goods, the buyer is entitled to inspect before payment since the goods are then "available for inspection". Proof of usage is not necessary to establish this right, but if inspection before payment is disputed the contrary must be established by usage or by an explicit contract term to that effect.

For the same reason, that the goods are available for inspection, a term calling for payment against storage documents or a delivery order does not normally bar the buyer's right to inspection before payment under subsection (3)(b). This result is reinforced by the buyer's right under subsection (1) to inspect goods which have been appropriated with notice to him.

6. Under subsection (4) an agreed place or method of inspection is generally held to be intended as exclusive. However, where compliance with such an agreed inspection term becomes impossible, the question is basically one of intention. If the parties clearly intend that the method of inspection named is to be a necessary condition without which the entire deal is to fail, the contract is at an end if that method becomes impossible. On the other hand, if the parties merely seek to indicate a convenient and reliable method but do not intend to give up the deal in the event of its failure, any reasonable method of inspection may be substituted under this Article.

Since the purpose of an agreed place of inspection is only to make sure at that point whether or not the goods will be thrown back, the "exclusive" feature of the named place is satisfied under this Article if the buyer's failure to inspect there is held to be an acceptance with the knowledge of such defects as inspection would have revealed within the section on waiver of buyer's objections by failure to particularize. Revocation of the acceptance is limited to the situations stated in the section pertaining to that subject. The reasonable time within which to give notice of defects within the section on notice of breach begins to run from the point of the "acceptance."

7. Clauses on time of inspection are commonly clauses which limit the time in which the buyer must inspect and give notice of defects. Such clauses are therefore governed by the section of this Article which requires that such a time limitation must be reasonable.

8. Inspection under this Article is not to be regarded as a "condition precedent to the passing of title" so that risk until inspection remains on the seller. Under subsection (4) such an approach cannot be sustained. Issues between the buyer and seller are settled in this Article almost wholly by special provisions and not by the technical determination of the locus of the title. Thus "inspection as a condition to the passing of title" becomes a concept almost without meaning. However, in peculiar circumstances inspection may still have some of the consequences hitherto sought and obtained under that concept.

9. "Inspection" under this section has to do with the buyer's check-up on whether the seller's performance is in accordance with a contract previously made and is not to be confused with the "examination" of the goods or of a sample or model of them at the time of contracting which may affect the warranties involved in the contract.

Cross References:

Generally: Sections 2–310(b), 2–321(3) and 2–606(1)(b).

Point 1: Section 2–607.

Point 2: Sections 2–501 and 2–502.

Point 4: Section 2–715.

Point 5: Section 2–321(3).

Point 6: Sections 2–606 to 2–608.

Point 7: Section 1–204.

Point 8: Comment to Section 2–401.

Point 9: Section 2–316(3)(b).

Definitional Cross References:

"Buyer". Section 2–103.

"Conform". Section 2–106.

"Contract". Section 1–201.

"Contract for sale". Section 2–106.

"Document of title". Section 1–201.

"Goods". Section 2–105.

"Party". Section 1–201.

"Presumed". Section 1–201.

"Reasonable time". Section 1–204.

"Rights". Section 1–201.

"Seller". Section 2–103.

"Send". Section 1–201.

"Term". Section 1–201.

§ 2.514. When Documents Deliverable on Acceptance; When on Payment

Unless otherwise agreed documents against which a draft is drawn are to be delivered to the drawee on acceptance of the draft if it is payable more than three days after presentment; otherwise, only on payment.

Acts 1967, 60th Leg., p. 2343, ch. 785, § 1, eff. Sept. 1, 1967.

Uniform Commercial Code Comment

Prior Uniform Statutory Provision:

Section 41, Uniform Bills of Lading Act.

Changes: Rewritten.

Purposes of Changes: To make the provision one of general application so that:

1. It covers any document against which a draft may be drawn, whatever may be the form of the document, and applies to interpret the action of a seller or consignor insofar as it may affect the rights and duties of any buyer, consignee or financing agency concerned with the paper. Supplementary or corresponding provisions are found in Sections 4–503 and 5–112.

2. An "arrival" draft is a sight draft within the purpose of this section.

Cross References:

Point 1: See Sections 2–502, 2–505(2), 2–507(2), 2–512, 2–513, 2–607 concerning protection of rights of buyer and seller, and 4–503 and 5–112 on delivery of documents.

Definitional Cross References:

"Delivery". Section 1–201.

"Draft". Section 3–104.

§ 2.515. Preserving Evidence of Goods in Dispute

In furtherance of the adjustment of any claim or dispute

(1) either party on reasonable notification to the other and for the purpose of ascertaining the facts and preserving evidence has the right to inspect, test and sample the goods including such of them as may be in the possession or control of the other; and

(2) the parties may agree to a third party inspection or survey to determine the conformity or condition of the goods and may agree that the findings shall be binding upon them in any subsequent litigation or adjustment.

Acts 1967, 60th Leg., p. 2343, ch. 785, § 1, eff. Sept. 1, 1967.

Uniform Commercial Code Comment

Prior Uniform Statutory Provision:

None.

Purposes:

1. To meet certain serious problems which arise when there is a dispute as to the quality of the goods and thereby perhaps to aid the parties in reaching a settlement, and to further the use of devices which will promote certainty as to the condition of the goods, or at least aid in preserving evidence of their condition.

2. Under paragraph (a), to afford either party an opportunity for preserving evidence, whether or not agreement has been reached, and thereby to reduce uncertainty in any litigation and, in turn perhaps, to promote agreement.

Paragraph (a) does not conflict with the provisions on the seller's right to resell rejected goods or the buyer's similar right. Apparent conflict between these provisions which will be suggested in certain circumstances is to be resolved by requiring prompt action by the parties. Nor does paragraph (a) impair the effect of a term for payment before inspection. Short of such defects as amount to fraud or substantial failure of consideration, non-conformity is neither an excuse nor a defense to an action for non-acceptance of documents. Normally, therefore, until the buyer has made payment, inspected and rejected the goods, there is no occasion or use for the rights under paragraph (a).

3. Under paragraph (b), to provide for third party inspection upon the agreement of the parties, thereby opening the door to amicable adjustments based upon the findings of such third parties.

The use of the phrase "conformity or condition" makes it clear that the parties' agreement may range from a complete settlement of all aspects of the dispute by a third party to the use of a third party merely to determine and record the condition of the goods so that they can be resold or used to reduce the stake in controversy. "Conformity", at one end of the scale of possible issues, includes the whole question of interpretation of the agreement and its legal effect, the state of the goods in regard to quality and condition, whether any defects are due to factors which operate at the risk of the buyer, and the degree of nonconformity where that may be material. "Condition", at the other end of the scale, includes nothing but the degree of damage or deterioration which the goods show. Paragraph (b) is intended to reach any point in the gamut which the parties may agree upon.

The principle of the section on reservation of rights reinforces this paragraph in simplifying such adjustments as the parties wish to make in partial settlement while reserving their rights as to any further points. Paragraph (b) also suggests the use of arbitration, where desired, of any points left open, but nothing in this section is intended to repeal or amend any statute governing arbitration. Where any question arises as to the extent of the parties' agreement under the paragraph, the presumption should be that it was meant to extend only to the relation between the contract description and the goods as delivered, since that is what a craftsman in the trade would normally be expected to report upon. Finally, a written and authenticated report of inspection or tests by a third party, whether or not sampling has been practicable, is entitled to be admitted as evidence under this Act, for it is a third party document.

Cross References:

Point 2: Sections 2–513(3), 2–706 and 2–711(2) and Article 5.

Point 3: Sections 1–202 and 1–207.

Definitional Cross References:

"Conform". Section 2–106.

"Goods". Section 2–105.

"Notification". Section 1–201.

"Party". Section 1–201.

SUBCHAPTER F. BREACH, REPUDIATION AND EXCUSE

§ 2.601. Buyer's Rights on Improper Delivery

Subject to the provisions of this chapter on breach in installment contracts (Section 2.612) and unless otherwise agreed under the sections on contractual limitations of remedy (Sections 2.718 and 2.719), if the goods or the tender of delivery fail in any respect to conform to the contract, the buyer may

(1) reject the whole; or

(2) accept the whole; or

(3) accept any commercial unit or units and reject the rest.

Acts 1967, 60th Leg., p. 2343, ch. 785, § 1, eff. Sept. 1, 1967.

Uniform Commercial Code Comment

Prior Uniform Statutory Provision:

No one general equivalent provision but numerous provisions, dealing with situations of non-conformity where buyer may accept or reject, including Sections 11, 44 and 69(1), Uniform Sales Act.

Changes: Partial acceptance in good faith is recognized and the buyer's remedies on the contract for breach of warranty and the like, where the buyer has returned the goods after transfer of title, are no longer barred.

Purposes of Changes: To make it clear that:

1. A buyer accepting a non-conforming tender is not penalized by the loss of any remedy otherwise open to him. This policy extends to cover and regulate the acceptance of a part of any lot improperly tendered in any case where the price can reasonably be apportioned. Partial acceptance is permitted whether the part of the goods accepted conforms or not. The only limitation on partial acceptance is that good faith and commercial reasonableness must be used to avoid undue impairment of the value of the remaining portion of the goods. This is the reason for the insistence on the "commercial unit" in paragraph (c). In this respect, the test is not only what unit has been the basis of contract, but whether the partial acceptance produces so materially adverse an effect on the remainder as to constitute bad faith.

2. Acceptance made with the knowledge of the other party is final. An original refusal to accept may be withdrawn by a later acceptance if the seller has indicated that he is holding the tender open. However, if the buyer attempts to accept, either in whole or in part, after his original rejection has caused the seller to arrange for other disposition of the goods, the buyer must answer for any ensuing damage since the next section provides that any exercise of ownership after rejection is wrongful as against the seller. Further, he is liable even though the seller may choose to treat his action as acceptance rather than conversion, since the damage flows from the misleading notice. Such arrangements for resale or other disposition of the goods by the seller must be viewed as within the normal contemplation of a buyer who has given notice of rejection. However, the buyer's attempts in good faith to dispose of defective goods where the seller has failed to give instructions within a reasonable time are not to be regarded as an acceptance.

Cross References:

Sections 2–602(2)(a), 2–612, 2–718 and 2–719.

Definitional Cross References:

"Buyer". Section 2–103.

"Commercial unit". Section 2–105.

"Conform". Section 2–106.

"Contract". Section 1–201.

"Goods". Section 2–105.

"Installment contract". Section 2–612.

"Rights". Section 1–201.

§ 2.602. Manner and Effect of Rightful Rejection

(a) Rejection of goods must be within a reasonable time after their delivery or tender. It is ineffective unless the buyer seasonably notifies the seller.

(b) Subject to the provisions of the two following sections on rejected goods (Sections 2.603 and 2.604),

(1) after rejection any exercise of ownership by the buyer with respect to any commercial unit is wrongful as against the seller; and

(2) if the buyer has before rejection taken physical possession of goods in which he does not have a security interest under the provisions of this chapter (Subsection (c) of Section 2.711), he is under a duty after rejection to hold them with reasonable care at the seller's disposition for a time sufficient to permit the seller to remove them; but

(3) the buyer has no further obligations with regard to goods rightfully rejected.

(c) The seller's rights with respect to goods wrongfully rejected are governed by the provisions of this chapter on Seller's remedies in general (Section 2.703).

Acts 1967, 60th Leg., p. 2343, ch. 785, § 1, eff. Sept. 1, 1967.

Uniform Commercial Code Comment

Prior Uniform Statutory Provision:

Section 50, Uniform Sales Act.

Changes: Rewritten.

Purposes of Changes: To make it clear that:

1. A tender or delivery of goods made pursuant to a contract of sale, even though wholly non-conforming, requires affirmative action by the buyer to avoid acceptance. Under subsection (1), therefore, the buyer is given a reasonable time to notify the seller of his rejection, but without such seasonable notification his rejection is ineffective. The sections of this Article dealing with inspection of goods must be read in connection with the buyer's reasonable time for action under this subsection. Contract provisions limiting the time for rejection fall within the rule of the section on "Time" and are effective if the time set gives the buyer a reasonable time for discovery of defects. What constitutes a due "notifying" of rejection by the buyer to the seller is defined in Section 1–201.

2. Subsection (2) lays down the normal duties of the buyer upon rejection, which flow from the relationship of the parties. Beyond his duty to hold the goods with reasonable care for the buyer's [seller's] disposition, this section continues the policy of prior uniform legislation in generally relieving the buyer from any duties with respect to them, except when the circumstances impose the limited obligation of salvage upon him under the next section.

3. The present section applies only to rightful rejection by the buyer. If the seller has made a tender which in all respects conforms to the contract, the buyer has a positive duty to accept and his failure to do so constitutes a "wrongful rejection" which gives the seller immediate remedies for breach. Subsection (3) is included here to emphasize the sharp distinction between the rejection of an improper tender and the non-acceptance which is a breach by the buyer.

4. The provisions of this section are to be appropriately limited or modified when a negotiation is in process.

Cross References:

Point 1: Sections 1–201, 1–204(1) and (3), 2–512(2), 2–513(1) and 2–606(1)(b).

Point 2: Section 2–603(1).

Point 3: Section 2–703.

Definitional Cross References:

"Buyer". Section 2–103.

"Commercial unit". Section 2–105.

"Goods". Section 2–105.

"Merchant". Section 2–104.

"Notifies". Section 1–201.

"Reasonable time". Section 1–204.

"Remedy". Section 1–201.

"Rights". Section 1–201.

"Seasonably". Section 1–204.

"Security interest". Section 1–201.

"Seller". Section 2–103.

§ 2.603. Merchant Buyer's Duties as to Rightfully Rejected Goods

(a) Subject to any security interest in the buyer (Subsection (c) of Section 2.711), when the seller has no agent or place of business at the market of rejection a merchant buyer is under a duty after rejection of goods in his possession or control to follow any reasonable instructions received from the seller with respect to the goods and in the absence of such instructions to make reasonable efforts to sell them for the seller's account if they are perishable or threaten to decline in value speedily. Instructions are not reasonable if on demand indemnity for expenses is not forthcoming.

(b) When the buyer sells goods under Subsection (a), he is entitled to reimbursement from the seller or out of the proceeds for reasonable expenses of caring for and selling them, and if the expenses include no selling commission then to such commission as is usual in the trade or if there is none to a reasonable sum not exceeding ten per cent on the gross proceeds.

(c) In complying with this section the buyer is held only to good faith and good faith conduct hereunder is neither acceptance nor conversion nor the basis of an action for damages.

Acts 1967, 60th Leg., p. 2343, ch. 785, § 1, eff. Sept. 1, 1967.

Uniform Commercial Code Comment

Prior Uniform Statutory Provision:

None.

Purposes:

1. This section recognizes the duty imposed upon the merchant buyer by good faith and commercial practice to follow any reasonable instructions of the seller as to reshipping, storing, delivery to a third party, reselling or the like. Subsection (1) goes further and extends the duty to include the making of reasonable efforts to effect a salvage sale where the value of the goods is threatened and the seller's instructions do not arrive in time to prevent serious loss.

2. The limitations on the buyer's duty to resell under subsection (1) are to be liberally construed. The buyer's duty to resell under this section arises from commercial necessity and thus is present only when the seller has "no agent or place of business at the market of rejection". A financing agency which is acting in behalf of the seller in handling the documents rejected by the buyer is sufficiently the seller's agent to lift the burden of salvage resale from the buyer. (See provisions of Sections 4–503 and 5–112 on bank's duties with respect to rejected documents.) The buyer's duty to resell is extended only to goods in his "possession or control", but these are intended as words of wide, rather than narrow, import. In effect, the measure of

the buyer's "control" is whether he can practicably effect control without undue commercial burden.

3. The explicit provisions for reimbursement and compensation to the buyer in subsection (2) are applicable and necessary only where he is not acting under instructions from the seller. As provided in subsection (1) the seller's instructions to be "reasonable" must on demand of the buyer include indemnity for expenses.

4. Since this section makes the resale of perishable goods an affirmative duty in contrast to a mere right to sell as under the case law, subsection (3) makes it clear that the buyer is liable only for the exercise of good faith in determining whether the value of the goods is sufficiently threatened to justify a quick resale or whether he has waited a sufficient length of time for instructions, or what a reasonable means and place of resale is.

5. A buyer who fails to make a salvage sale when his duty to do so under this section has arisen is subject to damages pursuant to the section on liberal administration of remedies.

Cross References:

Point 2: Sections 4–503 and 5–112.

Point 5: Section 1–106. Compare generally Section 2–706.

Definitional Cross References:

"Buyer". Section 2–103.

"Good faith". Section 1–201.

"Goods". Section 2–105.

"Merchant". Section 2–104.

"Security interest". Section 1–201.

"Seller". Section 2–103.

§ 2.604. Buyer's Options as to Salvage of Rightfully Rejected Goods

Subject to the provisions of the immediately preceding section on perishables if the seller gives no instructions within a reasonable time after notification of rejection the buyer may store the rejected goods for the seller's account or reship them to him or resell them for the seller's account with reimbursement as provided in the preceding section. Such action is not acceptance or conversion.

Acts 1967, 60th Leg., p. 2343, ch. 785, § 1, eff. Sept. 1, 1967.

Uniform Commercial Code Comment

Prior Uniform Statutory Provision:

None.

Purposes:

The basic purpose of this section is twofold: on the one hand it aims at reducing the stake in dispute and on the other at avoiding the pinning of a technical "acceptance" on a buyer who has taken steps towards realization on or preservation of the goods in good faith. This section is essentially a salvage section and the buyer's right to act under it is conditioned upon (1) non-conformity of the goods, (2) due notification of rejection to the seller under the section on manner of rejection, and (3) the absence of any instructions from the seller which the merchant-buyer has a duty to follow under the preceding section.

This section is designed to accord all reasonable leeway to a rightfully rejecting buyer acting in good faith. The listing of what the buyer may do in the absence of instructions from the seller is intended to be not exhaustive but merely illustrative. This is not a "merchant's" section and the options are pure options given to merchant and non-merchant buyers alike. The merchant-buyer, however, may in some instances be under a duty rather than an option to resell under the provisions of the preceding section.

Cross References:

Sections 2–602(1), and 2–603(1) and 2–706.

Definitional Cross References:

"Buyer". Section 2–103.

"Notification". Section 1–201.

"Reasonable time". Section 1–204.

"Seller". Section 2–103.

§ 2.605. Waiver of Buyer's Objections by Failure to Particularize

(a) The buyer's failure to state in connection with rejection a particular defect which is ascertainable by reasonable inspection precludes him from relying on the unstated defect to justify rejection or to establish breach

(1) where the seller could have cured it if stated seasonably; or

(2) between merchants when the seller has after rejection made a request in writing for a full and final written statement of all defects on which the buyer proposes to rely.

(b) Payment against documents made without reservation of rights precludes recovery of the payment for defects apparent in the documents.

Acts 1967, 60th Leg., p. 2343, ch. 785, § 1, eff. Sept. 1, 1967. Amended by Acts 2005, 79th Leg., ch. 122, § 11, eff. Sept. 1, 2005.

Uniform Commercial Code Comment

Prior Uniform Statutory Provision:

None.

Purposes:

1. The present section rests upon a policy of permitting the buyer to give a quick and informal notice of defects in a tender without penalizing him for omissions in his statement, while at the same time protecting a seller who is reasonably misled by the buyer's failure to state curable defects.

2. Where the defect in a tender is one which could have been cured by the seller, a buyer who merely rejects the

delivery without stating his objections to it is probably acting in commercial bad faith and seeking to get out of a deal which has become unprofitable. Subsection (1)(a), following the general policy of this Article which looks to preserving the deal wherever possible, therefore insists that the seller's right to correct his tender in such circumstances be protected.

3. When the time for cure is past, subsection (1)(b) makes it plain that a seller is entitled upon request to a final statement of objections upon which he can rely. What is needed is that he make clear to the buyer exactly what is being sought. A formal demand under paragraph (b) will be sufficient in the case of a merchant-buyer.

4. Subsection (2) applies to the particular case of documents the same principle which the section on effects of acceptance applies to the case of goods. The matter is dealt with in this section in terms of "waiver" of objections rather than of right to revoke acceptance, partly to avoid any confusion with the problems of acceptance of goods and partly because defects in documents which are not taken as grounds for rejection are generally minor ones. The only defects concerned in the present subsection are defects in the documents which are apparent. This rule applies to both tangible and electronic documents of title. Where payment is required against the documents they must be inspected before payment, and the payment then constitutes acceptance of the documents. Under the section dealing with this problem, such acceptance of the documents does not constitute an acceptance of the goods or impair any options or remedies of the buyer for their improper delivery. Where the documents are delivered without requiring such contemporary action as payment from the buyer, the reason of the next section on what constitutes acceptance of goods, applies. Their acceptance by non-objection is therefore postponed until after a reasonable time for their inspection. In either situation, however, the buyer "waives" only the defects apparent in the documents.

Cross References:

Point 2: Section 2–508.

Point 4: Sections 2–512(2), 2–606(1)(b), 2–607(2).

Definitional Cross References:

"Between merchants". Section 2–104.

"Buyer". Section 2–103.

"Seasonably". Section 1–204.

"Seller". Section 2–103.

"Writing" and "written". Section 1–201.

Sections 31 and 32 of Acts 2005, 79th Leg., ch. 122 provide:

"Sec. 31. This Act applies to a document of title that is issued or a bailment that arises on or after the effective date of this Act. This Act does not apply to a document of title that is issued or a bailment that arises before the effective date of this Act even if the document of title or bailment would be subject to this Act if the document of title had been issued or bailment had arisen after the effective date of this Act. This Act does not apply to a right of action that has accrued before the effective date of this Act.

"Sec. 32. A document of title issued or a bailment that arises before the effective date of this Act and the rights, obligations, and interests flowing from that document or bailment are governed by any statute or other rule amended or repealed by this Act as if amendment or repeal had not occurred and may be terminated, completed, consummated, or enforced under that statute or other rule."

§ 2.606. What Constitutes Acceptance of Goods

(a) Acceptance of goods occurs when the buyer

(1) after a reasonable opportunity to inspect the goods signifies to the seller that the goods are conforming or that he will take or retain them in spite of their non-conformity; or

(2) fails to make an effective rejection (Subsection (a) of Section 2.602), but such acceptance does not occur until the buyer has had a reasonable opportunity to inspect them; or

(3) does any act inconsistent with the seller's ownership; but if such act is wrongful as against the seller it is an acceptance only if ratified by him.

(b) Acceptance of a part of any commercial unit is acceptance of that entire unit.

Acts 1967, 60th Leg., p. 2343, ch. 785, § 1, eff. Sept. 1, 1967.

Uniform Commercial Code Comment

Prior Uniform Statutory Provision:

Section 48, Uniform Sales Act.

Changes: Rewritten, the qualification in paragraph (c) and subsection (2) being new; otherwise the general policy of the prior legislation is continued.

Purpose of Changes and New Matter: To make it clear that:

1. Under this Article "acceptance" as applied to goods means that the buyer, pursuant to the contract, takes particular goods which have been appropriated to the contract as his own, whether or not he is obligated to do so, and whether he does so by words, action, or silence when it is time to speak. If the goods conform to the contract, acceptance amounts only to the performance by the buyer of one part of his legal obligation.

2. Under this Article acceptance of goods is always acceptance of identified goods which have been appropriated to the contract or are appropriated by the contract. There is no provision for "acceptance of title" apart from acceptar e in general, since acceptance of title is not material under this Article to the detailed rights and duties of the parties. (See Section 2–401). The refinements of the older law between acceptance of goods and of title become unnecessary in view of the provisions of the sections on effect and revocation of acceptance, on effects of identification and on risk of loss, and those sections which free the seller's and buyer's remedies from the complications and confusions caused by the question of whether title has or has not passed to the buyer before breach.

3. Under paragraph (a), payment made after tender is always one circumstance tending to signify acceptance of the goods but in itself it can never be more than one circumstance and is not conclusive. Also, a conditional communica-

tion of acceptance always remains subject to its expressed conditions.

4. Under paragraph (c), any action taken by the buyer, which is inconsistent with his claim that he has rejected the goods, constitutes an acceptance. However, the provisions of paragraph (c) are subject to the sections dealing with rejection by the buyer which permit the buyer to take certain actions with respect to the goods pursuant to his options and duties imposed by those sections, without effecting an acceptance of the goods. The second clause of paragraph (c) modifies some of the prior case law and makes it clear that "acceptance" in law based on the wrongful act of the acceptor is acceptance only as against the wrongdoer and then only at the option of the party wronged.

In the same manner in which a buyer can bind himself, despite his insistence that he is rejecting or has rejected the goods, by an act inconsistent with the seller's ownership under paragraph (c), he can obligate himself by a communication of acceptance despite a prior rejection under paragraph (a). However, the sections on buyer's rights on improper delivery and on the effect of rightful rejection, make it clear that after he once rejects a tender, paragraph (a) does not operate in favor of the buyer unless the seller has re-tendered the goods or has taken affirmative action indicating that he is holding the tender open. See also Comment 2 to Section 2–601.

5. Subsection (2) supplements the policy of the section on buyer's rights on improper delivery, recognizing the validity of a partial acceptance but insisting that the buyer exercise this right only as to whole commercial units.

Cross References:

Point 2: Sections 2–401, 2–509, 2–510, 2–607, 2–608 and Part 7.

Point 4: Sections 2–601 through 2–604.

Point 5: Section 2–601.

Definitional Cross References:

"Buyer". Section 2–103.

"Commercial unit". Section 2–105.

"Goods". Section 2–105.

"Seller". Section 2–103.

§ 2.607. Effect of Acceptance; Notice of Breach; Burden of Establishing Breach After Acceptance; Notice of Claim or Litigation to Person Answerable Over

(a) The buyer must pay at the contract rate for any goods accepted.

(b) Acceptance of goods by the buyer precludes rejection of the goods accepted and if made with knowledge of a non-conformity cannot be revoked because of it unless the acceptance was on the reasonable assumption that the non-conformity would be seasonably cured but acceptance does not of itself impair any other remedy provided by this chapter for non-conformity.

(c) Where a tender has been accepted

(1) the buyer must within a reasonable time after he discovers or should have discovered any breach notify the seller of breach or be barred from any remedy; and

(2) if the claim is one for infringement or the like (Subsection (c) of Section 2.312) and the buyer is sued as a result of such a breach he must so notify the seller within a reasonable time after he receives notice of the litigation or be barred from any remedy over for liability established by the litigation.

(d) The burden is on the buyer to establish any breach with respect to the goods accepted.

(e) Where the buyer is sued for breach of a warranty or other obligation for which his seller is answerable over

(1) he may give his seller written notice of the litigation. If the notice states that the seller may come in and defend and that if the seller does not do so he will be bound in any action against him by his buyer by any determination of fact common to the two litigations, then unless the seller after seasonable receipt of the notice does come in and defend he is so bound.

(2) if the claim is one for infringement or the like (Subsection (c) of Section 2.312) the original seller may demand in writing that his buyer turn over to him control of the litigation including settlement or else be barred from any remedy over and if he also agrees to bear all expense and to satisfy any adverse judgment, then unless the buyer after seasonable receipt of the demand does turn over control the buyer is so barred.

(f) The provisions of Subsections (c), (d) and (e) apply to any obligation of a buyer to hold the seller harmless against infringement or the like (Subsection (c) of Section 2.312).

Acts 1967, 60th Leg., p. 2343, ch. 785, § 1, eff. Sept. 1, 1967.

Uniform Commercial Code Comment

Prior Uniform Statutory Provision:

Subsection (1)—Section 41, Uniform Sales Act; Subsections (2) and (3)—Sections 49 and 69, Uniform Sales Act.

Changes: Rewritten.

Purposes of Changes: To continue the prior basic policies with respect to acceptance of goods while making a number of minor though material changes in the interest of simplicity and commercial convenience so that:

1. Under subsection (1), once the buyer accepts a tender the seller acquires a right to its price on the contract terms.

In cases of partial acceptance, the price of any part accepted is, if possible, to be reasonably apportioned, using the type of apportionment familiar to the courts in quantum valebant cases, to be determined in terms of "the contract rate," which is the rate determined from the bargain in fact (the agreement) after the rules and policies of this Article have been brought to bear.

2. Under subsection (2) acceptance of goods precludes their subsequent rejection. Any return of the goods thereafter must be by way of revocation of acceptance under the next section. Revocation is unavailable for a non-conformity known to the buyer at the time of acceptance, except where the buyer has accepted on the reasonable assumption that the non-conformity would be seasonably cured.

3. All other remedies of the buyer remain unimpaired under subsection (2). This is intended to include the buyer's full rights with respect to future installments despite his acceptance of any earlier non-conforming installment.

4. The time of notification is to be determined by applying commercial standards to a merchant buyer. "A reasonable time" for notification from a retail consumer is to be judged by different standards so that in his case it will be extended, for the rule of requiring notification is designed to defeat commercial bad faith, not to deprive a good faith consumer of his remedy.

The content of the notification need merely be sufficient to let the seller know that the transaction is still troublesome and must be watched. There is no reason to require that the notification which saves the buyer's rights under this section must include a clear statement of all the objections that will be relied on by the buyer, as under the section covering statements of defects upon rejection (Section 2–605). Nor is there reason for requiring the notification to be a claim for damages or of any threatened litigation or other resort to a remedy. The notification which saves the buyer's rights under this Article need only be such as informs the seller that the transaction is claimed to involve a breach, and thus opens the way for normal settlement through negotiation.

5. Under this Article various beneficiaries are given rights for injuries sustained by them because of the seller's breach of warranty. Such a beneficiary does not fall within the reason of the present section in regard to discovery of defects and the giving of notice within a reasonable time after acceptance, since he has nothing to do with acceptance. However, the reason of this section does extend to requiring the beneficiary to notify the seller that an injury has occurred. What is said above, with regard to the extended time for reasonable notification from the lay consumer after the injury is also applicable here; but even a beneficiary can be properly held to the use of good faith in notifying, once he has had time to become aware of the legal situation.

6. Subsection (4) unambiguously places the burden of proof to establish breach on the buyer after acceptance. However, this rule becomes one purely of procedure when the tender accepted was non-conforming and the buyer has given the seller notice of breach under subsection (3). For subsection (2) makes it clear that acceptance leaves unimpaired the buyer's right to be made whole, and that right can be exercised by the buyer not only by way of cross-claim for damages, but also by way of recoupment in diminution or extinction of the price.

7. Subsections (3)(b) and (5)(b) give a warrantor against infringement an opportunity to defend or compromise third-party claims or be relieved of his liability. Subsection (5)(a) codifies for all warranties the practice of voucher to defend. Compare Section 3–803. Subsection (6) makes these provisions applicable to the buyer's liability for infringement under Section 2–312.

8. All of the provisions of the present section are subject to any explicit reservation of rights.

Cross References:

Point 1: Section 1–201.

Point 2: Section 2–608.

Point 4: Sections 1–204 and 2–605.

Point 5: Section 2–318.

Point 6: Section 2–717.

Point 7: Sections 2–312 and 3–803.

Point 8: Section 1–207.

Definitional Cross References:

"Burden of establishing". Section 1–201.

"Buyer". Section 2–103.

"Conform". Section 2–106.

"Contract". Section 1–201.

"Goods". Section 2–105.

"Notifies". Section 1–201.

"Reasonable time". Section 1–204.

"Remedy". Section 1–201.

"Seasonably". Section 1–204.

§ 2.608. Revocation of Acceptance in Whole or in Part

(a) The buyer may revoke his acceptance of a lot or commercial unit whose non-conformity substantially impairs its value to him if he has accepted it

(1) on the reasonable assumption that its non-conformity would be cured and it has not been seasonably cured; or

(2) without discovery of such non-conformity if his acceptance was reasonably induced either by the difficulty of discovery before acceptance or by the seller's assurances.

(b) Revocation of acceptance must occur within a reasonable time after the buyer discovers or should have discovered the ground for it and before any substantial change in condition of the goods which is not caused by their own defects. It is not effective until the buyer notifies the seller of it.

(c) A buyer who so revokes has the same rights and duties with regard to the goods involved as if he had rejected them.

Acts 1967, 60th Leg., p. 2343, ch. 785, § 1, eff. Sept. 1, 1967.

Uniform Commercial Code Comment

Prior Uniform Statutory Provision:

Section 69(1)(d), (3), (4) and (5), Uniform Sales Act.

Changes: Rewritten.

Purposes of Changes: To make it clear that:

1. Although the prior basic policy is continued, the buyer is no longer required to elect between revocation of acceptance and recovery of damages for breach. Both are now available to him. The non-alternative character of the two remedies is stressed by the terms used in the present section. The section no longer speaks of "rescission," a term capable of ambiguous application either to transfer of title to the goods or to the contract of sale and susceptible also of confusion with cancellation for cause of an executed or executory portion of the contract. The remedy under this section is instead referred to simply as "revocation of acceptance" of goods tendered under a contract for sale and involves no suggestion of "election" of any sort.

2. Revocation of acceptance is possible only where the non-conformity substantially impairs the value of the goods to the buyer. For this purpose the test is not what the seller had reason to know at the time of contracting; the question is whether the non-conformity is such as will in fact cause a substantial impairment of value to the buyer though the seller had no advance knowledge as to the buyer's particular circumstances.

3. "Assurances" by the seller under paragraph (b) of subsection (1) can rest as well in the circumstances or in the contract as in explicit language used at the time of delivery. The reason for recognizing such assurances is that they induce the buyer to delay discovery. These are the only assurances involved in paragraph (b). Explicit assurances may be made either in good faith or bad faith. In either case any remedy accorded by this Article is available to the buyer under the section on remedies for fraud.

4. Subsection (2) requires notification of revocation of acceptance within a reasonable time after discovery of the grounds for such revocation. Since this remedy will be generally resorted to only after attempts at adjustment have failed, the reasonable time period should extend in most cases beyond the time in which notification of breach must be given, beyond the time for discovery of non-conformity after acceptance and beyond the time for rejection after tender. The parties may by their agreement limit the time for notification under this section, but the same sanctions and considerations apply to such agreements as are discussed in the comment on manner and effect of rightful rejection.

5. The content of the notice under subsection (2) is to be determined in this case as in others by considerations of good faith, prevention of surprise, and reasonable adjustment. More will generally be necessary than the mere notification of breach required under the preceding section. On the other hand the requirements of the section on waiver of buyer's objections do not apply here. The fact that quick notification of trouble is desirable affords good ground for being slow to bind a buyer by his first statement. Following the general policy of this Article, the requirements of the content of notification are less stringent in the case of a non-merchant buyer.

6. Under subsection (2) the prior policy is continued of seeking substantial justice in regard to the condition of goods restored to the seller. Thus the buyer may not revoke his acceptance if the goods have materially deteriorated except by reason of their own defects. Worthless goods, however, need not be offered back and minor defects in the articles reoffered are to be disregarded.

7. The policy of the section allowing partial acceptance is carried over into the present section and the buyer may revoke his acceptance, in appropriate cases, as to the entire lot or any commercial unit thereof.

Cross References:

Point 3: Section 2–721.

Point 4: Sections 1–204, 2–602 and 2–607.

Point 5: Sections 2–605 and 2–607.

Point 7: Section 2–601.

Definitional Cross References:

"Buyer". Section 2–103.

"Commercial unit". Section 2–105.

"Conform". Section 2–106.

"Goods". Section 2–105.

"Lot". Section 2–105.

"Notifies". Section 1–201.

"Reasonable time". Section 1–204.

"Rights". Section 1–201.

"Seasonably". Section 1–204.

"Seller". Section 2–103.

§ 2.609. Right to Adequate Assurance of Performance

(a) A contract for sale imposes an obligation on each party that the other's expectation of receiving due performance will not be impaired. When reasonable grounds for insecurity arise with respect to the performance of either party the other may in writing demand adequate assurance of due performance and until he receives such assurance may if commercially reasonable suspend any performance for which he has not already received the agreed return.

(b) Between merchants the reasonableness of grounds for insecurity and the adequacy of any assurance offered shall be determined according to commercial standards.

(c) Acceptance of any improper delivery or payment does not prejudice the aggrieved party's right to demand adequate assurance of future performance.

(d) After receipt of a justified demand failure to provide within a reasonable time not exceeding thirty days such assurance of due performance as is adequate under the circumstances of the particular case is a repudiation of the contract.

Acts 1967, 60th Leg., p. 2343, ch. 785, § 1, eff. Sept. 1, 1967.

Uniform Commercial Code Comment

Prior Uniform Statutory Provision:

See Sections 53, 54(1)(b), 55 and 63(2), Uniform Sales Act.

Purposes:

1. The section rests on the recognition of the fact that the essential purpose of a contract between commercial men is actual performance and they do not bargain merely for a promise, or for a promise plus the right to win a lawsuit and that a continuing sense of reliance and security that the promised performance will be forthcoming when due, is an important feature of the bargain. If either the willingness or the ability of a party to perform declines materially between the time of contracting and the time for performance, the other party is threatened with the loss of a substantial part of what he has bargained for. A seller needs protection not merely against having to deliver on credit to a shaky buyer, but also against having to procure and manufacture the goods, perhaps turning down other customers. Once he has been given reason to believe that the buyer's performance has become uncertain, it is an undue hardship to force him to continue his own performance. Similarly, a buyer who believes that the seller's deliveries have become uncertain cannot safely wait for the due date of performance when he has been buying to assure himself of materials for his current manufacturing or to replenish his stock of merchandise.

2. Three measures have been adopted to meet the needs of commercial men in such situations. First, the aggrieved party is permitted to suspend his own performance and any preparation therefor, with excuse for any resulting necessary delay, until the situation has been clarified. "Suspend performance" under this section means to hold up performance pending the outcome of the demand, and includes also the holding up of any preparatory action. This is the same principle which governs the ancient law of stoppage and seller's lien, and also of excuse of a buyer from prepayment if the seller's actions manifest that he cannot or will not perform. (Original Act, Section 63(2).)

Secondly, the aggrieved party is given the right to require adequate assurance that the other party's performance will be duly forthcoming. This principle is reflected in the familiar clauses permitting the seller to curtail deliveries if the buyer's credit becomes impaired, which when held within the limits of reasonableness and good faith actually express no more than the fair business meaning of any commercial contract.

Third, and finally, this section provides the means by which the aggrieved party may treat the contract as broken if his reasonable grounds for insecurity are not cleared up within a reasonable time. This is the principle underlying the law of anticipatory breach, whether by way of defective part performance or by repudiation. The present section merges these three principles of law and commercial practice into a single theory of general application to all sales agreements looking to future performance.

3. Subsection (2) of the present section requires that "reasonable" grounds and "adequate" assurance as used in subsection (1) be defined by commercial rather than legal standards. The express reference to commercial standards carries no connotation that the obligation of good faith is not equally applicable here.

Under commercial standards and in accord with commercial practice, a ground for insecurity need not arise from or be directly related to the contract in question. The law as to "dependence" or "independence" of promises within a single contract does not control the application of the present section.

Thus a buyer who falls behind in "his account" with the seller, even though the items involved have to do with separate and legally distinct contracts, impairs the seller's expectation of due performance. Again, under the same test, a buyer who requires precision parts which he intends to use immediately upon delivery, may have reasonable grounds for insecurity if he discovers that his seller is making defective deliveries of such parts to other buyers with similar needs. Thus, too, in a situation such as arose in *Jay Dreher Corporation v. Delco Appliance Corporation*, 93 F.2d 275 (C.C.A.2, 1937), where a manufacturer gave a dealer an exclusive franchise for the sale of his product but on two or three occasions breached the exclusive dealing clause, although there was no default in orders, deliveries or payments under the separate sales contract between the parties, the aggrieved dealer would be entitled to suspend his performance of the contract for sale under the present section and to demand assurance that the exclusive dealing contract would be lived up to. There is no need for an explicit clause tying the exclusive franchise into the contract for the sale of goods since the situation itself ties the agreements together.

The nature of the sales contract enters also into the question of reasonableness. For example, a report from an apparently trustworthy source that the seller had shipped defective goods or was planning to ship them would normally give the buyer reasonable grounds for insecurity. But when the buyer has assumed the risk of payment before inspection of the goods, as in a sales contract on C.I.F. or similar cash against documents terms, that risk is not to be evaded by a demand for assurance. Therefore no ground for insecurity would exist under this section unless the report went to a ground which would excuse payment by the buyer.

4. What constitutes "adequate" assurance of due performance is subject to the same test of factual conditions. For example, where the buyer can make use of a defective delivery, a mere promise by a seller of good repute that he is giving the matter his attention and that the defect will not be repeated, is normally sufficient. Under the same circumstances, however, a similar statement by a known corner-cutter might well be considered insufficient without the

posting of a guaranty or, if so demanded by the buyer, a speedy replacement of the delivery involved. By the same token where a delivery has defects, even though easily curable, which interfere with easy use by the buyer, no verbal assurance can be deemed adequate which is not accompanied by replacement, repair, money-allowance, or other commercially reasonable cure.

A fact situation such as arose in *Corn Products Refining Co. v. Fasola*, 94 N.J.L. 181, 109 A. 505 (1920) offers illustration both of reasonable grounds for insecurity and "adequate" assurance. In that case a contract for the sale of oils on 30 days' credit, 2% off for payment within 10 days, provided that credit was to be extended to the buyer only if his financial responsibility was satisfactory to the seller. The buyer had been in the habit of taking advantage of the discount but at the same time that he failed to make his customary 10 day payment, the seller heard rumors, in fact false, that the buyer's financial condition was shaky. Thereupon, the seller demanded cash before shipment or security satisfactory to him. The buyer sent a good credit report from his banker, expressed willingness to make payments when due on the 30 day terms and insisted on further deliveries under the contract. Under this Article the rumors, although false, were enough to make the buyer's financial condition "unsatisfactory" to the seller under the contract clause. Moreover, the buyer's practice of taking the cash discounts is enough, apart from the contract clause, to lay a commercial foundation for suspicion when the practice is suddenly stopped. These matters, however, go only to the justification of the seller's demand for security, or his "reasonable grounds for insecurity".

The adequacy of the assurance given is not measured as in the type of "satisfaction" situation affected with intangibles, such as in personal service cases, cases involving a third party's judgment as final, or cases in which the whole contract is dependent on one party's satisfaction, as in a sale on approval. Here, the seller must exercise good faith and observe commercial standards. This Article thus approves the statement of the court in *James B. Berry's Sons Co. of Illinois v. Monark Gasoline & Oil Co., Inc.*, 32 F.2d 74 (C.C.A.8, 1929), that the seller's satisfaction under such a clause must be based upon reason and must not be arbitrary or capricious; and rejects the purely personal "good faith" test of the *Corn Products Refining Co.* case, which held that in the seller's sole judgment, if for *any* reason he was dissatisfied, he was entitled to revoke the credit. In the absence of the buyer's failure to take the 2% discount as was his custom, the banker's report given in that case would have been "adequate" assurance under this Act, regardless of the language of the "satisfaction" clause. However, the seller is reasonably entitled to feel insecure at a sudden expansion of the buyer's use of a credit term, and should be entitled either to security or to a satisfactory explanation.

The entire foregoing discussion as to adequacy of assurance by way of explanation is subject to qualification when repeated occasions for the application of this section arise. This Act recognizes that repeated delinquencies must be viewed as cumulative. On the other hand, commercial sense also requires that if repeated claims for assurance are made under this section, the basis for these claims must be increasingly obvious.

5. A failure to provide adequate assurance of performance and thereby to re-establish the security of expectation, results in a breach only "by repudiation" under subsection (4). Therefore, the possibility is continued of retraction of the repudiation under the section dealing with that problem, unless the aggrieved party has acted on the breach in some manner.

The thirty day limit on the time to provide assurance is laid down to free the question of reasonable time from uncertainty in later litigation.

6. Clauses seeking to give the protected party exceedingly wide powers to cancel or readjust the contract when ground for insecurity arises must be read against the fact that good faith is a part of the obligation of the contract and not subject to modification by agreement and includes, in the case of a merchant, the reasonable observance of commercial standards of fair dealing in the trade. Such clauses can thus be effective to enlarge the protection given by the present section to a certain extent, to fix the reasonable time within which requested assurance must be given, or to define adequacy of the assurance in any commercially reasonable fashion. But any clause seeking to set up arbitrary standards for action is ineffective under this Article. Acceleration clauses are treated similarly in the Articles on Commercial Paper and Secured Transactions.

Cross References:

Point 3: Section 1–203.

Point 5: Section 2–611.

Point 6: Sections 1–203 and 1–208 and Articles 3 and 9.

Definitional Cross References:

"Aggrieved party". Section 1–201.

"Between merchants". Section 2–104.

"Contract". Section 1–201.

"Contract for sale". Section 2–106.

"Party". Section 1–201.

"Reasonable time". Section 1–204.

"Rights". Section 1–201.

"Writing". Section 1–201.

§ 2.610. Anticipatory Repudiation

When either party repudiates the contract with respect to a performance not yet due the loss of which will substantially impair the value of the contract to the other, the aggrieved party may

(1) for a commercially reasonable time await performance by the repudiating party; or

(2) resort to any remedy for breach (Section 2.703 or Section 2.711), even though he has notified the repudiating party that he would await the latter's performance and has urged retraction; and

(3) in either case suspend his own performance or proceed in accordance with the provisions of this chapter on the seller's right to identify goods to the

contract notwithstanding breach or to salvage unfinished goods (Section 2.704).

Acts 1967, 60th Leg., p. 2343, ch. 785, § 1, eff. Sept. 1, 1967.

Uniform Commercial Code Comment

Prior Uniform Statutory Provision:

See Sections 63(2) and 65, Uniform Sales Act.

Purposes: To make it clear that:

1. With the problem of insecurity taken care of by the preceding section and with provision being made in this Article as to the effect of a defective delivery under an installment contract, anticipatory repudiation centers upon an overt communication of intention or an action which renders performance impossible or demonstrates a clear determination not to continue with performance.

Under the present section when such a repudiation substantially impairs the value of the contract, the aggrieved party may at any time resort to his remedies for breach, or he may suspend his own performance while he negotiates with, or awaits performance by, the other party. But if he awaits performance beyond a commercially reasonable time he cannot recover resulting damages which he should have avoided.

2. It is not necessary for repudiation that performance be made literally and utterly impossible. Repudiation can result from action which reasonably indicates a rejection of the continuing obligation. And, a repudiation automatically results under the preceding section on insecurity when a party fails to provide adequate assurance of due future performance within thirty days after a justifiable demand therefor has been made. Under the language of this section, a demand by one or both parties for more than the contract calls for in the way of counter-performance is not in itself a repudiation nor does it invalidate a plain expression of desire for future performance. However, when under a fair reading it amounts to a statement of intention not to perform except on conditions which go beyond the contract, it becomes a repudiation.

3. The test chosen to justify an aggrieved party's action under this section is the same as that in the section on breach in installment contracts—namely the substantial value of the contract. The most useful test of substantial value is to determine whether material inconvenience or injustice will result if the aggrieved party is forced to wait and receive an ultimate tender minus the part or aspect repudiated.

4. After repudiation, the aggrieved party may immediately resort to any remedy he chooses provided he moves in good faith (see Section 1–203). Inaction and silence by the aggrieved party may leave the matter open but it cannot be regarded as misleading the repudiating party. Therefore the aggrieved party is left free to proceed at any time with his options under this section, unless he has taken some positive action which in good faith requires notification to the other party before the remedy is pursued.

Cross References:

Point 1: Sections 2–609 and 2–612.

Point 2: Section 2–609.

Point 3: Section 2–612.

Point 4: Section 1–203.

Definitional Cross References:

"Aggrieved party". Section 1–201.

"Contract". Section 1–201.

"Party". Section 1–201.

"Remedy". Section 1–201.

§ 2.611. Retraction of Anticipatory Repudiation

(a) Until the repudiating party's next performance is due he can retract his repudiation unless the aggrieved party has since the repudiation cancelled or materially changed his position or otherwise indicated that he considers the repudiation final.

(b) Retraction may be by any method which clearly indicates to the aggrieved party that the repudiating party intends to perform, but must include any assurance justifiably demanded under the provisions of this chapter (Section 2.609).

(c) Retraction reinstates the repudiating party's rights under the contract with due excuse and allowance to the aggrieved party for any delay occasioned by the repudiation.

Acts 1967, 60th Leg., p. 2343, ch. 785, § 1, eff. Sept. 1, 1967.

Uniform Commercial Code Comment

Prior Uniform Statutory Provision:

None.

Purposes: To make it clear that:

1. The repudiating party's right to reinstate the contract is entirely dependent upon the action taken by the aggrieved party. If the latter has cancelled the contract or materially changed his position at any time after the repudiation, there can be no retraction under this section.

2. Under subsection (2) an effective retraction must be accompanied by any assurances demanded under the section dealing with right to adequate assurance. A repudiation is of course sufficient to give reasonable ground for insecurity and to warrant a request for assurance as an essential condition of the retraction. However, after a timely and unambiguous expression of retraction, a reasonable time for the assurance to be worked out should be allowed by the aggrieved party before cancellation.

Cross Reference:

Point 2: Section 2–609.

Definitional Cross References:

"Aggrieved party". Section 1–201.

"Cancellation". Section 2–106.

"Contract". Section 1–201.

"Party". Section 1–201.

"Rights". Section 1–201.

§ 2.612. "Installment Contract"; Breach

(a) An "installment contract" is one which requires or authorizes the delivery of goods in separate lots to be separately accepted, even though the contract contains a clause "each delivery is a separate contract" or its equivalent.

(b) The buyer may reject any installment which is non-conforming if the non-conformity substantially impairs the value of that installment and cannot be cured or if the non-conformity is a defect in the required documents; but if the non-conformity does not fall within Subsection (c) and the seller gives adequate assurance of its cure the buyer must accept that installment.

(c) Whenever non-conformity or default with respect to one or more installments substantially impairs the value of the whole contract there is a breach of the whole. But the aggrieved party reinstates the contract if he accepts a non-conforming installment without seasonably notifying of cancellation or if he brings an action with respect only to past installments or demands performance as to future installments.

Acts 1967, 60th Leg., p. 2343, ch. 785, § 1, eff. Sept. 1, 1967.

Uniform Commercial Code Comment

Prior Uniform Statutory Provision:

Section 45(2), Uniform Sales Act.

Changes: Rewritten.

Purposes of Changes: To continue prior law but to make explicit the more mercantile interpretation of many of the rules involved, so that:

1. The definition of an installment contract is phrased more broadly in this Article so as to cover installment deliveries tacitly authorized by the circumstances or by the option of either party.

2. In regard to the apportionment of the price for separate payment this Article applies the more liberal test of what can be apportioned rather than the test of what is clearly apportioned by the agreement. This Article also recognizes approximate calculation or apportionment of price subject to subsequent adjustment. A provision for separate payment for each lot delivered ordinarily means that the price is at least roughly calculable by units of quantity, but such a provision is not essential to an "installment contract." If separate acceptance of separate deliveries is contemplated, no generalized contrast between wholly "entire" and wholly "divisible" contracts has any standing under this Article.

3. This Article rejects any approach which gives clauses such as "each delivery is a separate contract" their legalistically literal effect. Such contracts nonetheless call for installment deliveries. Even where a clause speaks of "a separate contract for all purposes", a commercial reading of the language under the section on good faith and commercial standards requires that the singleness of the document and the negotiation, together with the sense of the situation, prevail over any uncommercial and legalistic interpretation.

4. One of the requirements for rejection under subsection (2) is non-conformity substantially impairing the value of the installment in question. However, an installment agreement may require accurate conformity in quality as a condition to the right to acceptance if the need for such conformity is made clear either by express provision or by the circumstances. In such a case the effect of the agreement is to define explicitly what amounts to substantial impairment of value impossible to cure. A clause requiring accurate compliance as a condition to the right to acceptance must, however, have some basis in reason, must avoid imposing hardship by surprise and is subject to waiver or to displacement by practical construction.

Substantial impairment of the value of an installment can turn not only on the quality of the goods but also on such factors as time, quantity, assortment, and the like. It must be judged in terms of the normal or specifically known purposes of the contract. The defect in required documents refers to such matters as the absence of insurance documents under a C.I.F. contract, falsity of a bill of lading, or one failing to show shipment within the contract period or to the contract destination. Even in such cases, however, the provisions on cure of tender apply if appropriate documents are readily procurable.

5. Under subsection (2) an installment delivery must be accepted if the non-conformity is curable and the seller gives adequate assurance of cure. Cure of non-conformity of an installment in the first instance can usually be afforded by an allowance against the price, or in the case of reasonable discrepancies in quantity either by a further delivery or a partial rejection. This Article requires reasonable action by a buyer in regard to discrepant delivery and good faith requires that the buyer make any reasonable minor outlay of time or money necessary to cure an overshipment by severing out an acceptable percentage thereof. The seller must take over a cure which involves any material burden; the buyer's obligation reaches only to cooperation. Adequate assurance for purposes of subsection (2) is measured by the same standards as under the section on right to adequate assurance of performance.

6. Subsection (3) is designed to further the continuance of the contract in the absence of an overt cancellation. The question arising when an action is brought as to a single installment only is resolved by making such action waive the right of cancellation. This involves merely a defect in one or more installments, as contrasted with the situation where there is a true repudiation within the section on anticipatory repudiation. Whether the non-conformity in any given installment justifies cancellation as to the future depends, not on whether such non-conformity indicates an intent or likelihood that the future deliveries will also be defective, but whether the non-conformity substantially impairs the value of the whole contract. If only the seller's security in regard to future installments is impaired, he has the right to demand adequate assurances of proper future performance but has not an immediate right to cancel the entire contract. It is clear under this Article, however, that defects in prior installments are cumulative in effect, so that acceptance does

not wash out the defect "waived." Prior policy is continued, putting the rule as to buyer's default on the same footing as that in regard to seller's default.

7. Under the requirement of seasonable notification of cancellation under subsection (3), a buyer who accepts a non-conforming installment which substantially impairs the value of the entire contract should properly be permitted to withhold his decision as to whether or not to cancel pending a response from the seller as to his claim for cure or adjustment. Similarly, a seller may withhold a delivery pending payment for prior ones, at the same time delaying his decision as to cancellation. A reasonable time for notifying of cancellation, judged by commercial standards under the section on good faith, extends of course to include the time covered by any reasonable negotiation in good faith. However, during this period the defaulting party is entitled, on request, to know whether the contract is still in effect, before he can be required to perform further.

Cross References:

Point 2: Sections 2–307 and 2–607.

Point 3: Section 1–203.

Point 5: Sections 2–208 and 2–609.

Point 6: Section 2–610.

Definitional Cross References:

"Action". Section 1–201.

"Aggrieved party". Section 1–201.

"Buyer". Section 2–103.

"Cancellation". Section 2–106.

"Conform". Section 2–106.

"Contract". Section 1–201.

"Lot". Section 2–105.

"Notifies". Section 1–201.

"Seasonably". Section 1–204.

"Seller". Section 2–103.

§ 2.613. Casualty to Identified Goods

Where the contract requires for its performance goods identified when the contract is made, and the goods suffer casualty without fault of either party before the risk of loss passes to the buyer, or in a proper case under a "no arrival, no sale" term (Section 2.324) then

(1) if the loss is total the contract is avoided; and

(2) if the loss is partial or the goods have so deteriorated as no longer to conform to the contract the buyer may nevertheless demand inspection and at his option either treat the contract as avoided or accept the goods with due allowance from the contract price for the deterioration or the deficiency in quantity but without further right against the seller.

Acts 1967, 60th Leg., p. 2343, ch. 785, § 1, eff. Sept. 1, 1967.

Uniform Commercial Code Comment

Prior Uniform Statutory Provision:

Sections 7 and 8, Uniform Sales Act.

Changes: Rewritten, the basic policy being continued but the test of a "divisible" or "indivisible" sale or contract being abandoned in favor of adjustment in business terms.

Purposes of Changes:

1. Where goods whose continued existence is presupposed by the agreement are destroyed without fault of either party, the buyer is relieved from his obligation but may at his option take the surviving goods at a fair adjustment. "Fault" is intended to include negligence and not merely wilful wrong. The buyer is expressly given the right to inspect the goods in order to determine whether he wishes to avoid the contract entirely or to take the goods with a price adjustment.

2. The section applies whether the goods were already destroyed at the time of contracting without the knowledge of either party or whether they are destroyed subsequently but before the risk of loss passes to the buyer. Where under the agreement, including of course usage of trade, the risk has passed to the buyer before the casualty, the section has no application. Beyond this, the essential question in determining whether the rules of this section are to be applied is whether the seller has or has not undertaken the responsibility for the continued existence of the goods in proper condition through the time of agreed or expected delivery.

3. The section on the term "no arrival, no sale" makes clear that delay in arrival, quite as much as physical change in the goods, gives the buyer the options set forth in this section.

Cross Reference:

Point 3: Section 2–324.

Definitional Cross References:

"Buyer". Section 2–103.

"Conform". Section 2–106.

"Contract". Section 1–201.

"Fault". Section 1–201.

"Goods". Section 2–105.

"Party". Section 1–201.

"Rights". Section 1–201.

"Seller". Section 2–103.

§ 2.614. Substituted Performance

(a) Where without fault of either party the agreed berthing, loading, or unloading facilities fail or an agreed type of carrier becomes unavailable or the agreed manner of delivery otherwise becomes commercially impracticable but a commercially reasonable substitute is available, such substitute performance must be tendered and accepted.

(b) If the agreed means or manner of payment fails because of domestic or foreign governmental regulation, the seller may withhold or stop delivery unless the buyer provides a means or manner of payment which is commercially a substantial equivalent. If delivery has already been taken, payment by the means or in the manner provided by the regulation discharges the buyer's obligation unless the regulation is discriminatory, oppressive or predatory.

Acts 1967, 60th Leg., p. 2343, ch. 785, § 1, eff. Sept. 1, 1967.

Uniform Commercial Code Comment

Prior Uniform Statutory Provision:

None.

Purposes:

1. Subsection (1) requires the tender of a commercially reasonable substituted performance where agreed to facilities have failed or become commercially impracticable. Under this Article, in the absence of specific agreement, the normal or usual facilities enter into the agreement either through the circumstances, usage of trade or prior course of dealing.

This section appears between Section 2–613 on casualty to identified goods and the next section on excuse by failure of presupposed conditions, both of which deal with excuse and complete avoidance of the contract where the occurrence or non-occurrence of a contingency which was a basic assumption of the contract makes the expected performance impossible. The distinction between the present section and those sections lies in whether the failure or impossibility of performance arises in connection with an incidental matter or goes to the very heart of the agreement. The differing lines of solution are contrasted in a comparison of *International Paper Co. v. Rockefeller,* 161 App.Div. 180, 146 N.Y.S. 371 (1914) and *Meyer v. Sullivan,* 40 Cal.App. 723, 181 P. 847 (1919). In the former case a contract for the sale of spruce to be cut from a particular tract of land was involved. When a fire destroyed the trees growing on that tract the seller was held excused since performance was impossible. In the latter case the contract called for delivery of wheat "f.o.b. Kosmos Steamer at Seattle." The war led to cancellation of that line's sailing schedule after space had been duly engaged and the buyer was held entitled to demand substituted delivery at the warehouse on the line's loading dock. Under this Article, of course, the seller would also be entitled, had the market gone the other way, to make a substituted tender in that manner.

There must, however, be a true commercial impracticability to excuse the agreed to performance and justify a substituted performance. When this is the case a reasonable substituted performance tendered by either party should excuse him from strict compliance with contract terms which do not go to the essence of the agreement.

2. The substitution provided in this section as between buyer and seller does not carry over into the obligation of a financing agency under a letter of credit, since such an agency is entitled to performance which is plainly adequate on its face and without need to look into commercial evidence outside of the documents. See Article 5, especially Sections 5–102, 5–103, 5–109, 5–110, 5–114.

3. Under subsection (2) where the contract is still executory on both sides, the seller is permitted to withdraw unless the buyer can provide him with a commercially equivalent return despite the governmental regulation. Where, however, only the debt for the price remains, a larger leeway is permitted. The buyer may pay in the manner provided by the regulation even though this may not be commercially equivalent provided that the regulation is not "discriminatory, oppressive or predatory."

Cross References:

Point 2: Article 5.

Definitional Cross References:

"Buyer". Section 2–103.

"Fault". Section 1–201.

"Party". Section 1–201.

"Seller". Section 2–103.

§ 2.615. Excuse by Failure of Presupposed Conditions

Except so far as a seller may have assumed a greater obligation and subject to the preceding section on substituted performance:

(1) Delay in delivery or non-delivery in whole or in part by a seller who complies with Subdivisions (2) and (3) is not a breach of his duty under a contract for sale if performance as agreed has been made impracticable by the occurrence of a contingency the non-occurrence of which was a basic assumption on which the contract was made or by compliance in good faith with any applicable foreign or domestic governmental regulation or order whether or not it later proves to be invalid.

(2) Where the causes mentioned in Subdivision (1) affect only a part of the seller's capacity to perform, he must allocate production and deliveries among his customers but may at his option include regular customers not then under contract as well as his own requirements for further manufacture. He may so allocate in any manner which is fair and reasonable.

(3) The seller must notify the buyer seasonably that there will be delay or non-delivery and, when allocation is required under Subdivision (2), of the estimated quota thus made available for the buyer.

Acts 1967, 60th Leg., p. 2343, ch. 785, § 1, eff. Sept. 1, 1967.

Uniform Commercial Code Comment

Prior Uniform Statutory Provision:

None.

Purposes:

1. This section excuses a seller from timely delivery of goods contracted for, where his performance has become commercially impracticable because of unforeseen supervening circumstances not within the contemplation of the parties at the time of contracting. The destruction of specific goods and the problem of the use of substituted performance on points other than delay or quantity, treated elsewhere in this Article, must be distinguished from the matter covered by this section.

2. The present section deliberately refrains from any effort at an exhaustive expression of contingencies and is to be interpreted in all cases sought to be brought within its scope in terms of its underlying reason and purpose.

3. The first test for excuse under this Article in terms of basic assumption is a familiar one. The additional test of commercial impracticability (as contrasted with "impossibility," "frustration of performance" or "frustration of the venture") has been adopted in order to call attention to the commercial character of the criterion chosen by this Article.

4. Increased cost alone does not excuse performance unless the rise in cost is due to some unforeseen contingency which alters the essential nature of the performance. Neither is a rise or a collapse in the market in itself a justification, for that is exactly the type of business risk which business contracts made at fixed prices are intended to cover. But a severe shortage of raw materials or of supplies due to a contingency such as war, embargo, local crop failure, unforeseen shutdown of major sources of supply or the like, which either causes a marked increase in cost or altogether prevents the seller from securing supplies necessary to his performance is within the contemplation of this section. (See *Ford & Sons, Ltd. v. Henry Leetham & Sons, Ltd.*, 21 Com.Cas. 55 (1915, K.B.D.).)

5. Where a particular source of supply is exclusive under the agreement and fails through casualty, the present section applies rather than the provision on destruction or deterioration of specific goods. The same holds true where a particular source of supply is shown by the circumstances to have been contemplated or assumed by the parties at the time of contracting. (See *Davis Co. v. Hoffmann-LaRoche Chemical Works*, 178 App.Div. 855, 166 N.Y.S. 179 (1917) and *International Paper Co. v. Rockefeller*, 161 App.Div. 180, 146 N.Y.S. 371 (1914).) There is no excuse under this section, however, unless the seller has employed all due measures to assure himself that his source will not fail. (See *Canadian Industrial Alcohol Co., Ltd. v. Dunbar Molasses Co.*, 258 N.Y. 194, 179 N.E. 383, 80 A.L.R. 1173 (1932) and *Washington Mfg. Co. v. Midland Lumber Co.*, 113 Wash. 593, 194 P. 777 (1921).)

In the case of failure of production by an agreed source for causes beyond the seller's control, the seller should, if possible, be excused since production by an agreed source is without more a basic assumption of the contract. Such excuse should not result in relieving the defaulting supplier from liability nor in dropping into the seller's lap an unearned bonus of damages over. The flexible adjustment machinery of this Article provides the solution under the provision on the obligation of good faith. A condition to his making good the claim of excuse is the turning over to the buyer of his rights against the defaulting source of supply to the extent of the buyer's contract in relation to which excuse is being claimed.

6. In situations in which neither sense nor justice is served by either answer when the issue is posed in flat terms of "excuse" or "no excuse," adjustment under the various provisions of this Article is necessary, especially the sections on good faith, on insecurity and assurance and on the reading of all provisions in the light of their purposes, and the general policy of this Act to use equitable principles in furtherance of commercial standards and good faith.

7. The failure of conditions which go to convenience or collateral values rather than to the commercial practicability of the main performance does not amount to a complete excuse. However, good faith and the reason of the present section and of the preceding one may properly be held to justify and even to require any needed delay involved in a good faith inquiry seeking a readjustment of the contract terms to meet the new conditions.

8. The provisions of this section are made subject to assumption of greater liability by agreement and such agreement is to be found not only in the expressed terms of the contract but in the circumstances surrounding the contracting, in trade usage and the like. Thus the exemptions of this section do not apply when the contingency in question is sufficiently foreshadowed at the time of contracting to be included among the business risks which are fairly to be regarded as part of the dickered terms, either consciously or as a matter of reasonable, commercial interpretation from the circumstances. (See *Madeirense Do Brasil, S.A. v. Stulman-Emrick Lumber Co.*, 147 F.2d 399 (C.C.A., 2 Cir., 1945).) The exemption otherwise present through usage of trade under the present section may also be expressly negated by the language of the agreement. Generally, express agreements as to exemptions designed to enlarge upon or supplant the provisions of this section are to be read in the light of mercantile sense and reason, for this section itself sets up the commercial standard for normal and reasonable interpretation and provides a minimum beyond which agreement may not go.

Agreement can also be made in regard to the consequences of exemption as laid down in paragraphs (b) and (c) and the next section on procedure on notice claiming excuse.

9. The case of a farmer who has contracted to sell crops to be grown on designated land may be regarded as falling either within the section on casualty to identified goods or this section, and he may be excused, when there is a failure of the specific crop, either on the basis of the destruction of identified goods or because of the failure of a basic assumption of the contract.

Exemption of the buyer in the case of a "requirements" contract is covered by the "Output and Requirements" section both as to assumption and allocation of the relevant risks. But when a contract by a manufacturer to buy fuel or raw material makes no specific reference to a particular venture and no such reference may be drawn from the circumstances, commercial understanding views it as a general deal in the general market and not conditioned on any assumption of the continuing operation of the buyer's plant. Even when notice is given by the buyer that the supplies are needed to fill a specific contract of a normal commercial kind, commercial understanding does not see such a supply contract as conditioned on the continuance of the buyer's further contract for outlet. On the other hand, where the buyer's contract is in reasonable commercial understanding conditioned on a definite and specific venture or assumption as, for instance, a war procurement subcontract known to be based on a prime contract which is subject to termination, or a supply contract for a particular construction venture, the reason of the present section may well apply and entitle the buyer to the exemption.

10. Following its basic policy of using commercial practicability as a test for excuse, this section recognizes as of equal significance either a foreign or domestic regulation and disregards any technical distinctions between "law," "regulation," "order" and the like. Nor does it make the present action of the seller depend upon the eventual judicial determination of the legality of the particular governmental action. The seller's good faith belief in the validity of the regulation is the test under this Article and the best evidence of his good faith is the general commercial acceptance of the regulation. However, governmental interference cannot excuse unless it truly "supervenes" in such a manner as to be beyond the seller's assumption of risk. And any action by the party claiming excuse which causes or colludes in inducing the governmental action preventing his performance would be in breach of good faith and would destroy his exemption.

11. An excused seller must fulfill his contract to the extent which the supervening contingency permits, and if the situation is such that his customers are generally affected he must take account of all in supplying one. Subsections (a) and (b), therefore, explicitly permit in any proration a fair and reasonable attention to the needs of regular customers who are probably relying on spot orders for supplies. Customers at different stages of the manufacturing process may be fairly treated by including the seller's manufacturing requirements. A fortiori, the seller may also take account of contracts later in date than the one in question. The fact that such spot orders may be closed at an advanced price causes no difficulty, since any allocation which exceeds normal past requirements will not be reasonable. However, good faith requires, when prices have advanced, that the seller exercise real care in making his allocations, and in case of doubt his contract customers should be favored and supplies prorated evenly among them regardless of price. Save for the extra care thus required by changes in the market, this section seeks to leave every reasonable business leeway to the seller.

Cross References:

Point 1: Sections 2–613 and 2–614.

Point 2: Section 1–102.

Point 5: Sections 1–203 and 2–613.

Point 6: Sections 1–102, 1–203 and 2–609.

Point 7: Section 2–614.

Point 8: Sections 1–201, 2–302 and 2–616.

Point 9: Sections 1–102, 2–306 and 2–613.

Definitional Cross References:

"Between merchants". Section 2–104.

"Buyer". Section 2–103.

"Contract". Section 1–201.

"Contract for sale". Section 2–106.

"Good faith". Section 1–201.

"Merchant". Section 2–104.

"Notifies". Section 1–201.

"Seasonably". Section 1–204.

"Seller". Section 2–103.

§ 2.616. Procedure on Notice Claiming Excuse

(a) Where the buyer receives notification of a material or indefinite delay or an allocation justified under the preceding section he may by written notification to the seller as to any delivery concerned, and where the prospective deficiency substantially impairs the value of the whole contract under the provisions of this chapter relating to breach of installment contracts (Section 2.612), then also as to the whole,

(1) terminate and thereby discharge any unexecuted portion of the contract; or

(2) modify the contract by agreeing to take his available quota in substitution.

(b) If after receipt of such notification from the seller the buyer fails so to modify the contract within a reasonable time not exceeding thirty days the contract lapses with respect to any deliveries affected.

(c) The provisions of this section may not be negated by agreement except insofar as the seller has assumed a greater obligation under the preceding section.

Acts 1967, 60th Leg., p. 2343, ch. 785, § 1, eff. Sept. 1, 1967.

Uniform Commercial Code Comment

Prior Uniform Statutory Provision:

None.

Purposes:

This section seeks to establish simple and workable machinery for providing certainty as to when a supervening and excusing contingency "excuses" the delay, "discharges" the contract, or may result in a waiver of the delay by the buyer. When the seller notifies, in accordance with the preceding section, claiming excuse, the buyer may acquiesce, in which case the contract is so modified. No consideration is necessary in a case of this kind to support such a modification. If the buyer does not elect so to modify the contract, he may terminate it and under subsection (2) his silence after receiving the seller's claim of excuse operates as such a termination. Subsection (3) denies effect to any contract clause made in advance of trouble which would require the buyer to stand ready to take delivery whenever the seller is excused from delivery by unforeseen circumstances.

Cross References:

Point 1: Sections 2–209 and 2–615.

Definitional Cross References:

"Buyer". Section 2–103.

"Contract". Section 1–201.

"Installment contract". Section 2–612.

"Notification". Section 1–201.

"Reasonable time". Section 1–204.

"Seller". Section 2–103.

"Termination". Section 2–106.

"Written". Section 1–201.

SUBCHAPTER G. REMEDIES

§ 2.701. Remedies for Breach of Collateral Contracts Not Impaired

Remedies for breach of any obligation or promise collateral or ancillary to a contract for sale are not impaired by the provisions of this chapter.

Acts 1967, 60th Leg., p. 2343, ch. 785, § 1, eff. Sept. 1, 1967.

Uniform Commercial Code Comment

Prior Uniform Statutory Provision:

None.

Purposes:

Whether a claim for breach of an obligation collateral to the contract for sale requires separate trial to avoid confusion of issues is beyond the scope of this Article; but contractual arrangements which as a business matter enter vitally into the contract should be considered a part thereof in so far as cross-claims or defenses are concerned.

Definitional Cross References:

"Contract for sale". Section 2–106.

"Remedy". Section 1–201.

§ 2.702. Seller's Remedies on Discovery of Buyer's Insolvency

(a) Where the seller discovers the buyer to be insolvent he may refuse delivery except for cash including payment for all goods theretofore delivered under the contract, and stop delivery under this chapter (Section 2.705).

(b) Where the seller discovers that the buyer has received goods on credit while insolvent he may reclaim the goods upon demand made within ten days after the receipt, but if misrepresentation of solvency has been made to the particular seller in writing within three months before delivery the ten day limitation does not apply. Except as provided in this subsection the seller may not base a right to reclaim goods on the buyer's fraudulent or innocent misrepresentation of solvency or of intent to pay.

(c) The seller's right to reclaim under Subsection (b) is subject to the rights of a buyer in ordinary course or other good faith purchaser or lien creditor under this chapter (Section 2.403). Successful reclamation of goods excludes all other remedies with respect to them.

Acts 1967, 60th Leg., p. 2343, ch. 785, § 1, eff. Sept. 1, 1967.

Uniform Commercial Code Comment

Prior Uniform Statutory Provision:

Subsection (1)—Sections 53(1)(b), 54(1)(c) and 57, Uniform Sales Act; Subsection (2)—none; Subsection (3)—Section 76(3), Uniform Sales Act.

Changes: Rewritten, the protection given to a seller who has sold on credit and has delivered goods to the buyer immediately preceding his insolvency being extended.

Purposes of Changes and New Matter: To make it clear that:

1. The seller's right to withhold the goods or to stop delivery except for cash when he discovers the buyer's insolvency is made explicit in subsection (1) regardless of the passage of title, and the concept of stoppage has been extended to include goods in the possession of any bailee who has not yet attorned to the buyer.

2. Subsection (2) takes as its base line the proposition that any receipt of goods on credit by an insolvent buyer amounts to a tacit business misrepresentation of solvency and therefore is fraudulent as against the particular seller. This Article makes discovery of the buyer's insolvency and demand within a ten day period a condition of the right to reclaim goods on this ground. The ten day limitation period operates from the time of receipt of the goods.

An exception to this time limitation is made when a written misrepresentation of solvency has been made to the particular seller within three months prior to the delivery. To fall within the exception the statement of solvency must be in writing, addressed to the particular seller and dated within three months of the delivery.

3. Subsection (3) subjects the right of reclamation to certain rights of third parties "under this Article (Section 2–403)." The rights so given priority of course include the rights given to purchasers from the buyer by Section 2–403(1) and (2). They also include other rights arising under Article 2, such as the rights of lien creditors of the buyer under Section 2–326(3) on consignment sales. Moreover, since Section 2–403(4) incorporates by reference rights given to other purchasers and to lien creditors by Articles 6, 7 and 9, such rights have the same priority. "Lien creditor" here has the same meaning as in Section 9–301(3). Thus if a seller retains an unperfected security interest, subordinate under Section 9–301(1)(b) to the rights of a levying creditor of the buyer, his right of reclamation under this section is also subject to the creditor's rights. Purchasers or lien creditors may also have rights not arising under this Article; under Section 1–103 such rights may have priority by virtue

of supplementary principles not displaced by this Section. See *In re Kravitz,* 278 F.2d 820 (3d Cir. 1960).

Because the right of the seller to reclaim goods under this section constitutes preferential treatment as against the buyer's other creditors, subsection (3) provides that such reclamation bars all his other remedies as to the goods involved.

Cross References:

Point 1: Sections 2–401 and 2–705.

Compare Section 2–502.

Definitional Cross References:

"Buyer". Section 2–103.

"Buyer in ordinary course of business". Section 1–201.

"Contract". Section 1–201.

"Good faith". Section 1–201.

"Goods". Section 2–105.

"Insolvent". Section 1–201.

"Person". Section 1–201.

"Purchaser". Section 1–201.

"Receipt" of goods. Section 2–103.

"Remedy". Section 1–201.

"Rights". Section 1–201.

"Seller". Section 2–103.

"Writing". Section 1–201.

§ 2.703. Seller's Remedies in General

Where the buyer wrongfully rejects or revokes acceptance of goods or fails to make a payment due on or before delivery or repudiates with respect to a part or the whole, then with respect to any goods directly affected and, if the breach is of the whole contract (Section 2.612), then also with respect to the whole undelivered balance, the aggrieved seller may

(1) withhold delivery of such goods;

(2) stop delivery by any bailee as hereafter provided (Section 2.705);

(3) proceed under the next section respecting goods still unidentified to the contract;

(4) resell and recover damages as hereafter provided (Section 2.706);

(5) recover damages for non-acceptance (Section 2.708) or in a proper case the price (Section 2.709);

(6) cancel.

Acts 1967, 60th Leg., p. 2343, ch. 785, § 1, eff. Sept. 1, 1967.

Uniform Commercial Code Comment

Prior Uniform Statutory Provisions: No comparable index section. See Section 53, Uniform Sales Act.

Purposes:

1. This section is an index section which gathers together in one convenient place all of the various remedies open to a seller for any breach by the buyer. This Article rejects any doctrine of election of remedy as a fundamental policy and thus the remedies are essentially cumulative in nature and include all of the available remedies for breach. Whether the pursuit of one remedy bars another depends entirely on the facts of the individual case.

2. The buyer's breach which occasions the use of the remedies under this section may involve only one lot or delivery of goods, or may involve all of the goods which are the subject matter of the particular contract. The right of the seller to pursue a remedy as to all the goods when the breach is as to only one or more lots is covered by the section on breach in installment contracts. The present section deals only with the remedies available after the goods involved in the breach have been determined by that section.

3. In addition to the typical case of refusal to pay or default in payment, the language in the preamble, "fails to make a payment due," is intended to cover the dishonor of a check on due presentment, or the non-acceptance of a draft, and the failure to furnish an agreed letter of credit.

4. It should also be noted that this Act requires its remedies to be liberally administered and provides that any right or obligation which it declares is enforceable by action unless a different effect is specifically prescribed (Section 1–106).

Cross References:

Point 2: Section 2–612.

Point 3: Section 2–325.

Point 4: Section 1–106.

Definitional Cross References:

"Aggrieved party". Section 1–201.

"Buyer". Section 2–103.

"Cancellation". Section 2–106.

"Contract". Section 1–201.

"Goods". Section 2–105.

"Remedy". Section 1–201.

"Seller". Section 2–103.

§ 2.704. Seller's Right to Identify Goods to the Contract Notwithstanding Breach or to Salvage Unfinished Goods

(a) An aggrieved seller under the preceding section may

(1) identify to the contract conforming goods not already identified if at the time he learned of the breach they are in his possession or control;

(2) treat as the subject of resale goods which have demonstrably been intended for the particular contract even though those goods are unfinished.

(b) Where the goods are unfinished an aggrieved seller may in the exercise of reasonable commercial judgment for the purposes of avoiding loss and of effective realization either complete the manufacture and wholly identify the goods to the contract or cease manufacture and resell for scrap or salvage value or proceed in any other reasonable manner.

Acts 1967, 60th Leg., p. 2343, ch. 785, § 1, eff. Sept. 1, 1967.

Uniform Commercial Code Comment

Prior Uniform Statutory Provisions:

Sections 63(3) and 64(4), Uniform Sales Act.

Changes: Rewritten, the seller's rights being broadened.

Purposes of Changes:

1. This section gives an aggrieved seller the right at the time of breach to identify to the contract any conforming finished goods, regardless of their resalability, and to use reasonable judgment as to completing unfinished goods. It thus makes the goods available for resale under the resale section, the seller's primary remedy, and in the special case in which resale is not practicable, allows the action for the price which would then be necessary to give the seller the value of his contract.

2. Under this Article the seller is given express power to complete manufacture or procurement of goods for the contract unless the exercise of reasonable commercial judgment as to the facts as they appear at the time he learns of the breach makes it clear that such action will result in a material increase in damages. The burden is on the buyer to show the commercially unreasonable nature of the seller's action in completing manufacture.

Cross References:

Sections 2–703 and 2–706.

Definitional Cross References:

"Aggrieved party". Section 1–201.

"Conforming". Section 2–106.

"Contract". Section 1–201.

"Goods". Section 2–105.

"Rights". Section 1–201.

"Seller". Section 2–103.

§ 2.705. Seller's Stoppage of Delivery in Transit or Otherwise

(a) The seller may stop delivery of goods in the possession of a carrier or other bailee when he discovers the buyer to be insolvent (Section 2.702) and may stop delivery of carload, truckload, planeload or larger shipments of express or freight when the buyer repudiates or fails to make a payment due before delivery or if for any other reason the seller has a right to withhold or reclaim the goods.

(b) As against such buyer the seller may stop delivery until

(1) receipt of the goods by the buyer; or

(2) acknowledgment to the buyer by any bailee of the goods except a carrier that the bailee holds the goods for the buyer; or

(3) such acknowledgment to the buyer by a carrier by reshipment or as a warehouse; or

(4) negotiation to the buyer of any negotiable document of title covering the goods.

(c)(1) To stop delivery the seller must so notify as to enable the bailee by reasonable diligence to prevent delivery of the goods.

(2) After such notification the bailee must hold and deliver the goods according to the directions of the seller but the seller is liable to the bailee for any ensuing charges or damages.

(3) If a negotiable document of title has been issued for goods the bailee is not obliged to obey a notification to stop until surrender of possession or control of the document.

(4) A carrier who has issued a non-negotiable bill of lading is not obliged to obey a notification to stop received from a person other than the consignor.

Acts 1967, 60th Leg., p. 2343, ch. 785, § 1, eff. Sept. 1, 1967. Amended by Acts 2005, 79th Leg., ch. 122, § 12, eff. Sept. 1, 2005.

Uniform Commercial Code Comment

Prior Uniform Statutory Provision:

Sections 57–59, Uniform Sales Act; see also Sections 12, 14 and 42, Uniform Bills of Lading Act and Sections 9, 11 and 49, Uniform Warehouse Receipts Act.

Changes: This section continues and develops the above sections of the Uniform Sales Act in the light of the other uniform statutory provisions noted.

Purposes: To make it clear that:

1. Subsection (1) applies the stoppage principle to other bailees as well as carriers.

It also expands the remedy to cover the situations, in addition to buyer's insolvency, specified in the subsection. But since stoppage is a burden in any case to carriers, and might be a very heavy burden to them if it covered all small shipments in all these situations, the right to stop for reasons other than insolvency is limited to carload, truckload, planeload or larger shipments. The seller shipping to a buyer of doubtful credit can protect himself by shipping C.O.D.

Where stoppage occurs for insecurity it is merely a suspension of performance, and if assurances are duly forthcoming from the buyer the seller is not entitled to resell or divert.

Improper stoppage is a breach by the seller if it effectively interferes with the buyer's right to due tender under the section on manner of tender of delivery. However, if the bailee obeys an unjustified order to stop he may also be liable to the buyer. The measure of his obligation is dependent on the provisions of the Documents of Title Article (Section 7–303). Subsection 3(b) therefore gives him a right of indemnity as against the seller in such a case.

2. "Receipt by the buyer" includes receipt by the buyer's designated representative, the sub-purchaser, when shipment is made direct to him and the buyer himself never receives the goods. It is entirely proper under this Article that the seller, by making such direct shipment to the sub-purchaser, be regarded as acquiescing in the latter's purchase and as thus barred from stoppage of the goods as against him.

As between the buyer and the seller, the latter's right to stop the goods at any time until they reach the place of final delivery is recognized by this section.

Under subsection (3)(c) and (d), the carrier is under no duty to recognize the stop order of a person who is a stranger to the carrier's contract. But the seller's right as against the buyer to stop delivery remains, whether or not the carrier is obligated to recognize the stop order. If the carrier does obey it, the buyer cannot complain merely because of that circumstance; and the seller becomes obligated under subsection (3)(b) to pay the carrier any ensuing damages or charges.

3. A diversion of a shipment is not a "reshipment" under subsection (2)(c) when it is merely an incident to the original contract of transportation. Nor is the procurement of "exchange bills" of lading which change only the name of the consignee to that of the buyer's local agent but do not alter the destination of a reshipment.

Acknowledgment by the carrier as a "warehouse" within the meaning of this Article requires a contract of a truly different character from the original shipment, a contract not in extension of transit but as a warehouse.

4. Subsection (3)(c) makes the bailee's obedience of a notification to stop conditional upon the surrender of possession or control of any outstanding negotiable document.

5. Any charges or losses incurred by the carrier in following the seller's orders, whether or not he was obligated to do so, fall to the seller's charge.

6. After an effective stoppage under this section the seller's rights in the goods are the same as if he had never made a delivery.

Cross References:

Sections 2–702 and 2–703.

Point 1: Sections 2–503 and 2–609, and Article 7.

Point 2: Section 2–103 and Article 7.

Definitional Cross References:

"Buyer". Section 2–103.

"Contract for sale". Section 2–106.

"Document of title". Section 1–201.

"Goods". Section 2–105.

"Insolvent". Section 1–201.

"Notification". Section 1–201.

"Receipt" of goods. Section 2–103.

"Rights". Section 1–201.

"Seller". Section 2–103.

Sections 31 and 32 of Acts 2005, 79th Leg., ch. 122 provide:

"Sec. 31. This Act applies to a document of title that is issued or a bailment that arises on or after the effective date of this Act. This Act does not apply to a document of title that is issued or a bailment that arises before the effective date of this Act even if the document of title or bailment would be subject to this Act if the document of title had been issued or bailment had arisen after the effective date of this Act. This Act does not apply to a right of action that has accrued before the effective date of this Act.

"Sec. 32. A document of title issued or a bailment that arises before the effective date of this Act and the rights, obligations, and interests flowing from that document or bailment are governed by any statute or other rule amended or repealed by this Act as if amendment or repeal had not occurred and may be terminated, completed, consummated, or enforced under that statute or other rule."

§ 2.706. Seller's Resale Including Contract for Resale

(a) Under the conditions stated in Section 2.703 on seller's remedies, the seller may resell the goods concerned or the undelivered balance thereof. Where the resale is made in good faith and in a commercially reasonable manner the seller may recover the difference between the resale price and the contract price together with any incidental damages allowed under the provisions of this chapter (Section 2.710), but less expenses saved in consequence of the buyer's breach.

(b) Except as otherwise provided in Subsection (c) or unless otherwise agreed resale may be at public or private sale including sale by way of one or more contracts to sell or of identification to an existing contract of the seller. Sale may be as a unit or in parcels and at any time and place and on any terms but every aspect of the sale including the method, manner, time, place and terms must be commercially reasonable. The resale must be reasonably identified as referring to the broken contract, but it is not necessary that the goods be in existence or that any or all of them have been identified to the contract before the breach.

(c) Where the resale is at private sale the seller must give the buyer reasonable notification of his intention to resell.

(d) Where the resale is at public sale

(1) only identified goods can be sold except where there is a recognized market for a public sale of futures in goods of the kind; and

(2) it must be made at a usual place or market for public sale if one is reasonably available and except in the case of goods which are perishable or threaten to decline in value speedily the seller must

give the buyer reasonable notice of the time and place of the resale; and

(3) if the goods are not to be within the view of those attending the sale the notification of sale must state the place where the goods are located and provide for their reasonable inspection by prospective bidders; and

(4) the seller may buy.

(e) A purchaser who buys in good faith at a resale takes the goods free of any rights of the original buyer even though the seller fails to comply with one or more of the requirements of this section.

(f) The seller is not accountable to the buyer for any profit made on any resale. A person in the position of a seller (Section 2.707) or a buyer who has rightfully rejected or justifiably revoked acceptance must account for any excess over the amount of his security interest, as hereinafter defined (Subsection (c) of Section 2.711).

Acts 1967, 60th Leg., p. 2343, ch. 785, § 1, eff. Sept. 1, 1967.

Uniform Commercial Code Comment

Prior Uniform Statutory Provision:

Section 60, Uniform Sales Act.

Changes: Rewritten.

Purposes of Changes: To simplify the prior statutory provision and to make it clear that:

1. The only condition precedent to the seller's right of resale under subsection (1) is a breach by the buyer within the section on the seller's remedies in general or insolvency. Other meticulous conditions and restrictions of the prior uniform statutory provision are disapproved by this Article and are replaced by standards of commercial reasonableness. Under this section the seller may resell the goods after any breach by the buyer. Thus, an anticipatory repudiation by the buyer gives rise to any of the seller's remedies for breach, and to the right of resale. This principle is supplemented by subsection (2) which authorizes a resale of goods which are not in existence or were not identified to the contract before the breach.

2. In order to recover the damages prescribed in subsection (1) the seller must act "in good faith and in a commercially reasonable manner" in making the resale. This standard is intended to be more comprehensive than that of "reasonable care and judgment" established by the prior uniform statutory provision. Failure to act properly under this section deprives the seller of the measure of damages here provided and relegates him to that provided in Section 2–708.

Under this Article the seller resells by authority of law, in his own behalf, for his own benefit and for the purpose of fixing his damages. The theory of a seller's agency is thus rejected.

3. If the seller complies with the prescribed standard of duty in making the resale, he may recover from the buyer the damages provided for in subsection (1). Evidence of market or current prices at any particular time or place is relevant only on the question of whether the seller acted in a commercially reasonable manner in making the resale.

The distinction drawn by some courts between cases where the title had not passed to the buyer and the seller had resold as owner, and cases where the title had passed and the seller had resold by virtue of his lien on the goods, is rejected.

4. Subsection (2) frees the remedy of resale from legalistic restrictions and enables the seller to resell in accordance with reasonable commercial practices so as to realize as high a price as possible in the circumstances. By "public" sale is meant a sale by auction. A "private" sale may be effected by solicitation and negotiation conducted either directly or through a broker. In choosing between a public and private sale the character of the goods must be considered and relevant trade practices and usages must be observed.

5. Subsection (2) merely clarifies the common law rule that the time for resale is a reasonable time after the buyer's breach, by using the language "commercially reasonable." What is such a reasonable time depends upon the nature of the goods, the condition of the market and the other circumstances of the case; its length cannot be measured by any legal yardstick or divided into degrees. Where a seller contemplating resale receives a demand from the buyer for inspection under the section of preserving evidence of goods in dispute, the time for resale may be appropriately lengthened.

On the question of the place for resale, subsection (2) goes to the ultimate test, the commercial reasonableness of the seller's choice as to the place for an advantageous resale. This Article rejects the theory that the seller is required to resell at the agreed place for delivery and that a resale elsewhere can be permitted only in exceptional cases.

6. The purpose of subsection (2) being to enable the seller to dispose of the goods to the best advantage, he is permitted in making the resale to depart from the terms and conditions of the original contract for sale to any extent "commercially reasonable" in the circumstances.

7. The provision of subsection (2) that the goods need not be in existence to be resold applies when the buyer is guilty of anticipatory repudiation of a contract for future goods, before the goods or some of them have come into existence. In such a case the seller may exercise the right of resale and fix his damages by "one or more contracts to sell" the quantity of conforming future goods affected by the repudiation. The companion provision of subsection (2) that resale may be made although the goods were not identified to the contract prior to the buyer's breach, likewise contemplates an anticipatory repudiation by the buyer but occurring after the goods are in existence. If the goods so identified conform to the contract, their resale will fix the seller's damages quite as satisfactorily as if they had been identified before the breach.

8. Where the resale is to be by private sale, subsection (3) requires that reasonable notification of the seller's intention to resell must be given to the buyer. The length of

notification of a private sale depends upon the urgency of the matter. Notification of the time and place of this type of sale is not required.

Subsection (4)(b) requires that the seller give the buyer reasonable notice of the time and place of a public resale so that he may have an opportunity to bid or to secure the attendance of other bidders. An exception is made in the case of goods "which are perishable or threaten to decline speedily in value."

9. Since there would be no reasonable prospect of competitive bidding elsewhere, subsection (4) requires that a public resale "must be made at a usual place or market for public sale if one is reasonably available;" i. e., a place or market which prospective bidders may reasonably be expected to attend. Such a market may still be "reasonably available" under this subsection, though at a considerable distance from the place where the goods are located. In such a case the expense of transporting the goods for resale is recoverable from the buyer as part of the seller's incidental damages under subsection (1). However, the question of availability is one of commercial reasonableness in the circumstances and if such "usual" place or market is not reasonably available, a duly advertised public resale may be held at another place if it is one which prospective bidders may reasonably be expected to attend, as distinguished from a place where there is no demand whatsoever for goods of the kind.

Paragraph (a) of subsection (4) qualifies the last sentence of subsection (2) with respect to resales of unidentified and future goods at public sale. If conforming goods are in existence the seller may identify them to the contract after the buyer's breach and then resell them at public sale. If the goods have not been identified, however, he may resell them at public sale only as "future" goods and only where there is a recognized market for public sale of futures in goods of the kind.

The provisions of paragraph (c) of subsection (4) are intended to permit intelligent bidding.

The provision of paragraph (d) of subsection (4) permitting the seller to bid and, of course, to become the purchaser, benefits the original buyer by tending to increase the resale price and thus decreasing the damages he will have to pay.

10. This Article departs in subsection (5) from the prior uniform statutory provision in permitting a good faith purchaser at resale to take a good title as against the buyer even though the seller fails to comply with the requirements of this section.

11. Under subsection (6), the seller retains profit, if any, without distinction based on whether or not he had a lien since this Article divorces the question of passage of title to the buyer from the seller's right of resale or the consequences of its exercise. On the other hand, where "a person in the position of a seller" or a buyer acting under the section on buyer's remedies, exercises his right of resale under the present section he does so only for the limited purpose of obtaining cash for his "security interest" in the goods. Once that purpose has been accomplished any excess in the resale price belongs to the seller to whom an accounting must be made as provided in the last sentence of subsection (6).

Cross References:

Point 1: Sections 2–610, 2–702 and 2–703.

Point 2: Section 1–201.

Point 3: Sections 2–708 and 2–710.

Point 4: Section 2–328.

Point 8: Section 2–104.

Point 9: Section 2–710.

Point 11: Sections 2–401, 2–707 and 2–711(3).

Definitional Cross References:

"Buyer". Section 2–103.
"Contract". Section 1–201.
"Contract for sale". Section 2–106.
"Good faith". Section 2–103.
"Goods". Section 2–105.
"Merchant". Section 2–104.
"Notification". Section 1–201.
"Person in position of seller". Section 2–707.
"Purchase". Section 1–201.
"Rights". Section 1–201.
"Sale". Section 2–106.
"Security interest". Section 1–201.
"Seller". Section 2–103.

§ 2.707. "Person in the Position of a Seller"

(a) A "person in the position of a seller" includes as against a principal an agent who has paid or become responsible for the price of goods on behalf of his principal or anyone who otherwise holds a security interest or other right in goods similar to that of a seller.

(b) A person in the position of a seller may as provided in this chapter withhold or stop delivery (Section 2.705) and resell (Section 2.706) and recover incidental damages (Section 2.710).

Acts 1967, 60th Leg., p. 2343, ch. 785, § 1, eff. Sept. 1, 1967.

Uniform Commercial Code Comment

Prior Uniform Statutory Provision:

Section 52(2), Uniform Sales Act.

Changes: Rewritten.

Purposes of Changes: To make it clear that:

In addition to following in general the prior uniform statutory provision, the case of a financing agency which has acquired documents by honoring a letter of credit for the buyer or by discounting a draft for the seller has been included in the term "a person in the position of a seller."

Cross References:

Article 5, Section 2–506.

Definitional Cross References:

"Consignee". Section 7–102.

"Consignor". Section 7–102.

"Goods". Section 2–105.

"Security interest". Section 1–201.

"Seller". Section 2–103.

§ 2.708. Seller's Damages for Non-Acceptance or Repudiation

(a) Subject to Subsection (b) and to the provisions of this chapter with respect to proof of market price (Section 2.723), the measure of damages for non-acceptance or repudiation by the buyer is the difference between the market price at the time and place for tender and the unpaid contract price together with any incidental damages provided in this chapter (Section 2.710), but less expenses saved in consequence of the buyer's breach.

(b) If the measure of damages provided in Subsection (a) is inadequate to put the seller in as good a position as performance would have done then the measure of damages is the profit (including reasonable overhead) which the seller would have made from full performance by the buyer, together with any incidental damages provided in this chapter (Section 2.710), due allowance for costs reasonably incurred and due credit for payments or proceeds of resale.

Acts 1967, 60th Leg., p. 2343, ch. 785, § 1, eff. Sept. 1, 1967.

Uniform Commercial Code Comment

Prior Uniform Statutory Provision:

Section 64, Uniform Sales Act.

Changes: Rewritten.

Purposes of Changes: To make it clear that:

1. The prior uniform statutory provision is followed generally in setting the current market price at the time and place for tender as the standard by which damages for non-acceptance are to be determined. The time and place of tender is determined by reference to the section on manner of tender of delivery, and to the sections on the effect of such terms as FOB, FAS, CIF, C & F, Ex Ship and No Arrival, No Sale.

In the event that there is no evidence available of the current market price at the time and place of tender, proof of a substitute market may be made under the section on determination and proof of market price. Furthermore, the section on the admissibility of market quotations is intended to ease materially the problem of providing competent evidence.

2. The provision of this section permitting recovery of expected profit including reasonable overhead where the standard measure of damages is inadequate, together with the new requirement that price actions may be sustained only where resale is impractical, are designed to eliminate the unfair and economically wasteful results arising under the older law when fixed price articles were involved. This section permits the recovery of lost profits in all appropriate cases, which would include all standard priced goods. The normal measure there would be list price less cost to the dealer or list price less manufacturing cost to the manufacturer. It is not necessary to a recovery of "profit" to show a history of earnings, especially if a new venture is involved.

3. In all cases the seller may recover incidental damages.

Cross References:

Point 1: Sections 2–319 through 2–324, 2–503, 2–723 and 2–724.

Point 2: Section 2–709.

Point 3: Section 2–710.

Definitional Cross References:

"Buyer". Section 2–103.

"Contract". Section 1–201.

"Seller". Section 2–103.

§ 2.709. Action for the Price

(a) When the buyer fails to pay the price as it becomes due the seller may recover, together with any incidental damages under the next section, the price

(1) of goods accepted or of conforming goods lost or damaged within a commercially reasonable time after risk of their loss has passed to the buyer; and

(2) of goods identified to the contract if the seller is unable after reasonable effort to resell them at a reasonable price or the circumstances reasonably indicate that such effort will be unavailing.

(b) Where the seller sues for the price he must hold for the buyer any goods which have been identified to the contract and are still in his control except that if resale becomes possible he may resell them at any time prior to the collection of the judgment. The net proceeds of any such resale must be credited to the buyer and payment of the judgment entitles him to any goods not resold.

(c) After the buyer has wrongfully rejected or revoked acceptance of the goods or has failed to make a payment due or has repudiated (Section 2.610), a seller who is held not entitled to the price under this section shall nevertheless be awarded damages for nonacceptance under the preceding section.

Acts 1967, 60th Leg., p. 2343, ch. 785, § 1, eff. Sept. 1, 1967.

Uniform Commercial Code Comment

Prior Uniform Statutory Provision:

Section 63, Uniform Sales Act.

Changes: Rewritten, important commercially needed changes being incorporated.

Purposes of Changes: To make it clear that:

1. Neither the passing of title to the goods nor the appointment of a day certain for payment is now material to a price action.

2. The action for the price is now generally limited to those cases where resale of the goods is impracticable except where the buyer has accepted the goods or where they have been destroyed after risk of loss has passed to the buyer.

3. This section substitutes an objective test by action for the former "not readily resalable" standard. An action for the price under subsection (1)(b) can be sustained only after a "reasonable effort to resell" the goods "at reasonable price" has actually been made or where the circumstances "reasonably indicate" that such an effort will be unavailing.

4. If a buyer is in default not with respect to the price, but on an obligation to make an advance, the seller should recover not under this section for the price as such, but for the default in the collateral (though coincident) obligation to finance the seller. If the agreement between the parties contemplates that the buyer will acquire, on making the advance, a security interest in the goods, the buyer on making the advance has such an interest as soon as the seller has rights in the agreed collateral. See Section 9–204.

5. "Goods accepted" by the buyer under subsection (1)(a) include only goods as to which there has been no justified revocation of acceptance, for such a revocation means that there has been a default by the seller which bars his rights under this section. "Goods lost or damaged" are covered by the section on risk of loss. "Goods identified to the contract" under subsection (1)(b) are covered by the section on identification and the section on identification notwithstanding breach.

6. This section is intended to be exhaustive in its enumeration of cases where an action for the price lies.

7. If the action for the price fails, the seller may nonetheless have proved a case entitling him to damages for non-acceptance. In such a situation, subsection (3) permits recovery of those damages in the same action.

Cross References:

Point 4: Section 1–106.

Point 5: Sections 2–501, 2–509, 2–510 and 2–704.

Point 7: Section 2–708.

Definitional Cross References:

"Action". Section 1–201.

"Buyer". Section 2–103.

"Conforming". Section 2–106.

"Contract". Section 1–201.

"Goods". Section 2–105.

"Seller". Section 2–103.

§ 2.710. Seller's Incidental Damages

Incidental damages to an aggrieved seller include any commercially reasonable charges, expenses or commissions incurred in stopping delivery, in the transportation, care and custody of goods after the buyer's breach, in connection with return or resale of the goods or otherwise resulting from the breach.

Acts 1967, 60th Leg., p. 2343, ch. 785, § 1, eff. Sept. 1, 1967.

Uniform Commercial Code Comment

Prior Uniform Statutory Provision:

See Sections 64 and 70, Uniform Sales Act.

Purposes: To authorize reimbursement of the seller for expenses reasonably incurred by him as a result of the buyer's breach. The section sets forth the principal normal and necessary additional elements of damage flowing from the breach but intends to allow all commercially reasonable expenditures made by the seller.

Definitional Cross References:

"Aggrieved party". Section 1–201.

"Buyer". Section 2–103.

"Goods". Section 2–105.

"Seller". Section 2–103.

§ 2.711. Buyer's Remedies in General; Buyer's Security Interest in Rejected Goods

(a) Where the seller fails to make delivery or repudiates or the buyer rightfully rejects or justifiably revokes acceptance then with respect to any goods involved, and with respect to the whole if the breach goes to the whole contract (Section 2.612), the buyer may cancel and whether or not he has done so may in addition to recovering so much of the price as has been paid

(1) "cover" and have damages under the next section as to all the goods affected whether or not they have been identified to the contract; or

(2) recover damages for non-delivery as provided in this chapter (Section 2.713).

(b) Where the seller fails to deliver or repudiates the buyer may also

(1) if the goods have been identified recover them as provided in this chapter (Section 2.502); or

(2) in a proper case obtain specific performance or replevy the goods as provided in this chapter (Section 2.716).

(c) On rightful rejection or justifiable revocation of acceptance a buyer has a security interest in goods in his possession or control for any payments made on their price and any expenses reasonably incurred in their inspection, receipt, transportation, care and custody and may hold such goods and resell them in like manner as an aggrieved seller (Section 2.706).

Acts 1967, 60th Leg., p. 2343, ch. 785, § 1, eff. Sept. 1, 1967.

Uniform Commercial Code Comment

Prior Uniform Statutory Provision:

No comparable index section; Subsection (3)—Section 69(5), Uniform Sales Act.

Changes: The prior uniform statutory provision is generally continued and expanded in Subsection (3).

Purposes of Changes and New Matter:

1. To index in this section the buyer's remedies, subsection (1) covering those remedies permitting the recovery of money damages, and subsection (2) covering those which permit reaching the goods themselves. The remedies listed here are those available to a buyer who has not accepted the goods or who has justifiably revoked his acceptance. The remedies available to a buyer with regard to goods finally accepted appear in the section dealing with breach in regard to accepted goods. The buyer's right to proceed as to all goods when the breach is as to only some of the goods is determined by the section on breach in installment contracts and by the section on partial acceptance.

Despite the seller's breach, proper retender of delivery under the section on cure of improper tender or replacement can effectively preclude the buyer's remedies under this section, except for any delay involved.

2. To make it clear in subsection (3) that the buyer may hold and resell rejected goods if he has paid a part of the price or incurred expenses of the type specified. "Paid" as used here includes acceptance of a draft or other time negotiable instrument or the signing of a negotiable note. His freedom of resale is coextensive with that of a seller under this Article except that the buyer may not keep any profit resulting from the resale and is limited to retaining only the amount of the price paid and the costs involved in the inspection and handling of the goods. The buyer's security interest in the goods is intended to be limited to the items listed in subsection (3), and the buyer is not permitted to retain such funds as he might believe adequate for his damages. The buyer's right to cover, or to have damages for non-delivery, is not impaired by his exercise of his right of resale.

3. It should also be noted that this Act requires its remedies to be liberally administered and provides that any right or obligation which it declares is enforceable by action unless a different effect is specifically prescribed (Section 1–106).

Cross References:

Point 1: Sections 2–508, 2–601(c), 2–608, 2–612 and 2–714.

Point 2: Section 2–706.

Point 3: Section 1–106.

Definitional Cross References:

"Aggrieved party". Section 1–201.

"Buyer". Section 2–103.

"Cancellation". Section 2–106.

"Contract". Section 1–201.

"Cover". Section 2–712.

"Goods". Section 2–105.

"Notifies". Section 1–201.

"Receipt" of goods. Section 2–103.

"Remedy". Section 1–201.

"Security interest". Section 1–201.

"Seller". Section 2–103.

§ 2.712. "Cover"; Buyer's Procurement of Substitute Goods

(a) After a breach within the preceding section the buyer may "cover" by making in good faith and without unreasonable delay any reasonable purchase of or contract to purchase goods in substitution for those due from the seller.

(b) The buyer may recover from the seller as damages the difference between the cost of cover and the contract price together with any incidental or consequential damages as hereinafter defined (Section 2.715), but less expenses saved in consequence of the seller's breach.

(c) Failure of the buyer to effect cover within this section does not bar him from any other remedy.

Acts 1967, 60th Leg., p. 2343, ch. 785, § 1, eff. Sept. 1, 1967.

Uniform Commercial Code Comment

Prior Uniform Statutory Provision:

None.

Purposes:

1. This section provides the buyer with a remedy aimed at enabling him to obtain the goods he needs thus meeting his essential need. This remedy is the buyer's equivalent of the seller's right to resell.

2. The definition of "cover" under subsection (1) envisages a series of contracts or sales, as well as a single contract or sale; goods not identical with those involved but commercially usable as reasonable substitutes under the circumstances of the particular case; and contracts on credit or delivery terms differing from the contract in breach, but again reasonable under the circumstances. The test of proper cover is whether at the time and place the buyer acted in good faith and in a reasonable manner, and it is immaterial that hindsight may later prove that the method of cover used was not the cheapest or most effective.

The requirement that the buyer must cover "without unreasonable delay" is not intended to limit the time necessary for him to look around and decide as to how he may best effect cover. The test here is similar to that generally used in this Article as to reasonable time and seasonable action.

3. Subsection (3) expresses the policy that cover is not a mandatory remedy for the buyer. The buyer is always free to choose between cover and damages for non-delivery under the next section.

However, this subsection must be read in conjunction with the section which limits the recovery of consequential damages to such as could not have been obviated by cover. Moreover, the operation of the section on specific performance of contracts for "unique" goods must be considered in this connection for availability of the goods to the particular buyer for his particular needs is the test for that remedy and inability to cover is made an express condition to the right of the buyer to replevy the goods.

4. This section does not limit cover to merchants, in the first instance. It is the vital and important remedy for the consumer buyer as well. Both are free to use cover: the domestic or non-merchant consumer is required only to act in normal good faith while the merchant buyer must also observe all reasonable commercial standards of fair dealing in the trade, since this falls within the definition of good faith on his part.

Cross References:

Point 1: Section 2–706.

Point 2: Section 1–204.

Point 3: Sections 2–713, 2–715 and 2–716.

Point 4: Section 1–203.

Definitional Cross References:

"Buyer". Section 2–103.

"Contract". Section 1–201.

"Good faith". Section 2–103.

"Goods". Section 2–105.

"Purchase". Section 1–201.

"Remedy". Section 1–201.

"Seller". Section 2–103.

§ 2.713. Buyer's Damages for Non-Delivery or Repudiation

(a) Subject to the provisions of this chapter with respect to proof of market price (Section 2.723), the measure of damages for non-delivery or repudiation by the seller is the difference between the market price at the time when the buyer learned of the breach and the contract price together with any incidental and consequential damages provided in this chapter (Section 2.715), but less expenses saved in consequence of the seller's breach.

(b) Market price is to be determined as of the place for tender or, in cases of rejection after arrival or revocation of acceptance, as of the place of arrival.

Acts 1967, 60th Leg., p. 2343, ch. 785, § 1, eff. Sept. 1, 1967.

Uniform Commercial Code Comment

Prior Uniform Statutory Provision:

Section 67(3), Uniform Sales Act.

Changes: Rewritten.

Purposes of Changes: To clarify the former rule so that:

1. The general baseline adopted in this section uses as a yardstick the market in which the buyer would have obtained cover had he sought that relief. So the place for measuring damages is the place of tender (or the place of arrival if the goods are rejected or their acceptance is revoked after reaching their destination) and the crucial time is the time at which the buyer learns of the breach.

2. The market or current price to be used in comparison with the contract price under this section is the price for goods of the same kind and in the same branch of trade.

3. When the current market price under this section is difficult to prove the section on determination and proof of market price is available to permit a showing of a comparable market price or, where no market price is available, evidence of spot sale prices is proper. Where the unavailability of a market price is caused by a scarcity of goods of the type involved, a good case is normally made for specific performance under this Article. Such scarcity conditions, moreover, indicate that the price has risen and under the section providing for liberal administration of remedies, opinion evidence as to the value of the goods would be admissible in the absence of a market price and a liberal construction of allowable consequential damages should also result.

4. This section carries forward the standard rule that the buyer must deduct from his damages any expenses saved as a result of the breach.

5. The present section provides a remedy which is completely alternative to cover under the preceding section and applies only when and to the extent that the buyer has not covered.

Cross References:

Point 3: Sections 1–106, 2–716 and 2–723.

Point 5: Section 2–712.

Definitional Cross References:

"Buyer". Section 2–103.

"Contract". Section 1–201.

"Seller". Section 2–103.

§ 2.714. Buyer's Damages for Breach in Regard to Accepted Goods

(a) Where the buyer has accepted goods and given notification (Subsection (c) of Section 2.607) he may recover as damages for any non-conformity of tender the loss resulting in the ordinary course of events from the seller's breach as determined in any manner which is reasonable.

(b) The measure of damages for breach of warranty is the difference at the time and place of acceptance between the value of the goods accepted and the value they would have had if they had been as warranted, unless special circumstances show proximate damages of a different amount.

(c) In a proper case any incidental and consequential damages under the next section may also be recovered.

Acts 1967, 60th Leg., p. 2343, ch. 785, § 1, eff. Sept. 1, 1967.

Uniform Commercial Code Comment

Prior Uniform Statutory Provision:

Section 69(6) and (7), Uniform Sales Act.

Changes: Rewritten.

Purposes of Changes:

1. This section deals with the remedies available to the buyer after the goods have been accepted and the time for revocation of acceptance has gone by. In general this section adopts the rule of the prior uniform statutory provision for measuring damages where there has been a breach of warranty as to goods accepted, but goes further to lay down an explicit provision as to the time and place for determining the loss.

The section on deduction of damages from price provides an additional remedy for a buyer who still owes part of the purchase price, and frequently the two remedies will be available concurrently. The buyer's failure to notify of his claim under the section on effects of acceptance, however, operates to bar his remedies under either that section or the present section.

2. The "non-conformity" referred to in subsection (1) includes not only breaches of warranties but also any failure of the seller to perform according to his obligations under the contract. In the case of such non-conformity, the buyer is permitted to recover for his loss "in any manner which is reasonable."

3. Subsection (2) describes the usual, standard and reasonable method of ascertaining damages in the case of breach of warranty but it is not intended as an exclusive measure. It departs from the measure of damages for non-delivery in utilizing the place of acceptance rather than the place of tender. In some cases the two may coincide, as where the buyer signifies his acceptance upon the tender. If, however, the non-conformity is such as would justify revocation of acceptance, the time and place of acceptance under this section is determined as of the buyer's decision not to revoke.

4. The incidental and consequential damages referred to in subsection (3), which will usually accompany an action brought under this section, are discussed in detail in the comment on the next section.

Cross References:

Point 1: Compare Section 2–711; Sections 2–607 and 2–717.

Point 2: Section 2–106.

Point 3: Sections 2–608 and 2–713.

Point 4: Section 2–715.

Definitional Cross References:

"Buyer". Section 2–103.

"Conform". Section 2–106.

"Goods". Section 1–201.

"Notification". Section 1–201.

"Seller". Section 2–103.

§ 2.715. Buyer's Incidental and Consequential Damages

(a) Incidental damages resulting from the seller's breach include expenses reasonably incurred in inspection, receipt, transportation and care and custody of goods rightfully rejected, any commercially reasonable charges, expenses or commissions in connection with effecting cover and any other reasonable expense incident to the delay or other breach.

(b) Consequential damages resulting from the seller's breach include

(1) any loss resulting from general or particular requirements and needs of which the seller at the time of contracting had reason to know and which could not reasonably be prevented by cover or otherwise; and

(2) injury to person or property proximately resulting from any breach of warranty.

Acts 1967, 60th Leg., p. 2343, ch. 785, § 1, eff. Sept. 1, 1967.

Uniform Commercial Code Comment

Prior Uniform Statutory Provisions: Subsection (2)(b)—Sections 69(7) and 70, Uniform Sales Act.

Changes: Rewritten.

Purposes of Changes and New Matter:

1. Subsection (1) is intended to provide reimbursement for the buyer who incurs reasonable expenses in connection with the handling of rightfully rejected goods or goods whose acceptance may be justifiably revoked, or in connection with effecting cover where the breach of the contract lies in non-conformity or non-delivery of the goods. The incidental damages listed are not intended to be exhaustive but are merely illustrative of the typical kinds of incidental damage.

2. Subsection (2) operates to allow the buyer, in an appropriate case, any consequential damages which are the result of the seller's breach. The "tacit agreement" test for the recovery of consequential damages is rejected. Although the older rule at common law which made the seller liable for all consequential damages of which he had "reason to know" in advance is followed, the liberality of that rule is modified by refusing to permit recovery unless the buyer could not reasonably have prevented the loss by cover or otherwise. Subparagraph (2) carries forward the provisions of the prior uniform statutory provision as to consequential damages resulting from breach of warranty, but modifies the rule by requiring first that the buyer attempt to minimize his damages in good faith, either by cover or otherwise.

3. In the absence of excuse under the section on merchant's excuse by failure of presupposed conditions, the seller

is liable for consequential damages in all cases where he had reason to know of the buyer's general or particular requirements at the time of contracting. It is not necessary that there be a conscious acceptance of an insurer's liability on the seller's part, nor is his obligation for consequential damages limited to cases in which he fails to use due effort in good faith.

Particular needs of the buyer must generally be made known to the seller while general needs must rarely be made known to charge the seller with knowledge.

Any seller who does not wish to take the risk of consequential damages has available the section on contractual limitation of remedy.

4. The burden of proving the extent of loss incurred by way of consequential damage is on the buyer, but the section on liberal administration of remedies rejects any doctrine of certainty which requires almost mathematical precision in the proof of loss. Loss may be determined in any manner which is reasonable under the circumstances.

5. Subsection (2)(b) states the usual rule as to breach of warranty, allowing recovery for injuries "proximately" resulting from the breach. Where the injury involved follows the use of goods without discovery of the defect causing the damage, the question of "proximate" cause turns on whether it was reasonable for the buyer to use the goods without such inspection as would have revealed the defects. If it was not reasonable for him to do so, or if he did in fact discover the defect prior to his use, the injury would not proximately result from the breach of warranty.

6. In the case of sale of wares to one in the business of reselling them, resale is one of the requirements of which the seller has reason to know within the meaning of subsection (2)(a).

Cross References:

Point 1: Section 2–608.

Point 3: Sections 1–203, 2–615 and 2–719.

Point 4: Section 1–106.

Definitional Cross References:

"Cover". Section 2–712.

"Goods". Section 1–201.

"Person". Section 1–201.

"Receipt" of goods. Section 2–103.

"Seller". Section 2–103.

§ 2.716. Buyer's Right to Specific Performance or Replevin

(a) Specific performance may be decreed where the goods are unique or in other proper circumstances.

(b) The decree for specific performance may include such terms and conditions as to payment of the price, damages, or other relief as the court may deem just.

(c) The buyer has a right of replevin for goods identified to the contract if after reasonable effort he is unable to effect cover for such goods or the circumstances reasonably indicate that such effort will be unavailing or if the goods have been shipped under reservation and satisfaction of the security interest in them has been made or tendered. In the case of goods bought for personal, family, or household purposes, the buyer's right of replevin vests upon acquisition of a special property, even if the seller had not then repudiated or failed to deliver.

Acts 1967, 60th Leg., p. 2343, ch. 785, § 1, eff. Sept. 1, 1967. Amended by Acts 1999, 76th Leg., ch. 414, § 2.18, eff. July 1, 2001.

Uniform Commercial Code Comment

1999 Amendment (effective July 1, 2001)

Prior Uniform Statutory Provision:

Section 68, Uniform Sales Act.

Changes:

Rephrased.

Purposes of Changes:

To make it clear that:

1. The present section continues in general prior policy as to specific performance and injunction against breach. However, without intending to impair in any way the exercise of the court's sound discretion in the matter, this Article seeks to further a more liberal attitude than some courts have shown in connection with the specific performance of contracts of sale.

2. In view of this Article's emphasis on the commercial feasibility of replacement, a new concept of what are "unique" goods is introduced under this section. Specific performance is no longer limited to goods which are already specific or ascertained at the time of contracting. The test of uniqueness under this section must be made in terms of the total situation which characterizes the contract. Output and requirements contracts involving a particular or peculiarly available source or market present today the typical commercial specific performance situation, as contrasted with contracts for the sale of heirlooms or priceless works of art which were usually involved in the older cases. However, uniqueness is not the sole basis of the remedy under this section for the relief may also be granted "in other proper circumstances" and inability to cover is strong evidence of "other proper circumstances".

3. The legal remedy of replevin is given to the buyer in cases in which cover is reasonably unavailable and goods have been identified to the contract. This is in addition to the buyer's right to recover identified goods under Section 2–502. For consumer goods, the buyer's right to replevin vests upon the buyer's acquisition of a special property, which occurs upon identification of the goods to the contract. See Section 2–501. Inasmuch as a secured party normally acquires no greater rights in its collateral that its debtor had or had power to convey, see Section 2–403(1)(first sentence), a buyer who acquires a right of replevin under subsection (3) will take free of a security interest created by the seller if it attaches to the goods after the goods have been identified to

the contract. The buyer will take free, even if the buyer does not buy in ordinary course and even if the security interest is perfected. Of course, to the extent that the buyer pays the price after the security interest attaches, the payments will constitute proceeds of the security interest.

4. This section is intended to give the buyer rights to the goods comparable to the seller's rights to the price.

5. If a negotiable document of title is outstanding, the buyer's right of replevin relates of course to the document not directly to the goods. See Article 7, especially Section 7–602.

Cross References:

Point 3: Section 2–502.

Point 4: Section 2–709.

Point 5: Article 7.

Definitional Cross References:

"Buyer". Section 2–103.

"Goods". Section 1–201.

"Rights". Section 1–201.

§ 2.717. Deduction of Damages from the Price

The buyer on notifying the seller of his intention to do so may deduct all or any part of the damages resulting from any breach of the contract from any part of the price still due under the same contract.

Acts 1967, 60th Leg., p. 2343, ch. 785, § 1, eff. Sept. 1, 1967.

Uniform Commercial Code Comment

Prior Uniform Statutory Provision:

See Section 69(1)(a), Uniform Sales Act.

Purposes:

1. This section permits the buyer to deduct from the price damages resulting from any breach by the seller and does not limit the relief to cases of breach of warranty as did the prior uniform statutory provision. To bring this provision into application the breach involved must be of the same contract under which the price in question is claimed to have been earned.

2. The buyer, however, must give notice of his intention to withhold all or part of the price if he wishes to avoid a default within the meaning of the section on insecurity and right to assurances. In conformity with the general policies of this Article, no formality of notice is required and any language which reasonably indicates the buyer's reason for holding up his payment is sufficient.

Cross Reference:

Point 2: Section 2–609.

Definitional Cross References:

"Buyer". Section 2–103.

"Notifies". Section 1–201.

§ 2.718. Liquidation or Limitation of Damages; Deposits

(a) Damages for breach by either party may be liquidated in the agreement but only at an amount which is reasonable in the light of the anticipated or actual harm caused by the breach, the difficulties of proof of loss, and the inconvenience or non-feasibility of otherwise obtaining an adequate remedy. A term fixing unreasonably large liquidated damages is void as a penalty.

(b) Where the seller justifiably withholds delivery of goods because of the buyer's breach, the buyer is entitled to restitution of any amount by which the sum of his payments exceeds

(1) the amount to which the seller is entitled by virtue of terms liquidating the seller's damages in accordance with Subsection (a), or

(2) in the absence of such terms, twenty percent of the value of the total performance for which the buyer is obligated under the contract or $500, whichever is smaller.

(c) The buyer's right to restitution under Subsection (b) is subject to offset to the extent that the seller establishes

(1) a right to recover damages under the provisions of this chapter other than Subsection (a), and

(2) the amount or value of any benefits received by the buyer directly or indirectly by reason of the contract.

(d) Where a seller has received payment in goods their reasonable value or the proceeds of their resale shall be treated as payments for the purposes of Subsection (b); but if the seller has notice of the buyer's breach before reselling goods received in part performance, his resale is subject to the conditions laid down in this chapter on resale by an aggrieved seller (Section 2.706).

Acts 1967, 60th Leg., p. 2343, ch. 785, § 1, eff. Sept. 1, 1967.

Uniform Commercial Code Comment

Prior Uniform Statutory Provision:

None.

Purposes:

1. Under subsection (1) liquidated damage clauses are allowed where the amount involved is reasonable in the light of the circumstances of the case. The subsection sets forth explicitly the elements to be considered in determining the reasonableness of a liquidated damage clause. A term fixing unreasonably large liquidated damages is expressly made void as a penalty. An unreasonably small amount would be

subject to similar criticism and might be stricken under the section on unconscionable contracts or clauses.

2. Subsection (2) refuses to recognize a forfeiture unless the amount of the payment so forfeited represents a reasonable liquidation of damages as determined under subsection (1). A special exception is made in the case of small amounts (20% of the price or $500, whichever is smaller) deposited as security. No distinction is made between cases in which the payment is to be applied on the price and those in which it is intended as security for performance. Subsection (2) is applicable to any deposit or down or part payment. In the case of a deposit or turn in of goods resold before the breach, the amount actually received on the resale is to be viewed as the deposit rather than the amount allowed the buyer for the trade in. However, if the seller knows of the breach prior to the resale of the goods turned in, he must make reasonable efforts to realize their true value, and this is assured by requiring him to comply with the conditions laid down in the section on resale by an aggrieved seller.

Cross References:

Point 1: Section 2–302.

Point 2: Section 2–706.

Definitional Cross References:

"Aggrieved party". Section 1–201.

"Agreement". Section 1–201.

"Buyer". Section 2–103.

"Goods". Section 2–105.

"Notice". Section 1–201.

"Party". Section 1–201.

"Remedy". Section 1–201.

"Seller". Section 2–103.

"Term". Section 1–201.

§ 2.719. Contractual Modification or Limitation of Remedy

(a) Subject to the provisions of Subsections (b) and (c) of this section and of the preceding section on liquidation and limitation of damages,

(1) the agreement may provide for remedies in addition to or in substitution for those provided in this chapter and may limit or alter the measure of damages recoverable under this chapter, as by limiting the buyer's remedies to return of the goods and repayment of the price or to repair and replacement of non-conforming goods or parts; and

(2) resort to a remedy as provided is optional unless the remedy is expressly agreed to be exclusive, in which case it is the sole remedy.

(b) Where circumstances cause an exclusive or limited remedy to fail of its essential purpose, remedy may be had as provided in this title.

(c) Consequential damages may be limited or excluded unless the limitation or exclusion is unconscionable. Limitation of consequential damages for injury to the person in the case of consumer goods is prima facie unconscionable but limitation of damages where the loss is commercial is not.

Acts 1967, 60th Leg., p. 2343, ch. 785, § 1, eff. Sept. 1, 1967.

Uniform Commercial Code Comment

Prior Uniform Statutory Provision:

None.

Purposes:

1. Under this section parties are left free to shape their remedies to their particular requirements and reasonable agreements limiting or modifying remedies are to be given effect.

However, it is of the very essence of a sales contract that at least minimum adequate remedies be available. If the parties intend to conclude a contract for sale within this Article they must accept the legal consequence that there be at least a fair quantum of remedy for breach of the obligations or duties outlined in the contract. Thus any clause purporting to modify or limit the remedial provisions of this Article in an unconscionable manner is subject to deletion and in that event the remedies made available by this Article are applicable as if the stricken clause had never existed. Similarly, under subsection (2), where an apparently fair and reasonable clause because of circumstances fails in its purpose or operates to deprive either party of the substantial value of the bargain, it must give way to the general remedy provisions of this Article.

2. Subsection (1)(b) creates a presumption that clauses prescribing remedies are cumulative rather than exclusive. If the parties intend the term to describe the sole remedy under the contract, this must be clearly expressed.

3. Subsection (3) recognizes the validity of clauses limiting or excluding consequential damages but makes it clear that they may not operate in an unconscionable manner. Actually such terms are merely an allocation of unknown or undeterminable risks. The seller in all cases is free to disclaim warranties in the manner provided in Section 2–316.

Cross References:

Point 1: Section 2–302.

Point 3: Section 2–316.

Definitional Cross References:

"Agreement". Section 1–201.

"Buyer". Section 2–103.

"Conforming". Section 2–106.

"Contract". Section 1–201.

"Goods". Section 2–105.

"Remedy". Section 1–201.

"Seller". Section 2–103.

§ 2.720. Effect of "Cancellation" or "Rescission" on Claims for Antecedent Breach

Unless the contrary intention clearly appears, expressions of "cancellation" or "rescission" of the contract or the like shall not be construed as a renunciation or discharge of any claim in damages for an antecedent breach.

Acts 1967, 60th Leg., p. 2343, ch. 785, § 1, eff. Sept. 1, 1967.

Uniform Commercial Code Comment

Prior Uniform Statutory Provision:

None.

Purpose:

This section is designed to safeguard a person holding a right of action from any unintentional loss of rights by the ill-advised use of such terms as "cancellation", "rescission", or the like. Once a party's rights have accrued they are not to be lightly impaired by concessions made in business decency and without intention to forego them. Therefore, unless the cancellation of a contract expressly declares that it is "without reservation of rights", or the like, it cannot be considered to be a renunciation under this section.

Cross Reference:

Section 1–107.

Definitional Cross References:

"Cancellation". Section 2–106.

"Contract". Section 1–201.

§ 2.721. Remedies for Fraud

Remedies for material misrepresentation or fraud include all remedies available under this chapter for non-fraudulent breach. Neither rescission or a claim for rescission of the contract for sale nor rejection or return of the goods shall bar or be deemed inconsistent with a claim for damages or other remedy.

Acts 1967, 60th Leg., p. 2343, ch. 785, § 1, eff. Sept. 1, 1967.

Uniform Commercial Code Comment

Prior Uniform Statutory Provision:

None.

Purposes:

To correct the situation by which remedies for fraud have been more circumscribed than the more modern and mercantile remedies for breach of warranty. Thus the remedies for fraud are extended by this section to coincide in scope with those for non-fraudulent breach. This section thus makes it clear that neither rescission of the contract for fraud nor rejection of the goods bars other remedies unless the circumstances of the case make the remedies incompatible.

Definitional Cross References:

"Contract for sale". Section 2–106.

"Goods". Section 1–201.

"Remedy". Section 1–201.

§ 2.722. Who Can Sue Third Parties for Injury to Goods

Where a third party so deals with goods which have been identified to a contract for sale as to cause actionable injury to a party to that contract

(1) a right of action against the third party is in either party to the contract for sale who has title to or a security interest or a special property or an insurable interest in the goods; and if the goods have been destroyed or converted a right of action is also in the party who either bore the risk of loss under the contract for sale or has since the injury assumed that risk as against the other;

(2) if at the time of the injury the party plaintiff did not bear the risk of loss as against the other party to the contract for sale and there is no arrangement between them for disposition of the recovery, his suit or settlement is, subject to his own interest, as a fiduciary for the other party to the contract;

(3) either party may with the consent of the other sue for the benefit of whom it may concern.

Acts 1967, 60th Leg., p. 2343, ch. 785, § 1, eff. Sept. 1, 1967.

Uniform Commercial Code Comment

Prior Uniform Statutory Provision:

None.

Purposes: To adopt and extend somewhat the principle of the statutes which provide for suit by the real party in interest. The provisions of this section apply only after identification of the goods. Prior to that time only the seller has a right of action. During the period between identification and final acceptance (except in the case of revocation of acceptance) it is possible for both parties to have the right of action. Even after final acceptance both parties may have the right of action if the seller retains possession or otherwise retains an interest.

Definitional Cross References:

"Action". Section 1–201.

"Buyer". Section 2–103.

"Contract for sale". Section 2–106.

"Goods". Section 2–105.

"Party". Section 1–201.

"Rights". Section 1–201.

"Security interest". Section 1–201.

§ 2.723. Proof of Market Price: Time and Place

(a) If an action based on anticipatory repudiation comes to trial before the time for performance with respect to some or all of the goods, any damages based on market price (Section 2.708 or Section 2.713) shall be determined according to the price of such goods prevailing at the time when the aggrieved party learned of the repudiation.

(b) If evidence of a price prevailing at the times or places described in this chapter is not readily available the price prevailing within any reasonable time before or after the time described or at any other place which in commercial judgment or under usage of trade would serve as a reasonable substitute for the one described may be used, making any proper allowance for the cost of transporting the goods to or from such other place.

(c) Evidence of a relevant price prevailing at a time or place other than the one described in this chapter offered by one party is not admissible unless and until he has given the other party such notice as the court finds sufficient to prevent unfair surprise.

Acts 1967, 60th Leg., p. 2343, ch. 785, § 1, eff. Sept. 1, 1967.

Uniform Commercial Code Comment

Prior Uniform Statutory Provision:

None.

Purposes: To eliminate the most obvious difficulties arising in connection with the determination of market price, when that is stipulated as a measure of damages by some provision of this Article. Where the appropriate market price is not readily available the court is here granted reasonable leeway in receiving evidence of prices current in other comparable markets or at other times comparable to the one in question. In accordance with the general principle of this Article against surprise, however, a party intending to offer evidence of such a substitute price must give suitable notice to the other party.

This section is not intended to exclude the use of any other reasonable method of determining market price or of measuring damages if the circumstances of the case make this necessary.

Definitional Cross References:

"Action". Section 1–201.

"Aggrieved party". Section 1–201.

"Goods". Section 2–105.

"Notifies". Section 1–201.

"Party". Section 1–201.

"Reasonable time". Section 1–204.

"Usage of trade". Section 1–205.

§ 2.724. Admissibility of Market Quotations

Whenever the prevailing price or value of any goods regularly bought and sold in any established commodity market is in issue, reports in official publications or trade journals or in newspapers or periodicals of general circulation published as the reports of such market shall be admissible in evidence. The circumstances of the preparation of such a report may be shown to affect its weight but not its admissibility.

Acts 1967, 60th Leg., p. 2343, ch. 785, § 1, eff. Sept. 1, 1967.

Uniform Commercial Code Comment

Prior Uniform Statutory Provision:

None.

Purposes: To make market quotations admissible in evidence while providing for a challenge of the material by showing the circumstances of its preparation.

No explicit provision as to the weight to be given to market quotations is contained in this section, but such quotations, in the absence of compelling challenge, offer an adequate basis for a verdict.

Market quotations are made admissible when the price or value of goods traded "in any established market" is in issue. The reason of the section does not require that the market be closely organized in the manner of a produce exchange. It is sufficient if transactions in the commodity are frequent and open enough to make a market established by usage in which one price can be expected to affect another and in which an informed report of the range and trend of prices can be assumed to be reasonably accurate.

This section does not in any way intend to limit or negate the application of similar rules of admissibility to other material, whether by action of the courts or by statute. The purpose of the present section is to assure a minimum of mercantile administration in this important situation and not to limit any liberalizing trend in modern law.

Definitional Cross Reference:

"Goods". Section 2–105.

§ 2.725. Statute of Limitations in Contracts for Sale

(a) An action for breach of any contract for sale must be commenced within four years after the cause of action has accrued. By the original agreement the parties may reduce the period of limitation to not less than one year but may not extend it.

(b) A cause of action accrues when the breach occurs, regardless of the aggrieved party's lack of knowledge of the breach. A breach of warranty occurs when tender of delivery is made, except that where a warranty explicitly extends to future performance of the goods and discovery of the breach must await the time of such performance the cause of action accrues when the breach is or should have been discovered.

(c) Where an action commenced within the time limited by Subsection (a) is so terminated as to leave available a remedy by another action for the same breach such other action may be commenced after the expiration of the time limited and within six months after the termination of the first action unless the termination resulted from voluntary discontinuance or from dismissal for failure or neglect to prosecute.

(d) This section does not alter the law on tolling of the statute of limitations nor does it apply to causes of action which have accrued before this title becomes effective.

Acts 1967, 60th Leg., p. 2343, ch. 785, § 1, eff. Sept. 1, 1967.

Uniform Commercial Code Comment

Prior Uniform Statutory Provision:

None.

Purposes: To introduce a uniform statute of limitations for sales contracts, thus eliminating the jurisdictional variations and providing needed relief for concerns doing business on a nationwide scale whose contracts have heretofore been governed by several different periods of limitation depending upon the state in which the transaction occurred. This Article takes sales contracts out of the general laws limiting the time for commencing contractual actions and selects a four year period as the most appropriate to modern business practice. This is within the normal commercial record keeping period.

Subsection (1) permits the parties to reduce the period of limitation. The minimum period is set at one year. The parties may not, however, extend the statutory period.

Subsection (2), providing that the cause of action accrues when the breach occurs, states an exception where the warranty extends to future performance.

Subsection (3) states the saving provision included in many state statutes and permits an additional short period for bringing new actions, where suits begun within the four year period have been terminated so as to leave a remedy still available for the same breach.

Subsection (4) makes it clear that this Article does not purport to alter or modify in any respect the law on tolling of the Statute of Limitations as it now prevails in the various jurisdictions.

Definitional Cross References:

"Action". Section 1–201.

"Aggrieved party". Section 1–201.

"Agreement". Section 1–201.

"Contract for sale". Section 2–106.

"Goods". Section 2–105.

"Party". Section 1–201.

"Remedy". Section 1–201.

"Term". Section 1–201.

"Termination". Section 2–106.

CHAPTER 2A. LEASES

SUBCHAPTER A. GENERAL PROVISIONS

SUBCHAPTER B. FORMATION AND CONSTRUCTION OF LEASE CONTRACT

SUBCHAPTER C. EFFECT OF LEASE CONTRACT

SUBCHAPTER A. GENERAL PROVISIONS

§ 2A.101. Short Title

This chapter shall be known and may be cited as the Uniform Commercial Code—Leases.

Added by Acts 1993, 73rd Leg., ch. 570, § 1, eff. Sept. 1, 1993.

Uniform Commercial Code Comment

Rationale for Codification:

There are several reasons for codifying the law with respect to leases of goods. An analysis of the case law as it applies to leases of goods suggests at least three significant issues to be resolved by codification. First, what is a lease? It is necessary to define lease to determine whether a transaction creates a lease or a security interest disguised as a lease. If the transaction creates a security interest disguised as a lease, the lessor will be required to file a financing statement or take other action to perfect its interest in the goods against third parties. There is no such requirement with respect to leases. Yet the distinction between a lease and a security interest disguised as a lease is not clear. Second, will the lessor be deemed to have made warranties to the lessee? If the transaction is a sale the express and implied warranties of Article 2 of the Uniform Commercial Code apply. However, the warranty law with respect to leases is uncertain. Third, what remedies are available to the lessor upon the lessee's default? If the transaction is a security interest disguised as a lease, the answer is stated in Part 5 of the Article on Secured Transactions (Article 9). There is no clear answer with respect to leases.

There are reasons to codify the law with respect to leases of goods in addition to those suggested by a review of the reported cases. The answer to this important question should not be limited to the issues raised in these cases. Is it not also proper to determine the remedies available to the lessee upon the lessor's default? It is, but that issue is not reached through a review of the reported cases. This is only one of the many issues presented in structuring, negotiating and documenting a lease of goods.

Statutory Analogue:

After it was decided to proceed with the codification project, the drafting committee of the National Conference of Commissioners on Uniform State Laws looked for a statutory analogue, gradually narrowing the focus to the Article on Sales (Article 2) and the Article on Secured Transactions (Article 9). A review of the literature with respect to the sale of goods reveals that Article 2 is predicated upon certain assumptions: Parties to the sales transaction frequently are without counsel; the agreement of the parties often is oral or evidenced by scant writings; obligations between the parties are bilateral; applicable law is influenced by the need to preserve freedom of contract. A review of the literature with respect to personal property security law reveals that Article 9 is predicated upon very different assumptions: Parties to a secured transaction regularly are represented by counsel; the agreement of the parties frequently is reduced to a writing, extensive in scope; the obligations between the parties are essentially unilateral; and applicable law seriously limits freedom of contract.

The lease is closer in spirit and form to the sale of goods than to the creation of a security interest. While parties to a lease are sometimes represented by counsel and their agreement is often reduced to a writing, the obligations of the parties are bilateral and the common law of leasing is dominated by the need to preserve freedom of contract. Thus the drafting committee concluded that Article 2 was the appropriate statutory analogue.

Issues:

The drafting committee then identified and resolved several issues critical to codification:

Scope: The scope of the Article was limited to leases (Section 2A–102). There was no need to include leases intended as security, *i.e.*, security interests disguised as leases, as they are adequately treated in Article 9. Further, even if leases intended as security were included, the need to preserve the distinction would remain, as policy suggests treatment significantly different from that accorded leases.

Definition of Lease: Lease was defined to exclude leases intended as security (Section 2A–103(1)(j)). Given the litigation to date a revised definition of security interest was suggested for inclusion in the Act. (Section 1–201(37)). This revision sharpens the distinction between leases and security interests disguised as leases.

Filing: The lessor was not required to file a financing statement against the lessee or take any other action to protect the lessor's interest in the goods (Section 2A–301). The refined definition of security interest will more clearly signal the need to file to potential lessors of goods. Those lessors who are concerned will file a protective financing statement (Section 9–408).

Warranties: All of the express and implied warranties of the Article on Sales (Article 2) were included (Sections 2A–210 through 2A–216), revised to reflect differences in lease transactions. The lease of goods is sufficiently similar to the sale of goods to justify this decision. Further, many courts have reached the same decision.

Certificate of Title Laws: Many leasing transactions involve goods subject to certificate of title statutes. To avoid conflict with those statutes, this Article is subject to them (Section 2A–104(1)(a)).

Consumer Leases: Many leasing transactions involve parties subject to consumer protection statutes or decisions. To avoid conflict with those laws this Article is subject to them to the extent provided in (Section 2A–104(1)(c) and (2)). Further, certain consumer protections have been incorporated in the Article.

Finance Leases: Certain leasing transactions substitute the supplier of the goods for the lessor as the party responsible to the lessee with respect to warranties and the like. The definition of finance lease (Section 2A–103(1)(g)) was developed to describe these transactions. Various sections of the Article implement the substitution of the supplier for the lessor, including Sections 2A–209 and 2A–407. No attempt was made to fashion a special rule where the finance lessor is an affiliate of the supplier of goods; this is to be developed by the courts, case by case.

Sale and Leaseback: Sale and leaseback transactions are becoming increasingly common. A number of state statutes treat transactions where possession is retained by the seller as fraudulent *per se* or *prima facie* fraudulent. That position is not in accord with modern practice and thus is changed by the Article "if the buyer bought for value and in good faith" (Section 2A–308(3)).

Remedies: The Article has not only provided for lessor's remedies upon default by the lessee (Sections 2A–523 through 2A–531), but also for lessee's remedies upon default by the lessor (Sections 2A–508 through 2A–522). This is a significant departure from Article 9, which provides remedies only for the secured party upon default by the debtor. This difference is compelled by the bilateral nature of the obligations between the parties to a lease.

Damages: Many leasing transactions are predicated on the parties' ability to stipulate an appropriate measure of damages in the event of default. The rule with respect to sales of goods (Section 2–718) is not sufficiently flexible to accommodate this practice. Consistent with the common law emphasis upon freedom to contract, the Article has created a revised rule that allows greater flexibility with respect to leases of goods (Section 2A–504(1)).

History:

This Article is a revision of the Uniform Personal Property Leasing Act, which was approved by the National Conference of Commissioners on Uniform State Laws in August, 1985. However, it was believed that the subject matter of the Uniform Personal Property Leasing Act would be better treated as an article of this Act. Thus, although the Conference promulgated the Uniform Personal Property Leasing Act as a Uniform Law, activity was held in abeyance to allow time to restate the Uniform Personal Property Leasing Act as Article 2A.

In August, 1986 the Conference approved and recommended this Article (including conforming amendments to Article 1 and Article 9) for promulgation as an amendment to this Act. In December, 1986 the Council of the American Law Institute approved and recommended this Article (including conforming amendments to Article 1 and Article 9), with official comments, for promulgation as an amendment to this Act. In March, 1987 the Permanent Editorial Board for the Uniform Commercial Code approved and recommended this Article (including conforming amendments to Article 1 and Article 9), with official comments, for promulgation as an amendment to this Act. In May, 1987 the American Law Institute approved and recommended this Article (including conforming amendments to Article 1 and Article 9), with official comments, for promulgation as an amendment to this Act. In August, 1987 the Conference confirmed its approval of the final text of this Article.

Upon its initial promulgation, Article 2A was rapidly enacted in several states, was introduced in a number of other states, and underwent bar association, law revision commission and legislative study in still further states. In that process debate emerged, principally sparked by the study of Article 2A by the California Bar Association, California's non-uniform amendments to Article 2A, and articles appearing in a symposium on Article 2A published after its promulgation in the Alabama Law Review. The debate chiefly centered on whether Article 2A had struck the proper balance or was clear enough concerning the ability of a lessor to grant a security interest in its leasehold interest and in the residual, priority between a secured party and the lessee, and the lessor's remedy structure under Article 2A.

This debate over issues on which reasonable minds could and did differ began to affect the enactment effort for Article 2A in a deleterious manner. Consequently, the Standby Committee for Article 2A, composed predominantly of the former members of the drafting committee, reviewed the legislative actions and studies in the various states, and opened a dialogue with the principal proponents of the non-uniform amendments. Negotiations were conducted in conjunction with, and were facilitated by, a study of the uniform Article and the non-uniform Amendments by the New York Law Revision Commission. Ultimately, a consensus was reached, which has been approved by the membership of the Conference, the Permanent Editorial Board, and the Council of the Institute. Rapid and uniform enactment of Article 2A is expected as a result of the completed amendments. The Article 2A experience reaffirms the essential viability of the procedures of the Conference and the Institute for creating and updating uniform state law in the commercial law area.

Relationship of Article 2A to Other Articles:

The Article on Sales provided a useful point of reference for codifying the law of leases. Many of the provisions of that Article were carried over, changed to reflect differences in style, leasing terminology or leasing practices. Thus, the official comments to those sections of Article 2 whose provisions were carried over are incorporated by reference in Article 2A, as well; further, any case law interpreting those provisions should be viewed as persuasive but not binding on a court when deciding a similar issue with respect to leases. Any change in the sequence that has been made when carrying over a provision from Article 2 should be viewed as a matter of style, not substance. This is not to suggest that in other instances Article 2A did not also incorporate substantially revised provisions of Article 2, Article 9 or otherwise where the revision was driven by a concern over the substance; but for the lack of a mandate, the drafting committee might well have made the same or a similar change in the statutory analogue. Those sections in Article 2A include Sections 2A–104, 2A–105, 2A–106, 2A–108(2) and (4), 2A–109(2), 2A–208, 2A–214(2) and (3)(a), 2A–216, 2A–303, 2A–306, 2A–503, 2A–504(3)(b), 2A–506(2), and 2A–515. For lack of relevance or significance not all of the provisions of Article 2 were incorporated in Article 2A.

This codification was greatly influenced by the fundamental tenet of the common law as it has developed with respect to leases of goods: freedom of the parties to contract. Note that, like all other Articles of this Act, the principles of construction and interpretation contained in Article 1 are applicable throughout Article 2A (Section 2A–103(4)). These principles include the ability of the parties to vary the effect of the provisions of Article 2A, subject to certain limitations including those that relate to the obligations of good faith, diligence, reasonableness and care (Section 1–102(3)). Consistent with those principles no negative inference is to be drawn by the episodic use of the phrase "unless otherwise agreed" in certain provisions of Article 2A. Section 1–102(4). Indeed, the contrary is true, as the general rule in the Act, including this Article, is that the effect of the Act's provisions may be varied by agreement. Section 1–102(3). This conclusion follows even where the statutory analogue contains the phrase and the correlative provision in Article 2A does not.

§ 2A.102. Scope

This chapter applies to any transaction, regardless of form, that creates a lease of goods. This chapter does not apply to a transaction that creates an interest in or lease of real estate, except to the extent that provision is made for leases of fixtures by Section 2A.309.

Added by Acts 1993, 73rd Leg., ch. 570, § 1, eff. Sept. 1, 1993.

Uniform Commercial Code Comment

Uniform Statutory Source: Section 9–102(1). Throughout this Article, unless otherwise stated, references to "Section" are to other sections of this Act.

Changes: Substantially revised.

Purposes: This Article governs transactions as diverse as the lease of a hand tool to an individual for a few hours and the leveraged lease of a complex line of industrial equipment to a multi-national organization for a number of years.

To achieve that end it was necessary to provide that this Article applies to any transaction, regardless of form, that creates a lease. Since lease is defined as a transfer of an interest in goods (Section 2A–103(1)(j)) and goods is defined to include fixtures (Section 2A–103(1)(h)), application is limited to the extent the transaction relates to goods, including fixtures. Further, since the definition of lease does not include a sale (Section 2–106(1)) or retention or creation of a security interest (Section 1–201(37)), application is further limited; sales and security interests are governed by other Articles of this Act.

Finally, in recognition of the diversity of the transactions to be governed, the sophistication of many of the parties to these transactions, and the common law tradition as it applies to the bailment for hire or lease, freedom of contract has been preserved. DeKoven, Proceedings After Default by the Lessee Under a True Lease of Equipment, in 1C P. Coogan, W. Hogan, D. Vagts, *Secured Transactions Under the Uniform Commercial Code,* § 29B.02[2] (1986). Thus, despite the extensive regulatory scheme established by this

Article, the parties to a lease will be able to create private rules to govern their transaction. Sections 2A–103(4) and 1–102(3). However, there are special rules in this Article governing consumer leases, as well as other state and federal statutes, that may further limit freedom of contract with respect to consumer leases.

A court may apply this Article by analogy to any transaction, regardless of form, that creates a lease of personal property other than goods, taking into account the expressed intentions of the parties to the transaction and any differences between a lease of goods and a lease of other property. Such application has precedent as the provisions of the Article on Sales (Article 2) have been applied by analogy to leases of goods. *E.g.*, Hawkland, *The Impact of the Uniform Commercial Code on Equipment Leasing*, 1972 Ill. L.F. 446; Murray, *Under the Spreading Analogy of Article 2 of the Uniform Commercial Code*, 39 Fordham L.Rev. 447 (1971). Whether such application would be appropriate for other bailments of personal property, gratuitous or for hire, should be determined by the facts of each case. *See Mieske v. Bartell Drug Co.*, 92 Wash.2d 40, 46–48, 593 P.2d 1308, 1312 (1979).

Further, parties to a transaction creating a lease of personal property other than goods, or a bailment of personal property may provide by agreement that this Article applies. Upholding the parties' choice is consistent with the spirit of this Article.

Cross References:

Sections 1–102(3), 1–201(37), Article 2, esp. Section 2–106(1), and Sections 2A–103(1)(h), 2A–103(1)(j) and 2A–103(4).

Definitional Cross Reference:

"Lease". Section 2A–103(1)(j).

State Bar Committee Comments

Chapter 2A is not intended to affect the existing and future judicial interpretations of the common law of this state relating to interests in or leases of real property, except to the extent the provisions of Section 2A.309 are applicable to leases of fixtures. A sentence to this effect has been added to Section 2A.102.

§ 2A.103. Definitions and Index of Definitions

(a) In this chapter unless the context otherwise requires:

(1) "Buyer in the ordinary course of business" means a person who in good faith and without knowledge that the sale to him or her is in violation of the ownership rights or security interest or leasehold interest of a third party in the goods buys in the ordinary course from a person in the business of selling goods of that kind but does not include a pawnbroker. "Buying" may be for cash or by exchange of other property or on secured or unsecured credit and includes acquiring goods or documents of title under a preexisting contract for sale but does not include a transfer in bulk or as security for or in total or partial satisfaction of a money debt.

(2) "Cancellation" occurs when either party puts an end to the lease contract for default by the other party.

(3) "Commercial unit" means a unit of goods as by commercial usage is a single whole for purposes of lease and division of which materially impairs its character or value on the market or in use. A commercial unit may be a single article, as a machine, or a set of articles, as a suite of furniture or a line of machinery, or a quantity, as a gross or carload, or any other unit treated in use or in the relevant market as a single whole.

(4) "Conforming" goods or performance under a lease contract means performance or goods that are in accordance with the obligations under the lease contract.

(5) "Consumer lease" means a lease that a lessor regularly engaged in the business of leasing or selling makes to a lessee who is an individual and who takes under the lease primarily for a personal, family, or household purpose, if the total payments to be made under the lease contract, excluding payments for options to renew or buy, do not exceed $25,000.

(6) "Fault" means a wrongful act, omission, breach, or default.

(7) "Finance lease" means a lease with respect to which:

(A) the lessor does not select, manufacture, or supply the goods;

(B) the lessor acquires the goods or the right to possession and use of the goods in connection with the lease; and

(C) one of the following occurs:

(i) the lessee receives a copy of the contract by which the lessor acquired the goods or the right to possession and use of the goods before signing the lease contract;

(ii) the lessee's approval of the contract by which the lessor acquired the goods or the right to possession and use of the goods is a condition to effectiveness of the lease contract;

(iii) the lessee, before signing the lease contract, receives an accurate and complete statement designating the promises and warranties, and any disclaimers of warranties, limitations or modifications of remedies, or liquidated damages, including those of a third party, such as the manufacturer of the goods, provided to the lessor by the person supplying the goods in connection with or as part of the contract by which the lessor acquired the goods or the right to possession and use of the goods; or

(iv) if the lease is not a consumer lease, the lessor, before the lessee signs the lease contract, informs the lessee in writing (a) of the identity of the person supplying the goods to the lessor, unless the lessee has selected that person and directed the lessor to acquire the goods or the right to possession and use of the goods from that person, (b) that the lessee is entitled under this chapter to the promises and warranties, including those of any third party, provided to the lessor by the person supplying the goods in connection with or as part of the contract by which the lessor acquired the goods or the right to possession and use of the goods, and (c) that the lessee may communicate with the person supplying the goods to the lessor and receive an accurate and complete statement of those promises and warranties, including any disclaimers and limitations of them or of remedies.

(8) "Goods" means all things that are moveable at the time of identification to the lease contract, or are fixtures (Section 2A.309), but the term does not include money, documents, instruments, accounts, chattel paper, general intangibles, or minerals or the like, including oil and gas, before extraction. The term also includes the unborn young of animals.

(9) "Installment lease contract" means a lease contract that authorizes or requires the delivery of goods in separate lots to be separately accepted, even though the lease contract contains the clause "each delivery is a separate lease" or its equivalent.

(10) "Lease" means a transfer of the right to possession and use of goods for a term in return for consideration, but a sale, including a sale on approval or a sale or return, or retention or creation of a security interest is not a lease. Unless the context clearly indicates otherwise, the term includes a sublease.

(11) "Lease agreement" means the bargain, with respect to the lease, of the lessor and the lessee in fact as found in their language or by implication from other circumstances including course of dealing or usage of trade or course of performance as provided by this chapter. Unless the context clearly indicates otherwise, the term includes a sublease agreement.

(12) "Lease contract" means the total legal obligation that results from the lease agreement as affected by this chapter and any other applicable rules of law. Unless the context clearly indicates otherwise, the term includes a sublease contract.

(13) "Leasehold interest" means the interest of the lessor or the lessee under a lease contract.

(14) "Lessee" means a person who acquires the right to possession and use of goods under a lease. Unless the context clearly indicates otherwise, the term includes a sublessee.

(15) "Lessee in ordinary course of business" means a person who in good faith and without knowledge that the lease to him or her is in violation of the ownership rights or security interest or leasehold interest of a third party in the goods, leases in ordinary course from a person in the business of selling or leasing goods of that kind but does not include a pawnbroker. "Leasing" may be for cash or by exchange of other property or on secured or unsecured credit and includes acquiring goods or documents of title under a preexisting lease contract but does not include a transfer in bulk or as security for or in total or partial satisfaction of a money debt.

(16) "Lessor" means a person who transfers the right to possession and use of goods under a lease. Unless the context clearly indicates otherwise, the term includes a sublessor.

(17) "Lessor's residual interest" means the lessor's interest in the goods after the expiration, termination, or cancellation of the lease contract.

(18) "Lien" means a charge against or interest in goods to secure payment of a debt or performance of an obligation, but the term does not include a security interest.

(19) "Lot" means a parcel or a single article that is the subject matter of a separate lease or delivery, whether or not it is sufficient to perform the lease contract.

(20) "Merchant lessee" means a lessee that is a merchant with respect to goods of the kind subject to the lease.

(21) "Present value" means the amount as of a date certain of one or more sums payable in the future, discounted to the date certain. The discount is determined by the interest rate specified by the parties if the rate was not manifestly unreasonable

at the time the transaction was entered into; otherwise, the discount is determined by a commercially reasonable rate that takes into account the facts and circumstances of each case at the time the transaction was entered into.

(22) "Purchase" includes taking by sale, lease, mortgage, security interest, pledge, gift, or any other voluntary transaction creating an interest in goods.

(23) "Sublease" means a lease of goods the right to possession and use of which was acquired by the lessor as a lessee under an existing lease.

(24) "Supplier" means a person from whom a lessor buys or leases goods to be leased under a finance lease.

(25) "Supply contract" means a contract under which a lessor buys or leases goods to be leased.

(26) "Termination" occurs when either party pursuant to a power created by agreement or law puts an end to the lease contract otherwise than for default.

(b) Other definitions applying to this chapter and the sections in which they appear are:

"Accessions". Section 2A.310(a).

"Construction mortgage". Section 2A.309(a)(4).

"Encumbrance". Section 2A.309(a)(5).

"Fixtures". Section 2A.309(a)(1).

"Fixture filing". Section 2A.309(a)(2).

"Purchase money lease". Section 2A.309(a)(3).

(c) The following definitions in other chapters apply to this chapter:

"Account". Section 9.102(a)(2).

"Between merchants". Section 2.104(c).

"Buyer". Section 2.103(a)(1).

"Chattel paper". Section 9.102(a)(11).

"Consumer goods". Section 9.102(a)(23).

"Document". Section 9.102(a)(30).

"Entrusting". Section 2.403(c).

"General intangible". Section 9.102(a)(42).

"Instrument". Section 9.102(a)(47).

"Merchant". Section 2.104(a).

"Mortgage". Section 9.102(a)(55).

"Pursuant to commitment". Section 9.102(a)(69).

"Receipt". Section 2.103(a)(3).

"Sale". Section 2.106(a).

"Sale on approval". Section 2.326.

"Sale or return". Section 2.326.

"Seller". Section 2.103(a)(4).

(d) In addition Chapter 1 contains general definitions and principles of construction and interpretation applicable throughout this chapter.

Added by Acts 1993, 73rd Leg., ch. 570, § 1, eff. Sept. 1, 1993. Amended by Acts 1999, 76th Leg., ch. 414, § 2.19, eff. July 1, 2001; Acts 2003, 78th Leg., ch. 542, § 4, eff. Sept. 1, 2003; Acts 2005, 79th Leg., ch. 122, § 13, eff. Sept. 1, 2005.

Uniform Commercial Code Comment

(a) "Buyer in ordinary course of business". Section 1–201(9).

(b) "Cancellation". Section 2–106(4). The effect of a cancellation is provided in Section 2A–505(1).

(c) "Commercial unit". Section 2–105(6).

(d) "Conforming". Section 2–106(2).

(e) "Consumer lease". New. This Article includes a subset of rules that applies only to consumer leases. Sections 2A–106, 2A–108(2), 2A–108(4), 2A–109(2), 2A–221, 2A–309, 2A–406, 2A–407, 2A–504(3)(b), and 2A–516(3)(b).

For a transaction to qualify as a consumer lease it must first qualify as a lease. Section 2A–103(1)(j). Note that this Article regulates the transactional elements of a lease, including a consumer lease; consumer protection statutes—, present and future—, and existing consumer protection decisions are unaffected by this Article. Section 2A–104(1)(c) and (2). Of course, Article 2A as state law also is subject to federal consumer protection law.

This definition is modeled after the definition of consumer lease in the Consumer Leasing Act, 15 U.S.C. § 1667 (1982), and in the Unif. Consumer Credit Code § 1.301(14), 7A U.L.A. 43 (1974). However, this definition of consumer lease differs from its models in several respects: the lessor can be a person regularly engaged either in the business of leasing or of selling goods, the lease need not be for a term exceeding four months, a lease primarily for an agricultural purpose is not covered, and whether there should be a limitation by dollar amount and its amount is left up to the individual states.

This definition focuses on the parties as well as the transaction. If a lease is within this definition, the lessor must be regularly engaged in the business of leasing or selling, and the lessee must be an individual not an organization; note that a lease to two or more individuals having a common interest through marriage or the like is not excluded as a lease to an organization under Section 1–201(28). The lessee must take the interest primarily for a personal, family or household purpose. If required by the enacting state, total payments under the lease contract, excluding payments for options to renew or buy, cannot exceed the figure designated.

(f) "Fault". Section 1–201(16).

(g) "Finance Lease". New. This Article includes a subset of rules that applies only to finance leases. Sections 2A–209, 2A–211(2), 2A–212(1), 2A–213, 2A–219(1), 2A–220(1)(a), 2A–221, 2A–405(c), 2A–407, 2A–516(2) and 2A–517(1)(a) and (2).

For a transaction to qualify as a finance lease it must first qualify as a lease. Section 2A–103(1)(j). Unless the lessor is comfortable that the transaction will qualify as a finance lease, the lease agreement should include provisions giving the lessor the benefits created by the subset of rules applicable to the transaction that qualifies as a finance lease under this Article.

A finance lease is the product of a three party transaction. The supplier manufactures or supplies the goods pursuant to the lessee's specification, perhaps even pursuant to a purchase order, sales agreement or lease agreement between the supplier and the lessee. After the prospective finance lease is negotiated, a purchase order, sales agreement, or lease agreement is entered into by the lessor (as buyer or prime lessee) or an existing order, agreement or lease is assigned by the lessee to the lessor, and the lessor and the lessee then enter into a lease or sublease of the goods. Due to the limited function usually performed by the lessor, the lessee looks almost entirely to the supplier for representations, covenants and warranties. If a manufacturer's warranty carries through, the lessee may also look to that. Yet, this definition does not restrict the lessor's function solely to the supply of funds; if the lessor undertakes or performs other functions, express warranties, covenants and the common law will protect the lessee.

This definition focuses on the transaction, not the status of the parties; to avoid confusion it is important to note that in other contexts, e.g., tax and accounting, the term finance lease has been used to connote different types of lease transactions, including leases that are disguised secured transactions. M. Rice, *Equipment Financing*, 62–71 (1981). A lessor who is a merchant with respect to goods of the kind subject to the lease may be a lessor under a finance lease. Many leases that are leases back to the seller of goods (Section 2A–308(3)) will be finance leases. This conclusion is easily demonstrated by a hypothetical. Assume that B has bought goods from C pursuant to a sales contract. After delivery to and acceptance of the goods by B, B negotiates to sell the goods to A and simultaneously to lease the goods back from A, on terms and conditions that, we assume, will qualify the transaction as a lease. Section 2A–103(1)(j). In documenting the sale and lease back, B assigns the original sales contract between B, as buyer, and C, as seller, to A. A review of these facts leads to the conclusion that the lease from A to B qualifies as a finance lease, as all three conditions of the definition are satisfied. Subparagraph (i) is satisfied as A, the lessor, had nothing to do with the selection, manufacture, or supply of the equipment. Subparagraph (ii) is satisfied as A, the lessor, bought the equipment at the same time that A leased the equipment to B, which certainly is in connection with the lease. Finally, subparagraph (iii) (A) is satisfied as A entered into the sales contract with B at the same time that A leased the equipment back to B. B, the lessee, will have received a copy of the sales contract in a timely fashion.

Subsection (i) requires the lessor to remain outside the selection, manufacture and supply of the goods; that is the rationale for releasing the lessor from most of its traditional liability. The lessor is not prohibited from possession, maintenance or operation of the goods, as policy does not require such prohibition. To insure the lessee's reliance on the supplier, and not on the lessor, subsection (ii) requires that the goods (where the lessor is the buyer of the goods) or that the right to possession and use of the goods (where the lessor is the prime lessee and the sublessor of the goods) be acquired in connection with the lease (or sublease) to qualify as a finance lease. The scope of the phrase "in connection with" is to be developed by the courts, case by case. Finally, as the lessee generally relies almost entirely upon the supplier for representations and covenants, and upon the supplier or a manufacturer, or both, for warranties with respect to the goods, subsection (iii) requires that one of the following occur: (A) the lessee receive a copy of the supply contract before signing the lease contract; (B) the lessee's approval of the supply contract is a condition to the effectiveness of the lease contract; (C) the lessee receive a statement describing the promises and warranties and any limitations relevant to the lessee before signing the lease contract; or (D) before signing the lease contract and except in a consumer lease, the lessee receive a writing identifying the supplier (unless the supplier was selected and required by the lessee) and the rights of the lessee under Section 2A–209, and advising the lessee a statement of promises and warranties is available from the supplier. Thus, even where oral supply orders or computer placed supply orders are compelled by custom and usage the transaction may still qualify as a finance lease if the lessee approves the supply contract before the lease contract is effective and such approval was a condition to the effectiveness of the lease contract. Moreover, where the lessor does not want the lessee to see the entire supply contract, including price information, the lessee may be provided with a separate statement of the terms of the supply contract relevant to the lessee; promises between the supplier and the lessor that do not affect the lessee need not be included. The statement can be a restatement of those terms or a copy of portions of the supply contract with the relevant terms clearly designated. Any implied warranties need not be designated, but a disclaimer or modification of remedy must be designated. A copy of any manufacturer's warranty is sufficient if that is the warranty provided. However, a copy of any Regulation M disclosure given pursuant to 12 C.F.R. § 213.4(g) concerning warranties in itself is not sufficient since those disclosures need only briefly identify express warranties and need not include any disclaimer of warranty.

If a transaction does not qualify as a finance lease, the parties may achieve the same result by agreement; no negative implications are to be drawn if the transaction does not qualify. Further, absent the application of special rules (fraud, duress, and the like), a lease that qualifies as a finance lease and is assigned by the lessor or the lessee to a third party does not lose its status as a finance lease under this Article. Finally, this Article creates no special rule where the lessor is an affiliate of the supplier; whether the transaction qualifies as a finance lease will be determined by the facts of each case.

(h) "Goods". Section 9–105(1)(h). See Section 2A–103(3) for reference to the definition of "Account", "Chattel paper", "Document", "General intangibles" and "Instrument". See Section 2A–217 for determination of the time and manner of identification.

(i) "Installment lease contract". Section 2–612(1).

(j) "Lease". New. There are several reasons to codify the law with respect to leases of goods. An analysis of the case law as it applies to leases of goods suggests at least several significant issues to be resolved by codification. First and foremost is the definition of a lease. It is necessary to define lease to determine whether a transaction creates a lease or a security interest disguised as a lease. If the transaction creates a security interest disguised as a lease, the transaction will be governed by the Article on Secured Transactions (Article 9) and the lessor will be required to file a financing statement or take other action to perfect its interest in the goods against third parties. There is no such requirement with respect to leases under the common law and, except with respect to leases of fixtures (Section 2A–309), this Article imposes no such requirement. Yet the distinction between a lease and a security interest disguised as a lease is not clear from the case law at the time of the promulgation of this Article. DeKoven, *Leases of Equipment: Puritan Leasing Company v. August, A Dangerous Decision*, 12 U.S.F. L.Rev. 257 (1978).

At common law a lease of personal property is a bailment for hire. While there are several definitions of bailment for hire, all require a thing to be let and a price for the letting. Thus, in modern terms and as provided in this definition, a lease is created when the lessee agrees to furnish consideration for the right to the possession and use of goods over a specified period of time. Mooney, *Personal Property Leasing: A Challenge*, 36 Bus.Law. 1605, 1607 (1981). Further, a lease is neither a sale (Section 2–106(1)) nor a retention or creation of a security interest (Section 1–201(37)). Due to extensive litigation to distinguish true leases from security interests, an amendment to Section 1–201(37) has been promulgated with this Article to create a sharper distinction.

This section as well as Section 1–201(37) must be examined to determine whether the transaction in question creates a lease or a security interest. The following hypotheticals indicate the perimeters of the issue. Assume that A has purchased a number of copying machines, new, for $1,000 each; the machines have an estimated useful economic life of three years. A advertises that the machines are available to rent for a minimum of one month and that the monthly rental is $100.00. A intends to enter into leases where A provides all maintenance, without charge to the lessee. Further, the lessee will rent the machine, month to month, with no obligation to renew. At the end of the lease term the lessee will be obligated to return the machine to A's place of business. This transaction qualifies as a lease under the first half of the definition, for the transaction includes a transfer by A to a prospective lessee of possession and use of the machine for a stated term, month to month. The machines are goods (Section 2A–103(1)(h)). The lessee is obligated to pay consideration in return, $100.00 for each month of the term.

However, the second half of the definition provides that a sale or a security interest is not a lease. Since there is no passing of title, there is no sale. Sections 2A–103(3) and 2–106(1). Under pre-Act security law this transaction would have created a bailment for hire or a true lease and not a conditional sale. *Da Rocha v. Macomber*, 330 Mass. 611, 614–15, 116 N.E.2d 139, 142 (1953). Under Section 1–201(37), as amended with the promulgation of this Article, the same result would follow. While the lessee is obligated to pay rent for the one month term of the lease, one of the other four conditions of the second paragraph of Section 1–201(37) must be met and none is. The term of the lease is one month and the economic life of the machine is 36 months; thus, subparagraph (a) of Section 1–201(37) is not now satisfied. Considering the amount of the monthly rent, absent economic duress or coercion, the lessee is not bound either to renew the lease for the remaining economic life of the goods or to become the owner. If the lessee did lease the machine for 36 months, the lessee would have paid the lessor $3,600 for a machine that could have been purchased for $1,000; thus, subparagraph (b) of Section 1–201(37) is not satisfied. Finally, there are no options; thus, subparagraphs (c) and (d) of Section 1–201(37) are not satisfied. This transaction creates a lease, not a security interest. However, with each renewal of the lease the facts and circumstances at the time of each renewal must be examined to determine if that conclusion remains accurate, as it is possible that a transaction that first creates a lease, later creates a security interest.

Assume that the facts are changed and that A requires each lessee to lease the goods for 36 months, with no right to terminate. Under pre-Act security law this transaction would have created a conditional sale, and not a bailment for hire or true lease. *Hervey v. Rhode Island Locomotive Works*, 93 U.S. 664, 672–73 (1876). Under this subsection, and Section 1–201(37), as amended with the inclusion of this Article in the Act, the same result would follow. The lessee's obligation for the term is not subject to termination by the lessee and the term is equal to the economic life of the machine.

Between these extremes there are many transactions that can be created. Some of the transactions have not been properly categorized by the courts in applying the 1978 and earlier Official Texts of Section 1–201(37). This subsection, together with Section 1–201(37), as amended with the promulgation of this Article, draws a brighter line, which should create a clearer signal to the professional lessor and lessee.

(k) "Lease agreement". This definition is derived from the first sentence of Section 1–201(3). Because the definition of lease is broad enough to cover future transfers, lease agreement includes an agreement contemplating a current or subsequent transfer. Thus it was not necessary to make an express reference to an agreement for the future lease of goods (Section 2–106(1)). This concept is also incorporated in the definition of lease contract. Note that the definition of lease does not include transactions in ordinary building materials that are incorporated into an improvement on land. Section 2A–309(2).

The provisions of this Article, if applicable, determine whether a lease agreement has legal consequences; otherwise the law of bailments and other applicable law determine the same. Sections 2A–103(4) and 1–103.

(*l*) "Lease contract". This definition is derived from the definition of contract in Section 1–201(11). Note that a lease contract may be for the future lease of goods, since this notion is included in the definition of lease.

(m) "Leasehold interest". New.

(n) "Lessee". New.

(*o*) "Lessee in ordinary course of business". Section 1–201(9).

(p) "Lessor". New.

(q) "Lessor's residual interest". New.

(r) "Lien". New. This term is used in Section 2A–307 (Priority of Liens Arising by Attachment or Levy on, Security Interests in, and Other Claims to Goods).

(s) "Lot". Section 2–105(5).

(t) "Merchant lessee". New. This term is used in Section 2A–511 (Merchant Lessee's Duties as to Rightfully Rejected Goods). A person may satisfy the requirement of dealing in goods of the kind subject to the lease as lessor, lessee, seller, or buyer.

(u) "Present value". New. Authorities agree that present value should be used to determine fairly the damages payable by the lessor or the lessee on default. *E.g.*, *Taylor v. Commercial Credit Equip. Corp.*, 170 Ga.App. 322, 316 S.E.2d 788 (Ct. App. 1984). Present value is defined to mean an amount that represents the discounted value as of a date certain of one or more sums payable in the future. This is a function of the economic principle that a dollar today is more valuable to the holder than a dollar payable in two years. While there is no question as to the principle, reasonable people would differ as to the rate of discount to apply in determining the value of that future dollar today. To minimize litigation, this Article allows the parties to specify the discount or interest rate, if the rate was not manifestly unreasonable at the time the transaction was entered into. In all other cases, the interest rate will be a commercially reasonable rate that takes into account the facts and circumstances of each case, as of the time the transaction was entered into.

(v) "Purchase". Section 1–201(32). This definition omits the reference to lien contained in the definition of purchase in Article 1 (Section 1–201(32)). This should not be construed to exclude consensual liens from the definition of purchase in this Article; the exclusion was mandated by the scope of the definition of lien in Section 2A–103(1)(r). Further, the definition of purchaser in this Article adds a reference to lease; as purchase is defined in Section 1–201(32) to include any other voluntary transaction creating an interest in property, this addition is not substantive.

(w) "Sublease". New.

(x) "Supplier". New.

(y) "Supply contract". New.

(z) "Termination". Section 2–106(3). The effect of a termination is provided in Section 2A–505(2).

State Bar Committee Comments

The definition of "goods" should include a mobile home that is to be permanently attached to a foundation provided the mobile home was movable at the time it was identified to the lease contract.

In the definition of "consumer lease," the dollar limitation of $25,000 was chosen to correspond with the $25,000 limitation in the Consumer Leasing Act (15 U.S.C. § 1667 (1982)), for lack of any empirical data from which to make a decision to increase or decrease the dollar limitation from $25,000. Eventually, inflation may warrant an increase from $25,000.

Sections 31 and 32 of Acts 2005, 79th Leg., ch. 122 provide:

"Sec. 31. This Act applies to a document of title that is issued or a bailment that arises on or after the effective date of this Act. This Act does not apply to a document of title that is issued or a bailment that arises before the effective date of this Act even if the document of title or bailment would be subject to this Act if the document of title had been issued or bailment had arisen after the effective date of this Act. This Act does not apply to a right of action that has accrued before the effective date of this Act.

"Sec. 32. A document of title issued or a bailment that arises before the effective date of this Act and the rights, obligations, and interests flowing from that document or bailment are governed by any statute or other rule amended or repealed by this Act as if amendment or repeal had not occurred and may be terminated, completed, consummated, or enforced under that statute or other rule."

§ 2A.104. Leases Subject to Other Laws

(a) A lease, although subject to this chapter, is also subject to any applicable:

(1) certificate of title statute of this state, including Chapter 501, Transportation Code, Chapter 31, Parks and Wildlife Code, and Subchapter E, Chapter 1201, Occupations Code;

(2) certificate of title statute of another jurisdiction (Section 2A.105); or

Text of subsec. (a)(3) effective until April 1, 2009

(3) consumer law of this state, both decisional and statutory, including, to the extent that they apply to a lease transaction, Chapters 17 and 35 of this code and Chapter 1201, Occupations Code.

Text of subsec. (a)(3) effective April 1, 2009

(3) consumer law of this state, both decisional and statutory, including, to the extent that they apply to a lease transaction:

(A) Titles 6, 7, 8, 9, and 14;

(B) Subtitle A, Title 11;

(C) Chapters 17, 53, 54, 72, 92, 101, 103, 305, 323, 522, 523, 602, 603, 604, and 2001;

(D) Section 65.017, Civil Practice and Remedies Code;

(E) Chapter 1201, Occupations Code; and

(F) Chapter 25, Transportation Code.

(b) In case of conflict between this chapter, other than Sections 2A.105, 2A.304(c) and 2A.305(c), and any statute or law referred to in Subsection (a), the statute or law controls.

(c) Failure to comply with any applicable statute has only the effect specified therein.

Added by Acts 1993, 73rd Leg., ch. 570, § 1, eff. Sept. 1, 1993. Amended by Acts 1997, 75th Leg., ch. 165, § 30.176, eff. Sept. 1, 1997; Acts 2003, 78th Leg., ch. 1276, § 14A.753, eff. Sept. 1, 2003; Acts 2007, 80th Leg., ch. 885, § 2.03, eff. April 1, 2009.

Uniform Commercial Code Comment

Uniform Statutory Source: Sections 9–203(4) and 9–302(3)(b) and (c).

Changes: Substantially revised.

Purposes:

1. This Article creates a comprehensive scheme for the regulation of transactions that create leases. Section 2A–102. Thus, the Article supersedes all prior legislation dealing with leases, except to the extent set forth in this Section.

2. Subsection (1) states the general rule that a lease, although governed by the scheme of this Article, also may be governed by certain other applicable laws. This may occur in the case of a consumer lease. Section 2A–103(1)(e). Those laws may be state statutes existing prior to enactment of Article 2A or passed afterward. In this case, it is desirable for this Article to specify which statute controls. Or the law may be a pre-existing consumer protection decision. This Article preserves such decisions. Or the law may be a statute of the United States. Such a law controls without any statement in this Article under applicable principles of preemption.

An illustration of a statute of the United States that governs consumer leases is the Consumer Leasing Act, 15 U.S.C. §§ 1667–1667(e) (1982) and its implementing regulation, Regulation M, 12 C.F.R. § 213 (1986); the statute mandates disclosures of certain lease terms, delimits the liability of a lessee in leasing personal property, and regulates the advertising of lease terms. An illustration of a state statute that governs consumer leases and which if adopted in the enacting state prevails over this Article is the Unif. Consumer Credit Code, which includes many provisions similar to those of the Consumer Leasing Act, *e.g.* Unif. Consumer Credit Code §§ 3.202, 3.209, 3.401, 7A U.L.A. 108–09, 115, 125 (1974), as well as provisions in addition to those of the Consumer Leasing Act, *e.g.*, Unif. Consumer Credit Code §§ 5.109–.111, 7A U.L.A. 171–76 (1974) (the right to cure a default). Such statutes may define consumer lease so as to govern transactions within and without the definition of consumer lease under this Article.

3. Under subsection (2), subject to certain limited exclusions, in case of conflict a statute or a decision described in subsection (1) prevails over this Article. For example, a provision like Unif. Consumer Credit Code § 5.112, 7A U.L.A. 176 (1974), limiting self-help repossession, prevails over Section 2A–525(3). A consumer protection decision rendered after the effective date of this Article may supplement its provisions. For example, in relation to Article 9 a court might conclude that an acceleration clause may not be enforced against an individual debtor after late payments have been accepted unless a prior notice of default is given. To the extent the decision establishes a general principle applicable to transactions other than secured transactions, it may supplement Section 2A–502.

4. Consumer protection in lease transactions is primarily left to other law. However, several provisions of this Article do contain special rules that may not be varied by agreement in the case of a consumer lease. *E.g.*, Sections 2A–106, 2A–108, and 2A–109(2). Were that not so, the ability of the parties to govern their relationship by agreement together with the position of the lessor in a consumer lease too often could result in a one-sided lease agreement.

5. In construing this provision the reference to statute should be deemed to include applicable regulations. A consumer protection decision is "final" on the effective date of this Article if it is not subject to appeal on that date or, if subject to appeal, is not later reversed on appeal. Of course, such a decision can be overruled by a later decision or superseded by a later statute.

Cross References:

Sections 2A–103(1)(e), 2A–106, 2A–108, 2A–109(2) and 2A–525(3).

Definitional Cross Reference:

"Lease". Section 2A–103(1)(j).

State Bar Committee Comments

Subsection (a)(3) clarifies that both decisional and statutory consumer laws are preserved as to leases. Rather than attempt to identify all such laws, the subsection references in a nonexclusive manner several important statutory sources to the extent they apply to lease transactions. The uniform version's confusing provision requiring a snapshot of existing consumer protection decisions at the time of adoption has been revised to defer to consumer law decisions, even those that are subsequent to the adoption of Chapter 2A. The reference to the Texas Consumer Credit Code is not intended to imply that a lease may be usurious. A true lease is generally not considered to be subject to the Texas usury statutes. *See, e.g., Transamerican Leasing Co. v. Three Bears, Inc.*, 586 S.W.2d 472 (Tex. 1979). Nevertheless, certain provisions of a lease may be subject to the Texas usury statutes—for example, a provision calling for interest on past due rental payments. *See, e.g., Whitehead Utilities, Inc. v. Emery Financial Corp.*, 697 S.W.2d 460 (Tex. App.—Beaumont, 1985).

§ 2A.105. Territorial Application of Chapter to Goods Covered by Certificate of Title

Subject to the provisions of Sections 2A.304(c) and 2A.305(c), with respect to goods covered by a certificate of title issued under a statute of this state or of another jurisdiction, compliance and the effect of compliance or noncompliance with a certificate of title statute are governed by the law (including the conflict of laws rules) of the jurisdiction issuing the certificate until the earlier of:

(1) surrender of the certificate; or

(2) four months after the goods are removed from that jurisdiction and thereafter until a new certificate of title is issued by another jurisdiction.

Added by Acts 1993, 73rd Leg., ch. 570, § 1, eff. Sept. 1, 1993.

Uniform Commercial Code Comment

Uniform Statutory Source: Section 9–103(2)(a) and (b).

Changes: Substantially revised. The provisions of the last sentence of Section 9–103(2)(b) have not been incorporated as it is superfluous in this context. The provisions of Section 9–103(2)(d) have not been incorporated because the problems dealt with are adequately addressed by this section and Sections 2A–304(3) and 305(3).

Purposes: The new certificate referred to in (b) must be permanent, not temporary. Generally, the lessor or creditor whose interest is indicated on the most recently issued certificate of title will prevail over interests indicated on certificates issued previously by other jurisdictions. This provision reflects a policy that it is reasonable to require holders of interests in goods covered by a certificate of title to police the goods or risk losing their interests when a new certificate of title is issued by another jurisdiction.

Cross References:

Sections 2A–304(3), 2A–305(3), 9–103(2)(b) and 9–103(2)(d).

Definitional Cross Reference:

"Goods". Section 2A–103(1)(h).

§ 2A.106. Limitation on Power of Parties to Consumer Lease to Choose Applicable Law and Judicial Forum

(a) If the law chosen by the parties to a consumer lease is that of a jurisdiction other than a jurisdiction in which the lessee resides at the time the lease agreement becomes enforceable or within 30 days thereafter or in which the goods are to be used, the choice is not enforceable.

(b) If the judicial forum chosen by the parties to a consumer lease is a forum located in a jurisdiction other than the jurisdiction in which the lessee in fact signed the lease agreement, resides at the commencement of the action, or resided at the time the lease contract became enforceable or in which the goods are in fact used by the lessee, the choice is not enforceable.

Added by Acts 1993, 73rd Leg., ch. 570, § 1, eff. Sept. 1, 1993.

Uniform Commercial Code Comment

Uniform Statutory Source: Unif. Consumer Credit Code § 1.201(8), 7A U.L.A. 36 (1974).

Changes: Substantially revised.

Purposes: There is a real danger that a lessor may induce a consumer lessee to agree that the applicable law will be a jurisdiction that has little effective consumer protection, or to agree that the applicable forum will be a forum that is inconvenient for the lessee in the event of litigation. As a result, this section invalidates these choice of law or forum clauses, except where the law chosen is that of the state of the consumer's residence or where the goods will be kept, or the forum chosen is one that otherwise would have jurisdiction over the lessee.

Subsection (1) limits potentially abusive choice of law clauses in consumer leases. The 30-day rule in subsection (1) was suggested by Section 9–103(1)(c). This section has no effect on choice of law clauses in leases that are not consumer leases. Such clauses would be governed by other law.

Subsection (2) prevents enforcement of potentially abusive jurisdictional consent clauses in consumer leases. By using the term judicial forum, this section does not limit selection of a nonjudicial forum, such as arbitration. This section has no effect on choice of forum clauses in leases that are not consumer leases; such clauses are, as a matter of current law, "prima facie valid". *The Bremen v. Zapata Off-Shore, Co.*, 407 U.S. 1, 10 (1972). Such clauses would be governed by other law, including the Model Choice of Forum Act (1968).

Cross Reference:

Section 9–103(1)(c).

Definitional Cross Reference:

"Consumer lease". Section 2A–103(1)(e).

"Goods". Section 2A–103(1)(h).

"Lease agreement". Section 2A–103(1)(k).

"Lessee". Section 2A–103(1)(n).

"Party". Section 1–201(29).

State Bar Committee Comments

Section 2A.106 does not apply to the choice of law or forum provisions of a supply contract. Other law, including Section 1.105, will govern the enforceability of such provisions. The choice of forum provisions have been narrowed from the uniform version in accord with existing Texas policy, as reflected in other Texas statutes.

§ 2A.107. Waiver or Renunciation of Claim or Right After Default

A claim or right arising out of an alleged default or breach of warranty may be discharged in whole or in part without consideration by a written waiver or renunciation signed and delivered by the aggrieved party.

Added by Acts 1993, 73rd Leg., ch. 570, § 1, eff. Sept. 1, 1993.

Uniform Commercial Code Comment

Uniform Statutory Source: Section 1–107.

Changes: Revised to reflect leasing practices and terminology. This clause is used throughout the official comments to this Article to indicate the scope of change in the provisions of the Uniform Statutory Source included in the section; these changes range from one extreme, *e.g.*, a significant difference in practice (a warranty as to merchantability is not implied in a finance lease (Section 2A–212)) to the other extreme, *e.g.*, a modest difference in style or terminology (the transaction governed is a lease not a sale (Section 2A–203)).

Cross References:

Sections 2A–203 and 2A–212.

Definitional Cross References:

"Aggrieved party". Section 1–201(2).

"Delivery". Section 1–201(14).

"Rights". Section 1–201(36).

"Signed". Section 1–201(39).

"Written". Section 1–201(46).

§ 2A.108. Unconscionability

(a) If the court as a matter of law finds a lease contract or any clause of a lease contract to have been unconscionable at the time it was made, the court may refuse to enforce the lease contract, or it may enforce the remainder of the lease contract without the unconscionable clause, or it may so limit the application of any unconscionable clause as to avoid any unconscionable result.

(b) With respect to a consumer lease, if the court as a matter of law finds that a lease contract or any clause of a lease contract has been induced by unconscionable conduct or that unconscionable conduct has occurred in the collection of a claim arising from a lease contract, the court may grant appropriate relief.

(c) Before making a finding of unconscionability under Subsection (a) or (b), the court, on its own motion or that of a party, shall afford the parties a reasonable opportunity to present evidence as to the setting, purpose, and effect of the lease contract or clause thereof or of the conduct.

(d) In an action in which the lessee claims unconscionability with respect to a consumer lease:

(1) if the court finds unconscionability under Subsection (a) or (b), the court shall award reasonable attorney's fees to the lessee;

(2) if the court does not find unconscionability and the lessee claiming unconscionability has brought or maintained an action he or she knew to be groundless, the court shall award reasonable attorney's fees to the party against whom the claim is made; and

(3) in determining attorney's fees, the amount of the recovery on behalf of the claimant under Subsections (a) and (b) is not controlling.

Added by Acts 1993, 73rd Leg., ch. 570, § 1, eff. Sept. 1, 1993.

Uniform Commercial Code Comment

Uniform Statutory Source: Section 2–302 and Unif. Consumer Credit Code § 5.108, 7A U.L.A. 167–69 (1974).

Changes: Subsection (1) is taken almost verbatim from the provisions of Section 2–302(1). Subsection (2) is suggested by the provisions of Unif. Consumer Credit Code § 5.108(1), (2), 7A U.L.A. 167 (1974). Subsection (3), taken from the provisions of Section 2–302(2), has been expanded to cover unconscionable conduct. Unif. Consumer Credit Code § 5.108(3), 7A U.L.A. 167 (1974). The provision for the award of attorney's fees to consumers, subsection (4), covers unconscionability under subsection (1) as well as (2). Subsection (4) is modeled on the provisions of Unif. Consumer Credit Code § 5.108(6), 7A U.L.A. 169 (1974).

Purposes: Subsections (1) and (3) of this section apply the concept of unconscionability reflected in the provisions of Section 2–302 to leases. *See Dillman & Assocs. v. Capitol Leasing Co.*, 110 Ill.App.3d 335, 342, 442 N.E.2d 311, 316 (App.Ct.1982). Subsection (3) omits the adjective "commercial" found in subsection 2–302(2) because subsection (3) is concerned with all leases and the relevant standard of conduct is determined by the context.

The balance of the section is modeled on the provisions of Unif. Consumer Credit Code § 5.108, 7A U.L.A. 167–69 (1974). Thus subsection (2) recognizes that a consumer lease or a clause in a consumer lease may not itself be unconscionable but that the agreement would never have been entered into if unconscionable means had not been employed to induce the consumer to agree. To make a statement to induce the consumer to lease the goods, in the expectation of invoking an integration clause in the lease to exclude the statement's admissibility in a subsequent dispute, may be unconscionable. Subsection (2) also provides a consumer remedy for unconscionable conduct, such as using or threatening to use force or violence, in the collection of a claim arising from a lease contract. These provisions are not exclusive. The remedies of this section are in addition to remedies otherwise available for the same conduct under other law, for example, an action in tort for abusive debt collection or under another statute of this State for such conduct. The reference to appropriate relief in subsection

(2) is intended to foster liberal administration of this remedy. Sections 2A–103(4) and 1–106(1).

Subsection (4) authorizes an award of reasonable attorney's fees if the court finds unconscionability with respect to a consumer lease under subsections (1) or (2). Provision is also made for recovery by the party against whom the claim was made if the court does not find unconscionability and does find that the consumer knew the action to be groundless. Further, subsection (4)(b) is independent of, and thus will not override, a term in the lease agreement that provides for the payment of attorney's fees.

Cross References:

Sections 1–106(1), 2–302 and 2A–103(4).

Definitional Cross Reference:

"Action". Section 1–201(1).

"Consumer lease". Section 2A–103(1)(e).

"Lease contract". Section 2A–103(1)(*l*).

"Lessee". Section 2A–103(1)(n).

"Party". Section 1–201(29).

§ 2A.109. Option to Accelerate at Will

(a) A term providing that one party or the party's successor in interest may accelerate payment or performance or require collateral or additional collateral "at will" or "when the party deems himself or herself insecure" or in words of similar import must be construed to mean that the party has power to do so only if the party in good faith believes that the prospect of payment or performance is impaired.

(b) With respect to a consumer lease, the burden of establishing good faith under Subsection (a) is on the party who exercises the power; otherwise the burden of establishing lack of good faith is on the party against whom the power has been exercised.

Added by Acts 1993, 73rd Leg., ch. 570, § 1, eff. Sept. 1, 1993.

Uniform Commercial Code Comment

Uniform Statutory Source: Section 1–208 and Unif. Consumer Credit Code § 5.109(2), 7A U.L.A. 171 (1974).

Purposes: Subsection (1) reflects modest changes in style to the provisions of the first sentence of Section 1–208.

Subsection (2), however, reflects a significant change in the provisions of the second sentence of Section 1–208 by creating a new rule with respect to a consumer lease. A lease provision allowing acceleration at the will of the lessor or when the lessor deems itself insecure is of critical importance to the lessee. In a consumer lease it is a provision that is not usually agreed to by the parties but is usually mandated by the lessor. Therefore, where its invocation depends not on specific criteria but on the discretion of the lessor, its use should be regulated to prevent abuse. Subsection (1) imposes a duty of good faith upon its exercises. Subsection (2) shifts the burden of establishing good faith to the lessor in the case of a consumer lease, but not otherwise.

Cross Reference:

Section 1–208

Definitional Cross Reference:

"Burden of establishing". Section 1–201(8).

"Consumer lease". Section 2A–103(1)(e).

"Good faith". Sections 1–201(19) and 2–103(1)(b).

"Party". Section 1–201(29).

"Term". Section 1–201(42).

§ 2A.110. Repealed by Acts 2001, 77th Leg., ch. 702, § 5, eff. Jan. 1, 2002

SUBCHAPTER B. FORMATION AND CONSTRUCTION OF LEASE CONTRACT

§ 2A.201. Statute of Frauds

(a) A lease contract is not enforceable by way of action or defense unless:

(1) the total payments to be made under the lease contract, excluding payments for options to renew or buy, are less than $1,000; or

(2) there is a writing, signed by the party against whom enforcement is sought or by that party's authorized agent, sufficient to indicate that a lease contract has been made between the parties and to describe the goods leased and the lease term.

(b) Any description of leased goods or of the lease term is sufficient and satisfies Subsection (a)(2), whether or not it is specific, if it reasonably identifies what is described.

(c) A writing is not insufficient because it omits or incorrectly states a term agreed upon, but the lease contract is not enforceable under Subsection (a)(2) beyond the lease term and the quantity of goods shown in the writing.

(d) A lease contract that does not satisfy the requirements of Subsection (a), but which is valid in other respects, is enforceable:

(1) if the goods are to be specially manufactured or obtained for the lessee and are not suitable for lease or sale to others in the ordinary course of the lessor's business, and the lessor, before notice of repudiation is received and under circumstances that reasonably indicate that the goods are for the lessee, has made either a substantial beginning of

their manufacture or commitments for their procurement;

(2) if the party against whom enforcement is sought admits in that party's pleading, testimony or otherwise in court that a lease contract was made, but the lease contract is not enforceable under this provision beyond the quantity of goods admitted;

(3) with respect to goods that have been received and accepted by the lessee; or

(4) if the lease contract would otherwise be enforceable under general principles of equitable estoppel, detrimental reliance or unjust enrichment.

(e) The lease term under a lease contract referred to in Subsection (d) is:

(1) if there is a writing signed by the party against whom enforcement is sought or by that party's authorized agent specifying the lease term, the term so specified;

(2) if the party against whom enforcement is sought admits in that party's pleading, testimony, or otherwise in court a lease term, the term so admitted; or

(3) a reasonable lease term.

Added by Acts 1993, 73rd Leg., ch. 570, § 1, eff. Sept. 1, 1993.

Uniform Commercial Code Comment

Uniform Statutory Source: Sections 2–201, 9–203(1) and 9–110.

Changes: This section is modeled on Section 2–201, with changes to reflect the differences between a lease contract and a contract for the sale of goods. In particular, subsection (1)(b) adds a requirement that the writing "describe the goods leased and the lease term", borrowing that concept, with revisions, from the provisions of Section 9–203(1)(a). Subsection (2), relying on the statutory analogue in Section 9–110, sets forth the minimum criterion for satisfying that requirement.

Purposes: The changes in this section conform the provisions of Section 2–201 to custom and usage in lease transactions. Section 2–201(2), stating a special rule between merchants, was not included in this section as the number of such transactions involving leases, as opposed to sales, was thought to be modest. Subsection (4) creates no exception for transactions where payment has been made and accepted. This represents a departure from the analogue, Section 2–201(3)(c). The rationale for the departure is grounded in the distinction between sales and leases. Unlike a buyer in a sales transaction, the lessee does not tender payment in full for goods delivered, but only payment of rent for one or more months. It was decided that, as a matter of policy, this act of payment is not a sufficient substitute for the required memorandum. Subsection (5) was needed to establish the criteria for supplying the lease term if it is omitted, as the lease contract may still be enforceable under subsection (4).

Cross References:

Sections 2–201, 9–110 and 9–203(1)(a).

Definitional Cross References:

"Action". Section 1–201(1).

"Agreed". Section 1–201(3).

"Buying". Section 2A–103(1)(a).

"Goods". Section 2A–103(1)(h).

"Lease". Section 2A–103(1)(j).

"Lease contract". Section 2A–103(1)(*l*).

"Lessee". Section 2A–103(1)(n).

"Lessor". Section 2A–103(1)(p).

"Notice". Section 1–201(25).

"Party". Section 1–201(29).

"Sale". Section 2–106(1).

"Signed". Section 1–201(39).

"Term". Section 1–201(42).

"Writing". Section 1–201(46).

State Bar Committee Comments

The provisions of Section 2A.201(d)(4) are new and have no parallel in Section 2.201. They are intended to resolve, in favor of the majority rule, the often litigated conflict between the statute of frauds and enforcement of a lease contract under certain equitable principles. *See Allied Grape Grocers v. Bronco Wire Co.*, 6 UCC Rep. 2d 1059, 249 Cal. Rptr. 872 (Ct. of App. [Fifth Dist.] 1988).

In the case of conflict between the provisions of Section 2A.201 and Section 26.01 of the Business and Commerce Code, the provisions of Section 2A.201 should control due to their more particular applicability to leases of goods.

§ 2A.202. Final Written Expression; Parol or Extrinsic Evidence

Terms with respect to which the confirmatory memoranda of the parties agree or which are otherwise set forth in a writing intended by the parties as a final expression of their agreement with respect to such terms as are included therein may not be contradicted by evidence of a prior agreement or of a contemporaneous oral agreement but may be explained or supplemented:

(1) by course of dealing or usage of trade or by course of performance; and

(2) by evidence of consistent additional terms unless the court finds the writing to have been

intended also as a complete and exclusive statement of the terms of the agreement.

Added by Acts 1993, 73rd Leg., ch. 570, § 1, eff. Sept. 1, 1993.

Uniform Commercial Code Comment

Uniform Statutory Source: Section 2–202.

Definitional Cross References:

"Agreement". Section 1–201(3).

"Course of dealing". Section 1–205.

"Party". Section 1–201(29).

"Term". Section 1–201(42).

"Usage of trade". Section 1–205.

"Writing". Section 1–201(46).

§ 2A.203. Seals Inoperative

The affixing of a seal to a writing evidencing a lease contract or an offer to enter into a lease contract does not render the writing a sealed instrument and the law with respect to sealed instruments does not apply to the lease contract or offer.

Added by Acts 1993, 73rd Leg., ch. 570, § 1, eff. Sept. 1, 1993.

Uniform Commercial Code Comment

Uniform Statutory Source: Section 2–203.

Changes: Revised to reflect leasing practices and terminology.

Definitional Cross References:

"Lease contract". Section 2A–103(1)(*l*).

"Writing". Section 1–201(46).

§ 2A.204. Formation in General

(a) A lease contract may be made in any manner sufficient to show agreement, including conduct by both parties which recognizes the existence of a lease contract.

(b) An agreement sufficient to constitute a lease contract may be found although the moment of its making is undetermined.

(c) Although one or more terms are left open, a lease contract does not fail for indefiniteness if the parties have intended to make a lease contract and there is a reasonably certain basis for giving an appropriate remedy.

Added by Acts 1993, 73rd Leg., ch. 570, § 1, eff. Sept. 1, 1993.

Uniform Commercial Code Comment

Uniform Statutory Source: Section 2–204.

Changes: Revised to reflect leasing practices and terminology.

Definitional Cross References:

"Agreement". Section 1–201(3).

"Lease contract". Section 2A–103(1)(*l*).

"Party". Section 1–201(29).

"Remedy". Section 1–201(34).

"Term". Section 1–201(42).

§ 2A.205. Firm Offers

An offer by a merchant to lease goods to or from another person in a signed writing that by its terms gives assurance it will be held open is not revocable, for lack of consideration, during the time stated or, if no time is stated, for a reasonable time, but in no event may the period of irrevocability exceed three months. Any such term of assurance on a form supplied by the offeree must be separately signed by the offeror.

Added by Acts 1993, 73rd Leg., ch. 570, § 1, eff. Sept. 1, 1993.

Uniform Commercial Code Comment

Uniform Statutory Source: Section 2–205.

Changes: Revised to reflect leasing practices and terminology.

Definitional Cross References:

"Goods". Section 2A–103(1)(h).

"Lease". Section 2A–103(1)(j).

"Merchant". Section 2–104(1).

"Person". Section 1–201(30).

"Reasonable time". Section 1–204(1) and (2).

"Signed". Section 1–201(39).

"Term". Section 1–201(42).

"Writing". Section 1–201(46).

§ 2A.206. Offer and Acceptance in Formation of Lease Contract

(a) Unless otherwise unambiguously indicated by the language or circumstances, an offer to make a lease contract must be construed as inviting acceptance in any manner and by any medium reasonable in the circumstances.

(b) If the beginning of a requested performance is a reasonable method of acceptance, an offeror who is not notified of acceptance within a reasonable time may treat the offer as having lapsed before acceptance.

Added by Acts 1993, 73rd Leg., ch. 570, § 1, eff. Sept. 1, 1993.

Uniform Commercial Code Comment

Uniform Statutory Source: Section 2–206(1)(a) and (2).

Changes: Revised to reflect leasing practices and terminology.

Definitional Cross References:

"Lease contract". Section 2A–103(1)(l).

"Notifies". Section 1–201(26).

"Reasonable time". Section 1–204(1) and (2).

§ 2A.207. Repealed by Acts 2003, 78th Leg., ch. 542, § 20, eff. Sept. 1, 2003.

§ 2A.208. Modification, Rescission and Waiver

(a) An agreement modifying a lease contract needs no consideration to be binding.

(b) A signed lease agreement that excludes modification or rescission except by a signed writing may not be otherwise modified or rescinded, but, except as between merchants, such a requirement on a form supplied by a merchant must be separately signed by the other party.

(c) Although an attempt at modification or rescission does not satisfy the requirements of Subsection (b), it may operate as a waiver.

(d) A party who has made a waiver affecting an executory portion of a lease contract may retract the waiver by reasonable notification received by the other party that strict performance will be required of any term waived, unless a retraction would be unjust in view of a material change of position in reliance on the waiver.

Added by Acts 1993, 73rd Leg., ch. 570, § 1, eff. Sept. 1, 1993.

Uniform Commercial Code Comment

Uniform Statutory Source: Section 2–209.

Changes: Revised to reflect leasing practices and terminology, except that the provisions of subsection 2–209(3) were omitted.

Purposes: Section 2–209(3) provides that "the requirements of the statute of frauds section of this Article (Section 2–201) must be satisfied if the contract as modified is within its provisions." This provision was not incorporated as it is unfair to allow an oral modification to make the entire lease contract unenforceable, *e.g.*, if the modification takes it a few dollars over the dollar limit. At the same time, the problem could not be solved by providing that the lease contract would still be enforceable in its pre-modification state (if it then satisfied the statute of frauds) since in some cases that might be worse than no enforcement at all. Resolution of the issue is left to the courts based on the facts of each case.

Cross References:

Sections 2–201 and 2–209.

Definitional Cross References:

"Agreement". Section 1–201(3).

"Between merchants". Section 2–104(3).

"Lease agreement". Section 2A–103(1)(k).

"Lease contract". Section 2A–103(1)(l).

"Merchant". Section 2–104(1).

"Notification". Section 1–201(26).

"Party". Section 1–201(29).

"Signed". Section 1–201(39).

"Term". Section 1–201(42).

"Writing". Section 1–201(46).

§ 2A.209. Lessee Under Finance Lease as Beneficiary of Supply Contract

(a) The benefit of a supplier's promises to the lessor under the supply contract and of all warranties, whether express or implied, including those of any third party provided in connection with or as part of the supply contract, extends to the lessee to the extent of the lessee's leasehold interest under a finance lease related to the supply contract, but is subject to the terms of the warranty and of the supply contract and all defenses or claims arising therefrom.

(b) The extension of the benefit of a supplier's promises and of warranties to the lessee (Section 2A.209(a)) does not:

(1) modify the rights and obligations of the parties to the supply contract, whether arising therefrom or otherwise; or

(2) impose any duty or liability under the supply contract on the lessee.

(c) Any modification or rescission of the supply contract by the supplier and the lessor is effective between the supplier and the lessee unless, before the modification or rescission, the supplier has received notice that the lessee has entered into a finance lease related to the supply contract. If the modification or rescission is effective between the supplier and the lessee, the lessor is deemed to have assumed, in addition to the obligations of the lessor to the lessee under the lease contract, promises of the supplier to the lessor and warranties that were so modified or rescinded as they existed and were available to the lessee before modification or rescission.

(d) In addition to the extension of the benefit of the supplier's promises and of warranties to the lessee under Subsection (a), the lessee retains all rights that the lessee may have against the supplier which arise from an agreement between the lessee and the supplier or under other law.

Added by Acts 1993, 73rd Leg., ch. 570, § 1, eff. Sept. 1, 1993.

Uniform Commercial Code Comment

Uniform Statutory Source: None.

Changes: This section is modeled on Section 9–318, the Restatement (Second) of Contracts §§ 302–315 (1981), and leasing practices. *See Earman Oil Co. v. Burroughs Corp.*, 625 F.2d 1291, 1296–97 (5th Cir. 1980).

Purposes:

1. The function performed by the lessor in a finance lease is extremely limited. Section 2A–103(1)(g). The lessee looks to the supplier of the goods for warranties and the like or, in some cases as to warranties, to the manufacturer if a warranty made by that person is passed on. That expectation is reflected in subsection (1), which is self-executing. As a matter of policy, the operation of this provision may not be excluded, modified or limited; however, an exclusion, modification, or limitation of any term of the supply contract or warranty, including any with respect to rights and remedies, and any defense or claim such as a statute of limitations, effective against the lessor as the acquiring party under the supply contract, is also effective against the lessee as the beneficiary designated under this provision. For example, the supplier is not precluded from excluding or modifying an express or implied warranty under a supply contract. Sections 2–312(2) and 2–316, or Section 2A–214. Further, the supplier is not precluded from limiting the rights and remedies of the lessor and from liquidating damages. Sections 2–718 and 2–719 or Sections 2A–503 and 2A–504. If the supply contract excludes or modifies warranties, limits remedies, or liquidates damages with respect to the lessor, such provisions are enforceable against the lessee as beneficiary. Thus, only selective discrimination against the beneficiaries designated under this section is precluded, *i.e.*, exclusion of the supplier's liability to the lessee with respect to warranties made to the lessor. This section does not affect the development of other law with respect to products liability.

2. Enforcement of this benefit is by action. Sections 2A–103(4) and 1–106(2).

3. The benefit extended by these provisions is not without a price, as this Article also provides in the case of a finance lease that is not a consumer lease that the lessee's promises to the lessor under the lease contract become irrevocable and independent upon the lessee's acceptance of the goods. Section 2A–407.

4. Subsection (2) limits the effect of subsection (1) on the supplier and the lessor by preserving, notwithstanding the transfer of the benefits of the supply contract to the lessee, all of the supplier's and the lessor's rights and obligations with respect to each other and others; it further absolves the lessee of any duties with respect to the supply contract that might have been inferred from the extension of the benefits thereof.

5. Subsections (2) and (3) also deal with difficult issues related to modification or rescission of the supply contract. Subsection (2) states a rule that determines the impact of the statutory extension of benefit contained in subsection (1) upon the relationship of the parties to the supply contract and, in a limited respect, upon the lessee. This statutory extension of benefit, like that contained in Sections 2A–216 and 2–318, is not a modification of the supply contract by the parties. Thus, subsection (3) states the rules that apply to a modification or rescission of the supply contract by the parties. Subsection (3) provides that a modification or rescission is not effective between the supplier and the lessee if, before the modification or rescission occurs, the supplier received notice that the lessee has entered into the finance lease. On the other hand, if the modification or rescission is effective, then to the extent of the modification or rescission of the benefit or warranty, the lessor by statutory dictate assumes an obligation to provide to the lessee that which the lessee would otherwise lose. For example, assume a reduction in an express warranty from four years to one year. No prejudice to the lessee may occur if the goods perform as agreed. If, however, there is a breach of the express warranty after one year and before four years pass, the lessor is liable. A remedy for any prejudice to the lessee because of the bifurcation of the lessee's recourse resulting from the action of the supplier and the lessor is left to resolution by the courts based on the facts of each case.

6. Subsection (4) makes it clear that the rights granted to the lessee by this section do not displace any rights the lessee otherwise may have against the supplier.

Cross References:

Sections 2A–103(1)(g), 2A–407 and 9–318.

Definitional Cross References:

"Action". Section 1–201(1).

"Finance lease". Section 2A–103(1)(g).

"Leasehold interest". Section 2A–103(1)(m).

"Lessee". Section 2A–103(1)(n).

"Lessor". Section 2A–103(1)(p).

"Notice". Section 1–201(25).

"Party". Section 1–201(29).

"Rights". Section 1–201(36).

"Supplier". Section 2A–103(1)(x).

"Supply contract". Section 2A–103(1)(y).

"Term". Section 1–201(42).

State Bar Committee Comments

In the case of a finance lease that is not a consumer lease, the uniform version has been revised to provide that the lessee's promises to the lessor under the lease contract may become irrevocable and independent upon the lessee's acceptance of the goods if the lease agreement so provides.

Section 2A.407(a). The enforceability of such a provision in any other lease should be determined by the facts of each case and other applicable law. Sections 2A.209 and 2A.407 carry no negative or positive implication on this issue of enforceability.

Because it is intended that the benefit of the implied warranty of fitness for a particular purpose be passed through to the finance lessee under the provisions of Section 2A.209(a), the finance lessee's "purpose" should be controlling when the supplier has knowledge of the finance lease arrangement and the finance lessee's intended use for the goods.

§ 2A.210. Express Warranties

(a) Express warranties by the lessor are created as follows:

(1) Any affirmation of fact or promise made by the lessor to the lessee that relates to the goods and becomes part of the basis of the bargain creates an express warranty that the goods will conform to the affirmation or promise.

(2) Any description of the goods which is made part of the basis of the bargain creates an express warranty that the goods will conform to the description.

(3) Any sample or model that is made part of the basis of the bargain creates an express warranty that the whole of the goods will conform to the sample or model.

(b) It is not necessary to the creation of an express warranty that the lessor use formal words, such as "warrant" or "guarantee," or that the lessor have a specific intention to make a warranty, but an affirmation merely of the value of the goods or a statement purporting to be merely the lessor's opinion or commendation of the goods does not create a warranty.

Added by Acts 1993, 73rd Leg., ch. 570, § 1, eff. Sept. 1, 1993.

Uniform Commercial Code Comment

Uniform Statutory Source: Section 2–313.

Changes: Revised to reflect leasing practices and terminology.

Purposes: All of the express and implied warranties of the Article on Sales (Article 2) are included in this Article, revised to reflect the differences between a sale of goods and a lease of goods. Sections 2A–210 through 2A–216. The lease of goods is sufficiently similar to the sale of goods to justify this decision. Hawkland, *The Impact of the Uniform Commercial Code on Equipment Leasing*, 1972 Ill.L.F. 446, 459–60. Many state and federal courts have reached the same conclusion.

Value of the goods, as used in subsection (2), includes rental value.

Cross References:

Article 2, esp. Section 2–313, and Sections 2A–210 through 2A–216.

Definitional Cross References:

"Conforming". Section 2A–103(1)(d).

"Goods". Section 2A–103(1)(h).

"Lessee". Section 2A–103(1)(n).

"Lessor". Section 2A–103(1)(p).

"Value". Section 1–201(44).

§ 2A.211. Warranties Against Interference and Against Infringement; Lessee's Obligation Against Infringement

(a) There is in a lease contract a warranty that for the lease term no person holds a claim to or interest in the goods that arose from an act or omission of the lessor other than a claim by way of infringement or the like, which will interfere with the lessee's enjoyment of its leasehold interest.

(b) Except in a finance lease there is in a lease contract by a lessor who is a merchant regularly dealing in goods of the kind a warranty that the goods are delivered free of the rightful claim of any person by way of infringement or the like.

(c) A lessee who furnishes specifications to a lessor or a supplier shall hold the lessor and the supplier harmless against a claim by way of infringement or the like that arises out of compliance with the specifications.

Added by Acts 1993, 73rd Leg., ch. 570, § 1, eff. Sept. 1, 1993.

Uniform Commercial Code Comment

Uniform Statutory Source: Section 2–312.

Changes: This section is modeled on the provisions of Section 2–312, with modifications to reflect the limited interest transferred by a lease contract and the total interest transferred by a sale. Section 2–312(2), which is omitted here, is incorporated in Section 2A–214. The warranty of quiet possession was abolished with respect to sales of goods. Section 2–312 official comment 1. Section 2A–211(1) reinstates the warranty of quiet possession with respect to leases. Inherent in the nature of the limited interest transferred by the lease—the right to possession and use of the goods—is the need of the lessee for protection greater than that afforded to the buyer. Since the scope of the protection is limited to claims or interests that arose from acts or omissions of the lessor, the lessor will be in position to evaluate the potential cost, certainly a far better position than that enjoyed by the lessee. Further, to the extent the market will allow, the lessor can attempt to pass on the anticipated additional cost to the lessee in the guise of higher rent.

Purposes: General language was chosen for subsection (1) that expresses the essence of the lessee's expectation: with an exception for infringement and the like, no person holding a claim or interest that arose from an act or omission of the lessor will be able to interfere with the lessee's use and enjoyment of the goods for the lease term. Subsection (2), like other similar provisions in later sections, excludes the finance lessor from extending this warranty; with few exceptions (Sections 2A–210 and 2A–211(1)), the lessee under a finance lease is to look to the supplier for warranties and the like or, in some cases as to warranties, to the manufacturer if a warranty made by that person is passed on. Subsections (2) and (3) are derived from Section 2–312(3). These subsections, as well as the analogue, should be construed so that applicable principles of law and equity supplement their provisions. Sections 2A–103(4) and 1–103.

Cross References:

Sections 2–312, 2–312(1), 2–312(2), 2–312 official comment 1, 2A–210, 2A–211(1) and 2A–214.

Definitional Cross References:

"Delivery". Section 1–201(14).

"Finance lease". Section 2A–103(1)(g).

"Goods". Section 2A–103(1)(h).

"Lease". Section 2A–103(1)(j).

"Lease contract". Section 2A–103(1)(*l*).

"Leasehold interest". Section 2A–103(1)(m).

"Lessee". Section 2A–103(1)(n).

"Lessor". Section 2A–103(1)(p).

"Merchant". Section 2–104(1).

"Person". Section 1–201(30).

"Supplier". Section 2A–103(1)(x).

§ 2A.212. Implied Warranty of Merchantability

(a) Except in a finance lease, a warranty that the goods will be merchantable is implied in a lease contract if the lessor is a merchant with respect to goods of that kind.

(b) Goods to be merchantable must be at least such as:

(1) pass without objection in the trade under the description in the lease agreement;

(2) in the case of fungible goods, are of fair average quality within the description;

(3) are fit for the ordinary purposes for which goods of that type are used;

(4) run, within the variation permitted by the lease agreement, of even kind, quality, and quantity within each unit and among all units involved;

(5) are adequately contained, packaged, and labeled as the lease agreement may require; and

(6) conform to any promises or affirmations of fact made on the container or label.

(c) Other implied warranties may arise from course of dealing or usage of trade.

Added by Acts 1993, 73rd Leg., ch. 570, § 1, eff. Sept. 1, 1993.

Uniform Commercial Code Comment

Uniform Statutory Source: Section 2–314.

Changes: Revised to reflect leasing practices and terminology. *E.g., Glenn Dick Equip. Co. v. Galey Constr., Inc.*, 97 Idaho 216, 225, 541 P.2d 1184, 1193 (1975) (implied warranty of merchantability (Article 2) extends to lease transactions).

Definitional Cross References:

"Conforming". Section 2A–103(1)(d).

"Course of dealing". Section 1–205.

"Finance lease". Section 2A–103(1)(g).

"Fungible". Section 1–201(17).

"Goods". Section 2A–103(1)(h).

"Lease agreement". Section 2A–103(1)(k).

"Lease contract". Section 2A–103(1)(*l*).

"Lessor". Section 2A–103(1)(p).

"Merchant". Section 2–104(1).

"Usage of trade". Section 1–205.

§ 2A.213. Implied Warranty of Fitness for Particular Purpose

Except in a finance lease, if the lessor at the time the lease contract is made has reason to know of any particular purpose for which the goods are required and that the lessee is relying on the lessor's skill or judgment to select or furnish suitable goods, there is in the lease contract an implied warranty that the goods will be fit for that purpose.

Added by Acts 1993, 73rd Leg., ch. 570, § 1, eff. Sept. 1, 1993.

Uniform Commercial Code Comment

Uniform Statutory Source: Section 2–315.

Changes: Revised to reflect leasing practices and terminology. *E.g., All-States Leasing Co. v. Bass*, 96 Idaho 873, 879, 538 P.2d 1177, 1183 (1975) (implied warranty of fitness for a particular purpose (Article 2) extends to lease transactions).

Definitional Cross References:

"Finance lease". Section 2A–103(1)(g).

"Goods". Section 2A–103(1)(h).

"Knows". Section 1–201(25).

"Lease contract". Section 2A–103(1)(*l*).

"Lessee". Section 2A–103(1)(n).

"Lessor". Section 2A–103(1)(p).

§ 2A.214. Exclusion or Modification of Warranties

(a) Words or conduct relevant to the creation of an express warranty and words or conduct tending to negate or limit a warranty must be construed whenever reasonable, as consistent with each other; but, subject to the provisions of Section 2A.202 on parol or extrinsic evidence, negation or limitation is inoperative to the extent that the construction is unreasonable.

(b) Subject to Subsection (c), to exclude or modify the implied warranty of merchantability or any part of it the language must mention "merchantability," be by a writing, and be conspicuous. Subject to Subsection (c), to exclude or modify an implied warranty of fitness the exclusion must be by a writing and be conspicuous. Language to exclude all implied warranties of fitness is sufficient if it is in writing, is conspicuous and states, for example, "There is no warranty that the goods will be fit for a particular purpose."

(c) Notwithstanding Subsection (b), but subject to Subsection (d):

(1) unless the circumstances indicate otherwise, all implied warranties are excluded by expressions like "as is," or "with all faults," or by other language that in common understanding calls the lessee's attention to the exclusion of warranties and makes plain that there is no implied warranty, if in writing and conspicuous;

(2) if the lessee before entering into the lease contract has examined the goods or the sample or model as fully as desired or has refused to examine the goods, there is no implied warranty with regard to defects that an examination ought in the circumstances to have revealed; and

(3) an implied warranty also may be excluded or modified by course of dealing, course of performance, or usage of trade.

(d) To exclude or modify a warranty against interference or against infringement (Section 2A.211) or any part of it, the language must be specific, be by a writing, and be conspicuous, unless the circumstances, including course of performance, course of dealing, or usage of trade, give the lessee reason to know that the goods are being leased subject to a claim or interest of any person.

Added by Acts 1993, 73rd Leg., ch. 570, § 1, eff. Sept. 1, 1993.

Uniform Commercial Code Comment

Uniform Statutory Source: Sections 2–316 and 2–312(2).

Changes: Subsection (2) requires that a disclaimer of the warranty of merchantability be conspicuous and in writing as is the case for a disclaimer of the warranty of fitness; this is contrary to the rule stated in Section 2–316(2) with respect to the disclaimer of the warranty of merchantability. This section also provides that to exclude or modify the implied warranty of merchantability, fitness or against interference or infringement the language must be in writing and conspicuous. There are, however, exceptions to the rule. *E.g.*, course of dealing, course of performance, or usage of trade may exclude or modify an implied warranty. Section 2A–214(3)(c). The analogue of Section 2–312(2) has been moved to subsection (4) of this section for a more unified treatment of disclaimers; there is no policy with respect to leases of goods that would justify continuing certain distinctions found in the Article on Sales (Article 2) regarding the treatment of the disclaimer of various warranties. *Compare* Sections 2–312(2) and 2–316(2). Finally, the example of a disclaimer of the implied warranty of fitness stated in subsection (2) differs from the analogue stated in Section 2–316(2); this example should promote a better understanding of the effect of the disclaimer.

Purposes: These changes were made to reflect leasing practices. *E.g., FMC Finance Corp. v. Murphree*, 632 F.2d 413, 418 (5th Cir.1980) (disclaimer of implied warranty under lease transactions must be conspicuous and in writing). The omission of the provisions of Section 2–316(4) was not substantive. Sections 2A–503 and 2A–504.

Cross References:

Article 2, esp. Sections 2–312(2) and 2–316, and Sections 2A–503 and 2A–504.

Definitional Cross References:

"Conspicuous". Section 1–201(10).

"Course of dealing". Section 1–205.

"Fault". Section 2A–103(1)(f).

"Goods". Section 2A–103(1)(h).

"Knows". Section 1–201(25).

"Lease". Section 2A–103(1)(j).

"Lease contract". Section 2A–103(1)(*l*).

"Lessee". Section 2A–103(1)(n).

"Person". Section 1–201(30).

"Usage of trade". Section 1–205.

"Writing". Section 1–201(46).

State Bar Committee Comments

Although the provisions of the Texas Deceptive Trade Practices and Consumer Protection Act, Business and Commerce Code Sections 17.40 *et seq.* (the "DTPA"), create a separate cause of action for a "consumer" for breaches of express or implied warranties, the warranties must be established independently of the DTPA because the DTPA itself does not create any warranties. *La Sara Grain v. First Nat. Bank of Mercedes*, 673 S.W.2d 558, 565

(Tex. 1984), *on remand,* 676 S.W.2d 183. The *La Sara* court stated that the implied warranties created by Sections 2.314 and 315 are actionable under the DTPA. Likewise, the implied warranties set forth in Sections 2A.211, 212 and 213 are actionable under the DTPA. With respect to a finance lease, the DTPA would provide to a finance lessee a separate cause of action for only the implied warranty of quiet enjoyment under Section 2A.211(a). Section 17.42 of the DTPA states that any waiver by a consumer of the provisions of the DTPA is unenforceable and void, except with respect to certain large business consumers. However, Texas cases have held that disclaimers of warranties under Chapter 2 of the Business and Commerce Code are enforceable despite DTPA § 17.42. *See McCrea v. Subilla Condominium Corp.*, 685 S.W.2d 755 (Tex. App.—Houston [1st Dist.] 1985, writ ref'd n.r.e.); *Ellmer v. Delaware Mini-Computer,* 665 S.W.2d 158, 160-161 (Tex. App.—Dallas [5th Dist.] 1983, no writ). As a consequence, if a lease contract under Chapter 2A properly disclaims any express and implied warranties under Section 2A.214, a breach of express or implied warranties under the DTPA or under Chapter 2A has been waived. However, a proper waiver of implied and express warranties under Section 2A.214 does not constitute an adequate waiver of a DTPA cause of action for false representations. *See McCrea*; *Metro For Truck Sales, Inc. v. Davis,* 709 S.W.2d 785 (Tex. App.—Fort Worth 1986) *on rehearing,* 711 S.W.2d 145 (writ ref'd n.r.e.).

§ 2A.215. Accumulation and Conflict of Warranties Express or Implied

Warranties, whether express or implied, must be construed as consistent with each other and as cumulative, but if that construction is unreasonable, the intention of the parties determines which warranty is dominant. In ascertaining that intention the following rules apply:

(1) exact or technical specifications displace an inconsistent sample or model or general language of description;

(2) a sample from an existing bulk displaces inconsistent general language of description; and

(3) express warranties displace inconsistent implied warranties other than an implied warranty of fitness for a particular purpose.

Added by Acts 1993, 73rd Leg., ch. 570, § 1, eff. Sept. 1, 1993.

Uniform Commercial Code Comment

Uniform Statutory Source: Section 2–317.

Definitional Cross Reference:

"Party". Section 1–201(29).

§ 2A.216. Third-Party Beneficiaries of Express and Implied Warranties

This chapter does not provide whether anyone other than a lessee may take advantage of an express or implied warranty of quality made to the lessee or whether the lessee or anyone entitled to take advantage of a warranty made to the lessee may sue a third party other than the immediate lessor, or the supplier in a finance lease, for deficiencies in the quality of the goods. These matters are left to the courts for their determination.

Added by Acts 1993, 73rd Leg., ch. 570, § 1, eff. Sept. 1, 1993.

Uniform Commercial Code Comment

Uniform Statutory Source: Section 2–318.

Changes: The provisions of Section 2–318 have been included in this section, modified in two respects: first, to reflect leasing practice, including the special practices of the lessor under a finance lease; second, to reflect and thus codify elements of the official comment to Section 2–318 with respect to the effect of disclaimers and limitations of remedies against third parties.

Purposes: Alternative A is based on the 1962 version of Section 2–318 and is least favorable to the injured person as the doctrine of privity imposed by other law is abrogated to only a limited extent. Alternatives B and C are based on later additions to Section 2–318 and are more favorable to the injured person. In determining which alternative to select, the state legislature should consider making its choice parallel to the choice it made with respect to Section 2–318, as interpreted by the courts.

The last sentence of each of Alternatives A, B and C does not preclude the lessor from excluding or modifying an express or implied warranty under a lease. Section 2A–214. Further, that sentence does not preclude the lessor from limiting the rights and remedies of the lessee and from liquidating damages. Sections 2A–503 and 2A–504. If the lease excludes or modifies warranties, limits remedies for breach, or liquidates damages with respect to the lessee, such provisions are enforceable against the beneficiaries designated under this section. However, this last sentence forbids selective discrimination against the beneficiaries designated under this section, *i.e.*, exclusion of the lessor's liability to the beneficiaries with respect to warranties made by the lessor to the lessee.

Other law, including the Article on Sales (Article 2), may apply in determining the extent to which a warranty to or for the benefit of the lessor extends to the lessee and third parties. This is in part a function of whether the lessor has bought or leased the goods.

This Article does not purport to change the development of the relationship of the common law, with respect to products liability, including strict liability in tort (as restated in Restatement (Second) of Torts, § 402A (1965)), to the provisions of this Act. *Compare Cline v. Prowler Indus. of Maryland,* 418 A.2d 968 (Del.1980) *and Hawkins Constr. Co.*

v. Matthews Co., 190 Neb. 546, 209 N.W.2d 643 (1973) *with Dippel v. Sciano*, 37 Wis.2d 443, 155 N.W.2d 55 (1967).

Cross References:

Article 2, esp. Section 2–318, and Sections 2A–214, 2A–503 and 2A–504.

Definitional Cross References:

"Goods". Section 2A–103(1)(h).

"Lessee". Section 2A–103(1)(n).

"Person". Section 1–201(30).

"Remedy". Section 1–201(34).

"Rights". Section 1–201(36).

State Bar Committee Comments

The uniform UCC Article 2A provisions of Section 2A.216 have been deleted in conformity with a similar deletion of the provisions of Section 2.318 of Chapter 2—Sales. The better policy, as reflected in these deletions, is to defer to the well developed common law on the issues covered by Section 2A.216.

§ 2A.217. Identification

Identification of goods as goods to which a lease contract refers may be made at any time and in any manner explicitly agreed to by the parties. In the absence of explicit agreement, identification occurs:

(1) when the lease contract is made if the lease contract is for a lease of goods that are existing and identified;

(2) when the goods are shipped, marked, or otherwise designated by the lessor as goods to which the lease contract refers, if the lease contract is for a lease of goods that are not existing and identified; or

(3) when the young are conceived, if the lease contract is for a lease of the unborn young of animals.

Added by Acts 1993, 73rd Leg., ch. 570, § 1, eff. Sept. 1, 1993.

Uniform Commercial Code Comment

Uniform Statutory Source: Section 2–501.

Changes: This section, together with Section 2A–218, is derived from the provisions of Section 2–501, with changes to reflect lease terminology; however, this section omits as irrelevant to leasing practice the treatment of special property.

Purposes: With respect to subsection (b) there is a certain amount of ambiguity in the reference to when goods are designated, *e.g.*, when the lessor is both selling and leasing goods to the same lessee/buyer and has marked goods for delivery but has not distinguished between those related to the lease contract and those related to the sales contract. As in Section 2–501(1)(b), this issue has been left to be resolved by the courts, case by case.

Cross References:

Sections 2–501 and 2A–218.

Definitional Cross References:

"Agreement". Section 1–201(3).

"Goods". Section 2A–103(1)(h).

"Lease". Section 2A–103(1)(j).

"Lease contract". Section 2A–103(1)(*l*).

"Lessor". Section 2A–103(1)(p).

"Party". Section 1–201(29).

§ 2A.218. Insurance and Proceeds

(a) A lessee obtains an insurable interest when existing goods are identified to the lease contract even though the goods identified are nonconforming and the lessee has an option to reject them.

(b) If a lessee has an insurable interest only by reason of the lessor's identification of the goods, the lessor, until default or insolvency or notification to the lessee that identification is final, may substitute other goods for those identified.

(c) Notwithstanding a lessee's insurable interest under Subsections (a) and (b), the lessor retains an insurable interest during the existence of the lease contract.

(d) Nothing in this section impairs any insurable interest recognized under any other statute or rule of law.

(e) The parties by agreement may determine that one or more parties have an obligation to obtain and pay for insurance covering the goods and by agreement may determine the beneficiary of the proceeds of the insurance.

Added by Acts 1993, 73rd Leg., ch. 570, § 1, eff. Sept. 1, 1993.

Uniform Commercial Code Comment

Uniform Statutory Source: Section 2–501.

Changes: This section, together with Section 2A–217, is derived from the provisions of Section 2–501, with changes and additions to reflect leasing practices and terminology.

Purposes: Subsection (2) states a rule allowing substitution of goods by the lessor under certain circumstances, until default or insolvency of the lessor, or until notification to the lessee that identification is final. Subsection (3) states a rule regarding the lessor's insurable interest that, by virtue of the difference between a sale and a lease, necessarily is different from the rule stated in Section 2–501(2) regarding the seller's insurable interest. For this purpose the option to buy shall be deemed to have been exercised by the lessee when the resulting sale is closed, not when the lessee gives notice to the lessor. Further, subsection (5) is new and reflects the common practice of shifting the responsibility and cost of insuring the goods between the parties to the lease transaction.

Cross References:

Sections 2–501, 2–501(2) and 2A–217.

Definitional Cross References:

"Agreement". Section 1–201(3).

"Buying". Section 2A–103(1)(a).

"Conforming". Section 2A–103(1)(d).

"Goods". Section 2A–103(1)(h).

"Insolvent". Section 1–201(23).

"Lease contract". Section 2A–103(1)(*l*).

"Lessee". Section 2A–103(1)(n).

"Lessor". Section 2A–103(1)(p).

"Notification". Section 1–201(26).

"Party". Section 1–201(29).

State Bar Committee Comments

Because of a perceived conflict with the provisions of Section 2.501(b) and because of the continuing residual interest of the lessor in the goods, subsection (c) has been revised to state the rule that a lessor's insurable interest continues during the existence of the lease contract. Whether the lessor has an insurable interest in the goods upon any transfer of title to the goods by virtue of the exercise of an option to purchase the goods by the lessee should be governed by the provisions of Section 2.501(b) and not Section 2A.218.

§ 2A.219. Risk of Loss

(a) Except in the case of a finance lease, risk of loss is retained by the lessor and does not pass to the lessee. In the case of a finance lease, risk of loss passes to the lessee.

(b) Subject to the provisions of this chapter on the effect of default on risk of loss (Section 2A.220), if risk of loss is to pass to the lessee and the time of passage is not stated, the following rules apply:

(1) If the lease contract requires or authorizes the goods to be shipped by carrier:

(A) and it does not require delivery at a particular destination, the risk of loss passes to the lessee when the goods are duly delivered to the carrier; but

(B) if it does require delivery at a particular destination and the goods are there duly tendered while in the possession of the carrier, the risk of loss passes to the lessee when the goods are there duly so tendered as to enable the lessee to take delivery.

(2) If the goods are held by a bailee to be delivered without being moved, the risk of loss passes to the lessee on acknowledgement by the bailee of the lessee's right to possession of the goods.

(3) In any case not within Subdivision (1) or (2), the risk of loss passes to the lessee on tender of delivery if the lessee is a merchant; otherwise the risk of loss passes to the lessee on the lessee's receipt of the goods.

Added by Acts 1993, 73rd Leg., ch. 570, § 1, eff. Sept. 1, 1993.

Uniform Commercial Code Comment

Uniform Statutory Source: Section 2–509(1) through (3).

Changes: Subsection (1) is new. The introduction to subsection (2) is new, but subparagraph (a) incorporates the provisions of Section 2–509(1); subparagraph (b) incorporates the provisions of Section 2–509(2) only in part, reflecting current practice in lease transactions.

Purposes: Subsection (1) states rules related to retention or passage of risk of loss consistent with current practice in lease transactions. The provisions of subsection (4) of Section 2–509 are not incorporated as they are not necessary. This section does not deal with responsibility for loss caused by the wrongful act of either the lesser or the lessee.

Cross References:

Sections 2–509(1), 2–509(2) and 2–509(4).

Definitional Cross References:

"Delivery". Section 1–201(14).

"Finance lease". Section 2A–103(1)(g).

"Goods". Section 2A–103(1)(h).

"Lease contract". Section 2A–103(1)(*l*).

"Lessee". Section 2A–103(1)(n).

"Lessor". Section 2A–103(1)(p).

"Merchant". Section 2–104(1).

"Receipt". Section 2–103(1)(c).

"Rights". Section 1–201(36).

"Supplier". Section 2A–103(1)(x).

State Bar Committee Comments

Section 2A.219(b)(3) has been revised from the uniform version. In establishing a default rule, the provisions of subsection (b)(3) should focus on the merchant status of the lessee in determining when risk of loss passes to the lessee. The uniform version may create unfair results when the lessee is not a merchant. A merchant lessee will likely have insurance to protect himself from casualty prior to receipt of the goods while a non-merchant lessee will likely not have such insurance.

§ 2A.220. Effect of Default on Risk of Loss

(a) Where risk of loss is to pass to the lessee and the time of passage is not stated:

(1) if a tender or delivery of goods so fails to conform to the lease contract as to give a right of rejection, the risk of their loss remains with the lessor, or, in the case of a finance lease, the supplier, until cure or acceptance; or

(2) if the lessee rightfully revokes acceptance, the lessee, to the extent of any deficiency in the lessee's effective insurance coverage, may treat the risk of loss as having remained with the lessor from the beginning.

(b) Whether or not risk of loss is to pass to the lessee, if the lessee as to conforming goods already identified to a lease contract repudiates or is otherwise in default under the lease contract, the lessor, or, in the case of a finance lease, the supplier, to the extent of any deficiency in the lessor's or the supplier's effective insurance coverage may treat the risk of loss as resting on the lessee for a commercially reasonable time.

Added by Acts 1993, 73rd Leg., ch. 570, § 1, eff. Sept. 1, 1993.

Uniform Commercial Code Comment

Uniform Statutory Source: Section 2–510.

Changes: Revised to reflect leasing practices and terminology. The rule in Section (1)(b) does not allow the lessee under a finance lease to treat the risk of loss as having remained with the supplier from the beginning. This is appropriate given the limited circumstances under which the lessee under a finance lease is allowed to revoke acceptance. Section 2A–517 and Section 2A–516 official comment.

Definitional Cross References:

"Conforming". Section 2A–103(1)(d).

"Delivery". Section 1–201(14).

"Finance lease". Section 2A–103(1)(g).

"Goods". Section 2A–103(1)(h).

"Lease contract". Section 2A–103(1)(*l*).

"Lessee". Section 2A–103(1)(n).

"Lessor". Section 2A–103(1)(p).

"Reasonable time". Section 1–204(1) and (2).

"Rights". Section 1–201(36).

"Supplier". Section 2A–103(1)(x).

§ 2A.221. Casualty to Identified Goods

If a lease contract requires goods identified when the lease contract is made, and the goods suffer casualty without fault of the lessee, the lessor or the supplier before delivery, or the goods suffer casualty before risk of loss passes to the lessee under the lease agreement or Section 2A.219:

(1) if the loss is total, the lease contract is avoided; and

(2) if the loss is partial or the goods have so deteriorated as to no longer conform to the lease contract, the lessee may nevertheless demand inspection and at the lessee's option either treat the lease contract as avoided or, except in a finance lease that is not a consumer lease, accept the goods with due allowance from the rent payable for the balance of the lease term for the deterioration or the deficiency in quantity but without further right against the lessor.

Added by Acts 1993, 73rd Leg., ch. 570, § 1, eff. Sept. 1, 1993.

Uniform Commercial Code Comment

Uniform Statutory Source: Section 2–613.

Changes: Revised to reflect leasing practices and terminology.

Purpose: Due to the vagaries of determining the amount of due allowance (Section 2–613(b), no attempt was made in subsection (b) to treat a problem unique to lease contracts and installment sales contracts: determining how to recapture the allowance, *e.g.*, application to the first or last rent payments or allocation, *pro rata*, to all rent payments.

Cross References:

Section 2–613.

Definitional Cross References:

"Conforming". Section 2A–103(1)(d).

"Consumer lease". Section 2A–103(1)(e).

"Delivery". Section 1–201(14).

"Fault". Section 2A–103(1)(f).

"Finance lease". Section 2A–103(1)(g).

"Goods". Section 2A–103(1)(h).

"Lease". Section 2A–103(1)(j).

"Lease agreement". Section 2A–103(1)(k).

"Lease contract". Section 2A–103(1)(*l*).

"Lessee". Section 2A–103(1)(n).

"Lessor". Section 2A–103(1)(p).

"Rights". Section 1–201(36).

"Supplier". Section 2A–103(1)(x).

SUBCHAPTER C. EFFECT OF LEASE CONTRACT

§ 2A.301. Enforceability of Lease Contract

Except as otherwise provided in this title, a lease contract is effective and enforceable according to its terms between the parties, against purchasers of the goods and against creditors of the parties.

Added by Acts 1993, 73rd Leg., ch. 570, § 1, eff. Sept. 1. 1993.

Uniform Commercial Code Comment

Uniform Statutory Source: Section 9–201.

Changes: The first sentence of Section 9–201 was incorporated, modified to reflect leasing terminology. The second sentence of Section 9–201 was eliminated as not relevant to leasing practices.

Purposes:

1. This section establishes a general rule regarding the validity and enforceability of a lease contract. The lease contract is effective and enforceable between the parties and against third parties. Exceptions to this general rule arise where there is a specific rule to the contrary in this Article. Enforceability is, thus, dependent upon the lease contract meeting the requirements of the Statute of Frauds provisions of Section 2A–201. Enforceability is also a function of the lease contract conforming to the principles of construction and interpretation contained in the Article on General Provisions (Article 1). Section 2A–103(4).

2. The effectiveness or enforceability of the lease contract is not dependent upon the lease contract or any financing statement or the like being filed or recorded; however, the priority of the interest of a lessor of fixtures with respect to the interests of certain third parties in such fixtures is subject to the provisions of the Article on Secured Transactions (Article 9). Section 2A–309. Prior to the adoption of this Article filing or recording was not required with respect to leases, only leases intended as security. The definition of security interest, as amended concurrently with the adoption of this Article, more clearly delineates leases and leases intended as security and thus signals the need to file. Section 1–201(37). Those lessors who are concerned about whether the transaction creates a lease or a security interest will continue to file a protective financing statement. Section 9–408. Coogan, Leasing and the Uniform Commercial Code, in *Equipment Leasing-Leveraged Leasing* 681, 744–46 (2d ed. 1980).

3. **Hypothetical:**

(a) In construing this section it is important to recognize its relationship to other sections in this Article. This is best demonstrated by reference to a hypothetical. Assume that on February 1 A, a manufacturer of combines and other farm equipment, leased a fleet of six combines to B, a corporation engaged in the business of farming, for a 12 month term. Under the lease agreement between A and B, A agreed to defer B's payment of the first two months' rent to April 1. On March 1 B recognized that it would need only four combines and thus subleased two combines to C for an 11 month term.

(b) This hypothetical raises a number of issues that are answered by the sections contained in this part. Since lease is defined to include sublease (Section 2A–103(1)(j) and (w)), this section provides that the prime lease between A and B and the sublease between B and C are enforceable in accordance with their terms, except as otherwise provided in this Article; that exception, in this case, is one of considerable scope.

(c) The separation of ownership, which is in A, and possession, which is in B with respect to four combines and which is in C with respect to two combines, is not relevant. Section 2A–302. A's interest in the six combines cannot be challenged simply because A parted with possession to B, who in turn parted with possession of some of the combines to C. Yet it is important to note that by the terms of Section 2A–302 this conclusion is subject to change if otherwise provided in this Article.

(d) B's entering the sublease with C raises an issue that is treated by this part. In a dispute over the leased combines A may challenge B's right to sublease. The rule is permissive as to transfers of interests under a lease contract, including subleases. Section 2A–303(2). However, the rule has two significant qualifications. If the prime lease contract between A and B prohibits B from subleasing the combines, or makes such a sublease an event of default, Section 2A–303(2) applies; thus, while B's interest under the prime lease may not be transferred under the sublease to C, A may have a remedy pursuant to Section 2A–303(5). Absent a prohibition or default provision in the prime lease contract A might be able to argue that the sublease to C materially increases A's risk; thus, while B's interest under the prime lease may be transferred under the sublease to C, A may have a remedy pursuant to Section 2A–303(5). Section 2A–303(5)(b)(ii).

(e) Resolution of this issue is also a function of the section dealing with the sublease of goods by a prime lessee (Section 2A–305). Subsection (1) of Section 2A–305, which is subject to the rules of Section 2A–303 stated above, provides that C takes subject to the interest of A under the prime lease between A and B. However, there are two exceptions. First, if B is a merchant (Sections 2A–103(3) and 2–104(1)) dealing in goods of that kind and C is a sublessee in the ordinary course of business (Sections 2A–103(1)(*o*) and 2A–103(1)(n)), C takes free of the prime lease between A and B. Second, if B has rejected the six combines under the prime lease with A, and B disposes of the goods by sublease to C, C takes free of the prime lease if C can establish good faith. Section 2A–511(4).

(f) If the facts of this hypothetical are expanded and we assume that the prime lease obligated B to maintain the combines, an additional issue may be presented. Prior to entering the sublease, B, in satisfaction of its maintenance covenant, brought the two combines that it desired to sublease to a local independent dealer of A's. The dealer did the requested work for B. C inspected the combines on the dealer's lot after the work was completed. C signed the sublease with B two days later. C, however, was prevented from taking delivery of the two combines as B refused to pay the dealer's invoice for the repairs. The dealer furnished the repair service to B in the ordinary course of the dealer's business. If under applicable law the dealer has a lien on repaired goods in the dealer's possession, the dealer's lien will take priority over B's and C's interests, and also should take priority over A's interest, depending upon the terms of the lease contract and the applicable law. Section 2A–306.

(g) Now assume that C is in financial straits and one of C's creditors obtains a judgment against C. If the creditor levies on C's subleasehold interest in the two combines, who will prevail? Unless the levying creditor also holds a lien covered by Section 2A–306, discussed above, the judgment creditor will take its interest subject to B's rights under the sublease and A's rights under the prime lease. Section 2A–307(1). The hypothetical becomes more complicated if we assume that B is in financial straits and B's creditor holds the judgment. Here the judgment creditor takes subject to the sublease unless the lien attached to the two combines before the sublease contract became enforceable. Section 2A–307(2)(a). However, B's judgment creditor cannot prime A's interest in the goods because, with respect to A, the judgment creditor is a creditor of B in its capacity as lessee under the prime lease between A and B. Thus, here the judgment creditor's interest is subject to the lease between A and B. Section 2A–307(1).

(h) Finally, assume that on April 1 B is unable to pay A the deferred rent then due under the prime lease, but that C is current in its payments under the sublease from B. What effect will B's default under the prime lease between A and B have on C's rights under the sublease between B and C? Section 2A–301 provides that a lease contract is effective against the creditors of either party. Since a lease contract includes a sublease contract (Section 2A–103(1)(*l*)), the sublease contract between B and C arguably could be enforceable against A, a prime lessor who has extended unsecured credit to B the prime lessee/sublessor, if the sublease contract meets the requirements of Section 2A–201. However, the rule stated in Section 2A–301 is subject to other provisions in this Article. Under Section 2A–305, C, as sublessee, would take subject to the prime lease contract in most cases. Thus, B's default under the prime lease will in most cases lead to A's recovery of the goods from C. Section 2A–523. A and C could provide otherwise by agreement. Section 2A–311. C's recourse will be to assert a claim for damages against B. Sections 2A–211(1) and 2A–508.

4. **Relationship Between Sections:** (a) As the analysis of the hypothetical demonstrates, Part 3 of the Article focuses on issues that relate to the enforceability of the lease contract (Sections 2A–301, 2A–302 and 2A–303) and to the priority of various claims to the goods subject to the lease contract (Sections 2A–304, 2A–305, 2A–306, 2A–307, 2A–308, 2A–309, 2A–310, and 2A–311).

(b) This section states a general rule of enforceability, which is subject to specific rules to the contrary stated elsewhere in the Article. Section 2A–302 negates any notion that the separation of title and possession is fraudulent as a rule of law. Finally, Section 2A–303 states rules with respect to the transfer of the lessor's interest (as well as the residual interest in the goods) or the lessee's interest under the lease contract. Qualifications are imposed as a function of various issues, including whether the transfer is the creation or enforcement of a security interest or one that is material to the other party to the lease contract. In addition, a system of rules is created to deal with the rights and duties among assignor, assignee and the other party to the lease contract.

(c) Sections 2A–304 and 2A–305 are twins that deal with good faith transferees of goods subject to the lease contract. Section 2A–304 creates a set of rules with respect to transfers by the lessor of goods subject to a lease contract; the transferee considered is a subsequent lessee of the goods. The priority dispute covered here is between the subsequent lessee and the original lessee of the goods (or persons claiming through the original lessee). Section 2A–305 creates a set of rules with respect to transfers by the lessee of goods subject to a lease contract; the transferees considered are buyers of the goods or sublessees of the goods. The priority dispute covered here is between the transferee and the lessor of the goods (or persons claiming through the lessor).

(d) Section 2A–306 creates a rule with respect to priority disputes between holders of liens for services or materials furnished with respect to goods subject to a lease contract and the lessor or the lessee under that contract. Section 2A–307 creates a rule with respect to priority disputes between the lessee and creditors of the lessor and priority disputes between the lessor and creditors of the lessee.

(e) Section 2A–308 creates a series of rules relating to allegedly fraudulent transfers and preferences. The most significant rule is that set forth in subsection (3) which validates sale-leaseback transactions if the buyer-lessor can establish that he or she bought for value and in good faith.

(f) Sections 2A–309 and 2A–310 create a series of rules with respect to priority disputes between various third parties and a lessor of fixtures or accessions, respectively, with respect thereto.

(g) Finally, Section 2A–311 allows parties to alter the statutory priorities by agreement.

Cross References:

Article 1, especially Section 1–201(37), and Sections 2–104(1), 2A–103(1)(j), 2A–103(1)(*l*), 2A–103(1)(n), 2A–103(1)(*o*) and 2A–103(1)(w), 2A–103(3), 2A–103(4), 2A–201, 2A–301 through 2A–303, 2A–303(2), 2A–303(5), 2A–304 through 2A–307, 2A–307(1), 2A–307(2)(a), 2A–308 through 2A–311, 2A–508, 2A–511(4), 2A–523, Article 9, especially Sections 9–201 and 9–408.

Definitional Cross References:

"Creditor". Section 1–201(12).

"Goods". Section 2A–103(1)(h).

"Lease contract". Section 2A–103(1)(*l*).

"Party". Section 1–201(29).

"Purchaser". Section 1–201(33).

"Term". Section 1–201(42).

§ 2A.302. Title to and Possession of Goods

Except as otherwise provided in this title, each provision of this chapter applies whether the lessor or a third party has title to the goods, and whether the lessor, the lessee, or a third party has possession of the goods, notwithstanding any statute or rule of law that possession or the absence of possession is fraudulent.

Added by Acts 1993, 73rd Leg., ch. 570, § 1, eff. Sept. 1, 1993.

Uniform Commercial Code Comment

Uniform Statutory Source: Section 9–202.

Changes: Section 9–202 was modified to reflect leasing terminology and to clarify the law of leases with respect to fraudulent conveyances or transfers.

Purposes: The separation of ownership and possession of goods between the lessor and the lessee (or a third party) has created problems under certain fraudulent conveyance statutes. *See, e.g., In re Ludlum Enters.*, 510 F.2d 996 (5th Cir.1975); *Suburbia Fed. Sav. & Loan Ass'n v. Bel-Air Conditioning Co.*, 385 So.2d 1151 (Fla.Dist.Ct.App.1980). This section provides, among other things, that separation of ownership and possession *per se* does not affect the enforceability of the lease contract. Sections 2A–301 and 2A–308.

Cross References:

Sections 2A–301, 2A–308 and 9–202.

Definitional Cross References:

"Goods". Section 2A–103(1)(h).

"Lessee". Section 2A–103(1)(n).

"Lessor". Section 2A–103(1)(p).

§ 2A.303. Alienability of Party's Interest Under Lease Contract or of Lessor's Residual Interest in Goods; Delegation of Performance; Transfer of Rights

(a) As used in this section, "creation of a security interest" includes the sale of a lease contract that is subject to Chapter 9 of this code, Secured Transactions, by reason of Section 9.109(a)(3).

(b) Except as provided in Section 9.407(c), a provision in a lease agreement which (1) prohibits the voluntary or involuntary transfer, including a transfer by sale, sublease, creation or enforcement of a security interest, or attachment, levy, or other judicial process, of an interest of a party under the lease contract or of the lessor's residual interest in the goods, or (2) makes such a transfer an event of default, gives rise to the rights and remedies provided in Subsection (d), but a transfer that is prohibited or is an event of default under the lease agreement is otherwise effective.

(c) A provision in a lease agreement which (1) prohibits a transfer of a right to damages for default with respect to the whole lease contract or of a right to payment arising out of the transferor's due performance of the transferor's entire obligation, or (2) makes such a transfer an event of default, is not enforceable, and such a transfer is not a transfer that materially impairs the prospect of obtaining return performance by, materially changes the duty of, or materially increases the burden or risk imposed on, the other party to the lease contract within the purview of Subsection (d).

(d) Subject to Section 9.407(c):

(1) if a transfer is made which is made an event of default under a lease agreement, the party to the lease contract not making the transfer, unless that party waives the default or otherwise agrees, has the rights and remedies described in Section 2A.501(b); and

(2) if Subdivision (1) is not applicable and if a transfer is made that (A) is prohibited under a lease agreement or (B) materially impairs the prospect of obtaining return performance by, materially changes the duty of, or materially increases the burden of risk imposed on, the other party to the lease contract, unless the party not making the transfer agrees at any time to the transfer in the lease contract or otherwise, then, except as limited by contract, (i) the transferor is liable to the party not making the transfer for damages caused by the transfer to the extent that the damages could not reasonably be prevented by the party not making the transfer and (ii) a court having jurisdiction may grant other appropriate relief, including cancellation of the lease contract or an injunction against the transfer.

(e) A transfer of "the lease" or of "all my rights under the lease," or a transfer in similar general terms, is a transfer of rights and, unless the language or the circumstances, as in a transfer for security, indicate the contrary, the transfer is a delegation of duties by the transferor to the transferee. Acceptance by the transferee constitutes a promise by the transferee to perform those duties. This promise is enforceable by either the transferor or the other party to the lease contract.

(f) Unless otherwise agreed by the lessor and the lessee, a delegation of performance does not relieve the transferor as against the other party of any duty to perform or of any liability for default.

(g) In a consumer lease, to prohibit the transfer of an interest of a party under the lease contract or to make a transfer an event of default, the language must be specific, by a writing, and conspicuous.

Added by Acts 1993, 73rd Leg., ch. 570, § 1, eff. Sept. 1, 1993. Amended by Acts 1999, 76th Leg., ch. 414, § 2.20, eff. July 1, 2001.

Uniform Commercial Code Comment

1999 Amendment (effective July 1, 2001)

Uniform Statutory Source: Sections 2–210 and 9–311.

Changes: The provisions of Sections 2–210 and 9–311 were incorporated in this section, with substantial modifications to reflect leasing terminology and practice and to harmonize the principles of the respective provisions, *i.e.*, limitations on delegation of performance on the one hand and alienability of rights on the other. In addition, unlike Section 2–210 which deals only with voluntary transfers, this section deals with involuntary as well as voluntary transfers. Moreover, the principle of Section 9–318(4) denying effectiveness to contractual terms prohibiting assignments of receivables due and to become due also is implemented.

Purposes:

1. Subsection (2) states a rule, consistent with Section 9–401(b), that voluntary and involuntary transfers of an interest of a party under the lease contract or of the lessor's residual interest, including by way of the creation or enforcement of a security interest, are effective, notwithstanding a provision in the lease agreement prohibiting the transfer or making the transfer an event of default. Although the transfers are effective, the provision in the lease agreement is nevertheless enforceable, but only as provided in subsection (4). Under subsection (4) the prejudiced party is limited to the remedies on "default under the lease contract" in this Article and, except as limited by this Article, as provided in the lease agreement, if the transfer has been made an event of default. Section 2A–501(2). Usually, there will be a specific provision to this effect or a general provision making a breach of a covenant an event of default. In those cases where the transfer is prohibited, but not made an event of default, the prejudiced party may recover damages; or, if the damage remedy would be ineffective adequately to protect that party, the court can order cancellation of the lease contract or enjoin the transfer. This rule that such provisions generally are enforceable is subject to subsection (3) and Section 9–407, which make such provisions unenforceable in certain instances.

2. Under Section 9–407, a provision in a lease agreement which prohibits the creation or enforcement of a security interest, including sales of lease contracts subject to Article 9 (Section 9–109(a)(3)), or makes it an event of default is generally not enforceable, reflecting the policy of Section 9–406 and former Section 9–318(4).

3. Subsection (3) is based upon Section 2–210(2) and Section 9–406. It makes unenforceable a prohibition against transfers of certain rights to payment or a provision making the transfer an event of default. It also provides that such transfers do not materially impair the prospect of obtaining return performance by, materially change the duty of, or materially increase the burden or risk imposed on, the other party to the lease contract so as to give rise to the rights and remedies stated in subsection (4). Accordingly, a transfer of a right to payment cannot be prohibited or made an event of default, or be one that materially impairs performance, changes duties or increases risk, if the right is already due or will become due without further performance being required by the party to receive payment. Thus, a lessor can transfer the right to future payments under the lease contract, including by way of a grant of a security interest, and the transfer will not give rise to the rights and remedies stated in subsection (4) if the lessor has no remaining performance under the lease contract. The mere fact that the lessor is obligated to allow the lessee to remain in possession and to use the goods as long as the lessee is not in default does not mean that there is remaining performance on the part of the lessor. Likewise, the fact that the lessor has potential liability under a "non-operating" lease contract for breaches of warranty does not mean that there is remaining performance. In contrast, the lessor would have remaining performance under a lease contract requiring the lessor to regularly maintain and service the goods or to provide "upgrades" of the equipment on a periodic basis in order to avoid obsolescence. The basic distinction is between a mere potential duty to respond which is not remaining performance, and an affirmative duty to render stipulated performance. Although the distinction may be difficult to draw in some cases, it is instructive to focus on the difference between "operating" and "non-operating" leases as generally understood in the marketplace. Even if there is remaining performance under a lease contract, a transfer for security of a right to payment that is made an event of default or that is in violation of a prohibition against transfer does not give rise to the rights and remedies under subsection (4) if it does not constitute an actual delegation of a material performance under Section 9–407.

4. The application of either the rule of Section 9–407 or the rule of subsection (3) to the grant by the lessor of a security interest in the lessor's right to future payment under the lease contract may produce the same result. Both provisions generally protect security transfers by the lessor in particular because the creation by the lessor of a security interest or the enforcement of that interest generally will not prejudice the lessee's rights if it does not result in a delegation of the lessor's duties. To the contrary, the receipt of loan proceeds or relief from the enforcement of an antecedent debt normally should enhance the lessor's ability to perform its duties under the lease contract. Nevertheless, there are circumstances where relief might be justified. For example, if ownership of the goods is transferred pursuant to enforcement of a security interest to a party whose ownership would prevent the lessee from continuing to possess the goods, relief might be warranted. See 49 U.S.C. § 1401(a) and (b) which places limitations on the operation of aircraft in the United States based on the citizenship or corporate qualification of the registrant.

5. Relief on the ground of material prejudice when the lease agreement does not prohibit the transfer or make it an event of default should be afforded only in extreme circumstances, considering the fact that the party asserting material prejudice did not insist upon a provision in the lease agreement that would protect against such a transfer.

6. Subsection (4) implements the rule of subsection (2). Subsection (2) provides that, even though a transfer is effec-

tive, a provision in the lease agreement prohibiting it or making it an event of default may be enforceable as provided in subsection (4). See *Brummond v. First National Bank of Clovis*, 656 P.2d 884, 35 U.C.C.Rep.Serv. (Callaghan) 1311 (N.Mex.1983), stating the analogous rule for Section 9–311. If the transfer prohibited by the lease agreement is made an event of default, then, under subsection (4)(a), unless the default is waived or there is an agreement otherwise, the aggrieved party has the rights and remedies referred to in Section 2A–501(2), viz. those in this Article and, except as limited in the Article, those provided in the lease agreement. In the unlikely circumstance that the lease agreement prohibits the transfer without making a violation of the prohibition an event of default or, even if there is no prohibition against the transfer, and the transfer is one that materially impairs performance, changes duties, or increases risk (for example, a sublease or assignment to a party using the goods improperly or for an illegal purpose), then subsection (4)(b) is applicable. In that circumstance, unless the party aggrieved by the transfer has otherwise agreed in the lease contract, such as by assenting to a particular transfer or to transfers in general, or agrees in some other manner, the aggrieved party has the right to recover damages from the transferor and a court may, in appropriate circumstances, grant other relief, such as cancellation of the lease contract or an injunction against the transfer.

7. If a transfer gives rise to the rights and remedies provided in subsection (4), the transferee as an alternative may propose, and the other party may accept, adequate cure or compensation for past defaults and adequate assurance of future due performance under the lease contract. Subsection (4) does not preclude any other relief that may be available to a party to the lease contract aggrieved by a transfer subject to an enforceable prohibition, such as an action for interference with contractual relations.

8. Subsection (7) requires that a provision in a consumer lease prohibiting a transfer, or making it an event of default, must be specific, written and conspicuous. See Section 1–201(10). This assists in protecting a consumer lessee against surprise assertions of default.

9. Subsection (5) is taken almost verbatim from the provisions of Section 2–210(5). The subsection states a rule of construction that distinguishes a commercial assignment, which substitutes the assignee for the assignor as to rights and duties, and an assignment for security or financing assignment, which substitutes the assignee for the assignor only as to rights. Note that the assignment for security or financing assignment is a subset of all security interests. Security interest is defined to include "any interest of a buyer of ____ chattel paper". Section 1–201(37). Chattel paper is defined to include a lease. Section 9–102. Thus, a buyer of leases is the holder of a security interest in the leases. That conclusion should not influence this issue, as the policy is quite different. Whether a buyer of leases is the holder of a commercial assignment, or an assignment for security or financing assignment should be determined by the language of the assignment or the circumstances of the assignment.

Cross References:

Sections 1–201(11), 1–201(37), 2–210, 2A–401, 9–102(1)(b), 9–104(f), 9–105(1)(a), 9–206, and 9–318.

Definitional Cross References:

"Agreed" and "Agreement". Section 1–201(3).

"Conspicuous". Section 1–201(10).

"Goods". Section 2A–103(1)(h).

"Lease". Section 2A–103(1)(j).

"Lease contract". Section 2A–103(1)(*l*).

"Lessee". Section 2A–103(1)(n).

"Lessor". Section 2A–103(1)(p).

"Lessor's residual interest". Section 2A–103(1)(q).

"Notice". Section 1–201(25).

"Party". Section 1–201(29).

"Person". Section 1–201(30).

"Reasonable time". Section 1–204(1) and (2).

"Rights". Section 1–201(36).

"Term". Section 1–201(42).

"Writing". Section 1–201(46).

§ 2A.304. Subsequent Lease of Goods by Lessor

(a) Subject to Section 2A.303 of this chapter, a subsequent lessee from a lessor of goods under an existing lease contract obtains, to the extent of the leasehold interest transferred, the leasehold interest in the goods that the lessor had or had power to transfer, and except as provided by Subsection (b) or Section 2A.527(d) takes subject to the existing lease contract. A lessor with voidable title has power to transfer a good leasehold interest to a good faith subsequent lessee for value, but only to the extent set forth in the preceding sentence. If goods have been delivered under a transaction of purchase, the lessor has that power even though:

(1) the lessor's transferor was deceived as to the identity of the lessor;

(2) the delivery was in exchange for a check which is later dishonored;

(3) it was agreed that the transaction was to be a "cash sale"; or

(4) the delivery was procured through fraud punishable as larcenous under the criminal law.

(b) A subsequent lessee in the ordinary course of business from a lessor who is a merchant dealing in goods of that kind to whom the goods were entrusted by the existing lessee of that lessor before the interest of the subsequent lessee became enforceable against that lessor obtains, to the extent of the leasehold interest transferred, all of that lessor's and the existing lessee's rights to the goods, and takes free of the existing lease contract.

(c) A subsequent lessee from the lessor of goods that are subject to an existing lease contract and are covered by a certificate of title issued under a statute of this state or of another jurisdiction takes no greater rights than those provided both by this section and by the certificate of title statute.

Added by Acts 1993, 73rd Leg., ch. 570, § 1, eff. Sept. 1, 1993.

Uniform Commercial Code Comment

Uniform Statutory Source: Section 2–403.

Changes: While Section 2–403 was used as a model for this section, the provisions of Section 2–403 were significantly revised to reflect leasing practices and to integrate this Article with certificate of title statutes.

Purposes:

1. This section must be read in conjunction with, as it is subject to, the provisions of Section 2A–303, which govern voluntary and involuntary transfers of rights and duties under a lease contract, including the lessor's residual interest in the goods.

2. This section must also be read in conjunction with Section 2–403. This section and Section 2A–305 are derived from Section 2–403, which states a unified policy on good faith purchases of goods. Given the scope of the definition of purchaser (Section 1–201(33)), a person who bought goods to lease as well as a person who bought goods subject to an existing lease from a lessor will take pursuant to Section 2–403. Further, a person who leases such goods from the person who bought them should also be protected under Section 2–403, first because the lessee's rights are derivative and second because the definition of purchaser should be interpreted to include one who takes by lease; no negative implication should be drawn from the inclusion of lease in the definition of purchase in this Article. Section 2A–103(1)(v).

3. There are hypotheticals that relate to an entrustee's unauthorized lease of entrusted goods to a third party that are outside the provisions of Sections 2–403, 2A–304 and 2A–305. Consider a sale of goods by M, a merchant, to B, a buyer. After paying for the goods B allows M to retain possession of the goods as B is short of storage. Before B calls for the goods M leases the goods to L, a lessee. This transaction is not governed by Section 2–403(2) as L is not a buyer in the ordinary course of business. Section 1–201(9). Further, this transaction is not governed by Section 2A–304(2) as B is not an existing lessee. Finally, this transaction is not governed by Section 2A–305(2) as B is not M's lessor. Section 2A–307(2) resolves the potential dispute between B, M and L. By virtue of B's entrustment of the goods to M and M's lease of the goods to L, B has a cause of action against M under the common law. Sections 2A–103(4) and 1–103. *See, e.g.*, Restatement (Second) of Torts §§ 222A–243. Thus, B is a creditor of M. Sections 2A–103(4) and 1–201(12). Section 2A–307(2) provides that B, as M's creditor, takes subject to M's lease to L. Thus, if L does not default under the lease, L's enjoyment and possession of the goods should be undisturbed. However, B is not without recourse. B's action should result in a judgment against M providing, among other things, a turnover of all proceeds arising from M's lease to L, as well as a transfer of all of M's right, title and interest as lessor under M's lease to L, including M's residual interest in the goods. Section 2A–103(1)(q).

4. Subsection (1) states a rule with respect to the leasehold interest obtained by a subsequent lessee from a lessor of goods under an existing lease contract. The interest will include such leasehold interest as the lessor has in the goods as well as the leasehold interest that the lessor had the power to transfer. Thus, the subsequent lessee obtains unimpaired all rights acquired under the law of agency, apparent agency, ownership or other estoppel, whether based upon statutory provisions or upon case law principles. Sections 2A–103(4) and 1–103. In general, the subsequent lessee takes subject to the existing lease contract, including the existing lessee's rights thereunder. Furthermore, the subsequent lease contract is, of course, limited by its own terms, and the subsequent lessee takes only to the extent of the leasehold interest transferred thereunder.

5. Subsection (1) further provides that a lessor with voidable title has power to transfer a good leasehold interest to a good faith subsequent lessee for value. In addition, subsections (1)(a) through (d) provide specifically for the protection of the good faith subsequent lessee for value in a number of specific situations which have been troublesome under prior law.

6. The position of an existing lessee who entrusts leased goods to its lessor is not distinguishable from the position of other entrusters. Thus, subsection (2) provides that the subsequent lessee in the ordinary course of business takes free of the existing lease contract between the lessor entrustee and the lessee entruster, if the lessor is a merchant dealing in goods of that kind. Further, the subsequent lessee obtains all of the lessor entrustee's and the lessee entruster's rights to the goods, but only to the extent of the leasehold interest transferred by the lessor entrustee. Thus, the lessor entrustee retains the residual interest in the goods. Section 2A–103(1)(q). However, entrustment by the existing lessee must have occurred before the interest of the subsequent lessee became enforceable against the lessor. Entrusting is defined in Section 2–403(3) and that definition applies here. Section 2A–103(3).

7. Subsection (3) states a rule with respect to a transfer of goods from a lessor to a subsequent lessee where the goods are subject to an existing lease and covered by a certificate of title. The subsequent lessee's rights are no greater than those provided by this section and the applicable certificate of title statute, including any applicable case law construing such statute. Where the relationship between the certificate of title statute and Section 2–403, the statutory analogue to this section, has been construed by a court, that construction is incorporated here. Sections 2A–103(4) and 1–102(1) and (2). The better rule is that the certificate of title statutes are in harmony with Section 2–403 and thus would be in harmony with this section. *E.g.*, *Atwood Chevrolet-Olds v. Aberdeen Mun. School Dist.*, 431 So.2d 926, 928, (Miss.1983); *Godfrey v. Gilsdorf*, 476 P.2d 3, 6, 86 Nev. 714, 718 (1970); *Martin v. Nager*, 192 N.J.Super. 189, 197–98, 469 A.2d 519, 523 (Super. Ct. Ch. Div. 1983). Where the certificate of title statute is silent on this issue of transfer, this section will control.

Cross References:

Sections 1–102, 1–103, 1–201(33), 2–403, 2A–103(1)(v), 2A–103(3), 2A–103(4), 2A–303 and 2A–305.

Definitional Cross References:

"Agreed". Section 1–201(3).

"Delivery". Section 1–201(14).

"Entrusting". Section 2–403(3).

"Good faith". Sections 1–201(19) and 2–103(1)(b).

"Goods". Section 2A–103(1)(h).

"Lease". Section 2A–103(1)(j).

"Lease contract". Section 2A–103(1)(*l*).

"Leasehold interest". Section 2A–103(1)(m).

"Lessee". Section 2A–103(1)(n).

"Lessee in the ordinary course of business". Section 2A–103(1)(*o*).

"Lessor". Section 2A–103(1)(p).

"Merchant". Section 2–104(1).

"Purchase". Section 2A–103(1)(v).

"Rights". Section 1–201(36).

"Value". Section 1–201(44).

State Bar Committee Comments

In the circumstances covered by subsection (c), the provisions of the certificate of title statute do not control over, but are of equal dignity with, the provisions of subsection (c). Section 2A.104(b).

§ 2A.305. Sale or Sublease of Goods by Lessee

(a) Subject to the provisions of Section 2A.303, a buyer or sublessee from the lessee of goods under an existing lease contract obtains, to the extent of the interest transferred, the leasehold interest in the goods that the lessee had or had power to transfer, and except as provided by Subsection (b) and Section 2A.511, takes subject to the existing lease contract. A lessee with a voidable leasehold interest has power to transfer a good leasehold interest to a good faith buyer for value or a good faith sublessee for value, but only to the extent set forth in the preceding sentence. When goods have been delivered under a transaction of lease the lessee has that power even though:

(1) the lessor was deceived as to the identity of the lessee;

(2) the delivery was in exchange for a check which is later dishonored; or

(3) the delivery was procured through fraud punishable as larcenous under the criminal law.

(b) A buyer in the ordinary course of business or a sublessee in the ordinary course of business from a lessee who is a merchant dealing in goods of that kind to whom the goods were entrusted by the lessor obtains, to the extent of the interest transferred, all of the lessor's and lessee's rights to the goods, and takes free of the existing lease contract.

(c) A buyer or sublessee from the lessee of goods that are subject to an existing lease contract and are covered by a certificate of title issued under a statute of this state or of another jurisdiction takes no greater rights than those provided both by this section and by the certificate of title statute.

Added by Acts 1993, 73rd Leg., ch. 570, § 1, eff. Sept. 1, 1993.

Uniform Commercial Code Comment

Uniform Statutory Source: Section 2–403.

Changes: While Section 2–403 was used as a model for this section, the provisions of Section 2–403 were significantly revised to reflect leasing practice and to integrate this Article with certificate of title statutes.

Purposes: This section, a companion to Section 2A–304, states the rule with respect to the leasehold interest obtained by a buyer or sublessee from a lessee of goods under an existing lease contract. *Cf.* Section 2A–304 official comment. Note that this provision is consistent with existing case law, which prohibits the bailee's transfer of title to a good faith purchaser for value under Section 2–403(1). *Rohweder v. Aberdeen Product. Credit Ass'n*, 765 F.2d 109 (8th Cir.1985).

Subsection (2) is also consistent with existing case law. *American Standard Credit, Inc. v. National Cement Co.*, 643 F.2d 248, 269–70 (5th Cir.1981); *but cf. Exxon Co., U.S.A. v. TLW Computer Indus.*, 37 U.C.C. Rep. Serv. (Callaghan) 1052, 1057–58 (D.Mass.1983). Unlike Section 2A–304(2), this subsection does not contain any requirement with respect to the time that the goods were entrusted to the merchant. In Section 2A–304(2) the competition is between two customers of the merchant lessor; the time of entrusting was added as a criterion to create additional protection to the customer who was first in time: the existing lessee. In subsection (2) the equities between the competing interests were viewed as balanced.

There appears to be some overlap between Section 2–403(2) and Section 2A–305(2) with respect to a buyer in the ordinary course of business. However, an examination of this Article's definition of buyer in the ordinary course of business (Section 2A–103(1)(a)) makes clear that this reference was necessary to treat entrusting in the context of a lease.

Subsection (3) states a rule of construction with respect to a transfer of goods from a lessee to a buyer or sublessee, where the goods are subject to an existing lease and covered by a certificate of title. *Cf.* Section 2A–304 official comment.

Cross References:

Sections 2–403, 2A–103(1)(a), 2A–304 and 2A–305(2).

Definitional Cross References:

"Buyer". Section 2–103(1)(a).

"Buyer in the ordinary course of business". Section 2A–103(1)(a).

"Delivery". Section 1–201(14).

"Entrusting". Section 2–403(3).

"Good faith". Sections 1–201(19) and 2–103(1)(b).

"Goods". Section 2A–103(1)(h).

"Lease". Section 2A–103(1)(j).

"Lease contract". Section 2A–103(1)(*l*).

"Leasehold interest". Section 2A–103(1)(m).

"Lessee". Section 2A–103(1)(n).

"Lessee in the ordinary course of business". Section 2A–103(1)(*o*).

"Lessor". Section 2A–103(1)(p).

"Merchant". Section 2–104(1).

"Rights". Section 1–201(36).

"Sale". Section 2–106(1).

"Sublease". Section 2A–103(1)(w).

"Value". Section 1–201(44).

State Bar Committee Comments

In the circumstances covered by subsection (c), the provisions of the certificate of title statute do not control over, but are of equal dignity with, the provisions of subsection (c). Section 2A.104(b).

§ 2A.306. Priority of Certain Liens Arising by Operation of Law

If a person in the ordinary course of the person's business furnishes services or materials with respect to goods subject to a lease contract, a lien upon those goods in the possession of that person given by statute or rule of law for those materials or services takes priority over any interest of the lessor or lessee under the lease contract or this chapter unless the lien is created by statute and the statute provides otherwise or unless the lien is created by rule of law and the rule of law provides otherwise.

Added by Acts 1993, 73rd Leg., ch. 570, § 1, eff. Sept. 1, 1993.

Uniform Commercial Code Comment

Uniform Statutory Source: Section 9–310.

Changes: The approach reflected in the provisions of Section 9–310 was included, but revised to conform to leasing terminology and to expand the exception to the special priority granted to protected liens to cover liens created by rule of law as well as those created by statute.

Purposes: This section should be interpreted to allow a qualified lessor or a qualified lessee to be the competing lienholder if the statute or rule of law so provides. The reference to statute includes applicable regulations and cases; these sources must be reviewed in resolving a priority dispute under this section.

Cross Reference:

Section 9–310.

Definitional Cross References:

"Goods". Section 2A–103(1)(h).

"Lease contract". Section 2A–103(1)(*l*).

"Lessee". Section 2A–103(1)(n).

"Lessor". Section 2A–103(1)(p).

"Lien". Section 2A–103(1)(r).

"Person". Section 1–201(30).

State Bar Committee Comments

The reference to "priority" in this section means that, in the circumstances prescribed by this section, the lien attaches to the prescribed goods and becomes a charge on the goods that is superior to the interests of both the lessee and the lessor in the goods, including the lessor's residual interest.

§ 2A.307. Priority of Liens Arising by Attachment or Levy on, Security Interests in, and Other Claims to Goods

(a) Except as otherwise provided in Section 2A.306, a creditor of a lessee takes subject to the lease contract.

(b) Except as otherwise provided in Subsection (c) and Sections 2A.306 and 2A.308, a creditor of a lessor takes subject to the lease contract unless the creditor holds a lien that attached to the goods before the lease contract became enforceable.

(c) Except as otherwise provided in Sections 9.317, 9.321, and 9.323, a lessee takes a leasehold interest subject to a security interest held by a creditor of the lessor.

Added by Acts 1993, 73rd Leg., ch. 570, § 1, eff. Sept. 1, 1993. Amended by Acts 1999, 76th Leg., ch. 414, § 2.21, eff. July 1, 2001.

Uniform Commercial Code Comment

1999 Amendment (effective July 1, 2001)

Uniform Statutory Source: None for subsection (1). Subsection (2) is derived from Section 9–301, and subsections (3) and (4) are derived from Section 9–307(1) and (3), respectively.

Changes: The provisions of Sections 9–301 and 9–307(1) and (3) were incorporated, and modified to reflect leasing terminology and the basic concepts reflected in this Article.

Purposes:

1. Subsection (1) states a general rule of priority that a creditor of the lessee takes subject to the lease contract. The term lessee (Section 2A–103(1)(n) includes sublessee.

Therefore, this subsection not only covers disputes between the prime lessor and a creditor of the prime lessee but also disputes between the prime lessor, or the sublessor, and a creditor of the sublessee. Section 2A–301 official comment 3(g). Further, by using the term creditor (Section 1–201(12)), this subsection will cover disputes with a general creditor, a secured creditor, a lien creditor and any representative of creditors. Section 2A–103(4).

2. Subsection (2) states a general rule of priority that a creditor of a lessor takes subject to the lease contract. Note the discussion above with regard to the scope of these rules. Section 2A–301 official comment 3(g). Thus, the section will not only cover disputes between the prime lessee and a creditor of the prime lessor but also disputes between the prime lessee, or the sublessee, and a creditor of the sublessor.

3. To take priority over the lease contract, and the interests derived therefrom, the creditor must come within the exception stated in subsection (2) or within one of the provisions of Article 9 mentioned in subsection (3). Subsection (2) provides that where the creditor holds a lien (Section 2A-103(1)(r)) that attached before the lease contract became enforceable (Section 2A–301), the creditor does not take subject to the lease. Subsection (3) provides that a lessee takes its leasehold interest subject to a security interest except as otherwise provided in Sections 9–317, 9–321, or 9–323.

4. The rules of this section operate in favor of whichever party to the lease contract may enforce it, even if one party perhaps may not, e.g., under Section 2A–201(1)(b).

5. The rules stated in subsections (2)(b) and (c), and the rule in subsection (3), are best understood by reviewing a hypothetical. Assume that a merchant engaged in the business of selling and leasing musical instruments obtained possession of a truck load of musical instruments on deferred payment terms from a supplier of musical instruments on January 6. To secure payment of such credit the merchant granted the supplier a security interest in the instruments; the security interest was perfected by filing on January 15. The merchant, as lessor, entered into a lease to an individual of one of the musical instruments supplied by the supplier; the lease became enforceable on January 10. Under subsection (2)(b) the lessee will prevail (assuming the lessee qualifies thereunder) unless subsection (c) provides otherwise. Under the rule stated in subsection (2)(c) a priority dispute between the supplier, as the lessor's secured creditor, and the lessee would be determined by ascertaining on January 10 (the day the lease became enforceable) the validity and perfected status of the security interest in the musical instrument and the enforceability of the lease contract by the lessee. Nothing more appearing, under the rule stated in subsection (2)(c), the supplier's security interest in the musical instrument would not have priority over the lease contract. Moreover, subsection (2) states that its rules are subject to the rules of subsections (3) and (4). Under this hypothetical the lessee should qualify as a "lessee in the ordinary course of business". Section 2A–103(1)(*o*). Subsection (3) also makes clear that the lessee in the ordinary course of business will win even if he or she knows of the existence of the supplier's security interest.

6. Subsections (3) and (4), which are modeled on the provisions of Section 9–307(1) and (3), respectively, state two exceptions to the priority rule stated in subsection (2) with respect to a creditor who holds a security interest. The lessee in the ordinary course of business will be treated in the same fashion as the buyer in the ordinary course of business, given a priority dispute with a secured creditor over goods subject to a lease contract.

Cross References:

Sections 1–201(12), 1–201(25), 1–201(37), 1–201(44), 2A–103(1)(n), 2A–103(1)(*o*), 2A–103(1)(r), 2A–103(4), 2A–201(1)(b), 2A–301 official comment 3(g), Article 9, especially Sections 9–301, 9–307(1) and 9–307(3).

Definitional Cross References:

"Creditor". Section 1–201(12).

"Goods". Section 2A–103(1)(h).

"Knowledge" and "Knows". Section 1–201(25).

"Lease". Section 2A–103(1)(j).

"Lease contract". Section 2A–103(1)(*l*).

"Leasehold interest". Section 2A–103(1)(m).

"Lessee". Section 2A–103(1)(n).

"Lessee in the ordinary course of business". Section 2A–103(1)(*o*).

"Lessor". Section 2A–103(1)(p).

"Lien". Section 2A–103(1)(r).

"Party". Section 1–201(29).

"Pursuant to commitment". Section 2A–103(3).

"Security interest". Section 1–201(37).

State Bar Committee Comments

The words "takes subject to the lease contract" mean that a creditor's lien or security interest can attach only to what the debtor (lessee) has. Whether the lien or security interest actually attaches to such interest of the debtor (lessee) is a question that must be answered by other law and is not intended to be covered by Chapter 2A.

§ 2A.308. Special Rights of Creditors

(a) A creditor of a lessor in possession of goods subject to a lease contract may treat the lease contract as void if as against the creditor retention of possession by the lessor is fraudulent or voids the lease contract under any statute or rule of law, but retention of possession in good faith and current course of trade by the lessor for a commercially reasonable time after the lease contract becomes enforceable is not fraudulent and does not void the lease contract.

(b) Nothing in this chapter impairs the rights of creditors of a lessor if the lease contract is made under circumstances which under any statute or rule of law apart from this chapter would constitute the transaction a fraudulent transfer or voidable preference.

(c) A creditor of a seller may treat a sale or an identification of goods to a contract for sale as void if as against the creditor retention of possession by the seller is fraudulent under any statute or rule of law, but retention of possession of the goods pursuant to a lease contract entered into by the seller as lessee and the buyer as lessor in connection with the sale or identification of the goods is not fraudulent if the buyer bought for value and in good faith.

Added by Acts 1993, 73rd Leg., ch. 570, § 1, eff. Sept. 1, 1993.

Uniform Commercial Code Comment

Uniform Statutory Source: Section 2–402(2) and (3)(b).

Changes: Rephrased and new material added to conform to leasing terminology and practice.

Purposes: Subsection (1) states a general rule of avoidance where the lessor has retained possession of goods if such retention is fraudulent under any statute or rule of law. However, the subsection creates an exception under certain circumstances for retention of possession of goods for a commercially reasonable time after the lease contract becomes enforceable.

Subsection (2) also preserves the possibility of an attack on the lease by creditors of the lessor if the lease was made in satisfaction of or as security for a pre-existing claim, and would constitute a fraudulent transfer or voidable preference under other law.

Finally, subsection (3) states a new rule with respect to sale-leaseback transactions, *i.e.*, transactions where the seller sells goods to a buyer but possession of the goods is retained by the seller pursuant to a lease contract between the buyer as lessor and the seller as lessee. Notwithstanding any statute or rule of law that would treat such retention as fraud, whether *per se, prima facie*, or otherwise, the retention is not fraudulent if the buyer bought for value (Section 1–201(44)) and in good faith (Sections 1–201(19) and 2–103(1)(b)). Section 2A–103(3) and (4). This provision overrides Section 2–402(2) to the extent it would otherwise apply to a sale-leaseback transaction.

Cross References:

Sections 1–201(19), 1–201(44), 2–402(2) and 2A–103(4).

Definitional Cross References:

"Buyer". Section 2–103(1)(a).

"Contract". Section 1–201(11).

"Creditor". Section 1–201(12).

"Good faith". Sections 1–201(19) and 2–103(1)(b).

"Goods". Section 2A–103(1)(h).

"Lease contract". Section 2A–103(1)(*l*).

"Lessee". Section 2A–103(1)(n).

"Lessor". Section 2A–103(1)(p).

"Money". Section 1–201(24).

"Reasonable time". Section 1–204(1) and (2).

"Rights". Section 1–201(36).

"Sale". Section 2–106(1).

"Seller". Section 2–103(1)(d).

"Value". Section 1–201(44).

State Bar Committee Comments

A portion of the uniform version of Section 2A.308(b), which adds as a condition to an attack on the lease by creditors of the lessor that the lease must be made in satisfaction of or as security for a pre-existing claim, has been deleted. Federal bankruptcy law will supersede Chapter 2A in any event. In addition, a violation of the Uniform Fraudulent Transfer Act, Chapter 25, Business and Commerce Code, should be sufficient alone, as a matter of policy, to permit an attack by the lessor's creditors.

§ 2A.309. Lessor's and Lessee's Rights When Goods Become Fixtures

(a) In this section:

(1) goods are "fixtures" when they become so related to particular real estate that an interest in them arises under real estate law;

(2) a "fixture filing" is the filing, in the office where a record of a mortgage on the real estate would be filed or recorded, of a financing statement covering goods that are or are to become fixtures and conforming to the requirements of Sections 9.502(a) and (b);

(3) a lease is a "purchase money lease" unless the lessee has possession or use of the goods or the right to possession or use of the goods before the lease agreement is enforceable;

(4) a mortgage is a "construction mortgage" to the extent it secures an obligation incurred for the construction of an improvement on land including the acquisition cost of the land, if the recorded writing so indicates; and

(5) "encumbrance" includes real estate mortgages and other liens on real estate and all other rights in real estate that are not ownership interests.

(b) Under this chapter a lease may be of goods that are fixtures or may continue in goods that become fixtures, but no lease exists under this chapter of ordinary building materials incorporated into an improvement on land.

(c) This chapter does not prevent the creation of a lease of fixtures pursuant to real estate law.

(d) The perfected interest of a lessor of fixtures has priority over a conflicting interest of an encumbrancer or owner of the real estate if:

(1) the lease is a purchase money lease, the conflicting interest of the encumbrancer or owner arises before the goods become fixtures, a fixture filing covering the fixtures is filed or recorded before the goods become fixtures or within 10 days thereafter, and the lessee has an interest of record in the real estate or is in possession of the real estate; or

(2) the interest of the lessor is perfected by a fixture filing before the interest of the encumbrancer or owner is of record, the lessor's interest has priority over any conflicting interest of a predecessor in title of the encumbrancer or owner, and the lessee has an interest of record in the real estate or is in possession of the real estate.

(e) The interest of a lessor of fixtures, whether or not perfected, has priority over the conflicting interest of an encumbrancer or owner of the real estate if:

(1) the fixtures are readily removable factory or office machines, readily removable equipment that is not primarily used or leased for use in the operation of the real estate, or readily removable replacements of domestic appliances that are goods subject to a consumer lease, and before the goods become fixtures the lease contract is enforceable; or

(2) the conflicting interest is a lien on the real estate obtained by legal or equitable proceedings after the lease contract is enforceable; or

(3) the encumbrancer or owner has consented in writing to the lease or has disclaimed an interest in the goods as fixtures; or

(4) the lessee has a right to remove the goods as against the encumbrancer or owner. If the lessee's right to remove terminates, the priority of the interest of the lessor continues for a reasonable time.

(f) Notwithstanding Subsection (d)(1) but otherwise subject to Subsections (d) and (e), the interest of a lessor of fixtures, including the lessor's residual interest, is subordinate to the conflicting interest of an encumbrancer of the real estate under a construction mortgage recorded before the goods become fixtures if the goods become fixtures before the completion of the construction. To the extent given to refinance a construction mortgage, the conflicting interest of an encumbrancer of the real estate under a mortgage has this priority to the same extent as the encumbrancer of the real estate under the construction mortgage.

(g) In cases not within the preceding subsections, priority between the interest of a lessor of fixtures, including the lessor's residual interest, and the conflicting interest of an encumbrancer or owner of the real estate who is not the lessee is determined by the priority rules governing conflicting interests in real estate.

(h) If the interest of a lessor of fixtures, including the lessor's residual interest, has priority over all conflicting interests of all owners and encumbrancers of the real estate, the lessor or the lessee may (1) on default, expiration, termination, or cancellation of the lease agreement but subject to the lease agreement and this chapter, or (2) if necessary to enforce other rights and remedies of the lessor or lessee under this chapter, remove the goods from the real estate, free and clear of all conflicting interests of all owners and encumbrancers of the real estate, but the lessor or lessee must reimburse any encumbrancer or owner of the real estate who is not the lessee and who has not otherwise agreed for the cost of repair of any physical injury, but not for any diminution in value of the real estate caused by the absence of the goods removed or by any necessity of replacing them. A person entitled to reimbursement may refuse permission to remove until the party seeking removal gives adequate security for the performance of this obligation.

(i) Even though the lease agreement does not create a security interest, the interest of a lessor of fixtures, including the lessor's residual interest, is perfected by filing a financing statement as a fixture filing for leased goods that are or are to become fixtures in accordance with the relevant provisions of Chapter 9.

Added by Acts 1993, 73rd Leg., ch. 570, § 1, eff. Sept. 1, 1993. Amended by Acts 1999, 76th Leg., ch. 414, § 2.22, eff. July 1, 2001.

Uniform Commercial Code Comment

Uniform Statutory Source: Section 9–313.

Changes: Revised to reflect leasing terminology and to add new material.

Purposes:

1. While Section 9–313 provided a model for this section, certain provisions were substantially revised.

2. Section 2A–309(1)(c), which is new, defines purchase money lease to exclude leases where the lessee had possession or use of the goods or the right thereof before the lease agreement became enforceable. This term is used in subsec-

tion (4)(a) as one of the conditions that must be satisfied to obtain priority over the conflicting interest of an encumbrancer or owner of the real estate.

3. Section 2A–309(4), which states one of several priority rules found in this section, deletes reference to office machines and the like (Section 9–313(4)(c)) as well as certain liens (Section 9–313(4)(d)). However, these items are included in subsection (5), another priority rule that is more permissive than the rule found in subsection (4) as it applies whether or not the interest of the lessor is perfected. In addition, subsection (5)(a) expands the scope of the provisions of Section 9–313(4)(c) to include readily removable equipment not primarily used or leased for use in the operation of real estate; the qualifier is intended to exclude from the expanded rule equipment integral to the operation of real estate, *e.g.*, heating and air conditioning equipment.

4. The rule stated in subsection (7) is more liberal than the rule stated in Section 9–313(7) in that issues of priority not otherwise resolved in this subsection are left for resolution by the priority rules governing conflicting interests in real estate, as opposed to the Section 9–313(7) automatic subordination of the security interest in fixtures. Note that, for the purpose of this section, where the interest of an encumbrancer or owner of the real estate is paramount to the intent of the lessor, the latter term includes the residual interest of the lessor.

5. The rule stated in subsection (8) is more liberal than the rule stated in Section 9–313(8) in that the right of removal is extended to both the lessor and the lessee and the occasion for removal includes expiration, termination or cancellation of the lease agreement, and enforcement of rights and remedies under this Article, as well as default. The new language also provides that upon removal the goods are free and clear of conflicting interests of owners and encumbrancers of the real estate.

6. Finally, subsection (9) provides a mechanism for the lessor of fixtures to perfect its interest by filing a financing statement under the provisions of the Article on Secured Transactions (Article 9), even though the lease agreement does not create a security interest. Section 1–201(37). The relevant provisions of Article 9 must be interpreted permissively to give effect to this mechanism as it implicitly expands the scope of Article 9 so that its filing provisions apply to transactions that create a lease of fixtures, even though the lease agreement does not create a security interest. This mechanism is similar to that provided in Section 2–326(3)(c) for the seller of goods on consignment, even though the consignment is not "intended as security". Section 1–201(37). Given the lack of litigation with respect to the mechanism created for consignment sales, this new mechanism should prove effective.

Cross References:

Sections 1–201(37), 2A–309(1)(c), 2A–309(4), Article 9, especially Sections 9–313, 9–313(4)(c), 9–313(4)(d), 9–313(7), 9–313(8) and 9–408.

Definitional Cross References:

"Agreed". Section 1–201(3).

"Cancellation". Section 2A–103(1)(b).

"Conforming". Section 2A–103(1)(d).

"Consumer lease". Section 2A–103(1)(e).

"Goods". Section 2A–103(1)(h).

"Lease". Section 2A–103(1)(j).

"Lease agreement". Section 2A–103(1)(k).

"Lease contract". Section 2A–103(1)(*l*).

"Lessee". Section 2A–103(1)(n).

"Lessor". Section 2A–103(1)(p).

"Lien". Section 2A–103(1)(r).

"Mortgage". Section 9–105(1)(j).

"Party". Section 1–201(29).

"Person". Section 1–201(30).

"Reasonable time". Section 1–204(1) and (2).

"Remedy". Section 1–201(34).

"Rights". Section 1–201(36).

"Security interest". Section 1–201(37).

"Termination". Section 2A–103(1)(z).

"Value". Section 1–201(44).

"Writing". Section 1–201(46).

§ 2A.310. Lessor's and Lessee's Rights When Goods Become Accessions

(a) Goods are "accessions" when they are installed in or affixed to other goods.

(b) The lessor's residual interest in the accessions and the interest of a lessor or a lessee under a lease contract entered into before the goods became accessions are superior to all interests in the whole except as stated in Subsection (d).

(c) The lessor's residual interest in the accessions and the interest of a lessor or a lessee under a lease contract entered into at the time or after the goods became accessions are superior to all subsequently acquired interests in the whole except as stated in Subsection (d) but are subordinate to interests in the whole existing at the time the lease contract was made unless the holders of such interests in the whole have in writing consented to the lease or disclaimed an interest in the goods as part of the whole.

(d) The lessor's residual interest in the accessions and the interest of a lessor or a lessee under a lease contract described by Subsection (b) or (c) are subordinate to the interest of:

(1) a buyer in the ordinary course of business or a lessee in the ordinary course of business of any interest in the whole acquired after the goods became accessions; or

(2) a creditor with a security interest in the whole perfected before the lease contract was made to the

extent that the creditor makes subsequent advances without knowledge of the lease contract.

(e) When under Subsections (b) or (c) and (d) a lessor or a lessee of accessions holds an interest that is superior to all interests in the whole, the lessor or the lessee may (1) on default, expiration, termination, or cancellation of the lease contract by the other party but subject to the provisions of the lease contract and this chapter, or (2) if necessary to enforce the lessor's or lessee's other rights and remedies under this chapter, remove the goods from the whole, free and clear of all interests in the whole, but the party must reimburse any holder of an interest in the whole who is not the lessee and who has not otherwise agreed for the cost of repair of any physical injury but not for any diminution in value of the whole caused by the absence of the goods removed or by any necessity for replacing them. A person entitled to reimbursement may refuse permission to remove until the party seeking removal gives adequate security for the performance of this obligation.

Added by Acts 1993, 73rd Leg., ch. 570, § 1, eff. Sept. 1, 1993.

Uniform Commercial Code Comment

Uniform Statutory Source: Section 9–314.

Changes: Revised to reflect leasing terminology and to add new material.

Purposes: Subsections (1) and (2) restate the provisions of subsection (1) of Section 9–314 to clarify the definition of accession and to add leasing terminology to the priority rule that applies when the lease is entered into before the goods become accessions. Subsection (3) restates the provisions of subsection (2) of Section 9–314 to add leasing terminology to the priority rule that applies when the lease is entered into on or after the goods become accessions. Unlike the rule with respect to security interests, the lease is merely subordinate, not invalid.

Subsection (4) creates two exceptions to the priority rules stated in subsections (2) and (3). Subsection (4) deletes the special priority rule found in the provisions of Section 9–314(3)(b) as the interests of the lessor and lessee are entitled to greater protection.

Finally, subsection (5) is modeled on the provisions of Section 9–314(4) with respect to removal of accessions, restated to reflect the parallel changes in Section 2A–309(8).

Neither this section nor Section 9–314 governs where the accession to the goods is not subject to the interest of a lessor or a lessee under a lease contract and is not subject to the interest of a secured party under a security agreement. This issue is to be resolved by the courts, case by case.

Cross References:

Sections 2A–309(8), 9–314(1), 9–314(2), 9–314(3)(b), 9–314(4).

Definitional Cross References:

"Agreed". Section 1–201(3).

"Buyer in the ordinary course of business". Section 2A–103(1)(a).

"Cancellation". Section 2A–103(1)(b).

"Creditor". Section 1–201(12).

"Goods". Section 2A–103(1)(h).

"Holder". Section 1–201(20).

"Knowledge". Section 1–201(25).

"Lease". Section 2A–103(1)(j).

"Lease contract". Section 2A–103(1)(*l*).

"Lessee". Section 2A–103(1)(n).

"Lessee in the ordinary course of business". Section 2A–103(1)(*o*).

"Lessor". Section 2A–103(1)(p).

"Party". Section 1–201(29).

"Person". Section 1–201(30).

"Remedy". Section 1–201(34).

"Rights". Section 1–201(36).

"Security interest". Section 1–201(37).

"Termination". Section 2A–103(1)(z).

"Value". Section 1–201(44).

"Writing". Section 1–201(46).

State Bar Committee Comments

Subsections (b), (c) and (d) of Section 2A.310 have been clarified to indicate that the lessor's residual interest is covered by the rules established by the section. This result was intended but not made clear by the uniform version.

SUBCHAPTER D. PERFORMANCE OF LEASE CONTRACT: REPUDIATED, SUBSTITUTED AND EXCUSED

§ 2A.401. Insecurity: Adequate Assurance of Performance

(a) A lease contract imposes an obligation on each party that the other's expectation of receiving due performance will not be impaired.

(b) If reasonable grounds for insecurity arise with respect to the performance of either party, the insecure party may demand in writing adequate assurance of due performance. Until the insecure party receives that assurance, if commercially reasonable, the insecure party may suspend any performance for which the party has not already received the agreed return.

(c) A repudiation of the lease contract occurs if assurance of due performance adequate under the circumstances of the particular case is not provided to the insecure party within a reasonable time, not to exceed 30 days after receipt of a demand by the other party.

(d) Between merchants, the reasonableness of grounds for insecurity and the adequacy of any assurance offered must be determined according to commercial standards.

(e) Acceptance of any nonconforming delivery or payment does not prejudice the aggrieved party's right to demand adequate assurance of future performance.

Added by Acts 1993, 73rd Leg., ch. 570, § 1, eff. Sept. 1, 1993.

Uniform Commercial Code Comment

Uniform Statutory Source: Section 2–609.

Changes: Revised to reflect leasing practices and terminology. Note that in the analogue to subsection (3) (Section 2–609(4)), the adjective "justified" modifies demand. The adjective was deleted here as unnecessary, implying no substantive change.

Definitional Cross References:

"Aggrieved party". Section 1–201(2).

"Agreed". Section 1–201(3).

"Between merchants". Section 2–104(3).

"Conforming". Section 2A–103(1)(d).

"Delivery". Section 1–201(14).

"Lease contract". Section 2A–103(1)(*l*).

"Party". Section 1–201(29).

"Reasonable time". Section 1–204(1) and (2).

"Receipt". Section 2–103(1)(c).

"Rights". Section 1–201(36).

"Writing". Section 1–201(46).

§ 2A.402. Anticipatory Repudiation

If either party repudiates a lease contract with respect to a performance not yet due under the lease contract, the loss of which performance will substantially impair the value of the lease contract to the other, the aggrieved party may:

(1) for a commercially reasonable time, await retraction of repudiation and performance by the repudiating party;

(2) make demand pursuant to Section 2A.401 and await assurance of future performance adequate under the circumstances of the particular case; or

(3) resort to any right or remedy on default under the lease contract or this chapter, even though the aggrieved party has notified the repudiating party that the aggrieved party would await the repudiating party's performance and assurance and has urged retraction. In addition, whether or not the aggrieved party is pursuing one of the foregoing remedies, the aggrieved party may suspend performance or, if the aggrieved party is the lessor, proceed in accordance with the provisions of this chapter on the lessor's right to identify goods to the lease contract notwithstanding default or to salvage unfinished goods (Section 2A.524).

Added by Acts 1993, 73rd Leg., ch. 570, § 1, eff. Sept. 1, 1993.

Uniform Commercial Code Comment

Uniform Statutory Source: Section 2–610.

Changes: Revised to reflect leasing practices and terminology.

Definitional Cross References:

"Aggrieved party". Section 1–201(2).

"Goods". Section 2A–103(1)(h).

"Lease contract". Section 2A–103(1)(*l*).

"Lessor". Section 2A–103(1)(p).

"Notifies". Section 1–201(26).

"Party". Section 1–201(29).

"Reasonable time". Section 1–204(1) and (2).

"Remedy". Section 1–201(34).

"Rights." Section 1–201(36).

"Value". Section 1–201(44).

§ 2A.403. Retraction of Anticipatory Repudiation

(a) Until the repudiating party's next performance is due, the repudiating party can retract the repudiation unless, since the repudiation, the aggrieved party has canceled the lease contract or materially changed the aggrieved party's position or otherwise indicated that the aggrieved party considers the repudiation final.

(b) Retraction may be by any method that clearly indicates to the aggrieved party that the repudiating party intends to perform under the lease contract and includes any assurance demanded under Section 2A.401.

(c) Retraction reinstates a repudiating party's rights under a lease contract with due excuse and allowance to the aggrieved party for any delay occasioned by the repudiation.

Added by Acts 1993, 73rd Leg., ch. 570, § 1, eff. Sept. 1, 1993.

Uniform Commercial Code Comment

Uniform Statutory Source: Section 2–611.

Changes: Revised to reflect leasing practices and terminology. Note that in the analogue to subsection (2) (Section 2–611(2)) the adjective "justifiably" modifies demanded. The adjective was deleted here (as it was in Section 2A–401) as unnecessary, implying no substantive change.

Definitional Cross References:

"Aggrieved party". Section 1–201(2).

"Cancellation". Section 2A–103(1)(b).

"Lease contract". Section 2A–103(1)(*l*).

"Party". Section 1–201(29).

"Rights". Section 1–201(36).

§ 2A.404. Substituted Performance

(a) If without fault of the lessee, the lessor and the supplier, the agreed berthing, loading, or unloading facilities fail or the agreed type of carrier becomes unavailable or the agreed manner of delivery otherwise becomes commercially impracticable, but a commercially reasonable substitute is available, the substitute performance must be tendered and accepted.

(b) If the agreed means or manner of payment fails because of domestic or foreign governmental regulation:

(1) the lessor may withhold or stop delivery or cause the supplier to withhold or stop delivery unless the lessee provides a means or manner of payment that is commercially a substantial equivalent; and

(2) if delivery has already been taken, payment by the means or in the manner provided by the regulation discharges the lessee's obligation unless the regulation is discriminatory, oppressive, or predatory.

Added by Acts 1993, 73rd Leg., ch. 570, § 1, eff. Sept. 1, 1993.

Uniform Commercial Code Comment

Uniform Statutory Source: Section 2–614.

Changes: Revised to reflect leasing practices and terminology.

Definitional Cross References:

"Agreed". Section 1–201(3).

"Delivery". Section 1–201(14).

"Fault". Section 2A–103(1)(f).

"Lessee". Section 2A–103(1)(n).

"Lessor". Section 2A–103(1)(p).

"Supplier". Section 2A–103(1)(x).

§ 2A.405. Excused Performance

Subject to Section 2A.404 on substituted performance, the following rules apply:

(1) Delay in delivery or nondelivery in whole or in part by a lessor or a supplier who complies with Subdivisions (2) and (3) is not a default under the lease contract if performance as agreed has been made impracticable by the occurrence of a contingency the nonoccurrence of which was a basic assumption on which the lease contract was made or by compliance in good faith with any applicable foreign or domestic governmental regulation or order, whether or not the regulation or order later proves to be invalid.

(2) If the causes mentioned in Subdivision (1) affect only part of the lessor's or the supplier's capacity to perform, the lessor or supplier shall allocate production and deliveries among the lessor's or supplier's customers but at the lessor's or supplier's option may include regular customers not then under contract for sale or lease as well as the lessor's or supplier's own requirements for further manufacture. The lessor or supplier may so allocate in any manner that is fair and reasonable.

(3) The lessor seasonably shall notify the lessee and in the case of a finance lease the supplier seasonably shall notify the lessor and the lessee, if known, that there will be delay or nondelivery and, if allocation is required under Subdivision (2), of the estimated quota made available for the lessee.

Added by Acts 1993, 73rd Leg., ch. 570, § 1, eff. Sept. 1, 1993.

Uniform Commercial Code Comment

Uniform Statutory Source: Section 2–615.

Changes: Revised to reflect leasing practices and terminology.

Definitional Cross References:

"Agreed". Section 1–201(3).

"Contract". Section 1–201(11).

"Delivery". Section 1–201(14).

"Finance lease". Section 2A–103(1)(g).

"Good faith". Sections 1–201(19) and 2–103(1)(b).

"Knows". Section 1–201(25).

"Lease". Section 2A–103(1)(j).

"Lease contract". Section 2A–103(1)(*l*).

"Lessee". Section 2A–103(1)(n).

"Lessor". Section 2A–103(1)(p).

"Notifies". Section 1–201(26).

"Sale". Section 2–106(1).

"Seasonably". Section 1–204(3).

"Supplier". Section 2A–103(1)(x).

§ 2A.406. Procedure on Excused Performance

(a) If the lessee receives notification of a material or indefinite delay or an allocation justified under Section 2A.405, the lessee may by written notification to the lessor as to any goods involved, and with respect to all of the goods if under an installment lease contract the value of the whole lease contract is substantially impaired (Section 2A.510):

(1) terminate the lease contract (Section 2A.505(b)); or

(2) except in a finance lease that is not a consumer lease, modify the lease contract by accepting the available quota in substitution, with due allowance from the rent payable for the balance of the lease term for the deficiency but without further right against the lessor.

(b) If, after receipt of a notification from the lessor under Section 2A.405, the lessee fails to modify the lease agreement within a reasonable time not exceeding 30 days, the lease contract lapses with respect to any deliveries affected.

Added by Acts 1993, 73rd Leg., ch. 570, § 1, eff. Sept. 1, 1993.

Uniform Commercial Code Comment

Uniform Statutory Source: Section 2–616(1) and (2).

Changes: Revised to reflect leasing practices and terminology. Note that subsection 1(a) allows the lessee under a lease, including a finance lease, the right to terminate the lease for excused performance (Sections 2A–404 and 2A–405). However, subsection 1(b), which allows the lessee the right to modify the lease for excused performance, excludes a finance lease that is not a consumer lease. This exclusion is compelled by the same policy that led to codification of provisions with respect to irrevocable promises. Section 2A–407.

Definitional Cross References:

"Consumer lease". Section 2A–103(1)(e).

"Delivery". Section 1–201(14).

"Finance lease". Section 2A–103(1)(g).

"Goods". Section 2A–103(1)(h).

"Installment lease contract". Section 2A–103(1)(i).

"Lease agreement". Section 2A–103(1)(k).

"Lease contract". Section 2A–103(1)(*l*).

"Lessee". Section 2A–103(1)(n).

"Lessor". Section 2A–103(1)(p).

"Notice". Section 1–201(25).

"Reasonable time". Section 1–204(1) and (2).

"Receipt". Section 2–103(1)(c).

"Rights". Section 1–201(36).

"Termination". Section 2A–103(1)(z).

"Value". Section 1–201(44).

"Written". Section 1–201(46).

§ 2A.407. Irrevocable Promises: Finance Leases

(a) In the case of a finance lease that is not a consumer lease, a term in the lease agreement that provides that the lessee's promises under the lease contract become irrevocable and independent upon the lessee's acceptance of the goods is enforceable.

(b) A promise that has become irrevocable and independent under Subsection (a):

(1) is effective and enforceable between the parties, and by or against third parties including assignees of the parties; and

(2) is not subject to cancellation, termination, modification, repudiation, excuse, or substitution without the consent of the party to whom the promise runs.

Added by Acts 1993, 73rd Leg., ch. 570, § 1, eff. Sept. 1, 1993.

Uniform Commercial Code Comment

Uniform Statutory Source: None.

Purposes:

1. This section extends the benefits of the classic "hell or high water" clause to a finance lease that is not a consumer lease. This section is self-executing; no special provision need be added to the contract. This section makes covenants in a finance lease irrevocable and independent due to the function of the finance lessor in a three party relationship: the lessee is looking to the supplier to perform the essential covenants and warranties. Section 2A–209. Thus, upon the lessee's acceptance of the goods the lessee's promises to the lessor under the lease contract become irrevocable and independent. The provisions of this section remain subject to the obligation of good faith (Sections 2A–103(4) and 1–203), and the lessee's revocation of acceptance (Section 2A–517).

2. The section requires the lessee to perform even if the lessor's performance after the lessee's acceptance is not in accordance with the lease contract; the lessee may, however, have and pursue a cause of action against the lessor, *e.g.*, breach of certain limited warranties (Sections 2A–210 and 2A–211(1)). This is appropriate because the benefit of the supplier's promises and warranties to the lessor under the supply contract and, in some cases, the warranty of a manufacturer who is not the supplier, is extended to the lessee under the finance lease. Section 2A–209. Despite this balance, this section excludes a finance lease that is a consumer lease. That a consumer be obligated to pay notwithstanding

defective goods or the like is a principle that is not tenable under case law (*Unico v. Owen*, 50 N.J. 101, 232 A.2d 405 (1967)), state statute (Unif. Consumer Credit Code §§ 3.403–.405, 7A U.L.A. 126–31 (1974), or federal statute (15 U.S.C. § 1666i (1982)).

3. The relationship of the three parties to a transaction that qualifies as a finance lease is best demonstrated by a hypothetical. A, the potential lessor, has been contracted by B, the potential lessee, to discuss the lease of an expensive line of equipment that B has recently placed an order for with C, the manufacturer of such goods. The negotiation is completed and A, as lessor, and B, as lessee, sign a lease of the line of equipment for a 60–month term. B, as buyer, assigns the purchase order with C to A. If this transaction creates a lease (Section 2A–103(1)(j)), this transaction should qualify as a finance lease. Section 2A–103(1)(g).

4. The line of equipment is delivered by C to B's place of business. After installation by C and testing by B, B accepts the goods by signing a certificate of delivery and acceptance, a copy of which is sent by B to A and C. One year later the line of equipment malfunctions and B falls behind in its manufacturing schedule.

5. Under this Article, because the lease is a finance lease, no warranty of fitness or merchantability is extended by A to B. Sections 2A–212(1) and 2A–213. Absent an express provision in the lease agreement, application of Section 2A–210 or Section 2A–211(1), or application of the principles of law and equity, including the law with respect to fraud, duress, or the like (Sections 2A–103(4) and 1–103), B has no claim against A. B's obligation to pay rent to A continues as the obligation became irrevocable and independent when B accepted the line of equipment (Section 2A–407(1)). B has no right of set-off with respect to any part of the rent still due under the lease. Section 2A–508(6). However, B may have another remedy. Despite the lack of privity between B and C (the purchase order with C having been assigned by B to A), B may have a claim against C. Section 2A–209(1).

6. This section does not address whether a "hell or high water" clause, *i.e.*, a clause that is to the effect of this section, is enforceable if included in a finance lease that is a consumer lease or a lease that is not a finance lease. That issue will continue to be determined by the facts of each case and other law which this section does not affect. Sections 2A–104, 2A–103(4), 9–206 and 9–318. However, with respect to finance leases that are not consumer leases courts have enforced "hell or high water" clauses. *In re O.P.M. Leasing Servs.*, 21 Bankr. 993, 1006 (Bankr. S.D.N.Y. 1982).

7. Subsection (2) further provides that a promise that has become irrevocable and independent under subsection (1) is enforceable not only between the parties but also against third parties. Thus, the finance lease can be transferred or assigned without disturbing enforceability. Further, subsection (2) also provides that the promise cannot, among other things, be cancelled or terminated without the consent of the lessor.

Cross References:

Sections 1–103, 1–203, 2A–103(1)(g), 2A–103(1)(j), 2A–103(4), 2A–104, 2A–209, 2A–209(1), 2A–210, 2A–211(1), 2A–212(1), 2A–213, 2A–517(1)(b), 9–206 and 9–318.

Definitional Cross References:

"Cancellation". Section 2A–103(1)(b).
"Consumer lease". Section 2A–103(1)(e).
"Finance lease". Section 2A–103(1)(g).
"Goods". Section 2A–103(1)(h).
"Lease contract". Section 2A–103(1)(*l*).
"Lessee". Section 2A–103(1)(n).
"Party". Section 1–201(29).
"Termination". Section 2A–103(1)(z).

State Bar Committee Comments

Section 2A.407(a) has been revised to provide that it not be self-executing; a special provision must be added to the finance lease contract to the effect that the covenants of the lessee in the finance lease become irrevocable and independent upon the lessee's acceptance of the goods. This is reasonable for policy reasons. A self-executing provision may produce surprise and unfair results in some circumstances.

This section carries no positive or negative implication as to the validity of such clauses in contexts where the section does not apply. The enforceability of such a clause in any other context will be determined by the facts of each case and other applicable law.

SUBCHAPTER E. DEFAULT

§ 2A.501. Default: Procedure

(a) Whether the lessor or the lessee is in default under a lease contract is determined by the lease agreement and this chapter.

(b) If the lessor or the lessee is in default under the lease contract, the party seeking enforcement has rights and remedies as provided in this chapter and, except as limited by this chapter, as provided in the lease agreement.

(c) If the lessor or the lessee is in default under the lease contract, the party seeking enforcement may reduce the party's claim to judgment or otherwise enforce the lease contract by self-help or any available judicial procedure or nonjudicial procedure, including administrative proceeding, arbitration, or the like, in accordance with this chapter.

(d) Except as otherwise provided by Section 1.305(a) or this chapter or the lease agreement, the rights and remedies referred to in Subsections (b) and (c) are cumulative.

(e) If the lease agreement covers both real property and goods, the party seeking enforcement may proceed under this subchapter as to the goods, or under other applicable law as to both the real property and the goods in accordance with that party's rights and remedies in respect of the real property, in which case this subchapter does not apply.

Added by Acts 1993, 73rd Leg., ch. 570, § 1, eff. Sept. 1, 1993. Amended by Acts 2003, 78th Leg., ch. 542, § 5, eff. Sept. 1, 2003.

Uniform Commercial Code Comment

Uniform Statutory Source: Section 9–501.

Changes: Substantially revised.

Purposes:

1. Subsection (1) is new and represents a departure from the Article on Secured Transactions (Article 9) as the subsection makes clear that whether a party to the lease agreement is in default is determined by this Article as well as the agreement. Sections 2A–508 and 2A–523. It further departs from Article 9 in recognizing the potential default of either party, a function of the bilateral nature of the obligations between the parties to the lease contract.

2. Subsection (2) is a version of the first sentence of Section 9–501(1), revised to reflect leasing terminology.

3. Subsection (3), an expansive version of the second sentence of Section 9–501(1), lists the procedures that may be followed by the party seeking enforcement; in effect, the scope of the procedures listed in subsection (3) is consistent with the scope of the procedures available to the foreclosing secured party.

4. Subsection (4) establishes that the parties' rights and remedies are cumulative. DeKoven, *Leases of Equipment: Puritan Leasing Company v. August, A Dangerous Decision*, 12 U.S.F.L.Rev. 257, 276–80 (1978). Cumulation, and largely unrestricted selection, of remedies is allowed in furtherance of the general policy of the Commercial Code, stated in Section 1–106, that remedies be liberally administered to put the aggrieved party in as good a position as if the other party had fully performed. Therefore, cumulation of, or selection among, remedies is available to the extent necessary to put the aggrieved party in as good a position as it would have been in had there been full performance. However, cumulation of, or selection among, remedies is not available to the extent that the cumulation or selection would put the aggrieved party in a better position than it would have been in had there been full performance by the other party.

5. Section 9–501(3), which, among other things, states that certain rules, to the extent they give rights to the debtor and impose duties on the secured party, may not be waived or varied, was not incorporated in this Article. Given the significance of freedom of contract in the development of the common law as it applies to bailments for hire and the lessee's lack of an equity of redemption, there was no reason to impose that restraint.

Cross References:

Sections 1–106, 2A–508, 2A–523, Article 9, especially Sections 9–501(1) and 9–501(3).

Definitional Cross References:

"Goods". Section 2A–103(1)(h).

"Lease agreement". Section 2A–103(1)(k).

"Lease contract". Section 2A–103(1)(*l*).

"Lessee". Section 2A–103(1)(n).

"Lessor". Section 2A–103(1)(p).

"Party". Section 1–201(29).

"Remedy". Section 1–201(34).

"Rights". Section 1–201(36).

State Bar Committee Comments

In determining whether a default exists, reference should also be made to all applicable laws and statutes. See Section 2A.104.

§ 2A.502. Notice After Default

Except as provided by this chapter or the lease agreement, the lessor or lessee in default under the lease contract is not entitled to notice of default or notice of enforcement from the other party to the lease agreement.

Added by Acts 1993, 73rd Leg., ch. 570, § 1, eff. Sept. 1, 1993.

Uniform Commercial Code Comment

Uniform Statutory Source: None.

Purposes: This section makes clear that absent agreement to the contrary or provision in this Article to the contrary, *e.g.*, Section 2A–516(3)(a), the party in default is not entitled to notice of default or enforcement. While a review of Part 5 of Article 9 leads to the same conclusion with respect to giving notice of default to the debtor, it is never stated. Although Article 9 requires notice of disposition and strict foreclosure, the different scheme of lessors' and lessees' rights and remedies developed under the common law, and codified by this Article, generally does not require notice of enforcement; furthermore, such notice is not mandated by due process requirements. However, certain sections of this Article do require notice. *E.g.*, Section 2A–517(2).

Cross References:

Sections 2A–516(3)(a), 2A–517(2), and Article 9, esp. Part 5.

Definitional Cross References:

"Lease agreement". Section 2A–103(1)(k).

"Lease contract". Section 2A–103(1)(*l*).

"Lessee". Section 2A–103(1)(n).

"Lessor". Section 2A–103(1)(p).

"Notice". Section 1–201(25).

"Party". Section 1–201(29).

§ 2A.503. Modification or Impairment of Rights and Remedies

(a) Except as otherwise provided in this chapter, the lease agreement may include rights and remedies for default in addition to or in substitution for those provided by this chapter and may limit or alter the measure of damages recoverable under this chapter.

(b) Resort to a remedy provided under this chapter or in the lease agreement is optional unless the remedy is expressly agreed to be exclusive. If circumstances cause an exclusive or limited remedy to fail its essential purpose, or provision for an exclusive remedy is unconscionable, remedy may be had as provided by this chapter.

(c) Consequential damages may be liquidated under Section 2A.504 or otherwise be limited, altered, or excluded unless the limitation, alteration, or exclusion is unconscionable. Liquidation, limitation, alteration, or exclusion of consequential damages for injury to the person in the case of consumer goods is prima facie unconscionable, but liquidation, limitation, alteration, or exclusion of damages where the loss is commercial is not prima facie unconscionable.

(d) Rights and remedies on default by the lessor or the lessee with respect to an obligation or promise collateral or ancillary to the lease contract are not impaired by this chapter.

Added by Acts 1993, 73rd Leg., ch. 570, § 1, eff. Sept. 1, 1993.

Uniform Commercial Code Comment

Uniform Statutory Source: Sections 2–719 and 2–701.

Changes: Rewritten to reflect lease terminology and to clarify the relationship between this section and Section 2A–504.

Purposes:

1. A significant purpose of this Part is to provide rights and remedies for those parties to a lease who fail to provide them by agreement or whose rights and remedies fail of their essential purpose or are unenforceable. However, it is important to note that this implies no restriction on freedom to contract. Sections 2A–103(4) and 1–102(3). Thus, subsection (1), a revised version of the provisions of Section 2–719(1), allows the parties to the lease agreement freedom to provide for rights and remedies in addition to or in substitution for those provided in this Article and to alter or limit the measure of damages recoverable under this Article. Except to the extent otherwise provided in this Article (*e.g.*, Sections 2A–105, 106 and 108(1) and (2)), this Part shall be construed neither to restrict the parties' ability to provide for rights and remedies or to limit or alter the measure of damages by agreement, nor to imply disapproval of rights and remedy schemes other than those set forth in this Part.

2. Subsection (2) makes explicit with respect to this Article what is implicit in Section 2–719 with respect to the Article on Sales (Article 2): if an exclusive remedy is held to be unconscionable, remedies under this Article are available. Section 2–719 official comment 1.

3. Subsection (3), a revision of Section 2–719(3), makes clear that consequential damages may also be liquidated. Section 2A–504(1).

4. Subsection (4) is a revision of the provisions of Section 2–701. This subsection leaves the treatment of default with respect to obligations or promises collateral or ancillary to the lease contract to other law. Sections 2A–103(4) and 1–103. An example of such an obligation would be that of the lessor to the secured creditor which has provided the funds to leverage the lessor's lease transaction; an example of such a promise would be that of the lessee, as seller, to the lessor, as buyer, in a sale-leaseback transaction.

Cross References:

Sections 1–102(3), 1–103, Article 2, especially Sections 2–701, 2–719, 2–719(1), 2–719(3), 2–719 official comment 1, and Sections 2A–103(4), 2A–105, 2A–106, 2A–108(1), 2A–108(2), and 2A–504.

Definitional Cross References:

"Agreed". Section 1–201(3).

"Consumer goods". Section 9–109(1).

"Lease agreement". Section 2A–103(1)(k).

"Lease contract". Section 2A–103(1)(*l*).

"Lessee". Section 2A–103(1)(n).

"Lessor". Section 2A–103(1)(p).

"Person". Section 1–201(30).

"Remedy". Section 1–201(34).

"Rights". Section 1–201(36).

State Bar Committee Comments

Section 2A.503(c) differs from Section 2.719(c) of Chapter 2 by expanding the presumption of unconscionability in the case of consumer goods to lease provisions attempting to liquidate, alter or exclude consequential damages for personal injury. The uniform version of Section 2A.503(c) fails to include liquidation.

§ 2A.504. Liquidation of Damages

(a) Damages payable by either party for default or any other act or omission, including indemnity for loss or diminution of anticipated tax benefits or loss or damage to lessor's residual interest, may be liquidated in the lease agreement but only at an amount or by a formula that is reasonable in light of the then anticipated harm caused by the default or other act or omission. In a consumer lease, a term fixing liquidated damages that are unreasonably large in light of the actual harm is unenforceable as a penalty.

(b) If the lease agreement provides for liquidation of damages, and such provision does not comply with Subsection (a) or such provision is an exclusive or limited remedy that circumstances cause to fail of its essential purpose, remedy may be had as provided in this chapter.

(c) If the lessor justifiably withholds or stops delivery of goods because of the lessee's default or insolvency (Section 2A.525 or 2A.526), the lessee is entitled to restitution of any amount by which the sum of the lessee's payments exceeds:

(1) the amount to which the lessor is entitled by virtue of terms liquidating the lessor's damages in accordance with Subsection (a); or

(2) in the absence of those terms, 20 percent of the then present value of the total rent the lessee was obligated to pay for the balance of the lease term, or, in the case of a consumer lease, the lesser of such amount or $500.

(d) A lessee's right to restitution under Subsection (c) is subject to offset to the extent the lessor establishes:

(1) a right to recover damages under the provisions of this chapter other than Subsection (a); and

(2) the amount of value of any benefits received by the lessee directly or indirectly by reason of the lease contract.

Added by Acts 1993, 73rd Leg., ch. 570, § 1, eff. Sept. 1, 1993.

Uniform Commercial Code Comment

Uniform Statutory Source: Sections 2–718(1), (2), (3) and 2–719(2).

Changes: Substantially rewritten.

Purposes: Many leasing transactions are predicated on the parties' ability to agree to an appropriate amount of damages or formula for damages in the event of default or other act or omission. The rule with respect to sales of goods (Section 2–718) may not be sufficiently flexible to accommodate this practice. Thus, consistent with the common law emphasis upon freedom to contract with respect to bailments for hire, this section has created a revised rule that allows greater flexibility with respect to leases of goods.

Subsection (1), a significantly modified version of the provisions of Section 2–718(1), provides for liquidation of damages in the lease agreement at an amount or by a formula. Section 2–718(1) does not by its express terms include liquidation by a formula; this change was compelled by modern leasing practice. Subsection (1), in a further expansion of Section 2–718(1), provides for liquidation of damages for default as well as any other act or omission.

A liquidated damages formula that is common in leasing practice provides that the sum of lease payments past due, accelerated future lease payments, and the lessor's estimated residual interest, less the net proceeds of disposition (whether by sale or re-lease) of the leased goods is the lessor's damages. Tax indemnities, costs, interest and attorney's fees are also added to determine the lessor's damages. Another common liquidated damages formula utilizes a periodic depreciation allocation as a credit to the aforesaid amount in mitigation of a lessor's damages. A third formula provides for a fixed number of periodic payments as a means of liquidating damages. Stipulated loss or stipulated damage schedules are also common. Whether these formulae are enforceable will be determined in the context of each case by applying a standard of reasonableness in light of the harm anticipated when the formula was agreed to. Whether the inclusion of these formulae will affect the classification of the transaction as a lease or a security interest is to be determined by the facts of each case. Section 1–201(37). *E.g., In re Noack,* 44 Bankr. 172, 174–75 (Bankr. E.D.Wis.1984).

This section does not incorporate two other tests that under sales law determine enforceability of liquidated damages, *i.e.*, difficulties of proof of loss and inconvenience or nonfeasibility of otherwise obtaining an adequate remedy. The ability to liquidate damages is critical to modern leasing practice; given the parties' freedom to contract at common law, the policy behind retaining these two additional requirements here was thought to be outweighed. Further, given the expansion of subsection (1) to enable the parties to liquidate the amount payable with respect to an indemnity for loss or diminution of anticipated tax benefits resulted in another change: the last sentence of Section 2–718(1), providing that a term fixing unreasonably large liquidated damages is void as a penalty, was also not incorporated. The impact of local, state and federal tax laws on a leasing transaction can result in an amount payable with respect to the tax indemnity many times greater than the original purchase price of the goods. By deleting the reference to unreasonably large liquidated damages the parties are free to negotiate a formula, restrained by the rule of reasonableness in this section. These changes should invite the parties to liquidate damages. Peters, *Remedies for Breach of Contracts Relating to the Sale of Goods Under the Uniform Commercial Code: A Roadmap for Article Two,* 73 Yale L.J. 199, 278 (1963).

Subsection (2), a revised version of Section 2–719(2), provides that if the liquidated damages provision is not enforceable or fails of its essential purpose, remedy may be had as provided in this Article.

Subsection (3)(b) of this section differs from subsection (2)(b) of Section 2–718; in the absence of a valid liquidated damages amount or formula the lessor is permitted to retain 20 percent of the present value of the total rent payable under the lease. The alternative limitation of $500 contained in Section 2–718 is deleted as unrealistically low with respect to a lease other than a consumer lease.

Cross References:

Sections 1–201(37), 2–718, 2–718(1), 2–718(2)(b) and 2–719(2).

Definitional Cross References:

"Consumer lease". Section 2A–103(1)(e).

"Delivery". Section 1–201(14).

"Goods". Section 2A–103(1)(h).

"Insolvent". Section 1–201(23).

"Lease agreement". Section 2A–103(1)(k).

"Lease contract". Section 2A–103(1)(*l*).

"Lessee". Section 2A–103(1)(n).

"Lessor". Section 2A–103(1)(p).

"Lessor's residual interest". Section 2A–103(1)(q).

"Party". Section 1–201(29).

"Present value". Section 2A–103(1)(u).

"Remedy". Section 1–201(34).

"Rights". Section 1–201(36).

"Term". Section 1–201(42).

"Value". Section 1–201(44).

State Bar Committee Comments

Section 2A.504(a) has been revised to add that, in a consumer lease, the liquidated damages may not be unreasonably large in relation to the actual damages. In a consumer lease, the increased likelihood of disparity of bargaining power and use of form leases may result in liquidated damage provisions that unfairly penalize the defaulting lessee and provide a windfall to the lessor. This danger outweighs the need for a liberalized liquidated damages rule in this context. The other provisions of Chapter 2A should provide adequate statutory remedies to an aggrieved lessor. The last sentence of subsection (a) adopts a rule requiring the liquidated damages to be within the reasonable range of actual damages, which by implication must not be impracticable to ascertain or to prove. This rule answers the dilemma presented by Section 2.718(a) and the Restatement (2d) of Contracts § 356 when faced with a situation where the actual damages may be readily proved to be much less than the liquidated damages. In consumer leases, prospective reasonableness is not sufficient; a rule favoring the principle of just compensation, which lies at the heart of the common law of contract damages and which abhors penalties that create windfalls, must be adopted at some expense to the principle of freedom of contract. *See* Anderson, *Damages Under the Uniform Commercial Code* § 13.01 *et seq.* (Callahan 1988).

§ 2A.505. Cancellation and Termination and Effect of Cancellation, Termination, Rescission, or Fraud on Rights and Remedies

(a) On cancellation of the lease contract, all obligations that are still executory on both sides are discharged, but any right based on prior default or performance survives, and the canceling party also retains any remedy for default of the whole lease contract or any unperformed balance.

(b) On termination of the lease contract, all obligations that are still executory on both sides are discharged but any right based on a prior default or performance survives.

(c) Unless the contrary intention clearly appears, expressions of "cancellation," "rescission," or the like of the lease contract may not be construed as a renunciation or discharge of any claim in damages for an antecedent default.

(d) Rights and remedies for material misrepresentation or fraud include all rights and remedies available under this chapter for default.

(e) Neither rescission nor a claim for rescission of the lease contract nor rejection or return of the goods may bar or be deemed inconsistent with a claim for damages or other right or remedy.

Added by Acts 1993, 73rd Leg., ch. 570, § 1, eff. Sept. 1, 1993.

Uniform Commercial Code Comment

Uniform Statutory Source: Sections 2–106(3) and (4), 2–720 and 2–721.

Changes: Revised to reflect leasing practices and terminology.

Definitional Cross References:

"Cancellation". Section 2A–103(1)(b).

"Goods". Section 2A–103(1)(h).

"Lease contract". Section 2A–103(1)(*l*).

"Party". Section 1–201(29).

"Remedy". Section 1–201(34).

"Rights". Section 1–201(36).

"Termination". Section 2A–103(1)(z).

§ 2A.506. Statute of Limitations

(a) An action for default under a lease contract, including breach of warranty or indemnity, must be commenced within four years after the cause of action accrued. By the original lease contract the parties may not expand such period of limitation but, except in the case of a consumer lease, may reduce the period of limitation to not less than one year.

(b) A cause of action for default accrues when the act or omission on which the default or breach of warranty is based is or should have been discovered by the aggrieved party. A cause of action for indemnity accrues:

(1) in the case of an indemnity against liability, when the act or omission on which the claim for indemnity is based is or should have been discovered by the indemnified party; or

(2) in the case of an indemnity against loss or damage, when the person indemnified makes payment thereof.

(c) If an action commenced within the time limited by Subsection (a) is so terminated as to leave available a remedy by another action for the same default or breach of warranty or indemnity, the other action may be commenced after the expiration of the time limited and within six months after the termination of the first action unless the termination resulted from voluntary discontinuance or from dismissal for failure or neglect to prosecute.

(d) This section does not alter the law on tolling of the statute of limitations nor does it apply to causes of action that have accrued before this chapter becomes effective.

Added by Acts 1993, 73rd Leg., ch. 570, § 1, eff. Sept. 1, 1993.

Uniform Commercial Code Comment

Uniform Statutory Source: Section 2–725.

Changes: Substantially rewritten.

Purposes: Subsection (1) does not incorporate the limitation found in Section 2–725(1) prohibiting the parties from extending the period of limitation. Breach of warranty and indemnity claims often arise in a lease transaction; with the passage of time such claims often diminish or are eliminated. To encourage the parties to commence litigation under these circumstances makes little sense.

Subsection (2) states two rules for determining when a cause of action accrues. With respect to default, the rule of Section 2–725(2) is not incorporated in favor of a more liberal rule of the later of the date when the default occurs or when the act or omission on which it is based is or should have been discovered. With respect to indemnity, a similarly liberal rule is adopted.

Cross References:

Sections 2–725(1) and 2–725(2).

Definitional Cross References:

"Action". Section 1–201(1).

"Aggrieved party". Section 1–201(2).

"Lease contract". Section 2A–103(1)(*l*).

"Party". Section 1–201(29).

"Remedy". Section 1–201(34).

"Termination". Section 2A–103(1)(z).

State Bar Committee Comments

Section 2A.506(b) has been revised to recognize the difference under the laws of this state between an indemnity against liability and an indemnity against loss or damage. In the case of an indemnity against liability, the cause of action accrues when the act or omission on which the claim for indemnity is based is or should have been discovered by the indemnified party. In the case of an indemnity against loss or damage, the cause of action does not accrue until the indemnified person makes payment of the loss or damage.

The provisions of the second sentence of Section 2A.506(a) with respect to non-consumer leases conflicts with Tex. Civ. Prac. & Rem. Code Section 16.070, which voids any contractual provision that establishes a limitations period of less than two years. The determination of which provision controls is left to the courts to be determined on a case-by-case basis. Nevertheless, this sentence has been revised to prohibit contractual expansion of the statute of limitation, which can lead to uncertainty, and to exclude consumer leases from the provision allowing a reduction in the statute of limitation.

§ 2A.507. Proof of Market Rent

(a) Damages based on market rent (Section 2A.519 or 2A.528) are determined according to the rent for the use of the goods concerned for a lease term identical to the remaining lease term of the original lease agreement and prevailing at the times specified in Sections 2A.519 and 2A.528.

(b) If evidence of rent for the use of the goods concerned for a lease term identical to the remaining lease term of the original lease agreement and prevailing at the times or places described in this chapter is not readily available, the rent prevailing within any reasonable time before or after the time described or at any other place or for a different lease term which in commercial judgment or under usage of trade would serve as a reasonable substitute for the one described may be used, making any proper allowance for the difference, including the cost of transporting the goods to or from the other place.

(c) Evidence of a relevant rent prevailing at a time or place or for a lease term other than the one described in this chapter offered by one party is not admissible unless and until the party has given the other party notice the court finds sufficient to prevent unfair surprise.

(d) If the prevailing rent or value of any goods regularly leased in any established market is in issue, reports in official publications or trade journals or in newspapers or periodicals of general circulation published as the reports of that market are admissible in evidence. The circumstances of the preparation of the report may be shown to affect its weight but not its admissibility.

Added by Acts 1993, 73rd Leg., ch. 570, § 1, eff. Sept. 1, 1993.

Uniform Commercial Code Comment

Uniform Statutory Source: Sections 2–723 and 2–724.

Changes: Revised to reflect leasing practices and terminology. Sections 2A–519 and 2A–528 specify the times as of which market rent is to be determined.

Definitional Cross References:

"Goods". Section 2A–103(1)(h).

"Lease". Section 2A–103(1)(j).

"Lease agreement". Section 2A–103(1)(k).

"Notice". Section 1–201(25).

"Party". Section 1–201(29).

"Reasonable time". Section 1–204(1) and (2).

"Usage of trade". Section 1–205.

"Value". Section 1–201(44).

§ 2A.508. Lessee's Remedies

(a) If a lessor fails to deliver the goods in conformity to the lease contract (Section 2A.509) or repudiates the lease contract (Section 2A.402), or a lessee rightfully rejects the goods (Section 2A.509) or justifiably revokes acceptance of the goods (Section 2A.517), then with respect to any goods involved, and with respect to all of the goods if under an installment lease contract and the value of the whole lease contract is substantially impaired (Section 2A.510), the lessor is in default under the lease contract and the lessee may:

(1) cancel the lease contract (Section 2A.505(a));

(2) recover so much of the rent and security as has been paid and is just under the circumstances;

(3) cover and recover damages as to all goods affected whether or not they have been identified to the lease contract (Sections 2A.518 and 2A.520), or recover damages for nondelivery (Sections 2A.519 and 2A.520); or

(4) exercise any other rights or pursue any other remedies provided in the lease contract.

(b) If a lessor fails to deliver the goods in conformity to the lease contract or repudiates the lease contract, the lessee may also:

(1) if the goods have been identified, recover them (Section 2A.522); or

(2) in a proper case, obtain specific performance, replevin, detinue, sequestration, claim and delivery, or the like for the goods (Section 2A.521).

(c) If a lessor is otherwise in default under a lease contract, the lessee may exercise the rights and pursue the remedies provided in the lease contract, which may include a right to cancel the lease, and in Section 2A.519(c).

(d) If a lessor has breached a warranty, whether express or implied, the lessee may recover damages (Section 2A.519(d)).

(e) On rightful rejection or justifiable revocation or acceptance, a lessee has a security interest in goods in the lessee's possession or control for any rent and security that has been paid and any expenses reasonably incurred in their inspection, receipt, transportation, and care and custody and may hold those goods and dispose of them in good faith and in a commercially reasonable manner, subject to Section 2A.527(e).

(f) Subject to the provisions of Section 2A.407, a lessee, on notifying the lessor of the lessee's intention to do so, may deduct all or part of the damages resulting from any default under the lease contract from any part of the rent still due under the same lease contract.

Added by Acts 1993, 73rd Leg., ch. 570, § 1, eff. Sept. 1, 1993.

Uniform Commercial Code Comment

Uniform Statutory Source: Sections 2–711 and 2–717.

Changes: Substantially rewritten.

Purposes:

1. This section is an index to Sections 2A–509 through 522 which set out the lessee's rights and remedies after the lessor's default. The lessor and the lessee can agree to modify the rights and remedies available under this Article; they can, among other things, provide that for defaults other than those specified in subsection (1) the lessee can exercise the rights and remedies referred to in subsection (1); and they can create a new scheme of rights and remedies triggered by the occurrence of the default. Sections 2A–103(4) and 1–102(3).

2. Subsection (1), a substantially rewritten version of the provisions of Section 2–711(1), lists three cumulative remedies of the lessee where the lessor has failed to deliver conforming goods or has repudiated the contract, or the lessee has rightfully rejected or justifiably revoked. Sections 2A–501(2) and (4). Subsection (1) also allows the lessee to exercise any contractual remedy. This Article rejects any general doctrine of election of remedy. To determine if one remedy bars another in a particular case is a function of whether the lessee has been put in as good a position as if the lessor had fully performed the lease agreement. Use of multiple remedies is barred only if the effect is to put the lessee in a better position than it would have been in had the lessor fully performed under the lease. Sections 2A–103(4), 2A–501(4), and 1–106(1). Subsection (1)(b), in recognition that no bright line can be created that would operate fairly in all installment lease cases and in recognition of the fact that a lessee may be able to cancel the lease (revoke acceptance of the goods) after the goods have been in use for some period

of time, does not require that all lease payments made by the lessee under the lease be returned upon cancellation. Rather, only such portion as is just of the rent and security payments made may be recovered. If a defect in the goods is discovered immediately upon tender to the lessee and the goods are rejected immediately, then the lessee should recover all payments made. If, however, for example, a 36-month equipment lease is terminated in the 12th month because the lessor has materially breached the contract by failing to perform its maintenance obligations, it may be just to return only a small part or none of the rental payments already made.

3. Subsection (2), a version of the provisions of Section 2–711(2) revised to reflect leasing terminology, lists two alternative remedies for the recovery of the goods by the lessee; however, each of these remedies is cumulative with respect to those listed in subsection (1).

4. Subsection (3) is new. It covers defaults which do not deprive the lessee of the goods and which are not so serious as to justify rejection or revocation of acceptance under subsection (1). It also covers defaults for which the lessee could have rejected or revoked acceptance of the goods but elects not to do so and retains the goods. In either case, a lessee which retains the goods is entitled to recover damages as stated in Section 2A–519(3). That measure of damages is "the loss resulting in the ordinary course of events from the lessor's default as determined in any manner that is reasonable together with incidental and consequential damages, less expenses saved in consequence of the lessor's breach."

5. Subsection (1)(d) and subsection (3) recognize that the lease agreement may provide rights and remedies in addition to or different from those which Article 2A provides. In particular, subsection (3) provides that the lease agreement may give the remedy of cancellation of the lease for defaults by the lessor that would not otherwise be material defaults which would justify cancellation under subsection (1). If there is a right to cancel, there is, of course, a right to reject or revoke acceptance of the goods.

6. Subsection (4) is new and merely adds to the completeness of the index by including a reference to the lessee's recovery of damages upon the lessor's breach of warranty; such breach may not rise to the level of a default by the lessor justifying revocation of acceptance. If the lessee properly rejects or revokes acceptance of the goods because of a breach of warranty, the rights and remedies are those provided in subsection (1) rather than those in Section 2A–519(4).

7. Subsection (5), a revised version of the provisions of Section 2–711(3), recognizes, on rightful rejection or justifiable revocation, the lessee's security interest in goods in its possession and control. Section 9–113, which recognized security interests arising under the Article on Sales (Article 2), was amended with the adoption of this Article to reflect the security interests arising under this Article. Pursuant to Section 2A–511(4), a purchaser who purchases goods from the lessee in good faith takes free of any rights of the lessor, or in the case of a finance lease the supplier. Such goods, however, must have been rightfully rejected and disposed of pursuant to Section 2A–511 or 2A–512. However, Section 2A–517(5) provides that the lessee will have the same rights and duties with respect to goods where acceptance has been revoked as with respect to goods rejected. Thus, Section 2A–511(4) will apply to the lessee's disposition of such goods.

8. Pursuant to Section 2A–527(5), the lessee must account to the lessor for the excess proceeds of such disposition, after satisfaction of the claim secured by the lessee's security interest.

9. Subsection (6), a slightly revised version of the provisions of Section 2–717, sanctions a right of set-off by the lessee, subject to the rule of Section 2A–407 with respect to irrevocable promises in a finance lease that is not a consumer lease, and further subject to an enforceable "hell or high water" clause in the lease agreement. Section 2A–407 official comment. No attempt is made to state how the set-off should occur; this is to be determined by the facts of each case.

10. There is no special treatment of the finance lease in this section. Absent supplemental principles of law and equity to the contrary, in the case of most finance leases, following the lessee's acceptance of the goods the lessee will have no rights or remedies against the lessor, because the lessor's obligations to the lessee are minimal. Sections 2A–210 and 2A–211(1). Since the lessee will look to the supplier for performance, this is appropriate. Section 2A–209.

Cross References:

Sections 1–102(3), 1–103, 1–106(1), Article 2, especially Sections 2–711, 2–717 and Sections 2A–103(4), 2A–209, 2A–210, 2A–211(1), 2A–407, 2A–501(2), 2A–501(4), 2A–509 through 2A–522, 2A–511(3), 2A–517(5), 2A–527(5) and Section 9–113.

Definitional Cross References:

"Conforming". Section 2A–103(1)(d).

"Delivery". Section 1–201(14).

"Good faith". Sections 1–201(19) and 2–103(1)(b).

"Goods". Section 2A–103(1)(h).

"Installment lease contract". Section 2A–103(1)(i).

"Lease contract". Section 2A–103(1)(*l*).

"Lessee". Section 2A–103(1)(n).

"Lessor". Section 2A–103(1)(p).

"Notifies". Section 1–201(26).

"Receipt". Section 2–103(1)(c).

"Remedy". Section 1–201(34).

"Rights". Section 1–201(36).

"Security interest". Section 1–201(37).

"Value". Section 1–201(44).

State Bar Committee Comments

The change to Section 2A.508(b)(2) is intended as a clarification. The remedy of replevin is the usual remedy in this state in these circumstances.

§ 2A.509. Lessee's Rights on Improper Delivery; Rightful Rejection

(a) Subject to the provisions of Section 2A.510 on default in installment lease contracts, if the goods or the tender or delivery fail in any respect to conform to the lease contract, the lessee may reject or accept the goods or accept any commercial unit or units and reject the rest of the goods.

(b) Rejection of goods is ineffective unless it is within a reasonable time after tender or delivery of the goods and the lessee seasonably notifies the lessor.

Added by Acts 1993, 73rd Leg., ch. 570, § 1, eff. Sept. 1, 1993.

Uniform Commercial Code Comment

Uniform Statutory Source: Sections 2–601 and 2–602(1).

Changes: Revised to reflect leasing practices and terminology.

Definitional Cross References:

"Commercial unit". Section 2A–103(1)(c).

"Conforming". Section 2A–103(1)(d).

"Delivery". Section 1–201(14).

"Goods". Section 2A–103(1)(h).

"Installment lease contract". Section 2A–103(1)(i).

"Lease contract". Section 2A–103(1)(*l*).

"Lessee". Section 2A–103(1)(n).

"Lessor". Section 2A–103(1)(p).

"Notifies". Section 1–201(26).

"Reasonable time". Section 1–204(1) and (2).

"Rights". Section 1–201(36).

"Seasonably". Section 1–204(3).

§ 2A.510. Installment Lease Contracts: Rejection and Default

(a) Under an installment lease contract a lessee may reject any delivery that is nonconforming if the nonconformity substantially impairs the value of that delivery and cannot be cured or the nonconformity is a defect in the required documents; but if the nonconformity does not fall within Subsection (b) and the lessor or the supplier gives adequate assurance of its cure, the lessee must accept the delivery.

(b) Whenever nonconformity or default with respect to one or more deliveries substantially impairs the value of the installment lease contract as a whole there is a default with respect to the whole. But the aggrieved party reinstates the installment lease contract as a whole if the aggrieved party accepts a nonconforming delivery without seasonably notifying of cancellation or brings an action with respect only to past deliveries or demands performance as to future deliveries.

Added by Acts 1993, 73rd Leg., ch. 570, § 1, eff. Sept. 1, 1993.

Uniform Commercial Code Comment

Uniform Statutory Source: Section 2–612.

Changes: Revised to reflect leasing practices and terminology.

Definitional Cross References:

"Action". Section 1–201(1).

"Aggrieved party". Section 1–201(2).

"Cancellation". Section 2A–103(1)(b).

"Conforming". Section 2A–103(1)(d).

"Delivery". Section 1–201(14).

"Installment lease contract". Section 2A–103(1)(i).

"Lessee". Section 2A–103(1)(n).

"Lessor". Section 2A–103(1)(p).

"Notifies". Section 1–201(26).

"Seasonably". Section 1–204(3).

"Supplier". Section 2A–103(1)(x).

"Value". Section 1–201(44).

§ 2A.511. Merchant Lessee's Duties as to Rightfully Rejected Goods

Subject to any security interest of a lessee (Section 2A.508(e)), if a lessor or a supplier has no agent or place of business at the market of rejection, a merchant lessee, after rejection of goods in the lessee's possession or control, shall follow any reasonable instructions received from the lessor or the supplier with respect to the goods. In the absence of those instructions, a merchant lessee shall make reasonable efforts to sell, lease, or otherwise dispose of the goods for the lessor's account if they threaten to decline in value speedily. Instructions are not reasonable if on demand indemnity for expenses is not forthcoming.

Added by Acts 1993, 73rd Leg., ch. 570, § 1, eff. Sept. 1, 1993.

Uniform Commercial Code Comment

Uniform Statutory Source: Sections 2–603 and 2–706(5).

Changes: Revised to reflect leasing practices and terminology. This section, by its terms, applies to merchants as well as others. Thus, in construing the section it is important to note that under this Act the term good faith is defined differently for merchants (Section 2–103(1)(b)) than for others (Section 1–201(19)). Section 2A–103(3) and (4).

Definitional Cross References:

"Action". Sections 1–201(1).

"Good faith". Sections 1–201(19) and 2–103(1)(b).

"Goods". Section 2A–103(1)(h).

"Lease". Section 2A–103(1)(j).

"Lessee". Section 2A–103(1)(n).

"Lessor". Section 2A–103(1)(p).

"Merchant lessee". Section 2A–103(1)(t).

"Purchaser". Section 1–201(33).

"Rights". Section 1–201(36).

"Security interest". Section 1–201(37).

"Supplier". Section 2A–103(1)(x).

"Value". Section 1–201(44).

State Bar Committee Comments

Most of the uniform version of Section 2A.511 has been moved to Section 2A.512. The moved provisions apply to all lessees and are not limited to merchant lessees. The title of Section 2A.511 is misleading when applied to the uniform version. After this change, the titles of Sections 2A.511 and 2A.512 are consistent with the respective section contents.

§ 2A.512. Lessee's Duties as to Rightfully Rejected Goods

(a) Except as otherwise provided with respect to goods that threaten to decline in value speedily (Section 2A.511) and subject to any security interest of a lessee (Section 2A.508(e)):

(1) the lessee, after rejection of goods in the lessee's possession, shall hold them with reasonable care at the lessor's or the supplier's disposition for a reasonable time after the lessee's seasonable notification of rejection;

(2) if the lessor or the supplier gives no instructions within a reasonable time after notification of rejection, the lessee may store the rejected goods for the lessor's or the supplier's account or ship them to the lessor or the supplier or dispose of them for the lessor's or the supplier's account with reimbursement in the manner provided by Subsection (d); but

(3) the lessee has no further obligations with regard to goods rightfully rejected.

(b) Action by the lessee pursuant to Subsection (a) is not acceptance or conversion.

(c) If a merchant lessee (Section 2A.511) or any other lessee disposes of goods, the lessee is entitled to reimbursement either from the lessor or the supplier or out of the proceeds for reasonable expenses of caring for and disposing of the goods and, if the expenses include no disposition commission, to such commission as is usual in the trade, or if there is none, to a reasonable sum not exceeding 10 percent of the gross proceeds.

(d) In complying with this section or Section 2A.511, the lessee is held only to good faith. Good faith conduct hereunder is neither acceptance or conversion nor the basis of an action for damages.

(e) A purchaser who purchases in good faith from a lessee pursuant to this section or Section 2A.511 takes the goods free of any rights of the lessor and the supplier even though the lessee fails to comply with one or more of the requirements of this chapter.

Added by Acts 1993, 73rd Leg., ch. 570, § 1, eff. Sept. 1, 1993.

Uniform Commercial Code Comment

Uniform Statutory Source: Sections 2–602(2)(b) and (c) and 2–604.

Changes: Substantially rewritten.

Purposes: The introduction to subsection (1) references goods that threaten to decline in value speedily and not perishables, the reference in Section 2–604, the statutory analogue. This is a change in style, not substance, as the first phrase includes the second. Subparagraphs (a) and (c) are revised versions of the provisions of Section 2–602(2)(b) and (c). Subparagraph (a) states the rule with respect to the lessee's treatment of goods in its possession following rejection; subparagraph (b) states the rule regarding such goods if the lessor or supplier then fails to give instructions to the lessee. If the lessee performs in a fashion consistent with subparagraphs (a) and (b), subparagraph (c) exonerates the lessee.

Cross References:

Sections 2–602(2)(b), 2–602(2)(c) and 2–604.

Definitional Cross References:

"Action". Section 1–201(1).

"Goods". Section 2A–103(1)(h).

"Lessee". Section 2A–103(1)(n).

"Lessor". Section 2A–103(1)(p).

"Notification". Section 1–201(26).

"Reasonable time". Section 1–204(1) and (2).

"Seasonably". Section 1–204(3).

"Security interest". Section 1–201(37).

"Supplier". Section 2A–103(1)(x).

"Value". Section 1–201(44).

State Bar Committee Comments

It is important to note that under Chapter 2A the term good faith is defined differently for merchants

(Section 2.103(a)(2)) than for others (Section 1.201(19)). Section 2A.103(c) and (d).

§ 2A.513. Cure by Lessor of Improper Tender or Delivery; Replacement

(a) If any tender or delivery by the lessor or the supplier is rejected because nonconforming and the time for performance has not yet expired, the lessor or the supplier may seasonably notify the lessee of the lessor's or the supplier's intention to cure and may then make a conforming delivery within the time provided by the lease contract.

(b) If the lessee rejects a nonconforming tender that the lessor or the supplier had reasonable grounds to believe would be acceptable with or without money allowance, the lessor or the supplier may have a further reasonable time to substitute a conforming tender if the lessor or supplier seasonably notifies the lessee.

Added by Acts 1993, 73rd Leg., ch. 570, § 1, eff. Sept. 1, 1993.

Uniform Commercial Code Comment

Uniform Statutory Source: Section 2–508.

Changes: Revised to reflect leasing practices and terminology.

Definitional Cross References:

"Conforming". Section 2A–103(1)(d).

"Delivery". Section 1–201(14).

"Lease contract". Section 2A–103(1)(*l*).

"Lessee". Section 2A–103(1)(n).

"Lessor". Section 2A–103(1)(p).

"Money". Section 1–201(24).

"Notifies". Section 1–201(26).

"Reasonable time". Section 1–204(1) and (2).

"Seasonably". Section 1–204(3).

"Supplier". Section 2A–103(1)(x).

§ 2A.514. Waiver of Lessee's Objections

(a) In rejecting goods, a lessee's failure to state a particular defect that is ascertainable by reasonable inspection precludes the lessee from relying on the defect to justify rejection or to establish default:

(1) if, stated seasonably, the lessor or the supplier could have cured it (Section 2A.513); or

(2) between merchants if the lessor or the supplier after rejection has made a request in writing for a full and final written statement of all defects on which the lessee proposes to rely.

(b) A lessee's failure to reserve rights when paying rent or other consideration against documents precludes recovery of the payment for defects apparent in the documents.

Added by Acts 1993, 73rd Leg., ch. 570, § 1, eff. Sept. 1, 1993. Amended by Acts 2005, 79th Leg., ch. 122, § 14, eff. Sept. 1, 2005.

Uniform Commercial Code Comment

Uniform Statutory Source: Section 2–605.

Changes: Revised to reflect leasing practices and terminology.

Purposes: The principles applicable to the commercial practice of payment against documents (subsection 2) are explained in official comment 4 to Section 2–605, the statutory analogue to this section.

Cross Reference:

Section 2–605 official comment 4.

Definitional Cross References:

"Between merchants". Section 2–104(3).

"Goods". Section 2A–103(1)(h).

"Lessee". Section 2A–103(1)(n).

"Lessor". Section 2A–103(1)(p).

"Rights". Section 1–201(36).

"Seasonably". Section 1–204(3).

"Supplier". Section 2A–103(1)(x).

"Writing". Section 1–201(46).

Sections 31 and 32 of Acts 2005, 79th Leg., ch. 122 provide:

"Sec. 31. This Act applies to a document of title that is issued or a bailment that arises on or after the effective date of this Act. This Act does not apply to a document of title that is issued or a bailment that arises before the effective date of this Act even if the document of title or bailment would be subject to this Act if the document of title had been issued or bailment had arisen after the effective date of this Act. This Act does not apply to a right of action that has accrued before the effective date of this Act.

"Sec. 32. A document of title issued or a bailment that arises before the effective date of this Act and the rights, obligations, and interests flowing from that document or bailment are governed by any statute or other rule amended or repealed by this Act as if amendment or repeal had not occurred and may be terminated, completed, consummated, or enforced under that statute or other rule."

§ 2A.515. Acceptance of Goods

(a) Acceptance of goods occurs after the lessee has had a reasonable opportunity to inspect the goods and:

(1) the lessee signifies or acts with respect to the goods in a manner that signifies to the lessor or the supplier that the goods are conforming or that the lessee will take or retain them in spite of their nonconformity; or

(2) the lessee fails to make an effective rejection of the goods (Section 2A.509(b)).

(b) Acceptance of a part of any commercial unit is acceptance of that entire unit.

Added by Acts 1993, 73rd Leg., ch. 570, § 1, eff. Sept. 1, 1993.

Uniform Commercial Code Comment

Uniform Statutory Source: Section 2–606.

Changes: The provisions of Section 2–606(1)(a) were substantially rewritten to provide that the lessee's conduct may signify acceptance. Further, the provisions of Section 2–606(1)(c) were not incorporated as irrelevant given the lessee's possession and use of the leased goods.

Cross References:

Sections 2–606(1)(a) and 2–606(1)(c).

Definitional Cross References:

"Commercial unit". Section 2A–103(1)(c).

"Conforming". Section 2A–103(1)(d).

"Goods". Section 2A–103(1)(h).

"Lessee". Section 2A–103(1)(n).

"Lessor". Section 2A–103(1)(p).

"Supplier". Section 2A–103(1)(x).

§ 2A.516. Effect of Acceptance of Goods; Notice of Default; Burden of Establishing Default After Acceptance; Notice of Claim or Litigation to Person Answerable Over

(a) A lessee must pay rent for any goods accepted in accordance with the lease contract, with due allowance for goods rightfully rejected or not delivered.

(b) A lessee's acceptance of goods precludes rejection of the goods accepted. In the case of a finance lease that is not a consumer lease, if made with knowledge of a nonconformity, acceptance cannot be revoked because of it. In any other case, if made with knowledge of a nonconformity, acceptance cannot be revoked because of it unless the acceptance was on the reasonable assumption that the nonconformity would be seasonably cured. Acceptance does not of itself impair any other remedy provided by this chapter or the lease agreement for nonconformity.

(c) If a tender has been accepted:

(1) within a reasonable time after the lessee discovers or should have discovered any default, the lessee shall notify the lessor and supplier, if any, or be barred from any remedy against the party not notified;

(2) within a reasonable time after the lessee receives notice of litigation for infringement or the like (Section 2A.211) the lessee shall notify the lessor or be barred from any remedy over for liability established by the litigation; and

(3) the burden is on the lessee to establish any default.

(d) If a lessee is sued for breach of a warranty or other obligation for which a lessor or a supplier is answerable over, the following apply:

(1) The lessee may give the lessor or the supplier, or both, written notice of the litigation. If the notice states that the person notified may come in and defend and that if the person notified does not do so that person will be bound in any action against that person by the lessee by any determination of fact common to both litigations, then unless the person notified after seasonable receipt of the notice does come in and defend that person is so bound.

(2) The lessor or the supplier may demand in writing that the lessee turn over control of the litigation including settlement if the claim is one for infringement or the like (Section 2A.211) or else be barred from any remedy over. If the demand states that the lessor or the supplier agrees to bear all expense and to satisfy any adverse judgment, then unless the lessee after seasonable receipt of the demand does turn over control the lessee is so barred.

(e) Subsections (c) and (d) apply to any obligation of a lessee to hold the lessor or the supplier harmless against infringement or the like (Section 2A.211).

(f) Subsection (c) shall not apply to a consumer lease.

Added by Acts 1993, 73rd Leg., ch. 570, § 1, eff. Sept. 1, 1993.

Uniform Commercial Code Comment

Uniform Statutory Source: Section 2–607.

Changes: Substantially revised.

Purposes:

1. Subsection (2) creates a special rule for finance leases, precluding revocation if acceptance is made with knowledge of nonconformity with respect to the lease agreement, as opposed to the supply agreement; this is not inequitable as the lessee has a direct claim against the supplier. Section 2A–209(1). Revocation of acceptance of a finance lease is permitted if the lessee's acceptance was without discovery of the nonconformity (with respect to the lease agreement, not the supply agreement) and was reasonably induced by the lessor's assurances. Section 2A–517(1)(b). Absent exclusion or modification, the lessor under a finance lease makes

certain warranties to the lessee. Sections 2A–210 and 2A–211(1). Revocation of acceptance is not prohibited even after the lessee's promise has become irrevocable and independent. Section 2A–407 official comment. Where the finance lease creates a security interest, the rule may be to the contrary. *General Elec. Credit Corp. of Tennessee v. Ger-Beck Mach. Co.*, 806 F.2d 1207 (3rd Cir.1986).

2. Subsection (3)(a) requires the lessee to give notice of default, within a reasonable time after the lessee discovered or should have discovered the default. In a finance lease, notice may be given either to the supplier, the lessor, or both, but remedy is barred against the party not notified. In a finance lease, the lessor is usually not liable for defects in the goods and the essential notice is to the supplier. While notice to the finance lessor will often not give any additional rights to the lessee, it would be good practice to give the notice since the finance lessor has an interest in the goods. Subsection (3)(a) does not use the term finance lease, but the definition of supplier is a person from whom a lessor buys or leases goods to be leased under a finance lease. Section 2A–103(1)(x). Therefore, there can be a "supplier" only in a finance lease. Subsection (4) applies similar notice rules as to lessors and suppliers if a lessee is sued for a breach of warranty or other obligation for which a lessor or supplier is answerable over.

3. Subsection (3)(b) requires the lessee to give the lessor notice of litigation for infringement or the like. There is an exception created in the case of a consumer lease. While such an exception was considered for a finance lease, it was not created because it was not necessary—the lessor in a finance lease does not give a warranty against infringement. Section 2A–211(2). Even though not required under subsection (3)(b), the lessee who takes under a finance lease should consider giving notice of litigation for infringement or the like to the supplier, because the lessee obtains the benefit of the suppliers' promises subject to the suppliers' defenses or claims. Sections 2A–209(1) and 2–607(3)(b).

Cross References:

Sections 2–607(3)(b), 2A–103(1)(x), 2A–209(1), 2A–210, 2A–211(1), 2A–211(2), 2A–407 official comment and 2A–517(1)(b).

Definitional Cross References:

"Action". Section 1–201(1).

"Agreement". Section 1–201(3).

"Burden of establishing". Section 1–201(8).

"Conforming". Section 2A–103(1)(d).

"Consumer lease". Section 2A–103(1)(e).

"Delivery". Section 1–201(14).

"Discover". Section 1–201(25).

"Finance lease". Section 2A–103(1)(g).

"Goods". Section 2A–103(1)(h).

"Knowledge". Section 1–201(25).

"Lease agreement". Section 2A–103(1)(k).

"Lease contract". Section 2A–103(1)(*l*).

"Lessee". Section 2A–103(1)(n).

"Lessor". Section 2A–103(1)(p).

"Notice". Section 1–201(25).

"Notifies". Section 1–201(26).

"Person". Section 1–201(30).

"Reasonable time". Section 1–204(1) and (2).

"Receipt". Section 2–103(1)(c).

"Remedy". Section 1–201(34).

"Seasonably". Section 1–204(3).

"Supplier". Section 2A–103(1)(x).

"Written". Section 1–201(46).

State Bar Committee Comments

The special revocation rules created for finance leases should not apply to consumer leases for reasons of policy and consistency with Section 2A.407. Section 2A.516(b) has been revised to exclude consumer leases from such special rules.

The notice required by Section 2A.516(c)(1) need not be formal. There is no reason to require that the notification which saves the lessee's rights under this section must include a clear statement of all the objections that will be relied on by the lessee, as under the section governing statements of defects upon rejection (Section 2A.514). Nor is there reason for requiring the notification to be a claim for damages or any threat in litigation or other resort to a remedy. This notification which saves the lessee's rights under Chapter 2A need only be such as informs the lessor or supplier that the transaction is claimed to involve a breach and thus opens the way for normal settlement through negotiation.

Pursuant to newly added Section 2A.516(f), subsection (c) does not apply to consumer leases. The rules governing the lessee's duty to give notice of default to the lessor or supplier in the case of a consumer lease will be determined by other laws. The failure to include consumer leases in subsection (c) carries no negative or positive implications as to the applicability of such laws; nor shall such failure in any way affect the interpretation of any such laws that are deemed applicable to consumer leases.

§ 2A.517. Revocation of Acceptance of Goods

(a) A lessee may revoke acceptance of a lot or commercial unit whose nonconformity substantially impairs its value to the lessee if the lessee has accepted it:

(1) except in the case of a finance lease that is not a consumer lease, on the reasonable assumption that its nonconformity would be cured and it has not been seasonably cured; or

(2) without discovery of the nonconformity if the lessee's acceptance was reasonably induced either by the lessor's assurances or, except in the case of a finance lease that is not a consumer lease, by the difficulty of discovery before acceptance.

(b) A lessee may revoke acceptance of a lot or commercial unit if the lessor defaults under the lease contract and the default substantially impairs the value of that lot or commercial unit to the lessee.

(c) If the lease agreement so provides, the lessee may revoke acceptance of a lot or commercial unit because of other defaults by the lessor.

(d) Revocation of acceptance must occur within a reasonable time after the lessee discovers or should have discovered the ground for it and before any substantial change in condition of the goods which is not caused by the nonconformity. Revocation is not effective until the lessee notifies the lessor.

(e) A lessee who so revokes has the same rights and duties with regard to the goods involved as if the lessee had rejected them.

Added by Acts 1993, 73rd Leg., ch. 570, § 1, eff. Sept. 1, 1993.

Uniform Commercial Code Comment

Uniform Statutory Source: Section 2–608.

Changes: Revised to reflect leasing practices and terminology. Note that in the case of a finance lease the lessee retains a limited right to revoke acceptance. Sections 2A–517(1)(b) and 2A–516 official comment. New subsections (2) and (3) added.

Purposes:

1. The section states the situations under which the lessee may return the goods to the lessor and cancel the lease. Subsection (2) recognizes that the lessor may have continuing obligations under the lease and that a default as to those obligations may be sufficiently material to justify revocation of acceptance of the leased items and cancellation of the lease by the lessee. For example, a failure by the lessor to fulfill its obligation to maintain leased equipment or to supply other goods which are necessary for the operation of the leased equipment may justify revocation of acceptance and cancellation of the lease.

2. Subsection (3) specifically provides that the lease agreement may provide that the lessee can revoke acceptance for defaults by the lessor which in the absence of such an agreement might not be considered sufficiently serious to justify revocation. That is, the parties are free to contract on the question of what defaults are so material that the lessee can cancel the lease.

Cross References:

Section 2A–516 official comment.

Definitional Cross References:

"Commercial unit". Section 2A–103(1)(c).

"Conforming". Section 2A–103(1)(d).

"Discover". Section 1–201(25).

"Finance lease". Section 2A–103(1)(g).

"Goods". Section 2A–103(1)(h).

"Lessee". Section 2A–103(1)(n).

"Lessor". Section 2A–103(1)(p).

"Lot". Section 2A–103(1)(s).

"Notifies". Section 1–201(26).

"Reasonable time". Section 1–204(1) and (2).

"Rights". Section 1–201(36).

"Seasonably". Section 1–204(3).

"Value". Section 1-201(44).

State Bar Committee Comments

Section 2A.517(a) has been revised to exclude consumer leases from the special revocation rules relating to finance leases for reasons of policy and consistency with Section 2A.407. Section 2A.517(b) has been revised to delete the exception for finance leases. Section 2A.407 will control over Section 2A.517(b) and prohibit revocation in the appropriate circumstances by a finance lessee who agrees that his promises are independent and irrevocable after acceptance.

§ 2A.518. Cover; Substitute Goods

(a) After default by a lessor under the lease contract of the type described by Section 2A.508(a), or, if agreed, after other default by the lessor, the lessee may cover by making any purchase or lease of or contract to purchase or lease goods in substitution for those due from the lessor.

(b) Except as otherwise provided with respect to damages liquidated in the lease agreement (Section 2A.504) or otherwise determined pursuant to agreement of the parties (Sections 1.302 and 2A.503), if a lessee's cover is by a lease agreement substantially similar to the original lease agreement and the new lease agreement is made in good faith and in a commercially reasonable manner, the lessee may recover from the lessor as damages (1) the present value, as of the date of the commencement of the term of the new lease agreement, of the rent under the new lease agreement applicable to that period of the new lease term which is comparable to the then remaining term of the original lease agreement minus the present value as of the same date of the total rent for the then remaining lease term of the original lease agreement, and (2) any incidental or consequential damages, less expenses saved as a consequence of the lessor's default.

(c) If the lessee's cover is by lease agreement that for any reason does not qualify for treatment under Subsection (b) or is by purchase or otherwise, the lessee may recover from the lessor as if the lessee had elected not to cover and Section 2A.519 governs.

Added by Acts 1993, 73rd Leg., ch. 570, § 1, eff. Sept. 1, 1993. Amended by Acts 2003, 78th Leg., ch. 542, § 6, eff. Sept. 1, 2003.

Uniform Commercial Code Comment

Uniform Statutory Source: Section 2–712.

Changes: Substantially revised.

Purposes:

1. Subsection (1) allows the lessee to take action to fix its damages after default by the lessor. Such action may consist of the lease of goods. The decision to cover is a function of commercial judgment, not a statutory mandate replete with sanctions for failure to comply. *Cf.* Section 9–507.

2. Subsection (2) states a rule for determining the amount of lessee's damages provided that there is no agreement to the contrary. The lessee's damages will be established using the new lease agreement as a measure if the following three criteria are met: (i) the lessee's cover is by lease agreement, (ii) the lease agreement is substantially similar to the original lease agreement, and (iii) such cover was effected in good faith, and in a commercially reasonable manner. Thus, the lessee will be entitled to recover from the lessor the present value, as of the date of commencement of the term of the new lease agreement, of the rent under the new lease agreement applicable to that period which is comparable to the then remaining term of the original lease agreement less the present value of the rent reserved for the remaining term under the original lease, together with incidental or consequential damages less expenses saved in consequence of the lessor's default. Consequential damages may include loss suffered by the lessee because of deprivation of the use of the goods during the period between the default and the acquisition of the goods under the new lease agreement. If the lessee's cover does not satisfy the criteria of subsection (2), Section 2A–519 governs.

3. Two of the three criteria to be met by the lessee are familiar, but the concept of the new lease agreement being substantially similar to the original lease agreement is not. Given the many variables facing a party who intends to lease goods and the rapidity of change in the market place, the policy decision was made not to draft with specificity. It was thought unwise to seek to establish certainty at the cost of fairness. Thus, the decision of whether the new lease agreement is substantially similar to the original will be determined case by case.

4. While the section does not draw a bright line, it is possible to describe some of the factors that should be considered in finding that a new lease agreement is substantially similar to the original. First, the goods subject to the new lease agreement should be examined. For example, in a lease of computer equipment the new lease might be for more modern equipment. However, it may be that at the time of the lessor's breach it was not possible to obtain the same type of goods in the market place. Because the lessee's remedy under Section 2A–519 is intended to place the lessee in essentially the same position as if he had covered, if goods similar to those to have been delivered under the original lease are not available, then the computer equipment in this hypothetical should qualify as a commercially reasonable substitute. See Section 2–712(1).

5. Second, the various elements of the new lease agreement should also be examined. Those elements include the presence or absence of options to purchase or release; the lessor's representations, warranties and covenants to the lessee, as well as those to be provided by the lessee to the lessor; and the services, if any, to be provided by the lessor or by the lessee. All of these factors allocate cost and risk between the lessor and the lessee and thus affect the amount of rent to be paid. If the differences between the original lease and the new lease can be easily valued, it would be appropriate for a court to adjust the difference in rental to take account of the difference between the two leases, find that the new lease is substantially similar to the old lease, and award cover damages under this section. If, for example, the new lease requires the lessor to insure the goods in the hands of the lessee, while the original lease required the lessee to insure, the usual cost of such insurance could be deducted from the rent due under the new lease before determining the difference in rental between the two leases.

6. Having examined the goods and the agreement, the test to be applied is whether, in light of these comparisons, the new lease agreement is substantially similar to the original lease agreement. These findings should not be made with scientific precision, as they are a function of economics, nor should they be made independently with respect to the goods and each element of the agreement, as it is important that a sense of commercial judgment pervade the finding. To establish the new lease as a proper measure of damage under subsection (2), these factors, taken as a whole, must result in a finding that the new lease agreement is substantially similar to the original.

7. A new lease can be substantially similar to the original lease even though its term extends beyond the remaining term of the original lease, so long as both (a) the lease terms are commercially comparable (*e.g.*, it is highly unlikely that a one-month rental and a five-year lease would reflect similar commercial realities), and (b) the court can fairly apportion a part of the rental payments under the new lease to that part of the term of the new lease which is comparable to the remaining lease term under the original lease. Also, the lease term of the new lease may be comparable to the term of the original lease even though the beginning and ending dates of the two leases are not the same. For example, a two-month lease of agricultural equipment for the months of August and September may be comparable to a two-month lease running from the 15th of August to the 15th of October if in the particular location two-month leases beginning on August 15th are basically interchangeable with two-month leases beginning August 1st. Similarly, the term of a one-year truck lease beginning on the 15th of January may be comparable to the term of a one-year truck lease beginning January 2d. If the lease terms are found to be comparable, the court may base cover damages on the entire difference between the costs under the two leases.

Cross References:

Sections 2–712(1), 2A–519 and 9–507.

Definitional Cross References:

"Agreement". Section 1–201(3).
"Contract". Section 1–201(11).
"Good faith". Sections 1–201(19) and 2–103(1)(b).
"Goods". Section 2A–103(1)(h).
"Lease". Section 2A–103(1)(j).
"Lease agreement". Section 2A–103(1)(k).
"Lease contract". Section 2A–103(1)(*l*).
"Lessee". Section 2A–103(1)(n).
"Lessor". Section 2A–103(1)(p).
"Party". Section 1–201(29).
"Present value". Section 2A–103(1)(u).
"Purchase". Section 2A–103(1)(v).

State Bar Committee Comments

The language of Section 2A.518 is not intended to prevent a lessee from covering with a substantially similar lease with respect to part of the goods and electing to obtain Section 2A.519 damages with respect to the remainder of the goods. The determination of whether a substantially similar lease has been reached in such circumstances must be left to a court to determine on a case-by-case basis.

§ 2A.519. Lessee's Damages for Nondelivery, Repudiation, Default, and Breach of Warranty in Regard to Accepted Goods

(a) Except as otherwise provided with respect to damages liquidated in the lease agreement (Section 2A.504) or otherwise determined pursuant to agreement of the parties (Sections 1.302 and 2A.503), if a lessee elects not to cover or a lessee elects to cover and the cover is by lease agreement that for any reason does not qualify for treatment under Section 2A.518(b) or is by purchase or otherwise, the measure of damages for nondelivery or repudiation by the lessor or for rejection or revocation of acceptance by the lessee is the present value, as of the date of the default, of the then market rent minus the present value as of the same date of the original rent, computed for the remaining lease term of the original lease agreement, together with incidental and consequential damages, less expenses saved in consequence of the lessor's default.

(b) Market rent is to be determined as of the place for tender or, in cases of rejection after arrival or revocation of acceptance, as of the place of arrival.

(c) Except as otherwise agreed, if the lessee has accepted goods and given notification (Section 2A.516(c)), the measure of damages for nonconforming tender or delivery or other default by a lessor is the loss resulting in the ordinary course of events from the lessor's default as determined in any manner that is reasonable together with incidental and consequential damages, less expenses saved in consequence of the lessor's default.

(d) Except as otherwise agreed, the measure of damages for breach of warranty is the present value at the time and place of acceptance of the difference between the value of the use of the goods accepted and the value if they had been as warranted for the lease term, unless special circumstances show proximate damages of a different amount, together with incidental and consequential damages, less expenses saved in consequence of the lessor's default or breach of warranty.

Added by Acts 1993, 73rd Leg., ch. 570, § 1, eff. Sept. 1, 1993. Amended by Acts 2003, 78th Leg., ch. 542, § 7, eff. Sept. 1, 2003.

Uniform Commercial Code Comment

Uniform Statutory Source: Sections 2–713 and 2–714.

Changes: Substantially revised.

Purposes:

1. Subsection (1), a revised version of the provisions of Section 2–713(1), states the basic rule governing the measure of lessee's damages for non-delivery or repudiation by the lessor or for rightful rejection or revocation of acceptance by the lessee. This measure will apply, absent agreement to the contrary, if the lessee does not cover or if the cover does not qualify under Section 2A–518. There is no sanction for cover that does not qualify.

2. The measure of damage is the present value, as of the date of default, of the market rent for the remaining term of the lease less the present value of the original rent for the remaining term of the lease, plus incidental and consequential damages less expenses saved in consequence of the default. Note that the reference in Section 2A–519(1) is to the date of default not to the date of an event of default. An event of default under a lease agreement becomes a default under a lease agreement only after the expiration of any relevant period of grace and compliance with any notice requirements under this Article and the lease agreement. American Bar Foundation, *Commentaries on Indentures*, § 5–1, at 216–217 (1971). Section 2A–501(1). This conclusion is also a function of whether, as a matter of fact or law, the event of default has been waived, suspended or cured. Sections 2A–103(4) and 1–103.

3. Subsection (2), a revised version of the provisions of Section 2–713(2), states the rule with respect to determining market rent.

4. Subsection (3), a revised version of the provisions of Section 2–714(1) and (3), states the measure of damages where goods have been accepted and acceptance is not revoked. The subsection applies both to defaults which occur at the inception of the lease and to defaults which occur subsequently, such as failure to comply with an obli-

gation to maintain the leased goods. The measure in essence is the loss, in the ordinary course of events, flowing from the default.

5. Subsection (4), a revised version of the provisions of Section 2–714(2), states the measure of damages for breach of warranty. The measure in essence is the present value of the difference between the value of the goods accepted and of the goods if they had been as warranted.

6. Subsections (1), (3) and (4) specifically state that the parties may by contract vary the damages rules stated in those subsections.

Cross References:

Sections 2–713(1), 2–713(2), 2–714 and Section 2A–518.

Definitional Cross References:

"Conforming". Section 2A–103(1)(d).

"Delivery". Section 1–201(14).

"Goods". Section 2A–103(1)(h).

"Lease". Section 2A–103(1)(j).

"Lease agreement". Section 2A–103(1)(k).

"Lessee". Section 2A–103(1)(n).

"Lessor". Section 2A–103(1)(p).

"Notification". Section 1–201(26).

"Present value". Section 2A–103(1)(u).

"Value". Section 1–201(44).

§ 2A.520. Lessee's Incidental and Consequential Damages

(a) Incidental damages resulting from a lessor's default include expenses reasonably incurred in inspection, receipt, transportation, and care and custody of goods rightfully rejected or goods the acceptance of which is justifiably revoked, any commercially reasonable charges, expenses or commissions in connection with effecting cover, and any other reasonable expense incident to the default.

(b) Consequential damages resulting from a lessor's default include:

(1) any loss resulting from general or particular requirements and needs of which the lessor at the time of contracting had reason to know and which could not reasonably be prevented by cover or otherwise; and

(2) injury to person or property proximately resulting from any breach of warranty.

Added by Acts 1993, 73rd Leg., ch. 570, § 1, eff. Sept. 1, 1993.

Uniform Commercial Code Comment

Uniform Statutory Source: Section 2–715.

Changes: Revised to reflect leasing terminology and practices.

Purposes: Subsection (1), a revised version of the provisions of Section 2–715(1), lists some examples of incidental damages resulting from a lessor's default; the list is not exhaustive. Subsection (1) makes clear that it applies not only to rightful rejection, but also to justifiable revocation.

Subsection (2), a revised version of the provisions of Section 2–715(2), lists some examples of consequential damages resulting from a lessor's default; the list is not exhaustive.

Cross References:

Section 2–715.

Definitional Cross References:

"Goods". Section 2A–103(1)(h).

"Knows". Section 1–201(25).

"Lessee". Section 2A–103(1)(n).

"Lessor". Section 2A–103(1)(p).

"Person". Section 1–201(30).

"Receipt". Section 2–103(1)(c).

§ 2A.521. Lessee's Right to Specific Performance, Replevin, and Other Remedies

(a) Specific performance may be decreed if the goods are unique or in other proper circumstances.

(b) A decree for specific performance may include the terms and conditions as to payment of the rent, damages, or other relief that the court deems just.

(c) A lessee has a right of replevin, detinue, sequestration, claim and delivery, or the like for goods identified to the lease contract if after reasonable effort the lessee is unable to effect cover for those goods or the circumstances reasonably indicate that the effort will be unavailing.

Added by Acts 1993, 73rd Leg., ch. 570, § 1, eff. Sept. 1, 1993.

Uniform Commercial Code Comment

Uniform Statutory Source: Section 2–716.

Changes: Revised to reflect leasing practices and terminology, and to expand the reference to the right of replevin in subsection (3) to include other similar rights of the lessee.

Definitional Cross References:

"Delivery". Section 1–201(14).

"Goods". Section 2A–103(1)(h).

"Lease contract". Section 2A–103(1)(*l*).

"Lessee". Section 2A–103(1)(n).

"Rights". Section 1–201(36).

"Term". Section 1–201(42).

State Bar Committee Comments

The revision to the title of Section 2A.521 is intended to clarify that other remedies are provided by the Section.

§ 2A.522. Lessee's Right to Goods on Lessor's Insolvency

(a) Subject to Subsection (b) and even though the goods have not been shipped, a lessee who has paid a part or all of the rent and security for goods identified to a lease contract (Section 2A.217) on making and keeping good a tender of any unpaid portion of the rent and security due under the lease contract may recover the goods identified from the lessor if the lessor becomes insolvent within 10 days after receipt of the first installment of rent and security.

(b) A lessee acquires the right to recover goods identified to a lease contract only if they conform to the lease contract.

Added by Acts 1993, 73rd Leg., ch. 570, § 1, eff. Sept. 1, 1993.

Uniform Commercial Code Comment

Uniform Statutory Source: Section 2–502.

Changes: Revised to reflect leasing practices and terminology.

Definitional Cross References:

"Conforming". Section 2A–103(1)(d).

"Goods". Section 2A–103(1)(h).

"Insolvent". Section 1–201(23).

"Lease contract". Section 2A–103(1)(*l*).

"Lessee". Section 2A–103(1)(n).

"Lessor". Section 2A–103(1)(p).

"Receipt". Section 2–103(1)(c).

"Rights". Section 1–201(36).

§ 2A.523. Lessor's Remedies

(a) If a lessee wrongfully rejects or revokes acceptance of goods or fails to make a payment when due or repudiates with respect to a part or the whole, then, with respect to any goods involved, and with respect to all of the goods if under an installment lease contract, the value of the whole lease contract is substantially impaired (Section 2A.510), the lessee is in default under the lease contract and the lessor may:

(1) cancel the lease contract (Section 2A.505(a));

(2) proceed respecting goods not identified to the lease contract (Section 2A.524);

(3) withhold delivery of the goods and take possession of goods previously delivered (Section 2A.525);

(4) stop delivery of the goods by any bailee (Section 2A.526);

(5) dispose of the goods and recover damages (Section 2A.527), or retain the goods and recover damages (Section 2A.528), or in a proper case recover rent (Section 2A.529); or

(6) exercise any other rights or pursue any other remedies provided in the lease contract.

(b) If a lessor does not fully exercise a right or obtain a remedy to which the lessor is entitled under Subsection (a), the lessor may recover the loss resulting in the ordinary course of events from the lessee's default as determined in any reasonable manner, together with incidental damages, less expenses saved in consequence of the lessee's default.

(c) If a lessee is otherwise in default under a lease contract, the lessor may exercise the rights and pursue the remedies provided in the lease contract, which may include a right to cancel the lease. In addition, unless otherwise provided in the lease contract:

(1) if the default substantially impairs the value of the lease contract to the lessor, the lessor may exercise the rights and pursue the remedies provided by Subsection (a) or (b); or

(2) if the default does not substantially impair the value of the lease contract to the lessor, the lessor may recover as provided by Subsection (b).

Added by Acts 1993, 73rd Leg., ch. 570, § 1, eff. Sept. 1, 1993.

Uniform Commercial Code Comment

Uniform Statutory Source: Section 2–703.

Changes: Substantially revised.

Purposes:

1. Subsection (1) is an index to Sections 2A–524 through 2A–531 and states that the remedies provided in those sections are available for the defaults referred to in subsection (1): wrongful rejection or revocation of acceptance, failure to make a payment when due, or repudiation. In addition, remedies provided in the lease contract are available. Subsection (2) sets out a remedy if the lessor does not pursue to completion a right or actually obtain a remedy available under subsection (1), and subsection (3) sets out statutory remedies for defaults not specifically referred to in subsection (1). Subsection (3) provides that, if any default by the lessee other than those specifically referred to in subsection (1) is material, the lessor can exercise the remedies provided in subsection (1) or (2); otherwise the available remedy is as provided in subsection (3). A lessor who has

brought an action seeking or has nonjudicially pursued one or more of the remedies available under subsection (1) may amend so as to claim or may nonjudicially pursue a remedy under subsection (2) unless the right or remedy first chosen has been pursued to an extent actually inconsistent with the new course of action. The intent of the provision is to reject the doctrine of election of remedies and to permit an alteration of course by the lessor unless such alteration would actually have an effect on the lessee that would be unreasonable under the circumstances. Further, the lessor may pursue remedies under both subsections (1) and (2) unless doing so would put the lessor in a better position than it would have been in had the lessee fully performed.

2. The lessor and the lessee can agree to modify the rights and remedies available under the Article; they can, among other things, provide that for defaults other than those specified in subsection (1) the lessor can exercise the rights and remedies referred to in subsection (1), whether or not the default would otherwise be held to substantially impair the value of the lease contract to the lessor; they can also create a new scheme of rights and remedies triggered by the occurrence of the default. Sections 2A–103(4) and 1–102(3).

3. Subsection (1), a substantially rewritten version of Section 2–703, lists various cumulative remedies of the lessor where the lessee wrongfully rejects or revokes acceptance, fails to make a payment when due, or repudiates. Section 2A–501(2) and (4). The subsection also allows the lessor to exercise any contractual remedy.

4. This Article rejects any general doctrine of election of remedy. Whether, in a particular case, one remedy bars another, is a function of whether lessor has been put in as good a position as if the lessee had fully performed the lease contract. Multiple remedies are barred only if the effect is to put the lessor in a better position than it would have been in had the lessee fully performed under the lease. Sections 2A–103(4), 2A–501(4), and 1–106(1).

5. **Hypothetical:** To better understand the application of subparagraphs (a) through (e), it is useful to review a hypothetical. Assume that A is a merchant in the business of selling and leasing new bicycles of various types. B is about to engage in the business of subleasing bicycles to summer residents of and visitors to an island resort. A, as lessor, has agreed to lease 60 bicycles to B. While there is one master lease, deliveries and terms are staggered. 20 bicycles are to be delivered by A to B's island location on June 1; the term of the lease of these bicycles is four months. 20 bicycles are to be delivered by A to B's island location on July 1; the term of the lease of these bicycles is three months. Finally, 20 bicycles are to be delivered by A to B's island location on August 1; the term of the lease of these bicycles is two months. B is obligated to pay rent to A on the 15th day of each month during the term for the lease. Rent is $50 per month, per bicycle. B has no option to purchase or release and must return the bicycles to A at the end of the term, in good condition, reasonable wear and tear excepted. Since the retail price of each bicycle is $400 and bicycles used in the retail rental business have a useful economic life of 36 months, this transaction creates a lease. Sections 2A–103(1)(j) and 1–201(37).

6. A's current inventory of bicycles is not large. Thus, upon signing the lease with B in February, A agreed to purchase 60 new bicycles from A's principal manufacturer, with special instructions to drop ship the bicycles to B's island location in accordance with the delivery schedule set forth in the lease.

7. The first shipment of 20 bicycles was received by B on May 21. B inspected the bicycles, accepted the same as conforming to the lease and signed a receipt of delivery and acceptance. However, due to poor weather that summer, business was terrible and B was unable to pay the rent due on June 15. Pursuant to the lease A sent B notice of default and proceeded to enforce his rights and remedies against B.

8. A's counsel first advised A that under Section 2A–510(2) and the terms of the lease B's failure to pay was a default with respect to the whole. Thus, to minimize A's continued exposure, A was advised to take possession of the bicycles. If A had possession of the goods A could refuse to deliver. Section 2A–525(1). However, the facts here are different. With respect to the bicycles in B's possession, A has the right to take possession of the bicycles, without breach of the peace. Section 2A–525(2). If B refuses to allow A access to the bicycles, A can proceed by action, including replevin or injunctive relief.

9. With respect to the 40 bicycles that have not been delivered, this Article provides various alternatives. First, assume that 20 of the remaining 40 bicycles have been manufactured and delivered by the manufacturer to a carrier for shipment to B. Given the size of the shipment, the carrier was using a small truck for the delivery and the truck had not yet reached the island ferry when the manufacturer (at the request of A) instructed the carrier to divert the shipment to A's place of business. A's right to stop delivery is recognized under these circumstances. Section 2A–526(1). Second, assume that the 20 remaining bicycles were in the process of manufacture when B defaulted. A retains the right (as between A as lessor and B as lessee) to exercise reasonable commercial judgment whether to complete manufacture or to dispose of the unfinished goods for scrap. Since A is not the manufacturer and A has a binding contract to buy the bicycles, A elected to allow the manufacturer to complete the manufacture of the bicycles, but instructed the manufacturer to deliver the completed bicycles to A's place of business. Section 2A–524(2).

10. Thus, so far A has elected to exercise the remedies referred to in subparagraphs (b) through (d) in subsection (1). None of these remedies bars any of the others because A's election and enforcement merely resulted in A's possession of the bicycles. Had B performed A would have recovered possession of the bicycles. Thus A is in the process of obtaining the benefit of his bargain. Note that A could exercise any other rights or pursue any other remedies provided in the lease contract (Section 2A–523(1)(f)), or elect to recover his loss due to the lessee's default under Section 2A–523(2).

11. A's counsel next would determine what action, if any, should be taken with respect to the goods. As stated in subparagraph (e) and as discussed fully in Section 2A–527(1) the lessor may, but has no obligation to, dispose of the goods by a substantially similar lease (indeed, the lessor has no obligation whatsoever to dispose of the goods at all) and

recover damages based on that action, but lessor will not be able to recover damages which put it in a better position than performance would have done, nor will it be able to recover damages for losses which it could have reasonably avoided. In this case, since A is in the business of leasing and selling bicycles, A will probably inventory the 60 bicycles for its retail trade.

12. A's counsel then will determine which of the various means of ascertaining A's damages against B are available. Subparagraph (e) catalogues each relevant section. First, under Section 2A–527(2) the amount of A's claim is computed by comparing the original lease between A and B with any subsequent lease of the bicycles but only if the subsequent lease is substantially similar to the original lease contract. While the section does not define this term, the official comment does establish some parameters. If, however, A elects to lease the bicycles to his retail trade, it is unlikely that the resulting lease will be substantially similar to the original, as leases to retail customers are considerably different from leases to wholesale customers like B. If, however, the leases were substantially similar, the damage claim is for accrued and unpaid rent to the beginning of the new lease, plus the present value as of the same date, of the rent reserved under the original lease for the balance of its term less the present value as of the same date of the rent reserved under the replacement lease for a term comparable to the balance of the term of the original lease, together with incidental damages less expenses saved in consequence of the lessee's default.

13. If the new lease is not substantially similar or if A elects to sell the bicycles or to hold the bicycles, damages are computed under Section 2A–528 or 2A–529.

14. If A elects to pursue his claim under Section 2A–528(1) the damage rule is the same as that stated in Section 2A–527(2) except that damages are measured from default if the lessee never took possession of the goods or from the time when the lessor did or could have regained possession and that the standard of comparison is not the rent reserved under a substantially similar lease entered into by the lessor but a market rent, as defined in Section 2A–507. Further, if the facts of this hypothetical were more elaborate A may be able to establish that the measure of damage under subsection (1) is inadequate to put him in the same position that B's performance would have, in which case A can claim the present value of his lost profits.

15. Yet another alternative for computing A's damage claim against B which will be available in some situations is recovery of the present value, as of entry of judgment, of the rent for the then remaining lease term under Section 2A–529. However, this formulation is not available if the goods have been repossessed or tendered back to A. For the 20 bicycles repossessed and the remaining 40 bicycles, A will be able to recover the present value of the rent only if A is unable to dispose of them, or circumstances indicate the effort will be unavailing. If A has prevailed in an action for the rent, at any time up to collection of a judgment by A against B, A might dispose of the bicycles. In such case A's claim for damages against B is governed by Section 2A–527 or 2A–528. Section 2A–529(3). The resulting recalculation of claim should reduce the amount recoverable by A against B and the lessor is required to cause an appropriate credit to be entered against the earlier judgment. However, the nature of the post-judgment proceedings to resolve this issue, and the sanctions for a failure to comply, if any, will be determined by other law.

16. Finally, if the lease agreement had so provided pursuant to subparagraph (f), A's claim against B would not be determined under any of these statutory formulae, but pursuant to a liquidated damages clause. Section 2A–504(1).

17. These various methods of computing A's damage claim against B are alternatives subject to Section 2A–501(4). However, the pursuit of any one of these alternatives is not a bar to, nor has it been barred by, A's earlier action to obtain possession of the 60 bicycles. These formulae, which vary as a function of an overt or implied mitigation of damage theory, focus on allowing A a recovery of the benefit of his bargain with B. Had B performed, A would have received the rent as well as the return of the 60 bicycles at the end of the term.

18. Finally, A's counsel should also advise A of his right to cancel the lease contract under subparagraph (a). Section 2A–505(1). Cancellation will discharge all existing obligations but preserve A's rights and remedies.

19. Subsection (2) recognizes that a lessor who is entitled to exercise the rights or to obtain a remedy granted by subsection (1) may choose not to do so. In such cases, the lessor can recover damages as provided in subsection (2). For example, for non-payment of rent, the lessor may decide not to take possession of the goods and cancel the lease, but rather to merely sue for the unpaid rent as it comes due plus lost interest or other damages "determined in any reasonable manner." Subsection (2) also negates any loss of alternative rights and remedies by reason of having invoked or commenced the exercise or pursuit of any one or more rights or remedies.

20. Subsection (3) allows the lessor access to a remedy scheme provided in this Article as well as that contained in the lease contract if the lessee is in default for reasons other than those stated in subsection (1). Note that the reference to this Article includes supplementary principles of law and equity, *e.g.*, fraud, misrepresentation and duress. Sections 2A–103(4) and 1–103.

21. There is no special treatment of the finance lease in this section. Absent supplementary principles of law to the contrary, in most cases the supplier will have no rights or remedies against the defaulting lessee. Section 2A–209(2)(ii). Given that the supplier will look to the lessor for payment, this is appropriate. However, there is a specific exception to this rule with respect to the right to identify goods to the lease contract. Section 2A–524(2). The parties are free to create a different result in a particular case. Sections 2A–103(4) and 1–102(3).

Cross References:

Sections 1–102(3), 1–103, 1–106(1), 1–201(37), 2–703, 2A–103(1)(j), 2A–103(4), 2A–209(2)(ii), 2A–501(4), 2A–504(1), 2A–505(1), 2A–507, 2A–510(2), 2A–524 through 2A–531, 2A–524(2), 2A–525(1), 2A–525(2), 2A–526(1), 2A–527(1), 2A–527(2), 2A–528(1) and 2A–529(3).

Definitional Cross References:

"Delivery". Section 1–201(14).

"Goods". Section 2A–103(1)(h).

"Installment lease contract". Section 2A–103(1)(i).

"Lease contract". Section 2A–103(1)(l).

"Lessee". Section 2A–103(1)(n).

"Lessor". Section 2A–103(1)(p).

"Remedy". Section 1–201(34).

"Rights". Section 1–201(36).

"Value". Section 1–201(44).

§ 2A.524. Lessor's Right to Identify Goods to Lease Contract

(a) A lessor aggrieved under Section 2A.523(a) may:

(1) identify to the lease contract conforming goods not already identified, if at the time the lessor learned of the default they were in the lessor's or the supplier's possession or control; and

(2) dispose of goods (Section 2A.527(a)) that demonstrably have been intended for the particular lease contract even though those goods are unfinished.

(b) If the goods are unfinished, in the exercise of reasonable commercial judgment for the purposes of avoiding loss and of effective realization, an aggrieved lessor or the supplier may either complete manufacture and wholly identify the goods to the lease contract or cease manufacture and lease, sell, or otherwise dispose of the goods for scrap or salvage value or proceed in any other reasonable manner.

Added by Acts 1993, 73rd Leg., ch. 570, § 1, eff. Sept. 1, 1993.

Uniform Commercial Code Comment

Uniform Statutory Source: Section 2–704.

Changes: Revised to reflect leasing practices and terminology.

Purposes: The remedies provided by this section are available to the lessor (i) if there has been a default by the lessee which falls within Section 2A–523(1) or 2A–523(3)(a), or (ii) if there has been any other default for which the lease contract gives the lessor the remedies provided by this section. Under "(ii)", the lease contract may give the lessor the remedies of identification and disposition provided by this section in various ways. For example, a lease provision might specifically refer to the remedies of identification and disposition, or it might refer to this section by number (i.e., 2A–524), or it might do so by a more general reference such as "all rights and remedies provided by Article 2A for default by the lessee."

Definitional Cross References:

"Aggrieved party". Section 1–201(2).

"Conforming". Section 2A–103(1)(d).

"Goods". Section 2A–103(1)(h).

"Learn". Section 1–201(25).

"Lease". Section 2A–103(1)(j).

"Lease contract". Section 2A–103(1)(l).

"Lessor". Section 2A–103(1)(p).

"Rights". Section 1–201(36).

"Supplier". Section 2A–103(1)(x).

"Value". Section 1–201(44).

§ 2A.525. Lessor's Right to Possession of Goods

(a) If a lessor discovers the lessee to be insolvent, the lessor may refuse to deliver the goods.

(b) After a default by the lessee under the lease contract of the type described by Section 2A.523(a) or (c)(1) or, if agreed, after other default by the lessee, the lessor has the right to take possession of the goods. If the lease contract so provides, the lessor may require the lessee to assemble the goods and make them available to the lessor at a place to be designated by the lessor which is reasonably convenient to both parties. Without removal, the lessor may render unusable any goods employed in trade or business, and may dispose of goods on the lessee's premises (Section 2A.527).

(c) The lessor may proceed under Subsection (b) without judicial process if that can be done without breach of the peace or the lessor may proceed by action.

Added by Acts 1993, 73rd Leg., ch. 570, § 1, eff. Sept. 1, 1993.

Uniform Commercial Code Comment

Uniform Statutory Source: Sections 2–702(1) and 9–503.

Changes: Substantially revised.

Purposes:

1. Subsection (1), a revised version of the provisions of Section 2–702(1), allows the lessor to refuse to deliver goods if the lessee is insolvent. Note that the provisions of Section 2–702(2), granting the unpaid seller certain rights of reclamation, were not incorporated in this section. Subsection (2) made this unnecessary.

2. Subsection (2), a revised version of the provisions of Section 9–503, allows the lessor, on a Section 2A–523(1) or 2A–523(3)(a) default by the lessee, the right to take possession of or reclaim the goods. Also, the lessor can contract for the right to take possession of the goods for other defaults by the lessee. Therefore, since the lessee's insolvency is an event of default in a standard lease agreement, subsection (2) is the functional equivalent of Section 2–702(2). Further, subsection (2) sanctions the classic crate and delivery clause obligating the lessee to assemble the goods and to make them available to the lessor. Finally, the lessor may

leave the goods in place, render them unusable (if they are goods employed in trade or business), and dispose of them on the lessee's premises.

3. Subsection (3), a revised version of the provisions of Section 9–503, allows the lessor to proceed under subsection (2) without judicial process, absent breach of the peace, or by action. Sections 2A–501(3), 2A–103(4) and 1–201(1). In the appropriate case action includes injunctive relief. *Clark Equipment Co. v. Armstrong Equip. Co.*, 431 F.2d 54 (5th Cir. 1970), *cert. denied*, 402 U.S. 909 (1971). This Section, as well as a number of other Sections in this Part, are included in the Article to codify the lessor's common law right to protect the lessor's reversionary interest in the goods. Section 2A–103(1)(q). These Sections are intended to supplement and not displace principles of law and equity with respect to the protection of such interest. Sections 2A–103(4) and 1–103. Such principles apply in many instances, *e.g.*, loss or damage to goods if risk of loss passes to the lessee, failure of the lessee to return goods to the lessor in the condition stipulated in the lease, and refusal of the lessee to return goods to the lessor after termination or cancellation of the lease. See also Section 2A–532.

Cross References:

Sections 1–106(2), 2–702(1), 2–702(2), 2A–103(4), 2A–501(3), 2A–532 and 9–503.

Definitional Cross References:

"Action". Section 1–201(1).

"Delivery". Section 1–201(14).

"Discover". Section 1–201(25).

"Goods". Section 2A–103(1)(h).

"Insolvent". Section 1–201(23).

"Lease contract". Section 2A–103(1)(*l*).

"Lessee". Section 2A–103(1)(n).

"Lessor". Section 2A–103(1)(p).

"Party". Section 1–201(29).

"Rights". Section 1–201(36).

§ 2A.526. Lessor's Stoppage of Delivery in Transit or Otherwise

(a) A lessor may stop delivery of goods in the possession of a carrier or other bailee if the lessor discovers the lessee to be insolvent and may stop delivery of carload, truckload, planeload, or larger shipments of express or freight if the lessee repudiates or fails to make a payment due before delivery, whether for rent, security or otherwise under the lease contract, or for any other reason the lessor has a right to withhold or take possession of the goods.

(b) In pursuing its remedies under Subsection (a), the lessor may stop delivery until:

(1) receipt of the goods by the lessee;

(2) acknowledgement to the lessee by any bailee of the goods, except a carrier, that the bailee holds the goods for the lessee; or

(3) such an acknowledgement to the lessee by a carrier via reshipment or as a warehouse.

(c)(1) To stop delivery, a lessor shall so notify as to enable the bailee by reasonable diligence to prevent delivery of the goods.

(2) After notification, the bailee shall hold and deliver the goods according to the directions of the lessor, but the lessor is liable to the bailee for any ensuing charges or damages.

(3) A carrier who has issued a nonnegotiable bill of lading is not obligated to obey a notification to stop received from a person other than the consignor.

Added by Acts 1993, 73rd Leg., ch. 570, § 1, eff. Sept. 1, 1993. Amended by Acts 2005, 79th Leg., ch. 122, § 15, eff. Sept. 1, 2005.

Uniform Commercial Code Comment

Uniform Statutory Source: Section 2–705.

Changes: Revised to reflect leasing practices and terminology.

Definitional Cross References:

"Bill of lading". Section 1–201(6).

"Delivery". Section 1–201(14).

"Discover". Section 1–201(25).

"Goods". Section 2A–103(1)(h).

"Insolvent". Section 1–201(23).

"Lease contract". Section 2A–103(1)(*l*).

"Lessee". Section 2A–103(1)(n).

"Lessor". Section 2A–103(1)(p).

"Notifies" and "Notification". Section 1–201(26).

"Person". Section 1–201(30).

"Receipt". Section 2–103(1)(c).

"Remedy". Section 1–201(34).

"Rights". Section 1–201(36).

Sections 31 and 32 of Acts 2005, 79th Leg., ch. 122 provide:

"Sec. 31. This Act applies to a document of title that is issued or a bailment that arises on or after the effective date of this Act. This Act does not apply to a document of title that is issued or a bailment that arises before the effective date of this Act even if the document of title or bailment would be subject to this Act if the document of title had been issued or bailment had arisen after the effective date of this Act. This Act does not apply to a right of action that has accrued before the effective date of this Act.

"Sec. 32. A document of title issued or a bailment that arises before the effective date of this Act and the rights, obligations, and interests flowing from that document or bailment are governed by any statute or other rule amended or repealed by this Act as if amendment or repeal had not occurred and may be terminated,

completed, consummated, or enforced under that statute or other rule."

§ 2A.527. Lessor's Rights to Dispose of Goods

(a) After a default by a lessee under the lease contract of the type described in Section 2A.523(a) or (c)(1) or after the lessor refuses to deliver or takes possession of goods (Section 2A.525 or 2A.526), or, if agreed, after other default by a lessee, the lessor may dispose of the goods concerned or the undelivered balance thereof by lease, sale or otherwise.

(b) Except as otherwise provided with respect to damages liquidated in the lease agreement (Section 2A.504) or otherwise determined pursuant to agreement of the parties (Sections 1.302 and 2A.503), if the disposition is by lease agreement substantially similar to the original lease agreement and the new lease agreement is made in good faith and in a commercially reasonable manner, the lessor may recover from the lessee as damages (1) accrued and unpaid rent as of the date of the commencement of the term of the new lease agreement, (2) the present value, as of the same date, of the total rent for the then remaining lease term of the original lease agreement minus the present value, as of the same date, of the rent under the new lease agreement applicable to that period of the new lease term which is comparable to the then remaining term of the original lease agreement, and (3) any incidental damages allowed under Section 2A.530, less expenses saved in consequence of the lessee's default.

(c) If the lessor's disposition is by lease agreement that for any reason does not qualify for treatment under Subsection (b), or is by sale or otherwise, the lessor may recover from the lessee as if the lessor had elected not to dispose of the goods and Section 2A.528 governs.

(d) A subsequent buyer or lessee who buys or leases from the lessor in good faith for value as a result of a disposition under this section takes the goods free of the original lease contract and any rights of the original lessee even though the lessor fails to comply with one or more of the requirements of this chapter.

(e) The lessor is not accountable to the lessee for any profit made on any disposition. A lessee who has rightfully rejected or justifiably revoked acceptance shall account to the lessor for any excess over the amount of the lessee's security interest (Section 2A.508(e)).

Added by Acts 1993, 73rd Leg., ch. 570, § 1, eff. Sept. 1, 1993. Amended by Acts 2003, 78th Leg., ch. 542, § 8, eff. Sept. 1, 2003.

Uniform Commercial Code Comment

Uniform Statutory Source: Section 2–706(1), (5) and (6).

Changes: Substantially revised.

Purposes:

1. Subsection (1), a revised version of the first sentence of subsection 2–706(1), allows the lessor the right to dispose of goods after a statutory or other material default by the lessee (even if the goods remain in the lessee's possession—Section 2A–525(2)), after the lessor refuses to deliver or takes possession of the goods, or, if agreed, after other contractual default. The lessor's decision to exercise this right is a function of a commercial judgment, not a statutory mandate replete with sanctions for failure to comply. *Cf.* Section 9–507. As the owner of the goods, in the case of a lessor, or as the prime lessee of the goods, in the case of a sublessor, compulsory disposition of the goods is inconsistent with the nature of the interest held by the lessor or the sublessor and is not necessary because the interest held by the lessee or the sublessee is not protected by a right of redemption under the common law or this Article. Subsection 2A–527(5).

2. The rule for determining the measure of damages recoverable by the lessor against the lessee is a function of several variables. If the lessor has elected to effect disposition under subsection (1) and such disposition is by lease that qualifies under subsection (2), the measure of damages set forth in subsection (2) will apply, absent agreement to the contrary. Sections 2A–504, 2A–103(4) and 1–102(3).

3. The lessor's damages will be established using the new lease agreement as a measure if the following three criteria are satisfied: (i) the lessor disposed of the goods by lease, (ii) the lease agreement is substantially similar to the original lease agreement, and (iii) such disposition was in good faith, and in a commercially reasonable manner. Thus, the lessor will be entitled to recover from the lessee the accrued and unpaid rent as of the date of commencement of the term of the new lease, and the present value, as of the same date, of the rent under the original lease for the then remaining term less the present value as of the same date of the rent under the new lease agreement applicable to the period of the new lease comparable to the remaining term under the original lease, together with incidental damages less expenses saved in consequence of the lessee's default. If the lessor's disposition does not satisfy the criteria of subsection (2), the lessor may calculate its claim against the lessee pursuant to Section 2A–528. Section 2A–523(1)(e).

4. Two of the three criteria to be met by the lessor are familiar, but the concept of the new lease agreement that is substantially similar to the original lease agreement is not. Given the many variables facing a party who intends to lease goods and the rapidity of change in the market place, the policy decision was made not to draft with specificity. It was thought unwise to seek to establish certainty at the cost of

fairness. The decision of whether the new lease agreement is substantially similar to the original will be determined case by case.

5. While the section does not draw a bright line, it is possible to describe some of the factors that should be considered in a finding that a new lease agreement is substantially similar to the original. The various elements of the new lease agreement should be examined. Those elements include the options to purchase or release; the lessor's representations, warranties and covenants to the lessee as well as those to be provided by the lessee to the lessor; and the services, if any, to be provided by the lessor or by the lessee. All of these factors allocate cost and risk between the lessor and the lessee and thus affect the amount of rent to be paid. These findings should not be made with scientific precision, as they are a function of economics, nor should they be made independently, as it is important that a sense of commercial judgment pervade the finding. *See* Section 2A–507(2). To establish the new lease as a proper measure of damage under subsection (2), these various factors, taken as a whole, must result in a finding that the new lease agreement is substantially similar to the original. If the differences between the original lease and the new lease can be easily valued, it would be appropriate for a court to find that the new lease is substantially similar to the old lease, adjust the difference in the rent between the two leases to take account of the differences, and award damages under this section. If, for example, the new lease requires the lessor to insure the goods in the hands of the lessee, while the original lease required the lessee to insure, the usual cost of such insurance could be deducted from rent due under the new lease before the difference in rental between the two leases is determined.

6. The following hypothetical illustrates the difficulty of providing a bright line. Assume that A buys a jumbo tractor for $1 million and then leases the tractor to B for a term of 36 months. The tractor is delivered to and is accepted by B on May 1. On June 1 B fails to pay the monthly rent to A. B returns the tractor to A, who immediately releases the tractor to C for a term identical to the term remaining under the lease between A and B. All terms and conditions under the lease between A and C are identical to those under the original lease between A and B, except that C does not provide any property damage or other insurance coverage, and B agreed to provide complete coverage. Coverage is expensive and difficult to obtain. It is a question of fact whether it is so difficult to adjust the recovery to take account of the difference between the two leases as to insurance that the second lease is not substantially similar to the original.

7. A new lease can be substantially similar to the original lease even though its term extends beyond the remaining term of the original lease, so long as both (a) the lease terms are commercially comparable (*e.g.*, it is highly unlikely that a one-month rental and a five-year lease would reflect similar realities), and (b) the court can fairly apportion a part of the rental payments under the new lease to that part of the term of the new lease which is comparable to the remaining lease term under the original lease. Also, the lease term of the new lease may be comparable to the remaining term of the original lease even though the beginning and ending dates of the two leases are not the same. For example, a two-month lease of agricultural equipment for the months of August and September may be comparable to a two-month lease running from the 15th of August to the 15th of October if in the particular location two-month leases beginning on August 15th are basically interchangeable with two-month leases beginning August 1st. Similarly, the term of a one-year truck lease beginning on the 15th of January may be comparable to the term of a one-year truck lease beginning January 2nd. If the lease terms are found to be comparable, the court may base cover damages on the entire difference between the costs under the two leases.

8. Subsection (3), which is new, provides that if the lessor's disposition is by lease that does not qualify under subsection (2), or is by sale or otherwise, Section 2A–528 governs.

9. Subsection (4), a revised version of subsection 2–706(5), applies to protect a subsequent buyer or lessee who buys or leases from the lessor in good faith and for value, pursuant to a disposition under this section. Note that by its terms, the rule in subsection 2A–304(1), which provides that the subsequent lessee takes subject to the original lease contract, is controlled by the rule stated in this subsection.

10. Subsection (5), a revised version of subsection 2–706(6), provides that the lessor is not accountable to the lessee for any profit made by the lessor on a disposition. This rule follows from the fundamental premise of the bailment for hire that the lessee under a lease of goods has no equity of redemption to protect.

Cross References:

Sections 1–102(3), 2–706(1), 2–706(5), 2–706(6), 2A–103(4), 2A–304(1), 2A–504, 2A–507(2), 2A–523(1)(e), 2A–525(2), 2A–527(5), 2A–528 and 9–507.

Definitional Cross References:

"Buyer" and "Buying". Section 2–103(1)(a).

"Delivery". Section 1–201(14).

"Good faith". Sections 1–201(19) and 2–103(1)(b).

"Goods". Section 2A–103(1)(h).

"Lease". Section 2A–103(1)(j).

"Lease contract". Section 2A–103(1)(*l*).

"Lessee". Section 2A–103(1)(n).

"Lessor". Section 2A–103(1)(p).

"Present value". Section 2A–103(1)(u).

"Rights". Section 1–201(36).

"Sale". Section 2–106(1).

"Security interest". Section 1–201(37).

"Value". Section 1–201(44).

§ 2A.528. Lessor's Damages for Nonacceptance, Failure to Pay, Repudiation, or Other Default

(a) Except as otherwise provided with respect to damages liquidated in the lease agreement (Section 2A.504) or otherwise determined pursuant to agreement of the parties (Sections 1.302 and 2A.503), if a lessor elects to retain the goods or a lessor elects to dispose of the goods and the disposition is by lease agreement that for any reason does not qualify for treatment under Section 2A.527(b) or is by sale or otherwise, the lessor may recover from the lessee as damages for a default of the type described in Section 2A.523(a) or (c)(1), or, if agreed, for other default of the lessee, (i) accrued and unpaid rent as of the date of default if the lessee has never taken possession of the goods, or, if the lessee has taken possession of the goods, as of the date the lessor repossesses the goods or an earlier date on which the lessee makes a tender of the goods to the lessor, (ii) the present value as of the date determined under clause (i) of the total rent for the then remaining lease term of the original lease agreement minus the present value as of the same date of the market rent at the place where the goods are located computed for the same lease term, and (iii) any incidental damages allowed under Section 2A.530, less expenses saved in consequence of the lessee's default.

(b) If the measure of damages provided in Subsection (a) is inadequate to put a lessor in as good a position as performance would have, the measure of damages is the present value of the profit, including reasonable overhead, the lessor would have made from full performance by the lessee, together with any incidental damages allowed under Section 2A.530, due allowance for costs reasonably incurred and due credit for payments or proceeds of disposition.

Added by Acts 1993, 73rd Leg., ch. 570, § 1, eff. Sept. 1, 1993. Amended by Acts 2003, 78th Leg., ch. 542, § 9, eff. Sept. 1, 2003.

Uniform Commercial Code Comment

Uniform Statutory Source: Section 2–708.

Changes: Substantially revised.

Purposes:

1. Subsection (1), a substantially revised version of Section 2–708(1), states the basic rule governing the measure of lessor's damages for a default described in Section 2A–523(1) or (3)(a), and, if agreed, for a contractual default. This measure will apply if the lessor elects to retain the goods (whether undelivered, returned by the lessee, or repossessed by the lessor after acceptance and default by the lessee) or if the lessor's disposition does not qualify under subsection 2A–527(2). Section 2A–527(3). Note that under some of these conditions, the lessor may recover damages from the lessee pursuant to the rule set forth in Section 2A–529. There is no sanction for disposition that does not qualify under subsection 2A–527(2). Application of the rule set forth in this section is subject to agreement to the contrary. Sections 2A–504, 2A–103(4) and 1–102(3).

2. If the lessee has never taken possession of the goods, the measure of damage is the accrued and unpaid rent as of the date of default together with the present value, as of the date of default, of the original rent for the remaining term of the lease less the present value as of the same date of market rent, and incidental damages, less expenses saved in consequence of the default. Note that the reference in Section 2A–528(1)(i) and (ii) is to the date of default not to the date of an event of default. An event of default under a lease agreement becomes a default under a lease agreement only after the expiration of any relevant period of grace and compliance with any notice requirements under this Article and the lease agreement. American Bar Foundation, *Commentaries on Indentures*, § 5–1, at 216–217 (1971). Section 2A–501(1). This conclusion is also a function of whether, as a matter of fact or law, the event of default has been waived, suspended or cured. Sections 2A–103(4) and 1–103. If the lessee has taken possession of the goods, the measure of damages is the accrued and unpaid rent as of the earlier of the time the lessor repossesses the goods or the time the lessee tenders the goods to the lessor plus the difference between the present value, as of the same time, of the rent under the lease for the remaining lease term and the present value, as of the same time, of the market rent.

3. Market rent will be computed pursuant to Section 2A–507.

4. Subsection (2), a somewhat revised version of the provisions of subsection 2–708(2), states a measure of damages which applies if the measure of damages in subsection (1) is inadequate to put the lessor in as good a position as performance would have. The measure of damage is the lessor's profit, including overhead, together with incidental damages, with allowance for costs reasonably incurred and credit for payments or proceeds of disposition. In determining the amount of due credit with respect to proceeds of disposition a proper value should be attributed to the lessor's residual interest in the goods. Sections 2A–103(1)(q) and 2A–507(4).

5. In calculating profit, a court should include any expected appreciation of the goods, *e.g.* the foal of a leased brood mare. Because this subsection is intended to give the lessor the benefit of the bargain, a court should consider any reasonable benefit or profit expected by the lessor from the performance of the lease agreement. *See Honeywell, Inc. v. Lithonia Lighting, Inc.*, 317 F.Supp. 406, 413 (N.D.Ga.1970); *Locks v. Wade*, 36 N.J.Super. 128, 131, 114 A.2d 875, 877 (Super.Ct.App.Div.1955). Further, in calculating profit the concept of present value must be given effect. *Taylor v. Commercial credit Equip. Corp.*, 170 Ga.App. 322, 316 S.E.2d 788 (Ct.App.1984). *See generally* Section 2A–103(1)(u).

Cross References:

Sections 1–102(3), 2–708, 2A–103(1)(u), 2A–402, 2A–504, 2A–507, 2A–527(2) and 2A–529.

Definitional Cross References:

"Agreement". Section 1–201(3).

"Goods". Section 2A–103(1)(h).

"Lease". Section 2A–103(1)(j).

"Lease agreement". Section 2A–103(1)(k).

"Lessee". Section 2A–103(1)(n).

"Lessor". Section 2A–103(1)(p).

"Party". Section 1–201(29).

"Present value". Section 2A–103(1)(u).

"Sale". Section 2–106(1).

§ 2A.529. Lessor's Action for the Rent

(a) After default by the lessee under the lease contract of the type described in Section 2A.523(a) or (c)(1), or, if agreed, after other default by the lessee, if the lessor complies with Subsection (b), the lessor may recover from the lessee as damages:

(1) for goods accepted by the lessee and not repossessed by or tendered to the lessor, and for conforming goods lost or damaged within a commercially reasonable time after risk of loss passes to the lessee (Section 2A.219), (i) accrued and unpaid rent as of the date of entry of judgment in favor of the lessor, (ii) the present value as of the same date of the rent for the then remaining lease term of the lease agreement, and (iii) any incidental damages allowed under Section 2A.530, less expenses saved in consequence of the lessee's default; and

(2) for goods identified to the lease contract if the lessor is unable after reasonable effort to dispose of them at a reasonable price or the circumstances reasonably indicate that effort will be unavailing, (i) accrued and unpaid rent as of the date of entry of judgment in favor of the lessor, (ii) the present value as of the same date of the rent for the then remaining lease term of the lease agreement, and (iii) any incidental damages allowed under Section 2A.530, less expenses saved in consequence of the lessee's default.

(b) Except as provided by Subsection (c) of this section, the lessor shall hold for the lessee for the remaining lease term of the lease agreement any goods that have been identified to the lease contract and are in the lessor's control.

(c) The lessor may dispose of the goods at any time before collection of the judgment for damages obtained pursuant to Subsection (a). If the disposition is before the end of the remaining lease term of the lease agreement, the lessor's recovery against the lessee for damages is governed by Section 2A.527 or 2A.528, and the lessor will cause an appropriate credit to be provided against any judgment for damages to the extent that the amount of the judgment exceeds the recovery available pursuant to Section 2A.527 or 2A.528.

(d) Payment of the judgment for damages obtained pursuant to Subsection (a) entitles the lessee to the use and possession of the goods not then disposed of for the remaining lease term of and in accordance with the lease agreement.

(e) After a lessee has wrongfully rejected or revoked acceptance of goods, has failed to pay rent then due, or has repudiated (Section 2A.402), a lessor who is held not entitled to rent under this section must nevertheless be awarded damages for nonacceptance under Section 2A.527 or 2A.528.

Added by Acts 1993, 73rd Leg., ch. 570, § 1, eff. Sept. 1, 1993.

Uniform Commercial Code Comment

Uniform Statutory Source: Section 2–709.

Changes: Substantially revised.

Purposes: 1. Absent a lease contract provision to the contrary, an action for the full unpaid rent (discounted to present value as of the time of entry of judgment as to rent due after that time) is available as to goods not lost or damaged only if the lessee retains possession of the goods or the lessor is or apparently will be unable to dispose of them at a reasonable price after reasonable effort. There is no general right in a lessor to recover the full rent from the lessee upon holding the goods for the lessee. If the lessee tenders goods back to the lessor, and the lessor refuses to accept the tender, the lessor will be limited to the damages it would have suffered had it taken back the goods. The rule in Article 2 that the seller can recover the price of accepted goods is rejected here. In a lease, the lessor always has a residual interest in the goods which the lessor usually realizes upon at the end of a lease term by either sale or a new lease. Therefore, it is not a substantial imposition on the lessor to require it to take back and dispose of the goods if the lessee chooses to tender them back before the end of the lease term: the lessor will merely do earlier what it would have done anyway, sell or relet the goods. Further, the lessee will frequently encounter substantial difficulties if the lessee attempts to sublet the goods for the remainder of the lease term. In contrast to the buyer who owns the entire interest in goods and can easily dispose of them, the lessee is selling only the right to use the goods under the terms of the lease and the sublessee must assume a relationship with the lessor. In that situation, it is usually more efficient to eliminate the original lessee as a middleman by allowing the lessee to return the goods to the lessor who can then redispose of them.

2. In some situations even where possession of the goods is reacquired, a lessor will be able to recover as damages the present value of the full rent due, not under this section, but under 2A–528(2) which allows a lost profit recovery if necessary to put the lessor in the position it would have been in had the lessee performed. Following is an example of such a case. A is a lessor of construction equipment and maintains a substantial inventory. B leases from A a backhoe for a period of two weeks at a rental of $1,000. After three days, B returns the backhoe and refuses to pay the rent. A has

five backhoes in inventory, including the one returned by B. During the next 11 days after the return by B of the backhoe, A rents no more than three backhoes at any one time and, therefore, always has two on hand. If B had kept the backhoe for the full rental period. A would have earned the full rental on that backhoe, plus the rental on the other backhoes it actually did rent during that period. Getting this backhoe back before the end of the lease term did not enable A to make any leases it would not otherwise have made. The only way to put A in the position it would have been in had the lessee fully performed is to give the lessor the full rentals. A realized no savings at all because the backhoe was returned early and might even have incurred additional expense if it was paying for parking space for equipment in inventory. A has no obligation to relet the backhoe for the benefit of B rather than leasing the backhoe or any other in inventory for its own benefit. Further, it is probably not reasonable to expect A to dispose of the backhoe by sale when it is returned in an effort to reduce damages suffered by B. Ordinarily, the loss of a two-week rental would not require A to reduce the size of its backhoe inventory. Whether A would similarly be entitled to full rentals as lost profit in a one-year lease of a backhoe is a question of fact: in any event the lessor, subject to mitigation of damages rules, is entitled to be put in as good a position as it would have been had the lessee fully performed the lease contract.

3. Under subsection (2) a lessor who is able and elects to sue for the rent due under a lease must hold goods not lost or damaged for the lessee. Subsection (3) creates an exception to the subsection (2) requirement. If the lessor disposes of those goods prior to collection of the judgment (whether as a matter of law or agreement), the lessor's recovery is governed by the measure of damages in Section 2A–527 if the disposition is by lease that is substantially similar to the original lease, or otherwise by the measure of damages in Section 2A–528. Section 2A–523 official comment.

4. Subsection (4), which is new, further reinforces the requisites of Subsection (2). In the event the judgment for damages obtained by the lessor against the lessee pursuant to subsection (1) is satisfied, the lessee regains the right to use and possession of the remaining goods for the balance of the original lease term; a partial satisfaction of the judgment creates no right in the lessee to use and possession of the goods.

5. The relationship between subsections (2) and (4) is important to understand. Subsection (2) requires the lessor to hold for the lessee identified goods in the lessor's possession. Absent agreement to the contrary, whether in the lease or otherwise, under most circumstances the requirement that the lessor hold the goods for the lessee for the term will mean that the lessor is not allowed to use them. Sections 2A–103(4) and 1–203. Further, the lessor's use of the goods could be viewed as a disposition of the goods that would bar the lessor from recovery under this section, remitting the lessor to the two preceding sections for a determination of the lessor's claim for damages against the lessee.

6. Subsection (5), the analogue of subsection 2–709(3), further reinforces the thrust of subsection (3) by stating that a lessor who is held not entitled to rent under this section has not elected a remedy; the lessor must be awarded damages under Sections 2A–527 and 2A–528. This is a function of two significant policies of this Article — that resort to a remedy is optional, unless expressly agreed to be exclusive (Section 2A–503(2)) and that rights and remedies provided in this Article generally are cumulative. (Section 2A–501(2) and (4)).

Cross References:

Sections 1–203, 2–709, 2–709(3), 2A–103(4), 2A–501(2), 2A–501(4), 2A–503(2), 2A–504, 2A–523(1)(e), 2A–525(2), 2A–527, 2A–528 and 2A–529(2).

Definitional Cross References:

"Action". Section 1–201(1).

"Conforming". Section 2A–103(1)(d).

"Goods". Section 2A–103(1)(h).

"Lease". Section 2A–103(1)(j).

"Lease agreement". Section 2A–103(1)(k).

"Lease contract". Section 2A–103(1)(*l*).

"Lessee". Section 2A–103(1)(n).

"Lessor". Section 2A–103(1)(p).

"Present value". Section 2A–103(1)(u).

"Reasonable time". Section 1–204(1) and (2).

§ 2A.530. Lessor's Incidental Damages

Incidental damages to an aggrieved lessor include any commercially reasonable charges, expenses, or commissions incurred in stopping delivery, in the transportation, care and custody of goods after the lessee's default, in connection with return or disposition of the goods, or otherwise resulting from the default.

Added by Acts 1993, 73rd Leg., ch. 570, § 1, eff. Sept. 1, 1993.

Uniform Commercial Code Comment

Uniform Statutory Source: Section 2–710.

Changes: Revised to reflect leasing practices and terminology.

Definitional Cross References:

"Aggrieved party". Section 1–201(2).

"Delivery". Section 1–201(14).

"Goods". Section 2A–103(1)(h).

"Lessee". Section 2A–103(1)(n).

"Lessor". Section 2A–103(1)(p).

§ 2A.531. Standing to Sue Third Parties for Injury to Goods

(a) If a third party so deals with goods that have been identified to a lease contract as to cause actionable injury to a party to the lease contract:

(1) the lessor has a right of action against the third party; and

(2) the lessee also has a right of action against the third party if the lessee:

(A) has a security interest in the goods;

(B) has an insurable interest in the goods;

(C) bears the risk of loss under the lease contract or has since the injury assumed that risk as against the lessor and the goods have been converted or destroyed.

(b) If at the time of the injury the party plaintiff did not bear the risk of loss as against the other party to the lease contract and there is no arrangement between them for disposition of the recovery, the party's suit or settlement, subject to the party's own interest, is as a fiduciary for the other party to the lease contract.

(c) Either party with the consent of the other may sue for the benefit of whom it may concern.

Added by Acts 1993, 73rd Leg., ch. 570, § 1, eff. Sept. 1, 1993.

Uniform Commercial Code Comment

Uniform Statutory Source: Section 2–722.

Changes: Revised to reflect leasing practices and terminology.

Definitional Cross References:

"Action". Section 1–201(1).

"Goods". Section 2A–103(1)(h).

"Lease contract". Section 2A–103(1)(*l*).

"Lessee". Section 2A–103(1)(n).

"Lessor". Section 2A–103(1)(p).

"Party". Section 1–201(29).

"Rights". Section 1–201(36).

"Security interest". Section 1–201(37).

§ 2A.532. Lessor's Rights to Residual Interest

In addition to any other recovery permitted by this chapter or other law, the lessor may recover from the lessee an amount that will fully compensate the lessor for any loss of or damage to the lessor's residual interest in the goods caused by the default of the lessee.

Added by Acts 1993, 73rd Leg., ch. 570, § 1, eff. Sept. 1, 1993.

Uniform Commercial Code Comment

Uniform Statutory Source: None.

This section recognizes the right of the lessor to recover under this Article (as well as under other law) from the lessee for failure to comply with the lease obligations as to the condition of leased goods when returned to the lessor, for failure to return the goods at the end of the lease, or for any other default which causes loss or injury to the lessor's residual interest in the goods.

CHAPTER 3. NEGOTIABLE INSTRUMENTS

SUBCHAPTER A. GENERAL PROVISIONS AND DEFINITIONS

SUBCHAPTER B. NEGOTIATION, TRANSFER, AND INDORSEMENT

SUBCHAPTER C. ENFORCEMENT OF INSTRUMENTS

Acts 1995, 74th Leg., ch. 921, § 1 amended Chapter 3 effective January 1, 1996. The former Chapter 3, Commercial Paper, consisting of §§ 3.101 to 3.805, was amended as Chapter 3, Negotiable Instruments, consisting of §§ 3.101 to 3.605.

SUBCHAPTER A. GENERAL PROVISIONS AND DEFINITIONS

§ 3.101. Short Title

This chapter may be cited as Uniform Commercial Code-Negotiable Instruments.

Amended by Acts 1995, 74th Leg., ch. 921, § 1, eff. Jan. 1, 1996.

§ 3.102. Subject Matter

(a) This chapter applies to negotiable instruments. It does not apply to money, to payment orders governed by Chapter 4A, or to securities governed by Chapter 8.

(b) If there is conflict between this chapter and Chapter 4 or 9, Chapters 4 and 9 govern.

(c) Regulations of the Board of Governors of the Federal Reserve System and operating circulars of the Federal Reserve Banks supersede any inconsistent provision of this chapter to the extent of the inconsistency.

Amended by Acts 1995, 74th Leg., ch. 921, § 1, eff. Jan. 1, 1996.

Uniform Commercial Code Comment

1. Former Article 3 had no provision affirmatively stating its scope. Former Section 3–103 was a limitation on scope. In revised Article 3, Section 3–102 states that Article 3 applies to "negotiable instruments," defined in Section 3–104. Section 3–104(b) also defines the term "instrument" as a synonym for "negotiable instrument." In most places Article 3 uses the shorter term "instrument." This follows the convention used in former Article 3.

2. The reference in former Section 3–103(1) to "documents of title" is omitted as superfluous because these documents contain no promise to pay money. The definition of "payment order" in Section 4A–103(a)(1)(iii) excludes drafts which are governed by Article 3. Section 3–102(a) makes clear that a payment order governed by Article 4A is not governed by Article 3. Thus, Article 3 and Article 4A are mutually exclusive.

Article 8 states in Section 8–103(d) that "A writing that is a security certificate is governed by this Article and not by Article 3, even though it also meets the requirements of that Article." Section 3–102(a) conforms to this provision. With respect to some promises or orders to pay money, there may be a question whether the promise or order is an instrument under Section 3–104(a) or a certificated security under Section 8–102(a)(4) and (15). Whether a writing is covered by Article 3 or Article 8 has important consequences. Among other things, under Section 8–207, the issuer of a certificated security may treat the registered owner as the owner for all purposes until the presentment for registration of a transfer. The issuer of a negotiable instrument, on the other hand, may discharge its obligation to pay the instrument only by paying a person entitled to enforce under Section 3–301. There are also important consequences to an indorser. An indorser of a security does not undertake the issuer's obligation or make any warranty that the issuer will honor the underlying obligation, while an indorser of a negotiable instrument becomes secondarily liable on the underlying obligation. *Amendments approved by the Permanent Editorial Board for Uniform Commercial Code November 4, 1995.*

Ordinarily the distinction between instruments and certificated securities in non-bearer form should be relatively clear. A certificated security under Article 8 must be in registered form (Section 8–102(a)(13)) so that it can be registered on the issuer's records. By contrast, registration plays no part in Article 3. The distinction between an instrument and a certificated security in bearer form may be somewhat more difficult and will generally lie in the economic functions of the two writings. Ordinarily, negotiable instruments under Article 3 will be separate and distinct instruments, while certificated securities under Article 8 will be either one of a class or series or by their terms divisible into a class or series (Section 8–102(a)(15)(ii)). Thus, a promissory note in bearer form could come under either Article 3 if it were simply an individual note, or under Article 8 if it were one of a series of notes or divisible into a series. An additional distinction is whether the instrument is of the type commonly dealt in on securities exchanges or markets or commonly recognized as a medium for investment (Section 8–102(a)(15)(iii)). Thus, a check written in bearer form (i.e., a check made payable to "cash") would not be a certificated security within Article 8 of the Uniform Commercial Code. *Amendments approved by the Permanent Editorial Board for Uniform Commercial Code November 4, 1995.*

Occasionally, a particular writing may fit the definition of both a negotiable instrument under Article 3 and of an investment security under Article 8. In such cases, the instrument is subject exclusively to the requirements of Article 8. Section 8–103(d) and Section 3–102(a). Amendments approved by the Permanent Editorial Board for Uniform Commercial Code November 4, 1995.

3. Although the terms of Article 3 apply to transactions by Federal Reserve Banks, federal preemption would make ineffective any Article 3 provision that conflicts with federal law. The activities of the Federal Reserve Banks are governed by regulations of the Federal Reserve Board and by operating circulars issued by the Reserve Banks themselves. In some instances, the operating circulars are issued pursuant to a Federal Reserve Board regulation. In other cases, the Reserve Bank issues the operating circular under its own authority under the Federal Reserve Act, subject to review by the Federal Reserve Board. Section 3–102(c) states that Federal Reserve Board regulations and operating circulars of the Federal Reserve Banks supersede any inconsistent provision of Article 3 to the extent of the inconsistency. Federal Reserve Board regulations, being valid exercises of regulatory authority pursuant to a federal statute, take precedence over state law if there is an inconsistency. *Childs v. Federal Reserve Bank of Dallas*, 719 F.2d 812 (5th Cir.1983), reh. den. 724 F.2d 127 (5th Cir.1984). Section 3–102(c) treats operating circulars as having the same effect whether issued under the Reserve Bank's own authority or under a Federal Reserve Board regulation. Federal statutes may also preempt Article 3. For example, the Expedited Funds Availability Act, 12 U.S.C. § 4001 et seq., provides that the Act and the regulations issued pursuant to the Act supersede any inconsistent provisions of the UCC. 12 U.S.C. § 4007(b).

4. In *Clearfield Trust Co. v. United States*, 318 U.S. 363 (1943), the Court held that if the United States is a party to an instrument, its rights and duties are governed by federal common law in the absence of a specific federal statute or regulation. In *United States v. Kimbell Foods, Inc.*, 440 U.S. 715 (1979), the Court stated a three-pronged test to ascertain whether the federal common-law rule should follow the state rule. In most instances courts under the *Kimbell* test have shown a willingness to adopt UCC rules in formulating federal common law on the subject. In *Kimbell* the Court adopted the priorities rules of Article 9.

5. In 1989 the United Nations Commission on International Trade Law completed a Convention on International Bills of Exchange and International Promissory Notes. If the United States becomes a party to this Convention, the Convention will preempt state law with respect to international bills and notes governed by the Convention. Thus, an international bill of exchange or promissory note that meets the definition of instrument in Section 3–104 will not be governed by Article 3 if it is governed by the Convention. That Convention applies only to bills and notes that indicate on their face that they involve cross-border transactions. It does not apply at all to checks. Convention Articles 1(3), 2(1), 2(2). Moreover, because it applies only if the bill or note specifically calls for application of the Convention, Convention Article 1, there is little chance that the Convention will apply accidentally to a transaction that the parties intended to be governed by this Article. *Amendments approved by the Permanent Editorial Board for Uniform Commercial Code November 2, 2002.*

§ 3.103. Definitions

(a) In this chapter:

(1) "Acceptor" means a drawee who has accepted a draft.

(2) Reserved.

(3) "Consumer transaction" means a transaction in which an individual incurs an obligation primarily for personal, family, or household purposes.

(4) "Drawee" means a person ordered in a draft to make payment.

(5) "Drawer" means a person who signs or is identified in a draft as a person ordering payment.

(6) Reserved.

(7) "Maker" means a person who signs or is identified in a note as a person undertaking to pay.

(8) "Order" means a written instruction to pay money signed by the person giving the instruction. The instruction may be addressed to any person, including the person giving the instruction, or to one or more persons jointly or in the alternative but not in succession. An authorization to pay is not an

order unless the person authorized to pay is also instructed to pay.

(9) "Ordinary care" in the case of a person engaged in business means observance of reasonable commercial standards, prevailing in the area in which the person is located, with respect to the business in which the person is engaged. In the case of a bank that takes an instrument for processing for collection or payment by automated means, reasonable commercial standards do not require the bank to examine the instrument if the failure to examine does not violate the bank's prescribed procedures and the bank's procedures do not vary unreasonably from general banking usage not disapproved by this chapter or Chapter 4.

(10) "Party" means a party to an instrument.

(11) "Principal obligor," with respect to an instrument, means the accommodated party or any other party to the instrument against whom a secondary obligor has recourse under this chapter.

(12) "Promise" means a written undertaking to pay money signed by the person undertaking to pay. An acknowledgment of an obligation by the obligor is not a promise unless the obligor also undertakes to pay the obligation.

(13) "Prove" with respect to a fact means to meet the burden of establishing the fact (Section 1.201(b)(8)).

(14) Reserved.

(15) "Remitter" means a person who purchases an instrument from its issuer if the instrument is payable to an identified person other than the purchaser.

(16) "Remotely-created item" means an item that is created by a third party, other than the payor bank, under the purported authority of the drawer of the item for the purpose of charging the drawer's account with a bank and that does not bear a handwritten signature purporting to be the signature of the drawer.

(17) "Secondary obligor," with respect to an instrument, means (A) an indorser or an accommodation party, (B) a drawer having the obligation described in Section 3.414(d), or (C) any other party to the instrument that has recourse against another party to the instrument pursuant to Section 3.116(b).

(b) Other definitions applying to this chapter and the sections in which they appear are:

"Acceptance"	Section 3.409.
"Accommodated party"	Section 3.419.
"Accommodation party"	Section 3.419.
"Account"	Section 4.104.
"Alteration"	Section 3.407.
"Anomalous indorsement"	Section 3.205.
"Blank indorsement"	Section 3.205.
"Cashier's check"	Section 3.104.
"Certificate of deposit"	Section 3.104.
"Certified check"	Section 3.409.
"Check"	Section 3.104.
"Consideration"	Section 3.303.
"Draft"	Section 3.104.
"Holder in due course"	Section 3.302.
"Incomplete instrument"	Section 3.115.
"Indorsement"	Section 3.204.
"Indorser"	Section 3.204.
"Instrument"	Section 3.104.
"Issue"	Section 3.105.
"Issuer"	Section 3.105.
"Negotiable instrument"	Section 3.104.
"Negotiation"	Section 3.201.
"Note"	Section 3.104.
"Payable at a definite time"	Section 3.108.
"Payable on demand"	Section 3.108.
"Payable to bearer"	Section 3.109.
"Payable to order"	Section 3.109.
"Payment"	Section 3.602.
"Person entitled to enforce"	Section 3.301.
"Presentment"	Section 3.501.
"Reacquisition"	Section 3.207.
"Special indorsement"	Section 3.205.
"Teller's check"	Section 3.104.
"Transfer of instrument"	Section 3.203.
"Traveler's check"	Section 3.104.
"Value"	Section 3.303.

(c) The following definitions in other chapters apply to this chapter:

"Banking day"	Section 4.104.
"Clearing house"	Section 4.104.
"Collecting bank"	Section 4.105.
"Depositary bank"	Section 4.105.
"Documentary draft"	Section 4.104.
"Intermediary bank"	Section 4.105.
"Item"	Section 4.104.
"Payor bank"	Section 4.105.
"Suspends payments"	Section 4.104.

(d) In addition, Chapter 1 contains general definitions and principles of construction and interpretation applicable throughout this chapter.

Amended by Acts 1995, 74th Leg., ch. 921, § 1, eff. Jan. 1, 1996; Acts 1997, 75th Leg., ch. 131, § 1, eff. Sept. 1, 1997; Acts 2003, 78th Leg., ch. 542, § 10, eff. Sept. 1, 2003; Acts 2005, 79th Leg., ch. 95, §§ 1, 2, eff. Sept. 1, 2005; Acts 2007, 80th Leg., ch. 427, §§ 1, 2, eff. Sept. 1, 2007.

Uniform Commercial Code Comment

1. Subsection (a) defines some common terms used throughout the Article that were not defined by former Article 3 and adds the definitions of "order" and "promise" found in former Section 3–102(1)(b) and (c).

2. The definition of "order" includes an instruction given by the signer to itself. The most common example of this kind of order is a cashier's check: a draft with respect to which the drawer and drawee are the same bank or branches of the same bank. Former Section 3–118(a) treated a cashier's check as a note. It stated "a draft drawn on the drawer is effective as a note." Although it is technically more correct to treat a cashier's check as a promise by the issuing bank to pay rather than an order to pay, a cashier's check is in the form of a check and it is normally referred to as a check. Thus, revised Article 3 follows banking practice in referring to a cashier's check as both a draft and a check rather than a note. Some insurance companies also follow the practice of issuing drafts in which the drawer draws on itself and makes the draft payable at or through a bank. These instruments are also treated as drafts. The obligation of the drawer of a cashier's check or other draft drawn on the drawer is stated in Section 3–412.

An order may be addressed to more than one person as drawee either jointly or in the alternative. The authorization of alternative drawees follows former Section 3–102(1)(b) and recognizes the practice of drawers, such as corporations issuing dividend checks, who for commercial convenience name a number of drawees, usually in different parts of the country. Section 3–501(b)(1) provides that presentment may be made to any one of multiple drawees. Drawees in succession are not permitted because the holder should not be required to make more than one presentment. Dishonor by any drawee named in the draft entitles the holder to rights of recourse against the drawer or indorsers.

3. The last sentence of subsection (a)(9) is intended to make it clear that an I.O.U. or other written acknowledgement of indebtedness is not a note unless there is also an undertaking to pay the obligation.

4. This Article now uses the broadened definition of good faith in revised Article 1. The definition in subsection (a)(4) is consistent with the The definition requires not only honesty in fact but also "observance of reasonable commercial standards of fair dealing." Although fair dealing is a broad term that must be defined in context, it is clear that it is concerned with the fairness of conduct rather than the care with which an act is performed. Failure to exercise ordinary care in conducting a transaction is an entirely different concept than failure to deal fairly in conducting the transaction. Both fair dealing and ordinary care, which is defined in Section 3–103(a)(7), are to be judged in the light of reasonable commercial standards, but those standards in each case are directed to different aspects of commercial conduct.

5. Subsection (a)(7) is a definition of ordinary care which is applicable not only to Article 3 but to Article 4 as well. See Section 4–104(c). The general rule is stated in the first sentence of subsection (a)(7) and it applies both to banks and to persons engaged in businesses other than banking. Ordinary care means observance of reasonable commercial standards of the relevant business prevailing in the area in which the person is located. The second sentence of subsection (a)(7) is a particular rule limited to the duty of a bank to examine an instrument taken by a bank for processing for collection or payment by automated means. This particular rule applies primarily to Section 4–406 and it is discussed in Comment 4 to that section. Nothing in Section 3–103(a)(7) is intended to prevent a customer from proving that the procedures followed by a bank are unreasonable, arbitrary, or unfair.

6. The definition of consumer account includes a joint account established by more than one individual. See Section 1–106(1).

§ 3.104. Negotiable Instrument

(a) Except as provided in Subsections (c) and (d), "negotiable instrument" means an unconditional promise or order to pay a fixed amount of money, with or without interest or other charges described in the promise or order, if it:

(1) is payable to bearer or to order at the time it is issued or first comes into possession of a holder;

(2) is payable on demand or at a definite time; and

(3) does not state any other undertaking or instruction by the person promising or ordering payment to do any act in addition to the payment of money, but the promise or order may contain:

(A) an undertaking or power to give, maintain, or protect collateral to secure payment;

(B) an authorization or power to the holder to confess judgment or realize on or dispose of collateral; or

(C) a waiver of the benefit of any law intended for the advantage or protection of an obligor.

(b) "Instrument" means a negotiable instrument.

(c) An order that meets all of the requirements of Subsection (a), except Subdivision (1), and otherwise falls within the definition of "check" in Subsection (f) is a negotiable instrument and a check.

(d) A promise or order other than a check is not an instrument if, at the time it is issued or first comes into possession of a holder, it contains a conspicuous statement, however expressed, to the effect that the promise or order is not negotiable or is not an instrument governed by this chapter.

(e) An instrument is a "note" if it is a promise and is a "draft" if it is an order. If an instrument falls within the definition of both "note" and "draft," a person entitled to enforce the instrument may treat it as either.

(f) "Check" means (i) a draft, other than a documentary draft, payable on demand and drawn on a bank or (ii) a cashier's check or teller's check. An instrument may be a check even though it is described on its face by another term, such as "money order."

(g) "Cashier's check" means a draft with respect to which the drawer and drawee are the same bank or branches of the same bank.

(h) "Teller's check" means a draft drawn by a bank:

(1) on another bank; or

(2) payable at or through a bank.

(i) "Traveler's check" means an instrument that:

(1) is payable on demand;

(2) is drawn on or payable at or through a bank;

(3) is designated by the term "traveler's check" or by a substantially similar term; and

(4) requires, as a condition to payment, a countersignature by a person whose specimen signature appears on the instrument.

(j) "Certificate of deposit" means an instrument containing an acknowledgment by a bank that a sum of money has been received by the bank and a promise by the bank to repay the sum of money. A certificate of deposit is a note of the bank.

(k) Repealed by Acts 2007, 80th Leg., ch. 427, § 4.

Amended by Acts 1995, 74th Leg., ch. 921, § 1, eff. Jan. 1, 1996; Acts 1997, 75th Leg., ch. 131, § 2, eff. Sept. 1, 1997; Acts 2007, 80th Leg., ch. 427, § 4, eff. Sept. 1, 2007.

Uniform Commercial Code Comment

1. The definition of "negotiable instrument" defines the scope of Article 3 since Section 3–102 states: "This Article applies to negotiable instruments." The definition in Section 3–104(a) incorporates other definitions in Article 3. An instrument is either a "promise," defined in Section 3–103(a)(9), or "order," defined in Section 3–103(a)(6). A promise is a written undertaking to pay money signed by the person undertaking to pay. An order is a written instruction to pay money signed by the person giving the instruction. Thus, the term "negotiable instrument" is limited to a signed writing that orders or promises payment of money. "Money" is defined in Section 1–201(24) and is not limited to United States dollars. It also includes a medium of exchange established by a foreign government or monetary units of account established by an intergovernmental organization or by agreement between two or more nations. Five other requirements are stated in Section 3–104(a): First, the promise or order must be "unconditional." The quoted term is explained in Section 3–106. Second, the amount of money must be "a fixed amount * * * with or without interest or other charges described in the promise or order." Section 3–112(b) relates to "interest." Third, the promise or order must be "payable to bearer or to order." The quoted phrase is explained in Section 3–109. An exception to this requirement is stated in subsection (c). Fourth, the promise or order must be payable "on demand or at a definite time." The quoted phrase is explained in Section 3–108. Fifth, the promise or order may not state "any other undertaking or instruction by the person promising or ordering payment to do any act in addition to the payment of money" with three exceptions. The quoted phrase is based on the first sentence of N.I.L. Section 5 which is the precursor of "no other promise, order, obligation or power given by the maker or drawer" appearing in former Section 3–104(1)(b). The words "instruction" and "undertaking" are used instead of "order" and "promise" that are used in the N.I.L. formulation because the latter words are defined terms that include only orders or promises to pay money. The three exceptions stated in Section 3–104(a)(3) are based on and are intended to have the same meaning as former Section 3–112(1)(b), (c), (d), and (e), as well as N.I.L. § 5(1), (2), and (3). Subsection (b) states that "instrument" means a "negotiable instrument." This follows former Section 3–102(1)(e) which treated the two terms as synonymous.

2. Unless subsection (c) applies, the effect of subsection (a)(1) and Section 3–102(a) is to exclude from Article 3 any promise or order that is not payable to bearer or to order. There is no provision in revised Article 3 that is comparable to former Section 3–805. The comment to former Section 3–805 states that the typical example of a writing covered by that section is a check reading "Pay John Doe." Such a check was governed by former Article 3 but there could not be a holder in due course of the check. Under Section 3–104(c) such a check is governed by revised Article 3 and there can be a holder in due course of the check. But subsection (c) applies only to checks. The comment to former Section 3–805 does not state any example other than the check to illustrate that section. Subsection (c) is based on the belief that it is good policy to treat checks, which are payment instruments, as negotiable instruments whether or not they contain the words "to the order of". These words are almost always pre-printed on the check form. Occasionally the drawer of a check may strike out these words before issuing the check. In the past some credit unions used check forms that did not contain the quoted words. Such check forms may still be in use but they are no longer common. Absence of the quoted words can easily be overlooked and should not affect the rights of holders who may pay money or give credit for a check without being aware that it is not in the conventional form.

Total exclusion from Article 3 of other promises or orders that are not payable to bearer or to order serves a useful purpose. It provides a simple device to clearly exclude a writing that does not fit the pattern of typical negotiable instruments and which is not intended to be a negotiable instrument. If a writing could be an instrument despite the absence of "to order" or "to bearer" language and a dispute arises with respect to the writing, it might be argued that the writing is a negotiable instrument because the other requirements of subsection (a) are somehow met. Even if the argument is eventually found to be without merit it can be used as a litigation ploy. Words making a promise or order payable to bearer or to order are the most distinguishing feature of a negotiable instrument and such words are frequently referred to as "words of negotiability." Article 3 is not meant to apply to contracts for the sale of goods or services or the sale or lease of real property or similar writings that may contain a promise to pay money. The use of words of negotiability in such contracts would be an aberration. Absence of the words precludes any argument that such contracts might be negotiable instruments.

An order or promise that is excluded from Article 3 because of the requirements of Section 3–104(a) may nevertheless be similar to a negotiable instrument in many respects. Although such a writing cannot be made a negotiable instrument within Article 3 by contract or conduct of its parties, nothing in Section 3–104 or in Section 3–102 is intended to mean that in a particular case involving such a writing a court could not arrive at a result similar to the result that would follow if the writing were a negotiable instrument. For example, a court might find that the obligor with respect to a promise that does not fall within Section 3–104(a) is precluded from asserting a defense against a bona fide purchaser. The preclusion could be based on estoppel or ordinary principles of contract. It does not depend upon the law of negotiable instruments. An example is stated in the paragraph following Case # 2 in Comment 4 to Section 3–302.

Moreover, consistent with the principle stated in Section 1–102(2)(b), the immediate parties to an order or promise that is not an instrument may provide by agreement that one or more of the provisions of Article 3 determine their rights and obligations under the writing. Upholding the parties' choice is not inconsistent with Article 3. Such an agreement may bind a transferee of the writing if the transferee has notice of it or the agreement arises from usage of trade and the agreement does not violate other law or public policy. An example of such an agreement is a provision that a transferee of the writing has the rights of a holder in due course stated in Article 3 if the transferee took rights under the writing in good faith, for value, and without notice of a claim or defense.

Even without an agreement of the parties to an order or promise that is not an instrument, it may be appropriate, consistent with the principles stated in Section 1–102(2), for a court to apply one or more provisions of Article 3 to the writing by analogy, taking into account the expectations of the parties and the differences between the writing and an instrument governed by Article 3. Whether such application is appropriate depends upon the facts of each case.

3. Subsection (d) allows exclusion from Article 3 of a writing that would otherwise be an instrument under subsection (a) by a statement to the effect that the writing is not negotiable or is not governed by Article 3. For example, a promissory note can be stamped with the legend NOT NEGOTIABLE. The effect under subsection (d) is not only to negate the possibility of a holder in due course, but to prevent the writing from being a negotiable instrument for any purpose. Subsection (d) does not, however, apply to a check. If a writing is excluded from Article 3 by subsection (d), a court could, nevertheless, apply Article 3 principles to it by analogy as stated in Comment 2.

4. Instruments are divided into two general categories: drafts and notes. A draft is an instrument that is an order. A note is an instrument that is a promise. Section 3–104(e). The term "bill of exchange" is not used in Article 3. It is generally understood to be a synonym for the term "draft." Subsections (f) through (j) define particular instruments that fall within the categories of draft and note. The term "draft," defined in subsection (e), includes a "check" which is defined in subsection (f). "Check" includes a share draft drawn on a credit union payable through a bank because the definition of bank (Section 4–104) includes credit unions. However, a draft drawn on an insurance payable through a bank is not a check because it is not drawn on a bank. "Money orders" are sold both by banks and non-banks. They vary in form and their form determines how they are treated in Article 3. The most common form of money order sold by banks is that of an ordinary check drawn by the purchaser except that the amount is machine impressed. That kind of money order is a check under Article 3 and is subject to a stop order by the purchaser-drawer as in the case of ordinary checks. The seller bank is the drawee and has no obligation to a holder to pay the money order. If a money order falls within the definition of a teller's check, the rules applicable to teller's checks apply. Postal money orders are subject to federal law. "Teller's check" is separately defined in subsection (h). A teller's check is always drawn by a bank and is usually drawn on another bank. In some cases a teller's check is drawn on a nonbank but is made payable at or through a bank. Article 3 treats both types of teller's check identically, and both are included in the definition of "check." A cashier's check, defined in subsection (g), is also included in the definition of "check." Traveler's checks are issued both by banks and nonbanks and may be in the form of a note or draft. Subsection (i) states the essential characteristics of a traveler's check. The requirement that the instrument be "drawn on or payable at or through a bank" may be satisfied without words on the instrument that identify a bank as drawee or paying agent so long as the instrument bears an appropriate routing number that identifies a bank as paying agent.

The definitions in Regulation CC § 229.2 of the terms "check," "cashier's check," "teller's check," and "traveler's check" are different from the definitions of those terms in Article 3.

Certificates of deposit are treated in former Article 3 as a separate type of instrument. In revised Article 3, Section 3–104(j) treats them as notes.

5. There are some differences between the requirements of Article 3 and the requirements included in Article 3 of the Convention on International Bills of Exchange and International Promissory Notes. Most obviously, the Convention does not include the limitation on extraneous undertakings set forth in Section 3–104(a)(3), and does not permit documents payable to bearer that would be permissible under Section 3–104(a)(1) and Section 3–109. See Convention Article 3. In most respects, however, the requirements of Section 3–104 and Article 3 of the Convention are quite similar. *Amendments approved by the Permanent Editorial Board for Uniform Commercial Code November 2, 2002.*

State Bar Committee Comments

Section 3.104 provides that instruments containing a variable interest rate may constitute "negotiable instruments". This result is consistent with existing Texas law. *See Amberboy v. Societe de Banque Privee*, 831 S.W.2d 793, 793–98 (Tex. 1992), *certified question accepted sub nom from Ackerman v. FDIC*, 930 F.2d 3, 4 (5th Cir. 1991) (holding that a promissory note is a negotiable instrument, as defined by the Texas Uniform Commercial Code, when the note requires interest to be charged at a rate that can be determined only by reference to a bank's published prime rate).

A "usury savings" provision in a note should not be considered a condition or a variation from a fixed amount of money for purposes of section 3.104(a). Usury savings provisions are commonplace in Texas notes, especially those having a variable interest rate, and, for policy purposes, should not jeopardize the negotiability of such notes.

The definitions of "teller's check" (§ 3.104(h)) and "cashier's check" (§ 3.104(g)) appear to be mutually exclusive. In fact, cashier's checks and teller's checks are a subset of a larger category of bank obligations on which the bank is liable as drawer. A teller's check is generally the bank's own check drawn on its account at another bank. A cashier's check is a check drawn by a bank on itself. However, the definition somewhat overlaps in the instance of a check drawn by a bank on itself but payable at or through another bank. This too is defined as a teller's check. The Texas Supreme Court has opined that a teller's check drawn on another bank is subject to a stop payment order but that payment may not be withheld or "stopped" on a cashier's check. *See, Guaranty Fed. Sav. Bank v. Horseshoe Operating Co.*, 793 S.W.2d 652 (Tex. 1990); *Wertz v. Richardson Heights Bank & Trust*, 495 S.W.2d 572 (Tex. 1973). In the case of a teller's check or a cashier's check, the customer of the drawer bank has no right to issue a valid stop payment order. But contrary to *Wertz*, the revisions to Chapter 3 assume that a bank may dishonor a cashier's check or a teller's check, whether payable at or through another bank or drawn on another bank. If the check drawer heeds its customer's requests and halts payment on the check, it remains liable on the check under section 3.411. *See* § 3.411 Official Comment; § 4.403 Official Comment 4.

Although section 3.104(a)(3) permits confessions of judgment and waivers of the benefit of any law intended for the protection of an obligor, these provisions should not be construed to supersede or revoke any provision of other Texas law that prohibits or makes ineffective any such provision in a promissory note or other instrument covered by such law. *See, e.g.*, Tex. Rev. Civ. Stat. Ann. art. 5069–3.20, 4.04 and 5.05 (Vernon 1987).

§ 3.105. Issue of Instrument

(a) "Issue" means the first delivery of an instrument by the maker or drawer, whether to a holder or nonholder, for the purpose of giving rights on the instrument to any person.

(b) An unissued instrument, or an unissued incomplete instrument that is completed, is binding on the maker or drawer, but nonissuance is a defense. An instrument that is conditionally issued or is issued for a special purpose is binding on the maker or drawer, but failure of the condition or special purpose to be fulfilled is a defense.

(c) "Issuer" applies to issued and unissued instruments and means a maker or drawer of an instrument.

Amended by Acts 1995, 74th Leg., ch. 921, § 1, eff. Jan. 1, 1996.

Uniform Commercial Code Comment

1. Under former Section 3–102(1)(a) "issue" was defined as the first delivery to a "holder or a remitter" but the term "remitter" was neither defined nor otherwise used. In revised Article 3, Section 3–105(a) defines "issue" more broadly to include the first delivery to anyone by the drawer or maker for the purpose of giving rights to anyone on the instrument. "Delivery" with respect to instruments is defined in Section 1–201(14) as meaning "voluntary transfer of possession."

2. Subsection (b) continues the rule that nonissuance, conditional issuance or issuance for a special purpose is a defense of the maker or drawer of an instrument. Thus, the defense can be asserted against a person other than a holder in due course. The same rule applies to nonissuance of an incomplete instrument later completed.

3. Subsection (c) defines "issuer" to include the signer of an unissued instrument for convenience of reference in the statute.

§ 3.106. Unconditional Promise or Order

(a) Except as provided in this section, for the purposes of Section 3.104(a), a promise or order is unconditional unless it states (i) an express condition to payment, (ii) that the promise or order is subject to or governed by another record, or (iii) that rights or obligations with respect to the promise or order are stated in another record. A reference to another record does not of itself make the promise or order conditional.

(b) A promise or order is not made conditional (i) by a reference to another record for a statement of rights with respect to collateral, prepayment, or acceleration, or (ii) because payment is limited to resort to a particular fund or source.

(c) If a promise or order requires, as a condition to payment, a countersignature by a person whose specimen signature appears on the promise or order, the condition does not make the promise or order conditional for the purposes of Section 3.104(a). If the person whose specimen signature appears on an instrument fails to countersign the instrument, the failure to countersign is a defense to the obligation of the issuer, but the failure does not prevent a transferee of the instrument from becoming a holder of the instrument.

(d) If a promise or order at the time it is issued or first comes into possession of a holder contains a statement, required by applicable statutory or administrative law, to the effect that the rights of a holder or transferee are subject to claims or defenses that the issuer could assert against the original payee, the promise or order is not thereby made conditional for the purposes of Section 3.104(a); but if the promise or order is an instrument, there cannot be a holder in due course of the instrument.

Amended by Acts 1995, 74th Leg., ch. 921, § 1, eff. Jan. 1, 1996; Acts 2005, 79th Leg., ch. 95, § 3, eff. Sept. 1, 2005.

Uniform Commercial Code Comment

1. This provision replaces former Section 3–105. Its purpose is to define when a promise or order fulfills the requirement in Section 3–104(a) that it be an "unconditional" promise or order to pay. Under Section 3–106(a) a promise or order is deemed to be unconditional unless one of the two tests of the subsection make the promise or order conditional. If the promise or order states an express condition to payment, the promise or order is not an instrument. For example, a promise states, "I promise to pay $100,000 to the order of John Doe if he conveys title to Blackacre to me." The promise is not an instrument because there is an express condition to payment. However, suppose a promise states, "In consideration of John Doe's promise to convey title to Blackacre I promise to pay $100,000 to the order of John Doe." That promise can be an instrument if Section 3–104 is otherwise satisfied. Although the recital of the executory promise of Doe to convey Blackacre might be read as an implied condition that the promise be performed, the condition is not an express condition as required by Section 3–106(a)(i). This result is consistent with former Section 3–105(1)(a) and (b). Former Section 3–105(1)(b) is not repeated in Section 3–106 because it is not necessary. It is an example of an implied condition. Former Section 3–105(1)(d), (e), and (f) and the first clause of former Section 3–105(1)(c) are other examples of implied conditions. They are not repeated in Section 3–106 because they are not necessary. The law is not changed.

Section 3–106(a)(ii) and (iii) carry forward the substance of former Section 3–105(2)(a). The only change is the use of "writing" instead of "agreement" and a broadening of the language that can result in conditionality. For example, a promissory note is not an instrument defined by Section 3–104 if it contains any of the following statements: 1. "This note is subject to a contract of sale dated April 1, 1990 between the payee and maker of this note." 2. "This note is subject to a loan and security agreement dated April 1, 1990 between the payee and maker of this note." 3. "Rights and obligations of the parties with respect to this note are stated in an agreement dated April 1, 1990 between the payee and maker of this note." It is not relevant whether any condition to payment is or is not stated in the writing to which reference is made. The rationale is that the holder of a negotiable instrument should not be required to examine another document to determine rights with respect to payment. But subsection (b)(i) permits reference to a separate writing for information with respect to collateral, prepayment, or acceleration.

Many notes issued in commercial transactions are secured by collateral, are subject to acceleration in the event of default, or are subject to prepayment, or acceleration does not prevent the note from being an instrument if the statement is in the note itself. See Section 3–104(a)(3) and Section 3–108(b). In some cases it may be convenient not to include a statement concerning collateral, prepayment, or acceleration in the note, but rather to refer to an accompanying loan agreement, security agreement or mortgage for that statement. Subsection (b)(i) allows a reference to the appropriate writing for a statement of these rights. For example, a note would not be made conditional by the following statement: "This note is secured by a security interest in collateral described in a security agreement dated April 1, 1990 between the payee and maker of this note. Rights and obligations with respect to the collateral are [stated in] [governed by] the security agreement." The bracketed words are alternatives, either of which complies.

Subsection (b)(ii) addresses the issues covered by former Section 3–105(1)(f), (g), and (h) and Section 3–105(2)(b). Under Section 3–106(a) a promise or order is not made conditional because payment is limited to payment from a particular source or fund. This reverses the result of former Section 3–105(2)(b). There is no cogent reason why the general credit of a legal entity must be pledged to have a negotiable instrument. Market forces determine the marketability of instruments of this kind. If potential buyers don't want promises or orders that are payable only from a particular source or fund, they won't take them, but Article 3 should apply.

2. Subsection (c) applies to traveler's checks or other instruments that may require a countersignature. Although the requirement of a countersignature is a condition to the obligation to pay, traveler's checks are treated in the commercial world as money substitutes and therefore should be governed by Article 3. The first sentence of subsection (c) allows a traveler's check to meet the definition of instrument by stating that the countersignature condition does not make it conditional for the purposes of Section 3–104. The second sentence states the effect of a failure to meet the condition. Suppose a thief steals a traveler's check and cashes it by skillfully imitating the specimen signature so that the countersignature appears to be authentic. The countersignature is for the purpose of identification of the owner of the instrument. It is not an indorsement. Subsection (c) provides that the failure of the owner to countersign does not prevent a transferee from becoming a holder. Thus, the merchant or bank that cashed the traveler's check becomes a holder when the traveler's check is taken. The forged countersignature is a defense to the obligation of the issuer to pay the instrument, and is included in defenses under Section 3–305(a)(2). These defenses may not be asserted

against a holder in due course. Whether a holder has notice of the defense is a factual question. If the countersignature is a very bad forgery, there may be notice. But if the merchant or bank cashed a traveler's check and the countersignature appeared to be similar to the specimen signature, there might not be notice that the countersignature was forged. Thus, the merchant or bank could be a holder in due course.

3. Subsection (d) concerns the effect of a statement to the effect that the rights of a holder or transferee are subject to claims and defenses that the issuer could assert against the original payee. The subsection applies only if the statement is required by Statutory or administrative law. The prime example is the Federal Trade Commission Rule (16 C.F.R. Part 433) preserving consumers' claims and defenses in consumer credit sales. The intent of the FTC rule is to make it impossible for there to be a holder in due course of a note bearing the FTC legend and undoubtedly that is the result. But, under former Article 3, the legend may also have had the unintended effect of making the note conditional, thus excluding the note from former Article 3 altogether. Subsection (d) is designed to make it possible to preclude the possibility of a holder in due course without excluding the instrument from Article 3. Most of the provisions of Article 3 are not affected by the holder-in-due-course doctrine and there is no reason why Article 3 should not apply to a note bearing the FTC legend if holder-in-due-course rights are not involved. Under subsection (d) the statement does not make the note conditional. If the note otherwise meets the requirements of Section 3–104(a) it is a negotiable instrument for all purposes except that there cannot be a holder in due course of the note. No particular form of legend or statement is required by subsection (d). The form of a particular legend or statement may be determined by the other statute or administrative law. For example, the FTC legend required in a note taken by the seller in a consumer sale of goods or services is tailored to that particular transaction and therefore uses language that is somewhat different from that stated in subsection (d), but the difference in expression does not affect the essential similarity of the message conveyed. The effect of the FTC legend is to make the rights of a holder or transferee subject to claims or defenses that the issuer could assert against the original payee of the note.

§ 3.107. Instrument Payable in Foreign Money

Unless the instrument otherwise provides, an instrument that states the amount payable in foreign money may be paid in the foreign money or in an equivalent amount in dollars calculated by using the current bank-offered spot rate at the place of payment for the purchase of dollars on the day on which the instrument is paid.

Amended by Acts 1995, 74th Leg., ch. 921, § 1, eff. Jan. 1, 1996.

Uniform Commercial Code Comment

The definition of instrument in Section 3–104 requires that the promise or order be payable in "money." That term is defined in Section 1–201(24) and is not limited to United States dollars. Section 3–107 states that an instrument payable in foreign money may be paid in dollars if the instrument does not prohibit it. It also states a conversion rate which applies in the absence of a different conversion rate stated in the instrument. The reference in former Section 3–107(1) to instruments payable in "currency" or "current funds" has been dropped as superfluous.

State Bar Committee Comments

The phrase "current bank-offered spot rate" is adopted from the Uniform Foreign Money Claims Act promulgated by the National Conference of Commissioners of Uniform Laws in 1989. If payment of an instrument is not made when due, this section takes no position on the date for conversion of any resulting judgment between United States dollars and the stated foreign currency. The correct conversion ratio between United States dollars and the stated foreign currency is one that enables the holder to receive sufficient U.S. dollars to allow it to acquire foreign currency in the amount stated in the instrument without suffering any loss on such conversion. As a consequence, the ratio is that which a bank is currently offering at the place of payment to customers who request it to purchase United States dollars and deliver the stated foreign currency. The purpose of this provision is to enable this conversion.

§ 3.108. Payable on Demand or at Definite Time

(a) A promise or order is "payable on demand" if it:

(1) states that it is payable on demand or at sight, or otherwise indicates that it is payable at the will of the holder; or

(2) does not state any time of payment.

(b) A promise or order is "payable at a definite time" if it is payable on elapse of a definite period of time after sight or acceptance or at a fixed date or dates or at a time or times readily ascertainable at the time the promise or order is issued, subject to rights of:

(1) prepayment;

(2) acceleration;

(3) extension at the option of the holder; or

(4) extension to a further definite time at the option of the maker or acceptor or automatically on or after a specified act or event.

(c) If an instrument, payable at a fixed date, is also payable on demand made before the fixed date, the instrument is payable on demand until the fixed date and, if demand for payment is not made before that date, becomes payable at a definite time on the fixed date.

Amended by Acts 1995, 74th Leg., ch. 921, § 1, eff. Jan. 1, 1996.

Uniform Commercial Code Comment

This section is a restatement of former Section 3–108 and Section 3–109. Subsection (b) broadens former Section 3–109 somewhat by providing that a definite time includes a time readily ascertainable at the time the promise or order is issued. Subsection (b)(iii) and (iv) restates former Section 3–109(1)(d). It adopts the generally accepted rule that a clause providing for extension at the option of the holder, even without a time limit, does not affect negotiability since the holder is given only a right which the holder would have without the clause. If the extension is to be at the option of the maker or acceptor or is to be automatic, a definite time limit must be stated or the time of payment remains uncertain and the order or promise is not a negotiable instrument. If a definite time limit is stated, the effect upon certainty of time of payment is the same as if the instrument were made payable at the ultimate date with a term providing for acceleration.

§ 3.109. Payable to Bearer or to Order

(a) A promise or order is payable to bearer if it:

(1) states that it is payable to bearer or to the order of bearer or otherwise indicates that the person in possession of the promise or order is entitled to payment;

(2) does not state a payee; or

(3) states that it is payable to or to the order of cash or otherwise indicates that it is not payable to an identified person.

(b) A promise or order that is not payable to bearer is payable to order if it is payable (i) to the order of an identified person, or (ii) to an identified person or order. A promise or order that is payable to order is payable to the identified person.

(c) An instrument payable to bearer may become payable to an identified person if it is specially indorsed pursuant to Section 3.205(a). An instrument payable to an identified person may become payable to bearer if it is indorsed in blank pursuant to Section 3.205(b).

Amended by Acts 1995, 74th Leg., ch. 921, § 1, eff. Jan. 1, 1996.

Uniform Commercial Code Comment

1. Under Section 3–104(a), a promise or order cannot be an instrument unless the instrument is payable to bearer or to order when it is issued or unless Section 3–104(c) applies. The terms "payable to bearer" and "payable to order" are defined in Section 3–109. The quoted terms are also relevant in determining how an instrument is negotiated. If the instrument is payable to bearer it can be negotiated by delivery alone. Section 3–201(b). An instrument that is payable to an identified person cannot be negotiated without the indorsement of the identified person. Section 3–201(b). An instrument payable to order is payable to an identified person. Section 3–109(b). Thus, an instrument payable to order requires the indorsement of the person to whose order the instrument is payable.

2. Subsection (a) states when an instrument is payable to bearer. An instrument is payable to bearer if it states that it is payable to bearer, but some instruments use ambiguous terms. For example, check forms usually have the words "to the order of" printed at the beginning of the line to be filled in for the name of the payee. If the drawer writes in the word "bearer" or "cash," the check reads "to the order of bearer" or "to the order of cash." In each case the check is payable to bearer. Sometimes the drawer will write the name of the payee "John Doe" but will add the words "or bearer." In that case the check is payable to bearer. Subsection (a). Under subsection (b), if an instrument is payable to bearer it can't be payable to order. This is different from former Section 3–110(3). An instrument that purports to be payable both to order and bearer states contradictory terms. A transferee of the instrument should be able to rely on the bearer term and acquire rights as a holder without obtaining the indorsement of the identified payee. An instrument is also payable to bearer if it does not state a payee. Instruments that do not state a payee are in most cases incomplete instruments. In some cases the drawer of a check may deliver or mail it to the person to be paid without filling in the line for the name of the payee. Under subsection (a) the check is payable to bearer when it is sent or delivered. It is also an incomplete instrument. This case is discussed in Comment 2 to Section 3–115. Subsection (a)(3) contains the words "otherwise indicates that it is not payable to an identified person." The quoted words are meant to cover uncommon cases in which an instrument indicates that it is not meant to be payable to a specific person. Such an instrument is treated like a check payable to "cash." The quoted words are not meant to apply to an instrument stating that it is payable to an identified person such as "ABC Corporation" if ABC Corporation is a nonexistent company. Although the holder of the check cannot be the nonexistent company, the instrument is not payable to bearer. Negotiation of such an instrument is governed by Section 3–404(b).

§ 3.110. Identification of Person to Whom Instrument is Payable

(a) The person to whom an instrument is initially payable is determined by the intent of the person, whether or not authorized, signing as, or in the name or behalf of, the issuer of the instrument. The instrument is payable to the person intended by the signer even if that person is identified in the instrument by a name or other identification that is not that of the intended person. If more than one person signs in the name or behalf of the issuer of an instrument and all the signers do not intend the same person as payee, the instrument is payable to any person intended by one or more of the signers.

(b) If the signature of the issuer of an instrument is made by automated means, such as a check-writing machine, the payee of the instrument is determined by the intent of the person who supplied the name or identification of the payee, whether or not authorized to do so.

(c) A person to whom an instrument is payable may be identified in any way, including by name, identifying number, office, or account number. For the purpose of determining the holder of an instrument, the following rules apply:

(1) If an instrument is payable to an account and the account is identified only by number, the instrument is payable to the person to whom the account is payable. If an instrument is payable to an account identified by number and by the name of a person, the instrument is payable to the named person, whether or not that person is the owner of the account identified by number.

(2) If an instrument is payable to:

(A) a trust, an estate, or a person described as trustee or representative of a trust or estate, the instrument is payable to the trustee, the representative, or a successor of either, whether or not the beneficiary or estate is also named;

(B) a person described as agent or similar representative of a named or identified person, the instrument is payable to the represented person, the representative, or a successor of the representative;

(C) a fund or organization that is not a legal entity, the instrument is payable to a representative of the members of the fund or organization; or

(D) an office or to a person described as holding an office, the instrument is payable to the named person, the incumbent of the office, or a successor to the incumbent.

(d) If an instrument is payable to two or more persons alternatively, it is payable to any of them and may be negotiated, discharged, or enforced by any or all of them in possession of the instrument. If an instrument is payable to two or more persons not alternatively, it is payable to all of them and may be negotiated, discharged, or enforced only by all of them. If an instrument payable to two or more persons is ambiguous as to whether it is payable to the persons alternatively, the instrument is payable to the persons alternatively.

Amended by Acts 1995, 74th Leg., ch. 921, § 1, eff. Jan. 1, 1996.

Uniform Commercial Code Comment

1. Section 3–110 states rules for determining the identity of the person to whom an instrument is initially payable if the instrument is payable to an identified person. This issue usually arises in a dispute over the validity of an indorsement in the name of the payee. Subsection (a) states the general rule that the person to whom an instrument is payable is determined by the intent of "the person, whether or not authorized, signing as, or in the name or behalf of, the issuer of the instrument." "Issuer" means the maker or drawer of the instrument. Section 3–105(c). If X signs a check as drawer of a check on X's account, the intent of X controls. If X, as President of Corporation, signs a check as President in behalf of Corporation as drawer, the intent of X controls. If X forges Y's signature as drawer of a check, the intent of X also controls. Under Section 3–103(a)(3), Y is referred to as the drawer of the check because the signing of Y's name identifies Y as the drawer. But since Y's signature was forged Y has no liability as drawer (Section 3–403(a)) unless some other provision of Article 3 or Article 4 makes Y liable. Since X, even though unauthorized, signed in the name of Y as issuer, the intent of X determines to whom the check is payable.

In the case of a check payable to "John Smith," since there are many people in the world named "John Smith" it is not possible to identify the payee of the check unless there is some further identification or the intention of the drawer is determined. Name alone is sufficient under subsection (a), but the intention of the drawer determines which John Smith is the person to whom the check is payable. The same issue is presented in cases of misdescriptions of the payee. The drawer intends to pay a person known to the drawer as John Smith. In fact that person's name is James Smith or John Jones or some other entirely different name. If the check identifies the payee as John Smith, it is nevertheless payable to the person intended by the drawer. That person may indorse the check in either the name John Smith or the person's correct name or in both names. Section 3–204(d). The intent of the drawer is also controlling in fictitious payee cases. Section 3–404(b). The last sentence of subsection (a) refers to rare cases in which the signature of an organization requires more than one signature and the persons signing on behalf of the organization do not all intend the same person as payee. Any person intended by a signer for the organization is the payee and an indorsement by that person is an effective indorsement.

Subsection (b) recognizes the fact that in a large number of cases there is no human signer of an instrument because the instrument, usually a check, is produced by automated means such as a check-writing machine. In that case, the relevant intent is that of the person who supplied the name of the payee. In most cases that person is an employee of the drawer, but in some cases the person could be an outsider who is committing a fraud by introducing names of payees of checks into the system that produces the checks.

A check-writing machine is likely to be operated by means of a computer in which is stored information as to name and address of the payee and the amount of the check. Access to the computer may allow production of fraudulent checks without knowledge of the organization that is the issuer of the check. Section 3–404(b) is also concerned with this issue. See Case #4 in Comment 2 to Section 3–404.

2. Subsection (c) allows the payee to be identified in any way including the various ways stated. Subsection (c)(1) relates to instruments payable to bank accounts. In some cases the account might be identified by name and number, and the name and number might refer to different persons. For example, a check is payable to "X Corporation Account No. 12345 in Bank of Podunk." Under the last sentence of subsection (c)(1), this check is payable to X Corporation and can be negotiated by X Corporation even if Account No. 12345 is some other person's account or the check is not deposited in that account. In other cases the payee is identified by an account number and the name of the owner of the account is not stated. For example, Debtor pays Creditor by issuing a check drawn on Payor Bank. The check is payable to a bank account owned by Creditor but identified only by number. Under the first sentence of subsection (c)(1) the check is payable to Creditor and, under Section 1–201(20), Creditor becomes the holder when the check is delivered. Under Section 3–201(b), further negotiation of the check requires the indorsement of Creditor. But under Section 4–205(a), if the check is taken by a depositary bank for collection, the bank may become a holder without the indorsement. Under Section 3–102(b), provisions of Article 4 prevail over those of Article 3. The depositary bank warrants that the amount of the check was credited to the payee's account.

3. Subsection (c)(2) replaces former Section 3–117 and subsection (1)(e), (f), and (g) of former Section 3–110. This provision merely determines who can deal with an instrument as a holder. It does not determine ownership of the instrument or its proceeds. Subsection (c)(2)(i) covers trusts and estates. If the instrument is payable to the trust or estate or to the trustee or representative of the trust or estate, the instrument is payable to the trustee or representative or any successor. Under subsection (c)(2)(ii), if the instrument states that it is payable to Doe, President of X Corporation, either Doe or X Corporation can be holder of the instrument. Subsection (c)(2)(iii) concerns informal organizations that are not legal entities such as unincorporated clubs and the like. Any representative of the members of the organization can act as holder. Subsection (c)(2)(iv) applies principally to instruments payable to public offices such as a check payable to County Tax Collector.

4. Subsection (d) replaces former Section 3–116. An instrument payable to X or Y is governed by the first sentence of subsection (d). An instrument payable to X and Y is governed by the second sentence of subsection (d). If an instrument is payable to X or Y, either is the payee and if either is in possession that person is the holder and the person entitled to enforce the instrument. Section 3–301. If an instrument is payable to X and Y, neither X nor Y acting alone is the person to whom the instrument is payable. Neither person, acting alone, can be the holder of the instrument. The instrument is "payable to an identified person." The "identified person" is X and Y acting jointly. Section 3–109(b) and Section 1–102(5)(a). Thus, under Section 1–201(20) X or Y, acting alone, cannot be the holder or the person entitled to enforce or negotiate the instrument because neither, acting alone, is the identified person stated in the instrument.

The third sentence of subsection (d) is directed to cases in which it is not clear whether an instrument is payable to multiple payees alternatively. In the case of ambiguity persons dealing with the instrument should be able to rely on the indorsement of a single payee. For example, an instrument payable to X and/or Y is treated like an instrument payable to X or Y.

§ 3.111. Place of Payment

Except as otherwise provided for items in Chapter 4, an instrument is payable at the place of payment stated in the instrument. If no place of payment is stated, an instrument is payable at the address of the drawee or maker stated in the instrument. If no address is stated, the place of payment is the place of business of the drawee or maker. If a drawee or maker has more than one place of business, the place of payment is any place of business of the drawee or maker chosen by the person entitled to enforce the instrument. If the drawee or maker has no place of business, the place of payment is the residence of the drawee or maker.

Amended by Acts 1995, 74th Leg., ch. 921, § 1, eff. Jan. 1, 1996.

Uniform Commercial Code Comment

If an instrument is payable at a bank in the United States, Section 3–501(b)(1) states that presentment must be made at the place of payment, i.e. the bank. The place of presentment of a check is governed by Regulation CC § 229.36.

§ 3.112. Interest

(a) Unless otherwise provided in the instrument:

(1) an instrument is not payable with interest; and

(2) interest on an interest-bearing instrument is payable from the date of the instrument.

(b) Interest may be stated in an instrument as a fixed or variable amount of money or it may be expressed as a fixed or variable rate or rates. The amount or rate of interest may be stated or described in the instrument in any manner and may require reference to information not contained in the instrument. If an instrument provides for interest, but the amount of interest payable cannot be ascertained from the description, interest is payable at the judgment rate in effect at the place of payment of the instrument and at the time interest first accrues, and the instrument shall not by virtue of this sentence be considered to violate the provisions of Title 4, Finance Code.[1]

Amended by Acts 1995, 74th Leg., ch. 921, § 1, eff. Jan. 1, 1996; Acts 1999, 76th Leg., ch. 62, § 7.45, eff. Sept. 1, 1999.

[1] V.T.C.A., Finance Code § 301.001 et seq.

Uniform Commercial Code Comment

1. Under Section 3–104(a) the requirement of a "fixed amount" applies only to principal. The amount of interest payable is that described in the instrument. If the description of interest in the instrument does not allow for the amount of interest to be ascertained, interest is payable at the judgment rate. Hence, if an instrument calls for interest, the amount of interest will always be determinable. If a variable rate of interest is prescribed, the amount of interest is ascertainable by reference to the formula or index described or referred to in the instrument. The last sentence of subsection (b) replaces subsection (d) of former Section 3–118.

2. The purpose of subsection (b) is to clarify the meaning of "interest" in the introductory clause of Section 3–104(a). It is not intended to validate a provision for interest in an instrument if that provision violates other law.

State Bar Committee Comments

The "judgment rate" for purposes of section 3.112(b) should be governed by article 5069–1.05 of Texas Revised Civil Statutes.

The application of the last sentence of subsection (b) to an instrument should not be misinterpreted to result in a violation of Texas usury law. *See* Tex. Rev. Civ. Stat. Ann. art. 5069–1.03 (permitting six percent interest where no specified rate of interest is agreed upon by the parties). Special nonuniform language has been added to the end of this sentence to eliminate the possibility of misinterpretation. The result is consistent with the majority of existing Texas case law. *See, e.g., Bailey, Vought, Robertson & Co. v. Remington Inv., Inc.*, 888 S.W.2d 860, 866 (Tex. App.—Dallas 1994, n.w.h.).

Section 3.112 specifies that the provisions of a negotiable instrument may contain interest at a variable amount of money or expressed at a variable rate or rates. Consequently, variable interest rate instruments may be negotiable instruments under Chapter 3. This result is consistent with existing Texas law. *Amberboy v. Societe de Banque Privee*, 831 S.W.2d 793, 793–98 (Tex. 1992), *certified question accepted sub nom. from Ackerman v. FDIC*, 930 F.2d 3, 4 (5th Cir. 1991).

§ 3.113. Date of Instrument

(a) An instrument may be antedated or postdated. The date stated determines the time of payment if the instrument is payable at a fixed period after date. Except as provided in Section 4.401(c), an instrument payable on demand is not payable before the date of the instrument.

(b) If an instrument is undated, its date is the date of its issue or, in the case of an unissued instrument, the date it first comes into possession of a holder.

Amended by Acts 1995, 74th Leg., ch. 921, § 1, eff. Jan. 1, 1996.

Uniform Commercial Code Comment

This section replaces former Section 3–114. Subsections (1) and (3) of former Section 3–114 are deleted as unnecessary. Section 3–113(a) is based in part on subsection (2) of former Section 3–114. The rule that a demand instrument is not payable before the date of the instrument is subject to Section 4–401(c) which allows the payor bank to pay a postdated check unless the drawer has notified the bank of the postdating pursuant to a procedure prescribed in that subsection. With respect to an undated instrument, the date is the date of issue.

§ 3.114. Contradictory Terms of Instrument

If an instrument contains contradictory terms, typewritten terms prevail over printed terms, handwritten terms prevail over both, and words prevail over numbers.

Amended by Acts 1995, 74th Leg., ch. 921, § 1, eff. Jan. 1, 1996.

Uniform Commercial Code Comment

Section 3–114 replaces subsections (b) and (c) of former Section 3–118.

§ 3.115. Incomplete Instrument

(a) "Incomplete instrument" means a signed writing, whether or not issued by the signer, the contents of which show at the time of signing that it is incomplete but that the signer intended it to be completed by the addition of words or numbers.

(b) Subject to Subsection (c), if an incomplete instrument is an instrument under Section 3.104, it may be enforced according to its terms if it is not completed, or according to its terms as augmented by completion. If an incomplete instrument is not an instrument under Section 3.104, but, after completion, the requirements of Section 3.104 are met, the instrument may be enforced according to its terms as augmented by completion.

(c) If words or numbers are added to an incomplete instrument without authority of the signer, there is an alteration of the incomplete instrument under Section 3.407.

(d) The burden of establishing that words or numbers were added to an incomplete instrument without authority of the signer is on the person asserting the lack of authority.

Amended by Acts 1995, 74th Leg., ch. 921, § 1, eff. Jan. 1, 1996.

Uniform Commercial Code Comment

1. This section generally carries forward the rules set out in former Section 3–115. The term "incomplete instrument" applies both to an "instrument," i.e. a writing meeting all the requirements of Section 3–104, and to a writing intended to be an instrument that is signed but lacks some element of an instrument. The test in both cases is whether the contents show that it is incomplete and that the signer intended that additional words or numbers be added.

2. If an incomplete instrument meets the requirements of Section 3–104 and is not completed it may be enforced in accordance with its terms. Suppose, in the following two cases, that a note delivered to the payee is incomplete solely because a space on the pre-printed note form for the due date is not filled in:

Case #1. If the incomplete instrument is never completed, the note is payable on demand. Section 3–108(a)(ii). However, if the payee and the maker agreed to a due date, the maker may have a defense under Section 3–117 if demand for payment is made before the due date agreed to by the parties.

Case #2. If the payee completes the note be filling in the due date agreed to by the parties, the note is payable on the due date stated. However, if the due date filled in was not the date agreed to by the parties there is an alteration of the note. Section 3–407 governs the case.

Suppose Debtor pays Creditor by giving Creditor a check on which the space for the name of the payee is left blank. The check is an instrument but it is incomplete. The check is enforceable in its incomplete form and it is payable to bearer because it does not state a payee. Section 3–109(a)(2). Thus, Creditor is a holder of the check. Normally in this kind of case Creditor would simply fill in the space with Creditor's name. When that occurs the check becomes payable to the Creditor.

3. In some cases the incomplete instrument does not meet the requirements of Section 3–104. An example is a check with the amount not filled in. The check cannot be enforced until the amount is filled in. If the payee fills in an amount authorized by the drawer the check meets the requirements of Section 3–104 and is enforceable as completed. If the payee fills in an unauthorized amount there is an alteration of the check and Section 3–407 applies.

4. Section 3–302(a)(1) also bears on the problem of incomplete instruments. Under that section a person cannot be a holder in due course of the instrument if it is so incomplete as to call into question its validity. Subsection (d) of Section 3–115 is based on the last clause of subsection (2) of former Section 3–115.

§ 3.116. Joint and Several Liability; Contribution

(a) Except as otherwise provided in the instrument, two or more persons who have the same liability on an instrument as makers, drawers, acceptors, indorsers who indorse as joint payees, or anomalous indorsers are jointly and severally liable in the capacity in which they sign.

(b) Except as provided in Section 3.419(e) or by agreement of the affected parties, a party having joint and several liability who pays the instrument is entitled to receive from any party having the same joint and several liability contribution in accordance with applicable law.

(c) Repealed by Acts 2005, 79th Leg., ch. 95, § 21.

Amended by Acts 1995, 74th Leg., ch. 921, § 1, eff. Jan. 1, 1996; Acts 2005, 79th Leg., ch. 95, § 21, eff. Sept. 1, 2005.

Uniform Commercial Code Comment

1. Subsection (a) replaces subsection (e) of former Section 3–118. Subsection (b) states contribution rights of parties with joint and several liability by referring to applicable law. But subsection (b) is subject to Section 3–419(f). If one of the parties with joint and several liability is an accommodation party and the other is the accommodated party, Section 3–419(f) applies. Because one of the joint and several obligors may have recourse against the other joint and several obligor under subsection (b), each party that is jointly and severally liable under subsection (a) is a secondary obligor in part and a principal obligor in part, as those terms are defined in Section 3–103(a). Accordingly, Section 3–605 determines the effect of a release, an extension of time, or a modification of the obligation of one of the joint and several obligors, as well as the effect of an impairment of collateral provided by one of those obligors.

2. Indorsers normally do not have joint and several liability. Rather, an earlier indorser has liability to a later indorser. But indorsers can have joint and several liability in two cases. If an instrument is payable to two payees jointly, both payees must indorse. The indorsement is a joint indorsement and the indorsers have joint and several liability and subsection (b) applies. The other case is that of two or more anomalous indorsers. The term is defined in Section 3–205(d). An anomalous indorsement normally indicates that the indorser signed as an accommodation party. If more than one accommodation party indorses a note as an accommodation to the maker, the indorsers have joint and several liability and subsection (b) applies.

§ 3.117. Other Agreements Affecting Instrument

Subject to applicable law regarding exclusion of proof of contemporaneous or previous agreements, the obligation of a party to an instrument to pay the instrument may be modified, supplemented, or nullified by a separate agreement of the obligor and a person entitled to enforce the instrument, if the instrument is issued or the obligation is incurred in reliance on the agreement or as part of the same transaction giving rise to the agreement. To the extent an obligation is modified, supplemented, or nullified by an agreement under this section, the agreement is a defense to the obligation.

Amended by Acts 1995, 74th Leg., ch. 921, § 1, eff. Jan. 1, 1996.

Uniform Commercial Code Comment

1. The separate agreement might be a security agreement or mortgage or it might be an agreement that contradicts the terms of the instrument. For example, a person may be induced to sign an instrument under an agreement that the signer will not be liable on the instrument unless certain conditions are met. Suppose X requested credit from Creditor who is willing to give the credit only if an acceptable accommodation party will sign the note of X as co-maker. Y agrees to sign as co-maker on the condition that Creditor also obtain the signature of Z as co-maker. Creditor agrees and Y signs as co-maker with X. Creditor fails to obtain the signature of Z on the note. Under Sections 3–412 and 3–419(b), Y is obliged to pay the note, but Section 3–117 applies. In this case, the agreement modifies the terms of the note by stating a condition to the obligation of Y to pay the note. This case is essentially similar to a case in which a maker of a note is induced to sign the note by fraud of the holder. Although the agreement that Y not be liable on the note unless Z also signs may not have been fraudulently made, a subsequent attempt by Creditor to require Y to pay the note in violation of the agreement is a bad faith act. Section 3–117, in treating the agreement as a defense, allows Y to assert the agreement against Creditor, but the defense would not be good against a subsequent holder in due course of the note that took it without notice of the agreement. If there cannot be a holder in due course because of Section 3–106(d), a subsequent holder that took the note in good faith, for value and without knowledge of the agreement would not be able to enforce the liability of Y. This result is consistent with the risk that a holder not in due course takes with respect to fraud in inducing issuance of an instrument.

2. The effect of merger or integration clauses to the effect that a writing is intended to be the complete and exclusive statement of the terms of the agreement or that the agreement is not subject to conditions is left to the supplementary law of the jurisdiction pursuant to Section 1–103. Thus, in the case discussed in Comment 1, whether Y is permitted to prove the condition to Y's obligation to pay the note is determined by that law. Moreover, nothing in this section is intended to validate an agreement which is fraudulent or void as against public policy, as in the case of a note given to deceive a bank examiner.

§ 3.118. Statute of Limitations

(a) Except as provided in Subsection (e), an action to enforce the obligation of a party to pay a note payable at a definite time must be commenced within six years after the due date or dates stated in the note or, if a due date is accelerated, within six years after the accelerated due date.

(b) Except as provided in Subsection (d) or (e), if demand for payment is made to the maker of a note payable on demand, an action to enforce the obligation of a party to pay the note must be commenced within six years after the demand. If no demand for payment is made to the maker, an action to enforce the note is barred if neither principal nor interest on the note has been paid for a continuous period of 10 years.

(c) Except as provided in Subsection (d), an action to enforce the obligation of a party to an unaccepted draft to pay the draft must be commenced within three years after dishonor of the draft or 10 years after the date of the draft, whichever period expires first.

(d) An action to enforce the obligation of the acceptor of a certified check or the issuer of a teller's check, cashier's check, or traveler's check must be commenced within three years after demand for payment is made to the acceptor or issuer, as the case may be.

(e) An action to enforce the obligation of a party to a certificate of deposit to pay the instrument must be commenced within six years after demand for payment is made to the maker, but if the instrument states a due date and the maker is not required to pay before that date, the six-year period begins when a demand for payment is in effect and the due date has passed.

(f) An action to enforce the obligation of a party to pay an accepted draft, other than a certified check, must be commenced:

(1) within six years after the due date or dates stated in the draft or acceptance if the obligation of the acceptor is payable at a definite time; or

(2) within six years after the date of the acceptance if the obligation of the acceptor is payable on demand.

(g) Unless governed by other law regarding claims for indemnity or contribution, the following actions must be commenced within three years after the cause of action accrues:

(1) an action for conversion of an instrument, an action for money had and received, or like action based on conversion;

(2) an action for breach of warranty; or

(3) an action to enforce an obligation, duty, or right arising under this chapter and not governed by this section.

(h) This section does not apply to an action involving a real property lien covered by Section 16.035 or 16.036, Civil Practice and Remedies Code.

(i) A right of action of a public institution of higher education or the Texas Higher Education Coordinating Board is not barred by this section.

Amended by Acts 1995, 74th Leg., ch. 921, § 1, eff. Jan. 1, 1996; Acts 1997, 75th Leg., ch. 219, § 4, eff. May 23, 1997; Acts 2001, 77th Leg., ch. 279, § 1, eff. May 22, 2001.

Uniform Commercial Code Comment

1. Section 3–118 differs from former Section 3–122, which states when a cause of action accrues on an instrument. Section 3–118 does not define when a cause of action accrues. Accrual of a cause of action is stated in other sections of Article 3 such as those that state the various obligations of parties to an instrument. The only purpose of Section 3–118 is to define the time within which an action to enforce an obligation, duty, or right arising under Article 3 must be commenced. Section 3–118 does not attempt to state all rules with respect to a statute of limitations. For example, the circumstances under which the running of a limitations period may be tolled is left to other law pursuant to Section 1–103.

2. The first six subsections apply to actions to enforce an obligation of any party to an instrument to pay the instrument. This changes present law in that indorsers who may become liable on an instrument after issue are subject to a period of limitations running from the same date as that of the maker or drawer. Subsections (a) and (b) apply to notes. If the note is payable at a definite time, a six-year limitations period starts at the due date of the note, subject to prior acceleration. If the note is payable on demand, there are two limitations periods. Although a note payable on demand could theoretically be called a day after it was issued, the normal expectation of the parties is that the note will remain outstanding until there is some reason to call it. If the law provides that the limitations period does not start until demand is made, the cause of action to enforce it may never be barred. On the other hand, if the limitations period starts when demand for payment may be made, i.e. at any time after the note was issued, the payee of a note on which interest or portions of principal are being paid could lose the right to enforce the note even though it was treated as a continuing obligation by the parties. Some demand notes are not enforced because the payee has forgiven the debt. This is particularly true in family and other noncommercial transactions. A demand note found after the death of the payee may be presented for payment many years after it was issued. The maker may be a relative and it may be difficult to determine whether the note represents a real or a forgiven debt. Subsection (b) is designed to bar notes that no longer represent a claim to payment and to require reasonably prompt action to enforce notes on which there is default. If a demand for payment is made to the maker, a six-year limitations period starts to run when demand is made. The second sentence of subsection (b) bars an action to enforce a demand note if no demand has been made on the note and no payment of interest or principal has been made for a continuous period of 10 years. This covers the case of a note that does not bear interest or a case in which interest due on the note has not been paid. This kind of case is likely to be a family transaction in which a failure to demand payment may indicate that the holder did not intend to enforce the obligation but neglected to destroy the note. A limitations period that bars stale claims in this kind of case is appropriate if the period is relatively long.

3. Subsection (c) applies primarily to personal uncertified checks. Checks are payment instruments rather than credit instruments. The limitations period expires three years after the date of dishonor or 10 years after the date of the check, whichever is earlier. Teller's checks, cashier's checks, certified checks, and traveler's checks are treated differently under subsection (d) because they are commonly treated as cash equivalents. A great delay in presenting a cashier's check for payment in most cases will occur because the check was mislaid during that period. The person to whom traveler's checks are issued may hold them indefinitely as a safe form of cash for use in an emergency. There is no compelling reason for barring the claim of the owner of the cashier's check or traveler's check. Under subsection (d) the claim is never barred because the three-year limitations period does not start to run until demand for payment is made. The limitations period in subsection (d) in effect applies only to cases in which there is a dispute about the legitimacy of the claim of the person demanding payment.

4. Subsection (e) covers certificates of deposit. The limitations period of six years doesn't start to run until the depositor demands payment. Most certificates of deposit are payable on demand even if they state a due date. The effect of a demand for payment before maturity is usually that the bank will pay, but that a penalty will be assessed against the depositor in the form of a reduction in the amount of interest that is paid. Subsection (e) also provides for cases in which the bank has no obligation to pay until the due date. In that case the limitations period doesn't start to run until there is a demand for payment in effect and the due date has passed.

5. Subsection (f) applies to accepted drafts other than certified checks. When a draft is accepted it is in effect turned into a note of the acceptor. In almost all cases the acceptor will agree to pay at a definite time. Subsection (f) states that in that case the six-year limitations period starts to run on the due date. In the rare case in which the obligation of the acceptor is payable on demand, the six-year limitations period starts to run at the date of the acceptance.

6. Subsection (g) covers warranty and conversion cases and other actions to enforce obligations or rights arising under Article 3. A three-year period is stated and subsection (g) follows general law in stating that the period runs from the time the cause of action accrues. Since the traditional term "cause of action" may have been replaced in some states by "claim for relief" or some equivalent term, the words "cause of action" have been bracketed to indicate that the words may be replaced by an appropriate substitute to conform to local practice.

7. One of the most significant differences between this Article and the Convention on International Bills of Ex-

change and International Promissory Notes is that the statute of limitation under the Convention generally is only four years, rather than the six years provided by this section. See Convention Article 84. *Amendments approved by the Permanent Editorial Board for Uniform Commercial Code November 2, 2002.*

State Bar Committee Comments

With respect to actions on instruments covered by this Act, the statute of limitations provisions of section 3.118 should be interpreted to supersede, because of their particularity, any conflicting statute of limitations of general applicability under Texas law. *See, e.g.*, Tex. Civ. Prac. & Rem. Code Ann. §§ 16.003, 16.004 (Vernon 1986).

Because Chapter 3 only applies to negotiable instruments, actions on non-negotiable instruments will not be governed by the provisions of section 3.118 but will be governed by other Texas statutes of limitation. *See, e.g.*, Tex. Civ. Prac. and Rem. Code Ann. §§ 16.003(a), 16.004(a)(3) (Vernon 1986). On the other hand, because of their particular nature, the statute of limitations provisions of sections 16.035 and 16.036 of the Texas Civil Practice and Remedies Code, relating to actions with respect to debts secured by liens on real property, and section 51.003 of the Texas Property Code, relating to actions to recover deficiencies after nonjudicial foreclosures, should be interpreted to control, in appropriate circumstances, over the provisions of section 3.118.

By virtue of Texas Business and Commerce Code § 1.103, existing Texas law permitting parties to extend, waive or shorten limitations periods should also apply to the limitation periods set forth in section 3.118. *See, e.g.*, Tex. Civ. Prac. & Rem. Code Ann. § 16.065, 16.070 (Vernon 1986 and Supp. 1994); *see also Fuqua v. Fuqua*, 750 S.W.2d 238, 241 (Tex. App.—Dallas 1988, writ denied);

Prior Texas case law applicable to demand notes had held that the limitations period began to run on the date the note was made. *See, e.g., G & R Inv. v. Nance*, 683 S.W.2d 727, 728 (Tex. App.—Houston [14th Dist.] 1984, writ ref'd n.r.e.). Section 3.118(b) changes this rule to commence the 6–year limitations period upon the date of demand. If no demand is made, the 10–year limitations period commences upon the date of the last payment of principal or interest.

During the initial years after the enactment of section 3.118, courts should look to existing Texas case law that arose after the change in the two-year limitations period to a four-year limitations period for oral debts for guidance on when to apply section 3.118 to negotiable instruments that predated the effective date. These cases generally provide that if the shorter limitations period had not run on the effective date of the new act, the longer limitations period applied because the defense of limitations would not become a vested right until the limitations period had actually run. *See, e.g., National Mar–Kit, Inc. v. Forrest*, 687 S.W.2d 457, 460 (Tex. App.—Houston [14th Dist.] 1985, no writ).

With respect to actions for conversion of instruments, the 3–year limitations period provided by subsection (g) supersedes the 2–year limitations period provided by section 16.003 of the Civil Practices and Remedies Code. *See* Tex. Bus. & Com. Code Ann. § 3.420 (Tex. UCC) (Vernon 1994). Nothing in section 3.118 is intended to change existing Texas case law as to when a cause of action for conversion accrues. *See, e.g., Lyco Acquisition 1984 v. First Nat'l Bank*, 860 S.W.2d 117, 199 (Tex. App.—Amarillo 1993, writ denied); *Southwest Bank & Trust v. Bankers Commercial Life Ins.*, 563 S.W.2d 329, 331 (Tex. Civ. App.—Dallas 1978, writ ref'd. n.r.e.) (holding that the discovery rule does not apply to toll the statute of limitations where a bank is sued for conversion on a forged indorsement, absent the bank's fraudulent concealment).

§ 3.119. Notice of Right to Defend Action

In an action for breach of an obligation for which a third person is answerable over pursuant to this chapter or Chapter 4, the defendant may give the third person notice of the litigation in a record, and the person notified may then give similar notice to any other person who is answerable over. If the notice states (i) that the person notified may come in and defend, and (ii) that failure to do so will bind the person notified in an action later brought by the person giving the notice as to any determination of fact common to the two litigations, the person notified is so bound unless after seasonable receipt of the notice the person notified does come in and defend.

Amended by Acts 1995, 74th Leg., ch. 921, § 1, eff. Jan. 1, 1996; Acts 2005, 79th Leg., ch. 95, § 4, eff. Sept. 1, 2005.

Uniform Commercial Code Comment

This section is a restatement of former Section 3–803.

State Bar Committee Comments

Section 3.119 is intended to supplement, not to displace, existing procedures for interpleader or joinder of parties. The section conforms to the analogous provision in section 2.607. It extends to such liabilities as those arising from forged indorsements even though not "on the instrument," and is intended to make it clear that the notification is not effective until received. In *Hartford Accident & Indem. Co. v. First Nat'l Bank & Trust Co.*, 22 N.E.2d 324 (N.Y. 1939), the common-law doctrine of "vouching in" was held inapplicable where the party notified had no direct liability to the party giving the notice. In that case the drawer of a check, sued by the payee whose indorsement had been forged, gave notice to a collecting bank. In a second action the drawee was held liable to the drawer; but in an action by the drawee for judgment against the collecting bank the determinations of fact in the first action were held not conclusive. This section does not disturb this result; the section is limited to cases where the person notified is "answerable over" to the person giving the notice.

§§ 3.120 to 3.122. Deleted by Acts 1995, 74th Leg., ch. 921, § 1, eff. Jan. 1, 1996

SUBCHAPTER B. NEGOTIATION, TRANSFER, AND INDORSEMENT

§ 3.201. Negotiation

(a) "Negotiation" means a transfer of possession, whether voluntary or involuntary, of an instrument by a person other than the issuer to a person who thereby becomes its holder.

(b) Except for negotiation by a remitter, if an instrument is payable to an identified person, negotiation requires transfer of possession of the instrument and its indorsement by the holder. If an instrument is payable to bearer, it may be negotiated by transfer of possession alone.

Amended by Acts 1995, 74th Leg., ch. 921, § 1, eff. Jan. 1, 1996.

Uniform Commercial Code Comment

1. Subsections (a) and (b) are based in part on subsection (1) of former Section 3–202. A person can become holder of an instrument when the instrument is issued to that person, or the status of holder can arise as the result of an event that occurs after issuance. "Negotiation" is the term used in Article 3 to describe this post-issuance event. Normally, negotiation occurs as the result of a voluntary transfer of possession of an instrument by a holder to another person who becomes the holder as a result of the transfer. Negotiation always requires a change in possession of the instrument because nobody can be a holder without possessing the instrument, either directly or through an agent. But in some cases the transfer of possession is involuntary and in some cases the person transferring possession is not a holder. In defining "negotiation" former Section 3–202(1) used the word "transfer," an undefined term, and "delivery," defined in Section 1–201(14) to mean voluntary change of possession. Instead, subsections (a) and (b) use the term "transfer of possession" and, subsection (a) states that negotiation can occur by an involuntary transfer of possession. For example, if an instrument is payable to bearer and it is stolen by Thief or is found by Finder, Thief or Finder becomes the holder of the instrument when possession is obtained. In this case there is an involuntary transfer of possession that results in negotiation to Thief or Finder.

2. In most cases negotiation occurs by a transfer of possession by a holder or remitter. Remitter transactions usually involve a cashier's or teller's check. For example, Buyer buys goods from Seller and pays for them with a cashier's check of Bank that Buyer buys from Bank. The check is issued by Bank when it is delivered to Buyer, regardless of whether the check is payable to Buyer or to Seller. Section 3–105(a). If the check is payable to Buyer, negotiation to Seller is done by delivery of the check to Seller after it is indorsed by Buyer. It is more common, however, that the check when issued will be payable to Seller. In that case Buyer is referred to as the "remitter." Section 3–103(a)(11). The remitter, although not a party to the check, is the owner of the check until ownership is transferred to Seller by delivery. This transfer is a negotiation because Seller becomes the holder of the check when Seller obtains possession. In some cases Seller may have acted fraudulently in obtaining possession of the check. In those cases Buyer may be entitled to rescind the transfer to Seller because of the fraud and assert a claim of ownership to the check under Section 3–306 against Seller or a subsequent transferee of the check. Section 3–202(b) provides for rescission of negotiation, and that provision applies to rescission by a remitter as well as by a holder.

3. Other sections of Article 3 may modify the rule stated in the first sentence of subsection (b). See for example, Sections 3–404, 3–405 and 3–406.

§ 3.202. Negotiation Subject to Rescission

(a) Negotiation is effective even if obtained:

(1) from an infant, a corporation exceeding its powers, or a person without capacity;

(2) by fraud, duress, or mistake; or

(3) in breach of duty or as part of an illegal transaction.

(b) To the extent permitted by other law, negotiation may be rescinded or may be subject to other remedies, but those remedies may not be asserted against a subsequent holder in due course or a person paying the instrument in good faith and without knowledge of facts that are a basis for rescission or other remedy.

Amended by Acts 1995, 74th Leg., ch. 921, § 1, eff. Jan. 1, 1996.

Uniform Commercial Code Comment

1. This section is based on former Section 3–207. Subsection (2) of former Section 3–207 prohibited rescission of a negotiation against holders in due course. Subsection (b) of Section 3–202 extends this protection to payor banks.

2. Subsection (a) applies even though the lack of capacity or the illegality, is of a character which goes to the essence of the transaction and makes it entirely void. It is inherent in the character of negotiable instruments that any person in possession of an instrument which by its terms is payable to that person or to bearer is a holder and may be dealt with by anyone as a holder. The principle finds its most extreme application in the well settled rule that a holder in due course may take the instrument even from a thief and be protected against the claim of the rightful owner. The policy of

subsection (a) is that any person to whom an instrument is negotiated is a holder until the instrument has been recovered from that person's possession. The remedy of a person with a claim to an instrument is to recover the instrument by replevin or otherwise; to impound it or to enjoin its enforcement, collection or negotiation; to recover its proceeds from the holder; or to intervene in any action brought by the holder against the obligor. As provided in Section 3–305(c), the claim of the claimant is not a defense to the obligor unless the claimant defends the action.

3. There can be no rescission or other remedy against a holder in due course or a person who pays in good faith and without notice, even though the prior negotiation may have been fraudulent or illegal in its essence and entirely void. As against any other party the claimant may have any remedy permitted by law. This section is not intended to specify what that remedy may be, or to prevent any court from imposing conditions or limitations such as prompt action or return of the consideration received. All such questions are left to the law of the particular jurisdiction. Section 3–202 gives no right that would not otherwise exist. The section is intended to mean that any remedies afforded by other law are cut off only by a holder in due course.

§ 3.203. Transfer of Instrument; Rights Acquired by Transfer

(a) An instrument is transferred when it is delivered by a person other than its issuer for the purpose of giving to the person receiving delivery the right to enforce the instrument.

(b) Transfer of an instrument, whether or not the transfer is a negotiation, vests in the transferee any right of the transferor to enforce the instrument, including any right as a holder in due course. The transferee cannot acquire rights of a holder in due course by a transfer, directly or indirectly, from a holder in due course if the transferee engaged in fraud or illegality affecting the instrument.

(c) Unless otherwise agreed, if an instrument is transferred for value and the transferee does not become a holder because of lack of indorsement by the transferor, the transferee has a specifically enforceable right to the unqualified indorsement of the transferor, but negotiation of the instrument does not occur until the indorsement is made.

(d) If a transferor purports to transfer less than the entire instrument, negotiation of the instrument does not occur. The transferee obtains no rights under this chapter and has only the rights of a partial assignee.

Amended by Acts 1995, 74th Leg., ch. 921, § 1, eff. Jan. 1, 1996.

Uniform Commercial Code Comment

1. Section 3–203 is based on former Section 3–201 which stated that a transferee received such rights as the transferor had. The former section was confusing because some rights of the transferor are not vested in the transferee unless the transfer is a negotiation. For example, a transferee that did not become the holder could not negotiate the instrument, a right that the transferor had. Former Section 3-201 did not define "transfer." Subsection (a) defines transfer by limiting it to cases in which possession of the instrument is delivered for the purpose of giving to the person receiving delivery the right to enforce the instrument.

Although transfer of an instrument might mean in a particular case that title to the instrument passes to the transferee, that result does not follow in all cases. The right to enforce an instrument and ownership of the instrument are two different concepts. A thief who steals a check payable to bearer becomes the holder of the check and a person entitled to enforce it, but does not become the owner of the check. If the thief transfers the check to a purchaser the transferee obtains the right to enforce the check. If the purchaser is not a holder in due course, the owner's claim to the check may be asserted against the purchaser. Ownership rights in instruments may be determined by principles of the law of property, independent of Article 3, which do not depend upon whether the instrument was transferred under Section 3–203. Moreover, a person who has an ownership right in an instrument might not be a person entitled to enforce the instrument. For example, suppose X is the owner and holder of an instrument payable to X. X sells the instrument to Y but is unable to deliver immediate possession to Y. Instead, X signs a document conveying all of X's right, title, and interest in the instrument to Y. Although the document may be effective to give Y a claim to ownership of the instrument, Y is not a person entitled to enforce the instrument until Y obtains possession of the instrument. No transfer of the instrument occurs under Section 3–203(a) until it is delivered to Y.

An instrument is a reified right to payment. The right is represented by the instrument itself. The right to payment is transferred by delivery of possession of the instrument "by a person other than its issuer for the purpose of giving to the person receiving delivery the right to enforce the instrument." The quoted phrase excludes issue of an instrument, defined in Section 3–105, and cases in which a delivery of possession is for some purpose other than transfer of the right to enforce. For example, if a check is presented for payment by delivering the check to the drawee, no transfer of the check to the drawee occurs because there is no intent to give the drawee the right to enforce the check.

2. Subsection (b) states that transfer vests in the transferee any right of the transferor to enforce the instrument "including any right as a holder in due course." If the transferee is not a holder because the transferor did not indorse, the transferee is nevertheless a person entitled to enforce the instrument under Section 3–301 if the transferor was a holder at the time of transfer. Although the transferee is not a holder, under subsection (b) the transferee obtained the rights of the transferor as holder. Because the transferee's rights are derivative of the transferor's rights, those rights must be proved. Because the transferee is not a

holder, there is no presumption under Section 3–308 that the transferee, by producing the instrument, is entitled to payment. The instrument, by its terms, is not payable to the transferee and the transferee must account for possession of the unindorsed instrument by proving the transaction through which the transferee acquired. it. Proof of a transfer to the transferee by a holder is proof that the transferee has acquired the rights of a holder. At that point the transferee is entitled to the presumption under Section 3–308.

Under subsection (b) a holder in due course that transfers an instrument transfers those rights as a holder in due course to the purchaser. The policy is to assure the holder in due course a free market for the instrument. There is one exception to this rule stated in the concluding clause of subsection (b). A person who is party to fraud or illegality affecting the instrument is not permitted to wash the instrument clean by passing it into the hands of a holder in due course and then repurchasing it.

3. Subsection (c) applies only to a transfer for value. It applies only if the instrument is payable to order or specially indorsed to the transferor. The transferee acquires, in the absence of a contrary agreement, the specifically enforceable right to the indorsement of the transferor. Unless otherwise agreed, it is a right to the general indorsement of the transferor with full liability as indorser, rather than to an indorsement without recourse. The question may arise if the transferee has paid in advance and the indorsement is omitted fraudulently or through oversight. A transferor who is willing to indorse only without recourse or unwilling to indorse at all should make those intentions clear before transfer. The agreement of the transferee to take less than an unqualified indorsement need not be an express one, and the understanding may be implied from conduct, from past practice, or from the circumstances of the transaction. Subsection (c) provides that there is no negotiation of the instrument until the indorsement by the transferor is made. Until that time the transferee does not become a holder, and if earlier notice of a defense or claim is received, the transferee does not qualify as a holder in due course under Section 3–302.

4. The operation of Section 3–203 is illustrated by the following cases. In each case Payee, by fraud, induced Maker to issue a note to Payee. The fraud is a defense to the obligation of Maker to pay the note under Section 3–305(a)(2).

Case #1. Payee negotiated the note to X who took as a holder in due course. After the instrument became overdue X negotiated the note to Y who had notice of the fraud. Y succeeds to X's rights as a holder in due course and takes free of Maker's defense of fraud.

Case #2. Payee negotiated the note to X who took as a holder in due course. Payee then repurchased the note from X. Payee does not succeed to X's rights as a holder in due course and is subject to Maker's defense of fraud.

Case #3. Payee negotiated the note to X who took as a holder in due course. X sold the note to Purchaser who received possession. The note, however, was indorsed to X and X failed to indorse it. Purchaser is a person entitled to enforce the instrument under Section 3–301 and succeeds to the rights of X as holder in due course. Purchaser is not a holder, however, and under Section 3–308 Purchaser will have to prove the transaction with X under which the rights of X as holder in due course were acquired.

Case #4. Payee sold the note to Purchaser who took for value, in good faith and without notice of the defense of Maker. Purchaser received possession of the note but Payee neglected to indorse it. Purchaser became a person entitled to enforce the instrument but did not become the holder because of the missing indorsement. If Purchaser received notice of the defense of Maker before obtaining the indorsement of Payee, Purchaser cannot become a holder in due course because at the time notice was received the note had not been negotiated to Purchaser. If indorsement by Payee was made after Purchaser received notice, Purchaser had notice of the defense when it became the holder.

5. Subsection (d) restates former Section 3–202(3). The cause of action on an instrument cannot be split. Any indorsement which purports to convey to any party less than the entire amount of the instrument is not effective for negotiation. This is true of either "Pay A one-half," or "Pay A two-thirds and B one-third." Neither A nor B becomes a holder. On the other hand an indorsement reading merely "Pay A and B" is effective, since it transfers the entire cause of action to A and B as tenants in common. An indorsement purporting to convey less than the entire instrument does, however, operate as a partial assignment of the cause of action. Subsection (d) makes no attempt to state the legal effect of such an assignment, which is left to other law. A partial assignee of an instrument has rights only to the extent the applicable law gives rights, either at law or in equity, to a partial assignee.

6. The rules for transferring instruments set out in this section are similar to the rules in Article 13 of the Convention on International Bills of Exchange and International Promissory Notes. *Amendments approved by the Permanent Editorial Board for Uniform Commercial Code November 2, 2002.*

§ 3.204. Indorsement

(a) "Indorsement" means a signature, other than that of a signer as maker, drawer, or acceptor, that alone or accompanied by other words is made on an instrument for the purpose of (i) negotiating the instrument, (ii) restricting payment of the instrument, or (iii) incurring indorser's liability on the instrument, but regardless of the intent of the signer, a signature and its accompanying words is an indorsement unless the accompanying words, terms of the instrument, place of the signature, or other circumstances unambiguously indicate that the signature was made for a purpose other than indorsement. For the purpose of determining whether a signature is made on an instrument, a paper affixed to the instrument is a part of the instrument.

(b) "Indorser" means a person who makes an indorsement.

(c) For the purpose of determining whether the transferee of an instrument is a holder, an indorsement that transfers a security interest in the instrument is effective as an unqualified indorsement of the instrument.

(d) If an instrument is payable to a holder under a name that is not the name of the holder, indorsement may be made by the holder in the name stated in the instrument or in the holder's name or both, but signature in both names may be required by a person paying or taking the instrument for value or collection.

Amended by Acts 1995, 74th Leg., ch. 921, § 1, eff. Jan. 1, 1996.

Uniform Commercial Code Comment

1. Subsection (a) is a definition of "indorsement," a term which was not defined in former Article 3. Indorsement is defined in terms of the purpose of the signature. If a blank or special indorsement is made to give rights as a holder to a transferee the indorsement is made for the purpose of negotiating the instrument. Subsection (a)(i). If the holder of a check has an account in the drawee bank and wants to be sure that payment of the check will be made by credit to the holder's account, the holder can indorse the check by signing the holder's name with the accompanying words "for deposit only" before presenting the check for payment to the drawee bank. In that case the purpose of the quoted words is to restrict payment of the instrument. Subsection (a)(ii). If X wants to guarantee payment of a note signed by Y as maker, X can do so by signing X's name to the back of the note as an indorsement. This indorsement is known as an anomalous indorsement (Section 3–205(d)) and is made for the purpose of incurring indorser's liability on the note. Subsection (a)(iii). In some cases an indorsement may serve more than one purpose. For example, if the holder of a check deposits it to the holder's account in a depositary bank for collection and indorses the check by signing the holder's name with the accompanying words "for deposit only" the purpose of the indorsement is both to negotiate the check to the depositary bank and to restrict payment of the check.

The "but" clause of the first sentence of subsection (a) elaborates on former Section 3–402. In some cases it may not be clear whether a signature was meant to be that of an indorser, a party to the instrument in some other capacity such as drawer, maker or acceptor, or a person who was not signing as a party. The general rule is that a signature is an indorsement if the instrument does not indicate an unambiguous intent of the signer not to sign as an indorser. Intent may be determined by words accompanying the signature, the place of signature, or other circumstances. For example, suppose a depositary bank gives cash for a check properly indorsed by the payee. The bank requires the payee's employee to sign the back of the check as evidence that the employee received the cash. If the signature consists only of the initials of the employee it is not reasonable to assume that it was meant to be an indorsement. If there was a full signature but accompanying words indicated that it was meant as a receipt for the cash given for the check, it is not an indorsement. If the signature is not qualified in any way and appears in the place normally used for indorsements, it may be an indorsement even though the signer intended the signature to be a receipt. To take another example, suppose the drawee of a draft signs the draft on the back in the space usually used for indorsements. No words accompany the signature. Since the drawee has no reason to sign a draft unless the intent is to accept the draft, the signature is effective as an acceptance. Custom and usage may be used to determine intent. For example, by long-established custom and usage, a signature in the lower right hand corner of an instrument indicates an intent to sign as the maker of a note or the drawer of a draft. Any similar clear indication of an intent to sign in some other capacity or for some other purpose may establish that a signature is not an indorsement. For example, if the owner of a traveler's check countersigns the check in the process of negotiating it, the countersignature is not an indorsement. The countersignature is a condition to the issuer's obligation to pay and its purpose is to provide a means of verifying the identity of the person negotiating the traveler's check by allowing comparison of the specimen signature and the countersignature. The countersignature is not necessary for negotiation and the signer does not incur indorser's liability. See Comment 2 to Section 3–106.

The last sentence of subsection (a) is based on subsection (2) of former Section 3–202. An indorsement on an allonge is valid even though there is sufficient space on the instrument for an indorsement.

2. Assume that Payee indorses a note to Creditor as security for a debt. Under subsection (b) of Section 3–203 Creditor takes Payee's rights to enforce or transfer the instrument subject to the limitations imposed by Article 9. Subsection (c) of Section 3–204 makes clear that Payee's indorsement to Creditor, even though it mentions creation of a security interest, is an unqualified indorsement that gives to Creditor the right to enforce the note as its holder.

3. Subsection (d) is a restatement of former Section 3–203. Section 3–110(a) states that an instrument is payable to the person intended by the person signing as or in the name or behalf of the issuer even if that person is identified by a name that is not the true name of the person. In some cases the name used in the instrument is a misspelling of the correct name and in some cases the two names may be entirely different. The payee may indorse in the name used in the instrument, in the payee's correct name, or in both. In each case the indorsement is effective. But because an indorsement in a name different from that used in the instrument may raise a question about its validity and an indorsement in a name that is not the correct name of the payee may raise a problem of identifying the indorser, the accepted commercial practice is to indorse in both names. Subsection (d) allows a person paying or taking the instrument for value or collection to require indorsement in both names.

§ 3.205. Special Indorsement; Blank Indorsement; Anomalous Indorsement

(a) If an indorsement is made by the holder of an instrument, whether payable to an identified person or payable to bearer, and the indorsement identifies a person to whom it makes the instrument payable, it is a "special indorsement." When specially indorsed, an instrument becomes payable to the identified person and may be negotiated only by the indorsement of that person. The principles stated in Section 3.110 apply to special indorsements.

(b) If an indorsement is made by the holder of an instrument and it is not a special indorsement, it is a "blank indorsement." When indorsed in blank, an instrument becomes payable to bearer and may be negotiated by transfer of possession alone until specially indorsed.

(c) The holder may convert a blank indorsement that consists only of a signature into a special indorsement by writing, above the signature of the indorser, words identifying the person to whom the instrument is made payable.

(d) "Anomalous indorsement" means an indorsement made by a person who is not the holder of the instrument. An anomalous indorsement does not affect the manner in which the instrument may be negotiated.

Amended by Acts 1995, 74th Leg., ch. 921, § 1, eff. Jan. 1, 1996.

Uniform Commercial Code Comment

1. Subsection (a) is based on subsection (1) of former Section 3–204. It states the test of a special indorsement to be whether the indorsement identifies a person to whom the instrument is payable. Section 3–110 states rules for identifying the payee of an instrument. Section 3–205(a) incorporates the principles stated in Section 3–110 in identifying an indorsee. The language of Section 3–110 refers to language used by the issuer of the instrument. When that section is used with respect to an indorsement, Section 3–110 must be read as referring to the language used by the indorser.

2. Subsection (b) is based on subsection (2) of former Section 3–204. An indorsement made by the holder is either a special or blank indorsement. If the indorsement is made by a holder and is not a special indorsement, it is a blank indorsement. For example, the holder of an instrument, intending to make a special indorsement, writes the words "Pay to the order of" without completing the indorsement by writing the name of the indorsee. The holder's signature appears under the quoted words. The indorsement is not a special indorsement because it does not identify a person to whom it makes the instrument payable. Since it is not a special indorsement it is a blank indorsement and the instrument is payable to bearer. The result is analogous to that of a check in which the name of the payee is left blank by the drawer. In that case the check is payable to bearer. See the last paragraphs of Comment 2 to Section 3–115.

A blank indorsement is usually the signature of the indorser on the back of the instrument without other words. Subsection (c) is based on subsection (3) of former Section 3–204. A "restrictive indorsement" described in Section 3–206 can be either a blank indorsement or a special indorsement. "Pay to T, in trust for B" is a restrictive indorsement. It is also a special indorsement because it identifies T as the person to whom the instrument is payable. "For deposit only" followed by the signature of the payee of a check is a restrictive indorsement. It is also a blank indorsement because it does not identify the person to whom the instrument is payable.

3. The only effect of an "anomalous indorsement," defined in subsection (d), is to make the signer liable on the instrument as an indorser. Such an indorsement is normally made by an accommodation party. Section 3–419.

4. Articles 14 and 16 of the Convention on International Bills of Exchange and International Promissory Notes includes similar rules for blank and special indorsements. *Amendments approved by the Permanent Editorial Board for Uniform Commercial Code November 2, 2002.*

§ 3.206. Restrictive Indorsement

(a) An indorsement limiting payment to a particular person or otherwise prohibiting further transfer or negotiation of the instrument is not effective to prevent further transfer or negotiation of the instrument.

(b) An indorsement stating a condition to the right of the indorsee to receive payment does not affect the right of the indorsee to enforce the instrument. A person paying the instrument or taking it for value or collection may disregard the condition, and the rights and liabilities of that person are not affected by whether the condition has been fulfilled.

(c) If an instrument bears an indorsement (i) described in Section 4.201(b), or (ii) in blank or to a particular bank using the words "for deposit" or "for collection," or other words indicating a purpose of having the instrument collected by a bank for the indorser or for a particular account, the following rules apply:

(1) a person, other than a bank, who purchases the instrument when so indorsed converts the instrument unless the amount paid for the instrument is received by the indorser or applied consistently with the indorsement;

(2) a depositary bank that purchases the instrument or takes it for collection when so indorsed converts the instrument unless the amount paid by

the bank with respect to the instrument is received by the indorser or applied consistently with the indorsement;

(3) a payor bank that is also the depositary bank or that takes the instrument for immediate payment over the counter from a person other than a collecting bank converts the instrument unless the proceeds of the instrument are received by the indorser or applied consistently with the indorsement; and

(4) except as otherwise provided in Subdivision (3), a payor bank or intermediary bank may disregard the indorsement and is not liable if the proceeds of the instrument are not received by the indorser or applied consistently with the indorsement.

(d) Except for an indorsement covered by Subsection (c), if an instrument bears an indorsement using words to the effect that payment is to be made to the indorsee as agent, trustee, or other fiduciary for the benefit of the indorser or another person, the following rules apply:

(1) unless there is notice of breach of fiduciary duty as provided in Section 3.307, a person who purchases the instrument from the indorsee or takes the instrument from the indorsee for collection or payment may pay the proceeds of payment or the value given for the instrument to the indorsee without regard to whether the indorsee violates a fiduciary duty to the indorser; and

(2) a subsequent transferee of the instrument or person who pays the instrument is neither given notice nor otherwise affected by the restriction in the indorsement unless the transferee or payor knows that the fiduciary dealt with the instrument or its proceeds in breach of fiduciary duty.

(e) The presence on an instrument of an indorsement to which this section applies does not prevent a purchaser of the instrument from becoming a holder in due course of the instrument unless the purchaser is a converter under Subsection (c) or has notice or knowledge of breach of fiduciary duty as stated in Subsection (d).

(f) In an action to enforce the obligation of a party to pay the instrument, the obligor has a defense if payment would violate an indorsement to which this section applies and the payment is not permitted by this section.

Amended by Acts 1995, 74th Leg., ch. 921, § 1, eff. Jan. 1, 1996.

Uniform Commercial Code Comment

1. This section replaces former Sections 3–205 and 3–206 and clarifies the law of restrictive indorsements.

2. Subsection (a) provides that an indorsement that purports to limit further transfer or negotiation is ineffective to prevent further transfer or negotiation. If a payee indorses "Pay A only," A may negotiate the instrument to subsequent holders who may ignore the restriction on the indorsement. Subsection (b) provides that an indorsement that states a condition to the right of a holder to receive payment is ineffective to condition payment. Thus if a payee indorses "Pay A if A ships goods complying with our contract," the right of A to enforce the instrument is not affected by the condition. In the case of a note, the obligation of the maker to pay A is not affected by the indorsement. In the case of a check, the drawee can pay A without regard to the condition, and if the check is dishonored the drawer is liable to pay A. If the check was negotiated by the payee to A in return for a promise to perform a contract and the promise was not kept, the payee would have a defense or counterclaim against A if the check were dishonored and A sued the payee as indorser, but the payee would have that defense or counterclaim whether or not the condition to the right of A was expressed in the indorsement. Former Section 3–206 treated a conditional indorsement like indorsements for deposit or collection. In revised Article 3, Section 3–206(b) rejects that approach and makes the conditional indorsement ineffective with respect to parties other than the indorser and indorsee. Since the indorsements referred to in subsections (a) and (b) are not effective as restrictive indorsements, they are no longer described as restrictive indorsements.

3. The great majority of restrictive indorsements are those that fall within subsection (c) which continues previous law. The depositary bank or the payor bank, if it takes the check for immediate payment over the counter, must act consistently with the indorsement, but an intermediary bank or payor bank that takes the check from a collecting bank is not affected by the indorsement. Any other person is also bound by the indorsement. For example, suppose a check is payable to X, who indorses in blank but writes above the signature the words "For deposit only." The check is stolen and is cashed at a grocery store by the thief. The grocery store indorses the check and deposits it in Depositary Bank. The account of the grocery store is credited and the check is forwarded to Payor Bank which pays the check. Under subsection (c), the grocery store and Depositary Bank are converters of the check because X did not receive the amount paid for the check. Payor Bank and any intermediary bank in the collection process are not liable to X. This Article does not displace the law of waiver as it may apply to restrictive indorsements. The circumstances under which a restrictive indorsement may be waived by the person who made it is not determined by this Article.

4. Subsection (d) replaces subsection (4) of former Section 3–206. Suppose Payee indorses a check "Pay to T in trust for B." T indorses in blank and delivers it to (a) Holder for value; (b) Depositary Bank for collection; or (c) Payor Bank for payment. In each case these takers can safely pay T so long as they have no notice under Section 3–307 of any breach of fiduciary duty that T may be committing. For example, under subsection (b)* of Section 3–307

these takers have notice of a breach of trust if the check was taken in any transaction known by the taker to be for T's personal benefit. Subsequent transferees of the check from Holder or Depositary Bank are not affected by the restriction unless they have knowledge that T dealt with the check in breach of trust.

5. Subsection (f) allows a restrictive indorsement to be used as a defense by a person obliged to pay the instrument if that person would be liable for paying in violation of the indorsement.

* Previous incorrect reference corrected by Permanent Editorial Board action November 1992.

§ 3.207. Reacquisition

Reacquisition of an instrument occurs if it is transferred to a former holder, by negotiation or otherwise. A former holder who reacquires the instrument may cancel indorsements made after the reacquirer first became a holder of the instrument. If the cancellation causes the instrument to be payable to the reacquirer or to bearer, the reacquirer may negotiate the instrument. An indorser whose indorsement is canceled is discharged, and the discharge is effective against any subsequent holder.

Amended by Acts 1995, 74th Leg., ch. 921, § 1, eff. Jan. 1, 1996.

Uniform Commercial Code Comment

Section 3–207 restates former Section 3–208. Reacquisition refers to cases in which a former holder reacquires the instrument either by negotiation from the present holder or by a transfer other than negotiation. If the reacquisition is by negotiation, the former holder reacquires the status of holder. Although Section 3–207 allows the holder to cancel all indorsements made after the holder first acquired holder status, cancellation is not necessary. Status of holder is not affected whether or not cancellation is made. But if the reacquisition is not the result of negotiation the former holder can obtain holder status only by striking the former holder's indorsement and any subsequent indorsements. The latter case is an exception to the general rule that if an instrument is payable to an identified person, the indorsement of that person is necessary to allow a subsequent transferee to obtain the status of holder. Reacquisition without indorsement by the person to whom the instrument is payable is illustrated by two examples:

Case #1. X, a former holder, buys the instrument from Y, the present holder. Y delivers the instrument to X but fails to indorse it. Negotiation does not occur because the transfer of possession did not result in X's becoming holder. Section 3–201(a). The instrument by its terms is payable to Y, not to X. But X can obtain the status of holder by striking X's indorsement and all subsequent indorsements. When these indorsements are struck, the instrument by its terms is payable either to X or to bearer, depending upon how X originally became holder. In either case X becomes holder. Section 1–201(20).

Case #2. X, the holder of an instrument payable to X, negotiates it to Y by special indorsement. The negotiation is part of an underlying transaction between X and Y. The underlying transaction is rescinded by agreement of X and Y, and Y returns the instrument without Y's indorsement. The analysis is the same as that in Case #1. X can obtain holder status by canceling X's indorsement to Y.

In Case #1 and Case #2, X acquired ownership of the instrument after reacquisition, but X's title was clouded because the instrument by its terms was not payable to X. Normally, X can remedy the problem by obtaining Y's indorsement, but in some cases X may not be able to conveniently obtain that indorsement. Section 3–207 is a rule of convenience which relieves X of the burden of obtaining an indorsement that serves no substantive purpose. The effect of cancellation of any indorsement under Section 3–207 is to nullify it. Thus, the person whose indorsement is canceled is relieved of indorser's liability. Since cancellation is notice of discharge, discharge is effective even with respect to the rights of a holder in due course. Sections 3–601 and 3–604.

§ 3.208. Deleted by Acts 1995, 74th Leg., ch. 921, § 1, eff. Jan. 1, 1996

SUBCHAPTER C. ENFORCEMENT OF INSTRUMENTS

§ 3.301. Person Entitled to Enforce Instrument

"Person entitled to enforce" an instrument means (i) the holder of the instrument, (ii) a nonholder in possession of the instrument who has the rights of a holder, or (iii) a person not in possession of the instrument who is entitled to enforce the instrument pursuant to Section 3.309 or 3.418(d). A person may be a person entitled to enforce the instrument even though the person is not the owner of the instrument or is in wrongful possession of the instrument.

Amended by Acts 1995, 74th Leg., ch. 921, § 1, eff. Jan. 1, 1996.

Uniform Commercial Code Comment

This section replaces former Section 3–301 that stated the rights of a holder. The rights stated in former Section 3–301 to transfer, negotiate, enforce, or discharge an instrument are stated in other sections of Article 3. In revised Article 3, Section 3–301 defines "person entitled to enforce" an instrument. The definition recognizes that enforcement is not limited to holders. The quoted phrase includes a person enforcing a lost or stolen instrument. Section 3–309. It also includes a person in possession of an instrument who is not a holder. A nonholder in possession of an instrument includes a person that acquired rights of a holder by subrogation or under Section 3–203(a). It also includes both a remitter that has received an instrument from the issuer but has not yet transferred or negotiated the instrument to another person and also any other person who under applicable law is a successor to the holder or otherwise acquires the holder's rights. *Amendments approved by the Permanent Editorial Board for Uniform Commercial Code November 2, 2002.*

§ 3.302. Holder in Due Course

(a) Subject to Subsection (c) and Section 3.106(d), "holder in due course" means the holder of an instrument if:

(1) the instrument when issued or negotiated to the holder does not bear such apparent evidence of forgery or alteration or is not otherwise so irregular or incomplete as to call into question its authenticity; and

(2) the holder took the instrument:

(A) for value;

(B) in good faith;

(C) without notice that the instrument is overdue or has been dishonored or that there is an uncured default with respect to payment of another instrument issued as part of the same series;

(D) without notice that the instrument contains an unauthorized signature or has been altered;

(E) without notice of any claim to the instrument described in Section 3.306; and

(F) without notice that any party has a defense or claim in recoupment described in Section 3.305(a).

(b) Notice of discharge of a party, other than discharge in an insolvency proceeding, is not notice of a defense under Subsection (a), but discharge is effective against a person who became a holder in due course with notice of the discharge. Public filing or recording of a document does not of itself constitute notice of a defense, claim in recoupment, or claim to the instrument.

(c) Except to the extent a transferor or predecessor in interest has rights as a holder in due course, a person does not acquire rights of a holder in due course of an instrument taken:

(1) by legal process or by purchase in an execution, bankruptcy, or creditor's sale or similar proceeding;

(2) by purchase as part of a bulk transaction not in ordinary course of business of the transferor; or

(3) as the successor in interest to an estate or other organization.

(d) If, under Section 3.303(a)(1), the promise of performance that is the consideration for an instrument has been partially performed, the holder may assert rights as a holder in due course of the instrument only to the fraction of the amount payable under the instrument equal to the value of the partial performance divided by the value of the promised performance.

(e) If (i) the person entitled to enforce an instrument has only a security interest in the instrument, and (ii) the person obliged to pay the instrument has a defense, claim in recoupment, or claim to the instrument that may be asserted against the person who granted the security interest, the person entitled to enforce the instrument may assert rights as a holder in due course only to an amount payable under the instrument that, at the time of enforcement of the instrument, does not exceed the amount of the unpaid obligation secured.

(f) To be effective, notice must be received at a time and in a manner that gives a reasonable opportunity to act on it.

(g) This section is subject to any law limiting status as a holder in due course in particular classes of transactions.

Amended by Acts 1995, 74th Leg., ch. 921, § 1, eff. Jan. 1, 1996.

Uniform Commercial Code Comment

1. Subsection (a)(1) is a return to the N.I.L. rule that the taker of an irregular or incomplete instrument is not a person the law should protect against defenses of the obligor or claims of prior owners. This reflects a policy choice against extending the holder in due course doctrine to an instrument that is so incomplete or irregular "as to call into question its authenticity." The term "authenticity" is used to make it clear that the irregularity or incompleteness must indicate that the instrument may not be what it purports to be. Persons who purchase or pay such instruments should do so at their own risk. Under subsection (1) of former Section 3–304, irregularity or incompleteness gave a purchaser notice of a claim or defense. But it was not clear from that provision whether the claim or defense had to be related to the irregularity or incomplete aspect of the instrument. This ambiguity is not present in subsection (a)(1).

2. Subsection (a)(2) restates subsection (1) of former Section 3–302. Section 3–305(a) makes a distinction between defenses to the obligation to pay an instrument and claims in recoupment by the maker or drawer that may be asserted to reduce the amount payable on the instrument. Because of this distinction, which was not made in former Article 3, the reference in subsection (a)(2)(vi) is to both a defense and a claim in recoupment. Notice of forgery or alteration is stated separately because forgery and alteration are not technically defenses under subsection (a) of Section 3–305.

3. Discharge is also separately treated in the first sentence of subsection (b). Except for discharge in an insolvency proceeding, which is specifically stated to be a real

defense in Section 3–305(a)(1), discharge is not expressed in Article 3 as a defense and is not included in Section 3–305(a)(2). Discharge is effective against anybody except a person having rights of a holder in due course who took the instrument without notice of the discharge. Notice of discharge does not disqualify a person from becoming a holder in due course. For example, a check certified after it is negotiated by the payee may subsequently be negotiated to a holder. If the holder had notice that the certification occurred after negotiation by the payee, the holder necessarily had notice of the discharge of the payee as indorser. Section 3–415(d). Notice of that discharge does not prevent the holder from becoming a holder in due course, but the discharge is effective against the holder. Section 3–601(b). Notice of a defense under Section 3–305(a)(1) of a maker, drawer or acceptor based on a bankruptcy discharge is different. There is no reason to give holder in due course status to a person with notice of that defense. The second sentence of subsection (b) is from former Section 3–304(5).

4. Professor Britton in his treatise Bills and Notes 309 (1961) stated: "A substantial number of decisions before the [N.I.L.] indicates that at common law there was nothing in the position of the payee as such which made it impossible for him to be a holder in due course." The courts were divided, however, about whether the payee of an instrument could be a holder in due course under the N.I.L.. Some courts read N.I.L. § 52(4) to mean that a person could be a holder in due course only if the instrument was "negotiated" to that person. N.I.L. § 30 stated that "an instrument is negotiated when it is transferred from one person to another in such manner as to constitute the transferee the holder thereof." Normally, an instrument is "issued" to the payee; it is not transferred to the payee. N.I.L. § 191 defined "issue" as the "first delivery of the instrument * * * to a person who takes it as a holder." Thus, some courts concluded that the payee never could be a holder in due course. Other courts concluded that there was no evidence that the N.I.L. was intended to change the common law rule that the payee could be a holder in due course. Professor Britton states on p. 318: "The typical situations which raise the [issue] are those where the defense of a maker is interposed because of fraud by a [maker who is] principal debtor * * * against a surety co-maker, or where the defense of fraud by a purchasing remitter is interposed by the drawer of the instrument against the good faith purchasing payee."

Former Section 3–302(2) stated: "A payee may be a holder in due course." This provision was intended to resolve the split of authority under the N.I.L. It made clear that there was no intent to change the common-law rule that allowed a payee to become a holder in due course. See Comment 2 to former Section 3–302. But there was no need to put subsection (2) in former Section 3–302 because the split in authority under the N.I.L. was caused by the particular wording of N.I.L. § 52(4). The troublesome language in that section was not repeated in former Article 3 nor is it repeated in revised Article 3. Former Section 3–302(2) has been omitted in revised Article 3 because it is surplusage and may be misleading. The payee of an instrument can be a holder in due course, but use of the holder-in-due-course doctrine by the payee of an instrument is not the normal situation.

The primary importance of the concept of holder in due course is with respect to assertion of defenses or claims in recoupment (Section 3–305) and of claims to the instrument (Section 3–306). The holder-in-due-course doctrine assumes the following case as typical. Obligor issues a note or check to Obligee. Obligor is the maker of the note or drawer of the check. Obligee is the payee. Obligor has some defense to Obligor's obligation to pay the instrument. For example, Obligor issued the instrument for goods that Obligee promised to deliver. Obligee never delivered the goods. The failure of Obligee to deliver the goods is a defense. Section 3–303(b). Although Obligor has a defense against Obligee, if the instrument is negotiated to Holder and the requirements of subsection (a) are met, Holder may enforce the instrument against Obligor free of the defense. Section 3–305(b). In the typical case the holder in due course is not the payee of the instrument. Rather, the holder in due course is an immediate or remote transferee of the payee. If Obligor in our example is the only obligor on the check or note, the holder-in-due-course doctrine is irrelevant in determining rights between Obligor and Obligee with respect to the instrument.

But in a small percentage of cases it is appropriate to allow the payee of an instrument to assert rights as a holder in due course. The cases are like those referred to in the quotation from Professor Britton referred to above, or other cases in which conduct of some third party is the basis of the defense of the issuer of the instrument. The following are examples:

Case #1. Buyer pays for goods bought from Seller by giving to Seller a cashier's check bought from Bank. Bank has a defense to its obligation to pay the check because Buyer bought the check from Bank with a check known to be drawn on an account with insufficient funds to cover the check. If Bank issued the check to Buyer as payee and Buyer indorsed it over to Seller, it is clear that Seller can be a holder in due course taking free of the defense if Seller had no notice of the defense. Seller is a transferee of the check. There is no good reason why Seller's position should be any different if Bank drew the check to the order of Seller as payee. in that case, when Buyer took delivery of the check from Bank, Buyer became the owner of the check even though Buyer was not the holder. Buyer was a remitter. Section 3–103(a)(11). At that point nobody was the holder. When Buyer delivered the check to Seller, ownership of the check was transferred to Seller who also became the holder. This is a negotiation. Section 3–201. The rights of Seller should not be affected by the fact that in one case the negotiation to Seller was by a holder and in the other case the negotiation was by a remitter. Moreover, it should be irrelevant whether Bank delivered the check to Buyer and Buyer delivered it to Seller or whether Bank delivered it directly to Seller. In either case Seller can be a holder in due course that takes free of Bank's defense.

Case #2. X fraudulently induces Y to join X in a spurious venture to purchase a business. The purchase is to be financed by a bank loan for part of the price. Bank lends money to X and Y by deposit in a joint account of X and Y who sign a note payable to Bank for the amount of the loan. X then withdraws the money from the joint account and absconds. Bank acted in good faith and without notice of the fraud of X against Y. Bank is payee of the note executed by Y, but its right to enforce the note against Y should not be affected by the fact that Y was induced to execute the note by the fraud of X. Bank can be a holder in due course that takes free of the defense of Y. Case #2 is similar to Case #1. In each case the payee of the instrument has given value to the person committing the fraud in exchange for the obligation of the person against whom the fraud was committed. In each case the payee was not party to the fraud and had no notice of it.

Suppose in Case #2 that the note does not meet the requirements of Section 3–104(a) and thus is not a negotiable instrument covered by Article 3. In that case, Bank cannot be a holder in due course but the result should be the same. Bank's rights are determined by general principles of contract law. Restatement Second, Contracts § 164(2) governs the case. If Y is induced to enter into a contract with Bank by a fraudulent misrepresentation by X, the contract is voidable by Y unless Bank "in good faith and without reason to know of the misrepresentation either gives value or relies materially on the transaction." Comment e to § 164(2) states:

> "This is the same principle that protects an innocent person who purchases goods or commercial paper in good faith, without notice and for value from one who obtained them from the original owner by a misrepresentation. See Uniform Commercial Code §§ 2–403(1), 3–305. In the cases that fall within [§ 164(2)], however, the innocent person deals directly with the recipient of the misrepresentation, which is made by one not a party to the contract."

The same result follows in Case #2 if Y had been induced to sign the note as an accommodation party (Section 3–419). If Y signs as co-maker of a note for the benefit of X, Y is a surety with respect to the obligation of X to pay the note but is liable as maker of the note to pay Bank. Section 3–419(b). If Bank is a holder in due course, the fraud of X cannot be asserted against Bank under Section 3–305(b). But the result is the same without resort to holder-in-due-course doctrine. If the note is not a negotiable instrument governed by Article 3, general rules of suretyship apply. Restatement, Security § 119 states that the surety (Y) cannot assert a defense against the creditor (Bank) based on the fraud of the principal (X) if the creditor "without knowledge of the fraud * * * extended credit to the principal on the security of the surety's promise * * *." The underlying principle of § 119 is the same as that of § 164(2) of Restatement Second, Contracts.

Case #3. Corporation draws a check payable to Bank. The check is given to an officer of Corporation who is instructed to deliver it to Bank in payment of a debt owed by Corporation to Bank. Instead, the officer, intending to defraud Corporation, delivers the check to Bank in payment of the officer's personal debt, or the check is delivered to Bank for deposit to the officer's personal account. If Bank obtains payment of the check, Bank has received funds of Corporation which have been used for the personal benefit of the officer. Corporation in this case will assert a claim to the proceeds of the check against Bank. If Bank was a holder in due course of the check it took the check free of Corporation's claim. Section 3–306. The issue in this case is whether Bank had notice of the claim when it took the check. If Bank knew that the officer was a fiduciary with respect to the check, the issue is governed by Section 3–307.

Case #4. Employer, who owed money to X, signed a blank check and delivered it to Secretary with instructions to complete the check by typing in X's name and the amount owed to X. Secretary fraudulently completed the check by typing in the name of Y, a creditor to whom Secretary owed money. Secretary then delivered the check to Y in payment of Secretary's debt. Y obtained payment of the check. This case is similar to Case #3. Since Secretary was authorized to complete the check, Employer is bound by Secretary's act in making the check payable to Y. The drawee bank properly paid the check. Y received funds of Employer which were used for the personal benefit of Secretary. Employer asserts a claim to these funds against Y. If Y is a holder in due course, Y takes free of the claim. Whether Y is a holder in due course depends upon whether Y had notice of Employer's claim.

5. Subsection (c) is based on former Section 3–302(3). Like former Section 3–302(3), subsection (c) is intended to state existing case law. It covers a few situations in which the purchaser takes an instrument under unusual circumstances. The purchaser is treated as a successor in interest to the prior holder and can acquire no better rights. But if the prior holder was a holder in due course, the purchaser obtains rights of a holder in due course.

Subsection (c) applies to a purchaser in an execution sale or sale in bankruptcy. It applies equally to an attaching creditor or any other person who acquires the instrument by legal process or to a representative, such as an executor, administrator, receiver or assignee for the benefit of creditors, who takes the instrument as part of an estate. Subsection (c) applies to bulk purchases lying outside of the ordinary course of business of the seller. For example, it applies to the purchase by one bank of a substantial part of the paper held by another bank which is threatened with insolvency and seeking to liquidate its assets. Subsection (c) would also apply when a new partnership takes over for value all of the assets of an old one after a new member has entered the firm, or to a reorganized or consolidated corporation taking over the assets of a predecessor.

In the absence of controlling state law to the contrary, subsection (c) applies to a sale by a state bank commissioner of the assets of an insolvent bank. However, subsection (c) may be preempted by federal law if the Federal Deposit Insurance Corporation takes over an insolvent bank. Under the governing federal law, the FDIC and similar financial institution insurers are given holder in due course status and that status is also acquired by their assignees under the shelter doctrine.

6. Subsections (d) and (e) clarify two matters not specifically addressed by former Article 3:

Case #5. Payee negotiates a $1,000 note to Holder who agrees to pay $900 for it. After paying $500, Holder learns that Payee defrauded Maker in the transaction giving rise to the note. Under subsection (d) Holder may assert rights as a holder in due course to the extent of $555.55 ($500 ÷ $900 = .555 × $1,000 = $555.55). This formula rewards Holder with a ratable portion of the bargained for profit.

Case #6. Payee negotiates a note of Maker for $1,000 to Holder as security for payment of Payee's debt to

Holder of $600. Maker has a defense which is good against Payee but of which Holder has no notice. Subsection (e) applies. Holder may assert rights as a holder in due course only to the extent of $600. Payee does not get the benefit of the holder-in-due-course status of Holder. With respect to $400 of the note, Maker may assert any rights that Maker has against Payee. A different result follows if the payee of a note negotiated it to a person who took it as a holder in due course and that person pledged the note as security for a debt. Because the defense cannot be asserted against the pledgor, the pledgee can assert rights as a holder in due course for the full amount of the note for the benefit of both the pledgor and the pledgee.

7. There is a large body of state statutory and case law restricting the use of the holder in due course doctrine in consumer transactions as well as some business transactions that raise similar issues. Subsection (g) subordinates Article 3 to that law and any other similar law that may evolve in the future. Section 3–106(d) also relates to statutory or administrative law intended to restrict use of the holder-in-due-course doctrine. See Comment 3 to Section 3–106.

8. The status of holder in due course resembles the status of protected holder under Article 29 of the Convention on International Bills of Exchange and International Promissory Notes. The requirements for being a protected holder under Article 29 generally track those of Section 3–302. *Amendments approved by the Permanent Editorial Board for Uniform Commercial Code November 2, 2002.*

§ 3.303. Value and Consideration

(a) An instrument is issued or transferred for value if:

(1) the instrument is issued or transferred for a promise of performance, to the extent the promise has been performed;

(2) the transferee acquires a security interest or other lien in the instrument other than a lien obtained by judicial proceeding;

(3) the instrument is issued or transferred as payment of, or as security for, an antecedent claim against any person, whether or not the claim is due;

(4) the instrument is issued or transferred in exchange for a negotiable instrument; or

(5) the instrument is issued or transferred in exchange for the incurring of an irrevocable obligation to a third party by the person taking the instrument.

(b) "Consideration" means any consideration sufficient to support a simple contract. The drawer or maker of an instrument has a defense if the instrument is issued without consideration. If an instrument is issued for a promise of performance, the issuer has a defense to the extent performance of the promise is due and the promise has not been performed. If an instrument is issued for value as stated in Subsection (a), the instrument is also issued for consideration.

Amended by Acts 1995, 74th Leg., ch. 921, § 1, eff. Jan. 1, 1996.

Uniform Commercial Code Comment

1. Subsection (a) is a restatement of former Section 3–303 and subsection (b) replaces former Section 3–408. The distinction between value and consideration in Article 3 is a very fine one. Whether an instrument is taken for value is relevant to the issue of whether a holder is a holder in due course. If an instrument is not issued for consideration the issuer has a defense to the obligation to pay the instrument. Consideration is defined in subsection (b) as "any consideration sufficient to support a simple contract." The definition of value in Section 1–201(44), which doesn't apply to Article 3, includes "any consideration sufficient to support a simple contract." Thus, outside Article 3, anything that is consideration is also value. A different rule applies in Article 3. Subsection (b) of Section 3–303 states that if an instrument is issued for value it is also issued for consideration.

Case # 1. X owes Y $1,000. The debt is not represented by a note. Later X issues a note to Y for the debt. Under subsection (a)(3) X's note is issued for value. Under subsection (b) the note is also issued for consideration whether or not, under contract law, Y is deemed to have given consideration for the note.

Case # 2. X issues a check to Y in consideration of Y's promise to perform services in the future. Although the executory promise is consideration for issuance of the check it is value only to the extent the promise is performed. Subsection (a)(1).

Case # 3. X issues a note to Y in consideration of Y's promise to perform services. If at the due date of the note Y's performance is not yet due, Y may enforce the note because it was issued for consideration. But if at the due date of the note, Y's performance is due and has not been performed, X has a defense. Subsection (b).

2. Subsection (a), which defines value, has primary importance in cases in which the issue is whether the holder of an instrument is a holder in due course and particularly to cases in which the issuer of the instrument has a defense to the instrument. Suppose Buyer and Seller signed a contract on April 1 for the sale of goods to be delivered on May 1. Payment of 50% of the price of the goods was due upon signing of the contract. On April 1 Buyer delivered to Seller a check in the amount due under the contract. The check was drawn by X to Buyer as payee and was indorsed to Seller. When the check was presented for payment to the drawee on April 2, it was dishonored because X had stopped payment. At that time Seller had not taken any action to perform the contract with Buyer. If X has a defense on the check, the defense can be asserted against Seller who is not a holder in due course because Seller did not give value for the check. Subsection (a)(1). The policy basis for subsection (a)(1) is that the holder who gives an executory promise of performance will not suffer an out-of-pocket loss to the

extent the executory promise is unperformed at the time the holder learns of dishonor of the instrument. When Seller took delivery of the check on April 1, Buyer's obligation to pay 50% of the price on that date was suspended, but when the check was dishonored on April 2 the obligation revived. Section 3–310(b). If payment for goods is due at or before delivery and the Buyer fails to make the payment, the Seller is excused from performing the promise to deliver the goods. Section 2–703. Thus, Seller is protected from an out-of-pocket loss even if the check is not enforceable. Holder-in-due-course status is not necessary to protect Seller.

3. Subsection (a)(2) equates value with the obtaining of a security interest or a nonjudicial lien in the instrument. The term "security interest" covers Article 9 cases in which an instrument is taken as collateral as well as bank collection cases in which a bank acquires a security interest under Section 4–210. The acquisition of a common-law or statutory banker's lien is also value under subsection (a)(2). An attaching creditor or other person who acquires a lien by judicial proceedings does not give value for the purposes of subsection (a)(2).

4. Subsection (a)(3) follows former Section 3–303(b) in providing that the holder takes for value if the instrument is taken in payment of or as security for an antecedent claim, even though there is no extension of time or other concession, and whether or not the claim is due. Subsection (a)(3) applies to any claim against any person; there is no requirement that the claim arise out of contract. In particular the provision is intended to apply to an instrument given in payment of or as security for the debt of a third person, even though no concession is made in return.

5. Subsection (a)(4) and (5) restate former Section 3–303(c). They state generally recognized exceptions to the rule that an executory promise is not value. A negotiable instrument is value because it carries the possibility of negotiation to a holder in due course, after which the party who gives it is obliged to pay. The same reasoning applies to any irrevocable commitment to a third person, such as a letter of credit issued when an instrument is taken.

6. The term "promise" in paragraph (a)(1) is used in the phrase 'promise of performance' and for that reason does not have the specialized meaning given that term in Section 3–103(a)(12). [see § 3.103(a)(9) in the Texas Uniform Commercial Code]. See Section 1–201 ("Changes from Former Law"). No inference should be drawn from the decision to use the phrase "promise of performance," although the phrase does include the word "promise," which has the specialized definition set forth in Section 3–103. Indeed, that is true even though "undertaking" is used instead of "promise" in Section 3–104(a)(3). See Section 3–104 comment 1 (explaining the use of the term "undertaking" in Section 3–104 to avoid use of the defined term "promise"). *Amendments approved by the Permanent Editorial Board for Uniform Commercial Code November 2, 2002.*

§ 3.304. Overdue Instrument

(a) An instrument payable on demand becomes overdue at the earliest of the following times:

(1) on the day after the day demand for payment is duly made;

(2) if the instrument is a check, 90 days after its date; or

(3) if the instrument is not a check, when the instrument has been outstanding for a period of time after its date that is unreasonably long under the circumstances of the particular case in light of the nature of the instrument and usage of the trade.

(b) With respect to an instrument payable at a definite time the following rules apply:

(1) if the principal is payable in installments and a due date has not been accelerated, the instrument becomes overdue on default under the instrument for nonpayment of an installment, and the instrument remains overdue until the default is cured;

(2) if the principal is not payable in installments and the due date has not been accelerated, the instrument becomes overdue on the day after the due date; and

(3) if a due date with respect to principal has been accelerated, the instrument becomes overdue on the day after the accelerated due date.

(c) Unless the due date of principal has been accelerated, an instrument does not become overdue if there is default in payment of interest but no default in payment of principal.

Amended by Acts 1995, 74th Leg., ch. 921, § 1, eff. Jan. 1, 1996.

Uniform Commercial Code Comment

1. To be a holder in due course, one must take without notice that an instrument is overdue. Section 3–302(a)(2)(iii). Section 3–304 replaces subsection (3) of former Section 3–304. For the sake of clarity it treats demand and time instruments separately. Subsection (a) applies to demand instruments. A check becomes stale after 90 days.

Under former Section 3–304(3)(c), a holder that took a demand note had notice that it was overdue if it was taken "more than a reasonable length time after its issue." In substitution for this test, subsection (a)(3) requires the trier of fact to look at both the circumstances of the particular case and the nature of the instrument and trade usage. Whether a demand note is stale may vary a great deal depending on the facts of the particular case.

2. Subsections (b) and (c) cover time instruments. They follow the distinction made under former Article 3 between defaults in payment of principal and interest. In subsection (b) installment instruments and single payment instruments are treated separately. If an installment is late, the instrument is overdue until the default is cured.

§ 3.305. Defenses and Claims in Recoupment

(a) Except as otherwise provided in this section, the right to enforce the obligation of a party to pay an instrument is subject to the following:

(1) a defense of the obligor based on:

(A) infancy of the obligor to the extent it is a defense to a simple contract;

(B) duress, lack of legal capacity, or illegality of the transaction that, under other law, nullifies the obligation of the obligor;

(C) fraud that induced the obligor to sign the instrument with neither knowledge nor reasonable opportunity to learn of its character or its essential terms; or

(D) discharge of the obligor in insolvency proceedings;

(2) a defense of the obligor stated in another section of this chapter or a defense of the obligor that would be available if the person entitled to enforce the instrument were enforcing a right to payment under a simple contract; and

(3) a claim in recoupment of the obligor against the original payee of the instrument if the claim arose from the transaction that gave rise to the instrument; but the claim of the obligor may be asserted against a transferee of the instrument only to reduce the amount owing on the instrument at the time the action is brought.

(b) The right of a holder in due course to enforce the obligation of a party to pay the instrument is subject to defenses of the obligor stated in Subsection (a)(1), but is not subject to defenses of the obligor stated in Subsection (a)(2) or claims in recoupment stated in Subsection (a)(3) against a person other than the holder.

(c) Except as provided in Subsection (d), in an action to enforce the obligation of a party to pay the instrument, the obligor may not assert against the person entitled to enforce the instrument a defense, claim in recoupment, or claim to the instrument (Section 3.306) of another person, but the other person's claim to the instrument may be asserted by the obligor if the other person is joined in the action and personally asserts the claim against the person entitled to enforce the instrument. An obligor is not obliged to pay the instrument if the person seeking enforcement of the instrument does not have rights of a holder in due course and the obligor proves that the instrument is a lost or stolen instrument.

(d) In an action to enforce the obligation of an accommodation party to pay an instrument, the accommodation party may assert against the person entitled to enforce the instrument any defense or claim in recoupment under Subsection (a) that the accommodated party could assert against the person entitled to enforce the instrument, except the defenses of discharge in insolvency proceedings, infancy, and lack of legal capacity.

(e) In a consumer transaction, if law other than this chapter requires that an instrument include a statement to the effect that the rights of a holder or transferee are subject to a claim or defense that the issuer could assert against the original payee, and the instrument does not include such a statement:

(1) the instrument has the same effect as if the instrument included such a statement;

(2) the issuer may assert against the holder or transferee all claims and defenses that would have been available if the instrument included such a statement; and

(3) the extent to which claims may be asserted against the holder or transferee is determined as if the instrument included such a statement.

If an instrument includes or is deemed to include a statement under this subsection, a holder or transferee who is liable under the statement to the issuer, but who is not the seller of the goods or services, shall be entitled to full indemnity from the seller for any liability under the statement incurred by the holder or transferee that results from the issuer's claims or defenses against the seller, plus reasonable attorney's fees. The provision in this section for express indemnity does not affect any right of indemnity, subrogation, or recovery to which a holder or transferee may be entitled under any rule, written contract, judicial decision, or other statute. This section is not intended to provide a holder or transferee indemnity from the seller with respect to the holder or transferee's direct liability to the issuer for the holder or transferee's own actionable misconduct unrelated to derivative liability under the statement.

(f) This section is subject to law other than this chapter that establishes a different rule for consumer transactions.

Amended by Acts 1995, 74th Leg., ch. 921, § 1, eff. Jan. 1, 1996; Acts 2005, 79th Leg., ch. 95, § 5, eff. Sept. 1, 2005.

Uniform Commercial Code Comment

1. Subsection (a) states the defenses to the obligation of a party to pay the instrument. Subsection (a)(1) states the "real defenses" that may be asserted against any person entitled to enforce the instrument.

Subsection (a)(1)(i) allows assertion of the defense of infancy against a holder in due course, even though the effect of the defense is to render the instrument voidable but not void. The policy is one of protection of the infant even at the expense of occasional loss to an innocent purchaser. No attempt is made to state when infancy is available as a defense or the conditions under which it may be asserted. In some jurisdictions it is held that an infant cannot rescind the transaction or set up the defense unless the holder is restored to the position held before the instrument was taken which, in the case of a holder in due course, is normally impossible. In other states an infant who has misrepresented age may be estopped to assert infancy. Such questions are left to other law, as an integral part of the policy of each state as to the protection of infants.

Subsection (a)(1)(ii) covers mental incompetence, guardianship, ultra vires acts or lack of corporate capacity to do business, or any other incapacity apart from infancy. Such incapacity is largely statutory. Its existence and effect is left to the law of each state. If under the state law the effect is to render the obligation of the instrument entirely null and void, the defense may be asserted against a holder in due course. If the effect is merely to render the obligation voidable at the election of the obligor, the defense is cut off.

Duress, which is also covered by subsection (a)(ii), is a matter of degree. An instrument signed at the point of a gun is void, even in the hands of a holder in due course. One signed under threat to prosecute the son of the maker for theft may be merely voidable, so that the defense is cut off. Illegality is most frequently a matter of gambling or usury, but may arise in other forms under a variety of statutes. The statutes differ in their provisions and the interpretations given them. They are primarily a matter of local concern and local policy. All such matters are therefore left to the local law. If under that law the effect of the duress or the illegality is to make the obligation entirely null and void, the defense may be asserted against a holder in due course. Otherwise it is cut off.

Subsection (a)(1)(iii) refers to "real" or "essential" fraud, sometimes called fraud in the essence or fraud in the factum, as effective against a holder in due course. The common illustration is that of the maker who is tricked into signing a note in the belief that it is merely a receipt or some other document. The theory of the defense is that the signature on the instrument is ineffective because the signer did not intend to sign such an instrument at all. Under this provision the defense extends to an instrument signed with knowledge that it is a negotiable instrument, but without knowledge of its essential terms. The test of the defense is that of excusable ignorance of the contents of the writing signed. The party must not only have been in ignorance, but must also have had no reasonable opportunity to obtain knowledge. In determining what is a reasonable opportunity all relevant factors are to be taken into account, including the intelligence, education, business experience, and ability to read or understand English of the signer. Also relevant is the nature of the representations that were made, whether the signer had good reason to rely on the representations or to have confidence in the person making them, the presence or absence of any third person who might read or explain the instrument to the signer, or any other possibility of obtaining independent information, and the apparent necessity, or lack of it, for acting without delay. Unless the misrepresentation meets this test, the defense is cut off by a holder in due course.

Subsection (a)(1)(iv) states specifically that the defense of discharge in insolvency proceedings is not cut off when the instrument is purchased by a holder in due course. "Insolvency proceedings" is defined in Section 1–201(22) and it includes bankruptcy whether or not the debtor is insolvent. Subsection (2)(e) of former Section 3–305 is omitted. The substance of that provision is stated in Section 3–601(b).

2. Subsection (a)(2) states other defenses that, pursuant to subsection (b), are cut off by a holder in due course. These defenses comprise those specifically stated in Article 3 and those based on common law contract principles. Article 3 defenses are nonissuance of the instrument, conditional issuance, and issuance for a special purpose (Section 3–105(b)); failure to countersign a traveler's check (Section 3–106(c)); modification of the obligation by a separate agreement (Section 3–117); payment that violates a restrictive indorsement (Section 3–206(f)); instruments issued without consideration or for which promised performance has not been given (Section 3–303(b)), and breach of warranty when a draft is accepted (Section 3–417(b)). The most prevalent common law defenses are fraud, misrepresentation or mistake in the issuance of the instrument. In most cases the holder in due course will be an immediate or remote transferee of the payee of the instrument. In most cases the holder-in-due-course doctrine is irrelevant if defenses are being asserted against the payee of the instrument, but in a small number of cases the payee of the instrument may be a holder in due course. Those cases are discussed in Comment 4 to Section 3–302.

Assume Buyer issues a note to Seller in payment of the price of goods that Seller fraudulently promises to deliver but which are never delivered. Seller negotiates the note to Holder who has no notice of the fraud. If Holder is a holder in due course, Holder is not subject to Buyer's defense of fraud. But in some cases an original party to the instrument is a holder in due course. For example, Buyer fraudulently induces Bank to issue a cashier's check to the order of Seller. The check is delivered by Bank to Seller, who has no notice of the fraud. Seller can be a holder in due course and can take the check free of Bank's defense of fraud. This case is discussed as Case # 1 in Comment 4 to Section 3–302. Former Section 3–305 stated that a holder in due course takes free of defenses of "any party to the instrument with whom the holder has not dealt." The meaning of this language was not at all clear and if read literally could have produced the wrong result. In the hypothetical case, it could be argued that Seller "dealt" with Bank because Bank delivered the check to Seller. But it is clear that Seller should take free of Bank's defense against Buyer regardless of whether Seller took delivery of the check from Buyer or from Bank. The quoted language is not included in Section 3–305. It is not necessary. If Buyer issues an instrument to

Seller and Buyer has a defense against Seller, that defense can obviously be asserted. Buyer and Seller are the only people involved. The holder-in-due-course doctrine has no relevance. The doctrine applies only to cases in which more than two parties are involved. Its essence is that the holder in due course does not have to suffer the consequences of a defense of the obligor on the instrument that arose from an occurrence with a third party.

3. Subsection (a)(3) is concerned with claims in recoupment which can be illustrated by the following example. Buyer issues a note to the order of Seller in exchange for a promise of Seller to deliver specified equipment. If Seller fails to deliver the equipment or delivers equipment that is rightfully rejected, Buyer has a defense to the note because the performance that was the consideration for the note was not rendered. Section 3–303(b). This defense is included in Section 3–305(a)(2). That defense can always be asserted against Seller. This result is the same as that reached under former Section 3–408.

But suppose Seller delivered the promised equipment and it was accepted by Buyer. The equipment, however, was defective. Buyer retained the equipment and incurred expenses with respect to its repair. In this case, Buyer does not have a defense under Section 3–303(b). Seller delivered the equipment and the equipment was accepted. Under Article 2, Buyer is obliged to pay the price of the equipment which is represented by the note. But Buyer may have a claim against Seller for breach of warranty. If Buyer has a warranty claim, the claim may be asserted against Seller as a counterclaim or as a claim in recoupment to reduce the amount owing on the note. It is not relevant whether Seller is or is not a holder in due course of the note or whether Seller knew or had notice that Buyer had the warranty claim. It is obvious that holder-in-due-course doctrine cannot be used to allow Seller to cut off a warranty claim that Buyer has against Seller. Subsection (b) specifically covers this point by stating that a holder in due course is not subject to a "claim in recoupment * * * against a person other than the holder."

Suppose Seller negotiates the note to Holder. If Holder had notice of Buyer's warranty claim at the time the note was negotiated to Holder, Holder is not a holder in due course (Section 3–302(a)(2)(iv)) and Buyer may assert the claim against Holder (Section 3–305(a)(3)) but only as a claim in recoupment, i.e. to reduce the amount owed on the note. If the warranty claim is $1,000 and the unpaid note is $10,000, Buyer owes $9,000 to Holder. If the warranty claim is more than the unpaid amount of the note, Buyer owes nothing to Holder, but Buyer cannot recover the unpaid amount of the warranty claim from Holder. If Buyer had already partially paid the note, Buyer is not entitled to recover the amounts paid. The claim can be used only as an offset to amounts owing on the note. If Holder had no notice of Buyer's claim and otherwise qualifies as a holder in due course, Buyer may not assert the claim against Holder. Section 3–305(b).

The result under Section 3–305 is consistent with the result reached under former Article 3, but the rules for reaching the result are stated differently. Under former Article 3 Buyer could assert rights against Holder only if Holder was not a holder in due course, and Holder's status depended upon whether Holder had notice of a defense by Buyer. Courts have held that Holder had that notice if Holder had notice of Buyer's warranty claim. The rationale under former Article 3 was "failure of consideration." This rationale does not distinguish between cases in which the seller fails to perform and those in which the buyer accepts the performance of seller but makes a claim against the seller because the performance is faulty. The term "failure of consideration" is subject to varying interpretations and is not used in Article 3. The use of the term "claim in recoupment" in Section 3–305(a)(3) is a more precise statement of the nature of Buyer's right against Holder. The use of the term does not change the law because the treatment of a defense under subsection (a)(2) and a claim in recoupment under subsection (a)(3) is essentially the same.

Under former Article 3, case law was divided on the issue of the extent to which an obligor on a note could assert against a transferee who is not a holder in due course a debt or other claim that the obligor had against the original payee of the instrument. Some courts limited claims to those that arose in the transaction that gave rise to the note. This is the approach taken in Section 3–305(a)(3). Other courts allowed the obligor on the note to use any debt or other claim, no matter how unrelated to the note, to offset the amount owed on the note. Under current judicial authority and non-UCC statutory law, there will be many cases in which a transferee of a note arising from a sale transaction will not qualify as a holder in due course. For example, applicable law may require the use of a note to which there cannot be a holder in due course. See Section 3–106(d) and Comment 3 to Section 3–106. It is reasonable to provide that the buyer should not be denied the right to assert claims arising out of the sale transaction. Subsection (a)(3) is based on the belief that it is not reasonable to require the transferee to bear the risk that wholly unrelated claims may also be asserted. The determination of whether a claim arose from the transaction that gave rise to the instrument is determined by law other than this Article and thus may vary as local law varies.

4. Subsection (c) concerns claims and defenses of a person other than the obligor on the instrument. It applies principally to cases in which an obligation is paid with the instrument of a third person. For example, Buyer buys goods from Seller and negotiates to Seller a cashier's check issued by Bank in payment of the price. Shortly after delivering the check to Seller, Buyer learns that Seller had defrauded Buyer in the sale transaction. Seller may enforce the check against Bank even though Seller is not a holder in due course. Bank has no defense to its obligation to pay the check and it may not assert defenses, claims in recoupment, or claims to the instrument of Buyer, except to the extent permitted by the "but" clause of the first sentence of subsection (c). Buyer may have a claim to the instrument under Section 3–306 based on a right to rescind the negotiation to Seller because of Seller's fraud. Section 3–202(b) and Comment 2 to Section 3–201. Bank cannot assert that claim unless Buyer is joined in the action in which Seller is trying to enforce payment of the check. In that case Bank may pay the amount of the check into court and the court will decide whether that amount belongs to Buyer or Seller. The last sentence of subsection (c) allows the issuer of an instrument such as a cashier's check to refuse payment in the rare case

in which the issuer can prove that the instrument is a lost or stolen instrument and the person seeking enforcement does not have rights of a holder in due course.

5. Subsection (d) applies to instruments signed for accommodation (Section 3–419) and this subsection equates the obligation of the accommodation party to that of the accommodated party. The accommodation party can assert whatever defense or claim the accommodated party had against the person enforcing the instrument. The only exceptions are discharge in bankruptcy, infancy and lack of capacity. The same rule does not apply to an indorsement by a holder of the instrument in negotiating the instrument. The indorser, as transferor, makes a warranty to the indorsee, as transferee, that no defense or claim in recoupment is good against the indorser. Section 3–416(a)(4). Thus, if the indorsee sues the indorser because of dishonor of the instrument, the indorser may not assert the defense or claim in recoupment of the maker or drawer against the indorsee.

Section 3–305(d) must be read in conjunction with Section 3–605, which provides rules (usually referred to as suretyship defenses) for determining when the obligation of an accommodation party is discharged, in whole or in part, because of some act or omission of a person entitled to enforce the instrument. To the extent a rule stated in Section 3–605 is inconsistent with Section 3–305(d), the Section 3–605 rule governs. For example, Section 3–605(a) provides rules for determining when and to what extent a discharge of the accommodated party under Section 3–604 will discharge the accommodation party. As explained in Comment 2 to Section 3–605, discharge of the accommodated party is normally part of a settlement under which the holder of a note accepts partial payment from an accommodated party who is financially unable to pay the entire amount of the note. If the holder then brings an action against the accommodation party to recover the remaining unpaid amount of the note, the accommodation party cannot use Section 3–305(d) to nullify Section 3–605(a) by asserting the discharge of the accommodated party as a defense. On the other hand, suppose the accommodated party is a buyer of goods who issued the note to the seller who took the note for the buyer's obligation to pay for the goods. Suppose the buyer has a claim for breach of warranty with respect to the goods against the seller and the warranty claim may be asserted against the holder of the note. The warranty claim is a claim in recoupment. If the holder and the accommodated party reach a settlement under which the holder accepts payment less than the amount of the note in full satisfaction of the note and the warranty claim, the accommodation party could defend an action on the note by the holder by asserting the accord and satisfaction under Section 3–305(d). There is no conflict with Section 3–605(a) because that provision is not intended to apply to settlement of disputed claims.

6. Subsection (e) is added to clarify the treatment of an instrument that omits the notice currently required by the Federal Trade Commission Rule related to certain consumer credit sales and consumer purchase money loans (16 C.F.R. Part 433). This subsection adopts the view that the instrument should be treated as if the language required by the FTC Rule were present. It is based on the language describing that rule in Section 3–106(d) and the analogous provision in Section 9–404(d).

7. Subsection (f) is modeled on Sections 9–403(e) and 9–404(c). It ensures that Section 3–305 is interpreted to accommodate relevant consumer-protection laws. The absence of such a provision from other sections in Article 3 should not justify any inference about the meaning of those sections.

8. Articles 28 and 30 of the Convention on International Bills of Exchange and International Promissory Notes includes a similar dichotomy, with a narrower group of defenses available against a protected holder under Articles 28(1) and 30 than are available under Article 28(2) against a holder that is not a protected holder.

State Bar Committee Comments

The *Official Text* fails to define the term "claim in recoupment". Based on the *Official Text* and the Official Comments contained therein, the term is intended to adopt the rule that the obligor may assert, only as an offset to amounts owing on the instrument, claims arising out of the same transaction with the original payee. As further guidance, Texas courts may look to the following two United States Fifth Circuit Court of Appeals cases: *FDIC v. Lattimore Land Corp.*, 656 F.2d 139, 143 (5th Cir. 1981), and *Frederick v. United States*, 386 F.2d 481, 488 (5th Cir. 1967).

§ 3.306. Claims to an Instrument

A person taking an instrument, other than a person having rights of a holder in due course, is subject to a claim of a property or possessory right in the instrument or its proceeds, including a claim to rescind a negotiation and to recover the instrument or its proceeds. A person having rights of a holder in due course takes free of the claim to the instrument.

Amended by Acts 1995, 74th Leg., ch. 921, § 1, eff. Jan. 1, 1996.

Uniform Commercial Code Comment

This section expands on the reference to "claims to" the instrument mentioned in former Sections 3–305 and 3–306. Claims covered by the section include not only claims to ownership but also any other claim of a property or possessory right. It includes the claim to a lien or the claim of a person in rightful possession of an instrument who was wrongfully deprived of possession. Also included is a claim based on Section 3–202(b) for rescission of a negotiation of the instrument by the claimant. Claims to an instrument under Section 3–306 are different from claims in recoupment referred to in Section 3–305(a)(3). The rule of this section is similar to the rule of Article 30(2) of the Convention on International Bills of Exchange and International Promissory Notes. *Amendments approved by the Permanent Editorial Board for Uniform Commercial Code November 2, 2002.*

§ 3.307. Notice of Breach of Fiduciary Duty

(a) In this section:

(1) "Fiduciary" means an agent, trustee, partner, corporate officer or director, or other representative owing a fiduciary duty with respect to an instrument.

(2) "Represented person" means the principal, beneficiary, partnership, corporation, or other person to whom the duty stated in Subdivision (1) is owed.

(b) If (i) an instrument is taken from a fiduciary for payment or collection or for value, (ii) the taker has knowledge of the fiduciary status of the fiduciary, and (iii) the represented person makes a claim to the instrument or its proceeds on the basis that the transaction of the fiduciary is a breach of fiduciary duty, the following rules apply:

(1) notice of breach of fiduciary duty by the fiduciary is notice of the claim of the represented person;

(2) in the case of an instrument payable to the represented person or the fiduciary as such, the taker has notice of the breach of fiduciary duty if the instrument is:

(A) taken in payment of or as security for a debt known by the taker to be the personal debt of the fiduciary;

(B) taken in a transaction known by the taker to be for the personal benefit of the fiduciary; or

(C) deposited to an account other than an account of the fiduciary, as such, or an account of the represented person;

(3) if an instrument is issued by the represented person or the fiduciary as such, and made payable to the fiduciary personally, the taker does not have notice of the breach of fiduciary duty unless the taker knows of the breach of fiduciary duty; and

(4) if an instrument is issued by the represented person or the fiduciary as such, to the taker as payee, the taker has notice of the breach of fiduciary duty if the instrument is:

(A) taken in payment of or as security for a debt known by the taker to be the personal debt of the fiduciary;

(B) taken in a transaction known by the taker to be for the personal benefit of the fiduciary; or

(C) deposited to an account other than an account of the fiduciary, as such, or an account of the represented person.

Amended by Acts 1995, 74th Leg., ch. 921, § 1, eff. Jan. 1, 1996.

Uniform Commercial Code Comment

1. This section states rules for determining when a person who has taken an instrument from a fiduciary has notice of a breach of fiduciary duty that occurs as a result of the transaction with the fiduciary. Former Section 3–304(2) and (4)(e) related to this issue, but those provisions were unclear in their meaning. Section 3–307 is intended to clarify the law by stating rules that comprehensively cover the issue of when the taker of an instrument has notice of breach of a fiduciary duty and thus notice of a claim to the instrument or its proceeds.

2. Subsection (a) defines the terms "fiduciary" and "represented person" and the introductory paragraph of subsection (b) describes the transaction to which the section applies. The basic scenario is one in which the fiduciary in effect embezzles money of the represented person by applying the proceeds of an instrument that belongs to the represented person to the personal use of the fiduciary. The person dealing with the fiduciary may be a depositary bank that takes the instrument for collection or a bank or other person that pays value for the instrument. The section also covers a transaction in which an instrument is presented for payment to a payor bank that pays the instrument by giving value to the fiduciary. Subsections (b)(2), (3), and (4) state rules for determining when the person dealing with the fiduciary has notice of breach of fiduciary duty. Subsection (b)(1) states that notice of breach of fiduciary duty is notice of the represented person's claim to the instrument or its proceeds.

Under Section 3–306, a person taking an instrument is subject to a claim to the instrument or its proceeds, unless the taker has rights of a holder in due course. Under Section 3–302(a)(2)(v), the taker cannot be a holder in due course if the instrument was taken with notice of a claim under Section 3–306. Section 3–307 applies to cases in which a represented person is asserting a claim because a breach of fiduciary duty resulted in a misapplication of the proceeds of an instrument. The claim of the represented person is a claim described in Section 3–306. Section 3–307 states rules for determining when a person taking an instrument has notice of the claim which will prevent assertion of rights as a holder in due course. It also states rules for determining when a payor bank pays an instrument with notice of breach of fiduciary duty.

Section 3–307(b) applies only if the person dealing with the fiduciary "has knowledge of the fiduciary status of the fiduciary." Notice which does not amount to knowledge is not enough to cause Section 3–307 to apply. "Knowledge" is defined in Section 1–201(25). In most cases, the "taker" referred to in Section 3–307 will be a bank or other organization. Knowledge of an organization is determined by the rules stated in Section 1–201(27). In many cases, the individual who receives and processes an instrument on behalf of the organization that is the taker of the instrument "for payment or collection or for value" is a clerk who has no knowledge of any fiduciary status of the person from whom the instrument is received. In such cases, Section 3–307 doesn't apply because, under Section 1–201(27), knowledge of the organization is determined by the knowledge of the "individual conducting that transaction," i.e. the clerk who receives and processes the instrument. Furthermore, paragraphs (2) and (4) each require that the person acting for the organization have knowledge of facts that indicate a breach of fiduciary duty. In the case of an instrument taken for deposit to an account, the knowledge is found in the fact that the deposit is made to an account other than that of the represented person or a fiduciary account for benefit of that person. In other cases the person acting for the organization must know that the instrument is taken in payment or as security for a personal debt of the fiduciary or for the personal benefit of the fiduciary. For example, if the instrument is being used to buy goods or services, the person acting for the organization must know that the goods or services are for the personal benefit of the fiduciary. The requirement that the taker have knowledge rather than notice is meant to limit Section 3–307 to relatively uncommon cases in which the person who deals with the fiduciary knows all the relevant facts: the fiduciary status and that the proceeds of the instrument are being used for the personal debt or benefit of the fiduciary or are being paid to an account that is not an account of the represented person or of the fiduciary, as such. Mere notice of these facts is not enough to put the taker on notice of the breach of fiduciary duty and does not give rise to any duty of investigation by the taker.

3. Subsection (b)(2) applies to instruments payable to the represented person or the fiduciary as such. For example, a check payable to Corporation is indorsed in the name of Corporation by Doe as its President. Doe gives the check to Bank as partial repayment of a personal loan that Bank had made to Doe. The check was indorsed either in blank or to Bank. Bank collects the check and applies the proceeds to reduce the amount owed on Doe's loan. If the person acting for Bank in the transaction knows that Doe is a fiduciary and that the check is being used to pay a personal obligation of Doe, subsection (b)(2) applies. If Corporation has a claim to the proceeds of the check because the use of the check by Doe was a breach of fiduciary duty, Bank has notice of the claim and did not take the check as a holder in due course. The same result follows if Doe had indorsed the check to himself before giving it to Bank. Subsection (b)(2) follows Uniform Fiduciaries Act § 4 in providing that if the instrument is payable to the fiduciary, as such, or to the represented person, the taker has notice of a claim if the instrument is negotiated for the fiduciary's personal debt. If fiduciary funds are deposited to a personal account of the fiduciary or to an account that is not an account of the represented person or of the fiduciary, as such, there is a split of authority concerning whether the bank is on notice of a breach of fiduciary duty. Subsection (b)(2)(iii) states that the bank is given notice of breach of fiduciary duty because of the deposit. The Uniform Fiduciaries Act § 9 states that the bank is not on notice unless it has knowledge of facts that makes its receipt of the deposit an act of bad faith.

The rationale of subsection (b)(2) is that it is not normal for an instrument payable to the represented person or the fiduciary, as such, to be used for the personal benefit of the fiduciary. It is likely that such use reflects an unlawful use of the proceeds of the instrument. If the fiduciary is entitled to compensation from the represented person for services rendered or for expenses incurred by the fiduciary the normal mode of payment is by a check drawn on the fiduciary account to the order of the fiduciary.

4. Subsection (b)(3) is based on Uniform Fiduciaries Act § 6 and applies when the instrument is drawn by the represented person or the fiduciary as such to the fiduciary personally. The term "personally" is used as it is used in the Uniform Fiduciaries Act to mean that the instrument is payable to the payee as an individual and not as a fiduciary. For example, Doe as President of Corporation writes a check on Corporation's account to the order of Doe personally. The check is then indorsed over to Bank as in Comment 3. In this case there is no notice of breach of fiduciary duty because there is nothing unusual about the transaction. Corporation may have owed Doe money for salary, reimbursement for expenses incurred for the benefit of Corporation, or for any other reason. If Doe is authorized to write checks on behalf of Corporation to pay debts of Corporation, the check is a normal way of paying a debt owed to Doe. Bank may assume that Doe may use the instrument for his personal benefit.

5. Subsection (b)(4) can be illustrated by a hypothetical case. Corporation draws a check payable to an organization. X, an officer or employee of Corporation, delivers the check to a person acting for the organization. The person signing the check on behalf of Corporation is X or another person. If the person acting for the organization in the transaction knows that X is a fiduciary, the organization is on notice of a claim by Corporation if it takes the instrument under the same circumstances stated in subsection (b)(2). If the organization is a bank and the check is taken in repayment of a personal loan of the bank to X, the case is like the case discussed in Comment 3. It is unusual for Corporation, the represented person, to pay a personal debt of Doe by issuing a check to the bank. It is more likely that the use of the check by Doe reflects an unlawful use of the proceeds of the check. The same analysis applies if the check is made payable to an organization in payment of goods or services. If the person acting for the organization knew of the fiduciary status of X and that the goods or services were for X's personal benefit, the organization is on notice of a claim by Corporation to the proceeds of the check. See the discussion in the last paragraph of Comment 2.

§ 3.308. Proof of Signatures and Status as Holder in Due Course

(a) In an action with respect to an instrument, the authenticity of, and authority to make, each signature on the instrument are admitted unless specifically denied in the pleadings. If the validity of a signature is denied in the pleadings, the burden of establishing validity is on the person claiming validity, but the signature is presumed to be authentic and authorized unless the action is to enforce the liability of the purported signer and the signer is dead or incompetent at the time of trial of the issue of validity of the signature. If an action to enforce the instrument is brought against a person as the undisclosed principal of a person who signed the instrument as a party to the instrument, the plaintiff has the burden of establishing that the defendant is liable on the instrument as a represented person under Section 3.402(a).

(b) If the validity of signatures is admitted or proved and there is compliance with Subsection (a), a plaintiff producing the instrument is entitled to payment if the plaintiff proves entitlement to enforce the instrument under Section 3.301, unless the defendant proves a defense or claim in recoupment. If a defense or claim in recoupment is proved, the right to payment of the plaintiff is subject to the defense or claim, except to the extent the plaintiff proves that the plaintiff has rights of a holder in due course that are not subject to the defense or claim.

Added by Acts 1995, 74th Leg., ch. 921, § 1, eff. Jan. 1, 1996.

Uniform Commercial Code Comment

1. Section 3–308 is a modification of former Section 3–307. The first two sentences of subsection (a) are a restatement of former Section 3–307(1). The purpose of the requirement of a specific denial in the pleadings is to give the plaintiff notice of the defendant's claim of forgery or lack of authority as to the particular signature, and to afford the plaintiff an opportunity to investigate and obtain evidence. If local rules of pleading permit, the denial may be on information and belief, or it may be a denial of knowledge or information sufficient to form a belief. It need not be under oath unless the local statutes or rules require verification. In the absence of such specific denial the signature stands admitted, and is not in issue. Nothing in this section is intended, however, to prevent amendment of the pleading in a proper case.

The question of the burden of establishing the signature arises only when it has been put in issue by specific denial. "Burden of establishing" is defined in Section 1–201. The burden is on the party claiming under the signature, but the signature is presumed to be authentic and authorized except as stated in the second sentence of subsection (a). "Presumed" is defined in Section 1–201 and means that until some evidence is introduced which would support a finding that the signature is forged or unauthorized, the plaintiff is not required to prove that it is valid. The presumption rests upon the fact that in ordinary experience forged or unauthorized signatures are very uncommon, and normally any evidence is within the control of, or more accessible to, the defendant. The defendant is therefore required to make some sufficient showing of the grounds for the denial before the plaintiff is required to introduce evidence. The defendant's evidence need not be sufficient to require a directed verdict, but it must be enough to support the denial by permitting a finding in the defendant's favor. Until introduction of such evidence the presumption requires a finding for the plaintiff. Once such evidence is introduced the burden of establishing the signature by a preponderance of the total evidence is on the plaintiff. The presumption does not arise if the action is to enforce the obligation of a purported signer who has died or become incompetent before the evidence is required, and so is disabled from obtaining or introducing it. "Action" is defined in Section 1–201 and includes a claim asserted against the estate of a deceased or an incompetent.

The last sentence of subsection (a) is a new provision that is necessary to take into account Section 3–402(a) that allows an undisclosed principal to be liable on an instrument signed by an authorized representative. In that case the person enforcing the instrument must prove that the undisclosed principal is liable.

2. Subsection (b) restates former Section 3–307(2) and (3). Once signatures are proved or admitted a holder, by mere production of the instrument, proves "entitlement to enforce the instrument" because under Section 3–301 a holder is a person entitled to enforce the instrument. Any other person in possession of an instrument may recover only if that person has the rights of a holder. Section 3–301. That person must prove a transfer giving that person such rights under Section 3–203(b) or that such rights were obtained by subrogation or succession.

If a plaintiff producing the instrument proves entitlement to enforce the instrument, either as a holder or a person with rights of a holder, the plaintiff is entitled to recovery unless the defendant proves a defense or claim in recoupment. Until proof of a defense or claim in recoupment is made, the issue as to whether the plaintiff has rights of a holder in due course does not arise. In the absence of a defense or claim in recoupment, any person entitled to enforce the instrument is entitled to recover. If a defense or claim in recoupment is proved, the plaintiff may seek to cut off the defense or claim in recoupment by proving that the plaintiff is a holder in due course or that the plaintiff has rights of a holder in due course under Section 3–203(b) or by subrogation or succession. All elements of Section 3–302(a) must be proved.

Nothing in this section is intended to say that the plaintiff must necessarily prove rights as a holder in due course. The plaintiff may elect to introduce no further evidence, in which case a verdict may be directed for the plaintiff or the defendant, or the issue of the defense or claim in recoupment may be left to the trier of fact, according to the weight and sufficiency of the defendant's evidence. The plaintiff may elect to rebut the defense or claim in recoupment by proof to the contrary, in which case a verdict may be directed for either party or the issue may be for the trier of fact. Subsection (b) means only that if the plaintiff claims the rights of a holder in due course against the defense or claim in recoupment, the plaintiff has the burden of proof on that issue.

State Bar Committee Comments

Section 3.308(a) specifies that a signature is presumed to be authentic and authorized unless the action was to enforce the liability of the purported signer and the signer is dead or incompetent "at the time of trial of the issue of validity of the signature." Section 3.308 is derived from former section 3.307, which stated this test in terms of "before proof is required" rather than at the time of trial. It was not the intent of the draftsmen of the *Official Text* to cause a change in this test by the revised wording. The test is not intended, for example, to apply differently with respect to a motion for summary judgment as opposed to an actual trial.

With respect to the meaning of the term "claim in recoupment," reference should be made to section 3.305.

§ 3.309. Enforcement of Lost, Destroyed, or Stolen Instrument

(a) A person who is not in possession of an instrument is entitled to enforce the instrument if:

(1) the person seeking to enforce the instrument:

(A) was entitled to enforce the instrument when loss of possession occurred; or

(B) has directly or indirectly acquired ownership of the instrument from a person who was entitled to enforce the instrument when loss of possession occurred;

(2) the loss of possession was not the result of a transfer by the person or a lawful seizure; and

(3) the person cannot reasonably obtain possession of the instrument because the instrument was destroyed, its whereabouts cannot be determined, or it is in the wrongful possession of an unknown person or a person that cannot be found or is not amenable to service of process.

(b) A person seeking enforcement of an instrument under Subsection (a) must prove the terms of the instrument and the person's right to enforce the instrument. If that proof is made, Section 3.308 applies to the case as if the person seeking enforcement had produced the instrument. The court may not enter judgment in favor of the person seeking enforcement unless it finds that the person required to pay the instrument is adequately protected against loss that might occur by reason of a claim by another person to enforce the instrument. Adequate protection may be provided by any reasonable means.

Added by Acts 1995, 74th Leg., ch. 921, § 1, eff. Jan. 1, 1996. Amended by Acts 2005, 79th Leg., ch. 95, § 6, eff. Sept. 1, 2005.

Uniform Commercial Code Comment

1. Section 3–309 is a modification of former Section 3–804. The rights stated are those of "a person entitled to enforce the instrument" at the time of loss rather than those of an "owner" as in former Section 3–804. Under subsection (b), judgment to enforce the instrument cannot be given unless the court finds that the defendant will be adequately protected against a claim to the instrument by a holder that may appear at some later time. The court is given discretion in determining how adequate protection is to be assured. Former Section 3–804 allowed the court to "require security indemnifying the defendant against loss." Under Section 3–309 adequate protection is a flexible concept. For example, there is substantial risk that a holder in due course may make a demand for payment if the instrument was payable to bearer when it was lost or stolen. On the other hand if the instrument was payable to the person who lost the instrument and that person did not indorse the instrument, no other person could be a holder of the instrument. In some cases there is risk of loss only if there is doubt about whether the facts alleged by the person who lost the instrument are true. Thus, the type of adequate protection that is reasonable in the circumstances may depend on the degree of certainty about the facts in the case.

2. Subsection (a) is intended to reject the result in Dennis Joslin Co. v. Robinson Broadcasting Corp., 977 F. Supp. 491 (D.D.C. 1997). A transferee of a lost instrument need prove only that its transferor was entitled to enforce, not that the transferee was in possession at the time the instrument was lost. The protections of subsection (a) should also be available when instruments are lost during transit, because whatever the precise status of ownership at the point of loss, either the sender or the receiver ordinarily would have been entitled to enforce the instrument during the course of transit. The amendments to subsection (a) are not intended to alter in any way the rules that apply to the preservation of checks in connection with truncation of any other expedited method of check collection or processing.

3. A security interest may attach to the right of a person not in possession of an instrument to enforce the instrument. Although the secured party may not be the owner of the instrument, the secured party may nevertheless be entitled to exercise its debtor's right to enforce the instrument by resorting to its collection rights under the circumstances described in Section 9–607. This section does not address whether the person required to pay the instrument owes any duty to a secured party that is not itself the owner of the instrument.

§ 3.310. Effect of Instrument on Obligation for Which Taken

(a) Unless otherwise agreed, if a certified check, cashier's check, or teller's check is taken for an obligation, the obligation is discharged to the same extent discharge would result if an amount of money equal to the amount of the instrument were taken in payment of the obligation. Discharge of the obligation does not affect any liability that the obligor may have as an indorser of the instrument.

(b) Unless otherwise agreed and except as provided in Subsection (a), if a note or an uncertified check is taken for an obligation, the obligation is suspended to the same extent the obligation would be discharged if an amount of money equal to the amount of the instrument were taken, and the following rules apply:

(1) In the case of an uncertified check, suspension of the obligation continues until dishonor of the check or until it is paid or certified. Payment or certification of the check results in discharge of the obligation to the extent of the amount of the check.

(2) In the case of a note, suspension of the obligation continues until dishonor of the note or until it is paid. Payment of the note results in discharge of the obligation to the extent of the payment.

(3) Except as provided in Subdivision (4), if the check or note is dishonored and the obligee of the obligation for which the instrument was taken is the person entitled to enforce the instrument, the obligee may enforce either the instrument or the obligation. In the case of an instrument of a third person that is negotiated to the obligee by the obligor, discharge of the obligor on the instrument also discharges the obligation.

(4) If the person entitled to enforce the instrument taken for an obligation is a person other than the obligee, the obligee may not enforce the obligation to the extent the obligation is suspended. If the obligee is the person entitled to enforce the instrument but no longer has possession of it because it was lost, stolen, or destroyed, the obligation may not be enforced to the extent of the amount payable on the instrument, and to that extent the obligee's rights against the obligor are limited to enforcement of the instrument.

(c) If an instrument other than one described in Subsection (a) or (b) is taken for an obligation, the effect is:

(1) that stated in Subsection (a) if the instrument is one for which a bank is liable as maker or acceptor; or

(2) that stated in Subsection (b) in any other case.

Added by Acts 1995, 74th Leg., ch. 921, § 1, eff. Jan. 1, 1996.

Uniform Commercial Code Comment

1. Section 3–310 is a modification of former Section 3–802. As a practical matter, application of former Section 3–802 was limited to cases in which a check or a note was given for an obligation. Subsections (a) and (b) of Section 3–310 are therefore stated in terms of checks and notes in the interests of clarity. Subsection (c) covers the rare cases in which some other instrument is given to pay an obligation.

2. Subsection (a) deals with the case in which a certified check, cashier's check or teller's check is given in payment of an obligation. In that case the obligation is discharged unless there is an agreement to the contrary. Subsection (a) drops the exception in former Section 3–802 for cases in which there is a right of recourse on the instrument against the obligor. Under former Section 3–802(1)(a) the obligation was not discharged if there was a right of recourse on the instrument against the obligor. Subsection (a) changes this result. The underlying obligation is discharged, but any right of recourse on the instrument is preserved.

3. Subsection (b) concerns cases in which an uncertified check or a note is taken for an obligation. The typical case is that in which a buyer pays for goods or services by giving the seller the buyer's personal check, or in which the buyer signs a note for the purchase price. Subsection (b) also applies to the uncommon cases in which a check or note of a third person is given in payment of the obligation. Subsection (b) preserves the rule under former Section 3–802(1)(b) that the buyer's obligation to pay the price is suspended, but subsection (b) spells out the effect more precisely. If the check or note is dishonored, the seller may sue on either the dishonored instrument or the contract of sale if the seller has possession of the instrument and is the person entitled to enforce it. If the right to enforce the instrument is held by somebody other than the seller, the seller can't enforce the right to payment of the price under the sales contract because that right is represented by the instrument which is enforceable by somebody else. Thus, if the seller sold the note or the check to a holder and has not reacquired it after dishonor, the only right that survives is the right to enforce the instrument. What that means is that even though the suspension of the obligation may end upon dishonor under paragraph (b)(1), the obligation is not revived in the circumstances described in paragraph (b)(4). *Amendments approved by the Permanent Editorial Board for Uniform Commercial Code November 2, 2002.*

The last sentence of subsection (b)(3) applies to cases in which an instrument of another person is indorsed over to the obligee in payment of the obligation. For example, Buyer delivers an uncertified personal check of X payable to the order of Buyer to Seller in payment of the price of goods. Buyer indorses the check over to Seller. Buyer is liable on the check as indorser. If Seller neglects to present the check for payment or to deposit it for collection within 30 days of the indorsement, Buyer's liability as indorser is discharged. Section 3–415(e). Under the last sentence of Section 3–310(b)(3) Buyer is also discharged on the obligation to pay for the goods.

4. There was uncertainty concerning the applicability of former Section 3–802 to the case in which the check given for the obligation was stolen from the payee, the payee's signature was forged, and the forger obtained payment. The last sentence of subsection (b)(4) addresses this issue. If the payor bank pays a holder, the drawer is discharged on the underlying obligation because the check was paid. Subsection (b)(1). If the payor bank pays a person not entitled to enforce the instrument, as in the hypothetical case, the suspension of the underlying obligation continues because the check has not been paid. Section 3–602(a). The payee's cause of action is against the depositary bank or payor bank in conversion under Section 3–420 or against the drawer under Section 3–309. In the latter case, the drawer's obligation under Section 3–414(b) is triggered by dishonor which occurs because the check is unpaid. Presentment for payment to the drawee is excused under Section 3–504(a)(i) and, under Section 3–502(e), dishonor occurs without presentment if the check is not paid. The payee cannot merely ignore the instrument and sue the drawer on the underlying contract. This would impose on the drawer the risk that the check when stolen was indorsed in blank or to bearer.

A similar analysis applies with respect to lost instruments that have not been paid. If a creditor takes a check of the debtor in payment of an obligation, the obligation is suspended under the introductory paragraph of subsection (b). If the creditor then loses the check, what are the creditor's rights? The creditor can request the debtor to issue a new check and in many cases, the debtor will issue a replacement check after stopping payment on the lost check. In that case both the debtor and creditor are protected. But the debtor is not obliged to issue a new check. If the debtor refuses to issue a replacement check, the last sentence of subsection (b)(4) applies. The creditor may not enforce the obligation of debtor for which the check was taken. The creditor may assert only rights on the check. The creditor can proceed under Section 3–309 to enforce the obligation of the debtor, as drawer, to pay the check.

5. Subsection (c) deals with rare cases in which other instruments are taken for obligations. If a bank is the obligor on the instrument, subsection (a) applies and the obligation is discharged. In any other case subsection (b) applies.

§ 3.311. Accord and Satisfaction by Use of Instrument

(a) Subsections (b)–(d) apply if a person against whom a claim is asserted proves that:

(1) that person in good faith tendered an instrument to the claimant as full satisfaction of the claim;

(2) the amount of the claim was unliquidated or subject to a bona fide dispute; and

(3) the claimant obtained payment of the instrument.

(b) Unless Subsection (c) applies, the claim is discharged if the person against whom the claim is asserted proves that the instrument or an accompanying written communication contained a conspicuous statement to the effect that the instrument was tendered as full satisfaction of the claim.

(c) Subject to Subsection (d), a claim is not discharged under Subsection (b) if either of the following applies:

(1) The claimant, if an organization, proves that:

(A) within a reasonable time before the tender, the claimant sent a conspicuous statement to the person against whom the claim is asserted that communications concerning disputed debts, including an instrument tendered as full satisfaction of a debt, are to be sent to a designated person, office, or place; and

(B) the instrument or accompanying communication was not received by that designated person, office, or place.

(2) The claimant, whether or not an organization, proves that within 90 days after payment of the instrument, the claimant tendered repayment of the amount of the instrument to the person against whom the claim is asserted. This subdivision does not apply if the claimant is an organization that sent a statement complying with Subdivision (1)(A).

(d) A claim is discharged if the person against whom the claim is asserted proves that within a reasonable time before collection of the instrument was initiated, the claimant, or an agent of the claimant having direct responsibility with respect to the disputed obligation, knew that the instrument was tendered in full satisfaction of the claim.

Added by Acts 1995, 74th Leg., ch. 921, § 1, eff. Jan. 1, 1996.

Uniform Commercial Code Comment

1. This section deals with an informal method of dispute resolution carried out by use of a negotiable instrument. In the typical case there is a dispute concerning the amount that is owed on a claim.

Case #1. The claim is for the price of goods or services sold to a consumer who asserts that he or she is not obliged to pay the full price for which the consumer was billed because of a defect or breach of warranty with respect to the goods or services.

Case #2. A claim is made on an insurance policy. The insurance company alleges that it is not liable under the policy for the amount of the claim.

In either case the person against whom the claim is asserted may attempt an accord and satisfaction of the disputed claim by tendering a check to the claimant for some amount less than the full amount claimed by the claimant. A statement will be included on the check or in a communication accompanying the check to the effect that the check is offered as full payment or full satisfaction of the claim. Frequently, there is also a statement to the effect that obtaining payment of the check is an agreement by the claimant to a settlement of the dispute for the amount tendered. Before enactment of revised Article 3, the case law was in conflict over the question of whether obtaining payment of the check had the effect of an agreement to the settlement proposed by the debtor. This issue was governed by a common law rule, but some courts hold that the common law was modified by former Section 1–207 which they interpreted as applying to full settlement checks.

2. Comment d. to Restatement of Contracts, Section 281 discusses the full satisfaction check and the applicable common law rule. In a case like Case #1, the buyer can propose a settlement of the disputed bill by a clear notation on the check indicating that the check is tendered as full satisfaction of the bill. Under the common law rule the seller, by obtaining payment of the check accepts the offer of compromise by the buyer. The result is the same if the seller adds a notation to the check indicating that the check is accepted under protest or in only partial satisfaction of the claim. Under the common law rule the seller can refuse the check or can accept it subject to the condition stated by the buyer, but the seller can't accept the check and refuse to be bound

by the condition. The rule applies only to an unliquidated claim or a claim disputed in good faith by the buyer. The dispute in the courts was whether Section 1–207 changed the common law rule. The Restatement states that section "need not be read as changing this well-established rule."

3. As part of the revision of Article 3, Section 1–207 has been amended to add subsection (2) stating that Section 1–207 "does not apply to an accord and satisfaction." Because of that amendment and revised Article 3, Section 3–311 governs full satisfaction checks. Section 3–311 follows the common law rule with some minor variations to reflect modern business conditions. In cases covered by Section 3–311 there will often be an individual on one side of the dispute and a business organization on the other. This section is not designed to favor either the individual or the business organization. In Case #1 the person seeking the accord and satisfaction is an individual. In Case #2 the person seeking the accord and satisfaction is an insurance company. Section 3–311 is based on a belief that the common law rule produces a fair result and that informal dispute resolution by full satisfaction checks should be encouraged.

4. Subsection (a) states three requirements for application of Section 3–311. "Good faith" in subsection (a)(i) is defined in Section 3–103(a)(4) as not only honesty in fact, but the observance of reasonable commercial standards of fair dealing. The meaning of "fair dealing" will depend upon the facts in the particular case. For example, suppose an insurer tenders a check in settlement of a claim for personal injury in an accident clearly covered by the insurance policy. The claimant is necessitous and the amount of the check is very small in relationship to the extent of the injury and the amount recoverable under the policy. If the trier of fact determines that the insurer was taking unfair advantage of the claimant, an accord and satisfaction would not result from payment of the check because of the absence of good faith by the insurer in making the tender. Another example of lack of good faith is found in the practice of some business debtors in routinely printing full satisfaction language on their check stocks so that all or a large part of the debts of the debtor are paid by checks bearing the full satisfaction language, whether or not there is any dispute with the creditor. Under such a practice the claimant cannot be sure whether a tender in full satisfaction is or is not being made. Use of a check on which full satisfaction language was affixed routinely pursuant to such a business practice may prevent an accord and satisfaction on the ground that the check was not tendered in good faith under subsection (a)(i).

Section 3–311 does not apply to cases in which the debt is a liquidated amount and not subject to a bona fide dispute. Subsection (a)(ii). Other law applies to cases in which a debtor is seeking discharge of such a debt by paying less than the amount owed. For the purpose of subsection (a)(iii) obtaining acceptance of a check is considered to be obtaining payment of the check.

The person seeking the accord and satisfaction must prove that the requirements of subsection (a) are met. If that person also proves that the statement required by subsection (b) was given, the claim is discharged unless subsection (c) applies. Normally the statement required by subsection (b) is written on the check. Thus, the canceled check can be used to prove the statement as well as the fact that the claimant obtained payment of the check. Subsection (b) requires a "conspicuous" statement that the instrument was tendered in full satisfaction of the claim. "Conspicuous" is defined in Section 1–201(10). The statement is conspicuous if "it is so written that a reasonable person against whom it is to operate ought to have noticed it." If the claimant can reasonably be expected to examine the check, almost any statement on the check should be noticed and is therefore conspicuous. In cases in which the claimant is an individual the claimant will receive the check and will normally indorse it. Since the statement concerning tender in full satisfaction normally will appear above the space provided for the claimant's indorsement of the check, the claimant "ought to have noticed" the statement.

5. Subsection (c)(1) is a limitation on subsection (b) in cases in which the claimant is an organization. It is designed to protect the claimant against inadvertent accord and satisfaction. If the claimant is an organization payment of the check might be obtained without notice to the personnel of the organization concerned with the disputed claim. Some business organizations have claims against very large numbers of customers. Examples are department stores, public utilities and the like. These claims are normally paid by checks sent by customers to a designated office at which clerks employed by the claimant or a bank acting for the claimant process the checks and record the amounts paid. If the processing office is not designed to deal with communications extraneous to recording the amount of the check and the account number of the customer, payment of a full satisfaction check can easily be obtained without knowledge by the claimant of the existence of the full satisfaction statement. This is particularly true if the statement is written on the reverse side of the check in the area in which indorsements are usually written. Normally, the clerks of the claimant have no reason to look at the reverse side of checks. Indorsement by the claimant normally is done by mechanical means or there may be no indorsement at all. Section 4–205(a). Subsection (c)(1) allows the claimant to protect itself by advising customers by a conspicuous statement that communications regarding disputed debts must be sent to a particular person, office, or place. The statement must be given to the customer within a reasonable time before the tender is made. This requirement is designed to assure that the customer has reasonable notice that the full satisfaction check must be sent to a particular place. The reasonable time requirement could be satisfied by a notice on the billing statement sent to the customer. If the full satisfaction check is sent to the designated destination and the check is paid, the claim is discharged. If the claimant proves that the check was not received at the designated destination the claim is not discharged unless subsection (d) applies.

6. Subsection (c)(2) is also designed to prevent inadvertent accord and satisfaction. It can be used by a claimant other than an organization or by a claimant as an alternative to subsection (c)(1). Some organizations may be reluctant to use subsection (c)(1) because it may result in confusion of customers that causes checks to be routinely sent to the special designated person, office, or place. Thus, much of the benefit of rapid processing of checks may be lost. An organization that chooses not to send a notice complying with subsection (c)(1)(i) may prevent an inadvertent accord and

satisfaction by complying with subsection (c)(2). If the claimant discovers that it has obtained payment of a full satisfaction check, it may prevent an accord and satisfaction if, within 90 days of the payment of the check, the claimant tenders repayment of the amount of the check to the person against whom the claim is asserted.

7. Subsection (c) is subject to subsection (d). If a person against whom a claim is asserted proves that the claimant obtained payment of a check known to have been tendered in full satisfaction of the claim by "the claimant or an agent of the claimant having direct responsibility with respect to the disputed obligation," the claim is discharged even if (i) the check was not sent to the person, office, or place required by a notice complying with subsection (c)(1), or (ii) the claimant tendered repayment of the amount of the check in compliance with subsection (c)(2).

A claimant knows that a check was tendered in full satisfaction of a claim when the claimant "has actual knowledge" of that fact. Section 1–201(25). Under Section 1–201(27), if the claimant is an organization, it has knowledge that a check was tendered in full satisfaction of the claim when that fact is

> "brought to the attention of the individual conducting that transaction, and in any event when it would have been brought to his attention if the organization had exercised due diligence. An organization exercises due diligence if it maintains reasonable routines for communicating significant information to the person conducting the transaction and there is reasonable compliance with the routines. Due diligence does not require an individual acting for the organization to communicate information unless such communication is part of his regular duties or unless he has reason to know of the transaction and that the transaction would be materially affected by the information."

With respect to an attempted accord and satisfaction the "individual conducting that transaction" is an employee or other agent of the organization having direct responsibility with respect to the dispute. For example, if the check and communication are received by a collection agency acting for the claimant to collect the disputed claim, obtaining payment of the check will result in an accord and satisfaction even if the claimant gave notice, pursuant to subsection (c)(1), that full satisfaction checks be sent to some other office. Similarly, if a customer asserting a claim for breach of warranty with respect to defective goods purchased in a retail outlet of a large chain store delivers the full satisfaction check to the manager of the retail outlet at which the goods were purchased, obtaining payment of the check will also result in an accord and satisfaction. On the other hand, if the check is mailed to the chief executive officer of the chain store subsection (d) would probably not be satisfied. The chief executive officer of a large corporation may have general responsibility for operations of the company, but does not normally have direct responsibility for resolving a small disputed bill to a customer. A check for a relatively small amount mailed to a high executive officer of a large organization is not likely to receive the executive's personal attention. Rather, the check would normally be routinely sent to the appropriate office for deposit and credit to the customer's account. If the check does receive the personal attention of the high executive officer and the officer is aware of the full-satisfaction language, collection of the check will result in an accord and satisfaction because subsection (d) applies. In this case the officer has assumed direct responsibility with respect to the disputed transaction.

If a full satisfaction check is sent to a lock box or other office processing checks sent to the claimant, it is irrelevant whether the clerk processing the check did or did not see the statement that the check was tendered as full satisfaction of the claim. Knowledge of the clerk is not imputed to the organization because the clerk has no responsibility with respect to an accord and satisfaction. Moreover, there is no failure of "due diligence" under Section 1–201(27) if the claimant does not require its clerks to look for full satisfaction statements on checks or accompanying communications. Nor is there any duty of the claimant to assign that duty to its clerks. Section 3–311(c) is intended to allow a claimant to avoid an inadvertent accord and satisfaction by complying with either subsection (c)(1) or (2) without burdening the check-processing operation with extraneous and wasteful additional duties.

8. In some cases the disputed claim may have been assigned to a finance company or bank as part of a financing arrangement with respect to accounts receivable. If the account debtor was notified of the assignment, the claimant is the assignee of the account receivable and the "agent of the claimant" in subsection (d) refers to an agent of the assignee.

State Bar Committee Comments

The language of subsection (d) is unclear in that, on its face, it purports to provide a general rule for discharge of a claim. Subsection (d) should have read "Subsection (c) does not apply if the person against. . . ." Subsection (d) should be construed as though it were worded in this manner. A careful reading of section 3.311 and its Official Comment should lead to no other interpretation.

§ 3.312. Lost, Destroyed, or Stolen Cashier's Check, Teller's Check, or Certified Check

(a) In this section:

(1) "Check" means a cashier's check, teller's check, or certified check.

(2) "Claimant" means a person who claims the right to receive the amount of a cashier's check, teller's check, or certified check that was lost, destroyed, or stolen.

(3) "Declaration of loss" means a statement, made in a record under penalty of perjury, to the effect that:

(A) the declarer lost possession of a check;

(B) the declarer is the drawer or payee of the check, in the case of a certified check, or the remitter or payee of the check, in the case of a cashier's check or teller's check;

(C) the loss of possession was not the result of a transfer by the declarer or a lawful seizure; and

(D) the declarer cannot reasonably obtain possession of the check because the check was destroyed, its whereabouts cannot be determined, or it is in the wrongful possession of an unknown person or a person that cannot be found or is not amenable to service of process.

(4) "Obligated bank" means the issuer of a cashier's check or teller's check or the acceptor of a certified check.

(b) A claimant may assert a claim to the amount of a check by a communication to the obligated bank describing the check with reasonable certainty and requesting payment of the amount of the check, if (i) the claimant is the drawer or payee of a certified check or the remitter or payee of a cashier's check or teller's check, (ii) the communication contains or is accompanied by a declaration of loss of the claimant with respect to the check, (iii) the communication is received at a time and in a manner affording the bank a reasonable time to act on it before the check is paid, and (iv) the claimant provides reasonable identification if requested by the obligated bank. Delivery of a declaration of loss is a warranty of the truth of the statements made in the declaration. If a claim is asserted in compliance with this subsection, the following rules apply:

(1) The claim becomes enforceable at the later of (i) the time the claim is asserted, or (ii) the 90th day following the date of the check, in the case of a cashier's check or teller's check, or the 90th day following the date of the acceptance, in the case of a certified check.

(2) Until the claim becomes enforceable, it has no legal effect and the obligated bank may pay the check or, in the case of a teller's check, may permit the drawee to pay the check. Payment to a person entitled to enforce the check discharges all liability of the obligated bank with respect to the check.

(3) If the claim becomes enforceable before the check is presented for payment, the obligated bank is not obliged to pay the check.

(4) When the claim becomes enforceable, the obligated bank becomes obliged to pay the amount of the check to the claimant if payment of the check has not been made to a person entitled to enforce the check. Subject to Section 4.302(a)(1), payment to the claimant discharges all liability of the obligated bank with respect to the check.

(c) If the obligated bank pays the amount of a check to a claimant under Subsection (b)(4) and the check is presented for payment by a person having rights of a holder in due course, the claimant is obliged to:

(1) refund the payment to the obligated bank if the check is paid; or

(2) pay the amount of the check to the person having rights of a holder in due course if the check is dishonored.

(d) If a claimant has the right to assert a claim under Subsection (b) and is also a person who is entitled to enforce a cashier's check, teller's check, or certified check that is lost, destroyed, or stolen, the claimant may assert rights with respect to the check under either this section or Section 3.309.

Added by Acts 1995, 74th Leg., ch. 921, § 1, eff. Jan. 1, 1996. Amended by Acts 2005, 79th Leg., ch. 95, § 7, eff. Sept. 1, 2005.

Uniform Commercial Code Comment

1. This section applies to cases in which a cashier's check, teller's check, or certified check is lost, destroyed, or stolen. In one typical case a customer of a bank closes his or her account and takes a cashier's check or teller's check of the bank as payment of the amount of the account. The customer may be moving to a new area and the check is to be used to open a bank account in that area. In such a case the check will normally be payable to the customer. In another typical case a cashier's check or teller's check is bought from a bank for the purpose of paying some obligation of the buyer of the check. In such a case the check may be made payable to the customer and then negotiated to the creditor by indorsement. But often, the payee of the check is the creditor. In the latter case the customer is a remitter. The section covers loss of the check by either the remitter or the payee. The section also covers loss of a certified check by either the drawer or payee.

Under Section 3–309 a person seeking to enforce a lost, destroyed, or stolen cashier's check or teller's check may be required by the court to give adequate protection to the issuing bank against loss that might occur by reason of the claim by another person to enforce the check. This might require the posting of an expensive bond for the amount of the check. The purpose of Section 3–312 is to offer a person who loses such a check a means of getting refund of the amount of the check within a reasonable period of time without the expense of posting a bond and with full protection of the obligated bank.

2. A claim to the amount of a lost, destroyed, or stolen cashier's check, teller's check, or certified check may be made under subsection (b) if the following requirements of that subsection are met. First, a claim may be asserted only by the drawer or payee of a certified check or the remitter or payee of a cashier's check or teller's check. An indorsee of a check is not covered because the indorsee is not an original

party to the check or a remitter. Limitation to an original party or remitter gives the obligated bank the ability to determine, at the time it becomes obligated on the check, the identity of the person or persons who can assert a claim with respect to the check. The bank is not faced with having to determine the rights of some person who was not a party to the check at that time or with whom the bank had not dealt. If a cashier's check is issued to the order of the person who purchased it from the bank and that person indorses it over to a third person who loses the check, the third person may assert rights to enforce the check under Section 3–309 but has no rights under Section 3–312.

Second, the claim must be asserted by a communication to the obligated bank describing the check with reasonable certainty and requesting payment of the amount of the check. "Obligated bank" is defined in subsection (a)(4). Third, the communication must be received in time to allow the obligated bank to act on the claim before the check is paid, and the claimant must provide reasonable identification if requested. Subsections (b)(iii) and (iv). Fourth, the communication must contain or be accompanied by a declaration of loss described in subsection (b). This declaration is an affidavit or other writing made under penalty of perjury alleging the loss, destruction, or theft of the check and stating that the declarer is a person entitled to assert a claim, i.e. the drawer or payee of a certified check or the remitter or payee of a cashier's check or teller's check.

A claimant who delivers a declaration of loss makes a warranty of the truth of the statements made in the declaration. The warranty is made to the obligated bank and anybody who has a right to enforce the check. If the declaration of loss falsely alleges loss of a cashier's check that did not in fact occur, a holder of the check who was unable to obtain payment because subsection (b)(3) and (4) caused the obligated bank to dishonor the check would have a cause of action against the declarer for breach of warranty.

The obligated bank may not impose additional requirements on the claimant to assert a claim under subsection (b). For example, the obligated bank may not require the posting of a bond or other form of security. Section 3–312(b) states the procedure for asserting claims covered by the section. Thus, procedures that may be stated in other law for stating claims to property do not apply and are displaced within the meaning of Section 1–103.

3. A claim asserted under subsection (b) does not have any legal effect, however, until the date it becomes enforceable, which cannot be earlier than 90 days after the date of a cashier's check or teller's check or 90 days after the date of acceptance of a certified check. Thus, if a lost check is presented for payment within the 90–day period, the bank may pay a person entitled to enforce the check without regard to the claim and is discharged of all liability with respect to the check. This ensures the continued utility of cashier's checks, teller's checks, and certified checks as cash equivalents. Virtually all such checks are presented for payment within 90 days.

If the claim becomes enforceable and payment has not been made to a person entitled to enforce the check, the bank becomes obligated to pay the amount of the check to the claimant. Subsection (b)(4). When the bank becomes obligated to pay the amount of the check to the claimant, the bank is relieved of its obligation to pay the check. Subsection (b)(3). Thus, any person entitled to enforce the check, including even a holder in due course, loses the right to enforce the check after a claim under subsection (b) becomes enforceable.

If the obligated bank pays the claimant under subsection (b)(4), the bank is discharged of all liability with respect to the check. The only exception is the unlikely case in which the obligated bank subsequently incurs liability under Section 4–302(a)(1) with respect to the check. For example, Obligated Bank is the issuer of a cashier's check and, after a claim becomes enforceable, it pays the claimant under subsection (b)(4). Later the check is presented to Obligated Bank for payment over the counter. Under subsection (b)(3), Obligated Bank is not obliged to pay the check and may dishonor the check by returning it to the person who presented it for payment. But the normal rules of check collection are not affected by Section 3–312. If Obligated Bank retains the check beyond midnight of the day of presentment without settling for it, it becomes accountable for the amount of the check under Section 4–302(a)(1) even though it had no obligation to pay the check.

An obligated bank that pays the amount of a check to a claimant under subsection (b)(4) is discharged of all liability on the check so long as the assertion of the claim meets the requirements of subsection (b) discussed in Comment 2. This is important in cases of fraudulent declarations of loss. For example, if the claimant falsely alleges a loss that in fact did not occur, the bank, subject to Section 1–203, may rely on the declaration of loss. On the other hand, a claim may be asserted only by a person described in subsection (b)(i). Thus, the bank is discharged under subsection (a)(4) only if it pays such a person. Although it is highly unlikely, it is possible that more than one person could assert a claim under subsection (b) to the amount of a check. Such a case could occur if one of the claimants makes a false declaration of loss. The obligated bank is not required to determine whether a claimant who complies with subsection (b) is acting wrongfully. The bank may utilize procedures outside this Article, such as interpleader, under which the conflicting claims may be adjudicated.

Although it is unlikely that a lost check would be presented for payment after the claimant was paid by the bank under subsection (b)(4), it is possible for it to happen. Suppose the declaration of loss by the claimant fraudulently alleged a loss that in fact did not occur. If the claimant negotiated the check, presentment for payment would occur shortly after negotiation in almost all cases. Thus, a fraudulent declaration of loss is not likely to occur unless the check is negotiated after the 90–day period has already expired or shortly before expiration. In such a case the holder of the check, who may not have noticed the date of the check, is not entitled to payment from the obligated bank if the check is presented for payment after the claim becomes enforceable. Subsection (b)(3). The remedy of the holder who is denied payment in that case is an action against the claimant under subsection (c) if the holder is a holder in due course, or for breach of warranty under subsection (b). The holder would also have common law remedies against the claimant under the law of restitution or fraud.

4. The following cases illustrate the operation of Section 3–312:

Case # 1. Obligated Bank (OB) certified a check drawn by its customer, Drawer (D), payable to Payee (P). Two days after the check was certified, D lost the check and then asserted a claim pursuant to subsection (b). The check had not been presented for payment when D's claim became enforceable 90 days after the check was certified. Under subsection (b)(1), at the time D's claim became enforceable OB became obliged to pay D the amount of the check. If the check is later presented for payment, OB may refuse to pay the check and has no obligation to anyone to pay the check. Any obligation owed by D to P, for which the check was intended as payment, is unaffected because the check was never delivered to P.

Case # 2. Obligated Bank (OB) issued a teller's check to Remitter (R) payable to Payee (P). R delivered the check to P in payment of an obligation. P lost the check and then asserted a claim pursuant to subsection (b). To carry out P's order, OB issued an order pursuant to Section 4–403(a) to the drawee of the teller's check to stop payment of the check effective on the 90th day after the date of the teller's check. The check was not presented for payment. On the 90th day after the date of the teller's check P's claim becomes enforceable and OB becomes obliged to pay P the amount of the check. As in Case # 1, OB has no further liability with respect to the check to anyone. When R delivered the check to P, R's underlying obligation to P was discharged under Section 3–310. Thus, R suffered no loss. Since P received the amount of the check, P also suffered no loss except with respect to the delay in receiving the amount of the check.

Case # 3. Obligated Bank (OB) issued a cashier's check to its customer, Payee (P). Two days after issue, the check was stolen from P who then asserted a claim pursuant to subsection (b). Ten days after issue, the check was deposited by X in an account in Depositary Bank (DB). X had found the check and forged the indorsement of P. DB promptly presented the check to OB and obtained payment on behalf of X. On the 90th day after the date of the check P's claim becomes enforceable and P is entitled to receive the amount of the check from OB. Subsection (b)(4). Although the check was presented for payment before P's claim became enforceable, OB is not discharged. Because of the forged indorsement X was not a holder and neither was OB. Thus, neither is a person entitled to enforce the check (Section 3–301) and OB is not discharged under Section 3–602(a). Thus, under subsection (b)(4), because OB did not pay a person entitled to enforce the check, OB must pay P. OB's remedy is against DB for breach of warranty under Section 4–208(a)(1). As an alternative to the remedy under Section 3–312, P could recover from DB for conversion under Section 3–420(a).

Case # 4. Obligated Bank (OB) issued a cashier's check to its customer, Payee (P). P made an unrestricted blank indorsement of the check and mailed the check to P's bank for deposit to P's account. The check was never received by P's bank. When P discovered the loss, P asserted a claim pursuant to subsection (b). X found the check and deposited it in X's account in Depositary Bank (DB) after indorsing the check. DB presented the check for payment before the end of the 90–day period after its date. OB paid the check. Because of the unrestricted blank indorsement by P, X became a holder of the check. DB also became a holder. Since the check was paid before P's claim became enforceable and payment was made to a person entitled to enforce the check, OB is discharged of all liability with respect to the check. Subsection (b)(2). Thus, P is not entitled to payment from OB. Subsection (b)(4) doesn't apply.

Case # 5. Obligated Bank (OB) issued a cashier's check to its customer, Payee (P). P made an unrestricted blank indorsement of the check and mailed the check to P's bank for deposit to P's account. The check was never received by P's bank. When P discovered the loss, P asserted a claim pursuant to subsection (b). At the end of the 90–day period after the date of the check, OB paid the amount of the check to P under subsection (b)(4). X then found the check and deposited it to X's account in Depositary Bank (DB). DB presented the check to OB for payment. OB is not obliged to pay the check. Subsection (b)(4). If OB dishonors the check, DB's remedy is to charge back X's account. Section 4–214(a). Although P, as an indorser, would normally have liability to DB under Section 3–415(a) because the check was dishonored, P is released from that liability under Section 3–415(e) because collection of the check was initiated more than 30 days after the indorsement. DB has a remedy only against X. A depositary bank that takes a cashier's check that cannot be presented for payment before expiration of the 90–day period after its date is on notice that the check might not be paid because of the possibility of a claim asserted under subsection (b) which would excuse the issuer of the check from paying the check. Thus, the depositary bank cannot safely release funds with respect to the check until it has assurance that the check has been paid. DB cannot be a holder in due course of the check because it took the check when the check was overdue. Section 3–304(a)(2). Thus, DB has no action against P under subsection (c).

Case # 6. Obligated Bank (OB) issued a cashier's check payable to bearer and delivered it to its customer, Remitter (R). R held the check for 90 days and then wrongfully asserted a claim to the amount of the check under subsection (b). The declaration of loss fraudulently stated that the check was lost. R received payment from OB under subsection (b)(4). R then negotiated the check to X for value. X presented the check to OB for payment. Although OB, under subsection (b)(2), was not obliged to pay the check, OB paid X by mistake. OB's teller did not notice that the check was more than 90 days old and was not aware that OB was not obliged to pay the check. If X took the check in good faith, OB may not recover from X. Section 3–418(c). OB's remedy is to recover from R for fraud or for breach of warranty in making a false declaration of loss. Subsection (b).

SUBCHAPTER D. LIABILITY OF PARTIES

§ 3.401. Signature

(a) A person is not liable on an instrument unless the person:

(1) signed the instrument; or

(2) is represented by an agent or representative who signed the instrument and the signature is binding on the represented person under Section 3.402.

(b) A signature may be made (i) manually or by means of a device or machine, and (ii) by the use of any name, including a trade or assumed name, or by a word, mark, or symbol executed or adopted by a person with present intention to authenticate a writing.

Amended by Acts 1995, 74th Leg., ch. 921, § 1, eff. Jan. 1, 1996.

Uniform Commercial Code Comment

1. Obligation on an instrument depends on a signature that is binding on the obligor. The signature may be made by the obligor personally or by an agent authorized to act for the obligor. Signature by agents is covered by Section 3–402. It is not necessary that the name of the obligor appear on the instrument, so long as there is a signature that binds the obligor. Signature includes an indorsement.

2. A signature may be handwritten, typed, printed or made in any other manner. It need not be subscribed, and may appear in the body of the instrument, as in the case of "I, John Doe, promise to pay * * *" without any other signature. It may be made by mark, or even by thumbprint. It may be made in any name, including any trade name or assumed name, however false and fictitious, which is adopted for the purpose. Parol evidence is admissible to identify the signer, and when the signer is identified the signature is effective. Indorsement in a name other than that of the indorser is governed by Section 3–204(d).

This section is not intended to affect any other law requiring a signature by mark to be witnessed, or any signature to be otherwise authenticated, or requiring any form of proof.

§ 3.402. Signature by Representative

(a) If a person acting, or purporting to act, as a representative signs an instrument by signing either the name of the represented person or the name of the signer, the represented person is bound by the signature to the same extent the represented person would be bound if the signature were on a simple contract. If the represented person is bound, the signature of the representative is the "authorized signature of the represented person" and the represented person is liable on the instrument, whether or not identified in the instrument.

(b) If a representative signs the name of the representative to an instrument and the signature is an authorized signature of the represented person, the following rules apply:

(1) If the form of the signature shows unambiguously that the signature is made on behalf of the represented person who is identified in the instrument, the representative is not liable on the instrument.

(2) Subject to Subsection (c), the representative is liable on the instrument to a holder in due course that took the instrument without notice that the representative was not intended to be liable on the instrument if (i) the form of the signature does not show unambiguously that the signature is made in a representative capacity, or (ii) the represented person is not identified in the instrument. With respect to any other person, the representative is liable on the instrument unless the representative proves that the original parties did not intend the representative to be liable on the instrument.

(c) If a representative signs the name of the representative as drawer of a check without indication of the representative status and the check is payable from an account of the represented person who is identified on the check, the signer is not liable on the check if the signature is an authorized signature of the represented person.

Amended by Acts 1995, 74th Leg., ch. 921, § 1, eff. Jan. 1, 1996.

Uniform Commercial Code Comment

1. Subsection (a) states when the represented person is bound on an instrument if the instrument is signed by a representative. If under the law of agency the represented person would be bound by the act of the representative in signing either the name of the represented person or that of the representative, the signature is the authorized signature of the represented person. Former Section 3–401(1) stated that "no person is liable on an instrument unless his signature appears thereon." This was interpreted as meaning that an undisclosed principal is not liable on an instrument. This interpretation provided an exception to ordinary agency law that binds an undisclosed principal on a simple contract.

It is questionable whether this exception was justified by the language of former Article 3 and there is no apparent policy justification for it. The exception is rejected by subsection (a) which returns to ordinary rules of agency. If P, the principal, authorized A, the agent, to borrow money on P's behalf and A signed A's name to a note without disclosing that the signature was on behalf of P, A is liable on the instrument. But if the person entitled to enforce the note can also prove that P authorized A to sign on P's behalf, why shouldn't P also be liable on the instrument? To recognize the liability of P takes nothing away from the utility of negotiable instruments. Furthermore, imposing liability on P has the merit of making it impossible to have an instrument on which nobody is liable even though it was authorized by P. That result could occur under former Section 3–401(1) if an authorized agent signed "as agent" but the note did not identify the principal. If the dispute was between the agent and the payee of the note, the agent could escape liability on the note by proving that the agent and the payee did not intend that the agent be liable on the note when the note was issued. Former Section 3–403(2)(b). Under the prevailing interpretation of former Section 3–401(1), the principal was not liable on the note under former Section 3–401(1) because the principal's name did not appear on the note. Thus, nobody was liable on the note even though all parties knew that the note was signed by the agent on behalf of the principal. Under Section 3–402(a) the principal would be liable on the note.

2. Subsection (b) concerns the question of when an agent who signs an instrument on behalf of a principal is bound on the instrument. The approach followed by former Section 3–403 was to specify the form of signature that imposed or avoided liability. This approach was unsatisfactory. There are many ways in which there can be ambiguity about a signature. It is better to state a general rule. Subsection (b)(1) states that if the form of the signature unambiguously shows that it is made on behalf of an identified represented person (for example, "P, by A, Treasurer") the agent is not liable. This is a workable standard for a court to apply. Subsection (b)(2) partly changes former Section 3–403(2). Subsection (b)(2) relates to cases in which the agent signs on behalf of a principal but the form of the signature does not fall within subsection (b)(1). The following cases are illustrative. In each case John Doe is the authorized agent of Richard Roe and John Doe signs a note on behalf of Richard Roe. In each case the intention of the original parties to the instrument is that Roe is to be liable on the instrument but Doe is not to be liable.

Case #1. Doe signs "John Doe" without indicating in the note that Doe is signing as agent. The note does not identify Richard Roe as the represented person.

Case #2. Doe signs "John Doe, Agent" but the note does not identify Richard Roe as the represented person.

Case #3. The name "Richard Roe" is written on the note and immediately below that name Doe signs "John Doe" without indicating that Doe signed as agent.

In each case Doe is liable on the instrument to a holder in due course without notice that Doe was not intended to be liable. In none of the cases does Doe's signature unambiguously show that Doe was signing as agent for an identified principal. A holder in due course should be able to resolve any ambiguity against Doe.

But the situation is different if a holder in due course is not involved. In each case Roe is liable on the note. Subsection (a). If the original parties to the note did not intend that Doe also be liable, imposing liability on Doe is a windfall to the person enforcing the note. Under subsection (b)(2) Doe is prima facie liable because his signature appears on the note and the form of the signature does not unambiguously refute personal liability. But Doe can escape liability by proving that the original parties did not intend that he be liable on the note. This is a change from former Section 3–403(2)(a).

A number of cases under former Article 3 involved situations in which an agent signed the agent's name to a note, without qualification and without naming the person represented, intending to bind the principal but not the agent. The agent attempted to prove that the other party had the same intention. Some of these cases involved mistake, and in some there was evidence that the agent may have been deceived into signing in that manner. In some of the cases the court refused to allow proof of the intention of the parties and imposed liability on the agent based on former Section 3–403(2)(a) even though both parties to the instrument may have intended that the agent not be liable. Subsection (b)(2) changes the result of those cases, and is consistent with Section 3–117 which allows oral or written agreements to modify or nullify apparent obligations on the instrument.

Former Section 3–403 spoke of the represented person being "named" in the instrument. Section 3–402 speaks of the represented person being "identified" in the instrument. This change in terminology is intended to reject decisions under former Section 3–403(2) requiring that the instrument state the legal name of the represented person.

3. Subsection (c) is directed at the check cases. It states that if the check identifies the represented person the agent who signs on the signature line does not have to indicate agency status. Virtually all checks used today are in personalized form which identify the person on whose account the check is drawn. In this case, nobody is deceived into thinking that the person signing the check is meant to be liable. This subsection is meant to overrule cases decided under former Article 3 such as Griffin v. Ellinger, 538 S.W.2d 97 (Texas 1976).

§ 3.403. Unauthorized Signature

(a) Unless otherwise provided in this chapter or Chapter 4, an unauthorized signature is ineffective except as the signature of the unauthorized signer in favor of a person who in good faith pays the instrument or takes it for value. An unauthorized signature may be ratified for all purposes of this chapter.

(b) If the signature of more than one person is required to constitute the authorized signature of an organization, the signature of the organization is unauthorized if one of the required signatures is lacking.

(c) The civil or criminal liability of a person who makes an unauthorized signature is not affected by any provision of this chapter that makes the unauthorized signature effective for the purposes of this chapter.

Amended by Acts 1995, 74th Leg., ch. 921, § 1, eff. Jan. 1, 1996.

Uniform Commercial Code Comment

1. "Unauthorized" signature is defined in Section 1–201(43) as one that includes a forgery as well as a signature made by one exceeding actual or apparent authority. Former Section 3–404(1) stated that an unauthorized signature was inoperative as the signature of the person whose name was signed unless that person "is precluded from

denying it." Under former Section 3–406 if negligence by the person whose name was signed contributed to an unauthorized signature, that person "is precluded from asserting the * * * lack of authority." Both of these sections were applied to cases in which a forged signature appeared on an instrument and the person asserting rights on the instrument alleged that the negligence of the purported signer contributed to the forgery. Since the standards for liability between the two sections differ, the overlap between the sections caused confusion. Section 3–403(a) deals with the problem by removing the preclusion language that appeared in former Section 3–404.

2. The except clause of the first sentence of subsection (a) states the generally accepted rule that the unauthorized signature, while it is wholly inoperative as that of the person whose name is signed, is effective to impose liability upon the signer or to transfer any rights that the signer may have in the instrument. The signer's liability is not in damages for breach of warranty of authority, but is full liability on the instrument in the capacity in which the signer signed. It is, however, limited to parties who take or pay the instrument in good faith; and one who knows that the signature is unauthorized cannot recover from the signer on the instrument.

3. The last sentence of subsection (a) allows an unauthorized signature to be ratified. Ratification is a retroactive adoption of the unauthorized signature by the person whose name is signed and may be found from conduct as well as from express statements. For example, it may be found from the retention of benefits received in the transaction with knowledge of the unauthorized signature. Although the forger is not an agent, ratification is governed by the rules and principles applicable to ratification of unauthorized acts of an agent.

Ratification is effective for all purposes of this Article. The unauthorized signature becomes valid so far as its effect as a signature is concerned. Although the ratification may relieve the signer of liability on the instrument, it does not of itself relieve the signer of liability to the person whose name is signed. It does not in any way affect the criminal law. No policy of the criminal law prevents a person whose name is forged to assume liability to others on the instrument by ratifying the forgery, but the ratification cannot affect the rights of the state. While the ratification may be taken into account with other relevant facts in determining punishment, it does not relieve the signer of criminal liability.

4. Subsection (b) clarifies the meaning of "unauthorized" in cases in which an instrument contains less than all of the signatures that are required as authority to pay a check. Judicial authority was split on the issue whether the one-year notice period under former Section 4–406(4) (now Section 4–406(f)) barred a customer's suit against a payor bank that paid a check containing less than all of the signatures required by the customer to authorize payment of the check. Some cases took the view that if a customer required that a check contain the signatures of both A and B to authorize payment and only A signed, there was no unauthorized signature within the meaning of that term in former Section 4–406(4) because A's signature was neither unauthorized nor forged. The other cases correctly pointed out that it was the customer's signature at issue and not that of A; hence, the customer's signature was unauthorized if all signatures required to authorize payment of the check were not on the check. Subsection (b) follows the latter line of cases. The same analysis applies if A forged the signature of B. Because the forgery is not effective as a signature of B, the required signature of B is lacking.

Subsection (b) refers to "the authorized signature of an organization." The definition of "organization" in Section 1–201(28) is very broad. It covers not only commercial entities but also "two or more persons having a joint or common interest." Hence subsection (b) would apply when a husband and wife are both required to sign an instrument.

§ 3.404. Impostors; Fictitious Payees

(a) If an impostor, by use of the mails or otherwise, induces the issuer of an instrument to issue the instrument to the impostor, or to a person acting in concert with the impostor, by impersonating the payee of the instrument or a person authorized to act for the payee, an indorsement of the instrument by any person in the name of the payee is effective as the indorsement of the payee in favor of a person who, in good faith, pays the instrument or takes it for value or for collection.

(b) If (i) a person whose intent determines to whom an instrument is payable (Section 3.110(a) or (b)) does not intend the person identified as payee to have any interest in the instrument, or (ii) the person identified as payee of an instrument is a fictitious person, the following rules apply until the instrument is negotiated by special indorsement:

(1) Any person in possession of the instrument is its holder.

(2) An indorsement by any person in the name of the payee stated in the instrument is effective as the indorsement of the payee in favor of a person who, in good faith, pays the instrument or takes it for value or for collection.

(c) Under Subsection (a) or (b), an indorsement is made in the name of a payee if:

(1) it is made in a name substantially similar to that of the payee; or

(2) the instrument, whether or not indorsed, is deposited in a depositary bank to an account in a name substantially similar to that of the payee.

(d) With respect to an instrument to which Subsection (a) or (b) applies, if a person paying the instrument or taking it for value or for collection fails to exercise ordinary care in paying or taking the instrument and that failure contributes to loss resulting from payment of the instrument, the person bearing the loss may recover from the person failing to exercise ordinary care to the extent the failure to exercise ordinary care contributed to the loss.

Amended by Acts 1995, 74th Leg., ch. 921, § 1, eff. Jan. 1, 1996.

Uniform Commercial Code Comment

1. Under former Article 3, the impostor cases were governed by former Section 3–405(1)(a) and the fictitious payee cases were governed by Section 3–405(1)(b). Section 3–404 replaces former Section 3–405(1)(a) and (b) and modifies the previous law in some respects. Former Section 3–405 was read by some courts to require that the indorsement be in the exact name of the named payee. Revised Article 3 rejects this result. Section 3–404(c) requires only that the indorsement be made in a name "substantially similar" to that of the payee. Subsection (c) also recognizes the fact that checks may be deposited without indorsement. Section 4–205(a).

Subsection (a) changes the former law in a case in which the impostor is impersonating an agent. Under former Section 3–405(1)(a), if Impostor impersonated Smith and induced the drawer to draw a check to the order of Smith, Impostor could negotiate the check. If Impostor impersonated Smith, the president of Smith Corporation, and the check was payable to the order of Smith Corporation, the section did not apply. See the last paragraph of Comment 2 to former Section 3–405. In revised Article 3, Section 3–404(a) gives Impostor the power to negotiate the check in both cases.

2. Subsection (b) is based in part on former Section 3–405(1)(b) and in part on N.I.L. § 9(3). It covers cases in which an instrument is payable to a fictitious or nonexisting person and to cases in which the payee is a real person but the drawer or maker does not intend the payee to have any interest in the instrument. Subsection (b) applies to any instrument, but its primary importance is with respect to checks of corporations and other organizations. It also applies to forged check cases. The following cases illustrate subsection (b):

Case #1. Treasurer is authorized to draw checks in behalf of Corporation. Treasurer fraudulently draws a check of Corporation payable to Supplier Co., a nonexistent company. Subsection (b) applies because Supplier Co. is a fictitious person and because Treasurer did not intend Supplier Co. to have any interest in the check. Under subsection (b)(1) Treasurer, as the person in possession of the check, becomes the holder of the check. Treasurer indorses the check in the name "Supplier Co." and deposits it in Depositary Bank. Under subsection (b)(2) and (c)(i), the indorsement is effective to make Depositary Bank the holder and therefore a person entitled to enforce the instrument. Section 3–301.

Case #2. Same facts as Case #1 except that Supplier Co. is an actual company that does business with Corporation. If Treasurer intended to steal the check when the check was drawn, the result in Case #2 is the same as the result in Case #1. Subsection (b) applies because Treasurer did not intend Supplier Co. to have any interest in the check. It does not make any difference whether Supplier Co. was or was not a creditor of Corporation when the check was drawn. If Treasurer did not decide to steal the check until after the check was drawn, the case is covered by Section 3–405 rather than Section 3–404(b), but the result is the same. See Case #6 in Comment 3 to Section 3–405.

Case #3. Checks of Corporation must be signed by two officers. President and Treasurer both sign a check of Corporation payable to Supplier Co., a company that does business with Corporation from time to time but to which Corporation does not owe any money. Treasurer knows that no money is owed to Supplier Co. and does not intend that Supplier Co. have any interest in the check. President believes that money is owed to Supplier Co. Treasurer obtains possession of the check after it is signed. Subsection (b) applies because Treasurer is "a person whose intent determines to whom an instrument is payable" and Treasurer does not intend Supplier Co. to have any interest in the check. Treasurer becomes the holder of the check and may negotiate it by indorsing it in the name "Supplier Co."

Case #4. Checks of Corporation are signed by a check-writing machine. Names of payees of checks produced by the machine are determined by information entered into the computer that operates the machine. Thief, a person who is not an employee or other agent of Corporation, obtains access to the computer and causes the check-writing machine to produce a check payable to Supplier Co., a non-existent company. Subsection (b)(ii) applies. Thief then obtains possession of the check. At that point Thief becomes the holder of the check because Thief is the person in possession of the instrument. Subsection (b)(1). Under Section 3–301 Thief, as holder, is the "person entitled to enforce the instrument" even though Thief does not have title to the check and is in wrongful possession of it. Thief indorses the check in the name "Supplier Co." and deposits it in an account in Depositary Bank which Thief opened in the name "Supplier Co." Depositary Bank takes the check in good faith and credits the "Supplier Co." account. Under subsection (b)(2) and (c)(i), the indorsement is effective. Depositary Bank becomes the holder and the person entitled to enforce the check. The check is presented to the drawee bank for payment and payment is made. Thief then withdraws the credit to the account. Although the check was issued without authority given by Corporation, the drawee bank is entitled to pay the check and charge Corporation's account if there was an agreement with Corporation allowing the bank to debit Corporation's account for payment of checks produced by the check-writing machine whether or not authorized. The indorsement is also effective if Supplier Co. is a real person. In that case subsection (b)(i) applies. Under Section 3–110(b) Thief is the person whose intent determines to whom the check is payable, and Thief did not intend Supplier Co. to have any interest in the check. When the drawee bank pays the check, there is no breach of warranty under Section 3–417(a)(1) or 4–208(a)(1) because Depositary Bank was a person entitled to enforce the check when it was forwarded for payment.

Case #5. Thief, who is not an employee or agent of Corporation, steals check forms of Corporation. John Doe is president of Corporation and is authorized to sign checks on behalf of Corporation as drawer. Thief draws a check in the name of Corporation as drawer by forging the signature of Doe. Thief makes the check payable to the order of Supplier Co. with the intention of stealing it. Whether Supplier Co. is a fictitious person or a real person, Thief becomes the holder of the check and the person entitled to enforce it. The analysis is the same as that in Case #4. Thief deposits the check in an account in Depositary Bank which Thief opened in the name "Supplier Co." Thief either indorses the check in a name other than "Supplier Co." or does not indorse the check at all. Under Section 4–205(a) a depositary bank may become holder of a check deposited to the account of a customer if the customer was a holder, whether or not the customer indorses. Subsection (c)(ii) treats deposit to an account in a name substantially similar to that of the payee as the equivalent of indorsement in the name of the payee. Thus, the deposit is an effective indorsement of the check. Depositary Bank becomes the holder of the check and the person entitled to enforce the check. If the check is paid by the drawee bank, there is no breach of warranty under Section 3–417(a)(1) or 4–208(a)(1) because Depositary Bank was a person entitled to enforce the check when it was forwarded for payment and, unless Depositary Bank knew about the forgery of Doe's signature, there is no breach of warranty under Section 3–417(a)(3) or 4–208(a)(3). Because the check was a forged check the drawee bank is not entitled to charge Corporation's account unless Section 3–406 or Section 4–406 applies.

3. In cases governed by subsection (a) the dispute will normally be between the drawer of the check that was obtained by the impostor and the drawee bank that paid it. The drawer is precluded from obtaining recredit of the drawer's account by arguing that the check was paid on a forged indorsement so long as the drawee bank acted in good faith in paying the check. Cases governed by subsection (b) are illustrated by Cases #1 through #5 in Comment 2. In Cases #1, #2, and #3 there is no forgery of the check, thus the drawer of the check takes the loss if there is no lack of good faith by the banks involved. Cases #4 and #5 are forged check cases. Depositary Bank is entitled to retain the proceeds of the check if it didn't know about the forgery. Under Section 3–418 the drawee bank is not entitled to recover from Depositary Bank on the basis of payment by mistake because Depositary Bank took the check in good faith and gave value for the check when the credit given for the check was withdrawn. And there is no breach of warranty under Section 3–417(a)(1) or (3) or 4–208(a)(1) or (3). Unless Section 3–406 applies the loss is taken by the drawee bank if a forged check is paid, and that is the result in Case #5. In Case #4 the loss is taken by Corporation, the drawer, because an agreement between Corporation and the drawee bank allowed the bank to debit Corporation's account despite the unauthorized use of the check-writing machine.

If a check payable to an impostor, fictitious payee, or payee not intended to have an interest in the check is paid, the effect of subsections (a) and (b) is to place the loss on the drawer of the check rather than on the drawee or the Depositary Bank that took the check for collection. Cases governed by subsection (a) always involve fraud, and fraud is almost always involved in cases governed by subsection (b). The drawer is in the best position to avoid the fraud and thus should take the loss. This is true in Case #1, Case #2, and Case #3. But in some cases the person taking the check might have detected the fraud and thus have prevented the loss by the exercise of ordinary care. In those cases, if that person failed to exercise ordinary care, it is reasonable that that person bear loss to the extent the failure contributed to the loss. Subsection (d) is intended to reach that result. It allows the person who suffers loss as a result of payment of the check to recover from the person who failed to exercise ordinary care. In Case #1, Case #2, and Case #3, the person suffering the loss is Corporation, the drawer of the check. In each case the most likely defendant is the depositary bank that took the check and failed to exercise ordinary care. In those cases, the drawer has a cause of action against the offending bank to recover a portion of the loss. The amount of loss to be allocated to each party is left to the trier of fact. Ordinary care is defined in Section 3–103(a)(7). An example of the type of conduct by a depositary bank that could give rise to recovery under subsection (d) is discussed in Comment 4 to Section 3–405. That comment addresses the last sentence of Section 3–405(b) which is similar to Section 3–404(d).

In Case #1, Case #2, and Case #3, there was no forgery of the drawer's signature. But cases involving checks payable to a fictitious payee or a payee not intended to have an interest in the check are often forged check cases as well. Examples are Case #4 and Case #5. Normally, the loss in forged check cases is on the drawee bank that paid the check. Case #5 is an example. In Case #4 the risk with respect to the forgery is shifted to the drawer because of the agreement between the drawer and the drawee bank. The doctrine that prevents a drawee bank from recovering payment with respect to a forged check if the payment was made to a person who took the check for value and in good faith is incorporated into Section 3–418 and Sections 3–417(a)(3) and 4–208(a)(3). This doctrine is based on the assumption that the depositary bank normally has no way of detecting the forgery because the drawer is not that bank's customer. On the other hand, the drawee bank, at least in some cases, may be able to detect the forgery by comparing the signature on the check with the specimen signature that the drawee has on file. But in some forged check cases the depositary bank is in a position to detect the fraud. Those cases typically involve a check payable to a fictitious payee or a payee not intended to have an interest in the check. Subsection (d) applies to those cases. If the depositary bank failed to exercise ordinary care and the failure substantially contributed to the loss, the drawer in Case #4 or the drawee bank in Case #5 has a cause of action against the depositary bank under subsection (d). Comment 4 to Section 3–405 can be used as a guide to the type of conduct that could give rise to recovery under Section 3–404(d).

State Bar Committee Comments

Subsection (d) has been revised from the *Official Text* to delete the word "substantially" located before the words "contributes to the loss resulting from payment of the instrument". Deletion of the word "substantially" eliminates an additional fact question of the degree of negligence for a trier of fact. A person contributing to the loss resulting from payment of the instrument by failing to exercise ordinary care in paying the instrument or taking it for value or for collection must pay the person bearing the loss to the extent his failure to exercise ordinary care contributed to the loss. The definition of "ordinary care" in section 3.103 has been expanded for banks to permit them not to examine each instrument in check processing. This change plus the retention of a "substantial contribution" standard would shift the balance of proof too far in favor of banks from a policy standpoint. As a consequence, in the interest of maintaining a more appropriate balance between banks and their customers, the deletion of the word "substantially" was made. This change conforms to a similar change made by the California legislature in adopting its version of UCC Articles 3 and 4.

§ 3.405. Employer's Responsibility for Fraudulent Indorsement by Employee

(a) In this section:

(1) "Employee" includes an independent contractor and employee of an independent contractor retained by the employer.

(2) "Fraudulent indorsement" means:

(A) in the case of an instrument payable to the employer, a forged indorsement purporting to be that of the employer; or

(B) in the case of an instrument with respect to which the employer is the issuer, a forged indorsement purporting to be that of the person identified as payee.

(3) "Responsibility" with respect to instruments means authority (i) to sign or indorse instruments on behalf of the employer, (ii) to process instruments received by the employer for bookkeeping purposes, for deposit to an account, or for other disposition, (iii) to prepare or process instruments for issue in the name of the employer, (iv) to supply information determining the names or addresses of payees of instruments to be issued in the name of the employer, (v) to control the disposition of instruments to be issued in the name of the employer, or (vi) to act otherwise with respect to instruments in a responsible capacity. "Responsibility" does not include authority that merely allows an employee to have access to instruments or blank or incomplete instrument forms that are being stored or transported or are part of incoming or outgoing mail, or similar access.

(b) For the purpose of determining the rights and liabilities of a person who, in good faith, pays an instrument or takes it for value or for collection, if an employer entrusted an employee with responsibility with respect to the instrument and the employee or a person acting in concert with the employee makes a fraudulent indorsement of the instrument, the indorsement is effective as the indorsement of the person to whom the instrument is payable if it is made in the name of that person. If the person paying the instrument or taking it for value or for collection fails to exercise ordinary care in paying or taking the instrument and that failure contributes to loss resulting from the fraud, the person bearing the loss may recover from the person failing to exercise ordinary care to the extent the failure to exercise ordinary care contributed to the loss.

(c) Under Subsection (b), an indorsement is made in the name of the person to whom an instrument is payable if:

(1) it is made in a name substantially similar to the name of that person; or

(2) the instrument, whether or not indorsed, is deposited in a depositary bank to an account in a name substantially similar to the name of that person.

Amended by Acts 1995, 74th Leg., ch. 921, § 1, eff. Jan. 1, 1996.

Uniform Commercial Code Comment

1. Section 3–405 is addressed to fraudulent indorsements made by an employee with respect to instruments with respect to which the employer has given responsibility to the employee. It covers two categories of fraudulent indorsements: indorsements made in the name of the employer to instruments payable to the employer and indorsements made in the name of payees of instruments issued by the employer. This section applies to instruments generally but normally the instrument will be a check. Section 3–405 adopts the principle that the risk of loss for fraudulent indorsements by employees who are entrusted with responsibility with respect to checks should fall on the employer rather than the bank that takes the check or pays it, if the bank was not negligent in the transaction. Section 3–405 is based on the belief that the employer is in a far better position to avoid the loss by care in choosing employees, in supervising them, and in adopting other measures to prevent forged indorsements on instruments payable to the employer or fraud in the issuance of instruments in the name of the employer. If the bank failed to exercise ordinary care, subsection (b) allows the employer to shift loss to the bank to the extent the bank's failure to exercise ordinary care contributed to the loss. "Ordinary care" is defined in Section 3–103(a)(9). The provision applies regardless of whether the employer is negligent.

The first category of cases governed by Section 3–405 are those involving indorsements made in the name of payees of instruments issued by the employer. In this category, Section 3–405 includes cases that were covered by former Section 3–405(1)(c). The scope of Section 3–405 in revised Article 3 is, however, somewhat wider. It covers some cases not covered by former Section 3–405(1)(c) in which the entrusted employee makes a forged indorsement to a check drawn by the employer. An example is Case #6 in Comment 3. Moreover, a larger group of employees is included in revised Section 3–405. The key provision is the definition of "responsibility" in subsection (a)(1) which identifies the kind of responsibility delegated to an employee which will cause the employer to take responsibility for the fraudulent acts of that employee. An employer can insure this risk by employee fidelity bonds.

The second category of cases governed by Section 3–405—fraudulent indorsements of the name of the employer to instruments payable to the employer—were covered in former Article 3 by Section 3–406. Under former Section 3–406, the employer took the loss only if negligence of the employer could be proved. Under revised Article 3, Section 3–406 need not be used with respect to forgeries of the employer's indorsement. Section 3–405 imposes the loss on the employer without proof of negligence.

2. With respect to cases governed by former Section 3–405(1)(c), Section 3–405 is more favorable to employers in one respect. The bank was entitled to the preclusion provided by former Section 3–405(1)(c) if it took the check in good faith. The fact that the bank acted negligently did not shift the loss to the bank so long as the bank acted in good faith. Under revised Section 3–405 the loss may be recovered from the bank to the extent the failure of the bank to exercise ordinary care contributed to the loss.

3. Section 3–404(b) and Section 3–405 both apply to cases of employee fraud. Section 3–404(b) is not limited to cases of employee fraud, but most of the cases to which it applies will be cases of employee fraud. The following cases illustrate the application of Section 3–405. In each case it is assumed that the bank that took the check acted in good faith and was not negligent.

Case #1. Janitor, an employee of Employer, steals a check for a very large amount payable to Employer after finding it on a desk in one of Employer's offices. Janitor forges Employer's indorsement on the check and obtains payment. Since Janitor was not entrusted with "responsibility" with respect to the check, Section 3–405 does not apply. Section 3–406 might apply to this case. The issue would be whether Employer was negligent in safeguarding the check. If not, Employer could assert that the indorsement was forged and bring an action for conversion against the depositary or payor bank under Section 3–420.

Case #2. X is Treasurer of Corporation and is authorized to write checks on behalf of Corporation by signing X's name as Treasurer. X draws a check in the name of Corporation and signs X's name as Treasurer. The check is made payable to X. X then indorses the check and obtains payment. Assume that Corporation did not owe any money to X and did not authorize X to write the check. Although the writing of the check was not authorized, Corporation is bound as drawer of the check because X had authority to sign checks on behalf of Corporation. This result follows from agency law and Section 3–402(a). Section 3–405 does not apply in this case because there is no forged indorsement. X was payee of the check so the indorsement is valid. Section 3–110(a).

Case #3. The duties of Employee, a bookkeeper, include posting the amounts of checks payable to Employer to the accounts of the drawers of the checks. Employee steals a check payable to Employer which was entrusted to Employee and forges Employer's indorsement. The check is deposited by Employee to an account in Depositary Bank which Employee opened in the same name as Employer, and the check is honored by the drawee bank. The indorsement is effective as Employer's indorsement because Employee's duties include processing checks for bookkeeping purposes. Thus, Employee is entrusted with "responsibility" with respect to the check. Neither Depositary Bank nor the drawee bank is liable to Employer for conversion of the check. The same result follows if Employee deposited the check in the account in Depositary Bank without indorsement. Section 4–205(a). Under subsection (c) deposit in a depositary bank in an account in a name substantially similar to that of Employer is the equivalent of an indorsement in the name of Employer.

Case #4. Employee's duties include stamping Employer's unrestricted blank indorsement on checks received by Employer and depositing them in Employer's bank account. After stamping Employer's unrestricted blank indorsement on a check, Employee steals the check and deposits it in Employee's personal bank account. Section 3–405 doesn't apply because there is no forged indorsement. Employee is authorized by Employer to indorse Employer's checks. The fraud by Employee is not the indorsement but rather the theft of the indorsed check. Whether Employer has a cause of action against the bank in which the check was deposited is determined by whether the bank had notice of the breach of fiduciary duty by Employee. The issue is determined under Section 3–307.

Case #5. The computer that controls Employer's check-writing machine was programmed to cause a check to be issued to Supplier Co. to which money was owed by Employer. The address of Supplier Co. was included in the information in the computer. Employee is an accounts payable clerk whose duties include entering information into the computer. Employee fraudulently changed the address of Supplier Co. in the computer data bank to an address of Employee. The check was subsequently produced by the check-writing machine and mailed to the address that Employee had entered into the computer. Employee obtained possession of the check, indorsed it in the name of Supplier Co, and deposited it to an account in Depositary Bank which Employee opened in the name "Supplier Co." The check was honored by the drawee bank. The indorsement is effective under Section 3–405(b) because Employee's duties allowed Employee to supply information determining the address of the payee of the check. An employee that is entrusted with duties that enable the employee to determine the address to which a check is to be sent controls the disposition of the check and facilitates forgery of the indorsement. The employer is held responsible. The drawee may debit the account of Employer for the amount of the check. There is no breach of warranty by Depositary Bank under Section 3–417(a)(1) or 4–208(a)(1).

Case #6. Treasurer is authorized to draw checks in behalf of Corporation. Treasurer draws a check of Corporation payable to Supplier Co., a company that sold goods to Corporation. The check was issued to pay the price of these goods. At the time the check was signed Treasurer had no intention of stealing the check. Later, Treasurer stole the check, indorsed it in the name "Supplier Co." and obtained payment by depositing it to an account in Depositary Bank which Treasurer opened in the name "Supplier Co.". The indorsement is effective under Section 3–405(b). Section 3–404(b) does not apply to this case.

Case #7. Checks of Corporation are signed by Treasurer in behalf of Corporation as drawer. Clerk's duties include the preparation of checks for issue by Corporation. Clerk prepares a check payable to the order of Supplier Co. for Treasurer's signature. Clerk fraudulently informs Treasurer that the check is needed to pay a debt owed to Supplier Co, a company that does business with Corporation. No money is owed to Supplier Co. and Clerk intends to steal the check. Treasurer signs it and returns it to Clerk for mailing. Clerk does not indorse the check but deposits it to an account in Depositary Bank which Clerk opened in the name "Supplier Co.". The check is honored by the drawee bank. Section 3–404(b)(i) does not apply to this case because Clerk, under Section 3–110(a), is not the person whose intent determines to whom the check is payable. But Section 3–405 does apply and it treats the deposit by Clerk as an effective indorsement by Clerk because Clerk was entrusted with responsibility with respect to the check. If Supplier Co. is a fictitious person Section 3–404(b)(ii) applies. But the result is the same. Clerk's deposit is treated as an effective indorsement of the check whether Supplier Co. is a fictitious or a real person or whether money was or was not owing to Supplier Co. The drawee bank may debit the account of Corporation for the amount of the check and there is no breach of warranty by Depositary Bank under Section 3–417(1)(a).

4. The last sentence of subsection (b) is similar to subsection (d) of Section 3–404 which is discussed in Comment 3 to Section 3–404. In Case #5, Case #6, or Case #7 the depositary bank may have failed to exercise ordinary care when it allowed the employee to open an account in the name "Supplier Co.," to deposit checks payable to "Supplier Co." in that account, or to withdraw funds from that account that were proceeds of checks payable to Supplier Co. Failure to exercise ordinary care is to be determined in the context of all the facts relating to the bank's conduct with respect to the bank's collection of the check. If the trier of fact finds that there was such a failure and that the failure substantially contributed to loss, it could find the depositary bank liable to the extent the failure contributed to the loss. The last sentence of subsection (b) can be illustrated by an example. Suppose in Case #5 that the check is not payable to an obscure "Supplier Co." but rather to a well-known national corporation. In addition, the check is for a very large amount of money. Before depositing the check, Employee opens an account in Depositary Bank in the name of the corporation and states to the person conducting the transaction for the bank that Employee is manager of a new office being opened by the corporation. Depositary Bank opens the account without requiring Employee to produce any resolutions of the corporation's board of directors or other evidence of authorization of Employee to act for the corporation. A few days later, the check is deposited, the account is credited, and the check is presented for payment. After Depositary Bank receives payment, it allows Employee to withdraw the credit by a wire transfer to an account in a bank in a foreign country. The trier of fact could find that Depositary Bank did not exercise ordinary care and that the failure to exercise ordinary care contributed to the loss suffered by Employer. The trier of fact could allow recovery by Employer from Depositary Bank for all or part of the loss suffered by Employer.

State Bar Committee Comments

The last sentence of subsection (b) has been revised in a manner similar to subsection 3.404(d) by deleting the word "substantially" before the words "contributes to the loss resulting from the fraud". As a consequence, a trier of fact could hold a bank liable if its failure to exercise ordinary care contributed to the loss suffered by an employer. The bank could be held liable for all or a part of the loss suffered by the employer depending upon the determination by the trier of facts of the extent of the loss caused by the bank's negligence. See the Texas Comment for section 3.404 for a discussion of the reasons why the deletion of the word "substantially" was effected.

§ 3.406. Negligence Contributing to Forged Signature or Alteration of Instrument

(a) A person whose failure to exercise ordinary care substantially contributes to an alteration of an instrument or to the making of a forged signature on an instrument is precluded from asserting the alteration or the forgery against a person who, in good faith, pays the instrument or takes it for value or for collection.

(b) Under Subsection (a), if the person asserting the preclusion fails to exercise ordinary care in paying or taking the instrument and that failure contributes to loss, the loss is allocated between the person precluded and the person asserting the preclusion according to the extent to which the failure of each to exercise ordinary care contributed to the loss.

(c) Under Subsection (a), the burden of proving failure to exercise ordinary care is on the person asserting the preclusion. Under Subsection (b), the burden of proving failure to exercise ordinary care is on the person precluded.

Amended by Acts 1995, 74th Leg., ch. 921, § 1, eff. Jan. 1, 1996.

Uniform Commercial Code Comment

1. Section 3–406(a) is based on former Section 3–406. With respect to alteration, Section 3–406 adopts the doctrine of *Young v. Grote*, 4 Bing. 253 (1827), which held that a drawer who so negligently draws an instrument as to facilitate its material alteration is liable to a drawee who pays the

altered instrument in good faith. Under Section 3–406 the doctrine is expanded to apply not only to drafts but to all instruments. It includes in the protected class any "person who, in good faith, pays the instrument or takes it for value or for collection." Section 3–406 rejects decisions holding that the maker of a note owes no duty of care to the holder because at the time the instrument is issued there is no contract between them. By issuing the instrument and "setting it afloat upon a sea of strangers" the maker or drawer voluntarily enters into a relation with later holders which justifies imposition of a duty of care. In this respect an instrument so negligently drawn as to facilitate alteration does not differ in principle from an instrument containing blanks which may be filled. Under Section 3–407 a person paying an altered instrument or taking it for value, in good faith and without notice of the alteration may enforce rights with respect to the instrument according to its original terms. If negligence of the obligor substantially contributes to an alteration, this section gives the holder or the payor the alternative right to treat the altered instrument as though it had been issued in the altered form.

No attempt is made to define particular conduct that will constitute "failure to exercise ordinary care [that] substantially contributes to an alteration." Rather, "ordinary care" is defined in Section 3–103(a)(7) in general terms. The question is left to the court or the jury for decision in the light of the circumstances in the particular case including reasonable commercial standards that may apply.

Section 3–406 does not make the negligent party liable in tort for damages resulting from the alteration. If the negligent party is estopped from asserting the alteration the person taking the instrument is fully protected because the taker can treat the instrument as having been issued in the altered form.

2. Section 3–406 applies equally to a failure to exercise ordinary care that substantially contributes to the making of a forged signature on an instrument. Section 3–406 refers to "forged signature" rather than "unauthorized signature" that appeared in former Section 3–406 because it more accurately describes the scope of the provision. Unauthorized signature is a broader concept that includes not only forgery but also the signature of an agent which does not bind the principal under the law of agency. The agency cases are resolved independently under agency law. Section 3–406 is not necessary in those cases.

The "substantially contributes" test of former Section 3–406 is continued in this section in preference to a "direct and proximate cause" test. The "substantially contributes" test is meant to be less stringent than a "direct and proximate cause" test. Under the less stringent test the preclusion should be easier to establish. Conduct "substantially contributes" to a material alteration or forged signature if it is a contributing cause of the alteration or signature and a substantial factor in bringing it about. The analysis of "substantially contributes" in former Section 3–406 by the court in *Thompson Maple Products v. Citizens National Bank of Corry*, 234 A.2d 32 (Pa.Super.Ct.1967), states what is intended by the use of the same words in revised Section 3–406(b). Since Section 3–404(d) and Section 3–405(b) also use the words "substantially contributes" the analysis of these words also applies to those provisions.

3. The following cases illustrate the kind of conduct that can be the basis of a preclusion under Section 3–406(a):

Case #1. Employer signs checks drawn on Employer's account by use of a rubber stamp of Employer's signature. Employer keeps the rubber stamp along with Employer's personalized blank check forms in an unlocked desk drawer. An unauthorized person fraudulently uses the check forms to write checks on Employer's account. The checks are signed by use of the rubber stamp. If Employer demands that Employer's account in the drawee bank be recredited because the forged check was not properly payable, the drawee bank may defend by asserting that Employer is precluded from asserting the forgery. The trier of fact could find that Employer failed to exercise ordinary care to safeguard the rubber stamp and the check forms and that the failure substantially contributed to the forgery of Employer's signature by the unauthorized use of the rubber stamp.

Case #2. An insurance company draws a check to the order of Sarah Smith in payment of a claim of a policyholder, Sarah Smith, who lives in Alabama. The insurance company also has a policyholder with the same name who lives in Illinois. By mistake, the insurance company mails the check to the Illinois Sarah Smith who indorses the check and obtains payment. Because the payee of the check is the Alabama Sarah Smith, the indorsement by the Illinois Sarah Smith is a forged indorsement. Section 3–110(a). The trier of fact could find that the insurance company failed to exercise ordinary care when it mailed the check to the wrong person and that the failure substantially contributed to the making of the forged indorsement. In that event the insurance company could be precluded from asserting the forged indorsement against the drawee bank that honored the check.

Case #3. A company writes a check for $10. The figure "10" and the word "ten" are typewritten in the appropriate spaces on the check form. A large blank space is left after the figure and the word. The payee of the check, using a typewriter with a typeface similar to that used on the check, writes the word "thousand" after the word "ten" and a comma and three zeros after the figure "10". The drawee bank in good faith pays $10,000 when the check is presented for payment and debits the account of the drawer in that amount. The trier of fact could find that the drawer failed to exercise ordinary care in writing the check and that the failure substantially contributed to the alteration. In that case the drawer is precluded from asserting the alteration against the drawee if the check was paid in good faith.

4. Subsection (b) differs from former Section 3–406 in that it adopts a concept of comparative negligence. If the person precluded under subsection (a) proves that the person asserting the preclusion failed to exercise ordinary care and that failure substantially contributed to the loss, the loss may be allocated between the two parties on a comparative negligence basis. In the case of a forged indorsement the litigation is usually between the payee of the check and the depositary bank that took the check for collection. An example is a case like Case #1 of Comment 3 to Section 3–405. If the trier of fact finds that Employer failed to exercise ordinary care in safeguarding the check and that the

failure substantially contributed to the making of the forged indorsement, subsection (a) of Section 3–406 applies. If Employer brings an action for conversion against the depositary bank that took the checks from the forger, the depositary bank could assert the preclusion under subsection (a). But suppose the forger opened an account in the depositary bank in a name identical to that of Employer, the payee of the check, and then deposited the check in the account. Subsection (b) may apply. There may be an issue whether the depositary bank should have been alerted to possible fraud when a new account was opened for a corporation shortly before a very large check payable to a payee with the same name is deposited. Circumstances surrounding the opening of the account may have suggested that the corporation to which the check was payable may not be the same as the corporation for which the account was opened. If the trier of fact finds that collecting the check under these circumstances was a failure to exercise ordinary care, it could allocate the loss between the depositary bank and Employer, the payee.

State Bar Committee Comments

Subsection (b) has been revised to delete the word "substantially" before the words "contributes to loss". This change mirrors a similar change in subsections 3.404(d) and 3.405(b). For a discussion of the reasons why this change was made, see the Texas Comment to section 3.404.

§ 3.407. Alteration

(a) "Alteration" means:

(1) an unauthorized change in an instrument that purports to modify in any respect the obligation of a party; or

(2) an unauthorized addition of words or numbers or other change to an incomplete instrument relating to the obligation of a party.

(b) Except as provided in Subsection (c), an alteration fraudulently made discharges a party whose obligation is affected by the alteration unless that party assents or is precluded from asserting the alteration. No other alteration discharges a party, and the instrument may be enforced according to its original terms.

(c) A payor bank or drawee paying a fraudulently altered instrument or a person taking it for value, in good faith and without notice of the alteration, may enforce rights with respect to the instrument:

(1) according to its original terms; or

(2) in the case of an incomplete instrument altered by unauthorized completion, according to its terms as completed.

Amended by Acts 1995, 74th Leg., ch. 921, § 1, eff. Jan. 1, 1996.

Uniform Commercial Code Comment

1. This provision restates former Section 3–407. Former Section 3–407 defined a "material" alteration as any alteration that changes the contract of the parties in any respect. Revised Section 3–407 refers to such a change as an alteration. As under subsection (2) of former Section 3–407, discharged because of alteration occurs only in the case of an alteration fraudulently made. There is no discharge if a blank is filled in the honest belief that it is authorized or if a change is made with a benevolent motive such as a desire to give the obligor the benefit of a lower interest rate. Changes favorable to the obligor are unlikely to be made with any fraudulent intent, but if such an intent is found the alteration may operate as a discharge.

Discharge is a personal defense of the party whose obligation is modified and anyone whose obligation is not affected is not discharged. But if an alteration discharges a party there is also discharge of any party having a right of recourse against the discharged party because the obligation of the party with the right of recourse is affected by the alteration. Assent to the alteration given before or after it is made will prevent the party from asserting the discharge. The phrase "or is precluded from asserting the alteration" in subsection (b) recognizes the possibility of an estoppel or other ground barring the defense which does not rest on assent.

2. Under subsection (c) a person paying a fraudulently altered instrument or taking it for value, in good faith and without notice of the alteration, is not affected by a discharge under subsection (b). The person paying or taking the instrument may assert rights with respect to the instrument according to its original terms or, in the case of an incomplete instrument that is altered by unauthorized completion, according to its terms as completed. If blanks are filled or an incomplete instrument is otherwise completed, subsection (c) places the loss upon the party who left the instrument incomplete by permitting enforcement in its completed form. This result is intended even though the instrument was stolen from the issuer and completed after the theft.

§ 3.408. Drawee Not Liable on Unaccepted Draft

A check or other draft does not of itself operate as an assignment of funds in the hands of the drawee available for its payment, and the drawee is not liable on the instrument until the drawee accepts it.

Amended by Acts 1995, 74th Leg., ch. 921, § 1, eff. Jan. 1, 1996.

Uniform Commercial Code Comment

1. This section is a restatement of former Section 3–409(1). Subsection (2) of former Section 3–409 is deleted as misleading and superfluous. Comment 3 says of subsection (2): "It is intended to make it clear that this section does not in any way affect any liability which may arise apart from the instrument." In reality subsection (2) did not make anything clear and was a source of confusion. If all it meant was that a bank that has not certified a check may engage in other conduct that might make it liable to a holder, it stated

the obvious and was superfluous. Section 1–103 is adequate to cover those cases.

2. Liability with respect to drafts may arise under other law. For example, Section 4–302 imposes liability on a payor bank for late return of an item.

§ 3.409. Acceptance of Draft; Certified Check

(a) "Acceptance" means the drawee's signed agreement to pay a draft as presented. It must be written on the draft and may consist of the drawee's signature alone. Acceptance may be made at any time and becomes effective when notification pursuant to instructions is given or the accepted draft is delivered for the purpose of giving rights on the acceptance to any person.

(b) A draft may be accepted although it has not been signed by the drawer, is otherwise incomplete, is overdue, or has been dishonored.

(c) If a draft is payable at a fixed period after sight and the acceptor fails to date the acceptance, the holder may complete the acceptance by supplying a date in good faith.

(d) "Certified check" means a check accepted by the bank on which it is drawn. Acceptance may be made as stated in Subsection (a) or by a writing on the check that indicates that the check is certified. The drawee of a check has no obligation to certify the check, and refusal to certify is not dishonor of the check.

Amended by Acts 1995, 74th Leg., ch. 921, § 1, eff. Jan. 1, 1996.

Uniform Commercial Code Comment

1. The first three subsections of Section 3–409 are a restatement of former Section 3–410. Subsection (d) adds a definition of certified check which is a type of accepted draft.

2. Subsection (a) states the generally recognized rule that the mere signature of the drawee on the instrument is a sufficient acceptance. Customarily the signature is written vertically across the face of the instrument, but since the drawee has no reason to sign for any other purpose a signature in any other place, even on the back of the instrument, is sufficient. It need not be accompanied by such words as "Accepted," "Certified," or "Good." It must not, however, bear any words indicating an intent to refuse to honor the draft. The last sentence of subsection (a) states the generally recognized rule that an acceptance written on the draft takes effect when the drawee notifies the holder or gives notice according to instructions.

3. The purpose of subsection (c) is to provide a definite date of payment if none appears on the instrument. An undated acceptance of a draft payable "thirty days after sight" is incomplete. Unless the acceptor writes in a different date the holder is authorized to complete the acceptance according to the terms of the draft by supplying a date of acceptance. Any date supplied by the holder is effective if made in good faith.

4. The last sentence of subsection (d) states the generally recognized rule that in the absence of agreement a bank is under no obligation to certify a check. A check is a demand instrument calling for payment rather than acceptance. The bank may be liable for breach of any agreement with the drawer, the holder, or any other person by which it undertakes to certify. Its liability is not on the instrument, since the drawee is not so liable until acceptance. Section 3–408. Any liability is for breach of the separate agreement.

§ 3.410. Acceptance Varying Draft

(a) If the terms of a drawee's acceptance vary from the terms of the draft as presented, the holder may refuse the acceptance and treat the draft as dishonored. In that case, the drawee may cancel the acceptance.

(b) The terms of a draft are not varied by an acceptance to pay at a particular bank or place in the United States, unless the acceptance states that the draft is to be paid only at that bank or place.

(c) If the holder assents to an acceptance varying the terms of a draft, the obligation of each drawer and indorser that does not expressly assent to the acceptance is discharged.

Amended by Acts 1995, 74th Leg., ch. 921, § 1, eff. Jan. 1, 1996.

Uniform Commercial Code Comment

1. This section is a restatement of former Section 3–412. It applies to conditional acceptances, acceptances for part of the amount, acceptances to pay at a different time from that required by the draft, or to the acceptance of less than all of the drawees. It applies to any other engagement changing the essential terms of the draft. If the drawee makes a varied acceptance the holder may either reject it or assent to it. The holder may reject by insisting on acceptance of the draft as presented. Refusal by the drawee to accept the draft as presented is dishonor. In that event the drawee is not bound by the varied acceptance and is entitled to have it canceled.

If the holder assents to the varied acceptance, the drawee's obligation as acceptor is according to the terms of the varied acceptance. Under subsection (c) the effect of the holder's assent is to discharge any drawer or indorser who does not also assent. The assent of the drawer or indorser must be affirmatively expressed. Mere failure to object within a reasonable time is not assent which will prevent the discharge.

2. Under subsection (b) an acceptance does not vary from the terms of the draft if it provides for payment at any particular bank or place in the United States unless the acceptance states that the draft is to be paid only at such

bank or place. Section 3–501(b)(1) states that if an instrument is payable at a bank in the United States presentment must be made at the place of payment (Section 3–111) which in this case is at the designated bank.

§ 3.411. Refusal to Pay Cashier's Checks, Teller's Checks, and Certified Checks

(a) In this section, "obligated bank" means the acceptor of a certified check or the issuer of a cashier's check or teller's check bought from the issuer.

(b) If the obligated bank wrongfully (i) refuses to pay a cashier's check or certified check, (ii) stops payment of a teller's check, or (iii) refuses to pay a dishonored teller's check, the person asserting the right to enforce the check is entitled to compensation for expenses and loss of interest resulting from the nonpayment and may recover consequential damages if the obligated bank refuses to pay after receiving notice of particular circumstances giving rise to the damages.

(c) Expenses or consequential damages under Subsection (b) are not recoverable if the refusal of the obligated bank to pay occurs because:

(1) the obligated bank suspends payments;

(2) the obligated bank asserts a claim or defense of the bank that it has reasonable grounds to believe is available against the person entitled to enforce the instrument;

(3) the obligated bank has a reasonable doubt whether the person demanding payment is the person entitled to enforce the instrument; or

(4) payment is prohibited by law.

Amended by Acts 1995, 74th Leg., ch. 921, § 1, eff. Jan. 1, 1996.

Uniform Commercial Code Comment

1. In some cases a creditor may require that the debt be paid by an obligation of a bank. The debtor may comply by obtaining certification of the debtor's check, but more frequently the debtor buys from a bank a cashier's check or teller's check payable to the creditor. The check is taken by the creditor as a cash equivalent on the assumption that the bank will pay the check. Sometimes, the debtor wants to retract payment by inducing the obligated bank not to pay. The typical case involves a dispute between the parties to the transaction in which the check is given in payment. In the case of a certified check or cashier's check, the bank can safely pay the holder of the check despite notice that there may be an adverse claim to the check (Section 3–602). It is also clear that the bank that sells a teller's check has no duty to order the bank on which it is drawn not to pay it. A debtor using any of these types of checks has no right to stop payment. Nevertheless, some banks will refuse payment as an accommodation to a customer. Section 3–411 is designed to discourage this practice.

2. The term "obligated bank" refers to the issuer of the cashier's check or teller's check and the acceptor of the certified check. If the obligated bank wrongfully refuses to pay, it is liable to pay for expenses and loss of interest resulting from the refusal to pay. There is no express provision for attorney's fees, but attorney's fees are not meant to be necessarily excluded. They could be granted because they fit within the language "expenses * * * resulting from the nonpayment." In addition the bank may be liable to pay consequential damages if it has notice of the particular circumstances giving rise to the damages.

3. Subsection (c) provides that expenses or consequential damages are not recoverable if the refusal to pay is because of the reasons stated. The purpose is to limit that recovery to cases in which the bank refuses to pay even though its obligation to pay is clear and it is able to pay. Subsection (b) applies only if the refusal to honor the check is wrongful. If the bank is not obliged to pay there is no recovery. The bank may assert any claim or defense that it has, but normally the bank would not have a claim or defense. In the usual case it is a remitter that is asserting a claim to the check on the basis of a rescission of negotiation to the payee under Section 3–202. See Comment 2 to Section 3–201. The bank can assert that claim if there is compliance with Section 3–305(c), but the bank is not protected from damages under subsection (b) if the claim of the remitter is not upheld. In that case, the bank is insulated from damages only if payment is enjoined under Section 3–602(b)(1). Subsection (c)(iii) refers to cases in which the bank may have a reasonable doubt about the identity of the person demanding payment. For example, a cashier's check is payable to "Supplier Co." The person in possession of the check presents it for payment over the counter and claims to be an officer of Supplier Co. The bank may refuse payment until it has been given adequate proof that the presentment in fact is being made for Supplier Co., the person entitled to enforce the check.

State Bar Committee Comments

Section 3.411 recognizes that banks may dishonor cashier's checks or teller's checks payable at or through another bank, or stop payment on teller's checks drawn on another bank, but attempts to discourage such dishonor or stoppage of payment by providing for consequential damages in appropriate circumstances. As to teller's checks drawn on another bank, these provisions are consistent with existing Texas case law that the drawer bank may stop payment on such a teller's check. *Guaranty Fed. Sav. Bank v. Horseshoe Operating Co.*, 793 S.W.2d 652 (Tex. 1990). This new section changes and clarifies Texas law by making it clear that drawer banks may also dishonor cashier's checks and teller's checks payable at or through another bank, although the bank's customer has no right to demand this action. The rule of *Wertz v. Richardson Heights Bank & Trust*, 495 S.W.2d 572 (Tex. 1973) is changed.

§ 3.412. Obligation of Issuer of Note or Cashier's Check

The issuer of a note or cashier's check or other draft drawn on the drawer is obliged to pay the instrument (i) according to its terms at the time it was issued or, if not issued, at the time it first came into possession of a holder, or (ii) if the issuer signed an incomplete instrument, according to its terms when completed, to the extent stated in Sections 3.115 and 3.407. The obligation is owed to a person entitled to enforce the instrument or to an indorser who paid the instrument under Section 3.415.

Amended by Acts 1995, 74th Leg., ch. 921, § 1, eff. Jan. 1, 1996.

Uniform Commercial Code Comment

1. The obligations of the maker, acceptor, drawer, and indorser are stated in four separate sections. Section 3–412 states the obligation of the maker of a note and is consistent with former Section 3–413(1). Section 3–412 also applies to the issuer of a cashier's check or other draft drawn on the drawer. Under former Section 3–118(a), since a cashier's check or other draft drawn on the drawer was "effective as a note," the drawer was liable under former Section 3–413(1) as a maker. Under Sections 3–103(a)(6) and 3–104(f) a cashier's check or other draft drawn on the drawer is treated as a draft to reflect common commercial usage, but the liability of the drawer is stated by Section 3–412 as being the same as that of the maker of a note rather than that of the drawer of a draft. Thus, Section 3–412 does not in substance change former law.

2. Under Section 3–105(b) nonissuance of either a complete or incomplete instrument is a defense by a maker or drawer against a person that is not a holder in due course.

3. The obligation of the maker may be modified in the case of alteration if, under Section 3–406, the maker is precluded from asserting the alteration.

4. The rule of this section is similar to the rule of Article 39 of the Convention on International Bills of Exchange and International Promissory Notes. *Amendments approved by the Permanent Editorial Board for Uniform Commercial Code November 2, 2002.*

§ 3.413. Obligation of Acceptor

(a) The acceptor of a draft is obliged to pay the draft (i) according to its terms at the time it was accepted, even though the acceptance states that the draft is payable "as originally drawn" or equivalent terms, (ii) if the acceptance varies the terms of the draft, according to the terms of the draft as varied, or (iii) if the acceptance is of a draft that is an incomplete instrument, according to its terms when completed, to the extent stated in Sections 3.115 and 3.407. The obligation is owed to a person entitled to enforce the draft or to the drawer or an indorser who paid the draft under Section 3.414 or 3.415.

(b) If the certification of a check or other acceptance of a draft states the amount certified or accepted, the obligation of the acceptor is that amount. The obligation of the acceptor is the amount of the instrument at the time it was taken by the holder in due course if:

(1) the certification or acceptance does not state an amount;

(2) the amount of the instrument is subsequently raised; and

(3) the instrument is then negotiated to a holder in due course.

Amended by Acts 1995, 74th Leg., ch. 921, § 1, eff. Jan. 1, 1996.

Uniform Commercial Code Comment

Subsection (a) is consistent with former Section 3–413(1). Subsection (b) has primary importance with respect to certified checks. It protects the holder in due course of a certified check that was altered after certification and before negotiation to the holder in due course. A bank can avoid liability for the altered amount by stating on the check the amount the bank agrees to pay. The subsection applies to other accepted drafts as well. The rule of this section is similar to the rule of Articles 41 of the Convention on International Bills of Exchange and International Promissory Notes. Articles 42 and 43 of the Convention include more detailed rules that in many respects do not have parallels in this Article. *Amendments approved by the Permanent Editorial Board for Uniform Commercial Code November 2, 2002.*

§ 3.414. Obligation of Drawer

(a) This section does not apply to cashier's checks or other drafts drawn on the drawer.

(b) If an unaccepted draft is dishonored, the drawer is obliged to pay the draft (i) according to its terms at the time it was issued or, if not issued, at the time it first came into possession of a holder, or (ii) if the drawer signed an incomplete instrument, according to its terms when completed, to the extent stated in Sections 3.115 and 3.407. The obligation is owed to a person entitled to enforce the draft or to an indorser who paid the draft under Section 3.415.

(c) If a draft is accepted by a bank, the drawer is discharged, regardless of when or by whom acceptance was obtained.

(d) If a draft is accepted and the acceptor is not a bank, the obligation of the drawer to pay the draft if the draft is dishonored by the acceptor is the same as the obligation of an indorser under Sections 3.415(a) and (c).

(e) If a draft states that it is drawn "without recourse" or otherwise disclaims liability of the drawer to pay the draft, the drawer is not liable under Subsection (b) to pay the draft if the draft is not a check. A disclaimer of the liability stated in Subsection (b) is not effective if the draft is a check.

(f) If (i) a check is not presented for payment or given to a depositary bank for collection within 30 days after its date, (ii) the drawee suspends payments after expiration of the 30-day period without paying the check, and (iii) because of the suspension of payments, the drawer is deprived of funds maintained with the drawee to cover payment of the check, the drawer to the extent deprived of funds may discharge its obligation to pay the check by assigning to the person entitled to enforce the check the rights of the drawer against the drawee with respect to the funds.

Amended by Acts 1995, 74th Leg., ch. 921, § 1, eff. Jan. 1, 1996.

Uniform Commercial Code Comment

1. Subsection (a) excludes cashier's checks because the obligation of the issuer of a cashier's check is stated in Section 3–412.

2. Subsection (b) states the obligation of the drawer on an unaccepted draft. It replaces former Section 3–413(2). The requirement under former Article 3 of notice of dishonor or protest has been eliminated. Under revised Article 3, notice of dishonor is necessary only with respect to indorser's liability. The liability of the drawer of an unaccepted draft is treated as a primary liability. Under former Section 3–102(1)(d) the term "secondary party" was used to refer to a drawer or indorser. The quoted term is not used in revised Article 3. The effect of a draft drawn without recourse is stated in subsection (e).

3. Under subsection (c) the drawer is discharged of liability on a draft accepted by a bank regardless of when acceptance was obtained. This changes former Section 3–411(1) which provided that the drawer is discharged only if the holder obtains acceptance. Holders that have a bank obligation do not normally rely on the drawer to guarantee the bank's solvency. A holder can obtain protection against the insolvency of a bank acceptor by a specific guaranty of payment by the drawer or by obtaining an indorsement by the drawer. Section 3–205(d).

4. Subsection (d) states the liability of the drawer if a draft is accepted by a drawee other than a bank and the acceptor dishonors. The drawer of an unaccepted draft is the only party liable on the instrument. The drawee has no liability on the draft. Section 3–408. When the draft is accepted, the obligations change. The drawee, as acceptor, becomes primarily liable and the drawer's liability is that of a person secondarily liable as a guarantor of payment. The drawer's liability is identical to that of an indorser, and subsection (d) states the drawer's liability that way. The drawer is liable to pay the person entitled to enforce the draft or any indorser that pays pursuant to Section 3–415. The drawer in this case is discharged if notice of dishonor is required by Section 3–503 and is not given in compliance with that section. A drawer that pays has a right of recourse against the acceptor. Section 3 413(a).

5. Subsection (e) does not permit the drawer of a check to avoid liability under subsection (b) by drawing the check without recourse. There is no legitimate purpose served by issuing a check on which nobody is liable. Drawing without recourse is effective to disclaim liability of the drawer if the draft is not a check. Suppose, in a documentary sale, Seller draws a draft on Buyer for the price of goods shipped to Buyer. The draft is payable upon delivery to the drawee of an order bill of lading covering the goods. Seller delivers the draft with the bill of lading to Finance Company that is named as payee of the draft. If Seller draws without recourse Finance Company takes the risk that Buyer will dishonor. If Buyer dishonors, Finance Company has no recourse against Seller but it can obtain reimbursement by selling the goods which it controls through the bill of lading.

6. Subsection (f) is derived from former Section 3–502(1)(b). It is designed to protect the drawer of a check against loss resulting from suspension of payments by the drawee bank when the holder of the check delays collection of the check. For example, X writes a check payable to Y for $1,000. The check is covered by funds in X's account in the drawee bank. Y delays initiation of collection of the check for more than 30 days after the date of the check. The drawee bank suspends payments after the 30-day period and before the check is presented for payment. If the $1,000 of funds in X's account have not been withdrawn, X has a claim for those funds against the drawee bank and, if subsection (e) were not in effect, X would be liable to Y on the check because the check was dishonored. Section 3–502(e). If the suspension of payments by the drawee bank will result in payment to X of less than the full amount of the $1,000 in the account or if there is a significant delay in payment to X, X will suffer a loss which would not have been suffered if Y had promptly initiated collection of the check. In most cases, X will not suffer any loss because of the existence of federal bank deposit insurance that covers accounts up to $100,000. Thus, subsection (e) has relatively little importance. There might be some cases, however, in which the account is not fully insured because it exceeds $100,000 or because the account doesn't qualify for deposit insurance. Subsection (f) retains the phrase "deprived of funds maintained with the drawee" appearing in former Section 3–502(1)(b). The quoted phrase applies if the suspension of payments by the drawee prevents the drawer from receiving the benefit of funds which would have paid the check if the holder had been timely in initiating collection. Thus, any significant delay in obtaining full payment of the funds is a deprivation of funds. The drawer can discharge drawer's liability by assigning rights against the drawee with respect to the funds to the holder.

7. The obligation of the drawer under this section is similar to the obligation of the drawer under Article 38 of the Convention on International Bills of Exchange and Interna-

tional Promissory Notes. *Amendments approved by the Permanent Editorial Board for Uniform Commercial Code November 2, 2002.*

§ 3.415. Obligation of Indorser

(a) Subject to Subsections (b), (c), (d), and (e) and to Section 3.419(d), if an instrument is dishonored, an indorser is obliged to pay the amount due on the instrument (i) according to the terms of the instrument at the time it was indorsed, or (ii) if the indorser indorsed an incomplete instrument, according to its terms when completed, to the extent stated in Sections 3.115 and 3.407. The obligation of the indorser is owed to a person entitled to enforce the instrument or to a subsequent indorser who paid the instrument under this section.

(b) If an indorsement states that it is made "without recourse" or otherwise disclaims liability of the indorser, the indorser is not liable under Subsection (a) to pay the instrument.

(c) If notice of dishonor of an instrument is required by Section 3.503 and notice of dishonor complying with that section is not given to an indorser, the liability of the indorser under Subsection (a) is discharged.

(d) If a draft is accepted by a bank after an indorsement is made, the liability of the indorser under Subsection (a) is discharged.

(e) If an indorser of a check is liable under Subsection (a) and the check is not presented for payment, or given to a depositary bank for collection, within 30 days after the day the indorsement was made, the liability of the indorser under Subsection (a) is discharged.

Amended by Acts 1995, 74th Leg., ch. 921, § 1, eff. Jan. 1, 1996.

Uniform Commercial Code Comment

1. Subsections (a) and (b) restate the substance of former Section 3–414(1). Subsection (2) of former Section 3–414 has been dropped because it is superfluous. Although notice of dishonor is not mentioned in subsection (a), it must be given in some cases to charge an indorser. It is covered in subsection (c). Regulation CC § 229.35(b) provides that a bank handling a check for collection or return is liable to a bank that subsequently handles the check to the extent the latter bank does not receive payment for the check. This liability applies whether or not the bank incurring the liability indorsed the check.

2. Section 3–503 states when notice of dishonor is required and how it must be given. If required notice of dishonor is not given in compliance with Section 3–503, subsection (c) of Section 3–415 states that the effect is to discharge the indorser's obligation.

3. Subsection (d) is similar in effect to Section 3–414(c) if the draft is accepted by a bank after the indorsement is made. See Comment 3 to Section 3–414. If a draft is accepted by a bank before the indorsement is made, the indorser incurs the obligation stated in subsection (a).

4. Subsection (e) modified former Sections 3–503(2)(b) and 3–502(1)(a) by stating a 30-day rather than a seven-day period, and stating it as an absolute rather than a presumptive period.

5. As stated in subsection (a), the obligation of an indorser to pay the amount due on the instrument is generally owed not only to a person entitled to enforce the instrument but also to a subsequent indorser who paid the instrument. But if the prior indorser and the subsequent indorser are both anomalous indorsers, this rule does not apply. In that case, Section 3–116 applies. Under Section 3–116(a), the anomalous indorsers are jointly and severally liable and if either pays the instrument the indorser who pays has a right of contribution against the other. Section 3–116(b). The right to contribution in Section 3–116(b) is subject to "agreement of the affected parties." Suppose the subsequent indorser can prove an agreement with the prior indorser under which the prior indorser agreed to treat the subsequent indorser as a guarantor of the obligation of the prior indorser. Rights of the two indorsers between themselves would be governed by the agreement. Under suretyship law, the subsequent indorser under such an agreement is referred to as a sub-surety. Under the agreement, if the subsequent indorser pays the instrument there is a right to reimbursement from the prior indorser; if the prior indorser pays the instrument, there is no right of recourse against the subsequent indorser. See PEB Commentary No. 11, dated February 10, 1994 [Appendix II at end of Volume 3B].

6. The rule of this section is similar to the rule of Article 44 of the Convention on International Bills of Exchange and International Promissory Notes. *Amendments approved by the Permanent Editorial Board for Uniform Commercial Code November 2, 2002.*

State Bar Committee Comments

Reference is made to section 3.116 which provides for special rules relating to indorsers who indorse as joint payees or anomalous indorsers. These parties are jointly and severally liable in the capacity in which they sign. Section 3.415 is not intended to govern the rights of contribution between these parties because contribution is explicitly governed by section 3.116.

§ 3.416. Transfer Warranties

(a) A person who transfers an instrument for consideration warrants to the transferee and, if the transfer is by indorsement, to any subsequent transferee that:

(1) the warrantor is a person entitled to enforce the instrument;

(2) all signatures on the instrument are authentic and authorized;

(3) the instrument has not been altered;

(4) the instrument is not subject to a defense or claim in recoupment of any party that can be asserted against the warrantor;

(5) the warrantor has no knowledge of any insolvency proceeding commenced with respect to the maker or acceptor or, in the case of an unaccepted draft, the drawer; and

(6) with respect to a remotely-created item, that the person on whose account the item is drawn authorized the issuance of the item in the amount for which the item is drawn.

(b) A person to whom the warranties under Subsection (a) are made and who took the instrument in good faith may recover from the warrantor as damages for breach of warranty an amount equal to the loss suffered as a result of the breach, but not more than the amount of the instrument plus expenses and loss of interest incurred as a result of the breach.

(c) The warranties stated in Subsection (a) cannot be disclaimed with respect to checks. Unless notice of a claim for breach of warranty is given to the warrantor within 30 days after the claimant has reason to know of the breach and the identity of the warrantor, the liability of the warrantor under Subsection (b) is discharged to the extent of any loss caused by the delay in giving notice of the claim.

(d) A cause of action for breach of warranty under this section accrues when the claimant has reason to know of the breach.

(e) If as to a particular item (1) a transferee (including a collecting bank) asserts a claim for breach of the warranty in Subsection (a)(6), but (2) under applicable law (including the applicable choice-of-law principles) that transferee would not make a warranty substantially similar to the warranty in Subsection (a)(6) if such transferee were a transferor, then that transferee would not receive the warranty in Subsection (a)(6) from any transferor.

Amended by Acts 1995, 74th Leg., ch. 921, § 1, eff. Jan. 1, 1996; Acts 1997, 75th Leg., ch. 131, § 3, eff. Sept. 1, 1997; Acts 2005, 79th Leg., ch. 95, § 8, eff. Sept. 1, 2005.

Uniform Commercial Code Comment

1. Subsection (a) is taken from subsection (2) of former Section 3–417. Subsections (3) and (4) of former Section 3–417 are deleted. Warranties under subsection (a) in favor of the immediate transferee apply to all persons who transfer an instrument for consideration whether or not the transfer is accompanied by indorsement. Any consideration sufficient to support a simple contract will support those warranties. If there is an indorsement the warranty runs with the instrument and the remote holder may sue the indorser-warrantor directly and thus avoid a multiplicity of suits.

2. Since the purpose of transfer (Section 3–203(a)) is to give the transferee the right to enforce the instrument, subsection (a)(1) is a warranty that the transferor is a person entitled to enforce the instrument (Section 3–301). Under Section 3–203(b) transfer gives the transferee any right of the transferor to enforce the instrument. Subsection (a)(1) is in effect a warranty that there are no unauthorized or missing indorsements that prevent the transferor from making the transferee a person entitled to enforce the instrument.

3. The rationale of subsection (a)(4) is that the transferee does not undertake to buy an instrument that is not enforceable in whole or in part, unless there is a contrary agreement. Even if the transferee takes as a holder in due course who takes free of the defense or claim in recoupment, the warranty gives the transferee the option of proceeding against the transferor rather than litigating with the obligor on the instrument the issue of the holder-in-due-course status of the transferee. Subsection (3) of former Section 3–417 which limits this warranty is deleted. The rationale is that while the purpose of a "no recourse" indorsement is to avoid a guaranty of payment, the indorsement does not clearly indicate an intent to disclaim warranties.

4. Under subsection (a)(5) the transferor does not warrant against difficulties of collection, impairment of the credit of the obligor or even insolvency. The transferee is expected to determine such questions before taking the obligation. If insolvency proceedings as defined in Section 1–201(22) have been instituted against the party who is expected to pay and the transferor knows it, the concealment of that fact amounts to a fraud upon the transferee, and the warranty against knowledge of such proceedings is provided accordingly.

5. Transfer warranties may be disclaimed with respect to any instrument except a check. Between the immediate parties disclaimer may be made by agreement. In the case of an indorser, disclaimer of transferor's liability, to be effective, must appear in the indorsement with words such as "without warranties" or some other specific reference to warranties. But in the case of a check, subsection (c) of Section 3–416 provides that transfer warranties cannot be disclaimed at all. In the check collection process the banking system relies on these warranties.

6. Subsection (b) states the measure of damages for breach of warranty. There is no express provision for attorney's fees, but attorney's fees are not meant to be necessarily excluded. They could be granted because they fit within the phrase "expenses * * * incurred as a result of the breach." The intention is to leave to other state law the issue as to when attorney's fees are recoverable.

7. Since the traditional term "cause of action" may have been replaced in some states by "claim for relief" or some equivalent term, the words "cause of action" in subsection (d) have been bracketed to indicate that the words may be replaced by an appropriate substitute to conform to local practice.

8. Subsection (a)(6) is based on a number of nonuniform amendments designed to address concerns about certain kinds of check fraud. The provision implements a limited rejection of Price v. Neal, 97 Eng. Rep. 871 (K.B. 1762), so that in certain circumstances (those involving remotely-created consumer items) the payor bank can use a warranty claim to absolve itself of responsibility for honoring an unauthorized item. The provision rests on the premise that monitoring by depositary banks can control this type of fraud more effectively than any practices readily available to payor banks. The provision expressly includes both the case in which the consumer does not authorize the item at all and also the case in which the consumer authorizes the item but in an amount different from the amount in which the item is drawn. Similar provisions appear in Sections 3–417, 4–207, and 4–208.

The provision supplements applicable federal law, which requires telemarketers who submit instruments for payment to obtain the customer's 'express verifiable authorization,' which may be either in writing or tape recorded and must be made available upon request to the customer's bank. Federal Trade Commission's Telemarketing Sales Rule, 16 C.F.R. § 310.3(a)(3), implementing the Telemarketing and Consumer Fraud and Abuse Prevention Act, 15 U.S.C. §§ 6101-6108. Some states also have consumer-protection laws governing authorization of instruments in telemarketing transactions. *See, e.g.,* 9 Vt. Stat. Ann. § 2464.

9. Article 45 of the Convention on International Bills of Exchange and International Promissory Notes includes warranties that are similar (except for the warranty in subsection (a)(6)).

§ 3.417. Presentment Warranties

(a) If an unaccepted draft is presented to the drawee for payment or acceptance and the drawee pays or accepts the draft, (i) the person obtaining payment or acceptance, at the time of presentment, and (ii) a previous transferor of the draft, at the time of transfer, warrant to the drawee making payment or accepting the draft in good faith that:

(1) the warrantor is, or was, at the time the warrantor transferred the draft, a person entitled to enforce the draft or authorized to obtain payment or acceptance of the draft on behalf of a person entitled to enforce the draft;

(2) the draft has not been altered;

(3) the warrantor has no knowledge that the signature of the drawer of the draft is unauthorized; and

(4) with respect to a remotely-created item, that the person on whose account the item is drawn authorized the issuance of the item in the amount for which the item is drawn.

(b) A drawee making payment may recover from any warrantor damages for breach of warranty equal to the amount paid by the drawee less the amount the drawee received or is entitled to receive from the drawer because of the payment. In addition, the drawee is entitled to compensation for expenses and loss of interest resulting from the breach. The right of the drawee to recover damages under this subsection is not affected by any failure of the drawee to exercise ordinary care in making payment. If the drawee accepts the draft, breach of warranty is a defense to the obligation of the acceptor. If the acceptor makes payment with respect to the draft, the acceptor is entitled to recover from any warrantor for breach of warranty the amounts stated in this subsection.

(c) If a drawee asserts a claim for breach of warranty under Subsection (a) based on an unauthorized indorsement of the draft or an alteration of the draft, the warrantor may defend by proving that the indorsement is effective under Section 3.404 or 3.405 or the drawer is precluded under Section 3.406 or 4.406 from asserting against the drawee the unauthorized indorsement or alteration.

(d) If (i) a dishonored draft is presented for payment to the drawer or an indorser, or (ii) any other instrument is presented for payment to a party obliged to pay the instrument, and (iii) payment is received, the following rules apply:

(1) The person obtaining payment and a prior transferor of the instrument warrant to the person making payment in good faith that the warrantor is, or was, at the time the warrantor transferred the instrument, a person entitled to enforce the instrument or authorized to obtain payment on behalf of a person entitled to enforce the instrument.

(2) The person making payment may recover from any warrantor for breach of warranty an amount equal to the amount paid plus expenses and loss of interest resulting from the breach.

(e) The warranties stated in Subsections (a) and (d) cannot be disclaimed with respect to checks. Unless notice of a claim for breach of warranty is given to the warrantor within 30 days after the claimant has reason to know of the breach and the identity of the warrantor, the liability of the warrantor under Subsection (b) or (d) is discharged to the extent of any loss caused by the delay in giving notice of the claim.

(f) A cause of action for breach of warranty under this section accrues when the claimant has reason to know of the breach.

(g) If as to a particular item (1) a transferee (including a collecting bank) asserts a claim for breach of the warranty in Subsection (a)(4), but (2) under applicable law (including the applicable choice-of-law principles) that transferee would not make a warranty substantially similar to the warranty in Subsection (a)(4) if such transferee were a transferor, then that transferee would not receive the warranty in Subsection (a)(4) from any transferor.

Amended by Acts 1995, 74th Leg., ch. 921, § 1, eff. Jan. 1, 1996; Acts 1997, 75th Leg., ch. 131, § 4, eff. Sept. 1, 1997; Acts 2005, 79th Leg., ch. 95, § 9, eff. Sept. 1, 2005.

Uniform Commercial Code Comment

1. This section replaces subsection (1) of former Section 3–417. The former provision was difficult to understand because it purported to state in one subsection all warranties given to any person paying any instrument. The result was a provision replete with exceptions that could not be readily understood except after close scrutiny of the language. In revised Section 3–417, presentment warranties made to drawees of uncertified checks and other unaccepted drafts are stated in subsection (a). All other presentment warranties are stated in subsection (d).

2. Subsection (a) states three warranties. Subsection (a)(1) in effect is a warranty that there are no unauthorized or missing indorsements. "Person entitled to enforce" is defined in Section 3–301. Subsection (a)(2) is a warranty that there is no alteration. Subsection (a)(3) is a warranty of no knowledge that there is a forged drawer's signature. Subsection (a) states that the warranties are made to the drawee and subsections (b) and (c) identify the drawee as the person entitled to recover for breach of warranty. There is no warranty made to the drawer under subsection (a) when presentment is made to the drawee. Warranty to the drawer is governed by subsection (d) and that applies only when presentment for payment is made to the drawer with respect to a dishonored draft. *In Sun 'N Sand, Inc. v. United California Bank*, 582 P.2d 920 (Cal.1978), the court held that under former Section 3–417(1) a warranty was made to the drawer of a check when the check was presented to the drawee for payment. The result in that case is rejected.

3. Subsection (a)(1) retains the rule that the drawee does not admit the authenticity of indorsements and subsection (a)(3) retains the rule of *Price v. Neal*, 3 Burr. 1354 (1762), that the drawee takes the risk that the drawer's signature is unauthorized unless the person presenting the draft has knowledge that the drawer's signature is unauthorized. Under subsection (a)(3) the warranty of no knowledge that the drawer's signature is unauthorized is also given by prior transferors of the draft.

4. Subsection (d) applies to presentment for payment in all cases not covered by subsection (a). It applies to presentment of notes and accepted drafts to any party obliged to pay the instrument, including an indorser, and to presentment of dishonored drafts if made to the drawer or an indorser. In cases covered by subsection (d), there is only one warranty and it is the same as that stated in subsection (a)(1). There are no warranties comparable to subsections (a)(2) and (a)(3) because they are appropriate only in the case of presentment to the drawee of an unaccepted draft. With respect to presentment of an accepted draft to the acceptor, there is no warranty with respect to alteration or knowledge that the signature of the drawer is unauthorized. Those warranties were made to the drawee when the draft was presented for acceptance (Section 3–417(a)(2) and (3)) and breach of that warranty is a defense to the obligation of the drawee as acceptor to pay the draft. If the drawee pays the accepted draft the drawee may recover the payment from any warrantor who was in breach of warranty when the draft was accepted. Section 3–417(b). Thus, there is no necessity for these warranties to be repeated when the accepted draft is presented for payment. Former Section 3–417(1)(b)(iii) and (c)(iii) are not included in revised Section 3–417 because they are unnecessary. Former Section 3–417(1)(c)(iv) is not included because it is also unnecessary. The acceptor should know what the terms of the draft were at the time acceptance was made.

If presentment is made to the drawer or maker, there is no necessity for a warranty concerning the signature of that person or with respect to alteration. If presentment is made to an indorser, the indorser had itself warranted authenticity of signatures and that the instrument was not altered. Section 3–416(a)(2) and (3).

5. The measure of damages for breach of warranty under subsection (a) is stated in subsection (b). There is no express provision for attorney's fees, but attorney's fees are not meant to be necessarily excluded. They could be granted because they fit within the language "expenses * * * resulting from the breach." Subsection (b) provides that the right of the drawee to recover for breach of warranty is not affected by a failure of the drawee to exercise ordinary care in paying the draft. This provision follows the result reached under former Article 3 in *Hartford Accident & Indemnity Co. v. First Pennsylvania Bank*, 859 F.2d 295 (3d Cir.1988).

6. Subsection (c) applies to checks and other unaccepted drafts. It gives to the warrantor the benefit of rights that the drawee has against the drawer under Section 3–404, 3–405, 3–406, or 4–406. If the drawer's conduct contributed to a loss from forgery or alteration, the drawee should not be allowed to shift the loss from the drawer to the warrantor.

7. The first sentence of subsection (e) recognizes that checks are normally paid by automated means and that payor banks rely on warranties in making payment. Thus, it is not appropriate to allow disclaimer of warranties appearing on checks that normally will not be examined by the payor bank. The second sentence requires a breach of warranty claim to be asserted within 30 days after the drawee learns of the breach and the identity of the warrantor.

8. Since the traditional term "cause of action" may have been replaced in some states by "claim for relief" or some equivalent term, the words "cause of action" in subsection (f) have been bracketed to indicate that the words may be replaced by an appropriate substitute to conform to local practice.

9. For discussion of subsection (a)(4), see Comment 8 to Section 3–416.

§ 3.418. Payment or Acceptance By Mistake

(a) Except as provided in Subsection (c), if the drawee of a draft pays or accepts the draft and the drawee acted on the mistaken belief that (i) payment of the draft had not been stopped pursuant to Section 4.403, or (ii) the signature of the drawer of the draft was authorized, the drawee may recover the amount of the draft from the person to whom or for whose benefit payment was made or, in the case of acceptance, may revoke the acceptance. Rights of the drawee under this subsection are not affected by failure of the drawee to exercise ordinary care in paying or accepting the draft.

(b) Except as provided in Subsection (c), if an instrument has been paid or accepted by mistake and the case is not covered by Subsection (a), the person paying or accepting may, to the extent permitted by the law governing mistake and restitution:

(1) recover the payment from the person to whom or for whose benefit payment was made; or

(2) in the case of acceptance, revoke the acceptance.

(c) The remedies provided by Subsection (a) or (b) may not be asserted against a person who took the instrument in good faith and for value or who in good faith changed position in reliance on the payment or acceptance. This subsection does not limit remedies provided by Section 3.417 or 4.407.

(d) Notwithstanding Section 4.215, if an instrument is paid or accepted by mistake and the payor or acceptor recovers payment or revokes acceptance under Subsection (a) or (b), the instrument is deemed not to have been paid or accepted and is treated as dishonored, and the person from whom payment is recovered has rights as a person entitled to enforce the dishonored instrument.

Amended by Acts 1995, 74th Leg., ch. 921, § 1, eff. Jan. 1, 1996.

Uniform Commercial Code Comment

1. This section covers payment or acceptance by mistake and replaces former Section 3–418. Under former Article 3, the remedy of a drawee that paid or accepted a draft by mistake was based on the law of mistake and restitution, but that remedy was not specifically stated. It was provided by Section 1–103. Former Section 3–418 was simply a limitation on the unstated remedy under the law of mistake and restitution. Under revised Article 3, Section 3–418 specifically states the right of restitution in subsections (a) and (b). Subsection (a) allows restitution in the two most common cases in which the problem is presented: payment or acceptance of forged checks and checks on which the drawer has stopped payment. If the drawee acted under a mistaken belief that the check was not forged or had not been stopped, the drawee is entitled to recover the funds paid or to revoke the acceptance whether or not the drawee acted negligently. But in each case, by virtue of subsection (c), the drawee loses the remedy if the person receiving payment or acceptance was a person who took the check in good faith and for value or who in good faith changed position in reliance on the payment or acceptance. Subsections (a) and (c) are consistent with former Section 3–418 and the rule of *Price v. Neal.* The result in the two cases covered by subsection (a) is that the drawee in most cases will not have a remedy against the person paid because there is usually a person who took the check in good faith and for value or who in good faith changed position in reliance on the payment or acceptance.

2. If a check has been paid by mistake and the payee receiving payment did not give value for the check or did not change position in reliance on the payment, the drawee bank is entitled to recover the amount of the check under subsection (a) regardless of how the check was paid. The drawee bank normally pays a check by a credit to an account of the collecting bank that presents the check for payment. The payee of the check normally receives the payment by a credit to the payee's account in the depositary bank. But in some cases the payee of the check may have received payment directly from the drawee bank by presenting the check for payment over the counter. In those cases the payee is entitled to receive cash, but the payee may prefer another form of payment such as a cashier's check or teller's check issued by the drawee bank. Suppose Seller contracted to sell goods to Buyer. The contract provided for immediate payment by Buyer and delivery of the goods 20 days after payment. Buyer paid by mailing a check for $10,000 drawn on Bank payable to Seller. The next day Buyer gave a stop payment order to Bank with respect to the check Buyer had mailed to Seller. A few days later Seller presented Buyer's check to Bank for payment over the counter and requested a cashier's check as payment. Bank issued and delivered a cashier's check for $10,000 payable to Seller. The teller failed to discover Buyer's stop order. The next day Bank discovered the mistake and immediately advised Seller of the facts. Seller refused to return the cashier's check and did not deliver any goods to Buyer.

Under Section 4–215, Buyer's check was paid by Bank at the time it delivered its cashier's check to Seller. See Comment 3 to Section 4–215. Bank is obliged to pay the cashier's check and has no defense to that obligation. The cashier's check was issued for consideration because it was issued in payment of Buyer's check. Although Bank has no defense on its cashier's check, it may have a right to recover $10,000, the amount of Buyer's check, from Seller under Section 3–418(a). Bank paid Buyer's check by mistake. Seller did not give value for Buyer's check because the promise to deliver goods to Buyer was never performed. Section 3–303(a)(1). And, on these facts, Seller did not change position in reliance on the payment of Buyer's check. Thus, the first sentence of Section 3–418(c) does not apply and Seller is obliged to return $10,000 to Bank. Bank is obliged to pay the cashier's check but it has a counterclaim against Seller based on its rights under Section 3–418(a). This claim can be asserted against Seller, but it cannot be asserted against some other person with rights of a holder in due course of the cashier's check. A person without rights of a holder in due course of the cashier's check would take subject to Bank's claim against Seller because it is a claim in recoupment. Section 3–305(a)(3).

If Bank recovers from Seller under Section 3–418(a), the payment of Buyer's check is treated as unpaid and dishonored. Section 3–418(d). One consequence is that Seller may enforce Buyer's obligation as drawer to pay the check. Section 3–414. Another consequence is that Seller's rights against Buyer on the contract of sale are also preserved. Under Section 3–310(b) Buyer's obligation to pay for the goods was suspended when Seller took Buyer's check and remains suspended until the check is either dishonored or paid. Under Section 3–310(b)(2) the obligation is discharged when the check is paid. Since Section 3–418(d) treats Buyer's check as unpaid and dishonored, Buyer's obligation is not discharged and suspension of the obligation terminates. Under Section 3–310(b)(3), Seller may enforce either the contract of sale or the check subject to defenses and claims of Buyer.

If Seller had released the goods to Buyer before learning about the stop order, Bank would have no recovery against Seller under Section 3–418(a) because Seller in that case gave value for Buyer's check. Section 3–418(c). In this case Bank's sole remedy is under Section 4–407 by subrogation.

3. Subsection (b) covers cases of payment or acceptance by mistake that are not covered by subsection (a). It directs courts to deal with those cases under the law governing mistake and restitution. Perhaps the most important class of cases that falls under subsection (b), because it is not covered by subsection (a), is that of payment by the drawee bank of a check with respect to which the bank has no duty to the drawer to pay either because the drawer has no account with the bank or because available funds in the drawer's account are not sufficient to cover the amount of the check. With respect to such a case, under Restatement of Restitution § 29, if the bank paid because of a mistaken belief that there were available funds in the drawer's account sufficient to cover the amount of the check, the bank is entitled to restitution. But § 29 is subject to Restatement of Restitution § 33 which denies restitution if the holder of the check receiving payment paid value in good faith for the check and had no reason to know that the check was paid by mistake when payment was received.

The result in some cases is clear. For example, suppose Father gives Daughter a check for $10,000 as a birthday gift. The check is drawn on Bank in which both Father and Daughter have accounts. Daughter deposits the check in her account in Bank. An employee of Bank, acting under the belief that there were available funds in Father's account to cover the check, caused Daughter's account to be credited for $10,000. In fact, Father's account was overdrawn and Father did not have overdraft privileges. Since Daughter received the check gratuitously there is clear unjust enrichment if she is allowed to keep the $10,000 and Bank is unable to obtain reimbursement from Father. Thus, Bank should be permitted to reverse the credit to Daughter's account. But this case is not typical. In most cases the remedy of restitution will not be available because the person receiving payment of the check will have given value for it in good faith.

In some cases, however, it may not be clear whether a drawee bank should have a right of restitution. For example, a check-kiting scheme may involve a large number of checks drawn on a number of different banks in which the drawer's credit balances are based on uncollected funds represented by fraudulently drawn checks. No attempt is made in Section 3–418 to state rules for determining the conflicting claims of the various banks that may be victimized by such a scheme. Rather, such cases are better resolved on the basis of general principles of law and the particular facts presented in the litigation.

4. The right of the drawee to recover a payment or to revoke an acceptance under Section 3–418 is not affected by the rules under Article 4 that determine when an item is paid. Even though a payor bank may have paid an item under Section 4–215, it may have a right to recover the payment under Section 3–418. *National Savings & Trust Co. v. Park Corp.*, 722 F.2d 1303 (6th Cir.1983), cert. denied, 466 U.S. 939 (1984), correctly states the law on the issue under former Article 3. Revised Article 3 does not change the previous law.

§ 3.419. Instruments Signed for Accommodation

(a) If an instrument is issued for value given for the benefit of a party to the instrument ("accommodated party") and another party to the instrument ("accommodation party") signs the instrument for the purpose of incurring liability on the instrument without being a direct beneficiary of the value given for the instrument, the instrument is signed by the accommodation party "for accommodation."

(b) An accommodation party may sign the instrument as maker, drawer, acceptor, or indorser. Subject to Subsection (d), the accommodation party is obliged to pay the instrument in the capacity in which the accommodation party signs. The obligation of an accommodation party may be enforced notwithstanding any statute of frauds and whether or not the accommodation party receives consideration for the accommodation.

(c) A person signing an instrument is presumed to be an accommodation party and there is notice that the instrument is signed for accommodation if the signature is an anomalous indorsement or is accompanied by words indicating that the signer is acting as surety or guarantor with respect to the obligation of another party to the instrument. Except as provided in Section 3.605, the obligation of an accommodation party to pay the instrument is not affected by the fact that the person enforcing the obligation had notice when the instrument was taken by that person that the accommodation party signed the instrument for accommodation.

(d) If the signature of a party to an instrument is accompanied by words indicating unambiguously that the party is guaranteeing collection rather than payment of the obligation of another party to the instrument, the signer is obliged to pay the amount due on the instrument to a person entitled to enforce the instrument only if:

(1) execution of judgment against the other party has been returned unsatisfied;

(2) the other party is insolvent or in an insolvency proceeding;

(3) the other party cannot be served with process; or

(4) it is otherwise apparent that payment cannot be obtained from the other party.

(e) If the signature of a party to an instrument is accompanied by words indicating that the party guarantees payment or the signer signs the instrument as an accommodation party in some other manner that does not unambiguously indicate an intention to guarantee collection rather than payment, the signer is obliged to pay the amount due on the instrument to a person entitled to enforce the instrument in the same circumstances as the accommodated party would be obliged, without prior resort to the accommodated party by the person entitled to enforce the instrument.

(f) An accommodation party who pays the instrument is entitled to reimbursement from the accommodated party and is entitled to enforce the instrument against the accommodated party. In proper circumstances, an accommodation party may obtain relief that requires the accommodated party to perform its obligations on the instrument. An accommodated party that pays the instrument has no right of recourse against, and is not entitled to contribution from, an accommodation party.

Amended by Acts 1995, 74th Leg., ch. 921, § 1, eff. Jan. 1, 1996; Acts 2005, 79th Leg., ch. 95, § 10, eff. Sept. 1, 2005.

Uniform Commercial Code Comment

1. Section 3–419 replaces former Sections 3–415 and 3–416. An accommodation party is a person who signs an instrument to benefit the accommodated party either by signing at the time value is obtained by the accommodated party or later, and who is not a direct beneficiary of the value obtained. An accommodation party will usually be a co-maker or anomalous indorser. Subsection (a) distinguishes between direct and indirect benefit. For example, if X cosigns a note of Corporation that is given for a loan to Corporation, X is an accommodation party if no part of the loan was paid to X or for X's direct benefit. This is true even though X may receive indirect benefit from the loan because X is employed by Corporation or is a stockholder of Corporation, or even if X is the sole stockholder so long as Corporation and X are recognized as separate entities.

2. It does not matter whether an accommodation party signs gratuitously either at the time the instrument is issued or after the instrument is in the possession of a holder. Subsection (b) of Section 3–419 takes the view stated in Comment 3 to former Section 3–415 that there need be no consideration running to the accommodation party: "The obligation of the accommodation party is supported by any consideration for which the instrument is taken before it is due. Subsection (2) is intended to change occasional decisions holding that there is no sufficient consideration where an accommodation party signs a note after it is in the hands of a holder who has given value. The [accommodation] party is liable to the holder in such a case even though there is no extension of time or other concession."

3. As stated in Comment 1, whether a person is an accommodation party is a question of fact. But it is almost always the case that a co-maker who signs with words of guaranty after the signature is an accommodation party. The same is true of an anomalous indorser. In either case a person taking the instrument is put on notice of the accommodation status of the co-maker or indorser. This is relevant to Section 3–605(h). But, under subsection (c), signing with words of guaranty or as an anomalous indorser also creates a presumption that the signer is an accommodation party. A party challenging accommodation party status would have to rebut this presumption by producing evidence that the signer was in fact a direct beneficiary of the value given for the instrument.

An accommodation party is always a surety. A surety who is not a party to the instrument, however, is not an accommodation party. For example, if M issues a note payable to the order of P, and S signs a separate contract in which S agrees to pay P the amount of the instrument if it is dishonored, S is a surety but is not an accommodation party. In such a case, S's rights and duties are determined under the general law of suretyship. In unusual cases two parties to an instrument may have a surety relationship that is not governed by Article 3 because the requirements of Section 3–419(a) are not met. In those cases the general law of suretyship applies to the relationship. See PEB Commentary No. 11, dated February 10, 1994 [Appendix II at end of Volume 3B].

4. Subsection (b) states that an accommodation party is liable on the instrument in the capacity in which the party signed the instrument. In most cases that capacity will be either that of a maker or indorser of a note. But subsection (d) provides a limitation on subsection (b). If the signature of the accommodation party is accompanied by words indicating unambiguously that the party is guaranteeing collection rather than payment of the instrument, liability is limited to that stated in subsection (d), which is based on former Section 3–416(2).

Former Article 3 was confusing because the obligation of a guarantor was covered both in Section 3–415 and in Section 3–416. The latter section suggested that a signature accompanied by words of guaranty created an obligation distinct from that of an accommodation party. Revised Article 3 eliminates that confusion by stating in Section 3–419 the obligation of a person who uses words of guaranty. Portions of former Section 3–416 are preserved. Former Section 3–416(2) is reflected in Section 3–419(d) and former Section 3–416(4) is reflected in Section 3–419(c). Words added to an anomalous indorsement indicating that payment of the instrument is guaranteed by the indorser do not change the liability of the indorser as stated in Section 3–415. This is a change from former Section 3–416(5). See PEB Commentary No. 11, supra.

5. Subsection (e) like former Section 3–415(5), provides that an accommodation party that pays the instrument is entitled to enforce the instrument against the accommodated party. Since the accommodation party that pays the instrument is entitled to enforce the instrument against the accommodated party, the accommodation party also obtains rights to any security interest or other collateral that secures payment of the instrument. Subsection (e) also provides that an accommodation party that pays the instrument is entitled to reimbursement from the accommodated party. See PEB Commentary No. 11, supra.

6. In occasional cases, the accommodation party might pay the instrument even though the accommodated party had a defense to its obligation that was available to the accommodation party under Section 3–305(d). In such cases, the accommodation party's right to reimbursement may conflict with the accommodated party's right to raise its defense. For example, suppose the accommodation party pays the instrument without being aware of the defense. In that case the accommodation party should be entitled to reimbursement. Suppose the accommodation party paid the instrument with knowledge of the defense. In that case, to the extent of the defense, reimbursement ordinarily would not be justified, but under some circumstances reimbursement may be justified depending upon the facts of the case. The resolution of this conflict is left to the general law of suretyship. Section 1–103. See PEB Commentary No. 11, supra.

7. Section 3–419, along with Section 3–116(a) and (b), Section 3–305(d) and Section 3–605, provides rules governing the rights of accommodation parties. In addition, except to the extent that it is displaced by provisions of this Article, the general law of suretyship also applies to the rights of accommodation parties. Section 1–103. See PEB Commentary No. 11, supra.

State Bar Committee Comments

Pursuant to section 1.103, revised Chapter 3 and section 3.419 should not be construed to displace the well developed principles of the common law of surety, including for example any right of exoneration, to the extent such principles are not directly in conflict with Chapter 3 or section 3.419.

§ 3.420. Conversion of Instrument

(a) The law applicable to conversion of personal property applies to instruments. An instrument is also converted if it is taken by transfer, other than a negotiation, from a person not entitled to enforce the instrument or a bank makes or obtains payment with respect to the instrument for a person not entitled to enforce the instrument or receive payment. An action for conversion of an instrument may not be brought by:

(1) the issuer or acceptor of the instrument; or

(2) a payee or indorsee who did not receive delivery of the instrument either directly or through delivery to an agent or a co-payee.

(b) In an action under Subsection (a), the measure of liability is presumed to be the amount payable on the instrument, but recovery may not exceed the amount of the plaintiff's interest in the instrument.

(c) A representative, other than a depositary bank, who has in good faith dealt with an instrument or its proceeds on behalf of one who was not the person entitled to enforce the instrument is not liable in conversion to that person beyond the amount of any proceeds that it has not paid out.

Added by Acts 1995, 74th Leg., ch. 921, § 1, eff. Jan. 1, 1996.

Uniform Commercial Code Comment

1. Section 3–420 is a modification of former Section 3–419. The first sentence of Section 3–420(a) states a general rule that the law of conversion applicable to personal property also applies to instruments. Paragraphs (a) and (b) of former Section 3–419(1) are deleted as inappropriate in cases of noncash items that may be delivered for acceptance or payment in collection letters that contain varying instructions as to what to do in the event of nonpayment on the day of delivery. It is better to allow such cases to be governed by the general law of conversion that would address the issue of when, under the circumstances prevailing, the presenter's right to possession has been denied. The second sentence of Section 3–420(a) states that an instrument is converted if it is taken by transfer other than a negotiation from a person not entitled to enforce the instrument or taken for collection or payment from a person not entitled to enforce the instrument or receive payment. This covers cases in which a depositary or payor bank takes an instrument bearing a forged indorsement. It also covers cases in which an instrument is payable to two persons and the two persons are not alternative payees, e.g., a check payable to John and Jane Doe. Under Section 3–110(d) the check can be negotiated or enforced only by both persons acting jointly. Thus, neither payee acting without the consent of the other, is a person entitled to enforce the instrument. If John indorses the check and Jane does not, the indorsement is not effective to allow negotiation of the check. If Depositary Bank takes the check for deposit to John's account, Depositary Bank is liable to Jane for conversion of the check if she did not consent to the transaction. John, acting alone, is not the person entitled to enforce the check because John is not the holder of the check. Section 3–110(d) and Comment 4 to Section 3–110. Depositary Bank does not get any greater rights under Section 4–205(1). If it acted for John as its customer,

it did not become holder of the check under that provision because John, its customer, was not a holder.

Under former Article 3, the cases were divided on the issue of whether the drawer of a check with a forged indorsement can assert rights against a depositary bank that took the check. The last sentence of Section 3–420(a) resolves the conflict by following the rule stated in *Stone & Webster Engineering Corp. v. First National Bank & Trust Co.*, 184 N.E.2d 358 (Mass.1962). There is no reason why a drawer should have an action in conversion. The check represents an obligation of the drawer rather than property of the drawer. The drawer has an adequate remedy against the payor bank for recredit of the drawer's account for unauthorized payment of the check.

There was also a split of authority under former Article 3 on the issue of whether a payee who never received the instrument is a proper plaintiff in a conversion action. The typical case was one in which a check was stolen from the drawer or in which the check was mailed to an address different from that of the payee and was stolen after it arrived at that address. The thief forged the indorsement of the payee and obtained payment by depositing the check to an account in a depositary bank. The issue was whether the payee could bring an action in conversion against the depositary bank or the drawee bank. In revised Article 3, under the last sentence of Section 3–420(a), the payee has no conversion action because the check was never delivered to the payee. Until delivery, the payee does not have any interest in the check. The payee never became the holder of the check nor a person entitled to enforce the check. Section 3–301. Nor is the payee injured by the fraud. Normally the drawer of a check intends to pay an obligation owed to the payee. But if the check is never delivered to the payee, the obligation owed to the payee is not affected. If the check falls into the hands of a thief who obtains payment after forging the signature of the payee as an indorsement, the obligation owed to the payee continues to exist after the thief receives payment. Since the payee's right to enforce the underlying obligation is unaffected by the fraud of the thief, there is no reason to give any additional remedy to the payee. The drawer of the check has no conversion remedy, but the drawee is not entitled to charge the drawer's account when the drawee wrongfully honored the check. The remedy of the drawee is against the depositary bank for breach of warranty under Section 3–417(a)(1) or 4–208(a)(1). The loss will fall on the person who gave value to the thief for the check.

The situation is different if the check is delivered to the payee. If the check is taken for an obligation owed to the payee, the last sentence of Section 3–310(b)(4) provides that the obligation may not be enforced to the extent of the amount of the check. The payee's rights are restricted to enforcement of the payee's rights in the instrument. In this event the payee is injured by the theft and has a cause of action for conversion.

The payee receives delivery when the check comes into the payee's possession, as for example when it is put into the payee's mailbox. Delivery to an agent is delivery to the payee. If a check is payable to more than one payee, delivery to one of the payees is deemed to be delivery to all of the payees. Occasionally, the person asserting a conversion cause of action is an indorsee rather that the original payee. If the check is stolen before the check can be delivered to the indorsee and the indorsee's indorsement is forged, the analysis is similar. For example, a check is payable to the order of A. A indorses it to B and puts it into an envelope addressed to B. The envelope is never delivered to B. Rather, Thief steals the envelope, forges B's indorsement to the check and obtains payment. Because the check was never delivered to B, the indorsee, B has no cause of action for conversion, but A does have such an action. A is the owner of the check. B never obtained rights in the check. If A intended to negotiate the check to B in payment of an obligation, that obligation was not affected by the conduct of Thief. B can enforce that obligation. Thief stole A's property not B's.

2. Subsection (2) of former Section 3–419 is amended because it is not clear why the former law distinguished between the liability of the drawee and that of other converters. Why should there be a conclusive presumption that the liability is face amount if a drawee refuses to pay or return an instrument or makes payment on a forged indorsement, while the liability of a maker who does the same thing is only presumed to be the face amount? Moreover, it was not clear under former Section 3–419(2) what face amount meant. If a note for $10,000 is payable in a year at 10% interest, it is common to refer to $10,000 as the face amount, but if the note is converted the loss to the owner also includes the loss of interest. In revised Article 3, Section 3–420(b), by referring to "amount payable on the instrument," allows the full amount due under the instrument to be recovered.

The "but" clause in subsection (b) addresses the problem of conversion actions in multiple payee checks. Section 3–110(d) states that an instrument cannot be enforced unless all payees join in the action. But an action for conversion might be brought by a payee having no interest or a limited interest in the proceeds of the check. This clause prevents such a plaintiff from receiving a windfall. An example is a check payable to a building contractor and a supplier of building material. The check is not payable to the payees alternatively. Section 3–110(d). The check is delivered to the contractor by the owner of the building. Suppose the contractor forges supplier's signature as an indorsement of the check and receives the entire proceeds of the check. The supplier should not, without qualification, be able to recover the entire amount of the check from the bank that converted the check. Depending upon the contract between the contractor and the supplier, the amount of the check may be due entirely to the contractor, in which case there should be no recovery, entirely to the supplier, in which case recovery should be for the entire amount, or part may be due to one and the rest to the other, in which case recovery should be limited to the amount due to the supplier.

3. Subsection (3) of former Section 3–419 drew criticism from the courts, that saw no reason why a depositary bank should have the defense stated in the subsection. *See Knesz v. Central Jersey Bank & Trust Co.*, 477 A.2d 806 (N.J.1984). The depositary bank is ultimately liable in the case of a forged indorsement check because of its warranty to the payor bank under Section 4–208(a)(1) and it is usually the most convenient defendant in cases involving multiple checks drawn on different banks. There is no basis for requiring the owner of the check to bring multiple actions against the

various payor banks and to require those banks to assert warranty rights against the depositary bank. In revised Article 3, the defense provided by Section 3–420(c) is limited to collecting banks other than the depositary bank. If suit is brought against both the payor bank and the depositary bank, the owner, of course, is entitled to but one recovery.

SUBCHAPTER E. DISHONOR

§ 3.501. Presentment

(a) "Presentment" means a demand made by or on behalf of a person entitled to enforce an instrument to:

(1) pay the instrument made to the drawee or a party obliged to pay the instrument or, in the case of a note or accepted draft payable at a bank, to the bank; or

(2) accept a draft made to the drawee.

(b) The following rules are subject to Chapter 4, agreement of the parties, and clearing-house rules and the like:

(1) Presentment may be made at the place of payment of the instrument and must be made at the place of payment if the instrument is payable at a bank in the United States. Presentment may be made by any commercially reasonable means, including an oral, written, or electronic communication. Presentment is effective:

(A) when the demand for payment or acceptance is received by the person to whom presentment is made; and

(B) if made to any one of two or more makers, acceptors, drawees, or other payors.

(2) On demand of the person to whom presentment is made, the person making presentment must:

(A) exhibit the instrument;

(B) give reasonable identification and, if presentment is made on behalf of another person, reasonable evidence of authority to do so; and

(C) sign a receipt on the instrument for any payment made or surrender the instrument if full payment is made.

(3) Without dishonoring the instrument, the party to whom presentment is made may:

(A) return the instrument for lack of a necessary indorsement; or

(B) refuse payment or acceptance for failure of the presentment to comply with the terms of the instrument, an agreement of the parties, or other applicable law or rule.

(4) The party to whom presentment is made may treat presentment as occurring on the next business day after the day of presentment if the party to whom presentment is made has established a cutoff hour not earlier than 2 p.m. for the receipt and processing of instruments presented for payment or acceptance and presentment is made after the cutoff hour.

Amended by Acts 1995, 74th Leg., ch. 921, § 1, eff. Jan. 1, 1996.

Uniform Commercial Code Comment

Subsection (a) defines presentment. Subsection (b)(1) states the place and manner of presentment. Electronic presentment is authorized. The communication of the demand for payment or acceptance is effective when received. Subsection (b)(2) restates former Section 3–505. Subsection (b)(2)(i) allows the person to whom presentment is made to require exhibition of the instrument, unless the parties have agreed otherwise as in an electronic presentment agreement. Former Section 3–507(3) is the antecedent of subsection (b)(3)(i). Since a payor must decide whether to pay or accept on the day of presentment, subsection (b)(4) allows the payor to set a cut-off hour for receipt of instruments presented.

§ 3.502. Dishonor

(a) Dishonor of a note is governed by the following rules:

(1) If the note is payable on demand, the note is dishonored if presentment is duly made to the maker and the note is not paid on the day of presentment.

(2) If the note is not payable on demand and is payable at or through a bank or the terms of the note require presentment, the note is dishonored if presentment is duly made and the note is not paid on the day it becomes payable or the day of presentment, whichever is later.

(3) If the note is not payable on demand and Subdivision (2) does not apply, the note is dishonored if it is not paid on the day it becomes payable.

(b) Dishonor of an unaccepted draft other than a documentary draft is governed by the following rules:

(1) If a check is duly presented for payment to the payor bank otherwise than for immediate payment over the counter, the check is dishonored if the payor bank makes timely return of the check or sends timely notice of dishonor or nonpayment un-

der Section 4.301 or 4.302, or becomes accountable for the amount of the check under Section 4.302.

(2) If a draft is payable on demand and Subdivision (1) does not apply, the draft is dishonored if presentment for payment is duly made to the drawee and the draft is not paid on the day of presentment.

(3) If a draft is payable on a date stated in the draft, the draft is dishonored if:

(A) presentment for payment is duly made to the drawee and payment is not made on the day the draft becomes payable or the day of presentment, whichever is later; or

(B) presentment for acceptance is duly made before the day the draft becomes payable and the draft is not accepted on the day of presentment.

(4) If a draft is payable on elapse of a period of time after sight or acceptance, the draft is dishonored if presentment for acceptance is duly made and the draft is not accepted on the day of presentment.

(c) Dishonor of an unaccepted documentary draft occurs according to the rules stated in Subsections (b)(2), (3), and (4), except that payment or acceptance may be delayed without dishonor until not later than the close of the third business day of the drawee following the day on which payment or acceptance is required by those subdivisions.

(d) Dishonor of an accepted draft is governed by the following rules:

(1) If the draft is payable on demand, the draft is dishonored if presentment for payment is duly made to the acceptor and the draft is not paid on the day of presentment.

(2) If the draft is not payable on demand, the draft is dishonored if presentment for payment is duly made to the acceptor and payment is not made on the day it becomes payable or the day of presentment, whichever is later.

(e) In any case in which presentment is otherwise required for dishonor under this section and presentment is excused under Section 3.504, dishonor occurs without presentment if the instrument is not duly accepted or paid.

(f) If a draft is dishonored because timely acceptance of the draft was not made and the person entitled to demand acceptance consents to a late acceptance, from the time of acceptance the draft is treated as never having been dishonored.

Amended by Acts 1995, 74th Leg., ch. 921, § 1, eff. Jan. 1, 1996.

Uniform Commercial Code Comment

1. Section 3–415 provides that an indorser is obliged to pay an instrument if the instrument is dishonored and is discharged if the indorser is entitled to notice of dishonor and notice is not given. Under Section 3–414, the drawer is obliged to pay an unaccepted draft if it is dishonored. The drawer, however, is not entitled to notice of dishonor except to the extent required in a case governed by Section 3–414(d). Part 5 tells when an instrument is dishonored (Section 3–502) and what it means to give notice of dishonor (Section 3–503). Often dishonor does not occur until presentment (Section 3–501), and frequently presentment and notice of dishonor are excused (Section 3–504).

2. In the great majority of cases presentment and notice of dishonor are waived with respect to notes. In most cases a formal demand for payment to the maker of the note is not contemplated. Rather, the maker is expected to send payment to the holder of the note on the date or dates on which payment is due. If payment is not made when due, the holder usually makes a demand for payment, but in the normal case in which presentment is waived, demand is irrelevant and the holder can proceed against indorsers when payment is not received. Under former Article 3, in the small minority of cases in which presentment and dishonor were not waived with respect to notes, the indorser was discharged from liability (former Section 3–502(1)(a)) unless the holder made presentment to the maker on the exact day the note was due (former Section 3–503(1)(c)) and gave notice of dishonor to the indorser before midnight of the third business day after dishonor (former Section 3–508(2)). These provisions are omitted from Revised Article 3 as inconsistent with practice which seldom involves face-to-face dealings.

3. Subsection (a) applies to notes. Subsection (a)(1) applies to notes payable on demand. Dishonor requires presentment, and dishonor occurs if payment is not made on the day of presentment. There is no change from previous Article 3. Subsection (a)(2) applies to notes payable at a definite time if the note is payable at or through a bank or, by its terms, presentment is required. Dishonor requires presentment, and dishonor occurs if payment is not made on the due date or the day of presentment if presentment is made after the due date. Subsection (a)(3) applies to all other notes. If the note is not paid on its due date it is dishonored. This allows holders to collect notes in ways that make sense commercially without having to be concerned about a formal presentment on a given day.

4. Subsection (b) applies to unaccepted drafts other than documentary drafts. Subsection (b)(1) applies to checks. Except for checks presented for immediate payment over the counter, which are covered by subsection (b)(2), dishonor occurs according to rules stated in Article 4. Those rules contemplate four separate situations that warrant discussion. The first two situations arise in the normal course of affairs, in which the drawee bank makes settlement for the amount

of the check to the presenting bank. In the first situation, the drawee bank under Section 4–301 recovers this settlement if it returns the check by its midnight deadline (Section 4-104). In that case the check is not paid and dishonor occurs under Section 3–502(b)(1). The second situation arises if the drawee bank has made such a settlement and does not return the check or give notice of dishonor or nonpayment within the midnight deadline. In that case, the settlement becomes final payment of the check under Section 4-215. Because the drawee bank already has paid such an item, it cannot be "accountable" for the item under the terms of Section 4–302(a)(1). Thus, no dishonor occurs regardless of whether the drawee bank retains the check indefinitely or for some reason returns the check after its midnight deadline.

The third and fourth situations arise less commonly, in cases in which the drawee bank does not settle for the check when it is received. Under Section 4–302 if the drawee bank is not also the depositary bank and retains the check without settling for it beyond midnight of the day it is presented for payment, the bank at that point becomes "accountable" for the amount of the check, i.e., it is obliged to pay the amount of the check. If the drawee bank is also the depositary bank, the bank becomes accountable for the amount of the check if the bank does not pay the check or return it or send notice of dishonor by its midnight deadline. Hence, if the drawee bank is also the depositary bank and does not either settle for the check when it is received (a settlement that would ripen into final payment if the drawee bank failed to take action to recover the settlement by its midnight deadline) or return the check or an appropriate notice by its midnight deadline, the drawee bank will become accountable for the amount of the check under Section 4–302. Thus, in all cases in which the drawee bank becomes accountable under Section 4–302, the check has not been paid (either by a settlement that became unrecoverable or otherwise) and thus, under Section 3–502(b)(1), the check is dishonored.

The fact that a bank that is accountable for the amount of the check under Section 4–302 is obliged to pay the check does not mean that the check has been paid. Indeed, because each of the paragraphs of Section 4–302(b) is limited by its terms to situations in which a bank has not paid the item, a drawee bank will be accountable under Section 4–302 only in situations in which it has not previously paid the check. Section 3–502(b)(1) reflects the view that a person presenting a check is entitled to payment, not just the ability to hold the drawee accountable under Section 4–302. If that payment is not made in a timely manner, the check is dishonored.

Regulation CC Section 229.36(d) provides that settlement between banks for the forward collection of checks is final. The relationship of that section to Articles 3 and 4 is discussed in the Commentary to that section. *Amendments approved by the Permanent Editorial Board for Uniform Commercial Code November 2, 2002.*

Subsection (b)(2) applies to demand drafts other than those governed by subsection (b)(1). It covers checks presented for immediate payment over the counter and demand drafts other than checks. Dishonor occurs if presentment for payment is made and payment is not made on the day of presentment.

Subsection (b)(3) and (4) applies to time drafts. An unaccepted time draft differs from a time note. The maker of a note knows that the note has been issued, but the drawee of a draft may not know that a draft has been drawn on it. Thus, with respect to drafts, presentment for payment or acceptance is required. Subsection (b)(3) applies to drafts payable on a date stated in the draft. Dishonor occurs if presentment for payment is made and payment is not made on the day the draft becomes payable or the day of presentment if presentment is made after the due date. The holder of an unaccepted draft payable on a stated date has the option of presenting the draft for acceptance before the day the draft becomes payable to establish whether the drawee is willing to assume liability by accepting. Under subsection (b)(3)(ii) dishonor occurs when the draft is presented and not accepted. Subsection (b)(4) applies to unaccepted drafts payable on elapse of a period of time after sight or acceptance. If the draft is payable 30 days after sight, the draft must be presented for acceptance to start the running of the 30–day period. Dishonor occurs if it is not accepted. The rules in subsection (b)(3) and (4) follow former Section 3–501(1)(a).

5. Subsection (c) gives drawees an extended period to pay documentary drafts because of the time that may be needed to examine the documents. The period prescribed is that given by Section 5–112 in cases in which a letter of credit is involved.

6. Subsection (d) governs accepted drafts. If the acceptor's obligation is to pay on demand the rule, stated in subsection (d)(1), is the same as for that of a demand note stated in subsection (a)(1). If the acceptor's obligation is to pay at a definite time the rule, stated in subsection (d)(2), is the same as that of a time note payable at a bank stated in subsection (b)(2).

7. Subsection (e) is a limitation on subsection (a)(1) and (2), subsection (b), subsection (c), and subsection (d). Each of those provisions states dishonor as occurring after presentment. If presentment is excused under Section 3–504, dishonor occurs under those provisions without presentment if the instrument is not duly accepted or paid.

8. Under subsection (b)(3)(ii) and (4) if a draft is presented for acceptance and the draft is not accepted on the day of presentment, there is dishonor. But after dishonor, the holder may consent to late acceptance. In that case, under subsection (f), the late acceptance cures the dishonor. The draft is treated as never having been dishonored. If the draft is subsequently presented for payment and payment is refused dishonor occurs at that time.

§ 3.503. Notice of Dishonor

(a) The obligation of an indorser stated in Section 3.415(a) and the obligation of a drawer stated in Section 3.414(d) may not be enforced unless:

(1) the indorser or drawer is given notice of dishonor of the instrument complying with this section; or

(2) notice of dishonor is excused under Section 3.504(b).

(b) Notice of dishonor may be given by any person; may be given by any commercially reasonable means, including an oral, written, or electronic communication; and is sufficient if it reasonably identifies the instrument and indicates that the instrument has been dishonored or has not been paid or accepted. Return of an instrument given to a bank for collection is sufficient notice of dishonor.

(c) Subject to Section 3.504(c), with respect to an instrument taken for collection by a collecting bank, notice of dishonor must be given (i) by the bank before midnight of the next banking day following the banking day on which the bank receives notice of dishonor of the instrument, or (ii) by any other person within 30 days following the day on which the person receives notice of dishonor. With respect to any other instrument, notice of dishonor must be given within 30 days following the day on which dishonor occurs.

Amended by Acts 1995, 74th Leg., ch. 921, § 1, eff. Jan. 1, 1996.

Uniform Commercial Code Comment

1. Subsection (a) is consistent with former Section 3–501(2)(a), but notice of dishonor is no longer relevant to the liability of a drawer except for the case of a draft accepted by an acceptor other than a bank. Comments 2 and 4 to Section 3–414. There is no reason why drawers should be discharged on instruments they draw until payment or acceptance. They are entitled to have the instrument presented to the drawee and dishonored (Section 3–414(b)) before they are liable to pay, but no notice of dishonor need be made to them as a condition of liability. Subsection (b), which states how notice of dishonor is given, is based on former Section 3–508(3).

2. Subsection (c) replaces former Section 3–508(2). It differs from that section in that it provides a 30–day period for a person other than a collecting bank to give notice of dishonor rather than the three-day period allowed in former Article 3. Delay in giving notice of dishonor may be excused under Section 3–504(c).

§ 3.504. Excused Presentment and Notice of Dishonor

(a) Presentment for payment or acceptance of an instrument is excused if:

(1) the person entitled to present the instrument cannot with reasonable diligence make presentment;

(2) the maker or acceptor has repudiated an obligation to pay the instrument or is dead or in insolvency proceedings;

(3) by the terms of the instrument presentment is not necessary to enforce the obligation of indorsers or the drawer;

(4) the drawer or indorser whose obligation is being enforced has waived presentment or otherwise has no reason to expect or right to require that the instrument be paid or accepted; or

(5) the drawer instructed the drawee not to pay or accept the draft or the drawee was not obligated to the drawer to pay the draft.

(b) Notice of dishonor is excused if (i) by the terms of the instrument notice of dishonor is not necessary to enforce the obligation of a party to pay the instrument, or (ii) the party whose obligation is being enforced waived notice of dishonor. A waiver of presentment is also a waiver of notice of dishonor.

(c) Delay in giving notice of dishonor is excused if the delay was caused by circumstances beyond the control of the person giving the notice and the person giving the notice exercised reasonable diligence after the cause of the delay ceased to operate.

Amended by Acts 1995, 74th Leg., ch. 921, § 1, eff. Jan. 1, 1996.

Uniform Commercial Code Comment

Section 3–504 is largely a restatement of former Section 3–511. Subsection (4) of former Section 3–511 is replaced by Section 3–502(f).

§ 3.505. Evidence of Dishonor

(a) The following are admissible as evidence and create a presumption of dishonor and of any notice of dishonor stated:

(1) a document regular in form as provided in Subsection (b) that purports to be a protest;

(2) a purported stamp or writing of the drawee, payor bank, or presenting bank on or accompanying the instrument stating that acceptance or payment has been refused unless reasons for the refusal are stated and the reasons are not consistent with dishonor;

(3) a book or record of the drawee, payor bank, or collecting bank that is kept in the usual course of business and that shows dishonor, even if there is no evidence of who made the entry.

(b) A protest is a certificate of dishonor made by a United States consul or vice consul, or a notary public or other person authorized to administer oaths by the law of the place where dishonor occurs. It may be made on information satisfactory to that person. The protest must identify the instrument and certify either that presentment has been made or, if not made, the reason why it was not made, and that the instrument has been dishonored by nonacceptance or nonpayment. The protest may also certify that notice of dishonor has been given to some or all parties.

Amended by Acts 1995, 74th Leg., ch. 921, § 1, eff. Jan. 1, 1996.

Uniform Commercial Code Comment

Protest is no longer mandatory and must be requested by the holder. Even if requested, protest is not a condition to the liability of indorsers or drawers. Protest is a service provided by the banking system to establish that dishonor has occurred. Like other services provided by the banking system, it will be available if market incentives, interbank agreements, or governmental regulations require it, but liabilities of parties no longer rest on it. Protest may be a requirement for liability on international drafts governed by foreign law which this Article cannot affect.

§ 3.506. Processing Fee by Holder of Payment Device

(a) For purposes of this section, "payment device" means any check, item, paper or electronic payment, or other payment device used as a medium for payment.

(b) On return of a payment device to the holder following dishonor of the payment device by a payor, the holder, the holder's assignee, agent, or representative, or any other person retained by the holder to seek collection of the face value of the dishonored payment device may charge the drawer or indorser a reasonable processing fee of not more than $30.

(c) A person may not charge a processing fee to a drawer or indorser under this section if the fee has been collected under Article 102.007(e) or 102.0071, Code of Criminal Procedure. If a processing fee has been collected under this section and the holder subsequently receives a fee collected under Article 102.007(e) or 102.0071, Code of Criminal Procedure, the holder shall immediately refund the fee previously collected from the drawer or indorser.

(d) Notwithstanding Subtitle B, Title 4, Finance Code, or any other law, a contract made under Subtitle B, Title 4, Finance Code, may provide that on return of a dishonored payment device given in payment under the contract, the holder may charge the obligor under the contract the processing fee authorized by this section, and the fee may be added to the unpaid balance owed under the contract. Interest may not be charged on the fee during the term of the contract.

(e) This section does not affect any right or remedy to which the holder of a payment device may be entitled under any rule, written contract, judicial decision, or other statute.

Added by Acts 2001, 77th Leg., ch. 1420, § 2.001(a), eff. Sept. 1, 2001; Amended by Acts 2003, 78th Leg., ch. 413, § 1, eff. Sept. 1, 2003; Acts 2005, 79th Leg., ch. 95, § 11, eff. Sept. 1, 2005.

§ 3.507. Delivery Notification Fee by Holder of Check or Similar Sight Order

(a) On return of a check or similar sight order to the holder following dishonor of the check or sight order by a payor and prior to the check or sight order being referred for prosecution, the holder, the holder's assignee, agent, or representative, or any other person retained by the holder to seek collection of the dishonored check or sight order may charge the drawer or indorser of the check or sight order the cost of delivery notification by registered or certified mail with return receipt requested under Section 31.06 or Section 32.41, Penal Code, as applicable.

(b) A person may not charge a delivery notification fee to a drawer or indorser under this section if the fee has been collected under Article 102.007(g), Code of Criminal Procedure. If a delivery notification fee has been collected under this section and the holder subsequently receives a fee collected under Article 102.007(g), Code of Criminal Procedure, the holder shall immediately refund the fee previously collected from the drawer or indorser.

(c) This section does not affect any right or remedy to which the holder of a check or similar sight order may be entitled under any rule, written contract, judicial decision, or other statute, including Section 3.506.

Added by Acts 2007, 80th Leg., ch. 976, § 4, eff. Sept. 1, 2007.

Section 5 of Acts 2007, 80th Leg., ch. 976 provides:

"The change in law made by this Act applies only to an offense committed on or after the effective date [Sept. 1, 2007] of this Act. An offense committed before the effective date of this Act is covered by the law in effect when the offense was committed, and the former law is continued in effect for that purpose. For purposes of this section, an offense was committed before the effective date of this Act if any element of the offense was committed before that date."

§§ 3.508 to 3.511. Deleted by Acts 1995, 74th Leg., ch. 921, § 1, eff. Jan. 1, 1996

SUBCHAPTER F. DISCHARGE AND PAYMENT

§ 3.601. Discharge and Effect of Discharge

(a) The obligation of a party to pay the instrument is discharged as stated in this chapter or by an act or agreement with the party that would discharge an obligation to pay money under a simple contract.

(b) Discharge of the obligation of a party is not effective against a person acquiring rights of a holder in due course of the instrument without notice of the discharge.

Amended by Acts 1995, 74th Leg., ch. 921, § 1, eff. Jan. 1, 1996.

Uniform Commercial Code Comment

Subsection (a) replaces subsections (1) and (2) of former Section 3–601. Subsection (b) restates former Section 3–602. Notice of discharge is not treated as notice of a defense that prevents holder in due course status. Section 3–302(b). Discharge is effective against a holder in due course only if the holder had notice of the discharge when holder in due course status was acquired. For example, if an instrument bearing a canceled indorsement is taken by a holder, the holder has notice that the indorser has been discharged. Thus, the discharge is effective against the holder even if the holder is a holder in due course.

§ 3.602. Payment

(a) Subject to Subsection (e), an instrument is paid to the extent payment is made by or on behalf of a party obliged to pay the instrument, and to a person entitled to enforce the instrument.

(b) Subject to Subsection (e), a note is paid to the extent payment is made by or on behalf of a party obliged to pay the note to a person that formerly was entitled to enforce the note only if at the time of the payment the party obliged to pay has not received adequate notification that the note has been transferred and that payment is to be made to the transferee. A notification is adequate only if it is signed by the transferor or the transferee, reasonably identifies the transferred note, and provides an address at which payments subsequently are to be made. Upon request, a transferee shall seasonably furnish reasonable proof that the note has been transferred. Unless the transferee complies with the request, a payment to the person that formerly was entitled to enforce the note is effective for purposes of Subsection (c) even if the party obliged to pay the note has received a notification under this subsection.

(c) Subject to Subsection (e), to the extent of a payment under Subsections (a) and (b), the obligation of the party obliged to pay the instrument is discharged even though payment is made with knowledge of a claim to the instrument under Section 3.306 by another person.

(d) Subject to Subsection (e), a transferee, or any party that has acquired rights in the instrument directly or indirectly from a transferee, including any such party that has rights as a holder in due course, is deemed to have notice of any payment that is made under Subsection (b) after the date that the note is transferred to the transferee but before the party obliged to pay the note receives adequate notification of the transfer.

(e) The obligation of a party to pay the instrument is not discharged under Subsections (a) through (d) if:

(1) a claim to the instrument under Section 3.306 is enforceable against the party receiving payment and:

(A) payment is made with knowledge by the payor that payment is prohibited by injunction or similar process of a court of competent jurisdiction; or

(B) in the case of an instrument other than a cashier's check, teller's check, or certified check, the party making payment accepted, from the person having a claim to the instrument, indemnity against loss resulting from refusal to pay the person entitled to enforce the instrument; or

(2) the person making payment knows that the instrument is a stolen instrument and pays a person it knows is in wrongful possession of the instrument.

(f) As used in this section, "signed," with respect to a record that is not a writing, includes the attachment to or logical association with the record of an electronic symbol, sound, or process with the present intent to adopt or accept the record.

Amended by Acts 1995, 74th Leg., ch. 921, § 1, eff. Jan. 1, 1996; Acts 2005, 79th Leg., ch. 95, § 12, eff. Sept. 1, 2005.

Uniform Commercial Code Comment

1. This section replaces former Section 3–603(1). The phrase "claim to the instrument" in subsection (a) means, by reference to Section 3–306, a claim of ownership or possession and not a claim in recoupment. Subsection (e)(1)(ii) is added to conform to Section 3–411. Section 3–411 is intended to discourage an obligated bank from refusing payment of a cashier's check, certified check or dishonored teller's check at the request of a claimant to the check who provided the bank with indemnity against loss. See Comment 1 to Section 3–411. An obligated bank that refuses payment under those circumstances not only remains liable on the check but may also be liable to the holder of the check for consequential damages. Section 3–602(e)(1)(ii) and Section 3–411, read together, change the rule of former Section 3–603(1) with respect to the obligation of the obligated bank on the check. Payment to the holder of a cashier's check, teller's check, or certified check discharges the obligation of the obligated

bank on the check to both the holder and the claimant even though indemnity has been given by the person asserting the claim. If the obligated bank pays the check in violation of an agreement with the claimant in connection with the indemnity agreement, any liability that the bank may have for violation of the agreement is not governed by Article 3, but is left to other law. This section continues the rule that the obligor is not discharged on the instrument if payment is made in violation of an injunction against payment. See Section 3–411(c)(iv).

2. Subsection (a) covers payments made in a traditional manner, to the person entitled to enforce the instrument. Subsection (b), which provides an alternative method of payment, deals with the situation in which a person entitled to enforce the instrument transfers the instrument without giving notice to parties obligated to pay the instrument. If that happens and one of those parties subsequently makes a payment to the transferor, the payment is effective even though it is not made to the person entitled to enforce the instrument. Unlike the earlier version of Section 3–602, this rule is consistent with Section 9–406(a), Restatement of Mortgages § 5.5, and Restatement of Contracts § 338(1).

3. In determining the party to whom a payment is made for purposes of this section, courts should look to traditional rules of agency. Thus, if the original payee of a note transfers ownership of the note to a third party but continues to service the obligation, the law of agency might treat payments made to the original payee as payments made to the third party.

4. Subsection (d) assures that the discharge provided by subsection (c) is effective against the transferee and those whose rights derive from the transferee. By deeming those persons to have notice of any payment made under subsection (b), subsection (d) gives those persons "notice of the discharge" within the meaning of Section 3–302(b). Accordingly, the discharge is effective against those persons, even if any of them has the rights of a holder in due course. Compare Section 3–601(b). The deemed notice provided by subsection (d) does not, however, prevent a person from becoming or acquiring the rights of, a holder in due course. See Section 3–302(b). Thus, such a person does not become subject to other defenses described in Section 3–305(a)(2), claims in recoupment described in Section 3–305(a)(3), or claims to the instrument under Section 3–306. A transferee can prevent payment to the transferor from discharging the obligation on the note by assuring that each person who is obligated on the note receives adequate notification pursuant to subsection (b) prior to making a payment. *Amendment approved by the Permanent Editorial Board for Uniform Commercial Code October 31, 2003.*

§ 3.603. Tender of Payment

(a) If tender of payment of an obligation to pay an instrument is made to a person entitled to enforce the instrument, the effect of tender is governed by principles of law applicable to tender of payment under a simple contract.

(b) If tender of payment of an obligation to pay an instrument is made to a person entitled to enforce the instrument and the tender is refused, there is discharge, to the extent of the amount of the tender, of the obligation of an indorser or accommodation party having a right of recourse with respect to the obligation to which the tender relates.

(c) If tender of payment of an amount due on an instrument is made to a person entitled to enforce the instrument, the obligation of the obligor to pay interest after the due date on the amount tendered is discharged. If presentment is required with respect to an instrument and the obligor is able and ready to pay on the due date at every place of payment stated in the instrument, the obligor is deemed to have made tender of payment on the due date to the person entitled to enforce the instrument.

Amended by Acts 1995, 74th Leg., ch. 921, § 1, eff. Jan. 1, 1996.

Uniform Commercial Code Comment

Section 3–603 replaces former Section 3–604. Subsection (a) generally incorporates the law of tender of payment applicable to simple contracts. Subsections (b) and (c) state particular rules. Subsection (b) replaces former Section 3–604(2). Under subsection (b) refusal of a tender of payment discharges any indorser or accommodation party having a right of recourse against the party making the tender. Subsection (c) replaces former Section 3–604(1) and (3).

§ 3.604. Discharge by Cancellation or Renunciation

(a) A person entitled to enforce an instrument, with or without consideration, may discharge the obligation of a party to pay the instrument:

(1) by an intentional voluntary act, such as surrender of the instrument to the party, destruction, mutilation, or cancellation of the instrument, cancellation or striking out of the party's signature, or the addition of words to the instrument indicating discharge; or

(2) by agreeing not to sue or otherwise renouncing rights against the party by a signed record.

(b) Cancellation or striking out of an indorsement pursuant to Subsection (a) does not affect the status and rights of a party derived from the indorsement.

(c) In this section, "signed," with respect to a record that is not a writing, includes the attachment to or logical association with the record of an electronic symbol, sound, or process with the present intent to adopt or accept the record.

Amended by Acts 1995, 74th Leg., ch. 921, § 1, eff. Jan. 1, 1996; Acts 2005, 79th Leg., ch. 95, § 13, eff. Sept. 1, 2005.

Uniform Commercial Code Comment

Section 3–604 replaces former Section 3–605.

§ 3.605. Discharge of Secondary Obligors

(a) If a person entitled to enforce an instrument releases the obligation of a principal obligor in whole or in part, and another party to the instrument is a secondary obligor with respect to the obligation of that principal obligor, the following rules apply:

(1) Any obligations of the principal obligor to the secondary obligor with respect to any previous payment by the secondary obligor are not affected. Unless the terms of the release preserve the secondary obligor's recourse, the principal obligor is discharged, to the extent of the release, from any other duties to the secondary obligor under this chapter.

(2) Unless the terms of the release provide that the person entitled to enforce the instrument retains the right to enforce the instrument against the secondary obligor, the secondary obligor is discharged to the same extent as the principal obligor from any unperformed portion of its obligation on the instrument. If the instrument is a check and the obligation of the secondary obligor is based on an indorsement of the check, the secondary obligor is discharged without regard to the language or circumstances of the discharge or other release.

(3) If the secondary obligor is not discharged under Subdivision (2), the secondary obligor is discharged to the extent of the value of the consideration for the release, and to the extent that the release would otherwise cause the secondary obligor a loss.

(b) If a person entitled to enforce an instrument grants a principal obligor an extension of the time at which one or more payments are due on the instrument and another party to the instrument is a secondary obligor with respect to the obligation of that principal obligor, the following rules apply:

(1) Any obligations of the principal obligor to the secondary obligor with respect to any previous payment by the secondary obligor are not affected. Unless the terms of the extension preserve the secondary obligor's recourse, the extension correspondingly extends the time for performance of any other duties owed to the secondary obligor by the principal obligor under this chapter.

(2) The secondary obligor is discharged to the extent that the extension would otherwise cause the secondary obligor a loss.

(3) To the extent that the secondary obligor is not discharged under Subdivision (2), the secondary obligor may perform its obligations to a person entitled to enforce the instrument as if the time for payment had not been extended or, unless the terms of the extension provide that the person entitled to enforce the instrument retains the right to enforce the instrument against the secondary obligor as if the time for payment had not been extended, treat the time for performance of its obligations as having been extended correspondingly.

(c) If a person entitled to enforce an instrument agrees, with or without consideration, to a modification of the obligation of a principal obligor other than a complete or partial release or an extension of the due date and another party to the instrument is a secondary obligor with respect to the obligation of that principal obligor, the following rules apply:

(1) Any obligations of the principal obligor to the secondary obligor with respect to any previous payment by the secondary obligor are not affected. The modification correspondingly modifies any other duties owed to the secondary obligor by the principal obligor under this chapter.

(2) The secondary obligor is discharged from any unperformed portion of its obligation to the extent that the modification would otherwise cause the secondary obligor a loss.

(3) To the extent that the secondary obligor is not discharged under Subdivision (2), the secondary obligor may satisfy its obligation on the instrument as if the modification had not occurred, or treat its obligation on the instrument as having been modified correspondingly.

(d) If the obligation of a principal obligor is secured by an interest in collateral, another party to the instrument is a secondary obligor with respect to that obligation, and a person entitled to enforce the instrument impairs the value of the interest in collateral, the obligation of the secondary obligor is discharged to the extent of the impairment. The value of an interest in collateral is impaired to the extent the value of the interest is reduced to an amount less than the amount of the recourse of the secondary obligor, or the reduction in value of the interest causes an increase in the amount by which the amount of the recourse exceeds the value of the interest. For purposes of this subsection, impairing the value of an interest in collateral includes failure to obtain or maintain perfection or recordation of the interest in collateral, release of collateral without substitution of collateral of equal value or equivalent reduction of the underlying obligation, failure to perform a duty to preserve the value of collateral owed, under Chapter 9 or other law, to a debtor or other person secondarily liable, and failure to comply with applicable law in disposing of or otherwise enforcing the interest in collateral.

(e) A secondary obligor is not discharged under Subsection (a)(3), (b), (c), or (d) unless the person entitled to enforce the instrument knows that the person is a secondary obligor or has notice under Section 3.419(c) that the instrument was signed for accommodation.

(f) A secondary obligor is not discharged under this section if the secondary obligor consents to the event or conduct that is the basis of the discharge, or the instrument or a separate agreement of the party provides for waiver of discharge under this section specifically or by general language indicating that parties waive defenses based on suretyship or impairment of collateral. Unless the circumstances indicate otherwise, consent by the principal obligor to an act that would lead to a discharge under this section constitutes consent to that act by the secondary obligor if the secondary obligor controls the principal obligor or deals with the person entitled to enforce the instrument on behalf of the principal obligor.

(g) A release or extension preserves a secondary obligor's recourse if the terms of the release or extension provide that:

(1) the person entitled to enforce the instrument retains the right to enforce the instrument against the secondary obligor; and

(2) the recourse of the secondary obligor continues as if the release or extension had not been granted.

(h) Except as otherwise provided in Subsection (i), a secondary obligor asserting discharge under this section has the burden of persuasion both with respect to the occurrence of the acts alleged to harm the secondary obligor and loss or prejudice caused by those acts.

(i) If the secondary obligor demonstrates prejudice caused by an impairment of its recourse, and the circumstances of the case indicate that the amount of loss is not reasonably susceptible of calculation or requires proof of facts that are not ascertainable, it is presumed that the act impairing recourse caused a loss or impairment equal to the liability of the secondary obligor on the instrument. In that event, the burden of persuasion as to any lesser amount of the loss is on the person entitled to enforce the instrument.

Amended by Acts 1995, 74th Leg., ch. 921, § 1, eff. Jan. 1, 1996; Acts 2005, 79th Leg., ch. 95, § 14, eff. Sept. 1, 2005; Acts 2007, 80th Leg., ch. 427, § 3, eff. Sept. 1, 2007.

Uniform Commercial Code Comment

1. This section contains rules that are applicable when a secondary obligor (as defined in Section 3–103(a)(17)) is a party to an instrument. These rules essentially parallel modern interpretations of the law of suretyship and guaranty that apply when a secondary obligor is not a party to an instrument. See generally *Restatement of the Law, Third, Suretyship and Guaranty* (1996). Of course, the rules in this section do not resolve all possible issues concerning the rights and duties of the parties. In the event that a situation is presented that is not resolved by this section (or the other related sections of this Article), the resolution may be provided by the general law of suretyship because, pursuant to Section 1–103, that law is applicable unless displaced by provisions of this Act.

2. Like the law of suretyship and guaranty, Section 3–605 provides secondary obligors with defenses that are not available to other parties to instruments. The general operation of Section 3–605, and its relationship to the law of suretyship and guaranty, can be illustrated by an example. Bank agrees to lend $10,000 to Borrower, but only if Backer also is liable for repayment of the loan. The parties could consummate that transaction in three different ways. First, if Borrower and Backer incurred those obligations with contracts not governed by this Article (such as a note that is not an instrument for purposes of this Article), the general law of suretyship and guaranty would be applicable. Under modern nomenclature, Bank is the 'obligee,' Borrower is the 'principal obligor,' and Backer is the 'secondary obligor.' See *Restatement of Suretyship and Guaranty* § 1. Then assume that Bank and Borrower agree to a modification of their rights and obligations after the note is signed. For example, they might agree that Borrower may repay the loan at some date after the due date, or that Borrower may discharge its repayment obligation by paying Bank $3,000 rather than $10,000. Alternatively, suppose that Bank releases collateral that Borrower has given to secure the loan. Under the law of suretyship and guaranty, the secondary obligor may be discharged under certain circumstances if these modifications of the obligations between Bank (the obligee) and Borrower (the principal obligor) are made without the consent of Backer (the secondary obligor). The rights that the secondary obligor has to a discharge of its liability in such cases commonly are referred to as suretyship defenses. The ex-

tent of the discharge depends upon the particular circumstances. See *Restatement of Suretyship and Guaranty* §§ 37, 39-44.

A second possibility is that the parties might decide to evidence the loan by a negotiable instrument. In that scenario, Borrower signs a note under which Borrower is obliged to pay $10,000 to the order of Bank on a due date stated in the note. Backer becomes liable for the repayment obligation by signing the note as a co-maker or indorser. In either case the note is signed for accommodation, Backer is an accommodation party, and Borrower is the accommodated party, See Section 3–419 (describing the obligations of accommodation parties). For purposes of Section 3–605, Backer is also a 'secondary obligor' and Borrower is a 'principal obligor,' as those terms are defined in Section 3–103. Because Backer is a party to the instrument, its rights to a discharge based on any modification of obligations between Bank and Borrower are governed by Section 3–605 rather than by the general law of suretyship and guaranty. Within Section 3–605, subsection (a) describes the consequences of a release of Borrower, subsection (b) describes the consequences of an extension of time, and subsection (c) describes the consequences of other modifications.

The third possibility is that Borrower would use an instrument governed by this Article to evidence its repayment obligation, but Backer's obligation would be created in some way other than by becoming party to the instrument. In that case, Backer's rights are determined by suretyship and guaranty law rather than by this Article. See Comment 3 to Section 3–419.

A person also can acquire secondary liability without having been a secondary obligor at the time that the principal obligation was created. For example, a transferee of real or personal property that assumes the obligation of the transferor as maker of a note secured by the property becomes by operation of law a principal obligor, with the transferor becoming a secondary obligor. *Restatement of Suretyship and Guaranty* § 2(e); *Restatement of Mortgages* § 5.1. Article 3 does not determine the effect of the release of the transferee in that case because the assuming transferee is not a 'party' to the instrument as defined in Section 3–103(a)(10). Section 3–605(a) does not apply then because the holder has not discharged the obligation of a 'principal obligor,' a term defined in Section 3–103(a)(11). Thus, the resolution of that question is governed by the law of suretyship. See *Restatement of Suretyship and Guaranty* § 39.

3. Section 3–605 is not, however, limited to the conventional situation of the accommodation party discussed in Comment 2. It also applies in four other situations. First, it applies to indorsers of notes who are not accommodation parties. Unless an indorser signs without recourse, the indorser's liability under Section 3–415(a) is functionally similar to that of a guarantor of payment. For example, if Bank in the second hypothetical discussed in Comment 2 indorsed the note and transferred it to Second Bank, Bank is liable to Second Bank in the event of dishonor of the note by Borrower. Section 3–415(a). Because of that secondary liability as indorser, Bank qualifies as a 'secondary obligor' under Section 3–103(a)(17) and has the same rights under Section 3–605 as an accommodation party.

Second, a similar analysis applies to the drawer of a draft that is accepted by a party that is not a bank. Under Section 3–414(d), that drawer has liability on the same terms as an indorser under Section 3–415(a). Thus, the drawer in that case is a 'secondary obligor' under Section 3–103(a)(17) and has rights under Section 3–605 to that extent.

Third, a similar principle justifies application of Section 3–605 to persons who indorse a check. Assume that Drawer draws a check to the order of Payee. Payee then indorses the check and transfers it to Transferee. If Transferee presents the check and it is dishonored, Transferee may recover from Drawer under Section 3–414 or Payee under Section 3–415. Because of that secondary liability as an indorser, Payee is a secondary obligor under Section 3–103(a)(17). As noted in Comment 4, below, however, Section 3–605(a)(3) will discharge indorsers of checks in some cases in which other secondary obligors will not be discharged by this section.

Fourth, this section also deals with the rights of co-makers of instruments, even when those co-makers do not qualify as accommodation parties. The co-makers' rights of contribution under Section 3–116 make each co-maker a secondary obligor to the extent of that right of contribution.

4. Subsection (a) is based on *Restatement of Suretyship and Guaranty* § 39. It addresses the effects of a release of the principal obligor by the person entitled to enforce the instrument. Paragraph (a)(1) governs the effect of that release on the principal obligor's duties to the secondary obligor; paragraphs (a)(2) and (a)(3) govern the effect of that release on the secondary obligor's duties to the person entitled to enforce the instrument.

With respect to the duties of the principal obligor, the release of course cannot affect obligations of the principal obligor with respect to payments that the secondary obligor already has made. But with respect to future payments by the secondary obligor, paragraph (a)(1) (based on *Restatement of Suretyship and Guaranty* § 39(a)) provides that the principal obligor is discharged, to the extent of the release, from any other duties to the secondary obligor. That rule is appropriate because otherwise the discharge granted to the principal obligor would be illusory: it would have obtained a release from a person entitled to enforce that instrument, but it would be directly liable for the same sum to the secondary obligor if the secondary obligor later complied with its secondary obligation to pay the instrument. This discharge does not occur, though, if the terms of the release effect a 'preservation of recourse' as described in subsection (g). See Comment 10, below.

The discharge under paragraph (a)(1) of the principal obligor's duties to the secondary obligor is broad, applying to all duties under this article. This includes not only the principal obligor's liability as a party to an instrument (as a maker, drawer or indorser under Sections 3–412 through 3–415) but also obligations under Sections 3–116 and 3–419.

Paragraph (a)(2) is based closely on *Restatement of Suretyship and Guaranty* § 39(b). It articulates a default rule that the release of a principal obligor also discharges the secondary obligor, to the extent of the release granted to the principal obligor, from any unperformed portion of its obligation on the instrument. The discharge of the secondary obligor under paragraph (a)(2) is phrased more narrowly than the discharge of the principal obligor is phrased under paragraph (a)(1) because, unlike principal obligors, the only obligations of secondary obligors in Article 3 are 'on the instrument' as makers or indorsers.

The parties can opt out of that rule by including a contrary statement in the terms of the release. The provision does not contemplate that any 'magic words' are necessary. Thus, discharge of the secondary obligor under paragraph (a)(2) is avoided not only if the terms of the release track the statutory language (e.g., the person entitled to enforce the instrument 'retains the right to enforce the instrument' against the secondary obligor), or if the terms of the release effect a preservation of recourse under subsection (g), but also if the terms of the release include a simple statement that the parties intend to 'release the principal obligor but not the secondary obligor' or that the person entitled to enforce the instrument 'reserves its rights' against the secondary obligor. At the same time, because paragraph (a)(2) refers to the 'terms of the release,' extrinsic circumstances cannot be used to establish that the parties intended the secondary obligor to remain obligated. If a release of the principal obligor includes such a provision, the secondary obligor is, nonetheless, discharged to the extent of the consideration that is paid for the release; that consideration is treated as a payment in partial satisfaction of the instrument.

Notwithstanding language in the release that prevents discharge of the secondary obligor under paragraph (a)(2), paragraph (a)(3) discharges the secondary obligor from its obligation to a person entitled to enforce the instrument to the extent that the release otherwise would cause the secondary obligor a loss. The rationale for that provision is that a release of the principal obligor changes the economic risk for which the secondary obligor contracted. This risk may be increased in two ways. First, by releasing the principal obligor, the person entitled to enforce the instrument has eliminated the likelihood of future payments by the principal obligor that would lessen the obligation of the secondary obligor. Second, unless the release effects a preservation of the secondary obligor's recourse, the release eliminates the secondary obligor's claims against the principal obligor with respect to any future payment by the secondary obligor. The discharge provided by this paragraph prevents that increased risk from causing the secondary obligor a loss. Moreover, permitting releases to be negotiated between the principal obligor and the person entitled to enforce the instrument without regard to the consequences to the secondary obligor would create an undue risk of opportunistic behavior by the obligee and principal obligor. That concern is lessened, and the discharge is not provided by paragraph (a)(3), if the secondary obligor has consented to the release or is deemed to have consented to it under subsection (f) (which presumes consent by a secondary obligor to actions taken by a principal obligor if the secondary obligor controls the principal obligor or deals with the person entitled to enforce the instrument on behalf of the principal obligor). See Comment 9, below.

Subsection (a) (and Restatement Section 39(b), the concepts of which it follows quite closely) is designed to facilitate negotiated workouts between a creditor and a principal obligor, so long as they are not at the expense of a secondary obligor who has not consented to the arrangement (either specifically or by waiving its rights to discharge under this section). Thus, for example, the provision facilitates an arrangement in which the principal obligor pays some portion of a guaranteed obligation, the person entitled to enforce the instrument grants a release to the principal obligor in exchange for that payment, and the person entitled to enforce the instrument pursues the secondary obligor for the remainder of the obligation. Under paragraph (a)(2), the person entitled to enforce the instrument may pursue the secondary obligor despite the release of the principal obligor so long as the terms of the release provide for this result. Under paragraph (a)(3), though, the secondary obligor will be protected against any loss it might suffer by reason of that release (if the secondary obligor has not waived discharge under subsection (f)). It should be noted that the obligee may be able to minimize the risk of such loss (and, thus, of the secondary obligor's discharge) by giving the secondary obligor prompt notice of the release even though such notice is not required.

The foregoing principles are illustrated by the following cases:

Case 1. D borrows $1000 from C. The repayment obligation is evidenced by a note issued by D, payable to the order of C. S is an accommodation indorser of the note. As the due date of the note approaches, it becomes obvious that D cannot pay the full amount of the note and may soon be facing bankruptcy. C, in order to collect as much as possible from D and lessen the need to seek recovery from S, agrees to release D from its obligation under the note in exchange for $100 in cash. The agreement to release D is silent as to the effect of the release on S. Pursuant to Section 3–605(a)(2), the release of D discharges S from its obligations to C on the note.

Case 2. Same facts as Case 1, except that the terms of the release provide that C retains its rights to enforce the instrument against S. D is discharged from its obligations to S pursuant to Section 3–605(a)(1), but S is not discharged from its obligations to C pursuant to Section 3–605(a)(2). However, if S could have recovered from D any sum it paid to C (had D not been discharged from its obligation to S), S has been harmed by the release and is discharged pursuant to Section 3–605(a)(3) to the extent of that harm.

Case 3. Same facts as Case 1, except that the terms of the release provide that C retains its rights to enforce the instrument against S and that S retains its recourse against D. Under subsection (g), the release effects a preservation of recourse. Thus, S is not discharged from its obligations to C pursuant to Section 3–605(a)(2) and D is not discharged from its obligations to S pursuant to Section 3–605(a)(1). Because S's claims against D are preserved, S will not suffer the kind of loss described in Case 2. If no other loss is suffered by S as a result of the release, S is not discharged pursuant to this section.

Case 4. Same facts as Case 3, except that D had made arrangements to work at a second job in order to earn the money to fulfill its obligations on the note. When C released D, however, D canceled the plans for the second job. While S still retains its recourse against D, S may be discharged from its obligation under the instrument to the extent that D's decision to forgo the second job causes S a loss because forgoing the job renders D unable to fulfill its obligations to S under Section 3–419.

Subsection (a) reflects a change from former Section 3–605(b), which provided categorically that the release of a principal obligor by the person entitled to enforce the instrument did not discharge a secondary obligor's obligation on the instrument and assumed that the release also did not discharge the principal obligor's obligations to the secondary obligor under Section 3–419. The rule under subsection (a) is much closer to the policy of the *Restatement of Suretyship and Guaranty* than was former Section 3–605(b). The change, however, is likely to affect only a narrow category of cases. First, as discussed above, Section 3–605 applies only to transactions in which the payment obligation is represented by a negotiable instrument, and, within that set of transactions, only to those transactions in which the secondary obligation is incurred by indorsement or cosigning, not to transactions that involve a separate document of guaranty. See Comment 2, above. Second, as provided in subsection (f), secondary obligors cannot obtain a discharge under subsection (a) in any transaction in which they have consented to the challenged conduct. Thus, subsection (a) will not apply to any transaction that includes a provision waiving suretyship defenses (a provision that is almost universally included in commercial loan documentation) or to any transaction in which the creditor obtains the consent of the secondary obligor at the time of the release.

The principal way in which subsection (a) goes beyond the policy of *Restatement* § 39 is with respect to the liability of indorsers of checks. Specifically, the last sentence of paragraph (a)(2) provides that a release of a principal obligor grants a complete discharge to the indorser of a check, without requiring the indorser to prove harm. In that particular context, it seems likely that continuing responsibility for the indorser often would be so inconsistent with the expectations of the parties as to create a windfall for the creditor and an unfair surprise for the indorser. Thus, the statute implements a simple rule that grants a complete discharge. The creditor, of course, can avoid that rule by contracting with the secondary obligor for a different result at the time that the creditor grants the release to the principal obligor.

Subsection (b) is based on *Restatement of Suretyship and Guaranty* § 40 and relates to extensions of the due date of the instrument. An extension of time to pay a note is often beneficial to the secondary obligor because the additional time may enable the principal obligor to obtain the funds to pay the instrument. In some cases, however, the extension may cause loss to the secondary obligor, particularly if deterioration of the financial condition of the principal obligor reduces the amount that the secondary obligor is able to recover on its right of recourse when default occurs. For example, suppose that the instrument is an installment note and the principal debtor is temporarily short of funds to pay a monthly installment. The payee agrees to extend the due date of the installment for a month or two to allow the debtor to pay when funds are available. Paragraph (b)(2) provides that an extension of time results in a discharge of the secondary obligor, but only to the extent that the secondary obligor proves that the extension caused loss. See subsection (h) (discussing the burden of proof under Section 3–605). Thus, if the extension is for a long period, the secondary obligor might be able to prove that during the period of extension the principal obligor became insolvent, reducing the value of the right of recourse of the secondary obligor. In such a case, paragraph (b)(2) discharges the secondary obligor to the extent of that harm. Although not required to notify the secondary obligor of the extension, the payee can minimize the risk of loss by the secondary obligor by giving the secondary obligor prompt notice of the extension; prompt notice can enhance the likelihood that the secondary obligor's right of recourse can remain valuable, and thus can limit the likelihood that the secondary obligor will suffer a loss because of the extension. See *Restatement of Suretyship and Guaranty* Section 38 comment b.

If the secondary obligor is not discharged under paragraph (b)(2) (either because it would not suffer a loss by reason of the extension or because it has waived its right to discharge pursuant to obligations of the secondary obligor. Consider the following cases:

Case 5. A borrows money from Lender and issues a note payable to the order of Lender that is due on April 1, 2002. B signs the note for accommodation at the request of Lender. B signed the note either as co-maker or as an anomalous indorser. In either case Lender subsequently makes an agreement with A extending the due date of A's obligation to pay the note to July 1, 2002. In either case B did not agree to the extension, and the extension did not address Lender's rights against B. Under paragraph (b)(1), A's obligations to B under this article are also extended to July 1, 2002. Under paragraph (b)(3), if B is not discharged, B may treat its obligations to Lender as also extended, or may pay the instrument on the original due date.

Case 6. Same facts as Case 5, except that the extension agreement includes a statement that the Lender retains its right to enforce the note against B on its original terms. Under paragraph (b)(3), B is liable on the original due date, but under paragraph (b)(1), A's obligations to B under Section 3–419 are not due until July 1, 2002.

Case 7. Same facts as Case 5, except that the extension agreement includes a statement that the Lender retains its right to enforce the note against B on its original terms and B retains its recourse against A as though no extension had been granted. Under paragraph (b)(3), B is liable on the original due date. Under paragraph (b)(1), A's obligations to B under Section 3–419 are not extended.

Under section 3–605(b), the results in Case 5 and Case 7 are identical to the results that follow from the law of suretyship and guaranty. See *Restatement of Suretyship and Guaranty* § 40. The situation in Case 6 is not specifically addressed in the Restatement, but the resolution in this Section is consistent with the concepts of suretyship and guaranty law as reflected in the Restatement. If the secondary obligor is called upon to pay on the due date, it may be difficult to quantify the extent to which the extension has impaired the right of recourse of the secondary obligor at that time. Still, the secondary obligor does have a right to make a claim against the obligee at that time. As a practical matter a suit making such a claim should establish the facts relevant to the extent of the impairment. *See Restatement of Suretyship and Guaranty* § 37(4).

As a practical matter, an extension of the due date will normally occur only when the principal obligor is unable to pay on the due date. The interest of the secondary obligor normally is to acquiesce in the willingness of the person entitled to enforce the instrument to wait for payment from the principal obligor rather than to pay right away and rely on an action against the principal obligor that may have little or no value. But in unusual cases the secondary obligor may prefer to pay the holder on the original due date so as to avoid continuing accrual of interest. In such cases the secondary obligor may do so. See paragraph (b)(3). If the terms of the extension provide that the person entitled to enforce the instrument retains its right to enforce the instrument against the secondary obligor on the original due date, though, those terms are effective and the secondary obligor may not delay payment until the extended due date. Unless the extension agreement effects a preservation of recourse, however, the secondary obligor may not proceed against the principal obligor under Section 3–419 until the extended due date. See paragraph (b)(1). To the extent that delay causes loss to the secondary obligor it is discharged under paragraph(b)(2).

Even in those cases in which a secondary obligor does not have a duty to pay the instrument on the original due date, it always has the right to pay the instrument on that date, and perhaps minimize its loss by doing so. The secondary obligor is not precluded, however, from asserting its rights to discharge under Section 3–605(b)(2) if it does not exercise that option. The critical issue is whether the extension caused the secondary obligor a loss by increasing the difference between its cost of performing its obligation on the instrument and the amount recoverable from the principal obligor under this Article. The decision by the secondary obligor not to exercise its option to pay on the original due date may, under the circumstances, be a factor to be considered in the determination of that issue, especially if the secondary obligor has been given prompt notice of the extension (as discussed above).

6. Subsection (c) is based on *Restatement of Suretyship and Guaranty* § 41. It is a residual provision, which applies to modifications of the obligation of the principal obligor that are not covered by subsection (a) and (b). Under subsection (c)(1), a modification of the obligation of the principal obligor on the instrument (other than a release covered by subsection (a) or an extension of the due date covered by subsection (b)), will correspondingly modify the duties of the principal obligor to the secondary obligor. Under subsection (c)(2), such a modification also will result in discharge of the secondary obligor to the extent the modification causes loss to the secondary obligor. To the extent that the secondary obligor is not discharged and the obligation changes the amount of money payable on the instrument, or the timing of such payment, subsection (c)(3) provides the secondary obligor with a choice: it may satisfy its obligation on the instrument as if the modification had not occurred, or it may treat its obligation to pay the instrument as having been modified in a manner corresponding to the modification of the principal obligor's obligation.

The following cases illustrate the application of subsection (c):

Case 8. Corporation borrows money from Lender and issues a note payable to Lender. X signs the note as an accommodation party for Corporation. The note refers to a loan agreement under which the note was issued, which states various events of default that allow Lender to accelerate the due date of the note. Among the events of default are breach of covenants not to incur debt beyond specified limits and not to engage in any line of business substantially different from that currently carried on by Corporation. Without consent of X, Lender agrees to modify the covenants to allow Corporation to enter into a new line of business that X considers to be risky, and to incur debt beyond the limits specified in the loan agreement to finance the new venture. This modification discharges X to the extent that the modification otherwise would cause X a loss.

Case 9. Corporation borrows money from Lender and issues a note payable to Lender in the amount of $100,000. X signs the note as an accommodation party for Corporation. The note calls for 60 equal monthly payments of interest and principal. Before the first payment is made, Corporation and Lender agree to modify the note by changing the repayment schedule to require four annual payments of interest only, followed by a fifth payment of interest and the entire $100,000 principal balance. To the extent that the modification does not discharge X, X has the option of fulfilling its obligation on the note in accordance with the original terms or the modified terms.

7. Subsection (d) is based on *Restatement of Suretyship and Guaranty* § 42 and deals with the discharge of secondary obligors by impairment of collateral. The last sentence of subsection (d) states four common examples of what is meant by impairment. Because it uses the term 'includes,' the provision allows a court to find impairment in other cases as well. There is extensive case law on impairment of collateral. The secondary obligor is discharged to the extent that the secondary obligor proves that impairment was caused by a person entitled to enforce the instrument. For example, assume that the payee of a secured note fails to perfect the security interest. The collateral is owned by the principal obligor who subsequently files in bankruptcy. As a result of the failure to perfect, the security interest is not enforceable in bankruptcy. If the payee were to obtain payment from the secondary obligor, the secondary obligor would be subrogated to the payee's security interest in the collateral under Section 3–419 and general principles of suretyship law. See *Restatement of Suretyship and Guaranty § 28(1)(c)*. In this situation, though, the value of the security interest is impaired completely because the security interest is unenforceable. Thus, the secondary obligor is discharged from its obligation on the note to the extent of that impairment. If the value of the collateral impaired is as much or more than the amount of the note, and if there will be no recovery on the note as an unsecured claim, there is a complete discharge. Subsection (d) applies whether the collateral is personalty or realty, whenever the obligation in question is in the form of a negotiable instrument.

8. Subsection (e) is based on former Section 3–605(h). The requirement of knowledge in the first clause is consistent with Section 9–628. The requirement of notice in the second clause is consistent with Section 3–419(c).

9. The importance of the suretyship defenses provided in Section 3–605 is greatly diminished by the fact that the right to discharge can be waived as provided in subsection (f). The waiver can be effectuated by a provision in the instrument or in a separate agreement. It is standard practice to include such a waiver of suretyship defenses in notes prepared by financial institutions or other commercial creditors. Thus, Section 3–605 will result in the discharge of an accommodation party on a note only in the occasional case in which the note does not include such a waiver clause and the person entitled to enforce the note nevertheless takes actions that would give rise to a discharge under this section without obtaining the consent of the secondary obligor.

Because subsection (f) by its terms applies only to a discharge 'under this section,' subsection (f) does not operate to waive a defense created by other law (such as the law governing enforcement of security interests under Article 9) that cannot be waived under that law. See, e.g., Section 9–602.

The last sentence of subsection (f) creates an inference of consent on the part of the secondary obligor whenever the secondary obligor controls the principal obligor or deals with the creditor on behalf of the principal obligor. That sentence is based on *Restatement of Suretyship and Guaranty* § 48(2).

Subsection (g) explains the criteria for determining whether the terms of a release or extension preserve the secondary obligor's recourse, a concept of importance in the application of subsections (a) and (b). First, the terms of the release or extension must provide that the person entitled to enforce the instrument retains the right to enforce the instrument against the secondary obligor. Second, the terms of the release or extension must provide that the recourse of the secondary obligor against the principal obligor continues as though the release or extension had not been granted. Those requirements are drawn from *Restatement of Suretyship and Guaranty* § 38.

11. Subsection (h) and (i) articulate rules for the burden of persuasion under Section 3–605. Those rules are based on *Restatement of Suretyship and Guaranty* § 49.

State Bar Committee Comments

Subsection (i) has been revised to delete the following language: "either specifically or by general language indicating the parties waive defenses based on suretyship or impairment of collateral." As a consequence, a waiver by an accommodation party or indorser must be specific in order to be enforceable and to prevent a discharge of the accommodation party or indorser.

A waiver of discharge enforceable under section 3.605(i) may not be enforceable as a waiver of a "debtor's" rights under Chapter 9. *See* Tex. Bus & Com. Code Ann. § 9.501(c) (Tex. UCC) (Vernon 1994). In any case of conflict, the policy considerations underlying section 9.501(c) and its prohibitions against certain waivers should entitle it to control over the provisions of section 3.605(i).

§ 3.606. Deleted by Acts 1995, 74th Leg., ch. 921, § 1, eff. Jan. 1, 1996

SUBCHAPTER G. ADVICE OF INTERNATIONAL SIGHT DRAFT [DELETED]

§ 3.701. Deleted by Acts 1995, 74th Leg., ch. 921, § 1, eff. Jan. 1, 1996

SUBCHAPTER H. MISCELLANEOUS [DELETED]

§§ 3.801 to 3.805. Deleted by Acts 1995, 74th Leg., ch. 921, § 1, eff. Jan. 1, 1996

CHAPTER 4. BANK DEPOSITS AND COLLECTIONS

SUBCHAPTER A. GENERAL PROVISIONS AND DEFINITIONS

Section

SUBCHAPTER B. COLLECTION OF ITEMS: DEPOSITARY AND COLLECTING BANKS

SUBCHAPTER C. COLLECTION OF ITEMS: PAYOR BANKS

SUBCHAPTER D. RELATIONSHIP BETWEEN PAYOR BANK AND ITS CUSTOMER

Acts 1995, 74th Leg., ch. 921, § 4 amended Chapter 4 effective January 1, 1996. The former Chapter 4, Bank Deposits and Collections, consisting of §§ 4.101 to 3.504, was amended as Chapter 4, Bank Deposits and Collections, also consisting of §§ 4.101 to 4.504.

SUBCHAPTER A. GENERAL PROVISIONS AND DEFINITIONS

§ 4.101. Short Title

This chapter may be cited as Uniform Commercial Code—Bank Deposits and Collections.

Acts 1967, 60th Leg., p. 2343, ch. 785, § 1, eff. Sept. 1, 1967. Amended by Acts 1995, 74th Leg., ch. 921, § 4, eff. Jan. 1, 1996.

Uniform Commercial Code Comment

1. The great number of checks handled by banks and the country-wide nature of the bank collection process require uniformity in the law of bank collections. There is needed a uniform statement of the principal rules of the bank collection process with ample provision for flexibility to meet the needs of the large volume handled and the changing needs and conditions that are bound to come with the years. This Article meets that need.

2. In 1950 at the time Article 4 was drafted, 6.7 billion checks were written annually. By the time of the 1990 revision of Article 4 annual volume was estimated by the American Bankers Association to be about 50 billion checks. The banking system could not have coped with this increase in check volume had it not developed in the late 1950s and early 1960s an automated system for check collection based on encoding checks with machine-readable information by Magnetic Ink Character Recognition (MICR). An important goal of the 1990 revision of Article 4 is to promote the efficiency of the check collection process by making the provisions of Article 4 more compatible with the needs of an automated system and, by doing so, increase the speed and lower the cost of check collection for those who write and receive checks. An additional goal of the 1990 revision of Article 4 is to remove any statutory barriers in the Article to the ultimate adoption of programs allowing the presentment of checks to payor banks by electronic transmission of information captured from the MICR line on the checks. The potential of these programs for saving the time and expense of transporting the huge volume of checks from depositary to payor banks is evident.

3. Article 4 defines rights between parties with respect to bank deposits and collections. It is not a regulatory statute. It does not regulate the terms of the bank-customer agreement, nor does it prescribe what constraints different jurisdictions may wish to impose on that relationship in the interest of consumer protection. The revisions in Article 4 are intended to create a legal frame-work that accommodates automation and truncation for the benefit of all bank customers. This may raise consumer problems which enacting jurisdictions may wish to address in individual legislation. For example, with respect to Section 4–401(c), jurisdictions may wish to examine their unfair and deceptive practices laws to determine whether they are adequate to protect drawers who postdate checks from unscrupulous practices that may arise on the part of persons who induce drawers to issue postdated checks in erroneous belief that the checks will not be immediately payable. Another example arises from the fact that under various truncation plans customers will no longer receive their cancelled checks and will no longer have the cancelled check to prove payment. Individual legislation might provide that a copy of a bank statement along with a copy of the check is prima facie evidence of payment.

§ 4.102. Applicability

(a) To the extent that items within this chapter are also within Chapters 3 and 8, they are subject to those chapters. If there is conflict, this chapter governs Chapter 3, but Chapter 8 governs this chapter.

(b) The liability of a bank for action or non-action with respect to an item handled by it for purposes of presentment, payment, or collection is governed by the law of the place where the bank is located. In the case of action or non-action by or at a branch or separate office of a bank, its liability is governed by the law of the place where the branch or separate office is located.

(c) Notwithstanding Section 1.301, the laws of this state govern a deposit contract between a bank and a consumer account holder if the branch or separate office of the bank that accepts the deposit contract is located in this state. For purposes of this subsection, "consumer account holder" means a natural person who holds a deposit account primarily for personal, family, or household purposes but does not include a natural person who holds an account for another in a professional capacity.

Acts 1967, 60th Leg., p. 2343, ch. 785, § 1, eff. Sept. 1, 1967. Amended by Acts 1995, 74th Leg., ch. 921, § 4, eff. Jan. 1, 1996; Acts 1999, 76th Leg., ch. 344, § 5.001, eff. Sept. 1, 1999; Acts 2003, 78th Leg., ch. 542, § 11, eff. Sept. 1, 2003.

Uniform Commercial Code Comment

1. The rules of Article 3 governing negotiable instruments, their transfer, and the contracts of the parties thereto apply to the items collected through banking channels wherever no specific provision is found in this Article. In the case of conflict, this Article governs. See Section 3–102(b).

Bonds and like instruments constituting investment securities under Article 8 may also be handled by banks for collection purposes. Various sections of Article 8 prescribe rules of transfer some of which (see Sections 8–108 and 8–304) may conflict with provisions of this Article (Sections 4–205, 4–207, and 4–208). In the case of conflict, Article 8 governs. Amendments approved by the Permanent Editorial Board for Uniform Commercial Code November 4, 1995.

Section 4–210 deals specifically with overlapping problems and possible conflicts between this Article and Article 9. However, similar reconciling provisions are not necessary in the case of Articles 5 and 7. Sections 4–301 and 4–302 are consistent with Section 5–112. In the case of Article 7 documents of title frequently accompany items but they are not themselves items. See Section 4–104(a)(9).

In *Clearfield Trust Co. v. United States*, 318 U.S. 363 (1943), the Court held that if the United States is a party to an instrument, its rights and duties are governed by federal common law in the absence of a specific federal statute or regulation. In *United States v. Kimbell Foods, Inc.*, 440 U.S. 715 (1979), the Court stated a three-pronged test to ascertain whether the federal common-law rule should follow the state rule. In most instances courts under the *Kimbell* test have shown a willingness to adopt UCC rules in formulating federal common law on the subject. In *Kimbell* the Court adopted the priorities rules of Article 9.

In addition, applicable federal law may supersede provisions of this Article. One federal law that does so is the Expedited Funds Availability Act, 12 U.S.C. § 4001 et seq., and its implementing Regulation CC, 12 CFR Pt. 229. In some instances this law is alluded to in the statute, e.g., Section 4–215(e) and (f). In other instances, although not referred to in this Article, the provisions of the EFAA and Regulation CC control with respect to checks. For example, except between the depositary bank and its customer, all settlements are final and not provisional (Regulation CC, Section 229.36(d)), and the midnight deadline may be extended (Regulation CC, Section 229.30(c)). The comments to this Article suggest in most instances the relevant Regulation CC provisions.

2. Subsection (b) is designed to state a workable rule for the solution of otherwise vexatious problems of the conflicts of laws:

a. The routine and mechanical nature of bank collections makes it imperative that one law govern the activities of one office of a bank. The requirement found in some cases that to hold an indorser notice must be given in accordance with the law of the place of indorsement, since that method of notice became an implied term of the indorser's contract, is more theoretical than practical.

b. Adoption of what is in essence a tort theory of the conflict of laws is consistent with the general theory of this Article that the basic duty of a collecting bank is one of good faith and and the exercise of ordinary care. Justification lies in the fact that, in using an ambulatory instrument, the drawer, payee, and indorsers must know that action will be taken with respect to it in other jurisdictions. This is especially pertinent with respect to the law of the place of payment.

c. The phrase "action or non-action with respect to any item handled by it for purposes of presentment, payment, or collection" is intended to make the conflicts rule of subsection (b) apply from the inception of the collection process of an item through all phases of deposit, forwarding, presentment, payment and remittance or credit of proceeds. Specifically the subsection applies to the initial act of a depositary bank in receiving an item and to the incidents of such receipt. The conflicts rule of *Weissman v. Banque de Bruxelles*, 254 N.Y. 488, 173 N.E. 835 (1930), is rejected. The subsection applies to questions of possible vicarious liability of a bank for action or non-action of sub-agents (see Section 4–202(c)), and tests these questions by the law of the state of the location of the bank which uses the sub-agent. The conflicts rule of *St. Nicholas Bank of New York v. State Nat. Bank*, 128 N.Y. 26, 27 N.E. 849, 13 L.R.A. 241 (1891), is rejected. The subsection applied to action or non-action of a payor bank in connection with handling an item (see Sections 4–215(a), 4–301, 4–302, 4–303) as well as action or non-action of a collecting bank (Sections 4–201 through 4–216); to action or non-action of a bank which suspends payment or is affected by another bank suspending payment (Section 4–216); to action or non-action of a bank with respect to an item under the rule of Part 4 of Article 4.

d. In a case in which subsection (b) makes this Article applicable, Section 4–103(a) leaves open the possibility of an agreement with respect to applicable law. This freedom of agreement follows the general policy of Section 1–105.

§ 4.103. Variation by Agreement; Measure of Damages; Action Constituting Ordinary Care

(a) The effect of the provisions of this chapter may be varied by agreement, but the parties to the agreement cannot disclaim a bank's responsibility for its lack of good faith or failure to exercise ordinary care or limit the measure of damages for the lack or failure. However, the parties may determine by agreement the standards by which the bank's responsibility is to be measured if those standards are not manifestly unreasonable.

(b) Federal Reserve regulations and operating circulars, clearing-house rules, and the like have the effect of agreements under Subsection (a), whether or not specifically assented to by all parties interested in items handled.

(c) Action or non-action approved by this chapter or pursuant to Federal Reserve regulations or operating circulars is the exercise of ordinary care and, in the absence of special instructions, action or non-action consistent with clearing-house rules and the like or with a general banking usage not disapproved by this chapter, is prima facie the exercise of ordinary care.

(d) The specification or approval of certain procedures by this chapter is not disapproval of other procedures that may be reasonable under the circumstances.

(e) The measure of damages for failure to exercise ordinary care in handling an item is the amount of the item reduced by an amount that could not have been realized by the exercise of ordinary care. If there is also bad faith, it includes any other damages the party suffered as a proximate consequence.

Acts 1967, 60th Leg., p. 2343, ch. 785, § 1, eff. Sept. 1, 1967. Amended by Acts 1995, 74th Leg., ch. 921, § 4, eff. Jan. 1, 1996.

Uniform Commercial Code Comment

1. Section 1–102 states the general principles and rules for variation of the effect of this Act by agreement and the limitations to this power. Section 4–103 states the specific rules for variation of Article 4 by agreement and also certain standards of ordinary care. In view of the technical complexity of the field of bank collections, the enormous number of items handled by banks, the certainty that there will be variations from the normal in each day's work in each bank, the certainty of changing conditions and the possibility of developing improved methods of collection to speed the process, it would be unwise to freeze present methods of operation by mandatory statutory rules. This section, therefore, permits within wide limits variation of the effect of provisions of the Article by agreement.

2. Subsection (a) confers blanket power to vary all provisions of the Article by agreements of the ordinary kind. The agreements may not disclaim a bank's responsibility for its own lack of good faith or failure to exercise ordinary care and may not limit the measure of damages for the lack or failure, but this subsection like Section 1–102(3) approves the practice of parties determining by agreement the standards by which the responsibility is to be measured. In the absence of a showing that the standards manifestly are unreasonable, the agreement controls. Owners of items and other interested parties are not affected by agreements under this subsection unless they are parties to the agreement or are bound by adoption, ratification, estoppel or the like.

As here used "agreement" has the meaning given to it by Section 1–201(3). The agreement may be direct, as between the owner and the depositary bank; or indirect, as in the case in which the owner authorizes a particular type of procedure and any bank in the collection chain acts pursuant to such authorization. It may be with respect to a single item; or to all items handled for a particular customer, e.g., a general agreement between the depositary bank and the customer at the time a deposit account is opened. Legends on deposit tickets, collection letters and acknowledgments of items, coupled with action by the affected party constituting acceptance, adoption, ratification, estoppel or the like, are agreements if they meet the tests of the definition of "agreement." See Section 1–201(3). *First Nat. Bank of Denver v. Federal Reserve Bank*, 6 F.2d 339 (8th Cir.1925) (deposit slip); *Jefferson County Bldg. Ass'n v. Southern Bank & Trust Co.*, 225 Ala. 25, 142 So. 66 (1932) (signature card and deposit slip); *Semingson v. Stock Yards Nat. Bank*, 162 Minn. 424, 203 N.W. 412 (1925) (passbook); *Farmers State Bank v. Union Nat. Bank*, 42 N.D. 449, 454, 173 N.W. 789, 790 (1919) (acknowledgment of receipt of item).

3. Subsection (a) (subject to its limitations with respect to good faith and ordinary care) goes far to meet the requirements of flexibility. However, it does not by itself confer fully effective flexibility. Since it is recognized that banks handle a great number of items every business day and that the parties interested in each item include the owner of the item, the drawer (if it is a check), all nonbank indorsers, the payor bank and from one to five or more collecting banks, it is obvious that it is impossible, practically, to obtain direct agreements from all of these parties on all items. In total, the interested parties constitute virtually every adult person and business organization in the United States. On the other hand they may become bound to agreements on the principle that collecting banks acting as agents have authority to make binding agreements with respect to items being handled. This conclusion was assumed but was not flatly decided in *Federal Reserve Bank of Richmond v. Malloy*, 264 U.S. 160, at 167, 44 S.Ct. 296, at 298, 68 L.Ed. 617, 31 A.L.R. 1261 (1924).

To meet this problem subsection (b) provides that official or quasi-official rules of collection, that is Federal Reserve regulations and operating circulars, clearing-house rules, and the like, have the effect of agreements under subsection (a), whether or not specifically assented to by all parties interested in items handled. Consequently, such official or quasi-official rules may, standing by themselves but subject to the good faith and ordinary care limitations, vary the effect of the provisions of Article 4.

Federal Reserve regulations. Various sections of the Federal Reserve Act (12 U.S.C. § 221 et seq.) authorize the Board of Governors of the Federal Reserve System to direct the Federal Reserve banks to exercise bank collection functions. For example, Section 16 (12 U.S.C. § 248(*o*)) authorizes the Board to require each Federal Reserve bank to exercise the functions of a clearing house for its members and Section 13 (12 U.S.C. § 342) authorizes each Federal Reserve bank to receive deposits from nonmember banks solely for the purposes of exchange or of collection. Under this statutory authorization the Board has issued Regulation J (Subpart A—Collection of Checks and Other Items). Under the supremacy clause of the Constitution, federal regulations prevail over state statutes. Moreover, the Expedited Funds Availability Act, 12 U.S.C. Section 4007(b) provides that the Act and Regulation CC, 12 CFR 229, supersede "any provision of the law of any State, including the Uniform Commercial Code as in effect in such State, which is inconsistent with this chapter or such regulations." See Comment 1 to Section 4–102.

Federal Reserve operating circulars. The regulations of the Federal Reserve Board authorize the Federal Reserve banks to promulgate operating circulars covering operating details. Regulation J, for example, provides that "Each Reserve Bank shall receive and handle items in accordance with this subpart, and shall issue operating circulars governing the details of its handling of items and other matters deemed appropriate by the Reserve Bank." This Article recognizes that "operating circulars" issued pursuant to the regulations and concerned with operating details as appropriate may, within their proper sphere, vary the effect of the Article.

Clearing-House Rules. Local clearing houses have long issued rules governing the details of clearing; hours of clearing, media of remittance, time for return of mis-sent items and the like. The case law has recognized these rules, within their proper sphere, as binding on affected parties and as appropriate sources for the courts to look to in filling out details of bank collection law. Subsection (b) in recognizing clearing-house rules as a means if preserving flexibility continues the sensible approach indicated in the cases. Included in the terms "clearing houses" are county and regional clearing houses as well as those within a single city or town. There is, of course, no intention of authorizing a local clearing house or a group of clearing houses to rewrite the basic law generally. The term "clearing-house rules" should be understood in the light of functions the clearing houses have exercised in the past.

And the like. This phrase is to be construed in the light of the foregoing. "Federal Reserve regulations and operating circulars" cover rules and regulations issued by public or quasi-public agencies under statutory authority. "Clearing-house rules" cover rules issued by a group of banks which have associated themselves to perform through a clearing house some of their collection, payment and clearing functions. Other agencies or associations of this kind may be established in the future whose rules and regulations could be appropriately looked on as constituting means of avoiding absolute statutory rigidity. The phrase "and the like" leaves open possibilities for future development. An agreement between a number of banks or even all the banks in an area simply because they are banks, would not of itself, by virtue of the phrase "and the like," meet the purposes and objectives of subsection (b).

4. Under this Article banks come under the general obligations of the use of good faith and the exercise of ordinary care. "Good faith" is defined in Section 1–201(b)(20). The term "ordinary care" is defined in Section 3–103(a)(7). These definitions are made to apply to Article 4 by Section 4–104(c). Section 4–202 states respects in which collecting banks must use ordinary care. Subsection (c) of Section 4–103 provides that action or non-action approved by the Article or pursuant to Federal Reserve regulations or operating circulars constitutes the exercise of ordinary care. Federal Reserve regulations and operating circulars constitute an affirmative standard of ordinary care equally with the provisions of Article 4 itself.

Subsection (c) further provides that, absent special instructions, action or non-action consistent with clearing-house rules and the like or with a general banking usage not disapproved by the Article, prima facie constitutes the exercise of ordinary care. Clearing-house rules and the phrase "and the like" have the significance set forth above in these Comments. The term "general banking usage" is not defined but should be taken to mean a general usage common to banks in the area concerned. See Section 1–205(2). In a case in which the adjective "general" is used, the intention is to require a usage broader than a mere practice between two or three banks but it is not intended to require anything as broad as a country-wide usage. A usage followed generally throughout a state, a substantial portion of a state, a metropolitan area or the like would certainly be sufficient. Consistently with the principle of Section 1–205(3), action or non-action consistent with clearing-house rules or the like or with banking usages prima facie constitutes the exercise of ordinary care. However, the phrase "in the absence of special instructions" affords owners of items an opportunity to prescribe other standards and although there may be no direct supervision or control of clearing houses or banking usages by official supervisory authorities, the confirmation of ordinary care by compliance with these standards is prima facie only, thus conferring on the courts the ultimate power to determine ordinary care in any case in which it should appear desirable to do so. The prima facie rule does, however, impose on the party contesting the standards to establish that they are unreasonable, arbitrary or unfair as used by the particular bank.

5. Subsection (d), in line with the flexible approach required for the bank collection process is designed to make clear that a novel procedure adopted by a bank is not to be considered unreasonable merely because that procedure is not specifically contemplated by this Article or by agreement, or because it has not yet been generally accepted as a bank usage. Changing conditions constantly call for new procedures and someone has to use the new procedure first. If this procedure is found to be reasonable under the circumstances, provided, of course, that it is not inconsistent with any provision of the Article or other law or agreement, the bank which has followed the new procedure should not be found to have failed in the exercise of ordinary care.

6. Subsection (e) sets forth a rule for determining the measure of damages for failure to exercise ordinary care which, under subsection (a), cannot be limited by agreement. In the absence of bad faith the maximum recovery is the amount of the item concerned. The term "bad faith" is not defined; the connotation is the absence of good faith (Section 3–103). When it is established that some part or all of the item could not have been collected even by the use of ordinary care the recovery is reduced by the amount that would have been in any event uncollectible. This limitation on recovery follows the case law. Finally, if bad faith is established the rule opens to allow the recovery of other damages, whose "proximateness" is to be tested by the ordinary rules applied in comparable cases. Of course, it continues to be as necessary under subsection (e) as it has been under ordinary common law principles that, before the

damage rule of the subsection becomes operative, liability of the bank and some loss to the customer or owner must be established.

§ 4.104. Definitions and Index of Definitions

(a) In this chapter, unless the context otherwise requires:

(1) "Account" means any deposit or credit account with a bank, including a demand, time, savings, passbook, share draft, or like account, other than an account evidenced by a certificate of deposit.

(2) "Afternoon" means the period of a day between noon and midnight.

(3) "Banking day" means the part of a day on which a bank is open to the public for carrying on substantially all of its banking functions.

(4) "Clearing house" means an association of banks or other payors regularly clearing items.

(5) "Customer" means a person having an account with a bank or for whom a bank has agreed to collect items, including a bank that maintains an account at another bank.

(6) "Documentary draft" means a draft to be presented for acceptance or payment if specified documents, certificated securities (Section 8.102) or instructions for uncertificated securities (Section 8.102), or other certificates, statements, or the like are to be received by the drawee or other payor before acceptance or payment of the draft.

(7) "Draft" means a draft as defined in Section 3.104 or an item, other than an instrument, that is an order.

(8) "Drawee" means a person ordered in a draft to make payment.

(9) "Item" means an instrument or a promise or order to pay money handled by a bank for collection or payment. The term does not include a payment order governed by Chapter 4A or a credit or debit card slip.

(10) "Midnight deadline" with respect to a bank is midnight on its next banking day following the banking day on which it receives the relevant item or notice or from which the time for taking action commences to run, whichever is later.

(11) "Settle" means to pay in cash, by clearing-house settlement, in a charge or credit or by remittance, or otherwise as agreed. A settlement may be either provisional or final.

(12) "Suspends payments" with respect to a bank means that it has been closed by order of the supervisory authorities, that a public officer has been appointed to take it over, or that it ceases or refuses to make payments in the ordinary course of business.

(b) Other definitions applying to this chapter and the sections in which they appear are:

"Agreement for electronic presentment"	Section 4.110.
"Collecting bank"	Section 4.105.
"Depositary bank"	Section 4.105.
"Intermediary bank"	Section 4.105.
"Payor bank"	Section 4.105.
"Presenting bank"	Section 4.105.
"Presentment notice"	Section 4.110.

(c) The following definitions in other chapters apply to this chapter:

"Acceptance"	Section 3.409.
"Alteration"	Section 3.407.
"Cashier's check"	Section 3.104.
"Certificate of deposit"	Section 3.104.
"Certified check"	Section 3.409.
"Check"	Section 3.104.
"Control"	Section 7.106.
"Holder in due course"	Section 3.302.
"Instrument"	Section 3.104.
"Notice of dishonor"	Section 3.503.
"Order"	Section 3.103.
"Ordinary care"	Section 3.103.
"Person entitled to enforce"	Section 3.301.
"Presentment"	Section 3.501.
"Promise"	Section 3.103.
"Prove"	Section 3.103.
"Record"	Section 1.201.
"Remotely–created item"	Section 3.103.
"Teller's check"	Section 3.104.
"Unauthorized signature"	Section 3.403.

(d) In addition, Chapter 1 contains general definitions and principles of construction and interpretation applicable throughout this chapter.

Acts 1967, 60th Leg., p. 2343, ch. 785, § 1, eff. Sept. 1, 1967. Amended by Acts 1995, 74th Leg., ch. 921, § 4, eff. Jan. 1, 1996; Acts 1995, 74th Leg., ch. 962, § 18, eff. Sept. 1, 1995; Acts 2003, 78th Leg., ch. 542, § 12, eff. Sept. 1, 2003; Acts 2005, 79th Leg., ch. 95, § 15, eff. Sept. 1, 2005; Acts 2005, 79th Leg., ch. 122, § 16, eff. Sept. 1, 2005.

Uniform Commercial Code Comment

1. Paragraph (a)(1): "Account" is defined to include both asset accounts in which a customer has deposited money and accounts from which a customer may draw on a line of credit. The limiting factor is that the account must be in a bank.

2. Paragraph (a)(3): "Banking day." Under this definition that part of a business day when a bank is open only for

limited functions, e.g., to receive deposits and cash checks, but with loan, bookkeeping and other departments closed, is not part of a banking day.

3. Paragraph (a)(4): "Clearing house." Occasionally express companies, governmental agencies and other nonbanks deal directly with a clearing house; hence the definition does not limit the term to an association of banks.

4. Paragraph (a)(5): "Customer." It is to be noted that this term includes a bank carrying an account with another bank as well as the more typical nonbank customer or depositor.

5. Paragraph (a)(6): "Documentary draft" applies even though the documents do not accompany the draft but are to be received by the drawee or other payor before acceptance or payment of the draft. Documents may be either in electronic or tangible form. See Article 5, Section 5–102, Comment 2 and Article 1, Section 1–201 (definition of "document of title").

6. Paragraph (a)(7): "Draft" is defined in Section 3–104 as a form of instrument. Since Article 4 applies to items that may not fall within the definition of instrument, the term is defined here to include an item that is a written order to pay money, even though the item may not qualify as an instrument. The term "order" is defined in Section 3–103.

7. Paragraph (a)(8): "Drawee" is defined in Section 3–103 in terms of an Article 3 draft which is a form of instrument. Here "drawee" is defined in terms of an Article 4 draft which includes items that may not be instruments.

8. Paragraph (a)(9): "Item" is defined broadly to include an instrument, as defined in Section 3–104, as well as promises or orders that may not be within the definition of "instrument." The terms "promise" and "order" are defined in Section 3–103. A promise is a written undertaking to pay money. An order is a written instruction to pay money. But see Section 4–110(c). Since bonds and other investment securities under Article 8 may be within the term "instrument" or "promise," they are items and when handled by banks for collection are subject to this Article. See Comment 1 to Section 4–102. The functional limitation on the meaning of this term is the willingness of the banking system to handle the instrument, undertaking or instruction for collection or payment.

9. Paragraph (a)(10): "Midnight deadline." The use of this phrase is an example of the more mechanical approach used in this Article. Midnight is selected as a termination point or time limit to obtain greater uniformity and definiteness than would be possible from other possible terminating points, such as the close of the banking day or business day.

10. Paragraph (a)(11): The term "settle" has substantial importance throughout Article 4. In the American Bankers Association Bank Collection Code, in deferred posting statutes, in Federal Reserve regulations and operating circulars, in clearing-house rules, in agreements between banks and customers and in legends on deposit tickets and collection letters, there is repeated reference to "conditional" or "provisional" credits or payments. Tied in with this concept of credits or payments being in some way tentative, has been a related but somewhat different problem as to when an item is "paid" or "finally paid" either to determine the relative priority of the item as against attachments, stop-payment orders and the like or in insolvency situations. There has been extensive litigation in the various states on these problems. To a substantial extent the confusion, the litigation and even the resulting court decisions fail to take into account that in the collection process some debits or credits are provisional or tentative and others are final and that very many debits or credits are provisional or tentative for awhile but later become final. Similarly, some cases fail to recognize that within a single bank, particularly a payor bank, each item goes through a series of processes and that in a payor bank most of these processes are preliminary to the basic act of payment or "final payment."

The term "settle" is used as a convenient term to characterize a broad variety of conditional, provisional, tentative and also final payments of items. Such a comprehensive term is needed because it is frequently difficult or unnecessary to determine whether a particular action is tentative or final or when a particular credit shifts from the tentative class to the final class. Therefore, its use throughout the Article indicates that in that particular context it is unnecessary or unwise to determine whether the debit or the credit or the payment is tentative or final. However, if qualified by the adjective "provisional" its tentative nature is intended, and if qualified by the adjective "final" its permanent nature is intended.

Examples of the various types of settlement contemplated by the term include payments in cash; the efficient but somewhat complicated process of payment through the adjustment and offsetting of balances through clearing houses; debit or credit entries in accounts between banks; the forwarding of various types of remittance instruments, sometimes to cover a particular item but more frequently to cover an entire group of items received on a particular day.

11. Paragraph (a)(12): "Suspends payments." This term is designed to afford an objective test to determine when a bank is no longer operating as a part of the banking system.

Sections 31 and 32 of Acts 2005, 79th Leg., ch. 122 provide:

"Sec. 31. This Act applies to a document of title that is issued or a bailment that arises on or after the effective date of this Act. This Act does not apply to a document of title that is issued or a bailment that arises before the effective date of this Act even if the document of title or bailment would be subject to this Act if the document of title had been issued or bailment had arisen after the effective date of this Act. This Act does not apply to a right of action that has accrued before the effective date of this Act.

"Sec. 32. A document of title issued or a bailment that arises before the effective date of this Act and the rights, obligations, and interests flowing from that document or bailment are governed by any statute or other rule amended or repealed by this Act as if amendment or repeal had not occurred and may be terminated, completed, consummated, or enforced under that statute or other rule."

§ 4.105. "Bank"; "Depositary Bank"; "Intermediary Bank"; "Collecting Bank"; "Payor Bank"; "Presenting Bank"

In this chapter:

(1) "Bank" means a person engaged in the business of banking, including a savings bank, savings and loan association, credit union, or trust company.

(2) "Depositary bank" means the first bank to take an item even though it is also the payor bank, unless the item is presented for immediate payment over the counter.

(3) "Payor bank" means a bank that is the drawee of a draft.

(4) "Intermediary bank" means a bank to which an item is transferred in course of collection except the depositary or payor bank.

(5) "Collecting bank" means a bank handling an item for collection except the payor bank.

(6) "Presenting bank" means a bank presenting an item except a payor bank.

Acts 1967, 60th Leg., p. 2343, ch. 785, § 1, eff. Sept. 1, 1967. Amended by Acts 1995, 74th Leg., ch. 921, § 4, eff. Jan. 1, 1996.

Uniform Commercial Code Comment

1. The definitions in general exclude a bank to which an item is issued, as this bank does not take by transfer except in the particular case covered in which the item is issued to payee for collection, as in the case in which a corporation is transferring balances from one account to another. Thus, the definition of "depositary bank" does not include the bank to which a check is made payable if a check is given in payment of a mortgage. This bank has the status of a payee under Article 3 on Negotiable Instruments and not that of a collecting bank.

2. Paragraph (1): "Bank" is defined in Section 1–201(4) as meaning "any person engaged in the business of banking." The definition in paragraph (1) makes clear that "bank" includes savings banks, savings and loan associations, credit unions and trust companies, in addition to the commercial banks commonly denoted by use of the term "bank."

3. Paragraph (2): A bank that takes an "on us" item for collection, for application to a customer's loan, or first handles the item for other reasons is a depositary bank even though it is also the payor bank. However, if the holder presents the item for immediate payment over the counter, the payor bank is not a depositary bank.

4. Paragraph (3): The definition of "payor bank" is clarified by use of the term "drawee." That term is defined in Section 4–104 as meaning "a person ordered in a draft to make payment." An "order" is defined in Section 3–103 as meaning "a written instruction to pay money . . . An authorization to pay is not an order unless the person authorized to pay is also instructed to pay." The definition of order is incorporated into Article 4 by Section 4–104(c). Thus a payor bank is one instructed to pay in the item. A bank does not become a payor bank by being merely authorized to pay or by being given an instruction to pay not contained in the item.

5. Paragraph (4): The term "intermediary bank" includes the last bank in the collection process if the drawee is not a bank. Usually the last bank is also a presenting bank.

§ 4.106. Payable Through or Payable at Bank; Collecting Bank

(a) If an item states that it is "payable through" a bank identified in the item, the item:

(1) designates the bank as a collecting bank and does not by itself authorize the bank to pay the item; and

(2) may be presented for payment only by or through the bank.

(b) If an item states that it is "payable at" a bank identified in the item, the item is equivalent to a draft drawn on the bank.

(c) If a draft names a nonbank drawee and it is unclear whether a bank named in the draft is a co-drawee or a collecting bank, the bank is a collecting bank.

Amended by Acts 1995, 74th Leg., ch. 921, § 4, eff. Jan. 1, 1996.

Uniform Commercial Code Comment

1. This section replaces former Sections 3–120 and 3–121. Some items are made "payable through" a particular bank. Subsection (a) states that such language makes the bank a collecting bank and not a payor bank. An item identifying a "payable through" bank can be presented for payment to the drawee only by the "payable through" bank. The item cannot be presented to the drawee over the counter for immediate payment or by a collecting bank other than the "payable through" bank.

2. Subsection (b) retains the alternative approach of the present law. Under Alternative A a note payable at a bank is the equivalent of a draft drawn on the bank and the midnight deadline provisions of Sections 4–301 and 4–302 apply. Under Alternative B a "payable at" bank is in the same position as a "payable through" bank under subsection (a).

3. Subsection (c) rejects the view of some cases that a bank named below the name of a drawee is itself a drawee. The commercial understanding is that this bank is a collecting bank and is not accountable under Section 4–302 for holding an item beyond its deadline. The liability of the bank is governed by Sections 4–202(a) and 4–103(e).

§ 4.107. Separate Office of a Bank

A branch or separate office of a bank is a separate bank for the purpose of computing the time within which and determining the place at or to which action may be taken or notices or orders must be given under this chapter and under Chapter 3.

Acts 1967, 60th Leg., p. 2343, ch. 785, § 1, eff. Sept. 1, 1967. Renumbered from § 4.106 and amended by Acts 1995, 74th Leg., ch. 921, § 4, eff. Jan. 1, 1996.

Uniform Commercial Code Comment

1. A rule with respect to the status of a branch or separate office of a bank as a part of any statute on bank collections is highly desirable if not absolutely necessary. However, practices in the operations of branches and separate offices vary substantially in the different states and it has not been possible to find any single rule that is logically correct, fair in all situations and workable under all different types of practices. The decision not to draft the section with greater specificity leaves to the courts the resolution of the issues arising under this section on the basis of the facts of each case.

2. In many states and for many purposes a branch or separate office of the bank should be treated as a separate bank. Many branches function as separate banks in the handling and payment of items and require time for doing so similar to that of a separate bank. This is particularly true if branch banking is permitted throughout a state or in different towns and cities. Similarly, if there is this separate functioning a particular branch or separate office is the only proper place for various types of action to be taken or orders or notices to be given. Examples include the drawing of a check on a particular branch by a customer whose account is carried at that branch; the presentment of that same check at that branch; the issuance of an order to the branch to stop payment on the check.

3. Section 1 of the American Bankers Association Bank Collection Code provided simply: "A branch or office of any such bank shall be deemed a bank." Although this rule appears to be brief and simple, as applied to particular sections of the ABA Code it produces illogical and, in some cases, unreasonable results. For example, under Section 11 of the ABA Code it seems anomalous for one branch of a bank to have charged an item to the account of the drawer and another branch to have the power to elect to treat the item as dishonored. Similar logical problems would flow from applying the same rule to Article 4. Warranties by one branch to another branch under Sections 4–207 and 4–208 (each considered a separate bank) do not make sense.

4. Assuming that it is not desirable to make each branch a separate bank for all purposes, this section provides that a branch or separate office is a separate bank for certain purposes. In so doing the single legal entity of the bank as a whole is preserved, thereby carrying with it the liability of the institution as a whole on such obligations as it may be under. On the other hand, in cases in which the Article provides a number of time limits for different types of action by banks, if a branch functions as a separate bank, it should have the time limits available to a separate bank. Similarly if in its relations to customers a branch functions as a separate bank, notices and orders with respect to accounts of customers of the branch should be given at the branch. For example, whether a branch has notice sufficient to affect its status as a holder in due course of an item taken by it should depend upon what notice that branch has received with respect to the item. Similarly the receipt of a stop-payment order at one branch should not be notice to another branch so as to impair the right of the second branch to be a holder in due course of the item, although in circumstances in which ordinary care requires the communication of a notice or order to the proper branch of a bank, the notice or order would be effective at the proper branch from the time it was or should have been received. See Section 1–201(27).

5. The bracketed language ("maintaining its own deposit ledger") in former Section 4–106 is deleted. Today banks keep records on customer accounts by electronic data storage. This has led most banks with branches to centralize to some degree their record keeping. The place where records are kept has little meaning if the information is electronically stored and is instantly retrievable at all branches of the bank. Hence, the inference to be drawn from the deletion of the bracketed language is that where record keeping is done is no longer an important factor in determining whether a branch is a separate bank.

§ 4.108. Time of Receipt of Items

(a) For the purpose of allowing time to process items, prove balances, and make the necessary entries on its books to determine its position for the day, a bank may fix an afternoon hour of two P.M. or later as a cutoff hour for the handling of money and items and the making of entries on its books.

(b) An item or deposit of money received on any day after a cutoff hour so fixed or after the close of the banking day may be treated as being received at the opening of the next banking day.

Acts 1967, 60th Leg., p. 2343, ch. 785, § 1, eff. Sept. 1, 1967. Renumbered from § 4.107 and amended by Acts 1995, 74th Leg., ch. 921, § 4, eff. Jan. 1, 1996.

Uniform Commercial Code Comment

1. Each of the huge volume of checks processed each day must go through a series of accounting procedures that consume time. Many banks have found it necessary to establish a cutoff hour to allow time for these procedures to be completed within the time limits imposed by Article 4. Subsection (a) approves a cutoff hour of this type provided it is not earlier than 2 P.M. Subsection (b) provides that if such a cutoff hour is fixed, items received after the cutoff hour may be treated as being received at the opening of the next banking day. If the number of items received either through the mail or over the counter tends to taper off radically as the afternoon hours progress, a 2 P.M. cutoff hour does not involve a large portion of the items received but at the same time permits a bank using such a cutoff hour to leave its doors open later in the afternoon without forcing into the evening the completion of its settling and proving process.

2. The provision in subsection (b) that items or deposits received after the close of the banking day may be treated as received at the opening of the next banking day is important in cases in which a bank closes at twelve or one o'clock, e.g., on a Saturday, but continues to receive some items by mail or over the counter if, for example, it opens Saturday evening for the limited purpose of receiving deposits and cashing checks.

§ 4.109. Delays

(a) Unless otherwise instructed, a collecting bank in a good faith effort to secure payment of a specific item drawn on a payor other than a bank, and with or without the approval of any person involved, may waive, modify, or extend time limits imposed or permitted by this title for a period not exceeding two additional banking days without discharge of drawers or indorsers or liability to its transferor or a prior party.

(b) Delay by a collecting bank or payor bank beyond time limits prescribed or permitted by this title or by instructions is excused if:

(1) the delay is caused by interruption of communication or computer facilities, suspension of payments by another bank, war, emergency conditions, failure of equipment, or other circumstances beyond the control of the bank; and

(2) the bank exercises such diligence as the circumstances require.

Acts 1967, 60th Leg., p. 2343, ch. 785, § 1, eff. Sept. 1, 1967. Renumbered from § 4.108 and amended by Acts 1995, 74th Leg., ch. 921, § 4, eff. Jan. 1, 1996.

Uniform Commercial Code Comment

1. Sections 4–202(b), 4–214, 4–301, and 4–302 prescribe various time limits for the handling of items. These are the limits of time within which a bank, in fulfillment of its obligation to exercise ordinary care, must handle items entrusted to it for collection or payment. Under Section 4–103 they may be varied by agreement or by Federal Reserve regulations or operating circular, clearing-house rules, or the like. Subsection (a) permits a very limited extension of these time limits. It authorizes a collecting bank to take additional time in attempting to collect drafts drawn on nonbank payors with or without the approval of any interested party. The right of a collecting bank to waive time limits under subsection (a) does not apply to checks. The two-day extension can only be granted in a good faith effort to secure payment and only with respect to specific items. It cannot be exercised if the customer instructs otherwise. Thus limited the escape provision should afford a limited degree of flexibility in special cases but should not interfere with the overall requirement and objective of speedy collections.

2. An extension granted under subsection (a) is without discharge of drawers or indorsers. It therefore extends the times for presentment or payment as specified in Article 3.

3. Subsection (b) is another escape clause from time limits. This clause operates not only with respect to time limits imposed by the Article itself but also time limits imposed by special instructions, by agreement or by Federal regulations or operating circulars, clearing-house rules or the like. The latter time limits are "permitted" by the Code. For example, a payor bank that fails to make timely return of a dishonored item may be accountable for the amount of the item. Subsection (b) excuses a bank from this liability when its failure to meet its midnight deadline resulted from, for example, a computer breakdown that was beyond the control of the bank, so long as the bank exercised the degree of diligence that the circumstances required. *In Port City State Bank v. American National Bank*, 486 F.2d 196 (10th Cir.1973), the court held that a bank exercised sufficient diligence to be excused under this subsection. If delay is sought to be excused under this subsection, the bank has the burden of proof on the issue of whether it exercised "such diligence as the circumstances require." The subsection is consistent with Regulation CC, Section 229.38(e).

§ 4.110. Electronic Presentment

(a) "Agreement for electronic presentment" means an agreement, clearing-house rule, or Federal Reserve regulation or operating circular providing that presentment of an item may be made by transmission of an image of an item or information describing the item ("presentment notice") rather than delivery of the item itself. The agreement may provide for procedures governing retention, presentment, payment, dishonor, and other matters concerning items subject to the agreement.

(b) Presentment of an item under an agreement for presentment is made when the presentment notice is received.

(c) If presentment is made by presentment notice, a reference to "item" or "check" in this chapter means the presentment notice unless the context otherwise indicates.

Added by Acts 1995, 74th Leg., ch. 921, § 4, eff. Jan. 1, 1996.

Uniform Commercial Code Comment

1. "An agreement for electronic presentment" refers to an agreement under which presentment may be made to a payor bank by a presentment notice rather than by presentment of the item. Under imaging technology now under development, the presentment notice might be an image of the item. The electronic presentment agreement may provide that the item may be retained by a depositary bank, other collecting bank, or even a customer of the depositary bank, or it may provide that the item will follow the presentment notice. The identifying characteristic of an electronic presentment agreement is that presentment occurs when the presentment notice is received. "An agreement for electronic presentment" does not refer to the common case of retention of items by payor banks because the item itself is presented to the payor bank in these cases. Payor bank check retention is a matter of agreement between payor banks and their customers. Provisions on payor bank check retention are found in Section 4–406(b).

2. The assumptions under which the electronic presentment amendments are based are as follows: No bank will participate in an electronic presentment program without an agreement. These agreements may be either bilateral (Sec-

tion 4–103(a)), under which two banks that frequently do business with each other may agree to depositary bank check retention, or multilateral (Section 4–103(b)), in which large segments of the banking industry may participate in such a program. In the latter case, federal or other uniform regulatory standards would likely supply the substance of the electronic presentment agreement, the application of which could be triggered by the use of some form of identifier on the item. Regulation CC, Section 229.36(c) authorizes truncation agreements but forbids them from extending return times or otherwise varying requirements of the part of Regulation CC governing check collection without the agreement of all parties interested in the check. For instance, an extension of return time could damage a depositary bank which must make funds available to its customers under mandatory availability schedules. The Expedited Funds Availability Act, 12 U.S.C. Section 4008(b)(2), directs the Federal Reserve Board to consider requiring that banks provide for check truncation.

3. The parties affected by an agreement for electronic presentment, with the exception of the customer, can be expected to protect themselves. For example, the payor bank can probably be expected to limit its risk of loss from drawer forgery by limiting the dollar amount of eligible items (Federal Reserve program), by reconcilement agreements (ABA Safekeeping program), by insurance (credit union share draft program), or by other means. Because agreements will exist, only minimal amendments are needed to make clear that the UCC does not prohibit electronic presentment.

§ 4.111. Statute of Limitations

An action to enforce an obligation, duty, or right arising under this chapter must be commenced within three years after the cause of action accrues.

Added by Acts 1995, 74th Leg., ch. 921, § 4, eff. Jan. 1, 1996.

Uniform Commercial Code Comment

This section conforms to the period of limitations set by Section 3–118(g) for actions for breach of warranty and to enforce other obligations, duties or rights arising under Article 3. Bracketing "cause of action" recognizes that some states use a different term, such as "claim for relief."

State Bar Committee Comments

The statute of limitations provisions of Section 4.111 only apply to an action to enforce an obligation, duty or right arising under Chapter 4. Other actions relating directly or indirectly to items covered by Chapter 4, or their payment or collection, will be governed by other law, including in particular section 3.118 of Chapter 3. To the extent such actions are not within the scope of section 3.118 because they do not relate to negotiable instruments, they will be governed by other Texas statutes of limitation. *See, e.g.*, Tex. Civ. Prac. & Rem. Code Ann. §§ 16.003(a), 16.004(a)(3) (Vernon 1986).

By virtue of section 1.103, existing Texas law permitting parties to extend, waive or shorten limitations periods should also apply to the limitations period set forth in section 4.111. *See, e.g.*, Tex. Civ. Prac. & Rem. Code Ann. §§ 16.065, 16.070 (Vernon 1986 & Supp. 1995); *Fuqua v. Fuqua*, 750 S.W.2d 238, 241 (Tex. App.—Dallas 1988, writ denied).

To the extent the three-year statute of limitations provided by Section 4.111 constitutes a lengthening of the statute of limitations provided by other Texas law, courts should look to existing Texas case law that arose after the change in the two-year limitations period to a four-year limitations period for an action on an oral debt. These cases generally provide that if the shorter limitations period had not run on the effective date of the new act, the longer limitations period applied because the defense of limitations would not become a vested right until the limitations period had actually run. *See, e.g.*, *National Mar-Kit, Inc. v. Forrest*, 687 S.W.2d 457, 460 (Tex. App.—Houston [14th Dist.] 1985, no writ).

§ 4.112. Payment of Check at Par

(a) Except as otherwise provided by Chapter 3 or this chapter, a payor bank shall pay a check drawn on it against an account with a sufficient balance at par without regard to whether the payee holds an account at the bank.

(b) This section does not prohibit a bank from requiring commercially reasonable verification of the payee's identity before settlement of the check.

(c) In addition to any remedy provided by law, the banking commissioner, in coordination with the Finance Commission of Texas, shall ensure that payor banks comply with the requirements of this section.

Added by Acts 2001, 77th Leg., ch. 699, § 20, eff. Sept. 1, 2001.

SUBCHAPTER B. COLLECTION OF ITEMS: DEPOSITARY AND COLLECTING BANKS

§ 4.201. Status of Collecting Bank as Agent and Provisional Status of Credits; Applicability of Chapter; Item Indorsed "Pay Any Bank"

(a) Unless a contrary intent clearly appears and before the time that a settlement given by a collecting bank for an item is or becomes final, the bank, with respect to the item, is an agent or sub-agent of the owner of the item and any settlement given for the item is provisional. This provision applies regardless of the form of indorsement or lack of indorsement and even though credit given for the item is subject to immediate withdrawal as of right or is in fact withdrawn; but the continuance of ownership of an item by its owner and any rights of the owner to proceeds of the item are subject to rights of a collecting bank, such as those resulting from outstanding advances on the item and rights of recoupment or setoff. If an item is handled by banks for purposes of presentment, payment, collection, or return, the relevant provisions of this chapter apply even though action of the parties clearly establishes that a particular bank has purchased the item and is the owner of it.

(b) After an item has been indorsed with the words "pay any bank" or the like, only a bank may acquire the rights of a holder until the item has been:

(1) returned to the customer initiating collection; or

(2) specially indorsed by a bank to a person who is not a bank.

Acts 1967, 60th Leg., p. 2343, ch. 785, § 1, eff. Sept. 1, 1967. Amended by Acts 1995, 74th Leg., ch. 921, § 4, eff. Jan. 1, 1996.

Uniform Commercial Code Comment

1. This section states certain basic rules of the bank collection process. One basic rule, appearing in the last sentence of subsection (a), is that, to the extent applicable, the provisions of the Article govern without regard to whether a bank handling an item owns the item or is an agent for collection. Historically, much time has been spent and effort expended in determining or attempting to determine whether a bank was a purchaser of an item or merely an agent for collection. See discussion of this subject and cases cited in 11 A.L.R. 1043, 16 A.L.R. 1084, 42 A.L.R. 492, 68 A.L.R. 725, 99 A.L.R. 486. See also Section 4 of the American Bankers Association Bank Collection Code. The general approach of Article 4, similar to that of other articles, is to provide, within reasonable limits, rules or answers to major problems known to exist in the bank collection process without regard to questions of status and ownership but to keep general principles such as status and ownership available to cover residual areas not covered by specific rules. In line with this approach, the last sentence of subsection (a) says in effect that Article 4 applies to practically every item moving through banks for the purpose of presentment, payment or collection.

2. Within this general rule of broad coverage, the first two sentences of subsection (a) state a rule of agency status. "Unless a contrary intent clearly appears" the status of a collecting bank is that of an agent or sub-agent for the owner of the item. Although as indicated in Comment 1 it is much less important under Article 4 to determine status than has been the case heretofore, status may have importance in some residual areas not covered by specific rules. Further, since status has been considered so important in the past, to omit all reference to it might cause confusion. The status of agency "applies regardless of the form of indorsement or lack of indorsement and even though credit given for the item is subject to immediate withdrawal as of right or is in fact withdrawn." Thus questions heretofore litigated as to whether ordinary indorsements "for deposit," "for collection" or in blank have the effect of creating an agency status or a purchase, no longer have significance in varying the prima facie rule of agency. Similarly, the nature of the credit given for an item or whether it is subject to immediate withdrawal as of right or is in fact withdrawn, does not alter the agency status. See A.L.R. references supra in Comment 1.

A contrary intent can change agency status but this must be clear. An example of a clear contrary intent would be if collateral papers established or the item bore a legend stating that the item was sold absolutely to the depositary bank.

3. The prima facie agency status of collecting banks is consistent with prevailing law and practice today. Section 2 of the American Bankers Association Bank Collection Code so provided. Legends on deposit tickets, collection letters and acknowledgments of items and Federal Reserve operating circulars consistently so provide. The status is consistent with rights of charge-back (Section 4–214 and Section 11 of the ABA Code) and risk of loss in the event of insolvency (Section 4–216 and Section 13 of the ABA Code). The right of charge-back with respect to checks is limited by Regulation CC, Section 226.36(d).

4. Affirmative statement of a prima facie agency status for collecting banks requires certain limitations and qualifications. Under current practices substantially all bank collections sooner or later merge into bank credits, at least if collection is effected. Usually, this takes place within a few days of the initiation of collection. An intermediary bank receives final collection and evidences the result of its collection by a "credit" on its books to the depositary bank. The depositary bank evidences the results of its collection by a "credit" in the account of its customer. As used in these instances the term "credit" clearly indicates a debtor-credit relationship. At some stage in the bank collection process the agency status of a collecting bank changes to that of debtor, a debtor of its customer. Usually at about the same time it also becomes a creditor for the amount of the item, a creditor of some intermediary, payor or other bank. Thus the collection is completed, all agency aspects are terminated and the identity of the item has become completely merged in bank accounts, that of the customer with the depositary bank and that of one bank with another.

Although Section 4–215(a) provides that an item is finally paid when the payor bank takes or fails to take certain action with respect to the item, the final payment of the item may or may not result in the simultaneous final settlement for the item in the case of all prior parties. If a series of provisional debits and credits for the item have been entered in accounts between banks, the final payment of the item by the payor bank may result in the automatic firming up of all these provisional debits and credits under Section 4–215(c), and the consequent receipt of final settlement for the item by each collecting bank and the customer of the depositary bank simultaneously with such action of the payor bank. However, if the payor bank or some intermediary bank accounts for the item with a remittance draft, the next prior bank usually does not receive final settlement for the item until the remittance draft finally clears. See Section 4–213(c). The first sentence of subsection (a) provides that the agency status of a collecting bank (whether intermediary or depositary) continues until the settlement given by it for the item is or becomes final. In the case of the series of provisional credits covered by Section 4–215(c), this could be simultaneously with the final payment of the item by the payor bank. In cases in which remittance drafts are used or in straight noncash collections, this would not be until the times specified in Sections 4–213(c) and 4–215(d). With respect to checks Regulation CC Sections 229.31(c), 229.32(b) and 229.36(d) provide that all settlements between banks are final in both the forward collection and return of checks.

Under Section 4–213(a) settlements for items may be made by any means agreed to by the parties. Since it is impossible to contemplate all the kinds of settlements that will be utilized, no attempt is made in Article 4 to provide when settlement is final in all cases. The guiding principle is that settlements should be final when the presenting person has received usable funds. Section 4–213(c) and (d) and Section 4–215(c) provide when final settlement occurs with respect to certain kinds of settlement, but these provisions are not intended to be exclusive.

A number of practical results flow from the rule continuing the agency status of a collecting bank until its settlement for the item is or becomes final, some of which are specifically set forth in this Article. One is that risk of loss continues in the owner of the item rather than the agent bank. See Section 4–214. Offsetting rights favorable to the owner are that pending such final settlement, the owner has the preference rights of Section 4–216 and the direct rights of Section 4–302 against the payor bank. It also follows from this rule that the dollar limitations of Federal Deposit Insurance are measured by the claim of the owner of the item rather than that of the collecting bank. With respect to checks, rights of the parties in insolvency are determined by Regulation CC Section 229.39 and the liability of a bank handling a check to a subsequent bank that does not receive payment because of suspension of payments by another bank is stated in Regulation CC Section 229.35(b).

5. In those cases in which some period of time elapses between the final payment of the item by the payor bank and the time that the settlement of the collecting bank is or becomes final, e.g., if the payor bank or an intermediary bank accounts for the item with a remittance draft or in straight noncash collections, the continuance of the agency status of the collecting bank necessarily carries with it the continuance of the owner's status as principal. The second sentence of subsection (a) provides that whatever rights the owner has to proceeds of the item are subject to the rights of collecting banks for outstanding advances on the item and other valid rights, if any. The rule provides a sound rule to govern cases of attempted attachment of proceeds of a noncash item in the hands of the payor bank as property of the absent owner. If a collecting bank has made an advance on an item which is still outstanding, its right to obtain reimbursement for this advance should be superior to the rights of the owner to the proceeds or to the rights of a creditor of the owner. An intentional crediting of proceeds of an item to the account of a prior bank known to be insolvent, for the purpose of acquiring a right of setoff, would not produce a valid setoff. See 8 Zollman, Banks and Banking (1936) Sec. 5443.

6. This section and Article 4 as a whole represent an intentional abandonment of the approach to bank collection problems appearing in Section 4 of the American Bankers Association Bank Collection Code. Because the tremendous volume of items handled makes impossible the examination by all banks of all indorsements on all items and thus in fact this examination is not made, except perhaps by depositary banks, it is unrealistic to base the rights and duties of all banks in the collection chain on variations in the form of indorsements. It is anomalous to provide throughout the ABA Code that the prima facie status of collecting banks is that of agent or sub-agent but in Section 4 to provide that subsequent holders (sub-agents) shall have the right to rely on the presumption that the bank of deposit (the primary agent) is the owner of the item. It is unrealistic, particularly in this background, to base rights and duties on status of agent or owner. Thus Section 4–201 makes the pertinent provisions of Article 4 applicable to substantially all items handled by banks for presentment, payment or collection, recognizes the prima facie status of most banks as agents, and then seeks to state appropriate limits and some attributes to the general rules so expressed.

7. Subsection (b) protects the ownership rights with respect to an item indorsed "pay any bank or banker" or in similar terms of a customer initiating collection or of any bank acquiring a security interest under Section 4–210, in the event the item is subsequently acquired under improper circumstances by a person who is not a bank and transferred by that person to another person, whether or not a bank. Upon return to the customer initiating collection of an item so indorsed, the indorsement may be cancelled (Section 3–207). A bank holding an item so indorsed may transfer the item out of banking channels by special indorsement; however, under Section 4–103(e), the bank would be liable to the owner of the item for any loss resulting therefrom if the transfer had been made in bad faith or with lack of ordinary care. If briefer and more simple forms of bank indorsements are developed under Section 4–206 (e.g., the use of bank transit numbers in lieu of present lengthy forms of bank indorsements), a depositary bank having the transit number "X100" could make subsection (b) operative by indorsements such as "Pay any bank—X100." Regulation CC Section 229.35(c) states the effect of an indorsement on a check by a bank.

§ 4.202. Responsibility for Collection or Return; When Action Timely

(a) A collecting bank must exercise ordinary care in:

(1) presenting an item or sending it for presentment;

(2) sending notice of dishonor or non-payment or returning an item other than a documentary draft to the bank's transferor after learning that the item has not been paid or accepted, as the case may be;

(3) settling for an item when the bank receives final settlement; and

(4) notifying its transferor of any loss or delay in transit within a reasonable time after discovery thereof.

(b) A collecting bank exercises ordinary care under Subsection (a) by taking proper action before its midnight deadline following receipt of an item, notice, or settlement. Taking proper action within a reasonably longer time may constitute the exercise of ordinary care, but the bank has the burden of establishing timeliness.

(c) Subject to Subsection (a)(1), a bank is not liable for the insolvency, neglect, misconduct, mistake, or default of another bank or person or for loss or destruction of an item in the possession of others or in transit.

Acts 1967, 60th Leg., p. 2343, ch. 785, § 1, eff. Sept. 1, 1967. Amended by Acts 1995, 74th Leg., ch. 921, § 4, eff. Jan. 1, 1996.

Uniform Commercial Code Comment

1. Subsection (a) states the basic responsibilities of a collecting bank. Of course, under Section 1–203 a collecting bank is subject to the standard requirement of good faith. By subsection (a) it must also use ordinary care in the exercise of its basic collection tasks. By Section 4–103(a) neither requirement may be disclaimed.

2. If the bank makes presentment itself, subsection (a)(1) requires ordinary care with respect both to the time and manner of presentment. (Sections 3–501 and 4–212.) If it forwards the item to be presented the subsection requires ordinary care with respect to routing (Section 4–204), and also in the selection of intermediary banks or other agents.

3. Subsection (a) describes types of basic action with respect to which a collecting bank must use ordinary care. Subsection (b) deals with the time for taking action. It first prescribes the general standard for timely action, namely, for items received on Monday, proper action (such as forwarding or presenting) on Monday or Tuesday is timely. Although under current "production line" operations banks customarily move items along on regular schedules substantially briefer than two days, the subsection states an outside time within which a bank may know it has taken timely action. To provide flexibility from this standard norm, the subsection further states that action within a reasonably longer time may be timely but the bank has the burden of proof. In the case of time items, action after the midnight deadline, but sufficiently in advance of maturity for proper presentation, is a clear example of a "reasonably longer time" that is timely. The standard of requiring action not later than Tuesday in the case of Monday items is also subject to possibilities of variation under the general provisions of Section 4–103, or under the special provisions regarding time of receipt of items (Section 4–108), and regarding delays (Section 4–109). This subsection (b) deals only with collecting banks. The time limits applicable to payor banks appear in Sections 4–301 and 4–302.

4. At common law the so-called New York collection rule subjected the initial collecting bank to liability for the actions of subsequent banks in the collection chain; the so-called Massachusetts rule was that each bank, subject to the duty of selecting proper intermediaries, was liable only for its own negligence. Subsection (c) adopts the Massachusetts rule. But since this is stated to be subject to subsection (a)(1) a collecting bank remains responsible for using ordinary care in selecting properly qualified intermediary banks and agents and in giving proper instructions to them. Regulation CC Section 229.36(d) states the liability of a bank during the forward collection of checks.

§ 4.203. Effect of Instructions

Subject to Chapter 3 concerning conversion of instruments (Section 3.420) and restrictive indorsements (Section 3.206), only a collecting bank's transferor can give instructions that affect the bank or constitute notice to it, and a collecting bank is not liable to prior parties for any action taken pursuant to the instructions or in accordance with any agreement with its transferor.

Acts 1967, 60th Leg., p. 2343, ch. 785, § 1, eff. Sept. 1, 1967. Amended by Acts 1995, 74th Leg., ch. 921, § 4, eff. Jan. 1, 1996.

Uniform Commercial Code Comment

This section adopts a "chain of command" theory which renders it unnecessary for an intermediary or collecting bank to determine whether its transferor is "authorized" to give the instructions. Equally the bank is not put on notice of any "revocation of authority" or "lack of authority" by notice received from any other person. The desirability of speed in the collection process and the fact that, by reason of advances made, the transferor may have the paramount interest in the item requires the rule.

The section is made subject to the provisions of Article 3 concerning conversion of instruments (Section 3–420) and restrictive indorsements (Section 3–206). Of course instructions from or an agreement with its transferor does not relieve a collecting bank of its general obligation to exercise good faith and ordinary care. See Section 4–103(a). If in any particular case a bank has exercised good faith and ordinary care and is relieved of responsibility by reason of instructions of or an agreement with its transferor, the owner of the item may still have a remedy for loss against the transferor (another bank) if such transferor has given wrongful instructions.

The rules of the section are applied only to collecting banks. Payor banks always have the problem of making proper payment of an item; whether such payment is proper should be based upon all of the rules of Articles 3 and 4 and all of the facts of any particular case, and should not be dependent exclusively upon instructions from or an agreement with a person presenting the item.

§ 4.204. Methods of Sending and Presenting; Sending Directly to Payor Bank

(a) A collecting bank shall send items by a reasonably prompt method, taking into consideration relevant instructions, the nature of the item, the number of those items on hand, the cost of collection involved, and the method generally used by it or others to present those items.

(b) A collecting bank may send:

(1) an item directly to the payor bank;

(2) an item to a non-bank payor if authorized by its transferor; and

(3) an item other than a documentary draft to a non-bank payor, if authorized by Federal Reserve regulation or operating circular, clearing-house rule, or the like.

(c) Presentment may be made by a presenting bank at a place where the payor bank or other payor has requested that presentment be made.

Acts 1967, 60th Leg., p. 2343, ch. 785, § 1, eff. Sept. 1, 1967. Amended by Acts 1995, 74th Leg., ch. 921, § 4, eff. Jan. 1, 1996.

Uniform Commercial Code Comment

1. Subsection (a) prescribes the general standards applicable to proper sending or forwarding of items. Because of the many types of methods available and the desirability of preserving flexibility any attempt to prescribe limited or precise methods is avoided.

2. Subsection (b)(1) codifies the practice of direct mail, express, messenger or like presentment to payor banks. The practice is now country-wide and is justified by the need for speed, the general responsibility of banks, Federal Deposit Insurance protection and other reasons.

3. Full approval of the practice of direct sending is limited to cases in which a bank is a payor. Since nonbank drawees or payors may be of unknown responsibility, substantial risks may be attached to placing in their hands the instruments calling for payments from them. This is obviously so in the case of documentary drafts. However, in some cities practices have long existed under clearing-house procedures to forward certain types of items to certain nonbank payors. Examples include insurance loss drafts drawn by field agents on home offices. For the purpose of leaving the door open to legitimate practices of this kind, subsection (b)(3) affirmatively approves direct sending of any item other than documentary drafts to any nonbank payor, if authorized by Federal Reserve regulation or operating circular, clearing-house rule or the like.

On the other hand subsection (b)(2) approves sending any item directly to a nonbank payor if authorized by a collecting bank's transferor. This permits special instructions or agreements out of the norm and is consistent with the "chain of command" theory of Section 4–203. However, if a transferor other than the owner of the item, e.g., a prior collecting bank, authorizes a direct sending to a nonbank payor, such transferor assumes responsibility for the propriety or impropriety of such authorization.

4. Section 3–501(b) provides where presentment may be made. This provision is expressly subject to Article 4. Section 4–204(c) specifically approves presentment by a presenting bank at any place requested by the payor bank or other payor. The time when a check is received by a payor bank for presentment is governed by Regulation CC Section 229.36(b).

§ 4.205. Depository Bank Holder of Unindorsed Item

If a customer delivers an item to a depositary bank for collection, the depositary bank:

(1) becomes a holder of the item at the time it receives the item for collection if the customer at the time of delivery was a holder of the item, whether or not the customer indorses the item, and, if the bank satisfies the other requirements of Section 3.302, the bank is a holder in due course; and

(2) warrants to collecting banks, the payor bank or other payor, and the drawer that the amount of the item was paid to the customer or deposited to the customer's account.

Acts 1967, 60th Leg., p. 2343, ch. 785, § 1, eff. Sept. 1, 1967. Amended by Acts 1995, 74th Leg., ch. 921, § 4, eff. Jan. 1, 1996.

Uniform Commercial Code Comment

Section 3–201(b) provides that negotiation of an instrument payable to order requires indorsement by the holder. The rule of former Section 4–205(1) was that the depositary bank may supply a missing indorsement of its customer unless the item contains the words "payee's indorsement required" or the like. The cases have differed on the status of the depositary bank as a holder if it fails to supply its customer's indorsement. *Marine Midland Bank, N.A. v. Price, Miller, Evans & Flowers*, 446 N.Y.S.2d 797 (N.Y.App.Div. 4th Dept. 1981), *rev'd*, 455 N.Y.S.2d 565 (N.Y.1982). It is common practice for depositary banks to receive unindorsed checks under so-called "lock-box" agreements from customers who receive a high volume of checks. No function would be served by requiring a depositary bank to run these items through a machine that would supply the customer's indorsement except to afford the drawer and the subsequent banks evidence that the proceeds of the item reached the customer's account. Paragraph (1) provides that the depositary bank becomes a holder when it takes the item for deposit if the depositor is a holder. Whether it supplies the customer's indorsement is immaterial. Paragraph (2) satisfies the need for a receipt of funds by the depositary bank by imposing on that bank a warranty that it paid the customer or deposited the item to the customer's account. This warranty runs not only to collecting banks and to the payor bank or nonbank drawee but also to the drawer, affording protection to these parties that the depositary bank received the item and applied it to the benefit of the holder.

State Bar Committee Comments

New section 4.205 raises the issue of whether a drawee bank may be liable for wrongful dishonor if it fails to pay a person who is entitled to enforce an instrument taken without indorsement of the depository bank's customer or containing an indorsement of questionable validity. Under section 3.501(b)(3), a payee bank need not, but may, pay on an item when an indorsement is missing or when a customer places a mark of questionable validity on an item. If it does not pay the item for lack of the necessary indorsement, under that section, the bank has not dishonored the item and may return the instrument for lack of the necessary indorsement.

§ 4.206. Transfer Between Banks

Any agreed method that identifies the transferor bank is sufficient for the item's further transfer to another bank.

Acts 1967, 60th Leg., p. 2343, ch. 785, § 1, eff. Sept. 1, 1967. Amended by Acts 1995, 74th Leg., ch. 921, § 4, eff. Jan. 1, 1996.

Uniform Commercial Code Comment

This section is designed to permit the simplest possible form of transfer from one bank to another, once an item gets in the bank collection chain, provided only identity of the transferor bank is preserved. This is important for tracing purposes and if recourse is necessary. However, since the responsibilities of the various banks appear in the Article it becomes unnecessary to have liability or responsibility depend on more formal indorsements. Simplicity in the form of transfer is conducive to speed. If the transfer is between banks, this section takes the place of the more formal requirements of Section 3–201.

§ 4.207. Transfer Warranties

(a) A customer or collecting bank that transfers an item and receives a settlement or other consideration warrants to the transferee and to any subsequent collecting bank that:

(1) the warrantor is a person entitled to enforce the item;

(2) all signatures on the item are authentic and authorized;

(3) the item has not been altered;

(4) the item is not subject to a defense or claim in recoupment (Section 3.305(a)) of any party that can be asserted against the warrantor;

(5) the warrantor has no knowledge of any insolvency proceeding commenced with respect to the maker or acceptor or, in the case of an unaccepted draft, the drawer; and

(6) with respect to a remotely-created item, that the person on whose account the item is drawn authorized the issuance of the item in the amount for which the item is drawn.

(b) If an item is dishonored, a customer or collecting bank transferring the item and receiving settlement or other consideration is obliged to pay the amount due on the item (i) according to the terms of the item at the time it was transferred, or (ii) if the transfer was of an incomplete item, according to its terms when completed as stated in Sections 3.115 and 3.407. The obligation of a transferor is owed to the transferee and to any subsequent collecting bank that takes the item in good faith. A transferor cannot disclaim its obligation under this subsection by an indorsement stating that it is made "without recourse" or otherwise disclaiming liability.

(c) A person to whom the warranties under Subsection (a) are made and who took the item in good faith may recover from the warrantor as damages for breach of warranty an amount equal to the loss suffered as a result of the breach, but not more than the amount of the item plus expenses and loss of interest incurred as a result of the breach.

(d) The warranties stated in Subsection (a) cannot be disclaimed with respect to checks. Unless notice of a claim for breach of warranty is given to the warrantor within 30 days after the claimant has reason to know of the breach and the identity of the warrantor, the warrantor is discharged to the extent of any loss caused by the delay in giving notice of the claim.

(e) A cause of action for breach of warranty under this section accrues when the claimant has reason to know of the breach.

(f) If the warranty under Subsection (a)(6) is not given by a transferor or collecting bank under applicable conflict of law rules, the warranty is not given to that transferor when that transferor is a transferee or to any prior collecting bank of that transferee.

Acts 1967, 60th Leg., p. 2343, ch. 785, § 1, eff. Sept. 1, 1967. Amended by Acts 1995, 74th Leg., ch. 921, § 4, eff. Jan. 1, 1996; Acts 1997, 75th Leg., ch. 131, § 5, eff. Sept. 1, 1997; Acts 2005, 79th Leg., ch. 95, § 16, eff. Sept. 1, 2005.

Uniform Commercial Code Comment

1. Except for subsection (b), this section conforms to Section 3–416 and extends its coverage to items. The substance of this section is discussed in the Comment to Section

3–416. Subsection (b) provides that customers or collecting banks that transfer items, whether by indorsement or not, undertake to pay the item if the item is dishonored. This obligation cannot be disclaimed by a "without recourse" indorsement or otherwise. With respect to checks, Regulation CC Section 229.34 states the warranties made by paying and returning banks.

2. For an explanation of subsection (a)(6), see comment 8 to Section 3–416.

§ 4.208. Presentment Warranties

(a) If an unaccepted draft is presented to the drawee for payment or acceptance and the drawee pays or accepts the draft, (i) the person obtaining payment or acceptance, at the time of presentment, and (ii) a previous transferor of the draft, at the time of transfer, warrant to the drawee that pays or accepts the draft in good faith that:

(1) the warrantor is, or was, at the time the warrantor transferred the draft, a person entitled to enforce the draft or authorized to obtain payment or acceptance of the draft on behalf of a person entitled to enforce the draft;

(2) the draft has not been altered;

(3) the warrantor has no knowledge that the signature of the purported drawer of the draft is unauthorized; and

(4) with respect to any remotely-created item, that the person on whose account the item is drawn authorized the issuance of the item in the amount for which the item is drawn.

(b) A drawee making payment may recover from a warrantor damages for breach of warranty equal to the amount paid by the drawee less the amount the drawee received or is entitled to receive from the drawer because of the payment. In addition, the drawee is entitled to compensation for expenses and loss of interest resulting from the breach. The right of the drawee to recover damages under this subsection is not affected by any failure of the drawee to exercise ordinary care in making payment. If the drawee accepts the draft, breach of warranty is a defense to the obligation of the acceptor. If the acceptor makes payment with respect to the draft, the acceptor is entitled to recover from a warrantor for breach of warranty the amounts stated in this subsection.

(c) If a drawee asserts a claim for breach of warranty under Subsection (a) based on an unauthorized indorsement of the draft or an alteration of the draft, the warrantor may defend by proving that the indorsement is effective under Section 3.404 or 3.405 or the drawer is precluded under Section 3.406 or 4.406 from asserting against the drawee the unauthorized indorsement or alteration.

(d) If (i) a dishonored draft is presented for payment to the drawer or an indorser, or (ii) any other item is presented for payment to a party obliged to pay the item, and the item is paid, the person obtaining payment and a prior transferor of the item warrant to the person making payment in good faith that the warrantor is, or was, at the time the warrantor transferred the item, a person entitled to enforce the item or authorized to obtain payment on behalf of a person entitled to enforce the item. The person making payment may recover from any warrantor for breach of warranty an amount equal to the amount paid plus expenses and loss of interest resulting from the breach.

(e) The warranties stated in Subsections (a) and (d) cannot be disclaimed with respect to checks. Unless notice of a claim for breach of warranty is given to the warrantor within 30 days after the claimant has reason to know of the breach and the identity of the warrantor, the warrantor is discharged to the extent of any loss caused by the delay in giving notice of the claim.

(f) A cause of action for breach of warranty under this section accrues when the claimant has reason to know of the breach.

(g) If as to a particular item (1) a transferee (including a collecting bank) asserts a claim for breach of the warranty under Subsection (a)(4), but (2) under applicable law (including the applicable choice-of-law principles) that transferee would not make a warranty substantially similar to the warranty in Subsection (a)(4) if such transferee were a transferor, then that transferee would not receive the warranty in Subsection (a)(4) from any transferor.

Amended by Acts 1995, 74th Leg., ch. 921, § 4, eff. Jan. 1, 1996; Acts 1997, 75th Leg., ch. 131, § 6, eff. Sept. 1, 1997; Acts 2005, 79th Leg., ch. 95, § 17, eff. Sept. 1, 2005.

Uniform Commercial Code Comment

1. This section conforms to Section 3–417 and extends its coverage to items. The substance of this section is discussed in the Comment to Section 3–417. "Draft" is defined in Section 4–104 as including an item that is an order to pay so as to make clear that the term "draft" in Article 4 may include items that are not instruments within Section 3–104.

2. For an explanation of subsection (a)(4), see comment 8 to Section 3–416.

§ 4.209. Encoding and Retention Warranties

(a) A person who encodes information on or with respect to an item after issue warrants to any subsequent collecting bank and to the payor bank or other payor that the information is correctly encoded. If the customer of a depositary bank encodes, that bank also makes the warranty.

(b) A person who undertakes to retain an item pursuant to an agreement for electronic presentment warrants to any subsequent collecting bank and to the payor bank or other payor that retention and presentment of the item comply with the agreement. If a customer of a depositary bank undertakes to retain an item, that bank also makes this warranty.

(c) A person to whom warranties are made under this section and who took the item in good faith may recover from the warrantor as damages for breach of warranty an amount equal to the loss suffered as a result of the breach, plus expenses and loss of interest incurred as a result of the breach.

Amended by Acts 1995, 74th Leg., ch. 921, § 4, eff. Jan. 1, 1996.

Uniform Commercial Code Comment

1. Encoding and retention warranties are included in Article 4 because they are unique to the bank collection process. These warranties are breached only by the person doing the encoding or retaining the item and not by subsequent banks handling the item. Encoding and check retention may be done by customers who are payees of a large volume of checks; hence, this section imposes warranties on customers as well as banks. If a customer encodes or retains, the depositary bank is also liable for any breach of this warranty.

2. A misencoding of the amount on the MICR line is not an alteration under Section 3–407(a) which defines alteration as changing the contract of the parties. If a drawer wrote a check for $2,500 and the depository bank encoded $25,000 on the MICR line, the payor bank could debit the drawer's account for only $2,500. This subsection would allow the payor bank to hold the depositary bank liable for the amount paid out over $2,500 without first pursuing the person who received payment. Intervening collecting banks would not be liable to the payor bank for the depositary bank's error. If a drawer wrote a check for $25,000 and the depositary bank encoded $2,500, the payor bank becomes liable for the full amount of the check. The payor bank's rights against the depositary bank depend on whether the payor bank has suffered a loss. Since the payor bank can debit the drawer's account for $25,000, the payor bank has a loss only to the extent that the drawer's account is less than the full amount of the check. There is no requirement that the payor bank pursue collection against the drawer beyond the amount in the drawer's account as a condition to the payor bank's action against the depositary bank for breach of warranty. See *Georgia Railroad Bank & Trust Co. v. First National Bank & Trust*, 229 S.E.2d 482 (Ga.App.1976), aff'd, 235 S.E.2d 1 (Ga.1977), and *First National Bank of Boston v. Fidelity Bank, National Association*, 724 F.Supp. 1168 (E.D.Pa.1989).

3. A person retaining items under an electronic presentment agreement (Section 4–110) warrants that it has complied with the terms of the agreement regarding its possession of the item and its sending a proper presentment notice. If the keeper is a customer, its depositary bank also makes this warranty.

§ 4.210. Security Interest of Collecting Bank in Items, Accompanying Documents and Proceeds

(a) A collecting bank has a security interest in an item and any accompanying documents or the proceeds of either:

(1) in case of an item deposited in an account, to the extent to which credit given for the item has been withdrawn or applied;

(2) in case of an item for which it has given credit available for withdrawal as of right, to the extent of the credit given, whether or not the credit is drawn upon or there is a right of charge-back; or

(3) if it makes an advance on or against the item.

(b) If credit given for several items received at one time or pursuant to a single agreement is withdrawn or applied in part, the security interest remains upon all the items, any accompanying documents, or the proceeds of either. For the purpose of this section, credits first given are first withdrawn.

(c) Receipt by a collecting bank of a final settlement for an item is a realization on its security interest in the item, accompanying documents, and proceeds. So long as the bank does not receive final settlement for the item or give up possession of the item or possession or control of the accompanying documents for purposes other than collection, the security interest continues to that extent and is subject to Chapter 9, but:

(1) no security agreement is necessary to make the security interest enforceable (Section 9.203(b)(3)(A));

(2) no filing is required to perfect the security interest; and

(3) the security interest has priority over conflicting perfected security interests in the item, accompanying documents, or proceeds.

Acts 1967, 60th Leg., p. 2343, ch. 785, § 1, eff. Sept. 1, 1967. Renumbered from § 4.208 and amended by Acts 1995, 74th Leg., ch. 921, § 4, eff. Jan. 1, 1996. Amended by Acts 1999, 76th Leg., ch. 414, § 2.23, eff. July 1, 2001; Acts 2005, 79th Leg., ch. 122, § 17, eff. Sept. 1, 2005.

Uniform Commercial Code Comment

1. Subsection (a) states a rational rule for the interest of a bank in an item. The customer of the depositary bank is normally the owner of the item and the several collecting banks are agents of the customer (Section 4–201). A collecting agent may properly make advances on the security of paper held for collection, and acquires at common law a possessory lien for these advances. Subsection (a) applies an analogous principle to a bank in the collection chain which extends credit on items in the course of collection. The bank has a security interest to the extent stated in this section. To the extent of its security interest it is a holder for value (Sections 3–303, 4–211) and a holder in due course if it satisfies the other requirements for that status (Section 3–302). Subsection (a) does not derogate from the banker's general common law lien or right of setoff against indebtedness owing in deposit accounts. See Section 1–103. Rather subsection (a) specifically implements and extends the principle as a part of the bank collection process.

2. Subsection (b) spreads the security interest of the bank over all items in a single deposit or received under a single agreement and a single giving of credit. It also adopts the "first-in, first-out" rule.

3. Collection statistics establish that the vast majority of items handled for collection are in fact collected. The first sentence of subsection (c) reflects the fact that in the normal case the bank's security interest is self-liquidating. The remainder of the subsection correlates the security interest with the provisions of Article 9, particularly for use in the cases of noncollection in which the security interest may be important.

Sections 31 and 32 of Acts 2005, 79th Leg., ch. 122 provide:

"Sec. 31. This Act applies to a document of title that is issued or a bailment that arises on or after the effective date of this Act. This Act does not apply to a document of title that is issued or a bailment that arises before the effective date of this Act even if the document of title or bailment would be subject to this Act if the document of title had been issued or bailment had arisen after the effective date of this Act. This Act does not apply to a right of action that has accrued before the effective date of this Act.

"Sec. 32. A document of title issued or a bailment that arises before the effective date of this Act and the rights, obligations, and interests flowing from that document or bailment are governed by any statute or other rule amended or repealed by this Act as if amendment or repeal had not occurred and may be terminated, completed, consummated, or enforced under that statute or other rule."

§ 4.211. When Bank Gives Value for Purposes of Holder in Due Course

For purposes of determining its status as a holder in due course, a bank has given value to the extent it has a security interest in an item, if the bank otherwise complies with the requirements of Section 3.302 on what constitutes a holder in due course.

Acts 1967, 60th Leg., p. 2343, ch. 785, § 1, eff. Sept. 1, 1967. Renumbered from § 4.209 and amended by Acts 1995, 74th Leg., ch. 921, § 4, eff. Jan. 1, 1996.

Uniform Commercial Code Comment

The section completes the thought of the previous section and makes clear that a security interest in an item is "value" for the purpose of determining the holder's status as a holder in due course. The provision is in accord with the prior law (N.I.L. Section 27) and with Article 3 (Section 3–303). The section does not prescribe a security interest under Section 4–210 as a test of "value" generally because the meaning of "value" under other Articles is adequately defined in Section 1–201.

§ 4.212. Presentment by Notice of Item Not Payable by, Through or at a Bank; Liability of Drawer or Indorser

(a) Unless otherwise instructed, a collecting bank may present an item not payable by, through, or at a bank by sending to the party to accept or pay a record providing notice that the bank holds the item for acceptance or payment. The notice must be sent in time to be received on or before the day when presentment is due, and the bank must meet any requirement of the party to accept or pay under Section 3.501 by the close of the bank's next banking day after it knows of the requirement.

(b) If presentment is made by notice and payment, acceptance, or request for compliance with a requirement under Section 3.501 is not received by the close of business on the day after maturity or, in the case of demand items, by the close of business on the third banking day after notice was sent, the presenting bank may treat the item as dishonored and charge any drawer or indorser by sending it notice of the facts.

Acts 1967, 60th Leg., p. 2343, ch. 785, § 1, eff. Sept. 1, 1967. Renumbered from § 4.210 and amended by Acts 1995, 74th Leg., ch. 921, § 4, eff. Jan. 1, 1996; Acts 2005, 79th Leg., ch. 95, § 18, eff. Sept. 1, 2005.

Uniform Commercial Code Comment

1. This section codifies a practice extensively followed in presentation of trade acceptances and documentary and other drafts drawn on nonbank payors. It imposes a duty on the payor to respond to the notice of the item if the item is not to be considered dishonored. Notice of such a dishonor charges drawers and indorsers. Presentment under this section is good presentment under Article 3. See Section 3–501.

2. A drawee not receiving notice is not, of course, liable to the drawer for wrongful dishonor.

3. A bank so presenting an instrument must be sufficiently close to the drawee to be able to exhibit the instrument on the day it is requested to do so or the next business day at the latest.

§ 4.213. Medium and Time of Settlement by Bank

(a) With respect to settlement by a bank, the medium and time of settlement may be prescribed by Federal Reserve regulations or circulars, clearing-house rules, and the like or by agreement. In the absence of such a prescription:

(1) the medium of settlement is cash or credit to an account in a Federal Reserve bank of or specified by the person to receive settlement; and

(2) the time of settlement is:

(A) with respect to tender of settlement by cash, a cashier's check, or a teller's check, when the cash or check is sent or delivered;

(B) with respect to tender of settlement by credit to an account in a Federal Reserve bank, when the credit is made;

(C) with respect to tender of settlement by a credit or debit to an account in a bank, when the credit or debit is made or, in the case of tender of settlement by authority to charge an account, when the authority is sent or delivered; or

(D) with respect to tender of settlement by a funds transfer, when payment is made pursuant to Section 4A.406(a) to the person receiving settlement.

(b) If the tender of settlement is not by a medium authorized by Subsection (a) or the time of settlement is not fixed by Subsection (a), a settlement does not occur until the tender of settlement is accepted by the person receiving settlement.

(c) If settlement for an item is made by cashier's check or teller's check and the person receiving settlement, before its midnight deadline:

(1) presents or forwards the check for collection, settlement is final when the check is finally paid; or

(2) fails to present or forward the check for collection, settlement is final at the midnight deadline of the person receiving settlement.

(d) If settlement for an item is made by giving authority to charge the account of the bank giving settlement in the bank receiving settlement, settlement is final when the charge is made by the bank receiving settlement if there are funds available in the account for the amount of the item.

Acts 1967, 60th Leg., p. 2343, ch. 785, § 1, eff. Sept. 1, 1967. Amended by Acts 1983, 68th Leg., p. 1531, ch. 290, § 4, eff. Aug. 29, 1983. Renumbered from § 4.211 and amended by Acts 1995, 74th Leg., ch. 921, § 4, eff. Jan. 1, 1996.

Uniform Commercial Code Comment

1. Subsection (a) sets forth the medium of settlement that the person receiving settlement must accept. In nearly all cases the medium of settlement will be determined by agreement or by Federal Reserve regulations and circulars, clearing-house rules, and the like. In the absence of regulations, rules or agreement, the person receiving settlement may demand cash or credit in a Federal Reserve bank. If the person receiving settlement does not have an account in a Federal Reserve bank, it may specify the account of another bank in a Federal Reserve bank. In the unusual case in which there is no agreement on the medium of settlement and the bank making settlement tenders settlement other than cash or Federal Reserve bank credit, no settlement has occurred under subsection (b) unless the person receiving settlement accepts the settlement tendered. For example, if a payor bank, without agreement, tenders a teller's check, the bank receiving the settlement may reject the check and return it to the payor bank or it may accept the check as settlement.

2. In several provisions of Article 4 the time that a settlement occurs is relevant. Subsection (a) sets out a general rule that the time of settlement, like the means of settlement, may be prescribed by agreement. In the absence of agreement, the time of settlement for tender of the common agreed media of settlement is that set out in subsection (a)(2). The time of settlement by cash, cashier's or teller's check or authority to charge an account is the time the cash, check or authority is sent, unless presentment is over the counter in which case settlement occurs upon delivery to the presenter. If there is no agreement on the time of settlement and the tender of settlement is not made by one of the media set out in subsection (a), under subsection (b) the time of settlement is the time the settlement is accepted by the person receiving settlement.

3. Subsections (c) and (d) are special provisions for settlement by remittance drafts and authority to charge an account in the bank receiving settlement. The relationship between final settlement and final payment under Section 4–215 is addressed in subsection (b) of Section 4–215. With respect to settlement by cashier's checks or teller's checks, other than in response to over-the-counter presentment, the bank receiving settlement can keep the risk that the check will not be paid on the bank tendering the check in settlement by acting to initiate collection of the check within the midnight deadline of the bank receiving settlement. If the bank fails to initiate settlement before its midnight deadline, final settlement occurs at the midnight deadline, and the bank receiving settlement assumes the risk that the check will not be paid. If there is no agreement that permits the bank tendering settlement to tender a cashier's or teller's check, subsection (b) allows the bank receiving the check to reject it, and, if it does, no settlement occurs. However, if the bank accepts the check, settlement occurs and the time of final settlement is governed by subsection (c).

With respect to settlement by tender of authority to charge the account of the bank making settlement in the bank receiving settlement, subsection (d) provides that final settlement does not take place until the account charged has available funds to cover the amount of the item. If there is no agreement that permits the bank tendering settlement to tender an authority to charge an account as settlement, subsection (b) allows the bank receiving the tender to reject it. However, if the bank accepts the authority, settlement occurs and the time of final settlement is governed by subsection (d).

§ 4.214. Right of Charge-Back or Refund; Liability of Collecting Bank; Return of Item

(a) If a collecting bank has made provisional settlement with its customer for an item and fails by reason of dishonor, suspension of payments by a bank, or otherwise to receive settlement for the item that is or becomes final, the bank may revoke the settlement given by it, charge back the amount of any credit given for the item to its customer's account, or obtain refund from its customer, whether or not it is able to return the item, if by its midnight deadline or within a longer reasonable time after it learns the facts it returns the item or sends notification of the facts. If the return or notice is delayed beyond the bank's midnight deadline or a longer reasonable time after it learns the facts, the bank may revoke the settlement, charge back the credit, or obtain refund from its customers, but it is liable for any loss resulting from the delay. These rights to revoke, charge-back, and obtain refund terminate if and when a settlement for the item received by the bank is or becomes final.

(b) A collecting bank returns an item when it is sent or delivered to the bank's customer or transferor or pursuant to its instructions.

(c) A depositary bank that is also the payor may charge-back the amount of an item to its customer's account or obtain refund in accordance with the section governing return of an item received by a payor bank for credit on its books (Section 4.301).

(d) The right to charge-back is not affected by:

(1) previous use of a credit given for the item; or

(2) failure by any bank to exercise ordinary care with respect to the item, but a bank so failing remains liable.

(e) A failure to charge-back or claim refund does not affect other rights of the bank against the customer or any other party.

(f) If credit is given in dollars as the equivalent of the value of an item payable in foreign money, the dollar amount of any charge-back or refund must be calculated on the basis of the bank-offered spot rate for the foreign money prevailing on the day when the person entitled to the charge-back or refund learns that it will not receive payment in ordinary course.

Acts 1967, 60th Leg., p. 2343, ch. 785, § 1, eff. Sept. 1, 1967. Renumbered from § 4.212 and amended by Acts 1995, 74th Leg., ch. 921, § 4, eff. Jan. 1, 1996.

Uniform Commercial Code Comment

1. Under current bank practice, in a major portion of cases banks make provisional settlement for items when they are first received and then await subsequent determination of whether the item will be finally paid. This is the principal characteristic of what are referred to in banking parlance as "cash items." Statistically, this practice of settling provisionally first and then awaiting final payment is justified because the vast majority of such cash items are finally paid, with the result that in this great preponderance of cases it becomes unnecessary for the banks making the provisional settlements to make any further entries. In due course the provisional settlements become final simply with the lapse of time. However, in those cases in which the item being collected is not finally paid or if for various reasons the bank making the provisional settlement does not itself receive final payment, provision is made in subsection (a) for the reversal of the provisional settlements, charge-back of provisional credits and the right to obtain refund.

2. Various causes of a bank's not receiving final payment, with the resulting right of charge-back or refund, are stated or suggested in subsection (a). These include dishonor of the original item; dishonor of a remittance instrument given for it; reversal of a provisional credit for the item; suspension of payments by another bank. The causes stated are illustrative; the right of charge-back or refund is stated to exist whether the failure to receive final payment in ordinary course arises through one of them "or otherwise."

3. The right of charge-back or refund exists if a collecting bank has made a provisional settlement for an item with its customer but terminates if and when a settlement received by the bank for the item is or becomes final. If the bank fails to receive such a final settlement the right of charge-back or refund must be exercised promptly after the bank learns the facts. The right exists (if so promptly exercised) whether or not the bank is able to return the item. The second sentence of subsection (a) adopts the view of *Appliance Buyers Credit Corp. v. Prospect National Bank*, 708 F.2d 290 (7th Cir.1983), that if the midnight deadline for returning an item or giving notice is not met, a collecting bank loses its rights only to the extent of damages for any loss resulting from the delay.

4. Subsection (b) states when an item is returned by a collecting bank. Regulation CC, Section 229.31 preempts this subsection with respect to checks by allowing direct return to the depositary bank. Because a returned check may follow a different path than in forward collection, settlement given for the check is final and not provisional except as between the depositary bank and its customer. Regulation CC Section 229.36(d). See also Regulations CC Sections 229.31(c) and 229.32(b). Thus owing to the federal preemption, this subsection applies only to noncheck items.

5. The rule of subsection (d) relating to charge-back (as distinguished from claim for refund) applies irrespective of

the cause of the nonpayment, and of the person ultimately liable for nonpayment. Thus charge-back is permitted even if nonpayment results from the depositary bank's own negligence. Any other rule would result in litigation based upon a claim for wrongful dishonor of other checks of the customer, with potential damages far in excess of the amount of the item. Any other rule would require a bank to determine difficult questions of fact. The customer's protection is found in the general obligation of good faith (Sections 1-203 and 4-103). If bad faith is established the customer's recovery "includes other damages, if any, suffered by the party as a proximate consequence" (Section 4-103(e); see also Section 4-402).

6. It is clear that the charge-back does not relieve the bank from any liability for failure to exercise ordinary care in handling the item. The measure of damages for such failure is stated in Section 4-103(e).

7. Subsection (f) states a rule fixing the time for determining the rate of exchange if there is a charge-back or refund of a credit given in dollars for an item payable in a foreign currency. Compare Section 3-107. Fixing such a rule is desirable to avoid disputes. If in any case the parties wish to fix a different time for determining the rate of exchange, they may do so by agreement.

§ 4.215. Final Payment of Item by Payor Bank; When Provisional Debits and Credits Become Final; When Certain Credits Become Available for Withdrawal

(a) An item is finally paid by a payor bank when the bank has first done any of the following:

(1) paid the item in cash;

(2) settled for the item without having a right to revoke the settlement under statute, clearing-house rule, or agreement; or

(3) made a provisional settlement for the item and failed to revoke the settlement in the time and manner permitted by statute, clearing-house rule, or agreement.

(b) If provisional settlement for an item does not become final, the item is not finally paid.

(c) If provisional settlement for an item between the presenting and payor banks is made through a clearing house or by debits or credits in an account between them, then to the extent that provisional debits or credits for the item are entered in accounts between the presenting and payor banks or between the presenting and successive prior collecting banks seriatim, they become final upon final payment of the item by the payor bank.

(d) If a collecting bank receives a settlement for an item that is or becomes final, the bank is accountable to its customer for the amount of the item, and any provisional credit given for the item in an account with its customer becomes final.

(e) Subject to (i) applicable law stating a time for availability of funds, and (ii) any right of the bank to apply the credit to an obligation of the customer, credit given by a bank for an item in a customer's account becomes available for withdrawal as of right if the bank:

(1) has received a provisional settlement for the item,—when the settlement becomes final and the bank has had a reasonable time to receive return of the item and the item has not been received within that time; or

(2) is both the depositary bank and the payor bank, and the item is finally paid,—at the opening of the bank's second banking day following receipt of the item.

(f) Subject to applicable law stating a time for availability of funds and any right of a bank to apply a deposit to an obligation of the depositor, a deposit of money becomes available for withdrawal as of right at the opening of the bank's next banking day after receipt of the deposit.

Acts 1967, 60th Leg., p. 2343, ch. 785, § 1, eff. Sept. 1, 1967. Amended by Acts 1985, 69th Leg., ch. 621, § 1, eff. June 14, 1985. Renumbered from § 4.213 and amended by Acts 1995, 74th Leg., ch. 921, § 4, eff. Jan. 1, 1996.

Uniform Commercial Code Comment

1. By the definition and use of the term "settle" (Section 4-104(a)(11)) this Article recognizes that various debits or credits, remittances, settlements or payments given for an item may be either provisional or final, that settlements sometimes are provisional and sometimes are final and sometimes are provisional for awhile but later become final. Subsection (a) defines when settlement for an item constitutes final payment.

Final payment of an item is important for a number of reasons. It is one of several factors determining the relative priorities between items and notices, stop-payment orders, legal process and setoffs (Section 4-303). It is the "end of the line" in the collection process and the "turn around" point commencing the return flow of proceeds. It is the point at which many provisional settlements become final. See Section 4-215(c). Final payment of an item by the payor bank fixes preferential rights under Section 4-216.

2. If an item being collected moves through several states, e.g., is deposited for collection in California, moves through two or three California banks to the Federal Reserve Bank of San Francisco, to the Federal Reserve Bank of Boston, to a payor bank in Maine, the collection process involves the eastward journey of the item from California to Maine and the westward journey of the proceeds from Maine to California. Subsection (a) recognizes that final payment

does not take place, in this hypothetical case, on the journey of the item eastward. It also adopts the view that neither does final payment occur on the journey westward because what in fact is journeying westward are *proceeds* of the item.

3. Traditionally and under various decisions payment in cash of an item by a payor bank has been considered final payment. Subsection (a)(1) recognizes and provides that payment of an item in cash by a payor bank is final payment.

4. Section 4–104(a)(11) defines "settle" as meaning "to pay in cash, by clearing-house settlement, in a charge or credit or by remittance, or otherwise as agreed. A settlement may be either provisional or final." Subsection (a)(2) of Section 4–215 provides that an item is finally paid by a payor bank when the bank has "settled for the item without having a right to revoke the settlement under statute, clearing-house rule or agreement." Former subsection (1)(b) is modified by subsection (a)(2) to make clear that a payor bank cannot make settlement provisional by unilaterally reserving a right to revoke the settlement. The right must come from a statute (e.g., Section 4–301), clearing-house rule or other agreement. Subsection (a)(2) provides in effect that if the payor bank finally settles for an item this constitutes final payment of the item. The subsection operates if nothing has occurred and no situation exists making the settlement provisional. If under statute, clearing-house rule or agreement, a right of revocation of the settlement exists, the settlement is provisional. Conversely, if there is an absence of a right to revoke under statute, clearing-house rule or agreement, the settlement is final and such final settlement constitutes final payment of the item.

A primary example of a statutory right on the part of the payor bank to revoke a settlement is the right to revoke conferred by Section 4–301. The underlying theory and reason for deferred posting statutes (Section 4–301) is to require a settlement on the date of receipt of an item but to keep that settlement provisional with the right to revoke prior to the midnight deadline. In any case in which Section 4–301 is applicable, any settlement by the payor bank is provisional solely by virtue of the statute, subsection (a)(2) of Section 4–215 does not operate, and such provisional settlement does not constitute final payment of the item. With respect to checks, Regulation CC Section 229.36(d) provides that settlement between banks for the forward collection of checks is final. The relationship of this provision to Article 4 is discussed in the Commentary to that section.

A second important example of a right to revoke a settlement is that arising under clearing-house rules. It is very common for clearing-house rules to provide that items exchanged and settled for in a clearing (e.g., before 10:00 a.m. on Monday) may be returned and the settlements revoked up to but not later than 2:00 p.m. on the same day (Monday) or under deferred posting at some hour on the next business day (e.g., 2:00 p.m. Tuesday). Under this type of rule the Monday morning settlement is provisional and being provisional does not constitute a final payment of the item.

An example of an agreement allowing the payor bank to revoke a settlement is a case in which the payor bank is also the depositary bank and has signed a receipt or duplicate deposit ticket or has made an entry in a passbook acknowledging receipt, for credit to the account of A, of a check drawn on it by B. If the receipt, deposit ticket, passbook or other agreement with A is to the effect that any credit so entered is provisional and may be revoked pending the time required by the payor bank to process the item to determine if it is in good form and there are funds to cover it, the agreement keeps the receipt or credit provisional and avoids its being either final settlement or final payment.

The most important application of subsection (a)(2) is that in which presentment of an item has been made over the counter for immediate payment. In this case Section 4–301(a) does not apply to make the settlement provisional, and final payment has occurred unless a rule or agreement provides otherwise.

5. Former Section 4–213(1)(c) provided that final payment occurred when the payor bank completed the "process of posting." The term was defined in former Section 4–109. In the present Article, Section 4–109 has been deleted and the process-of-posting test has been abandoned in Section 4–215(a) for determining when final payment is made. Difficulties in determining when the events described in former Section 4–109 take place make the process-of-posting test unsuitable for a system of automated check collection or electronic presentment.

6. The last sentence of former Section 4–213(1) is deleted as an unnecessary source of confusion. Initially the view that payor bank may be accountable for, that is, liable for the amount of, an item that it has already paid seems incongruous. This is particularly true in the light of the language formerly found in Section 4–302 stating that the payor bank can defend against liability for accountability by showing that it has already settled for the item. But, at least with respect to former Section 4–213(1)(c), such a provision was needed because under the process-of-posting test a payor bank may have paid an item without settling for it. Now that Article 4 has abandoned the process-of-posting test, the sentence is no longer needed. If the payor bank has neither paid the item nor returned it within its midnight deadline, the payor bank is accountable under Section 4–302.

7. Subsection (a)(3) covers the situation in which the payor bank makes a provisional settlement for an item, and this settlement becomes final at a later time by reason of the failure of the payor bank to revoke it in the time and manner permitted by statute, clearing-house rule or agreement. An example of this type of situation is the clearing-house settlement referred to in Comment 4. In the illustration there given if the time limit for the return of items received in the Monday morning clearing is 2:00 p.m. on Tuesday and the provisional settlement has not been revoked at that time in a manner permitted by the clearing-house rules, the provisional settlement made on Monday morning becomes final at 2:00 p.m. on Tuesday. Subsection (a)(3) provides specifically that in this situation the item is finally paid at 2:00 p.m. Tuesday. If on the other hand a payor bank receives an item in the mail on Monday and makes some provisional settlement for the item on Monday, it has until midnight on Tuesday to return the item or give notice and revoke any settlement under Section 4–301. In this situation subsection (a)(3) of Section 4–215 provides that if the provisional settlement made on Monday is not revoked before midnight on Tuesday as permitted by Section 4–301, the item is finally paid at midnight on Tuesday. With respect to checks, Regulation CC Section 229.30(c) allows an extension of the midnight

deadline under certain circumstances. If a bank does not expeditiously return a check liability may accrue under Regulation CC Section 229.38. For the relationship of that liability to responsibility under this Article, see Regulation CC Sections 229.30 and 229.38.

8. Subsection (b) relates final settlement to final payment under Section 4–215. For example, if a payor bank makes provisional settlement for an item by sending a cashier's or teller's check and that settlement fails to become final under Section 4–213(c), subsection (b) provides that final payment has not occurred. If the item is not paid, the drawer remains liable, and under Section 4–302(a) the payor bank is accountable unless it has returned the item before its midnight deadline. In this regard, subsection (b) is an exception to subsection (a)(3). Even if the payor bank has not returned an item by its midnight deadline there is still no final payment if provisional settlement had been made and settlement failed to become final. However, if presentment of the item was over the counter for immediate payment, final payment has occurred under Section 4–215(a)(2). Subsection (b) does not apply because the settlement was not provisional. Section 4–301(a). In this case the presenting person, often the payee of the item, has the right to demand cash or the cash equivalent of federal reserve credit. If the presenting person accepts another medium of settlement such as a cashier's or teller's check, the presenting person takes the risk that the payor bank may fail to pay a cashier's check because of insolvency or that the drawee of a teller's check may dishonor it.

9. Subsection (c) states the country-wide usage that when the item is finally paid by the payor bank under subsection (a) this final payment automatically without further action "firms up" other provisional settlements made for it. However, the subsection makes clear that this "firming up" occurs only if the settlement between the presenting and payor banks was made either through a clearing house or by debits and credits in accounts between them. It does not take place if the payor bank remits for the item by sending some form of remittance instrument. Further, the "firming up" continues only to the extent that provisional debits and credits are entered seriatim in accounts between banks which are successive to the presenting bank. The automatic "firming up" is broken at any time that any collecting bank remits for the item by sending a remittance draft, because final payment to the remittee then usually depends upon final payment of the remittance draft.

10. Subsection (d) states the general rule that if a collecting bank receives settlement for an item which is or becomes final, the bank is accountable to its customer for the amount of the item. One means of accounting is to remit to its customer the amount it has received on the item. If previously it gave to its customer a provisional credit for the item in an account its receipt of final settlement for the item "firms up" this provisional credit and makes it final. When this credit given by it so becomes final, in the usual case its agency status terminates and it becomes a debtor to its customer for the amount of the item. See Section 4–201(a). If the accounting is by a remittance instrument or authorization to charge further time will usually be required to complete its accounting (Section 4–213).

11. Subsection (e) states when certain credits given by a bank to its customer become available for withdrawal as of right. Subsection (e)(1) deals with the situation in which a bank has given a credit (usually provisional) for an item to its customer and in turn has received a provisional settlement for the item from an intermediary or payor bank to which it has forwarded the item. In this situation before the provisional credit entered by the collecting bank in the account of its customer becomes available for withdrawal as of right, it is not only necessary that the provisional settlement received by the bank for the item becomes final but also that the collecting bank has a reasonable time to receive return of the item and the item has not been received within that time. How much time is "reasonable" for these purposes will of course depend on the distance the item has to travel and the number of banks through which it must pass (having in mind not only travel time by regular lines of transmission but also the successive midnight deadlines of the several banks) and other pertinent facts. Also, if the provisional settlement received is some form of a remittance instrument or authorization to charge, the "reasonable" time depends on the identity and location of the payor of the remittance instrument, the means for clearing such instrument, and other pertinent facts. With respect to checks Regulation CC Sections 229.10–229.13 or similar applicable state law (Section 229.20) control. This is also time for the situation described in Comment 12.

12. Subsection (e)(2) deals with the situation of a bank that is both a depositary bank and a payor bank. The subsection recognizes that if A and B are both customers of a depositary-payor bank and A deposits B's check on the depositary-payor in A's account on Monday, time must be allowed to permit the check under the deferred posting rules of Section 4–301 to reach the bookkeeper for B's account at some time on Tuesday, and, if there are insufficient funds in B's account, to reverse or charge back the provisional credit in A's account. Consequently this provisional credit in A's account does not become available for withdrawal as of right until the opening of business on Wednesday. If it is determined on Tuesday that there are insufficient funds in B's account to pay the check, the credit to A's account can be reversed on Tuesday. On the other hand if the item is in fact paid on Tuesday, the rule of subsection (e)(2) is desirable to avoid uncertainty and possible disputes between the bank and its customer as to exactly what hour within the day the credit is available.

§ 4.216. Insolvency and Preference

(a) If an item is in or comes into the possession of a payor or collecting bank that suspends payment and the item has not been finally paid, the item must be returned by the receiver, trustee, or agent in charge of the closed bank to the presenting bank or the closed bank's customer.

(b) If a payor bank finally pays an item and suspends payments without making a settlement for the item with its customer or the presenting bank, which settlement is or becomes final, the owner of the item has a preferred claim against the payor bank.

(c) If a payor bank gives or a collecting bank gives or receives a provisional settlement for an item and thereafter suspends payments, the suspension does not prevent or interfere with the settlement's becoming final if the finality occurs automatically upon the lapse of certain time or the happening of certain events.

(d) If a collecting bank receives from subsequent parties settlement for an item, which settlement is or becomes final, and the bank suspends payments without making a settlement for the item with its customer, which settlement is or becomes final, the owner of the item has a preferred claim against the collecting bank.

Acts 1967, 60th Leg., p. 2343, ch. 785, § 1, eff. Sept. 1, 1967. Renumbered from § 4.214 and amended by Acts 1995, 74th Leg., ch. 921, § 4, eff. Jan. 1, 1996.

Uniform Commercial Code Comment

1. The underlying purpose of the provisions of this section is not to confer upon banks, holders of items or anyone else preferential positions in the event of bank failures over general depositors or any other creditors of the failed banks. The purpose is to fix as definitely as possible the cut-off point of time for the completion or cessation of the collection process in the case of items that happen to be in the process at the time a particular bank suspends payments. It must be remembered that in bank collections as a whole and in the handling of items by an individual bank, items go through a whole series of processes. It must also be remembered that at any particular point of time a particular bank (at least one of any size) is functioning as a depositary bank for some items, as an intermediary bank for others, as a presenting bank for still others and as a payor bank for still others, and that when it suspends payments it will have close to its normal load of items working through its various processes. For the convenience of receivers, owners of items, banks, and in fact substantially everyone concerned, it is recognized that at the particular moment of time that a bank suspends payment, a certain portion of the items being handled by it have progressed far enough in the bank collection process that it is preferable to permit them to continue the remaining distance, rather than to send them back and reverse the many entries that have been made or the steps that have been taken with respect to them. Therefore, having this background and these purposes in mind, the section states what items must be turned backward at the moment suspension intervenes and what items have progressed far enough that the collection process with respect to them continues, with the resulting necessary statement of rights of various parties flowing from this prescription of the cut-off time.

2. The rules stated are similar to those stated in the American Bankers Association Bank Collection Code, but with the abandonment of any theory of trust. On the other hand, some law previous to this Act may be relevant. See Note, Uniform Commercial Code: Stopping Payment of an Item Deposited with an Insolvent Depositary Bank, 40 Okla. L.Rev. 689 (1987). Although for practical purposes Federal Deposit Insurance affects materially the result of bank failures on holders of items and banks, no attempt is made to vary the rules of the section by reason of such insurance.

3. It is recognized that in view of *Jennings v. United States Fidelity & Guaranty Co.*, 294 U.S. 216, 55 S.Ct. 394, 79 L.Ed. 869, 99 A.L.R. 1248 (1935), amendment of the National Bank Act would be necessary to have this section apply to national banks. But there is no reason why it should not apply to others. See Section 1–108.

SUBCHAPTER C. COLLECTION OF ITEMS: PAYOR BANKS

§ 4.301. Deferred Posting; Recovery of Payment by Return of Items; Time of Dishonor; Return of Items by Payor Bank

(a) If a payor bank settles for a demand item other than a documentary draft presented otherwise than for immediate payment over the counter before midnight of the banking day of receipt, the payor bank may revoke the settlement and recover the settlement if, before it has made final payment and before its midnight deadline, it:

(1) returns the item;

(2) returns an image of the item, if the party to which the return is made has entered into an agreement to accept an image as a return of the item, and the image is returned in accordance with that agreement; or

(3) sends a record providing notice of dishonor or nonpayment if the item is unavailable for return.

(b) If a demand item is received by a payor bank for credit on its books, it may return the item or send notice of dishonor and may revoke any credit given or recover the amount thereof withdrawn by its customer, if it acts within the time limit and in the manner specified in Subsection (a).

(c) Unless previous notice of dishonor has been sent, an item is dishonored at the time when for purposes of dishonor it is returned or notice sent in accordance with this section.

(d) An item is returned:

(1) as to an item presented through a clearing house, when it is delivered to the presenting or last collecting bank or to the clearing house or is sent or delivered in accordance with clearing-house rules; or

(2) in all other cases, when it is sent or delivered to the bank's customer or transferor or pursuant to instructions.

Acts 1967, 60th Leg., p. 2343, ch. 785, § 1, eff. Sept. 1, 1967. Amended by Acts 1995, 74th Leg., ch. 921, § 4, eff. Jan. 1, 1996; Acts 2005, 79th Leg., ch. 95, § 19, eff. Sept. 1, 2005.

Uniform Commercial Code Comment

1. The term "deferred posting" appears in the caption of Section 4–301. This refers to the practice permitted by statute in most of the states before the UCC under which a payor bank receives items on one day but does not post the items to the customer's account until the next day. Items dishonored were then returned after the posting on the day after receipt. Under Section 4–301 the concept of "deferred posting" merely allows a payor bank that has settled for an item on the day of receipt to return a dishonored item on the next day before its midnight deadline, without regard to when the item was actually posted. With respect to checks Regulation CC Section 229.30(c) extends the midnight deadline under the UCC under certain circumstances. See the Commentary to Regulation CC Section 229.38(d) on the relationship between the UCC and Regulation CC on settlement.

2. The function of this section is to provide the circumstances under which a payor bank that has made timely settlement for an item may return the item and revoke the settlement so that it may recover any settlement made. These circumstances are: (1) the item must be a demand item other than a documentary draft; (2) the item must be presented otherwise than for immediate payment over the counter; and (3) the payor bank must return the item (or give notice if the item is unavailable for return) before its midnight deadline and before it has paid the item. With respect to checks, see Regulation CC Section 229.31(f) on notice in lieu of return and Regulation CC Section 229.33 as to the different requirement of notice of nonpayment. An instance of when an item may be unavailable for return arises under a collecting bank check retention plan under which presentment is made by a presentment notice and the item is retained by the collecting bank. Section 4–215(a)(2) provides that final payment occurs if the payor bank has settled for an item without a right to revoke the settlement under statute, clearing-house rule or agreement. In any case in which Section 4–301(a) is applicable, the payor bank has a right to revoke the settlement by statute; therefore, Section 4–215(a)(2) is inoperable, and the settlement is provisional. Hence, if the settlement is not over the counter and the payor bank settles in a manner that does not constitute final payment, the payor bank can revoke the settlement by returning the item before its midnight deadline.

3. The relationship of Section 4–301(a) to final settlement and final payment under Section 4–215 is illustrated by the following case. Depositary Bank sends by mail an item to Payor Bank with instructions to settle by remitting a teller's check drawn on a bank in the city where Depositary Bank is located. Payor Bank sends the teller's check on the day the item was presented. Having made timely settlement, under the deferred posting provisions of Section 4–301(a), Payor Bank may revoke that settlement by returning the item before its midnight deadline. If it fails to return the item before its midnight deadline, it has finally paid the item if the bank on which the teller's check was drawn honors the check. But if the teller's check is dishonored there has been no final settlement under Section 4–213(c) and no final payment under Section 4–215(b). Since the Payor Bank has neither paid the item nor made timely return, it is accountable for the item under Section 4–302(a).

4. The time limits for action imposed by subsection (a) are adopted by subsection (b) for cases in which the payor bank is also the depositary bank, but in this case the requirement of a settlement on the day of receipt is omitted.

5. Subsection (c) fixes a base point from which to measure the time within which notice of dishonor must be given. See Section 3–503.

6. Subsection (d) leaves banks free to agree upon the manner of returning items but establishes a precise time when an item is "returned." For definition of "sent" as used in paragraphs (1) and (2) see Section 1–201(38). Obviously the subsection assumes that the item has not been "finally paid" under Section 4–215(a). If it has been, this provision has no operation.

7. The fact that an item has been paid under proposed Section 4–215 does not preclude the payor bank from asserting rights of restitution or revocation under Section 3–418. *National Savings and Trust Co. v. Park Corp.*, 722 F.2d 1303 (6th Cir.1983), cert. denied, 466 U.S. 939 (1984), is the correct interpretation of the present law on this issue.

8. Paragraph (a)(2) is designed to facilitate electronic check-processing by authorizing the payor bank to return an image of the item instead of the actual item. It applies only when the payor bank and the party to which the return has been made have agreed that the payor bank can make such a return and when the return complies with the agreement. The purpose of the paragraph is to prevent third parties (such as the depositor of the check) from contending that the payor bank missed its midnight deadline because it failed to return the actual item in a timely manner. If the payor bank missed its midnight deadline, payment would have become final under Section 4–215 and the depositary bank would have lost its right of chargeback under Section 4–214. Of course, the depositary bank might enter into an agreement with its depositor to resolve that problem, but it is not clear that agreements by banks with their customers can resolve all such issues. In any event, paragraph (a)(2) should eliminate the need for such agreements. The provision rests on the premise that it is inappropriate to penalize a payor bank simply because it returns the actual item a few business days after the midnight deadline of the payor bank sent notice before that deadline to a collecting bank that had agreed to accept such notices.

Nothing in paragraph (a)(2) authorizes the payor bank to destroy the check.

§ 4.302. Payor Bank's Responsibility for Late Return of Item

(a) If an item is presented to and received by a payor bank, the bank is accountable for the amount of:

(1) a demand item, other than a documentary draft, whether properly payable or not, if the bank, in any case in which it is not also the depositary bank, retains the item beyond midnight of the banking day of receipt without settling for it or, whether or not it is also the depositary bank, does not pay or return the item or send notice of dishonor until after its midnight deadline; or

(2) any other properly payable item unless, within the time allowed for acceptance or payment of that item, the bank either accepts or pays the item or returns it and accompanying documents.

(b) The liability of a payor bank to pay an item pursuant to Subsection (a) is subject to defenses based on breach of a presentment warranty (Section 4.208) or proof that the person seeking enforcement of the liability presented or transferred the item for the purpose of defrauding the payor bank.

Acts 1967, 60th Leg., p. 2343, ch. 785, § 1, eff. Sept. 1, 1967. Amended by Acts 1995, 74th Leg., ch. 921, § 4, eff. Jan. 1, 1996.

Uniform Commercial Code Comment

1. Subsection (a)(1) continues the former law distinguishing between cases in which the payor bank is not also the depositary bank and those in which the payor bank is also the depositary bank ("on us" items). For "on us" items the payor bank is accountable if it retains the item beyond its midnight deadline without settling for it. If the payor bank is not the depositary bank it is accountable if it retains the item beyond midnight of the banking day of receipt without settling for it. It may avoid accountability either by settling for the item on the day of receipt and returning the item before its midnight deadline under Section 4–301 or by returning the item on the day of receipt. This rule is consistent with the deferred posting practice authorized by Section 4–301 which allows the payor bank to make provisional settlement for an item on the day of receipt and to revoke that settlement by returning the item on the next day. With respect to checks, Regulation CC Section 229.36(d) provides that settlements between banks for forward collection of checks are final when made. See the Commentary on that provision for its effect on the UCC.

2. If the settlement given by the payor bank does not become final, there has been no payment under Section 4–215(b), and the payor bank giving the failed settlement is accountable under subsection (a)(1) of Section 4–302. For instance, the payor bank makes provisional settlement by sending a teller's check that is dishonored. In such a case settlement is not final under Section 4–213(c) and no payment occurs under Section 4–215(b). Payor bank is accountable on the item. The general principle is that unless settlement provides the presenting bank with usable funds, settlement has failed and the payor bank is accountable for the amount of the item. On the other hand, if the payor bank makes a settlement for the item that becomes final under Section 4–215, the item has been paid and thus the payor bank is not accountable for the item under this Section. *Amendments approved by the Permanent Editorial Board for Uniform Commercial Code November 2, 2002.*

3. Subsection (b) is an elaboration of the deleted introductory language of former Section 4–302: "In the absence of a valid defense such as breach of a presentment warranty (subsection (1) of Section 4–207), settlement effected or the like . . . ." A payor bank can defend an action against it based on accountability by showing that the item contained a forged indorsement or a fraudulent alteration. Subsection (b) drops the ambiguous "or the like" language and provides that the payor bank may also raise the defense of fraud. Decisions that hold an accountable bank's liability to be "absolute" are rejected. A payor bank that makes a late return of an item should not be liable to a defrauder operating a check kiting scheme. In *Bank of Leumi Trust Co. v. Bally's Park Place Inc.*, 528 F.Supp. 349 (S.D.N.Y.1981), and *American National Bank v. Foodbasket*, 497 P.2d 546 (Wyo. 1972), banks that were accountable under Section 4–302 for missing their midnight deadline were successful in defending against parties who initiated collection knowing that the check would not be paid. The "settlement effected" language is deleted as unnecessary. If a payor bank is accountable for an item it is liable to pay it. If it has made final payment for an item, it is no longer accountable for the item.

§ 4.303. When Items Subject to Notice, Stop-Payment Order, Legal Process, or Setoff; Order in Which Items May be Charged or Certified

(a) Any knowledge, notice, or stop-payment order received by, legal process served upon, or setoff exercised by a payor bank comes too late to terminate, suspend, or modify the bank's right or duty to pay an item or to charge its customer's account for the item if the knowledge, notice, stop-payment order, or legal process is received or served and a reasonable time for the bank to act thereon expires or the setoff is exercised after the earliest of the following:

(1) the bank accepts or certifies the item;

(2) the bank pays the item in cash;

(3) the bank settles for the item without having a right to revoke the settlement under statute, clearing-house rule, or agreement;

(4) the bank becomes accountable for the amount of the item under Section 4.302 dealing with the payor bank's responsibility for late return of items; or

(5) with respect to checks, a cutoff hour not earlier than one hour after the opening of the next banking day after the banking day on which the bank received the check and not later than the close of that next banking day or, if no cutoff hour is

fixed, the close of the next banking day after the banking day on which the bank received the check.

(b) Subject to Subsection (a), items may be accepted, paid, certified, or charged to the indicated account of a bank's customer in any order and before or after the bank's regular banking hours. A bank is under no obligation to determine the time of day an item is received and without liability may withhold the amount thereof pending a determination of the effect, consequence or priority of any knowledge, notice, stop-payment order, or legal process concerning the same, or interplead such amount and the claimants thereto.

Acts 1967, 60th Leg., p. 2343, ch. 785, § 1, eff. Sept. 1, 1967. Amended by Acts 1985, 69th Leg., ch. 621, § 2, eff. June 14, 1985; Acts 1995, 74th Leg., ch. 921, § 4, eff. Jan. 1, 1996.

Uniform Commercial Code Comment

1. While a payor bank is processing an item presented for payment, it may receive knowledge or a legal notice affecting the item, such as knowledge or a notice that the drawer has filed a petition in bankruptcy or made an assignment for the benefit of creditors; may receive an order of the drawer stopping payment on the item; may have served on it an attachment of the account of the drawer; or the bank itself may exercise a right of setoff against the drawer's account. Each of these events affects the account of the drawer and may eliminate or freeze all or part of whatever balance is available to pay the item. Subsection (a) states the rule for determining the relative priorities between these various legal events and the item.

2. The rule is that if any one of several things has been done to the item or if it has reached any one of several stages in its processing at the time the knowledge, notice, stop-payment order or legal process is received or served and a reasonable time for the bank to act thereon expires or the setoff is exercised, the knowledge, notice, stop-payment order, legal process or setoff comes too late, the item has priority and a charge to the customer's account may be made and is effective. With respect to the effect of the customer's bankruptcy, the bank's rights are governed by Bankruptcy Code Section 542(c) which codifies the result of *Bank of Marin v. England*, 385 U.S. 99 (1966). Section 4–405 applies to the death or incompetence of the customer.

3. Once a payor bank has accepted or certified an item or has paid the item in cash, the event has occurred that determines priorities between the item and the various legal events usually described as the "four legals." Paragraphs (1) and (2) of subsection (a) so provide. If a payor bank settles for an item presented over the counter for immediate payment by a cashier's check or teller's check which the presenting person agrees to accept, paragraph (3) of subsection (a) would control and the event determining priority has occurred. Because presentment was over the counter, Section 4–301(a) does not apply to give the payor bank the statutory right to revoke the settlement. Thus the requirements of paragraph (3) have been met unless a clearing-house rule or agreement of the parties provides otherwise.

4. In the usual case settlement for checks is by entries in bank accounts. Since the process-of-posting test has been abandoned as inappropriate for automated check collection, the determining event for priorities is a given hour on the day after the item is received. (Paragraph (5) of subsection (a).) The hour may be fixed by the bank no earlier than one hour after the opening on the next banking day after the bank received the check and no later than the close of that banking day. If an item is received after the payor bank's regular Section 4–108 cutoff hour, it is treated as received the next banking day. If a bank receives an item after its regular cutoff hour on Monday and an attachment is levied at noon on Tuesday, the attachment is prior to the item if the bank had not before that hour taken the action described in paragraphs (1), (2), and (3) of subsection (a). The Commentary to Regulation CC Section 229.36(d) explains that even though settlement by a paying bank for a check is final for Regulation CC purposes, the paying bank's right to return the check before its midnight deadline under the UCC is not affected.

5. Another event conferring priority for an item and a charge to the customer's account based upon the item is stated by the language "become accountable for the amount of the item under Section 4–302 dealing with the payor bank's responsibility for late return of items." Expiration of the deadline under Section 4–302 with resulting accountability by the payor bank for the amount of the item, establishes priority of the item over notices, stop-payment orders, legal process or setoff.

6. In the case of knowledge, notice, stop-payment orders and legal process the effective time for determining whether they were received too late to affect the payment of an item and a charge to the customer's account by reason of such payment, is receipt plus a reasonable time for the bank to act on any of these communications. Usually a relatively short time is required to communicate to the accounting department advice of one of these events but certainly some time is necessary. Compare Sections 1–201(27) and 4–403. In the case of setoff the effective time is when the setoff is actually made.

7. As between one item and another no priority rule is stated. This is justified because of the impossibility of stating a rule that would be fair in all cases, having in mind the almost infinite number of combinations of large and small checks in relation to the available balance on hand in the drawer's account; the possible methods of receipt; and other variables. Further, the drawer has drawn all the checks, the drawer should have funds available to meet all of them and has no basis for urging one should be paid before another; and the holders have no direct right against the payor or bank in any event, unless of course, the bank has accepted, certified or finally paid a particular item, or has become liable for it under Section 4–302. Under subsection (b) the bank has the right to pay items for which it is itself liable ahead of those for which it is not.

State Bar Committee Comments

Because of the volume of checks required to be processed each day and the modern systems that have been developed to handle these check processing demands, it is difficult for a bank to determine the exact time of day and order of receipt of items, especially in relation to notices, service of process and stop payment orders. In addition, bank check processing services may continue beyond regular banking hours. As a consequence, non-uniform language was added to section 4.303(b) by the Texas legislature in 1985 (Acts 1985, 69th Leg., R.S. ch. 621, § 2, 1985 Tex. Gen. Laws 2308). This special Texas language eliminates the uncertainty of the point in time at which knowledge, notice, or stop-payment order received by, legal process served upon or setoff exercised by a payor bank is too late to be effective. Similar language has been added to revised section 4.303, following the words "in any order," to carry over such existing special Texas language and the improved policies created by such language.

Although the discretion given a bank by subsection (b) is great, the bank must continue to act in good faith in establishing its policies and procedures in this area. For example, a procedure designed to maximize the number of returned checks solely to increase returned check fees charged to customers would not be appropriate.

SUBCHAPTER D. RELATIONSHIP BETWEEN PAYOR BANK AND ITS CUSTOMER

§ 4.401. When Bank May Charge Customer's Account

(a) A bank may charge against the account of a customer an item that is properly payable from that account even though the charge creates an overdraft. An item is properly payable if it is authorized by the customer and is in accordance with any agreement between the customer and the bank.

(b) A customer is not liable for the amount of an overdraft if the customer neither signed the item nor benefited from the proceeds of the item.

(c) A bank may charge against the account of a customer a check that is otherwise properly payable from the account, even though payment was made before the date of the check, unless the customer has given notice to the bank of the postdating describing the check with reasonable certainty. The notice is effective for the period stated in Section 4.403(b) for stop-payment orders and must be received at such time and in such manner as to afford the bank a reasonable opportunity to act on it before the bank takes any action with respect to the check described in Section 4.303. If a bank charges against the account of a customer a check before the date stated in the notice of postdating, the bank is liable for damages for the loss resulting from its act. The loss may include damages for dishonor of subsequent items under Section 4.402.

(d) A bank that in good faith makes payment to a holder may charge the indicated account of its customer according to:

(1) the original terms of the altered item; or

(2) the terms of the completed item, even though the bank knows the item has been completed, unless the bank has notice that the completion was improper.

Acts 1967, 60th Leg., p. 2343, ch. 785, § 1, eff. Sept. 1, 1967. Amended by Acts 1995, 74th Leg., ch. 921, § 4, eff. Jan. 1, 1996.

Uniform Commercial Code Comment

1. An item is properly payable from a customer's account if the customer has authorized the payment and the payment does not violate any agreement that may exist between the bank and its customer. For an example of a payment held to violate an agreement with a customer, see *Torrance National Bank v. Enesco Federal Credit Union*, 285 P.2d 737 (Cal.App.1955). An item drawn for more than the amount of a customer's account may be properly payable. Thus under subsection (a) a bank may charge the customer's account for an item even though payment results in an overdraft. An item containing a forged drawer's signature or forged indorsement is not properly payable. Concern has arisen whether a bank may require a customer to execute a stop-payment order when the customer notifies the bank of the loss of an unindorsed or specially indorsed check. Since such a check cannot be properly payable from the customer's account, it is inappropriate for a bank to require stop-payment order in such a case.

2. Subsection (b) adopts the view of case authority holding that if there is more than one customer who can draw on an account, the nonsigning customer is not liable for an overdraft unless that person benefits from the proceeds of the item.

3. Subsection (c) is added because the automated check collection system cannot accommodate postdated checks. A check is usually paid upon presentment without respect to the date of the check. Under the former law, if a payor bank paid a postdated check before its stated date, it could not charge the customer's account because the check was not "properly payable." Hence, the bank might have been liable for wrongfully dishonoring subsequent checks of the drawer that would have been paid had the postdated check not been prematurely paid. Under subsection (c) a customer wishing to postdate a check must notify the payor bank of its postdating in time to allow the bank to act on the customer's notice before the bank has to commit itself to pay the check. If the bank fails to act on the customer's timely notice, it may be liable for damages for the resulting loss which may include damages for dishonor of subsequent items. This Act does not regulate fees that banks charge their customers for a notice of postdating or other services covered by the Act, but under principles of law such as unconscionability or good faith and fair dealing, courts have reviewed fees and the

bank's exercise of a discretion to set fees. *Perdue v. Crocker National Bank*, 38 Cal.3d 913 (1985) (unconscionability); *Best v. United Bank of Oregon*, 739 P.2d 554, 562-566 (1987) (good faith and fair dealing). In addition, Section 1–203 provides that every contract or duty within this Act imposes an obligation of good faith in its performance or enforcement.

4. Section 3–407(c) states that a payor bank or drawee which pays a fraudulently altered instrument in good faith and without notice of the alteration may enforce rights with respect to the instrument according to its original terms or, in the case of an incomplete instrument altered by unauthorized completion, according to its terms as completed. Section 4–401(d) follows the rule stated in Section 3–407(c) by applying it to an altered item and allows the bank to enforce rights with respect to the altered item by charging the customer's account.

§ 4.402. Bank's Liability to Customer for Wrongful Dishonor

(a) Except as otherwise provided by this chapter, a payor bank wrongfully dishonors an item if it dishonors an item that is properly payable, but a bank may dishonor an item that would create an overdraft unless it has agreed to pay the overdraft.

(b) A payor bank is liable to its customer for damages proximately caused by the wrongful dishonor of an item. Liability is limited to actual damages proved and may include damages for an arrest or prosecution of the customer or other consequential damages. Whether any consequential damages are proximately caused by the wrongful dishonor is a question of fact to be determined in each case.

(c) A payor bank's determination of the customer's account balance on which a decision to dishonor for insufficiency of available funds is based may be made at any time between the time the item is received by the payor bank and the time that the payor bank returns the item or gives notice in lieu of return, and no more than one determination need be made. If, at the election of the payor bank, a subsequent balance determination is made for the purpose of reevaluating the bank's decision to dishonor the item, the account balance at that time is determinative of whether a dishonor for insufficiency of available funds is wrongful.

Acts 1967, 60th Leg., p. 2343, ch. 785, § 1, eff. Sept. 1, 1967. Amended by Acts 1995, 74th Leg., ch. 921, § 4, eff. Jan. 1, 1996.

Uniform Commercial Code Comment

1. Subsection (a) states positively what has been assumed under the original Article: that if a bank fails to honor a properly payable item it may be liable to its customer for wrongful dishonor. Under subsection (b) the payor bank's wrongful dishonor of an item gives rise to a statutory cause of action. Damages may include consequential damages. Confusion has resulted from the attempts of courts to reconcile the first and second sentences of former Section 4–402. The second sentence implied that the bank was liable for some form of damages other than those proximately caused by the dishonor if the dishonor was other than by mistake. But nothing in the section described what these noncompensatory damages might be. Some courts have held that in distinguishing between mistaken dishonors and nonmistaken dishonors, the so-called "trader" rule has been retained that allowed a "merchant or trader" to recover substantial damages for wrongful dishonor without proof of damages actually suffered. Comment 3 to former Section 4–402 indicated that this was not the intent of the drafters. White & Summers, Uniform Commercial Code, Section 18–4 (1988), states: "The negative implication is that when wrongful dishonors occur not 'through mistake' but willfully, the court may impose damages greater than 'actual damages' . . . . Certainly the reference to 'mistake' in the second sentence of 4–402 invites a court to adopt the relevant pre-Code distinction." Subsection (b) by deleting the reference to mistake in the second sentence precludes any inference that Section 4–402 retains the "trader" rule. Whether a bank is liable for noncompensatory damages, such as punitive damages, must be decided by Section 1–103 and Section 1–106 ("by other rule of law").

2. Wrongful dishonor is different from "failure to exercise ordinary care in handling an item," and the measure of damages is that stated in this section, not that stated in Section 4–103(e). By the same token, if a dishonor comes within this section, the measure of damages of this section applies and not another measure of damages. If the wrongful refusal of the beneficiary's bank to make funds available from a funds transfer causes the beneficiary's check to be dishonored, no specific guidance is given as to whether recovery is under this section or Article 4A. In each case this issue must be viewed in its factual context, and it was thought unwise to seek to establish certainty at the cost of fairness.

3. The second and third sentences of the subsection (b) reject decisions holding that as a matter of law the dishonor of a check is not the "proximate cause" of the arrest and prosecution of the customer and leave to determination in each case as a question of fact whether the dishonor is or may be the "proximate cause."

4. Banks commonly determine whether there are sufficient funds in an account to pay an item after the close of banking hours on the day of presentment when they post debit and credit items to the account. The determination is made on the basis of credits available for withdrawal as of right or made available for withdrawal by the bank as an accommodation to its customer. When it is determined that payment of the item would overdraw the account, the item may be returned at any time before the bank's midnight deadline the following day. Before the item is returned new credits that are withdrawable as of right may have been added to the account. Subsection (c) eliminates uncertainty under Article 4 as to whether the failure to make a second determination before the item is returned on the day following presentment is a wrongful dishonor if new credits were

added to the account on that day that would have covered the amount of the check.

5. Section 4–402 has been construed to preclude an action for wrongful dishonor by a plaintiff other than the bank's customer. *Loucks v. Albuquerque National Bank*, 418 P.2d 191 (N.Mex. 1966). Some courts have allowed a plaintiff other than the customer to sue when the customer is a business entity that is one and the same with the individual or individuals operating it. *Murdaugh Volkswagen, Inc. v. First National Bank*, 801 F.2d 719 (4th Cir. 1986) and *Karsh v. American City Bank*, 113 Cal.App.3d 419, 169 Cal.Rptr. 851 (1980). However, where the wrongful dishonor impugns the reputation of an operator of the business, the issue is not merely, as the court in *Koger v. East First National Bank*, 443 So.2d 141 (Fla.App. 1983), put it, one of a literal versus a liberal interpretation of Section 4–402. Rather the issue is whether the statutory cause of action in Section 4–402 displaces, in accordance with Section 1–103, any cause of action that existed at common law in a person who is not the customer whose reputation was damaged. See *Marcum v. Security Trust and Savings Co.*, 221 Ala. 419, 129 So. 74 (1930). While Section 4–402 should not be interpreted to displace the latter cause of action, the section itself gives no cause of action to other than a "customer," however that definition is construed, and thus confers no cause of action on the holder of a dishonored item. *First American National Bank v. Commerce Union Bank*, 692 S.W.2d 642 (Tenn.App. 1985).

§ 4.403. Customer's Right to Stop Payment; Burden of Proof of Loss

(a) A customer or any person authorized to draw on the account if there is more than one person may stop payment of any item drawn on the customer's account or close the account by an order to the bank describing the item or account with reasonable certainty received at a time and in a manner that affords the bank a reasonable opportunity to act on it before any action by the bank with respect to the item described in Section 4.303. If the signature of more than one person is required to draw on an account, any of those persons may stop payment or close the account.

(b) A stop-payment order is effective for six months and is binding on the bank only if it is in a dated, authenticated record that describes the item with certainty. A stop-payment order may be renewed for additional six-month periods by an authenticated record given to the bank within a period during which the stop-payment order is effective.

(c) The burden of establishing the fact and amount of loss resulting from the payment of an item contrary to a stop-payment order or order to close an account is on the customer. The loss from payment of an item contrary to a stop-payment order may include damages for dishonor of subsequent items under Section 4.402.

Acts 1967, 60th Leg., p. 2343, ch. 785, § 1, eff. Sept. 1, 1967. Amended by Acts 1995, 74th Leg., ch. 921, § 4, eff. Jan. 1, 1996; Acts 2005, 79th Leg., ch. 95, § 20, eff. Sept. 1, 2005.

Uniform Commercial Code Comment

1. The position taken by this section is that stopping payment or closing an account is a service which depositors expect and are entitled to receive from banks notwithstanding its difficulty, inconvenience and expense. The inevitable occasional losses through failure to stop or close should be borne by the banks as a cost of the business of banking.

2. Subsection (a) follows the decisions holding that a payee or indorsee has no right to stop payment. This is consistent with the provision governing payment or satisfaction. See Section 3–602. The sole exception to this rule is found is Section 4–405 on payment after notice of death, by which any person claiming an interest in the account can stop payment.

3. Payment is commonly stopped only on checks; but the right to stop payment is not limited to checks, and extends to any item payable by any bank. If the maker of a note payable at a bank is in a position analogous to that of a drawer (Section 4–106) the maker may stop payment of the note. By analogy the rule extends to drawees other than banks.

4. A cashier's check or teller's check purchased by a customer whose account is debited in payment for the check is not a check drawn on the customer's account within the meaning of subsection (a); hence, a customer purchasing a cashier's check or teller's check has no right to stop payment of such a check under subsection (a). If a bank issuing a cashier's check or teller's check refuses to pay the check as an accommodation to its customer or for other reasons, its liability on the check is governed by Section 3–411. There is no right to stop payment after certification of a check or other acceptance of a draft, and this is true no matter who procures the certification. See Sections 3–411 and 4–303. The acceptance is the drawee's own engagement to pay, and it is not required to impair its credit by refusing payment for the convenience of the drawer.

5. Subsection (a) makes clear that if there is more than one person authorized to draw on a customer's account any one of them can stop payment of any check drawn on the account or can order the account closed. Moreover, if there is a customer, such as a corporation, that requires its checks to bear the signatures of more than one person, any of these persons may stop payment on a check. In describing the item, the customer, in the absence of a contrary agreement, must meet the standard of what information allows the bank under the technology then existing to identify the item with reasonable certainty.

6. Under subsection (b), a stop-payment order is effective after the order, whether written or oral, is received by the bank and the bank has a reasonable opportunity to act on it. If the order is written it remains in effect for six months from that time. If the order is oral it lapses after 14 days unless there is written confirmation. If there is written

confirmation within the 14-day period, the six-month period dates from the giving of the oral order. A stop-payment order may be renewed any number of times by written notice given during a six-month period while a stop order is in effect. A new stop-payment order may be given after a six-month period expires, but such a notice takes effect from the date given. When a stop-payment order expires it is as though the order had never been given, and the payor bank may pay the item in good faith under Section 4–404 even though a stop-payment order had once been given.

7. A payment in violation of an effective direction to stop payment is an improper payment, even though it is made by mistake or inadvertence. Any agreement to the contrary is invalid under Section 4–103(a) if in paying the item over the stop-payment order the bank has failed to exercise ordinary care. An agreement to the contrary which is imposed upon a customer as part of a standard form contract would have to be evaluated in the light of the general obligation of good faith. Sections 1–203 and 4–104(c). The drawee is, however, entitled to subrogation to prevent unjust enrichment (Section 4–407); retains common law defenses, e.g., that by conduct in recognizing the payment the customer has ratified the bank's action in paying over a stop-payment order (Section 1–103); and retains common law rights, e.g., to recover money paid under a mistake under Section 3–418. It has sometimes been said that payment cannot be stopped against a holder in due course, but the statement is inaccurate. The payment can be stopped but the drawer remains liable on the instrument to the holder in due course (Sections 3–305, 3–414) and the drawee, if it pays, becomes subrogated to the rights of the holder in due course against the drawer. Section 4–407. The relationship between Sections 4–403 and 4–407 is discussed in the comments to Section 4–407. Any defenses available against a holder in due course remain available to the drawer, but other defenses are cut off to the same extent as if the holder were bringing the action.

State Bar Committee Comments

Section 4.403(b) has been amended to carryover a special Texas change from the original uniform text of UCC section 4–403(2). This change reflects a longstanding Texas policy of requiring a written stop-payment order to obligate the bank to comply with its customer's instruction. Oral stop-payment orders raise uncertainties and significant questions of proof. For a discussion of the history of this Texas policy, *see* Millard H. Ruud, "The Texas Legislative History of the Uniform Commercial Code," 44 *Tex. L. Rev.* 597, 605–06 (1966).

§ 4.404. Bank Not Obligated to Pay Check More Than Six Months Old

A bank is under no obligation to a customer having a checking account to pay a check, other than a certified check, that is presented more than six months after its date, but it may charge its customer's account for a payment made thereafter in good faith.

Acts 1967, 60th Leg., p. 2343, ch. 785, § 1, eff. Sept. 1, 1967. Amended by Acts 1995, 74th Leg., ch. 921, § 4, eff. Jan. 1, 1996.

Uniform Commercial Code Comment

This section incorporates a type of statute that had been adopted in 26 jurisdictions before the Code. The time limit is set at six months because banking and commercial practice regards a check outstanding for longer than that period as stale, and a bank will normally not pay such a check without consulting the depositor. It is therefore not required to do so, but is given the option to pay because it may be in a position to know, as in the case of dividend checks, that the drawer wants payment made.

Certified checks are excluded from the section because they are the primary obligation of the certifying bank (Sections 3–409 and 3–413). The obligation runs directly to the holder of the check. The customer's account was presumable charged when the check was certified.

§ 4.405. Death or Incompetence of Customer

(a) A payor or collecting bank's authority to accept, pay, or collect an item or to account for proceeds of its collection, if otherwise effective, is not rendered ineffective by the incompetence of a customer of either bank existing at the time the item is issued or its collection is undertaken if the bank does not know of an adjudication of incompetence. Neither death nor incompetence of a customer revokes the authority to accept, pay, collect, or account until the bank knows of the fact of death or of an adjudication of incompetence and has reasonable opportunity to act on it.

(b) Even with knowledge, a bank may for 10 days after the date of death pay or certify checks drawn on or before that date unless ordered to stop payment by a person claiming an interest in the account.

Acts 1967, 60th Leg., p. 2343, ch. 785, § 1, eff. Sept. 1, 1967. Amended by Acts 1995, 74th Leg., ch. 921, § 4, eff. Jan. 1, 1996.

Uniform Commercial Code Comment

1. Subsection (a) follows existing decisions holding that a drawee (payor) bank is not liable for the payment of a check before it has notice of the death or incompetence of the drawer. The justice and necessity of the rule are obvious. A check is an order to pay which the bank must obey under penalty of possible liability for dishonor. Further, with the tremendous volume of items handled any rule that required banks to verify the continued life and competency of drawers would be completely unworkable.

One or both of these same reasons apply to other phases of the bank collection and payment process and the rule is made wide enough to apply to these other phases. It applies to all kinds of "items"; to "customers" who own items as well as "customers" who draw or make them; to the function of collecting items as well as the function of accepting or paying them; to the carrying out of instructions to account for proceeds even though these may involve transfers to third parties; to depositary and intermediary banks as well as payor banks; and to incompetency existing at the time of the issuance of an item or the commencement of the collection or payment process as well as to incompetency occurring thereafter. Further, the requirement of actual knowledge makes inapplicable the rule of some cases that an adjudication of incompetency is constructive notice to all the world because obviously it is as impossible for banks to keep posted on such adjudications (in the absence of actual knowledge) as it is to keep posted as to death of immediate or remote customers.

2. Subsection (b) provides a limited period after death during which a bank may continue to pay checks (as distinguished from other items) even though it has notice. The purpose of the provision, as of the existing statutes, is to permit holders of checks drawn and issued shortly before death to cash them without the necessity of filing a claim in probate. The justification is that these checks normally are given in immediate payment of an obligation, that there is almost never any reason why they should not be paid, and that filing in probate is a useless formality, burdensome to the holder, the executor, the court and the bank.

This section does not prevent an executor or administrator from recovering the payment from the holder of the check. It is not intended to affect the validity of any gift causa mortis or other transfer in contemplation of death, but merely to relieve the bank of liability for the payment.

3. Any surviving relative, creditor or other person who claims an interest in the account may give a direction to the bank not to pay checks, or not to pay a particular check. Such notice has the same effect as a direction to stop payment. The bank has no responsibility to determine the validity of the claim or even whether it is "colorable." But obviously anyone who has an interest in the estate, including the person named as executor in a will, even if the will has not yet been admitted to probate, is entitled to claim an interest in the account.

§ 4.406. Customer's Duty to Discover and Report Unauthorized Signature or Alteration

(a) A bank that sends or makes available to a customer a statement of account showing payment of items for the account shall either return or make available to the customer the items paid or provide information in the statement of account sufficient to allow the customer reasonably to identify the items paid. The statement of account provides sufficient information if the item is described by item number, amount, and date of payment. If the bank does not return the items, it shall provide in the statement of account the telephone number that the customer may call to request an item or a legible copy of the items pursuant to Subsection (b).

(b) If the items are not returned to the customer, the person retaining the items shall either retain the items or, if the items are destroyed, maintain the capacity to furnish legible copies of the items until the expiration of seven years after receipt of the items. A customer may request an item from the bank that paid the item, and that bank must provide in a reasonable time either the item or, if the item has been destroyed or is not otherwise obtainable, a legible copy of the item. A bank shall provide, on request and without charge to the customer, at least two items or a legible copy of the items with respect to each statement of account sent to the customer.

(c) If a bank sends or makes available a statement of account or items pursuant to Subsection (a), the customer must exercise reasonable promptness in examining the statement or the items to determine whether any payment was not authorized because of an alteration of an item or because a purported signature by or on behalf of the customer was not authorized. If, based on the statement or items provided, the customer should reasonably have discovered the unauthorized payment, the customer must promptly notify the bank of the relevant facts.

(d) If the bank proves that the customer failed, with respect to an item, to comply with the duties imposed on the customer by Subsection (c), the customer is precluded from asserting against the bank:

(1) the customer's unauthorized signature or any alteration on the item, if the bank also proves that it suffered a loss by reason of the failure; and

(2) the customer's unauthorized signature or alteration by the same wrongdoer on any other item paid in good faith by the bank if the payment was made before the bank received notice from the customer of the unauthorized signature or alteration and after the customer had been afforded a reasonable period of time, not exceeding 30 days, in which to examine the item or statement of account and notify the bank.

(e) If Subsection (d) applies and the customer proves that the bank failed to exercise ordinary care in paying the item and that the failure contributed to loss, the loss is allocated between the customer precluded and the bank asserting the preclusion according to the extent to which the failure of the customer to comply with Subsection (c) and the failure of the bank to exercise ordinary care contributed to the loss. If the customer proves that the bank did not pay the item in good faith, the preclusion under Subsection (d) does not apply.

(f) Without regard to care or lack of care of either the customer or the bank, a customer who does not within one year after the statement or items are made available to the customer (Subsection (a)) discover and report the customer's unauthorized signature on or any alteration on the item is precluded from asserting against the bank the unauthorized signature or alteration. If there is a preclusion under this subsection, the payor bank may not recover for breach of warranty under Section 4.208 with respect to the unauthorized signature or alteration to which the preclusion applies.

Acts 1967, 60th Leg., p. 2343, ch. 785, § 1, eff. Sept. 1, 1967. Amended by Acts 1995, 74th Leg., ch. 921, § 4, eff. Jan. 1, 1996.

Uniform Commercial Code Comment

1. Under subsection (a), if a bank that has paid a check or other item for the account of a customer makes available to the customer a statement of account showing payment of the item, the bank must either return the item to the customer or provide a description of the item sufficient to allow the customer to identify it. Under subsection (c), the customer has a duty to exercise reasonable promptness in examining the statement or the returned item to discover any unauthorized signature of the customer or any alteration and to promptly notify the bank if the customer should reasonably have discovered the unauthorized signature or alteration.

The duty stated in subsection (c) becomes operative only if the "bank sends or makes available a statement of account or items pursuant to subsection (a)." A bank is not under a duty to send a statement of account or the paid items to the customer; but, if it does not do so, the customer does not have any duties under subsection (c).

Under subsection (a), a statement of account must provide information "sufficient to allow the customer reasonably to identify the items paid." If the bank supplies its customer with an image of the paid item, it complies with this standard. But a safe harbor rule is provided. The bank complies with the standard of providing "sufficient information" if "the item is described by item number, amount, and date of payment." This means that the customer's duties under subsection (c) are triggered if the bank sends a statement of account complying with the safe harbor rule without returning the paid items. A bank does not have to return the paid items unless it has agreed with the customer to do so. Whether there is such an agreement depends upon the particular circumstances. See Section 1-201(3). If the bank elects to provide the minimum information that is "sufficient" under subsection (a) and, as a consequence, the customer could not "reasonably have discovered the unauthorized payment," there is no preclusion under subsection (d). If the customer made a record of the issued checks on the check stub or carbonized copies furnished by the bank in the checkbook, the customer should usually be able to verify the paid items shown on the statement of account and discover any unauthorized or altered checks. But there could be exceptional circumstances. For example, if a check is altered by changing the name of the payee, the customer could not normally detect the fraud unless the customer is given the paid check or the statement of account discloses the name of the payee of the altered check. If the customer could not "reasonably have discovered the unauthorized payment" under subsection (c) there would not be a preclusion under subsection (d).

The "safe harbor" provided by subsection (a) serves to permit a bank, based on the state of existing technology, to trigger the customer's duties under subsection (c) by providing a "statement of account showing payment of items" without having to return the paid items, in any case in which the bank has not agreed with the customer to return the paid items. The "safe harbor" does not, however, preclude a customer under subsection (d) from asserting its unauthorized signature or an alteration against a bank in those circumstances in which under subsection (c) the customer should not "reasonably have discovered the unauthorized payment." Whether the customer has failed to comply with its duties under subsection (c) is determined on a case-by-case basis.

The provision in subsection (a) that a statement of account contains "sufficient information if the item is described by item number, amount, and date of payment" is based upon the existing state of technology. This information was chosen because it can be obtained by the bank's computer from the check's MICR line without examination of the items involved. The other two items of information that the customer would normally want to know—the name of the payee and the date of the item—cannot currently be obtained from the MICR line. The safe harbor rule is important in determining the feasibility of payor or collecting bank check retention plans. A customer who keeps a record of checks written, e.g., on the check stubs or carbonized copies of the checks supplied by the bank in the checkbook, will usually have sufficient information to identify the items on the basis of item number, amount, and date of payment. But customers who do not utilize these record-keeping methods may not. The policy decision is that accommodating customers who do not keep adequate records is not as desirable as accommodating customers who keep more careful records. This policy results in less cost to the check collection system and thus to all customers of the system. It is expected that technological advances such as image processing may make it possible for banks to give customers more information in the future in a manner that is fully compatible with automation or truncation systems. At that time the Permanent Editorial Board may wish to make recommendations for an amendment revising the safe harbor requirements in the light of those advances.

2. Subsection (d) states the consequences of a failure by the customer to perform its duty under subsection (c) to report an alteration or the customer's unauthorized signature. Subsection (d)(1) applies to the unauthorized payment of the item to which the duty to report under subsection (c) applies. If the bank proves that the customer "should reasonably have discovered the unauthorized payment" (See Comment 1) and did not notify the bank, the customer is precluded from asserting against the bank the alteration or the customer's unauthorized signature if the bank proves that it suffered a loss as a result of the failure of the customer to perform its subsection (c) duty. Subsection (d)(2) applies to cases in which the customer fails to report an unauthorized signature or alteration with respect to an item in breach of the subsection (c) duty (See Comment 1) and the bank subsequently pays other items of the customer

with respect to which there is an alteration or unauthorized signature of the customer and the same wrongdoer is involved. If the payment of the subsequent items occurred after the customer has had a reasonable time (not exceeding 30 days) to report with respect to the first item and before the bank received notice of the unauthorized signature or alteration of the first item, the customer is precluded from asserting the alteration or unauthorized signature with respect to the subsequent items.

If the customer is precluded in a single or multiple item unauthorized payment situation under subsection (d), but the customer proves that the bank failed to exercise ordinary care in paying the item or items and that the failure substantially contributed to the loss, subsection (e) provides a comparative negligence test for allocating loss between the customer and the bank. Subsection (e) also states that, if the customer proves that the bank did not pay the item in good faith, the preclusion under subsection (d) does not apply.

Subsection (d)(2) changes former subsection (2)(b) by adopting a 30–day period in place of a 14–day period. Although the 14–day period may have been sufficient when the original version of Article 4 was drafted in the 1950s, given the much greater volume of checks at the time of the revision, a longer period was viewed as more appropriate. The rule of subsection (d)(2) follows pre-Code case law that payment of an additional item or items bearing an unauthorized signature or alteration by the same wrongdoer is a loss suffered by the bank traceable to the customer's failure to exercise reasonable care (See Comment 1) in examining the statement and notifying the bank of objections to it. One of the most serious consequences of failure of the customer to comply with the requirements of subsection (c) is the opportunity presented to the wrongdoer to repeat the misdeeds. Conversely, one of the best ways to keep down losses in this type of situation is for the customer to promptly examine the statement and notify the bank of an unauthorized signature or alteration so that the bank will be alerted to stop paying further items. Hence, the rule of subsection (d)(2) is prescribed, and to avoid dispute a specific time limit, 30 days, is designated for cases to which the subsection applies. These considerations are not present if there are no losses resulting from the payment of additional items. In these circumstances, a reasonable period for the customer to comply with its duties under subsection (c) would depend on the circumstances (Section 1–204(2)) and the subsection (d)(2) time limit should not be imported by analogy into subsection (c).

3. Subsection (b) applies if the items are not returned to the customer. Check retention plans may include a simple payor bank check retention plan or the kind of check retention plan that would be authorized by a truncation agreement in which a collecting bank or the payee may retain the items. Even after agreeing to a check retention plan, a customer may need to see one or more checks for litigation or other purposes. The customer's request for the check may always be made to the payor bank. Under subsection (b) retaining banks may destroy items but must maintain the capacity to furnish legible copies for seven years. A legible copy may include an image of an item. This Act does not define the length of the reasonable period of time for a bank to provide the check or copy of the check. What is reasonable depends on the capacity of the bank and the needs of the customer. This Act does not specify sanctions for failure to retain or furnish the items or legible copies; this is left to other laws regulating banks. See Comment 3 to Section 4–101. Moreover, this Act does not regulate fees that banks charge their customers for furnishing items or copies or other services covered by the Act, but under principles of law such as unconscionability or good faith and fair dealing, courts have reviewed fees and the bank's exercise of a discretion to set fees. *Perdue v. Crocker National Bank*, 38 Cal.3d 913 (1985) (unconscionability); *Best v. United Bank of Oregon*, 739 P.2d 554, 562–566 (1987) (good faith and fair dealing). In addition, Section 1–203 provides that every contract or duty within this Act imposes an obligation of good faith in its performance or enforcement.

4. Subsection (e) replaces former subsection (3) and poses a modified comparative negligence test for determining liability. See the discussion on this point in the Comments to Sections 3–404, 3–405, and 3–406. The term "good faith" is defined in Section 1–201(b)(20) as including "observance of reasonable commercial standards of fair dealing." The connotation of this standard is fairness and not absence of negligence.

The term "ordinary care" used in subsection (e) is defined in Section 3–103(a)(7), made applicable to Article 4 by Section 4–104(c), to provide that sight examination by a payor bank is not required if its procedure is reasonable and is commonly followed by other comparable banks in the area. The case law is divided on this issue. The definition of "ordinary care" in Section 3–103 rejects those authorities that hold, in effect, that failure to use sight examination is negligence as a matter of law. The effect of the definition of "ordinary care" on Section 4–406 is only to provide that in the small percentage of cases in which a customer's failure to examine its statement or returned items has led to loss under subsection (d) a bank should not have to share that loss solely because it has adopted an automated collection or payment procedure in order to deal with the great volume of items at a lower cost to all customers.

5. Several changes are made in former Section 4–406(5). First, former subsection (5) is deleted and its substance is made applicable only to the one-year notice preclusion in former subsection (4) (subsection (f)). Thus if a drawer has not notified the payor bank of an unauthorized check or material alteration within the one-year period, the payor bank may not choose to recredit the drawer's account and pass the loss to the collecting banks on the theory of breach of warranty. Second, the reference in former subsection (4) to unauthorized indorsements is deleted. Section 4–406 imposes no duties on the drawer to look for unauthorized indorsements. Section 4–111 sets out a statute of limitations allowing a customer a three-year period to seek a credit to an account improperly charged by payment of an item bearing an unauthorized indorsement. Third, subsection (c) is added to Section 4–208 to assure that if a depositary bank is sued for breach of a presentment warranty, it can defend by showing that the drawer is precluded by Section 3–406 or Section 4–406(c) and (d).

State Bar Committee Comments

The first sentence of subsection (e) has been revised in a manner similar to subsections 3.404(d), 3.405(b) and 3.406(b) by deleting the word "substantially" before the words "contributed to loss". As a consequence, the degree of the bank's failure to exercise ordinary care must not be decided in order to determine whether the comparative negligence standards should be applied to allocate the loss between the bank and the customer. See the Texas Comment for section 3.404 for a discussion of the reasons why the deletion of the word "substantially" was effected.

The last sentence of subsection (a) is a non-uniform change added in an effort to provide some protection to bank customers. The sentence requires banks to provide a telephone number on each statement of account that the customer may call to request an item or a legible copy thereof pursuant to the provisions of subsection (b).

The last sentence of subsection (b) is a non-uniform change that was added to provide some protection to bank customers that is not otherwise available under other provisions of revised Chapter 4 or other Texas law. The sentence requires a bank to provide at least two items or a legible copy thereof with respect to each statement of account sent to a customer, if the customer makes a request for the items. The bank must provide this service at no charge. This change is in response to the provisions of Chapter 4 permitting the depository bank to retain the originals of items and to make presentation via electronic information. This "truncation" process is an essential part of revised Chapter 4 and is intended to provide the means for increasing check processing efficiency and speed.

These changes to section 4.406 are based on similar changes made by the California legislature in adopting its version of UCC Articles 3 and 4.

§ 4.407. Payor Bank's Right to Subrogation on Improper Payment

If a payor bank has paid an item over the order of the drawer or maker to stop payment, or after an account has been closed, or otherwise under circumstances giving a basis for objection by the drawer or maker, to prevent unjust enrichment and only to the extent necessary to prevent loss to the bank by reason of its payment of the item, the payor bank is subrogated to the rights:

(1) of any holder in due course on the item against the drawer or maker;

(2) of the payee or any other holder of the item against the drawer or maker either on the item or under the transaction out of which the item arose; and

(3) of the drawer or maker against the payee or any other holder of the item with respect to the transaction out of which the item arose.

Acts 1967, 60th Leg., p. 2343, ch. 785, § 1, eff. Sept. 1, 1967. Amended by Acts 1995, 74th Leg., ch. 921, § 4, eff. Jan. 1, 1996.

Uniform Commercial Code Comment

1. Section 4–403 states that a stop-payment order or an order to close an account is binding on a bank. If a bank pays an item over such an order it is prima facie liable, but under subsection (c) of Section 4–403 the burden of establishing the fact and amount of loss from such payment is on the customer. A defense frequently interposed by a bank in an action against it for wrongful payment over a stop-payment order is that the drawer or maker suffered no loss because it would have been liable to a holder in due course in any event. On this argument some cases have held that payment cannot be stopped against a holder in due course. Payment can be stopped, but if it is, the drawer or maker is liable and the sound rule is that the bank is subrogated to the rights of the holder in due course. The preamble and paragraph (1) of this section state this rule.

2. Paragraph (2) also subrogates the bank to the rights of the payee or other holder against the drawer or maker either on the item or under the transaction out of which it arose. It may well be that the payee is not a holder in due course but still has good rights against the drawer. These may be on the check but also may not be as, for example, where the drawer buys goods from the payee and the goods are partially defective so that the payee is not entitled to the full price, but the goods are still worth a portion of the contract price. If the drawer retains the goods it is obligated to pay a part of the agreed price. If the bank has paid the check it should be subrogated to this claim of the payee against the drawer.

3. Paragraph (3) subrogates the bank to the rights of the drawer or maker against the payee or other holder with respect to the transaction out of which the item arose. If, for example, the payee was a fraudulent salesman inducing the drawer to issue a check for defective securities, and the bank pays the check over a stop-payment order but reimburses the drawer for such payment, the bank should have a basis for getting the money back from the fraudulent salesman.

4. The limitations of the preamble prevent the bank itself from getting any double recovery or benefits out of its subrogation rights conferred by the section.

5. The spelling out of the affirmative rights of the bank in this section does not destroy other existing rights (Section 1–103). Among others these may include the defense of a payor bank that by conduct in recognizing the payment a customer has ratified the bank's action in paying in disregard of a stop-payment order or right to recover money paid under a mistake.

SUBCHAPTER E. COLLECTION OF DOCUMENTARY DRAFTS

§ 4.501. Handling of Documentary Drafts; Duty to Send for Presentment and to Notify Customer of Dishonor

A bank that takes a documentary draft for collection shall present or send the draft and accompanying documents for presentment and, upon learning that the draft has not been paid or accepted in due course, shall seasonably notify its customer of the fact even though it may have discounted or bought the draft or extended credit available for withdrawal as of right.

Acts 1967, 60th Leg., p. 2343, ch. 785, § 1, eff. Sept. 1, 1967. Amended by Acts 1995, 74th Leg., ch. 921, § 4, eff. Jan. 1, 1996.

Uniform Commercial Code Comment

This section states the duty of a bank handling a documentary draft for a customer. "Documentary draft" is defined in Section 4–104. The duty stated exists even if the bank has bought the draft. This is because to the customer the draft normally represents an underlying commercial transaction, and if that is not going through as planned the customer should know it promptly. An electronic document of title may be presented through allowing access to the document or delivery of the document. Article 1, Section 1–201 (definition of "delivery").

§ 4.502. Presentment of "On Arrival" Drafts

If a draft or the relevant instructions require presentment "on arrival", "when goods arrive", or the like, the collecting bank need not present until in its judgment a reasonable time for arrival of the goods has expired. Refusal to pay or accept because the goods have not arrived is not dishonor; the bank must notify its transferor of the refusal but need not present the draft again until it is instructed to do so or learns of the arrival of the goods.

Acts 1967, 60th Leg., p. 2343, ch. 785, § 1, eff. Sept. 1, 1967. Amended by Acts 1995, 74th Leg., ch. 921, § 4, eff. Jan. 1, 1996.

Uniform Commercial Code Comment

The section is designed to establish a definite rule for "on arrival" drafts. The term includes not only drafts drawn payable "on arrival" but also drafts forwarded with instructions to present "on arrival." The term refers to the arrival of the relevant goods. Unless a bank has actual knowledge of the arrival of the goods, as for example, when it is the "notify" party on the bill of lading, the section only requires the exercise of such judgment in estimating time as a bank may be expected to have. Commonly the buyer-drawee will want the goods and will therefore call for the documents and take up the draft when they do arrive.

§ 4.503. Responsibility of Presenting Bank for Documents and Goods; Report of Reasons for Dishonor; Referee in Case of Need

Unless otherwise instructed and except as provided in Chapter 5, a bank presenting a documentary draft:

(1) must deliver the documents to the drawee on acceptance of the draft if it is payable more than three days after presentment; otherwise, only on payment; and

(2) upon dishonor, either in the case of presentment for acceptance or presentment for payment, may seek and follow instructions from any referee in case of need designated in the draft or, if the presenting bank does not choose to utilize the referee's services, it must use diligence and good faith to ascertain the reason for dishonor, must notify its transferor of the dishonor and of the results of its effort to ascertain the reasons therefor, and must request instructions.

However, the presenting bank is under no obligation with respect to goods represented by the documents except to follow any reasonable instructions seasonably received; it has a right to reimbursement for any expense incurred in following instructions and to prepayment of or indemnity for those expenses.

Acts 1967, 60th Leg., p. 2343, ch. 785, § 1, eff. Sept. 1, 1967. Amended by Acts 1995, 74th Leg., ch. 921, § 4, eff. Jan. 1, 1996.

Uniform Commercial Code Comment

1. This section states the rules governing, in the absence of instructions, the duty of the presenting bank in case either of honor or of dishonor of a documentary draft. The section should be read in connection with Section 2–514 on when documents are deliverable on acceptance, when on payment. In the case of a dishonor of the draft, the bank, subject to Section 4–504, must return possession or control of the documents to its principal.

2. If the draft is drawn under a letter of credit, Article 5 controls. See Sections 5–109 through 5–114.

§ 4.504. Privilege of Presenting Bank to Deal With Goods; Security Interest for Expenses

(a) A presenting bank that, following the dishonor of a documentary draft, has seasonably requested instructions but does not receive them within a reasonable time may store, sell, or otherwise deal with the goods in any reasonable manner.

(b) For its reasonable expenses incurred by action under Subsection (a) the presenting bank has a lien upon the goods or their proceeds, which may be foreclosed in the same manner as an unpaid seller's lien.

Acts 1967, 60th Leg., p. 2343, ch. 785, § 1, eff. Sept. 1, 1967. Amended by Acts 1995, 74th Leg., ch. 921, § 4, eff. Jan. 1, 1996.

Uniform Commercial Code Comment

The section gives the presenting bank, after dishonor, a privilege to deal with the goods in any commercially reasonable manner pending instructions from its transferor and, if still unable to communicate with its principal after a reasonable time, a right to realize its expenditures as if foreclosing on an unpaid seller's lien (Section 2–706). The provision includes situations in which storage of goods or other action becomes commercially necessary pending receipt of any requested instructions, even if the requested instructions are later received.

The "reasonable manner" referred to means one reasonable in the light of business factors and the judgment of a business man.

CHAPTER 4A. FUNDS TRANSFERS

SUBCHAPTER A. SUBJECT MATTER AND DEFINITIONS

SUBCHAPTER A. SUBJECT MATTER AND DEFINITIONS

§ 4A.101. Short Title

This chapter may be cited as Uniform Commercial Code—Funds Transfers.

Added by Acts 1993, 73rd Leg., ch. 570, § 7, eff. Sept. 1, 1993.

§ 4A.102. Subject Matter

Except as otherwise provided in Section 4A.108, this chapter applies to funds transfers defined in Section 4A.104.

Added by Acts 1993, 73rd Leg., ch. 570, § 7, eff. Sept. 1, 1993.

Uniform Commercial Code Comment

Article 4A governs a specialized method of payment referred to in the Article as a funds transfer but also commonly referred to in the commercial community as a wholesale wire transfer. A funds transfer is made by means of one or more payment orders. The scope of Article 4A is determined by the definitions of "payment order" and "funds transfer" found in Section 4A–103 and Section 4A–104.

The funds transfer governed by Article 4A is in large part a product of recent and developing technological changes. Before this Article was drafted there was no comprehensive body of law—statutory or judicial—that defined the juridical nature of a funds transfer or the rights and obligations flowing from payment orders. Judicial authority with respect to funds transfers is sparse, undeveloped and not uniform. Judges have had to resolve disputes by referring to general principles of common law or equity, or they have sought guidance in statutes such as Article 4 which are applicable to other payment methods. But attempts to define rights and obligations in funds transfers by general principles or by analogy to rights and obligations in negotiable instrument law or the law of check collection have not been satisfactory.

In the drafting of Article 4A, a deliberate decision was made to write on a clean slate and to treat a funds transfer as a unique method of payment to be governed by unique rules that address the particular issues raised by this method of payment. A deliberate decision was also made to use precise and detailed rules to assign responsibility, define behavioral norms, allocate risks and establish limits on liability, rather than to rely on broadly stated, flexible principles. In the drafting of these rules, a critical consideration was that the various parties to funds transfers need to be able to predict risk with certainty, to insure against risk, to adjust operational and security procedures, and to price funds transfer services appropriately. This consideration is particularly important given the very large amounts of money that are involved in funds transfers.

Funds transfers involve competing interests—those of the banks that provide funds transfer services and the commercial and financial organizations that use the services, as well as the public interest. These competing interests were represented in the drafting process and they were thoroughly considered. The rules that emerged represent a careful and delicate balancing of those interests and are intended to be the exclusive means of determining the rights, duties and liabilities of the affected parties in any situation covered by particular provisions of the Article. Consequently, resort to principles of law or equity outside of Article 4A is not appropriate to create rights, duties and liabilities inconsistent with those stated in this Article.

§ 4A.103. Payment Order—Definitions

(a) In this chapter:

(1) "Payment order" means an instruction of a sender to a receiving bank, transmitted orally, electronically, or in writing, to pay, or to cause another bank to pay, a fixed or determinable amount of money to a beneficiary if:

(A) the instruction does not state a condition of payment to the beneficiary other than the time of payment;

(B) the receiving bank is to be reimbursed by debiting an account of, or otherwise receiving payment from, the sender; and

(C) the instruction is transmitted by the sender directly to the receiving bank or to an agent, funds transfer system, or communication system for transmittal to the receiving bank.

(2) "Beneficiary" means the person to be paid by the beneficiary's bank.

(3) "Beneficiary's bank" means the bank identified in a payment order in which an account of the beneficiary is to be credited pursuant to the order or which otherwise is to make payment to the beneficiary if the order does not provide for payment to an account.

(4) "Receiving bank" means the bank to which the sender's instruction is addressed.

(5) "Sender" means the person giving the instruction to the receiving bank.

(b) If an instruction complying with Subsection (a)(1) is to make more than one payment to a beneficiary, the instruction is a separate payment order with respect to each payment.

(c) A payment order is issued when it is sent to the receiving bank.

Added by Acts 1993, 73rd Leg., ch. 570, § 7, eff. Sept. 1, 1993.

Uniform Commercial Code Comment

This section is discussed in the Comment following Section 4A–104.

§ 4A.104. Funds Transfer—Definitions

In this chapter:

(1) "Funds transfer" means the series of transactions, beginning with the originator's payment order, made for the purpose of making payment to the beneficiary of the order. The term includes any payment order issued by the originator's bank or an intermediary bank intended to carry out the originator's payment order. A funds transfer is completed by acceptance by the beneficiary's bank of a payment order for the benefit of the beneficiary of the originator's payment order.

(2) "Intermediary bank" means a receiving bank other than the originator's bank or the beneficiary's bank.

(3) "Originator" means the sender of the first payment order in a funds transfer.

(4) "Originator's bank" means:

(A) the receiving bank to which the payment order of the originator is issued if the originator is not a bank; or

(B) the originator if the originator is a bank.

Added by Acts 1993, 73rd Leg., ch. 570, § 7, eff. Sept. 1, 1993.

Uniform Commercial Code Comment

1. Article 4A governs a method of payment in which the person making payment (the "originator") directly transmits an instruction to a bank either to make payment to the person receiving payment (the "beneficiary") or to instruct some other bank to make payment to the beneficiary. The payment from the originator to the beneficiary occurs when the bank that is to pay the beneficiary becomes obligated to pay the beneficiary. There are two basic definitions: "Payment order" stated in Section 4A–103 and "Funds transfer" stated in Section 4A–104. These definitions, other related definitions, and the scope of Article 4A can best be understood in the context of specific fact situations. Consider the following cases:

Case #1. X, which has an account in Bank A, instructs that bank to pay $1,000,000 to Y's account in Bank A. Bank A carries out X's instruction by making a credit of $1,000,000 to Y's account and notifying Y that the credit is available for immediate withdrawal. The instruction by X to Bank A is a "payment order" which was issued when it was sent to Bank A. Section 4A–103(a)(1) and (c). X is the "sender" of the payment order and Bank A is the "receiving bank." Section 4A–103(a)(5) and (a)(4). Y is the "beneficiary" of the payment order and Bank A is the "beneficiary's bank." Section 4A–103(a)(2) and (a)(3). When Bank A notified Y of receipt of the payment order, Bank A "accepted" the payment order. Section 4A–209(b)(1). When Bank A accepted the order it incurred an obligation to Y to pay the amount of the order. Section 4A–404(a). When Bank A accepted X's order, X incurred an obligation to pay Bank A the amount of the order. Section 4A–402(b). Payment from X to Bank A would normally be made by a debit to X's account in Bank A. Section 4A–403(a)(3). At the time Bank A incurred the obligation to pay Y, payment of $1,000,000 by X to Y was also made. Section 4A–406(a). Bank A paid Y when it gave notice to Y of a withdrawable credit of $1,000,000 to Y's account. Section 4A–405(a). The overall transaction, which comprises the acts of X and Bank A, in which the payment by X to Y is accomplished is referred to as the "funds transfer." Section 4A–104(a). In this case only one payment order was involved in the funds transfer. A one-payment-order funds transfer is usually referred to as a "book transfer" because the payment is accomplished by the receiving bank's debiting the account of the sender and crediting the account of the beneficiary in the same bank. X, in addition to being the sender of the payment order to Bank A, is the "originator" of the funds transfer. Section 4A–104(c). Bank A is the "originator's bank" in the funds transfer as well as the beneficiary's bank. Section 4A–104(d).

Case #2. Assume the same facts as in Case #1 except that X instructs Bank A to pay $1,000,000 to Y's account in Bank B. With respect to this payment order, X is the sender, Y is the beneficiary, and Bank A is the receiving bank. Bank A carries out X's order by instructing Bank B to pay $1,000,000 to Y's account. This instruction is a payment order in which Bank A is the sender, Bank B is the receiving bank, and Y is the beneficiary. When Bank A issued its payment order to Bank B, Bank A "executed" X's order. Section 4A–301(a). In the funds transfer, X is the originator, Bank A is the originator's bank, and Bank B is the beneficiary's bank. When Bank A executed X's order, X incurred an obligation to pay Bank A the amount of the order. Section 4A–402(c). When Bank B accepts the payment order issued to it by Bank A, Bank B incurs an obligation to Y to pay the amount of the order (Section 4A–404(a)) and Bank A incurs an obligation to pay Bank B. Section 4A–402(b). Acceptance by Bank B also results in payment of $1,000,000 by X to Y. Section 4A–406(a). In this case two payment orders are involved in the funds transfer.

Case #3. Assume the same facts as in Case #2 except that Bank A does not execute X's payment order by issuing a payment order to Bank B. One bank will not normally act to carry out a funds transfer for another bank unless there is a preexisting arrangement between the banks for transmittal of payment orders and settlement of accounts. For example, if Bank B is a foreign bank with which Bank A has no relationship, Bank A can utilize a bank that is a correspondent of both Bank A and Bank B. Assume Bank A issues a payment order to Bank C to pay $1,000,000 to Y's account in Bank B. With respect to this order, Bank A is the sender, Bank C is the receiving bank, and Y is the beneficiary. Bank C will execute the payment order of Bank A by issuing a payment order to Bank B to pay $1,000,000 to Y's account in Bank B. With respect to Bank C's payment order, Bank C is the sender, Bank B is the receiving bank, and Y is the beneficiary. Payment of $1,000,000 by X to Y occurs when Bank B accepts the payment order issued to it by Bank C. In this case the funds transfer involves three payment orders. In the funds transfer, X is the originator, Bank A is the originator's bank, Bank B is the beneficiary's bank, and Bank C is an "intermediary bank." Section 4A–104(b). In some cases there may be more than one intermediary bank, and in those cases each intermediary bank is treated like Bank C in Case #3.

As the three cases demonstrate, a payment under Article 4A involves an overall transaction, the funds transfer, in which the originator, X, is making payment to the beneficiary, Y, but the funds transfer may encompass a series of payment orders that are issued in order to effect the payment initiated by the originator's payment order.

In some cases the originator and the beneficiary may be the same person. This will occur, for example, when a corporation orders a bank to transfer funds from an account of the corporation in that bank to another account of the corporation in that bank or in some other bank. In some funds transfers the first bank to issue a payment order is a bank that is executing a payment order of a customer that is not a bank. In this case the customer is the originator. In other cases, the first bank to issue a payment order is not acting for a customer, but is making a payment for its own account. In that event the first bank to issue a payment order is the originator as well as the originator's bank.

2. "Payment order" is defined in Section 4A–103(a)(1) as an instruction to a bank to pay, or to cause another bank to pay, a fixed or determinable amount of money. The bank to which the instruction is addressed is known as the "receiving bank." Section 4A–103(a)(4). "Bank" is defined in Section 4A–105(a)(2). The effect of this definition is to limit Article 4A to payments made through the banking system. A transfer of funds made by an entity outside the banking system is excluded. A transfer of funds through an entity other than a bank is usually a consumer transaction involving relatively small amounts of money and a single contract carried out by transfers of cash or a cash equivalent such as a check. Typically, the transferor delivers cash or a check to the company making the transfer, which agrees to pay a like amount to a person designated by the transferor. Transactions covered by Article 4A typically involve very large amounts of money in which several transactions involving several banks may be necessary to carry out the payment. Payments are normally made by debits or credits to bank accounts. Originators and beneficiaries are almost always business organizations and the transfers are usually made to pay obligations. Moreover, these transactions are frequently done on the basis of very short-term credit granted by the receiving bank to the sender of the payment order. Wholesale wire transfers involve policy questions that are distinct from those involved in consumer-based transactions by nonbanks.

3. Further limitations on the scope of Article 4A are found in the three requirements found in subparagraphs (i), (ii), and (iii) of Section 4A–103(a)(1). Subparagraph (i) states that the instruction to pay is a payment order only if it "does not state a condition to payment to the beneficiary other than time of payment." An instruction to pay a beneficiary sometimes is subject to a requirement that the beneficiary perform some act such as delivery of documents. For example, a New York bank may have issued a letter of credit in favor of X, a California seller of goods to be shipped to the New York bank's customer in New York. The terms of the letter of credit provide for payment to X if documents are presented to prove shipment of the goods. Instead of providing for presentment of the documents to the New York bank, the letter of credit states that they may be presented to a California bank that acts as an agent for payment. The New York bank sends an instruction to the California bank to pay X upon presentation of the required documents. The instruction is not covered by Article 4A because payment to the beneficiary is conditional upon receipt of shipping documents. The function of banks in a funds transfer under Article 4A is comparable to the role of banks in the collection and payment of checks in that it is essentially mechanical in nature. The low price and high speed that characterize funds transfers reflect this fact. Conditions to payment by the California bank other than time of payment impose responsibilities on that bank that go beyond those in Article 4A funds transfers. Although the payment by the New York bank to X under the letter of credit is not covered by Article 4A, if X is paid by the California bank, payment of the obligation of the New York bank to reimburse the California bank could be made by an Article 4A funds transfer. In such a case there is a distinction between the payment by the New York bank to X under the letter of credit and the payment by the New York bank to the California bank. For example, if the New York bank pays its reimbursement obligation to the California bank by a Fedwire naming the California bank as beneficiary (see Comment 1 to Section 4A–107), payment is made to the California bank rather than to X. That payment is governed by Article 4A and it could be made either before or after payment by the California bank to X. The payment by the New York bank to X under the letter of credit is not governed by Article 4A and it occurs when the California bank, as agent of the New York bank, pays X. No payment order was involved in that transaction. In this example, if the New York bank had erroneously sent an instruction to the California bank unconditionally instructing payment to X, the instruction would have been an Article 4A payment order. If the payment order was accepted (Section 4A–209(b)) by the California bank, a payment by the New York bank to X would have resulted (Section 4A–406(a)). But Article 4A would not prevent recovery of funds from X on the basis that X was not entitled to retain the funds under the law of mistake and restitution, letter of credit law or other applicable law.

4. Transfers of funds made through the banking system are commonly referred to as either "credit" transfers or "debit" transfers. In a credit transfer the instruction to pay is given by the person making payment. In a debit transfer the instruction to pay is given by the person receiving payment. The purpose of subparagraph (ii) of subsection (a)(1) of Section 4A–103 is to include credit transfers in Article 4A and to exclude debit transfers. All of the instructions to pay in the three cases described in Comment 1 fall within subparagraph (ii). Take Case #2 as an example. With respect to X's instruction given to Bank A, Bank A will be reimbursed by debiting X's account or otherwise receiving payment from X. With respect to Bank A's instruction to Bank B, Bank B will be reimbursed by receiving payment from Bank A. In a debit transfer, a creditor, pursuant to authority from the debtor, is enabled to draw on the debtor's bank account by issuing an instruction to pay to the debtor's bank. If the debtor's bank pays, it will be reimbursed by the debtor rather than by the person giving the instruction. For example, the holder of an insurance policy may pay premiums by authorizing the insurance company to order the policyholder's bank to pay the insurance company. The order to pay may be in the form of a draft covered by Article 3, or it might be an instruction to pay that is not an instrument under that Article. The bank receives reimbursement by debiting the policyholder's account. Or, a subsidiary corporation may make payments to its parent by authorizing the parent to order the subsidiary's bank to pay the parent from the subsidiary's account. These transactions are not covered by Article 4A because subparagraph (2) is not satisfied. Article 4A is limited to transactions in which the account to be debited by the receiving bank is that of the person in whose name the instruction is given.

If the beneficiary of a funds transfer is the originator of the transfer, the transfer is governed by Article 4A if it is a credit transfer in form. If it is in the form of a debit transfer it is not governed by Article 4A. For example, Corporation has accounts in Bank A and Bank B. Corporation instructs Bank A to pay to Corporation's account in Bank B. The funds transfer is governed by Article 4A.

Sometimes, Corporation will authorize Bank B to draw on Corporation's account in Bank A for the purpose of transferring funds into Corporation's account in Bank B. If Corporation also makes an agreement with Bank A under which Bank A is authorized to follow instructions of Bank B, as agent of Corporation, to transfer funds from Customer's account in Bank A, the instruction of Bank B is a payment order of Customer and is governed by Article 4A. This kind of transaction is known in the wire-transfer business as a "drawdown transfer." If Corporation does not make such an agreement with Bank A and Bank B instructs Bank A to make the transfer, the order is in form a debit transfer and is not governed by Article 4A. These debit transfers are normally ACH transactions in which Bank A relies on Bank B's warranties pursuant to ACH rules, including the warranty that the transfer is authorized.

5. The principal effect of subparagraph (iii) of subsection (a) of Section 4A–103 is to exclude from Article 4A payments made by check or credit card. In those cases the instruction of the debtor to the bank on which the check is drawn or to which the credit card slip is to be presented is contained in the check or credit card slip signed by the debtor. The instruction is not transmitted by the debtor directly to the debtor's bank. Rather, the instruction is delivered or otherwise transmitted by the debtor to the creditor who then presents it to the bank either directly or through bank collection channels. These payments are governed by Articles 3 and 4 and federal law. There are, however, limited instances in which the paper on which a check is printed can be used as the means of transmitting a payment order that is covered by Article 4A. Assume that Originator instructs Originator's Bank to pay $10,000 to the account of Beneficiary in Beneficiary's Bank. Since the amount of Originator's payment order is small, if Originator's Bank and Beneficiary's Bank do not have an account relationship, Originator's Bank may execute Originator's order by issuing a teller's check payable to Beneficiary's Bank for $10,000 along with instructions to credit Beneficiary's account in that amount. The instruction to Beneficiary's Bank to credit Beneficiary's account is a payment order. The check is the means by which Originator's Bank pays its obligation as sender of the payment order. The instruction of Originator's Bank to Beneficiary's Bank might be given in a letter accompanying the check or it may be written on the check itself. In either case the instruction to Beneficiary's Bank is a payment order but the check itself (which is an order to pay addressed to the drawee rather than to Beneficiary's Bank) is an instrument under Article 3 and is not a payment order. The check can be both the means by which Originator's Bank pays its obligation under § 4A–402(b) to Beneficiary's Bank and the means by which the instruction to Beneficiary's Bank is transmitted.

6. Most payments covered by Article 4A are commonly referred to as wire transfers and usually involve some kind of electronic transmission, but the applicability of Article 4A does not depend upon the means used to transmit the instruction of the sender. Transmission may be by letter or other written communication, oral communication or electronic communication. An oral communication is normally given by telephone. Frequently the message is recorded by the receiving bank to provide evidence of the transaction, but apart from problems of proof there is no need to record the oral instruction. Transmission of an instruction may be a direct communication between the sender and the receiving bank or through an intermediary such as an agent of the sender, a communication system such as international cable, or a funds transfer system such as CHIPS, SWIFT or an automated clearing house.

§ 4A.105. Other Definitions

(a) In this chapter:

(1) "Authorized account" means a deposit account of a customer in a bank designated by the customer as a source of payment of payment orders issued by the customer to the bank. If a customer does not so designate an account, any account of the customer is an authorized account if payment of a payment order from that account is not inconsistent with a restriction on the use of that account.

(2) "Bank" means a person engaged in the business of banking and includes a savings bank, savings and loan association, credit union, and trust company. A branch or separate office of a bank is a separate bank for purposes of this chapter.

(3) "Customer" means a person, including a bank, having an account with a bank or from whom a bank has agreed to receive payment orders.

(4) "Funds transfer business day" of a receiving bank means the part of a day during which the receiving bank is open for the receipt, processing, and transmittal of payment orders and cancellations and amendments of payment orders.

(5) "Funds transfer system" means a wire transfer network, automated clearinghouse, or other communication system of a clearinghouse or other association of banks through which a payment order by a bank may be transmitted to the bank to which the order is addressed.

(6) Reserved.

(7) "Prove" with respect to a fact means to meet the burden of establishing the fact (Section 1.201(b)(8)).

(b) Other definitions applying to this chapter and the sections in which they appear are:

(1) "Acceptance." Section 4A.209.

(2) "Beneficiary." Section 4A.103.

(3) "Beneficiary's bank." Section 4A.103.

(4) "Executed." Section 4A.301.

(5) "Execution date." Section 4A.301.

(6) "Funds transfer." Section 4A.104.

(7) "Funds transfer system rule." Section 4A.501.

(8) "Intermediary bank." Section 4A.104.

(9) "Originator." Section 4A.104.

(10) "Originator's bank." Section 4A.104.

(11) "Payment by beneficiary's bank to beneficiary." Section 4A.405.

(12) "Payment by originator to beneficiary." Section 4A.406.

(13) "Payment by sender to receiving bank." Section 4A.403.

(14) "Payment date." Section 4A.401.

(15) "Payment order." Section 4A.103.

(16) "Receiving bank." Section 4A.103.

(17) "Security procedure." Section 4A.201.

(18) "Sender." Section 4A.103.

(c) The following definitions in Chapter 4 apply to this chapter:

(1) "Clearinghouse." Section 4.104.

(2) "Item." Section 4.104.

(3) "Suspends payments." Section 4.104.

(d) In addition, Chapter 1 contains general definitions and principles of construction and interpretation applicable throughout this chapter.

Added by Acts 1993, 73rd Leg., ch. 570, § 7, eff. Sept. 1, 1993. Amended by Acts 2003, 78th Leg., ch. 542, § 13, eff. Sept. 1, 2003.

Uniform Commercial Code Comment

1. The definition of "bank" in subsection (a)(2) includes some institutions that are not commercial banks. The definition reflects the fact that many financial institutions now perform functions previously restricted to commercial banks, including acting on behalf of customers in funds transfers. Since many funds transfers involve payment orders to or from foreign countries the definition also covers foreign banks. The definition also includes Federal Reserve Banks. Funds transfers carried out by Federal Reserve Banks are described in Comments 1 and 2 to Section 4A–107.

2. Funds transfer business is frequently transacted by banks outside of general banking hours. Thus, the definition of banking day in Section 4–104(1)(c) cannot be used to describe when a bank is open for funds transfer business. Subsection (a)(4) defines a new term, "funds transfer business day," which is applicable to Article 4A. The definition states, "is open for the receipt, processing, and transmittal of payment orders and cancellations and amendments of payment orders." In some cases it is possible to electronically transmit payment orders and other communications to a receiving bank at any time. If the receiving bank is not open for the processing of an order when it is received, the communication is stored in the receiving bank's computer for retrieval when the receiving bank is open for processing. The use of the conjunctive makes clear that the defined term is limited to the period during which all functions of the receiving bank can be performed, i.e., receipt, processing, and transmittal of payment orders, cancellations and amendments.

3. Subsection (a)(5) defines "funds transfer system." The term includes a system such as CHIPS which provides for transmission of a payment order as well as settlement of the obligation of the sender to pay the order. It also includes automated clearing houses, operated by a clearing house or other association of banks, which process and transmit payment orders of banks to other banks. In addition the term includes organizations that provide only transmission services such as SWIFT. The definition also includes the wire transfer network and automated clearing houses of Federal Reserve Banks. Systems of the Federal Reserve Banks, however, are treated differently from systems of other associations of banks. Funds transfer systems other than systems of the Federal Reserve Banks are treated in Article 4A as a means of communication of payment orders between participating banks. Section 4A–206. The Comment to that section and the Comment to Section 4A–107 explain how Federal Reserve Banks function under Article 4A. Funds transfer systems are also able to promulgate rules binding on participating banks that, under Section 4A–501, may supplement or in some cases may even override provisions of Article 4A.

4. Subsection (d) incorporates definitions stated in Article 1 as well as principles of construction and interpretation stated in that Article. Included is Section 1–103. The last paragraph of the Comment to Section 4A–102 is addressed to the issue of the extent to which general principles of law and equity should apply to situations covered by provisions of Article 4A.

§ 4A.106. Time Payment Order is Received

(a) The time of receipt of a payment order or communication cancelling or amending a payment order is determined by the rules applicable to receipt of a notice stated in Section 1.202. A receiving bank may fix a cutoff time or times on a funds transfer business day for the receipt and processing of payment orders and communications cancelling or amending payment orders. Different cutoff times may apply to payment orders, cancellations, or amendments, or to different categories of payment orders, cancellations, or amendments. A cutoff time may apply to senders generally or different cutoff times may apply to different senders or categories of payment orders. If a payment order or communication cancelling or amending a payment order is received after the close of a funds transfer business day or after the appropriate cutoff time on a funds transfer business day, the receiving bank may treat the payment order or communication as received at the opening of the next funds transfer business day.

(b) If this chapter refers to an execution date or payment date or states a day on which a receiving bank is required to take action, and the date or day does not fall on a funds transfer business day, the next day that is a funds transfer business day is treated as the date or day stated, unless the contrary is stated in this chapter.

Added by Acts 1993, 73rd Leg., ch. 570, § 7, eff. Sept. 1, 1993. Amended by Acts 2003, 78th Leg., ch. 542, § 14, eff. Sept. 1, 2003.

Uniform Commercial Code Comment

The time that a payment order is received by a receiving bank usually defines the payment date or the execution date of a payment order. Section 4A–401 and Section 4A–301. The time of receipt of a payment order, or communication cancelling or amending a payment order is defined in subsection (a) by reference to the rules stated in Section 1–201(27). Thus, time of receipt is determined by the same rules that determine when a notice is received. Time of receipt, however, may be altered by a cut-off time.

§ 4A.107. Federal Reserve Regulations and Operating Circulars

Regulations of the Board of Governors of the Federal Reserve System and operating circulars of the Federal Reserve Banks supersede any inconsistent provision of this chapter to the extent of the inconsistency.

Added by Acts 1993, 73rd Leg., ch. 570, § 7, eff. Sept. 1, 1993.

Uniform Commercial Code Comment

1. Funds transfers under Article 4A may be made, in whole or in part, by payment orders through a Federal Reserve Bank in what is usually referred to as a transfer by Fedwire. If Bank A, which has an account in Federal Reserve Bank X, wants to pay $1,000,000 to Bank B, which has an account in Federal Reserve Bank Y, Bank A can issue an instruction to Reserve Bank X requesting a debit of $1,000,000 to Bank A's Reserve account and an equal credit to Bank B's Reserve account. Reserve Bank X will debit Bank A's account and will credit the account of Reserve Bank Y. Reserve Bank X will issue an instruction to Reserve Bank Y requesting a debit of $1,000,000 to the account of Reserve Bank X and an equal credit to Bank B's account in Reserve Bank Y. Reserve Bank Y will make the requested debit and credit and will give Bank B an advice of credit. The definition of "bank" in Section 4A–105(a)(2) includes both Reserve Bank X and Reserve Bank Y. Bank A's instruction to Reserve Bank X to pay money to Bank B is a payment order under Section 4A–103(a)(1). Bank A is the sender and Reserve Bank X is the receiving bank. Bank B is the beneficiary of Bank A's order and of the funds transfer. Bank A is the originator of the funds transfer and is also the originator's bank. Section 4A–104(c) and (d). Reserve Bank X, an intermediary bank under Section 4A–104(b), executes Bank A's order by sending a payment order to Reserve Bank Y instructing that bank to credit the Federal Reserve account of Bank B. Reserve Bank Y is the beneficiary's bank.

Suppose the transfer of funds from Bank A to Bank B is part of a larger transaction in which Originator, a customer of Bank A, wants to pay Beneficiary, a customer of Bank B. Originator issues a payment order to Bank A to pay $1,000,000 to the account of Beneficiary in Bank B. Bank A may execute Originator's order by means of Fedwire which simultaneously transfers $1,000,000 from Bank A to Bank B and carries a message instructing Bank B to pay $1,000,000 to the account of Y. The Fedwire transfer is carried out as described in the previous paragraph, except that the beneficiary of the funds transfer is Beneficiary rather than Bank B. Reserve Bank X and Reserve Bank Y are intermediary banks. When Reserve Bank Y advises Bank B of the credit to its Federal Reserve account it will also instruct Bank B to pay to the account of Beneficiary. The instruction is a payment order to Bank B which is the beneficiary's bank. When Reserve Bank Y advises Bank B of the credit to its Federal Reserve account Bank B receives payment of the payment order issued to it by Reserve Bank Y. Section 4A–403(a)(1). The payment order is automatically accepted by Bank B at the time it receives the payment order of Reserve Bank Y. Section 4A–209(b)(2). At the time of acceptance by Bank B payment by Originator to Beneficiary also occurs. Thus, in a Fedwire transfer, payment to the beneficiary's bank, acceptance by the beneficiary's bank and payment by the originator to the beneficiary all occur simultaneously by operation of law at the time the payment order to the beneficiary's bank is received.

If Originator orders payment to the account of Beneficiary in Bank C rather than Bank B, the analysis is somewhat modified. Bank A may not have any relationship with Bank C and may not be able to make payment directly to Bank C. In that case, Bank A could send a Fedwire instructing Bank B to instruct Bank C to pay Beneficiary. The analysis is the same as the previous case except that Bank B is an intermediary bank and Bank C is the beneficiary's bank.

2. A funds transfer can also be made through a Federal Reserve Bank in an automated clearing house transaction. In a typical case, Originator instructs Originator's Bank to pay to the account of Beneficiary in Beneficiary's Bank. Originator's instruction to pay a particular beneficiary is transmitted to Originator's Bank along with many other instructions for payment to other beneficiaries by many different beneficiary's banks. All of these instructions are contained in a magnetic tape or other electronic device. Transmission of instructions to the various beneficiary's banks requires that Originator's instructions be processed and repackaged with instructions of other originators so that all instructions to a particular beneficiary's bank are transmitted together to that bank. The repackaging is done in processing centers usually referred to as automated clearing houses. Automated clearing houses are operated either by Federal Reserve Banks or by other associations of banks. If Originator's Bank chooses to execute Originator's instructions by transmitting them to a Federal Reserve Bank for processing by the Federal Reserve Bank, the transmission to the Federal Reserve Bank results in the issuance of payment

orders by Originator's Bank to the Federal Reserve Bank, which is an intermediary bank. Processing by the Federal Reserve Bank will result in the issuance of payment orders by the Federal Reserve Bank to Beneficiary's Bank as well as payment orders to other beneficiary's banks making payments to carry out Originator's instructions.

3. Although the terms of Article 4A apply to funds transfers involving Federal Reserve Banks, federal preemption would make ineffective any Article 4A provision that conflicts with federal law. The payments activities of the Federal Reserve Banks are governed by regulations of the Federal Reserve Board and by operating circulars issued by the Reserve Banks themselves. In some instances, the operating circulars are issued pursuant to a Federal Reserve Board regulation. In other cases, the Reserve Bank issues the operating circular under its own authority under the Federal Reserve Act, subject to review by the Federal Reserve Board. Section 4A–107 states that Federal Reserve Board regulations and operating circulars of the Federal Reserve Banks supersede any inconsistent provision of Article 4A to the extent of the inconsistency. Federal Reserve Board regulations, being valid exercises of regulatory authority pursuant to a federal statute, take precedence over state law if there is an inconsistency. Childs v. Federal Reserve Bank of Dallas, 719 F.2d 812 (5th Cir. 1983), reh. den. 724 F.2d 127 (5th Cir. 1984). Section 4A–107 treats operating circulars as having the same effect whether issued under the Reserve Bank's own authority or under a Federal Reserve Board regulation.

§ 4A.108. Exclusion of Consumer Transactions Governed by Federal Law

This chapter does not apply to a funds transfer any part of which is governed by the Electronic Fund Transfer Act, 15 U.S.C. Sec. 1693 et seq., as amended from time to time.

Added by Acts 1993, 73rd Leg., ch. 570, § 7, eff. Sept. 1, 1993.

Uniform Commercial Code Comment

The Electronic Fund Transfer Act of 1978 is a federal statute that covers a wide variety of electronic funds transfers involving consumers. The types of transfers covered by the federal statute are essentially different from the wholesale wire transfers that are the primary focus of Article 4A. Section 4A–108 excludes a funds transfer from Article 4A if any part of the transfer is covered by the federal law. Existing procedures designed to comply with federal law will not be affected by Article 4A. The effect of Section 4A–108 is to make Article 4A and EFTA mutually exclusive. For example, if a funds transfer is to a consumer account in the beneficiary's bank and the funds transfer is made in part by use of Fedwire and in part by means of an automated clearing house, EFTA applies to the ACH part of the transfer but not to the Fedwire part. Under Section 4A–108, Article 4A does not apply to any part of the transfer. However, in the absence of any law to govern the part of the funds transfer that is not subject to EFTA, a court might apply appropriate principles from Article 4A by analogy.

[Sections 4A.109 to 4A.200 reserved for expansion]

SUBCHAPTER B. ISSUE AND ACCEPTANCE OF PAYMENT ORDER

§ 4A.201. Security Procedure

"Security procedure" means a procedure established by an agreement between a customer and a receiving bank for the purpose of (i) verifying that a payment order or communication amending or cancelling a payment order is that of the customer, or (ii) detecting error in the transmission or the content of the payment order or communication. A security procedure may require the use of algorithms or other codes, identifying words or numbers, encryption, callback procedures, or similar security devices. Comparison of a signature on a payment order or communication with an authorized specimen signature of the customer is not by itself a security procedure.

Added by Acts 1993, 73rd Leg., ch. 570, § 7, eff. Sept. 1, 1993.

Uniform Commercial Code Comment

A large percentage of payment orders and communications amending or cancelling payment orders are transmitted electronically and it is standard practice to use security procedures that are designed to assure the authenticity of the message. Security procedures can also be used to detect error in the content of messages or to detect payment orders that are transmitted by mistake as in the case of multiple transmission of the same payment order. Security procedures might also apply to communications that are transmitted by telephone or in writing. Section 4A–201 defines these security procedures. The definition of security procedure limits the term to a procedure "established by agreement of a customer and a receiving bank." The term does not apply to procedures that the receiving bank may follow unilaterally in processing payment orders. The question of whether loss that may result from the transmission of a spurious or erroneous payment order will be borne by the receiving bank or the sender or purported sender is affected by whether a security procedure was or was not in effect and whether there was or was not compliance with the procedure. Security procedures are referred to in Sections 4A–202 and 4A–203, which deal with authorized and verified payment orders, and Section 4A–205, which deals with erroneous payment orders.

§ 4A.202. Authorized and Verified Payment Orders

(a) A payment order received by the receiving bank is the authorized order of the person identified as sender if that person authorized the order or is otherwise bound by it under the law of agency.

(b) If a bank and its customer have agreed that the authenticity of payment orders issued to the bank in the name of the customer as sender will be verified pursuant to a security procedure, a payment order received by the receiving bank is effective as the order of the customer, whether or not authorized, if (i) the security procedure is a commercially reasonable method of providing security against unauthorized payment orders, and (ii) the bank proves that it accepted the payment order in good faith and in compliance with the security procedure and any written agreement or instruction of the customer restricting acceptance of payment orders issued in the name of the customer. The bank is not required to follow an instruction that violates a written agreement with the customer or notice of which is not received at a time and in a manner affording the bank a reasonable opportunity to act on it before the payment order is accepted.

(c) Commercial reasonableness of a security procedure is a question of law to be determined by considering the wishes of the customer expressed to the bank, the circumstances of the customer known to the bank, including the size, type, and frequency of payment orders normally issued by the customer to the bank, alternative security procedures offered to the customer, and security procedures in general use by customers and receiving banks similarly situated. A security procedure is deemed to be commercially reasonable if:

(1) the security procedure was chosen by the customer after the bank offered, and the customer refused, a security procedure that was commercially reasonable for the customer; and

(2) the customer expressly agreed in writing to be bound by any payment order, whether or not authorized, issued in its name and accepted by the bank in compliance with the security procedure chosen by the customer.

(d) The term "sender" in this chapter includes the customer in whose name a payment order is issued if the order is the authorized order of the customer under Subsection (a) or it is effective as the order of the customer under Subsection (b).

(e) This section applies to amendments and cancellations of payment orders to the same extent it applies to payment orders.

(f) Except as provided in this section and in Section 4A.203(a)(1), the rights and obligations arising under this section or Section 4A.203 may not be varied by agreement.

Added by Acts 1993, 73rd Leg., ch. 570, § 7, eff. Sept. 1, 1993.

Uniform Commercial Code Comment

This section is discussed in the Comment following Section 4A–203.

§ 4A.203. Unenforceability of Certain Verified Payment Orders

(a) If an accepted payment order is not, under Section 4A.202(a), an authorized order of a customer identified as sender, but is effective as an order of the customer pursuant to Section 4A.202(b), the following rules apply:

(1) By express written agreement, the receiving bank may limit the extent to which it is entitled to enforce or retain payment of the payment order.

(2) The receiving bank is not entitled to enforce or retain payment of the payment order if the customer proves that the order was not caused, directly or indirectly, by a person:

(A) entrusted at any time with duties to act for the customer with respect to payment orders or the security procedure; or

(B) who obtained access to transmitting facilities of the customer or who obtained, from a source controlled by the customer and without authority of the receiving bank, information facilitating breach of the security procedure, regardless of how the information was obtained or whether the customer was at fault. Information includes any access device, computer software, or the like.

(b) This section applies to amendments of payment orders to the same extent it applies to payment orders.

Added by Acts 1993, 73rd Leg., ch. 570, § 7, eff. Sept. 1, 1993.

Uniform Commercial Code Comment

1. Some person will always be identified as the sender of a payment order. Acceptance of the order by the receiving bank is based on a belief by the bank that the order was authorized by the person identified as the sender. If the receiving bank is the beneficiary's bank acceptance means that the receiving bank is obliged to pay the beneficiary. If the receiving bank is not the beneficiary's bank, acceptance means that the receiving bank has executed the sender's order and is obliged to pay the bank that accepted the order issued in execution of the sender's order. In either case the receiving bank may suffer a loss unless it is entitled to

enforce payment of the payment order that it accepted. If the person identified as the sender of the order refuses to pay on the ground that the order was not authorized by that person, what are the rights of the receiving bank? In the absence of a statute or agreement that specifically addresses the issue, the question usually will be resolved by the law of agency. In some cases, the law of agency works well. For example, suppose the receiving bank executes a payment order given by means of a letter apparently written by a corporation that is a customer of the bank and apparently signed by an officer of the corporation. If the receiving bank acts solely on the basis of the letter, the corporation is not bound as the sender of the payment order unless the signature was that of the officer and the officer was authorized to act for the corporation in the issuance of payment orders, or some other agency doctrine such as apparent authority or estoppel causes the corporation to be bound. Estoppel can be illustrated by the following example. Suppose P is aware that A, who is unauthorized to act for P, has fraudulently misrepresented to T that A is authorized to act for P. T believes A and is about to rely on the misrepresentation. If P does not notify T of the true facts although P could easily do so, P may be estopped from denying A's lack of authority. A similar result could follow if the failure to notify T is the result of negligence rather than a deliberate decision. Restatement, Second, Agency § 8B. Other equitable principles such as subrogation or restitution might also allow a receiving bank to recover with respect to an unauthorized payment order that it accepted. In Gatoil (U.S.A.), Inc. v. Forest Hill State Bank, 1 U.C.C. Rep.Serv.2d 171 (D.Md.1986), a joint venturer not authorized to order payments from the account of the joint venture, ordered a funds transfer from the account. The transfer paid a bona fide debt of the joint venture. Although the transfer was unauthorized the court refused to require recredit of the account because the joint venture suffered no loss. The result can be rationalized on the basis of subrogation of the receiving bank to the right of the beneficiary of the funds transfer to receive the payment from the joint venture.

But in most cases these legal principles give the receiving bank very little protection in the case of an authorized payment order. Cases like those just discussed are not typical of the way that most payment orders are transmitted and accepted, and such cases are likely to become even less common. Given the large amount of the typical payment order, a prudent receiving bank will be unwilling to accept a payment order unless it has assurance that the order is what it purports to be. This assurance is normally provided by security procedures described in Section 4A–201.

In a very large percentage of cases covered by Article 4A, transmission of the payment order is made electronically. The receiving bank may be required to act on the basis of a message that appears on a computer screen. Common law concepts of authority of agent to bind principal are not helpful. There is no way of determining the identity or the authority of the person who caused the message to be sent. The receiving bank is not relying on the authority of any particular person to act for the purported sender. The case is not comparable to payment of a check by the drawee bank on the basis of a signature that is forged. Rather, the receiving bank relies on a security procedure pursuant to which the authenticity of the message can be "tested" by various devices which are designed to provide certainty that the message is that of the sender identified in the payment order. In the wire transfer business the concept of "authorized" is different from that found in agency law. In that business a payment order is treated as the order of the person in whose name it is issued if it is properly tested pursuant to a security procedure and the order passes the test.

Section 4A–202 reflects the reality of the wire transfer business. A person in whose name a payment order is issued is considered to be the sender of the order if the order is "authorized" as stated in subsection (a) or if the order is "verified" pursuant to a security procedure in compliance with subsection (b). If subsection (b) does not apply, the question of whether the customer is responsible for the order is determined by the law of agency. The issue is one of actual or apparent authority of the person who caused the order to be issued in the name of the customer. In some cases the law of agency might allow the customer to be bound by an unauthorized order if conduct of the customer can be used to find an estoppel against the customer to deny that the order was unauthorized. If the customer is bound by the order under any of these agency doctrines, subsection (a) treats the order as authorized and thus the customer is deemed to be the sender of the order. In most cases, however, subsection (b) will apply. In that event there is no need to make an agency law analysis to determine authority. Under Section 4A–202, the issue of liability of the purported sender of the payment order will be determined by agency law only if the receiving bank did not comply with subsection (b).

2. The scope of Section 4A–202 can be illustrated by the following cases. *Case #1.* A payment order purporting to be that of Customer is received by Receiving Bank but the order was fraudulently transmitted by a person who had no authority to act for Customer. *Case #2.* An authentic payment order was sent by Customer, but before the order was received by Receiving Bank the order was fraudulently altered by an unauthorized person to change the beneficiary. *Case #3.* An authentic payment order was received by Receiving Bank, but before the order was executed by Receiving Bank a person who had no authority to act for Customer fraudulently sent a communication purporting to amend the order by changing the beneficiary. In each case Receiving Bank acted on the fraudulent communication by accepting the payment order. These cases are all essentially similar and they are treated identically by Section 4A–202. In each case Receiving Bank acted on a communication that it thought was authorized by Customer when in fact the communication was fraudulent. No distinction is made between Case #1 in which Customer took no part at all in the transaction and Case #2 and Case #3 in which an authentic order was fraudulently altered or amended by an unauthorized person. If subsection (b) does not apply, each case is governed by subsection (a). If there are no additional facts on which an estoppel might be found, Customer is not responsible in Case #1 for the fraudulently issued payment order, in Case #2 for the fraudulent alteration or in Case #3 for the fraudulent amendment. Thus, in each case Customer is not liable to pay the order and Receiving Bank takes the loss. The only remedy of Receiving Bank is to seek recovery from the person who received payment as beneficiary of the

fraudulent order. If there was verification in compliance with subsection (b), Customer will take the loss unless Section 4A–203 applies.

3. Subsection (b) of Section 4A–202 is based on the assumption that losses due to fraudulent payment orders can best be avoided by the use of commercially reasonable security procedures, and that the use of such procedures should be encouraged. The subsection is designed to protect both the customer and the receiving bank. A receiving bank needs to be able to rely on objective criteria to determine whether it can safely act on a payment order. Employees of the bank can be trained to "test" a payment order according to the various steps specified in the security procedure. The bank is responsible for the acts of these employees. Subsection (b)(ii) requires the bank to prove that it accepted the payment order in good faith and "in compliance with the security procedure." If the fraud was not detected because the bank's employee did not perform the acts required by the security procedure, the bank has not complied. Subsection (b)(ii) also requires the bank to prove that it complied with any agreement or instruction that restricts acceptance of payment orders issued in the name of the customer. A customer may want to protect itself by imposing limitations on acceptance of payment orders by the bank. For example, the customer may prohibit the bank from accepting a payment order that is not payable from an authorized account, that exceeds the credit balance in specified accounts of the customer, or that exceeds some other amount. Another limitation may relate to the beneficiary. The customer may provide the bank with a list of authorized beneficiaries and prohibit acceptance of any payment order to a beneficiary not appearing on the list. Such limitations may be incorporated into the security procedure itself or they may be covered by a separate agreement or instruction. In either case, the bank must comply with the limitations if the conditions stated in subsection (b) are met. Normally limitations on acceptance would be incorporated into an agreement between the customer and the receiving bank, but in some cases the instruction might be unilaterally given by the customer. If standing instructions or an agreement state limitations on the ability of the receiving bank to act, provision must be made for later modification of the limitations. Normally this would be done by an agreement that specifies particular procedures to be followed. Thus, subsection (b) states that the receiving bank is not required to follow an instruction that violates a written agreement. The receiving bank is not bound by an instruction unless it has adequate notice of it. Subsections (25), (26) and (27) of Section 1–201 apply.

Subsection (b)(i) assures that the interests of the customer will be protected by providing an incentive to a bank to make available to the customer a security procedure that is commercially reasonable. If a commercially reasonable security procedure is not made available to the customer, subsection (b) does not apply. The result is that subsection (a) applies and the bank acts at its peril in accepting a payment order that may be unauthorized. Prudent banking practice may require that security procedures be utilized in virtually all cases except for those in which personal contact between the customer and the bank eliminates the possibility of an unauthorized order. The burden of making available commercially reasonable security procedures is imposed on receiving banks because they generally determine what security procedures can be used and are in the best position to evaluate the efficacy of procedures offered to customers to combat fraud. The burden on the customer is to supervise its employees to assure compliance with the security procedure and to safeguard confidential security information and access to transmitting facilities so that the security procedure cannot be breached.

4. The principal issue that is likely to arise in litigation involving subsection (b) is whether the security procedure in effect when a fraudulent payment order was accepted was commercially reasonable. The concept of what is commercially reasonable in a given case is flexible. Verification entails labor and equipment costs that can vary greatly depending upon the degree of security that is sought. A customer that transmits very large numbers of payment orders in very large amounts may desire and may reasonably expect to be provided with state-of-the-art procedures that provide maximum security. But the expense involved may make use of a state-of-the-art procedure infeasible for a customer that normally transmits payment orders infrequently or in relatively low amounts. Another variable is the type of receiving bank. It is reasonable to require large money center banks to make available state-of-the-art security procedures. On the other hand, the same requirement may not be reasonable for a small country bank. A receiving bank might have several security procedures that are designed to meet the varying needs of different customers. The type of payment order is another variable. For example, in a wholesale wire transfer, each payment order is normally transmitted electronically and individually. A testing procedure will be individually applied to each payment order. In funds transfers to be made by means of an automated clearing house many payment orders are incorporated into an electronic device such as a magnetic tape that is physically delivered. Testing of the individual payment orders is not feasible. Thus, a different kind of security procedure must be adopted to take into account the different mode of transmission.

The issue of whether a particular security procedure is commercially reasonable is a question of law. Whether the receiving bank complied with the procedure is a question of fact. It is appropriate to make the finding concerning commercial reasonability a matter of law because security procedures are likely to be standardized in the banking industry and a question of law standard leads to more predictability concerning the level of security that a bank must offer to its customers. The purpose of subsection (b) is to encourage banks to institute reasonable safeguards against fraud but not to make them insurers against fraud. A security procedure is not commercially unreasonable simply because another procedure might have been better or because the judge deciding the question would have opted for a more stringent procedure. The standard is not whether the security procedure is the best available. Rather it is whether the procedure is reasonable for the particular customer and the particular bank, which is a lower standard. On the other hand, a security procedure that fails to meet prevailing standards of good banking practice applicable to the particular bank should not be held to be commercially reasonable. Subsection (c) states factors to be considered by the judge in making the determination of commercial reasonableness.

Sometimes an informed customer refuses a security procedure that is commercially reasonable and suitable for that customer and insists on using a higher-risk procedure because it is more convenient or cheaper. In that case, under the last sentence of subsection (c), the customer has voluntarily assumed the risk of failure of the procedure and cannot shift the loss to the bank. But this result follows only if the customer expressly agrees in writing to assume that risk. It is implicit in the last sentence of subsection (c) that a bank that accedes to the wishes of its customer in this regard is not acting in bad faith by so doing so long as the customer is made aware of the risk. In all cases, however, a receiving bank cannot get the benefit of subsection (b) unless it has made available to the customer a security procedure that is commercially reasonable and suitable for use by that customer. In most cases, the mutual interest of bank and customer to protect against fraud should lead to agreement to a security procedure which is commercially reasonable.

5. The effect of Section 4A–202(b) is to place the risk of loss on the customer if an unauthorized payment order is accepted by the receiving bank after verification by the bank in compliance with a commercially reasonable security procedure. An exception to this result is provided by Section 4A–203(a)(2). The customer may avoid the loss resulting from such a payment order if the customer can prove that the fraud was not committed by a person described in that subsection. Breach of a commercially reasonable security procedure requires that the person committing the fraud have knowledge of how the procedure works and knowledge of codes, identifying devices, and the like. That person may also need access to transmitting facilities through an access device or other software in order to breach the security procedure. This confidential information must be obtained either from a source controlled by the customer or from a source controlled by the receiving bank. If the customer can prove that the person committing the fraud did not obtain the confidential information from an agent or former agent of the customer or from a source controlled by the customer, the loss is shifted to the bank. "Prove" is defined in Section 4A–105(a)(7). Because of bank regulation requirements, in this kind of case there will always be a criminal investigation as well as an internal investigation of the bank to determine the probable explanation for the breach of security. Because a funds transfer fraud usually will involve a very large amount of money, both the criminal investigation and the internal investigation are likely to be thorough. In some cases there may be an investigation by bank examiners as well. Frequently, these investigations will develop evidence of who is at fault and the cause of the loss. The customer will have access to evidence developed in these investigations and that evidence can be used by the customer in meeting its burden of proof.

6. The effect of Section 4A–202(b) may also be changed by an agreement meeting the requirements of Section 4A–203(a)(1). Some customers may be unwilling to take all or part of the risk of loss with respect to unauthorized payment orders even if all of the requirements of Section 4A–202(b) are met. By virtue of Section 4A–203(a)(1), a receiving bank may assume all of the risk of loss with respect to unauthorized payment orders or the customer and bank may agree that losses from unauthorized payment orders are to be divided as provided in the agreement.

7. In a large majority of cases the sender of a payment order is a bank. In many cases in which there is a bank sender, both the sender and the receiving bank will be members of a funds transfer system over which the payment order is transmitted. Since Section 4A–202(f) does not prohibit a funds transfer system rule from varying rights and obligations under Section 4A–202, a rule of the funds transfer system can determine how loss due to an unauthorized payment order from a participating bank to another participating bank is to be allocated. A funds transfer system rule, however, cannot change the rights of a customer that is not a participating bank. § 4A–501(b). Section 4A–202(f) also prevents variation by agreement except to the extent stated.

§ 4A.204. Refund of Payment and Duty of Customer to Report With Respect to Unauthorized Payment Order

(a) If a receiving bank accepts a payment order issued in the name of its customer as sender which is (i) not authorized and not effective as the order of the customer under Section 4A.202, or (ii) not enforceable, in whole or in part, against the customer under Section 4A.203, the bank shall refund any payment of the payment order received from the customer to the extent the bank is not entitled to enforce payment and shall pay interest on the refundable amount calculated from the date the bank received payment to the date of the refund. However, the customer is not entitled to interest from the bank on the amount to be refunded if the customer fails to exercise ordinary care to determine that the order was not authorized by the customer and to notify the bank of the relevant facts within a reasonable time not exceeding 90 days after the date the customer received notification from the bank that the order was accepted or that the customer's account was debited with respect to the order. The bank is not entitled to any recovery from the customer on account of a failure by the customer to give notification as stated in this section.

(b) Reasonable time under Subsection (a) may be fixed by agreement as stated in Section 1.302(b), but the obligation of a receiving bank to refund payment as stated in Subsection (a) may not otherwise be varied by agreement.

Added by Acts 1993, 73rd Leg., ch. 570, § 7, eff. Sept. 1, 1993. Amended by Acts 2003, 78th Leg., ch. 542, § 15, eff. Sept. 1, 2003.

Uniform Commercial Code Comment

1. With respect to unauthorized payment orders, in a very large percentage of cases a commercially reasonable security procedure will be in effect. Section 4A–204 applies only to cases in which (i) no commercially reasonable security procedure is in effect, (ii) the bank did not comply with a

commercially reasonable security procedure that was in effect, (iii) the sender can prove, pursuant to Section 4A–203(a)(2), that the culprit did not obtain confidential security information controlled by the customer, or (iv) the bank, pursuant to Section 4A–203(a)(1) agreed to take all or part of the loss resulting from an unauthorized payment order. In each of these cases the bank takes the risk of loss with respect to an unauthorized payment order because the bank is not entitled to payment from the customer with respect to the order. The bank normally debits the customer's account or otherwise receives payment from the customer shortly after acceptance of the payment order. Subsection (a) of Section 4A–204 states that the bank must recredit the account or refund payment to the extent the bank is not entitled to enforce payment.

2. Section 4A–204 is designed to encourage a customer to promptly notify the receiving bank that it has accepted an unauthorized payment order. Since cases of unauthorized payment orders will almost always involve fraud, the bank's remedy is normally to recover from the beneficiary of the unauthorized order if the beneficiary was party to the fraud. This remedy may not be worth very much and it may not make any difference whether or not the bank promptly learns about the fraud. But in some cases prompt notification may make it easier for the bank to recover some part of its loss from the culprit. The customer will routinely be notified of the debit to its account with respect to an unauthorized order or will otherwise be notified of acceptance of the order. The customer has a duty to exercise ordinary care to determine that the order was unauthorized after it has received notification from the bank, and to advise the bank of the relevant facts within a reasonable time not exceeding 90 days after receipt of notification. Reasonable time is not defined and it may depend on the facts of the particular case. If a payment order for $1,000,000 is wholly unauthorized, the customer should normally discover it in far less than 90 days. If a $1,000,000 payment order was authorized but the name of the beneficiary was fraudulently changed, a much longer period may be necessary to discover the fraud. But in any event, if the customer delays more than 90 days the customer's duty has not been met. The only consequence of a failure of the customer to perform this duty is a loss of interest on the refund payable by the bank. A customer that acts promptly is entitled to interest from the time the customer's account was debited or the customer otherwise made payment. The rate of interest is stated in Section 4A–506. If the customer fails to perform the duty, no interest is recoverable for any part of the period before the bank learns that it accepted an unauthorized order. But the bank is not entitled to any recovery from the customer based on negligence for failure to inform the bank. Loss of interest is in the nature of a penalty on the customer designed to provide an incentive for the customer to police its account. There is no intention to impose a duty on the customer that might result in shifting loss from the unauthorized order to the customer.

§ 4A.205. Erroneous Payment Orders

(a) If an accepted payment order was transmitted pursuant to a security procedure for the detection of error and the payment order (i) erroneously instructed payment to a beneficiary not intended by the sender, (ii) erroneously instructed payment in an amount greater than the amount intended by the sender, or (iii) was an erroneously transmitted duplicate of a payment order previously sent by the sender, the following rules apply:

(1) If the sender proves that the sender or a person acting on behalf of the sender pursuant to Section 4A.206 complied with the security procedure and that the error would have been detected if the receiving bank had also complied, the sender is not obliged to pay the order to the extent stated in Subdivisions (2) and (3).

(2) If the funds transfer is completed on the basis of an erroneous payment order described in clause (i) or (iii) of Subsection (a), the sender is not obliged to pay the order and the receiving bank is entitled to recover from the beneficiary any amount paid to the beneficiary to the extent allowed by the law governing mistake and restitution.

(3) If the funds transfer is completed on the basis of a payment order described in clause (ii) of Subsection (a), the sender is not obliged to pay the order to the extent the amount received by the beneficiary is greater than the amount intended by the sender. In that case, the receiving bank is entitled to recover from the beneficiary the excess amount received to the extent allowed by the law governing mistake and restitution.

(b) If (i) the sender of an erroneous payment order described in Subsection (a) is not obliged to pay all or part of the order, and (ii) the sender receives notification from the receiving bank that the order was accepted by the bank or that the sender's account was debited with respect to the order, the sender has a duty to exercise ordinary care, on the basis of information available to the sender, to discover the error with respect to the order and to advise the bank of the relevant facts within a reasonable time, not exceeding 90 days, after the bank's notification was received by the sender. If the bank proves that the sender failed to perform that duty, the sender is liable to the bank for the loss the bank proves it incurred as a result of the failure, but the liability of the sender may not exceed the amount of the sender's order.

(c) This section applies to amendments to payment orders to the same extent it applies to payment orders.

Added by Acts 1993, 73rd Leg., ch. 570, § 7, eff. Sept. 1, 1993.

Uniform Commercial Code Comment

1. This section concerns error in the content or in the transmission of payment orders. It deals with three kinds of error. *Case #1.* The order identifies a beneficiary not intended by the sender. For example, Sender intends to wire funds to a beneficiary identified only by an account number. The wrong account number is stated in the order. *Case #2.* The error is in the amount of the order. For example, Sender intends to wire $1,000 to Beneficiary. Through error, the payment order instructs payment of $1,000,000. *Case #3.* A payment order is sent to the receiving bank and then, by mistake, the same payment order is sent to the receiving bank again. In Case #3, the receiving bank may have no way of knowing whether the second order is a duplicate of the first or is another order. Similarly, in Case #1 and Case #2, the receiving bank may have no way of knowing that the error exists. In each case, if this section does not apply and the funds transfer is completed, Sender is obliged to pay the order. Section 4A–402. Sender's remedy, based on payment by mistake, is to recover from the beneficiary that received payment.

Sometimes, however, transmission of payment orders of the sender to the receiving bank is made pursuant to a security procedure designed to detect one or more of the errors described above. Since "security procedure" is defined by Section 4A–201 as "a procedure established by agreement of a customer and a receiving bank for the purpose of * * * detecting error * * *," Section 4A–205 does not apply if the receiving bank and the customer did not agree to the establishment of a procedure for detecting error. A security procedure may be designed to detect an account number that is not one to which Sender normally makes payment. In that case, the security procedure may require a special verification that payment to the stated account number was intended. In the case of dollar amounts, the security procedure may require different codes for different dollar amounts. If a $1,000,000 payment order contains a code that is inappropriate for that amount, the error in amount should be detected. In the case of duplicate orders, the security procedure may require that each payment order be identified by a number or code that applies to no other order. If the number or code of each payment order received is registered in a computer base, the receiving bank can quickly identify a duplicate order. The three cases covered by this section are essentially similar. In each, if the error is not detected, some beneficiary will receive funds that the beneficiary was not intended to receive. If this section applies, the risk of loss with respect to the error of the sender is shifted to the bank which has the burden of recovering the funds from the beneficiary. The risk of loss is shifted to the bank only if the sender proves that the error would have been detected if there had been compliance with the procedure and that the sender (or an agent under Section 4A–206) complied. In the case of a duplicate order or a wrong beneficiary, the sender doesn't have to pay the order. In the case of an overpayment, the sender does not have to pay the order to the extent of the overpayment. If subsection (a)(1) applies, the position of the receiving bank is comparable to that of a receiving bank that erroneously executes a payment order as stated in Section 4A–303. However, failure of the sender to timely report the error is covered by Section 4A–205(b) rather than by Section 4A–304 which applies only to erroneous execution under Section 4A–303. A receiving bank to which the risk of loss is shifted by subsection (a)(1) or (2) is entitled to recover the amount erroneously paid to the beneficiary to the extent allowed by the law of mistake and restitution. Rights of the receiving bank against the beneficiary are similar to those of a receiving bank that erroneously executes a payment order as stated in Section 4A–303. Those rights are discussed in Comment 2 to Section 4A–303.

2. A security procedure established for the purpose of detecting error is not effective unless both sender and receiving bank comply with the procedure. Thus, the bank undertakes a duty of complying with the procedure for the benefit of the sender. This duty is recognized in subsection (a)(1). The loss with respect to the sender's error is shifted to the bank if the bank fails to comply with the procedure and the sender (or an agent under Section 4A–206) does comply. Although the customer may have been negligent in transmitting the erroneous payment order, the loss is put on the bank on a last-clear-chance theory. A similar analysis applies to subsection (b). If the loss with respect to an error is shifted to the receiving bank and the sender is notified by the bank that the erroneous payment order was accepted, the sender has a duty to exercise ordinary care to discover the error and notify the bank of the relevant facts within a reasonable time not exceeding 90 days. If the bank can prove that the sender failed in this duty it is entitled to compensation for the loss incurred as a result of the failure. Whether the bank is entitled to recover from the sender depends upon whether the failure to give timely notice would have made any difference. If the bank could not have recovered from the beneficiary that received payment under the erroneous payment order even if timely notice had been given, the sender's failure to notify did not cause any loss of the bank.

3. Section 4A–205 is subject to variation by agreement under Section 4A–501. Thus, if a receiving bank and its customer have agreed to a security procedure for detection of error, the liability of the receiving bank for failing to detect an error of the customer as provided in Section 4A–205 may be varied as provided in an agreement of the bank and the customer.

§ 4A.206. Transmission of Payment Order Through Funds Transfer or Other Communication System

(a) If a payment order addressed to a receiving bank is transmitted to a funds transfer system or other third-party communication system for transmittal to the bank, the system is deemed to be an agent of the sender for the purpose of transmitting the payment order to the bank. If there is a discrepancy between the terms of the payment order transmitted to the system and the terms of the payment order transmitted by the system to the bank, the terms of the payment order of the sender are those transmitted by the system. This section does not apply to a funds transfer system of the Federal Reserve Banks.

(b) This section applies to cancellations and amendments of payment orders to the same extent it applies to payment orders.

Added by Acts 1993, 73rd Leg., ch. 570, § 7, eff. Sept. 1, 1993.

Uniform Commercial Code Comment

1. A payment order may be issued to a receiving bank directly by delivery of a writing or electronic device or by an oral or electronic communication. If an agent of the sender is employed to transmit orders on behalf of the sender, the sender is bound by the order transmitted by the agent on the basis of agency law. Section 4A–206 is an application of that principle to cases in which a funds transfer or communication system acts as an intermediary in transmitting the sender's order to the receiving bank. The intermediary is deemed to be an agent of the sender for the purpose of transmitting payment orders and related messages for the sender. Section 4A–206 deals with error by the intermediary.

2. Transmission by an automated clearing house of an association of banks other than the Federal Reserve Banks is an example of a transaction covered by Section 4A–206. Suppose Originator orders Originator's Bank to cause a large number of payments to be made to many accounts in banks in various parts of the country. These payment orders are electronically transmitted to Originator's Bank and stored in an electronic device that is held by Originator's Bank. Or, transmission of the various payment orders is made by delivery to Originator's Bank of an electronic device containing the instruction to the bank. In either case the terms of the various payment orders by Originator are determined by the information contained in the electronic device. In order to execute the various orders, the information in the electronic device must be processed. For example, if some of the orders are for payments to accounts in Bank X and some to accounts in Bank Y, Originator's Bank will execute these orders of Originator by issuing a series of payment orders to Bank X covering all payments to accounts in that bank, and by issuing a series of payment orders to Bank Y covering all payments to accounts in that bank. The orders to Bank X may be transmitted together by means of an electronic device, and those to Bank Y may be included in another electronic device. Typically, this processing is done by an automated clearing house acting for a group of banks including Originator's Bank. The automated clearing house is a funds transfer system. Section 4A–105(a)(5). Originator's Bank delivers Originator's electronic device or transmits the information contained in the device to the funds transfer system for processing into payment orders of Originator's Bank to the appropriate beneficiary's banks. The processing may result in an erroneous payment order. Originator's Bank, by use of Originator's electronic device, may have given information to the funds transfer system instructing payment of $100,000 to an account in Bank X, but because of human error or an equipment malfunction the processing may have converted that instruction into an instruction to Bank X to make a payment of $1,000,000. Under Section 4A–206, Originator's Bank issued a payment order for $1,000,000 to Bank X when the erroneous information was sent to Bank X. Originator's Bank is responsible for the error of the automated clearing house. The liability of the funds transfer system that made the error is not governed by Article 4A. It is left to the law of contract, a funds transfer system rule, or other applicable law.

In the hypothetical case just discussed, if the automated clearing house is operated by a Federal Reserve Bank, the analysis is different. Section 4A–206 does not apply. Originator's Bank will execute Originator's payment orders by delivery or transmission of the electronic information to the Federal Reserve Bank for processing. The result is that Originator's Bank has issued payment orders to the Federal Reserve Bank which, in this case, is acting as an intermediary bank. When the Federal Reserve Bank has processed the information given to it by Originator's Bank it will issue payment orders to the various beneficiary's banks. If the processing results in an erroneous payment order, the Federal Reserve Bank has erroneously executed the payment order of Originator's Bank and the case is governed by Section 4A–303.

§ 4A.207. Misdescription of Beneficiary

(a) Subject to Subsection (b), if, in a payment order received by the beneficiary's bank, the name, bank account number, or other identification of the beneficiary refers to a nonexistent or unidentifiable person or account, no person has rights as a beneficiary of the order and acceptance of the order cannot occur.

(b) If a payment order received by the beneficiary's bank identifies the beneficiary both by name and by an identifying or bank account number and the name and number identify different persons, the following rules apply:

(1) Except as provided in Subsection (c), if the beneficiary's bank does not know that the name and number refer to different persons or if the funds transfer is processed by the beneficiary bank in a fully automated manner, it may rely on the number as the proper identification of the beneficiary of the order. The beneficiary's bank need not determine whether the name and number refer to the same person.

(2) If the beneficiary's bank pays the person identified by name or any individual processing the funds transfer on behalf of the beneficiary bank knows that the name and number identify different persons, no person has rights as beneficiary except the person paid by the beneficiary's bank if that person was entitled to receive payment from the originator of the funds transfer. If no person has rights as beneficiary, acceptance of the order cannot occur.

(c) If (i) a payment order described in Subsection (b) is accepted, (ii) the originator's payment order described the beneficiary inconsistently by name and number, and (iii) the beneficiary's bank pays the person identified by number as permitted by Subsection (b)(1), the following rules apply:

(1) If the originator is a bank, the originator is obliged to pay its order.

(2) If the originator is not a bank and proves that the person identified by number was not entitled to receive payment from the originator, the originator is not obliged to pay its order unless the originator's bank proves that the originator, before acceptance of the originator's order, had notice that payment of a payment order issued by the originator might be made by the beneficiary's bank on the basis of an identifying or bank account number even if it identifies a person different from the named beneficiary. Proof of notice may be made by any admissible evidence. The originator's bank satisfies the burden of proof if it proves that the originator, before the payment order was accepted, signed a writing stating the information to which the notice relates.

(d) In a case governed by Subsection (b)(1), if the beneficiary's bank rightfully pays the person identified by number and that person was not entitled to receive payment from the originator, the amount paid may be recovered from that person to the extent allowed by the law governing mistake and restitution as follows:

(1) If the originator is obliged to pay its payment order as stated in Subsection (c), the originator has the right to recover.

(2) If the originator is not a bank and is not obliged to pay its payment order, the originator's bank has the right to recover.

Added by Acts 1993, 73rd Leg., ch. 570, § 7, eff. Sept. 1, 1993.

Uniform Commercial Code Comment

1. Subsection (a) deals with the problem of payment orders issued to the beneficiary's bank for payment to nonexistent or unidentifiable persons or accounts. Since it is not possible in that case for the funds transfer to be completed, subsection (a) states that the order cannot be accepted. Under Section 4A–402(c), a sender of a payment order is not obliged to pay its order unless the beneficiary's bank accepts a payment order instructing payment to the beneficiary of that sender's order. Thus, if the beneficiary of a funds transfer is nonexistent or unidentifiable, each sender in the funds transfer that has paid its payment order is entitled to get its money back.

2. Subsection (b), which takes precedence over subsection (a), deals with the problem of payment orders in which the description of the beneficiary does not allow identification of the beneficiary because the beneficiary is described by name and by an identifying number or an account number and the name and number refer to different persons. A very large percentage of payment orders issued to the beneficiary's bank by another bank are processed by automated means using machines capable of reading orders on standard formats that identify the beneficiary by an identifying number or the number of a bank account. The processing of the order by the beneficiary's bank and the crediting of the beneficiary's account are done by use of the identifying or bank account number without human reading of the payment order itself. The process is comparable to that used in automated payment of checks. The standard format, however, may also allow the inclusion of the name of the beneficiary and other information which can be useful to the beneficiary's bank and the beneficiary but which plays no part in the process of payment. If the beneficiary's bank has both the account number and name of the beneficiary supplied by the originator of the funds transfer, it is possible for the beneficiary's bank to determine whether the name and number refer to the same person, but if a duty to make that determination is imposed on the beneficiary's bank the benefits of automated payment are lost. Manual handling of payment orders is both expensive and subject to human error. If payment orders can be handled on an automated basis there are substantial economies of operation and the possibility of clerical error is reduced. Subsection (b) allows banks to utilize automated processing by allowing banks to act on the basis of the number without regard to the name if the bank does not know that the name and number refer to different persons. "Know" is defined in Section 1–201(25) to mean actual knowledge, and Section 1–201(27) states rules for determining when an organization has knowledge of information received by the organization. The time of payment is the pertinent time at which knowledge or lack of knowledge must be determined.

Although the clear trend is for beneficiary's banks to process payment orders by automated means, Section 4A–207 is not limited to cases in which processing is done by automated means. A bank that processes by semi-automated means or even manually may rely on number as stated in Section 4A–207.

In cases covered by subsection (b) the erroneous identification would in virtually all cases be the identifying or bank account number. In the typical case the error is made by the originator of the funds transfer. The originator should know the name of the person who is to receive payment and can further identify that person by an address that would normally be known to the originator. It is not unlikely, however, that the originator may not be sure whether the identifying or account number refers to the person the originator intends to pay. Subsection (b)(1) deals with the typical case in which the beneficiary's bank pays on the basis of the account number and is not aware at the time of payment that the named beneficiary is not the holder of the account which was paid. In some cases the false number will be the result of error by the originator. In other cases fraud is involved. For example, Doe is the holder of shares in Mutual Fund. Thief, impersonating Doe, requests redemption of the shares and directs Mutual Fund to wire the redemption proceeds to Doe's account #12345 in Beneficiary's Bank. Mutual Fund originates a funds transfer by issuing a payment order to Originator's Bank to make the payment to Doe's account #12345 in Beneficiary's Bank.

Originator's Bank executes the order by issuing a conforming payment order to Beneficiary's Bank which makes payment to account #12345. That account is the account of Roe rather than Doe. Roe might be a person acting in concert with Thief or Roe might be an innocent third party. Assume that Roe is a gem merchant that agreed to sell gems to Thief who agreed to wire the purchase price to Roe's account in Beneficiary's Bank. Roe believed that the credit to Roe's account was a transfer of funds from Thief and released the gems to Thief in good faith in reliance on the payment. The case law is unclear on the responsibility of a beneficiary's bank in carrying out a payment order in which the identification of the beneficiary by name and number is conflicting. See Securities Fund Services, Inc. v. American National Bank, 542 F.Supp. 323 (N.D.Ill.1982) and Bradford Trust Co. v. Texas American Bank, 790 F.2d 407 (5th Cir.1986). Section 4A–207 resolves the issue.

If Beneficiary's Bank did not know about the conflict between the name and number, subsection (b)(1) applies. Beneficiary's Bank has no duty to determine whether there is a conflict and it may rely on the number as the proper identification of the beneficiary of the order. When it accepts the order, it is entitled to payment from Originator's Bank. Section 4A–402(b). On the other hand, if Beneficiary's Bank knew about the conflict between the name and number and nevertheless paid Roe, subsection (b)(2) applies. Under that provision, acceptance of the payment order of Originator's Bank did not occur because there is no beneficiary of that order. Since acceptance did not occur Originator's Bank is not obliged to pay Beneficiary's Bank. Section 4A–402(b). Similarly, Mutual Fund is excused from its obligation to pay Originator's Bank. Section 4A–402(c). Thus, Beneficiary's Bank takes the loss. Its only cause of action is against Thief. Roe is not obliged to return the payment to the beneficiary's bank because Roe received the payment in good faith and for value. Article 4A makes irrelevant the issue of whether Mutual Fund was or was not negligent in issuing its payment order.

3. Normally, subsection (b)(1) will apply to the hypothetical case discussed in Comment 2. Beneficiary's Bank will pay on the basis of the number without knowledge of the conflict. In that case subsection (c) places the loss on either Mutual Fund or Originator's Bank. It is not unfair to assign the loss to Mutual Fund because it is the person who dealt with the impostor and it supplied the wrong account number. It could have avoided the loss if it had not used an account number that it was not sure was that of Doe. Mutual Fund, however, may not have been aware of the risk involved in giving both name and number. Subsection (c) is designed to protect the originator, Mutual Fund, in this case. Under that subsection, the originator is responsible for the inconsistent description of the beneficiary if it had notice that the order might be paid by the beneficiary's bank on the basis of the number. If the originator is a bank, the originator always has that responsibility. The rationale is that any bank should know how payment orders are processed and paid. If the originator is not a bank, the originator's bank must prove that its customer, the originator, had notice. Notice can be proved by any admissible evidence, but the bank can always prove notice by providing the customer with a written statement of the required information and obtaining the customer's signature to the statement. That statement will then apply to any payment order accepted by the bank thereafter. The information need not be supplied more than once.

In the hypothetical case if Originator's Bank made the disclosure stated in the last sentence of subsection (c)(2), Mutual Fund must pay Originator's Bank. Under subsection (d)(1), Mutual Fund has an action to recover from Roe if recovery from Roe is permitted by the law governing mistake and restitution. Under the assumed facts Roe should be entitled to keep the money as a person who took it in good faith and for value since it was taken as payment for the gems. In that case, Mutual Fund's only remedy is against Thief. If Roe was not acting in good faith, Roe has to return the money to Mutual Fund. If Originator's Bank does not prove that Mutual Fund had notice as stated in subsection (c)(2), Mutual Fund is not required to pay Originator's Bank. Thus, the risk of loss falls on Originator's Bank whose remedy is against Roe or Thief as stated above. Subsection (d)(2).

State Bar Committee Comments

The test applied by Subsection 4A.207(b) depends on the knowledge of the beneficiary's bank with respect to the discrepancy between the name and number on a payment order. This test is difficult when a payment order is received and applied in a fully automated manner without review and approval by any person or persons. Questions may arise as to whether the bank knows or has reason to know of the discrepancy simply because its records assign a different number to the beneficiary's account. Because the processing of payment orders is fully automated for many banks and this automation should not be discouraged, the better rule would be to attribute knowledge to the beneficiary's bank if a person intervenes in the process and knows of the discrepancy. To cure this ambiguity, the Texas version of Subsection (b) has been revised in Subsection (1) to add language entitling a beneficiary bank to rely on the number as a proper identification of the beneficiary if the beneficiary bank processes funds transfers in a fully automated manner. In addition, Subsection (b)(2) is revised to provide that the knowledge of the beneficiary's bank must be that of an individual who processes the funds transfer on behalf of the beneficiary bank.

§ 4A.208. Misdescription of Intermediary Bank or Beneficiary's Bank

(a) This subsection applies to a payment order identifying an intermediary bank or the beneficiary's bank only by an identifying number.

(1) The receiving bank may rely on the number as the proper identification of the intermediary or beneficiary's bank and does not need to determine whether the number identifies a bank.

(2) The sender is obliged to compensate the receiving bank for any loss and expenses incurred by

the receiving bank as a result of its reliance on the number in executing or attempting to execute the order.

(b) This subsection applies to a payment order identifying an intermediary bank or the beneficiary's bank both by name and an identifying number if the name and number identify different persons.

(1) If the sender is a bank, the receiving bank may rely on the number as the proper identification of the intermediary or beneficiary's bank if the receiving bank, when it executes the sender's order, does not know that the name and number identify different persons. The receiving bank need not determine whether the name and number refer to the same person or whether the number refers to a bank. The sender is obliged to compensate the receiving bank for any loss and expenses incurred by the receiving bank as a result of its reliance on the number in executing or attempting to execute the order.

(2) If the sender is not a bank and the receiving bank proves that the sender, before the payment order was accepted, had notice that the receiving bank might rely on the number as the proper identification of the intermediary or beneficiary's bank even if it identifies a person different from the bank identified by name, the rights and obligations of the sender and the receiving bank are governed by Subsection (b)(1), as though the sender were a bank. Proof of notice may be made by any admissible evidence. The receiving bank satisfies the burden of proof if it proves that the sender, before the payment order was accepted, signed a writing stating the information to which the notice relates.

(3) Regardless of whether the sender is a bank, the receiving bank may rely on the name as the proper identification of the intermediary or beneficiary's bank if the receiving bank, at the time it executes the sender's order, does not know that the name and number identify different persons. The receiving bank need not determine whether the name and number refer to the same person.

(4) If the receiving bank knows that the name and number identify different persons, reliance on either the name or the number in executing the sender's payment order is a breach of the obligation stated in Section 4A.302(a)(1).

Added by Acts 1993, 73rd Leg., ch. 570, § 7, eff. Sept. 1, 1993.

Uniform Commercial Code Comment

1. This section addresses an issue similar to that addressed by Section 4A–207. Because of automation in the processing of payment orders, a payment order may identify the beneficiary's bank or an intermediary bank by an identifying number. The bank identified by number might or might not also be identified by name. The following two cases illustrate Section 4A–208(a) and (b):

Case #1. Originator's payment order to Originator's Bank identifies the beneficiary's bank as Bank A and instructs payment to Account #12345 in that bank. Originator's Bank executes Originator's order by issuing a payment order to Intermediary Bank. In the payment order of Originator's Bank the beneficiary's bank is identified as Bank A but is also identified by number, #67890. The identifying number refers to Bank B rather than Bank A. If processing by Intermediary Bank of the payment order of Originator's Bank is done by automated means, Intermediary Bank, in executing the order, will rely on the identifying number and will issue a payment order to Bank B rather than Bank A. If there is an Account #12345 in Bank B, the payment order of Intermediary Bank would normally be accepted and payment would be made to a person not intended by Originator. In this case, Section 4A–208(b)(1) puts the risk of loss on Originator's Bank. Intermediary Bank may rely on the number #67890 as the proper identification of the beneficiary's bank. Intermediary Bank has properly executed the payment order of Originator's Bank. By using the wrong number to describe the beneficiary's bank, Originator's Bank has improperly executed Originator's payment order because the payment order of Originator's Bank provides for payment to the wrong beneficiary, the holder of Account #12345 in Bank B rather than the holder of Account #12345 in Bank A. Section 4A–302(a)(1) and Section 4A–303(c). Originator's Bank is not entitled to payment from Originator but is required to pay Intermediary Bank. Section 4A–303(c) and Section 4A–402(c). Intermediary Bank is also entitled to compensation for any loss and expenses resulting from the error by Originator's Bank.

If there is no Account #12345 in Bank B, the result is that there is no beneficiary of the payment order issued by Originator's Bank and the funds transfer will not be completed. Originator's Bank is not entitled to payment from Originator and Intermediary Bank is not entitled to payment from Originator's Bank. Section 4A–402(c). Since Originator's Bank improperly executed Originator's payment order it may be liable for damages under Section 4A–305. As stated above, Intermediary Bank is entitled to compensation for loss and expenses resulting from the error by Originator's Bank.

Case #2. Suppose the same payment order by Originator to Originator's Bank as in Case #1. In executing the payment order Originator's Bank issues a payment order to Intermediary Bank in which the beneficiary's bank is identified only by number, #67890. That number does not refer to Bank A. Rather, it identifies a person that is not a bank. If processing by Intermediary Bank of the payment order of Originator's Bank is done by automated means, Intermediary Bank will rely on the number #67890 to identify the beneficiary's bank. Intermediary Bank has no duty to determine whether the number identifies a bank. The funds transfer cannot be completed in this case because no bank is identified as the beneficiary's bank. Subsection (a) puts the risk of loss on Originator's Bank. Originator's Bank is not entitled to payment from Originator. Section 4A–402(c). Originator's Bank has improperly executed Originator's payment order and may be liable for damages under Section 4A–305. Originator's Bank is obliged to compensate Intermediary Bank for loss and expenses resulting from the error by Originator's Bank.

Subsection (a) also applies if #67890 identifies a bank, but the bank is not Bank A. Intermediary Bank may rely on the number as the proper identification of the beneficiary's bank. If the bank to which Intermediary Bank sends its payment order accepts the order, Intermediary Bank is entitled to payment from Originator's Bank, but Originator's Bank is not entitled to payment from Originator. The analysis is similar to that in Case #1.

2. Subsection (b)(2) of Section 4A–208 addresses cases in which an erroneous identification of a beneficiary's bank or intermediary bank by name and number is made in a payment order of a sender that is not a bank. Suppose Originator issues a payment order to Originator's Bank that instructs that bank to use an intermediary bank identified as Bank A and by an identifying number, #67890. The identifying number refers to Bank B. Originator intended to identify Bank A as intermediary bank. If Originator's Bank relied on the number and issued a payment order to Bank B the rights of Originator's Bank depend upon whether the proof of notice stated in subsection (b)(2) is made by Originator's Bank. If proof is made, Originator's Bank's rights are governed by subsection (b)(1) of Section 4A–208. Originator's Bank is not liable for breach of Section 4A–302(a)(1) and is entitled to compensation from Originator for any loss and expenses resulting from Originator's error. If notice is not proved, Originator's Bank may not rely on the number in executing Originator's payment order. Since Originator's Bank does not get the benefit of subsection (b)(1) in that case, Originator's Bank improperly executed Originator's payment order and is in breach of the obligation stated in Section 4A–302(a)(1). If notice is not given, Originator's Bank can rely on the name if it is not aware of the conflict in name and number. Subsection (b)(3).

3. Although the principal purpose of Section 4A–208 is to accommodate automated processing of payment orders, Section 4A–208 applies regardless of whether processing is done by automation, semi-automated means or manually.

§ 4A.209. Acceptance of Payment Order

(a) Subject to Subsection (d), a receiving bank other than the beneficiary's bank accepts a payment order when it executes the order.

(b) Subject to Subsections (c) and (d), a beneficiary's bank accepts a payment order at the earliest of the following times:

(1) when the bank (i) pays the beneficiary as stated in Section 4A.405(a) or (b), or (ii) notifies the beneficiary of receipt of the order or that the account of the beneficiary has been credited with respect to the order unless the notice indicates that the bank is rejecting the order or that funds with respect to the order may not be withdrawn or used until receipt of payment from the sender of the order;

(2) when the bank receives payment of the entire amount of the sender's order pursuant to Section 4A.403(a)(1) or (2); or

(3) the opening of the next funds transfer business day of the bank following the payment date of the order if, at that time, the amount of the sender's order is fully covered by a withdrawable credit balance in an authorized account of the sender or the bank has otherwise received full payment from the sender, unless the order was rejected before that time or is rejected within (i) one hour after that time, or (ii) one hour after the opening of the next business day of the sender following the payment date if that time is later. If notice of rejection is received by the sender after the payment date and the authorized account of the sender does not bear interest, the bank is obliged to pay interest to the sender on the amount of the order for the number of days elapsing after the payment date to the day the sender receives notice or learns that the order was not accepted, counting that day as an elapsed day. If the withdrawable credit balance during that period falls below the amount of the order, the amount of interest payable is reduced accordingly.

(c) Acceptance of a payment order cannot occur before the order is received by the receiving bank. Acceptance does not occur under Subsection (b)(2) or (3) if the beneficiary of the payment order does not have an account with the receiving bank, the account has been closed, or the receiving bank is not permitted by law to receive credits for the beneficiary's account.

(d) A payment order issued to the originator's bank cannot be accepted until the payment date if the bank is the beneficiary's bank, or the execution date if the bank is not the beneficiary's bank. If the originator's bank executes the originator's payment order before the execution date or pays the beneficiary of the originator's payment order before the payment date and the payment order is subsequently canceled pursuant to Section 4A.211(b), the bank may recover from the beneficiary any payment received to the extent allowed by the law governing mistake and restitution.

Added by Acts 1993, 73rd Leg., ch. 570, § 7, eff. Sept. 1, 1993.

Uniform Commercial Code Comment

1. This section treats the sender's payment order as a request by the sender to the receiving bank to execute or pay the order and that request can be accepted or rejected by the receiving bank. Section 4A–209 defines when acceptance occurs. Section 4A–210 covers rejection. Acceptance of the payment order imposes an obligation on the receiving bank to the sender if the receiving bank is not the beneficiary's bank, or to the beneficiary if the receiving bank is the beneficiary's bank. These obligations are stated in Section 4A–302 and Section 4A–404.

2. Acceptance by a receiving bank other than the beneficiary's bank is defined in Section 4A–209(a). That subsection states the only way that a bank other than the beneficiary's bank can accept a payment order. A payment order to a bank other than the beneficiary's bank is, in effect, a request that the receiving bank execute the sender's order by issuing a payment order to the beneficiary's bank or to an intermediary bank. Normally, acceptance occurs at the time of execution, but there is an exception stated in subsection (d) and discussed in Comment 9. Execution occurs when the receiving bank "issues a payment order intended to carry out" the sender's order. Section 4A–301(a). In some cases the payment order issued by the receiving bank may not conform to the sender's order. For example, the receiving bank might make a mistake in the amount of its order, or the order might be issued to the wrong beneficiary's bank or for the benefit of the wrong beneficiary. In all of these cases there is acceptance of the sender's order by the bank when the receiving bank issues its order intended to carry out the sender's order, even though the bank's payment order does not in fact carry out the instruction of the sender. Improper execution of the sender's order may lead to liability to the sender for damages or it may mean that the sender is not obliged to pay its payment order. These matters are covered in Section 4A–303, Section 4A–305, and Section 4A–402.

3. A receiving bank has no duty to accept a payment order unless the bank makes an agreement, either before or after issuance of the payment order, to accept it, or acceptance is required by a funds transfer system rule. If the bank makes such an agreement it incurs a contractual obligation based on the agreement and may be held liable for breach of contract if a failure to execute violates the agreement. In many cases a bank will enter into an agreement with its customer to govern the rights and obligations of the parties with respect to payment orders issued to the bank by the customer or, in cases in which the sender is also a bank, there may be a funds transfer system rule that governs the obligations of a receiving bank with respect to payment orders transmitted over the system. Such agreements or rules can specify the circumstances under which a receiving bank is obliged to execute a payment order and can define the extent of liability of the receiving bank for breach of the agreement or rule. Section 4A–305(d) states the liability for breach of an agreement to execute a payment order.

4. In the case of a payment order issued to the beneficiary's bank, acceptance is defined in Section 4A–209(b). The function of a beneficiary's bank that receives a payment order is different from that of a receiving bank that receives a payment order for execution. In the typical case, the beneficiary's bank simply receives payment from the sender of the order, credits the account of the beneficiary and notifies the beneficiary of the credit. Acceptance by the beneficiary's bank does not create any obligation to the sender. Acceptance by the beneficiary's bank means that the bank is liable to the beneficiary for the amount of the order. Section 4A–404(a). There are three ways in which the beneficiary's bank can accept a payment order which are described in the following comments.

5. Under Section 4A–209(b)(1), the beneficiary's bank can accept a payment order by paying the beneficiary. In the normal case of crediting an account of the beneficiary, payment occurs when the beneficiary is given notice of the right to withdraw the credit, the credit is applied to a debt of the beneficiary, or "funds with respect to the order" are otherwise made available to the beneficiary. Section 4A–405(a). The quoted phrase covers cases in which funds are made available to the beneficiary as a result of receipt of a payment order for the benefit of the beneficiary but the release of funds is not expressed as payment of the order. For example, the beneficiary's bank might express a release of funds equal to the amount of the order as a "loan" that will be automatically repaid when the beneficiary's bank receives payment by the sender of the order. If the release of funds is designated as a loan pursuant to a routine practice of the bank, the release is conditional payment of the order rather than a loan, particularly if normal incidents of a loan such as the signing of a loan agreement or note and the payment of interest are not present. Such a release of funds is payment to the beneficiary under Section 4A–405(a). Under Section 4A–405(c) the bank cannot recover the money from the beneficiary if the bank does not receive payment from the sender of the payment order that it accepted. Exceptions to this rule are stated in § 4A–405(d) and (e). The beneficiary's bank may also accept by notifying the beneficiary that the order has been received. "Notifies" is defined in Section 1–201(26). In some cases a beneficiary's bank will receive a payment order during the day but settlement of the sender's obligation to pay the order will not occur until the end of the day. If the beneficiary's bank wants to defer incurring liability to the beneficiary until the beneficiary's bank receives payment, it can do so. The beneficiary's bank incurs no liability to the beneficiary with respect to a payment order that it receives until it accepts the order. If the bank does not accept pursuant to subsection (b)(1), acceptance does not occur until the end of the day when the beneficiary's bank receives settlement. If the sender settles, the payment order will be accepted under subsection (b)(2) and the funds will be released to the beneficiary the next morning. If the sender doesn't settle, no acceptance occurs. In either case the beneficiary's bank suffers no loss.

6. In most cases the beneficiary's bank will receive a payment order from another bank. If the sender is a bank and the beneficiary's bank receives payment from the sender by final settlement through the Federal Reserve System or a funds transfer system (Section 4A–403(a)(1)) or, less commonly, through credit to an account of the beneficiary's bank with the sender or another bank (Section 4A–403(a)(2)), acceptance by the beneficiary's bank occurs at the time payment is made. Section 4A–209(b)(2). A minor exception to this rule is stated in Section 4A–209(c). Section 4A–209(b)(2) results in automatic acceptance of payment orders issued to a beneficiary's bank by means of Fedwire

because the Federal Reserve account of the beneficiary's bank is credited and final payment is made to that bank when the payment order is received.

Subsection (b)(2) would also apply to cases in which the beneficiary's bank mistakenly pays a person who is not the beneficiary of the payment order issued to the beneficiary's bank. For example, suppose the payment order provides for immediate payment to Account #12345. The beneficiary's bank erroneously credits Account #12346 and notifies the holder of that account of the credit. No acceptance occurs in this case under subsection (b)(1) because the beneficiary of the order has not been paid or notified. The holder of Account #12345 is the beneficiary of the order issued to the beneficiary's bank. But acceptance will normally occur if the beneficiary's bank takes no other action, because the bank will normally receive settlement with respect to the payment order. At that time the bank has accepted because the sender paid its payment order. The bank is liable to pay the holder of Account #12345. The bank has paid the holder of Account #12346 by mistake, and has a right to recover the payment if the credit is withdrawn, to the extent provided in the law governing mistake and restitution.

7. Subsection (b)(3) covers cases of inaction by the beneficiary's bank. It applies whether or not the sender is a bank and covers a case in which the sender and the beneficiary both have accounts with the receiving bank and payment will be made by debiting the account of the sender and crediting the account of the beneficiary. Subsection (b)(3) is similar to subsection (b)(2) in that it bases acceptance by the beneficiary's bank on payment by the sender. Payment by the sender is effected by a debit to the sender's account if the account balance is sufficient to cover the amount of the order. On the payment date (Section 4A–401) of the order the beneficiary's bank will normally credit the beneficiary's account and notify the beneficiary of receipt of the order if it is satisfied that the sender's account balance covers the order or is willing to give credit to the sender. In some cases, however, the bank may not be willing to give credit to the sender and it may not be possible for the bank to determine until the end of the day on the payment date whether there are sufficient good funds in the sender's account. There may be various transactions during the day involving funds going into and out of the account. Some of these transactions may occur late in the day or after the close of the banking day. To accommodate this situation, subsection (b)(3) provides that the status of the account is determined at the opening of the next funds transfer business day of the beneficiary's bank after the payment date of the order. If the sender's account balance is sufficient to cover the order, the beneficiary's bank has a source of payment and the result in almost all cases is that the bank accepts the order at that time if it did not previously accept under subsection (b)(1). In rare cases, a bank may want to avoid acceptance under subsection (b)(3) by rejecting the order as discussed in Comment 8.

8. Section 4A–209 is based on a general principle that a receiving bank is not obliged to accept a payment order unless it has agreed or is bound by a funds transfer system rule to do so. Thus, provision is made to allow the receiving bank to prevent acceptance of the order. This principle is consistently followed if the receiving bank is not the beneficiary's bank. If the receiving bank is not the beneficiary's bank, acceptance is in the control of the receiving bank because it occurs only if the order is executed. But in the case of the beneficiary's bank acceptance can occur by passive receipt of payment under subsection (b)(2) or (3). In the case of a payment made by Fedwire acceptance cannot be prevented. In other cases the beneficiary's bank can prevent acceptance by giving notice of rejection to the sender before payment occurs under Section 4A–403(a)(1) or (2). A minor exception to the ability of the beneficiary's bank to reject is stated in Section 4A–502(c)(3).

Under subsection (b)(3) acceptance occurs at the opening of the next funds transfer business day of the beneficiary's bank following the payment date unless the bank rejected the order before that time or it rejects within one hour after that time. In some cases the sender and the beneficiary's bank may not be in the same time zone or the beginning of the business day of the sender and the funds transfer business day of the beneficiary's bank may not coincide. For example, the sender may be located in California and the beneficiary's bank in New York. Since in most cases notice of rejection would be communicated electronically or by telephone, it might not be feasible for the bank to give notice before one hour after the opening of the funds transfer business day in New York because at that hour, the sender's business day may not have started in California. For that reason, there are alternative deadlines stated in subsection (b)(3). In the case stated, the bank acts in time if it gives notice within one hour after the opening of the business day of the sender. But if the notice of rejection is received by the sender after the payment date, the bank is obliged to pay interest to the sender if the sender's account does not bear interest. In that case the bank had the use of funds of the sender that the sender could reasonably assume would be used to pay the beneficiary. The rate of interest is stated in Section 4A–506. If the sender receives notice on the day after the payment date the sender is entitled to one day's interest. If receipt of notice is delayed for more than one day, the sender is entitled to interest for each additional day of delay.

9. Subsection (d) applies only to a payment order by the originator of a funds transfer to the originator's bank and it refers to the following situation. On April 1, Originator instructs Bank A to make a payment on April 15 to the account of Beneficiary in Bank B. By mistake, on April 1, Bank A executes Originator's payment order by issuing a payment order to Bank B instructing immediate payment to Beneficiary. Bank B credited Beneficiary's account and immediately released the funds to Beneficiary. Under subsection (d) no acceptance by Bank A occurred on April 1 when Originator's payment order was executed because acceptance cannot occur before the execution date which in this case would be April 15 or shortly before that date. Section 4A–301(b). Under Section 4A–402(c), Originator is not obliged to pay Bank A until the order is accepted and that can't occur until the execution date. But Bank A is required to pay Bank B when Bank B accepted Bank A's order on April 1. Unless Originator and Beneficiary are the same person, in almost all cases Originator is paying a debt owed to Beneficiary and early payment does not injure Originator because Originator does not have to pay Bank A until the execution date. Section 4A–402(c). Bank A takes the interest loss. But suppose that on April 3, Originator concludes that no debt was owed to Beneficiary or that the debt was

less than the amount of the payment order. Under Section 4A–211(b) Originator can cancel its payment order if Bank A has not accepted. If early execution of Originator's payment order is acceptance, Originator can suffer a loss because cancellation after acceptance is not possible without the consent of Bank A and Bank B. Section 4A–211(c). If Originator has to pay Bank A, Originator would be required to seek recovery of the money from Beneficiary. Subsection (d) prevents this result and puts the risk of loss on Bank A by providing that the early execution does not result in acceptance until the execution date. Since on April 3 Originator's order was not yet accepted, Originator can cancel it under Section 4A–211(b). The result is that Bank A is not entitled to payment from Originator but is obliged to pay Bank B. Bank A has paid Beneficiary by mistake. If Originator's payment order is cancelled, Bank A becomes the originator of an erroneous funds transfer to Beneficiary. Bank A has the burden of recovering payment from Beneficiary on the basis of a payment by mistake. If Beneficiary received the money in good faith in payment of a debt owed to Beneficiary by Originator, the law of mistake and restitution may allow Beneficiary to keep all or part of the money received. If Originator owed money to Beneficiary, Bank A has paid Originator's debt and, under the law of restitution, which applies pursuant to Section 1–103, Bank A is subrogated to Beneficiary's rights against Originator on the debt.

If Bank A is the Beneficiary's bank and Bank A credited Beneficiary's account and released the funds to Beneficiary on April 1, the analysis is similar. If Originator's order is cancelled, Bank A has paid Beneficiary by mistake. The right of Bank A to recover the payment from Beneficiary is similar to Bank A's rights in the preceding paragraph.

§ 4A.210. Rejection of Payment Order

(a) A payment order is rejected by the receiving bank by a notice of rejection transmitted to the sender orally, electronically, or in writing. A notice of rejection need not use any particular words and is sufficient if it indicates that the receiving bank is rejecting the order or will not execute or pay the order. Rejection is effective when the notice is given if transmission is by a means that is reasonable under the circumstances. If notice of rejection is given by a means that is not reasonable, rejection is effective when the notice is received. If an agreement of the sender and receiving bank establishes the means to be used to reject a payment order:

(1) any means complying with the agreement is reasonable; and

(2) any means not complying is not reasonable unless no significant delay in receipt of the notice resulted from the use of the noncomplying means.

(b) This subsection applies if a receiving bank other than the beneficiary's bank fails to execute a payment order despite the existence on the execution date of a withdrawable credit balance in an authorized account of the sender sufficient to cover the order. If the sender does not receive notice of rejection of the order on the execution date and the authorized account of the sender does not bear interest, the bank is obliged to pay interest to the sender on the amount of the order for the number of days elapsing after the execution date to the earlier of the day the order is canceled pursuant to Section 4A.211(d) or the day the sender receives notice or learns that the order was not executed, counting the final day of the period as an elapsed day. If the withdrawable credit balance during that period falls below the amount of the order, the amount of interest is reduced accordingly.

(c) If a receiving bank suspends payments, all unaccepted payment orders issued to it are deemed rejected at the time the bank suspends payments.

(d) Acceptance of a payment order precludes a later rejection of the order. Rejection of a payment order precludes a later acceptance of the order.

Added by Acts 1993, 73rd Leg., ch. 570, § 7, eff. Sept. 1, 1993.

Uniform Commercial Code Comment

1. With respect to payment orders issued to a receiving bank other than the beneficiary's bank, notice of rejection is not necessary to prevent acceptance of the order. Acceptance can occur only if the receiving bank executes the order. Section 4A–209(a). But notice of rejection will routinely be given by such a bank in cases in which the bank cannot or is not willing to execute the order for some reason. There are many reasons why a bank doesn't execute an order. The payment order may not clearly instruct the receiving bank because of some ambiguity in the order or an internal inconsistency. In some cases, the receiving bank may not be able to carry out the instruction because of equipment failure, credit limitations on the receiving bank, or some other factor which makes proper execution of the order infeasible. In those cases notice of rejection is a means of informing the sender of the facts so that a corrected payment order can be transmitted or the sender can seek alternate means of completing the funds transfer. The other major reason for not executing an order is that the sender's account is insufficient to cover the order and the receiving bank is not willing to give credit to the sender. If the sender's account is sufficient to cover the order and the receiving bank chooses not to execute the order, notice of rejection is necessary to prevent liability to pay interest to the sender if the case falls within Section 4A–210(b) which is discussed in Comment 3.

2. A payment order to the beneficiary's bank can be accepted by inaction of the bank. Section 4A–209(b)(2) and (3). To prevent acceptance under those provisions it is necessary for the receiving bank to send notice of rejection before acceptance occurs. Subsection (a) of Section 4A–210 states the rule that rejection is accomplished by giving notice of rejection. This incorporates the definitions in Section 1–201(26). Rejection is effective when notice is given if it is

given by a means that is reasonable in the circumstances. Otherwise it is effective when the notice is received. The question of when rejection is effective is important only in the relatively few cases under subsection (b)(2) and (3) in which a notice of rejection is necessary to prevent acceptance. The question of whether a particular means is reasonable depends on the facts in a particular case. In a very large percentage of cases the sender and the receiving bank will be in direct electronic contact with each other and in those cases a notice of rejection can be transmitted instantaneously. Since time is of the essence in a large proportion of funds transfers, some quick means of transmission would usually be required, but this is not always the case. The parties may specify by agreement the means by which communication between the parties is to be made.

3. Subsection (b) deals with cases in which a sender does not learn until after the execution date that the sender's order has not been executed. It applies only to cases in which the receiving bank was assured of payment because the sender's account was sufficient to cover the order. Normally, the receiving bank will accept the sender's order if it is assured of payment, but there may be some cases in which the bank chooses to reject. Unless the receiving bank had obligated itself by agreement to accept, the failure to accept is not wrongful. There is no duty of the receiving bank to accept the payment order unless it is obliged to accept by express agreement. Section 4A–212. But even if the bank has not acted wrongfully, the receiving bank had the use of the sender's money that the sender could reasonably assume was to be the source of payment of the funds transfer. Until the sender learns that the order was not accepted the sender is denied the use of that money. Subsection (b) obliges the receiving bank to pay interest to the sender as restitution unless the sender receives notice of rejection on the execution date. The time of receipt of notice is determined pursuant to § 1–201(27). The rate of interest is stated in Section 4A–506. If the sender receives notice on the day after the execution date, the sender is entitled to one day's interest. If receipt of notice is delayed for more than one day, the sender is entitled to interest for each additional day of delay.

4. Subsection (d) treats acceptance and rejection as mutually exclusive. If a payment order has been accepted, rejection of that order becomes impossible. If a payment order has been rejected it cannot be accepted later by the receiving bank. Once notice of rejection has been given, the sender may have acted on the notice by making the payment through other channels. If the receiving bank wants to act on a payment order that it has rejected it has to obtain the consent of the sender. In that case the consent of the sender would amount to the giving of a second payment order that substitutes for the rejected first order. If the receiving bank suspends payments (Section 4–104(1)(k)), subsection (c) provides that unaccepted payment orders are deemed rejected at the time suspension of payments occurs. This prevents acceptance by passage of time under Section 4A–209(b)(3).

§ 4A.211. Cancellation and Amendment of Payment Order

(a) A communication of the sender of a payment order cancelling or amending the order may be transmitted to the receiving bank orally, electronically, or in writing. If a security procedure is in effect between the sender and the receiving bank, the communication is not effective to cancel or amend the order unless the communication is verified pursuant to the security procedure or the bank agrees to the cancellation or amendment.

(b) Subject to Subsection (a), a communication by the sender cancelling or amending a payment order is effective to cancel or amend the order if notice of the communication is received at a time and in a manner affording the receiving bank a reasonable opportunity to act on the communication before the bank accepts the payment order.

(c) After a payment order has been accepted, cancellation or amendment of the order is not effective unless the receiving bank agrees or a funds transfer system rule allows cancellation or amendment without agreement of the bank.

(1) With respect to a payment order accepted by a receiving bank other than the beneficiary's bank, cancellation or amendment is not effective unless a conforming cancellation or amendment of the payment order issued by the receiving bank is also made.

(2) With respect to a payment order accepted by the beneficiary's bank, cancellation or amendment is not effective unless the order was issued in execution of an unauthorized payment order or because of a mistake by a sender in the funds transfer which resulted in the issuance of a payment order (i) that is a duplicate of a payment order previously issued by the sender, (ii) that orders payment to a beneficiary not entitled to receive payment from the originator, or (iii) that orders payment in an amount greater than the amount the beneficiary was entitled to receive from the originator. If the payment order is canceled or amended, the beneficiary's bank is entitled to recover from the beneficiary any amount paid to the beneficiary to the extent allowed by the law governing mistake and restitution.

(d) An unaccepted payment order is canceled by operation of law at the close of the fifth funds transfer business day of the receiving bank after the execution date or payment date of the order.

(e) A canceled payment order cannot be accepted. If an accepted payment order is canceled, the acceptance is nullified and no person has any right or obligation based on the acceptance. Amendment of a payment order is deemed to be cancellation of the original order at the time of amendment and issue of a new payment order in the amended form at the same time.

(f) Unless otherwise provided in an agreement of the parties or in a funds transfer system rule, if the receiving bank, after accepting a payment order, agrees to cancellation or amendment of the order by the sender or is bound by a funds transfer system rule allowing cancellation or amendment without the bank's agreement, the sender, whether or not cancellation or amendment is effective, is liable to the bank for any loss and expenses, including reasonable attorney's fees, incurred by the bank as a result of the cancellation or amendment or attempted cancellation or amendment.

(g) A payment order is not revoked by the death or legal incapacity of the sender unless the receiving bank knows of the death or of an adjudication of incapacity by a court of competent jurisdiction and has reasonable opportunity to act before acceptance of the order.

(h) A funds transfer system rule is not effective to the extent it conflicts with Subsection (c)(2).

Added by Acts 1993, 73rd Leg., ch. 570, § 7, eff. Sept. 1, 1993.

Uniform Commercial Code Comment

1. This section deals with cancellation and amendment of payment orders. It states the conditions under which cancellation or amendment is both effective and rightful. There is no concept of wrongful cancellation or amendment of a payment order. If the conditions stated in this section are not met the attempted cancellation or amendment is not effective. If the stated conditions are met the cancellation or amendment is effective and rightful. The sender of a payment order may want to withdraw or change the order because the sender has had a change of mind about the transaction or because the payment order was erroneously issued or for any other reason. One common situation is that of multiple transmission of the same order. The sender that mistakenly transmits the same order twice wants to correct the mistake by cancelling the duplicate order. Or, a sender may have intended to order a payment of $1,000,000 but mistakenly issued an order to pay $10,000,000. In this case the sender might try to correct the mistake by cancelling the order and issuing another order in the proper amount. Or, the mistake could be corrected by amending the order to change it to the proper amount. Whether the error is corrected by amendment or cancellation and reissue the net result is the same. This result is stated in the last sentence of subsection (e).

2. Subsection (a) allows a cancellation or amendment of a payment order to be communicated to the receiving bank "orally, electronically, or in writing." The quoted phrase is consistent with the language of Section 4A–103(a) applicable to payment orders. Cancellations and amendments are normally subject to verification pursuant to security procedures to the same extent as payment orders. Subsection (a) recognizes this fact by providing that in cases in which there is a security procedure in effect between the sender and the receiving bank the bank is not bound by a communication cancelling or amending an order unless verification has been made. This is necessary to protect the bank because under subsection (b) a cancellation or amendment can be effective by unilateral action of the sender. Without verification the bank cannot be sure whether the communication was or was not effective to cancel or amend a previously verified payment order.

3. If the receiving bank has not yet accepted the order, there is no reason why the sender should not be able to cancel or amend the order unilaterally so long as the requirements of subsections (a) and (b) are met. If the receiving bank has accepted the order, it is possible to cancel or amend but only if the requirements of subsection (c) are met. First consider the case of a receiving bank other than the beneficiary's bank. If the bank has not yet accepted the order, the sender can unilaterally cancel or amend. The communication amending or cancelling the payment order must be received in time to allow the bank to act on it before the bank issues its payment order in execution of the sender's order. The time that the sender's communication is received is governed by Section 4A–106. If a payment order does not specify a delayed payment date or execution date, the order will normally be executed shortly after receipt. Thus, as a practical matter, the sender will have very little time in which to instruct cancellation or amendment before acceptance. In addition, a receiving bank will normally have cut-off times for receipt of such communications, and the receiving bank is not obliged to act on communications received after the cut-off hour. Cancellation by the sender after execution of the order by the receiving bank requires the agreement of the bank unless a funds transfer rule otherwise provides. Subsection (c). Although execution of the sender's order by the receiving bank does not itself impose liability on the receiving bank (under Section 4A–402 no liability is incurred by the receiving bank to pay its order until it is accepted), it would commonly be the case that acceptance follows shortly after issuance. Thus, as a practical matter, a receiving bank that has executed a payment order will incur a liability to the next bank in the chain before it would be able to act on the cancellation request of its customer. It is unreasonable to impose on the receiving bank a risk of loss with respect to a cancellation request without the consent of the receiving bank.

The statute does not state how or when the agreement of the receiving bank must be obtained for cancellation after execution. The receiving bank's consent could be obtained at the time cancellation occurs or it could be based on a preexisting agreement. Or, a funds transfer system rule could provide that cancellation can be made unilaterally by the sender. By virtue of that rule any receiving bank covered by the rule is bound. Section 4A–501. If the receiving bank has already executed the sender's order, the bank would not consent to cancellation unless the bank to which the receiving bank has issued its payment order consents to cancellation of that order. It makes no sense to allow cancellation of a payment order unless all subsequent payment orders in the funds transfer that were issued because of the cancelled payment order are also cancelled. Under subsection (c)(1), if a receiving bank consents to cancellation of the payment order after it is executed, the cancellation is not effective unless the receiving bank also cancels the payment order issued by the bank.

4. With respect to a payment order issued to the beneficiary's bank, acceptance is particularly important because it creates liability to pay the beneficiary, it defines when the originator pays its obligation to the beneficiary, and it defines when any obligation for which the payment is made is discharged. Since acceptance affects the rights of the originator and the beneficiary it is not appropriate to allow the beneficiary's bank to agree to cancellation or amendment except in unusual cases. Except as provided in subsection (c)(2), cancellation or amendment after acceptance by the beneficiary's bank is not possible unless all parties affected by the order agree. Under subsection (c)(2), cancellation or amendment is possible only in the four cases stated. The following examples illustrate subsection (c)(2):

Case #1. Originator's Bank executed a payment order issued in the name of its customer as sender. The order was not authorized by the customer and was fraudulently issued. Beneficiary's Bank accepted the payment order issued by Originator's Bank. Under subsection (c)(2) Originator's Bank can cancel the order if Beneficiary's Bank consents. It doesn't make any difference whether the payment order that Originator's Bank accepted was or was not enforceable against the customer under Section 4A–202(b). Verification under that provision is important in determining whether Originator's Bank or the customer has the risk of loss, but it has no relevance under Section 4A–211(c)(2). Whether or not verified, the payment order was not authorized by the customer. Cancellation of the payment order to Beneficiary's Bank causes the acceptance of Beneficiary's Bank to be nullified. Subsection (e). Beneficiary's Bank is entitled to recover payment from the beneficiary to the extent allowed by the law of mistake and restitution. In this kind of case the beneficiary is usually a party to the fraud who has no right to receive or retain payment of the order.

Case #2. Originator owed Beneficiary $1,000,000 and ordered Bank A to pay that amount to the account of Beneficiary in Bank B. Bank A issued a complying order to Bank B, but by mistake issued a duplicate order as well. Bank B accepted both orders. Under subsection (c)(2)(i) cancellation of the duplicate order could be made by Bank A with the consent of Bank B. Beneficiary has no right to receive or retain payment of the duplicate payment order if only $1,000,000 was owed by Originator to Beneficiary. If Originator owed $2,000,000 to Beneficiary, the law of restitution might allow Beneficiary to retain the $1,000,000 paid by Bank B on the duplicate order. In that case Bank B is entitled to reimbursement from Bank A under subsection (f).

Case #3. Originator owed $1,000,000 to X. Intending to pay X, Originator ordered Bank A to pay $1,000,000 to Y's account in Bank B. Bank A issued a complying payment order to Bank B which Bank B accepted by releasing the $1,000,000 to Y. Under subsection (c)(2)(ii) Bank A can cancel its payment order to Bank B with the consent of Bank B if Y was not entitled to receive payment from Originator. Originator can also cancel its order to Bank A with Bank A's consent. Subsection (c)(1). Bank B may recover the $1,000,000 from Y unless the law of mistake and restitution allows Y to retain some or all of the amount paid. If no debt was owed to Y, Bank B should have a right of recovery.

Case #4. Originator owed Beneficiary $10,000. By mistake Originator ordered Bank A to pay $1,000,000 to the account of Beneficiary in Bank B. Bank A issued a complying order to Bank B which accepted by notifying Beneficiary of its right to withdraw $1,000,000. Cancellation is permitted in this case under subsection (c)(2)(iii). If Bank B paid Beneficiary it is entitled to recover the payment except to the extent the law of mistake and restitution allows Beneficiary to retain payment. In this case Beneficiary might be entitled to retain $10,000, the amount of the debt owed to Beneficiary. If Beneficiary may retain $10,000, Bank B would be entitled to $10,000 from Bank A pursuant to subsection (f). In this case Originator also cancelled its order. Thus Bank A would be entitled to $10,000 from Originator pursuant to subsection (f).

5. Unless constrained by a funds transfer system rule, a receiving bank may agree to cancellation or amendment of the payment order under subsection (c) but is not required to do so regardless of the circumstances. If the receiving bank has incurred liability as a result of its acceptance of the sender's order, there are substantial risks in agreeing to cancellation or amendment. This is particularly true for a beneficiary's bank. Cancellation or amendment after acceptance by the beneficiary's bank can be made only in the four cases stated and the beneficiary's bank may not have any way of knowing whether the requirements of subsection (c) have been met or whether it will be able to recover payment from the beneficiary that received payment. Even with indemnity the beneficiary's bank may be reluctant to alienate its customer, the beneficiary, by denying the customer the funds. Subsection (c) leaves the decision to the beneficiary's bank unless the consent of the beneficiary's bank is not required under a funds transfer system rule or other interbank agreement. If a receiving bank agrees to cancellation or amendment under subsection (c)(1) or (2), it is automatically entitled to indemnification from the sender under subsection (f). The indemnification provision recognizes that a sender has no right to cancel a payment order after it is accepted by the receiving bank. If the receiving bank agrees to cancellation, it is doing so as an accommodation to the sender and it should not incur a risk of loss in doing so.

6. Acceptance by the receiving bank of a payment order issued by the sender is comparable to acceptance of an offer under the law of contracts. Under that law the death or legal incapacity of an offeror terminates the offer even though the offeree has no notice of the death or incapacity. Restatement Second, Contracts § 48. Comment a. to that section state that the "rule seems to be a relic of the obsolete view that a contract requires a 'meeting of minds,' and it is out of harmony with the modern doctrine that a manifestation of assent is effective without regard to actual mental assent." Subsection (g), which reverses the Restatement rule in the case of a payment order, is similar to Section 4–405(1) which applies to checks. Subsection (g) does not

address the effect of the bankruptcy of the sender of a payment order before the order is accepted, but the principle of subsection (g) has been recognized in Bank of Marin v. England, 385 U.S. 99 (1966). Although Bankruptcy Code Section 542(c) may not have been drafted with wire transfers in mind, its language can be read to allow the receiving bank to charge the sender's account for the amount of the payment order if the receiving bank executed it in ignorance of the bankruptcy.

7. Subsection (d) deals with stale payment orders. Payment orders normally are executed on the execution date or the day after. An order issued to the beneficiary's bank is normally accepted on the payment date or the day after. If a payment order is not accepted on its execution or payment date or shortly thereafter, it is probable that there was some problem with the terms of the order or the sender did not have sufficient funds or credit to cover the amount of the order. Delayed acceptance of such an order is normally not contemplated, but the order may not have been cancelled by the sender. Subsection (d) provides for cancellation by operation of law to prevent an unexpected delayed acceptance.

8. A funds transfer system rule can govern rights and obligations between banks that are parties to payment orders transmitted over the system even if the rule conflicts with Article 4A. In some cases, however, a rule governing a transaction between two banks can affect a third party in an unacceptable way. Subsection (h) deals with such a case. A funds transfer system rule cannot allow cancellation of a payment order accepted by the beneficiary's bank if the rule conflicts with subsection (c)(2). Because rights of the beneficiary and the originator are directly affected by acceptance, subsection (c)(2) severely limits cancellation. These limitations cannot be altered by funds transfer system rule.

§ 4A.212. Liability and Duty of Receiving Bank Regarding Unaccepted Payment Order

If a receiving bank fails to accept a payment order that it is obliged by express agreement to accept, the bank is liable for breach of the agreement to the extent provided in the agreement or in this chapter, but does not otherwise have any duty to accept a payment order or, before acceptance, to take any action, or refrain from taking action, with respect to the order except as provided in this chapter or by express agreement. Liability based on acceptance arises only when acceptance occurs as stated in Section 4A.209, and liability is limited to that provided in this chapter. A receiving bank is not the agent of the sender or beneficiary of the payment order it accepts, or of any other party to the funds transfer, and the bank owes no duty to any party to the funds transfer except as provided in this chapter or by express agreement.

Added by Acts 1993, 73rd Leg., ch. 570, § 7, eff. Sept. 1, 1993.

Uniform Commercial Code Comment

With limited exceptions stated in this Article, the duties and obligations of receiving banks that carry out a funds transfer arise only as a result of acceptance of payment orders or of agreements made by receiving banks. Exceptions are stated in Section 4A–209(b)(3) and Section 4A–210(b). A receiving bank is not like a collecting bank under Article 4. No receiving bank, whether it be an originator's bank, an intermediary bank or a beneficiary's bank, is an agent for any other party in the funds transfer.

[Sections 4A.213 to 4A.300 reserved for expansion]

SUBCHAPTER C. EXECUTION OF SENDER'S PAYMENT ORDER BY RECEIVING BANK

§ 4A.301. Execution and Execution Date

(a) A payment order is "executed" by the receiving bank when it issues a payment order intended to carry out the payment order received by the bank. A payment order received by the beneficiary's bank can be accepted but cannot be executed.

(b) "Execution date" of a payment order means the date on which the receiving bank may properly issue a payment order in execution of the sender's order. The execution date may be determined by instruction of the sender but cannot be earlier than the day the order is received and, unless otherwise determined, is the day the order is received. If the sender's instruction states a payment date, the execution date is the payment date or an earlier date on which execution is reasonably necessary to allow payment to the beneficiary on the payment date.

Added by Acts 1993, 73rd Leg., ch. 570, § 7, eff. Sept. 1, 1993.

Uniform Commercial Code Comment

1. The terms "executed," "execution" and "execution date" are used only with respect to a payment order to a receiving bank other than the beneficiary's bank. The beneficiary's bank can accept the payment order that it receives, but it does not execute the order. Execution refers to the act of the receiving bank in issuing a payment order "intended to carry out" the payment order that the bank received. A receiving bank has executed an order even if the order issued by the bank does not carry out the order received by the bank. For example, the bank may have erroneously issued an order to the wrong beneficiary, or in the wrong amount or to the wrong beneficiary's bank. In each of these cases execution has occurred but the execution is erroneous. Erroneous execution is covered in Section 4A–303.

2. "Execution date" refers to the time a payment order should be executed rather than the day it is actually executed. Normally the sender will not specify an execution date, but most payment orders are meant to be executed immedi-

ately. Thus, the execution date is normally the day the order is received by the receiving bank. It is common for the sender to specify a "payment date" which is defined in Section 4A–401 as "the day on which the amount of the order is payable to the beneficiary by the beneficiary's bank." Except for automated clearing house transfers, if a funds transfer is entirely within the United States and the payment is to be carried out electronically, the execution date is the payment date unless the order is received after the payment date. If the payment is to be carried out through an automated clearing house, execution may occur before the payment date. In an ACH transfer the beneficiary is usually paid one or two days after issue of the originator's payment order. The execution date is determined by the stated payment date and is a date before the payment date on which execution is reasonably necessary to allow payment on the payment date. A funds transfer system rule could also determine the execution date of orders received by the receiving bank if both the sender and the receiving bank are participants in the funds transfer system. The execution date can be determined by the payment order itself or by separate instructions of the sender or an agreement of the sender and the receiving bank. The second sentence of subsection (b) must be read in the light of Section 4A–106 which states that if a payment order is received after the cut-off time of the receiving bank it may be treated by the bank as received at the opening of the next funds transfer business day.

3. Execution on the execution date is timely, but the order can be executed before or after the execution date. Section 4A–209(d) and Section 4A–402(c) state the consequences of early execution and Section 4A–305(a) states the consequences of late execution.

§ 4A.302. Obligations of Receiving Bank in Execution of Payment Order

(a) Except as provided in Subsections (b) through (d), if the receiving bank accepts a payment order pursuant to Section 4A.209(a), the bank has the following obligations in executing the order:

(1) The receiving bank is obliged to issue, on the execution date, a payment order complying with the sender's order and to follow the sender's instructions concerning (i) any intermediary bank or funds transfer system to be used in carrying out the funds transfer, or (ii) the means by which payment orders are to be transmitted in the funds transfer. If the originator's bank issues a payment order to an intermediary bank, the originator's bank is obliged to instruct the intermediary bank according to the instruction of the originator. An intermediary bank in the funds transfer is similarly bound by an instruction given to it by the sender of the payment order it accepts.

(2) If the sender's instruction states that the funds transfer is to be carried out telephonically or by wire transfer or otherwise indicates that the funds transfer is to be carried out by the most expeditious means, the receiving bank is obliged to transmit its payment order by the most expeditious available means and to instruct any intermediary bank accordingly. If a sender's instruction states a payment date, the receiving bank is obliged to transmit its payment order at a time and by means reasonably necessary to allow payment to the beneficiary on the payment date or as soon thereafter as is feasible.

(b) Unless otherwise instructed, a receiving bank executing a payment order may (i) use any funds transfer system if use of that system is reasonable in the circumstances, and (ii) issue a payment order to the beneficiary's bank or to an intermediary bank through which a payment order conforming to the sender's order can expeditiously be issued to the beneficiary's bank if the receiving bank exercises ordinary care in the selection of the intermediary bank. A receiving bank is not required to follow an instruction of the sender designating a funds transfer system to be used in carrying out the funds transfer if the receiving bank, in good faith, determines that it is not feasible to follow the instruction or that following the instruction would unduly delay completion of the funds transfer.

(c) Unless Subsection (a)(2) applies or the receiving bank is otherwise instructed, the bank may execute a payment order by transmitting its payment order by first class mail or by any means reasonable in the circumstances. If the receiving bank is instructed to execute the sender's order by transmitting its payment order by a particular means, the receiving bank may issue its payment order by the means stated or by any means as expeditious as the means stated.

(d) Unless instructed by the sender, (i) the receiving bank may not obtain payment of its charges for services and expenses in connection with the execution of the sender's order by issuing a payment order in an amount equal to the amount of the sender's order less the amount of the charges, and (ii) may not instruct a subsequent receiving bank to obtain payment of its charges in the same amount.

Added by Acts 1993, 73rd Leg., ch. 570, § 7, eff. Sept. 1, 1993.

Uniform Commercial Code Comment

1. In the absence of agreement, the receiving bank is not obliged to execute an order of the sender. Section 4A–212. Section 4A–302 states the manner in which the receiving

bank may execute the sender's order if execution occurs. Subsection (a)(1) states the residual rule. The payment order issued by the receiving bank must comply with the sender's order and, unless some other rule is stated in the section, the receiving bank is obliged to follow any instruction of the sender concerning which funds transfer system is to be used, which intermediary banks are to be used, and what means of transmission is to be used. The instruction of the sender may be incorporated in the payment order itself or may be given separately. For example, there may be a master agreement between the sender and receiving bank containing instructions governing payment orders to be issued from time to time by the sender to the receiving bank. In most funds transfers, speed is a paramount consideration. A sender that wants assurance that the funds transfer will be expeditiously completed can specify the means to be used. The receiving bank can follow the instructions literally or it can use an equivalent means. For example, if the sender instructs the receiving bank to transmit by telex, the receiving bank could use telephone instead. Subsection (c). In most cases the sender will not specify a particular means but will use a general term such as "by wire" or "wire transfer" or "as soon as possible." These words signify that the sender wants a same-day transfer. In these cases the receiving bank is required to use a telephonic or electronic communication to transmit its order and is also required to instruct any intermediary bank to which it issues its order to transmit by similar means. Subsection (a)(2). In other cases, such as an automated clearing house transfer, a same-day transfer is not contemplated. Normally the sender's instruction or the context in which the payment order is received makes clear the type of funds transfer that is appropriate. If the sender states a payment date with respect to the payment order, the receiving bank is obliged to execute the order at a time and in a manner to meet the payment date if that is feasible. Subsection (a)(2). This provision would apply to many ACH transfers made to pay recurring debts of the sender. In other cases, involving relatively small amounts, time may not be an important factor and cost may be a more important element. Fast means, such as telephone or electronic transmission, are more expensive than slow means such as mailing. Subsection (c) states that in the absence of instructions the receiving bank is given discretion to decide. It may issue its payment order by first class mail or by any means reasonable in the circumstances. Section 4A–305 states the liability of a receiving bank for breach of the obligations stated in Section 4A–302.

2. Subsection (b) concerns the choice of intermediary banks to be used in completing the funds transfer, and the funds transfer system to be used. If the receiving bank is not instructed about the matter, it can issue an order directly to the beneficiary's bank or can issue an order to an intermediary bank. The receiving bank also has discretion concerning use of a funds transfer system. In some cases it may be reasonable to use either an automated clearing house system or a wire transfer system such as Fedwire or CHIPS. Normally, the receiving bank will follow the instruction of the sender in these matters, but in some cases it may be prudent for the bank not to follow instructions. The sender may have designated a funds transfer system to be used in carrying out the funds transfer, but it may not be feasible to use the designated system because of some impediment such as a computer breakdown which prevents prompt execution of the order. The receiving bank is permitted to use an alternate means of transmittal in a good faith effort to execute the order expeditiously. The same leeway is not given to the receiving bank if the sender designates an intermediary bank through which the funds transfer is to be routed. The sender's designation of that intermediary bank may mean that the beneficiary's bank is expecting to obtain a credit from that intermediary bank and may have relied on that anticipated credit. If the receiving bank uses another intermediary bank the expectations of the beneficiary's bank may not be realized. The receiving bank could choose to route the transfer to another intermediary bank and then to the designated intermediary bank if there was some reason such as a lack of a correspondent-bank relationship or a bilateral credit limitation, but the designated intermediary bank cannot be circumvented. To do so violates the sender's instructions.

3. The normal rule, under subsection (a)(1), is that the receiving bank, in executing a payment order, is required to issue a payment order that complies as to amount with that of the sender's order. In most cases the receiving bank issues an order equal to the amount of the sender's order and makes a separate charge for services and expenses in executing the sender's order. In some cases, particularly if it is an intermediary bank that is executing an order, charges are collected by deducting them from the amount of the payment order issued by the executing bank. If that is done, the amount of the payment order accepted by the beneficiary's bank will be slightly less than the amount of the originator's payment order. For example, Originator, in order to pay an obligation of $1,000,000 owed to Beneficiary, issues a payment order to Originator's Bank to pay $1,000,000 to the account of Beneficiary in Beneficiary's Bank. Originator's Bank issues a payment order to Intermediary Bank for $1,000,000 and debits Originator's account for $1,000,010. The extra $10 is the fee of Originator's Bank. Intermediary Bank executes the payment order of Originator's Bank by issuing a payment order to Beneficiary's Bank for $999,990, but under § 4A–402(c) is entitled to receive $1,000,000 from Originator's Bank. The $10 difference is the fee of Intermediary Bank. Beneficiary's Bank credits Beneficiary's account for $999,990. When Beneficiary's Bank accepts the payment order of Intermediary Bank the result is a payment of $999,990 from Originator to Beneficiary. Section 4A–406(a). If that payment discharges the $1,000,000 debt, the effect is that Beneficiary has paid the charges of Intermediary Bank and Originator has paid the charges of Originator's Bank. Subsection (d) of Section 4A–302 allows Intermediary Bank to collect its charges by deducting them from the amount of the payment order, but only if instructed to do so by Originator's Bank. Originator's Bank is not authorized to give that instruction to Intermediary Bank unless Originator authorized the instruction. Thus, Originator can control how the charges of Originator's Bank and Intermediary Bank are to be paid. Subsection (d) does not apply to charges of Beneficiary's Bank to Beneficiary.

In the case discussed in the preceding paragraph the $10 charge is trivial in relation to the amount of the payment and it may not be important to Beneficiary how the charge is paid. But it may be very important if the $1,000,000 obligation represented the price of exercising a right such as an option favorable to Originator and unfavorable to Beneficiary. Beneficiary might well argue that it was entitled to receive $1,000,000. If the option was exercised shortly before its expiration date, the result could be loss of the option benefit because the required payment of $1,000,000 was not made before the option expired. Section 4A–406(c) allows Originator to preserve the option benefit. The amount received by Beneficiary is deemed to be $1,000,000 unless Beneficiary demands the $10 and Originator does not pay it.

§ 4A.303. Erroneous Execution of Payment Order

(a) A receiving bank that (i) executes the payment order of the sender by issuing a payment order in an amount greater than the amount of the sender's order or (ii) issues a payment order in execution of the sender's order and then issues a duplicate order, is entitled to payment of the amount of the sender's order under Section 4A.402(c) if that subsection is otherwise satisfied. The bank is entitled to recover from the beneficiary of the erroneous order the excess payment received to the extent allowed by the law governing mistake and restitution.

(b) A receiving bank that executes the payment order of the sender by issuing a payment order in an amount less than the amount of the sender's order is entitled to payment of the amount of the sender's order under Section 4A.402(c) if (i) that subsection is otherwise satisfied and (ii) the bank corrects its mistake by issuing an additional payment order for the benefit of the beneficiary of the sender's order. If the error is not corrected, the issuer of the erroneous order is entitled to receive or retain payment from the sender of the order it accepted only to the extent of the amount of the erroneous order. This subsection does not apply if the receiving bank executes the sender's payment order by issuing a payment order in an amount less than the amount of the sender's order for the purpose of obtaining payment of its charges for services and expenses pursuant to instruction of the sender.

(c) If a receiving bank executes the payment order of the sender by issuing a payment order to a beneficiary different from the beneficiary of the sender's order and the funds transfer is completed on the basis of that error, the sender of the payment order that was erroneously executed and all previous senders in the funds transfer are not obliged to pay the payment orders they issued. The issuer of the erroneous order is entitled to recover from the beneficiary of the order the payment received to the extent allowed by the law governing mistake and restitution.

Added by Acts 1993, 73rd Leg., ch. 570, § 7, eff. Sept. 1, 1993.

Uniform Commercial Code Comment

1. Section 4A–303 states the effect of erroneous execution of a payment order by the receiving bank. Under Section 4A–402(c) the sender of a payment order is obliged to pay the amount of the order to the receiving bank if the bank executes the order, but the obligation to pay is excused if the beneficiary's bank does not accept a payment order instructing payment to the beneficiary of the sender's order. If erroneous execution of the sender's order causes the wrong beneficiary to be paid, the sender is not required to pay. If erroneous execution causes the wrong amount to be paid the sender is not obliged to pay the receiving bank an amount in excess of the amount of the sender's order. Section 4A–303 takes precedence over Section 4A–402(c) and states the liability of the sender and the rights of the receiving bank in various cases of erroneous execution.

2. Subsections (a) and (b) deal with cases in which the receiving bank executes by issuing a payment order in the wrong amount. If Originator ordered Originator's Bank to pay $1,000,000 to the account of Beneficiary in Beneficiary's Bank, but Originator's Bank erroneously instructed Beneficiary's Bank to pay $2,000,000 to Beneficiary's account, subsection (a) applies. If Beneficiary's Bank accepts the order of Originator's Bank, Beneficiary's Bank is entitled to receive $2,000,000 from Originator's Bank, but Originator's Bank is entitled to receive only $1,000,000 from Originator. Originator's Bank is entitled to recover the overpayment from Beneficiary to the extent allowed by the law governing mistake and restitution. Originator's Bank would normally have a right to recover the overpayment from Beneficiary, but in unusual cases the law of restitution might allow Beneficiary to keep all or part of the overpayment. For example, if Originator owed $2,000,000 to Beneficiary and Beneficiary received the extra $1,000,000 in good faith in discharge of the debt, Beneficiary may be allowed to keep it. In this case Originator's Bank has paid an obligation of Originator and under the law of restitution, which applies through Section 1–103, Originator's Bank would be subrogated to Beneficiary's rights against Originator on the obligation paid by Originator's Bank.

If Originator's Bank erroneously executed Originator's order by instructing Beneficiary's Bank to pay less than $1,000,000, subsection (b) applies. If Originator's Bank corrects its error by issuing another payment order to Beneficiary's Bank that results in payment of $1,000,000 to Beneficiary, Originator's Bank is entitled to payment of $1,000,000 from Originator. If the mistake is not corrected, Originator's Bank is entitled to payment from Originator only in the amount of the order issued by Originator's Bank.

3. Subsection (a) also applies to duplicate payment orders. Assume Originator's Bank properly executes Originator's $1,000,000 payment order and then by mistake issues a second $1,000,000 payment order in execution of Originator's order. If Beneficiary's Bank accepts both orders issued by Originator's Bank, Beneficiary's Bank is entitled to receive

$2,000,000 from Originator's Bank but Originator's Bank is entitled to receive only $1,000,000 from Originator. The remedy of Originator's Bank is the same as that of a receiving bank that executes by issuing an order in an amount greater than the sender's order. It may recover the overpayment from Beneficiary to the extent allowed by the law governing mistake and restitution and in a proper case as stated in Comment 2 may have subrogation rights if it is not entitled to recover from Beneficiary.

4. Suppose Originator instructs Originator's Bank to pay $1,000,000 to Account #12345 in Beneficiary's Bank. Originator's Bank erroneously instructs Beneficiary's Bank to pay $1,000,000 to Account #12346 and Beneficiary's Bank accepted. Subsection (c) covers this case. Originator is not obliged to pay its payment order, but Originator's Bank is required to pay $1,000,000 to Beneficiary's Bank. The remedy of Originator's Bank is to recover $1,000,000 from the holder of Account #12346 that received payment by mistake. Recovery based on the law of mistake and restitution is described in Comment 2.

§ 4A.304. Duty of Sender to Report Erroneously Executed Payment Order

If the sender of a payment order that is erroneously executed as stated in Section 4A.303 receives notification from the receiving bank that the order was executed or that the sender's account was debited with respect to the order, the sender has a duty to exercise ordinary care to determine, on the basis of information available to the sender, that the order was erroneously executed and to notify the bank of the relevant facts within a reasonable time not exceeding 90 days after the notification from the bank was received by the sender. If the sender fails to perform that duty, the bank is not obliged to pay interest on any amount refundable to the sender under Section 4A.402(d) for the period before the bank learns of the execution error. The bank is not entitled to any recovery from the sender on account of a failure by the sender to perform the duty stated in this section.

Added by Acts 1993, 73rd Leg., ch. 570, § 7, eff. Sept. 1, 1993.

Uniform Commercial Code Comment

This section is identical in effect to Section 4A–204 which applies to unauthorized orders issued in the name of a customer of the receiving bank. The rationale is stated in Comment 2 to Section 4A–204.

§ 4A.305. Liability for Late or Improper Execution or Failure to Execute Payment Order

(a) If a funds transfer is completed but execution of a payment order by the receiving bank in breach of Section 4A.302 of this chapter results in delay in payment to the beneficiary, the bank is obliged to pay interest to either the originator or the beneficiary of the funds transfer for the period of delay caused by the improper execution. Except as provided by Subsection (c), additional damages are not recoverable.

(b) If execution of a payment order by a receiving bank in breach of Section 4A.302 results in (i) noncompletion of the funds transfer, (ii) failure to use an intermediary bank designated by the originator, or (iii) issuance of a payment order that does not comply with the terms of the payment order of the originator, the bank is liable to the originator for its expenses in the funds transfer and for incidental expenses and interest losses, to the extent not covered by Subsection (a) of this section, resulting from the improper execution. Except as provided by Subsection (c), additional damages are not recoverable.

(c) In addition to the amounts payable under Subsections (a) and (b), damages, including consequential damages, are recoverable to the extent provided in an express written agreement of the receiving bank.

(d) If a receiving bank fails to execute a payment order it was obliged by express agreement to execute, the receiving bank is liable to the sender for its expenses in the transaction and for incidental expenses and interest losses resulting from the failure to execute. Additional damages, including consequential damages, are recoverable to the extent provided in an express written agreement of the receiving bank, but are not otherwise recoverable.

(e) Reasonable attorney's fees are recoverable if demand for compensation under Subsection (a) or (b) is made and refused before an action is brought on the claim. If a claim is made for breach of an agreement under Subsection (d) and the agreement does not provide for damages, reasonable attorney's fees are recoverable if demand for compensation under Subsection (d) of this section is made and refused before an action is brought on the claim.

(f) Except as provided by this section, the liability of a receiving bank under Subsections (a) and (b) of this section may not be varied by agreement.

Added by Acts 1993, 73rd Leg., ch. 570, § 7, eff. Sept. 1, 1993.

Uniform Commercial Code Comment

1. Subsection (a) covers cases of delay in completion of a funds transfer resulting from an execution by a receiving bank in breach of Section 4A–302(a). The receiving bank is

obliged to pay interest on the amount of the order for the period of the delay. The rate of interest is stated in Section 4A–506. With respect to wire transfers (other than ACH transactions) within the United States, the expectation is that the funds transfer will be completed the same day. In those cases, the originator can reasonably expect that the originator's account will be debited on the same day as the beneficiary's account is credited. If the funds transfer is delayed, compensation can be paid either to the originator or to the beneficiary. The normal practice is to compensate the beneficiary's bank to allow that bank to compensate the beneficiary by back-valuing the payment by the number of days of delay. Thus, the beneficiary is in the same position that it would have been in if the funds transfer had been completed on the same day. Assume on Day 1, Originator's Bank issues its payment order to Intermediary Bank which is received on that day. Intermediary Bank does not execute that order until Day 2 when it issues an order to Beneficiary's Bank which is accepted on that day. Intermediary Bank complies with subsection (a) by paying one day's interest to Beneficiary's Bank for the account of Beneficiary.

2. Subsection (b) applies to cases of breach of Section 4A–302 involving more than mere delay. In those cases the bank is liable for damages for improper execution but they are limited to compensation for interest losses and incidental expenses of the sender resulting from the breach, the expenses of the sender in the funds transfer and attorney's fees. This subsection reflects the judgment that imposition of consequential damages on a bank for commission of an error is not justified.

The leading common law case on the subject of consequential damages is *Evra Corp. v. Swiss Bank Corp.*, 673 F.2d 951 (7th Cir.1982), in which Swiss Bank, an intermediary bank, failed to execute a payment order. Because the beneficiary did not receive timely payment the originator lost a valuable ship charter. The lower court awarded the originator $2.1 million for lost profits even though the amount of the payment order was only $27,000. The Seventh Circuit reversed, in part on the basis of the common law rule of *Hadley v. Baxendale* that consequential damages may not be awarded unless the defendant is put on notice of the special circumstances giving rise to them. Swiss Bank may have known that the originator was paying the shipowner for the hire of a vessel but did not know that a favorable charter would be lost if the payment was delayed. "Electronic payments are not so unusual as to automatically place a bank on notice of extraordinary consequences if such a transfer goes awry. Swiss Bank did not have enough information to infer that if it lost a $27,000 payment order it would face liability in excess of $2 million." 673 F.2d at 956.

If *Evra* means that consequential damages can be imposed if the culpable bank has notice of particular circumstances giving rise to the damages, it does not provide an acceptable solution to the problem of bank liability for consequential damages. In the typical case transmission of the payment order is made electronically. Personnel of the receiving bank that process payment orders are not the appropriate people to evaluate the risk of liability for consequential damages in relation to the price charged for the wire transfer service. Even if notice is received by higher level management personnel who could make an appropriate decision whether the risk is justified by the price, liability based on notice would require evaluation of payment orders on an individual basis. This kind of evaluation is inconsistent with the high-speed, low-price, mechanical nature of the processing system that characterizes wire transfers. Moreover, in *Evra* the culpable bank was an intermediary bank with which the originator did not deal. Notice to the originator's bank would not bind the intermediary bank, and it seems impractical for the originator's bank to convey notice of this kind to intermediary banks in the funds transfer. The success of the wholesale wire transfer industry has largely been based on its ability to effect payment at low cost and great speed. Both of the these essential aspects of the modern wire transfer system would be adversely affected by a rule that imposed on banks liability for consequential damages. A banking industry amicus brief in *Evra* stated: "Whether banks can continue to make EFT services available on a widespread basis, by charging reasonable rates, depends on whether they can do so without incurring unlimited consequential risks. Certainly, no bank would handle for $3.25 a transaction entailing potential liability in the millions of dollars."

As the court in *Evra* also noted, the originator of the funds transfer is in the best position to evaluate the risk that a funds transfer will not be made on time and to manage that risk by issuing a payment order in time to allow monitoring of the transaction. The originator, by asking the beneficiary, can quickly determine if the funds transfer has been completed. If the originator has sent the payment order at a time that allows a reasonable margin for correcting error, no loss is likely to result if the transaction is monitored. The other published cases on this issue reach the *Evra* result. *Central Coordinates, Inc. v. Morgan Guaranty Trust Co.*, 40 U.C.C. Rep. Serv. 1340 (N.Y.Sup.Ct.1985), and *Gatoil (U.S.A.), Inc. v. Forest Hill State Bank*, 1 U.C.C. Rep.Serv.2d 171 (D.Md. 1986).

Subsection (c) allows the measure of damages in subsection (b) to be increased by an express written agreement of the receiving bank. An originator's bank might be willing to assume additional responsibilities and incur additional liability in exchange for a higher fee.

3. Subsection (d) governs cases in which a receiving bank has obligated itself by express agreement to accept payment orders of a sender. In the absence of such an agreement there is no obligation by a receiving bank to accept a payment order. Section 4A–212. The measure of damages for breach of an agreement to accept a payment order is the same as that stated in subsection (b). As in the case of subsection (b), additional damages, including consequential damages, may be recovered to the extent stated in an express written agreement of the receiving bank.

4. Reasonable attorney's fees are recoverable only in cases in which damages are limited to statutory damages stated in subsection (a), (b) and (d). If additional damages are recoverable because provided for by an express written agreement, attorney's fees are not recoverable. The rationale is that there is no need for statutory attorney's fees in the latter case, because the parties have agreed to a measure of damages which may or may not provide for attorney's fees.

5. The effect of subsection (f) is to prevent reduction of a receiving bank's liability under Section 4A–305.

[Sections 4A.306 to 4A.400 reserved for expansion]

SUBCHAPTER D. PAYMENT

§ 4A.401. Payment Date

"Payment date" of a payment order means the day on which the amount of the order is payable to the beneficiary by the beneficiary's bank. The payment date may be determined by instruction of the sender but cannot be earlier than the day the order is received by the beneficiary's bank and, unless otherwise determined, is the day the order is received by the beneficiary's bank.

Added by Acts 1993, 73rd Leg., ch. 570, § 7, eff. Sept. 1, 1993.

Uniform Commercial Code Comment

"Payment date" refers to the day the beneficiary's bank is to pay the beneficiary. The payment date may be expressed in various ways so long as it indicates the day the beneficiary is to receive payment. For example, in ACH transfers the payment date is the equivalent of "settlement date" or "effective date." Payment date applies to the payment order issued to the beneficiary's bank, but a payment order issued to a receiving bank other than the beneficiary's bank may also state a date for payment to the beneficiary. In the latter case, the statement of a payment date is to instruct the receiving bank concerning time of execution of the sender's order. Section 4A–301(b).

§ 4A.402. Obligation of Sender to Pay Receiving Bank

(a) This section is subject to Sections 4A.205 and 4A.207.

(b) With respect to a payment order issued to the beneficiary's bank, acceptance of the order by the bank obliges the sender to pay the bank the amount of the order, but payment is not due until the payment date of the order.

(c) This subsection is subject to Subsection (e) and to Section 4A.303. With respect to a payment order issued to a receiving bank other than the beneficiary's bank, acceptance of the order by the receiving bank obliges the sender to pay the bank the amount of the sender's order. Payment by the sender is not due until the execution date of the sender's order. The obligation of that sender to pay its payment order is excused if the funds transfer is not completed by acceptance by the beneficiary's bank of a payment order instructing payment to the beneficiary of that sender's payment order.

(d) If the sender of a payment order pays the order and was not obliged to pay all or part of the amount paid, the bank receiving payment is obliged to refund payment to the extent the sender was not obliged to pay. Except as provided by Sections 4A.204 and 4A.304, interest is payable on the refundable amount from the date of payment.

(e) If a funds transfer is not completed as provided by Subsection (c) and an intermediary bank is obliged to refund payment as provided by Subsection (d) but is unable to do so because not permitted by applicable law or because the bank suspends payments, a sender in the funds transfer that executed a payment order in compliance with an instruction, as provided by Section 4A.302(a)(1), to route the funds transfer through that intermediary bank is entitled to receive or retain payment from the sender of the payment order that it accepted. The first sender in the funds transfer that issued an instruction requiring routing through that intermediary bank is subrogated to the right of the bank that paid the intermediary bank to a refund as stated in Subsection (d).

(f) The right of the sender of a payment order to be excused from the obligation to pay the order as stated in Subsection (c) or to receive a refund under Subsection (d) may not be varied by agreement.

Added by Acts 1993, 73rd Leg., ch. 570, § 7, eff. Sept. 1, 1993.

Uniform Commercial Code Comment

1. Subsection (b) states that the sender of a payment order to the beneficiary's bank must pay the order when the beneficiary's bank accepts the order. At that point the beneficiary's bank is obliged to pay the beneficiary. Section 4A–404(a). The last clause of subsection (b) covers a case of premature acceptance by the beneficiary's bank. In some funds transfers, notably automated clearing house transfers, a beneficiary's bank may receive a payment order with a payment date after the day the order is received. The beneficiary's bank might accept the order before the payment date by notifying the beneficiary of receipt of the order. Although the acceptance obliges the beneficiary's bank to pay the beneficiary, payment is not due until the payment date. The last clause of subsection (b) is consistent with that result. The beneficiary's bank is also not entitled to payment from the sender until the payment date.

2. Assume that Originator instructs Bank A to order immediate payment to the account of Beneficiary in Bank B. Execution of Originator's payment order by Bank A is acceptance under Section 4A–209(a). Under the second sentence of Section 4A–402(c) the acceptance creates an obligation of Originator to pay Bank A the amount of the order.

The last clause of that sentence deals with attempted funds transfers that are not completed. In that event the obligation of the sender to pay its payment order is excused. Originator makes payment to Beneficiary when Bank B, the beneficiary's bank, accepts a payment order for the benefit of Beneficiary. Section 4A–406(a). If that acceptance by Bank B does not occur, the funds transfer has miscarried because Originator has not paid Beneficiary. Originator doesn't have to pay its payment order, and if it has already paid it is entitled to refund of the payment with interest. The rate of interest is stated in Section 4A–506. This "money-back guarantee" is an important protection of Originator. Originator is assured that it will not lose its money if something goes wrong in the transfer. For example, risk of loss resulting from payment to the wrong beneficiary is borne by some bank, not by Originator. The most likely reason for noncompletion is a failure to execute or an erroneous execution of a payment order by Bank A or an intermediary bank. Bank A may have issued its payment order to the wrong bank or it may have identified the wrong beneficiary in its order. The money-back guarantee is particularly important to Originator if noncompletion of the funds transfer is due to the fault of an intermediary bank rather than Bank A. In that case Bank A must refund payment to Originator, and Bank A has the burden of obtaining refund from the intermediary bank that it paid.

Subsection (c) can result in loss if an intermediary bank suspends payments. Suppose Originator instructs Bank A to pay to Beneficiary's account in Bank B and to use Bank C as an intermediary bank. Bank A executes Originator's order by issuing a payment order to Bank C. Bank A pays Bank C. Bank C fails to execute the order of Bank A and suspends payments. Under subsections (c) and (d), Originator is not obliged to pay Bank A and is entitled to refund from Bank A of any payment that it may have made. Bank A is entitled to a refund from Bank C, but Bank C is insolvent. Subsection (e) deals with this case. Bank A was required to issue its payment order to Bank C because Bank C was designated as an intermediary bank by Originator. Section 4A–302(a)(1). In this case Originator takes the risk of insolvency of Bank C. Under subsection (e), Bank A is entitled to payment from Originator and Originator is subrogated to the right of Bank A under subsection (d) to refund of payment from Bank C.

3. A payment order is not like a negotiable instrument on which the drawer or maker has liability. Acceptance of the order by the receiving bank creates an obligation of the sender to pay the receiving bank the amount of the order. That is the extent of the sender's liability to the receiving bank and no other person has any rights against the sender with respect to the sender's order.

§ 4A.403. Payment by Sender to Receiving Bank

(a) Payment of the sender's obligation under Section 4A.402 to pay the receiving bank occurs as follows:

(1) If the sender is a bank, payment occurs when the receiving bank receives final settlement of the obligation through a Federal Reserve Bank or through a funds transfer system.

(2) If the sender is a bank and the sender (i) credited an account of the receiving bank with the sender, or (ii) caused an account of the receiving bank in another bank to be credited, payment occurs when the credit is withdrawn or, if not withdrawn, at midnight of the day on which the credit is withdrawable and the receiving bank learns of that fact.

(3) If the receiving bank debits an account of the sender with the receiving bank, payment occurs when the debit is made to the extent the debit is covered by a withdrawable credit balance in the account.

(b) If the sender and receiving bank are members of a funds transfer system that nets obligations multilaterally among participants, the receiving bank receives final settlement when settlement is complete in accordance with the rules of the system. The obligation of the sender to pay the amount of a payment order transmitted through the funds transfer system may be satisfied, to the extent permitted by the rules of the system, by setting off and applying against the sender's obligation the right of the sender to receive payment from the receiving bank of the amount of any other payment order transmitted to the sender by the receiving bank through the funds transfer system. The aggregate balance of obligations owed by each sender to each receiving bank in the funds transfer system may be satisfied, to the extent permitted by the rules of the system, by setting off and applying against that balance the aggregate balance of obligations owed to the sender by other members of the system. The aggregate balance is determined after the right of setoff stated in the second sentence of this subsection has been exercised.

(c) If two banks transmit payment orders to each other under an agreement that settlement of the obligations of each bank to the other under Section 4A.402 will be made at the end of the day or other period, the total amount owed with respect to all orders transmitted by one bank shall be set off against the total amount owed with respect to all orders transmitted by the other bank. To the extent of the setoff, each bank has made payment to the other.

(d) In a case not covered by Subsection (a), the time when payment of the sender's obligation under Section 4A.402(b) or (c) occurs is governed by applicable principles of law that determine when an obligation is satisfied.

Added by Acts 1993, 73rd Leg., ch. 570, § 7, eff. Sept. 1, 1993.

Uniform Commercial Code Comment

1. This section defines when a sender pays the obligation stated in Section 4A–402. If a group of two or more banks engage in funds transfers with each other, the participating banks will sometimes be senders and sometimes receiving banks. With respect to payment orders other than Fedwires, the amounts of the various payment orders may be credited and debited to accounts of one bank with another or to a clearing house account of each bank and amounts owed and amounts due are netted. Settlement is made through a Federal Reserve Bank by charges to the Federal Reserve accounts of the net debtor banks and credits to the Federal Reserve accounts of the net creditor banks. In the case of Fedwires the sender's obligation is settled by a debit to the Federal Reserve account of the sender and a credit to the Federal Reserve account of the receiving bank at the time the receiving bank receives the payment order. Both of these cases are covered by subsection (a)(1). When the Federal Reserve settlement becomes final the obligation of the sender under Section 4A–402 is paid.

2. In some cases a bank does not settle an obligation owed to another bank through a Federal Reserve Bank. This is the case if one of the banks is a foreign bank without access to the Federal Reserve payment system. In this kind of case, payment is usually made by credits or debits to accounts of the two banks with each other or to accounts of the two banks in a third bank. Suppose Bank B has an account in Bank A. Bank A advises Bank B that its account in Bank A has been credited $1,000,000 and that the credit is immediately withdrawable. Bank A also instructs Bank B to pay $1,000,000 to the account of Beneficiary in Bank B. This case is covered by subsection (a)(2). Bank B may want to immediately withdraw this credit. For example, it might do so by instructing Bank A to debit the account and pay some third party. Payment by Bank A to Bank B of Bank A's payment order occurs when the withdrawal is made. Suppose Bank B does not withdraw the credit. Since Bank B is the beneficiary's bank, one of the effects of receipt of payment by Bank B is that acceptance of Bank A's payment order automatically occurs at the time of payment. Section 4A–209(b)(2). Acceptance means that Bank B is obliged to pay $1,000,000 to Beneficiary. Section 4A–404(a). Subsection (a)(2) of Section 4A–403 states that payment does not occur until midnight if the credit is not withdrawn. This allows Bank B an opportunity to reject the order if it does not have time to withdraw the credit to its account and it is not willing to incur the liability to Beneficiary before it has use of the funds represented by the credit.

3. Subsection (a)(3) applies to a case in which the sender (bank or nonbank) has a funded account in the receiving bank. If Sender has an account in Bank and issues a payment order to Bank, Bank can obtain payment from Sender by debiting the account of Sender, which pays its Section 4A–402 obligation to Bank when the debit is made.

4. Subsection (b) deals with multilateral settlements made through a funds transfer system and is based on the CHIPS settlement system. In a funds transfer system such as CHIPS, which allows the various banks that transmit payment orders over the system to settle obligations at the end of each day, settlement is not based on individual payment orders. Each bank using the system engages in funds transfers with many other banks using the system. Settlement for any participant is based on the net credit or debit position of that participant with all other banks using the system. Subsection (b) is designed to make clear that the obligations of any sender are paid when the net position of that sender is settled in accordance with the rules of the funds transfer system. This provision is intended to invalidate any argument, based on common-law principles, that multilateral netting is not valid because mutuality of obligation is not present. Subsection (b) dispenses with any mutuality of obligation requirements. Subsection (c) applies to cases in which two banks send payment orders to each other during the day and settle with each other at the end of the day or at the end of some other period. It is similar to subsection (b) in that it recognizes that a sender's obligation to pay a payment order is satisfied by a setoff. The obligations of each bank as sender to the other as receiving bank are obligations of the bank itself and not as representative of customers. These two sections are important in the case of insolvency of a bank. They make clear that liability under Section 4A–402 is based on the net position of the insolvent bank after setoff.

5. Subsection (d) relates to the uncommon case in which the sender doesn't have an account relationship with the receiving bank and doesn't settle through a Federal Reserve Bank. An example would be a customer that pays over the counter for a payment order that the customer issues to the receiving bank. Payment would normally be by cash, check or bank obligation. When payment occurs is determined by law outside Article 4A.

§ 4A.404. Obligation of Beneficiary's Bank to Pay and Give Notice to Beneficiary

(a) Subject to Sections 4A.211(e) and 4A.405(d) and (e), if a beneficiary's bank accepts a payment order, the bank is obliged to pay the amount of the order to the beneficiary of the order. Payment is due on the payment date of the order, but if acceptance occurs on the payment date after the close of the funds transfer business day of the bank, payment is due on the next funds transfer business day. If the bank refuses to pay after demand by the beneficiary and receipt of notice of particular circumstances that will give rise to consequential damages as a result of nonpayment, the beneficiary may recover damages resulting from the refusal to pay to the extent the bank had notice of the damages, unless the bank proves that it did not pay because of a reasonable doubt concerning the right of the beneficiary to payment.

(b) If a payment order accepted by the beneficiary's bank instructs payment to an account of the beneficiary, the bank is obliged to notify the beneficiary of receipt of the order before midnight of the next funds transfer business day following the payment date. If the payment order does not instruct payment to an account of the beneficiary, the bank is required to notify the beneficiary only if notice is required by the order. Notice may be given by first class mail or any other means reasonable in the circumstances. If the bank fails to give the required notice, the bank is obliged to pay interest to the beneficiary on the amount of the payment order from the day notice should have been given until the day the beneficiary learned of receipt of the payment order by the bank. No other damages are recoverable. Reasonable attorney's fees are recoverable if demand for interest is made and refused before an action is brought on the claim.

(c) The right of a beneficiary to receive payment and damages as stated in Subsection (a) may not be varied by agreement or a funds transfer system rule. The right of a beneficiary to be notified as stated in Subsection (b) may be varied by agreement of the beneficiary or by a funds transfer system rule if the beneficiary is notified of the rule before initiation of the funds transfer.

Added by Acts 1993, 73rd Leg., ch. 570, § 7, eff. Sept. 1, 1993.

Uniform Commercial Code Comment

1. The first sentence of subsection (a) states the time when the obligation of the beneficiary's bank arises. The second and third sentences state when the beneficiary's bank must make funds available to the beneficiary. They also state the measure of damages for failure, after demand, to comply. Since the Expedited Funds Availability Act, 12 U.S.C. 4001 et seq., also governs funds availability in a funds transfer, the second and third sentences of subsection (a) may be subject to preemption by that Act.

2. Subsection (a) provides that the beneficiary of an accepted payment order may recover consequential damages if the beneficiary's bank refuses to pay the order after demand by the beneficiary if the bank at that time had notice of the particular circumstances giving rise to the damages. Such damages are recoverable only to the extent the bank had "notice of the damages." The quoted phrase requires that the bank have notice of the general type or nature of the damages that will be suffered as a result of the refusal to pay and their general magnitude. There is no requirement that the bank have notice of the exact or even the approximate amount of the damages, but if the amount of damages is extraordinary the bank is entitled to notice of that fact. For example, in *Evra Corp. v. Swiss Bank Corp.*, 673 F.2d 951 (7th Cir.1982), failure to complete a funds transfer of only $27,000 required to retain rights to a very favorable ship charter resulted in a claim for more than $2,000,000 of consequential damages. Since it is not reasonably foreseeable that a failure to make a relatively small payment will result in damages of this magnitude, notice is not sufficient if the beneficiary's bank has notice only that the $27,000 is necessary to retain rights on a ship charter. The bank is entitled to notice that an exceptional amount of damages will result as well. For example, there would be adequate notice if the bank had been made aware that damages of $1,000,000 or more might result.

3. Under the last clause of subsection (a) the beneficiary's bank is not liable for damages if its refusal to pay was "because of a reasonable doubt concerning the right of the beneficiary to payment." Normally there will not be any question about the right of the beneficiary to receive payment. Normally, the bank should be able to determine whether it has accepted the payment order and, if it has been accepted, the first sentence of subsection (a) states that the bank is obliged to pay. There may be uncommon cases, however, in which there is doubt whether acceptance occurred. For example, if acceptance is based on receipt of payment by the beneficiary's bank under Section 4A–403 (a)(1) or (2), there may be cases in which the bank is not certain that payment has been received. There may also be cases in which there is doubt about whether the person demanding payment is the person identified in the payment order as beneficiary of the order.

The last clause of subsection (a) does not apply to cases in which a funds transfer is being used to pay an obligation and a dispute arises between the originator and the beneficiary concerning whether the obligation is in fact owed. For example, the originator may try to prevent payment to the beneficiary by the beneficiary's bank by alleging that the beneficiary is not entitled to payment because of fraud against the originator or a breach of contract relating to the obligation. The fraud or breach of contract claim of the originator may be grounds for recovery by the originator from the beneficiary after the beneficiary is paid, but it does not affect the obligation of the beneficiary's bank to pay the beneficiary. Unless the payment order has been cancelled pursuant to Section 4A–211(c), there is no excuse for refusing to pay the beneficiary and, in a proper case, the refusal may result in consequential damages. Except in the case of a book transfer, in which the beneficiary's bank is also the originator's bank, the originator of a funds transfer cannot cancel a payment order to the beneficiary's bank, with or without the consent of that bank, because the originator is not the sender of that order. Thus, the beneficiary's bank may safely ignore any instruction by the originator to withhold payment to the beneficiary.

4. Subsection (b) states the duty of the beneficiary's bank to notify the beneficiary of receipt of the order. If acceptance occurs under Section 4A–209(b)(1) the beneficiary is normally notified. Thus, subsection (b) applies primarily to cases in which acceptance occurs under Section 4A–209(b)(2) or (3). Notice under subsection (b) is not required if the person entitled to the notice agrees or a funds transfer system rule provides that notice is not required and the beneficiary is given notice of the rule. In ACH transactions the normal practice is not to give notice to the beneficiary unless notice is requested by the beneficiary. This practice

can be continued by adoption of a funds transfer system rule. Subsection (a) is not subject to variation by agreement or by a funds transfer system rule.

§ 4A.405. Payment by Beneficiary's Bank to Beneficiary

(a) If the beneficiary's bank credits an account of the beneficiary of a payment order, payment of the bank's obligation under Section 4A.404(a) occurs when and to the extent:

(1) the beneficiary is notified of the right to withdraw the credit;

(2) the bank lawfully applies the credit to a debt of the beneficiary; or

(3) funds with respect to the order are otherwise made available to the beneficiary by the bank.

(b) If the beneficiary's bank does not credit an account of the beneficiary of a payment order, the time when payment of the bank's obligation under Section 4A.404(a) occurs is governed by principles of law that determine when an obligation is satisfied.

(c) Except as provided by Subsections (d) and (e), if the beneficiary's bank pays the beneficiary of a payment order under a condition to payment or agreement of the beneficiary giving the bank the right to recover payment from the beneficiary if the bank does not receive payment of the order, the condition to payment or agreement is not enforceable.

(d) A funds transfer system rule may provide that payments made to beneficiaries of funds transfers through the system are provisional until receipt of payment by the beneficiary's bank of the payment order is accepted. A beneficiary's bank that makes a payment that is provisional under the rule is entitled to refund from the beneficiary if (i) the rule requires that both the beneficiary and the originator be given notice of the provisional nature of the payment before the funds transfer is initiated, (ii) the beneficiary, the beneficiary's bank and the originator's bank agreed to be bound by the rule, and (iii) the beneficiary's bank did not receive payment of the payment order that it accepted. If the beneficiary is obliged to refund payment to the beneficiary's bank, acceptance of the payment order by the beneficiary's bank is nullified and no payment by the originator of the funds transfer to the beneficiary occurs under Section 4A.406.

(e) This subsection applies to a funds transfer that includes a payment order transmitted over a funds transfer system that (i) nets obligations multilaterally among participants, and (ii) has in effect a loss-sharing agreement among participants for the purpose of providing funds necessary to complete settlement of the obligations of one or more participants that do not meet their settlement obligations. If the beneficiary's bank in the funds transfer accepts a payment order and the system fails to complete settlement pursuant to its rules with respect to any payment order in the funds transfer:

(1) the acceptance by the beneficiary's bank is nullified and no person has any right or obligation based on the acceptance;

(2) the beneficiary's bank is entitled to recover payment from the beneficiary;

(3) no payment by the originator to the beneficiary occurs under Section 4A.406; and

(4) subject to Section 4A.402(e), each sender in the funds transfer is excused from its obligation to pay its payment order under Section 4A.402(c) because the funds transfer has not been completed.

Added by Acts 1993, 73rd Leg., ch. 570, § 7, eff. Sept. 1, 1993.

Uniform Commercial Code Comment

1. This section defines when the beneficiary's bank pays the beneficiary and when the obligation of the beneficiary's bank under Section 4A–404 to pay the beneficiary is satisfied. In almost all cases the bank will credit an account of the beneficiary when it receives a payment order. In the typical case the beneficiary is paid when the beneficiary is given notice of the right to withdraw the credit. Subsection (a)(i). In some cases payment might be made to the beneficiary not by releasing funds to the beneficiary, but by applying the credit to a debt of the beneficiary. Subsection (a)(ii). In this case the beneficiary gets the benefit of the payment order because a debt of the beneficiary has been satisfied. The two principal cases in which payment will occur in this manner are setoff by the beneficiary's bank and payment of the proceeds of the payment order to a garnishing creditor of the beneficiary. These cases are discussed in Comment 2 to Section 4A–502.

2. If a beneficiary's bank releases funds to the beneficiary before it receives payment from the sender of the payment order, it assumes the risk that the sender may not pay the sender's order because of suspension of payments or other reason. Subsection (c). As stated in Comment 5 to Section 4A–209, the beneficiary's bank can protect itself against this risk by delaying acceptance. But if the bank accepts the order it is obliged to pay the beneficiary. If the beneficiary's bank has given the beneficiary notice of the right to withdraw a credit made to the beneficiary's account, the beneficiary has received payment from the bank. Once payment has been made to the beneficiary with respect to an obligation incurred by the bank under Section 4A–404(a), the payment cannot be recovered by the beneficiary's bank unless subsection (d) or (e) applies. Thus, a right to withdraw a credit cannot be revoked if the right to withdraw constitut-

ed payment of the bank's obligation. This principle applies even if funds were released as a "loan" (see Comment 5 to Section 4A-209), or were released subject to a condition that they would be repaid in the event the bank does not receive payment from the sender of the payment order, or the beneficiary agreed to return the payment if the bank did not receive payment from the sender.

3. Subsection (c) is subject to an exception stated in subsection (d) which is intended to apply to automated clearing house transfers. ACH transfers are made in batches. A beneficiary's bank will normally accept, at the same time and as part of a single batch, payment orders with respect to many different originator's banks. Comment 2 to Section 4A-206. The custom in ACH transactions is to release funds to the beneficiary early on the payment date even though settlement to the beneficiary's bank does not occur until later in the day. The understanding is that payments to beneficiaries are provisional until the beneficiary's bank receives settlement. This practice is similar to what happens when a depositary bank releases funds with respect to a check forwarded for collection. If the check is dishonored the bank is entitled to recover the funds from the customer. ACH transfers are widely perceived as check substitutes. Section 4A-405(d) allows the funds transfer system to adopt a rule making payments to beneficiaries provisional. If such a rule is adopted, a beneficiary's bank that releases funds to the beneficiary will be able to recover the payment if it doesn't receive payment of the payment order that it accepted. There are two requirements with respect to the funds transfer system rule. The beneficiary, the beneficiary's bank and the originator's bank must all agree to be bound by the rule and the rule must require that both the beneficiary and the originator be given notice of the provisional nature of the payment before the funds transfer is initiated. There is no requirement that the notice be given with respect to a particular funds transfer. Once notice of the provisional nature of the payment has been given, the notice is effective for all subsequent payments to or from the person to whom the notice was given. Subsection (d) provides only that the funds transfer system rule must require notice to the beneficiary and the originator. The beneficiary's bank will know what the rule requires, but it has no way of knowing whether the originator's bank complied with the rule. Subsection (d) does not require proof that the originator received notice. If the originator's bank failed to give the required notice and the originator suffered as a result, the appropriate remedy is an action by the originator against the originator's bank based on that failure. But the beneficiary's bank will not be able to get the benefit of subsection (d) unless the beneficiary had notice of the provisional nature of the payment because subsection (d) requires an agreement by the beneficiary to be bound by the rule. Implicit in an agreement to be bound by a rule that makes a payment provisional is a requirement that notice be given of what the rule provides. The notice can be part of the agreement or separately given. For example, notice can be given by providing a copy of the system's operating rules.

With respect to ACH transfers made through a Federal Reserve Bank acting as an intermediary bank, the Federal Reserve Bank is obliged under Section 4A-402(b) to pay a beneficiary's bank that accepts the payment order. Unlike Fedwire transfers, under current ACH practice a Federal Reserve Bank that processes a payment order does not obligate itself to pay if the originator's bank fails to pay the Federal Reserve Bank. It is assumed that the Federal Reserve will use its right of preemption which is recognized in Section 4A-107 to disclaim the Section 4A-402(b) obligation in ACH transactions if it decides to retain the provisional payment rule.

4. Subsection (e) is another exception to subsection (c). It refers to funds transfer systems having loss-sharing rules described in the subsection. CHIPS has proposed a rule that fits the description. Under the CHIPS loss-sharing rule the CHIPS banks will have agreed to contribute funds to allow the system to settle for payment orders sent over the system during the day in the event that one or more banks are unable to meet their settlement obligations. Subsection (e) applies only if CHIPS fails to settle despite the loss-sharing rule. Since funds under the loss-sharing rule will be instantly available to CHIPS and will be in an amount sufficient to cover any failure that can be reasonably anticipated, it is extremely unlikely that CHIPS would ever fail to settle. Thus, subsection (e) addresses an event that should never occur. If that event were to occur, all payment orders made over the system would be cancelled under the CHIPS rule. Thus, no bank would receive settlement, whether or not a failed bank was involved in a particular funds transfer. Subsection (e) provides that each funds transfer in which there is a payment order with respect to which there is a settlement failure is unwound. Acceptance by the beneficiary's bank in each funds transfer is nullified. The consequences of nullification are that the beneficiary has no right to receive or retain payment by the beneficiary's bank, no payment is made by the originator to the beneficiary and each sender in the funds transfer is, subject to Section 4A-402(e), not obliged to pay its payment order and is entitled to refund under Section 4A-402(d) if it has already paid.

§ 4A.406. Payment by Originator to Beneficiary; Discharge of Underlying Obligation

(a) Subject to Sections 4A.211(e) and 4A.405(d) and (e), the originator of a funds transfer pays the beneficiary of the originator's payment order:

(1) at the time a payment order for the benefit of the beneficiary is accepted by the beneficiary's bank in the funds transfer; and

(2) in an amount equal to the amount of the order accepted by the beneficiary's bank, but not more than the amount of the originator's order.

(b) If payment under Subsection (a) is made to satisfy an obligation, the obligation is discharged to the same extent discharge would result from payment to the beneficiary of the same amount in money, unless (i) the payment under Subsection (a) of this section was made by a means prohibited by the contract of the beneficiary with respect to the obligation, (ii) the beneficiary, within a reasonable time after receiving notice of receipt of the order by the beneficiary's bank, notified the originator of the beneficiary's refusal of the payment, (iii) funds with respect to the order were not withdrawn by the beneficiary or applied to a debt of the beneficiary, and (iv) the beneficiary would suffer a loss that could reasonably have been avoided if payment had been made by a means complying with the contract. If payment by the originator does not result in discharge under this section, the originator is subrogated to the rights of the beneficiary to receive payment from the beneficiary's bank under Section 4A.404(a).

(c) For the purpose of determining whether discharge of an obligation occurs under Subsection (b), if the beneficiary's bank accepts a payment order in an amount equal to the amount of the originator's payment order less charges of one or more receiving banks in the funds transfer, payment to the beneficiary is deemed to be in the amount of the originator's order unless upon demand by the beneficiary the originator does not pay the beneficiary the amount of the deducted charges.

(d) Rights of the originator or of the beneficiary of a funds transfer under this section may be varied only by agreement of the originator and the beneficiary.

Added by Acts 1993, 73rd Leg., ch. 570, § 7, eff. Sept. 1, 1993.

Uniform Commercial Code Comment

1. Subsection (a) states the fundamental rule of Article 4A that payment by the originator to the beneficiary is accomplished by providing to the beneficiary the obligation of the beneficiary's bank to pay. Since this obligation arises when the beneficiary's bank accepts a payment order, the originator pays the beneficiary at the time of acceptance and in the amount of the payment order accepted.

2. In a large percentage of funds transfers, the transfer is made to pay an obligation of the originator. Subsection (a) states that the beneficiary is paid by the originator when the beneficiary's bank accepts a payment order for the benefit of the beneficiary. When that happens the effect under subsection (b) is to substitute the obligation of the beneficiary's bank for the obligation of the originator. The effect is similar to that under Article 3 if a cashier's check payable to the beneficiary had been taken by the beneficiary. Normally, payment by funds transfer is sought by the beneficiary because it puts money into the hands of the beneficiary more quickly. As a practical matter the beneficiary and the originator will nearly always agree to the funds transfer in advance. Under subsection (b) acceptance by the beneficiary's bank will result in discharge of the obligation for which payment was made unless the beneficiary had made a contract with respect to the obligation which did not permit payment by the means used. Thus, if there is no contract of the beneficiary with respect to the means of payment of the obligation, acceptance by the beneficiary's bank of a payment order to the account of the beneficiary can result in discharge.

3. Suppose Beneficiary's contract stated that payment of an obligation owed by Originator was to be made by a cashier's check of Bank A. Instead Originator paid by a funds transfer to Beneficiary's account in Bank B. Bank B accepted a payment order for the benefit of Beneficiary by immediately notifying Beneficiary that the funds were available for withdrawal. Before Beneficiary had a reasonable opportunity to withdraw the funds Bank B suspended payments. Under the unless clause of subsection (b) Beneficiary is not required to accept the payment as discharging the obligation owed by Originator to Beneficiary if Beneficiary's contract means that Beneficiary was not required to accept payment by wire transfer. Beneficiary could refuse the funds transfer as payment of the obligation and could resort to rights under the underlying contract to enforce the obligation. The rationale is that Originator cannot impose the risk of Bank B's insolvency on Beneficiary if Beneficiary had specified another means of payment that did not entail that risk. If Beneficiary is required to accept Originator's payment, Beneficiary would suffer a loss that would not have occurred if payment had been made by a cashier's check on Bank A, and Bank A has not suspended payments. In this case Originator will have to pay twice. It is obliged to pay the amount of its payment order to the bank that accepted it and has to pay the obligation it owes to Beneficiary which has not been discharged. Under the last sentence of subsection (b) Originator is subrogated to Beneficiary's right to receive payment from Bank B under Section 4A–404(a).

4. Suppose Beneficiary's contract called for payment by a Fedwire transfer to Bank B, but the payment order accepted by Bank B was not a Fedwire transfer. Before the funds were withdrawn by Beneficiary, Bank B suspended payments. The sender of the payment order to Bank B paid the amount of the order to Bank B. In this case the payment by Originator did not comply with Beneficiary's contract, but the noncompliance did not result in a loss to Beneficiary as required by subsection (b)(iv). A Fedwire transfer avoids the risk of insolvency of the sender of the payment order to Bank B, but it does not affect the risk that Bank B will suspend payments before withdrawal of the funds by Beneficiary. Thus, the unless clause of subsection (b) is not applicable and the obligation owed to Beneficiary is discharged.

5. Charges of receiving banks in a funds transfer normally are nominal in relationship to the amount being paid by the originator to the beneficiary. Wire transfers are normally agreed to in advance and the parties may agree concerning how these charges are to be divided between the parties. Subsection (c) states a rule that applies in the absence of agreement. In some funds transfers charges of banks that execute payment orders are collected by deducting the charges from the amount of the payment order issued by the bank, i.e. the bank issues a payment order that is slightly less than the amount of the payment order that is being executed. The process is described in Comment 3 to Section 4A–302. The result in such a case is that the payment order accepted by the beneficiary's bank will be slightly less than the amount of the originator's order. Subsection (c) recognizes the principle that a beneficiary is entitled to full payment of a debt paid by wire transfer as a condition to

discharge. On the other hand, Subsection (c) prevents a beneficiary from denying the originator the benefit of the payment by asserting that discharge did not occur because deduction of bank charges resulted in less than full payment. The typical case is one in which the payment is made to exercise a valuable right such as an option which is unfavorable to the beneficiary. Subsection (c) allows discharge notwithstanding the deduction unless the originator fails to reimburse the beneficiary for the deducted charges after demand by the beneficiary.

[Sections 4A.407 to 4A.500 reserved for expansion]

SUBCHAPTER E. MISCELLANEOUS PROVISIONS

§ 4A.501. Variation by Agreement and Effect of Funds Transfer System Rule

(a) Except as otherwise provided in this chapter, the rights and obligations of a party to a funds transfer may be varied by agreement of the affected party.

(b) "Funds transfer system rule" means a rule of an association of banks (i) governing transmission of payment orders by means of a funds transfer system of the association or rights and obligations with respect to those orders, or (ii) to the extent the rule governs rights and obligations between banks that are parties to a funds transfer in which a Federal Reserve Bank, acting as an intermediary bank, sends a payment order to the beneficiary's bank. Except as otherwise provided in this chapter, a funds transfer system rule governing rights and obligations between participating banks using the system may be effective even if the rule conflicts with this chapter and indirectly affects another party to the funds transfer who does not consent to the rule. A funds transfer system rule may also govern rights and obligations of parties other than participating banks using the system to the extent stated in Sections 4A.404(c), 4A.405(d), and 4A.507(c).

Added by Acts 1993, 73rd Leg., ch. 570, § 7, eff. Sept. 1, 1993.

Uniform Commercial Code Comment

1. This section is designed to give some flexibility to Article 4A. Funds transfer system rules govern rights and obligations between banks that use the system. They may cover a wide variety of matters such as form and content of payment orders, security procedures, cancellation rights and procedures, indemnity rights, compensation rules for delays in completion of a funds transfer, time and method of settlement, credit restrictions with respect to senders of payment orders and risk allocation with respect to suspension of payments by a participating bank. Funds transfer system rules can be very effective in supplementing the provisions of Article 4A and in filling gaps that may be present in Article 4A. To the extent they do not conflict with Article 4A there is no problem with respect to their effectiveness. In that case they merely supplement Article 4A. Section 4A–501 goes further. It states that unless the contrary is stated, funds transfer system rules can override provisions of Article 4A. Thus, rights and obligations of a sender bank and a receiving bank with respect to each other can be different from that stated in Article 4A to the extent a funds transfer system rule applies. Since funds transfer system rules are defined as those governing the relationship between participating banks, a rule can have a direct effect only on participating banks. But a rule that affects the conduct of a participating bank may indirectly affect the rights of nonparticipants such as the originator or beneficiary of a funds transfer, and such a rule can be effective even though it may affect nonparticipants without their consent. For example, a rule might prevent execution of a payment order or might allow cancellation of a payment order with the result that a funds transfer is not completed or is delayed. But a rule purporting to define rights and obligations of nonparticipants in the system would not be effective to alter Article 4A rights because the rule is not within the definition of funds transfer system rule. Rights and obligations arising under Article 4A may also be varied by agreement of the affected parties, except to the extent Article 4A otherwise provides. Rights and obligations arising under Article 4A can also be changed by Federal Reserve regulations and operating circulars of Federal Reserve Banks. Section 4A–107.

2. Subsection (b)(ii) refers to ACH transfers. Whether an ACH transfer is made through an automated clearing house of a Federal Reserve Bank or through an automated clearing house of another association of banks, the rights and obligations of the originator's bank and the beneficiary's bank are governed by uniform rules adopted by various associations of banks in various parts of the nation. With respect to transfers in which a Federal Reserve Bank acts as intermediary bank these rules may be incorporated, in whole or in part, in operating circulars of the Federal Reserve Bank. Even if not so incorporated these rules can still be binding on the association banks. If a transfer is made through a Federal Reserve Bank, the rules are effective under subsection (b)(ii). If the transfer is not made through a Federal Reserve Bank, the association rules are effective under subsection (b)(i).

§ 4A.502. Creditor Process Served on Receiving Bank; Setoff by Beneficiary's Bank

(a) As used in this section, "creditor process" means levy, attachment, garnishment, notice of lien, sequestration, or similar process issued by or on behalf of a creditor or other claimant with respect to an account.

(b) This subsection applies to creditor process with respect to an authorized account of the sender of a payment order if the creditor process is served on the receiving bank. For the purpose of determining rights with respect to the creditor process, if the receiving bank accepts the payment order, the balance in the authorized account is deemed to be reduced by the amount of the payment order to the extent the bank did not otherwise receive payment of the order, unless the creditor process is served at a time and in a manner affording the bank a reasonable opportunity to act on it before the bank accepts the payment order.

(c) If a beneficiary's bank has received a payment order for payment to the beneficiary's account in the bank the following rules apply:

(1) The bank may credit the beneficiary's account, and the amount credited may be set off against an obligation owed by the beneficiary to the bank or may be applied to satisfy creditor process served on the bank with respect to the account.

(2) The bank may credit the beneficiary's account and allow withdrawal of the amount credited unless creditor process with respect to the account is served at a time and in a manner affording the bank a reasonable opportunity to act to prevent withdrawal.

(3) If creditor process with respect to the beneficiary's account has been served and the bank has had a reasonable opportunity to act on it, the bank may not reject the payment order except for a reason unrelated to the service of process.

(d) Creditor process with respect to a payment by the originator to the beneficiary pursuant to a funds transfer may be served only on the beneficiary's bank with respect to the debt owed by that bank to the beneficiary. Any other bank served with the creditor process is not obliged to act with respect to the process.

Added by Acts 1993, 73rd Leg., ch. 570, § 7, eff. Sept. 1, 1993.

Uniform Commercial Code Comment

1. When a receiving bank accepts a payment order, the bank normally receives payment from the sender by debiting an authorized account of the sender. In accepting the sender's order the bank may be relying on a credit balance in the account. If creditor process is served on the bank with respect to the account before the bank accepts the order but the bank employee responsible for the acceptance was not aware of the creditor process at the time the acceptance occurred, it is unjust to the bank to allow the creditor process to take the credit balance on which the bank may have relied. Subsection (b) allows the bank to obtain payment from the sender's account in this case. Under that provision, the balance in the sender's account to which the creditor process applies is deemed to be reduced by the amount of the payment order unless there was sufficient time for notice of the service of creditor process to be received by personnel of the bank responsible for the acceptance.

2. Subsection (c) deals with payment orders issued to the beneficiary's bank. The bank may credit the beneficiary's account when the order is received, but under Section 4A–404(a) the bank incurs no obligation to pay the beneficiary until the order is accepted pursuant to Section 4A–209(b). Thus, before acceptance, the credit to the beneficiary's account is provisional. But under Section 4A–209(b) acceptance occurs if the beneficiary's bank pays the beneficiary pursuant to Section 4A–405(a). Under that provision, payment occurs if the credit to the beneficiary's account is applied to a debt of the beneficiary. Subsection (c)(1) allows the bank to credit the beneficiary's account with respect to a payment order and to accept the order by setting off the credit against an obligation owed to the bank or applying the credit to creditor process with respect to the account.

Suppose a beneficiary's bank receives a payment order for the benefit of a customer. Before the bank accepts the order, the bank learns that creditor process has been served on the bank with respect to the customer's account. Normally there is no reason for a beneficiary's bank to reject a payment order, but if the beneficiary's account is garnished, the bank may be faced with a difficult choice. If it rejects the order, the garnishing creditor's potential recovery of funds of the beneficiary is frustrated. It may be faced with a claim by the creditor that the rejection was a wrong to the creditor. If the bank accepts the order, the effect is to allow the creditor to seize funds of its customer, the beneficiary. Subsection (c)(3) gives the bank no choice in this case. It provides that it may not favor its customer over the creditor by rejecting the order. The beneficiary's bank may rightfully reject only if there is an independent basis for rejection.

3. Subsection (c)(2) is similar to subsection (b). Normally the beneficiary's bank will release funds to the beneficiary shortly after acceptance or it will accept by releasing funds. Since the bank is bound by a garnishment order served before funds are released to the beneficiary, the bank might suffer a loss if funds were released without knowledge that a garnishment order had been served. Subsection (c)(2) protects the bank if it did not have adequate notice of the garnishment when the funds were released.

4. A creditor may want to reach funds involved in a funds transfer. The creditor may try to do so by serving process on the originator's bank, an intermediary bank or the beneficiary's bank. The purpose of subsection (d) is to guide the creditor and the court as to the proper method of reaching the funds involved in a funds transfer. A creditor of the originator can levy on the account of the originator in the originator's bank before the funds transfer is initiated, but that levy is subject to the limitations stated in subsection (b). The creditor of the originator cannot reach any other funds because no property of the originator is being transferred. A creditor of the beneficiary cannot levy on property of the originator and until the funds transfer is completed by acceptance by the beneficiary's bank of a payment order for the benefit of the beneficiary, the beneficiary has no property interest in the funds transfer which the beneficiary's creditor can reach. A creditor of the beneficiary that wants to reach the funds to be received by the beneficiary must serve

creditor process on the beneficiary's bank to reach the obligation of the beneficiary's bank to pay the beneficiary which arises upon acceptance by the beneficiary's bank under Section 4A–404(a).

5. "Creditor process" is defined in subsection (a) to cover a variety of devices by which a creditor of the holder of a bank account or a claimant to a bank account can seize the account. Procedure and nomenclature varies widely from state to state. The term used in Section 4A–502 is a generic term.

§ 4A.503. Injunction or Restraining Order With Respect to Funds Transfer

For proper cause and in compliance with applicable law, a court may restrain (i) a person from issuing a payment order to initiate a funds transfer, (ii) an originator's bank from executing the payment order of the originator, or (iii) the beneficiary's bank from releasing funds to the beneficiary or the beneficiary from withdrawing the funds. A court may not otherwise restrain a person from issuing a payment order, paying or receiving payment of a payment order, or otherwise acting with respect to a funds transfer.

Added by Acts 1993, 73rd Leg., ch. 570, § 7, eff. Sept. 1, 1993.

Uniform Commercial Code Comment

This section is related to Section 4A–502(d) and to Comment 4 to Section 4A–502. It is designed to prevent interruption of a funds transfer after it has been set in motion. The initiation of a funds transfer can be prevented by enjoining the originator or the originator's bank from issuing a payment order. After the funds transfer is completed by acceptance of a payment order by the beneficiary's bank, that bank can be enjoined from releasing funds to the beneficiary or the beneficiary can be enjoined from withdrawing the funds. No other injunction is permitted. In particular, intermediary banks are protected, and injunctions against the originator and the originator's bank are limited to issuance of a payment order. Except for the beneficiary's bank, nobody can be enjoined from paying a payment order, and no receiving bank can be enjoined from receiving payment from the sender of the order that it accepted.

§ 4A.504. Order in Which Items and Payment Orders May be Charged to Account; Order of Withdrawals From Account

(a) If a receiving bank has received more than one payment order of the sender or one or more payment orders and other items that are payable from the sender's account, the bank may charge the sender's account with respect to the various orders and items in any sequence.

(b) In determining whether a credit to an account has been withdrawn by the holder of the account or applied to a debt of the holder of the account, credits first made to the account are first withdrawn or applied.

Added by Acts 1993, 73rd Leg., ch. 570, § 7, eff. Sept. 1, 1993.

Uniform Commercial Code Comment

1. Subsection (a) concerns priority among various obligations that are to be paid from the same account. A customer may have written checks on its account with the receiving bank and may have issued one or more payment orders payable from the same account. If the account balance is not sufficient to cover all of the checks and payment orders, some checks may be dishonored and some payment orders may not be accepted. Although there is no concept of wrongful dishonor of a payment order in Article 4A in the absence of an agreement to honor by the receiving bank, some rights and obligations may depend on the amount in the customer's account. Section 4A–209(b)(3) and Section 4A–210(b). Whether dishonor of a check is wrongful also may depend upon the balance in the customer's account. Under subsection (a), the bank is not required to consider the competing items and payment orders in any particular order. Rather it may charge the customer's account for the various items and orders in any order. Suppose there is $12,000 in the customer's account. If a check for $5,000 is presented for payment and the bank receives a $10,000 payment order from the customer, the bank could dishonor the check and accept the payment order. Dishonor of the check is not wrongful because the account balance was less than the amount of the check after the bank charged the account $10,000 on account of the payment order. Or, the bank could pay the check and not execute the payment order because the amount of the order is not covered by the balance in the account.

2. Subsection (b) follows Section 4–208(b) in using the first-in-first-out rule for determining the order in which credits to an account are withdrawn.

§ 4A.505. Preclusion of Objection to Debit of Customer's Account

If a receiving bank has received payment from its customer with respect to a payment order issued in the name of the customer as sender and accepted by the bank, and the customer received notification reasonably identifying the order, the customer is precluded from asserting that the bank is not entitled to retain the payment unless the customer notifies the bank of the customer's objection to the payment within one year after the notification was received by the customer.

Added by Acts 1993, 73rd Leg., ch. 570, § 7, eff. Sept. 1, 1993.

Uniform Commercial Code Comment

This section is in the nature of a statute of repose for objecting to debits made to the customer's account. A receiving bank that executes payment orders of a customer may have received payment from the customer by debiting the customer's account with respect to a payment order that the customer was not required to pay. For example, the payment order may not have been authorized or verified pursuant to Section 4A–202 or the funds transfer may not have been completed. In either case the receiving bank is obliged to refund the payment to the customer and this obligation to refund payment cannot be varied by agreement. Section 4A–204 and Section 4A–402. Refund may also be required if the receiving bank is not entitled to payment from the customer because the bank erroneously executed a payment order. Section 4A–303. A similar analysis applies to that case. Section 4A–402(d) and (f) require refund and the obligation to refund may not be varied by agreement. Under 4A–505, however, the obligation to refund may not be asserted by the customer if the customer has not objected to the debiting of the account within one year after the customer received notification of the debit.

§ 4A.506. Rate of Interest

(a) If, under this chapter, a receiving bank is obliged to pay interest with respect to a payment order issued to the bank, the amount payable may be determined (i) by agreement of the sender and receiving bank, or (ii) by funds transfer system rule if the payment order is transmitted through a funds transfer system.

(b) If the amount of interest is not determined by an agreement or rule as stated in Subsection (a), the amount is calculated by multiplying the applicable Federal Funds rate by the amount on which interest is payable, and then multiplying the product by the number of days for which interest is payable. The applicable Federal Funds rate is the average of the Federal Funds rates published by the Federal Reserve Bank of New York for each of the days for which interest is payable divided by 360. The Federal Funds rate for any day on which a published rate is not available is the same as the published rate for the next preceding day for which there is a published rate. If a receiving bank that accepted a payment order is required to refund payment to the sender of the order because the funds transfer was not completed, but the failure to complete was not due to any fault by the bank, the interest payable is reduced by a percentage equal to the reserve requirement on deposits of the receiving bank.

Added by Acts 1993, 73rd Leg., ch. 570, § 7, eff. Sept. 1, 1993.

Uniform Commercial Code Comment

1. A receiving bank is required to pay interest on the amount of a payment order received by the bank in a number of situations. Sometimes the interest is payable to the sender and in other cases it is payable to either the originator or the beneficiary of the funds transfer. The relevant provisions are Section 4A–204(a), Section 4A–209(b)(3), Section 4A–210(b), Section 4A–305(a), Section 4A–402(d) and Section 4A–404(b). The rate of interest may be governed by a funds transfer system rule or by agreement as stated in subsection (a). If subsection (a) doesn't apply, the rate is determined under subsection (b). Subsection (b) is illustrated by the following example. A bank is obliged to pay interest on $1,000,000 for three days, July 3, July 4, and July 5. The published Fed Funds rate is .082 for July 3 and .081 for July 5. There is no published rate for July 4 because that day is not a banking day. The rate for July 3 applies to July 4. The applicable Fed Funds rate is .08167 (the average of .082, .082, and .081) divided by 360 which equals .0002268. The amount of interest payable is $1,000,000 × .0002268 × 3 = $680.40.

2. In some cases, interest is payable in spite of the fact that there is no fault by the receiving bank. The last sentence of subsection (b) applies to those cases. For example, a funds transfer might not be completed because the beneficiary's bank rejected the payment order issued to it by the originator's bank or an intermediary bank. Section 4A–402(c) provides that the originator is not obliged to pay its payment order and Section 4A–402(d) provides that the originator's bank must refund any payment received plus interest. The requirement to pay interest in this case is not based on fault by the originator's bank. Rather, it is based on restitution. Since the originator's bank had the use of the originator's money, it is required to pay the originator for the value of that use. The value of that use is not determined by multiplying the interest rate by the refundable amount because the originator's bank is required to deposit with the Federal Reserve a percentage of the bank's deposits as a reserve requirement. Since that deposit does not bear interest, the bank had use of the refundable amount reduced by a percentage equal to the reserve requirement. If the reserve requirement is 12%, the amount of interest payable by the bank under the formula stated in subsection (b) is reduced by 12%.

§ 4A.507. Choice of Law

(a) The following rules apply unless the affected parties otherwise agree or Subsection (c) applies:

(1) The rights and obligations between the sender of a payment order and the receiving bank are governed by the law of the jurisdiction in which the receiving bank is located.

(2) The rights and obligations between the beneficiary's bank and the beneficiary are governed by the law of the jurisdiction in which the beneficiary's bank is located.

(3) The issue of when payment is made pursuant to a funds transfer by the originator to the beneficiary is governed by the law of the jurisdiction in which the beneficiary's bank is located.

(b) If the parties described by each subdivision of Subsection (a) have made an agreement selecting the law of a particular jurisdiction to govern rights and obligations between each other, the law of that jurisdiction governs those rights and obligations as to matters of construction and interpretation, whether or not the payment order or the funds transfer bears a reasonable relation to that jurisdiction, and as to validity, to the extent permitted by Section 1.301 of this code.

(c) A funds transfer system rule may select the law of a particular jurisdiction to govern (i) rights and obligations between participating banks with respect to payment orders transmitted or processed through the system, or (ii) the rights and obligations of some or all parties to a funds transfer any part of which is carried out by means of the system. A choice of law made pursuant to clause (i) is binding on participating banks. A choice of law made pursuant to clause (ii) is binding on the originator, other sender, or a receiving bank having notice that the funds transfer system might be used in the funds transfer and of the choice of law by the system when the originator, other sender, or receiving bank issued or accepted a payment order. The beneficiary of a funds transfer is bound by the choice of law if, when the funds transfer is initiated, the beneficiary has notice that the funds transfer system might be used in the funds transfer and of the choice of law by the system. The law of a jurisdiction selected pursuant to this Subsection (c) may govern, as to matters of construction and interpretation, whether or not the law bears a reasonable relation to the matter in issue.

(d) In the event of inconsistency between an agreement under Subsection (b) and a choice-of-law rule under Subsection (c), the agreement under Subsection (b) prevails.

(e) If a funds transfer is made by use of more than one funds transfer system and there is inconsistency between choice-of law rules of the systems, the matter in issue is governed by the law of the selected jurisdiction that has the most significant relationship to the matter in issue.

Added by Acts 1993, 73rd Leg., ch. 570, § 7, eff. Sept. 1, 1993. Amended by Acts 2003, 78th Leg., ch. 542, § 16, eff. Sept. 1, 2003.

Uniform Commercial Code Comment

1. Funds transfers are typically interstate or international in character. If part of a funds transfer is governed by Article 4A and another part is governed by other law, the rights and obligations of parties to the funds transfer may be unclear because there is no clear consensus in various jurisdictions concerning the juridical nature of the transaction. Unless all of a funds transfer is governed by a single law it may be very difficult to predict the result if something goes wrong in the transfer. Section 4A–507 deals with this problem. Subsection (b) allows parties to a funds transfer to make a choice-of-law agreement. Subsection (c) allows a funds transfer system to select the law of a particular jurisdiction to govern funds transfers carried out by means of the system. Subsection (a) states residual rules if no choice of law has occurred under subsection (b) or subsection (c).

2. Subsection (a) deals with three sets of relationships. Rights and obligations between the sender of a payment order and the receiving bank are governed by the law of the jurisdiction in which the receiving bank is located. If the receiving bank is the beneficiary's bank the rights and obligations of the beneficiary are also governed by the law of the jurisdiction in which the receiving bank is located. Suppose Originator, located in Canada, sends a payment order to Originator's Bank located in a state in which Article 4A has been enacted. The order is for payment to an account of Beneficiary in a bank in England. Under subsection (a)(1), the rights and obligations of Originator and Originator's Bank toward each other are governed by Article 4A if an action is brought in a court in the Article 4A state. If an action is brought in a Canadian court, the conflict of laws issue will be determined by Canadian law which might or might not apply the law of the state in which Originator's Bank is located. If that law is applied, the execution of Originator's order will be governed by Article 4A, but with respect to the payment order of Originator's Bank to the English bank, Article 4A may or may not be applied with respect to the rights and obligations between the two banks. The result may depend upon whether action is brought in a court in the state in which Originator's Bank is located or in an English court. Article 4A is binding only on a court in a state that enacts it. It can have extraterritorial effect only to the extent courts of another jurisdiction are willing to apply it. Subsection (c) also bears on the issues discussed in this Comment.

Under Section 4A–406 payment by the originator to the beneficiary of the funds transfer occurs when the beneficiary's bank accepts a payment order for the benefit of the beneficiary. A jurisdiction in which Article 4A is not in effect may follow a different rule or it may not have a clear rule. Under Section 4A–507(a)(3) the issue is governed by the law of the jurisdiction in which the beneficiary's bank is located. Since the payment to the beneficiary is made through the beneficiary's bank it is reasonable that the issue of when payment occurs be governed by the law of the jurisdiction in which the bank is located. Since it is difficult in many cases to determine where a beneficiary is located, the location of the beneficiary's bank provides a more certain rule.

3. Subsection (b) deals with choice-of-law agreements and it gives maximum freedom of choice. Since the law of funds transfers is not highly developed in the case law there may be a strong incentive to choose the law of a jurisdiction in which Article 4A is in effect because it provides a greater degree of certainty with respect to the rights of various parties. With respect to commercial transactions, it is often said that "[u]niformity and predictability based upon commercial convenience are the prime considerations in making the choice of governing law ...." R. Leflar, American Conflicts Law, § 185 (1977). Subsection (b) is derived in part from recently enacted choice-of-law rules in the States of New York and California. N.Y. Gen. Obligations Law 5–1401 (McKinney's 1989 Supp.) and California Civil Code § 1646.5. This broad endorsement of freedom of contract is an enhancement of the approach taken by Restatement (Second) of Conflict of Laws § 187(b) (1971). The Restatement recognizes the basic right of freedom of contract, but the freedom granted the parties may be more limited than the freedom granted here. Under the formulation of the Restatement, if there is no substantial relationship to the jurisdiction whose law is selected and there is no "other" reasonable basis for the parties' choice, then the selection of the parties need not be honored by a court. Further, if the choice is violative of a fundamental policy of a state which has a materially greater interest than the chosen state, the selection could be disregarded by a court. Those limitations are not found in subsection (b).

4. Subsection (c) may be the most important provision in regard to creating uniformity of law in funds transfers. Most rights stated in Article 4A regard parties who are in privity of contract such as originator and beneficiary, sender and receiving bank, and beneficiary's bank and beneficiary. Since they are in privity they can make a choice of law by agreement. But that is not always the case. For example, an intermediary bank that improperly executes a payment order is not in privity with either the originator or the beneficiary. The ability of a funds transfer system to make a choice of law by rule is a convenient way of dispensing with individual agreements and to cover cases in which agreements are not feasible. It is probable that funds transfer systems will adopt a governing law to increase the certainty of commercial transactions that are effected over such systems. A system rule might adopt the law of an Article 4A state to govern transfers on the system in order to provide a consistent, unitary, law governing all transfers made on the system. To the extent such system rules develop, individual choice-of-law agreements become unnecessary.

Subsection (c) has broad application. A system choice of law applies not only to rights and obligations between banks that use the system, but may also apply to other parties to the funds transfer so long as some part of the transfer was carried out over the system. The originator and any other sender or receiving bank in the funds transfer is bound if at the time it issues or accepts a payment order it had notice that the funds transfer involved use of the system and that the system chose the law of a particular jurisdiction. Under Section 4A–107, the Federal Reserve by regulation could make a similar choice of law to govern funds transfers carried out by use of Federal Reserve Banks. Subsection (d) is a limitation on subsection (c). If parties have made a choice-of-law agreement that conflicts with a choice of law made under subsection (c), the agreement prevails.

5. Subsection (e) addresses the case in which a funds transfer involves more than one funds transfer system and the systems adopt conflicting choice-of-law rules. The rule that has the most significant relationship to the matter at issue prevails. For example, each system should be able to make a choice of law governing payment orders transmitted over that system without regard to a choice of law made by another system.

State Bar Committee Comments

The provisions of Section 4A.507(b) represent a dramatic departure from existing common law and other Texas statutes and could have substantial unforeseen consequences if one or more states pass legislation that changes the rules set forth in Chapter 4A. If all states adopt Chapter 4A, this provision should have little impact or danger, except in international transactions. Some commentators have questioned the constitutionality of the kind of choice of law provisions embodied in Section 4A.507(b). The better position is to defer to the general rules set forth in Section 1.105 with respect to the validity of contractual provisions, but permit parties to agree as to the laws of a jurisdiction with respect to matters of construction and interpretation. Section 4A.507(b) has been amended to correspond to this position.

CHAPTER 5. LETTERS OF CREDIT

Section

Acts 1999, 76th Leg., ch. 4, § 1 amended Chapter 5 effective September 1, 1999. The former Chapter 5, Letters of Credit, consisting of §§ 5.101 to 5.117, was amended as Chapter 5, Letters of Credit, consisting of §§ 5.101 to 5.118.

DISPOSITION TABLE

Showing where the subject matter of provisions contained in former Chapter 5, Letters of Credit, may be found in Chapter 5, Letters of Credit, as amended by Acts 1999, 76th Leg., ch. 4, § 1.

Former Section	Amended Section
5.101	5.101
5.102	5.103(a)
5.103	5.102, 5.106(a)
5.104	5.102(a)(6), (14), 5.104
5.105	5.105
5.106	5.106
5.107	5.107
5.108	—
5.109	5.108
5.110	—
5.111	5.110
5.112	5.102(a)(12), 5.108(b), (c), (h)
5.113	—
5.114	5.108(a), (i), 5.109(a)
5.115	5.111
5.116	5.112, 5.114
5.117	—

§ 5.101. Short Title

This chapter may be cited as Uniform Commercial Code—Letters of Credit.

Amended by Acts 1999, 76th Leg., ch. 4, § 1, eff. Sept. 1, 1999.

Uniform Commercial Code Comment

The Official Comment to the original Section 5–101 was a remarkably brief inaugural address. Noting that letters of credit had not been the subject of statutory enactment and that the law concerning them had been developed in the cases, the Comment stated that Article 5 was intended "within its limited scope" to set an independent theoretical frame for the further development of letters of credit. That statement addressed accurately conditions as they existed when the statement was made, nearly half a century ago. Since Article 5 was originally drafted, the use of letters of credit has expanded and developed, and the case law concerning these developments is, in some respects, discordant.

Revision of Article 5 therefore has required reappraisal both of the statutory goals and of the extent to which particular statutory provisions further or adversely affect achievement of those goals.

The statutory goal of Article 5 was originally stated to be: (1) to set a substantive theoretical frame that describes the function and legal nature of letters of credit; and (2) to preserve procedural flexibility in order to accommodate further development of the efficient use of letters of credit. A letter of credit is an idiosyncratic form of undertaking that supports performance of an obligation incurred in a separate financial, mercantile, or other transaction or arrangement. The objectives of the original and revised Article 5 are best achieved (1) by defining the peculiar characteristics of a letter of credit that distinguish it and the legal consequences of its use from other forms of assurance such as secondary guarantees, performance bonds, and insurance policies, and from ordinary contracts, fiduciary engagements, and escrow arrangements; and (2) by preserving flexibility through variation by agreement in order to respond to and accommodate developments in custom and usage that are not inconsistent with the essential definitions and substantive mandates of the statute. No statute can, however, prescribe the manner in which such substantive rights and duties are to be enforced or imposed without risking stultification of wholesome developments in the letter of credit mechanism. Letter of credit law should remain responsive to commercial reality and in particular to the customs and expectations of the international banking and mercantile community. Courts should read the terms of this article in a manner consistent with these customs and expectations.

The subject matter in Article 5, letters of credit, may also be governed by an international convention that is now being drafted by UNCITRAL, the draft Convention on Independent Guarantees and Standby Letters of Credit. The Uniform Customs and Practice is an international body of trade practice that is commonly adopted by international and domestic letters of credit and as such is the "law of the transaction" by agreement of the parties. Article 5 is consistent with and was influenced by the rules in the existing version of the UCP. In addition to the UCP and the international convention, other bodies of law apply to letters of credit. For example, the federal bankruptcy law applies to letters of credit with respect to applicants and beneficiaries that are in bankruptcy; regulations of the Federal Reserve Board and the Comptroller of the Currency lay out requirements for banks that issue letters of credit and describe how letters of credit are to be treated for calculating asset risk and for the purpose of loan limitations. In addition there is an array of anti-boycott and other similar laws that may affect the issuance and performance of letters of credit. All of these laws are beyond the scope of Article 5, but in certain circumstances they will override Article 5.

§ 5.102. Definitions

(a) in this chapter:

(1) "Adviser" means a person who, at the request of the issuer, a confirmer, or another adviser, notifies or requests another adviser to notify the beneficiary that a letter of credit has been issued, confirmed, or amended.

(2) "Applicant" means a person at whose request or for whose account a letter of credit is issued. The term includes a person who requests an issuer to issue a letter of credit on behalf of another if the person making the request undertakes an obligation to reimburse the issuer.

(3) "Beneficiary" means a person who under the terms of a letter of credit is entitled to have its complying presentation honored. The term in-

cludes a person to whom drawing rights have been transferred under a transferable letter of credit.

(4) "Confirmer" means a nominated person who undertakes, at the request or with the consent of the issuer, to honor a presentation under a letter of credit issued by another.

(5) "Dishonor" of a letter of credit means failure timely to honor or to take an interim action, such as acceptance of a draft, that may be required by the letter of credit.

(6) "Document" means a draft or other demand, document of title, investment security, certificate, invoice, or other record, statement, or representation of fact, law, right, or opinion (i) that is presented in a written or other medium permitted by the letter of credit or, unless prohibited by the letter of credit, by the standard practice referred to in Section 5.108(e); and (ii) that is capable of being examined for compliance with the terms and conditions of the letter of credit. A document may not be oral.

(7) "Good faith" means honesty in fact in the conduct or transaction concerned.

(8) "Honor" of a letter of credit means performance of the issuer's undertaking in the letter of credit to pay or deliver an item of value. Unless the letter of credit otherwise provides, "honor" occurs:

(A) upon payment;

(B) if the letter of credit provides for acceptance, upon acceptance of a draft and, at maturity, its payment; or

(C) if the letter of credit provides for incurring a deferred obligation, upon incurring the obligation and, at maturity, its performance.

(9) "Issuer" means a bank or other person that issues a letter of credit, but does not include an individual who makes an engagement for personal, family, or household purposes.

(10) "Letter of credit" means a definite undertaking that satisfies the requirements of Section 5.104 by an issuer to a beneficiary at the request or for the account of an applicant or, in the case of a financial institution, to itself or for its own account, to honor a documentary presentation by payment or delivery of an item of value.

(11) "Nominated person" means a person whom the issuer:

(A) designates or authorizes to pay, accept, negotiate, or otherwise give value under a letter of credit; and

(B) undertakes by agreement or custom and practice to reimburse.

(12) "Presentation" means delivery of a document to an issuer or nominated person for honor or giving of value under a letter of credit.

(13) "Presenter" means a person making a presentation as or on behalf of a beneficiary or nominated person.

(14) "Record" means information that is inscribed on a tangible medium or that is stored in an electronic or other medium and is retrievable in perceivable form.

(15) "Successor of a beneficiary" means a person who succeeds to substantially all of the rights of a beneficiary by operation of law, including a corporation with or into which the beneficiary has been merged or consolidated, an administrator, an executor, a personal representative, a trustee in bankruptcy, a debtor in possession, a liquidator, and a receiver.

(b) Definitions in other chapters of this code applying to this chapter and the sections in which they appear are:

"Accept" or "Acceptance".	Section 3.409.
"Value".	Sections 3.303 and 4.211.

(c) Chapter 1 contains certain additional general definitions and principles of construction and interpretation applicable throughout this chapter.

Amended by Acts 1999, 76th Leg., ch. 4, § 1, eff. Sept. 1, 1999.

Uniform Commercial Code Comment

1. Since no one can be a confirmer unless that person is a nominated person as defined in Section 5–102(a)(11), those who agree to "confirm" without the designation or authorization of the issuer are not confirmers under Article 5. Nonetheless, the undertakings to the beneficiary of such persons may be enforceable by the beneficiary as letters of credit issued by the "confirmer" for its own account or as guarantees or contracts outside of Article 5.

2. The definition of "document" contemplates and facilitates the growing recognition of electronic and other nonpaper media as "documents," however, for the time being, data in those media constitute documents only in certain circumstances. For example, a facsimile received by an issuer would be a document only if the letter of credit explicitly permitted it, if the standard practice authorized it and the letter did not prohibit it, or the agreement of the issuer and beneficiary permitted it. The fact that data transmitted in a nonpaper

(unwritten) medium can be recorded on paper by a recipient's computer printer, facsimile machine, or the like does not under current practice render the data so transmitted a "document." A facsimile or S.W.I.F.T. message received directly by the issuer is in an electronic medium when it crosses the boundary of the issuer's place of business. One wishing to make a presentation by facsimile (an electronic medium) will have to procure the explicit agreement of the issuer (assuming that the standard practice does not authorize it). Article 5 contemplates that electronic documents may be presented under a letter of credit and the provisions of this Article should be read to apply to electronic documents as well as tangible documents. An electronic document of title is delivered through the voluntary transfer of control. Article 1, Section 1–201 (definition of "delivery"). See Article 7, Section 7–106 on control of an electronic document. Where electronic transmissions are authorized neither by the letter of credit nor by the practice, the beneficiary may transmit the data electronically to its agent who may be able to put it in written form and make a conforming presentation. Cf. Article 7, Section 7–105 on reissuing an electronic document in a tangible medium.

3. "Good faith" continues in revised Article 5 to be defined as "honesty in fact." "Observance of reasonable standards of fair dealing" has not been added to the definition. The narrower definition of "honesty in fact" reinforces the "independence principle" in the treatment of "fraud," "strict compliance," "preclusion," and other tests affecting the performance of obligations that are unique to letters of credit. This narrower definition—which does not include "fair dealing"—is appropriate to the decision to honor or dishonor a presentation of documents specified in a letter of credit. The narrower definition is also appropriate for other parts of revised Article 5 where greater certainty of obligations is necessary and is consistent with the goals of speed and low cost. It is important that U.S. letters of credit have continuing vitality and competitiveness in international transactions.

For example, it would be inconsistent with the "independence" principle if any of the following occurred: (i) the beneficiary's failure to adhere to the standard of "fair dealing" in the underlying transaction or otherwise in presenting documents were to provide applicants and issuers with an "unfairness" defense to dishonor even when the documents complied with the terms of the letter of credit; (ii) the issuer's obligation to honor in "strict compliance in accordance with standard practice" were changed to "reasonable compliance" by use of the "fair dealing" standard, or (iii) the preclusion against the issuer (Section 5–108(d)) were modified under the "fair dealing" standard to enable the issuer later to raise additional deficiencies in the presentation. The rights and obligations arising from presentation, honor, dishonor and reimbursement, are independent and strict, and thus "honesty in fact" is an appropriate standard.

The contract between the applicant and beneficiary is not governed by Article 5, but by applicable contract law, such as Article 2 or the general law of contracts. "Good faith" in that contract is defined by other law, such as Section 2–103(1)(b) or Restatement of Contracts 2d, § 205, which incorporate the principle of "fair dealing" in most cases, or a State's common law or other statutory provisions that may apply to that contract.

The contract between the applicant and the issuer (sometimes called the "reimbursement" agreement) is governed in part by this article (e.g., Sections 5–108(i), 5–111(b), and 5–103(c)) and partly by other law (e.g., the general law of contracts). The definition of good faith in Section 5–102(a)(7) applies only to the extent that the reimbursement contract is governed by provisions in this article; for other purposes good faith is defined by other law.

4. Payment and acceptance are familiar modes of honor. A third mode of honor, incurring an unconditional obligation, has legal effects similar to an acceptance of a time draft but does not technically constitute an acceptance. The practice of making letters of credit available by "deferred payment undertaking" as now provided in UCP 500 has grown up in other countries and spread to the United States. The definition of "honor" will accommodate that practice.

5. The exclusion of consumers from the definition of "issuer" is to keep creditors from using a letter of credit in consumer transactions in which the consumer might be made the issuer and the creditor would be the beneficiary. If that transaction were recognized under Article 5, the effect would be to leave the consumer without defenses against the creditor. That outcome would violate the policy behind the Federal Trade Commission Rule in 16 CFR Part 433. In a consumer transaction, an individual cannot be an issuer where that person would otherwise be either the principal debtor or a guarantor.

6. The label on a document is not conclusive; certain documents labelled "guarantees" in accordance with European (and occasionally, American) practice are letters of credit. On the other hand, even documents that are labelled "letter of credit" may not constitute letters of credit under the definition in Section 5–102(a). When a document labelled a letter of credit requires the issuer to pay not upon the presentation of documents, but upon the determination of an extrinsic fact such as applicant's failure to perform a construction contract, and where that condition appears on its face to be fundamental and would, if ignored, leave no obligation to the issuer under the document labelled letter of credit, the issuer's undertaking is not a letter of credit. It is probably some form of suretyship or other contractual arrangement and may be enforceable as such. See Sections 5–102(a)(10) and 5–103(d). Therefore, undertakings whose fundamental term requires an issuer to look beyond documents and beyond conventional reference to the clock, calendar, and practices concerning the form of various documents are not governed by Article 5. Although Section 5–108(g) recognizes that certain nondocumentary conditions can be included in a letter of credit without denying the undertaking the status of letter of credit, that section does not apply to cases where the nondocumentary condition is fundamental to the issuer's obligation. The rules in Sections 5–102(a)(10), 5–103(d), and 5–108(g) approve the conclusion in *Wichita Eagle & Beacon Publishing Co. v. Pacific Nat. Bank*, 493 F.2d 1285 (9th Cir.1974).

The adjective "definite" is taken from the UCP. It approves cases that deny letter of credit status to documents that are unduly vague or incomplete. See, e.g., *Transparent Products Corp. v. Paysaver Credit Union*, 864 F.2d 60 (7th Cir.1988). Note, however, that no particular phrase or label is necessary to establish a letter of credit. It is sufficient if the undertaking of the issuer shows that it is intended to be a letter of credit. In most cases the parties' intention will be indicated by a label on the undertaking itself indicating that it is a "letter of credit," but no such language is necessary.

A financial institution may be both the issuer and the applicant or the issuer and the beneficiary. Such letters are sometimes issued by a bank in support of the bank's own lease obligations or on behalf of one of its divisions as an applicant or to one of its divisions as beneficiary, such as an overseas branch. Because wide use of letters of credit in which the issuer and the applicant or the issuer and the beneficiary are the same would endanger the unique status of letters of credit, only financial institutions are authorized to issue them.

In almost all cases the ultimate performance of the issuer under a letter of credit is the payment of money. In rare cases the issuer's obligation is to deliver stock certificates or the like. The definition of letter of credit in Section 5–102(a)(10) contemplates those cases.

7. Under the UCP any bank is a nominated bank where the letter of credit is "freely negotiable." A letter of credit might also nominate by the following: "We hereby engage with the drawer, indorsers, and bona fide holders of drafts drawn under and in compliance with the terms of this credit that the same will be duly honored on due presentation" or "available with any bank by negotiation." A restricted negotiation credit might be "available with x bank by negotiation" or the like.

Several legal consequences may attach to the status of nominated person. First, when the issuer nominates a person, it is authorizing that person to pay or give value and is authorizing the beneficiary to make presentation to that person. Unless the letter of credit provides otherwise, the beneficiary need not present the documents to the issuer before the letter of credit expires; it need only present those documents to the nominated person. Secondly, a nominated person that gives value in good faith has a right to payment from the issuer despite fraud. Section 5–109(a)(1).

8. A "record" must be in or capable of being converted to a perceivable form. For example, an electronic message recorded in a computer memory that could be printed from that memory could constitute a record. Similarly, a tape recording of an oral conversation could be a record.

9. Absent a specific agreement to the contrary, documents of a beneficiary delivered to an issuer or nominated person are considered to be presented under the letter of credit to which they refer, and any payment or value given for them is considered to be made under that letter of credit. As the court held in *Alaska Textile Co. v. Chase Manhattan Bank, N.A.*, 982 F.2d 813, 820 (2d Cir.1992), it takes a "significant showing" to make the presentation of a beneficiary's documents for "collection only" or otherwise outside letter of credit law and practice.

10. Although a successor of a beneficiary is one who succeeds "by operation of law," some of the successions contemplated by Section 5–102(a)(15) will have resulted from voluntary action of the beneficiary such as merger of a corporation. Any merger makes the successor corporation the "successor of a beneficiary" even though the transfer occurs partly by operation of law and partly by the voluntary action of the parties. The definition excludes certain transfers, where no part of the transfer is "by operation of law"—such as the sale of assets by one company to another.

11. "Draft" in Article 5 does not have the same meaning it has in Article 3. For example, a document may be a draft under Article 5 even though it would not be a negotiable instrument, and therefore would not qualify as a draft under Section 3–104(e).

State Bar Committee Comments

BA Commercial Corp. v. Hynutek, Inc., 705 S.W.2d 713, 715 (Tex. App.—Dallas 1986, no writ) refused to recognize as a letter of credit a "Standby Guarantee of Payment" that had been issued by a nonbank. This case might be decided differently under Revised Chapter 5. Neither the label of a document nor its issue by a nonbank is dispositive. The key issue is whether there is a definite undertaking to honor a documentary presentation by either payment or delivery of an item of value. See Revised § 5.102(a)(9) and (10).

Texas cases have recognized that a fundamental nondocumentary condition precludes the existence of a letter of credit. See, e.g., *Gunn-Olson-Stordahl Joint Venture v. Early Bank*, 748 S.W.2d 316, 318–20 (Tex. App.—Eastland, writ den. 1988) (writing requiring investigation of whether the person to be paid had performed the underlying contract was a guaranty rather than a letter of credit). The Revised § 5.102(a)(10) definition of "letter of credit" reflects this limitation upon the scope of Revised Chapter 5.

In *Temple Eastex, Inc. v. Addison Bank*, 672 S.W.2d 793, 797–98 (Tex.1984), which involved a letter of credit that required presentation of a "sight draft" but did not define the term, the record evidence of custom and usage in the banking industry established that a demand letter would suffice. Revised § 5.108(a) and (e) codify this holding by making the standard practice of financial institutions regularly issuing letters of credit determine whether a presentation of documents appears on its face to comply strictly with the terms and conditions of a letter of credit. On the other hand, Revised Chapter 5 rejects the *Temple-Eastex* position that ordinary principles of contract construction can be as important as the custom and usage of financial institutions in determining whether strict compliance exists. 672 S.W.2d at 798. Under Revised § 5.108(a) and (e), the standard practice of financial institutions regularly issuing letters of credit is the principal determinant of strict compliance.

§ 5.103. Scope

(a) This chapter applies to letters of credit and to certain rights and obligations arising out of transactions involving letters of credit.

(b) The statement of a rule in this chapter does not by itself require, imply, or negate application of the same or a different rule to a situation not provided for, or to a person not specified, in this chapter.

(c) With the exception of this subsection, Subsections (a) and (d), Sections 5.102(a)(9) and (10), Section 5.106(d), Section 5.110(c), and Section 5.114(d) and except to the extent prohibited in Sections 1.302 and 5.117(d), the effect of this chapter may be varied by agreement or by a provision stated or incorporated by reference in an undertaking. A term in an agreement or undertaking generally excusing liability or generally limiting remedies for failure to perform obligations is not sufficient to vary obligations prescribed by this chapter.

(d) Rights and obligations of an issuer to a beneficiary or a nominated person under a letter of credit are independent of the existence, performance, or nonperformance of a contract or arrangement out of which the letter of credit arises or which underlies it, including contracts or arrangements between the issuer and the applicant and between the applicant and the beneficiary.

Amended by Acts 1999, 76th Leg., ch. 4, § 1, eff. Sept. 1, 1999; Acts 2003, 78th Leg., ch. 542, § 17, eff. Sept. 1, 2003.

Uniform Commercial Code Comment

1. Sections 5–102(a)(10) and 5–103 are the principal limits on the scope of Article 5. Many undertakings in commerce and contract are similar, but not identical to the letter of credit. Principal among those are "secondary," "accessory," or "suretyship" guarantees. Although the word "guarantee" is sometimes used to describe an independent obligation like that of the issuer of a letter of credit (most often in the case of European bank undertakings but occasionally in the case of undertakings of American banks), in the United States the word "guarantee" is more typically used to describe a suretyship transaction in which the "guarantor" is only secondarily liable and has the right to assert the underlying debtor's defenses. This article does not apply to secondary or accessory guarantees and it is important to recognize the distinction between letters of credit and those guarantees. It is often a defense to a secondary or accessory guarantor's liability that the underlying debt has been discharged or that the debtor has other defenses to the underlying liability. In letter of credit law, on the other hand, the independence principle recognized throughout Article 5 states that the issuer's liability is independent of the underlying obligation. That the beneficiary may have breached the underlying contract and thus have given a good defense on that contract to the applicant against the beneficiary is no defense for the issuer's refusal to honor. Only staunch recognition of this principle by the issuers and the courts will give letters of credit the continuing vitality that arises from the certainty and speed of payment under letters of credit. To that end, it is important that the law not carry into letter of credit transactions rules that properly apply only to secondary guarantees or to other forms of engagement.

2. Like all of the provisions of the Uniform Commercial Code, Article 5 is supplemented by Section 1–103 and, through it, by many rules of statutory and common law. Because this article is quite short and has no rules on many issues that will affect liability with respect to a letter of credit transaction, law beyond Article 5 will often determine rights and liabilities in letter of credit transactions. Even within letter of credit law, the article is far from comprehensive; it deals only with "certain" rights of the parties. Particularly with respect to the standards of performance that are set out in Section 5–108, it is appropriate for the parties and the courts to turn to customs and practice such as the Uniform Customs and Practice for Documentary Credits, currently published by the International Chamber of Commerce as I.C.C. Pub. No. 500 (hereafter UCP). Many letters of credit specifically adopt the UCP as applicable to the particular transaction. Where the UCP are adopted but conflict with Article 5 and except where variation is prohibited, the UCP terms are permissible contractual modifications under Sections 1–102(3) and 5–103(c). See Section 5–116(c). Normally Article 5 should not be considered to conflict with practice except when a rule explicitly stated in the UCP or other practice is different from a rule explicitly stated in Article 5.

Except by choosing the law of a jurisdiction that has not adopted the Uniform Commercial Code, it is not possible entirely to escape the Uniform Commercial Code. Since incorporation of the UCP avoids only "conflicting" Article 5 rules, parties who do not wish to be governed by the nonconflicting provisions of Article 5 must normally either adopt the law of a jurisdiction other than a State of the United States or state explicitly the rule that is to govern. When rules of custom and practice are incorporated by reference, they are considered to be explicit terms of the agreement or undertaking.

Neither the obligation of an issuer under Section 5–108 nor that of an adviser under Section 5–107 is an obligation of the kind that is invariable under Section 1–102(3). Section 5–103(c) and Comment 1 to Section 5–108 make it clear that the applicant and the issuer may agree to almost any provision establishing the obligations of the issuer to the applicant. The last sentence of subsection (c) limits the power of the issuer to achieve that result by a nonnegotiated disclaimer or limitation of remedy.

What the issuer could achieve by an explicit agreement with its applicant or by a term that explicitly defines its duty, it cannot accomplish by a general disclaimer. The restriction on disclaimers in the last sentence of subsection (c) is based more on procedural than on substantive unfairness. Where, for example, the reimbursement agreement provides explicitly that the issuer need not examine any documents, the applicant understands the risk it has undertaken. A term in a reimbursement agreement which states generally that an issuer will not be liable unless it has acted in "bad faith" or committed "gross negligence" is ineffective under Section 5–103(c). On the other hand, less general terms such as terms that permit issuer reliance on an oral or electronic message believed in good faith to have been received from the applicant or terms that entitle an issuer to reimbursement when it honors a "substantially" though not "strictly" complying presentation, are effective. In each case the question is whether the disclaimer or limitation is sufficiently clear and explicit in reallocating a liability or risk that is allocated differently under a variable Article 5 provision.

Of course, no term in a letter of credit, whether incorporated by reference to practice rules or stated specifically, can free an issuer from a conflicting contractual obligation to its applicant. If, for example, an issuer promised its applicant that it would pay only against an inspection certificate of a particular company but failed to require such a certificate in its letter of credit or made the requirement only a nondocumentary condition that had to be disregarded, the issuer might be obliged to pay the beneficiary even though its payment might violate its contract with its applicant.

3. Parties should generally avoid modifying the definitions in Section 5–102. The effect of such an agreement is almost inevitably unclear. To say that something is a "guarantee" in the typical domestic transaction is to say that the parties intend that particular legal rules apply to it. By acknowledging that something is a guarantee, but asserting that it is to be treated as a "letter of credit," the parties leave a court uncertain about where the rules on guarantees stop and those concerning letters of credit begin.

State Bar Committee Comments

Texas cases have recognized the independence of an issuer's obligation to honor a letter of credit from the transaction that gave rise to the letter of credit. See, e.g., *Republic National Bank v. Northwest National Bank*, 578 S.W.2d 109, 114–16 (Tex.1978) (an issuer is obligated to honor a conforming presentation of documents without regard to an underlying contract). Revised § 5.103(d) codifies this principle. Revised § 5.103(c), which lists the provisions of Revised Chapter 5 that are not subject to waiver, has been amended to add § 5.110(c), a Texas non-uniform amendment.

§ 5.104. Formal Requirements

A letter of credit, confirmation, advice, transfer, amendment, or cancellation may be issued in any form that is a record and is authenticated:

(1) by a signature; or

(2) in accordance with the agreement of the parties or the standard practice referred to in Section 5.108(e).

Amended by Acts 1999, 76th Leg., ch. 4, § 1, eff. Sept. 1, 1999.

Uniform Commercial Code Comment

1. Neither Section 5–104 nor the definition of letter of credit in Section 5–102(a)(10) requires inclusion of all the terms that are normally contained in a letter of credit in order for an undertaking to be recognized as a letter of credit under Article 5. For example, a letter of credit will typically specify the amount available, the expiration date, the place where presentation should be made, and the documents that must be presented to entitle a person to honor. Undertakings that have the formalities required by Section 5–104 and meet the conditions specified in Section 5–102(a)(10) will be recognized as letters of credit even though they omit one or more of the items usually contained in a letter of credit.

2. The authentication specified in this section is authentication only of the identity of the issuer, confirmer, or adviser.

An authentication agreement may be by system rule, by standard practice, or by direct agreement between the parties. The reference to practice is intended to incorporate future developments in the UCP and other practice rules as well as those that may arise spontaneously in commercial practice.

3. Many banking transactions, including the issuance of many letters of credit, are now conducted mostly by electronic means. For example, S.W.I.F.T. is currently used to transmit letters of credit from issuing to advising banks. The letter of credit text so transmitted may be printed at the advising bank, stamped "original" and provided to the beneficiary in that form. The printed document may then be used as a way of controlling and recording payments and of recording and authorizing assignments of proceeds or transfers of rights under the letter of credit. Nothing in this section should be construed to conflict with that practice.

To be a record sufficient to serve as a letter of credit or other undertaking under this section, data must have a durability consistent with that function. Because consideration is not required for a binding letter of credit or similar undertaking (Section 5–105) yet those undertakings are to be strictly construed (Section 5–108), parties to a letter of credit transaction are especially dependent on the continued availability of the terms and conditions of the letter of credit or other undertaking. By declining to specify any particular medium in which the letter of credit must be established or communicated, Section 5–104 leaves room for future developments.

§ 5.105. Consideration

Consideration is not required to issue, amend, transfer, or cancel a letter of credit, advice, or confirmation.

Amended by Acts 1999, 76th Leg., ch. 4, § 1, eff. Sept. 1, 1999.

Uniform Commercial Code Comment

It is not to be expected that any issuer will issue its letter of credit without some form of remuneration. But it is not expected that the beneficiary will know what the issuer's remuneration was or whether in fact there was any identifiable remuneration in a given case. And it might be difficult for the beneficiary to prove the issuer's remuneration. This section dispenses with this proof and is consistent with the position of Lord Mansfield in *Pillans v. Van Mierop*, 97 Eng.Rep. 1035 (K.B. 1765) in making consideration irrelevant.

§ 5.106. Issuance, Amendment, Cancellation, and Duration

(a) A letter of credit is issued and becomes enforceable according to its terms against the issuer when the issuer sends or otherwise transmits it to the person requested to advise or to the beneficiary. A letter of credit is revocable only if it so provides.

(b) After a letter of credit is issued, rights and obligations of a beneficiary, applicant, confirmer, and issuer are not affected by an amendment or cancellation to which that person has not consented except to the extent the letter of credit provides that it is revocable or that the issuer may amend or cancel the letter of credit without that consent.

(c) If there is no stated expiration date or other provision that determines its duration, a letter of credit expires one year after its stated date of issuance or, if no date is stated, after the date on which it is issued.

(d) A letter of credit that states that it is perpetual expires five years after its stated date of issuance or, if no date is stated, after the date on which it is issued.

Amended by Acts 1999, 76th Leg., ch. 4, § 1, eff. Sept. 1, 1999.

Uniform Commercial Code Comment

1. This section adopts the position taken by several courts, namely that letters of credit that are silent as to revocability are irrevocable. See, e.g., *Weyerhaeuser Co. v. First Nat. Bank*, 27 UCC Rep.Serv. 777 (S.D. Iowa 1979); West Va. Hous. Dev. Fund v. Sroka, 415 F.Supp. 1107 (W.D.Pa.1976). This is the position of the current UCP (500). Given the usual commercial understanding and purpose of letters of credit, revocable letters of credit offer unhappy possibilities for misleading the parties who deal with them.

2. A person can consent to an amendment by implication. For example, a beneficiary that tenders documents for honor that conform to an amended letter of credit but not to the original letter of credit has probably consented to the amendment. By the same token an applicant that has procured the issuance of a transferable letter of credit has consented to its transfer and to performance under the letter of credit by a person to whom the beneficiary's rights are duly transferred. If some, but not all of the persons involved in a letter of credit transaction consent to performance that does not strictly conform to the original letter of credit, those persons assume the risk that other nonconsenting persons may insist on strict compliance with the original letter of credit. Under subsection (b) those not consenting are not bound. For example, an issuer might agree to amend its letter of credit or honor documents presented after the expiration date in the belief that the applicant has consented or will consent to the amendment or will waive presentation after the original expiration date. If that belief is mistaken, the issuer is bound to the beneficiary by the terms of the letter of credit as amended or waived, even though it may be unable to recover from the applicant.

In general, the rights of a recognized transferee beneficiary cannot be altered without the transferee's consent, but the same is not true of the rights of assignees of proceeds from the beneficiary. When the beneficiary makes a complete transfer of its interest that is effective under the terms for transfer established by the issuer, adviser, or other party controlling transfers, the beneficiary no longer has an interest in the letter of credit, and the transferee steps into the shoes of the beneficiary as the one with rights under the letter of credit. Section 5–102(a)(3). When there is a partial transfer, both the original beneficiary and the transferee beneficiary have an interest in performance of the letter of credit and each expects that its rights will not be altered by amendment unless it consents.

The assignee of proceeds under a letter of credit from the beneficiary enjoys no such expectation. Notwithstanding an assignee's notice to the issuer of the assignment of proceeds, the assignee is not a person protected by subsection (b). An assignee of proceeds should understand that its rights can be changed or completely extinguished by amendment or cancellation of the letter of credit. An assignee's claim is precarious, for it depends entirely upon the continued existence of the letter of credit and upon the beneficiary's preparation and presentation of documents that would entitle the beneficiary to honor under Section 5–108.

3. The issuer's right to cancel a revocable letter of credit does not free it from a duty to reimburse a nominated person who has honored, accepted, or undertaken a deferred obligation prior to receiving notice of the amendment or cancellation. Compare UCP Article 8.

4. Although all letters of credit should specify the date on which the issuer's engagement expires, the failure to specify an expiration date does not invalidate the letter of credit, or diminish or relieve the obligation of any party with respect to the letter of credit. A letter of credit that may be revoked or terminated at the discretion of the issuer by notice to the beneficiary is not "perpetual."

§ 5.107. Confirmer, Nominated Person, and Adviser

(a) A confirmer is directly obligated on a letter of credit and has the rights and obligations of an issuer to the extent of its confirmation. The confirmer also has rights against and obligations to the issuer as if the issuer were an applicant and the confirmer had issued the letter of credit at the request and for the account of the issuer.

(b) A nominated person who is not a confirmer is not obligated to honor or otherwise give value for a presentation.

(c) A person requested to advise may decline to act as an adviser. An adviser that is not a confirmer is not obligated to honor or give value for a presentation.

An adviser undertakes to the issuer and to the beneficiary accurately to advise the terms of the letter of credit, confirmation, amendment, or advice received by that person and undertakes to the beneficiary to check the apparent authenticity of the request to advise. Even if the advice is inaccurate, the letter of credit, confirmation, or amendment is enforceable as issued.

(d) A person who notifies a transferee beneficiary of the terms of a letter of credit, confirmation, amendment, or advice has the rights and obligations of an adviser under Subsection (c). The terms in the notice to the transferee beneficiary may differ from the terms in any notice to the transferor beneficiary to the extent permitted by the letter of credit, confirmation, amendment, or advice received by the person who so notifies.

Amended by Acts 1999, 76th Leg., ch. 4, § 1, eff. Sept. 1, 1999.

Uniform Commercial Code Comment

1. A confirmer has the rights and obligations identified in Section 5–108. Accordingly, unless the context otherwise requires, the terms "confirmer" and "confirmation" should be read into this article wherever the terms "issuer" and "letter of credit" appear.

A confirmer that has paid in accordance with the terms and conditions of the letter of credit is entitled to reimbursement by the issuer even if the beneficiary committed fraud (see Section 5–109(a)(1)(ii)) and, in that sense, has greater rights against the issuer than the beneficiary has. To be entitled to reimbursement from the issuer under the typical confirmed letter of credit, the confirmer must submit conforming documents, but the confirmer's presentation to the issuer need not be made before the expiration date of the letter of credit.

A letter of credit confirmation has been analogized to a guarantee of issuer performance, to a parallel letter of credit issued by the confirmer for the account of the issuer or the letter of credit applicant or both, and to a back-to-back letter of credit in which the confirmer is a kind of beneficiary of the original issuer's letter of credit. Like letter of credit undertakings, confirmations are both unique and flexible, so that no one of these analogies is perfect, but unless otherwise indicated in the letter of credit or confirmation, a confirmer should be viewed by the letter of credit issuer and the beneficiary as an issuer of a parallel letter of credit for the account of the original letter of credit issuer. Absent a direct agreement between the applicant and a confirmer, normally the obligations of a confirmer are to the issuer not the applicant, but the applicant might have a right to injunction against a confirmer under Section 5–109 or warranty claim under Section 5–110, and either might have claims against the other under Section 5–117.

2. No one has a duty to advise until that person agrees to be an adviser or undertakes to act in accordance with the instructions of the issuer. Except where there is a prior agreement to serve or where the silence of the adviser would be an acceptance of an offer to contract, a person's failure to respond to a request to advise a letter of credit does not in and of itself create any liability, nor does it establish a relationship of issuer and adviser between the two. Since there is no duty to advise a letter of credit in the absence of a prior agreement, there can be no duty to advise it timely or at any particular time. When the adviser manifests its agreement to advise by actually doing so (as is normally the case), the adviser cannot have violated any duty to advise in a timely way. This analysis is consistent with the result of *Sound of Market Street v. Continental Bank International*, 819 F.2d 384 (3d Cir.1987) which held that there is no such duty. This section takes no position on the reasoning of that case, but does not overrule the result. By advising or agreeing to advise a letter of credit, the adviser assumes a duty to the issuer and to the beneficiary accurately to report what it has received from the issuer, but, beyond determining the apparent authenticity of the letter, an adviser has no duty to investigate the accuracy of the message it has received from the issuer. "Checking" the apparent authenticity of the request to advise means only that the prospective adviser must attempt to authenticate the message (e.g., by "testing" the telex that comes from the purported issuer), and if it is unable to authenticate the message must report that fact to the issuer and, if it chooses to advise the message, to the beneficiary. By proper agreement, an adviser may disclaim its obligation under this section.

3. An issuer may issue a letter of credit which the adviser may advise with different terms. The issuer may then believe that it has undertaken a certain engagement, yet the text in the hands of the beneficiary will contain different terms, and the beneficiary would not be entitled to honor if the documents it submitted did not comply with the terms of the letter of credit as originally issued. On the other hand, if the adviser also confirmed the letter of credit, then as a confirmer it will be independently liable on the letter of credit as advised and confirmed. If in that situation the beneficiary's ultimate presentation entitled it to honor under the terms of the confirmation but not under those in the original letter of credit, the confirmer would have to honor but might not be entitled to reimbursement from the issuer.

4. When the issuer nominates another person to "pay," "negotiate," or otherwise to take up the documents and give value, there can be confusion about the legal status of the nominated person. In rare cases the person might actually be an agent of the issuer and its act might be the act of the issuer itself. In most cases the nominated person is not an agent of the issuer and has no authority to act on the issuer's behalf. Its "nomination" allows the beneficiary to present to it and earns it certain rights to payment under Section 5–109 that others do not enjoy. For example, when an issuer issues a "freely negotiable credit," it contemplates that banks or others might take up documents under that credit and advance value against them, and it is agreeing to pay those persons but only if the presentation to the issuer made by the nominated person complies with the credit. Usually there will be no agreement to pay, negotiate, or to serve in any other capacity by the nominated person, therefore the nominated person will have the right to decline to take the documents. It may return them or agree merely to act as a

forwarding agent for the documents but without giving value against them or taking any responsibility for their conformity to the letter of credit.

§ 5.108. Issuer's Rights and Obligations

(a) Except as otherwise provided in Section 5.109, an issuer shall honor a presentation that, as determined by the standard practice referred to in Subsection (e), appears on its face strictly to comply with the terms and conditions of the letter of credit. Except as otherwise provided in Section 5.113 and unless otherwise agreed with the applicant, an issuer shall dishonor a presentation that does not appear so to comply.

(b) An issuer has a reasonable time after presentation, but not beyond the end of the seventh business day of the issuer after the date of its receipt of documents:

(1) to honor;

(2) if the letter of credit provides for honor to be completed more than seven business days after presentation, to accept a draft or incur a deferred obligation; or

(3) to give notice to the presenter of discrepancies in the presentation.

(c) Except as otherwise provided in Subsection (d), an issuer is precluded from asserting as a basis for dishonor any discrepancy if timely notice is not given or any discrepancy not stated in the notice if timely notice is given.

(d) Failure to give the notice specified in Subsection (b) or to mention fraud, forgery, or expiration in the notice does not preclude the issuer from asserting as a basis for dishonor fraud or forgery as described in Section 5.109(a) or expiration of the letter of credit before presentation.

(e) An issuer shall observe standard practice of financial institutions that regularly issue letters of credit. Determination of the issuer's observance of the standard practice is a matter of interpretation for the court. The court shall offer the parties a reasonable opportunity to present evidence of the standard practice.

(f) An issuer is not responsible for:

(1) the performance or nonperformance of the underlying contract, arrangement, or transaction;

(2) an act or omission of others; or

(3) observance or knowledge of the usage of a particular trade other than the standard practice referred to in Subsection (e).

(g) If an undertaking constituting a letter of credit under Section 5.102(a)(10) contains nondocumentary conditions, an issuer shall disregard the nondocumentary conditions and treat them as if they were not stated.

(h) An issuer that has dishonored a presentation shall return the documents or hold them at the disposal of, and send advice to that effect to, the presenter.

(i) An issuer that has honored a presentation as permitted or required by this chapter:

(1) is entitled to be reimbursed by the applicant in immediately available funds not later than the date of its payment of funds;

(2) takes the documents free of claims of the beneficiary or presenter;

(3) is precluded from asserting a right of recourse on a draft under Sections 3.414 and 3.415;

(4) except as otherwise provided in Sections 5.110 and 5.117, is precluded from restitution of money paid or other value given by mistake to the extent the mistake concerns discrepancies in the documents or tender that are apparent on the face of the presentation; and

(5) is discharged to the extent of its performance under the letter of credit unless the issuer honored a presentation in which a required signature of a beneficiary was forged.

Amended by Acts 1999, 76th Leg., ch. 4, § 1, eff. Sept. 1, 1999.

Uniform Commercial Code Comment

1. This section combines some of the duties previously included in Sections 5–114 and 5–109. Because a confirmer has the rights and duties of an issuer, this section applies equally to a confirmer and an issuer. See Section 5–107(a).

The standard of strict compliance governs the issuer's obligation to the beneficiary and to the applicant. By requiring that a "presentation" appear strictly to comply, the section requires not only that the documents themselves appear on their face strictly to comply, but also that the other terms of the letter of credit such as those dealing with the time and place of presentation are strictly complied with. Typically, a letter of credit will provide that presentation is timely if made to the issuer, confirmer, or any other nominated person prior to expiration of the letter of credit. Accordingly, a nominated person that has honored a demand or otherwise given value before expiration will have a right to reimbursement from the issuer even though presentation to the issuer is made after the expiration of the letter of credit.

Conversely, where the beneficiary negotiates documents to one who is not a nominated person, the beneficiary or that person acting on behalf of the beneficiary must make presentation to a nominated person, confirmer, or issuer prior to the expiration date.

This section does not impose a bifurcated standard under which an issuer's right to reimbursement might be broader than a beneficiary's right to honor. However, the explicit deference to standard practice in Section 5–108(a) and (e) and elsewhere expands issuers' rights of reimbursement where that practice so provides. Also, issuers can and often do contract with their applicants for expanded rights of reimbursement. Where that is done, the beneficiary will have to meet a more stringent standard of compliance as to the issuer than the issuer will have to meet as to the applicant. Similarly, a nominated person may have reimbursement and other rights against the issuer based on this article, the UCP, bank-to-bank reimbursement rules, or other agreement or undertaking of the issuer. These rights may allow the nominated person to recover from the issuer even when the nominated person would have no right to obtain honor under the letter of credit.

The section adopts strict compliance, rather than the standard that commentators have called "substantial compliance," the standard arguably applied in *Banco Español de Credito v. State Street Bank and Trust Company*, 385 F.2d 230 (1st Cir.1967) and *Flagship Cruises Ltd. v. New England Merchants Nat. Bank*, 569 F.2d 699 (1st Cir.1978). Strict compliance does not mean slavish conformity to the terms of the letter of credit. For example, standard practice (what issuers do) may recognize certain presentations as complying that an unschooled layman would regard as discrepant. By adopting standard practice as a way of measuring strict compliance, this article indorses the conclusion of the court in *New Braunfels Nat. Bank v. Odiorne*, 780 S.W.2d 313 (Tex. Ct.App. 1989) (beneficiary could collect when draft requested payment on "Letter of Credit No. 86–122–5" and letter of credit specified "Letter of Credit No. 86–122–S" holding strict compliance does not demand oppressive perfectionism). The section also indorses the result in *Tosco Corp. v. Federal Deposit Ins. Corp.*, 723 F.2d 1242 (6th Cir.1983). The letter of credit in that case called for "drafts Drawn under Bank of Clarksville Letter of Credit Number 105." The draft presented stated "drawn under Bank of Clarksville, Clarksville, Tennessee letter of Credit No. 105." The court correctly found that despite the change of upper case "L" to a lower case "l" and the use of the word "No." instead of "Number," and despite the addition of the words "Clarksville, Tennessee," the presentation conformed. Similarly a document addressed by a foreign person to General Motors as "Jeneral Motors" would strictly conform in the absence of other defects.

Identifying and determining compliance with standard practice are matters of interpretation for the court, not for the jury. As with similar rules in Sections 4A–202(c) and 2–302, it is hoped that there will be more consistency in the outcomes and speedier resolution of disputes if the responsibility for determining the nature and scope of standard practice is granted to the court, not to a jury. Granting the court authority to make these decisions will also encourage the salutary practice of courts' granting summary judgment in circumstances where there are no significant factual disputes. The statute encourages outcomes such as *American Coleman Co. v. Intrawest Bank*, 887 F.2d 1382 (10th Cir. 1989), where summary judgment was granted.

In some circumstances standards may be established between the issuer and the applicant by agreement or by custom that would free the issuer from liability that it might otherwise have. For example, an applicant might agree that the issuer would have no duty whatsoever to examine documents on certain presentations (e.g., those below a certain dollar amount). Where the transaction depended upon the issuer's payment in a very short time period (e.g., on the same day or within a few hours of presentation), the issuer and the applicant might agree to reduce the issuer's responsibility for failure to discover discrepancies. By the same token, an agreement between the applicant and the issuer might permit the issuer to examine documents exclusively by electronic or electro-optical means. Neither those agreements nor others like them explicitly made by issuers and applicants violate the terms of Section 5–108(a) or (b) or Section 5–103(c).

2. Section 5–108(a) balances the need of the issuer for time to examine the documents against the possibility that the examiner (at the urging of the applicant or for fear that it will not be reimbursed) will take excessive time to search for defects. What is a "reasonable time" is not extended to accommodate an issuer's procuring a waiver from the applicant. See Article 14c of the UCP.

Under both the UCC and the UCP the issuer has a reasonable time to honor or give notice. The outside limit of that time is measured in business days under the UCC and in banking days under the UCP, a difference that will rarely be significant. Neither business nor banking days are defined in Article 5, but a court may find useful analogies in Regulation CC, 12 CFR 229.2, in state law outside of the Uniform Commercial Code, and in Article 4.

Examiners must note that the seven-day period is not a safe harbor. The time within which the issuer must give notice is the lesser of a reasonable time or seven business days. Where there are few documents (as, for example, with the mine run standby letter of credit), the reasonable time would be less than seven days. If more than a reasonable time is consumed in examination, no timely notice is possible. What is a "reasonable time" is to be determined by examining the behavior of those in the business of examining documents, mostly banks. Absent prior agreement of the issuer, one could not expect a bank issuer to examine documents while the beneficiary waited in the lobby if the normal practice was to give the documents to a person who had the opportunity to examine those together with many others in an orderly process. That the applicant has not yet paid the issuer or that the applicant's account with the issuer is insufficient to cover the amount of the draft is not a basis for extension of the time period.

This section does not preclude the issuer from contacting the applicant during its examination; however, the decision to honor rests with the issuer, and it has no duty to seek a waiver from the applicant or to notify the applicant of receipt of the documents. If the issuer dishonors a conforming presentation, the beneficiary will be entitled to the remedies under Section 5–111, irrespective of the applicant's views.

Even though the person to whom presentation is made cannot conduct a reasonable examination of documents within the time after presentation and before the expiration date, presentation establishes the parties' rights. The beneficiary's right to honor or the issuer's right to dishonor arises upon presentation at the place provided in the letter of credit even though it might take the person to whom presentation has been made several days to determine whether honor or dishonor is the proper course. The issuer's time for honor or giving notice of dishonor may be extended or shortened by a term in the letter of credit. The time for the issuer's performance may be otherwise modified or waived in accordance with Section 5–106.

The issuer's time to inspect runs from the time of its "receipt of documents." Documents are considered to be received only when they are received at the place specified for presentation by the issuer or other party to whom presentation is made. "Receipt of documents" when documents of title are presented must be read in light of the definition of "delivery" in Article 1, Section 1–201 and the definition of "presentment" in Section 5–102(a)(12).

Failure of the issuer to act within the time permitted by subsection (b) constitutes dishonor. Because of the preclusion in subsection (c) and the liability that the issuer may incur under Section 5–111 for wrongful dishonor, the effect of such a silent dishonor may ultimately be the same as though the issuer had honored, i.e., it may owe damages in the amount drawn but unpaid under the letter of credit.

3. The requirement that the issuer send notice of the discrepancies or be precluded from asserting discrepancies is new to Article 5. It is taken from the similar provision in the UCP and is intended to promote certainty and finality.

The section thus substitutes a strict preclusion principle for the doctrines of waiver and estoppel that might otherwise apply under Section 1–103. It rejects the reasoning in *Flagship Cruises Ltd. v. New England Merchants' Nat. Bank*, 569 F.2d 699 (1st Cir.1978) and *Wing On Bank Ltd. v. American Nat. Bank & Trust Co.*, 457 F.2d 328 (5th Cir. 1972) where the issuer was held to be estopped only if the beneficiary relied on the issuer's failure to give notice.

Assume, for example, that the beneficiary presented documents to the issuer shortly before the letter of credit expired, in circumstances in which the beneficiary could not have cured any discrepancy before expiration. Under the reasoning of *Flagship* and *Wing On*, the beneficiary's inability to cure, even if it had received notice, would absolve the issuer of its failure to give notice. The virtue of the preclusion obligation adopted in this section is that it forecloses litigation about reliance and detriment.

Even though issuers typically give notice of the discrepancy of tardy presentation when presentation is made after the expiration of a credit, they are not required to give that notice and the section permits them to raise late presentation as a defect despite their failure to give that notice.

4. To act within a reasonable time, the issuer must normally give notice without delay after the examining party makes its decision. If the examiner decides to dishonor on the first day, it would be obliged to notify the beneficiary shortly thereafter, perhaps on the same business day. This rule accepts the reasoning in cases such as *Datapoint Corp. v. M & I Bank*, 665 F.Supp. 722 (W.D.Wis.1987) and *Esso Petroleum Canada, Div. of Imperial Oil, Ltd. v. Security Pacific Bank*, 710 F.Supp. 275 (D.Or.1989).

The section deprives the examining party of the right simply to sit on a presentation that is made within seven days of expiration. The section requires the examiner to examine the documents and make a decision and, having made a decision to dishonor, to communicate promptly with the presenter. Nevertheless, a beneficiary who presents documents shortly before the expiration of a letter of credit runs the risk that it will never have the opportunity to cure any discrepancies.

5. Confirmers, other nominated persons, and collecting banks acting for beneficiaries can be presenters and, when so, are entitled to the notice provided in subsection (b). Even nominated persons who have honored or given value against an earlier presentation of the beneficiary and are themselves seeking reimbursement or honor need notice of discrepancies in the hope that they may be able to procure complying documents. The issuer has the obligations imposed by this section whether the issuer's performance is characterized as "reimbursement" of a nominated person or as "honor."

6. In many cases a letter of credit authorizes presentation by the beneficiary to someone other than the issuer. Sometimes that person is identified as a "payor" or "paying bank," or as an "acceptor" or "accepting bank," in other cases as a "negotiating bank," and in other cases there will be no specific designation. The section does not impose any duties on a person other than the issuer or confirmer, however a nominated person or other person may have liability under this article or at common law if it fails to perform an express or implied agreement with the beneficiary.

7. The issuer's obligation to honor runs not only to the beneficiary but also to the applicant. It is possible that an applicant who has made a favorable contract with the beneficiary will be injured by the issuer's wrongful dishonor. Except to the extent that the contract between the issuer and the applicant limits that liability, the issuer will have liability to the applicant for wrongful dishonor under Section 5–111 as a matter of contract law. A good faith extension of the time in Section 5–108(b) by agreement between the issuer and beneficiary binds the applicant even if the applicant is not consulted or does not consent to the extension.

The issuer's obligation to dishonor when there is no apparent compliance with the letter of credit runs only to the applicant. No other party to the transaction can complain if the applicant waives compliance with terms or conditions of the letter of credit or agrees to a less stringent standard for compliance than that supplied by this article. Except as otherwise agreed with the applicant, an issuer may dishonor a noncomplying presentation despite an applicant's waiver.

Waiver of discrepancies by an issuer or an applicant in one or more presentations does not waive similar discrepancies in a future presentation. Neither the issuer nor the beneficiary can reasonably rely upon honor over past waivers as a basis for concluding that a future defective presentation will justify honor. The reasoning of *Courtaulds of North America Inc. v. North Carolina Nat. Bank*, 528 F.2d 802 (4th Cir.1975) is accepted and that expressed in *Schweibish v. Pontchartrain*

State Bank, 389 So.2d 731 (La.App.1980) and *Titanium Metals Corp. v. Space Metals, Inc.*, 529 P.2d 431 (Utah 1974) is rejected.

8. The standard practice referred to in subsection (e) includes (i) international practice set forth in or referenced by the Uniform Customs and Practice, (ii) other practice rules published by associations of financial institutions, and (iii) local and regional practice. It is possible that standard practice will vary from one place to another. Where there are conflicting practices, the parties should indicate which practice governs their rights. A practice may be overridden by agreement or course of dealing. See Section 1–205(4).

9. The responsibility of the issuer under a letter of credit is to examine documents and to make a prompt decision to honor or dishonor based upon that examination. Nondocumentary conditions have no place in this regime and are better accommodated under contract or suretyship law and practice. In requiring that nondocumentary conditions in letters of credit be ignored as surplusage, Article 5 remains aligned with the UCP (see UCP 500 Article 13c), approves cases like *Pringle-Associated Mortgage Corp. v. Southern National Bank*, 571 F.2d 871, 874 (5th Cir.1978), and rejects the reasoning in cases such as *Sherwood & Roberts, Inc. v. First Security Bank*, 682 P.2d 149 (Mont. 1984).

Subsection (g) recognizes that letters of credit sometimes contain nondocumentary terms or conditions. Conditions such as a term prohibiting "shipment on vessels more than 15 years old," are to be disregarded and treated as surplusage. Similarly, a requirement that there be an award by a "duly appointed arbitrator" would not require the issuer to determine whether the arbitrator had been "duly appointed." Likewise a term in a standby letter of credit that provided for differing forms of certification depending upon the particular type of default does not oblige the issuer independently to determine which kind of default has occurred. These conditions must be disregarded by the issuer. Where the nondocumentary conditions are central and fundamental to the issuer's obligation (as for example a condition that would require the issuer to determine in fact whether the beneficiary had performed the underlying contract or whether the applicant had defaulted) their inclusion may remove the undertaking from the scope of Article 5 entirely. See Section 5–102(a)(10) and Comment 6 to Section 5–102.

Subsection (g) would not permit the beneficiary or the issuer to disregard terms in the letter of credit such as place, time, and mode of presentation. The rule in subsection (g) is intended to prevent an issuer from deciding or even investigating extrinsic facts, but not from consulting the clock, the calendar, the relevant law and practice, or its own general knowledge of documentation or transactions of the type underlying a particular letter of credit.

Even though nondocumentary conditions must be disregarded in determining compliance of a presentation (and thus in determining the issuer's duty to the beneficiary), an issuer that has promised its applicant that it will honor only on the occurrence of those nondocumentary conditions may have liability to its applicant for disregarding the conditions.

10. Subsection (f) condones an issuer's ignorance of "any usage of a particular trade"; that trade is the trade of the applicant, beneficiary, or others who may be involved in the underlying transaction. The issuer is expected to know usage that is commonly encountered in the course of document examination. For example, an issuer should know the common usage with respect to documents in the maritime shipping trade but would not be expected to understand synonyms used in a particular trade for product descriptions appearing in a letter of credit or an invoice.

11. Where the issuer's performance is the delivery of an item of value other than money, the applicant's reimbursement obligation would be to make the "item of value" available to the issuer.

12. An issuer is entitled to reimbursement from the applicant after honor of a forged or fraudulent drawing if honor was permitted under Section 5–109(a).

13. The last clause of Section 5–108(i)(5) deals with a special case in which the fraud is not committed by the beneficiary, but is committed by a stranger to the transaction who forges the beneficiary's signature. If the issuer pays against documents on which a required signature of the beneficiary is forged, it remains liable to the true beneficiary. This principle is applicable to both electronic and tangible documents.

State Bar Committee Comments

Texas cases have required that a presentation of documents "strictly comply" with the terms and conditions of a letter of credit for a beneficiary to be entitled to honor. See, e.g., *Temple-Eastex Inc. v. Addison Bank*, 672 S.W.2d 793, 795 (Tex.1984). Revised § 5.108(a) codifies this principle. Official Comment 1 (fourth paragraph) to Revised § 5.108 also expressly indorses the conclusion of *New Braunfels National Bank v. Odiorne*, 780 S.W.2d 313, 316–18 (Tex. App.—Austin 1989, writ den.), that strict compliance does not demand "an oppressive perfectionism". The court of appeals held that a draft misidentifying Letter of Credit "Number 86–122–S" as "Number 86–122–5" strictly complied with the identifying legend required by the letter of credit. Because the original letter of credit was presented with the draft, it would have been obvious to a document examiner that the draft contained an irrelevant typographical error.

The aspect of Revised § 5.108(c) generally precluding an issuer from justifying dishonor with discrepancies omitted from a timely statement of defects is consistent with the result reached under Texas law in *Apex Oil Co. v. Archem Co.*, 770 F.2d 1353, 1356–57 (5th Cir.1985). However, the waiver and estoppel analysis of *Apex Oil* is no longer relevant. Statutory preclusion exists under Revised Chapter 5 whether or not a beneficiary has changed position in reliance upon an issuer's conduct.

An issuer's observance of the standard practice of financial institutions regularly issuing letters of credit is a matter of interpretation for the court under Revised § 5.108(e). Whether a presentation of documents strictly complies with the terms and conditions of a letter of credit also is generally treated as a matter of law for the court under Texas case law. *Westwind Exploration v. Homestate Savings Association*, 696 S.W.2d 378, 381 (Tex.1985).

§ 5.109. Fraud and Forgery

(a) If a presentation is made that appears on its face strictly to comply with the terms and conditions of the letter of credit, but a required document is forged or materially fraudulent, or honor of the presentation would facilitate a material fraud by the beneficiary on the issuer or applicant:

(1) the issuer shall honor the presentation if honor is demanded by:

(A) a nominated person who has given value in good faith and without notice of forgery or material fraud;

(B) a confirmer who has honored its confirmation in good faith;

(C) a holder in due course of a draft drawn under the letter of credit that was taken after acceptance by the issuer or nominated person; or

(D) an assignee of the issuer's or nominated person's deferred obligation that was taken for value and without notice of forgery or material fraud after the obligation was incurred by the issuer or nominated person; and

(2) the issuer, acting in good faith, may honor or dishonor the presentation in any other case.

(b) If an applicant claims that a required document is forged or materially fraudulent or that honor of the presentation would facilitate a material fraud by the beneficiary on the issuer or applicant, a court of competent jurisdiction may temporarily or permanently enjoin the issuer from honoring a presentation or grant similar relief against the issuer or other persons only if the court finds that:

(1) the relief is not prohibited under the law applicable to an accepted draft or deferred obligation incurred by the issuer;

(2) a beneficiary, issuer, or nominated person who may be adversely affected is adequately protected against loss that it may suffer because the relief is granted;

(3) all of the conditions to entitle a person to the relief under the law of this state have been met; and

(4) on the basis of the information submitted to the court, the applicant is more likely than not to succeed under its claim of forgery or material fraud and the person demanding honor does not qualify for protection under Subsection (a)(1).

Amended by Acts 1999, 76th Leg., ch. 4, § 1, eff. Sept. 1, 1999.

Uniform Commercial Code Comment

1. This recodification makes clear that fraud must be found either in the documents or must have been committed by the beneficiary on the issuer or applicant. See *Cromwell v. Commerce & Energy Bank*, 464 So.2d 721 (La.1985).

Secondly, it makes clear that fraud must be "material." Necessarily courts must decide the breadth and width of "materiality." The use of the word requires that the fraudulent aspect of a document be material to a purchaser of that document or that the fraudulent act be significant to the participants in the underlying transaction. Assume, for example, that the beneficiary has a contract to deliver 1,000 barrels of salad oil. Knowing that it has delivered only 998, the beneficiary nevertheless submits an invoice showing 1,000 barrels. If two barrels in a 1,000 barrel shipment would be an insubstantial and immaterial breach of the underlying contract, the beneficiary's act, though possibly fraudulent, is not materially so and would not justify an injunction. Conversely, the knowing submission of those invoices upon delivery of only five barrels would be materially fraudulent. The courts must examine the underlying transaction when there is an allegation of material fraud, for only by examining that transaction can one determine whether a document is fraudulent or the beneficiary has committed fraud and, if so, whether the fraud was material.

Material fraud by the beneficiary occurs only when the beneficiary has no colorable right to expect honor and where there is no basis in fact to support such a right to honor. The section indorses articulations such as those stated in *Intraworld Indus. v. Girard Trust Bank*, 336 A.2d 316 (Pa.1975), *Roman Ceramics Corp. v. People's Nat. Bank*, 714 F.2d 1207 (3d Cir.1983), and similar decisions and embraces certain decisions under Section 5–114 that relied upon the phrase "fraud in the transaction." Some of these decisions have been summarized as follows in *Ground Air Transfer, Inc. v. Westate's Airlines, Inc.*, 899 F.2d 1269, 1272–73 (1st Cir.1990):

> We have said throughout that courts may not "*normally*" issue an injunction because of an important exception to the general "no injunction" rule. The exception, as we also explained in Itek, 730 F.2d at 24–25, concerns "fraud" so serious as to make it obviously pointless and unjust to permit the beneficiary to obtain the money. Where the circumstances "*plainly*" show that the underlying contract forbids the beneficiary to call a letter of credit, Itek, 730 F.2d at 24; where they show that the contract deprives the beneficiary of even a "*colorable*" right to do so, id., at 25; where the contract and circumstances reveal that the beneficiary's demand for payment has "absolutely no basis in fact," id.; see Dynamics Corp. of America, 356 F.Supp. at 999; where the beneficiary's conduct has "so vitiated the entire transaction that the legitimate purposes of the independence of the issuer's obligation would no longer be served," Itek, 730 F.2d at 25 (quoting *Roman Ceramics Corp. v. Peoples National Bank*, 714 F.2d 1207, 1212 n.12,

1215 (3d Cir.1983) (quoting Intraworld Indus., 336 A.2d at 324–25)); *then* a court may enjoin payment.

2. Subsection (a)(2) makes clear that the issuer may honor in the face of the applicant's claim of fraud. The subsection also makes clear what was not stated in former Section 5–114, that the issuer may dishonor and defend that dishonor by showing fraud or forgery of the kind stated in subsection (a). Because issuers may be liable for wrongful dishonor if they are unable to prove forgery or material fraud, presumably most issuers will choose to honor despite applicant's claims of fraud or forgery unless the applicant procures an injunction. Merely because the issuer has a right to dishonor and to defend that dishonor by showing forgery or material fraud does not mean it has a duty to the applicant to dishonor. The applicant's normal recourse is to procure an injunction, if the applicant is unable to procure an injunction, it will have a claim against the issuer only in the rare case in which it can show that the issuer did not honor in good faith.

3. Whether a beneficiary can commit fraud by presenting a draft under a clean letter of credit (one calling only for a draft and no other documents) has been much debated. Under the current formulation it would be possible but difficult for there to be fraud in such a presentation. If the applicant were able to show that the beneficiary were committing material fraud on the applicant in the underlying transaction, then payment would facilitate a material fraud by the beneficiary on the applicant and honor could be enjoined. The courts should be skeptical of claims of fraud by one who has signed a "suicide" or clean credit and thus granted a beneficiary the right to draw by mere presentation of a draft.

4. The standard for injunctive relief is high, and the burden remains on the applicant to show, by evidence and not by mere allegation, that such relief is warranted. Some courts have enjoined payments on letters of credit on insufficient showing by the applicant. For example, in *Griffin Cos. v. First Nat. Bank*, 374 N.W.2d 768 (Minn.App.1985), the court enjoined payment under a standby letter of credit, basing its decision on plaintiff's allegation, rather than competent evidence, of fraud.

There are at least two ways to prohibit injunctions against honor under this section after acceptance of a draft by the issuer. First is to define honor (see Section 5–102(a)(8)) in the particular letter of credit to occur upon acceptance and without regard to later payment of the acceptance. Second is explicitly to agree that the applicant has no right to an injunction after acceptance—whether or not the acceptance constitutes honor.

5. Although the statute deals principally with injunctions against honor, it also cautions against granting "similar relief" and the same principles apply when the applicant or issuer attempts to achieve the same legal outcome by injunction against presentation (see *Ground Air Transfer, Inc. v. Westates Airlines, Inc.*, 899 F.2d 1269 (1st Cir.1990)), interpleader, declaratory judgment, or attachment. These attempts should face the same obstacles that face efforts to enjoin the issuer from paying. Expanded use of any of these devices could threaten the independence principle just as much as injunctions against honor. For that reason courts should have the same hostility to them and place the same restrictions on their use as would be applied to injunctions against honor. Courts should not allow the "sacred cow of equity to trample the tender vines of letter of credit law."

6. Section 5–109(a)(1) also protects specified third parties against the risk of fraud. By issuing a letter of credit that nominates a person to negotiate or pay, the issuer (ultimately the applicant) induces that nominated person to give value and thereby assumes the risk that a draft drawn under the letter of credit will be transferred to one with a status like that of a holder in due course who deserves to be protected against a fraud defense.

7. The "loss" to be protected against—by bond or otherwise under subsection (b)(2)—includes incidental damages. Among those are legal fees that might be incurred by the beneficiary or issuer in defending against an injunction action.

State Bar Committee Comments

The special fraud and forgery rules of Revised § 5.109 apply to presentations of documents that, on their face, appear to comply strictly with the terms and conditions of a letter of credit. See Revised § 5.109(a). Apparent alterations of required terms that are not authenticated by the originators of the documents preclude strict compliance. See *Champion International Corp. v. Continental National Bank*, 715 S.W.2d 128, 130 (Tex. App.—San Antonio 1986, writ ref'd n.r.e.) (unauthorized alterations in invoices that, as issued, did not satisfy the conditions of the letter of credit justified dishonor of the draft presented with the invoices).

Both *Philipp Brothers, Inc. v. Oil Country Specialists Ltd.*, 787 S.W.2d 38, 40 (Tex.1990)(per curiam), and Official Comment 1 (third paragraph) to Revised § 5.109 indorse the following test for the type of fraud that justifies an injunction against honor:

> [F]raud in which the wrongdoing of the beneficiary has so vitiated the entire transaction that the legitimate purposes of the independence of the issuer's obligation would no longer be served.
>
> *Intraworld Industries, Inc. v. Girard Trust Bank*, 336 A.2d 316, 324–25 (Pa.1975).

Goldome Credit Corp. v. University Square Apts., 828 S.W.2d 505, 509–10 (Tex. App.—Amarillo 1992, no writ), contains the following summary of the general Texas prerequisites to temporary injunctive relief that apply under Revised § 5.109(b)(3): Relief must be limited to preserving the status quo; and the plaintiff must prove: (1) a threat of imminent, irreparable harm; (2) a benefit to the plaintiff from temporary relief that outweighs the harm to the defendant and to the public; and (3) a likelihood of prevailing on the merits. *GATX Leasing Corporation v. DBM Drilling Corporation*, 657 S.W.2d 178, 180 (Tex.App—San Antonio 1983, no writ), says the requirements traditionally include a showing by the applicant of irreparable injury, the lack of an adequate remedy at law, and the likelihood of prevailing on the merits.

§ 5.110. Warranties

(a) If its presentation is honored, the beneficiary warrants:

(1) to the issuer, any other person to whom presentation is made, and the applicant that there is no fraud or forgery of the kind described in Section 5.109(a); and

(2) to the applicant that the drawing does not violate any agreement between the applicant and beneficiary or any other agreement intended by them to be augmented by the letter of credit.

(b) The warranties in Subsection (a) are in addition to warranties arising under Chapters 3, 4, 7, and 8 because of the presentation or transfer of documents covered by any of those chapters.

(c) Notwithstanding any agreement or term to the contrary, the warranties in Subsection (a) do not arise until the issuer honors the letter of credit.

Amended by Acts 1999, 76th Leg., ch. 4, § 1, eff. Sept. 1, 1999.

Uniform Commercial Code Comment

1. Since the warranties in subsection (a) are not given unless a letter of credit has been honored, no breach of warranty under this subsection can be a defense to dishonor by the issuer. Any defense must be based on Section 5–108 or 5–109 and not on this section. Also, breach of the warranties by the beneficiary in subsection (a) cannot excuse the applicant's duty to reimburse.

2. The warranty in Section 5–110(a)(2) assumes that payment under the letter of credit is final. It does not run to the issuer, only to the applicant. In most cases the applicant will have a direct cause of action for breach of the underlying contract. This warranty has primary application in standby letters of credit or other circumstances where the applicant is not a party to an underlying contract with the beneficiary. It is not a warranty that the statements made on the presentation of the documents presented are truthful nor is it a warranty that the documents strictly comply under Section 5–108(a). It is a warranty that the beneficiary has performed all the acts expressly and implicitly necessary under any underlying agreement to entitle the beneficiary to honor. If, for example, an underlying sales contract authorized the beneficiary to draw only upon "due performance" and the beneficiary drew even though it had breached the underlying contract by delivering defective goods, honor of its draw would break the warranty. By the same token, if the underlying contract authorized the beneficiary to draw only upon actual default or upon its or a third party's determination of default by the applicant and if the beneficiary drew in violation of its authorization, then upon honor of its draw the warranty would be breached. In many cases, therefore, the documents presented to the issuer will contain inaccurate statements (concerning the goods delivered or concerning default or other matters), but the breach of warranty arises not because the statements are untrue but because the beneficiary's drawing violated its express or implied obligations in the underlying transaction.

3. The damages for breach of warranty are not specified in Section 5–111. Courts may find damage analogies in Section 2–714 in Article 2 and in warranty decisions under Articles 3 and 4.

Unlike wrongful dishonor cases—where the damages usually equal the amount of the draw—the damages for breach of warranty will often be much less than the amount of the draw, sometimes zero. Assume a seller entitled to draw only on proper performance of its sales contract. Assume it breaches the sales contract in a way that gives the buyer a right to damages but no right to reject. The applicant's damages for breach of the warranty in subsection (a)(2) are limited to the damages it could recover for breach of the contract of sale. Alternatively assume an underlying agreement that authorizes a beneficiary to draw only the "amount in default." Assume a default of $200,000 and a draw of $500,000. The damages for breach of warranty would be no more than $300,000.

State Bar Committee Comments

Under Revised § 5.110(a)(2), by obtaining honor a beneficiary makes an implied warranty to an applicant that the draw does not violate either any underlying agreement between the applicant and the beneficiary or any other agreement intended by both the applicant and the beneficiary to be augmented by the letter of credit. Examination of these agreements in order to determine whether the warranty has been breached is consistent with the independence principle, which applies prior to honor, and with the result in *Sun Marine Terminals, Inc. v. Artoc Bank & Trust*, 797 S.W.2d 7, 11–12 (Tex.1990).

Section 5.110(c) has been added as a Texas nonuniform amendment that is consistent with the policy of the Official Text of Revised Article 5. See the preamble to Revised § 5.110(a). The nonuniform amendment precludes waiver of the fundamental principle that a beneficiary's warranties do not arise until an issuer honors a letter of credit. Consequently an issuer cannot utilize breach of warranty by a beneficiary as a justification for dishonor. What is said here applies also to a confirmer. Since a confirmer has the rights and obligations of an issuer (§ 5.107(a)) this nonuniform amendment contemplates that a confirmer might honor a letter of credit, and in that event the warranties in this section would arise in favor of the confirmer. But the warranties would not arise until the confirmer had honored the credit, and that condition would be nonwaivable. Upon reimbursing the confirmer the issuer would also have the benefit of these warranties. See § 5.107, comment 1.

§ 5.111. Remedies

(a) If an issuer wrongfully dishonors or repudiates its obligation to pay money under a letter of credit before presentation, the beneficiary, successor, or nominated person presenting on its own behalf may recover from the issuer the amount that is the subject of the dishonor or repudiation. If the issuer's obligation under the letter of credit is not for the payment of money, the claimant may obtain specific performance or, at the claimant's election, recover an amount equal to the value of performance from the issuer. In either case, the claimant may also recover incidental but not consequential damages. The claimant is not obligated to take action to avoid damages that might be due from the issuer under this subsection. If, although not obligated to do so, the claimant avoids damages, the claimant's recovery from the issuer must be reduced by the amount of damages avoided. The issuer has the burden of proving the amount of damages avoided. In the case of repudiation the claimant need not present any document.

(b) If an issuer wrongfully dishonors a draft or demand presented under a letter of credit or honors a draft or demand in breach of its obligation to the applicant, the applicant may recover damages resulting from the breach, including incidental but not consequential damages, less any amount saved as a result of the breach.

(c) If an adviser or nominated person other than a confirmer breaches an obligation under this chapter or an issuer breaches an obligation not covered in Subsection (a) or (b), a person to whom the obligation is owed may recover damages resulting from the breach, including incidental but not consequential damages, less any amount saved as a result of the breach. To the extent of the confirmation, a confirmer has the liability of an issuer specified in this subsection and Subsections (a) and (b).

(d) An issuer, nominated person, or adviser who is found liable under Subsection (a), (b), or (c) shall pay interest on the amount owed thereunder from the date of wrongful dishonor or other appropriate date.

(e) Reasonable attorney's fees and other expenses of litigation may be awarded to the prevailing party in an action in which a remedy is sought under this chapter.

(f) Damages that would otherwise be payable by a party for breach of an obligation under this chapter may be liquidated by agreement or undertaking, but only in an amount or by a formula that is reasonable in light of the harm anticipated.

Amended by Acts 1999, 76th Leg., ch. 4, § 1, eff. Sept. 1, 1999.

Uniform Commercial Code Comment

1. The right to specific performance is new. The express limitation on the duty of the beneficiary to mitigate damages adopts the position of certain courts and commentators. Because the letter of credit depends upon speed and certainty of payment, it is important that the issuer not be given an incentive to dishonor. The issuer might have an incentive to dishonor if it could rely on the burden of mitigation falling on the beneficiary, (to sell goods and sue only for the difference between the price of the goods sold and the amount due under the letter of credit). Under the scheme contemplated by Section 5–111(a), the beneficiary would present the documents to the issuer. If the issuer wrongfully dishonored, the beneficiary would have no further duty to the issuer with respect to the goods covered by documents that the issuer dishonored and returned. The issuer thus takes the risk that the beneficiary will let the goods rot or be destroyed. Of course the beneficiary may have a duty of mitigation to the applicant arising from the underlying agreement, but the issuer would not have the right to assert that duty by way of defense or setoff. See Section 5–117(d). If the beneficiary sells the goods covered by dishonored documents or if the beneficiary sells a draft after acceptance but before dishonor by the issuer, the net amount so gained should be subtracted from the amount of the beneficiary's damages—at least where the damage claim against the issuer equals or exceeds the damage suffered by the beneficiary. If, on the other hand, the beneficiary suffers damages in an underlying transaction in an amount that exceeds the amount of the wrongfully dishonored demand (e.g., where the letter of credit does not cover 100 percent of the underlying obligation), the damages avoided should not necessarily be deducted from the beneficiary's claim against the issuer. In such a case, the damages would be the lesser of (i) the amount recoverable in the absence of mitigation (that is, the amount that is subject to the dishonor or repudiation plus any incidental damages) and (ii) the damages remaining after deduction for the amount of damages actually avoided.

A beneficiary need not present documents as a condition of suit for anticipatory repudiation, but if a beneficiary could never have obtained documents necessary for a presentation conforming to the letter of credit, the beneficiary cannot recover for anticipatory repudiation of the letter of credit. *Doelger v. Battery Park Bank*, 201 A.D. 515, 194 N.Y.S. 582 (1922) and *Decor by Nikkei Int'l, Inc. v. Federal Republic of Nigeria*, 497 F.Supp. 893 (S.D.N.Y.1980), *aff'd*, 647 F.2d 300 (2d Cir.1981), *cert. denied*, 454 U.S. 1148 (1982). The last sentence of subsection (c) does not expand the liability of a confirmer to persons to whom the confirmer would not otherwise be liable under Section 5–107.

Almost all letters of credit, including those that call for an acceptance, are "obligations to pay money" as that term is used in Section 5–111(a).

2. What damages "result" from improper honor is for the courts to decide. Even though an issuer pays a beneficiary in violation of Section 5–108(a) or of its contract with the applicant, it may have no liability to an applicant. If the underlying contract has been fully performed, the applicant may not have been damaged by the issuer's breach. Such a case would occur when *A* contracts for goods at $100 per ton, but, upon delivery, the market value of conforming goods has

decreased to $25 per ton. If the issuer pays over discrepancies, there should be no recovery by *A* for the price differential if the issuer's breach did not alter the applicant's obligation under the underlying contract, i.e., to pay $100 per ton for goods now worth $25 per ton. On the other hand, if the applicant intends to resell the goods and must itself satisfy the strict compliance requirements under a second letter of credit in connection with its sale, the applicant may be damaged by the issuer's payment despite discrepancies because the applicant itself may then be unable to procure honor on the letter of credit where it is the beneficiary, and may be unable to mitigate its damages by enforcing its rights against others in the underlying transaction. Note that an issuer found liable to its applicant may have recourse under Section 5-117 by subrogation to the applicant's claim against the beneficiary or other persons.

One who inaccurately advises a letter of credit breaches its obligation to the beneficiary, but may cause no damage. If the beneficiary knows the terms of the letter of credit and understands the advice to be inaccurate, the beneficiary will have suffered no damage as a result of the adviser's breach.

3. Since the confirmer has the rights and duties of an issuer, in general it has an issuer's liability, see subsection (c). The confirmer is usually a confirming bank. A confirming bank often also plays the role of an adviser. If it breaks its obligation to the beneficiary, the confirming bank may have liability as an issuer or, depending upon the obligation that was broken, as an adviser. For example, a wrongful dishonor would give it liability as an issuer under Section 5-111(a). On the other hand a confirming bank that broke its obligation to advise the credit but did not commit wrongful dishonor would be treated under Section 5-111(c).

4. Consequential damages for breach of obligations under this article are excluded in the belief that these damages can best be avoided by the beneficiary or the applicant and out of the fear that imposing consequential damages on issuers would raise the cost of the letter of credit to a level that might render it uneconomic. *A fortiori* punitive and exemplary damages are excluded, however, this section does not bar recovery of consequential or even punitive damages for breach of statutory or common law duties arising outside of this article.

5. The section does not specify a rate of interest. It leaves the setting of the rate to the court. It would be appropriate for a court to use the rate that would normally apply in that court in other situations where interest is imposed by law.

6. The court must award attorney's fees to the prevailing party, whether that party is an applicant, a beneficiary, an issuer, a nominated person, or adviser. Since the issuer may be entitled to recover its legal fees and costs from the applicant under the reimbursement agreement, allowing the issuer to recover those fees from a losing beneficiary may also protect the applicant against undeserved losses. The party entitled to attorneys' fees has been described as the "prevailing party." Sometimes it will be unclear which party "prevailed," for example, where there are multiple issues and one party wins on some and the other party wins on others. Determining which is the prevailing party is in the discretion of the court. Subsection (e) authorizes attorney's fees in all actions where a remedy is sought "under this article." It applies even when the remedy might be an injunction under Section 5-109 or when the claimed remedy is otherwise outside of Section 5-111. Neither an issuer nor a confirmer should be treated as a "losing" party when an injunction is granted to the applicant over the objection of the issuer or confirmer; accordingly neither should be liable for fees and expenses in that case.

"Expenses of litigation" is intended to be broader than "costs." For example, expense of litigation would include travel expenses of witnesses, fees for expert witnesses, and expenses associated with taking depositions.

7. For the purposes of Section 5-111(f) "harm anticipated" must be anticipated at the time when the agreement that includes the liquidated damage clause is executed or at the time when the undertaking that includes the clause is issued. See Section 2A-504.

State Bar Committee Comments

East Girard Savings Association v. Citizens National Bank & Trust, 593 F.2d 598, 603-04 (5th Cir.1979), holds under Texas law that, without proof of resulting loss, a beneficiary is entitled to recover from an issuer the amount withheld in a wrongful dishonor, plus incidental damages, but that the attorney's fees incurred by a beneficiary in suing an issuer for wrongful dishonor are not incidental damages. Revised § 5-111(a) codifies the Fifth Circuit's holding that the proper recovery is for the amount wrongfully withheld plus incidental damages. Although Revised § 5-111(e) expressly authorizes the award of reasonable attorney's fees and other expenses of litigation to a prevailing party in addition to damages, a Texas nonuniform amendment makes the award by a court of attorney's fees and other litigation expenses discretionary rather than mandatory.

§ 5.112. Transfer of Letter of Credit

(a) Except as otherwise provided in Section 5.113, unless a letter of credit provides that it is transferable, the right of a beneficiary to draw or otherwise demand performance under a letter of credit may not be transferred.

(b) Even if a letter of credit provides that it is transferable, the issuer may refuse to recognize or carry out a transfer if:

(1) the transfer would violate applicable law; or

(2) the transferor or transferee has failed to comply with any requirement stated in the letter of credit or any other requirement relating to transfer imposed by the issuer which is within the standard practice referred to in Section 5.108(e) or is otherwise reasonable under the circumstances.

Amended by Acts 1999, 76th Leg., ch. 4, § 1, eff. Sept. 1, 1999.

Uniform Commercial Code Comment

1. In order to protect the applicant's reliance on the designated beneficiary, letter of credit law traditionally has forbidden the beneficiary to convey to third parties its right to draw or demand payment under the letter of credit. Subsection (a) codifies that rule. The term "transfer" refers to the beneficiary's conveyance of that right. Absent incorporation of the UCP (which make elaborate provision for partial transfer of a commercial letter of credit) or similar trade practice and absent other express indication in the letter of credit that the term is used to mean something else, a term in the letter of credit indicating that the beneficiary has the right to transfer should be taken to mean that the beneficiary may convey to a third party its right to draw or demand payment. Even in that case, the issuer or other person controlling the transfer may make the beneficiary's right to transfer subject to conditions, such as timely notification, payment of a fee, delivery of the letter of credit to the issuer or other person controlling the transfer, or execution of appropriate forms to document the transfer. A nominated person who is not a confirmer has no obligation to recognize a transfer.

The power to establish "requirements" does not include the right absolutely to refuse to recognize transfers under a transferable letter of credit. An issuer who wishes to retain the right to deny all transfers should not issue transferable letters of credit or should incorporate the UCP. By stating its requirements in the letter of credit an issuer may impose any requirement without regard to its conformity to practice or reasonableness. Transfer requirements of issuers and nominated persons must be made known to potential transferors and transferees to enable those parties to comply with the requirements. A common method of making such requirements known is to use a form that indicates the information that must be provided and the instructions that must be given to enable the issuer or nominated person to comply with a request to transfer.

2. The issuance of a transferable letter of credit with the concurrence of the applicant is *ipso facto* an agreement by the issuer and applicant to permit a beneficiary to transfer its drawing right and permit a nominated person to recognize and carry out that transfer without further notice to them. In international commerce, transferable letters of credit are often issued under circumstances in which a nominated person or adviser is expected to facilitate the transfer from the original beneficiary to a transferee and to deal with that transferee. In those circumstances it is the responsibility of the nominated person or adviser to establish procedures satisfactory to protect itself against double presentation or dispute about the right to draw under the letter of credit. Commonly such a person will control the transfer by requiring that the original letter of credit be given to it or by causing a paper copy marked as an original to be issued where the original letter of credit was electronic. By keeping possession of the original letter of credit the nominated person or adviser can minimize or entirely exclude the possibility that the original beneficiary could properly procure payment from another bank. If the letter of credit requires presentation of the original letter of credit itself, no other payment could be procured. In addition to imposing whatever requirements it considers appropriate to protect itself against double payment the person that is facilitating the transfer has a right to charge an appropriate fee for its activity.

"Transfer" of a letter of credit should be distinguished from "assignment of proceeds." The former is analogous to a novation or a substitution of beneficiaries. It contemplates not merely payment to but also performance by the transferee. For example, under the typical terms of transfer for a commercial letter of credit, a transferee could comply with a letter of credit transferred to it by signing and presenting its own draft and invoice. An assignee of proceeds, on the other hand, is wholly dependent on the presentation of a draft and invoice signed by the beneficiary.

By agreeing to the issuance of a transferable letter of credit, which is not qualified or limited, the applicant may lose control over the identity of the person whose performance will earn payment under the letter of credit.

§ 5.113. Transfer by Operation of Law

(a) A successor of a beneficiary may consent to amendments, sign and present documents, and receive payment or other items of value in the name of the beneficiary without disclosing its status as a successor.

(b) A successor of a beneficiary may consent to amendments, sign and present documents, and receive payment or other items of value in its own name as the disclosed successor of the beneficiary. Except as otherwise provided in Subsection (e), an issuer shall recognize a disclosed successor of a beneficiary as beneficiary in full substitution for its predecessor upon compliance with the requirements for recognition by the issuer of a transfer of drawing rights by operation of law under the standard practice referred to in Section 5.108(e) or, in the absence of such a practice, compliance with other reasonable procedures sufficient to protect the issuer.

(c) An issuer is not obliged to determine whether a purported successor is a successor of a beneficiary or whether the signature of a purported successor is genuine or authorized.

(d) Honor of a purported successor's apparently complying presentation under Subsection (a) or (b) has the consequences specified in Section 5.108(i) even if the purported successor is not the successor of a beneficiary. Documents signed in the name of the beneficiary or of a disclosed successor by a person who is neither the beneficiary nor the successor of the beneficiary are forged documents for the purposes of Section 5.109.

(e) An issuer whose rights of reimbursement are not covered by Subsection (d) or substantially similar law and any confirmer or nominated person may decline to recognize a presentation under Subsection (b).

(f) A beneficiary whose name is changed after the issuance of a letter of credit has the same rights and obligations as a successor of a beneficiary under this section.

Amended by Acts 1999, 76th Leg., ch. 4, § 1, eff. Sept. 1, 1999.

Uniform Commercial Code Comment

This section affirms the result in Pastor v. Nat. Republic Bank of Chicago, 76 Ill.2d 139, 390 N.E.2d 894 (Ill. 1979) and Federal Deposit Insurance Co. v. Bank of Boulder, 911 F.2d 1466 (10th Cir. 1990). Both electronic and tangible documents may be signed.

An issuer's requirements for recognition of a successor's status might include presentation of a certificate of merger, a court order appointing a bankruptcy trustee or receiver, a certificate of appointment as bankruptcy trustee, or the like. The issuer is entitled to rely upon such documents which on their face demonstrate that presentation is made by a successor of a beneficiary. It is not obliged to make an independent investigation to determine the fact of succession.

State Bar Committee Comments

Temple–Eastex Inc. v. Addison Bank, 672 S.W.2d 793, 796 (Tex.1984), held that an issuer committed wrongful dishonor in not recognizing that the Texas Business Corporation Act entitled a corporation that was the sole shareholder and statutory distributee of a voluntarily dissolved corporation to draw upon a letter of credit designating the dissolved corporation as beneficiary. Moreover, the statutory distributee could make the draw under its own name rather than in the name of the dissolved corporation.

Revised Chapter 5 modifies this aspect of *Temple–Eastex*. Under Revised § 5.113(b) an issuer can insist that a successor by operation of law presenting documents in its own name comply with the requirements for recognition of a transfer of drawing rights imposed by the standard practice of financial institutions regularly issuing letters of credit. In the absence of relevant standard practice, an issuer can require reasonable safeguards to protect itself from loss. On the facts of *Temple–Eastex*, reasonable safeguards could include requiring presentation of the dissolved corporation's articles of dissolution and the certificate of dissolution issued by the Texas Secretary of State.

§ 5.114. Assignment of Proceeds

(a) In this section, "proceeds of a letter of credit" means the cash, check, accepted draft, or other item of value paid or delivered upon honor or giving of value by the issuer or any nominated person under the letter of credit. The term does not include a beneficiary's drawing rights or documents presented by the beneficiary.

(b) A beneficiary may assign its right to part or all of the proceeds of a letter of credit. The beneficiary may do so before presentation as a present assignment of its right to receive proceeds contingent upon its compliance with the terms and conditions of the letter of credit.

(c) An issuer or nominated person need not recognize an assignment of proceeds of a letter of credit until it consents to the assignment.

(d) An issuer or nominated person has no obligation to give or withhold its consent to an assignment of proceeds of a letter of credit, but consent may not be unreasonably withheld if the assignee possesses and exhibits the letter of credit and presentation of the letter of credit is a condition to honor.

(e) Rights of a transferee beneficiary or nominated person are independent of the beneficiary's assignment of the proceeds of a letter of credit and are superior to the assignee's right to the proceeds.

(f) Neither the rights recognized by this section between an assignee and an issuer, transferee beneficiary, or nominated person nor the issuer's or nominated person's payment of proceeds to an assignee or a third person affect the rights between the assignee and any person other than the issuer, transferee beneficiary, or nominated person. The mode of creating and perfecting a security interest in or granting an assignment of a beneficiary's rights to proceeds is governed by Chapter 9 or other law. Against persons other than the issuer, transferee beneficiary, or nominated person, the rights and obligations arising upon the creation of a security interest or other assignment of a beneficiary's right to proceeds and its perfection are governed by Chapter 9 or other law.

Amended by Acts 1999, 76th Leg., ch. 4, § 1, eff. Sept. 1, 1999.

Uniform Commercial Code Comment

1. Subsection (b) expressly validates the beneficiary's present assignment of letter of credit proceeds if made after the credit is established but before the proceeds are realized. This section adopts the prevailing usage—"assignment of proceeds"—to an assignee. That terminology carries with it no implication, however, that an assignee acquires no interest until the proceeds are paid by the issuer. For example, an "assignment of the right to proceeds" of a letter of credit for purposes of security that meets the requirements of Section 9–203(b) would constitute the present creation of a security interest in a "letter-of-credit right." This security interest

can be perfected by control (Section 9–107). Although subsection (a) explains the meaning of " 'proceeds' of a letter of credit," it should be emphasized that those proceeds also may be Article 9 proceeds of other collateral. For example, if a seller of inventory receives a letter of credit to support the account that arises upon the sale, payments made under the letter of credit are Article 9 proceeds of the inventory, account, and any document of title covering the inventory. Thus, the secured party who had a perfected security interest in that inventory, account, or document has a perfected security interest in the proceeds collected under the letter of credit, so long as they are identifiable cash proceeds (Section 9–315(a), (d)). This perfection is continuous, regardless of whether the secured party perfected a security interest in the right to letter of credit proceeds.

2. An assignee's rights to enforce an assignment of proceeds against an issuer and the priority of the assignee's rights against a nominated person or transferee beneficiary are governed by Article 5. Those rights and that priority are stated in subsections (c), (d), and (e). Note also that Section 4–210 gives first priority to a collecting bank that has given value for a documentary draft.

3. By requiring that an issuer or nominated person consent to the assignment of proceeds of a letter of credit, subsections (c) and (d) follow more closely recognized national and international letter of credit practices than did prior law. In most circumstances, it has always been advisable for the assignee to obtain the consent of the issuer in order better to safeguard its right to the proceeds. When notice of an assignment has been received, issuers normally have required signatures on a consent form. This practice is reflected in the revision. By unconditionally consenting to such an assignment, the issuer or nominated person becomes bound, subject to the rights of the superior parties specified in subsection (e), to pay to the assignee the assigned letter of credit proceeds that the issuer or nominated person would otherwise pay to the beneficiary or another assignee.

Where the letter of credit must be presented as a condition to honor and the assignee holds and exhibits the letter of credit to the issuer or nominated person, the risk to the issuer or nominated person of having to pay twice is minimized. In such a situation, subsection (d) provides that the issuer or nominated person may not unreasonably withhold its consent to the assignment.

§ 5.115. Statute of Limitations

An action to enforce a right or obligation arising under this chapter must be commenced within one year after the expiration date of the relevant letter of credit or one year after the cause of action accrues, whichever occurs later. A cause of action accrues when the breach occurs, regardless of the aggrieved party's lack of knowledge of the breach.

Amended by Acts 1999, 76th Leg., ch. 4, § 1, eff. Sept. 1, 1999.

Uniform Commercial Code Comment

1. This section is based upon Sections 4–111 and 2–725(2).

2. This section applies to all claims for which there are remedies under Section 5–111 and to other claims made under this article, such as claims for breach of warranty under Section 5–110. Because it covers all claims under Section 5–111, the statute of limitations applies not only to wrongful dishonor claims against the issuer but also to claims between the issuer and the applicant arising from the reimbursement agreement. These might be for reimbursement (issuer v. applicant) or for breach of the reimbursement contract by wrongful honor (applicant v. issuer).

3. The statute of limitations, like the rest of the statute, applies only to a letter of credit issued on or after the effective date and only to transactions, events, obligations, or duties arising out of or associated with such a letter. If a letter of credit was issued before the effective date and an obligation on that letter of credit was breached after the effective date, the complaining party could bring its suit within the time that would have been permitted prior to the adoption of Section 5–115 and would not be limited by the terms of Section 5–115.

§ 5.116. Choice of Law and Forum

(a) The liability of an issuer, nominated person, or adviser for action or omission is governed by the law of the jurisdiction chosen by an agreement in the form of a record signed or otherwise authenticated by the affected parties in the manner provided in Section 5.104 or by a provision in the person's letter of credit, confirmation, or other undertaking. The jurisdiction whose law is chosen need not bear any relation to the transaction.

(b) Unless Subsection (a) applies, the liability of an issuer, nominated person, or adviser for action or omission is governed by the law of the jurisdiction in which the person is located. The person is considered to be located at the address indicated in the person's undertaking. If more than one address is indicated, the person is considered to be located at the address from which the person's undertaking was issued. For the purpose of jurisdiction, choice of law, and recognition of interbranch letters of credit, but not enforcement of a judgment, all branches of a bank are considered separate juridical entities, and a bank is considered to be located at the place where its relevant branch is considered to be located under this subsection.

(c) Except as otherwise provided in this subsection, the liability of an issuer, nominated person, or adviser is governed by any rules of custom or practice, such as the Uniform Customs and Practice for Documentary Credits, to which the letter of credit, confirmation, or other undertaking is expressly made subject. If (i) this chapter would govern the liability of an issuer, nominated person, or adviser under Subsection (a) or (b), (ii) the relevant undertaking incorporates rules of custom or practice, and (iii) there is conflict between this chapter and those rules as applied to that undertaking, those rules govern except to the extent of any conflict with the nonvariable provisions specified in Section 5.103(c).

(d) If there is conflict between this chapter and Chapter 3, 4, 4A, or 9, this chapter governs.

(e) The forum for settling disputes arising out of an undertaking within this chapter may be chosen in the manner and with the binding effect that governing law may be chosen in accordance with Subsection (a).

Amended by Acts 1999, 76th Leg., ch. 4, § 1, eff. Sept. 1, 1999.

Uniform Commercial Code Comment

1. Although it would be possible for the parties to agree otherwise, the law normally chosen by agreement under subsection (a) and that provided in the absence of agreement under subsection (b) is the substantive law of a particular jurisdiction not including the choice of law principles of that jurisdiction. Thus, two parties, an issuer and an applicant, both located in Oklahoma might choose the law of New York. Unless they agree otherwise, the section anticipates that they wish the substantive law of New York to apply to their transaction and they do not intend that a New York choice of law principle might direct a court to Oklahoma law. By the same token, the liability of an issuer located in New York is governed by New York substantive law—in the absence of agreement—even in circumstances in which choice of law principles found in the common law of New York might direct one to the law of another State. Subsection (b) states the relevant choice of law principles and it should not be subordinated to some other choice of law rule. Within the States of the United States *renvoi* will not be a problem once every jurisdiction has enacted Section 5–116 because every jurisdiction will then have the same choice of law rule and in a particular case all choice of law rules will point to the same substantive law.

Subsection (b) does not state a choice of law rule for the "liability of an applicant." However, subsection (b) does state a choice of law rule for the liability of an issuer, nominated person, or adviser, and since some of the issues in suits by applicants against those persons involve the "liability of an issuer, nominated person, or adviser," subsection (b) states the choice of law rule for those issues. Because an issuer may have liability to a confirmer both as an issuer (Section 5–108(a), Comment 5 to Section 5–108) and as an applicant (Section 5–107(a), Comment 1 to Section 5–107, Section 5–108(i)), subsection (b) may state the choice of law rule for some but not all of the issuer's liability in a suit by a confirmer.

2. Because the confirmer or other nominated person may choose different law from that chosen by the issuer or may be located in a different jurisdiction and fail to choose law, it is possible that a confirmer or nominated person may be obligated to pay (under their law) but will not be entitled to payment from the issuer (under its law). Similarly, the rights of an unreimbursed issuer, confirmer, or nominated person against a beneficiary under Section 5–109, 5–110, or 5–117, will not necessarily be governed by the same law that applies to the issuer's or confirmer's obligation upon presentation. Because the UCP and other practice are incorporated in most international letters of credit, disputes arising from different legal obligations to honor have not been frequent. Since Section 5–108 incorporates standard practice, these problems should be further minimized—at least to the extent that the same practice is and continues to be widely followed.

3. This section does not permit what is now authorized by the nonuniform Section 5–102(4) in New York. Under the current law in New York a letter of credit that incorporates the UCP is not governed in any respect by Article 5. Under revised Section 5–116 letters of credit that incorporate the UCP or similar practice will still be subject to Article 5 in certain respects. First, incorporation of the UCP or other practice does not override the nonvariable terms of Article 5. Second, where there is no conflict between Article 5 and the relevant provision of the UCP or other practice, both apply. Third, practice provisions incorporated in a letter of credit will not be effective if they fail to comply with Section 5–103(c). Assume, for example, that a practice provision purported to free a party from any liability unless it were "grossly negligent" or that the practice generally limited the remedies that one party might have against another. Depending upon the circumstances, that disclaimer or limitation of liability might be ineffective because of Section 5–103(c).

Even though Article 5 is generally consistent with UCP 500, it is not necessarily consistent with other rules or with versions of the UCP that may be adopted after Article 5's revision, or with other practices that may develop. Rules of practice incorporated in the letter of credit or other undertaking are those in effect when the letter of credit or other undertaking is issued. Except in the unusual cases discussed in the immediately preceding paragraph, practice adopted in a letter of credit will override the rules of Article 5 and the parties to letter of credit transactions must be familiar with practice (such as future versions of the UCP) that is explicitly adopted in letters of credit.

4. In several ways Article 5 conflicts with and overrides similar matters governed by Articles 3 and 4. For example, "draft" is more broadly defined in letter of credit practice than under Section 3–104. The time allowed for honor and the required notification of reasons for dishonor are different in letter of credit practice than in the handling of documentary and other drafts under Articles 3 and 4.

5. Subsection (e) must be read in conjunction with existing law governing subject matter jurisdiction. If the local law restricts a court to certain subject matter jurisdiction not including letter of credit disputes, subsection (e) does not authorize parties to choose that forum. For example, the parties' agreement under Section 5–116(e) would not confer jurisdiction on a probate court to decide a letter of credit case.

If the parties choose a forum under subsection (e) and if—because of other law—that forum will not take jurisdiction, the parties' agreement or undertaking should then be construed (for the purpose of forum selection) as though it did not contain a clause choosing a particular forum. That result is necessary to avoid sentencing the parties to eternal purgatory where neither the chosen State nor the State which would have jurisdiction but for the clause will take jurisdiction—the former in disregard of the clause and the latter in honor of the clause.

§ 5.117. Subrogation of Issuer, Applicant, and Nominated Person

(a) An issuer that honors a beneficiary's presentation is subrogated to the rights of the beneficiary to the same extent as if the issuer were a secondary obligor of the underlying obligation owed to the beneficiary and of the applicant to the same extent as if the issuer were the secondary obligor of the underlying obligation owed to the applicant.

(b) An applicant that reimburses an issuer is subrogated to the rights of the issuer against any beneficiary, presenter, or nominated person to the same extent as if the applicant were the secondary obligor of the obligations owed to the issuer and has the rights of subrogation of the issuer to the rights of the beneficiary stated in Subsection (a).

(c) A nominated person who pays or gives value against a draft or demand presented under a letter of credit is subrogated to the rights of:

(1) the issuer against the applicant to the same extent as if the nominated person were a secondary obligor of the obligation owed to the issuer by the applicant;

(2) the beneficiary to the same extent as if the nominated person were a secondary obligor of the underlying obligation owed to the beneficiary; and

(3) the applicant to the same extent as if the nominated person were a secondary obligor of the underlying obligation owed to the applicant.

(d) Notwithstanding any agreement or term to the contrary, the rights of subrogation stated in Subsections (a) and (b) do not arise until the issuer honors the letter of credit or otherwise pays, and the rights in Subsection (c) do not arise until the nominated person pays or otherwise gives value. Until then, the issuer, the nominated person, and the applicant do not derive under this section present or prospective rights forming the basis of a claim, defense, or excuse.

Amended by Acts 1999, 76th Leg., ch. 4, § 1, eff. Sept. 1, 1999.

Uniform Commercial Code Comment

1. By itself this section does not grant any right of subrogation. It grants only the right that would exist if the person seeking subrogation "were a secondary obligor." (The term "secondary obligor" refers to a surety, guarantor, or other person against whom or whose property an obligee has recourse with respect to the obligation of a third party. See Restatement of the Law Third, Suretyship and Guaranty § 1 (1996).) If the secondary obligor would not have a right to subrogation in the circumstances in which one is claimed under this section, none is granted by this section. In effect, the section does no more than to remove an impediment that some courts have found to subrogation because they conclude that the issuer's or other claimant's rights are "independent" of the underlying obligation. If, for example, a secondary obligor would not have a subrogation right because its payment did not fully satisfy the underlying obligation, none would be available under this section. The section indorses the position of Judge Becker in *Tudor Development Group, Inc. v. United States Fidelity and Guaranty*, 968 F.2d 357 (3rd Cir.1991).

2. To preserve the independence of the letter of credit obligation and to insure that subrogation not be used as an offensive weapon by an issuer or others, the admonition in subsection (d) must be carefully observed. Only one who has completed its performance in a letter of credit transaction can have a right to subrogation. For example, an issuer may not dishonor and then defend its dishonor or assert a setoff on the ground that it is subrogated to another person's rights. Nor may the issuer complain after honor that its subrogation rights have been impaired by any good faith dealings between the beneficiary and the applicant or any other person. Assume, for example, that the beneficiary under a standby letter of credit is a mortgagee. If the mortgagee were obliged to issue a release of the mortgage upon payment of the underlying debt (by the issuer under the letter of credit), that release might impair the issuer's rights of subrogation, but the beneficiary would have no liability to the issuer for having granted that release.

§ 5.118. Security Interest of Issuer or Nominated Person

(a) An issuer or nominated person has a security interest in a document presented under a letter of credit to the extent that the issuer or nominated person honors or gives value for the presentation.

(b) So long as and to the extent that an issuer or nominated person has not been reimbursed or has not otherwise recovered the value given with respect to a security interest in a document under Subsection (a), the security interest continues and is subject to Chapter 9, but:

(1) a security agreement is not necessary to make the security interest enforceable under Section 9.203(b)(3);

(2) if the document is presented in a medium other than a written or other tangible medium, the security interest is perfected; and

(3) if the document is presented in a written or other tangible medium and is not a certificated security, chattel paper, a document of title, an instrument, or a letter of credit, the security interest is perfected and has priority over a conflicting security interest in the document so long as the debtor does not have possession of the document.

Added by Acts 1999, 76th Leg., ch. 414, § 2.24, eff. July 1, 2001.

Uniform Commercial Code Comment

1. This section gives the issuer of a letter of credit or a nominated person thereunder an automatic perfected security interest in a "document" (as that term is defined in Section 5–102(a)(6)). The security interest arises only if the document is presented to the issuer or nominated person under the letter of credit and only to the extent of the value that is given. This security interest is analogous to that awarded to a collecting bank under Section 4–210. Subsection (b) contains special rules governing the security interest arising under this section. In all other respects, a security interest arising under this section is subject to Article 9. See Section 9–109. Thus, for example, a security interest arising under this section may give rise to a security interest in proceeds under Section 9–315.

2. Subsection (b)(1) makes a security agreement unnecessary to the creation of a security interest under this section. Under subsection (b)(2), a security interest arising under this section is perfected if the document is presented in a medium other than a written or tangible medium. Documents that are written and that are not an otherwise-defined type of collateral under Article 9 (e.g., an invoice or inspection certificate) may be goods, in which an issuer or nominated person could perfect its security interest by possession. Because the definition of document in Section 5–102(a)(6) includes records (e.g., electronic records) that may not be goods, subsection (b)(2) provides for automatic perfection (i.e., without filing or possession).

Under subsection (b)(3), if the document (i) is in a written or tangible medium, (ii) is not a certificated security, chattel paper, a document of title, an instrument, or a letter of credit, and (iii) is not in the debtor's possession, the security interest is perfected and has priority over a conflicting security interest. If the document is a type of tangible collateral that subsection (b)(3) excludes from its perfection and priority rules, the issuer or nominated person must comply with the normal method of perfection (e.g., possession of an instrument) and is subject to the applicable Article 9 priority rules. Documents to which subsection (b)(3) applies may be important to an issuer or nominated person. For example, a confirmer who pays the beneficiary must be assured that its rights to all documents are not impaired. It will find it necessary to present all of the required documents to the issuer in order to be reimbursed. Moreover, when a nominated person sends documents to an issuer in connection with of the nominated person's reimbursement, that activity is not a collection, enforcement, or disposition of collateral under Article 9.

One purpose of this section is to protect an issuer or nominated person from claims of a beneficiary's creditors. It is a fallback provision inasmuch as issuers and nominated persons frequently may obtain and perfect security interests under the usual Article 9 rules, and, in many cases, the documents will be owned by the issuer, nominated person, or applicant.

CHAPTER 6. BULK TRANSFERS [REPEALED]

§§ 6.101 to 6.111. Repealed by Acts 1993, 73rd Leg., ch. 570, § 16, eff. Sept. 1, 1993

CHAPTER 7. DOCUMENTS OF TITLE

SUBCHAPTER A. GENERAL PROVISIONS

SUBCHAPTER B. WAREHOUSE RECEIPTS: SPECIAL PROVISIONS

SUBCHAPTER C. BILLS OF LADING: SPECIAL PROVISIONS

Acts 2005, 79th Leg., ch. 122, § 1 amended chapter 7.

SUBCHAPTER A. GENERAL PROVISIONS

Acts 2005, 79th Leg., ch. 122, § 1 made substantial textual revisions to Chapter 7, comprising mainly gender neutral references and word order; minor changes to substantive law focused on the facilitation of electronic commerce, by providing for electronic documents of title by expanding the "document of title" definition.

§ 7.101. Short Title

This chapter may be cited as Uniform Commercial Code—Documents of Title.

Acts 1967, 60th Leg., p. 2343, ch. 785, § 1, eff. Sept. 1, 1967. Amended by Acts 2005, 79th Leg., ch. 122, § 1, eff. Sept. 1, 2005.

Uniform Commercial Code Comment

Prior Uniform Statutory Provision: Former Section 7–101.

Changes: Revised for style only.

This Article is a revision of the 1962 Official Text with Comments as amended since 1962. The 1962 Official Text was a consolidation and revision of the Uniform Warehouse Receipts Act and the Uniform Bills of Lading Act, and embraced the provisions of the Uniform Sales Act relating to negotiation of documents of title.

This Article does not contain the substantive criminal provisions found in the Uniform Warehouse Receipts and Bills of Lading Acts. These criminal provisions are inappropriate to a Commercial Code, and for the most part duplicate portions of the ordinary criminal law relating to frauds. This revision deletes the former Section 7–105 that provided that courts could apply a rule from Parts 2 and 3 by analogy to a situation not explicitly covered in the provisions on warehouse receipts or bills of lading when it was appropriate. This is, of course, an unexceptional proposition and need not be stated explicitly in the statute. Thus former Section 7–105 has been deleted. Whether applying a rule by analogy to a situation is appropriate depends upon the facts of each case.

The Article does not attempt to define the tort liability of bailees, except to hold certain classes of bailees to a minimum standard of reasonable care. For important classes of bailees, liabilities in case of loss, damages or destruction, as well as other legal questions associated with particular documents of title, are governed by federal statutes, international treaties, and in some cases regulatory state laws, which supersede the provisions of this Article in case of inconsistency. See Section 7–103.

Sections 31 and 32 of Acts 2005, 79th Leg., ch. 122 provide:

"Sec. 31. This Act applies to a document of title that is issued or a bailment that arises on or after the effective date of this Act. This Act does not apply to a document of title that is issued or a bailment that arises before the effective date of this Act even if the document of title or bailment would be subject to this Act if the document of title had been issued or bailment had arisen after the effective date of this Act. This Act does not apply to a right of action that has accrued before the effective date of this Act.

"Sec. 32. A document of title issued or a bailment that arises before the effective date of this Act and the rights, obligations, and interests flowing from that document or bailment are governed by any statute or other rule amended or repealed by this Act as if amendment or repeal had not occurred and may be terminated, completed, consummated, or enforced under that statute or other rule."

§ 7.102. Definitions and Index of Definitions

(a) In this chapter, unless the context otherwise requires:

(1) "Bailee" means a person that by a warehouse receipt, bill of lading, or other document of title acknowledges possession of goods and contracts to deliver them.

(2) "Carrier" means a person that issues a bill of lading.

(3) "Consignee" means a person named in a bill of lading to which or to whose order the bill promises delivery.

(4) "Consignor" means a person named in a bill of lading as the person from which the goods have been received for shipment.

(5) "Delivery order" means a record that contains an order to deliver goods directed to a warehouse, carrier, or other person that in the ordinary course of business issues warehouse receipts or bills of lading.

(6) [Reserved.]

(7) "Goods" means all things that are treated as movable for the purposes of a contract for storage or transportation.

(8) "Issuer" means a bailee that issues a document of title or, in the case of an unaccepted delivery order, the person that orders the possessor of goods to deliver. The term includes a person for which an agent or employee purports to act in issuing a document if the agent or employee has real or apparent authority to issue documents, even if the issuer did not receive any goods, the goods were misdescribed, or in any other respect the agent or employee violated the issuer's instructions.

(9) "Person entitled under the document" means the holder, in the case of a negotiable document of title, or the person to which delivery of the goods is to be made by the terms of, or pursuant to instructions in a record under, a nonnegotiable document of title.

(10) [Reserved.]

(11) "Shipper" means a person that enters into a contract of transportation with a carrier.

(12) "Sign" means, with present intent to authenticate or adopt a record:

(A) to execute or adopt a tangible symbol; or

(B) to attach to or logically associate with the record an electronic sound, symbol, or process.

(13) "Warehouse" means a person engaged in the business of storing goods for hire.

(b) Definitions in other chapters applying to this chapter and the sections in which they appear are:

(1) "Contract for sale," Section 2.106.

(2) "Lessee in ordinary course of business," Section 2A.103.

(3) " 'Receipt' of goods," Section 2.103.

(c) In addition, Chapter 1 contains general definitions and principles of construction and interpretation applicable throughout this chapter.

Acts 1967, 60th Leg., p. 2343, ch. 785, § 1, eff. Sept. 1, 1967. Amended by Acts 2005, 79th Leg., ch. 122, § 1, eff. Sept. 1, 2005.

Uniform Commercial Code Comment

Prior Uniform Statutory Provision: Former Section 7–102.

Changes: New definitions of "carrier," "good faith," "record," "sign," and "shipper." Other definitions revised to accommodate electronic mediums.

Purposes:

1. "Bailee" is used in this Article as a blanket term to designate carriers, warehousemen and others who normally issue documents of title on the basis of goods which they have received. The definition does not, however, require actual possession of the goods. If a bailee acknowledges possession when it does not have possession, the bailee is bound by sections of this Article which declare the "bailee's" obligations. (See definition of "Issuer" in this section and Sections 7–203 and 7–301 on liability in case of non-receipt.) A "carrier" is one type of bailee and is defined as a person that issues a bill of lading. A "shipper" is a person who enters into the contract of transportation with the carrier. The definitions of "bailee," "consignee," "consignor," "goods", and "issuer", are unchanged in substance from prior law. "Document of title" is defined in Article 1, and may be in either tangible or electronic form.

2. The definition of warehouse receipt contained in the general definitions section of this Act (Section 1–201) does not require that the issuing warehouse be "lawfully engaged" in business or for profit. The warehouse's compliance with applicable state regulations such as the filing of a bond has no bearing on the substantive issues dealt with in this Article. Certainly the issuer's violations of law should not diminish its responsibility on documents the issuer has put in commercial circulation. But it is still essential that the business be storing goods "for hire" (Section 1–201 and this section). A person does not become a warehouse by storing its own goods.

3. When a delivery order has been accepted by the bailee it is for practical purposes indistinguishable from a warehouse receipt. Prior to such acceptance there is no basis for imposing obligations on the bailee other than the ordinary obligation of contract which the bailee may have assumed to the depositor of the goods. Delivery orders may be either electronic or tangible documents of title. See definition of "document of title" in Section 1–201.

4. The obligation of good faith imposed by this Article and by Article 1, Section 1–304 includes the observance of reasonable commercial standards of fair dealing.

5. The definitions of "record" and "sign" are included to facilitate electronic mediums. See comment 9 to Section 9–102 discussing "record" and the comment to amended Section 2–103 discussing "sign."

6. "Person entitled under the document" is moved from former Section 7–403.

7. These definitions apply in this Article unless the context otherwise requires. The "context" is intended to refer to the context in which the defined term is used in the Uniform Commercial Code. The definition applies whenever the defined term is used unless the context in which the defined term is used in the statute indicates that the term was not used in its defined sense. See comment to Section 1-201.

Cross References:

Point 1: Sections 1-201, 7-203 and 7-301.

Point 2: Sections 1-201 and 7-203.

Point 3: Section 1-201.

Point 4: Section 1-304.

Point 5: Section 9-102 and 2-103.

See general comment to document of title in Section 1-201.

Definitional Cross References:

"Bill of lading". Section 1-201.

"Contract". Section 1-201.

"Contract for sale". Section 2-106.

"Delivery". Section 1-201.

"Document of title". Section 1-201.

"Person". Section 1-201.

"Purchase". Section 1-201.

"Receipt of goods". Section 2-103.

"Right". Section 1-201.

"Warehouse receipt". Section 1-201.

Sections 31 and 32 of Acts 2005, 79th Leg., ch. 122 provide:

"Sec. 31. This Act applies to a document of title that is issued or a bailment that arises on or after the effective date of this Act. This Act does not apply to a document of title that is issued or a bailment that arises before the effective date of this Act even if the document of title or bailment would be subject to this Act if the document of title had been issued or bailment had arisen after the effective date of this Act. This Act does not apply to a right of action that has accrued before the effective date of this Act.

"Sec. 32. A document of title issued or a bailment that arises before the effective date of this Act and the rights, obligations, and interests flowing from that document or bailment are governed by any statute or other rule amended or repealed by this Act as if amendment or repeal had not occurred and may be terminated, completed, consummated, or enforced under that statute or other rule."

§ 7.103. Relation of Article to Treaty or Statute

(a) This chapter is subject to any treaty or statute of the United States or a regulatory statute of this state to the extent the treaty, statute, or regulatory statute is applicable.

(b) This chapter does not repeal or modify any law prescribing the form or contents of a document of title or the services or facilities to be afforded by a bailee, or otherwise regulating a bailee's businesses in respects not specifically treated in this chapter. However, violation of these laws does not affect the status of a document of title that otherwise complies with the definition of a document of title.

(c) This chapter modifies, limits, and supersedes the federal Electronic Signatures in Global and National Commerce Act (15 U.S.C. Section 7001 et seq.) but does not modify, limit, or supersede Section 101(c) of that Act (15 U.S.C. Section 7001(c)) or authorize electronic delivery of any of the notices described in Section 103(b) of that Act (15 U.S.C. Section 7003(b)).

Text of subsec. (d) effective until April 1, 2009

(d) To the extent there is a conflict between Chapter 43 and this chapter, this chapter governs.

Text of subsec. (d) effective April 1, 2009

(d) To the extent there is a conflict between Chapter 322 and this chapter, this chapter governs.

Acts 1967, 60th Leg., p. 2343, ch. 785, § 1, eff. Sept. 1, 1967. Amended by Acts 2005, 79th Leg., ch. 122, § 1, eff. Sept. 1, 2005; Acts 2007, 80th Leg., ch. 885, § 2.04, eff. April 1, 2009.

Uniform Commercial Code Comment

Prior Uniform Statutory Provision: Former Sections 7-103 and 10-104.

Changes: Deletion of references to tariffs and classifications; incorporation of former Section 10-104 into subsection (b), provide for intersection with federal and state law governing electronic transactions.

Purposes:

1. To make clear what would of course be true without the Section, that applicable Federal law is paramount.

2. To make clear also that regulatory state statutes (such as those fixing or authorizing a commission to fix rates and prescribe services, authorizing different charges for goods of different values, and limiting liability for loss to the declared value on which the charge was based) are not affected by the Article and are controlling on the matters which they cover unless preempted by federal law. The reference in former Section 7-103 to tariffs, classifications, and regulations filed or issued pursuant to regulatory state statutes has been deleted as inappropriate in the modern era of diminished regulation of carriers and warehouses. If a regulatory scheme requires a carrier or warehouse to issue a tariff or classification, that tariff or classification would be given effect via the state regulatory scheme that this Article recognizes as controlling. Permissive tariffs or classifications would not displace the provisions of this act, pursuant to this section, but may be given effect through the ability of parties to incorporate those terms by reference into their agreement.

3. The document of title provisions of this act supplement the federal law and regulatory state law governing bailees. This Article focuses on the commercial importance and usage of documents of title. State ex. rel Public Service Commission v. Gunkelman & Sons, Inc., 219 N.W.2d 853 (N.D. 1974).

4. Subsection (c) is included to make clear the interrelationship between the federal Electronic Signatures in Global

and National Commerce Act and this article and the conforming amendments to other articles of the Uniform Commercial Code promulgated as part of the revision of this article. Section 102 of the federal act allows a State statute to modify, limit, or supersede the provisions of Section 101 of the federal act. See the comments to Revised Article 1, Section 1–108.

5. Subsection (d) makes clear that once this article is in effect, its provisions regarding electronic commerce and regarding electronic documents of title control in the event there is a conflict with the provisions of the Uniform Electronic Transactions Act or other applicable state law governing electronic transactions.

Cross References:

Sections 1–108, 7–201, 7–202, 7–204, 7–206, 7–309, 7–401, 7–403.

Definitional Cross Reference:

"Bill of lading". Section 1–201.

Sections 31 and 32 of Acts 2005, 79th Leg., ch. 122 provide:

"Sec. 31. This Act applies to a document of title that is issued or a bailment that arises on or after the effective date of this Act. This Act does not apply to a document of title that is issued or a bailment that arises before the effective date of this Act even if the document of title or bailment would be subject to this Act if the document of title had been issued or bailment had arisen after the effective date of this Act. This Act does not apply to a right of action that has accrued before the effective date of this Act.

"Sec. 32. A document of title issued or a bailment that arises before the effective date of this Act and the rights, obligations, and interests flowing from that document or bailment are governed by any statute or other rule amended or repealed by this Act as if amendment or repeal had not occurred and may be terminated, completed, consummated, or enforced under that statute or other rule."

§ 7.104. Negotiable and Nonnegotiable Document of Title

(a) A document of title is negotiable if by its terms the goods are to be delivered to bearer or to the order of a named person.

(b) A document of title other than one described in Subsection (a) is nonnegotiable. A bill of lading that states that the goods are consigned to a named person is not made negotiable by a provision that the goods are to be delivered only against an order in a record signed by the same or another named person.

(c) A document of title is nonnegotiable if, at the time it is issued, the document has a conspicuous legend, however expressed, that it is nonnegotiable.

Acts 1967, 60th Leg., p. 2343, ch. 785, § 1, eff. Sept. 1, 1967. Amended by Acts 2005, 79th Leg., ch. 122, § 1, eff. Sept. 1, 2005.

Uniform Commercial Code Comment

Prior Uniform Statutory Provision: Former Section 7–104.

Changes: Subsection (a) is revised to reflect modern style and trade practice. Subsection (b) is revised for style and medium neutrality. Subsection (c) is new.

Purposes:

1. This Article deals with a class of commercial paper representing commodities in storage or transportation. This "commodity paper" is to be distinguished from what might be called "money paper" dealt with in the Article of this Act on Commercial Paper (Article 3) and "investment paper" dealt with in the Article of this Act on Investment Securities (Article 8). The class of "commodity paper" is designated "document of title" following the terminology of the Uniform Sales Act Section 76. Section 1–201. The distinctions between negotiable and nonnegotiable documents in this section makes the most important subclassification employed in the Article, in that the holder of negotiable documents may acquire more rights than its transferor had (See Section 7–502). The former Section 7–104, which provided that a document of title was negotiable if it runs to a named person or assigns if such designation was recognized in overseas trade, has been deleted as not necessary in light of current commercial practice.

A document of title is negotiable only if it satisfies this section. "Deliverable on proper indorsement and surrender of this receipt" will not render a document negotiable. Bailees often include such provisions as a means of insuring return of nonnegotiable receipts for record purposes. Such language may be regarded as insistence by the bailee upon a particular kind of receipt in connection with delivery of the goods. Subsection (a) makes it clear that a document is not negotiable which provides for delivery to order or bearer only if written instructions to that effect are given by a named person. Either tangible or electronic documents of title may be negotiable if the document meets the requirement of this section.

2. Subsection (c) is derived from Section 3–104(d). Prior to issuance of the document of title, an issuer may stamp or otherwise provide by a notation on the document that it is nonnegotiable even if the document would otherwise comply with the requirement of subsection (a). Once issued as a negotiable document of title, the document cannot be changed from a negotiable document to a nonnegotiable document. A document of title that is nonnegotiable cannot be made negotiable by stamping or providing a notation that the document is negotiable. The only way to make a document of title negotiable is to comply with subsection (a). A negotiable document of title may fail to be duly negotiated if the negotiation does not comply with the requirements for "due negotiation" stated in Section 7–501.

Cross Reference: Sections 7–501 and 7–502.

Definitional Cross References:

"Bearer". Section 1–201.

"Bill of lading". Section 1–201.

"Delivery". Section 1–201.

"Document of title". Section 1–201.

"Person". Section 1–201.

"Sign". Section 7–102

"Warehouse receipt". Section 1–201.

Sections 31 and 32 of Acts 2005, 79th Leg., ch. 122 provide:

"Sec. 31. This Act applies to a document of title that is issued or a bailment that arises on or after the effective date of this Act. This Act does not apply to a document of title that is issued or a bailment that arises before the effective date of this Act even if the document of title or bailment would be subject to this Act if the document of title had been issued or bailment had arisen after the effective date of this Act. This Act does not apply to a right of action that has accrued before the effective date of this Act.

"Sec. 32. A document of title issued or a bailment that arises before the effective date of this Act and the rights, obligations, and interests flowing from that document or bailment are governed by any statute or other rule amended or repealed by this Act as if amendment or repeal had not occurred and may be terminated, completed, consummated, or enforced under that statute or other rule."

§ 7.105. Reissuance in Alternative Medium

(a) Upon request of a person entitled under an electronic document of title, the issuer of the electronic document may issue a tangible document of title as a substitute for the electronic document if:

(1) the person entitled under the electronic document surrenders control of the document to the issuer; and

(2) the tangible document when issued contains a statement that it is issued in substitution for the electronic document.

(b) Upon issuance of a tangible document of title in substitution for an electronic document of title in accordance with Subsection (a):

(1) the electronic document ceases to have any effect or validity; and

(2) the person that procured issuance of the tangible document warrants to all subsequent persons entitled under the tangible document that the warrantor was a person entitled under the electronic document when the warrantor surrendered control of the electronic document to the issuer.

(c) Upon request of a person entitled under a tangible document of title, the issuer of the tangible document may issue an electronic document of title as a substitute for the tangible document if:

(1) the person entitled under the tangible document surrenders possession of the document to the issuer; and

(2) the electronic document when issued contains a statement that it is issued in substitution for the tangible document.

(d) Upon issuance of the electronic document of title in substitution for a tangible document of title in accordance with Subsection (c):

(1) the tangible document ceases to have any effect or validity; and

(2) the person that procured issuance of the electronic document warrants to all subsequent persons entitled under the electronic document that the warrantor was a person entitled under the tangible document when the warrantor surrendered possession of the tangible document to the issuer.

Amended by Acts 2005, 79th Leg., ch. 122, § 1, eff. Sept. 1, 2005.

Uniform Commercial Code Comment

Prior Uniform Statutory Provisions: None.

Other relevant law: UNCITRAL Draft Instrument on the Carriage of Goods by SeaTransport Law.

Purpose:

1. This section allows for documents of title issued in one medium to be reissued in another medium. This section applies to both negotiable and nonnegotiable documents. This section sets forth minimum requirements for giving the reissued document effect and validity. The issuer is not required to issue a document in an alternative medium and if the issuer chooses to do so, it may impose additional requirements. Because a document of title imposes obligations on the issuer of the document, it is imperative for the issuer to be the one who issues the substitute document in order for the substitute document to be effective and valid.

2. The request must be made to the issuer by the person entitled to enforce the document of title (Section 7–102(a)(9)) and that person must surrender possession or control of the original document to the issuer. The reissued document must have a notation that it has been issued as a substitute for the original document. These minimum requirements must be met in order to give the substitute document effect and validity. If these minimum requirements are not met for issuance of a substitute document of title, the original document of title continues to be effective and valid. Section 7–402. However, if the minimum requirements imposed by this section are met, in addition to any other requirements that the issuer may impose, the substitute document will be the document that is effective and valid.

3. To protect parties who subsequently take the substitute document of title, the person who procured issuance of the substitute document warrants that it was a person entitled under the original document at the time it surrendered possession or control of the original document to the issuer. This warranty is modeled after the warranty found in Section 4–209.

Cross Reference:

Sections 7–106, 7–402 and 7–601.

Definitional Cross Reference:

"Person entitled to enforce," Section 7–102.

Sections 31 and 32 of Acts 2005, 79th Leg., ch. 122 provide:

"Sec. 31. This Act applies to a document of title that is issued or a bailment that arises on or after the effective date of this Act. This Act does not apply to a document of title that is issued or a bailment that arises before the effective date of this Act even if the document of title or bailment would be subject to this Act if the document of title had been issued or bailment had arisen after the effective date of this Act. This Act does not apply to a right of action that has accrued before the effective date of this Act.

"Sec. 32. A document of title issued or a bailment that arises before the effective date of this Act and the rights, obligations, and interests flowing from that document or bailment are governed by any statute or other rule amended or repealed by this Act as if amendment or repeal had not occurred and may be terminated, completed, consummated, or enforced under that statute or other rule."

§ 7.106. Control of Electronic Document of Title

(a) A person has control of an electronic document of title if a system employed for evidencing the transfer of interests in the electronic document reliably establishes that person as the person to which the electronic document was issued or transferred.

(b) A system satisfies Subsection (a), and a person is deemed to have control of an electronic document of title, if the document is created, stored, and assigned in such a manner that:

(1) a single authoritative copy of the document exists which is unique, identifiable, and, except as otherwise provided in Subdivisions (4), (5), and (6), unalterable;

(2) the authoritative copy identifies the person asserting control as:

(A) the person to which the document was issued; or

(B) if the authoritative copy indicates that the document has been transferred, the person to which the document was most recently transferred;

(3) the authoritative copy is communicated to and maintained by the person asserting control or its designated custodian;

(4) copies or amendments that add or change an identified assignee of the authoritative copy can be made only with the consent of the person asserting control;

(5) each copy of the authoritative copy and any copy of a copy is readily identifiable as a copy that is not the authoritative copy; and

(6) any amendment of the authoritative copy is readily identifiable as authorized or unauthorized.

Added by Acts 2005, 79th Leg., ch. 122, § 1, eff. Sept. 1, 2005.

Uniform Commercial Code Comment

Prior Uniform Statutory Provision: Uniform Electronic Transactions Act Section 16.

Purpose:

1. The section defines "control" for electronic documents of title and derives its rules from the Uniform Electronic Transactions Act § 16 on transferrable records. Unlike UETA § 16, however, a document of title may be reissued in an alternative medium pursuant to Section 7–105. At any point in time in which a document of title is in electronic form, the control concept of this section is relevant. As under UETA § 16, the control concept embodied in this section provides the legal framework for developing systems for electronic documents of title.

2. Control of an electronic document of title substitutes for the concept of indorsement and possession in the tangible document of title context. See Section 7-501. A person with a tangible document of title delivers the document by voluntarily transferring possession and a person with an electronic document of title delivers the document by voluntarily transferring control. (Delivery is defined in Section 1–201).

3. Subsection (a) sets forth the general rule that the "system employed for evidencing the transfer of interests in the electronic document reliably establishes that person as the person to which the electronic document was issued or transferred." The key to having a system that satisfies this test is that identity of *the* person to which the document was issued or transferred must be reliably established. Of great importance to the functioning of the control concept is to be able to demonstrate, at any point in time, *the person* entitled under the electronic document. For example, a carrier may issue an electronic bill of lading by having the required information in a database that is encrypted and accessible by virtue of a password. If the computer system in which the required information is maintained identifies the person as *the* person to which the electronic bill of lading was issued or transferred, that person has control of the electronic document of title. That identification may be by virtue of passwords or other encryption methods. Registry systems may satisfy this test. For example, see the electronic warehouse receipt system established pursuant to 7 C.F.R. Part 735. This Article leaves to the market place the development of sufficient technologies and business practices that will meet the test.

An electronic document of title is evidenced by a record consisting of information stored in an electronic medium. Section 1–201. For example, a record in a computer database could be an electronic document of title assuming that it otherwise meets the definition of document of title. To the extent that third parties wish to deal in paper mediums, Section 7–105 provides a mechanism for exiting the electronic environment by having the issuer reissue the document of title in a tangible medium. Thus if a person entitled to enforce an electronic document of title causes the information in the record to be printed onto paper without the issuer's involvement in issuing the document of title pursuant to Section 7–105, that paper is not a document of title.

4. Subsection (a) sets forth the general test for control. Subsection (b) sets forth a safe harbor test that if satisfied, results in control under the general test in subsection (a). The test in subsection (b) is also used in Section 9–105 although Section 9–105 does not include the general test of subsection (a). Under subsection (b), at any point in time, a party should be able to identify the single authoritative copy

which is unique and identifiable as the authoritative copy. This does not mean that once created that the authoritative copy need be static and never moved or copied from its original location. To the extent that backup systems exist which result in multiple copies, the key to this idea is that at any point in time, the one authoritative copy needs to be unique and identifiable.

Parties may not by contract provide that control exists. The test for control is a factual test that depends upon whether the general test in subsection (a) or the safe harbor in subsection (b) is satisfied.

5. Article 7 has historically provided for rights under documents of title and rights of transferees of documents of title as those rights relate to the goods covered by the document. Third parties may possess or have control of documents of title. While misfeasance or negligence in failure to transfer or misdelivery of the document by those third parties may create serious issues, this Article has never dealt with those issues as it relates to tangible documents of title, preferring to leave those issues to the law of contracts, agency and tort law. In the electronic document of title regime, third party registry systems are just beginning to develop. It is very difficult to write rules regulating those third parties without some definitive sense of how the third party registry systems will be structured. Systems that are evolving to date tend to be "closed" systems in which all participants must sign on to the master agreement which provides for rights as against the registry system as well as rights among the members. In those closed systems, the document of title never leaves the system so the parties rely upon the master agreement as to rights against the registry for its failures in dealing with the document. This article contemplates that those "closed" systems will continue to evolve and that the control mechanism in this statute provides a method for the participants in the closed system to achieve the benefits of obtaining control allowed by this article.

This article also contemplates that parties will evolve open systems where parties need not be subject to a master agreement. In an open system a party that is expecting to obtain rights through an electronic document may not be a party to the master agreement. To the extent that open systems evolve by use of the control concept contained in this section, the law of contracts, agency, and torts as it applies to the registry's misfeasance or negligence concerning the transfer of control of the electronic document will allocate the risks and liabilities of the parties as that other law now does so for third parties who hold tangible documents and fail to deliver the documents.

Cross Reference:

Sections 7–105 and 7–501.

Definitional Cross–References:

"Delivery". 1–201.

"Document of title". 1–201.

Sections 31 and 32 of Acts 2005, 79th Leg., ch. 122 provide:

"Sec. 31. This Act applies to a document of title that is issued or a bailment that arises on or after the effective date of this Act. This Act does not apply to a document of title that is issued or a bailment that arises before the effective date of this Act even if the document of title or bailment would be subject to this Act if the document of title had been issued or bailment had arisen after the effective date of this Act. This Act does not apply to a right of action that has accrued before the effective date of this Act.

"Sec. 32. A document of title issued or a bailment that arises before the effective date of this Act and the rights, obligations, and interests flowing from that document or bailment are governed by any statute or other rule amended or repealed by this Act as if amendment or repeal had not occurred and may be terminated, completed, consummated, or enforced under that statute or other rule."

SUBCHAPTER B. WAREHOUSE RECEIPTS: SPECIAL PROVISIONS

Acts 2005, 79th Leg., ch. 122, § 1 amended chapter 7.

§ 7.201. Person That May Issue a Warehouse Receipt; Storage Under Bond

(a) A warehouse receipt may be issued by any warehouse.

(b) If goods, including distilled spirits and agricultural commodities, are stored under a statute requiring a bond against withdrawal or a license for the issuance of receipts in the nature of warehouse receipts, a receipt issued for the goods is deemed to be a warehouse receipt even if issued by a person that is the owner of the goods and is not a warehouse.

Acts 1967, 60th Leg., p. 2343, ch. 785, § 1, eff. Sept. 1, 1967. Amended by Acts 2005, 79th Leg., ch. 122, § 1, eff. Sept. 1, 2005.

Uniform Commercial Code Comment

Prior Uniform Statutory Provision: Former Section 7–201.

Changes: Update for style only.

Purposes:

It is not intended by re-enactment of subsection (a) to repeal any provisions of special licensing or other statutes regulating who may become a warehouse. Limitations on the transfer of the receipts and criminal sanctions for violation of such limitations are not impaired. Section 7–103. Compare Section 7–401(4) on the liability of the issuer in such cases. Subsection (b) covers receipts issued by the owner for whiskey or other goods stored in bonded warehouses under such statutes as 26 U.S.C. Chapter 51.

Cross References:

Sections 7–103, 7–401.

Definitional Cross References:

"Warehouse receipt". Section 1–201.

"Warehouse". Section 7–102.

Sections 31 and 32 of Acts 2005, 79th Leg., ch. 122 provide:

"Sec. 31. This Act applies to a document of title that is issued or a bailment that arises on or after the effective date of this Act. This Act does not apply to a document of title that is issued or a bailment that arises before the effective date of this Act even if the document of title or bailment would be subject to this Act if the document of title had been issued or bailment had arisen after the effective date of this Act. This Act does not apply to a right of action that has accrued before the effective date of this Act.

"Sec. 32. A document of title issued or a bailment that arises before the effective date of this Act and the rights, obligations, and interests flowing from that document or bailment are governed by any statute or other rule amended or repealed by this Act as if amendment or repeal had not occurred and may be terminated, completed, consummated, or enforced under that statute or other rule."

§ 7.202. Form of Warehouse Receipt

(a) A warehouse receipt need not be in any particular form.

(b) Unless a warehouse receipt provides for each of the following, the warehouse is liable for damages caused to a person injured by its omission:

(1) the location of the warehouse facility where the goods are stored;

(2) the date of issue of the receipt;

(3) the unique identification code of the receipt;

(4) a statement whether the goods received will be delivered to the bearer, to a named person, or to a named person or its order;

(5) the rate of storage and handling charges, but if goods are stored under a field warehousing arrangement, a statement of that fact is sufficient on a nonnegotiable receipt;

(6) a description of the goods or the packages containing them;

(7) the signature of the warehouse or its agent;

(8) if the receipt is issued for goods that the warehouse owns, either solely, jointly, or in common with others, the fact of that ownership; and

(9) a statement of the amount of advances made and of liabilities incurred for which the warehouse claims a lien or security interest, but if the precise amount of advances made or of liabilities incurred is, at the time of the issue of the receipt, unknown to the warehouse or to its agent that issued the receipt, a statement of the fact that advances have been made or liabilities incurred and the purpose of the advances or liabilities is sufficient.

(c) A warehouse may insert in its receipt any terms that are not contrary to this title and do not impair its obligation of delivery under Section 7.403 or its duty of care under Section 7.204. Any contrary provisions are ineffective.

Acts 1967, 60th Leg., p. 2343, ch. 785, § 1, eff. Sept. 1, 1967. Amended by Acts 2005, 79th Leg., ch. 122, § 1, eff. Sept. 1, 2005.

Uniform Commercial Code Comment

Prior Uniform Statutory Provision: Former Section 7–202.

Changes: Language is updated to accommodate electronic commerce and to reflect modern style.

Purposes:

1. This section does not displace any particular legislation that requires other terms in a warehouse receipt or that may require a particular form of a warehouse receipt. This section does not require that a warehouse receipt be issued. A warehouse receipt that is issued need not contain any of the terms listed in subsection (b) in order to qualify as a warehouse receipt as long as the receipt falls within the definition of "warehouse receipt" in Article 1. Thus the title has been changed to eliminate the phrase "essential terms" as provided in prior law. The only consequence of a warehouse receipt not containing any term listed in subsection (b) is that a person injured by a term's omission has a right as against the warehouse for harm caused by the omission. Cases, such as In re Celotex Corp., 134 B. R. 993 (Bankr. M.D. Fla. 1991), that held that in order to have a valid warehouse receipt all of the terms listed in this section must be contained in the receipt, are disapproved.

2. The unique identification code referred to in subsection (b)(3) can include any combination of letters, number, signs, and/or symbols that provide a unique identification. Whether an electronic or tangible warehouse receipt contains a signature will be resolved with the definition of sign in Section 7–102.

Cross References: Sections 7–103 and 7–401.

Definitional Cross References:

"Bearer". Section 1–201.

"Delivery". Section 1–201.

"Goods". Section 7–102.

"Person". Section 1–201.

"Security interest". Section 1–201.

"Sign". Section 7–102.

"Term". Section 1–201.

"Warehouse receipt". Section 1–201.

"Warehouse". Section 7–102.

Sections 31 and 32 of Acts 2005, 79th Leg., ch. 122 provide:

"Sec. 31. This Act applies to a document of title that is issued or a bailment that arises on or after the effective date of this Act. This Act does not apply to a document of title that is issued or a bailment that arises before the effective date of this Act even if the document of title or bailment would be subject to this Act if the document of title had been issued or bailment had arisen after the effective date of this Act. This Act does not apply to a right of action that has accrued before the effective date of this Act.

"Sec. 32. A document of title issued or a bailment that arises before the effective date of this Act and the rights, obligations, and interests flowing from that document or bailment are governed by any statute or other rule amended or repealed by this Act as if amendment or repeal had not occurred and may be terminated, completed, consummated, or enforced under that statute or other rule."

§ 7.203. Liability for Nonreceipt or Misdescription

A party to or purchaser for value in good faith of a document of title, other than a bill of lading, that relies upon the description of the goods in the document may recover from the issuer damages caused by the nonreceipt or misdescription of the goods, except to the extent that:

(1) the document conspicuously indicates that the issuer does not know whether all or part of the goods in fact were received or conform to the description, such as a case in which the description is in terms of marks or labels or kind, quantity, or condition, or the receipt or description is qualified by "contents, condition, and quality unknown," "said to contain," or words of similar import, if the indication is true; or

(2) the party or purchaser otherwise has notice of the nonreceipt or misdescription.

Acts 1967, 60th Leg., p. 2343, ch. 785, § 1, eff. Sept. 1, 1967. Amended by Acts 2005, 79th Leg., ch. 122, § 1, eff. Sept. 1, 2005.

Uniform Commercial Code Comment

Prior Uniform Statutory Provision: Former Section 7–203.

Changes: Changes to this section are for style only.

Purpose:

This section is a simplified restatement of existing law as to the method by which a bailee may avoid responsibility for the accuracy of descriptions which are made by or in reliance upon information furnished by the depositor. The issuer is liable on documents issued by an agent, contrary to instructions of its principal, without receiving goods. No disclaimer of the latter liability is permitted.

Cross Reference: Section 7–301.

Definitional Cross References:

"Conspicuous". Section 1–201.

"Document of title". Section 1–201.

"Goods". Section 7–102.

"Good Faith". Section 1–201. [7–102]

"Issuer". Section 7–102.

"Notice". Section 1–202.

"Party". Section 1–201.

"Purchaser". Section 1–201.

"Receipt of goods". Section 2–103.

"Value". Section 1–204.

Sections 31 and 32 of Acts 2005, 79th Leg., ch. 122 provide:

"Sec. 31. This Act applies to a document of title that is issued or a bailment that arises on or after the effective date of this Act. This Act does not apply to a document of title that is issued or a bailment that arises before the effective date of this Act even if the document of title or bailment would be subject to this Act if the document of title had been issued or bailment had arisen after the effective date of this Act. This Act does not apply to a right of action that has accrued before the effective date of this Act.

"Sec. 32. A document of title issued or a bailment that arises before the effective date of this Act and the rights, obligations, and interests flowing from that document or bailment are governed by any statute or other rule amended or repealed by this Act as if amendment or repeal had not occurred and may be terminated, completed, consummated, or enforced under that statute or other rule."

§ 7.204. Duty of Care; Contractual Limitation of Warehouse's Liability

(a) A warehouse is liable for damages for loss of or injury to the goods caused by its failure to exercise care with regard to the goods that a reasonably careful person would exercise under similar circumstances. However, unless otherwise agreed, the warehouse is not liable for damages that could not have been avoided by the exercise of that care.

(b) Damages may be limited by a term in the warehouse receipt or storage agreement limiting the amount of liability in case of loss or damage beyond which the warehouse is not liable. Such a limitation is not effective with respect to the warehouse's liability for conversion to its own use. The warehouse's liability, on request of the bailor in a record at the time of signing such storage agreement or within a reasonable time after receipt of the warehouse receipt, may be increased on part or all of the goods covered by the storage agreement or the warehouse receipt. In this event, increased rates may be charged based on an increased valuation of the goods.

(c) Reasonable provisions as to the time and manner of presenting claims and commencing actions based on the bailment may be included in the warehouse receipt or storage agreement.

Acts 1967, 60th Leg., p. 2343, ch. 785, § 1, eff. Sept. 1, 1967. Amended by Acts 2005, 79th Leg., ch. 122, § 1, eff. Sept. 1, 2005.

Uniform Commercial Code Comment

Prior Uniform Statutory Provision: Former Section 7–204.

Changes: Updated to reflect modern, standard commercial practices.

Purposes of Changes:

1. Subsection (a) continues the rule without change from former Section 7–204 on the warehouse's obligation to exercise reasonable care.

2. Former Section 7–204(2) required that the term limiting damages do so by setting forth a specific liability per article or item or of a value per unit of weight. This requirement has been deleted as out of step with modern industry

practice. Under subsection (b) a warehouse may limit its liability for damages for loss of or damage to the goods by a term in the warehouse receipt or storage agreement without the term constituting an impermissible disclaimer of the obligation of reasonable care. The parties cannot disclaim by contract the warehouse's obligation of care. Section 1–302. For example, limitations based upon per unit of weight, per package, per occurrence, or per receipt as well as limitations based upon a multiple of the storage rate may be commercially appropriate. As subsection (d) makes clear, the states or the federal government may supplement this section with more rigid standards of responsibility for some or all bailees.

3. Former Section 7–204(2) also provided that an increased rate can not be charged if contrary to a tariff. That language has been deleted. If a tariff is required under state or federal law, pursuant to Section 7–103(a), the tariff would control over the rule of this section allowing an increased rate. The provisions of a non-mandatory tariff may be incorporated by reference in the parties' agreement. See Comment 2 to Section 7–103. Subsection (c) deletes the reference to tariffs for the same reason that the reference has been omitted in subsection (b).

4. As under former Section 7–204(2), subsection (b) provides that a limitation of damages is ineffective if the warehouse has converted the goods to its own use. A mere failure to redeliver the goods is not conversion to the warehouse's own use. See Adams v. Ryan & Christie Storage, Inc., 563 F. Supp. 409 (E.D. Pa. 1983) aff'd 725 F.2d 666 (3rd Cir. 1983). Cases such as I.C.C. Metals Inc. v. Municipal Warehouse Co., 409 N.E. 2d 849 (N.Y. Ct. App. 1980) holding that mere failure to redeliver results in a presumption of conversion to the warehouse's own use are disapproved. "Conversion to its own use" is narrower than the idea of conversion generally. Cases such as Lipman v. Peterson, 575 P.2d 19 (Kan. 1978) holding to the contrary are disapproved.

5. Storage agreements commonly establish the contractual relationship between warehouses and depositors who have an on-going relationship. The storage agreement may allow for the movement of goods into and out of a warehouse without the necessity of issuing or amending a warehouse receipt upon each entry or exit of goods from the warehouse.

Cross References: Sections 1–302, 7–103, 7–309 and 7–403.

Definitional Cross References:

"Goods". Section 7–102.

"Reasonable time". Section 1–204.

"Sign". Section 7–102.

"Term". Section 1–201.

"Value". Section 1–204.

"Warehouse receipt". Section 1–201.

"Warehouse". Section 7–102.

Sections 31 and 32 of Acts 2005, 79th Leg., ch. 122 provide:

"Sec. 31. This Act applies to a document of title that is issued or a bailment that arises on or after the effective date of this Act. This Act does not apply to a document of title that is issued or a bailment that arises before the effective date of this Act even if the document of title or bailment would be subject to this Act if the document of title had been issued or bailment had arisen after the effective date of this Act. This Act does not apply to a right of action that has accrued before the effective date of this Act.

"Sec. 32. A document of title issued or a bailment that arises before the effective date of this Act and the rights, obligations, and interests flowing from that document or bailment are governed by any statute or other rule amended or repealed by this Act as if amendment or repeal had not occurred and may be terminated, completed, consummated, or enforced under that statute or other rule."

§ 7.205. Title Under Warehouse Receipt Defeated in Certain Cases

A buyer in ordinary course of business of fungible goods sold and delivered by a warehouse that is also in the business of buying and selling such goods takes the goods free of any claim under a warehouse receipt even if the receipt is negotiable and has been duly negotiated.

Acts 1967, 60th Leg., p. 2343, ch. 785, § 1, eff. Sept. 1, 1967. Amended by Acts 2005, 79th Leg., ch. 122, § 1, eff. Sept. 1, 2005.

Uniform Commercial Code Comment

Prior Uniform Statutory Provision: Former Section 7–205.

Changes: Changes for style only.

Purposes:

1. The typical case covered by this section is that of the warehouse-dealer in grain, and the substantive question at issue is whether in case the warehouse becomes insolvent the receipt holders shall be able to trace and recover grain shipped to farmers and other purchasers from the elevator. This was possible under the old acts, although courts were eager to find estoppels to prevent it. The practical difficulty of tracing fungible grain means that the preservation of this theoretical right adds little to the commercial acceptability of negotiable grain receipts, which really circulate on the credit of the warehouse. Moreover, on default of the warehouse, the receipt holders at least share in what grain remains, whereas retaking the grain from a good faith cash purchaser reduces the purchaser completely to the status of general creditor in a situation where there was very little the purchaser could do to guard against the loss. Compare 15 U.S.C. Section 714p enacted in 1955.

2. This provision applies to both negotiable and nonnegotiable warehouse receipts. The concept of due negotiation is provided for in 7–501. The definition of "buyer in ordinary course" is in Article 1 and provides, among other things, that a buyer must either have possession or a right to obtain the goods under Article 2 in order to be a buyer in ordinary course. This section requires actual delivery of the fungible goods to the buyer in ordinary course. Delivery requires voluntary transfer of possession of the fungible goods to the buyer. See amended Section 2–103. This section is not satisfied by the delivery of the document of title to the buyer in ordinary course.

Cross References: Sections 2–403 and 9–320.

Definitional Cross References:

"Buyer in ordinary course of business". Section 1–201.

"Delivery". Section 1–201.

"Duly negotiate". Section 7–501.

"Fungible" goods. Section 1–201.

"Goods". Section 7–102.

"Value". Section 1–204.

"Warehouse receipt". Section 1–201.

"Warehouse". Section 7–102.

Sections 31 and 32 of Acts 2005, 79th Leg., ch. 122 provide:

"Sec. 31. This Act applies to a document of title that is issued or a bailment that arises on or after the effective date of this Act. This Act does not apply to a document of title that is issued or a bailment that arises before the effective date of this Act even if the document of title or bailment would be subject to this Act if the document of title had been issued or bailment had arisen after the effective date of this Act. This Act does not apply to a right of action that has accrued before the effective date of this Act.

"Sec. 32. A document of title issued or a bailment that arises before the effective date of this Act and the rights, obligations, and interests flowing from that document or bailment are governed by any statute or other rule amended or repealed by this Act as if amendment or repeal had not occurred and may be terminated, completed, consummated, or enforced under that statute or other rule."

§ 7.206. Termination of Storage at Warehouse's Option

(a) A warehouse, by giving notice to the person on whose account the goods are held and any other person known to claim an interest in the goods, may require payment of any charges and removal of the goods from the warehouse at the termination of the period of storage fixed by the document of title or, if a period is not fixed, within a stated period not less than 30 days after the warehouse gives notice. If the goods are not removed before the date specified in the notice, the warehouse may sell them pursuant to Section 7.210.

(b) If a warehouse in good faith believes that goods are about to deteriorate or decline in value to less than the amount of its lien within the time provided in Subsection (a) and Section 7.210, the warehouse may specify in the notice given under Subsection (a) any reasonable shorter time for removal of the goods and, if the goods are not removed, may sell them at public sale held not less than one week after a single advertisement or posting.

(c) If, as a result of a quality or condition of the goods of which the warehouse did not have notice at the time of deposit, the goods are a hazard to other property, the warehouse facilities, or other persons, the warehouse may sell the goods at public or private sale without advertisement or posting on reasonable notification to all persons known to claim an interest in the goods. If the warehouse, after a reasonable effort, is unable to sell the goods, it may dispose of them in any lawful manner and does not incur liability by reason of that disposition.

(d) A warehouse shall deliver the goods to any person entitled to them under this chapter upon due demand made at any time before sale or other disposition under this section.

(e) A warehouse may satisfy its lien from the proceeds of any sale or disposition under this section but shall hold the balance for delivery on the demand of any person to which the warehouse would have been bound to deliver the goods.

Acts 1967, 60th Leg., p. 2343, ch. 785, § 1, eff. Sept. 1, 1967. Amended by Acts 2005, 79th Leg., ch. 122, § 1, eff. Sept. 1, 2005.

Uniform Commercial Code Comment

Prior Uniform Statutory Provision: Former Section 7–206.

Changes: Changes for style.

Purposes:

1. This section provides for three situations in which the warehouse may terminate storage for reasons other then enforcement of its lien as permitted by Section 7–210. Most warehousing is for an indefinite term, the bailor being entitled to delivery on reasonable demand. It is necessary to define the warehouse's power to terminate the bailment, since it would be commercially intolerable to allow warehouses to order removal of the goods on short notice. The thirty day period provided where the document does not carry its own period of termination corresponds to commercial practice of computing rates on a monthly basis. The right to terminate under subsection (a) includes a right to require payment of "any charges", but does not depend on the existence of unpaid charges.

2. In permitting expeditious disposition of perishable and hazardous goods the pre-Code Uniform Warehouse Receipts Act, Section 34, made no distinction between cases where the warehouse knowingly undertook to store such goods and cases where the goods were discovered to be of that character subsequent to storage. The former situation presents no such emergency as justifies the summary power of removal and sale. Subsections (b) and (c) distinguish between the two situations. The reason of this section should apply if the goods become hazardous during the course of storage. The process for selling the goods described in Section 7–210 governs the sale of goods under this section except as provided in subsections (b) and (c) for the situations described in those subsections respectively.

3. Protection of its lien is the only interest which the warehouse has to justify summary sale of perishable goods which are not hazardous. This same interest must be recognized when the stored goods, although not perishable, decline in market value to a point which threatens the warehouse's security.

4. The right to order removal of stored goods is subject to provisions of the public warehousing laws of some states forbidding warehouses from discriminating among custom-

ers. Nor does the section relieve the warehouse of any obligation under the state laws to secure the approval of a public official before disposing of deteriorating goods. Such regulatory statutes and the regulations under them remain in force and operative. Section 7–103.

Cross References: Sections 7–103 and 7–403.

Definitional Cross References:

"Delivery". Section 1–201.

"Document of title". Section 1–102.

"Good faith". Section 1–201 [7–102].

"Goods". Section 7–102.

"Notice". Section 1–202.

"Notification". Section 1–202.

"Person". Section 1–201.

"Reasonable time". Section 1–205.

"Value". Section 1–204.

"Warehouse". Section 7–102.

Sections 31 and 32 of Acts 2005, 79th Leg., ch. 122 provide:

"Sec. 31. This Act applies to a document of title that is issued or a bailment that arises on or after the effective date of this Act. This Act does not apply to a document of title that is issued or a bailment that arises before the effective date of this Act even if the document of title or bailment would be subject to this Act if the document of title had been issued or bailment had arisen after the effective date of this Act. This Act does not apply to a right of action that has accrued before the effective date of this Act.

"Sec. 32. A document of title issued or a bailment that arises before the effective date of this Act and the rights, obligations, and interests flowing from that document or bailment are governed by any statute or other rule amended or repealed by this Act as if amendment or repeal had not occurred and may be terminated, completed, consummated, or enforced under that statute or other rule."

§ 7.207. Goods Must be Kept Separate; Fungible Goods

(a) Unless the warehouse receipt provides otherwise, a warehouse shall keep separate the goods covered by each receipt so as to permit at all times identification and delivery of those goods. However, different lots of fungible goods may be commingled.

(b) If different lots of fungible goods are commingled, the goods are owned in common by the persons entitled thereto and the warehouse is severally liable to each owner for that owner's share. If, because of overissue, a mass of fungible goods is insufficient to meet all the receipts the warehouse has issued against it, the persons entitled include all holders to which overissued receipts have been duly negotiated.

Acts 1967, 60th Leg., p. 2343, ch. 785, § 1, eff. Sept. 1, 1967. Amended by Acts 2005, 79th Leg., ch. 122, § 1, eff. Sept. 1, 2005.

Uniform Commercial Code Comment

Prior Uniform Statutory Provision: Former Section 7–207.

Changes: Changes for style only.

Purposes:

No change of substance is made from former Section 7–207. Holders to whom overissued receipts have been duly negotiated shall share in a mass of fungible goods. Where individual ownership interests are merged into claims on a common fund, as is necessarily the case with fungible goods, there is no policy reason for discriminating between successive purchasers of similar claims.

Definitional Cross References:

"Delivery". Section 1–201.

"Duly negotiate". Section 7–501.

"Fungible goods". Section 1–201.

"Goods". Section 7–102.

"Holder". Section 1–201.

"Person". Section 1–201.

"Warehouse receipt". Section 1–201.

"Warehouse". Section 7–102.

Sections 31 and 32 of Acts 2005, 79th Leg., ch. 122 provide:

"Sec. 31. This Act applies to a document of title that is issued or a bailment that arises on or after the effective date of this Act. This Act does not apply to a document of title that is issued or a bailment that arises before the effective date of this Act even if the document of title or bailment would be subject to this Act if the document of title had been issued or bailment had arisen after the effective date of this Act. This Act does not apply to a right of action that has accrued before the effective date of this Act.

"Sec. 32. A document of title issued or a bailment that arises before the effective date of this Act and the rights, obligations, and interests flowing from that document or bailment are governed by any statute or other rule amended or repealed by this Act as if amendment or repeal had not occurred and may be terminated, completed, consummated, or enforced under that statute or other rule."

§ 7.208. Altered Warehouse Receipts

If a blank in a negotiable tangible warehouse receipt has been filled in without authority, a good faith purchaser for value and without notice of the lack of authority may treat the insertion as authorized. Any other unauthorized alteration leaves any tangible or electronic warehouse receipt enforceable against the issuer according to its original tenor.

Acts 1967, 60th Leg., p. 2343, ch. 785, § 1, eff. Sept. 1, 1967. Amended by Acts 2005, 79th Leg., ch. 122, § 1, eff. Sept. 1, 2005.

Uniform Commercial Code Comment

Prior Uniform Statutory Provision: Former Section 7–208.

Changes: To accommodate electronic documents of title.

Purpose:

1. The execution of tangible warehouse receipts in blank is a dangerous practice. As between the issuer and an innocent purchaser the risks should clearly fall on the former. The purchaser must have purchased the tangible negotiable warehouse receipt in good faith and for value to be protected under the rule of the first sentence which is a limited exception to the general rule in the second sentence. Electronic document of title systems should have protection against unauthorized access and unauthorized changes. See 7–106. Thus the protection for good faith purchasers found in the first sentence is not necessary in the context of electronic documents.

2. Under the second sentence of this section, an unauthorized alteration whether made with or without fraudulent intent does not relieve the issuer of its liability on the warehouse receipt as originally executed. The unauthorized alteration itself is of course ineffective against the warehouse. The rule stated in the second sentence applies to both tangible and electronic warehouse receipts.

Definitional Cross References:

"Good faith". Section 1–201 [7–102].

"Issuer". Section 7–102.

"Notice". Section 1–202.

"Purchaser". Section 1–201.

"Value". Section 1–204.

"Warehouse receipt". Section 1–201.

Sections 31 and 32 of Acts 2005, 79th Leg., ch. 122 provide:

"Sec. 31. This Act applies to a document of title that is issued or a bailment that arises on or after the effective date of this Act. This Act does not apply to a document of title that is issued or a bailment that arises before the effective date of this Act even if the document of title or bailment would be subject to this Act if the document of title had been issued or bailment had arisen after the effective date of this Act. This Act does not apply to a right of action that has accrued before the effective date of this Act.

"Sec. 32. A document of title issued or a bailment that arises before the effective date of this Act and the rights, obligations, and interests flowing from that document or bailment are governed by any statute or other rule amended or repealed by this Act as if amendment or repeal had not occurred and may be terminated, completed, consummated, or enforced under that statute or other rule."

§ 7.209. Lien of Warehouse

(a) A warehouse has a lien against the bailor on the goods covered by a warehouse receipt or storage agreement or on the proceeds thereof in its possession for charges for storage or transportation, including demurrage and terminal charges, insurance, labor, or other charges, present or future, in relation to the goods, and for expenses necessary for preservation of the goods or reasonably incurred in their sale pursuant to law. If the person on whose account the goods are held is liable for similar charges or expenses in relation to other goods whenever deposited and it is stated in the warehouse receipt or storage agreement that a lien is claimed for charges and expenses in relation to other goods, the warehouse also has a lien against the goods covered by the warehouse receipt or storage agreement or on the proceeds thereof in its possession for those charges and expenses, whether or not the other goods have been delivered by the warehouse. However, as against a person to which a negotiable warehouse receipt is duly negotiated, a warehouse's lien is limited to charges in an amount or at a rate specified in the warehouse receipt or, if no charges are so specified, to a reasonable charge for storage of the specific goods covered by the receipt subsequent to the date of the receipt.

(b) The warehouse may also reserve a security interest under Chapter 9 against the bailor for the maximum amount specified on the receipt for charges other than those specified in Subsection (a), such as for money advanced and interest. A security interest is governed by Chapter 9.

(c) A warehouse's lien for charges and expenses under Subsection (a) or a security interest under Subsection (b) is also effective against any person that so entrusted the bailor with possession of the goods that a pledge of them by the bailor to a good faith purchaser for value would have been valid. However, the lien or security interest is not effective against a person that before issuance of a document of title had a legal interest or a perfected security interest in the goods and that did not:

(1) deliver or entrust the goods or any document covering the goods to the bailor or the bailor's nominee with actual or apparent authority to ship, store, or sell; or with power to obtain delivery under Section 7.403; or with power of disposition under Section 2.403, 2A.304(a)(2), 2A.305(a)(2), or 9.320 or other statute or rule of law; or

(2) acquiesce in the procurement by the bailor or its nominee of any document.

(d) A warehouse's lien on household goods for charges and expenses in relation to the goods under Subsection (a) is also effective against all persons if the depositor was the legal possessor of the goods at the time of deposit. In this subsection, "household goods" means furniture, furnishings, or personal effects used by the depositor in a dwelling.

(e) A warehouse loses its lien on any goods that it voluntarily delivers or unjustifiably refuses to deliver.

Acts 1967, 60th Leg., p. 2343, ch. 785, § 1, eff. Sept. 1, 1967. Amended by Acts 1971, 62nd Leg., p. 3048, ch. 1010, § 1, eff. June 15, 1971; Acts 2005, 79th Leg., ch. 122, § 1, eff. Sept. 1, 2005.

Uniform Commercial Code Comment

Prior Uniform Statutory Provision: Former Sections 7–209 and 7–503.

Changes: Expanded to recognize warehouse lien when a warehouse receipt is not issued but goods are covered by a storage agreement.

Purposes:

1. Subsection (a) defines the warehouse's statutory lien. Other than allowing a warehouse to claim a lien under this section when there is a storage agreement and not a warehouse receipt, this section remains unchanged in substance from former Section 7–209(1). Under the first sentence, a specific lien attaches automatically without express notation on the receipt or storage agreement with regard to goods stored under the receipt or the storage agreement. That lien is limited to the usual charges arising out of a storage transaction.

Example 1: Bailor stored goods with a warehouse and the warehouse issued a warehouse receipt. A lien against those goods arose as set forth in subsection (a), the first sentence, for the charges for storage and the other expenses of those goods. The warehouse may enforce its lien under Section 7–210 as against the bailor. Whether the warehouse receipt is negotiable or nonnegotiable is not important to the warehouse's rights as against the bailor.

Under the second sentence, by notation on the receipt or storage agreement, the lien can be made a general lien extending to like charges in relation to other goods. Both the specific lien and general lien are as to goods in the possession of the warehouse and extend to proceeds from the goods as long as the proceeds are in the possession of the warehouse. The same rules apply whether the receipt is negotiable or non-negotiable.

Example 2: Bailor stored goods (lot A) with a warehouse and the warehouse issued a warehouse receipt for those goods. In the warehouse receipt it is stated that the warehouse will also have a lien on goods covered by the warehouse receipt for storage charges and the other expenses for any other goods that are stored with the warehouse by the bailor. The statement about the lien on other goods does not specify an amount or a rate. Bailor then stored other goods (lot B) with the warehouse. Under subsection (a), first sentence, the warehouse has a lien on the specific goods (lot A) covered by the warehouse receipt. Under subsection (a), second sentence, the warehouse has a lien on the goods in lot A for the storage charges and the other expenses arising from the goods in lot B. That lien is enforceable as against the bailor regardless of whether the receipt is negotiable or nonnegotiable.

Under the third sentence, if the warehouse receipt is negotiable, the lien as against a holder of that receipt by due negotiation is limited to the amount or rate specified on the receipt for the specific lien or the general lien, or, if none is specified, to a reasonable charge for storage of the specific goods covered by the receipt for storage after the date of the receipt.

Example 3: Same facts as Example 1 except that the warehouse receipt is negotiable and has been duly negotiated (Section 7–501) to a person other than the bailor. Under the last sentence of subsection (a), the warehouse may enforce its lien against the bailor's goods stored in the warehouse as against the person to whom the negotiable warehouse receipt has been duly negotiated. Section 7–502. That lien is limited to the charges or rates specified in the receipt or a reasonable charge for storage as stated in the last sentence of subsection (a).

Example 4: Same facts as Example 2 except that the warehouse receipt is negotiable and has been duly negotiated (Section 7–501) to a person other than the bailor. Under the last sentence of subsection (a), the lien on lot A goods for the storage charges and the other expenses arising from storage of lot B goods is not enforceable as against the person to whom the receipt has been duly negotiated. Without a statement of a specified amount or rate for the general lien, the warehouse's general lien is not enforceable as against the person to whom the negotiable document has been duly negotiated. However, the warehouse lien for charges and expenses related to storage of lot A goods is still enforceable as against the person to whom the receipt was duly negotiated.

Example 5. Same facts as Examples 2 and 4 except the warehouse had stated on the negotiable warehouse receipt a specified amount or rate for the general lien on other goods (lot B). Under the last sentence of subsection (a), the general lien on lot A goods for the storage charges and the other expenses arising from storage of lot B goods is enforceable as against the person to whom the receipt has been duly negotiated.

2. Subsection (b) provides for a security interest based upon agreement. Such a security interest arises out of relations between the parties other than bailment for storage or transportation, as where the bailee assumes the role of financier or performs a manufacturing operation, extending credit in reliance upon the goods covered by the receipt. Such a security interest is not a statutory lien. Compare Sections 9–109 and 9–333. It is governed in all respects by Article 9, except that subsection (b) requires that the receipt specify a maximum amount and limits the security interest to the amount specified. A warehouse could also take a security interest to secure its charges for storage and the other expenses listed in subsection (a) to protect these claims upon the loss of the statutory possessory warehouse lien if the warehouse loses possession of the goods as provided in subsection (e).

Example 6: Bailor stores goods with a warehouse and the warehouse issues a warehouse receipt that states that the warehouse is taking a security interest in the bailed goods for charges of storage, expenses, for money advanced, for manufacturing services rendered, and all other obligations that the bailor may owe the warehouse. That is a security interest covered in all respects by Article 9. Subsection (b). As allowed by this section, a warehouse may rely upon its statutory possessory lien to protect its charges for storage and the other expenses related to storage. For those storage charges covered by the statutory possessory lien, the warehouse is not required to use a security interest under subsection (b).

3. Subsections (a) and (b) validate the lien and security interest "against the bailor." Under basic principles of derivative rights as provided in Section 7–504, the warehouse lien

is also valid as against parties who obtain their rights from the bailor except as otherwise provided in subsection (a), third sentence, or subsection (c).

Example 7: Bailor stores goods with a warehouse and the warehouse issues a nonnegotiable warehouse receipt that also claims a general lien in other goods stored with the warehouse. A lien on the bailed goods for the charges for storage and the other expenses arises under subsection (a). Bailor notifies the warehouse that the goods have been sold to Buyer and the bailee acknowledges that fact to the Buyer. Section 2–503. The warehouse lien for storage of those goods is effective against Buyer for both the specific lien and the general lien. Section 7–504.

Example 8: Bailor stores goods with a warehouse and the warehouse issues a nonnegotiable warehouse receipt. A lien on the bailed goods for the charges for storage and the other expenses arises under subsection (a). Bailor grants a security interest in the goods while the goods are in the warehouse's possession to Secured Party (SP) who properly perfects a security interest in the goods. See Revised 9–312(d). The warehouse lien is superior in priority over SP's security interest. See Revised 9–203(b)(2) (debtor can grant a security interest to the extent of debtor's rights in the collateral).

Example 9: Bailor stores goods with a warehouse and the warehouse issues a negotiable warehouse receipt. A lien on the bailed goods for the charges for storage and the other expenses arises under subsection (a). Bailor grants a security interest in the negotiable document to SP. SP properly perfects its interest in the negotiable document by taking possession through a 'due negotiation.' Revised 9–312(c). SP's security interest is subordinate to the warehouse lien. Section 7–209(a), third sentence. Given that bailor's rights are subject to the warehouse lien, the bailor cannot grant to the SP greater rights than the bailor has under Section 9–203(b)(2), perfection of the security interest in the negotiable document and the goods covered by the document through SP's filing of a financing statement should not give a different result.

As against third parties who have interests in the goods prior to the storage with the warehouse, subsection (c) continues the rule under the prior uniform statutory provision that to validate the lien or security interest of the warehouse, the owner must have entrusted the goods to the depositor, and that the circumstances must be such that a pledge by the depositor to a good faith purchaser for value would have been valid. Thus the owner's interest will not be subjected to a lien or security interest arising out of a deposit of its goods by a thief. The warehouse may be protected because of the actual, implied or apparent authority of the depositor, because of a Factor's Act, or because of other circumstances which would protect a bona fide pledgee, unless those circumstances are denied effect under the second sentence of subsection (c). The language of Section 7–503 is brought into subsection (c) for purposes of clarity. The comments to Section 7–503 are helpful in interpreting delivery, entrustment or acquiescence.

Where the third party is the holder of a security interest, obtained prior to the issuance of a negotiable warehouse receipt, the rights of the warehouse depend on the priority given to a hypothetical bona fide pledgee by Article 9, particularly Section 9–322. Thus the special priority granted to statutory liens by Section 9–333 does not apply to liens under subsection (a) of this section, since subsection (c), second sentence, "expressly provides otherwise" within the meaning of Section 9–333.

As to household goods, however, subsection (d) makes the warehouse's lien "for charges and expenses in relation to the goods" effective against all persons if the depositor was the legal possessor. The purpose of the exception is to permit the warehouse to accept household goods for storage in sole reliance on the value of the goods themselves, especially in situations of family emergency.

Example 10: Bailor grants a perfected security interest in the goods to SP prior to storage of the goods with the warehouse. Bailor then stores goods with the warehouse and the warehouse issues a warehouse receipt for the goods. A warehouse lien on the bailed goods for the charges for storage or other expenses arises under subsection (a). The warehouse lien is not effective as against SP unless SP entrusted the goods to the bailor with actual or apparent authority to ship store, or sell the goods or with power of disposition under subsection (c)(1) or acquiesced in the bailor's procurement of a document of title under subsection (c)(2). This result obtains whether the receipt is negotiable or nonnegotiable.

Example 11: Sheriff who had lawfully repossessed household goods in an eviction action stored the goods with a warehouse. A lien on the bailed goods arises under subsection (a). The lien is effective as against the owner of the goods. Subsection (d).

4. As under previous law, this section creates a statutory possessory lien in favor of the warehouse on the goods stored with the warehouse or on the proceeds of the goods. The warehouse loses its lien if it loses possession of the goods or the proceeds. Subsection (e).

5. Where goods have been stored under a non-negotiable warehouse receipt and are sold by the person to whom the receipt has been issued, frequently the goods are not withdrawn by the new owner. The obligations of the seller of the goods in this situation are set forth in Section 2–503(4) on tender of delivery and include procurement of an acknowledgment by the bailee of the buyer's right to possession of the goods. If a new receipt is requested, such an acknowledgment can be withheld until storage charges have been paid or provided for. The statutory lien for charges on the goods sold, granted by the first sentence of subsection (a), continues valid unless the bailee gives it up. See Section 7–403. But once a new receipt is issued to the buyer, the buyer becomes "the person on whose account the goods are held" under the second sentence of subsection (a); unless the buyer undertakes liability for charges in relation to other goods stored by the seller, there is no general lien against the buyer for such charges. Of course, the bailee may preserve the general lien in such a case either by an arrangement by which the buyer "is liable for" such charges, or by reserving a security interest under subsection (b).

6. A possessory warehouse lien arises as provided under subsection (a) if the parties to the bailment have a storage agreement or a warehouse receipt is issued. In the modern warehouse, the bailor and the bailee may enter into a master contract governing the bailment with the bailee and bailor keeping track of the goods stored pursuant to the master

contract by notation on their respective books and records and the parties send notification via electronic communication as to what goods are covered by the master contract. Warehouse receipts are not issued. See Comment 4 to Section 7–204. There is no particular form for a warehouse receipt and failure to contain any of the terms listed in Section 7–202 does not deprive the warehouse of its lien that arises under subsection (a). See the comment to Section 7–202.

Cross References:

Point 1: Sections 7–501 and 7–502.

Point 2: Sections 9–109 and 9–333.

Point 3: Sections 2–503, 7–503, 7–504, 9–203, 9–312, and 9–322.

Point 4: Sections 2–503, 7–501, 7–502, 7–504, 9–312, 9–331, 9–333, 9–401.

Point 5: Sections 2–503 and 7–403.

Point 6: Sections 7–202 and 7–204.

Definitional Cross References:

"Delivery". Section 1–201.

"Document of Title". Section 1–201

"Goods". Section 7–102.

"Money". Section 1–201.

"Person". Section 1–201.

"Purchaser". Section 1–201.

"Right". Section 1–201.

"Security interest". Section 1–201.

"Value". Section 1–204.

"Warehouse receipt". Section 1–201.

"Warehouse". Section 7–102.

Sections 31 and 32 of Acts 2005, 79th Leg., ch. 122 provide:

"Sec. 31. This Act applies to a document of title that is issued or a bailment that arises on or after the effective date of this Act. This Act does not apply to a document of title that is issued or a bailment that arises before the effective date of this Act even if the document of title or bailment would be subject to this Act if the document of title had been issued or bailment had arisen after the effective date of this Act. This Act does not apply to a right of action that has accrued before the effective date of this Act.

"Sec. 32. A document of title issued or a bailment that arises before the effective date of this Act and the rights, obligations, and interests flowing from that document or bailment are governed by any statute or other rule amended or repealed by this Act as if amendment or repeal had not occurred and may be terminated, completed, consummated, or enforced under that statute or other rule."

§ 7.210. Enforcement of Warehouse's Lien

(a) Except as otherwise provided in Subsection (b), a warehouse's lien may be enforced by public or private sale of the goods, in bulk or in packages, at any time or place and on any terms that are commercially reasonable, after notifying all persons known to claim an interest in the goods. The notification must include a statement of the amount due, the nature of the proposed sale, and the time and place of any public sale. The fact that a better price could have been obtained by a sale at a different time or in a different method from that selected by the warehouse is not of itself sufficient to establish that the sale was not made in a commercially reasonable manner. The warehouse has sold in a commercially reasonable manner if the warehouse sells the goods in the usual manner in any recognized market therefor, sells at the price current in that market at the time of the sale, or has otherwise sold in conformity with commercially reasonable practices among dealers in the type of goods sold. A sale of more goods than apparently necessary to be offered to ensure satisfaction of the obligation is not commercially reasonable, except in cases covered by the preceding sentence.

(b) A warehouse's lien on goods, other than goods stored by a merchant in the course of its business, may be enforced only if the following requirements are satisfied:

(1) All persons known to claim an interest in the goods must be notified.

(2) The notification must include an itemized statement of the claim, a description of the goods subject to the lien, a demand for payment within a specified time not less than 10 days after receipt of the notification, and a conspicuous statement that unless the claim is paid within that time the goods will be advertised for sale and sold by auction at a specified time and place.

(3) The sale must conform to the terms of the notification.

(4) The sale must be held at the nearest suitable place to where the goods are held or stored.

(5) After the expiration of the time given in the notification, an advertisement of the sale must be published once a week for two weeks consecutively in a newspaper of general circulation where the sale is to be held. The advertisement must include a description of the goods, the name of the person on whose account the goods are being held, and the time and place of the sale. The sale must take place at least 15 days after the first publication. If there is no newspaper of general circulation where the sale is to be held, the advertisement must be posted at least 10 days before the sale in not less than six conspicuous places in the neighborhood of the proposed sale.

(c) Before any sale pursuant to this section, any person claiming a right in the goods may pay the amount necessary to satisfy the lien and the reasonable expenses incurred in complying with this section. In that event, the goods may not be sold but must be retained by the warehouse subject to the terms of the receipt and this chapter.

(d) A warehouse may buy at any public sale held pursuant to this section.

(e) A purchaser in good faith of goods sold to enforce a warehouse's lien takes the goods free of any rights of persons against which the lien was valid, despite the warehouse's noncompliance with this section.

(f) A warehouse may satisfy its lien from the proceeds of any sale pursuant to this section but shall hold the balance, if any, for delivery on demand to any person to which the warehouse would have been bound to deliver the goods.

(g) The rights provided by this section are in addition to all other rights allowed by law to a creditor against a debtor.

(h) If a lien is on goods stored by a merchant in the course of its business, the lien may be enforced in accordance with Subsection (a) or (b).

(i) A warehouse is liable for damages caused by failure to comply with the requirements for sale under this section and, in case of wilful violation, is liable for conversion.

Acts 1967, 60th Leg., p. 2343, ch. 785, § 1, eff. Sept. 1, 1967. Amended by Acts 2005, 79th Leg., ch. 122, § 1, eff. Sept. 1, 2005.

Uniform Commercial Code Comment

Prior Uniform Statutory Provision: Former Section 7–210.

Changes: Update to accommodate electronic commerce and for style.

Purposes:

1. Subsection (a) makes "commercial reasonableness" the standard for foreclosure proceedings in all cases except noncommercial storage with a warehouse. The latter category embraces principally storage of household goods by private owners; and for such cases the detailed provisions as to notification, publication and public sale are retained in subsection (b) with one change. The requirement in former Section 7-210(2)(b) that the notification must be sent in person or by registered or certified mail has been deleted. Notification may be sent by any reasonable means as provided in Section 1–202. The swifter, more flexible procedure of subsection (a) is appropriate to commercial storage. Compare seller's power of resale on breach by buyer under the provisions of the Article on Sales (Section 2–706). Commercial reasonableness is a flexible concept that allows for a wide variety of actions to satisfy the rule of this section, including electronic means of posting and sale.

2. The provisions of subsections (d) and (e) permitting the bailee to bid at public sales and confirming the title of purchasers at foreclosure sales are designed to secure more bidding and better prices and remain unchanged from former Section 7–210.

3. A warehouses may have recourse to an interpleader action in appropriate circumstances. See Section 7–603.

4. If a warehouse has both a warehouse lien and a security interest, the warehouse may enforce both the lien and the security interest simultaneously by using the procedures of Article 9. Section 7–210 adopts as its touchstone "commercial reasonableness" for the enforcement of a warehouse lien. Following the procedures of Article 9 satisfies "commercial reasonableness."

Cross Reference: Sections 2–706, 7–403, 7–603 and Part 6 of Article 9.

Definitional Cross References:

"Bill of lading". Section 1–201.

"Conspicuous". Section 1–201.

"Creditor". Section 1–201.

"Delivery". Section 1–201.

"Document of Title". Section 1–201.

"Good faith". Section 1–201 [7–102].

"Goods". Section 7–102.

"Notification". Section 1–202.

"Notifies". Section 1–202.

"Person". Section 1–201.

"Purchaser". Section 1–201.

"Rights". Section 1–201.

"Term". Section 1–201.

"Warehouse". Section 7–102.

Sections 31 and 32 of Acts 2005, 79th Leg., ch. 122 provide:

"Sec. 31. This Act applies to a document of title that is issued or a bailment that arises on or after the effective date of this Act. This Act does not apply to a document of title that is issued or a bailment that arises before the effective date of this Act even if the document of title or bailment would be subject to this Act if the document of title had been issued or bailment had arisen after the effective date of this Act. This Act does not apply to a right of action that has accrued before the effective date of this Act.

"Sec. 32. A document of title issued or a bailment that arises before the effective date of this Act and the rights, obligations, and interests flowing from that document or bailment are governed by any statute or other rule amended or repealed by this Act as if amendment or repeal had not occurred and may be terminated, completed, consummated, or enforced under that statute or other rule."

SUBCHAPTER C. BILLS OF LADING: SPECIAL PROVISIONS

Acts 2005, 79th Leg., ch. 122, § 1 amended chapter 7.

§ 7.301. Liability for Nonreceipt or Misdescription; "Said to Contain"; "Shipper's Load and Count"; Improper Handling

(a) A consignee of a nonnegotiable bill of lading which has given value in good faith, or a holder to which a negotiable bill has been duly negotiated, relying upon the description of the goods in the bill or upon the date shown in the bill, may recover from the issuer damages caused by the misdating of the bill or the nonreceipt or misdescription of the goods, except to the extent that the document of title indicates that the issuer does not know whether any part or all of the goods in fact were received or conform to the description, such as in a case in which the description is in terms of marks or labels or kind, quantity, or condition, or the receipt or description is qualified by "contents or condition of contents of packages unknown," "said to contain," "shipper's weight, load and count," or words of similar import, if that indication is true.

(b) If goods are loaded by the issuer of the bill of lading, the issuer shall count the packages of goods if shipped in packages and ascertain the kind and quantity if shipped in bulk and words such as "shipper's weight, load and count," or words of similar import indicating that the description was made by the shipper are ineffective except as to goods concealed by packages.

(c) If bulk goods are loaded by a shipper that makes available to the issuer of the bill of lading adequate facilities for weighing those goods, the issuer shall ascertain the kind and quantity within a reasonable time after receiving the shipper's request in a record to do so. In that case, "shipper's weight" or words of similar import are ineffective.

(d) The issuer, by including in the bill of lading the words "shipper's weight, load and count," or words of similar import, may indicate that the goods were loaded by the shipper, and, if that statement is true, the issuer is not liable for damages caused by the improper loading. However, omission of such words does not imply liability for damages caused by improper loading.

(e) A shipper guarantees to the issuer the accuracy at the time of shipment of the description, marks, labels, number, kind, quantity, condition, and weight, as furnished by the shipper, and the shipper shall indemnify the issuer against damage caused by inaccuracies in those particulars. This right of the issuer to that indemnity does not limit its responsibility or liability under the contract of carriage to any person other than the shipper.

Acts 1967, 60th Leg., p. 2343, ch. 785, § 1, eff. Sept. 1, 1967. Amended by Acts 2005, 79th Leg., ch. 122, § 1, eff. Sept. 1, 2005.

Uniform Commercial Code Comment

Prior Uniform Statutory Provision: Former Section 7–301.

Changes: Changes for clarity, style and to recognize deregulation in the transportation industry.

Purposes:

1. This section continues the rules from former Section 7–301 with one substantive change. The obligations of the issuer of the bill of lading under former subsections (2) and (3) were limited to issuers who were common carriers. Subsections (b) and (c) apply the same rules to all issuers not just common carriers. This section is compatible with the policies stated in the federal Bills of Lading Act, 49 U.S.C. § 80113 (2000).

2. The language of the pre-Code Uniform Bills of Lading Act suggested that a carrier is ordinarily liable for damage caused by improper loading, but may relieve itself of liability by disclosing on the bill that shipper actually loaded. A more accurate statement of the law is that the carrier is not liable for losses caused by act or default of the shipper, which would include improper loading. D. H. Overmyer Co. v. Nelson Brantley Glass Go., 168 S.E.2d 176 (Ga. Ct. App. 1969). There was some question whether under pre-Code law a carrier was liable even to a good faith purchaser of a negotiable bill for such losses, if the shipper's faulty loading in fact caused the loss. Subsection (d) permits the carrier to bar, by disclosure of shipper's loading, liability to a good faith purchaser. There is no implication that decisions such as Modern Tool Corp. v. Pennsylvania R. Co., 100 F.Supp. 595 (D.N.J.1951), are disapproved.

3. This section is a restatement of existing law as to the method by which a bailee may avoid responsibility for the accuracy of descriptions which are made by or in reliance upon information furnished by the depositor or shipper. The wording in this section–"contents or condition of contents of packages unknown" or "shipper's weight, load and count"–to indicate that the shipper loaded the goods or that the carrier does not know the description, condition, or contents of the loaded packages continues to be appropriate as commonly understood in the transportation industry. The reasons for this wording are as important in 2002 as when the prior section initially was approved. The issuer is liable on documents issued by an agent, contrary to instructions of his principal, without receiving goods. No disclaimer of this liability is permitted since it is not a matter either of the care of the goods or their description.

4. The shipper's erroneous report to the carrier concerning the goods may cause damage to the carrier. Subsection (e) therefore provides appropriate indemnity.

5. The word "freight" in the former Section 7–301 has been changed to "goods" to conform to international and domestic land transport usage in which "freight" means the price paid for carriage of the goods and not the goods themselves. Hence, changing the word "freight" to the word

"goods" is a clarifying change that fits both international and domestic practice.

Cross References: Sections 7–203, 7–309 and 7–501.

Definitional Cross References:

"Bill of lading". Section 1–201.

"Consignee". Section 7–102.

"Document of Title". Section 1–201.

"Duly negotiate". Section 7–501.

"Good faith". Section 1–201. [7–102].

"Goods". Section 7–102.

"Holder". Section 1–201.

"Issuer". Section 7–102.

"Notice". Section 1–202.

"Party". Section 1–201.

"Purchaser." Section 1–201.

"Receipt of Goods". Section 2–103.

"Value". Section 1–204.

Sections 31 and 32 of Acts 2005, 79th Leg., ch. 122 provide:

"Sec. 31. This Act applies to a document of title that is issued or a bailment that arises on or after the effective date of this Act. This Act does not apply to a document of title that is issued or a bailment that arises before the effective date of this Act even if the document of title or bailment would be subject to this Act if the document of title had been issued or bailment had arisen after the effective date of this Act. This Act does not apply to a right of action that has accrued before the effective date of this Act.

"Sec. 32. A document of title issued or a bailment that arises before the effective date of this Act and the rights, obligations, and interests flowing from that document or bailment are governed by any statute or other rule amended or repealed by this Act as if amendment or repeal had not occurred and may be terminated, completed, consummated, or enforced under that statute or other rule."

§ 7.302. Through Bills of Lading and Similar Documents of Title

(a) The issuer of a through bill of lading or other document of title embodying an undertaking to be performed in part by a person acting as its agent or by a performing carrier is liable to any person entitled to recover on the document for any breach by the other person or the performing carrier of its obligation under the document. However, to the extent that the bill covers an undertaking to be performed overseas or in territory not contiguous to the continental United States or an undertaking including matters other than transportation, this liability for breach by the other person or the performing carrier may be varied by agreement of the parties.

(b) If goods covered by a through bill of lading or other document of title embodying an undertaking to be performed in part by a person other than the issuer are received by that person, the person is subject, with respect to its own performance while the goods are in its possession, to the obligation of the issuer. The person's obligation is discharged by delivery of the goods to another person pursuant to the document and does not include liability for breach by any other person or by the issuer.

(c) The issuer of a through bill of lading or other document of title described in Subsection (a) is entitled to recover from the performing carrier, or other person in possession of the goods when the breach of the obligation under the document occurred:

(1) the amount it may be required to pay to any person entitled to recover on the document for the breach, as may be evidenced by any receipt, judgment, or transcript of judgment; and

(2) the amount of any expense reasonably incurred by the issuer in defending any action commenced by any person entitled to recover on the document for the breach.

Acts 1967, 60th Leg., p. 2343, ch. 785, § 1, eff. Sept. 1, 1967. Amended by Acts 2005, 79th Leg., ch. 122, § 1, eff. Sept. 1, 2005.

Uniform Commercial Code Comment

Prior Uniform Statutory Provision: Former Section 7–302.

Changes: To conform to current terminology and for style.

Purposes:

1. This section continues the rules from former Section 7–302 without substantive change. The term "performing carrier" is substituted for the term "connecting carrier" to conform the terminology of this section with terminology used in recent UNCITRAL and OAS proposals concerning transportation and through bills of lading. This change in terminology is not substantive. This section is compatible with liability on carriers under federal law. See 49 U.S.C. §§ 11706, 14706 and 15906.

The purpose of this section is to subject the initial carrier under a through bill to suit for breach of the contract of carriage by any performing carrier and to make it clear that any such performing carrier holds the goods on terms which are defined by the document of title even though such performing carrier did not issue the document. Since the performing carrier does hold the goods on the terms of the document, it must honor a proper demand for delivery or a diversion order just as the original bailee would have to. Similarly it has the benefits of the excuses for non-delivery and limitations of liability provided for the original bailee who issued the bill. Unlike the original bailee-issuer, the performing carrier's responsibility is limited to the period while the goods are in its possession. The section does not impose any obligation to issue through bills.

2. The reference to documents other than through bills looks to the possibility that multi-purpose documents may come into use, e.g., combination warehouse receipts and bills of lading. As electronic documents of title come into common usage, storage documents (e.g. warehouse receipts) and

transportation documents (e.g. bills of lading) may merge seamlessly into one electronic document that can serve both the storage and transportation segments of the movement of goods.

3. Under subsection (a) the issuer of a through bill of lading may become liable for the fault of another person. Subsection (c) gives the issuer appropriate rights of recourse.

4. Despite the broad language of subsection (a), Section 7–302 is subject to preemption by federal laws and treaties. Section 7–103. The precise scope of federal preemption in the transportation sector is a question determined under federal law.

Cross reference: Section 7–103

Definitional Cross References:

"Agreement". Section 1–201.

"Bailee". Section 7–102.

"Bill of lading". Section 1–201.

"Delivery". Section 1–201.

"Document of title". Section 1–201.

"Goods". Section 7–102.

"Issuer". Section 7–102.

"Party". Section 1–201.

"Person". Section 1–201.

Sections 31 and 32 of Acts 2005, 79th Leg., ch. 122 provide:

"Sec. 31. This Act applies to a document of title that is issued or a bailment that arises on or after the effective date of this Act. This Act does not apply to a document of title that is issued or a bailment that arises before the effective date of this Act even if the document of title or bailment would be subject to this Act if the document of title had been issued or bailment had arisen after the effective date of this Act. This Act does not apply to a right of action that has accrued before the effective date of this Act.

"Sec. 32. A document of title issued or a bailment that arises before the effective date of this Act and the rights, obligations, and interests flowing from that document or bailment are governed by any statute or other rule amended or repealed by this Act as if amendment or repeal had not occurred and may be terminated, completed, consummated, or enforced under that statute or other rule."

§ 7.303. Diversion; Reconsignment; Change of Instructions

(a) Unless the bill of lading otherwise provides, a carrier may deliver the goods to a person or destination other than that stated in the bill or may otherwise dispose of the goods, without liability for misdelivery, on instructions from:

(1) the holder of a negotiable bill;

(2) the consignor on a nonnegotiable bill even if the consignee has given contrary instructions;

(3) the consignee on a nonnegotiable bill in the absence of contrary instructions from the consignor, if the goods have arrived at the billed destination or if the consignee is in possession of the tangible bill or in control of the electronic bill; or

(4) the consignee on a nonnegotiable bill, if the consignee is entitled as against the consignor to dispose of the goods.

(b) Unless instructions described in Subsection (a) are included in a negotiable bill of lading, a person to which the bill is duly negotiated may hold the bailee according to the original terms.

Acts 1967, 60th Leg., p. 2343, ch. 785, § 1, eff. Sept. 1, 1967. Amended by Acts 2005, 79th Leg., ch. 122, § 1, eff. Sept. 1, 2005.

Uniform Commercial Code Comment

Prior Uniform Statutory Provision: Former Section 7–303.

Changes: To accommodate electronic documents and for style.

Purposes:

1. Diversion is a very common commercial practice which defeats delivery to the consignee originally named in a bill of lading. This section continues former Section 7–303's safe harbor rules for carriers in situations involving diversion and adapts those rules to electronic documents of title. This section works compatibly with Section 2–705. Carriers may as a business matter be willing to accept instructions from consignees in which case the carrier will be liable for misdelivery if the consignee was not the owner or otherwise empowered to dispose of the goods under subsection (a)(4). The section imposes no duty on carriers to undertake diversion. The carrier is of course subject to the provisions of mandatory filed tariffs as provided in Section 7–103.

2. It should be noted that the section provides only an immunity for carriers against liability for "misdelivery." It does not, for example, defeat the title to the goods which the consignee-buyer may have acquired from the consignor-seller upon delivery of the goods to the carrier under a nonnegotiable bill of lading. Thus if the carrier, upon instructions from the consignor, returns the goods to the consignor, the consignee may recover the goods from the consignor or the consignor's insolvent estate. However, under certain circumstances, the consignee's title may be defeated by diversion of the goods in transit to a different consignee. The rights that arise between the consignor-seller and the consignee-buyer out of a contract for the sale of goods are governed by Article 2.

Cross References:

Point 1: Sections 2–705 and 7–103.

Point 2: Article 2, Sections 7–403 and 7–504(3).

Definitional Cross References:

"Bailee". Section 7–102.

"Bill of lading". Section 1–201.

"Carrier". Section 7–102

"Consignee". Section 7–102.

"Consignor". Section 7–102.

"Delivery". Section 1–201.

"Goods". Section 7–102.

"Holder". Section 1–201.

"Notice". Section 1–202.

"Person". Section 1–201.

"Purchaser". Section 1–201.

"Term". Section 1–201.

Sections 31 and 32 of Acts 2005, 79th Leg., ch. 122 provide:

"Sec. 31. This Act applies to a document of title that is issued or a bailment that arises on or after the effective date of this Act. This Act does not apply to a document of title that is issued or a bailment that arises before the effective date of this Act even if the document of title or bailment would be subject to this Act if the document of title had been issued or bailment had arisen after the effective date of this Act. This Act does not apply to a right of action that has accrued before the effective date of this Act.

"Sec. 32. A document of title issued or a bailment that arises before the effective date of this Act and the rights, obligations, and interests flowing from that document or bailment are governed by any statute or other rule amended or repealed by this Act as if amendment or repeal had not occurred and may be terminated, completed, consummated, or enforced under that statute or other rule."

§ 7.304. Tangible Bills of Lading in Set

(a) Except as customary in international transportation, a tangible bill of lading may not be issued in a set of parts. The issuer is liable for damages caused by violation of this subsection.

(b) If a tangible bill of lading is lawfully issued in a set of parts, each of which contains an identification code and is expressed to be valid only if the goods have not been delivered against any other part, the whole of the parts constitutes one bill.

(c) If a tangible negotiable bill of lading is lawfully issued in a set of parts and different parts are negotiated to different persons, the title of the holder to which the first due negotiation is made prevails as to both the document of title and the goods even if any later holder may have received the goods from the carrier in good faith and discharged the carrier's obligation by surrendering its part.

(d) A person that negotiates or transfers a single part of a tangible bill of lading issued in a set is liable to holders of that part as if it were the whole set.

(e) The bailee is obliged to deliver in accordance with Subchapter D [1] against the first presented part of a tangible bill of lading lawfully issued in a set. Delivery in this manner discharges the bailee's obligation on the whole bill.

Acts 1967, 60th Leg., p. 2343, ch. 785, § 1, eff. Sept. 1, 1967. Amended by Acts 2005, 79th Leg., ch. 122, § 1, eff. Sept. 1, 2005.

[1] V.T.C.A., Bus. & C. § 7.401 et seq.

Uniform Commercial Code Comment

Prior Uniform Statutory Provision: Former Section 7–304.

Changes: To limit bills in a set to tangible bills of lading and to use terminology more consistent with modern usage.

Purposes:

1. Tangible bills of lading in a set are still used in some nations in international trade. Consequently, a tangible bill of lading part of a set could be at issue in a lawsuit that might come within Article 7. The statement of the legal effect of a lawfully issued set is in accord with existing commercial law relating to maritime and other international tangible bills of lading. This law has been codified in the Hague and Warsaw Conventions and in the Carriage of Goods by Sea Act, the provisions of which would ordinarily govern in situations where bills in a set are recognized by this Article. Tangible bills of lading in a set are prohibited in domestic trade.

2. Electronic bills of lading in domestic or international trade will not be issued in a set given the requirements of control necessary to deliver the bill to another person. An electronic bill of lading will be a single, authoritative copy. Section 7–106. Hence, this section differentiates between electronic bills of lading and tangible bills of lading. This section does not prohibit electronic data messages about goods in transit because these electronic data messages are not the issued bill of lading. Electronic data messages contain information for the carrier's management and handling of the cargo but this information for the carrier's use is not the issued bill of lading.

Cross Reference: Section 7–103, 7–303 and 7–106.

Definitional Cross References:

"Bailee". Section 7–102.

"Bill of lading". Section 1–201.

"Delivery". Section 1–201.

"Document of title". Section 1–201.

"Duly negotiate". Section 7–501.

"Good faith". Section 1–201. [7–102].

"Goods". Section 7–102.

"Holder". Section 1–201.

"Issuer". Section 7–102.

"Person". Section 1–201.

"Receipt of goods". Section 2–103.

Sections 31 and 32 of Acts 2005, 79th Leg., ch. 122 provide:

"Sec. 31. This Act applies to a document of title that is issued or a bailment that arises on or after the effective date of this Act. This Act does not apply to a document of title that is issued or a bailment that arises before the effective date of this Act even if the document of title or bailment would be subject to this Act if the document of title had been issued or bailment had arisen after the effective date of this Act. This Act does not apply to a right of action that has accrued before the effective date of this Act.

"Sec. 32. A document of title issued or a bailment that arises before the effective date of this Act and the rights, obligations, and interests flowing from that document or bailment are governed by any statute or other rule amended or repealed by this Act as if amendment or repeal had not occurred and may be terminated, completed, consummated, or enforced under that statute or other rule."

§ 7.305. Destination Bills

(a) Instead of issuing a bill of lading to the consignor at the place of shipment, a carrier, at the request of the consignor, may procure the bill to be issued at destination or at any other place designated in the request.

(b) Upon request of any person entitled as against a carrier to control the goods while in transit and on surrender of possession or control of any outstanding bill of lading or other receipt covering the goods, the issuer, subject to Section 7.105, may procure a substitute bill to be issued at any place designated in the request.

Acts 1967, 60th Leg., p. 2343, ch. 785, § 1, eff. Sept. 1, 1967. Amended by Acts 2005, 79th Leg., ch. 122, § 1, eff. Sept. 1, 2005.

Uniform Commercial Code Comment

Prior Uniform Statutory Provision: Former Section 7–305.

Changes: To accommodate electronic bills of lading and for style.

Purposes:

1. Subsection (a) continues the rules of former Section 7–305(1) without substantive change. This proposal is designed to facilitate the use of order bills in connection with fast shipments. Use of order bills on high speed shipments is impeded by the fact that the goods may arrive at destination before the documents, so that no one is ready to take delivery from the carrier. This is especially inconvenient for carriers by truck and air, who do not have terminal facilities where shipments can be held to await the consignee's appearance. Order bills would be useful to take advantage of bank collection. This may be preferable to C.O.D. shipment in which the carrier, e.g. a truck driver, is the collecting and remitting agent. Financing of shipments under this plan would be handled as follows: seller at San Francisco delivers the goods to an airline with instructions to issue a bill in New York to a named bank. Seller receives a receipt embodying this undertaking to issue a destination bill. Airline wires its New York freight agent to issue the bill as instructed by the seller. Seller wires the New York bank a draft on buyer. New York bank indorses the bill to buyer when the buyer honors the draft. Normally seller would act through its own bank in San Francisco, which would extend credit in reliance on the airline's contract to deliver a bill to the order of its New York correspondent. This section is entirely permissive; it imposes no duty to issue such bills. Whether a performing carrier will act as issuing agent is left to agreement between carriers.

2. Subsection (b) continues the rule from former Section 7–305(2) with accommodation for electronic bills of lading. If the substitute bill changes from an electronic to a tangible medium or vice versa, the issuance of the substitute bill must comply with Section 7–105 to give the substitute bill validity and effect.

Cross Reference: Section 7–105.

Definitional Cross References:

"Bill of lading". Section 1–201.

"Consignor". Section 7–102.

"Goods". Section 7–102.

"Issuer". Section 7–102.

"Receipt of goods". Section 2–103.

Sections 31 and 32 of Acts 2005, 79th Leg., ch. 122 provide:

"Sec. 31. This Act applies to a document of title that is issued or a bailment that arises on or after the effective date of this Act. This Act does not apply to a document of title that is issued or a bailment that arises before the effective date of this Act even if the document of title or bailment would be subject to this Act if the document of title had been issued or bailment had arisen after the effective date of this Act. This Act does not apply to a right of action that has accrued before the effective date of this Act.

"Sec. 32. A document of title issued or a bailment that arises before the effective date of this Act and the rights, obligations, and interests flowing from that document or bailment are governed by any statute or other rule amended or repealed by this Act as if amendment or repeal had not occurred and may be terminated, completed, consummated, or enforced under that statute or other rule."

§ 7.306. Altered Bills of Lading

An unauthorized alteration or filling in of a blank in a bill of lading leaves the bill enforceable according to its original tenor.

Acts 1967, 60th Leg., p. 2343, ch. 785, § 1, eff. Sept. 1, 1967. Amended by Acts 2005, 79th Leg., ch. 122, § 1, eff. Sept. 1, 2005.

Uniform Commercial Code Comment

Prior Uniform Statutory Provision: Former Section 7–306.

Changes: None

Purposes:

An unauthorized alteration or filling in of a blank, whether made with or without fraudulent intent, does not relieve the issuer of its liability on the document as originally executed. This section applies to both tangible and electronic bills of lading, applying the same rule to both types of bills of lading. The control concept of Section 7–106 requires that any changes to the electronic document of title be readily identifiable as authorized or unauthorized. Section 7–306 should be compared to Section 7–208 where a different rule applies to the unauthorized filling in of a blank for tangible warehouse receipts.

Cross Reference: Sections 7–106 and 7–208.

Definitional Cross References:

"Bill of lading". Section 1–201.

"Issuer". Section 7–102.

Sections 31 and 32 of Acts 2005, 79th Leg., ch. 122 provide:

"Sec. 31. This Act applies to a document of title that is issued or a bailment that arises on or after the effective date of this Act. This Act does not apply to a document of title that is issued or a bailment that arises before the effective date of this Act even if the document of title or bailment would be subject to this Act if the document of title had been issued or bailment had arisen after the effective date of this Act. This Act does not apply to a right of action that has accrued before the effective date of this Act.

"Sec. 32. A document of title issued or a bailment that arises before the effective date of this Act and the rights, obligations, and interests flowing from that document or bailment are governed by any statute or other rule amended or repealed by this Act as if amendment or repeal had not occurred and may be terminated, completed, consummated, or enforced under that statute or other rule."

§ 7.307. Lien of Carrier

(a) A carrier has a lien on the goods covered by a bill of lading or on the proceeds thereof in its possession for charges after the date of the carrier's receipt of the goods for storage or transportation, including demurrage and terminal charges, and for expenses necessary for preservation of the goods incident to their transportation or reasonably incurred in their sale pursuant to law. However, against a purchaser for value of a negotiable bill of lading, a carrier's lien is limited to charges stated in the bill or the applicable tariffs or, if no charges are stated, a reasonable charge.

(b) A lien for charges and expenses under Subsection (a) on goods that the carrier was required by law to receive for transportation is effective against the consignor or any person entitled to the goods unless the carrier had notice that the consignor lacked authority to subject the goods to those charges and expenses. Any other lien under Subsection (a) is effective against the consignor and any person that permitted the bailor to have control or possession of the goods unless the carrier had notice that the bailor lacked authority.

(c) A carrier loses its lien on any goods that it voluntarily delivers or unjustifiably refuses to deliver.

Acts 1967, 60th Leg., p. 2343, ch. 785, § 1, eff. Sept. 1, 1967. Amended by Acts 2005, 79th Leg., ch. 122, § 1, eff. Sept. 1, 2005.

Uniform Commercial Code Comment

Prior Uniform Statutory Provision: Former Section 7–307.

Changes: Expanded to cover proceeds of the goods transported.

Purposes:

1. The section is intended to give carriers a specific statutory lien for charges and expenses similar to that given to warehouses by the first sentence of Section 7–209(a) and extends that lien to the proceeds of the goods as long as the carrier has possession of the proceeds. But because carriers do not commonly claim a lien for charges in relation to other goods or lend money on the security of goods in their hands, provisions for a general lien or a security interest similar to those in Section 7–209(a) and (b) are omitted. Carriers may utilize Article 9 to obtain a security interest and become a secured party or a carrier may agree to limit its lien rights in a transportation agreement with the shipper. As the lien given by this section is specific, and the storage or transportation often preserves or increases the value of the goods, subsection (b) validates the lien against anyone who permitted the bailor to have possession of the goods. Where the carrier is required to receive the goods for transportation, the owner's interest may be subjected to charges and expenses arising out of deposit of his goods by a thief. The crucial mental element is the carrier's knowledge or reason to know of the bailor's lack of authority. If the carrier does not know or have reason to know of the bailor's lack of authority, the carrier has a lien under this section against any person so long as the conditions of subsection (b) are satisfied. In light of the crucial mental element, Sections 7–307 and 9–333 combine to give priority to a carrier's lien over security interests in the goods. In this regard, the judicial decision in In re Sharon Steel Corp., 25 U.C.C. Rep.2d 503, 176 B.R. 384 (W.D. Pa. 1995) is correct and is the controlling precedent.

2. The reference to charges in this section means charges relating to the bailment relationship for transportation. Charges does not mean that the bill of lading must state a specific rate or a specific amount. However, failure to state a specific rate or a specific amount has legal consequences under the second sentence of subsection (a).

3. The carrier's specific lien under this section is a possessory lien. See subsection (c). Part 3 of Article 7 does not require any particular form for a bill of lading. The carrier's lien arises when the carrier has issued a bill of lading.

Cross References:

Point 1: Sections 7–209, 9–109 and 9–333.

Point 3. Section 7–202 and 7–209.

Definitional Cross References:

"Bill of lading". Section 1–201.

"Carrier". Section 7–102.

"Consignor". Section 7–102.

"Delivery". Section 1–201.

"Goods". Section 7–102.

"Person". Section 1–201.

"Purchaser". Section 1–201.

"Value". Section 1–204.

Sections 31 and 32 of Acts 2005, 79th Leg., ch. 122 provide:

"Sec. 31. This Act applies to a document of title that is issued or a bailment that arises on or after the effective date of this Act. This Act does not apply to a document of title that is issued or a bailment that arises before the effective date of this Act even if the document of title or bailment would be subject to this Act if the document of title had been issued or bailment had arisen after the effective date of this Act. This Act does not apply to a right of action that has accrued before the effective date of this Act.

"Sec. 32. A document of title issued or a bailment that arises before the effective date of this Act and the rights, obligations, and interests flowing from that document or bailment are governed by any statute or other rule amended or repealed by this Act as if amendment or repeal had not occurred and may be terminated, completed, consummated, or enforced under that statute or other rule."

§ 7.308. Enforcement of Carrier's Lien

(a) A carrier's lien on goods may be enforced by public or private sale of the goods, in bulk or in packages, at any time or place and on any terms that are commercially reasonable, after notifying all persons known to claim an interest in the goods. The notification must include a statement of the amount due, the nature of the proposed sale, and the time and place of any public sale. The fact that a better price could have been obtained by a sale at a different time or in a different method from that selected by the carrier is not of itself sufficient to establish that the sale was not made in a commercially reasonable manner. The carrier has sold goods in a commercially reasonable manner if the carrier sells the goods in the usual manner in any recognized market therefor, sells at the price current in that market at the time of the sale, or has otherwise sold in conformity with commercially reasonable practices among dealers in the type of goods sold. A sale of more goods than apparently necessary to be offered to ensure satisfaction of the obligation is not commercially reasonable, except in cases covered by the preceding sentence.

(b) Before any sale pursuant to this section, any person claiming a right in the goods may pay the amount necessary to satisfy the lien and the reasonable expenses incurred in complying with this section. In that event, the goods may not be sold but must be retained by the carrier, subject to the terms of the bill of lading and this chapter.

(c) A carrier may buy at any public sale pursuant to this section.

(d) A purchaser in good faith of goods sold to enforce a carrier's lien takes the goods free of any rights of persons against which the lien was valid, despite the carrier's noncompliance with this section.

(e) A carrier may satisfy its lien from the proceeds of any sale pursuant to this section but shall hold the balance, if any, for delivery on demand to any person to which the carrier would have been bound to deliver the goods.

(f) The rights provided by this section are in addition to all other rights allowed by law to a creditor against a debtor.

(g) A carrier's lien may be enforced pursuant to either Subsection (a) or the procedure set forth in Section 7.210(b).

(h) A carrier is liable for damages caused by failure to comply with the requirements for sale under this section and, in case of wilful violation, is liable for conversion.

Acts 1967, 60th Leg., p. 2343, ch. 785, § 1, eff. Sept. 1, 1967. Amended by Acts 1983, 68th Leg., p. 1532, ch. 290, § 5, eff. Aug. 29, 1983; Acts 2005, 79th Leg., ch. 122, § 1, eff. Sept. 1, 2005.

Uniform Commercial Code Comment

Prior Uniform Statutory Provision: Former Section 7–308.

Changes: To conform language to modern usage and for style.

Purposes:

This section is intended to give the carrier an enforcement procedure of its lien coextensive with that given the warehouse in cases other than those covering noncommercial storage by the warehouse. See Section 7–210 and comments.

Cross Reference: Section 7–210.

Definitional Cross References:

"Bill of lading". Section 1–201.

"Carrier". Section 7–102.

"Creditor". Section 1–201.

"Delivery". Section 1–201.

"Good faith". Section 1–201. [7–102]

"Goods". Section 7–102.

"Notification". Section 1–202.

"Notifies". Section 1–202.

"Person". Section 1–201.

"Purchaser". Section 1–201.

"Rights". Section 1–201.

"Term". Section 1–201.

Sections 31 and 32 of Acts 2005, 79th Leg., ch. 122 provide:

"Sec. 31. This Act applies to a document of title that is issued or a bailment that arises on or after the effective date of this Act. This Act does not apply to a document of title that is issued or a bailment that arises before the effective date of this Act even if the document of title or bailment would be subject to this Act if the document of title had been issued or bailment had arisen after the effective date of this Act. This Act does not apply to a right of action that has accrued before the effective date of this Act.

"Sec. 32. A document of title issued or a bailment that arises before the effective date of this Act and the rights, obligations, and interests flowing from that document or bailment are governed by any statute or other rule amended or repealed by this Act as if amendment or repeal had not occurred and may be terminated, completed, consummated, or enforced under that statute or other rule."

§ 7.309. Duty of Care; Contractual Limitation of Carrier's Liability

(a) A carrier that issues a bill of lading, whether negotiable or nonnegotiable, shall exercise the degree of care in relation to the goods which a reasonably careful person would exercise under similar circumstances. This subsection does not affect any statute, regulation, or rule of law that imposes liability upon a common carrier for damages not caused by its negligence.

(b) Damages may be limited by a term in the bill of lading or in a transportation agreement that the carrier's liability may not exceed a value stated in the bill or transportation agreement if the carrier's rates are dependent upon value and the consignor is afforded an opportunity to declare a higher value and is advised of the opportunity. However, such a limitation is not effective with respect to the carrier's liability for conversion to its own use.

(c) Reasonable provisions as to the time and manner of presenting claims and commencing actions based on the shipment may be included in a bill of lading or a transportation agreement.

Acts 1967, 60th Leg., p. 2343, ch. 785, § 1, eff. Sept. 1, 1967. Amended by Acts 2005, 79th Leg., ch. 122, § 1, eff. Sept. 1, 2005.

Uniform Commercial Code Comment

Prior Uniform Statutory Provision: Former Section 7–309.

Changes: References to tariffs eliminated because of deregulation, adding reference to transportation agreements, and for style.

Purposes:

1. A bill of lading may also serve as the contract between the carrier and the bailor. Parties in their contract should be able to limit the amount of damages for breach of that contract including breach of the duty to take reasonable care of the goods. The parties cannot disclaim by contract the carrier's obligation of care. Section 1–302.

Federal statutes and treaties for air, maritime and rail transport may alter the standard of care. These federal statutes and treaties preempt this section when applicable. Section 7–103. Subsection (a) does not impair any rule of law imposing the liability of an insurer on a common carrier in intrastate commerce. Subsection (b), however, applies to the common carrier's liability as an insurer as well as to liability based on negligence. Subsection (b) allows the term limiting damages to appear either in the bill of lading or in the parties' transportation agreement. Compare 7–204(b). Subsection (c) allows the parties to agree to provisions regarding time and manner of presenting claims or commencing actions if the provisions are either in the bill of lading or the transportation agreement. Compare 7–204(c). Transportation agreements are commonly used to establish agreed terms between carriers and shippers that have an on-going relationship.

2. References to public tariffs in former Section 7–309(2) and (3) have been deleted in light of the modern era of deregulation. See Comment 2 to Section 7-103. If a tariff is required under state or federal law, pursuant to Section 7–103(a), the tariff would control over the rule of this section. As governed by contract law, parties may incorporate by reference the limits on the amount of damages or the reasonable provisions as to the time and manner of presenting claims set forth in applicable tariffs, e.g. a maximum unit value beyond which goods are not taken or a disclaimer of responsibility for undeclared articles of extraordinary value.

3. As under former Section 7–309(2), subsection (b) provides that a limitation of damages is ineffective if the carrier has converted the goods to its own use. A mere failure to redeliver the goods is not conversion to the carrier's own use. "Conversion to its own use" is narrower than the idea of conversion generally. Art Masters Associates, Ltd. v. United Parcel Service, 77 N.Y.2d 200, 567 N.E.2d 226 (1990); *See*, Kemper Ins. Co. v. Fed. Ex. Corp., 252 F.3d 509 (1st Cir), *cert. denied* 534 U.S. 1020 (2001) (opinion interpreting federal law).

4. As used in this section, damages may include damages arising from delay in delivery. Delivery dates and times are often specified in the parties' contract. See Section 7–403.

Cross Reference: Sections 1–302, 7–103, 7–204, 7–403.

Definitional Cross References:

"Action". Section 1–201.

"Bill of lading". Section 1–201.

"Carrier". Section 7–102.

"Consignor". Section 7–102.

"Document of Title". Section 1–102.

"Goods". Section 7–102.

"Value". Section 1–204.

Sections 31 and 32 of Acts 2005, 79th Leg., ch. 122 provide:

"Sec. 31. This Act applies to a document of title that is issued or a bailment that arises on or after the effective date of this Act. This Act does not apply to a document of title that is issued or a bailment that arises before the effective date of this Act even if the document of title or bailment would be subject to this Act if the document of title had been issued or bailment had arisen after the effective date of this Act. This Act does not apply to a right of action that has accrued before the effective date of this Act.

"Sec. 32. A document of title issued or a bailment that arises before the effective date of this Act and the rights, obligations, and interests flowing from that document or bailment are governed by any statute or other rule amended or repealed by this Act as if amendment or repeal had not occurred and may be terminated, completed, consummated, or enforced under that statute or other rule."

SUBCHAPTER D. WAREHOUSE RECEIPTS AND BILLS OF LADING: GENERAL OBLIGATIONS

Acts 2005, 79th Leg., ch. 122, § 1 amended chapter 7.

§ 7.401. Irregularities in Issue of Receipt or Bill or Conduct of Issuer

The obligations imposed by this chapter on an issuer apply to a document of title even if:

(1) the document does not comply with the requirements of this chapter or of any other statute, rule, or regulation regarding its issue, form, or content;

(2) the issuer violated laws regulating the conduct of its business;

(3) the goods covered by the document were owned by the bailee when the document was issued; or

(4) the person issuing the document is not a warehouse but the document purports to be a warehouse receipt.

Acts 1967, 60th Leg., p. 2343, ch. 785, § 1, eff. Sept. 1, 1967. Amended by Acts 2005, 79th Leg., ch. 122, § 1, eff. Sept. 1, 2005.

Uniform Commercial Code Comment

Prior Uniform Statutory Provision: Former Section 7–401.

Changes: Changes for style only.

Purposes:

The bailee's liability on its document despite non-receipt or misdescription of the goods is affirmed in Sections 7–203 and 7–301. The purpose of this section is to make it clear that regardless of irregularities a document which falls within the definition of document of title imposes on the issuer the obligations stated in this Article. For example, a bailee will not be permitted to avoid its obligation to deliver the goods (Section 7–403) or its obligation of due care with respect to them (Sections 7–204 and 7–309) by taking the position that no valid "document" was issued because it failed to file a statutory bond or did not pay stamp taxes or did not disclose the place of storage in the document. Tate v. Action Moving & Storage, Inc., 383 S.E.2d 229 (N.C. App. 1989), *rev. denied* 389 S.E.2d 104 (N.C. 1990). Sanctions against violations of statutory or administrative duties with respect to documents should be limited to revocation of license or other measures prescribed by the regulation imposing the duty. See Section 7–103.

Cross References: Sections 7–103, 7–203, 7–204, 7–301, 7–309.

Definitional Cross References:

"Bailee". Section 7–102.

"Document of title". Section 1–201.

"Goods". Section 7–102.

"Issuer". Section 7–102.

"Person". Section 1–201.

"Warehouse receipt". Section 1–201.

"Warehouse". Section 7–102.

Sections 31 and 32 of Acts 2005, 79th Leg., ch. 122 provide:

"Sec. 31. This Act applies to a document of title that is issued or a bailment that arises on or after the effective date of this Act. This Act does not apply to a document of title that is issued or a bailment that arises before the effective date of this Act even if the document of title or bailment would be subject to this Act if the document of title had been issued or bailment had arisen after the effective date of this Act. This Act does not apply to a right of action that has accrued before the effective date of this Act.

"Sec. 32. A document of title issued or a bailment that arises before the effective date of this Act and the rights, obligations, and interests flowing from that document or bailment are governed by any statute or other rule amended or repealed by this Act as if amendment or repeal had not occurred and may be terminated, completed, consummated, or enforced under that statute or other rule."

§ 7.402. Duplicate Document of Title; Overissue

A duplicate or any other document of title purporting to cover goods already represented by an outstanding document of the same issuer does not confer any right in the goods, except as provided in the case of tangible bills of lading in a set of parts, overissue of documents for fungible goods, substitutes for lost, stolen, or destroyed documents, or substitute documents issued pursuant to Section 7.105. The issuer is liable for damages caused by its overissue or failure to identify a duplicate document by a conspicuous notation.

Acts 1967, 60th Leg., p. 2343, ch. 785, § 1, eff. Sept. 1, 1967. Amended by Acts 2005, 79th Leg., ch. 122, § 1, eff. Sept. 1, 2005.

Uniform Commercial Code Comment

Prior Uniform Statutory Provision: Former Section 7–402.

Changes: Changes to accommodate electronic documents.

Purposes:

1. This section treats a duplicate which is not properly identified as a duplicate like any other overissue of documents: a purchaser of such a document acquires no title but only a cause of action for damages against the person that made the deception possible, except in the cases noted in the section. But parts of a tangible bill lawfully issued in a set of parts are not "overissue" (Section 7–304). Of course, if the issuer has clearly indicated that a document is a duplicate so that no one can be deceived by it, and in fact the duplicate is a correct copy of the original, the issuer is not liable for preparing and delivering such a duplicate copy.

Section 7–105 allows documents of title to be reissued in another medium. Re-issuance of a document in an alternative medium under Section 7–105 requires that the original document be surrendered to the issuer in order to make the substitute document the effective document. If the substitute document is not issued in compliance with section 7–105, then the document should be treated as a duplicate under this section.

2. The section applies to nonnegotiable documents to the extent of providing an action for damages for one who acquires an unmarked duplicate from a transferor who knew the facts and would therefore have had no cause of action against the issuer of the duplicate. Ordinarily the transferee of a nonnegotiable document acquires only the rights of its transferor.

3. Overissue is defined so as to exclude the common situation where two valid documents of different issuers are outstanding for the same goods at the same time. Thus freight forwarders commonly issue bills of lading to their customers for small shipments to be combined into carload shipments for which the railroad will issue a bill of lading to

the forwarder. So also a warehouse receipt may be outstanding against goods, and the holder of the receipt may issue delivery orders against the same goods. In these cases dealings with the subsequently issued documents may be effective to transfer title; e.g. negotiation of a delivery order will effectively transfer title in the ordinary case where no dishonesty has occurred and the goods are available to satisfy the orders. Section 7–503 provides for cases of conflict between documents of different issuers.

Cross References:

Point 1: Sections 7–105, 7–207, 7–304, and 7–601.

Point 3: Section 7–503.

Definitional Cross References:

"Bill of lading". Section 1–201.

"Conspicuous". Section 1–201.

"Document of title". Section 1–201.

"Fungible goods." Section 1–201.

"Goods". Section 7–102.

"Issuer". Section 7–102.

"Right". Section 1–201.

Sections 31 and 32 of Acts 2005, 79th Leg., ch. 122 provide:

"Sec. 31. This Act applies to a document of title that is issued or a bailment that arises on or after the effective date of this Act. This Act does not apply to a document of title that is issued or a bailment that arises before the effective date of this Act even if the document of title or bailment would be subject to this Act if the document of title had been issued or bailment had arisen after the effective date of this Act. This Act does not apply to a right of action that has accrued before the effective date of this Act.

"Sec. 32. A document of title issued or a bailment that arises before the effective date of this Act and the rights, obligations, and interests flowing from that document or bailment are governed by any statute or other rule amended or repealed by this Act as if amendment or repeal had not occurred and may be terminated, completed, consummated, or enforced under that statute or other rule."

§ 7.403. Obligation of Warehouse or Carrier to Deliver; Excuse

(a) A bailee shall deliver the goods to a person entitled under a document of title if the person complies with Subsections (b) and (c), unless and to the extent that the bailee establishes any of the following:

(1) delivery of the goods to a person whose receipt was rightful as against the claimant;

(2) damage to or delay, loss, or destruction of the goods for which the bailee is not liable;

(3) previous sale or other disposition of the goods in lawful enforcement of a lien or on a warehouse's lawful termination of storage;

(4) the exercise by a seller of its right to stop delivery pursuant to Section 2.705 or by a lessor of its right to stop delivery pursuant to Section 2A.526;

(5) a diversion, reconsignment, or other disposition pursuant to Section 7.303;

(6) release, satisfaction, or any other fact affording a personal defense against the claimant; or

(7) any other lawful excuse.

(b) A person claiming goods covered by a document of title shall satisfy the bailee's lien if the bailee so requests or the bailee is prohibited by law from delivering the goods until the charges are paid.

(c) Unless a person claiming the goods is one against which the document of title does not confer a right under Section 7.503(a):

(1) the person claiming under a document shall surrender possession or control of any outstanding negotiable document covering the goods for cancellation or indication of partial deliveries; and

(2) the bailee shall cancel the document or conspicuously indicate in the document the partial delivery or be liable to any person to which the document is duly negotiated.

Acts 1967, 60th Leg., p. 2343, ch. 785, § 1, eff. Sept. 1, 1967. Amended by Acts 2005, 79th Leg., ch. 122, § 1, eff. Sept. 1, 2005.

Uniform Commercial Code Comment

Prior Uniform Statutory Provision: Former Section 7–403.

Changes: Definition in former Section 7–403(4) moved to Section 7–102; bracketed language in former Section 7–403(1)(b) deleted; added cross reference to Section 2A–526; changes for style.

Purposes:

1. The present section, following former Section 7–403, is constructed on the basis of stating what previous deliveries or other circumstances operate to excuse the bailee's normal obligation on the document. Accordingly, "justified" deliveries under the pre-Code uniform acts now find their place as "excuse" under subsection (a).

2. The principal case covered by subsection (a)(1) is delivery to a person whose title is paramount to the rights represented by the document. For example, if a thief deposits stolen goods in a warehouse facility and takes a negotiable receipt, the warehouse is not liable on the receipt if it has surrendered the goods to the true owner, even though the receipt is held by a good faith purchaser. See Section 7–503(a). However, if the owner entrusted the goods to a person with power of disposition, and that person deposited the goods and took a negotiable document, the owner receiving delivery would not be rightful as against a holder to whom the negotiable document was duly negotiated, and delivery to the owner would not give the bailee a defense against such a holder. See Sections 7–502(a)(2), 7–503(a)(1).

3. Subsection (a)(2) amounts to a cross reference to all the tort law that determines the varying responsibilities and standards of care applicable to commercial bailees. A restatement of this tort law would be beyond the scope of this Act. Much of the applicable law as to responsibility of bailees for

the preservation of the goods and limitation of liability in case of loss has been codified for particular classes of bailees in interstate and foreign commerce by federal legislation and treaty and for intrastate carriers and other bailees by the regulatory state laws preserved by Section 7–103. In the absence of governing legislation the common law will prevail subject to the minimum standard of reasonable care prescribed by Sections 7–204 and 7–309 of this Article.

The bracketed language found in former Section 7–403(1)(b) has been deleted thereby leaving the allocations of the burden of going forward with the evidence and the burden of proof to the procedural law of the various states.

Subsection (a)(4) contains a cross reference to both the seller's and the lessor's rights to stop delivery under Article 2 and Article 2A respectively.

4. As under former Section 7–403, there is no requirement that a request for delivery must be accompanied by a formal tender of the amount of the charges due. Rather, the bailee must request payment of the amount of its lien when asked to deliver, and only in case this request is refused is it justified in declining to deliver because of nonpayment of charges. Where delivery without payment is forbidden by law, the request is treated as implicit. Such a prohibition reflects a policy of uniformity to prevent discrimination by failure to request payment in particular cases. Subsection (b) must be read in conjunction with the priorities given to the warehouse lien and the carrier lien under Section 7–209 and 7–307, respectively. If the parties are in dispute about whether the request for payment of the lien is legally proper, the bailee may have recourse to interpleader. See Section 7–603.

5. Subsection (c) states the obvious duty of a bailee to take up a negotiable document or note partial deliveries conspicuously thereon, and the result of failure in that duty. It is subject to only one exception, that stated in subsection (a)(1) of this section and in Section 7–503(a). Subsection (c) is limited to cases of delivery to a claimant; it has no application, for example, where goods held under a negotiable document are lawfully sold to enforce the bailee's lien.

6. When courts are considering subsection (a)(7), "any other lawful excuse," among others, refers to compliance with court orders under Sections 7–601, 7–602 and 7–603.

Cross References:

Point 2: Sections 7–502 and 7–503.

Point 3: Sections 2–705, 2A–526, 7–103, 7–204, and 7–309 and 10–103.

Point 4: Sections 7–209, 7–307 and 7–603.

Point 5: Section 7–503(1).

Point 6: Sections 7–601, 7–602, and 7–603.

Definitional Cross References:

"Bailee". Section 7–102.

"Conspicuous". Section 1–201

"Delivery". Section 1–201.

"Document of title". Section 1–201.

"Duly negotiate". Section 7–501.

"Goods". Section 7–102.

"Lessor". Section 2A–103.

"Person". Section 1–201.

"Receipt of goods". Section 2–103.

"Right". Section 1–201.

"Terms". Section 1–201.

"Warehouse". Section 7–102.

Sections 31 and 32 of Acts 2005, 79th Leg., ch. 122 provide:

"Sec. 31. This Act applies to a document of title that is issued or a bailment that arises on or after the effective date of this Act. This Act does not apply to a document of title that is issued or a bailment that arises before the effective date of this Act even if the document of title or bailment would be subject to this Act if the document of title had been issued or bailment had arisen after the effective date of this Act. This Act does not apply to a right of action that has accrued before the effective date of this Act.

"Sec. 32. A document of title issued or a bailment that arises before the effective date of this Act and the rights, obligations, and interests flowing from that document or bailment are governed by any statute or other rule amended or repealed by this Act as if amendment or repeal had not occurred and may be terminated, completed, consummated, or enforced under that statute or other rule."

§ 7.404. No Liability for Good Faith Delivery Pursuant to Document of Title

A bailee that in good faith has received goods and delivered or otherwise disposed of the goods according to the terms of a document of title or pursuant to this chapter is not liable for the goods even if:

(1) the person from which the bailee received the goods did not have authority to procure the document or to dispose of the goods; or

(2) the person to which the bailee delivered the goods did not have authority to receive the goods.

Acts 1967, 60th Leg., p. 2343, ch. 785, § 1, eff. Sept. 1, 1967. Amended by Acts 2005, 79th Leg., ch. 122, § 1, eff. Sept. 1, 2005.

Uniform Commercial Code Comment

Prior Uniform Statutory Provision: Former Section 7–404.

Changes: Changes reflect the definition of good faith in Section 1–201 [7–102] and for style.

Purposes:

This section uses the test of good faith, as defined in Section 1–201 [7–102], to continue the policy of former Section 7–404. Good faith now means "honesty in fact and the observance of reasonable commercial standards of fair dealing." The section states explicitly that the common law rule of "innocent conversion" by unauthorized "intermeddling" with another's property is inapplicable to the operations of commercial carriers and warehousemen that in good faith perform obligations that they have assumed and that generally they are under a legal compulsion to assume. The section applies to delivery to a fraudulent holder of a valid document as well as to delivery to the holder of an invalid document. Of course, in appropriate circumstances, a bailee may use interpleader or other dispute resolution process. See Section 7–603.

Cross Reference: Section 7–603.

Definitional Cross References:

"Bailee". Section 7–102.

"Delivery". Section 1–201.

"Document of title". Section 1–201.

"Good faith". Section 1–201. [7–102].

"Goods". Section 7–102.

"Person". Section 1–201.

"Receipt of goods". Section 2–103.

"Term". Section 1–201.

Sections 31 and 32 of Acts 2005, 79th Leg., ch. 122 provide:

"Sec. 31. This Act applies to a document of title that is issued or a bailment that arises on or after the effective date of this Act. This Act does not apply to a document of title that is issued or a bailment that arises before the effective date of this Act even if the document of title or bailment would be subject to this Act if the document of title had been issued or bailment had arisen after the effective date of this Act. This Act does not apply to a right of action that has accrued before the effective date of this Act.

"Sec. 32. A document of title issued or a bailment that arises before the effective date of this Act and the rights, obligations, and interests flowing from that document or bailment are governed by any statute or other rule amended or repealed by this Act as if amendment or repeal had not occurred and may be terminated, completed, consummated, or enforced under that statute or other rule."

SUBCHAPTER E. WAREHOUSE RECEIPTS AND BILLS OF LADING: NEGOTIATION AND TRANSFER

Acts 2005, 79th Leg., ch. 122, § 1 amended chapter 7.

§ 7.501. Form of Negotiation and Requirements of Due Negotiation

(a) The following rules apply to a negotiable tangible document of title:

(1) If the document's original terms run to the order of a named person, the document is negotiated by the named person's indorsement and delivery. After the named person's indorsement in blank or to bearer, any person may negotiate the document by delivery alone.

(2) If the document's original terms run to bearer, it is negotiated by delivery alone.

(3) If the document's original terms run to the order of a named person and it is delivered to the named person, the effect is the same as if the document had been negotiated.

(4) Negotiation of the document after it has been indorsed to a named person requires indorsement by the named person as well as delivery.

(5) A document is duly negotiated if it is negotiated in the manner stated in this subsection to a holder that purchases it in good faith, without notice of any defense against or claim to it on the part of any person, and for value, unless it is established that the negotiation is not in the regular course of business or financing or involves receiving the document in settlement or payment of a monetary obligation.

(b) The following rules apply to a negotiable electronic document of title:

(1) If the document's original terms run to the order of a named person or to bearer, the document is negotiated by delivery of the document to another person. Indorsement by the named person is not required to negotiate the document.

(2) If the document's original terms run to the order of a named person and the named person has control of the document, the effect is the same as if the document had been negotiated.

(3) A document is duly negotiated if it is negotiated in the manner stated in this subsection to a holder that purchases it in good faith, without notice of any defense against or claim to it on the part of any person, and for value, unless it is established that the negotiation is not in the regular course of business or financing or involves taking delivery of the document in settlement or payment of a monetary obligation.

(c) Indorsement of a nonnegotiable document of title neither makes it negotiable nor adds to the transferee's rights.

(d) The naming in a negotiable bill of lading of a person to be notified of the arrival of the goods does not limit the negotiability of the bill or constitute notice to a purchaser of the bill of any interest of that person in the goods.

Acts 1967, 60th Leg., p. 2343, ch. 785, § 1, eff. Sept. 1, 1967. Amended by Acts 2005, 79th Leg., ch. 122, § 1, eff. Sept. 1, 2005.

Uniform Commercial Code Comment

Prior Uniform Statutory Provision: Former Section 7–501.

Changes: To accommodate negotiable electronic documents of title.

Purpose:

1. Subsection (a) has been limited to tangible negotiable documents of title but otherwise remains unchanged in substance from the rules in former Section 7–501. Subsection (b) is new and applies to negotiable electronic documents of title. Delivery of a negotiable electronic document is through

voluntary transfer of control. Section 1–201 definition of "delivery." The control concept as applied to negotiable electronic documents of title is the substitute for both possession and indorsement as applied to negotiable tangible documents of title. Section 7–106.

Article 7 does not separately define the term "duly negotiated." However, the elements of "duly negotiated" are set forth in subsection (a)(5) for tangible documents and (b)(3) for electronic documents. As under former Section 7–501, in order to effect a "due negotiation" the negotiation must be in the "regular course of business or financing" in order to transfer greater rights than those held by the person negotiating. The foundation of the mercantile doctrine of good faith purchase for value has always been, as shown by the case situations, the furtherance and protection of the regular course of trade. The reason for allowing a person, in bad faith or in error, to convey away rights which are not its own has from the beginning been to make possible the speedy handling of that great run of commercial transactions which are patently usual and normal.

There are two aspects to the usual and normal course of mercantile dealings, namely, the person making the transfer and the nature of the transaction itself. The first question which arises is: Is the transferor a person with whom it is reasonable to deal as having full powers? In regard to documents of title the only holder whose possession or control appears, commercially, to be in order is almost invariably a person in the trade. No commercial purpose is served by allowing a tramp or a professor to "duly negotiate" an order bill of lading for hides or cotton not their own, and since such a transfer is obviously not in the regular course of business, it is excluded from the scope of the protection of subsections (a)(5) or (b)(3).

The second question posed by the "regular course" qualification is: Is the transaction one which is normally proper to pass full rights without inquiry, even though the transferor itself may not have such rights to pass, and even though the transferor may be acting in breach of duty? In raising this question the "regular course" criterion has the further advantage of limiting, the effective wrongful disposition to transactions whose protection will really further trade. Obviously, the snapping up of goods for quick resale at a price suspiciously below the market deserves no protection as a matter of policy: it is also clearly outside the range of regular course.

Any notice on the document sufficient to put a merchant on inquiry as to the "regular course" quality of the transaction will frustrate a "due negotiation". Thus irregularity of the document or unexplained staleness of a bill of lading may appropriately be recognized as negating a negotiation in "regular" course.

A pre-existing claim constitutes value, and "due negotiation" does not require "new value." A usual and ordinary transaction in which documents are received as security for credit previously extended may be in "regular" course, even though there is a demand for additional collateral because the creditor "deems himself insecure." But the matter has moved out of the regular course of financing if the debtor is thought to be insolvent, the credit previously extended is in effect cancelled, and the creditor snatches a plank in the shipwreck under the guise of a demand for additional collateral. Where a money debt is "paid" in commodity paper, any question of "regular" course disappears, as the case is explicitly excepted from "due negotiation".

2. Negotiation under this section may be made by any holder no matter how the holder acquired possession or control of the document.

3. Subsections (a)(3) and (b)(2) make explicit a matter upon which the intent of the pre-Code law was clear but the language somewhat obscure: a negotiation results from a delivery to a banker or buyer to whose order the document has been taken by the person making the bailment. There is no presumption of irregularity in such a negotiation; it may very well be in "regular course."

4. This Article does not contain any provision creating a presumption of due negotiation to, and full rights in, a holder of a document of title akin to that created by Uniform Commercial Code Article 3. But the reason of the provisions of this Act (Section 1–307) on the prima facie authenticity and accuracy of third party documents, joins with the reason of the present section to work such a presumption in favor of any person who has power to make a due negotiation. It would not make sense for this Act to authorize a purchaser to indulge the presumption of regularity if the courts were not also called upon to do so. Allocations of the burden of going forward with the evidence and the burden of proof are left to the procedural law of the various states.

5. Subsections (c) and (d) are unchanged from prior law and apply to both tangible and electronic documents of title.

Cross References: Sections 1–307, 7–502 and 7–503.

Definitional Cross References:

"Bearer". Section 1–201.

"Control". Section 7–106.

"Delivery". Section 1–201.

"Document of title". Section 1–201.

"Good faith". Section 1–201 [7–102].

"Holder". Section 1–201.

"Notice". Section 1–202.

"Person". Section 1–201.

"Purchase". Section 1–201.

"Rights". Section 1–201.

"Term". Section 1–201.

"Value". Section 1–204.

Sections 31 and 32 of Acts 2005, 79th Leg., ch. 122 provide:

"Sec. 31. This Act applies to a document of title that is issued or a bailment that arises on or after the effective date of this Act. This Act does not apply to a document of title that is issued or a bailment that arises before the effective date of this Act even if the document of title or bailment would be subject to this Act if the document of title had been issued or bailment had arisen after the effective date of this Act. This Act does not apply to a right of action that has accrued before the effective date of this Act.

"Sec. 32. A document of title issued or a bailment that arises before the effective date of this Act and the rights, obligations, and interests flowing from that document or bailment are governed by any statute or other rule amended or repealed by this Act as if amendment or repeal had not occurred and may be terminated, completed, consummated, or enforced under that statute or other rule."

§ 7.502. Rights Acquired by Due Negotiation

(a) Subject to Sections 7.205 and 7.503, a holder to which a negotiable document of title has been duly negotiated acquires thereby:

(1) title to the document;

(2) title to the goods;

(3) all rights accruing under the law of agency or estoppel, including rights to goods delivered to the bailee after the document was issued; and

(4) the direct obligation of the issuer to hold or deliver the goods according to the terms of the document free of any defense or claim by the issuer except those arising under the terms of the document or under this chapter. In the case of a delivery order, the bailee's obligation accrues only upon the bailee's acceptance of the delivery order and the obligation acquired by the holder is that the issuer and any indorser will procure the acceptance of the bailee.

(b) Subject to Section 7.503, title and rights acquired by due negotiation are not defeated by any stoppage of the goods represented by the document of title or by surrender of the goods by the bailee and are not impaired even if:

(1) the due negotiation or any prior due negotiation constituted a breach of duty;

(2) any person has been deprived of possession of a negotiable tangible document or control of a negotiable electronic document by misrepresentation, fraud, accident, mistake, duress, loss, theft, or conversion; or

(3) a previous sale or other transfer of the goods or document has been made to a third person.

Acts 1967, 60th Leg., p. 2343, ch. 785, § 1, eff. Sept. 1, 1967. Amended by Acts 2005, 79th Leg., ch. 122, § 1, eff. Sept. 1, 2005.

Uniform Commercial Code Comment

Prior Uniform Statutory Provision: Former Section 7–502.

Changes: To accommodate electronic documents of title and for style.

Purpose:

1. This section applies to both tangible and electronic documents of title. The elements of duly negotiated, which constitutes a due negotiation, are set forth in Section 7–501. The several necessary qualifications of the broad principle that the holder of a document acquired in a due negotiation is the owner of the document and the goods have been brought together in the next section (Section 7–503).

2. Subsection (a)(3) covers the case of "feeding" of a duly negotiated document by subsequent delivery to the bailee of such goods as the document falsely purported to cover; the bailee in such case is estopped as against the holder of the document.

3. The explicit statement in subsection (a)(4) of the bailee's direct obligation to the holder precludes the defense that the document in question was "spent" after the carrier had delivered the goods to a previous holder. But the holder is subject to such defenses as non-negligent destruction even though not apparent on the document. The sentence on delivery orders applies only to delivery orders in negotiable form which have been duly negotiated. On delivery orders, see also Section 7–503(b) and Comment.

4. Subsection (b) continues the law which gave full effect to the issuance or due negotiation of a negotiable document. The subsection adds nothing to the effect of the rules stated in subsection (a), but it has been included since such explicit reference was provided under former Section 7–502 to preserve the right of a purchaser by due negotiation. The listing is not exhaustive. The language"any stoppage" is included lest an inference be drawn that a stoppage of the goods before or after transit might cut off or otherwise impair the purchaser's rights.

Cross References: Sections 7–103, 7–205, 7–403, 7–501, and 7–503.

Definitional Cross References:

"Bailee". Section 7–102.

"Control". Section 7–106.

"Delivery". Section 1–201.

"Delivery order". Section 7–102.

"Document of title". Section 1–201.

"Duly negotiate". Section 7–501.

"Fungible". Section 1–201.

"Goods". Section 7–102.

"Holder". Section 1–201.

"Issuer". Section 7–102.

"Person". Section 1–201.

"Rights". Section 1–201.

"Term". Section 1–201.

"Warehouse receipt". Section 1–201.

Sections 31 and 32 of Acts 2005, 79th Leg., ch. 122 provide:

"Sec. 31. This Act applies to a document of title that is issued or a bailment that arises on or after the effective date of this Act. This Act does not apply to a document of title that is issued or a bailment that arises before the effective date of this Act even if the document of title or bailment would be subject to this Act if the document of title had been issued or bailment had arisen after the effective date of this Act. This Act does not apply to a right of action that has accrued before the effective date of this Act.

"Sec. 32. A document of title issued or a bailment that arises before the effective date of this Act and the rights, obligations, and interests flowing from that document or bailment are governed by any statute or other rule amended or repealed by this Act as if amendment or repeal had not occurred and may be terminated, completed, consummated, or enforced under that statute or other rule."

§ 7.503. Document of Title to Goods Defeated in Certain Cases

(a) A document of title confers no right in goods against a person that before issuance of the document had a legal interest or a perfected security interest in the goods and that did not:

(1) deliver or entrust the goods or any document covering the goods to the bailor or the bailor's nominee with actual or apparent authority to ship, store, or sell; with power to obtain delivery under Section 7.403; or with power of disposition under Section 2.403, 2A.304(a)(2), 2A.305(a)(2), or 9.320 or other statute or rule of law; or

(2) acquiesce in the procurement by the bailor or its nominee of any document.

(b) Title to goods based upon an unaccepted delivery order is subject to the rights of any person to which a negotiable warehouse receipt or bill of lading covering the goods has been duly negotiated. That title may be defeated under Section 7.504 to the same extent as the rights of the issuer or a transferee from the issuer.

(c) Title to goods based upon a bill of lading issued to a freight forwarder is subject to the rights of any person to which a bill issued by the freight forwarder is duly negotiated. However, delivery by the carrier in accordance with Subchapter D pursuant to its own bill of lading discharges the carrier's obligation to deliver.

Amended by Acts 1999, 76th Leg., ch. 414, § 2.25, eff. July 1, 2001; Acts 2005, 79th Leg., ch. 122, § 1, eff. Sept. 1, 2005.

Uniform Commercial Code Comment

Prior Uniform Statutory Provision: Former Section 7–503.

Changes: Changes to cross-reference to Article 2A and for style.

Purposes:

1. In general it may be said that the title of a purchaser by due negotiation prevails over almost any interest in the goods which existed prior to the procurement of the document of title if the possession of the goods by the person obtaining the document derived from any action by the prior claimant which introduced the goods into the stream of commerce or carried them along that stream. A thief of the goods cannot indeed by shipping or storing them to the thief's own order acquire power to transfer them to a good faith purchaser. Nor can a tenant or mortgagor defeat any rights of a landlord or mortgagee which have been perfected under the local law merely by wrongfully shipping or storing a portion of the crop or other goods. However, "acquiescence" by the landlord or mortgagee does not require active consent under subsection (a)(2) and knowledge of the likelihood of storage or shipment with no objection or effort to control it is sufficient to defeat the landlord's or the mortgagee's rights as against one who takes by due negotiation of a negotiable document. In re Sharon Steel, 176 B.R. 384 (Bankr. W.D. Pa. 1995); In re R.V. Segars Co, 54 B.R. 170 (Bankr. S.C. 1985); In re Jamestown Elevators, Inc., 49 B.R. 661 (Bankr. N.D. 1985).

On the other hand, where goods are delivered to a factor for sale, even though the factor has made no advances and is limited in its duty to sell for cash, the goods are "entrusted" to the factor "with actual ... authority ... to sell" under subsection (a)(1), and if the factor procures a negotiable document of title it can transfer the owner's interest to a purchaser by due negotiation. Further, where the factor is in the business of selling, goods entrusted to it simply for safekeeping or storage may be entrusted under circumstances which give the factor "apparent authority to ship, store or sell" under subsection (a)(1), or power of disposition under Section 2–403, 2A–304(2), 2A–305(2), 7–205, 9–320, or 9–321(c) or under a statute such as the earlier Factors Acts, or under a rule of law giving effect to apparent ownership. See Section 1–103.

Persons having an interest in goods also frequently deliver or entrust them to agents or servants other than factors for the purpose of shipping or warehousing or under circumstances reasonably contemplating such action. This Act is clear that such persons assume full risk that the agent to whom the goods are so delivered may ship or store in breach of duty, take a document to the agent's own order and then proceed to misappropriate the negotiable document of title that embodies the goods. This Act makes no distinction between possession or mere custody in such situations and finds no exception in the case of larceny by a bailee or the like. The safeguard in such situations lies in the requirement that a due negotiation can occur only "in the regular course of business or financing" and that the purchase be in good faith and without notice. See Section 7–501. Documents of title have no market among the commercially inexperienced and the commercially experienced do not take them without inquiry from persons known to be truck drivers or petty clerks even though such persons purport to be operating in their own names.

Again, where the seller allows a buyer to receive goods under a contract for sale, though as a "conditional delivery" or under "cash sale" terms and on explicit agreement for immediate payment, the buyer thereby acquires power to defeat the seller's interest by transfer of the goods to certain good faith purchasers. See Section 2–403. Both in policy and under the language of subsection (a)(1) that same power must be extended to accomplish the same result if the buyer procures a negotiable document of title to the goods and duly negotiates it.

This comment 1 should be considered in interpreting delivery, entrustment or acquiescence in application of Section 7–209.

2. Under subsection (a) a delivery order issued by a person having no right in or power over the goods is ineffective unless the owner acts as provided in subsection (a)(1) or (2). Thus the rights of a transferee of a non-negotiable warehouse receipt can be defeated by a delivery order subsequently issued by the transferor only if the transferee "deliv-

ers or entrusts" to the "person procuring" the delivery order or "acquiesces" in that person's procurement. Similarly, a second delivery order issued by the same issuer for the same goods will ordinarily be subject to the first, both under this section and under Section 7–402. After a delivery order is validly issued but before it is accepted, it may nevertheless be defeated under subsection (b) in much the same way that the rights of a transferee may be defeated under Section 7–504. For example, a buyer in ordinary course from the issuer may defeat the rights of the holder of a prior delivery order if the bailee receives notification of the buyer's rights before notification of the holder's rights. Section 7–504(b)(2). But an accepted delivery order has the same effect as a document issued by the bailee.

3. Under subsection (c) a bill of lading issued to a freight forwarder is subordinated to the freight forwarder's document of title, since the bill on its face gives notice of the fact that a freight forwarder is in the picture and the freight forwarder has in all probability issued a document of title. But the carrier is protected in following the terms of its own bill of lading.

Cross References:

Point 1: Sections 1–103, 2–403, 2A–304(2), 2A–305(2), 7–205, 7–209, 7–501, 9–320, 9–321(c), and 9–331.

Point 2: Sections 7–402 and 7–504.

Point 3: Sections 7–402, 7–403 and 7–404.

Definitional Cross References:

"Bill of lading". Section 1–201.

"Contract for sale". Section 2–106.

"Delivery". Section 1–201.

"Delivery order". Section 7–102.

"Document of title". Section 1–201.

"Duly negotiate". Section 7–501.

"Goods". Section 7–102.

"Person". Section 1–201.

"Right". Section 1–201.

"Warehouse receipt". Section 1–201.

Sections 31 and 32 of Acts 2005, 79th Leg., ch. 122 provide:

"Sec. 31. This Act applies to a document of title that is issued or a bailment that arises on or after the effective date of this Act. This Act does not apply to a document of title that is issued or a bailment that arises before the effective date of this Act even if the document of title or bailment would be subject to this Act if the document of title had been issued or bailment had arisen after the effective date of this Act. This Act does not apply to a right of action that has accrued before the effective date of this Act.

"Sec. 32. A document of title issued or a bailment that arises before the effective date of this Act and the rights, obligations, and interests flowing from that document or bailment are governed by any statute or other rule amended or repealed by this Act as if amendment or repeal had not occurred and may be terminated, completed, consummated, or enforced under that statute or other rule."

§ 7.504. Rights Acquired in Absence of Due Negotiation; Effect of Diversion; Stoppage of Delivery

(a) A transferee of a document of title, whether negotiable or nonnegotiable, to which the document has been delivered but not duly negotiated, acquires the title and rights that its transferor had or had actual authority to convey.

(b) In the case of a nonnegotiable document of title, until but not after the bailee receives notice of the transfer, the rights of the transferee may be defeated:

(1) by those creditors of the transferor that could treat the transfer as void under Section 2.402 or 2A.308;

(2) by a buyer from the transferor in ordinary course of business if the bailee has delivered the goods to the buyer or received notification of the buyer's rights;

(3) by a lessee from the transferor in ordinary course of business if the bailee has delivered the goods to the lessee or received notification of the lessee's rights; or

(4) as against the bailee, by good faith dealings of the bailee with the transferor.

(c) A diversion or other change of shipping instructions by the consignor in a nonnegotiable bill of lading which causes the bailee not to deliver the goods to the consignee defeats the consignee's title to the goods if the goods have been delivered to a buyer in ordinary course of business or a lessee in ordinary course of business and in any event defeats the consignee's rights against the bailee.

(d) Delivery of the goods pursuant to a nonnegotiable document of title may be stopped by a seller under Section 2.705 or a lessor under Section 2A.526, subject to the requirements of due notification in those sections. A bailee honoring the seller's or lessor's instructions is entitled to be indemnified by the seller or lessor against any resulting loss or expense.

Acts 1967, 60th Leg., p. 2343, ch. 785, § 1, eff. Sept. 1, 1967. Amended by Acts 2005, 79th Leg., ch. 122, § 1, eff. Sept. 1, 2005.

Uniform Commercial Code Comment

Prior Uniform Statutory Provision: Former Section 7–504.

Changes: To include cross-references to Article 2A and for style.

Purposes:

1. Under the general principles controlling negotiable documents, it is clear that in the absence of due negotiation a transferor cannot convey greater rights than the transferor has, even when the negotiation is formally perfect. This section recognizes the transferor's power to transfer rights which the transferor has or has "actual authority to convey." Thus, where a negotiable document of title is being transferred the operation of the principle of estoppel is not recognized, as contrasted with situations involving the transfer of the goods themselves. (Compare Section 2–403 on good faith purchase of goods.) This section applies to both tangible and electronic documents of title.

A necessary part of the price for the protection of regular dealings with negotiable documents of title is an insistence that no dealing which is in any way irregular shall be recognized as a good faith purchase of the document or of any rights pertaining to it. So, where the transfer of a negotiable document fails as a negotiation because a requisite indorsement is forged or otherwise missing, the purchaser in good faith and for value may be in the anomalous position of having less rights, in part, than if the purchaser had purchased the goods themselves. True, the purchaser's rights are not subject to defeat by attachment of the goods or surrender of them to the purchaser's transferor (contrast subsection (b)); but on the other hand, the purchaser cannot acquire enforceable rights to control or receive the goods over the bailee's objection merely by giving notice to the bailee. Similarly, a consignee who makes payment to its consignor against a straight bill of lading can thereby acquire the position of a good faith purchaser of goods under provisions of the Article of this Act on Sales (Section 2–403), whereas the same payment made in good faith against an unendorsed order bill would not have such effect. The appropriate remedy of a purchaser in such a situation is to regularize its status by compelling indorsement of the document (see Section 7–506).

2. As in the case of transfer—as opposed to "due negotiation"—of negotiable documents, subsection (a) empowers the transferor of a nonnegotiable document to transfer only such rights as the transferor has or has "actual authority" to convey. In contrast to situations involving the goods themselves the operation of estoppel or agency principles is not here recognized to enable the transferor to convey greater rights than the transferor actually has. Subsection (b) makes it clear, however, that the transferee of a nonnegotiable document may acquire rights greater in some respects than those of his transferor by giving notice of the transfer to the bailee. New subsection (b)(3) provides for the rights of a lessee in the ordinary course.

Subsection (b)(2) & (3) require delivery of the goods. Delivery of the goods means the voluntary transfer of physical possession of the goods. See amended 2–103.

3. Subsection (c) is in part a reiteration of the carrier's immunity from liability if it honors instructions of the consignor to divert, but there is added a provision protecting the title of the substituted consignee if the latter is a buyer in ordinary course of business. A typical situation would be where a manufacturer, having shipped a lot of standardized goods to A on nonnegotiable bill of lading, diverts the goods to customer B who pays for them. Under pre-Code passage-of-title-by-appropriation doctrine A might reclaim the goods from B. However, no consideration of commercial policy supports this involvement of an innocent third party in the default of the manufacturer on his contract to A; and the common commercial practice of diverting goods in transit suggests a trade understanding in accordance with this subsection. The same result should obtain if the substituted consignee is a lessee in ordinary course. The extent of the lessee's interest in the goods is less than a buyer's interest in the goods. However, as against the first consignee and the lessee in ordinary course as the substituted consignee, the lessee's rights in the goods as granted under the lease are superior to the first consignee's rights.

4. Subsection (d) gives the carrier an express right to indemnity where the carrier honors a seller's request to stop delivery.

5. Section 1–202 gives the bailee protection, if due diligence is exercised where the bailee's organization has not had time to act on a notification.

Cross References:

Point 1: Sections 2–403 and 7–506.

Point 2: Sections 2–403 and 2A–304.

Point 3: Sections 7-303, 7–403(a)(5) and 7–404.

Point 4: Sections 2–705 and 7–403(a)(4).

Point 5: Section 1–202.

Definitional Cross References:

"Bailee". Section 7-102.

"Bill of lading". Section 1-201.

"Buyer in ordinary course of business". Section 1–201.

"Consignee". Section 7-102.

"Consignor". Section 7-102.

"Creditor". Section 1–201.

"Delivery". Section 1-201.

"Document of Title". Section 1–201.

"Duly negotiate". Section 7–501.

"Good faith". Section 1-201. [7-102].

"Goods". Section 7-102.

"Honor". Section 1-201.

"Lessee in ordinary course". Section 2A–103.

"Notification" Section 1–202.

"Purchaser". Section 1-201.

"Rights". Section 1–201.

Sections 31 and 32 of Acts 2005, 79th Leg., ch. 122 provide:

"Sec. 31. This Act applies to a document of title that is issued or a bailment that arises on or after the effective date of this Act. This Act does not apply to a document of title that is issued or a bailment that arises before the effective date of this Act even if the document of title or bailment would be subject to this Act if the document of title had been issued or bailment had arisen after the effective date of this Act. This Act does not apply to a right of action that has accrued before the effective date of this Act.

"Sec. 32. A document of title issued or a bailment that arises before the effective date of this Act and the rights, obligations, and interests flowing from that document or bailment are governed by any statute or other rule amended or repealed by this Act as if amendment or repeal had not occurred and may be terminated,

completed, consummated, or enforced under that statute or other rule."

§ 7.505. Indorser Not Guarantor for Other Parties

The indorsement of a tangible document of title issued by a bailee does not make the indorser liable for any default by the bailee or previous indorsers.

Acts 1967, 60th Leg., p. 2343, ch. 785, § 1, eff. Sept. 1, 1967. Amended by Acts 2005, 79th Leg., ch. 122, § 1, eff. Sept. 1, 2005.

Uniform Commercial Code Comment

Prior Uniform Statutory Provision: Former Section 7–505.

Changes: Limited to tangible documents of title.

Purposes:

This section is limited to tangible documents of title as the concept of indorsement is irrelevant to electronic documents of title. Electronic documents of title will be transferred by delivery of control. Section 7–106. The indorsement of a tangible document of title is generally understood to be directed towards perfecting the transferee's rights rather than towards assuming additional obligations. The language of the present section, however, does not preclude the one case in which an indorsement given for value guarantees future action, namely, that in which the bailee has not yet become liable upon the document at the time of the indorsement. Under such circumstances the indorser, of course, engages that appropriate honor of the document by the bailee will occur. See Section 7–502(a)(4) as to negotiable delivery orders. However, even in such a case, once the bailee attorns to the transferee, the indorser's obligation has been fulfilled and the policy of this section excludes any continuing obligation on the part of the indorser for the bailee's ultimate actual performance.

Cross Reference: Sections 7–106 and 7–502.

Definitional Cross References:

"Bailee". Section 7–102.

"Document of title". Section 1–201.

"Party". Section 1–201.

Sections 31 and 32 of Acts 2005, 79th Leg., ch. 122 provide:

"Sec. 31. This Act applies to a document of title that is issued or a bailment that arises on or after the effective date of this Act. This Act does not apply to a document of title that is issued or a bailment that arises before the effective date of this Act even if the document of title or bailment would be subject to this Act if the document of title had been issued or bailment had arisen after the effective date of this Act. This Act does not apply to a right of action that has accrued before the effective date of this Act.

"Sec. 32. A document of title issued or a bailment that arises before the effective date of this Act and the rights, obligations, and interests flowing from that document or bailment are governed by any statute or other rule amended or repealed by this Act as if amendment or repeal had not occurred and may be terminated, completed, consummated, or enforced under that statute or other rule."

§ 7.506. Delivery Without Indorsement; Right to Compel Indorsement

The transferee of a negotiable tangible document of title has a specifically enforceable right to have its transferor supply any necessary indorsement, but the transfer becomes a negotiation only as of the time the indorsement is supplied.

Acts 1967, 60th Leg., p. 2343, ch. 785, § 1, eff. Sept. 1, 1967. Amended by Acts 2005, 79th Leg., ch. 122, § 1, eff. Sept. 1, 2005.

Uniform Commercial Code Comment

Prior Uniform Statutory Provision: Former Section 7–506.

Changes: Limited to tangible documents of title.

Purposes:

1. This section is limited to tangible documents of title as the concept of indorsement is irrelevant to electronic documents of title. Electronic documents of title will be transferred by delivery of control. Section 7–106. From a commercial point of view the intention to transfer a tangible negotiable document of title which requires an indorsement for its transfer, is incompatible with an intention to withhold such indorsement and so defeat the effective use of the document. Further, the preceding section and the Comment thereto make it clear that an indorsement generally imposes no responsibility on the indorser.

2. Although this section provides that delivery of a tangible document of title without the necessary indorsement is effective as a transfer, the transferee, of course, has not regularized its position until such indorsement is supplied. Until this is done the transferee cannot claim rights under due negotiation within the requirements of this Article (Section 7–501(a)(5)) on "due negotiation". Similarly, despite the transfer to the transferee of the transferor's title, the transferee cannot demand the goods from the bailee until the negotiation has been completed and the document is in proper form for surrender. See Section 7–403(c).

Cross References:

Point 1: Sections 7–106 and 7–505.

Point 2: Sections 7–501(a)(5) and 7–403(c).

Definitional Cross References:

"Document of title". Section 1–201.

"Rights". Section 1–201.

Sections 31 and 32 of Acts 2005, 79th Leg., ch. 122 provide:

"Sec. 31. This Act applies to a document of title that is issued or a bailment that arises on or after the effective date of this Act. This Act does not apply to a document of title that is issued or a bailment that arises before the effective date of this Act even if the document of title or bailment would be subject to this Act if the document of title had been issued or bailment had arisen after the effective date of this Act. This Act does not apply to a right of action that has accrued before the effective date of this Act.

"Sec. 32. A document of title issued or a bailment that arises before the effective date of this Act and the rights, obligations, and interests flowing from that document or bailment are governed by any statute or other rule amended or repealed by this Act as if amendment or repeal had not occurred and may be terminated,

completed, consummated, or enforced under that statute or other rule."

§ 7.507. Warranties on Negotiation or Delivery of Document of Title

If a person negotiates or delivers a document of title for value, otherwise than as a mere intermediary under Section 7.508, unless otherwise agreed, the transferor warrants to its immediate purchaser only in addition to any warranty made in selling or leasing the goods that:

(1) the document is genuine;

(2) the transferor does not have knowledge of any fact that would impair the document's validity or worth; and

(3) the negotiation or delivery is rightful and fully effective with respect to the title to the document and the goods it represents.

Acts 1967, 60th Leg., p. 2343, ch. 785, § 1, eff. Sept. 1, 1967. Amended by Acts 2005, 79th Leg., ch. 122, § 1, eff. Sept. 1, 2005.

Uniform Commercial Code Comment

Prior Uniform Statutory Provision: Former Section 7–507.

Changes: Substitution of the word "delivery" for the word "transfer," reference leasing transactions and style.

Purposes:

1. Delivery of goods by use of a document of title does not limit or displace the ordinary obligations of a seller or lessor as to any warranties regarding the goods that arises under other law. If the transfer of documents attends or follows the making of a contract for the sale or lease of goods, the general obligations on warranties as to the goods (Sections 2–312 through 2–318 and Sections 2A–210 through 2A–316) are brought to bear as well as the special warranties under this section.

2. The limited warranties of a delivering or collecting intermediary, including a collecting bank, are stated in Section 7–508.

Cross References:

Point 1: Sections 2–312 through 2–318 and 2A–310–through 2A–316.

Point 2: Section 7–508.

Definitional Cross References:

"Delivery". Section 1–201.

"Document of title". Section 1–201.

"Genuine". Section 1–201.

"Goods". Section 7–102.

"Person". Section 1–201.

"Purchaser". Section 1–201.

"Value". Section 1–204.

Sections 31 and 32 of Acts 2005, 79th Leg., ch. 122 provide:

"Sec. 31. This Act applies to a document of title that is issued or a bailment that arises on or after the effective date of this Act. This Act does not apply to a document of title that is issued or a bailment that arises before the effective date of this Act even if the document of title or bailment would be subject to this Act if the document of title had been issued or bailment had arisen after the effective date of this Act. This Act does not apply to a right of action that has accrued before the effective date of this Act.

"Sec. 32. A document of title issued or a bailment that arises before the effective date of this Act and the rights, obligations, and interests flowing from that document or bailment are governed by any statute or other rule amended or repealed by this Act as if amendment or repeal had not occurred and may be terminated, completed, consummated, or enforced under that statute or other rule."

§ 7.508. Warranties of Collecting Bank as to Documents of Title

A collecting bank or other intermediary known to be entrusted with documents of title on behalf of another or with collection of a draft or other claim against delivery of documents warrants by the delivery of the documents only its own good faith and authority even if the collecting bank or other intermediary has purchased or made advances against the claim or draft to be collected.

Acts 1967, 60th Leg., p. 2343, ch. 785, § 1, eff. Sept. 1, 1967. Amended by Acts 2005, 79th Leg., ch. 122, § 1, eff. Sept. 1, 2005.

Uniform Commercial Code Comment

Prior Uniform Statutory Provision: Former Section 7–508.

Changes: Changes for style only.

Purposes:

1. To state the limited warranties given with respect to the documents accompanying a documentary draft.

2. In warranting its authority a collecting bank or other intermediary only warrants its authority from its transferor. See Section 4–203. It does not warrant the genuineness or effectiveness of the document. Compare Section 7–507.

3. Other duties and rights of banks handling documentary drafts for collection are stated in Article 4, Part 5. On the meaning of draft, see Section 4–104 and Section 5–102, comment 11.

Cross References:

Sections 4–104, 4–203, 4–501 through 4–504, 5–102, and 7–507.

Definitional Cross References:

"Collecting bank". Section 4–105.

"Delivery". Section 1–201.

"Document of title". Section 1–102.

"Documentary draft". Section 4–104.

"Intermediary bank". Section 4–105.

"Good faith". Section 1–201 [7–102.]

Sections 31 and 32 of Acts 2005, 79th Leg., ch. 122 provide:

"Sec. 31. This Act applies to a document of title that is issued or a bailment that arises on or after the effective date of this Act. This Act does not apply to a document of title that is issued or a bailment that arises before the effective date of this Act even if the document of title or bailment would be subject to this Act if the document of title had been issued or bailment had arisen after the effective date of this Act. This Act does not apply to a right of action that has accrued before the effective date of this Act.

"Sec. 32. A document of title issued or a bailment that arises before the effective date of this Act and the rights, obligations, and interests flowing from that document or bailment are governed by any statute or other rule amended or repealed by this Act as if amendment or repeal had not occurred and may be terminated, completed, consummated, or enforced under that statute or other rule."

§ 7.509. Adequate Compliance With Commercial Contract

Whether a document of title is adequate to fulfill the obligations of a contract for sale, a contract for lease, or the conditions of a letter of credit is determined by Chapter 2, 2A, or 5.

Acts 1967, 60th Leg., p. 2343, ch. 785, § 1, eff. Sept. 1, 1967. Amended by Acts 2005, 79th Leg., ch. 122, § 1, eff. Sept. 1, 2005.

Uniform Commercial Code Comment

Prior Uniform Statutory Provision: Former Section 7–509.

Changes: To reference Article 2A.

Purposes:

To cross-refer to the Articles of this Act which deal with the substantive issues of the type of document of title required under the contract entered into by the parties.

Cross References: Articles 2, 2A and 5.

Definitional Cross References:

"Contract for sale". Section 2–106.

"Document of title". Section 1–201.

"Lease". Section 2A–103.

Sections 31 and 32 of Acts 2005, 79th Leg., ch. 122 provide:

"Sec. 31. This Act applies to a document of title that is issued or a bailment that arises on or after the effective date of this Act. This Act does not apply to a document of title that is issued or a bailment that arises before the effective date of this Act even if the document of title or bailment would be subject to this Act if the document of title had been issued or bailment had arisen after the effective date of this Act. This Act does not apply to a right of action that has accrued before the effective date of this Act.

"Sec. 32. A document of title issued or a bailment that arises before the effective date of this Act and the rights, obligations, and interests flowing from that document or bailment are governed by any statute or other rule amended or repealed by this Act as if amendment or repeal had not occurred and may be terminated, completed, consummated, or enforced under that statute or other rule."

SUBCHAPTER F. WAREHOUSE RECEIPTS AND BILLS OF LADING: MISCELLANEOUS PROVISIONS

Acts 2005, 79th Leg., ch. 122, § 1 amended chapter 7.

§ 7.601. Lost, Stolen, or Destroyed Documents of Title

(a) If a document of title is lost, stolen, or destroyed, a court may order delivery of the goods or issuance of a substitute document and the bailee may without liability to any person comply with the order. If the document was negotiable, a court may not order delivery of the goods or issuance of a substitute document without the claimant's posting security unless it finds that any person that may suffer loss as a result of nonsurrender of possession or control of the document is adequately protected against the loss. If the document was nonnegotiable, the court may require security. The court may also order payment of the bailee's reasonable costs and attorney's fees in any action under this subsection.

(b) A bailee that without court order delivers goods to a person claiming under a missing negotiable document of title is liable to any person injured thereby. If the delivery is not in good faith, the bailee is liable for conversion. Delivery in good faith is not conversion if the claimant posts security with the bailee in an amount at least double the value of the goods at the time of posting to indemnify any person injured by the delivery that files a notice of claim within one year after the delivery.

Acts 1967, 60th Leg., p. 2343, ch. 785, § 1, eff. Sept. 1, 1967. Amended by Acts 2005, 79th Leg., ch. 122, § 1, eff. Sept. 1, 2005.

Uniform Commercial Code Comment

Prior Uniform Statutory Provision: Former Section 7–601.

Changes: To accommodate electronic documents; to provide flexibility to courts similar to the flexibility in Section 3–309; to update to the modern era of deregulation; and for style.

Purposes:

1. Subsection (a) authorizes courts to order compulsory delivery of the goods or compulsory issuance of a substitute document. Compare Section 7–402. Using language similar to that found in Section 3–309, courts are given discretion as to what is adequate protection when the lost, stolen or destroyed document was negotiable or whether security should be required when the lost, stolen or destroyed document was nonnegotiable. In determining whether a party is adequately protected against loss in the case of a negotiable document, the court should consider the likelihood that the party will

suffer a loss. The court is also given discretion as to the bailee's costs and attorney fees. The rights and obligations of a bailee under this section depend upon whether the document of title is lost, stolen or destroyed and is in addition to the ability of the bailee to bring an action for interpleader. See Section 7–603.

2. Courts have the authority under this section to order a substitute document for either tangible or electronic documents. If the substitute document will be in a different medium than the original document, the court should fashion its order in light of the requirements of Section 7–105.

3. Subsection (b) follows prior Section 7–601 in recognizing the legality of the well established commercial practice of bailees making delivery in good faith when they are satisfied that the claimant is the person entitled under a missing (i.e. lost, stolen, or destroyed) negotiable document. Acting without a court order, the bailee remains liable on the original negotiable document and, to avoid conversion liability, the bailee may insist that the claimant provide an indemnity bond. Cf. Section 7–403.

4. Claimants on non-negotiable instruments are permitted to avail themselves of the subsection (a) procedure because straight (non-negotiable) bills of lading sometimes contain provisions that the goods shall not be delivered except upon production of the bill. If the carrier should choose to insist upon production of the bill, the consignee should have some means of compelling delivery on satisfactory proof of entitlement. Without a court order, a bailee may deliver, subject to Section 7–403, to a person claiming goods under a non-negotiable document that the same person claims is lost, stolen, or destroyed.

5. The bailee's lien should be protected when a court orders delivery of the goods pursuant to this section.

Cross References:

Point 1: Sections 3–309, 7–402 and 7–603.

Point 2: Section 7–105.

Point 3: Section 7–403.

Point 4: Section 7–403.

Point 5: Sections 7–209 and 7–307.

Definitional Cross References:

"Bailee". Section 7–102.

"Delivery". Section 1–201.

"Document of title". Section 1–201.

"Good faith". Section 1–201 [7–102].

"Goods". Section 7–102.

"Person". Section 1–201.

Sections 31 and 32 of Acts 2005, 79th Leg., ch. 122 provide:

"Sec. 31. This Act applies to a document of title that is issued or a bailment that arises on or after the effective date of this Act. This Act does not apply to a document of title that is issued or a bailment that arises before the effective date of this Act even if the document of title or bailment would be subject to this Act if the document of title had been issued or bailment had arisen after the effective date of this Act. This Act does not apply to a right of action that has accrued before the effective date of this Act.

"Sec. 32. A document of title issued or a bailment that arises before the effective date of this Act and the rights, obligations, and interests flowing from that document or bailment are governed by any statute or other rule amended or repealed by this Act as if amendment or repeal had not occurred and may be terminated, completed, consummated, or enforced under that statute or other rule."

§ 7.602. Attachment of Goods Covered by Negotiable Document of Title

Unless a document of title was originally issued upon delivery of the goods by a person that did not have power to dispose of them, a lien does not attach by virtue of any judicial process to goods in the possession of a bailee for which a negotiable document of title is outstanding unless possession or control of the document is first surrendered to the bailee or the document's negotiation is enjoined. The bailee may not be compelled to deliver the goods pursuant to process until possession or control of the document is surrendered to the bailee or to the court. A purchaser of the document for value without notice of the process or injunction takes free of the lien imposed by judicial process.

Acts 1967, 60th Leg., p. 2343, ch. 785, § 1, eff. Sept. 1, 1967. Amended by Acts 2005, 79th Leg., ch. 122, § 1, eff. Sept. 1, 2005.

Uniform Commercial Code Comment

Prior Uniform Statutory Provisions: Former Section 7–602.

Changes: Changes to accommodate electronic documents of title and for style.

Purposes:

1. The purpose of the section is to protect the bailee from conflicting claims of the document of title holder and the judgment creditors of the person who deposited the goods. The rights of the former prevail unless, in effect, the judgment creditors immobilize the negotiable document of title through the surrender of possession of a tangible document or control of an electronic document. However, if the document of title was issued upon deposit of the goods by a person who had no power to dispose of the goods so that the document is ineffective to pass title, judgment liens are valid to the extent of the debtor's interest in the goods.

2. The last sentence covers the possibility that the holder of a document who has been enjoined from negotiating it will violate the injunction by negotiating to an innocent purchaser for value. In such case the lien will be defeated.

Cross Reference:

Sections 7–106 and 7–501 through 7–503.

Definitional Cross References:

"Bailee". Section 7–102.

"Delivery". Section 1–201.

"Document of title". Section 1–201.

"Goods". Section 7–102.

"Notice". Section 1–202.

"Person". Section 1–201.

"Purchase". Section 1–201.

"Value". Section 1–204.

Sections 31 and 32 of Acts 2005, 79th Leg., ch. 122 provide:

"Sec. 31. This Act applies to a document of title that is issued or a bailment that arises on or after the effective date of this Act. This Act does not apply to a document of title that is issued or a bailment that arises before the effective date of this Act even if the document of title or bailment would be subject to this Act if the document of title had been issued or bailment had arisen after the effective date of this Act. This Act does not apply to a right of action that has accrued before the effective date of this Act.

"Sec. 32. A document of title issued or a bailment that arises before the effective date of this Act and the rights, obligations, and interests flowing from that document or bailment are governed by any statute or other rule amended or repealed by this Act as if amendment or repeal had not occurred and may be terminated, completed, consummated, or enforced under that statute or other rule."

§ 7.603. Conflicting Claims; Interpleader

If more than one person claims title to or possession of the goods, the bailee is excused from delivery until the bailee has a reasonable time to ascertain the validity of the adverse claims or to commence an action for interpleader. The bailee may assert an interpleader either in defending an action for nondelivery of the goods or by original action.

Acts 1967, 60th Leg., p. 2343, ch. 785, § 1, eff. Sept. 1, 1967. Amended by Acts 2005, 79th Leg., ch. 122, § 1, eff. Sept. 1, 2005.

Uniform Commercial Code Comment

Prior Uniform Statutory Provisions: Former Section 7–603.

Changes: Changes for style only.

Purposes:

1. The section enables a bailee faced with conflicting claims to the goods to compel the claimants to litigate their claims with each other rather than with the bailee. The bailee is protected from legal liability when the bailee complies with court orders from the interpleader. *See e.g.* Northwestern National Sales, Inc. v. Commercial Cold Storage, Inc., 162 Ga. App. 741, 293 S.E.2d. 30 (1982).

2. This section allows the bailee to bring an interpleader action but does not provide an exclusive basis for allowing interpleader. If either state or federal procedural rules allow an interpleader in other situations, the bailee may commence an interpleader under those rules. Even in an interpleader to which this section applies, the state or federal process of interpleader applies to the bailee's action for interpleader. For example, state or federal interpleader statutes or rules may permit a bailee to protect its lien or to seek attorney's fees and costs in the interpleader action.

Cross reference:

Point 1: Section 7–403.

Definitional Cross References:

"Action". Section 1–201.

"Bailee". Section 7–102.

"Delivery". Section 1–201.

"Goods". Section 7–102.

"Person". Section 1–201.

"Reasonable time". Section 1–205.

Sections 31 and 32 of Acts 2005, 79th Leg., ch. 122 provide:

"Sec. 31. This Act applies to a document of title that is issued or a bailment that arises on or after the effective date of this Act. This Act does not apply to a document of title that is issued or a bailment that arises before the effective date of this Act even if the document of title or bailment would be subject to this Act if the document of title had been issued or bailment had arisen after the effective date of this Act. This Act does not apply to a right of action that has accrued before the effective date of this Act.

"Sec. 32. A document of title issued or a bailment that arises before the effective date of this Act and the rights, obligations, and interests flowing from that document or bailment are governed by any statute or other rule amended or repealed by this Act as if amendment or repeal had not occurred and may be terminated, completed, consummated, or enforced under that statute or other rule."

CHAPTER 8. INVESTMENT SECURITIES

SUBCHAPTER A. SHORT TITLE AND GENERAL MATTERS

Section

SUBCHAPTER B. ISSUE AND ISSUER

Acts 1995, 74th Leg., ch. 962, § 1, amended Chapter 8 effective September 1, 1995. The former Chapter 8, Investment Securities, consisting of §§ 8.101 to 8.408, was amended as Chapter 8, Investment Securities, consisting of §§ 8.101 to 8.511.

DISPOSITION TABLE

Showing where the subject matter of provisions contained in former Chapter 8 may be found in Chapter 8 as amended by Acts 1995, 74th Leg., ch. 962, § 1.

Former Section	Amended Section
8.101	8.101
8.102	8.102
8.103	8.209
8.104	8.102, 8.210
8.105	8.114
8.106	8.110
8.201	8.201
8.202	8.202
8.203	8.203
8.204	8.204
8.205	8.205
8.206	8.206
8.207	8.207
8.208	8.208
8.301	8.302
8.302	8.102, 8.303
8.303	8.102
8.304	8.105, 8.115
8.305	8.105
8.306	8.108
8.307	8.304
8.308	8.102, 8.107, 8.304
8.309	8.304
8.310	8.304
8.311	8.404
8.312	8.306
8.313	8.102
8.316	8.307
8.317	8.112
8.318	8.115
8.319	8.313
8.320	8.313
8.321	8.313
8.401	8.401
8.402	8.402
8.403	8.403
8.404	8.404
8.405	8.405
8.406	8.407
8.407	—
8.408	—

SUBCHAPTER A. SHORT TITLE AND GENERAL MATTERS

§ 8.101. Short Title

This chapter may be cited as Uniform Commercial Code—Investment Securities.

Amended by Acts 1995, 74th Leg., ch. 962, § 1, eff. Sept. 1, 1995.

§ 8.102. Definitions

(a) In this chapter:

(1) "Adverse claim" means a claim that a claimant has a property interest in a financial asset and that it is a violation of the rights of the claimant for another person to hold, transfer, or deal with the financial asset.

(2) "Bearer form," as applied to a certificated security, means a form in which the security is payable to the bearer of the security certificate according to its terms but not by reason of an indorsement.

(3) "Broker" means a person defined as a broker or dealer under the federal securities laws, but without excluding a bank acting in that capacity.

(4) "Certificated security" means a security that is represented by a certificate.

(5) "Clearing corporation" means:

(A) a person that is registered as a "clearing agency" under the federal securities laws;

(B) a federal reserve bank; or

(C) any other person that provides clearance or settlement services with respect to financial assets that would require it to register as a clearing agency under the federal securities laws but for an exclusion or exemption from the registration requirement, if its activities as a clearing corporation, including promulgation of rules, are subject to regulation by a federal or state governmental authority.

(6) "Communicate" means to:

(A) send a signed writing; or

(B) transmit information by any mechanism agreed on by the persons transmitting and receiving the information.

(7) "Entitlement holder" means a person identified in the records of a securities intermediary as the person having a security entitlement against the securities intermediary. If a person acquires a security entitlement by virtue of Section 8.501(b)(2) or (3), that person is the entitlement holder.

(8) "Entitlement order" means a notification communicated to a securities intermediary directing transfer or redemption of a financial asset to which the entitlement holder has a security entitlement.

(9) "Financial asset," except as otherwise provided in Section 8.103, means:

(A) a security;

(B) an obligation of a person or a share, participation, or other interest in a person or in property or an enterprise of a person that is, or is of a type, dealt in or traded on financial markets or that is recognized in any area in which it is issued or dealt in as a medium for investment; or

(C) any property that is held by a securities intermediary for another person in a securities account if the securities intermediary has expressly agreed with the other person that the property is to be treated as a financial asset under this chapter.

As context requires, the term means either the interest itself or the means by which a person's claim to it is evidenced, including a certificated or uncertificated security, a security certificate, or a security entitlement.

(10) Reserved.

(11) "Indorsement" means a signature that alone or accompanied by other words is made on a security certificate in registered form or on a separate document for the purpose of assigning, transferring, or redeeming the security or granting a power to assign, transfer, or redeem it.

(12) "Instruction" means a notification communicated to the issuer of an uncertificated security that directs that the transfer of the security be registered or that the security be redeemed.

(13) "Registered form," as applied to a certificated security, means a form in which:

(A) the security certificate specifies a person entitled to the security; and

(B) a transfer of the security may be registered on books maintained for that purpose by or on behalf of the issuer, or the security certificate so states.

(14) "Securities intermediary" means:

(A) a clearing corporation; or

(B) a person, including a bank or broker, that in the ordinary course of its business maintains securities accounts for others and is acting in that capacity.

(15) "Security," except as otherwise provided in Section 8.103, means an obligation of an issuer or a share, participation, or other interest in an issuer or in property or an enterprise of an issuer:

(A) that is represented by a security certificate in bearer or registered form, or the transfer of which may be registered on books maintained for that purpose by or on behalf of the issuer;

(B) that is one of a class or series or by its terms is divisible into a class or series of shares, participations, interests, or obligations; and

(C) that:

(i) is, or is of a type, dealt in or traded on securities exchanges or securities markets; or

(ii) is a medium for investment and by its terms expressly provides that it is a security governed by this chapter.

(16) "Security certificate" means a certificate representing a security.

(17) "Security entitlement" means the rights and property interest of an entitlement holder with respect to a financial asset specified in Subchapter E.[1]

(18) "Uncertificated security" means a security that is not represented by a certificate.

(b) Other definitions applying to this chapter and the sections in which they appear are:

Appropriate person	Section 8.107
Control	Section 8.106
Delivery	Section 8.301
Investment company security	Section 8.103
Issuer	Section 8.201
Overissue	Section 8.210
Protected purchaser	Section 8.303
Securities account	Section 8.501

(c) In addition, Chapter 1 contains general definitions and principles of construction and interpretation applicable throughout this chapter.

(d) The characterization of a person, business, or transaction for purposes of this chapter does not determine the characterization of the person, business, or transaction for purposes of any other law, regulation, or rule.

Amended by Acts 1995, 74th Leg., ch. 962, § 1, eff. Sept. 1, 1995; Acts 2003, 78th Leg., ch. 542, § 18, eff. Sept. 1, 2003.

[1]V.T.C.A., Bus. & C. § 8.501 et seq.

Uniform Commercial Code Comment

1. "Adverse claim." The definition of the term "adverse claim" has two components. First, the term refers only to property interests. Second, the term means not merely that a person has a property interest in a financial asset but that it is a violation of the claimant's property interest for the other person to hold or transfer the security or other financial asset.

The term adverse claim is not, of course, limited to ownership rights, but extends to other property interests established by other law. A security interest, for example, would be an adverse claim with respect to a transferee from the debtor since any effort by the secured party to enforce the security interest against the property would be an interference with the transferee's interest.

The definition of adverse claim in the prior version of Article 8 might have been read to suggest that any wrongful action concerning a security, even a simple breach of contract, gave rise to an adverse claim. Insofar as such cases as *Fallon v. Wall Street Clearing Corp.*, 586 N.Y.S.2d 953, 182 A.D.2d 245, (1992) and *Pentech Intl. v. Wall St. Clearing Co.*, 983 F.2d 441 (2d Cir. 1993), were based on that view, they are rejected by the new definition which explicitly limits the term adverse claim to property interests. Suppose, for example, that A contracts to sell or deliver securities to B, but fails to do so and instead sells or pledges the securities to C. B, the promisee, has an action against A for breach of contract, but absent unusual circumstances the action for breach would not give rise to a property interest in the securities. Accordingly, B does not have an adverse claim. An adverse claim might, however, be based upon principles of equitable remedies that give rise to property claims. It would, for example, cover a right established by other law to rescind a transaction in which securities were transferred. Suppose, for example, that A holds securities and is induced by B's fraud to transfer them to B. Under the law of contract or restitution, A may have a right to rescind the transfer, which gives A a property claim to the securities. If so, A has an adverse claim to the securities in B's hands. By contrast, if B had committed no fraud, but had merely committed a breach of contract in connection with the transfer from A to B, A may have only a right to damages for breach, not a right to rescind. In that case, A would not have an adverse claim to the securities in B's hands.

2. "Bearer form." The definition of "bearer form" has remained substantially unchanged since the early drafts of the original version of Article 8. The requirement that the certificate be payable to bearer by its terms rather than by an indorsement has the effect of preventing instruments governed by other law, such as chattel paper or Article 3 negotiable instruments, from being inadvertently swept into the Article 8 definition of security merely by virtue of blank indorsements. Although the other elements of the definition of security in Section 8–102(a)(14) probably suffice for that purpose in any event, the language used in the prior version of Article 8 has been retained.

3. "Broker." Broker is defined by reference to the definitions of broker and dealer in the federal securities laws. The only difference is that banks, which are excluded from the federal securities law definition, are included in the Article 8 definition when they perform functions that would bring them within the federal securities law definition if it did not have the clause excluding banks. The definition covers both those who act as agents ("brokers" in securities parlance) and those who act as principals ("dealers" in securities parlance). Since the definition refers to persons "defined" as brokers or dealers under the federal securities law, rather than to persons required to "register" as brokers or dealers under the federal securities law, it covers not only registered brokers and dealers but also those exempt from the registration requirement, such as purely intrastate brokers. The only substantive rules that turn on the defined term broker are one provision of the section on warranties, Section 8–108(i), and the special perfection rule in Article 9

for security interests granted by brokers or securities intermediaries, Section 9–309(10).

4. "Certificated security." The term "certificated security" means a security that is represented by a security certificate.

5. "Clearing corporation." The definition of clearing corporation limits its application to entities that are subject to a rigorous regulatory framework. Accordingly, the definition includes only federal reserve banks, persons who are registered as "clearing agencies" under the federal securities laws (which impose a comprehensive system of regulation of the activities and rules of clearing agencies), and other entities subject to a comparable system of regulatory oversight.

6. "Communicate." The term "communicate" assures that the Article 8 rules will be sufficiently flexible to adapt to changes in information technology. Sending a signed writing always suffices as a communication, but the parties can agree that a different means of transmitting information is to be used. Agreement is defined in Section 1–201(3) as "the bargain of the parties in fact as found in their language or by implication from other circumstances including course of dealing or usage of trade or course of performance." Thus, use of an information transmission method might be found to be authorized by agreement, even though the parties have not explicitly so specified in a formal agreement. The term communicate is used in Sections 8–102(a)(7) (definition of entitlement order), 8–102(a)(11) (definition of instruction), and 8–403 (demand that issuer not register transfer).

7. "Entitlement holder." This term designates those who hold financial assets through intermediaries in the indirect holding system. Because many of the rules of Part 5 impose duties on securities intermediaries in favor of entitlement holders, the definition of entitlement holder is, in most cases, limited to the person specifically designated as such on the records of the intermediary. The last sentence of the definition covers the relatively unusual cases where a person may acquire a security entitlement under Section 8–501 even though the person may not be specifically designated as an entitlement holder on the records of the securities intermediary.

A person may have an interest in a security entitlement, and may even have the right to give entitlement orders to the securities intermediary with respect to it, even though the person is not the entitlement holder. For example, a person who holds securities through a securities account in its own name may have given discretionary trading authority to another person, such as an investment adviser. Similarly, the control provisions in Section 8–106 and the related provisions in Article 9 are designed to facilitate transactions in which a person who holds securities through a securities account uses them as collateral in an arrangement where the securities intermediary has agreed that if the secured party so directs the intermediary will dispose of the positions. In such arrangements, the debtor remains the entitlement holder but has agreed that the secured party can initiate entitlement orders. Moreover, an entitlement holder may be acting for another person as a nominee, agent, trustee, or in another capacity. Unless the entitlement holder is itself acting as a securities intermediary for the other person, in which case the other person would be an entitlement holder with respect to the securities entitlement, the relationship between an entitlement holder and another person for whose benefit the entitlement holder holds a securities entitlement is governed by other law.

8. "Entitlement order." This term is defined as a notification communicated to a securities intermediary directing transfer or redemption of the financial asset to which an entitlement holder has a security entitlement. The term is used in the rules for the indirect holding system in a fashion analogous to the use of the terms "indorsement" and "instruction" in the rules for the direct holding system. If a person directly holds a certificated security in registered form and wishes to transfer it, the means of transfer is an indorsement. If a person directly holds an uncertificated security and wishes to transfer it, the means of transfer is an instruction. If a person holds a security entitlement, the means of disposition is an entitlement order. An entitlement order includes a direction under Section 8–508 to the securities intermediary to transfer a financial asset to the account of the entitlement holder at another financial intermediary or to cause the financial asset to be transferred to the entitlement holder in the direct holding system (e.g., the delivery of a securities certificate registered in the name of the former entitlement holder). As noted in Comment 7, an entitlement order need not be initiated by the entitlement holder in order to be effective, so long as the entitlement holder has authorized the other party to initiate entitlement orders. See Section 8–107(b).

9. "Financial asset." The definition of "financial asset," in conjunction with the definition of "securities account" in Section 8–501, sets the scope of the indirect holding system rules of Part 5 of Revised Article 8. The Part 5 rules apply not only to securities held through intermediaries, but also to other financial assets held through intermediaries. The term financial asset is defined to include not only securities but also a broader category of obligations, shares, participations, and interests.

Having separate definitions of security and financial asset makes it possible to separate the question of the proper scope of the traditional Article 8 rules from the question of the proper scope of the new indirect holding system rules. Some forms of financial assets should be covered by the indirect holding system rules of Part 5, but not by the rules of Parts 2, 3, and 4. The term financial asset is used to cover such property. Because the term security entitlement is defined in terms of financial assets rather than securities, the rules concerning security entitlements set out in Part 5 of Article 8 and in Revised Article 9 apply to the broader class of financial assets.

The fact that something does or could fall within the definition of financial asset does not, without more, trigger Article 8 coverage. The indirect holding system rules of Revised Article 8 apply only if the financial asset is in fact held in a securities account, so that the interest of the person who holds the financial asset through the securities account is a security entitlement. Thus, questions of the scope of the indirect holding system rules cannot be framed as "Is such-and-such a 'financial asset' under Article 8?" Rather, one must analyze whether the relationship between an institution and a person on whose behalf the institution holds an asset falls within the scope of the term securities account as defined in Section 8–501. That question turns in large measure on whether it makes sense to apply the Part 5 rules to the relationship.

The term financial asset is used to refer both to the underlying asset and the particular means by which ownership of that asset is evidenced. Thus, with respect to a certificated security, the term financial asset may, as context requires, refer either to the interest or obligation of the issuer or to the security certificate representing that interest or obligation. Similarly, if a person holds a security or other financial asset through a securities account, the term financial asset may, as context requires, refer either to the underlying asset or to the person's security entitlement.

10. "Good faith." Good faith is defined in Article 8 for purposes of the application to Article 8 of Section 1–203, which provides that "Every contract or duty within this Act imposes an obligation of good faith in its performance or enforcement." The sole function of the good faith definition in Revised Article 8 is to give content to the Section 1–203 obligation as it applies to contracts and duties that are governed by Article 8. The standard is one of "reasonable commercial standards of fair dealing." The reference to commercial standards makes clear that assessments of conduct are to be made in light of the commercial setting. The substantive rules of Article 8 have been drafted to take account of the commercial circumstances of the securities holding and processing system. For example, Section 8–115 provides that a securities intermediary acting on an effective entitlement order, or a broker or other agent acting as a conduit in a securities transaction, is not liable to an adverse claimant, unless the claimant obtained legal process or the intermediary acted in collusion with the wrongdoer. This, and other similar provisions, see Sections 8–404 and 8–503(e), do not depend on notice of adverse claims, because it would impair rather than advance the interest of investors in having a sound and efficient securities clearance and settlement system to require intermediaries to investigate the propriety of the transactions they are processing. The good faith obligation does not supplant the standards of conduct established in provisions of this kind.

In Revised Article 8, the definition of good faith is not germane to the question whether a purchaser takes free from adverse claims. The rules on such questions as whether a purchaser who takes in suspicious circumstances is disqualified from protected purchaser status are treated not as an aspect of good faith but directly in the rules of Section 8–105 on notice of adverse claims.

11. "Indorsement" is defined as a signature made on a security certificate or separate document for purposes of transferring or redeeming the security. The definition is adapted from the language of Section 8–308(1) of the prior version and from the definition of indorsement in the Negotiable Instruments Article, see Section 3–204(a). The definition of indorsement does not include the requirement that the signature be made by an appropriate person or be authorized. Those questions are treated in the separate substantive provision on whether the indorsement is effective, rather than in the definition of indorsement. See Section 8–107.

12. "Instruction" is defined as a notification communicated to the issuer of an uncertificated security directing that transfer be registered or that the security be redeemed. Instructions are the analog for uncertificated securities of indorsements of certificated securities.

13. "Registered form." The definition of "registered form" is substantially the same as in the prior version of Article 8. Like the definition of bearer form, it serves primarily to distinguish Article 8 securities from instruments governed by other law, such as Article 3.

14. "Securities intermediary." A "securities intermediary" is a person that in the ordinary course of its business maintains securities accounts for others and is acting in that capacity. The most common examples of securities intermediaries would be clearing corporations holding securities for their participants, banks acting as securities custodians, and brokers holding securities on behalf of their customers. Clearing corporations are listed separately as a category of securities intermediary in subparagraph (i) even though in most circumstances they would fall within the general definition in subparagraph (ii). The reason is to simplify the analysis of arrangements such as the NSCC–DTC system in which NSCC performs the comparison, clearance, and netting function, while DTC acts as the depository. Because NSCC is a registered clearing agency under the federal securities laws, it is a clearing corporation and hence a securities intermediary under Article 8, regardless of whether it is at any particular time or in any particular aspect of its operations holding securities on behalf of its participants.

The terms securities intermediary and broker have different meanings. Broker means a person engaged in the business of buying and selling securities, as agent for others or as principal. Securities intermediary means a person maintaining securities accounts for others. A stockbroker, in the colloquial sense, may or may not be acting as a securities intermediary.

The definition of securities intermediary includes the requirement that the person in question is "acting in the capacity" of maintaining securities accounts for others. This is to take account of the fact that a particular entity, such as a bank, may act in many different capacities in securities transactions. A bank may act as a transfer agent for issuers, as a securities custodian for institutional investors and private investors, as a dealer in government securities, as a lender taking securities as collateral, and as a provider of general payment and collection services that might be used in connection with securities transactions. A bank that maintains securities accounts for its customers would be a securities intermediary with respect to those accounts; but if it takes a pledge of securities from a borrower to secure a loan, it is not thereby acting as a securities intermediary with respect to the pledged securities, since it holds them for its own account rather than for a customer. In other circumstances, those two functions might be combined. For example, if the bank is a government securities dealer it may maintain securities accounts for customers and also provide the customers with margin credit to purchase or carry the securities, in much the same way that brokers provide margin loans to their customers.

15. "Security." The definition of "security" has three components. First, there is the subparagraph (i) test that the interest or obligation be fully transferable, in the sense that the issuer either maintains transfer books or the obligation or interest is represented by a certificate in bearer or

registered form. Second, there is the subparagraph (ii) test that the interest or obligation be divisible, that is, one of a class or series, as distinguished from individual obligations of the sort governed by ordinary contract law or by Article 3. Third, there is the subparagraph (iii) functional test, which generally turns on whether the interest or obligation is, or is of a type, dealt in or traded on securities markets or securities exchanges. There is, however, an "opt-in" provision in subparagraph (iii) which permits the issuer of any interest or obligation that is "a medium of investment" to specify that it is a security governed by Article 8.

The divisibility test of subparagraph (ii) applies to the security—that is, the underlying intangible interest—not the means by which that interest is evidenced. Thus, securities issued in book-entry only form meet the divisibility test because the underlying intangible interest is divisible via the mechanism of the indirect holding system. This is so even though the clearing corporation is the only eligible direct holder of the security.

The third component, the functional test in subparagraph (iii), provides flexibility while ensuring that the Article 8 rules do not apply to interests or obligations in circumstances so unconnected with the securities markets that parties are unlikely to have thought of the possibility that Article 8 might apply. Subparagraph (iii)(A) covers interests or obligations that either are dealt in or traded on securities exchanges or securities markets, or are of a type dealt in or traded on securities exchanges or securities markets. The "is dealt in or traded on" phrase eliminates problems in the characterization of new forms of securities which are to be traded in the markets, even though no similar type has previously been dealt in or traded in the markets. Subparagraph (iii)(B) covers the broader category of media for investment, but it applies only if the terms of the interest or obligation specify that it is an Article 8 security. This opt-in provision allows for deliberate expansion of the scope of Article 8.

Section 8–103 contains additional rules on the treatment of particular interests as securities or financial assets.

16. "Security certificate." The term "security" refers to the underlying asset, e.g., 1000 shares of common stock of Acme, Inc. The term "security certificate" refers to the paper certificates that have traditionally been used to embody the underlying intangible interest.

17. "Security entitlement" means the rights and property interest of a person who holds securities or other financial assets through a securities intermediary. A security entitlement is both a package of personal rights against the securities intermediary and an interest in the property held by the securities intermediary. A security entitlement is not, however, a specific property interest in any financial asset held by the securities intermediary or by the clearing corporation through which the securities intermediary holds the financial asset. See Sections 8–104(c) and 8–503. The formal definition of security entitlement set out in subsection (a)(17) of this section is a cross-reference to the rules of Part 5. In a sense, then, the entirety of Part 5 is the definition of security entitlement. The Part 5 rules specify the rights and property interest that comprise a security entitlement.

18. "Uncertificated security." The term "uncertificated security" means a security that is not represented by a security certificate. For uncertificated securities, there is no need to draw any distinction between the underlying asset and the means by which a direct holder's interest in that asset is evidenced. Compare "certificated security" and "security certificate."

Definitional Cross References:

"Agreement" Section 1–201(3)

"Bank" Section 1–201(4)

"Person" Section 1–201(30)

"Send" Section 1–201(38)

"Signed" Section 1–201(39)

"Writing" Section 1–201(46)

§ 8.103. Rules for Determining Whether Certain Obligations and Interests are Securities or Financial Assets

(a) A share or similar equity interest issued by a corporation, business trust, joint stock company, or similar entity is a security.

(b) An investment company security is a security. "Investment company security" means a share or similar equity interest issued by an entity that is registered as an investment company under the federal investment company laws, an interest in a unit investment trust that is so registered, or a face-amount certificate issued by a face-amount certificate company that is so registered. "Investment company security" does not include an insurance policy or endowment policy or annuity contract issued by an insurance company.

(c) An interest in a partnership or limited liability company is not a security unless it is dealt in or traded on securities exchanges or in securities markets, its terms expressly provide that it is a security governed by this chapter, or it is an investment company security. However, an interest in a partnership or limited liability company is a financial asset if it is held in a securities account.

(d) A writing that is a security certificate is governed by this chapter and not by Chapter 3, even though it also meets the requirements of that chapter. However, a negotiable instrument governed by Chapter 3 is a financial asset if it is held in a securities account.

(e) An option or similar obligation issued by a clearing corporation to its participants is not a security, but is a financial asset.

(f) A commodity contract, as defined in Section 9.102(a)(15), is not a security or a financial asset.

(g) A document of title, as defined in Section 1.201(b)(16), is not a financial asset unless Section 8.102(a)(9)(C) applies.

Amended by Acts 1995, 74th Leg., ch. 962, § 1, eff. Sept. 1, 1995; Acts 1999, 76th Leg., ch. 414, § 2.26, eff. July 1, 2001; Acts 2005, 79th Leg., ch. 122, § 18, eff. Sept. 1, 2005.

Uniform Commercial Code Comment

1. This section contains rules that supplement the definitions of "financial asset" and "security" in Section 8–102. The Section 8–102 definitions are worded in general terms, because they must be sufficiently comprehensive and flexible to cover the wide variety of investment products that now exist or may develop. The rules in this section are intended to foreclose interpretive issues concerning the application of the general definitions to several specific investment products. No implication is made about the application of the Section 8–102 definitions to investment products not covered by this section.

2. Subsection (a) establishes an unconditional rule that ordinary corporate stock is a security. That is so whether or not the particular issue is dealt in or traded on securities exchanges or in securities markets. Thus, shares of closely held corporations are Article 8 securities.

3. Subsection (b) establishes that the Article 8 term "security" includes the various forms of the investment vehicles offered to the public by investment companies registered as such under the federal Investment Company Act of 1940, as amended. This clarification is prompted principally by the fact that the typical transaction in shares of open-end investment companies is an issuance or redemption, rather than a transfer of shares from one person to another as is the case with ordinary corporate stock. For similar reasons, the definitions of indorsement, instruction, and entitlement order in Section 8–102 refer to "redemptions" as well as "transfers," to ensure that the Article 8 rules on such matters as signature guaranties, Section 8–306, assurances, Sections 8–402 and 8–507, and effectiveness, Section 8–107, apply to directions to redeem mutual fund shares. The exclusion of insurance products is needed because some insurance company separate accounts are registered under the Investment Company Act of 1940, but these are not traded under the usual Article 8 mechanics.

4. Subsection (c) is designed to foreclose interpretive questions that might otherwise be raised by the application of the "of a type" language of Section 8–102(a)(15)(iii) to partnership interests. Subsection (c) establishes the general rule that partnership interests or shares of limited liability companies are not Article 8 securities unless they are in fact dealt in or traded on securities exchanges or in securities markets. The issuer, however, may explicitly "opt-in" by specifying that the interests or shares are securities governed by Article 8. Partnership interests or shares of limited liability companies are included in the broader term "financial asset." Thus, if they are held through a securities account, the indirect holding system rules of Part 5 apply, and the interest of a person who holds them through such an account is a security entitlement.

5. Subsection (d) deals with the line between Article 3 negotiable instruments and Article 8 investment securities. It continues the rule of the prior version of Article 8 that a writing that meets the Article 8 definition is covered by Article 8 rather than Article 3, even though it also meets the definition of negotiable instrument. However, subsection (d) provides that an Article 3 negotiable instrument is a "financial asset" so that the indirect holding system rules apply if the instrument is held through a securities intermediary. This facilitates making items such as money market instruments eligible for deposit in clearing corporations.

6. Subsection (e) is included to clarify the treatment of investment products such as traded stock options, which are treated as financial assets but not securities. Thus, the indirect holding system rules of Part 5 apply, but the direct holding system rules of Parts 2, 3, and 4 do not.

7. Subsection (f) excludes commodity contracts from all of Article 8. However, under Article 9, commodity contracts are included in the definition of "investment property." Therefore, the Article 9 rules on security interests in investment property do apply to security interests in commodity positions. See Section 9–102 and Comment 6 thereto. "Commodity contract" is defined in Section 9–102(a)(15).

8. Subsection (g) allows a document of title to be a financial asset and thus subject to the indirect holding system rules of Part 5 only to the extent that the intermediary and the person entitled under the document agree to do so. This is to prevent the inadvertent application of the Part 5 rules to intermediaries who may hold either electronic or tangible documents of title.

Sections 31 and 32 of Acts 2005, 79th Leg., ch. 122 provide:

"Sec. 31. This Act applies to a document of title that is issued or a bailment that arises on or after the effective date of this Act. This Act does not apply to a document of title that is issued or a bailment that arises before the effective date of this Act even if the document of title or bailment would be subject to this Act if the document of title had been issued or bailment had arisen after the effective date of this Act. This Act does not apply to a right of action that has accrued before the effective date of this Act.

"Sec. 32. A document of title issued or a bailment that arises before the effective date of this Act and the rights, obligations, and interests flowing from that document or bailment are governed by any statute or other rule amended or repealed by this Act as if amendment or repeal had not occurred and may be terminated, completed, consummated, or enforced under that statute or other rule."

§ 8.104. Acquisition of Security or Financial Asset or Interest Therein

(a) A person acquires a security or an interest therein under this chapter if:

(1) the person is a purchaser to whom a security is delivered pursuant to Section 8.301; or

(2) the person acquires a security entitlement to the security pursuant to Section 8.501.

(b) A person acquires a financial asset, other than a security, or an interest therein, under this chapter, if the person acquires a security entitlement to the financial asset.

(c) A person who acquires a security entitlement to a security or other financial asset has the rights specified in Subchapter E,[1] but is a purchaser of any security, security entitlement, or other financial asset held by the securities intermediary only to the extent provided in Section 8.503.

(d) Unless the context shows that a different meaning is intended, a person who is required by other law, regulation, rule, or agreement to transfer, deliver, present, surrender, exchange, or otherwise put in the possession of another person a security or financial asset satisfies that requirement by causing the other person to acquire an interest in the security or financial asset pursuant to Subsection (a) or (b).

Amended by Acts 1995, 74th Leg., ch. 962, § 1, eff. Sept. 1, 1995.

[1] V.T.C.A., Bus. & C. § 8.501 et seq.

Uniform Commercial Code Comment

1. This section lists the ways in which interests in securities and other financial assets are acquired under Article 8. In that sense, it describes the scope of Article 8. Subsection (a) describes the two ways that a person may acquire a security or interest therein under this Article: (1) by delivery (Section 8–301), and (2) by acquiring a security entitlement. Each of these methods is described in detail in the relevant substantive provisions of this Article. Part 3, beginning with the definition of "delivery" in Section 8–301, describes how interests in securities are acquired in the direct holding system. Part 5, beginning with the rules of Section 8–501 on how security entitlements are acquired, describes how interests in securities are acquired in the indirect holding system.

Subsection (b) specifies how a person may acquire an interest under Article 8 in a financial asset other than a security. This Article deals with financial assets other than securities only insofar as they are held in the indirect holding system. For example, a bankers' acceptance falls within the definition of "financial asset," so if it is held through a securities account the entitlement holder's right to it is a security entitlement governed by Part 5. The bankers' acceptance itself, however, is a negotiable instrument governed by Article 3, not by Article 8. Thus, the provisions of Parts 2, 3, and 4 of this Article that deal with the rights of direct holders of securities are not applicable. Article 3, not Article 8, specifies how one acquires a direct interest in a bankers' acceptance. If a bankers' acceptance is delivered to a clearing corporation to be held for the account of the clearing corporation's participants, the clearing corporation becomes the holder of the bankers' acceptance under the Article 3 rules specifying how negotiable instruments are transferred. The rights of the clearing corporation's participants, however, are governed by Part 5 of this Article.

2. The distinction in usage in Article 8 between the term "security" (and its correlatives "security certificate" and "uncertificated security") on the one hand, and "security entitlement" on the other, corresponds to the distinction between the direct and indirect holding systems. For example, with respect to certificated securities that can be held either directly or through intermediaries, obtaining possession of a security certificate and acquiring a security entitlement are both means of holding the underlying security. For many other purposes, there is no need to draw a distinction between the means of holding. For purposes of commercial law analysis, however, the form of holding may make a difference. Where an item of property can be held in different ways, the rules on how one deals with it, including how one transfers it or how one grants a security interest in it, differ depending on the form of holding.

Although a security entitlement is means of holding the underlying security or other financial asset, a person who has a security entitlement does not have any direct claim to a specific asset in the possession of the securities intermediary. Subsection (c) provides explicitly that a person who acquires a security entitlement is a "purchaser" of any security, security entitlement, or other financial asset held by the securities intermediary only in the sense that under Section 8–503 a security entitlement is treated as a *sui generis* form of property interest.

3. Subsection (d) is designed to ensure that parties will retain their expected legal rights and duties under Revised Article 8. One of the major changes made by the revision is that the rules for the indirect holding system are stated in terms of the "security entitlements" held by investors, rather than speaking of them as holding direct interests in securities. Subsection (d) is designed as a translation rule to eliminate problems of co-ordination of terminology, and facilitate the continued use of systems for the efficient handling of securities and financial assets through securities intermediaries and clearing corporations. The efficiencies of a securities intermediary or clearing corporation are, in part, dependent on the ability to transfer securities credited to securities accounts in the intermediary or clearing corporation to the account of an issuer, its agent, or other person by book entry in a manner that permits exchanges, redemptions, conversions, and other transactions (which may be governed by preexisting or new agreements, constitutional documents, or other instruments) to occur and to avoid the need to withdraw from immobilization in an intermediary or clearing corporation physical securities in order to deliver them for such purposes. Existing corporate charters, indentures and like documents may require the "presentation," "surrender," "delivery," or "transfer" of securities or security certificates for purposes of exchange, redemption, conversion or other reason. Likewise, documents may use a wide variety of terminology to describe, in the context for example of a tender or exchange offer, the means of putting the offeror or the issuer or its agent in possession of the security. Subsection (d) takes the place of provisions of prior law which could be used to reach the legal conclusion that book-entry transfers are equivalent to physical delivery to the person to whose account the book entry is credited.

§ 8.105. Notice of Adverse Claim

(a) A person has notice of an adverse claim if:

(1) the person knows of the adverse claim;

(2) the person is aware of facts sufficient to indicate that there is a significant probability that the adverse claim exists and deliberately avoids information that would establish the existence of the adverse claim; or

(3) the person has a duty, imposed by statute or regulation, to investigate whether an adverse claim exists, and the investigation so required would establish the existence of the adverse claim.

(b) Having knowledge that a financial asset or interest therein is or has been transferred by a representative imposes no duty of inquiry into the rightfulness of a transaction and is not notice of an adverse claim. However, a person who knows that a representative has transferred a financial asset or interest therein in a transaction that is, or whose proceeds are being used, for the individual benefit of the representative or otherwise in breach of duty has notice of an adverse claim.

(c) An act or event that creates a right to immediate performance of the principal obligation represented by a security certificate or sets a date on or after which the certificate is to be presented or surrendered for redemption or exchange does not itself constitute notice of an adverse claim except in the case of a transfer more than:

(1) one year after a date set for presentment or surrender for redemption or exchange; or

(2) six months after a date set for payment of money against presentation or surrender of the certificate, if money was available for payment on that date.

(d) A purchaser of a certificated security has notice of an adverse claim if the security certificate:

(1) whether in bearer or registered form, has been indorsed "for collection" or "for surrender" or for some other purpose not involving transfer; or

(2) is in bearer form and has on it an unambiguous statement that it is the property of a person other than the transferor, but the mere writing of a name on the certificate is not such a statement.

(e) Filing of a financing statement under Chapter 9 is not notice of an adverse claim to a financial asset.

Amended by Acts 1995, 74th Leg., ch. 962, § 1, eff. Sept. 1, 1995.

Uniform Commercial Code Comment

1. The rules specifying whether adverse claims can be asserted against persons who acquire securities or security entitlements, Sections 8–303, 8–502, and 8–510, provide that one is protected against an adverse claim only if one takes without notice of the claim. This section defines notice of an adverse claim.

The general Article 1 definition of "notice" in Section 1–201(25)—which provides that a person has notice of a fact if "from all the facts and circumstances known to him at the time in question he has reason to know that it exists"—does not apply to the interpretation of "notice of adverse claims." The Section 1–201(25) definition of "notice" does, however, apply to usages of that term and its cognates in Article 8 in contexts other than notice of adverse claims.

2. This section must be interpreted in light of the definition of "adverse claim" in Section 8–102(a)(1). "Adverse claim" does not include all circumstances in which a third party has a property interest in securities, but only those situations where a security is transferred in violation of the claimant's property interest. Therefore, awareness that someone other than the transferor has a property interest is not notice of an adverse claim. The transferee must be aware that the transfer violates the other party's property interest. If A holds securities in which B has some form of property interest, and A transfers the securities to C, C may know that B has an interest, but infer that A is acting in accordance with A's obligations to B. The mere fact that C knew that B had a property interest does not mean that C had notice of an adverse claim. Whether C had notice of an adverse claim depends on whether C had sufficient awareness that A was acting in violation of B's property rights. The rule in subsection (b) is a particularization of this general principle.

3. Paragraph (a)(1) provides that a person has notice of an adverse claim if the person has knowledge of the adverse claim. Knowledge is defined in Section 1–201(25) as actual knowledge.

4. Paragraph (a)(2) provides that a person has notice of an adverse claim if the person is aware of a significant probability that an adverse claim exists and deliberately avoids information that might establish the existence of the adverse claim. This is intended to codify the "willful blindness" test that has been applied in such cases. See *May v. Chapman*, 16 M. & W. 355, 153 Eng. Rep. 1225 (1847); *Goodman v. Simonds*, 61 U.S. 343 (1857).

The first prong of the willful blindness test of paragraph (a)(2) turns on whether the person is aware facts sufficient to indicate that there is a significant probability that an adverse claim exists. The "awareness" aspect necessarily turns on the actor's state of mind. Whether facts known to a person make the person aware of a "significant probability" that an adverse claim exists turns on facts about the world and the conclusions that would be drawn from those facts, taking account of the experience and position of the person in question. A particular set of facts might indicate a significant probability of an adverse claim to a professional with considerable experience in the usual methods and procedures by which securities transactions are conducted, even though the same facts would not indicate a significant probability of an adverse claim to a non-professional.

The second prong of the willful blindness test of paragraph (a)(2) turns on whether the person "deliberately avoids information" that would establish the existence of the adverse claim. The test is the character of the person's response to the information the person has. The question is whether the person deliberately failed to seek further information because of concern that suspicions would be confirmed.

Application of the "deliberate avoidance" test to a transaction by an organization focuses on the knowledge and the actions of the individual or individuals conducting the transaction on behalf of the organization. Thus, an organization that purchases a security is not willfully blind to an adverse claim unless the officers or agents who conducted that purchase transaction are willfully blind to the adverse claim. Under the two prongs of the willful blindness test, the individual or individuals conducting a transaction must know of facts indicating a substantial probability that the adverse claim exists and deliberately fail to seek further information that might confirm or refute the indication. For this purpose, information known to individuals within an organization who are not conducting or aware of a transaction, but not forwarded to the individuals conducting the transaction, is not pertinent in determining whether the individuals conducting the transaction had knowledge of a substantial probability of the existence of the adverse claim. Cf. Section 1–201(27). An organization may also "deliberately avoid information" if it acts to preclude or inhibit transmission of pertinent information to those individuals responsible for the conduct of purchase transactions.

5. Paragraph (a)(3) provides that a person has notice of an adverse claim if the person would have learned of the adverse claim by conducting an investigation that is required by other statute or regulation. This rule applies only if there is some other statute or regulation that explicitly requires persons dealing with securities to conduct some investigation. The federal securities laws require that brokers and banks, in certain specified circumstances, check with a stolen securities registry to determine whether securities offered for sale or pledge have been reported as stolen. If securities that were listed as stolen in the registry are taken by an institution that failed to comply with requirement to check the registry, the institution would be held to have notice of the fact that they were stolen under paragraph (a)(3). Accordingly, the institution could not qualify as a protected purchaser under Section 8–303. The same result has been reached under the prior version of Article 8. See *First Nat'l Bank of Cicero v. Lewco Securities*, 860 F.2d 1407 (7th Cir. 1988).

6. Subsection (b) provides explicitly for some situations involving purchase from one described or identifiable as a representative. Knowledge of the existence of the representative relation is not enough in itself to constitute "notice of an adverse claim" that would disqualify the purchaser from protected purchaser status. A purchaser may take a security on the inference that the representative is acting properly. Knowledge that a security is being transferred to an individual account of the representative or that the proceeds of the transaction will be paid into that account is not sufficient to constitute "notice of an adverse claim," but knowledge that the proceeds will be applied to the personal indebtedness of the representative is. See *State Bank of Binghamton v. Bache*, 162 Misc. 128, 293 N.Y.S. 667 (1937).

7. Subsection (c) specifies whether a purchaser of a "stale" security is charged with notice of adverse claims, and therefore disqualified from protected purchaser status under Section 8–303. The fact of "staleness" is viewed as notice of certain defects after the lapse of stated periods, but the maturity of the security does not operate automatically to affect holders' rights. The periods of time here stated are shorter than those appearing in the provisions of this Article on staleness as notice of defects or defenses of an issuer (Section 8–203) since a purchaser who takes a security after funds or other securities are available for its redemption has more reason to suspect claims of ownership than issuer's defenses. An owner will normally turn in a security rather than transfer it at such a time. Of itself, a default never constitutes notice of a possible adverse claim. To provide otherwise would not tend to drive defaulted securities home and would serve only to disrupt current financial markets where many defaulted securities are actively traded. Unpaid or overdue coupons attached to a bond do not bring it within the operation of this subsection, though they may be relevant under the general test of notice of adverse claims in subsection (a).

8. Subsection (d) provides the owner of a certificated security with a means of protection while a security certificate is being sent in for redemption or exchange. The owner may endorse it "for collection" or "for surrender," and this constitutes notice of the owner's claims, under subsection (d).

§ 8.106. Control

(a) A purchaser has control of a certificated security in bearer form if the certificated security is delivered to the purchaser.

(b) A purchaser has control of a certificated security in registered form if the certificated security is delivered to the purchaser and:

(1) the certificate is indorsed to the purchaser or in blank by an effective indorsement; or

(2) the certificate is registered in the name of the purchaser, on original issue or registration of transfer by the issuer.

(c) A purchaser has control of an uncertificated security if:

(1) the uncertificated security is delivered to the purchaser; or

(2) the issuer has agreed that it will comply with instructions originated by the purchaser without further consent by the registered owner.

(d) A purchaser has control of a security entitlement if:

(1) the purchaser becomes the entitlement holder;

(2) the securities intermediary has agreed that it will comply with entitlement orders originated by the purchaser without further consent by the entitlement holder; or

(3) another person has control of the security entitlement on behalf of the purchaser or, having previously acquired control of the security entitlement, acknowledges that it has control on behalf of the purchaser.

(e) If an interest in a security entitlement is granted by the entitlement holder to the entitlement holder's own securities intermediary, the securities intermediary has control.

(f) A purchaser who has satisfied the requirements of Subsection (c) or (d) has control, even if the registered owner in the case of Subsection (c) or the entitlement holder in the case of Subsection (d) retains the right to make substitutions for the uncertificated security or security entitlement, to originate instructions or entitlement orders to the issuer or securities intermediary, or otherwise to deal with the uncertificated security or security entitlement.

(g) An issuer or a securities intermediary may not enter into an agreement of the kind described in Subsection (c)(2) or (d)(2) without the consent of the registered owner or entitlement holder, but an issuer or a securities intermediary is not required to enter into such an agreement even though the registered owner or entitlement holder so directs. An issuer or securities intermediary that has entered into such an agreement is not required to confirm the existence of the agreement to another party unless requested to do so by the registered owner or entitlement holder.

Amended by Acts 1995, 74th Leg., ch. 962, § 1, eff. Sept. 1, 1995; Acts 1999, 76th Leg., ch. 414, § 2.27, eff. July 1, 2001.

Uniform Commercial Code Comment

1. The concept of "control" plays a key role in various provisions dealing with the rights of purchasers, including secured parties. See Sections 8–303 (protected purchasers); 8–503(e) (purchasers from securities intermediaries); 8–510 (purchasers of security entitlements from entitlement holders); 9–314 (perfection of security interests); 9–328 (priorities among conflicting security interests).

Obtaining "control" means that the purchaser has taken whatever steps are necessary, given the manner in which the securities are held, to place itself in a position where it can have the securities sold, without further action by the owner.

2. Subsection (a) provides that a purchaser obtains "control" with respect to a certificated security in bearer form by taking "delivery," as defined in Section 8–301. Subsection (b) provides that a purchaser obtains "control" with respect to a certificated security in registered form by taking "delivery," as defined in Section 8–301, provided that the security certificate has been indorsed to the purchaser or in blank. Section 8–301 provides that delivery of a certificated security occurs when the purchaser obtains possession of the security certificate, or when an agent for the purchaser (other than a securities intermediary) either acquires possession or acknowledges that the agent holds for the purchaser.

3. Subsection (c) specifies the means by which a purchaser can obtain control over uncertificated securities which the transferor holds directly. Two mechanisms are possible.

Under subsection (c)(1), securities can be "delivered" to a purchaser. Section 8–301(b) provides that "delivery" of an uncertificated security occurs when the purchaser becomes the registered holder. So far as the issuer is concerned, the purchaser would then be entitled to exercise all rights of ownership. See Section 8–207. As between the parties to a purchase transaction, however, the rights of the purchaser are determined by their contract. Cf. Section 9–202. Arrangements covered by this paragraph are analogous to arrangements in which bearer certificates are delivered to a secured party—so far as the issuer or any other parties are concerned, the secured party appears to be the outright owner, although it is in fact holding as collateral property that belongs to the debtor.

Under subsection (c)(2), a purchaser has control if the issuer has agreed to act on the instructions of the purchaser, even though the owner remains listed as the registered owner. The issuer, of course, would be acting wrongfully against the registered owner if it entered into such an agreement without the consent of the registered owner. Subsection (g) makes this point explicit. The subsection (c)(2) provision makes it possible for issuers to offer a service akin to the registered pledge device of the 1978 version of Article 8, without mandating that all issuers offer that service.

4. Subsection (d) specifies the means by which a purchaser can obtain control of a security entitlement. Three mechanisms are possible, analogous to those provided in subsection (c) for uncertificated securities. Under subsection (d)(1), a purchaser has control if it is the entitlement holder. This subsection would apply whether the purchaser holds through the same intermediary that the debtor used, or has the securities position transferred to its own intermediary. Subsection (d)(2) provides that a purchaser has control if the securities intermediary has agreed to act on entitlement orders originated by the purchaser if no further consent by the entitlement holder is required. Under subsection (d)(2), control may be achieved even though the original entitlement holder remains as the entitlement holder. Finally, a purchaser may obtain control under subsection (d)(3) if another person has control and the person acknowledges that it has control on the purchaser's behalf. Control under subsection (d)(3) parallels the delivery of certificated securities and uncertificated securities under Section 8–301. Of course, the acknowledging person cannot be the debtor.

This section specifies only the minimum requirements that such an arrangement must meet to confer "control"; the details of the arrangement can be specified by agreement. The arrangement might cover all of the positions in a particular account or subaccount, or only specified positions. There is no requirement that the control party's right to give entitlement orders be exclusive. The arrangement might provide that only the control party can give entitlement orders, or that either the entitlement holder or the control party can give entitlement orders. See subsection (f).

The following examples illustrate the application of subsection (d):

Example 1. Debtor grants Alpha Bank a security interest in a security interest in a security entitlement that includes 1000 shares of XYZ Co. stock that Debtor holds through an account with Able & Co. Alpha also has an account with Able. Debtor instructs Able to transfer the shares to Alpha, and Able does so by crediting the shares to Alpha's account. Alpha has control of the 1000 shares under subsection (d)(1). Although Debtor may have become the beneficial owner of the new securities entitlement, as between Debtor and Alpha, Able has agreed to act on Alpha's entitlement orders because, as between Able and Alpha, Alpha has become the entitlement holder. See Section 8–506.

Example 2. Debtor grants Alpha Bank a security interest in a security entitlement that includes 1000 shares of XYZ Co. stock that Debtor holds through an account with Able & Co. Alpha does not have an account with Able. Alpha uses Beta as its securities custodian. Debtor instructs Able to transfer the shares to Beta, for the account of Alpha, and Able does so. Alpha has control of the 1000 shares under subsection (d)(1). As in Example 1, although Debtor may have become the beneficial owner of the new securities entitlement, as between Debtor and Alpha, Beta has agreed to act on Alpha's entitlement orders because, as between Beta and Alpha, Alpha has become the entitlement holder.

Example 3. Debtor grants Alpha Bank a security interest in a security entitlement that includes 1000 shares of XYZ Co. stock that Debtor holds through an account with Able & Co. Debtor, Able, and Alpha enter into an agreement under which Debtor will continue to receive dividends and distributions, and will continue to have the right to direct dispositions, but Alpha also has the right to direct dispositions. Alpha has control of the 1000 shares under subsection (d)(2).

Example 4. Able & Co., a securities dealer, grants Alpha Bank a security interest in a security entitlement that includes 1000 shares of XYZ Co. stock that Able holds through an account with Clearing Corporation. Able causes Clearing Corporation to transfer the shares into Alpha's account at Clearing Corporation. As in Example 1, Alpha has control of the 1000 shares under subsection (d)(1).

Example 5. Able & Co., a securities dealer, grants Alpha Bank a security interest in a security entitlement that includes 1000 shares of XYZ Co. stock that Able holds through an account with Clearing Corporation. Alpha does not have an account with Clearing Corporation. It holds its securities through Beta Bank, which does have an account with Clearing Corporation. Able causes Clearing Corporation to transfer the shares into Beta's account at Clearing Corporation. Beta credits the position to Alpha's account with Beta. As in Example 2, Alpha has control of the 1000 shares under subsection (d)(1).

Example 6. Able & Co. a securities dealer, grants Alpha Bank a security interest in a security entitlement that includes 1000 shares of XYZ Co. stock that Able holds through an account with Clearing Corporation. Able causes Clearing Corporation to transfer the shares into a pledge account, pursuant to an agreement under which Able will continue to receive dividends, distributions, and the like, but Alpha has the right to direct dispositions. As in Example 3, Alpha has control of the 1000 shares under subsection (d)(2).

Example 7. Able & Co. a securities dealer, grants Alpha Bank a security interest in a security entitlement that includes 1000 shares of XYZ Co. stock that Able holds through an account with Clearing Corporation. Able, Alpha, and Clearing Corporation enter into an agreement under which Clearing Corporation will act on instructions from Alpha with respect to the XYZ Co. stock carried in Able's account, but Able will continue to receive dividends, distributions, and the like, and will also have the right to direct dispositions. As in Example 3, Alpha has control of the 1000 shares under subsection (d)(2).

Example 8. Able & Co. a securities dealer, holds a wide range of securities through its account at Clearing Corporation. Able enters into an arrangement with Alpha Bank pursuant to which Alpha provides financing to Able secured by securities identified as the collateral on lists provided by Able to Alpha on a daily or other periodic basis. Able, Alpha, and Clearing Corporation enter into an agreement under which Clearing Corporation agrees that if at any time Alpha directs Clearing Corporation to do so, Clearing Corporation will transfer any securities from Able's account at Alpha's instructions. Because Clearing Corporation has agreed to act on Alpha's instructions with respect to any securities carried in Able's account, at the moment that Alpha's security interest attaches to securities listed by Able, Alpha obtains control of those securities under subsection (d)(2). There is no requirement that Clearing Corporation be informed of which securities Able has pledged to Alpha.

Example 9. Debtor grants Alpha Bank a security interest in a security entitlement that includes 1000 shares of XYZ Co. stock that Debtor holds through an account with Able & Co. Beta Bank agrees with Alpha to act as Alpha's collateral agent with respect to the security entitlement. Debtor, Able, and Beta enter into an agreement under which Debtor will continue to receive dividends and distributions, and will continue to have the right to direct dispositions, but Beta also has the right to direct dispositions. Because Able has agreed that it will comply with entitlement orders originated by Beta without further consent by Debtor, Beta has control of the security entitlement (see Example 3). Because Beta has control on behalf of Alpha, Alpha also has control under subsection (d)(3). It is not necessary for Able to enter into an agreement directly with Alpha or for Able to be aware of Beta's agency relationship with Alpha.

5. For a purchaser to have "control" under subsection (c)(2) or (d)(2), it is essential that the issuer or securities intermediary, as the case may be, actually be a party to the agreement. If a debtor gives a secured party a power of attorney authorizing the secured party to act in the name of the debtor, but the issuer or securities intermediary does not specifically agree to this arrangement, the secured party does not have "control" within the meaning of subsection (c)(2) or (d)(2) because the issuer or securities intermediary is not a party to the agreement. The secured party does not have control under subsection (c)(1) or (d)(1) because, al-

though the power of attorney might give the secured party authority to act on the debtor's behalf as an agent, the secured party has not actually become the registered owner or entitlement holder.

6. Subsection (e) provides that if an interest in a security entitlement is granted by an entitlement holder to the securities intermediary through which the security entitlement is maintained, the securities intermediary has control. A common transaction covered by this provision is a margin loan from a broker to its customer.

7. The term "control" is used in a particular defined sense. The requirements for obtaining control are set out in this section. The concept is not to be interpreted by reference to similar concepts in other bodies of law. In particular, the requirements for "possession" derived from the common law of pledge are not to be used as a basis for interpreting subsection (c)(2) or (d)(2). Those provisions are designed to supplant the concepts of "constructive possession" and the like. A principal purpose of the "control" concept is to eliminate the uncertainty and confusion that results from attempting to apply common law possession concepts to modern securities holding practices.

The key to the control concept is that the purchaser has the ability to have the securities sold or transferred without further action by the transferor. There is no requirement that the powers held by the purchaser be exclusive. For example, in a secured lending arrangement, if the secured party wishes, it can allow the debtor to retain the right to make substitutions, to direct the disposition of the uncertificated security or security entitlement, or otherwise to give instructions or entitlement orders. (As explained in Section 8-102, Comment 8, an entitlement order includes a direction under Section 8-508 to the securities intermediary to transfer a financial asset to the account of the entitlement holder at another financial intermediary or to cause the financial asset to be transferred to the entitlement holder in the direct holding system (e.g., by delivery of a securities certificate registered in the name of the former entitlement holder).) Subsection (f) is included to make clear the general point stated in subsections (c) and (d) that the test of control is whether the purchaser has obtained the requisite power, not whether the debtor has retained other powers. There is no implication that retention by the debtor of powers other than those mentioned in subsection (f) is inconsistent with the purchaser having control. Nor is there a requirement that the purchaser's powers be unconditional, provided that further consent of the entitlement holder is not a condition.

Example 10. Debtor grants to Alpha Bank and to Beta Bank a security interest in a security entitlement that includes 1000 shares of XYZ Co. stock that Debtor holds through an account with Able & Co. By agreement among the parties, Alpha's security interest is senior and Beta's is junior. Able agrees to act on the entitlement orders of either Alpha or Beta. Alpha and Beta each has control under subsection (d)(2). Moreover, Beta has control notwithstanding a term of Able's agreement to the effect that Able's obligation to act on Beta's entitlement orders is conditioned on Alpha's consent. The crucial distinction is that Able's agreement to act on Beta's entitlement orders is not conditioned on Debtor's further consent.

Example 11. Debtor grants to Alpha Bank a security interest in a security entitlement that includes 1000 shares of XYZ Co. stock that Debtor holds through an account with Able & Co. Able agrees to act on the entitlement orders of Alpha, but Alpha's right to give entitlement orders to the securities intermediary is conditioned on the Debtor's default. Alternatively, Alpha's right to give entitlement orders is conditioned upon Alpha's statement to Able that Debtor is in default. Because Able's agreement to act on Alpha's entitlement orders is not conditioned on Debtor's further consent, Alpha has control of the securities entitlement under either alternative.

In many situations, it will be better practice for both the securities intermediary and the purchaser to insist that any conditions relating in any way to the entitlement holder be effective only as between the purchaser and the entitlement holder. That practice would avoid the risk that the securities intermediary could be caught between conflicting assertions of the entitlement holder and the purchaser as to whether the conditions in fact have been met. Nonetheless, the existence of unfulfilled conditions effective against the intermediary would not preclude the purchaser from having control.

§ 8.107. Whether Indorsement, Instruction, or Entitlement Order is Effective

(a) "Appropriate person" means:

(1) with respect to an indorsement, the person specified by a security certificate or by an effective special indorsement to be entitled to the security;

(2) with respect to an instruction, the registered owner of an uncertificated security;

(3) with respect to an entitlement order, the entitlement holder;

(4) if the person designated in Subdivision (1), (2), or (3) is deceased, the designated person's successor taking under other law or the designated person's personal representative acting for the estate of the decedent; or

(5) if the person designated in Subdivision (1), (2), or (3) lacks capacity, the designated person's guardian, conservator, or other similar representative who has power under other law to transfer the security or financial asset.

(b) An indorsement, instruction, or entitlement order is effective if:

(1) it is made by the appropriate person;

(2) it is made by a person who has power under the law of agency to transfer the security or financial asset on behalf of the appropriate person, including, in the case of an instruction or entitlement order, a person who has control under Section 8.106(c)(2) or (d)(2); or

(3) the appropriate person has ratified it or is otherwise precluded from asserting its ineffectiveness.

(c) An indorsement, instruction, or entitlement order made by a representative is effective even if:

(1) the representative has failed to comply with a controlling instrument or with the law of the state having jurisdiction of the representative relationship, including any law requiring the representative to obtain court approval of the transaction; or

(2) the representative's action in making the indorsement, instruction, or entitlement order or using the proceeds of the transaction is otherwise a breach of duty.

(d) If a security is registered in the name of or specially indorsed to a person described as a representative, or if a securities account is maintained in the name of a person described as a representative, an indorsement, instruction, or entitlement order made by the person is effective even though the person is no longer serving in the described capacity.

(e) Effectiveness of an indorsement, instruction, or entitlement order is determined as of the date the indorsement, instruction, or entitlement order is made, and an indorsement, instruction, or entitlement order does not become ineffective by reason of any later change of circumstances.

Amended by Acts 1995, 74th Leg., ch. 962, § 1, eff. Sept. 1, 1995.

Uniform Commercial Code Comment

1. This section defines two concepts, "appropriate person" and "effective." Effectiveness is a broader concept than appropriate person. For example, if a security or securities account is registered in the name of Mary Roe, Mary Roe is the "appropriate person," but an indorsement, instruction, or entitlement order made by John Doe is "effective" if, under agency or other law, Mary Roe is precluded from denying Doe's authority. Treating these two concepts separately facilitates statement of the rules of Article 8 that state the legal effect of an indorsement, instruction, or entitlement order. For example, a securities intermediary is protected against liability if it acts on an effective entitlement order, but has a duty to comply with an entitlement order only if it is originated by an appropriate person. See Sections 8–115 and 8–507.

One important application of the "effectiveness" concept is in the direct holding system rules on the rights of purchasers. A purchaser of a certificated security in registered form can qualify as a protected purchaser who takes free from adverse claims under Section 8–303 only if the purchaser obtains "control." Section 8–106 provides that a purchaser of a certificated security in registered form obtains control if there has been an "effective" indorsement.

2. Subsection (a) provides that the term "appropriate person" covers two categories: (1) the person who is actually designated as the person entitled to the security or security entitlement, and (2) the successor or legal representative of that person if that person has died or otherwise lacks capacity. Other law determines who has power to transfer a security on behalf of a person who lacks capacity. For example, if securities are registered in the name of more than one person and one of the designated persons dies, whether the survivor is the appropriate person depends on the form of tenancy. If the two were registered joint tenants with right of survivorship, the survivor would have that power under other law and thus would be the "appropriate person." If securities are registered in the name of an individual and the individual dies, the law of decedents' estates determines who has power to transfer the decedent's securities. That would ordinarily be the executor or administrator, but if a "small estate statute" permits a widow to transfer a decedent's securities without administration proceedings, she would be the appropriate person. If the registration of a security or a securities account contains a designation of a death beneficiary under the Uniform Transfer on Death Security Registration Act or comparable legislation, the designated beneficiary would, under that law, have power to transfer upon the person's death and so would be the appropriate person. Article 8 does not contain a list of such representatives, because any list is likely to become outdated by developments in other law.

3. Subsection (b) sets out the general rule that an indorsement, instruction, or entitlement order is effective if it is made by the appropriate person or by a person who has power to transfer under agency law or if the appropriate person is precluded from denying its effectiveness. The control rules in Section 8–106 provide for arrangements where a person who holds securities through a securities intermediary, or holds uncertificated securities directly, enters into a control agreement giving the secured party the right to initiate entitlement orders of instructions. Paragraph 2 of subsection (b) states explicitly that an entitlement order or instruction initiated by a person who has obtained such a control agreement is "effective."

Subsections (c), (d), and (e) supplement the general rule of subsection (b) on effectiveness. The term "representative," used in subsections (c) and (d), is defined in Section 1–201(35).

4. Subsection (c) provides that an indorsement, instruction, or entitlement order made by a representative is effective even though the representative's action is a violation of duties. The following example illustrates this subsection:

> *Example 1.* Certificated securities are registered in the name of John Doe. Doe dies and Mary Roe is appointed executor. Roe indorses the security certificate and transfers it to a purchaser in a transaction that is a violation of her duties as executor.

Roe's indorsement is effective, because Roe is the appropriate person under subsection (a)(4). This is so even though Roe's transfer violated her obligations as executor. The policies of free transferability of securities that underlie Article 8 dictate that neither a purchaser to whom Roe transfers the securities nor the issuer who registers transfer should be required to investigate the terms of the will to determine whether Roe is acting properly. Although Roe's indorsement is effective under this section, her breach of duty may be such that her beneficiary has an adverse claim to the securities that Roe transferred. The question whether that adverse claim can be asserted against purchasers is governed not by this section but by Section 8–303. Under Section 8–404, the issuer has no duties to an adverse claimant unless the claimant obtains legal process enjoining the issuer from registering transfer.

5. Subsection (d) deals with cases where a security or a securities account is registered in the name of a person specifically designated as a representative. The following example illustrates this subsection:

Example 2. Certificated securities are registered in the name of "John Jones, trustee of the Smith Family Trust." John Jones is removed as trustee and Martha Moe is appointed successor trustee. The securities, however, are not reregistered, but remain registered in the name of "John Jones, trustee of the Smith Family Trust." Jones indorses the security certificate and transfers it to a purchaser.

Subsection (d) provides that an indorsement by John Jones as trustee is effective even though Jones is no longer serving in that capacity. Since the securities were registered in the name of "John Jones, trustee of the Smith Family Trust," a purchaser, or the issuer when called upon to register transfer, should be entitled to assume without further inquiry that Jones has the power to act as trustee for the Smith Family Trust.

Note that subsection (d) does not apply to a case where the security or securities account is registered in the name of principal rather than the representative as such. The following example illustrates this point:

Example 3. Certificated securities are registered in the name of John Doe. John Doe dies and Mary Roe is appointed executor. The securities are not reregistered in the name of Mary Roe as executor. Later, Mary Roe is removed as executor and Martha Moe is appointed as her successor. After being removed, Mary Roe indorses the security certificate that is registered in the name of John Doe and transfers it to a purchaser.

Mary Roe's indorsement is not made effective by subsection (d), because the securities were not registered in the name of Mary Roe as representative. A purchaser or the issuer registering transfer should be required to determine whether Roe has power to act for John Doe. Purchasers and issuers can protect themselves in such cases by requiring signature guaranties. See Section 8–306.

6. Subsection (e) provides that the effectiveness of an indorsement, instruction, or entitlement order is determined as of the date it is made. The following example illustrates this subsection:

Example 4. Certificated securities are registered in the name of John Doe. John Doe dies and Mary Roe is appointed executor. Mary Roe indorses the security certificate that is registered in the name of John Doe and transfers it to a purchaser. After the indorsement and transfer, but before the security certificate is presented to the issuer for registration of transfer, Mary Roe is removed as executor and Martha Moe is appointed as her successor.

Mary Roe's indorsement is effective, because at the time Roe indorsed she was the appropriate person under subsection (a)(4). Her later removal as executor does not render the indorsement ineffective. Accordingly, the issuer would not be liable for registering the transfer. See Section 8–404.

§ 8.108. Warranties in Direct Holding

(a) A person who transfers a certificated security to a purchaser for value warrants to the purchaser, and an indorser, if the transfer is by indorsement, warrants to any subsequent purchaser, that:

(1) the certificate is genuine and has not been materially altered;

(2) the transferor or indorser does not know of any fact that might impair the validity of the security;

(3) there is no adverse claim to the security;

(4) the transfer does not violate any restriction on transfer;

(5) if the transfer is by indorsement, the indorsement is made by an appropriate person, or if the indorsement is by an agent, the agent has actual authority to act on behalf of the appropriate person; and

(6) the transfer is otherwise effective and rightful.

(b) A person who originates an instruction for registration of transfer of an uncertificated security to a purchaser for value warrants to the purchaser that:

(1) the instruction is made by an appropriate person, or if the instruction is by an agent, the agent has actual authority to act on behalf of the appropriate person;

(2) the security is valid;

(3) there is no adverse claim to the security; and

(4) at the time the instruction is presented to the issuer:

(A) the purchaser will be entitled to the registration of transfer;

(B) the transfer will be registered by the issuer free from all liens, security interests, restrictions, and claims other than those specified in the instruction;

(C) the transfer will not violate any restriction on transfer; and

(D) the requested transfer will otherwise be effective and rightful.

(c) A person who transfers an uncertificated security to a purchaser for value and does not originate an instruction in connection with the transfer warrants that:

(1) the uncertificated security is valid;

(2) there is no adverse claim to the security;

(3) the transfer does not violate any restriction on transfer; and

(4) the transfer is otherwise effective and rightful.

(d) A person who indorses a security certificate warrants to the issuer that:

(1) there is no adverse claim to the security; and

(2) the indorsement is effective.

(e) A person who originates an instruction for registration of transfer of an uncertificated security warrants to the issuer that:

(1) the instruction is effective; and

(2) at the time the instruction is presented to the issuer the purchaser will be entitled to the registration of transfer.

(f) A person who presents a certificated security for registration of transfer or for payment or exchange warrants to the issuer that the person is entitled to the registration, payment, or exchange, but a purchaser for value and without notice of adverse claims to whom transfer is registered warrants only that the person has no knowledge of any unauthorized signature in a necessary indorsement.

(g) If a person acts as agent of another in delivering a certificated security to a purchaser, the identity of the principal was known to the person to whom the certificate was delivered, and the certificate delivered by the agent was received by the agent from the principal or received by the agent from another person at the direction of the principal, the person delivering the security certificate warrants only that the delivering person has authority to act for the principal and does not know of any adverse claim to the certificated security.

(h) A secured party who redelivers a security certificate received, or after payment and on order of the debtor delivers the security certificate to another person, makes only the warranties of an agent under Subsection (g).

(i) Except as otherwise provided in Subsection (g), a broker acting for a customer makes to the issuer and a purchaser the warranties provided in Subsections (a)–(f). A broker that delivers a security certificate to its customer, or causes its customer to be registered as the owner of an uncertificated security, makes to the customer the warranties provided in Subsection (a) or (b), and has the rights and privileges of a purchaser under this section. The warranties of and in favor of the broker acting as an agent are in addition to applicable warranties given by and in favor of the customer.

Amended by Acts 1995, 74th Leg., ch. 962, § 1, eff. Sept. 1, 1995.

Uniform Commercial Code Comment

1. Subsections (a), (b), and (c) deal with warranties by security transferors to purchasers. Subsections (d) and (e) deal with warranties by security transferors to issuers. Subsection (f) deals with presentment warranties.

2. Subsection (a) specifies the warranties made by a person who transfers a certificated security to a purchaser for value. Paragraphs (3), (4), and (5) make explicit several key points that are implicit in the general warranty of paragraph (6) that the transfer is effective and rightful. Subsection (b) sets forth the warranties made to a purchaser for value by one who originates an instruction. These warranties are quite similar to those made by one transferring a certificated security, subsection (a), the principal difference being the absolute warranty of validity. If upon receipt of the instruction the issuer should dispute the validity of the security, the burden of proving validity is upon the transferor. Subsection (c) provides for the limited circumstances in which an uncertificated security could be transferred without an instruction, see Section 8–301(b)(2). Subsections (d) and (e) give the issuer the benefit of the warranties of an indorser or originator on those matters not within the issuer's knowledge.

3. Subsection (f) limits the warranties made by a purchaser for value without notice whose presentation of a security certificate is defective in some way but to whom the issuer does register transfer. The effect is to deny the issuer a remedy against such a person unless at the time of presentment the person had knowledge of an unauthorized signature in a necessary indorsement. The issuer can protect itself by refusing to make the transfer or, if it registers the transfer before it discovers the defect, by pursuing its remedy against a signature guarantor.

4. Subsection (g) eliminates all substantive warranties in the relatively unusual case of a delivery of certificated security by an agent of a disclosed principal where the agent delivers the exact certificate that it received from or for the principal. Subsection (h) limits the warranties given by a secured party who redelivers a certificate. Subsection (i) specifies the warranties of brokers in the more common scenarios.

5. Under Section 1–102(3) the warranty provisions apply "unless otherwise agreed" and the parties may enter into express agreements to allocate the risks of possible defects. Usual estoppel principles apply with respect to transfers of both certificated and uncertificated securities whenever the

purchaser has knowledge of the defect, and these warranties will not be breached in such a case.

§ 8.109. Warranties in Indirect Holding

(a) A person who originates an entitlement order to a securities intermediary warrants to the securities intermediary that:

(1) the entitlement order is made by an appropriate person, or if the entitlement order is by an agent, the agent has actual authority to act on behalf of the appropriate person; and

(2) there is no adverse claim to the security entitlement.

(b) A person who delivers a security certificate to a securities intermediary for credit to a securities account or originates an instruction with respect to an uncertificated security directing that the uncertificated security be credited to a securities account makes to the securities intermediary the warranties specified in Section 8.108(a) or (b).

(c) If a securities intermediary delivers a security certificate to its entitlement holder or causes its entitlement holder to be registered as the owner of an uncertificated security, the securities intermediary makes to the entitlement holder the warranties specified in Section 8.108(a) or (b).

Added by Acts 1995, 74th Leg., ch. 962, § 1, eff. Sept. 1, 1995.

Uniform Commercial Code Comment

1. Subsection (a) provides that a person who originates an entitlement order warrants to the securities intermediary that the order is authorized, and warrants the absence of adverse claims. Subsection (b) specifies the warranties that are given when a person who holds securities directly has the holding converted into indirect form. A person who delivers a certificate to a securities intermediary or originates an instruction for an uncertificated security gives to the securities intermediary the transfer warranties under Section 8–108. If the securities intermediary in turn delivers the certificate to a higher level securities intermediary, it gives the same warranties.

2. Subsection (c) states the warranties that a securities intermediary gives when a customer who has been holding securities in an account with the securities intermediary requests that certificates be delivered or that uncertificated securities be registered in the customer's name. The warranties are the same as those that brokers make with respect to securities that the brokers sell to or buy on behalf of the customers. See Section 8–108(i).

3. As with the Section 8–108 warranties, the warranties specified in this section may be modified by agreement under Section 1–102(3).

§ 8.110. Applicability; Choice of Law

(a) The local law of the issuer's jurisdiction, as specified in Subsection (d), governs:

(1) the validity of a security;

(2) the rights and duties of the issuer with respect to registration of transfer;

(3) the effectiveness of registration of transfer by the issuer;

(4) whether the issuer owes any duties to an adverse claimant to a security; and

(5) whether an adverse claim can be asserted against a person to whom transfer of a certificated or uncertificated security is registered or a person who obtains control of an uncertificated security.

(b) The local law of the securities intermediary's jurisdiction, as specified in Subsection (e), governs:

(1) acquisition of a security entitlement from the securities intermediary;

(2) the rights and duties of the securities intermediary and entitlement holder arising out of a security entitlement;

(3) whether the securities intermediary owes any duties to an adverse claimant to a security entitlement; and

(4) whether an adverse claim can be asserted against a person who acquires a security entitlement from the securities intermediary or a person who purchases a security entitlement or interest therein from an entitlement holder.

(c) The local law of the jurisdiction in which a security certificate is located at the time of delivery governs whether an adverse claim can be asserted against a person to whom the security certificate is delivered.

(d) "Issuer's jurisdiction" means the jurisdiction under which the issuer of the security is organized or, if permitted by the law of that jurisdiction, the law of another jurisdiction specified by the issuer. An issuer organized under the law of this state may specify the law of another jurisdiction as the law governing the matters specified in Subsections (a)(2)–(5).

(e) The following rules determine a securities intermediary's jurisdiction for purposes of this section:

(1) If an agreement between the securities intermediary and its entitlement holder governing the securities account expressly provides that a particular jurisdiction is the securities intermediary's jurisdiction for purposes of this subchapter, this chapter,

or this title, that jurisdiction is the securities intermediary's jurisdiction.

(2) If Subdivision (1) does not apply and an agreement between the securities intermediary and its entitlement holder governing the securities account expressly provides that the agreement is governed by the law of a particular jurisdiction, that jurisdiction is the securities intermediary's jurisdiction.

(3) If neither Subdivision (1) nor Subdivision (2) applies and an agreement between the securities intermediary and its entitlement holder governing the securities account expressly provides that the securities account is maintained at an office in a particular jurisdiction, that jurisdiction is the securities intermediary's jurisdiction.

(4) If none of the preceding subdivisions applies, the securities intermediary's jurisdiction is the jurisdiction in which the office identified in an account statement as the office serving the entitlement holder's account is located.

(5) If none of the preceding subdivisions applies, the securities intermediary's jurisdiction is the jurisdiction in which the chief executive office of the securities intermediary is located.

(f) A securities intermediary's jurisdiction is not determined by:

(1) the physical location of certificates representing financial assets;

(2) the jurisdiction in which is organized the issuer of the financial asset with respect to which an entitlement holder has a security entitlement; or

(3) the location of facilities for data processing or other recordkeeping concerning the account.

Added by Acts 1995, 74th Leg., ch. 962, § 1, eff. Sept. 1, 1995. Amended by Acts 1999, 76th Leg., ch. 414, § 2.28, eff. July 1, 2001.

Uniform Commercial Code Comment

1. This section deals with applicability and choice of law issues concerning Article 8. The distinction between the direct and indirect holding systems plays a significant role in determining the governing law. An investor in the direct holding system is registered on the books of the issuer and/or has possession of a security certificate. Accordingly, the jurisdiction of incorporation of the issuer or location of the certificate determine the applicable law. By contrast, an investor in the indirect holding system has a security entitlement, which is a bundle of rights against the securities intermediary with respect to a security, rather than a direct interest in the underlying security. Accordingly, in the rules for the indirect holding system, the jurisdiction of incorporation of the issuer of the underlying security or the location of any certificates that might be held by the intermediary or a higher tier intermediary, do not determine the applicable law.

The phrase "local law" refers to the law of a jurisdiction other than its conflict of laws rules. See Restatement (Second) of Conflict of Laws § 4.

2. Subsection (a) provides that the law of an issuer's jurisdiction governs certain issues where the substantive rules of Article 8 determine the issuer's rights and duties. Paragraph (1) of subsection (a) provides that the law of the issuer's jurisdiction governs the validity of the security. This ensures that a single body of law will govern the questions addressed in Part 2 of Article 8, concerning the circumstances in which an issuer can and cannot assert invalidity as a defense against purchasers. Similarly, paragraphs (2), (3), and (4) of subsection (a) ensure that the issuer will be able to look to a single body of law on the questions addressed in Part 4 of Article 8, concerning the issuer's duties and liabilities with respect to registration of transfer.

Paragraph (5) of subsection (a) applies the law of an issuer's jurisdiction to the question whether an adverse claim can be asserted against a purchaser to whom transfer has been registered, or who has obtained control over an uncertificated security. Although this issue deals with the rights of persons other than the issuer, the law of the issuer's jurisdiction applies because the purchasers to whom the provision applies are those whose protection against adverse claims depends on the fact that their interests have been recorded on the books of the issuer.

The principal policy reflected in the choice of law rules in subsection (a) is that an issuer and others should be able to look to a single body of law on the matters specified in subsection (a), rather than having to look to the law of all of the different jurisdictions in which security holders may reside. The choice of law policies reflected in this subsection do not require that the body of law governing all of the matters specified in subsection (a) be that of the jurisdiction in which the issuer is incorporated. Thus, subsection (d) provides that the term "issuer's jurisdiction" means the jurisdiction in which the issuer is organized, or, if permitted by that law, the law of another jurisdiction selected by the issuer. Subsection (d) also provides that issuers organized under the law of a State which adopts this Article may make such a selection, except as to the validity issue specified in paragraph (1). The question whether an issuer can assert the defense of invalidity may implicate significant policies of the issuer's jurisdiction of incorporation. See, e.g., Section 8–202 and Comments thereto.

Although subsection (a) provides that the issuer's rights and duties concerning registration of transfer are governed by the law of the issuer's jurisdiction, other matters related to registration of transfer, such as appointment of a guardian for a registered owner or the existence of agency relationships, might be governed by another jurisdiction's law. Neither this section nor Section 1–105 deals with what law governs the appointment of the administrator or executor; that question is determined under generally applicable choice of law rules.

3. Subsection (b) provides that the law of the securities intermediary's jurisdiction governs the issues concerning the

indirect holding system that are dealt with in Article 8. Paragraphs (1) and (2) cover the matters dealt with in the Article 8 rules defining the concept of security entitlement and specifying the duties of securities intermediaries. Paragraph (3) provides that the law of the security intermediary's jurisdiction determines whether the intermediary owes any duties to an adverse claimant. Paragraph (4) provides that the law of the security intermediary's jurisdiction determines whether adverse claims can be asserted against entitlement holders and others.

Subsection (e) determines what is a "securities intermediary's jurisdiction." The policy of subsection (b) is to ensure that a securities intermediary and all of its entitlement holders can look to a single, readily identifiable body of law to determine their rights and duties. Accordingly, subsection (e) sets out a sequential series of tests to facilitate identification of that body of law. Paragraph (1) of subsection (e) permits specification of the securities intermediary's jurisdiction by agreement. In the absence of such a specification, the law chosen by the parties to govern the securities account determines the securities intermediary's jurisdiction. See paragraph (2). Because the policy of this section is to enable parties to determine, in advance and with certainty, what law will apply to transactions governed by this Article, the validation of the parties' selection of governing law by agreement is not conditioned upon a determination that the jurisdiction whose law is chosen bear a "reasonable relation" to the transaction. See Section 4A–507; compare Section 1–105(1). That is also true with respect to the similar provisions in subsection (d) of this section and in Section 9–305. The remaining paragraphs in subsection (e) contain additional default rules for determining the securities intermediary's jurisdiction.

4. Subsection (c) provides a choice of law rule for adverse claim issues that may arise in connection with delivery of security certificates in the direct holding system. It applies the law of the place of delivery. If a certificated security issued by an Idaho corporation is sold, and the sale is settled by physical delivery of the certificate from Seller to Buyer in New York, under subsection (c), New York law determines whether Buyer takes free from adverse claims. The domicile of Seller, Buyer, and any adverse claimant is irrelevant.

5. The following examples illustrate how a court in a jurisdiction which has enacted this section would determine the governing law:

Example 1. John Doe, a resident of Kansas, maintains a securities account with Able & Co. Able is incorporated in Delaware. Its chief executive offices are located in Illinois. The office where Doe transacts business with Able is located in Missouri. The agreement between Doe and Able specifies that Illinois is the securities intermediary's (Able's) jurisdiction. Through the account, Doe holds securities of a Colorado corporation, which Able holds through Clearing Corporation. The rules of Clearing Corporation provide that the rights and duties of Clearing Corporation and its participants are governed by New York law. Subsection (a) specifies that a controversy concerning the rights and duties as between the issuer and Clearing Corporation is governed by Colorado law. Subsections (b) and (e) specify that a controversy concerning the rights and duties as between the Clearing Corporation and Able is governed by New York law, and that a controversy concerning the rights and duties as between Able and Doe is governed by Illinois law.

Example 2. Same facts as to Doe and Able as in Example 1. Through the account, Doe holds securities of a Senegalese corporation, which Able holds through Clearing Corporation. Clearing Corporation's operations are located in Belgium, and its rules and agreements with its participants provide that they are governed by Belgian law. Clearing Corporation holds the securities through a custodial account at the Paris branch office of Global Bank, which is organized under English law. The agreement between Clearing Corporation and Global Bank provides that it is governed by French law. Subsection (a) specifies that a controversy concerning the rights and duties as between the issuer and Global Bank is governed by Senegalese law. Subsections (b) and (e) specify that a controversy concerning the rights and duties as between Global Bank and Clearing Corporation is governed by French law, that a controversy the rights and duties as between Clearing Corporation and Able is governed by Belgian law, and that a controversy concerning the rights and duties as between Able and Doe is governed by Illinois law.

6. To the extent that this section does not specify the governing law, general choice of law rules apply. For example, suppose that in either of the examples in the preceding Comment, Doe enters into an agreement with Roe, also a resident of Kansas, in which Doe agrees to transfer all of his interests in the securities held through Able to Roe. Article 8 does not deal with whether such an agreement is enforceable or whether it gives Roe some interest in Doe's security entitlement. This section specifies what jurisdiction's law governs the issues that are dealt with in Article 8. Article 8, however, does specify that securities intermediaries have only limited duties with respect to adverse claims. See Section 8–115. Subsection (b)(3) of this section provides that Illinois law governs whether Able owes any duties to an adverse claimant. Thus, if Illinois has adopted Revised Article 8, Section 8–115 as enacted in Illinois determines whether Roe has any rights against Able.

7. The choice of law provisions concerning security interests in securities and security entitlements are set out in Section 9–305.

§ 8.111. Clearing Corporation Rules

A rule adopted by a clearing corporation governing rights and obligations among the clearing corporation and its participants in the clearing corporation is effective even if the rule conflicts with this chapter and affects another party who does not consent to the rule.

Added by Acts 1995, 74th Leg., ch. 962, § 1, eff. Sept. 1, 1995.

Uniform Commercial Code Comment

1. The experience of the past few decades shows that securities holding and settlement practices may develop rapidly, and in unforeseeable directions. Accordingly, it is

desirable that the rules of Article 8 be adaptable both to ensure that commercial law can conform to changing practices and to ensure that commercial law does not operate as an obstacle to developments in securities practice. Even if practices were unchanging, it would not be possible in a general statute to specify in detail the rules needed to provide certainty in the operations of the clearance and settlement system.

The provisions of this Article and Article 1 on the effect of agreements provide considerable flexibility in the specification of the details of the rights and obligations of participants in the securities holding system by agreement. See Sections 8–504 through 8–509, and Section 1–102(3) and (4). Given the magnitude of the exposures involved in securities transactions, however, it may not be possible for the parties in developing practices to rely solely on private agreements, particularly with respect to matters that might affect others, such as creditors. For example, in order to be fully effective, rules of clearing corporations on the finality or reversibility of securities settlements must not only bind the participants in the clearing corporation but also be effective against their creditors. Section 8–111 provides that clearing corporation rules are effective even if they indirectly affect third parties, such as creditors of a participant. This provision does not, however, permit rules to be adopted that would govern the rights and obligations of third parties other than as a consequence of rules that specify the rights and obligations of the clearing corporation and its participants.

2. The definition of clearing corporation in Section 8–102 covers only federal reserve banks, entities registered as clearing agencies under the federal securities laws, and others subject to comparable regulation. The rules of registered clearing agencies are subject to regulatory oversight under the federal securities laws.

§ 8.112. Creditor's Legal Process

(a) The interest of a debtor in a certificated security may be reached by a creditor only by actual seizure of the security certificate by the officer making the attachment or levy, except as otherwise provided in Subsection (d). However, a certificated security for which the certificate has been surrendered to the issuer may be reached by a creditor by legal process on the issuer.

(b) The interest of a debtor in an uncertificated security may be reached by a creditor only by legal process on the issuer at its chief executive office in the United States, except as otherwise provided in Subsection (d).

(c) The interest of a debtor in a security entitlement may be reached by a creditor only by legal process on the securities intermediary with whom the debtor's securities account is maintained, except as otherwise provided in Subsection (d).

(d) The interest of a debtor in a certificated security for which the certificate is in the possession of a secured party, or in an uncertificated security registered in the name of a secured party, or in a security entitlement maintained in the name of a secured party may be reached by a creditor by legal process on the secured party.

(e) A creditor whose debtor is the owner of a certificated security, uncertificated security, or security entitlement is entitled to aid from a court of competent jurisdiction, by injunction or otherwise, in reaching the certificated security, uncertificated security, or security entitlement or in satisfying the claim by means allowed at law or in equity in regard to property that cannot readily be reached by other legal process.

Added by Acts 1995, 74th Leg., ch. 962, § 1, eff. Sept. 1, 1995.

Uniform Commercial Code Comment

1. In dealing with certificated securities the instrument itself is the vital thing, and therefore a valid levy cannot be made unless all possibility of the certificate's wrongfully finding its way into a transferee's hands has been removed. This can be accomplished only when the certificate is in the possession of a public officer, the issuer, or an independent third party. A debtor who has been enjoined can still transfer the security in contempt of court. See *Overlock v. Jerome–Portland Copper Mining Co.*, 29 Ariz. 560, 243 P. 400 (1926). Therefore, although injunctive relief is provided in subsection (e) so that creditors may use this method to gain control of the certificated security, the security certificate itself must be reached to constitute a proper levy whenever the debtor has possession.

2. Subsection (b) provides that when the security is uncertificated and registered in the debtor's name, the debtor's interest can be reached only by legal process upon the issuer. The most logical place to serve the issuer would be the place where the transfer records are maintained, but that location might be difficult to identify, especially when the separate elements of a computer network might be situated in different places. The chief executive office is selected as the appropriate place by analogy to Section 9–307(b)(3). See Comment 2 to that section. This section indicates only how attachment is to be made, not when it is legally justified. For that reason there is no conflict between this section and *Shaffer v. Heitner*, 433 U.S. 186 (1977).

3. Subsection (c) provides that a security entitlement can be reached only by legal process upon the debtor's security intermediary. Process is effective only if directed to the debtor's own security intermediary. If Debtor holds securities through Broker, and Broker in turn holds through Clearing Corporation, Debtor's property interest is a security entitlement against Broker. Accordingly, Debtor's creditor cannot reach Debtor's interest by legal process directed to the Clearing Corporation. See also Section 8–115.

4. Subsection (d) provides that when a certificated security, an uncertificated security, or a security entitlement is controlled by a secured party, the debtor's interest can be

reached by legal process upon the secured party. This section does not attempt to provide for rights as between the creditor and the secured party, as, for example, whether or when the secured party must liquidate the security.

§ 8.113. Statute of Frauds Inapplicable

A contract or modification of a contract for the sale or purchase of a security is enforceable whether or not there is a writing signed or record authenticated by a party against whom enforcement is sought, even if the contract or modification is not capable of performance within one year of its making.

Added by Acts 1995, 74th Leg., ch. 962, § 1, eff. Sept. 1, 1995.

Uniform Commercial Code Comment

This section provides that the statute of frauds does not apply to contracts for the sale of securities, reversing prior law which had a special statute of frauds in Section 8–319 (1978). With the increasing use of electronic means of communication, the statute of frauds is unsuited to the realities of the securities business. For securities transactions, whatever benefits a statute of frauds may play in filtering out fraudulent claims are outweighed by the obstacles it places in the development of modern commercial practices in the securities business.

§ 8.114. Evidentiary Rules Concerning Certificated Securities

The following rules apply in an action on a certificated security against the issuer:

(1) Unless specifically denied in the pleadings, each signature on a security certificate or in a necessary indorsement is admitted.

(2) If the effectiveness of a signature is put in issue, the burden of establishing effectiveness is on the party claiming under the signature, but the signature is presumed to be genuine or authorized.

(3) If signatures on a security certificate are admitted or established, production of the certificate entitles a holder to recover on it unless the defendant establishes a defense or a defect going to the validity of the security.

(4) If it is shown that a defense or defect exists, the plaintiff has the burden of establishing that the plaintiff, or some person under whom the plaintiff claims, is a person against whom the defense or defect cannot be asserted.

Added by Acts 1995, 74th Leg., ch. 962, § 1, eff. Sept. 1, 1995.

Uniform Commercial Code Comment

This section adapts the rules of negotiable instruments law concerning procedure in actions on instruments, see Section 3–308, to actions on certificated securities governed by this Article. An "action on a security" includes any action or proceeding brought against the issuer to enforce a right or interest that is part of the security, such as an action to collect principal or interest or a dividend, or to establish a right to vote or to receive a new security under an exchange offer or plan of reorganization. This section applies only to certificated securities; actions on uncertificated securities are governed by general evidentiary principles.

§ 8.115. Securities Intermediary and Others Not Liable to Adverse Claimant

A securities intermediary that has transferred a financial asset pursuant to an effective entitlement order, or a broker or other agent or bailee that has dealt with a financial asset at the direction of its customer or principal, is not liable to a person having an adverse claim to the financial asset, unless the securities intermediary, or broker or other agent or bailee:

(1) took the action after it had been served with an injunction, restraining order, or other legal process enjoining it from doing so issued by a court of competent jurisdiction and had a reasonable opportunity to act on the injunction, restraining order, or other legal process;

(2) acted in collusion with the wrongdoer in violating the rights of the adverse claimant; or

(3) in the case of a security certificate that has been stolen, acted with notice of the adverse claim.

Added by Acts 1995, 74th Leg., ch. 962, § 1, eff. Sept. 1, 1995.

Uniform Commercial Code Comment

1. Other provisions of Article 8 protect certain purchasers against adverse claims, both for the direct holding system and the indirect holding system. See Sections 8–303 and 8–502. This section deals with the related question of the possible liability of a person who acted as the "conduit" for a securities transaction. It covers both securities intermediaries—the "conduits" in the indirect holding system—and brokers or other agents or bailees—the "conduits" in the direct holding system. The following examples illustrate its operation:

Example 1. John Doe is a customer of the brokerage firm of Able & Co. Doe delivers to Able a certificate for 100 shares of XYZ Co. common stock, registered in Doe's name and properly indorsed, and asks the firm to sell it for him. Able does so. Later, John Doe's spouse Mary Doe brings an action against Able asserting that Able's action was wrongful against her because the XYZ Co. stock was marital property in which she had an interest, and John Doe was acting wrongfully against her in transferring the securities.

Example 2. Mary Roe is a customer of the brokerage firm of Baker & Co. and holds her securities through a securities account with Baker. Roe instructs Baker to sell 100 shares of XYZ Co. common stock that she carried in her account. Baker does so. Later, Mary Roe's spouse John Roe brings an action against Baker asserting that Baker's action was wrongful against him because the XYZ Co. stock was marital property in which he had an interest, and Mary Roe was acting wrongfully against him in transferring the securities.

Under common law conversion principles, Mary Doe might be able to assert that Able & Co. is liable to her in Example 1 for exercising dominion over property inconsistent with her rights in it. On that or some similar theory John Roe might assert that Baker is liable to him in Example 2. Section 8–115 protects both Able and Baker from liability.

2. The policy of this section is similar to that of many other rules of law that protect agents and bailees from liability as innocent converters. If a thief steals property and ships it by mail, express service, or carrier, to another person, the recipient of the property does not obtain good title, even though the recipient may have given value to the thief and had no notice or knowledge that the property was stolen. Accordingly, the true owner can recover the property from the recipient or obtain damages in a conversion or similar action. An action against the postal service, express company, or carrier presents entirely different policy considerations. Accordingly, general tort law protects agents or bailees who act on the instructions of their principals or bailors. See Restatement (Second) of Torts § 235. See also UCC Section 7–404.

3. Except as provided in paragraph 3, this section applies even though the securities intermediary, or the broker or other agent or bailee, had notice or knowledge that another person asserts a claim to the securities. Consider the following examples:

Example 3. Same facts as in Example 1, except that before John Doe brought the XYZ Co. security certificate to Able for sale, Mary Doe telephoned or wrote to the firm asserting that she had an interest in all of John Doe's securities and demanding that they not trade for him.

Example 4. Same facts as in Example 2, except that before Mary Roe gave an entitlement order to Baker to sell the XYZ Co. securities from her account, John Roe telephoned or wrote to the firm asserting that he had an interest in all of Mary Roe's securities and demanding that they not trade for her.

Section 8–115 protects Able and Baker from liability. The protections of Section 8–115 do not depend on the presence or absence of notice of adverse claims. It is essential to the securities settlement system that brokers and securities intermediaries be able to act promptly on the directions of their customers. Even though a firm has notice that someone asserts a claim to a customer's securities or security entitlements, the firm should not be placed in the position of having to make a legal judgment about the validity of the claim at the risk of liability either to its customer or to the third party for guessing wrong. Under this section, the broker or securities intermediary is privileged to act on the instructions of its customer or entitlement holder, unless it has been served with a restraining order or other legal process enjoining it from doing so. This is already the law in many jurisdictions. For example a section of the New York Banking Law provides that banks need not recognize any adverse claim to funds or securities on deposit with them unless they have been served with legal process. N.Y. Banking Law § 134. Other sections of the UCC embody a similar policy. See Sections 3–602, 5–114(2)(b).

Paragraph (1) of this section refers only to a court order enjoining the securities intermediary or the broker or other agent or bailee from acting at the instructions of the customer. It does not apply to cases where the adverse claimant tells the intermediary or broker that the customer has been enjoined, or shows the intermediary or broker a copy of a court order binding the customer.

Paragraph (3) takes a different approach in one limited class of cases, those where a customer sells stolen certificated securities through a securities firm. Here the policies that lead to protection of securities firms against assertions of other sorts of claims must be weighed against the desirability of having securities firms guard against the disposition of stolen securities. Accordingly, paragraph (3) denies protection to a broker, custodian, or other agent or bailee who receives a stolen security certificate from its customer, if the broker, custodian, or other agent or bailee had notice of adverse claims. The circumstances that give notice of adverse claims are specified in Section 8–105. The result is that brokers, custodians, and other agents and bailees face the same liability for selling stolen certificated securities that purchasers face for buying them.

4. As applied to securities intermediaries, this section embodies one of the fundamental principles of the Article 8 indirect holding system rules—that a securities intermediary owes duties only to its own entitlement holders. The following examples illustrate the operation of this section in the multi-tiered indirect holding system:

Example 5. Able & Co., a broker-dealer, holds 50,000 shares of XYZ Co. stock in its account at Clearing Corporation. Able acquired the XYZ shares from another firm, Baker & Co., in a transaction that Baker contends was tainted by fraud, giving Baker a right to rescind the transaction and recover the XYZ shares from Able. Baker sends notice to Clearing Corporation stating that Baker has a claim to the 50,000 shares of XYZ Co. in Able's account. Able then initiates an entitlement order directing Clearing Corporation to transfer the 50,000 shares of XYZ Co. to another firm in settlement of a trade. Under Section 8–115, Clearing Corporation is privileged to comply with Able's entitlement order, without fear of liability to Baker. This is so even though Clearing Corporation has notice of Baker's claim, unless Baker obtains a court order enjoining Clearing Corporation from acting on Able's entitlement order.

Example 6. Able & Co., a broker-dealer, holds 50,000 shares of XYZ Co. stock in its account at Clearing Corporation. Able initiates an entitlement order directing Clearing Corporation to transfer the 50,000 shares of XYZ Co. to another firm in settlement of a trade. That trade was made by Able for its own account, and the proceeds were devoted to its own use. Able becomes insolvent, and it is discovered that Able has a shortfall in the shares of XYZ Co. stock that it should have been carrying for its customers. Able's customers bring an action against Clearing Corporation asserting that Clearing Corporation acted wrongfully in transferring the XYZ shares on Able's order because those were shares that should have been held by Able for its customers. Under Section 8-115, Clearing Corporation is not liable to Able's customers, because Clearing Corporation acted on an effective entitlement order of its own entitlement holder, Able. Clearing Corporation's protection against liability does not depend on the presence or absence of notice or knowledge of the claim by Clearing Corporation.

5. If the conduct of a securities intermediary or a broker or other agent or bailee rises to a level of complicity in the wrongdoing of its customer or principal, the policies that favor protection against liability do not apply. Accordingly, paragraph (2) provides that the protections of this section do not apply if the securities intermediary or broker or other agent or bailee acted in collusion with the customer or principal in violating the rights of another person. The collusion test is intended to adopt a standard akin to the tort rules that determine whether a person is liable as an aider or abettor for the tortious conduct of a third party. See Restatement (Second) of Torts § 876.

Knowledge that the action of the customer is wrongful is a necessary but not sufficient condition of the collusion test. The aspect of the role of securities intermediaries and brokers that Article 8 deals with is the clerical or ministerial role of implementing and recording the securities transactions that their customers conduct. Faithful performance of this role consists of following the instructions of the customer. It is not the role of the record-keeper to police whether the transactions recorded are appropriate, so mere awareness that the customer may be acting wrongfully does not itself constitute collusion. That, of course, does not insulate an intermediary or broker from responsibility in egregious cases where its action goes beyond the ordinary standards of the business of implementing and recording transactions, and reaches a level of affirmative misconduct in assisting the customer in the commission of a wrong.

§ 8.116. Securities Intermediary as Purchaser for Value

A securities intermediary that receives a financial asset and establishes a security entitlement to the financial asset in favor of an entitlement holder is a purchaser for value of the financial asset. A securities intermediary that acquires a security entitlement to a financial asset from another securities intermediary acquires the security entitlement for value if the securities intermediary acquiring the security entitlement establishes a security entitlement to the financial asset in favor of an entitlement holder.

Added by Acts 1995, 74th Leg., ch. 962, § 1, eff. Sept. 1, 1995.

Uniform Commercial Code Comment

1. This section is intended to make explicit two points that, while implicit in other provisions, are of sufficient importance to the operation of the indirect holding system that they warrant explicit statement. First, it makes clear that a securities intermediary that receives a financial asset and establishes a security entitlement in respect thereof in favor of an entitlement holder is a "purchaser" of the financial asset that the securities intermediary received. Second, it makes clear that by establishing a security entitlement in favor of an entitlement holder a securities intermediary gives value for any corresponding financial asset that the securities intermediary receives or acquires from another party, whether the intermediary holds directly or indirectly.

In many cases a securities intermediary that receives a financial asset will also be transferring value to the person from whom the financial asset was received. That, however, is not always the case. Payment may occur through a different system than settlement of the securities side of the transaction, or the securities might be transferred without a corresponding payment, as when a person moves an account from one securities intermediary to another. Even though the securities intermediary does not give value to the transferor, it does give value by incurring obligations to its own entitlement holder. Although the general definition of value in Section 1-201(44)(d) should be interpreted to cover the point, this section is included to make this point explicit.

2. The following examples illustrate the effect of this section:

Example 1. Buyer buys 1000 shares of XYZ Co. common stock through Buyer's broker Able & Co. to be held in Buyer's securities account. In settlement of the trade, the selling broker delivers to Able a security certificate in street name, indorsed in blank, for 1000 shares XYZ Co. stock, which Able holds in its vault. Able credits Buyer's account for securities in that amount. Section 8-116 specifies that Able is a purchaser of the XYZ Co. stock certificate, and gave value for it. Thus, Able can obtain the benefit of Section 8-303, which protects purchasers for value, if it satisfies the other requirements of that section.

Example 2. Buyer buys 1000 shares XYZ Co. common stock through Buyer's broker Able & Co. to be held in Buyer's securities account. The trade is settled by crediting 1000 shares XYZ Co. stock to Able's account at Clearing Corporation. Able credits Buyer's account for securities in that amount. When Clearing Corporation credits Able's account, Able acquires a security entitlement under Section 8-501. Section 8-116 specifies that Able acquired this security entitlement for value. Thus, Able can obtain the benefit of Section 8-502, which protects persons who acquire security entitlements for value, if it satisfies the other requirements of that section.

Example 3. Thief steals a certificated bearer bond from Owner. Thief sends the certificate to his broker Able & Co. to be held in his securities account, and Able credits Thief's account for the bond. Section 8-116 specifies that Able is a purchaser of the bond and gave value for it. Thus, Able can obtain the benefit of Section 8-303, which protects purchasers for value, if it satisfies the other requirements of that section.

SUBCHAPTER B. ISSUE AND ISSUER

§ 8.201. Issuer

(a) With respect to an obligation on or a defense to a security, "issuer" includes a person that:

(1) places or authorizes the placing of its name on a security certificate, other than as authenticating trustee, registrar, transfer agent, or the like, to evidence a share, participation, or other interest in its property or in an enterprise or to evidence its duty to perform an obligation represented by the certificate;

(2) creates a share, participation, or other interest in its property or in an enterprise, or undertakes an obligation, that is an uncertificated security;

(3) directly or indirectly creates a fractional interest in its rights or property, if the fractional interest is represented by a security certificate; or

(4) becomes responsible for, or in place of, another person described as an issuer in this section.

(b) With respect to an obligation on or defense to a security, a guarantor is an issuer to the extent of its guaranty, whether or not its obligation is noted on a security certificate.

(c) With respect to a registration of a transfer, "issuer" means a person on whose behalf transfer books are maintained.

Amended by Acts 1995, 74th Leg., ch. 962, § 1, eff. Sept. 1, 1995.

Uniform Commercial Code Comment

1. The definition of "issuer" in this section functions primarily to describe the persons whose defenses may be cut off under the rules in Part 2. In large measure it simply tracks the language of the definition of security in Section 8–102(a)(15).

2. Subsection (b) distinguishes the obligations of a guarantor as issuer from those of the principal obligor. However, it does not exempt the guarantor from the impact of subsection (d) of Section 8–202. Whether or not the obligation of the guarantor is noted on the security is immaterial. Typically, guarantors are parent corporations, or stand in some similar relationship to the principal obligor. If that relationship existed at the time the security was originally issued the guaranty would probably have been noted on the security. However, if the relationship arose afterward, e.g., through a purchase of stock or properties, or through merger or consolidation, probably the notation would not have been made. Nonetheless, the holder of the security is entitled to the benefit of the obligation of the guarantor.

3. Subsection (c) narrows the definition of "issuer" for purposes of Part 4 of this Article (registration of transfer). It is supplemented by Section 8–407.

§ 8.202. Issuer's Responsibility and Defenses; Notice of Defect or Defense

(a) Even against a purchaser for value and without notice, the terms of a certificated security include terms stated on the certificate and terms made part of the security by reference on the certificate to another instrument, indenture, or document or to a constitution, statute, ordinance, rule, regulation, order, or the like to the extent the terms referred to do not conflict with terms stated on the certificate. A reference under this subsection does not of itself charge a purchaser for value with notice of a defect going to the validity of the security, even if the certificate expressly states that a person accepting it admits notice. The terms of an uncertificated security include those stated in any instrument, indenture, or document or in a constitution, statute, ordinance, rule, regulation, order, or the like pursuant to which the security is issued.

(b) The following rules apply if an issuer asserts that a security is not valid:

(1) A security other than one issued by a government or governmental subdivision, agency, or instrumentality, even though issued with a defect going to its validity, is valid in the hands of a purchaser for value and without notice of the particular defect unless the defect involves a violation of a constitutional provision. In that case, the security is valid in the hands of a purchaser for value and without notice of the defect, other than a purchaser who takes by original issue.

(2) Subdivision (1) applies to an issuer that is a government or governmental subdivision, agency, or instrumentality only if:

(A) there has been substantial compliance with the legal requirements governing the issue; or

(B) the issuer has received a substantial consideration for the issue as a whole or for the particular security and a stated purpose of the issue is one for which the issuer has power to borrow money or issue the security.

(c) Except as otherwise provided in Section 8.205, lack of genuineness of a certificated security is a complete defense, even against a purchaser for value and without notice.

(d) All other defenses of the issuer of a security, including nondelivery and conditional delivery of a certificated security, are ineffective against a purchaser for value who has taken the certificated security without notice of the particular defense.

(e) This section does not affect the right of a party to cancel a contract for a security "when, as and if issued" or "when distributed" in the event of a material change in the character of the security that is the subject of the contract or in the plan or arrangement pursuant to which the security is to be issued or distributed.

(f) If a security is held by a securities intermediary against whom an entitlement holder has a security entitlement with respect to the security, the issuer may not assert any defense that the issuer could not assert if the entitlement holder held the security directly.

Amended by Acts 1995, 74th Leg., ch. 962, § 1, eff. Sept. 1, 1995.

Uniform Commercial Code Comment

1. In this Article the rights of the purchaser for value without notice are divided into two aspects, those against the issuer, and those against other claimants to the security. Part 2 of this Article, and especially this section, deal with rights against the issuer.

Subsection (a) states, in accordance with the prevailing case law, the right of the issuer (who prepares the text of the security) to include terms incorporated by adequate reference to an extrinsic source, so long as the terms so incorporated do not conflict with the stated terms. Thus, the standard practice of referring in a bond or debenture to the trust indenture under which it is issued without spelling out its necessarily complex and lengthy provisions is approved. Every stock certificate refers in some manner to the charter or articles of incorporation of the issuer. At least where there is more than one class of stock authorized applicable corporation codes specifically require a statement or summary as to preferences, voting powers and the like. References to constitutions, statutes, ordinances, rules, regulations or orders are not so common, except in the obligations of governments or governmental agencies or units; but where appropriate they fit into the rule here stated.

Courts have generally held that an issuer is estopped from denying representations made in the text of a security. *Delaware-New Jersey Ferry Co. v. Leeds*, 21 Del.Ch. 279, 186 A. 913 (1936). Nor is a defect in form or the invalidity of a security normally available to the issuer as a defense. *Bonini v. Family Theatre Corporation*, 327 Pa. 273, 194 A. 498 (1937); *First National Bank of Fairbanks v. Alaska Airmotive*, 119 F.2d 267 (C.C.A.Alaska 1941).

2. The rule in subsection (a) requiring that the terms of a security be noted or referred to on the certificate is based on practices and expectations in the direct holding system for certificated securities. This rule does not express a general rule or policy that the terms of a security are effective only if they are communicated to beneficial owners in some particular fashion. Rather, subsection (a) is based on the principle that a purchaser who does obtain a certificate is entitled to assume that the terms of the security have been noted or referred to on the certificate. That policy does not come into play in a securities holding system in which purchasers do not take delivery of certificates.

The provisions of subsection (a) concerning notation of terms on security certificates are necessary only because paper certificates play such an important role for certificated securities that a purchaser should be protected against assertion of any defenses or rights that are not noted on the certificate. No similar problem exists with respect to uncertificated securities. The last sentence of subsection (a) is, strictly speaking, unnecessary, since it only recognizes the fact that the terms of an uncertificated security are determined by whatever other law or agreement governs the security. It is included only to preclude any inference that uncertificated securities are subject to any requirement analogous to the requirement of notation of terms on security certificates.

The rule of subsection (a) applies to the indirect holding system only in the sense that if a certificated security has been delivered to the clearing corporation or other securities intermediary, the terms of the security should be noted or referred to on the certificate. If the security is uncertificated, that principle does not apply even at the issuer-clearing corporation level. The beneficial owners who hold securities through the clearing corporation are bound by the terms of the security, even though they do not actually see the certificate. Since entitlement holders in an indirect holding system have not taken delivery of certificates, the policy of subsection (a) does not apply.

3. The penultimate sentence of subsection (a) and all of subsection (b) embody the concept that it is the duty of the issuer, not of the purchaser, to make sure that the security complies with the law governing its issue. The penultimate sentence of subsection (a) makes clear that the issuer cannot, by incorporating a reference to a statute or other document, charge the purchaser with notice of the security's invalidity. Subsection (b) gives to a purchaser for value without notice of the defect the right to enforce the security against the issuer despite the presence of a defect that otherwise would render the security invalid. There are three circumstances in which a purchaser does not gain such rights: first, if the defect involves a violation of constitutional provisions, these rights accrue only to a subsequent purchaser, that is, one who takes other than by original issue. This Article leaves to the law of each particular State the rights of a purchaser on original issue of a security with a constitutional defect. No negative implication is intended by the explicit grant of rights to a subsequent purchaser.

Second, governmental issuers are distinguished in subsection (b) from other issuers as a matter of public policy, and additional safeguards are imposed before governmental issues are validated. Governmental issuers are estopped from asserting defenses only if there has been substantial compliance with the legal requirements governing the issue or if substantial consideration has been received and a stated purpose of the issue is one for which the issuer has power to borrow money or issue the security. The purpose of the substantial compliance requirement is to make certain that a mere technicality as, e.g., in the manner of publishing election notices, shall not be a ground for depriving an innocent purchaser of rights in the security. The policy is here adopted of such cases as *Tommie v. City of Gadsden*, 229 Ala. 521, 158 So. 763 (1935), in which minor discrepancies in the form of the election ballot used were overlooked and the bonds were declared valid since there had been substantial compliance with the statute.

A long and well established line of federal cases recognizes the principle of estoppel in favor of purchasers for value without notices where municipalities issue bonds containing recitals of compliance with governing constitutional and statutory provisions, made by the municipal authorities entrusted with determining such compliance. *Chaffee County v. Potter*, 142 U.S. 355 (1892); *Oregon v. Jennings*, 119 U.S. 74 (1886); *Gunnison County Commissioners v. Rollins*, 173 U.S. 255 (1898). This rule has been qualified, however, by requiring that the municipality have power to issue the security. *Anthony v. County of Jasper*, 101 U.S. 693 (1879); *Town of South Ottawa v. Perkins*, 94 U.S. 260 (1876). This section follows the case law trend, simplifying the rule by setting up two conditions for an estoppel against a governmental issuer: (1) substantial consideration given, and (2) power in the issuer to borrow money or issue the security for the stated purpose. As a practical matter the problem of policing governmental issuers has been alleviated by the present practice of requiring legal opinions as to the validity of the issue. The bulk of the case law on this point is nearly 100 years old and it may be assumed that the question now seldom arises.

Section 8–210, regarding overissue, provides the third exception to the rule that an innocent purchase for value takes a valid security despite the presence of a defect that would otherwise give rise to invalidity. See that section and its Comment for further explanation.

4. Subsection (e) is included to make clear that this section does not affect the presently recognized right of either party to a "when, as and if" or "when distributed" contract to cancel the contract on substantial change.

5. Subsection (f) has been added because the introduction of the security entitlement concept requires some adaptation of the Part 2 rules, particularly those that distinguish between purchasers who take by original issue and subsequent purchasers. The basic concept of Part 2 is to apply to investment securities the principle of negotiable instruments law that an obligor is precluded from asserting most defenses against purchasers for value without notice. Section 8–202 describes in some detail which defenses issuers can raise against purchasers for value and subsequent purchasers for value. Because these rules were drafted with the direct holding system in mind, some interpretive problems might be presented in applying them to the indirect holding. For example, if a municipality issues a bond in book-entry only form, the only direct "purchaser" of that bond would be the clearing corporation. The policy of precluding the issuer from asserting defenses is, however, equally applicable. Subsection (f) is designed to ensure that the defense preclusion rules developed for the direct holding system will also apply to the indirect holding system.

"(a) This Act does not affect an action or proceeding commenced before this Act takes effect [Sept. 1, 1995].

"(b) If a security interest in a security is perfected under Chapter 8, Business & Commerce Code, on the date this Act takes effect, and the action by which the security interest was perfected would suffice to perfect a security interest under Chapter 9, Business & Commerce Code, as amended by this Act, no further action is required to continue perfection. If a security interest in a security is perfected under Chapter 8, Business & Commerce Code, on the date this Act takes effect but the action by which the security interest was perfected would not suffice to perfect a security interest under Chapter 9, Business & Commerce Code, as amended by this Act, the security interest remains perfected until January 1, 1996, and continues perfected on and after that date if appropriate action to perfect under Chapter 9, Business & Commerce Code, as amended by this Act is taken before January 1, 1996. If a security interest is perfected under Chapter 8, Business & Commerce Code, on the date this Act takes effect and the security interest can be perfected by filing under Chapter 9, Business & Commerce Code, as amended by this Act, a financing statement signed by the secured party instead of the debtor may be filed before January 1, 1996, to continue perfection or filed on or after that date to perfect."

§ 8.203. Staleness as Notice of Defect or Defense

After an act or event, other than a call that has been revoked, creating a right to immediate performance of the principal obligation represented by a certificated security or setting a date on or after which the security is to be presented or surrendered for redemption or exchange, a purchaser is charged with notice of any defect in its issue or defense of the issuer if the act or event:

(1) requires the payment of money, the delivery of a certificated security, the registration of transfer of an uncertificated security, or any of them on presentation or surrender of the security certificate, the money or security is available on the date set for payment or exchange, and the purchaser takes the security more than one year after that date; or

(2) is not covered by Subdivision (1) and the purchaser takes the security more than two years after the date set for surrender or presentation or the date on which performance became due.

Amended by Acts 1995, 74th Leg., ch. 962, § 1, eff. Sept. 1, 1995.

Uniform Commercial Code Comment

1. The problem of matured or called securities is here dealt with in terms of the effect of such events in giving notice of the issuer's defenses and not in terms of "negotiability". The substance of this section applies only to certificated securities because certificates may be transferred to a purchaser by delivery after the security has matured, been called, or become redeemable or exchangeable. It is contemplated that uncertificated securities which have matured or been called will merely be canceled on the books of the issuer and the proceeds sent to the registered owner. Uncertificated securities which have become redeemable or exchangeable, at the option of the owner, may be transferred to a purchaser, but the transfer is effectuated only by registration

of transfer, thus necessitating communication with the issuer. If defects or defenses in such securities exist, the issuer will necessarily have the opportunity to bring them to the attention of the purchaser.

2. The fact that a security certificate is in circulation long after it has been called for redemption or exchange must give rise to the question in a purchaser's mind as to why it has not been surrendered. After the lapse of a reasonable period of time a purchaser can no longer claim "no reason to know" of any defects or irregularities in its issue. Where funds are available for the redemption the security certificate is normally turned in more promptly and a shorter time is set as the "reasonable period" than is set where funds are not available.

Defaulted certificated securities may be traded on financial markets in the same manner as unmatured and undefaulted instruments and a purchaser might not be placed upon notice of irregularity by the mere fact of default. An issuer, however, should at some point be placed in a position to determine definitely its liability on an invalid or improper issue, and for this purpose a security under this section becomes "stale" two years after the default. A different rule applies when the question is notice not of issuer's defenses but of claims of ownership. Section 8–105 and Comment.

3. Nothing in this section is designed to extend the life of preferred stocks called for redemption as "shares of stock" beyond the redemption date. After such a call, the security represents only a right to the funds set aside for redemption.

§ 8.204. Effect of Issuer's Restriction on Transfer

A restriction on transfer of a security imposed by the issuer, even if otherwise lawful, is ineffective against a person without knowledge of the restriction unless:

(1) the security is certificated and the restriction is noted conspicuously on the security certificate; or

(2) the security is uncertificated and the registered owner has been notified of the restriction.

Amended by Acts 1995, 74th Leg., ch. 962, § 1, eff. Sept. 1, 1995.

Uniform Commercial Code Comment

1. Restrictions on transfer of securities are imposed by issuers in a variety of circumstances and for a variety of purposes, such as to retain control of a close corporation or to ensure compliance with federal securities laws. Other law determines whether such restrictions are permissible. This section deals only with the consequences of failure to note the restriction on a security certificate.

This section imposes no bar to enforcement of a restriction on transfer against a person who has actual knowledge of it.

2. A restriction on transfer of a certificated security is ineffective against a person without knowledge of the restriction unless the restriction is noted conspicuously on the certificate. The word "noted" is used to make clear that the restriction need not be set forth in full text. Refusal by an issuer to register a transfer on the basis of an unnoted restriction would be a violation of the issuer's duty to register under Section 8–401.

3. The policy of this section is the same as in Section 8–202. A purchaser who takes delivery of a certificated security is entitled to rely on the terms stated on the certificate. That policy obviously does not apply to uncertificated securities. For uncertificated securities, this section requires only that the registered owner has been notified of the restriction. Suppose, for example, that A is the registered owner of an uncertificated security, and that the issuer has notified A of a restriction on transfer. A agrees to sell the security to B, in violation of the restriction. A completes a written instruction directing the issuer to register transfer to B, and B pays A for the security at the time A delivers the instruction to B. A does not inform B of the restriction, and B does not otherwise have notice or knowledge of it at the time B pays and receives the instruction. B presents the instruction to the issuer, but the issuer refuses to register the transfer on the grounds that it would violate the restriction. The issuer has complied with this section, because it did notify the registered owner A of the restriction. The issuer's refusal to register transfer is not wrongful. B has an action against A for breach of transfer warranty, see Section 8–108(b)(4)(iii). B's mistake was treating an uncertificated security transaction in the fashion appropriate only for a certificated security. The mechanism for transfer of uncertificated securities is registration of transfer on the books of the issuer; handing over an instruction only initiates the process. The purchaser should make arrangements to ensure that the price is not paid until it knows that the issuer has or will register transfer.

4. In the indirect holding system, investors neither take physical delivery of security certificates nor have uncertificated securities registered in their names. So long as the requirements of this section have been satisfied at the level of the relationship between the issuer and the securities intermediary that is a direct holder, this section does not preclude the issuer from enforcing a restriction on transfer. See Section 8–202(a) and Comment 2 thereto.

5. This section deals only with restrictions imposed by the issuer. Restrictions imposed by statute are not affected. See *Quiner v. Marblehead Social Co.*, 10 Mass. 476 (1813); *Madison Bank v. Price*, 79 Kan. 289, 100 P. 280 (1909); *Healey v. Steele Center Creamery Ass'n*, 115 Minn. 451, 133 N.W. 69 (1911). Nor does it deal with private agreements between stockholders containing restrictive covenants as to the sale of the security.

§ 8.205. Effect of Unauthorized Signature on Security Certificate

An unauthorized signature placed on a security certificate before or in the course of issue is ineffective, but the signature is effective in favor of a purchaser for value of the certificated security if the purchaser is without notice of the lack of authority and the signing has been done by:

(1) an authenticating trustee, registrar, transfer agent, or other person entrusted by the issuer with

the signing of the security certificate or of similar security certificates or with the immediate preparation for signing of any of them; or

(2) an employee of the issuer, or of any of the persons listed in Subdivision (1), entrusted with responsible handling of the security certificate.

Amended by Acts 1995, 74th Leg., ch. 962, § 1, eff. Sept. 1, 1995.

Uniform Commercial Code Comment

1. The problem of forged or unauthorized signatures may arise where an employee of the issuer, transfer agent, or registrar has access to securities which the employee is required to prepare for issue by affixing the corporate seal or by adding a signature necessary for issue. This section is based upon the issuer's duty to avoid the negligent entrusting of securities to such persons. Issuers have long been held responsible for signatures placed upon securities by parties whom they have held out to the public as authorized to prepare such securities. See *Fifth Avenue Bank of New York v. The Forty–Second & Grand Street Ferry Railroad Co.*, 137 N.Y. 231, 33 N.E. 378, 19 L.R.A. 331, 33 Am.St.Rep. 712 (1893); *Jarvis v. Manhattan Beach Co.*, 148 N.Y. 652, 43 N.E. 68, 31 L.R.A. 776, 51 Am.St.Rep. 727 (1896). The "apparent authority" concept of some of the case-law, however, is here extended and this section expressly rejects the technical distinction, made by courts reluctant to recognize forged signatures, between cases where forgers sign signatures they are authorized to sign under proper circumstances and those in which they sign signatures they are never authorized to sign. *Citizens' & Southern National Bank v. Trust Co. of Georgia*, 50 Ga.App. 681, 179 S.E. 278 (1935). Normally the purchaser is not in a position to determine which signature a forger, entrusted with the preparation of securities, has "apparent authority" to sign. The issuer, on the other hand, can protect itself against such fraud by the careful selection and bonding of agents and employees, or by action over against transfer agents and registrars who in turn may bond their personnel.

2. The issuer cannot be held liable for the honesty of employees not entrusted, directly or indirectly, with the signing, preparation, or responsible handling of similar securities and whose possible commission of forgery it has no reason to anticipate. The result in such cases as *Hudson Trust Co. v. American Linseed Co.*, 232 N.Y. 350, 134 N.E. 178 (1922), and *Dollar Savings Fund & Trust Co. v. Pittsburgh Plate Glass Co.*, 213 Pa. 307, 62 A. 916, 5 Ann.Cas. 248 (1906) is here adopted.

3. This section is not concerned with forged or unauthorized indorsements, but only with unauthorized signatures of issuers, transfer agents, etc., placed upon security certificates during the course of their issue. The protection here stated is available to all purchasers for value without notice and not merely to subsequent purchasers.

§ 8.206. Completion or Alteration of Security Certificate

(a) If a security certificate contains the signatures necessary to its issue or transfer but is incomplete in any other respect:

(1) any person may complete it by filling in the blanks as authorized; and

(2) even if the blanks are incorrectly filled in, the security certificate as completed is enforceable by a purchaser who took it for value and without notice of the incorrectness.

(b) A complete security certificate that has been improperly altered, even if fraudulently, remains enforceable, but only according to its original terms.

Amended by Acts 1995, 74th Leg., ch. 962, § 1, eff. Sept. 1, 1995.

Uniform Commercial Code Comment

1. The problem of forged or unauthorized signatures necessary for the issue or transfer of a security is not involved here, and a person in possession of a blank certificate is not, by this section, given authority to fill in blanks with such signatures. Completion of blanks left in a transfer instruction is dealt with elsewhere (Section 8–305(a)).

2. Blanks left upon issue of a security certificate are the only ones dealt with here, and a purchaser for value without notice is protected. A purchaser is not in a good position to determine whether blanks were completed by the issuer or by some person not authorized to complete them. On the other hand the issuer can protect itself by not placing its signature on the writing until the blanks are completed or, if it does sign before all blanks are completed, by carefully selecting the agents and employees to whom it entrusts the writing after authentication. With respect to a security certificate that is completed by the issuer but later is altered, the issuer has done everything it can to protect the purchaser and thus is not charged with the terms as altered. However, it is charged according to the original terms, since it is not thereby prejudiced. If the completion or alteration is obviously irregular, the purchaser may not qualify as a purchaser who took without notice under this section.

3. Only the purchaser who physically takes the certificate is directly protected. However, a transferee may receive protection indirectly through Section 8–302(a).

4. The protection granted a purchaser for value without notice under this section is modified to the extent that an overissue may result where an incorrect amount is inserted into a blank (Section 8–210).

§ 8.207. Rights and Duties of Issuer With Respect to Registered Owners

(a) Before due presentment for registration of transfer of a certificated security in registered form or of an instruction requesting registration of transfer of an uncertificated security, the issuer or indenture trustee may treat the registered owner as the person exclusively entitled to vote, receive notifications, and otherwise exercise all the rights and powers of an owner.

(b) This chapter does not affect the liability of the registered owner of a security for a call, assessment, or the like.

Amended by Acts 1995, 74th Leg., ch. 962, § 1, eff. Sept. 1, 1995.

Uniform Commercial Code Comment

1. Subsection (a) states the issuer's right to treat the registered owner of a security as the person entitled to exercise all the rights of an owner. This right of the issuer is limited by the provisions of Part 4 of this article. Once there has been due presentation for registration of transfer, the issuer has a duty to register ownership in the name of the transferee. Section 8–401. Thus its right to treat the old registered owner as exclusively entitled to the rights of ownership must cease.

The issuer may under this section make distributions of money or securities to the registered owners of securities without requiring further proof of ownership, provided that such distributions are distributable to the owners of all securities of the same issue and the terms of the security do not require surrender of a security certificate as a condition of payment or exchange. Any such distribution shall constitute a defense against a claim for the same distribution by a person, even if that person is in possession of the security certificate and is a protected purchaser of the security. See PEB Commentary No. 4, dated March 10, 1990.

2. Subsection (a) is permissive and does not require that the issuer deal exclusively with the registered owner. It is free to require proof of ownership before paying out dividends or the like if it chooses to. *Barbato v. Breeze Corporation*, 128 N.J.L. 309, 26 A.2d 53 (1942).

3. This section does not operate to determine who is finally entitled to exercise voting and other rights or to receive payments and distributions. The parties are still free to incorporate their own arrangements as to these matters in seller-purchaser agreements which may be definitive as between them.

4. No change in existing state laws as to the liability of registered owners for calls and assessments is here intended; nor is anything in this section designed to estop record holders from denying ownership when assessments are levied if they are otherwise entitled to do so under state law. See *State ex rel. Squire v. Murfey, Blosson & Co.*, 131 Ohio St. 289, 2 N.E.2d 866 (1936); *Willing v. Delaplaine*, 23 F.Supp. 579 (1937).

5. No interference is intended with the common practice of closing the transfer books or taking a record date for dividend, voting, and other purposes, as provided for in by-laws, charters, and statutes.

§ 8.208. Effect of Signature of Authenticating Trustee, Registrar, or Transfer Agent

(a) A person signing a security certificate as authenticating trustee, registrar, transfer agent, or the like warrants to a purchaser for value of the certificated security, if the purchaser is without notice of a particular defect, that:

(1) the certificate is genuine;

(2) the person's own participation in the issue of the security is within the person's capacity and within the scope of the authority received by the person from the issuer; and

(3) the person has reasonable grounds to believe that the certificated security is in the form and within the amount the issuer is authorized to issue.

(b) Unless otherwise agreed, a person signing under Subsection (a) does not assume responsibility for the validity of the security in other respects.

Amended by Acts 1995, 74th Leg., ch. 962, § 1, eff. Sept. 1, 1995.

Uniform Commercial Code Comment

1. The warranties here stated express the current understanding and prevailing case law as to the effect of the signatures of authenticating trustees, transfer agents, and registrars. See *Jarvis v. Manhattan Beach Co.*, 148 N.Y. 652, 43 N.E. 68, 31 L.R.A. 776, 51 Am.St.Rep. 727 (1896). Although it has generally been regarded as the particular obligation of the transfer agent to determine whether securities are in proper form as provided by the by-laws and Articles of Incorporation, neither a registrar nor an authenticating trustee should properly place a signature upon a certificate without determining whether it is at least regular on its face. The obligations of these parties in this respect have therefore been made explicit in terms of due care. See *Feldmeier v. Mortgage Securities, Inc.*, 34 Cal.App.2d 201, 93 P.2d 593 (1939).

2. Those cases which hold that an authenticating trustee is not liable for any defect in the mortgage or property which secures the bond or for any fraudulent misrepresentations made by the issuer are not here affected since these matters do not involve the genuineness or proper form of the security. *Ainsa v. Mercantile Trust Co.*, 174 Cal. 504, 163 P. 898 (1917); *Tschetinian v. City Trust Co.*, 186 N.Y. 432, 79 N.E. 401 (1906); *Davidge v. Guardian Trust Co. of New York*, 203 N.Y. 331, 96 N.E. 751 (1911).

3. The charter or an applicable statute may affect the capacity of a bank or other corporation undertaking to act as an authenticating trustee, registrar, or transfer agent. See, for example, the Federal Reserve Act (U.S.C.A., Title 12, Banks and Banking, Section 248) under which the Board of Governors of the Federal Reserve Bank is authorized to grant special permits to National Banks permitting them to act as trustees. Such corporations are therefore held to certify as to their legal capacity to act as well as to their authority.

4. Authenticating trustees, registrars, and transfer agents have normally been held liable for an issue in excess of the authorized amount. *Jarvis v. Manhattan Beach Co.*, supra; *Mullen v. Eastern Trust & Banking Co.*, 108 Me. 498, 81 A. 948 (1911). In imposing upon these parties a duty of due care with respect to the amount they are authorized to

help issue, this section does not necessarily validate the security, but merely holds persons responsible for the excess issue liable in damages for any loss suffered by the purchaser.

5. Aside from questions of genuineness and excess issue, these parties are not held to certify as to the validity of the security unless they specifically undertake to do so. The case law which has recognized a unique responsibility on the transfer agent's part to testify as to the validity of any security which it countersigns is rejected.

6. This provision does not prevent a transfer agent or issuer from agreeing with a registrar of stock to protect the registrar in respect of the genuineness and proper form of a security certificate signed by the issuer or the transfer agent or both. Nor does it interfere with proper indemnity arrangements between the issuer and trustees, transfer agents, registrars, and the like.

7. An unauthorized signature is a signature for purposes of this section if and only if it is made effective by Section 8–205.

§ 8.209. Issuer's Lien

A lien in favor of an issuer on a certificated security is valid against a purchaser only if the right of the issuer to the lien is noted conspicuously on the security certificate.

Added by Acts 1995, 74th Leg., ch. 962, § 1, eff. Sept. 1, 1996.

Uniform Commercial Code Comment

This section is similar to Sections 8–202 and 8–204 which require that the terms of a certificated security and any restriction on transfer imposed by the issuer be noted on the security certificate. This section differs from those two sections in that the purchaser's knowledge of the issuer's claim is irrelevant. "Noted" makes clear that the text of the lien provisions need not be set forth in full. However, this would not override a provision of an applicable corporation code requiring statement in haec verba. This section does not apply to uncertificated securities. It applies to the indirect holding system in the same fashion as Sections 8–202 and 8–204, see Comment 2 to Section 8–202.

Section 21 of Acts 1995, 74th Leg., ch. 962, as amended by Acts 1997, 75th Leg., ch. 165, § 3.01, provides:

"(a) This Act does not affect an action or proceeding commenced before this Act takes effect [Sept. 1, 1995].

"(b) If a security interest in a security is perfected under Chapter 8, Business & Commerce Code, on the date this Act takes effect, and the action by which the security interest was perfected would suffice to perfect a security interest under Chapter 9, Business & Commerce Code, as amended by this Act, no further action is required to continue perfection. If a security interest in a security is perfected under Chapter 8, Business & Commerce Code, on the date this Act takes effect but the action by which the security interest was perfected would not suffice to perfect a security interest under Chapter 9, Business & Commerce Code, as amended by this Act, the security interest remains perfected until January 1, 1996, and continues perfected on and after that date if appropriate action to perfect under Chapter 9, Business & Commerce Code, as amended by this Act is taken before January 1, 1996. If a security interest is perfected under Chapter 8, Business & Commerce Code, on the date this Act takes effect and the security interest can be perfected by filing under Chapter 9, Business & Commerce Code, as amended by this Act, a financing statement signed by the secured party instead of the debtor may be filed before January 1, 1996, to continue perfection or filed on or after that date to perfect."

§ 8.210. Overissue

(a) In this section, "overissue" means the issue of securities in excess of the amount the issuer has corporate power to issue, but an overissue does not occur if appropriate action has cured the overissue.

(b) Except as otherwise provided in Subsections (c) and (d), the provisions of this chapter that validate a security or compel its issue or reissue do not apply to the extent that validation, issue, or reissue would result in overissue.

(c) If an identical security not constituting an overissue is reasonably available for purchase, a person entitled to issue or validation may compel the issuer to purchase the security and deliver it if certificated or register its transfer if uncertificated, against surrender of any security certificate the person holds.

(d) If a security is not reasonably available for purchase, a person entitled to issue or validation may recover from the issuer the price the person or the last purchaser for value paid for it with interest from the date of the person's demand.

Added by Acts 1995, 74th Leg., ch. 962, § 1, eff. Sept. 1, 1995.

Uniform Commercial Code Comment

1. Deeply embedded in corporation law is the conception that "corporate power" to issue securities stems from the statute, either general or special, under which the corporation is organized. Corporation codes universally require that the charter or articles of incorporation state, at least as to capital shares, maximum limits in terms of number of shares or total dollar capital. Historically, special incorporation statutes are similarly drawn and sometimes similarly limit the face amount of authorized debt securities. The theory is that issue of securities in excess of the authorized amounts is prohibited. See, for example, *McWilliams v. Geddes & Moss Undertaking Co.*, 169 So. 894 (1936, La.); *Crawford v. Twin City Oil Co.*, 216 Ala. 216, 113 So. 61 (1927); *New York and New Haven R.R. Co. v. Schuyler*, 34 N.Y. 30 (1865). This conception persists despite modern corporation codes under which, by action of directors and stockholders, additional shares can be authorized by charter amendment and thereafter issued. This section does not give a person entitled to validation, issue, or reissue of a security, the right to compel amendment of the charter to authorize additional shares. Therefore, in a case where issue of an additional security would require charter amendment, the plaintiff is limited to the two alternate remedies set forth in subsections (c) and (d). The last clause of subsection (a), which is added in

Revised Article 8, does, however, recognize that under modern conditions, overissue may be a relatively minor technical problem that can be cured by appropriate action under governing corporate law.

2. Where an identical security is reasonably available for purchase, whether because traded on an organized market, or because one or more security owners may be willing to sell at a not unreasonable price, the issuer, although unable to issue additional shares, will be able to purchase them and may be compelled to follow that procedure. *West v. Tintic Standard Mining Co.*, 71 Utah 158, 263 P. 490 (1928).

3. The right to recover damages from an issuer who has permitted an overissue to occur is well settled. *New York and New Haven R.R. Co. v. Schuyler*, 34 N.Y. 30 (1865). The measure of such damages, however, has been open to question, some courts basing them upon the value of stock at the time registration is refused; some upon the value at the time of trial; and some upon the highest value between the time of refusal and the time of trial. *Allen v. South Boston Railroad*, 150 Mass. 200, 22 N.E. 917, 5 L.R.A. 716, 15 Am.St.Rep. 185 (1889); *Commercial Bank v. Kortright*, 22 Wend. (N.Y.) 348 (1839). The purchase price of the security to the last purchaser who gave value for it is here adopted as being the fairest means of reducing the possibility of speculation by the purchaser. Interest may be recovered as the best available measure of compensation for delay.

SUBCHAPTER C. TRANSFER OF CERTIFICATED AND UNCERTIFICATED SECURITIES

§ 8.301. Delivery

(a) Delivery of a certificated security to a purchaser occurs when:

(1) the purchaser acquires possession of the security certificate;

(2) another person, other than a securities intermediary, either acquires possession of the security certificate on behalf of the purchaser or, having previously acquired possession of the certificate, acknowledges that it holds for the purchaser; or

(3) a securities intermediary acting on behalf of the purchaser acquires possession of the security certificate, only if the certificate is in registered form and is (i) registered in the name of the purchaser, (ii) payable to the order of the purchaser, or (iii) specially indorsed to the purchaser by an effective indorsement and has not been indorsed to the securities intermediary or in blank.

(b) Delivery of an uncertificated security to a purchaser occurs when:

(1) the issuer registers the purchaser as the registered owner, on original issue or registration of transfer; or

(2) another person, other than a securities intermediary, either becomes the registered owner of the uncertificated security on behalf of the purchaser or, having previously become the registered owner, acknowledges that it holds for the purchaser.

Amended by Acts 1995, 74th Leg., ch. 962, § 1, eff. Sept. 1, 1995; Acts 1999, 76th Leg., ch. 414, § 2.29, eff. July 1, 2001.

Uniform Commercial Code Comment

1. This section specifies the requirements for "delivery" of securities. Delivery is used in Article 8 to describe the formal steps necessary for a purchaser to acquire a direct interest in a security under this Article. The concept of delivery refers to the implementation of a transaction, not the legal categorization of the transaction which is consummated by delivery. Issuance and transfer are different kinds of transaction, though both may be implemented by delivery. Sale and pledge are different kinds of transfers, but both may be implemented by delivery.

2. Subsection (a) defines delivery with respect to certificated securities. Paragraph (1) deals with simple cases where purchasers themselves acquire physical possession of certificates. Paragraphs (2) and (3) of subsection (a) specify the circumstances in which delivery to a purchaser can occur although the certificate is in the possession of a person other than the purchaser. Paragraph (2) contains the general rule that a purchaser can take delivery through another person, so long as the other person is actually acting on behalf of the purchaser or acknowledges that it is holding on behalf of the purchaser. Paragraph (2) does not apply to acquisition of possession by a securities intermediary, because a person who holds securities through a securities account acquires a security entitlement, rather than having a direct interest. See Section 8-501. Subsection (a)(3) specifies the limited circumstances in which delivery of security certificates to a securities intermediary is treated as a delivery to the customer. Note that delivery is a method of perfecting a security interest in a certificated security. See Section 9-313(a), (e).

3. Subsection (b) defines delivery with respect to uncertificated securities. Use of the term "delivery" with respect to uncertificated securities, does, at least on first hearing, seem a bit solecistic. The word "delivery" is, however, routinely used in the securities business in a broader sense than manual tradition. For example, settlement by entries on the books of a clearing corporation is commonly called "delivery," as in the expression "delivery versus payment." The diction of this section has the advantage of using the same term for uncertificated securities as for certificated securities, for which delivery is conventional usage. Paragraph (1) of subsection (b) provides that delivery occurs when the purchaser becomes the registered owner of an uncertificated security, either upon original issue or registration of transfer. Paragraph (2) provides for delivery of an uncertificated security through a third person, in a fashion analogous to subsection (a)(2).

§ 8.302. Rights of Purchaser

(a) Except as otherwise provided in Subsections (b) and (c), a purchaser of a certificated or uncertificated security acquires all rights in the security that the transferor had or had power to transfer.

(b) A purchaser of a limited interest acquires rights only to the extent of the interest purchased.

(c) A purchaser of a certificated security who as a previous holder had notice of an adverse claim does not improve its position by taking from a protected purchaser.

Amended by Acts 1995, 74th Leg., ch. 962, § 1, eff. Sept. 1, 1995; Acts 1999, 76th Leg., ch. 414, § 2.30, eff. July 1, 2001.

Uniform Commercial Code Comment

1. Subsection (a) provides that if purchaser of a certificated or uncertificated security acquires all rights that the transferor had or had power to transfer. This statement of the familiar "shelter" principle is qualified by the exceptions that a purchaser of a limited interest acquires only that interest, subsection (b), and that a person who does not qualify as a protected purchaser cannot improve its position by taking from a subsequent protected purchaser, subsection (c).

2. Although this section provides that a purchaser acquires a property interest in a certificated or uncertificated security, it does not state that a person can acquire an interest in a security only by purchase. Article 8 also is not a comprehensive codification of all of the law governing the creation or transfer of interests in securities by purchase. For example, the grant of a security interest is a transfer of a property interest, but the formal steps necessary to effectuate such a transfer are governed by Article 9 not by Article 8. Under the Article 9 rules, a security interest in a certificated or uncertificated security can be created by execution of a security agreement under Section 9–203 and can be perfected by filing. A transfer of an Article 9 security interest can be implemented by an Article 8 delivery, but need not be.

Similarly, Article 8 does not determine whether a property interest in certificated or uncertificated security is acquired under other law, such as the law of gifts, trusts, or equitable remedies. Nor does Article 8 deal with transfers by operation of law. For example, transfers from decedent to administrator, from ward to guardian, and from bankrupt to trustee in bankruptcy are governed by other law as to both the time they occur and the substance of the transfer. The Article 8 rules do, however, determine whether the issuer is obligated to recognize the rights that a third party, such as a transferee, may acquire under other law. See Sections 8–207, 8–401, and 8–404.

§ 8.303. Protected Purchaser

(a) "Protected purchaser" means a purchaser of a certificated or uncertificated security, or of an interest therein, who:

(1) gives value;

(2) does not have notice of any adverse claim to the security; and

(3) obtains control of the certificated or uncertificated security.

(b) In addition to acquiring the rights of a purchaser, a protected purchaser also acquires its interest in the security free of any adverse claim.

Amended by Acts 1995, 74th Leg., ch. 962, § 1, eff. Sept. 1, 1995.

Uniform Commercial Code Comment

1. Subsection (a) lists the requirements that a purchaser must meet to qualify as a "protected purchaser." Subsection (b) provides that a protected purchaser takes its interest free from adverse claims. "Purchaser" is defined broadly in Section 1–201. A secured party as well as an outright buyer can qualify as a protected purchaser. Also, "purchase" includes taking by issue, so a person to whom a security is originally issued can qualify as a protected purchaser.

2. To qualify as a protected purchaser, a purchaser must give value, take without notice of any adverse claim, and obtain control. Value is used in the broad sense defined in Section 1–201(44). See also Section 8–116 (securities intermediary as purchaser for value). Adverse claim is defined in Section 8–102(a)(1). Section 8–105 specifies whether a purchaser has notice of an adverse claim. Control is defined in Section 8–106. To qualify as a protected purchaser there must be a time at which all of the requirements are satisfied. Thus if a purchaser obtains notice of an adverse claim before giving value or satisfying the requirements for control, the purchaser cannot be a protected purchaser. See also Section 8–304(d).

The requirement that a protected purchaser obtain control expresses the point that to qualify for the adverse claim cut-off rule a purchaser must take through a transaction that is implemented by the appropriate mechanism. By contrast, the rules in Part 2 provide that any purchaser for value of a security without notice of a defense may take free of the issuer's defense based on that defense. See Section 8–202.

3. The requirements for control differ depending on the form of the security. For securities represented by bearer certificates, a purchaser obtains control by delivery. See Sections 8–106(a) and 8–301(a). For securities represented by certificates in registered form, the requirements for control are: (1) delivery as defined in Section 8–301(b), plus (2) either an effective indorsement or registration of transfer by the issuer. See Section 8–106(b). Thus, a person who takes through a forged indorsement does not qualify as a protected purchaser by virtue of the delivery alone. If, however, the purchaser presents the certificate to the issuer for registration of transfer, and the issuer registers transfer over the forged indorsement, the purchaser can qualify as a protected purchaser of the new certificate. If the issuer registers transfer on a forged indorsement, the true owner will be able to recover from the issuer for wrongful registration, see Section 8–404, unless the owner's delay in notifying the issuer of a loss or theft of the certificate results in preclusion under Section 8–406.

For uncertificated securities, a purchaser can obtain control either by delivery, see Sections 8–106(c)(1) and 8–301(b), or by obtaining an agreement pursuant to which the issuer agrees to act on instructions from the purchaser without further consent from the registered owner, see Section 8–106(c)(2). The control agreement device of Section 8–106(c)(2) takes the place of the "registered pledge" concept of the 1978 version of Article 8. A secured lender who obtains a control agreement under Section 8–106(c)(2) can qualify as a protected purchaser of an uncertificated security.

4. This section states directly the rules determining whether one takes free from adverse claims without using the phrase "good faith." Whether a person who takes under suspicious circumstances is disqualified is determined by the rules of Section 8–105 on notice of adverse claims. The term "protected purchaser," which replaces the term "bona fide purchaser" used in the prior version of Article 8, is derived from the term "protected holder" used in the Convention on International Bills and Notes prepared by the United Nations Commission on International Trade Law ("UNCITRAL").

§ 8.304. Indorsement

(a) An indorsement may be in blank or special. An indorsement in blank includes an indorsement to bearer. A special indorsement specifies to whom a security is to be transferred or who has power to transfer it. A holder may convert a blank indorsement to a special indorsement.

(b) An indorsement purporting to be only of part of a security certificate representing units intended by the issuer to be separately transferable is effective to the extent of the indorsement.

(c) An indorsement, whether special or in blank, does not constitute a transfer until delivery of the certificate on which it appears or, if the indorsement is on a separate document, until delivery of both the document and the certificate.

(d) If a security certificate in registered form has been delivered to a purchaser without a necessary indorsement, the purchaser may become a protected purchaser only when the indorsement is supplied. However, against a transferor, a transfer is complete on delivery and the purchaser has a specifically enforceable right to have any necessary indorsement supplied.

(e) An indorsement of a security certificate in bearer form may give notice of an adverse claim to the certificate, but it does not otherwise affect a right to registration that the holder possesses.

(f) Unless otherwise agreed, a person making an indorsement assumes only the obligations provided in Section 8.108 and not an obligation that the security will be honored by the issuer.

Amended by Acts 1995, 74th Leg., ch. 962, § 1, eff. Sept. 1, 1995.

Uniform Commercial Code Comment

1. By virtue of the definition of indorsement in Section 8–102 and the rules of this section, the simplified method of indorsing certificated securities previously set forth in the Uniform Stock Transfer Act is continued. Although more than one special indorsement on a given security certificate is possible, the desire for dividends or interest, as the case may be, should operate to bring the certificate home for registration of transfer within a reasonable period of time. The usual form of assignment which appears on the back of a stock certificate or in a separate "power" may be filled up either in the form of an assignment, a power of attorney to transfer, or both. If it is not filled up at all but merely signed, the indorsement is in blank. If filled up either as an assignment or as a power of attorney to transfer, the indorsement is special.

2. Subsection (b) recognizes the validity of a "partial" indorsement, e.g., as to fifty shares of the one hundred represented by a single certificate. The rights of a transferee under a partial indorsement to the status of a protected purchaser are left to the case law.

3. Subsection (c) deals with the effect of an indorsement without delivery. There must be a voluntary parting with control in order to effect a valid transfer of a certificated security as between the parties. *Levey v. Nason*, 279 Mass. 268, 181 N.E. 193 (1932), and *National Surety Co. v. Indemnity Insurance Co. of North America*, 237 App.Div. 485, 261 N.Y.S. 605 (1933). The provision in Section 10 of the Uniform Stock Transfer Act that an attempted transfer without delivery amounts to a promise to transfer is omitted. Even under that Act the effect of such a promise was left to the applicable law of contracts, and this Article by making no reference to such situations intends to achieve a similar result. With respect to delivery there is no counterpart to subsection (d) on right to compel indorsement, such as is envisaged in *Johnson v. Johnson*, 300 Mass. 24, 13 N.E.2d 788 (1938), where the transferee under a written assignment was given the right to compel a transfer of the certificate.

4. Subsection (d) deals with the effect of delivery without indorsement. As between the parties the transfer is made complete upon delivery, but the transferee cannot become a protected purchaser until indorsement is made. The indorsement does not operate retroactively, and notice may intervene between delivery and indorsement so as to prevent the transferee from becoming a protected purchaser. Although a purchaser taking without a necessary indorsement may be subject to claims of ownership, any issuer's defense of which the purchaser had no notice at the time of delivery will be cut off, since the provisions of this Article protect all purchasers for value without notice (Section 8–202).

The transferee's right to compel an indorsement where a security certificate has been delivered with intent to transfer is recognized in the case law. See *Coats v. Guaranty Bank & Trust Co.*, 170 La. 871, 129 So. 513 (1930). A proper indorsement is one of the requisites of transfer which a purchaser of a certificated security has a right to obtain (Section 8–307). A purchaser may not only compel an indorsement under that section but may also recover for any reasonable expense incurred by the transferor's failure to respond to the demand for an indorsement.

5. Subsection (e) deals with the significance of an indorsement on a security certificate in bearer form. The concept of indorsement applies only to registered securities. A purported indorsement of bearer paper is normally of no effect. An indorsement "for collection," "for surrender" or the like, charges a purchaser with notice of adverse claims (Section 8–105(d)) but does not operate beyond this to interfere with any right the holder may otherwise possess to have the security registered.

6. Subsection (f) makes clear that the indorser of a security certificate does not warrant that the issuer will honor the underlying obligation. In view of the nature of investment securities and the circumstances under which they are normally transferred, a transferor cannot be held to warrant as to the issuer's actions. As a transferor the indorser, of course, remains liable for breach of the warranties set forth in this Article (Section 8–108).

§ 8.305. Instruction

(a) If an instruction has been originated by an appropriate person but is incomplete in any other respect, any person may complete it as authorized and the issuer may rely on it as completed, even though it has been completed incorrectly.

(b) Unless otherwise agreed, a person initiating an instruction assumes only the obligations imposed by Section 8.108 and not an obligation that the security will be honored by the issuer.

Amended by Acts 1995, 74th Leg., ch. 962, § 1, eff. Sept. 1, 1995.

Uniform Commercial Code Comment

1. The term instruction is defined in Section 8–102(a)(12) as a notification communicated to the issuer of an uncertificated security directing that transfer be registered. Section 8–107 specifies who may initiate an effective instruction.

Functionally, presentation of an instruction is quite similar to the presentation of an indorsed certificate for reregistration. Note that instruction is defined in terms of "communicate," see Section 8–102(a)(6). Thus, the instruction may be in the form of a writing signed by the registered owner or in any other form agreed upon by the issuer and the registered owner. Allowing nonwritten forms of instructions will permit the development and employment of means of transmitting instructions electronically.

When a person who originates an instruction leaves a blank and the blank later is completed, subsection (a) gives the issuer the same rights it would have had against the originating person had that person completed the blank. This is true regardless of whether the person completing the instruction had authority to complete it. Compare Section 8–206 and its Comment, dealing with blanks left upon issue.

2. Subsection (b) makes clear that the originator of an instruction, like the indorser of a security certificate, does not warrant that the issuer will honor the underlying obligation, but does make warranties as a transferor under Section 8–108.

§ 8.306. Effect of Guaranteeing Signature, Indorsement, or Instruction

(a) A person who guarantees a signature of an indorser of a security certificate warrants that at the time of signing:

(1) the signature was genuine;

(2) the signer was an appropriate person to indorse or, if the signature is by an agent, the agent had actual authority to act on behalf of the appropriate person; and

(3) the signer had legal capacity to sign.

(b) A person who guarantees a signature of the originator of an instruction warrants that at the time of signing:

(1) the signature was genuine;

(2) the signer was an appropriate person to originate the instruction or, if the signature is by an agent, the agent had actual authority to act on behalf of the appropriate person, if the person specified in the instruction as the registered owner was, in fact, the registered owner, as to which fact the signature guarantor does not make a warranty; and

(3) the signer had legal capacity to sign.

(c) A person who specially guarantees the signature of an originator of an instruction makes the warranties of a signature guarantor under Subsection (b) and also warrants that at the time the instruction is presented to the issuer:

(1) the person specified in the instruction as the registered owner of the uncertificated security will be the registered owner; and

(2) the transfer of the uncertificated security requested in the instruction will be registered by the issuer free from all liens, security interests, restrictions, and claims other than those specified in the instruction.

(d) A guarantor under Subsections (a) and (b) or a special guarantor under Subsection (c) does not otherwise warrant the rightfulness of the transfer.

(e) A person who guarantees an indorsement of a security certificate makes the warranties of a signature guarantor under Subsection (a) and also warrants the rightfulness of the transfer in all respects.

(f) A person who guarantees an instruction requesting the transfer of an uncertificated security makes the warranties of a special signature guarantor under Subsection (c) and also warrants the rightfulness of the transfer in all respects.

(g) An issuer may not require a special guaranty of signature, a guaranty of indorsement, or a guaranty of instruction as a condition to registration of transfer.

(h) The warranties under this section are made to a person taking or dealing with the security in reliance on the guaranty, and the guarantor is liable to the person for loss resulting from their breach. An indorser or originator of an instruction whose signature, indorsement, or instruction has been guaranteed is liable to a guarantor for any loss suffered by the guarantor as a result of breach of the warranties of the guarantor.

Amended by Acts 1995, 74th Leg., ch. 962, § 1, eff. Sept. 1, 1995.

Uniform Commercial Code Comment

1. Subsection (a) provides that a guarantor of the signature of the indorser of a security certificate warrants that the signature is genuine, that the signer is an appropriate person or has actual authority to indorse on behalf of the appropriate person, and that the signer has legal capacity. Subsection (b) provides similar, though not identical, warranties for the guarantor of a signature of the originator of an instruction for transfer of an uncertificated security.

Appropriate person is defined in Section 8–107(a) to include a successor or person who has power under other law to act for a person who is deceased or lacks capacity. Thus if a certificate registered in the name of Mary Roe is indorsed by Jane Doe as executor of Mary Roe, a guarantor of the signature of Jane Doe warrants that she has power to act as executor.

Although the definition of appropriate person in Section 8–107(a) does not itself include an agent, an indorsement by an agent is effective under Section 8–107(b) if the agent has authority to act for the appropriate person. Accordingly, this section provides an explicit warranty of authority for agents.

2. The rationale of the principle that a signature guarantor warrants the authority of the signer, rather than simply the genuineness of the signature, was explained in the leading case of *Jennie Clarkson Home for Children v. Missouri, K. & T. R. Co.*, 182 N.Y. 47, 74 N.E. 571, 70 A.L.R. 787 (1905), which dealt with a guaranty of the signature of a person indorsing on behalf of a corporation. "If stock is held by an individual who is executing a power of attorney for its transfer, the member of the exchange who signs as a witness thereto guaranties not only the genuineness of the signature affixed to the power of attorney, but that the person signing is the individual in whose name the stock stands. With reference to stock standing in the name of a corporation, which can only sign a power of attorney through its authorized officers or agents, a different situation is presented. If the witnessing of the signature of the corporation is only that of the signature of a person who signs for the corporation, then the guaranty is of no value, and there is nothing to protect purchasers or the companies who are called upon to issue new stock in the place of that transferred from the frauds of persons who have signed the names of corporations without authority. If such is the only effect of the guaranty, purchasers and transfer agents must first go to the corporation in whose name the stock stands and ascertain whether the individual who signed the power of attorney had authority to so do. This will require time, and in many cases will necessitate the postponement of the completion of the purchase by the payment of the money until the facts can be ascertained. The broker who is acting for the owner has an opportunity to become acquainted with his customer, and may readily before sale ascertain, in case of a corporation, the name of the officer who is authorized to execute the power of attorney. It was therefore, we think, the purpose of the rule to cast upon the broker who witnesses the signature the duty of ascertaining whether the person signing the name of the corporation had authority to so do, and making the witness a guarantor that it is the signature of the corporation in whose name the stock stands."

3. Subsection (b) sets forth the warranties that can reasonably be expected from the guarantor of the signature of the originator of an instruction, who, though familiar with the signer, does not have any evidence that the purported owner is in fact the owner of the subject uncertificated security. This is in contrast to the position of the person guaranteeing a signature on a certificate who can see a certificate in the signer's possession in the name of or indorsed to the signer or in blank. Thus, the warranty in paragraph (2) of subsection (b) is expressly conditioned on the actual registration's conforming to that represented by the originator. If the signer purports to be the owner, the guarantor under paragraph (2), warrants only the identity of the signer. If, however, the signer is acting in a representative capacity, the guarantor warrants both the signer's identity and authority to act for the purported owner. The issuer needs no warranty as to the facts of registration because those facts can be ascertained from the issuer's own records.

4. Subsection (c) sets forth a "special guaranty of signature" under which the guarantor additionally warrants both registered ownership and freedom from undisclosed defects of record. The guarantor of the signature of an indorser of a security certificate effectively makes these warranties to a purchaser for value on the evidence of a clean certificate issued in the name of the indorser, indorsed to the indorser or indorsed in blank. By specially guaranteeing under subsection (c), the guarantor warrants that the instruction will, when presented to the issuer, result in the requested registration free from defects not specified.

5. Subsection (d) makes clear that the warranties of a signature guarantor are limited to those specified in this section and do not include a general warranty of rightfulness. On the other hand subsections (e) and (f) provide that a person guaranteeing an indorsement or an instruction does warrant that the transfer is rightful in all respects.

6. Subsection (g) makes clear what can be inferred from the combination of Sections 8–401 and 8–402, that the issuer may not require as a condition to transfer a guaranty of the indorsement or instruction nor may it require a special signature guaranty.

7. Subsection (h) specifies to whom the warranties in this section run, and also provides that a person who gives a guaranty under this section has an action against the indorser or originator for any loss suffered by the guarantor.

§ 8.307. Purchaser's Right to Requisites for Registration of Transfer

Unless otherwise agreed, the transferor of a security on due demand shall supply the purchaser with proof of authority to transfer or with any other requisite necessary to obtain registration of the transfer of the security, but if the transfer is not for value, a transferor need not comply unless the purchaser pays the necessary expenses. If the transferor fails within a reasonable time to comply with the demand, the purchaser may reject or rescind the transfer.

Amended by Acts 1995, 74th Leg., ch. 962, § 1, eff. Sept. 1, 1995.

Uniform Commercial Code Comment

1. Because registration of the transfer of a security is a matter of vital importance, a purchaser is here provided with the means of obtaining such formal requirements for registration as signature guaranties, proof of authority, transfer tax stamps and the like. The transferor is the one in a position to supply most conveniently whatever documentation may be requisite for registration of transfer, and the duty to do so upon demand within a reasonable time is here stated affirmatively. If an essential item is peculiarly within the province of the transferor so that the transferor is the only one who can obtain it, the purchaser may specifically enforce the right to obtain it. Compare Section 8–304(d). If a transfer is not for value the transferor need not pay expenses.

2. If the transferor's duty is not performed the transferee may reject or rescind the contract to transfer. The transferee is not bound to do so. An action for damages for breach of contract may be preferred.

§§ 8.308 to 8.321. Deleted by Acts 1995, 74th Leg., ch. 962, § 1, eff. Sept. 1, 1995

SUBCHAPTER D. REGISTRATION

§ 8.401. Duty of Issuer to Register Transfer

(a) If a certificated security in registered form is presented to an issuer with a request to register transfer or an instruction is presented to an issuer with a request to register transfer of an uncertificated security, the issuer shall register the transfer as requested if:

(1) under the terms of the security the person seeking registration of transfer is eligible to have the security registered in its name;

(2) the indorsement or instruction is made by the appropriate person or by an agent who has actual authority to act on behalf of the appropriate person;

(3) reasonable assurance is given that the indorsement or instruction is genuine and authorized (Section 8.402);

(4) any applicable law relating to the collection of taxes has been complied with;

(5) the transfer does not violate any restriction on transfer imposed by the issuer in accordance with Section 8.204;

(6) a demand that the issuer not register transfer has not become effective under Section 8.403, or the issuer has complied with Section 8.403(b) but no legal process or indemnity bond is obtained as provided in Section 8.403(d); and

(7) the transfer is in fact rightful or is to a protected purchaser.

(b) If an issuer is under a duty to register a transfer of a security, the issuer is liable to a person presenting a certificated security or an instruction for registration or to the person's principal for loss resulting from unreasonable delay in registration or failure or refusal to register the transfer.

Amended by Acts 1995, 74th Leg., ch. 962, § 1, eff. Sept. 1, 1995.

Uniform Commercial Code Comment

1. This section states the duty of the issuer to register transfers. A duty exists only if certain preconditions exist. If any of the preconditions do not exist, there is no duty to register transfer. If an indorsement on a security certificate is a forgery, there is no duty. If an instruction to transfer an uncertificated security is not originated by an appropriate person, there is no duty. If there has not been compliance with applicable tax laws, there is no duty. If a security certificate is properly indorsed but nevertheless the transfer is in fact wrongful, there is no duty unless the transfer is to a protected purchaser (and the other preconditions exist).

This section does not constitute a mandate that the issuer must establish that all preconditions are met before the issuer registers a transfer. The issuer may waive the reasonable assurances specified in paragraph (a)(3). If it has confidence in the responsibility of the persons requesting transfer, it may ignore questions of compliance with tax laws. Although an issuer has no duty if the transfer is wrongful, the issuer has no duty to inquire into adverse claims, see Section 8–404.

2. By subsection (b) the person entitled to registration may not only compel it but may hold the issuer liable in damages for unreasonable delay.

3. Section 8–201(c) provides that with respect to registration of transfer, "issuer" means the person on whose behalf transfer books are maintained. Transfer agents, registrars or the like within the scope of their respective functions have rights and duties under this Part similar to those of the issuer. See Section 8–407.

§ 8.402. Assurance That Indorsement or Instruction is Effective

(a) An issuer may require the following assurance that each necessary indorsement or each instruction is genuine and authorized:

(1) in all cases, a guaranty of the signature of the person making an indorsement or originating an instruction, including, in the case of an instruction, reasonable assurance of identity;

(2) if the indorsement is made or the instruction is originated by an agent, appropriate assurance of actual authority to sign;

(3) if the indorsement is made or the instruction is originated by a fiduciary pursuant to Section 8.107(a)(4) or (5), appropriate evidence of appointment or incumbency;

(4) if there is more than one fiduciary, reasonable assurance that all who are required to sign have done so; and

(5) if the indorsement is made or the instruction is originated by a person not covered by another provision of this subsection, assurance appropriate to the case corresponding as nearly as may be to the provisions of this subsection.

(b) An issuer may elect to require reasonable assurance beyond that specified in this section.

(c) In this section:

(1) "Appropriate evidence of appointment or incumbency" means:

(A) in the case of a fiduciary appointed or qualified by a court, a certificate issued by or under the direction or supervision of the court or an officer thereof and dated within 60 days before the date of presentation for transfer; or

(B) in any other case, a copy of a document showing the appointment or a certificate issued by or on behalf of a person reasonably believed by an issuer to be responsible or, in the absence of that document or certificate, other evidence the issuer reasonably considers appropriate.

(2) "Guaranty of the signature" means a guaranty signed by or on behalf of a person reasonably believed by the issuer to be responsible. An issuer may adopt standards with respect to responsibility if they are not manifestly unreasonable.

Amended by Acts 1995, 74th Leg., ch. 962, § 1, eff. Sept. 1, 1995

Uniform Commercial Code Comment

1. An issuer is absolutely liable for wrongful registration of transfer if the indorsement or instruction is ineffective. See Section 8–404. Accordingly, an issuer is entitled to require such assurance as is reasonable under the circumstances that all necessary indorsements are effective, and thus to minimize its risk. This section establishes the requirements the issuer may make in terms of documentation which, except in the rarest of instances, should be easily furnished. Subsection (b) provides that an issuer may require additional assurances if that requirement is reasonable under the circumstances, but if the issuer demands more than reasonable assurance that the instruction or the necessary indorsements are genuine and authorized, the presenter may refuse the demand and sue for improper refusal to register. Section 8–401(b).

2. Under subsection (a)(1), the issuer may require in all cases a guaranty of signature. See Section 8–306. When an instruction is presented the issuer always may require reasonable assurance as to the identity of the originator. Subsection (c) allows the issuer to require that the person making these guaranties be one reasonably believed to be responsible, and the issuer may adopt standards of responsibility which are not manifestly unreasonable. Regulations under the federal securities laws, however, place limits on the requirements transfer agents may impose concerning the responsibility of eligible signature guarantors. See 17 CFR 240.17Ad–15.

3. This section, by paragraphs (2) through (5) of subsection (a), permits the issuer to seek confirmation that the indorsement or instruction is genuine and authorized. The permitted methods act as a double check on matters which are within the warranties of the signature guarantor. See Section 8–306. Thus, an agent may be required to submit a power of attorney, a corporation to submit a certified resolution evidencing the authority of its signing officer to sign, an executor or administrator to submit the usual "short-form certificate," etc. But failure of a fiduciary to obtain court approval of the transfer or to comply with other requirements does not make the fiduciary's signature ineffective. Section 8–107(c). Hence court orders and other controlling instruments are omitted from subsection (a).

Subsection (a)(3) authorizes the issuer to require "appropriate evidence" of appointment or incumbency, and subsection (c) indicates what evidence will be "appropriate". In the case of a fiduciary appointed or qualified by a court that evidence will be a court certificate dated within sixty days before the date of presentation, subsection (c)(2)(i). Where the fiduciary is not appointed or qualified by a court, as in the case of a successor trustee, subsection (c)(2)(ii) applies. In that case, the issuer may require a copy of a trust instrument or other document showing the appointment, or it may require the certificate of a responsible person. In the absence of such a document or certificate, it may require other appropriate evidence. If the security is registered in the name of the fiduciary as such, the person's signature is effective even though the person is no longer serving in that capacity, see Section 8–107(d), hence no evidence of incumbency is needed.

4. Circumstances may indicate that a necessary signature was unauthorized or was not that of an appropriate person. Such circumstances would be ignored at risk of absolute liability. To minimize that risk the issuer may properly exercise the option given by subsection (b) to require assurance beyond that specified in subsection (a). On the other hand, the facts at hand may reflect only on the rightfulness of the transfer. Such facts do not create a duty of inquiry, because the issuer is not liable to an adverse claimant unless the claimant obtains legal process. See Section 8–404.

§ 8.403. Demand That Issuer Not Register Transfer

(a) A person who is an appropriate person to make an indorsement or originate an instruction may demand that the issuer not register transfer of a security by communicating to the issuer a notification that identifies the registered owner and the issue of which the security is a part and provides an address for communications directed to the person making the demand. The demand is effective only if it is received by the issuer at a time and in a manner affording the issuer reasonable opportunity to act on it.

(b) If a certificated security in registered form is presented to an issuer with a request to register transfer or an instruction is presented to an issuer with a request to register transfer of an uncertificated security after a demand that the issuer not register transfer has become effective, the issuer shall promptly communicate to (i) the person who initiated the demand at the address provided in the demand and (ii) the person who presented the security for registration of transfer or initiated the instruction requesting registration of transfer a notification stating that:

(1) the certificated security has been presented for registration of transfer or the instruction for registration of transfer of the uncertificated security has been received;

(2) a demand that the issuer not register transfer had previously been received; and

(3) the issuer will withhold registration of transfer for a period of time stated in the notification in order to provide the person who initiated the demand an opportunity to obtain legal process or an indemnity bond.

(c) The period described in Subsection (b)(3) may not exceed 30 days after the date of communication of the notification. A shorter period may be specified by the issuer if it is not manifestly unreasonable.

(d) An issuer is not liable to a person who initiated a demand that the issuer not register transfer for any loss the person suffers as a result of registration of a transfer pursuant to an effective indorsement or instruction if the person who initiated the demand does not, within the time stated in the issuer's communication, either:

(1) obtain an appropriate injunction, restraining order, or other process from a court of competent jurisdiction enjoining the issuer from registering the transfer; or

(2) file with the issuer an indemnity bond, sufficient in the issuer's judgment to protect the issuer and any transfer agent, registrar, or other agent of the issuer involved from any loss it or they may suffer by refusing to register the transfer.

(e) This section does not relieve an issuer from liability for registering transfer pursuant to an indorsement or instruction that was not effective.

Amended by Acts 1995, 74th Leg., ch. 962, § 1, eff. Sept. 1, 1995.

Uniform Commercial Code Comment

1. The general rule under this Article is that if there has been an effective indorsement or instruction, a person who contends that registration of the transfer would be wrongful should not be able to interfere with the registration process merely by sending notice of the assertion to the issuer. Rather, the claimant must obtain legal process. See Section 8–404. Section 8–403 is an exception to this general rule. It permits the registered owner—but not third parties—to demand that the issuer not register a transfer.

2. This section is intended to alleviate the problems faced by registered owners of certificated securities who lose or misplace their certificates. A registered owner who realizes that a certificate may have been lost or stolen should promptly report that fact to the issuer, lest the owner be precluded from asserting a claim for wrongful registration. See Section 8–406. The usual practice of issuers and transfer agents is that when a certificate is reported as lost, the owner is notified that a replacement can be obtained if the owner provides an indemnity bond. See Section 8–405. If the registered owner does not plan to transfer the securities, the owner might choose not to obtain a replacement, particularly if the owner suspects that the certificate has merely been misplaced.

Under this section, the owner's notification that the certificate has been lost would constitute a demand that the issuer not register transfer. No indemnity bond or legal process is necessary. If the original certificate is presented for registration of transfer, the issuer is required to notify the registered owner of that fact, and defer registration of transfer for a stated period. In order to prevent undue delay in the process of registration, the stated period may not exceed thirty days. This gives the registered owner an opportunity to either obtain legal process or post an indemnity bond and thereby prevent the issuer from registering transfer.

3. Subsection (e) makes clear that this section does not relieve an issuer from liability for registering a transfer pursuant to an ineffective indorsement. An issuer's liability for wrongful registration in such cases does not depend on the presence or absence of notice that the indorsement was ineffective. Registered owners who are confident that they neither indorsed the certificates, nor did anything that would preclude them from denying the effectiveness of another's indorsement, see Sections 8–107(b) and 8–406, might prefer to pursue their rights against the issuer for wrongful registration rather than take advantage of the opportunity to post a bond or seek a restraining order when notified by the issuer under this section that their lost certificates have been presented for registration in apparently good order.

§ 8.404. Wrongful Registration

(a) Except as otherwise provided in Section 8.406, an issuer is liable for wrongful registration of transfer if the issuer has registered a transfer of a security to a person not entitled to it, and the transfer was registered:

(1) pursuant to an ineffective indorsement or instruction;

(2) after a demand that the issuer not register transfer became effective under Section 8.403(a) and the issuer did not comply with Section 8.403(b);

(3) after the issuer had been served with an appropriate injunction, restraining order, or other process from a court of competent jurisdiction enjoining it from registering the transfer, and the issuer had a reasonable opportunity to act on the injunction, restraining order, or other legal process; or

(4) by an issuer acting in collusion with the wrongdoer.

(b) An issuer that is liable for wrongful registration of transfer under Subsection (a) on demand shall provide the person entitled to the security with a like certificated or uncertificated security and any payments or distributions that the person did not receive as a result of the wrongful registration. If an overissue would result, the issuer's liability to provide the person with a like security is governed by Section 8.210.

(c) Except as otherwise provided in Subsection (a) or in a law relating to the collection of taxes, an issuer is not liable to an owner or other person suffering loss as a result of the registration of a transfer of a security if registration was made pursuant to an effective indorsement or instruction.

Amended by Acts 1995, 74th Leg., ch. 962, § 1, eff. Sept. 1, 1995.

Uniform Commercial Code Comment

1. Subsection (a)(1) provides that an issuer is liable if it registers transfer pursuant to an indorsement or instruction that was not effective. For example, an issuer that registers transfer on a forged indorsement is liable to the registered owner. The fact that the issuer had no reason to suspect that the indorsement was forged or that the issuer obtained the ordinary assurances under Section 8–402 does not relieve the issuer from liability. The reason that issuers obtain signature guaranties and other assurances is that they are liable for wrongful registration.

Subsection (b) specifies the remedy for wrongful registration. Pre–Code cases established the registered owner's right to receive a new security where the issuer had wrongfully registered a transfer, but some cases also allowed the registered owner to elect between an equitable action to compel issue of a new security and an action for damages. Cf. *Casper v. Kalt–Zimmers Mfg. Co.*, 159 Wis. 517, 149 N.W. 754 (1914). Article 8 does not allow such election. The true owner of a certificated security is required to take a new security except where an overissue would result and a similar security is not reasonably available for purchase. See Section 8–210. The true owner of an uncertificated security is entitled and required to take restoration of the records to their proper state, with a similar exception for overissue.

2. Read together, subsections (c) and (a) have the effect of providing that an issuer has no duties to an adverse claimant unless the claimant serves legal process on the issuer to enjoin registration. Issuers, or their transfer agents, perform a record-keeping function for the direct holding system that is analogous to the functions performed by clearing corporations and securities intermediaries in the indirect holding system. This section applies to the record-keepers for the direct holding system the same standard that Section 8–115 applies to the record-keepers for the indirect holding system. Thus, issuers are not liable to adverse claimants merely on the basis of notice. As in the case of the analogous rules for the indirect holding system, the policy of this section is to protect the right of investors to have their securities transfers processed without the disruption or delay that might result if the record-keepers risked liability to third parties. It would be undesirable to apply different standards to the direct and indirect holding systems, since doing so might operate as a disincentive to the development of a book-entry direct holding system.

3. This section changes prior law under which an issuer could be held liable, even though it registered transfer on an effective indorsement or instruction, if the issuer had in some fashion been notified that the transfer might be wrongful against a third party, and the issuer did not appropriately

discharge its duty to inquire into the adverse claim. See Section 8–403 (1978).

The rule of former Section 8–403 was anomalous inasmuch as Section 8–207 provides that the issuer is entitled to "treat the registered owner as the person exclusively entitled to vote, receive notifications, and otherwise exercise all the rights and powers of an owner." Under Section 8–207, the fact that a third person notifies the issuer of a claim does not preclude the issuer from treating the registered owner as the person entitled to the security. See *Kerrigan v. American Orthodontics Corp.*, 960 F.2d 43 (7th Cir. 1992). The change made in the present version of Section 8–404 ensures that the rights of registered owners and the duties of issuers with respect to registration of transfer will be protected against third-party interference in the same fashion as other rights of registered ownership.

§ 8.405. Replacement of Lost, Destroyed, or Wrongfully Taken Security Certificate

(a) If an owner of a certificated security, whether in registered or bearer form, claims that the certificate has been lost, destroyed, or wrongfully taken, the issuer shall issue a new certificate if the owner:

(1) so requests before the issuer has notice that the certificate has been acquired by a protected purchaser;

(2) files with the issuer a sufficient indemnity bond; and

(3) satisfies other reasonable requirements imposed by the issuer.

(b) If, after the issue of a new security certificate, a protected purchaser of the original certificate presents it for registration of transfer, the issuer shall register the transfer unless an overissue would result. In that case, the issuer's liability is governed by Section 8.210. In addition to any rights on the indemnity bond, an issuer may recover the new certificate from a person to whom it was issued or any person taking under that person, except a protected purchaser.

Amended by Acts 1995, 74th Leg., ch. 962, § 1, eff. Sept. 1, 1995.

Uniform Commercial Code Comment

1. This section enables the owner to obtain a replacement of a lost, destroyed or stolen certificate, provided that reasonable requirements are satisfied and a sufficient indemnity bond supplied.

2. Where an "original" security certificate has reached the hands of a protected purchaser, the registered owner—who was in the best position to prevent the loss, destruction or theft of the security certificate—is now deprived of the new security certificate issued as a replacement. This changes the pre-UCC law under which the original certificate was ineffective after the issue of a replacement except insofar as it might represent an action for damages in the hands of a purchaser for value without notice. *Keller v. Eureka Brick Mach. Mfg. Co.*, 43 Mo.App. 84, 11 L.R.A. 472 (1890). Where both the original and the new certificate have reached protected purchasers the issuer is required to honor both certificates unless an overissue would result and the security is not reasonably available for purchase. See Section 8–210. In the latter case alone, the protected purchaser of the original certificate is relegated to an action for damages. In either case, the issuer itself may recover on the indemnity bond.

§ 8.406. Obligation to Notify Issuer of Lost, Destroyed, or Wrongfully Taken Security Certificate

If a security certificate has been lost, apparently destroyed, or wrongfully taken, and the owner fails to notify the issuer of that fact within a reasonable time after the owner has notice of it and the issuer registers a transfer of the security before receiving notification, the owner may not assert against the issuer a claim for registering the transfer under Section 8.404 or a claim to a new security certificate under Section 8.405.

Amended by Acts 1995, 74th Leg., ch. 962, § 1, eff. Sept. 1, 1995.

Uniform Commercial Code Comment

An owner who fails to notify the issuer within a reasonable time after the owner knows or has reason to know of the loss or theft of a security certificate is estopped from asserting the ineffectiveness of a forged or unauthorized indorsement and the wrongfulness of the registration of the transfer. If the lost certificate was indorsed by the owner, then the registration of the transfer was not wrongful under Section 8–404, unless the owner made an effective demand that the issuer not register transfer under Section 8–403.

§ 8.407. Authenticating Trustee, Transfer Agent, and Registrar

A person acting as authenticating trustee, transfer agent, registrar, or other agent for an issuer in the registration of a transfer of its securities, in the issue of new security certificates or uncertificated securities, or in the cancellation of surrendered security certificates has the same obligation to the holder or owner of a certificated or uncertificated security with regard to the particular functions performed as the issuer has in regard to those functions.

Amended by Acts 1995, 74th Leg., ch. 962, § 1, eff. Sept. 1, 1995.

Uniform Commercial Code Comment

1. Transfer agents, registrars, and the like are here expressly held liable both to the issuer and to the owner for wrongful refusal to register a transfer as well as for wrongful registration of a transfer in any case within the scope of their respective functions where the issuer would itself be liable. Those cases which have regarded these parties solely as agents of the issuer and have therefore refused to recognize their liability to the owner for mere non-feasance, i.e., refusal to register a transfer, are rejected. *Hulse v. Consolidated Quicksilver Mining Corp.*, 65 Idaho 768, 154 P.2d 149 (1944); *Nicholson v. Morgan*, 119 Misc. 309, 196 N.Y.Supp. 147 (1922); *Lewis v. Hargadine–McKittrick Dry Goods Co.*, 305 Mo. 396, 274 S.W. 1041 (1924).

2. The practice frequently followed by authenticating trustees of issuing certificates of indebtedness rather than authenticating duplicate certificates where securities have been lost or stolen became obsolete in view of the provisions of Section 8–405, which makes express provision for the issue of substitute securities. It is not a breach of trust or lack of due diligence for trustees to authenticate new securities. Cf. *Switzerland General Ins. Co. v. N.Y.C. & H.R.R. Co.*, 152 App.Div. 70, 136 N.Y.S. 726 (1912).

§ 8.408. Deleted by Acts 1995, 74th Leg., ch. 962, § 1, eff. Sept. 1, 1995

SUBCHAPTER E. SECURITY ENTITLEMENTS

§ 8.501. Securities Account; Acquisition of Security Entitlement From Securities Intermediary

(a) "Securities account" means an account to which a financial asset is or may be credited in accordance with an agreement under which the person maintaining the account undertakes to treat the person for whom the account is maintained as entitled to exercise the rights that comprise the financial asset.

(b) Except as otherwise provided in Subsections (d) and (e), a person acquires a security entitlement if a securities intermediary:

(1) indicates by book entry that a financial asset has been credited to the person's securities account;

(2) receives a financial asset from the person or acquires a financial asset for the person and, in either case, accepts it for credit to the person's securities account; or

(3) becomes obligated under other law, regulation, or rule to credit a financial asset to the person's securities account.

(c) If a condition of Subsection (b) has been met, a person has a security entitlement even though the securities intermediary does not itself hold the financial asset.

(d) If a securities intermediary holds a financial asset for another person, and the financial asset is registered in the name of, payable to the order of, or specially indorsed to the other person and has not been indorsed to the securities intermediary or in blank, the other person is treated as holding the financial asset directly rather than as having a security entitlement with respect to the financial asset.

(e) Issuance of a security is not establishment of a security entitlement.

Added by Acts 1995, 74th Leg., ch. 962, § 1, eff. Sept. 1, 1995.

Uniform Commercial Code Comment

1. Part 5 rules apply to security entitlements, and Section 8–501(b) provides that a person has a security entitlement when a financial asset has been credited to a "securities account." Thus, the term "securities account" specifies the type of arrangements between institutions and their customers that are covered by Part 5. A securities account is a consensual arrangement in which the intermediary undertakes to treat the customer as entitled to exercise the rights that comprise the financial asset. The consensual aspect is covered by the requirement that the account be established pursuant to agreement. The term agreement is used in the broad sense defined in Section 1–201(3). There is no requirement that a formal or written agreement be signed.

As the securities business is presently conducted, several significant relationships clearly fall within the definition of a securities account, including the relationship between a clearing corporation and its participants, a broker and customers who leave securities with the broker, and a bank acting as securities custodian and its custodial customers. Given the enormous variety of arrangements concerning securities that exist today, and the certainty that new arrangements will evolve in the future, it is not possible to specify all of the arrangements to which the term does and does not apply.

Whether an arrangement between a firm and another person concerning a security or other financial asset is a "securities account" under this Article depends on whether the firm has undertaken to treat the other person as entitled to exercise the rights that comprise the security or other financial asset. Section 1–102, however, states the fundamental principle of interpretation that the Code provisions should be construed and applied to promote their underlying purposes and policies. Thus, the question whether a given arrangement is a securities account should be decided not by dictionary analysis of the words of the definition taken out of context, but by considering whether it promotes the objectives of Article 8 to include the arrangement within the term securities account.

The effect of concluding that an arrangement is a securities account is that the rules of Part 5 apply. Accordingly, the definition of "securities account" must be interpreted in light of the substantive provisions in Part 5, which describe the core features of the type of relationship for which the commercial law rules of Revised Article 8 concerning security entitlements were designed. There are many arrangements between institutions and other persons concerning securities or other financial assets which do not fall within the definition of "securities account" because the institutions have not undertaken to treat the other persons as entitled to exercise the ordinary rights of an entitlement holder specified in the Part 5 rules. For example, the term securities account does not cover the relationship between a bank and its depositors or the relationship between a trustee and the beneficiary of an ordinary trust, because those are not relationships in which the holder of a financial asset has undertaken to treat the other as entitled to exercise the rights that comprise the financial asset in the fashion contemplated by the Part 5 rules.

In short, the primary factor in deciding whether an arrangement is a securities account is whether application of the Part 5 rules is consistent with the expectations of the parties to the relationship. Relationships not governed by Part 5 may be governed by other parts of Article 8 if the relationship gives rise to a new security, or may be governed by other law entirely.

2. Subsection (b) of this section specifies what circumstances give rise to security entitlements. Paragraph (1) of subsection (b) sets out the most important rule. It turns on the intermediary's conduct, reflecting a basic operating assumption of the indirect holding system that once a securities intermediary has acknowledged that it is carrying a position in a financial asset for its customer or participant, the intermediary is obligated to treat the customer or participant as entitled to the financial asset. Paragraph (1) does not attempt to specify exactly what accounting, record-keeping, or information transmission steps suffice to indicate that the intermediary has credited the account. That is left to agreement, trade practice, or rule in order to provide the flexibility necessary to accommodate varying or changing accounting and information processing systems. The point of paragraph (1) is that once an intermediary has acknowledged that it is carrying a position for the customer or participant, the customer or participant has a security entitlement. The precise form in which the intermediary manifests that acknowledgment is left to private ordering.

Paragraph (2) of subsection (b) sets out a different operational test, turning not on the intermediary's accounting system but on the facts that accounting systems are supposed to represent. Under paragraph (b)(2) a person has a security entitlement if the intermediary has received and accepted a financial asset for credit to the account of its customer or participant. For example, if a customer of a broker or bank custodian delivers a security certificate in proper form to the broker or bank to be held in the customer's account, the customer acquires a security entitlement. Paragraph (b)(2) also covers circumstances in which the intermediary receives a financial asset from a third person for credit to the account of the customer or participant. Paragraph (b)(2) is not limited to circumstances in which the intermediary receives security certificates or other financial assets in physical form. Paragraph (b)(2) also covers circumstances in which the intermediary acquires a security entitlement with respect to a financial asset which is to be credited to the account of the intermediary's own customer. For example, if a customer transfers her account from Broker A to Broker B, she acquires security entitlements against Broker B once the clearing corporation has credited the positions to Broker B's account. It should be noted, however, that paragraph (b)(2) provides that a person acquires a security entitlement when the intermediary not only receives but also accepts the financial asset for credit to the account. This limitation is included to take account of the fact that there may be circumstances in which an intermediary has received a financial asset but is not willing to undertake the obligations that flow from establishing a security entitlement. For example, a security certificate which is sent to an intermediary may not be in proper form, or may represent a type of financial asset which the intermediary is not willing to carry for others. It should be noted that in all but extremely unusual cases, the circumstances covered by paragraph (2) will also be covered by paragraph (1), because the intermediary will have credited the positions to the customer's account.

Paragraph (3) of subsection (b) sets out a residual test, to avoid any implication that the failure of an intermediary to make the appropriate entries to credit a position to a customer's securities account would prevent the customer from acquiring the rights of an entitlement holder under Part 5. As is the case with the paragraph (2) test, the paragraph (3) test would not be needed for the ordinary cases, since they are covered by paragraph (1).

3. In a sense, Section 8–501(b) is analogous to the rules set out in the provisions of Sections 8–313(1)(d) and 8–320 of the prior version of Article 8 that specified what acts by a securities intermediary or clearing corporation sufficed as a transfer of securities held in fungible bulk. Unlike the prior version of Article 8, however, this section is not based on the idea that an entitlement holder acquires rights only by virtue of a "transfer" from the securities intermediary to the entitlement holder. In the indirect holding system, the significant fact is that the securities intermediary has undertaken to treat the customer as entitled to the financial asset. It is up to the securities intermediary to take the necessary steps to ensure that it will be able to perform its undertaking. It is, for example, entirely possible that a securities intermediary might make entries in a customer's account reflecting that customer's acquisition of a certain security at a time when the securities intermediary did not itself happen to hold any units of that security. The person from whom the securities intermediary bought the security might have failed to deliver and it might have taken some time to clear up the problem, or there may have been an operational gap in time between the crediting of a customer's account and the receipt of securities from another securities intermediary. The entitlement holder's rights against the securities intermediary do not depend on whether or when the securities intermediary acquired its interests. Subsection (c) is intended to make this point clear. Subsection (c) does not mean that the intermediary is free to create security entitlements without itself holding sufficient financial assets to satisfy its entitlement holders. The duty of a securities intermediary to maintain sufficient assets is governed by Section 8–504 and regulatory law. Subsection (c) is included only to make it clear the question whether a person has acquired a security entitlement does not depend on whether the intermediary has complied with that duty.

4. Part 5 of Article 8 sets out a carefully designed system of rules for the indirect holding system. Persons who hold securities through brokers or custodians have security entitlements that are governed by Part 5, rather than being treated as the direct holders of securities. Subsection (d) specifies the limited circumstance in which a customer who leaves a financial asset with a broker or other securities intermediary has a direct interest in the financial asset, rather than a security entitlement.

The customer can be a direct holder only if the security certificate, or other financial asset, is registered in the name of, payable to the order of, or specially indorsed to the customer, and has not been indorsed by the customer to the securities intermediary or in blank. The distinction between those circumstances where the customer can be treated as direct owner and those where the customer has a security entitlement is essentially the same as the distinction drawn under the federal bankruptcy code between customer name securities and customer property. The distinction does not turn on any form of physical identification or segregation. A customer who delivers certificates to a broker with blank indorsements or stock powers is not a direct holder but has a security entitlement, even though the broker holds those certificates in some form of separate safe-keeping arrangement for that particular customer. The customer remains the direct holder only if there is no indorsement or stock power so that further action by the customer is required to place the certificates in a form where they can be transferred by the broker.

The rule of subsection (d) corresponds to the rule set out in Section 8–301(a)(3) specifying when acquisition of possession of a certificate by a securities intermediary counts as "delivery" to the customer.

5. Subsection (e) is intended to make clear that Part 5 does not apply to an arrangement in which a security is issued representing an interest in underlying assets, as distinguished from arrangements in which the underlying assets are carried in a securities account. A common mechanism by which new financial instruments are devised is that a financial institution that holds some security, financial instrument, or pool thereof, creates interests in that asset or pool which are sold to others. In many such cases, the interests so created will fall within the definition of "security" in Section 8–102(a)(15). If so, then by virtue of subsection (e) of Section 8–501, the relationship between the institution that creates the interests and the persons who hold them is not a security entitlement to which the Part 5 rules apply. Accordingly, an arrangement such as an American depositary receipt facility which creates freely transferable interests in underlying securities will be issuance of a security under Article 8 rather than establishment of a security entitlement to the underlying securities.

The subsection (e) rule can be regarded as an aspect of the definitional rules specifying the meaning of securities account and security entitlement. Among the key components of the definition of security in Section 8–102(a)(15) are the "transferability" and "divisibility" tests. Securities, in the Article 8 sense, are fungible interests or obligations that are intended to be tradable. The concept of security entitlement under Part 5 is quite different. A security entitlement is the package of rights that a person has against the person's own intermediary with respect to the positions carried in the person's securities account. That package of rights is not, as such, something that is traded. When a customer sells a security that she had held through a securities account, her security entitlement is terminated; when she buys a security that she will hold through her securities account, she acquires a security entitlement. In most cases, settlement of a securities trade will involve termination of one person's security entitlement and acquisition of a security entitlement by another person. That transaction, however, is not a "transfer" of the same entitlement from one person to another. That is not to say that an entitlement holder cannot transfer an interest in her security entitlement as such; granting a security interest in a security entitlement is such a transfer. On the other hand, the nature of a security entitlement is that the intermediary is undertaking duties only to the person identified as the entitlement holder.

§ 8.502. Assertion of Adverse Claim Against Entitlement Holder

An action based on an adverse claim to a financial asset, whether framed in conversion, replevin, constructive trust, equitable lien, or other theory, may not be asserted against a person who acquires a security entitlement under Section 8.501 for value and without notice of the adverse claim.

Added by Acts 1995, 74th Leg., ch. 962, § 1, eff. Sept. 1, 1995.

Uniform Commercial Code Comment

1. The section provides investors in the indirect holding system with protection against adverse claims by specifying that no adverse claim can be asserted against a person who acquires a security entitlement under Section 8–501 for value and without notice of the adverse claim. It plays a role in the indirect holding system analogous to the rule of the direct holding system that protected purchasers take free from adverse claims (Section 8–303).

This section does not use the locution "takes free from adverse claims" because that could be confusing as applied to the indirect holding system. The nature of indirect holding system is that an entitlement holder has an interest in common with others who hold positions in the same financial asset through the same intermediary. Thus, a particular entitlement holder's interest in the financial assets held by its intermediary is necessarily "subject to" the interests of others. See Section 8–503. The rule stated in this section might have been expressed by saying that a person who acquires a security entitlement under Section 8–501 for value and without notice of adverse claims takes "that security entitlement" free from adverse claims. That formulation has not been used, however, for fear that it would be misinterpreted as suggesting that the person acquires a right to the underlying financial assets that could not be affected by the competing rights of others claiming through common or higher tier intermediaries. A security entitlement is a complex bundle of rights. This section does not deal with the question of what rights are in the bundle. Rather, this section provides that once a person has acquired the bundle, someone else cannot take it away on the basis of assertion that the transaction in which the security entitlement was created involved a violation of the claimant's rights.

2. Because securities trades are typically settled on a net basis by book-entry movements, it would ordinarily be impossible for anyone to trace the path of any particular security, no matter how the interest of parties who hold through intermediaries is described. Suppose, for example, that S has a 1000 share position in XYZ common stock through an account with a broker, Able & Co. S's identical twin impersonates S and directs Able to sell the securities. That same day, B places an order with Baker & Co., to buy 1000 shares of XYZ common stock. Later, S discovers the wrongful act and seeks to recover "her shares." Even if S can show that, at the stage of the trade, her sell order was matched with B's buy order, that would not suffice to show that "her shares" went to B. Settlement between Able and Baker occurs on a net basis for all trades in XYZ that day; indeed Able's net position may have been such that it received rather than delivered shares in XYZ through the settlement system.

In the unlikely event that this was the only trade in XYZ common stock executed in the market that day, one could follow the shares from S's account to B's account. The plaintiff in an action in conversion or similar legal action to enforce a property interest must show that the defendant has an item of property that belongs to the plaintiff. In this example, B's security entitlement is not the same item of property that formerly was held by S, it is a new package of rights that B acquired against Baker under Section 8-501. Principles of equitable remedies might, however, provide S with a basis for contending that if the position B received was the traceable product of the wrongful taking of S's property by S's twin, a constructive trust should be imposed on B's property in favor of S. See G. Palmer, The Law of Restitution § 2.14. Section 8-502 ensures that no such claims can be asserted against a person, such as B in this example, who acquires a security entitlement under Section 8-501 for value and without notice, regardless of what theory of law or equity is used to describe the basis of the assertion of the adverse claim.

In the above example, S would ordinarily have no reason to pursue B unless Able is insolvent and S's claim will not be satisfied in the insolvency proceedings. Because S did not give an entitlement order for the disposition of her security entitlement, Able must recredit her account for the 1000 shares of XYZ common stock. See Section 8-507(b).

3. The following examples illustrate the operation of Section 8-502:

Example 1. Thief steals bearer bonds from Owner. Thief delivers the bonds to Broker for credit to Thief's securities account, thereby acquiring a security entitlement under Section 8-501(b). Under other law, Owner may have a claim to have a constructive trust imposed on the security entitlement as the traceable product of the bonds that Thief misappropriated. Because Thief was himself the wrongdoer, Thief obviously had notice of Owner's adverse claim. Accordingly, Section 8-502 does not preclude Owner from asserting an adverse claim against Thief.

Example 2. Thief steals bearer bonds from Owner. Thief owes a personal debt to Creditor. Creditor has a securities account with Broker. Thief agrees to transfer the bonds to Creditor as security for or in satisfaction of his debt to Creditor. Thief does so by sending the bonds to Broker for credit to Creditor's securities account. Creditor thereby acquires a security entitlement under Section 8-501(b). Under other law, Owner may have a claim to have a constructive trust imposed on the security entitlement as the traceable product of the bonds that Thief misappropriated. Creditor acquired the security entitlement for value, since Creditor acquired it as security for or in satisfaction of Thief's debt to Creditor. See Section 1-201(44). If Creditor did not have notice of Owner's claim, Section 8-502 precludes any action by Owner against Creditor, whether framed in constructive trust or other theory. Section 8-105 specifies what counts as notice of an adverse claim.

Example 3. Father, as trustee for Son, holds XYZ Co. shares in a securities account with Able & Co. In violation of his fiduciary duties, Father sells the XYZ Co. shares and uses the proceeds for personal purposes. Father dies, and his estate is insolvent. Assume—implausibly—that Son is able to trace the XYZ Co. shares and show that the "same shares" ended up in Buyer's securities account with Baker & Co. Section 8-502 precludes any action by Son against Buyer, whether framed in constructive trust or other theory, provided that Buyer acquired the security entitlement for value and without notice of adverse claims.

Example 4. Debtor holds XYZ Co. shares in a securities account with Able & Co. As collateral for a loan from Bank, Debtor grants Bank a security interest in the security entitlement to the XYZ Co. shares. Bank perfects by a method which leaves Debtor with the ability to dispose of the shares. See Section 9-312. In violation of the security agreement, Debtor sells the XYZ Co. shares and absconds with the proceeds. Assume. In violation of the security agreement, Debtor sells the XYZ Co. shares and absconds with the proceeds. Assume-implausibly-that Bank is able to trace the XYZ Co. shares and show that the "same shares" ended up in Buyer's securities account with Baker & Co. Section 8-502 precludes any action by Bank against Buyer, whether framed in constructive trust or other theory, provided that Buyer acquired the security entitlement for value and without notice of adverse claims.

Example 5. Debtor owns controlling interests in various public companies, including Acme and Ajax. Acme owns 60% of the stock of another public company, Beta. Debtor causes the Beta stock to be pledged to Lending Bank as collateral for Ajax's debt. Acme holds the Beta stock through an account with a securities custodian, C Bank, which in turn holds through Clearing Corporation. Lending Bank is also a Clearing Corporation participant. The pledge of the Beta stock is implemented by Acme instructing C Bank to instruct Clearing Corporation to debit C Bank's account and credit Lending Bank's account. Acme and Ajax both become insolvent. The Beta stock is still valuable. Acme's liquidator asserts that the pledge of the Beta stock for Ajax's debt was wrongful as against Acme and seeks to recover the Beta stock from Lending Bank. Because the pledge was implemented by an outright transfer into Lending Bank's account at Clearing Corporation, Lending Bank acquired a security entitlement to the Beta stock under Section 8-501. Lending

Bank acquired the security entitlement for value, since it acquired it as security for a debt. See Section 1–201(44). If Lending Bank did not have notice of Acme's claim, Section 8–502 will preclude any action by Acme against Lending Bank, whether framed in constructive trust or other theory.

Example 6. Debtor grants Alpha Co. a security interest in a security entitlement that includes 1000 shares of XYZ Co. stock that Debtor holds through an account with Able & Co. Alpha also has an account with Able. Debtor instructs Able to transfer the shares to Alpha, and Able does so by crediting the shares to Alpha's account. Alpha has control of the 1000 shares under Section 8–106(d). (The facts to this point are identical to those in Section 8–106, Comment 4, Example 1, except that Alpha Co. was Alpha Bank.) Alpha next grants Beta Co. a security interest in the 1000 shares included in Alpha's security entitlement. See Section 9–207(c)(3). Alpha instructs Able to transfer the shares to Gamma Co., Beta's custodian. Able does so, and Gamma credits the 1000 shares to Beta's account. Beta now has control under Section 8–106(d). By virtue of Debtor's explicit permission or by virtue of the permission inherent in Debtor's creation of a security interest in favor of Alpha and Alpha's resulting power to grant a security interest under Section 9–207, Debtor has no adverse claim to assert against Beta, assuming implausibly that Debtor could "trace" an interest to the Gamma account. Moreover, even. if Debtor did hold an adverse claim, if Beta did not have notice of Debtor's claim, Section 8–502 will preclude any action by Debtor against Beta, whether framed in constructive trust or other theory.

4. Although this section protects entitlement holders against adverse claims, it does not protect them against the risk that their securities intermediary will not itself have sufficient financial assets to satisfy the claims of all of its entitlement holders. Suppose that Customer A holds 1000 shares of XYZ Co. stock in an account with her broker, Able & Co. Able in turn holds 1000 shares of XYZ Co. through its account with Clearing Corporation, but has no other positions in XYZ Co. shares, either for other customers or for its own proprietary account. Customer B places an order with Able for the purchase of 1000 shares of XYZ Co. stock, and pays the purchase price. Able credits B's account with a 1000 share position in XYZ Co. stock, but Able does not itself buy any additional XYZ Co. shares. Able fails, having only 1000 shares to satisfy the claims of A and B. Unless other insolvency law establishes a different distributional rule, A and B would share the 1000 shares held by Able pro rata, without regard to the time that their respective entitlements were established. See Section 8–503(b). Section 8–502 protects entitlement holders, such as A and B, against adverse claimants. In this case, however, the problem that A and B face is not that someone is trying to take away their entitlements, but that the entitlements are not worth what they thought. The only role that Section 8–502 plays in this case is to preclude any assertion that A has some form of claim against B by virtue of the fact that Able's establishment of an entitlement in favor of B diluted A's rights to the limited assets held by Able.

§ 8.503. Property Interest of Entitlement Holder in Financial Asset Held by Securities Intermediary

(a) To the extent necessary for a securities intermediary to satisfy all security entitlements with respect to a particular financial asset, all interests in that financial asset held by the securities intermediary are held by the securities intermediary for the entitlement holders, are not property of the securities intermediary, and are not subject to claims of creditors of the securities intermediary, except as otherwise provided in Section 8.511.

(b) An entitlement holder's property interest with respect to a particular financial asset under Subsection (a) is a pro rata property interest in all interests in that financial asset held by the securities intermediary, without regard to the time the entitlement holder acquired the security entitlement or the time the securities intermediary acquired the interest in that financial asset.

(c) An entitlement holder's property interest with respect to a particular financial asset under Subsection (a) may be enforced against the securities intermediary only by exercise of the entitlement holder's rights under Sections 8.505–8.508.

(d) An entitlement holder's property interest with respect to a particular financial asset under Subsection (a) may be enforced against a purchaser of the financial asset or interest therein only if:

(1) insolvency proceedings have been initiated by or against the securities intermediary;

(2) the securities intermediary does not have sufficient interests in the financial asset to satisfy the security entitlements of all of its entitlement holders to that financial asset;

(3) the securities intermediary violated its obligations under Section 8.504 by transferring the financial asset or interest therein to the purchaser; and

(4) the purchaser is not protected under Subsection (f).

(e) The trustee or other liquidator, acting on behalf of all entitlement holders having security entitlements with respect to a particular financial asset, may recover the financial asset, or interest therein, from the purchaser. If the trustee or other liquidator elects not to pursue that right, an entitlement holder whose security entitlement remains unsatisfied has the right to recover its interest in the financial asset from the purchaser.

(f) An action based on the entitlement holder's property interest with respect to a particular financial asset under Subsection (a), whether framed in conversion, replevin, constructive trust, equitable lien, or other theory, may not be asserted against any purchaser of a financial asset or interest therein who gives value, obtains control, and does not act in collusion with the securities intermediary in violating the securities intermediary's obligations under Section 8.504.

Added by Acts 1995, 74th Leg., ch. 962, § 1, eff. Sept. 1, 1995.

Uniform Commercial Code Comment

1. This section specifies the sense in which a security entitlement is an interest in the property held by the securities intermediary. It expresses the ordinary understanding that securities that a firm holds for its customers are not general assets of the firm subject to the claims of creditors. Since securities intermediaries generally do not segregate securities in such fashion that one could identify particular securities as the ones held for customers, it would not be realistic for this section to state that "customers' securities" are not subject to creditors' claims. Rather subsection (a) provides that to the extent necessary to satisfy all customer claims, all units of that security held by the firm are held for the entitlement holders, are not property of the securities intermediary, and are not subject to creditors' claims, except as otherwise provided in Section 8–511.

An entitlement holder's property interest under this section is an interest with respect to a specific issue of securities or financial assets. For example, customers of a firm who have positions in XYZ common stock have security entitlements with respect to the XYZ common stock held by the intermediary, while other customers who have positions in ABC common stock have security entitlements with respect to the ABC common stock held by the intermediary.

Subsection (b) makes clear that the property interest described in subsection (a) is an interest held in common by all entitlement holders who have entitlements to a particular security or other financial asset. Temporal factors are irrelevant. One entitlement holder cannot claim that its rights to the assets held by the intermediary are superior to the rights of another entitlement holder by virtue of having acquired those rights before, or after, the other entitlement holder. Nor does it matter whether the intermediary had sufficient assets to satisfy all entitlement holders' claims at one point, but no longer does. Rather, all entitlement holders have a pro rata interest in whatever positions in that financial asset the intermediary holds.

Although this section describes the property interest of entitlement holders in the assets held by the intermediary, it does not necessarily determine how property held by a failed intermediary will be distributed in insolvency proceedings. If the intermediary fails and its affairs are being administered in an insolvency proceeding, the applicable insolvency law governs how the various parties having claims against the firm are treated. For example, the distributional rules for stockbroker liquidation proceedings under the Bankruptcy Code and Securities Investor Protection Act ("SIPA") provide that all customer property is distributed pro rata among all customers in proportion to the dollar value of their total positions, rather than dividing the property on an issue by issue basis. For intermediaries that are not subject to the Bankruptcy Code and SIPA, other insolvency law would determine what distributional rule is applied.

2. Although this section recognizes that the entitlement holders of a securities intermediary have a property interest in the financial assets held by the intermediary, the incidents of this property interest are established by the rules of Article 8, not by common law property concepts. The traditional Article 8 rules on certificated securities were based on the idea that a paper certificate could be regarded as a nearly complete reification of the underlying right. The rules on transfer and the consequences of wrongful transfer could then be written using the same basic concepts as the rules for physical chattels. A person's claim of ownership of a certificated security is a right to a specific identifiable physical object, and that right can be asserted against any person who ends up in possession of that physical certificate, unless cut off by the rules protecting purchasers for value without notice. Those concepts do not work for the indirect holding system. A security entitlement is not a claim to a specific identifiable thing; it is a package of rights and interests that a person has against the person's securities intermediary and the property held by the intermediary. The idea that discrete objects might be traced through the hands of different persons has no place in the Revised Article 8 rules for the indirect holding system. The fundamental principles of the indirect holding system rules are that an entitlement holder's own intermediary has the obligation to see to it that the entitlement holder receives all of the economic and corporate rights that comprise the financial asset, and that the entitlement holder can look only to that intermediary for performance of the obligations. The entitlement holder cannot assert rights directly against other persons, such as other intermediaries through whom the intermediary holds the positions, or third parties to whom the intermediary may have wrongfully transferred interests, except in extremely unusual circumstances where the third party was itself a participant in the wrongdoing. Subsections (c) through (e) reflect these fundamental principles.

Subsection (c) provides that an entitlement holder's property interest can be enforced against the intermediary only by exercise of the entitlement holder's rights under Sections 8–505 through 8–508. These are the provisions that set out the duty of an intermediary to see to it that the entitlement holder receives all of the economic and corporate rights that comprise the security. If the intermediary is in insolvency proceedings and can no longer perform in accordance with the ordinary Part 5 rules, the applicable insolvency law will determine how the intermediary's assets are to be distributed.

Subsections (d) and (e) specify the limited circumstances in which an entitlement holder's property interest can be asserted against a third person to whom the intermediary transferred a financial asset that was subject to the entitlement holder's claim when held by the intermediary. Subsection (d) provides that the property interest of entitlement holders cannot be asserted against any transferee except in the circumstances therein specified. So long as the intermediary is solvent, the entitlement holders must look to the intermediary to satisfy their claims. If the intermediary does not hold financial assets corresponding to the entitlement holders' claims, the intermediary has the duty to acquire them. See Section 8–504. Thus, paragraphs (1), (2), and (3) of subsection (d) specify that the only occasion in which the entitlement holders can pursue transferees is when the intermediary is unable to perform its obligation, and the transfer to the transferee was a violation of those obligations. Even in that case, a transferee who gave value and obtained control is protected by virtue of the rule in subsection (e), unless the transferee acted in collusion with the intermediary.

Subsections (d) and (e) have the effect of protecting transferees from an intermediary against adverse claims arising out of assertions by the intermediary's entitlement holders that the intermediary acted wrongfully in transferring the financial assets. These rules, however, operate in a slightly different fashion than traditional adverse claim cut-off rules. Rather than specifying that a certain class of transferee takes free from all claims, subsections (d) and (e) specify the circumstances in which this particular form of claim can be asserted against a transferee. Revised Article 8 also contains general adverse claim cut-off rules for the indirect holding system. See Sections 8–502 and 8–510. The rule of subsections (d) and (e) takes precedence over the general cut-off rules of those sections, because Section 8–503 itself defines and sets limits on the assertion of the property interest of entitlement holders. Thus, the question whether entitlement holders' property interest can be asserted as an adverse claim against a transferee from the intermediary is governed by the collusion test of Section 8–503(e), rather than by the "without notice" test of Sections 8–502 and 8–510.

3. The limitations that subsections (c) through (e) place on the ability of customers of a failed intermediary to recover securities or other financial assets from transferees are consistent with the fundamental policies of investor protection that underlie this Article and other bodies of law governing the securities business. The commercial law rules for the securities holding and transfer system must be assessed from the forward-looking perspective of their impact on the vast number of transactions in which no wrongful conduct occurred or will occur, rather than from the *post hoc* perspective of what rule might be most advantageous to a particular class of persons in litigation that might arise out of the occasional case in which someone has acted wrongfully. Although one can devise hypothetical scenarios where particular customers might find it advantageous to be able to assert rights against someone other than the customers' own intermediary, commercial law rules that permitted customers to do so would impair rather than promote the interest of investors and the safe and efficient operation of the clearance and settlement system. Suppose, for example, that Intermediary A transfers securities to B, that Intermediary A acted wrongfully as against its customers in so doing, and that after the transaction Intermediary A did not have sufficient securities to satisfy its obligations to its entitlement holders. Viewed solely from the standpoint of the customers of Intermediary A, it would seem that permitting the property to be recovered from B, would be good for investors. That, however, is not the case. B may itself be an intermediary with its own customers, or may be some other institution through which individuals invest, such as a pension fund or investment company. There is no reason to think that rules permitting customers of an intermediary to trace and recover securities that their intermediary wrongfully transferred work to the advantage of investors in general. To the contrary, application of such rules would often merely shift losses from one set of investors to another. The uncertainties that would result from rules permitting such recoveries would work to the disadvantage of all participants in the securities markets.

The use of the collusion test in Section 8–503(e) furthers the interests of investors generally in the sound and efficient operation of the securities holding and settlement system. The effect of the choice of this standard is that customers of a failed intermediary must show that the transferee from whom they seek to recover was affirmatively engaged in wrongful conduct, rather than casting on the transferee any burden of showing that the transferee had no awareness of wrongful conduct by the failed intermediary. The rule of Section 8–503(e) is based on the long-standing policy that it is undesirable to impose upon purchasers of securities any duty to investigate whether their sellers may be acting wrongfully.

Rather than imposing duties to investigate, the general policy of the commercial law of the securities holding and transfer system has been to eliminate legal rules that might induce participants to conduct investigations of the authority of persons transferring securities on behalf of others for fear that they might be held liable for participating in a wrongful transfer. The rules in Part 4 of Article 8 concerning transfers by fiduciaries provide a good example. Under *Lowry v. Commercial & Farmers' Bank*, 15 F. Cas. 1040 (C.C.D. Md. 1848) (No. 8551), an issuer could be held liable for wrongful transfer if it registered transfer of securities by a fiduciary under circumstances where it had any reason to believe that the fiduciary may have been acting improperly. In one sense that seems to be advantageous for beneficiaries who might be harmed by wrongful conduct by fiduciaries. The consequence of the *Lowry* rule, however, was that in order to protect against risk of such liability, issuers developed the practice of requiring extensive documentation for fiduciary stock transfers, making such transfers cumbersome and time consuming. Accordingly, the rules in Part 4 of Article 8, and in the prior fiduciary transfer statutes, were designed to discourage transfer agents from conducting investigations into the rightfulness of transfers by fiduciaries.

The rules of Revised Article 8 implement for the indirect holding system the same policies that the rules on protected purchasers and registration of transfer adopt for the direct holding system. A securities intermediary is, by definition, a person who is holding securities on behalf of other persons. There is nothing unusual or suspicious about a transaction in which a securities intermediary sells securities that it was holding for its customers. That is exactly what securities intermediaries are in business to do. The interests of customers of securities intermediaries would not be served by a rule that required counterparties to transfers from securities intermediaries to investigate whether the intermediary was acting wrongfully against its customers. Quite the contrary, such a rule would impair the ability of securities intermediaries to perform the function that customers want.

The rules of Section 8–503(c) through (e) apply to transferees generally, including pledgees. The reasons for treating pledgees in the same fashion as other transferees are discussed in the Comments to Section 8–511. The statement in subsection (a) that an intermediary holds financial assets for customers and not as its own property does not, of course, mean that the intermediary lacks power to transfer the financial assets to others. For example, although Article 9 provides that for a security interest to attach the debtor must either have "rights" in the collateral or the power to transfer "rights" in the collateral to a secured party, see Section 9–203, the fact that an intermediary is holding a financial asset in a form that permits ready transfer means that it has such rights, even if the intermediary is acting wrongfully against its entitlement holders in granting the security interest. The question whether the secured party takes subject to the entitlement holder's claim in such a case is governed by Section 8–511, which is an application to secured transactions of the general principles expressed in subsections (d) and (e) of this section.

§ 8.504. Duty of Securities Intermediary to Maintain Financial Asset

(a) A securities intermediary shall promptly obtain and thereafter maintain a financial asset in a quantity corresponding to the aggregate of all security entitlements it has established in favor of its entitlement holders with respect to that financial asset. The securities intermediary may maintain those financial assets directly or through one or more other securities intermediaries.

(b) Except to the extent otherwise agreed on by its entitlement holder, a securities intermediary may not grant any security interests in a financial asset it is obligated to maintain pursuant to Subsection (a).

(c) A securities intermediary satisfies the duty in Subsection (a) if:

(1) the securities intermediary acts with respect to the duty as agreed on by the entitlement holder and the securities intermediary; or

(2) in the absence of agreement, the securities intermediary exercises due care in accordance with reasonable commercial standards to obtain and maintain the financial asset.

(d) This section does not apply to a clearing corporation that is itself the obligor of an option or similar obligation to which its entitlement holders have security entitlements.

Added by Acts 1995, 74th Leg., ch. 962, § 1, eff. Sept. 1, 1995.

Uniform Commercial Code Comment

1. This section expresses one of the core elements of the relationships for which the Part 5 rules were designed, to wit, that a securities intermediary undertakes to hold financial assets corresponding to the security entitlements of its entitlement holders. The locution "shall promptly obtain and shall thereafter maintain" is taken from the corresponding regulation under federal securities law, 17 C.F.R. § 240.15c3–3. This section recognizes the reality that as the securities business is conducted today, it is not possible to identify particular securities as belonging to customers as distinguished from other particular securities that are the firm's own property. Securities firms typically keep all securities in fungible form, and may maintain their inventory of a particular security in various locations and forms, including physical securities held in vaults or in transit to transfer agents, and book entry positions at one or more clearing corporations. Accordingly, this section states that a securities intermediary shall maintain a quantity of financial assets corresponding to the aggregate of all security entitlements it has established. The last sentence of subsection (a) provides explicitly that the securities intermediary may hold directly or indirectly. That point is implicit in the use of the term "financial asset," inasmuch as Section 8–102(a)(9) provides that the term "financial asset" may refer either to the underlying asset or the means by which it is held, including both security certificates and security entitlements.

2. Subsection (b) states explicitly a point that is implicit in the notion that a securities intermediary must maintain financial assets corresponding to the security entitlements of its entitlement holders, to wit, that it is wrongful for a securities intermediary to grant security interests in positions that it needs to satisfy customers' claims, except as authorized by the customers. This statement does not determine the rights of a secured party to whom a securities intermediary wrongfully grants a security interest; that issue is governed by Sections 8–503 and 8–511.

Margin accounts are common examples of arrangements in which an entitlement holder authorizes the securities intermediary to grant security interests in the positions held for the entitlement holder. Securities firms commonly obtain the funds needed to provide margin loans to their customers by "rehypothecating" the customers' securities. In order to facilitate rehypothecation, agreements between margin customers and their brokers commonly authorize the broker to commingle securities of all margin customers for rehypothecation to the lender who provides the financing. Brokers commonly rehypothecate customer securities having a value somewhat greater than the amount of the loan made to the customer, since the lenders who provide the necessary financing to the broker need some cushion of protection against the risk of decline in the value of the rehypothecated securities. The extent and manner in which a firm may rehypothecate customers' securities are determined by the agreement between the intermediary and the entitlement holder and by applicable regulatory law. Current regulations under the federal securities laws require that brokers obtain the explicit consent of customers before pledging customer securities or commingling different customers' securities for pledge. Federal regulations also limit the extent to which a broker may rehypothecate customer securities to 110% of the aggregate amount of the borrowings of all customers.

3. The statement in this section that an intermediary must obtain and maintain financial assets corresponding to the aggregate of all security entitlements it has established is intended only to capture the general point that one of the key elements that distinguishes securities accounts from other relationships, such as deposit accounts, is that the intermediary undertakes to maintain a direct correspondence between the positions it holds and the claims of its customers. This section is not intended as a detailed specification of precisely how the intermediary is to perform this duty, nor whether there may be special circumstances in which an intermediary's general duty is excused. Accordingly, the general statement of the duties of a securities intermediary in this and the following sections is supplemented by two other provisions. First, each of Sections 8–504 through 8–508 contains an "agreement/due care" provision. Second, Section 8–509 sets out general qualifications on the duties stated in these sections, including the important point that compliance with corresponding regulatory provisions constitutes compliance with the Article 8 duties.

4. The "agreement/due care" provision in subsection (c) of this section is necessary to provide sufficient flexibility to accommodate the general duty stated in subsection (a) to the wide variety of circumstances that may be encountered in the modern securities holding system. For the most common forms of publicly traded securities, the modern depository-based indirect holding system has made the likelihood of an actual loss of securities remote, though correctable errors in accounting or temporary interruptions of data processing facilities may occur. Indeed, one of the reasons for the evolution of book-entry systems is to eliminate the risk of loss or destruction of physical certificates. There are, however, some forms of securities and other financial assets which must still be held in physical certificated form, with the attendant risk of loss or destruction. Risk of loss or delay may be a more significant consideration in connection with foreign securities. An American securities intermediary may well be willing to hold a foreign security in a securities account for its customer, but the intermediary may have relatively little choice of or control over foreign intermediaries through which the security must in turn be held. Accordingly, it is common for American securities intermediaries to disclaim responsibility for custodial risk of holding through foreign intermediaries.

Subsection (c)(1) provides that a securities intermediary satisfies the duty stated in subsection (a) if the intermediary acts with respect to that duty in accordance with the agreement between the intermediary and the entitlement holder. Subsection (c)(2) provides that if there is no agreement on the matter, the intermediary satisfies the subsection (a) duty if the intermediary exercises due care in accordance with reasonable commercial standards to obtain and maintain the financial asset in question. This formulation does not state that the intermediary has a universally applicable statutory duty of due care. Section 1–102(3) provides that statutory duties of due care cannot be disclaimed by agreement, but the "agreement/due care" formula contemplates that there may be particular circumstances where the parties do not wish to create a specific duty of due care, for example, with respect to foreign securities. Under subsection (c)(1), compliance with the agreement constitutes satisfaction of the subsection (a) duty, whether or not the agreement provides that the intermediary will exercise due care.

In each of the sections where the "agreement/due care" formula is used, it provides that entering into an agreement and performing in accordance with that agreement is a method by which the securities intermediary may satisfy the statutory duty stated in that section. Accordingly, the general obligation of good faith performance of statutory and contract duties, see Sections 1–203 and 8–102(a)(10), would apply to such an agreement. It would not be consistent with the obligation of good faith performance for an agreement to purport to establish the usual sort of arrangement between an intermediary and entitlement holder, yet disclaim altogether one of the basic elements that define that relationship. For example, an agreement stating that an intermediary assumes no responsibilities whatsoever for the safekeeping any of the entitlement holder's securities positions would not be consistent with good faith performance of the intermediary's duty to obtain and maintain financial assets corresponding to the entitlement holder's security entitlements.

To the extent that no agreement under subsection (c)(1) has specified the details of the intermediary's performance of the subsection (a) duty, subsection (c)(2) provides that the intermediary satisfies that duty if it exercises due care in accordance with reasonable commercial standards. The duty of care includes both care in the intermediary's own operations and care in the selection of other intermediaries through whom the intermediary holds the assets in question. The statement of the obligation of due care is meant to incorporate the principles of the common law under which the specific actions or precautions necessary to meet the obligation of care are determined by such factors as the nature and value of the property, the customs and practices of the business, and the like.

5. This section necessarily states the duty of a securities intermediary to obtain and maintain financial assets only at the very general and abstract level. For the most part, these matters are specified in great detail by regulatory law. Broker-dealers registered under the federal securities laws are subject to detailed regulation concerning the safeguarding of customer securities. See 17 C.F.R. § 240.15c3–3. Section 8–509(a) provides explicitly that if a securities intermediary complies with such regulatory law, that constitutes compliance with Section 8–504. In certain circumstances, these rules permit a firm to be in a position where it temporarily lacks a sufficient quantity of financial assets to satisfy all customer claims. For example, if another firm has failed to make a delivery to the firm in settlement of a trade, the firm is permitted a certain period of time to clear up the problem before it is obligated to obtain the necessary securities from some other source.

6. Subsection (d) is intended to recognize that there are some circumstances, where the duty to maintain a sufficient quantity of financial assets does not apply because the inter-

mediary is not holding anything on behalf of others. For example, the Options Clearing Corporation is treated as a "securities intermediary" under this Article, although it does not itself hold options on behalf of its participants. Rather, it becomes the issuer of the options, by virtue of guaranteeing the obligations of participants in the clearing corporation who have written or purchased the options cleared through it. See Section 8–103(e). Accordingly, the general duty of an intermediary under subsection (a) does not apply, nor would other provisions of Part 5 that depend upon the existence of a requirement that the securities intermediary hold financial assets, such as Sections 8–503 and 8–508.

§ 8.505. Duty of Securities Intermediary With Respect to Payments and Distributions

(a) A securities intermediary shall take action to obtain a payment or distribution made by the issuer of a financial asset. A securities intermediary satisfies the duty if:

(1) the securities intermediary acts with respect to the duty as agreed on by the entitlement holder and the securities intermediary; or

(2) in the absence of agreement, the securities intermediary exercises due care in accordance with reasonable commercial standards to attempt to obtain the payment or distribution.

(b) A securities intermediary is obligated to its entitlement holder for a payment or distribution made by the issuer of a financial asset if the payment or distribution is received by the securities intermediary.

Added by Acts 1995, 74th Leg., ch. 962, § 1, eff. Sept. 1, 1995.

Uniform Commercial Code Comment

1. One of the core elements of the securities account relationships for which the Part 5 rules were designed is that the securities intermediary passes through to the entitlement holders the economic benefit of ownership of the financial asset, such as payments and distributions made by the issuer. Subsection (a) expresses the ordinary understanding that a securities intermediary will take appropriate action to see to it that any payments or distributions made by the issuer are received. One of the main reasons that investors make use of securities intermediaries is to obtain the services of a professional in performing the record-keeping and other functions necessary to ensure that payments and other distributions are received.

2. Subsection (a) incorporates the same "agreement/due care" formula as the other provisions of Part 5 dealing with the duties of a securities intermediary. See Comment 4 to Section 8–504. This formulation permits the parties to specify by agreement what action, if any, the intermediary is to take with respect to the duty to obtain payments and distributions. In the absence of specification by agreement, the intermediary satisfies the duty if the intermediary exercises due care in accordance with reasonable commercial standards. The provisions of Section 8–509 also apply to the Section 8–505 duty, so that compliance with applicable regulatory requirements constitutes compliance with the Section 8–505 duty.

3. Subsection (b) provides that a securities intermediary is obligated to its entitlement holder for those payments or distributions made by the issuer that are in fact received by the intermediary. It does not deal with the details of the time and manner of payment. Moreover, as with any other monetary obligation, the obligation to pay may be subject to other rights of the obligor, by way of set-off counterclaim or the like. Section 8–509(c) makes this point explicit.

§ 8.506. Duty of Securities Intermediary to Exercise Rights as Directed by Entitlement Holder

A securities intermediary shall exercise rights with respect to a financial asset if directed to do so by an entitlement holder. A securities intermediary satisfies the duty if:

(1) the securities intermediary acts with respect to the duty as agreed on by the entitlement holder and the securities intermediary; or

(2) in the absence of agreement, the securities intermediary either places the entitlement holder in a position to exercise the rights directly or exercises due care in accordance with reasonable commercial standards to follow the direction of the entitlement holder.

Added by Acts 1995, 74th Leg., ch. 962, § 1, eff. Sept. 1, 1995.

Uniform Commercial Code Comment

1. Another of the core elements of the securities account relationships for which the Part 5 rules were designed is that although the intermediary may, by virtue of the structure of the indirect holding system, be the party who has the power to exercise the corporate and other rights that come from holding the security, the intermediary exercises these powers as representative of the entitlement holder rather than at its own discretion. This characteristic is one of the things that distinguishes a securities account from other arrangements where one person holds securities "on behalf of" another, such as the relationship between a mutual fund and its shareholders or a trustee and its beneficiary.

2. The fact that the intermediary exercises the rights of security holding as representative of the entitlement holder does not, of course, preclude the entitlement holder from conferring discretionary authority upon the intermediary. Arrangements are not uncommon in which investors do not wish to have their intermediaries forward proxy materials or other information. Thus, this section provides that the intermediary shall exercise corporate and other rights "if directed to do so" by the entitlement holder. Moreover, as with the other Part 5 duties, the "agreement/due care" formulation is used in stating how the intermediary is to perform this duty.

This section also provides that the intermediary satisfies the duty if it places the entitlement holder in a position to exercise the rights directly. This is to take account of the fact that some of the rights attendant upon ownership of the security, such as rights to bring derivative and other litigation, are far removed from the matters that intermediaries are expected to perform.

3. This section, and the two that follow, deal with the aspects of securities holding that are related to investment decisions. For example, one of the rights of holding a particular security that would fall within the purview of this section would be the right to exercise a conversion right for a convertible security. It is quite common for investors to confer discretionary authority upon another person, such as an investment adviser, with respect to these rights and other investment decisions. Because this section, and the other sections of Part 5, all specify that a securities intermediary satisfies the Part 5 duties if it acts in accordance with the entitlement holder's agreement, there is no inconsistency between the statement of duties of a securities intermediary and these common arrangements.

4. Section 8–509 also applies to the Section 8–506 duty, so that compliance with applicable regulatory requirements constitutes compliance with this duty. This is quite important in this context, since the federal securities laws establish a comprehensive system of regulation of the distribution of proxy materials and exercise of voting rights with respect to securities held through brokers and other intermediaries. By virtue of Section 8–509(a), compliance with such regulatory requirement constitutes compliance with the Section 8–506 duty.

§ 8.507. Duty of Securities Intermediary to Comply with Entitlement Order

(a) A securities intermediary shall comply with an entitlement order if the entitlement order is originated by the appropriate person, the securities intermediary has had reasonable opportunity to assure itself that the entitlement order is genuine and authorized, and the securities intermediary has had reasonable opportunity to comply with the entitlement order. A securities intermediary satisfies the duty if:

(1) the securities intermediary acts with respect to the duty as agreed on by the entitlement holder and the securities intermediary; or

(2) in the absence of agreement, the securities intermediary exercises due care in accordance with reasonable commercial standards to comply with the entitlement order.

(b) If a securities intermediary transfers a financial asset pursuant to an ineffective entitlement order, the securities intermediary shall reestablish a security entitlement in favor of the person entitled to it and pay or credit any payments or distributions that the person did not receive as a result of the wrongful transfer. If the securities intermediary does not reestablish a security entitlement, the securities intermediary is liable to the entitlement holder for damages.

Added by Acts 1995, 74th Leg., ch. 962, § 1, eff. Sept. 1, 1995.

Uniform Commercial Code Comment

1. Subsection (a) of this section states another aspect of duties of securities intermediaries that make up security entitlements—the securities intermediary's duty to comply with entitlement orders. One of the main reasons for holding securities through securities intermediaries is to enable rapid transfer in settlement of trades. Thus the right to have one's orders for disposition of the security entitlement honored is an inherent part of the relationship. Subsection (b) states the correlative liability of a securities intermediary for transferring a financial asset from an entitlement holder's account pursuant to an entitlement order that was not effective.

2. The duty to comply with entitlement orders is subject to several qualifications. The intermediary has a duty only with respect to an entitlement order that is in fact originated by the appropriate person. Moreover, the intermediary has a duty only if it has had reasonable opportunity to assure itself that the order is genuine and authorized, and reasonable opportunity to comply with the order. The same "agreement/due care" formula is used in this section as in the other Part 5 sections on the duties of intermediaries, and the rules of Section 8–509 apply to the Section 8–507 duty.

3. Appropriate person is defined in Section 8–107. In the usual case, the appropriate person is the entitlement holder, see Section 8–107(a)(3). Entitlement holder is defined in Section 8–102(a)(7) as the person "identified in the records of a securities intermediary as the person having a security entitlement." Thus, the general rule is that an intermediary's duty with respect to entitlement orders runs only to the person with whom the intermediary has established a relationship. One of the basic principles of the indirect holding system is that securities intermediaries owe duties only to their own customers. See also Section 8–115. The only situation in which a securities intermediary has a duty to comply with entitlement orders originated by a person other than the person with whom the intermediary established a relationship is covered by Section 8–107(a)(4) and (a)(5), which provide that the term "appropriate person" includes the successor or personal representative of a decedent, or the custodian or guardian of a person who lacks capacity. If the entitlement holder is competent, another person does not fall within the defined term "appropriate person" merely by virtue of having power to act as an agent for the entitlement holder. Thus, an intermediary is not required to determine at its peril whether a person who purports to be authorized to act for an entitlement holder is in fact authorized to do so. If an entitlement holder wishes to be able to act through agents, the entitlement holder can establish appropriate arrangements in advance with the securities intermediary.

One important application of this principle is that if an entitlement holder grants a security interest in its security entitlements to a third-party lender, the intermediary owes no duties to the secured party, unless the intermediary has entered into a "control" agreement in which it agrees to act on entitlement orders originated by the secured party. See Section 8–106. Even though the security agreement or some other document may give the secured party authority to act as agent for the debtor, that would not make the secured party an "appropriate person" to whom the security intermediary owes duties. If the entitlement holder and securities intermediary have agreed to such a control arrangement, then the intermediary's action in following instructions from the secured party would satisfy the subsection (a) duty. Although an agent, such as the secured party in this example, is not an "appropriate person," an entitlement order is "effective" if originated by an authorized person. See Section 8–107(a) and (b). Moreover, Section 8–507(a) provides that the intermediary satisfies its duty if it acts in accordance with the entitlement holder's agreement.

4. Subsection (b) provides that an intermediary is liable for a wrongful transfer if the entitlement order was "ineffective." Section 8–107 specifies whether an entitlement order is effective. An "effective entitlement order" is different from an "entitlement order originated by an appropriate person." An entitlement order is effective under Section 8–107(b) if it is made by the appropriate person, or by a person who has power to act for the appropriate person under the law of agency, or if the appropriate person has ratified the entitlement order or is precluded from denying its effectiveness. Thus, although a securities intermediary does not have a duty to act on an entitlement order originated by the entitlement holder's agent, the intermediary is not liable for wrongful transfer if it does so.

Subsection (b), together with Section 8–107, has the effect of leaving to other law most of the questions of the sort dealt with by Article 4A for wire transfers of funds, such as allocation between the securities intermediary and the entitlement holder of the risk of fraudulent entitlement orders.

5. The term entitlement order does not cover all directions that a customer might give a broker concerning securities held through the broker. Article 8 is not a codification of all of the law of customers and stockbrokers. Article 8 deals with the settlement of securities trades, not the trades. The term entitlement order does not refer to instructions to a broker to make trades, that is, enter into contracts for the purchase or sale of securities. Rather, the entitlement order is the mechanism of transfer for securities held through intermediaries, just as indorsements and instructions are the mechanism for securities held directly. In the ordinary case the customer's direction to the broker to deliver the securities at settlement is implicit in the customer's instruction to the broker to sell. The distinction is, however, significant in that this section has no application to the relationship between the customer and broker with respect to the trade itself. For example, assertions by a customer that it was damaged by a broker's failure to execute a trading order sufficiently rapidly or in the proper manner are not governed by this Article.

§ 8.508. Duty of Securities Intermediary to Change Entitlement Holder's Position to Other Form of Security Holding

A securities intermediary shall act at the direction of an entitlement holder to change a security entitlement into another available form of holding for which the entitlement holder is eligible or to cause the financial asset to be transferred to a securities account of the entitlement holder with another securities intermediary. A securities intermediary satisfies the duty if:

(1) the securities intermediary acts as agreed on by the entitlement holder and the securities intermediary; or

(2) in the absence of agreement, the securities intermediary exercises due care in accordance with reasonable commercial standards to follow the direction of the entitlement holder.

Added by Acts 1995, 74th Leg., ch. 962, § 1, eff. Sept. 1, 1995.

Uniform Commercial Code Comment

1. This section states another aspect of the duties of securities intermediaries that make up security entitlements—the obligation of the securities intermediary to change an entitlement holder's position into any other form of holding for which the entitlement holder is eligible or to transfer the entitlement holder's position to an account at another intermediary. This section does not state unconditionally that the securities intermediary is obligated to turn over a certificate to the customer or to cause the customer to be registered on the books of the issuer, because the customer may not be eligible to hold the security directly. For example, municipal bonds are now commonly issued in "book-entry only" form, in which the only entity that the issuer will register on its own books is a depository.

If security certificates in registered form are issued for the security, and individuals are eligible to have the security registered in their own name, the entitlement holder can request that the intermediary deliver or cause to be delivered to the entitlement holder a certificate registered in the name of the entitlement holder or a certificate indorsed in blank or specially indorsed to the entitlement holder. If security certificates in bearer form are issued for the security, the entitlement holder can request that the intermediary deliver or cause to be delivered a certificate in bearer form. If the security can be held by individuals directly in uncertificated form, the entitlement holder can request that the security be registered in its name. The specification of this duty does not determine the pricing terms of the agreement in which the duty arises.

2. The same "agreement/due care" formula is used in this section as in the other Part 5 sections on the duties of intermediaries. So too, the rules of Section 8–509 apply to the Section 8–508 duty.

§ 8.509. Specification of Duties of Securities Intermediary by Other Statute or Regulation; Manner of Performance of Duties of Securities Intermediary and Exercise of Rights of Entitlement Holder

(a) If the substance of a duty imposed on a securities intermediary by Sections 8.504–8.508 is the subject of another statute, regulation, or rule, compliance with that statute, regulation, or rule satisfies the duty.

(b) To the extent that specific standards for the performance of the duties of a securities intermediary or the exercise of the rights of an entitlement holder are not specified by another statute, regulation, or rule or by agreement between the securities intermediary and the entitlement holder, the securities intermediary shall perform its duties and the entitlement holder shall exercise its rights in a commercially reasonable manner.

(c) The obligation of a securities intermediary to perform the duties imposed by Sections 8.504–8.508 is subject to:

(1) rights of the securities intermediary arising out of a security interest under a security agreement with the entitlement holder or otherwise; and

(2) rights of the securities intermediary under another law, regulation, rule, or agreement to withhold performance of its duties as a result of unfulfilled obligations of the entitlement holder to the securities intermediary.

(d) Sections 8.504–8.508 do not require a securities intermediary to take any action that is prohibited by another statute, regulation, or rule.

Added by Acts 1995, 74th Leg., ch. 962, § 1, eff. Sept. 1, 1995.

Uniform Commercial Code Comment

This Article is not a comprehensive statement of the law governing the relationship between broker-dealers or other securities intermediaries and their customers. Most of the law governing that relationship is the common law of contract and agency, supplemented or supplanted by regulatory law. This Article deals only with the most basic commercial/property law principles governing the relationship. Although Sections 8–504 through 8–508 specify certain duties of securities intermediaries to entitlement holders, the point of these sections is to identify what it means to have a security entitlement, not to specify the details of performance of these duties.

For many intermediaries, regulatory law specifies in great detail the intermediary's obligations on such matters as safekeeping of customer property, distribution of proxy materials, and the like. To avoid any conflict between the general statement of duties in this Article and the specific statement of intermediaries' obligations in such regulatory schemes, subsection (a) provides that compliance with applicable regulation constitutes compliance with the duties specified in Sections 8–504 through 8–508.

§ 8.510. Rights of Purchaser of Security Entitlement From Entitlement Holder

(a) In a case not covered by the priority rules in Chapter 9 or the rules stated in Subsection (c), an action based on an adverse claim to a financial asset or security entitlement, whether framed in conversion, replevin, constructive trust, equitable lien, or other theory, may not be asserted against a person who purchases a security entitlement, or an interest therein, from an entitlement holder if the purchaser gives value, does not have notice of the adverse claim, and obtains control.

(b) If an adverse claim could not have been asserted against an entitlement holder under Section 8.502, the adverse claim cannot be asserted against a person who purchases from the entitlement holder a security entitlement or an interest therein.

(c) In a case not covered by the priority rules in Chapter 9, a purchaser for value of a security entitlement, or an interest therein, who obtains control has priority over a purchaser of a security entitlement, or an interest therein, who does not obtain control. Except as otherwise provided in Subsection (d), purchasers who have control rank according to priority in time of:

(1) the purchaser's becoming the person for whom the securities account, in which the security entitlement is carried, is maintained, if the purchaser obtained control under Section 8.106(d)(1);

(2) the securities intermediary's agreement to comply with the purchaser's entitlement orders with respect to security entitlements carried or to be carried in the securities account in which the security entitlement is carried, if the purchaser obtained control under Section 8.106(d)(2); or

(3) if the purchaser obtained control through another person under Section 8.106(d)(3), the time on which priority would be based under this subsection if the other person were the secured party.

(d) A securities intermediary as purchaser has priority over a conflicting purchaser who has control unless otherwise agreed on by the securities intermediary.

Added by Acts 1995, 74th Leg., ch. 962, § 1, eff. Sept. 1, 1995. Amended by Acts 1999, 76th Leg., ch. 414, § 2.31, eff. July 1, 2001.

Uniform Commercial Code Comment

1. This section specifies certain rules concerning the rights of persons who purchase interests in security entitle-

ments from entitlement holders. The rules of this section are provided to take account of cases where the purchaser's rights are derivative from the rights of another person who is and continues to be the entitlement holder.

2. Subsection (a) provides that no adverse claim can be asserted against a purchaser of an interest in a security entitlement if the purchaser gives value, obtains control, and does not have notice of the adverse claim. The primary purpose of this rule is to give adverse claim protection to persons who take security interests in security entitlements and obtain control, but do not themselves become entitlement holders.

The following examples illustrate subsection (a):

Example 1. X steals a certificated bearer bond from Owner. X delivers the certificate to Able & Co. for credit to X's securities account. Later, X borrows from Bank and grants bank a security interest in the security entitlement. Bank obtains control under Section 8–106(d)(2) by virtue of an agreement in which Able agrees to comply with entitlement orders originated by Bank. X absconds.

Example 2. Same facts as in Example 1, except that Bank does not obtain a control agreement. Instead, Bank perfects by filing a financing statement.

In both of these examples, when X deposited the bonds X acquired a security entitlement under Section 8–501. Under other law, Owner may be able to have a constructive trust imposed on the security entitlement as the traceable product of the bonds that X misappropriated. X granted a security interest in that entitlement to Bank. Bank was a purchaser of an interest in the security entitlement from X. In Example 1, although Bank was not a person who acquired a security entitlement from the intermediary, Bank did obtain control. If Bank did not have notice of Owner's claim, Section 8–510(a) precludes Owner from asserting an adverse claim against Bank. In Example 2, Bank had a perfected security interest, but did not obtain control. Accordingly, Section 8–510(a) does not preclude Owner from asserting its adverse claim against Bank.

3. Subsection (b) applies to the indirect holding system a limited version of the "shelter principle." The following example illustrates the relatively limited class of cases for which it may be needed:

Example 3. Thief steals a certificated bearer bond from Owner. Thief delivers the certificate to Able & Co. for credit to Thief's securities account. Able forwards the certificate to a clearing corporation for credit to Able's account. Later Thief instructs Able to sell the positions in the bonds. Able sells to Baker & Co., acting as broker for Buyer. The trade is settled by book-entries in the accounts of Able and Baker at the clearing corporation, and in the accounts of Thief and Buyer at Able and Baker respectively. Owner may be able to reconstruct the trade records to show that settlement occurred in such fashion that the "same bonds" that were carried in Thief's account at Able are traceable into Buyer's account at Baker. Buyer later decides to donate the bonds to Alma Mater University and executes an assignment of its rights as entitlement holder to Alma Mater.

Buyer had a position in the bonds, which Buyer held in the form of a security entitlement against Baker. Buyer then made a gift of the position to Alma Mater. Although Alma Mater is a purchaser, Section 1–201(33), it did not give value. Thus, Alma Mater is a person who purchased a security entitlement, or an interest therein, from an entitlement holder (Buyer). Buyer was protected against Owner's adverse claim by the Section 8–502 rule. Thus, by virtue of Section 8–510(b), Owner is also precluded from asserting an adverse claim against Alma Mater.

4. Subsection (c) specifies a priority rule for cases where an entitlement holder transfers conflicting interests in the same security entitlement to different purchasers. It follows the same principle as the Article 9 priority rule for investment property, that is, control trumps noncontrol. Indeed, the most significant category of conflicting "purchasers" may be secured parties. Priority questions for security interests, however, are governed by the rules in Article 9. Subsection (c) applies only to cases not covered by the Article 9 rules. It is intended primarily for disputes over conflicting claims arising out of repurchase agreement transactions that are not covered by the other rules set out in Articles 8 and 9.

The following example illustrates subsection (c):

Example 4. Dealer holds securities through an account at Alpha Bank. Alpha Bank in turns holds through a clearing corporation account. Dealer transfers securities to RP1 in a "hold in custody" repo transaction. Dealer then transfers the same securities to RP2 in another repo transaction. The repo to RP2 is implemented by transferring the securities from Dealer's regular account at Alpha Bank to a special account maintained by Alpha Bank for Dealer and RP2. The agreement among Dealer, RP2, and Alpha Bank provides that Dealer can make substitutions for the securities but RP2 can direct Alpha Bank to sell any securities held in the special account. Dealer becomes insolvent. RP1 claims a prior interest in the securities transferred to RP2.

In this example Dealer remained the entitlement holder but agreed that RP2 could initiate entitlement orders to Dealer's security intermediary, Alpha Bank. If RP2 had become the entitlement holder, the adverse claim rule of Section 8–502 would apply. Even if RP2 does not become the entitlement holder, the arrangement among Dealer, Alpha Bank, and RP2 does suffice to give RP2 control. Thus, under Section 8–510(c), RP2 has priority over RP1, because RP2 is a purchaser who obtained control, and RP1 is a purchaser who did not obtain control. The same result could be reached under Section 8–510(a) which provides that RP1's earlier in time interest cannot be asserted as an adverse claim against RP2. The same result would follow under the Article 9 priority rules if the interests of RP1 and RP2 are characterized as "security interests," see Section 9–328(1). The main point of the rules of Section 8–510(c) is to ensure that there will be clear rules to cover the conflicting claims of RP1 and RP2 without characterizing their interests as Article 9 security interests.

The priority rules in Article 9 for conflicting security interests also include a default temporal priority rule for cases where multiple secured parties have obtained control but omitted to specify their respective rights by agreement. See Section 9–328(2) and Comment 5 to Section 9328. Because the purchaser priority rule in Section 8–510(c) is intended to track the Article 9 priority rules, it too has a temporal priority rule for cases where multiple nonsecured party purchasers have obtained control but omitted to specify their respective rights by agreement. The rule is patterned on Section 9–328(2).

5. If a securities intermediary itself is a purchaser, subsection (d) provides that it has priority over the interest of another purchaser who has control. Article 9 contains a similar rule. See Section 9–328(3).

§ 8.511. Priority Among Security Interests and Entitlement Holders

(a) Except as otherwise provided in Subsections (b) and (c), if a securities intermediary does not have sufficient interests in a particular financial asset to satisfy both its obligations to entitlement holders who have security entitlements to that financial asset and its obligation to a creditor of the securities intermediary who has a security interest in that financial asset, the claims of entitlement holders, other than the creditor, have priority over the claim of the creditor.

(b) A claim of a creditor of a securities intermediary who has a security interest in a financial asset held by a securities intermediary has priority over claims of the securities intermediary's entitlement holders who have security entitlements with respect to that financial asset if the creditor has control over the financial asset.

(c) If a clearing corporation does not have sufficient financial assets to satisfy both its obligations to entitlement holders who have security entitlements with respect to a financial asset and its obligation to a creditor of the clearing corporation who has a security interest in that financial asset, the claim of the creditor has priority over the claims of entitlement holders.

Added by Acts 1995, 74th Leg., ch. 962, § 1, eff. Sept. 1, 1995.

Uniform Commercial Code Comment

1. This section sets out priority rules for circumstances in which a securities intermediary fails leaving an insufficient quantity of securities or other financial assets to satisfy the claims of its entitlement holders and the claims of creditors to whom it has granted security interests in financial assets held by it. Subsection (a) provides that entitlement holders' claims have priority except as otherwise provided in subsection (b), and subsection (b) provides that the secured creditor's claim has priority if the secured creditor obtains control, as defined in Section 8–106. The following examples illustrate the operation of these rules.

Example 1. Able & Co., a broker, borrows from Alpha Bank and grants Alpha Bank a security interest pursuant to a written agreement which identifies certain securities that are to be collateral for the loan, either specifically or by category. Able holds these securities in a clearing corporation account. Able becomes insolvent and it is discovered that Able holds insufficient securities to satisfy the claims of customers who have paid for securities that they held in accounts with Able and the collateral claims of Alpha Bank. Alpha Bank's security interest in the security entitlements that Able holds through the clearing corporation account may be perfected under the automatic perfection rule of Section 9–309(10), but Alpha Bank did not obtain control under Section 8–106. Thus, under Section 8–511(a) the entitlement holders' claims have priority over Alpha Bank's claim.

Example 2. Able & Co., a broker, borrows from Beta Bank and grants Beta Bank a security interest in securities that Able holds in a clearing corporation account. Pursuant to the security agreement, the securities are debited from Alpha's account and credited to Beta's account in the clearing corporation account. Able becomes insolvent and it is discovered that Able holds insufficient securities to satisfy the claims of customers who have paid for securities that they held in accounts with Able and the collateral claims of Alpha Bank. Although the transaction between Able and Beta took the form of an outright transfer on the clearing corporation's books, as between Able and Beta, Able remains the owner and Beta has a security interest. In that respect the situation is no different than if Able had delivered bearer bonds to Beta in pledge to secure a loan. Beta's security interest is perfected, and Beta obtained control. See Sections 8–106 and 9–314. Under Section 8–511(b), Beta Bank's security interest has priority over claims of Able's customers.

The result in Example 2 is an application to this particular setting of the general principle expressed in Section 8–503, and explained in the Comments thereto, that the entitlement holders of a securities intermediary cannot assert rights against third parties to whom the intermediary has wrongfully transferred interests, except in extremely unusual circumstances where the third party was itself a participant in the transferor's wrongdoing. Under subsection (b) the claim of a secured creditor of a securities intermediary has priority over the claims of entitlement holders if the secured creditor has obtained control. If, however, the secured creditor acted in collusion with the intermediary in violating the intermediary's obligation to its entitlement holders, then under Section 8–503(e), the entitlement holders, through their representative in insolvency proceedings, could recover the interest from the secured creditor, that is, set aside the security interest.

2. The risk that investors who hold through an intermediary will suffer a loss as a result of a wrongful pledge by the intermediary is no different than the risk that the intermediary might fail and not have the securities that it was supposed to be holding on behalf of its customers, either because the securities were never acquired by the intermediary or because the intermediary wrongfully sold securities that should have been kept to satisfy customers' claims. Investors are protected against that risk by the regulatory regimes under which securities intermediaries operate. Intermediaries are required to maintain custody, through clearing corporation accounts or in other approved locations, of their customers' securities and are prohibited from using customers' securities in their own business activities. Securities firms who are carrying both customer and proprietary posi-

tions are not permitted to grant blanket liens to lenders covering all securities which they hold, for their own account or for their customers. Rather, securities firms designate specifically which positions they are pledging. Under SEC Rules 8c–1 and 15c2–1, customers' securities can be pledged only to fund loans to customers, and only with the consent of the customers. Customers' securities cannot be pledged for loans for the firm's proprietary business; only proprietary positions can be pledged for proprietary loans. SEC Rule 15c3–3 implements these prohibitions in a fashion tailored to modern securities firm accounting systems by requiring brokers to maintain a sufficient inventory of securities, free from any liens, to satisfy the claims of all of their customers for fully paid and excess margin securities. Revised Article 8 mirrors that requirement, specifying in Section 8–504 that a securities intermediary must maintain a sufficient quantity of investment property to satisfy all security entitlements, and may not grant security interests in the positions it is required to hold for customers, except as authorized by the customers.

If a failed brokerage has violated the customer protection regulations and does not have sufficient securities to satisfy customers' claims, its customers are protected against loss from a shortfall by the Securities Investor Protection Act ("SIPA"). Securities firms required to register as brokers or dealers are also required to become members of the Securities Investor Protection Corporation ("SIPC"), which provides their customers with protection somewhat similar to that provided by FDIC and other deposit insurance programs for bank depositors. When a member firm fails, SIPC is authorized to initiate a liquidation proceeding under the provisions of SIPA. If the assets of the securities firm are insufficient to satisfy all customer claims, SIPA makes contributions to the estate from a fund financed by assessments on its members to protect customers against losses up to $500,000 for cash and securities held at member firms.

Article 8 is premised on the view that the important policy of protecting investors against the risk of wrongful conduct by their intermediaries is sufficiently treated by other law.

3. Subsection (c) sets out a special rule for secured financing provided to enable clearing corporations to complete settlement. In order to permit clearing corporations to establish liquidity facilities where necessary to ensure completion of settlement, subsection (c) provides a priority for secured lenders to such clearing corporations. Subsection (c) does not turn on control because the clearing corporation may be the top tier securities intermediary for the securities pledged, so that there may be no practicable method for conferring control on the lender.

CHAPTER 9. SECURED TRANSACTIONS

SUBCHAPTER A. SHORT TITLE, DEFINITIONS, AND GENERAL CONCEPTS

SUBCHAPTER B. EFFECTIVENESS OF SECURITY AGREEMENT; ATTACHMENT OF SECURITY INTEREST; RIGHTS OF PARTIES TO SECURITY AGREEMENT

SUBCHAPTER C. PERFECTION AND PRIORITY

Acts 1999, 76th Leg., ch. 414, § 1.01, amended Chapter 9 effective July 1, 2001. The former Chapter 9, Secured Transactions; Sales of Accounts and Chattel Paper, consisting of §§ 9.101 to 9.507, was amended as Chapter 9, Secured Transactions, consisting of §§ 9.101 to 9.709.

DISPOSITION TABLE

Showing where the subject matter of provisions contained in former Chapter 9, Secured Transactions; Sales of Accounts and Chattel Paper, may be found in Chapter 9, Secured Transactions, as amended by Acts 1999, 76th Leg., ch. 414, § 1.01.

Former Section	Amended Section
9.101	9.101
9.102	9.109
9.103	9.301, 9.305 to 9.307, 9.316, 9.337
9.104	9.109
9.105	9.102
9.106	9.102
9.107	9.103
9.108	—
9.109	9.102
9.110	9.108
9.111	—
9.112	—
9.113	9.110
9.114	—
9.115	9.106
9.116	9.206
9.201	9.201
9.202	9.202
9.203	9.203
9.204	9.204
9.205	9.205
9.206	9.403
9.207	9.207
9.208	9.210
9.301	9.317, 9.323
9.302	9.309 to 9.311
9.303	9.308
9.304	9.312
9.305	9.313
9.306	9.315
9.307	9.320
9.308	9.330
9.309	9.331
9.310	9.333
9.311	9.401
9.312	9.322, 9.324
9.313	9.334, 9.604
9.314	9.335
9.315	9.336
9.316	9.339
9.317	9.402
9.318	9.404, 9.406
9.319	9.343
9.401	9.501

Former Section	Amended Section
9.402	9.502, 9.503, 9.504, 9.506, 9.507, 9.512
9.403	9.515, 9.516, 9.519, 9.522, 9.525
9.404	9.513
9.405	9.514, 9.519
9.406	9.512
9.407	9.523
9.408	9.505
9.409	—
9.4095	9.525
9.410	—
9.411	9.526
9.412	9.5185
9.501	9.601 to 9.604
9.502	9.607, 9.608
9.503	9.609
9.504	9.610, 9.611, 9.615, 9.617, 9.618, 9.624
9.505	9.620, 9.621, 9.624
9.506	9.623, 9.624
9.507	9.625, 9.627
—	9.104
—	9.105
—	9.107
—	9.208
—	9.209
—	9.302
—	9.303
—	9.304
—	9.314
—	9.318
—	9.319
—	9.321
—	9.325 to 9.329
—	9.332
—	9.338
—	9.340 to 9.342
—	9.408 and 9.409
—	9.503
—	9.508 to 9.511
—	9.517 and 9.518
—	9.520
—	9.522
—	9.524
—	9.527
—	9.605 and 9.606
—	9.612 to 9.614
—	9.616
—	9.619
—	9.626
—	9.628

SUBCHAPTER A. SHORT TITLE, DEFINITIONS, AND GENERAL CONCEPTS

§ 9.101. Short Title

This chapter may be cited as Uniform Commercial Code—Secured Transactions.

Amended by Acts 1999, 76th Leg., ch. 414, § 1.01, eff. July 1, 2001.

Uniform Commercial Code Comment

1. **Source.** This Article supersedes former Uniform Commercial Code (UCC) Article 9. As did its predecessor, it provides a comprehensive scheme for the regulation of security interests in personal property and fixtures. For the most part this Article follows the general approach and retains much of the terminology of former Article 9. In addition to describing many aspects of the operation and interpretation of this Article, these Comments explain the material changes that this Article makes to former Article 9. Former Article 9 superseded the wide variety of pre-UCC security devices. Unlike the Comments to former Article 9, however, these Comments dwell very little on the pre-UCC state of the law. For that reason, the Comments to former Article 9 will remain of substantial historical value and interest. They also will remain useful in understanding the background and general conceptual approach of this Article.

Citations to "Bankruptcy Code Section ____" in these Comments are to Title 11 of the United States Code as in effect on December 31, 1998.

2. **Background and History.** In 1990, the Permanent Editorial Board for the UCC with the support of its sponsors, The American Law Institute and the National Conference of Commissioners on Uniform State Laws, established a committee to study Article 9 of the UCC. The study committee issued its report as of December 1, 1992, recommending the creation of a drafting committee for the revision of Article 9 and also recommending numerous specific changes to Article 9. Organized in 1993, a drafting committee met fifteen times from 1993 to 1998. This Article was approved by its sponsors in 1998.

3. **Reorganization and Renumbering; Captions; Style.** This Article reflects a substantial reorganization of former Article 9 and renumbering of most sections. New Part 4 deals with several aspects of third-party rights and duties that are unrelated to perfection and priority. Some of these were covered by Part 3 of former Article 9. Part 5 deals with filing (covered by former Part 4) and Part 6 deals with default and enforcement (covered by former Part 5). Appendix I contains conforming revisions to other articles of the UCC, and Appendix II contains model provisions for production-money priority.

This Article also includes headings for the subsections as an aid to readers. Unlike section captions, which are part of the UCC, see Section 1–109, subsection headings are not a part of the official text itself and have not been approved by the sponsors. Each jurisdiction in which this Article is introduced may consider whether to adopt the headings as a part of the statute and whether to adopt a provision clarifying the effect, if any, to be given to the headings. This Article also has been conformed to current style conventions.

4. **Summary of Revisions.** Following is a brief summary of some of the more significant revisions of Article 9 that are included in this Article.

a. **Scope of Article 9.** This Article expands the scope of Article 9 in several respects.

Deposit accounts. Section 9–109 includes within this Article's scope deposit accounts as original collateral, except in consumer transactions. Former Article 9 dealt with deposit accounts only as proceeds of other collateral.

Sales of payment intangibles and promissory notes. Section 9–109 also includes within the scope of this Article most sales of "payment intangibles" (defined in Section 9–102 as general intangibles under which an account debtor's principal obligation is monetary) and "promissory notes" (also defined in Section 9–102). Former Article 9 included sales of accounts and chattel paper, but not sales of payment intangibles or promissory notes. In its inclusion of sales of payment intangibles and promissory notes, this Article continues the drafting convention found in former Article 9; it provides that the sale of accounts, chattel paper, payment intangibles, or promissory notes creates a "security interest." The definition of "account" in Section 9–102 also has been expanded to include various rights to payment that were general intangibles under former Article 9.

Health-care-insurance receivables. Section 9–109 narrows Article 9's exclusion of transfers of interests in insurance policies by carving out of the exclusion "health-care-insurance receivables" (defined in Section 9–102). A health-care-insurance receivable is included within the definition of "account" in Section 9–102.

Nonpossessory statutory agricultural liens. Section 9–109 also brings nonpossessory statutory agricultural liens within the scope of Article 9.

Consignments. Section 9–109 provides that "true" consignments–bailments for the purpose of sale by the bailee–are security interests covered by Article 9, with certain exceptions. See Section 9–102 (defining "consignment"). Currently, many consignments are subject to Article 9's filing requirements by operation of former Section 2–326.

Supporting obligations and property securing rights to payment. This Article also addresses explicitly (i) obligations, such as guaranties and letters of credit, that support payment or performance of collateral such as accounts, chattel paper, and payment intangibles, and (ii) any property (including real property) that secures a right to payment or performance that is subject to an Article 9 security interest. See Sections 9–203, 9–308.

Commercial tort claims. Section 9–109 expands the scope of Article 9 to include the assignment of commercial tort claims by narrowing the exclusion of tort claims generally. However, this Article continues to exclude tort claims for bodily injury and other non-business tort claims of a natural person. See Section 9–102 (defining "commercial tort claim").

Transfers by States and governmental units of States. Section 9–109 narrows the exclusion of transfers by States and their governmental units. It excludes only transfers covered by another statute (other than a statute generally applicable to security interests) to the extent the statute governs the creation, perfection, priority, or enforcement of security interests.

Nonassignable general intangibles, promissory notes, health-care-insurance receivables, and letter-of-credit rights. This Article enables a security interest to attach to letter-of-credit rights, health-care-insurance receivables, promissory notes, and general intangibles, including contracts, permits, licenses, and franchises, notwithstanding a contractual or statutory prohibition against or limitation on assignment. This Article explicitly protects third parties against any adverse effect of the creation or attempted enforcement of the security interest. See Sections 9–408, 9–409.

Subject to Sections 9–408 and 9–409 and two other exceptions (Sections 9–406, concerning accounts, chattel paper, and payment intangibles, and 9–407, concerning interests in leased goods), Section 9–401 establishes a baseline rule that the inclusion of transactions and collateral within the scope of Article 9 has no effect on non-Article 9 law dealing with the alienability or inalienability of property. For example, if a commercial tort claim is nonassignable under other applicable law, the fact that a security interest in the claim is within the scope of Article 9 does not override the other applicable law's effective prohibition of assignment.

b. **Duties of Secured Party.** This Article provides for expanded duties of secured parties.

Release of control. Section 9–208 imposes upon a secured party having control of a deposit account, investment property, or a letter-of-credit right the duty to release control when there is no secured obligation and no commitment to give value. Section 9–209 contains analogous provisions when an account debtor has been notified to pay a secured party.

Information. Section 9–210 expands a secured party's duties to provide the debtor with information concerning collateral and the obligations that it secures.

Default and enforcement. Part 6 also includes some additional duties of secured parties in connection with default and enforcement. See, e.g., Section 9–616 (duty to explain calculation of deficiency or surplus in a consumer-goods transaction).

c. **Choice of Law.** The choice-of-law rules for the law governing perfection, the effect of perfection or nonperfection, and priority are found in Part 3, Subpart 1 (Sections 9–301 through 9–307). See also Section 9–316.

Where to file: Location of debtor. This Article changes the choice-of-law rule governing perfection (i.e., where to file) for most collateral to the law of the jurisdiction where the debtor is located. See Section 9–301. Under former Article 9, the jurisdiction of the debtor's location governed only perfection and priority of a security interest in accounts, general intangibles, mobile goods, and, for purposes of perfection by filing, chattel paper and investment property.

Determining debtor's location. As a baseline rule, Section 9–307 follows former Section 9–103, under which the location of the debtor is the debtor's place of business (or chief executive office, if the debtor has more than one place of business). Section 9–307 contains three major exceptions. First, a "registered organization," such as a corporation or limited liability company, is located in the State under whose law the debtor is organized, e.g., a corporate debtor's State of incorporation. Second, an individual debtor is located at his or her principal residence. Third, there are special rules for determining the location of the United States and registered organizations organized under the law of the United States.

Location of non-U.S. debtors. If, applying the foregoing rules, a debtor is located in a jurisdiction whose law does not require public notice as a condition of perfection of a nonpossessory security interest, the entity is deemed located in the

District of Columbia. See Section 9–307. Thus, to the extent that this Article applies to non-U.S. debtors, perfection could be accomplished in many cases by a domestic filing.

Priority. For tangible collateral such as goods and instruments, Section 9–301 provides that the law applicable to priority and the effect of perfection or nonperfection will remain the law of the jurisdiction where the collateral is located, as under former Section 9–103 (but without the confusing "last event" test). For intangible collateral, such as accounts, the applicable law for priority will be that of the jurisdiction in which the debtor is located.

Possessory security interests; agricultural liens. Perfection, the effect of perfection or nonperfection, and priority of a possessory security interest or an agricultural lien are governed by the law of the jurisdiction where the collateral subject to the security interest or lien is located. See Sections 9–301, 9–302.

Goods covered by certificates of title; deposit accounts; letter-of-credit rights; investment property. This Article includes several refinements to the treatment of choice-of-law matters for goods covered by certificates of title. See Section 9–303. It also provides special choice-of-law rules, similar to those for investment property under current Articles 8 and 9, for deposit accounts (Section 9–304), investment property (Section 9–305), and letter-of-credit rights (Section 9–306).

Change in applicable law. Section 9–316 addresses perfection following a change in applicable law.

d. **Perfection.** The rules governing perfection of security interests and agricultural liens are found in Part 3, Subpart 2 (Sections 9–308 through 9–316).

Deposit accounts; letter-of-credit rights. With certain exceptions, this Article provides that a security interest in a deposit account or a letter-of-credit right may be perfected *only* by the secured party's acquiring "control" of the deposit account or letter-of-credit right. See Sections 9–312, 9–314. Under Section 9–104, a secured party has "control" of a deposit account when, with the consent of the debtor, the secured party obtains the depositary bank's agreement to act on the secured party's instructions (including when the secured party becomes the account holder) or when the secured party is itself the depositary bank. The control requirements are patterned on Section 8–106, which specifies the requirements for control of investment property. Under Section 9–107, "control" of a letter-of-credit right occurs when the issuer or nominated person consents to an assignment of proceeds under Section 5–114.

Electronic chattel paper. Section 9–102 includes a new defined term: "electronic chattel paper." Electronic chattel paper is a record or records consisting of information stored in an electronic medium (i.e., it is not written). Perfection of a security interest in electronic chattel paper may be by control or filing. See Sections 9–105 (*sui generis* definition of control of electronic chattel paper), 9–312 (perfection by filing), 9–314 (perfection by control).

Investment property. The perfection requirements for "investment property" (defined in Section 9–102), including perfection by control under Section 9–106, remain substantially unchanged. However, a new provision in Section 9–314 is designed to ensure that a secured party retains control in "repledge" transactions that are typical in the securities markets.

Instruments, agricultural liens, and commercial tort claims. This Article expands the types of collateral in which a security interest may be perfected by filing to include instruments. See Section 9–312. Agricultural liens and security interests in commercial tort claims also are perfected by filing, under this Article. See Sections 9–308, 9–310.

Sales of payment intangibles and promissory notes. Although former Article 9 covered the outright sale of accounts and chattel paper, sales of most other types of receivables also are financing transactions to which Article 9 should apply. Accordingly, Section 9–102 expands the definition of "account" to include many types of receivables (including "health-care-insurance receivables," defined in Section 9–102) that former Article 9 classified as "general intangibles." It thereby subjects to Article 9's filing system sales of more types of receivables than did former Article 9. Certain sales of payment intangibles–primarily bank loan participation transactions–should not be subject to the Article 9 filing rules. These transactions fall in a residual category of collateral, "payment intangibles" (general intangibles under which the account debtor's principal obligation is monetary), the sale of which is exempt from the filing requirements of Article 9. See Sections 9–102, 9–109, 9–309 (perfection upon attachment). The perfection rules for sales of promissory notes are the same as those for sales of payment intangibles.

Possessory security interests. Several provisions of this Article address aspects of security interests involving a secured party or a third party who is in possession of the collateral. In particular, Section 9–313 resolves a number of uncertainties under former Section 9–305. It provides that a security interest in collateral in the possession of a third party is perfected when the third party acknowledges in an authenticated record that it holds for the secured party's benefit. Section 9–313 also provides that a third party need not so acknowledge and that its acknowledgment does not impose any duties on it, unless it otherwise agrees. A special rule in Section 9–313 provides that if a secured party already is in possession of collateral, its security interest remains perfected by possession if it delivers the collateral to a third party and the collateral is accompanied by instructions to hold it for the secured party or to redeliver it to the secured party. Section 9–313 also clarifies the limited circumstances under which a security interest in goods covered by a certificate of title may be perfected by the secured party's taking possession.

Automatic perfection. Section 9–309 lists various types of security interests as to which no public-notice step is required for perfection (e.g., purchase-money security interests in consumer goods other than automobiles). This automatic perfection also extends to a transfer of a health-care-insurance receivable *to* a health-care provider. Those transfers normally will be made by natural persons who receive health-care services; there is little value in requiring filing for perfection in that context. Automatic perfection also applies to security interests created by sales of payment intangibles and promissory notes. Section 9–308 provides that a perfected security interest in collateral supported by a "supporting obligation" (such as an account supported by a guaranty) also is a perfected security interest in the supporting obligation, and that a perfected security interest in an obligation secured by a security interest or lien on property (e.g., a real-property mortgage) also is a perfected security interest in the security interest or lien.

e. **Priority; Special Rules for Banks and Deposit Accounts.** The rules governing priority of security interests and agricultural liens are found in Part 3, Subpart 3 (Sections 9–317 through 9–342). This Article includes several new priority rules and some special rules relating to banks and deposit accounts (Sections 9–340 through 9–342).

Purchase-money security interests: General; consumer-goods transactions; inventory. Section 9–103 substantially rewrites the definition of purchase-money security interest (PMSI) (although the term is not formally "defined"). The substantive changes, however, apply only to non-consumer-goods transactions. (Consumer transactions and consumer-goods transactions are discussed below in Comment 4.j.) For non-consumer-goods transactions, Section 9–103 makes clear that a security interest in collateral may be (to some extent) both a PMSI as well as a non-PMSI, in accord with the "dual status" rule applied by some courts under former Article 9 (thereby rejecting the "transformation" rule). The definition provides an even broader conception of a PMSI in inventory, yielding a result that accords with private agreements entered into in response to the uncertainty under former Article 9. It also treats consignments as purchase-money security interests in inventory. Section 9–324 revises the PMSI priority rules, but for the most part without material change in substance. Section 9–324 also clarifies the priority rules for competing PMSIs in the same collateral.

Purchase-money security interests in livestock; agricultural liens. Section 9–324 provides a special PMSI priority, similar to the inventory PMSI priority rule, for livestock. Section 9–322 (which contains the baseline first-to-file-or-perfect priority rule) also recognizes special non-Article 9 priority rules for agricultural liens, which can override the baseline first-in-time rule.

Purchase-money security interests in software. Section 9–324 contains a new priority rule for a software purchase-money security interest.

Investment property. The priority rules for investment property are substantially similar to the priority rules found in former Section 9–115, which was added in conjunction with the 1994 revisions to UCC Article 8. Under Section 9–328, if a secured party has control of investment property (Sections 8–106, 9–106), its security interest is senior to a security interest perfected in another manner (e.g., by filing). Also under Section 9–328, security interests perfected by control generally rank according to the time that control is obtained or, in the case of a security entitlement or a commodity contract carried in a commodity account, the time when the control arrangement is entered into. This is a change from former Section 9–115, under which the security interests ranked equally. However, as between a securities intermediary's security interest in a security entitlement that it maintains for the debtor and a security interest held by another secured party, the securities intermediary's security interest is senior.

Deposit accounts. This Article's priority rules applicable to deposit accounts are found in Section 9–327. They are patterned on and are similar to those for investment property in former Section 9–115 and Section 9–328 of this Article. Under Section 9–327, if a secured party has control of a deposit account, its security interest is senior to a security interest perfected in another manner (i.e., as cash proceeds). Also under Section 9–327, security interests perfected by control rank according to the time that control is obtained, but as between a depositary bank's security interest and one held by another secured party, the depositary bank's security interest is senior. A corresponding rule in Section 9–340 makes a depositary bank's right of set-off generally senior to a security interest held by another secured party. However, if the other secured party becomes the depositary bank's customer with respect to the deposit account, then its security interest is senior to the depositary bank's security interest and right of set-off. Sections 9–327, 9–340.

Letter-of-credit rights. The priority rules for security interests in letter-of-credit rights are found in Section 9–329. They are somewhat analogous to those for deposit accounts. A security interest perfected by control has priority over one perfected in another manner (i.e., as a supporting obligation for the collateral in which a security interest is perfected). Security interests in a letter-of-credit right perfected by control rank according to the time that control is obtained. However, the rights of a transferee beneficiary or a nominated person are independent and superior to the extent provided in Section 5–114. See Section 9–109(c)(4).

Chattel paper and instruments. Section 9–330 is the successor to former Section 9–308. As under former Section 9–308, differing priority rules apply to purchasers of chattel paper who give new value and take possession (or, in the case of electronic chattel paper, obtain control) of the collateral depending on whether a conflicting security interest in the collateral is claimed merely as proceeds. The principal change relates to the role of knowledge and the effect of an indication of a previous assignment of the collateral. Section 9–330 also affords priority to purchasers of instruments who take possession in good faith and without knowledge that the purchase violates the rights of the competing secured party. In addition, to qualify for priority, purchasers of chattel paper, but not of instruments, must purchase in the ordinary course of business.

Proceeds. Section 9–322 contains new priority rules that clarify when a special priority of a security interest in collateral continues or does not continue with respect to proceeds of the collateral. Other refinements to the priority rules for proceeds are included in Sections 9–324 (purchase-money security interest priority) and 9–330 (priority of certain purchasers of chattel paper and instruments).

Miscellaneous priority provisions. This Article also includes (i) clarifications of selected good-faith-purchase and similar issues (Sections 9–317, 9–331); (ii) new priority rules to deal with the "double debtor" problem arising when a debtor creates a security interest in collateral acquired by the debtor subject to a security interest created by another person (Section 9–325); (iii) new priority rules to deal with the problems created when a change in corporate structure or the like results in a new entity that has become bound by the original debtor's after-acquired property agreement (Section 9–326); (iv) a provision enabling most transferees of funds from a deposit account or money to take free of a security interest (Section 9–332); (v) substantially rewritten and refined priority rules dealing with accessions and commingled goods (Sections 9–335, 9–336); (vi) revised priority rules for security interests in goods covered by a certificate of title (Section 9–337); and (vii) provisions designed to ensure that security interests in deposit accounts will not extend to most transferees of funds on deposit or payees from deposit accounts and will not otherwise "clog" the payments system (Sections 9–341, 9–342).

Model provisions relating to production-money security interests. Appendix II to this Article contains model definitions and priority rules relating to "production-money security interests" held by secured parties who give new value used in the production of crops. Because no consensus emerged on the wisdom of these provisions during the drafting process, the sponsors make no recommendation on whether these model provisions should be enacted.

f. **Proceeds.** Section 9–102 contains an expanded definition of "proceeds" of collateral which includes additional rights and property that arise out of collateral, such as distributions on account of collateral and claims arising out of the loss or nonconformity of, defects in, or damage to collateral. The term also includes collections on account of "supporting obligations," such as guarantees.

g. **Part 4: Additional Provisions Relating to Third–Party Rights.** New Part 4 contains several provisions relating to the relationships between certain third parties and the parties to secured transactions. It contains new Sections 9–401 (replacing former Section 9–311) (alienability of debtor's rights), 9–402 (replacing former Section 9–317) (secured party not obligated on debtor's contracts), 9–403 (replacing former Section 9–206) (agreement not to assert defenses against assignee), 9–404, 9–405, and 9–406 (replacing former Section 9–318) (rights acquired by assignee, modification of assigned contract, discharge of account debtor, restrictions on assignment of account, chattel paper, promissory note, or payment intangible ineffective), 9–407 (replacing some provisions of former Section 2A–303) (restrictions on creation or enforcement of security interest in leasehold interest or lessor's residual interest ineffective). It also contains new Sections 9–408 (restrictions on assignment of promissory notes, health-care-insurance receivables ineffective, and certain general intangibles ineffective) and 9–409 (restrictions on assignment of letter-of-credit rights ineffective), which are discussed above.

h. **Filing.** Part 5 (formerly Part 4) of Article 9 has been substantially rewritten to simplify the statutory text and to deal with numerous problems of interpretation and implementation that have arisen over the years.

Medium-neutrality. This Article is "medium-neutral"; that is, it makes clear that parties may file and otherwise communicate with a filing office by means of records communicated and stored in media other than on paper.

Identity of person who files a record; authorization. Part 5 is largely indifferent as to the person who effects a filing. Instead, it addresses whose authorization is necessary for a person to file a record with a filing office. The filing scheme does not contemplate that the identity of a "filer" will be a part of the searchable records. This approach is consistent with, and a necessary aspect of, eliminating signatures or other evidence of authorization from the system (except to the extent that filing offices may choose to employ authentication procedures in connection with electronic communications). As long as the appropriate person authorizes the filing, or, in the case of a termination statement, the debtor is entitled to the termination, it is largely insignificant whether the secured party or another person files any given record.

Section 9–509 collects in one place most of the rules that determine when a record may be filed. In general, the debtor's authorization is required for the filing of an initial financing statement or an amendment that adds collateral. With one further exception, a secured party of record's authorization is required for the filing of other amendments. The exception arises if a secured party has failed to provide a termination statement that is required because there is no outstanding secured obligation or commitment to give value. In that situation, a debtor is authorized to file a termination statement indicating that it has been filed by the debtor.

Financing statement formal requisites. The formal requisites for a financing statement are set out in Section 9–502. A financing statement must provide the name of the debtor and the secured party and an indication of the collateral that it covers. Sections 9–503 and 9–506 address the sufficiency of a name provided on a financing statement and clarify when a debtor's name is correct and when an incorrect name is insufficient. Section 9–504 addresses the indication of collateral covered. Under Section 9–504, a super-generic description (e.g.,"all assets" or "all personal property") in a financing statement is a sufficient indication of the collateral. (Note, however, that a super-generic description is inadequate for purposes of a security agreement. See Sections 9–108, 9–203.) To facilitate electronic filing, this Article does not require that the debtor's signature or other authorization appear on a financing statement. Instead, it prohibits the filing of unauthorized financing statements and imposes liability upon those who violate the prohibition. See Sections 9–509, 9–626.

Filing-office operations. Part 5 contains several provisions governing filing operations. First, it prohibits the filing office from rejecting an initial financing statement or other record for a reason other than one of the few that are specified. See Sections 9–520, 9–516. Second, the filing office is obliged to link all subsequent records (e.g., assignments, continuation statements, etc.) to the initial financing statement to which they relate. See Section 9–519. Third, the filing office may delete a financing statement and related records from the files no earlier than one year after lapse (lapse normally is five years after the filing date), and then only if a continuation statement has not been filed. See Sections 9–515, 9–519, 9–522. Thus, a financing statement and related records would be discovered by a search of the files even after the filing of a termination statement. This approach helps eliminate filing-office discretion and also eases problems associated with multiple secured parties and multiple partial assignments. Fourth, Part 5 mandates performance standards for filing offices. See Sections 9–519, 9–520, 9–523. Fifth, it provides for the promulgation of filing-office rules to deal with details best left out of the statute and requires the filing office to submit periodic reports. See Sections 9–526, 9–527.

Correction of records: Defaulting or missing secured parties and fraudulent filings. In some areas of the country, serious problems have arisen from fraudulent financing statements that are filed against public officials and other persons. This Article addresses the fraud problem by providing the opportunity for a debtor to file a termination statement when a secured party wrongfully refuses or fails to provide a termination statement. See Section 9–509. This opportunity also addresses the problem of secured parties that simply disappear through mergers or liquidations. In addition, Section 9–518 affords a statutory method by which a debtor who believes that a filed record is inaccurate or was wrongfully filed may indicate that fact in the files by filing a correction statement, albeit without affecting the efficacy, if any, of the challenged record.

Extended period of effectiveness for certain financing statements. Section 9–515 contains an exception to the usual rule that financing statements are effective for five years unless a continuation statement is filed to continue the effectiveness for another five years. Under that section, an initial financing statement filed in connection with a "public-finance transaction" or a "manufactured-home transaction" (terms defined in Section 9–102) is effective for 30 years.

National form of financing statement and related forms. Section 9–521 provides for uniform, national written forms of financing statements and related written records that must be accepted by a filing office that accepts written records.

i. **Default and Enforcement.** Part 6 of Article 9 extensively revises former Part 5. Provisions relating to enforcement of consumer-goods transactions and consumer transactions are discussed in Comment 4.j.

Debtor, secondary obligor; waiver. Section 9–602 clarifies the identity of persons who have rights and persons to whom a secured party owes specified duties under Part 6. Under that section, the rights and duties are enjoyed by and run to the "debtor," defined in Section 9–102 to mean any person with a non-lien property interest in collateral, and to any "obligor." However, with one exception (Section 9–616, as it relates to a consumer obligor), the rights and duties concerned affect non-debtor obligors only if they are "secondary obligors." "Secondary obligor" is defined in Section 9–102 to include one who is secondarily obligated on the secured obligation, e.g., a guarantor, or one who has a right of recourse against the debtor or another obligor with respect to an obligation secured by collateral. However, under Section 9–628, the secured party is relieved from any duty or liability to any person unless the secured party knows that the person is a debtor or obligor. Resolving an issue on which courts disagreed under former Article 9, this Article generally prohibits waiver by a secondary obligor of its rights and a secured party's duties under Part 6. See Section 9–602. However, Section 9–624 permits a secondary obligor or debtor to waive the right to notification of disposition of collateral and, in a non-consumer transaction, the right to redeem collateral, if the secondary obligor or debtor agrees to do so after default.

Rights of collection and enforcement of collateral. Section 9–607 explains in greater detail than former 9–502 the rights of a secured party who seeks to collect or enforce collateral, including accounts, chattel paper, and payment intangibles. It also sets forth the enforcement rights of a depositary bank holding a security interest in a deposit account maintained with the depositary bank. Section 9–607 relates solely to the rights of a secured party vis-a-vis a debtor with respect to collections and enforcement. It does not affect the rights or duties of third parties, such as account debtors on collateral, which are addressed elsewhere (e.g., Section 9–406). Section 9–608 clarifies the manner in which proceeds of collection or enforcement are to be applied.

Disposition of collateral: Warranties of title. Section 9–610 imposes on a secured party who disposes of collateral the warranties of title, quiet possession, and the like that are otherwise applicable under other law. It also provides rules for the exclusion or modification of those warranties.

Disposition of collateral: Notification, application of proceeds, surplus and deficiency, other effects. Section 9–611 requires a secured party to give notification of a disposition of collateral to other secured parties and lienholders who have filed financing statements against the debtor covering the collateral. (That duty was eliminated by the 1972 revisions to Article 9.) However, that section relieves the secured party from that duty when the secured party undertakes a search of the records and a report of the results is unreasonably delayed. Section 9–613, which applies only to non-consumer transactions, specifies the contents of a sufficient notification of disposition and provides that a notification sent 10 days or more before the earliest time for disposition is sent within a reasonable time. Section 9–615 addresses the application of proceeds of disposition, the entitlement of a debtor to any surplus, and the liability of an obligor for any deficiency. Section 9–619 clarifies the effects of a disposition by a secured party, including the rights of transferees of the collateral.

Rights and duties of secondary obligor. Section 9–618 provides that a secondary obligor obtains the rights and assumes the duties of a secured party if the secondary obligor receives an assignment of a secured obligation, agrees to assume the secured party's rights and duties upon a transfer to it of collateral, or becomes subrogated to the rights of the secured party with respect to the collateral. The assumption, transfer, or subrogation is not a disposition of collateral under Section 9–610, but it does relieve the former secured party of further duties. Former Section 9–504(5) did not address whether a secured party was relieved of its duties in this situation.

Transfer of record or legal title. Section 9–619 contains a new provision making clear that a transfer of record or legal title to a secured party is not of itself a disposition under Part 6. This rule applies regardless of the circumstances under which the transfer of title occurs.

Strict foreclosure. Section 9–620, unlike former Section 9–505, permits a secured party to accept collateral in partial satisfaction, as well as full satisfaction, of the obligations secured. This right of strict foreclosure extends to intangible as well as tangible property. Section 9–622 clarifies the effects of an acceptance of collateral on the rights of junior claimants. It rejects the approach taken by some courts–deeming a secured party to have constructively retained collateral in satisfaction of the secured obligations–in the case of a secured party's unreasonable delay in the disposition of collateral. Instead, unreasonable delay is relevant when determining whether a disposition under Section 9–610 is commercially reasonable.

Effect of noncompliance: "Rebuttable presumption" test. Section 9–626 adopts the "rebuttable presumption" test for the failure of a secured party to proceed in accordance with certain provisions of Part 6. (As discussed in Comment 4.j., the test does not necessarily apply to consumer transactions.) Under this approach, the deficiency claim of a noncomplying secured party is calculated by crediting the obligor with the greater of the actual net proceeds of a disposition and the amount of net proceeds that would have been realized if the disposition had been conducted in accordance with Part 6 (e.g., in a commercially reasonable manner). For non-consumer transactions, Section 9–626 rejects the "absolute bar" test that some courts have imposed; that approach bars a noncomplying secured party from recovering any deficiency, regardless of the loss (if any) the debtor suffered as a consequence of the noncompliance.

"Low-price" dispositions: Calculation of deficiency and surplus. Section 9–615(f) addresses the problem of procedurally regular dispositions that fetch a low price. Subsection (f) provides a special method for calculating a deficiency if the proceeds of a disposition of collateral to a secured party, a person related to the secured party, or a secondary obligor are "significantly below the range of proceeds that a complying disposition to a person other than the secured party, a person related to the secured party, or a secondary obligor would have brought." ("Person related to" is defined in Section 9–102.) In these situations there is reason to suspect that there may be inadequate incentives to obtain a better price. Consequently, instead of calculating a deficiency (or surplus) based on the actual net proceeds, the deficiency (or surplus) would be calculated based on the proceeds that would have been received in a disposition to person other than the secured party, a person related to the secured party, or a secondary obligor.

j. **Consumer Goods, Consumer–Goods Transactions, and Consumer Transactions.** This Article (including the accompanying conforming revisions (see Appendix I)) includes several special rules for "consumer goods," "consumer transactions," and "consumer-goods transactions." Each term is defined in Section 9–102.

(i) Revised Sections 2–502 and 2–716 provide a buyer of consumer goods with enhanced rights to possession of the goods, thereby accelerating the opportunity to achieve "buyer in ordinary course of business" status under Section 1–201.

(ii) Section 9–103(e) (allocation of payments for determining extent of purchase-money status), (f) (purchase-money status not affected by cross-collateralization, refinancing, restructuring, or the like), and (g) (secured party has burden of establishing extent of purchase-money status) do not apply to consumer-goods transactions. Sections 9–103 also provides that the limitation of those provisions to transactions other than consumer-goods transactions leaves to the courts the proper rules for consumer-goods transactions and prohibits the courts from drawing inferences from that limitation.

(iii) Section 9–108 provides that in a consumer transaction a description of consumer goods, a security entitlement, securities account, or commodity account "only by [UCC-defined] type of collateral" is not a sufficient collateral description in a security agreement.

(iv) Sections 9–403 and 9–404 make effective the Federal Trade Commission's anti-holder-in-due-course rule (when applicable), 16 C.F.R. Part 433, even in the absence of the required legend.

(v) The 10–day safe-harbor for notification of a disposition provided by Section 9–612 does not apply in a consumer transaction.

(vi) Section 9–613 (contents and form of notice of disposition) does not apply to a consumer-goods transaction.

(vii) Section 9–614 contains special requirements for the contents of a notification of disposition and a safe-harbor, "plain English" form of notification, for consumer-goods transactions.

(viii) Section 9–616 requires a secured party in a consumer-goods transaction to provide a debtor with a notification of how it calculated a deficiency at the time it first undertakes to collect a deficiency.

(ix) Section 9–620 prohibits partial strict foreclosure with respect to consumer goods collateral and, unless the debtor agrees to waive the requirement in an authenticated record after default, in certain cases requires the secured party to dispose of consumer goods collateral which has been repossessed.

(x) Section 9–626 ("rebuttable presumption" rule) does not apply to a consumer transaction. Section 9–626 also provides that its limitation to transactions other than consumer transactions leaves to the courts the proper rules for consumer transactions and prohibits the courts from drawing inferences from that limitation.

k. **Good Faith.** Section 9–102 contains a new definition of "good faith" that includes not only "honesty in fact" but also "the observance of reasonable commercial standards of fair dealing." The definition is similar to the ones adopted in connection with other, recently completed revisions of the UCC.

l. **Transition Provisions.** Part 7 (Sections 9–701 through 9–709) contains transition provisions. Transition from former Article 9 to this Article will be particularly challenging in view of its expanded scope, its modification of choice-of-law rules for perfection and priority, and its expansion of the methods of perfection.

m. **Conforming and Related Amendments to Other UCC Articles.** Appendix I contains several proposed revisions to the provisions and Comments of other UCC articles. For the most part the revisions are explained in the Comments to the proposed revisions. Cross-references in other UCC articles to sections of Article 9 also have been revised.

Article 1. Revised Section 1–201 contains revisions to the definitions of "buyer in ordinary course of business," "purchaser," and "security interest."

Articles 2 and 2A. Sections 2–210, 2–326, 2–502, 2–716, 2A–303, and 2A–307 have been revised to address the intersection between Articles 2 and 2A and Article 9.

Article 5. New Section 5–118 is patterned on Section 4–210. It provides for a security interest in documents presented under a letter of credit in favor of the issuer and a nominated person on the letter of credit.

Article 8. Revisions to Section 8–106, which deals with "control" of securities and security entitlements, conform it to Section 8–302, which deals with "delivery." Revisions to Section 8–110, which deals with a "securities intermediary's jurisdiction," conform it to the revised treatment of a "commodity intermediary's jurisdiction" in Section 9–305. Sections 8–301 and 8–302 have been revised for clarification. Section 8–510 has been revised to conform it to the revised priority rules of Section 9–328. Several Comments in Article 8 also have been revised.

§ 9.102. Definitions and Index of Definitions

(a) In this chapter:

(1) "Accession" means goods that are physically united with other goods in such a manner that the identity of the original goods is not lost.

(2) "Account," except as used in "account for," means a right to payment of a monetary obligation, whether or not earned by performance, (i) for property that has been or is to be sold, leased, licensed, assigned, or otherwise disposed of, (ii) for services rendered or to be rendered, (iii) for a policy of insurance issued or to be issued, (iv) for a secondary obligation incurred or to be incurred, (v) for energy provided or to be provided, (vi) for the use or hire of a vessel under a charter or other contract, (vii) arising out of the use of a credit or charge card or information contained on or for use with the card, or (viii) as winnings in a lottery or other game of chance operated or sponsored by a state, governmental unit of a state, or person licensed or authorized to operate the game by a state or governmental unit of a state. The term includes health-care-insurance receivables. The term does not include (i) rights to payment evidenced by chattel paper or an instrument, (ii) commercial tort claims, (iii) deposit accounts, (iv) investment property, (v) letter-of-credit rights or letters of credit, or (vi) rights to payment for money or funds advanced or sold, other than rights arising out of the use of a credit or charge card or information contained on or for use with the card.

(3) "Account debtor" means a person obligated on an account, chattel paper, or general intangible. The term does not include persons obligated to pay a negotiable instrument, even if the instrument constitutes part of chattel paper.

(4) "Accounting," except as used in "accounting for," means a record:

(A) authenticated by a secured party;

(B) indicating the aggregate unpaid secured obligations as of a date not more than 35 days earlier or 35 days later than the date of the record; and

(C) identifying the components of the obligations in reasonable detail.

(5) "Agricultural lien" means an interest in farm products:

(A) that secures payment or performance of an obligation for:

(i) goods or services furnished in connection with a debtor's farming operation; or

(ii) rent on real property leased by a debtor in connection with its farming operation;

(B) that is created by statute in favor of a person that:

(i) in the ordinary course of its business furnished goods or services to a debtor in connection with a debtor's farming operation; or

(ii) leased real property to a debtor in connection with the debtor's farming operation; and

(C) whose effectiveness does not depend on the person's possession of the personal property.

(6) "As-extracted collateral" means:

(A) oil, gas, or other minerals that are subject to a security interest that:

(i) is created by a debtor having an interest in the minerals before extraction; and

(ii) attaches to the minerals as extracted; or

(B) accounts arising out of the sale at the wellhead or minehead of oil, gas, or other minerals in which the debtor had an interest before extraction.

(7) "Authenticate" means:

(A) to sign; or

(B) to execute or otherwise adopt a symbol, or encrypt or similarly process a record in whole or in part, with the present intent of the authenticating person to identify the person and adopt or accept a record.

(8) "Bank" means an organization that is engaged in the business of banking. The term includes savings banks, savings and loan associations, credit unions, and trust companies.

(9) "Cash proceeds" means proceeds that are money, checks, deposit accounts, or the like.

(10) "Certificate of title" means a certificate of title with respect to which a statute provides for the security interest in question to be indicated on the certificate as a condition or result of the security

interest's obtaining priority over the rights of a lien creditor with respect to the collateral.

(11) "Chattel paper" means a record or records that evidence both a monetary obligation and a security interest in specific goods, a security interest in specific goods and software used in the goods, a security interest in specific goods and license of software used in the goods, a lease of specific goods, or a lease of specific goods and license of software used in the goods. In this subdivision, "monetary obligation" means a monetary obligation secured by the goods or owed under a lease of the goods and includes a monetary obligation with respect to software used in the goods. The term does not include (i) charters or other contracts involving the use or hire of a vessel or (ii) records that evidence a right to payment arising out of the use of a credit or charge card or information contained on or for use with the card. If a transaction is evidenced by records that include an instrument or series of instruments, the group of records taken together constitutes chattel paper.

(12) "Collateral" means the property subject to a security interest or agricultural lien. The term includes:

(A) proceeds to which a security interest attaches;

(B) accounts, chattel paper, payment intangibles, and promissory notes that have been sold; and

(C) goods that are the subject of a consignment.

(13) "Commercial tort claim" means a claim arising in tort with respect to which:

(A) the claimant is an organization; or

(B) the claimant is an individual and the claim:

(i) arose in the course of the claimant's business or profession; and

(ii) does not include damages arising out of personal injury to or the death of an individual.

(14) "Commodity account" means an account maintained by a commodity intermediary in which a commodity contract is carried for a commodity customer.

(15) "Commodity contract" means a commodity futures contract, an option on a commodity futures contract, a commodity option, or another contract if the contract or option is:

(A) traded on or subject to the rules of a board of trade that has been designated as a contract market for such a contract pursuant to federal commodities laws; or

(B) traded on a foreign commodity board of trade, exchange, or market and is carried on the books of a commodity intermediary for a commodity customer.

(16) "Commodity customer" means a person for which a commodity intermediary carries a commodity contract on its books.

(17) "Commodity intermediary" means a person that:

(A) is registered as a futures commission merchant under federal commodities law; or

(B) in the ordinary course of its business provides clearance or settlement services for a board of trade that has been designated as a contract market pursuant to federal commodities law.

(18) "Communicate" means:

(A) to send a written or other tangible record;

(B) to transmit a record by any means agreed upon by the persons sending and receiving the record; or

(C) in the case of transmission of a record to or by a filing office, to transmit a record by any means prescribed by filing-office rule.

(19) "Consignee" means a merchant to which goods are delivered in a consignment.

(20) "Consignment" means a transaction, regardless of its form, in which a person delivers goods to a merchant for the purpose of sale and:

(A) the merchant:

(i) deals in goods of that kind under a name other than the name of the person making delivery;

(ii) is not an auctioneer; and

(iii) is not generally known by its creditors to be substantially engaged in selling the goods of others;

(B) with respect to each delivery, the aggregate value of the goods is $1,000 or more at the time of delivery;

(C) the goods are not consumer goods immediately before delivery;

(D) the transaction does not create a security interest that secures an obligation; and

(E) the transaction does not involve delivery of a work of art to an art dealer or delivery of a sound recording to a distributor if Chapter 2101, Occupations Code, applies to the delivery.

(21) "Consignor" means a person that delivers goods to a consignee in a consignment.

(22) "Consumer debtor" means a debtor in a consumer transaction.

(23) "Consumer goods" means goods that are used or bought for use primarily for personal, family, or household purposes.

(24) "Consumer-goods transaction" means a consumer transaction in which:

(A) an individual incurs an obligation primarily for personal, family, or household purposes; and

(B) a security interest in consumer goods secures the obligation.

(25) "Consumer obligor" means an obligor who is an individual and who incurred the obligation as part of a transaction entered into primarily for personal, family, or household purposes.

(26) "Consumer transaction" means a transaction in which (i) an individual incurs an obligation primarily for personal, family, or household purposes, (ii) a security interest secures the obligation, and (iii) the collateral is held or acquired primarily for personal, family, or household purposes. The term includes consumer-goods transactions.

(27) "Continuation statement" means an amendment of a financing statement that:

(A) identifies, by its file number, the initial financing statement to which it relates; and

(B) indicates that it is a continuation statement for, or that it is filed to continue the effectiveness of, the identified financing statement.

(28) "Debtor" means:

(A) a person having an interest, other than a security interest or other lien, in the collateral, whether or not the person is an obligor;

(B) a seller of accounts, chattel paper, payment intangibles, or promissory notes; or

(C) a consignee.

(29) "Deposit account" means a demand, time, savings, passbook, or similar account maintained with a bank. The term includes a nonnegotiable certificate of deposit. The term does not include investment property or accounts evidenced by an instrument.

(30) "Document" means a document of title or a receipt of the type described in Section 7.201(b).

(31) "Electronic chattel paper" means chattel paper evidenced by a record or records consisting of information stored in an electronic medium.

(32) "Encumbrance" means a right, other than an ownership interest, in real property. The term includes mortgages and other liens on real property.

(33) "Equipment" means goods other than inventory, farm products, or consumer goods.

(34) "Farm products" means goods, other than standing timber, with respect to which the debtor is engaged in a farming operation and which are:

(A) crops grown, growing, or to be grown, including:

(i) crops produced on trees, vines, and bushes; and

(ii) aquatic goods produced in aquacultural operations;

(B) livestock, born or unborn, including aquatic goods produced in aquacultural operations;

(C) supplies used or produced in a farming operation; or

(D) products of crops or livestock in their unmanufactured states.

(35) "Farming operation" means raising, cultivating, propagating, fattening, grazing, or any other farming, livestock, or aquacultural operation.

(36) "File number" means the number assigned to an initial financing statement pursuant to Section 9.519(a).

(37) "Filing office" means an office designated in Section 9.501 as the place to file a financing statement.

(38) "Filing-office rule" means a rule adopted pursuant to Section 9.526.

(39) "Financing statement" means a record or records composed of an initial financing statement and any filed record relating to the initial financing statement.

(40) "Fixture filing" means the filing of a financing statement covering goods that are or are to become fixtures and satisfying Sections 9.502(a) and (b). The term includes the filing of a financing statement covering goods of a transmitting utility that are or are to become fixtures.

(41) "Fixtures" means goods that have become so related to particular real property that an interest in them arises under the real property law of the state in which the real property is situated.

(42) "General intangible" means any personal property, including things in action, other than accounts, chattel paper, commercial tort claims, deposit accounts, documents, goods, instruments, investment property, letter-of-credit rights, letters of credit, money, and oil, gas, or other minerals before extraction. The term includes payment intangibles and software.

(43) Reserved.

(44) "Goods" means all things that are movable when a security interest attaches. The term includes (i) fixtures, (ii) standing timber that is to be cut and removed under a conveyance or contract for sale, (iii) the unborn young of animals, (iv) crops grown, growing, or to be grown, even if the crops are produced on trees, vines, or bushes, and (v) manufactured homes. The term also includes a computer program embedded in goods and any supporting information provided in connection with a transaction relating to the program if (i) the program is associated with the goods in such a manner that it customarily is considered part of the goods, or (ii) by becoming the owner of the goods, a person acquires a right to use the program in connection with the goods. The term does not include a computer program embedded in goods that consist solely of the medium in which the program is embedded. The term also does not include accounts, chattel paper, commercial tort claims, deposit accounts, documents, general intangibles, instruments, investment property, letter-of-credit rights, letters of credit, money, or oil, gas, or other minerals before extraction.

(45) "Governmental unit" means a subdivision, agency, department, county, parish, municipality, or other unit of the government of the United States, a state, or a foreign country. The term includes an organization having a separate corporate existence if the organization is eligible to issue debt on which interest is exempt from income taxation under the laws of the United States.

(46) "Health care insurance receivable" means an interest in or claim under a policy of insurance that is a right to payment of a monetary obligation for health care goods or services provided or to be provided.

(47) "Instrument" means a negotiable instrument or any other writing that evidences a right to the payment of a monetary obligation, is not itself a security agreement or lease, and is of a type that in ordinary course of business is transferred by delivery with any necessary indorsement or assignment. The term does not include (i) investment property, (ii) letters of credit, (iii) writings that evidence a right to payment arising out of the use of a credit or charge card or information contained on or for use with the card, or (iv) nonnegotiable certificates of deposit.

(48) "Inventory" means goods, other than farm products, that:

(A) are leased by a person as lessor;

(B) are held by a person for sale or lease or to be furnished under a contract of service;

(C) are furnished by a person under a contract of service; or

(D) consist of raw materials, work in process, or materials used or consumed in a business.

(49) "Investment property" means a security, whether certificated or uncertificated, security entitlement, securities account, commodity contract, or commodity account.

(50) "Jurisdiction of organization," with respect to a registered organization, means the jurisdiction under whose law the organization is organized.

(51) "Letter-of-credit right" means a right to payment or performance under a letter of credit, whether or not the beneficiary has demanded or is at the time entitled to demand payment or performance. The term does not include the right of a beneficiary to demand payment or performance under a letter of credit.

(52) "Lien creditor" means:

(A) a creditor that has acquired a lien on the property involved by attachment, levy, or the like;

(B) an assignee for benefit of creditors from the time of assignment;

(C) a trustee in bankruptcy from the date of the filing of the petition; or

(D) a receiver in equity from the time of appointment.

(53) "Manufactured home" means a structure, transportable in one or more sections, that, in the traveling mode, is eight body feet or more in width or 40 body feet or more in length, or, when erected on site, is 320 or more square feet, and that is built on a permanent chassis and designed to be used as a dwelling with or without a permanent foundation when connected to the required utilities, and includes the plumbing, heating, air-conditioning, and electrical systems contained therein. The term in-

cludes any structure that meets all of the requirements of this subdivision except the size requirements and with respect to which the manufacturer voluntarily files a certification required by the United States secretary of housing and urban development and complies with the standards established under Title 42 of the United States Code.

(54) "Manufactured-home transaction" means a secured transaction:

(A) that creates a purchase-money security interest in a manufactured home, other than a manufactured home held as inventory; or

(B) in which a manufactured home, other than a manufactured home held as inventory, is the primary collateral.

(55) "Mortgage" means a consensual interest in real property, including fixtures, that secures payment or performance of an obligation.

(56) "New debtor" means a person that becomes bound as debtor under Section 9.203(d) by a security agreement previously entered into by another person.

(57) "New value" means (i) money, (ii) money's worth in property, services, or new credit, or (iii) release by a transferee of an interest in property previously transferred to the transferee. The term does not include an obligation substituted for another obligation.

(58) "Noncash proceeds" means proceeds other than cash proceeds.

(59) "Nonnegotiable certificate of deposit" means a writing signed by a bank that:

(A) states on its face that it is a certificate of deposit, as defined in Section 3.104, or receipt for a book entry;

(B) contains an acknowledgement that a sum of money has been received by the bank, with an express or implied agreement that the bank will repay the sum of money; and

(C) is not a negotiable instrument.

(60) "Obligor" means a person that, with respect to an obligation secured by a security interest in or an agricultural lien on the collateral, (i) owes payment or other performance of the obligation, (ii) has provided property other than the collateral to secure payment or other performance of the obligation, or (iii) is otherwise accountable in whole or in part for payment or other performance of the obligation. The term does not include issuers or nominated persons under a letter of credit.

(61) "Original debtor," except as used in Section 9.310(c), means a person that, as debtor, entered into a security agreement to which a new debtor has become bound under Section 9.203(d).

(62) "Payment intangible" means a general intangible under which the account debtor's principal obligation is a monetary obligation.

(63) "Person related to," with respect to an individual, means:

(A) the spouse of the individual;

(B) a brother, brother-in-law, sister, or sister-in-law of the individual;

(C) an ancestor or lineal descendant of the individual or the individual's spouse; or

(D) any other relative, by blood or marriage, of the individual or the individual's spouse who shares the same home with the individual.

(64) "Person related to," with respect to an organization, means:

(A) a person directly or indirectly controlling, controlled by, or under common control with the organization;

(B) an officer or director of, or a person performing similar functions with respect to, the organization;

(C) an officer or director of, or a person performing similar functions with respect to, a person described in Paragraph (A);

(D) the spouse of an individual described in Paragraph (A), (B), or (C); or

(E) an individual who is related by blood or marriage to an individual described in Paragraph (A), (B), (C), or (D) and shares the same home with the individual.

(65) "Proceeds," except as used in Section 9.609(b), means the following property:

(A) whatever is acquired upon the sale, lease, license, exchange, or other disposition of collateral;

(B) whatever is collected on, or distributed on account of, collateral;

(C) rights arising out of collateral;

(D) to the extent of the value of collateral, claims arising out of the loss, nonconformity, or interference with the use of, defects or infringement of rights in, or damage to the collateral; or

(E) to the extent of the value of collateral and to the extent payable to the debtor or the secured party, insurance payable by reason of the loss or nonconformity of, defects or infringement of rights in, or damage to the collateral.

(66) "Promissory note" means an instrument that evidences a promise to pay a monetary obligation, does not evidence an order to pay, and does not contain an acknowledgement by a bank that the bank has received for deposit a sum of money or funds.

(67) "Proposal" means a record authenticated by a secured party that includes the terms on which the secured party is willing to accept collateral in full or partial satisfaction of the obligation it secures pursuant to Sections 9.620, 9.621, and 9.622.

(68) "Public-finance transaction" means a secured transaction in connection with which:

(A) debt securities are issued;

(B) all or a portion of the securities issued have an initial stated maturity of at least 20 years; and

(C) the debtor, obligor, secured party, account debtor or other person obligated on collateral, assignor or assignee or a secured obligation, or assignor or assignee of a security interest is a state or a governmental unit of a state.

(69) "Pursuant to commitment," with respect to an advance made or other value given by a secured party, means pursuant to the secured party's obligation, whether or not a subsequent event of default or other event not within the secured party's control has relieved or may relieve the secured party from its obligation.

(70) "Record," except as used in "for record," "of record," "record or legal title," and "record owner," means information that is inscribed on a tangible medium or that is stored in an electronic or other medium and is retrievable in perceivable form.

(71) "Registered organization" means an organization organized solely under the law of a single state or the United States and as to which the state or the United States must maintain a public record showing the organization to have been organized.

(72) "Secondary obligor" means an obligor to the extent that:

(A) the obligor's obligation is secondary; or

(B) the obligor has a right of recourse with respect to an obligation secured by collateral against the debtor, another obligor, or property of either.

(73) "Secured party" means:

(A) a person in whose favor a security interest is created or provided for under a security agreement, whether or not any obligation to be secured is outstanding;

(B) a person that holds an agricultural lien;

(C) a consignor;

(D) a person to which accounts, chattel paper, payment intangibles, or promissory notes have been sold;

(E) a trustee, indenture trustee, agent, collateral agent, or other representative in whose favor a security interest or agricultural lien is created or provided for; or

(F) a person that holds a security interest arising under Section 2.401, 2.505, 2.711(c), 2A.508(e), 4.210, or 5.118.

(74) "Security agreement" means an agreement that creates or provides for a security interest.

(75) "Send," in connection with a record or notification, means:

(A) to deposit in the mail, deliver for transmission, or transmit by any other usual means of communication, with postage or cost of transmission provided for, addressed to any address reasonable under the circumstances; or

(B) to cause the record or notification to be received within the time that it would have been received if properly sent under Paragraph (A).

(76) "Software" means a computer program and any supporting information provided in connection with a transaction relating to the program. The term does not include a computer program that is included in the definition of "goods."

(77) "State" means a state of the United States, the District of Columbia, Puerto Rico, the United States Virgin Islands, or any territory or insular possession subject to the jurisdiction of the United States.

(78) "Supporting obligation" means a letter-of-credit right or secondary obligation that supports the payment or performance of an account, chattel paper, a document, a general intangible, an instrument, or investment property.

(79) "Tangible chattel paper" means chattel paper evidenced by a record or records consisting of information that is inscribed on a tangible medium.

(80) "Termination statement" means an amendment of a financing statement that:

(A) identifies, by its file number, the initial financing statement to which it relates; and

(B) indicates either that it is a termination statement or that the identified financing statement is no longer effective.

(81) "Transmitting utility" means a person primarily engaged in the business of:

(A) operating a railroad, subway, street railway, or trolley bus;

(B) transmitting communications electrically, electromagnetically, or by light;

(C) transmitting goods by pipeline or sewer; or

(D) transmitting or producing and transmitting electricity, steam, gas, or water.

(b) The following definitions in other chapters apply to this chapter:

"Applicant"	Section 5.102.
"Beneficiary"	Section 5.102.
"Broker"	Section 8.102.
"Certificated security"	Section 8.102.
"Check"	Section 3.104.
"Clearing corporation"	Section 8.102.
"Contract for sale"	Section 2.106.
"Control" (with respect to a document of title)	Section 7.106.
"Customer"	Section 4.104.
"Entitlement holder"	Section 8.102.
"Financial asset"	Section 8.102.
"Holder in due course"	Section 3.302.
"Issuer" (with respect to a letter of credit or letter-of-credit right)	Section 5.102.
"Issuer" (with respect to a security)	Section 8.201.
"Lease"	Section 2A.103.
"Lease agreement"	Section 2A.103.
"Lease contract"	Section 2A.103.
"Leasehold interest"	Section 2A.103.
"Lessee"	Section 2A.103.
"Lessee in ordinary course of business"	Section 2A.103.
"Lessor"	Section 2A.103.
"Lessor's residual interest"	Section 2A.103.
"Letter of credit"	Section 5.102.
"Merchant"	Section 2.104.
"Negotiable instrument"	Section 3.104.
"Nominated person"	Section 5.102.
"Note"	Section 3.104.
"Proceeds of a letter of credit"	Section 5.114.
"Prove"	Section 3.103.
"Sale"	Section 2.106.
"Securities account"	Section 8.501.
"Securities intermediary"	Section 8.102.
"Security"	Section 8.102.
"Security certificate"	Section 8.102.
"Security entitlement"	Section 8.102.
"Uncertificated security"	Section 8.102.

(c) Chapter 1 contains general definitions and principles of construction and interpretation applicable throughout this chapter.

Amended by Acts 1999, 76th Leg., ch. 414, § 1.01, eff. July 1, 2001; Acts 2001, 77th Leg., ch. 705, § 1, eff. June 13, 2001; Acts 2001, 77th Leg., ch. 1420, § 14.728, eff. Sept. 1, 2001; Acts 2003, 78th Leg., ch. 542, § 19, eff. Sept. 1, 2003; Acts 2003, 78th Leg., ch. 917, §§ 1, 2, eff. Sept. 1, 2003; Acts 2005, 79th Leg., ch. 122, § 19, eff. May 27, 2005; Acts 2005, 79th Leg., ch. 233, § 3, eff. Sept. 1, 2005.

Uniform Commercial Code Comment

1. **Source.** All terms that are defined in Article 9 and used in more than one section are consolidated in this section. Note that the definition of "security interest" is found in Section 1–201, not in this Article, and has been revised. See Appendix I. Many of the definitions in this section are new; many others derive from those in former Section 9–105. The following Comments also indicate other sections of former Article 9 that defined (or explained) terms.

2. **Parties to Secured Transactions.**

a. **"Debtor"; "Obligor"; "Secondary Obligor."** Determining whether a person was a "debtor" under former Section 9–105(1)(d) required a close examination of the context in which the term was used. To reduce the need for this examination, this Article redefines "debtor" and adds new defined terms, "secondary obligor" and "obligor." In the context of Part 6 (default and enforcement), these definitions distinguish among three classes of persons: (i) those persons who may have a stake in the proper enforcement of a security interest by virtue of their non-lien property interest (typically, an ownership interest) in the collateral, (ii) those persons who may have a stake in the proper enforcement of the security interest because of their obligation to pay the secured debt, and (iii) those persons who have an obligation to pay the secured debt but have no stake in the proper enforcement of the security interest. Persons in the first class are debtors. Persons in the second class are secondary obligors if any portion of the obligation is secondary or if the obligor has a right of recourse against the debtor or another obligor with respect to an obligation secured by collateral. One must consult the law of suretyship to determine whether an obligation is secondary. The Restatement (3d), Suretyship and Guaranty § 1 (1996), contains a useful explanation of the concept. Obligors in the third class are neither debtors nor secondary obligors. With one exception (Section 9–616, as it relates to a consumer obligor), the rights and duties provided by Part 6 affect non-debtor obligors only if they are "secondary obligors."

By including in the definition of "debtor" all persons with a property interest (other than a security interest in or other lien on collateral), the definition includes transferees of collateral, whether or not the secured party knows of the transfer or the transferee's identity. Exculpatory provisions in Part 6 protect the secured party in that circumstance. See Sections 9–605 and 9–628. The definition renders unnecessary former Section 9–112, which governed situations in which collateral was not owned by the debtor. The definition also includes a "consignee," as defined in this section, as well as a seller of accounts, chattel paper, payment intangibles, or promissory notes.

Secured parties and other lienholders are excluded from the definition of "debtor" because the interests of those parties normally derive from and encumber a debtor's interest. However, if in a *separate* secured transaction a secured party grants, *as debtor*, a security interest in its own interest (i.e., its security interest and any obligation that it secures), the secured party is a debtor *in that transaction*. This typically occurs when a secured party with a security interest in specific goods assigns chattel paper.

Consider the following examples:

Example 1: Behnfeldt borrows money and grants a security interest in her Miata to secure the debt. Behnfeldt is a debtor and an obligor.

Example 2: Behnfeldt borrows money and grants a security interest in her Miata to secure the debt. Bruno co-signs a negotiable note as maker. As before, Behnfeldt is the debtor and an obligor. As an accommodation party (see Section 3–419), Bruno is a secondary obligor. Bruno has this status even if the note states that her obligation is a primary obligation and that she waives all suretyship defenses.

Example 3: Behnfeldt borrows money on an unsecured basis. Bruno co-signs the note and grants a security interest in her Honda to secure her obligation. Inasmuch as Behnfeldt does not have a property interest in the Honda, Behnfeldt is not a debtor. Having granted the security interest, Bruno is the debtor. Because Behnfeldt is a principal obligor, she is not a secondary obligor. Whatever the outcome of enforcement of the security interest against the Honda or Bruno's secondary obligation, Bruno will look to Behnfeldt for her losses. The enforcement will not affect Behnfeldt's aggregate obligations.

When the principal obligor (borrower) and the secondary obligor (surety) each has granted a security interest in different collateral, the status of each is determined by the collateral involved.

Example 4: Behnfeldt borrows money and grants a security interest in her Miata to secure the debt. Bruno co-signs the note and grants a security interest in her Honda to secure her obligation. When the secured party enforces the security interest in Behnfeldt's Miata, Behnfeldt is the debtor, and Bruno is a secondary obligor. When the secured party enforces the security interest in the Honda, Bruno is the "debtor." As in Example 3, Behnfeldt is an obligor, but not a secondary obligor.

b. **"Secured Party."** The secured party is the person in whose favor the security interest has been created, as determined by reference to the security agreement. This definition controls, among other things, which person has the duties and potential liability that Part 6 imposes upon a secured party. The definition of "secured party" also includes a "consignee," a person to which accounts, chattel paper, payment intangibles, or promissory notes have been sold, and the holder of an agricultural lien.

The definition of "secured party" clarifies the status of various types of representatives. Consider, for example, a multi-bank facility under which Bank A, Bank B, and Bank C are lenders and Bank A serves as the collateral agent. If the security interest is granted to the banks, then they are the secured parties. If the security interest is granted to Bank A as collateral agent, then Bank A is the secured party.

c. **Other Parties.** A "consumer obligor" is defined as the obligor in a consumer transaction. Definitions of "new debtor" and "original debtor" are used in the special rules found in Sections 9–326 and 9–508.

3. **Definitions Relating to Creation of a Security Interest.**

a. **"Collateral."** As under former Section 9–105, "collateral" is the property subject to a security interest and includes accounts and chattel paper that have been sold. It has been expanded in this Article. The term now explicitly includes proceeds subject to a security interest. It also reflects the broadened scope of the Article. It includes property subject to an agricultural lien as well as payment intangibles and promissory notes that have been sold.

b. **"Security Agreement."** The definition of "security agreement" is substantially the same as under former Section 9–105–an agreement that creates or provides for a security interest. However, the term frequently was used colloquially in former Article 9 to refer to the document or writing that contained a debtor's security agreement. This Article eliminates that usage, reserving the term for the more precise meaning specified in the definition.

Whether an agreement creates a security interest depends not on whether the parties intend that the law *characterize* the transaction as a security interest but rather on whether the transaction falls within the definition of "security interest" in Section 1–201. Thus, an agreement that the parties characterize as a "lease" of goods may be a "security agreement," notwithstanding the parties' stated intention that the law treat the transaction as a lease and not as a secured transaction.

4. **Goods-Related Definitions.**

a. **"Goods"; "Consumer Goods"; "Equipment"; "Farm Products"; "Farming Operation"; "Inventory."** The definition of "goods" is substantially the same as the definition in former Section 9–105. This Article also retains the four mutually-exclusive "types" of collateral that consist of goods: "consumer goods," "equipment," "farm products," and "inventory." The revisions are primarily for clarification.

The classes of goods are mutually exclusive. For example, the same property cannot simultaneously be both equipment and inventory. In borderline cases–a physician's car or a farmer's truck that might be either consumer goods or equipment–the principal use to which the property is put is determinative. Goods can fall into different classes at different times. For example, a radio may be inventory in the hands of a dealer and consumer goods in the hands of a consumer. As under former Article 9, goods are "equipment" if they do not fall into another category.

The definition of "consumer goods" follows former Section 9–109. The classification turns on whether the debtor uses or bought the goods for use "primarily for personal, family, or household purposes."

Goods are inventory if they are leased by a lessor or held by a person for sale or lease. The revised definition of "inventory" makes clear that the term includes goods leased by the debtor to others as well as goods held for lease. (The same result should have obtained under the former definition.) Goods to be furnished or furnished under a service contract, raw materials, and work in process also are inventory. Implicit in the definition is the criterion that the sales or leases are or will be in the ordinary course of business. For example, machinery used in manufacturing is equipment, not inventory, even though it is the policy of the debtor to sell machinery when it becomes obsolete or worn. Inventory also includes goods that are consumed in a business (e.g., fuel used in operations). In general, goods used in a business are equipment if they are fixed assets or have, as identifiable units, a relatively long period of use, but are inventory, even though not held for sale or lease, if they are used up or consumed in a short period of time in producing a product or providing a service.

Goods are "farm products" if the debtor is engaged in farming operations with respect to the goods. Animals in a herd of livestock are covered whether the debtor acquires them by purchase or as a result of natural increase. Products of crops or livestock remain farm products as long as they have not been subjected to a manufacturing process. The terms "crops" and "livestock" are not defined. The new definition of "farming operations" is for clarification only.

Crops, livestock, and their products cease to be "farm products" when the debtor ceases to be engaged in farming operations with respect to them. If, for example, they come into the possession of a marketing agency for sale or distribution or of a manufacturer or processor as raw materials, they become inventory. Products of crops or livestock, even though they remain in the possession of a person engaged in farming operations, lose their status as farm products if they are subjected to a manufacturing process. What is and what is not a manufacturing operation is not specified in this Article. At one end of the spectrum, some processes are so closely connected with farming–such as pasteurizing milk or boiling sap to produce maple syrup or sugar–that they would not constitute manufacturing. On the other hand an extensive canning operation would be manufacturing. Once farm products have been subjected to a manufacturing operation, they normally become inventory.

The revised definition of "farm products" clarifies the distinction between crops and standing timber and makes clear that aquatic goods produced in aquacultural operations may be either crops or livestock. Although aquatic goods that are vegetable in nature often would be crops and those that are animal would be livestock, this Article leaves the courts free to classify the goods on a case-by-case basis. See Section 9–324, Comment 11.

The definitions of "goods" and "software" are also mutually exclusive. Computer programs usually constitute "software," and, as such, are not "goods" as this Article uses the terms. However, under the circumstances specified in the definition of "goods," computer programs embedded in goods are part of the "goods" and are not "software."

b. **"Accession"; "Manufactured Home"; "Manufactured–Home Transaction."** Other specialized definitions of goods include "accession" (see the special priority and enforcement rules in Section 9–335), and "manufactured home" (see Section 9–515, permitting a financing statement in a "manufactured-home transaction" to be effective for 30 years). The definition of "manufactured home" borrows from the federal Manufactured Housing Act, 42 U.S.C. §§ 5401 *et seq.*, and is intended to have the same meaning.

c. **"As–Extracted Collateral."** Under this Article, oil, gas, and other minerals that have not been extracted from the ground are treated as real property, to which this Article does not apply. Upon extraction, minerals become personal property (goods) and eligible to be collateral under this Article. See the definition of "goods," which excludes "oil, gas, and other minerals before extraction." To take account of financing practices reflecting the shift from real to personal property, this Article contains special rules for perfecting security interests in minerals which attach upon extraction and in accounts resulting from the sale of minerals at the wellhead or minehead. See, e.g., Sections 9–301(4) (law governing perfection and priority); 9–501 (place of filing), 9–502 (contents of financing statement), 9–519 (indexing of records). The new term, "as-extracted collateral," refers to the minerals and related accounts to which the special rules apply. The term "at the wellhead" encompasses arrangements based on a sale of the produce at the moment that it issues from the ground and is measured, without technical distinctions as to whether title passes at the "Christmas tree" of a well, the far side of a gathering tank, or at some other point. The term "at . . . the minehead" is comparable.

The following examples explain the operation of these provisions.

Example 5: Debtor owns an interest in oil that is to be extracted. To secure Debtor's obligations to Lender, Debtor enters into an authenticated agreement granting Lender an interest in the oil. Although Lender may acquire an interest in the oil under real-property law, Lender does not acquire a security interest under this Article until the oil becomes personal property, i.e., until is extracted and becomes "goods" to which this Article applies. Because Debtor had an interest in the oil before extraction and Lender's security interest attached to the oil as extracted, the oil is "as-extracted collateral."

Example 6: Debtor owns an interest in oil that is to be extracted and contracts to sell the oil to Buyer at the wellhead. In an authenticated agreement, Debtor agrees to sell to Lender the right to payment from Buyer. This right to payment is an account that constitutes "as-extracted collateral." If Lender then resells the account to Financer, Financer acquires a security interest. However, inasmuch as the debtor-seller in that transaction, Lender, had no interest in the oil before extraction, Financer's collateral (the account it owns) is not "as-extracted collateral."

Example 7: Under the facts of Example 6, before extraction, Buyer grants a security interest in the oil to Bank. Although Bank's security interest attaches when the oil is extracted, Bank's security interest is not in "as-extracted collateral," inasmuch as its debtor, Buyer, did not have an interest in the oil before extraction.

5. **Receivables-related Definitions.**

a. **"Account"; "Health–Care–Insurance Receivable"; "As–Extracted Collateral."** The definition of "account" has been expanded and reformulated. It is no longer limited to rights to payment relating to goods or services. Many categories of rights to payment that were classified as general intangibles under former Article 9 are accounts under this Article. Thus, if they are sold, a financing statement must be filed to perfect the buyer's interest in them. Among the types of property that are expressly excluded from the definition is "a right to payment for money or funds advanced or sold." As defined in Section 1–201, "money" is limited essentially to currency. As used in the exclusion from the definition of "account," however, "funds" is a broader concept (although the term is not defined). For example, when a bank-lender credits a borrower's deposit account for the amount of a loan, the bank's advance of funds is not a transaction giving rise to an account.

The definition of "health-care-insurance receivable" is new. It is a subset of the definition of "account." However, the rules generally applicable to account debtors on accounts do not apply to insurers obligated on health-care-insurance receivables. See Sections 9–404(e), 9–405(d), 9–406(i).

Note that certain accounts also are "as-extracted collateral." See Comment 4.c., Examples 6 and 7.

b. **"Chattel Paper"; "Electronic Chattel Paper"; "Tangible Chattel Paper."** "Chattel paper" consists of a monetary obligation together with a security interest in or a lease of specific goods if the obligation and security interest or lease are evidenced by "a record or records." The definition has been expanded from that found in former Article 9 to include records that evidence a monetary obligation and a security interest in specific goods and software used in the goods, *a security interest in specific goods and license of software used in the goods, or a lease of specific goods and license of software used in the goods. The expanded definition covers transactions in which the debtor's or lessee's monetary obligation includes amounts owed with respect to software used in the goods. The monetary obligation with respect to the software need not be owed under a license from the secured party or lessor, and the secured party or lessor need not be a party to the license transaction itself. Among the types of monetary obligations that are included in "chattel paper" are amounts that have been advanced by the secured party or lessor to enable the debtor or lessee to acquire or obtain financing for a license of the software used in the goods.** The definition also makes clear that rights to payment arising out of credit-card transactions are not chattel paper.

Charters of vessels are expressly excluded from the definition of chattel paper; they are accounts. The term "charter" as used in this section includes bareboat charters, time charters, successive voyage charters, contracts of affreightment, contracts of carriage, and all other arrangements for the use of vessels.

Under former Section 9–105, only if the evidence of an obligation consisted of "a writing or writings" could an obligation qualify as chattel paper. In this Article, traditional, written chattel paper is included in the definition of "tangible chattel paper." "Electronic chattel paper" is chattel paper that is stored in an electronic medium instead of in tangible form. The concept of an electronic medium should be construed liberally to include electrical, digital, magnetic, optical, electromagnetic, or any other current or similar emerging technologies.

The definition of electronic chattel paper does not dictate that it be created in any particular fashion. For example, a record consisting of a tangible writing may be converted to electronic form (e.g., by creating electronic images of a signed writing). Or, records may be initially created and executed in electronic form (e.g., a lessee might authenticate an electronic record of a lease that is then stored in electronic form). In either case the resulting records are electronic chattel paper. **Amendments in italics approved by the Permanent Editorial Board for Uniform Commercial Code October 20, 1999.*

c. **"Instrument"; "Promissory Note."** The definition of "instrument" includes a negotiable instrument. As under former Section 9–105, it also includes any other right to payment of a monetary obligation that is evidenced by a writing of a type that in ordinary course of business is transferred by delivery (and, if necessary, an indorsement or assignment). Except in the case of chattel paper, the fact that an instrument is secured by a security interest or encumbrance on property does not change the character of the instrument as such or convert the combination of the instrument and collateral into a separate classification of personal property. The definition makes clear that rights to payment arising out of credit-card transactions are not instruments. The definition of "promissory note" is new, necessitated by the inclusion of sales of promissory notes within the scope of Article 9. It explicitly excludes obligations arising out of "orders" to pay (e.g., checks) as opposed to "promises" to pay. See Section 3–104.

d. **"General Intangible"; "Payment Intangible."** "General intangible" is the residual category of personal property, including things in action, that is not included in the other defined types of collateral. Examples are various categories of intellectual property and the right to payment of a loan of funds that is not evidenced by chattel paper or an instrument. As used in the definition of "general intangible," "things in action" includes rights that arise under a license of intellectual property, including the right to exploit the intellectual property without liability for infringement. The definition has been revised to exclude commercial tort claims, deposit accounts, and letter-of-credit rights. Each of the three is a separate type of collateral. One important consequence of this exclusion is that tortfeasors (commercial tort claims), banks (deposit accounts), and persons obligated on letters of credit (letter-of-credit rights) are not "account debtors" having the rights and obligations set forth in Sections 9–404, 9–405, and 9–406. In particular, tortfeasors, banks, and persons obligated on letters of credit are not obligated to pay an assignee (secured party) upon receipt of the notification described in Section 9–404(a). See Comment 5.h. Another important consequence relates to the adequacy of the description in the security agreement. See Section 9–108.

"Payment intangible" is a subset of the definition of "general intangible." The sale of a payment intangible is subject to this Article. See Section 9–109(a)(3). Virtually any intangible right could give rise to a right to payment of money once one hypothesizes, for example, that the account debtor is in breach of its obligation. The term "payment intangible," however, embraces only those general intangibles "under which the account debtor's *principal* obligation is a monetary obligation." (Emphasis added.)

In classifying intangible collateral, a court should begin by identifying the particular rights that have been assigned. The account debtor (promisor) under a particular contract may owe several types of monetary obligations as well as other, nonmonetary obligations. If the promisee's right to payment of money is assigned separately, the right is an account or payment intangible, depending on how the account debtor's obligation arose. When all the promisee's rights are assigned together, an account, a payment intangible, and a general intangible all may be involved, depending on the nature of the rights.

A right to the payment of money is frequently buttressed by ancillary covenants, such as covenants in a purchase agreement, note, or mortgage requiring insurance on the collateral or forbidding removal of the collateral, or covenants to preserve the creditworthiness of the promisor, such as covenants restricting dividends and the like. This Article does not treat these ancillary rights separately from the rights to payment to which they relate. For example, attachment and perfection of an assignment of a right to payment of a monetary obligation, whether it be an account or payment intangible, also carries these ancillary rights.

Every "payment intangible" is also a "general intangible." Likewise, "software" is a "general intangible" for purposes of this Article. See Comment 25. Accordingly, except as otherwise provided, statutory provisions applicable to general intangibles apply to payment intangibles and software.

e. **"Letter-of-Credit Right."** The term "letter-of-credit right" embraces the rights to payment and performance under a letter of credit (defined in Section 5–102). However, it does not include a beneficiary's right to demand payment or performance. Transfer of those rights to a transferee beneficiary is governed by Article 5. See Sections 9–107, Comment 4, and 9–329, Comments 3 and 4.

f. **"Supporting Obligation."** This new term covers the most common types of credit enhancements–suretyship obligations (including guarantees) and letter-of-credit rights that support one of the types of collateral specified in the definition. As explained in Comment 2.a., suretyship law determines whether an obligation is "secondary" for purposes of this definition. Section 9–109 generally excludes from this Article transfers of interests in insurance policies. However, the regulation of a secondary obligation as an insurance product does not necessarily mean that it is a "policy of insurance" for purposes of the exclusion in Section 9–109. Thus, this Article may cover a secondary obligation (as a supporting obligation), even if the obligation is issued by a regulated insurance company and the obligation is subject to regulation as an "insurance" product.

This Article contains rules explicitly governing attachment, perfection, and priority of security interests in supporting obligations. See Sections 9–203, 9–308, 9–310, and 9–322. These provisions reflect the principle that a supporting obligation is an incident of the collateral it supports.

Collections of or other distributions under a supporting obligation are "proceeds" of the supported collateral as well as "proceeds" of the supporting obligation itself. See Section 9–102 (defining "proceeds") and Comment 13.b. As such, the collections and distributions are subject to the priority rules applicable to proceeds generally. See Section 9–322. However, under the special rule governing security interests in a letter-of-credit right, a secured party's failure to obtain control (Section 9–107) of a letter-of-credit right supporting collateral may leave its security interest exposed to a priming interest of a party who does take control. See Section 9–329 (security interest in a letter-of-credit right perfected by control has priority over a conflicting security interest).

g. **"Commercial Tort Claim."** This term is new. A tort claim may serve as original collateral under this Article only if it is a "commercial tort claim." See Section 9–109(d). Although security interests in commercial tort claims are within its scope, this Article does not override other applicable law restricting the assignability of a tort claim. See Section 9–401. A security interest in a tort claim also may exist under this Article if the claim is proceeds of other collateral.

h. **"Account Debtor."** An "account debtor" is a person obligated on an account, chattel paper, or general intangible. The account debtor's obligation often is a monetary obligation; however, this is not always the case. For example, if a franchisee uses its rights under a franchise agreement (a general intangible) as collateral, then the franchisor is an "account debtor." As a general matter, Article 3, and not Article 9, governs obligations on negotiable instruments. Accordingly, the definition of "account debtor" excludes obligors on negotiable instruments constituting part of chattel paper. The principal effect of this change from the definition in former Article 9 is that the rules in Sections 9–403, 9–404, 9–405, and 9–406, dealing with the rights of an assignee and duties of an account debtor, do not apply to an assignment of chattel paper in which the obligation to pay is evidenced by a negotiable instrument. (Section 9–406(d), however, does apply to promissory notes, including negotiable promissory notes.) Rather, the assignee's rights are governed by Article 3. Similarly, the duties of an obligor on a nonnegotiable instrument are governed by non-Article 9 law unless the nonnegotiable instrument is a part of chattel paper, in which case the obligor is an account debtor.

i. **Receivables Under Government Entitlement Programs.** This Article does not contain a defined term that encompasses specifically rights to payment or performance under the many and varied government entitlement programs. Depending on the nature of a right under a program, it could be an account, a payment intangible, a general intangible other than a payment intangible, or another type of collateral. The right also might be proceeds of collateral (e.g., crops).

6. **Investment-Property-Related Definitions: "Commodity Account"; "Commodity Contract"; "Commodity Customer"; "Commodity Intermediary"; "Investment Property."** These definitions are substantially the same as the corresponding definitions in former Section 9–115. "Investment property" includes securities, both certificated and uncertificated, securities accounts, security entitlements, commodity accounts, and commodity contracts. The term investment property includes a "securities account" in order to facilitate transactions in which a debtor wishes to create a security interest in all of the investment positions held

through a particular account rather than in particular positions carried in the account. Former Section 9–115 was added in conjunction with Revised Article 8 and contained a variety of rules applicable to security interests in investment property. These rules have been relocated to the appropriate sections of Article 9. See, e.g., Sections 9–203 (attachment), 9–314 (perfection by control), 9–328 (priority).

The terms "security," "security entitlement," and related terms are defined in Section 8–102, and the term "securities account" is defined in Section 8–501. The terms "commodity account," "commodity contract," "commodity customer," and "commodity intermediary" are defined in this section. Commodity contracts are not "securities" or "financial assets" under Article 8. See Section 8–103(f). Thus, the relationship between commodity intermediaries and commodity customers is not governed by the indirect-holding-system rules of Part 5 of Article 8. For securities, Article 9 contains rules on security interests, and Article 8 contains rules on the rights of transferees, including secured parties, on such matters as the rights of a transferee if the transfer was itself wrongful and gives rise to an adverse claim. For commodity contracts, Article 9 establishes rules on security interests, but questions of the sort dealt with in Article 8 for securities are left to other law.

The indirect-holding-system rules of Article 8 are sufficiently flexible to be applied to new developments in the securities and financial markets, where that is appropriate. Accordingly, the definition of "commodity contract" is narrowly drafted to ensure that it does not operate as an obstacle to the application of the Article 8 indirect-holding-system rules to new products. The term "commodity contract" covers those contracts that are traded on or subject to the rules of a designated contract market and foreign commodity contracts that are carried on the books of American commodity intermediaries. The effect of this definition is that the category of commodity contracts that are excluded from Article 8 but governed by Article 9 is essentially the same as the category of contracts that fall within the exclusive regulatory jurisdiction of the federal Commodity Futures Trading Commission.

Commodity contracts are different from securities or other financial assets. A person who enters into a commodity futures contract is not buying an asset having a certain value and holding it in anticipation of increase in value. Rather the person is entering into a contract to buy or sell a commodity at set price for delivery at a future time. That contract may become advantageous or disadvantageous as the price of the commodity fluctuates during the term of the contract. The rules of the commodity exchanges require that the contracts be marked to market on a daily basis; that is, the customer pays or receives any increment attributable to that day's price change. Because commodity customers may incur obligations on their contracts, they are required to provide collateral at the outset, known as "original margin," and may be required to provide additional amounts, known as "variation margin," during the term of the contract.

The most likely setting in which a person would want to take a security interest in a commodity contract is where a lender who is advancing funds to finance an inventory of a physical commodity requires the borrower to enter into a commodity contract as a hedge against the risk of decline in the value of the commodity. The lender will want to take a security interest in both the commodity itself and the hedging commodity contract. Typically, such arrangements are structured as security interests in the entire commodity account in which the borrower carries the hedging contracts, rather than in individual contracts.

One important effect of including commodity contracts and commodity accounts in Article 9 is to provide a clearer legal structure for the analysis of the rights of commodity clearing organizations against their participants and futures commission merchants against their customers. The rules and agreements of commodity clearing organizations generally provide that the clearing organization has the right to liquidate any participant's positions in order to satisfy obligations of the participant to the clearing corporation. Similarly, agreements between futures commission merchants and their customers generally provide that the futures commission merchant has the right to liquidate a customer's positions in order to satisfy obligations of the customer to the futures commission merchant.

The main property that a commodity intermediary holds as collateral for the obligations that the commodity customer may incur under its commodity contracts is not other commodity contracts carried by the customer but the other property that the customer has posted as margin. Typically, this property will be securities. The commodity intermediary's security interest in such securities is governed by the rules of this Article on security interests in securities, not the rules on security interests in commodity contracts or commodity accounts.

Although there are significant analytic and regulatory differences between commodities and securities, the development of commodity contracts on financial products in the past few decades has resulted in a system in which the commodity markets and securities markets are closely linked. The rules on security interests in commodity contracts and commodity accounts provide a structure that may be essential in times of stress in the financial markets. Suppose, for example that a firm has a position in a securities market that is hedged by a position in a commodity market, so that payments that the firm is obligated to make with respect to the securities position will be covered by the receipt of funds from the commodity position. Depending upon the settlement cycles of the different markets, it is possible that the firm could find itself in a position where it is obligated to make the payment with respect to the securities position before it receives the matching funds from the commodity position. If cross-margining arrangements have not been developed between the two markets, the firm may need to borrow funds temporarily to make the earlier payment. The rules on security interests in investment property would facilitate the use of positions in one market as collateral for loans needed to cover obligations in the other market.

7. **Consumer-Related Definitions: "Consumer Debtor"; "Consumer Goods"; "Consumer-goods transaction"; "Consumer Obligor"; "Consumer Transaction."** The definition of "consumer goods" (discussed above) is substantially the same as the definition in former Section 9–109. The definitions of "consumer debtor," "consumer obligor," "consumer-goods transaction," and "consumer transaction" have

been added in connection with various new (and old) consumer-related provisions and to designate certain provisions that are inapplicable in consumer transactions.

"Consumer-goods transaction" is a subset of "consumer transaction." Under each definition, both the obligation secured and the collateral must have a personal, family, or household purpose. However, "mixed" business and personal transactions also may be characterized as a consumer-goods transaction or consumer transaction. Subparagraph (A) of the definition of consumer-goods transactions and clause (i) of the definition of consumer transaction are primary purposes tests. Under these tests, it is necessary to determine the primary purpose of the obligation or obligations secured. Subparagraph (B) and clause (iii) of these definitions are satisfied if any of the collateral is consumer goods, in the case of a consumer-goods transaction, or "is held or acquired primarily for personal, family, or household purposes," in the case of a consumer transaction. The fact that some of the obligations secured or some of the collateral for the obligation does not satisfy the tests (e.g., some of the collateral is acquired for a business purpose) does not prevent a transaction from being a "consumer transaction" or "consumer-goods transaction."

8. **Filing-Related Definitions: "Continuation Statement"; "File Number"; "Filing Office"; "Filing-office Rule"; "Financing Statement"; "Fixture Filing"; "Manufactured–Home Transaction"; "New Debtor"; "Original Debtor"; "Public–Finance Transaction"; "Termination Statement"; "Transmitting Utility."** These definitions are used exclusively or primarily in the filing-related provisions in Part 5. Most are self-explanatory and are discussed in the Comments to Part 5. A financing statement filed in a manufactured-home transaction or a public-finance transaction may remain effective for 30 years instead of the 5 years applicable to other financing statements. See Section 9–515(b). The definitions relating to medium neutrality also are significant for the filing provisions. See Comment 9.

The definition of "transmitting utility" has been revised to embrace the business of transmitting communications generally to take account of new and future types of communications technology. The term designates a special class of debtors for whom separate filing rules are provided in Part 5, thereby obviating the many local fixture filings that would be necessary under the rules of Section 9–501 for a far-flung public-utility debtor. A transmitting utility will not necessarily be regulated by or operating as such in a jurisdiction where fixtures are located. For example, a utility might own transmission lines in a jurisdiction, although the utility generates no power and has no customers in the jurisdiction.

9. **Definitions Relating to Medium Neutrality.**

a. **"Record."** In many, but not all, instances, the term "record" replaces the term "writing" and "written." A "record" includes information that is in intangible form (e.g., electronically stored) as well as tangible form (e.g., written on paper). Given the rapid development and commercial adoption of modern communication and storage technologies, requirements that documents or communications be "written," "in writing," or otherwise in tangible form do not necessarily reflect or aid commercial practices.

A "record" need not be permanent or indestructible, but the term does not include any oral or other communication that is not stored or preserved by any means. The information must be stored on paper or in some other medium. Information that has not been retained other than through human memory does not qualify as a record. Examples of current technologies commercially used to communicate or store information include, but are not limited to, magnetic media, optical discs, digital voice messaging systems, electronic mail, audio tapes, and photographic media, as well as paper. "Record" is an inclusive term that includes all of these methods of storing or communicating information. Any "writing" is a record. A record may be authenticated. See Comment 9.b. A record may be created without the knowledge or intent of a particular person.

Like the terms "written" or "in writing," the term "record" does not establish the purposes, permitted uses, or legal effect that a record may have under any particular provision of law. Whatever is filed in the Article 9 filing system, including financing statements, continuation statements, and termination statements, whether transmitted in tangible or intangible form, would fall within the definition. However, in some instances, statutes or filing-office rules may require that a paper record be filed. In such cases, even if this Article permits the filing of an electronic record, compliance with those statutes or rules is necessary. Similarly, a filer must comply with a statute or rule that requires a particular type of encoding or formatting for an electronic record.

This Article sometimes uses the terms "for record," "of record," "record or legal title," and "record owner." Some of these are terms traditionally used in real-property law. The definition of "record" in this Article now explicitly excepts these usages from the defined term. Also, this Article refers to a record that is filed or recorded in real-property recording systems to record a mortgage as a "record of a mortgage." This usage recognizes that the defined term "mortgage" means an interest in real property; it does not mean the record that evidences, or is filed or recorded with respect to, the mortgage.

b. **"Authenticate"; "Communicate"; "Send."** The terms "authenticate" and "authenticated" generally replace "sign" and "signed." "Authenticated" replaces and broadens the definition of "signed," in Section 1–201, to encompass authentication of all records, not just writings. (References to authentication of, e.g., an agreement, demand, or notification mean, of course, authentication of a record containing an agreement, demand, or notification.) The terms "communicate" and "send" also contemplate the possibility of communication by nonwritten media. These definitions include the act of transmitting both tangible and intangible records. The definition of "send" replaces, for purposes of this Article, the corresponding term in Section 1–201. The reference to "usual means of communication" in that definition contemplates an inquiry into the appropriateness of the method of transmission used in the particular circumstances involved.

10. **Scope-Related Definitions.**

a. **Expanded Scope of Article: "Agricultural Lien"; "Consignment"; "Payment Intangible"; "Promissory Note."** These new definitions reflect the expanded scope of Article 9, as provided in Section 9–109(a).

b. **Reduced Scope of Exclusions: "Governmental Unit"; "Health-Care–Insurance Receivable"; "Commercial Tort Claims."** These new definitions reflect the reduced scope of the exclusions, provided in Section 9–109(c) and (d), of transfers by governmental debtors and assignments of interests in insurance policies and commercial tort claims.

11. **Choice-of-Law–Related Definitions: "Certificate of Title"; "Governmental Unit"; "Jurisdiction of Organization"; "Registered Organization"; "State."** These new definitions reflect the changes in the law governing perfection and priority of security interests and agricultural liens provided in Part 3, Subpart 1.

Not every organization that may provide information about itself in the public records is a "registered organization." For example, a general partnership is not a "registered organization," even if it files a statement of partnership authority under Section 303 of the Uniform Partnership Act (1994) or an assumed name ("dba") certificate. This is because the State under whose law the partnership is organized is not required to maintain a public record showing that the partnership has been organized. In contrast, corporations, limited liability companies, and limited partnerships are "registered organizations."

12. **Deposit-Account–Related Definitions: "Deposit Account"; "Bank."** The revised definition of "deposit account" incorporates the definition of "bank," which is new. The definition derives from the definitions of "bank" in Sections 4–105(1) and 4A–105(a)(2), which focus on whether the organization is "engaged in the business of banking."

Deposit accounts evidenced by Article 9 "instruments" are excluded from the term "deposit account." In contrast, former Section 9–105 excluded from the former definition "an account evidenced by a certificate of deposit." The revised definition clarifies the proper treatment of nonnegotiable or uncertificated certificates of deposit. Under the definition, an uncertificated certificate of deposit would be a deposit account (assuming there is no writing evidencing the bank's obligation to pay) whereas a nonnegotiable certificate of deposit would be a deposit account only if it is not an "instrument" as defined in this section (a question that turns on whether the nonnegotiable certificate of deposit is "of a type that in ordinary course of business is transferred by delivery with any necessary indorsement or assignment.")

A deposit account evidenced by an instrument is subject to the rules applicable to instruments generally. As a consequence, a security interest in such an instrument cannot be perfected by "control" (see Section 9–104), and the special priority rules applicable to deposit accounts (see Sections 9–327 and 9–340) do not apply.

The term "deposit account" does not include "investment property," such as securities and security entitlements. Thus, the term also does not include shares in a money-market mutual fund, even if the shares are redeemable by check.

13. **Proceeds-Related Definitions: "Cash Proceeds"; "Noncash Proceeds"; "Proceeds."** The revised definition of "proceeds" expands the definition beyond that contained in former Section 9–306 and resolves ambiguities in the former section.

a. **Distributions on Account of Collateral.** The phrase "whatever is collected on, or distributed on account of, collateral," in subparagraph (B), is broad enough to cover cash or stock dividends distributed on account of securities or other investment property that is original collateral. Compare former Section 9–306 ("Any payments or distributions made with respect to investment property collateral are proceeds."). This section rejects the holding of *Hastie v. FDIC*, 2 F.3d 1042 (10th Cir.1993) (postpetition cash dividends on stock subject to a prepetition pledge are not "proceeds" under Bankruptcy Code Section 552(b)), to the extent the holding relies on the Article 9 definition of "proceeds."

b. **Distributions on Account of Supporting Obligations.** Under subparagraph (B), collections on and distributions on account of collateral consisting of various credit-support arrangements ("supporting obligations," as defined in Section 9–102) also are proceeds. Consequently, they are afforded treatment identical to proceeds collected from or distributed by the obligor on the underlying (supported) right to payment or other collateral. Proceeds of supporting obligations also are proceeds of the underlying rights to payment or other collateral.

c. **Proceeds of Proceeds.** The definition of "proceeds" no longer provides that proceeds of proceeds are themselves proceeds. That idea is expressed in the revised definition of "collateral" in Section 9–102. No change in meaning is intended.

d. **Proceeds Received by Person Who Did Not Create Security Interest.** When collateral is sold subject to a security interest and the buyer then resells the collateral, a question arose under former Article 9 concerning whether the "debtor" had "received" what the buyer received on resale and, therefore, whether those receipts were "proceeds" under former Section 9–306(2). This Article contains no requirement that property be "received" by the debtor for the property to qualify as proceeds. It is necessary only that the property be traceable, directly or indirectly, to the original collateral.

e. **Cash Proceeds and Noncash Proceeds.** The definition of "cash proceeds" is substantially the same as the corresponding definition in former Section 9–306. The phrase "and the like" covers property that is functionally equivalent to "money, checks, or deposit accounts," such as some money-market accounts that are securities or part of securities entitlements. Proceeds other than cash proceeds are noncash proceeds.

14. **Consignment-Related Definitions: "Consignee"; "Consignment"; "Consignor."** The definition of "consignment" excludes, in subparagraphs (B) and (C), transactions for which filing would be inappropriate or of insufficient benefit to justify the costs. A consignment excluded from the application of this Article by one of those subparagraphs may still be a true consignment; however, it is governed by non-Article 9 law. The definition also excludes, in subparagraph (D), what have been called "consignments intended for security." These "consignments" are not bailments but secured transactions. Accordingly, all of Article 9 applies to them. See Sections 1–201(37), 9–109(a)(1). The "consignor" is the person who delivers goods to the "consignee" in a consignment.

The definition of "consignment" requires that the goods be delivered "to a merchant for the purpose of sale." If the goods are delivered for another purpose as well, such as milling or processing, the transaction is a consignment nonetheless because a purpose of the delivery is "sale." On the other hand, if a merchant-processor-bailee will not be selling the goods itself but will be delivering to buyers to which the owner-bailor agreed to sell the goods, the transaction would not be a consignment.

15. **"Accounting."** This definition describes the record and information that a debtor is entitled to request under Section 9–210.

16. **"Document."** The definition of "document" incorporates both tangible and electronic documents of title. See Section 1–201(b)16 and Comment 16.

17. **"Encumbrance"; "Mortgage."** The definitions of "encumbrance" and "mortgage" are unchanged in substance from the corresponding definitions in former Section 9–105. They are used primarily in the special real-property-related priority and other provisions relating to crops, fixtures, and accessions.

18. **"Fixtures."** This definition is unchanged in substance from the corresponding definition in former Section 9–313. See Section 9–334 (priority of security interests in fixtures and crops).

19. **"Good Faith."** This Article expands the definition of "good faith" to include "the observance of reasonable commercial standards of fair dealing." The definition in this section applies when the term is used in this Article, and the same concept applies in the context of this Article for purposes of the obligation of good faith imposed by Section 1–203. See subsection (c).

20. **"Lien Creditor"** This definition is unchanged in substance from the corresponding definition in former Section 9–301.

21. **"New Value."** This Article deletes former Section 9–108. Its broad formulation of new value, which embraced the taking of after-acquired collateral for a pre-existing claim, was unnecessary, counterintuitive, and ineffective for its original purpose of sheltering after-acquired collateral from attack as a voidable preference in bankruptcy. The new definition derives from Bankruptcy Code Section 547(a). The term is used with respect to temporary perfection of security interests in instruments, certificated securities, or negotiable documents under Section 9–312(e) and with respect to chattel paper priority in Section 9–330.

22. **"Person Related To."** Section 9–615 provides a special method for calculating a deficiency or surplus when "the secured party, a person related to the secured party, or a secondary obligor" acquires the collateral at a foreclosure disposition. Separate definitions of the term are provided with respect to an individual secured party and with respect to a secured party that is an organization. The definitions are patterned on the corresponding definition in Section 1.301(32) of the Uniform Consumer Credit Code (1974).

23. **"Proposal."** This definition describes a record that is sufficient to propose to retain collateral in full or partial satisfaction of a secured obligation. See Sections 9–620, 9–621, 9–622.

24. **"Pursuant to Commitment."** This definition is unchanged in substance from the corresponding definition in former Section 9–105. It is used in connection with special priority rules applicable to future advances. See Section 9–323.

25. **"Software."** The definition of "software" is used in connection with the priority rules applicable to purchase-money security interests. See Sections 9–103, 9–324. Software, like a payment intangible, is a type of general intangible for purposes of this Article. See Comment 4.a., above, regarding the distinction between "goods" and "software."

26. **Terminology: "Assignment" and "Transfer."** In numerous provisions, this Article refers to the "assignment" or the "transfer" of property interests. These terms and their derivatives are not defined. This Article generally follows common usage by using the terms "assignment" and "assign" to refer to transfers of rights to payment, claims, and liens and other security interests. It generally uses the term "transfer" to refer to other transfers of interests in property. Except when used in connection with a letter-of-credit transaction (see Section 9–107, Comment 4), no significance should be placed on the use of one term or the other. Depending on the context, each term may refer to the assignment or transfer of an outright ownership interest or to the assignment or transfer of a limited interest, such as a security interest.

State Bar Committee Comment

1. **Consignments.** Subparagraph (E) is a non-uniform amendment to Section 9.102(a)(20). The Artists' Consignment Act (formerly Article 9018, Vernon's Texas Civil Statutes) has been codified in the Occupations Code at Sections 2101.001–2101.003. It provides that "a work of art delivered to an art dealer for exhibition or sale and the proceeds from the dealer's sale of the work of art are not subject to a claim, lien, or security interest of a creditor of the dealer." Art dealers frequently obtain works of art from artists under a true consignment arrangement in which the dealer does not purchase the artwork from the artist but is given the authority to sell it on the artist's behalf and the obligation to remit some portion of the sale proceeds to the artist. Dealers are reluctant to purchase the work outright and thus take the risk that it will resell. However, it may be difficult to tell if a particular transaction is a true consignment (a bailment coupled with an agency) or a "sale or return" (where the dealer buys the artwork, but if it does not resell the artist will repurchase it), especially if the dealer is permitted to postpone paying for the work until it resells. The Artists' Consignment Act recognizes the utility of these arrangements and also recognizes that many artists are likely to be unaware of the possibility that their artwork delivered to the dealer might be subject to the claims of the dealer's creditors under Section 2.326(b). (Goods delivered in a "sale or return" transaction are subject to the claims of creditors of the buyer taking such a delivery.) The Artists' Consignment Act protects the artist consignor (or the artist's estate) by reversing the outcome of Section 2.326(b) where artworks are delivered to a dealer. Section 2.326 was amended when the Artists' Consignment Act was adopted to add Subsection 2.326(c)(4), which provides that transactions covered by the Artists' Consignment Act are not subject to

Section 2.326. Subsection 9.102(a)(20)(E) preserves this protection by excepting transactions covered by the Artists' Consignment Act from the definition of "consignment" in Chapter 9. The effect of the exception is that the transactions covered by the Artists' Consignment Act are not within the scope of Chapter 9; therefore, the artist is not treated as a secured party and need not file a financing statement to protect his or her rights from the claims of the dealer's creditors.

2. **Deposit accounts.** The middle sentence of Subsection 9.102(a)(29) is a nonuniform addition including nonnegotiable certificates of deposit in the definition of "deposit account." In the 1997 amendments to Chapter 9 a nonnegotiable certificate of deposit was included in the nonuniform definition of "instrument" in former Subsection 9.105(a)(9). Perfection of a security interest in a nonnegotiable certificate of deposit under those 1997 amendments was by possession as defined in the nonuniform addition to former Section 9.304(a): "Possession of a nonnegotiable certificate of deposit in which the secured party is the issuer of the document is established when the issuer places a restriction on withdrawals from the account on its records that evidences the document." Although revised Chapter 9 removes nonnegotiable certificates of deposit from the definition of "instrument" (Section 9.102(a)(47)) and inserts them into the definition of "deposit account," the effect is to permit perfection of security interests in nonnegotiable CD's by "control" as explained in revised Section 9.104, a method analogous to the restriction of withdrawals under the 1997 amendments. This makes unnecessary the analysis discussed in the second paragraph of Official Comment 12. Perfection of a security interest in a nonnegotiable certificate of deposit is subject to the rules of perfection of an interest in a deposit account found in Sections 9.304 and 9.312. This is designed to remove the controversy with respect to the nature of these items and adapt to the continuing and increasing use of electronic and other media for record keeping and other purposes. Nonnegotiable certificates of deposit encompass certificates that do not meet the test of a negotiable instrument, including those which may be labeled as nonnegotiable, and those which may be merely book entry (uncertificated). Book entry "certificates of deposit" are described in account agreements and appropriate disclosures but modern banking practice has moved away from the use of formal certificates for what is otherwise known as "time deposits" or "time accounts." See also the definitions in Regulation D, 12 C.F.R. sec. 204.2(c) and Regulation DD, 12 C.F.R. sec. 230.2(u). The term "deposit accounts" does not include "instruments." Since negotiable certificates of deposit are instruments, their treatment is unaffected by this nonuniform definition of deposit accounts.

3. **Instrument.** The last sentence of Subsection 9.102(a)(47) contains a nonuniform provision excluding nonnegotiable certificates of deposit from the definition of "instrument." The immediately preceding paragraph of this State Bar Committee Comment (dealing with deposit accounts) explains this provision.

4. **Nonnegotiable certificate of deposit.** Subsection 9.102(a)(59) is a nonuniform definition first incorporated by the Legislature in 1997 in pre-revised Section 9.105(a)(14) in order to provide Chapter 9 coverage for security interests in such personal property assets. Paragraph 2 of this State Bar Committee Comment explains the treatment. As a result of the insertion of this nonuniform definition the remaining terms in Section 9.102(a) bear a number one digit higher than in the official text.

§ 9.103. Purchase-Money Security Interest; Application of Payments; Burden of Establishing

(a) In this section:

(1) "Purchase-money collateral" means goods or software that secures a purchase-money obligation incurred with respect to that collateral.

(2) "Purchase-money obligation" means an obligation of an obligor incurred as all or part of the price of the collateral or for value given to enable the debtor to acquire rights in or the use of the collateral if the value is in fact so used.

(b) A security interest in goods is a purchase-money security interest:

(1) to the extent that the goods are purchase-money collateral with respect to that security interest;

(2) if the security interest is in inventory that is or was purchase-money collateral, also to the extent that the security interest secures a purchase-money obligation incurred with respect to other inventory in which the secured party holds or held a purchase-money security interest; and

(3) also to the extent that the security interest secures a purchase-money obligation incurred with respect to software in which the secured party holds or held a purchase-money security interest.

(c) A security interest in software is a purchase-money security interest to the extent that the security interest also secures a purchase-money obligation incurred with respect to goods in which the secured party holds or held a purchase-money security interest if:

(1) the debtor acquired its interest in the software in an integrated transaction in which it acquired an interest in the goods; and

(2) the debtor acquired its interest in the software for the principal purpose of using the software in the goods.

(d) The security interest of a consignor in goods that are the subject of a consignment is a purchase-money security interest in inventory.

(e) In a transaction other than a consumer-goods transaction, if the extent to which a security interest is a purchase-money security interest depends on the application of a payment to a particular obligation, the payment must be applied:

(1) in accordance with any reasonable method of application to which the parties agree;

(2) in the absence of the parties' agreement to a reasonable method, in accordance with any intention of the obligor manifested at or before the time of payment; or

(3) in the absence of an agreement to a reasonable method and a timely manifestation of the obligor's intention, in the following order:

(A) to obligations that are not secured; and

(B) if more than one obligation is secured, to obligations secured by purchase-money security interests in the order in which those obligations were incurred.

(f) In a transaction other than a consumer-goods transaction, a purchase-money security interest does not lose its status as such, even if:

(1) the purchase-money collateral also secures an obligation that is not a purchase-money obligation;

(2) collateral that is not purchase-money collateral also secures the purchase-money obligation; or

(3) the purchase-money obligation has been renewed, refinanced, consolidated, or restructured.

(g) In a transaction other than a consumer-goods transaction, a secured party claiming a purchase-money security interest has the burden of establishing the extent to which the security interest is a purchase-money security interest.

(h) The limitation of the rules in Subsections (e), (f), and (g) to transactions other than consumer-goods transactions is intended to leave to the court the determination of the proper rules in consumer-goods transactions. The court may not infer from that limitation the nature of the proper rule in consumer-goods transactions and may continue to apply established approaches.

Amended by Acts 1999, 76th Leg., ch. 414, § 1.01, eff. July 1, 2001.

Uniform Commercial Code Comment

1. **Source.** Former Section 9–107.

2. **Scope of This Section.** Under Section 9–309(1), a purchase-money security interest in consumer goods is perfected when it attaches. Sections 9–317 and 9–324 provide special priority rules for purchase-money security interests in a variety of contexts. This section explains when a security interest enjoys purchase-money status.

3. **"Purchase–Money Collateral"; "Purchase–Money Obligation"; "Purchase–Money Security Interest."** Subsection (a) defines "purchase-money collateral" and "purchase-money obligation." These terms are essential to the description of what constitutes a purchase-money security interest under subsection (b). As used in subsection (a)(2), the definition of "purchase-money obligation," the "price" of collateral or the "value given to enable" includes obligations for expenses incurred in connection with acquiring rights in the collateral, sales taxes, duties, finance charges, interest, freight charges, costs of storage in transit, demurrage, administrative charges, expenses of collection and enforcement, attorney's fees, and other similar obligations.

The concept of "purchase-money security interest" requires a close nexus between the acquisition of collateral and the secured obligation. Thus, a security interest does not qualify as a purchase-money security interest if a debtor acquires property on unsecured credit and subsequently creates the security interest to secure the purchase price.

4. **Cross-Collateralization of Purchase–Money Security Interests in Inventory.** Subsection (b)(2) deals with the problem of cross-collateralized purchase-money security interests in inventory. Consider a simple example:

Example: Seller (S) sells an item of inventory (Item–1) to Debtor (D), retaining a security interest in Item–1 to secure Item–1's price and all other obligations, existing and future, of D to S. S then sells another item of inventory to D (Item–2), again retaining a security interest in Item–2 to secure Item–2's price as well as all other obligations of D to S. D then pays to S Item–1's price. D then sells Item–2 to a buyer in ordinary course of business, who takes Item–2 free of S's security interest.

Under subsection (b)(2), S's security interest in *Item–1* securing *Item–2's unpaid price* would be a purchase-money security interest. This is so because S has a purchase-money security interest in Item–1, Item–1 secures the price of (a "purchase-money obligation incurred with respect to") Item–2 ("other inventory"), and Item–2 itself was subject to a purchase-money security interest. Note that, to the extent Item–1 secures the price of Item–2, S's security interest in Item–1 would not be a purchase-money security interest under subsection (b)(1). The security interest in Item–1 is a purchase-money security interest under subsection (b)(1) only to the extent that Item–1 is "purchase-money collateral," i.e., only to the extent that Item–1 "secures a purchase-money obligation incurred with respect to that collateral" (i.e., Item–1). See subsection (a)(1).

5. **Purchase-Money Security Interests in Goods and Software.** Subsections (b) and (c) limit purchase-money security interests to security interests in goods, including fixtures, and software. Otherwise, no change in meaning from former Section 9–107 is intended. The second sentence of former Section 9–115(5)(f) made the purchase-money priority rule (former Section 9–312(4)) inapplicable to investment property. This section's limitation makes that provision unnecessary.

Subsection (c) describes the limited circumstances under which a security interest in goods may be accompanied by a purchase-money security interest in software. The software must be acquired by the debtor in a transaction integrated with the transaction in which the debtor acquired the goods, and the debtor must acquire the software for the principal purpose of using the software in the goods. "Software" is defined in Section 9–102.

6. **Consignments.** Under former Section 9–114, the priority of the consignor's interest is similar to that of a purchase-money security interest. Subsection (d) achieves this result more directly, by defining the interest of a "consignor," defined in Section 9–102, to be a purchase-money security interest in inventory for purposes of this Article. This drafting convention obviates any need to set forth special priority rules applicable to the interest of a consignor. Rather, the priority of the consignor's interest as against the rights of lien creditors of the consignee, competing secured parties, and purchasers of the goods from the consignee can be determined by reference to the priority rules generally applicable to inventory, such as Sections 9–317, 9–320, 9–322, and 9–324. For other purposes, including the rights and duties of the consignor and consignee as between themselves, the consignor would remain the owner of goods under a bailment arrangement with the consignee. See Section 9–319.

7. **Provisions Applicable Only to Non–Consumer–Goods Transactions.**

a. **"Dual–Status" Rule.** For transactions other than consumer-goods transactions, this Article approves what some cases have called the "dual-status" rule, under which a security interest may be a purchase-money security interest to some extent and a non-purchase-money security interest to some extent. (Concerning consumer-goods transactions, see subsection (h) and Comment 8.) Some courts have found this rule to be explicit or implicit in the words "to the extent," found in former Section 9–107 and continued in subsections (b)(1) and (b)(2). The rule is made explicit in subsection (e). For non-consumer-goods transactions, this Article rejects the "transformation" rule adopted by some cases, under which any cross-collateralization, refinancing, or the like destroys the purchase-money status entirely.

Consider, for example, what happens when a $10,000 loan secured by a purchase-money security interest is refinanced by the original lender, and, as part of the transaction, the debtor borrows an additional $2,000 secured by the collateral. Subsection (f) resolves any doubt that the security interest remains a purchase-money security interest. Under subsection (b), however, it enjoys purchase-money status only to the extent of $10,000.

b. **Allocation of Payments.** Continuing with the example, if the debtor makes a $1,000 payment on the $12,000 obligation, then one must determine the extent to which the security interest remains a purchase-money security interest–$9,000 or $10,000. Subsection (e)(1) expresses the overriding principle, applicable in cases other than consumer-goods transactions, for determining the extent to which a security interest is a purchase-money security interest under these circumstances: freedom of contract, as limited by principle of reasonableness. An unconscionable method of application, for example, is not a reasonable one and so would not be given effect under subsection (e)(1). In the absence of agreement, subsection (e)(2) permits the obligor to determine how payments should be allocated. If the obligor fails to manifest its intention, obligations that are not secured will be paid first. (As used in this Article, the concept of "obligations that are not secured" means obligations for which the debtor has not created a security interest. This concept is different from and should not be confused with the concept of an "unsecured claim" as it appears in Bankruptcy Code Section 506(a).) The obligor may prefer this approach, because unsecured debt is likely to carry a higher interest rate than secured debt. A creditor who would prefer to be secured rather than unsecured also would prefer this approach.

After the unsecured debt is paid, payments are to be applied first toward the obligations secured by purchase-money security interests. In the event that there is more than one such obligation, payments first received are to be applied to obligations first incurred. See subsection (e)(3). Once these obligations are paid, there are no purchase-money security interests and no additional allocation rules are needed.

Subsection (f) buttresses the dual-status rule by making it clear that (in a transaction other than a consumer-goods transaction) cross-collateralization and renewals, refinancings, and restructurings do not cause a purchase-money security interest to lose its status as such. The statutory terms "renewed," "refinanced," and "restructured" are not defined. Whether the terms encompass a particular transaction depends upon whether, under the particular facts, the purchase-money character of the security interest fairly can be said to survive. Each term contemplates that an identifiable portion of the purchase-money obligation could be traced to the new obligation resulting from a renewal, refinancing, or restructuring.

c. **Burden of Proof.** As is the case when the extent of a security interest is in issue, under subsection (g) the secured party claiming a purchase-money security interest in a transaction other than a consumer-goods transaction has the burden of establishing whether the security interest retains its purchase-money status. This is so whether the determination is to be made following a renewal, refinancing, or restructuring or otherwise.

8. **Consumer-Goods Transactions; Characterization Under Other Law.** Under subsection (h), the limitation of subsections (e), (f), and (g) to transactions other than consumer-goods transactions leaves to the court the determination of the proper rules in consumer-goods transactions. Subsection (h) also instructs the court not to draw any inference from this limitation as to the proper rules for

consumer-goods transactions and leaves the court free to continue to apply established approaches to those transactions.

This section addresses only whether a security interest is a "purchase-money security interest" under this Article, primarily for purposes of perfection and priority. See, e.g., Sections 9–317, 9–324. In particular, its adoption of the dual-status rule, allocation of payments rules, and burden of proof standards for non-consumer-goods transactions is not intended to affect or influence characterizations under other statutes. Whether a security interest is a "purchase-money security interest" under other law is determined by that law. For example, decisions under Bankruptcy Code Section 522(f) have applied both the dual-status and the transformation rules. The Bankruptcy Code does not expressly adopt the state law definition of "purchase-money security interest." Where federal law does not defer to this Article, this Article does not, and could not, determine a question of federal law.

State Bar Committee Comment

As noted in Official Comment 7, Revised Article 9 rejects the so-called "transformation rule" and adopts the so-called "dual status" rule, under which a security interest does not automatically lose its purchase money status through the inclusion of an after-acquired property clause or a future advance clause in the security agreement. This does not change existing Texas law. See *Borg–Warner Acceptance Corp. v. Tascosa National Bank,* 784 S.W.2d 129 (Tex. App.—Amarillo 1990, writ denied).

§ 9.104. Control of Deposit Account

(a) A secured party has control of a deposit account if:

(1) the secured party is the bank with which the deposit account is maintained;

(2) the debtor, secured party, and bank have agreed in an authenticated record that the bank will comply with instructions originated by the secured party directing disposition of the funds in the deposit account without further consent by the debtor; or

(3) the secured party becomes the bank's customer with respect to the deposit account.

(b) A secured party that has satisfied Subsection (a) has control, even if the debtor retains the right to direct the disposition of funds from the deposit account.

Amended by Acts 1999, 76th Leg., ch. 414, § 1.01, eff. July 1, 2001; Acts 2001, 77th Leg., ch. 705, § 2, eff. June 13, 2001.

Uniform Commercial Code Comment

1. **Source.** New; derived from Section 8–106.

2. **Why "Control" Matters.** This section explains the concept of "control" of a deposit account. "Control" under this section may serve two functions. First, "control . . . pursuant to the debtor's agreement" may substitute for an authenticated security agreement as an element of attachment. See Section 9–203(b)(3)(D). Second, when a deposit account is taken as original collateral, the only method of perfection is obtaining control under this section. See Section 9–312(b)(1).

3. **Requirements for "Control."** This section derives from Section 8–106 of Revised Article 8, which defines "control" of securities and certain other investment property. Under subsection (a)(1), the bank with which the deposit account is maintained has control. The effect of this provision is to afford the bank automatic perfection. No other form of public notice is necessary; all actual and potential creditors of the debtor are always on notice that the bank with which the debtor's deposit account is maintained may assert a claim against the deposit account.

Under subsection (a)(2), a secured party may obtain control by obtaining the bank's authenticated agreement that it will comply with the secured party's instructions without further consent by the debtor. The analogous provision in Section 8–106 does not require that the agreement be authenticated. An agreement to comply with the secured party's instructions suffices for "control" of a deposit account under this section even if the bank's agreement is subject to specified conditions, e.g., that the secured party's instructions are accompanied by a certification that the debtor is in default. (Of course, if the condition is the *debtor's* further consent, the statute explicitly provides that the agreement would *not* confer control.) See revised Section 8–106, Comment 7.

Under subsection (a)(3), a secured party may obtain control by becoming the bank's "customer," as defined in Section 4–104. As the customer, the secured party would enjoy the right (but not necessarily the exclusive right) to withdraw funds from, or close, the deposit account. See Sections 4–401(a), 4–403(a).

Although the arrangements giving rise to control may themselves prevent, or may enable the secured party at its discretion to prevent, the debtor from reaching the funds on deposit, subsection (b) makes clear that the debtor's ability to reach the funds is not inconsistent with "control."

Perfection by control is not available for bank accounts evidenced by an instrument (e.g., certain certificates of deposit), which by definition are "instruments" and not "deposit accounts." See Section 9–102 (defining "deposit account" and "instrument").

§ 9.105. Control of Electronic Chattel Paper

A secured party has control of electronic chattel paper if the record or records comprising the chattel paper are created, stored, and assigned in such a manner that:

(1) a single authoritative copy of the record or records exists that is unique, identifiable and, except as otherwise provided in Subdivisions (4), (5), and (6), unalterable;

(2) the authoritative copy identifies the secured party as the assignee of the record or records;

(3) the authoritative copy is communicated to and maintained by the secured party or its designated custodian;

(4) copies or revisions that add or change an identified assignee of the authoritative copy can be made only with the participation of the secured party;

(5) each copy of the authoritative copy and any copy of a copy is readily identifiable as a copy that is not the authoritative copy; and

(6) any revision of the authoritative copy is readily identifiable as an authorized or unauthorized revision.

Amended by Acts 1999, 76th Leg., ch. 414, § 1.01, eff. July 1, 2001.

Uniform Commercial Code Comment

1. **Source.** New.

2. **"Control" of Electronic Chattel Paper.** This Article covers security interests in "electronic chattel paper," a new term defined in Section 9–102. This section governs how "control" of electronic chattel paper may be obtained. A secured party's control of electronic chattel paper (i) may substitute for an authenticated security agreement for purposes of attachment under Section 9–203, (ii) is a method of perfection under Section 9–314, and (iii) is a condition for obtaining special, non-temporal priority under Section 9–330. Because electronic chattel paper cannot be transferred, assigned, or possessed in the same manner as tangible chattel paper, a special definition of control is necessary. In descriptive terms, this section provides that control of electronic chattel paper is the functional equivalent of possession of "tangible chattel paper" (a term also defined in Section 9–102).

3. **"Authoritative Copy" of Electronic Chattel Paper.** One requirement for establishing control is that a particular copy be an "authoritative copy." Although other copies may exist, they must be distinguished from the authoritative copy. This may be achieved, for example, through the methods of authentication that are used or by business practices involving the marking of any additional copies. When tangible chattel paper is converted to electronic chattel paper, in order to establish that a copy of the electronic chattel paper is the authoritative copy it may be necessary to show that the tangible chattel paper no longer exists or has been permanently marked to indicate that it is not the authoritative copy.

4. **Development of Control Systems.** This Article leaves to the marketplace the development of systems and procedures, through a combination of suitable technologies and business practices, for dealing with control of electronic chattel paper in a commercial context. However, achieving control under this section requires more than the agreement of interested persons that the elements of control are satisfied. For example, paragraph (4) contemplates that control requires that it be a physical impossibility (or sufficiently unlikely or implausible so as to approach practical impossibility) to add or change an identified assignee without the participation of the secured party (or its authorized representative). It would not be enough for the assignor merely to agree that it will not change the identified assignee without the assignee-secured party's consent. However, the standards applied to determine whether a party is in control of electronic chattel paper should not be more stringent than the standards now applied to determine whether a party is in possession of tangible chattel paper. Control of electronic chattel paper contemplates systems or procedures such that the secured party must take some action (either directly or through its designated custodian) to effect a change or addition to the authoritative copy. But just as a secured party does not lose possession of tangible chattel paper merely by virtue of the possibility that a person acting on its behalf *could* wrongfully redeliver the chattel paper to the debtor, so control of electronic chattel paper would not be defeated by the possibility that the secured party's interest *could* be subverted by the wrongful conduct of a person (such as a custodian) acting on its behalf.

Systems that evolve for control of electronic chattel paper may or may not involve a third party custodian of the relevant records. However, this section and the concept of control of electronic chattel paper are not based on the same concepts as are control of deposit accounts (Section 9–104), security entitlements, a type of investment property (Section 9–106), and letter-of-credit rights (Section 9–107). The rules for control of that collateral are based on existing market practices and legal and regulatory regimes for institutions such as banks and securities intermediaries. Analogous practices for electronic chattel paper are developing nonetheless. The flexible approach adopted by this section, moreover, should not impede the development of these practices and, eventually, legal and regulatory regimes, which may become analogous to those for, e.g., investment property.

§ 9.106. Control of Investment Property

(a) A person has control of a certificated security, uncertificated security, or security entitlement as provided in Section 8.106.

(b) A secured party has control of a commodity contract if:

(1) the secured party is the commodity intermediary with which the commodity contract is carried; or

(2) the commodity customer, secured party, and commodity intermediary have agreed that the commodity intermediary will apply any value distributed on account of the commodity contract as directed by the secured party without further consent by the commodity customer.

(c) A secured party having control of all security entitlements or commodity contracts carried in a securities account or commodity account has control over the securities account or commodity account.

Amended by Acts 1999, 76th Leg., ch. 414, § 1.01, eff. July 1, 2001.

Uniform Commercial Code Comment

1. **Source.** Former Section 9–115(e).

2. **"Control" Under Article 8.** For an explanation of "control" of securities and certain other investment property, see Section 8–106, Comments 4 and 7.

3. **"Control" of Commodity Contracts.** This section, as did former Section 9–115(1)(e), contains provisions relating to control of commodity contracts which are analogous to those in Section 8–106 for other types of investment property.

4. **Securities Accounts and Commodity Accounts.** For drafting convenience, control with respect to a securities account or commodity account is defined in terms of obtaining control over the security entitlements or commodity contracts. Of course, an agreement that provides that (without further consent of the debtor) the securities intermediary or commodity intermediary will honor instructions from the secured party concerning a securities account or commodity account described as such is sufficient. Such an agreement necessarily implies that the intermediary will honor instructions concerning all security entitlements or commodity contracts carried in the account and thus affords the secured party control of all the security entitlements or commodity contracts.

§ 9.107. Control of Letter-Of-Credit Right

A secured party has control of a letter-of-credit right to the extent of any right to payment or performance by the issuer or any nominated person if the issuer or nominated person has consented to an assignment of proceeds of the letter of credit under Section 5.114(c) or otherwise applicable law or practice.

Amended by Acts 1999, 76th Leg., ch. 414, § 1.01, eff. July 1, 2001.

Uniform Commercial Code Comment

1. **Source.** New.

2. **"Control" of Letter-of-Credit Right.** Whether a secured party has control of a letter-of-credit right may determine the secured party's priority as against competing secured parties. See Section 9–329. This section provides that a secured party acquires control of a letter-of-credit right by receiving an assignment if the secured party obtains the consent of the issuer or any nominated person, such as a confirmer or negotiating bank, under Section 5–114 or other applicable law or practice. Because both issuers and nominated persons may give or be obligated to give value under a letter of credit, this section contemplates that a secured party obtains control of a letter-of-credit right with respect to the issuer or a particular nominated person only to the extent that the issuer or that nominated person consents to the assignment. For example, if a secured party obtains control to the extent of an issuer's obligation but fails to obtain the consent of a nominated person, the secured party does not have control to the extent that the nominated person gives value. In many cases the person or persons who will give value under a letter of credit will be clear from its terms. In other cases, prudence may suggest obtaining consent from more than one person. The details of the consenting issuer's or nominated person's duties to pay or otherwise render performance to the secured party are left to the agreement of the parties.

3. **"Proceeds of a Letter of Credit."** Section 5–114 follows traditional banking terminology by referring to a letter of credit beneficiary's assignment of its right to receive payment thereunder as an assignment of the "proceeds of a letter of credit." However, as the seller of goods can assign its right to receive payment (an "account") before it has been earned by delivering the goods to the buyer, so the beneficiary of a letter of credit can assign its contingent right to payment before the letter of credit has been honored. See Section 5–114(b). If the assignment creates a security interest, the security interest can be perfected at the time it is created. An assignment of, including the creation of a security interest in, a letter-of-credit right is an assignment of a present interest.

4. **"Transfer" vs. "Assignment."** Letter-of-credit law and practice distinguish the "transfer" of a letter of credit from an "assignment." Under a transfer, the transferee itself becomes the beneficiary and acquires the right to draw. Whether a new, substitute credit is issued or the issuer advises the transferee of its status as such, the transfer constitutes a novation under which the transferee is the new, substituted beneficiary (but only to the extent of the transfer, in the case of a partial transfer).

Section 5–114(e) provides that the rights of a transferee beneficiary or nominated person are independent of the beneficiary's assignment of the proceeds of a letter of credit and are superior to the assignee's right to the proceeds. For this reason, transfer does not appear in this Article as a means of control or perfection. Section 9–109(c)(4) recognizes the independent and superior rights of a transferee beneficiary under Section 5–114(e); this Article does not apply to the rights of a transferee beneficiary or nominated person to the extent that those rights are independent and superior under Section 5–114.

5. **Supporting Obligation: Automatic Attachment and Perfection.** A letter-of-credit right is a type of "supporting obligation," as defined in Section 9–102. Under Sections 9–203 and 9–308, a security interest in a letter-of-credit right automatically attaches and is automatically perfected if the security interest in the supported obligation is a perfected security interest. However, unless the secured party has control of the letter-of-credit right or itself becomes a transferee beneficiary, it cannot obtain any rights against the issuer or a nominated person under Article 5. Consequently, as a practical matter, the secured party's rights would be limited to its ability to locate and identify proceeds distributed by the issuer or nominated person under the letter of credit.

§ 9.108. Sufficiency of Description

(a) Except as otherwise provided in Subsections (c), (d), and (e), a description of personal or real property is sufficient, whether or not it is specific, if it reasonably identifies what is described.

(b) Except as otherwise provided in Subsection (d), a description of collateral reasonably identifies the collateral if it identifies the collateral by:

(1) specific listing;

(2) category;

(3) except as otherwise provided in Subsection (e), a type of collateral defined in this title;

(4) quantity;

(5) computational or allocational formula or procedure; or

(6) except as otherwise provided in Subsection (c), any other method, if the identity of the collateral is objectively determinable.

(c) A description of collateral as "all the debtor's assets" or "all the debtor's personal property" or using words of similar import does not reasonably identify the collateral.

(d) Except as otherwise provided in Subsection (e), a description of a security entitlement, securities account, or commodity account is sufficient if it describes:

(1) the collateral by those terms or as investment property; or

(2) the underlying financial asset or commodity contract.

(e) A description only by type of collateral defined in this title is an insufficient description of:

(1) a commercial tort claim; or

(2) in a consumer transaction, consumer goods, a security entitlement, a securities account, or a commodity account.

Amended by Acts 1999, 76th Leg., ch. 414, § 1.01, eff. July 1, 2001.

Uniform Commercial Code Comment

1. **Source.** Former Sections 9–110, 9–115(3).

2. **General Rules.** Subsection (a) retains substantially the same formulation as former Section 9–110. Subsection (b) expands upon subsection (a) by indicating a variety of ways in which a description might reasonably identify collateral. Whereas a provision similar to subsection (b) was applicable only to investment property under former Section 9–115(3), subsection (b) applies to all types of collateral, subject to the limitation in subsection (d). Subsection (b) is subject to subsection (c), which follows prevailing case law and adopts the view that an "all assets" or "all personal property" description for purposes of a *security agreement* is *not* sufficient. Note, however, that under Section 9–504, a *financing statement* sufficiently indicates the collateral if it "covers all assets or all personal property."

The purpose of requiring a description of collateral in a security agreement under Section 9–203 is evidentiary. The test of sufficiency of a description under this section, as under former Section 9–110, is that the description do the job assigned to it: make possible the identification of the collateral described. This section rejects any requirement that a description is insufficient unless it is exact and detailed (the so-called "serial number" test).

3. **After-Acquired Collateral.** Much litigation has arisen over whether a description in a security agreement is sufficient to include after-acquired collateral if the agreement does not explicitly so provide. This question is one of contract interpretation and is not susceptible to a statutory rule (other than a rule to the effect that it is a question of contract interpretation). Accordingly, this section contains no reference to descriptions of after-acquired collateral.

4. **Investment Property.** Under subsection (d), the use of the wrong Article 8 terminology does not render a description invalid (e.g., a security agreement intended to cover a debtor's "security entitlements" is sufficient if it refers to the debtor's "securities"). Note also that given the broad definition of "securities account" in Section 8–501, a security interest in a securities account also includes all other rights of the debtor against the securities intermediary arising out of the securities account. For example, a security interest in a securities account would include credit balances due to the debtor from the securities intermediary, whether or not they are proceeds of a security entitlement. Moreover, describing collateral as a securities account is a simple way of describing all of the security entitlements carried in the account.

5. **Consumer Investment Property; Commercial Tort Claims.** Subsection (e) requires greater specificity of description in order to prevent debtors from inadvertently encumbering certain property. Subsection (e) requires that a description by defined "type" of collateral alone of a commercial tort claim or, in a consumer transaction, of a security entitlement, securities account, or commodity account, is not sufficient. For example, "all existing and after-acquired investment property" or "all existing and after-acquired security entitlements," without more, would be insufficient in a consumer transaction to describe a security entitlement, securities account, or commodity account. The reference to "*only* by type" in subsection (e) means that a description is sufficient if it satisfies subsection (a) and contains a descriptive component beyond the "type" alone. Moreover, if the collateral consists of a securities account or commodity account, a description of the account is sufficient to cover all existing and future security entitlements or commodity contracts carried in the account. See Section 9–203(h), (i).

Under Section 9–204, an after-acquired collateral clause in a security agreement will not reach future commercial tort claims. It follows that when an effective security agreement covering a commercial tort claim is entered into the claim already will exist. Subsection (e) does not require a description to be specific. For example, a description such as "all tort claims arising out of the explosion of debtor's factory" would suffice, even if the exact amount of the claim, the theory on which it may be based, and the identity of the tortfeasor(s) are not described.

§ 9.109. Scope

(a) Except as otherwise provided in Subsections (c), (d), and (e), this chapter applies to:

(1) a transaction, regardless of its form, that creates a security interest in personal property or fixtures by contract;

(2) an agricultural lien;

(3) a sale of accounts, chattel paper, payment intangibles, or promissory notes;

(4) a consignment;

(5) a security interest arising under Section 2.401, 2.505, 2.711(c), or 2A.508(e), as provided in Section 9.110; and

(6) a security interest arising under Section 4.210 or 5.118.

(b) The application of this chapter to a security interest in a secured obligation is not affected by the fact that the obligation is itself secured by a transaction or interest to which this chapter does not apply.

(c) This chapter does not apply to the extent that:

(1) a statute, regulation, or treaty of the United States preempts this chapter;

(2) another statute of this state expressly governs the creation, perfection, priority, or enforcement of a security interest created by this state or a governmental unit of this state;

(3) a statute of another state, a foreign country, or a governmental unit of another state or a foreign country, other than a statute generally applicable to security interests, expressly governs creation, perfection, priority, or enforcement of a security interest created by the state, country, or governmental unit; or

(4) the rights of a transferee beneficiary or nominated person under a letter of credit are independent and superior under Section 5.114.

(d) This chapter does not apply to:

(1) a landlord's lien, other than an agricultural lien;

(2) a lien, other than an agricultural lien, given by statute or other rule of law for services or materials, but Section 9.333 applies with respect to priority of the lien;

(3) an assignment of a claim for wages, salary, or other compensation of an employee;

(4) a sale of accounts, chattel paper, payment intangibles, or promissory notes as part of a sale of the business out of which they arose;

(5) an assignment of accounts, chattel paper, payment intangibles, or promissory notes that is for the purpose of collection only;

(6) an assignment of a right to payment under a contract to an assignee that is also obligated to perform under the contract;

(7) an assignment of a single account, payment intangible, or promissory note to an assignee in full or partial satisfaction of a preexisting indebtedness;

(8) a transfer of an interest in or an assignment of a claim under a policy of insurance, other than an assignment by or to a health care provider of a health-care-insurance receivable and any subsequent assignment of the right to payment, but Sections 9.315 and 9.322 apply with respect to proceeds and priorities in proceeds;

(9) an assignment of a right represented by a judgment, other than a judgment taken on a right to payment that was collateral;

(10) a right of recoupment or set-off, but:

(A) Section 9.340 applies with respect to the effectiveness of rights of recoupment or set-off against deposit accounts; and

(B) Section 9.404 applies with respect to defenses or claims of an account debtor;

(11) the creation or transfer of an interest in or lien on real property, including a lease or rents thereunder, the interest of a vendor or vendee in a contract for deed to purchase an interest in real property, or the interest of an optionor or optionee in an option to purchase an interest in real property, except to the extent that provision is made for:

(A) liens on real property in Sections 9.203 and 9.308;

(B) fixtures in Section 9.334;

(C) fixture filings in Sections 9.501, 9.502, 9.512, 9.516, and 9.519; and

(D) security agreements covering personal and real property in Section 9.604;

(12) an assignment of a claim arising in tort, other than a commercial tort claim, but Sections 9.315 and 9.322 apply with respect to proceeds and priorities in proceeds; or

(13) an assignment of a deposit account, other than a nonnegotiable certificate of deposit, in a consumer transaction, but Sections 9.315 and 9.322 apply with respect to proceeds and priorities in proceeds.

(e) The application of this chapter to the sale of accounts, chattel paper, payment intangibles, or promissory notes is not to recharacterize that sale as a transaction to secure indebtedness but to protect purchasers of those assets by providing a notice filing system. For all purposes, in the absence of fraud or intentional misrepresentation, the parties' characterization of a transaction as a sale of such assets shall be conclusive that the transaction is a sale and is not a secured transaction and that title, legal and equitable, has passed to the party characterized as the purchaser of those assets regardless of whether the secured party has any recourse against the debtor, whether the debtor is entitled to any surplus, or any other term of the parties' agreement.

Amended by Acts 1999, 76th Leg., ch. 414, § 1.01, eff. July 1, 2001.

Uniform Commercial Code Comment

1. **Source.** Former Sections 9–102, 9–104.

2. **Basic Scope Provision.** Subsection (a)(1) derives from former Section 9–102(1) and (2). These subsections have been combined and shortened. No change in meaning is intended. Under subsection (a)(1), all consensual security interests in personal property and fixtures are covered by this Article, except for transactions excluded by subsections (c) and (d). As to which transactions give rise to a "security interest," the definition of that term in Section 1–201 must be consulted. When a security interest is created, this Article applies regardless of the form of the transaction or the name that parties have given to it.

3. **Agricultural Liens.** Subsection (a)(2) is new. It expands the scope of this Article to cover agricultural liens, as defined in Section 9–102.

4. **Sales of Accounts, Chattel Paper, Payment Intangibles, Promissory Notes, and Other Receivables.** Under subsection (a)(3), as under former Section 9–102, this Article applies to sales of accounts and chattel paper. This approach generally has been successful in avoiding difficult problems of distinguishing between transactions in which a receivable secures an obligation and those in which the receivable has been sold outright. In many commercial financing transactions the distinction is blurred.

Subsection (a)(3) expands the scope of this Article by including the sale of a "payment intangible" (defined in Section 9–102 as "a general intangible under which the account debtor's principal obligation is a monetary obligation") and a "promissory note" (also defined in Section 9–102). To a considerable extent, this Article affords these transactions treatment identical to that given sales of accounts and chattel paper. In some respects, however, sales of payment intangibles and promissory notes are treated differently from sales of other receivables. See, e.g., Sections 9–309 (automatic perfection upon attachment), 9–408 (effect of restrictions on assignment). By virtue of the expanded definition of "account" (defined in Section 9–102), this Article now covers sales of (and other security interests in) "health-care-insurance receivables" (also defined in Section 9–102). Although this Article occasionally distinguishes between outright sales of receivables and sales that secure an obligation, neither this Article nor the definition of "security interest" (Section 1–201(37)) delineates how a particular transaction is to be classified. That issue is left to the courts.

5. **Transfer of Ownership in Sales of Receivables.** A "sale" of an account, chattel paper, a promissory note, or a payment intangible includes a sale of a right in the receivable, such as a sale of a participation interest. The term also includes the sale of an enforcement right. For example, a "[p]erson entitled to enforce" a negotiable promissory note (Section 3–301) may sell its ownership rights in the instrument. See Section 3–203, Comment 1 ("Ownership rights in instruments may be determined by principles of the law of property, independent of Article 3, which do not depend upon whether the instrument was transferred under Section 3–203."). Also, the right under Section 3–309 to enforce a lost, destroyed, or stolen negotiable promissory note may be sold to a purchaser who could enforce that right by causing the seller to provide the proof required under that section. This Article rejects decisions reaching a contrary result, e.g., *Dennis Joslin Co. v. Robinson Broadcasting*, 977 F.Supp. 491 (D.D.C.1997).

Nothing in this section or any other provision of Article 9 prevents the transfer of full and complete ownership of an account, chattel paper, an instrument, or a payment intangible in a transaction of sale. However, as mentioned in Comment 4, neither this Article nor the definition of "security interest" in Section 1–201 provides rules for distinguishing sales transactions from those that create a security interest securing an obligation. This Article applies to both types of transactions. The principal effect of this coverage is to apply this Article's perfection and priority rules to these sales transactions. Use of terminology such as "security interest," "debtor," and "collateral" is merely a drafting convention adopted to reach this end, and its use has no relevance to distinguishing sales from other transactions. See PEB Commentary No. 14.

Following a debtor's outright sale and transfer of ownership of a receivable, the debtor-seller retains no legal or equitable rights in the receivable that has been sold. See Section 9–318(a). This is so whether or not the buyer's security interest is perfected. (A security interest arising from the sale of a promissory note or payment intangible is perfected upon attachment without further action. See Section 9–309.) However, if the buyer's interest in accounts or chattel paper is unperfected, a subsequent lien creditor, perfected secured party, or qualified buyer can reach the sold receivable and achieve priority over (or take free of) the buyer's unperfected security interest under Section 9–317. This is so not because the seller of a receivable retains rights in the property sold; it does not. Nor is this so because the seller of a receivable is a "debtor" and the buyer of a receivable is a "secured party" under this Article (they are).

It is so for the simple reason that Sections 9–318(b), 9–317, and 9–322 make it so, as did former Sections 9–301 and 9–312. Because the buyer's security interest is unperfected, for purposes of determining the rights of creditors of and purchasers for value from the debtor-seller, under Section 9–318(b) the debtor-seller is deemed to have the rights and title it sold. Section 9–317 subjects the buyer's unperfected interest in accounts and chattel paper to that of the debtor-seller's lien creditor and other persons who qualify under that section.

6. **Consignments.** Subsection (a)(4) is new. This Article applies to every "consignment." The term, defined in Section 9–102, includes many but not all "true" consignments (i.e., bailments for the purpose of sale). If a transaction is a "sale or return," as defined in revised Section 2–326, it is not a "consignment." In a "sale or return" transaction, the buyer becomes the owner of the goods, and the seller may obtain an enforceable security interest in the goods only by satisfying the requirements of Section 9–203.

Under common law, creditors of a bailee were unable to reach the interest of the bailor (in the case of a consignment, the consignor-owner). Like former Section 2–326 and former Article 9, this Article changes the common-law result; however, it does so in a different manner. For purposes of determining the rights and interests of third-party creditors of, and purchasers of the goods from, the consignee, but not for other purposes, such as remedies of the consignor, the consignee is deemed to acquire under this Article whatever rights and title the consignor had or had power to transfer. See Section 9–319. The interest of a consignor is defined to be a security interest under revised Section 1–201(37), more specifically, a purchase-money security interest in the consignee's inventory. See Section 9–103(d). Thus, the rules pertaining to lien creditors, buyers, and attachment, perfection, and priority of competing security interests apply to consigned goods. The relationship between the consignor and consignee is left to other law. Consignors also have no duties under Part 6. See Section 9–601(g).

Sometimes parties characterize transactions that secure an obligation (other than the bailee's obligation to returned bailed goods) as "consignments." These transactions are not "consignments" as contemplated by Section 9–109(a)(4). See Section 9–102. This Article applies also to these transactions, by virtue of Section 9–109(a)(1). They create a security interest within the meaning of the first sentence of Section 1–201(37).

This Article does not apply to bailments for sale that fall outside the definition of "consignment" in Section 9–102 and that do not create a security interest that secures an obligation.

7. **Security Interest in Obligation Secured by Non–Article 9 Transaction.** Subsection (b) is unchanged in substance from former Section 9–102(3). The following example provides an illustration.

Example 1: O borrows $10,000 from M and secures its repayment obligation, evidenced by a promissory note, by granting to M a mortgage on O's land. This Article does not apply to the creation of the real-property mortgage. However, if M sells the promissory note to X or gives a security interest in the note to secure M's own obligation to X, this Article applies to the security interest thereby created in favor of X. The security interest in the promissory note is covered by this Article even though the note is secured by a real-property mortgage. Also, X's security interest in the note gives X an attached security interest in the mortgage lien that secures the note and, if the security interest in the note is perfected, the security interest in the mortgage lien likewise is perfected. See Sections 9–203, 9–308.

It also follows from subsection (b) that an attempt to obtain or perfect a security interest in a secured obligation by complying with non-Article 9 law, as by an assignment of record of a real-property mortgage, would be ineffective. Finally, it is implicit from subsection (b) that one cannot obtain a security interest in a lien, such as a mortgage on real property, that is not also coupled with an equally effective security interest in the secured obligation. This Article rejects cases such as In re *Maryville Savings & Loan Corp.*, 743 F.2d 413 (6th Cir.1984), clarified on reconsideration, 760 F.2d 119 (1985).

8. **Federal Preemption.** Former Section 9–104(a) excluded from Article 9 "a security interest subject to any statute of the United States, to the extent that such statute governs the rights of parties to and third parties affected by transactions in particular types of property." Some (erroneously) read the former section to suggest that Article 9 sometimes deferred to federal law even when federal law did not preempt Article 9. Subsection (c)(1) recognizes explicitly that this Article defers to federal law only when and to the extent that it must–i.e., when federal law preempts it.

9. **Governmental Debtors.** Former Section 9–104(e) excluded transfers by governmental debtors. It has been revised and replaced by the exclusions in new paragraphs (2) and (3) of subsection (c). These paragraphs reflect the view that Article 9 should apply to security interests created by a State, foreign country, or a "governmental unit" (defined in Section 9–102) of either except to the extent that another statute governs the issue in question. Under paragraph (2), this Article defers to all statutes of the forum State. (A forum cannot determine whether it should consult the choice-of-law rules in the forum's UCC unless it first determines that its UCC applies to the transaction before it.) Paragraph (3) defers to statutes of another State or a foreign country only to the extent that those statutes contain rules applicable specifically to security interests created by the governmental unit in question.

Example 2: A New Jersey state commission creates a security interest in favor of a New York bank. The validity of the security interest is litigated in New York. The relevant security agreement provides that it is governed by New York law. To the extent that a New Jersey statute contains rules peculiar to creation of security interests by governmental units generally, to creation of security interests by state commissions, or to creation of security interests by this particular state commission, then that law will govern. On the other hand, to the extent that New Jersey law provides that security interests created by governmental units, state commissions, or this state commission are governed by the law generally applicable to secured transactions (i.e., New Jersey's Article 9), then New York's Article 9 will govern.

Example 3: An airline that is an instrumentality of a foreign country creates a security interest in favor of a New

York bank. The analysis used in the previous example would apply here. That is, if the matter is litigated in New York, New York law would govern except to the extent that the foreign country enacted a statute applicable to security interests created by governmental units generally or by the airline specifically.

The fact that New York law applies does not necessarily mean that perfection is accomplished by filing in New York. Rather, it means that the court should apply New York's Article 9, including its choice-of-law provisions. Under New York's Section 9–301, perfection is governed by the law of the jurisdiction in which the debtor is located. Section 9–307 determines the debtor's location for choice-of-law purposes.

If a transaction does not bear an appropriate relation to the forum State, then that State's Article 9 will not apply, regardless of whether the transaction would be excluded by paragraph (3).

Example 4: A Belgian governmental unit grants a security interest in its equipment to a Swiss secured party. The equipment is located in Belgium. A dispute arises and, for some reason, an action is brought in a New Mexico state court. Inasmuch as the transaction bears no "appropriate relation" to New Mexico, New Mexico's UCC, including its Article 9, is inapplicable. See Section 1–105(1). New Mexico's Section 9–109(c) on excluded transactions should not come into play. Even if the parties agreed that New Mexico law would govern, the parties' agreement would not be effective because the transaction does not bear a "reasonable relation" to New Mexico. See Section 1–105(1).

Conversely, Article 9 will come into play only if the litigation arises in a UCC jurisdiction or if a foreign choice-of-law rule leads a foreign court to apply the law of a UCC jurisdiction. For example, if issues concerning a security interest granted by a foreign airline to a New York bank are litigated overseas, the court may be bound to apply the law of the debtor's jurisdiction and not New York's Article 9.

10. **Certain Statutory and Common–Law Liens; Interests in Real Property.** With few exceptions (nonconsensual agricultural liens being one), this Article applies only to consensual security interests in personal property. Following former Section 9–104(b) and (j), paragraphs (1) and (11) of subsection (d) exclude landlord's liens and leases and most other interests in or liens on real property. These exclusions generally reiterate the limitations on coverage (i.e., "by contract," "in personal property and fixtures") made explicit in subsection (a)(1). Similarly, most jurisdictions provide special liens to suppliers of many types of services and materials, either by statute or by common law. With the exception of agricultural liens, it is not necessary for this Article to provide general codification of this lien structure, which is determined in large part by local conditions and which is far removed from ordinary commercial financing. As under former Section 9–104(c), subsection (d)(2) excludes these suppliers' liens (other than agricultural liens) from this Article. However, Section 9–333 provides a rule for determining priorities between certain possessory suppliers' liens and security interests covered by this Article.

11. **Wage and Similar Claims.** As under former Section 9–104(d), subsection (d)(3) excludes assignments of claims for wages and the like from this Article. These assignments present important social issues that other law addresses. The Federal Trade Commission has ruled that, with some exceptions, the taking of an assignment of wages or other earnings is an unfair act or practice under the Federal Trade Commission Act. See 16 C.F.R. Part 444. State statutes also may regulate such assignments.

12. **Certain Sales and Assignments of Receivables; Judgments.** In general this Article covers security interests in (including sales of) accounts, chattel paper, payment intangibles, and promissory notes. Paragraphs (4), (5), (6), and (7) of subsection (d) exclude from the Article certain sales and assignments of receivables that, by their nature, do not concern commercial financing transactions. These paragraphs add to the exclusions in former Section 9–104(f) analogous sales and assignments of payment intangibles and promissory notes. For similar reasons, subsection (d)(9) retains the exclusion of assignments of judgments under former Section 9–104(h) (other than judgments taken on a right to payment that itself was collateral under this Article).

13. **Insurance.** Subsection (d)(8) narrows somewhat the broad exclusion of interests in insurance policies under former Section 9–104(g). This Article now covers assignments by or to a health-care provider of "health-care-insurance receivables" (defined in Section 9–102).

14. **Set-Off.** Subsection (d)(10) adds two exceptions to the general exclusion of set-off rights from Article 9 under former Section 9–104(i). The first takes account of new Section 9–340, which regulates the effectiveness of a set-off against a deposit account that stands as collateral. The second recognizes Section 9–404, which affords the obligor on an account, chattel paper, or general intangible the right to raise claims and defenses against an assignee (secured party).

15. **Tort Claims.** Subsection (d)(12) narrows somewhat the broad exclusion of transfers of tort claims under former Section 9–104(k). This Article now applies to assignments of "commercial tort claims" (defined in Section 9–102) as well as to security interests in tort claims that constitute proceeds of other collateral (e.g., a right to payment for negligent destruction of the debtor's inventory). Note that once a claim arising in tort has been settled and reduced to a contractual obligation to pay, the right to payment becomes a payment intangible and ceases to be a claim arising in tort.

This Article contains two special rules governing creation of a security interest in tort claims. First, a description of collateral in a security agreement as "all tort claims" is insufficient to meet the requirement for attachment. See Section 9–108(e). Second, no security interest attaches under an after-acquired property clause to a tort claim. See Section 9–204(b). In addition, this Article does not determine whom the tortfeasor must pay to discharge its obligation. Inasmuch as a tortfeasor is not an "account debtor," the rules governing waiver of defenses and discharge of an obligation by an obligor (Sections 9–403, 9–404, 9–405, and 9–406) are inapplicable to tort-claim collateral.

16. **Deposit Accounts.** Except in consumer transactions, deposit accounts may be taken as original collateral under this Article. Under former Section 9–104(*l*), deposit accounts were excluded as original collateral, leaving security interests in deposit accounts to be governed by the common law. The common law is nonuniform, often difficult to discover and comprehend, and frequently costly to implement. As a

consequence, debtors who wished to use deposit accounts as collateral sometimes were precluded from doing so as a practical matter. By excluding deposit accounts from the Article's scope as original collateral in consumer transactions, subsection (d)(13) leaves those transactions to law other than this Article. However, in both consumer and non-consumer transactions, sections 9–315 and 9–322 apply to deposit accounts as proceeds and with respect to priorities in proceeds.

This Article contains several safeguards to protect debtors against inadvertently encumbering deposit accounts and to reduce the likelihood that a secured party will realize a windfall from a debtor's deposit accounts. For example, because "deposit account" is a separate type of collateral, a security agreement covering general intangibles will not adequately describe deposit accounts. Rather, a security agreement must reasonably identify the deposit accounts that are the subject of a security interest, e.g., by using the term "deposit accounts." See Section 9–108. To perfect a security interest in a deposit account as original collateral, a secured party (other than the bank with which the deposit account is maintained) must obtain "control" of the account either by obtaining the bank's authenticated agreement or by becoming the bank's customer with respect to the deposit account. See Sections 9–312(b)(1), 9–104. Either of these steps requires the debtor's consent.

This Article also contains new rules that determine which State's law governs perfection and priority of a security interest in a deposit account (Section 9–304), priority of conflicting security interests in and set-off rights against a deposit account (Sections 9–327, 9–340), the rights of transferees of funds from an encumbered deposit account (Section 9–332), the obligations of the bank (Section 9–341), enforcement of security interests in a deposit account (Section 9–607(c)), and the duty of a secured party to terminate control of a deposit account (Section 9–208(b)).

State Bar Committee Comment

1. **Deposit accounts and security interests in consumer nonnegotiable certificates of deposit.** Texas has declined to follow the complete exclusion (other than for proceeds and priorities in proceeds) of consumer deposit accounts from coverage by the Code. Revised Chapter 9 applies to a security interest in a nonnegotiable certificate of deposit in a consumer transaction as provided in the nonuniform added language of Subsection 9.109(d)(13). This permits more consumers to access credit, generally on more beneficial terms, by utilizing assets for which no immediate use or demand is expected while not depriving them of immediately available funds for daily needs. The creation, perfection, priority and foreclosure of such an interest is governed by the provisions of Chapter 9. Revised Chapter 9 also applies to negotiable certificates of deposit, which are instruments rather than deposit accounts. The common law outside of Chapter 9 continues to govern original security interests in consumer deposit accounts other than nonnegotiable certificates of deposit. See State Bar Committee Comment to Section 9.102.

2. **Sales of accounts, chattel paper, payment intangibles and promissory notes.** Official Comment 4 acknowledges that it has been a difficult problem "distinguishing between transactions in which a receivable secures an obligation and those in which the receivable has been sold outright. In many commercial financing transactions the distinction is blurred. Although this Article occasionally distinguishes between outright sales of receivables and sales that secure an obligation, neither this Article nor the definition of 'security interest' (Section 1–201(37) delineates how a particular transaction is to be classified. That issue is left to the courts."

The blurring of the distinction may occur, for example, in a transaction where the receivable is sold outright to the purchaser but the seller may be contractually obligated to repurchase the receivable if it goes into default or may have a contractual right to receive a share of the benefits of owning the asset. If the parties to a transaction want the transfer of accounts, chattel paper, payment intangibles, or promissory notes to be treated as an outright sale, Subsection (e) provides a safe harbor such that, unless there is fraud or intentional misrepresentation, transfers of accounts, chattel paper, payment intangibles, or promissory notes will be treated as sales for all purposes if the parties express their intent for that result by identifying transfers as sales, even though the transferor may have the contractual obligation to reassume a portion of the risks or the contractual right to receive a share of the benefits from the assets being sold. This nonuniform amendment is a retention of language incorporated by the Legislature in 1997 in former Subsections 9.102(a)(2) and 9.102(d). Absent fraud or intentional misrepresentation, it is intended to furnish certainty in commercial transactions where the parties specify the intended treatment of the transfers contemplated by those transactions by providing that the characterization of the parties will be conclusive and not subject to recharacterization by the courts. Whether the parties call the transaction an outright sale or a transfer to secure an obligation, Chapter 9 still applies as explained in Official Comment 5.

One context in which it has been important in Texas for the parties to identify a transaction clearly as an outright sale rather than a secured transaction is the rather broad sweep of the usury laws. The risk that existed in the past that a sale of a receivable might be recharacterized by a court as a transfer of a security interest to secure a loan, even though the parties did not intend a loan, was addressed in this nonuniform section. A loan would be subject to usury laws while a sale would not. Another context where the nature of the transaction has been equally important is securitization of receivables, a transaction in which the receivables are sold to a buyer who pools them and issues bonds or other financial obligations backed by the receivables. The value of these bonds or other financial obligations and the rights of the investors purchasing them would be adversely affected by recharacterizing the sale of the receivables as a loan secured by a security interest in the receivables. This non-uniform provision also addresses this concern.

§ 9.110. Security Interests Arising Under Chapter 2 or 2A

A security interest arising under Section 2.401, 2.505, 2.711(c), or 2A.508(e) is subject to this chapter. However, until the debtor obtains possession of the goods:

(1) the security interest is enforceable, even if Section 9.203(b)(3) has not been satisfied;

(2) filing is not required to perfect the security interest;

(3) the rights of the secured party after default by the debtor are governed by Chapter 2 or 2A; and

(4) the security interest has priority over a conflicting security interest created by the debtor.

Amended by Acts 1999, 76th Leg., ch. 414, § 1.01, eff. July 1, 2001.

§§ 9.111 to 9.116. Deleted by Acts 1999, 76th Leg., ch. 414, § 1.01, eff. July 1, 2001

SUBCHAPTER B. EFFECTIVENESS OF SECURITY AGREEMENT; ATTACHMENT OF SECURITY INTEREST; RIGHTS OF PARTIES TO SECURITY AGREEMENT

§ 9.201. General Effectiveness of Security Agreement

(a) Except as otherwise provided by this title, a security agreement is effective according to its terms between the parties, against purchasers of the collateral, and against creditors.

(b) A transaction subject to this chapter is subject to any applicable rule of law that establishes a different rule for consumers and to:

(1) Title 4, Finance Code; and

(2) Subchapter E, Chapter 17.

(c) In case of conflict between this chapter and a rule of law, statute, or regulation described in Subsection (b), the rule of law, statute, or regulation controls. Failure to comply with a statute or regulation described in Subsection (b) has only the effect the statute or regulation specifies.

(d) This chapter does not:

(1) validate any rate, charge, agreement, or practice that violates a rule of law, statute, or regulation described in Subsection (b); or

(2) extend the application of the rule of law, statute, or regulation to a transaction not otherwise subject to it.

Amended by Acts 1999, 76th Leg., ch. 414, § 1.01, eff. July 1, 2001.

Uniform Commercial Code Comment

1. **Source.** Former Sections 9–201, 9–203(4).

2. **Effectiveness of Security Agreement.** Subsection (a) provides that a security agreement is generally effective. With certain exceptions, a security agreement is effective between the debtor and secured party and is likewise effective against third parties. Note that "security agreement" is used here (and elsewhere in this Article) as it is defined in Section 9–102: "an agreement that creates or provides for a security interest." It follows that subsection (a) does not provide that every term or provision contained in a record that contains a security agreement or that is so labeled is effective. Properly read, former Section 9–201 was to the same effect. Exceptions to the general rule of subsection (a) arise where there is an overriding provision in this Article or any other Article of the UCC. For example, Section 9–317 subordinates unperfected security interests to lien creditors and certain buyers, and several provisions in Part 3 subordinate some security interests to other security interests and interests of purchasers.

3. **Law, Statutes, and Regulations Applicable to Certain Transactions.** Subsection (b) makes clear that certain transactions, although subject to this Article, also are subject to other applicable laws relating to consumers or specified in that subsection. Subsection (c) provides that the other law is controlling in the event of a conflict, and that a violation of other law does not *ipso facto* constitute a violation of this Article. Subsection (d) provides that this Article does not validate violations under or extend the application of the other applicable laws.

§ 9.202. Title to Collateral Immaterial

Except as otherwise provided with respect to consignments or sales of accounts, chattel paper, payment intangibles, or promissory notes, the provisions of this chapter with regard to rights and obligations apply whether title to collateral is in the secured party or the debtor.

Amended by Acts 1999, 76th Leg., ch. 414, § 1.01, eff. July 1, 2001.

Uniform Commercial Code Comment

1. **Source.** Former Section 9–202.

2. **Title Immaterial.** The rights and duties of parties to a secured transaction and affected third parties are provided in this Article without reference to the location of "title" to the

collateral. For example, the characteristics of a security interest that secures the purchase price of goods are the same whether the secured party appears to have retained title or the debtor appears to have obtained title and then conveyed title or a lien to the secured party.

3. **When Title Matters.**

a. **Under This Article.** This section explicitly acknowledges two circumstances in which the effect of certain Article 9 provisions turns on ownership (title). First, in some respects sales of accounts, chattel paper, payment intangibles, and promissory notes receive special treatment. See, e.g., Sections 9–207(a), 9–210(b), 9–615(e). Buyers of receivables under former Article 9 were treated specially, as well. See, e.g., former Section 9–502(2). Second, the remedies of a consignor under a true consignment and, for the most part, the remedies of a buyer of accounts, chattel paper, payment intangibles, or promissory notes are determined by other law and not by Part 6. See Section 9–601(g).

b. **Under Other Law.** This Article does not determine which line of interpretation (e.g., title theory or lien theory, retained title or conveyed title) should be followed in cases in which the applicability of another rule of law depends upon who has title. If, for example, a revenue law imposes a tax on the "legal" owner of goods or if a corporation law makes a vote of the stockholders prerequisite to a corporation "giving" a security interest but not if it acquires property "subject" to a security interest, this Article does not attempt to define whether the secured party is a "legal" owner or whether the transaction "gives" a security interest for the purpose of such laws. Other rules of law or the agreement of the parties determines the location and source of title for those purposes.

§ 9.203. Attachment and Enforceability of Security Interest; Proceeds; Supporting Obligations; Formal Requisites

(a) A security interest attaches to collateral when it becomes enforceable against the debtor with respect to the collateral, unless an agreement expressly postpones the time of attachment.

(b) Except as otherwise provided in Subsections (c)–(j), a security interest is enforceable against the debtor and third parties with respect to the collateral only if:

(1) value has been given;

(2) the debtor has rights in the collateral or the power to transfer rights in the collateral to a secured party; and

(3) one of the following conditions is met:

(A) the debtor has authenticated a security agreement that provides a description of the collateral and, if the security interest covers timber to be cut, a description of the land concerned;

(B) the collateral is not a certificated security and is in the possession of the secured party under Section 9.313 pursuant to the debtor's security agreement;

(C) the collateral is a certificated security in registered form and the security certificate has been delivered to the secured party under Section 8.301 pursuant to the debtor's security agreement; or

(D) the collateral is deposit accounts, electronic chattel paper, investment property, letter-of-credit rights, or electronic documents, and the secured party has control under Section 7.106, 9.104, 9.105, 9.106, or 9.107 pursuant to the debtor's security agreement.

(c) Subsection (b) is subject to Section 4.210 on the security interest of a collecting bank, Section 5.118 on the security interest of a letter-of-credit issuer or nominated person, Section 9.110 on a security interest arising under Chapter 2 or 2A, and Section 9.206 on security interests in investment property.

(d) A person becomes bound as debtor by a security agreement entered into by another person if, by operation of law other than this chapter or by contract:

(1) the security agreement becomes effective to create a security interest in the person's property; or

(2) the person becomes generally obligated for the obligations of the other person, including the obligation secured under the security agreement, and acquires or succeeds to all or substantially all of the assets of the other person.

(e) If a new debtor becomes bound as debtor by a security agreement entered into by another person:

(1) the agreement satisfies Subsection (b)(3) with respect to existing or after-acquired property of the new debtor to the extent the property is described in the agreement; and

(2) another agreement is not necessary to make a security interest in the property enforceable.

(f) The attachment of

a security interest in collateral gives the secured party the rights to proceeds provided by Section 9.315 and is also attachment of a security interest in a supporting obligation for the collateral.

(g) The attachment of a security interest in a right to payment or performance secured by a security interest or other lien on personal or real property is also attachment of a security interest in the security interest, mortgage, or other lien.

(h) The attachment of a security interest in a securities account is also attachment of a security interest in the security entitlements carried in the securities account.

(i) The attachment of a security interest in a commodity account is also attachment of a security interest in the commodity contracts carried in the commodity account.

(j) If a secured party holds a security interest that applies under this chapter to minerals, including oil and gas, upon their extraction and the security interest also qualifies under applicable law as a lien on those minerals before their extraction, the security interest before and after production is a single continuous and uninterrupted lien on the property. This subsection is a statement of the law of this state as it existed before the effective date of this subsection and applies with respect to minerals, including oil and gas, regardless of when the minerals were extracted.

Amended by Acts 1999, 76th Leg., ch. 414, § 1.01, eff. July 1, 2001; Acts 2005, 79th Leg., ch. 122, § 20, eff. Sept. 1, 2005.

Uniform Commercial Code Comment

1. **Source.** Former Sections 9–203, 9–115(2), (6).

2. **Creation, Attachment, and Enforceability.** Subsection (a) states the general rule that a security interest attaches to collateral only when it becomes enforceable against the debtor. Subsection (b) specifies the circumstances under which a security interest becomes enforceable. Subsection (b) states three basic prerequisites to the existence of a security interest: value (paragraph (1)), rights or power to transfer rights in collateral (paragraph (2)), and agreement plus satisfaction of an evidentiary requirement (paragraph (3)). When all of these elements exist, a security interest becomes enforceable between the parties and attaches under subsection (a). Subsection (c) identifies certain exceptions to the general rule of subsection (b).

3. **Security Agreement; Authentication.** Under subsection (b)(3), enforceability requires the debtor's security agreement and compliance with an evidentiary requirement in the nature of a Statute of Frauds. Paragraph (3)(A) represents the most basic of the evidentiary alternatives, under which the debtor must authenticate a security agreement that provides a description of the collateral. Under Section 9–102, a "security agreement" is "an agreement that creates or provides for a security interest." Neither that definition nor the requirement of paragraph (3)(A) rejects the deeply rooted doctrine that a bill of sale, although absolute in form, may be shown in fact to have been given as security. Under this Article, as under prior law, a debtor may show by parol evidence that a transfer purporting to be absolute was in fact for security. Similarly, a self-styled "lease" may serve as a security agreement if the agreement creates a security interest. See Section 1–201(37) (distinguishing security interest from lease).

4. **Possession, Delivery, or Control Pursuant to Security Agreement.** The other alternatives in subsection (b)(3) dispense with the requirement of an authenticated security agreement and provide alternative evidentiary tests. Under paragraph (3)(B), the secured party's possession substitutes for the debtor's authentication under paragraph (3)(A) if the secured party's possession is "pursuant to the debtor's security agreement." That phrase refers to the debtor's agreement to the secured party's possession for the purpose of creating a security interest. The phrase should not be confused with the phrase "debtor has authenticated a security agreement," used in paragraph (3)(A), which contemplates the debtor's authentication of a record. In the unlikely event that possession is obtained without the debtor's agreement, possession would not suffice as a substitute for an authenticated security agreement. However, once the security interest has become enforceable and has attached, it is not impaired by the fact that the secured party's possession is maintained without the agreement of a subsequent debtor (e.g., a transferee). Possession as contemplated by Section 9–313 is possession for purposes of subsection (b)(3)(B), even though it may not constitute possession "pursuant to the debtor's agreement" and consequently might not serve as a substitute for an authenticated security agreement under subsection (b)(3)(A). Subsection (b)(3)(C) provides that delivery of a certificated security to the secured party under Section 8–301 pursuant to the debtor's security agreement is sufficient as a substitute for an authenticated security agreement. Similarly, under subsection (b)(3)(D), control of investment property, a deposit account, electronic chattel paper, a letter-of-credit right, or electronic documents satisfies the evidentiary test if control is pursuant to the debtor's security agreement.

5. **Collateral Covered by Other Statute or Treaty.** One evidentiary purpose of the formal requisites stated in subsection (b) is to minimize the possibility of future disputes as to the terms of a security agreement (e.g., as to the property that stands as collateral for the obligation secured). One should distinguish the evidentiary functions of the formal requisites of attachment and enforceability (such as the requirement that a security agreement contain a description of the collateral) from the more limited goals of "notice filing" for financing statements under Part 5, explained in Section 9–502, Comment 2. When perfection is achieved by compliance with the requirements of a statute or treaty described in Section 9–311(a), such as a federal recording act or a certificate-of-title statute, the manner of describing the collateral in a registry imposed by the statute or treaty may or may not be adequate for purposes of this section and Section 9–108. However, the description contained in the security agreement, not the description in a public registry or on a certificate of title, controls for purposes of this section.

6. **Debtor's Rights; Debtor's Power to Transfer Rights.** Subsection (b)(2) conditions attachment on the debtor's having "rights in the collateral or the power to transfer rights in the collateral to a secured party." A debtor's limited rights in collateral, short of full ownership, are sufficient for a security interest to attach. However, in accordance with basic personal property conveyancing principles, the baseline rule is that a security interest attaches only to

whatever rights a debtor may have, broad or limited as those rights may be.

Certain exceptions to the baseline rule enable a debtor to transfer, and a security interest to attach to, greater rights than the debtor has. See Part 3, Subpart 3 (priority rules). The phrase, "or the power to transfer rights in the collateral to a secured party," accommodates those exceptions. In some cases, a debtor may have power to transfer another person's rights only to a class of transferees that excludes secured parties. See, e.g., Section 2–403(2) (giving certain merchants power to transfer an entruster's rights to a buyer in ordinary course of business). Under those circumstances, the debtor would not have the power to create a security interest in the other person's rights, and the condition in subsection (b)(2) would not be satisfied.

7. **New Debtors.** Subsection (e) makes clear that the enforceability requirements of subsection (b)(3) are met when a new debtor becomes bound under an original debtor's security agreement. If a new debtor becomes bound as debtor by a security agreement entered into by another person, the security agreement satisfies the requirement of subsection (b)(3) as to the existing and after-acquired property of the new debtor to the extent the property is described in the agreement.

Subsection (d) explains when a new debtor becomes bound. Persons who become bound under paragraph (2) are limited to those who both become primarily liable for the original debtor's obligations and succeed to (or acquire) its assets. Thus, the paragraph excludes sureties and other secondary obligors as well as persons who become obligated through veil piercing and other non-successorship doctrines. In many cases, paragraph (2) will exclude successors to the assets and liabilities of a division of a debtor. See also Section 9–508, Comment 3.

8. **Supporting Obligations.** Under subsection (f), a security interest in a "supporting obligation" (defined in Section 9–102) automatically follows from a security interest in the underlying, supported collateral. This result was implicit under former Article 9. Implicit in subsection (f) is the principle that the secured party's interest in a supporting obligation extends to the supporting obligation only to the extent that it supports the collateral in which the secured party has a security interest. Complex issues may arise, however, if a supporting obligation supports many separate obligations of a particular account debtor and if the supported obligations are separately assigned as security to several secured parties. The problems may be exacerbated if a supporting obligation is limited to an aggregate amount that is less than the aggregate amount of the obligations it supports. This Article does not contain provisions dealing with competing claims to a limited supporting obligation. As under former Article 9, the law of suretyship and the agreements of the parties will control.

9. **Collateral Follows Right to Payment or Performance.** Subsection (g) codifies the common-law rule that a transfer of an obligation secured by a security interest or other lien on personal or real property also transfers the security interest or lien. See Restatement (3d), Property (Mortgages) § 5.4(a) (1997). See also Section 9–308(e) (analogous rule for perfection).

10. **Investment Property.** Subsections (h) and (i) make clear that attachment of a security interest in a securities account or commodity account is also attachment in security entitlements or commodity contracts carried in the accounts.

State Bar Committee Comment

The nonuniform amendment added by Subsection (j) is a retention of the rule incorporated in former Subsection 9.203(c) when the Legislature amended the statute in 1991. That amendment merely codified a rule that was already the established law in Texas. Although the language in the retained provision has been stylistically improved, there is no intent to change the law as it has historically existed. This provision is explained and applied in *In re Hawn*, 149 B.R. 450 (S.D.Tex.1993); aff'd in part, *Hawn v. American Nat. Bank*, 1996 WL 142521 (S.D.Tex.1996) (not reported in F.Supp.), where the secured party had a deed of trust lien on the oil and gas while in the ground and a UCC security interest in the oil and gas when produced. Both liens were created in the same writing which was duly filed so as to perfect both the real property mortgage and the UCC security interest, thus resulting in a "single continuous security interest that attaches while the minerals are in the ground and continues after extraction." That continuous security interest primed an IRS lien perfected later, both as to the minerals in the ground and after severance.

Sections 31 and 32 of Acts 2005, 79th Leg., ch. 122 provide:

"Sec. 31. This Act applies to a document of title that is issued or a bailment that arises on or after the effective date of this Act. This Act does not apply to a document of title that is issued or a bailment that arises before the effective date of this Act even if the document of title or bailment would be subject to this Act if the document of title had been issued or bailment had arisen after the effective date of this Act. This Act does not apply to a right of action that has accrued before the effective date of this Act.

"Sec. 32. A document of title issued or a bailment that arises before the effective date of this Act and the rights, obligations, and interests flowing from that document or bailment are governed by any statute or other rule amended or repealed by this Act as if amendment or repeal had not occurred and may be terminated, completed, consummated, or enforced under that statute or other rule."

§ 9.204. After-Acquired Property; Future Advances

(a) Except as provided in Subsection (b), a security agreement may create or provide for a security interest in after-acquired collateral.

(b) A security interest does not attach under a term constituting an after-acquired property clause to:

(1) consumer goods, other than an accession when given as additional security, unless the debtor acquires rights in them within 10 days after the secured party gives value; or

(2) a commercial tort claim.

(c) A security agreement may provide that collateral secures, or that accounts, chattel paper, payment intangibles, or promissory notes are sold in connection with, future advances or other value, whether or not the advances or value are given pursuant to commitment.

Amended by Acts 1999, 76th Leg., ch. 414, § 1.01, eff. July 1, 2001.

Uniform Commercial Code Comment

1. **Source.** Former Section 9–204.

2. **After-Acquired Property; Continuing General Lien.** Subsection (a) makes clear that a security interest arising by virtue of an after-acquired property clause is no less valid than a security interest in collateral in which the debtor has rights at the time value is given. A security interest in after-acquired property is not merely an "equitable" interest; no further action by the secured party–such as a supplemental agreement covering the new collateral–is required. This section adopts the principle of a "continuing general lien" or "floating lien." It validates a security interest in the debtor's existing and (upon acquisition) future assets, even though the debtor has liberty to use or dispose of collateral without being required to account for proceeds or substitute new collateral. See Section 9–205. Subsection (a), together with subsection (c), also validates "cross-collateral" clauses under which collateral acquired at any time secures advances whenever made.

3. **After-Acquired Consumer Goods.** Subsection (b)(1) makes ineffective an after-acquired property clause covering consumer goods (defined in Section 9–109), except as accessions (see Section 9–335), acquired more than 10 days after the secured party gives value. Subsection (b)(1) is unchanged in substance from the corresponding provision in former Section 9–204(2).

4. **Commercial Tort Claims.** Subsection (b)(2) provides that an after-acquired property clause in a security agreement does not reach future commercial tort claims. In order for a security interest in a tort claim to attach, the claim must be in existence when the security agreement is authenticated. In addition, the security agreement must describe the tort claim with greater specificity than simply "all tort claims." See Section 9–108(e).

5. **Future Advances; Obligations Secured.** Under subsection (c) collateral may secure future as well as past or present advances if the security agreement so provides. This is in line with the policy of this Article toward security interests in after-acquired property under subsection (a). Indeed, the parties are free to agree that a security interest secures any obligation whatsoever. Determining the obligations secured by collateral is solely a matter of construing the parties' agreement under applicable law. This Article rejects the holdings of cases decided under former Article 9 that applied other tests, such as whether a future advance or other subsequently incurred obligation was of the same or a similar type or class as earlier advances and obligations secured by the collateral.

6. **Sales of Receivables.** Subsections (a) and (c) expressly validate after-acquired property and future advance clauses not only when the transaction is for security purposes but also when the transaction is the sale of accounts, chattel paper, payment intangibles, or promissory notes . . This result was implicit under former Article 9.

7. **Financing Statements.** The effect of after-acquired property and future advance clauses as components of a security agreement should not be confused with the requirements applicable to financing statements under this Article's system of perfection by notice filing. The references to after-acquired property clauses and future advance clauses in this section are limited to security agreements. There is no need to refer to after-acquired property or future advances or other obligations secured in a financing statement. See Section 9–502, Comment 2.

State Bar Committee Comment

Subsection (b) states that if the collateral is consumer goods other than accessions, the security interest will not attach under an after-acquired property clause unless the debtor acquires rights in the collateral within ten days after the secured party gives value. Even if the debtor timely acquires rights in the consumer goods in accordance with subsection (b), the act of taking a security interest in consumer goods may violate other statutes or regulations. See, e.g., 12 C.F.R. § 227.13 (making it an unfair act or practice under the Federal Trade Commission Act for a bank to secure repayment of a consumer credit obligation with a non-possessory, non-purchase money, security interest in household goods); 16 C.F.R. § 444.2 (making it an unfair act or practice under the Federal Trade Commission Act for a lender or retail installment seller to secure repayment of an extension of credit to a consumer with a non-possessory, non-purchase money, security interest in household goods).

§ 9.205. Use or Disposition of Collateral Permissible

(a) A security interest is not invalid or fraudulent against creditors solely because:

(1) the debtor has the right or ability to:

(A) use, commingle, or dispose of all or part of the collateral, including returned or repossessed goods;

(B) collect, compromise, enforce, or otherwise deal with collateral;

(C) accept the return of collateral or make repossessions; or

(D) use, commingle, or dispose of proceeds; or

(2) the secured party fails to require the debtor to account for proceeds or replace collateral.

(b) This section does not relax the requirements of possession if attachment, perfection, or enforcement of a security interest depends upon possession of the collateral by the secured party.

Amended by Acts 1999, 76th Leg., ch. 414, § 1.01, eff. July 1, 2001.

Uniform Commercial Code Comment

1. **Source.** Former Section 9–205.

2. **Validity of Unrestricted "Floating Lien."** This Article expressly validates the "floating lien" on shifting collateral. See Sections 9–201, 9–204 and Comment 2. This section provides that a security interest is not invalid or fraudulent by reason of the debtor's liberty to dispose of the collateral without being required to account to the secured party for proceeds or substitute new collateral. As did former Section 9–205, this section repeals the rule of *Benedict v. Ratner*, 268 U.S. 353 (1925), and other cases which held such arrangements void as a matter of law because the debtor was given unfettered dominion or control over collateral. The *Benedict* rule did not effectively discourage or eliminate security transactions in inventory and receivables. Instead, it forced financing arrangements to be self-liquidating. Although this section repeals *Benedict*, the filing and other perfection requirements (see Part 3, Subpart 2, and Part 5) provide for public notice that overcomes any potential misleading effects of a debtor's use and control of collateral. Moreover, nothing in this section prevents the debtor and secured party from agreeing to procedures by which the secured party polices or monitors collateral or to restrictions on the debtor's dominion. However, this Article leaves these matters to agreement based on business considerations, not on legal requirements.

3. **Possessory Security Interests.** Subsection (b) makes clear that this section does not relax the requirements for perfection by possession under Section 9–313. If a secured party allows the debtor access to and control over collateral its security interest may be or become unperfected.

4. **Permissible Freedom for Debtor to Enforce Collateral.** Former Section 9–205 referred to a debtor's "liberty. . to collect or compromise accounts or chattel paper." This section recognizes the broader rights of a debtor to "enforce," as well as to "collect" and "compromise" collateral. This section's reference to collecting, compromising, and enforcing "collateral" instead of "accounts or chattel paper" contemplates the many other types of collateral that a debtor may wish to "collect, compromise, or enforce": e.g., deposit accounts, documents, general intangibles, instruments, investment property, and letter-of-credit rights.

§ 9.206. Security Interest Arising in Purchase or Delivery of Financial Asset

(a) A security interest in favor of a securities intermediary attaches to a person's security entitlement if:

(1) the person buys a financial asset through the securities intermediary in a transaction in which the person is obligated to pay the purchase price to the securities intermediary at the time of the purchase; and

(2) the securities intermediary credits the financial asset to the buyer's securities account before the buyer pays the securities intermediary.

(b) The security interest described in Subsection (a) secures the person's obligation to pay for the financial asset.

(c) A security interest in favor of a person that delivers a certificated security or other financial asset represented by a writing attaches to the security or other financial asset if:

(1) the security or other financial asset:

(A) in the ordinary course of business is transferred by delivery with any necessary indorsement or assignment; and

(B) is delivered under an agreement between persons in the business of dealing with such securities or financial assets; and

(2) the agreement calls for delivery against payment.

(d) The security interest described in Subsection (c) secures the obligation to make payment for the delivery.

Amended by Acts 1999, 76th Leg., ch. 414, § 1.01, eff. July 1, 2001.

Uniform Commercial Code Comment

1. **Source.** Former 9–116.

2. **Codification of "Broker's Lien."** Depending upon a securities intermediary's arrangements with its entitlement holders, the securities intermediary may treat the entitlement holder as entitled to financial assets before the entitlement holder has actually made payment for them. For example, many brokers permit retail customers to pay for financial assets by check. The broker may not receive final payment of the check until several days after the broker has credited the customer's securities account for the financial assets. Thus, the customer will have acquired a security entitlement prior to payment. Subsection (a) provides that, in such circumstances, the securities intermediary has a security interest in the entitlement holder's security entitlement. Under subsection (b) the security interest secures the customer's obligation to pay for the financial asset in question. Subsections (a) and (b) codify and adapt to the indirect holding system the so-called "broker's lien," which has long been recognized. See Restatement, Security § 12.

3. **Financial Assets Delivered Against Payment.** Subsection (c) creates a security interest in favor of persons who deliver certificated securities or other financial assets in physical form, such as money market instruments, if the agreed payment is not received. In some arrangements for settlement of transactions in physical financial assets, the seller's securities custodian will deliver physical certificates to the buyer's securities custodian and receive a time-stamped delivery receipt. The buyer's securities custodian

will examine the certificate to ensure that it is in good order, and that the delivery matches a trade in which the buyer has instructed the seller to deliver to that custodian. If all is in order, the receiving custodian will settle with the delivering custodian through whatever funds settlement system has been agreed upon or is used by custom and usage in that market. The understanding of the trade, however, is that the delivery is conditioned upon payment, so that if payment is not made for any reason, the security will be returned to the deliverer. Subsection (c) clarifies the rights of persons making deliveries in such circumstances. It provides the person making delivery with a security interest in the securities or other financial assets; under subsection (d), the security interest secures the seller's right to receive payment for the delivery. Section 8–301 specifies when delivery of a certificated security occurs; that section should be applied as well to other financial assets as well for purposes of this section.

4. **Automatic Attachment and Perfection.** Subsections (a) and (c) refer to attachment of a security interest. Attachment under this section has the same incidents (enforceability, right to proceeds, etc.) as attachment under Section 9–203. This section overrides the general attachment rules in Section 9–203. See Section 9–203(c). A securities intermediary's security interest under subsection (a) is perfected by control without further action. See Section 8–106 (control); 9–314 (perfection). Security interests arising under subsection (c) are automatically perfected. See Section 9–309(9).

§ 9.207. Rights and Duties of Secured Party Having Possession or Control Of Collateral

(a) Except as otherwise provided in Subsection (d), a secured party shall use reasonable care in the custody and preservation of collateral in the secured party's possession. In the case of chattel paper or an instrument, reasonable care includes taking necessary steps to preserve rights against prior parties unless otherwise agreed.

(b) Except as otherwise provided in Subsection (d), if a secured party has possession of collateral:

(1) reasonable expenses, including the cost of insurance and payment of taxes or other charges, incurred in the custody, preservation, use, or operation of the collateral are chargeable to the debtor and are secured by the collateral;

(2) the risk of accidental loss or damage is on the debtor to the extent of any deficiency in any effective insurance coverage;

(3) the secured party shall keep the collateral identifiable, but fungible collateral may be commingled; and

(4) the secured party may use or operate the collateral:

(A) for the purpose of preserving the collateral or its value;

(B) as permitted by an order of a court having competent jurisdiction; or

(C) except in the case of consumer goods, in the manner and to the extent agreed by the debtor.

(c) Except as otherwise provided in Subsection (d), a secured party having possession of collateral or control of collateral under Section 7.106, 9.104, 9.105, 9.106, or 9.107:

(1) may hold as additional security any proceeds, except money or funds, received from the collateral;

(2) shall apply money or funds received from the collateral to reduce the secured obligation, unless remitted to the debtor; and

(3) may create a security interest in the collateral.

(d) If the secured party is a buyer of accounts, chattel paper, payment intangibles, or promissory notes or a consignor:

(1) Subsection (a) does not apply unless the secured party is entitled under an agreement:

(A) to charge back uncollected collateral; or

(B) otherwise to full or limited recourse against the debtor or a secondary obligor based on the nonpayment or other default of an account debtor or other obligor on the collateral; and

(2) Subsections (b) and (c) do not apply.

Amended by Acts 1999, 76th Leg., ch. 414, § 1.01, eff. July 1, 2001; Acts 2005, 79th Leg., ch. 122, § 21, eff. Sept. 1, 2005.

Uniform Commercial Code Comment

1. **Source.** Former Section 9–207.

2. **Duty of Care for Collateral in Secured Party's Possession.** Like former section 9–207, subsection (a) imposes a duty of care, similar to that imposed on a pledgee at common law, on a secured party in possession of collateral. See Restatement, Security §§ 17, 18. In many cases a secured party in possession of collateral may satisfy this duty by notifying the debtor of action that should be taken and allowing the debtor to take the action itself. If the secured party itself takes action, its reasonable expenses may be added to the secured obligation. The revised definitions of "collateral," "debtor," and "secured party" in Section 9–102 make this section applicable to collateral subject to an agricultural lien if the collateral is in the lienholder's possession. Under Section 1–102 the duty to exercise reasonable care may not be disclaimed by agreement, although under that section the parties remain free to determine by agreement standards that are not manifestly unreasonable as to what constitutes reasonable care. Unless otherwise agreed, for a secured party in possession of chattel paper or an instru-

ment, reasonable care includes the preservation of rights against prior parties. The secured party's right to have instruments or documents indorsed or transferred to it or its order is dealt with in the relevant sections of Articles 3, 7, and 8. See Sections 3–201, 7–506, 8–304(d).

3. **Specific Rules When Secured Party in Possession or Control of Collateral.** Subsections (b) and (c) provide rules following common-law precedents which apply unless the parties otherwise agree. The rules in subsection (b) apply to typical issues that may arise while a secured party is in possession of collateral, including expenses, insurance, and taxes, risk of loss or damage, identifiable and fungible collateral, and use or operation of collateral. Subsection (c) contains rules that apply in certain circumstances that may arise when a secured party is in either possession or control of collateral. These circumstances include the secured party's receiving proceeds from the collateral and the secured party's creation of a security interest in the collateral.

4. **Applicability Following Default.** This section applies when the secured party has possession of collateral either before or after default. See Sections 9–601(b), 9–609. Subsection (b)(4)(C) limits agreements concerning the use or operation of collateral to collateral other than consumer goods. Under Section 9–602(1), a debtor cannot waive or vary that limitation.

5. **"Repledges" and Right of Redemption.** Subsection (c)(3) eliminates the qualification in former Section 9–207 to the effect that the terms of a "repledge" may not "impair" a debtor's "right to redeem" collateral. The change is primarily for clarification. There is no basis on which to draw from subsection (c)(3) any inference concerning the debtor's right to redeem the collateral. The debtor enjoys that right under Section 9–623; this section need not address it. For example, if the collateral is a negotiable note that the secured party (SP–1) repledges to SP–2, nothing in this section suggests that the debtor (D) does not retain the right to redeem the note upon payment to SP–1 of all obligations secured by the note. But, as explained below, the debtor's unimpaired right to redeem as against the debtor's original secured party nevertheless may not be enforceable as against the new secured party.

In resolving questions that arise from the creation of a security interest by SP–1, one must take care to distinguish D's rights against SP–1 from D's rights against SP–2. Once D discharges the secured obligation, D becomes entitled to the note; SP–1 has no legal basis upon which to withhold it. If, as a practical matter, SP–1 is unable to return the note because SP–2 holds it as collateral for SP–1's unpaid debt, then SP–1 is liable to D under the law of conversion.

Whether SP–2 would be liable to D depends on the relative priority of SP–2's security interest and D's interest. By permitting SP–1 to create a security interest in the collateral (repledge), subsection (c)(3) provides a statutory power for SP–1 to give SP–2 a security interest (subject, of course, to any agreement by SP–1 not to give a security interest). In the vast majority of cases where repledge rights are significant, the security interest of the second secured party, SP–2 in the example, will be senior to the debtor's interest. By virtue of the debtor's consent or applicable legal rules, SP–2 typically would cut off D's rights in investment property or be immune from D's claims. See Sections 9–331, 3–306 (holder in due course), 8–303 (protected purchaser), 8–502 (acquisition of a security entitlement), 8–503(e) (action by entitlement holder). Moreover, the expectations and business practices in some markets, such as the securities markets, are such that D's consent to SP–2's taking free of D's rights inheres in D's creation of SP–1's security interest which gives rise to SP–1's power under this section. In these situations, D would have no right to recover the collateral or recover damages from SP–2. Nevertheless, D would have a damage claim against SP–1 if SP–1 had given a security interest to SP–2 in breach of its agreement with D. Moreover, if SP–2's security interest secures an amount that is less than the amount secured by SP–1's security interest (granted by D), then D's exercise of its right to redeem would provide value sufficient to discharge SP–1's obligations to SP–2.

For the most part this section does not change the law under former Section 9–207, although eliminating the reference to the debtor's right of redemption may alter the secured party's right to repledge in one respect. Former Section 9–207 could have been read to limit the secured party's statutory right to repledge collateral to repledge transactions in which the collateral did not secure a greater obligation than that of the original debtor. Inasmuch as this is a matter normally dealt with by agreement between the debtor and secured party, any change would appear to have little practical effect.

6. **"Repledges" of Investment Property.** The following example will aid the discussion of "repledges" of investment property.

Example. Debtor grants Alpha Bank a security interest in a security entitlement that includes 1000 shares of XYZ Co. stock that Debtor holds through an account with Able & Co. Alpha does not have an account with Able. Alpha uses Beta Bank as its securities custodian. Debtor instructs Able to transfer the shares to Beta, for the account of Alpha, and Able does so. Beta then credits Alpha's account. Alpha has control of the security entitlement for the 1000 shares under Section 8–106(d). (These are the facts of Example 2, Section 8–106, Comment 4.) Although, as between Debtor and Alpha, Debtor may have become the beneficial owner of the new securities entitlement with Beta, Beta has agreed to act on Alpha's entitlement orders because, as between Beta and Alpha, Alpha has become the entitlement holder.

Next, Alpha grants Gamma Bank a security interest in the security entitlement with Beta that includes the 1000 shares of XYZ Co. stock. In order to afford Gamma control of the entitlement, Alpha instructs Beta to transfer the stock to Gamma's custodian, Delta Bank, which credits Gamma's account for 1000 shares. At this point Gamma holds its securities entitlement for its benefit as well as that of its debtor, Alpha. Alpha's derivative rights also are for the benefit of Debtor.

In many, probably most, situations and at any particular point in time, it will be impossible for Debtor or Alpha to "trace" Alpha's "repledge" to any particular securities entitlement or financial asset of Gamma or anyone else. Debtor would retain, of course, a right to redeem the collateral from Alpha upon satisfaction of the secured obligation. However, in the absence of a traceable interest, Debtor would retain only a personal claim against Alpha in the event Alpha failed to restore the security entitlement to Debtor. Moreover, even in the unlikely event that Debtor could trace a property interest, in the context of the financial markets, normally the operation of this section, Debtor's explicit agreement to permit Alpha to create a senior security interest, or legal rules permitting Gamma to cut off Debtor's rights or become immune from Debtor's claims would effectively subordinate Debtor's interest to the holder of a security interest created by Alpha. And, under the shelter principle, all subsequent transferees would obtain interests to which Debtor's interest also would be subordinate.

7. **Buyers of Chattel Paper and Other Receivables; Consignors.** This section has been revised to reflect the fact that a seller of accounts, chattel paper, payment intangibles, or promissory notes retains no interest in the collateral and so is not disadvantaged by the secured party's noncompliance with the requirements of this section. Accordingly, subsection (d) provides that subsection (a) applies only to security interests that secure an obligation and to sales of receivables in which the buyer has recourse against the debtor. (Of course, a buyer of accounts or payment intangibles could not have "possession" of original collateral, but might have possession of proceeds, such as promissory notes or checks.) The meaning of "recourse" in this respect is limited to recourse arising out of the account debtor's failure to pay or other default.

Subsection (d) makes subsections (b) and (c) inapplicable to buyers of accounts, chattel paper, payment intangibles, or promissory notes and consignors. Of course, there is no reason to believe that a buyer of receivables or a consignor could not, for example, create a security interest or otherwise transfer an interest in the collateral, regardless of who has possession of the collateral. However, this section leaves the rights of those owners to law other than Article 9.

Sections 31 and 32 of Acts 2005, 79th Leg., ch. 122 provide:

"Sec. 31. This Act applies to a document of title that is issued or a bailment that arises on or after the effective date of this Act. This Act does not apply to a document of title that is issued or a bailment that arises before the effective date of this Act even if the document of title or bailment would be subject to this Act if the document of title had been issued or bailment had arisen after the effective date of this Act. This Act does not apply to a right of action that has accrued before the effective date of this Act.

"Sec. 32. A document of title issued or a bailment that arises before the effective date of this Act and the rights, obligations, and interests flowing from that document or bailment are governed by any statute or other rule amended or repealed by this Act as if amendment or repeal had not occurred and may be terminated, completed, consummated, or enforced under that statute or other rule."

§ 9.208. Additional Duties of Secured Party Having Control of Collateral

(a) This section applies to cases in which there is no outstanding secured obligation and the secured party is not committed to make advances, incur obligations, or otherwise give value.

(b) Within 10 days after receiving an authenticated demand by the debtor:

(1) a secured party having control of a deposit account under Section 9.104(a)(2) shall send to the bank with which the deposit account is maintained an authenticated statement that releases the bank from any further obligation to comply with instructions originated by the secured party;

(2) a secured party having control of a deposit account under Section 9.104(a)(3) shall:

(A) pay the debtor the balance on deposit in the deposit account; or

(B) transfer the balance on deposit into a deposit account in the debtor's name;

(3) a secured party, other than a buyer, having control of electronic chattel paper under Section 9.105 shall:

(A) communicate the authoritative copy of the electronic chattel paper to the debtor or its designated custodian;

(B) if the debtor designates a custodian that is the designated custodian with which the authoritative copy of the electronic chattel paper is maintained for the secured party, communicate to the custodian an authenticated record releasing the designated custodian from any further obligation to comply with instructions originated by the secured party and instructing the custodian to comply with instructions originated by the debtor; and

(C) take appropriate action to enable the debtor or its designated custodian to make copies of or revisions to the authoritative copy that add or change an identified assignee of the authoritative copy without the consent of the secured party;

(4) a secured party having control of investment property under Section 8.106(d)(2) or 9.106(b) shall send to the securities intermediary or commodity intermediary with which the security entitlement or commodity contract is maintained an authenticated record that releases the securities intermediary or commodity intermediary from any further obligation to comply with entitlement orders or directions originated by the secured party;

(5) a secured party having control of a letter-of-credit right under Section 9.107 shall send to each person having an unfulfilled obligation to pay or deliver proceeds of the letter of credit to the secured party an authenticated release from any further obligation to pay or deliver proceeds of the letter of credit to the secured party; and

(6) a secured party having control of an electronic document shall:

(A) give control of the electronic document to the debtor or its designated custodian;

(B) if the debtor designates a custodian that is the designated custodian with which the authoritative copy of the electronic document is maintained for the secured party, communicate to the custodian an authenticated record releasing the designated custodian from any further obligation to comply with instructions originated by the secured party and instructing the custodian to comply with instructions originated by the debtor; and

(C) take appropriate action to enable the debtor or its designated custodian to make copies of or revisions to the authoritative copy which add or change an identified assignee of the authoritative copy without the consent of the secured party.

Amended by Acts 1999, 76th Leg., ch. 414, § 1.01, eff. July 1, 2001; Acts 2005, 79th Leg., ch. 122, § 22, eff. Sept. 1, 2005.

Uniform Commercial Code Comment

1. **Source.** New.

2. **Scope and Purpose.** This section imposes duties on a secured party who has control of a deposit account, electronic chattel paper, investment property, a letter-of-credit right, or electronic documents of title. The duty to terminate the secured party's control is analogous to the duty to file a termination statement, imposed by Section 9–513. Under subsection (a), it applies only when there is no outstanding secured obligation and the secured party is not committed to give value. The requirements of this section can be varied by agreement under Section 1–102(3). For example, a debtor could by contract agree that the secured party may comply with subsection (b) by releasing control more than 10 days after demand. Also, duties under this section should not be read to conflict with the terms of the collateral itself. For example, if the collateral is a time deposit account, subsection (b)(2) should not require a secured party with control to make an early withdrawal of the funds (assuming that were possible) in order to pay them over to the debtor or put them in an account in the debtor's name.

3. **Remedy for Failure to Relinquish Control.** If a secured party fails to comply with the requirements of subsection (b), the debtor has the remedy set forth in Section 9–625(e). This remedy is identical to that applicable to failure to provide or file a termination statement under Section 9–513.

4. **Duty to Relinquish Possession.** Although Section 9–207 addresses directly the duties of a secured party in possession of collateral, that section does not require the secured party to relinquish possession when the secured party ceases to hold a security interest. Under common law, absent agreement to the contrary, the failure to relinquish possession of collateral upon satisfaction of the secured obligation would constitute a conversion. Inasmuch as problems apparently have not surfaced in the absence of statutory duties under former Article 9 and the common-law duty appears to have been sufficient, this Article does not impose a statutory duty to relinquish possession.

Sections 31 and 32 of Acts 2005, 79th Leg., ch. 122 provide:

"Sec. 31. This Act applies to a document of title that is issued or a bailment that arises on or after the effective date of this Act. This Act does not apply to a document of title that is issued or a bailment that arises before the effective date of this Act even if the document of title or bailment would be subject to this Act if the document of title had been issued or bailment had arisen after the effective date of this Act. This Act does not apply to a right of action that has accrued before the effective date of this Act.

"Sec. 32. A document of title issued or a bailment that arises before the effective date of this Act and the rights, obligations, and interests flowing from that document or bailment are governed by any statute or other rule amended or repealed by this Act as if amendment or repeal had not occurred and may be terminated, completed, consummated, or enforced under that statute or other rule."

§ 9.209. Duties of Secured Party if Account Debtor Has Been Notified of Assignment

(a) Except as otherwise provided in Subsection (c), this section applies if:

(1) there is no outstanding secured obligation; and

(2) the secured party is not committed to make advances, incur obligations, or otherwise give value.

(b) Within 10 days after receiving an authenticated demand by the debtor, a secured party shall send to an account debtor that has received notification of an assignment to the secured party as assignee under Section 9.406(a) an authenticated record that releases the account debtor from any further obligation to the secured party.

(c) This section does not apply to an assignment constituting the sale of an account, chattel paper, or payment intangible.

Added by Acts 1999, 76th Leg., ch. 414, § 1.01, eff. July 1, 2001.

Uniform Commercial Code Comment

1. **Source.** New.

2. **Scope and Purpose.** Like Sections 9–208 and 9–513, which require a secured party to relinquish control of collateral and to file or provide a termination statement for a financing statement, this section requires a secured party to free up collateral when there no longer is any outstanding secured obligation or any commitment to give value in the future. This section addresses the case in which account debtors have been notified to pay a secured party to whom the receivables have been assigned. It requires the secured party (assignee) to inform the account debtors that they no longer are obligated to make payment to the secured party. See subsection (b). It does not apply to account debtors whose obligations on an account, chattel paper, or payment intangible have been sold. See subsection (c).

§ 9.210. Request for Accounting; Request Regarding List of Collateral or Statement of Account

(a) In this section:

(1) "Request" means a record of a type described in Subdivision (2), (3), or (4).

(2) "Request for an accounting" means a record authenticated by a debtor requesting that the recipient provide an accounting of the unpaid obligations secured by collateral and reasonably identifying the transaction or relationship that is the subject of the request.

(3) "Request regarding a list of collateral" means a record authenticated by a debtor requesting that the recipient approve or correct a list of what the debtor believes to be the collateral securing an obligation and reasonably identifying the transaction or relationship that is the subject of the request.

(4) "Request regarding a statement of account" means a record authenticated by a debtor requesting that the recipient approve or correct a statement indicating what the debtor believes to be the aggregate amount of unpaid obligations secured by collateral as of a specified date and reasonably identifying the transaction or relationship that is the subject of the request.

(b) Subject to Subsections (c), (d), (e), and (f), a secured party, other than a buyer of accounts, chattel paper, payment intangibles, or promissory notes or a consignor, shall comply with a request within 14 days after receipt:

(1) in the case of a request for an accounting, by authenticating and sending to the debtor an accounting; and

(2) in the case of a request regarding a list of collateral or a request regarding a statement of account, by authenticating and sending to the debtor an approval or correction.

(c) A secured party that claims a security interest in all of a particular type of collateral owned by the debtor may comply with a request regarding a list of collateral by sending to the debtor an authenticated record including a statement to that effect within 14 days after receipt.

(d) A person that receives a request regarding a list of collateral, claims no interest in the collateral when it receives the request, and claimed an interest in the collateral at an earlier time shall comply with the request within 14 days after receipt by sending to the debtor an authenticated record:

(1) disclaiming any interest in the collateral; and

(2) if known to the recipient, providing the name and mailing address of any assignee of or successor to the recipient's interest in the collateral.

(e) A person that receives a request for an accounting or a request regarding a statement of account, claims no interest in the obligations when it receives the request, and claimed an interest in the obligations at an earlier time shall comply with the request within 14 days after receipt by sending to the debtor an authenticated record:

(1) disclaiming any interest in the obligations; and

(2) if known to the recipient, providing the name and mailing address of any assignee of or successor to the recipient's interest in the obligations.

(f) A debtor is entitled without charge to one response to a request under this section during any six-month period. The secured party may require payment of a charge not exceeding $25 for each additional response.

Added by Acts 1999, 76th Leg., ch. 414, § 1.01, eff. July 1, 2001. Amended by Acts 2001, 77th Leg., ch. 705, § 3, eff. June 13, 2001.

Uniform Commercial Code Comment

1. **Source.** Former Section 9–208.

2. **Scope and Purpose.** This section provides a procedure whereby a debtor may obtain from a secured party information about the secured obligation and the collateral in which the secured party may claim a security interest. It clarifies and resolves some of the issues that arose under former Section 9–208 and makes information concerning the secured indebtedness readily available to debtors, both before and after default. It applies to agricultural lien transactions (see the definitions of "debtor," "secured party," and "collateral" in Section 9–102), but generally not to sales of receivables. See subsection (b).

3. **Requests by Debtors Only.** A financing statement filed under Part 5 may disclose only that a secured party may have a security interest in specified types of collateral. In most cases the financing statement will contain no indication of the obligation (if any) secured, whether any security interest actually exists, or the particular property subject to a security interest. Because creditors of and prospective purchasers from a debtor may have legitimate needs for more detailed information, it is necessary to provide a procedure under which the secured party will be required to provide information. On the other hand, the secured party should not be under a duty to disclose any details of the debtor's financial affairs to any casual inquirer or competitor who may inquire. For this reason, this section gives the

right to request information to the debtor only. The debtor may submit a request in connection with negotiations with subsequent creditors and purchasers, as well as for the purpose of determining the status of its credit relationship or demonstrating which of its assets are free of a security interest.

4. **Permitted Types of Requests for Information.** Subsection (a) contemplates that a debtor may request three types of information by submitting three types of "requests" to the secured party. First, the debtor may request the secured party to prepare and send an "accounting" (defined in Section 9–102). Second, the debtor may submit to the secured party a list of collateral for the secured party's approval or correction. Third, the debtor may submit to the secured party for its approval or correction a statement of the aggregate amount of unpaid secured obligations. Inasmuch as a secured party may have numerous transactions and relationships with a debtor, each request must identify the relevant transactions or relationships. Subsections (b) and (c) require the secured party to respond to a request within 14 days following receipt of the request.

5. **Recipients Claiming No Interest in the Transaction.** A debtor may be unaware that a creditor with whom it has dealt has assigned its security interest or the secured obligation. Subsections (d) and (e) impose upon recipients of requests under this section the duty to inform the debtor that they claim no interest in the collateral or secured obligation, respectively, and to inform the debtor of the name and mailing address of any known assignee or successor. As under subsections (b) and (c), a response to a request under subsection (d) or (e) is due 14 days following receipt.

6. **Waiver; Remedy for Failure to Comply.** The debtor's rights under this section may not be waived or varied. See Section 9–602(2). Section 9–625 sets forth the remedies for noncompliance with the requirements of this section.

7. **Limitation on Free Responses to Requests.** Under subsection (f), during a six-month period a debtor is entitled to receive from the secured party one free response to a request. The debtor is not entitled to a free response to *each* type of request (i.e., three free responses) during a six-month period.

SUBCHAPTER C. PERFECTION AND PRIORITY

§ 9.301. Law Governing Perfection and Priority of Security Interests

Except as otherwise provided in Sections 9.303 through 9.306, the following rules determine the law governing perfection, the effect of perfection or nonperfection, and the priority of a security interest in collateral:

(1) Except as otherwise provided in this section, while a debtor is located in a jurisdiction, the local law of that jurisdiction governs perfection, the effect of perfection or nonperfection, and the priority of a security interest in collateral.

(2) While collateral is located in a jurisdiction, the local law of that jurisdiction governs perfection, the effect of perfection or nonperfection, and the priority of a possessory security interest in that collateral.

(3) Except as otherwise provided in Subdivision (4), while tangible negotiable documents, goods, instruments, money, or tangible chattel paper is located in a jurisdiction, the local law of that jurisdiction governs:

(A) perfection of a security interest in the goods by filing a fixture filing;

(B) perfection of a security interest in timber to be cut; and

(C) the effect of perfection or nonperfection and the priority of a nonpossessory security interest in the collateral.

(4) The local law of the jurisdiction in which the wellhead or minehead is located governs perfection, the effect of perfection or nonperfection, and the priority of a security interest in as-extracted collateral.

Amended by Acts 1999, 76th Leg., ch. 414, § 1.01, eff. July 1, 2001; Acts 2005, 79th Leg., ch. 122, § 23, eff. Sept. 1, 2005.

Uniform Commercial Code Comment

1. **Source.** Former Sections 9–103(1)(a), (b), 9–103(3)(a), (b), 9–103(5), substantially modified.

2. **Scope of This Subpart.** Part 3, Subpart 1 (Sections 9–301 through 9–307) contains choice-of-law rules similar to those of former Section 9–103. Former Section 9–103 generally addresses which State's law governs "perfection and the effect of perfection or non-perfection of" security interests. See, e.g., former Section 9–103(1)(b). This Article follows the broader and more precise formulation in former Section 9–103(6)(b), which was revised in connection with the promulgation of Revised Article 8 in 1994: "perfection, the effect of perfection or non-perfection, and the priority of" security interests. Priority, in this context, subsumes all of the rules in Part 3, including "cut off" or "take free" rules such as Sections 9–317(b), (c), and (d), 9–320(a), (b), and (d), and 9–332. This subpart does not address choice of law for other purposes. For example, the law applicable to issues such as attachment, validity, characterization (e.g., true lease or security interest), and enforcement is governed by the rules in Section 1–105; that governing law typically is specified in the same agreement that contains the security agreement. And, another jurisdiction's law may govern other third-party matters addressed in this Article. See Section 9–401, Comment 3.

3. **Scope of Referral.** In designating the jurisdiction whose law governs, this Article directs the court to apply only the substantive ("local") law of a particular jurisdiction and not its choice-of-law rules.

Example 1: Litigation over the priority of a security interest in accounts arises in State X. State X has adopted the official text of this Article, which provides that priority is determined by the local law of the jurisdiction in which the debtor is located. See Section 9–301(1). The debtor is located in State Y. Even if State Y has retained former Article 9 or enacted a nonuniform choice-of-law rule (e.g., one that provides that perfection is governed by the law of State Z), a State X court should look only to the substantive law of State Y and disregard State Y's choice-of-law rule. State Y's substantive law (e.g., its Section 9–501) provides that financing statements should be filed in a filing office in State Y. Note, however, that if the identical perfection issue were to be litigated in State Y, the court would look to State Y's former Section 9–103 or nonuniform 9–301 and conclude that a filing in State Y is ineffective.

Example 2: In the preceding Example, assume that State X has adopted the official text of this Article, and State Y has adopted a nonuniform Section 9–301(1) under which perfection is governed by the whole law of State X, including its choice-of-law rules. If litigation occurs in State X, the court should look to the substantive law of State Y, which provides that financing statements are to be filed in a filing office in State Y. If litigation occurs in State Y, the court should look to the law of State X, whose choice-of-law rule requires that the court apply the substantive law of State Y. Thus, regardless of the jurisdiction in which the litigation arises, the financing statement should be filed in State Y.

4. **Law Governing Perfection: General Rule.** Paragraph (1) contains the general rule: the law governing perfection of security interests in both tangible and intangible collateral, whether perfected by filing or automatically, is the law of the jurisdiction of the debtor's location, as determined under Section 9–307.

Paragraph (1) substantially simplifies the choice-of-law rules. Former Section 9–103 contained different choice-of-law rules for different types of collateral. Under Section 9–301(1), the law of a single jurisdiction governs perfection with respect to most types of collateral, both tangible and intangible. Paragraph (1) eliminates the need for former Section 9–103(1)(c), which concerned purchase-money security interests in tangible collateral that is intended to move from one jurisdiction to the other. It is likely to reduce the frequency of cases in which the governing law changes after a financing statement is properly filed. (Presumably, debtors change their own location less frequently than they change the location of their collateral.) The approach taken in paragraph (1) also eliminates some difficult priority issues and the need to distinguish between "mobile" and "ordinary" goods, and it reduces the number of filing offices in which secured parties must file or search when collateral is located in several jurisdictions.

5. **Law Governing Perfection: Exceptions.** The general rule is subject to several exceptions. It does not apply to goods covered by a certificate of title (see Section 9–303), deposit accounts (see Section 9–304), investment property (see Section 9–305), or letter-of-credit rights (see Section 9–306). Nor does it apply to possessory security interests, i.e., security interests that the secured party has perfected by taking possession of the collateral (see paragraph (2)), security interests perfected by filing a fixture filing (see subparagraph (3)(A)), security interests in timber to be cut (subparagraph (3)(B)), or security interests in as-extracted collateral (see paragraph (4)).

a. **Possessory Security Interests.** Paragraph (2) applies to possessory security interests and provides that perfection is governed by the local law of the jurisdiction in which the collateral is located. This is the rule of former Section 9–103(1)(b), except paragraph (2) eliminates the troublesome "last event" test of former law.

The distinction between nonpossessory and possessory security interests creates the potential for the same jurisdiction to apply two different choice-of-law rules to determine perfection in the same collateral. For example, were a secured party in possession of an instrument or a tangible document to relinquish possession in reliance on temporary perfection, the applicable law immediately would change from that of the location of the collateral to that of the location of the debtor. The applicability of two different choice-of-law rules for perfection is unlikely to lead to any material practical problems. The perfection rules of one Article 9 jurisdiction are likely to be identical to those of another. Moreover, under paragraph (3), the relative priority of competing security interests in tangible collateral is resolved by reference to the law of the jurisdiction in which the collateral is located, regardless of how the security interests are perfected.

b. **Fixtures.** Application of the general rule in paragraph (1) to perfection of a security interest in fixtures would yield strange results. For example, perfection of a security interest in fixtures located in Arizona and owned by a Delaware corporation would be governed by the law of Delaware. Although Delaware law would send one to a filing office in Arizona for the place to file a financing statement as a fixture filing, see Section 9–501, Delaware law would not take account of local, nonuniform, real-property filing and recording requirements that Arizona law might impose. For this reason, paragraph (3)(A) contains a special rule for security interests perfected by a fixture filing; the law of the jurisdiction in which the fixtures are located governs perfection, including the formal requisites of a fixture filing. Under paragraph (3)(C), the same law governs priority. Fixtures are "goods" as defined in Section 9–102.

c. **Timber to Be Cut.** Application of the general rule in paragraph (1) to perfection of a security interest in timber to be cut would yield undesirable results analogous to those described with respect to fixtures. Paragraph (3)(B) adopts a similar solution: perfection is governed by the law of the jurisdiction in which the timber is located. As with fixtures, under paragraph (3)(C), the same law governs priority. Timber to be cut also is "goods" as defined in Section 9–102.

Paragraph (3)(B) applies only to "timber to be cut," not to timber that has been cut. Consequently, once the timber is cut, the general choice-of-law rule in paragraph (1) becomes applicable. To ensure continued perfection, a secured party should file in both the jurisdiction in which the timber to be cut is located and in the state where the debtor is located. The former filing would be with the office in which a real property mortgage would be filed, and the latter would be a central filing. See Section 9–501.

d. **As-Extracted Collateral.** Paragraph (4) adopts the rule of former Section 9–103(5) with respect to certain security interests in minerals and related accounts. Like security interests in fixtures perfected by filing a fixture filing, security interests in minerals that are as-extracted collateral are perfected by filing in the office designated for the filing or recording of a mortgage on the real property. For the same reasons, the law governing perfection and priority is the law of the jurisdiction in which the wellhead or minehead is located.

6. **Change in Law Governing Perfection.** When the debtor changes its location to another jurisdiction, the jurisdiction whose law governs perfection under paragraph (1) changes, as well. Similarly, the law governing perfection of a possessory security interest in collateral under paragraph (2) changes when the collateral is removed to another jurisdiction. Nevertheless, these changes will not result in an immediate loss of perfection. See Section 9–316(a), (b).

7. **Law Governing Effect of Perfection and Priority: Goods, Documents, Instruments, Money, Negotiable Documents, and Tangible Chattel Paper.** Under former Section 9–103, the law of a single jurisdiction governed both questions of perfection and those of priority. This Article generally adopts that approach. See paragraph (1). But the approach may create problems if the debtor and collateral are located in different jurisdictions. For example, assume a security interest in equipment located in Pennsylvania is perfected by filing in Illinois, where the debtor is located. If the law of the jurisdiction in which the debtor is located were to govern priority, then the priority of an execution lien on goods located in Pennsylvania would be governed by rules enacted by the Illinois legislature.

To address this problem, paragraph (3)(C) divorces questions of perfection from questions of "the effect of perfection or nonperfection and the priority of a security interest." Under paragraph (3)(C), the rights of competing claimants to tangible collateral are resolved by reference to the law of the jurisdiction in which the collateral is located. A similar bifurcation applied to security interests in investment property under former Section 9–103(6). See Section 9–305.

Paragraph (3)(C) applies the law of the situs to determine priority only with respect to goods (including fixtures), instruments, money, tangible negotiable documents, and tangible chattel paper. Compare former Section 9–103(1), which applied the law of the location of the collateral to documents, instruments, and "ordinary" (as opposed to "mobile") goods. This Article does not distinguish among types of goods. The ordinary/mobile goods distinction appears to address concerns about where to file and search, rather than concerns about priority. There is no reason to preserve this distinction under the bifurcated approach.

Particularly serious confusion may arise when the choice-of-law rules of a given jurisdiction result in each of two competing security interests in the same collateral being governed by a different priority rule. The potential for this confusion existed under former Section 9–103(4) with respect to chattel paper: Perfection by possession was governed by the law of the location of the paper, whereas perfection by filing was governed by the law of the location of the debtor. Consider the mess that would have been created if the language or interpretation of former Section 9–308 were to differ in the two relevant States, or if one of the relevant jurisdictions (e.g., a foreign country) had not adopted Article 9. The potential for confusion could have been exacerbated when a secured party perfected both by taking possession in the State where the collateral is located (State A) and by filing in the State where the debtor is located (State B)–a common practice for some chattel paper financers. By providing that the law of the jurisdiction in which the collateral is located governs priority, paragraph (3) substantially diminishes this problem.

8. **Non-U.S. Debtors.** This Article applies the same choice-of-law rules to all debtors, foreign and domestic. For example, it adopts the bifurcated approach for determining the law applicable to security interests in goods and other tangible collateral. See Comment 5.a., above. The Article contains a new rule specifying the location of non-U.S. debtors for purposes of this Part. The rule appears in Section 9–307 and is explained in the Comments to that section. Former Section 9–103(3)(c), which contained a special choice-of-law rule governing security interests created by debtors located in a non-U.S. jurisdiction, proved unsatisfactory and was deleted.

Sections 31 and 32 of Acts 2005, 79th Leg., ch. 122 provide:

"Sec. 31. This Act applies to a document of title that is issued or a bailment that arises on or after the effective date of this Act. This Act does not apply to a document of title that is issued or a bailment that arises before the effective date of this Act even if the document of title or bailment would be subject to this Act if the document of title had been issued or bailment had arisen after the effective date of this Act. This Act does not apply to a right of action that has accrued before the effective date of this Act.

"Sec. 32. A document of title issued or a bailment that arises before the effective date of this Act and the rights, obligations, and interests flowing from that document or bailment are governed by any statute or other rule amended or repealed by this Act as if amendment or repeal had not occurred and may be terminated, completed, consummated, or enforced under that statute or other rule."

§ 9.302. Law Governing Perfection and Priority of Agricultural Liens

While farm products are located in a jurisdiction, the local law of that jurisdiction governs perfection, the effect of perfection or nonperfection, and the priority of an agricultural lien on the farm products.

Amended by Acts 1999, 76th Leg., ch. 414, § 1.01, eff. July 1, 2001.

Uniform Commercial Code Comment

1. **Source.** New.

2. **Agricultural Liens.** This section provides choice-of-law rules for agricultural liens on farm products. Perfection, the effect of perfection or nonperfection, and priority all are governed by the law of the jurisdiction in which the farm products are located. Other choice-of-law rules, including Section 1–105, determine which jurisdiction's law governs other matters, such as the secured party's rights on default. See Section 9–301, Comment 2. Inasmuch as no agricultural lien on proceeds arises under this Article, this section does not expressly apply to proceeds of agricultural liens. However, if another statute creates an agricultural lien on proceeds, it may be appropriate for courts to apply the choice-of-law rule in this section to determine priority in the proceeds.

§ 9.303. Law Governing Perfection and Priority of Security Interests in Goods Covered by a Certificate of Title

(a) This section applies to goods covered by a certificate of title, even if there is no other relationship between the jurisdiction under whose certificate of title the goods are covered and the goods or the debtor.

(b) Goods become covered by a certificate of title when a valid application for the certificate of title and the applicable fee are delivered to the appropriate authority. Goods cease to be covered by a certificate of title at the earlier of the time the certificate of title ceases to be effective under the law of the issuing jurisdiction or the time the goods become covered subsequently by a certificate of title issued by another jurisdiction.

(c) The local law of the jurisdiction under whose certificate of title the goods are covered governs perfection, the effect of perfection or nonperfection, and the priority of a security interest in goods covered by a certificate of title from the time the goods become covered by the certificate of title until the goods cease to be covered by the certificate of title.

Amended by Acts 1999, 76th Leg., ch. 414, § 1.01, eff. July 1, 2001.

Uniform Commercial Code Comment

1. **Source.** Former Section 9–103(2)(a), (b), substantially revised.

2. **Scope of This Section.** This section applies to "goods covered by a certificate of title." The new definition of "certificate of title" in Section 9–102 makes clear that this section applies not only to certificate-of-title statutes under which perfection occurs upon notation of the security interest on the certificate but also to those that contemplate notation but provide that perfection is achieved by another method, e.g., delivery of designated documents to an official. Subsection (a), which is new, makes clear that this section applies to certificates of a jurisdiction having no other contacts with the goods or the debtor. This result comports with most of the reported cases on the subject and with contemporary business practices in the trucking industry.

3. **Law Governing Perfection and Priority.** Subsection (c) is the basic choice-of-law rule for goods covered by a certificate of title. Perfection and priority of a security interest are governed by the law of the jurisdiction under whose certificate of title the goods are covered from the time the goods become covered by the certificate of title until the goods cease to be covered by the certificate of title.

Normally, under the law of the relevant jurisdiction, the perfection step would consist of compliance with that jurisdiction's certificate-of-title statute and a resulting notation of the security interest on the certificate of title. See Section 9–311(b). In the typical case of an automobile or over-the-road truck, a person who wishes to take a security interest in the vehicle can ascertain whether it is subject to any security interests by looking at the certificate of title. But certificates of title cover certain types of goods in some States but not in others. A secured party who does not realize this may extend credit and attempt to perfect by filing in the jurisdiction in which the debtor is located. If the goods had been titled in another jurisdiction, the lender would be unperfected.

Subsection (b) explains when goods become covered by a certificate of title and when they cease to be covered. Goods may become covered by a certificate of title, even though no certificate of title has issued. Former Section 9–103(2)(b) provided that the law of the jurisdiction issuing the certificate ceases to apply upon "surrender" of the certificate. This Article eliminates the concept of "surrender." However, if the certificate is surrendered in conjunction with an appropriate application for a certificate to be issued by another jurisdiction, the law of the original jurisdiction ceases to apply because the goods became covered subsequently by a certificate of title from another jurisdiction. Alternatively, the law of the original jurisdiction ceases to apply when the certificate "ceases to be effective" under the law of that jurisdiction. Given the diversity in certificate-of-title statutes, the term "effective" is not defined.

4. **Continued Perfection.** The fact that the law of one State ceases to apply under subsection (b) does not mean that a security interest perfected under that law becomes unperfected automatically. In most cases, the security interest will remain perfected. See Section 9–316(d), (e). Moreover, a perfected security interest may be subject to defeat by certain buyers and secured parties. See Section 9–337.

5. **Inventory.** Compliance with a certificate-of-title statute generally is *not* the method of perfecting security interests in inventory. Section 9–311(d) provides that a security interest created in inventory held by a person in the business of selling goods of that kind is subject to the normal filing rules; compliance with a certificate-of-title statute is not necessary or effective to perfect the security interest. Most certificate-of-title statutes are in accord.

The following example explains the subtle relationship between this rule and the choice-of-law rules in Section 9–303 and former Section 9–103(2):

Example: Goods are located in State A and covered by a certificate of title issued under the law of State A. The State A certificate of title is "clean"; it does not reflect a security interest. Owner takes the goods to State B and sells (trades in) the goods to Dealer, who is in the business of selling goods of that kind and is located (within the meaning of Section 9–307) in State B. As is customary, Dealer retains the duly assigned State A certificate of title pending resale of the goods. Dealer's inventory financer, SP, obtains a security interest in the goods under its after-acquired property clause.

Under Section 9–311(d) of both State A and State B, Dealer's inventory financer, SP, must perfect by filing instead of complying with a certificate-of-title statute. If Section 9–303 were read to provide that the law applicable to perfection of SP's security interest is that of State A, because the goods are covered by a State A certificate, then SP would be required to file in State A under State A's Section 9–501. That result would be anomalous, to say the least, since the principle underlying Section 9–311(d) is that the inventory should be treated as ordinary goods.

Section 9–303 (and former Section 9–103(2)) should be read as providing that the law of State B, not State A, applies. A court looking to the forum's Section 9–303(a) would find that Section 9–303 applies only if two conditions are met: (i) the goods are covered by the certificate as explained in Section 9–303(b), i.e., application had been made for a State (here, State A) to issue a certificate of title covering the goods and (ii) the certificate is a "certificate of title" as defined in Section 9–102, i.e., "a statute provides for the security interest in question to be indicated on the certificate as a condition or result of the security interest's obtaining priority over the rights of a lien creditor." Stated otherwise, Section 9–303 applies only when compliance with a certificate-of-title statute, and not filing, is the appropriate method of perfection. Under the law of State A, *for purposes of perfecting SP's security interest in the dealer's inventory*, the proper method of perfection is filing–not compliance with State A's certificate-of-title statute. For that reason, the goods are not covered by a "certificate of title," and the second condition is not met. Thus, Section 9–303 does not apply to the goods. Instead, Section 9–301 applies, and the applicable law is that of State B, where the debtor (dealer) is located.

6. **External Constraints on This Section.** The need to coordinate Article 9 with a variety of nonuniform certificate-of-title statutes, the need to provide rules to take account of situations in which multiple certificates of title are outstanding with respect to particular goods, and the need to govern the transition from perfection by filing in one jurisdiction to perfection by notation in another all create pressure for a detailed and complex set of rules. In an effort to minimize complexity, this Article does not attempt to coordinate Article 9 with the entire array of certificate-of-title statutes. In particular, Sections 9–303, 9–311, and 9–316(d) and (e) assume that the certificate-of-title statutes to which they apply do not have relation-back provisions (i.e., provisions under which perfection is deemed to occur at a time earlier than when the perfection steps actually are taken). A Legislative Note to Section 9–311 recommends the elimination of relation-back provisions in certificate-of-title statutes affecting perfection of security interests.

Ideally, at any given time, only one certificate of title is outstanding with respect to particular goods. In fact, however, sometimes more than one jurisdiction issues more than one certificate of title with respect to the same goods. This situation results from defects in certificate-of-title laws and the interstate coordination of those laws, not from deficiencies in this Article. As long as the possibility of multiple certificates of title remains, the potential for innocent parties to suffer losses will continue. At best, this Article can identify clearly which innocent parties will bear the losses in familiar fact patterns.

§ 9.304. Law Governing Perfection and Priority of Security Interests in Deposit Accounts

(a) The local law of a bank's jurisdiction governs perfection, the effect of perfection or nonperfection, and the priority of a security interest in a deposit account maintained with that bank.

(b) The following rules determine a bank's jurisdiction for purposes of this subchapter:

(1) If an agreement between the bank and its customer governing the deposit account expressly provides that a particular jurisdiction is the bank's jurisdiction for purposes of this subchapter, this chapter, or this title, that jurisdiction is the bank's jurisdiction.

(2) If Subdivision (1) does not apply and an agreement between the bank and its customer governing the deposit account expressly provides that the agreement is governed by the law of a particular jurisdiction, that jurisdiction is the bank's jurisdiction.

(3) If neither Subdivision (1) nor Subdivision (2) applies and an agreement between the bank and its customer governing the deposit account expressly provides that the deposit account is maintained at an office in a particular jurisdiction, that jurisdiction is the bank's jurisdiction.

(4) If none of the preceding subdivisions applies, the bank's jurisdiction is the jurisdiction in which the office identified in an account statement as the office serving the customer's account is located.

(5) If none of the preceding subdivisions applies, the bank's jurisdiction is the jurisdiction in which the chief executive office of the bank is located.

Amended by Acts 1999, 76th Leg., ch. 414, § 1.01, eff. July 1, 2001; Acts 2003, 78th Leg., ch. 917, § 3, eff. Sept. 1, 2003.

Uniform Commercial Code Comment

1. **Source.** New; derived from Section 8–110(e) and former Section 9–103(6).

2. **Deposit Accounts.** Under this section, the law of the "bank's jurisdiction" governs perfection and priority of a security interest in deposit accounts. Subsection (b) contains rules for determining the "bank's jurisdiction." The substance of these rules is substantially similar to that of the rules determining the "security intermediary's jurisdiction" under former Section 8–110(e), except that subsection (b)(1) provides more flexibility than the analogous provision in former Section 8–110(e)(1). Subsection (b)(1) permits the parties to choose the law of one jurisdiction to govern perfection and priority of security interests and a different governing law for other purposes. The parties' choice is effective, even if the jurisdiction whose law is chosen bears no relationship to the parties or the transaction. Section 8–110(e)(1) has been conformed to subsection (b)(1) of this section, and Section 9–305(b)(1), concerning a commodity intermediary's jurisdiction, makes a similar departure from former Section 9–103(6)(e)(i).

3. **Change in Law Governing Perfection.** When the bank's jurisdiction changes, the jurisdiction whose law governs perfection under subsection (a) changes, as well. Nevertheless, the change will not result in an immediate loss of perfection. See Section 9–316(f), (g).

§ 9.305. Law Governing Perfection and Priority of Security Interests in Investment Property

(a) Except as otherwise provided in Subsection (c), the following rules apply:

(1) While a security certificate is located in a jurisdiction, the local law of that jurisdiction governs perfection, the effect of perfection or nonperfection, and the priority of a security interest in the certificated security represented thereby.

(2) The local law of the issuer's jurisdiction as specified in Section 8.110(d) governs perfection, the effect of perfection or nonperfection, and the priority of a security interest in an uncertificated security.

(3) The local law of the securities intermediary's jurisdiction as specified in Section 8.110(e) governs perfection, the effect of perfection or nonperfection, and the priority of a security interest in a security entitlement or securities account.

(4) The local law of the commodity intermediary's jurisdiction governs perfection, the effect of perfection or nonperfection, and the priority of a security interest in a commodity contract or commodity account.

(b) The following rules determine a commodity intermediary's jurisdiction for purposes of this subchapter:

(1) If an agreement between the commodity intermediary and commodity customer governing the commodity account expressly provides that a particular jurisdiction is the commodity intermediary's jurisdiction for purposes of this subchapter, this chapter, or this title, that jurisdiction is the commodity intermediary's jurisdiction.

(2) If Subdivision (1) does not apply and an agreement between the commodity intermediary and commodity customer governing the commodity account expressly provides that the agreement is governed by the law of a particular jurisdiction, that jurisdiction is the commodity intermediary's jurisdiction.

(3) If neither Subdivision (1) nor Subdivision (2) applies and an agreement between the commodity intermediary and commodity customer governing the commodity account expressly provides that the commodity account is maintained at an office in a particular jurisdiction, that jurisdiction is the commodity intermediary's jurisdiction.

(4) If none of the preceding subdivisions applies, the commodity intermediary's jurisdiction is the jurisdiction in which the office identified in an account statement as the office serving the commodity customer's account is located.

(5) If none of the preceding subdivisions applies, the commodity intermediary's jurisdiction is the jurisdiction in which the chief executive office of the commodity intermediary is located.

(c) The local law of the jurisdiction in which the debtor is located governs:

(1) perfection of a security interest in investment property by filing;

(2) automatic perfection of a security interest in investment property created by a broker or securities intermediary; and

(3) automatic perfection of a security interest in a commodity contract or commodity account created by a commodity intermediary.

Amended by Acts 1999, 76th Leg., ch. 414, § 1.01, eff. July 1, 2001.

Uniform Commercial Code Comment

1. **Source.** Former Section 9–103(6).

2. **Investment Property: General Rules.** This section specifies choice-of-law rules for perfection and priority of security interests in investment property. Subsection (a)(1) covers security interests in certificated securities. Subsection (a)(2) covers security interests in uncertificated securities. Subsection (a)(3) covers security interests in security entitlements and securities accounts. Subsection (a)(4) covers security interests in commodity contracts and commodity accounts. The approach of each of these paragraphs is essentially the same. They identify the jurisdiction's law that governs questions of perfection and priority by using the same principles that Article 8 uses to determine other questions concerning that form of investment property. Thus, for certificated securities, the law of the jurisdiction in which the certificate is located governs. Cf. Section 8–110(c). For uncertificated securities, the law of the issuer's jurisdiction governs. Cf. Section 8–110(a). For security entitlements and securities accounts, the law of the securities intermediary's jurisdiction governs. Cf. Section 8–110(b). For commodity contracts and commodity accounts, the law of the commodity intermediary's jurisdiction governs. Because commodity contracts and commodity accounts are not governed by Article 8, subsection (b) contains rules that specify the commodity intermediary's jurisdiction. These are analogous to the rules in Section 8–110(e) specifying a securities

intermediary's jurisdiction. Subsection (b)(1) affords the parties greater flexibility than did former Section 9–103(6)(3). See also Section 9–304(b) (bank's jurisdiction); Revised Section 8–110(e)(1) (securities intermediary's jurisdiction).

3. **Investment Property: Exceptions.** Subsection (c) establishes an exception to the general rules set out in subsection (a). It provides that perfection of a security interest by filing, automatic perfection of a security interest in investment property created by a debtor who is a broker or securities intermediary (see Section 9–309(10)), and automatic perfection of a security interest in a commodity contract or commodity account of a debtor who is a commodity intermediary (see Section 9–309(11)) are governed by the law of the jurisdiction in which the debtor is located, as determined under Section 9–307.

4. **Examples:** The following examples illustrate the rules in this section:

Example 1: A customer residing in New Jersey maintains a securities account with Able & Co. The agreement between the customer and Able specifies that it is governed by Pennsylvania law but expressly provides that the law of California is Able's jurisdiction for purposes of the Uniform Commercial Code. Through the account the customer holds securities of a Massachusetts corporation, which Able holds through a clearing corporation located in New York. The customer obtains a margin loan from Able. Subsection (a)(3) provides that California law–the law of the securities intermediary's jurisdiction–governs perfection and priority of the security interest, even if California has no other relationship to the parties or the transaction.

Example 2: A customer residing in New Jersey maintains a securities account with Able & Co. The agreement between the customer and Able specifies that it is governed by Pennsylvania law. Through the account the customer holds securities of a Massachusetts corporation, which Able holds through a clearing corporation located in New York. The customer obtains a loan from a lender located in Illinois. The lender takes a security interest and perfects by obtaining an agreement among the debtor, itself, and Able, which satisfies the requirement of Section 8–106(d)(2) to give the lender control. Subsection (a)(3) provides that Pennsylvania law–the law of the securities intermediary's jurisdiction–governs perfection and priority of the security interest, even if Pennsylvania has no other relationship to the parties or the transaction.

Example 3: A customer residing in New Jersey maintains a securities account with Able & Co. The agreement between the customer and Able specifies that it is governed by Pennsylvania law. Through the account, the customer holds securities of a Massachusetts corporation, which Able holds through a clearing corporation located in New York. The customer borrows from SP–1, and SP–1 files a financing statement in New Jersey. Later, the customer obtains a loan from SP–2. SP–2 takes a security interest and perfects by obtaining an agreement among the debtor, itself, and Able, which satisfies the requirement of Section 8–106(d)(2) to give the SP–2 control. Subsection (c) provides that perfection of SP–1's security interest by filing is governed by the location of the debtor, so the filing in New Jersey was appropriate. Subsection (a)(3), however, provides that Pennsylvania law–the law of the securities intermediary's jurisdiction–governs all other questions of perfection and priority. Thus, Pennsylvania law governs perfection of SP–2's security interest, and Pennsylvania law also governs the priority of the security interests of SP–1 and SP–2.

5. **Change in Law Governing Perfection.** When the issuer's jurisdiction, the securities intermediary's jurisdiction, or commodity intermediary's jurisdiction changes, the jurisdiction whose law governs perfection under subsection (a) changes, as well. Similarly, the law governing perfection of a possessory security interest in a certificated security changes when the collateral is removed to another jurisdiction, see subsection (a)(1), and the law governing perfection by filing changes when the debtor changes its location. See subsection (c). Nevertheless, these changes will not result in an immediate loss of perfection. See Section 9–316.

§ 9.306. Law Governing Perfection and Priority of Security Interests in Letter-Of-Credit Rights

(a) Subject to Subsection (c), the local law of the issuer's jurisdiction or a nominated person's jurisdiction governs perfection, the effect of perfection or nonperfection, and the priority of a security interest in a letter-of-credit right if the issuer's jurisdiction or nominated person's jurisdiction is a state.

(b) For purposes of this subchapter, an issuer's jurisdiction or nominated person's jurisdiction is the jurisdiction whose law governs the liability of the issuer or nominated person with respect to the letter-of-credit right as provided in Section 5.116.

(c) This section does not apply to a security interest that is perfected only under Section 9.308(d).

Amended by Acts 1999, 76th Leg., ch. 414, § 1.01, eff. July 1, 2001.

Uniform Commercial Code Comment

1. **Source.** New; derived in part from Section 8–110(e) and former Section 9–103(6).

2. ***Sui Generis* Treatment.** This section governs the applicable law for perfection and priority of security interests in letter-of-credit rights, other than a security interest perfected only under Section 9–308(d) (i.e., as a supporting obligation). The treatment differs substantially from that provided in Section 9–304 for deposit accounts. The basic rule is that the law of the issuer's or nominated person's (e.g., confirmer's) jurisdiction, derived from the terms of the letter of credit itself, controls perfection and priority, but only if the issuer's or nominated person's jurisdiction is a State, as defined in Section 9–102. If the issuer's or nominated person's jurisdiction is not a State, the baseline rule of Section 9–301 applies–perfection and priority are governed by the law of the debtor's location, determined under Section 9–307. Export transactions typically involve a foreign issuer and a domestic nominated person, such as a confirmer, located in a State. The principal goal of this section is to reduce the likelihood that perfection and priority would be

governed by the law of a foreign jurisdiction in a transaction that is essentially domestic from the standpoint of the debtor-beneficiary, its creditors, and a domestic nominated person.

3. **Issuer's or Nominated Person's Jurisdiction.** Subsection (b) defers to the rules established under Section 5–116 for determination of an issuer's or nominated person's jurisdiction.

Example: An Italian bank issues a letter of credit that is confirmed by a New York bank. The beneficiary is a Connecticut corporation. The letter of credit provides that the issuer's liability is governed by Italian law, and the confirmation provides that the confirmer's liability is governed by the law of New York. Under Sections 9–306(b) and 5–116(a), Italy is the issuer's jurisdiction and New York is the confirmer's (nominated person's) jurisdiction. Because the confirmer's jurisdiction is a State, the law of New York governs perfection and priority of a security interest in the beneficiary's letter-of-credit right against the confirmer. See Section 9–306(a). However, because the issuer's jurisdiction is not a State, the law of that jurisdiction does not govern. See Section 9–306(a). Rather, the choice-of-law rule in Section 9–301(1) applies to perfection and priority of a security interest in the beneficiary's letter-of-credit right against the issuer. Under that section, perfection and priority are governed by the law of the jurisdiction in which the debtor (beneficiary) is located. That jurisdiction is Connecticut. See Section 9–307.

4. **Scope of this Section.** This section specifies only the law governing perfection, the effect of perfection or nonperfection, and priority of security interests. Section 5–116 specifies the law governing the liability of, and Article 5 (or other applicable law) deals with the rights and duties of, an issuer or nominated person. Perfection, nonperfection, and priority have no effect on those rights and duties.

5. **Change in Law Governing Perfection.** When the issuer's jurisdiction, or nominated person's jurisdiction changes, the jurisdiction whose law governs perfection under subsection (a) changes, as well. Nevertheless, this change will not result in an immediate loss of perfection. See Section 9–316(f), (g).

§ 9.307. Location of Debtor

(a) In this section, "place of business" means a place where a debtor conducts its affairs.

(b) Except as otherwise provided in this section, the following rules determine a debtor's location:

(1) A debtor who is an individual is located at the individual's principal residence.

(2) A debtor that is an organization and has only one place of business is located at its place of business.

(3) A debtor that is an organization and has more than one place of business is located at its chief executive office.

(c) Subsection (b) applies only if a debtor's residence, place of business, or chief executive office, as applicable, is located in a jurisdiction whose law generally requires information concerning the existence of a nonpossessory security interest to be made generally available in a filing, recording, or registration system as a condition or result of the security interest's obtaining priority over the rights of a lien creditor with respect to the collateral. If Subsection (b) does not apply, the debtor is located in the District of Columbia.

(d) A person that ceases to exist, have a residence, or have a place of business continues to be located in the jurisdiction specified by Subsections (b) and (c).

(e) A registered organization that is organized under the law of a state is located in that state.

(f) Except as otherwise provided in Subsection (i), a registered organization that is organized under the law of the United States and a branch or agency of a bank that is not organized under the law of the United States or a state are located:

(1) in the state that the law of the United States designates, if the law designates a state of location;

(2) in the state that the registered organization, branch, or agency designates, if the law of the United States authorizes the registered organization, branch, or agency to designate its state of location; or

(3) in the District of Columbia, if neither Subdivision (1) nor Subdivision (2) applies.

(g) A registered organization continues to be located in the jurisdiction specified by Subsection (e) or (f) notwithstanding:

(1) the suspension, revocation, forfeiture, or lapse of the registered organization's status as such in its jurisdiction of organization; or

(2) the dissolution, winding up, or cancellation of the existence of the registered organization.

(h) The United States is located in the District of Columbia.

(i) A branch or agency of a bank that is not organized under the law of the United States or a state is located in the state in which the branch or agency is licensed, if all branches and agencies of the bank are licensed in only one state.

(j) A foreign air carrier under the Federal Aviation Act of 1958, as amended, is located at the designated office of the agent upon which service of process may be made on behalf of the carrier.

(k) This section applies only for purposes of this subchapter.

Amended by Acts 1999, 76th Leg., ch. 414, § 1.01, eff. July 1, 2001.

Uniform Commercial Code Comment

1. **Source.** Former Section 9–103(3)(d), substantially revised.

2. **General Rules.** As a general matter, the location of the debtor determines the jurisdiction whose law governs perfection of a security interest. See Sections 9–301(1), 9–305(c). It also governs priority of a security interest in certain types of intangible collateral, such as accounts, electronic chattel paper, and general intangibles. This section determines the location of the debtor for choice-of-law purposes, but not for other purposes. See subsection (k).

Subsection (b) states the general rules: An individual debtor is deemed to be located at the individual's principal residence with respect to both personal and business assets. Any other debtor is deemed to be located at its place of business if it has only one, or at its chief executive office if it has more than one place of business.

As used in this section, a "place of business" means a place where the debtor conducts its affairs. See subsection (a). Thus, every organization, even eleemosynary institutions and other organizations that do not conduct "for profit" business activities, has a "place of business." Under subsection (d), a person who ceases to exist, have a residence, or have a place of business continues to be located in the jurisdiction determined by subsection (b).

The term "chief executive office" is not defined in this Section or elsewhere in the Uniform Commercial Code. "Chief executive office" means the place from which the debtor manages the main part of its business operations or other affairs. This is the place where persons dealing with the debtor would normally look for credit information, and is the appropriate place for filing. With respect to most multistate debtors, it will be simple to determine which of the debtor's offices is the "chief executive office." Even when a doubt arises, it would be rare that there could be more than two possibilities. A secured party in such a case may protect itself by perfecting under the law of each possible jurisdiction.

Similarly, the term "principal residence" is not defined. If the security interest in question is a purchase-money security interest in consumer goods which is perfected upon attachment, see Section 9–309(1), the choice of law may make no difference. In other cases, when a doubt arises, prudence may dictate perfecting under the law of each jurisdiction that might be the debtor's "principal residence."

The general rule is subject to several exceptions, each of which is discussed below.

3. **Non-U.S. Debtors.** Under the general rules of this section, a non-U.S. debtor normally would be located in a foreign jurisdiction and, as a consequence, foreign law would govern perfection. When foreign law affords no public notice of security interests, the general rule yields unacceptable results.

Accordingly, subsection (c) provides that the normal rules for determining the location of a debtor (i.e., the rules in subsection (b)) apply only if they yield a location that is "a jurisdiction whose law generally requires information concerning the existence of a nonpossessory security interest to be made generally available in a filing, recording, or registration system as a condition or result of the security interest's obtaining priority over the rights of a lien creditor with respect to the collateral." The phrase "generally requires" is meant to include legal regimes that generally require notice in a filing or recording system as a condition of perfecting nonpossessory security interests, but which permit perfection by another method (e.g., control, automatic perfection, temporary perfection) in limited circumstances. A jurisdiction that has adopted this Article or an earlier version of this Article is such a jurisdiction. If the rules in subsection (b) yield a jurisdiction whose law does not generally require notice in a filing or registration system, the debtor is located in the District of Columbia.

Example 1: Debtor is an English corporation with 7 offices in the United States and its chief executive office in London, England. Debtor creates a security interest in its accounts. Under subsection (b)(3), Debtor would be located in England. However, subsection (c) provides that subsection (b) applies only if English law generally conditions perfection on giving public notice in a filing, recording, or registration system. Otherwise, Debtor is located in the District of Columbia. Under Section 9–301(1), perfection, the effect of perfection, and priority are governed by the law of the jurisdiction of the debtor's location–here, England or the District of Columbia (depending on the content of English law).

Example 2: Debtor is an English corporation with 7 offices in the United States and its chief executive office in London, England. Debtor creates a security interest in equipment located in London. Under subsection (b)(3) Debtor would be located in England. However, subsection (c) provides that subsection (b) applies only if English law generally conditions perfection on giving public notice in a filing, recording, or registration system. Otherwise, Debtor is located in the District of Columbia. Under Section 9–301(1), perfection is governed by the law of the jurisdiction of the debtor's location, whereas, under Section 9–301(3), the law of the jurisdiction in which the collateral is located–here, England–governs priority.

The foregoing discussion assumes that each transaction bears an appropriate relation to the forum State. In the absence of an appropriate relation, the forum State's entire UCC, including the choice-of-law provisions in Article 9 (Sections 9–301 through 9–307), will not apply. See Section 9–109, Comment 9.

4. **Registered Organizations Organized Under Law of a State.** Under subsection (e), a registered organization (e.g., a corporation or limited partnership) organized under the law of a "State" (defined in Section 9–102) is located in its State of organization. Subsection (g) makes clear that events affecting the status of a registered organization, such as the dissolution of a corporation or revocation of its charter, do not affect its location for purposes of subsection (e). Howev-

er, certain of these events may result in, or be accompanied by, a transfer of collateral from the registered organization to another debtor. This section does not determine whether a transfer occurs, nor does it determine the legal consequences of any transfer.

Determining the registered organization-debtor's location by reference to the jurisdiction of organization could provide some important side benefits for the filing systems. A jurisdiction could structure its filing system so that it would be impossible to make a mistake in a registered organization-debtor's name on a financing statement. For example, a filer would be informed if a filed record designated an incorrect corporate name for the debtor. Linking filing to the jurisdiction of organization also could reduce pressure on the system imposed by transactions in which registered organizations cease to exist–as a consequence of merger or consolidation, for example. The jurisdiction of organization might prohibit such transactions unless steps were taken to ensure that existing filings were refiled against a successor or terminated by the secured party.

5. **Registered Organizations Organized Under Law of United States; Branches and Agencies of Banks Not Organized Under Law of United States.** Subsection (f) specifies the location of a debtor that is a registered organization organized under the law of the United States. It defers to the law of the United States, to the extent that that law determines, or authorizes the debtor to determine, the debtor's location. Thus, if the law of the United States designates a particular State as the debtor's location, that State is the debtor's location for purposes of this Article's choice-of-law rules. Similarly, if the law of the United States authorizes the registered organization to designate its State of location, the State that the registered organization designates is the State in which it is located for purposes of this Article's choice-of-law rules. In other cases, the debtor is located in the District of Columbia.

In some cases, the law of the United States authorizes the registered organization to designate a main office, home office, or other comparable office. See, e.g., 12 U.S.C. §§ 22 and 1464(a); 12 C.F.R. § 552.3. Designation of such an office constitutes the designation of the State of location for purposes of Section 9–307(f)(2).

Subsection (f) also specifies the location of a branch or agency in the United States of a foreign bank that has one or more branches or agencies in the United States. The law of the United States authorizes a foreign bank (or, on behalf of the bank, a federal regulatory agency) to designate a single home state for all of the foreign bank's branches and agencies in the United States. See 12 U.S.C. § 3103(c) and 12 C.F.R. § 211.22. The designated State constitutes the State of location for the branch or agency for purposes of Section 9–307(f): however if all of the foreign bank's branches or agencies that are in the United States are licensed in only one State, the branches and agencies are located in that State. See subsection (i).

In cases not governed by subsection (f) or (i), the location of a foreign bank is determined by subsections (b) and (c).

Subsection (f) also determines the location of branches and agencies of banks that are not organized under the law of the United States or a State. However, if all the branches and agencies of the bank are licensed only in one State, then they are located in that State. See subsection (i).

6. **United States.** To the extent that Article 9 governs (see Sections 1–105, 9–109(c)), the United States is located in the District of Columbia for purposes of this Article's choice-of-law rules. See subsection (h).

7. **Foreign Air Carriers.** Subsection (j) follows former Section 9–103(3)(d). To the extent that it is applicable, the Convention on the International Recognition of Rights in Aircraft (Geneva Convention) supersedes state legislation on this subject, as set forth in Section 9–311(b), but some nations are not parties to that Convention.

§ 9.308. When Security Interest or Agricultural Lien is Perfected; Continuity of Perfection

(a) Except as otherwise provided in this section and Section 9.309, a security interest is perfected if it has attached and all of the applicable requirements for perfection in Sections 9.310 through 9.316 have been satisfied. A security interest is perfected when it attaches if the applicable requirements are satisfied before the security interest attaches.

(b) An agricultural lien is perfected if it has become effective and all of the applicable requirements for perfection in Section 9.310 have been satisfied. An agricultural lien is perfected when it becomes effective if the applicable requirements are satisfied before the agricultural lien becomes effective.

(c) A security interest or agricultural lien is perfected continuously if it is originally perfected by one method under this chapter and is later perfected by another method under this chapter, without an intermediate period when it was unperfected.

(d) Perfection of a security interest in collateral also perfects a security interest in a supporting obligation for the collateral.

(e) Perfection of a security interest in a right to payment or performance also perfects a security interest in a security interest, mortgage, or other lien on personal or real property securing the right.

(f) Perfection of a security interest in a securities account also perfects a security interest in the security entitlements carried in the securities account.

(g) Perfection of a security interest in a commodity account also perfects a security interest in the commodity contracts carried in the commodity account.

Amended by Acts 1999, 76th Leg., ch. 414, § 1.01, eff. July 1, 2001.

Uniform Commercial Code Comment

1. **Source.** Former Sections 9–303, 9–115(2).

2. **General Rule.** This Article uses the term "attach" to describe the point at which property becomes subject to a security interest. The requisites for attachment are stated in Section 9–203. When it attaches, a security interest may be either perfected or unperfected. "Perfected" means that the security interest has attached and the secured party has taken all the steps required by this Article as specified in Sections 9–310 through 9–316. A perfected security interest may still be or become subordinate to other interests. See, e.g., Sections 9–320, 9–322. However, in general, after perfection the secured party is protected against creditors and transferees of the debtor and, in particular, against any representative of creditors in insolvency proceedings instituted by or against the debtor. See, e.g., Section 9–317.

Subsection (a) explains that the time of perfection is when the security interest has attached and any necessary steps for perfection, such as taking possession or filing, have been taken. The "except" clause refers to the perfection-upon-attachment rules appearing in Section 9–309. It also reflects that other subsections of this section, e.g., subsection (d), contain automatic-perfection rules. If the steps for perfection have been taken in advance, as when the secured party files a financing statement before giving value or before the debtor acquires rights in the collateral, then the security interest is perfected when it attaches.

3. **Agricultural Liens.** Subsection (b) is new. It describes the elements of perfection of an agricultural lien.

4. **Continuous Perfection.** The following example illustrates the operation of subsection (c):

Example 1: Debtor, an importer, creates a security interest in goods that it imports and the documents of title that cover the goods. The secured party, Bank, takes possession of a tangible negotiable bill of lading covering certain imported goods and thereby perfects its security interest in the bill of lading and the goods. See Sections 9–313(a), 9–312(c)(1). Bank releases the bill of lading to the debtor for the purpose of procuring the goods from the carrier and selling them. Under Section 9–312(f), Bank continues to have a perfected security interest in the document and goods for 20 days. Bank files a financing statement covering the collateral before the expiration of the 20–day period. Its security interest now continues perfected for as long as the filing is good.

If the successive stages of Bank's security interest succeed each other without an intervening gap, the security interest is "perfected continuously," and the date of perfection is when the security interest first became perfected (i.e., when Bank received possession of the tangible bill of lading). If, however, there is a gap between stages–for example, if Bank does not file until after the expiration of the 20–day period specified in Section 9–312(f) and leaves the collateral in the debtor's possession–then, the chain being broken, the perfection is no longer continuous. The date of perfection would now be the date of filing (after expiration of the 20–day period). Bank's security interest would be vulnerable to any interests arising during the gap period which under Section 9–317 take priority over an unperfected security interest.

5. **Supporting Obligations.** Subsection (d) is new. It provides for automatic perfection of a security interest in a supporting obligation for collateral if the security interest in the collateral is perfected. This is unlikely to effect any change in the law prior to adoption of this Article.

Example 2: Buyer is obligated to pay Debtor for goods sold. Buyer's president guarantees the obligation. Debtor creates a security interest in the right to payment (account) in favor of Lender. Under Section 9–203(f), the security interest attaches to Debtor's rights under the guarantee (supporting obligation). Under subsection (d), perfection of the security interest in the account constitutes perfection of the security interest in Debtor's rights under the guarantee.

6. **Rights to Payment Secured by Lien.** Subsection (e) is new. It deals with the situation in which a security interest is created in a right to payment that is secured by a security interest, mortgage, or other lien.

Example 3: Owner gives to Mortgagee a mortgage on Blackacre to secure a loan. Owner's obligation to pay is evidenced by a promissory note. In need of working capital, Mortgagee borrows from Financer and creates a security interest in the note in favor of Financer. Section 9–203(g) adopts the traditional view that the mortgage follows the note; i.e., the transferee of the note acquires the mortgage, as well. This subsection adopts a similar principle: perfection of a security interest in the right to payment constitutes perfection of a security interest in the mortgage securing it.

An important consequence of the rules in Section 9–203(g) and subsection (e) is that, by acquiring a perfected security interest in a mortgage (or other secured) note, the secured party acquires a security interest in the mortgage (or other lien) that is senior to the rights of a person who becomes a lien creditor of the mortgagee (Article 9 debtor). See Section 9–317(a)(2). This result helps prevent the separation of the mortgage (or other lien) from the note.

Under this Article, attachment and perfection of a security interest in a secured right to payment do not of themselves affect the obligation to pay. For example, if the obligation is evidenced by a negotiable note, then Article 3 dictates the person whom the maker must pay to discharge the note and any lien securing it. See Section 3–602. If the right to payment is a payment intangible, then Section 9–406 determines whom the account debtor must pay.

Similarly, this Article does not determine who has the power to release a mortgage of record. That issue is determined by real-property law.

7. **Investment Property.** Subsections (f) and (g) follow former Section 9–115(2).

§ 9.309. Security Interest Perfected Upon Attachment

The following security interests are perfected when they attach:

(1) a purchase money security interest in consumer goods, except as otherwise provided in Section 9.311(b) with respect to consumer goods that

are subject to a statute or treaty described in Section 9.311(a);

(2) an assignment of accounts or payment intangibles that does not by itself or in conjunction with other assignments to the same assignee transfer a significant part of the assignor's outstanding accounts or payment intangibles;

(3) a sale of a payment intangible;

(4) a sale of a promissory note;

(5) a security interest created by the assignment of a health-care-insurance receivable to the provider of the health care goods or services;

(6) a security interest arising under Section 2.401, 2.505, 2.711(c), or 2A.508(e), until the debtor obtains possession of the collateral;

(7) a security interest of a collecting bank arising under Section 4.210;

(8) a security interest of an issuer or nominated person arising under Section 5.118;

(9) a security interest arising in the delivery of a financial asset under Section 9.206(c);

(10) a security interest in investment property created by a broker or securities intermediary;

(11) a security interest in a commodity contract or a commodity account created by a commodity intermediary;

(12) an assignment for the benefit of all the creditors of the transferor and subsequent transfers by the assignee thereunder;

(13) a security interest created by an assignment of a beneficial interest in a decedent's estate; and

(14) a sale by an individual of an account that is a right to payment of winnings in a lottery or other game of chance.

Amended by Acts 1999, 76th Leg., ch. 414, § 1.01, eff. July 1, 2001; Acts 2003, 78th Leg., ch. 917, § 4, eff. Sept. 1, 2003.

Uniform Commercial Code Comment

1. **Source.** Derived from former Sections 9–302(1), 9–115(4)(c), (d), 9–116.

2. **Automatic Perfection.** This section contains the perfection-upon-attachment rules previously located in former Sections 9–302(1), 9–115(4)(c), (d), and 9–116. Rather than continue to state the rule by indirection, this section explicitly provides for perfection upon attachment.

3. **Purchase-Money Security Interest in Consumer Goods.** Former Section 9–302(1)(d) has been revised and appears here as paragraph (1). No filing or other step is required to perfect a purchase-money security interest in consumer goods, other than goods, such as automobiles, that are subject to a statute or treaty described in Section 9–311(a). However, filing is required to perfect a non-purchase-money security interest in consumer goods and is necessary to prevent a buyer of consumer goods from taking free of a security interest under Section 9–320(b). A fixture filing is required for priority over conflicting interests in fixtures to the extent provided in Section 9–334.

4. **Rights to Payment.** Paragraph (2) expands upon former Section 9–302(1)(e) by affording automatic perfection to certain assignments of payment intangibles as well as accounts. The purpose of paragraph (2) is to save from *ex post facto* invalidation casual or isolated assignments–assignments which no one would think of filing. Any person who regularly takes assignments of any debtor's accounts or payment intangibles should file. In this connection Section 9–109(d)(4) through (7), which excludes certain transfers of accounts, chattel paper, payment intangibles, and promissory notes from this Article, should be consulted.

Paragraphs (3) and (4), which are new, afford automatic perfection to sales of payment intangibles and promissory notes, respectively. They reflect the practice under former Article 9. Under that Article, filing a financing statement did not affect the rights of a buyer of payment intangibles or promissory notes, inasmuch as the former Article did not cover those sales. To the extent that the exception in paragraph (2) covers outright sales of payment intangibles, which automatically are perfected under paragraph (3), the exception is redundant.

Paragraph (14), which is new, affords automatic perfection to sales by individuals of an "account" (as defined in Section 9–102) consisting of the right to winnings in a lottery or other game of chance. Payments on these accounts typically extend for periods of twenty years or more. It would be unduly burdensome for the secured party, who would have no other reason to maintain contact with the seller, to monitor the seller's whereabouts for such a length of time. This paragraph was added in 2001. It applies to a sale of an account described in it, even if the sale was entered into before the effective date of the paragraph. However, if the relative priorities of conflicting claims to the account were established before the paragraph took effect, Article 9 as in effect immediately prior to the date the paragraph took effect determines priority.

5. **Health-Care-Insurance Receivables.** Paragraph (5) extends automatic perfection to assignments of health-care-insurance receivables if the assignment is made to the health-care provider that provided the health-care goods or services. The primary effect is that, when an individual assigns a right to payment under an insurance policy to the person who provided health-care goods or services, the provider has no need to file a financing statement against the individual. The normal filing requirements apply to other assignments of health-care-insurance receivables covered by this Article, e.g., assignments from the health-care provider to a financer.

6. **Investment Property.** Paragraph (9) replaces the last clause of former Section 9–116(2), concerning security interests that arise in the delivery of a financial asset.

Paragraphs (10) and (11) replace former Section 9–115(4)(c) and (d), concerning secured financing of securities and commodity firms and clearing corporations. The former sections indicated that, with respect to certain security interests created by a securities intermediary or commodity intermediary, "[t]he filing of a financing statement ... has no effect for purposes of perfection or priority with respect to that security interest." No change in meaning is intended by the deletion of the quoted phrase.

Secured financing arrangements for securities firms are currently implemented in various ways. In some circumstances, lenders may require that the transactions be structured as "hard pledges," where the securities are transferred on the books of a clearing corporation from the debtor's account to the lender's account or to a special pledge account for the lender where they cannot be disposed of without the specific consent of the lender. In other circumstances, lenders are content with so-called "agreement to pledge" or "agreement to deliver" arrangements, where the debtor retains the positions in its own account, but reflects on its books that the positions have been hypothecated and promises that the securities will be transferred to the secured party's account on demand.

The perfection and priority rules of this Article are designed to facilitate current secured financing arrangements for securities firms as well as to provide sufficient flexibility to accommodate new arrangements that develop in the future. Hard pledge arrangements are covered by the concept of control. See Sections 9–314, 9–106, 8–106. Non-control secured financing arrangements for securities firms are covered by the automatic perfection rule of paragraph (10). Before the 1994 revision of Articles 8 and 9, agreement to pledge arrangements could be implemented under a provision that a security interest in securities given for new value under a written security agreement was perfected without filing or possession for a period of 21 days. Although the security interests were temporary in legal theory, the financing arrangements could, in practice, be continued indefinitely by rolling over the loans at least every 21 days. Accordingly, a knowledgeable creditor of a securities firm realizes that the firm's securities may be subject to security interests that are not discoverable from any public records. The automatic-perfection rule of paragraph (10) makes it unnecessary to engage in the purely formal practice of rolling over these arrangements every 21 days.

In some circumstances, a clearing corporation may be the debtor in a secured financing arrangement. For example, a clearing corporation that settles delivery-versus-payment transactions among its participants on a net, same-day basis relies on timely payments from all participants with net obligations due to the system. If a participant that is a net debtor were to default on its payment obligation, the clearing corporation would not receive some of the funds needed to settle with participants that are net creditors to the system. To complete end-of-day settlement after a payment default by a participant, a clearing corporation that settles on a net, same-day basis may need to draw on credit lines and pledge securities of the defaulting participant or other securities pledged by participants in the clearing corporation to secure such drawings. The clearing corporation may be the top-tier securities intermediary for the securities pledged, so that it would not be practical for the lender to obtain control. Even where the clearing corporation holds some types of securities through other intermediaries, however, the clearing corporation is unlikely to be able to complete the arrangements necessary to convey "control" over the securities to be pledged in time to complete settlement in a timely manner. However, the term "securities intermediary" is defined in Section 8–102(a)(14) to include clearing corporations. Thus, the perfection rule of paragraph (10) applies to security interests in investment property granted by clearing corporations.

7. **Beneficial Interests in Trusts.** Under former Section 9–302(1)(c), filing was not required to perfect a security interest created by an assignment of a beneficial interest in a trust. Because beneficial interests in trusts are now used as collateral with greater frequency in commercial transactions, under this Article filing is required to perfect a security interest in a beneficial interest.

8. **Assignments for Benefit of Creditors.** No filing or other action is required to perfect an assignment for the benefit of creditors. These assignments are not financing transactions, and the debtor ordinarily will not be engaging in further credit transactions.

§ 9.310. When Filing Required to Perfect Security Interest or Agricultural Lien; Security Interests and Agricultural Liens to Which Filing Provisions Do Not Apply

(a) Except as otherwise provided in Subsection (b) and Section 9.312(b), a financing statement must be filed to perfect all security interests and agricultural liens.

(b) The filing of a financing statement is not necessary to perfect a security interest:

(1) that is perfected under Section 9.308(d), (e), (f), or (g);

(2) that is perfected under Section 9.309 when it attaches;

(3) in property subject to a statute, regulation, or treaty described in Section 9.311(a);

(4) in goods in possession of a bailee that is perfected under Section 9.312(d)(1) or (2);

(5) in certificated securities, documents, goods, or instruments which is perfected without filing, control or possession under Section 9.312(e), (f), or (g);

(6) in collateral in the secured party's possession under Section 9.313;

(7) in a certificated security that is perfected by delivery of the security certificate to the secured party under Section 9.313;

(8) in deposit accounts, electronic chattel paper, electronic documents, investment property, or letter-of-credit rights that is perfected by control under Section 9.314;

(9) in proceeds that is perfected under Section 9.315;

(10) that is perfected under Section 9.316; or

(11) in oil or gas production or their proceeds under Section 9.343.

(c) If a secured party assigns a perfected security interest or agricultural lien, a filing under this Chapter is not required to continue the perfected status of the security interest against creditors of and transferees from the original debtor.

Amended by Acts 1999, 76th Leg., ch. 414, § 1.01, eff. July 1, 2001; Acts 2005, 79th Leg., ch. 122, § 24, eff. Sept. 1, 2005.

Uniform Commercial Code Comment

1. **Source.** Former Section 9–302(1), (2).

2. **General Rule.** Subsection (a) establishes a central Article 9 principle: Filing a financing statement is necessary for perfection of security interests and agricultural liens. However, filing is not necessary to perfect a security interest that is perfected by another permissible method, see subsection (b), nor does filing ordinarily perfect a security interest in a deposit account, letter-of-credit right, or money. See Section 9–312(b). Part 5 of the Article deals with the office in which to file, mechanics of filing, and operations of the filing office.

3. **Exemptions from Filing.** Subsection (b) lists the security interests for which filing is not required as a condition of perfection, because they are perfected automatically upon attachment (subsections (b)(2) and (b)(9)) or upon the occurrence of another event (subsections (b)(1), (b)(5), and (b)(9)), because they are perfected under the law of another jurisdiction (subsection (b)(10)), or because they are perfected by another method, such as by the secured party's taking possession or control (subsections (b)(3), (b)(4), (b)(5), (b)(6), (b)(7), and (b)(8)).

4. **Assignments of Perfected Security Interests.** Subsection (c) concerns assignment of a perfected security interest or agricultural lien. It provides that no filing is necessary in connection with an assignment by a secured party to an assignee in order to maintain perfection as against creditors of and transferees from the original debtor.

Example 1: Buyer buys goods from Seller, who retains a security interest in them. After Seller perfects the security interest by filing, Seller assigns the perfected security interest to X. The security interest, in X's hands and without further steps on X's part, continues perfected against *Buyer's* transferees and creditors.

Example 2: Dealer creates a security interest in specific equipment in favor of Lender. After Lender perfects the security interest in the equipment by filing, Lender assigns the chattel paper (which includes the perfected security interest in Dealer's equipment) to X. The security interest in the equipment, in X's hands and without further steps on X's part, continues perfected against *Dealer's* transferees and creditors. However, regardless of whether Lender made the assignment to secure Lender's obligation to X or whether the assignment was an outright sale of the chattel paper, the assignment creates a security interest in the chattel paper in favor of X. Accordingly, X must take whatever steps may be required for perfection in order to be protected against *Lender's* transferees and creditors with respect to the chattel paper.

Subsection (c) applies not only to an assignment of a security interest perfected by filing but also to an assignment of a security interest perfected by a method other than by filing, such as by control or by possession. Although subsection (c) addresses explicitly only the absence of an additional filing requirement, the same result normally will follow in the case of an assignment of a security interest perfected by a method other than by filing. For example, as long as possession of collateral is maintained by an assignee or by the assignor or another person on behalf of the assignee, no further perfection steps need be taken on account of the assignment to continue perfection as against creditors and transferees of the original debtor. Of course, additional action may be required for perfection of the assignee's interest as against creditors and transferees of the *assignor*.

Similarly, subsection (c) applies to the assignment of a security interest perfected by compliance with a statute, regulation, or treaty under Section 9–311(b), such as a certificate-of-title statute. Unless the statute expressly provides to the contrary, the security interest will remain perfected against creditors of and transferees from the original debtor, even if the assignee takes no action to cause the certificate of title to reflect the assignment or to cause its name to appear on the certificate of title. See PEB Commentary No. 12, which discusses this issue under former Section 9–302(3). Compliance with the statute is "equivalent to filing" under Section 9–311(b).

Sections 31 and 32 of Acts 2005, 79th Leg., ch. 122 provide:

"Sec. 31. This Act applies to a document of title that is issued or a bailment that arises on or after the effective date of this Act. This Act does not apply to a document of title that is issued or a bailment that arises before the effective date of this Act even if the document of title or bailment would be subject to this Act if the document of title had been issued or bailment had arisen after the effective date of this Act. This Act does not apply to a right of action that has accrued before the effective date of this Act.

"Sec. 32. A document of title issued or a bailment that arises before the effective date of this Act and the rights, obligations, and interests flowing from that document or bailment are governed by any statute or other rule amended or repealed by this Act as if amendment or repeal had not occurred and may be terminated, completed, consummated, or enforced under that statute or other rule."

§ 9.311. Perfection of Security Interests in Property Subject to Certain Statutes, Regulations, and Treaties

(a) Except as otherwise provided in Subsection (d), the filing of a financing statement is not necessary or effective to perfect a security interest in property subject to:

(1) a statute, regulation, or treaty of the United States whose requirements for a security interest's obtaining priority over the rights of a lien creditor with respect to the property preempt Section 9.310(a);

Text of subsec. (a)(2) effective until April 1, 2009

(2) the following statutes of this state: Chapter 501, Transportation Code,[1] relating to the certificates of title for motor vehicles; Subchapter B–1, Chapter 31, Parks and Wildlife Code,[2] relating to the certificates of title for vessels and outboard motors; Chapter 1201, Occupations Code, relating to the documents of title for manufactured homes; or Subchapter A, Chapter 35,[3] relating to utility security instruments; or

Text of subsec. (a)(2) effective April 1, 2009

(2) the following statutes of this state: Chapter 501, Transportation Code, relating to the certificates of title for motor vehicles; Subchapter B–1, Chapter 31, Parks and Wildlife Code, relating to the certificates of title for vessels and outboard motors; Chapter 1201, Occupations Code, relating to the documents of title for manufactured homes; or Chapter 261, relating to utility security instruments; or

(3) a certificate of title statute of another jurisdiction that provides for a security interest to be indicated on the certificate as a condition or result of the security interest's obtaining priority over the rights of a lien creditor with respect to the property.

(b) Compliance with the requirements of a statute, regulation, or treaty described in Subsection (a) for obtaining priority over the rights of a lien creditor is equivalent to the filing of a financing statement under this Chapter. Except as otherwise provided in Subsection (d) and Sections 9.313 and 9.316(d) and (e) for goods covered by a certificate of title, a security interest in property subject to a statute, regulation, or treaty described in Subsection (a) may be perfected only by compliance with those requirements, and a security interest so perfected remains perfected notwithstanding a change in the use or transfer of possession of the collateral.

(c) Except as otherwise provided in Subsection (d) and Sections 9.316(d) and (e), duration and renewal of perfection of a security interest perfected by compliance with the requirements prescribed by a statute, regulation, or treaty described in Subsection (a) are governed by the statute, regulation, or treaty. In other respects, the security interest is subject to this Chapter.

(d) During any period in which collateral subject to a statute specified in Subsection (a)(2) is inventory held for sale or lease by a person or leased by that person as lessor and that person is in the business of selling goods of that kind, this section does not apply to a security interest in that collateral created by that person.

Amended by Acts 1999, 76th Leg., ch. 414, § 1.01, eff. July 1, 2001; Acts 2001, 77th Leg., ch. 705, § 4, eff. June 13, 2001; Acts 2003, 78th Leg., ch. 1276, § 14A.754, eff. Sept. 1, 2003; Acts 2007, 80th Leg., ch. 885, § 2.05, eff. April 1, 2009.

[1] V.T.C.A., Transportation Code § 501.001 et seq.

[2] V.T.C.A., Parks and Wildlife Code § 31.045 et seq.

[3] V.T.C.A., Bus. & C. § 35.01 et seq.

Uniform Commercial Code Comment

1. **Source.** Former Section 9–302(3), (4).

2. **Federal Statutes, Regulations, and Treaties.** Subsection (a)(1) exempts from the filing provisions of this Article transactions as to which a system of filing–state or federal–has been established under federal law. Subsection (b) makes clear that when such a system exists, perfection of a relevant security interest can be achieved only through compliance with that system (i.e., filing under this Article is not a permissible alternative).

An example of the type of federal statute referred to in subsection (a)(1) is 49 U.S.C. §§ 44107–11, for civil aircraft of the United States. The Assignment of Claims Act of 1940, as amended, provides for notice to contracting and disbursing officers and to sureties on bonds but does not establish a national filing system and therefore is not within the scope of subsection (a)(1). An assignee of a claim against the United States may benefit from compliance with the Assignment of Claims Act. But regardless of whether the assignee complies with that Act, the assignee must file under this Article in order to perfect its security interest against creditors and transferees of its assignor.

Subsection (a)(1) provides explicitly that the filing requirement of this Article defers only to federal statutes, regulations, or treaties whose requirements for a security interest's obtaining priority over the rights of a lien creditor preempt Section 9–310(a). The provision eschews reference to the term "perfection," inasmuch as Section 9–308 specifies the meaning of that term and a preemptive rule may use other terminology.

3. **State Statutes.** Subsections (a)(2) and (3) exempt from the filing requirements of this Article transactions covered by State certificate-of-title statutes covering motor vehicles and the like. The description of certificate-of-title statutes in subsections (a)(2) and (a)(3) tracks the language of the definition of "certificate of title" in Section 9–102. For a discussion of the operation of state certificate-of-title statutes in interstate contexts, see the Comments to Section 9–303.

Some states have enacted central filing statutes with respect to secured transactions in kinds of property that are of special importance in the local economy. Subsection (a)(2) defers to these statutes with respect to filing for that property.

4. **Inventory Covered by Certificate of Title.** Under subsection (d), perfection of a security interest in the invento-

ry of a person in the business of selling goods of that kind is governed by the normal perfection rules, even if the inventory is subject to a certificate-of-title statute. Compliance with a certificate-of-title statute is both unnecessary and ineffective to perfect a security interest in inventory to which this subsection applies. Thus, a secured party who finances an automobile dealer that is in the business of selling and leasing its inventory of automobiles can perfect a security interest in all the automobiles by filing a financing statement but not by compliance with a certificate-of-title statute.

Subsection (d), and thus the filing and other perfection provisions of this Article, does not apply to inventory that is subject to a certificate-of-title statute and is of a kind that the debtor is not in the business of selling. For example, if goods are subject to a certificate-of-title statute and the debtor is in the business of leasing but not of selling, goods of that kind, the other subsections of this section govern perfection of a security interest in the goods. The fact that the debtor eventually sells the goods does not, of itself, mean that the debtor "is in the business of selling goods of that kind."

The filing and other perfection provisions of this Article apply to goods subject to a certificate-of-title statute only "during any period in which collateral is inventory held for sale or lease or leased." If the debtor takes goods of this kind out of inventory and uses them, say, as equipment, a filed financing statement would not remain effective to perfect a security interest.

5. **Compliance with Perfection Requirements of Other Statute.** Subsection (b) makes clear that compliance with the perfection requirements (i.e., the requirements for obtaining priority over a lien creditor), but not other requirements, of a statute, regulation, or treaty described in subsection (a) is sufficient for perfection under this Article. Perfection of a security interest under such a statute, regulation, or treaty has all the consequences of perfection under this Article.

The interplay of this section with certain certificate-of-title statutes may create confusion and uncertainty. For example, statutes under which perfection does not occur until a certificate of title is issued will create a gap between the time that the goods are covered by the certificate under Section 9–303 and the time of perfection. If the gap is long enough, it may result in turning some unobjectionable transactions into avoidable preferences under Bankruptcy Code Section 547. (The preference risk arises if more than 10 days (or 20 days, in the case of a purchase-money security interest) passes between the time a security interest attaches (or the debtor receives possession of the collateral, in the case of a purchase-money security interest) and the time it is perfected.) Accordingly, the Legislative Note to this section instructs the legislature to amend the applicable certificate-of-title statute to provide that perfection occurs upon receipt by the appropriate State official of a properly tendered application for a certificate of title on which the security interest is to be indicated.

Under some certificate-of-title statutes, including the Uniform Motor Vehicle Certificate of Title and Anti–Theft Act, perfection generally occurs upon delivery of specified documents to a state official but may, under certain circumstances, relate back to the time of attachment. This relation-back feature can create great difficulties for the application of the rules in Sections 9–303 and 9–311(b). Accordingly, the Legislative Note also recommends to legislatures that they remove any relation-back provisions from certificate-of-title statutes affecting security interests.

6. **Compliance with Perfection Requirements of Other Statute as Equivalent to Filing.** Under Subsection (b), compliance with the perfection requirements (i.e., the requirements for obtaining priority over a lien creditor) of a statute, regulation, or treaty described in subsection (a) "is equivalent to the filing of a financing statement."

The quoted phrase appeared in former Section 9–302(3). Its meaning was unclear, and many questions arose concerning the extent to which and manner in which Article 9 rules referring to "filing" were applicable to perfection by compliance with a certificate-of-title statute. This Article takes a variety of approaches for applying Article 9's filing rules to compliance with other statutes and treaties. First, as discussed above in Comment 5, it leaves the determination of some rules, such as the rule establishing time of perfection (Section 9–516(a)), to the other statutes themselves. Second, this Article explicitly applies some Article 9 filing rules to perfection under other statutes or treaties. See, e.g., Section 9–505. Third, this Article makes other Article 9 rules applicable to security interests perfected by compliance with another statute through the "equivalent to ... filing" provision in the first sentence of Section 9–311(b). The third approach is reflected for the most part in occasional Comments explaining how particular rules apply when perfection is accomplished under Section 9–311(b). See, e.g., Section 9–310, Comment 4; Section 9–315, Comment 6; Section 9–317, Comment 8. The absence of a Comment indicating that a particular filing provision applies to perfection pursuant to Section 9–311(b) does not mean the provision is inapplicable.

7. **Perfection by Possession of Goods Covered by Certificate-of-Title Statute.** A secured party who holds a security interest perfected under the law of State A in goods that subsequently are covered by a State B certificate of title may face a predicament. Ordinarily, the secured party will have four months under State B's Section 9–316(c) and (d) in which to (re)perfect as against a purchaser of the goods by having its security interest noted on a State B certificate. This procedure is likely to require the cooperation of the debtor and any competing secured party whose security interest has been noted on the certificate. Comment 4(e) to former Section 9–103 observed that "that cooperation is not likely to be forthcoming from an owner who wrongfully procured the issuance of a new certificate not showing the out-of-state security interest, or from a local secured party finding himself in a priority contest with the out-of-state secured party." According to that Comment, "[t]he only solution for the out-of-state secured party under present certificate of title statutes seems to be to reperfect by possession, i.e., by repossessing the goods." But the "solution" may not have worked: Former Section 9–302(4) provided that a security interest in property subject to a certificate-of-title statute "can be perfected only by compliance therewith."

Sections 9–316(d) and (e), 9–311(c), and 9–313(b) of this Article resolve the conflict by providing that a security interest that remains perfected solely by virtue of Section

9–316(e) can be (re)perfected by the secured party's taking possession of the collateral. These sections contemplate only that taking possession of goods covered by a certificate of title will work as a method of perfection. None of these sections creates a right to take possession. Section 9–609 and the agreement of the parties define the secured party's right to take possession.

State Bar Committee Comment

Utility security instruments. The filing of utility security instruments (which includes mortgages, deeds of trust, and security agreements) may be governed by Texas Business & Commerce Code, Chapter 35, Subchapter A, Sections 35.01–35.09. In order to be subject to those provisions the utility must elect to subject itself by making certain that the title page of the security instrument contains a conspicuous statement: "This Instrument Grants A Security Interest By A Utility." Section 35.015. Such a security instrument, whose contents satisfy the requirements of Section 35.02(b), is to be filed in the office of the Secretary of State. Section 35.02(a). Utilities are a special class of debtor for which the ordinary filing rules may be a problem, especially where the collateral is fixtures such as pipelines or power lines. Requiring a local filing in each county where such fixtures may be located would be cumbersome and needlessly expensive. The Texas statutory scheme for such utilities has been to permit such security instruments to be filed in one "central" office, and that is also the approach of revised Chapter 9. Section 9.501(b). In Texas these arrangements are made in part in nonuniform fashion by the provisions of Chapter 35. However, Subsection 35.02(d) states that Chapter 9 governs the priorities and remedies for security interests perfected under Chapter 35.

§ 9.312. Perfection of Security Interests in Chattel Paper, Deposit Accounts, Documents, and Goods Covered by Documents, Instruments, Investment Property, Letter-Of-Credit Rights, and Money; Perfection by Permissive Filing; Temporary Perfection Without Filing or Transfer of Possession

(a) A security interest in chattel paper, negotiable documents, instruments, or investment property may be perfected by filing.

(b) Except as otherwise provided in Sections 9.315(c) and (d) for proceeds:

(1) a security interest in a deposit account may be perfected only by control under Section 9.314;

(2) and except as otherwise provided in Section 9.308(d), a security interest in a letter-of-credit right may be perfected only by control under Section 9.314; and

(3) a security interest in money may be perfected only by the secured party's taking possession under Section 9.313.

(c) While goods are in the possession of a bailee that has issued a negotiable document covering the goods:

(1) a security interest in the goods may be perfected by perfecting a security interest in the document; and

(2) a security interest perfected in the document has priority over any security interest that becomes perfected in the goods by another method during that time.

(d) While goods are in the possession of a bailee that has issued a nonnegotiable document covering the goods, a security interest in the goods may be perfected by:

(1) issuance of a document in the name of the secured party;

(2) the bailee's receipt of notification of the secured party's interest; or

(3) filing as to the goods.

(e) A security interest in certificated securities, negotiable documents, or instruments is perfected without filing or the taking of possession or control for a period of 20 days from the time it attaches to the extent that it arises for new value given under an authenticated security agreement.

(f) A perfected security interest in a negotiable document or goods in possession of a bailee, other than one that has issued a negotiable document for the goods, remains perfected for 20 days without filing if the secured party makes available to the debtor the goods or documents representing the goods for the purpose of:

(1) ultimate sale or exchange; or

(2) loading, unloading, storing, shipping, transshipping, manufacturing, processing, or otherwise dealing with them in a manner preliminary to their sale or exchange.

(g) A perfected security interest in a certificated security or instrument remains perfected for 20 days without filing if the secured party delivers the security certificate or instrument to the debtor for the purpose of:

(1) ultimate sale or exchange; or

(2) presentation, collection, enforcement, renewal, or registration of transfer.

(h) After the 20-day period specified in Subsection (e), (f), or (g) expires, perfection depends upon compliance with this chapter.

Amended by Acts 1999, 76th Leg., ch. 414, § 1.01, eff. July 1, 2001; Acts 2005, 79th Leg., ch. 122, § 25, eff. Sept. 1, 2005.

Uniform Commercial Code Comment

1. **Source.** Former Section 9–304, with additions and some changes.

2. **Instruments.** Under subsection (a), a security interest in instruments may be perfected by filing. This rule represents an important change from former Article 9, under which the secured party's taking possession of an instrument was the only method of achieving long-term perfection. The rule is likely to be particularly useful in transactions involving a large number of notes that a debtor uses as collateral but continues to collect from the makers. A security interest perfected by filing is subject to defeat by certain subsequent purchasers (including secured parties). Under Section 9–330(d), purchasers for value who take possession of an instrument without knowledge that the purchase violates the rights of the secured party generally would achieve priority over a security interest in the instrument perfected by filing. In addition, Section 9–331 provides that filing a financing statement does not constitute notice that would preclude a subsequent purchaser from becoming a holder in due course and taking free of all claims under Section 3–306.

3. **Chattel Paper; Negotiable Documents.** Subsection (a) further provides that filing is available as a method of perfection for security interests in chattel paper and negotiable documents. Tangible chattel paper is sometimes delivered to the assignee, and sometimes left in the hands of the assignor for collection. Subsection (a) allows the assignee to perfect its security interest by filing in the latter case. Alternatively, the assignee may perfect by taking possession. See Section 9–313(a). An assignee of electronic chattel paper may perfect by taking control. See Sections 9–314(a), 9–105. The security interest of an assignee who takes possession or control may qualify for priority over a competing security interest perfected by filing. See Section 9–330.

Negotiable documents may be, and usually are, delivered to the secured party. See Article 1, Section 1–201 (definition of "delivery"). The secured party's taking possession of a tangible document or control of an electronic document will suffice as a perfection step. See Sections 9–313(a), 9–314 and 7–106. However, as is the case with chattel paper, a security interest in a negotiable document may be perfected by filing.

4. **Investment Property.** A security interest in investment property, including certificated securities, uncertificated securities, security entitlements, and securities accounts, may be perfected by filing. However, security interests created by brokers, securities intermediaries, or commodity intermediaries are automatically perfected; filing is of no effect. See Section 9–309(10), (11). A security interest in all kinds of investment property also may be perfected by control, see Sections 9–314, 9–106, and a security interest in a certificated security also may be perfected by the secured party's taking delivery under Section 8–301. See Section 9–313(a). A security interest perfected only by filing is subordinate to a conflicting security interest perfected by control or delivery. See Section 9–328(1), (5). Thus, although filing is a permissible method of perfection, a secured party who perfects by filing takes the risk that the debtor has granted or will grant a security interest in the same collateral to another party who obtains control. Also, perfection by filing would not give the secured party protection against other types of adverse claims, since the Article 8 adverse claim cut-off rules require control. See Section 8–510.

5. **Deposit Accounts.** Under new subsection (b)(1), the only method of perfecting a security interest in a deposit account as original collateral is by control. Filing is ineffective, except as provided in Section 9–315 with respect to proceeds. As explained in Section 9–104, "control" can arise as a result of an agreement among the secured party, debtor, and bank, whereby the bank agrees to comply with instructions of the secured party with respect to disposition of the funds on deposit, even though the debtor retains the right to direct disposition of the funds. Thus, subsection (b)(1) takes an intermediate position between certain non-UCC law, which conditions the effectiveness of a security interest on the secured party's enjoyment of such dominion and control over the deposit account that the debtor is unable to dispose of the funds, and the approach this Article takes to securities accounts, under which a secured party who is unable to reach the collateral without resort to judicial process may perfect by filing. By conditioning perfection on "control," rather than requiring the secured party to enjoy absolute dominion to the exclusion of the debtor, subsection (b)(1) permits perfection in a wide variety of transactions, including those in which the secured party actually relies on the deposit account in extending credit and maintains some meaningful dominion over it, but does not wish to deprive the debtor of access to the funds altogether.

6. **Letter-of-Credit Rights.** Letter-of-credit rights commonly are "supporting obligations," as defined in Section 9–102. Perfection as to the related account, chattel paper, document, general intangible, instrument, or investment property will perfect as to the letter-of-credit rights. See Section 9–308(d). Subsection (b)(2) provides that, in other cases, a security interest in a letter-of-credit right may be perfected only by control. "Control," for these purposes, is explained in Section 9–107.

7. **Goods Covered by Document of Title.** Subsection (c) applies to goods in the possession of a bailee who has issued a negotiable document covering the goods. Subsection (d) applies to goods in the possession of a bailee who has issued a nonnegotiable document of title, including a document of title that is "non-negotiable" under Section 7–104. Section 9–313 governs perfection of a security interest in goods in the possession of a bailee who has not issued a document of title.

Subsection (c) clarifies the perfection and priority rules in former Section 9–304(2). Consistently with the provisions of Article 7, subsection (c) takes the position that, as long as a negotiable document covering goods is outstanding, title to the goods is, so to say, locked up in the document. Accordingly, a security interest in goods covered by a negotiable document may be perfected by perfecting a security interest in the document. The security interest also may be perfected by another method, e.g., by filing. The priority rule in subsection (c) governs only priority between (i) a security interest in goods which is perfected by perfecting in the document and (ii) a security interest in the goods which becomes perfected by another method while the goods are covered by the document.

Example 1: While wheat is in a grain elevator and covered by a negotiable warehouse receipt, Debtor creates a security interest in the wheat in favor of SP–1 and SP–2. SP–1 perfects by filing a financing statement covering "wheat." Thereafter, SP–2 perfects by filing a financing statement describing the warehouse receipt. Subsection (c)(1) provides that SP–2's security interest is perfected. Subsection (c)(2) provides that SP–2's security interest is senior to SP–1's.

Example 2: The facts are as in Example 1, but SP–1's security interest attached and was perfected before the goods were delivered to the grain elevator. Subsection (c)(2) does not apply, because SP–1's security interest did not become perfected during the time that the wheat was in the possession of a bailee. Rather, the first-to-file-or-perfect priority rule applies. See Section 9–322.

A secured party may become "a holder to whom a negotiable document of title has been duly negotiated" under Section 7–501. If so, the secured party acquires the rights specified by Article 7. Article 9 does not limit those rights, which may include the right to priority over an earlier-perfected security interest. See Section 9–331(a).

Subsection (d) takes a different approach to the problem of goods covered by a nonnegotiable document. Here, title to the goods is not looked on as being locked up in the document, and the secured party may perfect its security interest directly in the goods by filing as to them. The subsection provides two other methods of perfection: issuance of the document in the secured party's name (as consignee of a straight bill of lading or the person to whom delivery would be made under a non-negotiable warehouse receipt) and receipt of notification of the secured party's interest by the bailee. Perfection under subsection (d) occurs when the bailee receives notification of the secured party's interest in the goods, regardless of who sends the notification. Receipt of notification is effective to perfect, regardless of whether the bailee responds. Unlike former Section 9–304(3), from which it derives, subsection (d) does not apply to goods in the possession of a bailee who has not issued a document of title. Section 9–313(c) covers that case and provides that perfection by possession as to goods not covered by a document requires the bailee's acknowledgment.

8. **Temporary Perfection Without Having First Otherwise Perfected.** Subsection (e) follows former Section 9–304(4) in giving perfected status to security interests in certificated securities, instruments, and negotiable documents for a short period (reduced from 21 to 20 days, which is the time period generally applicable in this Article), although there has been no filing and the collateral is in the debtor's possession or control. The 20–day temporary perfection runs from the date of attachment. There is no limitation on the purpose for which the debtor is in possession, but the secured party must have given "new value" (defined in Section 9–102) under an authenticated security agreement.

9. **Maintaining Perfection After Surrendering Possession.** There are a variety of legitimate reasons–many of them are described in subsections (f) and (g)–why certain types of collateral must be released temporarily to a debtor. No useful purpose would be served by cluttering the files with records of such exceedingly short term transactions.

Subsection (f) affords the possibility of 20–day perfection in negotiable documents and goods in the possession of a bailee but not covered by a negotiable document. Subsection (g) provides for 20–day perfection in certificated securities and instruments. These subsections derive from former Section 9–305(5). However, the period of temporary perfection has been reduced from 21 to 20 days, which is the time period generally applicable in this Article, and "enforcement" has been added in subsection (g) as one of the special and limited purposes for which a secured party can release an instrument or certificated security to the debtor and still remain perfected. The period of temporary perfection runs from the date a secured party who already has a perfected security interest turns over the collateral to the debtor. There is no new value requirement, but the turnover must be for one or more of the purposes stated in subsection (f) or (g). The 20–day period may be extended by perfecting as to the collateral by another method before the period expires. However, if the security interest is not perfected by another method until after the 20–day period expires, there will be a gap during which the security interest is unperfected.

Temporary perfection extends only to the negotiable document or goods under subsection (f) and only to the certificated security or instrument under subsection (g). It does not extend to proceeds. If the collateral is sold, the security interest will continue in the proceeds for the period specified in Section 9–315.

Subsections (f) and (g) deal only with perfection. Other sections of this Article govern the priority of a security interest in goods after surrender of possession or control of the document covering them. In the case of a purchase-money security interest in inventory, priority may be conditioned upon giving notification to a prior inventory financer. See Section 9–324.

§ 9.313. When Possession by or Delivery To Secured Party Perfects Security Interest Without Filing

(a) Except as otherwise provided in Subsection (b), a secured party may perfect a security interest in tangible negotiable documents, goods, instruments, money, or tangible chattel paper by taking possession of the collateral. A secured party may perfect a security interest in certificated securities by taking delivery of the certificated securities under Section 8.301.

(b) With respect to goods covered by a certificate of title issued by this state, a secured party may perfect a security interest in the goods by taking possession of the goods only in the circumstances described in Section 9.316(d).

(c) With respect to collateral other than certificated securities and goods covered by a document, a secured party takes possession of collateral in the possession of a person other than the debtor, the secured party, or a lessee of the collateral from the debtor in the ordinary course of the debtor's business when:

(1) the person in possession authenticates a record acknowledging that it holds possession of the collateral for the secured party's benefit; or

(2) the person takes possession of the collateral after having authenticated a record acknowledging that it will hold possession of collateral for the secured party's benefit.

(d) If perfection of a security interest depends upon possession of the collateral by a secured party, perfection occurs no earlier than the time the secured party takes possession and continues only while the secured party retains possession.

(e) A security interest in a certificated security in registered form is perfected by delivery when delivery of the certificated security occurs under Section 8.301 and remains perfected by delivery until the debtor obtains possession of the security certificate.

(f) A person in possession of collateral is not required to acknowledge that it holds possession for a secured party's benefit.

(g) If a person acknowledges that it holds possession for the secured party's benefit:

(1) the acknowledgment is effective under Subsection (c) or Section 8.301(a), even if the acknowledgment violates the rights of a debtor; and

(2) unless the person otherwise agrees or law other than this chapter otherwise provides, the person does not owe any duty to the secured party and is not required to confirm the acknowledgment to another person.

(h) A secured party having possession of collateral does not relinquish possession by delivering the collateral to a person other than the debtor or a lessee of the collateral from the debtor in the ordinary course of the debtor's business if the person was instructed before the delivery or is instructed contemporaneously with the delivery:

(1) to hold possession of the collateral for the secured party's benefit; or

(2) to redeliver the collateral to the secured party.

(i) A secured party does not relinquish possession, even if a delivery under Subsection (h) violates the rights of a debtor. A person to which collateral is delivered under Subsection (h) does not owe any duty to the secured party and is not required to confirm the delivery to another person unless the person otherwise agrees or law other than this chapter otherwise provides.

Amended by Acts 1999, 76th Leg., ch. 414, § 1.01, eff. July 1, 2001; Acts 2005, 79th Leg., ch. 122, § 26, eff. Sept. 1, 2005.

Uniform Commercial Code Comment

1. **Source.** Former Sections 9–305, 9–115(6).

2. **Perfection by Possession.** As under the common law of pledge, no filing is required by this Article to perfect a security interest if the secured party takes possession of the collateral. See Section 9–310(b)(6).

This section permits a security interest to be perfected by the taking of possession only when the collateral is goods, instruments, tangible negotiable documents, money, or tangible chattel paper. Accounts, commercial tort claims, deposit accounts, investment property, letter-of-credit rights, letters of credit, and oil, gas, or other minerals before extraction are excluded. (But see Comment 6, below, regarding certificated securities.) A security interest in accounts and payment intangibles–property not ordinarily represented by any writing whose delivery operates to transfer the right to payment–may under this Article be perfected only by filing. This rule would not be affected by the fact that a security agreement or other record described the assignment of such collateral as a "pledge." Section 9–309(2) exempts from filing certain assignments of accounts or payment intangibles which are out of the ordinary course of financing. These exempted assignments are perfected when they attach. Similarly, under Section 9–309(3), sales of payment intangibles are automatically perfected.

3. **"Possession."** This section does not define "possession." It adopts the general concept as it developed under former Article 9. As under former Article 9, in determining whether a particular person has possession, the principles of agency apply. For example, if the collateral is in possession of an agent of the secured party for the purposes of possessing on behalf of the secured party, and if the agent is not also an agent of the debtor, the secured party has taken actual possession, and subsection (c) does not apply. Sometimes a person holds collateral both as an agent of the secured party and as an agent of the debtor. The fact of dual agency is not of itself inconsistent with the secured party's having taken possession (and thereby having rendered subsection (c) inapplicable). The debtor cannot qualify as an agent for the secured party for purposes of the secured party's taking possession. And, under appropriate circumstances, a court may determine that a person in possession is so closely connected to or controlled by the debtor that the debtor has retained effective possession, even though the person may have agreed to take possession on behalf of the secured party. If so, the person's taking possession would not constitute the secured party's taking possession and would not be sufficient for perfection. See also Section 9–205(b). In a

typical escrow arrangement, where the escrowee has possession of collateral as agent for both the secured party and the debtor, the debtor's relationship to the escrowee is not such as to constitute retention of possession by the debtor.

4. **Goods in Possession of Third Party: Perfection.** Former Section 9–305 permitted perfection of a security interest by notification to a bailee in possession of collateral. This Article distinguishes between goods in the possession of a bailee who has issued a document of title covering the goods and goods in the possession of a third party who has not issued a document. Section 9–312(c) or (d) applies to the former, depending on whether the document is negotiable. Section 9–313(c) applies to the latter. It provides a method of perfection by possession when the collateral is possessed by a third person who is not the secured party's agent.

Notification of a third person does not suffice to perfect under Section 9–313(c). Rather, perfection does not occur unless the third person authenticates an acknowledgment that it holds possession of the collateral for the secured party's benefit. Compare Section 9–312(d), under which receipt of notification of the security party's interest by a bailee holding goods covered by a nonnegotiable document is sufficient to perfect, even if the bailee does not acknowledge receipt of the notification. A third person may acknowledge that it will hold for the secured party's benefit goods to be received in the future. Under these circumstances, perfection by possession occurs when the third person obtains possession of the goods.

Under subsection (c), acknowledgment of notification by a "lessee . . . in . . . ordinary course of . . . business" (defined in Section 2A–103) does not suffice for possession. The section thus rejects the reasoning of *In re Atlantic Systems, Inc.*, 135 B.R. 463 (Bankr. S.D.N.Y.1992) (holding that notification to debtor-lessor's lessee sufficed to perfect security interest in leased goods). See Steven O. Weise, *Perfection by Possession: The Need for an Objective Test*, 29 Idaho Law Rev. 705 (1992–93) (arguing that lessee's possession in ordinary course of debtor-lessor's business does not provide adequate public notice of possible security interest in leased goods). Inclusion of a per se rule concerning lessees is not meant to preclude a court, under appropriate circumstances, from determining that a third person is so closely connected to or controlled by the debtor that the debtor has retained effective possession. If so, the third person's acknowledgment would not be sufficient for perfection.

In some cases, it may be uncertain whether a person who has possession of collateral is an agent of the secured party or a non-agent bailee. Under those circumstances, prudence might suggest that the secured party obtain the person's acknowledgment to avoid litigation and ensure perfection by possession regardless of how the relationship between the secured party and the person is characterized.

5. **No Relation Back.** Former Section 9–305 provided that a security interest is perfected by possession from the time possession is taken "without a relation back." As the Comment to former Section 9–305 observed, the relation-back theory, under which the taking of possession was deemed to relate back to the date of the original security agreement, has had little vitality since the 1938 revision of the Federal Bankruptcy Act. The theory is inconsistent with former Article 9 and with this Article. See Section 9–313(d). Accordingly, this Article deletes the quoted phrase as unnecessary. Where a pledge transaction is contemplated, perfection dates only from the time possession is taken, although a security interest may attach, unperfected. The only exceptions to this rule are the short, 20–day periods of perfection provided in Section 9–312(e), (f), and (g), during which a debtor may have possession of specified collateral in which there is a perfected security interest.

6. **Certificated Securities.** The second sentence of subsection (a) reflects the traditional rule for perfection of a security interest in certificated securities. Compare Section 9–115(6) (1994 Official Text); Sections 8–321, 8–313(1)(a) (1978 Official Text); Section 9–305 (1972 Official Text). It has been modified to refer to "delivery" under Section 8–301. Corresponding changes appear in Section 9–203(b).

Subsection (e), which is new, applies to a secured party in possession of security certificates or another person who has taken delivery of security certificates and holds them for the secured party's benefit under Section 8–301. See Comment 8.

Under subsection (e), a possessory security interest in a certificated security remains perfected until the debtor obtains possession of the security certificate. This rule is analogous to that of Section 9–314(c), which deals with perfection of security interests in investment property by control. See Section 9–314, Comment 3.

7. **Goods Covered by Certificate of Title.** Subsection (b) is necessary to effect changes to the choice-of-law rules governing goods covered by a certificate of title. These changes are described in the Comments to Section 9–311. Subsection (b), like subsection (a), does not create a right to take possession. Rather, it indicates the circumstances under which the secured party's taking possession of goods covered by a certificate of title is effective to perfect a security interest in the goods: the goods become covered by a certificate of title issued by this State at a time when the security interest is perfected by any method under the law of another jurisdiction.

8. **Goods in Possession of Third Party: No Duty to Acknowledge; Consequences of Acknowledgment.** Subsections (f) and (g) are new and address matters as to which former Article 9 was silent. They derive in part from Section 8–106(g). Subsection (f) provides that a person in possession of collateral is not required to acknowledge that it holds for a secured party. Subsection (g)(1) provides that an acknowledgment is effective even if wrongful as to the debtor. Subsection (g)(2) makes clear that an acknowledgment does not give rise to any duties or responsibilities under this Article. Arrangements involving the possession of goods are hardly standardized. They include bailments for services to be performed on the goods (such as repair or processing), for use (leases), as security (pledges), for carriage, and for storage. This Article leaves to the agreement of the parties and to any other applicable law the imposition of duties and responsibilities upon a person who acknowledges under subsection (c). For example, by acknowledging, a third party does not become obliged to act on the secured party's direction or to remain in possession of the collateral unless it agrees to do so or other law so provides.

9. **Delivery to Third Party by Secured Party.** New subsections (h) and (i) address the practice of mortgage warehouse lenders. These lenders typically send mortgage

notes to prospective purchasers under cover of letters advising the prospective purchasers that the lenders hold security interests in the notes. These lenders relied on notification to maintain perfection under former 9–305. Requiring them to obtain authenticated acknowledgments from each prospective purchaser under subsection (c) could be unduly burdensome and disruptive of established practices. Under subsection (h), when a secured party in possession itself delivers the collateral to a third party, instructions to the third party would be sufficient to maintain perfection by possession; an acknowledgment would not be necessary. Under subsection (i), the secured party does not relinquish possession by making a delivery under subsection (h), even if the delivery violates the rights of the debtor. That subsection also makes clear that a person to whom collateral is delivered under subsection (h) does not owe any duty to the secured party and is not required to confirm the delivery to another person unless the person otherwise agrees or law other than this Article provides otherwise.

Sections 31 and 32 of Acts 2005, 79th Leg., ch. 122 provide:

"Sec. 31. This Act applies to a document of title that is issued or a bailment that arises on or after the effective date of this Act. This Act does not apply to a document of title that is issued or a bailment that arises before the effective date of this Act even if the document of title or bailment would be subject to this Act if the document of title had been issued or bailment had arisen after the effective date of this Act. This Act does not apply to a right of action that has accrued before the effective date of this Act.

"Sec. 32. A document of title issued or a bailment that arises before the effective date of this Act and the rights, obligations, and interests flowing from that document or bailment are governed by any statute or other rule amended or repealed by this Act as if amendment or repeal had not occurred and may be terminated, completed, consummated, or enforced under that statute or other rule."

§ 9.314. Perfection by Control

(a) A security interest in investment property, deposit accounts, letter-of-credit rights, electronic chattel paper, or electronic documents may be perfected by control of the collateral under Section 7.106, 9.104, 9.105, 9.106, or 9.107.

(b) A security interest in deposit accounts, electronic chattel paper, letter-of-credit rights, or electronic documents is perfected by control under Section 7.106, 9.104, 9.105, or 9.107 when the secured party obtains control and remains perfected by control only while the secured party retains control.

(c) A security interest in investment property is perfected by control under Section 9.106 from the time the secured party obtains control and remains perfected by control until:

(1) the secured party does not have control; and

(2) one of the following occurs:

(A) if the collateral is a certificated security, the debtor has or acquires possession of the security certificate;

(B) if the collateral is an uncertificated security, the issuer has registered or registers the debtor as the registered owner; or

(C) if the collateral is a security entitlement, the debtor is or becomes the entitlement holder.

Amended by Acts 1999, 76th Leg., ch. 414, § 1.01, eff. July 1, 2001; Acts 2005, 79th Leg., ch. 122, § 27, eff. Sept. 1, 2005.

Uniform Commercial Code Comment

1. **Source.** Substantially new; derived in part from former Section 9–115(4).

2. **Control.** This section provides for perfection by control with respect to investment property, deposit accounts, letter-of-credit rights, electronic chattel paper, and electronic documents. For explanations of how a secured party takes control of these types of collateral, see Sections 9–104 through 9–107 and Section 7–106. Subsection (b) explains when a security interest is perfected by control and how long a security interest remains perfected by control. Like Section 9–313(d) and for the same reasons, subsection (b) makes no reference to the doctrine of "relation back." See Section 9–313, Comment 5. As to an electronic document that is reissued in a tangible medium, Section 7–105, a secured party that is perfected by control in the electronic document should file as to the document before relinquishing control in order to maintain continuous perfection in the document. See Section 9–308.

3. **Investment Property.** Subsection (c) provides a special rule for investment property. Once a secured party has control, its security interest remains perfected by control until the secured party ceases to have control and the debtor receives possession of collateral that is a certificated security, becomes the registered owner of collateral that is an uncertificated security, or becomes the entitlement holder of collateral that is a security entitlement. The result is particularly important in the "repledge" context. See Section 9–207, Comment 5.

In a transaction in which a secured party who has control grants a security interest in investment property or sells outright the investment property, by virtue of the debtor's consent or applicable legal rules, a purchaser from the secured party typically will cut off the debtor's rights in the investment property or be immune from the debtor's claims. See Section 9–207, Comments 5 and 6. If the investment property is a security, the debtor normally would retain no interest in the security following the purchase from the secured party, and a claim of the debtor against the secured party for redemption (Section 9–623) or otherwise with respect to the security would be a purely personal claim. If the investment property transferred by the secured party is a financial asset in which the debtor had a security entitlement credited to a securities account maintained with the secured party as a securities intermediary, the debtor's claim against the secured party could arise as a part of its securities account notwithstanding its personal nature. (This claim would be analogous to a "credit balance" in the securities account, which is a component of the securities account even though it is a personal claim against the intermediary.) In the case in which the debtor may retain an interest in investment property notwithstanding a repledge or sale by the secured party, subsection (c) makes clear that the security interest will remain perfected by control.

Sections 31 and 32 of Acts 2005, 79th Leg., ch. 122 provide:

"Sec. 31. This Act applies to a document of title that is issued or a bailment that arises on or after the effective date of this Act. This Act does not apply to a document of title that is issued or a bailment that arises before the effective date of this Act even if the document of title or bailment would be subject to this Act if the document of title had been issued or bailment had arisen after the effective date of this Act. This Act does not apply to a right of action that has accrued before the effective date of this Act.

"Sec. 32. A document of title issued or a bailment that arises before the effective date of this Act and the rights, obligations, and interests flowing from that document or bailment are governed by any statute or other rule amended or repealed by this Act as if amendment or repeal had not occurred and may be terminated, completed, consummated, or enforced under that statute or other rule."

§ 9.315. Secured Party's Rights on Disposition of Collateral and in Proceeds

(a) Except as otherwise provided in this chapter and Section 2.403(b):

(1) a security interest or agricultural lien continues in collateral notwithstanding sale, lease, license, exchange, or other disposition thereof unless the secured party authorized the disposition free of the security interest or agricultural lien; and

(2) a security interest attaches to any identifiable proceeds of collateral.

(b) Proceeds that are commingled with other property are identifiable proceeds:

(1) if the proceeds are goods, to the extent provided by Section 9.336; and

(2) if the proceeds are not goods, to the extent that the secured party identifies the proceeds by a method of tracing, including application of equitable principles, that is permitted under law other than this chapter with respect to commingled property of the type involved.

(c) A security interest in proceeds is a perfected security interest if the interest in the original collateral was perfected.

(d) A perfected security interest in proceeds becomes unperfected on the 21st day after the security interest attaches to receipt of the proceeds unless:

(1) the following conditions are satisfied:

(A) a filed financing statement covers the original collateral;

(B) the proceeds are collateral in which a security interest may be perfected by filing in the office in which the financing statement has been filed; and

(C) the proceeds are not acquired with cash proceeds;

(2) the proceeds are identifiable cash proceeds; or

(3) the security interest in the proceeds is perfected other than under Subsection (c) when the security interest attaches to the proceeds or within 20 days thereafter.

(e) If a filed financing statement covers the original collateral, a security interest in proceeds that remains perfected under Subsection (d)(1) becomes unperfected at the later of:

(1) when the effectiveness of the filed financing statement lapses under Section 9.515 or is terminated under Section 9.513; or

(2) the 21st day after the security interest attaches to the proceeds.

Amended by Acts 1999, 76th Leg., ch. 414, § 1.01, eff. July 1, 2001.

Uniform Commercial Code Comment

1. **Source.** Former Section 9–306.

2. **Continuation of Security Interest or Agricultural Lien Following Disposition of Collateral.** Subsection (a)(1), which derives from former Section 9–306(2), contains the general rule that a security interest survives disposition of the collateral. In these cases, the secured party may repossess the collateral from the transferee or, in an appropriate case, maintain an action for conversion. The secured party may claim both any proceeds and the original collateral but, of course, may have only one satisfaction.

In many cases, a purchaser or other transferee of collateral will take free of a security interest, and the secured party's only right will be to proceeds. For example, the general rule does not apply, and a security interest does not continue in collateral, if the secured party authorized the disposition, in the agreement that contains the security agreement or otherwise. Subsection (a)(1) adopts the view of PEB Commentary No. 3 and makes explicit that the authorized disposition to which it refers is an authorized disposition "free of" the security interest or agricultural lien. The secured party's right to proceeds under this section or under the express terms of an agreement does not in itself constitute an authorization of disposition. The change in language from former Section 9–306(2) is not intended to address the frequently litigated situation in which the effectiveness of the secured party's consent to a disposition is conditioned upon the secured party's receipt of the proceeds. In that situation, subsection (a) leaves the determination of authorization to the courts, as under former Article 9.

This Article contains several provisions under which a transferee takes free of a security interest or agricultural lien. For example, Section 9–317 states when transferees take free of unperfected security interests; Sections 9–320 and 9–321 on goods, 9–321 on general intangibles, 9–330 on chattel paper and instruments, and 9–331 on negotiable instruments, negotiable documents, and securities state when purchasers of such collateral take free of a security interest, even though perfected and even though the disposition was not authorized. Section 9–332 enables most transferees (including non-purchasers) of funds from a deposit account and most transferees of money to take free of a perfected security interest in the deposit account or money.

Likewise, the general rule that a security interest survives disposition does not apply if the secured party entrusts goods collateral to a merchant who deals in goods of that kind and the merchant sells the collateral to a buyer in ordinary course of business. Section 2–403(2) gives the merchant the power to transfer all the secured party's rights to the buyer, even if the sale is wrongful as against the secured party. Thus, under subsection (a)(1), an entrusting secured party runs the same risk as any other entruster.

3. **Secured Party's Right to Identifiable Proceeds.** Under subsection (a)(2), which derives from former Section 9–306(2), a security interest attaches to any identifiable "proceeds," as defined in Section 9–102. See also Section 9–203(f). Subsection (b) is new. It indicates when proceeds commingled with other property are identifiable proceeds and permits the use of whatever methods of tracing other law permits with respect to the type of property involved. Among the "equitable principles" whose use other law may permit is the "lowest intermediate balance rule." See Restatement (2d), Trusts § 202.

4. **Automatic Perfection in Proceeds: General Rule.** Under subsection (c), a security interest in proceeds is a perfected security interest if the security interest in the original collateral was perfected. This Article extends the period of automatic perfection in proceeds from 10 days to 20 days. Generally, a security interest in proceeds becomes unperfected on the 21st day after the security interest attaches to the proceeds. See subsection (d). The loss of perfected status under subsection (d) is prospective only. Compare, e.g., Section 9–515(c) (deeming security interest unperfected retroactively).

5. **Automatic Perfection in Proceeds: Proceeds Acquired with Cash Proceeds.** Subsection (d)(1) derives from former Section 9–306(3)(a). It carries forward the basic rule that a security interest in proceeds remains perfected beyond the period of automatic perfection if a filed financing statement covers the original collateral (e.g., inventory) and the proceeds are collateral in which a security interest may be perfected by filing in the office where the financing statement has been filed (e.g., equipment). A different rule applies if the proceeds are acquired with cash proceeds, as is the case if the original collateral (inventory) is sold for cash (cash proceeds) that is used to purchase equipment (proceeds). Under these circumstances, the security interest in the equipment proceeds remains perfected only if the description in the filed financing indicates the type of property constituting the proceeds (e.g., "equipment").

This section reaches the same result but takes a different approach. It recognizes that the treatment of proceeds acquired with cash proceeds under former Section 9–306(3)(a) essentially was superfluous. In the example, had the filing covered "equipment" as well as "inventory," the security interest in the proceeds would have been perfected under the usual rules governing after-acquired equipment (see former Sections 9–302, 9–303); paragraph (3)(a) added only an exception to the general rule. Subsection (d)(1)(C) of this section takes a more direct approach. It makes the general rule of continued perfection inapplicable to proceeds acquired with cash proceeds, leaving perfection of a security interest in those proceeds to the generally applicable perfection rules under subsection (d)(3).

Example 1: Lender perfects a security interest in Debtor's inventory by filing a financing statement covering "inventory." Debtor sells the inventory and deposits the buyer's check into a deposit account. Debtor draws a check on the deposit account and uses it to pay for equipment. Under the "lowest intermediate balance rule," which is a permitted method of tracing in the relevant jurisdiction, see Comment 3, the funds used to pay for the equipment were identifiable proceeds of the inventory. Because the proceeds (equipment) were acquired with cash proceeds (deposit account), subsection (d)(1) does not extend perfection beyond the 20–day automatic period.

Example 2: Lender perfects a security interest in Debtor's inventory by filing a financing statement covering "all debtor's property." As in Example 1, Debtor sells the inventory, deposits the buyer's check into a deposit account, draws a check on the deposit account, and uses the check to pay for equipment. Under the "lowest intermediate balance rule," which is a permitted method of tracing in the relevant jurisdiction, see Comment 3, the funds used to pay for the equipment were identifiable proceeds of the inventory. Because the proceeds (equipment) were acquired with cash proceeds (deposit account), subsection (d)(1) does not extend perfection beyond the 20–day automatic period. However, because the financing statement is sufficient to perfect a security interest in debtor's equipment, under subsection (d)(3) the security interest in the equipment proceeds remains perfected beyond the 20–day period.

6. **Automatic Perfection in Proceeds: Lapse or Termination of Financing Statement During 20–Day Period; Perfection Under Other Statute or Treaty.** Subsection (e) provides that a security interest in proceeds perfected under subsection (d)(1) ceases to be perfected when the financing statement covering the original collateral lapses or is terminated. If the lapse or termination occurs before the 21st day after the security interest attaches, however, the security interest in the proceeds remains perfected until the 21st day. Section 9–311(b) provides that compliance with the perfection requirements of a statute or treaty described in Section 9–311(a) "is equivalent to the filing of a financing statement." It follows that collateral subject to a security interest perfected by such compliance under Section 9–311(b) is covered by a "filed financing statement" within the meaning of Section 9–315(d) and (e).

7. **Automatic Perfection in Proceeds: Continuation of Perfection in Cash Proceeds.** Former Section 9–306(3)(b) provided that if a filed financing statement covered original collateral, a security interest in identifiable cash proceeds of the collateral remained perfected beyond the ten-day period of automatic perfection. Former Section 9–306(3)(c) contained a similar rule with respect to identifiable cash proceeds of investment property. Subsection (d)(2) extends the benefits of former Sections 9–306(3)(b) and (3)(c) to identifi-

able cash proceeds of all types of original collateral in which a security interest is perfected by any method. Under subsection (d)(2), if the security interest in the original collateral was perfected, a security interest in identifiable cash proceeds will remain perfected indefinitely, regardless of whether the security interest in the original collateral remains perfected. In many cases, however, a purchaser or other transferee of the cash proceeds will take free of the perfected security interest. See, e.g., Sections 9–330(d) (purchaser of check), 9–331 (holder in due course of check), 9–332 (transferee of money or funds from a deposit account).

8. **Insolvency Proceedings; Returned and Repossessed Goods.** This Article deletes former Section 9–306(4), which dealt with proceeds in insolvency proceedings. Except as otherwise provided by the Bankruptcy Code, the debtor's entering into bankruptcy does not affect a secured party's right to proceeds.

This Article also deletes former Section 9–306(5), which dealt with returned and repossessed goods. Section 9–330, Comments 9 to 11 explain and clarify the application of priority rules to returned and repossessed goods as proceeds of chattel paper.

9. **Proceeds of Collateral Subject to Agricultural Lien.** This Article does not determine whether a lien extends to proceeds of farm products encumbered by an agricultural lien. If, however, the proceeds are themselves farm products on which an "agricultural lien" (defined in Section 9–102) arises under other law, then the agricultural-lien provisions of this Article apply to the agricultural lien on the proceeds in the same way in which they would apply had the farm products not been proceeds.

§ 9.316. Continued Perfection of Security Interest Following Change in Governing Law

(a) A security interest perfected pursuant to the law of the jurisdiction designated in Section 9.301(1) or 9.305(c) remains perfected until the earliest of:

(1) the time perfection would have ceased under the law of that jurisdiction;

(2) the expiration of four months after a change of the debtor's location to another jurisdiction; or

(3) the expiration of one year after a transfer of collateral to a person that thereby becomes a debtor and is located in another jurisdiction.

(b) If a security interest described in Subsection (a) becomes perfected under the law of the other jurisdiction before the earliest time or event described in that subsection, it remains perfected thereafter. If the security interest does not become perfected under the law of the other jurisdiction before the earliest time or event, it becomes unperfected and is deemed never to have been perfected as against a purchaser of the collateral for value.

(c) A possessory security interest in collateral, other than goods covered by a certificate of title and as-extracted collateral consisting of goods, remains continuously perfected if:

(1) the collateral is located in one jurisdiction and subject to a security interest perfected under the law of that jurisdiction;

(2) thereafter the collateral is brought into another jurisdiction; and

(3) upon entry into the other jurisdiction, the security interest is perfected under the law of the other jurisdiction.

(d) Except as otherwise provided in Subsection (e), a security interest in goods covered by a certificate of title that is perfected by any method under the law of another jurisdiction when the goods become covered by a certificate of title from this state remains perfected until the security interest would have become unperfected under the law of the other jurisdiction had the goods not become so covered.

(e) A security interest described in Subsection (d) becomes unperfected as against a purchaser of the goods for value and is deemed never to have been perfected as against a purchaser of the goods for value if the applicable requirements for perfection under Section 9.311(b) or 9.313 are not satisfied before the earlier of:

(1) the time the security interest would have become unperfected under the law of the other jurisdiction had the goods not become covered by a certificate of title from this State; or

(2) the expiration of four months after the goods had become so covered.

(f) A security interest in deposit accounts, letter-of-credit rights, or investment property that is perfected under the law of the bank's jurisdiction, the issuer's jurisdiction, a nominated person's jurisdiction, the securities intermediary's jurisdiction, or the commodity intermediary's jurisdiction, as applicable, remains perfected until the earlier of:

(1) the time the security interest would have become unperfected under the law of that jurisdiction; or

(2) the expiration of four months after a change of the applicable jurisdiction to another jurisdiction.

(g) If a security interest described in Subsection (f) becomes perfected under the law of the other jurisdiction before the earlier of the time or the end of the period described in that subsection, it remains perfected thereafter. If the security interest does not become perfected under the law of the other jurisdiction before the earlier of that time or the end of that period, it becomes unperfected and is deemed never to have been perfected as against a purchaser of the collateral for value.

Amended by Acts 1999, 76th Leg., ch. 414, § 1.01, eff. July 1, 2001.

Uniform Commercial Code Comment

1. **Source.** Former Section 9–103(1)(d), (2)(b), (3)(e), as modified.

2. **Continued Perfection.** This section deals with continued perfection of security interests that have been perfected under the law of another jurisdiction. The fact that the law of a particular jurisdiction ceases to govern perfection under Sections 9–301 through 9–307 does not necessarily mean that a security interest perfected under that law automatically becomes unperfected. To the contrary: This section generally provides that a security interest perfected under the law of one jurisdiction remains perfected for a fixed period of time (four months or one year, depending on the circumstances), even though the jurisdiction whose law governs perfection changes. However, cessation of perfection under the law of the original jurisdiction cuts short the fixed period. The four-month and one-year periods are long enough for a secured party to discover in most cases that the law of a different jurisdiction governs perfection and to reperfect (typically by filing) under the law of that jurisdiction. If a secured party properly reperfects a security interest before it becomes unperfected under subsection (a), then the security interest remains perfected continuously thereafter. See subsection (b).

Example 1: Debtor is a general partnership whose chief executive office is in Pennsylvania. Lender perfects a security interest in Debtor's equipment by filing in Pennsylvania on May 15, 2002. On April 1, 2005, without Lender's knowledge, Debtor moves its chief executive office to New Jersey. Lender's security interest remains perfected for four months after the move. See subsection (a)(2).

Example 2: Debtor is a general partnership whose chief executive office is in Pennsylvania. Lender perfects a security interest in Debtor's equipment by filing in Pennsylvania on May 15, 2002. On April 1, 2007, without Lender's knowledge, Debtor moves its chief executive office to New Jersey. Lender's security interest remains perfected only through May 14, 2007, when the effectiveness of the filed financing statement lapses. See subsection (a)(1). Although, under these facts, Lender would have only a short period of time to discover that Debtor had relocated and to reperfect under New Jersey law, Lender could have protected itself by filing a continuation statement in Pennsylvania before Debtor relocated. By doing so, Lender would have prevented lapse and allowed itself the full four months to discover Debtor's new location and refile there or, if Debtor is in default, to perfect by taking possession of the equipment.

Example 3: Under the facts of Example 2, Lender files a financing statement in New Jersey before the effectiveness of the Pennsylvania financing statement lapses. Under subsection (b), Lender's security interest is continuously perfected beyond May 14, 2007, for a period determined by New Jersey's Article 9.

Subsection (a)(3) allows a one-year period in which to reperfect. The longer period is necessary, because, even with the exercise of due diligence, the secured party may be unable to discover that the collateral has been transferred to a person located in another jurisdiction.

Example 4: Debtor is a Pennsylvania corporation. Lender perfects a security interest in Debtor's equipment by filing in Pennsylvania. Debtor's shareholders decide to "reincorporate" in Delaware. They form a Delaware corporation (Newcorp) into which they merge Debtor. The merger effectuates a transfer of the collateral from Debtor to Newcorp, which thereby becomes a debtor and is located in another jurisdiction. Under subsection (a)(3), the security interest remains perfected for one year after the merger. If a financing statement is filed in Delaware against Newcorp within the year following the merger, then the security interest remains perfected thereafter for a period determined by Delaware's Article 9.

Note that although Newcorp is a "new debtor" as defined in Section 9–102, the application of subsection (a)(3) is not limited to transferees who are new debtors. Note also that, under Section 9–507, the financing statement naming Debtor remains effective even though Newcorp has become the debtor.

This section addresses security interests that are perfected (i.e., that have attached and as to which any required perfection step has been taken) before the debtor changes its location. As the following example explains, this section does not apply to security interests that have not attached before the location changes.

Example 5: Debtor is a Pennsylvania corporation. Debtor grants to Lender a security interest in Debtor's existing and after-acquired inventory. Lender perfects by filing in Pennsylvania. Debtor's shareholders decide to "reincorporate" in Delaware. They form a Delaware corporation (Newcorp) into which they merge Debtor. By virtue of the merger, Newcorp becomes bound by Debtor's security agreement. See Section 9–203. After the merger, Newcorp acquires inventory to which Lender's security interest attaches. Because Newcorp is located in Delaware, Delaware law governs perfection of a security interest in Newcorp's inventory. See Sections 9–301, 9–307. Having failed to perfect under Delaware law, Lender holds an unperfected security interest in the inventory acquired by Newcorp after the merger. The same result follows regardless of the name of the Delaware corporation (i.e., even if the Delaware corporation and Debtor have the same name). A different result would occur if Debtor and Newcorp were incorporated in the same state. See Section 9–508, Comment 4.

3. **Retroactive Unperfection.** Subsection (b) sets forth the consequences of the failure to reperfect before perfection ceases under subsection (a): the security interest becomes unperfected prospectively and, as against purchasers for value, including buyers and secured parties, but not as against donees or lien creditors, retroactively. The rule applies to agricultural liens, as well. See also Section 9–515 (taking the same approach with respect to lapse). Although this approach creates the potential for circular priorities, the

alternative–retroactive unperfection against lien creditors–would create substantial and unjustifiable preference risks.

Example 6: Under the facts of Example 4, six months after the merger, Buyer bought from Newcorp some equipment formerly owned by Debtor. At the time of the purchase, Buyer took subject to Lender's perfected security interest, of which Buyer was unaware. See Section 9–315(a)(1). However, subsection (b) provides that if Lender fails to reperfect in Delaware within a year after the merger, its security interest becomes unperfected and is deemed never to have been perfected against Buyer. Having given value and received delivery of the equipment without knowledge of the security interest and before it was perfected, Buyer would take free of the security interest. See Section 9–317(b).

Example 7: Under the facts of Example 4, one month before the merger, Debtor created a security interest in certain equipment in favor of Financer, who perfected by filing in Pennsylvania. At that time, Financer's security interest is subordinate to Lender's. See Section 9–322(a)(1). Financer reperfects by filing in Delaware within a year after the merger, but Lender fails to do so. Under subsection (b), Lender's security interest is deemed never to have been perfected against Financer, a purchaser for value. Consequently, under Section 9–322(a)(2), Financer's security interest is now senior.

Of course, the expiration of the time period specified in subsection (a) does not of itself prevent the secured party from later reperfecting under the law of the new jurisdiction. If the secured party does so, however, there will be a gap in perfection, and the secured party may lose priority as a result. Thus, in Example 7, if Lender perfects by filing in Delaware more than one year under the merger, it will have a new date of filing and perfection for purposes of Section 9–322(a)(1). Financer's security interest, whose perfection dates back to the filing in Pennsylvania under subsection (b), will remain senior.

4. **Possessory Security Interests.** Subsection (c) deals with continued perfection of possessory security interests. It applies not only to security interests perfected solely by the secured party's having taken possession of the collateral. It also applies to security interests perfected by a method that includes as an element of perfection the secured party's having taken possession, such as perfection by taking delivery of a certificated security in registered form, see Section 9–313(a), and perfection by obtaining control over a certificated security. See Section 9–314(a).

5. **Goods Covered by Certificate of Title.** Subsections (d) and (e) address continued perfection of a security interest in goods covered by a certificate of title. The following examples explain the operation of those subsections.

Example 8: Debtor's automobile is covered by a certificate of title issued by Illinois. Lender perfects a security interest in the automobile by complying with Illinois' certificate-of-title statute. Thereafter, Debtor applies for a certificate of title in Indiana. Six months thereafter, Creditor acquires a judicial lien on the automobile. Under Section 9–303(b), Illinois law ceases to govern perfection; rather, once Debtor delivers the application and applicable fee to the appropriate Indiana authority, Indiana law governs. Nevertheless, under Indiana's Section 9–316(d), Lender's security interest remains perfected until it would become unperfected under Illinois law had no certificate of title been issued by Indiana. (For example, Illinois' certificate-of-title statute may provide that the surrender of an Illinois certificate of title in connection with the issuance of a certificate of title by another jurisdiction causes a security interest noted thereon to become unperfected.) If Lender's security interest remains perfected, it is senior to Creditor's judicial lien.

Example 9: Under the facts in Example 8, five months after Debtor applies for an Indiana certificate of title, Debtor sells the automobile to Buyer. Under subsection (e)(2), because Lender did not reperfect within the four months after the goods became covered by the Indiana certificate of title, Lender's security interest is deemed never to have been perfected against Buyer. Under Section 9–317(b), Buyer is likely to take free of the security interest. Lender could have protected itself by perfecting its security interest either under Indiana's certificate-of-title statute, see Section 9–311, or, if it had a right to do so under an agreement or Section 9–609, by taking possession of the automobile. See Section 9–313(b).

The results in Examples 8 and 9 do not depend on the fact that the original perfection was achieved by notation on a certificate of title. Subsection (d) applies regardless of the method by which a security interest is perfected under the law of another jurisdiction when the goods became covered by a certificate of title from this State.

Section 9–337 affords protection to a limited class of persons buying or acquiring a security interest in the goods while a security interest is perfected under the law of another jurisdiction but after this State has issued a clean certificate of title.

6. **Deposit Accounts, Letter-of-Credit Rights, and Investment Property.** Subsections (f) and (g) address changes in the jurisdiction of a bank, issuer of an uncertificated security, issuer of or nominated person under a letter of credit, securities intermediary, and commodity intermediary. The provisions are analogous to those of subsections (a) and (b).

7. **Agricultural Liens.** This section does not apply to agricultural liens.

Example 10: Supplier holds an agricultural lien on corn. The lien arises under an Iowa statute. Supplier perfects by filing a financing statement in Iowa, where the corn is located. See Section 9–302. Debtor stores the corn in Missouri. Assume the Iowa agricultural lien survives or an agricultural lien arises under Missouri law (matters that this Article does not govern). Once the corn is located in Missouri, Missouri becomes the jurisdiction whose law governs perfection. See Section 9–302. Thus, the agricultural lien will not be perfected unless Supplier files a financing statement in Missouri.

§ 9.317. Interests That Take Priority Over or Take Free of Security Interest or Agricultural Lien

(a) A security interest or agricultural lien is subordinate to the rights of:

(1) a person entitled to priority under Section 9.322; and

(2) except as otherwise provided in Subsection (e), a person that becomes a lien creditor before the earlier of the time:

(A) the security interest or agricultural lien is perfected; or

(B) one of the conditions specified in Section 9.203(b)(3) is met and a financing statement covering the collateral is filed.

(b) Except as otherwise provided in Subsection (e), a buyer, other than a secured party, of tangible chattel paper, tangible documents, goods, instruments, or a security certificate takes free of a security interest or agricultural lien if the buyer gives value and receives delivery of the collateral without knowledge of the security interest or agricultural lien and before it is perfected.

(c) Except as otherwise provided in Subsection (e), a lessee of goods takes free of a security interest or agricultural lien if the lessee gives value and receives delivery of the collateral without knowledge of the security interest or agricultural lien and before it is perfected.

(d) A licensee of a general intangible or a buyer, other than a secured party, of accounts, electronic chattel paper, electronic documents, general intangibles, or investment property other than a certificated security takes free of a security interest if the licensee or buyer gives value without knowledge of the security interest and before it is perfected.

(e) Except as otherwise provided in Sections 9.320 and 9.321, if a person files a financing statement with respect to a purchase-money security interest before or within 20 days after the debtor receives delivery of the collateral, the security interest takes priority over the rights of a buyer, lessee, or lien creditor that arise between the time the security interest attaches and the time of filing.

Amended by Acts 1999, 76th Leg., ch. 414, § 1.01, eff. July 1, 2001; Acts 2001, 77th Leg., ch. 705, § 6, eff. June 13, 2001; Acts 2005, 79th Leg., ch. 122, § 28, eff. Sept. 1, 2005.

Uniform Commercial Code Comment

1. **Source.** Former Sections 9–301, 2A–307(2).

2. **Scope of This Section.** As did former Section 9–301, this section lists the classes of persons who take priority over, or take free of, an unperfected security interest. Section 9–308 explains when a security interest or agricultural lien is "perfected." A security interest that has attached (see Section 9–203) but as to which a required perfection step has not been taken is "unperfected." Certain provisions have been moved from former Section 9–301. The definition of "lien creditor" now appears in Section 9–102, and the rules governing priority in future advances are found in Section 9–323.

3. **Competing Security Interests.** Section 9–322 states general rules for determining priority among conflicting security interests and refers to other sections that state special rules of priority in a variety of situations. The security interests given priority under Section 9–322 and the other sections to which it refers take priority in general even over a perfected security interest. *A fortiori* they take priority over an unperfected security interest. **Amendments in italics approved by the Permanent Editorial Board for Uniform Commercial Code October 20, 1999.*

4. **Filed but Unattached Security Interest vs. Lien Creditor.** Under former Section 9–301(1)(b), a lien creditor's rights had priority over an unperfected security interest. Perfection required attachment (former Section 9–303) and attachment required the giving of value (former Section 9–203). It followed that, if a secured party had filed a financing statement but the debtor had not entered into a security agreement and value had not yet been given, an intervening lien creditor whose lien arose after filing but before attachment of the security interest acquired rights that are senior to those of the secured party who later gives value. This result comported with the *nemo dat* concept: When the security interest attached, the collateral was already subject to the judicial lien.

On the other hand, this approach treated the first secured advance differently from all other advances, even in circumstances in which a security agreement covering the collateral had been entered into before the judicial lien attached. The special rule for future advances in former Section 9–301(4) (substantially reproduced in Section 9–323(b)) afforded priority to a discretionary advance made by a secured party within 45 days after the lien creditor's rights arose as long as the secured party was "perfected" when the lien creditor's lien arose–i.e., as long as the advance was not the first one and an earlier advance had been made.

Subsection (a)(2) revises former Section 9–301(1)(b) and, in appropriate cases, treats the first advance the same as subsequent advances. More specifically, a judicial lien that arises after the security-agreement condition of Section 9–203(b)(3) is satisfied and a financing statement is filed, but before the security interest attaches and becomes perfected is subordinate to all advances secured by the security interest, even the first advance, except as otherwise provided in Section 9–323(b). However, if the security interest becomes unperfected (e.g., because the effectiveness of the filed financing statement lapses) before the judicial lien arises, the security interest is subordinate. If a financing statement is filed but a security interest does not attach, then no priority contest arises. The lien creditor has the only enforceable claim to the property.

5. **Security Interest of Consignor or Receivables Buyer vs. Lien Creditor.** Section 1–201(37) defines "security interest" to include the interest of most true consignors of goods and the interest of most buyers of certain receivables (accounts, chattel paper, payment intangibles, and promissory

notes). A consignee of goods or a seller of accounts or chattel paper each is deemed to have rights in the collateral which a lien creditor may reach, as long as the competing security interest of the consignor or buyer is unperfected. This is so even though, as between the consignor and the debtor-consignee, the latter has only limited rights, and, as between the buyer and debtor-seller, the latter does not have any rights in the collateral. See Sections 9–318 (seller), 9–319 (consignee). Security interests arising from sales of payment intangibles and promissory notes are automatically perfected. See Section 9–309. Accordingly, a subsequent judicial lien always would be subordinate to the rights of a buyer of those types of receivables.

6. **Purchasers Other Than Secured Parties.** Subsections (b), (c), and (d) afford priority over an unperfected security interest to certain purchasers (other than secured parties) of collateral. They derive from former Sections 9–301(1)(c), 2A–307(2), and 9–301(d). Former Section 9–301(1)(c) and (1)(d) provided that unperfected security interests are "subordinate" to the rights of certain purchasers. But, as former Comment 9 suggested, the practical effect of subordination in this context is that the purchaser takes free of the security interest. To avoid any possible misinterpretation, subsections (b) and (d) of this section use the phrase "takes free."

Subsection (b) governs goods, as well as intangibles of the type whose transfer is effected by physical delivery of the representative piece of paper (tangible chattel paper, tangible documents, instruments, and security certificates). To obtain priority, a buyer must both give value and receive delivery of the collateral without knowledge of the existing security interest and before perfection. Even if the buyer gave value without knowledge and before perfection, the buyer would take subject to the security interest if perfection occurred before physical delivery of the collateral to the buyer. Subsection (c) contains a similar rule with respect to lessees of goods. Note that a lessee of goods in ordinary course of business takes free of all security interests created by the lessor, even if perfected. See Section 9–321.

Normally, there will be no question when a buyer of tangible chattel paper, tangible documents, instruments, or security certificates "receives delivery" of the property. See Section 1–201 (defining "delivery"). However, sometimes a buyer or lessee of goods, such as complex machinery, takes delivery of the goods in stages and completes assembly at its own location. Under those circumstances, the buyer or lessee "receives delivery" within the meaning of subsections (b) and (c) when, after an inspection of the portion of the goods remaining with the seller or lessor, it would be apparent to a potential lender to the seller or lessor that another person might have an interest in the goods.

The rule of subsection (b) obviously is not appropriate where the collateral consists of intangibles and there is no representative piece of paper whose physical delivery is the only or the customary method of transfer. Therefore, with respect to such intangibles (accounts, electronic chattel paper, electronic documents, general intangibles, and investment property other than certificated securities), subsection (d) gives priority to any buyer who gives value without knowledge, and before perfection, of the security interest. A licensee of a general intangible takes free of an unperfected security interest in the general intangible under the same circumstances. Note that a licensee of a general intangible in ordinary course of business takes rights under a nonexclusive license free of security interests created by the licensor, even if perfected. See Section 9–321.

Unless Section 9–109 excludes the transaction from this Article, a buyer of accounts, chattel paper, payment intangibles, or promissory notes is a "secured party" (defined in Section 9–102), and subsections (b) and (d) do not determine priority of the security interest created by the sale. Rather, the priority rules generally applicable to competing security interests apply. See Section 9–322.

7. **Agricultural Liens.** Subsections (a), (b), and (c) subordinate unperfected agricultural liens in the same manner in which they subordinate unperfected security interests.

8. **Purchase-Money Security Interests.** Subsection (e) derives from former Section 9–301(2). It provides that, if a purchase-money security interest is perfected by filing no later than 20 days after the debtor receives delivery of the collateral, the security interest takes priority over the rights of buyers, lessees, or lien creditors which arise between the time the security interest attaches and the time of filing. Subsection (e) differs from former Section 9–301(2) in two significant respects. First, subsection (e) protects a purchase-money security interest against all buyers and lessees, not just against transferees in bulk. Second, subsection (e) conditions this protection on filing within 20, as opposed to ten, days after delivery.

Section 9–311(b) provides that compliance with the perfection requirements of a statute or treaty described in Section 9–311(a) "is equivalent to the filing of a financing statement." It follows that a person who perfects a security interest in goods covered by a certificate of title by complying with the perfection requirements of an applicable certificate-of-title statute "files a financing statement" within the meaning of subsection(e).

State Bar Committee Comment

As noted in Official Comment 8, subsection (e) changes the grace period from ten days to twenty days. This change does not affect Texas law, as former section 9.301(b) already provided a twenty-day grace period.

§ 9.318. No Interest Retained in Right to Payment That is Sold; Rights and Title of Seller of Account or Chattel Paper With Respect to Creditors and Purchasers

(a) A debtor that has sold an account, chattel paper, payment intangible, or promissory note does not retain a legal or equitable interest in the collateral sold.

(b) For purposes of determining the rights of creditors of, and purchasers for value of an account or chattel paper from, a debtor that has sold an account or chattel paper, while the buyer's security interest is unperfected, the debtor is deemed to have rights and title to the account or chattel paper identical to those the debtor sold.

Amended by Acts 1999, 76th Leg., ch. 414, § 1.01, eff. July 1, 2001.

Uniform Commercial Code Comment

1. **Source.** New.

2. **Sellers of Accounts, Chattel Paper, Payment Intangibles, and Promissory Notes.** Section 1–201(37) defines "security interest" to include the interest of a buyer of accounts, chattel paper, payment intangibles, or promissory notes. See also Section 9–109(a) and Comment 5. Subsection (a) makes explicit what was implicit, but perfectly obvious, under former Article 9: The fact that a sale of an account or chattel paper gives rise to a "security interest" does not imply that the seller retains an interest in the property that has been sold. To the contrary, a seller of an account or chattel paper retains no interest whatsoever in the property to the extent that it has been sold. Subsection (a) also applies to sales of payment intangibles and promissory notes, transactions that were not covered by former Article 9. Neither this Article nor the definition of "security interest" in Section 1–201 provides rules for distinguishing sales transactions from those that create a security interest securing an obligation.

3. **Buyers of Accounts and Chattel Paper.** Another aspect of sales of accounts and chattel paper also was implicit, and equally obvious, under former Article 9: If the buyer's security interest is unperfected, then for purposes of determining the rights of certain third parties, the seller (debtor) is deemed to have all rights and title that the seller sold. The seller is deemed to have these rights even though, as between the parties, it has sold all its rights to the buyer. Subsection (b) makes this explicit. As a consequence of subsection (b), if the buyer's security interest is unperfected, the seller can transfer, and the creditors of the seller can reach, the account or chattel paper as if it had not been sold.

Example: Debtor sells accounts or chattel paper to Buyer–1 and retains no interest in them. Buyer–1 does not file a financing statement. Debtor then sells the same receivables to Buyer–2. Buyer–2 files a proper financing statement. Having sold the receivables to Buyer–1, Debtor would not have any rights in the collateral so as to permit Buyer–2's security (ownership) interest to attach. Nevertheless, under this section, for purposes of determining the rights of purchasers for value from Debtor, Debtor is deemed to have the rights that Debtor sold. Accordingly, Buyer–2's security interest attaches, is perfected by the filing, and, under Section 9–322, is senior to Buyer–1's interest.

4. **Effect of Perfection.** If the security interest of a buyer of accounts or chattel paper is perfected the usual result would take effect: transferees from and creditors of the seller could not acquire an interest in the sold accounts or chattel paper. The same result generally would occur if payment intangibles or promissory notes were sold, inasmuch as the buyer's security interest is automatically perfected under Section 9–309. However, in certain circumstances a purchaser who takes possession of a promissory note will achieve priority, under Sections 9–330 or 9–331, over the security interest of an earlier buyer of the promissory note. It necessarily follows that the seller in those circumstances retains the power to transfer the promissory note, as if it had not been sold, to a purchaser who obtains priority under either of those sections. See Section 9–203(b)(3), Comment 6.

§ 9.319. Rights and Title of Consignee With Respect to Creditors and Purchasers

(a) Except as otherwise provided in Subsection (b), for purposes of determining the rights of creditors of, and purchasers for value of goods from, a consignee, while the goods are in the possession of the consignee, the consignee is deemed to have rights and title to the goods identical to those the consignor had or had power to transfer.

(b) For purposes of determining the rights of a creditor of a consignee, law other than this chapter determines the rights and title of a consignee while goods are in the consignee's possession if, under this subchapter, a perfected security interest held by the consignor would have priority over the rights of the creditor.

Amended by Acts 1999, 76th Leg., ch. 414, § 1.01, eff. July 1, 2001.

Uniform Commercial Code Comment

1. **Source.** New.

2. **Consignments.** This section takes an approach to consignments similar to that taken by Section 9–318 with respect to buyers of accounts and chattel paper. Revised Section 1–201(37) defines "security interest" to include the interest of a consignor of goods under many true consignments. Section 9–319(a) provides that, for purposes of determining the rights of certain third parties, the consignee is deemed to acquire all rights and title that the consignor had, if the consignor's security interest is unperfected. The consignee acquires these rights even though, as between the parties, it purchases a limited interest in the goods (as would be the case in a true consignment, under which the consignee acquires only the interest of a bailee). As a consequence of this section, creditors of the consignee can acquire judicial liens and security interests in the goods.

Insofar as creditors of the consignee are concerned, this Article to a considerable extent reformulates the former law, which appeared in former Sections 2–326 and 9–114, without changing the results. However, neither Article 2 nor former Article 9 specifically addresses the rights of non-ordinary course buyers from the consignee. Former Section 9–114 contained priority rules applicable to security interests in consigned goods. Under this Article, the priority rules for purchase-money security interests in inventory apply to consignments. See Section 9–103(d). Accordingly, a special section containing priority rules for consignments no longer is needed. Section 9–317 determines whether the rights of a judicial lien creditor are senior to the interest of the consignor, Sections 9–322 and 9–324 govern competing security interests in consigned goods, and Sections 9–317, 9–315, and 9–320 determine whether a buyer takes free of the consignor's interest.

The following example explains the operation of this section:

Example 1: SP–1 delivers goods to Debtor in a transaction constituting a "consignment" as defined in Section 9–102. SP–1 does not file a financing statement. Debtor then grants a security interest in the goods to SP–2. SP–2 files a proper financing statement. Assuming Debtor is a mere bailee, as in a "true" consignment, Debtor would not have any rights in the collateral (beyond those of a bailee) so as to permit SP–2's security interest to attach to any greater rights. Nevertheless, under this section, for purposes of determining the rights of Debtor's creditors, Debtor is deemed to acquire SP–1's rights. Accordingly, SP–2's security interest attaches, is perfected by the filing, and, under Section 9–322, is senior to SP–1's interest.

3. **Effect of Perfection.** Subsection (b) contains a special rule with respect to consignments that are perfected. If application of this Article would result in the consignor having priority over a competing creditor, then other law determines the rights and title of the consignee.

Example 2: SP–1 delivers goods to Debtor in a transaction constituting a "consignment" as defined in Section 9–102. SP–1 files a proper financing statement. Debtor then grants a security interest in the goods to SP–2. Under Section 9–322, SP–1's security interest is senior to SP–2's. Subsection (b) indicates that, for purposes of determining SP–2's rights, other law determines the rights and title of the consignee. If, for example, a consignee obtains only the special property of a bailee, then SP–2's security interest would attach only to that special property.

Example 3: SP–1 obtains a security interest in all Debtor's existing and after-acquired inventory. SP–1 perfects its security interest with a proper filing. Then SP–2 delivers goods to Debtor in a transaction constituting a "consignment" as defined in Section 9–102. SP–2 files a proper financing statement but does not send notification to SP–1 under Section 9–324(b). Accordingly, SP–2's security interest is junior to SP–1's under Section 9–322(a). Under Section 9–319(a), Debtor is deemed to have the consignor's rights and title, so that SP–1's security interest attaches to SP–2's ownership interest in the goods. Thereafter, Debtor grants a security interest in the goods to SP–3, and SP–3 perfects by filing. Because SP–2's perfected security interest is senior to SP–3's under Section 9–322(a), Section 9–319(b) applies: Other law determines Debtor's rights and title to the goods insofar as SP–3 is concerned, and SP–3's security interest attaches to those rights.

§ 9.320. Buyers of Goods

(a) Except as otherwise provided by Subsection (e), a buyer in ordinary course of business, other than a person buying farm products from a person engaged in farming operations, takes free of a security interest created by the buyer's seller, even if the security interest is perfected and the buyer knows of its existence.

(b) Except as otherwise provided in Subsection (e), a buyer of goods from a person who used or bought the goods for use primarily for personal, family, or household purposes takes free of a security interest, even if perfected, if the buyer buys:

(1) without knowledge of the security interest;

(2) for value;

(3) primarily for the buyer's personal, family, or household purposes; and

(4) before the filing of a financing statement covering the goods.

(c) To the extent that it affects the priority of a security interest over a buyer of goods under Subsection (b), the period of effectiveness of a filing made in the jurisdiction in which the seller is located is governed by Sections 9.316(a) and (b).

(d) A buyer in ordinary course of business buying oil, gas, or other minerals at the wellhead or minehead or after extraction takes free of an interest arising out of an encumbrance.

(e) Subsections (a) and (b) do not affect a security interest in goods in the possession of the secured party under Section 9.313.

Added by Acts 1999, 76th Leg., ch. 414, § 1.01, eff. July 1, 2001.

Uniform Commercial Code Comment

1. **Source.** Former Section 9–307.

2. **Scope of This Section.** This section states when buyers of goods take free of a security interest even though perfected. Of course, a buyer who takes free of a perfected security interest takes free of an unperfected one. Section 9–317 should be consulted to determine what purchasers, in addition to the buyers covered in this section, take free of an unperfected security interest. Article 2 states general rules on purchase of goods from a seller with defective or voidable title (Section 2–403).

3. **Buyers in Ordinary Course.** Subsection (a) derives from former Section 9–307(1). The definition of "buyer in ordinary course of business" in Section 1–201 restricts its application to buyers "from a person, other than a pawnbroker, in the business of selling goods of that kind." Thus subsection (a) applies primarily to inventory collateral. The subsection further excludes from its operation buyers of "farm products"(defined in Section 9–102) from a person engaged in farming operations. The buyer in ordinary course of business is defined as one who buys goods "in good faith, without knowledge that the sale violates the rights of another person and in the ordinary course." Subsection (a) provides that such a buyer takes free of a security interest, even though perfected, and even though the buyer knows the security interest exists. Reading the definition together with the rule of law results in the buyer's taking free if the buyer merely knows that a security interest covers the goods but

taking subject if the buyer knows, in addition, that the sale violates a term in an agreement with the secured party.

As did former Section 9–307(1), subsection (a) applies only to security interests created by the seller of the goods to the buyer in ordinary course. However, under certain circumstances a buyer in ordinary course who buys goods that were encumbered with a security interest created by a person other than the seller may take free of the security interest, as Example 2 explains. See also Comment 6, below.

Example 1: Manufacturer, who is in the business of manufacturing appliances, owns manufacturing equipment subject to a perfected security interest in favor of Lender. Manufacturer sells the equipment to Dealer, who is in the business of buying and selling used equipment. Buyer buys the equipment from Dealer. Even if Buyer qualifies as a buyer in the ordinary course of business, Buyer does not take free of Lender's security interest under subsection (a), because Dealer did not create the security interest; Manufacturer did.

Example 2: Manufacturer, who is in the business of manufacturing appliances, owns manufacturing equipment subject to a perfected security interest in favor of Lender. Manufacturer sells the equipment to Dealer, who is in the business of buying and selling used equipment. Lender learns of the sale but does nothing to assert its security interest. Buyer buys the equipment from Dealer. Inasmuch as Lender's acquiescence constitutes an "entrusting" of the goods to Dealer within the meaning of Section 2–403(3) Buyer takes free of Lender's security interest under Section 2–403(2) if Buyer qualifies as a buyer in ordinary course of business.

4. **Buyers of Farm Products.** This section does not enable a buyer of farm products to take free of a security interest created by the seller, even if the buyer is a buyer in ordinary course of business. However, a buyer of farm products may take free of a security interest under Section 1324 of the Food Security Act of 1985, 7 U.S.C. § 1631.

5. **Buyers of Consumer Goods.** Subsection (b), which derives from former Section 9–307(2), deals with buyers of collateral that the debtor-seller holds as "consumer goods" (defined in Section 9–102). Under Section 9–309(1), a purchase-money interest in consumer goods, except goods that are subject to a statute or treaty described in Section 9–311(a) (such as automobiles that are subject to a certificate-of-title statute), is perfected automatically upon attachment. There is no need to file to perfect. Under subsection (b) a buyer of consumer goods takes free of a security interest, even though perfected, if the buyer buys (1) without knowledge of the security interest, (2) for value, (3) primarily for the buyer's own personal, family, or household purposes, and (4) before a financing statement is filed.

As to purchase money-security interests which are perfected without filing under Section 9–309(1): A secured party may file a financing statement, although filing is not required for perfection. If the secured party does file, all buyers take subject to the security interest. If the secured party does not file, a buyer who meets the qualifications stated in the preceding paragraph takes free of the security interest.

As to security interests for which a perfection step is required: This category includes all non-purchase-money security interests, and all security interests, whether or not purchase-money, in goods subject to a statute or treaty described in Section 9–311(a), such as automobiles covered by a certificate-of-title statute. As long as the required perfection step has not been taken and the security interest remains unperfected, not only the buyers described in subsection (b) but also the purchasers described in Section 9–317 will take free of the security interest. After a financing statement has been filed or the perfection requirements of the applicable certificate-of-title statute have been complied with (compliance is the equivalent of filing a financing statement; see Section 9–311(b)), all subsequent buyers, under the rule of subsection (b), are subject to the security interest.

The rights of a buyer under subsection (b) turn on whether a financing statement has been filed against consumer goods. Occasionally, a debtor changes his or her location after a filing is made. Subsection (c), which derives from former Section 9–103(1)(d)(iii), deals with the continued effectiveness of the filing under those circumstances. It adopts the rules of Sections 9–316(a) and (b). These rules are explained in the Comments to that section.

6. **Authorized Dispositions.** The limitations that subsections (a) and (b) impose on the persons who may take free of a security interest apply of course only to unauthorized sales by the debtor. If the secured party authorized the sale in an express agreement or otherwise, the buyer takes free under Section 9–315(a) without regard to the limitations of this section. (That section also states the right of a secured party to the proceeds of a sale, authorized or unauthorized.) Moreover, the buyer also takes free if the secured party waived or otherwise is precluded from asserting its security interest against the buyer. See Section 1–103.

7. **Oil, Gas, and Other Minerals.** Under subsection (d), a buyer in ordinary course of business of minerals at the wellhead or minehead or after extraction takes free of a security interest created by the seller. Specifically, it provides that qualified buyers take free not only of Article 9 security interests but also of interests "arising out of an encumbrance." As defined in Section 9–102, the term "encumbrance" means "a right, other than an ownership interest, in real property." Thus, to the extent that a mortgage encumbers minerals not only before but also after extraction, subsection (d) enables a buyer in ordinary course of the minerals to take free of the mortgage. This subsection does not, however, enable these buyers to take free of interests arising out of ownership interests in the real property. This issue is significant only in a minority of states. Several of them have adopted special statutes and nonuniform amendments to Article 9 to provide special protections to mineral owners, whose interests often are highly fractionalized in the case of oil and gas. See Terry I. Cross, *Oil and Gas Product Liens—Statutory Security Interests for Producers and Royalty Owners Under the Statutes of Kansas, New Mexico, Oklahoma, Texas and Wyoming*, 50 Consumer Fin. L. Q. Rep. 418 (1996). Inasmuch as a complete resolution of the issue would require the addition of complex provisions to this Article, and there are good reasons to believe that a uniform solution would not be feasible, this Article leaves its resolution to other legislation.

8. **Possessory Security Interests.** Subsection (e) is new. It rejects the holding of *Tanbro Fabrics Corp. v. Deering*

Milliken, Inc., 350 N.E.2d 590 (N.Y.1976) and, together with Section 9–317(b), prevents a buyer of goods collateral from taking free of a security interest if the collateral is in the possession of the secured party. "The secured party" referred in subsection (e) is the holder of the security interest referred to in subsection (a) or (b). Section 9–313 determines whether a secured party is in possession for purposes of this section. Under some circumstances, Section 9–313 provides that a secured party is in possession of collateral even if the collateral is in the physical possession of a third party.

§ 9.321. Licensee of General Intangible and Lessee of Goods in Ordinary Course of Business

(a) In this section, "licensee in ordinary course of business" means a person that becomes a licensee of a general intangible in good faith, without knowledge that the license violates the rights of another person in the general intangible, and in the ordinary course from a person in the business of licensing general intangibles of that kind. A person becomes a licensee in the ordinary course if the license to the person comports with the usual or customary practices in the kind of business in which the licensor is engaged or with the licensor's own usual or customary practices.

(b) A licensee in ordinary course of business takes its rights under a nonexclusive license free of a security interest in the general intangible created by the licensor, even if the security interest is perfected and the licensee knows of its existence.

(c) A lessee in ordinary course of business takes its leasehold interest free of a security interest in the goods created by the lessor, even if the security interest is perfected and the lessee knows of its existence.

Added by Acts 1999, 76th Leg., ch. 414, § 1.01, eff. July 1, 2001.

Uniform Commercial Code Comment

1. **Source.** Derived from Sections 2A–103(1)(*o*), 2A–307(3).

2. **Licensee in Ordinary Course.** Like the analogous rules in Section 9–320(a) with respect to buyers in ordinary course and subsection (c) with respect to lessees in ordinary course, the new rule in subsection (b) reflects the expectations of the parties and the marketplace: a licensee under a nonexclusive license takes subject to a security interest unless the secured party authorizes the license free of the security interest or other, controlling law such as that of this section (protecting ordinary-course licensees) dictates a contrary result. See Sections 9–201, 9–315. The definition of "licensee in ordinary course of business" in subsection (a) is modeled upon that of "buyer in ordinary course of business."

3. **Lessee in Ordinary Course.** Subsection (c) contains the rule formerly found in Section 2A–307(3). The rule works in the same way as that of Section 9–320(a).

§ 9.322. Priorities Among Conflicting Security Interests in and Agricultural Liens On Same Collateral

(a) Except as otherwise provided in this section, priority among conflicting security interests and agricultural liens in the same collateral is determined according to the following rules:

(1) Conflicting perfected security interests and agricultural liens rank according to priority in time of filing or perfection. Priority dates from the earlier of the time a filing covering the collateral is first made or the security interest or agricultural lien is first perfected, if there is no period thereafter when there is neither filing nor perfection.

(2) A perfected security interest or agricultural lien has priority over a conflicting unperfected security interest or agricultural lien.

(3) The first security interest or agricultural lien to attach or become effective has priority if conflicting security interests and agricultural liens are unperfected.

(b) For the purposes of Subsection (a)(1):

(1) the time of filing or perfection as to a security interest in collateral is also the time of filing or perfection as to a security interest in proceeds; and

(2) the time of filing or perfection as to a security interest in collateral supported by a supporting obligation is also the time of filing or perfection as to a security interest in the supporting obligation.

(c) Except as otherwise provided in Subsection (f), a security interest in collateral that qualifies for priority over a conflicting security interest under Section 9.327, 9.328, 9.329, 9.330, or 9.331 also has priority over a conflicting security interest in:

(1) any supporting obligation for the collateral; and

(2) proceeds of the collateral if:

(A) the security interest in proceeds is perfected;

(B) the proceeds are cash proceeds or of the same type as the collateral; and

(C) in the case of proceeds that are proceeds of proceeds, all intervening proceeds are cash proceeds, proceeds of the same type as the collateral, or an account relating to the collateral.

(d) Subject to Subsection (e) and except as otherwise provided in Subsection (f), if a security interest in chattel paper, deposit accounts, negotiable documents, instruments, investment property, or letter-of-credit rights is perfected by a method other than filing, conflicting perfected security interests in proceeds of the collateral rank according to priority in time of filing.

(e) Subsection (d) applies only if the proceeds of the collateral are not cash proceeds, chattel paper, negotiable documents, instruments, investment property, or letter-of-credit rights.

(f) Subsections (a)–(e) are subject to:

(1) Subsection (g) and the other provisions of this subchapter;

(2) Section 4.210 with respect to a security interest of a collecting bank;

(3) Section 5.118 with respect to a security interest of an issuer or nominated person; and

(4) Section 9.110 with respect to a security interest arising under Chapter 2 or 2A.

(g) A perfected agricultural lien on collateral has priority over a conflicting security interest in or agricultural lien on the same collateral if the statute creating the agricultural lien so provides.

Added by Acts 1999, 76th Leg., ch. 414, § 1.01, eff. July 1, 2001.

Uniform Commercial Code Comment

1. **Source.** Former Section 9–312(5), (6).

2. **Scope of This Section.** In a variety of situations, two or more people may claim a security interest in the same collateral. This section states general rules of priority among conflicting security interests. As subsection (f) provides, the general rules in subsections (a) through (e) are subject to the rule in subsection (g) governing perfected agricultural liens and to the other rules in this Part of this Article. Rules that override this section include those applicable to purchase-money security interests (Section 9–324) and those qualifying for special priority in particular types of collateral. See, e.g., Section 9–327 (deposit accounts); Section 9–328 (investment property); Section 9–329 (letter-of-credit rights); Section 9–330 (chattel paper and instruments); Section 9–334 (fixtures). In addition, the general rules of sections (a) through (e) are subject to priority rules governing security interests arising under Articles 2, 2A, 4, and 5.

3. **General Rules.** Subsection (a) contains three general rules. Subsection (a)(1) governs the priority of competing perfected security interests. Subsection (a)(2) governs the priority of competing security interests if one is perfected and the other is not. Subsection (a)(3) governs the priority of competing unperfected security interests. The rules may be regarded as adaptations of the idea, deeply rooted at common law, of a race of diligence among creditors. The first two rules are based on precedence in the time as of which the competing secured parties either filed their financing statements or obtained perfected security interests. Under subsection (a)(1), the first secured party who files or perfects has priority. Under subsection (a)(2), which is new, a perfected security interest has priority over an unperfected one. Under subsection (a)(3), if both security interests are unperfected, the first to attach has priority. Note that Section 9–709(b) may affect the application of subsection (a) to a filing that occurred before the effective date of this Article and which would be ineffective to perfect a security interest under former Article 9 but effective under this Article.

4. **Competing Perfected Security Interests.** When there is more than one perfected security interest, the security interests rank according to priority in time of filing or perfection. "Filing," of course, refers to the filing of an effective financing statement. "Perfection" refers to the acquisition of a perfected security interest, i.e., one that has attached and as to which any required perfection step has been taken. See Sections 9–308 and 9–309.

Example 1: On February 1, A files a financing statement covering a certain item of Debtor's equipment. On March 1, B files a financing statement covering the same equipment. On April 1, B makes a loan to Debtor and obtains a security interest in the equipment. On May 1, A makes a loan to Debtor and obtains a security interest in the same collateral. A has priority even though B's loan was made earlier and was perfected when made. It makes no difference whether A knew of B's security interest when A made its advance.

The problem stated in Example 1 is peculiar to a notice-filing system under which filing may occur before the security interest attaches (see Section 9–502). The justification for determining priority by order of filing lies in the necessity of protecting the filing system–that is, of allowing the first secured party who has filed to make subsequent advances without each time having to check for subsequent filings as a condition of protection. Note, however, that this first-to-file protection is not absolute. For example, Section 9–324 affords priority to certain purchase-money security interests, even if a competing secured party was the first to file or perfect.

Example 2: A and B make non-purchase-money advances secured by the same collateral. The collateral is in Debtor's possession, and neither security interest is perfected when the second advance is made. Whichever secured party first perfects its security interest (by taking possession of the collateral or by filing) takes priority. It makes no difference whether that secured party knows of the other security interest at the time it perfects its own.

The rule of subsection (a)(1), affording priority to the first to file or perfect, applies to security interests that are perfected by any method, including temporarily (Section 9–312) or upon attachment (Section 9–309), even though there may be no notice to creditors or subsequent purchasers and notwithstanding any common-law rule to the contrary. The form of the claim to priority, i.e., filing or perfection, may shift from time to time, and the rank will be based on the first filing or perfection as long as there is no intervening period without filing or perfection. See Section 9–308(c).

Example 3: On October 1, A acquires a temporarily perfected (20–day) security interest, unfiled, in a tangible negotiable document in the debtor's possession under Section 9–312(e). On October 5, B files and thereby perfects a security interest that previously had attached to the same document. On October 10, A files. A has priority, even after the 20–day period expires, regardless of whether A knows of B's security interest when A files. A was the first to perfect and maintained continuous perfection or filing since the start of the 20–day period. However, the perfection of A's security interest extends only "to the extent it arises for new value given." To the extent A's security interest secures advances made by A beyond the 20–day period, its security interest would be subordinate to B's, inasmuch as B was the first to file.

In general, the rule in subsection (a)(1) does not distinguish among various advances made by a secured party. The priority of every advance dates from the earlier of filing or perfection. However, in rare instances, the priority of an advance dates from the time the advance is made. See Example 3 and Section 9–323.

5. **Priority in After–Acquired Property.** The application of the priority rules to after-acquired property must be considered separately for each item of collateral. Priority does not depend only on time of perfection but may also be based on priority in filing before perfection.

Example 4: On February 1, A makes advances to Debtor under a security agreement covering "all Debtor's machinery, both existing and after-acquired." A promptly files a financing statement. On April 1, B takes a security interest in all Debtor's machinery, existing and after-acquired, to secure an outstanding loan. The following day, B files a financing statement. On May 1, Debtor acquires a new machine. When Debtor acquires rights in the new machine, both A and B acquire security interests in the machine simultaneously. Both security interests are perfected simultaneously. However, A has priority because A filed before B.

When after-acquired collateral is encumbered by more than one security interest, one of the security interests often is a purchase-money security interest that is entitled to special priority under Section 9–324.

6. **Priority in Proceeds: General Rule.** Subsection (b)(1) follows former Section 9–312(6). It provides that the baseline rules of subsection (a) apply generally to priority conflicts in proceeds except where otherwise provided (e.g., as in subsections (c) through (e)). Under Section 9–203, attachment cannot occur (and therefore, under Section 9–308, perfection cannot occur) as to particular collateral until the collateral itself comes into existence and the debtor has rights in it. Thus, a security interest in proceeds of original collateral does not attach and is not perfected until the proceeds come into existence and the debtor acquires rights in them.

Example 5: On April 1, Debtor authenticates a security agreement granting to A a security interest in all Debtor's existing and after-acquired inventory. The same day, A files a financing statement covering inventory. On May 1, Debtor authenticates a security agreement granting B a security interest in all Debtor's existing and future accounts. On June 1, Debtor sells inventory to a customer on 30–day unsecured credit. When Debtor acquires the account, B's security interest attaches to it and is perfected by B's financing statement. At the very same time, A's security interest attaches to the account as proceeds of the inventory and is automatically perfected. See Section 9–315. Under subsection (b) of this section, for purposes of determining A's priority in the account, the time of filing as to the original collateral (April 1, as to inventory) is also the time of filing as to proceeds (account). Accordingly, A's security interest in the account has priority over B's. Of course, had B filed its financing statement before A filed (e.g., on March 1), then B would have priority in the accounts.

Section 9–324 governs the extent to which a special purchase-money priority in goods or software carries over into the proceeds of the original collateral.

7. **Priority in Proceeds: Special Rules.** Subsections (c), (d), and (e), which are new, provide additional priority rules for proceeds of collateral in situations where the temporal (first-in-time) rules of subsection (a)(1) are not appropriate. These new provisions distinguish what these Comments refer to as "non-filing collateral" from what they call "filing collateral." As used in these Comments, non-filing collateral is collateral of a type for which perfection may be achieved by a method other than filing (possession or control, mainly) and for which secured parties who so perfect generally do not expect or need to conduct a filing search. More specifically, non-filing collateral is chattel paper, deposit accounts, negotiable documents, instruments, investment property, and letter-of-credit rights. Other collateral–accounts, commercial tort claims, general intangibles, goods, nonnegotiable documents, and payment intangibles–is filing collateral.

8. **Proceeds of Non–Filing Collateral: Non–Temporal Priority.** Subsection (c)(2) provides a baseline priority rule for proceeds of non-filing collateral which applies if the secured party has taken the steps required for non-temporal priority over a conflicting security interest in non-filing collateral (e.g., control, in the case of deposit accounts, letter-of-credit rights, investment property, and in some cases, electronic negotiable documents, section 9–331). This rule determines priority in proceeds of non-filing collateral whether or not there exists an actual conflicting security interest in the original non-filing collateral. Under subsection (c)(2), the priority in the original collateral continues in proceeds if the security interest in proceeds is perfected and the proceeds are cash proceeds or non-filing proceeds "of the same type" as the original collateral. As used in subsection (c)(2), "type" means a type of collateral defined in the Uniform Commercial Code and should be read broadly. For example, a security is "of the same type" as a security entitlement (i.e., investment property), and a promissory note is "of the same type" as a draft (i.e., an instrument).

Example 6: SP–1 perfects its security interest in investment property by filing. SP–2 perfects subsequently by taking control of a certificated security. Debtor receives cash proceeds of the security (e.g., dividends deposited into Debtor's deposit account). If the first-to-file-or-perfect rule of subsection (a)(1) were applied, SP–1's security interest in the cash proceeds would be senior, although SP–2's security interest continues perfected under Section 9–315 beyond the 20–day period of automatic perfection. This was the result under former Article 9. Under subsection (c), however, SP–2's security interest is senior.

Note that a different result would obtain in Example 6 (i.e., SP–1's security interest would be senior) if SP–1 were to obtain control of the deposit-account proceeds. This is so because subsection (c) is subject to subsection (f), which in turn provides that the priority rules under subsections (a) through (e) are subject to "the other provisions of this part." One of those "other provisions" is Section 9–327, which affords priority to a security interest perfected by control. See Section 9–327(1).

Example 7: SP–1 perfects its security interest in investment property by filing. SP–2 perfects subsequently by taking control of a certificated security. Debtor receives proceeds of the security consisting of a new certificated security issued as a stock dividend on the original collateral. Although the new security is of the same type as the original collateral (i.e., investment property), once the 20–day period of automatic perfection expires (see Section 9–315(d)), SP–2's security interest is unperfected. (SP–2 has not filed or taken delivery or control, and no temporary-perfection rule applies.) Consequently, once the 20–day period expires, subsection (c) does not confer priority, and, under subsection (a)(2), SP–1's security interest in the security is senior. This was the result under former Article 9.

Example 8: SP–1 perfects its security interest in investment property by filing. SP–2 perfects subsequently by taking control of a certificated security and also by filing against investment property. Debtor receives proceeds of the security consisting of a new certificated security issued as a stock dividend of the collateral. Because the new security is of the same type as the original collateral (i.e., investment property) and (unlike Example 7) SP–2's security interest is perfected by filing, SP–2's security interest is senior under subsection (c). If the new security were redeemed by the issuer upon surrender and yet another security were received by Debtor, SP–2's security interest would continue to enjoy priority under subsection (c). The new security would be proceeds of proceeds.

Example 9: SP–1 perfects its security interest in investment property by filing. SP–2 subsequently perfects its security interest in investment property by taking control of a certificated security and also by filing against investment property. Debtor receives proceeds of the security consisting of a dividend check that it deposits to a deposit account. Because the check and the deposit account are cash proceeds, SP–1's and SP–2's security interests in the cash proceeds are perfected under Section 9–315 beyond the 20–day period of automatic perfection. However, SP–2's security interest is senior under subsection (c).

Example 10: SP–1 perfects its security interest in investment property by filing. SP–2 perfects subsequently by taking control of a certificated security and also by filing against investment property. Debtor receives an instrument as proceeds of the security. (Assume that the instrument is not cash proceeds.) Because the instrument is not of the same type as the original collateral (i.e., investment property), SP–2's security interest, although perfected by filing, does not achieve priority under subsection (c). Under the first-to-file-or-perfect rule of subsection (a)(1), SP–1's security interest in the proceeds is senior.

The proceeds of proceeds are themselves proceeds. See Section 9–102 (defining "proceeds" and "collateral"). Sometimes competing security interests arise in proceeds that are several generations removed from the original collateral. As the following example explains, the applicability of subsection (c) may turn on the nature of the intervening proceeds.

Example 11: SP–1 perfects its security interest in Debtor's deposit account by obtaining control. Thereafter, SP–2 files against inventory, (presumably) searches, finds no indication of a conflicting security interest, and advances against Debtor's existing and after-acquired inventory. Debtor uses funds from the deposit account to purchase inventory, which SP–1 can trace as identifiable proceeds of its security interest in Debtor's deposit account, and which SP–2 claims as original collateral. The inventory is sold and the proceeds deposited into *another* deposit account, as to which SP–1 has not obtained control. Subsection (c) does not govern priority in this other deposit account. This deposit account is cash proceeds and is also the same type of collateral as SP–1's original collateral, as required by subsections (c)(2)(A) and (B). However, SP–1's security interest does not satisfy subsection (c)(2)(C) because the inventory proceeds, which intervened between the original deposit account and the deposit account constituting the proceeds at issue, are not cash proceeds, proceeds of the same type as the collateral (original deposit account), or an account relating to the collateral. Stated otherwise, once proceeds other than cash proceeds, proceeds of the same type as the original collateral, or an account relating to the original collateral intervene in the chain of proceeds, priority under subsection (c) is thereafter unavailable. The special priority rule in subsection (d) also is inapplicable to this case. See Comment 9, Example 13, below. Instead, the general first-to-file-or-perfect rule of subsections (a) and (b) apply. Under that rule, SP–1 has priority unless its security interest in the inventory proceeds became unperfected under Section 9–315(d). Had SP–2 filed against inventory before SP–1 obtained control of the original deposit account, the SP–2 would have had priority even if SP–1's security interest in the inventory proceeds remained perfected.

9. **Proceeds of Non–Filing Collateral: Special Temporal Priority.** Under subsections (d) and (e), if a security interest in non-filing collateral is perfected by a method other than filing (e.g., control or possession), it does not retain its priority over a conflicting security interest in proceeds that are filing collateral. Moreover, it is not entitled to priority in proceeds under the first-to file-or-perfect rule of subsections (a)(1) and (b). Instead, under subsection (d), priority is determined by a new first-to-file rule.

Example 12: SP–1 perfects its security interest in Debtor's deposit account by obtaining control. Thereafter, SP–2 files against equipment, (presumably) searches, finds no indication of a conflicting security interest, and advances against Debtor's equipment. SP–1 then files against Debtor's equipment. Debtor uses funds from the deposit account to purchase equipment, which SP–1 can trace as proceeds of its security interest in Debtor's deposit account. If the first-to-file-or-perfect rule were applied, SP–1's security interest would be senior under subsections (a)(1) and (b), because it was the first to perfect in the original collateral and there was no period during which its security interest was unperfected. Under subsection (d), however, SP–2's security interest would be senior because it filed first. This corresponds with the likely expectations of the parties.

Note that under subsection (e), the first-to-file rule of subsection (d) applies only if the proceeds in question are other than non-filing collateral (i.e., if the proceeds are filing collateral). If the proceeds are non-filing collateral, either the first-to-file-or-perfect rule under subsections (a) and (b) or the non-temporal priority rule in subsection (c) would apply, depending on the facts.

Example 13: SP–1 perfects its security interest in Debtor's deposit account by obtaining control. Thereafter, SP–2 files against inventory, (presumably) searches, finds no indication of a conflicting security interest, and advances against Debtor's existing and after-acquired inventory. Debtor uses funds from the deposit account to purchase inventory, which SP–1 can trace as identifiable proceeds of its security interest in Debtor's deposit account, and which SP–2 claims as original collateral. The inventory is sold and the proceeds deposited into *another* deposit account, as to which SP–1 has not obtained control. As discussed above in Comment 8, Example 11, subsection (c) does not govern priority in this deposit account. Subsection (d) also does not govern, because the proceeds at issue (the deposit account) are cash proceeds. See subsection (e). Rather, the general rules of subsections (a) and (b) govern.

10. **Priority in Supporting Obligations.** Under subsections (b)(2) and (c)(1), a security interest having priority in collateral also has priority in a supporting obligation for that collateral. However, the rules in these subsections are subject to the special rule in Section 9–329 governing the priority of security interests in a letter-of-credit right. See subsection (f). Under Section 9–329, a secured party's failure to obtain control (Section 9–107) of a letter-of-credit right that serves as supporting collateral leaves its security interest exposed to a priming interest of a party who does take control.

11. **Unperfected Security Interests.** Under subsection (a)(3), if conflicting security interests are unperfected, the first to attach has priority. This rule may be of merely theoretical interest, inasmuch as it is hard to imagine a situation where the case would come into litigation without either secured party's having perfected its security interest. If neither security interest had been perfected at the time of the filing of a petition in bankruptcy, ordinarily neither would be good against the trustee in bankruptcy under the Bankruptcy Code.

12. **Agricultural Liens.** Statutes other than this Article may purport to grant priority to an agricultural lien as against a conflicting security interest or agricultural lien. Under subsection (g), if another statute grants priority to an agricultural lien, the agricultural lien has priority only if the same statute creates the agricultural lien and the agricultural lien is perfected. Otherwise, subsection (a) applies the same priority rules to an agricultural lien as to a security interest, regardless of whether the agricultural lien conflicts with another agricultural lien or with a security interest.

Inasmuch as no agricultural lien on proceeds arises under this Article, subsections (b) through (e) do not apply to proceeds of agricultural liens. However, if an agricultural lien has priority under subsection (g) and the statute creating the agricultural lien gives the secured party a lien on proceeds of the collateral subject to the lien, a court should apply the principle of subsection (g) and award priority in the proceeds to the holder of the perfected agricultural lien.

§ 9.323. Future Advances

(a) Except as otherwise provided in Subsection (c), for purposes of determining the priority of a perfected security interest under Section 9.322(a)(1), perfection of the security interest dates from the time an advance is made to the extent that the security interest secures an advance that:

(1) is made while the security interest is perfected only:

(A) under Section 9.309 when it attaches; or

(B) temporarily under Section 9.312(e), (f), or (g); and

(2) is not made pursuant to a commitment entered into before or while the security interest is perfected by a method other than under Section 9.309 or 9.312(e), (f), or (g).

(b) Except as otherwise provided in Subsection (c), a security interest is subordinate to the rights of a person that becomes a lien creditor to the extent that the security interest secures an advance made more than 45 days after the person becomes a lien creditor unless the advance is made:

(1) without knowledge of the lien; or

(2) pursuant to a commitment entered into without knowledge of the lien.

(c) Subsections (a) and (b) do not apply to a security interest held by a secured party that is a buyer of accounts, chattel paper, payment intangibles, or promissory notes or a consignor.

(d) Except as otherwise provided in Subsection (e), a buyer of goods other than a buyer in ordinary course of business takes free of a security interest to the extent that it secures advances made after the earlier of:

(1) the time the secured party acquires knowledge of the buyer's purchase; or

(2) 45 days after the purchase.

(e) Subsection (d) does not apply if the advance is made pursuant to a commitment entered into without knowledge of the buyer's purchase and before the expiration of the 45-day period.

(f) Except as otherwise provided in Subsection (g), a lessee of goods, other than a lessee in ordinary course of business, takes the leasehold interest free of a security interest to the extent that it secures advances made after the earlier of:

(1) the time the secured party acquires knowledge of the lease; or

(2) 45 days after the lease contract becomes enforceable.

(g) Subsection (f) does not apply if the advance is made pursuant to a commitment entered into without knowledge of the lease and before the expiration of the 45-day period.

Added by Acts 1999, 76th Leg., ch. 414, § 1.01, eff. July 1, 2001. Amended by Acts 2001, 77th Leg., ch. 705, § 7, eff. June 13, 2001.

Uniform Commercial Code Comment

1. **Source.** Former Sections 9–312(7), 9–301(4), 9–307(3), 2A–307(4).

2. **Scope of This Section.** A security agreement may provide that collateral secures future advances. See Section 9–204(c). This section collects all of the special rules dealing with the priority of advances made by a secured party after a third party acquires an interest in the collateral. Subsection (a) applies when the third party is a competing secured party. It replaces and clarifies former Section 9–312(7). Subsection (b) deals with lien creditors and replaces former Section 9–301(4). Subsections (d) and (e) deal with buyers and replace former Section 9–307(3). Subsections (f) and (g) deal with lessees and replace former Section 2A–307(4).

3. **Competing Security Interests.** Under a proper reading of the first-to-file-or-perfect rule of Section 9–322(a)(1) (and former Section 9–312(5)), it is abundantly clear that the time when an advance is made plays no role in determining priorities among conflicting security interests except when a financing statement was not filed and the advance is the giving of value as the last step for attachment and perfection. Thus, a secured party takes subject to all advances secured by a competing security interest having priority under Section 9–322(a)(1). This result generally obtains regardless of how the competing security interest is perfected and regardless of whether the advances are made "pursuant to commitment" (Section 9–102). Subsection (a) of this section states the only other instance when the time of an advance figures in the priority scheme in Section 9–322: when the security interest is perfected only automatically under Section 9–309 or temporarily under Section 9–312(e), (f), or (g), and the advance is not made pursuant to a commitment entered into while the security interest was perfected by another method. Thus, an advance has priority from the date it is made only in the rare case in which it is made without commitment and while the security interest is perfected only temporarily under Section 9–312.

The new formulation in subsection (a) clarifies the result when the initial advance is paid and a new ("future") advance is made subsequently. Under former Section 9–312(7), the priority of the new advance turned on whether it was "made while a security interest is perfected." This section resolves any ambiguity by omitting the quoted phrase.

Example 1: On February 1, A makes an advance secured by machinery in the debtor's possession and files a financing statement. On March 1, B makes an advance secured by the same machinery and files a financing statement. On April 1, A makes a further advance, under the original security agreement, against the same machinery. A was the first to file and so, under the first-to-file-or-perfect rule of Section 9–322(a)(1), A's security interest has priority over B's, both as to the February 1 and as to the April 1 advance. It makes no difference whether A knows of B's intervening advance when A makes the second advance. Note that, as long as A was the first to file or perfect, A would have priority with respect to both advances if either A or B had perfected by taking possession of the collateral. Likewise, A would have priority if A's April 1 advance was not made under the original agreement with the debtor, but was under a new agreement.

Example 2: On October 1, A acquires a temporarily perfected (20–day) security interest, unfiled, in a tangible negotiable document in the debtor's possession under Section 9–312(e) or (f). The security interest secures an advance made on that day as well as future advances. On October 5, B files and thereby perfects a security interest that previously had attached to the same document. On October 8, A makes an additional advance. On October 10, A files. Under Section 9–322(a)(1), because A was the first to perfect and maintained continuous perfection or filing since the start of the 20–day period, A has priority, even after the 20–day period expires. See Section 9–322, Comment 4, Example 3. However, under this section, for purposes of Section 9–322(a)(1), to the extent A's security interest secures the October 8 advance, the security interest was perfected on October 8. Inasmuch as B perfected on October 5, B has priority over the October 8 advance.

The rule in subsection (a) is more liberal toward the priority of future advances than the corresponding rules applicable to intervening lien creditors (subsection (b)), buyers (subsections (d) and (e)), and lessees (subsections (f) and (g)).

4. **Competing Lien Creditors.** Subsection (b) replaces former Section 9–301(4) and addresses the rights of a "lien creditor," as defined in Section 9–102. *Under Section 9–317(a)(2), a security interest is senior to the rights of* **a** person who becomes a lien creditor, unless the person becomes a lien creditor before the security interest is perfected and before a financing statement covering the collateral is filed ***and Section 9–203(b)(3) is satisfied***. *Subsection (b) of this section* eliminates the erroneous implication of former law by providing that a perfected provides that a *security interest is subordinate to those rights* to the extent that the specified circumstances occur. *Subsection (b) does not elevate the priority of a security interest that is subordinate to the rights of a lien creditor under Section 9–317(a)(2); it only subordinates.**

As under former Section 9–301(4), a secured party's knowledge does not cut short the 45–day period during which future advances can achieve priority over an intervening lien creditor's interest. Rather, because of the impact of the rule in subsection (b) on the question whether the security interest for future advances is "protected" under Section 6323(c)(2) and (d) of the Internal Revenue Code as amended by the Federal Tax Lien Act of 1966, the priority of the security interest for future advances over a lien creditor is made absolute for 45 days regardless of knowledge of the secured party concerning the lien. If, however, the advance is made after the 45 days, the advance will not have priority unless it was made or committed without knowledge of the lien. **Amendments in italics approved by the Permanent Editorial Board for Uniform Commercial Code October 20, 1999.*

5. **Sales of Receivables; Consignments.** Subsections (a) and (b) do not apply to outright sales of accounts, chattel paper, payment intangibles, or promissory notes, nor do they apply to consignments.

6. **Competing Buyers and Lessees.** Under subsections (d) and (e), a buyer will not take subject to a security interest to the extent it secures advances made after the secured party has knowledge that the buyer has purchased the collateral or more than 45 days after the purchase unless the advances were made pursuant to a commitment entered into before the expiration of the 45–day period and without knowledge of the purchase. Subsections (f) and (g) provide an analogous rule for lessees. Of course, a buyer in ordinary course who takes free of the security interest under Section 9–320 and a lessee in ordinary course who takes free under Section 9–321 are not subject to any future advances. Subsections (d) and (e) replace former Section 9–307(3), and subsections (f) and (g) replace former Section 2A–307(4). No change in meaning is intended.

§ 9.324. Priority of Purchase-Money Security Interests

(a) Except as otherwise provided in Subsection (g), a perfected purchase-money security interest in goods other than inventory or livestock has priority over a conflicting security interest in the same goods, and, except as otherwise provided in Section 9.327, a perfected security interest in its identifiable proceeds also has priority, if the purchase-money security interest is perfected when the debtor receives possession of the collateral or within 20 days thereafter.

(b) Subject to Subsection (c) and except as otherwise provided in Subsection (g), a perfected purchase-money security interest in inventory has priority over a conflicting security interest in the same inventory, has priority over a conflicting security interest in chattel paper or an instrument constituting proceeds of the inventory and in proceeds of the chattel paper, if so provided in Section 9.330, and, except as otherwise provided in Section 9.327, also has priority in identifiable cash proceeds of the inventory to the extent the identifiable cash proceeds are received on or before the delivery of the inventory to a buyer, if:

(1) the purchase-money security interest is perfected when the debtor receives possession of the inventory;

(2) except where excused by Section 9.343 (oil and gas production), the purchase-money secured party sends an authenticated notification to the holder of the conflicting security interest;

(3) the holder of the conflicting security interest receives any required notification within five years before the debtor receives possession of the inventory; and

(4) the notification states that the person sending the notification has or expects to acquire a purchase-money security interest in inventory of the debtor and describes the inventory.

(c) Subsections (b)(2)–(4) apply only if the holder of the conflicting security interest had filed a financing statement covering the same types of inventory:

(1) if the purchase-money security interest is perfected by filing, before the date of the filing; or

(2) if the purchase-money security interest is temporarily perfected without filing or possession under Section 9.312(f), before the beginning of the 20-day period under that subsection.

(d) Subject to Subsection (e) and except as otherwise provided in Subsection (g), a perfected purchase-money security interest in livestock that are farm products has priority over a conflicting security interest in the same livestock, and, except as otherwise provided in Section 9.327, a perfected security interest in their identifiable proceeds and identifiable products in their unmanufactured states also has priority, if:

(1) the purchase-money security interest is perfected when the debtor receives possession of the livestock;

(2) the purchase-money secured party sends an authenticated notification to the holder of the conflicting security interest;

(3) the holder of the conflicting security interest receives the notification within six months before the debtor receives possession of the livestock; and

(4) the notification states that the person sending the notification has or expects to acquire a purchase-money security interest in livestock of the debtor and describes the livestock.

(e) Subsections (d)(2)–(4) apply only if the holder of the conflicting security interest had filed a financing statement covering the same types of livestock:

(1) if the purchase-money security interest is perfected by filing, before the date of the filing; or

(2) if the purchase-money security interest is temporarily perfected without filing or possession

under Section 9.312(f), before the beginning of the 20-day period under that subsection.

(f) Except as otherwise provided in Subsection (g), a perfected purchase-money security interest in software has priority over a conflicting security interest in the same collateral, and, except as otherwise provided in Section 9.327, a perfected security interest in its identifiable proceeds also has priority, to the extent that the purchase-money security interest in the goods in which the software was acquired for use has priority in the goods and proceeds of the goods under this section.

(g) If more than one security interest qualifies for priority in the same collateral under Subsection (a), (b), (d), or (f):

(1) a security interest securing an obligation incurred as all or part of the price of the collateral has priority over a security interest securing an obligation incurred for value given to enable the debtor to acquire rights in or the use of collateral; and

(2) in all other cases, Section 9.322(a) applies to the qualifying security interests.

Added by Acts 1999, 76th Leg., ch. 414, § 1.01, eff. July 1, 2001.

Uniform Commercial Code Comment

1. **Source.** Former Section 9–312(3), (4).

2. **Priority of Purchase–Money Security Interests.** This section contains the priority rules applicable to purchase-money security interests, as defined in Section 9–103. It affords a special, non-temporal priority to those purchase-money security interests that satisfy the statutory conditions. In most cases, priority will be over a security interest asserted under an after-acquired property clause. See Section 9–204 on the extent to which security interests in after-acquired property are validated.

A purchase-money security interest can be created only in goods and software. See Section 9–103. Section 9–324(a), which follows former Section 9–312(4), contains the general rule for purchase-money security interests in goods. It is subject to subsections (b) and (c), which derive from former Section 9–312(3) and apply to purchase-money security interests in inventory, and subsections (d) and (e), which apply to purchase-money security interests in livestock that are farm products. Subsection (f) applies to purchase-money security interests in software. Subsection (g) deals with the relatively unusual case in which a debtor creates two purchase money security interests in the same collateral and both security interests qualify for special priority under one of the other subsections.

Former Section 9–312(2) contained a rule affording special priority to those who provided secured credit that enabled a debtor to produce crops. This rule proved unworkable and has been eliminated from this Article. Instead, model Section 9–324A contains a revised production-money priority rule. That section is a model, not uniform, provision. The sponsors of the UCC have taken no position as to whether it should be enacted, instead leaving the matter for state legislatures to consider if they are so inclined.

3. **Purchase-Money Priority in Goods Other Than Inventory and Livestock.** Subsection (a) states a general rule applicable to all types of goods except inventory and farm-products livestock: the purchase-money interest takes priority if it is perfected when the debtor receives possession of the collateral or within 20 days thereafter. (As to the 20–day "grace period," compare Section 9–317(e). Former Sections 9–312(4) and 9–301(2) contained a 10–day grace period.) The perfection requirement means that the purchase-money secured party either has filed a financing statement before that time or has a temporarily perfected security interest in goods covered by documents under Section 9–312(e) and (f) which is continued in a perfected status by filing before the expiration of the 20–day period specified in that section. A purchase-money security interest qualifies for priority under subsection (a), even if the purchase-money secured party knows that a conflicting security interest has been created and/or that the holder of the conflicting interest has filed a financing statement covering the collateral.

Normally, there will be no question when "the debtor receives possession of the collateral" for purposes of subsection (a). However, sometimes a debtor buys goods and takes possession of them in stages, and then assembly and testing are completed (by the seller or debtor-buyer) at the debtor's location. Under those circumstances, the buyer "takes possession" within the meaning of subsection (a) when, after an inspection of the portion of the goods in the debtor's possession, it would be apparent to a potential lender to the debtor that the debtor has acquired an interest in the goods taken as a whole.

A similar issue concerning the time when "the debtor receives possession" arises when a person acquires possession of goods under a transaction that is not governed by this Article and then later agrees to buy the goods on secured credit. For example, a person may take possession of goods as lessee under a lease contract and then exercise an option to purchase the goods from the lessor on secured credit. Under Section 2A–307(1), creditors of the lessee generally take subject to the lease contract; filing a financing statement against the lessee is unnecessary to protect the lessor's leasehold or residual interest. Once the lease is converted to a security interest, filing a financing statement is necessary to protect the seller's (former lessor's) security interest. Accordingly, the 20–day period in subsection (a) does not commence until the goods become "collateral" (defined in Section 9–102), i.e., until they are subject to a security interest.

4. **Purchase-Money Security Interests in Inventory.** Subsections (b) and (c) afford a means by which a purchase-money security interest in inventory can achieve priority over an earlier-filed security interest in the same collateral. To achieve priority, the purchase-money security interest must be perfected when the debtor receives possession of the inventory. For a discussion of when "the debtor receives

possession," see Comment 3, above. The 20–day grace period of subsection (a) does not apply.

The arrangement between an inventory secured party and its debtor typically requires the secured party to make periodic advances against incoming inventory or periodic releases of old inventory as new inventory is received. A fraudulent debtor may apply to the secured party for advances even though it has already given a purchase-money security interest in the inventory to another secured party. For this reason, subsections (b)(2) through (4) and (c) impose a second condition for the purchase-money security interest's achieving priority: the purchase-money secured party must give notification to the holder of a conflicting security interest who filed against the same item or type of inventory before the purchase-money secured party filed or its security interest became perfected temporarily under Section 9–312(e) or (f). The notification requirement protects the non-purchase-money inventory secured party in such a situation: if the inventory secured party has received notification, it presumably will not make an advance; if it has not received notification (or if the other security interest does not qualify as purchase-money), any advance the inventory secured party may make ordinarily will have priority under Section 9–322. Inasmuch as an arrangement for periodic advances against incoming goods is unusual outside the inventory field, subsection (a) does not contain a notification requirement.

5. **Notification to Conflicting Inventory Secured Party: Timing.** Under subsection (b)(3), the perfected purchase-money security interest achieves priority over a conflicting security interest only if the holder of the conflicting security interest receives a notification within five years before the debtor receives possession of the purchase-money collateral. If the debtor never receives possession, the five-year period never begins, and the purchase-money security interest has priority, even if notification is not given. However, where the purchase-money inventory financing began by the purchase-money secured party's possession of a negotiable document of title, to retain priority the secured party must give the notification required by subsection (b) at or before the usual time, i.e., when the debtor gets possession of the inventory, even though the security interest remains perfected for 20 days under Section 9–312(e) or (f).

Some people have mistakenly read former Section 9–312(3)(b) to require, as a condition of purchase-money priority in inventory, that the purchase-money secured party give the notification before it files a financing statement. Read correctly, the "before" clauses compare (i) the time when the holder of the conflicting security interest filed a financing statement with (ii) the time when the purchase-money security interest becomes perfected by filing or automatically perfected temporarily. Only if (i) occurs before (ii) must notification be given to the holder of the conflicting security interest. Subsection (c) has been rewritten to clarify this point.

6. **Notification to Conflicting Inventory Secured Party: Address.** Inasmuch as the address provided as that of the secured party on a filed financing statement is an "address that is reasonable under the circumstances," the holder of a purchase-money security interest may satisfy the requirement to "send" notification to the holder of a conflicting security interest in inventory by sending a notification to that address, even if the address is or becomes incorrect. See Section 9–102 (definition of "send"). Similarly, because the address is "held out by [the holder of the conflicting security interest] as the place for receipt of such communications [i.e., communications relating to security interests]," the holder is deemed to have "received" a notification delivered to that address. See Section 1–201(26).

7. **Consignments.** Subsections (b) and (c) also determine the priority of a consignor's interest in consigned goods as against a security interest in the goods created by the consignee. Inasmuch as a consignment subject to this Article is defined to be a purchase-money security interest, see Section 9–103(d), no inference concerning the nature of the transaction should be drawn from the fact that a consignor uses the term "security interest" in its notice under subsection (b)(4). Similarly, a notice stating that the consignor has delivered or expects to deliver goods, properly described, "on consignment" meets the requirements of subsection (b)(4), even if it does not contain the term "security interest," and even if the transaction subsequently is determined to be a security interest. Cf. Section 9–505 (use of "consignor" and "consignee" in financing statement).

8. **Priority in Proceeds: General.** When the purchase-money secured party has priority over another secured party, the question arises whether this priority extends to the proceeds of the original collateral. Subsections (a), (d), and (f) give an affirmative answer, but only as to proceeds in which the security interest is perfected (see Section 9–315). Although this qualification did not appear in former Section 9–312(4), it was implicit in that provision.

In the case of inventory collateral under subsection (b), where financing frequently is based on the resulting accounts, chattel paper, or other proceeds, the special priority of the purchase-money secured interest carries over into only certain types of proceeds. As under former Section 9–312(3), the purchase-money priority in inventory under subsection (b) carries over into identifiable cash proceeds (defined in Section 9–102) received on or before the delivery of the inventory to a buyer.

As a general matter, also like former Section 9–312(3), the purchase-money priority in inventory does *not* carry over into proceeds consisting of accounts or chattel paper. Many parties financing inventory are quite content to protect their first-priority security interest in the inventory itself. They realize that when the inventory is sold, someone else will be financing the resulting receivables (accounts or chattel paper), and the priority for inventory will not run forward to the receivables constituting the proceeds. Indeed, the cash supplied by the receivables financer often will be used to pay the inventory financing. In some situations, the party financing the inventory on a purchase-money basis makes contractual arrangements that the proceeds of receivables financing by another be devoted to paying off the inventory security interest.

However, the purchase-money priority in inventory *does* carry over to proceeds consisting of chattel paper and its proceeds (and also to instruments) to the extent provided in Section 9–330. Under Section 9–330(e), the holder of a purchase-money security interest in inventory is deemed to give new value for proceeds consisting of chattel paper.

Taken together, Sections 9–324(b) and 9–330(e) enable a purchase-money inventory secured party to obtain priority in chattel paper constituting proceeds of the inventory, even if the secured party does not actually give new value for the chattel paper, provided the purchase-money secured party satisfies the other conditions for achieving priority.

When the proceeds of original collateral (goods or software) consist of a deposit account, Section 9–327 governs priority to the extent it conflicts with the priority rules of this section.

9. **Priority in Accounts Constituting Proceeds of Inventory.** The application of the priority rules in subsection (b) is shown by the following examples:

Example 1: Debtor creates a security interest in its existing and after-acquired inventory in favor of SP–1, who files a financing statement covering inventory. SP–2 subsequently takes a purchase-money security interest in certain inventory and, under subsection (b), achieves priority in this inventory over SP–1. This inventory is then sold, producing accounts. Accounts are not cash proceeds, and so the special purchase-money priority in the inventory does not control the priority in the accounts. Rather, the first-to-file-or-perfect rule of Section 9–322(a)(1) applies. The time of SP–1's filing as to the inventory is also the time of filing as to the accounts under Section 9–322 (b). Assuming that each security interest in the accounts proceeds remains perfected under Section 9–315, SP–1 has priority as to the accounts.

Example 2: In Example 1, if SP–2 had filed directly against accounts, the date of that filing as to accounts would be compared with the date of SP–1's filing as to the inventory. The first filed would prevail under Section 9–322(a)(1).

Example 3: If SP–3 had filed against accounts in Example 1 before either SP–1 or SP–2 filed against inventory, SP–3's filing against accounts would have priority over the filings of SP–1 and SP–2. This result obtains even though the filings against inventory are effective to continue the perfected status of SP–1's and SP–2's security interest in the accounts beyond the 20–day period of automatic perfection. See Section 9–315. SP–1's and SP–2's position as to the inventory does not give them a claim to accounts (as proceeds of the inventory) which is senior to someone who has filed earlier against accounts. If, on the other hand, either SP–1's or SP–2's filing against the inventory preceded SP–3's filing against accounts, SP–1 or SP–2 would outrank SP–3 as to the accounts.

10. **Purchase-Money Security Interests in Livestock.** New subsections (d) and (e) provide a purchase-money priority rule for farm-products livestock. They are patterned on the purchase-money priority rule for inventory found in subsections (b) and (c) and include a requirement that the purchase-money secured party notify earlier-filed parties. Two differences between subsections (b) and (d) are noteworthy. First, unlike the purchase-money inventory lender, the purchase-money livestock lender enjoys priority in *all* proceeds of the collateral. Thus, under subsection (d), the purchase-money secured party takes priority in accounts over an earlier-filed accounts financer. Second, subsection (d) affords priority in certain products of the collateral as well as proceeds.

11. **Purchase-Money Security Interests in Aquatic Farm Products.** Aquatic goods produced in aquacultural operations (e.g., catfish raised on a catfish farm) are farm products. See Section 9–102 (definition of "farm products"). The definition does not indicate whether aquatic goods are "crops," as to which the model production money security interest priority in Section 9–324A applies, or "livestock," as to which the purchase-money priority in subsection (d) of this section applies. This Article leaves courts free to determine the classification of particular aquatic goods on a case-by-case basis, applying whichever priority rule makes more sense in the overall context of the debtor's business.

12. **Purchase-Money Security Interests in Software.** Subsection (f) governs the priority of purchase-money security interests in software. Under Section 9–103(c), a purchase-money security interest arises in software only if the debtor acquires its interest in the software for the principal purpose of using the software in goods subject to a purchase-money security interest. Under subsection (f), a purchase-money security interest in software has the same priority as the purchase-money security interest in the goods in which the software was acquired for use. This priority is determined under subsections (b) and (c) (for inventory) or (a) (for other goods).

13. **Multiple Purchase–Money Security Interests.** New subsection (g) governs priority among multiple purchase-money security interests in the same collateral. It grants priority to purchase-money security interests securing the price of collateral (i.e., created in favor of the seller) over purchase-money security interests that secure enabling loans. Section 7.2(c) of the Restatement (3d) of the Law of Property (Mortgages) (1997) adopts this rule with respect to real property mortgages. As Comment *d* to that section explains:

> the equities favor the vendor. Not only does the vendor part with specific real estate rather than money, but the vendor would never relinquish it at all except on the understanding that the vendor will be able to use it to satisfy the obligation to pay the price. This is the case even though the vendor may know that the mortgagor is going to finance the transaction in part by borrowing from a third party and giving a mortgage to secure that obligation. In the final analysis, the law is more sympathetic to the vendor's hazard of losing real estate previously owned than to the third party lender's risk of being unable to collect from an interest in real estate that never previously belonged to it.

The first-to-file-or-perfect rule of Section 9–322 applies to multiple purchase-money security interests securing enabling loans.

State Bar Committee Comment

As noted in Official Comment 3, subsection (a) changes the grace period from ten days to twenty days. This change does not affect Texas law, as former section 9.312(d) already provided a twenty-day grace period.

§ 9.325. Priority of Security Interests in Transferred Collateral

(a) Except as otherwise provided in Subsection (b), a security interest created by a debtor is subordinate to a security interest in the same collateral created by another person if:

(1) the debtor acquired the collateral subject to the security interest created by the other person;

(2) the security interest created by the other person was perfected when the debtor acquired the collateral; and

(3) there is no period thereafter when the security interest is unperfected.

(b) Subsection (a) subordinates a security interest only if the security interest:

(1) otherwise would have priority solely under Section 9.322(a) or 9.324; or

(2) arose solely under Section 2.711(c) or 2A.508(e).

Added by Acts 1999, 76th Leg., ch. 414, § 1.01, eff. July 1, 2001.

Uniform Commercial Code Comment

1. **Source.** New.

2. **"Double Debtor Problem."** This section addresses the "double debtor" problem, which arises when a debtor acquires property that is subject to a security interest created by another debtor.

3. **Taking Subject to Perfected Security Interest.** Consider the following scenario:

Example 1: A owns an item of equipment subject to a perfected security interest in favor of SP–A. A sells the equipment to B, not in the ordinary course of business. B acquires its interest subject to SP–A's security interest. See Sections 9–201, 9–315(a)(1). Under this section, if B creates a security interest in the equipment in favor of SP–B, SP–B's security interest is subordinate to SP–A's security interest, even if SP–B filed against B before SP–A filed against A, and even if SP–B took a purchase-money security interest. Normally, SP–B could have investigated the source of the equipment and discovered SP–A's filing before making an advance against the equipment, whereas SP–A had no reason to search the filings against someone other than its debtor, A.

4. **Taking Subject to Unperfected Security Interest.** This section applies only if the security interest in the transferred collateral was perfected when the transferee acquired the collateral. See subsection (a)(2). If this condition is not met, then the normal priority rules apply.

Example 2: A owns an item of equipment subject to an unperfected security interest in favor of SP–A. A sells the equipment to B, who gives value and takes delivery of the equipment without knowledge of the security interest. B takes free of the security interest. See Section 9–317(b). If B then creates a security interest in favor of SP–B, no priority issue arises; SP–B has the only security interest in the equipment.

Example 3: The facts are as in Example 2, except that B knows of SP–A's security interest and therefore takes the equipment subject to it. If B creates a security interest in the equipment in favor of SP–B, this section does not determine the relative priority of the security interests. Rather, the normal priority rules govern. If SP–B perfects its security interest, then, under Section 9–322(a)(2), SP–A's unperfected security interest will be junior to SP–B's perfected security interest. The award of priority to SP–B is premised on the belief that SP–A's failure to file could have misled SP–B.

5. **Taking Subject to Perfected Security Interest that Becomes Unperfected.** This section applies only if the security interest in the transferred collateral did not become unperfected at any time after the transferee acquired the collateral. See subsection (a)(3). If this condition is not met, then the normal priority rules apply.

Example 4: As in Example 1, A owns an item of equipment subject to a perfected security interest in favor of SP–A. A sells the equipment to B, not in the ordinary course of business. B acquires its interest subject to SP–A's security interest. See Sections 9–201, 9–315(a)(1). B creates a security interest in favor of SP–B, and SP–B perfects its security interest. This section provides that SP–A's security interest is senior to SP–B's. However, if SP–A's financing statement lapses while SP–B's security interest is perfected, then the normal priority rules would apply, and SP–B's security interest would become senior to SP–A's security interest. See Sections 9–322(a)(2), 9–515(c).

6. **Unusual Situations.** The appropriateness of the rule of subsection (a) is most apparent when it works to subordinate security interests having priority under the basic priority rules of Section 9–322(a) or the purchase-money priority rules of Section 9–324. The rule also works properly when applied to the security interest of a buyer under Section 2–711(3) or a lessee under Section 2A–508(5). However, subsection (a) may provide an inappropriate resolution of the "double debtor" problem in some of the wide variety of other contexts in which the problem may arise. Although subsection (b) limits the application of subsection (a) to those cases in which subordination is known to be appropriate, courts should apply the rule in other settings, if necessary to promote the underlying purposes and policies of the Uniform Commercial Code. See Section 1–103(a).

§ 9.326. Priority of Security Interests Created by New Debtor

(a) Subject to Subsection (b), a security interest created by a new debtor that is perfected by a filed financing statement that is effective solely under Section 9.508 in collateral in which a new debtor has or acquires rights is subordinate to a security interest in the same collateral that is perfected other than by a filed financing statement that is effective solely under Section 9.508.

(b) The other provisions of this subchapter determine the priority among conflicting security interests in the same collateral perfected by filed financing statements that are effective solely under Section 9.508. However, if the security agreements to which a new debtor became bound as debtor were not entered into by the same original debtor, the conflicting security interests rank according to priority in time of the new debtor's having become bound.

Added by Acts 1999, 76th Leg., ch. 414, § 1.01, eff. July 1, 2001.

Uniform Commercial Code Comment

1. **Source.** New.

2. **Subordination of Security Interests Created by New Debtor.** This section addresses the priority contests that may arise when a new debtor becomes bound by the security agreement of an original debtor and each debtor has a secured creditor.

Subsection (a) subordinates the original debtor's secured party's security interest perfected against the new debtor solely under Section 9–508. The security interest is subordinated to security interests in the same collateral perfected by another method, e.g., by filing against the new debtor. As used in this section, "a filed financing statement that is effective solely under Section 9–508" refers to a financing statement filed against the *original debtor* that continues to be effective under Section 9–508. It does not encompass a new initial financing statement providing the name of the new debtor, even if the initial financing statement is filed to maintain the effectiveness of a financing statement under the circumstances described in Section 9–508(b). Nor does it encompass a financing statement filed against the original debtor which remains effective against collateral transferred by the original debtor to the new debtor. See Section 9–508(c). Concerning priority contests involving transferred collateral, see Sections 9–325 and 9–507.

Example 1: SP–X holds a perfected-by-filing security interest in X Corp's existing and after-acquired inventory, and SP–Z holds a perfected-by-possession security interest in an item of Z Corp's inventory. Z Corp becomes bound as debtor by X Corp's security agreement (e.g., Z Corp buys X Corp's assets and assumes its security agreement). See Section 9–203(d). Under Section 9–508, SP–X's financing statement is effective to perfect a security interest in the item of inventory in which Z Corp has rights. However, subsection (a) provides that SP–X's security interest is subordinate to SP–Z's, regardless of whether SP–X's financing statement was filed before SP–Z perfected its security interest.

Example 2: SP–X holds a perfected-by-filing security interest in X Corp's existing and after-acquired inventory, and SP–Z holds a perfected-by-filing security interest in Z Corp's existing and after-acquired inventory. Z Corp becomes bound as debtor by X Corp's security agreement. Subsequently, Z Corp acquires a new item of inventory. Under Section 9–508, SP–X's financing statement is effective to perfect a security interest in the new item of inventory in which Z Corp has rights. However, because SP–Z's security interest was perfected by another method, subsection (a) provides that SP–X's security interest is subordinate to SP–Z's, regardless of which financing statement was filed first. This would be the case even if SP–Z filed after Z Corp became bound by X Corp's security agreement.

3. **Other Priority Rules.** Subsection (b) addresses the priority among security interests created by the original debtor (X Corp). By invoking the other priority rules of this subpart, as applicable, subsection (b) preserves the relative priority of security interests created by the original debtor.

Example 3: Under the facts of Example 2, SP–Y also holds a perfected-by-filing security interest in X Corp's existing and after-acquired inventory. SP–Y filed after SP–X. Inasmuch as both SP–X's and SP–Y's security interests in inventory acquired by Z Corp after it became bound are perfected solely under Section 9–508, the normal priority rules determine their relative priorities. Under the "first-to-file-or-perfect" rule of Section 9–322(a)(1), SP–X has priority over SP–Y.

Example 4: Under the facts of Example 3, after Z Corp became bound by X Corp's security agreement, SP–Y promptly filed a new initial financing statement against Z Corp. At that time, SP–X's security interest was perfected only by virtue of its original filing against X Corp which was "effective solely under Section 9–508." Because SP–Y's security interest no longer is perfected by a financing statement that is "effective solely under Section 9–508," this section does not apply to the priority contest. Rather, the normal priority rules apply. Under Section 9–322, because SP–Y's financing statement was filed *against Z Corp*, the new debtor, before SP–X's, SP–Y's security interest is senior to that of SP–X. Similarly, the normal priority rules would govern priority between SP–Y and SP–Z.

The second sentence of subsection (b) effectively limits the applicability of the first sentence to situations in which a new debtor has become bound by more than one security agreement entered into by the *same* original debtor. When the new debtor has become bound by security agreements entered into by *different* original debtors, the second sentence provides that priority is based on priority in time of the new debtor's becoming bound.

Example 5: Under the facts of Example 2, SP–W holds a perfected-by-filing security interest in W Corp's existing and after-acquired inventory. After Z Corp became bound by X Corp's security agreement in favor of SP–X, Z Corp became bound by W Corp's security agreement. Under subsection (b), SP–W's security interest in inventory acquired by Z Corp is subordinate to that of SP–X, because Z Corp became bound under SP–X's security agreement before it became bound under SP–W's security agreement. This is the result regardless of which financing statement (SP–X's or SP–W's) was filed first.

The second sentence of subsection (b) reflects the generally accepted view that priority based on the first-to-file rule is inappropriate for resolving priority disputes when the filings were made against different debtors. Like subsection (a) and the first sentence of subsection (b), however, the second sentence of subsection (b) relates only to priority conflicts among security interests perfected by filed financing statements that are "effective solely under Section 9–508."

Example 6: Under the facts of Example 5, after Z Corp became bound by W Corp's security agreement, SP–W promptly filed a new initial financing statement against Z Corp. At that time, SP–X's security interest was perfected only pursuant to its original filing against X Corp which was "effective solely under Section 9–508." Because SP–W's security interest is not perfected by a financing statement that is "effective solely under Section 9–508," this section does not apply to the priority contest. Rather, the normal priority rules apply. Under Section 9–322, because SP–W's financing statement was the first to be filed *against Z Corp*, the new debtor, SP–W's security interest is senior to that of SP–X. Similarly, the normal priority rules would govern priority between SP–W and SP–Z.

§ 9.327. Priority of Security Interests in Deposit Account

The following rules govern priority among conflicting security interests in the same deposit account:

(1) A security interest held by a secured party having control of the deposit account under Section 9.104 has priority over a conflicting security interest held by a secured party that does not have control.

(2) Except as otherwise provided in Subdivisions (3) and (4), security interests perfected by control under Section 9.314 rank according to priority in time of obtaining control.

(3) Except as otherwise provided in Subdivision (4), a security interest held by the bank with which the deposit account is maintained has priority over a conflicting security interest held by another secured party.

(4) A security interest perfected by control under Section 9.104(a)(3) has priority over a security interest held by the bank with which the deposit account is maintained.

Added by Acts 1999, 76th Leg., ch. 414, § 1.01, eff. July 1, 2001.

Uniform Commercial Code Comment

1. **Source.** New; derived from former Section 9–115(5).

2. **Scope of This Section.** This section contains the rules governing the priority of conflicting security interests in deposit accounts. It overrides conflicting priority rules. See Sections 9–322(f)(1), 9–324(a), (b), (d), (f). This section does not apply to accounts evidenced by an instrument (e.g., certain certificates of deposit), which by definition are not "deposit accounts."

3. **Control.** Under paragraph (1), security interests perfected by control (Sections 9–314, 9–104) take priority over those perfected otherwise, e.g., as identifiable cash proceeds under Section 9–315. Secured parties for whom the deposit account is an integral part of the credit decision will, at a minimum, insist upon the right to immediate access to the deposit account upon the debtor's default (i.e., control). Those secured parties for whom the deposit account is less essential will not take control, thereby running the risk that the debtor will dispose of funds on deposit (either outright or for collateral purposes) after default but before the account can be frozen by court order or the secured party can obtain control.

Paragraph (2) governs the case (expected to be very rare) in which a bank enters into a Section 9–104(a)(2) control agreement with more than one secured party. It provides that the security interests rank according to time of obtaining control. If the bank is solvent and the control agreements are well drafted, the bank will be liable to each secured party, and the priority rule will have no practical effect.

4. **Priority of Bank.** Under paragraph (3), the security interest of the bank with which the deposit account is maintained normally takes priority over all other conflicting security interests in the deposit account, regardless of whether the deposit account constitutes the competing secured party's original collateral or its proceeds. A rule of this kind enables banks to extend credit to their depositors without the need to examine either the public record or their own records to determine whether another party might have a security interest in the deposit account.

A secured party who takes a security interest in the deposit account as original collateral can protect itself against the results of this rule in one of two ways. It can take control of the deposit account by becoming the bank's customer. Under paragraph (4), this arrangement operates to subordinate the bank's security interest. Alternatively, the secured party can obtain a subordination agreement from the bank. See Section 9–339.

A secured party who claims the deposit account as proceeds of other collateral can reduce the risk of becoming junior by obtaining the debtor's agreement to deposit proceeds into a specific cash-collateral account and obtaining the agreement of that bank to subordinate all its claims to those of the secured party. But if the debtor violates its agreement and deposits funds into a deposit account other than the cash-collateral account, the secured party risks being subordinated.

5. **Priority in Proceeds of, and Funds Transferred from, Deposit Account.** The priority afforded by this section does not extend to proceeds of a deposit account. Rather, Section 9–322(c) through (e) and the provisions referred to in Section 9–322(f) govern priorities in proceeds of a deposit account. Section 9–315(d) addresses continuation of perfection in proceeds of deposit accounts. As to funds transferred from a deposit account that serves as collateral, see Section 9–332.

§ 9.328. Priority of Security Interests in Investment Property

The following rules govern priority among conflicting security interests in the same investment property:

(1) A security interest held by a secured party having control of investment property under Section

9.106 has priority over a security interest held by a secured party that does not have control of the investment property.

(2) Except as otherwise provided in Subdivisions (3) and (4), conflicting security interests held by secured parties each of which has control under Section 9.106 rank according to priority in time of:

(A) if the collateral is a security, obtaining control;

(B) if the collateral is a security entitlement carried in a securities account and:

(i) if the secured party obtained control under Section 8.106(d)(1), the secured party's becoming the person for which the securities account is maintained;

(ii) if the secured party obtained control under Section 8.106(d)(2), the securities intermediary's agreement to comply with the secured party's entitlement orders with respect to security entitlements carried or to be carried in the securities account; or

(iii) if the secured party obtained control through another person under Section 8.106(d)(3), the time on which priority would be based under this subdivision if the other person were the secured party; or

(C) if the collateral is a commodity contract carried with a commodity intermediary, the satisfaction of the requirement for control specified in Section 9.106(b)(2) with respect to commodity contracts carried or to be carried with the commodity intermediary.

(3) A security interest held by a securities intermediary in a security entitlement or a securities account maintained with the securities intermediary has priority over a conflicting security interest held by another secured party.

(4) A security interest held by a commodity intermediary in a commodity contract or a commodity account maintained with the commodity intermediary has priority over a conflicting security interest held by another secured party.

(5) A security interest in a certificated security in registered form that is perfected by taking delivery under Section 9.313(a) and not by control under Section 9.314 has priority over a conflicting security interest perfected by a method other than control.

(6) Conflicting security interests created by a broker, securities intermediary, or commodity intermediary that are perfected without control under Section 9.106 rank equally.

(7) In all other cases, priority among conflicting security interests in investment property is governed by Sections 9.322 and 9.323.

Added by Acts 1999, 76th Leg., ch. 414, § 1.01, eff. July 1, 2001.

Uniform Commercial Code Comment

1. **Source.** Former Section 9–115(5).

2. **Scope of This Section.** This section contains the rules governing the priority of conflicting security interests in investment property. Paragraph (1) states the most important general rule–that a secured party who obtains control has priority over a secured party who does not obtain control. Paragraphs (2) through (4) deal with conflicting security interests each of which is perfected by control. Paragraph (5) addresses the priority of a security interest in a certificated security which is perfected by delivery but not control. Paragraph (6) deals with the relatively unusual circumstance in which a broker, securities intermediary, or commodity intermediary has created conflicting security interests none of which is perfected by control. Paragraph (7) provides that the general priority rules of Sections 9–322 and 9–323 apply to cases not covered by the specific rules in this section. The principal application of this residual rule is that the usual first in time of filing rule applies to conflicting security interests that are perfected only by filing. Because the control priority rule of paragraph (1) provides for the ordinary cases in which persons purchase securities on margin credit from their brokers, there is no need for special rules for purchase-money security interests. See also Section 9–103 (limiting purchase-money collateral to goods and software).

3. **General Rule: Priority of Security Interest Perfected by Control.** Under paragraph (1), a secured party who obtains control has priority over a secured party who does not obtain control. The control priority rule does not turn on either temporal sequence or awareness of conflicting security interests. Rather, it is a structural rule, based on the principle that a lender should be able to rely on the collateral without question if the lender has taken the necessary steps to assure itself that it is in a position where it can foreclose on the collateral without further action by the debtor. The control priority rule is necessary because the perfection rules provide considerable flexibility in structuring secured financing arrangements. For example, at the "retail" level, a secured lender to an investor who wants the full measure of protection can obtain control, but the creditor may be willing to accept the greater measure of risk that follows from perfection by filing. Similarly, at the "wholesale" level, a lender to securities firms can leave the collateral with the debtor and obtain a perfected security interest under the automatic perfection rule of Section 9–309(10), but a lender who wants to be entirely sure of its position will want to obtain control. The control priority rule of paragraph (1) is an essential part of this system of flexibility. It is feasible to provide more than one method of perfecting security interests only if the rules ensure that those who take the necessary steps to obtain the full measure of protection do not run the risk of subordination to those who have not taken such steps. A secured party who is unwilling to run the risk that

the debtor has granted or will grant a conflicting control security interest should not make a loan without obtaining control of the collateral.

As applied to the retail level, the control priority rule means that a secured party who obtains control has priority over a conflicting security interest perfected by filing without regard to inquiry into whether the control secured party was aware of the filed security interest. Prior to the 1994 revisions to Articles 8 and 9, Article 9 did not permit perfection of security interests in securities by filing. Accordingly, parties who deal in securities never developed a practice of searching the UCC files before conducting securities transactions. Although filing is now a permissible method of perfection, in order to avoid disruption of existing practices in this business it is necessary to give perfection by filing a different and more limited effect for securities than for some other forms of collateral. The priority rules are not based on the assumption that parties who perfect by the usual method of obtaining control will search the files. Quite the contrary, the control priority rule is intended to ensure that, with respect to investment property, secured parties who do obtain control are entirely unaffected by filings. To state the point another way, perfection by filing is intended to affect only general creditors or other secured creditors who rely on filing. The rule that a security interest perfected by filing can be primed by a control security interest, without regard to awareness, is a consequence of the system of perfection and priority rules for investment property. These rules are designed to take account of the circumstances of the securities markets, where filing is not given the same effect as for some other forms of property. No implication is made about the effect of filing with respect to security interests in other forms of property, nor about other Article 9 rules, e.g., Section 9–330, which govern the circumstances in which security interests in other forms of property perfected by filing can be primed by subsequent perfected security interests.

The following examples illustrate the application of the priority rule in paragraph (1):

Example 1: Debtor borrows from Alpha and grants Alpha a security interest in a variety of collateral, including all of Debtor's investment property. At that time Debtor owns 1000 shares of XYZ Co. stock for which Debtor has a certificate. Alpha perfects by filing. Later, Debtor borrows from Beta and grants Beta a security interest in the 1000 shares of XYZ Co. stock. Debtor delivers the certificate, properly indorsed, to Beta. Alpha and Beta both have perfected security interests in the XYZ Co. stock. Beta has control, see Section 8–106(b)(1), and hence has priority over Alpha.

Example 2: Debtor borrows from Alpha and grants Alpha a security interest in a variety of collateral, including all of Debtor's investment property. At that time Debtor owns 1000 shares of XYZ Co. stock, held through a securities account with Able & Co. Alpha perfects by filing. Later, Debtor borrows from Beta and grants Beta a security interest in the 1000 shares of XYZ Co. stock. Debtor instructs Able to have the 1000 shares transferred through the clearing corporation to Custodian Bank, to be credited to Beta's account with Custodian Bank. Alpha and Beta both have perfected security interests in the XYZ Co. stock. Beta has control, see Section 8–106(d)(1), and hence has priority over Alpha.

Example 3: Debtor borrows from Alpha and grants Alpha a security interest in a variety of collateral, including all of Debtor's investment property. At that time Debtor owns 1000 shares of XYZ Co. stock, which is held through a securities account with Able & Co. Alpha perfects by filing. Later, Debtor borrows from Beta and grants Beta a security interest in the 1000 shares of XYZ Co. stock. Debtor, Able, and Beta enter into an agreement under which Debtor will continue to receive dividends and distributions, and will continue to have the right to direct dispositions, but Beta will also have the right to direct dispositions and receive the proceeds. Alpha and Beta both have perfected security interests in the XYZ Co. stock (more precisely, in the Debtor's security entitlement to the financial asset consisting of the XYZ Co. stock). Beta has control, see Section 8–106(d)(2), and hence has priority over Alpha.

Example 4: Debtor borrows from Alpha and grants Alpha a security interest in a variety of collateral, including all of Debtor's investment property. At that time Debtor owns 1000 shares of XYZ Co. stock, held through a securities account with Able & Co. Alpha perfects by filing. Debtor's agreement with Able & Co. provides that Able has a security interest in all securities carried in the account as security for any obligations of Debtor to Able. Debtor incurs obligations to Able and later defaults on the obligations to Alpha and Able. Able has control by virtue of the rule of Section 8–106(e) that if a customer grants a security interest to its own intermediary, the intermediary has control. Since Alpha does not have control, Able has priority over Alpha under the general control priority rule of paragraph (1).

4. **Conflicting Security Interests Perfected by Control: Priority of Securities Intermediary or Commodity Intermediary.** Paragraphs (2) through (4) govern the priority of conflicting security interests each of which is perfected by control. The following example explains the application of the rules in paragraphs (3) and (4):

Example 5: Debtor holds securities through a securities account with Able & Co. Debtor's agreement with Able & Co. provides that Able has a security interest in all securities carried in the account as security for any obligations of Debtor to Able. Debtor borrows from Beta and grants Beta a security interest in 1000 shares of XYZ Co. stock carried in the account. Debtor, Able, and Beta enter into an agreement under which Debtor will continue to receive dividends and distributions and will continue to have the right to direct dispositions, but Beta will also have the right to direct dispositions and receive the proceeds. Debtor incurs obligations to Able and later defaults on the obligations to Beta and Able. Both Beta and Able have control, so the general control priority rule of paragraph (1) does not apply. Compare Example 4. Paragraph (3) provides that a security interest held by a securities intermediary in positions of its own customer has priority over a conflicting security interest of an external lender, so Able has priority over Beta. (Paragraph (4) contains a parallel rule for commodity intermediaries.) The agreement among Able, Beta, and Debtor could, of course, determine the relative priority of the security interests of Able and Beta, see Section 9–339, but the fact that the intermediary has agreed to act on the instructions of a secured party such as Beta does not itself imply any agreement by the intermediary to subordinate.

5. **Conflicting Security Interests Perfected by Control: Temporal Priority.** Former Section 9–115 introduced into Article 9 the concept of conflicting security interests that rank equally. Paragraph (2) of this section governs priority in those circumstances in which more than one secured party (other than a broker, securities intermediary, or commodity intermediary) has control. It replaces the equal-priority rule for conflicting security interests in investment property with a temporal rule. For securities, both certificated and uncertificated, under paragraph (2)(A) priority is based on the time that control is obtained. For security entitlements carried in securities accounts, the treatment is more complex. Paragraph (2)(B) bases priority on the timing of the steps taken to achieve control. The following example illustrates the application of paragraph (2).

Example 6: Debtor borrows from Alpha and grants Alpha a security interest in a variety of collateral, including all of Debtor's investment property. At that time Debtor owns a security entitlement that includes 1000 shares of XYZ Co. stock that Debtor holds through a securities account with Able & Co. Debtor, Able, and Alpha enter into an agreement under which Debtor will continue to receive dividends and distributions, and will continue to have the right to direct dispositions, but Alpha will also have the right to direct dispositions and receive the proceeds. Later, Debtor borrows from Beta and grants Beta a security interest in all its investment property, existing and after-acquired. Debtor, Able, and Beta enter into an agreement under which Debtor will continue to receive dividends and distributions, and will continue to have the right to direct dispositions, but Beta will also have the right to direct dispositions and receive the proceeds. Alpha and Beta both have perfected-by-control security interests in the security entitlement to the XYZ Co. stock by virtue of their agreements with Able. See Sections 9–314(a), 9–106(a), 8–106(d)(2). Under paragraph (2)(B)(ii), the priority of each security interest dates from the time of the secured party's agreement with Able. Because Alpha's agreement was first in time, Alpha has priority. This priority applies equally to security entitlements to financial assets credited to the account after the agreement was entered into.

The priority rule is analogous to "first-to-file" priority under Section 9–322 with respect to after-acquired collateral. Paragraphs (2)(B)(i) and (2)(B)(iii) provide similar rules for security entitlements as to which control is obtained by other methods, and paragraph (2)(C) provides a similar rule for commodity contracts carried in a commodity account. Section 8–510 also has been revised to provide a temporal priority conforming to paragraph (2)(B).

6. **Certificated Securities.** A long-standing practice has developed whereby secured parties whose collateral consists of a security evidenced by a security certificate take possession of the security certificate. If the security certificate is in bearer form, the secured party's acquisition of possession constitutes "delivery" under Section 8–301(a)(1), and the delivery constitutes "control" under Section 8–106(a). Comment 5 discusses the priority of security interests perfected by control of investment property.

If the security certificate is in registered form, the secured party will not achieve control over the security unless the security certificate contains an appropriate indorsement or is (re)registered in the secured party's name. See Section 8–106(b). However, the secured party's acquisition of possession constitutes "delivery" of the security certificate under Section 8–301 and serves to perfect the security interest under Section 9–313(a), even if the security certificate has not been appropriately indorsed and has not been (re)registered in the secured party's name. A security interest perfected by this method has priority over a security interest perfected other than by control (e.g., by filing). See paragraph (5).

The priority rule stated in paragraph (5) may seem anomalous, in that it can afford less favorable treatment to purchasers who buy collateral outright that to those who take a security interest in it. For example, a buyer of a security certificate would cut off a security interest perfected by filing only if the buyer achieves the status of a protected purchaser under Section 8–303. The buyer would not be a protected purchaser, for example, if it does not obtain "control" under Section 8–106 (e.g., if it fails to obtain a proper indorsement of the certificate) or if it had notice of an adverse claim under Section 8–105. The apparent anomaly disappears, however, when one understands the priority rule not as one intended to protect careless or guilty parties, but as one that eliminates the need to conduct a search of the public records only insofar as necessary to serve the needs of the securities markets.

7. **Secured Financing of Securities Firms.** Priority questions concerning security interests granted by brokers and securities intermediaries are governed by the general control-beats-non-control priority rule of paragraph (1), as supplemented by the special rules set out in paragraphs (2) (temporal priority–first to control), (3) (special priority for securities intermediary), and (6) (equal priority for non-control). The following examples illustrate the priority rules as applied to this setting.

Example 7: Able & Co., a securities dealer, enters into financing arrangements with two lenders, Alpha Bank and Beta Bank. In each case the agreements provide that the lender will have a security interest in the securities identified on lists provided to the lender on a daily basis, that the debtor will deliver the securities to the lender on demand, and that the debtor will not list as collateral any securities which the debtor has pledged to any other lender. Upon Able's insolvency it is discovered that Able has listed the same securities on the collateral lists provided to both Alpha and Beta. Alpha and Beta both have perfected security interests under the automatic-perfection rule of Section 9–309(10). Neither Alpha nor Beta has control. Paragraph (6) provides that the security interests of Alpha and Beta rank equally, because each of them has a non-control security interest granted by a securities firm. They share pro-rata.

Example 8: Able enters into financing arrangements, with Alpha Bank and Beta Bank as in Example 7. At some point, however, Beta decides that it is unwilling to continue to provide financing on a non-control basis. Able directs the clearing corporation where it holds its principal inventory of securities to move specified securities into Beta's account. Upon Able's insolvency it is discovered that a list of collateral provided to Alpha includes securities that had been moved to Beta's account. Both Alpha and Beta have perfected security interests; Alpha under the automatic-perfection rule of Section 9–309(10), and Beta under that rule and also the perfection-by-control rule in Section 9–314(a). Beta has control but Alpha does not. Beta has priority over Alpha under paragraph (1).

Example 9: Able & Co. carries its principal inventory of securities through Clearing Corporation, which offers a "shared control" facility whereby a participant securities firm can enter into an arrangement with a lender under which the securities firm will retain the power to trade and otherwise direct dispositions of securities carried in its account, but Clearing Corporation agrees that, at any time the lender so directs, Clearing Corporation will transfer any securities from the firm's account to the lender's account or otherwise dispose of them as directed by the lender. Able enters into financing arrangements with two lenders, Alpha and Beta, each of which obtains such a control agreement from Clearing Corporation. The agreement with each lender provides that Able will designate specific securities as collateral on lists provided to the lender on a daily or other periodic basis, and that it will not pledge the same securities to different lenders. Upon Able's insolvency, it is discovered that Able has listed the same securities on the collateral lists provided to both Alpha and Beta. Both Alpha and Beta have control over the disputed securities. Paragraph (2) awards priority to whichever secured party first entered into the agreement with Clearing Corporation.

8. **Relation to Other Law.** Section 1–103 provides that "unless displaced by particular provisions of this Act, the principles of law and equity ... shall supplement its provisions." There may be circumstances in which a secured party's action in acquiring a security interest that has priority under this section constitutes conduct that is wrongful under other law. Though the possibility of such resort to other law may provide an appropriate "escape valve" for cases of egregious conduct, care must be taken to ensure that this does not impair the certainty and predictability of the priority rules. Whether a court may appropriately look to other law to impose liability upon or estop a secured party from asserting its Article 9 priority depends on an assessment of the secured party's conduct under the standards established by such other law as well as a determination of whether the particular application of such other law is displaced by the UCC.

Some circumstances in which other law is clearly displaced by the UCC rules are readily identifiable. Common law "first in time, first in right" principles, or correlative tort liability rules such as common law conversion principles under which a purchaser may incur liability to a person with a prior property interest without regard to awareness of that claim, are necessarily displaced by the priority rules set out in this section since these rules determine the relative ranking of security interests in investment property. So too, Article 8 provides protections against adverse claims to certain purchasers of interests in investment property. In circumstances where a secured party not only has priority under Section 9–328, but also qualifies for protection against adverse claims under Section 8–303, 8–502, or 8–510, resort to other law would be precluded.

In determining whether it is appropriate in a particular case to look to other law, account must also be taken of the policies that underlie the commercial law rules on securities markets and security interests in securities. A principal objective of the 1994 revision of Article 8 and the provisions of Article 9 governing investment property was to ensure that secured financing transactions can be implemented on a simple, timely, and certain basis. One of the circumstances that led to the revision was the concern that uncertainty in the application of the rules on secured transactions involving securities and other financial assets could contribute to systemic risk by impairing the ability of financial institutions to provide liquidity to the markets in times of stress. The control priority rule is designed to provide a clear and certain rule to ensure that lenders who have taken the necessary steps to establish control do not face a risk of subordination to other lenders who have not done so.

The control priority rule does not turn on an inquiry into the state of a secured party's awareness of potential conflicting claims because a rule under which a person's rights depended on that sort of after-the-fact inquiry could introduce an unacceptable measure of uncertainty. If an inquiry into awareness could provide a complete and satisfactory resolution of the problem in all cases, the priority rules of this section would have incorporated that test. The fact that they do not necessarily means that resort to other law based solely on that factor is precluded, though the question whether a control secured party induced or encouraged its financing arrangement with actual knowledge that the debtor would be violating the rights of another secured party may, in some circumstances, appropriately be treated as a factor in determining whether the control party's action is the kind of egregious conduct for which resort to other law is appropriate.

§ 9.329. Priority of Security Interests in Letter-Of-Credit Right

The following rules govern priority among conflicting security interests in the same letter-of-credit right:

(1) A security interest held by a secured party having control of the letter-of-credit right under Section 9.107 has priority to the extent of its control over a conflicting security interest held by a secured party that does not have control.

(2) Security interests perfected by control under Section 9.314 rank according to priority in time of obtaining control.

Added by Acts 1999, 76th Leg., ch. 414, § 1.01, eff. July 1, 2001.

Uniform Commercial Code Comment

1. **Source.** New; loosely modeled after former Section 9–115(5).

2. **General Rule.** Paragraph (1) awards priority to a secured party who perfects a security interest directly in letter-of-credit rights (i.e., one that takes an assignment of proceeds and obtains consent of the issuer or any nominated person under Section 5–114(c)) over another conflicting secu-

rity interest (i.e., one that is perfected automatically in the letter-of-credit rights as supporting obligations under Section 9–308(d)). This is consistent with international letter-of-credit practice and provides finality to payments made to recognized assignees of letter-of-credit proceeds. If an issuer or nominated person recognizes multiple security interests in a letter-of-credit right, resulting in multiple parties having control (Section 9–107), under paragraph (2) the security interests rank according to the time of obtaining control.

3. **Drawing Rights; Transferee Beneficiaries.** Drawing under a letter of credit is personal to the beneficiary and requires the beneficiary to perform the conditions for drawing under the letter of credit. Accordingly, a beneficiary's grant of a security interest in a letter of credit includes the beneficiary's "letter-of-credit right" as defined in Section 9–102 and the right to "proceeds of [the] letter of credit" as defined in Section 5–114(a), but does not include the right to demand payment under the letter of credit.

Section 5–114(e) provides that the "[r]ights of a transferee beneficiary or nominated person are independent of the beneficiary's assignment of the proceeds of a letter of credit and are superior to the assignee's right to the proceeds." To the extent the rights of a transferee beneficiary or nominated person are independent and superior, this Article does not apply. See Section 9–109(c).

Under Article 5, there is in effect a novation upon the transfer with the issuer becoming bound on a new, independent obligation to the transferee. The rights of nominated persons and transferee beneficiaries under a letter of credit include the right to demand payment from the issuer. Under Section 5–114(e), their rights to payment are independent of their obligations to the beneficiary (or original beneficiary) and superior to the rights of assignees of letter-of-credit proceeds (Section 5–114(c)) and others claiming a security interest in the beneficiary's (or original beneficiary's) letter-of-credit rights.

A transfer of drawing rights under a transferable letter of credit establishes independent Article 5 rights in the transferee and does not create or perfect an Article 9 security interest in the transferred drawing rights. The definition of "letter-of-credit right" in Section 9–102 excludes a beneficiary's drawing rights. The exercise of drawing rights by a transferee beneficiary may breach a contractual obligation of the transferee to the original beneficiary concerning when and how much the transferee may draw or how it may use the funds received under the letter of credit. If, for example, drawing rights are transferred to support a sale or loan from the transferee to the original beneficiary, then the transferee would be obligated to the original beneficiary under the sale or loan agreement to account for any drawing and for the use of any funds received. The transferee's obligation would be governed by the applicable law of contracts or restitution.

4. **Secured Party–Transferee Beneficiaries.** As described in Comment 3, drawing rights under letters of credit are transferred in many commercial contexts in which the transferee is not a secured party claiming a security interest in an underlying receivable supported by the letter of credit. Consequently, a transfer of a letter of credit is not a method of "perfection" of a security interest. The transferee's independent right to draw under the letter of credit and to receive and retain the value thereunder (in effect, priority) is not based on Article 9 but on letter-of-credit law and the terms of the letter of credit. Assume, however, that a secured party does hold a security interest in a receivable that is owned by a beneficiary-debtor and supported by a transferable letter of credit. Assume further that the beneficiary-debtor causes the letter of credit to be transferred to the secured party, the secured party draws under the letter of credit, and, upon the issuer's payment to the secured party-transferee, the underlying account debtor's obligation to the original beneficiary-debtor is satisfied. In this situation, the payment to the secured party-transferee is proceeds of the receivable collected by the secured party-transferee. Consequently, the secured party-transferee would have certain duties to the debtor and third parties under Article 9. For example, it would be obliged to collect under the letter of credit in a commercially reasonable manner and to remit any surplus pursuant to Sections 9–607 and 9–608.

This scenario is problematic under letter-of-credit law and practice, inasmuch as a transferee beneficiary collects in its own right arising from its own performance. Accordingly, under Section 5–114, the independent and superior rights of a transferee control over any inconsistent duties under Article 9. A transferee beneficiary may take a transfer of drawing rights to avoid reliance on the original beneficiary's credit and collateral, and it may consider any Article 9 rights superseded by its Article 5 rights. Moreover, it will not always be clear (i) whether a transferee beneficiary has a security interest in the underlying collateral, (ii) whether any security interest is senior to the rights of others, or (iii) whether the transferee beneficiary is aware that it holds a security interest. There will be clear cases in which the role of a transferee beneficiary as such is merely incidental to a conventional secured financing. There also will be cases in which the existence of a security interest may have little to do with the position of a transferee beneficiary as such. In dealing with these cases and less clear cases involving the possible application of Article 9 to a nominated person or a transferee beneficiary, the right to demand payment under a letter of credit should be distinguished from letter-of-credit rights. The courts also should give appropriate consideration to the policies and provisions of Article 5 and letter-of-credit practice as well as Article 9.

§ 9.330. Priority of Purchaser of Chattel Paper or Instrument

(a) A purchaser of chattel paper has priority over a security interest in the chattel paper that is claimed merely as proceeds of inventory subject to a security interest if:

(1) in good faith and in the ordinary course of the purchaser's business, the purchaser gives new value and takes possession of the chattel paper or obtains control of the chattel paper under Section 9.105; and

(2) the chattel paper does not indicate that it has been assigned to an identified assignee other than the purchaser.

(b) A purchaser of chattel paper has priority over a security interest in the chattel paper that is claimed other than merely as proceeds of inventory subject to a security interest if the purchaser gives new value and takes possession of the chattel paper or obtains control of the chattel paper under Section 9.105 in good faith, in the ordinary course of the purchaser's business, and without knowledge that the purchase violates the rights of the secured party.

(c) Except as otherwise provided in Section 9.327, a purchaser having priority in chattel paper under Subsection (a) or (b) also has priority in proceeds of the chattel paper to the extent that:

(1) Section 9.322 provides for priority in the proceeds; or

(2) the proceeds consist of the specific goods covered by the chattel paper or cash proceeds of the specific goods, even if the purchaser's security interest in the proceeds is unperfected.

(d) Except as otherwise provided in Section 9.331(a), a purchaser of an instrument has priority over a security interest in the instrument perfected by a method other than possession if the purchaser gives value and takes possession of the instrument in good faith and without knowledge that the purchase violates the rights of the secured party.

(e) For purposes of Subsections (a) and (b), the holder of a purchase-money security interest in inventory gives new value for chattel paper constituting proceeds of the inventory.

(f) For purposes of Subsections (b) and (d), if chattel paper or an instrument indicates that it has been assigned to an identified secured party other than the purchaser, a purchaser of the chattel paper or instrument has knowledge that the purchase violates the rights of the secured party.

Added by Acts 1999, 76th Leg., ch. 414, § 1.01, eff. July 1, 2001.

Uniform Commercial Code Comment

1. **Source.** Former Section 9–308.

2. **Non-Temporal Priority.** This Article permits a security interest in chattel paper or instruments to be perfected either by filing or by the secured party's taking possession. This section enables secured parties and other purchasers of chattel paper (both electronic and tangible) and instruments to obtain priority over earlier-perfected security interests.

3. **Chattel Paper.** Subsections (a) and (b) follow former Section 9–308 in distinguishing between earlier-perfected security interests in chattel paper that is claimed merely as proceeds of inventory subject to a security interest and chattel paper that is claimed other than merely as proceeds. Like former Section 9–308, this section does not elaborate upon the phrase "merely as proceeds." For an elaboration, see PEB Commentary No. 8.

This section makes explicit the "good faith" requirement and retains the requirements of "the ordinary course of the purchaser's business" and the giving of "new value" as conditions for priority. Concerning the last, this Article deletes former Section 9–108 and adds to Section 9–102 a completely different definition of the term "new value." Under subsection (e), the holder of a purchase-money security interest in inventory is deemed to give "new value" for chattel paper constituting the proceeds of the inventory. Accordingly, the purchase-money secured party may qualify for priority in the chattel paper under subsection (a) or (b), whichever is applicable, even if it does not make an additional advance against the chattel paper.

If a possessory security interest in tangible chattel paper or a perfected-by-control security interest in electronic chattel paper does not qualify for priority under this section, it may be subordinate to a perfected-by-filing security interest under Section 9–322(a)(1).

4. **Possession.** The priority afforded by this section turns in part on whether a purchaser "takes possession" of tangible chattel paper. Similarly, the governing law provisions in Section 9–301 address both "possessory" and "nonpossessory" security interests. Two common practices have raised particular concerns. First, in some cases the parties create more than one copy or counterpart of chattel paper evidencing a single secured obligation or lease. This practice raises questions as to which counterpart is the "original" and whether it is necessary for a purchaser to take possession of all counterparts in order to "take possession" of the chattel paper. Second, parties sometimes enter into a single "master" agreement. The master agreement contemplates that the parties will enter into separate "schedules" from time to time, each evidencing chattel paper. Must a purchaser of an obligation or lease evidenced by a single schedule also take possession of the master agreement as well as the schedule in order to "take possession" of the chattel paper?

The problem raised by the first practice is easily solved. The parties may in the terms of their agreement and by designation on the chattel paper identify only one counterpart as the original chattel paper for purposes of taking possession of the chattel paper. Concerns about the second practice also are easily solved by careful drafting. Each schedule should provide that it incorporates the terms of the master agreement, not the other way around. This will make it clear that each schedule is a "stand alone" document.

5. **Chattel Paper Claimed Merely as Proceeds.** Subsection (a) revises the rule in former Section 9–308(b) to eliminate reference to what the purchaser knows. Instead, a purchaser who meets the possession or control, ordinary course, and new value requirements takes priority over a competing security interest unless the chattel paper itself indicates that it has been assigned to an identified assignee other than the purchaser. Thus subsection (a) recognizes

the common practice of placing a "legend" on chattel paper to indicate that it has been assigned. This approach, under which the chattel paper purchaser who gives new value in ordinary course can rely on possession of unlegended, tangible chattel paper without any concern for other facts that it may know, comports with the expectations of both inventory and chattel paper financers.

6. **Chattel Paper Claimed Other Than Merely as Proceeds.** Subsection (b) eliminates the requirement that the purchaser take without knowledge that the "specific paper" is subject to the security interest and substitutes for it the requirement that the purchaser take "without knowledge that the purchase violates the rights of the secured party." This standard derives from the definition of "buyer in ordinary course of business" in Section 1–201(9). The source of the purchaser's knowledge is irrelevant. Note, however, that "knowledge" means "actual knowledge." Section 1–201(25).

In contrast to a junior secured party in accounts, who may be required in some special circumstances to undertake a search under the "good faith" requirement, see Comment 5 to Section 9–331, a purchaser of chattel paper under this section is not required as a matter of good faith to make a search in order to determine the existence of prior security interests. There may be circumstances where the purchaser undertakes a search nevertheless, either on its own volition or because other considerations make it advisable to do so, e.g., where the purchaser also is purchasing accounts. Without more, a purchaser of chattel paper who has seen a financing statement covering the chattel paper or who knows that the chattel paper is encumbered with a security interest, does not have knowledge that its purchase violates the secured party's rights. However, if a purchaser sees a statement in a financing statement to the effect that a purchase of chattel paper from the debtor would violate the rights of the filed secured party, the purchaser would have such knowledge. Likewise, under new subsection (f), if the chattel paper itself indicates that it had been assigned to an identified secured party other than the purchaser, the purchaser would have wrongful knowledge for purposes of subsection (b), thereby preventing the purchaser from qualifying for priority under that subsection, even if the purchaser did not have actual knowledge. In the case of tangible chattel paper, the indication normally would consist of a written legend on the chattel paper. In the case of electronic chattel paper, this Article leaves to developing market and technological practices the manner in which the chattel paper would indicate an assignment.

7. **Instruments.** Subsection (d) contains a special priority rule for instruments. Under this subsection, a purchaser of an instrument has priority over a security interest perfected by a method other than possession (e.g., by filing, temporarily under Section 9–312(e) or (g), as proceeds under Section 9–315(d), or automatically upon attachment under Section 9–309(4) if the security interest arises out of a sale of the instrument) if the purchaser gives value and takes possession of the instrument in good faith and without knowledge that the purchase violates the rights of the secured party. Generally, to the extent subsection (d) conflicts with Section 3–306, subsection (d) governs. See Section 3–102(b). For example, notice of a conflicting security interest precludes a purchaser from becoming a holder in due course under Section 3–302 and thereby taking free of all claims to the instrument under Section 3–306. However, a purchaser who takes even with knowledge of the security interest qualifies for priority under subsection (d) if it takes without knowledge that the purchase violates the rights of the holder of the security interest. Likewise, a purchaser qualifies for priority under subsection (d) if it takes for "value" as defined in Section 1–201, even if it does not take for "value" as defined in Section 3–303.

Subsection (d) is subject to Section 9–331(a), which provides that Article 9 does not limit the rights of a holder in due course under Article 3. Thus, in the rare case in which the purchaser of an instrument qualifies for priority under subsection (d), but another person has the rights of a holder in due course of the instrument, the other person takes free of the purchaser's claim. See Section 3–306.

The rule in subsection (d) is similar to the rules in subsections (a) and (b), which govern priority in chattel paper. The observations in Comment 6 concerning the requirement of good faith and the phrase "without knowledge that the purchase violates the rights of the secured party" apply equally to purchasers of instruments. However, unlike a purchaser of chattel paper, to qualify for priority under this section a purchaser of an instrument need only give "value" as defined in Section 1–201; it need not give "new value." Also, the purchaser need not purchase the instrument in the ordinary course of its business.

Subsection (d) applies to checks as well as notes. For example, to collect and retain checks that are proceeds (collections) of accounts free of a senior secured party's claim to the same checks, a junior secured party must satisfy the good-faith requirement (honesty in fact and the observance of reasonable commercial standards of fair dealing) of this subsection. This is the same good-faith requirement applicable to holders in due course. See Section 9–331, Comment 5.

8. **Priority in Proceeds of Chattel Paper.** Subsection (c) sets forth the two circumstances under which the priority afforded to a purchaser of chattel paper under subsection (a) or (b) extends also to proceeds of the chattel paper. The first is if the purchaser would have priority under the normal priority rules applicable to proceeds. The second, which the following Comments discuss in greater detail, is if the proceeds consist of the specific goods covered by the chattel paper. Former Article 9 generally was silent as to the priority of a security interest in proceeds when a purchaser qualifies for priority under Section 9–308 (but see former Section 9–306(5)(b), concerning returned and repossessed goods).

9. **Priority in Returned and Repossessed Goods.** Returned and repossessed goods may constitute proceeds of chattel paper. The following Comments explain the treatment of returned and repossessed goods as proceeds of chattel paper. The analysis is consistent with that of PEB Commentary No. 5, which these Comments replace, and is based upon the following example:

Example: SP–1 has a security interest in all the inventory of a dealer in goods (Dealer); SP–1's security interest is perfected by filing. Dealer sells some of its inventory to a buyer in the ordinary course of business (BIOCOB) pursuant to a conditional sales contract (chattel paper) that does not indicate that it has been assigned to SP–1. SP–2 purchases the chattel paper from Dealer and takes possession of the paper in good faith, in the ordinary course of business, and without knowledge that the purchase violates the rights of SP–1. Subsequently, BIOCOB returns the goods to Dealer because they are defective. Alternatively, Dealer acquires possession of the goods following BIOCOB's default.

10. **Assignment of Non–Lease Chattel Paper.**

a. **Loan by SP–2 to Dealer Secured by Chattel Paper (or Functional Equivalent Pursuant to Recourse Arrangement).**

(1) **Returned Goods.** If BIOCOB returns the goods to Dealer for repairs, Dealer is merely a bailee and acquires thereby no meaningful rights in the goods to which SP–1's security interest could attach. (Although SP–1's security interest could attach to Dealer's interest as a bailee, that interest is not likely to be of any particular value to SP–1.) Dealer is the owner of the *chattel paper* (i.e., the owner of a right to payment secured by a security interest in the goods); SP–2 has a security interest in the chattel paper, as does SP–1 (as proceeds of the goods under Section 9–315). Under Section 9–330, SP–2's security interest in the chattel paper is senior to that of SP–1. SP–2 enjoys this priority regardless of whether, or when, SP–2 filed a financing statement covering the chattel paper. Because chattel paper and goods represent different types of collateral, Dealer does not have any meaningful interest in *goods* to which either SP–1's or SP–2's security interest could attach in order to secure Dealer's obligations to either creditor. See Section 9–102 (defining "chattel paper" and "goods").

Now assume that BIOCOB returns the goods to Dealer under circumstances whereby Dealer once again becomes the owner of the goods. This would be the case, for example, if the goods were defective and BIOCOB was entitled to reject or revoke acceptance of the goods. See Sections 2–602 (rejection), 2–608 (revocation of acceptance). Unless BIOCOB has waived its defenses as against assignees of the chattel paper, SP–1's and SP–2's rights against BIOCOB would be subject to BIOCOB's claims and defenses. See Sections 9–403, 9–404. SP–1's security interest would attach again because the returned goods would be proceeds of the chattel paper. Dealer's acquisition of the goods easily can be characterized as "proceeds" consisting of an "in kind" collection on or distribution on account of the chattel paper. See Section 9–102 (definition of "proceeds"). Assuming that SP–1's security interest is perfected by filing against the goods and that the filing is made in the same office where a filing would be made against the chattel paper, SP–1's security interest in the goods would remain perfected beyond the 20–day period of automatic perfection. See Section 9–315(d).

Because Dealer's newly reacquired interest in the goods is proceeds of the chattel paper, SP–2's security interest also would attach in the goods as proceeds. If SP–2 had perfected its security interest in the chattel paper by filing (again, assuming that filing against the chattel paper was made in the same office where a filing would be made against the goods), SP–2's security interest in the reacquired goods would be perfected beyond 20 days. See Section 9–315(d). However, if SP–2 had relied only on its possession of the chattel paper for perfection and had not filed against the chattel paper or the goods, SP–2's security interest would be unperfected after the 20–day period. See Section 9–315(d). Nevertheless, SP–2's unperfected security interest in the goods would be senior to SP–1's security interest under Section 9–330(c). The result in this priority contest is not affected by SP–2's acquiescence or non-acquiescence in the return of the goods to Dealer.

(2) **Repossessed Goods.** As explained above, Dealer owns the chattel paper covering the goods, subject to security interests in favor of SP–1 and SP–2. In Article 9 parlance, Dealer has an interest in chattel paper, not goods. If Dealer, SP–1, or SP–2 repossesses the goods upon BIOCOB's default, whether the repossession is rightful or wrongful as among Dealer, SP–1, or SP–2, Dealer's interest will not change. The location of goods and the party who possesses them does not affect the fact that Dealer's interest is in chattel paper, not goods. The goods continue to be owned by BIOCOB. SP–1's security interest in the goods does not attach until such time as Dealer reacquires an interest (other than a bare possessory interest) in the goods. For example, Dealer might buy the goods at a foreclosure sale from SP–2 (whose security interest in the chattel paper is senior to that of SP–1); that disposition would cut off BIOCOB's rights in the goods. Section 9–617.

In many cases the matter would end upon sale of the goods to Dealer at a foreclosure sale and there would be no priority contest between SP–1 and SP–2; Dealer would be unlikely to buy the goods under circumstances whereby SP–2 would retain its security interest. There can be exceptions, however. For example, Dealer may be obliged to purchase the goods from SP–2 and SP–2 may be obliged to convey the goods to Dealer, but Dealer may fail to pay SP–2. Or, one could imagine that SP–2, like SP–1, has a general security interest in the inventory of Dealer. In the latter case, SP–2 should not receive the benefit of any special priority rule, since its interest in no way derives from priority under Section 9–330. In the former case, SP–2's security interest in the goods reacquired by Dealer is senior to SP–1's security interest under Section 9–330.

b. **Dealer's Outright Sale of Chattel Paper to SP–2.** Article 9 also applies to a transaction whereby SP–2 buys the chattel paper in an outright sale transaction without recourse against Dealer. Sections 1–201(37), 9–109(a). Although Dealer does not, in such a transaction, retain any residual ownership interest in the chattel paper, the chattel paper constitutes proceeds of the goods to which SP–1's security interest will attach and continue following the sale of the goods. Section 9–315(a). Even though Dealer has not retained any interest in the chattel paper, as discussed above BIOCOB subsequently may return the goods to Dealer under circumstances whereby Dealer reacquires an interest in the goods. The priority contest between SP–1 and SP–2 will be resolved as discussed above; Section 9–330 makes no distinction among purchasers of chattel paper on the basis of whether the purchaser is an outright buyer of chattel paper or one whose security interest secures an obligation of Dealer.

11. **Assignment of Lease Chattel Paper.** As defined in Section 9–102, "chattel paper" includes not only writings that evidence security interests in specific goods but also those that evidence true leases of goods.

The analysis with respect to lease chattel paper is similar to that set forth above with respect to non-lease chattel paper. It is complicated, however, by the fact that, unlike the case of chattel paper arising out of a sale, Dealer retains a residual interest in the *goods*. See Section 2A-103(1)(q) (defining "lessor's residual interest"); *In re Leasing Consultants, Inc.*, 486 F.2d 367 (2d Cir.1973) (lessor's residual interest under true lease is an interest in goods and is a separate type of collateral from lessor's interest in the lease). If Dealer leases goods to a "lessee in ordinary course of business" (LIOCOB), then LIOCOB takes its interest under the lease (i.e., its "leasehold interest") free of the security interest of SP-1. See Sections 2A-307(3), 2A-103(1)(m) (defining "leasehold interest"), (1)(*o*) (defining "lessee in ordinary course of business"). SP-1 would, however, retain its security interest in the residual interest. In addition, SP-1 would acquire an interest in the lease chattel paper as proceeds. If Dealer then assigns the lease chattel paper to SP-2, Section 9-330 gives SP-2 priority over SP-1 with respect to the chattel paper, *but not* with respect to the residual interest in the *goods*. Consequently, assignees of lease chattel paper typically take a security interest in and file against the lessor's residual interest in goods, expecting their priority in the goods to be governed by the first-to-file-or-perfect rule of Section 9-322.

If the goods are returned to Dealer, other than upon expiration of the lease term, then the security interests of both SP-1 and SP-2 normally would attach to the goods as proceeds of the chattel paper. (If the goods are returned to Dealer at the expiration of the lease term and the lessee has made all payments due under the lease, however, then Dealer no longer has any rights under the chattel paper. Dealer's interest in the goods consists solely of its residual interest, as to which SP-2 has no claim.) This would be the case, for example, when the lessee rescinds the lease or when the lessor recovers possession in the exercise of its remedies under Article 2A. See, e.g., Section 2A-525. If SP-2 enjoyed priority in the chattel paper under Section 9-330, then SP-2 likewise would enjoy priority in the returned goods as proceeds. This does not mean that SP-2 necessarily is entitled to the entire value of the returned goods. The value of the goods represents the sum of the present value of (i) the value of their use for the term of the lease and (ii) the value of the residual interest. SP-2 has priority in the former, but SP-1 ordinarily would have priority in the latter. Thus, an allocation of a portion of the value of the goods to each component may be necessary. Where, as here, one secured party has a security interest in the lessor's residual interest and another has a priority security interest in the chattel paper, it may be advisable for the conflicting secured parties to establish a method for making such an allocation and otherwise to determine their relative rights in returned goods by agreement.

§ 9.331. Priority of Rights of Purchasers of Instruments, Documents, and Securities Under Other Chapters; Priority of Interests in Financial Assets and Security Entitlements Under Chapter 8

(a) This chapter does not limit the rights of a holder in due course of a negotiable instrument, a holder to which a negotiable document of title has been duly negotiated, or a protected purchaser of a security. These holders or purchasers take priority over an earlier security interest, even if perfected, to the extent provided in Chapters 3, 7, and 8.

(b) This chapter does not limit the rights of or impose liability on a person to the extent that the person is protected against the assertion of a claim under Chapter 8.

(c) Filing under this chapter does not constitute notice of a claim or defense to the holders, or purchasers, or persons described in Subsections (a) and (b).

Added by Acts 1999, 76th Leg., ch. 414, § 1.01, eff. July 1, 2001. Amended by Acts 2001, 77th Leg., ch. 705, § 8, eff. June 13, 2001.

Uniform Commercial Code Comment

1. **Source.** Former Section 9-309.

2. **"Priority."** In some provisions, this Article distinguishes between claimants that take collateral free of a security interest (in the sense that the security interest no longer encumbers the collateral) and those that take an interest in the collateral that is senior to a surviving security interest. See, e.g., Section 9-317. Whether a holder or purchaser referred to in this section takes free or is senior to a security interest depends on whether the purchaser is a buyer of the collateral or takes a security interest in it. The term "priority" is meant to encompass both scenarios, as it does in Section 9-330.

3. **Rights Acquired by Purchasers.** The rights to which this section refers are set forth in Sections 3-305 and 3-306 (holder in due course), 7-502 (holder to whom a negotiable document of title has been duly negotiated), and 8-303 (protected purchaser). The holders and purchasers referred to in this section do not always take priority over a security interest. See, e.g., Section 7-503 (affording paramount rights to certain owners and secured parties as against holder to whom a negotiable document of title has been duly negotiated). Accordingly, this section adds the clause, "to the extent provided in Articles 3, 7, and 8" to former Section 9-309.

4. **Financial Assets and Security Entitlements.** New subsection (b) provides explicit protection for those who deal with financial assets and security entitlements and who are immunized from liability under Article 8. See, e.g., Sections 8-502, 8-503(e), 8-510, 8-511. The new subsection makes explicit in Article 9 what is implicit in former Article 9 and explicit in several provisions of Article 8. It does not change the law.

5. **Collections by Junior Secured Party.** Under this section, a secured party with a junior security interest in receivables (accounts, chattel paper, promissory notes, or payment intangibles) may collect and retain the proceeds of those receivables free of the claim of a senior secured party to the same receivables, if the junior secured party is a holder in due course of the proceeds. In order to qualify as a holder in due course, the junior must satisfy the requirements of Section 3-302, which include taking in "good faith." This means that the junior not only must act "honestly" but also must observe "reasonable commercial standards of fair

dealing" under the particular circumstances. See Section 9–102(a). Although "good faith" does not impose a general duty of inquiry, e.g., a search of the records in filing offices, there may be circumstances in which "reasonable commercial standards of fair dealing" would require such a search.

Consider, for example, a junior secured party in the business of financing or buying accounts who fails to undertake a search to determine the existence of prior security interests. Because a search, under the usages of trade of that business, would enable it to know or learn upon reasonable inquiry that collecting the accounts violated the rights of a senior secured party, the junior may fail to meet the good-faith standard. See *Utility Contractors Financial Services, Inc. v. Amsouth Bank, NA*, 985 F.2d 1554 (11th Cir.1993). Likewise, a junior secured party who collects accounts when it knows or should know under the particular circumstances that doing so would violate the rights of a senior secured party, because the debtor had agreed not to grant a junior security interest in, or sell, the accounts, may not meet the good-faith test. Thus, if a junior secured party conducted or should have conducted a search and a financing statement filed on behalf of the senior secured party states such a restriction, the junior's collection would not meet the good-faith standard. On the other hand, if there was a course of performance between the senior secured party and the debtor which placed no such restrictions on the debtor and allowed the debtor to collect and use the proceeds without any restrictions, the junior secured party may then satisfy the requirements for being a holder in due course. This would be more likely in those circumstances where the junior secured party was providing additional financing to the debtor on an on-going basis by lending against or buying the accounts and had no notice of any restrictions against doing so. Generally, the senior secured party would not be prejudiced because the practical effect of such payment to the junior secured party is little different than if the debtor itself had made the collections and subsequently paid the secured party from the debtor's general funds. Absent collusion, the junior secured party would take the funds free of the senior security interests. See Section 9–332. In contrast, the senior secured party is likely to be prejudiced if the debtor is going out of business and the junior secured party collects the accounts by notifying the account debtors to make payments directly to the junior. Those collections may not be consistent with "reasonable commercial standards of fair dealing."

Whether the junior secured party qualifies as a holder in due course is fact-sensitive and should be decided on a case-by-case basis in the light of those circumstances. Decisions such as *Financial Management Services Inc. v. Familian*, 905 P.2d 506 (Ariz. App.Div.1995) (finding holder in due course status) could be determined differently under this application of the good-faith requirement.

The concepts addressed in this Comment are also applicable to junior secured parties as purchasers of instruments under Section 9–330(d). See Section 9–330, Comment 7.

§ 9.332. Transfer of Money; Transfer of Funds From Deposit Account

(a) A transferee of money takes the money free of a security interest unless the transferee acts in collusion with the debtor in violating the rights of the secured party.

(b) A transferee of funds from a deposit account takes the funds free of a security interest in the deposit account unless the transferee acts in collusion with the debtor in violating the rights of the secured party.

Added by Acts 1999, 76th Leg., ch. 414, § 1.01, eff. July 1, 2001.

Uniform Commercial Code Comment

1. **Source.** New.

2. **Scope of This Section.** This section affords broad protection to transferees who take funds from a deposit account and to those who take money. The term "transferee" is not defined; however, the debtor itself is not a transferee. Thus this section does not cover the case in which a debtor withdraws money (currency) from its deposit account or the case in which a bank debits an encumbered account and credits another account it maintains for the debtor.

A transfer of funds from a deposit account, to which subsection (b) applies, normally will be made by check, by funds transfer, or by debiting the debtor's deposit account and crediting another depositor's account.

Example 1: Debtor maintains a deposit account with Bank A. The deposit account is subject to a perfected security interest in favor of Lender. Debtor draws a check on the account, payable to Payee. Inasmuch as the check is not the proceeds of the deposit account (it is an order to pay funds from the deposit account), Lender's security interest in the deposit account does not give rise to a security interest in the check. Payee deposits the check into its own deposit account, and Bank A pays it. Unless Payee acted in collusion with Debtor in violating Lender's rights, Payee takes the funds (the credits running in favor of Payee) free of Lender's security interest. This is true regardless of whether Payee is a holder in due course of the check and even if Payee gave no value for the check.

Example 2: Debtor maintains a deposit account with Bank A. The deposit account is subject to a perfected security interest in favor of Lender. At Bank B's suggestion, Debtor moves the funds from the account at Bank A to Debtor's deposit account with Bank B. Unless Bank B acted in collusion with Debtor in violating Lender's rights, Bank B takes the funds (the credits running in favor of Bank B) free from Lender's security interest. See subsection (b). However, inasmuch as the deposit account maintained with Bank B constitutes the proceeds of the deposit account at Bank A, Lender's security interest would attach to that account as proceeds. See Section 9–315.

Subsection (b) also would apply if, in the example, Bank A debited Debtor's deposit account in exchange for the issuance of Bank A's cashier's check. Lender's security interest would attach to the cashier's check as proceeds of the deposit account, and the rules applicable to instruments would govern any competing claims to the cashier's check. See, e.g., Sections 3–306, 9–322, 9–330, 9–331.

If Debtor withdraws money (currency) from an encumbered deposit account and transfers the money to a third party, then subsection (a), to the extent not displaced by federal law relating to money, applies. It contains the same rule as subsection (b).

Subsection (b) applies to *transfers of funds from* a deposit account; it does not apply to *transfers of the deposit account* itself or of an interest therein. For example, this section does not apply to the creation of a security interest in a deposit account. Competing claims to the deposit account itself are dealt with by other Article 9 priority rules. See Sections 9–317(a), 9–327, 9–340, 9–341. Similarly, a corporate merger normally would not result in a transfer of funds from a deposit account. Rather, it might result in a transfer of the deposit account itself. If so, the normal rules applicable to transferred collateral would apply; this section would not.

3. **Policy.** Broad protection for transferees helps to ensure that security interests in deposit accounts do not impair the free flow of funds. It also minimizes the likelihood that a secured party will enjoy a claim to whatever the transferee purchases with the funds. Rules concerning recovery of payments traditionally have placed a high value on finality. The opportunity to upset a completed transaction, or even to place a completed transaction in jeopardy by bringing suit against the transferee of funds, should be severely limited. Although the giving of value usually is a prerequisite for receiving the ability to take free from third-party claims, where payments are concerned the law is even more protective. Thus, Section 3–418(c) provides that, even where the law of restitution otherwise would permit recovery of funds paid by mistake, no recovery may be had from a person "who in good faith changed position in reliance on the payment." Rather than adopt this standard, this section eliminates all reliance requirements whatsoever. Payments made by mistake are relatively rare, but payments of funds from encumbered deposit accounts (e.g., deposit accounts containing collections from accounts receivable) occur with great regularity. In most cases, unlike payment by mistake, no one would object to these payments. In the vast proportion of cases, the transferee probably would be able to show a change of position in reliance on the payment. This section does not put the transferee to the burden of having to make this proof.

4. **"Bad Actors."** To deal with the question of the "bad actor," this section borrows "collusion" language from Article 8. See, e.g., Sections 8–115, 8–503(e). This is the most protective (i.e., least stringent) of the various standards now found in the UCC. Compare, e.g., Section 1–201(9) ("without knowledge that the sale ... is in violation of the ... security interest"); Section 1–201(19) ("honesty in fact in the conduct or transaction concerned"); Section 3–302(a)(2)(v) ("without notice of any claim").

5. **Transferee Who Does Not Take Free.** This section sets forth the circumstances under which certain transferees of money or funds take free of security interests. It does not determine the rights of a transferee who does not take free of a security interest.

Example 3: The facts are as in Example 2, but, in wrongfully moving the funds from the deposit account at Bank A to Debtor's deposit account with Bank B, Debtor acts in collusion with Bank B. Bank B does not take the funds free of Lender's security interest under this section. If Debtor grants a security interest to Bank B, Section 9–327 governs the relative priorities of Lender and Bank B. Under Section 9–327(3), Bank B's security interest in the Bank B deposit account is senior to Lender's security interest in the deposit account as proceeds. However, Bank B's senior security interest does not protect Bank B against any liability to Lender that might arise from Bank B's wrongful conduct.

§ 9.333. Priority of Certain Liens Arising by Operation of Law

(a) In this section, "possessory lien" means an interest, other than a security interest or an agricultural lien:

(1) that secures payment or performance of an obligation for services or materials furnished with respect to goods by a person in the ordinary course of the person's business;

(2) that is created by statute or rule of law in favor of the person; and

(3) whose effectiveness depends on the person's possession of the goods.

(b) A possessory lien on goods has priority over a security interest in the goods unless the lien is created by a statute that expressly provides otherwise.

Added by Acts 1999, 76th Leg., ch. 414, § 1.01, eff. July 1, 2001.

Uniform Commercial Code Comment

1. **Source.** Former Section 9–310.

2. **"Possessory Liens."** This section governs the relative priority of security interests arising under this Article and "possessory liens," i.e., common-law and statutory liens whose effectiveness depends on the lienor's possession of goods with respect to which the lienor provided services or furnished materials in the ordinary course of its business. As under former Section 9–310, the possessory lien has priority over a security interest unless the possessory lien is created by a statute that expressly provides otherwise. If the statute creating the possessory lien is silent as to its priority relative to a security interest, this section provides a rule of interpretation that the possessory lien takes priority, even if the statute has been construed judicially to make the possessory lien subordinate.

§ 9.334. Priority of Security Interests in Fixtures and Crops

(a) A security interest under this chapter may be created in goods that are fixtures or may continue in goods that become fixtures. A security interest does not exist under this chapter in ordinary building materials incorporated into an improvement on land.

(b) This chapter does not prevent creation of an encumbrance upon fixtures under real property law.

(c) In cases not governed by Subsections (d)–(h), a security interest in fixtures is subordinate to a conflicting interest of an encumbrancer or owner of the related real property other than the debtor.

(d) Except as otherwise provided in Subsection (h), a perfected security interest in fixtures has priority over the conflicting interest of an encumbrancer or owner of the real property if the debtor has an interest of record in or is in possession of the real property and:

(1) the security interest is a purchase-money security interest;

(2) the interest of the encumbrancer or owner arises before the goods become fixtures; and

(3) the security interest is perfected by a fixture filing before the goods become fixtures or within 20 days thereafter.

(e) A perfected security interest in fixtures has priority over a conflicting interest of an encumbrancer or owner of the real property if:

(1) the debtor has an interest of record in the real property or is in possession of the real property and the security interest:

(A) is perfected by a fixture filing before the interest of the encumbrancer or owner is of record; and

(B) has priority over any conflicting interest of a predecessor in title of the encumbrancer or owner;

(2) before the goods become fixtures, the security interest is perfected by any method permitted by this chapter and the fixtures are readily removable:

(A) factory or office machines;

(B) equipment that is not primarily used or leased for use in the operation of the real property; or

(C) replacements of domestic appliances that are consumer goods;

(3) the conflicting interest is a lien on the real property obtained by legal or equitable proceedings after the security interest was perfected by any method permitted by this chapter; or

(4) the security interest is:

(A) created in a manufactured home in a manufactured-home transaction; and

(B) perfected pursuant to a statute described in Section 9.311(a)(2).

(f) A security interest in fixtures, whether or not perfected, has priority over the conflicting interest of an encumbrancer or owner of the real property if:

(1) the encumbrancer or owner has, in an authenticated record, consented to the security interest or disclaimed an interest in the goods as fixtures; or

(2) the debtor has a right to remove the goods as against the encumbrancer or owner.

(g) The priority of the security interest under Subsection (f)(2) continues for a reasonable time if the debtor's right to remove the goods as against the encumbrancer or owner terminates.

(h) A mortgage is a construction mortgage to the extent that it secures an obligation incurred for the construction of an improvement on land, including the acquisition cost of the land, if a recorded record of the mortgage so indicates. Except as otherwise provided in Subsections (e) and (f), a security interest in fixtures is subordinate to a construction mortgage if a record of the mortgage is recorded before the goods become fixtures before the completion of the construction. A mortgage has this priority to the same extent as a construction mortgage to the extent that it is given to refinance a construction mortgage.

(i) A perfected security interest in crops growing on real property has priority over a conflicting interest of an encumbrancer or owner of the real property if the debtor has an interest of record in or is in possession of the real property.

Added by Acts 1999, 76th Leg., ch. 414, § 1.01, eff. July 1, 2001. Amended by Acts 2001, 77th Leg., ch. 705, § 9, eff. June 13, 2001.

Uniform Commercial Code Comment

1. **Source.** Former Section 9–313.

2. **Scope of This Section.** This section contains rules governing the priority of security interests in fixtures and crops as against persons who claim an interest in real property. Priority contests with other Article 9 security interests are governed by the other priority rules of this Article. The provisions with respect to fixtures follow those of former Section 9–313. However, they have been rewritten to conform to Section 2A–309 and to prevailing style conventions. Subsections (i) and (j), which apply to crops, are new.

3. **Security Interests in Fixtures.** Certain goods that are the subject of personal-property (chattel) financing become so affixed or otherwise so related to real property that they become part of the real property. These goods are called "fixtures." See Section 9–102 (definition of "fixtures"). Some fixtures retain their personal-property nature: a security interest under this Article may be created in fixtures and may continue in goods that become fixtures. See subsection (a). However, if the goods are ordinary building materials

incorporated into an improvement on land, no security interest in them exists. Rather, the priority of claims to the building materials are determined by the law governing claims to real property.

Thus, this section recognizes three categories of goods: (1) those that retain their chattel character entirely and are not part of the real property; (2) ordinary building materials that have become an integral part of the real property and cannot retain their chattel character for purposes of finance; and (3) an intermediate class that has become real property for certain purposes, but as to which chattel financing may be preserved.

To achieve priority under certain provisions of this section, a security interest must be perfected by making a "fixture filing" (defined in Section 9–102) in the real-property records. Because the question whether goods have become fixtures often is a difficult one under applicable real-property law, a secured party may make a fixture filing as a precaution. Courts should not infer from a fixture filing that the secured party concedes that the goods are or will become fixtures.

4. **Priority in Fixtures: General.** In considering priority problems under this section, one must first determine whether real-property claimants per se have an interest in the crops or fixtures as part of real property. If not, it is immaterial, so far as concerns real property parties as such, whether a security interest arising under this Article is perfected or unperfected. In no event does a real-property claimant (e.g., owner or mortgagee) acquire an interest in a "pure" chattel just because a security interest therein is unperfected. If on the other hand real-property law gives real-property parties an interest in the goods, a conflict arises and this section states the priorities.

5. **Priority in Fixtures: Residual Rule.** Subsection (c) states the residual priority rule, which applies only if one of the other rules does not: A security interest in fixtures is subordinate to a conflicting interest of an encumbrancer or owner of the related real property other than the debtor.

6. **Priority in Fixtures: First to File or Record.** Subsection (e)(1), which follows former Section 9–313(4)(b), contains the usual priority rule of conveyancing, that is, the first to file or record prevails. In order to achieve priority under this rule, however, the security interest must be perfected by a "fixture filing" (defined in Section 9–102), i.e., a filing for record in the real property records and indexed therein, so that it will be found in a real-property search .. The condition in subsection (e)(1)(B), that the security interest must have had priority over any conflicting interest of a predecessor in title of the conflicting encumbrancer or owner, appears to limit to the first-in-time principle. However, this apparent limitation is nothing other than an expression of the usual rule that a person must be entitled to transfer what he has. Thus, if the fixture security interest is subordinate to a mortgage, it is subordinate to an interest of an assignee of the mortgage, even though the assignment is a later recorded instrument. Similarly if the fixture security interest is subordinate to the rights of an owner, it is subordinate to a subsequent grantee of the owner and likewise subordinate to a subsequent mortgagee of the owner.

7. **Priority in Fixtures: Purchase–Money Security Interests.** Subsection (d), which follows former Section 9–313(4)(a), contains the principal exception to the first-to-file-or-record rule of subsection (e)(1). It affords priority to purchase-money security interests in fixtures as against *prior* recorded real-property interests, provided that the purchase-money security interest is filed as a fixture filing in the real-property records before the goods become fixtures or within 20 days thereafter. This priority corresponds to the purchase-money priority under Section 9–324(a).

It should be emphasized that this purchase-money priority with the 20–day grace period for filing is limited to rights against real-property interests that arise *before* the goods become fixtures. There is no such priority with the 20–day grace period as against real-property interests that arise subsequently. The fixture security interest can defeat subsequent real-property interests only if it is filed first and prevails under the usual conveyancing rule in subsection (e)(1) or one of the other rules in this section.

8. **Priority in Fixtures: Readily Removable Goods.** Subsection (e)(2), which derives from Section 2A–309 and former Section 9–313(4)(d), contains another exception to the usual first-to-file-or-perfect rule. It affords priority to the holders of security interests in certain types of readily removable goods–factory and office machines, equipment that is not primarily used or leased for use in the operation of the real property, and (as discussed below) certain replacements of domestic appliances. This rule is made necessary by the confusion in the law as to whether certain machinery, equipment, and appliances become fixtures. It protects a secured party who, perhaps in the mistaken belief that the readily removable goods will not become fixtures, makes a UCC filing (or otherwise perfects under this Article) rather than making a fixture filing.

Frequently, under applicable law, goods of the type described in subsection (e)(2) will not be considered to have become part of the real property. In those cases, the fixture security interest does not conflict with a real-property interest, and resort to this section is unnecessary. However, if the goods have become part of the real property, subsection (e)(2) enables a fixture secured party to take priority over a conflicting real-property interest if the fixture security interest is perfected by a fixture filing or by any other method permitted by this Article. If perfection is by fixture filing, the fixture security interest would have priority over subsequently recorded real-property interests under subsection (e)(1) and, if the fixture security interest is a purchase-money security interest (a likely scenario), it would also have priority over most real property interests under the purchase-money priority of subsection (d). Note, however, that unlike the purchase-money priority rule in subsection (d), the priority rules in subsection (e) override the priority given to a construction mortgage under subsection (h).

The rule in subsection (e)(2) is limited to readily removable replacements of domestic appliances. It does not apply to original installations. Moreover, it is limited to appliances that are "consumer goods" (defined in Section 9–102) in the hands of the debtor. The principal effect of the rule is to make clear that a secured party financing occasional replacements of domestic appliances in noncommercial, owner-occupied contexts need not concern itself with real-property descriptions or records; indeed, for a purchase-money replacement of consumer goods, perfection without any filing will be possible. See Section 9–309(1).

9. **Priority in Fixtures: Judicial Liens.** Subsection (e)(3), which follows former Section 9–313(4)(d), adopts a first-in-time rule applicable to conflicts between a fixture security interest and a lien on the real property obtained by legal or equitable proceedings. Such a lien is subordinate to an earlier-perfected security interest, regardless of the method by which the security interest was perfected. Judgment creditors generally are not reliance creditors who search real-property records. Accordingly, a perfected fixture security interest takes priority over a subsequent judgment lien or other lien obtained by legal or equitable proceedings, even if no evidence of the security interest appears in the relevant real-property records. Subsection (e)(3) thus protects a perfected fixture security interest from avoidance by a trustee in bankruptcy under Bankruptcy Code Section 544(a), regardless of the method of perfection.

10. **Priority in Fixtures: Manufactured Homes.** A manufactured home may become a fixture. New subsection (e)(4) contains a special rule granting priority to certain security interests created in a "manufactured home" as part of a "manufactured-home transaction" (both defined in Section 9–102). Under this rule, a security interest in a manufactured home that becomes a fixture has priority over a conflicting interest of an encumbrancer or owner of the real property if the security interest is perfected under a certificate-of-title statute (see Section 9–311). Subsection (e)(4) is only one of the priority rules applicable to security interests in a manufactured home that becomes a fixture. Thus, a security interest in a manufactured home which does not qualify for priority under this subsection may qualify under another.

11. **Priority in Fixtures: Construction Mortgages.** The purchase-money priority presents a difficult problem in relation to construction mortgages. The latter ordinarily will have been recorded even before the commencement of delivery of materials to the job, and therefore would take priority over fixture security interests were it not for the purchase-money priority. However, having recorded first, the holder of a construction mortgage reasonably expects to have first priority in the improvement built using the mortgagee's advances. Subsection (g) expressly gives priority to the construction mortgage recorded before the filing of the purchase-money security interest in fixtures. A refinancing of a construction mortgage has the same priority as the construction mortgage itself. The phrase "an obligation incurred for the construction of an improvement" covers both optional advances and advances pursuant to commitment. Both types of advances have the same priority under subsection (g).

The priority under this subsection applies only to goods that become fixtures during the construction period leading to the completion of the improvement. The construction priority will not apply to additions to the building made long after completion of the improvement, even if the additions are financed by the real-property mortgagee under an open-end clause of the construction mortgage. In such case, subsections (d), (e), and (f) govern.

Although this subsection affords a construction mortgage priority over a purchase-money security interest that otherwise would have priority under subsection (d), the subsection is subject to the priority rules in subsections (e) and (f). Thus, a construction mortgage may be junior to a fixture security interest perfected by a fixture filing before the construction mortgage was recorded. See subsection (e)(1).

12. **Crops.** Growing crops are "goods" in which a security interest may be created and perfected under this Article. In some jurisdictions, a mortgage of real property may cover crops, as well. In the event that crops are encumbered by both a mortgage and an Article 9 security interest, subsection (i) provides that the security interest has priority. States whose real-property law provides otherwise should either amend that law directly or override it by enacting subsection (j).

§ 9.335. Accessions

(a) A security interest may be created in an accession and continues in collateral that becomes an accession.

(b) If a security interest is perfected when the collateral becomes an accession, the security interest remains perfected in the collateral.

(c) Except as otherwise provided in Subsection (d), the other provisions of this subchapter determine the priority of a security interest in an accession.

(d) A security interest in an accession is subordinate to a security interest in the whole that is perfected by compliance with the requirements of a certificate-of-title statute under Section 9.311(b).

(e) After default, subject to Subchapter F, a secured party may remove an accession from other goods if the security interest in the accession has priority over the claims of every person having an interest in the whole.

(f) A secured party that removes an accession from other goods under Subsection (e) shall promptly reimburse any holder of a security interest or other lien on, or owner of, the whole or the other goods, other than the debtor, for the cost of repair of any physical injury to the whole or the other goods. The secured party need not reimburse the holder or owner for any diminution in value of the whole or the other goods caused by the absence of the accession removed or by any necessity for replacing it. A person entitled to reimbursement may refuse permission to remove until the secured party gives adequate assurance for the performance of the obligation to reimburse.

Added by Acts 1999, 76th Leg., ch. 414, § 1.01, eff. July 1, 2001.

Uniform Commercial Code Comment

1. **Source.** Former Section 9–314.

2. **"Accession."** This section applies to an "accession," as defined in Section 9–102, regardless of the cost or difficulty

of removing the accession from the other goods, and regardless of whether the original goods have come to form an integral part of the other goods. This section does not apply to goods whose identity has been lost. Goods of that kind are "commingled goods" governed by Section 9–336. Neither this section nor the following one addresses the case of collateral that changes form without the addition of other goods.

3. **"Accession" vs. "Other Goods."** This section distinguishes among the "accession," the "other goods," and the "whole." The last term refers to the combination of the "accession" and the "other goods." If one person's collateral becomes physically united with another person's collateral, each is an "accession."

Example 1: SP–1 holds a security interest in the debtor's tractors (which are not subject to a certificate-of-title statute), and SP–2 holds a security interest in a particular tractor engine. The engine is installed in a tractor. From the perspective of SP–1, the tractor becomes an "accession" and the engine is the "other goods." From the perspective of SP–2, the engine is the "accession" and the tractor is the "other goods." The completed tractor–tractor cum engine–constitutes the "whole."

4. **Scope.** This section governs only a few issues concerning accessions. Subsection (a) contains rules governing continuation of a security interest in an accession. Subsection (b) contains a rule governing continued perfection of a security interest in goods that become an accession. Subsection (d) contains a special priority rule governing accessions that become part of a whole covered by a certificate of title. Subsections (e) and (f) govern enforcement of a security interest in an accession.

5. **Matters Left to Other Provisions of This Article: Attachment and Perfection.** Other provisions of this Article often govern accession-related issues. For example, this section does not address whether a secured party acquires a security interest in the whole if its collateral becomes an accession. Normally this will turn on the description of the collateral in the security agreement.

Example 2: Debtor owns a computer subject to a perfected security interest in favor of SP–1. Debtor acquires memory and installs it in the computer. Whether SP–1's security interest attaches to the memory depends on whether the security agreement covers it.

Similarly, this section does not determine whether perfection against collateral that becomes an accession is effective to perfect a security interest in the whole. Other provisions of this Article, including the requirements for indicating the collateral covered by a financing statement, resolve that question.

6. **Matters Left to Other Provisions of This Article: Priority.** With one exception, concerning goods covered by a certificate of title (see subsection (d)), the other provisions of this Part, including the rules governing purchase-money security interests, determine the priority of most security interests in an accession, including the relative priority of a security interest in an accession and a security interest in the whole. See subsection (c).

Example 3: Debtor owns an office computer subject to a security interest in favor of SP–1. Debtor acquires memory and grants a perfected security interest in the memory to SP–2. Debtor installs the memory in the computer, at which time (one assumes) SP–1's security interest attaches to the memory. The first-to-file-or-perfect rule of Section 9–322 governs priority in the memory. If, however, SP–2's security interest is a purchase-money security interest, Section 9–324(a) would afford priority in the memory to SP–2, regardless of which security interest was perfected first.

7. **Goods Covered by Certificate of Title.** This section does govern the priority of a security interest in an accession that is or becomes part of a whole that is subject to a security interest perfected by compliance with a certificate-of-title statute. Subsection (d) provides that a security interest in the whole, perfected by compliance with a certificate-of-title statute, takes priority over a security interest in the accession. It enables a secured party to rely upon a certificate of title without having to check the UCC files to determine whether any components of the collateral may be encumbered. The subsection imposes a corresponding risk upon those who finance goods that may become part of goods covered by a certificate of title. In doing so, it reverses the priority that appeared reasonable to most pre-UCC courts.

Example 4: Debtor owns an automobile subject to a security interest in favor of SP–1. The security interest is perfected by notation on the certificate of title. Debtor buys tires subject to a perfected-by-filing purchase-money security interest in favor of SP–2 and mounts the tires on the automobile's wheels. If the security interest in the automobile attaches to the tires, then SP–1 acquires priority over SP–2. The same result would obtain if SP–1's security interest attached to the automobile and was perfected after the tires had been mounted on the wheels.

§ 9.336. Commingled Goods

(a) In this section, "commingled goods" means goods that are physically united with other goods in such a manner that their identity is lost in a product or mass.

(b) A security interest does not exist in commingled goods as such. However, a security interest may attach to a product or mass that results when goods become commingled goods.

(c) If collateral becomes commingled goods, a security interest attaches to the product or mass.

(d) If a security interest in collateral is perfected before the collateral becomes commingled goods, the security interest that attaches to the product or mass under Subsection (c) is perfected.

(e) Except as otherwise provided in Subsection (f), the other provisions of this subchapter determine the priority of a security interest that attaches to the product or mass under Subsection (c).

(f) If more than one security interest attaches to the product or mass under Subsection (c), the following rules determine priority:

(1) A security interest that is perfected under Subsection (d) has priority over a security interest that is unperfected at the time the collateral becomes commingled goods.

(2) If more than one security interest is perfected under Subsection (d), the security interests rank equally in proportion to the value of the collateral at the time it became commingled goods.

Added by Acts 1999, 76th Leg., ch. 414, § 1.01, eff. July 1, 2001. Amended by Acts 2001, 77th Leg., ch. 705, § 10, eff. June 13, 2001.

Uniform Commercial Code Comment

1. **Source.** Former Section 9–315.

2. **"Commingled Goods."** Subsection (a) defines "commingled goods." It is meant to include not only goods whose identity is lost through manufacturing or production (e.g., flour that has become part of baked goods) but also goods whose identity is lost by commingling with other goods from which they cannot be distinguished (e.g., ball bearings).

3. **Consequences of Becoming "Commingled Goods."** By definition, the identity of the original collateral cannot be determined once the original collateral becomes commingled goods. Consequently, the security interest in the specific original collateral alone is lost once the collateral becomes commingled goods, and no security interest in the original collateral can be created thereafter except as a part of the resulting product or mass. See subsection (b).

Once collateral becomes commingled goods, the secured party's security interest is transferred from the original collateral to the product or mass. See subsection (c). If the security interest in the original collateral was perfected, the security interest in the product or mass is a perfected security interest. See subsection (d). This perfection continues until lapse.

4. **Priority of Perfected Security Interests That Attach Under This Section.** This section governs the priority of competing security interests in a product or mass only when both security interests arise under this section. In that case, if both security interests are perfected by operation of this section (see subsections (c) and (d)), then the security interests rank equally, in proportion to the value of the collateral at the time it became commingled goods. See subsection (f)(2).

Example 1: SP–1 has a perfected security interest in Debtor's eggs, which have a value of $300 and secure a debt of $400, and SP–2 has a perfected security interest in Debtor's flour, which has a value of $500 and secures a debt of $700. Debtor uses the flour and eggs to make cakes, which have a value of $1000. The two security interests rank equally and share in the ratio of 3:5. Applying this ratio to the entire value of the product, SP–1 would be entitled to $375 (i.e., 3/8 x $1000), and SP–2 would be entitled to $625 (i.e., 5/8 x $1000).

Example 2: Assume the facts of Example 1, except that SP–1's collateral, worth $300, secures a debt of $200. Recall that, if the cake is worth $1000, then applying the ratio of 3:5 would entitle SP–1 to $375 and SP–2 to $625. However, SP–1 is not entitled to collect from the product more than it is owed. Accordingly, SP–1's share would be only $200, SP–2 would receive the remaining value, up to the amount it is owed ($700).

Example 3: Assume that the cakes in the previous examples have a value of only $600. Again, the parties share in the ratio of 3:5. If, as in Example 1, SP–1 is owed $400, then SP–1 is entitled to $225 (i.e., 3/8 x $600), and SP–2 is entitled to $375 (i.e., 5/8 x $600). Debtor receives nothing. If, however, as in Example 2, SP–1 is owed only $200, then SP–2 receives $400.

The results in the foregoing examples remain the same, regardless of whether SP–1 or SP–2 (or each) has a purchase-money security interest.

5. **Perfection: Unperfected Security Interests.** The rule explained in the preceding Comment applies only when both security interests in original collateral are perfected when the goods become commingled goods. If a security interest in original collateral is unperfected at the time the collateral becomes commingled goods, subsection (f)(1) applies.

Example 4: SP–1 has a perfected security interest in the debtor's eggs, and SP–2 has an unperfected security interest in the debtor's flour. Debtor uses the flour and eggs to make cakes. Under subsection (c), both security interests attach to the cakes. But since SP–1's security interest was perfected at the time of commingling and SP–2's was not, only SP–1's security interest in the cakes is perfected. See subsection (d). Under subsection (f)(1) and Section 9–322(a)(2), SP–1's perfected security interest has priority over SP–2's unperfected security interest.

If both security interests are unperfected, the rule of Section 9–322(a)(3) would apply.

6. **Multiple Security Interests.** On occasion, a single input may be encumbered by more than one security interest. In those cases, the multiple secured parties should be treated like a single secured party for purposes of determining their collective share under subsection (f)(2). The normal priority rules would determine how that share would be allocated between them. Consider the following example, which is a variation on Example 1 above:

Example 5: SP–1A has a perfected, first-priority security interest in Debtor's eggs. SP–1B has a perfected, second-priority security interest in the same collateral. The eggs have a value of $300. Debtor owes $200 to SP–1A and $200 to SP–1B. SP–2 has a perfected security interest in Debtor's flour, which has a value of $500 and secures a debt of $600. Debtor uses the flour and eggs to make cakes, which have a value of $1000.

For purposes of subsection (f)(2), SP–1A and SP–1B should be treated like a single secured party. The collective security interest would rank equally with that of SP–2. Thus, the secured parties would share in the ratio of 3 (for SP–1A and SP–1B combined) to 5 (for SP–2). Applying this ratio to the entire value of the product, SP–1A and SP–1B in the aggregate would be entitled to $375 (i.e., 3/8 x $1000), and SP–2 would be entitled to $625 (i.e., 5/8 x $1000).

SP–1A and SP–1B would share the $375 in accordance with their priority, as established under other rules. Inasmuch as SP–1A has first priority, it would receive $200, and SP–1B would receive $175.

7. **Priority of Security Interests That Attach Other Than by Operation of This Section.** Under subsection (e), the normal priority rules determine the priority of a security interest that attaches to the product or mass other than by operation of this section. For example, assume that SP–1 has a perfected security interest in Debtor's existing and after-acquired baked goods, and SP–2 has a perfected security interest in Debtor's flour. When the flour is processed into cakes, subsections (c) and (d) provide that SP–2 acquires a perfected security interest in the cakes. If SP–1 filed against the baked goods before SP–2 filed against the flour, then SP–1 will enjoy priority in the cakes. See Section 9–322 (first-to-file-or-perfect). But if SP–2 filed against the flour before SP–1 filed against the baked goods, then SP–2 will enjoy priority in the cakes to the extent of its security interest.

§ 9.337. Priority of Security Interests in Goods Covered by Certificate of Title

If, while a security interest in goods is perfected by any method under the law of another jurisdiction, this state issues a certificate of title that does not show that the goods are subject to the security interest or contain a statement that they may be subject to security interests not shown on the certificate:

(1) a buyer of the goods, other than a person in the business of selling goods of that kind, takes free of the security interest if the buyer gives value and receives delivery of the goods after issuance of the certificate and without knowledge of the security interest; and

(2) the security interest is subordinate to a conflicting security interest in the goods that attaches, and is perfected under Section 9.311(b), after issuance of the certificate and without the conflicting secured party's knowledge of the security interest.

Added by Acts 1999, 76th Leg., ch. 414, § 1.01, eff. July 1, 2001.

Uniform Commercial Code Comment

1. **Source.** Derived from former Section 9–103(2)(d).

2. **Protection for Buyers and Secured Parties.** This section affords protection to certain good-faith purchasers for value who are likely to have relied on a "clean" certificate of title, i.e., one that neither shows that the goods are subject to a particular security interest nor contains a statement that they may be subject to security interests not shown on the certificate. Under this section, a buyer can take free of, and the holder of a conflicting security interest can acquire priority over, a security interest that is perfected by any method under the law of another jurisdiction. The fact that the security interest has been reperfected by possession under Section 9–313 does not of itself disqualify the holder of a conflicting security interest from protection under paragraph (2).

§ 9.338. Priority of Security Interest or Agricultural Lien Perfected by Filed Financing Statement Providing Certain Incorrect Information

If a security interest or agricultural lien is perfected by a filed financing statement providing information described in Section 9.516(b)(5) that is incorrect at the time the financing statement is filed:

(1) the security interest or agricultural lien is subordinate to a conflicting perfected security interest in the collateral to the extent that the holder of the conflicting security interest gives value in reasonable reliance upon the incorrect information; and

(2) a purchaser, other than a secured party, of the collateral takes free of the security interest or agricultural lien to the extent that, in reasonable reliance upon the incorrect information, the purchaser gives value and, in the case of tangible chattel paper, tangible documents, goods, instruments, or a security certificate, receives delivery of the collateral.

Added by Acts 1999, 76th Leg., ch. 414, § 1.01, eff. July 1, 2001. Amended by Acts 2005, 79th Leg., ch. 122, § 29, eff. Sept. 1, 2005.

Uniform Commercial Code Comment

1. **Source.** New.

2. **Effect of Incorrect Information in Financing Statement.** Section 9–520(a) requires the filing office to reject financing statements that do not contain information concerning the debtor as specified in Section 9–516(b)(5). An error in this information does not render the financing statement ineffective. On rare occasions, a subsequent purchaser of the collateral (i.e., a buyer or secured party) may rely on the misinformation to its detriment. This section subordinates a security interest or agricultural lien perfected by an effective, but flawed, financing statement to the rights of a buyer or holder of a perfected security interest to the extent that, in reasonable reliance on the incorrect information, the purchaser gives value and, in the case of tangible collateral, receives delivery of the collateral. A purchaser who has not made itself aware of the information in the filing office with respect to the debtor cannot act in "reasonable reliance" upon incorrect information.

3. **Relationship to Section 9–507.** This section applies to financing statements that contain information that is incorrect at the time of filing and imposes a small risk of subordination on the filer. In contrast, Section 9–507 deals with financing statements containing information that is cor-

rect at the time of filing but which becomes incorrect later. Except as provided in Section 9–507 with respect to changes in the debtor's name, an otherwise effective financing statement does not become ineffective if the information contained in it becomes inaccurate.

Sections 31 and 32 of Acts 2005, 79th Leg., ch. 122 provide:

"Sec. 31. This Act applies to a document of title that is issued or a bailment that arises on or after the effective date of this Act. This Act does not apply to a document of title that is issued or a bailment that arises before the effective date of this Act even if the document of title or bailment would be subject to this Act if the document of title had been issued or bailment had arisen after the effective date of this Act. This Act does not apply to a right of action that has accrued before the effective date of this Act.

"Sec. 32. A document of title issued or a bailment that arises before the effective date of this Act and the rights, obligations, and interests flowing from that document or bailment are governed by any statute or other rule amended or repealed by this Act as if amendment or repeal had not occurred and may be terminated, completed, consummated, or enforced under that statute or other rule."

§ 9.339. Priority Subject to Subordination

This chapter does not preclude subordination by agreement by a person entitled to priority.

Added by Acts 1999, 76th Leg., ch. 414, § 1.01, eff. July 1, 2001.

Uniform Commercial Code Comment

1. **Source.** Former Section 9–316.

2. **Subordination by Agreement.** The preceding sections deal elaborately with questions of priority. This section makes it entirely clear that a person entitled to priority may effectively agree to subordinate its claim. Only the person entitled to priority may make such an agreement: a person's rights cannot be adversely affected by an agreement to which the person is not a party.

§ 9.340. Effectiveness of Right of Recoupment or Set-Off Against Deposit Account

(a) Except as otherwise provided in Subsection (c), a bank with which a deposit account is maintained may exercise any right of recoupment or set-off against a secured party that holds a security interest in the deposit account.

(b) Except as otherwise provided in Subsection (c), the application of this chapter to a security interest in a deposit account does not affect a right of recoupment or set-off of the secured party as to a deposit account maintained with the secured party.

(c) The exercise by a bank of a set-off against a deposit account is ineffective against a secured party that holds a security interest in the deposit account that is perfected by control under Section 9.104(a)(3), if the set-off is based on a claim against the debtor.

Added by Acts 1999, 76th Leg., ch. 414, § 1.01, eff. July 1, 2001.

Uniform Commercial Code Comment

1. **Source.** New; subsection (b) is based on a nonuniform Illinois amendment.

2. **Set-off vs. Security Interest.** This section resolves the conflict between a security interest in a deposit account and the bank's rights of recoupment and set-off.

Subsection (a) states the general rule and provides that the bank may effectively exercise rights of recoupment and set-off against the secured party. Subsection (c) contains an exception: if the secured party has control under Section 9–104(a)(3) (i.e., if it has become the bank's customer), then any set-off exercised by the bank against a debt owed by the debtor (as opposed to a debt owed to the bank by the secured party) is ineffective. The bank may, however, exercise its recoupment rights effectively. This result is consistent with the priority rule in Section 9–327(4), under which the security interest of a bank in a deposit account is subordinate to that of a secured party who has control under Section 9–104(a)(3).

This section deals with rights of set-off and recoupment that a bank may have under other law. It does not create a right of set-off or recoupment, nor is it intended to override any limitations or restrictions that other law imposes on the exercise of those rights.

3. **Preservation of Set–Off Right.** Subsection (b) makes clear that a bank may hold both a right of set-off against, and an Article 9 security interest in, the same deposit account. By holding a security interest in a deposit account, a bank does not impair any right of set-off it would otherwise enjoy. This subsection does not pertain to accounts evidenced by an instrument (e.g., certain certificates of deposit), which are excluded from the definition of "deposit accounts."

§ 9.341. Bank's Rights and Duties With Respect to Deposit Account

Except as otherwise provided in Section 9.340(c), and unless the bank otherwise agrees in an authenticated record, a bank's rights and duties with respect to a deposit account maintained with the bank are not terminated, suspended, or modified by:

(1) the creation, attachment, or perfection of a security interest in the deposit account;

(2) the bank's knowledge of the security interest; or

(3) the bank's receipt of instructions from the secured party.

Added by Acts 1999, 76th Leg., ch. 414, § 1.01, eff. July 1, 2001.

Uniform Commercial Code Comment

1. **Source.** New.

2. **Free Flow of Funds.** This section is designed to prevent security interests in deposit accounts from impeding the free flow of funds through the payment system. Subject to two exceptions, it leaves the bank's rights and duties with respect to the deposit account and the funds on deposit unaffected by the creation or perfection of a security interest or by the bank's knowledge of the security interest. In addition, the section permits the bank to ignore the instructions of the secured party unless it had agreed to honor them or unless other law provides to the contrary. A secured party who wishes to deprive the debtor of access to funds on deposit or to appropriate those funds for itself needs to obtain the agreement of the bank, utilize the judicial process, or comply with procedures set forth in other law. Section 4–303(a), concerning the effect of notice on a bank's right and duty to pay items, is not to the contrary. That section addresses only whether an otherwise effective notice comes too late; it does not determine whether a timely notice is otherwise effective.

3. **Operation of Rule.** The general rule of this section is subject to Section 9–340(c), under which a bank's right of set-off may not be exercised against a deposit account in the secured party's name if the right is based on a claim against the debtor. This result reflects current law in many jurisdictions and does not appear to have unduly disrupted banking practices or the payments system. The more important function of this section, which is not impaired by Section 9–340, is the bank's right to follow the debtor's (customer's) instructions (e.g., by honoring checks, permitting withdrawals, etc.) until such time as the depository institution is served with judicial process or receives instructions with respect to the funds on deposit from a secured party who has control over the deposit account.

4. **Liability of Bank.** This Article does not determine whether a bank that pays out funds from an encumbered deposit is liable to the holder of a security interest. Although the fact that a secured party has control over the deposit account and the manner by which control was achieved may be relevant to the imposition of liability, whatever rule applies generally when a bank pays out funds in which a third party has an interest would determine liability to a secured party. Often, this rule is found in a non-UCC adverse claim statute.

5. **Certificates of Deposit.** This section does not address the obligations of banks that issue instruments evidencing deposits (e.g., certain certificates of deposit).

§ 9.342. Bank's Right to Refuse to Enter Into or Disclose Existence of Control Agreement

This chapter does not require a bank to enter into an agreement of the kind described in Section 9.104(a)(2), even if its customer so requests or directs. A bank that has entered into such an agreement is not required to confirm the existence of the agreement to another person unless requested to do so by its customer.

Added by Acts 1999, 76th Leg., ch. 414, § 1.01, eff. July 1, 2001.

Uniform Commercial Code Comment

1. **Source.** New; derived from Section 8–106(g).

2. **Protection for Bank.** This section protects banks from the need to enter into agreements against their will and from the need to respond to inquiries from persons other than their customers.

§ 9.343. Oil and Gas Interests: Security Interest Perfected Without Filing; Statutory Lien

(a) This section provides a security interest in favor of interest owners, as secured parties, to secure the obligations of the first purchaser of oil and gas production, as debtor, to pay the purchase price. An authenticated record giving the interest owner a right under real property law operates as a security agreement created under this chapter. The act of the first purchaser in signing an agreement to purchase oil or gas production, in issuing a division order, or in making any other voluntary communication to the interest owner or any governmental agency recognizing the interest owner's right operates as an authentication of a security agreement in accordance with Section 9.203(b) for purposes of this chapter.

(b) The security interest provided by this section is perfected automatically without the filing of a financing statement. If the interest of the secured party is evidenced by a deed, mineral deed, reservation in either, oil or gas lease, assignment, or any other such record recorded in the real property records of a county clerk, that record is effective as a filed financing statement for purposes of this chapter, but no fee is required except a fee that is otherwise required by the county clerk, and there is no requirement of refiling every five years to maintain effectiveness of the filing.

(c) The security interest exists in oil and gas production, and also in the identifiable proceeds of that production owned by, received by, or due to the first purchaser:

(1) for an unlimited time if:

(A) the proceeds are oil or gas production, inventory of raw, refined, or manufactured oil or gas production, or rights to or products of any of those, although the sale of those proceeds by a first purchaser to a buyer in the ordinary course of business as provided in Subsection (e) cuts off the security interest in those proceeds;

(B) the proceeds are accounts, chattel paper, instruments, documents, or payment intangibles; or

(C) the proceeds are cash proceeds, as defined in Section 9.102; and

(2) for the length of time provided in Section 9.315 for all other proceeds.

(d) This section creates a lien that secures the payment of all taxes that are or should be withheld or paid by the first purchaser and a lien that secures the rights of any person who would be entitled to a security interest under Subsection (a) except for lack of any adoption of a security agreement by the first purchaser or a lack of possession or record required by Section 9.203 for the security interest to be enforceable.

(e) The security interests and liens created by this section have priority over any purchaser who is not a buyer in the ordinary course of the first purchaser's business, but are cut off by the sale to a buyer from the first purchaser who is in the ordinary course of the first purchaser's business under Section 9.320(a). But in either case, whether or not the buyer from the first purchaser is in ordinary course, a security interest will continue in the proceeds of the sale by the first purchaser as provided in Subsection (c).

(f) The security interests and all liens created by this section have the following priorities over other Chapter 9 security interests:

(1) A security interest created by this section is treated as a purchase-money security interest for purposes of determining its relative priority under Section 9.324 over other security interests not provided for by this section. A holder of a security interest created under this section is not required to give the written notice every five years as provided in Section 9.324(b)(3) to have purchase-money priority over a security interest with a prior financing statement covering inventory.

(2) A statutory lien is subordinate to all other perfected Chapter 9 security interests and has priority over unperfected Chapter 9 security interests and the lien creditors, buyers, and transferees mentioned in Section 9.317.

(g) The security interests and liens created by this section have the following priorities among themselves:

(1) If a record effective as a filed financing statement under Subsection (b) exists, the security interests perfected by that record have priority over a security interest automatically perfected without filing under Subsection (b). If several security interests perfected by records exist, they have the same priority among themselves as established by real property law for interests in oil and gas in place. If real property law establishes no priority among them, they share priority pro rata.

(2) A security interest perfected automatically without filing under Subsection (b) has priority over a lien created under Subsection (d).

(3) A nontax lien under Subsection (d) has priority over a lien created under that subsection that secures the payment of taxes.

(h) The priorities for statutory liens mentioned in Section 9.333 do not apply to any security interest or statutory lien created by this section. But if a pipeline common carrier has a statutory or tariff lien that is effective and enforceable against a trustee in bankruptcy and not invalidated by the Federal Tax Lien Act, that lien has priority over the security interests and statutory liens created by this section.

(i) If oil or gas production in which there are security interests or statutory liens created by this section is commingled with inventory or other production, the rules of Section 9.336 apply.

(j) A security interest or statutory lien created by this section remains effective against the debtor and perfected against the debtor's creditors even if assigned, regardless of whether the assignment is perfected against the assignor's creditors. If a deed, mineral deed, assignment of oil and gas lease, or other such record evidencing the assignment is filed in the real property records of the county, it will have the same effect as filing an amended financing statement under Section 9.514.

(k) This section does not impair an operator's right to set-off or withhold funds from other interest owners as security for or in satisfaction of any debt or security interest. In case of a dispute between an operator and another interest owner, a good faith tender of funds by anyone to the person who the operator and other interest owner agree on, to a person who otherwise shows himself or herself to be the one entitled to the funds, or to a court of competent jurisdiction in the event of litigation or bankruptcy operates as a tender of the funds to both.

(*l*) A first purchaser who acts in good faith may terminate an interest owner's security interest or statutory lien under this section by paying, or by making and keeping open a tender of, the amount the first purchaser believes to be due to the interest owner:

(1) if the interest owner's rights are to oil or gas production or its proceeds, either to the operator alone, in which event the operator is considered the first purchaser, or to some combination of the interest owner and the operator, as the first purchaser chooses;

(2) whatever the nature of the production to which the interest owner has rights, to the person that the interest owner agreed to or acquiesced in; or

(3) to a court of competent jurisdiction in the event of litigation or bankruptcy.

(m) A person who buys from a first purchaser can ensure that the person buys free and clear of an interest owner's security interest or statutory lien under this section:

(1) by buying in the ordinary course of the first purchaser's business from the first purchaser under Section 9.320(a);

(2) by obtaining the interest owner's consent to the sale under Section 9.315(a)(1);

(3) by ensuring that the first purchaser has paid the interest owner or, provided that gas production is involved, or the interest owner has so agreed or acquiesced, by ensuring that the first purchaser has paid the interest owner's operator; or

(4) by ensuring that the person or the first purchaser or some other person has withheld funds sufficient to pay amounts in dispute and has maintained a tender of those funds to whoever shows himself or herself to be the person entitled.

(n) If a tender under Subsection (m)(4) that is valid thereafter fails, the security interest and liens governed by this section remain effective.

(*o*) In addition to the usual remedy of sequestration available to secured parties, and the remedies given in Subchapter F, [1] the holders of security interests and liens created by this section have available to them, to the extent constitutionally permitted, the remedies of replevin, attachment, and garnishment to assist them in realizing upon their rights.

(p) The rights of any person claiming under a security interest or lien created by this section are governed by the other provisions of this chapter except to the extent that this section necessarily displaces those provisions. This section does not invalidate or otherwise affect the interests of any person in any real property before severance of any oil or gas production.

(q) The security interest created under Subsections (a) and (b) do not apply to proceeds of gas production that have been withheld, in cash or account form, by a purchaser under Section 201.204(c), Tax Code.

(r) In this section:

(1) "Oil and gas production" means any oil, natural gas, condensate of either, natural gas liquids, other gaseous, liquid, or dissolved hydrocarbons, sulfur, or helium, or other substance produced as a by-product or adjunct to their production, or any combination of these, which is severed, extracted, or produced from the ground, the seabed, or other submerged lands within the jurisdiction of this state. Any such substance, including recoverable or recovered natural gas liquids, that is transported to or in a natural gas pipeline or natural gas gathering system, or otherwise transported or sold for use as natural gas, or is transported or sold for the extraction of helium or natural gas liquids is "gas production." Any such substance that is transported or sold to persons and for purposes not included in the foregoing natural gas definition is "oil production."

(2) "Interest owner" means a person owning an entire or fractional interest of any kind or nature in oil or gas production at the time of severance, or a person who has an express, implied, or constructive right to receive a monetary payment determined by the value of oil or gas production or by the amount of production.

(3) "First purchaser" means the first person that purchases oil or gas production from an operator or interest owner after the production is severed, or an operator that receives production proceeds from a third-party purchaser who acts in good faith under a division order or other agreement authenticated by the operator under which the operator collects proceeds of production on behalf of other interest owners. To the extent the operator receives proceeds attributable to the interest of other interest owners from a third-party purchaser who acts in good faith under a division order or other agreement authenticated by such operator, the operator is considered to be the first purchaser of the production for all purposes under this section, notwith-

standing the characterization of other persons as first purchasers under other laws or regulations. To the extent the operator has not received from the third-party purchaser proceeds attributable to the operator's interest and the interest of other interest owners, the operator is not considered the first purchaser for the purposes of this section and is entitled to all rights and benefits under this section. Nothing in this section impairs or affects any rights otherwise held by a royalty owner to take its share of oil in kind or receive payment directly from a third-party purchaser for the royalty owner's share of oil production with or without a previously made agreement.

(4) "Operator" means a person engaged in the business of severing oil or gas production from the ground, whether for the person alone, only for other persons, or for the person and others.

Added by Acts 1999, 76th Leg., ch. 414, § 1.01, eff. July 1, 2001.

[1] V.T.C.A., Bus. & C. § 9.601 et seq.

State Bar Committee Comment

1. **Source.** Former Section 9.319.

2. **History.** The 68th Legislature added the nonuniform predecessor of this section to Chapter 9 in 1983 (1983 Tex. Gen. Laws, ch. 807, sec. 1, eff. Aug. 29, 1983) and modest amendments were made in 1987 (1987 Tex. Gen. Laws, ch. 601, secs. 1 & 2, eff. Sept. 1, 1987). Except for stylistic changes, renumbering of statutory cross-references, and rephrasing (e.g., references to "authenticated record" instead of "signed security agreement"), the substantive content of former Section 9.319 has been carried over into this section as a nonuniform amendment to revised Chapter 9.

3. **Purpose.** As originally published in Vernon's Texas Bus. & Com. Code Ann. in 1984, the former sec. 9.319 included an "Official Comment" by Mr. Colin Kaufman, primary author of the nonuniform sec. 9.319, who was then teaching at St. Mary's University School of Law. That comment still reflects the purpose of this nonuniform provision and is quoted in full immediately below. Bracketed material in the comment updates some of the statutory references that have been renumbered since publication of the original comment.

OFFICIAL COMMENT

By

Professor Colin Kaufman, St. Mary's University, for the Conference Committee Report on House Bill No. 846 (Chapter 807) of the 68th Legislature

1. Although real estate law governs rights to oil and gas in place as between owners, operators and first purchasers, it can give no Article Nine security interest in the goods after severance. This section fills that lack. There is a New Mexico statute which addressed similar problems. This section gives interest owners rights to oil production in the hands of a "first purchaser" and his transferees. An "operator" is not a first purchaser unless in addition to acting as lessee or agent in operating a lease (including producing and storing oil production), he agrees to buy production from an interest owner. An operator must do something inconsistent with agency status to be a first purchaser.

2. The greatest problems to be solved in a statute like this are presented by federal law. Revised Statutes Sec. 3466 [now 31 U.S.C. sec. 3713] applies in insolvency proceedings, the Bankruptcy Code applies in case of bankruptcy, and the Federal Tax Lien Act applies also. All these statutes distinguish in their application between consensual security interests and statutory liens. Therefore state law should draw the same distinction.

3. Some interests in oil and gas leases are not necessarily reflected by a writing, but exist by virtue of resulting or constructive trusts. See e.g. *Gaines v. Hamman,* 358 S.W.2d 557 (Tex.1962). Sec. 9.203 makes a writing necessary to create a consensual Article 9 security interest unless there is possession by the secured party. Subsection (d) solves that problem by giving a statutory lien. A statutory lien is also given for severance and other taxes due to the state.

4. Although Article Nine security interests take their collateral before the priority rules of Sec. 507 of the Bankruptcy Code come into play, statutory liens for taxes are given a much lower position. The legislative history to Sec. 724(b) of the Bankruptcy Code shows that Congress intended such liens to come between the fifth and sixth priority categories of Sec. 507. A circular priority problem arises if state law tries to place statutory liens ahead of security interests, while bankruptcy law makes statutory liens inferior to certain unsecured debts and expenses of administration. A possible solution is for both security interests and statutory liens to lose to the trustee in bankruptcy. Cf. *In re Quaker City Uniform Co.,* 238 F.2d 155 (3d Cir. 1956), *cert. denied* 352 U.S. 1030. This section avoids the problem by adopting the same priority as would apply in bankruptcy. Also, Congress intended consensual security interests to have rights superior to the government under Revised Statute 3466 [now 31 U.S.C. sec. 3713] and the Federal Tax Lien Act, while leaving most statutory liens subject to the requirements of "choateness". *United States v. Kimbell Foods, Inc.,* 440 U.S. 715, 99 S.Ct. 1448, 59 L.Ed.2d 711 (1979). This makes it necessary for all the consensual security interests recognized by this section to have priority over all the statutory liens recognized by it, if circular priority problems are to be avoided. Pipeline common carriers, who have a lien accompanied by possession, are sometimes said to have a lien effective against their customers' trustee in bankruptcy and valid in case of a federal tax lien filing. If this view is accurate, such a lien

will continue to enjoy the priority which Section 9.310 of this code provides. Under *Kimbell Foods,* a priority over the federal tax lien will probably be recognized as superior to federal rights under Revised Statute 3466 [now 31 U.S.C. sec. 3713].

5. It is fair to give these interest holders and non-tax statutory liens the same priority in the inventory produced that they would have if they went through all the motions required to get the best rights they can under Article 9, i.e., a purchase money security interest in inventory, in the oil and gas accounts mentioned in Sec. 9.103(e) [now 9.102(a)(6)] of Article 9, and in those proceeds which they would think of taking an interest in. This section gives them these rights without making them go through the motions. Their relation to the transaction is already well understood. Requiring them to follow Article 9's requirements would add nothing to the understanding of others. People in the business of dealing with operators and "first purchasers" are substantially aware that royalty owners and the like always exist and have a claim to the production. No unfair surprise will result if their claim also extends to proceeds. Their identities can be discovered through the realty records in most cases. Where rights exist in people who cannot be discovered from such records, those rights are almost invariably shares in or fractions of rights which are disclosed. Thus another secured party lending on the security of a first purchaser's inventory may be in doubt as to who is owed money by the first purchaser, but he is seldom in doubt as to how much the first purchaser might owe all persons claiming an Article 9 security interest or a statutory lien under this section. Since only purchase money interests get rights under this section, other secured parties lending to first purchasers do not have to worry about future advances or later loans reducing the value of collateral available to them, as they might ordinarily worry in the usual case governed by Sec. 9.312 [now 9.322, 9.323 and 9.324].

6. Article 9 treats a sale or other absolute assignment of an account or chattel paper as an Article 9 "secured transaction". See Section 9.102(a)(2) [now 9.109(a)(2); see also 9.109(e)]. Although the 1972 amendments made some exceptions to this rule to deal with the problems of cases like *Spurlin v. Sloan,* 368 S.W.2d 314 (Kentucky 1963), see Section 9.104(f) [now 9.109(d)(4)–(7)], generally this means that the assignment by the interest owner of his "account" or "chattel paper" rights to payment for his share of the production are treated for Article 9 purposes as a secured transaction by which the interest owner is the debtor and the assignee is the secured party. If the assignee does not get a filed financing statement to perfect this second "secured transaction", then the assignor's creditors can defeat him, even though the underlying assigned rights include a security interest perfected without filing under Subsection (b). This problem is raised by cases like *General Electric Credit Corp. v. Bankers Commercial Corp.,* 244 Ark. 984, 429 S.W.2d 60 (1968). This section provides that failure to perfect the second "secured transaction" will not affect the perfection and validity of the underlying assigned security interest.

7. Subsection (g)(1) makes the "automatic perfection" security interests inferior as against third parties to those which are also "filing" (recorded) security interests. This carries out the policy behind the recording statute, which requires recording in the real estate records for an interest in realty to have maximum protection against third parties. This provision merely carries that real estate priority forward as a priority in the oil produced, and also as a priority in proceeds. It is not intended to alter any rights which the holder of an unrecorded writing may have against the one who gave him that writing, or against any other holder of a recorded interest. Likewise the section does not alter the rights of anyone claiming against the holder of a recorded interest under a theory of resulting or constructive trust or some other theory which does not require a writing.

8. This section deals with security interests and liens given to secure valid debts. It does not deal with the concept, "what is a valid debt." This is a problem not addressed by Article 9 at all. This section is not intended to displace or harm any right of set off or other rule of law limiting the extent of the debt secured by this section. See Section 9.104(i) [now 9.109(d)(10)] excluding rights of set off from the scope of Article 9. This section is intended to assure that honest interest owners get what is due them, not to assure that dishonest interest owners will have any greater ability to avoid paying their own debts to their operators.

9. This section's provisions on who can be paid to avoid the interest owner's security interest or statutory lien reflect existing practice. The prevailing practice in the gas industry has been for the use of 100% division orders. Gas interest owners have not yet gone unpaid. So it seemed an undue burden to change historic ways of doing business to require gas pipeline companies and gathering systems to insist on paying individual interest owners directly. Such direct payments are much more common in oil sales. Direct payments would be a new way of doing business for very few first purchasers of oil, though they might have to extend existing ways of doing business to new transactions. Disruption of existing arrangements is unlikely because this section allows payment to someone else (the operator) to discharge the interest owner's security interest or statutory lien whenever the interest owner acquiesced in or agreed to this style of doing business. The agreement between the interest owner and the operator providing for an operator's lien will probably be the most common agreement by which an interest owner agrees for someone else to collect his money. Of course such a situation is not the only kind of arrangement this section makes effective; the interest owner could agree with the first pur-

chaser or someone further downstream just as effectively.

4. **Research References.** Cynthia G. Grinstead, *The Effect of Texas U.C.C. Section 9.319 on Oil and Gas Secured Transactions,* 63 Tex.L.Rev. 311 (1984); Terry I. Cross & Jason T. Barnes, *Oil and Gas Liens & Foreclosures—A Multi-State Perspective,* 51 Okla.L.Rev. 175 (1998).

SUBCHAPTER D. RIGHTS OF THIRD PARTIES

§ 9.401. Alienability of Debtor's Rights

(a) Except as otherwise provided in Subsection (b) and Sections 9.406, 9.407, 9.408, and 9.409, whether a debtor's rights in collateral may be voluntarily or involuntarily transferred is governed by law other than this chapter.

(b) An agreement between the debtor and secured party that prohibits a transfer of the debtor's rights in collateral or makes the transfer a default does not prevent the transfer from taking effect.

Amended by Acts 1999, 76th Leg., ch. 414, § 1.01, eff. July 1, 2001.

Uniform Commercial Code Comment

1. **Source.** Former Section 9–311.

2. **Scope of This Part.** This Part deals with several issues affecting third parties (i.e., parties other than the debtor and the secured party). These issues are not addressed in Part 3, Subpart 3, which deals with priorities. This Part primarily addresses the rights and duties of account debtors and other persons obligated on collateral who are not, themselves, parties to a secured transaction.

3. **Governing Law.** There was some uncertainty under former Article 9 as to which jurisdiction's law (usually, which jurisdiction's version of Article 9) applied to the matters that this Part addresses. Part 3, Subpart 1, does not determine the law governing these matters because they do not relate to perfection, the effect of perfection or nonperfection, or priority. However, it might be inappropriate for a designation of applicable law by a debtor and secured party under Section 1–105 to control the law applicable to an independent transaction or relationship between the debtor and an account debtor.

Consider an example under Section 9–408.

Example 1: State X has adopted this Article; former Article 9 is the law of State Y. A general intangible (e.g., a franchise agreement) between a debtor-franchisee, D, and an account debtor-franchisor, AD, is governed by the law of State Y. D grants to SP a security interest in its rights under the franchise agreement. The franchise agreement contains a term prohibiting D's assignment of its rights under the agreement. D and SP agree that their secured transaction is governed by the law of State X. Under State X's Section 9–408, the restriction on D's assignment is ineffective to prevent the creation, attachment, or perfection of SP's security interest. State Y's former Section 9–318(4), however, does not address restrictions on the creation of security interests in general intangibles other than general intangibles for money due or to become due. Accordingly, it does not address restrictions on the assignment to SP of D's rights under the franchise agreement. The non-Article–9 law of State Y, which does address restrictions, provides that the prohibition on assignment is effective.

This Article does not provide a specific answer to the question of which State's law applies to the restriction on assignment in the example. However, assuming that under non-UCC choice-of-law principles the effectiveness of the restriction would be governed by the law of State Y, which governs the franchise agreement, the fact that State X's Article 9 governs the secured transaction between SP and D would not override the otherwise applicable law governing the agreement. Of course, to the extent that jurisdictions eventually adopt identical versions of this Article and courts interpret it consistently, the inability to identify the applicable law in circumstances such as those in the example may be inconsequential.

4. **Inalienability Under Other Law.** Subsection (a) addresses the question whether property necessarily is transferable by virtue of its inclusion (i.e., its eligibility as collateral) within the scope of Article 9. It gives a negative answer, subject to the identified exceptions. The substance of subsection (a) was implicit under former Article 9.

5. **Negative Pledge Covenant.** Subsection (b) is an exception to the general rule in subsection (a). It makes clear that in secured transactions under this Article the debtor has rights in collateral (whether legal title or equitable) which it can transfer and which its creditors can reach. It is best explained with an example.

Example 2: A debtor, D, grants to SP a security interest to secure a debt in excess of the value of the collateral. D agrees with SP that it will not create a subsequent security interest in the collateral and that any security interest purportedly granted in violation of the agreement will be void. Subsequently, in violation of its agreement with SP, D purports to grant a security interest in the same collateral to another secured party.

Subsection (b) validates D's creation of the subsequent (prohibited) security interest, which might even achieve priority over the earlier security interest. See Comment 7. However, unlike some other provisions of this Part, such as Section 9–406, subsection (b) does not provide that the agreement restricting assignment itself is "ineffective." Consequently, the debtor's breach may create a default.

6. **Rights of Lien Creditors.** Difficult problems may arise with respect to attachment, levy, and other judicial procedures under which a debtor's creditors may reach collateral subject to a security interest. For example, an obligation may be secured by collateral worth many times the amount of the obligation. If a lien creditor has caused all or a portion of the collateral to be seized under judicial process, it may be difficult to determine the amount of the debtor's "equity" in the collateral that has been seized. The section leaves resolution of this problem to the courts. The doctrine of marshaling may be appropriate.

7. **Sale of Receivables.** If a debtor sells an account, chattel paper, payment intangible, or promissory note outright, as against the buyer the debtor has no remaining rights to transfer. If, however, the buyer fails to perfect its interest, then solely insofar as the rights of certain third parties are concerned, the debtor is deemed to retain its rights and title. See Section 9–318. The debtor has the power to convey these rights to a subsequent purchaser. If the subsequent purchaser (buyer or secured lender) perfects its interest, it will achieve priority over the earlier, unperfected purchaser. See Section 9–322(a)(1).

§ 9.402. Secured Party Not Obligated on Contract of Debtor or in Tort

The existence of a security interest, agricultural lien, or authority given to a debtor to dispose of or use collateral, without more, does not subject a secured party to liability in contract or tort for the debtor's acts or omissions.

Amended by Acts 1999, 76th Leg., ch. 414, § 1.01, eff. July 1, 2001.

Uniform Commercial Code Comment

1. **Source.** Former Section 9–317.

2. **Nonliability of Secured Party.** This section, like former Section 9–317, rejects theories on which a secured party might be held liable on a debtor's contracts or in tort merely because a security interest exists or because the debtor is entitled to dispose of or use collateral. This section expands former Section 9–317 to cover agricultural liens.

§ 9.403. Agreement Not to Assert Defenses Against Assignee

(a) In this section, "value" has the meaning provided in Section 3.303(a).

(b) Except as otherwise provided in this section, an agreement between an account debtor and an assignor not to assert against an assignee any claim or defense that the account debtor may have against the assignor is enforceable by an assignee that takes an assignment:

(1) for value;

(2) in good faith;

(3) without notice of a claim of a property or possessory right to the property assigned; and

(4) without notice of a defense or claim in recoupment of the type that may be asserted against a person entitled to enforce a negotiable instrument under Section 3.305(a).

(c) Subsection (b) does not apply to defenses of a type that may be asserted against a holder in due course of a negotiable instrument under Section 3.305(b).

(d) In a consumer transaction, if a record evidences the account debtor's obligation, law other than this chapter requires that the record include a statement to the effect that the rights of an assignee are subject to claims or defenses that the account debtor could assert against the original obligee, and the record does not include such a statement:

(1) the record has the same effect as if the record included such a statement; and

(2) the account debtor may assert against an assignee those claims and defenses that would have been available if the record included such a statement.

(e) This section is subject to law other than this chapter that establishes a different rule for an account debtor who is an individual and who incurred the obligation primarily for personal, family, or household purposes.

(f) Except as otherwise provided in Subsection (d), this section does not displace law other than this chapter that gives effect to an agreement by an account debtor not to assert a claim or defense against an assignee.

Amended by Acts 1999, 76th Leg., ch. 414, § 1.01, eff. July 1, 2001.

Uniform Commercial Code Comment

1. **Source.** Former Section 9–206.

2. **Scope and Purpose.** Subsection (b), like former Section 9–206, generally validates an agreement between an account debtor and an assignor that the account debtor will not assert against an assignee claims and defenses that it may have against the assignor. These agreements are typical in installment sale agreements and leases. However, this section expands former Section 9–206 to apply to all account debtors; it is not limited to account debtors that have bought or leased goods. This section applies only to the obligations of an "account debtor," as defined in Section 9–102. Thus, it does not determine the circumstances under which and the extent to which a person who is obligated on a negotiable instrument is disabled from asserting claims and defenses. Rather, Article 3 must be consulted. See, e.g., Sections 3–305, 3–306. Article 3 governs even when the negotiable instrument constitutes part of chattel paper. See Section 9–102 (an obligor on a negotiable instrument constituting part of chattel paper is not an "account debtor").

3. **Conditions of Validation; Relationship to Article 3.** Subsection (b) validates an account debtor's agreement only if the assignee takes an assignment for value, in good faith, and without notice of conflicting claims to the property assigned or of certain claims or defenses of the account debtor. Like former Section 9–206, this section is designed

to put the assignee in a position that is no better and no worse than that of a holder in due course of a negotiable instrument under Article 3. However, former Section 9–206 left open certain issues, e.g., whether the section incorporated the special Article 3 definition of "value" in Section 3–303 or the generally applicable definition in Section 1–201(44). Subsection (a) addresses this question; it provides that "value" has the meaning specified in Section 3–303(a). Similarly, subsection (c) provides that subsection (b) does not validate an agreement with respect to defenses that could be asserted against a holder in due course under Section 3–305(b) (the so-called "real" defenses). In 1990, the definition of "holder in due course" (Section 3–302) and the articulation of the rights of a holder in due course (Sections 3–305 and 3–306) were revised substantially. This section tracks more closely the rules of Sections 3–302, 3–305, and 3–306.

4. **Relationship to Terms of Assigned Property.** Former Section 9–206(2), concerning warranties accompanying the sale of goods, has been deleted as unnecessary. This Article does not regulate the terms of the account, chattel paper, or general intangible that is assigned, except insofar as the account, chattel paper, or general intangible itself creates a security interest (as often is the case with chattel paper). Thus, Article 2, and not this Article, determines whether a seller of goods makes or effectively disclaims warranties, even if the sale is secured. Similarly, other law, and not this Article, determines the effectiveness of an account debtor's undertaking to pay notwithstanding, and not to assert, any defenses or claims against an assign*or*–e.g., a "hell-or-high-water" provision in the underlying agreement that is assigned. If other law gives effect to this undertaking, then, under principles of *nemo dat*, the undertaking would be enforceable by the assignee (secured party). If other law prevents the assignor from enforcing the undertaking, this section nevertheless might permit the assignee to do so. The right of the assignee to enforce would depend upon whether, under the particular facts, the account debtor's undertaking fairly could be construed as an agreement that falls within the scope of this section and whether the assignee meets the requirements of this section.

5. **Relationship to Federal Trade Commission Rule.** Subsection (d) is new. It applies to rights evidenced by a record that is required to contain, but does not contain, the notice set forth in Federal Trade Commission Rule 433, 16 C.F.R. Part 433 (the "Holder-in-Due–Course Regulations"). Under this subsection, an assignee of such a record takes subject to the consumer account debtor's claims and defenses to the same extent as it would have if the writing had contained the required notice. Thus, subsection (d) effectively renders waiver-of-defense clauses ineffective in the transactions with consumers to which it applies.

6. **Relationship to Other Law.** Like former Section 9–206(1), this section takes no position on the enforceability of waivers of claims and defenses by consumer account debtors, leaving that question to other law. However, the reference to "law other than this article" in subsection (e) encompasses administrative rules and regulations; the reference in former Section 9–206(1) that it replaces ("statute or decision") arguably did not.

This section does not displace other law that gives effect to a non-consumer account debtor's agreement not to assert defenses against an assignee, even if the agreement would not qualify under subsection (b). See subsection (f). It validates, but does not invalidate, agreements made by a non-consumer account debtor. This section also does not displace other law to the extent that the other law permits an assignee, who takes an assignment with notice of a claim of a property or possessory right, a defense, or a claim in recoupment, to enforce an account debtor's agreement not to assert claims and defenses against the assign*or* (e.g., a "hell-or-high-water" agreement). See Comment 4. It also does not displace an assignee's right to assert that an account debtor is estopped from asserting a claim or defense. Nor does this section displace other law with respect to waivers of potential future claims and defenses that are the subject of an agreement between the account debtor and the assign*ee*. Finally, it does not displace Section 1–107, concerning waiver of a breach that allegedly already has occurred.

§ 9.404. Rights Acquired by Assignee; Claims and Defenses Against Assignee

(a) Unless an account debtor has made an enforceable agreement not to assert defenses or claims, and subject to Subsections (b)–(e), the rights of an assignee are subject to:

(1) all terms of the agreement between the account debtor and assignor and any defense or claim in recoupment arising from the transaction that gave rise to the contract; and

(2) any other defense or claim of the account debtor against the assignor that accrues before the account debtor receives a notification of the assignment authenticated by the assignor or the assignee.

(b) Subject to Subsection (c) and except as otherwise provided in Subsection (d), the claim of an account debtor against an assignor may be asserted against an assignee under Subsection (a) only to reduce the amount the account debtor owes.

(c) This section is subject to law other than this chapter that establishes a different rule for an account debtor who is an individual and who incurred the obligation primarily for personal, family, or household purposes.

(d) In a consumer transaction, if a record evidences the account debtor's obligation, law other than this chapter requires that the record include a statement to the effect that the account debtor's recovery against an assignee with respect to claims and defenses against the assignor may not exceed amounts paid by the account debtor under the record, and the record does not include such a statement, the extent to which a claim of an account debtor against the assignor may be asserted against an assignee is determined as if the record included such a statement.

(e) This section does not apply to an assignment of a health-care-insurance receivable.

Amended by Acts 1999, 76th Leg., ch. 414, § 1.01, eff. July 1, 2001.

Uniform Commercial Code Comment

1. **Source.** Former Section 9–318(1).

2. **Purpose; Rights of Assignee in General.** Subsection (a), like former Section 9–318(1), provides that an assignee generally takes an assignment subject to defenses and claims of an account debtor. Under subsection (a)(1), if the account debtor's defenses on an assigned claim arise from the transaction that gave rise to the contract with the assignor, it makes no difference whether the defense or claim accrues before or after the account debtor is notified of the assignment. Under subsection (a)(2), the assignee takes subject to other defenses or claims only if they accrue before the account debtor has been notified of the assignment. Of course, an account debtor may waive its right to assert defenses or claims against an assignee under Section 9–403 or other applicable law. Subsection (a) tracks Section 3–305(a)(3) more closely than its predecessor.

3. **Limitation on Affirmative Claims.** Subsection (b) is new. It limits the claim that the account debtor may assert against an assignee. Borrowing from Section 3–305(a)(3) and cases construing former Section 9–318, subsection (b) generally does not afford the account debtor the right to an affirmative recovery from an assignee.

4. **Consumer Account Debtors; Relationship to Federal Trade Commission Rule.** Subsections (c) and (d) also are new. Subsection (c) makes clear that the rules of this section are subject to other law establishing special rules for consumer account debtors. An "account debtor who is an individual" as used in subsection (c) includes individuals who are jointly or jointly and severally obligated. Subsection (d) applies to rights evidenced by a record that is required to contain, but does not contain, the notice set forth in Federal Trade Commission Rule 433, 16 C.F.R. Part 433 (the "Holder-in-Due-Course Regulations"). Under subsection (d), a consumer account debtor has the same right to an affirmative recovery from an assignee of such a record as the consumer would have had against the assignee had the record contained the required notice.

5. **Scope; Application to "Account Debtor."** This section deals only with the rights and duties of "account debtors"–and for the most part only with account debtors on accounts, chattel paper, and payment intangibles. Subsection (e) provides that the obligation of an insurer with respect to a health-care-insurance receivable is governed by other law. References in this section to an "account debtor" include account debtors on collateral that is proceeds. Neither this section nor any other provision of this Article, including Sections 9–408 and 9–409, provides analogous regulation of the rights and duties of other obligors on collateral, such as the maker of a negotiable instrument (governed by Article 3), the issuer of or nominated person under a letter of credit (governed by Article 5), or the issuer of a security (governed by Article 8). Article 9 leaves those rights and duties untouched; however, Section 9–409 deals with the special case of letters of credit. When chattel paper is composed in part of a negotiable instrument, the obligor on the instrument is not an "account debtor," and Article 3 governs the rights of the assignee of the chattel paper with respect to the issues that this section addresses. See, e.g., Section 3–601 (dealing with discharge of an obligation to pay a negotiable instrument).

§ 9.405. Modification of Assigned Contract

(a) A modification of or substitution for an assigned contract is effective against an assignee if made in good faith. The assignee acquires corresponding rights under the modified or substituted contract. The assignment may provide that the modification or substitution is a breach of contract by the assignor. This subsection is subject to Subsections (b)–(d).

(b) Subsection (a) applies to the extent that:

(1) the right to payment or a part thereof under an assigned contract has not been fully earned by performance; or

(2) the right to payment or a part thereof has been fully earned by performance and the account debtor has not received notification of the assignment under Section 9.406(a).

(c) This section is subject to law other than this chapter that establishes a different rule for an account debtor who is an individual and who incurred the obligation primarily for personal, family, or household purposes.

(d) This section does not apply to an assignment of a health-care-insurance receivable.

Amended by Acts 1999, 76th Leg., ch. 414, § 1.01, eff. July 1, 2001.

Uniform Commercial Code Comment

1. **Source.** Former Section 9–318(2).

2. **Modification of Assigned Contract.** The ability of account debtors and assignors to modify assigned contracts can be important, especially in the case of government contracts and complex contractual arrangements (e.g., construction contracts) with respect to which modifications are customary. Subsections (a) and (b) provide that good-faith modifications of assigned contracts are binding against an assignee to the extent that (i) the right to payment has not been fully earned or (ii) the right to payment has been earned and notification of the assignment has not been given to the account debtor. Former Section 9–318(2) did not validate modifications of fully-performed contracts under any circumstances, whether or not notification of the assignment had been given to the account debtor. Subsection (a) protects the interests of assignees by (i) limiting the effectiveness of modifications to those made in good faith, (ii) affording the assignee with corresponding rights under the contract as modified, and (iii) recognizing that the modifica-

tion may be a breach of the assignor's agreement with the assignee.

3. **Consumer Account Debtors.** Subsection (c) is new. It makes clear that the rules of this section are subject to other law establishing special rules for consumer account debtors.

4. **Account Debtors on Health-Care-Insurance Receivables.** Subsection (d) also is new. It provides that this section does not apply to an assignment of a health-care-insurance receivable. The obligation of an insurer with respect to a health-care-insurance receivable is governed by other law.

§ 9.406. Discharge of Account Debtor; Notification of Assignment; Identification and Proof of Assignment; Restrictions on Assignment of Accounts, Chattel Paper, Payment Intangibles, and Promissory Notes Ineffective

(a) Subject to Subsections (b)–(i), an account debtor on an account, chattel paper, or a payment intangible may discharge its obligation by paying the assignor until, but not after, the account debtor receives a notification, authenticated by the assignor or the assignee, that the amount due or to become due has been assigned and that payment is to be made to the assignee. After receipt of the notification, the account debtor may discharge its obligation by paying the assignee and may not discharge the obligation by paying the assignor.

(b) Subject to Subsection (h), notification is ineffective under Subsection (a):

(1) if it does not reasonably identify the rights assigned;

(2) to the extent that an agreement between an account debtor and a seller of a payment intangible limits the account debtor's duty to pay a person other than the seller and the limitation is effective under law other than this chapter; or

(3) at the option of an account debtor, if the notification notifies the account debtor to make less than the full amount of any installment or other periodic payment to the assignee, even if:

(A) only a portion of the account, chattel paper, or payment intangible has been assigned to that assignee;

(B) a portion has been assigned to another assignee; or

(C) the account debtor knows that the assignment to that assignee is limited.

(c) Subject to Subsection (h), if requested by the account debtor, an assignee shall seasonably furnish reasonable proof that the assignment has been made. Unless the assignee complies, the account debtor may discharge its obligation by paying the assignor, even if the account debtor has received a notification under Subsection (a).

(d) Except as otherwise provided in Subsection (e) and Sections 2A.303 and 9.407, and subject to Subsection (h), a term in an agreement between an account debtor and an assignor or in a promissory note is ineffective to the extent that it:

(1) prohibits, restricts, or requires the consent of the account debtor or person obligated on the promissory note to the assignment or transfer of, or the creation, attachment, perfection, or enforcement of a security interest in, the account, chattel paper, payment intangible, or promissory note; or

(2) provides that the assignment or transfer or the creation, attachment, perfection, or enforcement of the security interest may give rise to a default, breach, right of recoupment, claim, defense, termination, right of termination, or remedy under the account, chattel paper, payment intangible, or promissory note.

(e) Subsection (d) does not apply to the sale of a payment intangible or promissory note.

(f) Except as otherwise provided in Sections 2A.303 and 9.407, and subject to Subsections (h) and (i), a rule of law, statute, or regulation that prohibits, restricts, or requires the consent of a government, governmental body or official, or account debtor to the assignment or transfer of, or creation of a security interest in, an account or chattel paper is ineffective to the extent that the rule of law, statute, or regulation:

(1) prohibits, restricts, or requires the consent of the government, governmental body or official, or account debtor to the assignment or transfer of, or the creation, attachment, perfection, or enforcement of a security interest in, the account or chattel paper; or

(2) provides that the assignment or transfer or the creation, attachment, perfection, or enforcement of the security interest may give rise to a default, breach, right of recoupment, claim, defense, termination, right of termination, or remedy under the account or chattel paper.

(g) Subject to Subsection (h), an account debtor may not waive or vary its option under Subsection (b)(3).

(h) This section is subject to law other than this chapter that establishes a different rule for an account debtor who is an individual and who incurred the obligation primarily for personal, family, or household purposes.

(i) This section does not apply to an assignment of a health-care-insurance receivable.

Amended by Acts 1999, 76th Leg., ch. 414, § 1.01, eff. July 1, 2001; Acts 2001, 77th Leg., ch. 705, § 11, eff. June 13, 2001.

Uniform Commercial Code Comment

1. **Source.** Former Section 9–318(3), (4).

2. **Account Debtor's Right to Pay Assignor Until Notification.** Subsection (a) provides the general rule concerning an account debtor's right to pay the assignor until the account debtor receives appropriate notification. The revision makes clear that once the account debtor receives the notification, the account debtor cannot discharge its obligation by paying the assignor. It also makes explicit that payment to the assignor before notification, or payment to the assignee after notification, discharges the obligation. No change in meaning from former Section 9–318 is intended. Nothing in this section conditions the effectiveness of a notification on the identity of the person who gives it. An account debtor that doubts whether the right to payment has been assigned may avail itself of the procedures in subsection (c). See Comment 4.

An effective notification under subsection (a) must be authenticated. This requirement normally could be satisfied by sending notification on the notifying person's letterhead or on a form on which the notifying person's name appears. In each case the printed name would be a symbol adopted by the notifying person for the purpose of identifying the person and adopting the notification. See Section 9–102 (defining "authenticate").

Subsection (a) applies only to account debtors on accounts, chattel paper, and payment intangibles. (Section 9–102 defines the term "account debtor" more broadly, to include those obligated on all general intangibles.) Although subsection (a) is more precise than its predecessor, it probably does not change the rule that applied under former Article 9. Former Section 9–318(3) referred to the account debtor's obligation to "pay," indicating that the subsection was limited to account debtors on accounts, chattel paper, and other payment obligations.

3. **Limitations on Effectiveness of Notification.** Subsection (b) contains some special rules concerning the effectiveness of a notification under subsection (a).

Subsection (b)(1) tracks former Section 9–318(3) by making ineffective a notification that does not reasonably identify the rights assigned. A reasonable identification need not identify the right to payment with specificity, but what is reasonable also is not left to the arbitrary decision of the account debtor. If an account debtor has doubt as to the adequacy of a notification, it may not be safe in disregarding the notification unless it notifies the assignee with reasonable promptness as to the respects in which the account debtor considers the notification defective.

Subsection (b)(2), which is new, applies only to sales of payment intangibles. It makes a notification ineffective to the extent that other law gives effect to an agreement between an account debtor and a seller of a payment intangible that limits the account debtor's duty to pay a person other than the seller. Payment intangibles are substantially less fungible than accounts and chattel paper. In some (e.g., commercial bank loans), account debtors customarily and legitimately expect that they will not be required to pay any person other than the financial institution that has advanced funds.

It has become common in financing transactions to assign interests in a single obligation to more than one assignee. Requiring an account debtor that owes a single obligation to make multiple payments to multiple assignees would be unnecessarily burdensome. Thus, under subsection (b)(3), an account debtor that is notified to pay an assignee less than the full amount of any installment or other periodic payment has the option to treat the notification as ineffective, ignore the notice, and discharge the assigned obligation by paying the assignor. Some account debtors may not realize that the law affords them the right to ignore certain notices of assignment with impunity. By making the notification ineffective at the account debtor's option, subsection (b)(3) permits an account debtor to pay the assignee in accordance with the notice and thereby to satisfy its obligation *pro tanto*. Under subsection (g), the rights and duties created by subsection (b)(3) cannot be waived or varied.

4. **Proof of Assignment.** Subsection (c) links payment with discharge, as in subsection (a). It follows former Section 9–318(3) in referring to the right of the account debtor to pay the assignor if the requested proof of assignment is not seasonably forthcoming. Even if the proof is not forthcoming, the notification of assignment would remain effective, so that, in the absence of reasonable proof of the assignment, the account debtor could discharge the obligation by paying either the assignee or the assignor. Of course, if the assignee did not in fact receive an assignment, the account debtor cannot discharge its obligation by paying a putative assignee who is a stranger. The observations in Comment 3 concerning the reasonableness of an identification of a right to payment also apply here. An account debtor that questions the adequacy of proof submitted by an assignee would be well advised to promptly inform the assignee of the defects.

An account debtor may face another problem if its obligation becomes due while the account debtor is awaiting reasonable proof of the assignment that it has requested from the assignee. This section does not excuse the account debtor from timely compliance with its obligations. Consequently, an account debtor that has received a notification of assignment and who has requested reasonable proof of the assignment may discharge its obligation by paying the assignor at the time (or even earlier if reasonably necessary to avoid risk of default) when a payment is due, even if the account debtor has not yet received a response to its request for proof. On the other hand, after requesting reasonable proof of the assignment, an account debtor may not discharge its obligation by paying the assignor substantially in advance of the time that the payment is due unless the assignee has failed to provide the proof seasonably.

5. **Contractual Restrictions on Assignment.** Former Section 9–318(4) rendered ineffective an agreement between an account debtor and an assignor which prohibited assignment of an account (whether outright or to secure an obligation) or prohibited a security assignment of a general intangible for the payment of money due or to become due. Subsection (d) essentially follows former Section 9–318(4), but expands the rule of free assignability to chattel paper (subject to Sections 2A–303 and 9–407) and promissory notes and explicitly overrides both restrictions and prohibitions of assignment. The policies underlying the ineffectiveness of contractual restrictions under this section build on common-law developments that essentially have eliminated legal restrictions on assignments of rights to payment as security and other assignments of rights to payment such as accounts and chattel paper. Any that might linger for accounts and chattel paper are addressed by new subsection (f). See Comment 6.

Former Section 9–318(4) did not apply to a sale of a payment intangible (as described in the former provision, "a general intangible for money due or to become due") but did apply to an assignment of a payment intangible for security. Subsection (e) continues this approach and also makes subsection (d) inapplicable to sales of promissory notes. Section 9–408 addresses anti-assignment clauses with respect to sales of payment intangibles and promissory notes.

Like former Section 9–318(4), subsection (d) provides that anti-assignment clauses are "ineffective." The quoted term means that the clause is of no effect whatsoever; the clause does not prevent the assignment from taking effect between the parties and the prohibited assignment does not constitute a default under the agreement between the account debtor and assignor. However, subsection (d) does not override terms that do not directly prohibit, restrict, or require consent to an assignment but which might, nonetheless, present a practical impairment of the assignment. Properly read, however, subsection (d) reaches only covenants that prohibit, restrict, or require consents to assignments; it does not override all terms that might "impair" an assignment in fact.

Example: Buyer enters into an agreement with Seller to buy equipment that Seller is to manufacture according to Buyer's specifications. Buyer agrees to make a series of prepayments during the construction process. In return, Seller agrees to set aside the prepaid funds in a special account and to use the funds solely for the manufacture of the designated equipment. Seller also agrees that it will not assign any of its rights under the sale agreement with Buyer. Nevertheless, Seller grants to Secured Party a security interest in its accounts. Seller's anti-assignment agreement is ineffective under subsection (d); its agreement concerning the use of prepaid funds, which is not a restriction or prohibition on assignment, is not. However, if Secured Party notifies Buyer to make all future payments directly to Secured Party, Buyer will be obliged to do so under subsection (a) if it wishes the payments to discharge its obligation. Unless Secured Party releases the funds to Seller so that Seller can comply with its use-of-funds covenant, Seller will be in breach of that covenant.

In the example, there appears to be a plausible business purpose for the use-of-funds covenant. However, a court may conclude that a covenant with no business purpose other than imposing an impediment to an assignment actually is a direct restriction that is rendered ineffective by subsection (d).

6. **Legal Restrictions on Assignment.** Former Section 9–318(4), like subsection (d) of this section, addressed only contractual restrictions on assignment. The former section was grounded on the reality that legal, as opposed to contractual, restrictions on assignments of rights to payment had largely disappeared. New subsection (f) codifies this principle of free assignability for accounts and chattel paper. For the most part the discussion of contractual restrictions in Comment 5 applies as well to legal restrictions rendered ineffective under subsection (f).

7. **Multiple Assignments.** This section, like former Section 9–318, is not a complete codification of the law of assignments of rights to payment. In particular, it is silent concerning many of the ramifications for an account debtor in cases of multiple assignments of the same right. For example, an assignor might assign the same receivable to multiple assignees (which assignments could be either inadvertent or wrongful). Or, the assignor could assign the receivable to assignee–1, which then might re-assign it to assignee–2, and so forth. The rights and duties of an account debtor in the face of multiple assignments and in other circumstances not resolved in the statutory text are left to the common-law rules. See, e.g., Restatement (2d), Contracts §§ 338(3), 339. The failure of former Article 9 to codify these rules does not appear to have caused problems.

8. **Consumer Account Debtors.** Subsection (h) is new. It makes clear that the rules of this section are subject to other law establishing special rules for consumer account debtors.

9. **Account Debtors on Health–Care–Insurance Receivables.** Subsection (i) also is new. The obligation of an insurer with respect to a health-care-insurance receivable is governed by other law. Section 9–408 addresses contractual and legal restrictions on the assignment of a health-care-insurance receivable.

§ 9.407. Restrictions on Creation or Enforcement of Security Interest in Leasehold Interest or in Lessor's Residual Interest

(a) Except as otherwise provided in Subsection (b), a term in a lease agreement is ineffective to the extent that it:

(1) prohibits, restricts, or requires the consent of a party to the lease to the assignment or transfer of, or the creation, attachment, perfection, or enforcement of a security interest in, an interest of a party under the lease contract or in the lessor's residual interest in the goods; or

(2) provides that the assignment or transfer or the creation, attachment, perfection, or enforcement of the security interest may give rise to a default, breach, right of recoupment, claim, defense, termination, right of termination, or remedy under the lease.

(b) Except as otherwise provided in Section 2A.303(g), a term described in Subsection (a)(2) is effective to the extent that there is:

(1) a transfer by the lessee of the lessee's right of possession or use of the goods in violation of the term; or

(2) a delegation of a material performance of either party to the lease contract in violation of the term.

(c) The creation, attachment, perfection, or enforcement of a security interest in the lessor's interest under the lease contract or the lessor's residual interest in the goods is not a transfer that materially impairs the lessee's prospect of obtaining return performance or materially changes the duty of or materially increases the burden or risk imposed on the lessee within the purview of Section 2A.303(d) unless, and then only to the extent that, enforcement actually results in a delegation of material performance of the lessor.

Amended by Acts 1999, 76th Leg., ch. 414, § 1.01, eff. July 1, 2001; Acts 2001, 77th Leg., ch. 705, § 12, eff. June 13, 2001.

Uniform Commercial Code Comment

1. **Source.** Section 2A–303.

2. **Restrictions on Assignment Generally Ineffective.** Under subsection (a), as under former Section 2A–303(3), a term in a lease agreement which prohibits or restricts the creation of a security interest generally is ineffective. This reflects the general policy of Section 9–406(d) and former Section 9–318(4). This section has been conformed in several respects to analogous provisions in Sections 9–406, 9–408, and 9–409, including the substitution of "ineffective" for "not enforceable" and the substitution of "*assignment or transfer of, or the** creation, attachment, perfection, or enforcement of a security interest" for "creation or enforcement of a security interest." **Amendments in italics approved by the Permanent Editorial Board for Uniform Commercial Code October 20, 1999.*

3. **Exceptions for Certain Transfers and Delegations.** Subsection (b) provides exceptions to the general ineffectiveness of restrictions under subsection (a). A term that other wise is ineffective under subsection (a)(2) is effective to the extent that a lessee transfers its right to possession and use of goods or if either party delegates material performance of the lease contract in violation of the term. However, under subsection (c), as under former Section 2A–303(3), a lessor's creation of a security interest in its interest in a lease contract or its residual interest in the leased goods is not a material impairment under Section 2A–303(4) (former Section 2A–303(5)), absent an actual delegation of the lessor's material performance. The terms of the lease contract determine whether the lessor, in fact, has any remaining obligations to perform. If it does, it is then necessary to determine whether there has been an actual delegation of "material performance." See Section 2A–303, Comments 3 and 4.

§ 9.408. Restrictions on Assignment of Promissory Notes, Health-Care-Insurance Receivables, and Certain General Intangibles Ineffective

(a) Except as otherwise provided in Subsection (b), a term in a promissory note or in an agreement between an account debtor and a debtor that relates to a health-care-insurance receivable or a general intangible, including a contract, permit, license, or franchise, and which term prohibits, restricts, or requires the consent of the person obligated on the promissory note or the account debtor to, the assignment or transfer of, or creation, attachment, or perfection of a security interest in, the promissory note, health-care-insurance receivable, or general intangible, is ineffective to the extent that the term:

(1) would impair the creation, attachment, or perfection of a security interest; or

(2) provides that the assignment or transfer or the creation, attachment, or perfection of the security interest may give rise to a default, breach, right of recoupment, claim, defense, termination, right of termination, or remedy under the promissory note, health-care-insurance receivable, or general intangible.

(b) Subsection (a) applies to a security interest in a payment intangible or promissory note only if the security interest arises out of a sale of the payment intangible or promissory note.

(c) A rule of law, statute, or regulation that prohibits, restricts, or requires the consent of a government, governmental body or official, person obligated on a promissory note, or account debtor to the assignment or transfer of, or creation of a security interest in, a promissory note, health-care-insurance receivable, or general intangible, including a contract, permit, license, or franchise between an account debtor and a debtor, is ineffective to the extent that the rule of law, statute, or regulation:

(1) would impair the creation, attachment, or perfection of a security interest; or

(2) provides that the assignment or transfer or the creation, attachment, or perfection of the security interest may give rise to a default, breach, right of recoupment, claim, defense, termination, right of termination, or remedy under the promissory note, health-care-insurance receivable, or general intangible.

(d) To the extent that a term in a promissory note or in an agreement between an account debtor and a debtor that relates to a health-care-insurance receivable or general intangible or a rule of law, statute, or regulation described in Subsection (c) would be effective under law other than this chapter but is ineffective under Subsection (a) or (c), the creation, attachment, or perfection of a security interest in the promissory note, health-care-insurance receivable, or general intangible:

(1) is not enforceable against the person obligated on the promissory note or the account debtor;

(2) does not impose a duty or obligation on the person obligated on the promissory note or the account debtor;

(3) does not require the person obligated on the promissory note or the account debtor to recognize the security interest, pay or render performance to the secured party, or accept payment or performance from the secured party;

(4) does not entitle the secured party to use or assign the debtor's rights under the promissory note, health-care-insurance receivable, or general intangible, including any related information or materials furnished to the debtor in the transaction giving rise to the promissory note, health-care-insurance receivable, or general intangible;

(5) does not entitle the secured party to use, assign, possess, or have access to any trade secrets or confidential information of the person obligated on the promissory note or the account debtor; and

(6) does not entitle the secured party to enforce the security interest in the promissory note, health-care-insurance receivable, or general intangible.

Amended by Acts 1999, 76th Leg., ch. 414, § 1.01, eff. July 1, 2001; Acts 2001, 77th Leg., ch. 705, § 13, eff. June 13, 2001.

Uniform Commercial Code Comment

1. **Source.** New.

2. **Free Assignability.** This section makes ineffective any attempt to restrict the assignment of a general intangible, health-care-insurance receivable, or promissory note, whether the restriction appears in the terms of a promissory note or the agreement between an account debtor and a debtor (subsection (a)) or in a rule of law, including a statute or governmental rule or regulation (subsection (c)). This result allows the creation, attachment, and perfection of a security interest in a general intangible, such as an agreement for the nonexclusive license of software, as well as sales of certain receivables, such as a health-care-insurance receivable (which is an "account"), payment intangible, or promissory note, without giving rise to a default or breach by the assignor or from triggering a remedy of the account debtor or person obligated on a promissory note. This enhances the ability of certain debtors to obtain credit. On the other hand, subsection (d) protects the other party–the "account debtor" on a general intangible or the person obligated on a promissory note–from adverse effects arising from the security interest. It leaves the account debtor's or obligated person's rights and obligations unaffected in all material respects if a restriction rendered ineffective by subsection (a) or (c) would be effective under law other than Article 9.

Example 1: A term of an agreement for the nonexclusive license of computer software prohibits the licensee from assigning any of its rights as licensee with respect to the software. The agreement also provides that an attempt to assign rights in violation of the restriction is a default entitling the licensor to terminate the license agreement. The licensee, as debtor, grants to a secured party a security interest in its rights under the license and in the computers in which it is installed. Under this section, the term prohibiting assignment and providing for a default upon an attempted assignment is ineffective to prevent the creation, attachment, or perfection of the security interest or entitle the licensor to terminate the license agreement. However, under subsection (d), the secured party (absent the licensor's agreement) is not entitled to enforce the license or to use, assign, or otherwise enjoy the benefits of the licensed software, and the licensor need not recognize (or pay any attention to) the secured party. Even if the secured party takes possession of the computers on the debtor's default, the debtor would remain free to remove the software from the computer, load it on another computer, and continue to use it, if the license so permits. If the debtor does not remove the software, other law may require the secured party to remove it before disposing of the computer. Disposition of the software with the computer could violate an effective prohibition on enforcement of the security interest. See subsection (d).

3. **Nature of Debtor's Interest.** Neither this section nor any other provision of this Article determines whether a debtor has a property interest. The definition of the term "security interest" provides that it is an "interest in personal property." See Section 1–201(37). Ordinarily, a debtor can create a security interest in collateral only if it has "rights in the collateral." See Section 9–203(b). Other law determines whether a debtor has a property interest ("rights in the collateral") and the nature of that interest. For example, the nonexclusive license addressed in Example 1 may not create any property interest whatsoever in the intellectual property (e.g., copyright) that underlies the license and that effectively enables the licensor to grant the license. The debtor's property interest may be confined solely to its interest in the promises made by the licensor in the license agreement (e.g., a promise not to sue the debtor for its use of the software).

4. **Scope: Sales of Payment Intangibles and Other General Intangibles; Assignments Unaffected by this Section.** Subsections (a) and (c) render ineffective restrictions on assignments only "to the extent" that the assignments restrict the "creation, attachment, or perfection of a security interest," including sales of payment intangibles and promissory notes. This section does not render ineffective a restriction on an assignment that does not create a security interest. For example, if the debtor in Comment 2, Example 1 purported to assign the license to another entity that would use the computer software itself, other law would govern the effectiveness of the anti-assignment provisions.

Subsection (a) applies to a security interest in payment intangibles only if the security interest arises out of sale of the payment intangibles. Contractual restrictions directed to security interests in payment intangibles which secure an obligation are subject to Section 9–406(d). Subsection (a) also deals with sales of promissory notes which also create security interests. See Section 9–109(a). Subsection (c) deals with all security interests in payment intangibles or promissory notes, whether or not arising out of a sale.

Subsection (a) does not render ineffective any term, and subsection (c) does not render ineffective any law, statute or regulation, that restricts outright sales of general intangibles other than payment intangibles. They deal only with restrictions on security interests. The only sales of general intangibles that create security interests are sales of payment intangibles.

5. **Terminology: "Account Debtor"; "Person Obligated on a Promissory Note."** This section uses the term "account debtor" as it is defined in Section 9–102. The term refers to the party, other than the debtor, to a general intangible, including a permit, license, franchise, or the like, and the person obligated on a health-care-insurance receivable, which is a type of account. The definition of "account debtor" does not limit the term to persons who are obligated to *pay* under a general intangible. Rather, the term includes all persons who are obligated on a general intangible, including those who are obligated to render performance in exchange for payment. In some cases, e.g., the creation of a security interest in a franchisee's rights under a franchise agreement, the principal payment obligation may be owed *by* the debtor (franchisee) *to* the account debtor (franchisor). This section also refers to a "person obligated on a promissory note," inasmuch as those persons do not fall within the definition of "account debtor."

Example 2: A licensor and licensee enter into an agreement for the nonexclusive license of computer software. The licensee's interest in the license agreement is a general intangible. If the licensee grants to a secured party a security interest in its rights under the license agreement, the licensee is the debtor and the licensor is the account debtor. On the other hand, if the licensor grants to a secured party a security interest in its right to payment (an account) under the license agreement, the licensor is the debtor and the licensee is the account debtor.

6. **Effects on Account Debtors and Persons Obligated on Promissory Notes.** Subsections (a) and (c) affect two classes of persons. These subsections affect account debtors on general intangibles and health-care-insurance receivables and persons obligated on promissory notes. Subsection (c) also affects governmental entities that enact or determine rules of law. *However, subsection (d) ensures that these affected persons are not affected adversely.* That provision removes any burdens or adverse effects on these persons for which any rational basis could exist to restrict the effectiveness of an assignment or to exercise any remedies. For this reason, the effects of subsections (a) and (c) are immaterial insofar as those persons are concerned.

Subsection (a) does not override terms that do not directly prohibit, restrict, or require consent to an assignment but which might, nonetheless, present a practical impairment of the assignment. Properly read, however, this section, like Section 9–406(d), reaches only covenants that prohibit, restrict, or require consents to assignments; it does not override all terms that might "impair" an assignment in fact.

Example 3: A licensor and licensee enter into an agreement for the nonexclusive license of valuable business software. The license agreement includes terms (i) prohibiting the licensee from assigning its rights under the license, (ii) prohibiting the licensee from disclosing to anyone certain information relating to the software and the licensor, and (iii) deeming prohibited assignments and prohibited disclosures to be defaults. The licensee wishes to obtain financing and, in exchange, is willing to grant a security interest in its rights under the license agreement. The secured party, reasonably, refuses to extend credit unless the licensee discloses the information that it is prohibited from disclosing under the license agreement. The secured party cannot determine the value of the proposed collateral in the absence of this information. Under this section, the terms of the license prohibiting the assignment (grant of the security interest) and making the assignment a default are ineffective. However, the nondisclosure covenant is not a term that prohibits the assignment or creation of a security interest in the license. Consequently, the nondisclosure term is enforceable even though the *practical* effect is to restrict the licensee's ability to use its rights under the license agreement as collateral.

The nondisclosure term also would be effective in the factual setting of Comment 2, Example 1. If the secured party's possession of the computers loaded with software would put it in a position to discover confidential information that the debtor was prohibited from disclosing, the licensor should be entitled to enforce its rights against the secured party. Moreover, the licensor could have required the debtor to obtain the secured party's agreement that (i) it would immediately return all copies of software loaded on the computers and that (ii) it would not examine or otherwise acquire any information contained in the software. This section does not prevent an account debtor from protecting by agreement its independent interests that are unrelated to the "creation, attachment, or perfection" of a security interest. In Example 1, moreover, the secured party is not in possession of copies of software by virtue of its security interest or in connection with enforcing its security interest *in the debtor's license of the software.* Its possession is incidental to its possession of the computers, in which it has a security interest. Enforcing against the secured party a restriction relating to the software in no way interferes with its security interest in the computers.

7. **Effect in Assignor's Bankruptcy.** This section could have a substantial effect if the assignor enters bankruptcy. Roughly speaking, Bankruptcy Code Section 552 invalidates security interests in property acquired after a bankruptcy petition is filed, except to the extent that the postpetition property constitutes proceeds of prepetition collateral.

Example 4: A debtor is the owner of a cable television franchise that, under applicable law, cannot be assigned without the consent of the municipal franchisor. A lender wishes to extend credit to the debtor, provided that the credit is secured by the debtor's "going business" value. To secure the loan, the debtor grants a security interest in all its existing and after-acquired property. The franchise represents the principal value of the business. The municipality refuses to consent to any assignment for collateral purposes. If other law were given effect, the security interest in the franchise would not attach; and if the debtor were to enter bankruptcy and sell the business, the secured party would receive but a fraction of the business's value. Under this section, however, the security interest would attach to the franchise. As a result, the security interest would attach to the proceeds of any sale of the franchise while a bankruptcy is pending. However, this section would protect the interests of the municipality by preventing the secured party from enforcing its security interest to the detriment of the municipality.

8. **Effect Outside of Bankruptcy.** The principal effects of this section will take place outside of bankruptcy. Compared to the relatively few debtors that enter bankruptcy, there are many more that do not. By making available previously unavailable property as collateral, this section should enable debtors to obtain additional credit. For purposes of determining whether to extend credit, under some circumstances a secured party may ascribe value to the collateral to which its security interest has attached, even if this section precludes the secured party from enforcing the security interest without the agreement of the account debtor or person obligated on the promissory note. This may be the case where the secured party sees a likelihood of obtaining that agreement in the future. This may also be the case where the secured party anticipates that the collateral will give rise to a type of proceeds as to which this section would not apply.

Example 5: Under the facts of Example 4, the debtor does not enter bankruptcy. Perhaps in exchange for a fee, the municipality agrees that the debtor may transfer the franchise to a buyer. As consideration for the transfer, the debtor receives from the buyer its check for part of the purchase price and its promissory note for the balance. The security interest attaches to the check and promissory note as proceeds. See Section 9–315(a)(2). This section does not apply to the security interest in the check, which is not a promissory note, health-care-insurance receivable, or general intangible. Nor does it apply to the security interest in the promissory note, inasmuch as it was not sold to the secured party.

9. **Contrary Federal Law.** This section does not override federal law to the contrary. However, it does reflect an important policy judgment that should provide a template for future federal law reforms.

§ 9.409. Restrictions on Assignment of Letter-Of-Credit Rights Ineffective

(a) A term in a letter of credit or a rule of law, statute, regulation, custom, or practice applicable to the letter of credit that prohibits, restricts, or requires the consent of an applicant, issuer, or nominated person to a beneficiary's assignment of or creation of a security interest in a letter-of-credit right is ineffective to the extent that the term or rule of law, statute, regulation, custom, or practice:

(1) would impair the creation, attachment, or perfection of a security interest in the letter-of-credit right; or

(2) provides that the assignment or the creation, attachment, or perfection of the security interest may give rise to a default, breach, right of recoupment, claim, defense, termination, right of termination, or remedy under the letter-of-credit right.

(b) To the extent that a term in a letter of credit is ineffective under Subsection (a) but would be effective under law other than this chapter or a custom or practice applicable to the letter of credit, to the transfer of a right to draw or otherwise demand performance under the letter of credit, or to the assignment of a right to proceeds of the letter of credit, the creation, attachment, or perfection of a security interest in the letter-of-credit right:

(1) is not enforceable against the applicant, issuer, nominated person, or transferee beneficiary;

(2) imposes no duties or obligations on the applicant, issuer, nominated person, or transferee beneficiary; and

(3) does not require the applicant, issuer, nominated person, or transferee beneficiary to recognize the security interest, pay or render performance to the secured party, or accept payment or other performance from the secured party.

Amended by Acts 1999, 76th Leg., ch. 414, § 1.01, eff. July 1, 2001; Acts 2001, 77th Leg., ch. 705, § 14, eff. June 13, 2001.

Uniform Commercial Code Comment

1. **Source.** New.

2. **Purpose and Relevance.** This section, patterned on Section 9–408, limits the effectiveness of attempts to restrict the creation, attachment, or perfection of a security interest in letter-of-credit rights, whether the restriction appears in the letter of credit or a rule of law, custom, or practice applicable to the letter of credit. It protects the creation, attachment, and perfection of a security interest while preventing these events from giving rise to a default or breach by the assignor or from triggering a remedy or defense of

the issuer or other person obligated on a letter of credit. Letter-of-credit rights are a type of supporting obligation. See Section 9–102. Under Sections 9–203 and 9–308, a security interest in a supporting obligation attaches and is perfected automatically if the security interest in the supported obligation attaches and is perfected. See Section 9–107, Comment 5. The automatic attachment and perfection under Article 9 would be anomalous or misleading if, under other law (e.g., Article 5), a restriction on transfer or assignment were effective to block attachment and perfection.

3. **Relationship to Letter-of-Credit Law.** Although restrictions on an assignment of a letter of credit are ineffective to prevent creation, attachment, and perfection of a security interest, subsection (b) protects the issuer and other parties from any adverse effects of the security interest by preserving letter-of-credit law and practice that limits the right of a beneficiary to transfer its right to draw or otherwise demand performance (Section 5–112) and limits the obligation of an issuer or nominated person to recognize a beneficiary's assignment of letter-of-credit proceeds (Section 5–114). Thus, this section's treatment of letter-of-credit rights differs from this Article's treatment of instruments and investment property. Moreover, under Section 9–109(c)(4), this Article does not apply to the extent that the rights of a transferee beneficiary or nominated person are independent and superior under Section 5–114, thereby preserving the "independence principle" of letter-of-credit law.

§§ 9.4095 to 9.412. Deleted by Acts 1999, 76th Leg., ch. 414, § 1.01, eff. July 1, 2001

SUBCHAPTER E. FILING

§ 9.501. Filing Office

(a) Except as otherwise provided in Subsection (b), if the local law of this state governs perfection of a security interest or agricultural lien, the office in which to file a financing statement to perfect the security interest or agricultural lien is:

(1) the office designated for the filing or recording of a record of a mortgage on the related real property, if:

(A) the collateral is as-extracted collateral or timber to be cut; or

(B) the financing statement is filed as a fixture filing and the collateral is goods that are or are to become fixtures; or

(2) the office of the Secretary of State, in all other cases, including a case in which the collateral is goods that are or are to become fixtures and the financing statement is not filed as a fixture filing.

(b) The office in which to file a financing statement to perfect a security interest in collateral, including fixtures, of a transmitting utility is the office of the Secretary of State. The financing statement also constitutes a fixture filing as to the collateral indicated in the financing statement that is or is to become fixtures.

Amended by Acts 1999, 76th Leg., ch. 414, § 1.01, eff. July 1, 2001.

Uniform Commercial Code Comment

1. **Source.** Derived from former Section 9–401.

2. **Where to File.** Subsection (a) indicates where in a given State a financing statement is to be filed. Former Article 9 afforded each State three alternative approaches, depending on the extent to which the State desires central filing (usually with the Secretary of State), local filing (usually with a county office), or both. As Comment 1 to former Section 9–401 observed, "The principal advantage of state-wide filing is ease of access to the credit information which the files exist to provide. Consider for example the national distributor who wishes to have current information about the credit standing of the thousands of persons he sells to on credit. The more completely the files are centralized on a state-wide basis, the easier and cheaper it becomes to procure credit information; the more the files are scattered in local filing units, the more burdensome and costly." Local filing increases the net costs of secured transactions also by increasing uncertainty and the number of required filings. Any benefit that local filing may have had in the 1950's is now insubstantial. Accordingly, this Article dictates central filing for most situations, while retaining local filing for real-estate-related collateral and special filing provisions for transmitting utilities.

3. **Minerals and Timber.** Under subsection (a)(1), a filing in the office where a record of a mortgage on the related real property would be filed will perfect a security interest in as-extracted collateral. Inasmuch as the security interest does not attach until extraction, the filing continues to be effective after extraction. A different result occurs with respect to timber to be cut, however. Unlike as-extracted collateral, standing timber may be goods before it is cut. See Section 9–102 (defining "goods"). Once cut, however, it is no longer timber *to be* cut, and the filing in the real-property-mortgage office ceases to be effective. The timber then becomes ordinary goods, and filing in the office specified in subsection (a)(2) is necessary for perfection. Note also that after the timber is cut the law of the debtor's location, not the location of the timber, governs perfection under Section 9–301.

4. **Fixtures.** There are two ways in which a secured party may file a financing statement to perfect a security interest in goods that are or are to become fixtures. It may file in the Article 9 records, as with most other goods. See subsection (a)(2). Or it may file the financing statement as a "fixture filing," defined in Section 9–102, in the office in which a record of a mortgage on the related real property would be filed. See subsection(a)(1)(B).

5. **Transmitting Utilities.** The usual filing rules do not apply well for a transmitting utility (defined in Section 9–102). Many pre-UCC statutes provided special filing rules for railroads and in some cases for other public utilities, to avoid the requirements for filing with legal descriptions in

every county in which such debtors had property. Former Section 9–401(5) recreated and broadened these provisions, and subsection (b) follows this approach. The nature of the debtor will inform persons searching the record as to where to make a search.

§ 9.502. Contents of Financing Statement; Record of Mortgage as Financing Statement; Time of Filing Financing Statement

(a) Subject to Subsection (b), a financing statement is sufficient only if it:

(1) provides the name of the debtor;

(2) provides the name of the secured party or a representative of the secured party; and

(3) indicates the collateral covered by the financing statement.

(b) Except as otherwise provided in Section 9.501(b), to be sufficient, a financing statement that covers as-extracted collateral or timber to be cut, or that is filed as a fixture filing and covers goods that are or are to become fixtures, must satisfy Subsection (a) and also:

(1) indicate that it covers this type of collateral;

(2) indicate that it is to be filed for record in the real property records;

(3) provide a description of the real property to which the collateral is related sufficient to give constructive notice of a mortgage under the law of this state if the description were contained in a record of the mortgage of the real property; and

(4) if the debtor does not have an interest of record in the real property, provide the name of a record owner.

(c) A record of a mortgage is effective, from the date of recording, as a financing statement filed as a fixture filing or as a financing statement covering as-extracted collateral or timber to be cut only if:

(1) the record indicates the goods or accounts that it covers;

(2) the goods are or are to become fixtures related to the real property described in the record or the collateral is related to the real property described in the record and is as-extracted collateral or timber to be cut;

(3) the record satisfies the requirements for a financing statement in this section other than an indication that it is to be filed in the real property records; and

(4) the record is duly recorded.

(d) A financing statement may be filed before a security agreement is made or a security interest otherwise attaches.

Amended by Acts 1999, 76th Leg., ch. 414, § 1.01, eff. July 1, 2001.

Uniform Commercial Code Comment

1. **Source.** Former Section 9–402(1), (5), (6).

2. **"Notice Filing."** This section adopts the system of "notice filing." What is required to be filed is not, as under pre-UCC chattel mortgage and conditional sales acts, the security agreement itself, but only a simple record providing a limited amount of information (financing statement). The financing statement may be filed before the security interest attaches or thereafter. See subsection (d). See also Section 9–308(a) (contemplating situations in which a financing statement is filed before a security interest attaches).

The notice itself indicates merely that a person may have a security interest in the collateral indicated. Further inquiry from the parties concerned will be necessary to disclose the complete state of affairs. Section 9–210 provides a statutory procedure under which the secured party, at the debtor's request, may be required to make disclosure. However, in many cases, information may be forthcoming without the need to resort to the formalities of that section.

Notice filing has proved to be of great use in financing transactions involving inventory, accounts, and chattel paper, because it obviates the necessity of refiling on each of a series of transactions in a continuing arrangement under which the collateral changes from day to day. However, even in the case of filings that do not necessarily involve a series of transactions (e.g., a loan secured by a single item of equipment), a financing statement is effective to encompass transactions under a security agreement not in existence and not contemplated at the time the notice was filed, if the indication of collateral in the financing statement is sufficient to cover the collateral concerned. Similarly, a financing statement is effective to cover after-acquired property of the type indicated and to perfect with respect to future advances under security agreements, regardless of whether after-acquired property or future advances are mentioned in the financing statement and even if not in the contemplation of the parties at the time the financing statement was authorized to be filed.

3. **Debtor's Signature; Required Authorization.** Subsection (a) sets forth the simple formal requirements for an effective financing statement. These requirements are: (1) the debtor's name; (2) the name of a secured party or representative of the secured party; and (3) an indication of the collateral.

Whereas former Section 9–402(1) required the debtor's signature to appear on a financing statement, this Article contains no signature requirement. The elimination of the signature requirement facilitates paperless filing. (However, as PEB Commentary No. 15 indicates, a paperless financing statement was sufficient under former Article 9.) Elimination of the signature requirement also makes the exceptions provided by former Section 9–402(2) unnecessary.

The fact that this Article does not require that an authenticating symbol be contained in the public record does not mean that all filings are authorized. Rather, Section 9–509(a) entitles a person to file an initial financing statement, an amendment that adds collateral, or an amendment that adds a debtor only if the debtor authorizes the filing, and Section 9–509(d) entitles a person other than the debtor to file a termination statement only if the secured party of record authorizes the filing. Of course, a filing has legal effect only to the extent it is authorized. See Section 9–510.

Law other than this Article, including the law with respect to ratification of past acts, generally determines whether a person has the requisite authority to file a record under this Article. See Sections 1–103 and 9–509, Comment 3. However, under Section 9–509(b), the debtor's authentication of (or becoming bound by) a security agreement *ipso facto* constitutes the debtor's authorization of the filing of a financing statement covering the collateral described in the security agreement. The secured party need not obtain a separate authorization.

Section 9–625 provides a remedy for unauthorized filings. Making an unauthorized filing also may give rise to civil or criminal liability under other law. In addition, this Article contains provisions that assist in the discovery of unauthorized filings and the amelioration of their practical effect. For example, Section 9–518 provides a procedure whereby a person may add to the public record a statement to the effect that a financing statement indexed under the person's name was wrongfully filed, and Section 9–509(d) entitles any person to file a termination statement if the secured party of record fails to comply with its obligation to file or send one to the debtor, the debtor authorizes the filing, and the termination statement so indicates. However, the filing office is neither obligated nor permitted to inquire into issues of authorization. See Section 9–520(a).

4. **Certain Other Requirements.** Subsection (a) deletes other provisions of former Section 9–402(1) because they seems unwise (real-property description for financing statements covering crops), unnecessary (adequacy of copies of financing statements), or both (copy of security agreement as financing statement). In addition, the filing office must reject a financing statement lacking certain other information formerly required as a condition of perfection (e.g., an address for the debtor or secured party). See Sections 9–516(b), 9–520(a). However, if the filing office accepts the record, it is effective nevertheless. See Section 9–520(c).

5. **Real-Property-Related Filings.** Subsection (b) contains the requirements for financing statements filed as fixture filings and financing statements covering timber to be cut or minerals and minerals-related accounts constituting as-extracted collateral. A description of the related real property must be sufficient to reasonably identify it. See Section 9–108. This formulation rejects the view that the real property description must be by metes and bounds, or otherwise conforming to traditional real-property practice in conveyancing, but, of course, the incorporation of such a description by reference to the recording data of a deed, mortgage or other instrument containing the description should suffice under the most stringent standards. The proper test is that a description of real property must be sufficient so that the financing statement will fit into the real-property search system and be found by a real-property searcher. Under the optional language in subsection (b)(3), the test of adequacy of the description is whether it would be adequate in a record of a mortgage of the real property. As suggested in the Legislative Note, more detail may be required if there is a tract indexing system or a land registration system.

If the debtor does not have an interest of record in the real property, a real-property-related financing statement must show the name of a record owner, and Section 9–519(d) requires the financing statement to be indexed in the name of that owner. This requirement also enables financing statements covering as-extracted collateral or timber to be cut and financing statements filed as fixture filings to fit into the real-property search system.

6. **Record of Mortgage Effective as Financing Statement.** Subsection (c) explains when a record of a mortgage is effective as a financing statement filed as a fixture filing or to cover timber to be cut or as-extracted collateral. Use of the term "record of a mortgage" recognizes that in some systems the record actually filed is not the record pursuant to which a mortgage is created. Moreover, "mortgage" is defined in Section 9–102 as an "interest in real property," not as the record that creates or evidences the mortgage or the record that is filed in the public recording systems. A record creating a mortgage may also create a security interest with respect to fixtures (or other goods) in conformity with this Article. A single agreement creating a mortgage on real property and a security interest in chattels is common and useful for certain purposes. Under subsection (c), the recording of the record evidencing a mortgage (if it satisfies the requirements for a financing statement) constitutes the filing of a financing statement as to the fixtures (but not, of course, as to other goods). Section 9–515(g) makes the usual five-year maximum life for financing statements inapplicable to mortgages that operate as fixture filings under Section 9–502(c). Such mortgages are effective for the duration of the real-property recording.

Of course, if a combined mortgage covers chattels that are not fixtures, a regular financing statement filing is necessary with respect to the chattels, and subsection (c) is inapplicable. Likewise, a financing statement filed as a "fixture filing" is not effective to perfect a security interest in personal property other than fixtures.

In some cases it may be difficult to determine whether goods are or will become fixtures. Nothing in this Part prohibits the filing of a "precautionary" fixture filing, which would provide protection in the event goods are determined to be fixtures. The fact of filing should not be a factor in the determining whether goods are fixtures. Cf. Section 9–505(b).

§ 9.503. Name of Debtor and Secured Party

(a) A financing statement sufficiently provides the name of the debtor:

(1) if the debtor is a registered organization, only if the financing statement provides the name of the debtor indicated on the debtor's formation documents that are filed of public record in the debtor's

jurisdiction of organization to create the registered organization and that show the debtor to have been organized, including any amendments to those documents for the express purpose of amending the debtor's name;

(2) if the debtor is a decedent's estate, only if the financing statement provides the name of the decedent and indicates that the debtor is an estate;

(3) if the debtor is a trust or a trustee acting with respect to property held in trust, only if the financing statement:

(A) provides the name specified for the trust in its organic documents or, if no name is specified, provides the name of the settlor and additional information sufficient to distinguish the debtor from other trusts having one or more of the same settlors; and

(B) indicates, in the debtor's name or otherwise, that the debtor is a trust or is a trustee acting with respect to property held in trust;

(4) if the debtor is an individual, if the financing statement provides the individual's name shown on the individual's driver's license or identification certificate issued by the individual's state of residence; and

(5) in other cases:

(A) if the debtor has a name, only if the financing statement provides the individual or organizational name of the debtor; and

(B) if the debtor does not have a name, only if the financing statement provides the names of the partners, members, associates, or other persons comprising the debtor.

(b) A financing statement that provides the name of the debtor in accordance with Subsection (a) is not rendered ineffective by the absence of:

(1) a trade name or other name of the debtor; or

(2) unless required under Subsection (a)(4)(B), names of partners, members, associates, or other persons comprising the debtor.

(c) A financing statement that provides only the debtor's trade name does not sufficiently provide the name of the debtor.

(d) Failure to indicate the representative capacity of a secured party or representative of a secured party does not affect the sufficiency of a financing statement.

(e) A financing statement may provide the name of more than one debtor and the name of more than one secured party.

Amended by Acts 1999, 76th Leg., ch. 414, § 1.01, eff. July 1, 2001; Acts 2007, 80th Leg., ch. 565, § 1, eff. June 16, 2007.

Uniform Commercial Code Comment

1. **Source.** Subsections (a)(4)(A), (b), and (c) derive from former Section 9–402(7); otherwise, new.

2. **Debtor's Name.** The requirement that a financing statement provide the debtor's name is particularly important. Financing statements are indexed under the name of the debtor, and those who wish to find financing statements search for them under the debtor's name. Subsection (a) explains what the debtor's name is for purposes of a financing statement. If the debtor is a "registered organization" (defined in Section 9–102 so as to ordinarily include corporations, limited partnerships, and limited liability companies), then the debtor's name is the name shown on the public records of the debtor's "jurisdiction of organization" (also defined in Section 9–102). Subsections (a)(2) and (a)(3) contain special rules for decedent's estates and common-law trusts.

Subsection (a)(4)(A) essentially follows the first sentence of former Section 9–402(7). Section 1–201(28) defines the term "organization," which appears in subsection (a)(4), very broadly, to include all legal and commercial entities as well as associations that lack the status of a legal entity. Thus, the term includes corporations, partnerships of all kinds, business trusts, limited liability companies, unincorporated associations, personal trusts, governments, and estates. If the organization has a name, that name is the correct name to put on a financing statement. If the organization does not have a name, then the financing statement should name the individuals or other entities who comprise the organization.

Together with subsections (b) and (c), subsection (a) reflects the view prevailing under former Article 9 that the actual individual or organizational name of the debtor on a financing statement is both necessary and sufficient, whether or not the financing statement provides trade or other names of the debtor and, if the debtor has a name, whether or not the financing statement provides the names of the partners, members, or associates who comprise the debtor.

Note that, even if the name provided in an initial financing statement is correct, the filing office nevertheless must reject the financing statement if it does not identify an individual debtor's last name (e.g., if it is not clear whether the debtor's name is Perry Mason or Mason Perry). See Section 9–516(b)(3)(C).

3. **Secured Party's Name.** New subsection (d) makes clear that when the secured party is a representative, a financing statement is sufficient if it names the secured party, whether or not it indicates any representative capacity. Similarly, a financing statement that names a representative of the secured party is sufficient, even if it does not indicate the representative capacity.

Example: Debtor creates a security interest in favor of Bank X, Bank Y, and Bank Z, but not to their representative, the collateral agent (Bank A). The collateral agent is not itself a secured party. See Section 9–102. Under Sections 9–502(a) and 9–503(d), however, a financing statement is effective if it names as secured party Bank A and not the actual secured parties, even if it omits Bank A's representative capacity.

Each person whose name is provided in an initial financing statement as the name of the secured party or representative of the secured party is a secured party of record. See Section 9–511.

4. **Multiple Names.** Subsection (e) makes explicit what is implicit under former Article 9: a financing statement may provide the name of more than one debtor and secured party. See Section 1–102(5)(a) (words in the singular include the plural). With respect to records relating to more than one debtor, see Section 9–520(d). With respect to financing statements providing the name of more than one secured party, see Sections 9–509(e) and 9–510(b).

§ 9.504. Indication of Collateral

A financing statement sufficiently indicates the collateral that it covers if the financing statement provides:

(1) a description of the collateral pursuant to Section 9.108; or

(2) an indication that the financing statement covers all assets or all personal property.

Amended by Acts 1999, 76th Leg., ch. 414, § 1.01, eff. July 1, 2001; Acts 2001, 77th Leg., ch. 705, § 15, eff. June 13, 2001.

Uniform Commercial Code Comment

1. **Source.** Former Section 9–402(1).

2. **Indication of Collateral.** To comply with Section 9–502(a), a financing statement must "indicate" the collateral it covers. A financing statement sufficiently indicates collateral claimed to be covered by the financing statement if it satisfies the purpose of conditioning perfection on the filing of a financing statement, i.e., if it provides notice that a person may have a security interest in the collateral claimed. See Section 9–502, Comment 2. In particular, an indication of collateral that would have satisfied the requirements of former Section 9–402(*l*) (i.e., "a statement indicating the types, or describing the items, of collateral") suffices under Section 9–502(a). An indication may satisfy the requirements of Section 9–502(a), even if it would not have satisfied the requirements of former Section 9–402(*l*).

This section provides two safe harbors. Under paragraph (*l*), a "description" of the collateral (as the term is explained in Section 9–108) suffices as an indication for purposes of the sufficiency of a financing statement.

Debtors sometimes create a security interest in all, or substantially all, of their assets. To accommodate this practice, paragraph (2) expands the class of sufficient collateral references to embrace "an indication that the financing statement covers all assets or all personal property." If the property in question belongs to the debtor and is personal property, any searcher will know that the property is covered by the financing statement. Of course, regardless of its breadth, a financing statement has no effect with respect to property indicated but to which a security interest has not attached. Note that a broad statement of this kind (e.g., "all debtor's personal property") would not be a sufficient "description" for purposes of a security agreement. See Sections 9–203(b)(3)(A), 9–108. It follows that a somewhat narrower description than "all assets," e.g., "all assets other than automobiles," is sufficient for purposes of this section, even if it does not suffice for purposes of a security agreement.

§ 9.505. Filing and Compliance With Other Statutes and Treaties for Consignments, Leases, Other Bailments, and Other Transactions

(a) A consignor, lessor, or other bailor of goods, a licensor, or a buyer of a payment intangible or promissory note may file a financing statement, or may comply with a statute or treaty described in Section 9.311(a), using the terms "consignor," "consignee," "lessor," "lessee," "bailor," "bailee," "licensor," "licensee," "owner," "registered owner," "buyer," or "seller," or words of similar import, instead of the terms "secured party" and "debtor."

(b) This subchapter applies to the filing of a financing statement under Subsection (a) and, as appropriate, to compliance that is equivalent to filing a financing statement under Section 9.311(b), but the filing or compliance is not of itself a factor in determining whether the collateral secures an obligation. If it is determined for another reason that the collateral secures an obligation, a security interest held by the consignor, lessor, bailor, licensor, owner, or buyer that attaches to the collateral is perfected by the filing or compliance.

Amended by Acts 1999, 76th Leg., ch. 414, § 1.01, eff. July 1, 2001.

Uniform Commercial Code Comment

1. **Source.** Former Section 9–408.

2. **Precautionary Filing.** Occasionally, doubts arise concerning whether a transaction creates a relationship to which this Article or its filing provisions apply. For example, questions may arise over whether a "lease" of equipment in fact creates a security interest or whether the "sale" of payment intangibles in fact secures an obligation, thereby requiring action to perfect the security interest. This section, which derives from former Section 9–408, affords the option of filing of a financing statement with appropriate changes of terminology but without affecting the substantive question of classification of the transaction.

3. **Changes from Former Section 9–408.** This section expands the rule of Section 9–408 to embrace more generally other bailments and transactions, as well as sales transac-

tions, primarily sales of payment intangibles and promissory notes. It provides the same benefits for compliance with a statute or treaty described in Section 9–311(a) that former Section 9–408 provided for filing, in connection with the use of terms such as "lessor," "consignor," etc. The references to "owner" and "registered owner" are intended to address, for example, the situation where a putative lessor is the registered owner of an automobile covered by a certificate of title and the transaction is determined to create a security interest. Although this section provides that the security interest is perfected, the relevant certificate-of-title statute may expressly provide to the contrary or may be ambiguous. If so, it may be necessary or advisable to amend the certificate-of-title statute to ensure that perfection of the security interest will be achieved.

As does Section 1–201, former Article 9 referred to transactions, including leases and consignments, "intended as security." This misleading phrase created the erroneous impression that the parties to a transaction can dictate how the law will classify it (e.g., as a bailment or as a security interest) and thus affect the rights of third parties. This Article deletes the phrase wherever it appears. Subsection (b) expresses the principle more precisely by referring to a security interest that "secures an obligation."

4. **Consignments.** Although a "true" consignment is a bailment, the filing and priority provisions of former Article 9 applied to "true" consignments. See former Sections 2–326(3), 9–114. A consignment "intended as security" created a security interest that was in all respects subject to former Article 9. This Article subsumes most true consignments under the rubric of "security interest." See Sections 9–102 (definition of "consignment"), 9–109(a)(4), 1–201(37) (definition of "security interest"). Nevertheless, it maintains the distinction between a (true) "consignment," as to which only certain aspects of Article 9 apply, and a so-called consignment that actually "secures an obligation," to which Article 9 applies in full. The revisions to this section reflect the change in terminology.

§ 9.506. Effect of Errors or Omissions

(a) A financing statement substantially satisfying the requirements of this subchapter is effective, even if it has minor errors or omissions, unless the errors or omissions make the financing statement seriously misleading.

(b) Except as otherwise provided in Subsection (c), a financing statement that fails sufficiently to provide the name of the debtor in accordance with Section 9.503(a) is seriously misleading.

(c) If a search of the records of the filing office under the debtor's correct name, using the filing office's standard search logic, if any, would disclose a financing statement that fails sufficiently to provide the name of the debtor in accordance with Section 9.503(a), the name provided does not make the financing statement seriously misleading.

(d) For purposes of Section 9.508(b), the "debtor's correct name" in Subsection (c) means the correct name of the new debtor.

Amended by Acts 1999, 76th Leg., ch. 414, § 1.01, eff. July 1, 2001.

Uniform Commercial Code Comment

1. **Source.** Former Section 9–402(8).

2. **Errors.** Like former Section 9–402(8), subsection (a) is in line with the policy of this Article to simplify formal requisites and filing requirements. It is designed to discourage the fanatical and impossibly refined reading of statutory requirements in which courts occasionally have indulged themselves. Subsection (a) provides the standard applicable to indications of collateral. Subsections (b) and (c), which are new, concern the effectiveness of financing statements in which the debtor's name is incorrect. Subsection (b) contains the general rule: a financing statement that fails sufficiently to provide the debtor's name in accordance with Section 9–503(a) is seriously misleading as a matter of law. Subsection (c) provides an exception: If the financing statement nevertheless would be discovered in a search under the debtor's correct name, using the filing office's standard search logic, if any, then as a matter of law the incorrect name does not make the financing statement seriously misleading. A financing statement that is seriously misleading under this section is ineffective even if it is disclosed by (i) using a search logic other than that of the filing office to search the official records, or (ii) using the filing office's standard search logic to search a data base other than that of the filing office.

In addition to requiring the debtor's name and an indication of the collateral, Section 9–502(a) requires a financing statement to provide the name of the secured party or a representative of the secured party. Inasmuch as searches are not conducted under the secured party's name, and no filing is needed to continue the perfected status of security interest after it is assigned, an error in the name of the secured party or its representative will not be seriously misleading. However, in an appropriate case, an error of this kind may give rise to an estoppel in favor of a particular holder of a conflicting claim to the collateral. See Section 1–103.

3. **New Debtors.** Subsection (d) provides that, in determining the extent to which a financing statement naming an original debtor is effective against a new debtor, the sufficiency of the financing statement should be tested against the name of the new debtor.

§ 9.507. Effect of Certain Events on Effectiveness of Financing Statement

(a) A filed financing statement remains effective with respect to collateral that is sold, exchanged, leased, licensed, or otherwise disposed of and in which a security interest or agricultural lien continues, even if the secured party knows of or consents to the disposition.

(b) Except as otherwise provided in Subsection (c) and Section 9.508, a financing statement is not rendered ineffective if, after the financing statement is filed, the information provided in the financing statement becomes seriously misleading under Section 9.506.

(c) If a debtor so changes its name that a filed financing statement becomes seriously misleading under Section 9.506:

(1) the financing statement is effective to perfect a security interest in collateral acquired by the debtor before, or within four months after, the change; and

(2) the financing statement is not effective to perfect a security interest in collateral acquired by the debtor more than four months after the change, unless an amendment to the financing statement that renders the financing statement not seriously misleading is filed within four months after the change.

Amended by Acts 1999, 76th Leg., ch. 414, § 1.01, eff. July 1, 2001.

Uniform Commercial Code Comment

1. **Source.** Former Section 9–402(7).

2. **Scope of Section.** This section deals with situations in which the information in a proper financing statement becomes inaccurate after the financing statement is filed. Compare Section 9–338, which deals with situations in which a financing statement contains a particular kind of information concerning the debtor (i.e., the information described in Section 9–516(b)(5)) that is incorrect at the time it is filed.

3. **Post-Filing Disposition of Collateral.** Under subsection (a), a financing statement remains effective even if the collateral is sold or otherwise disposed of. This subsection clarifies the third sentence of former Section 9–402(7) by providing that a financing statement remains effective following the disposition of collateral only when the security interest or agricultural lien continues in that collateral. This result is consistent with the conclusion of PEB Commentary No. 3. Normally, a security interest does continue after disposition of the collateral. See Section 9–315(a). Law other than this Article determines whether an agricultural lien survives disposition of the collateral.

As a consequence of the disposition, the collateral may be owned by a person other than the debtor against whom the financing statement was filed. Under subsection (a), the secured party remains perfected even if it does not correct the public record. For this reason, any person seeking to determine whether a debtor owns collateral free of security interests must inquire as to the debtor's source of title and, if circumstances seem to require it, search in the name of a former owner. Subsection (a) addresses only the sufficiency of the information contained in the financing statement. A disposition of collateral may result in loss of perfection for other reasons. See Section 9–316.

Example: Dee Corp. is an Illinois corporation. It creates a security interest in its equipment in favor of Secured Party. Secured Party files a proper financing statement in Illinois. Dee Corp. sells an item of equipment to Bee Corp., a Pennsylvania corporation, subject to the security interest. The security interest continues, see Section 9–315(a), and remains perfected, see Section 9–507(a), notwithstanding that the financing statement is filed under "D" (for Dee Corp.) and not under "B." However, because Bee Corp. is located in Pennsylvania and not Illinois, see Section 9–307, unless Secured Party perfects under Pennsylvania law within one year after the transfer, its security interest will become unperfected and will be deemed to have been unperfected against purchasers of the collateral. See Section 9–316.

4. **Other Post-Filing Changes.** Subsection (b) provides that, as a general matter, post-filing changes that render a financing statement inaccurate and seriously misleading have no effect on a financing statement. The financing statement remains effective. It is subject to two exceptions: Section 9–508 and Section 9–507(c). Section 9–508 addresses the effectiveness of a financing statement filed against an original debtor when a new debtor becomes bound by the original debtor's security agreement. It is discussed in the Comments to that section. Section 9–507(c) addresses a "pure" change of the debtor's name, i.e., a change that does not implicate a new debtor. It clarifies former Section 9–402(7). If a name change renders a filed financing statement seriously misleading, the financing statement, unless amended to provide the debtor's new correct name, is effective only to perfect a security interest in collateral acquired by the debtor before, or within four months after, the change. If an amendment that provides the new correct name is filed within four months after the change, the financing statement as amended would be effective also with respect to collateral acquired more than four months after the change. If an amendment that provides the new correct name is filed more than four months after the change, the financing statement as amended would be effective also with respect to collateral acquired more than four months after the change, but only from the time of the filing of the amendment.

§ 9.508. Effectiveness of Financing Statement if New Debtor Becomes Bound by Security Agreement

(a) Except as otherwise provided in this section, a filed financing statement naming an original debtor is effective to perfect a security interest in collateral in which a new debtor has or acquires rights to the extent that the financing statement would have been effective had the original debtor acquired rights in the collateral.

(b) If the difference between the name of the original debtor and that of the new debtor causes a filed financing statement that is effective under Subsection (a) to be seriously misleading under Section 9.506:

(1) the financing statement is effective to perfect a security interest in collateral acquired by the new debtor before, and within four months after, the new debtor becomes bound under Section 9.203(d); and

(2) the financing statement is not effective to perfect a security interest in collateral acquired by the new debtor more than four months after the new debtor becomes bound under Section 9.203(d) unless an initial financing statement providing the name of the new debtor is filed before the expiration of that time.

(c) This section does not apply to collateral as to which a filed financing statement remains effective against the new debtor under Section 9.507(a).

Added by Acts 1999, 76th Leg., ch. 414, § 1.01, eff. July 1, 2001.

Uniform Commercial Code Comment

1. **Source.** New.

2. **The Problem.** Section 9–203(d) and (e) and this section deal with situations where one party (the "new debtor") becomes bound as debtor by a security agreement entered into by another person (the "original debtor"). These situations often arise as a consequence of changes in business structure. For example, the original debtor may be an individual debtor who operates a business as a sole proprietorship and then incorporates it. Or, the original debtor may be a corporation that is merged into another corporation. Under both former Article 9 and this Article, collateral that is transferred in the course of the incorporation or merger normally would remain subject to a perfected security interest. See Sections 9–315(a), 9–507(a). Former Article 9 was less clear with respect to whether an after-acquired property clause in a security agreement signed by the original debtor would be effective to create a security interest in property acquired by the new corporation or the merger survivor and, if so, whether a financing statement filed against the original debtor would be effective to perfect the security interest. This section and Sections 9–203(d) and (e) are a clarification.

3. **How New Debtor Becomes Bound.** Normally, a security interest is unenforceable unless the debtor has authenticated a security agreement describing the collateral. See Section 9–203(b). New Section 9–203(e) creates an exception, under which a security agreement entered into by one person is effective with respect to the property of another. This exception comes into play if a "new debtor" becomes bound as debtor by a security agreement entered into by another person (the "original debtor"). (The quoted terms are defined in Section 9–102.) If a new debtor does become bound, then the security agreement entered into by the original debtor satisfies the security-agreement requirement of Section 9–203(b)(3) as to existing or after-acquired property of the new debtor to the extent the property is described in the security agreement. In that case, no other agreement is necessary to make a security interest enforceable in that property. See Section 9–203(e).

Section 9–203(d) explains when a new debtor becomes bound by an original debtor's security agreement. Under Section 9–203(d)(1), a new debtor becomes bound as debtor if, by contract or operation of other law, the security agreement becomes effective to create a security interest in the new debtor's property. For example, if the applicable corporate law of mergers provides that when A Corp merges into B Corp, B Corp becomes a debtor under A Corp's security agreement, then B Corp would become bound as debtor following such a merger. Similarly, B Corp would become bound as debtor if B Corp contractually assumes A's obligations under the security agreement.

Under certain circumstances, a new debtor becomes bound for purposes of this Article even though it would not be bound under other law. Under Section 9–203(d)(2), a new debtor becomes bound when, by contract or operation of other law, it (i) becomes obligated not only for the secured obligation but also generally for the obligations of the original debtor and (ii) acquires or succeeds to substantially all the assets of the original debtor. For example, some corporate laws provide that, when two corporations merge, the surviving corporation succeeds to the assets of its merger partner and "has all liabilities" of both corporations. In the case where, for example, A Corp merges into B Corp (and A Corp ceases to exist), some people have questioned whether A Corp's grant of a security interest in its existing and after-acquired property becomes a "liability" of B Corp, such that B Corp's existing and after-acquired property becomes subject to a security interest in favor of A Corp's lender. Even if corporate law were to give a negative answer, under Section 9–203(d)(2), B Corp would become bound for purposes of Section 9–203(e) and this section. The "substantially all of the assets" requirement of Section 9–203(d)(2) excludes sureties and other secondary obligors as well as persons who become obligated through veil piercing and other non-successorship doctrines. In most cases, it will exclude successors to the assets and liabilities of a division of a debtor.

4. **When Financing Statement Effective Against New Debtor.** Subsection (a) provides that a filing against the original debtor generally is effective to perfect a security interest in collateral that a new debtor has at the time it becomes bound by the original debtor's security agreement and collateral that it acquires after the new debtor becomes bound. Under subsection (b), however, if the filing against the original debtor is seriously misleading as to the new debtor's name, the filing is effective as to collateral acquired by the new debtor more than four months after the new debtor becomes bound only if a person files during the four-month period an initial financing statement providing the name of the new debtor. Compare Section 9–507(c) (four-month period of effectiveness with respect to collateral acquired by a debtor after the debtor changes its name). Moreover, if the original debtor and the new debtor are located in different jurisdictions, a filing against the original debtor would not be effective to perfect a security interest in collateral that the new debtor acquires or has acquired from a person other than the original debtor. See Example 5, Section 9–316, Comment 2.

5. **Transferred Collateral.** This section does not apply to collateral transferred by the original debtor to a new debtor. See subsection (c). Under those circumstances, the filing against the original debtor continues to be effective until it lapses or perfection is lost for another reason. See Sections 9–316, 9–507(a).

6. **Priority.** Section 9–326 governs the priority contest between a secured creditor of the original debtor and a secured creditor of the new debtor.

§ 9.509. Persons Entitled to File a Record

(a) A person may file an initial financing statement, amendment that adds collateral covered by a financing statement, or amendment that adds a debtor to a financing statement only if:

(1) the debtor authorizes the filing in an authenticated record or pursuant to Subsection (b) or (c); or

(2) the person holds an agricultural lien that has become effective at the time of filing and the financing statement covers only collateral in which the person holds an agricultural lien.

(b) By authenticating or becoming bound as debtor by a security agreement, a debtor or new debtor authorizes the filing of an initial financing statement, and an amendment, covering:

(1) the collateral described in the security agreement; and

(2) property that becomes collateral under Section 9.315(a)(2), whether or not the security agreement expressly covers proceeds.

(c) By acquiring collateral in which a security interest or agricultural lien continues under Section 9.315(a)(1), a debtor authorizes the filing of an initial financing statement, and an amendment, covering the collateral and property that becomes collateral under Section 9.315(a)(2).

(d) A person may file an amendment other than an amendment that adds collateral covered by a financing statement or an amendment that adds a debtor to a financing statement only if:

(1) the secured party of record authorizes the filing; or

(2) the amendment is a termination statement for a financing statement as to which the secured party of record has failed to file or send a termination statement as required by Section 9.513(a) or (c), the debtor authorizes the filing, and the termination statement indicates that the debtor authorized it to be filed.

(e) If there is more than one secured party of record for a financing statement, each secured party of record may authorize the filing of an amendment under Subsection (d).

Added by Acts 1999, 76th Leg., ch. 414, § 1.01, eff. July 1, 2001. Amended by Acts 2001, 77th Leg., ch. 705, § 16, eff. June 13, 2001.

Uniform Commercial Code Comment

1. **Source.** New.

2. **Scope and Approach of This Section.** This section collects in one place most of the rules determining whether a record may be filed. Section 9–510 explains the extent to which a filed record is effective. Under these sections, the identity of the person who effects a filing is immaterial. The filing scheme contemplated by this Part does not contemplate that the identity of a "filer" will be a part of the searchable records. This is consistent with, and a necessary aspect of, eliminating signatures or other evidence of authorization from the system. (Note that the 1972 amendments to this Article eliminated the requirement that a financing statement contain the signature of the secured party.) As long as the appropriate person authorizes the filing, or, in the case of a termination statement, the debtor is entitled to the termination, it is insignificant whether the secured party or another person files any given record. The question of authorization is one for the court, not the filing office. However, a filing office may choose to employ authentication procedures in connection with electronic communications, e.g., to verify the identity of a filer who seeks to charge the filing fee.

3. **Unauthorized Filings.** Records filed in the filing office do not require signatures for their effectiveness. Subsection (a)(1) substitutes for the debtor's signature on a financing statement the requirement that the debtor authorize in an authenticated record the filing of an initial financing statement or an amendment that adds collateral. Also, under subsection (a)(1), if an amendment adds a debtor, the debtor who is added must authorize the amendment. A person who files an unauthorized record in violation of subsection (a)(1) is liable under Section 9–625(b) and (e) for actual and statutory damages. Of course, a filed financing statement is ineffective to perfect a security interest if the filing is not authorized. See Section 9–510(a). Law other than this Article, including the law with respect to ratification of past acts, generally determines whether a person has the requisite authority to file a record under this section. See Sections 1–103, 9–502, Comment 3. This Article applies to other issues, such as the priority of a security interest perfected by the filing of a financing statement.

4. ***Ipso Facto* Authorization.** Under subsection (b), the authentication of a security agreement *ipso facto* constitutes the debtor's authorization of the filing of a financing statement covering the collateral described in the security agreement. The secured party need not obtain a separate authorization. Similarly, a new debtor's becoming bound by a security agreement *ipso facto* constitutes the new debtor's authorization of the filing of a financing statement covering the collateral described in the security agreement by which the new debtor has become bound. And, under subsection (c), the acquisition of collateral in which a security interest

continues after disposition under Section 9–315(a)(1) *ipso facto* constitutes an authorization to file an initial financing statement against the person who acquired the collateral. The authorization to file an initial financing statement also constitutes an authorization to file a record covering actual proceeds of the original collateral, even if the security agreement is silent as to proceeds.

Example 1: Debtor authenticates a security agreement creating a security interest in Debtor's inventory in favor of Secured Party. Secured Party files a financing statement covering inventory and accounts. The financing statement is authorized insofar as it covers inventory and unauthorized insofar as it covers accounts.

Example 2: Debtor authenticates a security agreement creating a security interest in Debtor's inventory in favor of Secured Party. Secured Party files a financing statement covering inventory. Debtor sells some inventory, deposits the buyer's payment into a deposit account, and withdraws the funds to purchase equipment. As long as the equipment can be traced to the inventory, the security interest continues in the equipment. See Section 9–315(a)(2). However, because the equipment was acquired with cash proceeds, the financing statement becomes ineffective to perfect the security interest in the equipment on the 21st day after the security interest attaches to the equipment unless Secured Party continues perfection beyond the 20–day period by filing a financing statement against the equipment or amending the filed financing statement to cover equipment. See Section 9–315(d). Debtor's authentication of the security agreement authorizes the filing of an initial financing statement or amendment covering the equipment, which is "property that becomes collateral under Section 9–315(a)(2)." See Section 9–509(b)(2).

5. **Agricultural Liens.** Under subsection (a)(2), the holder of an agricultural lien may file a financing statement covering collateral subject to the lien without obtaining the debtor's authorization. Because the lien arises as matter of law, the debtor's consent is not required. A person who files an unauthorized record in violation of this subsection is liable under Section 9–625(e) for a statutory penalty and damages.

6. **Amendments; Termination Statements Authorized by Debtor.** Most amendments may not be filed unless the secured party of record, as determined under Section 9–511, authorizes the filing. See subsection (d)(1). However, under subsection (d)(2), the authorization of the secured party of record is not required for the filing of a termination statement if the secured party of record failed to send or file a termination statement as required by Section 9–513, the debtor authorizes it to be filed, and the termination statement so indicates.

7. **Multiple Secured Parties of Record.** Subsection (e) deals with multiple secured parties of record. It permits each secured party of record to authorize the filing of amendments. However, Section 9–510(b) protects the rights and powers of one secured party of record from the effects of filings made by another secured party of record. See Section 9–510, Comment 3.

8. **Successor to Secured Party of Record.** A person may succeed to the powers of the secured party of record by operation of other law, e.g., the law of corporate mergers. In that case, the successor has the power to authorize filings within the meaning of this section.

§ 9.510. Effectiveness of Filed Record

(a) A filed record is effective only to the extent that it was filed by a person that may file it under Section 9.509.

(b) A record authorized by one secured party of record does not affect the financing statement with respect to another secured party of record.

(c) A continuation statement that is not filed within the six-month period prescribed by Section 9.515(d) is ineffective.

Added by Acts 1999, 76th Leg., ch. 414, § 1.01, eff. July 1, 2001.

Uniform Commercial Code Comment

1. **Source.** New.

2. **Ineffectiveness of Unauthorized or Overbroad Filings.** Subsection (a) provides that a filed financing statement is effective only to the extent it was filed by a person entitled to file it.

Example 1: Debtor authorizes the filing of a financing statement covering inventory. Under Section 9–509, the secured party may file a financing statement covering only inventory; it may not file a financing statement covering other collateral. The secured party files a financing statement covering inventory and equipment. This section provides that the financing statement is effective only to the extent the secured party may file it. Thus, the financing statement is effective to perfect a security interest in inventory but ineffective to perfect a security interest in equipment.

3. **Multiple Secured Parties of Record.** Section 9–509(e) permits any secured party of record to authorize the filing of most amendments. Subsection (b) of this section prevents a filing authorized by one secured party of record from affecting the rights and powers of another secured party of record without the latter's consent.

Example 2: Debtor creates a security interest in favor of A and B. The filed financing statement names A and B as the secured parties. An amendment deleting some collateral covered by the financing statement is filed pursuant to B's authorization. Although B's security interest in the deleted collateral becomes unperfected, A's security interest remains perfected in all the collateral.

Example 3: Debtor creates a security interest in favor of A and B. The financing statement names A and B as the secured parties. A termination statement is filed pursuant to B's authorization. Although the effectiveness of the financing statement terminates with respect to B's security interest, A's rights are unaffected. That is, the financing statement continues to be effective to perfect A's security interest.

4. **Continuation Statements.** A continuation statement may be filed only within the six months immediately before

lapse. See Section 9–515(d). The filing office is obligated to reject a continuation statement that is filed outside the six-month period. See Sections 9–520(a), 9–516(b)(7). Subsection (c) provides that if the filing office fails to reject a continuation statement that is not filed in a timely manner, the continuation statement is ineffective nevertheless.

§ 9.511. Secured Party of Record

(a) A secured party of record with respect to a financing statement is a person whose name is provided as the name of the secured party or a representative of the secured party in an initial financing statement that has been filed. If an initial financing statement is filed under Section 9.514(a), the assignee named in the initial financing statement is the secured party of record with respect to the financing statement.

(b) If an amendment of a financing statement that provides the name of a person as a secured party or a representative of a secured party is filed, the person named in the amendment is a secured party of record. If an amendment is filed under Section 9.514(b), the assignee named in the amendment is a secured party of record.

(c) A person remains a secured party of record until the filing of an amendment of the financing statement that deletes the person.

Added by Acts 1999, 76th Leg., ch. 414, § 1.01, eff. July 1, 2001.

Uniform Commercial Code Comment

1. **Source.** New.

2. **Secured Party of Record.** This new section explains how the secured party of record is to be determined. If SP–1 is named as the secured party in an initial financing statement, it is the secured party of record. Similarly, if an initial financing statement reflects a total assignment from SP–0 to SP–1, then SP–1 is the secured party of record. See subsection (a). If, subsequently, an amendment is filed assigning SP–1's status to SP–2, then SP–2 becomes the secured party of record in place of SP–1. The same result obtains if a subsequent amendment deletes the reference to SP–1 and substitutes therefor a reference to SP–2. If, however, a subsequent amendment adds SP–2 as a secured party but does not purport to remove SP–1 as a secured party, then SP–2 and SP–1 each is a secured party of record. See subsection (b). An amendment purporting to remove the only secured party of record without providing a successor is ineffective. See Section 9–512(e). At any point in time, all effective records that comprise a financing statement must be examined to determine the person or persons that have the status of secured party of record.

3. **Successor to Secured Party of Record.** Application of other law may result in a person succeeding to the powers of a secured party of record. For example, if the secured party of record (A) merges into another corporation (B) and the other corporation (B) survives, other law may provide that B has all of A's powers. In that case, B is authorized to take all actions under this Part that A would have been authorized to take. Similarly, acts taken by a person who is authorized under generally applicable principles of agency to act on behalf of the secured party of record are effective under this Part.

State Bar Committee Comment

The reference in Comment 3 to application of other law resulting in a person or entity succeeding to the powers of a secured party of record specifically encompasses, without limitation, sales by regulatory authorities, such as the FDIC and the Insurance Commission, of assets of entities subject to their jurisdiction.

§ 9.512. Amendment of Financing Statement

(a) Subject to Section 9.509, a person may add or delete collateral covered by, continue or terminate the effectiveness of, or, subject to Subsection (e), otherwise amend the information provided in a financing statement by filing an amendment that:

(1) identifies, by its file number, the initial financing statement to which the amendment relates; and

(2) if the amendment relates to an initial financing statement filed or recorded in a filing office described in Section 9.501(a)(1), provides the information specified in Section 9.502(b).

(b) Except as otherwise provided in Section 9.515, the filing of an amendment does not extend the period of effectiveness of the financing statement.

(c) A financing statement that is amended by an amendment that adds collateral is effective as to the added collateral only from the date of the filing of the amendment.

(d) A financing statement that is amended by an amendment that adds a debtor is effective as to the added debtor only from the date of the filing of the amendment.

(e) An amendment is ineffective to the extent it:

(1) purports to delete all debtors and fails to provide the name of a debtor to be covered by the financing statement; or

(2) purports to delete all secured parties of record and fails to provide the name of a new secured party of record.

(f) A secured party may change the name or mailing address of the secured party in more than one financing statement by filing a master amendment setting forth the name of the secured party and file number of each financing statement and the new name or mailing address of the secured party. The secured party must also provide filing information in computer-readable form prescribed by the Secretary of State.

Added by Acts 1999, 76th Leg., ch. 414, § 1.01, eff. July 1, 2001.

Uniform Commercial Code Comment

1. **Source.** Former 9–402(4).

2. **Changes to Financing Statements.** This section addresses changes to financing statements, including addition and deletion of collateral. Although termination statements, assignments, and continuation statements are types of amendment, this Article follows former Article 9 and contains separate sections containing additional provisions applicable to particular types of amendments. See Section 9–513 (termination statements); 9–514 (assignments); 9–515 (continuation statements). One should not infer from this separate treatment that this Article requires a separate amendment to accomplish each change. Rather, a single amendment would be legally sufficient to, e.g., add collateral and continue the effectiveness of the financing statement.

3. **Amendments.** An amendment under this Article may identify only the information contained in a financing statement that is to be changed; alternatively, it may take the form of an amended and restated financing statement. The latter would state, for example, that the financing statement "is amended and restated to read as follows: . . ." References in this Part to an "amended financing statement" are to a financing statement as amended by an amendment using either technique.

This section revises former Section 9–402(4) to permit secured parties of record to make changes in the public record without the need to obtain the debtor's signature. However, the filing of an amendment that adds collateral or adds a debtor must be authorized by the debtor or it will not be effective. See Sections 9–509(a), 9–510(a).

4. **Amendment Adding Debtor.** An amendment that adds a debtor is effective, provided that the added debtor authorizes the filing. See Section 9–509(a). However, filing an amendment adding a debtor to a previously filed financing statement affords no advantage over filing an initial financing statement against that debtor and may be disadvantageous. With respect to the added debtor, for purposes of determining the priority of the security interest, the time of filing is the time of the filing of the amendment, not the time of the filing of the initial financing statement. See subsection (d). However, the effectiveness of the financing statement lapses with respect to added debtor at the time it lapses with respect to the original debtor. See subsection (b).

5. **Deletion of All Debtors or Secured Parties of Record.** Subsection (e) assures that there will be a debtor and secured party of record for every financing statement.

Example: A filed financing statement names A and B as secured parties of record and covers inventory and equipment. An amendment deletes equipment and purports to delete A and B as secured parties of record without adding a substitute secured party. The amendment is ineffective to the extent it purports to delete the secured parties of record but effective with respect to the deletion of collateral. As a consequence, the financing statement, as amended, covers only inventory, but A and B remain as secured parties of record.

State Bar Committee Comment

Subsection (f) carries forward the master amendment filing concept of former Section 9.410(b) while incorporating the broadened scope of the revisions by deleting the requirement of a written statement signed by the secured party of record in each financing statement. The language specifically facilitates the medium-neutral revisions relating to filing of the master amendment without need for a signed paper original or copy of the electronic document. The definition of secured party is found in Section 9.102(73) and the definition of secured party of record is found in Section 9.511. See especially Official Comment 3 and State Bar Committee Comment to Section 9.511. Filing fees for master amendments are specified in Section 9.525(f).

§ 9.513. Termination Statement

(a) A secured party shall cause the secured party of record for a financing statement to file a termination statement for the financing statement if the financing statement covers consumer goods and:

(1) there is no obligation secured by the collateral covered by the financing statement and no commitment to make an advance, incur an obligation, or otherwise give value; or

(2) the debtor did not authorize the filing of the initial financing statement.

(b) To comply with Subsection (a), a secured party shall cause the secured party of record to file the termination statement:

(1) within one month after there is no obligation secured by the collateral covered by the financing statement and no commitment to make advances, incur an obligation, or otherwise give value; or

(2) if earlier, within 20 days after the secured party receives an authenticated demand from a debtor.

(c) In cases not governed by Subsection (a), within 20 days after a secured party receives an authenticated demand from a debtor, the secured party shall cause the secured party of record for a financing statement to send the debtor a termination statement for the financing statement or file the termination statement in the filing office if:

(1) except in the case of a financing statement covering accounts or chattel paper that has been sold or goods that are the subject of a consignment, there is no obligation secured by the collateral covered by the financing statement and no commitment to make an advance, incur an obligation, or otherwise give value;

(2) the financing statement covers accounts or chattel paper that has been sold but as to which the account debtor or other person obligated has discharged its obligation;

(3) the financing statement covers goods that were the subject of a consignment to the debtor but are not in the debtor's possession; or

(4) the debtor did not authorize the filing of the initial financing statement.

(d) Except as otherwise provided in Section 9.510, upon the filing of a termination statement with the filing office, the financing statement to which the termination statement relates ceases to be effective. Except as otherwise provided in Section 9.510, for purposes of Sections 9.519(g), 9.522(a), and 9.523(c), the filing with the filing office of a termination statement relating to a financing statement that indicates that the debtor is a transmitting utility also causes the effectiveness of the financing statement to lapse.

Added by Acts 1999, 76th Leg., ch. 414, § 1.01, eff. July 1, 2001. Amended by Acts 2001, 77th Leg., ch. 705, § 17, eff. June 13, 2001.

Uniform Commercial Code Comment

1. **Source.** Former Section 9–404.

2. **Duty to File or Send.** This section specifies when a secured party must cause the secured party of record to file or send to the debtor a termination statement for a financing statement. Because most financing statements expire in five years unless a continuation statement is filed (Section 9–515), no compulsion is placed on the secured party to file a termination statement unless demanded by the debtor, except in the case of consumer goods. Because many consumers will not realize the importance to them of clearing the public record, an affirmative duty is put on the secured party in that case. But many purchase-money security interests in consumer goods will not be filed, except for motor vehicles. See Section 9–309(1). Under Section 9–311(b), compliance with a certificate-of-title statute is "equivalent to the filing of a financing statement under this article." Thus, this section applies to a certificate of title unless the section is superseded by a certificate-of-title statute that contains a specific rule addressing a secured party's duty to cause a notation of a security interest to be removed from a certificate of title. In the context of a certificate of title, however, the secured party could comply with this section by causing the removal itself or providing the debtor with documentation sufficient to enable the debtor to effect the removal.

Subsections (a) and (b) apply to a financing statement covering consumer goods. Subsection (c) applies to other financing statements. Subsection (a) and (c) each makes explicit what was implicit under former Article 9: If the debtor did not authorize the filing of a financing statement in the first place, the secured party of record should file or send a termination statement. The liability imposed upon a secured party that fails to comply with subsection (a) or (c) is identical to that imposed for the filing of an unauthorized financing statement or amendment. See Section 9–625(e).

3. **"Bogus" Filings.** A secured party's duty to send a termination statement arises when the secured party "receives" an authenticated demand from the debtor. In the case of an unauthorized financing statement, the person named as debtor in the financing statement may have no relationship with the named secured party and no reason to know the secured party's address. Inasmuch as the address in the financing statement is "held out by [the person named as secured party in the financing statement] as the place for receipt of such communications [i.e., communications relating to security interests]," the putative secured party is deemed to have "received" a notification delivered to that address. See Section 1–201(26). If a termination statement is not forthcoming, the person named as debtor itself may authorize the filing of a termination statement, which will be effective if it indicates that the person authorized it to be filed. See Sections 9–509(d)(2), 9–510(c).

4. **Buyers of Receivables.** Applied literally, former Section 9–404(1) would have required many buyers of receivables to file a termination statement immediately upon filing a financing statement because "there is no outstanding secured obligation and no commitment to make advances, incur obligations, or otherwise give value." Subsections (c)(1) and (2) remedy this problem. While the security interest of a buyer of accounts or chattel paper (B–1) is perfected, the debtor is not deemed to retain an interest in the sold receivables and thus could transfer no interest in them to another buyer (B–2) or to a lien creditor (LC). However, for purposes of determining the rights of the debtor's creditors and certain purchasers of accounts or chattel paper from the debtor, while B–1's security interest is unperfected, the debtor-seller is deemed to have rights in the sold receivables, and a competing security interest or judicial lien may attach to those rights. See Sections 9–318, 9–109, Comment 5. Suppose that B–1's security interest in certain accounts and chattel paper is perfected by filing, but the effectiveness of the financing statement lapses. Both before and after lapse, B–1 collects some of the receivables. After lapse, LC acquires a lien on the accounts and chattel paper. B–1's unperfected security interest in the accounts and chattel paper is subordinate to LC's rights. See Section 9–317(a)(2). But collections on accounts and chattel paper are not "accounts" or "chattel paper." Even if B–1's security interest in the accounts and chattel paper is or becomes unperfected, neither the debtor nor LC acquires rights to the collections that B–1 collects (and owns) before LC acquires a lien.

5. **Effect of Filing.** Subsection (d) states the effect of filing a termination statement: the related financing statement ceases to be effective. If one of several secured parties of record files a termination statement, subsection (d) applies only with respect to the rights of the person who authorized the filing of the termination statement. See Section

9–510(b). The financing statement remains effective with respect to the rights of the others. However, even if a financing statement is *terminated* (and thus no longer is effective) with respect to all secured parties of record, the financing statement, including the termination statement, will remain of record until at least one year after it *lapses* with respect to all secured parties of record. See Section 9–519(g).

§ 9.514. Assignment of Powers of Secured Party of Record

(a) Except as otherwise provided in Subsection (c), an initial financing statement may reflect an assignment of all of the secured party's power to authorize an amendment to the financing statement by providing the name and mailing address of the assignee as the name and address of the secured party.

(b) Except as otherwise provided in Subsection (c), a secured party of record may assign of record all or a part of its power to authorize an amendment to a financing statement by filing in the filing office an amendment of the financing statement that:

(1) identifies, by its file number, the initial financing statement to which it relates;

(2) provides the name of the assignor; and

(3) provides the name and mailing address of the assignee.

(c) An assignment of record of a security interest in a fixture covered by a record of a mortgage that is effective as a financing statement filed as a fixture filing under Section 9.502(c) may be made only by an assignment of record of the mortgage in the manner provided by law of this state other than this chapter.

(d) A secured party of record may assign of record all of the secured party's rights under more than one financing statement filed with the Secretary of State by filing a master assignment setting forth the name of the secured party of record and file number of each financing statement and the name and mailing address of the assignee. The secured party must also provide filing information in computer-readable form prescribed by the Secretary of State.

Added by Acts 1999, 76th Leg., ch. 414, § 1.01, eff. July 1, 2001.

Uniform Commercial Code Comment

1. **Source.** Former Section 9–405.

2. **Assignments.** This section provides a permissive device whereby a secured party of record may effectuate an assignment of its power to affect a financing statement. It may also be useful for a secured party who has assigned all or part of its security interest or agricultural lien and wishes to have the fact noted of record, so that inquiries concerning the transaction would be addressed to the assignee. See Section 9–502, Comment 2. Upon the filing of an assignment, the assignee becomes the "secured party of record" and may authorize the filing of a continuation statement, termination statement, or other amendment. Note that under Section 9–310(c) no filing of an assignment is required as a condition of continuing the perfected status of the security interest against creditors and transferees of the original debtor. However, if an assignment is not filed, the assignor remains the secured party of record, with the power (even if not the right) to authorize the filing of effective amendments. See Sections 9–511(c), 9–509(d).

Where a record of a mortgage is effective as a financing statement filed as a fixture filing (Section 9–502(c)), then an assignment of record of the security interest may be made only in the manner in which an assignment of record of the mortgage may be made under local real-property law.

3. **Comparison to Prior Law.** Most of the changes reflected in this section are for clarification or to embrace medium-neutral drafting. As a general matter, this section preserves the opportunity given by former Section 9–405 to assign a security interest of record in one of two different ways. Under subsection (a), a secured party may assign all of its power to affect a financing statement by naming an assignee in the initial financing statement. The secured party of record may accomplish the same result under subsection (b) by making a subsequent filing. Subsection (b) also may be used for an assignment of only some of the secured party of record's power to affect a financing statement, e.g., the power to affect the financing statement as it relates to particular items of collateral or as it relates to an undivided interest in a security interest in all the collateral. An initial financing statement may not be used to change the secured party of record under these circumstances. However, an amendment adding the assignee as a secured party of record may be used.

State Bar Committee Comment

Subsection (d) carries forward the master assignment concept of former Section 9.410(a). It incorporates the medium-neutral revisions of the drafters so that written originals or copies signed by the secured party of record need not be obtained. The definition of secured party is found in Section 9.102(73) and the definition of secured party of record is found in Section 9.511. See especially Official Comment 3 and State Bar Committee Comment to Section 9.511. Filing fees for a master assignment are specified in Section 9.525(f).

§ 9.515. Duration and Effectiveness of Financing Statement; Effect of Lapsed Financing Statement

(a) Except as otherwise provided in Subsections (b)–(g), a filed financing statement is effective for a period of five years after the date of filing.

(b) Except as otherwise provided in Subsections (e), (f), and (g), an initial financing statement filed in connection with a public-finance transaction or manufactured-home transaction is effective for a period of 30 years after the date of filing if it indicates that it is filed in connection with a public-finance transaction or manufactured-home transaction.

(c) The effectiveness of a filed financing statement lapses on the expiration of the period of its effectiveness unless before the lapse a continuation statement is filed pursuant to Subsection (d). Upon lapse, a financing statement ceases to be effective and any security interest or agricultural lien that was perfected by the financing statement becomes unperfected, unless the security interest is perfected otherwise. If the security interest or agricultural lien becomes unperfected upon lapse, it is deemed never to have been perfected as against a purchaser of the collateral for value.

(d) A continuation statement may be filed only within six months before the expiration of the five-year period specified in Subsection (a) or the 30-year period specified in Subsection (b), whichever is applicable.

(e) Except as otherwise provided in Section 9.510, upon timely filing of a continuation statement, the effectiveness of the initial financing statement continues for a period of five years commencing on the day on which the financing statement would have become ineffective in the absence of the filing. Upon the expiration of the five-year period, the financing statement lapses in the same manner as provided in Subsection (c), unless, before the lapse, another continuation statement is filed pursuant to Subsection (d). Succeeding continuation statements may be filed in the same manner to continue the effectiveness of the initial financing statement.

(f) If a debtor is a transmitting utility and a filed financing statement so indicates, the financing statement is effective until a termination statement is filed.

(g) A record of a mortgage that is effective as a financing statement filed as a fixture filing or as a financing statement covering as-extracted collateral or timber to be cut under Section 9.502(c) remains effective as a financing statement filed as a fixture filing or as a financing statement covering as-extracted collateral or timber to be cut until the mortgage is released or satisfied of record or its effectiveness otherwise terminates as to the real property.

Added by Acts 1999, 76th Leg., ch. 414, § 1.01, eff. July 1, 2001. Amended by Acts 2003, 78th Leg., ch. 917, § 5, eff. Sept. 1, 2003.

Uniform Commercial Code Comment

1. **Source.** Former Section 9–403(2), (3), (6).

2. **Period of Financing Statement's Effectiveness.** Subsection (a) states the general rule: a financing statement is effective for a five-year period unless its effectiveness is continued under this section or terminated under Section 9–513. Subsection (b) provides that if the financing statement relates to a public-finance transaction or a manufactured-home transaction and so indicates, the financing statement is effective for 30 years. These financings typically extend well beyond the standard, five-year period. Under subsection (f), a financing statement filed against a transmitting utility remains effective indefinitely, until a termination statement is filed. Likewise, under subsection (g), a mortgage effective as a fixture filing remains effective until its effectiveness terminates under real-property law.

3. **Lapse.** When the period of effectiveness under subsection (a) or (b) expires, the effectiveness of the financing statement lapses. The last sentence of subsection (c) addresses the effect of lapse. The deemed retroactive unperfection applies only with respect to purchasers for value; unlike former Section 9–403(2), it does not apply with respect to lien creditors.

Example 1: SP–1 and SP–2 both hold security interests in the same collateral. Both security interests are perfected by filing. SP–1 filed first and has priority under Section 9–322(a)(1). The effectiveness of SP–1's filing lapses. As long as SP–2's security interest remains perfected thereafter, SP–2 is entitled to priority over SP–1's security interest, which is deemed never to have been perfected as against a purchaser for value (SP–2). See Section 9–322(a)(2).

Example 2: SP holds a security interest perfected by filing. On July 1, LC acquires a judicial lien on the collateral. Two weeks later, the effectiveness of the financing statement lapses. Although the security interest becomes unperfected upon lapse, it was perfected when LC acquired its lien. Accordingly, notwithstanding the lapse, the perfected security interest has priority over the rights of LC, who is not a purchaser. See Section 9–317(a)(2).

4. **Effect of Debtor's Bankruptcy.** Under former Section 9–403(2), lapse was tolled if the debtor entered bankruptcy or another insolvency proceeding. Nevertheless, being unaware that insolvency proceedings had been commenced, filing offices routinely removed records from the files as if lapse had not been tolled. Subsection (c) deletes the former tolling provision and thereby imposes a new burden on the secured party: to be sure that a financing statement does not lapse during the debtor's bankruptcy. The secured party can prevent lapse by filing a continuation statement, even without first obtaining relief from the automatic stay. See Bankruptcy Code Section 362(b)(3). Of course, if the debtor enters bankruptcy before lapse, the provisions of this Article with respect to lapse would

be of no effect to the extent that federal bankruptcy law dictates a contrary result (e.g., to the extent that the Bankruptcy Code determines rights as of the date of the filing of the bankruptcy petition).

5. **Continuation Statements.** Subsection (d) explains when a continuation statement may be filed. A continuation statement filed at a time other than that prescribed by subsection (d) is ineffective, see Section 9–510(c), and the filing office may not accept it. See Sections 9–520(a), 9–516(b). Subsection (e) specifies the effect of a continuation statement and provides for successive continuation statements.

§ 9.516. What Constitutes Filing; Effectiveness of Filing

(a) Except as otherwise provided in Subsection (b), communication of a record to a filing office and tender of the filing fee or acceptance of the record by the filing office constitutes filing.

(b) Filing does not occur with respect to a record that a filing office refuses to accept because:

(1) the record is not communicated by a method or medium of communication authorized by the filing office;

(2) an amount equal to or greater than the applicable filing fee is not tendered;

(3) the filing office is unable to index the record because:

(A) in the case of an initial financing statement, the record does not provide a name for the debtor;

(B) in the case of an amendment or correction statement, the record:

(i) does not identify the initial financing statement as required by Section 9.512 or 9.518, as applicable; or

(ii) identifies an initial financing statement whose effectiveness has lapsed under Section 9.515;

(C) in the case of an initial financing statement that provides the name of a debtor identified as an individual or an amendment that provides a name of a debtor identified as an individual that was not previously provided in the financing statement to which the record relates, the record does not identify the debtor's last name; or

(D) in the case of a record filed or recorded in the filing office described in Section 9.501(a)(1), the record does not provide the name of the debtor and a sufficient description of the real property to which it relates;

(4) in the case of an initial financing statement or an amendment that adds a secured party of record, the record does not provide a name and mailing address for the secured party of record;

(5) in the case of an initial financing statement or an amendment that provides a name of a debtor that was not previously provided in the financing statement to which the amendment relates, the record does not:

(A) provide a mailing address for the debtor;

(B) indicate whether the debtor is an individual or an organization; or

(C) if the financing statement indicates that the debtor is an organization, provide:

(i) a type of organization for the debtor;

(ii) a jurisdiction of organization for the debtor; or

(iii) an organizational identification number for the debtor or indicate that the debtor has none;

(6) in the case of an assignment reflected in an initial financing statement under Section 9.514(a) or an amendment filed under Section 9.514(b), the record does not provide a name and mailing address for the assignee;

(7) in the case of a continuation statement, the record is not filed within the six-month period prescribed by Section 9.515(d); or

(8) the record is not on an industry standard form, including a national standard form or a form approved by the International Association of Commercial Administrators, adopted by rule by the secretary of state.

(c) For purposes of Subsection (b):

(1) a record does not provide information if the filing office is unable to read or decipher the information; and

(2) a record that does not indicate that it is an amendment or identify an initial financing statement to which it relates, as required by Section 9.512, 9.514, or 9.518, is an initial financing statement.

(d) A record that is communicated to the filing office with tender of the filing fee, but that the filing office refuses to accept for a reason other than one set forth in Subsection (b), is effective as a filed record except as against a purchaser of the collateral that gives value in reasonable reliance upon the absence of the record from the files.

Added by Acts 1999, 76th Leg., ch. 414, § 1.01, eff. July 1, 2001. Amended by Acts 2003, 78th Leg., ch. 748, § 1, eff. Jan. 1, 2004; Acts 2007, 80th Leg., ch. 565, § 2, eff. June 16, 2007.

Uniform Commercial Code Comment

1. **Source.** Subsection (a): former Section 9–403(1); the remainder is new.

2. **What Constitutes Filing.** Subsection (a) deals generically with what constitutes filing of a record, including an initial financing statement and amendments of all kinds (e.g., assignments, termination statements, and continuation statements). It follows former Section 9–403(1), under which either acceptance of a record by the filing office or presentation of the record and tender of the filing fee constitutes filing.

3. **Effectiveness of Rejected Record.** Subsection (b) provides an exclusive list of grounds upon which the filing office may reject a record. See Section 9–520(a). Although some of these grounds would also be grounds for rendering a filed record ineffective (e.g., an initial financing statement does not provide a name for the debtor), many others would not be (e.g., an initial financing statement does not provide a mailing address for the debtor or secured party of record). Neither this section nor Section 9–520 requires or authorizes the filing office to determine, or even consider, the accuracy of information provided in a record. For example, the State A filing office may not reject under subsection (b)(5)(C) an initial financing statement indicating that the debtor is a State A corporation and providing a three-digit organizational identification number, even if all State A organizational identification numbers contain at least five digits and two letters. Some organizations that are not registered organizations (such as foreign corporations) have a readily determinable jurisdiction of organization. When that is not the case, with respect to an organization that is not a registered organization, for purposes of this section, the debtor's jurisdiction of organization is any jurisdiction that bears a reasonable relation to the debtor, such as the jurisdiction stated in any organizational document or agreement for the debtor as the jurisdiction under whose law the organization is formed or as the jurisdiction whose law is the governing law, or the jurisdiction in which the debtor is located under Section 9–307(b) (i.e., its place of business or its chief executive office). Thus, for purposes of this section, more than one jurisdiction may qualify as the debtor's jurisdiction of organization. See Comment 9.

A financing statement or other record that is communicated to the filing office but which the filing office refuses to accept provides no public notice, regardless of the reason for the rejection. However, this section distinguishes between records that the filing office rightfully rejects and those that it wrongfully rejects. A filer is able to prevent a rightful rejection by complying with the requirements of subsection (b). No purpose is served by giving effect to records that justifiably never find their way into the system, and subsection (b) so provides.

Subsection (d) deals with the filing office's unjustified refusal to accept a record. Here, the filer is in no position to prevent the rejection and as a general matter should not be prejudiced by it. Although wrongfully rejected records generally are effective, subsection (d) contains a special rule to protect a third-party purchaser of the collateral (e.g., a buyer or competing secured party) who gives value in reliance upon the apparent absence of the record from the files. As against a person who searches the public record and reasonably relies on what the public record shows, subsection (d) imposes upon the filer the risk that a record failed to make its way into the filing system because of the filing office's wrongful rejection of it. (Compare Section 9–517, under which a mis-indexed financing statement is fully effective.) This risk is likely to be small, particularly when a record is presented electronically, and the filer can guard against this risk by conducting a post-filing search of the records. Moreover, Section 9–520(b) requires the filing office to give prompt notice of its refusal to accept a record for filing.

4. **Method or Medium of Communication.** Rejection pursuant to subsection (b)(1) for failure to communicate a record properly should be understood to mean noncompliance with procedures relating to security, authentication, or other communication-related requirements that the filing office may impose. Subsection (b)(1) does not authorize a filing office to impose additional substantive requirements. See Section 9–520, Comment 2.

5. **Address for Secured Party of Record.** Under subsection (b)(4) and Section 9–520(a), the lack of a mailing address for the secured party of record requires the filing office to reject an initial financing statement. The failure to include an address for the secured party of record no longer renders a financing statement ineffective. See Section 9–502(a). The function of the address is not to identify the secured party of record but rather to provide an address to which others can send required notifications, e.g., of a purchase-money security interest in inventory or of the disposition of collateral. Inasmuch as the address shown on a filed financing statement is an "address that is reasonable under the circumstances," a person required to send a notification to the secured party may satisfy the requirement by sending a notification to that address, even if the address is or becomes incorrect. See Section 9–102 (definition of "send"). Similarly, because the address is "held out by [the secured party] as the place for receipt of such communications [i.e., communications relating to security interests]," the secured party is deemed to have received a notification delivered to that address. See Section 1–201(26).

6. **Uncertainty Concerning Individual Debtor's Last Name.** Subsection (b)(3)(C) requires the filing office to reject an initial financing statement or amendment adding an individual debtor if the office cannot index the record because it does not identify the debtor's last name (e.g., it is unclear whether the debtor's name is Elton John or John Elton).

7. **Inability of Filing Office to Read or Decipher Information.** Under subsection (c)(1), if the filing office cannot read or decipher information, the information is not provided by a record for purposes of subsection (b).

8. **Classification of Records.** For purposes of subsection (b), a record that does not indicate it is an amendment or identify an initial financing statement to which it relates is

deemed to be an initial financing statement. See subsection (c)(2).

9. **Effectiveness of Rejectable But Unrejected Record.** Section 9–520(a) requires the filing office to refuse to accept an initial financing statement for a reason set forth in subsection (b). However, if the filing office accepts such a financing statement nevertheless, the financing statement generally is effective if it complies with the requirements of Section 9–502(a) and (b). See Section 9–520(c). Similarly, an otherwise effective financing statement generally remains so even though the information in the financing statement becomes incorrect. See Section 9–507(b).

§ 9.517. Effect of Indexing Errors

The failure of the filing office to index a record or to correctly index information contained in a record does not affect the effectiveness of the filed record.

Added by Acts 1999, 76th Leg., ch. 414, § 1.01, eff. July 1, 2001. Amended by Acts 2007, 80th Leg., ch. 565, § 3, eff. June 16, 2007.

Uniform Commercial Code Comment

1. **Source.** New.

2. **Effectiveness of Mis–Indexed Records.** This section provides that the filing office's error in mis-indexing a record does not render ineffective an otherwise effective record. As did former Section 9–401, this section imposes the risk of filing-office error on those who search the files rather than on those who file.

§ 9.518. Claim Concerning Inaccurate or Wrongfully Filed Record

(a) Any person named as a debtor or a secured party may file a correction statement with respect to a record if the person believes that the record is inaccurate or was wrongfully filed.

(b) A correction statement must:

(1) identify the record to which it relates by the file number assigned to the initial financing statement to which the record relates;

(2) indicate that it is a correction statement; and

(3) provide the basis for the person's belief that the record is inaccurate and indicate the manner in which the person believes the record should be amended to cure any inaccuracy or provide the basis for the person's belief that the record was wrongfully filed.

(c) The filing of a correction statement does not affect the effectiveness of an initial financing statement or other filed record.

(d) Filing of a correction statement is not effective as an amendment to a filed financing statement and is not sufficient to effect a change in the manner in which the filing office has indexed a financing statement or information contained in a financing statement.

Added by Acts 1999, 76th Leg., ch. 414, § 1.01, eff. July 1, 2001. Amended by Acts 2007, 80th Leg., ch. 565, § 4, eff. June 16, 2007.

Uniform Commercial Code Comment

1. **Source.** New.

2. **Correction Statements.** Former Article 9 did not afford a nonjudicial means for a debtor to correct a financing statement or other record that was inaccurate or wrongfully filed. Subsection (a) affords the debtor the right to file a correction statement. Among other requirements, the correction statement must provide the basis for the debtor's belief that the public record should be corrected. See subsection (b). These provisions, which resemble the analogous remedy in the Fair Credit Reporting Act, 15 U.S.C. § 1681i, afford an aggrieved person the opportunity to state its position on the public record. They do not permit an aggrieved person to change the legal effect of the public record. Thus, although a filed correction statement becomes part of the "financing statement," as defined in Section 9–102, the filing does not affect the effectiveness of the initial financing statement or any other filed record. See subsection (c).

This section does not displace other provisions of this Article that impose liability for making unauthorized filings or failing to file or send a termination statement (see Section 9–625(e)), nor does it displace any available judicial remedies.

3. **Resort to Other Law.** This Article cannot provide a satisfactory or complete solution to problems caused by misuse of the public records. The problem of "bogus" filings is not limited to the UCC filing system but extends to the real-property records, as well. A summary judicial procedure for correcting the public record and criminal penalties for those who misuse the filing and recording systems are likely to be more effective and put less strain on the filing system than provisions authorizing or requiring action by filing and recording offices.

§ 9.5185. Fraudulent Filing

(a) A person may not intentionally or knowingly present for filing or cause to be presented for filing a financing statement that the person knows:

(1) is forged;

(2) contains a material false statement; or

(3) is groundless.

(b) A person who violates Subsection (a) is liable to the owner of property covered by the financing statement for:

(1) the greater of $5,000 or the owner's actual damages;

(2) court costs; and

(3) reasonable attorney's fees.

(c) A person who violates Subsection (a) also may be prosecuted under Section 37.101, Penal Code.

(d) An owner of property covered by a fraudulent financing statement described in Subsection (a) also may file suit in a court of suitable jurisdiction requesting specific relief, including, but not limited to, release of the fraudulent financing statement. A successful plaintiff is entitled to reasonable attorney's fees and costs of court assessed against the person who filed the fraudulent financing statement. If the person who filed the fraudulent financing statement cannot be located or is a fictitious person, the owner of the property may serve the known or unknown defendant through publication in a newspaper of general circulation in the county in which the suit is brought.

Added by Acts 1999, 76th Leg., ch. 414, § 1.01, eff. July 1, 2001.

State Bar Committee Comment

This nonuniform provision is a retention of former Section 9.412, which was added by the Texas legislature to Chapter 9 in 1995. Disgruntled individuals were filing completely fraudulent financing statements against USDA officers, particularly those representing the Farmers Home Administration, simply to tie up such officers' credit and create the maximum amount of personal aggravation for such individuals. These filings were not based on any kind of a relationship whatsoever and were simply intended to harass and cause personal harm and inconvenience to government officers. A fraudulent filing was defined as one in which the person knows that the financing statement is either forged, contains a material false statement, or is groundless. An action is created if a person intentionally or knowingly presented for filing or caused to be presented for filing a fraudulent financing statement. Certain remedies were provided in that bill, including civil liability, criminal sanctions, and a remedy for removing the false evidence of a lien.

Subsequently in 1997 House Bill 1185 (companion Senate Bill 424) was enacted to further respond to what had become an epidemic problem. The Senate bill analysis digest includes the following:

Currently, individuals and organizations have begun to take action based on their refusal to recognize the authority and sovereignty of the government of the State of Texas. These entities have filed fraudulent judgment liens issued by so-called "common law courts" and fraudulent documents purporting to create liens or claims on personal and real property with the Secretary of State and many county and district court clerks throughout the state. Many of the filings have been against the State of Texas and public officers and employees, as well as private individuals. These filings have clogged the channels of commerce and have amounted to harassment and intimidation of both public officials and ordinary citizens. This bill provides both civil and criminal remedies for those against whom such fraudulent filings have been made.

Section 17 of this bill repeals the criminal sanctions in Section 9.412 [now 9.5185], but inserts other criminal remedies for not only personal property fraudulent filings but also real property and judgment lien fraudulent filings.

Subsection (c) is inserted as a reminder of possible criminal liability. Texas Penal Code Section 37.101 is entitled "Fraudulent Filing of Financing Statement."

§ 9.519. Numbering, Maintaining, and Indexing Records; Communicating Information Provided in Records

(a) For each record filed in a filing office, the filing office shall:

(1) assign a unique number to the filed record;

(2) create a record that bears the number assigned to the filed record and the date and time of filing;

(3) maintain the filed record for public inspection; and

(4) index the filed record in accordance with Subsections (c), (d), and (e).

(b) Except as provided in Subsection (i), a file number assigned after January 1, 2002, must include a digit that:

(1) is mathematically derived from or related to the other digits of the file number; and

(2) aids the filing office in determining whether a number communicated as the file number includes a single-digit or transpositional error.

(c) Except as otherwise provided in Subsections (d) and (e), the filing office shall:

(1) index an initial financing statement according to the name of the debtor and index all filed records relating to the initial financing statement in a manner that associates with one another an initial financing statement and all filed records relating to the initial financing statement; and

(2) index a record that provides a name of a debtor that was not previously provided in the financing statement to which the record relates also according to the name that was not previously provided.

(d) If a financing statement is filed as a fixture filing or covers as-extracted collateral or timber to be cut, it must be filed for record and the filing office shall index it:

(1) under the names of the debtor and of each owner of record shown on the financing statement as if they were the mortgagors under a mortgage of the real property described; and

(2) to the extent that the law of this state provides for indexing of records of mortgages under the name of the mortgagee, under the name of the secured party as if the secured party were the mortgagee thereunder, or, if indexing is by description, as if the financing statement were a record of a mortgage of the real property described.

(e) If a financing statement is filed as a fixture filing or covers as-extracted collateral or timber to be cut, the filing office shall index an assignment filed under Section 9.514(a) or an amendment filed under Section 9.514(b):

(1) under the name of the assignor as grantor; and

(2) to the extent that the law of this state provides for indexing a record of the assignment of a mortgage under the name of the assignee, under the name of the assignee.

(f) The filing office shall maintain a capability:

(1) to retrieve a record by the name of the debtor and by the file number assigned to the initial financing statement to which the record relates; and

(2) to associate and retrieve with one another an initial financing statement and each filed record relating to the initial financing statement.

(g) The filing office may not remove a debtor's name from the index until one year after the effectiveness of a financing statement naming the debtor lapses under Section 9.515 with respect to all secured parties of record.

(h) Except as provided in Subsection (i), the filing office shall perform the acts required by Subsections (a)–(e) at the time and in the manner prescribed by filing-office rule, but not later than two business days after the filing office receives the record in question.

(i) Subsections (b) and (h) do not apply to a filing office described in Section 9.501(a)(1).

Added by Acts 1999, 76th Leg., ch. 414, § 1.01, eff. July 1, 2001.

Uniform Commercial Code Comment

1. **Source.** Former Sections 9–403(4), (7), 9–405(2).

2. **Filing Office's Duties.** Subsections (a) through (e) set forth the duties of the filing office with respect to filed records. Subsection (h), which is new, imposes a minimum standard of performance for those duties. Prompt indexing is crucial to the effectiveness of any filing system. An accepted but un-indexed record affords no public notice. Subsection (f) requires the filing office to maintain appropriate storage and retrieval facilities, and subsection (g) contains minimum requirements for the retention of records.

3. **File Number.** Subsection (a)(1) requires the filing office to assign a unique number to each filed record. That number is the "file number" only if the record is an initial financing statement. See Section 9–102.

4. **Time of Filing.** Subsection (a)(2) and Section 9–523 refer to the "date and time" of filing. The statutory text does not contain any instructions to a filing office as to how the time of filing is to be determined. The method of determining or assigning a time of filing is an appropriate matter for filing-office rules to address.

5. **Related Records.** Subsections (c) and (f) are designed to ensure that an initial financing statement and all filed records relating to it are associated with one another, indexed under the name of the debtor, and retrieved together. To comply with subsection (f), a filing office (other than a real-property recording office in a State that enacts subsection (f), Alternative B) must be capable of retrieving records in each of two ways: by the name of the debtor and by the file number of the initial financing statement to which the record relates.

6. **Prohibition on Deleting Names from Index.** This Article contemplates that the filing office will not delete the name of a debtor from the index until at least one year passes after the effectiveness of the financing statement lapses as to all secured parties of record. See subsection (g). This rule applies even if the filing office accepts an amendment purporting to delete or modify the name of a debtor or terminate the effectiveness of the financing statement. If an amendment provides a modified name for a debtor, the amended name should be added to the index, see subsection (c)(2), but the pre-amendment name should remain in the index.

Compared to former Article 9, the rule in subsection (g) increases the amount of information available to those who search the public records. The rule also contemplates that searchers–not the filing office–will determine the significance and effectiveness of filed records.

§ 9.520. Acceptance and Refusal to Accept Record

(a) A filing office shall refuse to accept a record for filing for a reason set forth in Section 9.516(b) and may refuse to accept a record for filing only for a reason set forth in Section 9.516(b).

(b) If a filing office refuses to accept a record for filing, it shall communicate to the person that presented the record the fact of and reason for the refusal and the date and time the record would have been filed had the filing office accepted it. The communication must be made at the time and in the manner prescribed by filing-office rule, but in the case of a filing office described in Section 9.501(a)(2), in no event more than two business days after the filing office receives the record.

(c) A filed financing statement satisfying Sections 9.502(a) and (b) is effective, even if the filing office is required to refuse to accept it for filing under Subsection (a). However, Section 9.338 applies to a filed financing statement providing information described in Section 9.516(b)(5) that is incorrect at the time the financing statement is filed.

(d) If a record communicated to a filing office provides information that relates to more than one debtor, this subchapter applies as to each debtor separately.

Added by Acts 1999, 76th Leg., ch. 414, § 1.01, eff. July 1, 2001.

Uniform Commercial Code Comment

1. **Source.** New.

2. **Refusal to Accept Record for Filing.** In some States, filing offices considered themselves obligated by former Article 9 to review the form and content of a financing statement and to refuse to accept those that they determine are legally insufficient. Some filing offices imposed requirements for or conditions to filing that do not appear in the statute. Under this section, the filing office is not expected to make legal judgments and is not permitted to impose additional conditions or requirements.

Subsection (a) both prescribes and limits the bases upon which the filing office must and may reject records by reference to the reasons set forth in Section 9–516(b). For the most part, the bases for rejection are limited to those that prevent the filing office from dealing with a record that it receives–because some of the requisite information (e.g., the debtor's name) is missing or cannot be deciphered, because the record is not communicated by a method (e.g., it is MIME-rather than UU-encoded) or medium (e.g., it is written rather than electronic) that the filing office accepts, or because the filer fails to tender an amount equal to or greater than the filing fee.

3. **Consequences of Accepting Rejectable Record.** Section 9–516(b) includes among the reasons for rejecting an initial financing statement the failure to give certain information that is not required as a condition of effectiveness. In conjunction with Section 9–516(b)(5), this section requires the filing office to refuse to accept a financing statement that is legally sufficient to perfect a security interest under Section 9–502 but does not contain a mailing address for the debtor, does not disclose whether the debtor is an individual or an organization (e.g., a partnership or corporation) or, if the debtor is an organization, does not give certain specified information concerning the organization. The information required by Section 9–516(b)(5) assists searchers in weeding out "false positives," i.e., records that a search reveals but which do not pertain to the debtor in question. It assists filers by helping to ensure that the debtor's name is correct and that the financing statement is filed in the proper jurisdiction.

If the filing office accepts a financing statement that does not give this information at all, the filing is fully effective. Section 9–520(c). The financing statement also generally is effective if the information is given but is incorrect; however, Section 9–338 affords protection to buyers and holders of perfected security interests who give value in reasonable reliance upon the incorrect information.

4. **Filing Office's Duties with Respect to Rejected Record.** Subsection (b) requires the filing office to communicate the fact of rejection and the reason therefor within a fixed period of time. Inasmuch as a rightfully rejected record is ineffective and a wrongfully rejected record is not fully effective, prompt communication concerning any rejection is important.

5. **Partial Effectiveness of Record.** Under subsection (d), the provisions of this Part apply to each debtor separately. Thus, a filing office may reject an initial financing statement or other record as to one named debtor but accept it as to the other.

Example: An initial financing statement is communicated to the filing office. The financing statement names two debtors, John Smith and Jane Smith. It contains all of the information described in Section 9–516(b)(5) with respect to John but lacks some of the information with respect to Jane. The filing office must accept the financing statement with respect to John, reject it with respect to Jane, and notify the filer of the rejection.

§ 9.521. Repealed by Acts 2003, 78th Leg., ch. 748, § 3, eff. Jan. 1, 2004

§ 9.5211. Uniform Form of Written Financing Statement and Amendment

(a) Except as provided by Section 9.516(b), a filing office that accepts written records may not refuse to accept a written initial financing statement on an industry standard form, including a national standard form or a form approved by the International Association of Commercial Administrators, adopted by rule by the secretary of state.

(b) Except as provided by Section 9.516(b), a filing office that accepts written records may not refuse to accept a written record on an industry standard form, including a national standard form or a form approved by the International Association of Commercial Administrators, adopted by rule by the secretary of state.

Added by Acts 2003, 78th Leg., ch. 748, § 2, eff. Jan. 1, 2004.

§ 9.522. Maintenance and Destruction of Records

(a) The filing office shall maintain a record of the information provided in a filed financing statement for at least one year after the effectiveness of the financing statement has lapsed under Section 9.515 with respect to all secured parties of record. The record must be retrievable by using the name of the debtor and by using the file number assigned to the initial financing statement to which the record relates.

(b) Except to the extent that a statute governing disposition of public records provides otherwise, the filing office immediately may destroy any written record evidencing a financing statement. However, if the filing office destroys a written record, it shall maintain another record of the financing statement that complies with Subsection (a).

Added by Acts 1999, 76th Leg., ch. 414, § 1.01, eff. July 1, 2001.

§ 9.523. Information From Filing Office; Sale or License of Records

(a) If a person that files a written record requests an acknowledgment of the filing, the filing office shall send to the person an image of the record showing the number assigned to the record pursuant to Section 9.519(a)(1) and the date and time of the filing of the record. However, if the person furnishes a copy of the record to the filing office, the filing office may instead:

(1) note upon the copy the number assigned to the record pursuant to Section 9.519(a)(1) and the date and time of the filing of the record; and

(2) send the copy to the person.

(b) If a person files a record other than a written record, the filing office shall communicate to the person an acknowledgment that provides:

(1) the information in the record;

(2) the number assigned to the record pursuant to Section 9.519(a)(1); and

(3) the date and time of the filing of the record.

(c) The filing office shall communicate or otherwise make available in a record the following information to any person that requests it:

(1) whether there is on file on a date and time specified by the filing office, but not a date earlier than three business days before the filing office receives the request, any financing statement that:

(A) designates a particular debtor or, if the request so states, designates a particular debtor at the address specified in the request;

(B) has not lapsed under Section 9.515 with respect to all secured parties of record; and

(C) if the request so states, has lapsed under Section 9.515 and a record of which is maintained by the filing office under Section 9.522(a);

(2) the date and time of filing of each financing statement; and

(3) the information provided in each financing statement.

(d) In complying with its duty under Subsection (c), the filing office may communicate information in any medium. However, if requested, the filing office shall communicate information by issuing its written certificate.

(e) The filing office shall perform the acts required by Subsections (a)–(d) at the time and in the manner prescribed by filing-office rule, but not later than two business days after the filing office receives the request.

(f) At least weekly, the Secretary of State shall offer to sell or license to the public on a nonexclusive basis, in bulk, copies of all records filed with the Secretary under this subchapter, in every medium from time to time available to the Secretary.

Added by Acts 1999, 76th Leg., ch. 414, § 1.01, eff. July 1, 2001.

Uniform Commercial Code Comment

1. **Source.** Former Section 9–407; subsections (d) and (e) are new.

2. **Filing Office's Duty to Provide Information.** Former Section 9–407, dealing with obtaining information from the filing office, was bracketed to suggest to legislatures that its enactment was optional. Experience has shown that the method by which interested persons can obtain information concerning the public records should be uniform. Accordingly, the analogous provisions of this Article are not in brackets.

Most of the other changes from former Section 9–407 are for clarification, to embrace medium-neutral drafting, or to impose standards of performance on the filing office.

3. **Acknowledgments of Filing.** Subsections (a) and (b) require the filing office to acknowledge the filing of a record. Under subsection (a), the filing office is required to acknowledge the filing of a written record only upon request of the filer. Subsection (b) requires the filing office to acknowledge the filing of a non-written record even in the absence of a request from the filer.

4. **Response to Search Request.** Subsection (c)(3) requires the filing office to provide "the information contained in each financing statement" to a person who requests it. This requirement can be satisfied by providing copies, images, or reports. The requirement does not in any manner inhibit the filing office from also offering to provide less than all of the information (presumably for a lower fee) to a person who asks for less. Thus, subsection (c) accommo-

dates the practice of providing only the type of record (e.g., initial financing statement, continuation statement), number assigned to the record, date and time of filing, and names and addresses of the debtor and secured party when a requesting person asks for no more (i.e., when the person does not ask for copies of financing statements). In contrast, the filing office's obligation under subsection (b) to provide an acknowledgment containing "the information contained in the record" is not defined by a customer's request. Thus unless the filer stipulates otherwise, to comply with subsection (b) the filing office's acknowledgment must contain all of the information in a record.

Subsection (c) assures that a minimum amount of information about filed records will be available to the public. It does not preclude a filing office from offering additional services.

5. **Lapsed and Terminated Financing Statements.** This section reflects the policy that terminated financing statements will remain part of the filing office's data base. The filing office may remove from the data base only lapsed financing statements, and then only when at least a year has passed after lapse. See Section 9–519(g). Subsection (c)(1)(C) requires a filing office to conduct a search and report as to lapsed financing statements that have not been removed from the data base, when requested.

6. **Search by Debtor's Address.** Subsection (c)(1)(A) contemplates that, by making a single request, a searcher will receive the results of a search of the entire public record maintained by any given filing office. Addition of the bracketed language in subsection (c)(1)(A) would permit a search report limited to financing statements showing a particular address for the debtor, but only if the search request is so limited. With or without the bracketed language, this subsection does not permit the filing office to compel a searcher to limit a request by address.

7. **Medium of Communication; Certificates.** Former Article 9 provided that the filing office respond to a request for information by providing a certificate. The principle of medium-neutrality would suggest that the statute not require a written certificate. Subsection (d) follows this principle by permitting the filing office to respond by communicating "in any medium." By permitting communication "in any medium," subsection (d) is not inconsistent with a system in which persons other than filing office staff conduct searches of the filing office's (computer) records.

Some searchers find it necessary to introduce the results of their search into evidence. Because official written certificates might be introduced into evidence more easily than official communications in another medium, subsection (d) affords States the option of requiring the filing office to issue written certificates upon request. The alternative bracketed language in subsection (d) recognizes that some States may prefer to permit the filing office to respond in another medium, as long as the response can be admitted into evidence in the courts of that State without extrinsic evidence of its authenticity.

8. **Performance Standard.** The utility of the filing system depends on the ability of searchers to get current information quickly. Accordingly, subsection (e) requires that the filing office respond to a request for information no later than two business days after it receives the request. The information contained in the response must be current as of a date no earlier than three business days before the filing office receives the request. See subsection (c)(1). The failure of the filing office to comply with performance standards, such as subsection (e), has no effect on the private rights of persons affected by the filing of records.

9. **Sales of Records in Bulk.** Subsection (f), which is new, mandates that the appropriate official or the filing office sell or license the filing records to the public in bulk, on a nonexclusive basis, in every medium available to the filing office. The details of implementation are left to filing-office rules.

§ 9.524. Delay by Filing Office

Delay by the filing office beyond a time limit prescribed by this subchapter is excused if:

(1) the delay is caused by interruption of communication or computer facilities, war, emergency conditions, failure of equipment, or other circumstances beyond control of the filing office; and

(2) the filing office exercises reasonable diligence under the circumstances.

Added by Acts 1999, 76th Leg., ch. 414, § 1.01, eff. July 1, 2001.

Uniform Commercial Code Comment

Source. New; derived from Section 4–109.

§ 9.525. Fees

(a) Except as otherwise provided in Subsections (e) and (f), the fee for filing and indexing a record under this subchapter, other than an initial financing statement of the kind described in Subsection (b), is:

(1) $15 if the record is communicated in writing and consists of one or two pages;

(2) $30 if the record is communicated in writing and consists of more than two pages; and

(3) $5 if the record is communicated by another medium authorized by filing-office rule.

(b) Except as otherwise provided in Subsection (e), the fee for filing and indexing an initial financing statement of the following kinds is:

(1) $60 if the financing statement indicates that it is filed in connection with a public-finance transaction; and

(2) $60 if the financing statement indicates that it is filed in connection with a manufactured-home transaction.

(c) The number of names required to be indexed does not affect the amount of the fee in Subsections (a) and (b).

(d) The fee for responding to a request for information from the filing office, including for communicating whether there is on file any financing statement naming a particular debtor, is:

(1) $15 if the request is communicated in writing; and

(2) an amount established by the filing office if the request is communicated by another medium authorized by filing-office rule.

(e) This section does not require a fee with respect to a record of a mortgage that is effective as a financing statement filed as a fixture filing or as a financing statement covering as-extracted collateral or timber to be cut under Section 9.502(c). However, the recording and satisfaction fees that otherwise would be applicable to the record of the mortgage apply.

(f) The filing fee for filing, indexing, and furnishing filing data about a statement of master amendment under Section 9.512(f) or master assignment under Section 9.514(d) is $500 plus 50 cents for each financing statement covered by the master statement in excess of 50.

Added by Acts 1999, 76th Leg., ch. 414, § 1.01, eff. July 1, 2001. Amended by Acts 2001, 77th Leg., ch. 705, § 18, eff. June 13, 2001.

Uniform Commercial Code Comment

1. **Source.** Various sections of former Part 4.

2. **Fees.** This section contains all fee requirements for filing, indexing, and responding to requests for information. Uniformity in the fee structure (but not necessarily in the amount of fees) makes this Article easier for secured parties to use and reduces the likelihood that a filed record will be rejected for failure to pay at least the correct amount of the fee. See Section 9–516(b)(2).

The costs of processing electronic records are less than those with respect to written records. Accordingly, this section mandates a lower fee as an incentive to file electronically and imposes the additional charge (if any) for multiple debtors only with respect to written records. When written records are used, this Article encourages the use of the uniform forms in Section 9–521. The fee for filing these forms should be no greater than the fee for other written records.

To make the relevant information included in a filed record more accessible once the record is found, this section mandates a higher fee for longer written records than for shorter ones. Finally, recognizing that financing statements naming more than one debtor are most often filed against a husband and wife, any additional charge for multiple debtors applies to records filed with respect to more than two debtors, rather than with respect to more than one.

§ 9.526. Filing-Office Rules

(a) The Secretary of State shall adopt and publish rules to implement this chapter. The filing-office rules must be consistent with this chapter.

(b) To keep the filing-office rules and practices of the filing office in harmony with the rules and practices of filing offices in other jurisdictions that enact substantially this subchapter, and to keep the technology used by the filing office compatible with the technology used by filing offices in other jurisdictions that enact substantially this subchapter, the Secretary of State, so far as is consistent with the purposes, policies, and provisions of this chapter, in adopting, amending, and repealing filing-office rules, shall:

(1) consult with filing offices in other jurisdictions that enact substantially this subchapter;

(2) consult the most recent version of the Model Administrative Rules promulgated by the International Association of Corporation Administrators or any successor organization; and

(3) take into consideration the rules and practices of, and the technology used by, filing offices in other jurisdictions that enact substantially this subchapter.

Added by Acts 1999, 76th Leg., ch. 414, § 1.01, eff. July 1, 2001.

Uniform Commercial Code Comment

1. **Source.** New; subsection (b) derives in part from the Uniform Consumer Credit Code (1974).

2. **Rules Required.** Operating a filing office is a complicated business, requiring many more rules and procedures than this Article can usefully provide. Subsection (a) requires the adoption of rules to carry out the provisions of Article 9. The filing-office rules must be consistent with the provisions of the statute and adopted in accordance with local procedures. The publication requirement informs secured parties about filing-office practices, aids secured parties in evaluating filing-related risks and costs, and promotes regularity of application within the filing office.

3. **Importance of Uniformity.** In today's national economy, uniformity of the policies and practices of the filing offices will reduce the costs of secured transactions substantially. The International Association of Corporate Administrators (IACA), referred to in subsection (b), is an organization whose membership includes filing officers from every State. These individuals are responsible for the proper functioning of the Article 9 filing system and have worked diligently to develop model filing-office rules, with a view toward efficiency and uniformity.

Although uniformity is an important desideratum, subsection (a) affords considerable flexibility in the adoption of filing-office rules. Each State may adopt a version of subsection (a) that reflects the desired relationship between the statewide filing office described in Section 9–501(a)(2) and the local filing offices described in Section 9–501(a)(1) and that takes into account the practices of its filing offices. Subsection (a) need not designate a single official or agency to adopt rules applicable to all filing offices, and the rules applicable to the statewide filing office need not be identical to those applicable to the local filing office. For example, subsection (a) might provide for the statewide filing office to adopt filing-office rules, and, if not prohibited by other law, the filing office might adopt one set of rules for itself and another for local offices. Or, subsection (a) might designate one official or agency to adopt rules for the statewide filing office and another to adopt rules for local filing offices.

§ 9.527. Duty to Report

The Secretary of State shall report before January 1 of each odd-numbered year to the Legislature on the operation of the filing office. The report must contain a statement of the extent to which:

(1) the filing-office rules are not in harmony with the rules of filing offices in other jurisdictions that enact substantially this subchapter and the reasons for these variations; and

(2) the filing-office rules are not in harmony with the most recent version of the Model Administrative Rules promulgated by the International Association of Corporation Administrators, or any successor organization, and the reasons for these variations.

Added by Acts 1999, 76th Leg., ch. 414, § 1.01, eff. July 1, 2001.

Uniform Commercial Code Comment

1. **Source.** New; derived in part from the Uniform Consumer Credit Code (1974).

2. **Duty to Report.** This section is designed to promote compliance with the standards of performance imposed upon the filing office and with the requirement that the filing office's policies, practices, and technology be consistent and compatible with the policies, practices, and technology of other filing offices.

SUBCHAPTER F. DEFAULT

§ 9.601. Rights After Default; Judicial Enforcement; Consignor or Buyer of Accounts, Chattel Paper, Payment Intangibles, or Promissory Notes

(a) After default, a secured party has the rights provided in this subchapter and, except as otherwise provided in Section 9.602, those provided by agreement of the parties. A secured party:

(1) may reduce a claim to judgment, foreclose, or otherwise enforce the claim, security interest, or agricultural lien by any available judicial procedure; and

(2) if the collateral is documents, may proceed either as to the documents or as to the goods they cover.

(b) A secured party in possession of collateral or control of collateral under Section 7.106, 9.104, 9.105, 9.106, or 9.107 has the rights and duties provided in Section 9.207.

(c) The rights under Subsections (a) and (b) are cumulative and may be exercised simultaneously.

(d) Except as otherwise provided in Subsection (g) and Section 9.605, after default, a debtor and an obligor have the rights provided in this subchapter and by agreement of the parties.

(e) If a secured party has reduced its claim to judgment, the lien of any levy that may be made upon the collateral by virtue of an execution based upon the judgment relates back to the earliest of:

(1) the date of the perfection of the security interest or agricultural lien in the collateral;

(2) the date of filing a financing statement covering the collateral; or

(3) any date specified in a statute under which the agricultural lien was created.

(f) A sale pursuant to an execution is a foreclosure of the security interest or agricultural lien by judicial procedure within the meaning of this section. A secured party may purchase at the sale and thereafter hold the collateral free of any other requirements of this chapter.

(g) Except as otherwise provided in Section 9.607(c), this subchapter imposes no duties upon a secured party that is a consignor or is a buyer of accounts, chattel paper, payment intangibles, or promissory notes.

Added by Acts 1999, 76th Leg., ch. 414, § 1.01, eff. July 1, 2001. Amended by Acts 2005, 79th Leg., ch. 122, § 30, eff. Sept. 1, 2005.

Uniform Commercial Code Comment

1. **Source.** Former Section 9–501(1), (2), (5).

2. **Enforcement: In General.** The rights of a secured party to enforce its security interest in collateral after the debtor's default are an important feature of a secured trans-

action. (Note that the term "rights," as defined in Section 1–201, includes "remedies.") This Part provides those rights as well as certain limitations on their exercise for the protection of the defaulting debtor, other creditors, and other affected persons. However, subsections (a) and (d) make clear that the rights provided in this Part do not exclude other rights provided by agreement.

3. **When Remedies Arise.** Under subsection (a) the secured party's rights arise "[a]fter default." As did former Section 9–501, this Article leaves to the agreement of the parties the circumstances giving rise to a default. This Article does not determine whether a secured party's post-default conduct can constitute a waiver of default in the face of an agreement stating that such conduct shall not constitute a waiver. Rather, it continues to leave to the parties' agreement, as supplemented by law other than this Article, the determination whether a default has occurred or has been waived. See Section 1–103.

4. **Possession of Collateral; Section 9–207.** After a secured party takes possession of collateral following a default, there is no longer any distinction between a security interest that before default was nonpossessory and a security interest that was possessory before default, as under a common-law pledge. This Part generally does not distinguish between the rights of a secured party with a nonpossessory security interest and those of a secured party with a possessory security interest. However, Section 9–207 addresses rights and duties with respect to collateral in a secured party's possession. Under subsection (b) of this section, Section 9–207 applies not only to possession before default but also to possession after default. Subsection (b) also has been conformed to Section 9–207, which, unlike former Section 9–207, applies to secured parties having control of collateral.

5. **Cumulative Remedies.** Former Section 9–501(1) provided that the secured party's remedies were cumulative, but it did not explicitly provide whether the remedies could be exercised simultaneously. Subsection (c) permits the simultaneous exercise of remedies if the secured party acts in good faith. The liability scheme of Subpart 2 affords redress to an aggrieved debtor or obligor. Moreover, permitting the simultaneous exercise of remedies under subsection (c) does not override any non-UCC law, including the law of tort and statutes regulating collection of debts, under which the simultaneous exercise of remedies in a particular case constitutes abusive behavior or harassment giving rise to liability.

6. **Judicial Enforcement.** Under subsection (a) a secured party may reduce its claim to judgment or foreclose its interest by any available procedure outside this Article under applicable law. Subsection (e) generally follows former Section 9–501(5). It makes clear that any judicial lien that the secured party may acquire against the collateral effectively is a continuation of the original security interest (if perfected) and not the acquisition of a new interest or a transfer of property on account of a preexisting obligation. Under former Section 9–501(5), the judicial lien was stated to relate back to the date of perfection of the security interest. Subsection (e), however, provides that the lien relates back to the earlier of the date of filing or the date of perfection. This provides a secured party who enforces a security interest by judicial process with the benefit of the "first-to-file-or-perfect" priority rule of Section 9–322(a)(1).

7. **Agricultural Liens.** Part 6 provides parallel treatment for the enforcement of agricultural liens and security interests. Because agricultural liens are statutory rather than consensual, this Article does draw a few distinctions between these liens and security interests. Under subsection (e), the statute creating an agricultural lien would govern whether and the date to which an execution lien relates back. Section 9–606 explains when a "default" occurs in the agricultural lien context.

8. **Execution Sales.** Subsection (f) also follows former Section 9–501(5). It makes clear that an execution sale is an appropriate method of foreclosure contemplated by this Part. However, the sale is governed by other law and not by this Article, and the limitations under Section 9–610 on the right of a secured party to purchase collateral do not apply.

9. **Sales of Receivables; Consignments.** Subsection (g) provides that, except as provided in Section 9–607(c), the duties imposed on secured parties do not apply to buyers of accounts, chattel paper, payment intangibles, or promissory notes. Although denominated "secured parties," these buyers own the entire interest in the property sold and so may enforce their rights without regard to the seller ("debtor") or the seller's creditors. Likewise, a true consignor may enforce its ownership interest under other law without regard to the duties that this Part imposes on secured parties. Note, however, that Section 9–615 governs cases in which a consignee's secured party (other than a consignor) is enforcing a security interest that is senior to the security interest (i.e., ownership interest) of a true consignor.

State Bar Committee Comment

A default may permit the secured party to exercise its rights under an acceleration clause. Before exercising its rights under an acceleration clause, a secured party must present the promissory note to the maker and notify the maker of the secured party's intent to accelerate and the secured party's acceleration, unless the maker has waived its right to presentment, notice of intent to accelerate, and notice of acceleration in a clear and unequivocal manner. See *Shumway v. Horizon Credit Corp.*, 801 S.W.2d 890 (Tex. 1991).

Sections 31 and 32 of Acts 2005, 79th Leg., ch. 122 provide:

"Sec. 31. This Act applies to a document of title that is issued or a bailment that arises on or after the effective date of this Act. This Act does not apply to a document of title that is issued or a bailment that arises before the effective date of this Act even if the document of title or bailment would be subject to this Act if the document of title had been issued or bailment had arisen after the effective date of this Act. This Act does not apply to a right of action that has accrued before the effective date of this Act.

"Sec. 32. A document of title issued or a bailment that arises before the effective date of this Act and the rights, obligations, and interests flowing from that document or bailment are governed by any statute or other rule amended or repealed by this Act as if amendment or repeal had not occurred and may be terminated, completed, consummated, or enforced under that statute or other rule."

§ 9.602. Waiver and Variance of Rights and Duties

Except as otherwise provided in Section 9.624, to the extent that they give rights to a debtor or obligor and impose duties on a secured party, the debtor or obligor may not waive or vary the rules stated in the following listed sections:

(1) Section 9.207(b)(4)(C), which deals with use and operation of the collateral by the secured party;

(2) Section 9.210, which deals with requests for an accounting and requests concerning a list of collateral and statement of account;

(3) Section 9.607(c), which deals with collection and enforcement of collateral;

(4) Sections 9.608(a) and 9.615(c) to the extent that they deal with application or payment of noncash proceeds of collection, enforcement, or disposition;

(5) Sections 9.608(a) and 9.615(d) to the extent that they require accounting for or payment of surplus proceeds of collateral;

(6) Section 9.609 to the extent that it imposes upon a secured party that takes possession of collateral without judicial process the duty to do so without breach of the peace;

(7) Sections 9.610(b), 9.611, 9.613, and 9.614, which deal with disposition of collateral;

(8) Section 9.615(f), which deals with calculation of a deficiency or surplus when a disposition is made to the secured party, a person related to the secured party, or a secondary obligor;

(9) Section 9.616, which deals with explanation of the calculation of a surplus or deficiency;

(10) Sections 9.620, 9.621, and 9.622, which deal with acceptance of collateral in satisfaction of obligation;

(11) Section 9.623, which deals with redemption of collateral;

(12) Section 9.624, which deals with permissible waivers; and

(13) Sections 9.625 and 9.626, which deal with the secured party's liability for failure to comply with this chapter.

Added by Acts 1999, 76th Leg., ch. 414, § 1.01, eff. July 1, 2001.

Uniform Commercial Code Comment

1. **Source.** Former Section 9–501(3).

2. **Waiver: In General.** Section 1–102(3) addresses which provisions of the UCC are mandatory and which may be varied by agreement. With exceptions relating to good faith, diligence, reasonableness, and care, immediate parties, as between themselves, may vary its provisions by agreement. However, in the context of rights and duties after default, our legal system traditionally has looked with suspicion on agreements that limit the debtor's rights and free the secured party of its duties. As stated in former Section 9–501, Comment 4, "no mortgage clause has ever been allowed to clog the equity of redemption." The context of default offers great opportunity for overreaching. The suspicious attitudes of the courts have been grounded in common sense. This section, like former Section 9–501(3), codifies this long-standing and deeply rooted attitude. The specified rights of the debtor and duties of the secured party may not be waived or varied except as stated. Provisions that are not specified in this section are subject to the general rules in Section 1–102(3).

3. **Nonwaivable Rights and Duties.** This section revises former Section 9–501(3) by restricting the ability to waive or modify additional specified rights and duties: (i) duties under Section 9–207(b)(4)(C), which deals with the use and operation of consumer goods, (ii) the right to a response to a request for an accounting, concerning a list of collateral, or concerning a statement of account (Section 9–210), (iii) the duty to collect collateral in a commercially reasonable manner (Section 9–607), (iv) the implicit duty to refrain from a breach of the peace in taking possession of collateral under Section 9–609, (v) the duty to apply noncash proceeds of collection or disposition in a commercially reasonable manner (Sections 9–608 and 9–615), (vi) the right to a special method of calculating a surplus or deficiency in certain dispositions to a secured party, a person related to secured party, or a secondary obligor (Section 9–615), (vii) the duty to give an explanation of the calculation of a surplus or deficiency (Section 9–616), (viii) the right to limitations on the effectiveness of certain waivers (Section 9–624), and (ix) the right to hold a secured party liable for failure to comply with this Article (Sections 9–625 and 9–626). For clarity and consistency, this Article uses the term "waive or vary" instead of "renounc[e] or modify[]," which appeared in former Section 9–504(3).

This section provides generally that the specified rights and duties "may not be waived or varied." However, it does not restrict the ability of parties to agree to settle, compromise, or renounce claims for past conduct that may have constituted a violation or breach of those rights and duties, even if the settlement involves an express "waiver."

4. **Waiver by Debtors and Obligors.** The restrictions on waiver contained in this section apply to obligors as well as debtors. This resolves a question under former Article 9 as to whether secondary obligors, assuming that they were "debtors" for purposes of former Part 5, were permitted to waive, under the law of suretyship, rights and duties under that Part.

5. **Certain Post-Default Waivers.** Section 9–624 permits post-default waivers in limited circumstances. These waivers must be made in agreements that are authenticated. Under Section 1–201, an " 'agreement' means the bargain of the parties in fact." In considering waivers under Section 9–624

and analogous agreements in other contexts, courts should carefully scrutinize putative agreements that appear in records that also address many additional or unrelated matters.

State Bar Committee Comment

Section 9.610(b) requires every aspect of a disposition to be "commercially reasonable." Section 9.602(7) references Section 9.610(b) as a statute that creates a rule that may not be waived or varied by a debtor or an obligor. Section 9.602(7) will change the result in *Steinberg v. Cinema N' Drafthouse Systems, Inc.*, 28 F.3d 23 (5th Cir. 1994) (permitting guarantor to waive duty of commercial reasonableness), but will conform to the result in *Rabinowitz v. The Cadle Company II, Inc.*, 993 S.W.2d 796 (Tex. Civ. App.—Dallas 1999) (concluding guarantor could not waive duty of commercial reasonableness).

§ 9.603. Agreement on Standards Concerning Rights and Duties

(a) The parties may determine by agreement the standards measuring the fulfillment of the rights of a debtor or obligor and the duties of a secured party under a rule stated in Section 9.602 if the standards are not manifestly unreasonable.

(b) Subsection (a) does not apply to the duty under Section 9.609 to refrain from breaching the peace.

Added by Acts 1999, 76th Leg., ch. 414, § 1.01, eff. July 1, 2001.

Uniform Commercial Code Comment

1. **Source.** Former Section 9–501(3).

2. **Limitation on Ability to Set Standards.** Subsection (a), like former Section 9–501(3), permits the parties to set standards for compliance with the rights and duties under this Part if the standards are not "manifestly unreasonable." Under subsection (b), the parties are not permitted to set standards measuring fulfillment of the secured party's duty to take collateral without breaching the peace.

§ 9.604. Procedure if Security Agreement Covers Real Property or Fixtures

(a) If a security agreement covers both personal and real property, a secured party may proceed:

(1) under this subchapter as to the personal property without prejudicing any rights with respect to the real property; or

(2) as to both the personal property and the real property in accordance with the rights with respect to the real property, in which case the other provisions of this subchapter do not apply.

(b) Subject to Subsection (c), if a security agreement covers goods that are or become fixtures, a secured party may proceed:

(1) under this subchapter; or

(2) in accordance with the rights with respect to real property, in which case the other provisions of this subchapter do not apply.

(c) Subject to the other provisions of this subchapter, if a secured party holding a security interest in fixtures has priority over all owners and encumbrancers of the real property, the secured party, after default, may remove the collateral from the real property.

(d) A secured party that removes collateral shall promptly reimburse any encumbrancer or owner of the real property, other than the debtor, for the cost of repair of any physical injury caused by the removal. The secured party need not reimburse the encumbrancer or owner for any diminution in value of the real property caused by the absence of the goods removed or by any necessity of replacing them. A person entitled to reimbursement may refuse permission to remove until the secured party gives adequate assurance for the performance of the obligation to reimburse.

Added by Acts 1999, 76th Leg., ch. 414, § 1.01, eff. July 1, 2001.

Uniform Commercial Code Comment

1. **Source.** Former Sections 9–501(4), 9–313(8).

2. **Real-Property–Related Collateral.** The collateral in many transactions consists of both real and personal property. In the interest of simplicity, speed, and economy, subsection (a), like former Section 9–501(4), permits (but does not require) the secured party to proceed as to both real and personal property in accordance with its rights and remedies with respect to the real property. Subsection (a) also makes clear that a secured party who exercises rights under Part 6 with respect to personal property does not prejudice any rights under real-property law.

This Article does not address certain other real-property-related problems. In a number of States, the exercise of remedies by a creditor who is secured by both real property and non-real property collateral is governed by special legal rules. For example, under some anti-deficiency laws, creditors risk loss of rights against personal property collateral if they err in enforcing their rights against the real property. Under a "one-form-of-action" rule (or rule against splitting a cause of action), a creditor who judicially enforces a real property mortgage and does not proceed in the same action to enforce a security interest in personalty may (among other consequences) lose the right to proceed against the personalty. Although statutes of this kind create impediments to enforcement of security interests, this Article does not override these limitations under other law.

3. **Fixtures.** Subsection (b) is new. It makes clear that a security interest in fixtures may be enforced either under real-property law or under any of the applicable provisions of Part 6, including sale or other disposition either before or after removal of the fixtures (see subsection (c)). Subsection (b) also serves to overrule cases holding that a secured party's only remedy after default is the removal of the fixtures from the real property. See, e.g., *Maplewood Bank & Trust v. Sears, Roebuck & Co.*, 625 A.2d 537 (N.J.Super. Ct. App.Div.1993).

Subsection (c) generally follows former Section 9–313(8). It gives the secured party the right to remove fixtures under certain circumstances. A secured party whose security interest in fixtures has priority over owners and encumbrancers of the real property may remove the collateral from the real property. However, subsection (d) requires the secured party to reimburse any owner (other than the debtor) or encumbrancer for the cost of repairing any physical injury caused by the removal. This right to reimbursement is implemented by the last sentence of subsection (d), which gives the owner or encumbrancer a right to security or indemnity as a condition for giving permission to remove.

§ 9.605. Unknown Debtor or Secondary Obligor

A secured party does not owe a duty based on its status as secured party:

(1) to a person that is a debtor or obligor, unless the secured party knows:

(A) that the person is a debtor or obligor;

(B) the identity of the person; and

(C) how to communicate with the person; or

(2) to a secured party or lienholder that has filed a financing statement against a person, unless the secured party knows:

(A) that the person is a debtor; and

(B) the identity of the person.

Added by Acts 1999, 76th Leg., ch. 414, § 1.01, eff. July 1, 2001.

Uniform Commercial Code Comment

1. **Source.** New.

2. **Duties to Unknown Persons.** This section relieves a secured party from duties owed to a debtor or obligor, if the secured party does not know about the debtor or obligor. Similarly, it relieves a secured party from duties owed to a secured party or lienholder who has filed a financing statement against the debtor, if the secured party does not know about the debtor. For example, a secured party may be unaware that the original debtor has sold the collateral subject to the security interest and that the new owner has become the debtor. If so, the secured party owes no duty to the new owner (debtor) or to a secured party who has filed a financing statement against the new owner. This section should be read in conjunction with the exculpatory provisions in Section 9–628. Note that it relieves a secured party not only from duties arising under this Article but also from duties arising under other law by virtue of the secured party's status as such under this Article, unless the other law otherwise provides.

§ 9.606. Time of Default for Agricultural Lien

For purposes of this subchapter, a default occurs in connection with an agricultural lien at the time the secured party becomes entitled to enforce the lien in accordance with the statute under which it was created.

Added by Acts 1999, 76th Leg., ch. 414, § 1.01, eff. July 1, 2001.

Uniform Commercial Code Comment

1. **Source.** New.

2. **Time of Default.** Remedies under this Part become available upon the debtor's "default." See Section 9–601. This section explains when "default" occurs in the agricultural-lien context. It requires one to consult the enabling statute to determine when the lienholder is entitled to enforce the lien.

§ 9.607. Collection and Enforcement By Secured Party

(a) If so agreed, and in any event after default, a secured party:

(1) may notify an account debtor or other person obligated on collateral to make payment or otherwise render performance to or for the benefit of the secured party;

(2) may take any proceeds to which the secured party is entitled under Section 9.315;

(3) may enforce the obligations of an account debtor or other person obligated on collateral and exercise the rights of the debtor with respect to the obligation of the account debtor or other person obligated on collateral to make payment or otherwise render performance to the debtor, and with respect to any property that secures the obligations of the account debtor or other person obligated on the collateral;

(4) if it holds a security interest in a deposit account perfected by control under Section 9.104(a)(1), may apply the balance of the deposit account to the obligation secured by the deposit account; and

(5) if it holds a security interest in a deposit account perfected by control under Section

9.104(a)(2) or (3), may instruct the bank to pay the balance of the deposit account to or for the benefit of the secured party.

(b) If necessary to enable a secured party to exercise under Subsection (a)(3) the right of a debtor to enforce a mortgage nonjudicially, the secured party may record in the office in which a record of the mortgage is recorded:

(1) a copy of the security agreement that creates or provides for a security interest in the obligation secured by the mortgage; and

(2) the secured party's sworn affidavit in recordable form stating that:

(A) a default has occurred; and

(B) the secured party is entitled to enforce the mortgage nonjudicially.

(c) A secured party shall proceed in a commercially reasonable manner if the secured party:

(1) undertakes to collect from or enforce an obligation of an account debtor or other person obligated on collateral; and

(2) is entitled to charge back uncollected collateral or otherwise to full or limited recourse against the debtor or a secondary obligor.

(d) A secured party may deduct from the collections made pursuant to Subsection (c) reasonable expenses of collection and enforcement, including reasonable attorney's fees and legal expenses incurred by the secured party.

(e) This section does not determine whether an account debtor, bank, or other person obligated on collateral owes a duty to a secured party.

Added by Acts 1999, 76th Leg., ch. 414, § 1.01, eff. July 1, 2001.

Uniform Commercial Code Comment

1. **Source.** Former Section 9–502; subsections (b), (d), and (e) are new.

2. **Collections: In General.** Collateral consisting of rights to payment is not only the most liquid asset of a typical debtor's business but also is property that may be collected without any interruption of the debtor's business This situation is far different from that in which collateral is inventory or equipment, whose removal may bring the business to a halt. Furthermore, problems of valuation and identification, present with collateral that is tangible personal property, frequently are not as serious in the case of rights to payment and other intangible collateral. Consequently, this section, like former Section 9–502, recognizes that financing through assignments of intangibles lacks many of the complexities that arise after default in other types of financing. This section allows the assignee to liquidate collateral by collecting whatever may become due on the collateral, whether or not the method of collection contemplated by the security arrangement before default was direct (i.e., payment by the account debtor to the assignee, "notification" financing) or indirect (i.e., payment by the account debtor to the assignor, "nonnotification" financing).

3. **Scope.** The scope of this section is broader than that of former Section 9–502. It applies not only to collections from account debtors and obligors on instruments but also to enforcement more generally against all persons obligated on collateral. It explicitly provides for the secured party's enforcement of the debtor's rights in respect of the account debtor's (and other third parties') obligations and for the secured party's enforcement of supporting obligations with respect to those obligations. (Supporting obligations are components of the collateral under Section 9–203(f).) The rights of a secured party under subsection (a) include the right to enforce claims that the debtor may enjoy against others. For example, the claims might include a breach-of-warranty claim arising out of a defect in equipment that is collateral or a secured party's action for an injunction against infringement of a patent that is collateral. Those claims typically would be proceeds of original collateral under Section 9–315.

4. **Collection and Enforcement Before Default.** Like Part 6 generally, this section deals with the rights and duties of secured parties following default. However, as did former Section 9–502 with respect to collection rights, this section also applies to the collection and enforcement rights of secured parties even if a default has not occurred, as long as the debtor has so agreed. It is not unusual for debtors to agree that secured parties are entitled to collect and enforce rights against account debtors prior to default.

5. **Collections by Junior Secured Party.** A secured party who holds a security interest in a right to payment may exercise the right to collect and enforce under this section, even if the security interest is subordinate to a conflicting security interest in the same right to payment. Whether the junior secured party has priority in the collected proceeds depends on whether the junior secured party qualifies for priority as a purchaser of an instrument (e.g., the account debtor's check) under Section 9–330(d), as a holder in due course of an instrument under Sections 3–305 and 9–331(a), or as a transferee of money under Section 9–332(a). See Sections 9–330, Comment 7; 9–331, Comment 5; and 9–332.

6. **Relationship to Rights and Duties of Persons Obligated on Collateral.** This section permits a secured party to collect and enforce obligations included in collateral in its capacity as a secured party. It is not necessary for a secured party first to become the owner of the collateral pursuant to a disposition or acceptance. However, the secured party's rights, as between it and the debtor, to collect from and enforce collateral against account debtors and others obligated on collateral under subsection (a) are subject to Section 9–341, Part 4, and other applicable law. *Neither this section nor former Section 9–502 should be understood to regulate the duties of an account debtor or other person obligated on collateral.* Subsection (e) makes this explicit. For example, the secured party may be unable to exercise the debtor's rights under an instrument if the

debtor is in possession of the instrument, or under a nontransferable letter of credit if the debtor is the beneficiary. Unless a secured party has control over a letter-of-credit right and is entitled to receive payment or performance from the issuer or a nominated person under Article 5, its remedies with respect to the letter-of-credit right may be limited to the recovery of any identifiable proceeds from the debtor. This section establishes only the baseline rights of the secured party *vis-a-vis the debtor*—the secured party is entitled to enforce and collect after default or earlier if so agreed.

7. **Deposit Account Collateral.** Subsections (a)(4) and (5) set forth the self-help remedy for a secured party whose collateral is a deposit account. Subsection (a)(4) addresses the rights of a secured party that is the bank with which the deposit account is maintained. That secured party automatically has control of the deposit account under Section 9–104(a)(1). After default, and otherwise if so agreed, the bank/secured party may apply the funds on deposit to the secured obligation.

If a security interest of a third party is perfected by control (Section 9–104(a)(2) or (a)(3)), then after default, and otherwise if so agreed, the secured party may instruct the bank to pay out the funds in the account. If the third party has control under Section 9–104(a)(3), the depositary institution is obliged to obey the instruction because the secured party is its customer. See Section 4–401. If the third party has control under Section 9–104(a)(2), the control agreement determines the depositary institution's obligation to obey.

If a security interest in a deposit account is unperfected, or is perfected by filing by virtue of the proceeds rules of Section 9–315, the depositary institution ordinarily owes no obligation to obey the secured party's instructions. See Section 9–341. To reach the funds without the debtor's cooperation, the secured party must use an available judicial procedure.

8. **Rights Against Mortgagor of Real Property.** Subsection (b) addresses the situation in which the collateral consists of a mortgage note (or other obligation secured by a mortgage on real property). After the debtor's (mortgagee's) default, the secured party (assignee) may wish to proceed with a nonjudicial foreclosure of the mortgage securing the note but may be unable to do so because it has not become the assignee of record. The assignee/secured party may not have taken a recordable assignment at the commencement of the transaction (perhaps the mortgage note in question was one of hundreds assigned to the secured party as collateral). Having defaulted, the mortgagee may be unwilling to sign a recordable assignment. This section enables the secured party (assignee) to become the assignee of record by recording in the applicable real-property records the security agreement and an affidavit certifying default. Of course, the secured party's rights derive from those of its debtor. Subsection (b) would not entitle the secured party to proceed with a foreclosure unless the mortgagor also were in default or the debtor (mortgagee) otherwise enjoyed the right to foreclose.

9. **Commercial Reasonableness.** Subsection (c) provides that the secured party's collection and enforcement rights under subsection (a) must be exercised in a commercially reasonable manner. These rights include the right to settle and compromise claims against the account debtor. The secured party's failure to observe the standard of commercial reasonableness could render it liable to an aggrieved person under Section 9–625, and the secured party's recovery of a deficiency would be subject to Section 9–626. Subsection (c) does not apply if, as is characteristic of most sales of accounts, chattel paper, payment intangibles, and promissory notes, the secured party (buyer) has no right of recourse against the debtor (seller) or a secondary obligor. However, if the secured party does have a right of recourse, the commercial-reasonableness standard applies to collection and enforcement even though the assignment to the secured party was a "true" sale. The obligation to proceed in a commercially reasonable manner arises because the collection process affects the extent of the seller's recourse liability, not because the seller retains an interest in the sold collateral (the seller does not). Concerning classification of a transaction, see Section 9–109, Comment 4.

10. **Attorney's Fees and Legal Expenses.** The phrase "reasonable attorney's fees and legal expenses," which appears in subsection (d), includes only those fees and expenses incurred in proceeding against account debtors or other third parties. The secured party's right to recover these expenses from the collections arises automatically under this section. The secured party also may incur other attorney's fees and legal expenses in proceeding against the debtor or obligor. Whether the secured party has a right to recover those fees and expenses depends on whether the debtor or obligor has agreed to pay them, as is the case with respect to attorney's fees and legal expenses under Sections 9–608(a)(1)(A) and 9–615(a)(1). The parties also may agree to allocate a portion of the secured party's overhead to collection and enforcement under subsection (d) or Section 9–608(a).

§ 9.608. Application of Proceeds of Collection or Enforcement; Liability for Deficiency and Right to Surplus

(a) If a security interest or agricultural lien secures payment or performance of an obligation, the following rules apply:

(1) A secured party shall apply or pay over for application the cash proceeds of collection or enforcement under Section 9.607 in the following order to:

(A) the reasonable expenses of collection and enforcement and, to the extent provided for by agreement and not prohibited by law, reasonable attorney's fees and legal expenses incurred by the secured party;

(B) the satisfaction of obligations secured by the security interest or agricultural lien under which the collection or enforcement is made; and

(C) the satisfaction of obligations secured by any subordinate security interest in or other lien on the collateral subject to the security interest or agricultural lien under which the collection or enforcement is made if the secured party receives an authenticated demand for proceeds before distribution of the proceeds is completed.

(2) If requested by a secured party, a holder of a subordinate security interest or other lien shall furnish reasonable proof of the interest or lien within a reasonable time. Unless the holder complies, the secured party need not comply with the holder's demand under Subdivision (1)(C).

(3) A secured party need not apply or pay over for application noncash proceeds of collection and enforcement under Section 9.607 unless the failure to do so would be commercially unreasonable. A secured party that applies or pays over for application noncash proceeds shall do so in a commercially reasonable manner.

(4) A secured party shall account to and pay a debtor for any surplus, and the obligor is liable for any deficiency.

(b) If the underlying transaction is a sale of accounts, chattel paper, payment intangibles, or promissory notes, the debtor is not entitled to any surplus, and the obligor is not liable for any deficiency.

Added by Acts 1999, 76th Leg., ch. 414, § 1.01, eff. July 1, 2001. Amended by Acts 2001, 77th Leg., ch. 705, § 19, eff. June 13, 2001.

Uniform Commercial Code Comment

1. **Source.** Subsection (a) is new; subsection (b) derives from former Section 9–502(2).

2. **Modifications of Prior Law.** Subsections (a) and (b) modify former Section 9–502(2) by explicitly providing for the application of proceeds recovered by the secured party in substantially the same manner as provided in Section 9–615(a) and (e) for dispositions of collateral.

3. **Surplus and Deficiency.** Subsections (a)(4) and (b) omit, as unnecessary, the references contained in former Section 9–502(2) to agreements varying the baseline rules on surplus and deficiency. The parties are always free to agree that an obligor will not be liable for a deficiency, even if the collateral secures an obligation, and that an obligor is liable for a deficiency, even if the transaction is a sale of receivables. For parallel provisions, see Section 9–615(d) and (e).

4. **Noncash Proceeds.** Subsection (a)(3) addresses the situation in which an enforcing secured party receives noncash proceeds.

Example: An enforcing secured party receives a promissory note from an account debtor who is unable to pay an account when it is due. The secured party accepts the note in exchange for extending the date on which the account debtor's obligation is due. The secured party may wish to credit its debtor (the assignor) with the principal amount of the note upon receipt of the note, but probably will prefer to credit the debtor only as and when the note is paid.

Under subsection (a)(3), the secured party is under no duty to apply the note or its value to the outstanding obligation unless its failure to do so would be commercially unreasonable. If the secured party does apply the note to the outstanding obligation, however, it must do so in a commercially reasonable manner. The parties may provide for the method of application of noncash proceeds by agreement, if the method is not manifestly unreasonable. See Section 9–603. This section does not explain when the failure to apply noncash proceeds would be commercially unreasonable; it leaves that determination to case-by-case adjudication. In the example, the secured party appears to have accepted the account debtor's note in order to increase the likelihood of payment and decrease the likelihood that the account debtor would dispute its obligation. Under these circumstances, it may well be commercially reasonable for the secured party to credit its debtor's obligations only as and when cash proceeds are collected from the account debtor, especially given the uncertainty that attends the account debtor's eventual payment. For an example of a secured party's receipt of noncash proceeds in which it may well be commercially unreasonable for the secured party to delay crediting its debtor's obligations with the value of noncash proceeds, see Section 9–615, Comment 3.

When the secured party is not required to "apply or pay over for application noncash proceeds," the proceeds nonetheless remain collateral subject to this Article. If the secured party were to dispose of them, for example, appropriate notification would be required (see Section 9–611), and the disposition would be subject to the standards provided in this Part (see Section 9–610). Moreover, a secured party in possession of the noncash proceeds would have the duties specified in Section 9–207.

5. **No Effect on Priority of Senior Security Interest.** The application of proceeds required by subsection (a) does not affect the priority of a security interest in collateral which is senior to the interest of the secured party who is collecting or enforcing collateral under Section 9–607. Although subsection (a) imposes a duty to apply proceeds to the enforcing secured party's expenses and to the satisfaction of the secured obligations owed to it and to subordinate secured parties, that duty applies only among the enforcing secured party and those persons. Concerning the priority of a junior secured party who collects and enforces collateral, see Section 9–607, Comment 5.

§ 9.609. Secured Party's Right to Take Possession After Default

(a) After default, a secured party:

(1) may take possession of the collateral; and

(2) without removal, may render equipment unusable and dispose of collateral on the debtor's premises under Section 9.610.

(b) A secured party may proceed under Subsection (a):

(1) pursuant to judicial process; or

(2) without judicial process, if it proceeds without breach of the peace.

(c) If so agreed, and in any event after default, a secured party may require the debtor to assemble the collateral and make it available to the secured party at a place to be designated by the secured party that is reasonably convenient to both parties.

Added by Acts 1999, 76th Leg., ch. 414, § 1.01, eff. July 1, 2001.

Uniform Commercial Code Comment

1. **Source.** Former Section 9–503.

2. **Secured Party's Right to Possession.** This section follows former Section 9–503 and earlier uniform legislation. It provides that the secured party is entitled to take possession of collateral after default.

3. **Judicial Process; Breach of Peace.** Subsection (b) permits a secured party to proceed under this section without judicial process if it does so "without breach of the peace." Although former Section 9–503 placed the same condition on a secured party's right to take possession of collateral, subsection (b) extends the condition to the right provided in subsection (a)(2) as well. Like former Section 9–503, this section does not define or explain the conduct that will constitute a breach of the peace, leaving that matter for continuing development by the courts. In considering whether a secured party has engaged in a breach of the peace, however, courts should hold the secured party responsible for the actions of others taken on the secured party's behalf, including independent contractors engaged by the secured party to take possession of collateral.

This section does not authorize a secured party who repossesses without judicial process to utilize the assistance of a law-enforcement officer. A number of cases have held that a repossessing secured party's use of a law-enforcement officer without benefit of judicial process constituted a failure to comply with former Section 9–503.

4. **Damages for Breach of Peace.** Concerning damages that may be recovered based on a secured party's breach of the peace in connection with taking possession of collateral, see Section 9–625, Comment 3.

5. **Multiple Secured Parties.** More than one secured party may be entitled to take possession of collateral under this section. Conflicting rights to possession among secured parties are resolved by the priority rules of this Article. Thus, a senior secured party is entitled to possession as against a junior claimant. Non-UCC law governs whether a junior secured party in possession of collateral is liable to the senior in conversion. Normally, a junior who refuses to relinquish possession of collateral upon the demand of a secured party having a superior possessory right to the collateral would be liable in conversion.

6. **Secured Party's Right to Disable and Dispose of Equipment on Debtor's Premises.** In the case of some collateral, such as heavy equipment, the physical removal from the debtor's plant and the storage of the collateral pending disposition may be impractical or unduly expensive. This section follows former Section 9–503 by providing that, in lieu of removal, the secured party may render equipment unusable or may dispose of collateral on the debtor's premises. Unlike former Section 9–503, however, this section explicitly conditions these rights on the debtor's default. Of course, this section does not validate unreasonable action by a secured party. Under Section 9–610, all aspects of a disposition must be commercially reasonable.

7. **Debtor's Agreement to Assemble Collateral.** This section follows former Section 9–503 also by validating a debtor's agreement to assemble collateral and make it available to a secured party at a place that the secured party designates. Similar to the treatment of agreements to permit collection prior to default under Section 9–607 and former 9–502, however, this section validates these agreements whether or not they are conditioned on the debtor's default. For example, a debtor might agree to make available to a secured party, from time to time, any instruments or negotiable documents that the debtor receives on account of collateral. A court should not infer from this section's validation that a debtor's agreement to assemble and make available collateral would not be enforceable under other applicable law.

8. **Agreed Standards.** Subject to the limitation imposed by Section 9–603(b), this section's provisions concerning agreements to assemble and make available collateral and a secured party's right to disable equipment and dispose of collateral on a debtor's premises are likely topics for agreement on standards as contemplated by Section 9–603.

State Bar Committee Comment

Official Comment 3 states: "In considering whether a secured party has engaged in a breach of the peace ... courts should hold the secured party responsible for the actions of others taken on the secured party's behalf, including independent contractors engaged by the secured party to take possession of collateral." The Texas Supreme Court has held that the duty to avoid breaching the peace cannot be delegated and that a secured party remains liable for a breach of the peace committed by its independent contractor. See *MBank El Paso, N.A. v. Sanchez,* 836 S.W.2d 151 (Tex. 1992).

§ 9.610. Disposition of Collateral After Default

(a) After default, a secured party may sell, lease, license, or otherwise dispose of any or all of the collateral in its present condition or following any commercially reasonable preparation or processing.

(b) Every aspect of a disposition of collateral, including the method, manner, time, place, and other terms, must be commercially reasonable. If commercially reasonable, a secured party may dispose of collateral by public or private proceedings, by one or more contracts, as a unit or in parcels, and at any time and place and on any terms.

(c) A secured party may purchase collateral:

(1) at a public disposition; or

(2) at a private disposition only if the collateral is of a kind that is customarily sold on a recognized market or the subject of widely distributed standard price quotations.

(d) A contract for sale, lease, license, or other disposition includes the warranties relating to title, possession, quiet enjoyment, and the like that by operation of law accompany a voluntary disposition of property of the kind subject to the contract.

(e) A secured party may disclaim or modify warranties under Subsection (d):

(1) in a manner that would be effective to disclaim or modify the warranties in a voluntary disposition of property of the kind subject to the contract of disposition; or

(2) by communicating to the purchaser a record evidencing the contract for disposition and including an express disclaimer or modification of the warranties.

(f) A record is sufficient to disclaim warranties under Subsection (e) if it indicates "There is no warranty relating to title, possession, quiet enjoyment, or the like in this disposition" or uses words of similar import.

Added by Acts 1999, 76th Leg., ch. 414, § 1.01, eff. July 1, 2001.

Uniform Commercial Code Comment

1. **Source.** Former Section 9–504(1), (3)

2. **Commercially Reasonable Dispositions.** Subsection (a) follows former Section 9–504 by permitting a secured party to dispose of collateral in a commercially reasonable manner following a default. Although subsection (b) permits both public and private dispositions, "every aspect of a disposition . . . must be commercially reasonable." This section encourages private dispositions on the assumption that they frequently will result in higher realization on collateral for the benefit of all concerned. Subsection (a) does not restrict dispositions to sales; collateral may be sold, leased, licensed, or otherwise disposed. Section 9–627 provides guidance for determining the circumstances under which a disposition is "commercially reasonable."

3. **Time of Disposition.** This Article does not specify a period within which a secured party must dispose of collateral. This is consistent with this Article's policy to encourage private dispositions through regular commercial channels. It may, for example, be prudent not to dispose of goods when the market has collapsed. Or, it might be more appropriate to sell a large inventory in parcels over a period of time instead of in bulk. Of course, under subsection (b) every aspect of a disposition of collateral must be commercially reasonable. This requirement explicitly includes the "method, manner, time, place and other terms." For example, if a secured party does not proceed under Section 9–620 and holds collateral for a long period of time without disposing of it, and if there is no good reason for not making a prompt disposition, the secured party may be determined not to have acted in a "commercially reasonable" manner. See also Section 1–203 (general obligation of good faith).

4. **Pre-Disposition Preparation and Processing.** Former Section 9–504(1) appeared to give the secured party the choice of disposing of collateral either "in its then condition or following any commercially reasonable preparation or processing." Some courts held that the "commercially reasonable" standard of former Section 9–504(3) nevertheless could impose an affirmative duty on the secured party to process or prepare the collateral prior to disposition. Subsection (a) retains the substance of the quoted language. Although courts should not be quick to impose a duty of preparation or processing on the secured party, subsection (a) does not grant the secured party the right to dispose of the collateral "in its then condition" under *all* circumstances. A secured party may not dispose of collateral "in its then condition" when, taking into account the costs and probable benefits of preparation or processing and the fact that the secured party would be advancing the costs at its risk, it would be commercially unreasonable to dispose of the collateral in that condition.

5. **Disposition by Junior Secured Party.** Disposition rights under subsection (a) are not limited to first-priority security interests. Rather, any secured party as to whom there has been a default enjoys the right to dispose of collateral under this subsection. The exercise of this right by a secured party whose security interest is subordinate to that of another secured party does not of itself constitute a conversion or otherwise give rise to liability in favor of the holder of the senior security interest. Section 9–615 addresses application of the proceeds of a disposition by a junior secured party. Under Section 9–615(a), a junior secured party owes no obligation to apply the proceeds of disposition to the satisfaction of obligations secured by a senior security interest. Section 9–615(g) builds on this general rule by protecting certain juniors from claims of a senior concerning cash proceeds of the disposition. Even if a senior were to have a non-Article 9 claim to proceeds of a junior's disposition, Section 9–615(g) would protect a junior that acts in good faith and without knowledge that its actions violate the rights of a senior party. Because the disposition by a junior would not cut off a senior's security interest or other lien (see Section 9–617), in many (probably most) cases the junior's receipt of the cash proceeds would not violate the rights of the senior.

The holder of a senior security interest is entitled, by virtue of its priority, to take possession of collateral from the junior secured party and conduct its own disposition, provided that the senior enjoys the right to take possession of the collateral from the debtor. See Section 9–609. The holder of a junior security interest normally must notify the senior secured party of an impending disposition. See Section 9–611. Regardless of whether the senior receives a notification from the junior, the junior's disposition does not of itself discharge the senior's security interest. See Section 9–617. Unless the senior secured party has authorized the disposition free and clear of its security interest, the senior's security interest ordinarily will survive the disposition by the junior and continue under Section 9–315(a). If the senior enjoys the right to repossess the collateral from the debtor, the senior likewise may recover the collateral from the transferee.

When a secured party's collateral is encumbered by another security interest or other lien, one of the claimants may seek to invoke the equitable doctrine of marshaling. As explained by the Supreme Court, that doctrine "rests upon the principle that a creditor having two funds to satisfy his debt, may not by his application of them to his demand, defeat another creditor, who may resort to only one of the funds." *Meyer v. United States*, 375 U.S. 233, 236 (1963), quoting *Sowell v. Federal Reserve Bank*, 268 U.S. 449, 456–57 (1925). The purpose of the doctrine is "to prevent the arbitrary action of a senior lienor from destroying the rights of a junior lienor or a creditor having less security." Id. at 237. Because it is an equitable doctrine, marshaling "is applied only when it can be equitably fashioned as to all of the parties" having an interest in the property. Id. This Article leaves courts free to determine whether marshaling is appropriate in any given case. See Section 1–103.

6. **Security Interests of Equal Rank.** Sometimes two security interests enjoy the same priority. This situation may arise by contract, e.g., pursuant to "equal and ratable" provisions in indentures, or by operation of law. See Section 9–328(6). This Article treats a security interest having equal priority like a senior security interest in many respects. Assume, for example, that SP–X and SP–Y enjoy equal priority, SP–W is senior to them, and SP–Z is junior. If SP–X disposes of the collateral under this section, then (i) SP–W's and SP–Y's security interests survive the disposition but SP–Z's does not, see Section 9–617, and (ii) neither SP–W nor SP–Y is entitled to receive a distribution of proceeds, but SP–Z is. See Section 9–615(a)(3).

When one considers the ability to obtain possession of the collateral, a secured party with equal priority is unlike a senior secured party. As the senior secured party, SP–W should enjoy the right to possession as against SP–X. See Section 9–609, Comment 5. If SP–W takes possession and disposes of the collateral under this section, it is entitled to apply the proceeds to satisfy its secured claim. SP–Y, however, should not have such a right to take possession from SP–X; otherwise, once SP–Y took possession from SP–X, SP–X would have the right to get possession from SP–Y, which would be obligated to redeliver possession to SP–X, and so on. Resolution of this problem is left to the parties and, if necessary, the courts.

7. **Public vs. Private Dispositions.** This Part maintains two distinctions between "public" and other dispositions: (i) the secured party may buy at the former, but normally not at the latter (Section 9–610(c)), and (ii) the debtor is entitled to notification of "the time and place of a public disposition" and notification of "the time after which" a private disposition or other intended disposition is to be made (Section 9–613(1)(E)). It does not retain the distinction under former Section 9–504(4), under which transferees in a noncomplying public disposition could lose protection more easily than transferees in other noncomplying dispositions. Instead, Section 9–617(b) adopts a unitary standard. Although the term is not defined, as used in this Article, a "public disposition" is one at which the price is determined after the public has had a meaningful opportunity for competitive bidding. "Meaningful opportunity" is meant to imply that some form of advertisement or public notice must precede the sale (or other disposition) and that the public must have access to the sale (disposition).

8. **Investment Property.** Dispositions of investment property may be regulated by the federal securities laws. Although a "public" disposition of securities under this Article may implicate the registration requirements of the Securities Act of 1933, it need not do so. A disposition that qualifies for a "private placement" exemption under the Securities Act of 1933 nevertheless may constitute a "public" disposition within the meaning of this section. Moreover, the "commercially reasonable" requirements of subsection (b) need not prevent a secured party from conducting a foreclosure sale without the issuer's compliance with federal registration requirements.

9. **"Recognized Market."** A "recognized market," as used in subsection (c) and Section 9–611(d), is one in which the items sold are fungible and prices are not subject to individual negotiation. For example, the New York Stock Exchange is a recognized market. A market in which prices are individually negotiated or the items are not fungible is not a recognized market, even if the items are the subject of widely disseminated price guides or are disposed of through dealer auctions.

10. **Relevance of Price.** While not itself sufficient to establish a violation of this Part, a low price suggests that a court should scrutinize carefully all aspects of a disposition to ensure that each aspect was commercially reasonable. Note also that even if the disposition is commercially reasonable, Section 9–615(f) provides a special method for calculating a deficiency or surplus if (i) the transferee in the disposition is the secured party, a person related to the secured party, or a secondary obligor, and (ii) the amount of proceeds of the disposition is significantly below the range of proceeds that a complying disposition to a person other than the secured party, a person related to the secured party, or a secondary obligor would have brought.

11. **Warranties.** Subsection (d) affords the transferee in a disposition under this section the benefit of any title, possession, quiet enjoyment, and similar warranties that would have accompanied the disposition by operation of non-Article 9 law had the disposition been conducted under other circumstances. For example, the Article 2 warranty of title would apply to a sale of goods, the analogous warranties of Article 2A would apply to a lease of goods, and any common-law warranties of title would apply to dispositions of other types of collateral. See, e.g., Restatement (2d), Contracts § 333 (warranties of assignor).

Subsection (e) explicitly provides that these warranties can be disclaimed either under other applicable law or by communicating a record containing an express disclaimer. The record need not be written, but an oral communication would not be sufficient. See Section 9–102 (definition of "record"). Subsection (f) provides a sample of wording that will effectively exclude the warranties in a disposition under this section, whether or not the exclusion would be effective under non-Article 9 law.

The warranties incorporated by subsection (d) are those relating to "title, possession, quiet enjoyment, and the like." Depending on the circumstances, a disposition under this section also may give rise to other statutory or implied warranties, e.g., warranties of quality or fitness for purpose. Law other than this Article determines whether such other warranties apply to a disposition under this section. Other law also determines issues relating to disclaimer of such warranties. For example, a foreclosure sale of a car by a car dealer could give rise to an implied warranty of merchantability (Section 2–314) unless effectively disclaimed or modified (Section 2–316).

This section's approach to these warranties conflicts with the former Comment to Section 2–312. This Article rejects the baseline assumption that commercially reasonable dispositions under this section are out of the ordinary commercial course or peculiar. The Comment to Section 2–312 has been revised accordingly.

§ 9.611. Notification Before Disposition of Collateral

(a) In this section, "notification date" means the earlier of the date on which:

(1) a secured party sends to the debtor and any secondary obligor an authenticated notification of disposition; or

(2) the debtor and any secondary obligor waive the right to notification.

(b) Except as otherwise provided in Subsection (d), a secured party that disposes of collateral under Section 9.610 shall send to the persons specified in Subsection (c) a reasonable authenticated notification of disposition.

(c) To comply with Subsection (b), the secured party shall send an authenticated notification of disposition to:

(1) the debtor;

(2) any secondary obligor; and

(3) if the collateral is other than consumer goods:

(A) any other person from which the secured party has received, before the notification date, an authenticated notification of a claim of an interest in the collateral;

(B) any other secured party or lienholder that, 10 days before the notification date, held a security interest in or other lien on the collateral perfected by the filing of a financing statement that:

(i) identified the collateral;

(ii) was indexed under the debtor's name as of that date; and

(iii) was filed in the office in which to file a financing statement against the debtor covering the collateral as of that date; and

(C) any other secured party that, 10 days before the notification date, held a security interest in the collateral perfected by compliance with a statute, regulation, or treaty described in Section 9.311(a).

(d) Subsection (b) does not apply if the collateral is perishable or threatens to decline speedily in value or is of a type customarily sold on a recognized market.

(e) A secured party complies with the requirement for notification prescribed by Subsection (c)(3)(B) if:

(1) not later than 20 days or earlier than 30 days before the notification date, the secured party requests, in a commercially reasonable manner, information concerning financing statements indexed under the debtor's name in the office indicated in Subsection (c)(3)(B); and

(2) before the notification date, the secured party:

(A) did not receive a response to the request for information; or

(B) received a response to the request for information and sent an authenticated notification of disposition to each secured party or other lienholder named in that response whose financing statement covered the collateral.

Added by Acts 1999, 76th Leg., ch. 414, § 1.01, eff. July 1, 2001.

Uniform Commercial Code Comment

1. **Source.** Former Section 9–504(3).

2. **Reasonable Notification.** This section requires a secured party who wishes to dispose of collateral under Section 9–610 to send "a reasonable authenticated notification of disposition" to specified interested persons, subject to certain exceptions. The notification must be reasonable as to the manner in which it is sent, its timeliness (i.e., a reasonable time before the disposition is to take place), and its content. See Sections 9–612 (timeliness of notification), 9–613 (contents of notification generally), 9–614 (contents of notification in consumer-goods transactions).

3. **Notification to Debtors and Secondary Obligors.** This section imposes a duty to send notification of a disposition not only to the debtor but also to any secondary obligor. Subsections (b) and (c) resolve an uncertainty under former Article 9 by providing that secondary obligors (sureties) are entitled to receive notification of an intended disposition of collateral, regardless of who created the security interest in the collateral. If the surety created the security interest, it would be the debtor. If it did not, it would be a secondary obligor. (This Article also resolves the question of the secondary obligor's ability to waive, pre-default, the right to notification–waiver generally is not permitted. See Section 9–602.) Section 9–605 relieves a secured party from any duty to send notification to a debtor or secondary obligor unknown to the secured party.

Under subsection (b), the principal obligor (borrower) is not always entitled to notification of disposition.

Example: Behnfeldt borrows on an unsecured basis, and Bruno grants a security interest in her car to secure the debt. Behnfeldt is a primary obligor, not a secondary obligor. As such, she is not entitled to notification of disposition under this section.

4. **Notification to Other Secured Parties.** Prior to the 1972 amendments to Article 9, former Section 9–504(3) required the enforcing secured party to send reasonable notification of the disposition:

> except in the case of consumer goods to any other person who has a security interest in the collateral and who has duly filed a financing statement indexed in the name of the debtor in this State or who is known by the secured party to have a security interest in the collateral.

The 1972 amendments eliminated the duty to give notice to secured parties other than those from whom the foreclosing secured party had received written notice of a claim of an interest in the collateral.

Many of the problems arising from dispositions of collateral encumbered by multiple security interests can be ameliorated or solved by informing all secured parties of an intended disposition and affording them the opportunity to work with one another. To this end, subsection (c)(3)(B) expands the duties of the foreclosing secured party to include the duty to notify (and the corresponding burden of searching the files to discover) certain competing secured parties. The subsection imposes a search burden that in some cases may be greater than the pre–1972 burden on foreclosing secured parties but certainly is more modest than that faced by a new secured lender.

To determine who is entitled to notification, the foreclosing secured party must determine the proper office for filing a financing statement as of a particular date, measured by reference to the "notification date," as defined in subsection (a). This determination requires reference to the choice-of-law provisions of Part 3. The secured party must ascertain whether any financing statements covering the collateral and indexed under the debtor's name, as the name existed as of that date, in fact were filed in that office. The foreclosing secured party generally need not notify secured parties whose effective financing statements have become more difficult to locate because of changes in the location of the debtor, proceeds rules, or changes in the debtor's name.

Under subsection (c)(3)(C), the secured party also must notify a secured party who has perfected a security interest by complying with a statute or treaty described in Section 9–311(a), such as a certificate-of-title statute.

Subsection (e) provides a "safe harbor" that takes into account the delays that may be attendant to receiving information from the public filing offices. It provides, generally, that the secured party will be deemed to have satisfied its notification duty under subsection (c)(3)(B) if it requests a search from the proper office at least 20 but not more than 30 days before sending notification to the debtor and if it also sends a notification to all secured parties (and other lienholders) reflected on the search report. The secured party's duty under subsection (c)(3)(B) also will be satisfied if the secured party requests but does not receive a search report before the notification is sent to the debtor. Thus, if subsection (e) applies, a secured party who is entitled to notification under subsection (c)(3)(B) has no remedy against a foreclosing secured party who does not send the notification. The foreclosing secured party has complied with the notification requirement. Subsection (e) has no effect on the requirements of the other paragraphs of subsection (c). For example, if the foreclosing secured party received a notification from the holder of a conflicting security interest in accordance with subsection (c)(3)(A) but failed to send to the holder a notification of the disposition, the holder of the conflicting security interest would have the right to recover any loss under Section 9–625(b).

5. **Authentication Requirement.** Subsections (b) and (c) explicitly provide that a notification of disposition must be "authenticated." Some cases read former Section 9–504(3) as validating oral notification.

6. **Second Try.** This Article leaves to judicial resolution, based upon the facts of each case, the question whether the requirement of "reasonable notification" requires a "second try," i.e., whether a secured party who sends notification and learns that the debtor did not receive it must attempt to locate the debtor and send another notification.

7. **Recognized Market; Perishable Collateral.** New subsection (d) makes it clear that there is no obligation to give notification of a disposition in the case of perishable collateral or collateral customarily sold on a recognized market (e.g., marketable securities). Former Section 9–504(3) might be read (incorrectly) to relieve the secured party from its duty to notify a debtor but not from its duty to notify other secured parties in connection with dispositions of such collateral.

8. **Failure to Conduct Notified Disposition.** Nothing in this Article prevents a secured party from electing not to conduct a disposition after sending a notification. Nor does this Article prevent a secured party from electing to send a revised notification if its plans for disposition change. This assumes, however, that the secured party acts in good faith, the revised notification is reasonable, and the revised plan for disposition and any attendant delay are commercially reasonable.

9. **Waiver.** A debtor or secondary obligor may waive the right to notification under this section only by a post-default authenticated agreement. See Section 9–624(a).

State Bar Committee Comment

This section requires the secured party to send "authenticated" notification, which, as noted in Official Comment 5, invalidates oral notification. The "authentication" requirement will change the result in cases that have permitted a secured party to satisfy its duty to send "reasonable notification" under former section 9.504(c) by providing oral notice. See, e.g., *Beltran v. Groos Bank, N.A., 755 S.W.2d 944 (Tex. App.—San Antonio 1988, no writ)* (upholding oral notice to guarantor); *MBank Dallas N.A. v. Sunbelt Mfg., Inc., 710 S.W.2d 633 (Tex. App.—Dallas 1986, writ ref'd n.r.e.)* (upholding oral notice to debtor).

§ 9.612. Timeliness of Notification Before Disposition of Collateral

(a) Except as otherwise provided in Subsection (b), whether a notification is sent within a reasonable time is a question of fact.

(b) In a transaction other than a consumer transaction, a notification of disposition sent after default and 10 days or more before the earliest time of disposition set forth in the notification is sent within a reasonable time before the disposition.

Added by Acts 1999, 76th Leg., ch. 414, § 1.01, eff. July 1, 2001.

Uniform Commercial Code Comment

1. **Source.** New.

2. **Reasonable Notification.** Section 9–611(b) requires the secured party to send a "reasonable authenticated notification." Under that section, as under former Section 9–504(3), one aspect of a reasonable notification is its timeliness. This generally means that the notification must be sent at a reasonable time in advance of the date of a public disposition or the date after which a private disposition is to be made. A notification that is sent so near to the disposition date that a notified person could not be expected to act on or take account of the notification would be unreasonable.

3. **Timeliness of Notification: Safe Harbor.** The 10–day notice period in subsection (b) is intended to be a "safe harbor" and not a minimum requirement. To qualify for the "safe harbor" the notification must be sent after default. A notification also must be sent in a commercially reasonable manner. See Section 9–611(b) ("reasonable authenticated notification"). These requirements prevent a secured party from taking advantage of the "safe harbor" by, for example, giving the debtor a notification at the time of the original extension of credit or sending the notice by surface mail to a debtor overseas.

§ 9.613. Contents and Form of Notification Before Disposition of Collateral: General

Except in a consumer-goods transaction, the following rules apply:

(1) The contents of a notification of disposition are sufficient if the notification:

(A) describes the debtor and the secured party;

(B) describes the collateral that is the subject of the intended disposition;

(C) states the method of intended disposition;

(D) states that the debtor is entitled to an accounting of the unpaid indebtedness and states the charge, if any, for an accounting; and

(E) states the time and place of a public disposition or the time after which any other disposition is to be made.

(2) Whether the contents of a notification that lacks any of the information specified in Subdivision (1) are nevertheless sufficient is a question of fact.

(3) The contents of a notification providing substantially the information specified in Subdivision (1) are sufficient, even if the notification includes:

(A) information not specified by that subdivision; or

(B) minor errors that are not seriously misleading.

(4) A particular phrasing of the notification is not required.

(5) The following form of notification and the form appearing in Section 9.614(3), when completed, each provide sufficient information:

To: __________ [*Name of debtor, obligor, or other person to which the notification is sent*]

NOTIFICATION OF DISPOSITION OF COLLATERAL

From: __________ [*Name, address, and telephone number of secured party*]

Name of Debtor(s): __________ [*Include only if debtor(s) are not an addressee*]

[*For a public disposition:*]

We will sell [or lease or license, *as applicable*] the [*describe collateral*] [to the highest qualified bidder] in public as follows:

Day and Date: __________

Time: __________

Place: __________

[*For a private disposition:*]

We will sell [or lease or license, *as applicable*] the __________[*describe collateral*] privately sometime after __________ [*day and date*].

You are entitled to an accounting of the unpaid indebtedness secured by the property that we intend to sell [or lease or license, *as applicable*] [for a charge of $___]. You may request an accounting by calling us at __________ [*telephone number*].

Added by Acts 1999, 76th Leg., ch. 414, § 1.01, eff. July 1, 2001. Amended by Acts 2001, 77th Leg., ch. 705, § 20, eff. June 13, 2001.

Uniform Commercial Code Comment

1. **Source.** New.

2. **Contents of Notification.** To comply with the "reasonable authenticated notification" requirement of Section 9–611(b), the contents of a notification must be reasonable. Except in a consumer-goods transaction, the contents of a notification that includes the information set forth in paragraph (1) are sufficient as a matter of law, unless the parties agree otherwise. (The reference to "time" of disposition means here, as it did in former Section 9–504(3), not only the hour of the day but also the date.) Although a secured party may choose to include additional information concerning the transaction or the debtor's rights and obligations, no additional information is required unless the parties agree otherwise. A notification that lacks some of the information set forth in paragraph (1) nevertheless may be sufficient if found to be reasonable by the trier of fact, under paragraph (2). A properly completed sample form of notification in paragraph (5) or in Section 9–614(a)(3) is an example of a notification that would contain the information set forth in paragraph (1). Under paragraph (4), however, no particular phrasing of the notification is required.

§ 9.614. Contents and Form of Notification Before Disposition of Collateral: Consumer-Goods Transaction

In a consumer-goods transaction, the following rules apply:

(1) A notification of disposition must provide the following information:

(A) the information specified in Section 9.613(1);

(B) a description of any liability for a deficiency of the person to which the notification is sent;

(C) a telephone number from which the amount that must be paid to the secured party to redeem the collateral under Section 9.623 is available; and

(D) a telephone number or mailing address from which additional information concerning the disposition and the obligation secured is available.

(2) A particular phrasing of the notification is not required.

(3) The following form of notification, when completed, provides sufficient information:

__________ [Name and address of secured party]

__________ [Date]

NOTICE OF OUR PLAN TO SELL PROPERTY

__________ [Name and address of any obligor who is also a debtor]

Subject: __________ [Identification of Transaction]

We have your __________ [describe collateral], because you broke promises in our agreement.

[For a public disposition:]

We will sell __________ [describe collateral] at public sale. A sale could include a lease or license. The sale will be held as follows:

Date:__________

Time:__________

Place:__________

You may attend the sale and bring bidders if you want.

[For a private disposition:]

We will sell __________ [describe collateral] at private sale sometime after __________ [date]. A sale could include a lease or license.

The money that we get from the sale (after paying our costs) will reduce the amount you owe. If we get less money than you owe, you __________ [will or will not, as applicable] still owe us the difference. If we get more money than you owe, you will get the extra money, unless we must pay it to someone else.

You can get the property back at any time before we sell it by paying us the full amount you owe (not just the past due payments), including our expenses. To learn the exact amount you must pay, call us at __________ [telephone number].

If you want us to explain to you in writing how we have figured the amount that you owe us, you may call us at __________ [telephone number] [or write us at __________ [secured party's address] __________] and request a written explanation. [We will charge you $__________ for the explanation if we sent you another written explanation of the amount you owe us within the last six months.]

If you need more information about the sale call us at __________ [telephone number] [or write us at __________ [secured party's address] __________].

We are sending this notice to the following other people who have an interest in __________ [describe collateral] or who owe money under your agreement:

__________ [Names of all other debtors and obligors, if any]

(4) A notification in the form of Subdivision (3) is sufficient, even if additional information appears at the end of the form.

(5) A notification in the form of Subdivision (3) is sufficient, even if it includes errors in information not required by Subdivision (1), unless the error is misleading with respect to rights arising under this chapter.

(6) If a notification under this section is not in the form of Subdivision (3), law other than this chapter determines the effect of including information not required by Subdivision (1).

Added by Acts 1999, 76th Leg., ch. 414, § 1.01, eff. July 1, 2001.

Uniform Commercial Code Comment

1. **Source.** New.

2. **Notification in Consumer–Goods Transactions.** Paragraph (1) sets forth the information required for a reasonable notification in a consumer-goods transaction. A notification that lacks any of the information set forth in paragraph (1) is insufficient as a matter of law. Compare Section 9–613(2), under which the trier of fact may find a notification to be sufficient even if it lacks some information listed in paragraph (1) of that section.

3. **Safe-Harbor Form of Notification; Errors in Information.** Although paragraph (2) provides that a particular phrasing of a notification is not required, paragraph (3) specifies a safe-harbor form that, when properly completed, satisfies paragraph (1). Paragraphs (4), (5), and (6) contain special rules applicable to erroneous and additional information. Under paragraph (4), a notification in the safe-harbor form specified in paragraph (3) is not rendered insufficient if it contains additional information at the end of the form. Paragraph (5) provides that non-misleading errors in information contained in a notification are permitted if the safe-harbor form is used *and if the errors are in information not required by paragraph (1).* Finally, if a notification is in a form other than the paragraph (3) safe-harbor form, other law determines the effect of including in the notification information other than that required by paragraph (1).

§ 9.615. Application of Proceeds of Disposition; Liability for Deficiency and Right to Surplus

(a) A secured party shall apply or pay over for application the cash proceeds of disposition under Section 9.610 in the following order to:

(1) the reasonable expenses of retaking, holding, preparing for disposition, processing, and disposing and, to the extent provided for by agreement and not prohibited by law, reasonable attorney's fees and legal expenses incurred by the secured party;

(2) the satisfaction of obligations secured by the security interest or agricultural lien under which the disposition is made;

(3) the satisfaction of obligations secured by any subordinate security interest in or other subordinate lien on the collateral if:

(A) the secured party receives from the holder of the subordinate security interest or other lien an authenticated demand for proceeds before distribution of the proceeds is completed; and

(B) in a case in which a consignor has an interest in the collateral, the subordinate security interest or other lien is senior to the interest of the consignor; and

(4) a secured party that is a consignor of the collateral if the secured party receives from the consignor an authenticated demand for proceeds before distribution of the proceeds is completed.

(b) If requested by a secured party, a holder of a subordinate security interest or other lien shall furnish reasonable proof of the interest or lien within a reasonable time. Unless the holder does so, the secured party need not comply with the holder's demand under Subsection (a)(3).

(c) A secured party need not apply or pay over for application noncash proceeds of disposition under Section 9.610 unless the failure to do so would be commercially unreasonable. A secured party that applies or pays over for application noncash proceeds shall do so in a commercially reasonable manner.

(d) If the security interest under which a disposition is made secures payment or performance of an obligation, after making the payments and applications required by Subsection (a) and permitted by Subsection (c):

(1) unless Subsection (a)(4) requires the secured party to apply or pay over cash proceeds to a consignor, the secured party shall account to and pay a debtor for any surplus; and

(2) the obligor is liable for any deficiency.

(e) If the underlying transaction is a sale of accounts, chattel paper, payment intangibles, or promissory notes:

(1) the debtor is not entitled to any surplus; and

(2) the obligor is not liable for any deficiency.

(f) The surplus or deficiency following a disposition is calculated based on the amount of proceeds that would have been realized in a disposition complying with this subchapter to a transferee other than the secured party, a person related to the secured party, or a secondary obligor if:

(1) the transferee in the disposition is the secured party, a person related to the secured party, or a secondary obligor; and

(2) the amount of proceeds of the disposition is significantly below the range of proceeds that a complying disposition to a person other than the secured party, a person related to the secured party, or a secondary obligor would have brought.

(g) A secured party that receives cash proceeds of a disposition in good faith and without knowledge that the receipt violates the rights of the holder of a security interest or other lien that is not subordinate to the security interest or agricultural lien under which the disposition is made:

(1) takes the cash proceeds free of the security interest or other lien;

(2) is not obligated to apply the proceeds of the disposition to the satisfaction of obligations secured by the security interest or other lien; and

(3) is not obligated to account to or pay the holder of the security interest or other lien for any surplus.

Added by Acts 1999, 76th Leg., ch. 414, § 1.01, eff. July 1, 2001. Amended by Acts 2001, 77th Leg., ch. 705, § 21, eff. June 13, 2001.

Uniform Commercial Code Comment

1. **Source.** Former Section 9–504(1), (2).

2. **Application of Proceeds.** This section contains the rules governing application of proceeds and the debtor's liability for a deficiency following a disposition of collateral. Subsection (a) sets forth the basic order of application. The proceeds are applied first to the expenses of disposition, second to the obligation secured by the security interest that is being enforced, and third, in the specified circumstances, to interests that are subordinate to that security interest.

Subsections (a) and (d) also address the right of a consignor to receive proceeds of a disposition by a secured party whose interest is senior to that of the consignor. Subsection (a) requires the enforcing secured party to pay excess proceeds first to subordinate secured parties or lienholders whose interests are senior to that of a consignor and, finally, to a consignor. Inasmuch as a consignor is the owner of the collateral, secured parties and lienholders whose interests are junior to the consignor's interest will not be entitled to any proceeds. In like fashion, under subsection (d)(1) the debtor is not entitled to a surplus when the enforcing secured party is required to pay over proceeds to a consignor.

3. **Noncash Proceeds.** Subsection (c) addresses the application of noncash proceeds of a disposition, such as a note or lease. The explanation in Section 9–608, Comment 4, generally applies to this subsection.

Example: A secured party in the business of selling or financing automobiles takes possession of collateral (an automobile) following its debtor's default. The secured party decides to sell the automobile in a private disposition under Section 9–610 and sends appropriate notification under Section 9–611. After undertaking its normal credit investigation and in accordance with its normal credit policies, the secured party sells the automobile on credit, on terms typical of the credit terms normally extended by the secured party in the ordinary course of its business. The automobile stands as collateral for the remaining balance of the price. The noncash proceeds received by the secured party are chattel paper. The secured party may wish to credit its debtor (the assignor) with the principal amount of the chattel paper or may wish to credit the debtor only as and when the payments are made on the chattel paper by the buyer.

Under subsection (c), the secured party is under no duty to apply the noncash proceeds (here, the chattel paper) or their value to the secured obligation unless its failure to do so would be commercially unreasonable. If a secured party elects to apply the chattel paper to the outstanding obligation, however, it must do so in a commercially reasonable manner. The facts in the example indicate that it would be commercially unreasonable for the secured party to fail to apply the value of the chattel paper to the original debtor's secured obligation. Unlike the example in Comment 4 to Section 9–608, the noncash proceeds received in this example are of the type that the secured party regularly generates in the ordinary course of its financing business in nonforeclosure transactions. The original debtor should not be exposed to delay or uncertainty in this situation. Of course, there will be many situations that fall between the examples presented in the Comment to Section 9–608 and in this Comment. This Article leaves their resolution to the court based on the facts of each case.

One would expect that where noncash proceeds are or may be material, the secured party and debtor would agree to more specific standards in an agreement entered into before or after default. The parties may agree to the method of application of noncash proceeds if the method is not manifestly unreasonable. See Section 9–603.

When the secured party is not required to "apply or pay over for application noncash proceeds," the proceeds nonetheless remain collateral subject to this Article. See Section 9–608, Comment 4.

4. **Surplus and Deficiency.** Subsection (d) deals with surplus and deficiency. It revises former Section 9–504(2) by imposing an explicit requirement that the secured party "pay" the debtor for any surplus, while retaining the secured party's duty to "account." Inasmuch as the debtor may not be an obligor, subsection (d) provides that the obligor (not the debtor) is liable for the deficiency. The special rule governing surplus and deficiency when receivables have been sold likewise takes into account the distinction between a debtor and an obligor. Subsection (d) also addresses the situation in which a consignor has an interest that is subordinate to the security interest being enforced.

5. **Collateral Under New Ownership.** When the debtor sells collateral subject to a security interest, the original

debtor (creator of the security interest) is no longer a debtor inasmuch as it no longer has a property interest in the collateral; the buyer is the debtor. See Section 9–102. As between the debtor (buyer of the collateral) and the original debtor (seller of the collateral), the debtor (buyer) normally would be entitled to the surplus following a disposition. Subsection (d) therefore requires the secured party to pay the surplus to the debtor (buyer), not to the original debtor (seller) with which it has dealt. But, because this situation typically arises as a result of the debtor's wrongful act, this Article does not expose the secured party to the risk of determining ownership of the collateral. If the secured party does not know about the buyer and accordingly pays the surplus to the original debtor, the exculpatory provisions of this Article exonerate the secured party from liability to the buyer. See Sections 9–605, 9–628(a), (b). If a debtor sells collateral *free* of a security interest, as in a sale to a buyer in ordinary course of business (see Section 9–320(a)), the property is no longer collateral and the buyer is not a debtor.

6. **Certain "Low–Price" Dispositions.** Subsection (f) provides a special method for calculating a deficiency or surplus when the secured party, a person related to the secured party (defined in Section 9–102), or a secondary obligor acquires the collateral at a foreclosure disposition. It recognizes that when the foreclosing secured party or a related party is the transferee of the collateral, the secured party sometimes lacks the incentive to maximize the proceeds of disposition. As a consequence, the disposition may comply with the procedural requirements of this Article (e.g., it is conducted in a commercially reasonable manner following reasonable notice) but nevertheless fetch a low price.

Subsection (f) adjusts for this lack of incentive. If the proceeds of a disposition of collateral to a secured party, a person related to the secured party, or a secondary obligor are "significantly below the range of proceeds that a complying disposition to a person other than the secured party, a person related to the secured party, or a secondary obligor would have brought," then instead of calculating a deficiency (or surplus) based on the actual net proceeds, the calculation is based upon the amount that would have been received in a commercially reasonable disposition to a person other than the secured party, a person related to the secured party, or a secondary obligor. Subsection (f) thus rejects the view that the secured party's receipt of such a price necessarily constitutes noncompliance with Part 6. However, such a price may suggest the need for greater judicial scrutiny. See Section 9–610, Comment 10.

7. **"Person Related To."** Section 9–102 defines "person related to." That term is a key element of the system provided in subsection (f) for low-price dispositions. One part of the definition applies when the secured party is an individual, and the other applies when the secured party is an organization. The definition is patterned closely on the corresponding definition in Section 1.301(32) of the Uniform Consumer Credit Code.

§ 9.616. Explanation of Calculation of Surplus or Deficiency

(a) In this section:

(1) "Explanation" means a writing that:

(A) states the amount of the surplus or deficiency;

(B) provides an explanation in accordance with Subsection (c) of how the secured party calculated the surplus or deficiency;

(C) states, if applicable, that future debits, credits, charges, including additional credit service charges or interest, rebates, and expenses may affect the amount of the surplus or deficiency; and

(D) provides a telephone number or mailing address from which additional information concerning the transaction is available.

(2) "Request" means a record:

(A) authenticated by a debtor or consumer obligor;

(B) requesting that the recipient provide an explanation; and

(C) sent after disposition of the collateral under Section 9.610.

(b) In a consumer-goods transaction in which the debtor is entitled to a surplus or a consumer obligor is liable for a deficiency under Section 9.615, the secured party shall:

(1) send an explanation to the debtor or consumer obligor, as applicable, after the disposition and:

(A) before or when the secured party accounts to the debtor and pays any surplus or first makes written demand on the consumer obligor after the disposition for payment of the deficiency; and

(B) within 14 days after receipt of a request; or

(2) in the case of a consumer obligor who is liable for a deficiency, within 14 days after receipt of a request, send to the consumer obligor a record waiving the secured party's right to a deficiency.

(c) To comply with Subsection (a)(1)(B), a writing must provide the following information in the following order:

(1) the aggregate amount of obligations secured by the security interest under which the disposition was made and, if the amount reflects a rebate of unearned interest or credit service charge, an indication of that fact, calculated as of a specified date:

(A) if the secured party takes or receives possession of the collateral after default, not more than 35 days before the secured party takes or receives possession; or

(B) if the secured party takes or receives possession of the collateral before default or does not take possession of the collateral, not more than 35 days before the disposition;

(2) the amount of proceeds of the disposition;

(3) the aggregate amount of the obligations after deducting the amount of proceeds;

(4) the amount, in the aggregate or by type, and types of expenses, including expenses of retaking, holding, preparing for disposition, processing, and disposing of the collateral, and attorney's fees secured by the collateral which are known to the secured party and relate to the current disposition;

(5) the amount, in the aggregate or by type, and types of credits, including rebates of interest or credit service charges, to which the obligor is known to be entitled and which are not reflected in the amount in Subdivision (1); and

(6) the amount of the surplus or deficiency.

(d) A particular phrasing of the explanation is not required. An explanation complying substantially with the requirements of Subsection (a) is sufficient, even if it includes minor errors that are not seriously misleading.

(e) A debtor or consumer obligor is entitled without charge to one response to a request under this section during any six-month period in which the secured party did not send to the debtor or consumer obligor an explanation pursuant to Subsection (b)(1). The secured party may require payment of a charge not exceeding $25 for each additional response.

Added by Acts 1999, 76th Leg., ch. 414, § 1.01, eff. July 1, 2001.

Uniform Commercial Code Comment

1. **Source.** New.

2. **Duty to Send Information Concerning Surplus or Deficiency.** This section reflects the view that, in every consumer-goods transaction, the debtor or obligor is entitled to know the amount of a surplus or deficiency and the basis upon which the surplus or deficiency was calculated. Under subsection (b)(1), a secured party is obligated to provide this information (an "explanation," defined in subsection (a)(1)) no later than the time that it accounts for and pays a surplus or the time of its first written attempt to collect the deficiency. The obligor need not make a request for an accounting in order to receive an explanation. A secured party who does not attempt to collect a deficiency in writing or account for and pay a surplus has no obligation to send an explanation under subsection (b)(1) and, consequently, cannot be liable for noncompliance.

A debtor or secondary obligor need not wait until the secured party commences written collection efforts in order to receive an explanation of how a deficiency or surplus was calculated. Subsection (b)(2) obliges the secured party to send an explanation within 14 days after it receives a "request" (defined in subsection (a)(2)).

3. **Explanation of Calculation of Surplus or Deficiency.** Subsection (c) contains the requirements for how a calculation of a surplus or deficiency must be explained in order to satisfy subsection (a)(1)(B). It gives a secured party some discretion concerning rebates of interest or credit service charges. The secured party may include these rebates in the aggregate amount of obligations secured, under subsection (c)(1), or may include them with other types of rebates and credits under subsection (c)(5). Rebates of interest or credit service charges are the only types of rebates for which this discretion is provided. If the secured party provides an explanation that includes rebates of precomputed interest, its explanation must so indicate. The expenses and attorney's fees to be described pursuant to subsection (c)(4) are those relating to the most recent disposition, not those that may have been incurred in connection with earlier enforcement efforts and which have been resolved by the parties.

4. **Liability for Noncompliance.** A secured party who fails to comply with subsection (b)(2) is liable for any loss caused plus $500. See Section 9–625(b), (c), (e)(6). A secured party who fails to send an explanation under subsection (b)(1) is liable for any loss caused plus, if the noncompliance was "part of a pattern, or consistent with a practice of noncompliance," $500. See Section 9–625(b), (c), (e)(5). However, a secured party who fails to comply with this section is not liable for statutory minimum damages under Section 9–625(c)(2). See Section 9–628(d).

§ 9.617. Rights of Transferee of Collateral

(a) A secured party's disposition of collateral after default:

(1) transfers to a transferee for value all of the debtor's rights in the collateral;

(2) discharges the security interest under which the disposition is made; and

(3) discharges any subordinate security interest or other subordinate lien.

(b) A transferee that acts in good faith takes free of the rights and interests described in Subsection (a), even if the secured party fails to comply with this chapter or the requirements of any judicial proceeding.

(c) If a transferee does not take free of the rights and interests described in Subsection (a), the transferee takes the collateral subject to:

(1) the debtor's rights in the collateral;

(2) the security interest or agricultural lien under which the disposition is made; and

(3) any other security interest or other lien.

Added by Acts 1999, 76th Leg., ch. 414, § 1.01, eff. July 1, 2001.

Uniform Commercial Code Comment

1. **Source.** Former Section 9–504(4).

2. **Title Taken by Good–Faith Transferee.** Subsection (a) sets forth the rights acquired by persons who qualify under subsection (b)–transferees who act in good faith. Such a person is a "transferee," inasmuch as a buyer at a foreclosure sale does not meet the definition of "purchaser" in Section 1–201 (the transfer is not, vis-a-vis the debtor, "voluntary"). By virtue of the expanded definition of the term "debtor" in Section 9–102, subsection (a) makes clear that the ownership interest of a person who bought the collateral subject to the security interest is terminated by a subsequent disposition under this Part. Such a person is a debtor under this Article. Under former Article 9, the result arguably was the same, but the statute was less clear. Under subsection (a), a disposition normally discharges the security interest being foreclosed and any subordinate security interests and other liens.

A disposition has the effect specified in subsection (a), even if the secured party fails to comply with this Article. An aggrieved person (e.g., the holder of a subordinate security interest to whom a notification required by Section 9–611 was not sent) has a right to recover any loss under Section 9–625(b).

3. **Unitary Standard in Public and Private Dispositions.** Subsection (b) now contains a unitary standard that applies to transferees in both private and public dispositions—acting in good faith. However, this change from former Section 9–504(4) should not be interpreted to mean that a transferee acts in good faith even though it has knowledge of defects or buys in collusion, standards applicable to public dispositions under the former section. Properly understood, those standards were specific examples of the absence of good faith.

4. **Title Taken by Nonqualifying Transferee.** Subsection (c) specifies the consequences for a transferee who does not qualify for protection under subsections (a) and (b) (i.e., a transferee who does not act in good faith). The transferee takes subject to the rights of the debtor, the enforcing secured party, and other security interests or other liens.

§ 9.618. Rights and Duties of Certain Secondary Obligors

(a) A secondary obligor acquires the rights and becomes obligated to perform the duties of the secured party after the secondary obligor:

(1) receives an assignment of a secured obligation from the secured party;

(2) receives a transfer of collateral from the secured party and agrees to accept the rights and assume the duties of the secured party; or

(3) is subrogated to the rights of a secured party with respect to collateral.

(b) An assignment, transfer, or subrogation described in Subsection (a):

(1) is not a disposition of collateral under Section 9.610; and

(2) relieves the secured party of further duties under this chapter.

Added by Acts 1999, 76th Leg., ch. 414, § 1.01, eff. July 1, 2001.

Uniform Commercial Code Comment

1. **Source.** Former Section 9–504(5).

2. **Scope of This Section.** Under this section, assignments of secured obligations and other transactions (regardless of form) that function like assignments of secured obligations are not dispositions to which Part 6 applies. Rather, they constitute assignments of rights and (occasionally) delegations of duties. Application of this section may require an investigation into the agreement of the parties, which may not be reflected in the words of the repurchase agreement (e.g., when the agreement requires a recourse party to "purchase the collateral" but contemplates that the purchaser will then conduct an Article 9 foreclosure disposition).

This section, like former Section 9–504(5), does not constitute a general and comprehensive rule for allocating rights and duties upon assignment of a secured obligation. Rather, it applies only in situations involving a secondary obligor described in subsection (a). In other contexts, the agreement of the parties and applicable law other than Article 9 determine whether the assignment imposes upon the assignee any duty to the debtor and whether the assignor retains its duties to the debtor after the assignment.

Subsection (a)(1) applies when there has been an assignment of an obligation that is secured at the time it is assigned. Thus, if a secondary obligor acquires the collateral at a disposition under Section 9–610 and simultaneously or subsequently discharges the unsecured deficiency claim, subsection (a)(1) is not implicated. Similarly, subsection (a)(3) applies only when the secondary obligor is subrogated to the secured party's rights with respect to collateral. Thus, this subsection will not be implicated if a secondary obligor discharges the debtor's unsecured obligation for a post-disposition deficiency. Similarly, if the secured party disposes of some of the collateral and the secondary obligor thereafter discharges the remaining obligation, subsection (a) applies only with respect to rights and duties concerning the remaining collateral, and, under subsection (b), the subrogation is not a disposition *of the remaining collateral.*

As discussed more fully in Comment 3, a secondary obligor may receive a transfer of collateral in a disposition under Section 9–610 in exchange for a payment that is applied against the secured obligation. However, a secondary obligor who pays and receives a transfer of collateral does not necessarily become subrogated to the rights of the secured party as contemplated by subsection (a)(3). Only to the extent the secondary obligor makes a payment in satisfaction of its secondary obligation would it become subrogated. To the extent its payment constitutes the price of the collateral in a Section 9–610 disposition by the secured party, the secondary obligor would not be subrogated. Thus, if the amount paid by the secondary obligor for the collateral in a Section 9–610 disposition is itself insufficient to discharge the secured obligation, but the secondary obligor makes an additional payment that satisfies the remaining balance, the secondary obligor would be subrogated to the secured party's deficiency claim. However, the duties of the secured party *as such* would have come to an end with respect to that collateral. In some situations the capacity in which the payment is made may be unclear. Accordingly, the parties should in their relationship provide clear evidence of the nature and circumstances of the payment by the secondary obligor.

3. **Transfer of Collateral to Secondary Obligor.** It is possible for a secured party to transfer collateral to a secondary obligor in a transaction that is a disposition under Section 9–610 and that establishes a surplus or deficiency under Section 9–615. Indeed, this Article includes a special rule, in Section 9–615(f), for establishing a deficiency in the case of some dispositions to, *inter alia*, secondary obligors. This Article rejects the view, which some may have ascribed to former Section 9–504(5), that a transfer of collateral to a recourse party can *never* constitute a disposition of collateral which discharges a security interest. Inasmuch as a secured party could itself buy collateral at its own public sale, it makes no sense to prohibit a recourse party ever from buying at the sale.

4. **Timing and Scope of Obligations.** Under subsection (a), a recourse party acquires rights and incurs obligations only "after" one of the specified circumstances occurs. This makes clear that when a successor assignee, transferee, or subrogee becomes obligated it does not assume any liability for earlier actions or inactions of the secured party whom it has succeeded unless it agrees to do so. Once the successor becomes obligated, however, it is responsible for complying with the secured party's duties thereafter. For example, if the successor is in possession of collateral, then it has the duties specified in Section 9–207.

Under subsection (b), the same event (assignment, transfer, or subrogation) that gives rise to rights to, and imposes obligations on, a successor relieves its predecessor of any further duties under this Article. For example, if the security interest is enforced after the secured obligation is assigned, the assignee–but not the assignor–has the duty to comply with this Part. Similarly, the assignment does not excuse the assignor from liability for failure to comply with duties that arose before the event or impose liability on the assignee for the assignor's failure to comply.

§ 9.619. Transfer of Record or Legal Title

(a) In this section, "transfer statement" means a record authenticated by a secured party stating:

(1) that the debtor has defaulted in connection with an obligation secured by specified collateral;

(2) that the secured party has exercised its post-default remedies with respect to the collateral;

(3) that, by reason of the exercise, a transferee has acquired the rights of the debtor in the collateral; and

(4) the name and mailing address of the secured party, debtor, and transferee.

(b) A transfer statement entitles the transferee to the transfer of record of all rights of the debtor in the collateral specified in the statement in any official filing, recording, registration, or certificate-of-title system covering the collateral. If a transfer statement is presented with the applicable fee and request form to the official or office responsible for maintaining the system, the official or office shall:

(1) accept the transfer statement;

(2) promptly amend its records to reflect the transfer; and

(3) if applicable, issue a new appropriate certificate of title in the name of the transferee.

(c) A transfer of the record or legal title to collateral to a secured party under Subsection (b) or otherwise is not of itself a disposition of collateral under this chapter and does not of itself relieve the secured party of its duties under this chapter.

Added by Acts 1999, 76th Leg., ch. 414, § 1.01, eff. July 1, 2001.

Uniform Commercial Code Comment

1. **Source.** New.

2. **Transfer of Record or Legal Title.** Potential buyers of collateral that is covered by a certificate of title (e.g., an automobile) or is subject to a registration system (e.g., a copyright) typically require as a condition of their purchase that the certificate or registry reflect their ownership. In many cases, this condition can be met only with the consent of the record owner. If the record owner is the debtor and, as may be the case after the default, the debtor refuses to cooperate, the secured party may have great difficulty disposing of the collateral.

Subsection (b) provides a simple mechanism for obtaining record or legal title, for use primarily when other law does not provide one. Of course, use of this mechanism will not be effective to clear title to the extent that subsection (b) is preempted by federal law. Subsection (b) contemplates a transfer of record or legal title to a third party, following a secured party's exercise of its disposition or acceptance remedies under this Part, as well as a transfer by a debtor to a secured party prior to the secured party's exercise of those remedies. Under subsection (c), a transfer of record or legal title (under subsection (b) or under other law) to a secured party prior to the exercise of those remedies merely puts the secured party in a position to pass legal or record title to a transferee at foreclosure. A secured party who has obtained record or legal title retains its duties with respect to enforcement of its security interest, and the debtor retains its rights as well.

3. **Title-Clearing Systems Under Other Law.** Applicable non-UCC law (e.g., a certificate-of-title statute, federal registry rules, or the like) may provide a means by which the secured party may obtain or transfer record or legal title for the purpose of a disposition of the property under this Article. The mechanism provided by this section is in addition to any title-clearing provision under law other than this Article.

§ 9.620. Acceptance of Collateral in Full or Partial Satisfaction of Obligation; Compulsory Disposition of Collateral

(a) Except as otherwise provided in Subsection (g), a secured party may accept collateral in full or partial satisfaction of the obligation it secures only if:

(1) the debtor consents to the acceptance under Subsection (c);

(2) the secured party does not receive, within the time set forth in Subsection (d), a notification of objection to the proposal authenticated by:

(A) a person to which the secured party was required to send a proposal under Section 9.621; or

(B) any other person, other than the debtor, holding an interest in the collateral subordinate to the security interest that is the subject of the proposal;

(3) if the collateral is consumer goods, the collateral is not in the possession of the debtor when the debtor consents to the acceptance; and

(4) Subsection (e) does not require the secured party to dispose of the collateral or the debtor waives the requirement pursuant to Section 9.624.

(b) A purported or apparent acceptance of collateral under this section is ineffective unless:

(1) the secured party consents to the acceptance in an authenticated record or sends a proposal to the debtor; and

(2) the conditions of Subsection (a) are met.

(c) For purposes of this section:

(1) a debtor consents to an acceptance of collateral in partial satisfaction of the obligation it secures only if the debtor agrees to the terms of the acceptance in a record authenticated after default; and

(2) a debtor consents to an acceptance of collateral in full satisfaction of the obligation it secures only if the debtor agrees to the terms of the acceptance in a record authenticated after default or the secured party:

(A) sends to the debtor after default a proposal that is unconditional or subject only to a condition that collateral not in the possession of the secured party be preserved or maintained;

(B) in the proposal, proposes to accept collateral in full satisfaction of the obligation it secures; and

(C) does not receive a notification of objection authenticated by the debtor within 20 days after the proposal is sent.

(d) To be effective under Subsection (a)(2), a notification of objection must be received by the secured party:

(1) in the case of a person to which the proposal was sent pursuant to Section 9.621, within 20 days after notification was sent to that person; and

(2) in other cases:

(A) within 20 days after the last notification was sent pursuant to Section 9.621; or

(B) if a notification was not sent, before the debtor consents to the acceptance under Subsection (c).

(e) A secured party that has taken possession of collateral shall dispose of the collateral pursuant to Section 9.610 within the time specified in Subsection (f) if:

(1) 60 percent of the cash price has been paid in the case of a purchase-money security interest in consumer goods; or

(2) 60 percent of the principal amount of the obligation secured has been paid in the case of a non-purchase-money security interest in consumer goods.

(f) To comply with Subsection (e), the secured party shall dispose of the collateral:

(1) within 90 days after taking possession; or

(2) within any longer period to which the debtor and all secondary obligors have agreed in an agreement to that effect entered into and authenticated after default.

(g) In a consumer transaction, a secured party may not accept collateral in partial satisfaction of the obligation it secures.

Added by Acts 1999, 76th Leg., ch. 414, § 1.01, eff. July 1, 2001.

Uniform Commercial Code Comment

1. **Source.** Former Section 9–505.

2. **Overview.** This section and the two sections following deal with strict foreclosure, a procedure by which the secured party acquires the debtor's interest in the collateral without the need for a sale or other disposition under Section 9–610. Although these provisions derive from former Section 9–505, they have been entirely reorganized and substantially rewritten. The more straightforward approach taken in this Article eliminates the fiction that the secured party always will present a "proposal" for the retention of collateral and the debtor will have a fixed period to respond. By eliminating the need (but preserving the possibility) for proceeding in that fashion, this section eliminates much of the awkwardness of former Section 9–505. It reflects the belief that strict foreclosures should be encouraged and often will produce better results than a disposition for all concerned.

Subsection (a) sets forth the conditions necessary to an effective acceptance (formerly, retention) of collateral in full or partial satisfaction of the secured obligation. Section 9–621 requires in addition that a secured party who wishes to proceed under this section notify certain other persons who have or claim to have an interest in the collateral. Unlike the failure to meet the conditions in subsection (a), under Section 9–622(b) the failure to comply with the notification requirement of Section 9–621 does not render the acceptance of collateral ineffective. Rather, the acceptance can take effect notwithstanding the secured party's noncompliance. A person to whom the required notice was not sent has the right to recover damages under Section 9–625(b). Section 9–622(a) sets forth the effect of an acceptance of collateral.

3. **Conditions to Effective Acceptance.** Subsection (a) contains the conditions necessary to the effectiveness of an acceptance of collateral. Subsection (a)(1) requires the debtor's consent. Under subsections (c)(1) and (c)(2), the debtor may consent by agreeing to the acceptance in writing after default. Subsection (c)(2) contains an alternative method by which to satisfy the debtor's-consent condition in subsection (a)(1). It follows the proposal-and-objection model found in former Section 9–505: The debtor consents if the secured party sends a proposal to the debtor and does not receive an objection within 20 days. Under subsection (c)(1), however, that silence is not deemed to be consent with respect to acceptances in partial satisfaction. Thus, a secured party who wishes to conduct a "partial strict foreclosure" must obtain the debtor's agreement in a record authenticated after default. In all other respects, the conditions necessary to an effective partial strict foreclosure are the same as those governing acceptance of collateral in full satisfaction.

The time when a debtor consents to a strict foreclosure is significant in several circumstances under this section and the following one. See Sections 9–620(a)(1), (d)(2), 9–621(a)(1), (a)(2), (a)(3). For purposes of determining the time of consent, a debtor's conditional consent constitutes consent.

Subsection (a)(2) contains the second condition to the effectiveness of an acceptance under this section–the absence of a timely objection from a person holding a junior interest in the collateral or from a secondary obligor. Any junior party–secured party or lienholder–is entitled to lodge an objection to a proposal, even if that person was not entitled to notification under Section 9–621. Subsection (d), discussed below, indicates when an objection is timely.

Subsections (a)(3) and (a)(4) contain special rules for transactions in which consumers are involved. See Comment 12.

4. **Proposals.** Section 9–102 defines the term "proposal." It is necessary to send a "proposal" to the debtor only if the debtor does not agree to an acceptance in an authenticated record as described in subsection (c)(1) or (c)(2). Section 9–621(a) determines whether it is necessary to send a proposal to third parties. A proposal need not take any particular form as long as it sets forth the terms under which the secured party is willing to accept collateral in satisfaction. A proposal to accept collateral should specify the amount (or a means of calculating the amount, such as by including a per diem accrual figure) of the secured obligations to be satisfied, state the conditions (if any) under which the proposal may be revoked, and describe any other applicable conditions. Note, however, that a conditional proposal generally requires the debtor's agreement in order to take effect. See subsection (c).

5. **Secured Party's Agreement; No "Constructive" Strict Foreclosure.** The conditions of subsection (a) relate to actual or implied consent by the debtor and any secondary obligor or holder of a junior security interest or lien. To ensure that the debtor cannot unilaterally cause an acceptance of collateral, subsection (b) provides that compliance with these conditions is necessary but not sufficient to cause an acceptance of collateral. Rather, under subsection (b), acceptance does not occur unless, in addition, the secured party consents to the acceptance in an authenticated record or sends to the debtor a proposal. For this reason, a mere delay in collection or disposition of collateral does not constitute a "constructive" strict foreclosure. Instead, delay is a factor relating to whether the secured party acted in a commercially reasonable manner for purposes of Section 9–607 or 9–610. A debtor's voluntary surrender of collateral to a secured party and the secured party's acceptance of possession of the collateral does not, of itself, necessarily raise an implication that the secured party intends or is proposing to accept the collateral in satisfaction of the secured obligation under this section.

6. **When Acceptance Occurs.** This section does not impose any formalities or identify any steps that a secured party must take in order to accept collateral once the conditions of subsections (a) and (b) have been met. Absent facts or circumstances indicating a contrary intention, the fact that the conditions have been met provides a sufficient indication that the secured party has accepted the collateral on the terms to which the secured party has consented or proposed and the debtor has consented or failed to object. Following a proposal, acceptance of the collateral normally is automatic upon the secured party's becoming bound and the time for objection passing. As a matter of good business practice, an enforcing secured party may wish to memorialize its acceptance following a proposal, such as by notifying the debtor that the strict foreclosure is effective or by placing a written record to that effect in its files. The secured party's agreement to accept collateral is self-executing and cannot be breached. The secured party is bound by its agreement to accept collateral and by any proposal to which the debtor consents.

7. **No Possession Requirement.** This section eliminates the requirement in former Section 9–505 that the secured party be "in possession" of collateral. It clarifies that intangible collateral, which cannot be possessed, may be subject to a strict foreclosure under this section. However, under subsection (a)(3), if the collateral is consumer goods, acceptance does not occur unless the debtor is not in possession.

8. **When Objection Timely.** Subsection (d) explains when an objection is timely and thus prevents an acceptance of collateral from taking effect. An objection by a person to which notification was sent under Section 9–621 is effective if it is received by the secured party within 20 days from the date the notification was sent to that person. Other objecting parties (i.e., third parties who are not entitled to notification) may object at any time within 20 days after the last notification is sent under Section 9–621. If no such notification is sent, third parties must object before the debtor agrees to the acceptance in writing or is deemed to have consented by silence. The former may occur any time after default, and the latter requires a 20–day waiting period. See subsection (c).

9. **Applicability of Other Law.** This section does not purport to regulate all aspects of the transaction by which a secured party may become the owner of collateral previously owned by the debtor. For example, a secured party's acceptance of a motor vehicle in satisfaction of secured obligations may require compliance with the applicable motor vehicle certificate-of-title law. State legislatures should conform those laws so that they mesh well with this section and Section 9–610, and courts should construe those laws and this section harmoniously. A secured party's acceptance of collateral in the possession of the debtor also may implicate statutes dealing with a seller's retention of possession of goods sold.

10. **Accounts, Chattel Paper, Payment Intangibles, and Promissory Notes.** If the collateral is accounts, chattel paper, payment intangibles, or promissory notes, then a secured party's acceptance of the collateral in satisfaction of secured obligations would constitute a sale to the secured party. That sale normally would give rise to a new security interest (the ownership interest) under Sections 1–201(37) and 9–109. In the case of accounts and chattel paper, the new security interest would remain perfected by a filing that was effective to perfect the secured party's original security interest. In the case of payment intangibles or promissory notes, the security interest would be perfected when it attaches. See Section 9–309. However, the procedures for acceptance of collateral under this section satisfy all necessary formalities and a new security agreement authenticated by the debtor would not be necessary.

11. **Role of Good Faith.** Section 1–203 imposes an obligation of good faith on a secured party's enforcement under this Article. This obligation may not be disclaimed by agreement. See Section 1–102. Thus, a proposal and acceptance made under this section in bad faith would not be effective. For example, a secured party's proposal to accept marketable securities worth $1,000 in full satisfaction of indebtedness in the amount of $100, made in the hopes that the debtor might inadvertently fail to object, would be made in bad faith. On the other hand, in the normal case proposals and acceptances should be not second-guessed on the basis of the "value" of the collateral involved. Disputes about valuation or even a clear excess of collateral value over the amount of obligations satisfied do not necessarily demonstrate the absence of good faith.

12. **Special Rules in Consumer Cases.** Subsection (e) imposes an obligation on the secured party to dispose of consumer goods under certain circumstances. Subsection (f) explains when a disposition that is required under subsection (e) is timely. An effective acceptance of collateral cannot occur if subsection (e) requires a disposition unless the debtor waives this requirement pursuant to Section 9–624(b). Moreover, a secured party who takes possession of collateral and unreasonably delays disposition violates subsection (e), if applicable, and may also violate Section 9–610 or other provisions of this Part. Subsection (e) eliminates as superfluous the express statutory reference to "conversion" found in former Section 9–505. Remedies available under other law, including conversion, remain available under this Article in appropriate cases. See Sections 1–103, 1–106.

Subsection (g) prohibits the secured party in consumer transactions from accepting collateral in partial satisfaction of the obligation it secures. If a secured party attempts an acceptance in partial satisfaction in a consumer transaction, the attempted acceptance is void.

State Bar Committee Comment

As noted in Official Comment 5, this section prohibits an "involuntary" or "constructive" strict foreclosure. This will change the result in cases that have held that a secured party's conduct could result in an involuntary strict foreclosure and a corresponding waiver of any deficiency claim. See, e.g., *In re Boyd,* 73 B.R. 122 (Bankr. N.D. Tex. 1987) (finding bank employee's use of repossessed boat manifested intent to keep collateral and forgive debt); *Tanenbaum v. Economics Laboratory, Inc.,* 628 S.W.2d 769 (Tex. 1982) (holding creditor's decision to scrap repossessed restaurant equipment amounted to strict foreclosure).

§ 9.621. Notification of Proposal to Accept Collateral

(a) A secured party that desires to accept collateral in full or partial satisfaction of the obligation it secures shall send its proposal to:

(1) any person from which the secured party has received, before the debtor consented to the acceptance, an authenticated notification of a claim of an interest in the collateral;

(2) any other secured party or lienholder that, 10 days before the debtor consented to the acceptance, held a security interest in or other lien on the collateral perfected by the filing of a financing statement that:

(A) identified the collateral;

(B) was indexed under the debtor's name as of that date; and

(C) was filed in the office or offices in which to file a financing statement against the debtor covering the collateral as of that date; and

(3) any other secured party that, 10 days before the debtor consented to the acceptance, held a security interest in the collateral perfected by compliance with a statute, regulation, or treaty described in Section 9.311(a).

(b) A secured party that desires to accept collateral in partial satisfaction of the obligation it secures shall send its proposal to any secondary obligor in addition to the persons described in Subsection (a).

Added by Acts 1999, 76th Leg., ch. 414, § 1.01, eff. July 1, 2001.

Uniform Commercial Code Comment

1. **Source.** Former Section 9–505.

2. **Notification Requirement.** Subsection (a) specifies three classes of competing claimants to whom the secured party must send notification of its proposal: (i) those who notify the secured party that they claim an interest in the collateral, (ii) holders of certain security interests and liens who have filed against the debtor, and (iii) holders of certain security interests who have perfected by compliance with a statute (including a certificate-of-title statute), regulation, or treaty described in Section 9–311(a). With regard to (ii), see Section 9–611, Comment 4. Subsection (b) also requires notification to any secondary obligor if the proposal is for acceptance in partial satisfaction.

Unlike Section 9–611, this section contains no "safe harbor," which excuses an enforcing secured party from notifying certain secured parties and other lienholders. This is because, unlike Section 9–610, which requires that a disposition of collateral be commercially reasonable, Section 9–620 permits the debtor and secured party to set the amount of credit the debtor will receive for the collateral subject only to the requirement of good faith. An effective acceptance discharges subordinate security interests and other subordinate liens. See Section 9–622. If collateral is subject to several liens securing debts much larger than the value of the collateral, the debtor may be disinclined to refrain from consenting to an acceptance by the holder of the senior security interest, even though, had the debtor objected and the senior disposed of the collateral under Section 9–610, the collateral may have yielded more than enough to satisfy the senior security interest (but not enough to satisfy all the liens). Accordingly, this section imposes upon the enforcing secured party the risk of the filing office's errors and delay. The holder of a security interest who is entitled to notification under this section but does not receive it has the right to recover under Section 9–625(b) any loss resulting from the enforcing secured party's noncompliance with this section.

§ 9.622. Effect of Acceptance of Collateral

(a) A secured party's acceptance of collateral in full or partial satisfaction of the obligation it secures:

(1) discharges the obligation to the extent consented to by the debtor;

(2) transfers to the secured party all of a debtor's rights in the collateral;

(3) discharges the security interest or agricultural lien that is the subject of the debtor's consent and any subordinate security interest or other subordinate lien; and

(4) terminates any other subordinate interest.

(b) A subordinate interest is discharged or terminated under Subsection (a), even if the secured party fails to comply with this chapter.

Added by Acts 1999, 76th Leg., ch. 414, § 1.01, eff. July 1, 2001.

Uniform Commercial Code Comment

1. **Source.** New.

2. **Effect of Acceptance.** Subsection (a) specifies the effect of an acceptance of collateral in full or partial satisfaction of the secured obligation. The acceptance to which it refers is an effective acceptance. If a purported acceptance is ineffective under Section 9–620, e.g., because the secured party receives a timely objection from a person entitled to notification, then neither this subsection nor subsection (b) applies. Paragraph (1) expresses the fundamental consequence of accepting collateral in full or partial satisfaction of the secured obligation–the obligation is discharged to the extent consented to by the debtor. Unless otherwise agreed, the obligor remains liable for any deficiency. Paragraphs (2) through (4) indicate the effects of an acceptance on various property rights and interests. Paragraph (2) follows Section 9–617(a) in providing that the secured party acquires "all of a debtor's rights in the collateral." Under paragraph (3), the effect of strict foreclosure on holders of junior security interests and other liens is the same regardless of whether the collateral is accepted in full or partial satisfaction of the secured obligation: all junior encumbrances are discharged. Paragraph (4) provides for the termination of other subordinate interests.

Subsection (b) makes clear that subordinate interests are discharged under subsection (a) regardless of whether the secured party complies with this Article. Thus, subordinate interests are discharged regardless of whether a proposal was required to be sent or, if required, was sent. However, a secured party's failure to send a proposal or otherwise to comply with this Article may subject the secured party to liability under Section 9–625.

§ 9.623. Right to Redeem Collateral

(a) A debtor, any secondary obligor, or any other secured party or lienholder may redeem collateral.

(b) To redeem collateral, a person shall tender:

(1) fulfillment of all obligations secured by the collateral; and

(2) the reasonable expenses and attorneys' fees described in Section 9.615(a)(1).

(c) A redemption may occur at any time before a secured party:

(1) has collected collateral under Section 9.607;

(2) has disposed of collateral or entered into a contract for its disposition under Section 9.610; or

(3) has accepted collateral in full or partial satisfaction of the obligation it secures under Section 9.622.

Added by Acts 1999, 76th Leg., ch. 414, § 1.01, eff. July 1, 2001.

Uniform Commercial Code Comment

1. **Source.** Former Section 9–506.

2. **Redemption Right.** Under this section, as under former Section 9–506, the debtor or another secured party may redeem collateral as long as the secured party has not collected (Section 9–607), disposed of or contracted for the disposition of (Section 9–610), or accepted (Section 9–620) the collateral. Although this section generally follows former Section 9–506, it extends the right of redemption to holders of nonconsensual liens. To redeem the collateral a person must tender fulfillment of all obligations secured, plus certain expenses. If the entire balance of a secured obligation has been accelerated, it would be necessary to tender the entire balance. A tender of fulfillment obviously means more than a new promise to perform an existing promise. It requires payment in full of all monetary obligations then due and performance in full of all other obligations then matured. If unmatured secured obligations remain, the security interest continues to secure them (i.e., as if there had been no default).

3. **Redemption of Remaining Collateral Following Partial Enforcement.** Under Section 9–610 a secured party may make successive dispositions of portions of its collateral. These dispositions would not affect the debtor's, another secured party's, or a lienholder's right to redeem the remaining collateral.

4. **Effect of "Repledging."** Section 9–207 generally permits a secured party having possession or control of collateral to create a security interest in the collateral. As explained in the Comments to that section, the debtor's right (as opposed to its practical ability) to redeem collateral is not affected by, and does not affect, the priority of a security interest created by the debtor's secured party.

State Bar Committee Comment

Official Comment 2 states: "To redeem the collateral a person must tender fulfillment of all obligations secured, plus certain expenses. If the entire balance of a secured obligation has been accelerated, it would be necessary to tender the entire balance." Before exercising its rights under an acceleration clause, a secured party must present the promissory note to the maker and notify the maker of the secured party's intent to accelerate and the secured party's acceleration, unless the maker has waived its right to presentment, notice of intent to accelerate, and notice of acceleration in a clear and unequivocal manner. See *Shumway v. Horizon Credit Corp.*, 801 S.W.2d 890 (Tex. 1991).

§ 9.624. Waiver

(a) A debtor or secondary obligor may waive the right to notification of disposition of collateral under Section 9.611 only by an agreement to that effect entered into and authenticated after default.

(b) A debtor may waive the right to require disposition of collateral under Section 9.620(e) only by an agreement to that effect entered into and authenticated after default.

(c) Except in a consumer-goods transaction, a debtor or secondary obligor may waive the right to redeem collateral under Section 9.623 only by an agreement to that effect entered into and authenticated after default.

Added by Acts 1999, 76th Leg., ch. 414, § 1.01, eff. July 1, 2001.

Uniform Commercial Code Comment

1. **Source.** Former Sections 9–504(3), 9–505, 9–506.

2. **Waiver.** This section is a limited exception to Section 9–602, which generally prohibits waiver by debtors and obligors. It makes no provision for waiver of the rule prohibiting a secured party from buying at its own private disposition. Transactions of this kind are equivalent to "strict foreclosures" and are governed by Sections 9–620, 9–621, and 9–622.

§ 9.625. Remedies For Secured Party's Failure to Comply With Chapter

(a) If it is established that a secured party is not proceeding in accordance with this chapter, a court may order or restrain collection, enforcement, or disposition of collateral on appropriate terms and conditions.

(b) Subject to Subsections (c), (d), and (f), a person is liable for damages in the amount of any loss caused by a failure to comply with this chapter. Loss caused by a failure to comply may include loss resulting from the debtor's inability to obtain, or increased costs of, alternative financing.

(c) Except as otherwise provided in Section 9.628:

(1) a person that, at the time of the failure, was a debtor, was an obligor, or held a security interest in or other lien on the collateral may recover damages under Subsection (b) for its loss; and

(2) if the collateral is consumer goods, a person that was a debtor or a secondary obligor at the time a secured party failed to comply with this subchapter may recover for that failure in any event an amount not less than the credit service charge plus 10 percent of the principal amount of the obligation or the time price differential plus 10 percent of the cash price.

(d) A debtor whose deficiency is eliminated under Section 9.626 may recover damages for the loss of any surplus. However, a debtor or secondary obligor whose deficiency is eliminated or reduced under Section 9.626 may not otherwise recover under Subsection (b) for noncompliance with the provisions of this subchapter relating to collection, enforcement, disposition, or acceptance.

(e) In addition to any damages recoverable under Subsection (b), the debtor, consumer obligor, or person named as a debtor in a filed record, as applicable, may recover $500 in each case from a person that:

(1) fails to comply with Section 9.208;

(2) fails to comply with Section 9.209;

(3) files a record that the person is not entitled to file under Section 9.509(a);

(4) fails to cause the secured party of record to file or send a termination statement as required by Section 9.513(a) or (c);

(5) fails to comply with Section 9.616(b)(1) and whose failure is part of a pattern, or consistent with a practice, of noncompliance; or

(6) fails to comply with Section 9.616(b)(2).

(f) A debtor or consumer obligor may recover damages under Subsection (b) and, in addition, $500 in each case from a person that, without reasonable cause, fails to comply with a request under Section 9.210. A recipient of a request under Section 9.210 that never claimed an interest in the collateral or obligations that are the subject of a request under that section has a reasonable excuse for failure to comply with the request within the meaning of this subsection.

(g) If a secured party fails to comply with a request regarding a list of collateral or a statement of account under Section 9.210, the secured party may claim a security interest only as shown in the list or statement included in the request as against a person that is reasonably misled by the failure.

Added by Acts 1999, 76th Leg., ch. 414, § 1.01, eff. July 1, 2001. Amended by Acts 2001, 77th Leg., ch. 705, § 22, eff. June 13, 2001.

Uniform Commercial Code Comment

1. **Source.** Former Section 9–507.

2. **Remedies for Noncompliance; Scope.** Subsections (a) and (b) provide the basic remedies afforded to those aggrieved by a secured party's failure to comply with this Article. Like all provisions that create liability, they are subject to Section 9–628, which should be read in conjunction with Section 9–605. The principal limitations under this Part on a secured party's right to enforce its security interest against collateral are the requirements that it proceed in good faith (Section 1–203), in a commercially reasonable manner (Sections 9–607 and 9–610), and, in most cases, with reasonable notification (Sections 9–611 through 9–614). Following former Section 9–507, under subsection (a) an aggrieved person may seek injunctive relief, and under subsection (b) the person may recover damages for losses caused by noncompliance. Unlike former Section 9–507, however, subsections (a) and (b) are not limited to noncompliance with provisions of this Part of Article 9. Rather, they apply to noncompliance with any provision of this Article. The change makes this section applicable to noncompliance with Sections 9–207 (duties of secured party in possession of collateral), 9–208 (duties of secured party having control over deposit account), 9–209 (duties of secured party if account debtor has been notified of an assignment), 9–210 (duty to comply with request for accounting, etc.), 9–509(a) (duty to refrain from filing unauthorized financing statement), and 9–513(a) or (c) (duty to provide termination statement). Subsection (a) also modifies the first sentence of former Section 9–507(1) by adding the references to "collection" and "enforcement." Subsection (c)(2), which gives a minimum damage recovery in consumer-goods transactions, applies only to noncompliance with the provisions of this Part.

3. **Damages for Noncompliance with This Article.** Subsection (b) sets forth the basic remedy for failure to comply with the requirements of this Article: a damage recovery in the amount of loss caused by the noncompliance. Subsection (c) identifies who may recover under subsection (b). It affords a remedy to any aggrieved person who is a debtor or obligor. However, a principal obligor who is not a debtor may recover damages only for noncompliance with Section 9–616, inasmuch as none of the other rights and duties in this Article run in favor of such a principal obligor. Such a principal obligor could not suffer any loss or damage on account of noncompliance with rights or duties of which it is not a beneficiary. Subsection (c) also affords a remedy to an aggrieved person who holds a competing security interest or other lien, regardless of whether the aggrieved person is entitled to notification under Part 6. The remedy is available even to holders of senior security interests and other liens. The exercise of this remedy is subject to the normal rules of pleading and proof. A person who has delegated the duties of a secured party but who remains obligated to perform them is liable under this subsection. The last sentence of

subsection (d) eliminates the possibility of double recovery or other over-compensation arising out of a reduction or elimination of a deficiency under Section 9–626, based on noncompliance with the provisions of this Part relating to collection, enforcement, disposition, or acceptance. Assuming no double recovery, a debtor whose deficiency is eliminated under Section 9–626 may pursue a claim for a surplus. Because Section 9–626 does not apply to consumer transactions, the statute is silent as to whether a double recovery or other over-compensation is possible in a consumer transaction.

Damages for violation of the requirements of this Article, including Section 9–609, are those reasonably calculated to put an eligible claimant in the position that it would have occupied had no violation occurred. See Section 1–106. Subsection (b) supports the recovery of actual damages for committing a breach of the peace in violation of Section 9–609, and principles of tort law supplement this subsection. See Section 1–103. However, to the extent that damages in tort compensate the debtor for the same loss dealt with by this Article, the debtor should be entitled to only one recovery.

4. **Minimum Damages in Consumer-Goods Transactions.** Subsection (c)(2) provides a minimum, statutory, damage recovery for a debtor and secondary obligor in a consumer-goods transaction. It is patterned on former Section 9–507(1) and is designed to ensure that every noncompliance with the requirements of Part 6 in a consumer-goods transaction results in liability, regardless of any injury that may have resulted. Subsection (c)(2) leaves the treatment of statutory damages as it was under former Article 9. A secured party is not liable for statutory damages under this subsection more than once with respect to any one secured obligation (see Section 9–628(e)), nor is a secured party liable under this subsection for failure to comply with Section 9–616 (see Section 9–628(d)).

Following former Section 9–507(1), this Article does not include a definition or explanation of the terms "credit service charge," "principal amount," "time-price differential," or "cash price," as used in subsection (c)(2). It leaves their construction and application to the court, taking into account the subsection's purpose of providing a minimum recovery in consumer-goods transactions.

5. **Supplemental Damages.** Subsections (e) and (f) provide damages that supplement the recovery, if any, under subsection (b). Subsection (e) imposes an additional $500 liability upon a person who fails to comply with the provisions specified in that subsection, and subsection (f) imposes like damages on a person who, without reasonable excuse, fails to comply with a request for an accounting or a request regarding a list of collateral or statement of account under Section 9–210. However, under subsection (f), a person has a reasonable excuse for the failure if the person never claimed an interest in the collateral or obligations that were the subject of the request.

6. **Estoppel.** Subsection (g) limits the extent to which a secured party who fails to comply with a request regarding a list of collateral or statement of account may claim a security interest.

§ 9.626. Action in Which Deficiency or Surplus is in Issue

(a) In an action arising from a transaction, other than a consumer transaction, in which the amount of a deficiency or surplus is in issue, the following rules apply:

(1) A secured party need not prove compliance with the provisions of this subchapter relating to collection, enforcement, disposition, or acceptance unless the debtor or a secondary obligor places the secured party's compliance in issue.

(2) If the secured party's compliance is placed in issue, the secured party has the burden of establishing that the collection, enforcement, disposition, or acceptance was conducted in accordance with this subchapter.

(3) Except as otherwise provided in Section 9.628, if a secured party fails to prove that the collection, enforcement, disposition, or acceptance was conducted in accordance with the provisions of this subchapter relating to collection, enforcement, disposition, or acceptance, the liability of a debtor or a secondary obligor for a deficiency is limited to an amount by which the sum of the secured obligation, expenses, and attorney's fees exceeds the greater of:

(A) the proceeds of the collection, enforcement, disposition, or acceptance; or

(B) the amount of proceeds that would have been realized had the noncomplying secured party proceeded in accordance with the provisions of this subchapter relating to collection, enforcement, disposition, or acceptance.

(4) For purposes of Subdivision (3)(B), the amount of proceeds that would have been realized is equal to the sum of the secured obligation, expenses, and attorney's fees unless the secured party proves that the amount is less than that sum.

(5) If a deficiency or surplus is calculated under Section 9.615(f), the debtor or obligor has the burden of establishing that the amount of proceeds of the disposition is significantly below the range of prices that a complying disposition to a person other than the secured party, a person related to the secured party, or a secondary obligor would have brought.

(b) The limitation of the rules in Subsection (a) to transactions other than consumer transactions is intended to leave to the court the determination of the proper rules in consumer transactions. The court may not infer from that limitation the nature of the proper rule in consumer transactions and may continue to apply established approaches.

Added by Acts 1999, 76th Leg., ch. 414, § 1.01, eff. July 1, 2001.

Uniform Commercial Code Comment

1. **Source.** New.

2. **Scope.** The basic damage remedy under Section 9–625(b) is subject to the special rules in this section for transactions other than consumer transactions. This section addresses situations in which the amount of a deficiency or surplus is in issue, i.e., situations in which the secured party has collected, enforced, disposed of, or accepted the collateral. It contains special rules applicable to a determination of the amount of a deficiency or surplus. Because this section affects a person's liability for a deficiency, it is subject to Section 9–628, which should be read in conjunction with Section 9–605. The rules in this section apply only to noncompliance in connection with the "collection, enforcement, disposition, or acceptance" under Part 6. For other types of noncompliance with Part 6, the general liability rule of Section 9–625(b)–recovery of actual damages–applies. Consider, for example, a repossession that does not comply with Section 9–609 for want of a default. The debtor's remedy is under Section 9–625(b). In a proper case, the secured party also may be liable for conversion under non-UCC law. If the secured party thereafter disposed of the collateral, however, it would violate Section 9–610 at that time, and this section would apply.

3. **Rebuttable Presumption Rule.** Subsection (a) establishes the rebuttable presumption rule for transactions other than consumer transactions. Under paragraph (1), the secured party need not prove compliance with the relevant provisions of this Part as part of its prima facie case. If, however, the debtor or a secondary obligor raises the issue (in accordance with the forum's rules of pleading and practice), then the secured party bears the burden of proving that the collection, enforcement, disposition, or acceptance complied. In the event the secured party is unable to meet this burden, then paragraph (3) explains how to calculate the deficiency. Under this rebuttable presumption rule, the debtor or obligor is to be credited with the greater of the actual proceeds of the disposition or the proceeds that would have been realized had the secured party complied with the relevant provisions. If a deficiency remains, then the secured party is entitled to recover it. The references to "the secured obligation, expenses, and attorney's fees" in paragraphs (3) and (4) embrace the application rules in Sections 9–608(a) and 9–615(a).

Unless the secured party proves that compliance with the relevant provisions would have yielded a smaller amount, under paragraph (4) the amount that a complying collection, enforcement, or disposition would have yielded is deemed to be equal to the amount of the secured obligation, together with expenses and attorney's fees. Thus, the secured party may not recover any deficiency unless it meets this burden.

4. **Consumer Transactions.** Although subsection (a) adopts a version of the rebuttable presumption rule for transactions other than consumer transactions, with certain exceptions Part 6 does not specify the effect of a secured party's noncompliance in consumer transactions. (The exceptions are the provisions for the recovery of damages in Section 9–625.) Subsection (b) provides that the limitation of subsection (a) to transactions other than consumer transactions is intended to leave to the court the determination of the proper rules in consumer transactions. It also instructs the court not to draw any inference from the limitation as to the proper rules for consumer transactions and leaves the court free to continue to apply established approaches to those transactions.

Courts construing former Section 9–507 disagreed about the consequences of a secured party's failure to comply with the requirements of former Part 5. Three general approaches emerged. Some courts have held that a noncomplying secured party may not recover a deficiency (the "absolute bar" rule). A few courts held that the debtor can offset against a claim to a deficiency all damages recoverable under former Section 9–507 resulting from the secured party's noncompliance (the "offset" rule). A plurality of courts considering the issue held that the noncomplying secured party is barred from recovering a deficiency unless it overcomes a rebuttable presumption that compliance with former Part 5 would have yielded an amount sufficient to satisfy the secured debt. In addition to the nonuniformity resulting from court decisions, some States enacted special rules governing the availability of deficiencies.

5. **Burden of Proof When Section 9–615(f) Applies.** In a non-consumer transaction, subsection (a)(5) imposes upon a debtor or obligor the burden of proving that the proceeds of a disposition are so low that, under Section 9–615(f), the actual proceeds should not serve as the basis upon which a deficiency or surplus is calculated. Were the burden placed on the secured party, then debtors might be encouraged to challenge the price received in every disposition to the secured party, a person related to the secured party, or a secondary obligor.

6. **Delay in Applying This Section.** There is an inevitable delay between the time a secured party engages in a noncomplying collection, enforcement, disposition, or acceptance and the time of a subsequent judicial determination that the secured party did not comply with Part 6. During the interim, the secured party, believing that the secured obligation is larger than it ultimately is determined to be, may continue to enforce its security interest in collateral. If some or all of the secured indebtedness ultimately is discharged under this section, a reasonable application of this section would impose liability on the secured party for the amount of any excess, unwarranted recoveries but would not make the enforcement efforts wrongful.

State Bar Committee Comment

Official Comment 3 states: "Subsection (a) establishes the refutable presumption rule for transactions other than consumer transactions." With respect to any transaction other than a consumer transaction, this is a change in Texas law, which has followed the "absolute bar" rule (a rule that bars a noncomplying secured party from collecting any deficiency). See *Tanenbaum v. Economics Laboratory, Inc.*, 628 S.W.2d 769 (Tex. 1982). The "absolute bar" rule remains the law in Texas in consumer transactions. Under subsection (a), a secured party is not required to prove compliance with the default provisions unless the debtor or a secondary obligor places the secured party's compliance in issue. This is a change in Texas law. In *Greathouse v. Charter National Bank–Southwest,* 851 S.W.2d 173 (Tex. 1992), the Texas Supreme Court held that a secured party in a deficiency suit must plead that its disposition of the collateral was commercially reasonable. The secured party may plead specifically or by averring generally that all conditions precedent have been performed or have occurred. If the secured party pleads generally, then the secured party is required to prove that the collateral disposition was commercially reasonable only if the debtor specifically denies it in his answer. Under *Greathouse,* if the secured party pleads specifically, then the secured party must prove its allegations. But under subsection (a), a secured party may plead specifically and yet not be required to prove compliance unless the debtor or a secondary obligor places the secured party's compliance in issue. As this section applies to transactions other than consumer transactions, *Greathouse* remains unchanged and continues to be the law in Texas in consumer transactions.

§ 9.627. Determination of Whether Conduct Was Commercially Reasonable

(a) The fact that a greater amount could have been obtained by a collection, enforcement, disposition, or acceptance at a different time or in a different method from that selected by the secured party is not of itself sufficient to preclude the secured party from establishing that the collection, enforcement, disposition, or acceptance was made in a commercially reasonable manner.

(b) A disposition of collateral is made in a commercially reasonable manner if the disposition is made:

(1) in the usual manner on any recognized market;

(2) at the price current in any recognized market at the time of the disposition; or

(3) otherwise in conformity with reasonable commercial practices among dealers in the type of property that was the subject of the disposition.

(c) A collection, enforcement, disposition, or acceptance is commercially reasonable if it has been approved:

(1) in a judicial proceeding;

(2) by a bona fide creditors' committee;

(3) by a representative of creditors; or

(4) by an assignee for the benefit of creditors.

(d) Approval under Subsection (c) need not be obtained, and lack of approval does not mean that the collection, enforcement, disposition, or acceptance is not commercially reasonable.

Added by Acts 1999, 76th Leg., ch. 414, § 1.01, eff. July 1, 2001.

Uniform Commercial Code Comment

1. **Source.** Former Section 9–507(2).

2. **Relationship of Price to Commercial Reasonableness.** Some observers have found the notion contained in subsection (a) (derived from former Section 9–507(2)) (the fact that a better price could have been obtained does not establish lack of commercial reasonableness) to be inconsistent with that found in Section 9–610(b) (derived from former Section 9–504(3)) (every aspect of the disposition, including its terms, must be commercially reasonable). There is no such inconsistency. While not itself sufficient to establish a violation of this Part, a low price suggests that a court should scrutinize carefully all aspects of a disposition to ensure that each aspect was commercially reasonable.

The law long has grappled with the problem of dispositions of personal and real property which comply with applicable procedural requirements (e.g., advertising, notification to interested persons, etc.) but which yield a price that seems low. This Article addresses that issue in Section 9–615(f). That section applies only when the transferee is the secured party, a person related to the secured party, or a secondary obligor. It contains a special rule for calculating a deficiency or surplus in a complying disposition that yields a price that is "significantly below the range of proceeds that a complying disposition to a person other than the secured party, a person related to the secured party, or a secondary obligor would have brought."

3. **Determination of Commercial Reasonableness; Advance Approval.** It is important to make clear the conduct and procedures that are commercially reasonable and to provide a secured party with the means of obtaining, by court order or negotiation with a creditors' committee or a representative of creditors, advance approval of a proposed method of enforcement as commercially reasonable. This section contains rules that assist in that determination and provides for advance approval in appropriate situations. However, none of the specific methods of disposition specified in subsection (b) is required or exclusive.

4. **"Recognized Market."** As in Sections 9–610(c) and 9–611(d), the concept of a "recognized market" in subsections (b)(1) and (2) is quite limited; it applies only to markets in which there are standardized price quotations for property that is essentially fungible, such as stock exchanges.

§ 9.628. Nonliability and Limitation on Liability of Secured Party; Liability of Secondary Obligor

(a) Unless a secured party knows that a person is a debtor or obligor, knows the identity of the person, and knows how to communicate with the person:

(1) the secured party is not liable to the person, or to a secured party or lienholder that has filed a financing statement against the person, for failure to comply with this chapter; and

(2) the secured party's failure to comply with this chapter does not affect the liability of the person for a deficiency.

(b) A secured party is not liable because of its status as secured party:

(1) to a person that is a debtor or obligor, unless the secured party knows:

(A) that the person is a debtor or obligor;

(B) the identity of the person; and

(C) how to communicate with the person; or

(2) to a secured party or lienholder that has filed a financing statement against a person, unless the secured party knows:

(A) that the person is a debtor; and

(B) the identity of the person.

(c) A secured party is not liable to any person, and a person's liability for a deficiency is not affected, because of any act or omission arising out of the secured party's reasonable belief that a transaction is not a consumer-goods transaction or a consumer transaction or that goods are not consumer goods, if the secured party's belief is based on its reasonable reliance on:

(1) a debtor's representation concerning the purpose for which collateral was to be used, acquired, or held; or

(2) an obligor's representation concerning the purpose for which a secured obligation was incurred.

(d) A secured party is not liable to any person under Section 9.625(c)(2) for its failure to comply with Section 9.616.

(e) A secured party is not liable under Section 9.625(c)(2) more than once with respect to any one secured obligation.

Added by Acts 1999, 76th Leg., ch. 414, § 1.01, eff. July 1, 2001.

Uniform Commercial Code Comment

1. **Source.** New.

2. **Exculpatory Provisions.** Subsections (a), (b), and (c) contain exculpatory provisions that should be read in conjunction with Section 9–605. Without this group of provisions, a secured party could incur liability to unknown persons and under circumstances that would not allow the secured party to protect itself. The broadened definition of the term "debtor" underscores the need for these provisions.

If a secured party reasonably, but mistakenly, believes that a consumer transaction or consumer-goods transaction is a non-consumer transaction or non-consumer-goods transaction, and if the secured party's belief is based on its reasonable reliance on a representation of the type specified in subsection (c)(1) or (c)(2), then this Article should be applied as if the facts reasonably believed and the representation reasonably relied upon were true. For example, if a secured party reasonably believed that a transaction was a non-consumer transaction and its belief was based on reasonable reliance on the debtor's representation that the collateral secured an obligation incurred for business purposes, the secured party is not liable to any person, and the debtor's liability for a deficiency is not affected, because of any act or omission of the secured party which arises out of the reasonable belief. Of course, if the secured party's belief is not reasonable or, even if reasonable, is not based on reasonable reliance on the debtor's representation, this limitation on liability is inapplicable.

3. **Inapplicability of Statutory Damages to Section 9–616.** Subsection (d) excludes noncompliance with Section 9–616 entirely from the scope of statutory damage liability under Section 9–625(c)(2).

4. **Single Liability for Statutory Minimum Damages.** Subsection (e) ensures that a secured party will incur statutory damages only once in connection with any one secured obligation.

SUBCHAPTER G. TRANSITION PROVISIONS

§ 9.701. Effective Date of Revisions

(a) In this subchapter, "revision" means the revision of this chapter enacted by the 76th Legislature, Regular Session, 1999.

(b) The revision takes effect July 1, 2001.

Reenacted from Acts 1999, 76th Leg., ch. 414 and amended by Acts 2001, 77th Leg., ch. 705, § 23, eff. June 13, 2001.

Uniform Commercial Code Comment

A uniform law as complex as Article 9 necessarily gives rise to difficult problems and uncertainties during the transition to the new law. As is customary for uniform laws, this Article is based on the general assumption that all States will have enacted substantially identical versions. While always important, uniformity is essential to the success of this Article. If former Article 9 is in effect in some jurisdictions, and this Article is in effect in others, horrendous complications may arise. For example, the proper place in which to file to perfect a security interest (and thus the status of a particular security interest as perfected or unperfected) would depend on whether the matter was litigated in a State in which former Article 9 was in effect or a State in which this Article was in effect. Accordingly, this section contemplates that States will adopt a uniform effective date for this Article. Any one State's failure to adopt the uniform effective date will greatly increase the cost and uncertainty surrounding the transition.

Other problems arise from transactions and relationships that were entered into under former Article 9 or under non-UCC law and which remain outstanding on the effective date of this Article. The difficulties arise primarily because this Article expands the scope of former Article 9 to cover additional types of collateral and transactions and because it provides new methods of perfection for some types of collateral, different priority rules, and different choice-of-law rules governing perfection and priority. This Section and the other sections in this Part address primarily this second set of problems.

§ 9.702. Saving Clause

(a) Except as otherwise provided in this subchapter, this chapter, as revised, applies to a transaction or lien within its scope, even if the transaction or lien was entered into or created before the revision takes effect.

(b) Except as otherwise provided in Subsection (c) and Sections 9.703–9.709:

(1) transactions and liens that were not governed by this chapter, as it existed immediately before the effective date of the revision, were validly entered into or created before the effective date of the revision, and would be subject to this chapter, as revised, if they had been entered into or created on or after the effective date of the revision, and the rights, duties, and interests flowing from those transactions and liens remain valid on and after the effective date of the revision; and

(2) the transactions and liens may be terminated, completed, consummated, and enforced as required or permitted by this chapter, as revised, or by the law that otherwise would apply if the revision had not taken effect.

(c) The revision does not affect an action, case, or proceeding commenced before the effective date of the revision.

Reenacted from Acts 1999, 76th Leg., ch. 414, § 3.02 and amended by Acts 2001, 77th Leg., ch. 705, § 23, eff. June 13, 2001.

Uniform Commercial Code Comment

1. **Pre-Effective-Date Transactions.** Subsection (a) contains the general rule that this Article applies to transactions, security interests, and other liens within its scope (see Section 9–109), even if the transaction or lien was entered into or created before the effective date. Thus, secured transactions entered into under former Article 9 must be terminated, completed, consummated, and enforced under this Article. Subsection (b) is an exception to the general rule. It applies to valid, pre-effective-date transactions and liens that were not governed by former Article 9 but would be governed by this Article if they had been entered into or created after this Article takes effect. Under subsection (b), these valid transactions, such as the creation of agricultural liens and security interests in commercial tort claims, retain their validity under this Article and may be terminated, completed, consummated, and enforced under this Article. However, these transactions also may be terminated, completed, consummated, and enforced by the law that otherwise would apply had this Article not taken effect.

2. **Judicial Proceedings Commenced Before Effective Date.** As is usual in transition provisions, subsection (c) provides that this Article does not affect litigation pending on the effective date.

§ 9.703. Security Interest Perfected Before Effective Date

(a) A security interest that is enforceable immediately before the effective date of the revision and would have priority over the rights of a person that becomes a lien creditor at that time is a perfected security interest under this chapter, as revised, if, on the effective date of the revision, the applicable requirements for enforceability and perfection under this chapter, as revised, are satisfied without further action.

(b) Except as otherwise provided in Section 9.705, if, immediately before the revision takes effect, a security interest is enforceable and would have priority over the rights of a person that becomes a lien creditor at that time, but the applicable requirements for enforceability or perfection under this chapter, as revised, are not satisfied when the revision takes effect, the security interest:

(1) is a perfected security interest until July 1, 2002;

(2) remains enforceable after June 30, 2002, only if the security interest becomes enforceable under Section 9.203, as revised, before July 1, 2002; and

(3) remains perfected after June 30, 2002, only if the applicable requirements for perfection under this chapter, as revised, are satisfied before July 1, 2002.

Reenacted from Acts 1999, 76th Leg., ch. 414, § 3.03 and amended by Acts 2001, 77th Leg., ch. 705, § 23, eff. June 13, 2001.

Uniform Commercial Code Comment

1. **Perfected Security Interests Under Former Article 9 and This Article.** This section deals with security interests that are perfected (i.e., that are enforceable and have priority over the rights of a lien creditor) under former Article 9 or

other applicable law immediately before this Article takes effect. Subsection (a) provides, not surprisingly, that if the security interest would be a perfected security interest under this Article (i.e., if the transaction satisfies this Article's requirements for enforceability (attachment) and perfection), no further action need be taken for the security interest to be a perfected security interest.

2. **Security Interests Enforceable and Perfected Under Former Article 9 but Unenforceable or Unperfected Under This Article.** Subsection (b) deals with security interests that are enforceable and perfected under former Article 9 or other applicable law immediately before this Article takes effect but do not satisfy the requirements for enforceability (attachment) or perfection under this Article. Except as otherwise provided in Section 9–705, these security interests are perfected security interests for one year after the effective date. If the security interest satisfies the requirements for attachment and perfection within that period, the security interest remains perfected thereafter. If the security interest satisfies only the requirements for attachment within that period, the security interest becomes unperfected at the end of the one-year period.

Example 1: A pre-effective-date security agreement in a consumer transaction covers "all securities accounts." The security interest is properly perfected. The collateral description was adequate under former Article 9 (see former Section 9–115(3)) but is insufficient under this Article (see Section 9–108(e)(2)). Unless the debtor authenticates a new security agreement describing the collateral other than by "type" (or Section 9–203(b)(3) otherwise is satisfied) within the one-year period following the effective date, the security interest becomes unenforceable at the end of that period.

Other examples under former Article 9 or other applicable law that may be effective as attachment or enforceability steps but may be ineffective under this Article include an oral agreement to sell a payment intangible or possession by virtue of a notification to a bailee under former Section 9–305. Neither the oral agreement nor the notification would satisfy the revised Section 9–203 requirements for attachment.

Example 2: A pre-effective-date possessory security interest in instruments is perfected by a bailee's receipt of notification under former 9–305. The bailee has not, however, acknowledged that it holds for the secured party's benefit under revised Section 9–313. Unless the bailee authenticates a record acknowledging that it holds for the secured party (or another appropriate perfection step is taken) within the one-year period following the effective date, the security interest becomes unperfected at the end of that period.

3. **Interpretation of Pre–Effective–Date Security Agreements.** Section 9–102 defines "security agreement" as "an agreement that creates or provides for a security interest." Under Section 1–201(3), an "agreement" is a "bargain of the parties in fact." If parties to a pre-effective-date security agreement describe the collateral by using a term defined in former Article 9 in one way and defined in this Article in another way, in most cases it should be presumed that the bargain of the parties contemplated the meaning of the term under former Article 9.

Example 3: A pre-effective-date security agreement covers "all accounts" of a debtor. As defined under former Article 9, an "account" did not include a right to payment for lottery winnings. These rights to payment are "accounts" under this Article, however. The agreement of the parties presumptively created a security interest in "accounts" as defined in former Article 9. A different result might be appropriate, for example, if the security agreement explicitly contemplated future changes in the Article 9 definitions of types of collateral-e.g., " 'Accounts' means 'accounts' as defined in the UCC Article 9 of [State X], as that definition may be amended from time to time." Whether a different approach is appropriate in any given case depends on the bargain of the parties, as determined by applying ordinary principles of contract construction.

§ 9.704. Security Interest Unperfected Before Effective Date

A security interest that is enforceable immediately before the revision takes effect but that would be subordinate to the rights of a person that becomes a lien creditor at that time:

(1) remains an enforceable security interest until July 1, 2002;

(2) remains enforceable after June 30, 2002, if the security interest becomes enforceable under Section 9.203, as revised, before July 1, 2002; and

(3) becomes perfected:

(A) without further action, when the revision takes effect, if the applicable requirements for perfection under this chapter, as revised, are satisfied before or at that time; or

(B) when the applicable requirements for perfection are satisfied if the requirements are satisfied after the revision takes effect.

Reenacted from Acts 1999, 76th Leg., ch. 414, § 3.04 and amended by Acts 2001, 77th Leg., ch. 705, § 23, eff. June 13, 2001.

Uniform Commercial Code Comment

This section deals with security interests that are enforceable but unperfected (i.e., subordinate to the rights of a person who becomes a lien creditor) under former Article 9 or other applicable law immediately before this Article takes effect. These security interests remain enforceable for one year after the effective date, and thereafter if the appropriate steps for attachment under this Article are taken before the one-year period expires. (This section's treatment of enforceability is the same as that of Section 9–703.) The security interest becomes a perfected security interest on the effective date if, at that time, the security interest satisfies the requirements for perfection under this Article. If the security interest does not satisfy the requirements for perfection until sometime thereafter, it becomes a perfected security interest at that later time.

Example: A security interest has attached under former Article 9 but is unperfected because the filed financing statement covers "all of debtor's personal property" and controlling case law in the applicable jurisdiction has determined that this identification of collateral in a financing statement is insufficient. Upon the effective date of this Article, the financing statement becomes sufficient under Section 9–504(2). On that date the security interest becomes perfected. (This assumes, of course, that the financing statement is filed in the proper filing office under this Article.)

§ 9.705. Effectiveness of Action Taken Before Effective Date

(a) If action, other than the filing of a financing statement, is taken before the revision takes effect and the action would have resulted in priority of a security interest over the rights of a person that becomes a lien creditor had the security interest become enforceable before the revision takes effect, the action is effective to perfect a security interest that attaches under this chapter, as revised, within one year after the effective date of the revision. An attached security interest becomes unperfected on July 1, 2002, unless the security interest becomes a perfected security interest under this chapter, as revised, before that date.

(b) The filing of a financing statement before the effective date of the revision is effective to perfect a security interest to the extent the filing would satisfy the applicable requirements for perfection under this chapter, as revised.

(c) The revision does not render ineffective an effective financing statement that, before the effective date of the revision, is filed and satisfies the applicable requirements for perfection under the law of the jurisdiction governing perfection as provided in Section 9.103, as it existed immediately before the effective date of the revision. However, except as otherwise provided in Subsections (d), (e), and (g) and Section 9.706, the financing statement ceases to be effective at the earlier of:

(1) the time the financing statement would have ceased to be effective under the law of the jurisdiction in which it is filed; or

(2) June 30, 2006.

(d) The filing of a continuation statement after the revision takes effect does not continue the effectiveness of the financing statement filed before the revision takes effect. However, upon the timely filing of a continuation statement after the revision takes effect and in accordance with the law of the jurisdiction governing perfection as provided in Subchapter C,[1] as revised, the effectiveness of a financing statement filed in the same office in that jurisdiction before the revision takes effect continues for the period provided by the law of that jurisdiction.

(e) Subsection (c)(2) applies to a financing statement that, before the revision takes effect, is filed against a transmitting utility and satisfies the applicable requirements for perfection under the law of the jurisdiction governing perfection as provided in Section 9.103, as it existed immediately before the effective date of the revision, only to the extent that Subchapter C, as revised, provides that the law of a jurisdiction other than the jurisdiction in which the financing statement is filed governs perfection of a security interest in collateral covered by the financing statement.

(f) A financing statement that includes a financing statement filed before the revision takes effect and a continuation statement filed after the revision takes effect is effective only to the extent that it satisfies the requirements of Subchapter E,[2] as revised, for an initial financing statement.

(g) Subsection (c)(2) does not apply to a financing statement that was filed before July 1, 2001, in the proper office in this state pursuant to Section 9.401, as that section existed immediately before July 1, 2001, and as to which the proper filing office was not changed pursuant to Section 9.501 of the revision. The lapse date of such a financing statement is the day when the financing statement would have ceased to be effective under Section 9.403(b), as that section existed immediately before July 1, 2001. On timely filing of a continuation statement within six months before that lapse date, the effectiveness of the financing statement continues for another period of five years commencing on the lapse date, and succeeding continuation statements may be filed within six months before the expiration of the five-year period and each additional five-year period to continue the effectiveness of the financing statement.

Reenacted from Acts 1999, 76th Leg., ch. 414, § 3.05 and amended by Acts 2001, 77th Leg., ch. 705, § 23, eff. June 13, 2001; Acts 2007, 80th Leg., ch. 565, § 5, eff. June 16, 2007.

[1] V.T.C.A., Bus. & C. § 9.301 et seq.

[2] V.T.C.A., Bus. & C. § 9.501 et seq.

Uniform Commercial Code Comment

1. **General.** This section addresses primarily the situation in which the perfection step is taken under former Article 9 or other applicable law before the effective date of this Article, but the security interest does not attach until after that date.

2. **Perfection Other Than by Filing.** Subsection (a) applies when the perfection step is a step other than the filing of a financing statement. If the step that would be a valid perfection step under former Article 9 or other law is taken before this Article takes effect, and if a security interest attaches within one year after this Article takes effect, then the security interest becomes a perfected security interest upon attachment. However, the security interest becomes unperfected one year after the effective date unless the requirements for attachment and perfection under this Article are satisfied within that period.

3. **Perfection by Filing: Ineffective Filings Made Effective.** Subsection (b) deals with financing statements that were filed under former Article 9 and which would not have perfected a security interest under the former Article (because, e.g., they did not accurately describe the collateral or were filed in the wrong place), but which would perfect a security interest under this Article. Under subsection (b), such a financing statement is effective to perfect a security interest to the extent it complies with this Article. Subsection (b) applies regardless of the reason for the filing. For example, a secured party need not wait until the effective date to respond to the change this Article makes with respect to the jurisdiction whose law governs perfection of certain security interests. Rather, a secured party may wish to prepare for this change by filing a financing statement before the effective date in the jurisdiction whose law governs perfection under this Article. When this Article takes effect, the filing becomes effective to perfect a security interest (assuming the filing satisfies the perfection requirements of this Article). Note, however, that Section 9–706 determines whether a financing statement filed before the effective date operates to continue the effectiveness of a financing statement filed in another office before the effective date.

4. **Perfection by Filing: Change in Applicable Law.** Subsection (c) provides that a financing statement filed in the proper jurisdiction under former Section 9–103 remains effective for all purposes, despite the fact that Part 3 of this Article would require filing of a financing statement in a different jurisdiction. This means that, during the early years of this Article's effectiveness, it may be necessary to search the files not only in the jurisdiction whose law governs perfection under this Article but also (if different) in the jurisdiction(s) whose law governed perfection under former Article 9. To limit this burden, subsection (c) provides that a financing statement filed in the jurisdiction determined by former Section 9–103 becomes ineffective at the earlier of the time it would become ineffective under the law of that jurisdiction or June 30, 2006. The June 30, 2006, limitation addresses some nonuniform versions of former Article 9 that extended the effectiveness of a financing statement beyond five years. Note that a financing statement filed before the effective date may remain effective beyond June 30, 2006, if subsection (d) (concerning continuation statements) or (e) (concerning transmitting utilities) or Section 9–706 (concerning initial financing statements that operate to continue pre-effective-date financing statements) so provides.

Subsection (c) is an exception to Section 9–703(b). Under the general rule in Section 9–703(b), a security interest that is enforceable and perfected on the effective date of this Article is a perfected security interest for one year after this Article takes effect, even if the security interest is not enforceable under this Article and the applicable requirements for perfection under this Article have not been met. However, in some cases subsection (c) may shorten the one-year period of perfection; in others, if the security interest is enforceable under Section 9–203, it may extend the period of perfection. A financing statement that remains effective under subsection (c) may be amended (but generally may not be continued) after this Article takes effect by filing an amendment in the office where the financing statement was filed.

Example 1: On July 3, 1996, D, a State X corporation, creates a security interest in certain manufacturing equipment located in State Y. On July 6, 1996, SP perfects a security interest in the equipment under former Article 9 by filing in the office of the State Y Secretary of State. See former Section 9–103(1)(b). This Article takes effect in States X and Y on July 1, 2001. Under Section 9–705(c), the financing statement remains effective for the first five days of July, 2001, after which it lapses. See former Section 9–403. Had SP continued the effectiveness of the financing statement by filing a continuation statement in State Y under former Article 9 before July 1, 2001, the financing statement would have remained effective to perfect the security interest through June 30, 2006. See subsection (c)(2). Alternatively, SP could have filed an initial financing statement in State X under subsection (b) or Section 9–706 before the State Y financing statement lapsed. Had SP done so, the security interest would have remained perfected without interruption until the State X financing statement lapsed.

5. **Continuing Effectiveness of Filed Financing Statement.** A financing statement filed before the effective date of this Article may be continued only by filing in the State and office designated by this Article. This result is accomplished in the following manner: Subsection (d) indicates that, as a general matter, a continuation statement filed after the effective date of this Article does not continue the effectiveness of a financing statement filed under the law designated by former Section 9–103. Instead, an initial financing statement must be filed under Section 9–706. The second sentence of subsection (d) contains an exception to the general rule. It provides that a continuation statement is effective to continue the effectiveness of a financing statement filed before this Article takes effect if this Article prescribes not only the same jurisdiction but also the same filing office.

Example 2: On November 8, 2000, D, a State X corporation, creates a security interest in certain manufacturing equipment located in State Y. On November 15, 2000, SP perfects a security interest in the equipment under former Article 9 by filing in office of the State Y Secretary of State. See former Section 9–103(1)(b). This Article takes effect in States X and Y on July 1, 2001. Under Section 9–705(c), the financing statement ceases to be effective in November, 2005, when it lapses. See Section 9–515. Under this Article, the law of D's location (State X, see Section 9–307) governs perfection. See Section 9–301. Thus, the filing of a continuation statement in State Y after the effective date would not continue the effectiveness of the financing statement. See subsection (d). However, the effectiveness of the financing statement could be continued under Section 9–706.

Example 3: The facts are as in Example 2, except that D is a State Y corporation. Assume State Y adopted former

Section 9–401(1) (second alternative). State Y law governs perfection under Part 3 of this Article. (See Sections 9–301, 9–307.) Under the second sentence of subsection (d), the timely filing of a continuation statement in accordance with the law of State Y continues the effectiveness of the financing statement.

Example 4: The facts are as in Example 3, except that the collateral is equipment used in farming operations and, in accordance with former Section 9–401(1) (second alternative) as enacted in State Y, the financing statement was filed in State Y, in the office of the Shelby County Recorder of Deeds. Under this Article, a continuation statement must be filed in the office of the State Y Secretary of State. See Section 9–501(a)(2). Under the second sentence of subsection (d), the timely filing of a continuation statement in accordance with the law of State Y operates to continue a pre-effective-date financing statement only if the continuation statement is filed in the same office as the financing statement. Accordingly, the continuation statement is not effective in this case, but the financing statement may be continued under Section 9–706.

Example 5: The facts are as in Example 3, except that State Y enacted former Section 9–401(1) (third alternative). As required by former Section 9–401(1), SP filed financing statements in both the office of the State Y Secretary of State and the office of the Shelby County Recorder of Deeds. Under this Article, a continuation statement must be filed in the office of the State Y Secretary of State. See Section 9–501(a)(2). The timely filing of a continuation statement in that office after this Article takes effect would be effective to continue the effectiveness of the financing statement (and thus continue the perfection of the security interest), even if the financing statement filed with the County Recorder lapses.

6. **Continuation Statements.** In some cases, this Article reclassifies collateral covered by a financing statement filed under former Article 9. For example, collateral consisting of the right to payment for real property sold would be a "general intangible" under the former Article but an "account" under this Article. To continue perfection under those circumstances, a continuation statement must comply with the normal requirements for a continuation statement. See Section 9–515. In addition, the pre-effective-date financing statement and continuation statement, taken together, must satisfy the requirements of this Article concerning the sufficiency of the debtor's name, secured party's name, and indication of collateral. See subsection (f).

Example 6: A pre-effective-date financing statement covers "all general intangibles" of a debtor. As defined under former Article 9, a "general intangible," would include rights to payment for lottery winnings. These rights to payment are "accounts" under this Article, however. A post-effective-date continuation statement will not continue the effectiveness of the pre-effective-date financing statement with respect to lottery winnings unless it amends the indication of collateral covered to include lottery winnings (e.g., by adding "accounts," "rights to payment for lottery winnings," or the like). If the continuation statement does not amend the indication of collateral, the continuation statement will be effective to continue the effectiveness of the financing statement only with respect to "general intangibles" as defined in this Article.

Example 7: The facts are as in Example 6, except that the pre-effective-date financing statement covers "all accounts and general intangibles." Even though rights to payment for lottery winnings are "general intangibles" under former Article 9 and "accounts" under this Article, a post-effective-date continuation statement would continue the effectiveness of the pre-effective-date financing statement with respect to lottery winnings. There would be no need to amend the indication of collateral covered, inasmuch as the indication ("accounts") satisfies the requirements of this Article.

§ 9.706. When Initial Financing Statement Suffices to Continue Effectiveness of Financing Statement

(a) The filing of an initial financing statement in the office specified in Section 9.501, as revised, continues the effectiveness of a financing statement filed before the revision takes effect if:

(1) the filing of an initial financing statement in that office would be effective to perfect a security interest under this chapter, as revised;

(2) the pre-effective-date financing statement was filed in an office in another state or another office in this state; and

(3) the initial financing statement satisfies Subsection (c).

(b) The filing of an initial financing statement under Subsection (a) continues the effectiveness of the pre-effective-date financing statement:

(1) if the initial financing statement is filed before the revision takes effect, for the period provided in Section 9.403, as it existed immediately before the effective date of the revision, with respect to a financing statement; and

(2) if the initial financing statement is filed after the revision takes effect, for the period provided in Section 9.515, as revised, with respect to an initial financing statement.

(c) To be effective for purposes of Subsection (a), an initial financing statement must:

(1) satisfy the requirements of Subchapter E, [1] as revised, for an initial financing statement;

(2) identify the pre-effective-date financing statement by indicating the office in which the financing statement was filed and providing the dates of filing and file numbers, if any, of the financing statement and of the most recent continuation statement filed with respect to the financing statement; and

(3) indicate that the pre-effective-date financing statement remains effective.

Reenacted from Acts 1999, 76th Leg., ch. 414, § 3.06 and amended by Acts 2001, 77th Leg., ch. 705, § 23, eff. June 13, 2001.

[1] V.T.C.A., Bus. & C. § 9.501 et seq.

Uniform Commercial Code Comment

1. **Continuation of Financing Statements Not Filed in Proper Filing Office Under This Article.** This section deals with continuing the effectiveness of financing statements that are filed in the proper State and office under former Article 9, but which would be filed in the wrong State or in the wrong office of the proper State under this Article. Section 9–705(d) provides that, under these circumstances, filing a continuation statement after the effective date of this Article in the office designated by former Article 9 would not be effective. This section provides the means by which the effectiveness of such a financing statement can be continued if this Article governs perfection under the applicable choice-of-law rule: filing an initial financing statement in the office specified by Section 9–501.

Although it has the effect of continuing the effectiveness of a pre-effective-date financing statement, an initial financing statement described in this section is not a continuation statement. Rather, it is governed by the rules applicable to initial financing statements. (However, the debtor need not authorize the filing. See Section 9–708.) Unlike a continuation statement, the initial financing statement described in this section may be filed any time during the effectiveness of the pre-effective-date financing statement-even before this Article is enacted-and not only within the six months immediately prior to lapse. In contrast to a continuation statement, which extends the lapse date of a filed financing statement for five years, the initial financing statement has its own lapse date, which bears no relation to the lapse date of the pre-effective-date financing statement whose effectiveness the initial financing statement continues. See subsection (b).

As subsection (a) makes clear, the filing of an initial financing statement under this section continues the effectiveness of a pre-effective-date financing statement. If the effectiveness of a pre-effective-date financing statement lapses before the initial financing statement is filed, the effectiveness of the pre-effective-date financing statement cannot be continued. Rather, unless the security interest is perfected otherwise, there will be a period during which the security interest is unperfected before becoming perfected again by the filing of the initial financing statement under this section.

If an initial financing statement is filed under this section before the effective date of this Article, it takes effect when this Article takes effect (assuming that it is ineffective under former Article 9). Note, however, that former Article 9 determines whether the filing office is obligated to accept such an initial financing statement. For the reason given in the preceding paragraph, an initial financing statement filed before the effective date of this Article does not continue the effectiveness of a pre-effective-date financing statement unless the latter remains effective on the effective date of this Article. Thus, for example, if the effectiveness of the pre-effective-date financing statement lapses before this Article takes effect, the initial financing statement would not continue its effectiveness.

2. **Requirements of Initial Financing Statement Filed in Lieu of Continuation Statement.** Subsection (c) sets forth the requirements for the initial financing statement under subsection (a). These requirements are needed to inform searchers that the initial financing statement operates to continue a financing statement filed elsewhere and to enable searchers to locate and discover the attributes of the other financing statement. A single initial financing statement may continue the effectiveness of more than one financing statement filed before this Article's effective date. See Section 1–102(5)(a) (words in the singular include the plural). If under this Article the collateral is of a type different from its type under former Article 9–as would be the case, e.g., with a right to payment of lottery winnings (a "general intangible" under former Article 9 and an "account" under this Article), then subsection (c) requires that the initial financing statement indicate the type under this Article.

§ 9.707. Amendment of Pre-Effective-Date Financing Statement

(a) In this section, "pre-effective-date financing statement" means a financing statement filed before the revision takes effect.

(b) After the revision takes effect, a person may add or delete collateral covered by, continue or terminate the effectiveness of, or otherwise amend the information provided in a pre-effective-date financing statement only in accordance with the law of the jurisdiction governing perfection as provided in Subchapter C.[1] However, the effectiveness of a pre-effective-date financing statement also may be terminated in accordance with the law of the jurisdiction in which the financing statement is filed.

(c) Except as otherwise provided in Subsection (d), if the law of this state governs perfection of a security interest, the information in a pre-effective-date financing statement may be amended after the revision takes effect only if:

(1) the pre-effective-date financing statement and an amendment are filed in the office specified in Section 9.501;

(2) an amendment is filed in the office specified in Section 9.501 concurrently with, or after the filing in that office of, an initial financing statement that satisfies Section 9.706(c); or

(3) an initial financing statement that provides the information as amended and satisfies Section 9.706(c) is filed in the office specified in Section 9.501.

(d) If the law of this state governs perfection of a security interest, the effectiveness of a pre-effective-date financing statement may be continued only under Sections 9.705(d) and (f) or Section 9.706.

(e) Whether or not the law of this state governs perfection of a security interest, the effectiveness of a pre-effective-date financing statement filed in this state may be terminated after the revision takes effect by filing a termination statement in the office in which the pre-effective-date financing statement is filed, unless an initial financing statement that satisfies Section 9.706(c) has been filed in the office specified by the law of the jurisdiction governing perfection as provided in Subchapter C as the office in which to file a financing statement.

Reenacted from Acts 1999, 76th Leg., ch. 414, and amended by Acts 2001, 77th Leg., ch. 705, § 23, eff. June 13, 2001.

[1] V.T.C.A., Bus. & C. § 9.301 et seq.

Uniform Commercial Code Comment

1. **Scope of This Section.** This section addresses post-effective-date amendments to pre-effective-date financing statements.

2. **Applicable Law.** Determining how to amend a pre-effective-date financing statement requires one first to determine the jurisdiction whose law applies. Subsection (b) provides that, as a general matter, post-effective-date amendments to pre-effective-date financing statements are effective only if they are accomplished in accordance with the substantive (or local) law of the jurisdiction governing perfection under Part 3 of this Article. However, under certain circumstances, the effectiveness of a financing statement may be terminated in accordance with the substantive law of the jurisdiction in which the financing statement is filed. See Comment 5, below.

Example 1: D is a corporation organized under the law of State Y. It owns equipment located in State X. Under former Article 9, SP properly perfected a security interest in the equipment by filing a financing statement in State X. Under this Article, the law of State Y governs perfection of the security interest. See Sections 9–301, 9–307. After this Article takes effect, SP wishes to amend the financing statement to reflect a change in D's name. Under subsection (b), the financing statement may be amended in accordance with the law of State Y, i.e., in accordance with subsection (c) as enacted in State Y.

Example 2: The facts are as in Example 1, except that SP wishes to terminate the effectiveness of the State X filing. The first sentence of subsection (b) provides that the financing statement may be terminated after the effective date of this Article in accordance with the law of State Y, i.e., in accordance with subsection (c) as enacted in State Y. However, the second sentence provides that the financing statement also may be terminated in accordance with the law of the jurisdiction in which it is filed, i.e., in accordance with subsection (e) as enacted in State X. If the pre-effective-date financing statement is filed in the jurisdiction whose law governs perfection (here, State Y), then both sentences would designate the law of State Y as applicable to the termination of the financing statement. That is, the financing statement could be terminated in accordance with subsection (c) or (e) as enacted in State Y.

3. **Method of Amending.** Subsection (c) provides three methods of effectuating a post-effective-date amendment to a pre-effective-date financing statement. Under subsection (c)(1), if the financing statement is filed in the jurisdiction and office determined by this Article, then an effective amendment may be filed in the same office.

Example 3: D is a corporation organized under the law of State Z. It owns equipment located in State Z. Before the effective date of this Article, SP perfected a security interest in the equipment by filing in two offices in State Z, a local filing office and the office of the Secretary of State. See former Section 9–401(1) (third alternative). State Z enacts this Article and specifies in Section 9–501 that a financing statement covering equipment is to be filed in the office of the Secretary of State. SP wishes to assign its power as secured party of record. Under subsection (b), the substantive law of State Z applies. Because the pre-effective-date financing statement is filed in the office specified in subsection (c)(1) as enacted by State Z, SP may effectuate the assignment by filing an amendment under Section 9–514 with the office of the Secretary of State. SP need not amend the local filing, and the priority of the security interest perfected by the filing of the financing statement would not be affected by the failure to amend the local filing.

If a pre-effective-date financing statement is filed in an office other than the one specified by Section 9–501 of the relevant jurisdiction, then ordinarily an amendment filed in that office is ineffective. (Subsection (e) provides an exception for termination statements.) Rather, the amendment must be effectuated by a filing in the jurisdiction and office determined by this Article. That filing may consist of an initial financing statement followed by an amendment, an initial financing statement together with an amendment, or an initial financing statement that indicates the information provided in the financing statement, as amended. Subsection (c)(2) encompasses the first two options; subsection (c)(3) contemplates the last. In each instance, the initial financing statement must satisfy Section 9–706(c).

4. **Continuation.** Subsection (d) refers to the two methods by which a secured party may continue the effectiveness of a pre-effective-date financing statement under this Part. The Comments to Sections 9–705 and 9–706 explain these methods.

5. **Termination.** The effectiveness of a pre-effective-date financing statement may be terminated pursuant to subsection (c). This section also provides an alternative method for accomplishing this result: filing a termination statement in the office in which the financing statement is filed. The alternative method becomes unavailable once an initial financing statement that relates to the pre-effective-date financing statement and satisfies Section 9–706(c) is filed in the jurisdiction and office determined by this Article.

Example 4: The facts are as in Example 1, except that SP wishes to terminate a financing statement filed in State X. As explained in Example 1, the financing statement may be amended in accordance with the law of the jurisdiction governing perfection under this Article, i.e., in accordance with the substantive law of State Y. As enacted in State Y, subsection (c)(1) is inapplicable because the financing statement was not filed in the State Y filing office specified in Section 9–501. Under subsection (c)(2), the financing statement may be amended by filing in the State Y filing office an initial financing statement followed by a termination statement. The filing of an initial financing statement together with a termination statement also would be legally sufficient under subsection (c)(2), but Section 9–512(a)(1) may render this method impractical. The financing statement also may be amended under subsection (c)(3), but the resulting initial financing statement is likely to be very confusing. In each instance, the initial financing statement must satisfy Section 9–706(c). Applying the law of State Y, subsection (e) is inapplicable, because the financing statement was not filed in "this State," i.e., State Y.

This section affords another option to SP. Subsection (b) provides that the effectiveness of a financing statement may be terminated either in accordance with the law of the jurisdiction governing perfection (here, State Y) or in accordance with the substantive law of the jurisdiction in which the financing statement is filed (here, State X). Applying the law of State X, the financing statement is filed in "this State," i.e., State X, and subsection (e) applies. Accordingly, the effectiveness of the financing statement can be terminated by filing a termination statement in the State X office in which the financing statement is filed, unless an initial financing statement that relates to the financing statement and satisfies Section 9–706(c) as enacted in State X has been filed in the jurisdiction and office determined by this Article (here, the State Y filing office).

§ 9.708. Persons Entitled to File Initial Financing Statement or Continuation Statement

A person may file an initial financing statement or a continuation statement under this subchapter if:

(1) the secured party of record authorizes the filing; and

(2) the filing is necessary under this subchapter:

(A) to continue the effectiveness of a financing statement filed before the revision takes effect; or

(B) to perfect or continue the perfection of a security interest.

Reenacted from Acts 1999, 76th Leg., ch. 414, § 3.07 and amended by Acts 2001, 77th Leg., ch. 705, § 23, eff. June 13, 2001.

Uniform Commercial Code Comment

This section permits a secured party to file an initial financing statement or continuation statement necessary under this Part to continue the effectiveness of a financing statement filed before this Article takes effect or to perfect or otherwise continue the perfection of a security interest. Because a filing described in this section typically operates to continue the effectiveness of a financing statement whose filing the debtor already has authorized, this section does not require authorization from the debtor.

§ 9.709. Priority

(a) This chapter, as revised, determines the priority of conflicting claims to collateral. However, if the relative priorities of the claims were established before the revision takes effect, this chapter, as it existed before the effective date of the revision, determines priority.

(b) For purposes of Section 9.322(a), as revised, the priority of a security interest that becomes enforceable under Section 9.203, as revised, dates from the time the revision takes effect if the security interest is perfected under this chapter, as revised, by the filing of a financing statement before the revision takes effect that would not have been effective to perfect the security interest under this chapter, as it existed immediately before the effective date of the revision. This subsection does not apply to conflicting security interests each of which is perfected by the filing of such a financing statement.

Reenacted from Acts 1999, 76th Leg., ch. 414, § 3.08 and amended by Acts 2001, 77th Leg., ch. 705, § 23, eff. June 13, 2001.

Uniform Commercial Code Comment

1. **Law Governing Priority.** Ordinarily, this Article determines the priority of conflicting claims to collateral. However, when the relative priorities of the claims were established before this Article takes effect, former Article 9 governs.

Example 1: In 1999, SP–1 obtains a security interest in a right to payment for goods sold ("account"). SP–1 fails to file a financing statement. This Article takes effect on July 1, 2001. Thereafter, on August 1, 2001, D creates a security interest in the same account in favor of SP–2, who files a financing statement. This Article determines the relative priorities of the claims. SP–2's security interest has priority under Section 9–322(a)(1).

Example 2: In 1999, SP–1 obtains a security interest in a right to payment for goods sold ("account"). SP–1 fails to file a financing statement. In 2000, D creates a security interest in the same account in favor of SP–2, who likewise fails to file a financing statement. This Article takes effect on July 1, 2001. Because the relative priorities of the security interests were established before the effective date of this Article, former Article 9 governs priority, and SP–1's security interest has priority under former Section 9–312(5)(b).

Example 3: The facts are as in Example 2, except that, on August 1, 2001, SP–2 files a proper financing statement under this Article. Until August 1, 2001, the relative priorities of the security interests were established before the effective date of this Article, as in Example 2. However, by taking the affirmative step of filing a financing statement, SP–2 established anew the relative priority of the conflicting claims after the effective date. Thus, this Article determines priority. SP–2's security interest has priority under Section 9–322(a)(1).

As Example 3 illustrates, relative priorities that are "established" before the effective date do not necessarily remain unchanged following the effective date. Of course, unlike priority contests among unperfected security interests, some priorities are established permanently, e.g., the rights of a buyer of property who took free of a security interest under former Article 9.

One consequence of the rule in subsection (a) is that the mere taking effect of this Article does not of itself adversely affect the priority of conflicting claims to collateral.

Example 4: In 1999, SP–1 obtains a security interest in a right to payment for lottery winnings (a "general intangible" as defined in former Article 9 but an "account" as defined in this Article). SP–1's security interest is unperfected because its filed financing statement covers only "accounts." In 2000, D creates a security interest in the same right to payment in favor of SP–2, who files a financing statement covering "accounts and general intangibles." Before this Article takes effect on July 1, 2001, SP–2's perfected security interest has priority over SP–1's unperfected security interest under former 9–312(5). Because the relative priorities of the security interests were established before the effective date of this Article, former Article 9 continues to govern priority after this Article takes effect. Thus, SP–2's priority is not adversely affected by this Article's having taken effect.

Note that were this Article to govern priority, SP–2 would become subordinated to SP–1 under Section 9–322(a)(1), even though nothing changes other than this Article's having taken effect. Under Section 9–704, SP–1's security interest would become perfected; the financing statement covering "accounts" adequately covers the lottery winnings and complies with the other perfection requirements of this Article, e.g., it is filed in the proper office.

Example 5: In 1999, SP–1 obtains a security interest in a right to payment for lottery winnings-a "general intangible" (as defined under former Article 9). SP–1's security interest is unperfected because its filed financing statement covers only "accounts." In 2000, D creates a security interest in the same right to payment in favor of SP–2, who makes the same mistake and also files a financing statement covering only "accounts." Before this Article takes effect on July 1, 2001, SP–1's unperfected security interest has priority over SP–2's unperfected security interest, because SP–1's security interest was the first to attach. See former Section 9–312(5)(b). Because the relative priorities of the security interests were established before the effective date of this Article, former Article 9 continues to govern priority after this Article takes effect. Although Section 9–704 makes both security interests perfected for purposes of this Article, both are unperfected under former Article 9, which determines their relative priorities.

2. **Financing Statements Ineffective Under Former Article 9 but Effective Under This Article.** If this Article determines priority, subsection (b) may apply. It deals with the case in which a filing that occurs before the effective date of this Article would be ineffective to perfect a security interest under former Article 9 but effective under this Article. For purposes of Section 9–322(a), the priority of a security interest that attaches after this Article takes effect and is perfected in this manner dates from the time this Article takes effect.

Example 6: In 1999, SP–1 obtains a security interest in D's existing and after-acquired instruments and files a financing statement covering "instruments." In 2000, D grants a security interest in its existing and after-acquired accounts in favor of SP–2, who files a financing statement covering "accounts." After this Article takes effect on July 1, 2001, one of D's account debtors gives D a negotiable note to evidence its obligation to pay an overdue account. Under the first-to-file-or-perfect rule in Section 9–322(a), SP–1 would have priority in the instrument, which constitutes SP–2's proceeds. SP–1's filing in 1999 was earlier than SP–2's in 2000. However, subsection (b) provides that, for purposes of Section 9–322(a), SP–1's priority dates from the time this Article takes effect (July 1, 2001). Under Section 9–322(b), SP–2's priority with respect to the proceeds (instrument) dates from its filing as to the original collateral (accounts). Accordingly, SP–2's security interest would be senior.

Subsection (b) does not apply to conflicting security interests each of which is perfected by a pre-effective-date filing that was not effective under former Article 9 but is effective under this Article.

Example 7: In 1999, SP–1 obtains a security interest in D's existing and after-acquired instruments and files a financing statement covering "instruments." In 2000, D grants a security interest in its existing and after-acquired instruments in favor of SP–2, who files a financing statement covering "instruments." After this Article takes effect on July 1, 2001, one of D's account debtors gives D a negotiable note to evidence its obligation to pay an overdue account. Under the first-to-file-or-perfect rule in Section 9–322(a), SP–1 would have priority in the instrument. Both filings are effective under this Article, see Section 9–705(b), and SP–1's filing in 1999 was earlier than SP–2's in 2000. Subsection (b) does not change this result.

[Chapter 10 reserved for expansion]

CHAPTER 11. EFFECTIVE DATE AND TRANSITION PROVISIONS—1973 AMENDMENTS

§ 11.101. Effective Date

This Act [1] (referred to as the "1973 amendments") takes effect on January 1, 1974.

Added by Acts 1973, 63rd Leg., p. 1030, ch. 400, § 6, eff. Jan. 1, 1974.

[1] Acts 1973, 63rd Leg., p. 1030, ch. 400.

§ 11.102. Preservation of Old Transition Provisions

The provisions of Article 10 of the Uniform Commercial Code, as amended, shall continue to apply to the amended code, and for this purpose this code as amended shall be considered one continuous statute.

Added by Acts 1973, 63rd Leg., p. 1030, ch. 400, § 6, eff. Jan. 1, 1974.

§ 11.103. Transition to 1973 Amendments—General Rule

Transactions validly entered into after June 30, 1966, and before January 1, 1974, and which were subject to the provisions of this title and which would be subject to the 1973 amendments if they had been entered into on or after January 1, 1974, and the rights, duties and interests flowing from such transactions remain valid on and after the latter date and may be terminated, completed, consummated or enforced as required or permitted by the 1973 amendments. Security interests arising out of such transactions which are perfected when the 1973 amendments become effective shall remain perfected until they lapse as provided in the code as amended, and may be continued as permitted by the code as amended, except as stated in Section 11.105.

Added by Acts 1973, 63rd Leg., p. 1030, ch. 400, § 6, eff. Jan. 1, 1974.

§ 11.104. Transition Provision on Change of Requirement of Filing

A security interest for the perfection of which filing or the taking of possession was required under this code and which attached prior to January 1, 1974, but was not perfected shall be deemed perfected on January 1, 1974, if this code as amended permits perfection without filing or authorizes filing in the office or offices where a prior ineffective filing was made.

Added by Acts 1973, 63rd Leg., p. 1030, ch. 400, § 6, eff. Jan. 1, 1974.

§ 11.105. Transition Provision on Change of Place of Filing

(a) A financing statement or continuation statement filed prior to January 1, 1974, which shall not have lapsed prior to January 1, 1974, shall remain effective for the period provided in the code before January 1, 1974, but not less than five years after the filing.

(b) With respect to any collateral, other than fixtures or minerals or the like (including oil and gas) or accounts subject to Subsection (e) of Section 9.103, which are covered by a financing statement or security agreement filed as a financing statement or continuation statement filed prior to January 1, 1974, and which shall not have lapsed prior to January 1, 1974, acquired by the debtor on or after January 1, 1974, any effective financing statement or security agreement filed as a financing statement or continuation statement described in this section and purporting to cover such after-acquired collateral shall apply only if the filing or filings are in the office or offices that would be appropriate to perfect the security interests in the new collateral under the code with its 1973 amendments.

(c) The effectiveness of any financing statement or continuation statement filed prior to January 1, 1974, may be continued by a continuation statement as permitted by this code with 1973 amendments, except that if this code with 1973 amendments, requires a filing or a filing for record in an office where there was no previous financing statement, a new financing statement conforming to Section 11.106 shall be filed or filed for record in that office.

(d) If the filing for record of a mortgage would have been effective as to the types of collateral enumerated in Subsection (f) of Section 9.402 if the 1973 amendments had been in effect on the date of the filing for record of the mortgage, the mortgage shall be deemed effective as such a filing as to the types of collateral enumerated in Subsection (f) of Section 9.402 of this code, as amended, on January 1, 1974.

Added by Acts 1973, 63rd Leg., p. 1030, ch. 400, § 6, eff. Jan. 1, 1974. Amended by Acts 1975, 64th Leg., p. 943, ch. 353, §§ 10, 11, eff. June 19, 1975.

§ 11.106. Required Refilings

(a) If a security interest is perfected or has priority when the 1973 amendments take effect as to all persons or as to certain persons without any filing or recording, and if the filing of a financing statement would be required for the perfection or priority of the security interest against those persons under the 1973 amendments, the perfection and priority rights of the security interest continue until January 1, 1977. The perfection will then lapse unless a financing statement is filed as provided in Subsection (d) or unless the security interest is perfected otherwise than by filing.

(b) If a security interest is perfected when the 1973 amendments take effect under a law other than this title which requires no further filing, refiling or recording to continue its perfection, perfection continues until and will lapse on January 1, 1977, unless a financing statement is filed as provided in Subsection (d) or unless the security interest is perfected otherwise than by filing, or unless under Subsection (c) of Section 9.302 the other law continues to govern filing.

(c) If a security interest is perfected by a filing, refiling or recording under a law repealed by this Act which required further filing, refiling or recording to continue its perfection, perfection continues and will lapse on the date provided by the law so repealed for such further filing, refiling or recording unless a financing statement is filed as provided in Subsection (d) or unless the security interest is perfected otherwise than by filing.

(d) A financing statement may be filed within six months before the perfection of a security interest would otherwise lapse. Any such financing statement may be signed by either the debtor or the secured party. It must identify the security agreement, statement or notice (however denominated in any statute or other law repealed or modified by this Act), state the office where and the date when the last filing, refiling or recording, if any, was made with respect thereto, and the filing number, if any, or book and page, if any, of recording and further state that the security agreement, statement or notice, however denominated, in another filing office under this title or under any statute or other law repealed or modified by this Act is still effective. Section 9.401 and Section 9.103 determine the proper place to file such a financing statement. Except as specified in this subsection, the provisions of Section 9.403(c) for continuation statements apply to such a financing statement.

Added by Acts 1973, 63rd Leg., p. 1030, ch. 400, § 6, eff. Jan. 1, 1974.

§ 11.107. Transition Provisions as to Priorities

Except as otherwise provided in this chapter, this title as it existed before the 1973 amendments took effect shall apply to any questions of priority if the positions of the parties were fixed prior to January 1, 1974. In other cases questions of priority shall be determined by this title with 1973 amendments.

Added by Acts 1973, 63rd Leg., p. 1030, ch. 400, § 6, eff. Jan. 1, 1974.

§ 11.108. Presumption That Rule of Law Continues Unchanged

Unless a change in law has clearly been made, the provisions of this title with 1973, 1975, and 1977 amendments shall be deemed declaratory of the meaning of the title.

Added by Acts 1973, 63rd Leg., p. 1030, ch. 400, § 6, eff. Jan. 1, 1974. Amended by Acts 1975, 64th Leg., p. 944, ch. 353, § 12, eff. June 19, 1975; Acts 1977, 65th Leg., p. 334, ch. 163, § 5, eff. Aug. 29, 1977.

[Chapters 12 to 14 reserved for expansion]

TITLE 2. COMPETITION AND TRADE PRACTICES

CHAPTER 15. MONOPOLIES, TRUSTS AND CONSPIRACIES IN RESTRAINT OF TRADE

SUBCHAPTER A. GENERAL PROVISIONS AND PROHIBITED RESTRAINTS

Section

SUBCHAPTER B. PROCEDURE AND EVIDENCE

SUBCHAPTER C. ENFORCEMENT

SUBCHAPTER D. RECOVERY OF DAMAGES PURSUANT TO FEDERAL ANTITRUST LAWS

SUBCHAPTER E. COVENANTS NOT TO COMPETE

SUBCHAPTER A. GENERAL PROVISIONS AND PROHIBITED RESTRAINTS

§ 15.01. Title of Act

This Act shall be known and may be cited as the Texas Free Enterprise and Antitrust Act of 1983.

Amended by Acts 1983, 68th Leg., p. 3010, ch. 519, § 1, eff. Aug. 29, 1983.

§ 15.02. Applicability of Provisions

(a) The provisions of this Act are cumulative of each other and of any other provision of law of this state in effect relating to the same subject. Among other things, the provisions of this Act preserve the constitutional and common law authority of the attorney general to bring actions under state and federal law.

(b) If any of the provisions of this Act are held invalid, the remainder shall not be affected as a result; nor shall the application of the provision held invalid to persons or circumstances other than those as to which it is held invalid be affected as a result.

Amended by Acts 1983, 68th Leg., p. 3010, ch. 519, § 1, eff. Aug. 29, 1983.

§ 15.03. Definitions

Except as otherwise provided in Subsection (a) of Section 15.10 of this Act, for purposes of this Act:

(1) The term "attorney general" means the Attorney General of Texas or any assistant attorney general acting under the direction of the Attorney General of Texas.

(2) The term "goods" means any property, tangible or intangible, real, personal, or mixed, and any article, commodity, or other thing of value, including insurance.

(3) The term "person" means a natural person, proprietorship, partnership, corporation, municipal corporation, association, or any other public or private group, however organized, but does not include the State of Texas, its departments, and its administrative agencies or a community center operating under Subchapter A, Chapter 534, Health and Safety Code.[1]

(4) The term "services" means any work or labor, including without limitation work or labor furnished in connection with the sale, lease, or repair of goods.

(5) The terms "trade" and "commerce" mean the sale, purchase, lease, exchange, or distribution of any goods or services; the offering for sale, purchase, lease, or exchange of any goods or services; the advertising of any goods or services; the business of insurance; and all other economic activity undertaken in whole or in part for the purpose of financial gain involving or relating to any goods or services.

Amended by Acts 1983, 68th Leg., p. 3010, ch. 519, § 1, eff. Aug. 29, 1983; Acts 1991, 72nd Leg., ch. 242, § 6.01, eff. Sept. 1, 1991; Acts 1995, 74th Leg., ch. 601, § 2, eff. Sept. 1, 1995.

[1] V.T.C.A., Health & Safety Code § 534.001 et seq.

§ 15.04. Purpose and Construction

The purpose of this Act is to maintain and promote economic competition in trade and commerce occurring wholly or partly within the State of Texas and to provide the benefits of that competition to consumers in the state. The provisions of this Act shall be construed to accomplish this purpose and shall be construed in harmony with federal judicial interpretations of comparable federal antitrust statutes to the extent consistent with this purpose.

Amended by Acts 1983, 68th Leg., p. 3010, ch. 519, § 1, eff. Aug. 29, 1983; Acts 1991, 72nd Leg., ch. 242, § 6.02, eff. Sept. 1, 1991.

§ 15.05. Unlawful Practices

(a) Every contract, combination, or conspiracy in restraint of trade or commerce is unlawful.

(b) It is unlawful for any person to monopolize, attempt to monopolize, or conspire to monopolize any part of trade or commerce.

(c) It is unlawful for any person to sell, lease, or contract for the sale or lease of any goods, whether patented or unpatented, for use, consumption, or resale or to fix a price for such use, consumption, or resale or to discount from or rebate upon such price, on the condition, agreement, or understanding that the purchaser or lessee shall not use or deal in the goods of a competitor or competitors of the seller or lessor, where the effect of the condition, agreement, or understanding may be to lessen competition substantially in any line of trade or commerce.

(d) It is unlawful for any person to acquire, directly or indirectly, the whole or any part of the stock or other share capital or the assets of any other person or persons, where the effect of such acquisition may be to lessen competition substantially in any line of trade or commerce.

This subsection shall not be construed:

(1) to prohibit the purchase of stock or other share capital of another person where the purchase is made solely for investment and does not confer control of that person in a manner that could substantially lessen competition;

(2) to prevent a corporation from forming subsidiary or parent corporations for the purpose of conducting its immediately lawful business, or any natural and legitimate branch extensions of such business, or from owning and holding all or a part of the stock or other share capital of a subsidiary, or transferring all or part of its stock or other share capital to be owned and held by a parent, where the effect of such a transaction is not to lessen competition substantially;

(3) to affect or impair any right previously legally acquired; or

(4) to apply to transactions duly consummated pursuant to authority given by any statute of this state or of the United States or pursuant to authority or approval given by any regulatory agency of this state or of the United States under any constitutional or statutory provisions vesting the agency with such power.

(e) It is unlawful for an employer and a labor union or other organization to agree or combine so that:

(1) a person is denied the right to work for an employer because of membership or nonmembership in the labor union or other organization; or

(2) membership or nonmembership in the labor union or other organization is made a condition of obtaining or keeping a job with the employer.

(f) It is not unlawful for:

(1) employees to agree to quit their employment or to refuse to deal with tangible personal property of their immediate employer, unless their refusal to deal with tangible personal property of their immediate employer is intended to induce or has the effect of inducing that employer to refrain from buying or otherwise acquiring tangible personal property from a person; or

(2) persons to agree to refer for employment a migratory worker who works on seasonal crops if the referral is made irrespective of whether or not the worker belongs to a labor union or organization.

(g) Nothing in this section shall be construed to prohibit activities that are exempt from the operation of the federal antitrust laws, 15 U.S.C. Section 1 et seq., except that an exemption otherwise available under the McCarran-Ferguson Act (15 U.S.C. Sections 1011–1015) does not serve to exempt activities under this Act. Nothing in this section shall apply to actions required or affirmatively approved by any statute of this state or of the United States or by a regulatory agency of this state or of the United States duly acting under any constitutional or statutory authority vesting the agency with such power.

(h) In any lawsuit alleging a contract, combination, or conspiracy to fix prices, evidence of uniform prices alone shall not be sufficient to establish a violation of Subsection (a) of Section 15.05.

(i) In determining whether a restraint related to the sale or delivery of professional services is reasonable, except in cases involving price fixing, or other per se violations, the court may consider, but shall not reach its decision solely on the basis of, criteria which include: (1) whether the activities involved maintain or improve the quality of such services to benefit the public interest; (2) whether the activities involved limit or reduce the cost of such services to benefit the public interest. For purposes of this subsection, the term "professional services" means services performed by any licensed accountant, physician, or professional engineer in connection with his or her professional employment or practice.

Amended by Acts 1983, 68th Leg., p. 3010, ch. 519, § 1, eff. Aug. 29, 1983; Acts 1991, 72nd Leg., ch. 242, § 6.02, eff. Sept. 1, 1991.

§ 15.06. Repealed by Acts 1983, 68th Leg., p. 3010, ch. 519, § 1, eff. Aug. 29, 1983

[Sections 15.07 to 15.09 reserved for expansion]

SUBCHAPTER B. PROCEDURE AND EVIDENCE

§ 15.10. Civil Investigative Demands

(a) Definitions. For purposes of this section:

(1) The terms "antitrust investigation" and "investigation" mean any inquiry conducted by the attorney general for the purpose of ascertaining whether any person is or has been engaged in or is actively preparing to engage in activities which may constitute an antitrust violation.

(2) The term "antitrust violation" means any act or omission in violation of any of the prohibitions contained in Section 15.05 of this Act or in violation of any of the antitrust laws set forth in Subsection (a) of Section 12 of Title 15, the United States Code.

(3) The terms "civil investigative demand" and "demand" mean any demand issued by the attorney general under Subsection (b) of this section.

(4) The terms "documentary material" and "material" include the original or any identical copy and all nonidentical copies of any contract, agreement, book, booklet, brochure, pamphlet, catalog, magazine, notice, announcement, circular, bulletin, instruction, minutes, agenda, study, analysis, report, graph, map, chart, table, schedule, note, letter, telegram, telephone or other message, product of discovery, magnetic or electronic recording, and any other written, printed, or recorded matter.

(5) The term "person" means a natural person, proprietorship, partnership, corporation, municipal corporation, association, or any other public or private group, however organized, and includes any person acting under color or authority of state law.

(6) The term "product of discovery" includes without limitation the original or duplicate of any deposition, interrogatory, document, thing, result of the inspection of land or other property, examination, or admission obtained by any method of discovery in any judicial or administrative proceeding of an adversarial nature; any digest, analysis, selection, compilation, or other derivation thereof, and any index or manner of access thereto.

(b) Authority to Issue Demand. Whenever the attorney general has reason to believe that any person may be in possession, custody, or control of any documentary material or may have any information relevant to a civil antitrust investigation, the attorney general may, prior to the institution of a civil proceeding, issue in writing and serve upon such person a civil investigative demand requiring the person to produce such documentary material for inspection and copying, to answer in writing written interrogatories, to give oral testimony, or to provide any combination of such material, answers, and testimony; provided, however, that the attorney general may not issue and serve a demand for documentary material upon a proprietorship or partnership whose annual gross income does not exceed $5 million.

(c) Contents of Demand.

(1) Each demand shall describe the nature of the activities that are the subject of the investigation and shall set forth each statute and section of that statute that may have been or may be violated as a result of such activities. Each demand shall advise the person upon whom the demand is to be served that the person has the right to object to the demand as provided for in this section.

(2) Each demand for production of documentary material shall:

(A) describe the class or classes of material to be produced with reasonable specificity so that the material demanded is fairly identified;

(B) prescribe a return date or dates which will provide a reasonable period of time within which the material is to be produced; and

(C) identify the individual or individuals acting on behalf of the attorney general to whom the material is to be made available for inspection and copying.

(3) Each demand for answers to written interrogatories shall:

(A) propound the interrogatories with definiteness and certainty;

(B) prescribe a date or dates by which answers to interrogatories shall be submitted; and

(C) identify the individual or individuals acting on behalf of the attorney general to whom the answers should be submitted.

(4) Each demand for the giving of oral testimony shall:

(A) prescribe a reasonable date, time, and place at which the testimony shall begin; and

(B) identify the individual or individuals acting on behalf of the attorney general who will conduct the examination.

(5) No demand for any product of discovery may be returned until 20 days after the attorney general serves a copy of the demand upon the person from whom the discovery was obtained.

(d) Protected Material and Information.

(1) A demand may require the production of documentary material, the submission of answers to written interrogatories, or the giving of oral testimony only if the material or information sought would be discoverable under the Texas Rules of Civil Procedure or other state law relating to discovery.

(2) Any demand for a product of discovery supercedes any inconsistent order, rule, or provision of law (other than this subchapter) preventing or restraining disclosure of such product of discovery; provided, however, that voluntary disclosure of a product of discovery under this section does not constitute a waiver of any right or privilege, including any right or privilege which may be invoked to

resist discovery of trial preparation materials, to which the person making the disclosure may be entitled.

(e) Service; Proof of Service.

(1) Service of any demand or of any petition filed under Subsection (f) or (h) of this section may be made upon any natural person by delivering a duly executed copy of the demand or petition to the person to be served or by mailing such copy by registered or certified mail, return receipt requested, to such person at his or her residence or principal office or place of business.

(2) Service of any demand or of any petition filed under Subsection (f) or (h) of this section may be made upon any person other than a natural person by delivering a duly executed copy of the demand or petition to a person to whom delivery would be appropriate under state law if the demand or petition were process in a civil suit.

(3) A verified return by the individual serving any demand or any petition filed under Subsection (f) or (h) setting forth the manner of service shall be proof of such service. In the case of service by registered or certified mail, the return shall be accompanied by the return post office receipt of delivery of the demand or petition.

(f) Petition for Order Modifying or Setting Aside Demand. At any time before the return date specified in a demand or within 20 days after the demand has been served, whichever period is shorter, the person who has been served and, in the case of a demand for a product of discovery, the person from whom the discovery was obtained may file a petition for an order modifying or setting aside the demand in the district court in the county of the person's residence or principal office or place of business or in a district court of Travis County. Any such petition shall specify each ground upon which the petitioner relies in seeking the relief sought. The petition may be based upon any failure of such demand to comply with the provisions of this section or upon any constitutional or other legal right or privilege of the petitioner. The petitioner shall serve a copy of the petition upon the attorney general. The attorney general may submit an answer to the petition. In ruling on the petition, the court shall presume absent evidence to the contrary that the attorney general issued the demand in good faith and within the scope of his or her authority.

(g) Compliance With Demand.

(1) A person on whom a demand is served shall comply with the terms of the demand unless otherwise provided by court order.

(2) The time for compliance with the demand in whole or in part shall not run during the pendency of any petition filed under Subsection (f) of this section; provided, however, that the petitioner shall comply with any portions of the demand not sought to be modified or set aside.

(3) Documentary Material.

(A) Any person upon whom any demand for the production of documentary material has been duly served under this section shall make such material available to the attorney general for inspection and copying during normal business hours on the return date specified in the demand at the person's principal office or place of business or as otherwise may be agreed upon by the person and the attorney general. The attorney general shall bear the expense of any copying. The person may substitute copies for originals of all or part of the requested documents so long as the originals are made available for inspection. The person shall indicate in writing which if any of the documents produced contain trade secrets or confidential information.

(B) The production of documentary material in response to any demand shall be made under a sworn certificate in such form as the demand designates by a natural person having knowledge of the facts and circumstances relating to such production to the effect that all of the requested material in the possession, custody, or control of the person to whom the demand is directed has been produced.

(4) Interrogatories.

(A) Each interrogatory in any demand duly served under this section shall be answered separately and fully in writing, unless it is objected to, in which case the basis for the objection shall be set forth in lieu of an answer. The person shall indicate in writing which if any of the answers contain trade secrets or confidential information.

(B) Answers to interrogatories shall be submitted under a sworn certificate in such form as the related demand designates by a natural person having knowledge of the facts and circumstances relating to the preparation of the answers to the effect that all of the requested information in the possession, custody, control, or knowledge of the person to whom the demand is directed has been set forth fully and accurately.

(5) Oral Examination.

(A) The examination of any person pursuant to a demand for oral testimony duly served under this section shall be taken before any person authorized to administer oaths and affirmations by the laws of Texas or the United States. The person before whom the testimony is to be taken shall put the witness on oath or affirmation and shall personally or by someone acting under his or her direction and in his or her presence record the witness's testimony. At the expense of the attorney general, the testimony shall be taken stenographically and may be transcribed.

(B) The oral testimony of any person taken pursuant to a demand served under this section shall be taken in the county where the person resides, is found, transacts business, or in such other place as may be agreed upon by the person and the attorney general.

(C) Any person compelled to appear under a demand for oral testimony under this section may be accompanied, represented, and advised by counsel. Counsel may advise such person in confidence, either upon the request of such person or upon counsel's own initiative, with respect to any question arising in connection with the examination.

(D) The individual conducting the examination on behalf of the attorney general shall exclude from the place of examination all other persons except the person being examined, the person's counsel, the counsel of the person to whom the demand has been issued, the person before whom the testimony is to be taken, any stenographer taking the testimony, and any persons assisting the individual conducting the examination.

(E) During the examination, the person being examined or his or her counsel may object on the record to any question, in whole or in part, and shall briefly state for the record the reason for the objection. An objection may properly be made, received, and entered upon the record when it is claimed that such person is entitled to refuse to answer the question on grounds of any constitutional or other legal right or privilege, including the privilege against self-incrimination. Neither such person nor his or her counsel shall otherwise object to or refuse to answer any question or interrupt the oral examination. If the person refuses to answer any question, the attorney general may petition the district court in the county where the examination is being conducted for an order compelling the person to answer the question.

(F) If and when the testimony has been fully transcribed, the person before whom the testimony was taken shall promptly transmit the transcript of the testimony to the witness and a copy of the transcript to the attorney general. The witness shall have a reasonable opportunity to examine the transcript and make any changes in form or substance accompanied by a statement of the reasons for such changes. The witness shall then sign and return the transcript, unless he or she is ill, cannot be found, refuses to sign, or in writing waives the signing. If the witness does not sign the transcript within 15 days of receiving it, the person before whom the testimony has been given shall sign it and state on the record the reason, if known, for the witness's failure to sign. The officer shall then certify on the transcript that the witness was duly sworn and that the transcript is a true record of the testimony given by the witness and promptly transmit a copy of the certified transcript to the attorney general.

(G) Upon request, the attorney general shall furnish a copy of the certified transcript to the witness.

(H) The witness shall be entitled to the same fees and mileage that are paid to witnesses in the district courts of Texas.

(h) Failure To Comply With Demand.

(1) Petition for Enforcement. Whenever any person fails to comply with any demand duly served on such person under this section, the attorney general may file in the district court in the county in which the person resides, is found, or transacts business and serve on the person a petition for an order of the court for enforcement of this section. If the person transacts business in more than one county, the petition shall be filed in the county of the person's principal office or place of business in the state or in any other county as may be agreed upon by the person and the attorney general.

(2) Deliberate Noncompliance. Any person, who, with intent to avoid, evade, or prevent compliance in whole or part with a demand issued under this section, removes from any place, conceals, withholds, destroys, mutilates, alters, or by any other means falsifies any documentary material or otherwise provides inaccurate information is guilty of a misdemeanor and on conviction is punishable by a

fine of not more than $5,000 or by confinement in county jail for not more than one year or by both.

(i) Disclosure and Use of Material and Information.

(1) Except as provided in this section or ordered by a court for good cause shown, no documentary material, answers to interrogatories, or transcripts of oral testimony, or copies or contents thereof, shall be available for examination or used by any person without the consent of the person who produced the material, answers, or testimony and, in the case of any product of discovery, of the person from whom the discovery was obtained.

(2) The attorney general may make available for inspection or prepare copies of documentary material, answers to interrogatories, or transcripts of oral testimony in his or her possession as he or she determines may be required by the state in the course of any investigation or a judicial proceeding in which the state is a party.

(3) The attorney general may make available for inspection or prepare copies of documentary material, answers to interrogatories, or transcripts of oral testimony in his or her possession as he or she determines may be required for official use by any officer of the State of Texas or of the United States charged with the enforcement of the laws of the State of Texas or the United States; provided that any material disclosed under this subsection may not be used for criminal law enforcement purposes.

(4) Upon request, the attorney general shall make available copies of documentary material, answers to interrogatories, and transcripts of oral testimony for inspection by the person who produced such material or information and, in the case of a product of discovery, the person from whom the discovery was obtained or by any duly authorized representative of the person, including his or her counsel.

(5) Not later than 15 days prior to disclosing any documentary material or answers to written interrogatories designated as containing trade secrets or confidential information under this subsection, the attorney general shall notify the person who produced the material of the attorney general's intent to make such disclosure. The person who produced the documentary material or answers to written interrogatories may petition a district court in any county of this state in which the person resides, does business, or maintains its principal office for a protective order limiting the terms under which the attorney general may disclose such trade secrets or confidential information.

(6) Upon written request, the attorney general shall return documentary material produced under this section in connection with an antitrust investigation to the person who produced it whenever:

(A) any case or proceeding before any court arising out of the investigation has been completed; or

(B) the attorney general has decided after completing an examination and analysis of such material not to institute any case or proceeding before a court in connection with the investigation.

(j) Jurisdiction. Whenever any petition is filed in the district court in any county as provided for in this section, the court shall have jurisdiction to hear and determine the matter presented and to enter any order or orders required to implement the provisions of this section. Any final order is subject to appeal. Failure to comply with any final order entered by a court under this section is punishable by the court as a contempt of the order.

(k) Nonexclusive Procedures. Nothing in this section shall preclude the attorney general from using procedures not specified in the section in conducting an antitrust investigation; provided, however, that in conducting such an investigation, the attorney general shall use the procedures set forth in this section in lieu of those set forth in Article 1302–5.01 through Article 1302–5.06, Texas Miscellaneous Corporation Laws Act.

Added by Acts 1983, 68th Leg., p. 3019, ch. 519, § 2, eff. Aug. 29, 1983.

§ 15.11. Party to Suit May Subpoena Witness

(a) A party to a suit brought to enforce any of the prohibitions in Section 15.05 of this Act or to enforce the laws conserving natural resources may apply to the clerk of the court in which the suit is pending to subpoena a witness located anywhere in the state. On receipt of the application, the clerk shall issue the subpoena applied for but may not issue more than five subpoenas for a party without first obtaining the court's written approval.

(b) A witness subpoenaed under Subsection (a) of this section who fails to appear and testify in compliance with the subpoena is guilty of contempt of court and may be fined not more than $100 and attached and imprisoned in the county jail until he or she appears in court and testifies as required.

Added by Acts 1983, 68th Leg., p. 3019, ch. 519, § 2, eff. Aug. 29, 1983.

§ 15.12. Additional Procedures

In addition to the procedures set forth in this subchapter, the attorney general and any other party to a suit brought by the attorney general to enforce any of the prohibitions in Section 15.05 of this Act may request discovery and production of documents and other things, serve written interrogatories, and subpoena and depose witnesses in accordance with the applicable provisions of the Texas Rules of Civil Procedure and other state law relating to discovery.

Amended by Acts 1983, 68th Leg., p. 3019, ch. 519, § 2, eff. Aug. 29, 1983.

§ 15.13. Immunity from Criminal Prosecution

(a) Application by Attorney General. If a person upon whom an investigative demand or request for discovery has been properly served pursuant to Section 15.10, 15.11, or 15.12 of this Act refuses or is likely to refuse to comply with the demand or request on the basis of his or her privilege against self-incrimination, the attorney general may apply to a district court in the county in which the person is located for an order granting the person immunity from prosecution and compelling the person's compliance with the demand or request.

(b) Order Granting Immunity and Compelling Testimony and Production. Upon receipt of an application filed under Subsection (a) of this section, the court may issue an order granting the person immunity from prosecution and requiring the person to comply with the demand or request notwithstanding his or her claim of privilege. The order shall explain the scope of protection afforded by it.

(c) Effectiveness of Order. An order may be issued under Subsection (b) of this section prior to the assertion of the privilege against self-incrimination but shall not be effective until the person to whom it is directed asserts the privilege and is informed of the order.

(d) Compliance with Order. A person who has been informed of an order issued by a court under this section compelling his or her testimony or production of material may not refuse to comply with the order on the basis of his or her privilege against self-incrimination. A person who complies with the order may not be criminally prosecuted for or on account of any act, transaction, matter, or thing about which he or she is ordered to testify or produce unless the alleged offense is perjury or failure to comply with the order. Failure to comply with the order may be punished by the court as contempt of the order.

Amended by Acts 1983, 68th Leg., p. 3019, ch. 519, § 2, eff. Aug. 29, 1983.

§§ 15.14, 15.15. Repealed by Acts 1983, 68th Leg., p. 3019, ch. 519, § 2, eff. Aug. 29, 1983

§ 15.16. Declaratory Judgment Action

(a) A person (other than a foreign corporation not having a permit or certificate of authority to do business in this state) uncertain of whether or not his or her action or proposed action violates or will violate the prohibitions contained in Section 15.05 of this Act may file suit against the state for declaratory judgment, citing this section as authority, in one of the Travis County district courts.

(b) Citation and all process in the suit shall be served on the attorney general, who shall represent the state. The petition shall describe in detail the person's action or proposed action and all other relevant facts, and the court in its declaratory judgment shall fully recite the action or proposed action and other facts considered.

(c) A declaratory judgment granted under this section which rules that action or proposed action does not violate the prohibitions contained in Section 15.05 of this Act:

(1) shall be strictly construed and may not be extended by implication to an action or fact not recited in the judgment;

(2) does not bind the state with reference to a person not a party to the suit in which the judgment was granted; and

(3) does not estop the state from subsequently establishing a violation of the prohibitions contained in Section 15.05 of this Act based on an action or fact not recited in the declaratory judgment, which action or fact, when combined with an action or fact recited in the judgment, constitutes a violation of the prohibitions contained in Section 15.05 of this Act.

(d) A person filing suit under this section shall pay all costs of the suit.

Amended by Acts 1983, 68th Leg., p. 3019, ch. 519, § 2, eff. Aug. 29, 1983.

§§ 15.17 to 15.19. Repealed by Acts 1983, 68th Leg., p. 3019, ch. 519, § 2, eff. Aug. 29, 1983

SUBCHAPTER C. ENFORCEMENT

§ 15.20. Civil Suits by the State

(a) Suit to Collect Civil Fine. The attorney general may file suit in district court in Travis County or in any county in the State of Texas in which any of the named defendants resides, does business, or maintains its principal office on behalf of the State of Texas to collect a civil fine from any person, other than a municipal corporation, whom the attorney general believes has violated any of the prohibitions in Subsection (a), (b), or (c) of Section 15.05 of this Act. Every person adjudged to have violated any of these prohibitions shall pay a fine to the state not to exceed $1 million if a corporation, or, if any other person, $100,000.

(b) Suit for Injunctive Relief. The attorney general may file suit against any person, other than a municipal corporation, in district court in Travis County, or in any county in the State of Texas in which any of the named defendants resides, does business, or maintains its principal office on behalf of the State of Texas to enjoin temporarily or permanently any activity or contemplated activity that violates or threatens to violate any of the prohibitions in Section 15.05 of this Act. In any such suit, the court shall apply the same principles as those generally applied by courts of equity in suits for injunctive relief against threatened conduct that would cause injury to business or property. In any such suit in which the state substantially prevails on the merits, the state shall be entitled to recover the cost of suit.

Upon finding a violation of the prohibition against acquiring the stock, share capital, or assets of a person in Subsection (d) of Section 15.05 of this Act, the court shall, upon further finding that no other remedy will eliminate the lessening of competition, order the divestiture or other disposition of the stock, share capital, or assets and shall prescribe a reasonable time, manner, and degree of the divestiture or other disposition.

(c) No suit filed under Subsection (a) or (b) of this section may be transferred to another county except on order of the court.

(d) Nothing in this section shall be construed to limit the constitutional or common law authority of the attorney general to bring actions under state and federal law.

Amended by Acts 1983, 68th Leg., p. 3034, ch. 519, § 3, eff. Aug. 29, 1983.

§ 15.21. Suits by Injured Persons or Governmental Entities

(a) Suit to Recover Damages.

(1) Any person or governmental entity, including the State of Texas and any of its political subdivisions or tax-supported institutions, whose business or property has been injured by reason of any conduct declared unlawful in Subsection (a), (b), or (c) of Section 15.05 of this Act may sue any person, other than a municipal corporation, in district court in any county of this state in which any of the named defendants resides, does business, or maintains its principal office or in any county in which any of the named plaintiffs resided at the time the cause of action or any part thereof arose and shall recover actual damages sustained, interest on actual damages for the period beginning on the date of service of such person's pleading setting forth a claim under the antitrust laws and ending on the date of judgment (the rate of such interest to be in accordance with Texas law regarding postjudgment interest rates and the amount of interest to be adjusted by the court if it finds that the award of all or part of such interest is unjust in the circumstances), and the cost of suit, including a reasonable attorney's fee; provided, however, that if the trier of fact finds that the unlawful conduct was willful or flagrant, it shall increase the recovery to threefold the damages sustained and the cost of suit, including a reasonable attorney's fee; provided that interest on actual damages as specified above may not be recovered when recovered damages are increased threefold.

(2) Any person or governmental entity who obtains a judgment for damages under 15 U.S.C. Section 15 or any other provision of federal law comparable to this subsection may not recover damages in a suit under this subsection based on substantially the same conduct that was the subject of the federal suit.

(3) On a finding by the court that an action under this section was groundless and brought in bad faith or for the purpose of harassment, the court shall award to the defendant or defendants a reasonable attorney's fee, court costs, and other reasonable expenses of litigation.

(b) Suit for Injunctive Relief. Any person or governmental entity, including the State of Texas and any of its political subdivisions or tax-supported institutions, whose business or property is threatened with injury by reason of anything declared unlawful in Subsection (a), (b), or (c) of Section 15.05 of this Act may sue any person, other than a municipal corporation, in district court in any county of this state in which any of the named defendants resides, does business, or maintains its principal office or in any county in which any of the named plaintiffs resided at the time the cause of action or any part thereof arose to enjoin the unlawful practice temporarily or permanently. In any such suit, the court shall apply the same principles as those generally applied by courts of equity in suits for injunctive relief against threatened conduct that would cause injury to business or property. In any such suit in which the plaintiff substantially prevails on the merits, the plaintiff shall be entitled to recover the cost of suit, including a reasonable attorney's fee based on the fair market value of the attorney services used.

(c) Copies of Complaints to Attorney General. Any person or governmental entity filing suit under this section shall mail a copy of the complaint to the Attorney General of Texas. The attorney general as representative of the public may intervene in the action by filing a notice of intervention with the court before which the action is pending and serving copies of the notice on all parties to the action. The penalty for failure to comply with this subsection shall be a monetary fine not in excess of $200. The attorney general may file suit to recover the fine on behalf of the state in the district court in which the private suit has been brought.

Amended by Acts 1983, 68th Leg., p. 3034, ch. 519, § 3, eff. Aug. 29, 1983.

§ 15.22. Criminal Suits

(a) Every person, other than a municipal corporation, who acts in violation of any of the prohibitions in Subsection (a) or (b) of Section 15.05 of this Act shall be deemed guilty of a felony and upon conviction shall be punished by confinement in the Texas Department of Corrections for a term of not more than three years or by a fine not to exceed $5,000 or by both.

(b) A district attorney or criminal district attorney may file criminal suit to enforce the provisions in Subsection (a) of this section in district court in Travis County or in any county in which any of the acts that allegedly have contributed to a violation of any of the prohibitions in Subsections (a) and (b) of Section 15.05 of this Act are alleged to have occurred or to be occurring.

Amended by Acts 1983, 68th Leg., p. 3034, ch. 519, § 3, eff. Aug. 29, 1983.

[Section 15.23 reserved for expansion]

§ 15.24. Judgment in Favor of the State Evidence in Action

A final judgment rendered in an action brought under Section 15.20 or 15.22 of this Act to the effect that a defendant or defendants have violated any of the prohibitions in Section 15.05 of this Act is prima facie evidence against such defendant or defendants in any action brought under Section 15.21 as to all matters with respect to which the judgment would be an estoppel between the parties to the suit. This section shall not apply to consent judgments or decrees entered before any testimony has been taken.

Added by Acts 1983, 68th Leg., p. 3034, ch. 519, § 3, eff. Aug. 29, 1983.

§ 15.25. Limitation of Actions

(a) Any suit to recover damages under Section 15.21 of this Act is barred unless filed within four years after the cause of action accrued or within one year after the conclusion of any action brought by the state under Section 15.20 or 15.22 of this Act based in whole or in part on the same conduct, whichever is longer. For the purpose of this subsection, a cause of action for a continuing violation is considered to accrue at any and all times during the period of the violation.

(b) No suit under this Act shall be barred on the grounds that the activity or conduct complained of in any way affects or involves interstate or foreign commerce. It is the intent of the legislature to exercise its powers to the full extent consistent with the constitutions of the State of Texas and the United States.

Added by Acts 1983, 68th Leg., p. 3034, ch. 519, § 3, eff. Aug. 29, 1983.

§ 15.26. Jurisdiction

Whenever any suit or petition is filed in the district court in any county in the State of Texas as provided for in Section 15.10, 15.20, 15.21, or 15.22 of this Act, the court shall have jurisdiction and venue to hear and determine the matter presented and to enter any order or orders required to implement the provisions of this Act. Once suit is properly filed, it may be transferred to another county upon order of the court for good cause shown.

Added by Acts 1983, 68th Leg., p. 3034, ch. 519, § 3, eff. Aug. 29, 1983.

[Section 15.27 reserved for expansion]

§§ 15.28 to 15.34. Repealed by Acts 1983, 68th Leg., p. 3034, ch. 519, § 3, eff. Aug. 29, 1983

SUBCHAPTER D. RECOVERY OF DAMAGES PURSUANT TO FEDERAL ANTITRUST LAWS

§ 15.40. Authority, Powers, and Duties of Attorney General

(a) The attorney general may bring an action on behalf of the state or of any of its political subdivisions or tax supported institutions to recover the damages provided for by the federal antitrust laws, Title 15, United States Code,[1] provided that the attorney general shall notify in writing any political subdivision or tax supported institution of his intention to bring any such action on its behalf, and at any time within 30 days thereafter, such political subdivision or tax supported institution may, by formal resolution of its governing body or as otherwise specifically provided by applicable law, withdraw the authority of the attorney general to bring the intended action. In any action brought pursuant to this section on behalf of any political subdivision or tax supported institution of the state, the state shall retain for deposit in the general revenue fund of the State Treasury, out of the proceeds, if any, resulting from such action, an amount equal to the expense incurred by the state in the investigation and prosecution of such action.

(b) In any action brought by the attorney general pursuant to the federal antitrust laws for the recovery of damages by the estate[2] or any of its political subdivisions or tax supported institutions, in addition to his other powers and authority the attorney general may enter into contracts relating to the investigation and the prosecution of such action with any other party who could bring a similar action or who has brought such an action for the recovery of damages and with whom the attorney general finds it advantageous to act jointly, or to share common expenses or to cooperate in any manner relative to such action. In any such action the attorney general may undertake, among other things, either to render legal services as special counsel to, or to obtain the legal services of special counsel from, any department or agency of the United States, any other state or any department or agency thereof, any county, city, public corporation or public district of this state or of any other state, that has brought or intends to bring a similar action for the recovery of damages, or their duly authorized legal representatives in such action.

Added by Acts 1969, 61st Leg., p. 1708, ch. 559, § 1, eff. June 10, 1969.

[1] 15 U.S.C.A. § 15 et seq.

[2] So enrolled in bill; probably should read "state".

SUBCHAPTER E. COVENANTS NOT TO COMPETE

§ 15.50. Criteria for Enforceability of Covenants Not to Compete

(a) Notwithstanding Section 15.05 of this code, and subject to any applicable provision of Subsection (b), a covenant not to compete is enforceable if it is ancillary to or part of an otherwise enforceable agreement at the time the agreement is made to the extent that it contains limitations as to time, geographical area, and scope of activity to be restrained that are reasonable and do not impose a greater restraint than is necessary to protect the goodwill or other business interest of the promisee.

(b) A covenant not to compete is enforceable against a person licensed as a physician by the Texas State Board of Medical Examiners if such covenant complies with the following requirements:

(1) the covenant must:

(A) not deny the physician access to a list of his patients whom he had seen or treated within one year of termination of the contract or employment;

(B) provide access to medical records of the physician's patients upon authorization of the patient and any copies of medical records for a reasonable fee as established by the Texas State Board of Medical Examiners under Section 159.008, Occupations Code; and

(C) provide that any access to a list of patients or to patients' medical records after termination of the contract or employment shall not require such list or records to be provided in a format different than that by which such records are maintained except by mutual consent of the parties to the contract;

(2) the covenant must provide for a buy out of the covenant by the physician at a reasonable price or, at the option of either party, as determined by a mutually agreed upon arbitrator or, in the case of

an inability to agree, an arbitrator of the court whose decision shall be binding on the parties; and

(3) the covenant must provide that the physician will not be prohibited from providing continuing care and treatment to a specific patient or patients during the course of an acute illness even after the contract or employment has been terminated.

Added by Acts 1989, 71st Leg., ch. 1193, § 1, eff. Aug. 28, 1989. Amended by Acts 1993, 73rd Leg., ch. 965, § 1, eff. Sept. 1, 1993; Acts 1999, 76th Leg., ch. 1574, § 1, eff. Sept. 1, 1999; Acts 2001, 77th Leg., ch. 1420, § 14.729, eff. Sept. 1, 2001.

§ 15.51. Procedures and Remedies in Actions to Enforce Covenants not to Compete

(a) Except as provided in Subsection (c) of this section, a court may award the promisee under a covenant not to compete damages, injunctive relief, or both damages and injunctive relief for a breach by the promisor of the covenant.

(b) If the primary purpose of the agreement to which the covenant is ancillary is to obligate the promisor to render personal services, for a term or at will, the promisee has the burden of establishing that the covenant meets the criteria specified by Section 15.50 of this code. If the agreement has a different primary purpose, the promisor has the burden of establishing that the covenant does not meet those criteria. For the purposes of this subsection, the "burden of establishing" a fact means the burden of persuading the triers of fact that the existence of the fact is more probable than its nonexistence.

(c) If the covenant is found to be ancillary to or part of an otherwise enforceable agreement but contains limitations as to time, geographical area, or scope of activity to be restrained that are not reasonable and impose a greater restraint than is necessary to protect the goodwill or other business interest of the promisee, the court shall reform the covenant to the extent necessary to cause the limitations contained in the covenant as to time, geographical area, and scope of activity to be restrained to be reasonable and to impose a restraint that is not greater than necessary to protect the goodwill or other business interest of the promisee and enforce the covenant as reformed, except that the court may not award the promisee damages for a breach of the covenant before its reformation and the relief granted to the promisee shall be limited to injunctive relief. If the primary purpose of the agreement to which the covenant is ancillary is to obligate the promisor to render personal services, the promisor establishes that the promisee knew at the time of the execution of the agreement that the covenant did not contain limitations as to time, geographical area, and scope of activity to be restrained that were reasonable and the limitations imposed a greater restraint than necessary to protect the goodwill or other business interest of the promisee, and the promisee sought to enforce the covenant to a greater extent than was necessary to protect the goodwill or other business interest of the promisee, the court may award the promisor the costs, including reasonable attorney's fees, actually and reasonably incurred by the promisor in defending the action to enforce the covenant.

Added by Acts 1989, 71st Leg., ch. 1193, § 1, eff. Aug. 28, 1989. Amended by Acts 1993, 73rd Leg., ch. 965, § 2, eff. Sept. 1, 1993.

§ 15.52. Preemption of Other Law

The criteria for enforceability of a covenant not to compete provided by Section 15.50 of this code and the procedures and remedies in an action to enforce a covenant not to compete provided by Section 15.51 of this code are exclusive and preempt any other criteria for enforceability of a covenant not to compete or procedures and remedies in an action to enforce a covenant not to compete under common law or otherwise.

Added by Acts 1993, 73rd Leg., ch. 965, § 3, eff. Sept. 1, 1993.

CHAPTER 16. TRADEMARKS

SUBCHAPTER A. GENERAL PROVISIONS

Section

SUBCHAPTER A. GENERAL PROVISIONS

§ 16.01. Definitions

(a) In this chapter, unless the context requires a different definition,

(1) "applicant" means the person applying for registration of a mark under this chapter and includes his legal representative, successor, assignee, and predecessor in title to the mark sought to be registered;

(2) "mark" includes service mark and trademark;

(3) "registrant" means the person to whom a registration has been issued under this chapter and includes his legal representative, successor, assignee, and predecessor in title to the registration;

(4) "service mark" means a word, name, symbol, device, slogan or any combination thereof which, whether registered or not, has been adopted and used by a person to identify his services and distinguish them from the services of others, and includes the titles, designations, character names, and distinctive features of broadcast or other advertising;

(5) "trademark" means a word, name, symbol, device, slogan or any combination thereof which, whether registered or not, has been adopted and used by a person to identify his goods and distinguish them from the goods manufactured or sold by others; and

(6) "trade name" includes individual name, surname, firm name, corporate name, and lawfully adopted name or title used by a person to identify his business, vocation, or occupation.

(b) This chapter does not apply to the registration or use of livestock brands or other indicia of ownership of goods which do not qualify as a "mark" as defined in this chapter.

Acts 1967, 60th Leg., p. 2343, ch. 785, § 1.

§ 16.02. When Mark Considered to be Used

(a) A mark is considered to be used in this state in connection with goods when

(1) it is placed on

(A) the goods;

(B) containers of the goods;

(C) displays associated with the goods; or

(D) tags or labels affixed to the goods; and

(2) the goods are sold, displayed for sale, or otherwise publicly distributed in this state.

(b) A mark is considered to be used in this state in connection with services when

(1) it is used or displayed in this state in connection with selling or advertising the services; and

(2) the services are rendered in this state.

Acts 1967, 60th Leg., p. 2343, ch. 785, § 1.

[Sections 16.03 to 16.07 reserved for expansion]

SUBCHAPTER B. REGISTRATION OF MARK

§ 16.08. Registrable Marks

(a) A mark in actual use in connection with the applicant's goods or services, which distinguishes his goods or services from those of others, is registrable unless it

(1) is, or includes matter which is, immoral, deceptive, or scandalous;

(2) may disparage, or falsely suggest a connection with, or bring into contempt or disrepute

(A) a person, whether living or dead;

(B) an institution;

(C) a belief; or

(D) a national symbol;

(3) depicts or simulates the flag, coat of arms, or other insignia of

(A) the United States;

(B) a state;

(C) a municipality; or

(D) a foreign nation;

(4) is or includes the name, signature, or portrait of a living individual who has not consented in writing to its registration;

(5) is

(A) merely descriptive or deceptively misdescriptive of the applicant's goods or services;

(B) primarily geographically descriptive or deceptively misdescriptive of the applicant's goods or services; or

(C) primarily merely a surname; or

(6) is likely to cause confusion or mistake, or to deceive, because, when applied to the applicant's goods or services, it resembles another person's unabandoned mark registered in this state.

(b) Subsection (a)(5) of this section does not prevent the registration of a mark that has become distinctive as applied to the applicant's goods or services. The secretary of state may accept as evidence that a mark has become distinctive as applied to the applicant's goods or services proof of substantially exclusive and continuous use of the mark by the applicant in this state for the five years next preceding the date on which the applicant filed his application for registration.

(c) A trade name is not registrable under this chapter. However, if a trade name is also a service mark or trademark, as defined in this chapter, it is registrable as a service mark or trademark.

Acts 1967, 60th Leg., p. 2343, ch. 785, § 1.

§ 16.09. Classification of Goods and Services

(a) The secretary of state shall adopt rules establishing a classification of goods and services for the convenient administration of this chapter. The classifications established do not limit or expand an applicant's or registrant's rights. To the extent practicable, the classification of goods and services should conform to the classification adopted by the United States Patent and Trademark Office.

(b) An applicant may include in a single application for registration of a mark all goods or services in connection with which the mark is actually being used and which are in a single class. An applicant may not include in a single application for registration goods or services which are not in a single class.

Acts 1967, 60th Leg., p. 2343, ch. 785, § 1. Amended by Acts 1989, 71st Leg., ch. 865, § 1, eff. Sept. 1, 1989; Acts 2003, 78th Leg., ch. 168, § 1, eff. Sept. 1, 2003.

§ 16.10. Application for Registration

(a) Subject to the limitations prescribed by this chapter, a person may file an application to register a mark in the office of the secretary of state on a form prescribed by the secretary of state.

(b) The applicant shall include in the application:

(1) the name and business address of the applicant;

(2) if the applicant is a corporation, limited partnership, limited liability company, or other business entity, the state of incorporation or organization;

(3) an appointment of the secretary of state as the applicant's agent for service of process only in suits relating to the registration which may be issued if the applicant:

(A) is or becomes a:

(i) nonresident individual, partnership, or association; or

(ii) foreign corporation, limited partnership, or limited liability company without a certificate of authority to do business in this state; or

(B) cannot be found in this state;

(4) the names or a description of the goods or services in connection with which the mark is being used;

(5) the manner in which the mark is being used in connection with the goods or services;

(6) the class in which the applicant believes the goods or services belong;

(7) the date on which the applicant first used the mark anywhere in connection with the goods or services;

(8) the date on which the applicant first used the mark in this state in connection with the goods or services;

(9) a statement that the applicant is the owner of the mark, and that, to the best of the applicant's knowledge, no other person is entitled to use the mark in this state:

(A) in the identical form used by the applicant; or

(B) in a form that is likely, when used in connection with the goods or services, to cause confusion or mistake, or to deceive, because of its resemblance to the mark used by the applicant;

(10) a narrative description of the mark; and

(11) such additional information or documents as the secretary of state may reasonably require.

(c) The applicant shall:

(1) prepare and file the application and a copy of the application with the secretary of state; and

(2) submit as part of the application to the secretary of state:

(A) two identical specimens or facsimiles of the mark as actually used, one specimen or facsimile with the original application and one specimen or facsimile with the copy;

(B) a drawing of the mark that complies with any requirement specified by the secretary of state; and

(C) an application fee of $50 payable to the secretary of state.

(d) The applicant or the applicant's agent shall sign the application.

Acts 1967, 60th Leg., p. 2343, ch. 785, § 1. Amended by Acts 1979, 66th Leg., p. 233, ch. 120, § 47, eff. May 9, 1979; Acts 1983, 68th Leg., p. 313, ch. 69, § 6, eff. Sept. 1, 1983; Acts 1987, 70th Leg., ch. 1007, § 6, eff. June 19, 1987; Acts 1997, 75th Leg., ch. 248, § 1, eff. Sept. 1, 1997.

§ 16.105. Examination of Application

(a) On the filing of an application for registration and payment of the application fee, the secretary of state shall examine the application for compliance with this chapter.

(b) The applicant shall provide to the secretary of state additional pertinent information requested by the secretary of state.

(c) The secretary of state shall examine applications in the order in which the applications are filed, including applications concurrently processed for registration of the same or confusingly similar marks used in connection with the same or similar goods or services.

Added by Acts 1997, 75th Leg., ch. 248, § 2, eff. Sept. 1, 1997.

§ 16.106. Amendment to Application

(a) The applicant may make an amendment to the application as reasonably requested by the secretary of state or in response to a rejection or objection to the registration by the secretary of state.

(b) An amendment to the application, other than an amendment to the date on which the applicant first uses the mark, may be made by the applicant's agent. The secretary of state may require the applicant to execute and submit a new application instead of making an amendment.

(c) An amendment to the application made to the date on which the applicant first used the mark may not specify a date of use that is after the date on which the application was filed.

Added by Acts 1997, 75th Leg., ch. 248, § 2, eff. Sept. 1, 1997.

§ 16.107. Disclaimer of Unregistrable Component

The secretary of state may require the applicant to disclaim or the applicant may voluntarily disclaim an unregistrable component of a mark that is otherwise registrable. A disclaimer may not prejudice or affect the:

(1) rights of the applicant or registrant in the disclaimed matter; or

(2) rights of the applicant or registrant to make an application to register a mark if the disclaimed matter is distinctive of the goods or services of the applicant or registrant.

Added by Acts 1997, 75th Leg., ch. 248, § 2, eff. Sept. 1, 1997.

§ 16.108. Concurrent Applications for Same or Similar Mark

(a) When concurrently processing applications for the same or confusingly similar marks used in connection with the same or similar goods or services, the secretary of state shall give priority to the application that was filed first. If the previously filed application is registered, the secretary of state shall reject the other application.

(b) The applicant may bring an action for cancellation of the previously issued registration on the ground that the applicant has a prior or superior right to the mark under this chapter.

Added by Acts 1997, 75th Leg., ch. 248, § 2, eff. Sept. 1, 1997.

§ 16.109. Denial of Registration

(a) If the secretary of state finds that the applicant is not entitled to register the mark, the secretary of state shall:

(1) notify the applicant of the reason for the denial of the application; and

(2) give the applicant a reasonable amount of time as prescribed by the secretary of state in which to:

(A) issue a response to the denial; or

(B) amend the application.

(b) The applicant may repeat the examination procedures described by Subsection (a) until the earlier of:

(1) the expiration of the period prescribed by the secretary of state under Subsection (a)(2); or

(2) the date on which the secretary of state finally refuses registration of the application.

(c) If the secretary of state finally refuses registration of the mark, the applicant may seek a review of the decision of the secretary of state in accordance with the procedures prescribed by this chapter.

Added by Acts 1997, 75th Leg., ch. 248, § 2, eff. Sept. 1, 1997.

§ 16.11. Registration by Secretary of State

If the application satisfies the requirements of this chapter, and the application fee has been paid, the secretary of state shall:

(1) endorse on the original and the copy of the application:

(A) the word "filed"; and

(B) the date on which the application was filed;

(2) file the original in his office;

(3) issue a certificate of registration evidencing registration on the date on which the application was filed;

(4) attach the copy to the certificate of registration; and

(5) deliver the certificate of registration with the attached copy of the application to the applicant.

Acts 1967, 60th Leg., p. 2343, ch. 785, § 1. Amended by Acts 1979, 66th Leg., p. 233, ch. 120, § 48, eff. May 9, 1979; Acts 1997, 75th Leg., ch. 248, § 3, eff. Sept. 1, 1997.

§ 16.12. Term of Registration

(a) The registration of a mark under this chapter is effective for a term of 10 years from the date of registration.

(b) Repealed by Acts 1997, 75th Leg., ch. 248, § 8, eff. Sept. 1, 1997.

Acts 1967, 60th Leg., p. 2343, ch. 785, § 1. Amended by Acts 1997, 75th Leg., ch. 248, § 8, eff. Sept. 1, 1997.

§ 16.13. Notice of Expiration of Registration

(a) During the period beginning 12 months and ending 6 months before the day a registration expires, the secretary of state shall, by writing to the last known address of the registrant under this chapter or under a prior act, notify the registrant of the necessity for renewing or reregistering under Section 16.14 of this code.

(b) Neither the secretary of state's failure to notify a registrant nor the registrant's nonreceipt of a notice under Subsection (a) of this section

(1) extends the term of a registration; or

(2) excuses the registrant's failure to renew or reregister.

Acts 1967, 60th Leg., p. 2343, ch. 785, § 1.

§ 16.14. Renewal of Registration and Reregistration

(a) The registration of a mark under this chapter may be renewed for an additional 10-year term by filing a renewal application within six months before the day the registration expires. The registrant shall submit to the secretary of state:

(1) a renewal application stating that:

(A) the mark is still in use in this state; or

(B) nonuse of the mark in this state:

(i) is due to special circumstances which excuse the nonuse; and

(ii) is not due to an intention to abandon the mark in this state; and

(2) a renewal application fee of $25 payable to the secretary of state.

(b) A registrant may renew a registration under Subsection (a) of this section for successive terms of 10 years.

(c) Repealed by Acts 1997, 75th Leg., ch. 248, § 8, eff. Sept. 1, 1997.

(d) The renewal application must be signed by the registrant or the registrant's agent.

Acts 1967, 60th Leg., p. 2343, ch. 785, § 1. Amended by Acts 1983, 68th Leg., p. 313, ch. 69, § 7, eff. Sept. 1, 1983; Acts 1997, 75th Leg., ch. 248, §§ 4, 8, eff. Sept. 1, 1997.

§ 16.15. Record, Notice, and Proof of Registration

(a) The secretary of state shall keep for public examination a record of all:

(1) marks registered, reregistered, or renewed under this chapter;

(2) assignments recorded under Section 16.18 of this code; and

(3) other instruments recorded under Section 16.19 of this code.

(b) Registration of a mark under this chapter is constructive notice throughout this state of the registrant's claim of ownership of the mark throughout this state.

(c) A certificate of registration issued by the secretary of state under this chapter, or a copy of it certified by the secretary of state, is admissible in evidence as prima facie proof of

(1) the validity of the registration;

(2) the registrant's ownership of the mark; and

(3) the registrant's exclusive right to use the mark in commerce in this state in connection with the goods or services specified in the certificate, subject to any conditions and limitations stated in the certificate.

Acts 1967, 60th Leg., p. 2343, ch. 785, § 1. Amended by Acts 1997, 75th Leg., ch. 248, § 5, eff. Sept. 1, 1997.

§ 16.16. Cancellation of Registration

(a) The secretary of state shall cancel

(1) all registrations in force before May 2, 1962, which are more than 10 years old and which have not been reregistered under Section 16.14(c) of this code;

(2) a registration on receipt of a voluntary request for cancellation from the registrant under this chapter or under a prior act as identified by the records of the secretary of state;

(3) registrations granted under this chapter and not renewed under Section 16.14(a) of this code;

(4) a registration concerning which a district or appellate court has rendered a final judgment, which has become unappealable, cancelling the registration or finding that

(A) the registered mark has been abandoned;

(B) the registrant under this chapter or under a prior act is not the owner of the mark;

(C) the registration was granted contrary to the provisions of this chapter;

(D) the registration was obtained fraudulently; or

(E) the registered mark has become incapable of serving as a mark.

(b) The clerk of the court whose final judgment cancels a registration or makes any of the findings specified in Subsection (a)(4) of this section shall, when the judgment becomes unappealable, transmit a certified copy of it to the secretary of state.

Acts 1967, 60th Leg., p. 2343, ch. 785, § 1.

§ 16.17. Assignment of Mark and Registration

(a) A mark and its registration under this chapter are assignable with the goodwill of the business in which the mark is used, or with that part of the goodwill connected with the use of, and symbolized by, the mark.

(b) An assignment shall be made by duly executed written instrument.

Acts 1967, 60th Leg., p. 2343, ch. 785, § 1.

§ 16.18. Recordation of Assignment and Its Effect

(a) An assignment made under Section 16.17 of this code may be recorded with the secretary of state by

(1) filing with him

(A) the original assignment; and

(B) a duplicate original or legible photocopy on durable paper of the assignment; and

(2) paying him a fee of $10.

(b) If an assignment has been properly filed for record under Subsection (a) of this section, the secretary of state shall

(1) issue in the assignee's name a new certificate of registration for the remainder of the term of the mark's registration, reregistration, or last renewal;

(2) endorse on the original and duplicate original assignment or photocopy the

(A) words "Filed for record in the office of the Secretary of State, State of Texas"; and

(B) date on which the assignment was filed for record;

(3) file the duplicate original or photocopy of the assignment in his office; and

(4) return the endorsed original assignment to the assignee or his representative.

(c) The assignment of a mark registered under this chapter is void against a purchaser who purchases the mark for value after the assignment is made and without notice of it unless the assignment is recorded by the secretary of state

(1) within three months after the date of the assignment; or

(2) before the mark is purchased.

Acts 1967, 60th Leg., p. 2343, ch. 785, § 1. Amended by Acts 1983, 68th Leg., p. 314, ch. 69, § 8, eff. Sept. 1, 1983.

§ 16.19. Recordation of Other Instruments

(a) An instrument that is related to the ownership of a mark registered under this subchapter, including articles of merger or conversion or a document effecting a name change, may be recorded with the secretary of state by:

(1) filing a certified copy of the instrument; and

(2) paying a filing fee in the amount established for the filing of an assignment under Section 16.18.

(b) This section does not apply to the recording of a mortgage or a security interest or other instrument that is recordable under the Uniform Commercial Code.

(c) A license agreement related to a mark registered under this chapter may not be recorded under this section.

Added by Acts 1997, 75th Leg., ch. 248, § 6, eff. Sept. 1, 1997.

§ 16.20. Transfer of Mark; Change of Registrant's Name; Change of Address

(a) If ownership of a registered mark is transferred or a registrant's name is changed during the unexpired term of a registration, a new certificate of registration may be issued for the remainder of the unexpired term of the mark's registration in the name of the transferee or in the new name of the registrant upon the filing of an instrument under Section 16.19.

(b) The secretary of state may amend the trademark records of an effective registration to reflect a change of registrant address upon receipt of a statement signed by the registrant or the registrant's agent. The statement must set forth the name of the registrant of record, a description of the registered mark, the registration number issued by the secretary of state, and the registrant's new address.

Added by Acts 1997, 75th Leg., ch. 248, § 6, eff. Sept. 1, 1997. Amended by Acts 2003, 78th Leg., ch. 168, § 2, eff. Sept. 1, 2003.

§ 16.21. Powers of Secretary of State

(a) The secretary of state may adopt rules relating to the filing of documents under this subchapter.

(b) The secretary of state may prescribe forms for use in filing documents under this subchapter.

Added by Acts 1997, 75th Leg., ch. 248, § 6, eff. Sept. 1, 1997.

§ 16.22. Electronic Filings and Reproductions

(a) An application for renewal of trademark registration, an assignment under Section 16.17, or a transfer of ownership or change of registrant name under Section 16.19 may be submitted in an electronic format that is approved by the secretary of state. An instrument that is filed in accordance with this subsection is deemed to have complied with:

(1) the filing requirements of the section pursuant to which it is filed; and

(2) any requirement that the document be submitted as an originally signed instrument.

(b) All electronic acknowledgments and certificates required to be issued by the secretary of state for the instruments filed pursuant to Subsection (a) shall be considered issued or provided by the secretary of state on the initial transmission by the secretary of state of the acknowledgment or certificate required to be filed.

(c) Any certificate issued by the secretary of state concerning any instrument filed under this subchapter need not be on paper or reduced to printed form.

(d) If permitted by the rules adopted by the secretary of state, an original instrument required or authorized to be filed with the secretary of state under this subchapter may be a photographic, photostatic, facsimile, or similar reproduction of a signed instrument.

(e) All civil and criminal penalties applicable to the filing of documents under this chapter apply to all documents filed pursuant to this section.

Added by Acts 2003, 78th Leg., ch. 168, § 3, eff. Sept. 1, 2003.

[Section 16.23 reserved for expansion]

SUBCHAPTER C. COURT ACTION

§ 16.24. Review of Secretary of State's Decisions

(a) If the secretary of state takes final action refusing to register a mark under Section 16.109 or to renew the registration of a mark under Section 16.14, the applicant or registrant may file suit for review of the secretary of state's decision in one of the Travis County district courts.

(b) A suit filed under Subsection (a) of this section is tried de novo, as an appeal from a justice court to a county court, and

(1) every decision or action concerning an issue in the suit made or taken by the secretary of state before the suit was filed is void;

(2) the district court shall determine the issues in the suit as if no decision had been made or action taken by the secretary of state; and

(3) the district court may not apply in any form the substantial evidence rule in reviewing a decision or action of the secretary of state.

(c) The legislature declares that

(1) this section is not severable from the other sections of this chapter;

(2) it would not have enacted this chapter without this section; and

(3) this chapter is void if a court in a final judgment which becomes unappealable invalidates this section in whole or part.

Acts 1967, 60th Leg., p. 2343, ch. 785, § 1. Amended by Acts 1999, 76th Leg., ch. 1215, § 1, eff. Sept. 1, 1999.

§ 16.25. Suit to Cancel Registration

(a) A person who believes that he is or will be damaged by a registration under this chapter may sue to cancel the registration in a district court having venue.

(b) The clerk of a court in which suit is filed under Subsection (a) of this section shall transmit notice of the suit to the secretary of state, who shall place the notice in the registration file with proper notations and endorsements.

(c) When the registrant's agent for service of process is the secretary of state, the secretary of state shall forward notice of the suit by registered mail to the registrant at his last address of record.

(d) If the court finds that the losing party in a suit filed under Subsection (a) of this section should have known his position was without merit, the court may award the successful party his reasonable attorneys' fees and charge them as part of the costs against the losing party.

Acts 1967, 60th Leg., p. 2343, ch. 785, § 1.

§ 16.26. Infringement of Registered Mark

(a) Subject to Section 16.27 of this code, a person commits an infringement if, without the registrant's consent, he

(1) uses anywhere in this state a reproduction, counterfeit, copy, or colorable imitation of a mark registered under this chapter in connection with selling, offering for sale, or advertising goods or services when the use is likely to deceive or cause confusion or mistake as to the source or origin of the goods or services; or

(2) reproduces, counterfeits, copies, or colorably imitates a mark registered under this chapter and applies the reproduction, counterfeit, copy, or colorable imitation to a label, sign, print, package, wrapper, receptacle, or advertisement intended to be used in selling, leasing, distributing, or rendering goods or services in this state when the use is likely to deceive or cause confusion or mistake as to the source or origin of the goods or services.

(b) A registrant may sue for damages and to enjoin an infringement proscribed by Subsection (a) of this section in a district court having venue.

(c) If the district court determines that there has been an infringement, it shall enjoin the act of infringement and may

(1) require the infringer to pay the registrant all damages resulting from the acts of infringement and occurring from and after the date two years before the day the suit was filed; and

(2) order that the infringing reproductions, counterfeits, copies, or colorable imitations in the possession or under the control of the infringer be

(A) delivered to an officer of the court;

(B) delivered to the registrant; or

(C) destroyed.

(d) A registrant is entitled to recover damages under Subsection (c)(1) of this section only for an infringement that occurred during the period of time the infringer had actual knowledge of the registrant's mark.

Acts 1967, 60th Leg., p. 2343, ch. 785, § 1.

§ 16.27. Exceptions to Liability for Infringement

(a) No registration under this chapter adversely affects common law rights acquired prior to registration under this chapter. However, during any period when the registration of a mark under this chapter is in force and the registrant has not abandoned the mark, no common law rights as against the registrant of the mark may be acquired.

(b) The owner or operator of a radio or television station, or the owner or publisher of a newspaper, magazine, directory, or other publication, is not liable in that business under Section 16.26 of this code for the use of a registered mark furnished by one of his advertisers or customers.

Acts 1967, 60th Leg., p. 2343, ch. 785, § 1.

§ 16.28. Procuring Application or Registration by Fraud

(a) No person may procure for himself or another the filing of an application or the registration of a mark under this chapter by knowingly making a false or fraudulent representation or declaration, oral or written, or by any other fraudulent means.

(b) A person injured by the false or fraudulent procurement of an application or registration may sue the person who violated Subsection (a) of this section in a district court having venue and

(1) recover from him damages resulting from use of the fraudulently registered mark, plus costs of suit, including attorneys' fees; and

(2) have the registration cancelled.

Acts 1967, 60th Leg., p. 2343, ch. 785, § 1.

§ 16.29. Injury to Business Reputation or Trade Name or Mark

A person may bring an action to enjoin an act likely to injure a business reputation or to dilute the distinctive quality of a mark registered under this chapter or Title 15, U.S.C., or a mark or trade name valid at common law, regardless of whether there is competition between the parties or confusion as to the source of goods or services. An injunction sought under this section shall be obtained pursuant to Rule 680 et seq. of the Texas Rules of Civil Procedure.

Added by Acts 1989, 71st Leg., ch. 932, § 1, eff. June 14, 1989.

§ 16.30. Olympic Symbols

(a) Without the permission of the United States Olympic Committee, a person may not, for the purpose of trade, to induce the sale of goods or services, or to promote a theatrical exhibition, athletic performance, or competition, use:

(1) the symbol of the International Olympic Committee, consisting of five interlocking rings;

(2) the emblem of the United States Olympic Committee, consisting of an escutcheon having a blue chief and vertically extending red and white bars on the base with five interlocking rings displayed on the chief;

(3) a trademark, trade name, sign, symbol, or insignia falsely representing association with or authorization by the International Olympic Committee or the United States Olympic Committee; or

(4) the words "Olympic," "Olympiad," or "Citius Altius Fortius" or a combination or simulation of those words that tends to cause confusion or mistake, to deceive, or to suggest falsely a connection with the United States Olympic Committee or an Olympic activity.

(b) On violation of Subsection (a), the United States Olympic Committee is entitled to the remedies available to a registrant on infringement of a mark registered under this chapter.

Added by Acts 1995, 74th Leg., ch. 113, § 1, eff. Sept. 1, 1995.

§ 16.31. Criminal Penalty

(a) A person commits an offense if the person knowingly or intentionally signs and presents or causes to be presented for filing a document that may be or is required to be filed under this chapter and that:

(1) indicates that the person signing the document has the authority to act on behalf of an applicant or registrant when the person is not authorized to act on behalf of the applicant or registrant;

(2) contains a material false statement; or

(3) is forged.

(b) An offense under this section is a Class A misdemeanor unless the actor's intent is to defraud or harm another, in which event the offense is a state jail felony.

Added by Acts 1997, 75th Leg., ch. 248, § 7, eff. Sept. 1, 1997.

CHAPTER 17. DECEPTIVE TRADE PRACTICES

SUBCHAPTER A. GENERAL PROVISIONS

SUBCHAPTER A. GENERAL PROVISIONS

§ 17.01. Definitions

In this chapter, unless the context requires a different definition,

(1) "container" includes bale, barrel, bottle, box, cask, keg, and package; and

(2) "proprietary mark" includes word, name, symbol, device, and any combination of them in any form or arrangement, used by a person to identify his tangible personal property and distinguish it from the tangible personal property of another.

Acts 1967, 60th Leg., p. 2343, ch. 785, § 1.

[Sections 17.02 to 17.06 reserved for expansion]

SUBCHAPTER B. DECEPTIVE ADVERTISING, PACKING, SELLING, AND EXPORTING

§ 17.07. Repealed by Acts 1993, 73rd Leg., ch. 300, § 43(5), eff. Aug. 30, 1993

§ 17.08. Private Use of State Seal

(a) In this section:

(1) "Commercial purpose" means a purpose that is intended to result in a profit or other tangible benefit but does not include:

(A) official use of the state seal or a representation of the state seal in a state function;

(B) use of the state seal or a representation of the state seal for a political purpose by an elected official of this state;

(C) use of the state seal or a representation of the state seal in an encyclopedia, dictionary, book, journal, pamphlet, periodical, magazine, or newspaper incident to a description or history of seals, coats of arms, heraldry, or this state;

(D) use of the state seal or a representation of the state seal in a library, museum, or educational facility incident to descriptions or exhibits relating to seals, coats of arms, heraldry, or this state;

(E) use of the state seal or a representation of the state seal in a theatrical, motion-picture, television, or similar production for a historical, educational, or newsworthy purpose; or

(F) use of the state seal or a representation of the state seal for another historical, educational, or newsworthy purpose if authorized in writing by the secretary of state.

(2) "Representation of the state seal" includes a nonexact representation that the secretary of state determines is deceptively similar to the state seal.

(3) "Official use" means the use of the state seal by an officer or employee of this state in performing a state function.

(4) "State function" means a state governmental activity authorized or required by law.

(5) "State seal" means the state seal, the reverse of the state seal, and the state arms as defined by Sections 3101.001 and 3101.002, Government Code.

(b) Except as otherwise provided by this section, a person may not use a representation of the state seal:

(1) to advertise or publicize tangible personal property or a commercial undertaking; or

(2) for another commercial purpose.

(c) A person may use a representation of the state seal for a commercial purpose if the person obtains a license from the secretary of state for that use. The secretary of state, under the authority vested in the secretary as custodian of the seal under Article IV, Section 19, of the Texas Constitution, shall issue a license to a person who applies for a license on a form provided by the secretary of state and who pays the fees required under this section if the secretary of state determines that the use is in the best interests of the state and not detrimental to the image of the state. A license issued under this section expires one year after the date of issuance and may be renewed.

(d) The secretary of state shall adopt rules relating to the use of the state seal by a person licensed under this section. The secretary of state shall adopt the rules in the manner provided by Chapter 2001, Government Code.

(e) The application fee for a license under this section is $35. The license fee for an original or renewal license is $250. In addition to those fees, each licensee shall pay an amount equal to three percent of the licensee's annual gross receipts related to the licensed use in excess of $5,000 to the state as a royalty fee.

(f) A person licensed under this section shall maintain records relating to the licensee's use of the state seal in the manner required by the rules of the secretary of state. The secretary of state may examine the records during reasonable business hours to determine the licensee's compliance with this section. Each licensee shall display the license in a conspicuous manner in the licensee's office or place of business.

(g) The secretary of state may suspend or revoke a license issued under this section for failure to comply with this section or the rules adopted under this section. The secretary of state may bring a civil action to enjoin a violation of this section or the rules adopted under this section.

(h) A person who reproduces an official document bearing the state seal does not violate Subsection (b) of this section if the document is:

(1) reproduced in complete form; and

(2) used for a purpose related to the purpose for which the document was issued by the state.

(i) A person who violates a provision of Subsection (b) of this section commits an offense. An offense under this section is a Class C misdemeanor.

(j) A person who violates Subsection (b) of this section commits a separate offense each day that the person violates a provision of that subsection.

Acts 1967, 60th Leg., p. 2343, ch. 785, § 1. Amended by Acts 1985, 69th Leg., ch. 811, § 10, eff. Sept. 1, 1985; Acts 1993, 73rd Leg., ch. 300, § 8, eff. Aug. 30, 1993; Acts 1995, 74th Leg., ch. 76, § 5.95(49), eff. Sept. 1, 1995; Acts 2007, 80th Leg., ch. 921, § 2A.001, eff. Sept. 1, 2007.

§§ 17.09, 17.10. Repealed by Acts 1973, 63rd Leg., p. 995, ch. 399, § 3(d), eff. Jan. 1, 1974

§ 17.11. Deceptive Wholesale and Going-Out-Of-Business Advertising

(a) In Subsection (b) of this section, unless the context requires a different definition, "wholesaler" means a person who sells for the purpose of resale and not directly to a consuming purchaser.

(b) No person may wilfully misrepresent the nature of his business by using in selling or advertising the word manufacturer, wholesaler, retailer, or other word of similar meaning.

(c) No person may wilfully misrepresent the ownership of a business for the purpose of holding a liquidation sale, auction sale, or other sale which represents that the business is going out of business. A person who advertises a liquidation sale, auction sale, or going-out-of-business sale shall state the correct name and permanent address of the owner of the business in the advertising.

(d) A person who violates a provision of Subsection (b) or (c) of this section is guilty of a misdemeanor and upon conviction is punishable by a fine of not less than $100 nor more than $500.

Acts 1967, 60th Leg., p. 2343, ch. 785, § 1.

§ 17.12. Deceptive Advertising

(a) No person may disseminate a statement he knows materially misrepresents the cost or character of tangible personal property, a security, service, or anything he may offer for the purpose of

(1) selling, contracting to sell, otherwise disposing of, or contracting to dispose of the tangible personal property, security, service, or anything he may offer; or

(2) inducing a person to contract with regard to the tangible personal property, security, service, or anything he may offer.

(b) No person may solicit advertising in the name of a club, association, or organization without the written permission of such club, association, or organization or distribute any publication purporting to represent officially a club, association, or organization without the written authority of or a contract with such club, association, or organization and without listing in such publication the complete name and address of the club, association, or organization endorsing it.

(c) A person's proprietary mark appearing on or in a statement described in Subsection (a) of this section is prima facie evidence that the person disseminated the statement.

(d) A person who violates a provision of Subsection (a) or (b) of this Section is guilty of a misdemeanor and upon conviction is punishable by a fine of not less than $10 nor more than $200.

Acts 1967, 60th Leg., p. 2343, ch. 785, § 1. Amended by Acts 1969, 61st Leg., p. 2045, ch. 701, § 1, eff. June 12, 1969.

[Sections 17.13 to 17.17 reserved for expansion]

SUBCHAPTER C. REGULATING THE SALE OR TRANSFER OF SECONDHAND WATCHES

§ 17.18. Applicability of Subchapter to Secondhand Watches

(a) A watch is secondhand if its

(1) case, movement, or case and movement as a unit, has been previously sold or transferred to a person for his own use or the use of another;

(2) serial number, movement number, or other identification mark or number has been removed, altered, or covered up; or

(3) movement is more than one year old and has been repaired even though the watch has been returned to the seller or transferor for exchange or credit as described in Subsection (b)(1) of this section.

(b) A watch is not secondhand if

(1) after the sale or transfer described in Subsection (a)(1) of this section,

(A) the purchaser or transferee returns the watch to the seller or transferor for exchange or credit within one year from the date of sale or transfer to him;

(B) the seller or transferor keeps a written record showing

(i) the purchaser's or transferee's name;

(ii) the date of sale or transfer;

(iii) the serial number on the case and movement, if present; and

(iv) any proprietary mark;

(C) the record is kept for at least five years from the date of sale or transfer; and

(D) the record is open for inspection at the seller's or transferor's business address during business hours by

(i) the county or district attorney of the county in which the seller or transferor does business; or

(ii) his duly authorized representative; or

(2) its movement is merely cleaned, oiled, or recased.

(c) The provisions of Subsections (a) and (b) of this section do not apply to a pawnbroker's auction sale of unredeemed pledges.

Acts 1967, 60th Leg., p. 2343, ch. 785, § 1.

§ 17.19. Labeling Secondhand Watches

No person in the business of buying or selling watches may sell or exchange, offer to sell or exchange, possess, or display with intent to sell or exchange a secondhand watch unless he

(1) fastens to the watch a clearly written or printed tag bearing the word "secondhand"; and

(2) places the tag so the word "secondhand" is in plain sight at all times.

Acts 1967, 60th Leg., p. 2343, ch. 785, § 1.

§ 17.20. Content of Invoice for Secondhand Watch

(a) No person in the business of buying or selling watches may sell or transfer a secondhand watch unless he gives the purchaser or transferee a written invoice

(1) bearing the words "secondhand watch" in letters larger than any other letters on the invoice, except those of the letterhead; and

(2) listing the following items:

(A) the seller's or transferor's name and address;

(B) the purchaser's or transferee's name and address;

(C) the date of sale or transfer;

(D) the name of the watch or its manufacturer; and

(E) the serial number or proprietary mark on the watch or, if the serial number or proprietary mark has been removed, altered, or covered up, a statement to that effect.

(b) The seller or transferor shall keep on file a duplicate of the invoice required by Subsection (a) of this section for at least five years from the date of sale or transfer.

(c) The county or district attorney, or his authorized representative, of the county in which the seller or transferor does business may inspect the duplicate invoice described in Subsection (b) of this section

(1) during the seller's or transferor's business hours; and

(2) at the seller's or transferor's business address.

Acts 1967, 60th Leg., p. 2343, ch. 785, § 1.

§ 17.21. Advertising Watch as Secondhand

No person may advertise or display a secondhand watch for sale or exchange unless he clearly states in the advertisement or display that the watch is secondhand.

Acts 1967, 60th Leg., p. 2343, ch. 785, § 1.

§ 17.22. Criminal Penalty

A person, or his agent or employee, who violates a provision of Section 17.19, 17.20, or 17.21 of this code is guilty of a misdemeanor and upon conviction is punishable by imprisonment in the county jail for not more than 100 days or by a fine of not more than $500 or by both.

Acts 1967, 60th Leg., p. 2343, ch. 785, § 1.

[Sections 17.23 to 17.27 reserved for expansion]

SUBCHAPTER D. COUNTERFEITING OR CHANGING A REQUIRED MARK; MISUSE OF CONTAINER BEARING MARK

§ 17.28. Repealed by Acts 1973, 63rd Leg., p. 995, ch. 399, § 3(d), eff. Jan. 1, 1974

§ 17.29. Misusing Container; Evidence of Misuse and Container's Ownership

(a) In this section, unless the context requires a different definition, "container" also includes drink-dispensing fountain.

(b) Unless the owner of a reusable container bearing a proprietary mark (or one acting with the owner's written permission) agrees, no person may

(1) fill the container for sale or other commercial purpose;

(2) deface, cover up, or remove the proprietary mark from the container; or

(3) refuse to return the container to the owner if he requests its return.

(c) A person's wilful

(1) possession of a full or empty reusable container without the owner's permission is prima facie evidence of his violating a provision of Subsection (b) of this section;

(2) use, purchase, sale, or other disposition of a full or empty reusable container without the owner's permission is prima facie evidence of his violating a provision of Subsection (b) of this section; and

(3) breaking, damaging, or destroying a full or empty reusable container is prima facie evidence of his violating a provision of Subsection (b) of this section.

(d) In an action in which the ownership of a reusable container is in issue, a person's proprietary mark on the container is prima facie evidence that the person or his licensee owns the container.

(e) A person who violates a provision of Subsection (b) of this section is guilty of a misdemeanor and upon conviction is punishable by

(1) a fine of not less than $25 nor more than $50 for each violation concerning a drink-dispensing fountain; or

(2) a fine of not less than $5 nor more than $10 for each violation concerning any other container.

Acts 1967, 60th Leg., p. 2343, ch. 785, § 1.

§ 17.30. Misusing Dairy Container Bearing Proprietary Mark

(a) In this section, unless the context requires a different definition, "dairy container" includes butter box, ice cream can, ice cream tub, milk bottle, milk bottle case, milk can, and milk jar.

(b) Without the owner's consent, no person may

(1) fill with milk, cream, butter, or ice cream; damage; mutilate; or destroy a dairy container bearing the owner's commonly used proprietary mark; or

(2) wilfully refuse to return on request to the owner a dairy container bearing his commonly used proprietary mark.

(c) Without the owner's written consent, no person may

(1) deface or remove an owner's proprietary mark from a dairy container; or

(2) substitute on a dairy container his proprietary mark for that of the owner.

(d) A person's commonly used proprietary mark on a dairy container is prima facie evidence of that person's ownership of the container.

(e) A person who violates a provision of Subsection (b) or (c) of this section is guilty of a misdemeanor and upon conviction is punishable by a fine of not less than $10 nor more than $100.

Acts 1967, 60th Leg., p. 2343, ch. 785, § 1.

§ 17.31. Identification, Possession, and Use of Certain Containers

(a) In this section:

(1) "Bakery basket or tray" means a wire or plastic container that holds bread or other baked goods and is used by a distributor or retailer or an agent of a distributor or retailer to transport, store, or carry bakery products.

(2) "Container" means a bakery basket or tray, dairy case, egg basket, poultry box, or other container used to transport, store, or carry a product.

(3) "Dairy case" means a wire or plastic container that holds 16 quarts or more of beverage and is used by a distributor or retailer or an agent of a distributor or retailer to transport, store, or carry dairy products.

(4) "Egg basket" means a permanent type of container that contains four dozen or more shell eggs and is used by a distributor or retailer or an agent of a distributor or retailer to transport, store, or carry eggs.

(5) "Laundry cart" means a basket that is mounted on wheels and used in a coin-operated laundry or dry cleaning establishment by a customer or an attendant to transport laundry and laundry supplies.

(6) "Name or mark" means any permanently affixed or permanently stamped name or mark that is used for the purpose of identifying the owner of a shopping cart, laundry cart, or container.

(7) "Parking area" means a lot or other property provided by a retail establishment for the use of customers to park automobiles or other vehicles while doing business in that establishment.

(8) "Poultry box" means a permanent type of container that is used by a processor, distributor, retailer, or food service establishment or an agent of one of those persons to transport, store, or carry poultry.

(9) "Shopping cart" means a basket that is mounted on wheels, or a similar device, generally used in a retail establishment by a customer to transport goods of any kind.

(b) A person owning a shopping cart, laundry cart, or container may adopt and use a name or mark on the carts or containers.

(c) A person may not:

(1) use for any purpose outside the premises of the owner or an adjacent parking area, a container of another that is identified with or by any name or mark unless the use is authorized by the owner;

(2) sell or offer for sale a container of another that is identified with or by a name or mark unless the sale is authorized by the owner; or

(3) deface, obliterate, destroy, cover up, or otherwise remove or conceal a name or mark on a container of another without the written consent of the owner.

(d) A common carrier or contract carrier, unless engaged in the transporting of dairy products, eggs, and poultry to and from farms where they are produced, may not receive or transport a container marked with a name or mark unless the carrier has in the carrier's possession a bill of lading or invoice for the container.

(e) A person may not remove a container from the premises, parking area, or any other area of a processor, distributor, or retail establishment or from a delivery vehicle unless the person is legally authorized to do so, if:

(1) the container is marked on at least one side with a name or mark; and

(2) a notice to the public, warning that unauthorized use by a person other than the owner is punishable by law, is visibly displayed on the container.

(f) A person may not:

(1) remove a shopping cart or laundry cart from the premises or parking area of a retail establishment with intent to temporarily or permanently deprive the owner of the cart or the retailer of possession of the cart;

(2) remove a shopping cart or laundry cart, without written authorization from the owner of the cart, from the premises or parking area of any retail establishment;

(3) possess, without the written permission of the owner or retailer in lawful possession of the cart, a shopping cart or laundry cart outside the premises or parking lot of the retailer whose name or mark appears on the cart; or

(4) remove, obliterate, or alter a serial number, name, or mark affixed to a shopping cart or laundry cart.

(g) The requiring, taking, or accepting of a deposit on delivery of a container, shopping cart, or laundry cart is not considered a sale of the container or cart.

(h) A person who violates this section commits an offense. An offense under this section is a Class C misdemeanor. Each violation constitutes a separate offense.

(i) This section does not apply to the owner of a shopping cart, laundry cart, or container or to a customer or any other person who has written consent from the owner of a shopping cart, laundry cart, or container or from a retailer in lawful possession of the cart or container to remove it from the premises or the parking area of the retail establishment. For the purposes of this section, the term "written consent" includes tokens and other indicia of consent established by the owner of the carts or the retailer.

Added by Acts 1989, 71st Leg., ch. 724, § 1, eff. Sept. 1, 1989.

[Sections 17.32 to 17.40 reserved for expansion]

SUBCHAPTER E. DECEPTIVE TRADE PRACTICES AND CONSUMER PROTECTION

This Subchapter E was enacted by § 1 of Acts 1973, 63rd Leg., p. 322, ch. 143. Section 3 of the 1973 Act repealed Chapter 10 of Title 79, Vernon's Ann.Civ.St. arts. 5069–10.01 to 5069–10.08.

DISPOSITION TABLE

Showing where the subject matter of former Chapter 10 of Title 79, Revised Civil Statutes, is now covered in this Subchapter E.

Vernon's Ann. Civ.St. Article	Subchapter Section
5069–10.01(a)	17.45
5069–10.01(b)	17.46
5069–10.01(c)	17.45
5069–10.01(d)	17.45
5069–10.02	17.46
5069–10.03	17.49
5069–10.04	17.47
5069–10.05	17.58
5069–10.06	17.60
5069–10.07	17.61
5069–10.08	17.62

§ 17.41. Short Title

This subchapter may be cited as the Deceptive Trade Practices-Consumer Protection Act.

Added by Acts 1973, 63rd Leg., p. 322, ch. 143, § 1, eff. May 21, 1973.

§ 17.42. Waivers: Public Policy

(a) Any waiver by a consumer of the provisions of this subchapter is contrary to public policy and is unenforceable and void; provided, however, that a waiver is valid and enforceable if:

(1) the waiver is in writing and is signed by the consumer;

(2) the consumer is not in a significantly disparate bargaining position; and

(3) the consumer is represented by legal counsel in seeking or acquiring the goods or services.

(b) A waiver under Subsection (a) is not effective if the consumer's legal counsel was directly or indirectly identified, suggested, or selected by a defendant or an agent of the defendant.

(c) A waiver under this section must be:

(1) conspicuous and in bold-face type of at least 10 points in size;

(2) identified by the heading "Waiver of Consumer Rights," or words of similar meaning; and

(3) in substantially the following form:

"I waive my rights under the Deceptive Trade Practices-Consumer Protection Act, Section 17.41 et seq., Business & Commerce Code, a law that gives consumers special rights and protections. After consultation with an attorney of my own selection, I voluntarily consent to this waiver."

(d) The waiver required by Subsection (c) may be modified to waive only specified rights under this subchapter.

(e) The fact that a consumer has signed a waiver under this section is not a defense to an action brought by the attorney general under Section 17.47.

Added by Acts 1973, 63rd Leg., p. 322, ch. 143, § 1, eff. May 21, 1973. Amended by Acts 1981, 67th Leg., p. 863, ch. 307, § 1, eff. Aug. 31, 1981; Acts 1983, 68th Leg., p. 4943, ch. 883, § 1, eff. Aug. 29, 1983; Acts 1987, 70th Leg., ch. 167, § 5.02(6), eff. Sept. 1, 1987; Acts 1989, 71st Leg., ch. 380, § 1, eff. Sept. 1, 1989; Acts 1995, 74th Leg., ch. 414, § 1, eff. Sept. 1, 1995.

§ 17.43. Cumulative Remedies

The provisions of this subchapter are not exclusive. The remedies provided in this subchapter are in addition to any other procedures or remedies provided for in any other law; provided, however, that no recovery shall be permitted under both this subchapter and another law of both damages and penalties for the same act or practice. A violation of a provision of law other than this subchapter is not in and of itself a violation of this subchapter. An act or practice that is a violation of a provision of law other than this subchapter may be made the basis of an action under this subchapter if the act or practice is proscribed by a provision of this subchapter or is declared by such other law to be actionable under this subchapter. The provisions of this subchapter do not in any way preclude other political subdivisions of this state from dealing with deceptive trade practices.

Added by Acts 1973, 63rd Leg., p. 322, ch. 143, § 1, eff. May 21, 1973. Amended by Acts 1979, 66th Leg., p. 1327, ch. 603, § 1, eff. Aug. 27, 1979; Acts 1995, 74th Leg., ch. 414, § 1, eff. Sept. 1, 1995.

§ 17.44. Construction and Application

(a) This subchapter shall be liberally construed and applied to promote its underlying purposes, which are to protect consumers against false, misleading, and deceptive business practices, unconscionable actions, and breaches of warranty and to provide efficient and economical procedures to secure such protection.

(b) Chapter 27, Property Code, prevails over this subchapter to the extent of any conflict.

Added by Acts 1973, 63rd Leg., p. 322, ch. 143, § 1, eff. May 21, 1973. Amended by Acts 1995, 74th Leg., ch. 414, § 1, eff. Sept. 1, 1995.

§ 17.45. Definitions

As used in this subchapter:

(1) "Goods" means tangible chattels or real property purchased or leased for use.

(2) "Services" means work, labor, or service purchased or leased for use, including services furnished in connection with the sale or repair of goods.

(3) "Person" means an individual, partnership, corporation, association, or other group, however organized.

(4) "Consumer" means an individual, partnership, corporation, this state, or a subdivision or agency of this state who seeks or acquires by purchase or lease, any goods or services, except that the term does not include a business consumer that has assets of $25 million or more, or that is owned or controlled by a corporation or entity with assets of $25 million or more.

(5) "Unconscionable action or course of action" means an act or practice which, to a consumer's detriment, takes advantage of the lack of knowledge, ability, experience, or capacity of the consumer to a grossly unfair degree.

(6) "Trade" and "commerce" mean the advertising, offering for sale, sale, lease, or distribution of any good or service, of any property, tangible or intangible, real, personal, or mixed, and any other article, commodity, or thing of value, wherever situated, and shall include any trade or commerce directly or indirectly affecting the people of this state.

(7) "Documentary material" includes the original or a copy of any book, record, report, memorandum, paper, communication, tabulation, map, chart, photograph, mechanical transcription, or other tangible document or recording, wherever situated.

(8) "Consumer protection division" means the consumer protection division of the attorney general's office.

(9) "Knowingly" means actual awareness, at the time of the act or practice complained of, of the falsity, deception, or unfairness of the act or practice giving rise to the consumer's claim or, in an action brought under Subdivision (2) of Subsection (a) of Section 17.50, actual awareness of the act, practice, condition, defect, or failure constituting the breach of warranty, but actual awareness may be inferred where objective manifestations indicate that a person acted with actual awareness.

(10) "Business consumer" means an individual, partnership, or corporation who seeks or acquires by purchase or lease, any goods or services for commercial or business use. The term does not include this state or a subdivision or agency of this state.

(11) "Economic damages" means compensatory damages for pecuniary loss, including costs of repair and replacement. The term does not include exemplary damages or damages for physical pain and mental anguish, loss of consortium, disfigurement, physical impairment, or loss of companionship and society.

(12) "Residence" means a building:

(A) that is a single-family house, duplex, triplex, or quadruplex or a unit in a multiunit residential structure in which title to the individual units is transferred to the owners under a condominium or cooperative system; and

(B) that is occupied or to be occupied as the consumer's residence.

(13) "Intentionally" means actual awareness of the falsity, deception, or unfairness of the act or practice, or the condition, defect, or failure constituting a breach of warranty giving rise to the consumer's claim, coupled with the specific intent that the consumer act in detrimental reliance on the falsity or deception or in detrimental ignorance of the unfairness. Intention may be inferred from objective manifestations that indicate that the person acted intentionally or from facts showing that a defendant acted with flagrant disregard of prudent and fair business practices to the extent that the

defendant should be treated as having acted intentionally.

Added by Acts 1973, 63rd Leg., p. 322, ch. 143, § 1, eff. May 21, 1973. Amended by Acts 1975, 64th Leg., p. 149, ch. 62, § 1, eff. Sept. 1, 1975; Acts 1977, 65th Leg., p. 600, ch. 216, § 1, eff. May 23, 1977; Acts 1979, 66th Leg., p. 1327, ch. 603, § 2, eff. Aug. 27, 1979; Acts 1983, 68th Leg., p. 4943, ch. 883, §§ 2, 3, eff. Aug. 29, 1983; Acts 1995, 74th Leg., ch. 414, § 2, eff. Sept. 1, 1995; Acts 2007, 80th Leg., ch. 411, § 1, eff. Sept. 1, 2007.

§ 17.46. Deceptive Trade Practices Unlawful

(a) False, misleading, or deceptive acts or practices in the conduct of any trade or commerce are hereby declared unlawful and are subject to action by the consumer protection division under Sections 17.47, 17.58, 17.60, and 17.61 of this code.

(b) Except as provided in Subsection (d) of this section, the term "false, misleading, or deceptive acts or practices" includes, but is not limited to, the following acts:

(1) passing off goods or services as those of another;

(2) causing confusion or misunderstanding as to the source, sponsorship, approval, or certification of goods or services;

(3) causing confusion or misunderstanding as to affiliation, connection, or association with, or certification by, another;

(4) using deceptive representations or designations of geographic origin in connection with goods or services;

(5) representing that goods or services have sponsorship, approval, characteristics, ingredients, uses, benefits, or quantities which they do not have or that a person has a sponsorship, approval, status, affiliation, or connection which he does not;

(6) representing that goods are original or new if they are deteriorated, reconditioned, reclaimed, used, or secondhand;

(7) representing that goods or services are of a particular standard, quality, or grade, or that goods are of a particular style or model, if they are of another;

(8) disparaging the goods, services, or business of another by false or misleading representation of facts;

(9) advertising goods or services with intent not to sell them as advertised;

(10) advertising goods or services with intent not to supply a reasonable expectable public demand, unless the advertisements disclosed a limitation of quantity;

(11) making false or misleading statements of fact concerning the reasons for, existence of, or amount of price reductions;

(12) representing that an agreement confers or involves rights, remedies, or obligations which it does not have or involve, or which are prohibited by law;

(13) knowingly making false or misleading statements of fact concerning the need for parts, replacement, or repair service;

(14) misrepresenting the authority of a salesman, representative or agent to negotiate the final terms of a consumer transaction;

(15) basing a charge for the repair of any item in whole or in part on a guaranty or warranty instead of on the value of the actual repairs made or work to be performed on the item without stating separately the charges for the work and the charge for the warranty or guaranty, if any;

(16) disconnecting, turning back, or resetting the odometer of any motor vehicle so as to reduce the number of miles indicated on the odometer gauge;

(17) advertising of any sale by fraudulently representing that a person is going out of business;

(18) advertising, selling, or distributing a card which purports to be a prescription drug identification card issued under Section 4151.152, Insurance Code, in accordance with rules adopted by the commissioner of insurance, which offers a discount on the purchase of health care goods or services from a third party provider, and which is not evidence of insurance coverage, unless:

(A) the discount is authorized under an agreement between the seller of the card and the provider of those goods and services or the discount or card is offered to members of the seller;

(B) the seller does not represent that the card provides insurance coverage of any kind; and

(C) the discount is not false, misleading, or deceptive;

(19) using or employing a chain referral sales plan in connection with the sale or offer to sell of goods, merchandise, or anything of value, which uses the sales technique, plan, arrangement, or agreement in which the buyer or prospective buyer

is offered the opportunity to purchase merchandise or goods and in connection with the purchase receives the seller's promise or representation that the buyer shall have the right to receive compensation or consideration in any form for furnishing to the seller the names of other prospective buyers if receipt of the compensation or consideration is contingent upon the occurrence of an event subsequent to the time the buyer purchases the merchandise or goods;

(20) representing that a guarantee or warranty confers or involves rights or remedies which it does not have or involve, provided, however, that nothing in this subchapter shall be construed to expand the implied warranty of merchantability as defined in Sections 2.314 through 2.318 and Sections 2A.212 through 2A.216 to involve obligations in excess of those which are appropriate to the goods;

(21) promoting a pyramid promotional scheme, as defined by Section 17.461;

(22) representing that work or services have been performed on, or parts replaced in, goods when the work or services were not performed or the parts replaced;

(23) filing suit founded upon a written contractual obligation of and signed by the defendant to pay money arising out of or based on a consumer transaction for goods, services, loans, or extensions of credit intended primarily for personal, family, household, or agricultural use in any county other than in the county in which the defendant resides at the time of the commencement of the action or in the county in which the defendant in fact signed the contract; provided, however, that a violation of this subsection shall not occur where it is shown by the person filing such suit he neither knew or had reason to know that the county in which such suit was filed was neither the county in which the defendant resides at the commencement of the suit nor the county in which the defendant in fact signed the contract;

(24) failing to disclose information concerning goods or services which was known at the time of the transaction if such failure to disclose such information was intended to induce the consumer into a transaction into which the consumer would not have entered had the information been disclosed;

(25) using the term "corporation," "incorporated," or an abbreviation of either of those terms in the name of a business entity that is not incorporated under the laws of this state or another jurisdiction;

(26) selling, offering to sell, or illegally promoting an annuity contract under Chapter 22, Acts of the 57th Legislature, 3rd Called Session, 1962 (Article 6228a–5, Vernon's Texas Civil Statutes), with the intent that the annuity contract will be the subject of a salary reduction agreement, as defined by that Act, if the annuity contract is not an eligible qualified investment under that Act or is not registered with the Teacher Retirement System of Texas as required by Section 8A of that Act; or

(27) taking advantage of a disaster declared by the governor under Chapter 418, Government Code, by:

(A) selling or leasing fuel, food, medicine, or another necessity at an exorbitant or excessive price; or

(B) demanding an exorbitant or excessive price in connection with the sale or lease of fuel, food, medicine, or another necessity.

(c)(1) It is the intent of the legislature that in construing Subsection (a) of this section in suits brought under Section 17.47 of this subchapter the courts to the extent possible will be guided by Subsection (b) of this section and the interpretations given by the Federal Trade Commission and federal courts to Section 5(a)(1) of the Federal Trade Commission Act [15 U.S.C.A. § 45(a)(1)].

(2) In construing this subchapter the court shall not be prohibited from considering relevant and pertinent decisions of courts in other jurisdictions.

(d) For the purposes of the relief authorized in Subdivision (1) of Subsection (a) of Section 17.50 of this subchapter, the term "false, misleading, or deceptive acts or practices" is limited to the acts enumerated in specific subdivisions of Subsection (b) of this section.

Added by Acts 1973, 63rd Leg., p. 322, ch. 143, § 1, eff. May 21, 1973. Amended by Acts 1977, 65th Leg., p. 601, ch. 216, §§ 2, 3, eff. May 23, 1977; Acts 1977, 65th Leg., p. 892, ch. 336, § 1, eff. Aug. 29, 1977; Acts 1979, 66th Leg., p. 1327, ch. 603, § 3, eff. Aug. 27, 1979; Acts 1987, 70th Leg., ch. 280, § 1, eff. Sept. 1, 1987; Acts 1993, 73rd Leg., ch. 570, § 6, eff. Sept. 1, 1993; Acts 1995, 74th Leg., ch. 414, § 3, eff. Sept. 1, 1995; Acts 1995, 74th Leg., ch. 463, § 1, eff. Sept. 1, 1995; Acts 2001, 77th Leg., ch. 962, § 1, eff. Sept. 1, 2001; Acts 2001, 77th Leg., ch. 1229, § 27, eff. June 1, 2002; Acts 2003, 78th Leg., ch. 1276, § 4.001(a), eff. Sept. 1, 2003; Acts 2005, 79th Leg., ch. 728, § 11.101, eff. Sept. 1, 2005; Acts 2007, 80th Leg., ch. 1230, § 26, eff. Sept. 1, 2007.

Section 32 of Acts 2007, 80th Leg., ch. 1230 provides:

"Section 17.46(b), Business & Commerce Code, as amended by this Act, applies only to a cause of action that accrues on or after January 1, 2008. A cause of action that accrues before January 1, 2008, is governed by the law as it existed immediately before the effective date [Sept. 1, 2007] of this Act, and that law is continued in effect for that purpose."

§ 17.461. Pyramid Promotional Scheme

(a) In this section:

(1) "Compensation" means payment of money, a financial benefit, or another thing of value. The term does not include payment based on sale of a product to a person, including a participant, who purchases the product for actual use or consumption.

(2) "Consideration" means the payment of cash or the purchase of a product. The term does not include:

(A) a purchase of a product furnished at cost to be used in making a sale and not for resale;

(B) a purchase of a product subject to a repurchase agreement that complies with Subsection (b); or

(C) time and effort spent in pursuit of a sale or in a recruiting activity.

(3) "Participate" means to contribute money into a pyramid promotional scheme without promoting, organizing, or operating the scheme.

(4) "Product" means a good, a service, or intangible property of any kind.

(5) "Promoting a pyramid promotional scheme" means:

(A) inducing or attempting to induce one or more other persons to participate in a pyramid promotional scheme; or

(B) assisting another person in inducing or attempting to induce one or more other persons to participate in a pyramid promotional scheme, including by providing references.

(6) "Pyramid promotional scheme" means a plan or operation by which a person gives consideration for the opportunity to receive compensation that is derived primarily from a person's introduction of other persons to participate in the plan or operation rather than from the sale of a product by a person introduced into the plan or operation.

(b) To qualify as a repurchase agreement for the purposes of Subsection (a)(2)(B), an agreement must be an enforceable agreement by the seller to repurchase, on written request of the purchaser and not later than the first anniversary of the purchaser's date of purchase, all unencumbered products that are in an unused, commercially resalable condition at a price not less than 90 percent of the amount actually paid by the purchaser for the products being returned, less any consideration received by the purchaser for purchase of the products being returned. A product that is no longer marketed by the seller is considered resalable if the product is otherwise in an unused, commercially resalable condition and is returned to the seller not later than the first anniversary of the purchaser's date of purchase, except that the product is not considered resalable if before the purchaser purchased the product it was clearly disclosed to the purchaser that the product was sold as a nonreturnable, discontinued, seasonal, or special promotion item.

(c) A person commits an offense if the person contrives, prepares, establishes, operates, advertises, sells, or promotes a pyramid promotional scheme. An offense under this subsection is a state jail felony.

(d) It is not a defense to prosecution for an offense under this section that the pyramid promotional scheme involved both a franchise to sell a product and the authority to sell additional franchises if the emphasis of the scheme is on the sale of additional franchises.

Added by Acts 1995, 74th Leg., ch. 463, § 2, eff. Sept. 1, 1995.

§ 17.462. Listing of Business Location in Directory or Database

(a) A person may not misrepresent the geographical location of a business that derives 50 percent or more of its gross income from the sale or arranging for the sale of flowers or floral arrangements in the listing of the business in a telephone directory or other directory assistance database.

(b) A person is considered to misrepresent the geographical location of a business for purposes of Subsection (a) if the name of the business indicates that the business is located in a geographical area and:

(1) the business is not located within the geographical area indicated;

(2) the listing fails to identify the municipality and state of the business's geographical location; and

(3) a telephone call to the local telephone number listed in the directory or database routinely is forwarded or transferred to a location that is outside

the calling area covered by the directory or database in which the number is listed.

(c) A person may place a directory listing for a business described by Subsection (a) the name of which indicates that it is located in a geographical area that is different from the geographical area in which the business is located if a conspicuous notice in the listing states the municipality and state in which the business is located.

(d) This section does not apply to a publisher of a telephone directory or other publication or a provider of a directory assistance service publishing or providing information about another business.

(e) This section creates no duty and imposes no obligation upon anyone other than the business that is the subject of the advertisement or listing.

(f) A violation of this section is a false, misleading, or deceptive act or practice under this subchapter, and any public or private right or remedy prescribed by this subchapter may be used to enforce this section.

Added by Acts 2003, 78th Leg., ch. 138, § 1, eff. Sept. 1, 2003.

§ 17.47. Restraining Orders

(a) Whenever the consumer protection division has reason to believe that any person is engaging in, has engaged in, or is about to engage in any act or practice declared to be unlawful by this subchapter, and that proceedings would be in the public interest, the division may bring an action in the name of the state against the person to restrain by temporary restraining order, temporary injunction, or permanent injunction the use of such method, act, or practice.

Nothing herein shall require the consumer protection division to notify such person that court action is or may be under consideration. Provided, however, the consumer protection division shall, at least seven days prior to instituting such court action, contact such person to inform him in general of the alleged unlawful conduct. Cessation of unlawful conduct after such prior contact shall not render such court action moot under any circumstances, and such injunctive relief shall lie even if such person has ceased such unlawful conduct after such prior contact. Such prior contact shall not be required if, in the opinion of the consumer protection division, there is good cause to believe that such person would evade service of process if prior contact were made or that such person would destroy relevant records if prior contact were made, or that such an emergency exists that immediate and irreparable injury, loss, or damage would occur as a result of such delay in obtaining a temporary restraining order.

(b) An action brought under Subsection (a) of this section which alleges a claim to relief under this section may be commenced in the district court of the county in which the person against whom it is brought resides, has his principal place of business, has done business, or in the district court of the county where the transaction occurred, or, on the consent of the parties, in a district court of Travis County. The court may issue temporary restraining orders, temporary or permanent injunctions to restrain and prevent violations of this subchapter and such injunctive relief shall be issued without bond.

(c) In addition to the request for a temporary restraining order, or permanent injunction in a proceeding brought under Subsection (a) of this section, the consumer protection division may request, and the trier of fact may award, a civil penalty to be paid to the state in an amount of:

(1) not more than $20,000 per violation; and

(2) if the act or practice that is the subject of the proceeding was calculated to acquire or deprive money or other property from a consumer who was 65 years of age or older when the act or practice occurred, an additional amount of not more than $250,000.

(d) The court may make such additional orders or judgments as are necessary to compensate identifiable persons for actual damages or to restore money or property, real or personal, which may have been acquired by means of any unlawful act or practice. Damages may not include any damages incurred beyond a point two years prior to the institution of the action by the consumer protection division. Orders of the court may also include the appointment of a receiver or a sequestration of assets if a person who has been ordered by a court to make restitution under this section has failed to do so within three months after the order to make restitution has become final and nonappealable.

(e) Any person who violates the terms of an injunction under this section shall forfeit and pay to the state a civil penalty of not more than $10,000 per violation, not to exceed $50,000. In determining whether or not an injunction has been violated the court shall take into consideration the maintenance of procedures reasonably adapted to insure compliance with the injunction. For the purposes of this section, the district court issuing the injunction shall retain jurisdiction, and the cause shall be continued, and in these cases, the consumer protection division, or the district or county attorney with prior notice to the consumer protection division, acting in the name of the state, may petition for recovery of civil penalties under this section.

(f) An order of the court awarding civil penalties under Subsection (e) of this section applies only to violations of the injunction incurred prior to the awarding of the penalty order. Second or subsequent violations of an injunction issued under this section are subject to the same penalties set out in Subsection (e) of this section.

(g) In determining the amount of penalty imposed under Subsection (c), the trier of fact shall consider:

(1) the seriousness of the violation, including the nature, circumstances, extent, and gravity of any prohibited act or practice;

(2) the history of previous violations;

(3) the amount necessary to deter future violations;

(4) the economic effect on the person against whom the penalty is to be assessed;

(5) knowledge of the illegality of the act or practice; and

(6) any other matter that justice may require.

(h) In bringing or participating in an action under this subchapter, the consumer protection division acts in the name of the state and does not establish an attorney-client relationship with another person, including a person to whom the consumer protection division requests that the court award relief.

Added by Acts 1973, 63rd Leg., p. 322, ch. 143, § 1, eff. May 21, 1973. Amended by Acts 1977, 65th Leg., p. 602, ch. 216, § 4, eff. May 23, 1977; Acts 1985, 69th Leg., ch. 564, § 1, eff. Aug. 26, 1985; Acts 1989, 71st Leg., ch. 1082, § 8.01, eff. Jan. 1, 1991; Acts 1991, 72nd Leg., ch. 242, § 11.18, eff. Sept. 1, 1991; Acts 1997, 75th Leg., ch. 388, § 1, eff. May 28, 1997; Acts 2003, 78th Leg., ch. 360, § 1, eff. Sept. 1, 2003.

§ 17.48. Duty of District and County Attorney

(a) It is the duty of the district and county attorneys to lend to the consumer protection division any assistance requested in the commencement and prosecutions of action under this subchapter.

(b) A district or county attorney, with prior written notice to the consumer protection division, may institute and prosecute actions seeking injunctive relief under this subchapter, after complying with the prior contact provisions of Subsection (a) of Section 17.47 of this subchapter. On request, the consumer protection division shall assist the district or county attorney in any action taken under this subchapter. If an action is prosecuted by a district or county attorney alone, he shall make a full report to the consumer protection division including the final disposition of the matter. No district or county attorney may bring an action under this section against any licensed insurer or licensed insurance agent transacting business under the authority and jurisdiction of the State Board of Insurance unless first requested in writing to do so by the State Board of Insurance, the commissioner of insurance, or the consumer protection division pursuant to a request by the State Board of Insurance or commissioner of insurance.

Added by Acts 1973, 63rd Leg., p. 322, ch. 143, § 1, eff. May 21, 1973.

§ 17.49. Exemptions

(a) Nothing in this subchapter shall apply to the owner or employees of a regularly published newspaper, magazine, or telephone directory, or broadcast station, or billboard, wherein any advertisement in violation of this subchapter is published or disseminated, unless it is established that the owner or employees of the advertising medium have knowledge of the false, deceptive, or misleading acts or practices declared to be unlawful by this subchapter, or had a direct or substantial financial interest in the sale or distribution of the unlawfully advertised good or service. Financial interest as used in this section relates to an expectation which would be the direct result of such advertisement.

(b) Nothing in this subchapter shall apply to acts or practices authorized under specific rules or regulations promulgated by the Federal Trade Commission under Section 5(a)(1) of the Federal Trade Commission Act [15 U.S.C.A. 45(a)(1)]. The provisions of this subchapter do apply to any act or practice prohibited or not specifically authorized by a rule or regulation of the Federal Trade Commission. An act or practice is not specifically authorized if no rule or regulation has been issued on the act or practice.

(c) Nothing in this subchapter shall apply to a claim for damages based on the rendering of a professional service, the essence of which is the providing of advice, judgment, opinion, or similar professional skill. This exemption does not apply to:

(1) an express misrepresentation of a material fact that cannot be characterized as advice, judgment, or opinion;

(2) a failure to disclose information in violation of Section 17.46(b)(24);

(3) an unconscionable action or course of action that cannot be characterized as advice, judgment, or opinion;

(4) breach of an express warranty that cannot be characterized as advice, judgment, or opinion; or

(5) a violation of Section 17.46(b)(26).

(d) Subsection (c) applies to a cause of action brought against the person who provided the professional service and a cause of action brought against any entity that could be found to be vicariously liable for the person's conduct.

(e) Except as specifically provided by Subsections (b) and (h), Section 17.50, nothing in this subchapter shall apply to a cause of action for bodily injury or death or for the infliction of mental anguish.

(f) Nothing in the subchapter shall apply to a claim arising out of a written contract if:

(1) the contract relates to a transaction, a project, or a set of transactions related to the same project involving total consideration by the consumer of more than $100,000;

(2) in negotiating the contract the consumer is represented by legal counsel who is not directly or indirectly identified, suggested, or selected by the defendant or an agent of the defendant; and

(3) the contract does not involve the consumer's residence.

(g) Nothing in this subchapter shall apply to a cause of action arising from a transaction, a project, or a set of transactions relating to the same project, involving total consideration by the consumer of more than $500,000, other than a cause of action involving a consumer's residence.

(h) A person who violates Section 17.46(b)(26) is jointly and severally liable under that subdivision for actual damages, court costs, and attorney's fees. Subject to Chapter 41, Civil Practice and Remedies Code, exemplary damages may be awarded in the event of fraud or malice.

Added by Acts 1973, 63rd Leg., p. 322, ch. 143, § 1, eff. May 21, 1973. Amended by Acts 1995, 74th Leg., ch. 414, § 4, eff. Sept. 1, 1995; Acts 2001, 77th Leg., ch. 1229, § 28, eff. June 1, 2002; Acts 2003, 78th Leg., ch. 1276, § 4.001(b), eff. Sept. 1, 2003.

§ 17.50. Relief for Consumers

(a) A consumer may maintain an action where any of the following constitute a producing cause of economic damages or damages for mental anguish:

(1) the use or employment by any person of a false, misleading, or deceptive act or practice that is:

(A) specifically enumerated in a subdivision of Subsection (b) of Section 17.46 of this subchapter; and

(B) relied on by a consumer to the consumer's detriment;

(2) breach of an express or implied warranty;

(3) any unconscionable action or course of action by any person; or

(4) the use or employment by any person of an act or practice in violation of Chapter 541, Insurance Code.

(b) In a suit filed under this section, each consumer who prevails may obtain:

(1) the amount of economic damages found by the trier of fact. If the trier of fact finds that the conduct of the defendant was committed knowingly, the consumer may also recover damages for mental anguish, as found by the trier of fact, and the trier of fact may award not more than three times the amount of economic damages; or if the trier of fact finds the conduct was committed intentionally, the consumer may recover damages for mental anguish, as found by the trier of fact, and the trier of fact may award not more than three times the amount of damages for mental anguish and economic damages;

(2) an order enjoining such acts or failure to act;

(3) orders necessary to restore to any party to the suit any money or property, real or personal, which may have been acquired in violation of this subchapter; and

(4) any other relief which the court deems proper, including the appointment of a receiver or the revocation of a license or certificate authorizing a person to engage in business in this state if the judgment has not been satisfied within three months of the date of the final judgment. The court may not revoke or suspend a license to do business in this state or appoint a receiver to take over the affairs of a person who has failed to satisfy a judgment if the person is a licensee of or regulated by a state agency which has statutory authority to revoke or suspend a license or to appoint a receiver or trustee. Costs and fees of such receivership or other relief shall be assessed against the defendant.

(c) On a finding by the court that an action under this section was groundless in fact or law or brought in bad faith, or brought for the purpose of harassment, the court shall award to the defendant reasonable and necessary attorneys' fees and court costs.

(d) Each consumer who prevails shall be awarded court costs and reasonable and necessary attorneys' fees.

(e) In computing additional damages under Subsection (b), attorneys' fees, costs, and prejudgment interest may not be considered.

(f) A court may not award prejudgment interest applicable to:

(1) damages for future loss under this subchapter; or

(2) additional damages under Subsection (b).

(g) Chapter 41, Civil Practice and Remedies Code, does not apply to a cause of action brought under this subchapter.

(h) Notwithstanding any other provision of this subchapter, if a claimant is granted the right to bring a cause of action under this subchapter by another law, the claimant is not limited to recovery of economic damages only, but may recover any actual damages incurred by the claimant, without regard to whether the conduct of the defendant was committed intentionally. For the purpose of the recovery of damages for a cause of action described by this subsection only, a reference in this subchapter to economic damages means actual damages. In applying Subsection (b)(1) to an award of damages under this subsection, the trier of fact is authorized to award a total of not more than three times actual damages, in accordance with that subsection.

Added by Acts 1973, 63rd Leg., p. 322, ch. 143, § 1, eff. May 21, 1973. Amended by Acts 1977, 65th Leg., p. 603, ch. 216, § 5, eff. May 23, 1977; Acts 1979, 66th Leg., p. 1329, ch. 603, § 4, eff. Aug. 27, 1979; Acts 1989, 71st Leg., ch. 380, § 2, eff. Sept. 1, 1989; Acts 1995, 74th Leg., ch. 414, § 5, eff. Sept. 1, 1995; Acts 2005, 79th Leg., ch. 728, § 11.102, eff. Sept. 1, 2005.

§ 17.50A. Renumbered as V.T.C.A., Bus. & C. Code § 17.505 by Acts 1987, 70th Leg., ch. 167, § 5.02(4), eff. Sept. 1, 1987

§ 17.50B. Renumbered as V.T.C.A., Bus. & C. Code § 17.506 by Acts 1987, 70th Leg., ch. 167, § 5.02(5), eff. Sept. 1, 1987

§ 17.501. Consumer Protection Division Participation in Class Action

(a) A consumer filing an action under Section 17.50 that is to be maintained as a class action shall send to the consumer protection division:

(1) a copy of the notice required by Section 17.505(a), by registered or certified mail, at the same time the notice is given to the person complained against; and

(2) a copy of the petition in the action not later than the earlier of:

(A) the 30th day after the date the petition is filed; or

(B) the 10th day before the date of any hearing on class certification or a proposed settlement.

(b) The court shall abate the action for 60 days if the court finds that notice was not provided to the consumer protection division as required by Subsection (a).

(c) The court, on a showing of good cause, may allow the consumer protection division, as representative of the public, to intervene in an action to which this section applies. The consumer protection division shall file its motion for intervention with the court before which the action is pending and serve a copy of the motion on each party to the action.

Added by Acts 2003, 78th Leg., ch. 360, § 2, eff. Sept. 1, 2003.

§ 17.505. Notice; Inspection

(a) As a prerequisite to filing a suit seeking damages under Subdivision (1) of Subsection (b) of Section 17.50 of this subchapter against any person, a consumer shall give written notice to the person at least 60 days before filing the suit advising the person in reasonable detail of the consumer's specific complaint and the amount of economic damages, damages for mental anguish, and expenses, including attorneys' fees, if any, reasonably incurred by the consumer in asserting the claim against the defendant. During the 60-day period a written request to inspect, in a reasonable manner and at a reasonable time and place, the goods that are the subject of the consumer's action or claim may be presented to the consumer.

(b) If the giving of 60 days' written notice is rendered impracticable by reason of the necessity of filing suit in order to prevent the expiration of the statute of limitations or if the consumer's claim is asserted by way of counterclaim, the notice provided for in Subsection (a) of this section is not required, but the tender provided for by Subsection (d), Section 17.506 of this subchapter may be made within 60 days after service of the suit or counterclaim.

(c) A person against whom a suit is pending who does not receive written notice, as required by Subsection (a), may file a plea in abatement not later than the 30th day after the date the person files an original answer in the court in which the suit is pending. This subsection does not apply if Subsection (b) applies.

(d) The court shall abate the suit if the court, after a hearing, finds that the person is entitled to an abatement because notice was not provided as required by this section. A suit is automatically abated without the order of the court beginning on the 11th day after the date a plea in abatement is filed under Subsection (c) if the plea in abatement:

(1) is verified and alleges that the person against whom the suit is pending did not receive the written notice as required by Subsection (a); and

(2) is not controverted by an affidavit filed by the consumer before the 11th day after the date on which the plea in abatement is filed.

(e) An abatement under Subsection (d) continues until the 60th day after the date that written notice is served in compliance with Subsection (a).

Added by Acts 1977, 65th Leg., p. 604, ch. 216, § 6, eff. May 23, 1977. Amended by Acts 1979, 66th Leg., p. 1330, ch. 603, § 5, eff. Aug. 27, 1979. Renumbered from V.T.C.A., Bus. & C. Code § 17.50A and amended by Acts 1987, 70th Leg., ch. 167, § 5.02(4), (5), eff. Sept. 1, 1987. Amended by Acts 1989, 71st Leg., ch. 380, § 3, eff. Sept. 1, 1989; Acts 1995, 74th Leg., ch. 414, § 6, eff. Sept. 1, 1995.

§ 17.5051. Mediation

(a) A party may, not later than the 90th day after the date of service of a pleading in which relief under this subchapter is sought, file a motion to compel mediation of the dispute in the manner provided by this section.

(b) The court shall, not later than the 30th day after the date a motion under this section is filed, sign an order setting the time and place of the mediation.

(c) If the parties do not agree on a mediator, the court shall appoint the mediator.

(d) Mediation shall be held within 30 days after the date the order is signed, unless the parties agree otherwise or the court determines that additional time, not to exceed an additional 30 days, is warranted.

(e) Except as agreed to by all parties who have appeared in the action, each party who has appeared shall participate in the mediation and, except as provided by Subsection (f), shall share the mediation fee.

(f) A party may not compel mediation under this section if the amount of economic damages claimed is less than $15,000, unless the party seeking to compel mediation agrees to pay the costs of the mediation.

(g) Except as provided in this section, Section 154.023, Civil Practice and Remedies Code, and Subchapters C and D, Chapter 154, Civil Practice and Remedies Code,[1] apply to the appointment of a mediator and to the mediation process provided by this section.

(h) This section does not apply to an action brought by the attorney general under Section 17.47.

Added by Acts 1995, 74th Leg., ch. 414, § 7, eff. Sept. 1, 1995.

[1] V.T.C.A., Civil Practice & Remedies Code §§ 154.051 and 154.071 et seq.

§ 17.5052. Offers of Settlement

(a) A person who receives notice under Section 17.505 may tender an offer of settlement at any time during the period beginning on the date the notice is received and ending on the 60th day after that date.

(b) If a mediation under Section 17.5051 is not conducted, the person may tender an offer of settlement at any time during the period beginning on the date an original answer is filed and ending on the 90th day after that date.

(c) If a mediation under Section 17.5051 is conducted, a person against whom a claim under this subchapter is pending may tender an offer of settlement during the period beginning on the day after the date that the mediation ends and ending on the 20th day after that date.

(d) An offer of settlement tendered by a person against whom a claim under this subchapter is pending must include an offer to pay the following amounts of money, separately stated:

(1) an amount of money or other consideration, reduced to its cash value, as settlement of the consumer's claim for damages; and

(2) an amount of money to compensate the consumer for the consumer's reasonable and necessary attorneys' fees incurred as of the date of the offer.

(e) Unless both parts of an offer of settlement required under Subsection (d) are accepted by the consumer not later than the 30th day after the date the offer is made, the offer is rejected.

(f) A settlement offer tendered by a person against whom a claim under this subchapter is pending that complies with this section and that has been rejected by the consumer may be filed with the court with an affidavit certifying its rejection.

(g) If the court finds that the amount tendered in the settlement offer for damages under Subsection (d)(1) is the same as, substantially the same as, or more than the damages found by the trier of fact, the consumer may not recover as damages any amount in excess of the lesser of:

(1) the amount of damages tendered in the settlement offer; or

(2) the amount of damages found by the trier of fact.

(h) If the court makes the finding described by Subsection (g), the court shall determine reasonable and necessary attorneys' fees to compensate the consumer for attorneys' fees incurred before the date and time of the rejected settlement offer. If the court finds that the amount tendered in the settlement offer to compensate the consumer for attorneys' fees under Subsection (d)(2) is the same as, substantially the same as, or more than the amount of reasonable and necessary attorneys' fees incurred by the consumer as of the date of the offer, the consumer may not recover attorneys' fees greater than the amount of fees tendered in the settlement offer.

(i) If the court finds that the offering party could not perform the offer at the time the offer was made or that the offering party substantially misrepresented the cash value of the offer, Subsections (g) and (h) do not apply.

(j) If Subsection (g) does not apply, the court shall award as damages the amount of economic damages and damages for mental anguish found by the trier of fact, subject to Sections 17.50 and 17.501.[1] If Subsection (h) does not apply, the court shall award attorneys' fees as provided by Section 17.50(d).

(k) An offer of settlement is not an admission of engaging in an unlawful act or practice or liability under this subchapter. Except as otherwise provided by this section, an offer or a rejection of an offer may not be offered in evidence at trial for any purpose.

Added by Acts 1995, 74th Leg., ch. 414, § 7, eff. Sept. 1, 1995.

[1] So in enrolled bill; there was no V.T.C.A., Bus. & C. Code § 17.501 in effect when this section was adopted.

§ 17.506. Damages: Defenses

(a) In an action brought under Section 17.50 of this subchapter, it is a defense to the award of any damages or attorneys' fees if the defendant proves that before consummation of the transaction he gave reasonable and timely written notice to the plaintiff of the defendant's reliance on:

(1) written information relating to the particular goods or service in question obtained from official government records if the written information was false or inaccurate and the defendant did not know and could not reasonably have known of the falsity or inaccuracy of the information;

(2) written information relating to the particular goods or service in question obtained from another source if the information was false or inaccurate and the defendant did not know and could not reasonably have known of the falsity or inaccuracy of the information; or

(3) written information concerning a test required or prescribed by a government agency if the information from the test was false or inaccurate and the defendant did not know and could not reasonably have known of the falsity or inaccuracy of the information.

(b) In asserting a defense under Subdivision (1), (2), or (3) of Subsection (a) of Section 17.506 above, the defendant shall prove the written information was a producing cause of the alleged damage. A finding of one producing cause does not bar recovery if other conduct of the defendant not the subject of a defensive finding under Subdivision (1), (2), or (3) of Subsection (a) of Section 17.506 above was a producing cause of damages of the plaintiff.

(c) In a suit where a defense is asserted under Subdivision (2) of Subsection (a) of Section 17.506 above, suit may be asserted against the third party supplying the written information without regard to privity where the third party knew or should have reasonably foreseen that the information would be provided to a consumer; provided no double recovery may result.

(d) In an action brought under Section 17.50 of this subchapter, it is a defense to a cause of action if the defendant proves that he received notice from the consumer advising the defendant of the nature of the consumer's specific complaint and of the amount of economic damages, damages for mental anguish, and expenses, including attorneys' fees, if any, reasonably incurred by the consumer in asserting the claim against the defendant, and that within 30 days after the day on which the defendant received the notice the defendant tendered to the consumer:

(1) the amount of economic damages and damages for mental anguish claimed; and

(2) the expenses, including attorneys' fees, if any, reasonably incurred by the consumer in asserting the claim against the defendant.

Added by Acts 1979, 66th Leg., p. 1331, ch. 603, § 6, eff. Aug. 27, 1979. Renumbered from V.T.C.A., Bus. & C. Code § 17.50B and amended by Acts 1987, 70th Leg., ch. 167, § 5.02(5), eff. Sept. 1, 1987. Amended by Acts 1995, 74th Leg., ch. 414, § 8, eff. Sept. 1, 1995.

§§ 17.51 to 17.54. Repealed by Acts 1977, 65th Leg., p. 605, ch. 216, §§ 10 to 13, eff. May 23, 1977

§ 17.55. Promotional Material

If damages or civil penalties are assessed against the seller of goods or services for advertisements or promotional material in a suit filed under Section 17.47, 17.48, 17.50, or 17.51[1] of this subchapter, the seller of the goods or services has a cause of action against a third party for the amount of damages or civil penalties assessed against the seller plus attorneys' fees on a showing that:

(1) the seller received the advertisements or promotional material from the third party;

(2) the seller's only action with regard to the advertisements or promotional material was to disseminate the material; and

(3) the seller has ceased disseminating the material.

Added by Acts 1973, 63rd Leg., p. 322, ch. 143, § 1, eff. May 21, 1973.

[1] Repealed.

§ 17.55A. Renumbered as V.T.C.A., Bus. & C. Code § 17.555 by Acts 1987, 70th Leg., ch. 167, § 5.02(6), eff. Sept. 1, 1987

§ 17.555. Indemnity

A person against whom an action has been brought under this subchapter may seek contribution or indemnity from one who, under the statute law or at common law, may have liability for the damaging event of which the consumer complains. A person seeking indemnity as provided by this section may recover all sums that he is required to pay as a result of the action, his attorney's fees reasonable in relation to the amount of work performed in maintaining his action for indemnity, and his costs.

Added by Acts 1977, 65th Leg., p. 604, ch. 216, § 7, eff. May 23, 1977. Renumbered from § 17.55A by Acts 1987, 70th Leg., ch. 167, § 5.02(6), eff. Sept. 1, 1987.

§ 17.56. Venue

Text of section as amended by Acts 1995, 74th Leg., ch. 138, § 7.

Except as provided by Article 5.06–1(8), Insurance Code, an action brought which alleges a claim to relief under Section 17.50 of this subchapter shall be brought as provided by Chapter 15, Civil Practice and Remedies Code.

Added by Acts 1973, 63rd Leg., p. 322, ch. 143, § 1, eff. May 21, 1973. Amended by Acts 1977, 65th Leg., p. 604, ch. 216, § 8, eff. May 23, 1977; Acts 1979, 66th Leg., p. 1332, ch. 603, § 7, eff. Aug. 27, 1979; Acts 1995, 74th Leg., ch. 138, § 7, eff. Aug. 28, 1995.

For text of section as amended by Acts 1995, 74th Leg., ch. 414, § 9, see § 17.56, post.

§ 17.56. Venue

Text of section as amended by Acts 1995, 74th Leg., ch. 414, § 9.

An action brought under this subchapter may be brought:

(1) in any county in which venue is proper under Chapter 15, Civil Practice and Remedies Code; or

(2) in a county in which the defendant or an authorized agent of the defendant solicited the transaction made the subject of the action at bar.

Added by Acts 1973, 63rd Leg., p. 322, ch. 143, § 1, eff. May 21, 1973. Amended by Acts 1977, 65th Leg., p. 604, ch. 216, § 8, eff. May 23, 1977; Acts 1979, 66th Leg., p. 1332, ch. 603, § 7, eff. Aug. 27, 1979; Acts 1995, 74th Leg., ch. 414, § 9, eff. Sept. 1, 1995.

For text of section as amended by Acts 1995, 74th Leg., ch. 138, § 7, see § 17.56, ante.

§ 17.56A. Renumbered as V.T.C.A., Bus. & C. Code § 17.565 by Acts 1987, 70th Leg., ch. 167, § 5.02(7), eff. Sept. 1, 1987

§ 17.565. Limitation

All actions brought under this subchapter must be commenced within two years after the date on which the false, misleading, or deceptive act or practice occurred or within two years after the consumer discovered or in the exercise of reasonable diligence should have discovered the occurrence of the false, misleading, or deceptive act or practice. The period of limitation provided in this section may be extended for a period of 180 days if the plaintiff proves that failure timely to commence the action was caused by the defendant's knowingly engaging in conduct solely calculated to induce the plaintiff to refrain from or postpone the commencement of the action.

Added by Acts 1979, 66th Leg., p. 1332, ch. 603, § 8, eff. Aug. 27, 1979. Renumbered from V.T.C.A., Bus. & C. Code § 17.56A by Acts 1987, 70th Leg., ch. 167, § 5.02(7), eff. Sept. 1, 1987.

§ 17.57. Subpoenas

The clerk of a district court at the request of any party to a suit pending in his court which is brought under this subchapter shall issue a subpoena for any witness or witnesses who may be represented to reside within 100 miles of the courthouse of the county in which the suit is pending or who may be found within such distance at the time of trial. The clerk shall issue a separate subpoena and a copy thereof for each witness subpoenaed. When an action is pending in Travis County on the consent of the parties a subpoena may be issued for any witness or witnesses who may be represented to reside within 100 miles of the courthouse of a county in which the suit could otherwise have been brought or who may be found within such distance at the time of the trial.

Added by Acts 1973, 63rd Leg., p. 322, ch. 143, § 1, eff. May 21, 1973.

§ 17.58. Voluntary Compliance

(a) In the administration of this subchapter the consumer protection division may accept assurance of voluntary compliance with respect to any act or practice which violates this subchapter from any person who is engaging in, has engaged in, or is about to engage in the act or practice. The assurance shall be in writing and shall be filed with and subject to the approval of the district court in the county in which the alleged violator resides or does business or in the district court of Travis County.

(b) The acceptance of an assurance of voluntary compliance may be conditioned on the stipulation that the person in violation of this subchapter restore to any person in interest any money or property, real or personal, which may have been acquired by means of acts or practices which violate this subchapter.

(c) An assurance of voluntary compliance shall not be considered an admission of prior violation of this subchapter. However, unless an assurance has been rescinded by agreement of the parties or voided by a court for good cause, subsequent failure to comply with the terms of an assurance is prima facie evidence of a violation of this subchapter.

(d) Matters closed by the filing of an assurance of voluntary compliance may be reopened at any time. Assurances of voluntary compliance shall in no way affect individual rights of action under this subchapter, except that the rights of individuals with regard to money or property received pursuant to a stipulation in the voluntary compliance under Subsection (b) of this section are governed by the terms of the voluntary compliance.

Added by Acts 1973, 63rd Leg., p. 322, ch. 143, § 1, eff. May 21, 1973.

§ 17.59. Post Judgment Relief

(a) If a money judgment entered under this subchapter is unsatisfied 30 days after it becomes final and if the prevailing party has made a good faith attempt to obtain satisfaction of the judgment, the following presumptions exist with respect to the party against whom the judgment was entered:

(1) that the defendant is insolvent or in danger of becoming insolvent; and

(2) that the defendant's property is in danger of being lost, removed, or otherwise exempted from collection on the judgment; and

(3) that the prevailing party will be materially injured unless a receiver is appointed over the defendant's business; and

(4) that there is no adequate remedy other than receivership available to the prevailing party.

(b) Subject to the provisions of Subsection (a) of this section, a prevailing party may move that the defendant show cause why a receiver should not be appointed. Upon adequate notice and hearing, the court shall appoint a receiver over the defendant's business unless the defendant proves that all of the presumptions set forth in Subsection (a) of this section are not applicable.

(c) The order appointing a receiver must clearly state whether the receiver will have general power to manage and operate the defendant's business or have power to manage only a defendant's finances. The order shall limit the duration of the receivership to such time as the judgment or judgments awarded under this subchapter are paid in full. Where there are judgments against a defendant which have been awarded to more than one plaintiff, the court shall have discretion to take any action necessary to efficiently operate a receivership in order to accomplish the purpose of collecting the judgments.

Added by Acts 1973, 63rd Leg., p. 322, ch. 143, § 1, eff. May 21, 1973. Amended by Acts 1977, 65th Leg., p. 604, ch. 216, § 9, eff. May 23, 1977.

§ 17.60. Reports and Examinations

Whenever the consumer protection division has reason to believe that a person is engaging in, has engaged in, or is about to engage in any act or practice declared to be unlawful by this subchapter, or when it reasonably believes it to be in the public interest to conduct an investigation to ascertain whether any person is engaging in, has engaged in, or is about to engage in any such act or practice, an authorized member of the division may:

(1) require the person to file on the prescribed forms a statement or report in writing, under oath or otherwise, as to all the facts and circumstances concerning the alleged violation and such other data and information as the consumer protection division deems necessary;

(2) examine under oath any person in connection with this alleged violation;

(3) examine any merchandise or sample of merchandise deemed necessary and proper; and

(4) pursuant to an order of the appropriate court, impound any sample of merchandise that is produced in accordance with this subchapter and retain it in the possession of the division until the completion of all proceedings in connection with which the merchandise is produced.

Added by Acts 1973, 63rd Leg., p. 322, ch. 143, § 1, eff. May 21, 1973. Amended by Acts 1989, 71st Leg., ch. 1082, § 8.02, eff. Jan. 1, 1991; Acts 1991, 72nd Leg., ch. 242, § 11.19, eff. Sept. 1, 1991.

§ 17.61. Civil Investigative Demand

(a) Whenever the consumer protection division believes that any person may be in possession, custody, or control of the original copy of any documentary material relevant to the subject matter of an investigation of a possible violation of this subchapter, an authorized agent of the division may execute in writing and serve on the person a civil investigative demand requiring the person to produce the documentary material and permit inspection and copying.

(b) Each demand shall:

(1) state the statute and section under which the alleged violation is being investigated, and the general subject matter of the investigation;

(2) describe the class or classes of documentary material to be produced with reasonable specificity so as to fairly indicate the material demanded;

(3) prescribe a return date within which the documentary material is to be produced; and

(4) identify the persons authorized by the consumer protection division to whom the documentary material is to be made available for inspection and copying.

(c) A civil investigative demand may contain a requirement or disclosure of documentary material which would be discoverable under the Texas Rules of Civil Procedure.

(d) Service of any demand may be made by:

(1) delivering a duly executed copy of the demand to the person to be served or to a partner or to any officer or agent authorized by appointment or by law to receive service of process on behalf of that person;

(2) delivering a duly executed copy of the demand to the principal place of business in the state of the person to be served;

(3) mailing by registered mail or certified mail a duly executed copy of the demand addressed to the person to be served at the principal place of business in this state, or if the person has no place of business in this state, to his principal office or place of business.

(e) Documentary material demanded pursuant to this section shall be produced for inspection and copying during normal business hours at the principal office or place of business of the person served, or at other times and places as may be agreed on by the person served and the consumer protection division.

(f) No documentary material produced pursuant to a demand under this section, unless otherwise ordered by a court for good cause shown, shall be produced for inspection or copying by, nor shall its contents be disclosed to any person other than the authorized employee of the office of the attorney general without the consent of the person who produced the material.

The office of the attorney general shall prescribe reasonable terms and conditions allowing the documentary material to be available for inspection and copying by the person who produced the material or any duly authorized representative of that person. The office of the attorney general may use the documentary material or copies of it as it determines necessary in the enforcement of this subchapter, including presentation before any court. Any material which contains trade secrets shall not be presented except with the approval of the court in which the action is pending after adequate notice to the person furnishing the material.

(g) At any time before the return date specified in the demand, or within 20 days after the demand has been served, whichever period is shorter, a petition to extend the return date for, or to modify or set aside the demand, stating good cause, may be filed in the district court in the county where the parties reside, or a district court of Travis County.

(h) A person on whom a demand is served under this section shall comply with the terms of the demand unless otherwise provided by a court order.

(i) Personal service of a similar investigative demand under this section may be made on any person outside of this state if the person has engaged in conduct in violation of this subchapter. Such persons shall be deemed to have submitted themselves to the jurisdiction of this state within the meaning of this section.

Added by Acts 1973, 63rd Leg., p. 322, ch. 143, § 1, eff. May 21, 1973. Amended by Acts 1989, 71st Leg., ch. 1082, § 8.03, eff. Jan. 1, 1991; Acts 1991, 72nd Leg., ch. 242, § 11.20, eff. Sept. 1, 1991; Acts 2007, 80th Leg., ch. 411, § 2, eff. Sept. 1, 2007.

§ 17.62. Penalties

(a) Any person who, with intent to avoid, evade, or prevent compliance, in whole or in part, with Section 17.60 or 17.61 of this subchapter, removes from any place, conceals, withholds, or destroys, mutilates, alters, or by any other means falsifies any documentary material or merchandise or sample of merchandise is guilty of a misdemeanor and on conviction is punishable by a fine of not more than $5,000 or by confinement in the county jail for not more than one year, or both.

(b) If a person fails to comply with a directive of the consumer protection division under Section 17.60 of this subchapter or with a civil investigative demand for documentary material served on him under Section 17.61 of this subchapter, or if satisfactory copying or reproduction of the material cannot be done and the person refuses to surrender the material, the consumer protection division may file in the district court in the county in which the person resides, is found, or transacts business, and serve on the person, a petition for an order of the court for enforcement of Sections 17.60 and 17.61 of this subchapter. If the person transacts business in more than one county, the petition shall be filed in the county in which the person maintains his principal place of business, or in another county agreed on by the parties to the petition.

(c) When a petition is filed in the district court in any county under this section, the court shall have jurisdiction to hear and determine the matter presented and to enter any order required to carry into effect the provisions of Sections 17.60 and 17.61 of this subchapter. Any final order entered is subject to appeal to the Texas Supreme Court. Failure to comply with any final order entered under this section is punishable by contempt.

Added by Acts 1973, 63rd Leg., p. 322, ch. 143, § 1, eff. May 21, 1973.

§ 17.63. Application

The provisions of this subchapter apply only to acts or practices occurring after the effective date of this subchapter, except a right of action or power granted to the attorney general under Chapter 10, Title 79, Revised Civil Statutes of Texas, 1925, as amended,[1] prior to the effective date of this subchapter.

Added by Acts 1973, 63rd Leg., p. 322, ch. 143, § 1, eff. May 21, 1973.

[1] Vernon's Ann.Civ.St. art. 5069–10.01 et seq. (repealed).

SUBCHAPTER F. GOING OUT OF BUSINESS SALES

Subchapter F, as added by Acts 1985, 69th Leg., ch. 172, § 1, consists of §§ 17.81 to 17.93.

A former subchapter F, consisting of §§ 17.801 to 17.808, was repealed by Acts 1987, 70th Leg., ch. 167, art. 6, § 6.04. Such subchapter, added by Acts 1985, 69th Leg., ch. 117, § 7(a), had incorporated into the Business and Commerce Code, Acts 1967, 60th Leg., p. 1003, ch. 434, §§ 1 to 5, which had been classified as Vernon's Ann.P.C. (1925) art. 1137q, subsequently transferred by Acts 1973, 63rd Leg., p. 995, ch. 399, § 5, to Vernon's Ann.Civ.St. art. 9011, and repealed by § 7(b) of the 1985 Act.

For Subchapter G, Labeling, Advertising, and Sale of Kosher Foods, consisting of §§ 17.821 to 17.826, see Subchapter G, post.

§ 17.81. Definition

In this chapter "going out of business sale" means an offer to sell to the public, or the sale to the public of, goods, wares, and merchandise on the implied or direct representation by written or oral advertising that the sale is in anticipation of the termination of all of the operations of a business at all of its locations in a county and in all of the counties immediately adjacent to that county.

Added by Acts 1985, 69th Leg., ch. 172, § 1, eff. Sept. 1, 1985.

§ 17.82. Prohibited Conduct

(a) A person may not conduct a sale advertised with the phrase "going out of business," "closing out," "shutting doors forever," or "bankruptcy sale"; the word "foreclosure" or "bankruptcy"; or a similar phrase or word indicating that an enterprise is ceasing business unless the business is closing all of its operations in a county and in all of the counties immediately adjacent to that county and follows the procedures required by this subchapter.

(b) A person may not fraudulently represent that the person is conducting a going out of business sale.

Added by Acts 1985, 69th Leg., ch. 172, § 1, eff. Sept. 1, 1985.

§ 17.83. Original Inventory

(a) To conduct a going out of business sale, a person must file an original inventory with the chief appraiser of the appraisal district in which the person's principal place of business in the state is located. The original inventory must be accompanied by a filing fee of $20.

(b) The original inventory must include:

(1) the name and address of the owner of the goods, wares, or merchandise to be sold;

(2) the name and address of the owner of the defunct business, the former stock in trade of which is to be offered for sale, and the full name of the defunct business;

(3) a description of the place where the liquidation sale is to be held;

(4) a statement of the beginning and ending dates of the sale;

(5) a complete and detailed inventory of the goods, wares, and merchandise to be offered on the beginning date of the sale and the total cost of those items; and

(6) a complete and detailed list of the goods, wares, and merchandise to be added to the inventory after the beginning date of the sale and the total cost of those items.

Added by Acts 1985, 69th Leg., ch. 172, § 1, eff. Sept. 1, 1985. Amended by Acts 2001, 77th Leg., ch. 291, § 1, eff. Sept. 1, 2001.

§ 17.835. Notice of Filing of Original Inventory

Not later than the fifth business day after the date on which a person files an original inventory under Section 17.83, the chief appraiser shall send notice of the filing to the comptroller, the county clerk of the county in which the person's principal place of business in the state is located, and the tax collector for each of the taxing units that tax the property described in the original inventory.

Added by Acts 2001, 77th Leg., ch. 291, § 2, eff. Sept. 1, 2001.

§ 17.84. Permit

(a) After receiving an original inventory, the chief appraiser shall issue to the applicant a permit for a going out of business sale. The permit is valid for 120 days after the day that it is issued and is not renewable.

(b) The permit holder must post the permit in a conspicuous place at the location of the going out of business sale.

(c) Before advertising a going out of business sale, the permit holder shall deliver a copy of the permit to the person publishing or broadcasting the advertisement.

Added by Acts 1985, 69th Leg., ch. 172, § 1, eff. Sept. 1, 1985. Amended by Acts 2001, 77th Leg., ch. 291, § 3, eff. Sept. 1, 2001.

§ 17.85. Deadline for Orders

A person may not sell an item at a going out of business sale if the person ordered the item after the beginning date of the sale.

Added by Acts 1985, 69th Leg., ch. 172, § 1, eff. Sept. 1, 1985.

§ 17.86. Sale Inventory

Before the end of each 30-day period during the going out of business sale the permit holder shall file with the chief appraiser a sale inventory containing a complete and detailed list of the goods, wares, and merchandise listed in the original inventory that have not been sold before the date that the sale inventory is filed. A sale inventory must list items offered on the beginning date of the sale separately from the items added to the sale inventory after that date.

Added by Acts 1985, 69th Leg., ch. 172, § 1, eff. Sept. 1, 1985. Amended by Acts 2001, 77th Leg., ch. 291, § 4, eff. Sept. 1, 2001.

§ 17.87. Final Inventory

Within 30 days after the day that the going out of business sale ends, the permit holder shall file with the chief appraiser a final inventory. The final inventory must include:

(1) the name and address of the permit holder;

(2) a statement of the disposition of the items listed in the original inventory that were not sold during the going out of business sale and the name and address of any person purchasing those items after the ending date of the sale; and

(3) a description of the place where the sale was held.

Added by Acts 1985, 69th Leg., ch. 172, § 1, eff. Sept. 1, 1985. Amended by Acts 2001, 77th Leg., ch. 291, § 5, eff. Sept. 1, 2001.

§ 17.88. Disposition of Sale Items

After a permit expires, the permit holder may not sell at retail an item offered at the sale covered by the permit.

Added by Acts 1985, 69th Leg., ch. 172, § 1, eff. Sept. 1, 1985.

§ 17.89. Later Sales

A person may not conduct a going out of business sale beginning within two years after the ending date of the most recent going out of business sale conducted by the person.

Added by Acts 1985, 69th Leg., ch. 172, § 1, eff. Sept. 1, 1985.

§ 17.90. Form of Inventory

An inventory filed under this subchapter must be in the form of a sworn affidavit.

Added by Acts 1985, 69th Leg., ch. 172, § 1, eff. Sept. 1, 1985.

§ 17.91. Exceptions

This subchapter does not apply to:

(1) a sale conducted by a public officer as part of the officer's official duties;

(2) a sale for which an accounting must be made to a court of law;

(3) a sale conducted pursuant to an order of a court; or

(4) a foreclosure sale pursuant to a deed of trust or other lien.

Added by Acts 1985, 69th Leg., ch. 172, § 1, eff. Sept. 1, 1985.

§ 17.92. Penalty

(a) A person commits an offense if the person:

(1) conducts a sale in violation of Section 17.82 of this code;

(2) conducts a going out of business sale without a valid permit issued under Section 17.84 of this code;

(3) sells an item at a going out of business sale in violation of Section 17.85 of this code;

(4) fails to file an inventory required by Section 17.86 or 17.87 of this code; or

(5) sells an item at retail in violation of Section 17.88 of this code.

(b) An offense under this section is a Class A misdemeanor.

(c) Each day of violation constitutes a separate offense.

Added by Acts 1985, 69th Leg., ch. 172, § 1, eff. Sept. 1, 1985.

§ 17.93. Injunction

The attorney general may bring an action to enjoin a violation of this subchapter.

Added by Acts 1985, 69th Leg., ch. 172, § 1, eff. Sept. 1, 1985.

SUBCHAPTER G. LABELING, ADVERTISING, AND SALE OF KOSHER FOODS

Acts 1983, 68th Leg., p. 4847, ch. 855, §§ 1 to 6, classified as Vernon's Ann.Civ.St. art. 4476–10a, was repealed by § 8(b) of Acts 1985, 69th Leg., ch. 117, which by § 8(a) thereof incorporated the provisions of the 1983 Act into the Business and Commerce

Code by adding this Subchapter G, consisting of §§ 17.821 to 17.826.

For Subchapter F, Going Out of Business Sales, as added by Acts 1985, 69th Leg., ch. 172, § 1, consisting of §§ 17.81 to 17.93, see Subchapter F, ante.

§ 17.821. Definitions

In this chapter:

(1) "Kosher food" means food prepared and served in conformity with orthodox Jewish religious requirements.

(2) "Label" means a display of written, printed, or graphic matter on the immediate article or container of any food product.

(3) "Person" includes an individual, corporation, or association.

(4) "Restaurant" means a place where food is sold for on-premises consumption.

(5) "Retail store" means any retail grocery store, delicatessen, butcher shop, or other place where food is sold for off-premises consumption.

(6) "Sell" means to offer for sale, expose for sale, have in possession for sale, convey, exchange, barter, or trade.

Added by Acts 1985, 69th Leg., ch. 117, § 8(a), eff. Sept. 1, 1985.

§ 17.822. Meat Labeling

(a) If a person sells both kosher meat and nonkosher meat in the same retail store, the person shall clearly label each portion of kosher meat with the word "kosher." If unwrapped or unpackaged meat products are displayed for sale, the display case or container in which the meat is displayed must be clearly labeled with the word "kosher" or "nonkosher," as applicable.

(b) A person commits an offense if the person is required to label meat in accordance with this section and the person knowingly sells meat that is not labeled as provided in this section.

Added by Acts 1985, 69th Leg., ch. 117, § 8(a), eff. Sept. 1, 1985.

§ 17.823. Sale of Nonkosher Food

A person commits an offense if the person knowingly or intentionally sells at a restaurant or a retail store a food product that is represented as kosher food and is not kosher food and the person either knows the food is not kosher food or was reckless about determining whether or not the food is kosher food.

Added by Acts 1985, 69th Leg., ch. 117, § 8(a), eff. Sept. 1, 1985.

§ 17.824. Exception

It is an exception to the application of Subsection (b) of Section 17.822 or Section 17.823 of this code that a person describes or labels food as "kosher-style," and, if the description is written, the words "kosher" and "style" are of the same size type or script.

Added by Acts 1985, 69th Leg., ch. 117, § 8(a), eff. Sept. 1, 1985.

§ 17.825. Civil Remedy

A consumer aggrieved by a violation of this chapter may maintain a cause of action for damages in accordance with Section 17.50 of this code.

Added by Acts 1985, 69th Leg., ch. 117, § 8(a), eff. Sept. 1, 1985.

§ 17.826. Penalty

An offense under this chapter is punishable by the fine imposed for an offense under Subsection (d) of Section 17.12 of this code.

Added by Acts 1985, 69th Leg., ch. 117, § 8(a), eff. Sept. 1, 1985.

SUBCHAPTER H. SALE OF INDIAN ARTICLES

§ 17.851. Definitions

In this subchapter:

(1) "American Indian" or "Indian" means an individual who is an enrolled member of a federally or state recognized American Indian tribe, band, nation, rancheria, or pueblo or who is an Alaska Native and a member of an Alaska Native village or regional or village corporation as defined in or established under the Alaska Native Claims Settlement Act (43 U.S.C. Sec. 1601 et seq.).

(2) "Authentic Indian arts and crafts" means any product that:

(A) is Indian handcrafted; and

(B) is not made by machine or from unnatural materials, except stabilized or treated turquoise.

(3) "Nonauthentic Indian arts and crafts" means any product that is made to imitate or resemble authentic Indian arts and crafts and that:

(A) is not Indian handcrafted; or

(B) is made by machine or from unnatural materials, except stabilized or treated turquoise.

(4) "Indian handcrafted" means the skillful and expert use of the hands in making products solely by Indians within the United States, including the use of findings and hand tools and equipment for buffing, polishing, grinding, drilling, or sewing.

(5) "Made by machine" means the producing or reproducing of a product in mass production by mechanically stamping, casting, blanking, or weaving.

(6) "Findings" means an ingredient that adapts the product of which it is a part for wearing or display, including ceramic, glass, or silver beads, leather backing, binding material, bolo tie clips, tie bar clips, tie tac pins, earring pins, earring clips, earring screw backs, cuff link toggles, money clips, pin stems, combs, and chains.

(7) "Turquoise" means a hydrous copper sulphate containing aluminum salts plus iron.

(8) "Natural turquoise" means turquoise, exclusive of any backing material, the composition of which has not been chemically or otherwise altered.

(9) "Stabilized turquoise" means turquoise, excluding any backing material, that has been chemically hardened, but not adulterated so as to change the color of the natural mineral.

(10) "Treated turquoise" means turquoise, excluding any backing material, that has been altered to produce a change in the coloration of the natural mineral.

(11) "Simulated turquoise" means:

(A) reconstituted turquoise, which is turquoise dust or particles that are mixed with plastic resins and are compressed into a solid form so as to resemble natural turquoise; or

(B) imitation turquoise, which is any compound or mineral that is manufactured or treated so as to closely approximate turquoise in appearance.

Added by Acts 1989, 71st Leg., ch. 897, § 1, eff. Aug. 28, 1989.

§ 17.852. Inquiry as to Producer

(a) Each person selling or offering for sale authentic or nonauthentic Indian arts and crafts shall request the suppliers of those arts and crafts to disclose the methods used in producing those arts and crafts and to determine whether those arts and crafts are in fact authentic Indian arts and crafts.

(b) Each person selling or offering for sale turquoise shall request the suppliers of the turquoise to disclose the true nature of the turquoise.

Added by Acts 1989, 71st Leg., ch. 897, § 1, eff. Aug. 28, 1989.

§ 17.853. Unlawful Acts

A person may not:

(1) sell or offer for sale a product represented to be authentic Indian arts and crafts unless the product is in fact authentic Indian arts and crafts;

(2) sell or offer for sale any authentic Indian arts and crafts or nonauthentic Indian arts and crafts represented to be made of silver unless the product is made of coin silver or sterling silver;

(3) sell or offer for sale a product that is nonauthentic Indian arts and crafts unless the product is clearly labeled as to any characteristics that make it nonauthentic;

(4) sell or offer for sale any turquoise, mounted or unmounted, without a disclosure of the true nature of the turquoise; or

(5) sell or offer for sale art represented to be by an American Indian unless it is in fact produced by an American Indian.

Added by Acts 1989, 71st Leg., ch. 897, § 1, eff. Aug. 28, 1989.

§ 17.854. Penalty

A person who violates this subchapter commits an offense. An offense under this section is a Class B misdemeanor.

Added by Acts 1989, 71st Leg., ch. 897, § 1, eff. Aug. 28, 1989.

SUBCHAPTER I. LABELING, ADVERTISING, AND SALE OF HALAL FOODS

§ 17.881. Definitions

In this subchapter:

(1) "Halal," as applied to food, means food prepared and served in conformity with Islamic religious requirements according to a recognized Islamic authority.

(2) "Label" means a display of written, printed, or graphic matter on the immediate article or container of any food product.

(3) "Person" includes an individual, corporation, or association.

(4) "Restaurant" means a place where food is sold for on-premises consumption.

(5) "Retail store" means a retail grocery store, delicatessen, butcher shop, or other place where food is sold for off-premises consumption.

(6) "Sell" means to offer for sale, expose for sale, have in possession for sale, convey, exchange, barter, or trade.

Added by Acts 2003, 78th Leg., ch. 1013, § 1, eff. Sept. 1, 2003.

§ 17.882. Meat Labeling

(a) If a person sells both halal meat and nonhalal meat in the same retail store, the person shall clearly label each portion of halal meat with the word "halal." If an unwrapped or unpackaged meat product is displayed for sale, the display case or container in which the meat is displayed must be clearly labeled with the word "halal" or "nonhalal," as applicable.

(b) A person commits an offense if the person is required to label meat in accordance with this section and the person knowingly sells meat that is not labeled as provided in this section.

Added by Acts 2003, 78th Leg., ch. 1013, § 1, eff. Sept. 1, 2003.

§ 17.883. Sale of Nonhalal Food

A person commits an offense if the person knowingly or intentionally sells at a restaurant or a retail store a food product that is represented as halal food and is not halal food and the person either knows the food is not halal food or was reckless about determining whether or not the food is halal food.

Added by Acts 2003, 78th Leg., ch. 1013, § 1, eff. Sept. 1, 2003.

§ 17.884. Civil Remedy

A consumer aggrieved by a violation of this subchapter may maintain a cause of action for damages in accordance with Section 17.50.

Added by Acts 2003, 78th Leg., ch. 1013, § 1, eff. Sept. 1, 2003.

§ 17.885. Criminal Penalty

An offense under this subchapter is punishable by the fine imposed for an offense under Section 17.12(d).

Added by Acts 2003, 78th Leg., ch. 1013, § 1, eff. Sept. 1, 2003.

SUBCHAPTER J. PROTECTION FROM MISLEADING OR DECEPTIVE LIVE MUSICAL PERFORMANCES

§ 17.901. Definitions

In this subchapter:

(1) "Performing musical group" means a vocal or instrumental group seeking to engage in a live musical performance.

(2) "Recording group" means a vocal or instrumental group of which one or more members:

(A) has released a sound recording under that group's name for commercial purposes; and

(B) has a legal right to use or operate under the group's name without abandoning the name or affiliation with the group.

(3) "Sound recording" means musical, spoken, or other sounds recorded on a tangible medium, including a disc, tape, or phonograph record.

Added by Acts 2007, 80th Leg., ch. 595, § 1, eff. Sept. 1, 2007.

§ 17.902. Unauthorized Advertisement, Promotion, or Conduction of Certain Live Musical Performances

A person may not advertise, promote, or conduct a live musical performance in this state through the use of a false, deceptive, or misleading affiliation, connection, or association between a recording group and a performing musical group. An act is not considered a violation of this section if:

(1) the performing musical group is the authorized registrant and owner of a federal service mark for the recording group that is registered in the United States Patent and Trademark Office;

(2) at least one member of the performing musical group is or was a member of the recording group and that member has a legal right to use or operate under the name of the recording group without abandoning the name or affiliation with the recording group;

(3) the live musical performance is identified in all advertisements or other promotions for the event as being conducted as a "salute" or "tribute" to the recording group;

(4) the advertisement or promotion relates to a live musical performance that is to take place outside of this state; or

(5) the live musical performance is expressly authorized by each member of the recording group.

Added by Acts 2007, 80th Leg., ch. 595, § 1, eff. Sept. 1, 2007.

§ 17.903. Injunction; Restitution

(a) If the attorney general has reason to believe that a person is engaging in, has engaged in, or is about to engage in an act or practice that violates Section 17.902, and that proceedings would be in the public interest, the attorney general may bring an action in the name of the state against the person to restrain that act or practice by temporary or permanent injunction.

(b) The prosecuting attorney in the county in which a violation of Section 17.902 occurs, with prior written notice to the attorney general, may institute and prosecute an action seeking injunctive relief under this section. The prosecuting attorney shall make a full report to the attorney general regarding any action prosecuted by the prosecuting attorney under this subsection. The report must include a statement regarding the final disposition of the matter.

(c) When a court issues a permanent injunction to restrain and prevent a violation of Section 17.902, the court may make additional orders or judgments as necessary to restore money or other property that may have been acquired because of a violation of this subchapter.

Added by Acts 2007, 80th Leg., ch. 595, § 1, eff. Sept. 1, 2007.

§ 17.904. Civil Penalty

(a) A person who violates Section 17.902 is liable to the state for a civil penalty of not less than $5,000 or more than $15,000 for each violation. Each performance that violates Section 17.902 constitutes a separate violation.

(b) The attorney general or the prosecuting attorney in the county in which a violation occurs may bring suit to recover the civil penalty imposed under Subsection (a).

(c) The civil penalty provided by this section is in addition to injunctive relief or any other remedy that may be granted under Section 17.903.

Added by Acts 2007, 80th Leg., ch. 595, § 1, eff. Sept. 1, 2007.

CHAPTER 18. CREDIT SERVICES ORGANIZATIONS [REPEALED]

§§ 18.01 to 18.15. Repealed by Acts 1997, 75th Leg., ch. 1008, § 6(c), eff. Sept. 1, 1997

CHAPTER 19. FARM, INDUSTRIAL, OFF-ROAD CONSTRUCTION, FORESTRY HARVESTING EQUIPMENT, AND OUTDOOR POWER EQUIPMENT DEALER AGREEMENTS

Acts 2007, 80th Leg., ch. 885, § 2.47(a)(1) repeals this chapter effective April 1, 2009.

Acts 1999, 76th Leg., ch. 725, § 1 amended the chapter heading.

SUBCHAPTER A. GENERAL PROVISIONS

§ 19.01. Definitions

In this chapter:

(1) "Affiliated dealer" means a dealer in which a supplier has an ownership interest.

(2) "Controlling interest" means 50 percent or more of ownership or a managing interest in a dealership.

(3) "Current price" means an amount equal to the price listed in the supplier's printed price list in effect when a dealer agreement is terminated, less applicable trade and cash discounts.

(4) "Dealer cost" means an amount equal to the sum of the original invoice price that the dealer paid for inventory and the cost to the dealer of its delivery from the supplier to the dealer, less applicable discounts.

(5) "Dealer" means a person in the business of the retail sale of equipment. The term does not include a single line dealer primarily engaged in the retail sale and service of off-road construction and earth-moving equipment.

(6) "Dealer agreement" means an oral or written contract, of definite or indefinite duration, between a supplier and a dealer, that provides for the rights and obligations of the parties with respect to the purchase or sale of equipment.

(7) "Dealership" means the retail sale business engaged in by a dealer under a dealer agreement.

(8) "Equipment" means farm tractors, farm implements, utility tractors, industrial tractors, forklifts, material-handling equipment, forestry harvesting equipment, off-road construction equipment, and outdoor power equipment and the attachments to or repair parts for those items.

(9) "Inventory" means new or unused equipment that is provided by a supplier to a dealer under a dealer agreement and that was purchased within 30 months of the termination of the dealership or was listed in the supplier's current sales manual at the time of termination.

(10) "Outdoor power equipment" means any machinery operated by an engine or electric power and used in the landscaping or cultivation of land for nonagricultural purposes, and includes lawn and garden implements.

(11) "Supplier" means a person engaged in the manufacture, assembly, or wholesale distribution of equipment and the person's successors in interest, including a purchaser of assets or stock or a surviving corporation resulting from a merger, liquidation, or reorganization.

(12) "Single line dealer" means an individual, partnership, or corporation who:

(A) has purchased 75 percent or more of the dealer's total new product inventory from a single supplier under all agreements with that supplier; and

(B) has a total annual average sales volume in excess of $100 million for the preceding three years with that single supplier for the territory for which the dealer is responsible in this state.

Added by Acts 1991, 72nd Leg., ch. 119, § 1, eff. May 19, 1991. Amended by Acts 1999, 76th Leg., ch. 725, § 2, eff. Sept. 1, 1999; Acts 1999, 76th Leg., ch. 736, § 1, eff. Sept. 1, 1999.

Repeal

Acts 2007, 80th Leg., ch. 885, § 2.47(a)(1) repeals this section effective April 1, 2009.

§ 19.02. Actions for a Violation of Chapter

A person injured by a violation of this chapter may bring an action for:

(1) an injunction to prevent further violation;

(2) damages;

(3) reasonable attorney's fees; and

(4) costs.

Added by Acts 1991, 72nd Leg., ch. 119, § 1, eff. May 19, 1991.

Repeal

Acts 2007, 80th Leg., ch. 885, § 2.47(a)(1) repeals this section effective April 1, 2009.

§ 19.03. Security Interest

This chapter does not affect a supplier's security interest in inventory.

Added by Acts 1991, 72nd Leg., ch. 119, § 1, eff. May 19, 1991.

Repeal

Acts 2007, 80th Leg., ch. 885, § 2.47(a)(1) repeals this section effective April 1, 2009.

§ 19.04. Bulk Transfer Law

Chapter 6 of this code does not apply to a transaction between a supplier and dealer that is required by this chapter.

Added by Acts 1991, 72nd Leg., ch. 119, § 1, eff. May 19, 1991.

Repeal

Acts 2007, 80th Leg., ch. 885, § 2.47(a)(1) repeals this section effective April 1, 2009.

§ 19.05. No Waiver

An attempted waiver of a provision of this chapter is void.

Added by Acts 1991, 72nd Leg., ch. 119, § 1, eff. May 19, 1991.

Repeal

Acts 2007, 80th Leg., ch. 885, § 2.47(a)(1) repeals this section effective April 1, 2009.

[Sections 19.06 to 19.20 reserved for expansion]

SUBCHAPTER B. OPERATION OF DEALERSHIP

§ 19.21. Supplementary Agreement

A supplier may not coerce or compel a dealer to enter into a written or oral agreement supplementary to an existing dealer agreement with the supplier unless the supplementary agreement is imposed on all other similarly situated dealers in the state.

Added by Acts 1991, 72nd Leg., ch. 119, § 1, eff. May 19, 1991.

Repeal

Acts 2007, 80th Leg., ch. 885, § 2.47(a)(1) repeals this section effective April 1, 2009.

§ 19.22. Coerced Orders, Deliveries, or Refusals to Purchase

(a) A supplier may not coerce or compel a dealer to order or accept delivery of equipment with special features or accessories not included in the base list price of the equipment as publicly advertised by the supplier unless the special features or accessories are safety features or accessories required by the supplier or by applicable law.

(b) A supplier may not coerce or compel a dealer to refuse purchase of equipment manufactured by another equipment manufacturer.

Added by Acts 1991, 72nd Leg., ch. 119, § 1, eff. May 19, 1991. Amended by Acts 1999, 76th Leg., ch. 736, § 2, eff. Sept. 1, 1999.

Repeal

Acts 2007, 80th Leg., ch. 885, § 2.47(a)(1) repeals this section effective April 1, 2009.

§ 19.23. Equipment Represented as Available for Immediate Delivery

A supplier may not discriminate among dealers in the supplier's delivery, in reasonable quantities and within a reasonable time after receipt of a dealer's order, of equipment covered by the dealer agreement and specifically represented by the supplier as available for immediate delivery unless the discrimination is due to:

(1) the supplier's restrictions on extending credit to the dealer;

(2) the dealer's default under a dealership agreement; or

(3) an act of God, work stoppage or delay due to a strike or labor difficulty, bona fide shortage of materials, freight embargo, or other cause over which the supplier has no control.

Added by Acts 1991, 72nd Leg., ch. 119, § 1, eff. May 19, 1991.

Repeal

Acts 2007, 80th Leg., ch. 885, § 2.47(a)(1) repeals this section effective April 1, 2009.

§ 19.24. Late Delivery of Back-Ordered Seasonal Demand Item

(a) Unless the supplier notifies a dealer of the status of a back-ordered item before its actual shipment to the dealer, a dealer may reject the delivery of an item of equipment other than a part or attachment from a supplier if:

(1) the item has special value in a particular time of year because of predictable seasonable demand and is less marketable and less valuable after the seasonal demand period ends;

(2) the item was back-ordered and delivery is made after the seasonal demand period ends; and

(3) the dealer sends written notice of the rejection to the supplier before the 11th day after the delivery of the item.

(b) The supplier shall pay the costs of the return of an item the delivery of which is rejected under Subsection (a) of this section.

(c) A supplier may not coerce or compel a dealer to accept late delivery of back-ordered seasonal demand equipment other than parts or attachments.

Added by Acts 1991, 72nd Leg., ch. 119, § 1, eff. May 19, 1991.

Repeal

Acts 2007, 80th Leg., ch. 885, § 2.47(a)(1) repeals this section effective April 1, 2009.

§ 19.25. Sales to Affiliated Dealer

(a) Except as provided by Subsection (b) of this section, a supplier may not:

(1) sell or offer to sell new or unused equipment to an affiliated dealer at a price lower than the price for a sale of the same equipment, identically equipped, to a nonaffiliated dealer; or

(2) use a sales promotion plan or other program or device that results in a sale or offer of sale of new or unused equipment to an affiliated dealer at an actual price:

(A) lower than the price to a nonaffiliated dealer; or

(B) that is fixed and predetermined solely by the supplier.

(b) This section does not apply to sales made to a dealer for resale to:

(1) a unit or agency of the United States, this state, or any political subdivision of this state or the United States;

(2) a major fleet account; or

(3) an organization for testing or demonstrating the equipment.

Added by Acts 1991, 72nd Leg., ch. 119, § 1, eff. May 19, 1991.

Repeal

Acts 2007, 80th Leg., ch. 885, § 2.47(a)(1) repeals this section effective April 1, 2009.

§ 19.26. Transfer of Interest in Dealership

(a) A supplier may not prevent, by contract or otherwise, a dealer or any officer, member, partner, or stockholder of a dealer from selling or transferring a noncontrolling interest in the dealership to another party.

(b) A supplier may prevent a person from selling or transferring a controlling interest in a dealership without the supplier's written consent. A supplier may not unreasonably withhold the supplier's consent to a sale or transfer of a controlling interest in a dealership.

(c) A supplier and a dealer may provide by written agreement for succession rights to a controlling interest in a dealership on the death of an individual owning the controlling interest. If not otherwise determined by written agreement between the dealer and supplier, on the death of an individual owning a controlling interest, the family member of the individual to whom the interest passes by will or intestate succession may request that the supplier consent to a transfer of the ownership interest to the family member. The supplier shall consent to the transfer if the family member meets the reasonable financial, business experience, and character standards of the supplier. The supplier shall send a written response to the family member before the 91st day after the date of receipt of the family member's request, granting the supplier's consent or stating the supplier's refusal to consent and the specific reasons for the refusal.

(d) In this section, "family member" means an individual related within the second degree by consanguinity or affinity to an individual owning a controlling interest.

(e) Nothing in this section requires a supplier to continue a dealer agreement if the supplier determines that the dealer's area of responsibility or trade area lacks sufficient sales potential to reasonably support continuation of the agreement.

Added by Acts 1991, 72nd Leg., ch. 119, § 1, eff. May 19, 1991.

Repeal

Acts 2007, 80th Leg., ch. 885, § 2.47(a)(1) repeals this section effective April 1, 2009.

§ 19.27. Change in Competitive Circumstances

A supplier may not substantially change the competitive circumstances of a dealer agreement without cause.

Added by Acts 1991, 72nd Leg., ch. 119, § 1, eff. May 19, 1991.

Repeal

Acts 2007, 80th Leg., ch. 885, § 2.47(a)(1) repeals this section effective April 1, 2009.

§ 19.28. Warranty Claim

(a) This section applies to a warranty claim submitted by a dealer:

(1) while the dealer agreement is in effect; or

(2) after the termination of the dealer agreement, if the claim is for work performed before the effective date of the termination.

(b) Not later than the 30th day after the date a supplier receives a warranty claim from a dealer, the supplier shall accept or reject the claim. A claim not rejected before that deadline is deemed accepted.

(c) Not later than the 30th day after the date the claim is accepted or rejected, the supplier shall:

(1) pay an accepted claim; or

(2) send the dealer written notice of the grounds for rejection of a rejected claim.

(d) A supplier that pays a claim, including a supplier of an electric engine or motor, may not pay less than the hourly labor rate and other expenses involved in the work that the dealer regularly charges to a retail customer who does not assert a warranty and the dealer's net price plus 15 percent for parts. The number of hours of labor claimed may not exceed 1½ times the supplier's recommended hours for the repair involved.

(e) After payment of a claim, a supplier may not charge back, set off, or otherwise attempt to recover all or part of the amount of the claim unless:

(1) the claim was fraudulent;

(2) the work for which the claim was made was not properly performed or was unnecessary to comply with the warranty; or

(3) the dealer did not substantiate the claim according to the written requirements of the supplier in effect when the claim arose.

(f) A dealer or supplier authorized to sell new farm, industrial, or outdoor power equipment shall give the purchaser a written warranty agreement including replacement or cash refund. If the dealer determines the equipment cannot be made usable, the manufacturer is liable to the purchaser for the replacement or cash refund.

Added by Acts 1997, 75th Leg., ch. 1223, § 1, eff. Sept. 1, 1997.

Repeal

Acts 2007, 80th Leg., ch. 885, § 2.47(a)(1) repeals this section effective April 1, 2009.

[Sections 19.29 to 19.40 reserved for expansion]

SUBCHAPTER C. RENEWAL OR TERMINATION OF DEALER AGREEMENT

§ 19.41. Cause Required

A supplier may not terminate, cancel, or fail to renew a dealer agreement without cause.

Added by Acts 1991, 72nd Leg., ch. 119, § 1, eff. May 19, 1991.

Repeal

Acts 2007, 80th Leg., ch. 885, § 2.47(a)(1) repeals this section effective April 1, 2009.

§ 19.42. Renovation or Additional Space

A supplier may not require as a condition of renewal or extension of a dealer agreement that a dealer complete substantial renovation of the dealer's place of business or acquire new or additional space to serve as the dealer's place of business, unless the supplier:

(1) gives the dealer one year's written notice of the requirement, stating all grounds for the requirement; and

(2) provides the dealer a reasonable time to complete the renovation or acquisition.

Added by Acts 1991, 72nd Leg., ch. 119, § 1, eff. May 19, 1991.

Repeal

Acts 2007, 80th Leg., ch. 885, § 2.47(a)(1) repeals this section effective April 1, 2009.

§ 19.43. Return of Inventory

(a) If on termination of a dealer agreement the dealer delivers to the supplier or a person designated by the supplier the inventory that was purchased from the supplier and that is held by the dealer on the date of the termination, the supplier shall pay to the dealer:

(1) the dealer cost of new, unsold, undamaged, and complete farm tractors, farm implements, utility tractors, industrial tractors, forklifts, material-handling equipment, outdoor power equipment, forestry harvesting equipment, off-road construction equipment, and attachments returned by the dealer;

(2) an amount equal to 85 percent of the current price of new, undamaged repair parts returned by the dealer; and

(3) an amount equal to an additional five percent of the current price of new, undamaged repair parts returned by the dealer, unless the supplier performs the handling, packing, and loading of the parts, in which case no additional amount is required under this subdivision.

(b) Before returning inventory under this section and not later than the 120th day after the effective date of termination, the dealer shall submit to the supplier a list of the inventory the dealer intends to return, including to the extent possible each item's trade name, description, and serial number. Not later than the 60th day after the date the supplier receives the list, the supplier shall notify the dealer in writing of:

(1) each item that the supplier claims is not subject to reimbursement under this section; and

(2) the destination of each item the dealer is to deliver to a person designated by the supplier.

(c) The supplier may subtract from the sum due under Subsection (a) of this section the amount of debts owed by the dealer to the supplier. The supplier and dealer are each responsible for one-half of the cost of delivering the inventory to the supplier or to a person designated by the supplier, except that if the dealer delivers an item to a person designated by the supplier the dealer is not responsible for an amount that exceeds the amount for which the dealer would have been responsible if the item had been delivered to the supplier.

(d) The supplier shall pay the amount due under this section before the 91st day after the day that the supplier or person designated by the supplier receives inventory from the dealer and after the dealer has furnished proof that the inventory was purchased from the supplier.

(e) On payment of the amount due under this section, title to the inventory is transferred to the supplier or other person designated by the supplier.

(f) The supplier and dealer may by agreement alter the time limits provided by this section.

Added by Acts 1991, 72nd Leg., ch. 119, § 1, eff. May 19, 1991. Amended by Acts 1995, 74th Leg., ch. 922, § 1, eff. Sept. 1, 1995; Acts 1999, 76th Leg., ch. 725, § 3, eff. Sept. 1, 1999.

Repeal

Acts 2007, 80th Leg., ch. 885, § 2.47(a)(1) repeals this section effective April 1, 2009.

§ 19.44. Return of Data Processing Equipment and Specialized Repair Tools

(a) If on termination of a dealer agreement the dealer delivers to the supplier data processing or peripheral equipment, software, or specialized repair tools that the supplier required the dealer to purchase or lease, the supplier shall assume the dealer's lease responsibilities, for that equipment or software, if any, and pay to the dealer:

(1) an amount equal to the fair market value of the data processing equipment or software purchased by the dealer and delivered to the supplier; and

(2) an amount equal to 75 percent of the cost to the dealer of the specialized repair tools purchased by the dealer and delivered to the supplier.

(b) The supplier and dealer are each responsible for one-half of the cost of delivering the data processing equipment and software and specialized repair tools to the supplier.

(c) The supplier shall assume the lease responsibilities and pay the amount due under this section before the 61st day after the date that the supplier receives data processing equipment and software or specialized repair tools from the dealer.

(d) On payment of the amount due under this section, title or the right of possession to the data processing equipment or specialized repair tools purchased or leased by the dealer is transferred to the supplier.

Added by Acts 1991, 72nd Leg., ch. 119, § 1, eff. May 19, 1991.

Repeal

Acts 2007, 80th Leg., ch. 885, § 2.47(a)(1) repeals this section effective April 1, 2009.

§ 19.45. Exceptions

(a) A supplier is not required to repurchase:

(1) inventory:

(A) that the dealer orders after the dealer receives notice of the termination of the dealer agreement from the supplier; or

(B) for which the dealer cannot furnish evidence of clear title that is satisfactory to the supplier; or

(2) a repair part that:

(A) has a limited storage life and that was purchased from the supplier more than two years before the date of termination of the dealer agreement;

(B) is in a broken or damaged package;

(C) is usually sold as part of a set, if the part is separated from the set; or

(D) cannot be sold without reconditioning or repackaging.

(b) A supplier is not required to purchase or assume the lease responsibilities for:

(1) data processing equipment or software that the dealer purchased that was not specifically required by the supplier; or

(2) a specialized repair tool that:

(A) is not unique to the supplier's product line;

(B) is not in complete and salable condition; or

(C) was not purchased by the dealer within three years of the date of termination of the dealer agreement.

Added by Acts 1991, 72nd Leg., ch. 119, § 1, eff. May 19, 1991.

Repeal

Acts 2007, 80th Leg., ch. 885, § 2.47(a)(1) repeals this section effective April 1, 2009.

§ 19.46. Repealed by Acts 1997, 75th Leg., ch. 1223, § 2, eff. Sept. 1, 1997

§ 19.47. Late Payment

If a supplier does not make the payments required by this subchapter before the 61st day after the date that the supplier received the final shipment of the inventory, data processing equipment or software, or specialized repair tools from the dealer, the supplier is liable to the dealer for:

(1) the greater of the dealer cost or current price of the inventory;

(2) the cost to the dealer of the data processing equipment and software, and specialized repair tools;

(3) the expenses incurred by the dealer in returning the inventory, data processing equipment and software, and specialized repair tools to the supplier;

(4) interest on amounts due under Subdivisions (1) through (3) of this section, at the rate applicable to a judgment of a court of this state, for the period beginning on the 61st day after the date the supplier received the inventory, data processing equipment or software, or specialized repair tools;

(5) reasonable attorney's fees; and

(6) court costs.

Added by Acts 1991, 72nd Leg., ch. 119, § 1, eff. May 19, 1991.

Repeal

Acts 2007, 80th Leg., ch. 885, § 2.47(a)(1) repeals this section effective April 1, 2009.

CHAPTER 20. REGULATION OF CONSUMER CREDIT REPORTING AGENCIES

§ 20.01. Definitions

In this chapter:

(1) "Adverse action" includes:

(A) the denial of, increase in a charge for, or reduction in the amount of insurance for personal, family, or household purposes;

(B) the denial of employment or other decision made for employment purposes that adversely affects a current or prospective employee; or

(C) an action or determination with respect to a consumer's application for credit that is adverse to the consumer's interests.

(2) "Consumer" means an individual who resides in this state.

(3) "Consumer file" means all of the information about a consumer that is recorded and retained by a consumer reporting agency regardless of how the information is stored.

(4) "Consumer report" means a communication or other information by a consumer reporting agency relating to the credit worthiness, credit standing, credit capacity, debts, character, general reputation, personal characteristics, or mode of living of a consumer that is used or expected to be used or collected, wholly or partly, as a factor in establishing the consumer's eligibility for credit or insurance for personal, family, or household purposes, employment purposes, or other purpose authorized under Sections 603 and 604 of the Fair Credit Reporting Act (15 U.S.C. Sections 1681a and 1681b), as amended. The term does not include:

(A) a report containing information solely on a transaction between the consumer and the person making the report;

(B) an authorization or approval of a specific extension of credit directly or indirectly by the issuer of a credit card or similar device;

(C) a report in which a person who has been requested by a third party to make a specific extension of credit directly or indirectly to a consumer makes a decision with respect to the request, if the third party advises the consumer of the name and address of the person to whom the request was made and the person makes the disclosures that must be made under Section 615 of the Fair Credit Reporting Act (15 U.S.C. Section 1681m), as amended, to the consumer in the event of adverse action against the consumer;

(D) any communication of information described in this subdivision among persons related by common ownership or affiliated by corporate control; or

(E) any communication of other information among persons related by common ownership or affiliated by corporate control, if it is clearly and conspicuously disclosed to the consumer that the information may be communicated among such persons and the consumer is given the opportunity before the time that the information is initially communicated to direct that such information not be communicated among such persons.

(5) "Consumer reporting agency" means a person that regularly engages wholly or partly in the practice of assembling or evaluating consumer credit information or other information on consumers to furnish consumer reports to third parties for monetary fees, for dues, or on a cooperative nonprofit basis. The term does not include a business entity that provides only check verification or check guarantee services.

(6) "Investigative consumer report" means all or part of a consumer report in which information on the character, general reputation, personal charac-

teristics, or mode of living of a consumer is obtained through a personal interview with a neighbor, friend, or associate of the consumer or others with whom the consumer is acquainted or who may have knowledge concerning any such information. The term does not include specific factual information on a consumer's credit record obtained directly from a creditor of the consumer or from a consumer reporting agency when the information was obtained directly from a creditor of the consumer or from the consumer.

(7) "Security alert" means a notice placed on a consumer file that alerts a recipient of a consumer report involving that consumer file that the consumer's identity may have been used without the consumer's consent to fraudulently obtain goods or services in the consumer's name.

(8) "Security freeze" means a notice placed on a consumer file that prohibits a consumer reporting agency from releasing a consumer report relating to the extension of credit involving that consumer file without the express authorization of the consumer.

Added by Acts 1997, 75th Leg., ch. 1396, § 33(a), eff. Oct. 1, 1997. Amended by Acts 2003, 78th Leg., ch. 1326, § 1, eff. Sept. 1, 2003.

§ 20.02. Permissible Purposes; Prohibition; Use of Consumer's Social Security Number

(a) A consumer reporting agency may furnish a consumer report only:

(1) in response to a court order issued by a court with proper jurisdiction;

(2) in accordance with the written instructions of the consumer to whom the report relates; or

(3) to a person the agency has reason to believe:

(A) intends to use the information in connection with a transaction involving the extension of credit to, or review or collection of an account of, the consumer to whom the report relates;

(B) intends to use the information for employment purposes as authorized under the Fair Credit Reporting Act (15 U.S.C. Section 1681 et seq.), as amended, and regulations adopted under that Act;

(C) intends to use the information in connection with the underwriting of insurance involving the consumer as authorized under the Fair Credit Reporting Act (15 U.S.C. Section 1681 et seq.), as amended, and regulations adopted under that Act;

(D) intends to use the information in connection with a determination of the consumer's eligibility for a license or other benefit granted by a governmental entity required by law to consider an applicant's financial responsibility or status;

(E) has a legitimate business need for the information in connection with a business transaction involving the consumer; or

(F) intends to use the information for any purpose authorized under the Fair Credit Reporting Act (15 U.S.C. Section 1681 et seq.), as amended, and regulations adopted under that Act.

(b) A consumer reporting agency may not prohibit a user of a consumer report or investigative consumer report from disclosing the contents of the report or providing a copy of the report to the consumer to whom it relates at the consumer's request if adverse action against the consumer based wholly or partly on the report has been taken or is contemplated by the user of the report. A user of a consumer report or a consumer reporting agency may not be found liable or otherwise held responsible for a disclosed or copied report when acting under this subsection. The disclosure or copy of the report, by itself, does not make a user of the report a consumer reporting agency.

(c) If a consumer furnishes the consumer's social security number to a person for use in obtaining a consumer report, the person shall include the consumer's social security number with the request for the consumer report and shall include the social security number with all future reports of information regarding the consumer made by the person to a consumer reporting agency unless the person has reason to believe that the social security number is inaccurate.

Added by Acts 1997, 75th Leg., ch. 1396, § 33(a), eff. Oct. 1, 1997.

§ 20.021. Check Verification and Check Guarantee Services; Disclosures to Consumers

(a) In this section, "check verifier" means any business offering check verification or check guarantee services in this state.

(b) On request and proper identification provided by a consumer, a check verifier shall disclose to the consumer in writing all information pertaining to the consumer in the check verifier's files at the time of the request, including:

(1) the criteria used by the check verifier to reject a check from the consumer;

(2) a set of instructions describing how information is presented on the check verifier's written disclosure of the consumer file; and

(3) a toll-free number at which personnel are available to consumers during normal business hours for use in resolving a dispute if the consumer submits a written dispute to the check verifier.

(c) A check verifier may not charge a consumer for disclosing the information required under Subsection (b) if the check verifier has rejected a check from the consumer in the 30 days prior to the consumer's request for information. A check verifier may otherwise impose a reasonable charge on a consumer for the disclosure of information pertaining to the consumer in an amount not to exceed $8.

Added by Acts 2003, 78th Leg., ch. 1291, § 2, eff. Sept. 1, 2003. Renumbered from V.T.C.A., Bus. & C. Code § 20.11 by Acts 2005, 79th Leg., ch. 728, § 23.001(2), eff. Sept. 1, 2005.

§ 20.03. Disclosures to Consumers

(a) On request and proper identification provided by a consumer, a consumer reporting agency shall disclose to the consumer in writing all information pertaining to the consumer in the consumer reporting agency's files at the time of the request, including:

(1) the name of each person requesting credit information about the consumer during the preceding six months and the date of each request;

(2) a set of instructions describing how information is presented on the consumer reporting agency's written disclosure of the consumer file; and

(3) if the consumer reporting agency compiles and maintains files on a nationwide basis, a toll-free number at which personnel are available to consumers during normal business hours for use in resolving a dispute if the consumer submits a written dispute to the consumer reporting agency.

(b) The information must be disclosed in a clear, accurate manner that is understandable to a consumer.

(c) A consumer reporting agency shall provide a copy of the consumer's file to the consumer on the request of the consumer and on evidence of proper identification, as directed by the Fair Credit Reporting Act (15 U.S.C. Section 1681 et seq.), as amended, and regulations adopted under that Act.

(d) Any written disclosure to a consumer by a consumer reporting agency under this chapter must include a written statement that explains in clear and simple language the consumer's rights under this chapter and includes:

(1) the process for receiving a consumer report or consumer file;

(2) the process for requesting or removing a security alert or freeze;

(3) the toll-free telephone number for requesting a security alert;

(4) applicable fees;

(5) dispute procedures;

(6) the process for correcting a consumer file or report; and

(7) information on a consumer's right to bring an action in court or arbitrate a dispute.

Added by Acts 1997, 75th Leg., ch. 1396, § 33(a), eff. Oct. 1, 1997. Amended by Acts 2003, 78th Leg., ch. 1326, § 2, eff. Sept. 1, 2003.

§ 20.031. Requesting Security Alert

On a request in writing or by telephone and with proper identification provided by a consumer, a consumer reporting agency shall place a security alert on the consumer's consumer file not later than 24 hours after the date the agency receives the request. The security alert must remain in effect for not less than 45 days after the date the agency places the security alert on the file. There is no limit on the number of security alerts a consumer may request. At the end of a 45–day security alert, on request in writing or by telephone and with proper identification provided by the consumer, the agency shall provide the consumer with a copy of the consumer's file. A consumer may include with the security alert request a telephone number to be used by persons to verify the consumer's identity before entering into a transaction with the consumer.

Added by Acts 2003, 78th Leg., ch. 1326, § 3, eff. Sept. 1, 2003.

§ 20.032. Notification of Security Alert

A consumer reporting agency shall notify a person who requests a consumer report if a security alert is in effect for the consumer file involved in that report and include a verification telephone number for the consumer if the consumer has provided a number under Section 20.031.

Added by Acts 2003, 78th Leg., ch. 1326, § 3, eff. Sept. 1, 2003.

§ 20.033. Toll-free Security Alert Request Number

A consumer reporting agency shall maintain a toll-free telephone number that is answered at a minimum during normal business hours to accept security alert requests from consumers. If calls are not answered after normal business hours, an automated answering system shall record requests and calls shall be returned to the consumer not later than two hours after the time the normal business day begins on the next business day after the date the call was received.

Added by Acts 2003, 78th Leg., ch. 1326, § 3, eff. Sept. 1, 2003.

§ 20.034. Requesting Security Freeze

(a) On written request sent by certified mail that includes proper identification provided by a consumer, a consumer reporting agency shall place a security freeze on a consumer's consumer file not later than the fifth business day after the date the agency receives the request.

(b) On written request for a security freeze provided by a consumer under Subsection (a), a consumer reporting agency shall disclose to the consumer the process of placing, removing, and temporarily lifting a security freeze and the process for allowing access to information from the consumer's consumer file for a specific requester or period while the security freeze is in effect.

(c) A consumer reporting agency shall, not later than the 10th business day after the date the agency receives the request for a security freeze:

(1) send a written confirmation of the security freeze to the consumer; and

(2) provide the consumer with a unique personal identification number or password to be used by the consumer to authorize a removal or temporary lifting of the security freeze under Section 20.037.

(d) A consumer may request in writing a replacement personal identification number or password. The request must comply with the requirements for requesting a security freeze under Subsection (a). The consumer reporting agency shall not later than the third business day after the date the agency receives the request for a replacement personal identification number or password provide the consumer with a new unique personal identification number or password to be used by the consumer instead of the number or password that was provided under Subsection (c).

Added by Acts 2003, 78th Leg., ch. 1326, § 3, eff. Sept. 1, 2003. Amended by Acts 2007, 80th Leg., ch. 1143, § 1, eff. Sept. 1, 2007.

Section 5 of Acts 2007, 80th Leg., ch. 1143 provides:

"The change in law made by this Act applies only to a request for placement, removal, or temporary lifting of a security freeze on a consumer file that is made on or after the effective date of this Act. A request for placement, removal, or temporary lifting of a security freeze on a consumer file that is made before the effective date of this Act is governed by the law in effect on the date the request was made, and the former law is continued in effect for that purpose."

§ 20.035. Notification of Change

If a security freeze is in place, a consumer reporting agency shall notify the consumer in writing of a change in the consumer file to the consumer's name, date of birth, social security number, or address not later than 30 calendar days after the date the change is made. The agency shall send notification of a change of address to the new address and former address. This section does not require notice of an immaterial change, including a street abbreviation change or correction of a transposition of letters or misspelling of a word.

Added by Acts 2003, 78th Leg., ch. 1326, § 3, eff. Sept. 1, 2003.

§ 20.036. Notification of Security Freeze

A consumer reporting agency shall notify a person who requests a consumer report if a security freeze is in effect for the consumer file involved in that report.

Added by Acts 2003, 78th Leg., ch. 1326, § 3, eff. Sept. 1, 2003.

§ 20.037. Removal or Temporary Lifting of Security Freeze

(a) On a request in writing or by telephone and with proper identification provided by a consumer, including the consumer's personal identification number or password provided under Section 20.034, a consumer reporting agency shall remove a security freeze not later than the third business day after the date the agency receives the request.

(b) On a request in writing or by telephone and with proper identification provided by a consumer, including the consumer's personal identification number or password provided under Section 20.034, a consumer reporting agency, not later than the third business day after the date the agency receives the request, shall temporarily lift the security freeze for:

(1) a certain properly designated period; or

(2) a certain properly identified requester.

(c) A consumer reporting agency may develop procedures involving the use of a telephone, a facsimile machine, the Internet, or another electronic medium to receive and process a request from a consumer under this section.

(d) A consumer reporting agency shall remove a security freeze placed on a consumer file if the security freeze was placed due to a material misrepresentation of fact by the consumer. The consumer reporting agency shall notify the consumer in writing before removing the security freeze under this subsection.

(e) Repealed by Acts 2007, 80th Leg., ch. 1143, § 4.

Added by Acts 2003, 78th Leg., ch. 1326, § 3, eff. Sept. 1, 2003. Amended by Acts 2007, 80th Leg., ch. 1143, § 4, eff. Sept. 1, 2007.

Section 5 of Acts 2007, 80th Leg., ch. 1143 provides:

"The change in law made by this Act applies only to a request for placement, removal, or temporary lifting of a security freeze on a consumer file that is made on or after the effective date of this Act. A request for placement, removal, or temporary lifting of a security freeze on a consumer file that is made before the effective date of this Act is governed by the law in effect on the date the request was made, and the former law is continued in effect for that purpose."

§ 20.038. Exemption From Security Freeze

A security freeze does not apply to a consumer report provided to:

(1) a state or local governmental entity, including a law enforcement agency or court or private collection agency, if the entity, agency, or court is acting under a court order, warrant, subpoena, or administrative subpoena;

(2) a child support agency as defined by Section 101.004, Family Code, acting to investigate or collect child support payments or acting under Title IV–D of the Social Security Act (42 U.S.C. Section 651 et seq.);

(3) the Health and Human Services Commission acting under Section 531.102, Government Code;

(4) the comptroller acting to investigate or collect delinquent sales or franchise taxes;

(5) a tax assessor-collector acting to investigate or collect delinquent ad valorem taxes;

(6) a person for the purposes of prescreening as provided by the Fair Credit Reporting Act (15 U.S.C. Section 1681 et seq.), as amended;

(7) a person with whom the consumer has an account or contract or to whom the consumer has issued a negotiable instrument, or the person's subsidiary, affiliate, agent, assignee, prospective assignee, or private collection agency, for purposes related to that account, contract, or instrument;

(8) a subsidiary, affiliate, agent, assignee, or prospective assignee of a person to whom access has been granted under Section 20.037(b);

(9) a person who administers a credit file monitoring subscription service to which the consumer has subscribed;

(10) a person for the purpose of providing a consumer with a copy of the consumer's report on the consumer's request;

(11) a check service or fraud prevention service company that issues consumer reports:

(A) to prevent or investigate fraud; or

(B) for purposes of approving or processing negotiable instruments, electronic funds transfers, or similar methods of payment;

(12) a deposit account information service company that issues consumer reports related to account closures caused by fraud, substantial overdrafts, automated teller machine abuses, or similar negative information regarding a consumer to an inquiring financial institution for use by the financial institution only in reviewing a consumer request for a deposit account with that institution; or

(13) a consumer reporting agency that:

(A) acts only to resell credit information by assembling and merging information contained in a database of another consumer reporting agency or multiple consumer reporting agencies; and

(B) does not maintain a permanent database of credit information from which new consumer reports are produced.

Added by Acts 2003, 78th Leg., ch. 1326, § 3, eff. Sept. 1, 2003.

§ 20.0385. Applicability of Security Alert and Security Freeze

(a) The requirement under this chapter to place a security alert or security freeze on a consumer file does not apply to:

(1) a check service or fraud prevention service company that issues consumer reports:

(A) to prevent or investigate fraud; or

(B) for purposes of approving or processing negotiable instruments, electronic funds transfers, or similar methods of payment; or

(2) a deposit account information service company that issues consumer reports related to account closures caused by fraud, substantial overdrafts, automated teller machine abuses, or similar negative information regarding a consumer to an inquiring financial institution for use by the financial institution only in reviewing a consumer request for a deposit account with that institution.

(b) The requirement under this chapter to place a security freeze on a consumer file does not apply to a consumer reporting agency that:

(1) acts only to resell credit information by assembling and merging information contained in a database of another consumer reporting agency or multiple consumer reporting agencies; and

(2) does not maintain a permanent database of credit information from which new consumer reports are produced.

(c) Notwithstanding Section 20.12, a violation of a requirement under this chapter to place, temporarily lift, or remove a security freeze on a consumer file is not a false, misleading, or deceptive act or practice under Subchapter E, Chapter 17.

Added by Acts 2003, 78th Leg., ch. 1326, § 3, eff. Sept. 1, 2003. Amended by Acts 2007, 80th Leg., ch. 1143, § 2, eff. Sept. 1, 2007.

Section 5 of Acts 2007, 80th Leg., ch. 1143 provides:

"The change in law made by this Act applies only to a request for placement, removal, or temporary lifting of a security freeze on a consumer file that is made on or after the effective date of this Act. A request for placement, removal, or temporary lifting of a security freeze on a consumer file that is made before the effective date of this Act is governed by the law in effect on the date the request was made, and the former law is continued in effect for that purpose."

§ 20.039. Respect of Security Freeze

A consumer reporting agency shall honor a security freeze placed on a consumer file by another consumer reporting agency.

Added by Acts 2003, 78th Leg., ch. 1326, § 3, eff. Sept. 1, 2003.

§ 20.04. Charges for Certain Disclosures or Services

(a) Except as provided by Subsection (b), a consumer reporting agency may impose a reasonable charge on a consumer for the disclosure of information pertaining to the consumer or for placing a security freeze on a consumer file, temporarily lifting a security freeze for a designated period or for an identified requester, or removing a security freeze in accordance with this chapter. The amount of the charge for the disclosure of information pertaining to the consumer may not exceed $8. The amount of the charge for placing a security freeze on a consumer file, temporarily lifting a security freeze for a designated period, or removing a security freeze may not exceed $10 per request. The amount of the charge for temporarily lifting a security freeze for an identified requester may not exceed $12 per request. On January 1 of each year, a consumer reporting agency may increase the charge for disclosure to a consumer or for placing, temporarily lifting, or removing a security freeze. The increase, if any, must be based proportionally on changes to the Consumer Price Index for All Urban Consumers as determined by the United States Department of Labor with fractional changes rounded to the nearest 50 cents.

(b) A consumer reporting agency may not charge a fee for:

(1) a request by a consumer for a copy of the consumer's file:

(A) made not later than the 60th day after the date on which adverse action is taken against the consumer; or

(B) made on the expiration of a 45-day security alert;

(2) notification of the deletion of information that is found to be inaccurate or can no longer be verified sent to a person designated by the consumer, as prescribed by Section 611 of the Fair Credit Reporting Act (15 U.S.C. Section 1681i), as amended;

(3) a set of instructions for understanding the information presented on the consumer report;

(4) a toll-free telephone number that consumers may call to obtain additional assistance concerning the consumer report or to request a security alert;

(5) a request for a security alert made by a consumer; or

(6) the placement, temporary lifting, or removal of a security freeze at the request of a consumer who has submitted to the consumer reporting agency a copy of a valid police report, investigative report, or complaint involving the alleged commission of an offense under Section 32.51, Penal Code.

Added by Acts 1997, 75th Leg., ch. 1396, § 33(a), eff. Oct. 1, 1997. Amended by Acts 2003, 78th Leg., ch. 1326, § 4, eff. Sept. 1, 2003; Acts 2007, 80th Leg., ch. 1143, § 3, eff. Sept. 1, 2007.

Section 5 of Acts 2007, 80th Leg., ch. 1143 provides:

"The change in law made by this Act applies only to a request for placement, removal, or temporary lifting of a security freeze on a consumer file that is made on or after the effective date of this Act. A request for placement, removal, or temporary lifting of a security freeze on a consumer file that is made before the effective date of this Act is governed by the law in effect on the date the request was made, and the former law is continued in effect for that purpose."

§ 20.05. Reporting of Information Prohibited

(a) Except as provided by Subsection (b), a consumer reporting agency may not furnish a consumer report containing information related to:

(1) a case under Title 11 of the United States Code or under the federal Bankruptcy Act in which the date of entry of the order for relief or the date of adjudication predates the consumer report by more than 10 years;

(2) a suit or judgment in which the date of entry predates the consumer report by more than seven years or the governing statute of limitations, whichever is longer;

(3) a tax lien in which the date of payment predates the consumer report by more than seven years;

(4) a record of arrest, indictment, or conviction of a crime in which the date of disposition, release, or parole predates the consumer report by more than seven years; or

(5) another item or event that predates the consumer report by more than seven years.

(b) A consumer reporting agency may furnish a consumer report that contains information described by Subsection (a) if the information is provided in connection with:

(1) a credit transaction with a principal amount that is or may reasonably be expected to be $150,000 or more;

(2) the underwriting of life insurance for a face amount that is or may reasonably be expected to be $150,000 or more; or

(3) the employment of a consumer at an annual salary that is or may reasonably be expected to be $75,000 or more.

(b–1) A consumer reporting agency may furnish to a person a consumer report that contains information described by Subsection (a) if the information is needed by the person to avoid a violation of 18 U.S.C. Section 1033.

(c) A consumer reporting agency may not furnish medical information about a consumer in a consumer report that is being obtained for employment purposes or in connection with a credit, insurance, or direct marketing transaction unless the consumer consents to the furnishing of the medical information.

Added by Acts 1997, 75th Leg., ch. 1396, § 33(a), eff. Oct. 1, 1997. Amended by Acts 2005, 79th Leg., ch. 599, § 1, eff. June 17, 2005.

Section 2 of Acts 2005, 79th Leg., ch. 599 provides:

"This Act applies only to a consumer report furnished by a consumer reporting agency on or after the effective date of this Act. A consumer report furnished before the effective date of this Act is covered by the law in effect on the date the consumer report was furnished, and the former law is continued in effect for that purpose."

§ 20.06. Dispute Procedure

(a) If the completeness or accuracy of information contained in a consumer's file is disputed by the consumer and the consumer notifies the consumer reporting agency of the dispute, the agency shall reinvestigate the disputed information free of charge and record the current status of the disputed information not later than the 30th business day after the date on which the agency receives the notice. The consumer reporting agency shall provide the consumer with the option of notifying the agency of a dispute concerning the consumer's file by speaking directly to a representative of the agency during normal business hours.

(b) Not later than the fifth business day after the date on which a consumer reporting agency receives notice of a dispute from a consumer in accordance with Subsection (a), the agency shall provide notice of the dispute to each person who provided any information related to the dispute.

(c) A consumer reporting agency may terminate a reinvestigation of information disputed by a consumer under Subsection (a) if the agency reasonably determines that the dispute is frivolous or irrelevant. An agency that terminates a reinvestigation of disputed information under this subsection shall promptly notify the consumer of the termination and the reasons for the termination by mail, or if authorized by the consumer, by telephone. The presence of contradictory information in a consumer's file does not by itself constitute reasonable grounds for determining that the dispute is frivolous or irrelevant.

(d) If disputed information is found to be inaccurate or cannot be verified after a reinvestigation under Subsection (a), the consumer reporting agency, unless otherwise directed by the consumer, shall promptly delete the information from the consumer's file, revise the consumer file, and provide the revised consumer report to the consumer and to each person who requested the consumer report within the preceding six months. The consumer reporting agency may not report the inaccurate or unverified information in subsequent reports.

(e) Information deleted under Subsection (d) may not be reinserted in the consumer's file unless the person who furnishes the information to the consumer reporting agency reinvestigates and states in writing or by electronic record to the agency that the information is complete and accurate.

(f) A consumer reporting agency shall provide written notice of the results of a reinvestigation or reinsertion made under this section not later than the fifth business day after the date on which the reinvestigation or reinsertion has been completed. The notice must include:

(1) a statement that the reinvestigation is complete;

(2) a statement of the determination made by the agency on the completeness or accuracy of the disputed information;

(3) a copy of the consumer's file or consumer report and a description of the results of the reinvestigation;

(4) a statement that a description of the procedure used to determine the accuracy and completeness of the information shall be provided to the consumer by the agency on request, including the name, business address, and, if available, the telephone number of each person contacted in connection with the information;

(5) a statement that the consumer is entitled to add a statement to the consumer's file disputing the accuracy or completeness of the information as provided by Section 611 of the Fair Credit Reporting Act (15 U.S.C. Section 1681i), as amended; and

(6) a statement that the consumer may be entitled to dispute resolution as prescribed by this section, after the consumer receives the notice specified under this subsection.

(g) This section does not require a person who obtains a consumer report for resale to another person to alter or correct an inaccuracy in the consumer report if the report was not assembled or prepared by the person.

(h) This section applies to a business offering check verification or check guarantee services in this state.

Added by Acts 1997, 75th Leg., ch. 1396, § 33(a), eff. Oct. 1, 1997. Amended by Acts 2003, 78th Leg., ch. 851, § 3, eff. Sept. 1, 2003; Acts 2003, 78th Leg., ch. 1291, § 1, eff. Sept. 1, 2003.

§ 20.07. Correction of Inaccurate Information

(a) A consumer reporting agency shall provide a person who provides consumer credit information to the agency with the option of correcting previously reported inaccurate information by submitting the correction by facsimile or other automated means.

(b) The credit reporting agency which receives a correction shall have reasonable procedures to assure that previously reported inaccurate information in a consumer's file is corrected in a prompt and timely fashion.

Added by Acts 1997, 75th Leg., ch. 1396, § 33(a), eff. Oct. 1, 1997.

§ 20.08. Consumer's Right to File Action in Court or Arbitrate Disputes

(a) An action to enforce an obligation of a consumer reporting agency to a consumer under this chapter may be brought in any court as provided by the Fair Credit Reporting Act (15 U.S.C. Section 1681 et seq.), as amended, or, if agreed to by both parties, may be submitted to binding arbitration after the consumer has followed all dispute procedures in Section 20.06 and has received the notice specified in Section 20.06(f) in the manner provided by the rules of the American Arbitration Association.

(b) A decision rendered by an arbitrator under this section does not affect the validity of an obligation or debt owed by the consumer to any party.

(c) A prevailing party in an action or arbitration proceeding brought under this section shall be compensated for the party's attorney fees and costs of the proceeding as determined by the court or arbitration.

(d) A consumer may not submit to arbitration more than one action against a particular consumer reporting agency during any 120-day period.

(e) The results of an arbitration action brought against a consumer reporting agency doing business in this state shall be communicated in a timely manner to other consumer reporting agencies doing business in this state.

(f) If a determination is made in favor of a consumer after submission of a dispute to arbitration, the disputed adverse information in the consumer's file or record shall be removed or stricken in a timely manner. If the adverse information is not removed or stricken, the consumer may bring an action against the noncomplying agency under this section regardless of the 120-day waiting period required under this section.

Added by Acts 1997, 75th Leg., ch. 1396, § 33(a), eff. Oct. 1, 1997.

§ 20.09. Civil Liability

(a) A consumer reporting agency that wilfully violates this chapter is liable to the consumer against whom the violation occurs for the greater of three times the amount of actual damages to the consumer or $1,000, reasonable attorney fees, and court or arbitration costs.

(b) A consumer reporting agency that negligently violates this chapter is liable to the consumer against whom the violation occurs for the greater of the amount of actual damages to the consumer or $500, reasonable attorney fees, and court or arbitration costs. A consumer reporting agency is not considered to have negligently violated this chapter if, not later than the 30th day after the date on which the agency receives notice of a dispute from the consumer under Section 20.06 that clearly explains the nature and substance of the dispute, the agency completes the reinvestigation and sends the consumer and, at the request of the consumer, each person who received the consumer information written notification of the results of the reinvestigation in accordance with Section 20.06(f).

(c) In addition to liability imposed under Subsection (a), a consumer reporting agency that does not correct a consumer's file and consumer report before the 10th day after the date on which a judgment is entered against the agency because of inaccurate information contained in a consumer's file is also liable for $1,000 a day until the inaccuracy is corrected.

Added by Acts 1997, 75th Leg., ch. 1396, § 33(a), eff. Oct. 1, 1997.

§ 20.10. Remedies Cumulative

An action taken under this chapter does not prohibit a consumer from taking any other action authorized by law except that a credit reporting agency may not be subject to suit with respect to any issue that was the subject of an arbitration proceeding brought under Section 20.08.

Added by Acts 1997, 75th Leg., ch. 1396, § 33(a), eff. Oct. 1, 1997.

§ 20.11. Injunctive Relief; Civil Penalty

(a) The attorney general may file a suit against a person for:

(1) injunctive relief to prevent or restrain a violation of this chapter; or

(2) a civil penalty in an amount not to exceed $2,000 for each violation of this chapter.

(b) If the attorney general brings an action against a person under Subsection (a) and an injunction is granted against the person or the person is found liable for a civil penalty, the attorney general may recover reasonable expenses, court costs, investigative costs, and attorney's fees.

(c) Each day a violation continues or occurs is a separate violation for purposes of imposing a penalty under this section.

Added by Acts 2003, 78th Leg., ch. 1326, § 5, eff. Sept. 1, 2003.

§ 20.12. Deceptive Trade Practice

A violation of this chapter is a false, misleading, or deceptive act or practice under Subchapter E, Chapter 17.

Added by Acts 2003, 78th Leg., ch. 1326, § 5, eff. Sept. 1, 2003.

§ 20.13. Venue

An action brought under this chapter shall be filed in a district court:

(1) in Travis County;

(2) in any county in which the violation occurred; or

(3) in the county in which the victim resides, regardless of whether the alleged violator has resided, worked, or done business in the county in which the victim resides.

Added by Acts 2003, 78th Leg., ch. 1326, § 5, eff. Sept. 1, 2003.

[Chapters 21 and 22 reserved for expansion]

TITLE 3. INSOLVENCY, FRAUDULENT TRANSFERS, AND FRAUD

CHAPTER 23. ASSIGNMENTS FOR THE BENEFIT OF CREDITORS

SUBCHAPTER A. GENERAL PROVISIONS

SUBCHAPTER A. GENERAL PROVISIONS

§ 23.01. Definitions

In this chapter, unless the context requires a different definition,

(1) "assigned estate" means all the real and personal estate of an assigning debtor passing to the consenting creditors under an assignment by virtue of Section 23.02 or 23.09(b) of this code;

(2) "assignee" means an assignee for the benefit of creditors;

(3) "assigning debtor" means a person executing an assignment;

(4) "assignment" means a general assignment for the benefit of creditors made under this chapter;

(5) "consenting creditor" means a creditor who has consented to an assignment in one of the ways provided by Section 23.30 of this code; and

(6) "real and personal estate" does not include property exempt by law from execution.

Acts 1967, 60th Leg., p. 2343, ch. 785, § 1.

§ 23.02. Nature and Effect of Assignment

(a) A debtor may assign his real and personal estate under this chapter to an assignee for the benefit of the debtor's creditors.

(b) An assigning debtor shall provide in the assignment for distribution of all his real and personal estate to each consenting creditor in proportion to each consenting creditor's claim.

(c) Regardless of an expression to the contrary, an assignment passes all an assigning debtor's real and personal estate to each consenting creditor in proportion to each consenting creditor's claim.

Acts 1967, 60th Leg., p. 2343, ch. 785, § 1.

[Sections 23.03 to 23.07 reserved for expansion]

SUBCHAPTER B. THE ASSIGNMENT

§ 23.08. Form and Content of Assignment

(a) For an assignment to be valid,

(1) the assigning debtor must make the assignment in writing; and

(2) it must be proved or acknowledged and recorded in the manner provided by law for the conveyance of real estate.

(b) The assigning debtor shall attach to his assignment an inventory containing the following information:

(1) a list naming each creditor of the assigning debtor;

(2) the resident address, if known, of each creditor;

(3) the amount owed each creditor and the type of debt;

(4) the consideration for the debt and the place where the debt arose;

(5) a description of each existing judgment or security for the payment of the debt;

(6) a schedule of all the assigning debtor's real and personal estate at the date of the assignment;

(7) a description of

(A) each encumbrance on the real and personal estate; and

(B) each voucher and security relating to the estate; and

(8) the value of the estate.

(c) The assigning debtor shall sign the inventory required by Subsection (b) of this section and swear that it is just and true.

Acts 1967, 60th Leg., p. 2343, ch. 785, § 1.

§ 23.09. Fraud Does Not Defeat Assignment

(a) An assignment is not affected and a consenting creditor is not deprived of his proportionate share of the assigned estate by the fraudulent act or intent of the assigning debtor or assignee. A consenting creditor is a proper party to a suit filed to enforce a right under an assignment, or to protect an interest in an assigned estate.

(b) Except as to an innocent purchaser for value, a transfer of property made in contemplation of an assignment with an intent to defeat, delay, defraud, or give preference to a creditor is void and the property passes under the assignment rather than by the transfer.

(c) An assignee may sue to recover property transferred with an intent described in Subsection (b) of this section, and when the property is recovered, the assignee shall apply it for the benefit of the assigning debtor's creditors along with property belonging to the assigned estate already in the assignee's possession. If an assignee neglects or refuses to sue to recover property transferred with an intent described in Subsection (b) of this section, a creditor, after securing the assignee against cost or liability, may sue in the assignee's name to recover the property.

Acts 1967, 60th Leg., p. 2343, ch. 785, § 1.

§ 23.10. Assignment Discharges Debtor

If an assigning debtor makes an assignment, he is discharged from liability on the claim of a consenting creditor unless the consenting creditor does not receive at least one-third of the amount allowed on his claim against the assigned estate.

Acts 1967, 60th Leg., p. 2343, ch. 785, § 1.

[Sections 23.11 to 23.15 reserved for expansion]

SUBCHAPTER C. DUTIES AND RIGHTS OF ASSIGNEE

§ 23.16. Assignee's Qualifications, Duty to Record Assignment, and Bond

(a) An assignee shall be a resident of this state and a resident of the county in which the assigning debtor resides, or in which the assigning debtor's principal business was conducted.

(b) Immediately after the assignment instrument is executed and delivered to him, the assignee shall record it in the county of his residence and in each county in which there is real property conveyed to the assignee by the assignment.

(c) Within five days after delivery to him of the assignment instrument, the assignee shall execute a bond

(1) with a surety who must be approved by the judge of either the county or district court in the county of the assignee's residence;

(2) conditioned that he will perform faithfully his duties as assignee and distribute proportionately the net proceeds of the assigned estate to the consenting creditors entitled to it under the assignment;

(3) in an amount fixed by the county or district judge;

(4) payable to the state; and

(5) which inures to the benefit of the assigning debtor and each of the creditors.

(d) The assignee shall file the bond with the county clerk of the county in which the assigning debtor resides and then the assignee shall take possession of the assigned estate and carry out the assignment.

(e) An assignment is valid as against an assigning debtor or his creditors even though the assignee fails to execute and file a bond as required by Subsections (c) and (d) of this section.

Acts 1967, 60th Leg., p. 2343, ch. 785, § 1.

§ 23.17. Notice of Assignee's Appointment

(a) Within 30 days after an assignment is executed, the assignee shall publish notice of his appointment as assignee in a newspaper published in the county

(1) where the assigning debtor resides or where he operated his principal business before the assignment; or

(2) nearest the assigning debtor's residence or principal business if a newspaper is not published in the county of the assigning debtor's residence or principal business.

(b) The assignee shall publish notice of his appointment as assignee once each week for three consecutive weeks.

(c) The assignee shall notify by mail each of the assigning debtor's listed creditors of his appointment as assignee.

Acts 1967, 60th Leg., p. 2343, ch. 785, § 1.

§ 23.18. Replacement of Assignee

(a) A county or district court of the county in which the assignee resides shall remove or replace the assignee on application of the assigning debtor or a creditor, or on its own motion,

(1) if the court is satisfied that the assignee has not executed and filed the bond required by Sections 23.16(c) and (d) of this code;

(2) if the assignee refuses or fails to serve for any reason; or

(3) for good cause.

(b) On removal, resignation, or death of the assignee, the court shall appoint in writing a new assignee in term time or vacation.

(c) As soon as the new assignee executes and files a bond as required by Sections 23.16(c) and (d) of this code, he shall take possession of the assigned estate and carry out the assignment.

Acts 1967, 60th Leg., p. 2343, ch. 785, § 1.

§ 23.19. Assignee's Duty to Distribute Assigned Estate

Each time an assignee has enough money to pay 10 percent of the assigning debtor's debts, he shall distribute the money among the creditors entitled to receive it in proportion to their claims allowed under Section 23.31(b) of this code.

Acts 1967, 60th Leg., p. 2343, ch. 785, § 1.

§ 23.20. Discount of Claim Not Due and Allowance of Secured Claim

(a) The assignee may allow a claim which is not due at its present value by discounting it at the legal rate.

(b) If a creditor holds collateral to secure his claim worth less than his claim, the assignee may estimate the value of the collateral and allow the creditor as a claim against the assigned estate only the difference between the value of the collateral and the amount of the claim.

Acts 1967, 60th Leg., p. 2343, ch. 785, § 1.

§ 23.21. Assignee's Entitlement to Compensation

An assignee is entitled to reasonable compensation for his services and reimbursement for his necessary expenses, including an attorney's fee, all of which shall be fixed by the county or district court who approved his bond. The compensation, expenses, and attorney's fee fixed by the county or district court shall be paid out of the assigned estate.

Acts 1967, 60th Leg., p. 2343, ch. 785, § 1.

§ 23.22. Examination of Debtor or Other Person

(a) The court in which a proceeding involving an assigned estate has been filed may, after reasonable notice to each person concerned, compel any person to answer questions under oath on

(1) application of a creditor of the assigning debtor; or

(2) its own motion.

(b) The court may compel attendance and an answer to any question concerning the assigned estate by writ or order as in other cases. Questions asked and answers given during the examination shall be in writing, the person examined shall swear to and sign his answers before the clerk, and the questions and answers shall be filed with the clerk for use by anyone interested in the proceeding.

(c) The court shall charge the cost of the examination against the applicant or the assigned estate, as the court deems proper.

(d) The assigning debtor may not be prosecuted or punished for an answer given by him during the examination.

Acts 1967, 60th Leg., p. 2343, ch. 785, § 1.

§ 23.23. Assignee's Final Report and Discharge

(a) An assignee wishing to be discharged from his appointment shall prepare and file for record with the county clerk of the county in which his assignment is recorded a sworn report describing

(1) all property which came into his possession under the assignment; and

(2) how and to whom he distributed the property.

(b) The assignee shall also deposit in the registry of the court who approved his bond money belonging to the assigned estate still in his possession at the time he files his report under Subsection (a) of this section. The court shall distribute the money under this chapter to the consenting creditors and assignee and, in the case of surplus, to the nonconsenting creditors and assigning debtor.

Acts 1967, 60th Leg., p. 2343, ch. 785, § 1.

§ 23.24. Time Limit on Bringing Action Against Assignee

An action against an assignee based on his conduct in carrying out the assignment, as shown in his report filed under Section 23.23(a) of this code, must be brought within 12 months after the report is filed or the action is barred.

Acts 1967, 60th Leg., p. 2343, ch. 785, § 1.

[Sections 23.25 to 23.29 reserved for expansion]

SUBCHAPTER D. DUTIES AND RIGHTS OF CREDITORS

§ 23.30. Creditor's Consent to Assignment

(a) A creditor must inform the assignee in writing of his consent to the assignment within four months after the assignee gives the notice required by Section 23.17 of this code.

(b) If a creditor is not given actual notice of an assignment, but subsequently learns of the assignment, he may consent to the assignment at any time before the first distribution of the assigned estate is begun.

(c) Receipt by a creditor of payment for part of his claim from the assignee is conclusive evidence of the creditor's consent to the assignment.

(d) If a creditor does not consent to an assignment, he is not entitled to receive any of the assigned estate under the assignment.

Acts 1967, 60th Leg., p. 2343, ch. 785, § 1.

§ 23.31. Creditor's Proof and Assignee's Allowance of Claim

(a) Within six months after the first publication of notice of appointment required by Section 23.17 of this code, a consenting creditor must file with the assignee a statement, sworn to by the creditor, his agent, or attorney,

(1) describing the nature and amount of the creditor's claim against the assigning debtor; and

(2) stating that

(A) the claim is true;

(B) the debt is just; and

(C) all proper credits or offsets have been allowed against the claim.

(b) The assignee shall allow a claim filed under Subsection (a) of this section against the assigned estate unless he has good reason to believe the claim is not just and true.

(c) If a creditor does not file a statement in the time required by Subsection (a) of this section, he is not entitled to receive any of the assigned estate.

Acts 1967, 60th Leg., p. 2343, ch. 785, § 1.

§ 23.32. Creditor's Suit on Disputed Claim

(a) The assignee shall give any creditor a copy of any statement of claim filed under Section 23.31(a) of this code if the creditor requests a copy.

(b) Within eight months after the first publication of notice required by Section 23.17 of this code, an assigning debtor or creditor may sue to

(1) set aside an allowance made on a claim by the assignee; and

(2) restrain payment of the claim by the assignee.

Acts 1967, 60th Leg., p. 2343, ch. 785, § 1.

§ 23.33. Nonconsenting Creditor's Right to Surplus

If a creditor does not consent to an assignment, he may garnishee the assignee for the excess of the assigned estate remaining in the assignee's possession after the assignee has paid

(1) each consenting creditor the amount of his claim allowed under Section 23.31(b) of this code; and

(2) the expense of carrying out the assignment.

Acts 1967, 60th Leg., p. 2343, ch. 785, § 1.

CHAPTER 24. UNIFORM FRAUDULENT TRANSFER ACT

Section

This chapter, which consisted of §§ 24.01 to 24.05, was amended by Acts 1987, 70th Leg., ch. 1004, § 1, to read as provided for in §§ 24.001 to 24.013.

DISPOSITION TABLE

Showing where provisions of former Chapter 24 are now covered in amended Chapter 24.

Former Sections	Amended Sections
24.01	24.002
24.02(a)	24.005
24.02(b)	24.009
24.03	24.006
24.04	24.013
24.05	24.007, 24.008

§ 24.001. Short Title

This chapter may be cited as the Uniform Fraudulent Transfer Act.

Amended by Acts 1987, 70th Leg., ch. 1004, § 1, eff. Sept. 1, 1987.

§ 24.002. Definitions

In this chapter:

(1) "Affiliate" means:

(A) a person who directly or indirectly owns, controls, or holds with power to vote, 20 percent or more of the outstanding voting securities of the debtor, other than a person who holds the securities:

(i) as a fiduciary or agent without sole discretionary power to vote the securities; or

(ii) solely to secure a debt, if the person has not exercised the power to vote;

(B) a corporation 20 percent or more of whose outstanding voting securities are directly or indirectly owned, controlled, or held with power to vote, by the debtor or a person who directly or indirectly owns, controls, or holds, with power to vote, 20 percent or more of the outstanding voting securities of the debtor, other than a person who holds the securities:

(i) as a fiduciary or agent without sole power to vote the securities; or

(ii) solely to secure a debt, if the person has not in fact exercised the power to vote;

(C) a person whose business is operated by the debtor under a lease or other agreement, or a person substantially all of whose assets are controlled by the debtor; or

(D) a person who operates the debtor's business under a lease or other agreement or controls substantially all of the debtor's assets.

(2) "Asset" means property of a debtor, but the term does not include:

(A) property to the extent it is encumbered by a valid lien;

(B) property to the extent it is generally exempt under nonbankruptcy law; or

(C) an interest in property held in tenancy by the entireties to the extent it is not subject to process by a creditor holding a claim against only one tenant, under the law of another jurisdiction.

(3) "Claim" means a right to payment or property, whether or not the right is reduced to judgment, liquidated, unliquidated, fixed, contingent, matured, unmatured, disputed, undisputed, legal, equitable, secured, or unsecured.

(4) "Creditor" means a person, including a spouse, minor, person entitled to receive court or administratively ordered child support for the benefit of a child, or ward, who has a claim.

(5) "Debt" means a liability on a claim.

(6) "Debtor" means a person who is liable on a claim.

(7) "Insider" includes:

(A) if the debtor is an individual:

(i) a relative of the debtor or of a general partner of the debtor;

(ii) a partnership in which the debtor is a general partner;

(iii) a general partner in a partnership described in Subparagraph (ii) of this paragraph; or

(iv) a corporation of which the debtor is a director, officer, or person in control;

(B) if the debtor is a corporation:

(i) a director of the debtor;

(ii) an officer of the debtor;

(iii) a person in control of the debtor;

(iv) a partnership in which the debtor is a general partner;

(v) a general partner in a partnership described in Subparagraph (iv) of this paragraph; or

(vi) a relative of a general partner, director, officer, or person in control of the debtor;

(C) if the debtor is a partnership:

(i) a general partner in the debtor;

(ii) a relative of a general partner in, a general partner of, or a person in control of the debtor;

(iii) another partnership in which the debtor is a general partner;

(iv) a general partner in a partnership described in Subparagraph (iii) of this paragraph; or

(v) a person in control of the debtor;

(D) an affiliate, or an insider of an affiliate as if the affiliate were the debtor; and

(E) a managing agent of the debtor.

(8) "Lien" means a charge against or an interest in property to secure payment of a debt or performance of an obligation, and includes a security interest created by agreement, a judicial lien obtained by legal or equitable process or proceedings, a common-law lien, or a statutory lien.

(9) "Person" means an individual, partnership, corporation, association, organization, government or governmental subdivision or agency, business trust, estate, trust, or any other legal or commercial entity.

(10) "Property" means anything that may be the subject of ownership.

(11) "Relative" means an individual related by consanguinity within the third degree as determined by the common law, a spouse, or an individual related to a spouse within the third degree as so determined, and includes an individual in an adoptive relationship within the third degree.

(12) "Transfer" means every mode, direct or indirect, absolute or conditional, voluntary or involuntary, of disposing of or parting with an asset or an interest in an asset, and includes payment of money, release, lease, and creation of a lien or other encumbrance. The term does not include a transfer under a disclaimer filed under Section 37A, Texas Probate Code, or Section 112.010, Property Code.

(13) "Valid lien" means a lien that is effective against the holder of a judicial lien subsequently obtained by legal or equitable process or proceedings.

Amended by Acts 1987, 70th Leg., ch. 1004, § 1, eff. Sept. 1, 1987; Acts 1993, 73rd Leg., ch. 846, § 2, eff. Sept. 1, 1993; Acts 1997, 75th Leg., ch. 911, § 95, eff. Sept. 1, 1997.

§ 24.003. Insolvency

(a) A debtor is insolvent if the sum of the debtor's debts is greater than all of the debtor's assets at a fair valuation.

(b) A debtor who is generally not paying the debtor's debts as they become due is presumed to be insolvent.

(c) A partnership is insolvent under Subsection (a) of this section if the sum of the partnership's debts is greater than the aggregate, at a fair valuation, of all of the partnership's assets and the sum of the excess of the value of each general partner's nonpartnership assets over the partner's nonpartnership debts.

(d) Assets under this section do not include property that has been transferred, concealed, or removed with intent to hinder, delay, or defraud creditors or that has been transferred in a manner making the transfer voidable under this chapter.

(e) Debts under this section do not include an obligation to the extent it is secured by a valid lien on property of the debtor not included as an asset.

Amended by Acts 1987, 70th Leg., ch. 1004, § 1, eff. Sept. 1, 1987; Acts 1993, 73rd Leg., ch. 570, § 8, eff. Sept. 1, 1993.

§ 24.004. Value

(a) Value is given for a transfer or an obligation if, in exchange for the transfer or obligation, property is transferred or an antecedent debt is secured or satisfied, but value does not include an unperformed promise made otherwise than in the ordinary course of the promisor's business to furnish support to the debtor or another person.

(b) For the purposes of Sections 24.005(a)(2) and 24.006 of this code, a person gives a reasonably equivalent value if the person acquires an interest of the debtor in an asset pursuant to a regularly conducted, noncollusive foreclosure sale or execution of a power of sale for the acquisition or disposition of the interest of the debtor upon default under a mortgage, deed of trust, or security agreement.

(c) A transfer is made for present value if the exchange between the debtor and the transferee is intended by them to be contemporaneous and is in fact substantially contemporaneous.

(d) "Reasonably equivalent value" includes without limitation, a transfer or obligation that is within the range of values for which the transferor would have sold the assets in an arm's length transaction.

Amended by Acts 1987, 70th Leg., ch. 1004, § 1, eff. Sept. 1, 1987; Acts 1993, 73rd Leg., ch. 570, § 9, eff. Sept. 1, 1993.

§ 24.005. Transfers Fraudulent as to Present and Future Creditors

(a) A transfer made or obligation incurred by a debtor is fraudulent as to a creditor, whether the creditor's claim arose before or within a reasonable time after the transfer was made or the obligation was incurred, if the debtor made the transfer or incurred the obligation:

(1) with actual intent to hinder, delay, or defraud any creditor of the debtor; or

(2) without receiving a reasonably equivalent value in exchange for the transfer or obligation, and the debtor:

(A) was engaged or was about to engage in a business or a transaction for which the remaining assets of the debtor were unreasonably small in relation to the business or transaction; or

(B) intended to incur, or believed or reasonably should have believed that the debtor would incur, debts beyond the debtor's ability to pay as they became due.

(b) In determining actual intent under Subsection (a)(1) of this section, consideration may be given, among other factors, to whether:

(1) the transfer or obligation was to an insider;

(2) the debtor retained possession or control of the property transferred after the transfer;

(3) the transfer or obligation was concealed;

(4) before the transfer was made or obligation was incurred, the debtor had been sued or threatened with suit;

(5) the transfer was of substantially all the debtor's assets;

(6) the debtor absconded;

(7) the debtor removed or concealed assets;

(8) the value of the consideration received by the debtor was reasonably equivalent to the value of the asset transferred or the amount of the obligation incurred;

(9) the debtor was insolvent or became insolvent shortly after the transfer was made or the obligation was incurred;

(10) the transfer occurred shortly before or shortly after a substantial debt was incurred; and

(11) the debtor transferred the essential assets of the business to a lienor who transferred the assets to an insider of the debtor.

Amended by Acts 1987, 70th Leg., ch. 1004, § 1, eff. Sept. 1, 1987; Acts 1993, 73rd Leg., ch. 570, § 10, eff. Sept. 1, 1993.

§ 24.006. Transfers Fraudulent as to Present Creditors

(a) A transfer made or obligation incurred by a debtor is fraudulent as to a creditor whose claim arose before the transfer was made or the obligation was incurred if the debtor made the transfer or incurred the obligation without receiving a reasonably equivalent value in exchange for the transfer or obligation and the debtor was insolvent at that time or the debtor became insolvent as a result of the transfer or obligation.

(b) A transfer made by a debtor is fraudulent as to a creditor whose claim arose before the transfer was made if the transfer was made to an insider for an antecedent debt, the debtor was insolvent at that time, and the insider had reasonable cause to believe that the debtor was insolvent.

Amended by Acts 1987, 70th Leg., ch. 1004, § 1, eff. Sept. 1, 1987.

§ 24.007. When Transfer is Made or Obligation is Incurred

For the purposes of this chapter:

(1) a transfer is made:

(A) with respect to an asset that is real property other than a fixture, but including the interest of a seller or purchaser under a contract for the sale of the asset, when the transfer is so far perfected that a good faith purchaser of the asset from the debtor against whom applicable law permits the transfer to be perfected cannot acquire an interest in the asset that is superior to the interest of the transferee; and

(B) with respect to an asset that is not real property or that is a fixture, when the transfer is so far perfected that a creditor on a simple contract cannot acquire a judicial lien otherwise than under this chapter that is superior to the interest of the transferee;

(2) if applicable law permits the transfer to be perfected as provided in Subdivision (1) of this section and the transfer is not so perfected before the commencement of an action for relief under this chapter, the transfer is deemed made immediately before the commencement of the action;

(3) if applicable law does not permit the transfer to be perfected as provided in Subdivision (1) of this section, the transfer is made when it becomes effective between the debtor and the transferee;

(4) a transfer is not made until the debtor has acquired rights in the asset transferred; and

(5) an obligation is incurred:

(A) if oral, when it becomes effective between the parties; or

(B) if evidenced by a writing, when the writing executed by the obligor is delivered to or for the benefit of the obligee.

Amended by Acts 1987, 70th Leg., ch. 1004, § 1, eff. Sept. 1, 1987.

§ 24.008. Remedies of Creditors

(a) In an action for relief against a transfer or obligation under this chapter, a creditor, subject to the limitations in Section 24.009 of this code, may obtain:

(1) avoidance of the transfer or obligation to the extent necessary to satisfy the creditor's claim;

(2) an attachment or other provisional remedy against the asset transferred or other property of the transferee in accordance with the applicable Texas Rules of Civil Procedure and the Civil Practice and Remedies Code relating to ancillary proceedings; or

(3) subject to applicable principles of equity and in accordance with applicable rules of civil procedure:

(A) an injunction against further disposition by the debtor or a transferee, or both, of the asset transferred or of other property;

(B) appointment of a receiver to take charge of the asset transferred or of other property of the transferee; or

(C) any other relief the circumstances may require.

(b) If a creditor has obtained a judgment on a claim against the debtor, the creditor, if the court so orders, may levy execution on the asset transferred or its proceeds.

Amended by Acts 1987, 70th Leg., ch. 1004, § 1, eff. Sept. 1, 1987.

§ 24.009. Defenses, Liability, and Protection of Transferee

(a) A transfer or obligation is not voidable under Section 24.005(a)(1) of this code against a person who took in good faith and for a reasonably equivalent value or against any subsequent transferee or obligee.

(b) Except as otherwise provided in this section, to the extent a transfer is voidable in an action by a creditor under Section 24.008(a)(1) of this code, the creditor may recover judgment for the value of the asset transferred, as adjusted under Subsection (c) of this section, or the amount necessary to satisfy the creditor's claim, whichever is less. The judgment may be entered against:

(1) the first transferee of the asset or the person for whose benefit the transfer was made; or

(2) any subsequent transferee other than a good faith transferee who took for value or from any subsequent transferee.

(c)(1) Except as provided by Subdivision (2) of this subsection, if the judgment under Subsection (b) of this section is based upon the value of the asset transferred, the judgment must be for an amount equal to the value of the asset at the time of the transfer, subject to adjustment as the equities may require.

(2) The value of the asset transferred is not to be adjusted to include the value of improvements made by a good faith transferee, including:

(A) physical additions or changes to the asset transferred;

(B) repairs to the asset;

(C) payment of any tax on the asset;

(D) payment of any debt secured by a lien on the asset that is superior or equal to the rights of a voiding creditor under this chapter; and

(E) preservation of the asset.

(d)(1) Notwithstanding voidability of a transfer or an obligation under this chapter, a good faith transferee or obligee is entitled, at the transferee's or obligee's election, to the extent of the value given the debtor for the transfer or obligation, to:

(A) a lien, prior to the rights of a voiding creditor under this chapter, or a right to retain any interest in the asset transferred;

(B) enforcement of any obligation incurred; or

(C) a reduction in the amount of the liability on the judgment.

(2) Notwithstanding voidability of a transfer under this chapter, to the extent of the value of any improvements made by a good faith transferee, the good faith transferee is entitled to a lien on the asset transferred prior to the rights of a voiding creditor under this chapter

(e) A transfer is not voidable under Section 24.005(a)(2) or Section 24.006 of this code if the transfer results from:

(1) termination of a lease upon default by the debtor when the termination is pursuant to the lease and applicable law; or

(2) enforcement of a security interest in compliance with Chapter 9 of this code.[1]

(f) A transfer is not voidable under Section 24.006(b) of this code:

(1) to the extent the insider gave new value to or for the benefit of the debtor after the transfer was made unless the new value was secured by a valid lien;

(2) if made in the ordinary course of business or financial affairs of the debtor and the insider; or

(3) if made pursuant to a good-faith effort to rehabilitate the debtor and the transfer secured present value given for that purpose as well as an antecedent debt of the debtor.

Amended by Acts 1987, 70th Leg., ch. 1004, § 1, eff. Sept. 1, 1987; Acts 1993, 73rd Leg., ch. 570, § 11, eff. Sept. 1, 1993.

[1] V.T.C.A., Bus. & C. § 9.101 et seq.

§ 24.01. Deleted by Acts 1987, 70th Leg., ch. 1004, § 1, eff. Sept. 1, 1987

§ 24.010. Extinguishment of Cause of Action

(a) Except as provided by Subsection (b) of this section, a cause of action with respect to a fraudulent transfer or obligation under this chapter is extinguished unless action is brought:

(1) under Section 24.005(a)(1) of this code, within four years after the transfer was made or the obligation was incurred or, if later, within one year after the transfer or obligation was or could reasonably have been discovered by the claimant;

(2) under Section 24.005(a)(2) or 24.006(a) of this code, within four years after the transfer was made or the obligation was incurred; or

(3) under Section 24.006(b) of this code, within one year after the transfer was made.

(b) A cause of action on behalf of a spouse, minor, or ward with respect to a fraudulent transfer or obligation under this chapter is extinguished unless the action is brought:

(1) under Section 24.005(a) or 24.006(a) of this code, within two years after the cause of action accrues, or if later, within one year after the transfer or obligation was or could reasonably have been discovered by the claimant; or

(2) under Section 24.006(b) of this code within one year after the date the transfer was made.

(c) If a creditor entitled to bring an action under this chapter is under a legal disability when a time period prescribed by this section starts, the time of the disability is not included in the period. A disability that arises after the period starts does not suspend the running of the period. A creditor may not tack one legal disability to another to extend the period. For the purposes of this subsection, a creditor is under a legal disability if the creditor is:

(1) younger than 18 years of age, regardless of whether the person is married; or

(2) of unsound mind.

Amended by Acts 1987, 70th Leg., ch. 1004, § 1, eff. Sept. 1, 1987; Acts 1993, 73rd Leg., ch. 570, § 12, eff. Sept. 1, 1993.

§ 24.011. Supplementary Provisions

Unless displaced by the provisions of this chapter, the principles of law and equity, including the law merchant and the law relating to principal and agent, estoppel, laches, fraud, misrepresentation, duress, coercion, mistake, insolvency, or other validating or invalidating cause, supplement its provisions.

Amended by Acts 1987, 70th Leg., ch. 1004, § 1, eff. Sept. 1, 1987.

§ 24.012. Uniformity of Application and Construction

This chapter shall be applied and construed to effectuate its general purpose to make uniform the law with respect to the subject of this chapter among states enacting it.

Amended by Acts 1987, 70th Leg., ch. 1004, § 1, eff. Sept. 1, 1987.

§ 24.013. Costs

In any proceeding under this chapter, the court may award costs and reasonable attorney's fees as are equitable and just.

Added by Acts 2003, 78th Leg., ch. 420, § 1, eff. Sept. 1, 2003.

§§ 24.02 to 24.05. Deleted by Acts 1987, 70th Leg., ch. 1004, § 1, eff. Sept. 1, 1987

CHAPTER 25. PROPERTY UNDER LIEN [REPEALED]

§§ 25.01 to 25.03. Repealed by Acts 1973, 63rd Leg., p. 995, ch. 399, § 3(d), eff. Jan. 1, 1974

CHAPTER 26. STATUTE OF FRAUDS

Section

§ 26.01. Promise or Agreement Must Be in Writing

(a) A promise or agreement described in Subsection (b) of this section is not enforceable unless the promise or agreement, or a memorandum of it, is

(1) in writing; and

(2) signed by the person to be charged with the promise or agreement or by someone lawfully authorized to sign for him.

(b) Subsection (a) of this section applies to:

(1) a promise by an executor or administrator to answer out of his own estate for any debt or damage due from his testator or intestate;

(2) a promise by one person to answer for the debt, default, or miscarriage of another person;

(3) an agreement made on consideration of marriage or on consideration of nonmarital conjugal cohabitation;

(4) a contract for the sale of real estate;

(5) a lease of real estate for a term longer than one year;

(6) an agreement which is not to be performed within one year from the date of making the agreement;

(7) a promise or agreement to pay a commission for the sale or purchase of:

(A) an oil or gas mining lease;

(B) an oil or gas royalty;

(C) minerals; or

(D) a mineral interest; and

(8) an agreement, promise, contract, or warranty of cure relating to medical care or results thereof made by a physician or health care provider as defined in Section 74.001, Civil Practice and Remedies Code. This section shall not apply to pharmacists.

Acts 1967, 60th Leg., vol. 2, p. 2343, ch. 785, § 1. Amended by Acts 1977, 65th Leg., p. 2053, ch. 817, § 21.01, eff. Aug. 29, 1977; Acts 1987, 70th Leg., ch. 551, § 1, eff. Aug. 31, 1987; Acts 2005, 79th Leg., ch. 187, § 1, eff. Sept. 1, 2005.

Sections 2(a) and (b) of Acts 2005, 79th Leg., ch. 187 provide:

"(a) This Act applies only to a cause of action that accrues on or after the effective date of this Act. An action that accrued before the effective date of this Act is governed by the law applicable to the action immediately before the effective date of this Act, and that law is continued in effect for that purpose.

"(b) This Act applies only to an act, including an agreement, promise, contract, warranty, notice, request, disclosure, use of a consent form, or report, made or occurring on or after the effective date of this Act."

§ 26.02. Loan Agreement Must be in Writing

(a) In this section:

(1) "Financial institution" means a state or federally chartered bank, savings bank, savings and loan association, or credit union, a holding company, subsidiary, or affiliate of such an institution, or a lender approved by the United States Secretary of Housing and Urban Development for participation in a mortgage insurance program under the National Housing Act (12 U.S.C. Section 1701 et seq.).

(2) "Loan agreement" means one or more promises, promissory notes, agreements, undertakings, security agreements, deeds of trust or other documents, or commitments, or any combination of those actions or documents, pursuant to which a financial institution loans or delays repayment of or agrees to loan or delay repayment of money, goods, or another thing of value or to otherwise extend credit or make a financial accommodation. The term does not include a promise, promissory note, agreement, undertaking, document, or commitment relating to:

(A) a credit card or charge card; or

(B) an open-end account, as that term is defined by Section 301.002, Finance Code, intended or used primarily for personal, family, or household use.

(b) A loan agreement in which the amount involved in the loan agreement exceeds $50,000 in value is not enforceable unless the agreement is in writing and signed by the party to be bound or by that party's authorized representative.

(c) The rights and obligations of the parties to an agreement subject to Subsection (b) of this section shall be determined solely from the written loan agreement, and any prior oral agreements between the parties are superseded by and merged into the loan agreement.

(d) An agreement subject to Subsection (b) of this section may not be varied by any oral agreements or discussions that occur before or contemporaneously [1] with the execution of the agreement.

(e) In a loan agreement subject to Subsection (b) of this section, the financial institution shall give notice to the debtor or obligor of the provisions of Subsections (b) and (c) of this section. The notice must be in a separate document signed by the debtor or obligor or incorporated into one or more of the documents constituting the loan agreement. The notice must be in type that is boldface, capitalized, underlined, or otherwise set out from surrounding written material so as to be conspicuous. The notice must state substantially the following:

> "This written loan agreement represents the final agreement between the parties and may not be contradicted by evidence of prior, contemporaneous, or subsequent [2] oral agreements of the parties.
>
> "There are no unwritten oral agreements between the parties.

______________________	______________________
"Debtor or Obligor	Financial Institution"

(f) If the notice required by Subsection (e) of this section is not given on or before execution of the loan agreement or is not conspicuous, this section does not apply to the loan agreement, but the validity and enforceability of the loan agreement and the rights and obligations of the parties are not impaired or affected.

(g) All financial institutions shall conspicuously post notices that inform borrowers of the provisions of this section. The notices shall be located in such a manner and in places in the institutions so as to fully inform borrowers of the provisions of this section. The Finance Commission of Texas shall prescribe the language of the notice.

Added by Acts 1989, 71st Leg., ch. 831, § 1, eff. Sept. 1, 1989. Amended by Acts 1997, 75th Leg., ch. 1396, § 34, eff. Sept. 1, 1997; Acts 1999, 76th Leg., ch. 62, § 7.47, eff. Sept. 1, 1999.

[1] So in enrolled bill; subsec. (e) makes reference to prior, contemporaneous or subsequent agreements.

[2] So in enrolled bill; subsec. (d) makes reference to oral agreements before or contemporaneously with the execution of the agreement.

CHAPTER 27. FRAUD

Section

§ 27.01. Fraud in Real Estate and Stock Transactions

(a) Fraud in a transaction involving real estate or stock in a corporation or joint stock company consists of a

(1) false representation of a past or existing material fact, when the false representation is

(A) made to a person for the purpose of inducing that person to enter into a contract; and

(B) relied on by that person in entering into that contract; or

(2) false promise to do an act, when the false promise is

(A) material;

(B) made with the intention of not fulfilling it;

(C) made to a person for the purpose of inducing that person to enter into a contract; and

(D) relied on by that person in entering into that contract.

(b) A person who makes a false representation or false promise commits the fraud described in Subsection (a) of this section and is liable to the person defrauded for actual damages.

(c) A person who makes a false representation or false promise with actual awareness of the falsity thereof commits the fraud described in Subsection (a) of this section and is liable to the person defrauded for exemplary damages. Actual awareness may be inferred where objective manifestations indicate that a person acted with actual awareness.

(d) A person who (1) has actual awareness of the falsity of a representation or promise made by another person and (2) fails to disclose the falsity of the representation or promise to the person defrauded, and (3) benefits from the false representation or promise commits the fraud described in Subsection (a) of this section and is liable to the person defrauded for exemplary damages. Actual awareness may be inferred where objective manifestations indicate that a person acted with actual awareness.

(e) Any person who violates the provisions of this section shall be liable to the person defrauded for reasonable and necessary attorney's fees, expert witness fees, costs for copies of depositions, and costs of court.

Acts 1967, 60th Leg., vol. 2, p. 2343, ch. 785, § 1. Amended by Acts 1983, 68th Leg., p. 5208, ch. 949, §§ 1, 2, eff. Sept. 1, 1983.

§ 27.02. Certain Insurance Claims for Excessive Charges

(a) A person who sells goods or services commits an offense if:

(1) the person advertises or promises to provide the good or service and to pay:

(A) all or part of any applicable insurance deductible; or

(B) a rebate in an amount equal to all or part of any applicable insurance deductible;

(2) the good or service is paid for by the consumer from proceeds of a property or casualty insurance policy; and

(3) the person knowingly charges an amount for the good or service that exceeds the usual and customary charge by the person for the good or service by an amount equal to or greater than all or part of the applicable insurance deductible paid by the person to an insurer on behalf of an insured or remitted to an insured by the person as a rebate.

(b) A person who is insured under a property or casualty insurance policy commits an offense if the person:

(1) submits a claim under the policy based on charges that are in violation of Subsection (a) of this section; or

(2) knowingly allows a claim in violation of Subsection (a) of this section to be submitted, unless the person promptly notifies the insurer of the excessive charges.

(c) An offense under this section is a Class A misdemeanor.

Added by Acts 1989, 71st Leg., ch. 898, § 1, eff. Sept. 1, 1989.

[Chapters 28 to 32 reserved for expansion]

TITLE 4. MISCELLANEOUS COMMERCIAL PROVISIONS

As amended by Acts 2007, 80th Leg., ch. 885, § 2.01, effective April 1, 2009, Title 4 will read, "Business Opportunities and Agreements".

CHAPTER 33. FIDUCIARY SECURITY TRANSFERS [REPEALED]

§§ 33.01 to 33.10. Repealed by Acts 1995, 74th Leg., ch. 962, § 19, eff. Sept. 1, 1995

CHAPTER 34. PRINCIPAL AND SURETY

Acts 2007, 80th Leg., ch. 885, § 2.47(a)(1) repeals this chapter effective April 1, 2009.

§ 34.01. Definition of Surety

In this chapter, unless the context requires a different definition, "surety" includes endorser, guarantor, drawer of a draft which has been accepted, and every other form of suretyship, whether created by express contract or by operation of law.

Acts 1967, 60th Leg., p. 2343, ch. 785, § 1.

Repeal

Acts 2007, 80th Leg., ch. 885, § 2.47(a)(1) repeals this section effective April 1, 2009.

§ 34.02. Surety May Require Suit on Accrued Right of Action

(a) When a right of action has accrued on a contract for the payment of money or performance of an act, a surety on the contract may require by written notice that the obligee forthwith sue on the contract.

(b) A surety who gives notice to an obligee under Subsection (a) of this section is discharged from all liability on the contract if the obligee

(1) is not under legal disability; and either

(2) fails to sue on the contract during the first term of court after receiving the notice, or during the second term showing good cause for the delay; or

(3) fails to prosecute the suit to judgment and execution.

Acts 1967, 60th Leg., p. 2343, ch. 785, § 1.

Repeal

Acts 2007, 80th Leg., ch. 885, § 2.47(a)(1) repeals this section effective April 1, 2009.

§ 34.03. Levy First on Principal's Property

(a) If a judgment granted against two or more defendants finds a suretyship relation between or among them, the court shall order the sheriff to levy the execution

(1) first, against the principal's property which is located in the county where the judgment was granted;

(2) second, if the sheriff cannot find enough of the principal's property in the county to satisfy the execution, against so much of the principal's property as he finds; and

(3) third, against so much of the surety's property as is necessary to make up the balance of the amount shown in the writ of execution.

(b) The clerk shall note the order to the sheriff on the writ of execution.

Acts 1967, 60th Leg., p. 2343, ch. 785, § 1.

Repeal

Acts 2007, 80th Leg., ch. 885, § 2.47(a)(1) repeals this section effective April 1, 2009.

§ 34.04. Subrogation Rights of Surety

(a) A judgment is not discharged by a surety's payment of it in whole or part if the payment is compelled or, if voluntarily made, is applied to the judgment because of the suretyship relation.

(b) A surety who pays on a judgment as described in Subsection (a) of this section is subrogated to all of the judgment creditor's rights under the judgment. A subrogated surety is entitled

(1) to execution on the judgment against the principal's property for the amount of his payment, plus interest and costs; and

(2) if there is more than one surety, to execution on the judgment against both the principal's property and the property of his cosurety or cosureties for the amount his payment exceeded his proportionate share of the judgment, plus interest and costs.

(c) A subrogated surety seeking execution under Subsection (b) of this section shall apply for it to the clerk or court, and execution shall be levied, collected, and returned as in other cases.

Acts 1967, 60th Leg., p. 2343, ch. 785, § 1.

Repeal

Acts 2007, 80th Leg., ch. 885, § 2.47(a)(1) repeals this section effective April 1, 2009.

§ 34.05. Officer Compelled to Pay on Judgment Treated As Surety

(a) An officer has the rights of a surety provided in Section 34.04 of this code if compelled to pay a judgment in whole or part because of his default.

(b) An officer who fails to pay over money collected, or who wastes property levied on by him or in his possession, does not have the rights of a surety provided in Section 34.04 of this code.

Acts 1967, 60th Leg., p. 2343, ch. 785, § 1.

Repeal

Acts 2007, 80th Leg., ch. 885, § 2.47(a)(1) repeals this section effective April 1, 2009.

CHAPTER 35. MISCELLANEOUS

SUBCHAPTER A. FILING OF UTILITY SECURITY INSTRUMENTS

Section

SUBCHAPTER B. DUTIES OF RAILROAD COMMISSION AND CRIMINAL OFFENSES INVOLVING BILLS OF LADING

Acts 2007, 80th Leg., ch. 885, § 2.47(a)(1) repeals this chapter effective April 1, 2009. Without reference to this repeal, Acts 2007, 80th Leg. ch. 123, § 1 added § 35.42, Acts 2007, 80th Leg., ch. 130, § 1 added a Subchapter L, consisting of §§ 35.131 to 35.137, Acts 2007, 80th Leg., ch. 498, § 1 added § 35.521, and Acts 2007, 80th Leg., ch. 822, § 1 added a Subchapter L, consisting of §§ 35.151 to 35.157.

SUBCHAPTER A. FILING OF UTILITY SECURITY INSTRUMENTS

§ 35.01. Definitions

(a) In Sections 35.02–35.08 of this code, unless the context requires a different definition,

(1) "Security instrument" means a mortgage, deed of trust, security agreement or other instrument executed to secure the payment of a bond, note, or other obligation of a utility, or instruments supplementary or amendatory thereto (including any signed copy thereof); and

(2) "Utility" means a person engaged in this state in the

(A) generation, transmission, or distribution and sale of electric power;

(B) transportation, distribution and sale through a local distribution system of natural or other gas for domestic, commercial, industrial, or other use;

(C) ownership or operation of a pipeline for the transmission or sale of natural or other gas, natural gas liquids, crude oil or petroleum products to other pipeline companies, refineries, local distribution systems, municipalities, or industrial consumers;

(D) provision of telephone or telegraph service to others;

(E) production, transmission, or distribution and sale of steam or water;

(F) operation of a railroad; and

(G) the provision of sewer service to others.

(b) The definitions in Chapters 1 and 9 of this code also apply to this subchapter.

Acts 1967, 60th Leg., p. 2343, ch. 785, § 1. Amended by Acts 1967, 60th Leg., p. 1987, ch. 735, § 10; Acts 1973, 63rd Leg., p. 1032, ch. 400, § 7, eff. Jan. 1, 1974; Acts 1989, 71st Leg., ch. 49, § 1, eff. May 3, 1989.

Repeal

Acts 2007, 80th Leg., ch. 885, § 2.47(a)(1) repeals this section effective April 1, 2009.

§ 35.01A. Renumbered as § 35.015 by Acts 1987, 70th Leg., ch. 167, § 5.02(8), eff. Sept. 1, 1987

§ 35.015. Election to be Treated as a Utility

In this chapter:

(1) Any person who is a utility under the definition contained in Subdivision (2) of Subsection (a) of Section 35.01 above shall nevertheless not be considered to be a utility and subject to the requirements and benefits of Subchapter A of this chapter, unless and until such person files a security instrument with the secretary of state which states conspicuously on its title page: "This Instrument Grants A Security Interest By A Utility."

(2) An election by a utility to be covered by this subchapter shall only be effective for the collateral covered by the security instrument upon which the election is made and shall not be effective for other collateral unless a similar election is made for such collateral.

(3) Any person who executes a security instrument with respect to which no election is made to be treated as a utility as provided in Subsection (a) of this section shall be subject to other applicable requirements of law pertaining to the perfection of a lien or security interest in the collateral covered by such security instrument.

Added by Acts 1981, 67th Leg., p. 2935, ch. 778, § 1, eff. Aug. 31, 1981. Renumbered from § 35.01A by Acts 1987, 70th Leg., ch. 167, § 5.02(8), eff. Sept. 1, 1987.

Repeal

Acts 2007, 80th Leg., ch. 885, § 2.47(a)(1) repeals this section effective April 1, 2009.

§ 35.02. Filing Utility Security Instruments With Secretary of State; Perfection; Notice

(a) Payment of the statutory filing fee and deposit for filing in the office of the Secretary of State of a security instrument executed by a utility which states conspicuously on its title page: "This Instrument Grants A Security Interest By A Utility" shall, subject to the provisions of Subsection (b) of this section

(1) constitute perfection of a security interest created by the security instrument in any personal property (including goods which are, or are to become, fixtures) in which a security interest may be perfected by filing under Chapter 9 of this code, located in this state, and owned by the utility when the security instrument was executed or to be acquired by the utility after execution of the security instrument; and

(2) be taken and held as notice to all persons of the existence of such security instrument and the interest granted therein, as security, in any real property (or fixtures thereon, or to be placed thereon) located in this state and owned by the utility when the security instrument was executed or to be acquired by the utility after the execution of the security instrument; provided that the security instrument shall first be proven, acknowledged or certified as otherwise required by law for the recording of real property mortgages.

(b) For perfection or notice to be effective as to a particular item of property, the filed security instrument must

(1) identify the property by type, character, or description if it is presently owned personal property (including fixtures); provided that for such purposes, any description of personal property or real estate is sufficient whether or not it is specific if it reasonably identifies what is described;

(2) provide a description of the property if it is presently owned real property; and

(3) state conspicuously on its title page: "This Instrument Contains After-Acquired Property Provisions" if the property is to be acquired after the execution of the security instrument.

(c) Filing under this section satisfies any requirement of

(1) filing of the security instrument or a financing statement in the office of a county clerk where such would otherwise be necessary to perfect a security interest; and

(2) recording of the security instrument in the office of a county clerk where such would otherwise cause the security instrument to be effective and valid as to all creditors and subsequent purchasers for valuable consideration without notice.

(d) The provisions in Chapter 9 of this code pertaining to priorities and remedies shall apply to security interests in personal property (including fixtures) perfected under this section.

Acts 1967, 60th Leg., p. 2343, ch. 785, § 1. Amended by Acts 1973, 63rd Leg., p. 1032, ch. 400, § 7, eff. Jan. 1, 1974.

Repeal

Acts 2007, 80th Leg., ch. 885, § 2.47(a)(1) repeals this section effective April 1, 2009.

§ 35.03. Duration of Notice

The perfection or notice provided by any security instrument filed under Section 35.02 of this code is effective from the date of deposit for filing until the interest granted as security is released by the filing of a termination statement, or a release of all or a part of the property, signed by the secured party, and no renewal, refiling or continuation statement shall be required to continue such effectiveness.

Acts 1967, 60th Leg., p. 2343, ch. 785, § 1. Amended by Acts 1973, 63rd Leg., p. 1032, ch. 400, § 7, eff. Jan. 1, 1974.

Repeal

Acts 2007, 80th Leg., ch. 885, § 2.47(a)(1) repeals this section effective April 1, 2009.

§ 35.04. Notice of Name Change, Merger or Consolidation

(a) Where a utility changes its name or merges or consolidates with another person after the deposit for filing of a security instrument executed by it, a written statement of the name change, merger or consolidation shall promptly be deposited for filing in the office of the Secretary of State. Any such statement must be signed by the secured party and the utility, identify the appropriate security instrument by file number, and state the name of the utility after the name change, merger or consolidation.

(b) A security instrument deposited for filing before the name change, merger or consolidation is not effective to provide perfection or notice of interests granted as security under Section 35.02 of this Chapter in property acquired by the utility more than four months after the name change, merger or consolidation, unless the written statement is deposited for filing as required by Subsection (a) before the expiration of that time.

Acts 1967, 60th Leg., p. 2343, ch. 785, § 1. Amended by Acts 1973, 63rd Leg., p. 1032, ch. 400, § 7, eff. Jan. 1, 1974.

Repeal

Acts 2007, 80th Leg., ch. 885, § 2.47(a)(1) repeals this section effective April 1, 2009.

§ 35.05. Filing of Security Instruments and Statement of Name Change, Merger or Consolidation by Secretary of State; Fees

(a) The Secretary of State shall endorse upon any security instrument and any statement of name change, merger, or consolidation deposited for filing in his office, the day and hour of receipt and the file number assigned to it. Such endorsement shall, in the absence of other evidence, be conclusive proof of the time and fact of deposit for filing.

(b) The Secretary of State shall retain in his office all security instruments and statements of name change, merger, or consolidation deposited in his office and shall file such in adequate filing devices.

(c) The uniform fee for filing and indexing a security instrument, or an instrument supplementary or amendatory thereto, and a statement of name change, merger, or consolidation and for stamping a copy of such documents, furnished by the secured party or the utility, to show the date and place of filing shall be $25.

Acts 1967, 60th Leg., p. 2343, ch. 785, § 1. Amended by Acts 1973, 63rd Leg., p. 1032, ch. 400, § 7, eff. Jan. 1, 1974; Acts 1987, 70th Leg., ch. 1007, § 7, eff. June 19, 1987.

Repeal

Acts 2007, 80th Leg., ch. 885, § 2.47(a)(1) repeals this section effective April 1, 2009.

§ 35.06. Information From Secretary of State

Upon the request of any person, the Secretary of State shall issue his certificate showing whether there is on file on the date and hour stated therein, any presently effective security instrument naming a particular utility, and if there is, giving the date and hour of filing of such instrument and the names and addresses of each secured party therein. The uniform fee for such a certificate shall be $10.00 if the request for the certificate is in the standard form prescribed by the Secretary of State, and otherwise shall be $25.00. Upon request the Secretary of State shall furnish a copy of any filed security instrument for a uniform fee of $1.50 per page, but not less than $5.00 nor more than $100.00 per request concerning a particular utility.

Acts 1967, 60th Leg., p. 2343, ch. 785, § 1. Amended by Acts 1973, 63rd Leg., p. 1032, ch. 400, § 7, eff. Jan. 1, 1974; Acts 1989, 71st Leg., ch. 398, § 3, eff. Sept. 1, 1989.

Repeal

Acts 2007, 80th Leg., ch. 885, § 2.47(a)(1) repeals this section effective April 1, 2009.

§ 35.07. Recording of Notice in County of Real Property; Separate Index by County Clerk of Security Instruments and Continuation Statements

(a) If any security instrument filed with the office of the Secretary of State under Section 35.02 of this code grants an interest, as security, in any real property owned by the utility, a notice of utility security instrument affecting real property shall be recorded in the office of the county clerk in the county where the real property is located, stating

(1) the name of the utility which executed the security instrument;

(2) that a security instrument affecting real property in the county has been executed by the utility; and

(3) that such security instrument was filed, and other security instruments may be on file, in the office of the Secretary of State.

(b) It shall not be necessary to record a notice regarding other security instruments executed by the utility, and the notice recorded under Subsection (a) of this section shall be sufficient to provide notice of any and all other security instruments

(1) executed by the utility;

(2) filed in the office of the Secretary of State; and

(3) granting an interest, as security, in any real property, and fixtures thereto, located in the county where such notice was recorded.

(c) Notices recorded under Subsection (a) of this section shall be recorded and indexed by the county clerk in the same records and indices as are mortgages on real property.

(d) The county clerk shall maintain a separate index of utility security instruments and continuation statements recorded under prior law.

Acts 1967, 60th Leg., p. 2343, ch. 785, § 1. Amended by Acts 1973, 63rd Leg., p. 1032, ch. 400, § 7, eff. Jan. 1, 1974.

Repeal

Acts 2007, 80th Leg., ch. 885, § 2.47(a)(1) repeals this section effective April 1, 2009.

§ 35.08. Prior Perfected Liens; Refiling With Secretary of State

The perfection or notice provided by any security instrument covering any real or personal property located in this state which was heretofore filed or recorded in the office of the Secretary of State or the office of the county clerk of any county in this state continues effective until it would have lapsed under prior law or January 1, 1978, whichever occurs first; but it may be filed or refiled prior to such time in the office of the Secretary of State as provided in Section 35.02 of this code, and such filing or refiling shall continue the effectiveness as provided in Sections 35.02 and 35.03 of this code.

Acts 1967, 60th Leg., p. 2343, ch. 785, § 1. Amended by Acts 1973, 63rd Leg., p. 1032, ch. 400, § 7, eff. Jan. 1, 1974.

Repeal

Acts 2007, 80th Leg., ch. 885, § 2.47(a)(1) repeals this section effective April 1, 2009.

§ 35.09. Repealer

The following act and all other acts and parts of acts inconsistent herewith are hereby repealed:

Article 6645, Revised Civil Statutes of Texas, 1925, as amended.

Added by Acts 1973, 63rd Leg., p. 1032, ch. 400, § 7, eff. Jan. 1, 1974.

Repeal

Acts 2007, 80th Leg., ch. 885, § 2.47(a)(1) repeals this section effective April 1, 2009.

[Sections 35.10 to 35.13 reserved for expansion]

SUBCHAPTER B. DUTIES OF RAILROAD COMMISSION AND CRIMINAL OFFENSES INVOLVING BILLS OF LADING

§ 35.14. Definitions

In Sections 35.15–35.21 of this code, unless the context requires a different definition,

(1) "agent" includes officer, employee, and receiver;

(2) "airbill" means a document serving for air transportation as a bill of lading does for marine or rail transportation, and includes an air consignment note or air waybill;

(3) "bill of lading" means a document evidencing the receipt of goods for shipment issued by a person engaged in the business of transporting or forwarding goods, and includes an airbill;

(4) "common carrier" in Sections 35.15–35.17 of this code does not include a pipeline company or express company; and

(5) "goods" means all things which are treated as movable for the purposes of a contract of storage or transportation.

Acts 1967, 60th Leg., p. 2343, ch. 785, § 1.

Repeal

Acts 2007, 80th Leg., ch. 885, § 2.47(a)(1) repeals this section effective April 1, 2009.

§ 35.15. Duties of Railroad Commission

(a) The railroad commission shall

(1) prescribe forms, terms, and conditions for authenticating, certifying, or validating bills of lading issued by a common carrier;

(2) regulate the manner of issuing bills of lading by a common carrier; and

(3) take other action necessary to carry out the purposes of Chapter 7 of this code.

(b) After giving reasonable notice to interested common carriers and to the public, the railroad commission may amend a rule promulgated under Subsection (a) of this section.

Acts 1967, 60th Leg., p. 2343, ch. 785, § 1.

Repeal

Acts 2007, 80th Leg., ch. 885, § 2.47(a)(1) repeals this section effective April 1, 2009.

§ 35.16. Agent Wrongfully Failing to Issue Bill of Lading

(a) An agent of a common carrier may not after lawful demand fail or refuse to issue a bill of lading in accordance with Chapter 7 of this code or a rule of the railroad commission.

(b) An agent who violates a provision of Subsection (a) of this section is guilty of a misdemeanor and upon conviction is punishable by imprisonment in the county jail for not more than six months or by a fine of not more than $200 or by both.

Acts 1967, 60th Leg., p. 2343, ch. 785, § 1.

Repeal

Acts 2007, 80th Leg., ch. 885, § 2.47(a)(1) repeals this section effective April 1, 2009.

§ 35.17. Agent Issuing Fraudulent Bill of Lading

(a) An agent of a common carrier may not with intent to defraud a person

(1) issue a bill of lading;

(2) misdescribe in a bill of lading goods or their quantity described in the bill of lading; or

(3) issue a bill of lading without authority.

(b) An agent who violates a provision of Subsection (a) of this section is guilty of a felony and upon conviction is punishable by imprisonment in the penitentiary for not less than 2 nor more than 10 years.

Acts 1967, 60th Leg., p. 2343, ch. 785, § 1.

Repeal

Acts 2007, 80th Leg., ch. 885, § 2.47(a)(1) repeals this section effective April 1, 2009.

§ 35.18. Agent Issuing Duplicate Order Bill of Lading

(a) Except where customary in overseas transportation, an agent of a common carrier may not knowingly issue or aid in issuing an order bill of lading in duplicate or in a set of parts.

(b) An agent who violates a provision of Subsection (a) of this section is guilty of a felony and upon conviction is punishable by imprisonment in the penitentiary for not more than five years and by a fine of not more than $5,000.

Acts 1967, 60th Leg., p. 2343, ch. 785, § 1.

Repeal

Acts 2007, 80th Leg., ch. 885, § 2.47(a)(1) repeals this section effective April 1, 2009.

§ 35.19. Repealed by Acts 1973, 63rd Leg., p. 995, ch. 399, § 3(d), eff. Jan. 1, 1974

§ 35.20. Inducing Issuance of Fraudulent Bill of Lading

(a) A person may not with intent to defraud induce an agent of a common carrier to

(1) issue to him a bill of lading; or

(2) materially misrepresent in a bill of lading issued on behalf of the common carrier the quantity of goods described in the bill of lading.

(b) A person who violates a provision of Subsection (a) of this section is guilty of a felony and upon conviction is punishable by imprisonment in the penitentiary for not less than two nor more than five years.

Acts 1967, 60th Leg., p. 2343, ch. 785, § 1.

Repeal

Acts 2007, 80th Leg., ch. 885, § 2.47(a)(1) repeals this section effective April 1, 2009.

§ 35.21. Negotiating Fraudulent Bill of Lading

(a) A person may not with intent to defraud negotiate or transfer a bill of lading

(1) issued in violation of Chapter 7 of this code; or

(2) containing a false, material statement of fact.

(b) A person who violates a provision of Subsection (a) of this section is guilty of a felony and upon conviction is punishable by imprisonment in the penitentiary for not more than 10 years.

Acts 1967, 60th Leg., p. 2343, ch. 785, § 1.

Repeal

Acts 2007, 80th Leg., ch. 885, § 2.47(a)(1) repeals this section effective April 1, 2009.

[Sections 35.22 to 35.26 reserved for expansion]

SUBCHAPTER C. CRIMINAL OFFENSES INVOLVING WAREHOUSE RECEIPTS

§ 35.27. Definitions

In Sections 35.28–35.33 of this code, unless the context requires a different definition,

(1) "goods" means all things which are treated as movable for the purposes of a contract of storage or transportation;

(2) "issue" includes aiding in the issue of;

(3) "warehouseman" means a person engaged in the business of storing goods for hire; and

(4) "warehouse receipt" means a receipt issued by a person engaged in the business of storing goods for hire.

Acts 1967, 60th Leg., p. 2343, ch. 785, § 1.

Repeal

Acts 2007, 80th Leg., ch. 885, § 2.47(a)(1) repeals this section effective April 1, 2009.

§ 35.28. Warehouseman Issuing Fraudulent Warehouse Receipt

(a) A warehouseman, his officer, agent, or employee, may not with intent to defraud issue a warehouse receipt which contains a false statement of fact.

(b) A warehouseman, his officer, agent, or employee, who violates Subsection (a) of this section is guilty of a misdemeanor and upon conviction is punishable by imprisonment in the county jail for not more than one year or by a fine of not more than $1,000 or by both.

Acts 1967, 60th Leg., p. 2343, ch. 785, § 1.

Repeal

Acts 2007, 80th Leg., ch. 885, § 2.47(a)(1) repeals this section effective April 1, 2009.

§ 35.29. Warehouseman Failing to State His Ownership of Goods on Receipt

(a) A warehouseman, his officer, agent, or employee, may not knowingly issue a negotiable warehouse receipt describing goods the warehouseman owns and is storing (whether the warehouseman owns them solely, jointly, or in common) unless he states the warehouseman's ownership on the receipt.

(b) A warehouseman, his officer, agent, or employee, who violates Subsection (a) of this section is guilty of a misdemeanor and upon conviction is punishable by imprisonment in the county jail for not more than one year or by a fine of not more than $1,000.

Acts 1967, 60th Leg., p. 2343, ch. 785, § 1.

Repeal

Acts 2007, 80th Leg., ch. 885, § 2.47(a)(1) repeals this section effective April 1, 2009.

§ 35.30. Warehouseman Issuing Warehouse Receipt Without Goods

(a) A warehouseman, his officer, agent, or employee, may not issue a warehouse receipt if he knows at the time of issuance that the goods described in the warehouse receipt are not under his actual control.

(b) A warehouseman, his officer, agent, or employee, who violates Subsection (a) of this section is guilty of a felony and upon conviction is punishable by imprisonment in the penitentiary for not more than five years or by a fine of not more than $5,000 or by both.

Acts 1967, 60th Leg., p. 2343, ch. 785, § 1.

Repeal

Acts 2007, 80th Leg., ch. 885, § 2.47(a)(1) repeals this section effective April 1, 2009.

§ 35.31. Warehouseman Issuing Duplicate Warehouse Receipt

(a) A warehouseman, his officer, agent, or employee, may not issue a duplicate or additional negotiable warehouse receipt for goods if he knows at the time of issuance that a previously issued negotiable warehouse receipt describing those goods is outstanding and uncancelled.

(b) Subsection (a) of this section does not apply if

(1) the word "Duplicate" is plainly placed on the duplicate or additional negotiable warehouse receipt; or

(2) goods described in the outstanding and uncancelled negotiable warehouse receipt were delivered pursuant to court order on proof that the receipt was lost or destroyed.

(c) A warehouseman, his officer, agent, or employee, who violates Subsection (a) of this section is guilty of a felony and upon conviction is punishable by imprisonment in the penitentiary for not more than five years or by a fine of not more than $5,000 or by both.

Acts 1967, 60th Leg., p. 2343, ch. 785, § 1.

Repeal

Acts 2007, 80th Leg., ch. 885, § 2.47(a)(1) repeals this section effective April 1, 2009.

§ 35.32. Warehouseman Wrongfully Delivering Goods

(a) A warehouseman, his officer, agent, or employee, may not knowingly deliver goods described in a negotiable warehouse receipt and stored with him unless the receipt is surrendered to him at or before the time he delivers the goods.

(b) Subsection (a) of this section does not apply if the goods are

(1) delivered pursuant to court order on proof that the negotiable warehouse receipt describing them was lost or destroyed;

(2) lawfully sold to satisfy a warehouseman's lien; or

(3) disposed of because of their perishable or hazardous nature.

(c) A warehouseman, his officer, agent, or employee, who violates Subsection (a) of this section is guilty of a misdemeanor and upon conviction is punishable by imprisonment in the county jail for not more than one year or by a fine of not more than $1,000 or by both.

Acts 1967, 60th Leg., p. 2343, ch. 785, § 1.

Repeal

Acts 2007, 80th Leg., ch. 885, § 2.47(a)(1) repeals this section effective April 1, 2009.

§ 35.33. Failing to Disclose Ownership of Goods

(a) A person who obtains a negotiable warehouse receipt describing goods he does not own, or goods subject to a lien, may not with intent to defraud negotiate the receipt for value without disclosing his lack of ownership or the lien's existence.

(b) A person who violates a provision of Subsection (a) of this section is guilty of a misdemeanor and upon conviction is punishable by imprisonment in the county jail for not more than one year or by a fine of not more than $1,000 or by both.

Acts 1967, 60th Leg., p. 2343, ch. 785, § 1.

Repeal

Acts 2007, 80th Leg., ch. 885, § 2.47(a)(1) repeals this section effective April 1, 2009.

[Sections 35.34 to 35.38 reserved for expansion]

SUBCHAPTER D. MISCELLANEOUS

§ 35.39. Damages on Protested, Out-of-State Draft

The holder of a protested draft is entitled to damages equalling 10 percent of the amount of the draft, plus interest and costs of suit, if the

(1) draft was drawn by a merchant in this state on his agent or factor outside this state; and

(2) drawer's or indorser's liability on the draft has been fixed.

Acts 1967, 60th Leg., p. 2343, ch. 785, § 1.

Repeal

Acts 2007, 80th Leg., ch. 885, § 2.47(a)(1) repeals this section effective April 1, 2009.

§ 35.395. Delivery of Check Form

(a) In this section:

(1) "Addressee" means a person to whom a check form is sent.

(2) "Check form" means a device for the transmission or payment of money that:

(A) is not a negotiable instrument under Section 3.104;

(B) if completed would be a check as that term is described by Section 3.104; and

(C) is printed with information relating to the financial institution on which the completed check may be drawn.

(3) "Courier" means any entity that delivers parcels for a fee.

(4) "Check form provider" means a business that provides check forms to a customer for a personal or business account.

(b) When an addressee requests of a check form provider, courier delivery of a check form with signature required, and such service is available in the delivery area of the addressee, the entity making the arrangement for courier delivery pursuant to the request of the addressee must provide the addressee with the option to require that a signature of the addressee, or the representative of the addressee, be obtained on delivery. The option to require such a signature may be provided on a printed check form order form, on an electronic check form order form where check form orders are offered on the Internet, to an electronic mail address established for such purpose by the entity making the offer, or by another method reasonably calculated to effectively communicate the addressee's intent.

(c) An entity making the arrangement for the courier delivery of a check form to an addressee pursuant to the provisions of Subsection (b) shall notify the courier of the check form that the signature of the addressee is required for delivery under Subsection (b).

(d) If the addressee suffers a pecuniary loss through the use of check forms stolen at the time of delivery to the addressee, a civil penalty of up to a maximum amount of $1,000 per delivery may be levied upon:

(1) an entity that violates Subsection (b) or (c); or

(2) a courier who is properly notified under Subsection (c) that a signature is required for delivery, and delivers the check form without obtaining a signature of the addressee or a representative of the addressee.

(e) The attorney general may bring suit to recover a civil penalty imposed under this section. The attorney general may recover reasonable expenses incurred in obtaining a civil penalty under this subsection, including court costs, reasonable attorney's fees, investigative costs, witness fees, and deposition expenses.

Added by Acts 2005, 79th Leg., ch. 1202, § 1, eff. June 1, 2006.

Repeal

Acts 2007, 80th Leg., ch. 885, § 2.47(a)(1) repeals this section effective April 1, 2009.

§ 35.40. Identification of Patent Right Note or Lien

(a) A note or lien evidencing or securing the purchase price for a patent right or patent right territory must contain on its face a statement that it was given for a patent right or patent right territory.

(b) The statement required by Subsection (a) of this section

(1) is notice to a subsequent purchaser of the note or lien of all equities between the original parties to the note or lien; and

(2) subjects a subsequent holder of the note or lien to all defenses available against the original parties to the note or lien.

(c) A person selling a patent right or patent right territory may not take a note or lien evidencing or securing the purchase price for it without placing on the face of the note or lien the statement required by Subsection (a) of this section.

(d) A person who violates Subsection (c) of this section is guilty of a misdemeanor and upon conviction is punishable by a fine of not less than $25 nor more than $200.

Acts 1967, 60th Leg., p. 2343, ch. 785, § 1.

Repeal

Acts 2007, 80th Leg., ch. 885, § 2.47(a)(1) repeals this section effective April 1, 2009.

§ 35.41. Destruction of Die, Mold, or Form

(a) In this Act:

(1) "Owner" means an individual, firm, or corporation that holds title to a die, mold, or form.

(2) "Molder" means an individual, firm, or corporation that makes a die, mold, or form, or that uses a die, mold, or form to make another product.

(b) After the three-year period beginning on the day on which a die, mold, or form was last used or, if never used, on the day on which it was made, a molder in possession of the die, mold, or form may send notice to its owner of the molder's intent to destroy the die, mold, or form. Notice must be sent by registered mail, return receipt requested, to the last known address of the owner.

(c) If, before the 121st day after the day that the notice sent in accordance with Subsection (b) of this section is received, the owner does not take possession of the die, mold, or form or make arrangements with the molder for its removal or continued storage, the molder may destroy the die, mold, or form.

(d) On destruction of a die, mold, or form in accordance with this section, the owner's title to it ends.

(e) If a molder satisfies the requirements of this section, the molder may not be held criminally or civilly liable for the destruction of the die, mold, or form.

(f) This section does not prevent a molder that holds title to a die, mold or form from destroying it at any time.

Added by Acts 1983, 68th Leg., p. 4598, ch. 778, § 1, eff. Aug. 29, 1983.

Repeal

Acts 2007, 80th Leg., ch. 885, § 2.47(a)(1) repeals this section effective April 1, 2009.

§ 35.42. Reduction of Value or Expiration of Stored Value Card

(a) In this section:

(1) "Record" has the meaning assigned by Section 43.002, and includes a record that contains a microprocessor chip, magnetic strip, or other means of storing information.

(2) "Stored value card" means a record that evidences a promise made for monetary consideration by the seller or issuer of the record that goods or services will be provided to the owner of the record in the value shown in the record, that is prefunded, and the value of which is reduced on redemption. The term includes a gift card or gift certificate.

(3) "Use" of a stored value card includes a whole or partial redemption of or adding value to the card.

(b) This section does not apply to a stored value card that:

(1) is distributed by the issuer to a person under an awards, rewards, loyalty, incentive, rebate or promotional program and not issued or reloaded in exchange for money tendered by the cardholder;

(2) is sold below face value or donated to:

(A) an employee of the seller or issuer;

(B) a nonprofit or charitable organization; or

(C) an educational institution, for fund-raising purposes;

(3) is issued by a financial institution acting as a financial agent of the United States or this state;

(4) is issued as a prepaid calling card by a prepaid calling card company regulated under Section 55.253, Utilities Code;

(5) does not expire and for which the seller does not charge a fee other than a fee described in Subsection (d); or

(6) is issued by an air carrier holding a certificate of public convenience and necessity under Title 49, United States Code.

(c) This section does not apply to a stored value card issued by a federally insured financial institution, as defined by Section 201.101, Finance Code, for which the financial institution is primarily liable as the issuing principal.

(d) If disclosed as provided by Subsection (f), the issuer of a stored value card may impose and collect a reasonable handling fee in connection with the issuance of or adding of value to the card, a reasonable access fee for a card transaction conducted at an unmanned teller machine, as defined by Section 59.301, Finance Code, and a reasonable reissue or replacement charge if a lost or expired card is reissued or replaced.

(e) The issuer of a stored value card may impose or collect a periodic fee or other charge that causes the unredeemed balance of the card to decrease over time only if the fee is reasonable, is not assessed until after the first anniversary of the date the card is sold or issued, and is disclosed as provided by Subsection (f).

(f) An expiration date or policy, fee, or other material restriction or contract term applicable to a stored value card must be clearly and conspicuously disclosed to a person at the time the card is sold or issued to the person to enable the person to make an informed decision before the person purchases the card. A disclosure regarding expiration or a periodic fee that reduces the unredeemed value of the stored value card must also be legibly printed on the card. A stored value card that is sold without the disclosure as required by this section of an expiration date or policy, fee, or other material restriction or contract term applicable to the card is valid until redeemed or replaced.

(g) This section does not create a cause of action against a person who issues or sells a stored value card.

Added by Acts 2005, 79th Leg., ch. 81, § 1, eff. Sept. 1, 2005.

Repeal

Acts 2007, 80th Leg., ch. 885, § 2.47(a)(1) repeals this section effective April 1, 2009.

Section 6 of Acts 2005, 79th Leg., ch. 81 provides:

"The changes in law made by this Act apply only to a stored value card issued or activated on or after the effective date of this Act. A stored value card issued or activated before the effective date of this

Act is governed by the law in effect when the card was issued or activated, and the former law is continued in effect for that purpose."

§ 35.43. Consumer Rebate Response and Grace Period for Corrections

(a) In this section:

(1) "Consumer" means a person who obtains a product or service that is to be used primarily for personal, business, family, or household purposes.

(2) "Consumer rebate" means an offer to a consumer of cash, credit, or credit toward future purchases that is made in connection with a sale of a good or service to the consumer, is in an amount of $10 or more, and requires the consumer to mail or electronically submit a rebate request after the sale is completed. The term does not include:

(A) any promotion or incentive that is offered by a manufacturer to another company or organization that is not the consumer to help promote or place the product or service;

(B) a rebate that is redeemed at the time of purchase;

(C) any discount, cash, credit, or credit toward a future purchase that is automatically provided to a consumer without the need to submit a request for redemption;

(D) a rebate that is applied to a bill that the consumer becomes obligated to pay after the date the purchase is made;

(E) any refund that may be given to a consumer in accordance with a manufacturer or retailer's return, guarantee, adjustment, or warranty policies; or

(F) any manufacturer or retailer's frequent shopper customer reward program.

(3) "Properly completed" means that the consumer submitted the required information and documentation in the manner and by the deadline specified in the rebate offer and otherwise satisfied the terms and conditions of the rebate offer.

(b) Except as provided by Subsection (c), a person, including a manufacturer or retailer, who offers a rebate shall mail the amount of the rebate to the consumer or electronically pay the consumer the amount of the rebate within the time period promised in the rebate information provided to the consumer, or if silent, not later than the 30th day after the date the person receives a properly completed rebate request.

(c) If a consumer rebate offer is contingent on the consumer continuing to purchase a service for a minimum length of time, the time period in Subsection (b) begins on the later of:

(1) the date the consumer submits the rebate request; or

(2) the expiration date of the service period.

(d) If the person offering the rebate receives a rebate request that is timely submitted but not properly completed, the person shall:

(1) process the rebate in the manner provided by Subsection (b) as if the rebate request were properly completed; or

(2) notify the consumer, not later than the date specified by Subsection (b), of the reasons that the rebate request is not properly completed and the consumer's right to correct the deficiency within 30 days after the date of the notification.

(e) The notification under Subsection (d)(2) must be by mail, except that notification may be by e-mail if the consumer has agreed to be notified by e-mail.

(f) If the consumer corrects the deficiency stated in the notification under Subsection (d)(2) before the 31st day after the postmark date of the person's mailed notification to the consumer or the date the e-mail is received, if applicable, the person shall process the rebate in the manner provided by Subsection (b) for a properly completed request.

(g) This section does not impose any obligation on a person to pay a rebate to any consumer who is not eligible under the terms and conditions of the rebate offer or has not satisfied all of the terms and conditions of the rebate offer, if the person offering the rebate has complied with Subsections (d) and (e).

(h) A person offering a rebate has the right to reject a rebate request from a consumer who the person determines:

(1) is attempting to commit fraud;

(2) has already received the offered rebate; or

(3) is submitting proof of purchase that is not legitimate.

(i) A person making a determination under Subsection (h) shall notify the consumer within the time period provided by Subsection (d) that the person is considering rejecting, or has rejected, the rebate request and shall instruct the consumer of any actions that the consumer may take to cure the deficiency.

(j) If the person offering a rebate erroneously rejects a properly completed rebate request, the person shall pay the consumer as soon as practicable, but not later than 30 days, after the date the person learns of the error.

(k) For the purposes of this section, if a person who offers a rebate uses an independent entity to process the rebate, an act of the entity is considered to be an act of the person and receipt of a rebate request by the entity is considered receipt of the request by the person.

(*l*) A violation of this section is a deceptive trade practice in addition to the practices described by Subchapter E, Chapter 17, and is actionable by a consumer under that subchapter. Claims related to more than one consumer may not be joined in a single action brought for an alleged violation of this subchapter, unless all parties agree.

(m) A court may not certify an action brought under this section as a class action.

(n) A violation of this section is subject to an action by the office of the attorney general as provided by Section 17.46(a).

Added by Acts 2007, 80th Leg., ch. 123, § 1, eff. Sept. 1, 2007.

§ 35.44. Store Lease Contracts

(a) A provision of a lease contract that requires a store to be open when another store located in the same shopping center is open does not apply on Sunday unless the provision specifically states that it applies on Sunday.

(b) This section applies to a contract regardless of whether it was executed before or after this section took effect.

Added by Acts 1985, 69th Leg., ch. 220, § 4, eff. Sept. 1, 1985. Renumbered from V.T.C.A., Bus. & C. Code § 35.42 by Acts 1987, 70th Leg., ch. 167, § 5.01(a)(3), eff. Sept. 1, 1987.

Repeal

Acts 2007, 80th Leg., ch. 885, § 2.47(a)(1) repeals this section effective April 1, 2009.

§ 35.45. Delivery of Unsolicited Goods

(a) Unless otherwise agreed, if unsolicited goods are delivered to a person, the person:

(1) is entitled to refuse to accept delivery of the goods; and

(2) is not required to return the goods to the sender.

(b) If unsolicited goods are either addressed to or intended for the recipient, the goods are considered a gift to the recipient, who may use them or dispose of them in any manner without obligation to the sender.

(c) Unsolicited goods received due to a bona fide mistake must be returned, but the burden of proof of the error is on the sender.

(d) This section does not apply to goods substituted for goods ordered or solicited by the recipient.

Added by Acts 1985, 69th Leg., ch. 959, § 7, eff. Sept. 1, 1985. Renumbered from V.T.C.A. Bus. & C. Code § 35.42 by Acts 1987, 70th Leg., ch. 167, § 5.01(a)(3), eff. Sept. 1, 1987.

Repeal

Acts 2007, 80th Leg., ch. 885, § 2.47(a)(1) repeals this section effective April 1, 2009.

§ 35.455. Disclosures Required for Certain Consumer Contracts Solicited by Mail

(a) Unless the context requires a different definition, the definitions of Chapter 3 apply to this section.

(b) This section applies only to a person that solicits business in this state by mailing an individual a check or draft payable to the individual. This section does not apply to a financial institution as defined in Section 201.101, Finance Code, or an authorized lender as defined in Section 341.001, Finance Code, that sends a check or draft to an existing or prospective account holder authorizing the existing or prospective account holder to access an extension of credit.

(c) A person that makes an offer that the recipient may accept by endorsing and negotiating the check or draft shall clearly and conspicuously disclose on the check or draft, next to the place for endorsement, that by signing and negotiating the document the depositor agrees to pay for future goods or services as a result of this contract.

(d) If a person makes an offer under Subsection (c) that includes a free membership period, trial period, or other incentive with a time limit, and if the offer results in a contract unless the recipient cancels, rescinds, or revokes the offer by the end of the time period, the offeror shall send notice to the recipient, at least two weeks before debiting any account, of the recipient's obligation to cancel, rescind, revoke, or otherwise terminate the recipient's acceptance. The notice must be clear and conspicuous. If the offeror bills the consumer by mailing an invoice, notice may be included with the invoice.

(e) An offer is void if the offeror:

(1) does not make the disclosure required by Subsection (c);

(2) does not give notice as required by Subsection (d), if applicable; or

(3) provides an incentive with a time limit, including a free trial or membership period, that is less than two weeks.

(f) If an offer described by Subsection (c) does not contain the required disclosure, or is not followed by any notice required by Subsection (d), or if the offeror fails to honor the recipient's request to cancel made under the terms of the offer or as required by Subsection (d), the delivery of any goods or services to the recipient does not operate to form a contract between the offeror and the recipient.

(g) A violation of this section is a deceptive trade practice in addition to the practices described by Subchapter E, Chapter 17, and is actionable under that subchapter.

Added by Acts 2005, 79th Leg., ch. 596, § 1, eff. Sept. 1, 2005.

Repeal

Acts 2007, 80th Leg., ch. 885, § 2.47(a)(1) repeals this section effective April 1, 2009.

Section 2 of Acts 2005, 79th Leg., ch. 596 provides:

"Section 35.455, Business & Commerce Code, as added by this Act, applies only to a solicitation that is mailed on or after September 1, 2005. A solicitation that is mailed before September 1, 2005, is covered by the law in effect on the date the solicitation was mailed, and the former law is continued in effect for that purpose."

§ 35.46. Attaching Motor Vehicle Dealer's Name to Vehicle

(a) In this section:

(1) "Motor vehicle" has the meaning assigned by Section 541.201, Transportation Code.

(2) "Center high-mounted stop lamp" means a device that is mounted on the rear center line of a motor vehicle either in or on the rear window or within six inches from the rear window of the vehicle for the purpose of emitting a light when the vehicle's brakes are applied.

(3) "Overlay" means a transparent or semi-transparent covering placed over a center high-mounted stop lamp on which is impressed or imprinted a name, trade name, logotype, or other message that can be read by a person behind the vehicle when the lamp is illuminated.

(b) A person in the business of selling motor vehicles may not sell a motor vehicle with a center high-mounted stop lamp over which an overlay has been placed.

(c) A person who violates this section commits an offense. An offense under this section is a Class C misdemeanor.

Added by Acts 1987, 70th Leg., ch. 858, § 1, eff. Sept. 1, 1987. Amended by Acts 1997, 75th Leg., ch. 165, § 30.178, eff. Sept. 1, 1997.

Repeal

Acts 2007, 80th Leg., ch. 885, § 2.47(a)(1) repeals this section effective April 1, 2009.

§ 35.47. Certain Electronic Communications Made for Purpose of Sales

(a) A person may not make a telephone call or use an automatic dial announcing device to make a telephone call for the purpose of making a sale if:

(1) the person making the call or using the device knows or should have known that the called number is a mobile telephone for which the called person will be charged for that specific call; and

(2) the called person has not given consent to make such a call to the person calling or using the device or to the business enterprise for which the person is calling or using the device.

(b) A person may not make or cause to be made a transmission for the purpose of a solicitation or sale to a facsimile recording device or other telecopier for which the person or entity receiving the transmission will be charged for the transmission, unless the person or entity receiving the transmission has given, prior to the transmission, consent to make or cause to be made the transmission.

(c) A person may not make or cause to be made a transmission for the purpose of a solicitation or sale to a facsimile recording device after 11 p.m. and before 7 a.m.

(d) On complaint of a called person that Subsection (a), (b), or (c) of this section has been violated, the county or district attorney of the county in which the person resides shall investigate the complaint and file charges if appropriate. A telephone company serving the caller or called person is not responsible for investigating a complaint or keeping records relating to this section.

(e) A person who violates Subsection (a), (b), or (c) of this section commits an offense. An offense under this section is a Class C misdemeanor.

(f) A person who receives a communication that violates 47 U.S.C. Section 227, a regulation adopted under that provision, or this section may bring an action against the person who originates the communication in a court of this state for an injunction, damages in the amount provided by this subsection, or both. A plaintiff prevailing in an action for damages under this subsection is entitled to the greater of $500 for each violation or the person's actual damages, except that the court may increase the amount of the award to not more than the greater of $1,500 for each violation or three times the person's actual damages if the court finds that the defendant committed the violation knowingly or intentionally.

Added by Acts 1989, 71st Leg., ch. 783, § 1, eff. Sept. 1, 1989. Amended by Acts 1999, 76th Leg., ch. 635, § 1, eff. Sept. 1, 1999; Acts 2001, 77th Leg., ch. 1429, § 2, eff. Jan. 1, 2002.

Repeal

Acts 2007, 80th Leg., ch. 885, § 2.47(a)(1) repeals this section effective April 1, 2009.

§ 35.48. Retention and Disposal of Business Records

(a) In this section:

(1) "Business record" means letters, words, sounds, or numbers, or the equivalent of letters, words, sounds, or numbers, recorded in the operation of a business by:

(A) handwriting;

(B) typewriting;

(C) printing;

(D) photostat;

(E) photograph;

(F) magnetic impulse;

(G) mechanical or electronic recording;

(H) digitized optical image; or

(I) another form of data compilation.

(1–a) "Personal identifying information" means an individual's first name or initial and last name in combination with any one or more of the following items:

(A) date of birth;

(B) social security number or other government-issued identification number;

(C) mother's maiden name;

(D) unique biometric data, including the individual's fingerprint, voice print, and retina or iris image;

(E) unique electronic identification number, address, or routing code;

(F) telecommunication access device, including debit and credit card information; or

(G) financial institution account number or any other financial information.

(2) "Reproduction" means a counterpart of an original business record produced by:

(A) production from the same impression or the same matrix as the original;

(B) photograph, including an enlargement or miniature;

(C) mechanical or electronic rerecording;

(D) chemical reproduction;

(E) digitized optical image; or

(F) another technique that accurately reproduces the original.

(3) "Telecommunication access device" has the meaning assigned by Section 32.51, Penal Code.

(b) A business record required to be kept by state law may be destroyed at any time after the third anniversary of the date the record was created unless a law or regulation applicable to the business record prescribes a different retention period or procedure for disposal.

(c) A state law requiring retention of a business record is satisfied by retention of a reproduction of the business record.

(d) When a business disposes of a business record that contains personal identifying information of a customer of the business, the business shall modify, by shredding, erasing, or other means, the personal identifying information to make it unreadable or undecipherable.

(e) A business is considered to comply with Subsection (d) if the business contracts with a person engaged in the business of disposing of records for the modification of personal identifying information on behalf of the business in accordance with Subsection (d).

(f) A business that does not dispose of a business record of a customer in the manner required by Subsection (d) is liable for a civil penalty of up to $500 for each record. The attorney general may bring an action against the business to:

(1) recover the civil penalty;

(2) obtain any other remedy, including injunctive relief; and

(3) recover costs and reasonable attorney's fees incurred in bringing the action.

(g) A business that modifies a record as required by Subsection (d) in good faith is not liable for a civil penalty under Subsection (f) if the record is reconstructed, in whole or in part, through extraordinary means.

(h) Subsection (d) does not require a business to modify a record if:

(1) the business is required to retain the record under other law; or

(2) the record is historically significant and:

(A) there is no potential for identity theft or fraud while the record is in the custody of the business; or

(B) the record is transferred to a professionally managed historical repository.

(i) Subsection (d) does not apply to:

(1) a financial institution as defined by 15 U.S.C. Section 6809; or

(2) a covered entity as defined by Section 601.001 or 602.001, Insurance Code.

Added by Acts 1989, 71st Leg., ch. 955, § 1, eff. June 15, 1989. Renumbered from V.T.C.A. Bus. & C. Code § 35.47 by Acts 1990, 71st Leg., 6th C.S., ch. 12, § 2(2), eff. Sept. 6, 1990. Amended by Acts 1991, 72nd Leg., ch. 472, § 1, eff. Aug. 26, 1991; Acts 1995, 74th Leg., ch. 735, § 3, eff. Sept. 1, 1995; Acts 2005, 79th Leg., ch. 935, §§ 1 to 3, eff. Sept. 1, 2005.

Repeal

Acts 2007, 80th Leg., ch. 885, § 2.47(a)(1) repeals this section effective April 1, 2009.

Section 4 of Acts 2005, 79th Leg., ch. 935 provides:

"This Act applies to the disposal of business records without regard to whether the records were created before, on, or after the effective date of this Act."

§ 35.49. Other Remedies

(a) A person who sells, distributes, or manufactures cigarettes and who sustains direct economic or commercial injury as a result of a violation of Section 154.0415, Tax Code, or Section 48.015, Penal Code, may bring an action in good faith for appropriate injunctive relief.

(b) The remedy provided by this section is in addition to any other remedy provided by law.

Added by Acts 2001, 77th Leg., ch. 1104, § 5, eff. Sept. 1, 2001.

Repeal

Acts 2007, 80th Leg., ch. 885, § 2.47(a)(1) repeals this section effective April 1, 2009.

§ 35.50. Biometric Identifier

(a) In this section, "biometric identifier" means a retina or iris scan, fingerprint, voiceprint, or record of hand or face geometry.

(b) A person may not capture a biometric identifier of an individual for a commercial purpose unless the person:

(1) informs the individual before capturing the biometric identifier; and

(2) receives the individual's consent to capture the biometric identifier.

(c) A person who possesses a biometric identifier of an individual:

(1) may not sell, lease, or otherwise disclose the biometric identifier to another person unless:

(A) the individual consents to the disclosure;

(B) the disclosure completes a financial transaction requested or authorized by the individual;

(C) the disclosure is required or permitted by a federal statute or by a state statute other than Chapter 552, Government Code; or

(D) the disclosure is made by or to a law enforcement agency for a law enforcement purpose; and

(2) shall store, transmit, and protect from disclosure the biometric identifier using reasonable care and in a manner that is the same as or more protective than the manner in which the person stores, transmits, and protects the person's other confidential information.

(d) A person who violates this section is subject to a civil penalty of not more than $25,000 for each violation. The attorney general may institute an action to recover the civil penalty.

Added by Acts 2001, 77th Leg., ch. 634, § 1, eff. Sept. 1, 2001.

Repeal

Acts 2007, 80th Leg., ch. 885, § 2.47(a)(1) repeals this section effective April 1, 2009.

§ 35.51. Rights of Parties to Choose Law Applicable to Certain Transactions

(a) In this section:

(1) "Transaction" includes more than one substantially similar or related transaction entered into contemporaneously and having at least one common party.

(2) "Qualified transaction" means a transaction under which a party:

(A) pays or receives, or is obligated to pay or entitled to receive, consideration with an aggregate value of at least $1,000,000; or

(B) lends, advances, borrows, or receives, or is obligated to lend or advance or is entitled to borrow or receive, funds or credit with an aggregate value of at least $1,000,000.

(b) Except as provided by Subsection (e) or (f) of this section or Section 35.52 of this code, if the parties to a qualified transaction agree in writing that the law of a particular jurisdiction governs an issue relating to the transaction, including the validity or enforceability of an agreement relating to the transaction or a provision of the agreement, and the transaction bears a reasonable relation to that jurisdiction, the law, other than conflict of laws rules, of that jurisdiction governs the issue regardless of whether the application of that law is contrary to a fundamental or public policy of this state or of any other jurisdiction.

(c) Except as provided by Subsection (f) of this section and Section 35.52 of this code, if the parties to a qualified transaction agree in writing that the law of a particular jurisdiction governs the interpretation or construction of an agreement relating to the transaction or a provision of the agreement, the law, other than conflict of laws rules, of that jurisdiction governs that issue regardless of whether the transaction bears a reasonable relation to that jurisdiction.

(d) For purposes of this section, a transaction bears a reasonable relation to a particular jurisdiction if the transaction, the subject matter of the transaction, or a party to the transaction is reasonably related to that jurisdiction. A transaction bears a reasonable relation to a particular jurisdiction if:

(1) a party to the transaction is a resident of that jurisdiction;

(2) a party to the transaction has its place of business or, if that party has more than one place of business, its chief executive office or an office from which it conducts a substantial part of the negotiations relating to the transaction, in that jurisdiction;

(3) all or part of the subject matter of the transaction is located in that jurisdiction;

(4) a party to the transaction is required to perform a substantial part of its obligations relating to the transaction, such as delivering payments, in that jurisdiction; or

(5) a substantial part of the negotiations relating to the transaction, and the signing of an agreement relating to the transaction by a party to the transaction, occurred in that jurisdiction.

(e) Except as provided by Subsection (f) of this section or Section 35.52 of this code, if:

(1) the parties to a qualified transaction agree in writing that the law of a particular jurisdiction governs the validity or enforceability of an agreement relating to the transaction or a provision of the agreement;

(2) the transaction bears a reasonable relation to that jurisdiction; and

(3) a term of the agreement or of that provision is invalid or unenforceable under the law, other than conflict of laws rules, of that jurisdiction but is valid or enforceable under the law, other than conflict of laws rules, of the jurisdiction that has the most significant relation to the transaction, the subject matter of the transaction, and the parties, then:

(A) the law, other than conflict of laws rules, of the jurisdiction that has the most significant relation to the transaction, the subject matter of the transaction, and the parties governs the validity or enforceability of that term; and

(B) the law, other than conflict of laws rules, of the jurisdiction that the parties agree would govern the validity or enforceability of that agreement or of that provision governs the validity or enforceability of the other terms of that agreement or provision.

(f) Subsections (b)–(e) of this section do not apply to the determination of the law that governs:

(1) whether a transaction transfers or creates an interest in real property for security purposes or otherwise, the nature of an interest in real property that is transferred or created by a transaction, the method for foreclosure of a lien on real property, the nature of an interest in real property that results from foreclosure, or the manner and effect of recording or failing to record evidence of a

transaction that transfers or creates an interest in real property;

(2) the validity of a marriage or an adoption, whether a marriage has been terminated, or the effect of a marriage on property owned by a spouse at the time of the marriage or acquired by either spouse during the marriage;

(3) whether an instrument is a will, the rights of persons under a will, or the rights of persons in the absence of a will; or

(4) an issue that another statute of this state, or a statute of the United States, provides is governed by the law of a particular jurisdiction.

(g) Subsections (b)–(e) of this section apply to the determination of the law that governs an issue relating to a transaction involving real property other than those specified in Subsection (f)(1) of this section, including the validity or enforceability of an indebtedness incurred in consideration for the transfer of, or the payment of which is secured by a lien on, real property.

Added by Acts 1993, 73rd Leg., ch. 570, § 13, eff. Sept. 1, 1993.

Repeal

Acts 2007, 80th Leg., ch. 885, § 2.47(a)(1) repeals this section effective April 1, 2009.

§ 35.52. Law Applicable to Construction Contracts

(a) If a contract is principally for the construction or repair of improvements to real property located in this state and the contract contains a provision that makes the contract or any conflict arising under it subject to the law of another state, to litigation in the courts of another state, or to arbitration in another state, that provision is voidable by the party that is obligated by the contract to perform the construction or repair.

(b) A contract is principally for the construction or repair of improvements to real property located in this state if the contract obligates a party, as its principal obligation under the contract, to provide labor, or labor and materials, for the construction or repair of improvements to real property located in this state as a general contractor or subcontractor.

(c) A contract is not principally for the construction or repair of improvements to real property located in this state if:

(1) the contract is a partnership agreement or other agreement governing an entity or trust;

(2) the contract provides for a loan or other extension of credit and the party promising to construct or repair improvements does so as part of its agreements with the lender or other extender of credit; or

(3) the contract is for the management of real property or improvements and the obligation to construct or repair is part of that management.

(d) Subsections (b) and (c) of this section are not an exclusive list of situations in which a contract is or is not principally for the construction or repair of improvements to real property located in this state.

Added by Acts 1993, 73rd Leg., ch. 570, § 13, eff. Sept. 1, 1993.

Repeal

Acts 2007, 80th Leg., ch. 885, § 2.47(a)(1) repeals this section effective April 1, 2009.

§ 35.521. Agreement for Payment of Construction Subcontractor

(a) In this section:

(1) "Contingent payee" means a party to a contract with a contingent payment clause, other than an architect or engineer, whose receipt of payment is conditioned on the contingent payor's receipt of payment from another person.

(2) "Contingent payment clause" means a provision in a contract for construction management, or for the construction of improvements to real property or the furnishing of materials for the construction, that provides that the contingent payor's receipt of payment from another is a condition precedent to the obligation of the contingent payor to make payment to the contingent payee for work performed or materials furnished.

(3) "Contingent payor" means a party to a contract with a contingent payment clause that conditions payment by the party on the receipt of payment from another person.

(4) "Improvement" includes new construction, remodeling, or repair.

(5) "Obligor" means the person obligated to make payment to the contingent payor for an improvement.

(6) "Primary obligor" means the owner of the real property to be improved or repaired under the contract, or the contracting authority if the contract

is for a public project. A primary obligor may be an obligor.

(b) A contingent payor or its surety may not enforce a contingent payment clause to the extent that the obligor's nonpayment to the contingent payor is the result of the contractual obligations of the contingent payor not being met, unless the nonpayment is the result of the contingent payee's failure to meet the contingent payee's contractual requirements.

(c) Except as provided by Subsection (f), a contingent payor or its surety may not enforce a contingent payment clause as to work performed or materials delivered after the contingent payor receives written notice from the contingent payee objecting to the further enforceability of the contingent payment clause as provided by this section and the notice becomes effective as provided by Subsection (d). The contingent payee may send written notice only after the 45th day after the date the contingent payee submits a written request for payment to the contingent payor that is in a form substantially in accordance with the contingent payee's contract requirements for the contents of a regular progress payment request or an invoice.

(d) For purposes of Subsection (c), the written notice becomes effective on the latest of:

(1) the 10th day after the date the contingent payor receives the notice;

(2) the eighth day after the date interest begins to accrue against the obligor under:

(A) Section 28.004, Property Code, under a contract for a private project governed by Chapter 28, Property Code; or

(B) 31 U.S.C. Section 3903(a)(6), under a contract for a public project governed by 40 U.S.C. Section 3131; or

(3) the 11th day after the date interest begins to accrue against the obligor under Section 2251.025, Government Code, under a contract for a public project governed by Chapter 2251, Government Code.

(e) A notice given by a contingent payee under Subsection (c) does not prevent enforcement of a contingent payment clause if:

(1) the obligor has a dispute under Chapter 28, Property Code, Chapter 2251, Government Code, or 31 U.S.C. Chapter 39 as a result of the contingent payee's failure to meet the contingent payee's contractual requirements; and

(2) the contingent payor gives notice in writing to the contingent payee that the written notice given under Subsection (c) does not prevent enforcement of the contingent payment clause under this subsection and the contingent payee receives the notice under this subdivision not later than the later of:

(A) the fifth day before the date the written notice from the contingent payee under Subsection (c) becomes effective under Subsection (d); or

(B) the fifth day after the date the contingent payor receives the written notice from the contingent payee under Subsection (c).

(f) A written notice given by a contingent payee under Subsection (c) does not prevent the enforcement of a contingent payment clause to the extent that the funds are not collectible as a result of a primary obligor's successful assertion of a defense of sovereign immunity, if the contingent payor has exhausted all of its rights and remedies under its contract with the primary obligor and under Chapter 2251, Government Code. This subsection does not:

(1) create or validate a defense of sovereign immunity; or

(2) extend to a primary obligor a defense or right that did not exist before the effective date of this section.

(g) On receipt of payment by the contingent payee of the unpaid indebtedness giving rise to the written notice provided by the contingent payee under Subsection (c), the contingent payment clause is reinstated as to work performed or materials furnished after the receipt of the payment, subject to the provisions of this section.

(h) A contingent payor or its surety may not enforce a contingent payment clause if the contingent payor is in a sham relationship with the obligor, as described by the sham relationships in Section 53.026, Property Code.

(i) A contingent payment clause may not be used as a basis for invalidation of the enforceability or perfection of a mechanic's lien under Chapter 53, Property Code.

(j) A contingent payor or its surety may not enforce a contingent payment clause if the enforcement would be unconscionable. The party asserting that a contingent payment clause is unconscionable has the burden of proving that the clause is unconscionable.

(k) The enforcement of a contingent payment clause is not unconscionable if the contingent payor:

(1) proves that the contingent payor has exercised diligence in ascertaining and communicating in writing to the contingent payee, before the contract in which the contingent payment clause has been asserted becomes enforceable against the contingent payee, the financial viability of the primary obligor and the existence of adequate financial arrangements to pay for the improvements; and

(2) has done the following:

(A) made reasonable efforts to collect the amount owed to the contingent payor; or

(B) made or offered to make, at a reasonable time, an assignment by the contingent payor to the contingent payee of a cause of action against the obligor for the amounts owed to the contingent payee by the contingent payor and offered reasonable cooperation to the contingent payee's collection efforts, if the assigned cause of action is not subject to defenses caused by the contingent payor's action or failure to act.

(*l*) A cause of action brought on an assignment made under Subsection (k)(2)(B) is enforceable by a contingent payee against an obligor or a primary obligor.

(m) A contingent payor is considered to have exercised diligence for purposes of Subsection (k)(1) under a contract for a private project governed by Chapter 53, Property Code, if the contingent payee receives in writing from the contingent payor:

(1) the name, address, and business telephone number of the primary obligor;

(2) a description, legally sufficient for identification, of the property on which the improvements are being constructed;

(3) the name and address of the surety on any payment bond provided under Subchapter I, Chapter 53, Property Code, to which any notice of claim should be sent;

(4) if a loan has been obtained for the construction of improvements:

(A) a statement, furnished by the primary obligor and supported by reasonable and credible evidence from all applicable lenders, of the amount of the loan;

(B) a summary of the terms of the loan;

(C) a statement of whether there is foreseeable default of the primary obligor; and

(D) the name, address, and business telephone number of the borrowers and lenders; and

(5) a statement, furnished by the primary obligor and supported by reasonable and credible evidence from all applicable banks or other depository institutions, of the amount, source, and location of funds available to pay the balance of the contract amount if there is no loan or the loan is not sufficient to pay for all of the construction of the improvements.

(n) A contingent payor is considered to have exercised diligence for purposes of Subsection (k)(1) under a contract for a public project governed by Chapter 2253, Government Code, if the contingent payee receives in writing from the contingent payor:

(1) the name, address, and primary business telephone number of the primary obligor;

(2) the name and address of the surety on the payment bond provided to the primary obligor to which any notice of claim should be sent; and

(3) a statement from the primary obligor that funds are available and have been authorized for the full contract amount for the construction of the improvements.

(*o*) A contingent payor is considered to have exercised diligence for purposes of Subsection (k)(1) under a contract for a public project governed by 40 U.S.C. Section 3131 if the contingent payee receives in writing from the contingent payor:

(1) the name, address, and primary business telephone number of the primary obligor;

(2) the name and address of the surety on the payment bond provided to the primary obligor; and

(3) the name of the contracting officer, if known at the time of the execution of the contract.

(p) A primary obligor shall furnish the information described by Subsection (m) or (n), as applicable, to the contingent payor not later than the 30th day after the date the primary obligor receives a written request for the information. If the primary obligor fails to provide the information under the written request, the contingent payor, the contingent payee, and their sureties are relieved of the obligation to initiate or continue performance of the construction contracts of the contingent payor and contingent payee.

(q) The assertion of a contingent payment clause is an affirmative defense to a civil action for payment under a contract.

(r) This section does not affect a provision that affects the timing of a payment in a contract for construction management or for the construction of improvements to real property if the payment is to be made within a reasonable period.

(s) A person may not waive this section by contract or other means. A purported waiver of this section is void.

(t) An obligor or a primary obligor may not prohibit a contingent payor from allocating risk by means of a contingent payment clause.

(u) This section does not apply to a contract that is solely for:

(1) design services;

(2) the construction or maintenance of a road, highway, street, bridge, utility, water supply project, water plant, wastewater plant, water and wastewater distribution or conveyance facility, wharf, dock, airport runway or taxiway, drainage project, or related type of project associated with civil engineering construction; or

(3) improvements to or the construction of a structure that is a:

(A) detached single-family residence;

(B) duplex;

(C) triplex; or

(D) quadruplex.

Added by Acts 2007, 80th Leg., ch. 498, § 1, eff. Sept. 1, 2007.

§ 35.53. Notice of Law; Dispute Resolution Forum Applicable to Contract

(a) This section applies to a contract only if:

(1) the contract is for the sale, lease, exchange, or other disposition for value of goods for the price, rental, or other consideration of $50,000 or less;

(2) any element of the execution of the contract occurred in this state and a party to the contract is:

(A) an individual resident of this state; or

(B) an association or corporation created under the laws of this state or having its principal place of business in this state; and

(3) Section 1.301 of this code does not apply to the contract.

(b) If a contract to which this section applies contains a provision making the contract or any conflict arising under the contract subject to the laws of another state, to litigation in the courts of another state, or to arbitration in another state, the provisions must be set out conspicuously in print, type, or other form of writing that is bold-faced, capitalized, underlined, or otherwise set out in such a manner that a reasonable person against whom the provision may operate would notice. If the provision is not set out as provided by this subsection, the provision is voidable by a party against whom it is sought to be enforced.

(c) Repealed by Acts 1993, 73rd Leg., ch. 570, § 16(4), eff. Sept. 1, 1993.

Added by Acts 1987, 70th Leg., ch. 812, § 1, eff. Sept. 1, 1987. Amended by Acts 1989, 71st Leg., ch. 622, § 2, eff. Sept. 1, 1989; Acts 1989, 71st Leg., ch. 772, § 1, eff. Sept. 1, 1989; Acts 1991, 72nd Leg., ch. 840, § 1, eff. Aug. 26, 1991; Acts 1993, 73rd Leg., ch. 570, §§ 14, 16(4), eff. Sept. 1, 1993; Acts 2005, 79th Leg., ch. 728, § 2.001, eff. Sept. 1, 2005.

Repeal

Acts 2007, 80th Leg., ch. 885, § 2.47(a)(1) repeals this section effective April 1, 2009.

§ 35.531. Law Applicable to Contract Made Over Internet

(a) In this section, "Internet" means the largest nonproprietary nonprofit cooperative public computer network, popularly known as the Internet.

(b) Subject to Subsection (e), this section applies only to a contract made solely over the Internet between a person located in this state and a person located outside this state who does not maintain an office or agent in this state for doing business in this state.

(c) A contract to which this section applies is governed by the law of this state unless each party to the contract who is located in this state:

(1) is given notice that the law of the state in which another party to the contract is located applies to the contract; and

(2) agrees to the application of that state's law.

(d) A person asserting that the law of another state applies to a contract has the burden of proving that notice was given and agreement was obtained as provided by Subsection (c).

(e) Sections 1.301 and 35.53 do not apply to a contract to which this section applies. This section does not apply to a contract to which Section 35.51 applies.

Added by Acts 1999, 76th Leg., ch. 977, § 1, eff. Sept. 1, 1999. Amended by Acts 2005, 79th Leg., ch. 728, § 2.002, eff. Sept. 1, 2005.

Repeal

Acts 2007, 80th Leg., ch. 885, § 2.47(a)(1) repeals this section effective April 1, 2009.

§ 35.54. Use of Crime Victim or Motor Vehicle Accident Information for Certain Purposes Prohibited

(a) In this section:

(1) "Crime victim information" means information that is collected or prepared by a law enforcement agency that identifies or serves to identify a person who, according to the records of the law enforcement agency, may have been the victim of a crime in which physical injury to the person occurred or was attempted or in which the offender entered or attempted to enter the dwelling of the person.

(2) "Motor vehicle accident information" means information that is collected or prepared by a law enforcement agency that identifies or serves to identify a person who, according to the records of the law enforcement agency, may have been involved in a motor vehicle accident.

(b) A person who has possession of crime victim or motor vehicle accident information that the person obtained or knows was obtained from a law enforcement agency may not use the information to contact directly a person who is a crime victim or who was involved in a motor vehicle accident or a member of the person's family for the purpose of soliciting business from the person or family member and may not sell the information to another person for financial gain.

(c) The attorney general may bring an action against a person who violates Subsection (b) of this section pursuant to Section 17.47 of this code.

(d) A person who violates Subsection (b) of this section commits an offense. An offense under this subsection is a Class C misdemeanor unless the defendant has been previously convicted under this subsection more than two times, in which event the offense is a felony of the third degree.

Added by Acts 1989, 71st Leg., 1st C.S., ch. 4, § 1, eff. Jan. 1, 1990. Amended by Acts 1991, 72nd Leg., ch. 860, § 1, eff. Sept. 1, 1991.

Repeal

Acts 2007, 80th Leg., ch. 885, § 2.47(a)(1) repeals this section effective April 1, 2009.

§ 35.55. Sale of Items at Flea Market

(a) In this section, "flea market" means a location at which booths or similar spaces are rented or otherwise made available temporarily to two or more persons and at which the persons offer tangible personal property for sale.

(b) In addition to any other sanctions provided by law, a person commits an offense if the person sells or offers for sale at a flea market:

(1) infant formula or baby food of a type usually consumed by children younger than two years of age;

(2) a drug, as defined by Section 431.002, Health and Safety Code; or

(3) contact lenses, including disposable contact lenses.

(c) A person does not commit an offense under this section solely because the person provides spaces at a flea market.

(d) It is a defense to prosecution under Subsection (b) that:

(1) the person selling the item:

(A) is authorized in writing to sell the item at retail by the manufacturer of the item or the manufacturer's authorized distributor;

(B) the authorization states the person's name; and

(C) the person provides for examination the authorization to any person at the flea market who requests to see the authorization; or

(2) only a sample of the item or a catalog or brochure displaying the item was available at the flea market and the item sold was not delivered to the buyer at the flea market.

(e) A person commits an offense if the person provides to another person an authorization under Subsection (d)(1) and:

(1) the authorization is forged or contains a false statement; or

(2) the person displaying the authorization obtained the authorization by fraud.

(f) An offense under this section is a misdemeanor punishable by a fine of not more than $100.

(g) A law enforcement agency investigating a violation of this section shall maintain a record of the investigation. The record is public information.

(h) This section does not apply to the sale or offer for sale of a nutritional supplement or vitamin.

Added by Acts 1999, 76th Leg., ch. 694, § 1, eff. Sept. 1, 1999.

Repeal

Acts 2007, 80th Leg., ch. 885, § 2.47(a)(1) repeals this section effective April 1, 2009.

§ 35.56. Offense: Improperly Induced Appraisal for Mortgage Loan

(a) In this section:

(1) "Lender" means a person who lends money for or invests money in mortgage loans.

(2) "Mortgage loan" means a loan that is secured by a deed of trust, security deed, or other lien on real property.

(b) A lender commits an offense if in connection with a mortgage loan transaction the lender pays or offers to pay a person, including an individual licensed or certified by the Texas Appraiser Licensing and Certification Board or the Texas Real Estate Commission, a fee or other consideration for appraisal services and the payment:

(1) is contingent on a minimum, maximum, or pre-agreed estimate of value of property securing the loan; and

(2) interferes with the person's ability or obligation to provide an independent and impartial opinion of the property's value.

(c) An offense under this section is a Class A misdemeanor.

(d) Instructions given by a lender to a real estate appraiser regarding legal or other regulatory requirements for the appraisal of property, or any other communications between a lender or real estate appraiser necessary or appropriate under a law, regulation, or underwriting standard applicable to a real estate appraisal, do not constitute interference by a lender for purposes of Subsection (b)(2).

Added by Acts 2001, 77th Leg., ch. 839, § 1, eff. Sept. 1, 2001.

Repeal

Acts 2007, 80th Leg., ch. 885, § 2.47(a)(1) repeals this section effective April 1, 2009.

§ 35.57. Shipping Articles Without Inspection

(a) A person commits an offense if the person:

(1) exports from this state, or ships for the purpose of exportation to a state other than this state or to a foreign port, an article of commerce that by law of this state is required to be inspected by a public inspector; and

(2) does not have the article inspected as provided by law.

(b) An offense under this section is a misdemeanor punishable by a fine of not more than $100.

Added by Acts 2001, 77th Leg., ch. 1420, § 2.002(a), eff. Sept. 1, 2001. Renumbered from V.T.C.A., Bus. & C. Code § 35.49 by Acts 2003, 78th Leg., ch. 1275, § 2(2), eff. Sept. 1, 2003.

Repeal

Acts 2007, 80th Leg., ch. 885, § 2.47(a)(1) repeals this section effective April 1, 2009.

§ 35.58. Confidentiality of Social Security Number

Text of section as added by Acts 2003, 78th Leg., ch. 341, § 1

(a) A person may not print an individual's social security number on a card or other device required to access a product or service provided by the person unless the individual has requested in writing such printing. A person may not require a request for such printing as a condition to receipt of or access to a product or service provided by the person.

(b) A person who violates this section is liable to the state for a civil penalty in an amount not to exceed $500 for each violation. The attorney general or the prosecuting attorney in the county in which the violation occurs may bring suit to recover the civil penalty imposed under this section. The attorney general may bring an action in the name of the state to restrain or enjoin a person from violating this section.

(c) This section does not apply to:

(1) the collection, use, or release of a social security number that is required by state or federal law, including Chapter 552, Government Code; or

(2) the use of a social security number for internal verification or administrative purposes.

Added by Acts 2003, 78th Leg., ch. 341, § 1, eff. March 1, 2005.

For text of section as added by Acts 2003, 78th Leg., ch. 1326, § 6, see § 35.58, post.

Repeal

Acts 2007, 80th Leg., ch. 885, § 2.47(a)(1) repeals this section effective April 1, 2009.

§ 35.58. Confidentiality of Social Security Number

Text of section as added by Acts 2003, 78th Leg., ch. 1326, § 6

(a) A person, other than government or a governmental subdivision or agency, may not:

(1) intentionally communicate or otherwise make available to the general public an individual's social security number;

(2) display an individual's social security number on a card or other device required to access a product or service provided by the person;

(3) require an individual to transmit the individual's social security number over the Internet unless the connection with the Internet is secure or the number is encrypted;

(4) require an individual's social security number for access to an Internet website, unless a password or unique personal identification number or other authentication device is also required for access; or

(5) print an individual's social security number on any materials, except as provided by Subsection (f), that are sent by mail, unless state or federal law requires that the individual's social security number be included in the materials.

(b) A person that is using an individual's social security number before January 1, 2005, in a manner prohibited by Subsection (a) may continue that use if:

(1) the use is continuous; and

(2) the person provides annual disclosure to the individual, beginning January 1, 2006, stating that on written request from the individual the person will cease to use the individual's social security number in a manner prohibited by Subsection (a).

(c) A person, other than government or a governmental subdivision or agency, may not deny services to an individual because the individual makes a written request under Subsection (b).

(d) If a person receives a written request from an individual directing the person to stop using the individual's social security number in a manner prohibited by Subsection (a), the person shall comply with the request not later than the 30th day after the date the request is received. The person may not impose a fee or charge for complying with the request.

(e) This section does not apply to:

(1) the collection, use, or release of a social security number that is required by state or federal law, including Chapter 552, Government Code;

(2) the use of a social security number for internal verification or administrative purposes;

(3) documents that are recorded or required to be open to the public under Chapter 552, Government Code;

(4) court records; or

(5) an institution of higher education if the use of a social security number by the institution is regulated by Chapter 51, Education Code, or another provision of the Education Code.

(f) Subsection (a)(5) does not apply to an application or form sent by mail, including a document sent:

(1) as part of an application or enrollment process;

(2) to establish, amend, or terminate an account, contract, or policy; or

(3) to confirm the accuracy of a social security number.

Added by Acts 2003, 78th Leg., ch. 1326, § 6, eff. Jan. 1, 2005.

For text of section as added by Acts 2003, 78th Leg., ch. 341, § 1, see §§ 35.58, ante.

Repeal

Acts 2007, 80th Leg., ch. 885, § 2.47(a)(1) repeals this section effective April 1, 2009.

§ 35.581. Privacy Policy Necessary to Require Disclosure of Social Security Number

Text of section as added by Acts 2005, 79th Leg., ch. 198, § 1

(a) A person may not require an individual to disclose the individual's social security number to obtain goods or services from or enter into a business transaction with the person, unless the person:

(1) adopts a privacy policy;

(2) makes the privacy policy available to the individual; and

(3) maintains under the privacy policy the confidentiality and security of a social security number disclosed to the person.

(b) A privacy policy adopted under this section must include how personal information is collected, how and when the personal information is used, how the personal information is protected, who has access to the personal information, and how the personal information is disposed.

(c) This section does not apply to:

(1) a person who is required to maintain and disseminate a privacy policy under the Gramm–Leach–Bliley Act (15 U.S.C. Sections 6801 to 6809), the Family Educational Rights and Privacy Act (20 U.S.C. Section 1232g), or the Health Insurance Portability and Accountability Act of 1996 (42 U.S.C. Section 1320d et seq.);

(2) a covered entity under rules adopted by the commissioner of insurance relating to insurance consumer health information privacy or insurance consumer financial information privacy;

(3) a governmental body, as defined by Section 552.003, Government Code, other than a municipally owned utility;

(4) a person with respect to a loan transaction, if the person is not engaged in the business of making loans; or

(5) a person subject to Section 901.457, Occupations Code.

(d) A person who violates Subsection (a) is liable to the state for a civil penalty in an amount not to exceed $500 for each calendar month during which a violation occurs. The civil penalty may not be imposed for more than one violation that occurs in a month. The attorney general or the prosecuting attorney in the county in which the violation occurs may bring suit to recover the civil penalty imposed under this section.

(e) The attorney general may bring an action in the name of the state to restrain or enjoin a person from violating Subsection (a).

Added by Acts 2005, 79th Leg., ch. 198, § 1, eff. Sept. 1, 2005. Amended by Acts 2007, 80th Leg., ch. 93, § 1, eff. Sept. 1, 2007.

For text of section as added by Acts 2005, 79th Leg., ch. 946, § 1, see § 35.581, post.

Repeal

Acts 2007, 80th Leg., ch. 885, § 2.47(a)(1) repeals this section effective April 1, 2009.

§ 35.581. Merchant or Third Party Use of Consumer Driver's License or Social Security Numbers; Restrictions; Actions; Civil Penalty[1]

Text of section as added by Acts 2005, 79th Leg., ch. 946, § 1

(a) A merchant or a third party under contract with a merchant who requires a consumer returning an item of merchandise to provide the consumer's driver's license or social security number may use the number or numbers provided by the consumer solely for identification purposes if the consumer does not have a valid receipt for the item being returned and is seeking a cash, credit, or store credit refund.

(b) A merchant or third party under contract with a merchant may not disclose a consumer's driver's license or social security number to any other merchant or third party not involved in the initial transaction.

(c) A merchant or third party under contract with a merchant may only use a consumer's driver's license or social security number to monitor, investigate, or prosecute fraudulent return of merchandise.

(d) A merchant or third party under contract with a merchant shall destroy or arrange for the destruction of records containing the consumer's driver's license or social security number at the expiration of six months from the date of the last transaction.

(e) A person who violates this section is liable to the state for a civil penalty in an amount not to exceed $500 for each violation. The attorney general or the prosecuting attorney in the county in which the violation occurs may bring suit to recover the civil penalty imposed under this section.

(f) The attorney general may bring an action in the name of the state to restrain or enjoin a person from violating this section.

Added by Acts 2005, 79th Leg., ch. 946, § 1, eff. Sept. 1, 2005.

For text of section as added by Acts 2005, 79th Leg., ch. 198, § 1, see § 35.581, ante.

[1] Section heading editorially supplied.

Section 2 of Acts 2005, 79th Leg., ch. 946 provides:

"Section 35.581, Business & Commerce Code, as added by this Act, applies only to an item of merchandise that is returned on or after the effective date of this Act."

§ 35.585. Extension of Credit to Victim of Identity Theft

(a) In this section, "victim of identity theft" means an individual who has filed a criminal complaint alleging the commission of an offense under Section 32.51, Penal Code, other than a person who is convicted of an offense under Section 37.08, Penal Code, with respect to that complaint. A person who has been notified that an individual who has the capacity to contract has been the victim of identity theft may not deny the individual an extension of credit, including a loan, in the individual's name or restrict or limit the credit extended solely because the individual has been a victim of identity theft. This subsection does not prohibit a person from denying an individual an extension of credit for a reason other than because the individual has been a victim of identity theft.

(b) A license issued under Subtitle B, Title 4, Finance Code, that is held by a person who violates this section is subject to revocation or suspension under that subtitle.

Added by Acts 2005, 79th Leg., ch. 102, § 1, eff. Sept. 1, 2005.

Repeal

Acts 2007, 80th Leg., ch. 885, § 2.47(a)(1) repeals this section effective April 1, 2009.

§ 35.59. Verification of Consumer Identity

(a) In this section:

(1) "Consumer report" has the meaning assigned by Section 20.01.

(2) "Extension of credit" does not include an increase in the dollar limit of an existing open-end credit plan as defined by Regulation Z (12 C.F. R. Section 226.2), as amended, or any change to, or review of, an existing credit account.

(3) "Security alert" has the meaning assigned by Section 20.01.

(b) A person who receives notification of a security alert under Section 20.032 in connection with a request for a consumer report for the approval of a credit-based application, including an application for an extension of credit, a purchase, lease, or rental agreement for goods, or for an application for a noncredit-related service, may not lend money, extend credit, or authorize an application without taking reasonable steps to verify the consumer's identity.

(c) If a consumer has included with a security alert a specified telephone number to be used for identity verification purposes, a person who receives that number with a security alert must take reasonable steps to contact the consumer using that number before lending money, extending credit, or completing any purchase, lease, or rental of goods, or approving any noncredit-related services.

(d) If a person uses a consumer report to facilitate the extension of credit or for any other transaction on behalf of a subsidiary, affiliate, agent, assignee, or prospective assignee, that person, rather than the subsidiary, affiliate, agent, assignee, or prospective assignee, may verify the consumer's identity.

Added by Acts 2003, 78th Leg., ch. 1326, § 7, eff. Sept. 1, 2003.

Repeal

Acts 2007, 80th Leg., ch. 885, § 2.47(a)(1) repeals this section effective April 1, 2009.

§ 35.591. Notation of Forged Check

(a) In this section, "victim of identify theft" means a person who has filed with an appropriate law enforcement agency a criminal complaint alleging commission of an offense under Section 32.51, Penal Code.

(b) If a victim of identity theft closes an account at a financial institution as a result of the identity theft, notifies the financial institution that the identity theft is the reason for closing the account, provides the financial institution with a copy of the criminal complaint described by Subsection (a), and requests that the financial institution return checks with the notation "forgery," the financial institution shall process as forgeries the checks received after the customer takes those actions, in accordance with the financial institution's customary procedures.

(c) A victim of identity theft who requests that a financial institution return checks with the notation "forgery" as provided by Subsection (b):

(1) may not assert that the financial institution is liable under Section 4.402 for wrongfully dishonoring a check returned after the victim makes the request; and

(2) shall hold the financial institution harmless for acting in accordance with the victim's request.

Added by Acts 2005, 79th Leg., ch. 615, § 1, eff. Sept. 1, 2005.

Repeal

Acts 2007, 80th Leg., ch. 885, § 2.47(a)(1) repeals this section effective April 1, 2009.

§ 35.595. Notification to Check Verification Entities That Customer is Victim of Identity Theft

(a) In this section:

(1) "Check verification entity" means a consumer reporting agency that compiles and maintains, for businesses in this state, files on consumers on a nationwide basis regarding the consumers' check-writing history.

(2) "Financial institution" means a bank, savings association, savings bank, or credit union maintaining an office, branch, or agency office in this state.

(b) A financial institution shall submit the information as required by Subsection (c) if a customer notifies the financial institution that the customer was a victim of an offense under Section 32.51, Penal Code, requests that the financial institution close an account that has been compromised by the alleged offense, and presents to the financial institution:

(1) a copy of a police report of an offense under Section 32.51, Penal Code;

(2) a sworn statement by the person that the person was the victim of an offense under that section; and

(3) written authorization to submit the information required by Subsection (d) to the electronic notification system established under Section 11.309, Finance Code, for secure distribution to check verification entities.

(c) A financial institution that receives the documents required by Subsection (b), not later than the second business day after the date the customer provides the documents to the financial institution, shall submit the information required by Subsection (d) to the electronic notification system established under Section 11.309, Finance Code.

(d) The information submitted by a financial institution under Subsection (c) must include:

(1) the customer's name, address, phone number, date of birth, and driver's license number or government-issued identification number;

(2) the financial institution account number of any account that has been compromised by the alleged offense and has been closed in response to the alleged offense;

(3) the financial institution routing number; and

(4) the number on any check that has been lost, stolen, or compromised.

(e) A check verification entity shall maintain reasonable procedures, in accordance with rules adopted by the finance commission, to prevent the check verification entity from recommending acceptance or approval of a check or similar sight order drawn on an account identified in the notification if:

(1) the check verification entity receives notification through the electronic notification system; or

(2) a customer presents to the check verification entity:

(A) a copy of a police report of an offense under Section 32.51, Penal Code;

(B) a sworn statement by the person that the person was the victim of an offense under that section and that the person has requested that the financial institution close any account that has been compromised by the alleged offense; and

(C) the information described by Subsection (d).

(f) A financial institution or check verification entity, or an officer, director, employee, or agent of the institution or entity, is not liable for damages resulting from providing the notification required by Subsection (c) or failing to recommend acceptance or approval of a check or similar sight order under Subsection (e).

(g) The Finance Commission of Texas may adopt rules:

(1) to implement this section;

(2) to clarify the duties and responsibilities of a customer, financial institution, or check verification entity under this section; and

(3) to specify how an erroneous notification may be withdrawn, amended, or corrected.

Added by Acts 2007, 80th Leg., ch. 1044, § 1, eff. Sept. 1, 2007.

Section 3 of Acts 2007, 80th Leg., ch. 1044 provides:

"A financial institution is not required to comply with Section 35.595, Business & Commerce Code, as added by this Act, before March 1, 2008. "

§ 35.60. Identity Theft by Electronic Device

Text of section as added by Acts 2003, 78th Leg., ch. 649, § 1 and renumbered from V.T.C.A., Bus. & C. Code § 35.58 by Acts 2007, 80th Leg., ch. 921, § 17.001(6)

(a) In this section:

(1) "Payment card" means a credit card, a debit card, a check card, or any other card that is issued to an authorized user to purchase or obtain goods, services, money, or any other thing of value.

(2) "Re–encoder" means an electronic device that can be used to transfer encoded information from a magnetic strip on a payment card onto the magnetic strip of a different payment card.

(3) "Scanning device" means an electronic device used to access, read, scan, or store information encoded on the magnetic strip of a payment card.

(b) A person commits an offense if the person uses a scanning device or re-encoder to access, read, scan, store, or transfer information encoded on the magnetic strip of a payment card without the consent of an authorized user of the payment card and with intent to harm or defraud another.

(c) An offense under this section is a Class B misdemeanor.

(d) If conduct that constitutes an offense under this section also constitutes an offense under any other law, the actor may be prosecuted under this section or the other law.

Added by Acts 2003, 78th Leg., ch. 649, § 1, eff. Sept. 1, 2003. Renumbered from V.T.C.A., Bus. & C. Code § 35.58 by Acts 2007, 80th Leg., ch. 921, § 17.001(6), eff. Sept. 1, 2007.

For text of section as added by Acts 2005, 79th Leg., ch. 195, § 1, see § 35.60, post.

Repeal

Acts 2007, 80th Leg., ch. 885, § 2.47(a)(1) repeals this section effective April 1, 2009.

Acts 2005, 79th Leg., ch. 728, § 23.001, renumbered this section as § 35.60; however, this renumbering did not take effect pursuant to § 23.003 of ch. 728 which provided:

"If the number, letter, or designation assigned by Section 23.001 of this Act conflicts with a number, letter, or designation assigned by another Act of the 79th Legislature [Acts 2005, Ch. 195]: (1) the other Act controls and the change made by Section 23.001 of this Act has no effect; and (2) any cross-reference change made by Section 23.002 of this Act to conform to that change made by Section 23.001 of this Act has no effect."

§ 35.60. Warning Sign About Identity Theft for Restaurant or Bar Employees

Text of section as added by Acts 2005, 79th Leg., ch. 195, § 1

(a) In this section:

(1) "Credit card" means an identification card, plate, coupon, book, number, or any other device authorizing a designated person or bearer to obtain property or service on credit.

(2) "Debit card" means an identification card, plate, coupon, book, number, or any other device authorizing a designated person or bearer to communicate a request to an unmanned teller machine or a customer convenience terminal or obtain property or services by debit to an account at a financial institution.

(b) This section applies only to a restaurant or bar that accepts credit cards or debit cards from customers in the ordinary course of business.

(c) A restaurant or bar owner shall display in a prominent place on the premises of the restaurant or bar a sign stating in letters at least 1/2 inch high: "UNDER SECTION 32.51, PENAL CODE, IT IS A STATE JAIL FELONY (PUNISHABLE BY CONFINEMENT IN A STATE JAIL FOR NOT MORE THAN TWO YEARS) TO OBTAIN, POSSESS, TRANSFER, OR USE A CUSTOMER'S DEBIT CARD OR CREDIT CARD NUMBER WITHOUT THE CUSTOMER'S CONSENT."

(d) A restaurant or bar owner shall display the sign in English and in another language spoken by a substantial portion of the employees of the restaurant or bar as their familiar language.

(e) A restaurant or bar owner who fails to comply with this section commits an offense. An offense under this subsection is a misdemeanor punishable by a fine of not more than $25.

(f) It is a defense to prosecution under this section that the person charged produces to the court satisfactory evidence that the person displayed a sign as required by Subsection (c) not later than 48 hours after the person received a citation for an offense under Subsection (e). If the court is satisfied with the evidence produced by the person, the court shall dismiss the charge.

Added by Acts 2005, 79th Leg., ch. 195, § 1, eff. Sept. 1, 2005.

For text of section as added by Acts 2003, 78th Leg., ch. 649, § 1 and renumbered from V.T.C.A., Bus. & C. Code § 35.58 by Acts 2007, 80th Leg., ch. 921, § 17.001(6), see § 35.60, ante.

Repeal

Acts 2007, 80th Leg., ch. 885, § 2.47(a)(1) repeals this section effective April 1, 2009.

§ 35.61. Business Receipt Containing Credit Card or Debit Card Information

(a) This section does not apply to a transaction in which the sole means of recording a person's credit card or debit card account number on a receipt or other document evidencing the transaction is by handwriting or by an imprint or copy of the credit card or debit card.

(b) A person that accepts a credit card or debit card for the transaction of business may not print more than the last four digits of the credit card or debit card account number or the month and year of the credit card's or debit card's expiration date on a receipt or other document that evidences the transaction and that is provided to a cardholder.

(c) A person who provides, leases, or sells a cash register or other machine used to print receipts or other documents evidencing credit card or debit card transactions shall provide notice of the requirements of this section to the recipient, lessee, or buyer, as applicable, of the machine.

(d) A court may not certify an action brought under this section as a class action.

(e) A person who violates Subsection (b) is liable to the state for a civil penalty in an amount not to exceed $500 for each calendar month during which a violation occurs. The civil penalty may not be imposed for more than one violation that occurs in a month. The attorney general or the prosecuting attorney in the county in which the violation occurs may bring suit to recover the civil penalty imposed under this section.

(f) The attorney general may bring an action in the name of the state to restrain or enjoin a person from violating Subsection (b).

Added by Acts 2003, 78th Leg., ch. 808, § 1, eff. Sept. 1, 2003. Renumbered from V.T.C.A., Bus. & C. Code § 35.58 by Acts 2005, 79th Leg., ch. 728, § 23.001(4), eff. Sept. 1, 2005.

Repeal

Acts 2007, 80th Leg., ch. 885, § 2.47(a)(1) repeals this section effective April 1, 2009.

§ 35.62. Deletion of Certain Electronic Records Concerning a Customer Who Issues a Check

(a) This section applies only to a business that accepts checks from customers in the ordinary course of business.

(b) A business shall delete any electronic record indicating that a customer has issued a dishonored check or any other information except for the checking account number or bank routing transit number on which the business bases a refusal to accept a check from a customer not later than the 30th day after the date:

(1) the customer and the business agree that the information contained in the electronic record is incorrect; or

(2) the customer presents to the business:

(A) a report filed by the customer with a law enforcement agency stating that the dishonored check was unauthorized; and

(B) a written notice from the customer that the dishonored check was unauthorized.

(c) A business that violates Subsection (b) is liable to the state for a civil penalty of up to $1,000. The attorney general may sue to collect the penalty.

(d) The attorney general may recover reasonable expenses incurred in obtaining a civil penalty under Subsection (c), including court costs, reasonable attorney's fees, investigative costs, witness fees, and deposition expenses.

(e) In this section, "law enforcement agency" has the meaning assigned by Article 59.01, Code of Criminal Procedure.

(f) This section does not apply to a financial institution as defined by 31 U.S.C. Section 5312(a)(2), as amended.

Added by Acts 2005, 79th Leg., ch. 984, § 1, eff. Sept. 1, 2005.

Repeal

Acts 2007, 80th Leg., ch. 885, § 2.47(a)(1) repeals this section effective April 1, 2009.

SUBCHAPTER E. TERMINATION OF FARM AND INDUSTRIAL EQUIPMENT FRANCHISE [REPEALED]

§ 35.63. Sale of Plastic Bulk Merchandise Container

(a) In this section:

(1) "Plastic bulk merchandise container" means a plastic crate or shell used by a product producer, distributor, or retailer for the bulk transportation or storage of retail containers of milk, eggs, or bottled beverage products.

(2) "Proof of ownership" includes a bill of sale or other evidence showing that an item has been sold to the person possessing the item.

(b) A person who is in the business of recycling, shredding, or destroying plastic bulk merchandise containers, before purchasing five or more plastic bulk merchandise containers from the same person, shall:

(1) obtain from that person:

(A) proof of ownership for the containers; and

(B) a record that contains:

(i) the name, address, and telephone number of the person or the person's authorized representative;

(ii) the name and address of the buyer of the containers or any consignee of the containers;

(iii) a description of the containers, including the number of the containers to be sold; and

(iv) the date of the transaction; and

(2) verify the identity of the individual selling the containers or representing the seller from a driver's license or other government-issued identification card that includes the individual's photograph, and record the verification.

(c) A person shall retain a record obtained or made under this section until the first anniversary of the later of the date the containers are purchased or delivered.

(d) A person who violates Subsection (b) or (c) is liable to this state for a civil penalty of $10,000 for each violation.

(e) A person who is in the business of recycling, shredding, or destroying plastic bulk merchandise containers may not use an artifice to avoid the application of this section, including documenting purchases from the same person on the same day as multiple transactions. A person who violates this subsection is liable to this state for a civil penalty of $30,000 for each violation.

(f) The attorney general or appropriate prosecuting attorney may sue to collect a civil penalty under this section.

Added by Acts 2007, 80th Leg., ch. 307, § 1, eff. Sept. 1, 2007.

§ 35.64. Certain Uses of Name or Picture of Member of Armed Forces Prohibited

Text of section as added by Acts 2007, 80th Leg., ch. 182, § 1

(a) In this section:

(1) "Heir" means a surviving grandparent, parent, sibling, child, or grandchild of a deceased individual.

(2) "Personal representative" means an executor, independent executor, administrator, independent administrator, or temporary administrator, together with their successors.

(b) A person commits an offense if the person uses, in an advertisement for a commercial purpose, the name of an individual who is an active duty or former member of the United States armed forces, who is a member or former member of a reserve component of the United States armed forces, or who is a member or former member of the state military forces, as defined by Section 431.001, Government Code, or a picture of the individual in uniform in which the individual is clearly identifiable, without obtaining the consent of:

(1) the individual, if the individual is living; or

(2) the individual's surviving spouse or personal representative or a majority of the individual's adult heirs, if the individual is deceased.

(c) An offense under this section is a Class A misdemeanor.

(d) This section does not apply to a member of the print or broadcast media who uses a name or picture of an individual in a report of news to the public or an advertisement for that report.

Added by Acts 2007, 80th Leg., ch. 182, § 1, eff. Sept. 1, 2007.

For text of section as added by Acts 2007, 80th Leg., ch. 916, § 1, see § 35.64, post.

§ 35.64. Zip Code Verification in Credit Card Transaction

Text of section as added by Acts 2007, 80th Leg., ch. 916, § 1

(a) In this section:

(1) "Credit card" means a card or device issued under an agreement by which the issuer gives to a cardholder the right to obtain credit from the issuer or another person.

(2) "Credit card issuer" means a lender, including a financial institution, or a merchant that receives applications and issues credit cards to individuals.

(b) A business may require a customer who purchases a good or service from the business using a credit card to provide the customer's zip code to verify the customer's identity as provided by Subsection (c).

(c) A business that obtains a customer's zip code under Subsection (b) may electronically verify with the credit card issuer that the zip code matches any zip code that the credit card issuer has on file for the credit card.

(d) A business that obtains a customer's zip code under Subsection (b) may not retain the zip code in any form after the purchase of the good or service has been completed.

Added by Acts 2007, 80th Leg., ch. 916, § 1, eff. June 15, 2007.

For text of section as added by Acts 2007, 80th Leg., ch. 182, § 1, see § 35.64, ante.

§§ 35.65 to 35.68. Repealed by Acts 1991, 72nd Leg., ch. 119, § 2, eff. May 19, 1991

SUBCHAPTER F. RENTAL–PURCHASE AGREEMENTS

§ 35.71. Definitions

In this subchapter:

(1) "Advertisement" means a commercial message in any medium that directly or indirectly promotes or assists a rental-purchase agreement.

(2) "Cash price" means the price for which the merchant would have sold the merchandise to the consumer for cash on the date of the rental-purchase agreement.

(3) "Consumer" means an individual who leases personal property under a rental-purchase agreement.

(3–a) "Loss damage waiver" means a merchant's agreement not to hold a consumer liable for loss from all or part of any damage to merchandise.

(4) "Merchandise" means the personal property that is the subject of a rental-purchase agreement.

(5) "Merchant" means a person who, in the ordinary course of business, regularly leases, offers to lease, or arranges for the leasing of merchandise under a rental-purchase agreement, and includes a person who is assigned an interest in a rental-purchase agreement.

(6) "Rental-purchase agreement" means an agreement for the use of merchandise by a consumer for personal, family, or household purposes, for an initial period of four months or less that is automatically renewable with each payment after the initial period, and that permits the consumer to become the owner of the merchandise.

Added by Acts 1985, 69th Leg., ch. 209, § 1, eff. Sept. 1, 1985. Amended by Acts 2003, 78th Leg., ch. 816, § 24.001, eff. Sept. 1, 2003.

Repeal

Acts 2007, 80th Leg., ch. 885, § 2.47(a)(1) repeals this section effective April 1, 2009.

§ 35.72. Form

(a) A rental-purchase agreement must be written in plain English and in any other language used by the merchant in an advertisement related to the rental-purchase agreement. Numerical amounts must be stated in figures.

(b) Disclosures required by this subchapter must be printed or typed in each rental-purchase agreement in a size equal to at least 10-point bold-faced type. The attorney general shall provide a form agreement that may be used to satisfy the requirements of an agreement under this subchapter.

(c) A rental-purchase agreement may not contain a provision:

(1) requiring a confession of judgment;

(2) authorizing a merchant or an agent of the merchant to commit a breach of the peace in the repossession of merchandise;

(3) waiving a defense, counterclaim, or right the consumer may have against the merchant or an agent of the merchant;

(4) requiring the purchase of insurance or a loss damage waiver from the merchant to cover the merchandise;

(5) requiring the payment of a late charge or reinstatement fee unless a periodic payment is delinquent for more than seven days if the payment is due monthly, or is delinquent for more than three days if the payment is due more frequently than monthly, and the charge or fee is in an amount equal to not more than the lesser of 10 percent of the delinquent payment or $10, and not less than $5; or

(6) requiring a payment at the end of the scheduled rental-purchase term in excess of or in addition to a regular periodic payment in order to acquire ownership of the merchandise. In no event shall the consumer be required to pay a sum greater than

the total amount to be paid to acquire ownership, as disclosed in Subsection (g)(3) of this section.

(d) Only one late charge or reinstatement fee may be collected on a payment regardless of the period during which it remains in default.

(e) A rental-purchase agreement must provide that:

(1) a charge in addition to periodic payments, if any, must be reasonably related to the service performed; and

(2) a consumer who fails to make a timely payment may reinstate an agreement, without losing rights or options previously acquired, by taking the required action before the later of one week or half of the number of days in a regular payment period after the due date of the payment.

(f) Notice of the right to reinstate an agreement must be disclosed in the agreement. This subchapter does not prevent a merchant from attempting repossession of merchandise during the reinstatement period, and the consumer's right to reinstate an agreement does not expire because of such a repossession. If the merchandise is returned during the applicable reinstatement period, other than through judicial process, the right to reinstate the agreement shall be extended for a period of not less than 30 days after the date of the return of the merchandise. On reinstatement, the merchant shall provide the consumer with the same merchandise or substitute merchandise of comparable quality and condition. If substitute merchandise is provided, the merchant shall provide the consumer with the disclosures required in Subsection (g) of this section.

(g) A rental-purchase agreement must disclose:

(1) whether the merchandise is new or used;

(2) the amount and timing of payments;

(3) the total number of payments necessary and the total amount to be paid to acquire ownership of the merchandise;

(4) the amount and purpose of any payment, charge, or fee in addition to the regular periodic payments;

(5) whether the consumer is liable for loss or damage to the merchandise, and if so the maximum amount for which the consumer may be liable;

(6) that the consumer does not acquire ownership rights unless the consumer has complied with the ownership terms of the agreement; and

(7) the cash price of the merchandise.

Added by Acts 1985, 69th Leg., ch. 209, § 1, eff. Sept. 1, 1985. Amended by Acts 2003, 78th Leg., ch. 816, § 24.002, eff. Sept. 1, 2003; Acts 2005, 79th Leg., ch. 1346, § 1, eff. June 18, 2005.

Repeal

Acts 2007, 80th Leg., ch. 885, § 2.47(a)(1) repeals this section effective April 1, 2009.

Section 2 of Acts 2005, 79th Leg., ch. 1346 provides:

"The change in law made by this Act applies only to a rental-purchase agreement entered into on or after the effective date of this Act. A rental-purchase agreement entered into before the effective date of this Act is governed by the law in effect when the rental-purchase agreement was entered into, and the former law is continued in effect for that purpose."

§ 35.721. Loss Damage Waiver

(a) In addition to other charges permitted by this subchapter, a consumer may contract for a loss damage waiver. A loss damage waiver is not insurance.

(b) A merchant may not sell a loss damage waiver unless the consumer agrees to the waiver in writing. A merchant may not impose or require the purchase of a loss damage waiver as a mandatory charge.

(c) A loss damage waiver may exclude loss or damage to the merchandise that is caused by an unexplained disappearance or abandonment of the merchandise, or any other damage that is intentionally caused by the consumer or that results from the consumer's wilful or wanton misconduct.

(d) A loss damage waiver agreement must include a statement of the total charge for the loss damage waiver.

(e) A merchant may charge a periodic fee for a loss damage waiver that may not exceed 10 percent of the periodic rental payment.

(f) A contract that offers a loss damage waiver must include the following notice:

"This contract offers an optional loss damage waiver for an additional charge to cover your responsibility for loss of or damage to the merchandise. You do not have to purchase this coverage. Before deciding whether or not to purchase this loss damage waiver, you may consider whether your homeowners' or casualty insurance policy affords you coverage for loss of or damage to rental merchandise and the amount of the deductible you would pay under your policy."

(g) A merchant may not sell a loss damage waiver unless the form of the contract containing the waiver has been approved by the Texas Department of Licensing and Regulation.

(h) The Texas Commission of Licensing and Regulation shall by rule:

(1) provide the method for annual submission of all contracts, including amendments to a contract, that contain a loss damage waiver, for review by the Texas Department of Licensing and Regulation; and

(2) set a reasonable fee to be paid by the merchant for the review of contract forms under Subdivision (1) and for the administration of this subchapter by the Texas Department of Licensing and Regulation.

Added by Acts 2003, 78th Leg., ch. 816, § 24.003, eff. Sept. 1, 2003.

Repeal

Acts 2007, 80th Leg., ch. 885, § 2.47(a)(1) repeals this section effective April 1, 2009.

§ 35.722. Enforcement; Investigation; Hearing

(a) In this section:

(1) "Commission" means the Texas Commission of Licensing and Regulation.

(2) "Department" means the Texas Department of Licensing and Regulation.

(b) The department shall enforce Section 35.721 and may, as necessary, investigate a merchant who has one or more contracts that include a loss damage waiver.

(c) A person may file a complaint alleging a violation of Section 35.721 with the department. The department shall investigate the alleged violation on receipt of the complaint, and may inspect any record relevant to the complaint.

(d) If, as a result of an investigation, the department determines that a violation may have occurred, the commission shall provide an opportunity for a hearing in the manner provided for a contested case under Chapter 2001, Government Code.

(e) If, after opportunity for hearing, the commission determines that the merchant has violated Section 35.721, the commission may:

(1) impose an administrative penalty under Chapter 51, Occupations Code; or

(2) award the complainant damages in an amount up to the amount of the contract price for the merchandise.

Added by Acts 2003, 78th Leg., ch. 816, § 24.003, eff. Sept. 1, 2003.

Repeal

Acts 2007, 80th Leg., ch. 885, § 2.47(a)(1) repeals this section effective April 1, 2009.

§ 35.73. Advertisement

An advertisement for a rental-purchase agreement that refers to or states the amount of a payment or the right to acquire ownership of any one particular item under the agreement must clearly and conspicuously state:

(1) that the transaction advertised is a rental-purchase agreement;

(2) the total amount and number of payments necessary to acquire ownership; and

(3) that the consumer does not acquire ownership rights unless the merchandise is rented for a specified number of payment periods.

Added by Acts 1985, 69th Leg., ch. 209, § 1, eff. Sept. 1, 1985.

Repeal

Acts 2007, 80th Leg., ch. 885, § 2.47(a)(1) repeals this section effective April 1, 2009.

§ 35.74. Enforcement

(a) A consumer damaged by a violation of this subchapter by a merchant is entitled to recover from the merchant:

(1) actual damages;

(2) 25 percent of an amount equal to the total amount of payments required to obtain ownership of the merchandise involved, except that the amount recovered under this subdivision may not be less than $250 nor more than $1,000; and

(3) reasonable attorney's fees and court costs.

(b) A merchant is not liable under this section for a violation of this subchapter caused by the merchant's error if before the 31st day after the date the merchant discovers the error, and before an action under this section is filed or written notice of the error is received by the merchant from the consumer, the merchant gives the consumer written notice of the error and makes adjustments in the consumer's account as necessary to assure that the consumer will not be required to pay an amount in excess of the amount disclosed and that the agreement otherwise complies with this subchapter.

(c) A violation of this subchapter is a deceptive trade practice under Subchapter E of Chapter 17, Business & Commerce Code.[1]

Added by Acts 1985, 69th Leg., ch. 209, § 1, eff. Sept. 1, 1985.

[1] V.T.C.A., Bus. & C. § 17.41 et seq.

Repeal

Acts 2007, 80th Leg., ch. 885, § 2.47(a)(1) repeals this section effective April 1, 2009.

SUBCHAPTER G. SALES REPRESENTATIVES

§ 35.81. Definitions

In this subchapter:

(1) "Commission" means compensation paid a sales representative by a principal in an amount based on a percentage of the dollar amount of certain orders for or sales of the principal's product.

(2) "Principal" means a person who:

(A) manufactures, produces, imports, or distributes a product for sale;

(B) uses a sales representative to solicit orders for the product; and

(C) compensates the sales representative in whole or in part by commission.

(3) "Sales representative" means an independent contractor who solicits on behalf of a principal orders for the purchase at wholesale of the principal's product.

Added by Acts 1987, 70th Leg., ch. 318, § 1, eff. Sept. 1, 1987. Amended by Acts 1995, 74th Leg., ch. 714, § 1, eff. Sept. 1, 1995.

Repeal

Acts 2007, 80th Leg., ch. 885, § 2.47(a)(1) repeals this section effective April 1, 2009.

§ 35.82. Contract

A contract between a principal and a sales representative under which the sales representative is to solicit wholesale orders within this state must be in writing or in a computer-based medium and set forth the method by which the sales representative's commission is to be computed and paid. The principal shall provide the sales representative with a copy of the contract. A provision in the contract establishing venue for an action arising under the contract in a state other than this state is void.

Added by Acts 1987, 70th Leg., ch. 318, § 1, eff. Sept. 1, 1987. Amended by Acts 1995, 74th Leg., ch. 714, § 2, eff. Sept. 1, 1995.

Repeal

Acts 2007, 80th Leg., ch. 885, § 2.47(a)(1) repeals this section effective April 1, 2009.

§ 35.83. Payment in Absence of Contract

If a compensation agreement between a sales representative and a principal that does not comply with Section 35.82 is terminated, the principal shall pay all commissions due the sales representative within thirty working days after the date of the termination.

Added by Acts 1987, 70th Leg., ch. 318, § 1, eff. Sept. 1, 1987. Amended by Acts 1995, 74th Leg., ch. 714, § 2, eff. Sept. 1, 1995.

Repeal

Acts 2007, 80th Leg., ch. 885, § 2.47(a)(1) repeals this section effective April 1, 2009.

§ 35.84. Damages

A principal who fails to comply with a provision of a contract under Section 35.82 relating to payment of a commission or fails to pay a commission as required by Section 35.83 is liable to the sales representative in a civil action for three times the unpaid commission sustained by the sales representative plus reasonable attorney's fees and costs.

Added by Acts 1987, 70th Leg., ch. 318, § 1, eff. Sept. 1, 1987. Amended by Acts 1995, 74th Leg., ch. 714, § 2, eff. Sept. 1, 1995.

Repeal

Acts 2007, 80th Leg., ch. 885, § 2.47(a)(1) repeals this section effective April 1, 2009.

§ 35.85. Jurisdiction

A principal who is not a resident of this state and who enters into a contract subject to this subchapter is considered to be doing business in this state for purposes of the exercise of personal jurisdiction over the principal.

Added by Acts 1987, 70th Leg., ch. 318, § 1, eff. Sept. 1, 1987.

Repeal

Acts 2007, 80th Leg., ch. 885, § 2.47(a)(1) repeals this section effective April 1, 2009.

§ 35.86. Waiver

A provision of this subchapter may not be waived, whether by express waiver or by attempt to make a contract or agreement subject to the laws of another state. A waiver of a provision of this subchapter is void.

Added by Acts 1987, 70th Leg., ch. 318, § 1, eff. Sept. 1, 1987.

Repeal

Acts 2007, 80th Leg., ch. 885, § 2.47(a)(1) repeals this section effective April 1, 2009.

SUBCHAPTER H. PROTECTION OF SOUND OR IMAGE RECORDINGS OR PERFORMANCES

§ 35.91. Definitions

In this subchapter:

(1) "Fixed" means embodied in a recording or other tangible medium of expression, by or under the authority of the author, so that the matter embodied is sufficiently permanent or stable to permit it to be perceived, reproduced, or otherwise communicated for a period of more than transitory duration.

(2) "Live performance" means a recitation, rendering, or playing of a series of images, musical, spoken, or other sounds, or a combination of images and sounds, in an audible sequence.

(3) "Owner" means a person who owns the sounds fixed in a master phonograph record, master disc, master tape, master film, or other recording on which sound is or can be recorded and from which the transferred recorded sounds are directly or indirectly derived.

(4) "Recording" means a tangible medium on which sounds, images, or both are recorded or otherwise stored, including an original phonograph record, disc, tape, audio or video cassette, wire, film, or other medium now existing or developed later on which sounds, images, or both are or can be recorded or otherwise stored or a copy or reproduction that duplicates in whole or in part the original.

Added by Acts 1989, 71st Leg., ch. 339, § 1, eff. Sept. 1, 1989.

Repeal

Acts 2007, 80th Leg., ch. 885, § 2.47(a)(1) repeals this section effective April 1, 2009.

§ 35.92. Unauthorized Duplication

(a) A person commits an offense if the person:

(1) knowingly reproduces for sale or causes to be transferred any recording with intent to sell it or cause it to be sold or use it or cause it to be used for commercial advantage or private financial gain through public performance without the consent of the owner;

(2) transports within this state, for commercial advantage or private financial gain, a recording with the knowledge that the sounds have been reproduced or transferred without the consent of the owner; or

(3) advertises, offers for sale, sells, or rents, causes the sale, resale, or rental of or possesses for one or more of these purposes any recording that the person knows has been reproduced or transferred without the consent of the owner.

(b) An offense under this section is punishable by:

(1) a fine of not more than $250,000, imprisonment for not more than five years, or both, if:

(A) the offense involves at least 1,000 unauthorized recordings during a 180–day period; or

(B) the defendant has been previously convicted under this section;

(2) a fine of not more than $250,000, imprisonment for not more than two years, or both, if the offense involves more than 100 but less than 1,000 unauthorized recordings during a 180–day period; or

(3) a fine of not more than $25,000, confinement in the county jail for not more than one year, or both, for any other offense.

(c) This section does not affect the rights and remedies of a party in private litigation.

(d) This section applies only to recordings that were initially fixed before February 15, 1972. This section does not apply to any fees due ASCAP.

Added by Acts 1989, 71st Leg., ch. 339, § 1, eff. Sept. 1, 1989.

Repeal

Acts 2007, 80th Leg., ch. 885, § 2.47(a)(1) repeals this section effective April 1, 2009.

§ 35.93. Unauthorized Recording of Live Performance

(a) A person commits an offense if the person:

(1) for commercial advantage or private financial gain advertises, offers for sale, sells, rents, transports, causes the sale, resale, rental, or transportation of or possesses for one or more of these purposes a recording containing sounds of a live performance with the knowledge that the live performance has been recorded or fixed without the consent of the owner; or

(2) with the intent to sell for commercial advantage or private financial gain records or fixes or causes to be recorded or fixed on a recording a live performance with the knowledge that the live performance has been recorded or fixed without the consent of the owner.

(b) An offense under this section is punishable by:

(1) a fine of not more than $250,000, imprisonment for not more than five years, or both, if:

(A) the offense involves at least 1,000 unauthorized recordings embodying sound or at least 65 unauthorized audiovisual recordings during a 180–day period; or

(B) the defendant has been previously convicted under this section;

(2) a fine of not more than $250,000, imprisonment for not more than two years, or both, if the offense involves more than 100 but less than 1,000 unauthorized recordings embodying sound or more than seven but less than 65 unauthorized audiovisual recordings during a 180–day period; or

(3) a fine of not more than $25,000, confinement in the county jail for not more than one year, or both, for any other offense.

(c) In the absence of a written agreement or law to the contrary, the performer or performers of a live performance are presumed to own the rights to record or fix those sounds.

(d) For the purposes of this section, a person who is authorized to maintain custody and control over business records that reflect whether or not the owner of the live performance consented to having the live performance recorded or fixed is a proper witness in a proceeding regarding the issue of consent. A witness called pursuant to this section is subject to the rules of evidence relating to the competency of a witness to testify and the relevance and admissibility of the testimony offered.

(e) This section does not affect the rights and remedies of a party in private litigation.

Added by Acts 1989, 71st Leg., ch. 339, § 1, eff. Sept. 1, 1989.

Repeal

Acts 2007, 80th Leg., ch. 885, § 2.47(a)(1) repeals this section effective April 1, 2009.

§ 35.935. Unauthorized Operation of Recording Device in Motion Picture Theater

(a) In this section:

(1) "Audiovisual recording function" means the capability of a device to record or transmit a motion picture or any part of a motion picture by means of any technology now known or later developed.

(2) "Motion picture theater" means a movie theater, screening room, or other place primarily used to exhibit a motion picture.

(b) A person commits an offense if the person, with the intent to record a motion picture, knowingly operates the audiovisual recording function of any device in a motion picture theater, while the motion picture is being exhibited, without the consent of the owner of the theater.

(c) An offense under this section is a Class A misdemeanor, except that the offense is:

(1) a state jail felony if the person has been previously convicted one time of an offense under this section; or

(2) a felony of the third degree if the person has been previously convicted two or more times of an offense under this section.

(d) It is a defense to prosecution under this section that the audiovisual recording function of the device was operated solely for official law enforcement purposes.

(e) If conduct constituting an offense under this section also constitutes an offense under another law, the actor may be prosecuted under this section, the other law, or both.

(f) A person who reasonably believes that another has knowingly operated the audiovisual recording function of any device in a motion picture theater in violation of this section is privileged to detain that person in a reasonable manner and for a reasonable time to allow for the arrival of law enforcement authorities.

Added by Acts 2005, 79th Leg., ch. 46, § 1, eff. Sept. 1, 2005.

Repeal

Acts 2007, 80th Leg., ch. 885, § 2.47(a)(1) repeals this section effective April 1, 2009.

§ 35.94. Labeling

(a) A person commits an offense if, for commercial advantage or private financial gain, the person knowingly advertises, offers for sale, sells, rents, or transports, causes the sale, resale, rental, or transportation of, or possesses for any of these purposes a recording if the outside cover, box, or jacket of the recording does not clearly and conspicuously disclose the actual name and address of the manufacturer and the name of the performer or group.

(b) An offense under this section is punishable by:

(1) a fine of not more than $250,000, imprisonment for not more than five years, or both, if:

(A) the offense involves at least 65 unauthorized recordings during a 180–day period; or

(B) the defendant has been previously convicted under this section;

(2) a fine of not more than $250,000, imprisonment for not more than two years, or both, if the offense involves more than seven but less than 65 unauthorized recordings during a 180–day period; or

(3) a fine of not more than $25,000, confinement in the county jail for not more than one year, or both for any other offense.

(c) This section does not affect the rights and remedies of a party in private litigation.

Added by Acts 1989, 71st Leg., ch. 339, § 1, eff. Sept. 1, 1989.

Repeal

Acts 2007, 80th Leg., ch. 885, § 2.47(a)(1) repeals this section effective April 1, 2009.

§ 35.95. Forfeiture

If a person is convicted of a violation of this subchapter, the court in its judgment of conviction shall order the forfeiture and destruction or other disposition of:

(1) all recordings on which the conviction is based; and

(2) all implements, devices, and equipment used or intended to be used in the manufacture of the recordings on which the conviction is based.

Added by Acts 1989, 71st Leg., ch. 339, § 1, eff. Sept. 1, 1989.

Repeal

Acts 2007, 80th Leg., ch. 885, § 2.47(a)(1) repeals this section effective April 1, 2009.

§ 35.96. Remedies Cumulative

The penalties provided by this subchapter are in addition to any other penalties provided under any other law.

Added by Acts 1989, 71st Leg., ch. 339, § 1, eff. Sept. 1, 1989.

Repeal

Acts 2007, 80th Leg., ch. 885, § 2.47(a)(1) repeals this section effective April 1, 2009.

SUBCHAPTER I. PROVISION OF SOFTWARE OR SERVICES TO BLOCK OR SCREEN INTERNET MATERIAL

§ 35.101. Definitions

In this subchapter:

(1) "Freeware" means software that is distributed to a person free of charge regardless of whether use of the software is subject to certain restrictions.

(2) "Internet" means the largest nonproprietary nonprofit cooperative public computer network, popularly known as the Internet.

(3) "Interactive computer service" means any information service or system that provides or enables computer access by multiple users to the Internet.

(4) "Shareware" means copyrighted software in which the copyright owner sets certain conditions for its use and distribution, including requiring payment to the copyright owner after a person who has secured a copy of the software decides to use the software, regardless of whether the payment is for additional support or functionality for the software.

Added by Acts 1997, 75th Leg., ch. 303, § 1, eff. Sept. 1, 1997.

Repeal

Acts 2007, 80th Leg., ch. 885, § 2.47(a)(1) repeals this section effective April 1, 2009.

§ 35.102. Software or Services That Restrict Access to Certain Material on Internet

(a) A person who provides an interactive computer service to another person for a fee shall provide free of charge to each subscriber of the service in this state a link leading to fully functional shareware, freeware, or demonstration versions of software or to a service that, for at least one operating system, enables the subscriber to automatically block or screen material on the Internet.

(b) A provider is considered to be in compliance with this section if the provider places, on the provider's first page of world wide web text information accessible to a subscriber, a link leading to the software or a service described by Subsection (a). The identity of the link or other on-screen depiction of the link must appear set out from surrounding written or graphical material so as to be conspicuous.

(c) This section does not apply to the Department of Information Resources, in its capacity as the telecommunications provider for the state, and an institution of higher education, as that term is defined by Section 61.003, Education Code, that provides interactive computer service.

(d) A person who provides a link that complies with this section is not liable to a subscriber for any temporary inoperability of the link or for the effectiveness of the software or service that the person links to.

Added by Acts 1997, 75th Leg., ch. 303, § 1, eff. Sept. 1, 1997. Amended by Acts 2007, 80th Leg., ch. 937, § 2.01, eff. Sept. 1, 2007.

Repeal

Acts 2007, 80th Leg., ch. 885, § 2.47(a)(1) repeals this section effective April 1, 2009.

§ 35.103. Civil Penalty

(a) A person is liable to the state for a civil penalty of $2,000 for each day on which the person provides an interactive computer service for a fee but fails to provide a link to software or a service as required by Section 35.102. The aggregate civil penalty may not exceed $60,000.

(b) The attorney general may institute a suit to recover the civil penalty. Before filing suit, the attorney general shall give the person notice of the person's noncompliance and liability for a civil penalty. If the person complies with the requirements of Section 35.102 not later than the 30th day after the date of the notice, the violation is considered cured and the person is not liable for the civil penalty.

Added by Acts 1997, 75th Leg., ch. 303, § 1, eff. Sept. 1, 1997.

Repeal

Acts 2007, 80th Leg., ch. 885, § 2.47(a)(1) repeals this section effective April 1, 2009.

SUBCHAPTER J. WIRELESS COMMUNICATION FACILITY

§ 35.111. Definition

In this subchapter, "wireless communication facility" means an equipment enclosure, antenna, antenna support structure, and any associated facility used for the reception or transmittal of a radio frequency, microwave, or other signal for a commercial communications purpose.

Added by Acts 2003, 78th Leg., ch. 1222, § 2, eff. June 20, 2003.

Repeal

Acts 2007, 80th Leg., ch. 885, § 2.47(a)(1) repeals this section effective April 1, 2009.

§ 35.112. Notice of Construction

(a) A person proposing to construct a wireless communication facility that is taller than 100 feet shall, on or before the 30th day before the date the construction begins, mail a letter to each of the following:

(1) any airport located within three miles of the proposed facility location; and

(2) the Texas Agricultural Aviation Association.

(b) The letter must state:

(1) the legal description of the proposed site of construction, including a graphic depiction showing the location, height, longitude, latitude, pad size, roadway access, and proposed use of the wireless communication facility and location of any guy wires;

(2) at a minimum, the name, phone number, electronic mail address, if any, and mailing address of the person proposing construction of the wireless communication facility; and

(3) a phone number that is operational 24 hours a day, seven days a week, for emergency purposes.

Added by Acts 2003, 78th Leg., ch. 1222, § 2, eff. June 20, 2003.

Repeal

Acts 2007, 80th Leg., ch. 885, § 2.47(a)(1) repeals this section effective April 1, 2009.

§ 35.113. Exceptions

This subchapter does not apply to any structure whose main purpose is to provide electric service, a wireless communication facility used by an entity only for internal communications, a wireless communication facility constructed by a municipality, a wireless communication facility used for emergency communications, a radio or television reception antenna, a satellite or microwave parabolic antenna not used by a wireless communication service provider, a receive-only antenna, an antenna owned and operated by a federally licensed amateur radio station operator, a cable television company facility, a radio or television broadcasting facility, a colocation antenna, or a wireless communication facility installed for colocation purposes.

Added by Acts 2003, 78th Leg., ch. 1222, § 2, eff. June 20, 2003.

Repeal

Acts 2007, 80th Leg., ch. 885, § 2.47(a)(1) repeals this section effective April 1, 2009.

§ 35.114. Effect on Certain Ordinances

This subchapter does not preempt a local ordinance regulating a wireless communication facility.

Added by Acts 2003, 78th Leg., ch. 1222, § 2, eff. June 20, 2003.

Repeal

Acts 2007, 80th Leg., ch. 885, § 2.47(a)(1) repeals this section effective April 1, 2009.

SUBCHAPTER K. INTERNATIONAL MATCHMAKING ORGANIZATIONS

§ 35.121. Definitions

In this subchapter:

(1) "Basic rights information" means information applicable to a noncitizen, including information about human rights, immigration, and emergency assistance and resources.

(2) "Client" means a person who is a resident of the United States and who contracts with an international matchmaking organization to meet recruits.

(3) "Criminal history record information" means criminal history record information obtained from the Department of Public Safety under Subchapter F, Chapter 411, Government Code, and from the Federal Bureau of Investigation under Section 411.087, Government Code.

(4) "International matchmaking organization" means a corporation, partnership, sole proprietorship, or other legal entity that does business in the United States and offers to Texas residents dating, matrimonial, or social referral services involving recruits by:

(A) exchanging names, telephone numbers, addresses, or statistics;

(B) selecting photographs; or

(C) providing a social environment for introducing clients to recruits in a country other than the United States.

(5) "Marital history information" means a declaration of a person's current marital status, the number of times the person has been married, and whether any marriage occurred as a result of receiving services from an international matchmaking organization.

(6) "Recruit" means a person who is not a citizen or resident of the United States and who is recruited by an international matchmaking organization for the purpose of providing dating, matrimonial, or social referral services.

Added by Acts 2005, 79th Leg., ch. 728, § 2.003(a), eff. Sept. 1, 2005.

Repeal

Acts 2007, 80th Leg., ch. 885, § 2.47(a)(1) repeals this section effective April 1, 2009.

§ 35.122. Notice of Availability of Criminal History, Marital History, and Basic Rights Information

(a) An international matchmaking organization shall provide each recruit with the criminal history record information and marital history information of its clients and with basic rights information.

(b) The information under Subsection (a) must be:

(1) in the recruit's native language; and

(2) displayed in a manner that:

(A) separates the criminal history record information, the marital history information, and the basic rights information from any other information; and

(B) is highly noticeable.

Added by Acts 2005, 79th Leg., ch. 728, § 2.003(a), eff. Sept. 1, 2005.

Repeal

Acts 2007, 80th Leg., ch. 885, § 2.47(a)(1) repeals this section effective April 1, 2009.

§ 35.123. Providing Criminal History, Marital History, and Basic Rights Information

(a) An international matchmaking organization shall disseminate to a recruit the criminal history record information and marital history information of a client and the basic rights information not later than the 30th day after the date the international matchmaking organization receives the criminal history record information and the marital history information from the client.

(b) The international matchmaking organization shall provide the information to the recruit in the recruit's native language. The international matchmaking organization shall pay the costs incurred to translate the information.

Added by Acts 2005, 79th Leg., ch. 728, § 2.003(a), eff. Sept. 1, 2005.

Repeal

Acts 2007, 80th Leg., ch. 885, § 2.47(a)(1) repeals this section effective April 1, 2009.

§ 35.124. Obtaining Criminal History Record Information and Marital History Information

(a) The client shall:

(1) obtain a copy of the person's own criminal history record information;

(2) provide the criminal history record information to the international matchmaking organization; and

(3) provide to the international matchmaking organization the person's own marital history information.

(b) The international matchmaking organization shall require the client to affirm that the marital history information is complete and accurate and includes information regarding marriages, annulments, and dissolutions that occurred in another state or a foreign country.

(c) The international matchmaking organization may not provide any further services to the client or the recruit until the organization has:

(1) obtained the requested criminal history record information and marital history information; and

(2) provided the information to the recruit.

Added by Acts 2005, 79th Leg., ch. 728, § 2.003(a), eff. Sept. 1, 2005.

Repeal

Acts 2007, 80th Leg., ch. 885, § 2.47(a)(1) repeals this section effective April 1, 2009.

§ 35.125. Civil Penalty

(a) An international matchmaking organization that violates this subchapter is subject to a civil penalty not to exceed $20,000 for each violation.

(b) In determining the amount of the civil penalty, the court shall consider:

(1) any previous violations of this subchapter by the international matchmaking organization;

(2) the seriousness of the violation, including the nature, circumstances, extent, and gravity of the violation;

(3) the demonstrated good faith of the international matchmaking organization; and

(4) the amount necessary to deter future violations.

(c) The attorney general or the appropriate district or county attorney may bring an action under this section in the name of the state in a district court of Travis County or of a county in which any part of the violation occurs.

(d) A penalty collected under this section by the attorney general or a district or county attorney shall be deposited in the state treasury to the credit of the compensation to victims of crime fund under Article 56.34, Code of Criminal Procedure.

Added by Acts 2005, 79th Leg., ch. 728, § 2.003(a), eff. Sept. 1, 2005.

Repeal

Acts 2007, 80th Leg., ch. 885, § 2.47(a)(1) repeals this section effective April 1, 2009.

SUBCHAPTER L. CREDIT CARD MARKETING AT POSTSECONDARY EDUCATIONAL INSTITUTIONS

Subchapter L, Credit Card Marketing at Postsecondary Educational Institutions, consisting of §§ 35.131 to 35.137, was added by Acts 2007, 80th Leg., ch. 130, § 1.

For another Subchapter L, Protection of Customer Telephone Records, consisting of §§ 35.151 to 35.157, added by Acts 2007, 80th Leg., ch. 822, § 1, see § 35.151 et seq., post.

§ 35.131. Definitions

In this subchapter:

(1) "Campus credit card marketing activity":

(A) means any activity:

(i) conducted by an agent or employee of a credit card issuer on the campus of a postsecondary educational institution; and

(ii) designed to encourage and enable students to apply for a credit card; and

(B) includes the act of placing on the campus a display or poster together with a form that can be returned to the credit card issuer as a credit card application, even if an employee or agent of the credit card issuer is not present at the display.

(2) "Credit card" means a card or device issued under an agreement by which the issuer gives to a cardholder the right to obtain credit from the issuer or another person.

(3) "Credit card issuer" means a lender, including a financial institution, or a merchant that receives applications and issues credit cards to individuals.

(4) "Governing board" means the body charged with policy direction of any postsecondary educational institution, including a board of directors, a board of regents, a board of trustees, and an independent school district board that is charged with policy direction of a public junior college.

(5) "Postsecondary educational institution" means:

(A) an institution of higher education as defined by Section 61.003, Education Code;

(B) a private or independent institution of higher education as defined by Section 61.003, Education Code; or

(C) a private postsecondary educational institution as defined by Section 61.302, Education Code.

Added by Acts 2007, 80th Leg., ch. 130, § 1, eff. Sept. 1, 2007.

§ 35.132. Campus Credit Card Marketing Activity Outside Designated Location or Time Prohibited

(a) A credit card issuer may not engage in campus credit card marketing activities:

(1) outside of a campus location designated by the governing board of the postsecondary educational institution for that purpose in accordance with Subsection (b); or

(2) at a time other than a time designated by the governing board in accordance with Subsection (b).

(b) The governing board of a postsecondary educational institution may designate:

(1) one or more locations on campus where a credit card issuer may engage in campus credit card marketing activities; and

(2) one or more times during which a credit card issuer may engage in campus credit card marketing activities.

Added by Acts 2007, 80th Leg., ch. 130, § 1, eff. Sept. 1, 2007.

§ 35.133. Credit Card Issuer to Develop Financial Educational Material

A credit card issuer who conducts campus credit card marketing activities shall develop financial educational material in consultation with or subject to approval by the postsecondary educational institution. The financial educational material must include a clear and practical explanation of:

(1) effective money management skills, including how to develop and maintain a budget;

(2) key financial terms and phrases related to credit cards and personal debt management;

(3) credit educational materials and programs offered by the credit card issuer that are available to student cardholders after they have opened an account;

(4) resources to assist students in understanding credit reports and credit scores and the consequences of irresponsible credit card use; and

(5) the importance of responsible credit practices, including timely paying the minimum amount due each month and reducing costs by paying as much of the balance as possible.

Added by Acts 2007, 80th Leg., ch. 130, § 1, eff. Sept. 1, 2007.

§ 35.134. Credit Card Issuer to Provide Financial Educational Material

A credit card issuer that conducts campus credit card marketing activities shall:

(1) during the time that the credit card issuer conducts the credit card marketing activity on the campus, make available to students, on the campus, financial educational material developed under Section 35.133;

(2) make financial educational material similar to material developed under Section 35.133 available on the Internet; and

(3) provide to a student to whom a credit card is issued, at the time the credit card is provided to the student, financial educational material developed under Section 35.133.

Added by Acts 2007, 80th Leg., ch. 130, § 1, eff. Sept. 1, 2007.

§ 35.135. Restriction on Gifts or Incentives for Completing Credit Card Application

A credit card issuer may not offer a gift or other incentive in exchange for the completion of a credit card application as part of a campus credit card marketing activity unless the credit card issuer, at the time the credit card issuer provides a credit card application to an individual, provides financial educational material developed under Section 35.133 to the individual.

Added by Acts 2007, 80th Leg., ch. 130, § 1, eff. Sept. 1, 2007.

§ 35.136. Credit Card and Debt Education at New Student Orientation

The governing board of a postsecondary educational institution that has designated a location for campus credit card marketing activities under Section 35.132(b) shall also adopt a policy requiring a credit card and debt education and counseling session to be included in any orientation program for new students. The postsecondary educational institution may use existing educational materials prepared by nonprofit entities for purposes of the credit card and debt education and counseling session.

Added by Acts 2007, 80th Leg., ch. 130, § 1, eff. Sept. 1, 2007.

§ 35.137. Civil Penalty

A person who intentionally violates this subchapter is liable to the state for a civil penalty in an amount not to exceed $2,500 for each violation. The attorney general or the prosecuting attorney in the county in which the violation occurs may bring suit to recover the civil penalty imposed under this section.

Added by Acts 2007, 80th Leg., ch. 130, § 1, eff. Sept. 1, 2007.

SUBCHAPTER L. PROTECTION OF CUSTOMER TELEPHONE RECORDS

Subchapter L, Protection of Customer Telephone Records, consisting of §§ 35.151 to 35.157, was added by Acts 2007, 80th Leg., ch. 822, § 1.

For another Subchapter L, Credit Card Marketing at Postsecondary Educational Institutions, consisting of §§ 35.131 to 35.137, added by Acts 2007, 80th Leg., ch. 130, § 1, see § 35.131 et seq., ante.

§ 35.151. Definitions

In this subchapter:

(1) "Caller identification record" means a record that:

(A) is delivered electronically to the recipient of a telephone call simultaneously with the reception of the call; and

(B) indicates the telephone number from which the telephone call was made or other similar information regarding the call.

(2) "Telephone company" means a provider of commercial telephone services, or a provider that bills for those services, regardless of the technology used to provide that service, including landline, radio, wireless, microwave, satellite, Voice over Internet Protocol (VoIP), or other cable, broadband, or digital technology.

(3) "Telephone record" means a written, electronic, or oral record, other than a caller identification record collected and retained by or on behalf of a customer, created by a telephone company about a customer, that includes:

(A) the telephone number:

(i) dialed by a customer; or

(ii) of an incoming call made to a customer;

(B) the time a call was made to or by a customer;

(C) the duration of a call made to or by a customer; or

(D) the location from which a call was initiated or at which a call was received by a customer.

Added by Acts 2007, 80th Leg., ch. 822, § 1, eff. Sept. 1, 2007.

§ 35.152. Construction of Subchapter

This subchapter does not apply to expand the obligations or duties of a telephone company under federal or other state law to protect telephone records.

Added by Acts 2007, 80th Leg., ch. 822, § 1, eff. Sept. 1, 2007.

§ 35.153. Unauthorized or Fraudulent Procurement, Sale, or Receipt of Telephone Records

(a) A person commits an offense if the person:

(1) obtains, attempts to obtain, or conspires with another to obtain a telephone record of a resident of this state without the authorization of the resident to whom the record pertains by:

(A) making a statement the person knows to be false to an agent of a telephone company;

(B) making a statement the person knows to be false to a telephone company;

(C) fraudulently accessing the record through the telephone company's Internet website; or

(D) providing to a telephone company a document that the person knows:

(i) is fraudulent;

(ii) has been lost or stolen;

(iii) has been obtained by fraud; or

(iv) contains a false, fictitious, or fraudulent statement or representation;

(2) asks another person to obtain a telephone record of a resident of this state knowing that the record will be obtained in a manner prohibited by this section;

(3) sells, transfers, or attempts to sell or transfer a telephone record of a resident of this state without authorization of the resident to whom the record pertains; or

(4) offers to obtain or offers to sell a telephone record that has been or will be obtained without authorization from the resident to whom the record pertains.

(b) An offense under this section is a Class A misdemeanor, except that a fine shall not exceed $20,000.

(c) In addition to the penalties provided by Subsection (b), a person convicted of an offense under this section may be required to forfeit personal property used or intended to be used in violation of this section.

(d) In addition to the penalties provided by Subsections (b) and (c), a person convicted of an offense under this section shall be ordered to pay to a resident whose telephone record was obtained in a manner prohibited by this section an amount equal to the sum of:

(1) the greater of the resident's financial loss, if proof of the loss is submitted to the satisfaction of the court, or $1,000; and

(2) the amount of any financial gain received by the person as the direct result of the offense.

(e) An offense under this section may be prosecuted in:

(1) the county in which the customer whose telephone record is the subject of the prosecution resided at the time of the offense; or

(2) any county in which any part of the offense took place regardless of whether the defendant was ever present in the county.

(f) If venue lies in more than one county under Subsection (e), a defendant may be prosecuted in only one county for the same conduct.

(g) If conduct constituting an offense under this section also constitutes an offense under another section of this code or of any other law, including the Penal Code, the actor may be prosecuted under either section or under both sections.

(h) This section does not create a private right of action.

Added by Acts 2007, 80th Leg., ch. 822, § 1, eff. Sept. 1, 2007.

§ 35.154. Exceptions

Section 35.153 does not apply to:

(1) a person who acted pursuant to a valid court order, warrant, subpoena, or civil investigative demand;

(2) a telephone company that disclosed a telephone record:

(A) the disclosure of which is otherwise authorized by law;

(B) reasonably believing the disclosure was necessary to:

(i) provide service to a customer;

(ii) protect an individual from fraudulent, abusive, or unlawful use of a telephone record or telephone service; or

(iii) protect the rights or property of the company;

(C) to the National Center for Missing and Exploited Children in connection with a report submitted under 42 U.S.C. Section 13032;

(D) for purposes of testing the company's security procedures or systems for maintaining the confidentiality of customer information;

(E) to a governmental entity, if the company reasonably believed that an emergency involving danger of death or serious physical injury to a person justified disclosure of the information;

(F) in connection with the sale or transfer of all or part of the company's business, the purchase or acquisition of all or part of another company's business, or the migration of a customer from one telephone company to another telephone company;

(G) necessarily incident to the rendition of the service, to initiate, render, bill, and collect the customer's charges, or to protect the customer of those services and other carriers from fraudulent, abusive, or unlawful use of, or subscription to, such services; or

(H) while acting reasonably and in good faith, notwithstanding a later determination that the action was not authorized; or

(3) a person or a telephone company that acted in connection with the official duties of a 9-1-1 governmental entity or a public agency solely for purposes of delivering or assisting in the delivery of 9-1-1 emergency services and other emergency services.

Added by Acts 2007, 80th Leg., ch. 822, § 1, eff. Sept. 1, 2007.

§ 35.155. Deceptive Trade Practice; Enforcement

A violation of this subchapter is a false, misleading, or deceptive act or practice under Section 17.46 and is subject to action only by the consumer protection division of the attorney general's office as provided by Section 17.46(a).

Added by Acts 2007, 80th Leg., ch. 822, § 1, eff. Sept. 1, 2007.

§ 35.156. Consistency With Federal Law

This subchapter may not be construed in a manner that is inconsistent with 18 U.S.C. Section 1038, 47 U.S.C. Section 222, or any other applicable federal law or rule.

Added by Acts 2007, 80th Leg., ch. 822, § 1, eff. Sept. 1, 2007.

§ 35.157. Nonapplicability to Law Enforcement Agencies

This subchapter does not prohibit any lawfully authorized investigative, protective, or intelligence activity of a law enforcement agency of the United States, a state, or a political subdivision of a state or of an intelligence agency of the United States.

Added by Acts 2007, 80th Leg., ch. 822, § 1, eff. Sept. 1, 2007.

CHAPTER 36. ASSUMED BUSINESS OR PROFESSIONAL NAME

SUBCHAPTER A. GENERAL PROVISIONS

SUBCHAPTER B. ASSUMED BUSINESS OR PROFESSIONAL NAME CERTIFICATE

SUBCHAPTER C. CIVIL AND CRIMINAL PENALTIES

Acts 2007, 80th Leg., ch. 885, § 2.47(a)(1) repeals this chapter effective April 1, 2009.

SUBCHAPTER A. GENERAL PROVISIONS

§ 36.01. Short Title

This chapter may be cited as the Assumed Business or Professional Name Act.

Added by Acts 1977, 65th Leg., p. 1095, ch. 403, § 1, eff. Aug. 29, 1977.

Repeal

Acts 2007, 80th Leg., ch. 885, § 2.47(a)(1) repeals this section effective April 1, 2009.

§ 36.02. Definitions

In this chapter, unless the context otherwise requires:

(1) "Partnership" means a joint venture or general partnership other than a limited partnership or a registered limited liability partnership.

(2) "Company" means a real estate investment trust, joint-stock company, or any other business, professional, or other association or legal entity that is not incorporated other than a partnership, limited partnership, limited liability company, or registered limited liability partnership.

(3) "Corporation" means a domestic or foreign corporation, professional corporation, professional association, other corporation, or any other business, professional, or other association or legal entity that is incorporated.

(4) "Person" includes an individual, partnership, limited partnership, limited liability company, registered limited liability partnership, company, or corporation.

(5) "Representative" means a trustee, administrator, executor, independent executor, guardian, conservator, trustee in bankruptcy, receiver, or any other person appointed by a court or by trust or will to have custody of, take possession of, have title to, or otherwise be empowered to control the person or property of any person.

(6) "Estate" means the property of any person which is administered by a representative.

(7) "Assumed name" means:

(A) in the case of an individual, a name that does not include the surname of the individual;

(B) in the case of a partnership, a name that does not include the surname or other legal name of each joint venturer or general partner;

(C) in the case of an individual or a partnership, a name, including a surname, that suggests the existence of additional owners by including words such as "Company," "& Company," "& Son," "& Sons," "& Associates," "Brothers," and the like, but not words that merely describe the business or professional service being conducted or rendered;

(D) in the case of a limited partnership, any name other than the name stated in its certificate of limited partnership;

(E) in the case of a company, any name used by the company;

(F) in the case of a corporation, any name other than the name stated in its articles of incorporation or association or comparable document;

(G) in the case of a registered limited liability partnership, any name other than the name stated in its application filed with the office of the Secretary of State or comparable document; and

(H) in the case of a limited liability company, any name other than the name stated in its articles of organization or comparable document.

(8) "Registrant" means any person that has filed, or on whose behalf there has been filed, an assumed name certificate under the provisions of this chapter or other law.

(9) "Office" means, in the case of any person that is not an individual or that is a corporation which is not required to or does not maintain a registered office in this state, the principal office of such person and also its principal place of business if not the same as its principal office. In the case of a corporation, limited partnership, registered limited liability partnership, or limited liability company which is required to maintain a registered office in this state, "office" means the registered office and also its principal office if not the same as its registered office.

(10) "Address" means a post office address and also the street address if not the same as the post office address.

Added by Acts 1977, 65th Leg., p. 1095, ch. 403, § 1, eff. Aug. 29, 1977. Amended by Acts 1993, 73rd Leg., ch. 215, § 1.29, eff. Sept. 1, 1993.

Repeal

Acts 2007, 80th Leg., ch. 885, § 2.47(a)(1) repeals this section effective April 1, 2009.

§ 36.03. Exclusion of Insurance Companies

The provisions of this chapter shall not apply to any insurance company as described in Subchapter A, Chapter 805, Insurance Code, which is authorized to do business in this state except as such code shall specifically provide.

Added by Acts 1977, 65th Leg., p. 1096, ch. 403, § 1, eff. Aug. 29, 1977. Amended by Acts 2003, 78th Leg., ch. 1276, § 10A.506, eff. Sept. 1, 2003.

Repeal

Acts 2007, 80th Leg., ch. 885, § 2.47(a)(1) repeals this section effective April 1, 2009.

[Sections 36.04 to 36.09 reserved for expansion]

SUBCHAPTER B. ASSUMED BUSINESS OR PROFESSIONAL NAME CERTIFICATE

§ 36.10. For Unincorporated Business or Profession Other than a Limited Partnership, Registered Limited Liability Partnership, or Limited Liability Company

(a) Any person who regularly conducts business or renders professional services other than as a corporation, limited partnership, registered limited liability partnership, or limited liability company in this state under an assumed name shall file in the office of the county clerk in each county in which such person has or will maintain business or professional premises or, if no business or professional premises are or will be maintained in any county, in each county where such person conducts business or renders a professional service, a certificate setting forth:

(1) the assumed name under which such business or professional service is or is to be conducted or rendered;

(2) if the registrant is:

(A) an individual, his full name and residence address;

(B) a partnership, (i) the venture or partnership name, (ii) the venture or partnership office address, and (iii) the full name of each joint venturer or general partner and his residence address if he is an individual or its office address if not an individual;

(C) an estate, (i) the name of the estate, (ii) the estate's office address, if any, and (iii) the full name of each representative of the estate and his residence address if he is an individual or its office address if not an individual;

(D) a real estate investment trust, (i) the name of the trust, (ii) the address of the trust, (iii) the full name of each trustee manager and his residence address if he is an individual and its office address if not an individual; or

(E) a company other than a real estate investment trust, or a corporation, (i) the name of the company or corporation, (ii) the state, country, or other jurisdiction under the laws of which it was organized, incorporated, or associated, and (iii) its office address;

(3) the period, not to exceed 10 years, during which the assumed name will be used; and

(4) a statement specifying that the business or professional service that is or is to be conducted or rendered in the county under such assumed name is being or will be conducted or rendered as a proprietorship, sole practitioner, partnership, real estate investment trust, joint-stock company, or some other form of unincorporated business or professional association or entity, other than a limited partnership, limited liability company, or registered limited liability partnership, as the case may be.

(b) A certificate filed under Subsection (a) of this section shall be executed and acknowledged by each individual whose name is required to be stated therein or by his representative or attorney in fact, and in the case of any person not an individual the name of which is required to be stated therein, the certificate shall be executed and acknowledged under oath on behalf of such person by its representative or attorney in fact or by a joint venturer, general partner, trustee manager, officer, or anyone having comparable authority, as the case may be, of such person. Any certificate executed and acknowledged by an attorney in fact shall include a statement that such attorney in fact has been duly authorized in writing by his principal to execute and acknowledge the same.

Added by Acts 1977, 65th Leg., p. 1096, ch. 403, § 1, eff. Aug. 29, 1977. Amended by Acts 1993, 73rd Leg., ch. 215, § 1.30, eff. Sept. 1, 1993.

Repeal

Acts 2007, 80th Leg., ch. 885, § 2.47(a)(1) repeals this section effective April 1, 2009.

§ 36.11. For Incorporated Business or Profession, Limited Partnership, Registered Limited Liability Partnership, or Limited Liability Company

(a) Any corporation, limited partnership, registered limited liability partnership, or limited liability company which regularly conducts business or renders professional services in this state under an assumed name, or which may be required by law to use an assumed name in this state to conduct such business or render such services, shall file in the office of the Secretary of State and, (1) if such corporation, limited partnership, registered limited liability partnership, or limited liability company is required to maintain a registered office in this state, in the office of the county clerk of the county in which such registered office is located and of the county in which its principal office is located if within this state and not the same county where the registered office is located; or (2) if such corporation, limited partnership, registered limited liability partnership, or limited liability company is not required to or does not maintain a registered office in this state, in the office of the county clerk of the county in which its office within this state is located or if the corporation, limited partnership, registered limited liability partnership, or limited liability company is not incorporated, organized, or associated under the laws of this state, in the office of the county clerk of the county in which its principal place of business in this state is located if not the same as its office, a certificate setting forth:

(1) the assumed name under which such business or professional service is or is to be conducted or rendered;

(2) the name of the corporation, limited partnership, registered limited liability partnership, or limited liability company as stated in its articles of incorporation, association, or organization or in its certificate of limited partnership or application filed with the office of the Secretary of State, or other comparable document;

(3) the state, country, or other jurisdiction under the laws of which it was incorporated, organized, or associated and address of its registered or similar office in that state, country, or jurisdiction;

(4) the period, not to exceed 10 years, during which the assumed name will be used;

(5) a statement specifying that the entity is a business corporation, nonprofit corporation, professional corporation, professional association, or other type of corporation, limited partnership, registered limited liability partnership, limited liability company, or some other type of incorporated business, professional or other association, or legal entity;

(6) if the corporation, limited partnership, registered limited liability partnership, or limited liability company is required to maintain a registered office in this state, (A) the address of such registered office and the name of its registered agent at such address, and (B) the address of its principal office if not the same as that of its registered office in this state;

(7) if the corporation, limited partnership, registered limited liability partnership, or limited liability company is not required to or does not maintain a registered office in this state, its office address in this state and if the corporation, limited partnership, registered limited liability partnership, or limited liability company is not incorporated, organized, or associated under the laws of this state, the address of its place of business in this state and its office address elsewhere, if any; and

(8) the county or counties within the state where business or professional services are being or are to be conducted or rendered under such assumed name.

(b) A certificate filed in the office of the Secretary of State under Subsection (a) of this section shall be executed by an officer, general partner, member, manager, representative, or attorney in fact for the corporation, limited partnership, registered limited liability partnership, or limited liability company. A certificate executed by an attorney in fact shall include a statement that the attorney in fact has been duly authorized in writing by his principal to execute the same. A certificate filed in the office of the county clerk under Subsection (a) of this section shall be executed and acknowledged in the manner provided by Section 36.10(b) of this code for a certificate filed under that section.

(c) Nothing in this chapter shall require a corporation, limited partnership, registered limited liability partnership, or limited liability company or its shareholders, associates, partners, or members to file an assumed business or professional name certificate in order to conduct business or render a professional service within this state under the name of the corporation, limited partnership, registered limited liability partnership, or limited liability company as stated in its articles of incorporation, association, or organization, certificate of limited partnership, application filed with the office of the Secretary of State, or other comparable document.

(d) Notwithstanding Subsections (a)–(c) of this section, a limited partnership, registered limited liability partnership, or limited liability company that filed a certificate in compliance with Section 36.10 of this chapter before September 1, 1993, is not required to file a new certificate that complies with this section until the earlier of:

(1) the expiration of the period specified in the existing certificate during which the assumed name will be used; or

(2) a material change occurs in the information set forth in the existing certificate.

Added by Acts 1977, 65th Leg., p. 1097, ch. 403, § 1, eff. Aug. 29, 1977. Amended by Acts 1993, 73rd Leg., ch. 215, § 1.31, eff. Sept. 1, 1993; Acts 1999, 76th Leg., ch. 327, § 1, eff. Sept. 1, 1999.

Repeal

Acts 2007, 80th Leg., ch. 885, § 2.47(a)(1) repeals this section effective April 1, 2009.

§ 36.12. Material Change in Information; New Certificate

(a) Whenever an event occurs that causes the information in a certificate filed pursuant to this chapter by a person conducting business or rendering a professional service under an assumed name in this state to become materially misleading, a new certificate complying with Section 36.10 or Section 36.11 of this chapter, as the case may be, shall be filed in the office of the county clerk and of the Secretary of State, if applicable, in which an original or renewal certificate was filed. The new certificate shall be filed within 60 days after the occurrence of the events which necessitates its filing.

(b) An event that causes the information contained in a certificate filed under this chapter to become materially misleading includes such matters as:

(1) a change in the name, identity, entity, form of business or professional organization, or location of a registrant;

(2) in the case of a proprietorship or sole practitioner, a change in ownership;

(3) in the case of a partnership, the admission of a new partner or joint venturer or whenever any general partner or joint venturer ceases to be associated with the partnership; or

(4) in the case of a registrant that is required by law to maintain a registered or similar office and a registered or similar agent at such office, a change in the address of such office or identity of such agent.

(c) A new certificate filed under this section shall be effective for a term not to exceed 10 years from the date it is filed.

Added by Acts 1977, 65th Leg., p. 1098, ch. 403, § 1, eff. Aug. 29, 1977.

Repeal

Acts 2007, 80th Leg., ch. 885, § 2.47(a)(1) repeals this section effective April 1, 2009.

§ 36.13. Duration and Renewal of Certificate

(a) A certificate filed pursuant to this chapter in the office of the county clerk and of the Secretary of State, if applicable, by any person conducting business or rendering a professional service under an assumed name in this state shall be effective for a term not to exceed 10 years from the date the certificate is filed.

(b) At the end of the stated term, not to exceed 10 years, the certificate shall become null and void and of no effect, unless within six months prior to its expiration a renewal certificate complying with the provisions of this chapter for an original certificate shall be filed in the office of the county clerk and of the Secretary of State, if applicable.

(c) A registrant may renew a certificate under this section for any number of successive terms, but each such term shall not exceed 10 years in duration.

Added by Acts 1977, 65th Leg., p. 1099, ch. 403, § 1, eff. Aug. 29, 1977. Amended by Acts 1999, 76th Leg., ch. 327, § 2, eff. Sept. 1, 1999.

Repeal

Acts 2007, 80th Leg., ch. 885, § 2.47(a)(1) repeals this section effective April 1, 2009.

§ 36.14. Abandonment of Use of Assumed Business or Professional Name

(a) A registrant that has filed an assumed business or professional name certificate under this chapter which ceases to transact business or render professional services under the assumed name stated in such certificate in this state may file in the office of the county clerk and of the Secretary of State, if applicable, where such certificate has been filed, a statement of abandonment of use of a business or professional name setting forth:

(1) the assumed business or professional name being abandoned;

(2) the date on which the certificate was filed in the office in which such statement is being filed and any other filing office or offices, if any, where the certificate has been filed; and

(3) the registrant's name and residence or office address as would be required to be stated if the certificate were being presently filed.

(b) A statement filed under Subsection (a) of this section shall be executed and acknowledged in the same manner as would be required if the registrant were filing an assumed business or professional name certificate under this chapter.

Added by Acts 1977, 65th Leg., p. 1100, ch. 403, § 1, eff. Aug. 29, 1977.

Repeal

Acts 2007, 80th Leg., ch. 885, § 2.47(a)(1) repeals this section effective April 1, 2009.

§ 36.15. Index of Certificates; Filing Fees

Each county clerk and the Secretary of State shall keep an alphabetical index of all assumed names which have been filed in his office pursuant to the provisions of this chapter and of the persons filing the same. The county clerk shall receive a fee of $2 for filing each certificate or statement required or permitted to be filed pursuant to this chapter, plus a fee of 50 cents for each name to be indexed. The Secretary of State shall collect for the use of the state a fee of $25 for indexing and filing each certificate or statement required or permitted to be filed pursuant to this chapter. The Secretary of State shall collect for the use of the state a fee of $10 for filing each abandonment of use of assumed name. A copy of such certificate or statement duly certified to by the county clerk in whose office the same was filed or by the Secretary of State shall be presumptive evidence in all courts in this state of the facts therein contained.

Added by Acts 1977, 65th Leg., p. 1100, ch. 403, § 1, eff. Aug. 29, 1977. Amended by Acts 1981, 67th Leg., p. 752, ch. 284, § 1, eff. Aug. 31, 1981; Acts 1983, 68th Leg., p. 314, ch. 69, § 9, eff. Sept. 1, 1983.

Repeal

Acts 2007, 80th Leg., ch. 885, § 2.47(a)(1) repeals this section effective April 1, 2009.

§ 36.16. Prescribed Forms

The Secretary of State may prescribe the forms to be used for filing any assumed business or professional name certificate or statement that complies with this chapter in his office or in the office of any county clerk in this state. The use of such forms, however, shall not be mandatory unless otherwise specifically provided by law.

Added by Acts 1977, 65th Leg., p. 1100, ch. 403, § 1, eff. Aug. 29, 1977.

Repeal

Acts 2007, 80th Leg., ch. 885, § 2.47(a)(1) repeals this section effective April 1, 2009.

§ 36.17. Effect of Filing

Nothing in this chapter shall be construed to give a registrant of an assumed business or professional name any right to use the name when contrary to the common law or statutory law of unfair competition, unfair trade practices, common law copyright, or similar law. The mere filing of an assumed business or professional name certificate pursuant to this chapter shall not constitute actual use of the assumed name set out therein for purposes of determining priority of rights.

Added by Acts 1977, 65th Leg., p. 1100, ch. 403, § 1, eff. Aug. 29, 1977.

Repeal

Acts 2007, 80th Leg., ch. 885, § 2.47(a)(1) repeals this section effective April 1, 2009.

§ 36.18. Filing of Reproduction

The Secretary of State may accept for filing a photographic, photostatic, or similarly reproduced copy of a signed original document required or authorized to be filed in the office of the Secretary of State under this chapter. A signature on a document required or authorized to be filed in the office of the Secretary of State under this chapter may be a facsimile.

Added by Acts 1999, 76th Leg., ch. 327, § 3, eff. Sept. 1, 1999.

Repeal

Acts 2007, 80th Leg., ch. 885, § 2.47(a)(1) repeals this section effective April 1, 2009.

[Sections 36.19 to 36.24 reserved for expansion]

SUBCHAPTER C. CIVIL AND CRIMINAL PENALTIES

§ 36.25. Civil Penalties

Failure to comply with the provisions of this chapter by any person shall not impair the validity of any contract or act by such person nor prevent such person from defending any action or proceeding in any court of this state, but such person shall not maintain an action or proceeding in any court of this state arising out of a contract or act in which an assumed name was used until an original, new, or renewed assumed business or professional name certificate has been filed as required by this chapter. In an action or proceeding brought against a person that has not complied with this chapter, the plaintiff or other party bringing the suit or proceeding may recover, if the court shall so determine, expenses incurred, including attorney's fees, in locating and effecting service of process on such person.

Added by Acts 1977, 65th Leg., p. 1100, ch. 403, § 1, eff. Aug. 29, 1977.

Repeal

Acts 2007, 80th Leg., ch. 885, § 2.47(a)(1) repeals this section effective April 1, 2009.

§ 36.26. Criminal Penalty—General Violation

(a) A person conducting business or rendering a professional service in this state under an assumed name who intentionally violates a provision of this chapter commits an offense.

(b) An offense under this section is a Class A misdemeanor.

Added by Acts 1977, 65th Leg., p. 1101, ch. 403, § 1, eff. Aug. 29, 1977. Amended by Acts 1979, 66th Leg., p. 867, ch. 391, § 1, eff. Aug. 27, 1979; Acts 1999, 76th Leg., ch. 327, § 4, eff. Sept. 1, 1999.

Repeal

Acts 2007, 80th Leg., ch. 885, § 2.47(a)(1) repeals this section effective April 1, 2009.

§ 36.27. Criminal Penalty—Fraudulent Filing

(a) A person may not knowingly or intentionally sign and present for filing or cause to be presented for filing a document authorized or required to be filed under this chapter if the document:

(1) indicates that the person signing the document has the authority to act on behalf of the entity for which the document is presented and the person does not have that authority;

(2) contains a material false statement; or

(3) is forged.

(b) A person who violates Subsection (a) of this section commits an offense. An offense under this subsection is punishable as if it were an offense under Section 37.10, Penal Code.

Added by Acts 1999, 76th Leg., ch. 327, § 5, eff. Sept. 1, 1999.

Repeal

Acts 2007, 80th Leg., ch. 885, § 2.47(a)(1) repeals this section effective April 1, 2009.

CHAPTER 37. TELEPHONE SOLICITATION

Acts 2007, 80th Leg., ch. 885, § 2.47(a)(1) repeals this chapter effective April 1, 2009.

§ 37.01. Definitions

In this chapter:

(1) "Automated dialing announcing device" means automated equipment used for telephone solicitation or collection that is capable:

(A) of storing telephone numbers to be called or has a random or sequential number generator capable of producing numbers to be called; and

(B) alone or in conjunction with other equipment, of conveying a prerecorded or synthesized voice message to the number called without the use of a live operator.

(2) "Consumer" means a person who is solicited to purchase, lease, or receive a consumer good or service.

(3) "Consumer good or service" means:

(A) real property or tangible or intangible personal property that is normally used for personal, family, or household purposes, including personal property intended to be attached to or installed in any real property;

(B) a cemetery lot;

(C) a time-share estate; and

(D) a service related to real or personal property.

(4) "Consumer telephone call" means an unsolicited call made to a residential telephone number by a telephone solicitor to:

(A) solicit a sale of a consumer good or service;

(B) solicit an extension of credit for a consumer good or service; or

(C) obtain information that will or may be used to directly solicit a sale of a consumer good or service or to extend credit for the sale.

(5) "Telephone solicitor" means a person who makes or causes to be made a consumer telephone call, including a call made by an automated dialing device.

Added by Acts 1991, 72nd Leg., ch. 494, § 1, eff. Jan. 1, 1992.

Repeal

Acts 2007, 80th Leg., ch. 885, § 2.47(a)(1) repeals this section effective April 1, 2009.

§ 37.02. Solicitor Identity; Permissible Hours; Disconnect

(a) A telephone solicitor may not make a consumer telephone call to a consumer unless:

(1) the telephone solicitor identifies himself or herself by name and identifies the business on whose behalf the telephone solicitor is calling and the purpose of the call immediately after making contact with the consumer to whom the call is made;

(2) the telephone solicitor makes the call after 12 noon or before 9 p.m. on a Sunday or after 9 a.m. and before 9 p.m. on a weekday or a Saturday; and

(3) for those calls in which an automated dial announcing device is used, the device must disconnect the consumer's telephone line within the period provided by Section 55.126, Utilities Code, after termination of the call by either the telephone solicitor or the consumer.

(b) A consumer telephone call is not subject to the provisions of Subsection (a) of this section if the call is made:

(1) in response to the express request of the consumer;

(2) primarily in connection with an existing debt or contract for which payment or performance has not been completed at the time of the call; or

(3) to a consumer with whom the telephone solicitor has a prior or existing business relationship.

Added by Acts 1991, 72nd Leg., ch. 494, § 1, eff. Jan. 1, 1992. Amended by Acts 1999, 76th Leg., ch. 667, § 1, eff. Sept. 1, 1999.

Repeal

Acts 2007, 80th Leg., ch. 885, § 2.47(a)(1) repeals this section effective April 1, 2009.

§ 37.03. Charges to Consumer Credit Account

A person who sells consumer goods and services through the use of a telephone solicitor may not make or submit a charge to a consumer's credit card account unless:

(1) the seller provides that the consumer may receive a full refund for the return of undamaged and unused goods or a cancellation of services by providing notice to the seller not later than the seventh day after the date the consumer receives the goods or services and in which the seller will process:

(A) a refund not later than the 30th day after the date the seller receives the returned merchandise from the consumer;

(B) a full refund not later than the 30th day after the purchaser of services cancels an order for the purchase of services not performed or a pro rata refund for any services not yet performed for the consumer;

(2) the seller provides to the consumer a written contract fully describing the goods or services being offered, the total price to be charged, the name, address, and business phone of the seller, and any terms or conditions affecting the sale and receives from the consumer a signed copy of such contract; or

(3) the seller is an organization that qualifies for and has obtained an exemption from federal income tax from the Internal Revenue Service under Section 501(c)(3), Internal Revenue Code of 1986 (26 U.S.C. Section 501(c)(3)).

Added by Acts 1991, 72nd Leg., ch. 494, § 1, eff. Jan. 1, 1992.

Repeal

Acts 2007, 80th Leg., ch. 885, § 2.47(a)(1) repeals this section effective April 1, 2009.

§ 37.04. Enforcement

(a) The attorney general's office shall investigate a complaint relating to a violation of this chapter and may petition a district court for a temporary restraining order to restrain a continuing violation of this chapter and for the assessment of a civil penalty as provided by Section 37.05 of this code.

(b) A district court, on petition of the attorney general's office and on a finding by the court that a person is violating this chapter may, by injunction, prohibit a person from continuing a violation of this chapter or grant any other injunctive relief warranted by the facts.

(c) Venue for a suit brought under this chapter is in:

(1) the county in which the consumer telephone call originated;

(2) the county in which the consumer telephone call was received; or

(3) Travis County.

Added by Acts 1991, 72nd Leg., ch. 494, § 1, eff. Jan. 1, 1992.

Repeal

Acts 2007, 80th Leg., ch. 885, § 2.47(a)(1) repeals this section effective April 1, 2009.

§ 37.05. Civil Penalty

(a) A person who knowingly violates this chapter is liable for a civil penalty of not more than $10,000 for each violation.

(b) In addition to bringing an action for injunctive relief, the attorney general may also seek restitution and civil penalties as provided herein.

(c) A consumer injured by a violation of this chapter may bring any action for recovery of damages. The damages awarded may not be less than the amount paid by the buyer to the telephone solicitor, plus reasonable attorney fees and court costs.

Added by Acts 1991, 72nd Leg., ch. 494, § 1, eff. Jan. 1, 1992.

Repeal

Acts 2007, 80th Leg., ch. 885, § 2.47(a)(1) repeals this section effective April 1, 2009.

CHAPTER 38. REGULATION OF TELEPHONE SOLICITATION

SUBCHAPTER A. GENERAL PROVISIONS

Acts 2007, 80th Leg., ch. 885, § 2.47(a)(1) repeals this chapter effective April 1, 2009.

SUBCHAPTER A. GENERAL PROVISIONS

§ 38.001. Definitions

In this chapter:

(1) "Item" means property or service and includes a coupon book that is to be used with a business or company.

(2) "Owner" means a person who has control of or is entitled to, by ownership or other claim, at least 10 percent of the net income of a seller.

(3) "Purchaser" means a person who is:

(A) solicited to become or becomes obligated for the purchase or rental of an item; or

(B) offered the opportunity to claim or receive an item.

(4) "Salesperson" means a person employed or authorized by a seller to make a telephone solicitation.

(5) "Seller" means a person who makes a telephone solicitation on the person's own behalf.

(6) "Supervised financial institution" means a bank, trust company, savings and loan association, credit union, industrial loan company, personal property broker, consumer finance lender, commercial finance lender, insurer, or other financial institution that is subject to supervision by an official or agency of this state or the United States.

(7) "Telephone solicitation" means a telephone call initiated by a seller or salesperson to or from a person for the purpose of inducing the person to purchase, rent, claim, or receive an item. The term includes a call made by a purchaser in response to a solicitation sent by mail or made by any other means.

Added by Acts 1997, 75th Leg., ch. 1008, § 2, eff. Sept. 1, 1997.

Repeal

Acts 2007, 80th Leg., ch. 885, § 2.47(a)(1) repeals this section effective April 1, 2009.

§ 38.002. Making Telephone Solicitation

In this chapter, a person makes a telephone solicitation if the person effects or attempts to effect a telephone solicitation, including a solicitation initiated by an automatic dialing machine or a recorded message device.

Added by Acts 1997, 75th Leg., ch. 1008, § 2, eff. Sept. 1, 1997.

Repeal

Acts 2007, 80th Leg., ch. 885, § 2.47(a)(1) repeals this section effective April 1, 2009.

§ 38.003. Construction and Application

This chapter shall be liberally construed and applied to promote its underlying purpose to protect persons against false, misleading, or deceptive practices in the telephone solicitation business.

Added by Acts 1997, 75th Leg., ch. 1008, § 2, eff. Sept. 1, 1997.

Repeal

Acts 2007, 80th Leg., ch. 885, § 2.47(a)(1) repeals this section effective April 1, 2009.

[Sections 38.004 to 38.050 reserved for expansion]

SUBCHAPTER B. EXEMPTIONS

§ 38.051. Claim of Exemption

(a) In a civil proceeding alleging a violation of this chapter, the burden of proving an exemption is on the person claiming the exemption.

(b) In a criminal proceeding alleging a violation of this chapter, the burden of producing evidence to support a defense of an exemption is on the person claiming the exemption.

Added by Acts 1997, 75th Leg., ch. 1008, § 2, eff. Sept. 1, 1997.

Repeal

Acts 2007, 80th Leg., ch. 885, § 2.47(a)(1) repeals this section effective April 1, 2009.

§ 38.052. Exemptions Apply to Seller

The exemptions provided by this chapter apply only to a seller engaging in a telephone solicitation on the seller's own behalf.

Added by Acts 1997, 75th Leg., ch. 1008, § 2, eff. Sept. 1, 1997.

Repeal

Acts 2007, 80th Leg., ch. 885, § 2.47(a)(1) repeals this section effective April 1, 2009.

§ 38.053. Persons or Items Regulated by Other Law

This chapter does not apply to:

(1) a person offering or selling a security that has been qualified for sale under Section 7, The Securities Act (Article 581–7, Vernon's Texas Civil Statutes), or that is subject to an exemption under Section 5 or 6 of that Act;

(2) a publicly traded corporation registered with the Securities and Exchange Commission or the State Securities Board, or a subsidiary or agent of the corporation;

(3) a person licensed under the Insurance Code if the solicited transaction is governed by the Insurance Code;

(4) a supervised financial institution or parent, subsidiary, or affiliate of a supervised financial institution;

(5) a person or affiliate of a person whose business is regulated by the Public Utility Commission of Texas, except that this chapter applies to a person or affiliate of a person who is regulated by the Public Utility Commission of Texas only with respect to one or more automated dial announcing devices;

(6) a person subject to the control or licensing regulations of the Federal Communications Commission;

(7) a person selling a contractual plan regulated by the Federal Trade Commission trade regulation on use of negative option plans by sellers in commerce under 16 C.F.R. Part 425;

(8) a person subject to the filing requirements of Chapter 1803, Occupations Code; or

(9) a person soliciting a transaction regulated by the Commodity Futures Trading Commission if the person is registered or temporarily licensed for that activity with the Commodity Futures Trading Commission under the Commodity Exchange Act (7 U.S.C. Section 1 et seq.) and the registration or license has not expired or been suspended or revoked.

Added by Acts 1997, 75th Leg., ch. 1008, § 2, eff. Sept. 1, 1997. Amended by Acts 2001, 77th Leg., ch. 1420, § 14.730, eff. Sept. 1, 2001.

Repeal

Acts 2007, 80th Leg., ch. 885, § 2.47(a)(1) repeals this section effective April 1, 2009.

§ 38.054. Media and Subscription Services and Certain Catalogs

This chapter does not apply to:

(1) a person soliciting the sale of a subscription to:

(A) a daily or weekly newspaper of general circulation;

(B) a magazine or other periodical of general circulation; or

(C) a cable television service;

(2) a person selling merchandise under an arrangement in which the seller periodically ships the merchandise to a consumer who has consented in advance to receive the merchandise periodically; or

(3) a person who periodically issues and delivers catalogs to potential purchasers if the catalog:

(A) includes a written description or illustration and the sales price of each item offered for sale;

(B) includes at least 24 full pages of written material or illustrations;

(C) is distributed in more than one state; and

(D) has an annual circulation of at least 250,000 customers.

Added by Acts 1997, 75th Leg., ch. 1008, § 2, eff. Sept. 1, 1997.

Repeal

Acts 2007, 80th Leg., ch. 885, § 2.47(a)(1) repeals this section effective April 1, 2009.

§ 38.055. Certain Nonprofit and Educational Organizations

This chapter does not apply to an educational institution or organization or a nonprofit organization exempt from taxation under Section 501(c)(3), Internal Revenue Code of 1986.

Added by Acts 1997, 75th Leg., ch. 1008, § 2, eff. Sept. 1, 1997.

Repeal

Acts 2007, 80th Leg., ch. 885, § 2.47(a)(1) repeals this section effective April 1, 2009.

§ 38.056. Certain Commercial Sales

This chapter does not apply to a sale in which the purchaser is a business that intends to:

(1) resell the item purchased; or

(2) use the item purchased in a recycling, reuse, remanufacturing, or manufacturing process.

Added by Acts 1997, 75th Leg., ch. 1008, § 2, eff. Sept. 1, 1997.

Repeal

Acts 2007, 80th Leg., ch. 885, § 2.47(a)(1) repeals this section effective April 1, 2009.

§ 38.057. Food

This chapter does not apply to a person soliciting the sale of food.

Added by Acts 1997, 75th Leg., ch. 1008, § 2, eff. Sept. 1, 1997.

Repeal

Acts 2007, 80th Leg., ch. 885, § 2.47(a)(1) repeals this section effective April 1, 2009.

§ 38.058. Solicitation of Current or Former Customers

This chapter does not apply to:

(1) the solicitation of contracts for the maintenance or repair of items previously purchased from the person making the solicitation or on whose behalf the solicitation is made; or

(2) a person soliciting business from a former or current customer if the person has operated under the exact same business name for at least two years.

Added by Acts 1997, 75th Leg., ch. 1008, § 2, eff. Sept. 1, 1997.

Repeal

Acts 2007, 80th Leg., ch. 885, § 2.47(a)(1) repeals this section effective April 1, 2009.

§ 38.059. Promotions at Established Retail Sales Locations or at Consumer's Residence

This chapter does not apply to:

(1) a person soliciting:

(A) without intent to complete or obtain provisional acceptance of a sale during the telephone solicitation;

(B) who does not make the major sales presentation during the telephone solicitation but arranges for the major sales presentation to be made at a later face-to-face meeting between the salesperson and the purchaser; and

(C) who does not cause an individual to go to the prospective purchaser to collect payment for the purchase or to deliver an item purchased directly following the telephone solicitation; or

(2) a person who for at least two years has been operating under the same name as that used in connection with its telemarketing operations a retail establishment where consumer goods are displayed and offered for sale continuously if a majority of the person's business involves the buyers obtaining services or products at the person's retail establishment.

Added by Acts 1997, 75th Leg., ch. 1008, § 2, eff. Sept. 1, 1997.

Repeal

Acts 2007, 80th Leg., ch. 885, § 2.47(a)(1) repeals this section effective April 1, 2009.

§ 38.060. Certain Solicitation Services Having Predominately Exempt Customers

(a) This chapter does not apply to a person:

(1) who provides telephone solicitation services under contract to sellers;

(2) who has been operating continuously for at least three years under the same business name; and

(3) for whom at least 75 percent of the person's contracts are performed on behalf of other persons exempt under this section.

(b) Notwithstanding Section 38.052, the exemption provided by this section applies to a person providing telephone solicitation services to sellers.

Added by Acts 1997, 75th Leg., ch. 1008, § 2, eff. Sept. 1, 1997.

Repeal

Acts 2007, 80th Leg., ch. 885, § 2.47(a)(1) repeals this section effective April 1, 2009.

§ 38.061. Certain Isolated Solicitations

This chapter does not apply to a person engaging in a commercial telephone solicitation that is an isolated transaction and not done in the course of a pattern of repeated transactions of a similar nature.

Added by Acts 1997, 75th Leg., ch. 1008, § 2, eff. Sept. 1, 1997.

Repeal

Acts 2007, 80th Leg., ch. 885, § 2.47(a)(1) repeals this section effective April 1, 2009.

[Sections 38.062 to 38.100 reserved for expansion]

SUBCHAPTER C. REGISTRATION

§ 38.101. Registration Required

(a) A seller may not engage in telephone solicitation from a location in this state or to a purchaser located in this state without a registration certificate for the business location from which the solicitation is made.

(b) A separate registration certificate is required for each business location from which a solicitation is made.

Added by Acts 1997, 75th Leg., ch. 1008, § 2, eff. Sept. 1, 1997.

Repeal

Acts 2007, 80th Leg., ch. 885, § 2.47(a)(1) repeals this section effective April 1, 2009.

§ 38.102. Contents of Registration Statement; Verification; Public Information

(a) A seller must file a registration statement with the secretary of state to obtain a registration certificate.

(b) A registration statement must be in the form prescribed by the secretary of state and contain the information required by Subchapter D.[1]

(c) A registration statement must be verified by each principal of the seller and must specify the date and location of verification.

(d) The information included in or attached to a registration statement is public information.

(e) In this section, "principal" means an owner, an executive officer of a corporation, a general partner of a partnership, a sole proprietor, a trustee of a trust, or another individual with similar supervisory functions with respect to any person.

Added by Acts 1997, 75th Leg., ch. 1008, § 2, eff. Sept. 1, 1997.

[1] V.T.C.A., Bus. & C. § 38.151 et seq.

Repeal

Acts 2007, 80th Leg., ch. 885, § 2.47(a)(1) repeals this section effective April 1, 2009.

§ 38.103. Filing Fee

The filing fee for a registration statement is $200.

Added by Acts 1997, 75th Leg., ch. 1008, § 2, eff. Sept. 1, 1997.

Repeal

Acts 2007, 80th Leg., ch. 885, § 2.47(a)(1) repeals this section effective April 1, 2009.

§ 38.104. Issuance of Certificate of Registration

(a) The secretary of state shall issue a registration certificate and mail the certificate to the seller on receipt of:

(1) a completed registration statement;

(2) the registration statement filing fee;

(3) the security required by Section 38.107; and

(4) the consent regarding service of process required by Section 38.108.

(b) If the seller uses one registration statement to register more than one business location, the secretary of state shall issue a registration certificate for each business location and mail all the certificates to the principal business location shown on the registration statement.

Added by Acts 1997, 75th Leg., ch. 1008, § 2, eff. Sept. 1, 1997.

Repeal

Acts 2007, 80th Leg., ch. 885, § 2.47(a)(1) repeals this section effective April 1, 2009.

§ 38.105. Effective Date; Renewal

(a) A registration statement becomes effective on the date that the secretary of state issues the registration certificate.

(b) A registration statement is effective for one year and may be renewed annually by:

(1) filing a renewal registration statement with the information required by Subchapter D;[1] and

(2) paying the registration statement filing fee.

Added by Acts 1997, 75th Leg., ch. 1008, § 2, eff. Sept. 1, 1997.

[1] V.T.C.A., Bus. & C. § 38.151 et seq.

Repeal

Acts 2007, 80th Leg., ch. 885, § 2.47(a)(1) repeals this section effective April 1, 2009.

§ 38.106. Update Addendum Required

(a) A seller shall file with the secretary of state an addendum for each quarter after the effective date of the registration providing the required registration information for each salesperson who is soliciting or has solicited on behalf of the seller during the preceding quarter.

(b) A seller may comply with Subsection (a) by providing a copy of the "Employer's Quarterly Report" for employee wages the seller files with the Texas Workforce Commission.

(c) In addition to the quarterly addendum, if a material change in information submitted in a registration statement, other than the information described by Subsection (a), occurs before the date for renewal, a seller shall submit that information to the secretary of state by filing an addendum.

Added by Acts 1997, 75th Leg., ch. 1008, § 2, eff. Sept. 1, 1997.

Repeal

Acts 2007, 80th Leg., ch. 885, § 2.47(a)(1) repeals this section effective April 1, 2009.

§ 38.107. Security

(a) A registration statement filed under this chapter must be accompanied by:

(1) a bond executed by a corporate surety approved by the secretary of state and licensed to do business in this state;

(2) an irrevocable letter of credit issued for the benefit of the registrant by a supervised financial institution whose deposits are insured by an agency of the federal government; or

(3) a certificate of deposit in a supervised financial institution whose deposits are insured by an agency of the federal government, the principal of which may be withdrawn only on the order of the secretary of state.

(b) The bond, letter of credit, or certificate of deposit must be:

(1) in the amount of $10,000; and

(2) conditioned on the seller's compliance with this chapter.

Added by Acts 1997, 75th Leg., ch. 1008, § 2, eff. Sept. 1, 1997.

Repeal

Acts 2007, 80th Leg., ch. 885, § 2.47(a)(1) repeals this section effective April 1, 2009.

§ 38.108. Secretary of State as Seller's Agent to Receive Service

(a) A seller shall file with the secretary of state, in the form prescribed by the secretary of state, an irrevocable consent appointing the secretary of state to act as the seller's agent to receive service of process in a noncriminal suit, action, or proceeding against the seller or the seller's successor, executor, or administrator that may arise under this chapter if:

(1) an agent has not been designated under Section 38.151(15);

(2) the agent has resigned or died and a replacement has not been designated under Section 38.106; or

(3) the agent cannot with reasonable diligence be found at the designated address.

(b) Service on the secretary of state under this section has the same effect as service on the seller. Service on the secretary of state may be made by:

(1) leaving a copy of the process in the office of the secretary of state;

(2) promptly sending by first-class mail a notice of the service and a copy of the process to the seller's principal business location at the last address on file with the secretary of state; and

(3) filing the plaintiff's affidavit of compliance with this section in the case on or before the return date of the process, if any, or within an additional period that the court allows.

Added by Acts 1997, 75th Leg., ch. 1008, § 2, eff. Sept. 1, 1997.

Repeal

Acts 2007, 80th Leg., ch. 885, § 2.47(a)(1) repeals this section effective April 1, 2009.

[Sections 38.109 to 38.150 reserved for expansion]

SUBCHAPTER D. DISCLOSURES REQUIRED IN REGISTRATION STATEMENT

§ 38.151. Disclosure of Certain Names, Addresses, and Organizational Information

A registration statement must contain:

(1) the seller's name and the name under which the seller is doing or intends to do business, if different from the seller's name;

(2) the name of each parent and affiliated organization of the seller that:

(A) will engage in business transactions with purchasers relating to sales solicited by the seller; or

(B) accepts responsibility for statements made by, or acts of, the seller relating to sales solicited by the seller;

(3) the seller's business form and place of organization;

(4) if the seller is a corporation, a copy of its articles of incorporation and bylaws;

(5) if the seller is a partnership, a copy of the partnership agreement;

(6) if the seller is operating under an assumed business name, the location where the assumed name has been registered;

(7) for any parent or affiliated organization disclosed under Subdivision (2), the applicable information that is required of a seller under Subdivisions (3)–(6);

(8) the complete street address of each location of the seller, designating the principal location from which the seller will be conducting business;

(9) if the principal business location of the seller is not in this state, a designation of its main location in the state;

(10) a listing of each telephone number to be used by the seller and the address where each telephone using the number is located;

(11) the name and title of each of the seller's officers, directors, trustees, general and limited partners, sole proprietor, and owners, as applicable, and the name of each of those persons who has management responsibilities in connection with the seller's business activities;

(12) the complete address of the principal residence, the date of birth, and the number and state of issuance of the driver's license of each person whose name is disclosed under Subdivision (11);

(13) the name and principal residence address of each person the seller leaves in charge at each location from which the seller does business in this state and the business location at which each of these persons is or will be in charge;

(14) the name and principal residence address of each salesperson who solicits on behalf of the seller or a copy of the "Employer's Quarterly Report" for employee wages the seller files with the Texas Workforce Commission and the name the salesperson uses while soliciting;

(15) the name and address of the seller's agent in this state, other than the secretary of state, authorized to receive service of process; and

(16) the name and address of each financial institution with which banking or similar monetary transactions are made by the seller and the identification number of each of the seller's accounts in each institution.

Added by Acts 1997, 75th Leg., ch. 1008, § 2, eff. Sept. 1, 1997.

Repeal

Acts 2007, 80th Leg., ch. 885, § 2.47(a)(1) repeals this section effective April 1, 2009.

§ 38.152. Disclosure of Certain Convictions, Judgments, Orders, and Bankruptcies

(a) With respect to the seller and each person identified under Section 38.151(11) or (13), a registration statement must state the identity of each person:

(1) who has been convicted of or pleaded nolo contendere to:

(A) a felony or misdemeanor involving an alleged violation of this chapter; or

(B) fraud, theft, embezzlement, fraudulent conversion, or misappropriation of property;

(2) against whom a final judgment or order has been entered in a civil or administrative action, including a stipulated judgment or order, in which the complaint or petition alleged:

(A) acts constituting a violation of this chapter, fraud, theft, embezzlement, fraudulent conversion, or misappropriation of property;

(B) the use of untrue or misleading representations in an attempt to sell or dispose of property; or

(C) the use of unfair, unlawful, or deceptive business practices;

(3) who is subject to an injunction or restrictive court order relating to business activity as the result of an action brought by a federal, state, or local public agency, including an action affecting a vocational license; or

(4) who has, during the previous seven tax years:

(A) filed in bankruptcy;

(B) been adjudged a bankrupt;

(C) been reorganized due to insolvency; or

(D) been a principal, director, officer, trustee, general or limited partner of, or had management responsibilities for, a corporation, partnership, joint venture, or other business entity that has filed in bankruptcy, been adjudged a bankrupt, or been reorganized due to insolvency while the person held that position or within one year after the date on which the person last held that position.

(b) Under Subsections (a)(1), (2), and (3), the statement must identify the:

(1) court or administrative agency rendering the conviction, judgment, or order;

(2) docket number of the matter;

(3) date of conviction, judgment, or order; and

(4) name of the governmental agency, if any, that brought the action resulting in the conviction, judgment, or order.

(c) Under Subsection (a)(4), the statement must include the:

(1) name and location of the person filing in bankruptcy, adjudged a bankrupt, or reorganized due to insolvency;

(2) date of the filing, judgment, or reorganization order;

(3) court having jurisdiction; and

(4) docket number of the matter.

Added by Acts 1997, 75th Leg., ch. 1008, § 2, eff. Sept. 1, 1997.

Repeal

Acts 2007, 80th Leg., ch. 885, § 2.47(a)(1) repeals this section effective April 1, 2009.

§ 38.153. Disclosure of Certain Sales Information

The registration statement must be accompanied by:

(1) a description of the items the seller is offering for sale;

(2) a copy of all sales information and literature, including scripts, outlines, instructions, and information regarding the conduct of telephone solicitations, sample introductions, sample closings, product information, and contest or premium-award information, provided by the seller to salespersons or about which the seller informs salespersons;

(3) a copy of all written material the seller sends to any purchaser;

(4) if the seller represents or implies, or directs salespersons to represent or imply, to purchasers that the purchaser will receive a specific item, including a certificate that the purchaser must redeem to obtain the item described in the certificate, or one or more items from among designated items, whether the items are designated as gifts, premiums, bonuses, prizes, or otherwise:

(A) a list of the items described;

(B) the value of each item and the basis for the valuation;

(C) the price paid by the seller to its supplier for each item and the name, address, and telephone number of each item's supplier;

(D) if the purchaser is to receive fewer than all of the items described by the seller:

(i) the manner in which the seller decides which item a particular purchaser is to receive;

(ii) for each item, the odds of a single purchaser's receiving the item; and

(iii) the name and address of each recipient who has received, during the preceding 12 months or, if the seller has not been in business that long, during the period the seller has been in business, the item having the greatest value and the item with the smallest odds of being received; and

(E) all rules, regulations, and terms a purchaser must meet to receive the item;

(5) if the seller is offering an item that the seller does not manufacture or supply:

(A) the name, address, and telephone number of each of the seller's suppliers and a description of each item provided by the supplier;

(B) if the possession of the item is to be retained by the seller or will not be transferred to the purchaser until the purchaser has paid in full:

(i) the address of each location where the item will be kept;

(ii) if not kept on premises owned by the seller or at an address registered under Section 38.151(8) or (9), the name of the owner of the business at which the item will be kept; and

(iii) a copy of any contract or other document that evidences the seller's right to store the item at the address designated under Subparagraph (ii);

(C) if the seller is not selling the item from its own inventory but purchases the item to fill an order already taken from a purchaser, copies of all contracts or other documents evidencing the seller's ability to call on suppliers to fill the seller's orders;

(D) if the seller represents to purchasers that the seller has insurance or a surety bond relating to a purchaser's purchase of an item, a copy of each insurance policy and bond; and

(E) if the seller makes a representation as to the post-purchase earning or profit potential of an item, data to substantiate the claims made and, if the representation relates to previous sales made by the seller or a related entity, substantiating data based on the experiences of at least 50 percent of the persons who purchased that particular type of item from the seller or related entity during the preceding six months or, if the seller or related entity has not been in business that long, during the period the seller or related entity has been in business, including:

(i) the period the seller or related entity has been selling the particular type of item being offered;

(ii) the number of purchasers of the item from the seller or related entity known to the seller or related entity to have made at least the same earnings or profit as those represented; and

(iii) the percentage that the number disclosed under Subparagraph (ii) represents of the total number of purchasers from the seller or related entity of the particular type of item offered; and

(6) if the seller is offering to sell an interest in an oil, gas, or mineral field, well, or exploration site:

(A) the seller's ownership interest, if any, in each field, well, or site being offered for sale;

(B) the total number of interests to be sold in each field, well, or site being offered for sale; and

(C) if, in selling an interest in any particular field, well, or site, reference is made to an investigation of the field, well, or site by the seller or anyone else:

(i) the name, business address, telephone number, and professional credentials of the person who made the investigation; and

(ii) a copy of the report and other documents relating to the investigation prepared by the person.

Added by Acts 1997, 75th Leg., ch. 1008, § 2, eff. Sept. 1, 1997.

Repeal

Acts 2007, 80th Leg., ch. 885, § 2.47(a)(1) repeals this section effective April 1, 2009.

[Sections 38.154 to 38.200 reserved for expansion]

SUBCHAPTER E. ADDITIONAL INFORMATION FROM SELLER

§ 38.201. Information Posted or Available at Seller's Business Location

(a) A seller shall post the registration certificate in a conspicuous place at the location for which it is issued.

(b) A seller shall make available at each of the seller's business locations a copy of the entire registration statement and addenda, if any, for inspection by a purchaser or representative of a governmental agency.

(c) A seller shall post in close proximity to the registration certificate the name of each individual in charge of the location.

Added by Acts 1997, 75th Leg., ch. 1008, § 2, eff. Sept. 1, 1997.

Repeal

Acts 2007, 80th Leg., ch. 885, § 2.47(a)(1) repeals this section effective April 1, 2009.

§ 38.202. Disclosures to Prospective Purchasers

A seller shall, when the solicitation is made and before consummation of any sales transaction, provide to each purchaser:

(1) the complete street address of the location from which the salesperson is calling the purchaser and, if different, the complete street address of the seller's principal location;

(2) if the seller represents or implies that a purchaser will receive without charge a specified item or one item from among designated items, whether the items are designated as gifts, premiums, bonuses, prizes, or otherwise:

(A) the information required to be filed by Sections 38.153(4)(D)(i), (D)(ii), and (E), as appropriate; and

(B) the total number of individuals who have actually received from the seller during the preceding 12 months or, if the seller has not been in the business that long, during the period the seller has been in business the item having the greatest value and the item with the smallest odds of being received;

(3) if the seller is offering to sell an interest in an oil, gas, or mineral field, well, or exploration site, the information required by Section 38.153(6); and

(4) if the seller represents that an item is being offered at a price below that usually charged for the item, the name of the manufacturer of the item.

Added by Acts 1997, 75th Leg., ch. 1008, § 2, eff. Sept. 1, 1997.

Repeal

Acts 2007, 80th Leg., ch. 885, § 2.47(a)(1) repeals this section effective April 1, 2009.

§ 38.203. Reference to Compliance With Statute Prohibited

A seller may not make or authorize the making of a reference to its compliance with this chapter to a purchaser.

Added by Acts 1997, 75th Leg., ch. 1008, § 2, eff. Sept. 1, 1997.

Repeal

Acts 2007, 80th Leg., ch. 885, § 2.47(a)(1) repeals this section effective April 1, 2009.

[Sections 38.204 to 38.250 reserved for expansion]

SUBCHAPTER F. OFFENSES

§ 38.251. Violation of Chapter

(a) A person commits an offense if the person knowingly violates Section 38.101, 38.106, 38.201, 38.202, or 38.203. Each violation constitutes a separate offense.

(b) An offense under this section is a Class A misdemeanor.

Added by Acts 1997, 75th Leg., ch. 1008, § 2, eff. Sept. 1, 1997.

Repeal

Acts 2007, 80th Leg., ch. 885, § 2.47(a)(1) repeals this section effective April 1, 2009.

§ 38.252. Salesperson for Unregistered Seller

(a) A person commits an offense if the person knowingly acts as a salesperson on behalf of a seller who violates the registration requirements of this chapter. Each violation constitutes a separate offense.

(b) An offense under this section is a Class A misdemeanor.

Added by Acts 1997, 75th Leg., ch. 1008, § 2, eff. Sept. 1, 1997.

Repeal

Acts 2007, 80th Leg., ch. 885, § 2.47(a)(1) repeals this section effective April 1, 2009.

§ 38.253. Request of Credit Card Account Number or Checking Account Number After Offer of Free Item

(a) A seller commits an offense if the seller knowingly:

(1) represents or implies that a purchaser will receive without charge an item or service, regardless of whether designated as a gift, premium, bonus, prize, or otherwise; and

(2) requests a credit card account number or checking account number from the purchaser for the purpose of charging to the credit card account or debiting from the checking account an amount as a condition precedent to the purchaser's receipt of an item.

(b) An offense under this section is a Class A misdemeanor.

Added by Acts 1997, 75th Leg., ch. 1008, § 2, eff. Sept. 1, 1997.

Repeal

Acts 2007, 80th Leg., ch. 885, § 2.47(a)(1) repeals this section effective April 1, 2009.

[Sections 38.254 to 38.300 reserved for expansion]

SUBCHAPTER G. ENFORCEMENT

§ 38.301. Injunction

(a) The attorney general may bring suit to enjoin a person from violating this chapter.

(b) The attorney general shall notify the defendant of the alleged prohibited conduct not later than the seventh day before the date the suit is filed except that if the attorney general intends to request that the court issue a temporary restraining order notice is not required.

(c) The attorney general is entitled to recover all reasonable costs of prosecuting the case, including court costs and costs of investigation, depositions, witness fees, and attorney's fees.

Added by Acts 1997, 75th Leg., ch. 1008, § 2, eff. Sept. 1, 1997.

Repeal

Acts 2007, 80th Leg., ch. 885, § 2.47(a)(1) repeals this section effective April 1, 2009.

§ 38.302. Civil Penalties

(a) A person who violates this chapter is subject to a civil penalty of not more than $5,000 for each violation.

(b) A person who violates an injunction issued under Section 38.301 is liable to this state for a civil penalty of not more than $25,000 for each violation and not more than $50,000 for all violations of the injunction.

(c) The attorney general may bring suit to recover a civil penalty under Subsection (b) in the court that issued the original injunction.

(d) The party bringing the suit also is entitled to recover all reasonable costs of prosecuting the case, including court costs and costs of investigation, depositions, witness fees, and attorney's fees.

Added by Acts 1997, 75th Leg., ch. 1008, § 2, eff. Sept. 1, 1997.

Repeal

Acts 2007, 80th Leg., ch. 885, § 2.47(a)(1) repeals this section effective April 1, 2009.

§ 38.303. Deceptive Trade Practices

A violation of this chapter is a false, misleading, or deceptive act or practice under Subchapter E, Chapter 17,[1] and any public or private right or remedy prescribed by that subchapter may be used to enforce this chapter.

Added by Acts 1997, 75th Leg., ch. 1008, § 2, eff. Sept. 1, 1997.

[1] V.T.C.A., Bus. & C. § 17.41 et seq.

Repeal

Acts 2007, 80th Leg., ch. 885, § 2.47(a)(1) repeals this section effective April 1, 2009.

§ 38.304. Action to Recover Against Security

(a) A person who is injured by the bankruptcy of a seller or the seller's breach of an agreement entered into during a telephone solicitation may bring an action to recover against the bond, letter of credit, or certificate of deposit required under Section 38.107.

(b) The liability of the surety on a bond provided under Section 38.107 does not exceed the amount of the bond, regardless of the number of claims filed or the aggregate amount claimed. If the amount claimed exceeds the amount of the bond, the surety shall deposit the amount of the bond with the secretary of state for distribution to claimants entitled to recovery, and the surety is then relieved of all liability under the bond.

Added by Acts 1997, 75th Leg., ch. 1008, § 2, eff. Sept. 1, 1997.

Repeal

Acts 2007, 80th Leg., ch. 885, § 2.47(a)(1) repeals this section effective April 1, 2009.

§ 38.305. Waiver Prohibited

An attempted waiver of a provision of this chapter is void.

Added by Acts 1997, 75th Leg., ch. 1008, § 2, eff. Sept. 1, 1997.

Repeal

Acts 2007, 80th Leg., ch. 885, § 2.47(a)(1) repeals this section effective April 1, 2009.

CHAPTER 39. CANCELLATION OF CERTAIN CONSUMER TRANSACTIONS

Section

Acts 2007, 80th Leg., ch. 885, § 2.47(a)(1) repeals this chapter effective April 1, 2009.

§ 39.001. Definitions

In this chapter:

(1) "Consumer" means an individual who seeks or acquires real or personal property, services, money, or credit for personal, family, or household purposes.

(2) "Consumer transaction" means a transaction in which one or more of the parties is a consumer.

(3) "Merchant" means a party to a consumer transaction other than a consumer.

(4) "Merchant's place of business" means a merchant's main or permanent branch office or local address. For a state or national bank or savings and loan association, the term includes any approved branch and any registered loan production office.

Added by Acts 1997, 75th Leg., ch. 1008, § 3, eff. Sept. 1, 1997.

Repeal

Acts 2007, 80th Leg., ch. 885, § 2.47(a)(1) repeals this section effective April 1, 2009.

§ 39.002. Applicability of Chapter

(a) This chapter applies only to a consumer transaction in which the merchant or the merchant's agent engages in a personal solicitation of a sale to the consumer at a place other than the merchant's place of business, and the consumer's agreement or offer to purchase is given to the merchant or the merchant's agent at a place other than the merchant's place of business:

(1) for the purchase of goods or services for consideration that exceeds $25 payable in installments or in cash; or

(2) for the purchase of real property for consideration that exceeds $100 payable in installments or in cash.

(b) Notwithstanding Subsection (a), this chapter does not apply to:

(1) a purchase of farm equipment;

(2) an insurance sale regulated by the Texas Department of Insurance;

(3) a sale of goods or services made:

(A) under a preexisting revolving charge account or retail charge agreement; or

(B) after negotiations between the parties at a business establishment at a fixed location where goods or services are offered or exhibited for sale; or

(4) a sale of real property if:

(A) the purchaser is represented by a licensed attorney;

(B) the transaction is negotiated by a licensed real estate broker; or

(C) the transaction is negotiated at a place other than the consumer's residence by the person who owns the property.

Added by Acts 1997, 75th Leg., ch. 1008, § 3, eff. Sept. 1, 1997.

Repeal

Acts 2007, 80th Leg., ch. 885, § 2.47(a)(1) repeals this section effective April 1, 2009.

§ 39.003. Consumer's Right to Cancel

In addition to any other rights or remedies available, a consumer may cancel a consumer transaction to which this chapter applies not later than midnight of the third business day after the date the consumer signs an agreement or offer to purchase.

Added by Acts 1997, 75th Leg., ch. 1008, § 3, eff. Sept. 1, 1997.

Repeal

Acts 2007, 80th Leg., ch. 885, § 2.47(a)(1) repeals this section effective April 1, 2009.

§ 39.004. Notice by Merchant

(a) A merchant must provide a consumer with a complete receipt or copy of any contract pertaining to the consumer transaction at the time of its execution.

(b) The document provided under Subsection (a) must:

(1) be in the same language as that principally used in the oral sales presentation;

(2) show the date of the transaction;

(3) contain the name and address of the merchant; and

(4) contain in immediate proximity to the space reserved in the contract for the signature of the consumer, or on the front page of the receipt if a contract is not used, a statement in bold-faced type of a minimum size of 10 points in substantially the following form:

"YOU, THE BUYER, MAY CANCEL THIS TRANSACTION AT ANY TIME PRIOR TO MIDNIGHT OF THE THIRD BUSINESS DAY AFTER THE DATE OF THIS TRANSACTION. SEE THE ATTACHED NOTICE OF CANCELLATION FORM FOR AN EXPLANATION OF THIS RIGHT."

(c) The merchant must attach to the document provided under Subsection (a) a completed notice of cancellation form in duplicate. The form must:

(1) be easily detachable;

(2) be in the same language as the document provided under Subsection (a); and

(3) contain the following information and statements in 10-point bold-faced type:

"NOTICE OF CANCELLATION

(enter date of transaction)

"YOU MAY CANCEL THIS TRANSACTION, WITHOUT ANY PENALTY OR OBLIGATION, WITHIN THREE BUSINESS DAYS FROM THE ABOVE DATE.

"IF YOU CANCEL, ANY PROPERTY TRADED IN, ANY PAYMENTS MADE BY YOU UNDER THE CONTRACT OR SALE, AND ANY NEGOTIABLE INSTRUMENT EXECUTED BY YOU WILL BE RETURNED WITHIN 10 BUSINESS DAYS FOLLOWING RECEIPT BY THE MERCHANT OF YOUR CANCELLATION NOTICE, AND ANY SECURITY INTEREST ARISING OUT OF THE TRANSACTION WILL BE CANCELLED.

"IF YOU CANCEL, YOU MUST MAKE AVAILABLE TO THE MERCHANT AT YOUR RESIDENCE, IN SUBSTANTIALLY AS GOOD CONDITION AS WHEN RECEIVED, ANY GOODS DELIVERED TO YOU UNDER THIS CONTRACT OR SALE; OR YOU MAY IF YOU WISH, COMPLY WITH THE INSTRUCTIONS OF THE MERCHANT REGARDING THE RETURN SHIPMENT OF THE GOODS AT THE MERCHANT'S EXPENSE AND RISK.

"IF YOU DO NOT AGREE TO RETURN THE GOODS TO THE MERCHANT OR IF THE MERCHANT DOES NOT PICK THEM UP WITHIN 20 DAYS OF THE DATE OF YOUR NOTICE OF CANCELLATION, YOU MAY RETAIN OR DISPOSE OF THE GOODS WITHOUT ANY FURTHER OBLIGATION.

"TO CANCEL THIS TRANSACTION, MAIL OR DELIVER A SIGNED AND DATED COPY OF THIS CANCELLATION NOTICE OR ANY OTHER WRITTEN NOTICE, OR SEND A TELEGRAM, TO (name of merchant), AT (address of merchant's place of business) NOT LATER THAN MIDNIGHT OF (date).

I HEREBY CANCEL THIS TRANSACTION.

(date)

(buyer's signature) "

(d) The use of the forms and notices of the right to cancel prescribed by the Federal Trade Commission's trade-regulation rule providing a cooling-off period for door-to-door sales constitutes compliance with this section.

(e) A consumer transaction in which the contract price does not exceed $200 complies with the notice requirements of this section if:

(1) the consumer may at any time cancel the order, refuse to accept delivery of the goods without incurring any obligation to pay for them, or return the goods to the merchant and receive a full refund of the amount the consumer has paid; and

(2) the consumer's right to cancel the order, refuse delivery, or return the goods without obligation or charge at any time is clearly and conspicuously set forth on the face or reverse side of the sales ticket.

Added by Acts 1997, 75th Leg., ch. 1008, § 3, eff. Sept. 1, 1997.

Repeal

Acts 2007, 80th Leg., ch. 885, § 2.47(a)(1) repeals this section effective April 1, 2009.

§ 39.005. Merchant's Compensation

A merchant is not entitled to compensation for services performed under a consumer transaction if the consumer cancels the transaction under this chapter.

Added by Acts 1997, 75th Leg., ch. 1008, § 3, eff. Sept. 1, 1997.

Repeal

Acts 2007, 80th Leg., ch. 885, § 2.47(a)(1) repeals this section effective April 1, 2009.

§ 39.006. Retention of Goods or Real Property

Until a merchant has complied with this chapter, a consumer with possession of goods or right or title to real property delivered by the merchant:

(1) may retain possession of the goods or right or title to the real property; and

(2) has a lien on the goods or real property to the extent of any recovery to which the consumer is entitled.

Added by Acts 1997, 75th Leg., ch. 1008, § 3, eff. Sept. 1, 1997.

Repeal

Acts 2007, 80th Leg., ch. 885, § 2.47(a)(1) repeals this section effective April 1, 2009.

§ 39.007. Duty of Consumer

(a) Within a reasonable time after a cancellation under this chapter, the consumer on demand must tender to the merchant any goods or right or title to real property delivered by the merchant under the consumer transaction.

(b) The consumer is not obligated to tender goods at a place other than the consumer's residence.

(c) If the merchant fails to demand possession of the goods or the right or title to real property within a reasonable time after cancellation, the goods or real property become the property of the consumer without obligation to pay.

(d) Goods or real property in possession of the consumer are at the risk of the merchant, except that the consumer shall take reasonable care of the goods or the real property both before and for a reasonable time after cancellation.

(e) For purposes of this section, 20 days is presumed to be a reasonable time.

Added by Acts 1997, 75th Leg., ch. 1008, § 3, eff. Sept. 1, 1997.

Repeal

Acts 2007, 80th Leg., ch. 885, § 2.47(a)(1) repeals this section effective April 1, 2009.

§ 39.008. Violations

(a) A merchant may not:

(1) fail to include on both copies of the form described by Section 39.004(c):

(A) the name of the merchant;

(B) the address of the merchant's place of business;

(C) the date of the transaction; and

(D) a date not earlier than the third business day after the date of the transaction by which the consumer must give notice of cancellation;

(2) include in a contract or receipt pertaining to a consumer transaction a confession of judgment or a waiver of any of the rights to which the consumer is entitled under this chapter;

(3) at the time the consumer signs the contract or purchases the goods, services, or real property, fail to inform the consumer orally of the right to cancel the transaction;

(4) misrepresent in any manner the consumer's right to cancel;

(5) negotiate, transfer, sell, or assign any note or other evidence of indebtedness to a finance company or other third party before midnight of the fifth business day after the date the contract was signed or the goods or services were purchased;

(6) fail to notify the consumer before the end of the 10th business day after the date the merchant receives the notice of cancellation whether the merchant intends to repossess or to abandon any shipped or delivered goods; or

(7) fail or refuse to honor a valid cancellation under this chapter by a consumer and fail before the end of the 10th business day after the date the merchant receives the notice of cancellation to:

(A) refund all payments made under the contract or sale;

(B) return any goods or property traded in to the merchant in substantially the same condition as when received by the merchant;

(C) cancel and return any negotiable instrument executed by the consumer in connection with the contract of sale;

(D) take any action appropriate to terminate promptly any security interest created in the transaction; or

(E) restore improvements on real property to the same condition as when the merchant took title to or possession of the real property unless the consumer requests otherwise.

(b) A sale or contract entered into under a consumer transaction in violation of Subsection (a) is void.

(c) A merchant who violates a provision of this chapter is liable to the consumer for:

(1) any actual damages suffered by the consumer as a result of the violation;

(2) reasonable attorney's fees; and

(3) court costs.

(d) If the merchant fails to tender goods or property traded to the merchant in substantially the same condition as when received by the merchant, the consumer may elect to recover an amount equal to the trade-in allowance stated in the agreement.

(e) A violation of this chapter is a false, misleading, or deceptive act or practice as defined by Section 17.46(b). In addition to any remedy under this chapter, a remedy under Subchapter E, Chapter 17,[1] is also available for a violation of this chapter.

Added by Acts 1997, 75th Leg., ch. 1008, § 3, eff. Sept. 1, 1997.

[1] V.T.C.A., Bus. & C. § 17.41 et seq.

Repeal

Acts 2007, 80th Leg., ch. 885, § 2.47(a)(1) repeals this section effective April 1, 2009.

§ 39.009. Injunction

If the attorney general believes that a person is violating or about to violate this chapter, the attorney general may bring an action in the name of the state to restrain or enjoin the person from violating this chapter.

Added by Acts 1997, 75th Leg., ch. 1008, § 3, eff. Sept. 1, 1997.

Repeal

Acts 2007, 80th Leg., ch. 885, § 2.47(a)(1) repeals this section effective April 1, 2009.

CHAPTER 40. CONTESTS AND GIFT GIVEAWAYS

SUBCHAPTER A. GENERAL PROVISIONS

Acts 2007, 80th Leg., ch. 885, § 2.47(a)(1) repeals this chapter effective April 1, 2009.

SUBCHAPTER A. GENERAL PROVISIONS

§ 40.001. Short Title

This chapter may be cited as the Contest and Gift Giveaway Act.

Added by Acts 1997, 75th Leg., ch. 1008, § 4, eff. Sept. 1, 1997.

Repeal

Acts 2007, 80th Leg., ch. 885, § 2.47(a)(1) repeals this section effective April 1, 2009.

§ 40.002. Construction of Chapter

This chapter shall be interpreted to provide the maximum disclosure to, and fair treatment of, a person who enters a contest or gift giveaway through which the person is solicited to attend a sales presentation.

Added by Acts 1997, 75th Leg., ch. 1008, § 4, eff. Sept. 1, 1997.

Repeal

Acts 2007, 80th Leg., ch. 885, § 2.47(a)(1) repeals this section effective April 1, 2009.

§ 40.003. Definitions

(a) In this chapter:

(1) "Contest" means a promotional device in which:

(A) a person is offered, as an inducement to attend a sales presentation, a chance to win or receive a prize by complying with specified entry requirements;

(B) the chance to win any prize is determined by random selection; and

(C) all offered prizes are awarded.

(2) "Contest period" means the duration of a contest from the beginning date to the ending date.

(3) "Drawing" means a contest in which the recipient of a prize is determined from all of the entries received.

(4) "Entry form" means a card, letter, entry blank, token, or similar device that identifies a contestant by:

(A) name;

(B) number, letter, or symbol; or

(C) both name and number, letter, or symbol.

(5) "Gift" means an item of value that is offered, transferred, or given to a person as an inducement to attend a sales presentation but that is not offered, transferred, or awarded by chance through a contest. The term does not include a manufacturer's rebate or discount available to the public.

(6) "Major prize" means a prize that has an actual unit cost to the offeror of at least $250.

(7) "Matched contest" means a contest in which:

(A) winning numbers are preselected, printed on an entry form, and distributed to the public; and

(B) the numbers on the entry form are subsequently matched with the list of winning numbers at a sales location to determine prize eligibility.

(8) "Minor prize" means a prize that:

(A) has an actual unit cost to the offeror of less than $250; and

(B) is transferred to a person who:

(i) attends a sales presentation; and

(ii) is not the winner of a major prize.

(9) "Odds of winning" means a ratio in which:

(A) the numerator equals the actual number of units of an identified prize to be given away during a contest period; and

(B) the denominator equals the number of entry forms distributed or reasonably anticipated to be distributed during the contest period.

(10) "Offeror" means a person who solicits a person to attend a sales presentation.

(11) "Person" includes an individual, a corporation, a firm, and an association.

(12) "Prize" means an item of value that is offered, awarded, or given to a person through a contest. The term does not include a manufacturer's rebate or discount available to the public.

(13) "Sales presentation" means a transaction or occurrence in which a consumer is solicited to execute a contract that obligates the consumer to purchase goods or services as defined by Subchapter E, Chapter 17, [1] including:

(A) a "timeshare interest" as defined by Chapter 221, Property Code; and

(B) a "membership interest" as defined by Chapter 222, Property Code.

(14) "Winning number" includes a letter or other identifying symbol.

(b) For purposes of Subsection (a)(1)(B), a determination made by "random selection" does not include the method used by an offeror to identify any person who will be notified of an offer to win a prize.

Added by Acts 1997, 75th Leg., ch. 1008, § 4, eff. Sept. 1, 1997.

[1] V.T.C.A., Bus. & C. § 17.41 et seq.

Repeal

Acts 2007, 80th Leg., ch. 885, § 2.47(a)(1) repeals this section effective April 1, 2009.

§ 40.004. Exemption

This chapter does not apply to a sales presentation conducted in conjunction with a business seminar, trade show, convention, or other gathering at which representatives of business entities are the only individuals solicited to attend the sales presentation.

Added by Acts 1997, 75th Leg., ch. 1008, § 4, eff. Sept. 1, 1997.

Repeal

Acts 2007, 80th Leg., ch. 885, § 2.47(a)(1) repeals this section effective April 1, 2009.

§ 40.005. Determination of Retail Value of Prize or Gift

(a) The retail value of an item offered as a prize or gift is the price at which a substantial number of sales of the exact item of the same manufacturer, brand, model, and type have been made to members of the public by at least two principal retail outlets in this state during the six months preceding the offering of the prize or gift.

(b) If a substantial number of sales of a particular item have not been made in this state in the six months preceding the offering of the item described in the solicitation or if the offeror elects, the retail value of the item is the actual cost of the item to the offeror, net of any rebates, plus 200 percent.

(c) If a prize or gift involves lodging, airfare, a trip, or a recreational activity, the retail value is the retail sales price of that lodging, airfare, trip, or recreational activity to a member of the public who is not involved in a promotional or other discount transaction.

Added by Acts 1997, 75th Leg., ch. 1008, § 4, eff. Sept. 1, 1997.

Repeal

Acts 2007, 80th Leg., ch. 885, § 2.47(a)(1) repeals this section effective April 1, 2009.

§ 40.006. Raincheck Requirements

(a) Subject to Subsections (d)–(g), an offeror may not fail:

(1) in a gift offer to provide each gift as represented to each person who attends a sales presentation; or

(2) in a matched contest to award each prize as represented on the entry form to each person who presents a winning entry.

(b) Except as provided by Subsections (d)–(g), an offeror may not provide a coupon book, a discount book, or a certificate or voucher that entitles the holder to redeem the certificate or voucher for a gift or prize required to be available under this section.

(c) An offeror shall have available at the sales location a sufficient quantity of:

(1) each gift to meet the reasonable anticipated response to the offer; or

(2) each prize to meet the reasonable anticipated number of prize winners.

(d) If the response to an offer exceeds the number of gifts, or of major or minor prizes, available at the sales location, the offeror, at the time of the visit or, if a sales presentation is required, at the conclusion of the sales presentation, shall tender to the recipient of the offer a raincheck for the gift or prize represented in the offer. The offeror shall send that exact gift or prize to the recipient, without cost to the recipient, not later than the 14th day after the date on which the recipient visits the sales location or attends the sales presentation. The offeror shall obtain a return receipt from the shipper verifying that the gift or prize was delivered to the recipient.

(e) If, after the expiration of 14 days from the date of issuance of the raincheck, the offeror has failed to send the gift or minor prize, the offeror, not later than the 15th day after the date of issuance of the raincheck, shall send to the recipient of the raincheck a check or money order in the amount of $100 payable to the recipient. The offeror shall obtain a return receipt from the United States Postal Service that verifies that the check or money order was delivered to the recipient.

(f) If the offeror knows at the time the recipient of the offer visits the sales location or attends a sales presentation that the gift or minor prize will not be available within 14 days of the date of the visit or attendance, the offeror shall at the time of the visit or at the conclusion of the sales presentation tender to the recipient, by cash or check, the amount of $100.

(g) If the gift or prize involves lodging, airfare, a trip, or a recreational activity, the offeror may give the recipient a certificate that evidences the recipient's right to the gift or prize. The offeror may require a refundable deposit if the requirement of a deposit is fully disclosed.

Added by Acts 1997, 75th Leg., ch. 1008, § 4, eff. Sept. 1, 1997.

Repeal

Acts 2007, 80th Leg., ch. 885, § 2.47(a)(1) repeals this section effective April 1, 2009.

§ 40.007. Deposit Requirements

(a) If a gift or prize involves lodging, airfare, a trip, or a recreational activity, the offeror may require a refundable deposit if the requirement of a deposit is fully, clearly, and conspicuously disclosed.

(b) For purposes of this section, "refundable deposit" means a deposit that is required to be returned in its entirety to a consumer if:

(1) it is paid by the consumer for a reservation that is used by the consumer; or

(2) the consumer provides at least five possible reservation dates, none of which can be confirmed.

(c) A condition that restricts the refund of the deposit must be clearly and conspicuously disclosed in at least 10-point type on the solicitation.

Added by Acts 1997, 75th Leg., ch. 1008, § 4, eff. Sept. 1, 1997.

Repeal

Acts 2007, 80th Leg., ch. 885, § 2.47(a)(1) repeals this section effective April 1, 2009.

[Sections 40.008 to 40.030 reserved for expansion]

SUBCHAPTER B. GIFT OFFERS

§ 40.031. Application of Subchapter

This subchapter applies to a person who uses a gift as part of an advertising plan or program.

Added by Acts 1997, 75th Leg., ch. 1008, § 4, eff. Sept. 1, 1997.

Repeal

Acts 2007, 80th Leg., ch. 885, § 2.47(a)(1) repeals this section effective April 1, 2009.

§ 40.032. Full Disclosure Required

A gift is not prohibited in a legitimate trade promotion if the advertising regarding the promotion fully discloses any requirement of a purchase to be made or contractual obligation to be assumed to qualify for the gift.

Added by Acts 1997, 75th Leg., ch. 1008, § 4, eff. Sept. 1, 1997.

Repeal

Acts 2007, 80th Leg., ch. 885, § 2.47(a)(1) repeals this section effective April 1, 2009.

§ 40.033. Consideration to Offeror; Limitations

(a) An offeror may not notify a person that the person will receive a gift, a condition of receipt of which requires the person to pay consideration of any kind or a charge or expense to a person for the gift, unless the consideration, charge, or expense is fully, clearly, and conspicuously disclosed.

(b) An offeror may not charge a redemption fee or shipping fee even if full disclosure of the fee is made.

(c) In this section, "redemption or shipping fee" means any kind of consideration paid to the offeror. The term does not include a refundable deposit.

Added by Acts 1997, 75th Leg., ch. 1008, § 4, eff. Sept. 1, 1997.

Repeal

Acts 2007, 80th Leg., ch. 885, § 2.47(a)(1) repeals this section effective April 1, 2009.

§ 40.034. Limitation on Requirement of Purchase

An offeror may not notify a person that the person will receive a gift, a condition of receipt of which requires the person to purchase a good or service, unless at the time of notification the offeror clearly and conspicuously discloses that purchase of a good or service is required.

Added by Acts 1997, 75th Leg., ch. 1008, § 4, eff. Sept. 1, 1997.

Repeal

Acts 2007, 80th Leg., ch. 885, § 2.47(a)(1) repeals this section effective April 1, 2009.

§ 40.035. Limitation on Required Attendance at Sales Presentation

(a) An offeror may not notify a person that the person will receive a gift unless at the time of the notification the offeror clearly and conspicuously discloses:

(1) that attendance at the sales presentation is required;

(2) a description of the product or service being sold; and

(3) the approximate duration of the sales presentation.

(b) An item of value offered as an inducement to a person to attend a sales presentation constitutes a gift unless the item qualifies as a prize offered, transferred, or given through a contest.

Added by Acts 1997, 75th Leg., ch. 1008, § 4, eff. Sept. 1, 1997.

Repeal

Acts 2007, 80th Leg., ch. 885, § 2.47(a)(1) repeals this section effective April 1, 2009.

§ 40.036. Gift Offers; Prohibited Acts

A person may not:

(1) use the term "gift" or a similar term in a false, misleading, or deceptive manner;

(2) directly represent or imply that a gift promotion is a contest;

(3) in a gift promotion, use the term:

(A) "finalist," "major award winner," "grand prize recipient," "winner," "won," "will win," or "will be awarded" or use words or phrases of similar meaning that imply that a person is being solicited to enter or participate in a contest; or

(B) "sweepstakes" or "contest" or use words or phrases of similar meaning that imply that the respondent is being solicited to enter or has won a contest;

(4) fail to disclose the retail value of a gift;

(5) fail to disclose clearly and conspicuously in at least 10-point type that airfare, lodging, or both are not included as part of a prize that is a trip or recreational activity to the extent that either or both are not included;

(6) represent that a gift has a sponsor, approval, characteristic, ingredient, use, benefit, quantity, status, affiliation, connection, or identity that the gift does not have;

(7) represent that a gift is of a particular standard, quality, grade, style, or model if the gift is of another; or

(8) use a word or phrase that simulates or causes confusion with:

(A) a document issued by an officer of a court of any jurisdiction or that implies the offeror is sending a court or legal document; or

(B) the seal or name of a governmental entity, whether real or fictitious, or that implies that the offeror is a governmental entity.

Added by Acts 1997, 75th Leg., ch. 1008, § 4, eff. Sept. 1, 1997.

Repeal

Acts 2007, 80th Leg., ch. 885, § 2.47(a)(1) repeals this section effective April 1, 2009.

[Sections 40.037 to 40.060 reserved for expansion]

SUBCHAPTER C. MATCHED CONTESTS AND DRAWINGS

§ 40.061. Application of Subchapter

This subchapter applies to a person who uses a contest as part of an advertising plan or program.

Added by Acts 1997, 75th Leg., ch. 1008, § 4, eff. Sept. 1, 1997.

Repeal

Acts 2007, 80th Leg., ch. 885, § 2.47(a)(1) repeals this section effective April 1, 2009.

§ 40.062. Consideration to Offeror; Limitations

An offeror may not notify a person that the person has won a prize, will receive a prize, or has a chance to win or receive a prize, a condition of receipt of which requires the person to pay consideration of any kind or a charge or expense to a person for the prize except for:

(1) expenses incurred for travel to and from the sales location; or

(2) a refundable deposit authorized under Section 40.007.

Added by Acts 1997, 75th Leg., ch. 1008, § 4, eff. Sept. 1, 1997.

Repeal

Acts 2007, 80th Leg., ch. 885, § 2.47(a)(1) repeals this section effective April 1, 2009.

§ 40.063. Limitation on Requirement of Purchase

An offeror may not notify a person that the person has won a prize, will receive a prize, or has a chance to win or receive a prize, a condition of receipt of which requires the person to purchase a good or service unrelated to the prize.

Added by Acts 1997, 75th Leg., ch. 1008, § 4, eff. Sept. 1, 1997.

Repeal

Acts 2007, 80th Leg., ch. 885, § 2.47(a)(1) repeals this section effective April 1, 2009.

§ 40.064. Limitation on Required Attendance at Sales Presentation

An offeror may not notify a person that the person has won a prize, will receive a prize, or has a chance to win or receive a prize unless at the time of the notification the offeror clearly and conspicuously discloses:

(1) that attendance at the sales presentation is required;

(2) a description of the product or service being sold; and

(3) the approximate duration of the sales presentation.

Added by Acts 1997, 75th Leg., ch. 1008, § 4, eff. Sept. 1, 1997.

Repeal

Acts 2007, 80th Leg., ch. 885, § 2.47(a)(1) repeals this section effective April 1, 2009.

§ 40.065. Matched Contest Requirements

(a) The identity and number of the major prizes to be awarded in a matched contest shall be determined before the contest begins. That information shall be disclosed on each entry form distributed.

(b) Each major prize identified on an entry form shall be awarded.

(c) The contest period may not exceed 12 calendar months.

(d) If, during the contest period, a winning number is not presented or matched for a major prize, the offeror shall conduct a drawing from the names of those individuals who have attended a sales presentation during the contest period. The offeror shall conduct the drawing not later than the 60th day after the date on which the contest period ends. Each major prize identified on the entry forms distributed during the contest period that was not previously awarded shall be awarded at the time of the drawing.

Added by Acts 1997, 75th Leg., ch. 1008, § 4, eff. Sept. 1, 1997.

Repeal

Acts 2007, 80th Leg., ch. 885, § 2.47(a)(1) repeals this section effective April 1, 2009.

§ 40.066. Matched Contest; Prohibited Acts

(a) A person engaged in the preparation, promotion, sale, distribution, or use of a matched contest may not:

(1) use the term "prize" or another similar term in a false, misleading, or deceptive manner;

(2) fail to disclose the retail value of the prize;

(3) fail to disclose clearly and conspicuously in at least 10-point type that airfare, lodging, or both are not included as part of a prize that is a trip or recreational activity to the extent that either or both are not included;

(4) represent that a person solicited to enter a contest is a "finalist," "major award winner," "grand prize recipient," or "winner" or that a person has "won," "will win," or "will be awarded" or use words or phrases of similar meaning when a person is being solicited to enter or participate in a contest, unless the representation is true;

(5) represent that a prize has a sponsor, approval, characteristic, ingredient, use, benefit, quantity, status, affiliation, connection, or identity that the prize does not have;

(6) represent that a prize is of a particular standard, quality, grade, style, or model if the prize is of another;

(7) misrepresent the odds of winning a prize;

(8) misrepresent the rules or terms of participation in a contest;

(9) represent that:

(A) any number, ticket, coupon, symbol, or entry form confers or will confer an advantage on a person that another person does not have;

(B) a person is more likely to win a prize than another person; or

(C) a number, ticket, coupon, symbol, or entry form has some value that other entries do not have;

(10) fail to obtain a person's express written consent before using that person's name for a promotional purpose;

(11) use or distribute simulated checks or currency or other simulated items of value unless the words "SPECIMEN—NON-NEGOTIABLE" are clearly and conspicuously printed on those items in at least 18-point type;

(12) use a word or phrase that simulates or causes confusion with:

(A) a document issued by an officer of a court of any jurisdiction or that implies the offeror is sending a court or legal document; or

(B) the seal or name of a real or fictitious governmental entity or that implies that the offeror is a governmental entity.

(b) A person may not use a matched contest unless the person clearly and conspicuously discloses in writing in the offer:

(1) the fact that attendance at a sales presentation is required;

(2) the name and street address of the person who is soliciting attendance at a sales presentation;

(3) a description of the product or service being sold;

(4) each requirement, restriction, qualification, and other condition that must be satisfied for a person to enter a contest, including:

(A) any deadline by which the person must visit the location or attend the sales presentation to qualify to receive a prize; and

(B) the approximate duration of the sales presentation;

(5) a statement of the odds of winning each prize offered, expressed as a ratio in Arabic numerals;

(6) the geographical area or states in which the contest will be conducted;

(7) the beginning and ending dates of the contest period;

(8) the identity and address of each person responsible for the awarding of the prizes;

(9) the fact that all unclaimed prizes will be awarded by a drawing and the date of the drawing; and

(10) all other rules and terms of the contest.

Added by Acts 1997, 75th Leg., ch. 1008, § 4, eff. Sept. 1, 1997.

Repeal

Acts 2007, 80th Leg., ch. 885, § 2.47(a)(1) repeals this section effective April 1, 2009.

§ 40.067. Drawings; Prohibited Acts

(a) A person may not use a drawing unless the offeror clearly and conspicuously discloses in writing in the offer:

(1) a statement of the odds of winning each prize offered, expressed as a ratio in Arabic numerals;

(2) the exact prizes to be awarded in the contest;

(3) the beginning and ending dates of the contest period;

(4) the date on which the drawing will take place; and

(5) the location of the drawing.

(b) A person engaged in the preparation, promotion, sale, distribution, or use of a drawing may not:

(1) use the term "prize" or a similar term in a false, misleading, or deceptive manner;

(2) fail to provide the prize as represented at the conclusion of the drawing;

(3) fail to disclose the retail value of the prize;

(4) fail to disclose clearly and conspicuously in at least 10-point type that airfare, lodging, or both are not included in a prize that is a trip or recreational activity to the extent that either or both are not included;

(5) represent that a prize has a sponsor, approval, characteristic, ingredient, use, benefit, quantity, status, affiliation, connection, or identity that the prize does not have;

(6) represent that a prize is of a particular standard, quality, grade, style, or model if the prize is of another;

(7) misrepresent the odds of winning a prize; or

(8) misrepresent the rules or terms of participation in a contest.

(c) If the odds of winning cannot be determined because the total number of entries is not known, the offeror shall make a statement to the effect that the odds of winning depend on the total number of entries received.

Added by Acts 1997, 75th Leg., ch. 1008, § 4, eff. Sept. 1, 1997.

Repeal

Acts 2007, 80th Leg., ch. 885, § 2.47(a)(1) repeals this section effective April 1, 2009.

[Sections 40.068 to 40.090 reserved for expansion]

SUBCHAPTER D. CONTEST RECORDS

§ 40.091. Application of Subchapter

This subchapter applies to a person who uses a contest as part of an advertising plan or program.

Added by Acts 1997, 75th Leg., ch. 1008, § 4, eff. Sept. 1, 1997.

Repeal

Acts 2007, 80th Leg., ch. 885, § 2.47(a)(1) repeals this section effective April 1, 2009.

§ 40.092. General Contest Records; List of Winners

(a) For each contest other than a drawing, the offeror shall maintain until the second anniversary of the date on which all prizes have been awarded:

(1) a record of the identity and address of each person who is responsible for developing, creating, sponsoring, or implementing any part of the advertising plan or program;

(2) records that show that the winning numbers have been deposited in the mail or otherwise made available to recipients in accordance with the odds statement provided under Section 40.066(b);

(3) a copy of each contest solicitation;

(4) records adequate to disclose:

(A) the name and address of each contestant;

(B) the approximate date on which each contestant was sent the solicitation used in the contest;

(C) the number of major prizes awarded;

(D) the date on which each major prize was awarded;

(E) the name, brand, type, model number, and manufacturer of each prize offered;

(F) the method of computing the retail value of each prize;

(G) the method of selecting major prize winners;

(H) the name and address of each major prize winner; and

(I) the facts on which each representation or disclosure made in connection with the contest is based and from which the validity of the representation or disclosure can be determined.

(b) Postal receipt records, affidavits of mailing, and a list of winners or recipients of the major prizes satisfy the requirements of Subsection (a)(2).

Added by Acts 1997, 75th Leg., ch. 1008, § 4, eff. Sept. 1, 1997.

Repeal

Acts 2007, 80th Leg., ch. 885, § 2.47(a)(1) repeals this section effective April 1, 2009.

§ 40.093. Drawing Records; List of Winners

(a) For each drawing, the offeror shall maintain until the second anniversary of the date on which all major prizes have been awarded:

(1) a record of the identity and address of each person who is responsible for developing, creating, sponsoring, or implementing any part of the advertising plan or program;

(2) records that show that the winning entry for each major prize was selected entirely at random from all of the entries received;

(3) a copy of each contest solicitation; and

(4) records adequate to disclose:

(A) the total number of entries;

(B) the number of major prizes awarded;

(C) the date on which each major prize was awarded;

(D) the name, brand, type, model number, and manufacturer of each prize offered;

(E) the method of computing the retail value of each prize;

(F) the method of selecting winners; and

(G) the names and addresses of the winners.

(b) An affidavit from the person who conducted the drawing and a list of winners or recipients of the major prizes satisfies the requirements of Subsection (a)(2).

Added by Acts 1997, 75th Leg., ch. 1008, § 4, eff. Sept. 1, 1997.

Repeal

Acts 2007, 80th Leg., ch. 885, § 2.47(a)(1) repeals this section effective April 1, 2009.

§ 40.094. Disclosure on Request

At the end of the contest period, each person who conducts a contest shall provide to any person requesting the information:

(1) the names of all major prize winners; and

(2) the prizes won by each winner.

Added by Acts 1997, 75th Leg., ch. 1008, § 4, eff. Sept. 1, 1997.

Repeal

Acts 2007, 80th Leg., ch. 885, § 2.47(a)(1) repeals this section effective April 1, 2009.

§ 40.095. Records Available to Attorney General

The records required under this subchapter shall be made available to the attorney general not later than the 30th day after the date on which a written request for the records is received.

Added by Acts 1997, 75th Leg., ch. 1008, § 4, eff. Sept. 1, 1997.

Repeal

Acts 2007, 80th Leg., ch. 885, § 2.47(a)(1) repeals this section effective April 1, 2009.

[Sections 40.096 to 40.120 reserved for expansion]

SUBCHAPTER E. ENFORCEMENT

§ 40.121. Criminal Penalty

(a) A person commits an offense if the person knowingly violates this chapter.

(b) Except as provided by Subsection (c), an offense under this section is a Class B misdemeanor.

(c) An offense under this section is a:

(1) Class A misdemeanor if it is shown at the trial of the defendant that the violation occurred not later than the fifth anniversary of the date of a previous conviction under this section; or

(2) third degree felony if the violation was intentional and it is shown at the trial of the defendant that the violation occurred not later than the fifth anniversary of the earlier of the dates of two previous convictions under this section.

(d) Subsection (c)(2) does not apply to a violation of Subchapter D.[1]

(e) A person may not be prosecuted for more than one offense involving the same promotion, even if that promotion is mailed or distributed to more than one person or is used at more than one location.

Added by Acts 1997, 75th Leg., ch. 1008, § 4, eff. Sept. 1, 1997.

[1] V.T.C.A., Bus. & C. § 40.091 et seq.

Repeal

Acts 2007, 80th Leg., ch. 885, § 2.47(a)(1) repeals this section effective April 1, 2009.

§ 40.122. Deceptive Trade Practice

A violation of this chapter is a deceptive trade practice in addition to the practices described by Subchapter E, Chapter 17,[1] and is actionable under that subchapter.

Added by Acts 1997, 75th Leg., ch. 1008, § 4, eff. Sept. 1, 1997.

[1] V.T.C.A., Bus. & C. § 17.41 et seq.

Repeal

Acts 2007, 80th Leg., ch. 885, § 2.47(a)(1) repeals this section effective April 1, 2009.

CHAPTER 41. BUSINESS OPPORTUNITIES

SUBCHAPTER A. GENERAL PROVISIONS

Acts 2007, 80th Leg., ch. 885, § 2.47(a)(1) repeals this chapter effective April 1, 2009.

SUBCHAPTER A. GENERAL PROVISIONS

§ 41.001. Short Title

This chapter may be cited as the Business Opportunity Act.

Added by Acts 1997, 75th Leg., ch. 1008, § 5, eff. Sept. 1, 1997.

Repeal

Acts 2007, 80th Leg., ch. 885, § 2.47(a)(1) repeals this section effective April 1, 2009.

§ 41.002. Construction and Application

(a) This chapter shall be liberally construed and applied to:

(1) protect persons against false, misleading, or deceptive practices in the advertising, offering for

sale or lease, and sale or lease of business opportunities; and

(2) provide efficient and economical procedures to secure that protection.

(b) In construing this chapter, a court to the extent possible shall follow the interpretations given by the Federal Trade Commission and the federal courts to Section 5(a)(1), Federal Trade Commission Act (15 U.S.C. Section 45(a)(1)), and 16 C.F.R. Part 436 and their subsequent amendments.

Added by Acts 1997, 75th Leg., ch. 1008, § 5, eff. Sept. 1, 1997.

Repeal

Acts 2007, 80th Leg., ch. 885, § 2.47(a)(1) repeals this section effective April 1, 2009.

§ 41.003. Definitions

In this chapter:

(1) "Business opportunity contract" means an agreement that obligates or is intended to obligate a purchaser to a seller.

(2) "Buy-back" means a representation that implies that the purchaser's payment is protected from loss.

(3) "Designee" means a person who:

(A) is selected by a seller as a source of goods or services to be used by a purchaser in connection with a business opportunity; and

(B) gives consideration to the seller in connection with that selection or the disposition of goods or services to the purchaser.

(4) "Equipment" includes machines, electrical devices, video and audio devices, molds, display racks, vending machines, coin-operated game machines, machines that dispense products, and display units.

(5) "Initial consideration" means the total amount a purchaser is obligated to pay under a business opportunity contract before or at the time the equipment, supplies, products, or services are delivered or within six months after the date the purchaser begins operation of the business opportunity plan. The term means the total sale price if the contract states a specific total sale price for purchase of the business opportunity plan and the total sale price is to be paid as a down payment and one or more additional payments. The term does not include the not-for-profit sale for not more than $500 of sales demonstration materials, samples, and equipment.

(6) "Marketing program" means advice or training that is given to the purchaser by the seller or a person recommended by the seller pertaining to the sale of products, equipment, supplies, or services and that includes the preparation or provision of:

(A) promotional literature, brochures, pamphlets, or advertising materials;

(B) training regarding the promotion, operation, or management of the business opportunity; or

(C) operational, managerial, technical, or financial guidelines or assistance.

(7) "Product" includes any tangible personal property.

(8) "Purchaser" means a person who becomes or is solicited to become obligated on a business opportunity contract.

(9) "Secured investment" is synonymous with "buy-back" and has the meaning assigned by Subdivision (2).

(10) "Seller" means a principal or agent who sells or leases or offers to sell or lease a business opportunity.

(11) "Services" includes any assistance, guidance, direction, work, labor, or other services provided by the seller to initiate or maintain a business opportunity.

(12) "Supplies" includes materials used to produce, grow, breed, or make a product or item.

Added by Acts 1997, 75th Leg., ch. 1008, § 5, eff. Sept. 1, 1997.

Repeal

Acts 2007, 80th Leg., ch. 885, § 2.47(a)(1) repeals this section effective April 1, 2009.

§ 41.004. Business Opportunity; Exceptions

(a) In this chapter, "business opportunity" means a sale or lease for an initial consideration of more than $500 of products, equipment, supplies, or services that will be used by or for the purchaser to begin a business in which the seller represents that:

(1) the purchaser will earn or is likely to earn a profit in excess of the initial consideration paid by the purchaser; and

(2) the seller will:

(A) provide locations or assist the purchaser in finding locations for the use or operation of the products, equipment, supplies, or services on premises that are not owned or leased by the purchaser or seller;

(B) provide a sales, production, or marketing program; or

(C) buy back or is likely to buy back products, supplies, or equipment purchased or a product made, produced, fabricated, grown, or bred by the purchaser using in whole or in part the product, supplies, equipment, or services that the seller initially sold or leased or offered for sale or lease to the purchaser.

(b) In this chapter, "business opportunity" does not include:

(1) the sale or lease of an established and ongoing business or enterprise that has actively conducted business before the sale or lease, whether composed of one or more than one component business or enterprise, if the sale or lease represents an isolated transaction or series of transactions involving a bona fide change of ownership or control of the business or enterprise or liquidation of the business or enterprise;

(2) a contract or agreement in which a retailer of goods or services sells the inventory of one or more ongoing leased departments to a purchaser who is granted the right to sell the goods or services within or adjoining the retail business establishment as a department or division of the retail business establishment;

(3) a transaction regulated by the Motor Vehicle Board of the Texas Department of Transportation, Texas Department of Licensing and Regulation, Texas Department of Insurance, or Texas Real Estate Commission if engaged in by a person licensed by one of those agencies;

(4) a real estate syndication;

(5) a sale or lease to a business enterprise that also sells or leases equipment, products, and supplies or performs services:

(A) that are not supplied by the seller; and

(B) that the purchaser does not use with the equipment, products, supplies, or services of the seller;

(6) the offer or sale of a franchise as described by the Petroleum Marketing Practices Act (15 U.S.C. Section 2801 et seq.) and its subsequent amendments;

(7) the offer or sale of a business opportunity if the seller:

(A) has a net worth of at least $25 million according to the seller's audited balance sheet as of a date not earlier than the 13th month before the date of the transaction; or

(B) is at least 80-percent owned by another person who:

(i) in writing unconditionally guarantees performance by the person offering the plan; and

(ii) has a net worth of more than $25 million according to the person's most recent audited balance sheet as of a date not earlier than the 13th month before the date of the transaction; or

(8) an arrangement defined as a franchise by 16 C.F.R. Section 436.2(a) and its subsequent amendments if:

(A) the franchisor complies in all material respects in this state with 16 C.F.R. Part 436 and each order or other action of the Federal Trade Commission; and

(B) before offering for sale or selling a franchise in this state, a person files with the secretary of state a notice containing:

(i) the name of the franchisor;

(ii) the name under which the franchisor intends to do business; and

(iii) the franchisor's principal business address.

(c) The secretary of state shall prescribe the form of the notice described by Subsection (b)(8)(B).

Added by Acts 1997, 75th Leg., ch. 1008, § 5, eff. Sept. 1, 1997.

Repeal

Acts 2007, 80th Leg., ch. 885, § 2.47(a)(1) repeals this section effective April 1, 2009.

§ 41.005. Burden of Proof

A person who claims to be exempt from this chapter has the burden of proving the exemption.

Added by Acts 1997, 75th Leg., ch. 1008, § 5, eff. Sept. 1, 1997.

Repeal

Acts 2007, 80th Leg., ch. 885, § 2.47(a)(1) repeals this section effective April 1, 2009.

§ 41.006. Rules

The secretary of state may adopt rules to administer and enforce this chapter.

Added by Acts 1997, 75th Leg., ch. 1008, § 5, eff. Sept. 1, 1997.

Repeal

Acts 2007, 80th Leg., ch. 885, § 2.47(a)(1) repeals this section effective April 1, 2009.

§ 41.007. Filing Fee

The secretary of state may charge a reasonable fee to cover the costs incurred as a result of a filing required by Subchapter B [1] or Section 41.004 or 41.251.

Added by Acts 1997, 75th Leg., ch. 1008, § 5, eff. Sept. 1, 1997.

[1] V.T.C.A., Bus. & C. § 41.051 et seq.

Repeal

Acts 2007, 80th Leg., ch. 885, § 2.47(a)(1) repeals this section effective April 1, 2009.

§ 41.008. Recordkeeping

(a) A seller shall maintain a complete set of books, records, and accounts of business opportunity sales made by the seller.

(b) A document relating to a business opportunity sold or leased shall be maintained until the fourth anniversary of the date of the business opportunity contract.

Added by Acts 1997, 75th Leg., ch. 1008, § 5, eff. Sept. 1, 1997.

Repeal

Acts 2007, 80th Leg., ch. 885, § 2.47(a)(1) repeals this section effective April 1, 2009.

§ 41.009. Waiver

A waiver of this chapter is contrary to public policy and is unenforceable and void.

Added by Acts 1997, 75th Leg., ch. 1008, § 5, eff. Sept. 1, 1997.

Repeal

Acts 2007, 80th Leg., ch. 885, § 2.47(a)(1) repeals this section effective April 1, 2009.

[Sections 41.010 to 41.050 reserved for expansion]

SUBCHAPTER B. REGISTRATION OF BUSINESS OPPORTUNITY

§ 41.051. Filing of Disclosure Statement and List of Sellers

Before the sale or offer for sale, including advertising, of a business opportunity, the principal seller shall register the business opportunity with the secretary of state by filing:

(1) a copy of the disclosure statement required by Subchapter D; [1] and

(2) a list of the names and resident addresses of the individuals who sell or will sell the business opportunity for the principal seller.

Added by Acts 1997, 75th Leg., ch. 1008, § 5, eff. Sept. 1, 1997.

[1] V.T.C.A., Bus. & C. § 41.151 et seq.

Repeal

Acts 2007, 80th Leg., ch. 885, § 2.47(a)(1) repeals this section effective April 1, 2009.

§ 41.052. Updating of Information on File

(a) A disclosure statement on file must be updated through a new filing annually and whenever a material change occurs.

(b) The list of individuals who sell or will sell the business opportunity for the principal seller must be updated through a new filing every six months.

Added by Acts 1997, 75th Leg., ch. 1008, § 5, eff. Sept. 1, 1997.

Repeal

Acts 2007, 80th Leg., ch. 885, § 2.47(a)(1) repeals this section effective April 1, 2009.

§ 41.053. Filing of Copy of Bond or Notification of Account

A principal seller who is required to provide a bond or establish a trust account shall contemporaneously file with the secretary of state a copy of:

(1) the bond; or

(2) the formal notification by the depository that the trust account is established.

Added by Acts 1997, 75th Leg., ch. 1008, § 5, eff. Sept. 1, 1997.

Repeal

Acts 2007, 80th Leg., ch. 885, § 2.47(a)(1) repeals this section effective April 1, 2009.

§ 41.054. Use of Disclosure Document From Other Regulatory Agency

Instead of using a disclosure statement required by this chapter in a transaction with a purchaser or for purposes of filing with the secretary of state, a seller may use a copy of a similar document required by the State Securities Board, Securities and Exchange Commission, or Federal Trade Commission that contains all the information required to be disclosed by this chapter.

Added by Acts 1997, 75th Leg., ch. 1008, § 5, eff. Sept. 1, 1997.

Repeal

Acts 2007, 80th Leg., ch. 885, § 2.47(a)(1) repeals this section effective April 1, 2009.

[Sections 41.055 to 41.100 reserved for expansion]

SUBCHAPTER C. BOND, TRUST ACCOUNT, OR LETTER OF CREDIT

§ 41.101. Bond, Trust Account, or Letter of Credit Required

(a) Before a seller makes a representation described by Section 41.004(a)(1) or otherwise represents that the buyer is assured of making a profit from a business opportunity, the principal seller must:

(1) obtain a surety bond by a surety company authorized to do business in this state;

(2) establish a trust account; or

(3) obtain an irrevocable letter of credit.

(b) The bond, trust account, or irrevocable letter of credit must:

(1) be in an amount of not less than $25,000; and

(2) be in favor of this state.

Added by Acts 1997, 75th Leg., ch. 1008, § 5, eff. Sept. 1, 1997.

Repeal

Acts 2007, 80th Leg., ch. 885, § 2.47(a)(1) repeals this section effective April 1, 2009.

§ 41.102. Action Against Bond, Trust Account, or Letter of Credit

(a) A person may bring an action against the bond, trust account, or irrevocable letter of credit obtained or established under Section 41.101 to recover actual damages for:

(1) a violation of this chapter; or

(2) the seller's breach of:

(A) the business opportunity contract; or

(B) an obligation arising from a business opportunity sale.

(b) The aggregate liability of the surety, trustee, or issuer in actions under Subsection (a) may not exceed the amount of the bond, trust account, or irrevocable letter of credit.

Added by Acts 1997, 75th Leg., ch. 1008, § 5, eff. Sept. 1, 1997.

Repeal

Acts 2007, 80th Leg., ch. 885, § 2.47(a)(1) repeals this section effective April 1, 2009.

[Sections 41.103 to 41.150 reserved for expansion]

SUBCHAPTER D. DISCLOSURE STATEMENT

§ 41.151. Disclosure to Purchaser of Business Opportunity

A seller must provide a purchaser with a written disclosure statement that meets the requirements of this subchapter. The seller must provide the statement at least 10 business days before the earlier of:

(1) the date the purchaser signs a business opportunity contract; or

(2) the date the seller receives any consideration.

Added by Acts 1997, 75th Leg., ch. 1008, § 5, eff. Sept. 1, 1997.

Repeal

Acts 2007, 80th Leg., ch. 885, § 2.47(a)(1) repeals this section effective April 1, 2009.

§ 41.152. Cover Sheet of Disclosure Statement

(a) A disclosure statement must have a cover sheet that is entitled, in at least 12-point boldface capital letters, "DISCLOSURES REQUIRED BY TEXAS LAW." The following statement must appear below the title in at least 10-point boldface type: "The State of Texas has not reviewed and does not endorse, approve, recommend, or sponsor any business opportunity. The information contained in this disclosure has not been verified by the state. If you have any questions about this investment, see an attorney before you sign a contract or agreement."

(b) Only the title and required statement may appear on the cover sheet.

Added by Acts 1997, 75th Leg., ch. 1008, § 5, eff. Sept. 1, 1997.

Repeal

Acts 2007, 80th Leg., ch. 885, § 2.47(a)(1) repeals this section effective April 1, 2009.

§ 41.153. Contents: Names and Addresses

A disclosure statement must contain:

(1) the name of the seller;

(2) the names under which the seller has done, is doing, or intends to do business;

(3) the name of any parent or affiliated company that will engage in business transactions with the purchaser or that takes responsibility for statements made by the seller; and

(4) the names, addresses, and titles of:

(A) the seller's officers, directors, trustees, general partners, general managers, and principal executives;

(B) stockholders owning more than 20 percent of the stock shares of the seller; and

(C) any other persons responsible for the seller's business activities relating to the sale of business opportunities.

Added by Acts 1997, 75th Leg., ch. 1008, § 5, eff. Sept. 1, 1997.

Repeal

Acts 2007, 80th Leg., ch. 885, § 2.47(a)(1) repeals this section effective April 1, 2009.

§ 41.154. Contents: Sales Periods

A disclosure statement must state the period the seller has:

(1) sold business opportunities; and

(2) sold business opportunities involving the products, equipment, supplies, or services the seller is offering to the purchaser.

Repeal

Acts 2007, 80th Leg., ch. 885, § 2.47(a)(1) repeals this section effective April 1, 2009.

§ 41.155. Contents: Services Description

A disclosure statement must contain:

(1) a detailed description of the actual services the seller undertakes to perform for the purchaser; and

(2) if the seller promises to perform services in connection with the placement of equipment, products, or supplies at a location:

(A) the full nature of those services; and

(B) the nature of the agreements to be made with the owners or managers of that location.

Repeal

Acts 2007, 80th Leg., ch. 885, § 2.47(a)(1) repeals this section effective April 1, 2009.

§ 41.156. Contents: Financial Statement

A disclosure statement must contain a copy of a financial statement of the seller that:

(1) was prepared according to generally accepted accounting principles within the previous 13 months; and

(2) has been updated to reflect material changes in the seller's financial condition.

Added by Acts 1997, 75th Leg., ch. 1008, § 5, eff. Sept. 1, 1997.

Repeal

Acts 2007, 80th Leg., ch. 885, § 2.47(a)(1) repeals this section effective April 1, 2009.

§ 41.157. Contents: Training Description

If the seller promises training, the disclosure statement must contain a complete description of the training, the length of the training, and the cost of the training, including travel and lodging expenses, that the purchaser will be required to incur.

Added by Acts 1997, 75th Leg., ch. 1008, § 5, eff. Sept. 1, 1997.

Repeal

Acts 2007, 80th Leg., ch. 885, § 2.47(a)(1) repeals this section effective April 1, 2009.

§ 41.158. Contents: Security Description

If the seller is required to secure a bond or establish a trust account, the disclosure statement must contain the following statement:

(1) "As required by Texas law, the seller has secured a bond issued by ______, a surety company authorized to do business in this state. Before signing a contract to purchase this business oppor-

tunity, you should confirm the bond's status with the surety company."; or

(2) "As required by Texas law, the seller has established a trust account with ______. Before signing a contract to purchase this business opportunity, you should confirm with the bank or savings institution the current status of the trust account.".

Added by Acts 1997, 75th Leg., ch. 1008, § 5, eff. Sept. 1, 1997.

Repeal

Acts 2007, 80th Leg., ch. 885, § 2.47(a)(1) repeals this section effective April 1, 2009.

§ 41.159. Contents: Delivery Date

If the seller is required to deliver to the purchaser the product, equipment, or supplies necessary to begin substantial operation of the business and states a definite or approximate delivery date for the product, equipment, or supplies, the disclosure statement must contain the following statement: "If the seller fails to deliver the product, equipment, or supplies necessary to begin substantial operation of the business within 45 days of the delivery date stated in your contract, you may notify the seller in writing and cancel your contract."

Added by Acts 1997, 75th Leg., ch. 1008, § 5, eff. Sept. 1, 1997.

Repeal

Acts 2007, 80th Leg., ch. 885, § 2.47(a)(1) repeals this section effective April 1, 2009.

§ 41.160. Contents: Sales or Earnings Representation

If the seller makes a statement concerning sales or earnings that may be made through the business opportunity, the disclosure statement must contain a statement disclosing:

(1) the total number of purchasers of business opportunities involving the product, equipment, supplies, or services being offered who to the seller's knowledge have actually achieved sales of or received earnings in the amount or range specified not earlier than the third year before the date of the disclosure statement; and

(2) the total number of purchasers who purchased business opportunities involving the product, equipment, supplies, or services being offered not earlier than the third year before the date of the disclosure statement.

Added by Acts 1997, 75th Leg., ch. 1008, § 5, eff. Sept. 1, 1997.

Repeal

Acts 2007, 80th Leg., ch. 885, § 2.47(a)(1) repeals this section effective April 1, 2009.

§ 41.161. Contents: Legal Action History

(a) A disclosure statement must contain a statement disclosing which, if any, of the persons described by Section 41.153:

(1) has, at any time during the previous seven fiscal years:

(A) been convicted of a felony, or pleaded nolo contendere to a felony charge, involving fraud, embezzlement, fraudulent conversion, or misappropriation of property; or

(B) been held liable in a civil action resulting in a final judgment, or settled out of court a civil action, involving allegations of fraud, embezzlement, fraudulent conversion, or misappropriation of property, the use of untrue or misleading representations in an attempt to sell or dispose of property, or the use of unfair, unlawful, or deceptive business practices;

(2) is a party to a civil action involving allegations of fraud, embezzlement, fraudulent conversion, or misappropriation of property, the use of untrue or misleading representations in an attempt to sell or dispose of property, or the use of unfair, unlawful, or deceptive business practices; or

(3) is subject to an injunction or restrictive order relating to business activity as a result of an action brought by a public agency or department.

(b) A statement required by Subsection (a) must include:

(1) the identity and location of the court or agency;

(2) the date of conviction, judgment, or decision;

(3) the penalty imposed;

(4) the damages assessed;

(5) the terms of the settlement or order; and

(6) the date, nature, and issuer of each order or ruling.

Added by Acts 1997, 75th Leg., ch. 1008, § 5, eff. Sept. 1, 1997.

Repeal

Acts 2007, 80th Leg., ch. 885, § 2.47(a)(1) repeals this section effective April 1, 2009.

§ 41.162. Contents: Bankruptcy

(a) A disclosure statement must contain a statement disclosing which, if any, of the persons described by Section 41.153 has, at any time during the previous seven fiscal years:

(1) filed in bankruptcy;

(2) been adjudged bankrupt;

(3) been reorganized because of insolvency; or

(4) been a principal, director, executive officer, or partner of any other person that, during or not later than the first anniversary of the end of the period the person held the position in relation to the other person, filed in bankruptcy, was adjudged bankrupt, or was reorganized because of insolvency.

(b) A statement that is required by Subsection (a)(4) must include:

(1) the name and location of the person that filed in bankruptcy, was adjudged bankrupt, or was reorganized;

(2) the date of the filing, adjudication, or reorganization; and

(3) any other material facts relating to the filing, adjudication, or reorganization.

Added by Acts 1997, 75th Leg., ch. 1008, § 5, eff. Sept. 1, 1997.

Repeal

Acts 2007, 80th Leg., ch. 885, § 2.47(a)(1) repeals this section effective April 1, 2009.

§ 41.163. Contents: Contract Copy

A disclosure statement must contain a copy of the business opportunity contract that the seller uses as a matter of course and that will be presented to the purchaser at closing.

Added by Acts 1997, 75th Leg., ch. 1008, § 5, eff. Sept. 1, 1997.

Repeal

Acts 2007, 80th Leg., ch. 885, § 2.47(a)(1) repeals this section effective April 1, 2009.

[Sections 41.164 to 41.200 reserved for expansion]

SUBCHAPTER E. BUSINESS OPPORTUNITY CONTRACT

§ 41.201. Form of Business Opportunity Contract

A business opportunity contract must be in writing and include, in 10-point type or in handwriting of an equivalent size, the following:

(1) the terms of payment, including the initial consideration, down payment, and additional payments required;

(2) a detailed description of the acts or services the seller undertakes to perform for the purchaser;

(3) the seller's principal business address and the name and address of the seller's agent in this state authorized to receive service of process;

(4) the delivery date or, if the contract provides for staggered delivery times to the purchaser, the approximate delivery date of the products, equipment, or supplies the seller is to:

(A) deliver to the purchaser's home or business address; or

(B) place at locations owned or managed by persons other than the purchaser; and

(5) a complete description of the nature of the buy-back or security arrangement if the seller has represented orally or in writing when selling, leasing, soliciting, or offering a business opportunity that there is a buy-back or that the initial consideration is secured.

Added by Acts 1997, 75th Leg., ch. 1008, § 5, eff. Sept. 1, 1997.

Repeal

Acts 2007, 80th Leg., ch. 885, § 2.47(a)(1) repeals this section effective April 1, 2009.

§ 41.202. Delivery of Copies of Documents to Purchaser

A copy of the completed business opportunity contract and any other document the seller requires the purchaser to sign shall be given to the purchaser at the time the purchaser signs the contract.

Added by Acts 1997, 75th Leg., ch. 1008, § 5, eff. Sept. 1, 1997.

Repeal

Acts 2007, 80th Leg., ch. 885, § 2.47(a)(1) repeals this section effective April 1, 2009.

§ 41.203. Effect of Assignment of Business Opportunity Contract

An assignee of a business opportunity contract or of the seller's rights under the contract is subject to all equities, rights, and defenses of the purchaser against the seller.

Added by Acts 1997, 75th Leg., ch. 1008, § 5, eff. Sept. 1, 1997.

Repeal

Acts 2007, 80th Leg., ch. 885, § 2.47(a)(1) repeals this section effective April 1, 2009.

[Sections 41.204 to 41.250 reserved for expansion]

SUBCHAPTER F. TERMINATION OF BUSINESS OPPORTUNITY REGISTRATION

§ 41.251. Voluntary Termination of Business Opportunity Registration

The principal seller of a registered business opportunity may voluntarily terminate the business opportunity's registration with the secretary of state if:

(1) the registered business opportunity will no longer be offered in this state;

(2) the registered business opportunity has changed to the extent that it no longer meets the definition of a business opportunity under Section 41.004(a);

(3) the registered business opportunity has become exempt under Section 41.004(b); or

(4) the principal seller offering the registered business opportunity has ceased to exist as a legal entity.

Added by Acts 1997, 75th Leg., ch. 1008, § 5, eff. Sept. 1, 1997.

Repeal

Acts 2007, 80th Leg., ch. 885, § 2.47(a)(1) repeals this section effective April 1, 2009.

§ 41.252. Involuntary Termination of Business Opportunity Registration

(a) The secretary of state may terminate the registration of a business opportunity registered under Section 41.051 if the seller does not comply with the requirements governing the updating of filings under Section 41.052.

(b) The secretary of state must give the business opportunity registrant notice of the delinquency not later than the 31st day before the date of termination of the business opportunity registration under Subsection (a).

(c) The notice of delinquency must be given by certified mail addressed to the registered agent or the principal place of business of the business opportunity registrant noted in the latest filing made under this chapter.

(d) The secretary of state may adopt rules governing:

(1) the termination of a delinquent registration;

(2) the effective date of the termination; and

(3) the grace period, if any.

Added by Acts 1997, 75th Leg., ch. 1008, § 5, eff. Sept. 1, 1997.

Repeal

Acts 2007, 80th Leg., ch. 885, § 2.47(a)(1) repeals this section effective April 1, 2009.

[Sections 41.253 to 41.300 reserved for expansion]

SUBCHAPTER G. ENFORCEMENT

§ 41.301. Prohibited Acts

A seller may not:

(1) employ a representation, device, scheme, or artifice to deceive a purchaser;

(2) make an untrue statement of a material fact or omit to state a material fact in connection with the documents and information required to be furnished to the secretary of state or purchaser;

(3) represent that the business opportunity provides or will provide income or earning potential unless the seller:

(A) has documented data to substantiate the claims of income or earning potential; and

(B) discloses the data to the purchaser when the representation is made; or

(4) make a claim or representation in advertising or promotional material or in an oral sales presentation, solicitation, or discussion between the seller and the purchaser that is inconsistent with the information required to be disclosed by this chapter.

Added by Acts 1997, 75th Leg., ch. 1008, § 5, eff. Sept. 1, 1997.

Repeal

Acts 2007, 80th Leg., ch. 885, § 2.47(a)(1) repeals this section effective April 1, 2009.

§ 41.302. Deceptive Trade Practice

A violation of this chapter is a false, misleading, or deceptive act or practice under Section 17.46, Business & Commerce Code. A public or private right or remedy prescribed by Chapter 17, Business & Commerce Code, may be used to enforce this chapter.

Added by Acts 1997, 75th Leg., ch. 1008, § 5, eff. Sept. 1, 1997.

Repeal

Acts 2007, 80th Leg., ch. 885, § 2.47(a)(1) repeals this section effective April 1, 2009.

§ 41.303. Review and Suit by Attorney General

(a) The attorney general may review a disclosure statement filed with the secretary of state under Subchapter B.[1]

(b) If a disclosure statement fails to comply with this chapter, the attorney general may:

(1) notify the secretary of state and the seller in writing of the deficiency; and

(2) file suit to enjoin the seller from doing business until the failure to comply has been corrected.

(c) If the attorney general notifies the secretary of state under Subsection (b), the secretary of state shall:

(1) attach a copy of the notice from the attorney general to the front of the disclosure statement; and

(2) on inquiry of the status of the disclosure statement, disclose that a statement has been filed but that its correctness has been questioned by the attorney general.

Added by Acts 1997, 75th Leg., ch. 1008, § 5, eff. Sept. 1, 1997.

[1] V.T.C.A., Bus. & C. § 41.051 et seq.

Repeal

Acts 2007, 80th Leg., ch. 885, § 2.47(a)(1) repeals this section effective April 1, 2009.

CHAPTER 42. EUROPEAN UNION CURRENCY CONVERSION

Section

Acts 2007, 80th Leg., ch. 885, § 2.47(a)(1) repeals this chapter effective April 1, 2009.

§ 42.001. Definitions

In this chapter:

(1) "Euro" means the currency of the member states of the European Community, as amended by the Treaty on European Union. The term is abbreviated as EUR.

(2) "European currency unit" means the currency basket that is periodically used as the unit of account of the European Community, as defined by Regulation No. 3320/94 of the Council of the European Union and as referred to in Article 109g of the treaty establishing the European Community, as amended by the Treaty on European Union. The term is abbreviated as ECU.

(3) "Treaty on European Union" means the Treaty on European Union of February 7, 1992.

(4) "Introduction of the euro" means the periodic implementation of economic and monetary union in member states of the European Union in accordance with the Treaty on European Union.

Added by Acts 1999, 76th Leg., ch. 971, § 1, eff. June 18, 1999.

Repeal

Acts 2007, 80th Leg., ch. 885, § 2.47(a)(1) repeals this section effective April 1, 2009.

§ 42.002. Applicability of Chapter

(a) This chapter applies to each contract, security, and instrument, including a commercial contract, governed by the laws of this state.

(b) With respect to currency alteration, other than the introduction of the euro, this chapter does not create any negative inference or negative presumption regarding the validity or enforceability of a contract, security, or instrument denominated wholly or partly in a currency affected by the alteration.

Added by Acts 1999, 76th Leg., ch. 971, § 1, eff. June 18, 1999.

Repeal

Acts 2007, 80th Leg., ch. 885, § 2.47(a)(1) repeals this section effective April 1, 2009.

§ 42.003. Conflicts of Law

This chapter prevails to the extent of any conflict between this chapter and any other law of this state.

Added by Acts 1999, 76th Leg., ch. 971, § 1, eff. June 18, 1999.

Repeal

Acts 2007, 80th Leg., ch. 885, § 2.47(a)(1) repeals this section effective April 1, 2009.

§ 42.004. Continuity of Contract

(a) If a subject or medium of payment of a contract, security, or instrument is the European currency unit or a currency that has been substituted or replaced by the euro, the euro is a commercially reasonable substitute and substantial equivalent that may be:

(1) used in determining the value of the European currency unit or currency, as appropriate; or

(2) tendered, in each case, at the conversion rate specified in, and otherwise computed in accordance with, the regulations adopted by the Council of the European Union.

(b) A person may perform any obligation described by Subsection (a) in euros or in the currency or currencies originally designated in the contract, security, or instrument if that currency or those currencies remain legal tender, but the person may not perform those obligations in any other currency, regardless of whether that other currency:

(1) has been substituted or replaced by the euro; or

(2) is considered a denomination of the euro and has a fixed conversion rate with respect to the euro.

(c) The following occurrences are not considered a discharge of, do not excuse performance under, and do not give a party the right to unilaterally alter or terminate a contract, security, or instrument:

(1) the introduction of the euro;

(2) the tender of euros in connection with any obligation described by Subsection (a);

(3) the determination of the value of any obligation described by Subsection (a); or

(4) the computation or determination of the subject or medium of payment of a contract, security, or instrument with reference to an interest rate or any other basis that has been substituted or replaced because of the introduction of the euro and that is a commercially reasonable substitute and substantial equivalent.

Added by Acts 1999, 76th Leg., ch. 971, § 1, eff. June 18, 1999.

Repeal

Acts 2007, 80th Leg., ch. 885, § 2.47(a)(1) repeals this section effective April 1, 2009.

§ 42.005. Effect on Certain Agreements

This chapter does not alter or impair an agreement between parties that specifically relates to the introduction of the euro.

Added by Acts 1999, 76th Leg., ch. 971, § 1, eff. June 18, 1999.

Repeal

Acts 2007, 80th Leg., ch. 885, § 2.47(a)(1) repeals this section effective April 1, 2009.

CHAPTER 43. UNIFORM ELECTRONIC TRANSACTIONS ACT

Section

Section
43.251 to 43.253. Renumbered.

Acts 2007, 80th Leg., ch. 885, § 2.47(a)(1) repeals this chapter effective April 1, 2009.

Chapter 43, Uniform Electronic Transactions Act, consisting of §§ 43.001 to 43.020, was added by Acts 2001, 77th Leg., ch. 702, § 1.

Another Chapter 43, Sweepstakes, as added by Acts 2001, 77th Leg., ch. 1119, § 1, was renumbered as V.T.C.A., Bus. & C. Code, Chapter 45, §§ 45.001 to 45.004 by Acts 2003, 78th Leg., ch. 1275, § 2(4), and another Chapter 43, Telemarketing, as added by Acts 2001, 77th Leg., ch. 1429, § 1, was renumbered as V.T.C.A., Bus. & C. Code, Chapter 44, §§ 44.001 to 44.253 by Acts 2003, 78th Leg., ch. 1275, § 2(3).

State Bar Committee Comments included with the permission of the State Bar of Texas, Business Law Section.

State Bar Committee Comments

1. **General Effect of Chapter 43.** The effect of this chapter generally is to return to the control of state law certain matters which would otherwise be governed by the federal Electronic Signatures in Global and National Commerce Act (PL 106–229, 114 Stat. 464, June 30, 2000), also known as "E–SIGN," codified at 15 U.S.C. Sections 7001 *et seq.* E–SIGN prevents signatures, contracts, or records relating to any transaction affecting interstate or foreign commerce from being denied legal effect, validity, or enforceability *solely* because the signature, contract, or record is in electronic form or because an electronic record or signature was used in forming the contract. That same rule is the fundamental premise of this chapter enacted as Texas law. Chapter 43 does not substantively modify, limit, or supersede another law of this state, but rather imposes a procedural requirement that a record or signature may not be denied legal effect or enforceability solely because it is in electronic form. *See* Section 43.007 and its Official Comment 1. *See also* the State Bar Committee Comments to Section 43.007.

2. **Non-preemption by E–SIGN.** As stated in 15 U.S.C. Section 7002(a), E–SIGN generally preempts state laws that modify or contradict the basic federal provisions of 15 U.S.C. Section 7001 that signatures, contracts, or records relating to any transaction affecting interstate or foreign commerce may not be denied legal effect or enforceability solely because the signature, contract, or record is in electronic form or because an electronic record or signature was used in forming the contract. However, concerns regarding broad federal preemption of contracts law, a traditional area of state regulation, and support for the Uniform Electronic Transactions Act (UETA) led Congress to include specific preemption provisions and exceptions in E–SIGN at 15 U.S.C. Sections 7002 and 7003. Section 7002(a)(1) of E–SIGN generally permits the Uniform Electronic Transactions Act (UETA) as enacted by any state to supersede E–SIGN so long as that state enacts the uniform official text of UETA. Any specific exceptions the state enacts to the scope of its version of UETA are preempted to the extent inconsistent with E–SIGN. Additionally, E–SIGN would permit UETA (or any other state law, rule, or regulation specifying alternative procedures or requirements for using electronic records or signatures to establish valid contracts or records) to escape preemption as long as its requirements were consistent with E–SIGN and technologically neutral (15 U.S.C. Section 7002(a)(2)).

Chapter 43 is closely modeled on the official text of UETA with minimal changes or additions none of which are inconsistent with E–SIGN and all of which are technologically neutral. Non-substantive changes involving section numbers, cross-references, a delayed effective date, format, selection among optional provisions, and similar changes should not constitute departures from the official text of UETA sufficient to invoke preemption under 15 U.S.C. Section 7002(a). Sections 43.019 and 43.020 of this chapter are not part of the official text of UETA but are consistent with E–SIGN and are technologically neutral in keeping with 15 U.S.C. Section 7002(a)(2). Thus, even if this chapter were considered to specify alternative procedures or requirements for electronic signatures or records, it should not be preempted by E–SIGN.

Section 43.019, not contained in the official text of UETA, responds to the E–SIGN requirement, in 15 U.S.C. Section 7002(a)(2)(B), that state law must specifically refer to E–SIGN in order to supersede its provisions and avoid preemption.

3. **Continuing Relevance of E–SIGN.** E–SIGN continues to be relevant with respect to Texas law not governed by this chapter, such as the Texas Constitution or another law that is otherwise exempt from this chapter, to the extent such other law would purport to make signatures, contracts, and other records used in interstate or foreign commerce unenforceable on the sole grounds they are electronic. Further, the legislation enacting this chapter specifically preserves the effectiveness of E–SIGN Sections 7001(c) and 7003(b), which will continue to apply to electronic transactions otherwise governed by this chapter as a result of a savings provision in Acts 2001, 77th Leg., ch. 702, § 6, which reads:

(a) Notwithstanding Section 43.019, Business & Commerce Code, as added by this Act, Chapter 43, Business & Commerce Code, as added by this Act, does not modify, limit, or supersede the provisions of Section 101(c) or Section 103(b), Electronic Signatures in Global and National Commerce Act (15 U.S.C. Sections 7001 and 7003), as amended from time to time, and specifically does not authorize the electronic delivery of any notice of the type described by Section 103(b), Electronic Signatures in Global and National Commerce Act (15 U.S.C. Section 7003), as amended from time to time, including:

(1) any notice of:

(A) the cancellation or termination of utility services (including water, heat, and power);

(B) default, acceleration, repossession, foreclosure, or eviction, or the right to cure, under a credit agreement secured by, or a rental agreement for, a primary residence of an individual;

(C) the cancellation or termination of health insurance or benefits or life insurance benefits (excluding annuities); or

(D) recall of a product, or material failure of a product, that risks endangering health or safety; or

(2) any document required to accompany any transportation or handling of hazardous materials, pesticides, or other toxic or dangerous materials.

(b) If a federal regulatory agency under Section 104(d)(1), Electronic Signatures in Global and National Commerce Act (15 U.S.C. Section 7004), exempts a specified category or type of record from the requirements relating to consent in Section 101(c), Electronic Signatures in Global and National Commerce Act (15 U.S.C. Section 7001), or if a federal regulatory agency under Section 103(c)(2), Electronic Signatures in Global and National Commerce Act (15 U.S.C. Section 7003), removes an exception for a type of document from the application of Section 101, Electronic Signatures in Global and National Commerce Act (15 U.S.C. Section 7001), the regulatory agency of this state with jurisdiction over the subject matter with respect to which the federal action was taken may exempt the specified category or type of record from the application of Chapter 43, Business & Commerce Code, as added by this Act. An exemption under this subsection must be by rule or order of the state regulatory agency after notice and an opportunity for public comment.

For further discussion of the interaction between E–SIGN and UETA *Compare* Patricia Brumfield Fry, *A Preliminary Analysis of Federal and State Electronic Commerce Laws*, ELECTRONIC LAW & COMMERCE REPORT (BNA July 12, 2000), also available through the website of the National Conference of Commissioners on Uniform State Laws [www.nccusl.org], *with* Robert A. Wittie and Jane K. Winn, *Electronic Records and Signatures under the Federal E–Sign Legislation and the UETA*, 56 BUS. LAW. 293, 324–333 (2000).

4. Severability. Section 20 of the official text of UETA provides for severability but is omitted from this chapter. Section 311.032, Texas Government Code (part of the Code Construction Act) states the severability rule that applies to this chapter and is essentially identical to the omitted provision from UETA. Reference to the Code Construction Act of the Texas Government Code for such a severability provision should be considered a non-substantive change to the official text of UETA and is also consistent with E–SIGN. This approach to severability should not invoke preemption under 15 U.S.C. Section 7002(a).

§ 43.001. Short Title

This chapter may be cited as the Uniform Electronic Transactions Act.

Added by Acts 2001, 77th Leg., ch. 702, § 1, eff. Jan. 1, 2002.

Repeal

Acts 2007, 80th Leg., ch. 885, § 2.47(a)(1) repeals this section effective April 1, 2009.

§ 43.002. Definitions

In this chapter:

(1) "Agreement" means the bargain of the parties in fact, as found in their language or inferred from other circumstances and from rules, regulations, and procedures given the effect of agreements under laws otherwise applicable to a particular transaction.

(2) "Automated transaction" means a transaction conducted or performed, in whole or in part, by electronic means or electronic records, in which the acts or records of one or both parties are not reviewed by an individual in the ordinary course in forming a contract, performing under an existing contract, or fulfilling an obligation required by the transaction.

(3) "Computer program" means a set of statements or instructions to be used directly or indirectly in an information processing system in order to bring about a certain result.

(4) "Contract" means the total legal obligation resulting from the parties' agreement as affected by this chapter and other applicable law.

(5) "Electronic" means relating to technology having electrical, digital, magnetic, wireless, optical, electromagnetic, or similar capabilities.

(6) "Electronic agent" means a computer program or an electronic or other automated means used independently to initiate an action or respond to electronic records or performances in whole or in part, without review or action by an individual.

(7) "Electronic record" means a record created, generated, sent, communicated, received, or stored by electronic means.

(8) "Electronic signature" means an electronic sound, symbol, or process attached to or logically

associated with a record and executed or adopted by a person with the intent to sign the record.

(9) "Governmental agency" means an executive, legislative, or judicial agency, department, board, commission, authority, institution, or instrumentality of the federal government or of a state or of a county, municipality, or other political subdivision of a state.

(10) "Information" means data, text, images, sounds, codes, computer programs, software, databases, or the like.

(11) "Information processing system" means an electronic system for creating, generating, sending, receiving, storing, displaying, or processing information.

(12) "Record" means information that is inscribed on a tangible medium or that is stored in an electronic or other medium and is retrievable in perceivable form.

(13) "Security procedure" means a procedure employed for the purpose of verifying that an electronic signature, record, or performance is that of a specific person or for detecting changes or errors in the information in an electronic record. The term includes a procedure that requires the use of algorithms or other codes, identifying words or numbers, encryption, or callback or other acknowledgment procedures.

(14) "State" means a state of the United States, the District of Columbia, Puerto Rico, the United States Virgin Islands, or any territory or insular possession subject to the jurisdiction of the United States. The term includes an Indian tribe or band, or Alaskan native village, which is recognized by federal law or formally acknowledged by a state.

(15) "Transaction" means an action or set of actions occurring between two or more persons relating to the conduct of business, commercial, or governmental affairs.

Added by Acts 2001, 77th Leg., ch. 702, § 1, eff. Jan. 1, 2002.

Repeal

Acts 2007, 80th Leg., ch. 885, § 2.47(a)(1) repeals this section effective April 1, 2009.

State Bar Committee Comments

1. **"Governmental Agency" and "State Agency."** Section 43.002(9) provides a definition of "Governmental agency" to mean "an executive, legislative, or judicial agency, department, board, commission, authority, institution, or instrumentality of the federal government or of a state or of a county, municipality, or other political subdivision of a state." Sections 43.017(a) and 43.017(b) use the term "state agency" without defining it. The term "state agency" was substituted for the term "governmental agency of this State," in Section 43.017(a) of this chapter, and for the term "governmental agency," in Section 43.017(b) of this chapter, to exempt local government agencies from rules adopted under Section 43.017. The definition of "governmental agency" in Section 43.002(9) of this chapter would otherwise include a local government agency.

2. **Person.** The definition of "person" contained in Section 2(12) of UETA, is omitted from Section 43.002 of this chapter. The applicable definition of "person" is found in Section 311.005 of the Texas Government Code and applies to this Act. The Government Code definition of "person" is substantially the same as the definition omitted from this chapter and application of either definition should produce the same result on any given set of facts. Reference to the Code Construction Act of the Texas Government Code for the definition of "person" should be considered a non-substantive change to the official text of UETA and is also consistent with E–SIGN. This approach should not invoke preemption under 15 U.S.C. Section 7002(a).

§ 43.003. Scope

(a) Except as otherwise provided in Subsection (b), this chapter applies to electronic records and electronic signatures relating to a transaction.

(b) This chapter does not apply to a transaction to the extent it is governed by:

(1) a law governing the creation and execution of wills, codicils, or testamentary trusts; or

(2) the Uniform Commercial Code, other than Sections 1.107 and 1.206 and Chapters 2 and 2A.

(c) This chapter applies to an electronic record or electronic signature otherwise excluded from the application of this chapter under Subsection (b) when used for a transaction subject to a law other than those specified in Subsection (b).

(d) A transaction subject to this chapter is also subject to other applicable substantive law.

Added by Acts 2001, 77th Leg., ch. 702, § 1, eff. Jan. 1, 2002.

Repeal

Acts 2007, 80th Leg., ch. 885, § 2.47(a)(1) repeals this section effective April 1, 2009.

State Bar Committee Comments

1. **Uniform Enactment.** As enacted, Section 43.003(b) of this chapter does not contain any non-

uniform exception to the scope of UETA and does not therefore invoke the E–SIGN consistency test for preemption set forth in 15 U.S.C. Section 7002(a)(1).

2. **Electronic Records and Signatures in Real Estate Transactions.** As explained in item 3 of Official Comment 9 to this section, the fundamental rule of this chapter in Section 43.007 would permit the parties to a real estate transaction to conduct that transaction electronically where they so agreed. For example, Section 5.021 of the Property Code requires a conveyance of certain real estate interests to be in writing and subscribed by the conveyor. Pursuant to this chapter, a vendor and purchaser could now agree that vendor's deed or other instrument of conveyance would be delivered to the purchaser by e-mail or other electronic medium capable of retention by the purchaser at the time of receipt and that the subscription requirement would be met by an electronic subscription. *See* Sections 43.005 and 43.008. However, as the discussion of real estate transactions in the Official Comment of Section 43.003 suggests, such an electronic conveyance, effective between the parties, would not be recordable in the deed records of the particular county until the county had adopted an electronic filing system in accordance with Chapter 195, Local Government Code. Any electronic filing must comply with rules adopted by the Texas State Library and Archives Commission and must be made by an authorized filer as defined in Section 195.003, Local Government Code. Thus, until electronic filing of real estate conveyances in the proper records becomes possible, conveyances written on paper or other tangible, permanent medium suitable for recording under current practices will be preferable so that the purchaser's rights against third parties can be protected through the filing system. Electronic recording of conveyances will also require compliance with Section 43.011, which authorizes acknowledgments on electronic records, if the acknowledgment contains the electronic signature of the notary public, together with all other information required to be included by other applicable law. The acknowledgment will not be required to contain a seal. *See* Official Comment to Section 43.011.

§ 43.004. Prospective Application

This chapter applies to any electronic record or electronic signature created, generated, sent, communicated, received, or stored on or after January 1, 2002.

Added by Acts 2001, 77th Leg., ch. 702, § 1, eff. Jan. 1, 2002.

Repeal

Acts 2007, 80th Leg., ch. 885, § 2.47(a)(1) repeals this section effective April 1, 2009.

§ 43.005. Use of Electronic Records and Electronic Signatures; Variation by Agreement

(a) This chapter does not require a record or signature to be created, generated, sent, communicated, received, stored, or otherwise processed or used by electronic means or in electronic form.

(b) This chapter applies only to transactions between parties each of which has agreed to conduct transactions by electronic means. Whether the parties agree to conduct a transaction by electronic means is determined from the context and surrounding circumstances, including the parties' conduct.

(c) A party that agrees to conduct a transaction by electronic means may refuse to conduct other transactions by electronic means. The right granted by this subsection may not be waived by agreement.

(d) Except as otherwise provided in this chapter, the effect of any of its provisions may be varied by agreement. The presence in certain provisions of this chapter of the words "unless otherwise agreed," or words of similar import, does not imply that the effect of other provisions may not be varied by agreement.

(e) Whether an electronic record or electronic signature has legal consequences is determined by this chapter and other applicable law.

Added by Acts 2001, 77th Leg., ch. 702, § 1, eff. Jan. 1, 2002.

Repeal

Acts 2007, 80th Leg., ch. 885, § 2.47(a)(1) repeals this section effective April 1, 2009.

State Bar Committee Comments

1. **Applicability to Governmental Agencies.** This section applies to the question whether a governmental agency has agreed to conduct a transaction by electronic means, so long as the governmental agency has the power to make such an agreement.

2. **No Automatic Right.** While the Texas Uniform Electronic Transactions Act codified in this chapter removes barriers to the use of electronic records and electronic signatures in transactions, it does not confer an automatic right on one party to conduct a transaction by electronic means. In consensual transactions, *e.g.*, agreements, both parties must agree to conduct the transaction by electronic means. In recording or filing transactions, the person submitting the record to be filed or recorded does not have a right to submit the record electronically until the recipient has the technology and ability necessary to receive, access, store and retrieve the record in electronic format. The recipient

filing office may also have the right to require, or other law may require, that the record be submitted in a particular format. *See* Sections 43.008, 43.012(g), and 43.017, *and see* State Bar Committee Comment 2 of Section 43.003.

§ 43.006. Construction and Application

This chapter must be construed and applied:

(1) to facilitate electronic transactions consistent with other applicable law;

(2) to be consistent with reasonable practices concerning electronic transactions and with the continued expansion of those practices; and

(3) to effectuate its general purpose to make uniform the law with respect to the subject of this chapter among states enacting it.

Added by Acts 2001, 77th Leg., ch. 702, § 1, eff. Jan. 1, 2002.

Repeal

Acts 2007, 80th Leg., ch. 885, § 2.47(a)(1) repeals this section effective April 1, 2009.

§ 43.007. Legal Recognition of Electronic Records, Electronic Signatures, and Electronic Contracts

(a) A record or signature may not be denied legal effect or enforceability solely because it is in electronic form.

(b) A contract may not be denied legal effect or enforceability solely because an electronic record was used in its formation.

(c) If a law requires a record to be in writing, an electronic record satisfies the law.

(d) If a law requires a signature, an electronic signature satisfies the law.

Added by Acts 2001, 77th Leg., ch. 702, § 1, eff. Jan. 1, 2002.

Repeal

Acts 2007, 80th Leg., ch. 885, § 2.47(a)(1) repeals this section effective April 1, 2009.

State Bar Committee Comments

1. **No Automatic Right.** While the Texas Uniform Electronic Transactions Act codified in this chapter removes barriers to the use of electronic records and electronic signatures in transactions, it does not confer an automatic right on one party to conduct a transaction by electronic means. In consensual transactions, *e.g.*, agreements, both parties must agree to conduct the transaction by electronic means. Section 43.005(b). In recording or filing transactions, the person submitting the record to be filed or recorded does not have a right to submit the record electronically until the recipient has the technology and ability necessary to receive, access, store and retrieve the record in electronic format. The recipient filing office may also have the right to require, or other law may require, that the record be submitted in a particular format. *See* Sections 43.008, 43.012(g), and 43.017, *and see* State Bar Committee Comment 2 of Section 43.003.

2. **Effect on Texas Law.** According to Official Comment 1 this section states the fundamental premise of Chapter 43. Its effect on Texas law is illustrated by the following examples:

a. **Statute of Frauds.** Where there is a requirement in Texas law in the nature of a statute of frauds, UETA allows the requirement for a signed writing to be met by an electronic communication or electronic record satisfying the writing requirement and an electronic signature satisfying the signature requirement. The most obvious example would be Section 26.001 of the Texas Business and Commerce Code, the general Texas statute of frauds modeled on the original English act. The requirements of that statute may now be met electronically where the parties have agreed to conduct the transaction by electronic means.

b. **Written Communications.** Where a state statute specifies or requires written communications, that requirement can be satisfied by e-mail, but only where the parties have agreed to communicate electronically. For example, Section 93.005 of the Property Code requires the landlord to refund the security deposit to a commercial tenant who "provides notice" of the tenant's forwarding address, and Section 93.009(a) requires that this notice be in the form of a "written statement of the tenant's forwarding address." Subsection 43.008(a) should permit landlord and tenant to agree that tenant may furnish this information by e-mail and should validate the tenant's e-mailing the new address to the landlord so long as the e-mail is capable of retention by the landlord as required by that subsection.

c. **Requirement for Communication by a Specific Method.** Where a statute requires communication by a specific method, that separate statutory requirement controls. For example, Section 62.005 of the Property Code provides that notices required to be sent to real estate brokers in certain circumstances under Chapter 62 must be sent by certified mail, return receipt requested. That statute controls over Chapter 43 and thus electronic notice to the broker is not permitted to be effective even if the parties wish to agree otherwise. *See* Section 43.008, Official Comment 4.

d. **Variation by Agreement.** Certain statutes impose particular requirements for communicating information from one person to another but permit the statutory requirements to be varied by agreement of the parties. In effect the statutory requirements become default rules that apply in the absence of agreement otherwise. For example, subsection 93.002(e) of the Property Code provides that if a commercial tenant abandons the premises the landlord may store the tenant's property and may dispose of such property after delivering the appropriate notice to the tenant by certified mail. Subsection 93.002(f) of the same statute requires a landlord who changes the door lock on the premises of a commercial tenant to place a written notice on the tenant's front door advising where a new key may be obtained. However, subsection 93.002(h) of this statute states that "[a] lease supersedes this section to the extent of any conflict." This quoted provision appears to permit the landlord and commercial tenant to vary the notice requirements by agreeing to different terms in the lease. According to subsection 43.008(d) of this chapter and Official Comment 6, requirements for sending, formatting and the like, which are imposed by other law, may also be varied by agreement to the extent permitted by such other law. Thus, if landlord and tenant agree on some electronic form or method of giving the notices referred to, such as e-mail, their agreement and its enforcement is permitted under this chapter.

3. **Continuing Relevance of E–SIGN.** The potential effect of this chapter is limited by a savings provision in the enacting legislation, Acts 2001, 77th Leg., ch. 702, § 6, retaining the applicability of E–SIGN Sections 7001(c) and 7003(b). The savings provision is reproduced in State Bar Committee Comment 3 of Section 43.001.

§ 43.008. Provision of Information in Writing; Presentation of Records

(a) If parties have agreed to conduct a transaction by electronic means and a law requires a person to provide, send, or deliver information in writing to another person, the requirement is satisfied if the information is provided, sent, or delivered, as the case may be, in an electronic record capable of retention by the recipient at the time of receipt. An electronic record is not capable of retention by the recipient if the sender or its information processing system inhibits the ability of the recipient to print or store the electronic record.

(b) If a law other than this chapter requires a record (i) to be posted or displayed in a certain manner, (ii) to be sent, communicated, or transmitted by a specified method, or (iii) to contain information that is formatted in a certain manner, the following rules apply:

(1) the record must be posted or displayed in the manner specified in the other law;

(2) except as otherwise provided in Subsection (d)(2), the record must be sent, communicated, or transmitted by the method specified in the other law; and

(3) the record must contain the information formatted in the manner specified in the other law.

(c) If a sender inhibits the ability of a recipient to store or print an electronic record, the electronic record is not enforceable against the recipient.

(d) The requirements of this section may not be varied by agreement, but:

(1) to the extent a law other than this chapter requires information to be provided, sent, or delivered in writing but permits that requirement to be varied by agreement, the requirement under Subsection (a) that the information be in the form of an electronic record capable of retention may also be varied by agreement; and

(2) a requirement under a law other than this chapter to send, communicate, or transmit a record by first class mail may be varied by agreement to the extent permitted by the other law.

Added by Acts 2001, 77th Leg., ch. 702, § 1, eff. Jan. 1, 2002.

Repeal

Acts 2007, 80th Leg., ch. 885, § 2.47(a)(1) repeals this section effective April 1, 2009.

State Bar Committee Comments

1. **No Automatic Right.** While the Texas Uniform Electronic Transactions Act codified in this chapter removes barriers to the use of electronic records and electronic signatures in transactions, it does not confer an automatic right on one party to conduct a transaction by electronic means. In consensual transactions, *e.g.*, agreements, both parties must agree to conduct the transaction by electronic means. In recording or filing transactions, the person submitting the record to be filed or recorded does not have a right to submit the record electronically until the recipient has the technology and ability necessary to receive, access, store and retrieve the record in electronic format. The recipient filing office may also have the right to require, or other law may require, that the record be submitted in a particular format. *See* Sections 43.008, 43.012(g), and 43.017, *and see* State Bar Committee Comment 2 of Section 43.003.

2. **Electronic Records and Signatures in Real Estate Transactions.** As explained in Official Comment 3 to Section 43.003, the fundamental rule of this chapter in Section 43.007 would permit the parties to a real estate transaction to conduct that transaction electronically where they so agreed. For example, Section 5.021 of the Property Code requires a conveyance of certain real estate interests to be in writing and subscribed by the conveyor.

Pursuant to this chapter, a vendor and purchaser could now agree that vendor's deed or other instrument of conveyance would be delivered to the purchaser by e-mail or other electronic medium capable of retention by the purchaser at the time of receipt and that the subscription requirement would be met by an electronic subscription. *See* Sections 43.003 and 43.005. However, as the discussion of real estate transactions in State Bar Comment 2 of Section 43.003 suggests, such an electronic conveyance, effective between the parties, would not be recordable in the deed records of the particular county until the county had adopted an electronic filing system in accordance with Chapter 195, Local Government Code. Any electronic filing must comply with rules adopted by the Texas State Library and Archives Commission and must be made by an authorized filer as defined in Section 195.003, Local Government Code. Thus, until electronic filing of real estate conveyances in the proper records becomes possible, conveyances written on paper or other tangible, permanent medium suitable for recording under current practices will be preferable so that the purchaser's rights against third parties can be protected through the filing system. Electronic recording of conveyances will also require compliance with Section 43.011, which authorizes acknowledgments on electronic records, if the acknowledgment contains the electronic signature of the notary public, together with all other information required to be included by other applicable law. The acknowledgment will not be required to contain a seal. *See* Official Comment to Section 43.011.

3. **Local Government Code Filing Provisions.** The legislation enacting this chapter also amends certain Local Government Code provisions dealing with electronic filing. Specifically, Acts 2001, 77th Leg., ch. 702, § 2 reads:

Subsection (a), Section 191.009, Local Government Code, is amended to read as follows:

(a) A county clerk may accept instruments by electronic filing and record the instruments electronically if the filing or recording complies with the rules adopted by the Texas State Library and Archives Commission under Chapter 195. Such an instrument is an electronic record, as defined by Section 43.002, Business & Commerce Code.

Acts 2001, 77th Leg., ch. 702, § 3 reads:

Section 195.002, Local Government Code, is amended by adding Subsection (e) to read as follows:

(e) Notwithstanding Sections 43.017 and 43.018, Business & Commerce Code, a county clerk may accept any filed electronic record, as defined by Section 43.002, Business & Commerce Code, and may electronically record that record if the filing and recording of that record complies with rules adopted by the commission under this section.

Acts 2001, 77th Leg., ch. 702, § 4 reads:

Chapter 195, Local Government Code, is amended by adding Section 195.009 to read as follows:

Sec. 195.009. FILING. For purposes of this chapter, an instrument is filed with the county clerk when it is received by the county clerk, unless the county clerk rejects the filing within the time and manner provided by this chapter and rules adopted under this chapter.

§ 43.009. Attribution and Effect of Electronic Record and Electronic Signature

(a) An electronic record or electronic signature is attributable to a person if it was the act of the person. The act of the person may be shown in any manner, including a showing of the efficacy of any security procedure applied to determine the person to which the electronic record or electronic signature was attributable.

(b) The effect of an electronic record or electronic signature attributed to a person under Subsection (a) is determined from the context and surrounding circumstances at the time of its creation, execution, or adoption, including the parties' agreement, if any, and otherwise as provided by law.

Added by Acts 2001, 77th Leg., ch. 702, § 1, eff. Jan. 1, 2002.

Repeal

Acts 2007, 80th Leg., ch. 885, § 2.47(a)(1) repeals this section effective April 1, 2009.

§ 43.010. Effect of Change or Error

(a) If a change or error in an electronic record occurs in a transmission between parties to a transaction, the rules provided by this section apply.

(b) If the parties have agreed to use a security procedure to detect changes or errors and one party has conformed to the procedure, but the other party has not, and the nonconforming party would have detected the change or error had that party also conformed, the conforming party may avoid the effect of the changed or erroneous electronic record.

(c) In an automated transaction involving an individual, the individual may avoid the effect of an electronic record that resulted from an error made by the individual in dealing with the electronic agent of another person if the electronic agent did not provide an opportunity for the prevention or correction of the error and, at the time the individual learns of the error, the individual:

(1) promptly notifies the other person of the error and that the individual did not intend to be bound by the electronic record received by the other person;

(2) takes reasonable steps, including steps that conform to the other person's reasonable instructions, to return to the other person or, if instructed by the other person, to destroy the consideration received, if any, as a result of the erroneous electronic record; and

(3) has not used or received any benefit or value from the consideration, if any, received from the other person.

(d) If neither Subsection (b) nor Subsection (c) applies, the change or error has the effect provided by other law, including the law of mistake, and the parties' contract, if any.

(e) Subsections (c) and (d) may not be varied by agreement.

Added by Acts 2001, 77th Leg., ch. 702, § 1, eff. Jan. 1, 2002.

Repeal

Acts 2007, 80th Leg., ch. 885, § 2.47(a)(1) repeals this section effective April 1, 2009.

§ 43.011. Notarization and Acknowledgment

If a law requires a signature or record to be notarized, acknowledged, verified, or made under oath, the requirement is satisfied if the electronic signature of the person authorized to perform those acts, together with all other information required to be included by other applicable law, is attached to or logically associated with the signature or record.

Added by Acts 2001, 77th Leg., ch. 702, § 1, eff. Jan. 1, 2002.

Repeal

Acts 2007, 80th Leg., ch. 885, § 2.47(a)(1) repeals this section effective April 1, 2009.

State Bar Committee Comments

1. **Local Government Code Filing Provisions.** The legislation enacting this chapter also amends certain Local Government Code provisions dealing with electronic filing. These amendments are reproduced in State Bar Committee Comment 3 of Section 43.008.

2. **Electronic Records and Signatures in Real Estate Transactions.** As explained in item 3 of Official Comment 9 to Section 43.007, the fundamental rule of this chapter in Section 43.007 would permit the parties to a real estate transaction to conduct that transaction electronically where they so agreed. For example, Section 5.021 of the Property Code requires a conveyance of certain real estate interests to be in writing and subscribed by the conveyor. Pursuant to this Chapter, a vendor and purchaser could now agree that vendor's deed or other instrument of conveyance would be delivered to the purchaser by e-mail or other electronic medium capable of retention by the purchaser at the time of receipt and that the subscription requirement would be met by an electronic subscription. *See* Sections 43.005 and 43.008. However, as the discussion of real estate transactions in the Official Comment of Section 43.003 suggests, such an electronic conveyance, effective between the parties, would not be recordable in the deed records of the particular county until the county had adopted an electronic filing system in accordance with Chapter 195, Local Government Code. Any electronic filing must comply with rules adopted by the Texas State Library and Archives Commission and must be made by an authorized filer as defined in Section 195.003, Local Government Code. Thus, until electronic filing of real estate conveyances in the proper records becomes possible, conveyances written on paper or other tangible, permanent medium suitable for recording under current practices will be preferable so that the purchaser's rights against third parties can be protected through the filing system. Electronic recording of conveyances will also require compliance with Section 43.011, which authorizes acknowledgments on electronic records, if the acknowledgment contains the electronic signature of the notary public, together with all other information required to be included by other applicable law. The acknowledgment will not be required to contain a seal. *See* Official Comment to Section 43.011.

§ 43.012. Retention of Electronic Records; Originals

(a) If a law requires that a record be retained, the requirement is satisfied by retaining an electronic record of the information in the record which:

(1) accurately reflects the information set forth in the record after it was first generated in its final form as an electronic record or otherwise; and

(2) remains accessible for later reference.

(b) A requirement to retain a record in accordance with Subsection (a) does not apply to any information the sole purpose of which is to enable the record to be sent, communicated, or received.

(c) A person may satisfy Subsection (a) by using the services of another person if the requirements of that subsection are satisfied.

(d) If a law requires a record to be presented or retained in its original form, or provides consequences if the record is not presented or retained in its original form, that law is satisfied by an electronic record retained in accordance with Subsection (a).

(e) If a law requires retention of a check, that requirement is satisfied by retention of an electronic record of the information on the front and back of the check in accordance with Subsection (a).

(f) A record retained as an electronic record in accordance with Subsection (a) satisfies a law requiring a person to retain a record for evidentiary, audit, or like purposes, unless a law enacted after January 1, 2002, specifically prohibits the use of an electronic record for the specified purpose.

(g) This section does not preclude a governmental agency of this state from specifying additional requirements for the retention of a record subject to the agency's jurisdiction.

Added by Acts 2001, 77th Leg., ch. 702, § 1, eff. Jan. 1, 2002.

Repeal

Acts 2007, 80th Leg., ch. 885, § 2.47(a)(1) repeals this section effective April 1, 2009.

State Bar Committee Comments

1. **Local Government Code Filing Provisions.** The legislation enacting this chapter also amends certain Local Government Code provisions dealing with electronic filing. These amendments are reproduced in State Bar Committee Comment 3 of Section 43.008.

2. **Electronic Records and Signatures in Real Estate Transactions.** As explained in item 3 of Official Comment 9 to Section 43.007, the fundamental rule of this chapter in Section 43.007 would permit the parties to a real estate transaction to conduct that transaction electronically where they so agreed. For example, Section 5.021 of the Property Code requires a conveyance of certain real estate interests to be in writing and subscribed by the conveyor. Pursuant to this chapter, a vendor and purchaser could now agree that vendor's deed or other instrument of conveyance would be delivered to the purchaser by e-mail or other electronic medium capable of retention by the purchaser at the time of receipt and that the subscription requirement would be met by an electronic subscription. *See* Sections 43.005 and 43.008. However, as the discussion of real estate transactions in the Official Comment of Section 43.003 suggests, such an electronic conveyance, effective between the parties, would not be recordable in the deed records of the particular county until the county had adopted an electronic filing system in accordance with Chapter 195, Local Government Code. Any electronic filing must comply with rules adopted by the Texas State Library and Archives Commission and must be made by an authorized filer as defined in Section 195.003, Local Government Code. Thus, until electronic filing of real estate conveyances in the proper records becomes possible, conveyances written on paper or other tangible, permanent medium suitable for recording under current practices will be preferable so that the purchaser's rights against third parties can be protected through the filing system. Electronic recording of conveyances will also require compliance with Section 43.011, which authorizes acknowledgments on electronic records, if the acknowledgment contains the electronic signature of the notary public, together with all other information required to be included by other applicable law. The acknowledgment will not be required to contain a seal. *See* Official Comment to Section 43.011.

§ 43.013. Admissibility in Evidence

In a proceeding, evidence of a record or signature may not be excluded solely because it is in electronic form.

Added by Acts 2001, 77th Leg., ch. 702, § 1, eff. Jan. 1, 2002.

Repeal

Acts 2007, 80th Leg., ch. 885, § 2.47(a)(1) repeals this section effective April 1, 2009.

§ 43.014. Automated Transaction

(a) In an automated transaction, the rules provided by this section apply.

(b) A contract may be formed by the interaction of electronic agents of the parties, even if no individual was aware of or reviewed the electronic agents' actions or the resulting terms and agreements.

(c) A contract may be formed by the interaction of an electronic agent and an individual, acting on the individual's own behalf or for another person, including by an interaction in which the individual performs actions that the individual is free to refuse to perform and which the individual knows or has reason to know will cause the electronic agent to complete the transaction or performance.

(d) The terms of the contract are determined by the substantive law applicable to it.

Added by Acts 2001, 77th Leg., ch. 702, § 1, eff. Jan. 1, 2002.

Repeal

Acts 2007, 80th Leg., ch. 885, § 2.47(a)(1) repeals this section effective April 1, 2009.

§ 43.015. Time and Place of Sending and Receipt

(a) Unless otherwise agreed between the sender and the recipient, an electronic record is sent when it:

(1) is addressed properly or otherwise directed properly to an information processing system that the recipient has designated or uses for the purpose of receiving electronic records or information of the

type sent and from which the recipient is able to retrieve the electronic record;

(2) is in a form capable of being processed by that system; and

(3) enters an information processing system outside the control of the sender or of a person that sent the electronic record on behalf of the sender or enters a region of the information processing system designated or used by the recipient which is under the control of the recipient.

(b) Unless otherwise agreed between the sender and the recipient, an electronic record is received when:

(1) it enters an information processing system that the recipient has designated or uses for the purpose of receiving electronic records or information of the type sent and from which the recipient is able to retrieve the electronic record; and

(2) it is in a form capable of being processed by that system.

(c) Subsection (b) applies even if the place the information processing system is located is different from the place the electronic record is deemed to be received under Subsection (d).

(d) Unless otherwise expressly provided in the electronic record or agreed between the sender and the recipient, an electronic record is deemed to be sent from the sender's place of business and to be received at the recipient's place of business. For purposes of this subsection, the following rules apply:

(1) if the sender or the recipient has more than one place of business, the place of business of that person is the place having the closest relationship to the underlying transaction; and

(2) if the sender or the recipient does not have a place of business, the place of business is the sender's or the recipient's residence, as the case may be.

(e) An electronic record is received under Subsection (b) even if no individual is aware of its receipt.

(f) Receipt of an electronic acknowledgment from an information processing system described in Subsection (b) establishes that a record was received but, by itself, does not establish that the content sent corresponds to the content received.

(g) If a person is aware that an electronic record purportedly sent under Subsection (a), or purportedly received under Subsection (b), was not actually sent or received, the legal effect of the sending or receipt is determined by other applicable law. Except to the extent permitted by the other law, the requirements of this subsection may not be varied by agreement.

Added by Acts 2001, 77th Leg., ch. 702, § 1, eff. Jan. 1, 2002.

Repeal

Acts 2007, 80th Leg., ch. 885, § 2.47(a)(1) repeals this section effective April 1, 2009.

§ 43.016. Transferable Records

(a) In this section, "transferable record" means an electronic record that:

(1) would be a note under Chapter 3, or a document under Chapter 7, if the electronic record were in writing; and

(2) the issuer of the electronic record expressly has agreed is a transferable record.

(b) A person has control of a transferable record if a system employed for evidencing the transfer of interests in the transferable record reliably establishes that person as the person to which the transferable record was issued or transferred.

(c) A system satisfies Subsection (b), and a person is deemed to have control of a transferable record, if the transferable record is created, stored, and assigned in such a manner that:

(1) a single authoritative copy of the transferable record exists which is unique, identifiable, and, except as otherwise provided in Subdivisions (4), (5), and (6), unalterable;

(2) the authoritative copy identifies the person asserting control as:

(A) the person to which the transferable record was issued; or

(B) if the authoritative copy indicates that the transferable record has been transferred, the person to which the transferable record was most recently transferred;

(3) the authoritative copy is communicated to and maintained by the person asserting control or its designated custodian;

(4) copies or revisions that add or change an identified assignee of the authoritative copy can be made only with the consent of the person asserting control;

(5) each copy of the authoritative copy and any copy of a copy is readily identifiable as a copy that is not the authoritative copy; and

(6) any revision of the authoritative copy is readily identifiable as authorized or unauthorized.

(d) Except as otherwise agreed, a person having control of a transferable record is the holder, as defined in Section 1.201, of the transferable record and has the same rights and defenses as a holder of an equivalent record or writing under the Uniform Commercial Code, including, if the applicable statutory requirements under Section 3.302(a), 7.501, or 9.330 are satisfied, the rights and defenses of a holder in due course, a holder to which a negotiable document of title has been duly negotiated, or a purchaser, respectively. Delivery, possession, and indorsement are not required to obtain or exercise any of the rights under this subsection.

(e) Except as otherwise agreed, an obligor under a transferable record has the same rights and defenses as an equivalent obligor under equivalent records or writings under the Uniform Commercial Code.

(f) If requested by a person against which enforcement is sought, the person seeking to enforce the transferable record shall provide reasonable proof that the person is in control of the transferable record. Proof may include access to the authoritative copy of the transferable record and related business records sufficient to review the terms of the transferable record and to establish the identity of the person having control of the transferable record.

Added by Acts 2001, 77th Leg., ch. 702, § 1, eff. Jan. 1, 2002.

Repeal

Acts 2007, 80th Leg., ch. 885, § 2.47(a)(1) repeals this section effective April 1, 2009.

§ 43.017. Acceptance and Distribution of Electronic Records by Governmental Agencies

(a) Except as otherwise provided by Section 43.012(f), each state agency shall determine whether, and the extent to which, the agency will send and accept electronic records and electronic signatures to and from other persons and otherwise create, generate, communicate, store, process, use, and rely upon electronic records and electronic signatures.

(b) To the extent that a state agency uses electronic records and electronic signatures under Subsection (a), the Department of Information Resources and Texas State Library and Archives Commission, pursuant to their rulemaking authority under other law and giving due consideration to security, may specify:

(1) the manner and format in which the electronic records must be created, generated, sent, communicated, received, and stored and the systems established for those purposes;

(2) if electronic records must be signed by electronic means, the type of electronic signature required, the manner and format in which the electronic signature must be affixed to the electronic record, and the identity of, or criteria that must be met by, any third party used by a person filing a document to facilitate the process;

(3) control processes and procedures as appropriate to ensure adequate preservation, disposition, integrity, security, confidentiality, and auditability of electronic records; and

(4) any other required attributes for electronic records which are specified for corresponding nonelectronic records or reasonably necessary under the circumstances.

(c) Except as otherwise provided in Section 43.012(f), this chapter does not require a governmental agency of this state to use or permit the use of electronic records or electronic signatures.

Added by Acts 2001, 77th Leg., ch. 702, § 1, eff. Jan. 1, 2002.

Repeal

Acts 2007, 80th Leg., ch. 885, § 2.47(a)(1) repeals this section effective April 1, 2009.

State Bar Committee Comments

1. Official Section 17 of UETA not Enacted. Sections 17–19 of the official text of UETA are optional statutes for extending UETA to governmental agencies. Section 17 of official UETA by its terms would authorize state agencies to use electronic records and electronic signatures generally for intra-governmental purposes, and to convert written records and manual signatures to electronic records and electronic signatures. The section was considered unnecessary in light of existing laws, such as Chapters 2054 and 2177 of the Government Code, and is not included in this Act.

2. Source of this Section. Section 43.017 is based on Section 18 of the official text of UETA with slight modification. Section 43.017 affirms the rule-making authority vested in the Department of Information Resources and the Texas State Library and Archives Commission with respect to electronic signatures and records. The term "state agency" was substituted for the term "governmental agency of this State," in Section 43.017(a) of this chapter, and for the term "governmental agency", in Section 43.017(b) of this chapter, to exempt local agencies from rules adopted under Section 43.017. The definition of "governmental agency" in Section 43.002(9) of this chapter would otherwise include a local agency.

3. **Local Government Code Filing Provisions.** The legislation enacting this chapter also amends certain Local Government Code provisions dealing with electronic filing. These amendments are reproduced in State Bar Committee Comment 3 of Section 43.008.

§ 43.018. Interoperability

The Department of Information Resources may encourage and promote consistency and interoperability with similar requirements adopted by other governmental agencies of this and other states and the federal government and nongovernmental persons interacting with governmental agencies of this state. If appropriate, those standards may specify differing levels of standards from which governmental agencies of this state may choose in implementing the most appropriate standard for a particular application.

Added by Acts 2001, 77th Leg., ch. 702, § 1, eff. Jan. 1, 2002.

Repeal

Acts 2007, 80th Leg., ch. 885, § 2.47(a)(1) repeals this section effective April 1, 2009.

State Bar Committee Comment

Source of this Section. Sections 17–19 of the official text of UETA are optional statutes for extending UETA to governmental agencies. As explained in the State Bar Committee Comments to Section 43.017, Section 17 of the official text was not enacted and Section 18 of the official text is the source for Section 43.017. Section 43.018 is based on Section 19 of the official text of UETA.

State Bar Committee Comment

Source of this Section. Sections 17–19 of the official text of UETA are optional statutes for extending UETA to governmental agencies. As explained in the State Bar Committee Comments to Section 43.017, Section 17 of the official text was not enacted and Section 18 of the official text is the source for Section 43.017. Section 43.018 is based on Section 19 of the official text of UETA.

§ 43.019. Exemption to Preemption by Federal Electronic Signatures Act

This chapter modifies, limits, or supersedes the provisions of the Electronic Signatures in Global and National Commerce Act (15 U.S.C. Section 7001 et seq.) as authorized by Section 102 of that Act (15 U.S.C. Section 7002).

Added by Acts 2001, 77th Leg., ch. 702, § 1, eff. Jan. 1, 2002.

Repeal

Acts 2007, 80th Leg., ch. 885, § 2.47(a)(1) repeals this section effective April 1, 2009.

State Bar Committee Comments

1. **Required Reference to E–SIGN.** Section 43.019 is not contained in the official text of UETA. However, this section is responsive to the E–SIGN requirement, in 15 U.S.C. Section 7002(a)(2)(B), that state law must specifically reference E–SIGN in order to supersede its provisions and avoid preemption.

2. **Continuing Relevance of E–SIGN.** The potential effect of this chapter is limited by a savings provision in the enacting legislation, Acts 2001, 77th Leg., ch. 702, § 6, retaining the applicability of E–SIGN Sections 7001(c) and 7003(b). The savings provision is reproduced in State Bar Committee Comment 3 of Section 43.001.

3. **Official Text Section 19.** Sections 17–19 of the official text of UETA are optional statutes for extending UETA to governmental agencies. As explained in the State Bar Committee Comments to Section 43.017, Section 17 of the official text was not enacted and Section 18 of the official text is the source for Section 43.017. Section 43.018 is based on Section 19 of the official text of UETA.

State Bar Committee Comments

1. **Required Reference to E–SIGN.** Section 43.019 is not contained in the official text of UETA. However, this section is responsive to the E–SIGN requirement, in 15 U.S.C. Section 7002(a)(2)(B), that state law must specifically reference E–SIGN in order to supersede its provisions and avoid preemption.

2. **Continuing Relevance of E–SIGN.** The potential effect of this chapter is limited by a savings provision in the enacting legislation, Acts 2001, 77th Leg., ch. 702, § 6, retaining the applicability of E–SIGN Sections 7001(c) and 7003(b). The savings provision is reproduced in State Bar Committee Comment 3 of Section 43.001.

3. **Official Text Section 19.** Sections 17–19 of the official text of UETA are optional statutes for extending UETA to governmental agencies. As explained in the State Bar Committee Comments to Section 43.017, Section 17 of the official text was not enacted and Section 18 of the official text is the source for Section 43.017. Section 43.018 is based on Section 19 of the official text of UETA.

§ 43.020. Applicability of Penal Code

This chapter does not authorize any activity that is prohibited by the Penal Code.

Added by Acts 2001, 77th Leg., ch. 702, § 1, eff. Jan. 1, 2002.

Repeal

Acts 2007, 80th Leg., ch. 885, § 2.47(a)(1) repeals this section effective April 1, 2009.

State Bar Committee Comments

1. **Purpose and Effect.** Section 43.020 of this chapter is not contained in official UETA but has minimal substantive impact. This section purports to prevent this chapter from authorizing any act prohibited by the Penal Code, but this chapter would not otherwise authorize an act prohibited by the Penal Code. *See* Sections 43.003(d) and 43.005(e) of this chapter. Inclusion of this provision should not invoke preemption of Chapter 43 by E–SIGN. *See* State Bar Committee Comment 2 of Section 43.001, above.

2. **Severability.** Section 20 of the official text of UETA provides for severability but is omitted from this chapter. Section 311.032, Texas Government Code (part of the Code Construction Act) states the severability rule that applies to this chapter and is essentially identical to the omitted provision from UETA. Reference to the Code Construction Act of the Texas Government Code for such a severability provision should be considered a non-substantive change to the official text of UETA and is also consistent with E–SIGN. This approach to severability should not invoke preemption under 15 U.S.C. Section 7002(a).

State Bar Committee Comments

1. **Purpose and Effect.** Section 43.020 of this chapter is not contained in official UETA but has minimal substantive impact. This section purports to prevent this chapter from authorizing any act prohibited by the Penal Code, but this chapter would not otherwise authorize an act prohibited by the Penal Code. *See* Sections 43.003(d) and 43.005(e) of this chapter. Inclusion of this provision should not invoke preemption of Chapter 43 by E–SIGN. *See* State Bar Committee Comment 2 of Section 43.001, above.

2. **Severability.** Section 20 of the official text of UETA provides for severability but is omitted from this chapter. Section 311.032, Texas Government Code (part of the Code Construction Act) states the severability rule that applies to this chapter and is essentially identical to the omitted provision from UETA. Reference to the Code Construction Act of the Texas Government Code for such a severability provision should be considered a non-substantive change to the official text of UETA and is also consistent with E–SIGN. This approach to severability should not invoke preemption under 15 U.S.C. Section 7002(a).

§ 43.021. Certain Requirements Considered to be Recommendations

Any requirement of the Department of Information Resources or the Texas State Library and Archives Commission under this chapter that generally applies to one or more state agencies using electronic records or electronic signatures is considered to be a recommendation to the comptroller concerning the electronic records or electronic signatures used by the comptroller. The comptroller may adopt or decline to adopt the recommendation.

Added by Acts 2001, 77th Leg., ch. 1158, § 2, eff. Jan. 1, 2002. Renumbered from V.T.C.A., Bus. & C. Code § 43.020 by Acts 2003, 78th Leg., ch. 1275, § 2(5), eff. Sept. 1, 2003.

Repeal

Acts 2007, 80th Leg., ch. 885, § 2.47(a)(1) repeals this section effective April 1, 2009.

§§ 43.051, 43.052. Renumbered as V.T.C.A, Business and Commerce Code §§ 44.051 and 44.052 by Acts 2003, 78th Leg., ch. 1275, § 2(3), eff. Sept. 1, 2003

§§ 43.101 to 43.104. Renumbered as V.T.C.A, Business and Commerce Code §§ 44.101 to 44.104 by Acts 2003, 78th Leg., ch. 1275, § 2(3), eff. Sept. 1, 2003

§§ 43.151 to 43.153. Renumbered as V.T.C.A, Business and Commerce Code §§ 44.151 to 44.153 by Acts 2003, 78th Leg., ch. 1275, § 2(3), eff. Sept. 1, 2003

§§ 43.201, 43.202. Renumbered as V.T.C.A, Business and Commerce Code §§ 44.201 and 44.202 by Acts 2003, 78th Leg., ch. 1275, § 2(3), eff. Sept. 1, 2003

§§ 43.251 to 43.253. Renumbered as V.T.C.A, Business and Commerce Code §§ 44.251 to 44.253 by Acts 2003, 78th Leg., ch. 1275, § 2(3), eff. Sept. 1, 2003

CHAPTER 44. TELEMARKETING

SUBCHAPTER A. GENERAL PROVISIONS

Section

SUBCHAPTER B. CALLER IDENTIFICATION

Acts 2007, 80th Leg., ch. 885, § 2.47(a)(1) repeals this chapter effective April 1, 2009.

Acts 2001, 77th Leg., ch. 1429, § 1 added this Chapter, Telemarketing, consisting of V.T.C.A., Bus. & C. Code §§ 43.001 to 43.253. Acts 2003, 78th Leg., ch. 1275, § 2(3) renumbered this Chapter as Chapter 44, consisting of V.T.C.A., Bus. & C. Code §§ 44.001 to 44.253.

SUBCHAPTER A. GENERAL PROVISIONS

§ 44.001. Short Title

This chapter may be cited as the Texas Telemarketing Disclosure and Privacy Act.

Added by Acts 2001, 77th Leg., ch. 1429, § 1, eff. Jan. 1, 2002. Renumbered from V.T.C.A., Bus. & C. Code § 43.001 by Acts 2003, 78th Leg., ch. 1275, § 2(3), eff. Sept. 1, 2003.

Repeal

Acts 2007, 80th Leg., ch. 885, § 2.47(a)(1) repeals this section effective April 1, 2009.

§ 44.002. Definitions

In this chapter:

(1) "Caller identification service" means a service or device designed to provide the user of the service or device with the telephone number of an incoming telephone call.

(2) "Commission" means the Public Utility Commission of Texas.

(3) "Consumer good or service" means property of any kind that is normally used for personal, family, or household purposes. The term does not include a security, as defined by Section 4, The Securities Act (Article 581–4, Vernon's Texas Civil Statutes).

(4) "Established business relationship" means a prior or existing relationship of a person formed by a voluntary two-way communication between a person and a consumer regardless of whether consideration is exchanged, regarding consumer goods or services offered by the person, that has not been terminated by either party.

(5) "Facsimile recording device" means any device capable of receiving a facsimile transmission.

(6) "Facsimile solicitation" means a telemarketing call made by a transmission to a facsimile recording device.

(7) "Telemarketer" means a person who makes or causes to be made a telemarketing call.

(8) "State licensee" means a person licensed by a state agency under a law of this state that requires the person to obtain a license as a condition of engaging in a profession or business.

(9) "Telephone call" means a call or other transmission which is made to or received at a telephone number, including:

(A) a call made by an automated telephone dialing system;

(B) a transmission to a facsimile recording device; and

(C) a call or other transmission, including a transmission of a text or graphic message or of an image, to a mobile telephone number serviced by a provider of commercial mobile service, as defined by Section 332(d), Communications Act of 1934 (47 U.S.C. Section 151 et seq.), as amended, Federal Communications Commission rules, and the Omnibus Budget Reconciliation Act of 1993 (Pub. L. No. 103–66), as amended, except that the term does not include a transmission made to a mobile telephone number as part of an ad-based telephone service, in connection with which the telephone service customer has agreed with the service provider to receive the transmission.

Added by Acts 2001, 77th Leg., ch. 1429, § 1, eff. Jan. 1, 2002. Amended by Acts 2003, 78th Leg., ch. 399, § 1, eff. June 20, 2003. Renumbered from V.T.C.A., Bus. & C. Code § 43.002 by Acts 2003, 78th Leg., ch. 1275, § 2(3), eff. Sept. 1, 2003. Amended by Acts 2007, 80th Leg., ch. 206, § 1, eff. Sept. 1, 2007.

Repeal

Acts 2007, 80th Leg., ch. 885, § 2.47(a)(1) repeals this section effective April 1, 2009.

§ 44.003. Telemarketing Calls Governed by Chapter

(a) For the purposes of this chapter, a telemarketing call is an unsolicited telephone call made to:

(1) solicit a sale of a consumer good or service;

(2) solicit an extension of credit for a consumer good or service; or

(3) obtain information that may be used to solicit a sale of a consumer good or service or to extend credit for the sale.

(b) This chapter does not apply to a call made:

(1) by a consumer that is the result of a solicitation by a seller or telemarketer or in response to general media advertising by direct mail solicitations that clearly, conspicuously, and truthfully make all disclosures required by federal or state law;

(2) in connection with:

(A) an established business relationship; or

(B) a business relationship that has been terminated, if the call is made before the later of the date the first Texas no-call list in which the consumer's telephone number appears is published or one year after the date of termination;

(3) between a telemarketer and a business, other than by a facsimile solicitation, unless the business informed the telemarketer that the business does not wish to receive telemarketing calls from the telemarketer;

(4) to collect a debt; or

(5) by a state licensee if:

(A) the call is not made by an automated telephone dialing system;

(B) the solicited transaction is not completed until a face-to-face sales presentation by the seller and the consumer is not required to pay or authorize payment until after the presentation; and

(C) the consumer has not informed the telemarketer that the consumer does not wish to receive telemarketing calls from the telemarketer.

Added by Acts 2001, 77th Leg., ch. 1429, § 1, eff. Jan. 1, 2002. Renumbered from V.T.C.A., Bus. & C. Code § 43.003 by Acts 2003, 78th Leg., ch. 1275, § 2(3), eff. Sept. 1, 2003.

Repeal

Acts 2007, 80th Leg., ch. 885, § 2.47(a)(1) repeals this section effective April 1, 2009.

§ 44.004. Making Telemarketing Call

In this chapter, a person makes a telemarketing call if the person effects a telemarketing call on the person's own behalf or on behalf of another entity. A person makes a telemarketing call on behalf of another entity if, as a result of the telemarketing call, the other entity:

(1) can become entitled to receive money or other property of any kind from a sale solicited during the call; or

(2) can receive information that is obtained during the call and that is to be used for the purpose of:

(A) extending or offering to extend credit for a consumer good or service to the person solicited; or

(B) directly soliciting a sale of a consumer good or service or extending credit for the sale.

Added by Acts 2001, 77th Leg., ch. 1429, § 1, eff. Jan. 1, 2002. Renumbered from V.T.C.A., Bus. & C. Code § 43.004 by Acts 2003, 78th Leg., ch. 1275, § 2(3), eff. Sept. 1, 2003.

Repeal

Acts 2007, 80th Leg., ch. 885, § 2.47(a)(1) repeals this section effective April 1, 2009.

§ 44.005. Construction and Application

This chapter shall be liberally construed and applied to promote its underlying purpose to protect the public against false, misleading, abusive, or deceptive practices in the telemarketing business.

Added by Acts 2001, 77th Leg., ch. 1429, § 1, eff. Jan. 1, 2002. Renumbered from V.T.C.A., Bus. & C. Code § 43.005 by Acts 2003, 78th Leg., ch. 1275, § 2(3), eff. Sept. 1, 2003.

Repeal

Acts 2007, 80th Leg., ch. 885, § 2.47(a)(1) repeals this section effective April 1, 2009.

§ 44.006. **Waiver Prohibited**

An attempted waiver of a provision of this chapter is void.

Added by Acts 2001, 77th Leg., ch. 1429, § 1, eff. Jan. 1, 2002. Renumbered from V.T.C.A., Bus. & C. Code § 43.006 by Acts 2003, 78th Leg., ch. 1275, § 2(3), eff. Sept. 1, 2003.

Repeal

Acts 2007, 80th Leg., ch. 885, § 2.47(a)(1) repeals this section effective April 1, 2009.

[Sections 44.007 to 44.050 reserved for expansion]

SUBCHAPTER B. CALLER IDENTIFICATION

§ 44.051. **Prohibition on Interference With Caller Identification Service**

(a) A telemarketer may not, in making a telemarketing call, block the identity of the telephone number from which the telephone call is made to evade devices designed to identify telephone callers.

(b) A telemarketer may not:

(1) interfere with or circumvent the capability of a caller identification service to access or provide to the recipient of the telemarketing call any information regarding the call that the service is capable of providing; and

(2) fail to provide caller identification information in a manner that is accessible by a caller identification service, if the person has capability to provide the information in that manner.

(c) For purposes of this section, the use of telecommunications service or equipment that is incapable of transmitting caller identification information does not of itself constitute interference with or circumvention of the capability of a caller identification service to access or provide the information.

Added by Acts 2001, 77th Leg., ch. 1429, § 1, eff. Jan. 1, 2002. Renumbered from V.T.C.A., Bus. & C. Code § 43.051 by Acts 2003, 78th Leg., ch. 1275, § 2(3), eff. Sept. 1, 2003.

Repeal

Acts 2007, 80th Leg., ch. 885, § 2.47(a)(1) repeals this section effective April 1, 2009.

§ 44.052. **Enforcement; Penalties**

(a) Except as provided by Subsection (c), the commission shall receive and investigate complaints concerning violations of this subchapter and may assess an administrative penalty not to exceed $1,000 for each violation. If the complaint alleges that the person violating this subchapter is a telecommunications provider, as defined by Section 51.002, Utilities Code, the commission has exclusive jurisdiction over the violation alleged in the complaint, notwithstanding Subsection (b).

(b) Except as provided by Subsection (c), the attorney general may investigate violations of this subchapter and file civil enforcement actions seeking injunctive relief, attorney's fees, and civil penalties in an amount not to exceed $1,000 for each violation. If the court finds the defendant wilfully or knowingly violated this subchapter, the court may increase the amount of the civil penalties to an amount not to exceed $3,000 for each violation. A violation of this subchapter is subject to enforcement action by the attorney general's consumer protection division under Sections 17.47, 17.58, 17.60, and 17.61.

(c) A state agency that issues a license to a state licensee may receive and investigate complaints concerning violations of this subchapter by the state licensee, may assess an administrative penalty not to exceed $1,000 for each violation, and may order restitution of any monetary damages of the complainant. In addition, if the agency finds that the licensee wilfully or knowingly violated this subchapter, the agency may suspend or revoke the state licensee's license.

(d) Venue for an action under this subchapter is in Travis County.

Added by Acts 2001, 77th Leg., ch. 1429, § 1, eff. Jan. 1, 2002. Renumbered from V.T.C.A., Bus. & C. Code § 43.052 by Acts 2003, 78th Leg., ch. 1275, § 2(3), eff. Sept. 1, 2003.

Repeal

Acts 2007, 80th Leg., ch. 885, § 2.47(a)(1) repeals this section effective April 1, 2009.

[Sections 44.053 to 44.100 reserved for expansion]

SUBCHAPTER C. TEXAS NO-CALL LIST

§ 44.101. **Commission to Establish Texas No-call Lists**

(a) The commission shall establish and provide for the operation of a database to compile a list of names, zip codes, and telephone numbers of consumers in this state who object to receiving unsolicited telemarketing or telephone calls.

(b) The commission may contract with a private vendor to maintain the Texas no-call list if:

(1) the private vendor has maintained a no-call list database containing the names and telephone numbers of consumers who have previously requested to be added to a no-call list; and

(2) the contract requires the vendor to publish the Texas portion of the national no-call list in an electronic format to any telemarketer who agrees to use the Texas no-call list only for the purposes of updating the no-call list of that telemarketer by including in its list persons with whom the telemarketer does not have an established business relationship.

(c) The Texas no-call list is a combined list consisting of the name and telephone numbers of each consumer in this state who has requested to be on that list and of each person in the portion of the national do-not-call registry maintained by the United States government that relates to this state. The Texas no-call list shall be updated and published on January 1, April 1, July 1, and October 1 of each year. An entry on the Texas no-call list expires on the third anniversary of the date the entry is first published on the list. An entry may be renewed for successive three-year periods. The telephone number of the consumer on the Texas no-call list may be deleted from the list on the consumer's written request or if the telephone number of the consumer is changed. The commission may charge a person a reasonable amount not to exceed $3 for a request to place a telephone number on the Texas no-call list or to renew an entry on the list, except that the commission shall provide for a method of placement or renewal of an entry by use of the Internet at no charge. The commission shall develop and make available an Internet website at which a person may request that a telephone number be placed on the Texas no-call list and shall provide a toll-free telephone number and a mailing address that persons may call or write to obtain a copy of a form to request placement of a telephone number on the Texas no-call list. A private for-profit publisher of a residential telephone directory that is distributed to the public at minimal or no cost shall include in the directory a prominently displayed Internet website address, toll-free number, and mailing address established by the commission through which a person may request placement of a telephone number on the Texas no-call list or order a copy of the form to make this request.

(d) The commission or its designee may provide information on the Texas no-call list to the administrator of the national do-not-call registry and may allow placement of the names and telephone numbers contained on the Texas no-call list in the national do-not-call registry.

Added by Acts 2001, 77th Leg., ch. 1429, § 1, eff. Jan. 1, 2002. Amended by Acts 2003, 78th Leg., ch. 401, § 1, eff. June 20, 2003. Renumbered from V.T.C.A., Bus. & C. Code § 43.101 by Acts 2003, 78th Leg., ch. 1275, § 2(3), eff. Sept. 1, 2003. Amended by Acts 2005, 79th Leg., ch. 171, § 1, eff. May 27, 2005.

Repeal

Acts 2007, 80th Leg., ch. 885, § 2.47(a)(1) repeals this section effective April 1, 2009.

Section 4 of Acts 2005, 79th Leg., ch. 171 provides:

"A residential electric customer who on the effective date of this Act is enrolled on the list compiled under Section 39.1025, Utilities Code, remains on the list until the customer's enrollment expires. If the residential electric customer applies to renew enrollment on that list after the effective date of this Act, the customer shall be enrolled on the Texas no-call list established under Subchapter C, Chapter 44, Business & Commerce Code."

§ 44.102. Telemarketing of Persons on Texas No-call List; Enforcement; Penalties

(a) A telemarketer may not make a telemarketing call to a telephone number that has been published on the Texas no-call list more than 60 days after the telephone number appears on the then-current list.

(b) Except as provided by Subsection (d), the commission shall receive and investigate complaints concerning violations of this subchapter and may assess an administrative penalty not to exceed $1,000 for each violation. If the complaint alleges that the person violating this subchapter is a telecommunications provider, as defined by Section 51.002, Utilities Code, the commission has exclusive jurisdiction, notwithstanding Subsection (c), over the violation alleged in the complaint, except that this does not affect the right of a consumer to bring an action under Subsection (f).

(c) Except as provided in Subsection (d), the attorney general may investigate violations of this subchapter and file civil enforcement actions seeking injunctive relief, attorney's fees, and civil penalties in an amount not to exceed $1,000 for each violation. If the court finds the defendant wilfully or knowingly violated this subchapter, the court may increase the amount of the civil penalties to an amount not to exceed $3,000 for each violation. A violation of this subchapter is subject to enforcement action by the attorney general's consumer protection division under Sections 17.47, 17.58, 17.60, and 17.61.

(d) A state agency that issues a license to a state licensee shall receive and investigate complaints concerning violations of this subchapter by the state licensee, may assess an administrative penalty not to exceed $1,000 for each violation, and may order restitution of any monetary damages of the complainant. In addition, if the agency finds that the licensee wilfully or knowingly violated this subchapter, the agency may suspend or revoke the state licensee's license.

(e) Venue for an action based on a violation of this subchapter is in the county where the telemarketing call was made or received, or if brought by the attorney general, commission, or a state agency, in Travis County.

(f) For purposes of this subchapter, a consumer on the Texas no-call list is presumed to be adversely affected by a telemarketer who calls the consumer more than once and may bring a civil action based on the second or a subsequent violation of this subchapter if:

(1) the consumer has notified the telemarketer of the alleged violation and not later than the 30th day after the date of the call files a verified complaint setting forth the relevant facts surrounding the violation with the commission, the attorney general, or a state agency that licenses the person making the call; and

(2) the commission, attorney general, or state agency receiving the complaint fails to initiate an administrative action or a civil enforcement action, as appropriate, against the telemarketer named in the complaint before the 121st day after the date the complaint is filed.

(g) If the consumer brings an action based on violation of this section and the court finds that the defendant wilfully or knowingly violated this section, the court may award damages in an amount not to exceed $500 for each violation.

Added by Acts 2001, 77th Leg., ch. 1429, § 1, eff. Jan. 1, 2002. Renumbered from V.T.C.A., Bus. & C. Code § 43.102 by Acts 2003, 78th Leg., ch. 1275, § 2(3), eff. Sept. 1, 2003.

Repeal

Acts 2007, 80th Leg., ch. 885, § 2.47(a)(1) repeals this section effective April 1, 2009.

§ 44.103. Rules; Customer Information; Isolated Violation

(a) The commission may adopt rules to administer this subchapter. The commission shall adopt rules:

(1) requiring each local exchange telephone company and each commercial mobile service provider that provides commercial mobile service in this state to inform its customers of the requirements of this subchapter by annual inserts in billing statements mailed to customers, notification in a customer's electronic bill, notification printed on a customer's paper bill, notification sent free of charge by messaging service to a customer's mobile telephone number, or conspicuous publication of the notice in the consumer information pages of local telephone directories or other appropriate notice to consumers;

(2) providing that a telemarketing call made to a number on the Texas no-call list is not a violation of Section 44.102 if the telemarketing call is an isolated occurrence made by a person who has in place adequate procedures to comply with this subchapter; and

(3) providing for:

(A) the dissemination of the Texas no-call lists in formats, including electronic formats, commonly used by persons making telemarketing calls; and

(B) a fee for each such distribution not to exceed $75.

(b) In addition to requiring the notice under Subsection (a)(1), the commission may conduct educational programs designed to inform the public of their rights and telemarketers of their obligations under this subchapter.

(c) The commission shall include on its Internet website a notice explaining the application of the Texas no-call list to a call or other transmission, including a transmission of a text or graphic message or of an image, to a mobile telephone number.

Added by Acts 2001, 77th Leg., ch. 1429, § 1, eff. Jan. 1, 2002. Amended by Acts 2003, 78th Leg., ch. 399, § 2, eff. June 20, 2003. Renumbered from V.T.C.A., Bus. & C. Code § 43.103 and amended by Acts 2003, 78th Leg., ch. 1275, §§ 2(3), 3(1), eff. Sept. 1, 2003. Amended by Acts 2007, 80th Leg., ch. 206, § 2, eff. Sept. 1, 2007.

Repeal

Acts 2007, 80th Leg., ch. 885, § 2.47(a)(1) repeals this section effective April 1, 2009.

§ 44.104. Assistance of Department of Information Resources

On request of the commission, the Department of Information Resources shall assist the commission in administering this subchapter.

Added by Acts 2001, 77th Leg., ch. 1429, § 1, eff. Jan. 1, 2002. Renumbered from V.T.C.A., Bus. & C. Code § 43.104 by Acts 2003, 78th Leg., ch. 1275, § 2(3), eff. Sept. 1, 2003.

Repeal

Acts 2007, 80th Leg., ch. 885, § 2.47(a)(1) repeals this section effective April 1, 2009.

[Sections 44.105 to 44.150 reserved for expansion]

SUBCHAPTER D. FACSIMILE TRANSMISSIONS

§ 44.151. Notice in Facsimile Solicitation

In addition to the technical and procedural standards of federal statutes or regulations regarding telephone facsimile machines and transmissions, a person in this state who makes or causes to be made a facsimile solicitation shall include in the document transmitted or on a cover page to the document a statement, in at least 12–point type, stating:

(1) the correct and complete name of the person making the facsimile solicitation and street address of the location of the person's place of business; and

(2) a toll-free or local exchange accessible telephone number of the person that:

(A) is answered in the order in which calls are received by an individual capable of responding to inquiries from recipients of facsimile solicitations at all times after 9 a.m. and before 5 p.m. on each day except Saturday and Sunday; or

(B) automatically and immediately deletes the specified telephone number of the recipient.

Added by Acts 2001, 77th Leg., ch. 1429, § 1, eff. Jan. 1, 2002. Renumbered from V.T.C.A., Bus. & C. Code § 43.151 by Acts 2003, 78th Leg., ch. 1275, § 2(3), eff. Sept. 1, 2003.

Repeal

Acts 2007, 80th Leg., ch. 885, § 2.47(a)(1) repeals this section effective April 1, 2009.

§ 44.152. Acknowledgment Required; Transmission Prohibited

On receipt of oral or written notification from a recipient of a facsimile solicitation not to send any further facsimile transmissions to one or more telephone numbers specified by the recipient, the person making the facsimile solicitation:

(1) shall within 24 hours send the recipient a written acknowledgment of the recipient's notification; and

(2) may not make or cause to be made a transmission to a telephone number specified by the recipient, except for a single transmission to comply with Subdivision (1).

Added by Acts 2001, 77th Leg., ch. 1429, § 1, eff. Jan. 1, 2002. Renumbered from V.T.C.A., Bus. & C. Code § 43.152 by Acts 2003, 78th Leg., ch. 1275, § 2(3), eff. Sept. 1, 2003.

Repeal

Acts 2007, 80th Leg., ch. 885, § 2.47(a)(1) repeals this section effective April 1, 2009.

§ 44.153. Enforcement; Penalties

(a) Except as provided by Subsection (c), the commission shall receive and investigate complaints concerning violations of this subchapter and may assess an administrative penalty not to exceed $1,000 for each violation. If the complaint alleges that the person violating this subchapter is a telecommunications provider, as defined by Section 51.002, Utilities Code, the commission has exclusive jurisdiction, notwithstanding Subsection (b), over the violation alleged in the complaint, except that this does not affect the right of a consumer to bring an action under Subsection (e).

(b) Except as provided by Subsection (c), the attorney general may investigate violations of this subchapter and file civil enforcement actions seeking injunctive relief, attorney's fees, and civil penalties in an amount not to exceed $1,000 for each violation. If the court finds the defendant wilfully or knowingly violated this subchapter, the court may increase the amount of the civil penalties to an amount not to exceed $3,000 for each violation. A violation of this subchapter is subject to enforcement action by the attorney general's consumer protection division under Sections 17.47, 17.58, 17.60, and 17.61.

(c) A state agency that issues a license to a state licensee shall receive and investigate complaints concerning violations of this subchapter by the state licensee and may assess an administrative penalty not to exceed $1,000 for each violation. In addition, if the agency finds that the licensee wilfully or knowingly violated this subchapter, the agency may suspend or revoke the state licensee's license.

(d) Venue for an action based on a violation under this subchapter is in the county where the telemarketing call was made or received, or if brought by the attorney general, commission, or a state agency, in Travis County.

(e) A person may bring a private right of action based on a violation of this subchapter:

(1) to enjoin the violation; and

(2) for damages in an amount equal to the greater of:

(A) the person's actual monetary loss from the violation; or

(B) $500 for each violation; or

(C) for both an injunction and damages.

(f) If the court finds that the defendant wilfully or knowingly violated this section, the court may increase the amount of the award to an amount equal to not more than three times the amount available under Subsection (e)(2).

Added by Acts 2001, 77th Leg., ch. 1429, § 1, eff. Jan. 1, 2002. Renumbered from V.T.C.A., Bus. & C. Code § 43.153 by Acts 2003, 78th Leg., ch. 1275, § 2(3), eff. Sept. 1, 2003.

Repeal

Acts 2007, 80th Leg., ch. 885, § 2.47(a)(1) repeals this section effective April 1, 2009.

[Sections 44.154 to 44.200 reserved for expansion]

SUBCHAPTER E. REGULATORY REPORTS

§ 44.201. Report by Commission

Before December 31 of each even-numbered year, the commission shall submit a report to the lieutenant governor and speaker of the house of representatives. The report must contain for the two-year period ending August 31 of the year of the report:

(1) a statement of the number of telephone numbers included on the Texas no-call list, the number of no-call lists distributed, and the amount collected for those requests and for distribution;

(2) a list of complaints received by the commission concerning activities regulated by this chapter, itemized by type;

(3) a summary of any enforcement efforts made by the commission; and

(4) the commission's recommendations for any changes in this chapter.

Added by Acts 2001, 77th Leg., ch. 1429, § 1, eff. Jan. 1, 2002. Renumbered from V.T.C.A., Bus. & C. Code § 43.201 by Acts 2003, 78th Leg., ch. 1275, § 2(3), eff. Sept. 1, 2003.

Repeal

Acts 2007, 80th Leg., ch. 885, § 2.47(a)(1) repeals this section effective April 1, 2009.

§ 44.202. Report by Attorney General

Before December 31 of each even-numbered year, the attorney general shall submit a report to the lieutenant governor and speaker of the house of representatives. The report must contain for the two-year period ending August 31 of the year of the report:

(1) a list of complaints received by the attorney general concerning activities regulated by this chapter, itemized by type;

(2) a summary of any enforcement efforts made by the attorney general; and

(3) the attorney general's recommendations for any changes in this chapter.

Added by Acts 2001, 77th Leg., ch. 1429, § 1, eff. Jan. 1, 2002. Renumbered from V.T.C.A., Bus. & C. Code § 43.202 by Acts 2003, 78th Leg., ch. 1275, § 2(3), eff. Sept. 1, 2003.

Repeal

Acts 2007, 80th Leg., ch. 885, § 2.47(a)(1) repeals this section effective April 1, 2009.

[Sections 44.203 to 44.250 reserved for expansion]

SUBCHAPTER F. PROVISIONS APPLICABLE TO ADMINISTRATIVE PENALTIES

§ 44.251. Determination of Amount

The amount of an administrative penalty imposed under this chapter shall be based on:

(1) the seriousness of the violation, including the nature, circumstances, extent, and gravity of the violation;

(2) the history of previous violations;

(3) the amount necessary to deter a future violation;

(4) efforts to correct the violation; and

(5) any other matter that justice may require.

Added by Acts 2001, 77th Leg., ch. 1429, § 1, eff. Jan. 1, 2002. Renumbered from V.T.C.A., Bus. & C. Code § 43.251 by Acts 2003, 78th Leg., ch. 1275, § 2(3), eff. Sept. 1, 2003.

Repeal

Acts 2007, 80th Leg., ch. 885, § 2.47(a)(1) repeals this section effective April 1, 2009.

§ 44.252. Stay of Penalty

The enforcement of the penalty may be stayed during the time the order is under judicial review if the person pays the penalty to the clerk of the court or files a supersedeas bond with the court in the amount of the penalty. A person who cannot afford to pay the penalty or file the bond may stay the enforcement by filing an affidavit in the manner required by the Texas Rules of Civil Procedure for a party who cannot afford to file security for costs, subject to the right to contest the affidavit as provided by those rules.

Added by Acts 2001, 77th Leg., ch. 1429, § 1, eff. Jan. 1, 2002. Renumbered from V.T.C.A., Bus. & C. Code § 43.252 by Acts 2003, 78th Leg., ch. 1275, § 2(3), eff. Sept. 1, 2003.

Repeal

Acts 2007, 80th Leg., ch. 885, § 2.47(a)(1) repeals this section effective April 1, 2009.

§ 44.253. Contested Case

A proceeding to impose the penalty is considered to be a contested case under Chapter 2001, Government Code.

Added by Acts 2001, 77th Leg., ch. 1429, § 1, eff. Jan. 1, 2002. Renumbered V.T.C.A., Bus. & C. Code § 43.253 by Acts 2003, 78th Leg., ch. 1275, § 2(3), eff. Sept. 1, 2003.

Repeal

Acts 2007, 80th Leg., ch. 885, § 2.47(a)(1) repeals this section effective April 1, 2009.

CHAPTER 45. SWEEPSTAKES

Acts 2007, 80th Leg., ch. 885, § 2.47(a)(1) repeals this chapter effective April 1, 2009.

Acts 2001, 77th Leg., ch. 1119, § 1 added this Chapter, Sweepstakes, consisting of V.T.C.A., Bus. & C. Code §§ 43.001 to 43.004. Acts 2003, 78th Leg., ch. 1275, § 2(4) renumbered this Chapter as Chapter 45, consisting of V.T.C.A., Bus. & C. Code §§ 45.001 to 45.004.

§ 45.001. Definitions

In this chapter:

(1) "Catalogues" means promotional booklets listing merchandise for sale that are at least 24 pages long, have a circulation of at least 250,000, and either:

(A) require customers to go to a physical location to purchase the advertised items; or

(B) are published by a company that derives more than 50 percent of its total gross revenue from sales occurring at physical locations.

(2) "Conducting" a sweepstakes means distributing any material that promotes a sweepstakes, describes the prize or prizes, states one or more of the sweepstakes rules, includes any current or future opportunity to enter the sweepstakes, or provides any method for the recipient of the material to obtain additional information about the sweepstakes.

(3) "Credit card" means:

(A) a card that, if covered by Texas law, would be a lender credit card, as defined by Section 301.002, Finance Code; or

(B) a card that, if covered by Texas law, would be a lender credit card under Section 301.002, Finance Code, except that the obligations under the card are payable in full each month, not deferred, and no finance charge is assessed when the obligations are paid.

(4) "Debit card" means a card offered by an institution whose deposits are insured by the Federal Deposit Insurance Corporation or by another agency, corporation, or instrumentality chartered by the United States government.

(5) "Imply" means all methods and means by which an implication can be conveyed, including a statement, a question, a request, conduct, a graphic, a symbol, lettering, coloring, font size, font style, or formatting.

(6) "Magazines" and "newspapers" mean publications:

(A) in which more than 40 percent of the total column inches in each issue consist of advertising space purchased by companies other than the publisher, its affiliates, and the vendors for any of them; and

(B) for which more than 50 percent of the total number of copies distributed of each issue go to customers who paid for the copy.

(7) "Sweepstakes" means a contest that awards one or more prizes based on chance or the random selection of entries.

Added by Acts 2001, 77th Leg., ch. 1119, § 1, eff. Nov. 1, 2001. Renumbered from V.T.C.A., Bus. & C. Code § 43.001 by Acts 2003, 78th Leg., ch. 1275, § 2(4), eff. Sept. 1, 2003.

Repeal

Acts 2007, 80th Leg., ch. 885, § 2.47(a)(1) repeals this section effective April 1, 2009.

§ 45.002. Offenses

A person conducting a sweepstakes through the mail may not:

(1) require an individual to order or purchase a good or service, or promise to purchase a good or service in the future, to enter a sweepstakes;

(2) automatically enter an individual in a sweepstakes because the individual ordered or purchased a good or service or because the individual promised to order or purchase a good or service;

(3) solicit business using an order form or purchasing mechanism that has any role in the operation of a sweepstakes;

(4) use a mechanism for entering a sweepstakes that:

(A) has any connection to ordering or purchasing a good or service;

(B) is not identical for all individuals entering the sweepstakes; and

(C) does not have printed on the entry form in a font size at least as large as the largest font size used on the entry form the following language: "Buying Will Not Help You Win. Your chances of winning without making a purchase are the same as the chances of someone who purchases something. It is illegal to give any advantage to buyers in a sweepstakes.";

(5) solicit an individual to enter a sweepstakes by invitation or other opportunity and allow the individual to choose or indicate the preferred characteristics of a prize to be awarded in the sweepstakes, unless those choices:

(A) are made on the sweepstakes entry form; and

(B) do not appear on and are not connected in any way to an order form or other purchasing mechanism;

(6) offer through the mail any nonsweepstakes prize, gift, premium, giveaway, or skill contest during the 30-day period immediately following the last date on which the person conducted a sweepstakes through the mail;

(7) offer through the mail any opportunity to enter a sweepstakes during the 30-day period immediately following the last date on which the person conducted a sweepstakes through the mail;

(8) ask an individual for any information or any action by that individual that would be consistent with the individual winning a sweepstakes prize, unless the individual has won a sweepstakes prize;

(9) provide an individual who has not yet won the sweepstakes with any document or other item that simulates any event, circumstance, or condition connected with being the winner of the sweepstakes;

(10) send material accompanying or relating to a sweepstakes or an offer to enter a sweepstakes that states or implies that an individual must comply with a restriction or condition to enter the sweepstakes, unless all individuals entering the sweepstakes are required to comply with the identical restriction or condition;

(11) use a scratch-off device or any other game piece that suggests an element of chance or luck to convey information about a sweepstakes or an offer to enter a sweepstakes;

(12) send material accompanying or relating to a sweepstakes or an offer to enter a sweepstakes that:

(A) states or implies that an individual's chances of winning a prize in the sweepstakes are raised, lowered, or different in any way because of a factor or circumstance that has no relation to the manner in which a winner of the sweepstakes is selected;

(B) states or implies that a winner of a sweepstakes prize will be selected at a time or place or in a manner that is different from the actual time or place at which or manner in which a winner is selected;

(C) states or implies falsely that the individual receiving the advertisement has received any special treatment or personal attention from the offeror of the sweepstakes or any officer, employee, or agent of the offeror of the sweepstakes;

(D) states or implies that an individual who orders or purchases a good or service will receive a benefit in the sweepstakes or be treated differently in the sweepstakes compared with an individual who did not order or purchase a good or service;

(E) states or implies that an individual who does not order or purchase a good or service will suffer a disadvantage in the sweepstakes or be treated differently in the sweepstakes compared with an individual who ordered or purchased a good or service; or

(F) states that the recipient of the material:

(i) is a winner if the recipient is not a winner;

(ii) may be a winner;

(iii) will be a winner if certain conditions are met or if certain events occur in the future;

(iv) may be or will be among the group from which a winner will be selected; or

(v) has in any way a better chance than another individual of being chosen as a winner;

(13) publish or cause to be published different advertisements for the same sweepstakes that contain inconsistent descriptions of the grand prize awarded through the sweepstakes;

(14) award multiple prizes in a sweepstakes unless all prizes are awarded on the same date and through the same selection process;

(15) publish or cause to be published official rules of a sweepstakes that do not uniquely identify the prizes to be awarded and the date they will be awarded; or

(16) provide for entry by mail in a sweepstakes and use:

(A) more than one address to accept entries in the sweepstakes; or

(B) the address for entry in the sweepstakes for any purpose other than entry in the sweepstakes.

Added by Acts 2001, 77th Leg., ch. 1119, § 1, eff. Nov. 1, 2001. Renumbered from V.T.C.A., Bus. & C. Code § 43.002 by Acts 2003, 78th Leg., ch. 1275, § 2(4), eff. Sept. 1, 2003.

Repeal

Acts 2007, 80th Leg., ch. 885, § 2.47(a)(1) repeals this section effective April 1, 2009.

§ 45.003. Application of Chapter; Acts Not Prohibited

(a) This chapter does not apply to any sweepstakes that is conducted through advertisements or inserts in magazines, newspapers, or catalogues sent through the mail.

(b) This chapter does not apply to any charitable raffle regulated by Chapter 2002, Occupations Code.

(c) This chapter does not apply to any sweepstakes regulated by the Alcoholic Beverage Code.

(d) This chapter does not apply to any company regulated under the Public Utility Regulatory Act (Title 2, Utilities Code).[1]

(e) This chapter does not apply to any company that is an air carrier subject to Title 49 of the United States Code or to a nonprofit association of airmen who are subject to that title.

(f) This chapter does not apply to a drawing for the opportunity to participate in a hunting, fishing, or other recreational event conducted by the Parks and Wildlife Department.

(g) If the only use of the mail is for consumers to return their entry forms to the sponsor of the contest, then this chapter does not apply to that sweepstakes.

(h) This chapter does not prohibit a sweepstakes sponsor from making a statement in the official rules of the sweepstakes describing the method to be used in choosing a winner, and this chapter does not prohibit a sweepstakes sponsor from notifying the winner after the winner has been selected.

(i) This chapter does not prohibit a sweepstakes sponsor, after determining the winner, from obtaining an affidavit from the person selected to verify that the person is eligible to win the prize and has complied with the rules of the sweepstakes.

(j) This chapter does not apply to a sweepstakes conducted through the mail if the most valuable prize to be awarded is less than $50,000. The value of a prize is measured by the highest number among its face value, its fair market value, and its financial present value.

(k) Sections 45.002(3) and (4)(A) do not apply to a single sheet of paper that contains both a contest entry form and an order form if the order form is perforated or detachable and if the entry form must be separated from the order form and returned to an address different from the return address for the order form.

(*l*) Sections 45.002(2), (3), and (4) do not apply to a contest that is offered to promote a credit card or a debit card if the official rules of the contest provide that consumers are entered in the contest based on the number of purchases made or the amount of money spent. A person who did not qualify as an issuer as of January 1, 2001, is not eligible for the exceptions under this subsection.

(m) Sections 45.002(2), (3), and (4) do not apply to a company that is offering a sweepstakes in which the consumer must go to a physical location to obtain or use the goods or services that are being sold by the company offering the sweepstakes.

(n) This chapter does not apply to any sweepstakes that is promoting one or more food products that are regulated by the federal Food and Drug Administration or the United States Department of Agriculture.

(*o*) This chapter does not apply to any company whose primary business is the production, distribution, sale, and marketing of audiovisual entertainment works, products, or sound recordings. For purposes of this subsection, "primary business" means that 75 percent or more of a company's business is the production, distribution, sale, and marketing of audiovisual entertainment works, products, or sound recordings, and "production" means the systematic development, planning, and execution of creating the audiovisual works, products, or sound recordings. This chapter does not apply to a company that owns or operates a cable system, as that term is defined by 47 U.S.C. Section 522, as amended.

Added by Acts 2001, 77th Leg., ch. 1119, § 1, eff. Nov. 1, 2001. Amended by Acts 2003, 78th Leg., ch. 105, § 1, eff. May 20, 2003. Renumbered from V.T.C.A., Bus. & C. Code § 43.003 and amended by Acts 2003, 78th Leg., ch. 1275, §§ 2(4), 3(2), eff. Sept. 1, 2003.

[1] V.T.C.A., Utilities Code § 11.001 et seq.

Repeal

Acts 2007, 80th Leg., ch. 885, § 2.47(a)(1) repeals this section effective April 1, 2009.

§ 45.004. Civil Penalty

(a) The attorney general may initiate an action under this chapter by filing suit in a district court in Travis County or in any county in which a violation occurred.

(b) For each violation found, the court shall award the attorney general a civil penalty of not less than $5,000 or more than $50,000.

(c) If the material accompanying or relating to a sweepstakes or an offer to enter a sweepstakes contains multiple statements, implications, representations, or offers that are prohibited by this chapter, each statement, implication, representation, or offer is a separate violation and shall result in a separate civil penalty. Each individual who receives the material constitutes an additional and separate group of violations of this chapter.

(d) Any person who provides names or addresses of residents of this state that are used in conducting a sweepstakes that the person knows to be in violation of this chapter is liable for the cumulative civil penalties that result from the person's conduct. The liability of a person who provides names or addresses does not reduce the liability of the person who conducted the sweepstakes.

(e) If the attorney general substantially prevails, the court shall award the attorney general reasonable expenses incurred in recovering a civil penalty under this section, including court costs, reasonable attorney's fees, reasonable investigative costs, witness fees, and deposition expenses.

(f) A civil penalty recovered under this section shall be deposited in the state treasury.

(g) A court may also award injunctive relief or other equitable or ancillary relief that is reasonably necessary to prevent future violations of this chapter.

(h) This chapter does not create any private right of action for any person.

Added by Acts 2001, 77th Leg., ch. 1119, § 1, eff. Nov. 1, 2001. Renumbered from V.T.C.A., Bus. & C. Code § 43.004 by Acts 2003, 78th Leg., ch. 1275, § 2(4), eff. Sept. 1, 2003.

Repeal

Acts 2007, 80th Leg., ch. 885, § 2.47(a)(1) repeals this section effective April 1, 2009.

CHAPTER 46 ELECTRONIC MAIL SOLICITATION

Section

Acts 2007, 80th Leg., ch. 885, § 2.47(a)(1) repeals this chapter effective April 1, 2009.

Chapter 46, Electronic Mail Solicitation, consisting of §§ 46.001 to 46.011, was added by Acts 2003, 78th Leg., ch. 1053, § 1.

Another Chapter 46, Sexually Oriented Businesses, consisting of §§ 46.001 to 46.004, added by Acts 2003, 78th Leg., ch. 402, § 1, was renumbered as Chapter 47, consisting of V.T.C.A., Bus. & C. Code §§ 47.001 to 47.004, by Acts 2005, 79th Leg., ch. 728, § 23.001(5).

§ 46.001. Definitions

In this chapter:

(1) "Commercial electronic mail message" means an electronic mail message that advertises, offers for sale or lease, or promotes any goods, services, business opportunity, property, or any other article, commodity, or thing of value.

(2) "Electronic mail" means a message, file, or other information that is transmitted through a local, regional, or global computer network, regardless of whether the message, file, or other information is viewed, stored for retrieval at a later time, printed, or filtered by a computer program that is designed or intended to filter or screen those items.

(3) "Electronic mail service provider" means a person that:

(A) is qualified to do business in this state;

(B) is an intermediary in sending or receiving electronic mail; and

(C) provides an end user of an electronic mail service the ability to send or receive electronic mail.

(4) "Established business relationship" means a prior or existing relationship of a person formed by a voluntary two-way communication between a person and another person, regardless of whether consideration is exchanged, regarding products or services offered by one of the persons, that has not been terminated by either party.

(5) "Internet domain name" refers to a globally unique, hierarchical reference to an Internet host or service, assigned through a centralized Internet naming authority and composed of a series of character strings separated by periods with the rightmost string specifying the top of the hierarchy.

(6) "Obscene" has the meaning assigned by Section 43. 21, Penal Code.

(7) "Sender" means a person who initiates an electronic mail message.

(8) "Sexual conduct" has the meaning assigned by Section 43.25, Penal Code.

(9) "Unsolicited commercial electronic mail message" means a commercial electronic mail message sent without the consent of the recipient by a person with whom the recipient does not have an established business relationship. The term does not include electronic mail sent by an organization using electronic mail for the purpose of communicating exclusively with members, employees, or contractors of the organization.

Added by Acts 2003, 78th Leg., ch. 1053, § 1, eff. Sept. 1, 2003.

Repeal

Acts 2007, 80th Leg., ch. 885, § 2.47(a)(1) repeals this section effective April 1, 2009.

§ 46.002. Certain Electronic Mail Messages Prohibited

(a) A person may not intentionally transmit a commercial electronic mail message that:

(1) falsifies electronic mail transmission information or other routing information for an unsolicited commercial electronic mail message; or

(2) contains false, deceptive, or misleading information in the subject line.

(b) A person may not intentionally send a commercial electronic mail message that uses another person's Internet domain name without the other person's consent.

Added by Acts 2003, 78th Leg., ch. 1053, § 1, eff. Sept. 1, 2003.

Repeal

Acts 2007, 80th Leg., ch. 885, § 2.47(a)(1) repeals this section effective April 1, 2009.

§ 46.003. Unsolicited Electronic Mail Messages

(a) A person may not intentionally take any action to send an unsolicited commercial electronic mail message unless:

(1) "ADV:" is used as the first four characters in the subject line of the message or, if the message contains any obscene material or material depicting sexual conduct, "ADV: ADULT ADVERTISEMENT" is used as the first word in the subject line of the message; and

(2) the sender of the message or a person acting on behalf of the sender provides a functioning return electronic mail address to which a recipient may, at no cost to the recipient, send a reply requesting the removal of the recipient's electronic mail address from the sender's electronic mail list.

(b) A sender shall remove a person's electronic mail address from the sender's electronic mail list not later than the 3rd day after the date on which the sender receives a request for removal of that address under Subsection (a)(2).

Added by Acts 2003, 78th Leg., ch. 1053, § 1, eff. Sept. 1, 2003.

Repeal

Acts 2007, 80th Leg., ch. 885, § 2.47(a)(1) repeals this section effective April 1, 2009.

§ 46.004. Sale or Provision of Address on Electronic Mail List Prohibited

A sender or a person acting on behalf of the sender may not sell or otherwise provide the electronic mail address of a person who requests the removal of that address from the sender's electronic mail list under Section 46.003(a)(2), except as required by other law.

Added by Acts 2003, 78th Leg., ch. 1053, § 1, eff. Sept. 1, 2003.

Repeal

Acts 2007, 80th Leg., ch. 885, § 2.47(a)(1) repeals this section effective April 1, 2009.

§ 46.005. Criminal Penalty

A person commits an offense if the person intentionally takes any action to send a message containing obscene material or material depicting sexual conduct in violation of Section 46.003(a)(1). An offense under this section is a Class B misdemeanor.

Added by Acts 2003, 78th Leg., ch. 1053, § 1, eff. Sept. 1, 2003.

Repeal

Acts 2007, 80th Leg., ch. 885, § 2.47(a)(1) repeals this section effective April 1, 2009.

§ 46.006. Civil Penalty

(a) A person who violates this chapter other than Section 46.009 is liable to the state for a civil penalty in an amount not to exceed the lesser of:

(1) $10 for each unlawful message or action; or

(2) $25,000 for each day an unlawful message is received or an action is taken.

(b) The attorney general or the prosecuting attorney in the county in which the violation occurs may:

(1) bring suit to recover the civil penalty imposed under Subsection (a); and

(2) seek an injunction to prevent or restrain a violation of this chapter.

(c) The attorney general or the prosecuting attorney may recover reasonable expenses incurred in obtaining a civil penalty under this section, including court costs, reasonable attorney's fees, investigative costs, witness fees, and deposition expenses.

Added by Acts 2003, 78th Leg., ch. 1053, § 1, eff. Sept. 1, 2003.

Repeal

Acts 2007, 80th Leg., ch. 885, § 2.47(a)(1) repeals this section effective April 1, 2009.

§ 46.007. Deceptive Trade Practices

A violation of this chapter is a false, misleading, or deceptive act or practice under Subchapter E, Chapter 17, and any public or private right or remedy prescribed by that subchapter may be used to enforce this chapter, except as provided by Section 46.008(d).

Added by Acts 2003, 78th Leg., ch. 1053, § 1, eff. Sept. 1, 2003.

Repeal

Acts 2007, 80th Leg., ch. 885, § 2.47(a)(1) repeals this section effective April 1, 2009.

§ 46.008. Civil Liability

(a) A person injured by a violation of this chapter may bring an action to recover actual damages, including lost profits. A person who prevails in the action is entitled to reasonable attorney's fees and court costs.

(b) In lieu of actual damages, a person injured by a violation of this chapter arising from the transmission of an unsolicited or commercial electronic mail message, other than an electronic mail service provider, may recover the lesser of:

(1) $10 for each unlawful message; or

(2) $25,000 for each day the unlawful message is received.

(c) In lieu of actual damages, an electronic mail service provider injured by a violation of this chapter arising from the transmission of an unsolicited or commercial electronic mail message may recover the greater of:

(1) $10 for each unlawful message; or

(2) $25,000 for each day the unlawful message is received.

(d) A court may not certify an action brought under this chapter as a class action.

(e) At the request of a party to any action brought under this chapter, the court, in its discretion, may conduct a legal proceeding in such a manner as to protect the secrecy and security of the computer, computer network, computer data, computer program, and computer software involved to prevent a possible recurrence of the same or a similar act by another person and to protect any trade secrets of a party to the action.

Added by Acts 2003, 78th Leg., ch. 1053, § 1, eff. Sept. 1, 2003.

Repeal

Acts 2007, 80th Leg., ch. 885, § 2.47(a)(1) repeals this section effective April 1, 2009.

§ 46.009. Notice to Attorney General

(a) A person who brings an action under Section 46.008 shall give notice of the action to the attorney general by sending a copy of the petition by registered or certified mail not later than the 30th day after the date the petition was filed and at least 10 days before the date set for a hearing on the action.

(b) The attorney general may intervene in the action by:

(1) filing a notice of intervention with the court in which the action is pending; and

(2) serving each party to the action with a copy of the notice of intervention.

(c) A person who violates Subsection (a) is liable to the state for a civil penalty in an amount not to exceed $200 for each violation. The attorney general may bring suit to recover the civil penalty imposed under this subsection in the court in which the action is instituted.

Added by Acts 2003, 78th Leg., ch. 1053, § 1, eff. Sept. 1, 2003.

Repeal

Acts 2007, 80th Leg., ch. 885, § 2.47(a)(1) repeals this section effective April 1, 2009.

§ 46.010. Blocking of Commercial Electronic Mail Message

An electronic mail service provider may on its own initiative block the receipt or transmission through its service of any commercial electronic mail message that the provider reasonably believes is or will be sent in violation of this chapter if the provider:

(1) provides a process for the prompt, good faith resolution of disputes related to the blocking with senders of commercial electronic mail messages; and

(2) makes contact information publicly accessible on its Internet website for the purpose of dispute resolution.

Added by Acts 2003, 78th Leg., ch. 1053, § 1, eff. Sept. 1, 2003.

Repeal

Acts 2007, 80th Leg., ch. 885, § 2.47(a)(1) repeals this section effective April 1, 2009.

§ 46.011. Qualified Immunity

(a) In this section, "telecommunications utility" has the meaning assigned by Section 51.002, Utilities Code.

(b) A telecommunications utility or an electronic mail service provider may not be held liable under Section 46.002 or 46.003 and is not subject to the penalties provided under this chapter.

(c) A person injured by a violation of this chapter does not have a cause of action against a telecommunications utility or an electronic mail service provider under this chapter solely because the utility or provider:

(1) is an intermediary between the sender, or any person acting on behalf of the sender, and the recipient in the transmission of electronic mail that violates this chapter;

(2) provides transmission, routing, relaying, handling, or storing, through an automatic technical process, of an unsolicited commercial electronic mail message through the utility's or provider's computer network or facilities; or

(3) provides telecommunications services, information services, or other services used in the transmission of an electronic mail message that violates this chapter.

(d) An electronic mail service provider that provides for a dispute resolution process as described by Section 46.010 may not be held liable for blocking the receipt or transmission through its service of any commercial electronic mail message that the provider reasonably believes is or will be sent in violation of this chapter.

(e) A person may not be held liable under this chapter for a commercial electronic mail message that is sent as a result of an error or accidental transmission.

(f) A sender may not be held liable for the transmission of an electronic mail message that violates this chapter if the sender:

(1) contracts in good faith with an electronic mail service provider to transmit electronic mail messages for the sender; and

(2) has no reason to believe the electronic mail service provider will transmit any of the sender's messages in a manner that violates this chapter.

Added by Acts 2003, 78th Leg., ch. 1053, § 1, eff. Sept. 1, 2003.

Repeal

Acts 2007, 80th Leg., ch. 885, § 2.47(a)(1) repeals this section effective April 1, 2009.

CHAPTER 47. SEXUALLY ORIENTED BUSINESSES

SUBCHAPTER A. RESTRICTION ON OWNERS, OPERATORS, MANAGERS, OR EMPLOYEES OF SEXUALLY ORIENTED BUSINESSES

Acts 2007, 80th Leg., ch. 885, § 2.47(a)(1) repeals this chapter effective April 1, 2009. Without reference to this repeal, Acts 2007, 80th Leg., ch. 1206, § 3 added a Subchapter B, consisting of §§ 47.051 to 47.056.

This Chapter was added as Chapter 46, Sexually Oriented Businesses, consisting of V.T.C.A., Bus. & C. §§ 46.001 to 46.004, by Acts 2003, 78th Leg., ch. 402, § 1, and was renumbered as Chapter 47, consisting of §§ 47.001 to 47.004, by Acts 2005, 79th Leg., ch. 728, § 23.001(5).

SUBCHAPTER A. RESTRICTION ON OWNERS, OPERATORS, MANAGERS, OR EMPLOYEES OF SEXUALLY ORIENTED BUSINESSES

§ 47.001. Definitions

Text of section effective until January 1, 2008

In this chapter:

(1) "Sex offender" means a person who has been convicted of or placed on deferred adjudication for an offense for which a person is subject to registration under Chapter 62, Code of Criminal Procedure.

(2) "Sexually oriented business" has the meaning assigned by Section 243.002, Local Government Code.

Added by Acts 2003, 78th Leg., ch. 402, § 1, eff. Sept. 1, 2003. Renumbered from V.T.C.A., Bus. & C. Code § 46.001 by Acts 2005, 79th Leg., ch. 728, § 23.001(5), eff. Sept. 1, 2005.

For text of section effective January 1, 2008, see § 47.001, post

Repeal

Acts 2007, 80th Leg., ch. 885, § 2.47(a)(1) repeals this section effective April 1, 2009.

§ 47.001. Definitions

Text of section effective January 1, 2008

In this subchapter:

(1) "Sex offender" means a person who has been convicted of or placed on deferred adjudication for an offense for which a person is subject to registration under Chapter 62, Code of Criminal Procedure.

(2) "Sexually oriented business" has the meaning assigned by Section 243.002, Local Government Code.

Added by Acts 2003, 78th Leg., ch. 402, § 1, eff. Sept. 1, 2003. Renumbered from V.T.C.A., Bus. & C. Code § 46.001 by Acts 2005, 79th Leg., ch. 728, § 23.001(5), eff. Sept. 1, 2005. Amended by Acts 2007, 80th Leg., ch. 1206, § 2, eff. Jan. 1, 2008.

For text of section effective until January 1, 2008, see § 47.001, ante

Repeal

Acts 2007, 80th Leg., ch. 885, § 2.47(a)(1) repeals this section effective April 1, 2009.

§ 47.002. Prohibition on Ownership, Operation, or Management by or Employment of Sex Offender

(a) A sex offender may not own wholly or partly or serve as a director, officer, operator, manager, or employee of a sexually oriented business.

(b) A sexually oriented business may not contract with a person to operate or manage the business as an independent contractor or employ a person as an officer, operator, manager, or other employee if the business knows the person is a sex offender.

Added by Acts 2003, 78th Leg., ch. 402, § 1, eff. Sept. 1, 2003. Renumbered from V.T.C.A., Bus. & C. Code § 46.002 by Acts 2005, 79th Leg., ch. 728, § 23.001(5), eff. Sept. 1, 2005.

Repeal

Acts 2007, 80th Leg., ch. 885, § 2.47(a)(1) repeals this section effective April 1, 2009.

§ 47.003. Injunction

(a) The attorney general or the appropriate district or county attorney, in the name of the state, may bring an action for an injunction or other process against a person who is violating or threatening to violate Section 47.002. The action may be brought in a district court of Travis County or of a county in which any part of the violation or threatened violation occurs.

(b) The district court may grant any prohibitory or mandatory relief warranted by the facts, including a temporary restraining order, temporary injunction, or permanent injunction.

Added by Acts 2003, 78th Leg., ch. 402, § 1, eff. Sept. 1, 2003. Renumbered from V.T.C.A., Bus. & C. Code § 46.003 and amended by Acts 2005, 79th Leg., ch. 728, §§ 23.001(5), 23.002(2), eff. Sept. 1, 2005.

Repeal

Acts 2007, 80th Leg., ch. 885, § 2.47(a)(1) repeals this section effective April 1, 2009.

§ 47.004. Criminal Penalty

(a) A sex offender commits an offense if the offender violates Section 47.002(a).

(b) A sexually oriented business commits an offense if the business violates Section 47.002(b).

(c) An offense under this section is a Class A misdemeanor.

Added by Acts 2003, 78th Leg., ch. 402, § 1, eff. Sept. 1, 2003. Renumbered from V.T.C.A., Bus. & C. Code § 46.004 and amended by Acts 2005, 79th Leg., ch. 728, §§ 23.001(5), 23.002(3), eff. Sept. 1, 2005.

Repeal

Acts 2007, 80th Leg., ch. 885, § 2.47(a)(1) repeals this section effective April 1, 2009.

SUBCHAPTER B. FEE IMPOSED ON CERTAIN SEXUALLY ORIENTED BUSINESSES

§ 47.051. Definitions

Text of section effective January 1, 2008

In this subchapter:

(1) "Nude" means:

(A) entirely unclothed; or

(B) clothed in a manner that leaves uncovered or visible through less than fully opaque clothing any portion of the breasts below the top of the areola of the breasts, if the person is female, or any portion of the genitals or buttocks.

(2) "Sexually oriented business" means a nightclub, bar, restaurant, or similar commercial enterprise that:

(A) provides for an audience of two or more individuals live nude entertainment or live nude performances; and

(B) authorizes on-premises consumption of alcoholic beverages, regardless of whether the consumption of alcoholic beverages is under a license or permit issued under the Alcoholic Beverage Code.

Added by Acts 2007, 80th Leg., ch. 1206, § 3, eff. Jan. 1, 2008.

§ 47.052. Fee Based on Admissions; Records

Text of section effective January 1, 2008

(a) A fee is imposed on a sexually oriented business in an amount equal to $5 for each entry by each customer admitted to the business.

(b) A sexually oriented business shall record daily in the manner required by the comptroller the number of customers admitted to the business. The business shall maintain the records for the period required by the comptroller and make the records available for inspection and audit on request by the comptroller.

(c) This section does not require a sexually oriented business to impose a fee on a customer of the business. A business has discretion to determine the manner in which the business derives the money required to pay the fee imposed under this section.

Added by Acts 2007, 80th Leg., ch. 1206, § 3, eff. Jan. 1, 2008.

Section 8 of Acts 2007, 80th Leg., ch. 1206 provides:

"The fee imposed by Section 47.052, Business & Commerce Code, as added by this Act, applies only to a sexually oriented business with respect to the admission by the business of customers on or after the effective date of this Act."

§ 47.053. Remission of Fee; Submission of Reports

Text of section effective January 1, 2008

Each quarter, a sexually oriented business shall:

(1) remit the fee imposed by Section 47.052 to the comptroller in the manner prescribed by the comptroller; and

(2) file a report with the comptroller in the manner and containing the information required by the comptroller.

Added by Acts 2007, 80th Leg., ch. 1206, § 3, eff. Jan. 1, 2008.

§ 47.054. Allocation of Certain Revenue for Sexual Assault Programs

Text of section effective January 1, 2008

The comptroller shall deposit the first $25 million received from the fee imposed under this subchapter in a state fiscal biennium to the credit of the sexual assault program fund.

Added by Acts 2007, 80th Leg., ch. 1206, § 3, eff. Jan. 1, 2008.

§ 47.055. Allocation of Additional Revenue

Text of section effective January 1, 2008

(a) The comptroller shall deposit all amounts received from the fee imposed under this subchapter after the first $25 million in a state fiscal biennium in the Texas health opportunity pool established under Subchapter N, Chapter 531, Government Code. Money deposited in the pool under this section may be used only to provide health benefits coverage premium payment assistance to low-income persons through a premium payment assistance program developed under that subchapter.

(b) This section takes effect only if Senate Bill No. 10, Acts of the 80th Legislature, Regular Session, 2007, becomes law and the Texas health opportunity pool is established under that Act. If that Act does not become law, or that Act becomes law but the pool is not established, this section has no effect, and the revenue is deposited as provided by Section 47.0551.

Added by Acts 2007, 80th Leg., ch. 1206, § 3, eff. Jan. 1, 2008.

§ 47.0551. Allocation of Additional Revenue

Text of section effective January 1, 2008

(a) The comptroller shall deposit all amounts received from the fee imposed under this subchapter after the first $25 million in a state fiscal biennium to the credit of the premium payment assistance account. The premium payment assistance account is an account in the general revenue fund that may be appropriated to the Health and Human Services Commission only to provide health benefits coverage premium payment assistance to low-income persons through a program developed by the commission.

(b) This section takes effect only if Senate Bill No. 10, Acts of the 80th Legislature, Regular Session, 2007, does not become law, or that Act becomes law, but the Texas health opportunity pool is not established under that Act. If that Act becomes law and the pool is established, this section has no effect, and the revenue is deposited as provided by Section 47.055.

Added by Acts 2007, 80th Leg., ch. 1206, § 3, eff. Jan. 1, 2008.

§ 47.056. Administration, Collection, and Enforcement

Text of section effective January 1, 2008

The provisions of Subtitle B, Title 2, Tax Code, apply to the administration, payment, collection, and enforcement of the fee imposed by this chapter.

Added by Acts 2007, 80th Leg., ch. 1206, § 3, eff. Jan. 1, 2008.

CHAPTER 48. UNAUTHORIZED USE OF IDENTIFYING INFORMATION

SUBCHAPTER A. GENERAL PROVISIONS

SUBCHAPTER B. IDENTITY THEFT

Chapter 48, Unauthorized Use of Identifying Information, consisting of §§ 48.001 to 48.203, was added by Acts 2005, 79th Leg., ch. 294, § 1.

For another Chapter 48, Internet Fraud, consisting of §§ 48.001 to 48.006, added by Acts 2005, 79th Leg., ch. 544, § 1; and Chapter 48, Consumer Protection Against Computer Spyware Act, consisting of §§ 48.001 to 48.102, added by Acts 2005, 79th Leg., ch. 298, § 1, see §§ 48.001 et seq., post.

Acts 2007, 80th Leg., ch. 885, § 2.47(a)(2) repeals this chapter effective April 1, 2009.

SUBCHAPTER A. GENERAL PROVISIONS

§ 48.001. Short Title

This chapter may be cited as the Identity Theft Enforcement and Protection Act.

Added by Acts 2005, 79th Leg., ch. 294, § 2, eff. Sept. 1, 2005.

Repeal

Acts 2007, 80th Leg., ch. 885, § 2.47(a)(2) repeals this section effective April 1, 2009.

§ 48.002. Definitions

In this chapter:

(1) "Personal identifying information" means information that alone or in conjunction with other information identifies an individual, including an individual's:

(A) name, social security number, date of birth, or government-issued identification number;

(B) mother's maiden name;

(C) unique biometric data, including the individual's fingerprint, voice print, and retina or iris image;

(D) unique electronic identification number, address, or routing code; and

(E) telecommunication access device.

(2) "Sensitive personal information":

(A) means an individual's first name or first initial and last name in combination with any one or more of the following items, if the name and the items are not encrypted:

(i) social security number;

(ii) driver's license number or government-issued identification number; or

(iii) account number or credit or debit card number in combination with any required security code, access code, or password that would permit access to an individual's financial account; and

(B) does not include publicly available information that is lawfully made available to the general public from the federal government or a state or local government.

(3) "Telecommunication access device" has the meaning assigned by Section 32.51, Penal Code.

(4) "Victim" means a person whose identifying information is used by an unauthorized person.

Added by Acts 2005, 79th Leg., ch. 294, § 2, eff. Sept. 1, 2005.

Repeal

Acts 2007, 80th Leg., ch. 885, § 2.47(a)(2) repeals this section effective April 1, 2009.

[Sections 48.003 to 48.100 reserved for expansion]

SUBCHAPTER B. IDENTITY THEFT

§ 48.101. Unauthorized Use or Possession of Personal Identifying Information

(a) A person may not obtain, possess, transfer, or use personal identifying information of another person without the other person's consent and with intent to obtain a good, a service, insurance, an extension of credit, or any other thing of value in the other person's name.

(b) It is a defense to an action brought under this section that an act by a person:

(1) is covered by the Fair Credit Reporting Act (15 U.S.C. Section 1681 et seq.); and

(2) is in compliance with that Act and regulations adopted under that Act.

(c) This section does not apply to:

(1) a financial institution as defined by 15 U.S.C. Section 6809; or

(2) a covered entity as defined by Section 601.001 or 602.001, Insurance Code.

Added by Acts 2005, 79th Leg., ch. 294, § 2, eff. Sept. 1, 2005.

Repeal

Acts 2007, 80th Leg., ch. 885, § 2.47(a)(2) repeals this section effective April 1, 2009.

§ 48.102. Business Duty to Protect and Safeguard Sensitive Personal Information

(a) A business shall implement and maintain reasonable procedures, including taking any appropriate corrective action, to protect and safeguard from unlawful use or disclosure any sensitive personal information collected or maintained by the business in the regular course of business.

(b) A business shall destroy or arrange for the destruction of customer records containing sensitive personal information within the business's custody or control that are not to be retained by the business by:

(1) shredding;

(2) erasing; or

(3) otherwise modifying the sensitive personal information in the records to make the information unreadable or undecipherable through any means.

(c) This section does not apply to a financial institution as defined by 15 U.S.C. Section 6809.

Added by Acts 2005, 79th Leg., ch. 294, § 2, eff. Sept. 1, 2005.

Repeal

Acts 2007, 80th Leg., ch. 885, § 2.47(a)(2) repeals this section effective April 1, 2009.

§ 48.103. Notification Required Following Breach of Security of Computerized Data

(a) In this section, "breach of system security" means unauthorized acquisition of computerized data that compromises the security, confidentiality, or integrity of sensitive personal information maintained by a person. Good faith acquisition of sensitive personal information by an employee or agent of the person or business for the purposes of the person is not a breach of system security unless the sensitive personal information is used or disclosed by the person in an unauthorized manner.

(b) A person that conducts business in this state and owns or licenses computerized data that includes sensitive personal information shall disclose any breach of system security, after discovering or receiving notification of the breach, to any resident of this state whose sensitive personal information was, or is reasonably believed to have been, acquired by an unauthorized person. The disclosure shall be made as quickly as possible, except as provided by Subsection (d) or as necessary to determine the scope of the breach and restore the reasonable integrity of the data system.

(c) Any person that maintains computerized data that includes sensitive personal information that the person does not own shall notify the owner or license holder of the information of any breach of system security immediately after discovering the breach, if the sensitive personal information was, or is reasonably believed to have been, acquired by an unauthorized person.

(d) A person may delay providing notice as required by Subsections (b) and (c) at the request of a law enforcement agency that determines that the notification will impede a criminal investigation. The notification shall be made as soon as the law enforcement agency determines that it will not compromise the investigation.

(e) A person may give notice as required by Subsections (b) and (c) by providing:

(1) written notice;

(2) electronic notice, if the notice is provided in accordance with 15 U.S.C. Section 7001; or

(3) notice as provided by Subsection (f).

(f) If the person or business demonstrates that the cost of providing notice would exceed $250,000, the number of affected persons exceeds 500,000, or the person does not have sufficient contact information, the notice may be given by:

(1) electronic mail, if the person has an electronic mail address for the affected persons;

(2) conspicuous posting of the notice on the person's website; or

(3) notice published in or broadcast on major statewide media.

(g) Notwithstanding Subsection (e), a person that maintains its own notification procedures as part of an information security policy for the treatment of sensitive personal information that complies with the timing requirements for notice under this section complies with this section if the person notifies affected persons in accordance with that policy.

(h) If a person is required by this section to notify at one time more than 10,000 persons of a breach of system security, the person shall also notify, without unreasonable delay, all consumer reporting agencies, as defined by 15 U.S.C. Section 1681a, that maintain files on consumers on a nationwide basis, of the timing, distribution, and content of the notices.

Added by Acts 2005, 79th Leg., ch. 294, § 2, eff. Sept. 1, 2005.

Repeal

Acts 2007, 80th Leg., ch. 885, § 2.47(a)(2) repeals this section effective April 1, 2009.

[Sections 48.104 to 48.200 reserved for expansion]

SUBCHAPTER C. REMEDIES AND OFFENSES

§ 48.201. Civil Penalty; Injunction

(a) A person who violates this chapter is liable to the state for a civil penalty of at least $2,000 but not more than $50,000 for each violation. The attorney general may bring suit to recover the civil penalty imposed by this subsection.

(b) If it appears to the attorney general that a person is engaging in, has engaged in, or is about to engage in conduct that violates this chapter, the attorney general may bring an action in the name of this state against the person to restrain the violation by a temporary restraining order or a permanent or temporary injunction.

(c) An action brought under Subsection (b) shall be filed in a district court in Travis County or:

(1) in any county in which the violation occurred; or

(2) in the county in which the victim resides, regardless of whether the alleged violator has resided, worked, or done business in the county in which the victim resides.

(d) The plaintiff in an action under this section is not required to give a bond. The court may also grant any other equitable relief that the court considers appropriate to prevent any additional harm to a victim of identity theft or a further violation of this chapter or to satisfy any judgment entered against the defendant, including the issuance of an order to appoint a receiver, sequester assets, correct a public or private record, or prevent the dissipation of a victim's assets.

(e) The attorney general is entitled to recover reasonable expenses incurred in obtaining injunctive relief, civil penalties, or both, under this section, including reasonable attorney's fees, court costs, and investigatory costs. Amounts collected by the attorney general under this section shall be deposited in the general revenue fund and may be appropriated only for the investigation and prosecution of other cases under this chapter.

(f) The fees associated with an action under this section are the same as in a civil case, but the fees may be assessed only against the defendant.

Added by Acts 2005, 79th Leg., ch. 294, § 2, eff. Sept. 1, 2005.

Repeal

Acts 2007, 80th Leg., ch. 885, § 2.47(a)(2) repeals this section effective April 1, 2009.

§ 48.202. Court Order to Declare Individual a Victim of Identity Theft

(a) A person who is injured by a violation of Section 48.101 or who has filed a criminal complaint alleging commission of an offense under Section 32.51, Penal Code, may file an application with a district court for the issuance of a court order declaring that the person is a victim of identity theft. A person may file an application under this section regardless of whether the person is able to identify each person who allegedly transferred or used the person's identifying information in an unlawful manner.

(b) A person is presumed to be a victim of identity theft under this section if the person charged with an offense under Section 32.51, Penal Code, is convicted of the offense.

(c) After notice and hearing, if the court is satisfied by a preponderance of the evidence that the applicant has been injured by a violation of Section 48.101 or is the victim of an offense under Section 32.51, Penal Code, the court shall enter an order containing:

(1) a declaration that the person filing the application is a victim of identity theft resulting from a violation of Section 48.101 or an offense under Section 32.51, Penal Code, as appropriate;

(2) any known information identifying the violator or person charged with the offense;

(3) the specific personal identifying information and any related document used to commit the alleged violation or offense; and

(4) information identifying any financial account or transaction affected by the alleged violation or offense, including:

(A) the name of the financial institution in which the account is established or of the merchant involved in the transaction, as appropriate;

(B) any relevant account numbers;

(C) the dollar amount of the account or transaction affected by the alleged violation or offense; and

(D) the date of the alleged violation or offense.

(d) An order rendered under this section must be sealed because of the confidential nature of the information required to be included in the order. The order may be opened and the order or a copy of the order may be released only:

(1) to the proper officials in a civil proceeding brought by or against the victim arising or resulting from a violation of this chapter, including a proceeding to set aside a judgment obtained against the victim;

(2) to the victim for the purpose of submitting the copy of the order to a governmental entity or private business to:

(A) prove that a financial transaction or account of the victim was directly affected by a violation of this chapter or the commission of an offense under Section 32.51, Penal Code; or

(B) correct any record of the entity or business that contains inaccurate or false information as a result of the violation or offense;

(3) on order of the judge; or

(4) as otherwise required or provided by law.

(e) A court at any time may vacate an order issued under this section if the court finds that the application or any information submitted to the court by the applicant contains a fraudulent misrepresentation or a material misrepresentation of fact.

(f) A copy of an order provided to a person under Subsection (d)(1) must remain sealed throughout and after the civil proceeding. Information contained in a copy of an order provided to a governmental entity or business under Subsection (d)(2) is confidential and may not be released to another person except as otherwise required or provided by law.

Added by Acts 2005, 79th Leg., ch. 294, § 2, eff. Sept. 1, 2005.

Repeal

Acts 2007, 80th Leg., ch. 885, § 2.47(a)(2) repeals this section effective April 1, 2009.

§ 48.203. Deceptive Trade Practice

A violation of Section 48.101 is a deceptive trade practice actionable under Subchapter E, Chapter 17.

Added by Acts 2005, 79th Leg., ch. 294, § 2, eff. Sept. 1, 2005.

Repeal

Acts 2007, 80th Leg., ch. 885, § 2.47(a)(2) repeals this section effective April 1, 2009.

CHAPTER 48. INTERNET FRAUD

Acts 2007, 80th Leg., ch. 885, § 2.47(a)(4) repeals this chapter effective April 1, 2009.

Chapter 48, Internet Fraud, consisting of §§ 48.001 to 48.006, was added by Acts 2005, 79th Leg., ch. 544, § 1.

For another Chapter 48, Unauthorized Use of Identifying Information, consisting of §§ 48.001 to 48.203, added by Acts 2005, 79th Leg., ch. 294, § 1, see § 48.001 et seq., ante.

For another Chapter 48, Consumer Protection Against Computer Spyware Act, consisting of §§ 48.001 to 48.102, added by Acts 2005, 79th Leg., ch. 298, § 1, see § 48.001 et seq., post.

§ 48.001. Short Title

This chapter may be cited as the Anti–Phishing Act.

Added by Acts 2005, 79th Leg., ch. 544, § 1, eff. Sept. 1, 2005.

Repeal

Acts 2007, 80th Leg., ch. 885, § 2.47(a)(4) repeals this section effective April 1, 2009.

§ 48.002. Definitions

In this chapter:

(1) "Electronic mail" means a message, file, or other information that is transmitted through a local, regional, or global computer network, regardless of whether the message, file, or other information is viewed, stored for retrieval at a later time,

printed, or filtered by a computer program that is designed or intended to filter or screen those items.

(2) "Electronic mail address" means a destination, commonly expressed as a string of characters, to which electronic mail may be sent or delivered.

(3) "Identifying information" has the meaning assigned by Section 32.51, Penal Code.

(4) "Internet domain name" refers to a globally unique, hierarchical reference to an Internet host or service, assigned through a centralized Internet naming authority and composed of a series of character strings separated by periods with the rightmost string specifying the top of the hierarchy.

(5) "Web page" means a location that has a single uniform resource locator (URL) with respect to the world wide web or another location that can be accessed on the Internet.

Added by Acts 2005, 79th Leg., ch. 544, § 1, eff. Sept. 1, 2005.

Repeal

Acts 2007, 80th Leg., ch. 885, § 2.47(a)(4) repeals this section effective April 1, 2009.

§ 48.003. Creation of Web Page or Domain Name for Fraudulent Purposes

A person may not, with the intent to engage in conduct involving the fraudulent use or possession of another person's identifying information:

(1) create a web page or Internet domain name that is represented as a legitimate online business without the authorization of the registered owner of the business; and

(2) use that web page or a link to the web page, that domain name, or another site on the Internet to induce, request, or solicit another person to provide identifying information for a purpose that the other person believes is legitimate.

Added by Acts 2005, 79th Leg., ch. 544, § 1, eff. Sept. 1, 2005.

Repeal

Acts 2007, 80th Leg., ch. 885, § 2.47(a)(4) repeals this section effective April 1, 2009.

§ 48.004. Electronic Mail Fraud

A person may not, with the intent to engage in conduct involving the fraudulent use or possession of identifying information, send or cause to be sent to an electronic mail address held by a resident of this state an electronic mail message that:

(1) is falsely represented as being sent by a legitimate online business;

(2) refers or links the recipient of the message to a web page that is represented as being associated with the legitimate online business; and

(3) directly or indirectly induces, requests, or solicits the recipient of the electronic mail message to provide identifying information for a purpose that the recipient believes is legitimate.

Added by Acts 2005, 79th Leg., ch. 544, § 1, eff. Sept. 1, 2005.

Repeal

Acts 2007, 80th Leg., ch. 885, § 2.47(a)(4) repeals this section effective April 1, 2009.

Section 2 of Acts 2005, 79th Leg., ch. 544 provides:

"Section 48.004, Business & Commerce Code, as added by this Act, applies only to an electronic mail message that is sent on or after September 1, 2005."

§ 48.005. Civil Relief

(a) The following persons may bring a civil action against a person who violates this chapter:

(1) a person engaged in the business of providing Internet access service to the public who is adversely affected by the violation;

(2) an owner of a web page or trademark who is adversely affected by the violation; or

(3) the attorney general.

(b) A person bringing an action under this section may:

(1) seek injunctive relief to restrain the violator from continuing the violation;

(2) recover damages in an amount equal to the greater of:

(A) actual damages arising from the violation; or

(B) $100,000 for each violation of the same nature; or

(3) both seek injunctive relief and recover damages as provided by this subsection.

(c) The court may increase an award of actual damages in an action brought under this section to an amount not to exceed three times the actual damages sustained if the court finds that the violations have occurred with a frequency as to constitute a pattern or practice.

(d) A plaintiff who prevails in an action filed under this section is entitled to recover reasonable attorney's fees and court costs.

(e) For purposes of this section, violations are of the same nature if the violations consist of the same course of conduct or action, regardless of the number of times the conduct or act occurred.

Added by Acts 2005, 79th Leg., ch. 544, § 1, eff. Sept. 1, 2005.

Repeal

Acts 2007, 80th Leg., ch. 885, § 2.47(a)(4) repeals this section effective April 1, 2009.

§ 48.006. Applicability of Chapter

This chapter does not apply to a telecommunications provider's or Internet service provider's good faith transmission or routing of, or intermediate temporary storing or caching of, identifying information.

Added by Acts 2005, 79th Leg., ch. 544, § 1, eff. Sept. 1, 2005.

Repeal

Acts 2007, 80th Leg., ch. 885, § 2.47(a)(4) repeals this section effective April 1, 2009.

CHAPTER 48. CONSUMER PROTECTION AGAINST COMPUTER SPYWARE ACT

Acts 2007, 80th Leg., ch. 885, § 2.47(a)(3) repeals this chapter effective April 1, 2009.

Chapter 48, Consumer Protection Against Computer Spyware Act, consisting of §§ 48.001 to 48.102, was added by Acts 2005, 79th Leg., ch. 298, § 1.

For another Chapter 48, Unauthorized Use of Identifying Information, consisting of §§ 48.001 to 48.203, added by Acts 2005, 79th Leg., ch. 294, § 1; and Chapter 48, Internet Fraud, consisting of §§ 48.001 to 48.006, added by Acts 2005, 79th Leg., ch. 544, § 1, see §§ 48.001 et seq., ante.

SUBCHAPTER A. GENERAL PROVISIONS

§ 48.001. Short Title

This chapter may be cited as the Consumer Protection Against Computer Spyware Act.

Added by Acts 2005, 79th Leg., ch. 298, § 1, eff. Sept. 1, 2005.

Repeal

Acts 2007, 80th Leg., ch. 885, § 2.47(a)(3) repeals this section effective April 1, 2009.

§ 48.002. Definitions

In this chapter:

(1) "Advertisement" means a communication that includes the promotion of a commercial product or service, including communication on an Internet website operated for a commercial purpose.

(2) "Cause computer software to be copied" means to distribute or transfer computer software or a component of computer software. The term does not include:

(A) the transmission or routing of computer software or a component of the software;

(B) the provision of intermediate temporary storage or caching of software;

(C) the provision of a storage medium such as a compact disk;

(D) a website;

(E) the distribution of computer software by a third party through a computer server; or

(F) the provision of an information location tool, such as a directory, index, reference, pointer, or hypertext link, through which the user of a computer is able to locate computer software.

(3) "Computer software" means a sequence of instructions written in a programming language that is executed on a computer. The term does not include:

(A) a web page; or

(B) a data component of a web page that cannot be executed independently of that page.

(4) "Damage," with respect to a computer, means significant impairment to the integrity or availability of data, computer software, a system, or information.

(5) "Execute," with respect to computer software, means to perform a function or carry out instructions.

(6) "Keystroke–logging function" means a function of a computer software program that records all keystrokes made by a person using a computer and transfers that information from the computer to another person.

(7) "Owner or operator of a computer" means the owner or lessee of a computer or an individual using a computer with the authorization of the owner or lessee of the computer. If a computer was sold at retail, the phrase "owner of a computer" does not include the person who owned the computer before the date on which the computer was sold.

(8) "Person" means any individual, partnership, corporation, limited liability company, or other organization, or a combination of those organizations.

(9) "Personally identifiable information," with respect to an individual who is the owner or operator of a computer, means:

(A) first name or first initial in combination with last name;

(B) a home or other physical address, including street name;

(C) an electronic mail address;

(D) a credit or debit card number;

(E) a bank account number;

(F) a password or access code associated with a credit or debit card or bank account;

(G) a social security number, tax identification number, driver's license number, passport number, or other government-issued identification number; or

(H) any of the following information if the information alone or in combination with other information personally identifies the individual:

(i) account balances;

(ii) overdraft history; or

(iii) payment history.

Added by Acts 2005, 79th Leg., ch. 298, § 1, eff. Sept. 1, 2005.

Repeal

Acts 2007, 80th Leg., ch. 885, § 2.47(a)(3) repeals this section effective April 1, 2009.

§ 48.003. Applicability of Chapter

(a) Section 48.052, other than Subdivision (1) of that section, and Sections 48.053(4) and 48.055 do not apply to a telecommunications carrier, cable operator, computer hardware or software provider, or provider of information service or interactive computer service that monitors or has interaction with a subscriber's Internet or other network connection or service or a protected computer for:

(1) network or computer security purposes;

(2) diagnostics, technical support, or repair purposes;

(3) authorized updates of computer software or system firmware;

(4) authorized remote system management; or

(5) detection or prevention of unauthorized use of or fraudulent or other illegal activities in connection with a network, service, or computer software, including scanning for and removing software proscribed under this chapter.

(b) This chapter does not apply to:

(1) the use of a navigation device, any interaction with a navigation device, or the installation or use of computer software on a navigation device by a multichannel video programming distributor or video programmer in connection with the provision of multichannel video programming or other services offered over a multichannel video programming system if the provision of the programming or other service is subject to 47 U.S.C. Section 338(i) or 551; or

(2) the collection or disclosure of subscriber information by a multichannel video programming distributor or video programmer in connection with the provision of multichannel video programming or other services offered over a multichannel video programming system if the collection or disclosure of the information is subject to 47 U.S.C. Section 338(i) or 551.

(c) In this section, "multichannel video programming distributor" has the meaning assigned by 47 U.S.C. Section 522(13).

Added by Acts 2005, 79th Leg., ch. 298, § 1, eff. Sept. 1, 2005.

Repeal

Acts 2007, 80th Leg., ch. 885, § 2.47(a)(3) repeals this section effective April 1, 2009.

[Sections 48.004 to 48.050 reserved for expansion]

SUBCHAPTER B. PROHIBITED CONDUCT OR ACTIVITIES

§ 48.051. Unauthorized Collection or Culling of Personally Identifiable Information

If a person is not the owner or operator of the computer, the person may not knowingly cause computer software to be copied to a computer in this state and use the software to:

(1) collect, through intentionally deceptive means:

(A) personally identifiable information by using a keystroke-logging function; or

(B) personally identifiable information in a manner that correlates that information with information regarding all or substantially all of the websites visited by the owner or operator of the computer, other than websites operated by the person collecting the information; or

(2) cull, through intentionally deceptive means, the following kinds of personally identifiable information from the consumer's computer hard drive for a purpose wholly unrelated to any of the purposes of the software or service described to an owner or operator of the computer:

(A) a credit or debit card number;

(B) a bank account number;

(C) a password or access code associated with a credit or debit card number or a bank account;

(D) a social security number;

(E) account balances; or

(F) overdraft history.

Added by Acts 2005, 79th Leg., ch. 298, § 1, eff. Sept. 1, 2005.

Repeal

Acts 2007, 80th Leg., ch. 885, § 2.47(a)(3) repeals this section effective April 1, 2009.

§ 48.052. Unauthorized Access to or Modifications of Computer Settings; Computer Damage

If a person is not the owner or operator of the computer, the person may not knowingly cause computer software to be copied to a computer in this state and use the software to:

(1) modify, through intentionally deceptive means, a setting that controls:

(A) the page that appears when an Internet browser or a similar software program is launched to access and navigate the Internet;

(B) the default provider or web proxy used to access or search the Internet; or

(C) a list of bookmarks used to access web pages;

(2) take control of the computer by:

(A) accessing or using the computer's modem or Internet service to:

(i) cause damage to the computer;

(ii) cause the owner or operator of the computer to incur financial charges for a service not previously authorized by the owner or operator; or

(iii) cause a third party affected by the conduct to incur financial charges for a service not previously authorized by the third party; or

(B) opening, without the consent of the owner or operator of the computer, an advertisement that:

(i) is in the owner's or operator's Internet browser in a multiple, sequential, or stand-alone form; and

(ii) cannot be closed by an ordinarily reasonable person using the computer without closing the browser or shutting down the computer;

(3) modify settings on the computer that relate to access to or use of the Internet and protection of information for purposes of stealing personally identifiable information of the owner or operator of the computer; or

(4) modify security settings on the computer relating to access to or use of the Internet for purposes of causing damage to one or more computers.

Added by Acts 2005, 79th Leg., ch. 298, § 1, eff. Sept. 1, 2005.

Repeal

Acts 2007, 80th Leg., ch. 885, § 2.47(a)(3) repeals this section effective April 1, 2009.

§ 48.053. Unauthorized Interference With Installation or Disabling of Computer Software

If a person is not the owner or operator of the computer, the person may not knowingly cause computer software to be copied to a computer in this state and use the software to:

(1) prevent, through intentionally deceptive means, reasonable efforts of the owner or operator of the computer to block the installation or execution of or to disable computer software by causing computer software that the owner or operator has properly removed or disabled to automatically reinstall or reactivate on the computer;

(2) intentionally misrepresent to another that computer software will be uninstalled or disabled by the actions of the owner or operator of the computer;

(3) remove, disable, or render inoperative, through intentionally deceptive means, security, antispyware, or antivirus computer software installed on the computer;

(4) prevent the owner's or operator's reasonable efforts to block the installation of or to disable computer software by:

(A) presenting the owner or operator with an option to decline the installation of software knowing that, when the option is selected, the installation process will continue to proceed; or

(B) misrepresenting that software has been disabled;

(5) change the name, location, or other designation of computer software to prevent the owner from locating and removing the software; or

(6) create randomized or intentionally deceptive file names or random or intentionally deceptive directory folders, formats, or registry entries to avoid detection and prevent the owner from removing computer software.

Added by Acts 2005, 79th Leg., ch. 298, § 1, eff. Sept. 1, 2005.

Repeal

Acts 2007, 80th Leg., ch. 885, § 2.47(a)(3) repeals this section effective April 1, 2009.

§ 48.054. Knowing Violation

A person knowingly violates Section 48. 051, 48.052, or 48.053 if the person:

(1) acts with actual knowledge of the facts that constitute the violation; or

(2) consciously avoids information that would establish actual knowledge of those facts.

Added by Acts 2005, 79th Leg., ch. 298, § 1, eff. Sept. 1, 2005.

Repeal

Acts 2007, 80th Leg., ch. 885, § 2.47(a)(3) repeals this section effective April 1, 2009.

§ 48.055. Other Prohibited Conduct

If a person is not the owner or operator of the computer, the person may not:

(1) induce the owner or operator of a computer in this state to install a computer software component to the computer by intentionally misrepresenting the extent to which the installation is necessary for security or privacy reasons, to open or view text, or to play a particular type of musical or other content; or

(2) copy and execute or cause the copying and execution of a computer software component to a computer in this state in a deceptive manner with the intent of causing the owner or operator of the computer to use the component in a manner that violates this chapter.

Added by Acts 2005, 79th Leg., ch. 298, § 1, eff. Sept. 1, 2005.

Repeal

Acts 2007, 80th Leg., ch. 885, § 2.47(a)(3) repeals this section effective April 1, 2009.

§ 48.056. Deceptive Act or Omission

For purposes of this chapter, a person is considered to have acted through intentionally deceptive means if the person, with the intent to deceive an owner or operator of a computer:

(1) intentionally makes a materially false or fraudulent statement;

(2) intentionally makes a statement or uses a description that omits or misrepresents material information; or

(3) intentionally and materially fails to provide to the owner or operator any notice regarding the installation or execution of computer software.

Added by Acts 2005, 79th Leg., ch. 298, § 1, eff. Sept. 1, 2005.

Repeal

Acts 2007, 80th Leg., ch. 885, § 2.47(a)(3) repeals this section effective April 1, 2009.

[Sections 48.057 to 48.100 reserved for expansion]

SUBCHAPTER C. CIVIL REMEDIES

§ 48.101. Civil Relief

(a) The following persons, if adversely affected by the violation, may bring a civil action against a person who violates this chapter:

(1) a provider of computer software;

(2) an owner of a web page or trademark;

(3) a telecommunications carrier;

(4) a cable operator; or

(5) an Internet service provider.

(b) In addition to any other remedy provided by law and except as provided by Subsection (g), a person bringing an action under this section may:

(1) seek injunctive relief to restrain the violator from continuing the violation;

(2) recover damages in an amount equal to the greater of:

(A) actual damages arising from the violation; or

(B) $100,000 for each violation of the same nature; or

(3) both seek injunctive relief and recover damages as provided by this subsection.

(c) The court may increase an award of actual damages in an action brought under Subsection (b) to an amount not to exceed three times the actual damages sustained if the court finds that the violations have occurred with a frequency as to constitute a pattern or practice.

(d) A plaintiff who prevails in an action filed under Subsection (b) is entitled to recover reasonable attorney's fees and court costs.

(e) Each separate violation of this chapter is an actionable violation.

(f) For purposes of Subsection (b), violations are of the same nature if the violations consist of the same course of conduct or action, regardless of the number of times the conduct or act occurred.

(g) In the case of a violation of Section 48.052 that causes a telecommunications carrier or cable operator to incur costs for the origination, transport, or termination of a call triggered using the modem of a customer of the telecommunications carrier or cable operator as a result of the violation and in addition to any other remedy provided by law, a telecommunications carrier or cable operator bringing an action under this section may:

(1) apply to a court for an order to enjoin the violation;

(2) recover the charges the telecommunications carrier or cable operator is obligated to pay to a telecommunications carrier, cable operator, other provider of transmission capability, or an information service provider as a result of the violation, including charges for the origination, transport, or termination of the call;

(3) recover the costs of handling customer inquiries or complaints with respect to amounts billed for calls as a result of the violation;

(4) recover other costs, including court costs, and reasonable attorney's fees; or

(5) both apply for injunctive relief and recover charges and other costs as provided by this subsection.

Added by Acts 2005, 79th Leg., ch. 298, § 1, eff. Sept. 1, 2005.

Repeal

Acts 2007, 80th Leg., ch. 885, § 2.47(a)(3) repeals this section effective April 1, 2009.

§ 48.102. Civil Penalty; Injunction

(a) A person who violates this chapter is liable to the state for a civil penalty in an amount not to exceed $100,000 for each violation. The attorney general may bring suit to recover the civil penalty imposed by this subsection.

(b) If it appears to the attorney general that a person is engaging in, has engaged in, or is about to engage in conduct that violates this chapter, the attorney general may bring an action in the name of this state against the person to restrain the violation by a temporary restraining order or a permanent or temporary injunction.

(c) The attorney general is entitled to recover reasonable expenses incurred in obtaining injunctive relief, civil penalties, or both, under this section, including reasonable attorney's fees and court costs.

Added by Acts 2005, 79th Leg., ch. 298, § 1, eff. Sept. 1, 2005.

Repeal

Acts 2007, 80th Leg., ch. 885, § 2.47(a)(3) repeals this section effective April 1, 2009.

CHAPTER 51. BUSINESS OPPORTUNITIES

As amended by Acts 2007, 80th Leg., ch. 885, § 2.01, effective April 1, 2009, Title 4 will read, "Business Opportunities and Agreements".

Acts 2007, 80th Leg., ch. 885, § 2.01, added this chapter effective April 1, 2009.

SUBCHAPTER A. GENERAL PROVISIONS

§ 51.001. Short Title

This chapter may be cited as the Business Opportunity Act.

Added by Acts 2007, 80th Leg., ch. 885, § 2.01, eff. April 1, 2009.

§ 51.002. General Definitions

In this chapter:

(1) "Business opportunity contract" means an agreement that obligates or is intended to obligate a purchaser to a seller.

(2) "Buy-back" or "secured investment" means a representation that implies a purchaser's payment is protected from loss.

(3) "Equipment" includes electrical devices, video and audio devices, molds, display units, including display racks, and machines, including coin-operated game machines and vending and other machines that dispense products.

(4) "Initial consideration" means the total amount a purchaser is obligated to pay under a business opportunity contract before or at the time products, equipment, supplies, or services are delivered or within six months after the date the purchaser begins operation of the business opportunity plan. The term means the total sale price if the contract states a specific total sale price for purchase of the business opportunity plan and the total sale price is

to be paid as a down payment and one or more additional payments. The term does not include the not-for-profit sale of sales demonstration materials, samples, or equipment for not more than $500.

(5) "Marketing program" means advice or training that a seller or a person recommended by a seller gives to a purchaser regarding the sale of products, equipment, supplies, or services. The term includes the preparation or provision of:

(A) a brochure, pamphlet, or advertising material, including promotional literature;

(B) training regarding the promotion, operation, or management of a business opportunity; or

(C) operational, managerial, technical, or financial guidelines or assistance.

(6) "Product" includes tangible personal property.

(7) "Purchaser" means a person who becomes or is solicited to become obligated under a business opportunity contract.

(8) "Seller" means a principal or agent who sells or leases or offers to sell or lease a business opportunity.

(9) "Services" includes any assistance, guidance, direction, work, labor, or other services provided by a seller to initiate or maintain a business opportunity.

(10) "Supplies" includes materials used to make, produce, grow, or breed a product or item.

Added by Acts 2007, 80th Leg., ch. 885, § 2.01, eff. April 1, 2009.

§ 51.003. Definition of Business Opportunity

(a) In this chapter, "business opportunity" means a sale or lease for an initial consideration of more than $500 of products, equipment, supplies, or services that will be used by or for the purchaser to begin a business in which the seller represents that:

(1) the purchaser will earn or is likely to earn a profit in excess of the amount of the initial consideration the purchaser paid; and

(2) the seller will:

(A) provide a location or assist the purchaser in finding a location for the use or operation of the products, equipment, supplies, or services on premises that are not owned or leased by the purchaser or seller;

(B) provide a sales, production, or marketing program; or

(C) buy back or is likely to buy back products, equipment, or supplies purchased or products made, produced, grown, or bred by the purchaser using wholly or partly the products, equipment, supplies, or services that the seller initially sold or leased or offered for sale or lease to the purchaser.

(b) In this chapter, "business opportunity" does not include:

(1) the sale or lease of an established and ongoing business or enterprise that has actively conducted business before the sale or lease, whether composed of one or more than one component business or enterprise, if the sale or lease represents an isolated transaction or series of transactions involving a bona fide change of ownership or control of the business or enterprise or liquidation of the business or enterprise;

(2) a sale by a retailer of goods or services under a contract or other agreement to sell the inventory of one or more ongoing leased departments to a purchaser who is granted the right to sell the goods or services within or adjoining a retail business establishment as a department or division of the retail business establishment;

(3) a transaction that is:

(A) regulated by the Texas Department of Licensing and Regulation, the Texas Department of Insurance, the Texas Real Estate Commission, or the director of the Motor Vehicle Division of the Texas Department of Transportation; and

(B) engaged in by a person licensed by one of those agencies;

(4) a real estate syndication;

(5) a sale or lease to a business enterprise that also sells or leases products, equipment, or supplies or performs services:

(A) that are not supplied by the seller; and

(B) that the purchaser does not use with the seller's products, equipment, supplies, or services;

(6) the offer or sale of a franchise as described by the Petroleum Marketing Practices Act (15 U.S.C. Section 2801 et seq.) and its subsequent amendments;

(7) the offer or sale of a business opportunity if the seller:

(A) has a net worth of $25 million or more according to the seller's audited balance sheet as of a date not earlier than the 13th month before the date of the transaction; or

(B) is at least 80 percent owned by another person who:

(i) in writing unconditionally guarantees performance by the person offering the business opportunity plan; and

(ii) has a net worth of more than $25 million according to the person's most recent audited balance sheet as of a date not earlier than the 13th month before the date of the transaction; or

(8) an arrangement defined as a franchise by 16 C.F.R. Section 436.2(a) and its subsequent amendments if:

(A) the franchisor complies in all material respects in this state with 16 C.F.R. Part 436 and each order or other action of the Federal Trade Commission; and

(B) before offering for sale or selling a franchise in this state, a person files with the secretary of state a notice containing:

(i) the name of the franchisor;

(ii) the name under which the franchisor intends to transact business; and

(iii) the franchisor's principal business address.

(c) The secretary of state shall prescribe the form of the notice described by Subsection (b)(8)(B).

Added by Acts 2007, 80th Leg., ch. 885, § 2.01, eff. April 1, 2009.

§ 51.004. Liberal Construction and Application

(a) This chapter shall be liberally construed and applied to:

(1) protect persons against false, misleading, or deceptive practices in the advertising, offering for sale or lease, or sale or lease of business opportunities; and

(2) provide efficient and economical procedures to secure that protection.

(b) In construing this chapter, a court to the extent possible shall follow the interpretations given by the Federal Trade Commission and the federal courts to Section 5(a)(1), Federal Trade Commission Act (15 U.S.C. Section 45(a)(1)), and 16 C.F.R. Part 436 and their subsequent amendments.

Added by Acts 2007, 80th Leg., ch. 885, § 2.01, eff. April 1, 2009.

§ 51.005. Burden of Proof

A person who claims to be exempt from this chapter has the burden of proving the exemption.

Added by Acts 2007, 80th Leg., ch. 885, § 2.01, eff. April 1, 2009.

§ 51.006. Waiver

A waiver of this chapter is contrary to public policy and void.

Added by Acts 2007, 80th Leg., ch. 885, § 2.01, eff. April 1, 2009.

§ 51.007. Maintenance of Records

(a) A seller shall maintain a complete set of books, records, and accounts of business opportunity sales made by the seller.

(b) A document relating to a business opportunity sold or leased shall be maintained until the fourth anniversary of the date of the business opportunity contract.

Added by Acts 2007, 80th Leg., ch. 885, § 2.01, eff. April 1, 2009.

§ 51.008. Filing Fee

The secretary of state may charge a reasonable fee to cover the costs incurred as a result of a filing required by Subchapter B or Section 51.003 or 51.251.

Added by Acts 2007, 80th Leg., ch. 885, § 2.01, eff. April 1, 2009.

§ 51.009. Rules

The secretary of state may adopt rules to administer and enforce this chapter.

Added by Acts 2007, 80th Leg., ch. 885, § 2.01, eff. April 1, 2009.

[Sections 51.010 to 51.050 reserved for expansion]

SUBCHAPTER B. REGISTRATION OF BUSINESS OPPORTUNITY

§ 51.051. Filing of Disclosure Statements and List of Sellers

Before a sale or offer for sale, including advertising, of a business opportunity, the principal seller must register the business opportunity with the secretary of state by filing:

(1) a copy of the disclosure statement required by Subchapter D, except as provided by Section 51.053; and

(2) a list of the name and resident address of any individual who sells or will sell the business opportunity for the principal seller.

Added by Acts 2007, 80th Leg., ch. 885, § 2.01, eff. April 1, 2009.

§ 51.052. Updating of Information on File

(a) A copy of a disclosure statement filed under Section 51.051 must be updated through a new filing:

(1) annually; and

(2) when a material change occurs.

(b) The list filed under Section 51.051(2) must be updated through a new filing every six months.

Added by Acts 2007, 80th Leg., ch. 885, § 2.01, eff. April 1, 2009.

§ 51.053. Filing of Disclosure Document from Other Regulatory Agency

Instead of filing with the secretary of state a copy of a disclosure statement, a seller may file a copy of a similar document required by the State Securities Board, Securities and Exchange Commission, or Federal Trade Commission that contains all the information required to be disclosed by this chapter.

Added by Acts 2007, 80th Leg., ch. 885, § 2.01, eff. April 1, 2009.

§ 51.054. Filing of Copy of Bond or Notification of Account

A principal seller who is required to obtain a bond or establish a trust account under Subchapter C shall contemporaneously file with the secretary of state a copy of:

(1) the bond; or

(2) the formal notification by the depository that the trust account is established.

Added by Acts 2007, 80th Leg., ch. 885, § 2.01, eff. April 1, 2009.

[Sections 51.055 to 51.100 reserved for expansion]

SUBCHAPTER C. BOND, TRUST ACCOUNT, OR LETTER OF CREDIT

§ 51.101. Bond, Trust Account, or Letter of Credit Required

(a) Before a seller makes a representation described by Section 51.003(a)(1) or otherwise represents that the purchaser is assured of making a profit from a business opportunity, the principal seller must:

(1) obtain a surety bond from a surety company authorized to transact business in this state;

(2) establish a trust account; or

(3) obtain an irrevocable letter of credit.

(b) The bond, trust account, or irrevocable letter of credit must be:

(1) in an amount of $25,000 or more; and

(2) in favor of this state.

Added by Acts 2007, 80th Leg., ch. 885, § 2.01, eff. April 1, 2009.

§ 51.102. Action Against Bond, Trust Account, or Letter of Credit

(a) A person may bring an action against the bond, trust account, or irrevocable letter of credit obtained or established under Section 51.101 to recover actual damages for:

(1) a violation of this chapter; or

(2) the seller's breach of:

(A) the business opportunity contract; or

(B) an obligation arising from a business opportunity sale.

(b) The aggregate liability of the surety, trustee, or issuer in an action under Subsection (a) may not exceed the amount of the bond, trust account, or irrevocable letter of credit.

Added by Acts 2007, 80th Leg., ch. 885, § 2.01, eff. April 1, 2009.

[Sections 51.103 to 51.150 reserved for expansion]

SUBCHAPTER D. DISCLOSURE STATEMENT

§ 51.151. Disclosure to Purchaser of Business Opportunity

(a) Except as provided by Section 51.164, a seller must provide a purchaser with a written disclosure statement that meets the requirements of this subchapter.

(b) The seller must provide the disclosure statement at least 10 business days before the earlier of the date:

(1) the purchaser signs a business opportunity contract; or

(2) the seller receives any consideration.

Added by Acts 2007, 80th Leg., ch. 885, § 2.01, eff. April 1, 2009.

§ 51.152. Cover Sheet of Disclosure Statement

(a) A disclosure statement must have a cover sheet titled, in at least 12-point boldface capital letters, "DISCLOSURES REQUIRED BY TEXAS LAW." The following statement must appear below the title in at least 10-point boldface type: "The State of Texas has not reviewed and does not endorse, approve, recommend, or sponsor any business opportunity. The information contained in this disclosure has not been verified by the state. If you have any questions about this investment, see an attorney before you sign a contract or agreement."

(b) Only the title and required statement may appear on the cover sheet.

Added by Acts 2007, 80th Leg., ch. 885, § 2.01, eff. April 1, 2009.

§ 51.153. Contents: Names and Addresses

A disclosure statement must contain:

(1) the name of the seller;

(2) each name under which the seller has transacted, is transacting, or intends to transact business;

(3) the name of any parent or affiliated company that will engage in a business transaction with the purchaser or that takes responsibility for statements made by the seller; and

(4) the names, addresses, and titles of:

(A) the seller's officers, directors, trustees, general partners, general managers, and principal executives;

(B) shareholders owning more than 20 percent of the shares of the seller; and

(C) any other persons responsible for the seller's business activities relating to the sale of business opportunities.

Added by Acts 2007, 80th Leg., ch. 885, § 2.01, eff. April 1, 2009.

§ 51.154. Contents: Sales Periods

A disclosure statement must:

(1) specify the period during which the seller has sold business opportunities; and

(2) specify the period during which the seller has sold business opportunities involving the products, equipment, supplies, or services the seller is offering to the purchaser.

Added by Acts 2007, 80th Leg., ch. 885, § 2.01, eff. April 1, 2009.

§ 51.155. Contents: Services Description

A disclosure statement must contain:

(1) a detailed description of the actual services the seller undertakes to perform for the purchaser; and

(2) if the seller promises to perform services in connection with the placement of products, equipment, or supplies at a location:

(A) the full nature of those services; and

(B) the nature of any agreements to be made with the owners or managers of that location.

Added by Acts 2007, 80th Leg., ch. 885, § 2.01, eff. April 1, 2009.

§ 51.156. Contents: Updated Financial Statement

A disclosure statement must contain a copy of a financial statement of the seller that:

(1) was prepared according to generally accepted accounting principles within the previous 13 months; and

(2) has been updated to reflect any material change in the seller's financial condition.

Added by Acts 2007, 80th Leg., ch. 885, § 2.01, eff. April 1, 2009.

§ 51.157. Contents: Training Description

If the seller promises training, the disclosure statement must contain a complete description of the training, including:

(1) the length of the training; and

(2) any costs of the training that the purchaser will be required to incur, including travel and lodging expenses.

Added by Acts 2007, 80th Leg., ch. 885, § 2.01, eff. April 1, 2009.

§ 51.158. Contents: Security Description

If the seller is required to obtain a bond or establish a trust account, the disclosure statement must contain one of the following statements, as applicable:

(1) "As required by Texas law, the seller has secured a bond issued by ______, a surety company authorized to do business in this state. Before

signing a contract to purchase this business opportunity, you should confirm the bond's status with the surety company."; or

(2) "As required by Texas law, the seller has established a trust account with ______. Before signing a contract to purchase this business opportunity, you should confirm with the bank or savings institution the current status of the trust account."

Added by Acts 2007, 80th Leg., ch. 885, § 2.01, eff. April 1, 2009.

§ 51.159. Contents: Delivery Date; Cancellation of Contract

If the seller is required to deliver to the purchaser the product, equipment, or supplies necessary to begin substantial operation of the business and states a definite or approximate delivery date for the product, equipment, or supplies, the disclosure statement must contain the following statement: "If the seller fails to deliver the product, equipment, or supplies necessary to begin substantial operation of the business within 45 days of the delivery date stated in your contract, you may notify the seller in writing and cancel your contract."

Added by Acts 2007, 80th Leg., ch. 885, § 2.01, eff. April 1, 2009.

§ 51.160. Contents: Sales or Earnings Representation

If the seller makes a statement concerning sales or earnings that may be made through the business opportunity, the disclosure statement must contain a statement disclosing:

(1) the total number of purchasers of business opportunities involving the product, equipment, supplies, or services being offered who to the seller's knowledge have, not earlier than the third year before the date of the disclosure statement, actually achieved sales of or received earnings in the amount or range specified; and

(2) the total number of purchasers who, not earlier than the third year before the date of the disclosure statement, purchased business opportunities involving the product, equipment, supplies, or services being offered.

Added by Acts 2007, 80th Leg., ch. 885, § 2.01, eff. April 1, 2009.

§ 51.161. Contents: Legal Action History

(a) A disclosure statement must contain a statement disclosing any person described by Section 51.153 who:

(1) has, during the previous seven fiscal years:

(A) been convicted of a felony, or pleaded nolo contendere to a felony charge, involving fraud, embezzlement, fraudulent conversion, or misappropriation of property; or

(B) been held liable in a civil action resulting in a final judgment, or has settled out of court a civil action, involving:

(i) allegations of fraud, embezzlement, fraudulent conversion, or misappropriation of property;

(ii) the use of untrue or misleading representations in an attempt to sell or dispose of property; or

(iii) the use of unfair, unlawful, or deceptive business practices;

(2) is a party to a civil action involving:

(A) allegations of fraud, embezzlement, fraudulent conversion, or misappropriation of property;

(B) the use of untrue or misleading representations in an attempt to sell or dispose of property; or

(C) the use of unfair, unlawful, or deceptive business practices; or

(3) is subject to an injunction or restrictive order relating to business activity as a result of an action brought by a public agency or department.

(b) A statement required by Subsection (a) must include:

(1) the identity and location of any court or agency;

(2) the date of any entry of a plea of nolo contendere, conviction, judgment, or decision;

(3) any penalty imposed;

(4) any damages assessed;

(5) the terms of any settlement or order; and

(6) the date, nature, and issuer of any order or ruling.

Added by Acts 2007, 80th Leg., ch. 885, § 2.01, eff. April 1, 2009.

§ 51.162. Contents: Bankruptcy or Reorganization

(a) A disclosure statement must contain a statement disclosing any person described by Section 51.153 who has, during the previous seven fiscal years:

(1) filed in bankruptcy;

(2) been adjudged bankrupt;

(3) been reorganized because of insolvency; or

(4) been a principal, director, executive officer, or partner of any other person that, during or not later than the first anniversary of the end of the period the person held the position in relation to the other person, filed in bankruptcy, was adjudged bankrupt, or was reorganized because of insolvency.

(b) A statement required by Subsection (a)(4) must include:

(1) the name and location of the person who filed in bankruptcy, was adjudged bankrupt, or was reorganized;

(2) the date of the filing, adjudication, or reorganization; and

(3) any other material fact relating to the filing, adjudication, or reorganization.

Added by Acts 2007, 80th Leg., ch. 885, § 2.01, eff. April 1, 2009.

§ 51.163. Contents: Contract Copy

A disclosure statement must contain a copy of the business opportunity contract that the seller uses as a matter of course and that will be presented to the purchaser at closing.

Added by Acts 2007, 80th Leg., ch. 885, § 2.01, eff. April 1, 2009.

§ 51.164. Use of Disclosure Document From Other Regulatory Agency

Instead of providing a disclosure statement to a purchaser under this subchapter, a seller may provide a copy of a similar document required by the State Securities Board, Securities and Exchange Commission, or Federal Trade Commission that contains all the information required to be disclosed by this chapter.

Added by Acts 2007, 80th Leg., ch. 885, § 2.01, eff. April 1, 2009.

[Sections 51.165 to 51.200 reserved for expansion]

SUBCHAPTER E. BUSINESS OPPORTUNITY CONTRACT

§ 51.201. Form of Business Opportunity Contract

A business opportunity contract must be in writing and include, in 10–point type or in handwriting of an equivalent size, the following:

(1) the terms of payment, including the initial consideration, down payment, and additional payments required;

(2) a detailed description of the acts or services the seller undertakes to perform for the purchaser;

(3) the seller's principal business address;

(4) the name and address of the seller's agent in this state authorized to receive service of process;

(5) the delivery date or, if the contract provides for staggered delivery times to the purchaser, the approximate delivery date of the products, equipment, or supplies the seller is to:

(A) deliver to the purchaser's home or business address; or

(B) place at a location owned or managed by a person other than the purchaser; and

(6) a complete description of the nature of the buy-back or security arrangement if the seller has represented orally or in writing when selling, leasing, soliciting, or offering a business opportunity that there is a buy-back or that the initial consideration is secured.

Added by Acts 2007, 80th Leg., ch. 885, § 2.01, eff. April 1, 2009.

§ 51.202. Delivery of Copies of Documents to Purchaser

A copy of the completed business opportunity contract and any other document the seller requires the purchaser to sign shall be given to the purchaser at the time the purchaser signs the contract.

Added by Acts 2007, 80th Leg., ch. 885, § 2.01, eff. April 1, 2009.

§ 51.203. Effect of Assignment of Business Opportunity Contract

An assignee of a business opportunity contract or of the seller's rights under the contract is subject to all equities, rights, and defenses of the purchaser against the seller.

Added by Acts 2007, 80th Leg., ch. 885, § 2.01, eff. April 1, 2009.

[Sections 51.204 to 51.250 reserved for expansion]

SUBCHAPTER F. TERMINATION OF BUSINESS OPPORTUNITY REGISTRATION

§ 51.251. Voluntary Termination of Business Opportunity Registration

The principal seller of a registered business opportunity may voluntarily terminate the business opportunity's registration with the secretary of state if:

(1) the registered business opportunity will no longer be offered in this state;

(2) the registered business opportunity has changed to the extent that it no longer meets the definition of a business opportunity under Section 51.003(a);

(3) the registered business opportunity has become exempt under Section 51.003(b); or

(4) the principal seller offering the registered business opportunity ceases to exist as a legal entity.

Added by Acts 2007, 80th Leg., ch. 885, § 2.01, eff. April 1, 2009.

§ 51.252. Involuntary Termination of Business Opportunity Registration

(a) The secretary of state may terminate the registration of a business opportunity registered under Section 51.051 if the seller does not comply with Section 51.052.

(b) The secretary of state must give the business opportunity registrant notice of the delinquency not later than the 31st day before the date of termination of the business opportunity registration under Subsection (a).

(c) The notice of delinquency must be given by certified mail addressed to the registered agent or the principal place of business of the business opportunity registrant noted in the latest filing made under this chapter.

(d) The secretary of state may adopt rules governing:

(1) the termination of a delinquent registration;

(2) the effective date of the termination; and

(3) the grace period, if any.

Added by Acts 2007, 80th Leg., ch. 885, § 2.01, eff. April 1, 2009.

[Sections 51.253 to 51.300 reserved for expansion]

SUBCHAPTER G. ENFORCEMENT

§ 51.301. Prohibited Acts

A seller may not:

(1) employ a representation, device, scheme, or artifice to deceive a purchaser;

(2) make an untrue statement of a material fact or omit to state a material fact in connection with the documents and information required to be provided to the secretary of state or purchaser;

(3) represent that the business opportunity provides or will provide income or earning potential unless the seller:

(A) has documented data to substantiate the representation of income or earning potential; and

(B) discloses the data to the purchaser when the representation is made; or

(4) make a claim or representation that is inconsistent with the information required to be disclosed by this chapter in:

(A) advertising or other promotional material; or

(B) an oral sales presentation, solicitation, or discussion between the seller and the purchaser.

Added by Acts 2007, 80th Leg., ch. 885, § 2.01, eff. April 1, 2009.

§ 51.302. Deceptive Trade Practice; Remedies

(a) A violation of this chapter is a false, misleading, or deceptive act or practice under Section 17.46.

(b) A public or private right or remedy prescribed by Chapter 17 may be used to enforce this chapter.

Added by Acts 2007, 80th Leg., ch. 885, § 2.01, eff. April 1, 2009.

§ 51.303. Review and Suit by Attorney General

(a) The attorney general may review the copy of a disclosure statement filed with the secretary of state under Subchapter B.

(b) If the disclosure statement fails to comply with this chapter, the attorney general may:

(1) notify the secretary of state and the seller in writing of the deficiency; and

(2) file suit to enjoin the seller from transacting business until the failure to comply has been corrected.

(c) If the attorney general notifies the secretary of state under Subsection (b), the secretary of state shall:

(1) attach a copy of the notice to the front of the disclosure statement; and

(2) on inquiry of the status of the disclosure statement, disclose that a statement has been filed but that the attorney general has questioned the correctness of the statement.

Added by Acts 2007, 80th Leg., ch. 885, § 2.01, eff. April 1, 2009.

CHAPTER 52. INVENTION DEVELOPMENT SERVICES

As amended by Acts 2007, 80th Leg., ch. 885, § 2.01, effective April 1, 2009, Title 4 will read, "Business Opportunities and Agreements".

Acts 2007, 80th Leg., ch. 885, § 2.01 added this chapter effective April 1, 2009.

SUBCHAPTER A. GENERAL PROVISIONS

§ 52.001. Short Title

This chapter may be cited as the Regulation of Invention Development Services Act.

Added by Acts 2007, 80th Leg., ch. 885, § 2.01, eff. April 1, 2009.

§ 52.002. Definitions

In this chapter:

(1) "Customer" means:

(A) an individual who enters into a contract with an invention developer for invention development services; or

(B) a firm, partnership, corporation, or other entity that enters into a contract with an invention developer for invention development services and is not purchasing those services as an adjunct to the traditional commercial enterprises in which the entity engages as a business.

(2) "Invention" means a discovery, process, machine, design, formulation, product, concept, idea, or any combination of these, regardless of whether patentable.

(3) "Invention developer" means an individual, firm, partnership, or corporation, or an agent, employee, officer, partner, or independent contractor of one of those entities, who:

(A) performs or offers to perform invention development services for a customer; and

(B) is not:

(i) a federal, state, or local government department or agency;

(ii) a nonprofit, charitable, scientific, or educational organization organized under the Texas Non–Profit Corporation Act (Article 1396–1.01 et seq., Vernon's Texas Civil Statutes) or formed under Title 1 and Chapter 22, Business Organizations Code, or described by Section 170(b)(1)(A), Internal Revenue Code of 1986, as amended;

(iii) an attorney acting within the scope of the attorney's professional license;

(iv) a person registered to practice before the United States Patent and Trademark Office and acting within the scope of that person's professional license; or

(v) a person, firm, corporation, association, or other entity that does not charge a fee, including reimbursement for expenditures made or costs incurred by the entity, for invention development services other than payment made from a portion of the income a customer received by virtue of an act performed by the entity.

(4) "Invention development services" means an act done by or for an invention developer for the invention developer's procurement or attempted procurement of a licensee or buyer of an intellectual property right in an invention, including:

(A) evaluating, perfecting, marketing, or brokering an invention;

(B) performing a patent search; and

(C) preparing or prosecuting a patent application by a person not registered to practice before the United States Patent and Trademark Office.

Added by Acts 2007, 80th Leg., ch. 885, § 2.01, eff. April 1, 2009.

§ 52.003. Applicability of Chapter to Contract for Invention Development Services

This chapter applies to each contract under which an invention developer agrees to perform invention development services for a customer.

Added by Acts 2007, 80th Leg., ch. 885, § 2.01, eff. April 1, 2009.

§ 52.004. Waiver by Customer Prohibited

A waiver by a customer of a provision of this chapter is void.

Added by Acts 2007, 80th Leg., ch. 885, § 2.01, eff. April 1, 2009.

[Sections 52.005 to 52.050 reserved for expansion]

SUBCHAPTER B. FINANCIAL REQUIREMENTS OF INVENTION DEVELOPERS

§ 52.051. Bond Required

(a) Except as provided by Section 52.053, an invention developer performing or offering to perform invention development services in this state shall maintain a bond issued by a surety company authorized to transact business in this state.

(b) The principal amount of the bond must equal at least the greater of:

(1) five percent of the invention developer's gross income from the invention development business in this state during the invention developer's last fiscal year; or

(2) $25,000.

(c) The invention developer must file a copy of the bond with the secretary of state before the date the invention developer begins business in this state.

(d) Before the 91st day after the last day of the invention developer's fiscal year, the invention developer shall change the amount of the bond if necessary to conform with this section and Section 52.052.

Added by Acts 2007, 80th Leg., ch. 885, § 2.01, eff. April 1, 2009.

§ 52.052. Beneficiary of Bond; Claim Against Bond

(a) The bond required by Section 52.051 must be:

(1) in favor of this state; and

(2) for the benefit of any person who, after entering into a contract for invention development services with the invention developer, is damaged by fraud, dishonesty, or failure to provide the invention developer's services in performance of the contract.

(b) A person making a claim against the bond may bring an action against the invention developer and the surety. The aggregate liability of the surety to all persons for all breaches of conditions of the bond required by this section is limited to the amount of the bond.

Added by Acts 2007, 80th Leg., ch. 885, § 2.01, eff. April 1, 2009.

§ 52.053. Cash Deposit Instead of Bond

Instead of furnishing the bond required by Section 52.051, the invention developer may provide for, in an amount equal to the amount of the bond required:

(1) cash deposited with the secretary of state;

(2) a certificate of deposit payable to the secretary of state and issued by a bank that is:

(A) transacting business in this state; and

(B) insured by the Federal Deposit Insurance Corporation;

(3) an investment certificate of a share account assigned to the secretary of state and issued by a savings and loan association that is:

(A) transacting business in this state; and

(B) insured by the Federal Deposit Insurance Corporation; or

(4) a bearer bond issued by the United States government or this state.

Added by Acts 2007, 80th Leg., ch. 885, § 2.01, eff. April 1, 2009.

[Sections 52.054 to 52.100 reserved for expansion]

SUBCHAPTER C. INVENTION DEVELOPMENT SERVICES CONTRACT

§ 52.101. Written Contract Required; Customer Copy

(a) A contract for invention development services must be in writing.

(b) The invention developer shall give a copy of the contract to the customer at the time the customer signs the contract.

Added by Acts 2007, 80th Leg., ch. 885, § 2.01, eff. April 1, 2009.

§ 52.102. Mandatory Contract Terms

(a) A contract for invention development services must contain in boldfaced type of not less than 10–point size:

(1) the payment terms;

(2) the contract termination rights required by Section 52.104;

(3) a full, clear, and concise description of the specific acts or services that the invention developer agrees to perform for the customer;

(4) a statement of whether the invention developer agrees to construct, sell, or distribute one or more prototypes, models, or devices embodying the customer's invention;

(5) the full name and principal place of business of the invention developer;

(6) the name and principal place of business of any parent, subsidiary, or affiliated company that may engage in performing any of the invention development services;

(7) if the invention developer makes an oral or written representation of estimated or projected customer earnings, a statement of estimated or projected customer earnings and a description of the data on which the estimation or projection is based;

(8) the name and address of the custodian of all records and correspondence pertaining to the invention development services described by the contract;

(9) a statement that the invention developer:

(A) is required to maintain all records and correspondence relating to performance of the invention development services for the customer until the second anniversary of the date the contract expires; and

(B) on seven days' written notice will make the invention development services records and correspondence available to the customer or the customer's representative for review and copying at the customer's reasonable expense on the invention developer's premises during normal business hours; and

(10) a time schedule for performance of the invention development services, including an estimated date by which performance is expected to be completed.

(b) An invention developer is a fiduciary to the extent that the description of specific acts or services required by Subsection (a)(3) gives the invention developer discretion in determining which acts or services will be performed.

Added by Acts 2007, 80th Leg., ch. 885, § 2.01, eff. April 1, 2009.

§ 52.103. Multiple Contracts

If it is the invention developer's normal practice to seek more than one contract in connection with an invention or if the invention developer normally seeks to perform services in connection with an invention in more than one phase with the performance of each phase covered in one or more subsequent contracts, the invention developer shall give to the customer at the time the customer signs the first contract:

(1) a written statement describing that practice; and

(2) a written summary of the developer's normal terms, if any, for subsequent contracts, including the approximate amount of the developer's normal fees or other consideration that the developer may require from the customer.

Added by Acts 2007, 80th Leg., ch. 885, § 2.01, eff. April 1, 2009.

§ 52.104. Payment for Services; Option to Terminate Contract

(a) For purposes of this section, delivery of a promissory note, bill of exchange, or negotiable instrument of any kind to the invention developer or to a third party for the benefit of the invention developer is payment, regardless of the date or dates appearing on the instrument.

(b) Notwithstanding any contractual provision to the contrary, payment for invention development services may not be required, made, or received before the fourth working day after the date the customer receives a copy of the contract for invention development services signed by the invention developer and the customer.

(c) Until the payment for invention development services is made, the parties to the contract have the option to terminate the contract. The customer may exercise the option to terminate by refraining from making payment to the invention developer. The invention developer may exercise the option to terminate by giving to the customer a written notice of the invention developer's exercise of the option. The written notice becomes effective when the customer receives the notice.

Added by Acts 2007, 80th Leg., ch. 885, § 2.01, eff. April 1, 2009.

§ 52.105. Cover Notice Required

(a) A contract for invention development services must have attached a conspicuous and legible cover sheet that contains:

(1) the name, home address, office address, and local office address of the invention developer; and

(2) the following notice in boldfaced type of not less than 10–point size:

THIS CONTRACT BETWEEN YOU AND AN INVENTION DEVELOPER IS REGULATED BY THE STATE OF TEXAS' REGULATION OF INVENTION DEVELOPMENT SERVICES ACT. YOU ARE NOT PERMITTED OR REQUIRED TO MAKE ANY PAYMENTS UNDER THIS CONTRACT UNTIL FOUR (4) WORKING DAYS AFTER YOU SIGN THIS CONTRACT AND RECEIVE A COMPLETED COPY OF IT.

IF YOU ASSIGN EVEN A PARTIAL INTEREST IN THE INVENTION TO THE INVENTION DEVELOPER, THE INVENTION DEVELOPER MAY HAVE THE RIGHT TO SELL OR DISPOSE OF THE INVENTION WITHOUT YOUR CONSENT AND MAY NOT HAVE TO SHARE THE PROFITS WITH YOU.

THE TOTAL NUMBER OF CUSTOMERS WHO HAVE CONTRACTED WITH THE INVENTION DEVELOPER SINCE (year) IS (number). THE TOTAL NUMBER OF CUSTOMERS KNOWN BY THIS INVENTION DEVELOPER TO HAVE RECEIVED, BY VIRTUE OF THIS INVENTION DEVELOPER'S PERFORMANCE, AN AMOUNT OF MONEY IN EXCESS OF THE AMOUNT PAID BY THE CUSTOMER TO THIS INVENTION DEVELOPER IS (number).

YOU ARE ENCOURAGED TO CONSULT WITH A QUALIFIED ATTORNEY BEFORE SIGNING THIS CONTRACT. BY PROCEEDING WITHOUT THE ADVICE OF A QUALIFIED ATTORNEY, YOU COULD LOSE ANY RIGHTS YOU MIGHT HAVE IN YOUR IDEA OR INVENTION.

(b) The invention developer shall complete the cover sheet by providing the proper information in the blanks of the cover sheet. In the first blank the invention developer shall enter the later of the year that the invention developer began to transact business or May 7, 1981. The invention developer may round the numbers the invention developer enters in the last two blanks to the nearest 100 and, in computing the numbers, may exclude persons who have contracted with the invention developer during the three calendar months preceding the date of the contract. If the number to be inserted in the third blank is zero, the invention developer shall enter a zero in the blank.

(c) The cover sheet may not contain anything other than the information required by Subsection (a).

Added by Acts 2007, 80th Leg., ch. 885, § 2.01, eff. April 1, 2009.

§ 52.106. Quarterly Reports to Customer Required

At least once each calendar quarter during the term of a contract for invention development services, the invention developer shall deliver to the customer at the address specified in the contract a written report that identifies the contract and contains:

(1) a full, clear, and concise description of the services performed up to the date of the report and of the services to be performed; and

(2) the name and address of each person to whom the subject matter of the contract has been disclosed, the reason for each disclosure, the nature of the disclosure, and copies of all responses received as a result of those disclosures.

Added by Acts 2007, 80th Leg., ch. 885, § 2.01, eff. April 1, 2009.

[Sections 52.107 to 52.150 reserved for expansion]

SUBCHAPTER D. ENFORCEMENT

§ 52.151. Contract Voidable

A contract for invention development services is voidable at the option of the customer if the contract:

(1) does not substantially comply with this chapter; or

(2) was entered into in reliance on any false, fraudulent, or misleading information, representa-

tion, notice, or advertisement of the invention developer.

Added by Acts 2007, 80th Leg., ch. 885, § 2.01, eff. April 1, 2009.

§ 52.152. Private Cause of Action

(a) This section applies only to a customer who is injured by an invention developer's:

(1) violation of this chapter;

(2) false or fraudulent statement, representation, or omission of material fact; or

(3) failure to make all disclosures required by this chapter.

(b) A customer to whom this section applies may recover in a civil action against the invention developer:

(1) the greater of:

(A) the amount of any actual damages sustained by the customer; or

(B) $1,000;

(2) court costs; and

(3) attorney's fees.

Added by Acts 2007, 80th Leg., ch. 885, § 2.01, eff. April 1, 2009.

§ 52.153. Deceptive Trade Practice

The following acts, omissions, or failures by an invention developer constitute a deceptive trade practice under Chapter 17:

(1) a violation of this chapter;

(2) an omission of material fact; or

(3) a failure to make a disclosure required by this chapter.

Added by Acts 2007, 80th Leg., ch. 885, § 2.01, eff. April 1, 2009.

§ 52.154. Mutually Exclusive Remedies

Remedies available under Sections 52.152 and 52.153 are mutually exclusive.

Added by Acts 2007, 80th Leg., ch. 885, § 2.01, eff. April 1, 2009.

§ 52.155. Presumption of Injury

For purposes of Sections 52.152 and 52.153, a rebuttable presumption of injury is established by:

(1) a substantial violation of this chapter by an invention developer; or

(2) a customer's execution of a contract for invention development services in reliance on a false or fraudulent statement, representation, or an omission of material fact.

Added by Acts 2007, 80th Leg., ch. 885, § 2.01, eff. April 1, 2009.

§ 52.156. Enforcement by Attorney General

(a) The attorney general shall enforce this chapter.

(b) The attorney general may:

(1) recover a civil penalty not to exceed $2,000 for each violation of this chapter; and

(2) seek equitable relief to restrain a violation of this chapter.

Added by Acts 2007, 80th Leg., ch. 885, § 2.01, eff. April 1, 2009.

§ 52.157. Application of Other Laws

This chapter does not nullify or limit any obligation, right, or remedy that is applicable or available under the law of this state.

Added by Acts 2007, 80th Leg., ch. 885, § 2.01, eff. April 1, 2009.

CHAPTER 53. STORE LEASES

As amended by Acts 2007, 80th Leg., ch. 885, § 2.01, effective April 1, 2009, Title 4 will read, "Business Opportunities and Agreements".

Acts 2007, 80th Leg., ch. 885, § 2.01 added this chapter effective April 1, 2009.

§ 53.001. Store Lease Contract

(a) A provision of a lease contract that requires a store to be open when another store located in the same shopping center is open does not apply on Sunday unless the provision specifically states that it applies on Sunday.

(b) This section applies to a contract executed before or after September 1, 1985.

Added by Acts 2007, 80th Leg., ch. 885, § 2.01, eff. April 1, 2009.

CHAPTER 54. COMPENSATION AGREEMENTS FOR SALES REPRESENTATIVES

As amended by Acts 2007, 80th Leg., ch. 885, § 2.01, effective April 1, 2009, Title 4 will read, "Business Opportunities and Agreements".

Acts 2007, 80th Leg., ch. 885, § 2.01 added this chapter effective April 1, 2009.

§ 54.001. Definitions

In this chapter:

(1) "Commission" means compensation paid a sales representative by a principal in an amount based on a percentage of the dollar amount of certain orders for or sales of the principal's product.

(2) "Principal" means a person who:

(A) manufactures, produces, imports, or distributes a product for sale;

(B) uses a sales representative to solicit orders for the product; and

(C) compensates the sales representative wholly or partly by commission.

(3) "Sales representative" means an independent contractor who solicits, on behalf of a principal, orders for the purchase at wholesale of the principal's product.

Added by Acts 2007, 80th Leg., ch. 885, § 2.01, eff. April 1, 2009.

§ 54.002. Contract

(a) A contract between a principal and a sales representative under which the sales representative is to solicit wholesale orders within this state must:

(1) be in writing or in a computer-based medium; and

(2) state the method by which the sales representative's commission is to be computed and paid.

(b) The principal shall provide the sales representative with a copy of the contract.

(c) A provision in the contract establishing venue for an action arising under the contract in a state other than this state is void.

Added by Acts 2007, 80th Leg., ch. 885, § 2.01, eff. April 1, 2009.

§ 54.003. Payment on Termination of Certain Compensation Agreements

If a compensation agreement between a sales representative and a principal that does not comply with Section 54.002 is terminated, the principal shall pay all commissions due the sales representative not later than the 30th working day after the date of the termination.

Added by Acts 2007, 80th Leg., ch. 885, § 2.01, eff. April 1, 2009.

§ 54.004. Damages

A principal who fails to comply with a provision of a contract under Section 54.002 relating to payment of a commission or who fails to pay a commission as required by Section 54.003 is liable to the sales representative in a civil action for:

(1) three times the unpaid commission due the sales representative; and

(2) reasonable attorney's fees and costs.

Added by Acts 2007, 80th Leg., ch. 885, § 2.01, eff. April 1, 2009.

§ 54.005. Personal Jurisdiction

A principal who is not a resident of this state and who enters into a contract subject to this chapter is considered to be transacting business in this state for purposes of the exercise of personal jurisdiction over the principal.

Added by Acts 2007, 80th Leg., ch. 885, § 2.01, eff. April 1, 2009.

§ 54.006. Waiver

A provision of this chapter may not be waived, whether by an express waiver or by an attempt to make a contract or agreement subject to the laws of another state. A waiver of a provision of this chapter is void.

Added by Acts 2007, 80th Leg., ch. 885, § 2.01, eff. April 1, 2009.

CHAPTER 55. FARM, INDUSTRIAL, OFF-ROAD CONSTRUCTION, FORESTRY HARVESTING, AND OUTDOOR POWER EQUIPMENT DEALER AGREEMENTS

As amended by Acts 2007, 80th Leg., ch. 885, § 2.01, effective April 1, 2009, Title 4 will read, "Business Opportunities and Agreements".

Acts 2007, 80th Leg., ch. 885, § 2.01 added this chapter effective April 1, 2009.

SUBCHAPTER A. GENERAL PROVISIONS

§ 55.001. Definitions

In this chapter:

(1) "Controlling interest" means 50 percent or more ownership of or a managing interest in a dealership.

(2) "Current price" means an amount equal to the price listed in the supplier's printed price list in effect when a dealer agreement is terminated, less applicable trade and cash discounts.

(3) "Dealer" means a person in the business of the retail sale of equipment. The term does not include an individual, partnership, or corporation who:

(A) is primarily engaged in the retail sale and service of off-road construction and earth-moving equipment;

(B) has purchased 75 percent or more of the dealer's total new product inventory from a single supplier under all agreements with that supplier; and

(C) has a total annual average sales volume in excess of $100 million for the preceding three years with that single supplier for the territory for which the dealer is responsible in this state.

(4) "Dealer agreement" means an oral or written contract, of definite or indefinite duration, between a supplier and a dealer, that states the rights and obligations of the parties with respect to the purchase or sale of equipment.

(5) "Dealer cost" means an amount equal to the sum of the original invoice price that the dealer paid for inventory and the cost to the dealer of the inventory's delivery from the supplier to the dealer, less applicable discounts.

(6) "Dealership" means the retail sale business engaged in by a dealer under a dealer agreement.

(7) "Equipment" means farm tractors, farm implements, utility tractors, industrial tractors, forklifts, material-handling equipment, forestry harvesting equipment, off-road construction equipment, and outdoor power equipment and any attachments to or repair parts for those items.

(8) "Inventory" means new or unused equipment that is provided by a supplier to a dealer under a dealer agreement and that was:

(A) purchased within the 30–month period preceding the date of the termination of the dealership; or

(B) listed in the supplier's current sales manual on the date of termination.

(9) "Outdoor power equipment" means machinery operated by an engine or electric power and used in the landscaping or cultivation of land for nonagricultural purposes. The term includes lawn and garden implements.

(10) "Supplier" means:

(A) a person engaged in the manufacture, assembly, or wholesale distribution of equipment; or

(B) the person's successor in interest, including a purchaser of assets or stock and a surviving corporation resulting from a merger, liquidation, or reorganization.

Added by Acts 2007, 80th Leg., ch. 885, § 2.01, eff. April 1, 2009.

§ 55.002. Security Interest

This chapter does not affect a supplier's security interest in inventory.

Added by Acts 2007, 80th Leg., ch. 885, § 2.01, eff. April 1, 2009.

§ 55.003. Waiver of Chapter

An attempted waiver of a provision of this chapter is void.

Added by Acts 2007, 80th Leg., ch. 885, § 2.01, eff. April 1, 2009.

[Sections 55.004 to 55.050 reserved for expansion]

SUBCHAPTER B. PROVISIONS REGARDING DEALER AGREEMENT OR DEALERSHIP

§ 55.051. Supplementary Agreement

A supplier may not coerce or compel a dealer to enter into a written or oral agreement supplementing a dealer agreement with the supplier unless the supplementary agreement is imposed on all other similarly situated dealers in this state.

Added by Acts 2007, 80th Leg., ch. 885, § 2.01, eff. April 1, 2009.

§ 55.052. Change in Competitive Circumstances

A supplier may not substantially change the competitive circumstances of a dealer agreement without cause.

Added by Acts 2007, 80th Leg., ch. 885, § 2.01, eff. April 1, 2009.

§ 55.053. Interest in Dealership by Sale or Transfer

(a) A supplier may not prevent, by contract or otherwise, a dealer or an officer, member, partner, or shareholder of a dealer from selling or transferring a noncontrolling interest in the dealership to another person.

(b) A supplier may prevent a person from selling or transferring a controlling interest in a dealership without the supplier's written consent. A supplier may not unreasonably withhold the supplier's consent to a sale or transfer of a controlling interest.

Added by Acts 2007, 80th Leg., ch. 885, § 2.01, eff. April 1, 2009.

§ 55.054. Transfer of Controlling Interest in Dealership by Succession

(a) In this section, "family member" means an individual related within the second degree by consanguinity or affinity to an individual owning a controlling interest.

(b) A supplier and a dealer may provide by written agreement for succession rights to a controlling interest in a dealership on the death of an individual owning the controlling interest.

(c) If not otherwise determined by a written agreement between the dealer and supplier, on the death of an individual owning a controlling interest in a dealership, the family member to whom the interest passes by will or intestate succession may request that the supplier consent to a transfer of the ownership interest to the family member.

(d) The supplier shall consent to a transfer described by Subsection (c) if the family member meets the reasonable financial, business experience, and character standards of the supplier. Before the 91st day after the date the supplier receives the family member's request, the supplier shall send a written response to the family member that:

(1) grants the supplier's consent; or

(2) states the supplier's refusal to consent and the specific reasons for the refusal.

Added by Acts 2007, 80th Leg., ch. 885, § 2.01, eff. April 1, 2009.

§ 55.055. Continuation of Agreement

Section 55.053 or 55.054 does not require a supplier to continue a dealer agreement if the supplier determines that the dealer's area of responsibility or trade area lacks sufficient sales potential to reasonably support continuation of the agreement.

Added by Acts 2007, 80th Leg., ch. 885, § 2.01, eff. April 1, 2009.

§ 55.056. Cause Required for Termination

A supplier may not terminate, cancel, or fail to renew a dealer agreement without cause.

Added by Acts 2007, 80th Leg., ch. 885, § 2.01, eff. April 1, 2009.

§ 55.057. Renovation or Additional Space

A supplier may not require as a condition of renewal or extension of a dealer agreement that the dealer complete substantial renovation of the dealer's place of business or acquire new or additional space to serve as the dealer's place of business, unless the supplier gives the dealer:

(1) one year's written notice of the requirement that states all grounds for the requirement; and

(2) reasonable time to complete the renovation or acquisition.

Added by Acts 2007, 80th Leg., ch. 885, § 2.01, eff. April 1, 2009.

[Sections 55.058 to 55.100 reserved for expansion]

SUBCHAPTER C. WARRANTIES

§ 55.101. Applicability of Subchapter

This subchapter applies only to a warranty claim submitted by a dealer:

(1) while the dealer agreement is in effect; or

(2) after the termination of the dealer agreement, if the claim is for work performed before the effective date of the termination.

Added by Acts 2007, 80th Leg., ch. 885, § 2.01, eff. April 1, 2009.

§ 55.102. Acceptance or Rejection of Warranty Claim

(a) Not later than the 30th day after the date a supplier receives a warranty claim from a dealer, the supplier shall accept or reject the claim. A claim not rejected before that date is considered accepted.

(b) Not later than the 30th day after the date a warranty claim is accepted or rejected, the supplier shall:

(1) pay the accepted claim; or

(2) send the dealer written notice of the grounds for rejecting the claim.

(c) A supplier, including a supplier of an electric engine or motor, who pays a claim may not pay less than the hourly labor rate and other expenses involved in the work that the dealer regularly charges to a retail customer who does not assert a warranty and the dealer's net price plus 15 percent for parts. The number of hours of labor claimed may not exceed 1–1/2 times the supplier's recommended hours for the work.

Added by Acts 2007, 80th Leg., ch. 885, § 2.01, eff. April 1, 2009.

§ 55.103. Supplier's Recovery of Warranty Claim

After paying a warranty claim, a supplier may not charge back, set off, or otherwise attempt to recover all or part of the amount of the claim unless:

(1) the claim was fraudulent;

(2) the work for which the claim was made was not properly performed or was unnecessary to comply with the warranty; or

(3) the dealer did not substantiate the claim according to the supplier's written requirements in effect when the claim arose.

Added by Acts 2007, 80th Leg., ch. 885, § 2.01, eff. April 1, 2009.

§ 55.104. Purchaser's Warranty Agreement

A dealer or supplier authorized to sell new farm, industrial, or outdoor power equipment shall give the purchaser a written warranty agreement including replacement or cash refund. If the dealer determines the equipment cannot be made usable, the manufacturer is liable to the purchaser for the replacement or cash refund.

Added by Acts 2007, 80th Leg., ch. 885, § 2.01, eff. April 1, 2009.

[Sections 55.105 to 55.150 reserved for expansion]

SUBCHAPTER D. DELIVERY, SALE, AND RETURN OF EQUIPMENT

§ 55.151. Coerced Orders, Deliveries, or Refusals to Purchase Prohibited

A supplier may not coerce or compel a dealer to:

(1) order or accept delivery of equipment with a special feature or accessory not included in the base list price of the equipment as publicly advertised by the supplier unless the special feature or accessory is a safety feature or accessory required by the supplier or by applicable law; or

(2) refuse to purchase equipment manufactured by another manufacturer.

Added by Acts 2007, 80th Leg., ch. 885, § 2.01, eff. April 1, 2009.

§ 55.152. Discrimination Among Dealers

(a) A supplier may not discriminate among dealers in the supplier's delivery, in reasonable quantities and within a reasonable time after receipt of a dealer's order, of equipment covered by the dealer agreement and specifically represented by the supplier as available for immediate delivery.

(b) Subsection (a) does not apply if the discrimination is because of:

(1) the supplier's restrictions on extending credit to the dealer;

(2) the dealer's default under a dealership agreement; or

(3) an act of God, work stoppage or delay because of a strike or labor difficulty, bona fide shortage of materials, freight embargo, or other cause over which the supplier has no control.

Added by Acts 2007, 80th Leg., ch. 885, § 2.01, eff. April 1, 2009.

§ 55.153. Late Delivery of Back–Ordered Seasonal Demand Item

(a) Unless the supplier notifies a dealer of the status of a back-ordered item before shipment of the item to the dealer, a dealer may reject the delivery of an item of equipment other than a repair part or attachment from a supplier if:

(1) the item has special value in a particular time of year because of predictable seasonal demand and is less marketable and less valuable after the seasonal demand period ends;

(2) the item was back-ordered and delivery is made after the seasonal demand period ends; and

(3) the dealer sends written notice of the rejection to the supplier before the 11th day after the delivery of the item.

(b) The supplier shall pay the costs of the return of an item the delivery of which is rejected under Subsection (a).

(c) A supplier may not coerce or compel a dealer to accept late delivery of back-ordered seasonal demand equipment other than repair parts or attachments.

Added by Acts 2007, 80th Leg., ch. 885, § 2.01, eff. April 1, 2009.

§ 55.154. Sales to Affiliated Dealer

(a) In this section, "affiliated dealer" means a dealer in which a supplier has an ownership interest.

(b) Except as provided by Subsection (c), a supplier may not:

(1) sell or offer to sell new or unused equipment to an affiliated dealer at a price lower than the price for a sale of the same equipment, identically equipped, to a nonaffiliated dealer; or

(2) use a sales promotion plan or other program or device that results in a sale or offer of sale of new or unused equipment to an affiliated dealer at an actual price that is:

(A) lower than the price for a nonaffiliated dealer; or

(B) fixed and predetermined solely by the supplier.

(c) This section does not apply to sales made to a dealer for resale to:

(1) a unit, agency, or political subdivision of the United States or this state;

(2) a major fleet account; or

(3) an organization for testing or demonstrating the equipment.

Added by Acts 2007, 80th Leg., ch. 885, § 2.01, eff. April 1, 2009.

§ 55.155. Return of Inventory; Responsibility for Costs

(a) If on termination of a dealer agreement the dealer delivers to the supplier or a person designated by the supplier inventory purchased from the supplier and held by the dealer on the date of the termination, the supplier shall pay to the dealer:

(1) the dealer cost of new, unsold, undamaged, and complete equipment, other than repair parts, returned by the dealer; and

(2) an amount equal to:

(A) 85 percent of the current price of new, undamaged repair parts returned by the dealer, if the supplier handles, packs, and loads the parts; or

(B) 90 percent of the current price of new, undamaged repair parts returned by the dealer, if the supplier does not handle, pack, or load the parts.

(b) Before returning inventory under this section and not later than the 120th day after the effective date of termination, the dealer shall submit to the supplier a list of the inventory the dealer intends to return, including, to the extent possible, each item's trade name, description, and serial number. Not later than the 60th day after the date the supplier receives the list, the supplier shall notify the dealer in writing of:

(1) each item that the supplier claims is not subject to reimbursement under this section; and

(2) the destination for each item the dealer is to deliver to a person designated by the supplier.

(c) The supplier may subtract from the amount owed under Subsection (a) the amount of debt owed by the dealer to the supplier.

(d) The supplier and dealer are each responsible for one-half of the cost of delivering the inventory to the supplier or a person designated by the supplier, except that if the dealer delivers an item to a person designated by the supplier the dealer is not responsible for the amount that exceeds the amount for which the dealer would have been responsible if the item had been delivered to the supplier.

(e) The supplier shall pay the amount owed under this section:

(1) before the 91st day after the date the supplier or person designated by the supplier receives inventory from the dealer; and

(2) after the dealer has furnished proof that the inventory was purchased from the supplier.

(f) On payment of the amount owed under this section, title to the inventory is transferred to the supplier or person designated by the supplier.

(g) A supplier and dealer may by agreement alter the time limits provided by this section.

Added by Acts 2007, 80th Leg., ch. 885, § 2.01, eff. April 1, 2009.

§ 55.156. Return of Data Processing or Peripheral Equipment, Software, or Certain Tools; Responsibility for Costs

(a) If on termination of a dealer agreement the dealer delivers to the supplier data processing or peripheral equipment, software, or specialized repair tools that the supplier required the dealer to purchase or lease, the supplier shall:

(1) assume any responsibilities of the dealer under the lease for that equipment or software; and

(2) pay the dealer:

(A) an amount equal to the fair market value of the data processing or peripheral equipment or software purchased by the dealer and delivered to the supplier; and

(B) an amount equal to 75 percent of the cost to the dealer of the specialized repair tools purchased by the dealer and delivered to the supplier.

(b) The supplier and dealer are each responsible for one-half of the cost of delivering the data processing or peripheral equipment, software, or specialized repair tools to the supplier.

(c) The supplier shall assume the responsibilities under the lease and pay the amount required by this section before the 61st day after the date the supplier receives the data processing or peripheral equipment, software, or specialized repair tools.

(d) On payment of the amount required by this section, title or the right of possession to the data processing or peripheral equipment or specialized repair tools purchased or leased by the dealer is transferred to the supplier.

Added by Acts 2007, 80th Leg., ch. 885, § 2.01, eff. April 1, 2009.

§ 55.157. Supplier's Liability for Late Payment

A supplier who does not make a payment required by Section 55.155 or 55.156 before the 61st day after the date the supplier receives the final shipment of the inventory, data processing or peripheral equipment, software, or specialized repair tools from the dealer is liable to the dealer for:

(1) the greater of the dealer cost or current price of any inventory;

(2) any cost to the dealer of the data processing or peripheral equipment, software, or specialized repair tools;

(3) any expense incurred by the dealer in returning the inventory, data processing or peripheral equipment, software, or specialized repair tools to the supplier;

(4) interest on any amounts owed under Subdivision (1), (2), or (3), at the rate applicable to a judgment of a court of this state, beginning on the 61st day after the date the supplier received the inventory, data processing or peripheral equipment, software, or specialized repair tools;

(5) reasonable attorney's fees; and

(6) court costs.

Added by Acts 2007, 80th Leg., ch. 885, § 2.01, eff. April 1, 2009.

§ 55.158. Exceptions to Supplier's Repurchase, Purchase, or Assumption Responsibility

(a) A supplier is not required to repurchase:

(1) inventory:

(A) that the dealer orders after the dealer receives notice of the termination of the dealer agreement from the supplier; or

(B) for which the dealer cannot furnish evidence of clear title that is satisfactory to the supplier; or

(2) a repair part that:

(A) has a limited storage life and was purchased from the supplier more than two years before the date of termination of the dealer agreement;

(B) is in a broken or damaged package;

(C) is usually sold as part of a set, if the part is separated from the set; or

(D) cannot be sold without reconditioning or repackaging.

(b) A supplier is not required to purchase or assume the responsibilities under the lease for:

(1) data processing or peripheral equipment or software that the dealer purchased that was not specifically required by the supplier; or

(2) a specialized repair tool that:

(A) is not unique to the supplier's product line;

(B) is not in complete and salable condition; or

(C) was not purchased by the dealer within the three-year period preceding the date of termination of the dealer agreement.

Added by Acts 2007, 80th Leg., ch. 885, § 2.01, eff. April 1, 2009.

[Sections 55.159 to 55.200 reserved for expansion]

SUBCHAPTER E. ENFORCEMENT

§ 55.201. Action for Violation of Chapter

A person injured by a violation of this chapter may bring an action for:

(1) an injunction to prevent further violation;

(2) damages;

(3) reasonable attorney's fees; and

(4) costs.

Added by Acts 2007, 80th Leg., ch. 885, § 2.01, eff. April 1, 2009.

TITLE 5. REGULATION OF BUSINESSES AND SERVICES

Acts 2007, 80th Leg., ch. 885, § 2.01 added this Title effective April 1, 2009.

SUBTITLE A. GENERAL PRACTICES

CHAPTER 71. ASSUMED BUSINESS OR PROFESSIONAL NAME

SUBCHAPTER A. GENERAL PROVISIONS

Section

SUBCHAPTER B. REQUIREMENTS APPLICABLE TO CERTAIN UNINCORPORATED PERSONS

SUBCHAPTER C. REQUIREMENTS APPLICABLE TO INCORPORATED BUSINESS OR PROFESSION AND CERTAIN OTHER ENTITIES

SUBCHAPTER D. GENERAL PROVISIONS REGARDING ASSUMED NAME CERTIFICATE

SUBCHAPTER A. GENERAL PROVISIONS

§ 71.001. Short Title

This chapter may be cited as the Assumed Business or Professional Name Act.

Added by Acts 2007, 80th Leg., ch. 885, § 2.01, eff. April 1, 2009.

§ 71.002. Definitions

In this chapter:

(1) "Address" means:

(A) a post office address; and

(B) a street address, if the street address is not the same as the post office address.

(2) "Assumed name" means:

(A) for an individual, a name that does not include the surname of the individual;

(B) for a partnership, a name that does not include the surname or other legal name of each joint venturer or general partner;

(C) for an individual or a partnership, a name, including a surname, that suggests the existence of additional owners by including words such as "Company," "& Company," "& Son," "& Sons," "& Associates," "Brothers," and similar words, but not words that merely describe the business being conducted or the professional service being rendered;

(D) for a limited partnership, a name other than the name stated in its certificate of formation;

(E) for a company, a name used by the company;

(F) for a corporation, a name other than the name stated in its certificate of formation or a comparable document;

(G) for a registered limited liability partnership, a name other than the name stated in its application filed with the office of the secretary of state or a comparable document; and

(H) for a limited liability company, a name other than the name stated in its certificate of formation or a comparable document.

(3) "Certificate" means an assumed name certificate.

(4) "Company" means a real estate investment trust, a joint-stock company, or any other business, professional, or other association or legal entity that is not incorporated, other than a partnership, limited partnership, limited liability company, or registered limited liability partnership.

(5) "Corporation" means:

(A) a domestic or foreign corporation, professional corporation, professional association, or other corporation; or

(B) any other business, professional, or other association or legal entity that is incorporated.

(6) "Estate" means a person's property that is administered by a representative.

(7) "Office" means:

(A) for a person that is not an individual or that is a corporation that is not required to or does not maintain a registered office in this state, the person's:

(i) principal office; and

(ii) principal place of business if not the same as the person's principal office; and

(B) for a corporation, limited partnership, registered limited liability partnership, or limited liability company that is required to maintain a registered office in this state, the entity's:

(i) registered office; and

(ii) principal office if not the same as the entity's registered office.

(8) "Partnership" means a joint venture or general partnership other than a limited partnership or a registered limited liability partnership.

(9) "Person" includes an individual, partnership, limited partnership, limited liability company, registered limited liability partnership, company, or corporation.

(10) "Registrant" means a person who has filed, or on whose behalf there has been filed, a certificate under this chapter or other law.

(11) "Representative" means a trustee, administrator, executor, independent executor, guardian, conservator, trustee in bankruptcy, receiver, or other person appointed by a court or by trust or will to

have custody of, take possession of, have title to, or otherwise be empowered to control the person or property of any person.

Added by Acts 2007, 80th Leg., ch. 885, § 2.01, eff. April 1, 2009.

§ 71.003. Applicability of Chapter

(a) This chapter does not apply to an insurer authorized to engage in business in this state and described in Subchapter A, Chapter 805, Insurance Code, except as specifically provided by the Insurance Code.

(b) This chapter does not require a corporation, limited partnership, registered limited liability partnership, or limited liability company or its shareholders, associates, partners, or members to file a certificate to conduct business or render a professional service in this state under the name of the entity as stated in the certificate of formation, application filed with the office of the secretary of state, or other comparable document of the entity.

Added by Acts 2007, 80th Leg., ch. 885, § 2.01, eff. April 1, 2009.

[Sections 71.004 to 71.050 reserved for expansion]

SUBCHAPTER B. REQUIREMENTS APPLICABLE TO CERTAIN UNINCORPORATED PERSONS

§ 71.051. Certificate for Certain Unincorporated Persons

A person must file a certificate under this subchapter if the person regularly conducts business or renders a professional service in this state under an assumed name other than as a corporation, limited partnership, registered limited liability partnership, or limited liability company.

Added by Acts 2007, 80th Leg., ch. 885, § 2.01, eff. April 1, 2009.

§ 71.052. Contents of Certificate

The certificate must state:

(1) the assumed name under which the business is or is to be conducted or the professional service is or is to be rendered;

(2) if the registrant is:

(A) an individual, the individual's full name and residence address;

(B) a partnership:

(i) the venture or partnership name;

(ii) the venture or partnership office address;

(iii) the full name of each joint venturer or general partner; and

(iv) each joint venturer's or general partner's residence address if the venturer or partner is an individual or the joint venturer's or general partner's office address if the venturer or partner is not an individual;

(C) an estate:

(i) the name of the estate;

(ii) the estate's office address, if any;

(iii) the full name of each representative of the estate; and

(iv) each representative's residence address if the representative is an individual or the representative's office address if the representative is not an individual;

(D) a real estate investment trust:

(i) the name of the trust;

(ii) the address of the trust;

(iii) the full name of each trustee manager; and

(iv) each trustee manager's residence address if the trustee manager is an individual or the trustee manager's office address if the trustee manager is not an individual; or

(E) a company, other than a real estate investment trust, or a corporation:

(i) the name of the company or corporation;

(ii) the state, country, or other jurisdiction under the laws of which the company or corporation was organized or incorporated; and

(iii) the company's or corporation's office address;

(3) the period, not to exceed 10 years, during which the registrant will use the assumed name; and

(4) a statement specifying that the business that is or will be conducted or the professional service that is or will be rendered in the county under the assumed name is being or will be conducted or rendered as a proprietorship, sole practitioner, partnership, real estate investment trust, joint-stock company, or other form of unincorporated business or professional association or entity other than a limited partnership, limited liability company, or registered limited liability partnership.

Added by Acts 2007, 80th Leg., ch. 885, § 2.01, eff. April 1, 2009.

§ 71.053. Execution of Certificate

(a) The certificate must be executed and acknowledged:

(1) by each individual whose name is required to be stated in the certificate or the individual's representative or attorney-in-fact; and

(2) under oath on behalf of each person whose name is required to be stated in the certificate and who is not an individual, by:

(A) the person's representative or attorney-in-fact; or

(B) a joint venturer, general partner, trustee manager, officer, or other person having authority regarding the person comparable to the person's representative or attorney-in-fact.

(b) A certificate executed and acknowledged by an attorney-in-fact must include a statement that the attorney has been authorized in writing by the attorney's principal to execute and acknowledge the certificate.

Added by Acts 2007, 80th Leg., ch. 885, § 2.01, eff. April 1, 2009.

§ 71.054. Place of Filing

A person shall file the certificate in the office of the county clerk in each county in which the person:

(1) has or will maintain business or professional premises; or

(2) conducts business or renders a professional service, if the person does not or will not maintain business or professional premises in any county.

Added by Acts 2007, 80th Leg., ch. 885, § 2.01, eff. April 1, 2009.

[Sections 71.055 to 71.100 reserved for expansion]

SUBCHAPTER C. REQUIREMENTS APPLICABLE TO INCORPORATED BUSINESS OR PROFESSION AND CERTAIN OTHER ENTITIES

§ 71.101. Certificate for Incorporated Business or Profession, Limited Partnership, Registered Limited Liability Partnership, or Limited Liability Company

A corporation, limited partnership, registered limited liability partnership, or limited liability company must file a certificate under this subchapter if the entity:

(1) regularly conducts business or renders professional services in this state under an assumed name; or

(2) is required by law to use an assumed name in this state to conduct business or render professional services.

Added by Acts 2007, 80th Leg., ch. 885, § 2.01, eff. April 1, 2009.

§ 71.102. Contents of Certificate

The certificate must state:

(1) the assumed name under which the business is or is to be conducted or the professional service is or is to be rendered;

(2) the registrant's name as stated in the registrant's certificate of formation or application filed with the office of the secretary of state or other comparable document;

(3) the state, country, or other jurisdiction under the laws of which the registrant was incorporated or organized and the registrant's registered or similar office address in that state, country, or jurisdiction;

(4) the period, not to exceed 10 years, during which the registrant will use the assumed name;

(5) a statement specifying that the registrant is:

(A) a business corporation, nonprofit corporation, professional corporation, professional association, or other type of corporation;

(B) a limited partnership, registered limited liability partnership, or limited liability company; or

(C) another type of incorporated business, professional or other association, or legal entity;

(6) the address of:

(A) the registrant's:

(i) registered office in this state and the name of its registered agent at that address; and

(ii) principal office, if the principal office address is not the same as the registrant's registered office address in this state; or

(B) if the registrant is not required to or does not maintain a registered office in this state:

(i) the registrant's office in this state; and

(ii) the registrant's place of business in this state and any office of the registrant outside this state, if the registrant is not incorporated or organized under the laws of this state; and

(7) the county or counties in this state where the registrant is or will be conducting business or ren-

dering professional services under the assumed name.

Added by Acts 2007, 80th Leg., ch. 885, § 2.01, eff. April 1, 2009.

§ 71.103. Place of Filing

(a) The corporation, limited partnership, registered limited liability partnership, or limited liability company shall file the certificate in the office of the secretary of state and in the office or offices of each county clerk as specified by Subsection (b) or (c).

(b) Except as provided by Subsection (c), the entity shall file the certificate in the offices of the county clerk of the county in which the entity's:

(1) registered office is located; and

(2) principal office is located if the principal office is in this state and not in the same county where the registered office is located.

(c) If the entity is not required to or does not maintain a registered office in this state, the entity shall file the certificate:

(1) in the office of the county clerk of the county in which the entity's office in this state is located; or

(2) in the office of the county clerk of the county in which the entity's principal place of business in this state is located, if:

(A) the entity is not incorporated or organized under the laws of this state; and

(B) the county in which the entity's principal place of business in this state is located is not the same county where the entity's office is located.

Added by Acts 2007, 80th Leg., ch. 885, § 2.01, eff. April 1, 2009.

§ 71.104. Execution of Certificate

(a) A certificate filed in the secretary of state's office must be executed by an officer, general partner, member, manager, or representative of or attorney-in-fact for the registrant.

(b) A certificate filed in a county clerk's office must be executed and acknowledged in the manner provided by Section 71.053 for a certificate filed under that section.

(c) A certificate executed by an attorney-in-fact must include a statement that the attorney has been authorized in writing by the attorney's principal to execute the certificate.

Added by Acts 2007, 80th Leg., ch. 885, § 2.01, eff. April 1, 2009.

[Sections 71.105 to 71.150 reserved for expansion]

SUBCHAPTER D. GENERAL PROVISIONS REGARDING ASSUMED NAME CERTIFICATE

§ 71.151. Duration and Renewal of Certificate

(a) A certificate is effective for a term not to exceed 10 years from the date the certificate is filed.

(b) A certificate is void at the end of the certificate's stated term, unless within six months preceding the certificate's expiration date the registrant files in the office of a county clerk and the secretary of state, if applicable, a renewal certificate complying with the requirements of this chapter for an original certificate.

(c) A registrant may renew a certificate under this section for any number of successive terms, but each term may not exceed 10 years.

Added by Acts 2007, 80th Leg., ch. 885, § 2.01, eff. April 1, 2009.

§ 71.152. Material Change in Information; New Certificate

(a) Not later than the 60th day after an event occurs that causes the information in a certificate to become materially misleading, a registrant must file a new certificate complying with this chapter in the office in which the original or renewal certificate was filed.

(b) An event that causes the information in a certificate to become materially misleading includes:

(1) a change in the name, identity, entity, form of business or professional organization, or location of a registrant;

(2) for a proprietorship or sole practitioner, a change in ownership;

(3) for a partnership:

(A) the admission of a new partner or joint venturer; or

(B) the end of a general partner's or joint venturer's association with the partnership; or

(4) for a registrant required by law to maintain a registered office or similar office and a registered

agent or similar agent at that office, a change in the address of the office or in the identity of the agent.

(c) A new certificate filed under this section is effective for a term not to exceed 10 years from the date the certificate is filed.

Added by Acts 2007, 80th Leg., ch. 885, § 2.01, eff. April 1, 2009.

§ 71.153. Abandonment of Use of Business or Professional Name

(a) A registrant who has filed a certificate under this chapter and who ceases to conduct business or render professional services in this state under the assumed name stated in the certificate may file a statement of abandonment of use of the assumed name in the office in which the registrant's certificate was filed.

(b) The statement of abandonment of use of an assumed name must state:

(1) the assumed name being abandoned;

(2) the date on which the certificate was filed in the office in which the statement of abandonment is being filed and in any other office in which the certificate was filed; and

(3) the registrant's name and residence or office address as required for a certificate filed under this chapter.

(c) A statement of abandonment must be executed and acknowledged in the same manner as if the registrant were filing a certificate under this chapter.

Added by Acts 2007, 80th Leg., ch. 885, § 2.01, eff. April 1, 2009.

§ 71.154. Index of Certificates

(a) The secretary of state and each county clerk shall keep an alphabetical index of:

(1) all assumed names that have been filed in the office of the respective officer; and

(2) the persons filing the certificates.

(b) A copy of a certificate or statement is presumptive evidence in any court in this state of the facts contained in the copy if the copy is certified to by:

(1) the county clerk in whose office the certificate or statement was filed; or

(2) the secretary of state.

Added by Acts 2007, 80th Leg., ch. 885, § 2.01, eff. April 1, 2009.

§ 71.155. Filing Fees

(a) The county clerk shall collect a fee of:

(1) $2 for filing each certificate or statement required or permitted to be filed under this chapter; and

(2) 50 cents for each name to be indexed.

(b) The secretary of state shall collect for the use of this state a fee of:

(1) $25 for indexing and filing each certificate or statement required or permitted to be filed under this chapter; and

(2) $10 for filing each statement of abandonment of use of an assumed name.

Added by Acts 2007, 80th Leg., ch. 885, § 2.01, eff. April 1, 2009.

§ 71.156. Prescribed Forms

(a) The secretary of state may prescribe a form to be used for filing a certificate or statement that complies with this chapter in the secretary's office or in the office of any county clerk in this state.

(b) Unless otherwise specifically provided by law, the use of a form prescribed under this section is not mandatory.

Added by Acts 2007, 80th Leg., ch. 885, § 2.01, eff. April 1, 2009.

§ 71.157. Effect of Filing

(a) This chapter does not give a registrant a right to use the assumed name in violation of the common or statutory law of unfair competition or unfair trade practices, common law copyright, or similar law.

(b) The filing of a certificate under this chapter does not in itself constitute actual use of the assumed name stated in the certificate for purposes of determining priority of rights.

Added by Acts 2007, 80th Leg., ch. 885, § 2.01, eff. April 1, 2009.

§ 71.158. Filing of Reproduction

(a) The secretary of state may accept for filing a photographic, photostatic, or similar reproduction of a signed original document required or authorized to be filed in the secretary's office under this chapter.

(b) A signature on a document required or authorized to be filed in the secretary of state's office under this chapter may be a facsimile.

Added by Acts 2007, 80th Leg., ch. 885, § 2.01, eff. April 1, 2009.

[Sections 71.159 to 71.200 reserved for expansion]

SUBCHAPTER E. PENALTIES

§ 71.201. Civil Action; Sanction

(a) A person's failure to comply with this chapter does not impair the validity of any contract or act by the person or prevent the person from defending any action or proceeding in any court of this state, but the person may not maintain in a court of this state an action or proceeding arising out of a contract or act in which an assumed name was used until an original, new, or renewed certificate has been filed as required by this chapter.

(b) In an action or proceeding brought against a person who has not complied with this chapter, the court may award the plaintiff or other party bringing the action or proceeding expenses incurred, including attorney's fees, in locating and effecting service of process on the defendant.

Added by Acts 2007, 80th Leg., ch. 885, § 2.01, eff. April 1, 2009.

§ 71.202. Criminal Penalty: General Violation

(a) A person commits an offense if the person:

(1) conducts business or renders a professional service in this state under an assumed name; and

(2) intentionally violates this chapter.

(b) An offense under this section is a Class A misdemeanor.

Added by Acts 2007, 80th Leg., ch. 885, § 2.01, eff. April 1, 2009.

§ 71.203. Criminal Penalty: Fraudulent Filing

(a) A person may not knowingly or intentionally sign and present for filing or cause to be presented for filing a document authorized or required to be filed under this chapter that:

(1) indicates that the person signing the document has the authority to act on behalf of the entity for which the document is presented and the person does not have that authority;

(2) contains a material false statement; or

(3) is forged.

(b) A person commits an offense if the person violates Subsection (a). An offense under this subsection is punishable as if it were an offense under Section 37.10, Penal Code.

Added by Acts 2007, 80th Leg., ch. 885, § 2.01, eff. April 1, 2009.

CHAPTER 72. BUSINESS RECORDS

SUBCHAPTER A. DISPOSAL OF CERTAIN BUSINESS RECORDS

§ 72.001. Definitions

In this subchapter:

(1) "Business record" means letters, words, sounds, or numbers, or the equivalent of letters, words, sounds, or numbers, recorded in the operation of a business by:

(A) handwriting;

(B) typewriting;

(C) printing;

(D) photostat;

(E) photograph;

(F) magnetic impulse;

(G) mechanical or electronic recording;

(H) digitized optical image; or

(I) another form of data compilation.

(2) "Personal identifying information" means an individual's first name or initial and last name in combination with one or more of the following:

(A) date of birth;

(B) social security number or other government-issued identification number;

(C) mother's maiden name;

(D) unique biometric data, including the individual's fingerprint, voice data, or retina or iris image;

(E) unique electronic identification number, address, or routing code;

(F) telecommunication access device as defined by Section 32.51, Penal Code, including debit or credit card information; or

(G) financial institution account number or any other financial information.

(3) "Reproduction" means a counterpart of an original business record produced by:

(A) production from the same impression or the same matrix as the original;

(B) photography, including an enlargement or miniature;

(C) mechanical or electronic rerecording;

(D) chemical reproduction;

(E) digitized optical imaging; or

(F) another technique that accurately reproduces the original.

Added by Acts 2007, 80th Leg., ch. 885, § 2.01, eff. April 1, 2009.

§ 72.002. Destruction of Certain Business Records

(a) A business record required to be retained by a law of this state may be destroyed at any time after the third anniversary of the date the business record was created.

(b) Subsection (a) does not apply if a law or rule applicable to the business record prescribes a different retention period or procedure for disposal.

Added by Acts 2007, 80th Leg., ch. 885, § 2.01, eff. April 1, 2009.

§ 72.003. Retention of Reproduction of Business Records

A law of this state that requires retention of a business record is satisfied by retention of a reproduction of the original record.

Added by Acts 2007, 80th Leg., ch. 885, § 2.01, eff. April 1, 2009.

§ 72.004. Disposal of Business Records Containing Personal Identifying Information

(a) This section does not apply to:

(1) a financial institution as defined by 15 U.S.C. Section 6809; or

(2) a covered entity as defined by Section 601.001 or 602.001, Insurance Code.

(b) When a business disposes of a business record that contains personal identifying information of a customer of the business, the business shall modify, by shredding, erasing, or other means, the personal identifying information so as to make the information unreadable or undecipherable.

(c) A business is considered to comply with Subsection (b) if the business contracts with a person engaged in the business of disposing of records for the modification of personal identifying information on behalf of the business in accordance with that subsection.

(d) A business that disposes of a business record without complying with Subsection (b) is liable for a civil penalty in an amount not to exceed $500 for each business record. The attorney general may bring an action against the business to:

(1) recover the civil penalty;

(2) obtain any other remedy, including injunctive relief; and

(3) recover costs and reasonable attorney's fees incurred in bringing the action.

(e) A business that in good faith modifies a business record as required by Subsection (b) is not liable for a civil penalty under Subsection (d) if the business record is reconstructed, wholly or partly, through extraordinary means.

(f) Subsection (b) does not require a business to modify a business record if:

(1) the business is required to retain the business record under another law; or

(2) the business record is historically significant and:

(A) there is no potential for identity theft or fraud while the business retains custody of the business record; or

(B) the business record is transferred to a professionally managed historical repository.

Added by Acts 2007, 80th Leg., ch. 885, § 2.01, eff. April 1, 2009.

[Sections 72.005 to 72.050 reserved for expansion]

SUBCHAPTER B. DELETION OF CERTAIN RECORDS OR INFORMATION RELATING TO CUSTOMERS' CHECKS

§ 72.051. Required Deletion of Certain Electronic Records

(a) In this section, "law enforcement agency" has the meaning assigned by Article 59.01, Code of Criminal Procedure.

(b) This section applies only to a business that accepts checks from customers in the ordinary course of business. This section does not apply to a financial institution as defined by 31 U.S.C. Section 5312(a)(2), as amended.

(c) A business shall delete any electronic record indicating that a customer has issued a dishonored check or any other information except for a checking account number or bank routing transit number on which the business bases a refusal to accept a check from a customer. The record must be deleted not later than the 30th day after the date:

(1) the customer and the business agree that the information contained in the electronic record is incorrect; or

(2) the customer presents to the business:

(A) a copy of a report filed by the customer with a law enforcement agency stating that the dishonored check was unauthorized; and

(B) a written statement of the customer indicating that the dishonored check was unauthorized.

(d) A business that violates Subsection (c) is liable to this state for a civil penalty in an amount not to exceed $1,000. The attorney general may:

(1) bring an action to recover the civil penalty; and

(2) recover reasonable expenses incurred in recovering the penalty, including court costs, reasonable attorney's fees, investigative costs, witness fees, and deposition expenses.

Added by Acts 2007, 80th Leg., ch. 885, § 2.01, eff. April 1, 2009.

[Chapters 73 to 90 reserved for expansion]

SUBTITLE B. RENTAL PRACTICES

CHAPTER 91. PRIVATE PASSENGER VEHICLE RENTAL COMPANIES

SUBCHAPTER A. GENERAL PROVISIONS

§ 91.001. Definitions

In this chapter:

(1) "Authorized driver" means:

(A) the renter;

(B) a person whom the rental company expressly designates on the rental agreement as an authorized driver;

(C) the renter's spouse if the spouse:

(i) holds a driver's license; and

(ii) satisfies any minimum age requirement established by the rental company;

(D) an employer, employee, or coworker of the renter if the person:

(i) holds a driver's license;

(ii) satisfies any minimum age requirement established by the rental company; and

(iii) is engaged in a business activity with the renter at the time of the rental; or

(E) a person who:

(i) holds a driver's license; and

(ii) is driving directly to a medical or police facility under circumstances reasonably believed to constitute an emergency.

(2) "Damage" means damage to or loss of a rented vehicle, regardless of fault involved in the damage or loss. The term includes:

(A) theft and loss of use; and

(B) any cost incident to the damage or loss, including storage, impound, towing, and administrative charges.

(3) "Damage waiver" means a rental company's agreement not to hold an authorized driver liable for all or part of any damage to a rented vehicle.

(4) "Mandatory charge" means a charge for an item or service provided in connection with a rental transaction, other than a charge imposed by law:

(A) that is in addition to the base rental rate; and

(B) that the renter may not avoid or decline.

(5) "Private passenger vehicle" means a motor vehicle of the private passenger type, including a passenger van, primarily intended for private use.

(6) "Rental agreement" means an agreement for 30 days or less that states the terms governing the use of a private passenger vehicle rented by a rental company.

(7) "Rental company" means a person in the business of renting private passenger vehicles to the public for 30 days or less. The term does not include a person who holds a license under Chapter 2301, Occupations Code, and whose primary business activity is not renting private passenger vehicles.

(8) "Renter" means a person who obtains use of a private passenger vehicle from a rental company under a rental agreement.

Added by Acts 2007, 80th Leg., ch. 885, § 2.01, eff. April 1, 2009.

[Sections 91.002 to 91.050 reserved for expansion]

SUBCHAPTER B. DAMAGE WAIVERS AND MANDATORY CHARGES

§ 91.051. Written Agreement Required for Damage Waiver

A rental company may not sell a damage waiver unless the renter agrees to the damage waiver in writing at or before the time the rental agreement is executed.

Added by Acts 2007, 80th Leg., ch. 885, § 2.01, eff. April 1, 2009.

§ 91.052. Notice to Renter

(a) A rental company shall provide each renter who purchases a damage waiver, the charge for which is not included in the base rental rate, the following notice:

NOTICE: Your rental agreement offers, for an additional charge, an optional waiver to cover all or a part of your responsibility for damage to or loss of the vehicle. Before deciding whether to purchase the waiver, you may wish to determine whether your own automobile insurance or credit card agreement provides you coverage for rental vehicle damage or loss and determine the amount of the deductible under your own insurance coverage. The purchase of the waiver is not mandatory. The waiver is not insurance.

(b) The notice under Subsection (a) must be in at least 10–point type.

Added by Acts 2007, 80th Leg., ch. 885, § 2.01, eff. April 1, 2009.

§ 91.053. Posted Notice

In addition to providing the notice required by Section 91.052, a rental company shall post in a conspicuous location where the damage waiver is offered the following notice:

Notice to Texas Residents Regarding Damage Waivers

Your personal automobile insurance policy may or may not provide coverage for your responsibility for the loss of or damage to a rented vehicle during the rental term. Before deciding whether to purchase a damage waiver, you may wish to determine whether your automobile insurance policy provides you coverage for rental vehicle damage or loss. If you file a claim under your personal automobile insurance policy, your insurance company may choose to nonrenew your policy at your renewal date, but may do so only if you are at fault for the claim.

Added by Acts 2007, 80th Leg., ch. 885, § 2.01, eff. April 1, 2009.

§ 91.054. Prohibited Representations and Coercion

(a) An employee or agent of a rental company may not:

(1) make an oral or written representation that contradicts this chapter; or

(2) use coercive language or a coercive act in an attempt to persuade a renter to purchase a damage waiver.

(b) For purposes of this section, if the renter has declined the damage waiver, a further statement or question by the employee or agent that refers to the damage waiver, other than a statement made in conjunction with review of the rental agreement that the waiver has been declined, is considered coercive.

Added by Acts 2007, 80th Leg., ch. 885, § 2.01, eff. April 1, 2009.

§ 91.055. Mandatory Charge

(a) A rental company that includes a mandatory charge in a rental agreement shall prominently display and fully disclose the charge:

(1) separately on the face of the agreement; and

(2) in all of the rental company's price advertising, price quotes, price offers, and price displays, including displays in computerized reservation systems.

(b) A rental company may not impose or require the purchase of a damage waiver as a mandatory charge.

Added by Acts 2007, 80th Leg., ch. 885, § 2.01, eff. April 1, 2009.

§ 91.056. Voiding of Damage Waiver

A rental company may not void a damage waiver unless:

(1) an authorized driver causes the damage intentionally or by wilful and wanton misconduct;

(2) the damage arises out of use of the vehicle:

(A) by a person:

(i) who is not an authorized driver;

(ii) while under the influence of an intoxicant that impairs driving ability, including alcohol, an illegal drug, or a controlled substance; or

(iii) while engaged in commission of a crime other than a traffic infraction;

(B) to carry persons or property for hire;

(C) to push or tow anything;

(D) for driver's training;

(E) to engage in a speed contest; or

(F) outside the continental United States, unless the rental agreement specifically authorizes the use; or

(3) the rental company entered into the rental transaction based on fraudulent information supplied by the renter.

Added by Acts 2007, 80th Leg., ch. 885, § 2.01, eff. April 1, 2009.

[Sections 91.057 to 91.100 reserved for expansion]

SUBCHAPTER C. ENFORCEMENT PROVISIONS

§ 91.101. Civil Penalty

A rental company that violates this chapter is liable for a civil penalty in an amount of not less than $500 or more than $1,000 for each act of violation.

Added by Acts 2007, 80th Leg., ch. 885, § 2.01, eff. April 1, 2009.

§ 91.102. Injunction

A person injured or threatened with injury by a violation of this chapter may seek injunctive relief against the person committing or threatening to commit the violation.

Added by Acts 2007, 80th Leg., ch. 885, § 2.01, eff. April 1, 2009.

§ 91.103. Suit for Civil Penalty or Injunctive Relief

The attorney general or a county or district attorney may bring an action in the name of the state for a civil penalty under Section 91.101, injunctive relief under Section 91.102, or both.

Added by Acts 2007, 80th Leg., ch. 885, § 2.01, eff. April 1, 2009.

CHAPTER 92. RENTAL–PURCHASE AGREEMENTS

SUBCHAPTER A. GENERAL PROVISIONS

SUBCHAPTER A. GENERAL PROVISIONS

§ 92.001. Definitions

In this chapter:

(1) "Advertisement" means a commercial message in any medium that directly or indirectly promotes or assists a rental-purchase agreement.

(2) "Commission" means the Texas Commission of Licensing and Regulation.

(3) "Consumer" means an individual who leases personal property under a rental-purchase agreement.

(4) "Department" means the Texas Department of Licensing and Regulation.

(5) "Loss damage waiver" means a merchant's agreement to not hold a consumer liable for loss from all or part of any damage to merchandise.

(6) "Merchandise" means the personal property that is the subject of a rental-purchase agreement.

(7) "Merchant" means a person who, in the ordinary course of business, regularly leases, offers to lease, or arranges for the leasing of merchandise under a rental-purchase agreement. The term includes a person who is assigned an interest in a rental-purchase agreement.

(8) "Rental–purchase agreement" means an agreement under which a consumer may use merchandise for personal, family, or household purposes for an initial period of four months or less, and that:

(A) is automatically renewable with each payment after the initial period; and

(B) permits the consumer to become the owner of the merchandise.

Added by Acts 2007, 80th Leg., ch. 885, § 2.01, eff. April 1, 2009.

§ 92.002. Advertisement Requirements

An advertisement for a rental-purchase agreement that refers to or states the amount of a payment or the right to acquire ownership of any one particular item under the agreement must clearly and conspicuously state:

(1) that the transaction advertised is a rental-purchase agreement;

(2) the total amount and number of payments necessary to acquire ownership; and

(3) that the consumer does not acquire ownership rights unless the merchandise is rented for a specified number of payment periods.

Added by Acts 2007, 80th Leg., ch. 885, § 2.01, eff. April 1, 2009.

[Sections 92.003 to 92.050 reserved for expansion]

SUBCHAPTER B. FORM AND CONTENT OF AGREEMENTS

§ 92.051. Form of Agreement

(a) A rental-purchase agreement must be written in:

(1) plain English; and

(2) any other language used by the merchant in an advertisement related to the agreement.

(b) A numerical amount included in a rental-purchase agreement must be stated in figures.

(c) A disclosure required by this chapter must be printed or typed in each rental-purchase agreement in a size equal to at least 10–point boldfaced type.

(d) The attorney general shall provide a form agreement that may be used to satisfy the requirements of a rental-purchase agreement under this chapter.

Added by Acts 2007, 80th Leg., ch. 885, § 2.01, eff. April 1, 2009.

§ 92.052. Required Disclosures

(a) A rental-purchase agreement must disclose:

(1) whether the merchandise is new or used;

(2) the price for which the merchant would have sold the merchandise to the consumer for cash on the date of the agreement;

(3) the amount and timing of payments;

(4) the total number of payments necessary and the total amount to be paid to acquire ownership of the merchandise;

(5) that the consumer does not acquire ownership rights unless the consumer complies with the ownership terms of the agreement;

(6) the amount and purpose of any payment, charge, or fee in addition to the regular periodic payments; and

(7) whether the consumer is liable for loss or damage to the merchandise and, if so, the maximum amount for which the consumer may be liable.

(b) Notice of the right to reinstate the agreement must be disclosed in the agreement.

Added by Acts 2007, 80th Leg., ch. 885, § 2.01, eff. April 1, 2009.

§ 92.053. Other Required Provisions

A rental-purchase agreement must provide that:

(1) any charge in addition to periodic payments must be reasonably related to the service performed; and

(2) a consumer who fails to make a timely payment may reinstate an agreement, without losing any right or option previously acquired, by taking the required action before the later of:

(A) one week after the due date of the payment; or

(B) the number of days after the due date of the payment that is equal to half the number of days in a regular payment period.

Added by Acts 2007, 80th Leg., ch. 885, § 2.01, eff. April 1, 2009.

§ 92.054. Prohibited Provisions

(a) A rental-purchase agreement may not:

(1) require a consumer to:

(A) pay a late charge or reinstatement fee except as provided by Section 92.055(b);

(B) make a payment at the end of the scheduled rental-purchase term in excess of or in addition to a regular periodic payment to acquire ownership of the merchandise; or

(C) purchase insurance or a loss damage waiver from the merchant to cover the merchandise;

(2) require a confession of judgment;

(3) authorize a merchant or an agent of the merchant to commit a breach of the peace in repossessing merchandise; or

(4) waive a defense, counterclaim, or right the consumer may have against the merchant or an agent of the merchant.

(b) A consumer may not in any event be required to pay a sum greater than the total amount to be paid to acquire ownership of the merchandise as disclosed under Section 92.052(a)(4).

Added by Acts 2007, 80th Leg., ch. 885, § 2.01, eff. April 1, 2009.

§ 92.055. Restrictions on Late Charges and Reinstatement Fees

(a) Only one late charge or reinstatement fee may be collected on a payment regardless of the period during which the payment remains in default.

(b) A rental-purchase agreement may require the consumer to pay a late charge or reinstatement fee only if:

(1) a periodic payment is delinquent for more than:

(A) seven days, if the payment is due monthly; or

(B) three days, if the payment is due more frequently than monthly; and

(2) the charge or fee is in an amount not less than $5 and not more than the lesser of:

(A) $10; or

(B) 10 percent of the delinquent payment.

Added by Acts 2007, 80th Leg., ch. 885, § 2.01, eff. April 1, 2009.

[Sections 92.056 to 92.100 reserved for expansion]

SUBCHAPTER C. REPOSSESSION AND REINSTATEMENT

§ 92.101. Merchant's Repossession Right

This chapter does not prevent a merchant from attempting repossession of merchandise during the reinstatement period.

Added by Acts 2007, 80th Leg., ch. 885, § 2.01, eff. April 1, 2009.

§ 92.102. Effect of Repossession During Reinstatement Period

A consumer's right to reinstate a rental-purchase agreement is not affected by the merchant's repossession of the merchandise during the reinstatement period.

Added by Acts 2007, 80th Leg., ch. 885, § 2.01, eff. April 1, 2009.

§ 92.103. Effect on Reinstatement Period of Merchandise Return

If merchandise is returned during the applicable reinstatement period, other than through judicial process, the right to reinstate the rental-purchase agreement is extended for a period of not less than 30 days after the date of return.

Added by Acts 2007, 80th Leg., ch. 885, § 2.01, eff. April 1, 2009.

§ 92.104. Merchant's Duties on Reinstatement

(a) On reinstatement, the merchant shall provide the consumer with:

(1) the same merchandise; or

(2) substitute merchandise of comparable quality and condition.

(b) A merchant who provides the consumer with substitute merchandise shall also provide the consumer with the disclosures required by Section 92.052(a).

Added by Acts 2007, 80th Leg., ch. 885, § 2.01, eff. April 1, 2009.

[Sections 92.105 to 92.150 reserved for expansion]

SUBCHAPTER D. LOSS DAMAGE WAIVERS

§ 92.151. Contract for Waiver

In addition to other charges permitted by this chapter, a consumer may contract for a loss damage waiver.

Added by Acts 2007, 80th Leg., ch. 885, § 2.01, eff. April 1, 2009.

§ 92.152. Charge for Waiver

A merchant may charge a periodic fee for a loss damage waiver in an amount not to exceed 10 percent of the periodic rental payment.

Added by Acts 2007, 80th Leg., ch. 885, § 2.01, eff. April 1, 2009.

§ 92.153. Restrictions on Merchant Concerning Waiver

A merchant may not:

(1) sell a loss damage waiver unless:

(A) the department has approved the form of the contract containing the waiver; and

(B) the consumer agrees to the waiver in writing; or

(2) impose or require the purchase of a loss damage waiver as a mandatory charge.

Added by Acts 2007, 80th Leg., ch. 885, § 2.01, eff. April 1, 2009.

§ 92.154. Required Notice in Waiver

A contract that offers a loss damage waiver must include the following notice:

"This contract offers an optional loss damage waiver for an additional charge to cover your responsibility for loss of or damage to the merchandise. You do not have to purchase this coverage. Before deciding whether or not to purchase this loss damage waiver, you may consider whether your homeowners' or casualty insurance policy affords you coverage for loss of or damage to rental merchandise and the amount of the deductible you would pay under your policy."

Added by Acts 2007, 80th Leg., ch. 885, § 2.01, eff. April 1, 2009.

§ 92.155. Statement of Total Charge

A loss damage waiver agreement must include a statement of the total charge for the loss damage waiver.

Added by Acts 2007, 80th Leg., ch. 885, § 2.01, eff. April 1, 2009.

§ 92.156. Authorized Exclusions

A loss damage waiver may exclude:

(1) loss or damage to the merchandise that is caused by an unexplained disappearance or abandonment of the merchandise;

(2) damage that is intentionally caused by the consumer; or

(3) damage that results from the consumer's wilful or wanton misconduct.

Added by Acts 2007, 80th Leg., ch. 885, § 2.01, eff. April 1, 2009.

§ 92.157. Relationship to Insurance

A loss damage waiver is not insurance.

Added by Acts 2007, 80th Leg., ch. 885, § 2.01, eff. April 1, 2009.

§ 92.158. Rules for Review of Certain Contracts

The commission by rule shall provide the method for annually submitting to the department for review any contract, including any amendment to a contract, that contains a loss damage waiver.

Added by Acts 2007, 80th Leg., ch. 885, § 2.01, eff. April 1, 2009.

§ 92.159. Fees

The commission by rule shall set a reasonable fee to be paid by a merchant for:

(1) the review of a contract form under Section 92.158; and

(2) the administration of this chapter by the department.

Added by Acts 2007, 80th Leg., ch. 885, § 2.01, eff. April 1, 2009.

§ 92.160. Administrative Enforcement of Subchapter

(a) The department shall enforce this subchapter and, as necessary, may investigate a merchant who has one or more contracts that include a loss damage waiver.

(b) A person may file a complaint with the department alleging a violation of this subchapter. The department shall investigate the alleged violation on receipt of the complaint and may inspect any record relevant to the complaint.

(c) If, as a result of an investigation, the department determines that a violation may have occurred, the commission shall provide an opportunity for a hearing in the manner provided for a contested case under Chapter 2001, Government Code.

(d) If, after opportunity for hearing, the commission determines that the merchant has violated this subchapter, the commission may:

(1) impose an administrative penalty under Chapter 51, Occupations Code; or

(2) award the complainant damages in an amount not to exceed the amount of the contract price for the merchandise.

Added by Acts 2007, 80th Leg., ch. 885, § 2.01, eff. April 1, 2009.

[Sections 92.161 to 92.200 reserved for expansion]

SUBCHAPTER E. CIVIL ENFORCEMENT

§ 92.201. Action for Violation of Chapter

(a) A consumer damaged by a merchant's violation of this chapter is entitled to recover from the merchant:

(1) actual damages;

(2) an amount equal to 25 percent of the total amount of payments required to obtain ownership of the merchandise, except that the amount recovered under this subdivision may not be less than $250 or more than $1,000; and

(3) reasonable attorney's fees and court costs.

(b) A merchant is not liable under this section for a violation of this chapter caused by the merchant's error if, subject to Subsection (c), the merchant:

(1) provides the consumer written notice of the error; and

(2) makes adjustments in the consumer's account as necessary to ensure:

(A) the consumer will not be required to pay an amount in excess of the amount disclosed; and

(B) the agreement otherwise complies with this chapter.

(c) A merchant must take action under Subsection (b) before:

(1) the 31st day after the date the merchant discovers the error; and

(2) the merchant receives written notice of the error from the consumer or an action under this section is filed.

Added by Acts 2007, 80th Leg., ch. 885, § 2.01, eff. April 1, 2009.

§ 92.202. Deceptive Trade Practice

A violation of this chapter is a deceptive trade practice under Subchapter E, Chapter 17.

Added by Acts 2007, 80th Leg., ch. 885, § 2.01, eff. April 1, 2009.

[Chapters 93 to 100 reserved for expansion]

SUBTITLE C. BUSINESS OPERATIONS

CHAPTER 101. INTERNATIONAL MATCHMAKING ORGANIZATIONS

§ 101.001. Definitions

In this chapter:

(1) "Basic rights information" means information applicable to a noncitizen, including information about human rights, immigration, and emergency assistance and resources.

(2) "Client" means a person who is a resident of the United States and who contracts with an international matchmaking organization to meet recruits.

(3) "Criminal history record information" means criminal history record information obtained from the Department of Public Safety under Subchapter F, Chapter 411, Government Code, and from the Federal Bureau of Investigation under Section 411.087, Government Code.

(4) "International matchmaking organization" means a corporation, partnership, sole proprietorship, or other legal entity that does business in the United States and offers to residents of this state dating, matrimonial, or social referral services involving recruits by:

(A) exchanging names, telephone numbers, addresses, or statistics;

(B) selecting photographs; or

(C) providing a social environment for introducing clients to recruits in a country other than the United States.

(5) "Marital history information" means a declaration of a person's current marital status, the number of times the person has been married, and whether any marriage occurred as a result of receiving services from an international matchmaking organization.

(6) "Recruit" means a person who:

(A) is not a citizen or resident of the United States; and

(B) is recruited by an international matchmaking organization for the purpose of providing dating, matrimonial, or social referral services.

Added by Acts 2007, 80th Leg., ch. 885, § 2.01, eff. April 1, 2009.

§ 101.002. Providing Criminal History, Marital History, and Basic Rights Information

(a) An international matchmaking organization shall provide each recruit with the criminal history record information and marital history information of the organization's clients and with basic rights information.

(b) The information under Subsection (a) must:

(1) be in the recruit's native language; and

(2) be displayed in a manner that:

(A) separates the criminal history record information, the marital history information, and the basic rights information from any other information; and

(B) is highly noticeable.

Added by Acts 2007, 80th Leg., ch. 885, § 2.01, eff. April 1, 2009.

§ 101.003. Providing Additional Criminal History, Marital History, and Basic Rights Information

(a) An international matchmaking organization shall disseminate to a recruit the criminal history record information and marital history information of a client and the basic rights information not later than the 30th day after the date the organization receives the criminal history record information and the marital history information from the client.

(b) The international matchmaking organization shall provide the information to the recruit in the recruit's native language. The organization shall pay the costs incurred to translate the information.

Added by Acts 2007, 80th Leg., ch. 885, § 2.01, eff. April 1, 2009.

§ 101.004. Obtaining Criminal History Record Information and Marital History Information

(a) A client shall:

(1) obtain a copy of the client's own criminal history record information;

(2) provide the criminal history record information to the international matchmaking organization; and

(3) provide the client's own marital history information to the international matchmaking organization.

(b) The international matchmaking organization shall require the client to affirm that the marital history information is complete and accurate and includes information regarding marriages, annulments, and dissolutions that occurred in another state or a foreign country.

(c) The international matchmaking organization may not provide any further services to the client or the recruit until the organization has:

(1) obtained the requested criminal history record information and marital history information; and

(2) provided the information to the recruit.

Added by Acts 2007, 80th Leg., ch. 885, § 2.01, eff. April 1, 2009.

§ 101.005. Civil Penalty

(a) An international matchmaking organization that violates this chapter is subject to a civil penalty not to exceed $20,000 for each violation.

(b) In determining the amount of the civil penalty, the court shall consider:

(1) any previous violations of this chapter by the international matchmaking organization;

(2) the seriousness of the violation, including the nature, circumstances, extent, and gravity of the violation;

(3) the demonstrated good faith of the international matchmaking organization; and

(4) the amount necessary to deter future violations.

(c) The attorney general or the appropriate district or county attorney may bring an action under this section in the name of the state in a district court in:

(1) Travis County; or

(2) a county in which any part of the violation occurs.

(d) A penalty collected under this section by the attorney general or a district or county attorney shall be deposited in the state treasury to the credit of the compensation to victims of crime fund under Article 56.54, Code of Criminal Procedure.

Added by Acts 2007, 80th Leg., ch. 885, § 2.01, eff. April 1, 2009.

CHAPTER 102. SEXUALLY ORIENTED BUSINESSES

§ 102.001. Definitions

In this chapter:

(1) "Sex offender" means a person who has been convicted of or placed on deferred adjudication for an offense for which a person is subject to registration under Chapter 62, Code of Criminal Procedure.

(2) "Sexually oriented business" has the meaning assigned by Section 243.002, Local Government Code.

Added by Acts 2007, 80th Leg., ch. 885, § 2.01, eff. April 1, 2009.

§ 102.002. Prohibition on Certain Activities by Sex Offender in Relation to Business

A sex offender may not:

(1) wholly or partly own a sexually oriented business; or

(2) serve as a director, officer, operator, manager, or employee of a sexually oriented business.

Added by Acts 2007, 80th Leg., ch. 885, § 2.01, eff. April 1, 2009.

§ 102.003. Prohibition on Certain Activities by Business in Relation to Sex Offender

If a sexually oriented business knows that a person is a sex offender, the business may not:

(1) contract with that person to operate or manage the business as an independent contractor; or

(2) employ that person as an officer, operator, manager, or other employee.

Added by Acts 2007, 80th Leg., ch. 885, § 2.01, eff. April 1, 2009.

§ 102.004. Injunction or Other Relief

(a) The attorney general or appropriate district or county attorney, in the name of the state, may bring an action for an injunction or other process against a person who violates or threatens to violate Section 102.002 or 102.003.

(b) The action may be brought in a district court in:

(1) Travis County; or

(2) a county in which any part of the violation or threatened violation occurs.

(c) The court may grant any prohibitory or mandatory relief warranted by the facts, including a temporary restraining order, temporary injunction, or permanent injunction.

Added by Acts 2007, 80th Leg., ch. 885, § 2.01, eff. April 1, 2009.

§ 102.005. Criminal Penalties

(a) A sex offender commits an offense if the sex offender violates Section 102.002.

(b) A sexually oriented business commits an offense if the business violates Section 102.003.

(c) An offense under this section is a Class A misdemeanor.

Added by Acts 2007, 80th Leg., ch. 885, § 2.01, eff. April 1, 2009.

CHAPTER 103. APPRAISALS IMPROPERLY INDUCED BY MORTGAGE LENDERS

§ 103.001. Definitions

In this chapter:

(1) "Lender" means a person who lends money for or invests money in mortgage loans.

(2) "Mortgage loan" means a loan secured by a deed of trust, security deed, or other lien on real property.

Added by Acts 2007, 80th Leg., ch. 885, § 2.01, eff. April 1, 2009.

§ 103.002. Criminal Penalty

(a) A lender commits an offense if in connection with a mortgage loan transaction the lender pays or offers to pay a person, including an individual licensed or certified by the Texas Appraiser Licensing and Certification Board or the Texas Real Estate Commission, a fee or other consideration for appraisal services and the payment:

(1) is contingent on a minimum, maximum, or pre-agreed estimate of value of property securing the loan; and

(2) interferes with the person's ability or obligation to provide an independent and impartial opinion of the property's value.

(b) An offense under this section is a Class A misdemeanor.

(c) An instruction a lender gives to a real estate appraiser regarding a legal or other regulatory requirement for the appraisal of property, or any other communication between a lender or real estate appraiser necessary or appropriate under a law, regulation, or underwriting standard applicable to a real estate appraisal, does not constitute interference by a lender for purposes of Subsection (a)(2).

Added by Acts 2007, 80th Leg., ch. 885, § 2.01, eff. April 1, 2009.

CHAPTER 104. RESTRICTIONS ON CHARGES BY MOTOR FUEL FRANCHISORS

§ 104.001. Definitions

In this chapter:

(1) "Franchise":

(A) includes:

(i) a contract under which a distributor or retailer is authorized to occupy marketing premises in connection with the sale, consignment, or distribution of motor fuel under a trademark owned or controlled by a franchisor-refiner or by a refiner who supplies motor fuel to a distributor who authorizes the occupancy;

(ii) a contract relating to the supply of motor fuel to be sold, consigned, or distributed under a trademark owned or controlled by a refiner; and

(iii) the unexpired portion of any franchise transferred or assigned under the franchise provisions or any applicable provision of state or federal law authorizing the transfer or assignment regardless of the franchise provisions; and

(B) does not include a contract:

(i) that is made in the distribution of motor fuels through a card-lock or key-operated pumping system; and

(ii) to which a refiner or producer of the motor fuel is not a party.

(2) "Franchisee" means a distributor or retailer who is authorized under a franchise to use a trademark in connection with the sale, consignment, or distribution of motor fuel.

(3) "Franchisor" means a refiner or distributor who authorizes under a franchise the use of a trademark in connection with the sale, consignment, or distribution of motor fuel.

(4) "Motor fuel" includes diesel fuel and gasoline:

(A) delivered to a service station by a franchisor; and

(B) usable as a propellant of a motor vehicle.

Added by Acts 2007, 80th Leg., ch. 885, § 2.01, eff. April 1, 2009.

§ 104.002. Prohibited Fees, Charges, and Discounts

(a) For purposes of this section, wholesale price is computed by adding to the invoice price or purchase price per gallon charged to a franchisee who buys motor fuel any excise tax paid by the buyer and any reasonable freight charges paid by the buyer, and subtracting that portion of any refund, rebate, or subsidy not designed to offset the fee, charge, or discount described by this section.

(b) Except as provided by Subsection (c), a franchisor may not require a franchisee to pay to the franchisor a fee, charge, or discount for:

(1) honoring a credit card issued by the franchisor; or

(2) submitting to the franchisor, for payment or credit to the franchisee's account, documents or other evidence of indebtedness of the holder of a credit card issued by the franchisor.

(c) A franchisor may require a franchisee to pay the fee, charge, or discount if the franchisor, in consideration of competitive prices in the relevant market, has adjusted the wholesale prices charged or rebates credited to franchisees for motor fuel by amounts that on average for franchisees in this state substantially offset the fee, charge, or discount.

Added by Acts 2007, 80th Leg., ch. 885, § 2.01, eff. April 1, 2009.

§ 104.003. Civil Action

(a) A franchisee may bring a civil action against a franchisor who violates Section 104.002, without regard to the amount in controversy, in the district court in any county in which the franchisor or franchisee transacts business. An action under this section must be commenced and prosecuted not later than the second anniversary of the date the cause of action accrues against the franchisor.

(b) The court shall award to a franchisee who prevails in an action under this section:

(1) the amount of actual damages;

(2) equitable relief as determined by the court to be necessary to remedy the effects of the franchisor's violation of Section 104.002, including a declaratory judgment, permanent injunctive relief, and temporary injunctive relief; and

(3) court costs and attorney's fees that are reasonable in relation to the amount of work expended.

(c) In addition to the remedies provided under Subsection (b), on finding that the defendant wilfully and knowingly committed the violation, the trier of fact shall award not more than three times the amount of actual damages.

(d) In an action under this section, the franchisor has the burden of establishing the offset described by Section 104.002 as an affirmative defense.

Added by Acts 2007, 80th Leg., ch. 885, § 2.01, eff. April 1, 2009.

CHAPTER 105. REFUELING SERVICES FOR PERSONS WITH DISABILITIES

Section

§ 105.001. Definitions

(a) In this chapter:

(1) "Refueling service" means the service of pumping motor vehicle fuel into the fuel tank of a motor vehicle.

(2) "Service station" means a gasoline service station or other facility that offers gasoline or other motor vehicle fuel for sale to the public from the facility.

(b) In this chapter, with respect to the operation of a service station, "person" means an individual, firm, partnership, association, trustee, or corporation.

Added by Acts 2007, 80th Leg., ch. 885, § 2.01, eff. April 1, 2009.

§ 105.002. Applicability of Chapter

(a) This chapter applies to a service station that ordinarily provides pump island service, except that such a service station is not required to provide refueling service under this chapter during any regularly scheduled hours during which, for security reasons, the service station does not provide pump island service.

(b) This chapter does not apply to:

(1) a service station or other facility that:

(A) never provides pump island service; and

(B) has only remotely controlled pumps; or

(2) a refueling service used to provide liquefied gas, as defined by Section 162.001, Tax Code.

Added by Acts 2007, 80th Leg., ch. 885, § 2.01, eff. April 1, 2009.

§ 105.003. Refueling Services

(a) A person who operates a service station shall provide, on request, refueling service to a person with a disability who is the driver of a vehicle and displays:

(1) a license plate issued under Section 504.201 or 504.203, Transportation Code; or

(2) a disabled parking placard issued under Section 681.004, Transportation Code.

(b) The price charged for motor vehicle fuel provided under Subsection (a) may not exceed the price the service station would otherwise generally charge the public for the purchase of motor vehicle fuel without refueling service.

Added by Acts 2007, 80th Leg., ch. 885, § 2.01, eff. April 1, 2009.

§ 105.004. Notice

(a) The Department of Agriculture shall provide a notice that states the provisions of this chapter to each person who operates a service station.

(b) The Texas Department of Transportation shall provide a notice that states the provisions of this chapter to each person with a disability who is issued:

(1) license plates under Section 504.201, Transportation Code; or

(2) a disabled parking placard under Section 681.004, Transportation Code.

Added by Acts 2007, 80th Leg., ch. 885, § 2.01, eff. April 1, 2009.

§ 105.005. Offense; Penalty

(a) A person commits an offense if the person violates Section 105.003 and the person is:

(1) a manager responsible for setting the service policy of a service station subject to this chapter; or

(2) an employee acting independently against the established service policy of the service station.

(b) An offense under this section is a Class C misdemeanor.

Added by Acts 2007, 80th Leg., ch. 885, § 2.01, eff. April 1, 2009.

§ 105.006. Enforcement

In addition to enforcement by the prosecuting attorney who represents the state, this chapter may be enforced by the attorney general.

Added by Acts 2007, 80th Leg., ch. 885, § 2.01, eff. April 1, 2009.

TITLE 6. SALE OR TRANSFER OF GOODS

Acts 2007, 80th Leg., ch. 885, § 2.01 added this Title effective April 1, 2009.

CHAPTER 201. SALE OF ITEMS AT FLEA MARKETS

§ 201.001. Definition

In this chapter, "flea market" means a location at which booths or similar spaces are rented or otherwise made temporarily available to two or more persons and at which the persons offer tangible personal property for sale.

Added by Acts 2007, 80th Leg., ch. 885, § 2.01, eff. April 1, 2009.

§ 201.002. Inapplicability of Chapter to Certain Items

This chapter does not apply to the sale or offer for sale of a nutritional supplement or vitamin.

Added by Acts 2007, 80th Leg., ch. 885, § 2.01, eff. April 1, 2009.

§ 201.003. Sale of Certain Items Prohibited

(a) A person commits an offense if the person sells or offers for sale at a flea market:

(1) infant formula or baby food of a type usually consumed by children younger than two years of age;

(2) a drug, as defined by Section 431.002, Health and Safety Code; or

(3) contact lenses, including disposable contact lenses.

(b) It is a defense to prosecution under this section that the person selling the item:

(1) is authorized in writing to sell the item at retail by the manufacturer of the item or the manufacturer's authorized distributor and the authorization states the person's name; and

(2) provides the authorization for examination by any person at the flea market who requests to see the authorization.

(c) It is a defense to prosecution under this section that only a sample of the item or a catalog or brochure displaying the item was available at the flea market and the item sold was not delivered to the buyer at the flea market.

(d) An offense under this section is a misdemeanor punishable by a fine not to exceed $100.

(e) The penalty provided by this section is in addition to any other sanction provided by law.

Added by Acts 2007, 80th Leg., ch. 885, § 2.01, eff. April 1, 2009.

§ 201.004. Fraudulent Authorization for Sale of Certain Items at Retail

(a) A person commits an offense if the person provides to another person an authorization under Section 201.003(b) and:

(1) the authorization is forged or contains a false statement; or

(2) the person displaying the authorization obtained the authorization by fraud.

(b) An offense under this section is a misdemeanor punishable by a fine not to exceed $100.

Added by Acts 2007, 80th Leg., ch. 885, § 2.01, eff. April 1, 2009.

§ 201.005. Provision of Booth or Similar Space Not an Offense

A person does not commit an offense under this chapter solely because the person provides booths or similar spaces at a flea market.

Added by Acts 2007, 80th Leg., ch. 885, § 2.01, eff. April 1, 2009.

§ 201.006. Investigation Records Required

A law enforcement agency investigating a violation of this chapter shall maintain a record of the investigation. The record is public information.

Added by Acts 2007, 80th Leg., ch. 885, § 2.01, eff. April 1, 2009.

CHAPTER 202. SALES OF MOTOR VEHICLES WITH STOPLAMP COVERINGS

§ 202.001. Sale of Motor Vehicle with Certain Stoplamp Covering Prohibited

(a) In this section, "motor vehicle" has the meaning assigned by Section 541.201, Transportation Code.

(b) A person in the business of selling motor vehicles may not sell a motor vehicle with a transparent or semitransparent covering:

(1) placed over a stoplamp that is mounted on the rear center line of the vehicle either in or on the rear window or within six inches from the rear window of the vehicle for the purpose of emitting light when the vehicle's brakes are applied; and

(2) on which is impressed or imprinted a name, trade name, logotype, or other message that a person behind the vehicle can read when the stoplamp is illuminated.

(c) A person who violates this section commits an offense. An offense under this section is a Class C misdemeanor.

Added by Acts 2007, 80th Leg., ch. 885, § 2.01, eff. April 1, 2009.

CHAPTER 203. EXPORTING ARTICLES WITHOUT INSPECTION

§ 203.001. Criminal Penalty for Exporting Articles Without Required Inspection

(a) A person commits an offense if the person:

(1) exports from this state, or ships for the purpose of exportation to a state other than this state or to a foreign port, an article of commerce that by law of this state is required to be inspected by a public inspector; and

(2) does not have the article inspected as required by law.

(b) An offense under this section is a misdemeanor punishable by a fine not to exceed $100.

Added by Acts 2007, 80th Leg., ch. 885, § 2.01, eff. April 1, 2009.

TITLE 7. RECEIPTS, DOCUMENTS OF TITLE, AND OTHER INSTRUMENTS

Acts 2007, 80th Leg., ch. 885, § 2.01 added this Title effective April 1, 2009.

CHAPTER 251. WAREHOUSE RECEIPTS

§ 251.001. Definitions

In this chapter:

(1) "Goods" means all things treated as movable for purposes of a contract of storage or transportation.

(2) "Issue" includes aiding in the issuance of a warehouse receipt.

(3) "Warehouse receipt" means a receipt issued by a warehouseman.

(4) "Warehouseman" means a person engaged in the business of storing goods for hire. The term includes an officer, agent, or employee of a warehouseman.

Added by Acts 2007, 80th Leg., ch. 885, § 2.01, eff. April 1, 2009.

§ 251.002. Warehouseman Issuing Fraudulent Warehouse Receipt

(a) A warehouseman may not, with intent to defraud, issue a warehouse receipt that contains a false statement.

(b) A warehouseman who violates this section commits an offense. An offense under this section is a misdemeanor punishable by:

(1) confinement in the county jail for a term of not more than one year;

(2) a fine not to exceed $1,000; or

(3) both the fine and confinement.

Added by Acts 2007, 80th Leg., ch. 885, § 2.01, eff. April 1, 2009.

§ 251.003. Warehouseman Failing to State Warehouseman's Ownership of Goods on Receipt

(a) A warehouseman may not knowingly issue a negotiable warehouse receipt describing goods the warehouseman owns, whether solely, jointly, or in common, and is storing, unless the warehouseman states the warehouseman's ownership of the goods on the receipt.

(b) A warehouseman who violates this section commits an offense. An offense under this section is a misdemeanor punishable by:

(1) confinement in the county jail for a term of not more than one year; or

(2) a fine not to exceed $1,000.

Added by Acts 2007, 80th Leg., ch. 885, § 2.01, eff. April 1, 2009.

§ 251.004. Warehouseman Issuing Warehouse Receipt Without Control of Goods

(a) A warehouseman may not issue a warehouse receipt for goods if the warehouseman knows at the time of issuance that the goods described in the receipt are not under the warehouseman's control.

(b) A warehouseman who violates this section commits an offense. An offense under this section is a felony punishable by:

(1) imprisonment in the Texas Department of Criminal Justice for a term of not more than five years;

(2) a fine not to exceed $5,000; or

(3) both the fine and imprisonment.

Added by Acts 2007, 80th Leg., ch. 885, § 2.01, eff. April 1, 2009.

§ 251.005. Warehouseman Issuing Duplicate or Additional Warehouse Receipt

(a) A warehouseman may not issue a duplicate or additional negotiable warehouse receipt for goods if the warehouseman knows at the time of issuance that a previously issued negotiable warehouse receipt describing the goods is outstanding and uncanceled.

(b) This section does not apply if:

(1) the word "duplicate" is plainly placed on the duplicate or additional negotiable warehouse receipt; or

(2) goods described in the outstanding and uncanceled negotiable warehouse receipt were delivered under a court order on proof that the receipt was lost or destroyed.

(c) A warehouseman who violates this section commits an offense. An offense under this section is a felony punishable by:

(1) imprisonment in the Texas Department of Criminal Justice for a term of not more than five years;

(2) a fine not to exceed $5,000; or

(3) both the fine and imprisonment.

Added by Acts 2007, 80th Leg., ch. 885, § 2.01, eff. April 1, 2009.

§ 251.006. Warehouseman Wrongfully Delivering Goods

(a) A warehouseman may not knowingly deliver goods that are described in a negotiable warehouse receipt and stored with the warehouseman, unless the receipt is surrendered to the warehouseman at or before the time the warehouseman delivers the goods.

(b) This section does not apply if the goods are:

(1) delivered under a court order on proof that the negotiable warehouse receipt describing the goods was lost or destroyed;

(2) lawfully sold to satisfy a warehouseman's lien; or

(3) disposed of because of the perishable or hazardous nature of the goods.

(c) A warehouseman who violates this section commits an offense. An offense under this section is a misdemeanor punishable by:

(1) confinement in the county jail for a term of not more than one year;

(2) a fine not to exceed $1,000; or

(3) both the fine and confinement.

Added by Acts 2007, 80th Leg., ch. 885, § 2.01, eff. April 1, 2009.

§ 251.007. Failure to Disclose Lack of Ownership of Goods

(a) A person who obtains a negotiable warehouse receipt describing goods the person does not own may not, with intent to defraud, negotiate the receipt for value without disclosing the person's lack of ownership.

(b) A person who violates this section commits an offense. An offense under this section is a misdemeanor punishable by:

(1) confinement in the county jail for a term of not more than one year;

(2) a fine not to exceed $1,000; or

(3) both the fine and confinement.

Added by Acts 2007, 80th Leg., ch. 885, § 2.01, eff. April 1, 2009.

§ 251.008. Failure to Disclose Existence of Lien on Goods

(a) A person who obtains a negotiable warehouse receipt describing goods subject to a lien may not, with intent to defraud, negotiate the receipt for value without disclosing the lien's existence.

(b) A person who violates this section commits an offense. An offense under this section is a misdemeanor punishable by:

(1) confinement in the county jail for a term of not more than one year;

(2) a fine not to exceed $1,000; or

(3) both the fine and confinement.

Added by Acts 2007, 80th Leg., ch. 885, § 2.01, eff. April 1, 2009.

CHAPTER 252. BILLS OF LADING

§ 252.001. Definitions

In this chapter:

(1) "Agent" includes an officer, employee, or receiver.

(2) "Bill of lading" means a document evidencing the receipt of goods for shipment issued by a person engaged in the business of transporting or forwarding goods. The term includes an air consignment note, air waybill, or other document for air transportation comparable to a bill of lading for marine or rail transportation.

(3) "Goods" means all things treated as movable for purposes of a contract of storage or transportation.

Added by Acts 2007, 80th Leg., ch. 885, § 2.01, eff. April 1, 2009.

§ 252.002. Duties of Railroad Commission

(a) In this section, "common carrier" does not include a pipeline company or express company.

(b) The Railroad Commission of Texas shall:

(1) prescribe forms, terms, and conditions for authenticating, certifying, or validating bills of lading issued by a common carrier;

(2) regulate the manner by which a common carrier issues bills of lading; and

(3) take other action necessary to carry out the purposes of Chapter 7.

(c) After giving reasonable notice to interested common carriers and to the public, the railroad commission may amend a rule adopted under Subsection (b).

Added by Acts 2007, 80th Leg., ch. 885, § 2.01, eff. April 1, 2009.

§ 252.003. Agent Wrongfully Failing or Refusing to Issue Bill of Lading

(a) In this section, "common carrier" does not include a pipeline company or express company.

(b) An agent of a common carrier may not after lawful demand fail or refuse to issue a bill of lading in accordance with Chapter 7 or a rule of the railroad commission.

(c) An agent who violates this section commits an offense. An offense under this section is a misdemeanor punishable by:

(1) confinement in the county jail for a term of not more than six months;

(2) a fine not to exceed $200; or

(3) both the fine and confinement.

Added by Acts 2007, 80th Leg., ch. 885, § 2.01, eff. April 1, 2009.

§ 252.004. Agent Issuing Fraudulent Bill of Lading

(a) In this section, "common carrier" does not include a pipeline company or express company.

(b) An agent of a common carrier may not with intent to defraud a person:

(1) issue a bill of lading;

(2) incorrectly describe goods or the quantity of goods in a bill of lading; or

(3) issue a bill of lading without authority.

(c) An agent who violates this section commits an offense. An offense under this section is a felony punishable by imprisonment in the Texas Department of Criminal Justice for a term of not more than 10 years or less than two years.

Added by Acts 2007, 80th Leg., ch. 885, § 2.01, eff. April 1, 2009.

§ 252.005. Agent Issuing Order Bill of Lading in Duplicate or Set of Parts

(a) Except where customary in overseas transportation, an agent of a common carrier may not knowingly issue or aid in issuing an order bill of lading in duplicate or in a set of parts.

(b) An agent who violates this section commits an offense. An offense under this section is a felony punishable by:

(1) imprisonment in the Texas Department of Criminal Justice for a term of not more than five years; and

(2) a fine not to exceed $5,000.

Added by Acts 2007, 80th Leg., ch. 885, § 2.01, eff. April 1, 2009.

§ 252.006. Fraudulently Inducing Issuance of Bill of Lading

(a) A person may not, with intent to defraud, induce an agent of a common carrier to:

(1) issue to the person a bill of lading; or

(2) materially misrepresent in a bill of lading issued on behalf of the common carrier the quantity of goods described in the bill of lading.

(b) A person who violates this section commits an offense. An offense under this section is a felony punishable by imprisonment in the Texas Department of Criminal Justice for a term of not more than five years or less than two years.

Added by Acts 2007, 80th Leg., ch. 885, § 2.01, eff. April 1, 2009.

§ 252.007. Fraudulently Negotiating or Transferring Bill of Lading

(a) A person may not, with intent to defraud, negotiate or transfer a bill of lading that:

(1) is issued in violation of Chapter 7; or

(2) contains a false, material statement of fact.

(b) A person who violates this section commits an offense. An offense under this section is a felony punishable by imprisonment in the Texas Department of Criminal Justice for a term of not more than 10 years.

Added by Acts 2007, 80th Leg., ch. 885, § 2.01, eff. April 1, 2009.

CHAPTER 253. PROTESTED OUT-OF-STATE DRAFTS

§ 253.001. Damages on Protested Out-of-State Drafts

The holder of a protested draft is entitled to damages in an amount equal to 10 percent of the amount of the draft, plus interest and the costs of suit, if:

(1) the draft was drawn by a merchant in this state on the merchant's agent or factor outside this state; and

(2) the drawer's or indorser's liability on the draft has been fixed.

Added by Acts 2007, 80th Leg., ch. 885, § 2.01, eff. April 1, 2009.

CHAPTER 254. NOTE OR LIEN IDENTIFYING A PATENT RIGHT

§ 254.001. Identification of Patent Right

(a) A note or lien evidencing or securing the purchase price for a patent right or patent right territory must contain on the face of the note or lien a statement that the note or lien was given for a patent right or patent right territory.

(b) The statement required by Subsection (a):

(1) is notice to a subsequent purchaser of the note or lien of all equities between the original parties to the note or lien; and

(2) subjects a subsequent holder of the note or lien to all defenses available against the original parties to the note or lien.

Added by Acts 2007, 80th Leg., ch. 885, § 2.01, eff. April 1, 2009.

§ 254.002. Failure to Identify Patent Right; Criminal Penalty

(a) A person selling a patent right or patent right territory may not take a note or lien evidencing or securing the purchase price for the patent right or patent right territory without placing on the face of the note or lien the statement required by Section 254.001(a).

(b) A person who violates this section commits an offense. An offense under this section is a misdemeanor punishable by a fine of not less than $25 or more than $200.

Added by Acts 2007, 80th Leg., ch. 885, § 2.01, eff. April 1, 2009.

TITLE 8. SECURITY INSTRUMENTS

Acts 2007, 80th Leg., ch. 885, § 2.01 added this Title effective April 1, 2009.

CHAPTER 261. UTILITY SECURITY INSTRUMENTS

§ 261.001. Definitions

(a) In this chapter:

(1) "Utility" means a person engaged in this state in:

(A) generating, transmitting, or distributing and selling electric power;

(B) transporting, distributing, and selling, through a local distribution system, natural or other gas for domestic, commercial, industrial, or other use;

(C) owning or operating a pipeline to transmit or sell natural or other gas, natural gas liquids, crude oil, or petroleum products to another pipeline company or to a refinery, local distribution system, municipality, or industrial consumer;

(D) providing telephone or telegraph service to others;

(E) producing, transmitting, or distributing and selling steam or water;

(F) operating a railroad; or

(G) providing sewer service to others.

(2) "Utility security instrument" means:

(A) a mortgage, deed of trust, security agreement, or other instrument executed to secure payment of a bond, note, or other obligation of a utility; or

(B) an instrument that supplements or amends an instrument described by Paragraph (A), including a signed copy of the instrument.

(b) The definitions in Chapters 1 and 9 apply to this chapter.

Added by Acts 2007, 80th Leg., ch. 885, § 2.01, eff. April 1, 2009.

§ 261.002. Act Constituting Filing

For purposes of this chapter, a utility security instrument is filed when it is deposited for filing with the secretary of state.

Added by Acts 2007, 80th Leg., ch. 885, § 2.01, eff. April 1, 2009.

§ 261.003. Applicability of Chapter

A utility is subject to the requirements and entitled to the benefits of this chapter:

(1) only if the utility files with the secretary of state a utility security instrument that states conspicuously on its title page: "This Instrument Grants A Security Interest By A Utility"; and

(2) only with respect to collateral covered by a utility security instrument filed by the utility in accordance with Subdivision (1).

Added by Acts 2007, 80th Leg., ch. 885, § 2.01, eff. April 1, 2009.

§ 261.004. Filing Utility Security Instrument With Secretary of State: Perfection and Notice

(a) Subject to Subsection (b), the filing with the secretary of state of a utility security instrument executed by a utility and described by Section 261.003(1) and payment of the filing fee prescribed by Section 261.008:

(1) constitute perfection of a security interest created by the instrument in any personal property:

(A) in which a security interest may be perfected by filing under Chapter 9, including any goods that are or will become a fixture;

(B) that is located in this state; and

(C) that was owned by the utility when the instrument was executed or is to be acquired by the utility after the instrument is executed; and

(2) if the instrument is proven, acknowledged, or certified as otherwise required by law for the recording of real property mortgages, serve as notice to all persons of the existence of the instrument and the security interest granted by the instrument in any real property, or in any fixture on or to be placed on the property, that:

(A) is located in this state; and

(B) was owned by the utility when the instrument was executed or is to be acquired by the utility after the instrument is executed.

(b) For perfection or notice under Subsection (a) to be effective as to a particular item of property, the filed utility security instrument must:

(1) identify the property by type, character, or description if the property is presently owned personal property, including a fixture, and for that purpose any description of personal property or real property is sufficient, regardless of whether specific, if it reasonably identifies what is described;

(2) provide a description of the property if the property is presently owned real property; or

(3) if the property is to be acquired after the instrument is executed, state conspicuously on its title page: "This Instrument Contains After–Acquired Property Provisions."

(c) A filing under this section satisfies any requirement of:

(1) a filing of the utility security instrument or a financing statement in the office of a county clerk if that filing would otherwise be necessary to perfect a security interest; and

(2) a recording of the utility security instrument in the office of a county clerk if that recording would otherwise make the instrument effective as to all creditors and subsequent purchasers for valuable consideration without notice.

Added by Acts 2007, 80th Leg., ch. 885, § 2.01, eff. April 1, 2009.

§ 261.005. Duration of Perfection and Notice

The perfection and notice provided by the filing of a utility security instrument under Section 261.004 take effect on the date of filing and remain in effect without any renewal, refiling, or continuation statement until the interest granted as security is released by the filing of a termination statement, or a release of all or a part of the property, signed by the secured party.

Added by Acts 2007, 80th Leg., ch. 885, § 2.01, eff. April 1, 2009.

§ 261.006. Priorities and Remedies Applicable to Certain Perfected Security Interests

The provisions of Chapter 9 relating to priorities and remedies apply to security interests in personal property, including fixtures, perfected under Section 261.004.

Added by Acts 2007, 80th Leg., ch. 885, § 2.01, eff. April 1, 2009.

§ 261.007. Notice of Name Change, Merger, or Consolidation

(a) A utility that changes its name or merges or consolidates after filing a utility security instrument under Section 261.004 shall promptly file with the secretary of state a written statement of the name change, merger, or consolidation. The written statement must:

(1) be signed by the secured party and the utility;

(2) identify the appropriate utility security instrument by file number; and

(3) state the name of the utility after the name change, merger, or consolidation.

(b) Unless a written statement is filed under Subsection (a) not later than four months after the effective date of the name change, merger, or consolidations, the filing of a utility security instrument before the name change, merger, or consolidation does not constitute perfection or serve as notice under Section 261.004 of a security interest in property acquired by the utility more than four months after the name change, merger, or consolidation.

Added by Acts 2007, 80th Leg., ch. 885, § 2.01, eff. April 1, 2009.

§ 261.008. Endorsement and Filing by Secretary of State; Fees

(a) The secretary of state shall endorse on a utility security instrument and any statement of name change, merger, or consolidation filed with the secretary of state:

(1) the day and hour of receipt; and

(2) the assigned file number.

(b) In the absence of other evidence, an endorsement under Subsection (a) is conclusive proof of the time and fact of filing.

(c) The secretary of state shall file in adequate filing devices and retain in the secretary of state's office all utility security instruments and statements of name change, merger, or consolidation filed with the secretary of state.

(d) The secretary of state shall charge a $25 fee to:

(1) file and index:

(A) a utility security instrument;

(B) an instrument that supplements or amends a utility security instrument; or

(C) a statement of name change, merger, or consolidation; and

(2) stamp a copy of a document described by Subdivision (1), provided by the secured party or the utility, to indicate the date and place of filing.

Added by Acts 2007, 80th Leg., ch. 885, § 2.01, eff. April 1, 2009.

§ 261.009. Certificate of Filing; Fee

(a) On request of any person, the secretary of state shall issue a certificate that:

(1) indicates whether on the date and hour stated in the request, there is on file any presently effective utility security instrument naming a particular utility; and

(2) if there is, states:

(A) the date and hour the utility security instrument was filed; and

(B) the names and addresses of each secured party.

(b) The fee for a certificate under this section is:

(1) $10, if the request for the certificate is in the standard form prescribed by the secretary of state; or

(2) $25, if the request is not in the standard form.

Added by Acts 2007, 80th Leg., ch. 885, § 2.01, eff. April 1, 2009.

§ 261.010. Copy of Filed Utility Security Instrument; Fee

(a) On request and payment of the fee prescribed by Subsection (b), the secretary of state shall provide a person with a copy of any filed utility security instrument.

(b) The fee for a copy under this section is $1.50 per page, but may not be less than $5 or more than $100 for each request concerning a particular utility.

Added by Acts 2007, 80th Leg., ch. 885, § 2.01, eff. April 1, 2009.

§ 261.011. Notice of Utility Security Instrument Affecting Real Property

(a) If a utility security instrument filed with the secretary of state under Section 261.004 grants a security interest in real property owned by the utility, a notice of utility security instrument affecting real property must be recorded in the office of the county clerk in the county in which the real property is located. The notice must state:

(1) the name of the utility that executed the utility security instrument;

(2) that a utility security instrument affecting real property in the county has been executed by the utility; and

(3) that the utility security instrument was filed, and other security instruments may be on file, with the secretary of state.

(b) A notice recorded under Subsection (a) is sufficient to provide notice of any other security instrument filed with the secretary of state that:

(1) was executed by the utility; and

(2) grants a security interest in any real property located in the county in which the notice was recorded or in any fixture on the property.

(c) The county clerk shall record and index a notice described by Subsection (a) in the same records and indices as the clerk records and indexes mortgages on real property.

(d) The county clerk shall maintain a separate index of utility security instruments and continuation statements recorded under prior law.

Added by Acts 2007, 80th Leg., ch. 885, § 2.01, eff. April 1, 2009.

TITLE 9. APPLICABILITY OF LAW TO COMMERCIAL TRANSACTIONS

Acts 2007, 80th Leg., ch. 885, § 2.01 added this Title effective April 1, 2009.

CHAPTER 271. RIGHTS OF PARTIES TO CHOOSE LAW APPLICABLE TO CERTAIN TRANSACTIONS

§ 271.001. Definition

In this chapter, "qualified transaction" means a transaction under which a party:

(1) pays or receives, or is obligated to pay or is entitled to receive, consideration with an aggregate value of at least $1 million; or

(2) lends, advances, borrows, or receives, or is obligated to lend or advance or is entitled to borrow or receive, money or credit with an aggregate value of at least $1 million.

Added by Acts 2007, 80th Leg., ch. 885, § 2.01, eff. April 1, 2009.

§ 271.002. Substantially Similar or Related Transactions

For purposes of this chapter, two or more substantially similar or related transactions are considered a single transaction if the transactions:

(1) are entered into contemporaneously; and

(2) have at least one common party.

Added by Acts 2007, 80th Leg., ch. 885, § 2.01, eff. April 1, 2009.

§ 271.003. Conflict–of–Laws Rules

For purposes of this chapter, a reference to the law of a particular jurisdiction does not include that jurisdiction's conflict-of-laws rules.

Added by Acts 2007, 80th Leg., ch. 885, § 2.01, eff. April 1, 2009.

§ 271.004. Determination of Reasonable Relation of Transaction to Particular Jurisdiction

(a) For purposes of this chapter, a transaction bears a reasonable relation to a particular jurisdiction if the transaction, the subject matter of the transaction, or a party to the transaction is reasonably related to that jurisdiction.

(b) A transaction bears a reasonable relation to a particular jurisdiction if:

(1) a party to the transaction is a resident of that jurisdiction;

(2) a party to the transaction has the party's place of business or, if that party has more than one place of business, the party's chief executive office or an office from which the party conducts a substantial part of the negotiations relating to the transaction, in that jurisdiction;

(3) all or part of the subject matter of the transaction is located in that jurisdiction;

(4) a party to the transaction is required to perform in that jurisdiction a substantial part of the party's obligations relating to the transaction, such as delivering payments; or

(5) a substantial part of the negotiations relating to the transaction occurred in that jurisdiction and an agreement relating to the transaction was signed in that jurisdiction by a party to the transaction.

Added by Acts 2007, 80th Leg., ch. 885, § 2.01, eff. April 1, 2009.

§ 271.005. Law Governing Issue Relating to Qualified Transaction

(a) Except as provided by Section 271.007, 271.008(b), 271.009, 271.010, or 271.011 or by Chapter 272, the law of a particular jurisdiction governs an issue relating to a qualified transaction if:

(1) the parties to the transaction agree in writing that the law of that jurisdiction governs the issue, including the validity or enforceability of an agreement relating to the transaction or a provision of the agreement; and

(2) the transaction bears a reasonable relation to that jurisdiction.

(b) The law of a particular jurisdiction governs an issue described by this section regardless of whether the application of that law is contrary to a fundamental or public policy of this state or of any other jurisdiction.

Added by Acts 2007, 80th Leg., ch. 885, § 2.01, eff. April 1, 2009.

§ 271.006. Law Governing Interpretation or Construction of Agreement Relating to Qualified Transaction

Except as provided by Section 271.008(b), 271.009, 271.010, or 271.011 and by Chapter 272, if the parties to a qualified transaction agree in writing that the law of a particular jurisdiction governs the interpretation or construction of an agreement relating to the transaction or a provision of the agreement, the law of that jurisdiction governs that issue regardless of whether the transaction bears a reasonable relation to that jurisdiction.

Added by Acts 2007, 80th Leg., ch. 885, § 2.01, eff. April 1, 2009.

§ 271.007. Law Governing Validity or Enforceability of Term of Agreement Relating to Qualified Transaction

(a) Except as provided by Section 271.008(b), 271.009, 271.010, or 271.011 or by Chapter 272, this section applies if:

(1) the parties to a qualified transaction agree in writing that the law of a particular jurisdiction governs the validity or enforceability of an agreement relating to the transaction or a provision of the agreement;

(2) the transaction bears a reasonable relation to that jurisdiction; and

(3) a term of the agreement or of that provision is invalid or unenforceable under the law of that jurisdiction but is valid or enforceable under the law of the jurisdiction that has the most significant relation to the transaction, the subject matter of the transaction, and the parties.

(b) If this section applies:

(1) the law of the jurisdiction that has the most significant relation to the transaction, the subject matter of the transaction, and the parties governs the validity or enforceability of a term described by Subsection (a)(3); and

(2) the law of the jurisdiction that the parties agree would govern the validity or enforceability of the agreement or provision governs the validity or enforceability of the other terms of the agreement or provision.

Added by Acts 2007, 80th Leg., ch. 885, § 2.01, eff. April 1, 2009.

§ 271.008. Applicability to Certain Real Property Transactions; Exceptions

(a) Sections 271.004–271.007 apply to the determination of the law that governs an issue relating to a transaction involving real property other than a matter described by Subsection (b), including the validity or enforceability of an indebtedness incurred in consideration for the transfer of, or the payment of which is secured by a lien on, real property.

(b) Sections 271.004–271.007 do not apply to the determination of the law that governs:

(1) whether a transaction transfers or creates an interest in real property for security purposes or otherwise;

(2) the nature of an interest in real property that is transferred or created by a transaction;

(3) the method for foreclosure of a lien on real property;

(4) the nature of an interest in real property that results from foreclosure; or

(5) the manner and effect of recording or failing to record evidence of a transaction that transfers or creates an interest in real property.

Added by Acts 2007, 80th Leg., ch. 885, § 2.01, eff. April 1, 2009.

§ 271.009. Exception: Marriage or Adoption

Sections 271.004–271.007 do not apply to the determination of the law that governs:

(1) the validity of a marriage or an adoption;

(2) whether a marriage has been terminated; or

(3) the effect of a marriage on property owned by a spouse at the time of the marriage or acquired by either spouse during the marriage.

Added by Acts 2007, 80th Leg., ch. 885, § 2.01, eff. April 1, 2009.

§ 271.010. Exception: Decedent's Estate

Sections 271.004–271.007 do not apply to the determination of the law that governs:

(1) whether an instrument is a will;

(2) the rights of persons under a will; or

(3) the rights of persons in the absence of a will.

Added by Acts 2007, 80th Leg., ch. 885, § 2.01, eff. April 1, 2009.

§ 271.011. Exception: Other Statute Specifying Governing Law

Sections 271.004–271.007 do not apply to the determination of the law that governs an issue that another statute of this state or a statute of the United States provides is governed by the law of a particular jurisdiction.

Added by Acts 2007, 80th Leg., ch. 885, § 2.01, eff. April 1, 2009.

CHAPTER 272. LAW APPLICABLE TO CERTAIN CONTRACTS FOR CONSTRUCTION OR REPAIR OF REAL PROPERTY IMPROVEMENTS

§ 272.001. Voidable Contract Provision

(a) This section applies only to a contract that is principally for the construction or repair of an improvement to real property located in this state.

(b) If a contract contains a provision making the contract or any conflict arising under the contract subject to another state's law, litigation in the courts of another state, or arbitration in another state, that provision is voidable by the party obligated by the contract to perform the construction or repair.

Added by Acts 2007, 80th Leg., ch. 885, § 2.01, eff. April 1, 2009.

§ 272.002. Contract Principally for Construction or Repair of Real Property Improvements

(a) For purposes of this chapter, a contract is principally for the construction or repair of an improvement to real property located in this state if the contract obligates a party, as the party's principal obligation under the contract, to provide labor or labor and materials as a general contractor or subcontractor for the construction or repair of an improvement to real property located in this state.

(b) For purposes of this chapter, a contract is not principally for the construction or repair of an improvement to real property located in this state if the contract:

(1) is a partnership agreement or other agreement governing an entity or trust;

(2) provides for a loan or other extension of credit and the party promising to construct or repair the improvement is doing so as part of the party's agreements with the lender or other person who extends credit; or

(3) is for the management of real property or improvements and the obligation to construct or repair the improvement is part of that management.

(c) Subsections (a) and (b) do not provide an exclusive list of the situations in which a contract is or is not principally for the construction or repair of an improvement to real property located in this state.

Added by Acts 2007, 80th Leg., ch. 885, § 2.01, eff. April 1, 2009.

CHAPTER 273. LAW OR FORUM APPLICABLE TO CERTAIN CONTRACTS FOR DISPOSITION OF GOODS

§ 273.001. Contracts Subject to Chapter

This chapter applies to a contract only if:

(1) the contract is for the sale, lease, exchange, or other disposition for value of goods for the price, rental, or other consideration of $50,000 or less;

(2) any element of the contract's execution occurred in this state;

(3) a party to the contract is:

(A) an individual resident of this state; or

(B) an association or corporation that is created under the laws of this state or has its principal place of business in this state; and

(4) Section 1.301 does not apply to the contract.

Added by Acts 2007, 80th Leg., ch. 885, § 2.01, eff. April 1, 2009.

§ 273.002. Notice of Applicable Law or Forum

If a contract contains a provision making the contract or any conflict arising under the contract subject to another state's laws, litigation in the courts of another state, or arbitration in another state, that provision must be set out conspicuously in print, type, or other form of writing that is boldfaced, capitalized, underlined, or otherwise set out in such a manner that a reasonable person against whom the provision may operate would notice the provision.

Added by Acts 2007, 80th Leg., ch. 885, § 2.01, eff. April 1, 2009.

§ 273.003. Failure to Provide Notice

A contract provision that does not comply with Section 273.002 is voidable by a party against whom the provision is sought to be enforced.

Added by Acts 2007, 80th Leg., ch. 885, § 2.01, eff. April 1, 2009.

CHAPTER 274. LAW APPLICABLE TO CONTRACT MADE OVER INTERNET

§ 274.001. Definition

In this chapter, "Internet" means the largest nonproprietary nonprofit cooperative public computer network, popularly known as the Internet.

Added by Acts 2007, 80th Leg., ch. 885, § 2.01, eff. April 1, 2009.

§ 274.002. Applicability of Chapter; Exception

(a) Except as provided by Subsection (b), this chapter applies only to a contract made solely over the Internet between a person located in this state and a person located outside this state who does not maintain an office or agent in this state for transacting business in this state.

(b) This chapter does not apply to a contract to which Chapter 271 applies.

Added by Acts 2007, 80th Leg., ch. 885, § 2.01, eff. April 1, 2009.

§ 274.003. State Law Governing Contract; Burden of Proof

(a) A contract is governed by the law of this state unless each party to the contract who is located in this state:

(1) is given notice that the law of the state in which another party to the contract is located applies to the contract; and

(2) agrees to the application of that state's law.

(b) A person asserting that the law of another state governs a contract has the burden of proving that notice was given and agreement was obtained as specified by Subsection (a).

Added by Acts 2007, 80th Leg., ch. 885, § 2.01, eff. April 1, 2009.

§ 274.004. Applicability of Other Law to Contract

Section 1.031 and Chapter 273 do not apply to a contract to which this chapter applies.

Added by Acts 2007, 80th Leg., ch. 885, § 2.01, eff. April 1, 2009.

TITLE 10. USE OF TELECOMMUNICATIONS

Acts 2007, 80th Leg., ch. 885, § 2.01 added this Title effective April 1, 2009.

SUBTITLE A. TELEPHONES

CHAPTER 301. TELEPHONE SOLICITATION PRACTICES

SUBCHAPTER A. GENERAL PROVISIONS

§ 301.001. Definitions

In this chapter:

(1) "Automated dial announcing device" means automated equipment used for telephone solicitation or collection that can:

(A) store telephone numbers to be called or produce numbers to be called through use of a random or sequential number generator; and

(B) convey, alone or in conjunction with other equipment, a prerecorded or synthesized voice message to the number called without the use of a live operator.

(2) "Consumer" means a person who is solicited to purchase, lease, or receive a consumer good or service.

(3) "Consumer good or service" means:

(A) real property or tangible or intangible personal property that is normally used for personal, family, or household purposes, including:

(i) personal property intended to be attached to or installed in any real property;

(ii) a cemetery lot; and

(iii) a time-share estate; or

(B) a service related to real or personal property.

(4) "Consumer telephone call" means an unsolicited call made to a residential telephone number by a telephone solicitor to:

(A) solicit a sale of a consumer good or service;

(B) solicit an extension of credit for a consumer good or service; or

(C) obtain information that will or may be used to directly solicit a sale of a consumer good or service or to extend credit for the sale.

(5) "Telephone solicitor" means a person who makes or causes to be made a consumer telephone call, including a call made by an automated dial announcing device.

Added by Acts 2007, 80th Leg., ch. 885, § 2.01, eff. April 1, 2009.

[Sections 301.002 to 301.050 reserved for expansion]

SUBCHAPTER B. PERMITTED AND PROHIBITED PRACTICES

§ 301.051. Telephone Solicitation Requirements

(a) This section does not apply to a consumer telephone call made:

(1) in response to the express request of the consumer;

(2) primarily in connection with an existing debt or contract for which payment or performance has not been completed at the time of the call; or

(3) to a consumer with whom the telephone solicitor has a prior or existing business relationship.

(b) A telephone solicitor may not make a consumer telephone call to a consumer unless:

(1) the telephone solicitor, immediately after making contact with the consumer to whom the call is made, identifies:

(A) himself or herself by name;

(B) the business on whose behalf the telephone solicitor is calling; and

(C) the purpose of the call;

(2) the telephone solicitor makes the call after 12 noon and before 9 p.m. on a Sunday or after 9 a.m. and before 9 p.m. on a weekday or a Saturday; and

(3) for those calls in which an automated dial announcing device is used, the device disconnects the consumer's telephone line within the period specified by Section 55.126, Utilities Code, after either the telephone solicitor or the consumer terminates the call.

Added by Acts 2007, 80th Leg., ch. 885, § 2.01, eff. April 1, 2009.

§ 301.052. Charges to Consumer's Credit Card Account

A person who sells consumer goods or services through the use of a telephone solicitor may not make or submit a charge to a consumer's credit card account unless the seller:

(1) provides that:

(A) the consumer may receive a full refund for returning undamaged and unused goods or canceling services by providing notice to the seller not later than the seventh day after the date the consumer receives the goods or services; and

(B) the seller will process:

(i) a refund not later than the 30th day after the date the seller receives the returned goods from the consumer; or

(ii) a full refund not later than the 30th day after the date the consumer cancels an order for the purchase of services not performed or a pro rata refund for any services not yet performed for the consumer;

(2) provides to the consumer a written contract fully describing the goods or services being offered, the total price to be charged, the name, address, and business telephone number of the seller, and any terms affecting the sale and receives from the consumer a signed copy of the contract; or

(3) is an organization that qualifies for an exemption from federal income taxation under Section 501(c)(3), Internal Revenue Code of 1986, and has obtained that exemption from the Internal Revenue Service.

Added by Acts 2007, 80th Leg., ch. 885, § 2.01, eff. April 1, 2009.

[Sections 301.053 to 301.100 reserved for expansion]

SUBCHAPTER C. ENFORCEMENT

§ 301.101. Investigation by Attorney General's Office

The attorney general's office shall investigate a complaint relating to a violation of this chapter.

Added by Acts 2007, 80th Leg., ch. 885, § 2.01, eff. April 1, 2009.

§ 301.102. Injunctive Relief

(a) The attorney general's office may petition a district court for a temporary restraining order to restrain a continuing violation of this chapter.

(b) A district court, on petition of the attorney general's office and on finding that a person is violating this chapter, may:

(1) issue an injunction prohibiting the person from continuing the violation; or

(2) grant any other injunctive relief warranted by the facts.

Added by Acts 2007, 80th Leg., ch. 885, § 2.01, eff. April 1, 2009.

§ 301.103. Civil Penalty; Restitution

(a) A person who knowingly violates this chapter is liable for a civil penalty of not more than $10,000 for each violation.

(b) In addition to bringing an action for injunctive relief under Section 301.102, the attorney general's office may seek restitution and petition a district court for the assessment of a civil penalty as provided by this chapter.

Added by Acts 2007, 80th Leg., ch. 885, § 2.01, eff. April 1, 2009.

§ 301.104. Civil Action

A consumer injured by a violation of this chapter may bring an action for recovery of damages. The damages awarded may not be less than the amount the consumer paid the person who sold the consumer goods or services through the use of the telephone solicitor, plus reasonable attorney's fees and court costs.

Added by Acts 2007, 80th Leg., ch. 885, § 2.01, eff. April 1, 2009.

§ 301.105. Venue

Venue for an action brought under this chapter is in:

(1) the county in which the consumer telephone call originated;

(2) the county in which the consumer telephone call was received; or

(3) Travis County.

Added by Acts 2007, 80th Leg., ch. 885, § 2.01, eff. April 1, 2009.

CHAPTER 302. REGULATION OF TELEPHONE SOLICITATION

SUBCHAPTER A. GENERAL PROVISIONS

SUBCHAPTER B. EXEMPTIONS

SUBCHAPTER C. REGISTRATION

SUBCHAPTER D. DISCLOSURES REQUIRED IN REGISTRATION STATEMENT

SUBCHAPTER A. GENERAL PROVISIONS

§ 302.001. Definitions

In this chapter:

(1) "Item" means property or a service. The term includes a coupon book to be used with a business.

(2) "Owner" means a person who has control of or is entitled to, by ownership or other claim, at least 10 percent of a seller's net income.

(3) "Purchaser" means a person who:

(A) is solicited to become or becomes obligated for the purchase or rental of an item; or

(B) is offered an opportunity to claim or receive an item.

(4) "Salesperson" means a person who is employed or authorized by a seller to make a telephone solicitation.

(5) "Seller" means a person who makes a telephone solicitation on the person's own behalf.

(6) "Supervised financial institution" means a bank, trust company, savings and loan association, credit union, industrial loan company, personal property broker, consumer finance lender, commercial finance lender, insurer, or other financial institution that is subject to supervision by an official or agency of this state or the United States.

(7) "Telephone solicitation" means a telephone call a seller or salesperson initiates to induce a person to purchase, rent, claim, or receive an item. The term includes a telephone call a purchaser makes in response to a solicitation sent by mail or made by any other means.

Added by Acts 2007, 80th Leg., ch. 885, § 2.01, eff. April 1, 2009.

§ 302.002. Making Telephone Solicitation

For purposes of this chapter, a person makes a telephone solicitation if the person effects or attempts to effect a telephone solicitation, including a solicitation initiated by an automatic dialing machine or a recorded message device.

Added by Acts 2007, 80th Leg., ch. 885, § 2.01, eff. April 1, 2009.

§ 302.003. Liberal Construction and Application

This chapter shall be liberally construed and applied to promote its underlying purpose to protect persons against false, misleading, or deceptive practices in the telephone solicitation business.

Added by Acts 2007, 80th Leg., ch. 885, § 2.01, eff. April 1, 2009.

§ 302.004. Attempted Waiver Void

An attempted waiver of a provision of this chapter is void.

Added by Acts 2007, 80th Leg., ch. 885, § 2.01, eff. April 1, 2009.

[Sections 302.005 to 302.050 reserved for expansion]

SUBCHAPTER B. EXEMPTIONS

§ 302.051. Burden of Proof

(a) In a civil proceeding in which a violation of this chapter is alleged, a person who claims an exemption from the application of this chapter has the burden of proving the exemption.

(b) In a criminal proceeding in which a violation of this chapter is alleged, a person who claims an exemption from the application of this chapter as a defense to prosecution has the burden of producing evidence to support the defense.

Added by Acts 2007, 80th Leg., ch. 885, § 2.01, eff. April 1, 2009.

§ 302.052. Exemptions Apply Only to Sellers; Exception

Except as provided by Section 302.060, an exemption from the application of this chapter applies only to a seller.

Added by Acts 2007, 80th Leg., ch. 885, § 2.01, eff. April 1, 2009.

§ 302.053. Exemption: Persons Regulated by Other Law

This chapter does not apply to:

(1) a person offering or selling a security that has been qualified for sale under Section 7, The Securities Act (Article 581–7, Vernon's Texas Civil Statutes), or that is subject to an exemption under Section 5 or 6 of that Act;

(2) a publicly traded corporation registered with the Securities and Exchange Commission or the State Securities Board, or a subsidiary or agent of the corporation;

(3) a person who holds a license issued under the Insurance Code if the solicited transaction is governed by that code;

(4) a supervised financial institution or a parent, a subsidiary, or an affiliate of a supervised financial institution;

(5) a person whose business is regulated by the Public Utility Commission of Texas or an affiliate of that person, except that this chapter applies to such a person or affiliate only with respect to one or more automated dial announcing devices;

(6) a person subject to the control or licensing regulations of the Federal Communications Commission;

(7) a person selling a contractual plan regulated by the Federal Trade Commission trade regulation on use of negative option plans by sellers in commerce under 16 C.F.R. Part 425;

(8) a person subject to filing requirements under Chapter 1803, Occupations Code; or

(9) a person who:

(A) is soliciting a transaction regulated by the Commodity Futures Trading Commission; and

(B) is registered or holds a temporary license for the activity described by Paragraph (A) with the Commodity Futures Trading Commission under the Commodity Exchange Act (7 U.S.C. Section 1 et seq.), if the registration or license has not expired or been suspended or revoked.

Added by Acts 2007, 80th Leg., ch. 885, § 2.01, eff. April 1, 2009.

§ 302.054. Exemption: Persons Selling Media Subscriptions, Certain Merchandise, or Items From Certain Catalogs

This chapter does not apply to:

(1) a person soliciting the sale of a subscription to:

(A) a daily or weekly newspaper of general circulation;

(B) a magazine or other periodical of general circulation; or

(C) a cable television service;

(2) a person selling merchandise under an arrangement in which the seller periodically ships the merchandise to a consumer who has consented in advance to receive the merchandise periodically; or

(3) a person periodically issuing and delivering to purchasers catalogs that each:

(A) include a written description or illustration and the sales price of each item offered for sale;

(B) include at least 24 full pages of written material or illustrations;

(C) are distributed in more than one state; and

(D) have an annual circulation of at least 250,000 customers.

Added by Acts 2007, 80th Leg., ch. 885, § 2.01, eff. April 1, 2009.

§ 302.055. Exemption: Educational and Nonprofit Organizations

This chapter does not apply to an educational institution or organization or a nonprofit organization exempt from taxation under Section 501(c)(3), Internal Revenue Code of 1986.

Added by Acts 2007, 80th Leg., ch. 885, § 2.01, eff. April 1, 2009.

§ 302.056. Exemption: Certain Commercial Sales

This chapter does not apply to a sale in which the purchaser is a business that intends to:

(1) resell the item purchased; or

(2) use the item purchased in a recycling, reuse, remanufacturing, or manufacturing process.

Added by Acts 2007, 80th Leg., ch. 885, § 2.01, eff. April 1, 2009.

§ 302.057. Exemption: Person Soliciting Food Sales

This chapter does not apply to a person soliciting the sale of food.

Added by Acts 2007, 80th Leg., ch. 885, § 2.01, eff. April 1, 2009.

§ 302.058. Exemption: Solicitation of Former or Current Customers

This chapter does not apply to:

(1) the solicitation of a contract for the maintenance or repair of an item previously purchased from the person making the solicitation or on whose behalf the solicitation is made; or

(2) a person who:

(A) is soliciting business from a former or current customer; and

(B) has operated under the same business name for at least two years.

Added by Acts 2007, 80th Leg., ch. 885, § 2.01, eff. April 1, 2009.

§ 302.059. Exemption: Persons Who Make Certain Sales Presentations or Make Sales at Established Retail Locations

This chapter does not apply to:

(1) a person conducting a telephone solicitation who:

(A) does not intend to complete or obtain provisional acceptance of a sale during the telephone solicitation;

(B) does not make a major sales presentation during the telephone solicitation but arranges for a major sales presentation to be made face-to-face at a later meeting between the salesperson and the purchaser; and

(C) does not cause an individual to go to the purchaser to collect payment for the purchase or to deliver an item purchased directly following the telephone solicitation; or

(2) a person who for at least two years, under the same name as that used in connection with the person's telemarketing operations, has operated a retail establishment where consumer goods are displayed and offered for sale continuously, if a majority of the person's business involves buyers obtaining services or products at the retail establishment.

Added by Acts 2007, 80th Leg., ch. 885, § 2.01, eff. April 1, 2009.

§ 302.060. Exemption: Certain Persons Providing Telephone Solicitation Services Predominantly for Exempt Persons

This chapter does not apply to a person:

(1) who provides telephone solicitation services under contract to a seller;

(2) who has been operating continuously for at least three years under the same business name; and

(3) for whom at least 75 percent of the person's contracts are performed on behalf of other persons exempt from the application of this chapter under this section.

Added by Acts 2007, 80th Leg., ch. 885, § 2.01, eff. April 1, 2009.

§ 302.061. Exemption: Persons Conducting Certain Isolated Telephone Solicitations

This chapter does not apply to a person engaging in a telephone solicitation that:

(1) is an isolated transaction; and

(2) is not done in the course of a pattern of repeated transactions of a similar nature.

Added by Acts 2007, 80th Leg., ch. 885, § 2.01, eff. April 1, 2009.

[Sections 302.062 to 302.100 reserved for expansion]

SUBCHAPTER C. REGISTRATION

§ 302.101. Registration Certificate Required

(a) A seller may not make a telephone solicitation from a location in this state or to a purchaser located in this state unless the seller holds a registration certificate for the business location from which the telephone solicitation is made.

(b) A separate registration certificate is required for each business location from which a telephone solicitation is made.

Added by Acts 2007, 80th Leg., ch. 885, § 2.01, eff. April 1, 2009.

§ 302.102. Filing of Registration Statement; Public Information

(a) To obtain a registration certificate, a seller must file with the secretary of state a registration statement that:

(1) is in the form prescribed by the secretary of state;

(2) contains the information required by Subchapter D;

(3) is verified by each principal of the seller; and

(4) specifies the date and location of verification.

(b) Information included in or attached to a registration statement is public information.

(c) In this section, "principal" means an owner, an executive officer of a corporation, a general partner of a partnership, a sole proprietor, a trustee of a trust, or another individual with similar supervisory functions with respect to any person.

Added by Acts 2007, 80th Leg., ch. 885, § 2.01, eff. April 1, 2009.

§ 302.103. Issuance of Registration Certificate

(a) The secretary of state shall issue a registration certificate and mail the certificate to the seller when the secretary of state receives:

(1) a completed registration statement required by Section 302.102;

(2) the filing fee prescribed by Section 302.106;

(3) the security required by Section 302.107; and

(4) the consent regarding service of process required by Section 302.108.

(b) If the seller uses a single registration statement to register more than one business location, the secretary of state shall:

(1) issue a registration certificate for each business location; and

(2) mail all the certificates to the principal business location shown on the registration statement.

Added by Acts 2007, 80th Leg., ch. 885, § 2.01, eff. April 1, 2009.

§ 302.104. Effective Date of Registration Statement; Renewal

(a) A registration statement takes effect on the date the secretary of state issues the registration certificate and is effective for one year.

(b) A registration statement may be renewed annually by:

(1) filing a renewal registration statement containing the information required by Subchapter D; and

(2) paying the filing fee prescribed by Section 302.106.

Added by Acts 2007, 80th Leg., ch. 885, § 2.01, eff. April 1, 2009.

§ 302.105. Addenda Requirements

(a) For each quarter after the effective date of a registration statement, the seller shall file with the secretary of state an addendum providing the required registration information for each salesperson who is soliciting or has solicited on behalf of the seller during the preceding quarter.

(b) A seller may comply with Subsection (a) by filing with the secretary of state a copy of the "Employer's Quarterly Report" for employee wages that the seller files with the Texas Workforce Commission.

(c) In addition to filing the quarterly addendum, if a material change in information submitted in a registration statement, other than the information described by Subsection (a), occurs before the date for renewal, a seller shall submit that information to the secretary of state by filing an addendum.

Added by Acts 2007, 80th Leg., ch. 885, § 2.01, eff. April 1, 2009.

§ 302.106. Filing Fee

The filing fee for a registration statement is $200.

Added by Acts 2007, 80th Leg., ch. 885, § 2.01, eff. April 1, 2009.

§ 302.107. Security Requirements

A registration statement must be accompanied by security that:

(1) is in the amount of $10,000;

(2) is in the form of:

(A) a bond executed by a corporate security that:

(i) is approved by the secretary of state; and

(ii) holds a license to transact business in this state;

(B) an irrevocable letter of credit issued for the benefit of the registrant by a supervised financial institution whose deposits are insured by an agency of the federal government; or

(C) a certificate of deposit in a supervised financial institution whose deposits are insured by an agency of the federal government, the principal of which may be withdrawn only on the order of the secretary of state; and

(3) is conditioned on the seller's compliance with this chapter.

Added by Acts 2007, 80th Leg., ch. 885, § 2.01, eff. April 1, 2009.

§ 302.108. Appointment of Secretary of State as Agent for Service

(a) A seller shall file with the secretary of state, in the form prescribed by the secretary of state, an irrevocable consent appointing the secretary of state to act as the seller's agent to receive service of process in a noncriminal action or proceeding that may arise under this chapter against the seller or the seller's successor, executor, or administrator if:

(1) an agent has not been named under Section 302.151(15);

(2) the agent named under Section 302.151(15) has resigned or died and the name of a successor agent has not been submitted under Section 302.105; or

(3) the agent named under Section 302.151(15) cannot with reasonable diligence be found at the disclosed address.

(b) Service on the secretary of state under this section has the same effect as service on the seller. Service on the secretary of state may be made by:

(1) leaving a copy of the process in the office of the secretary of state;

(2) promptly sending by first class mail a notice of the service and a copy of the process to the seller's principal business location at the last address on file with the secretary of state; and

(3) filing the plaintiff's affidavit of compliance with this section in the action or proceeding on or before the return date of any process or within an additional period that the court allows.

Added by Acts 2007, 80th Leg., ch. 885, § 2.01, eff. April 1, 2009.

[Sections 302.109 to 302.150 reserved for expansion]

SUBCHAPTER D. DISCLOSURES REQUIRED IN REGISTRATION STATEMENT

§ 302.151. Disclosure of Certain Names, Addresses, Telephone Numbers, and Organizational Information

A registration statement must contain:

(1) the seller's name and, if different from the seller's name, the name under which the seller is transacting or intends to transact business;

(2) the name of each parent and affiliated organization of the seller that:

(A) will transact business with a purchaser relating to sales solicited by the seller; or

(B) accepts responsibility for statements made by, or acts of, the seller relating to sales solicited by the seller;

(3) the seller's:

(A) form of business; and

(B) place of organization;

(4) for a seller who is a corporation, a copy of the seller's certificate of formation and bylaws;

(5) for a seller who is a partnership, a copy of the partnership agreement;

(6) for a seller who is operating under an assumed business name, the location where the assumed name has been registered;

(7) for any parent or affiliated organization disclosed under Subdivision (2), the applicable information that is required of a seller under Subdivisions (3) through (6);

(8) the complete street address of each location of the seller, designating the principal location from which the seller will be transacting business;

(9) if the principal business location of the seller is not in this state, a designation of the seller's main location in this state;

(10) a listing of each telephone number to be used by the seller and the address where each telephone using the number is located;

(11) the name and title of each of the seller's officers, directors, trustees, general and limited partners, and owners, as applicable, and the name of each of those persons who has management responsibilities in connection with the seller's business activities;

(12) for each person whose name is disclosed under Subdivision (11) and for each seller who is a sole proprietor:

(A) the complete address of the person's principal residence;

(B) the person's date of birth; and

(C) the number of and state that issued the person's driver's license;

(13) the name and principal residence address of each person the seller leaves in charge at each location from which the seller transacts business in this state and the business location at which each of those persons is or will be in charge;

(14) the name and principal residence address of each salesperson who solicits on the seller's behalf or a copy of the "Employer's Quarterly Report" for employee wages the seller files with the Texas Workforce Commission and the name the salesperson uses while soliciting;

(15) the name and address of the seller's agent in this state, other than the secretary of state, who is authorized to receive service of process; and

(16) the name and address of each financial institution with which the seller makes banking or similar monetary transactions and the identification number of each of the seller's accounts in each institution.

Added by Acts 2007, 80th Leg., ch. 885, § 2.01, eff. April 1, 2009.

§ 302.152. Disclosure of Certain Convictions, Pleas, Judgments, Orders, Bankruptcies, and Reorganizations

(a) With respect to the seller and each person identified under Section 302.151(11) or (13), a registration statement must identify each person:

(1) who has been convicted of or pleaded nolo contendere to:

(A) an offense involving an alleged violation of this chapter; or

(B) fraud, theft, embezzlement, fraudulent conversion, or misappropriation of property;

(2) against whom a final judgment or order has been entered in a civil or administrative action, including a stipulated judgment or order, in which the complaint or petition alleged:

(A) acts constituting:

(i) a violation of this chapter; or

(ii) fraud, theft, embezzlement, fraudulent conversion, or misappropriation of property;

(B) the use of false or misleading representations in an attempt to sell or otherwise dispose of property; or

(C) the use of unfair, unlawful, or deceptive business practices;

(3) who is subject to an injunction or restrictive court order relating to business activity as the result of an action brought by a federal, state, or local public agency, including an action affecting a vocational license; or

(4) who, during the previous seven tax years:

(A) has filed in bankruptcy;

(B) has been adjudged a bankrupt;

(C) has been reorganized because of insolvency; or

(D) has been a principal, director, officer, trustee, or general or limited partner of, or had management responsibilities for, a corporation, partnership, joint venture, or other business entity that has filed in bankruptcy, been adjudged a bankrupt, or been reorganized because of insolvency while the person held that position or on or before the first anniversary of the date on which the person last held that position.

(b) For each person identified under Subsection (a)(1), (2), or (3), the statement must disclose:

(1) the court that received the plea of nolo contendere or the court or administrative agency that rendered the conviction, judgment, or order;

(2) the docket number of the matter;

(3) the date the plea of nolo contendere was received or the date of the conviction, judgment, or order; and

(4) the name of any government agency that brought the action resulting in the plea or the conviction, judgment, or order.

(c) For each person identified under Subsection (a)(4), the statement must disclose:

(1) the name and location of the person filing in bankruptcy, adjudged a bankrupt, or reorganized because of insolvency;

(2) the date of the filing, judgment, or reorganization order;

(3) the court having jurisdiction; and

(4) the docket number of the matter.

Added by Acts 2007, 80th Leg., ch. 885, § 2.01, eff. April 1, 2009.

§ 302.153. Disclosure of Certain Sales Information

(a) A registration statement must be accompanied by:

(1) a description of the items the seller is offering for sale;

(2) a copy of all sales information and literature, including scripts, outlines, instructions, and information regarding the conduct of telephone solicitations, sample introductions, sample closings, product information, and contest or premium-award information, that the seller provides to salespersons or about which the seller informs salespersons;

(3) a copy of all written material the seller sends to any purchaser; and

(4) as applicable, the information and documents specified by Subsections (b) through (h).

(b) If the seller represents or implies, or directs a salesperson to represent or imply, to a purchaser that the purchaser will receive a specific item, including a certificate that the purchaser must redeem to obtain the item described in the certificate, or one or more items from among designated items, regardless of whether the items are designated as gifts, premiums, bonuses, or prizes or otherwise, the registration statement must be accompanied by:

(1) a list of the items described;

(2) the value of each item and the basis for the valuation;

(3) the price the seller paid for each item to the seller's supplier and the name, address, and telephone number of each item's supplier;

(4) all rules and terms a purchaser must meet to receive the item; and

(5) if the purchaser will not receive all of the items described by the seller:

(A) the manner in which the seller decides which item a particular purchaser is to receive;

(B) for each item, the odds of a single purchaser receiving the item; and

(C) the name and address of each purchaser who has received, during the preceding 12 months, the item with the greatest value and the item with the lowest odds of being received.

(c) If the seller is offering an item that the seller does not manufacture or supply, the registration statement must be accompanied by:

(1) the name, address, and telephone number of each of the seller's suppliers;

(2) a description of each item provided by each supplier named in Subdivision (1); and

(3) as applicable, the information and documents specified by Subsections (d) through (g).

(d) If the seller is offering an item that the seller does not manufacture or supply and the possession of the item is to be retained by the seller or will not be transferred to the purchaser until the purchaser has paid in full, the registration statement must be accompanied by:

(1) the address of each location where the item will be kept;

(2) if the item is not kept on premises owned by the seller or at an address registered under Section 302.151(8) or (9), the name of the owner of the business at which the item will be kept; and

(3) a copy of any contract or other document that evidences the seller's right to store the item at the address designated under Subdivision (2).

(e) If the seller is offering an item that the seller does not manufacture or supply and the seller is not selling the item from the seller's own inventory but purchases the item to fill an order previously taken from a purchaser, the registration statement must be accompanied by a copy of each contract or other document that evidences the seller's ability to call on suppliers to fill the seller's orders.

(f) If the seller is offering an item that the seller does not manufacture or supply and the seller represents to purchasers that the seller has insurance or a surety bond relating to a purchaser's purchase of an item, the registration statement must be accompanied by a copy of each insurance policy or bond.

(g) If the seller is offering an item that the seller does not manufacture or supply and the seller makes a representation regarding the post-purchase earning or profit potential of an item, the registration statement must be accompanied by:

(1) data to substantiate the claims made; and

(2) if the representation relates to previous sales made by the seller or a related entity, substantiating data based on the experiences of at least 50 percent of purchasers of that particular type of item from the seller or related entity during the preceding six months, including:

(A) the period the seller or related entity has been selling the particular type of item being offered;

(B) the number of purchasers of the item known to the seller or related entity to have made at least the same earnings or profit as those represented; and

(C) the percentage that the number disclosed under Paragraph (B) represents of the total number of purchasers from the seller or related entity of the particular type of item offered.

(h) If the seller is offering to sell an interest in an oil, gas, or mineral field, well, or exploration site, the registration statement must be accompanied by:

(1) any ownership interest of the seller in each field, well, or site being offered for sale;

(2) the total number of interests to be sold in each field, well, or site being offered for sale; and

(3) if, in selling an interest in any particular field, well, or site, reference is made to an investigation of the field, well, or site by the seller or anyone else:

(A) the name, business address, telephone number, and professional credentials of the person who conducted the investigation; and

(B) a copy of the report and other documents relating to the investigation prepared by the person who conducted the investigation.

Added by Acts 2007, 80th Leg., ch. 885, § 2.01, eff. April 1, 2009.

[Sections 302.154 to 302.200 reserved for expansion]

SUBCHAPTER E. ADDITIONAL INFORMATION FROM SELLER

§ 302.201. Information Required to be Posted or Available at Seller's Business Location

(a) A seller shall post the registration certificate in a conspicuous place at the location for which the certificate is issued.

(b) A seller shall post in close proximity to the registration certificate the name of each individual in charge of the location.

(c) A seller shall make available at each of the seller's business locations a copy of the entire registration statement and any addenda for inspection by a purchaser or by a representative of a government agency.

Added by Acts 2007, 80th Leg., ch. 885, § 2.01, eff. April 1, 2009.

§ 302.202. Disclosures Required Before Purchase

When a telephone solicitation is made and before consummation of any sales transaction, a seller shall provide to each purchaser:

(1) the complete street address of the location from which the salesperson is calling the purchaser and, if different, the complete street address of the seller's principal location;

(2) if the seller represents or implies that a purchaser will receive without charge a specified item or one item from among designated items, regardless of whether the items are designated as gifts, premiums, bonuses, prizes, or otherwise:

(A) the information required to be filed by Sections 302.153(b)(4) and (5)(A) and (B), as appropriate; and

(B) the total number of individuals who have actually received from the seller during the preceding 12 months the item having the greatest value and the item with the smallest odds of being received;

(3) if the seller is offering to sell an interest in an oil, gas, or mineral field, well, or exploration site, the information required by Section 302.153(h); and

(4) if the seller represents that an item is being offered at a price below that usually charged for the item, the name of the item's manufacturer. (Bus. & Com. Code, Sec. 38.202.)

Added by Acts 2007, 80th Leg., ch. 885, § 2.01, eff. April 1, 2009.

§ 302.203. Reference to Compliance with Statute Prohibited

A seller may not make or authorize the making of a reference to the seller's compliance with this chapter to a purchaser.

Added by Acts 2007, 80th Leg., ch. 885, § 2.01, eff. April 1, 2009.

[Sections 302.204 to 302.250 reserved for expansion]

SUBCHAPTER F. OFFENSES

§ 302.251. Violation of Certain Provisions

(a) A person commits an offense if the person knowingly violates section 302.101, 302.105, 302.201, 302.202, or 302.203. Each violation constitutes a separate offense.

(b) An offense under this section is a Class A misdemeanor.

Added by Acts 2007, 80th Leg., ch. 885, § 2.01, eff. April 1, 2009.

§ 302.252. Acting as Salesperson for Unregistered Seller

(a) A person commits an offense if the person knowingly acts as a salesperson on behalf of a seller who violates the registration requirements of this chapter. Each violation constitutes a separate offense.

(b) An offense under this section is a Class A misdemeanor.

Added by Acts 2007, 80th Leg., ch. 885, § 2.01, eff. April 1, 2009.

§ 302.253. Request for Credit Card Account Number or Checking Account Number After Offer of Free Item

(a) A seller commits an offense if the seller knowingly:

(1) represents or implies that a purchaser will receive an item without charge, regardless of whether the item is designated as a gift, premium, bonus, or prize or otherwise; and

(2) requests a credit card account number or checking account number from the purchaser to charge to the credit card account or debit from the checking account an amount as a condition precedent to the purchaser's receipt of the item.

(b) An offense under this section is a Class A misdemeanor.

Added by Acts 2007, 80th Leg., ch. 885, § 2.01, eff. April 1, 2009.

[Sections 302.254 to 302.300 reserved for expansion]

SUBCHAPTER G. ENFORCEMENT

§ 302.301. Injunction

(a) The attorney general may bring an action to enjoin a person from violating this chapter.

(b) The attorney general shall notify the defendant of the alleged prohibited conduct not later than the seventh day before the date the action is filed, except that notice is not required if the attorney general intends to request that the court issue a temporary restraining order.

(c) The attorney general is entitled to recover all reasonable costs of prosecuting the action, including court costs and investigation costs, deposition expenses, witness fees, and attorney's fees.

Added by Acts 2007, 80th Leg., ch. 885, § 2.01, eff. April 1, 2009.

§ 302.302. Civil Penalties

(a) A person who violates this chapter is subject to a civil penalty of not more than $5,000 for each violation.

(b) A person who violates an injunction issued under Section 302.301 is liable to this state for a civil penalty of not more than:

(1) $25,000 for each violation of the injunction; and

(2) $50,000 for all violations of the injunction.

(c) The attorney general may bring an action to recover a civil penalty under Subsection (b) in the court that issued the original injunction.

(d) The party bringing the action also is entitled to recover all reasonable costs of prosecuting the action, including court costs and investigation costs, deposition expenses, witness fees, and attorney's fees.

Added by Acts 2007, 80th Leg., ch. 885, § 2.01, eff. April 1, 2009.

§ 302.303. Deceptive Trade Practices

(a) A violation of this chapter is a false, misleading, or deceptive act or practice under Subchapter E, Chapter 17.[1]

(b) A public or private right or remedy prescribed by Subchapter E, Chapter 17, may be used to enforce this chapter.

Added by Acts 2007, 80th Leg., ch. 885, § 2.01, eff. April 1, 2009.

[1] V.T.C.A., Bus. & C. Code § 17.41 et seq.

§ 302.304. Action to Recover Against Security

(a) A person injured by a seller's bankruptcy or by a seller's breach of an agreement entered into during a telephone solicitation may bring an action to recover against the security required under Section 302.107.

(b) The liability of the surety on a bond provided under Section 302.107 may not exceed the amount of the bond, regardless of the number of claims filed or the aggregate amount claimed. If the amount claimed exceeds the amount of the bond, the surety shall deposit the amount of the bond with the secretary of state for distribution to claimants entitled to recovery, and the surety is then relieved of all liability under the bond.

Added by Acts 2007, 80th Leg., ch. 885, § 2.01, eff. April 1, 2009.

CHAPTER 303. TELEPHONE SOLICITATION FOR CERTAIN LAW ENFORCEMENT–RELATED CHARITABLE ORGANIZATIONS

SUBCHAPTER A. GENERAL PROVISIONS

SUBCHAPTER A. GENERAL PROVISIONS

§ 303.001. Definitions

In this chapter:

(1) "Commercial telephone solicitor" means a person whom a law enforcement-related charitable organization retains to make a telephone solicitation, directly or through another person under the direction of the person retained. The term does not include a bona fide officer, director, or employee of, or volunteer for, a law enforcement-related charitable organization.

(2) "Contribution" means a promise to give or a gift of money or other property, credit, financial assistance, or another thing of any kind or value. The term does not include:

(A) volunteer services; or

(B) bona fide fees, dues, or assessments a member pays if membership is not conferred solely as consideration for making a contribution in response to a telephone solicitation.

(3) "Law enforcement-related charitable organization" means a person who solicits a contribution and is or purports to be established or operating for a charitable purpose relating to law enforcement. The term includes a nongovernmental law enforcement organization or publication and survivors of law enforcement officers killed in the line of duty. The term does not include a governmental law enforcement agency or organization.

(4) "Telephone solicitation" means the use of a telephone to solicit another person to make a charitable contribution to a law enforcement-related charitable organization.

Added by Acts 2007, 80th Leg., ch. 885, § 2.01, eff. April 1, 2009.

§ 303.002. Solicitation Governed by Chapter

The telephone solicitation of a contribution from a person in this state is considered to be engaging in telephone solicitation in this state regardless of where the solicitation originates.

Added by Acts 2007, 80th Leg., ch. 885, § 2.01, eff. April 1, 2009.

§ 303.003. Public Access to Certain Documents and Information

(a) Except as provided by subsection (b), a document required to be filed with the attorney general under this chapter is public information available to members of the public under Chapter 552, Government Code.

(b) A document that identifies the donors to a law enforcement-related charitable organization is confidential and not subject to disclosure.

Added by Acts 2007, 80th Leg., ch. 885, § 2.01, eff. April 1, 2009.

§ 303.004. Rules; Procedures; Forms

The attorney general may adopt rules, procedures, and forms necessary to administer and enforce this chapter.

Added by Acts 2007, 80th Leg., ch. 885, § 2.01, eff. April 1, 2009.

[Sections 303.005 to 303.050 reserved for expansion]

SUBCHAPTER B. REGISTRATION AND BOND REQUIREMENTS

§ 303.051. Record of Organizations

The attorney general shall maintain:

(1) a register of law enforcement-related charitable organizations subject to this chapter; and

(2) a registry of law enforcement-related charitable organizations that submit to the attorney general a completed registration statement containing the information required by Section 303.052.

Added by Acts 2007, 80th Leg., ch. 885, § 2.01, eff. April 1, 2009.

§ 303.052. Form and Content of Registration Statement

A registration statement under Section 303.051(2) must be submitted on a form the attorney general prescribes or approves and must contain:

(1) for each of the organization's offices, chapters, local units, branches, and affiliates:

(A) the legal name and each assumed name;

(B) the mailing address and street address; and

(C) each telephone number and facsimile number;

(2) the organization's employer identification number;

(3) the name, title, address, and telephone number of:

(A) the organization's executive director or other chief operating officer; and

(B) each of the organization's officers and directors;

(4) the name of each officer, director, or employee:

(A) whom the organization compensates or who has custody and control of the organization's money; and

(B) who has been convicted of or pleaded nolo contendere to:

(i) a felony; or

(ii) a misdemeanor involving fraud or the theft, misappropriation, misapplication, or misuse of another's property;

(5) for each person listed under Subdivision (4), a statement of:

(A) the offense; and

(B) the state, court, and date of each conviction or plea of nolo contendere;

(6) if the organization is a corporation, the date and state of incorporation;

(7) if the organization is not a corporation, the type of organization and date established;

(8) the date the organization began transacting business in this state;

(9) the name and address of the organization's registered agent in this state;

(10) a statement of the organization's charitable purposes;

(11) a list of the programs for which funds are solicited;

(12) the day and month on which the organization's fiscal year ends;

(13) a statement of whether the organization:

(A) is eligible to receive tax-deductible contributions under Section 170, Internal Revenue Code of 1986; and

(B) has applied for or been granted tax-exempt status by the Internal Revenue Service and, if so:

(i) the Internal Revenue Code of 1986 section on which the application was based;

(ii) the application date;

(iii) the date the exemption was granted or denied; and

(iv) a statement of whether or when the tax exemption has ever been denied, revoked, or modified;

(14) a statement that includes:

(A) the method of accounting used and the name, address, and telephone number of each of the organization's accountants and auditors;

(B) for the preceding 12 months:

(i) the total contributions received;

(ii) the total fund-raising costs, computed according to generally accepted accounting principles;

(iii) if the organization retained a commercial telephone solicitor:

(a) the name and address of each commercial telephone solicitor; and

(b) a written confirmation from each commercial telephone solicitor that it has complied with all state and local registration laws; and

(iv) the amount paid to commercial telephone solicitors; and

(C) a statement that:

(i) the organization has attempted in good faith to comply with each ordinance of a municipality or each order of a county in this state regarding telephone solicitation that has been filed with the attorney general; or

(ii) no ordinance or order described by Subparagraph (i) applies;

(15) if the organization files a federal tax return, a copy of:

(A) the organization's most recently filed Internal Revenue Service Form 990 and other federal tax returns;

(B) each supplement, amendment, and attachment to those returns; and

(C) each request for an extension to file any of those returns;

(16) if the organization does not file a federal tax return:

(A) a statement of the reason a return is not filed; and

(B) the organization's most recent financial statements, including audited financial statements, if any have been prepared; and

(17) a sworn statement verifying that the information contained in the registration statement and each attachment to the registration statement is true, correct, and complete to the best of the affiant's knowledge.

Added by Acts 2007, 80th Leg., ch. 885, § 2.01, eff. April 1, 2009.

§ 303.053. Initial Registration Statement

A law enforcement-related charitable organization shall file the organization's initial registration statement before the 10th working day before the date the organization begins telephone solicitation in this state.

Added by Acts 2007, 80th Leg., ch. 885, § 2.01, eff. April 1, 2009.

§ 303.054. Expiration of Registration; Renewal

(a) A law enforcement-related charitable organization's registration expires on the 15th day of the fifth month after the last day of the organization's fiscal year.

(b) The organization shall file a renewal registration statement on the form required under Section 303.052. The renewal registration statement must include the organization's name and employer identification number and any changes to information previously submitted to the attorney general. For an item on which there is no change from the previous year's registration statement, "no change" may be indicated.

Added by Acts 2007, 80th Leg., ch. 885, § 2.01, eff. April 1, 2009.

§ 303.055. Filing Fee

(a) An initial registration statement must be accompanied by a filing fee not to exceed $50.

(b) A renewal registration statement must be accompanied by a filing fee of $50.

Added by Acts 2007, 80th Leg., ch. 885, § 2.01, eff. April 1, 2009.

§ 303.056. Exemption: Volunteer

A volunteer authorized to solicit on behalf of a law enforcement-related charitable organization is not required to register under this chapter. (V.A.C.S. Art. 9023e, Sec. 4(f).)

Added by Acts 2007, 80th Leg., ch. 885, § 2.01, eff. April 1, 2009.

§ 303.057. Registration Does Not Imply Endorsement

(a) Registration under this chapter does not imply endorsement by this state or the attorney general.

(b) A law enforcement-related charitable organization may not state or imply that registration under this chapter is endorsement by this state or the attorney general.

Added by Acts 2007, 80th Leg., ch. 885, § 2.01, eff. April 1, 2009.

§ 303.058. Books and Records

(a) A law enforcement-related charitable organization required to file a registration statement shall maintain books and records of the organization's activities in this state. The books and records must be maintained:

(1) in a form that enables the organization to accurately provide the information required by this chapter; and

(2) until at least the third anniversary of the end of the period to which the registration statement relates.

(b) On written request of authorized personnel of the attorney general, the organization shall make the books and records available for inspection and copying by authorized personnel:

(1) at the organization's principal place of business not later than the 10th working day after the date of the request; or

(2) at another agreed place and time.

(c) The authority provided by this section is in addition to the attorney general's other statutory or common law audit or investigative authority.

Added by Acts 2007, 80th Leg., ch. 885, § 2.01, eff. April 1, 2009.

§ 303.059. Bond

A commercial telephone solicitor shall post with the secretary of state a surety bond that:

(1) is in the amount of $50,000; and

(2) is issued by a surety company authorized to transact business in this state.

Added by Acts 2007, 80th Leg., ch. 885, § 2.01, eff. April 1, 2009.

[Sections 303.060 to 303.100 reserved for expansion]

SUBCHAPTER C. SOLICITATION PRACTICES

§ 303.101. Deceptive Act or Practice

A person may not commit an unfair or deceptive act or practice in making a telephone solicitation for a law enforcement-related charitable organization.

Added by Acts 2007, 80th Leg., ch. 885, § 2.01, eff. April 1, 2009.

§ 303.102. Representation of Benefit to Survivors

A person may not represent to a person solicited that a contribution is to be used to benefit the survivors of a law enforcement officer killed in the line of duty unless:

(1) all of the contributions collected are used to benefit those survivors; or

(2) the person solicited is informed in writing of the percentage of the contribution that will directly benefit those survivors.

Added by Acts 2007, 80th Leg., ch. 885, § 2.01, eff. April 1, 2009.

§ 303.103. Notice of Disposition of Money

(a) If less than 90 percent of the contributions collected by a law enforcement-related charitable organization or commercial telephone solicitor are paid to a law enforcement-related charitable organization, the commercial telephone solicitor shall notify each person solicited by telephone, before accepting a contribution from the person, of:

(1) the percentage of the contributions that will be paid to the organization for which the contributions are being solicited; and

(2) the percentage of the contributions that the solicitor will retain.

(b) Information required to be disclosed under Subsection (a) shall also be included on any written statement mailed to the contributor.

Added by Acts 2007, 80th Leg., ch. 885, § 2.01, eff. April 1, 2009.

§ 303.104. Hours of Solicitation

A law enforcement-related charitable organization or commercial telephone solicitor may not make a telephone solicitation call unless the call is made after 9 a.m. and before 7 p.m., Monday through Friday.

Added by Acts 2007, 80th Leg., ch. 885, § 2.01, eff. April 1, 2009.

[Sections 303.105 to 303.150 reserved for expansion]

SUBCHAPTER D. VIOLATION; REMEDIES

§ 303.151. Notification of Noncompliance

If a law enforcement-related charitable organization does not file a document required by this chapter, files an incomplete or inaccurate document, or otherwise does not comply with this chapter, the attorney general shall notify the organization of the organization's noncompliance by first class mail sent to the organization's last reported address.

Added by Acts 2007, 80th Leg., ch. 885, § 2.01, eff. April 1, 2009.

§ 303.152. Violations Relating to Filing of Documents

(a) A law enforcement-related charitable organization violates this chapter if the organization:

(1) does not file complete documents before the 31st day after the date a notice under Section 303.151 is mailed; or

(2) with actual awareness files materially inaccurate documents.

(b) For purposes of Subsection (a)(2), actual awareness may be inferred from an objective manifestation that indicates that a person acted with actual awareness.

Added by Acts 2007, 80th Leg., ch. 885, § 2.01, eff. April 1, 2009.

§ 303.153. Remedies

(a) The attorney general may bring an action against a person who violates this chapter to:

(1) cancel or suspend the person's registration;

(2) obtain an injunction to restrain the person from continuing the violation;

(3) restrain the person from transacting business in this state while violating this chapter;

(4) impose a civil penalty of not more than $25,000 for each violation; or

(5) both obtain an injunction and impose a civil penalty.

(b) A person who violates an injunction issued under this section is liable to this state for a civil penalty of not less than $100,000.

(c) In an action that the attorney general successfully prosecutes under this chapter, the court may allow the attorney general to recover civil penalties and the reasonable costs, attorney's fees, and expenses, including investigative costs, witness fees, and deposition expenses, incurred in bringing the action.

(d) A remedy authorized by this chapter is in addition to any other procedure or remedy provided by another statutory law or common law.

Added by Acts 2007, 80th Leg., ch. 885, § 2.01, eff. April 1, 2009.

§ 303.154. Venue

An action under this chapter must be brought in:

(1) Travis County;

(2) the county in which the law enforcement-related charitable organization has its principal place of business or a fixed and established place of business at the time the action is brought; or

(3) the county in which solicitation occurred.

Added by Acts 2007, 80th Leg., ch. 885, § 2.01, eff. April 1, 2009.

CHAPTER 304. TELEMARKETING

SUBCHAPTER A. GENERAL PROVISIONS

§ 304.001. Short Title

This chapter may be cited as the texas telemarketing disclosure and privacy act.

Added by Acts 2007, 80th Leg., ch. 885, § 2.01, eff. April 1, 2009.

§ 304.002. Definitions

In this chapter:

(1) "Caller identification service or device" means a service or device designed to provide the user of

the service or device with the telephone number of an incoming telephone call.

(2) "Commission" means the Public Utility Commission of Texas.

(3) "Consumer good or service" means property of any kind that is normally used for personal, family, or household purposes. The term does not include a security, as defined by Section 4, The Securities Act (Article 581–4, Vernon's Texas Civil Statutes).

(4) "Established business relationship" means a relationship that:

(A) is formed by a voluntary two-way communication between a person and a consumer, regardless of whether consideration is exchanged;

(B) pertains to a consumer good or service offered by the person; and

(C) has not been terminated by either party.

(5) "Facsimile recording device" means a device capable of receiving a facsimile transmission.

(6) "Facsimile solicitation" means a telemarketing call made by a transmission to a facsimile recording device.

(7) "State licensee" means a person licensed by a state agency under a law of this state that requires the person to obtain a license as a condition of engaging in a profession or business.

(8) "Telemarketer" means a person who makes or causes to be made a telemarketing call.

(9) "Telemarketing call" means an unsolicited telephone call made to:

(A) solicit a sale of a consumer good or service;

(B) solicit an extension of credit for a consumer good or service; or

(C) obtain information that may be used to solicit a sale of a consumer good or service or to extend credit for the sale.

(10) "Telephone call" means a call or other transmission made to or received at a telephone number, including:

(A) a call made by an automated telephone dialing system;

(B) a transmission to a facsimile recording device; and

(C) a call to a mobile telephone number serviced by a provider of commercial mobile service, as defined by Section 332(d), Communications Act of 1934 (47 U.S.C. Section 151 et seq.), as amended, Federal Communications Commission rules, or the Omnibus Budget Reconciliation Act of 1993 (Pub. L. No. 103–66), as amended.

Added by Acts 2007, 80th Leg., ch. 885, § 2.01, eff. April 1, 2009.

§ 304.003. Making Telemarketing Call

For purposes of this chapter, a person makes a telemarketing call if the person effects a telemarketing call on the person's own behalf or on behalf of another entity. A person makes a telemarketing call on behalf of another entity if, as a result of the telemarketing call, the other entity can:

(1) become entitled to receive money or other property of any kind from a sale solicited during the call; or

(2) receive information obtained during the call to:

(A) extend or offer to extend to the person solicited credit for a consumer good or service; or

(B) directly solicit a sale of a consumer good or service or extend credit for the sale.

Added by Acts 2007, 80th Leg., ch. 885, § 2.01, eff. April 1, 2009.

§ 304.004. Inapplicability of Chapter to Certain Calls

This chapter does not apply to a call made:

(1) by a consumer:

(A) as the result of a solicitation by a seller or telemarketer; or

(B) in response to general media advertising by a direct mail solicitation that clearly, conspicuously, and truthfully makes all disclosures required by federal or state law;

(2) in connection with:

(A) an established business relationship; or

(B) a business relationship that has been terminated, if the call is made before the later of:

(i) the publication date of the first Texas no-call list in which the consumer's telephone number appears; or

(ii) the first anniversary of the date of termination;

(3) between a telemarketer and a business, other than by a facsimile solicitation, unless the business has informed the telemarketer that the business

does not wish to receive a telemarketing call from the telemarketer;

(4) to collect a debt; or

(5) by a state licensee if:

(A) the call is not made by an automated telephone dialing system;

(B) the solicited transaction is not completed until a face-to-face sales presentation by the seller occurs and the consumer is not required to pay or authorize payment until after the presentation; and

(C) the consumer has not informed the telemarketer that the consumer does not wish to receive a telemarketing call from the telemarketer.

Added by Acts 2007, 80th Leg., ch. 885, § 2.01, eff. April 1, 2009.

§ 304.005. Liberal Construction and Application

This chapter shall be liberally construed and applied to promote its underlying purpose to protect the public against false, misleading, abusive, or deceptive practices in the telemarketing business.

Added by Acts 2007, 80th Leg., ch. 885, § 2.01, eff. April 1, 2009.

§ 304.006. Attempted Waiver Void

An attempted waiver of a provision of this chapter is void.

Added by Acts 2007, 80th Leg., ch. 885, § 2.01, eff. April 1, 2009.

[Sections 304.007 to 304.050 reserved for expansion]

SUBCHAPTER B. TEXAS NO–CALL LIST

§ 304.051. Maintenance of Texas No–Call List

(a) The commission shall provide for the operation of a database to compile a list of names, zip codes, and telephone numbers of consumers in this state who object to receiving telemarketing calls or other unsolicited telephone calls.

(b) The Texas no-call list is a combined list consisting of the name and telephone numbers of:

(1) each consumer in this state who has requested to be on that list; and

(2) each person in the portion of the national do-not-call registry maintained by the United States government that relates to this state.

(c) The commission shall:

(1) make available an Internet website at which a person may request that a telephone number be placed on the Texas no-call list; and

(2) provide a toll-free telephone number and mailing address that a person may call or write to obtain a copy of a form to request placement of a telephone number on the Texas no-call list.

(d) The Texas no-call list shall be updated and published on January 1, April 1, July 1, and October 1 of each year.

(e) The commission may contract with a private vendor to maintain the Texas no-call list if the vendor has maintained a no-call list database containing the names and telephone numbers of consumers who have previously requested to be added to a no-call list. A contract under this subsection must require the vendor to publish the Texas portion of the national no-call list in an electronic format for any telemarketer who agrees to use the Texas no-call list only to update the telemarketer's no-call list to include those persons with whom the telemarketer does not have an established business relationship.

Added by Acts 2007, 80th Leg., ch. 885, § 2.01, eff. April 1, 2009.

§ 304.052. Telemarketing Call to Telephone Number on List Prohibited

A telemarketer may not make a telemarketing call to a telephone number published on the Texas no-call list more than 60 days after the date the telephone number appears on the current list.

Added by Acts 2007, 80th Leg., ch. 885, § 2.01, eff. April 1, 2009.

§ 304.053. Expiration, Renewal, and Deletion of Entry

(a) An entry on the texas no-call list expires on the third anniversary of the date the entry is first published on the list. An entry may be renewed for successive three-year periods.

(b) The telephone number of a consumer on the Texas no-call list may be deleted from the list if:

(1) the consumer makes a written request; or

(2) the telephone number of the consumer is changed.

Added by Acts 2007, 80th Leg., ch. 885, § 2.01, eff. April 1, 2009.

§ 304.054. Fee

(a) Except as provided by subsection (b), the commission may charge a person a reasonable amount not to exceed $3 for a request to place a telephone number on the Texas no-call list or to renew an entry on the list.

(b) The commission shall provide a method for placement or renewal of an entry by use of the Internet at no charge.

Added by Acts 2007, 80th Leg., ch. 885, § 2.01, eff. April 1, 2009.

§ 304.055. Publication in Telephone Directory

A private for-profit publisher of a residential telephone directory that is distributed to the public at minimal or no cost shall include in the directory a prominently displayed Internet website address, toll-free number, and mailing address established by the commission through which a person may request placement of a telephone number on the Texas no-call list or order a copy of the form to make that request.

Added by Acts 2007, 80th Leg., ch. 885, § 2.01, eff. April 1, 2009.

§ 304.056. Placement of Entries on National Do–Not–Call Registry

The commission or a person the commission designates may:

(1) provide information on the Texas no-call list to the administrator of the national do-not-call registry; and

(2) allow the names and telephone numbers on the Texas no-call list to be placed on the national do-not-call registry.

Added by Acts 2007, 80th Leg., ch. 885, § 2.01, eff. April 1, 2009.

§ 304.057. General Rulemaking Authority

The commission may adopt rules to administer this subchapter and subchapter f, other than sections 304.254, 304.255, 304.256, and 304.258, as that subchapter relates to the Texas no-call list.

Added by Acts 2007, 80th Leg., ch. 885, § 2.01, eff. April 1, 2009.

§ 304.058. Rules Regarding Isolated Calls

The commission shall adopt rules providing that a telemarketing call made to a telephone number on the Texas no-call list is not a violation of Section 304.052 if the telemarketing call:

(1) is an isolated occurrence; and

(2) is made by a person who has in place adequate procedures to comply with this subchapter.

Added by Acts 2007, 80th Leg., ch. 885, § 2.01, eff. April 1, 2009.

§ 304.059. Rules Regarding Public Notice

The commission shall adopt rules requiring each local exchange telephone company and each provider of commercial mobile service, as described by Section 304.002(10)(C), that provides commercial mobile service in this state to inform its customers of the requirements of this subchapter and Sections 304.251, 304.252, 304.253, 304.257, and 304.259, as those sections relate to the Texas no-call list, through:

(1) annual inserts in billing statements mailed to customers;

(2) notification:

(A) included in a customer's electronic bill;

(B) printed on a customer's paper bill;

(C) sent free of charge by messaging service to a customer's mobile telephone number; or

(D) conspicuously published in the consumer information pages of local telephone directories; or

(3) other appropriate means of notice.

Added by Acts 2007, 80th Leg., ch. 885, § 2.01, eff. April 1, 2009.

§ 304.060. Rules Regarding Dissemination of List

The commission shall adopt rules providing for:

(1) the distribution of the Texas no-call list in formats, including electronic formats, commonly used by persons making telemarketing calls; and

(2) a fee for each distribution, not to exceed $75.

Added by Acts 2007, 80th Leg., ch. 885, § 2.01, eff. April 1, 2009.

§ 304.061. Educational Programs

In addition to requiring the notice under section 304.059, the commission may conduct educational programs designed to inform members of the public of their rights and telemarketers of their obligations under this subchapter and Sections 304.251, 304.252,

304.253, 304.257, and 304.259, as those sections relate to the Texas no-call list.

Added by Acts 2007, 80th Leg., ch. 885, § 2.01, eff. April 1, 2009.

§ 304.062. Assistance of Department of Information Resources

On request of the commission, the department of information resources shall assist the commission in administering this subchapter.

Added by Acts 2007, 80th Leg., ch. 885, § 2.01, eff. April 1, 2009.

[Sections 304.063 to 304.100 reserved for expansion]

SUBCHAPTER C. FACSIMILE TRANSMISSIONS

§ 304.101. Notice in Facsimile Solicitation

In addition to complying with the technical and procedural standards established by federal statutes or regulations regarding telephone facsimile machines and transmissions, a person in this state who makes or causes to be made a facsimile solicitation shall include in the transmitted document or on a cover page to the document a statement, in at least 12–point type, containing:

(1) the complete name of the person making the facsimile solicitation and street address of the person's place of business; and

(2) a toll-free or local exchange accessible telephone number of the person that:

(A) is answered in the order in which calls are received by an individual capable of responding to inquiries from recipients of facsimile solicitations at all times after 9 a.m. and before 5 p.m. on each day except Saturday and Sunday; or

(B) automatically and immediately deletes the specified telephone number of the recipient.

Added by Acts 2007, 80th Leg., ch. 885, § 2.01, eff. April 1, 2009.

§ 304.102. Acknowledgment Required; Transmission Prohibited

On receiving oral or written notice from the recipient of a facsimile solicitation not to send any further facsimile transmissions to one or more specified telephone numbers, the person making the solicitation:

(1) shall within 24 hours after receiving the notice send the recipient of the solicitation written acknowledgment of the receipt; and

(2) other than a single transmission to comply with Subdivision (1), may not make or cause to be made a transmission to a telephone number specified by the recipient.

Added by Acts 2007, 80th Leg., ch. 885, § 2.01, eff. April 1, 2009.

[Sections 304.103 to 304.150 reserved for expansion]

SUBCHAPTER D. CALLER IDENTIFICATION

§ 304.151. Interference With Caller Identification Service or Device Prohibited

(a) In making a telemarketing call, a telemarketer may not block the identity of the telephone number from which the call is made to evade a device designed to identify a telephone caller.

(b) A telemarketer may not:

(1) interfere with or circumvent the capability of a caller identification service or device to access or provide to the recipient of the telemarketing call any information regarding the call that the service or device is capable of providing; or

(2) fail to provide caller identification information in a manner that is accessible by a caller identification service or device, if the telemarketer is capable of providing the information in that manner.

Added by Acts 2007, 80th Leg., ch. 885, § 2.01, eff. April 1, 2009.

§ 304.152. Exception: Use of Certain Service or Equipment

For purposes of section 304.151, use of a telecommunications service or telecommunications equipment that is incapable of transmitting caller identification information does not of itself constitute interference with or circumvention of the capability of a caller identification service or device to access or provide the information.

Added by Acts 2007, 80th Leg., ch. 885, § 2.01, eff. April 1, 2009.

[Sections 304.153 to 304.200 reserved for expansion]

SUBCHAPTER E. REGULATORY REPORTS

§ 304.201. Report By Commission

(a) Before december 31 of each even-numbered year, the commission shall submit a report to the lieutenant governor and the speaker of the house of representatives.

(b) The report must contain for the two-year period ending August 31 of the year of the report:

(1) a statement of:

(A) the number of telephone numbers included on the Texas no-call list;

(B) the number of no-call lists distributed; and

(C) the amount collected for requests to place telephone numbers and renew entries on the list and for distribution of the list;

(2) a list of complaints the commission received concerning activities regulated by this chapter, itemized by type;

(3) a summary of any enforcement efforts made by the commission; and

(4) the commission's recommendations for any changes to this chapter.

Added by Acts 2007, 80th Leg., ch. 885, § 2.01, eff. April 1, 2009.

§ 304.202. Report By Attorney General

(a) Before December 31 of each even-numbered year, the attorney general shall submit a report to the lieutenant governor and the speaker of the house of representatives.

(b) The report must contain for the two-year period ending August 31 of the year of the report:

(1) a list of complaints the attorney general received concerning activities regulated by this chapter, itemized by type;

(2) a summary of any enforcement efforts made by the attorney general; and

(3) the attorney general's recommendations for any changes to this chapter.

Added by Acts 2007, 80th Leg., ch. 885, § 2.01, eff. April 1, 2009.

[Sections 304.203 to 304.250 reserved for expansion]

SUBCHAPTER F. ENFORCEMENT

§ 304.251. Enforcement By Commission

(a) Except as provided by section 304.253, the commission shall receive and investigate complaints concerning violations of Subchapters B, C, and D and may impose an administrative penalty not to exceed $1,000 for each violation.

(b) Notwithstanding Section 304.252, if a complaint alleges that the person violating Subchapter B, C, or D is a telecommunications provider, as defined by Section 51.002, Utilities Code, the commission has exclusive jurisdiction over the violation alleged in the complaint.

Added by Acts 2007, 80th Leg., ch. 885, § 2.01, eff. April 1, 2009.

§ 304.252. Enforcement by Attorney General

(a) Except as provided by section 304.253, the attorney general may investigate violations of Subchapters B, C, and D[1] and file civil enforcement actions seeking:

(1) a civil penalty in an amount not to exceed $1,000 for each violation, except as provided by Subsection (b);

(2) injunctive relief; and

(3) attorney's fees.

(b) If the court finds the defendant wilfully or knowingly violated Subchapter B, C, or D, the court may increase the amount of the civil penalty to an amount not to exceed $3,000 for each violation.

(c) A violation of Subchapter B, C, or D is subject to enforcement action by the attorney general's consumer protection division under Sections 17.47, 17.58, 17.60, and 17.61.

Added by Acts 2007, 80th Leg., ch. 885, § 2.01, eff. April 1, 2009.

[1] V.T.C.A., Bus. & C. Code § 304.051 et seq., § 304.101 et seq. or § 304.151 et seq.

§ 304.253. Enforcement by Licensing Agency

(a) A state agency that issues a license to a state licensee shall:

(1) receive and investigate complaints concerning violations of Subchapters B and C by the state licensee; and

(2) may receive and investigate complaints concerning violations of Subchapter D by the state licensee.

(b) The state agency may:

(1) impose an administrative penalty not to exceed $1,000 for each violation;

(2) order restitution for any monetary damages of the complainant in the case of a violation of Subchapter B or D; and

(3) suspend or revoke the state licensee's license, if the agency finds that the licensee wilfully or knowingly violated Subchapter B, C, or D.

Added by Acts 2007, 80th Leg., ch. 885, § 2.01, eff. April 1, 2009.

§ 304.254. Determination of Amount of Administrative Penalty

The amount of an administrative penalty imposed under this subchapter must be based on:

(1) the seriousness of the violation, including the nature, circumstances, extent, and gravity of the violation;

(2) any history of previous violations;

(3) the amount necessary to deter a future violation;

(4) any effort to correct the violation; and

(5) any other matter that justice may require.

Added by Acts 2007, 80th Leg., ch. 885, § 2.01, eff. April 1, 2009.

§ 304.255. Stay of Administrative Penalty

(a) The enforcement of an administrative penalty imposed under this subchapter may be stayed during the time the order is under judicial review if the person on whom the penalty is imposed pays the penalty to the clerk of the court or files a supersedeas bond with the court in the amount of the penalty.

(b) A person who cannot afford to pay the penalty or file the bond may stay the enforcement by filing an affidavit in the manner required by the Texas Rules of Civil Procedure for a party who cannot afford to file security for costs, subject to the right to contest the affidavit as provided by those rules.

Added by Acts 2007, 80th Leg., ch. 885, § 2.01, eff. April 1, 2009.

§ 304.256. Contested Case

A proceeding to impose an administrative penalty under this subchapter is a contested case under chapter 2001, Government Code.

Added by Acts 2007, 80th Leg., ch. 885, § 2.01, eff. April 1, 2009.

§ 304.257. Private Action: Telemarketing Calls

(a) A consumer on the texas no-call list is presumed to be adversely affected by a telemarketer who calls the consumer more than once. The consumer may bring a civil action based on the second or a subsequent violation of Subchapter B if:

(1) the consumer has notified the telemarketer of the alleged violation;

(2) not later than the 30th day after the date of the call, the consumer files with the commission, the attorney general, or a state agency that licenses the person making the call a verified complaint stating the relevant facts surrounding the violation; and

(3) the commission, attorney general, or state agency receiving the complaint does not initiate an administrative action or a civil enforcement action, as appropriate, against the telemarketer named in the complaint before the 121st day after the date the complaint is filed.

(b) If the consumer brings an action based on a violation of Section 304.052 and the court finds that the defendant wilfully or knowingly violated that section, the court may award damages in an amount not to exceed $500 for each violation.

(c) Section 304.251(b) does not affect the right of a consumer to bring an action under Subsection (a).

Added by Acts 2007, 80th Leg., ch. 885, § 2.01, eff. April 1, 2009.

§ 304.258. Private Action: Facsimile Transmission

(a) A person may bring a civil action based on a violation of subchapter c:

(1) for damages in an amount equal to the greater of:

(A) the person's actual monetary loss from the violation; or

(B) $500 for each violation;

(2) to enjoin the violation; or

(3) for both damages and an injunction.

(b) If the court finds that the defendant wilfully or knowingly violated Subchapter C, the court may increase the amount of the damages awarded to an amount equal to not more than three times the amount available under Subsection (a)(1).

(c) Section 304.251(b) does not affect the right of a consumer to bring an action under Subsection (a).

Added by Acts 2007, 80th Leg., ch. 885, § 2.01, eff. April 1, 2009.

§ 304.259. Venue

(a) Venue for an action based on a violation of subchapter b or c is in:

(1) the county in which the telemarketing call was made or received; or

(2) Travis County, if the action is brought by the commission, the attorney general, or a state agency.

(b) Venue for an action under Subchapter D is in Travis County.

Added by Acts 2007, 80th Leg., ch. 885, § 2.01, eff. April 1, 2009.

CHAPTER 305. TELEPHONIC COMMUNICATIONS MADE FOR PURPOSE OF SOLICITATION

SUBCHAPTER A. PROHIBITED COMMUNICATIONS MADE FOR PURPOSE OF SOLICITATION

Section

SUBCHAPTER B. ENFORCEMENT

SUBCHAPTER A. PROHIBITED COMMUNICATIONS MADE FOR PURPOSE OF SOLICITATION

§ 305.001. Prohibited Telephone Calls

A person may not make a telephone call or use an automatic dial announcing device to make a telephone call for the purpose of making a sale if:

(1) the person making the call or using the device knows or should have known that the called number is a mobile telephone for which the called person will be charged for that specific call; and

(2) the called person has not consented to the making of such a call to the person calling or using the device or to the business enterprise for which the person is calling or using the device.

Added by Acts 2007, 80th Leg., ch. 885, § 2.01, eff. April 1, 2009.

§ 305.002. Prohibited Facsimile Transmissions: Charge to Recipient

A person may not make or cause to be made a transmission for the purpose of a solicitation or sale to a facsimile recording device or other telecopier for which the person receiving the transmission will be charged for the transmission, unless the person receiving the transmission has, before the transmission, consented to the making of the transmission.

Added by Acts 2007, 80th Leg., ch. 885, § 2.01, eff. April 1, 2009.

§ 305.003. Prohibited Facsimile Transmissions: Hours of Transmission

A person may not make or cause to be made a transmission for the purpose of a solicitation or sale to a facsimile recording device after 11 p.m. and before 7 a.m.

Added by Acts 2007, 80th Leg., ch. 885, § 2.01, eff. April 1, 2009.

[Sections 305.004 to 305.050 reserved for expansion]

SUBCHAPTER B. ENFORCEMENT

§ 305.051. Investigation

(a) On complaint of a called person that a person has violated section 305.001, 305.002, or 305.003, the county or district attorney of the county in which the called person resides shall investigate the complaint and file charges if appropriate.

(b) A telephone company serving the caller or called person is not responsible for investigating a complaint or keeping records relating to this chapter.

Added by Acts 2007, 80th Leg., ch. 885, § 2.01, eff. April 1, 2009.

§ 305.052. Criminal Penalty

(a) A person who violates section 305.001, 305.002, or 305.003 commits an offense.

(b) An offense under this section is a Class C misdemeanor.

Added by Acts 2007, 80th Leg., ch. 885, § 2.01, eff. April 1, 2009.

§ 305.053. Civil Action

(a) A person who receives a communication that violates 47 u.s.c. section 227, a regulation adopted under that provision, or Subchapter A may bring an action in this state against the person who originates the communication for:

(1) an injunction;

(2) damages in the amount provided by this section; or

(3) both an injunction and damages.

(b) A plaintiff who prevails in an action for damages under this section is entitled to the greater of:

(1) $500 for each violation; or

(2) the plaintiff's actual damages.

(c) If the court finds that the defendant committed the violation knowingly or intentionally, the court may increase the amount of the award of damages under Subsection (b) to not more than the greater of:

(1) $1,500 for each violation; or

(2) three times the plaintiff's actual damages.

Added by Acts 2007, 80th Leg., ch. 885, § 2.01, eff. April 1, 2009.

[Chapters 306 to 320 reserved for expansion]

SUBTITLE B. ELECTRONIC COMMUNICATIONS

CHAPTER 321. REGULATION OF CERTAIN ELECTRONIC MAIL

SUBCHAPTER A. GENERAL PROVISIONS

SUBCHAPTER A. GENERAL PROVISIONS

§ 321.001. Definitions

In This Chapter:

(1) "Commercial electronic mail message" means an electronic mail message that advertises, offers for sale or lease, or promotes any goods, services, business opportunity, property, or other article, commodity, or thing of value.

(2) "Electronic mail" means a message, file, or other information that is transmitted through a local, regional, or global computer network, regardless of whether the message, file, or information is viewed, stored for retrieval at a later time, printed, or filtered by a computer program that is designed or intended to filter or screen the message, file, or information.

(3) "Electronic mail service provider" means a person who:

(A) is authorized to transact business in this state;

(B) is an intermediary in transmitting or receiving electronic mail; and

(C) provides to an end user of an electronic mail service the ability to transmit or receive electronic mail.

(4) "Established business relationship" means a relationship that:

(A) is formed by a voluntary two-way communication between a person and another person, regardless of whether consideration is exchanged;

(B) pertains to a product or service offered by one of the persons; and

(C) has not been terminated by either person.

(5) "Obscene" has the meaning assigned by Section 43.21, Penal Code.

(6) "Sender" means a person who initiates an electronic mail message.

(7) "Sexual conduct" has the meaning assigned by Section 43.25, Penal Code.

(8) "Unsolicited commercial electronic mail message" means a commercial electronic mail message transmitted without the consent of the recipient by a person with whom the recipient does not have an established business relationship. The term does not include electronic mail transmitted by an organization using electronic mail to communicate exclusively with members, employees, or contractors of the organization.

Added by Acts 2007, 80th Leg., ch. 885, § 2.01, eff. April 1, 2009.

[Sections 321.002 to 321.050 reserved for expansion]

SUBCHAPTER B. PROHIBITED AND REQUIRED CONDUCT

§ 321.051. Transmission of Certain Commercial Electronic Mail Messages Prohibited

(a) In this section, "internet domain name" means a globally unique, hierarchical reference to an Internet host or service that is:

(1) assigned through a centralized Internet naming authority; and

(2) composed of a series of character strings separated by periods, with the right-most string specifying the top of the hierarchy.

(b) A person may not intentionally transmit a commercial electronic mail message that:

(1) is an unsolicited commercial electronic mail message and falsifies the electronic mail transmission or routing information;

(2) contains false, deceptive, or misleading information in the subject line; or

(3) uses another person's Internet domain name without the other person's consent.

Added by Acts 2007, 80th Leg., ch. 885, § 2.01, eff. April 1, 2009.

§ 321.052. Requirement for Transmission of Unsolicited Commercial Electronic Mail Messages

(a) A person may not intentionally take an action to transmit an unsolicited commercial electronic mail message unless:

(1) "ADV:" appears first in the subject line of the message or, if the message contains obscene material or material depicting sexual conduct, "ADV: ADULT ADVERTISEMENT" appears first in the subject line; and

(2) the sender or a person acting on behalf of the sender provides a functioning return electronic mail address to which a recipient of the message may, at no cost to the recipient, send a reply requesting the removal of the recipient's electronic mail address from the sender's electronic mail list.

(b) A sender shall remove a person's electronic mail address from the sender's electronic mail list not later than the third day after the date the sender receives a request for removal of that address under Subsection (a)(2).

Added by Acts 2007, 80th Leg., ch. 885, § 2.01, eff. April 1, 2009.

§ 321.053. Selling or Providing Certain Electronic Mail Addresses Prohibited

A sender or a person acting on behalf of a sender may not sell or otherwise provide to another the electronic mail address of a person who requests the removal of that address from the sender's electronic mail list as provided by Section 321.052(a)(2), except as required by other law.

Added by Acts 2007, 80th Leg., ch. 885, § 2.01, eff. April 1, 2009.

[Sections 321.054 to 321.100 reserved for expansion]

SUBCHAPTER C. ENFORCEMENT

§ 321.101. Transmission of Message Containing Obscene Material or Material Depicting Sexual Conduct; Criminal Penalty

(a) A person commits an offense if the person intentionally takes an action to transmit a message that contains obscene material or material depicting sexual conduct in violation of Section 321.052(a)(1).

(b) An offense under this section is a Class B misdemeanor.

Added by Acts 2007, 80th Leg., ch. 885, § 2.01, eff. April 1, 2009.

§ 321.102. Violation of Chapter: General Civil Penalty and Injunctive Relief

(a) A person who violates this chapter is liable to this state for a civil penalty in an amount not to exceed the lesser of:

(1) $10 for each unlawful message or unlawful action; or

(2) $25,000 for each day an unlawful message is received or each day an unlawful action is taken.

(b) The attorney general or a prosecuting attorney in the county in which the violation occurs may:

(1) bring an action to recover the civil penalty; and

(2) obtain an injunction to prevent or restrain a violation of this chapter.

(c) The attorney general or prosecuting attorney may recover reasonable expenses incurred in recovering the civil penalty, including court costs, reasonable attorney's fees, investigative costs, witness fees, and deposition expenses.

(d) Subsection (a) does not apply to a violation of Section 321.107(a).

Added by Acts 2007, 80th Leg., ch. 885, § 2.01, eff. April 1, 2009.

§ 321.103. Violation of Chapter: Deceptive Trade Practice

A violation of this chapter is a false, misleading, or deceptive act or practice under Subchapter E, Chapter 17,[1] and any public or private right or remedy prescribed by that subchapter may be used to enforce this chapter, except as provided by Section 321.109.

Added by Acts 2007, 80th Leg., ch. 885, § 2.01, eff. April 1, 2009.

[1] V.T.C.A., Bus. & C. Code § 17.41 et seq.

§ 321.104. Violation of Chapter: Civil Action for Damages

(a) A person injured by a violation of this chapter may bring an action to recover:

(1) actual damages, including lost profits; or

(2) an amount described by Section 321.105 or 321.106, as applicable.

(b) A person who prevails in the action is entitled to recover reasonable attorney's fees and court costs.

Added by Acts 2007, 80th Leg., ch. 885, § 2.01, eff. April 1, 2009.

§ 321.105. Alternative Recovery for Persons Other than Electronic Mail Service Providers

(a) In lieu of actual damages, a person injured by a violation of this chapter arising from the transmission of an unsolicited or commercial electronic mail message may recover an amount equal to the lesser of:

(1) $10 for each unlawful message; or

(2) $25,000 for each day the unlawful message is received.

(b) Subsection (a) does not apply to a person who is an electronic mail service provider.

Added by Acts 2007, 80th Leg., ch. 885, § 2.01, eff. April 1, 2009.

§ 321.106. Alternative Recovery for Electronic Mail Service Providers

In lieu of actual damages, an electronic mail service provider injured by a violation of this chapter arising from the transmission of an unsolicited or commercial electronic mail message may recover an amount equal to the greater of:

(1) $10 for each unlawful message; or

(2) $25,000 for each day the unlawful message is received.

Added by Acts 2007, 80th Leg., ch. 885, § 2.01, eff. April 1, 2009.

§ 321.107. Required Notice of Civil Action to Attorney General; Civil Penalty

(a) A person who brings an action under section 321.104 shall notify the attorney general of the action by mailing a copy of the petition by registered or certified mail not later than the 30th day after the date the petition is filed and at least 10 days before the date set for a hearing on the action.

(b) A person who violates Subsection (a) is liable to this state for a civil penalty in an amount not to exceed $200 for each violation. The attorney general may bring an action to recover the civil penalty in the court in which the action under Section 321.104 was brought.

Added by Acts 2007, 80th Leg., ch. 885, § 2.01, eff. April 1, 2009.

§ 321.108. Intervention in Civil Action by Attorney General

The attorney general may intervene in an action brought under section 321.104 by:

(1) filing a notice of intervention with the court in which the action is pending; and

(2) serving each party to the action with a copy of the notice of intervention.

Added by Acts 2007, 80th Leg., ch. 885, § 2.01, eff. April 1, 2009.

§ 321.109. Certification as Class Action Prohibited

A court may not certify an action brought under this chapter as a class action.

Added by Acts 2007, 80th Leg., ch. 885, § 2.01, eff. April 1, 2009.

§ 321.110. Protection of Secrecy or Security

At the request of a party to an action brought under this chapter, the court, in the court's discretion, may conduct a legal proceeding in a manner that protects:

(1) the secrecy and security of the computer, computer network, computer data, computer program, and computer software involved so as to prevent a possible recurrence of the same or a similar act by another person; or

(2) any trade secret of a party to the action.

Added by Acts 2007, 80th Leg., ch. 885, § 2.01, eff. April 1, 2009.

§ 321.111. Immunity From Liability: Commercial Electronic Mail Message Transmitted by Error or Accident

A person may not be held liable under this chapter for a commercial electronic mail message that is transmitted as a result of an error or accident.

Added by Acts 2007, 80th Leg., ch. 885, § 2.01, eff. April 1, 2009.

§ 321.112. Immunity From Liability: Telecommunications Utilities and Electronic Mail Service Providers

(a) In this section, "telecommunications utility" has the meaning assigned by Section 51.002, Utilities Code.

(b) A telecommunications utility or an electronic mail service provider may not be held liable under Section 321.051 or 321.052 and is not subject to a penalty provided by this chapter.

(c) A person injured by a violation of this chapter does not have a cause of action against a telecommunications utility or an electronic mail service provider under this chapter solely because the utility or service provider:

(1) is an intermediary between the sender, or a person acting on behalf of the sender, and the recipient in the transmission of electronic mail that violates this chapter;

(2) provides transmission, routing, relaying, handling, or storing, through an automatic technical process, of an unsolicited commercial electronic mail message through the utility's or service provider's computer network or facilities; or

(3) provides telecommunications services, information services, or other services used in the transmission of an electronic mail message that violates this chapter.

Added by Acts 2007, 80th Leg., ch. 885, § 2.01, eff. April 1, 2009.

§ 321.113. Qualified Immunity From Liability of Senders

A sender may not be held liable for the transmission of an electronic mail message that violates this chapter if the sender:

(1) contracts in good faith with an electronic mail service provider to transmit electronic mail messages for the sender; and

(2) has no reason to believe the electronic mail service provider will transmit any of the sender's electronic mail messages in violation of this chapter.

Added by Acts 2007, 80th Leg., ch. 885, § 2.01, eff. April 1, 2009.

§ 321.114. Authority to Block Certain Commercial Electronic Mail Messages; Qualified Immunity

(a) An electronic mail service provider may on its own initiative block the receipt or transmission through its service of any commercial electronic mail message that the service provider reasonably believes is or will be transmitted in violation of this chapter, if the service provider:

(1) provides a process for the prompt, good faith resolution of a dispute related to the blocking with the sender of the commercial electronic mail message; and

(2) makes contact information for the resolution of the dispute accessible to the public on the service provider's Internet website.

(b) An electronic mail service provider who complies with Subsection (a) may not be held liable for blocking the receipt or transmission through its service of any commercial electronic mail message that the service provider reasonably believes is or will be transmitted in violation of this chapter.

Added by Acts 2007, 80th Leg., ch. 885, § 2.01, eff. April 1, 2009.

CHAPTER 322. UNIFORM ELECTRONIC TRANSACTIONS ACT

Section

§ 322.001. Short Title

This chapter may be cited as the uniform electronic transactions act.

Added by Acts 2007, 80th Leg., ch. 885, § 2.01, eff. April 1, 2009.

§ 322.002. Definitions

In this chapter:

(1) "Agreement" means the bargain of the parties in fact, as found in their language or inferred from other circumstances and from rules, regulations, and procedures given the effect of agreements under laws otherwise applicable to a particular transaction.

(2) "Automated transaction" means a transaction conducted or performed, in whole or in part, by electronic means or electronic records, in which the acts or records of one or both parties are not reviewed by an individual in the ordinary course in forming a contract, performing under an existing contract, or fulfilling an obligation required by the transaction.

(3) "Computer program" means a set of statements or instructions to be used directly or indirectly in an information processing system in order to bring about a certain result.

(4) "Contract" means the total legal obligation resulting from the parties' agreement as affected by this chapter and other applicable law.

(5) "Electronic" means relating to technology having electrical, digital, magnetic, wireless, optical, electromagnetic, or similar capabilities.

(6) "Electronic agent" means a computer program or an electronic or other automated means used independently to initiate an action or respond to electronic records or performances in whole or in part, without review or action by an individual.

(7) "Electronic record" means a record created, generated, sent, communicated, received, or stored by electronic means.

(8) "Electronic signature" means an electronic sound, symbol, or process attached to or logically associated with a record and executed or adopted by a person with the intent to sign the record.

(9) "Governmental agency" means an executive, legislative, or judicial agency, department, board, commission, authority, institution, or instrumentality of the federal government or of a state or of a county, municipality, or other political subdivision of a state.

(10) "Information" means data, text, images, sounds, codes, computer programs, software, databases, or the like.

(11) "Information processing system" means an electronic system for creating, generating, sending, receiving, storing, displaying, or processing information.

(12) "Record" means information that is inscribed on a tangible medium or that is stored in an electronic or other medium and is retrievable in perceivable form.

(13) "Security procedure" means a procedure employed for the purpose of verifying that an electronic signature, record, or performance is that of a specific person or for detecting changes or errors in the information in an electronic record. The term

includes a procedure that requires the use of algorithms or other codes, identifying words or numbers, encryption, or callback or other acknowledgment procedures.

(14) "State" means a state of the United States, the District of Columbia, Puerto Rico, the United States Virgin Islands, or any territory or insular possession subject to the jurisdiction of the United States. The term includes an Indian tribe or band, or Alaskan native village, which is recognized by federal law or formally acknowledged by a state.

(15) "Transaction" means an action or set of actions occurring between two or more persons relating to the conduct of business, commercial, or governmental affairs.

Added by Acts 2007, 80th Leg., ch. 885, § 2.01, eff. April 1, 2009.

§ 322.003. Scope

(a) Except as otherwise provided in subsection (b), this chapter applies to electronic records and electronic signatures relating to a transaction.

(b) This chapter does not apply to a transaction to the extent it is governed by:

(1) a law governing the creation and execution of wills, codicils, or testamentary trusts; or

(2) the Uniform Commercial Code, other than Sections 1.107 and 1.206 and Chapters 2 and 2A.

(c) This chapter applies to an electronic record or electronic signature otherwise excluded from the application of this chapter under Subsection (b) when used for a transaction subject to a law other than those specified in Subsection (b).

(d) A transaction subject to this chapter is also subject to other applicable substantive law.

Added by Acts 2007, 80th Leg., ch. 885, § 2.01, eff. April 1, 2009.

§ 322.004. Prospective Application

This chapter applies to any electronic record or electronic signature created, generated, sent, communicated, received, or stored on or after January 1, 2002.

Added by Acts 2007, 80th Leg., ch. 885, § 2.01, eff. April 1, 2009.

§ 322.005. Use of Electronic Records and Electronic Signatures; Variation by Agreement

(a) This chapter does not require a record or signature to be created, generated, sent, communicated, received, stored, or otherwise processed or used by electronic means or in electronic form.

(b) This chapter applies only to transactions between parties each of which has agreed to conduct transactions by electronic means. Whether the parties agree to conduct a transaction by electronic means is determined from the context and surrounding circumstances, including the parties' conduct.

(c) A party that agrees to conduct a transaction by electronic means may refuse to conduct other transactions by electronic means. The right granted by this subsection may not be waived by agreement.

(d) Except as otherwise provided in this chapter, the effect of any of its provisions may be varied by agreement. The presence in certain provisions of this chapter of the words "unless otherwise agreed," or words of similar import, does not imply that the effect of other provisions may not be varied by agreement.

(e) Whether an electronic record or electronic signature has legal consequences is determined by this chapter and other applicable law.

Added by Acts 2007, 80th Leg., ch. 885, § 2.01, eff. April 1, 2009.

§ 322.006. Construction and Application

This chapter must be construed and applied:

(1) to facilitate electronic transactions consistent with other applicable law;

(2) to be consistent with reasonable practices concerning electronic transactions and with the continued expansion of those practices; and

(3) to effectuate its general purpose to make uniform the law with respect to the subject of this chapter among states enacting it.

Added by Acts 2007, 80th Leg., ch. 885, § 2.01, eff. April 1, 2009.

§ 322.007. Legal Recognition of Electronic Records, Electronic Signatures, and Electronic Contracts

(a) A record or signature may not be denied legal effect or enforceability solely because it is in electronic form.

(b) A contract may not be denied legal effect or enforceability solely because an electronic record was used in its formation.

(c) If a law requires a record to be in writing, an electronic record satisfies the law.

(d) If a law requires a signature, an electronic signature satisfies the law.

Added by Acts 2007, 80th Leg., ch. 885, § 2.01, eff. April 1, 2009.

§ 322.008. Provision of Information in Writing; Presentation of Records

(a) If parties have agreed to conduct a transaction by electronic means and a law requires a person to provide, send, or deliver information in writing to another person, the requirement is satisfied if the information is provided, sent, or delivered, as the case may be, in an electronic record capable of retention by the recipient at the time of receipt. An electronic record is not capable of retention by the recipient if the sender or its information processing system inhibits the ability of the recipient to print or store the electronic record.

(b) If a law other than this chapter requires a record (i) to be posted or displayed in a certain manner, (ii) to be sent, communicated, or transmitted by a specified method, or (iii) to contain information that is formatted in a certain manner, the following rules apply:

(1) the record must be posted or displayed in the manner specified in the other law;

(2) except as otherwise provided in Subsection (d)(2), the record must be sent, communicated, or transmitted by the method specified in the other law; and

(3) the record must contain the information formatted in the manner specified in the other law.

(c) If a sender inhibits the ability of a recipient to store or print an electronic record, the electronic record is not enforceable against the recipient.

(d) The requirements of this section may not be varied by agreement, but:

(1) to the extent a law other than this chapter requires information to be provided, sent, or delivered in writing but permits that requirement to be varied by agreement, the requirement under Subsection (a) that the information be in the form of an electronic record capable of retention may also be varied by agreement; and

(2) a requirement under a law other than this chapter to send, communicate, or transmit a record by first class mail may be varied by agreement to the extent permitted by the other law.

Added by Acts 2007, 80th Leg., ch. 885, § 2.01, eff. April 1, 2009.

§ 322.009. Attribution and Effect of Electronic Record and Electronic signature

(a) An electronic record or electronic signature is attributable to a person if it was the act of the person. The act of the person may be shown in any manner, including a showing of the efficacy of any security procedure applied to determine the person to which the electronic record or electronic signature was attributable.

(b) The effect of an electronic record or electronic signature attributed to a person under Subsection (a) is determined from the context and surrounding circumstances at the time of its creation, execution, or adoption, including the parties' agreement, if any, and otherwise as provided by law.

Added by Acts 2007, 80th Leg., ch. 885, § 2.01, eff. April 1, 2009.

§ 322.010. Effect of Change or Error

(a) If a change or error in an electronic record occurs in a transmission between parties to a transaction, the rules provided by this section apply.

(b) If the parties have agreed to use a security procedure to detect changes or errors and one party has conformed to the procedure, but the other party has not, and the nonconforming party would have detected the change or error had that party also conformed, the conforming party may avoid the effect of the changed or erroneous electronic record.

(c) In an automated transaction involving an individual, the individual may avoid the effect of an electronic record that resulted from an error made by the individual in dealing with the electronic agent of another person if the electronic agent did not provide an opportunity for the prevention or correction of the error and, at the time the individual learns of the error, the individual:

(1) promptly notifies the other person of the error and that the individual did not intend to be bound by the electronic record received by the other person;

(2) takes reasonable steps, including steps that conform to the other person's reasonable instructions, to return to the other person or, if instructed by the other person, to destroy the consideration received, if any, as a result of the erroneous electronic record; and

(3) has not used or received any benefit or value from the consideration, if any, received from the other person.

(d) If neither Subsection (b) nor Subsection (c) applies, the change or error has the effect provided by other law, including the law of mistake, and the parties' contract, if any.

(e) Subsections (c) and (d) may not be varied by agreement.

Added by Acts 2007, 80th Leg., ch. 885, § 2.01, eff. April 1, 2009.

§ 322.011. Notarization and Acknowledgment

If a law requires a signature or record to be notarized, acknowledged, verified, or made under oath, the requirement is satisfied if the electronic signature of the person authorized to perform those acts, together with all other information required to be included by other applicable law, is attached to or logically associated with the signature or record.

Added by Acts 2007, 80th Leg., ch. 885, § 2.01, eff. April 1, 2009.

§ 322.012. Retention of Electronic Records; Originals

(a) If a law requires that a record be retained, the requirement is satisfied by retaining an electronic record of the information in the record which:

(1) accurately reflects the information set forth in the record after it was first generated in its final form as an electronic record or otherwise; and

(2) remains accessible for later reference.

(b) A requirement to retain a record in accordance with Subsection (a) does not apply to any information the sole purpose of which is to enable the record to be sent, communicated, or received.

(c) A person may satisfy Subsection (a) by using the services of another person if the requirements of that subsection are satisfied.

(d) If a law requires a record to be presented or retained in its original form, or provides consequences if the record is not presented or retained in its original form, that law is satisfied by an electronic record retained in accordance with Subsection (a).

(e) If a law requires retention of a check, that requirement is satisfied by retention of an electronic record of the information on the front and back of the check in accordance with Subsection (a).

(f) A record retained as an electronic record in accordance with Subsection (a) satisfies a law requiring a person to retain a record for evidentiary, audit, or like purposes, unless a law enacted after January 1, 2002, specifically prohibits the use of an electronic record for the specified purpose.

(g) This section does not preclude a governmental agency of this state from specifying additional requirements for the retention of a record subject to the agency's jurisdiction.

Added by Acts 2007, 80th Leg., ch. 885, § 2.01, eff. April 1, 2009.

§ 322.013. Admissibility in Evidence

In a proceeding, evidence of a record or signature may not be excluded solely because it is in electronic form.

Added by Acts 2007, 80th Leg., ch. 885, § 2.01, eff. April 1, 2009.

§ 322.014. Automated Transaction

(a) In an automated transaction, the rules provided by this section apply.

(b) A contract may be formed by the interaction of electronic agents of the parties, even if no individual was aware of or reviewed the electronic agents' actions or the resulting terms and agreements.

(c) A contract may be formed by the interaction of an electronic agent and an individual, acting on the individual's own behalf or for another person, including by an interaction in which the individual performs actions that the individual is free to refuse to perform and which the individual knows or has reason to know will cause the electronic agent to complete the transaction or performance.

(d) The terms of the contract are determined by the substantive law applicable to it.

Added by Acts 2007, 80th Leg., ch. 885, § 2.01, eff. April 1, 2009.

§ 322.015. Time and Place of Sending and Receipt

(a) Unless otherwise agreed between the sender and the recipient, an electronic record is sent when it:

(1) is addressed properly or otherwise directed properly to an information processing system that the recipient has designated or uses for the purpose of receiving electronic records or information of the type sent and from which the recipient is able to retrieve the electronic record;

(2) is in a form capable of being processed by that system; and

(3) enters an information processing system outside the control of the sender or of a person that sent the electronic record on behalf of the sender or enters a region of the information processing system designated or used by the recipient which is under the control of the recipient.

(b) Unless otherwise agreed between the sender and the recipient, an electronic record is received when:

(1) it enters an information processing system that the recipient has designated or uses for the purpose of receiving electronic records or information of the type sent and from which the recipient is able to retrieve the electronic record; and

(2) it is in a form capable of being processed by that system.

(c) Subsection (b) applies even if the place the information processing system is located is different from the place the electronic record is deemed to be received under Subsection (d).

(d) Unless otherwise expressly provided in the electronic record or agreed between the sender and the recipient, an electronic record is deemed to be sent from the sender's place of business and to be received at the recipient's place of business. For purposes of this subsection, the following rules apply:

(1) if the sender or the recipient has more than one place of business, the place of business of that person is the place having the closest relationship to the underlying transaction; and

(2) if the sender or the recipient does not have a place of business, the place of business is the sender's or the recipient's residence, as the case may be.

(e) An electronic record is received under Subsection (b) even if no individual is aware of its receipt.

(f) Receipt of an electronic acknowledgment from an information processing system described in Subsection (b) establishes that a record was received but, by itself, does not establish that the content sent corresponds to the content received.

(g) If a person is aware that an electronic record purportedly sent under Subsection (a), or purportedly received under Subsection (b), was not actually sent or received, the legal effect of the sending or receipt is determined by other applicable law. Except to the extent permitted by the other law, the requirements of this subsection may not be varied by agreement.

Added by Acts 2007, 80th Leg., ch. 885, § 2.01, eff. April 1, 2009.

§ 322.016. Transferable Records

(a) In this section, "transferable record" means an electronic record that:

(1) would be a note under Chapter 3, or a document under Chapter 7, if the electronic record were in writing; and

(2) the issuer of the electronic record expressly has agreed is a transferable record.

(b) A person has control of a transferable record if a system employed for evidencing the transfer of interests in the transferable record reliably establishes that person as the person to which the transferable record was issued or transferred.

(c) A system satisfies Subsection (b), and a person is deemed to have control of a transferable record, if the transferable record is created, stored, and assigned in such a manner that:

(1) a single authoritative copy of the transferable record exists which is unique, identifiable, and, except as otherwise provided in Subdivisions (4), (5), and (6), unalterable;

(2) the authoritative copy identifies the person asserting control as:

(A) the person to which the transferable record was issued; or

(B) if the authoritative copy indicates that the transferable record has been transferred, the person to which the transferable record was most recently transferred;

(3) the authoritative copy is communicated to and maintained by the person asserting control or its designated custodian;

(4) copies or revisions that add or change an identified assignee of the authoritative copy can be made only with the consent of the person asserting control;

(5) each copy of the authoritative copy and any copy of a copy is readily identifiable as a copy that is not the authoritative copy; and

(6) any revision of the authoritative copy is readily identifiable as authorized or unauthorized.

(d) Except as otherwise agreed, a person having control of a transferable record is the holder, as defined in Section 1.201, of the transferable record and has the same rights and defenses as a holder of an equivalent record or writing under the Uniform Commercial Code, including, if the applicable statutory requirements under Section 3.302(a), 7.501, or 9.330 are satisfied, the rights and defenses of a holder in due course, a holder to which a negotiable document of title has been duly negotiated, or a purchaser, respectively. Delivery, possession, and indorsement are not required to obtain or exercise any of the rights under this subsection.

(e) Except as otherwise agreed, an obligor under a transferable record has the same rights and defenses as an equivalent obligor under equivalent records or writings under the Uniform Commercial Code.

(f) If requested by a person against which enforcement is sought, the person seeking to enforce the transferable record shall provide reasonable proof that the person is in control of the transferable record. Proof may include access to the authoritative copy of the transferable record and related business records sufficient to review the terms of the transferable record and to establish the identity of the person having control of the transferable record.

Added by Acts 2007, 80th Leg., ch. 885, § 2.01, eff. April 1, 2009.

§ 322.017. Acceptance and Distribution of Electronic Records by Governmental Agencies

(a) Except as otherwise provided by section 322.012(f), each state agency shall determine whether, and the extent to which, the agency will send and accept electronic records and electronic signatures to and from other persons and otherwise create, generate, communicate, store, process, use, and rely upon electronic records and electronic signatures.

(b) To the extent that a state agency uses electronic records and electronic signatures under Subsection (a), the Department of Information Resources and Texas State Library and Archives Commission, pursuant to their rulemaking authority under other law and giving due consideration to security, may specify:

(1) the manner and format in which the electronic records must be created, generated, sent, communicated, received, and stored and the systems established for those purposes;

(2) if electronic records must be signed by electronic means, the type of electronic signature required, the manner and format in which the electronic signature must be affixed to the electronic record, and the identity of, or criteria that must be met by, any third party used by a person filing a document to facilitate the process;

(3) control processes and procedures as appropriate to ensure adequate preservation, disposition, integrity, security, confidentiality, and auditability of electronic records; and

(4) any other required attributes for electronic records which are specified for corresponding nonelectronic records or reasonably necessary under the circumstances.

(c) Except as otherwise provided in Section 322.012(f), this chapter does not require a governmental agency of this state to use or permit the use of electronic records or electronic signatures.

Added by Acts 2007, 80th Leg., ch. 885, § 2.01, eff. April 1, 2009.

§ 322.018. Interoperability

The department of information resources may encourage and promote consistency and interoperability with similar requirements adopted by other governmental agencies of this and other states and the federal government and nongovernmental persons interacting with governmental agencies of this state. If appropriate, those standards may specify differing levels of standards from which governmental agencies of this state may choose in implementing the most appropriate standard for a particular application.

Added by Acts 2007, 80th Leg., ch. 885, § 2.01, eff. April 1, 2009.

§ 322.019. Exemption to Preemption by Federal Electronic Signatures Act

This chapter modifies, limits, or supersedes the provisions of the Electronic Signatures in Global and National Commerce Act (15 U.S.C. Section 7001 et seq.) as authorized by Section 102 of that Act (15 U.S.C. Section 7002).

Added by Acts 2007, 80th Leg., ch. 885, § 2.01, eff. April 1, 2009.

§ 322.020. Applicability of Penal Code

This chapter does not authorize any activity that is prohibited by the penal code.

Added by Acts 2007, 80th Leg., ch. 885, § 2.01, eff. April 1, 2009.

§ 322.021. Certain Requirements Considered to be Recommendations

Any requirement of the department of information resources or the texas state Library and Archives Commission under this chapter that generally applies to one or more state agencies using electronic records or electronic signatures is considered to be a recommendation to the comptroller concerning the electronic records or electronic signatures used by the comptroller. The comptroller may adopt or decline to adopt the recommendation.

Added by Acts 2007, 80th Leg., ch. 885, § 2.01, eff. April 1, 2009.

CHAPTER 323. PROVISION OF SOFTWARE OR SERVICES TO BLOCK OR SCREEN INTERNET MATERIAL

§ 323.001. Definitions

In this chapter:

(1) "Freeware" means software distributed to a person free of charge, regardless of whether use of the software is subject to certain restrictions.

(2) "Institution of higher education" has the meaning assigned by Section 61.003, Education Code.

(3) "Interactive computer service" means any information service or system that provides or enables computer access to the Internet by multiple users.

(4) "Internet" means the largest nonproprietary nonprofit cooperative public computer network, popularly known as the Internet.

(5) "Shareware" means copyrighted software for which the copyright owner sets certain conditions for the software's distribution and use, including requiring payment to the copyright owner after a person who has secured a copy of the software decides to use the software, regardless of whether the payment is for additional support or functionality of the software.

Added by Acts 2007, 80th Leg., ch. 885, § 2.01, eff. April 1, 2009.

§ 323.002. Software or Services That Restrict Access to Certain Internet Material

(a) This section does not apply to:

(1) the Department of Information Resources, in the department's capacity as the telecommunications provider for this state; or

(2) an institution of higher education that provides interactive computer service.

(b) A person who charges a fee to provide an interactive computer service shall provide free of charge to each subscriber of the service in this state a link leading to fully functional shareware, freeware, or a demonstration version of software or to a service that, for at least one operating system, enables the subscriber to automatically block or screen material on the Internet.

(c) A person who charges a fee to provide an interactive computer service is in compliance with this section if the person places, on the person's first page of world wide web text information accessible to a subscriber, a link leading to the software or service described by Subsection (b). The identity of the link or other on-screen depiction of the link must appear set out from surrounding written or graphical material so as to be conspicuous.

(d) A person who provides a link that complies with this section is not liable to a subscriber for any temporary inoperability of the link or for the effectiveness of the software or service to which the person links.

Added by Acts 2007, 80th Leg., ch. 885, § 2.01, eff. April 1, 2009.

§ 323.003. Civil Penalty

(a) A person is liable to this state for a civil penalty of $2,000 for each day the person violates section 323.002. The aggregate civil penalty may not exceed $60,000.

(b) The attorney general may bring an action against a person who violates Section 323.002 to recover the civil penalty. Before bringing the action, the attorney general shall give the person notice of the person's noncompliance and liability for a civil penalty. If the person complies with Section 323.002 not later than the 30th day after the date of the notice, the violation is cured and the person is not liable for the civil penalty.

Added by Acts 2007, 80th Leg., ch. 885, § 2.01, eff. April 1, 2009.

CHAPTER 324. CONSUMER PROTECTION AGAINST COMPUTER SPYWARE

SUBCHAPTER A. GENERAL PROVISIONS

SUBCHAPTER B. PROHIBITED CONDUCT OR ACTIVITIES

SUBCHAPTER C. CIVIL REMEDIES

SUBCHAPTER A. GENERAL PROVISIONS

§ 324.001. Short Title

This chapter may be cited as the consumer protection against computer spyware act.

Added by Acts 2007, 80th Leg., ch. 885, § 2.01, eff. April 1, 2009.

§ 324.002. Definitions

In this chapter:

(1) "Advertisement" means a communication that includes the promotion of a commercial product or service, including communication on an Internet website operated for a commercial purpose.

(2) "Computer software" means a sequence of instructions written in a programming language that is executed on a computer. The term does not include:

(A) a web page; or

(B) a data component of a web page that cannot be executed independently of that page.

(3) "Damage," with respect to a computer, means significant impairment to the integrity or availability of data, computer software, a system, or information.

(4) "Execute," with respect to computer software, means to perform a function or carry out instructions.

(5) "Keystroke-logging function" means a function of a computer software program that:

(A) records all keystrokes made by a person using a computer; and

(B) transfers that information from the computer to another person.

(6) "Owner or operator of a computer" means the owner or lessee of a computer or an individual using a computer with the authorization of the owner or lessee of the computer. The phrase "owner of a computer," with respect to a computer sold at retail, does not include a person who owned the computer before the date on which the computer was sold.

(7) "Person" means an individual, partnership, corporation, limited liability company, or other organization, or a combination of those organizations.

(8) "Personally identifiable information," with respect to an individual who is the owner or operator of a computer, means:

(A) a first name or first initial in combination with a last name;

(B) a home or other physical address, including street name;

(C) an electronic mail address;

(D) a credit or debit card number;

(E) a bank account number;

(F) a password or access code associated with a credit or debit card or bank account;

(G) a social security number, tax identification number, driver's license number, passport number, or other government-issued identification number; or

(H) any of the following information if the information alone or in combination with other information personally identifies the individual:

(i) account balances;

(ii) overdraft history; or

(iii) payment history.

Added by Acts 2007, 80th Leg., ch. 885, § 2.01, eff. April 1, 2009.

§ 324.003. Exceptions to Applicability of Chapter

(a) Section 324.052, other than subdivision (1) of that section, and sections 324.053(4) and 324.054 do not apply to a telecommunications carrier, cable operator, computer hardware or software provider, or provider of information service or interactive computer service that monitors or has interaction with a subscriber's Internet or other network connection or service or a protected computer for:

(1) a network or computer security purpose;

(2) diagnostics, technical support, or a repair purpose;

(3) an authorized update of computer software or system firmware;

(4) authorized remote system management; or

(5) detection or prevention of unauthorized use of or fraudulent or other illegal activity in connection with a network, service, or computer software, including scanning for and removing software proscribed under this chapter.

(b) This chapter does not apply to:

(1) the use of a navigation device, any interaction with a navigation device, or the installation or use of computer software on a navigation device by a multichannel video programming distributor, as defined by 47 U.S. C. Section 522(13), or video programmer in connection with the provision of multichannel video programming or other services offered over a multichannel video programming system if the provision of the programming or other service is subject to 47 U.S.C. Section 338(i) or 551; or

(2) the collection or disclosure of subscriber information by a multichannel video programming distributor, as defined by 47 U.S.C. Section 522(13), or video programmer in connection with the provision of multichannel video programming or other services offered over a multichannel video programming system if the collection or disclosure of the information is subject to 47 U.S.C. Section 338(i) or 551.

Added by Acts 2007, 80th Leg., ch. 885, § 2.01, eff. April 1, 2009.

§ 324.004. Causing Computer Software to be Copied

For purposes of this chapter, a person causes computer software to be copied if the person distributes or transfers computer software or a component of computer software. Causing computer software to be copied does not include:

(1) transmitting or routing computer software or a component of the software;

(2) providing intermediate temporary storage or caching of software;

(3) providing a storage medium such as a compact disk;

(4) a website;

(5) the distribution of computer software by a third party through a computer server; or

(6) providing an information location tool, such as a directory, index, reference, pointer, or hypertext link, through which the user of a computer is able to locate computer software.

Added by Acts 2007, 80th Leg., ch. 885, § 2.01, eff. April 1, 2009.

§ 324.005. Knowing Violation

A person knowingly violates section 324. 051, 324.052, or 324.053 if the person:

(1) acts with actual knowledge of the facts that constitute the violation; or

(2) consciously avoids information that would establish actual knowledge of those facts.

Added by Acts 2007, 80th Leg., ch. 885, § 2.01, eff. April 1, 2009.

§ 324.006. Intentionally Deceptive Means

For purposes of this chapter, a person is considered to have acted through intentionally deceptive means if the person, with the intent to deceive the owner or operator of a computer:

(1) intentionally makes a materially false or fraudulent statement;

(2) intentionally makes a statement or uses a description that omits or misrepresents material information; or

(3) intentionally and materially fails to provide to the owner or operator any notice regarding the installation or execution of computer software.

Added by Acts 2007, 80th Leg., ch. 885, § 2.01, eff. April 1, 2009.

[Sections 324.007 to 324.050 reserved for expansion]

SUBCHAPTER B. PROHIBITED CONDUCT OR ACTIVITIES

§ 324.051. Unauthorized Collection or Culling of Personally Identifiable Information

A person other than the owner or operator of the computer may not knowingly cause computer software to be copied to a computer in this state and use the software to:

(1) collect personally identifiable information through intentionally deceptive means:

(A) by using a keystroke-logging function; or

(B) in a manner that correlates that information with information regarding all or substantially all of the websites visited by the owner or operator of the computer, other than websites operated by the person collecting the information; or

(2) cull, through intentionally deceptive means, the following kinds of personally identifiable information from the consumer's computer hard drive for a purpose wholly unrelated to any of the purposes of the software or service described to an owner or operator of the computer:

(A) a credit or debit card number;

(B) a bank account number;

(C) a password or access code associated with a credit or debit card number or a bank account;

(D) a social security number;

(E) account balances; or

(F) overdraft history.

Added by Acts 2007, 80th Leg., ch. 885, § 2.01, eff. April 1, 2009.

§ 324.052. Unauthorized Access to or Modifications of Computer Settings; Computer Damage

A person other than the owner or operator of the computer may not knowingly cause computer software to be copied to a computer in this state and use the software to:

(1) modify, through intentionally deceptive means, a setting that controls:

(A) the page that appears when an Internet browser or a similar software program is launched to access and navigate the Internet;

(B) the default provider or web proxy used to access or search the Internet; or

(C) a list of bookmarks used to access web pages;

(2) take control of the computer by:

(A) accessing or using the computer's modem or Internet service to:

(i) cause damage to the computer;

(ii) cause the owner or operator of the computer to incur financial charges for a service the owner or operator did not previously authorize; or

(iii) cause a third party affected by the conduct to incur financial charges for a service the third party did not previously authorize; or

(B) opening, without the consent of the owner or operator of the computer, an advertisement that:

(i) is in the owner's or operator's Internet browser in a multiple, sequential, or stand-alone form; and

(ii) cannot be closed by an ordinarily reasonable person using the computer without closing the browser or shutting down the computer;

(3) modify settings on the computer that relate to access to or use of the Internet and protection of information for purposes of stealing personally identifiable information of the owner or operator of the computer; or

(4) modify security settings on the computer relating to access to or use of the Internet for purposes of causing damage to one or more computers.

Added by Acts 2007, 80th Leg., ch. 885, § 2.01, eff. April 1, 2009.

§ 324.053. Unauthorized Interference With Installation or Disabling of Computer Software

A person other than the owner or operator of the computer may not knowingly cause computer software to be copied to a computer in this state and use the software to:

(1) prevent, through intentionally deceptive means, reasonable efforts of the owner or operator of the computer to block the installation or execution of or to disable computer software by causing computer software that the owner or operator has

properly removed or disabled to automatically reinstall or reactivate on the computer;

(2) intentionally misrepresent to another that computer software will be uninstalled or disabled by the actions of the owner or operator of the computer;

(3) remove, disable, or render inoperative, through intentionally deceptive means, security, antispyware, or antivirus computer software installed on the computer;

(4) prevent reasonable efforts of the owner or operator to block the installation of or to disable computer software by:

(A) presenting the owner or operator with an option to decline the installation of software knowing that, when the option is selected, the installation process will continue to proceed; or

(B) misrepresenting that software has been disabled;

(5) change the name, location, or other designation of computer software to prevent the owner from locating and removing the software; or

(6) create randomized or intentionally deceptive file names or random or intentionally deceptive directory folders, formats, or registry entries to avoid detection and prevent the owner from removing computer software.

Added by Acts 2007, 80th Leg., ch. 885, § 2.01, eff. April 1, 2009.

§ 324.054. Other Prohibited Conduct

A person other than the owner or operator of the computer may not:

(1) induce the owner or operator of a computer in this state to install a computer software component to the computer by intentionally misrepresenting the extent to which the installation is necessary:

(A) for security or privacy reasons;

(B) to open or view text; or

(C) to play a particular type of musical or other content; or

(2) copy and execute or cause the copying and execution of a computer software component to a computer in this state in a deceptive manner with the intent to cause the owner or operator of the computer to use the component in a manner that violates this chapter.

Added by Acts 2007, 80th Leg., ch. 885, § 2.01, eff. April 1, 2009.

[Sections 324.055 to 324.100 reserved for expansion]

SUBCHAPTER C. CIVIL REMEDIES

§ 324.101. Private Action

(a) Any of the following persons, if adversely affected by the violation, may bring a civil action against a person who violates this chapter:

(1) a provider of computer software;

(2) an owner of a web page or trademark;

(3) a telecommunications carrier;

(4) a cable operator; or

(5) an Internet service provider.

(b) Each separate violation of this chapter is an actionable violation.

(c) In addition to any other remedy provided by law and except as provided by Subsection (g), a person who brings an action under this section may obtain:

(1) injunctive relief that restrains the violator from continuing the violation;

(2) subject to Subsection (d), damages in an amount equal to the greater of:

(A) actual damages arising from the violation; or

(B) $100,000 for each violation of the same nature; or

(3) both injunctive relief and damages.

(d) The court may increase the amount of an award of actual damages in an action brought under Subsection (c) to an amount not to exceed three times the amount of actual damages sustained if the court finds that the violation has reoccurred with sufficient frequency to constitute a pattern or practice.

(e) A plaintiff who prevails in an action brought under Subsection (c) is entitled to recover reasonable attorney's fees and court costs.

(f) For purposes of Subsection (c), violations are of the same nature if the violations consist of the same course of conduct or action, regardless of the number of times the conduct or act occurred.

(g) If a violation of Section 324.052 causes a telecommunications carrier or cable operator to incur costs for the origination, transport, or termination of a call triggered using the modem of a customer of the telecommunications carrier or cable operator as a result of the violation, the telecommunications carrier or cable operator may in addition to any other remedy provided by law:

(1) apply to a court for an order to enjoin the violation;

(2) recover the charges the telecommunications carrier or cable operator is obligated to pay to a telecommunications carrier, a cable operator, another provider of transmission capability, or an information service provider as a result of the violation, including charges for the origination, transport, or termination of the call;

(3) recover the costs of handling customer inquiries or complaints with respect to amounts billed for calls as a result of the violation;

(4) recover other costs, including court costs, and reasonable attorney's fees; or

(5) both apply for injunctive relief and recover charges and other costs as provided by this subsection.

Added by Acts 2007, 80th Leg., ch. 885, § 2.01, eff. April 1, 2009.

§ 324.102. Civil Penalty; Injunctive Relief

(a) A person who violates this chapter is liable to this state for a civil penalty in an amount not to exceed $100,000 for each violation. The attorney general may bring an action to recover the civil penalty imposed by this subsection.

(b) If it appears to the attorney general that a person is engaging in, has engaged in, or is about to engage in conduct that violates this chapter, the attorney general may bring an action in the name of the state against the person to restrain the violation by a temporary restraining order or by a permanent or temporary injunction.

(c) The attorney general is entitled to recover reasonable expenses incurred in obtaining civil penalties or injunctive relief, or both, under this section, including reasonable attorney's fees and court costs.

Added by Acts 2007, 80th Leg., ch. 885, § 2.01, eff. April 1, 2009.

CHAPTER 325. INTERNET FRAUD

Section

§ 325.001. Short Title

This chapter may be cited as the anti–phishing act.

Added by Acts 2007, 80th Leg., ch. 885, § 2.01, eff. April 1, 2009.

§ 325.002. Definitions

In this chapter:

(1) "Electronic mail" means a message, file, or other information that is transmitted through a local, regional, or global computer network, regardless of whether the message, file, or information is viewed, stored for retrieval at a later time, printed, or filtered by a computer program that is designed or intended to filter or screen the message, file, or information.

(2) "Electronic mail address" means a destination, commonly expressed as a string of characters, to which electronic mail may be sent or delivered.

(3) "Identifying information" has the meaning assigned by Section 32.51, Penal Code.

(4) "Internet domain name" refers to a globally unique, hierarchical reference to an Internet host or service that is:

(A) assigned through a centralized Internet naming authority; and

(B) composed of a series of character strings separated by periods with the right-most string specifying the top of the hierarchy.

(5) "Web page" means:

(A) a location that has a single uniform resource locator with respect to the world wide web; or

(B) another location that can be accessed on the Internet.

Added by Acts 2007, 80th Leg., ch. 885, § 2.01, eff. April 1, 2009.

§ 325.003. Inapplicability of Chapter

This chapter does not apply to a telecommunications provider's or internet service provider's good faith transmission or routing of, or intermediate temporary storing or caching of, identifying information.

Added by Acts 2007, 80th Leg., ch. 885, § 2.01, eff. April 1, 2009.

§ 325.004. Creation and Use of Web Page or Domain Name for Fraudulent Purpose Prohibited

A person may not, with the intent to engage in conduct involving the fraudulent use or possession of identifying information of another person:

(1) create a web page or Internet domain name that is represented as a legitimate online business without the authorization of the registered owner of that business; and

(2) use that web page or a link to that web page, that domain name, or another site on the Internet to induce, request, or solicit another person to provide identifying information for a purpose that the other person believes is legitimate.

Added by Acts 2007, 80th Leg., ch. 885, § 2.01, eff. April 1, 2009.

§ 325.005. Transmission of Fraudulent Electronic Mail Prohibited

A person may not, with the intent to engage in conduct involving the fraudulent use or possession of identifying information, send or cause to be sent to an electronic mail address held by a resident of this state an electronic mail message that:

(1) is falsely represented as being sent by a legitimate online business;

(2) refers or links the recipient to a web page that is represented as being associated with the legitimate online business; and

(3) directly or indirectly induces, requests, or solicits the recipient to provide identifying information for a purpose that the recipient believes is legitimate.

Added by Acts 2007, 80th Leg., ch. 885, § 2.01, eff. April 1, 2009.

§ 325.006. Civil Action for Injunctive Relief or Damages

(a) Any of the following persons may bring a civil action against a person who violates this chapter:

(1) a person who is engaged in the business of providing Internet access service to the public and is adversely affected by the violation;

(2) an owner of a web page or trademark who is adversely affected by the violation; or

(3) the attorney general.

(b) A person who brings an action under this section may obtain:

(1) injunctive relief that restrains the violator from continuing the violation;

(2) subject to Subsection (c), damages in an amount equal to the greater of:

(A) actual damages arising from the violation; or

(B) $100,000 for each violation of the same nature; or

(3) both injunctive relief and damages.

(c) The court may increase the amount of an award of actual damages in an action brought under this section to an amount not to exceed three times the actual damages sustained if the court finds that the violation has reoccurred with sufficient frequency to constitute a pattern or practice.

(d) A plaintiff who prevails in an action brought under this section is entitled to recover reasonable attorney's fees and court costs.

(e) For purposes of this section, violations are of the same nature if the violations consist of the same course of conduct or action, regardless of the number of times the conduct or act occurred.

Added by Acts 2007, 80th Leg., ch. 885, § 2.01, eff. April 1, 2009.

TITLE 11. PERSONAL IDENTITY INFORMATION

Acts 2007, 80th Leg., ch. 885, § 2.01 added this Title effective April 1, 2009.

SUBTITLE A. IDENTIFYING INFORMATION

CHAPTER 501. PROTECTION OF DRIVER'S LICENSE AND SOCIAL SECURITY NUMBERS

SUBCHAPTER A. CONFIDENTIALITY OF SOCIAL SECURITY NUMBERS

SUBCHAPTER B. PRIVACY POLICY TO PROTECT SOCIAL SECURITY NUMBERS

SUBCHAPTER A. CONFIDENTIALITY OF SOCIAL SECURITY NUMBERS

§ 501.001. Certain Uses of Social Security Number Prohibited

(a) A person, other than a government or a governmental subdivision or agency, may not:

(1) intentionally communicate or otherwise make available to the public an individual's social security number;

(2) display an individual's social security number on a card or other device required to access a product or service provided by the person;

(3) require an individual to transmit the individual's social security number over the Internet unless:

(1) the Internet connection is secure; or

(2) the social security number is encrypted;

(4) require an individual's social security number for access to an Internet website unless a password or unique personal identification number or other authentication device is also required for access; or

(5) except as provided by Subsection (f), print an individual's social security number on any material sent by mail, unless state or federal law requires that social security number to be included in the material.

(b) A person using an individual's social security number before January 1, 2005, in a manner prohibited by Subsection (a) may continue that use if:

(1) the use is continuous; and

(2) beginning January 1, 2006, the person provides to the individual an annual disclosure stating that, on written request from the individual, the person will stop using the individual's social security number in a manner prohibited by Subsection (a).

(c) A person, other than a government or a governmental subdivision or agency, may not deny a service to an individual because the individual makes a written request under Subsection (b)(2).

(d) If a person receives a written request from an individual directing the person to stop using the individual's social security number in a manner prohibited by Subsection (a), the person shall comply with the request not later than the 30th day after the date the request is received. The person may not impose a fee for complying with the request.

(e) This section does not apply to:

(1) the collection, use, or release of a social security number required by state or federal law, including Chapter 552, Government Code;

(2) the use of a social security number for internal verification or administrative purposes;

(3) a document that is recorded or required to be open to the public under Chapter 552, Government Code;

(4) a court record; or

(5) an institution of higher education if the use of a social security number by the institution is regulated by Chapter 51, Education Code, or another provision of the Education Code.

(f) Subsection (a)(5) does not apply to an application or form sent by mail, including a document sent:

(1) as part of an application or enrollment process;

(2) to establish, amend, or terminate an account, contract, or policy; or

(3) to confirm the accuracy of a social security number.

Added by Acts 2007, 80th Leg., ch. 885, § 2.01, eff. April 1, 2009.

§ 501.002. Certain Uses of Social Security Number Prohibited; Remedies

(a) A person may not print an individual's social security number on a card or other device required to access a product or service provided by the person unless the individual has requested in writing that printing. The person may not require a request for that printing as a condition of receipt of or access to a product or service provided by the person.

(b) A person who violates this section is liable to this state for a civil penalty in an amount not to exceed $500 for each violation. The attorney general or the prosecuting attorney in the county in which the violation occurs may bring an action to recover the civil penalty imposed under this section.

(c) The attorney general may bring an action in the name of the state to restrain or enjoin a person from violating this section.

(d) This section does not apply to:

(1) the collection, use, or release of a social security number required by state or federal law, including Chapter 552, Government Code; or

(2) the use of a social security number for internal verification or administrative purposes.

(e) This section applies to a card or other device issued in connection with an insurance policy only if the policy is delivered, issued for delivery, or renewed on or after March 1, 2005.

Added by Acts 2007, 80th Leg., ch. 885, § 2.01, eff. April 1, 2009.

[Sections 501.003 to 501.050 reserved for expansion]

SUBCHAPTER B. PRIVACY POLICY TO PROTECT SOCIAL SECURITY NUMBERS

§ 501.051. Inapplicability of Subchapter

This subchapter does not apply to:

(1) a person who is required to maintain and disseminate a privacy policy under:

(A) the Gramm–Leach–Bliley Act (15 U.S.C. Sections 6801 to 6809);

(B) the Family Educational Rights and Privacy Act of 1974 (20 U.S.C. Section 1232g); or

(C) the Health Insurance Portability and Accountability Act of 1996 (42 U.S.C. Section 1320d et seq.);

(2) a covered entity under rules adopted by the commissioner of insurance relating to insurance consumer health information privacy or insurance consumer financial information privacy;

(3) a governmental body, as defined by Section 552.003, Government Code, other than a municipally owned utility; or

(4) a person with respect to a loan transaction, if the person is not engaged in the business of making loans.

Added by Acts 2007, 80th Leg., ch. 885, § 2.01, eff. April 1, 2009.

§ 501.052. Privacy Policy Necessary to Require Disclosure of Social Security Number

(a) A person may not require an individual to disclose the individual's social security number to obtain goods or services from or enter into a business transaction with the person unless the person:

(1) adopts a privacy policy as provided by Subsection (b);

(2) makes the privacy policy available to the individual; and

(3) maintains under the privacy policy the confidentiality and security of the social security number disclosed to the person.

(b) A privacy policy adopted under this section must include:

(1) how personal information is collected;

(2) how and when the personal information is used;

(3) how the personal information is protected;

(4) who has access to the personal information; and

(5) the method of disposal of the personal information.

Added by Acts 2007, 80th Leg., ch. 885, § 2.01, eff. April 1, 2009.

§ 501.053. Civil Penalty; Injunction

(a) A person who violates section 501.052(a) is liable to this state for a civil penalty in an amount not to exceed $500 for each calendar month during which a violation occurs. The civil penalty may not be imposed for more than one violation that occurs in a month. The attorney general or the prosecuting attorney in the county in which the violation occurs may bring an action to recover the civil penalty imposed under this section.

(b) The attorney general may bring an action in the name of the state to restrain or enjoin a person from violating Section 501.052(a).

Added by Acts 2007, 80th Leg., ch. 885, § 2.01, eff. April 1, 2009.

[Sections 501.054 to 501.100 reserved for expansion]

SUBCHAPTER C. OTHER RESTRICTIONS TO PROTECT DRIVER'S LICENSE AND SOCIAL SECURITY NUMBERS

§ 501.101. Use of Consumer Driver's License or Social Security Number by Merchant or Certain Third Party

(a) A merchant or a third party under contract with a merchant who requires a consumer returning merchandise to provide the consumer's driver's license or social security number may use the number or numbers provided by the consumer solely for identification purposes if the consumer does not have a valid receipt for the item being returned and is seeking a cash, credit, or store credit refund.

(b) A merchant or a third party under contract with a merchant may not disclose a consumer's driver's license or social security number to any other third party, including a merchant, not involved in the initial transaction.

(c) A merchant or a third party under contract with a merchant may use a consumer's driver's license or social security number only to monitor, investigate, or prosecute fraudulent return of merchandise.

(d) A merchant or a third party under contract with a merchant shall destroy or arrange for the destruction of records containing the consumer's driver's license or social security number at the expiration of six months from the date of the last transaction.

Added by Acts 2007, 80th Leg., ch. 885, § 2.01, eff. April 1, 2009.

§ 501.102. Civil Penalty; Injunction

(a) A person who violates this subchapter is liable to this state for a civil penalty in an amount not to exceed $500 for each violation. The attorney general or the prosecuting attorney in the county in which the violation occurs may bring an action to recover the civil penalty imposed under this section.

(b) The attorney general may bring an action in the name of the state to restrain or enjoin a person from violating this subchapter.

Added by Acts 2007, 80th Leg., ch. 885, § 2.01, eff. April 1, 2009.

CHAPTER 502. PROTECTION OF IDENTIFYING FINANCIAL INFORMATION

§ 502.001. Warning Sign About Identity Theft for Restaurant or Bar Employees

(a) In this section:

(1) "Credit card" means an identification card, plate, coupon, book, or number or any other device authorizing a designated person or bearer to obtain property or service on credit.

(2) "Debit card" means an identification card, plate, coupon, book, or number or any other device authorizing a designated person or bearer to communicate a request to an unmanned teller machine or a customer convenience terminal or to obtain property or services by debit to an account at a financial institution.

(b) This section applies only to a restaurant or bar that accepts credit cards or debit cards from customers in the ordinary course of business.

(c) A restaurant or bar owner shall display in a prominent place on the premises of the restaurant or bar a sign stating in letters at least one-half inch high: "UNDER SECTION 32.51, PENAL CODE, IT IS A STATE JAIL FELONY (PUNISHABLE BY CONFINEMENT IN A STATE JAIL FOR NOT MORE THAN TWO YEARS) TO OBTAIN, POSSESS, TRANSFER, OR USE A CUSTOMER'S DEBIT CARD OR CREDIT CARD NUMBER WITHOUT THE CUSTOMER'S CONSENT."

(d) The restaurant or bar owner shall display the sign in English and in another language spoken by a substantial portion of the employees of the restaurant or bar as their familiar language.

(e) A restaurant or bar owner who fails to comply with this section commits an offense. An offense under this subsection is a misdemeanor punishable by a fine not to exceed $25.

(f) It is a defense to prosecution under Subsection (e) that the restaurant or bar owner charged with the offense produces to the court satisfactory evidence that the person displayed the sign required by Subsection (c) not later than 48 hours after the person received a citation for an offense under Subsection (e). If the court is satisfied with the evidence produced by the person, the court shall dismiss the charge.

Added by Acts 2007, 80th Leg., ch. 885, § 2.01, eff. April 1, 2009.

§ 502.002. Business Receipt Containing Credit Card or Debit Card Information

(a) A person who accepts a credit card or debit card for the transaction of business may not print on a receipt or other document that evidences the transaction and is provided to a cardholder more than the last four digits of the credit card or debit card account number or the month and year that the credit card or debit card expires.

(b) This section does not apply to a transaction in which the sole means of recording a person's credit card or debit card account number on a receipt or other document evidencing the transaction is by handwriting or an imprint or copy of the credit card or debit card.

(c) A person who provides, leases, or sells a cash register or other machine used to print a receipt or other document evidencing a credit card or debit card transaction shall provide notice of the requirements of this section to the recipient, lessee, or buyer, as applicable, of the machine.

(d) A person who violates Subsection (a) is liable to this state for a civil penalty in an amount not to exceed $500 for each calendar month in which a violation occurs. The civil penalty may not be imposed for more than one violation that occurs in a month. The attorney general or the prosecuting attorney in the county in which the violation occurs may bring an action to recover the civil penalty imposed under this section.

(e) The attorney general may bring an action in the name of the state to restrain or enjoin a person from violating Subsection (a).

(f) A court may not certify an action brought under this section as a class action.

Added by Acts 2007, 80th Leg., ch. 885, § 2.01, eff. April 1, 2009.

§ 502.003. Delivery of check form

(a) In this section:

(1) "Addressee" means a person to whom a check form is sent.

(2) "Check form" means a device for the transmission or payment of money that:

(A) is not a negotiable instrument under Section 3.104;

(B) if completed would be a check as defined by Section 3.104; and

(C) is printed with information relating to the financial institution on which the completed check may be drawn.

(3) "Check form provider" means a business that provides check forms to a customer for a personal or business account.

(4) "Courier" means an entity that delivers parcels for a fee.

(b) If an addressee requests that a check form provider employ courier delivery of a check form with signature required, and that service is available in the delivery area of the addressee, the entity arranging for courier delivery in compliance with the addressee's request must provide the addressee with the option to require that the signature of the addressee, or the representative of the addressee, be obtained on delivery.

(c) The option under Subsection (b) to require the signature of the addressee or representative may be provided:

(1) on a printed check form order form;

(2) on an electronic check form order form where check form orders are offered on the Internet;

(3) by electronic mail to an address established for that purpose by the entity making the offer; or

(4) by another method reasonably designed to effectively communicate the addressee's intent.

(d) An entity that arranges for the courier delivery of a check form to an addressee as requested under Subsection (b) shall notify the courier of the check form that the signature of the addressee or a representative of the addressee is required for delivery under that subsection.

(e) If the addressee suffers a pecuniary loss because of the use of a check form stolen at the time of delivery to the addressee, a civil penalty of not more than $1,000 for each delivery may be imposed on:

(1) an entity that violates Subsection (b), (c), or (d); or

(2) a courier that:

(A) is properly notified under Subsection (d) that a signature is required for delivery; and

(B) delivers the check form without obtaining the signature of the addressee or a representative of the addressee.

(f) The attorney general may bring an action to recover a civil penalty imposed under Subsection (e). The attorney general may recover reasonable expenses incurred in obtaining the civil penalty, including court costs, reasonable attorney's fees, investigative costs, witness fees, and deposition expenses.

Added by Acts 2007, 80th Leg., ch. 885, § 2.01, eff. April 1, 2009.

CHAPTER 503. BIOMETRIC IDENTIFIERS

§ 503.001. Capture or Use of Biometric Identifier

(a) In this section, "biometric identifier" means a retina or iris scan, fingerprint, voiceprint, or record of hand or face geometry.

(b) A person may not capture a biometric identifier of an individual for a commercial purpose unless the person:

(1) informs the individual before capturing the biometric identifier; and

(2) receives the individual's consent to capture the biometric identifier.

(c) A person who possesses a biometric identifier of an individual:

(1) may not sell, lease, or otherwise disclose the biometric identifier to another person unless:

(A) the individual consents to the disclosure;

(B) the disclosure completes a financial transaction that the individual requested or authorized;

(C) the disclosure is required or permitted by a federal statute or by a state statute other than Chapter 552, Government Code; or

(D) the disclosure is made by or to a law enforcement agency for a law enforcement purpose; and

(2) shall store, transmit, and protect from disclosure the biometric identifier using reasonable care and in a manner that is the same as or more protective than the manner in which the person stores, transmits, and protects any other confidential information the person possesses.

(d) A person who violates this section is subject to a civil penalty of not more than $25,000 for each violation. The attorney general may bring an action to recover the civil penalty.

Added by Acts 2007, 80th Leg., ch. 885, § 2.01, eff. April 1, 2009.

CHAPTER 504. PROHIBITED USE OF CRIME VICTIM OR MOTOR VEHICLE ACCIDENT INFORMATION

§ 504.001. Definitions

In this chapter:

(1) "Crime victim information" means information that:

(A) is collected or prepared by a law enforcement agency; and

(B) identifies or serves to identify a person who, according to a record of the agency, may have been the victim of a crime in which:

(i) physical injury to the person occurred or was attempted; or

(ii) the offender entered or attempted to enter the dwelling of the person.

(2) "Motor vehicle accident information" means information that:

(A) is collected or prepared by a law enforcement agency; and

(B) identifies or serves to identify a person who, according to a record of the agency, may have been involved in a motor vehicle accident.

Added by Acts 2007, 80th Leg., ch. 885, § 2.01, eff. April 1, 2009.

§ 504.002. Prohibition on Use for Solicitation or Sale of Information

(a) A person who possesses crime victim or motor vehicle accident information that the person obtained or knows was obtained from a law enforcement agency may not:

(1) use the information to contact directly any of the following persons for the purpose of soliciting business from the person:

(A) a crime victim;

(B) a person who was involved in a motor vehicle accident; or

(C) a member of the family of a person described by Paragraph (A) or (B); or

(2) sell the information to another person for financial gain.

(b) The attorney general may bring an action against a person who violates Subsection (a) pursuant to Section 17.47.

(c) A person commits an offense if the person violates Subsection (a). An offense under this subsection is a Class C misdemeanor unless the defendant has been previously convicted under this section three or more times, in which event the offense is a felony of the third degree.

Added by Acts 2007, 80th Leg., ch. 885, § 2.01, eff. April 1, 2009.

[Chapters 505 to 520 reserved for expansion]

SUBTITLE B. IDENTITY THEFT

CHAPTER 521. UNAUTHORIZED USE OF IDENTIFYING INFORMATION

SUBCHAPTER A. GENERAL PROVISIONS

SUBCHAPTER A. GENERAL PROVISIONS

§ 521.001. Short Title

This chapter may be cited as the identity theft enforcement and protection act.

Added by Acts 2007, 80th Leg., ch. 885, § 2.01, eff. April 1, 2009.

§ 521.002. Definitions

(a) In this chapter:

(1) "Personal identifying information" means information that alone or in conjunction with other information identifies an individual, including an individual's:

(A) name, social security number, date of birth, or government-issued identification number;

(B) mother's maiden name;

(C) unique biometric data, including the individual's fingerprint, voice print, and retina or iris image;

(D) unique electronic identification number, address, or routing code; and

(E) telecommunication access device as defined by Section 32.51, Penal Code.

(2) "Sensitive personal information" means, subject to Subsection (b), an individual's first name or first initial and last name in combination with any one or more of the following items, if the name and the items are not encrypted:

(A) social security number;

(B) driver's license number or government-issued identification number; or

(C) account number or credit or debit card number in combination with any required security code, access code, or password that would permit access to an individual's financial account.

(3) "Victim" means a person whose identifying information is used by an unauthorized person.

(b) For purposes of this chapter, the term "sensitive personal information" does not include publicly available information that is lawfully made available to the public from the federal government or a state or local government.

Added by Acts 2007, 80th Leg., ch. 885, § 2.01, eff. April 1, 2009.

[Sections 521.003 to 521.050 reserved for expansion]

SUBCHAPTER B. IDENTITY THEFT

§ 521.051. Unauthorized Use or Possession of Personal Identifying Information

(a) A person may not obtain, possess, transfer, or use personal identifying information of another person without the other person's consent and with intent to obtain a good, a service, insurance, an extension of credit, or any other thing of value in the other person's name.

(b) It is a defense to an action brought under this section that an act by a person:

(1) is covered by the Fair Credit Reporting Act (15 U.S.C. Section 1681 et seq.); and

(2) is in compliance with that Act and regulations adopted under that Act.

(c) This section does not apply to:

(1) a financial institution as defined by 15 U.S.C. Section 6809; or

(2) a covered entity as defined by Section 601.001 or 602.001, Insurance Code.

Added by Acts 2007, 80th Leg., ch. 885, § 2.01, eff. April 1, 2009.

§ 521.052. Business Duty to Protect Sensitive Personal Information

(a) A business shall implement and maintain reasonable procedures, including taking any appropriate corrective action, to protect from unlawful use or disclosure any sensitive personal information collected or maintained by the business in the regular course of business.

(b) A business shall destroy or arrange for the destruction of customer records containing sensitive personal information within the business's custody or control that are not to be retained by the business by:

(1) shredding;

(2) erasing; or

(3) otherwise modifying the sensitive personal information in the records to make the information unreadable or indecipherable through any means.

(c) This section does not apply to a financial institution as defined by 15 U.S.C. Section 6809.

Added by Acts 2007, 80th Leg., ch. 885, § 2.01, eff. April 1, 2009.

§ 521.053. Notification Required Following Breach of Security of Computerized Data

(a) In this section, "breach of system security" means unauthorized acquisition of computerized data that compromises the security, confidentiality, or integrity of sensitive personal information maintained by a person. Good faith acquisition of sensitive personal information by an employee or agent of the person for the purposes of the person is not a breach of system security unless the person uses or discloses the sensitive personal information in an unauthorized manner.

(b) A person who conducts business in this state and owns or licenses computerized data that includes sensitive personal information shall disclose any breach of system security, after discovering or receiving notification of the breach, to any resident of this state whose sensitive personal information was, or is reasonably believed to have been, acquired by an unauthorized person. The disclosure shall be made as quickly as possible, except as provided by Subsection (d) or as necessary to determine the scope of the breach and restore the reasonable integrity of the data system.

(c) Any person who maintains computerized data that includes sensitive personal information not owned by the person shall notify the owner or license holder of the information of any breach of system security immediately after discovering the breach, if the sensitive personal information was, or is reasonably believed to have been, acquired by an unauthorized person.

(d) A person may delay providing notice as required by Subsection (b) or (c) at the request of a law enforcement agency that determines that the notification will impede a criminal investigation. The notification shall be made as soon as the law enforcement agency determines that the notification will not compromise the investigation.

(e) A person may give notice as required by Subsection (b) or (c) by providing:

(1) written notice;

(2) electronic notice, if the notice is provided in accordance with 15 U. S.C. Section 7001; or

(3) notice as provided by Subsection (f).

(f) If the person required to give notice under Subsection (b) or (c) demonstrates that the cost of providing notice would exceed $250,000, the number of affected persons exceeds 500,000, or the person does not have sufficient contact information, the notice may be given by:

(1) electronic mail, if the person has electronic mail addresses for the affected persons;

(2) conspicuous posting of the notice on the person's website; or

(3) notice published in or broadcast on major statewide media.

(g) Notwithstanding Subsection (e), a person who maintains the person's own notification procedures as part of an information security policy for the treatment of sensitive personal information that complies with the timing requirements for notice under this section complies with this section if the person notifies affected persons in accordance with that policy.

(h) If a person is required by this section to notify at one time more than 10,000 persons of a breach of system security, the person shall also notify each consumer reporting agency, as defined by 15 U.S.C. Section 1681a, that maintains files on consumers on a nationwide basis, of the timing, distribution, and content of the notices. The person shall provide the notice required by this subsection without unreasonable delay.

Added by Acts 2007, 80th Leg., ch. 885, § 2.01, eff. April 1, 2009.

[Sections 521.054 to 521.100 reserved for expansion]

SUBCHAPTER C. COURT ORDER DECLARING INDIVIDUAL A VICTIM OF IDENTITY THEFT

§ 521.101. Application for Court Order to Declare Individual a Victim of Identity Theft

(a) A person who is injured by a violation of section 521.051 or who has filed a criminal complaint alleging commission of an offense under Section 32.51, Penal Code, may file an application with a district court for the issuance of an order declaring that the person is a victim of identity theft.

(b) A person may file an application under this section regardless of whether the person is able to identify each person who allegedly transferred or used the person's identifying information in an unlawful manner.

Added by Acts 2007, 80th Leg., ch. 885, § 2.01, eff. April 1, 2009.

§ 521.102. Presumption of Applicant's Status as Victim

An applicant under section 521.101 is presumed to be a victim of identity theft under this subchapter if the person charged with an offense under Section 32.51, Penal Code, is convicted of the offense.

Added by Acts 2007, 80th Leg., ch. 885, § 2.01, eff. April 1, 2009.

§ 521.103. Issuance of Order; Contents

(a) After notice and hearing, if the court is satisfied by a preponderance of the evidence that an applicant under Section 521.101 has been injured by a violation of Section 521.051 or is the victim of an offense under Section 32.51, Penal Code, the court shall enter an order declaring that the applicant is a victim of identity theft resulting from a violation of Section 521.051 or an offense under Section 32.51, Penal Code, as appropriate.

(b) An order under this section must contain:

(1) any known information identifying the violator or person charged with the offense;

(2) the specific personal identifying information and any related document used to commit the alleged violation or offense; and

(3) information identifying any financial account or transaction affected by the alleged violation or offense, including:

(A) the name of the financial institution in which the account is established or of the merchant involved in the transaction, as appropriate;

(B) any relevant account numbers;

(C) the dollar amount of the account or transaction affected by the alleged violation or offense; and

(D) the date of the alleged violation or offense.

Added by Acts 2007, 80th Leg., ch. 885, § 2.01, eff. April 1, 2009.

§ 521.104. Confidentiality of Order

(a) An order issued under section 521.103 must be sealed because of the confidential nature of the information required to be included in the order. The order may be opened and the order or a copy of the order may be released only:

(1) to the proper officials in a civil proceeding brought by or against the victim arising or resulting from a violation of this chapter, including a proceeding to set aside a judgment obtained against the victim;

(2) to the victim for the purpose of submitting the copy of the order to a governmental entity or private business to:

(A) prove that a financial transaction or account of the victim was directly affected by a violation of this chapter or the commission of an offense under Section 32.51, Penal Code; or

(B) correct any record of the entity or business that contains inaccurate or false information as a result of the violation or offense;

(3) on order of the judge; or

(4) as otherwise required or provided by law.

(b) A copy of an order provided to a person under Subsection (a)(1) must remain sealed throughout and after the civil proceeding.

(c) Information contained in a copy of an order provided to a governmental entity or business under Subsection (a)(2) is confidential and may not be released to another person except as otherwise required or provided by law.

Added by Acts 2007, 80th Leg., ch. 885, § 2.01, eff. April 1, 2009.

§ 521.105. Grounds for Vacating Order

A court at any time may vacate an order issued under section 521.103 if the court finds that the application filed under Section 521.101 or any information submitted to the court by the applicant contains a fraudulent misrepresentation or a material misrepresentation of fact.

Added by Acts 2007, 80th Leg., ch. 885, § 2.01, eff. April 1, 2009.

[Sections 521.106 to 521.150 reserved for expansion]

SUBCHAPTER D. REMEDIES

§ 521.151. Civil Penalty; Injunction

(a) A person who violates this chapter is liable to this state for a civil penalty of at least $2,000 but not more than $50,000 for each violation. The attorney general may bring an action to recover the civil penalty imposed under this subsection.

(b) If it appears to the attorney general that a person is engaging in, has engaged in, or is about to engage in conduct that violates this chapter, the attorney general may bring an action in the name of the state against the person to restrain the violation by a temporary restraining order or by a permanent or temporary injunction.

(c) An action brought under Subsection (b) must be filed in a district court in Travis County or:

(1) in any county in which the violation occurred; or

(2) in the county in which the victim resides, regardless of whether the alleged violator has resided, worked, or transacted business in the county in which the victim resides.

(d) The attorney general is not required to give a bond in an action under this section.

(e) In an action under this section, the court may grant any other equitable relief that the court considers appropriate to:

(1) prevent any additional harm to a victim of identity theft or a further violation of this chapter; or

(2) satisfy any judgment entered against the defendant, including issuing an order to appoint a receiver, sequester assets, correct a public or private record, or prevent the dissipation of a victim's assets.

(f) The attorney general is entitled to recover reasonable expenses, including reasonable attorney's fees, court costs, and investigatory costs, incurred in obtaining injunctive relief or civil penalties, or both, under this section. Amounts collected by the attorney general under this section shall be deposited in the general revenue fund and may be appropriated only for the investigation and prosecution of other cases under this chapter.

(g) The fees associated with an action under this section are the same as in a civil case, but the fees may be assessed only against the defendant.

Added by Acts 2007, 80th Leg., ch. 885, § 2.01, eff. April 1, 2009.

§ 521.152. Deceptive Trade Practice

A violation of section 521.051 is a deceptive trade practice actionable under Subchapter E, Chapter 17.[1]

Added by Acts 2007, 80th Leg., ch. 885, § 2.01, eff. April 1, 2009.

[1] V.T.C.A., Bus. & C. Code § 17.41 et seq.

CHAPTER 522. IDENTITY THEFT BY ELECTRONIC DEVICE

§ 522.001. Definitions

In this chapter:

(1) "Payment card" means a credit card, debit card, check card, or other card that is issued to an authorized user to purchase or obtain goods, services, money, or any other thing of value.

(2) "Re-encoder" means an electronic device that can be used to transfer encoded information from a magnetic strip on a payment card onto the magnetic strip of a different payment card.

(3) "Scanning device" means an electronic device used to access, read, scan, or store information encoded on the magnetic strip of a payment card.

Added by Acts 2007, 80th Leg., ch. 885, § 2.01, eff. April 1, 2009.

§ 522.002. Offense; Penalty

(a) A person commits an offense if the person uses a scanning device or re-encoder to access, read, scan, store, or transfer information encoded on the magnetic strip of a payment card without the consent of an authorized user of the payment card and with intent to harm or defraud another.

(b) An offense under this section is a Class B misdemeanor.

(c) If conduct that constitutes an offense under this section also constitutes an offense under any other law, the actor may be prosecuted under this section or the other law.

Added by Acts 2007, 80th Leg., ch. 885, § 2.01, eff. April 1, 2009.

CHAPTER 523. PROVISIONS RELATING TO VICTIMS OF IDENTITY THEFT

Section

§ 523.001. Extension of Credit to Victim of Identity Theft

(a) In this section, "victim of identity theft" means an individual who has filed a criminal complaint alleging the commission of an offense under Section 32.51, Penal Code, other than a person who is convicted of an offense under Section 37.08, Penal Code, with respect to that complaint.

(b) A person who has been notified that an individual has been the victim of identity theft may not deny the individual an extension of credit, including a loan, in the individual's name or restrict or limit the credit extended solely because the individual has been a victim of identity theft. This subsection does not prohibit a person from denying an individual an extension of credit for a reason other than the individual's having been a victim of identity theft, including by reason of the individual's lack of capacity to contract.

(c) A license issued under Subtitle B, Title 4, Finance Code, that is held by a person who violates this section is subject to revocation or suspension under that subtitle.

Added by Acts 2007, 80th Leg., ch. 885, § 2.01, eff. April 1, 2009.

§ 523.002. Verification of consumer identity

(a) In this section:

(1) "Consumer report" has the meaning assigned by Section 20.01.

(2) "Extension of credit" does not include:

(A) an increase in the dollar limit of an existing open-end credit plan as defined by federal Regulation Z (12 C.F.R. Section 226.2), as amended; or

(B) any change to, or review of, an existing credit account.

(3) "Security alert" has the meaning assigned by Section 20.01.

(b) A person who receives notification of a security alert under Section 20.032 in connection with a request for a consumer report for the approval of a credit-based application, including an application for an extension of credit, a purchase, lease, or rental agreement for goods, or for an application for a noncredit-related service, may not lend money, extend credit, or authorize an application without taking reasonable steps to verify the consumer's identity.

(c) If a consumer has included with a security alert a specified telephone number to be used for identity verification purposes, a person who receives that number with a security alert must take reasonable steps to contact the consumer using that number before lending money, extending credit, or completing any purchase, lease, or rental of goods, or approving any noncredit-related services.

(d) If a person uses a consumer report to facilitate the extension of credit or for any other transaction on behalf of a subsidiary, affiliate, agent, assignee, or prospective assignee, that person, rather than the subsidiary, affiliate, agent, assignee, or prospective assignee, may verify the consumer's identity.

Added by Acts 2007, 80th Leg., ch. 885, § 2.01, eff. April 1, 2009.

§ 523.003. Notation of Forged Check

(a) In this section, "victim of identity theft" means a person who has filed with an appropriate law enforcement agency a criminal complaint alleging commission of an offense under Section 32.51, Penal Code.

(b) A financial institution, in accordance with its customary procedures, shall process as forgeries checks received on the account of a victim of identity theft if the victim:

(1) closes the account at the financial institution as a result of the identity theft;

(2) notifies the financial institution that the identity theft is the reason for closing the account;

(3) provides the financial institution with a copy of the criminal complaint described by Subsection (a); and

(4) requests that the financial institution return checks with the notation "forgery."

(c) A victim of identity theft who requests that a financial institution return checks with the notation "forgery" as provided by Subsection (b):

(1) may not assert that the financial institution is liable under Section 4.402 for wrongfully dishonoring a check returned after the victim makes the request; and

(2) shall hold the financial institution harmless for acting in accordance with the victim's request.

Added by Acts 2007, 80th Leg., ch. 885, § 2.01, eff. April 1, 2009.

TITLE 12. RIGHTS AND DUTIES OF CONSUMERS AND MERCHANTS

Acts 2007, 80th Leg., ch. 885, § 2.01 added this Title effective April 1, 2009.

CHAPTER 601. CANCELLATION OF CERTAIN CONSUMER TRANSACTIONS

SUBCHAPTER A. GENERAL PROVISIONS

§ 601.001. Definitions

In this chapter:

(1) "Consumer" means an individual who seeks or acquires real property, money or other personal property, services, or credit for personal, family, or household purposes.

(2) "Consumer transaction" means a transaction between a merchant and one or more consumers.

(3) "Merchant" means a party to a consumer transaction other than a consumer.

(4) "Merchant's place of business" means a merchant's main or permanent branch office or local address. For a state or national bank or savings and loan association, the term includes an approved branch office and a registered loan production office.

Added by Acts 2007, 80th Leg., ch. 885, § 2.01, eff. April 1, 2009.

§ 601.002. Applicability of Chapter; Exception

(a) This chapter applies only to a consumer transaction in which:

(1) the merchant or the merchant's agent engages in a personal solicitation of a sale to the

consumer at a place other than the merchant's place of business;

(2) the consumer's agreement or offer to purchase is given to the merchant or the merchant's agent at a place other than the merchant's place of business; and

(3) the agreement or offer is for:

(A) the purchase of goods or services for consideration that exceeds $25, payable in installments or in cash; or

(B) the purchase of real property for consideration that exceeds $100, payable in installments or in cash.

(b) Notwithstanding Subsection (a), this chapter does not apply to:

(1) a purchase of farm equipment;

(2) an insurance sale regulated by the Texas Department of Insurance;

(3) a sale of goods or services made:

(A) under a preexisting revolving charge account or retail charge agreement; or

(B) after negotiations between the parties at a business establishment in a fixed location where goods or services are offered or exhibited for sale; or

(4) a sale of real property if:

(A) the purchaser is represented by a licensed attorney;

(B) the transaction is negotiated by a licensed real estate broker; or

(C) the transaction is negotiated at a place other than the consumer's residence by the person who owns the property.

Added by Acts 2007, 80th Leg., ch. 885, § 2.01, eff. April 1, 2009.

[Sections 601.003 to 601.050 reserved for expansion]

SUBCHAPTER B. CONSUMER'S RIGHT TO CANCEL TRANSACTION

§ 601.051. Consumer's Right to Cancel

In addition to any other rights or remedies available, a consumer may cancel a consumer transaction not later than midnight of the third business day after the date the consumer signs an agreement or offer to purchase.

Added by Acts 2007, 80th Leg., ch. 885, § 2.01, eff. April 1, 2009.

§ 601.052. Notice of Consumer's Right to Cancel Required

(a) A merchant must provide a consumer with a complete receipt or copy of a contract pertaining to the consumer transaction at the time of its execution.

(b) The document provided under Subsection (a) must:

(1) be in the same language as that principally used in the oral sales presentation;

(2) contain the date of the transaction;

(3) contain the name and address of the merchant; and

(4) contain a statement:

(A) in immediate proximity to the space reserved in the contract for the signature of the consumer or on the front page of the receipt if a contract is not used; and

(B) in boldfaced type of a minimum size of 10 points in substantially the following form:

"YOU, THE BUYER, MAY CANCEL THIS TRANSACTION AT ANY TIME PRIOR TO MIDNIGHT OF THE THIRD BUSINESS DAY AFTER THE DATE OF THIS TRANSACTION. SEE THE ATTACHED NOTICE OF CANCELLATION FORM FOR AN EXPLANATION OF THIS RIGHT."

Added by Acts 2007, 80th Leg., ch. 885, § 2.01, eff. April 1, 2009.

§ 601.053. Completed Cancellation Form Required

(a) A merchant that provides a document under section 601.052 must attach to the document a completed notice of cancellation form in duplicate. The form must:

(1) be easily detachable;

(2) be in the same language as the document provided under Section 601.052; and

(3) contain the following information and statements in 10–point boldfaced type:

"NOTICE OF CANCELLATION

(enter date of transaction)

"YOU MAY CANCEL THIS TRANSACTION, WITHOUT ANY PENALTY OR OBLIGATION, WITHIN THREE BUSINESS DAYS FROM THE ABOVE DATE.

"IF YOU CANCEL, ANY PROPERTY TRADED IN, ANY PAYMENTS MADE BY YOU UNDER THE CONTRACT OR SALE, AND ANY NEGOTIABLE INSTRUMENT EXECUTED BY YOU WILL BE RETURNED WITHIN 10 BUSINESS DAYS FOLLOWING RECEIPT BY THE MERCHANT OF YOUR CANCELLATION NOTICE, AND ANY SECURITY INTEREST ARISING OUT OF THE TRANSACTION WILL BE CANCELLED.

"IF YOU CANCEL, YOU MUST MAKE AVAILABLE TO THE MERCHANT AT YOUR RESIDENCE, IN SUBSTANTIALLY AS GOOD CONDITION AS WHEN RECEIVED, ANY GOODS DELIVERED TO YOU UNDER THIS CONTRACT OR SALE; OR YOU MAY IF YOU WISH, COMPLY WITH THE INSTRUCTIONS OF THE MERCHANT REGARDING THE RETURN SHIPMENT OF THE GOODS AT THE MERCHANT'S EXPENSE AND RISK.

"IF YOU DO NOT AGREE TO RETURN THE GOODS TO THE MERCHANT OR IF THE MERCHANT DOES NOT PICK THEM UP WITHIN 20 DAYS OF THE DATE OF YOUR NOTICE OF CANCELLATION, YOU MAY RETAIN OR DISPOSE OF THE GOODS WITHOUT ANY FURTHER OBLIGATION.

"TO CANCEL THIS TRANSACTION, MAIL OR DELIVER A SIGNED AND DATED COPY OF THIS CANCELLATION NOTICE OR ANY OTHER WRITTEN NOTICE, OR SEND A TELEGRAM, TO (name of merchant), AT (address of merchant's place of business) NOT LATER THAN MIDNIGHT OF (date).

I HEREBY CANCEL THIS TRANSACTION.

(date)

(buyer's signature)"

(b) A merchant may not fail to include on both copies of the form described by Subsection (a):

(1) the name of the merchant;

(2) the address of the merchant's place of business;

(3) the date of the transaction; and

(4) a date not earlier than the third business day after the date of the transaction by which the consumer must give notice of cancellation.

Added by Acts 2007, 80th Leg., ch. 885, § 2.01, eff. April 1, 2009.

§ 601.054. Use of Forms and Notices Prescribed by the Federal Trade Commission Authorized

The use of the forms and notices of the right to cancel prescribed by the Federal Trade Commission's trade-regulation rule providing a cooling-off period for door-to-door sales constitutes compliance with Sections 601.052 and 601.053.

Added by Acts 2007, 80th Leg., ch. 885, § 2.01, eff. April 1, 2009.

§ 601.055. Alternative Notice Authorized for Certain Consumer Transactions

A consumer transaction in which the contract price does not exceed $200 complies with the notice requirements of Sections 601.052 and 601.053 if:

(1) the consumer may at any time cancel the order, refuse to accept delivery of the goods without incurring any obligation to pay for the goods, or return the goods to the merchant and receive a full refund of the amount the consumer has paid; and

(2) the consumer's right to cancel the order, refuse delivery, or return the goods without obligation or charge at any time is clearly and conspicuously stated on the face or reverse side of the sales ticket.

Added by Acts 2007, 80th Leg., ch. 885, § 2.01, eff. April 1, 2009.

[Sections 601.056 to 601.100 reserved for expansion]

SUBCHAPTER C. RIGHTS AND DUTIES OF CONSUMER AND MERCHANT

§ 601.101. Merchant's Compensation

A merchant is not entitled to compensation for services performed under a consumer transaction canceled under this chapter.

Added by Acts 2007, 80th Leg., ch. 885, § 2.01, eff. April 1, 2009.

§ 601.102. Consumer's Retention of Goods or Title to Real Property Authorized

Until a merchant has complied with this chapter, a consumer with possession of goods or the right or title to real property delivered by the merchant:

(1) may retain possession of the goods or the right or title to the real property; and

(2) has a lien on the goods or real property to the extent of any recovery to which the consumer is entitled.

Added by Acts 2007, 80th Leg., ch. 885, § 2.01, eff. April 1, 2009.

§ 601.103. Consumer's Duties With Respect to Delivered Goods or Real Property

(a) Within a reasonable time after a cancellation under this chapter, the consumer must, on demand, tender to the merchant any goods or any right or title to real property delivered by the merchant under the consumer transaction.

(b) The consumer is not obligated to tender goods at a place other than the consumer's residence.

(c) If the merchant fails to demand possession of the goods or the right or title to real property within a reasonable time after cancellation, the goods or real property become the property of the consumer without obligation to pay.

(d) Goods or real property in possession of the consumer are at the risk of the merchant, except that the consumer shall take reasonable care of the goods or the real property both before and for a reasonable time after cancellation.

(e) For purposes of this section, 20 days is presumed to be a reasonable time.

Added by Acts 2007, 80th Leg., ch. 885, § 2.01, eff. April 1, 2009.

[Sections 601.104 to 601.150 reserved for expansion]

SUBCHAPTER D. PROHIBITED ACTS AND CONDUCT BY MERCHANT

§ 601.151. Confession of Judgment or Waiver of Rights

A merchant may not include in a contract or receipt pertaining to a consumer transaction a confession of judgment or a waiver of any of the rights to which the consumer is entitled under this chapter.

Added by Acts 2007, 80th Leg., ch. 885, § 2.01, eff. April 1, 2009.

§ 601.152. Failure to Inform or Misrepresentation of Right to Cancel

A merchant may not:

(1) at the time the consumer signs the contract pertaining to a consumer transaction or purchases the goods, services, or real property, fail to inform the consumer orally of the right to cancel the transaction; or

(2) misrepresent in any manner the consumer's right to cancel.

Added by Acts 2007, 80th Leg., ch. 885, § 2.01, eff. April 1, 2009.

§ 601.153. Transfer of Indebtedness During Certain Period

A merchant may not negotiate, transfer, sell, or assign a note or other evidence of indebtedness to a finance company or other third party before midnight of the fifth business day after the date the contract pertaining to a consumer transaction was signed or the goods or services were purchased.

Added by Acts 2007, 80th Leg., ch. 885, § 2.01, eff. April 1, 2009.

§ 601.154. Failure to Take Certain Actions Following Receipt of Notice of Cancellation

A merchant may not:

(1) fail to notify the consumer before the end of the 10th business day after the date the merchant receives the notice of cancellation whether the merchant intends to repossess or abandon any shipped or delivered goods;

(2) fail or refuse to honor a valid cancellation under this chapter by a consumer; or

(3) fail before the end of the 10th business day after the date the merchant receives a valid notice of cancellation to:

(A) refund all payments made under the contract or sale;

(B) return any goods or property traded in to the merchant in substantially the same condition as when received by the merchant;

(C) cancel and return a negotiable instrument executed by the consumer in connection with the contract of sale;

(D) take any action appropriate to terminate promptly any security interest created in the transaction; or

(E) restore improvements on real property to the same condition as when the merchant took title to or possession of the real property unless the consumer requests otherwise.

Added by Acts 2007, 80th Leg., ch. 885, § 2.01, eff. April 1, 2009.

[Sections 601.155 to 601.200 reserved for expansion]

SUBCHAPTER E. ENFORCEMENT

§ 601.201. Certain Sales or Contracts Void

A sale or contract entered into under a consumer transaction in violation of section 601.053(b) or Subchapter D is void.

Added by Acts 2007, 80th Leg., ch. 885, § 2.01, eff. April 1, 2009.

§ 601.202. Liability For Damages

A merchant who violates this chapter is liable to the consumer for:

(1) actual damages suffered by the consumer as a result of the violation;

(2) reasonable attorney's fees; and

(3) court costs.

Added by Acts 2007, 80th Leg., ch. 885, § 2.01, eff. April 1, 2009.

§ 601.203. Alternative Recovery Under Certain Circumstances

If the merchant fails to tender goods or property traded to the merchant in substantially the same condition as when received by the merchant, the consumer may elect to recover an amount equal to the trade-in allowance stated in the agreement.

Added by Acts 2007, 80th Leg., ch. 885, § 2.01, eff. April 1, 2009.

§ 601.204. Deceptive Trade Practice

A violation of this chapter is a false, misleading, or deceptive act or practice as defined by section 17.46(b). In addition to any remedy under this chapter, a remedy under Subchapter E, Chapter 17,[1] is also available for a violation of this chapter.

Added by Acts 2007, 80th Leg., ch. 885, § 2.01, eff. April 1, 2009.

[1] V.T.C.A., Bus. & C. Code § 17.41 et seq.

§ 601.205. Injunction

If the attorney general believes that a person is violating or about to violate this chapter, the attorney general may bring an action in the name of the state to restrain or enjoin the person from violating this chapter.

Added by Acts 2007, 80th Leg., ch. 885, § 2.01, eff. April 1, 2009.

CHAPTER 602. DELIVERY OF UNSOLICITED GOODS

Section

§ 602.001. Inapplicability of Chapter to Substituted Goods

This chapter does not apply to goods substituted for goods ordered or solicited by the recipient of the goods.

Added by Acts 2007, 80th Leg., ch. 885, § 2.01, eff. April 1, 2009.

§ 602.002. Actions Authorized on Delivery of Unsolicited Goods

Unless otherwise agreed, a person to whom unsolicited goods are delivered:

(1) is entitled to refuse to accept delivery of the goods; and

(2) is not required to return the goods to the sender.

Added by Acts 2007, 80th Leg., ch. 885, § 2.01, eff. April 1, 2009.

§ 602.003. Certain Unsolicited Goods Considered Gift

(a) Unsolicited goods that are addressed to or intended for the recipient are considered a gift to the recipient.

(b) The recipient may use or dispose of goods described by Subsection (a) in any manner without obligation to the sender.

Added by Acts 2007, 80th Leg., ch. 885, § 2.01, eff. April 1, 2009.

§ 602.004. Mistaken Delivery

A person who receives unsolicited goods as the result of a bona fide mistake shall return the goods. the sender has the burden of proof as to the mistake.

Added by Acts 2007, 80th Leg., ch. 885, § 2.01, eff. April 1, 2009.

CHAPTER 603. REGULATION OF CONSUMER CONTRACTS CREATED BY ACCEPTANCE OF CHECK OR OTHER DRAFT

SUBCHAPTER A. GENERAL PROVISIONS

§ 603.001. Definitions

Unless the context requires a different definition, the definitions provided by chapter 3 apply to this chapter.

Added by Acts 2007, 80th Leg., ch. 885, § 2.01, eff. April 1, 2009.

§ 603.002. Applicability of Chapter

(a) Except as provided by subsection (b), this chapter applies only to a person who solicits business in this state by mailing an individual a check or other draft payable to that individual.

(b) This chapter does not apply to a financial institution as defined by Section 201.101, Finance Code, or an authorized lender as defined by Section 341.001 of that code, that sends a check or other draft to an existing or prospective account holder authorizing that person to access an extension of credit.

Added by Acts 2007, 80th Leg., ch. 885, § 2.01, eff. April 1, 2009.

[Sections 603.003 to 603.050 reserved for expansion]

SUBCHAPTER B. REQUIRED DISCLOSURES AND NOTICES

§ 603.051. Required Disclosure on Check or Other Draft

(a) A person who makes an offer that the recipient may accept by endorsing and negotiating a check or other draft shall disclose on the check or other draft that by signing and negotiating the instrument, the depositor agrees to pay for future goods or services as a result of the contract.

(b) The disclosure required by Subsection (a) must be clear, conspicuous, and located on the check or other draft next to the place for endorsement.

Added by Acts 2007, 80th Leg., ch. 885, § 2.01, eff. April 1, 2009.

§ 603.052. Required Notice of Right to Terminate Acceptance of Offer

(a) If an offer described by section 603.051 includes a free membership period, trial period, or other incentive with a time limit, and if the offer results in a contract unless the recipient terminates the acceptance of the offer not later than the end of the time period, the offeror shall send notice to the recipient, at least two weeks before debiting any account, of the recipient's obligation to terminate the recipient's acceptance of the offer.

(b) The notice required by Subsection (a) must be clear and conspicuous. If the offeror bills the recipient by mailing an invoice, the notice may be included with the invoice.

Added by Acts 2007, 80th Leg., ch. 885, § 2.01, eff. April 1, 2009.

§ 603.053. Effect of Noncompliance

(a) An offer described by section 603.051 is void if the offeror:

(1) does not make the disclosure required by that section;

(2) does not send notice as required by Section 603.052, if applicable; or

(3) provides an incentive with a time limit, including a free membership period or trial period, that is less than two weeks in length.

(b) A delivery of goods or services to the recipient does not operate to form a contract between the offeror and the recipient if:

(1) the offer does not contain the disclosure required by Section 603.051;

(2) the offer is not followed by a notice required by Section 603.052, if applicable; or

(3) the offeror fails to honor the recipient's cancellation or termination of the acceptance of the

offer made under the terms of the offer or as required by Section 603.052.

Added by Acts 2007, 80th Leg., ch. 885, § 2.01, eff. April 1, 2009.

[Sections 603.054 to 603.100 reserved for expansion]

SUBCHAPTER C. ENFORCEMENT

§ 603.101. Deceptive Trade Practice

A violation of this chapter is a deceptive trade practice in addition to the practices described by Subchapter E, Chapter 17, and is actionable under that subchapter.

Added by Acts 2007, 80th Leg., ch. 885, § 2.01, eff. April 1, 2009.

CHAPTER 604. SALE OR ISSUANCE OF STORED VALUE CARD

SUBCHAPTER A. GENERAL PROVISIONS

§ 604.001. Definition of Stored Value Card

In this chapter, "stored value card":

(1) means a record, as defined by Section 322.002, including a record that contains a microprocessor chip, magnetic strip, or other means of storing information:

(A) that evidences a promise made for monetary consideration by the seller or issuer of the record that goods or services will be provided to the owner of the record in the value shown in the record;

(B) that is prefunded; and

(C) the value of which is reduced on redemption; and

(2) includes a gift card or gift certificate.

Added by Acts 2007, 80th Leg., ch. 885, § 2.01, eff. April 1, 2009.

§ 604.002. Inapplicability of Chapter

This chapter does not apply to a stored value card that:

(1) is issued by:

(A) a financial institution acting as a financial agent of the United States or this state;

(B) a federally insured financial institution, as defined by Section 201. 101, Finance Code, if the financial institution is primarily liable for the card as the issuing principal; or

(C) an air carrier holding a certificate of public convenience and necessity under Title 49, United States Code;

(2) is issued as a prepaid calling card by a prepaid calling card company regulated under Section 55.253, Utilities Code;

(3) is distributed by the issuer to a person under an awards, rewards, loyalty, incentive, rebate, or promotional program and is not issued or reloaded in exchange for money tendered by the cardholder;

(4) is sold below face value or donated to:

(A) an employee of the seller or issuer;

(B) a nonprofit or charitable organization; or

(C) an educational institution for fund-raising purposes; or

(5) does not expire and for which the seller does not charge a fee other than a fee described in Section 604.051.

Added by Acts 2007, 80th Leg., ch. 885, § 2.01, eff. April 1, 2009.

§ 604.003. Cause of Action Not Created

This chapter does not create a cause of action against a person who issues or sells a stored value card.

Added by Acts 2007, 80th Leg., ch. 885, § 2.01, eff. April 1, 2009.

[Sections 604.004 to 604.050 reserved for expansion]

SUBCHAPTER B. PERMISSIBLE FEES

§ 604.051. Fees and Charges Related to Issuance and Handling of Card

If disclosed as required by subchapter c, the issuer of a stored value card may impose and collect a reasonable:

(1) handling fee in connection with the issuance of or adding of value to the card;

(2) access fee for a card transaction conducted at an unmanned teller machine, as defined by Section 59.301, Finance Code; and

(3) reissue or replacement charge if an expired or lost card is reissued or replaced.

Added by Acts 2007, 80th Leg., ch. 885, § 2.01, eff. April 1, 2009.

§ 604.052. Fees or Charges That Decrease Unredeemed Balance of Card

The issuer of a stored value card may impose or collect a periodic fee or other charge that causes the unredeemed balance of the card to decrease over time only if the fee:

(1) is reasonable;

(2) is not assessed until after the first anniversary of the date the card is sold or issued; and

(3) is disclosed as required by Subchapter C.[1]

Added by Acts 2007, 80th Leg., ch. 885, § 2.01, eff. April 1, 2009.

[1] V.T.C.A., Bus. & C. Code § 604.101 et seq.

[Sections 604.053 to 604.100 reserved for expansion]

SUBCHAPTER C. REQUIRED DISCLOSURES

§ 604.101. Required Disclosure of Certain Matters Applicable to Card

An expiration date or policy, fee, or other material restriction or contract term applicable to a stored value card must be clearly and conspicuously disclosed at the time the card is sold or issued to a person to enable the person to make an informed decision before purchasing the card. (Bus. & Com. Code, Sec. 35.42(f) (part).)

Added by Acts 2007, 80th Leg., ch. 885, § 2.01, eff. April 1, 2009.

§ 604.102. Required Printing of Certain Disclosures

In addition to the disclosure required under section 604.101, a disclosure regarding the expiration of a stored value card or a periodic fee that reduces the unredeemed value of a stored value card must be legibly printed on the card.

Added by Acts 2007, 80th Leg., ch. 885, § 2.01, eff. April 1, 2009.

§ 604.103. Validity of card Sold Without Required Disclosures

A stored value card sold without the disclosure required by this subchapter of an expiration date or policy, fee, or other material restriction or contract term applicable to the card is valid until redeemed or replaced.

Added by Acts 2007, 80th Leg., ch. 885, § 2.01, eff. April 1, 2009.

TITLE 13. CONTESTS AND OTHER PROMOTIONS

Acts 2007, 80th Leg., ch. 885, § 2.01 added this Title effective April 1, 2009.

CHAPTER 621. CONTESTS AND GIFT GIVEAWAYS

SUBCHAPTER A. GENERAL PROVISIONS

Section

SUBCHAPTER B. GIFT OFFERS

SUBCHAPTER C. MATCHED CONTESTS AND DRAWINGS

SUBCHAPTER A. GENERAL PROVISIONS

§ 621.001. Short Title

This chapter may be cited as the contest and gift giveaway act.

Added by Acts 2007, 80th Leg., ch. 885, § 2.01, eff. April 1, 2009.

§ 621.002. Construction of Chapter

This chapter shall be interpreted to provide the maximum disclosure to, and fair treatment of, a person who enters a contest or gift giveaway through which the person is solicited to attend a sales presentation.

Added by Acts 2007, 80th Leg., ch. 885, § 2.01, eff. April 1, 2009.

§ 621.003. Definitions

(a) In this chapter:

(1) "Contest" means a promotional device in which:

(A) a person is offered, as an inducement to attend a sales presentation, a chance to win or receive a prize by complying with specified entry requirements;

(B) the winner or recipient of a prize is determined by random selection; and

(C) all offered prizes are awarded.

(2) "Contest period" means the duration of a contest from the beginning date to the ending date.

(3) "Drawing" means a contest in which the recipient of a prize is determined from all of the entries received.

(4) "Entry form" means a card, letter, entry blank, token, or similar device that identifies a contestant by:

(A) name;

(B) number, letter, or symbol; or

(C) both name and number, letter, or symbol.

(5) "Gift" means an item of value that is offered, transferred, or given to a person as an inducement to attend a sales presentation but that is not offered, transferred, or awarded through a contest. The term does not include a manufacturer's rebate or discount available to the public.

(6) "Major prize" means a prize that has an actual unit cost to the offeror of at least $250.

(7) "Matched contest" means a contest in which:

(A) the winning numbers are preselected, printed on an entry form, and distributed to the public; and

(B) the numbers printed on the entry forms are subsequently matched with the list of winning numbers at a sales location to determine prize eligibility.

(8) "Minor prize" means a prize that:

(A) has an actual unit cost to the offeror of less than $250; and

(B) is transferred to a person who:

(i) attends a sales presentation; and

(ii) is not the winner of a major prize.

(9) "Odds of winning" means a ratio in which:

(A) the numerator equals the actual number of units of an identified prize to be given away during a contest period; and

(B) the denominator equals the number of entry forms distributed or reasonably anticipated to be distributed during the contest period.

(10) "Offeror" means a person who solicits another person to attend a sales presentation.

(11) "Person" includes an individual, a corporation, a firm, and an association.

(12) "Prize" means an item of value that is offered, awarded, or given to a person through a contest. The term does not include a manufacturer's rebate or discount available to the public.

(13) "Sales presentation" means a transaction or occurrence in which a consumer is solicited to execute a contract that obligates the consumer to purchase goods or services as defined by Subchapter E, Chapter 17, including:

(A) a timeshare interest as defined by Section 221.002, Property Code; and

(B) a membership interest as defined by Section 222.003, Property Code.

(14) "Winning number" includes a letter or other identifying symbol.

(b) For purposes of Subsection (a)(1)(B), a determination made by random selection does not include the method used by an offeror to identify a person who will be notified of an offer to win a prize.

Added by Acts 2007, 80th Leg., ch. 885, § 2.01, eff. April 1, 2009.

§ 621.004. Inapplicability of Chapter to Certain Sales Presentations

This chapter does not apply to a sales presentation that is conducted in conjunction with a business seminar, trade show, convention, or other gathering if only representatives of business entities who attend the seminar, trade show, convention, or gathering are solicited to attend.

Added by Acts 2007, 80th Leg., ch. 885, § 2.01, eff. April 1, 2009.

§ 621.005. Determination of Retail Value of Prize or Gift

(a) The retail value of an item offered as a prize or gift is the price at which at least two principal retail outlets in this state have made a substantial number of sales of an identical item to members of the public during the six months preceding the offering of the prize or gift. The item sold by the principal retail outlets must be from the same manufacturer, and be of the same brand, model, and type, as the item offered as a prize or gift.

(b) If a substantial number of sales of a particular item offered as a prize or gift have not been made in this state during the six months preceding the offering of the item described in the solicitation or if the offeror elects, the retail value of the item is the actual cost of the item to the offeror, net of any rebates, plus 200 percent.

(c) If a prize or gift involves lodging, airfare, a trip, or a recreational activity, the retail value is the retail sales price of that lodging, airfare, trip, or recreational activity to a member of the public who is not involved in a promotional or other discount transaction.

Added by Acts 2007, 80th Leg., ch. 885, § 2.01, eff. April 1, 2009.

§ 621.006. Deposit Requirements

(a) In this section, "refundable deposit" means a deposit that is required to be returned in its entirety to a consumer if:

(1) it is paid by the consumer for a reservation used by the consumer; or

(2) the consumer provides at least five possible reservation dates, none of which can be confirmed.

(b) An offeror may require a refundable deposit for a gift or prize involving lodging, airfare, a trip, or a recreational activity if the deposit requirement is fully, clearly, and conspicuously disclosed.

(c) A condition that restricts the refund of the deposit must be clearly and conspicuously disclosed in at least 10–point type on the solicitation.

Added by Acts 2007, 80th Leg., ch. 885, § 2.01, eff. April 1, 2009.

[Sections 621.007 to 621.050 reserved for expansion]

SUBCHAPTER B. GIFT OFFERS

§ 621.051. Applicability of Subchapter

This subchapter applies to a person who uses a gift as part of an advertising plan or program.

Added by Acts 2007, 80th Leg., ch. 885, § 2.01, eff. April 1, 2009.

§ 621.052. Required Disclosures Relating to Gifts

(a) An offeror who notifies a person that the person will receive a gift shall, at the time of the notification, clearly and conspicuously disclose:

(1) that attendance at a sales presentation is required;

(2) the approximate duration of the sales presentation; and

(3) a description of the product or service being sold.

(b) A person shall disclose:

(1) the retail value of a gift; and

(2) clearly and conspicuously in at least 10-point type that airfare, lodging, or both are not included as part of a gift that is a trip or recreational activity to the extent that either or both are not included.

Added by Acts 2007, 80th Leg., ch. 885, § 2.01, eff. April 1, 2009.

§ 621.053. Prohibited acts relating to gifts

A person may not:

(1) use the term "gift" or a similar term in a false, misleading, or deceptive manner;

(2) directly represent or imply that a gift promotion is a contest;

(3) in a gift promotion, use the term:

(A) "finalist," "major award winner," "grand prize recipient," "winner," "won," "will win," or "will be awarded" or use words or phrases of similar meaning that imply that a person is being solicited to enter or participate in a contest; or

(B) "sweepstakes" or "contest" or use words or phrases of similar meaning that imply that a person is being solicited to enter or has won a contest;

(4) represent that a gift has a sponsor, approval, characteristic, ingredient, use, benefit, quantity, status, affiliation, connection, or identity that the gift does not have;

(5) represent that a gift is of a particular standard, quality, grade, style, or model if the gift is of another; or

(6) use a word or phrase that:

(A) simulates or causes confusion with a document issued by an officer of a court or with the seal or name of a real or fictitious governmental entity; or

(B) implies that the offeror is sending a court document or legal document or that the offeror is a governmental entity.

Added by Acts 2007, 80th Leg., ch. 885, § 2.01, eff. April 1, 2009.

§ 621.054. Limitations on Conditioning Gift on Payment of Consideration, Charge, or Expense

(a) In this section, "redemption or shipping fee" means any kind of consideration paid to the offeror. The term does not include a refundable deposit.

(b) Except as provided by Subsection (c), an offeror may notify a person that the person will receive a gift, the receipt of which is conditioned on the person paying consideration of any kind, paying a charge, or incurring an expense, only if the offeror fully, clearly, and conspicuously discloses the consideration, charge, or expense.

(c) An offeror may not charge a redemption or shipping fee for a gift regardless of whether full disclosure of the fee is made.

(d) A gift is not prohibited in a legitimate trade promotion if the advertising regarding the promotion fully discloses any contractual obligation to be assumed to qualify for the gift.

Added by Acts 2007, 80th Leg., ch. 885, § 2.01, eff. April 1, 2009.

§ 621.055. Limitations on Conditioning Gift on Purchase

(a) An offeror may notify a person that the person will receive a gift, the receipt of which is conditioned on the person purchasing a good or service, only if at the time of notification the offeror clearly and conspicuously discloses that purchase of a good or service is required.

(b) A gift is not prohibited in a legitimate trade promotion if the advertising regarding the promotion fully discloses any requirement of a purchase to be made to qualify for the gift.

Added by Acts 2007, 80th Leg., ch. 885, § 2.01, eff. April 1, 2009.

[Sections 621.056 to 621.100 reserved for expansion]

SUBCHAPTER C. MATCHED CONTESTS AND DRAWINGS

§ 621.101. Applicability of Subchapter

This subchapter applies to a person who uses a contest as part of an advertising plan or program.

Added by Acts 2007, 80th Leg., ch. 885, § 2.01, eff. April 1, 2009.

§ 621.102. Required Disclosures Relating to Prizes Generally

An offeror who notifies a person that the person has won a prize, will receive a prize, or has a chance to win or receive a prize shall, at the time of the notification, clearly and conspicuously disclose:

(1) that attendance at a sales presentation is required;

(2) the approximate duration of the sales presentation; and

(3) a description of the product or service being sold.

Added by Acts 2007, 80th Leg., ch. 885, § 2.01, eff. April 1, 2009.

§ 621.103. Requirements For Matched Contest

(a) The identity and number of the major prizes to be awarded in a matched contest must be:

(1) determined before the contest begins; and

(2) disclosed on each entry form distributed.

(b) Each major prize identified on an entry form for a matched contest shall be awarded.

(c) The contest period for a matched contest may not exceed 12 calendar months.

(d) If, during the contest period for a matched contest, a winning number is not presented or matched for a major prize, the offeror shall conduct a drawing from the names of those individuals who attended a sales presentation during the contest period. The offeror shall conduct the drawing not later than the 60th day after the date the contest period ends. Each major prize identified on the entry forms distributed during the contest period that was not previously awarded shall be awarded at the time of the drawing.

Added by Acts 2007, 80th Leg., ch. 885, § 2.01, eff. April 1, 2009.

§ 621.104. Required Disclosures Relating to Matched Contest

(a) A person who uses a matched contest shall clearly and conspicuously disclose in writing in the offer:

(1) that attendance at a sales presentation is required;

(2) the name and street address of the person who is soliciting attendance at a sales presentation;

(3) a description of the product or service being sold;

(4) each requirement, restriction, qualification, and other condition that must be satisfied for a person to enter the contest, including:

(A) any deadline by which the person must visit the location or attend the sales presentation to qualify to receive a prize; and

(B) the approximate duration of the sales presentation;

(5) a statement of the odds of winning each prize offered, expressed as a ratio in Arabic numerals;

(6) the geographical area or states in which the contest will be conducted;

(7) the beginning and ending dates of the contest period;

(8) the identity and address of each person responsible for awarding prizes;

(9) that all unclaimed prizes will be awarded by a drawing and the date of the drawing; and

(10) all other rules and terms of the contest.

(b) A person engaged in the preparation, promotion, sale, distribution, or use of a matched contest shall disclose:

(1) the retail value of a prize; and

(2) clearly and conspicuously in at least 10–point type that airfare, lodging, or both are not included as part of a prize that is a trip or recreational activity to the extent that either or both are not included.

Added by Acts 2007, 80th Leg., ch. 885, § 2.01, eff. April 1, 2009.

§ 621.105. Prohibited Acts Relating to Matched Contest

A person engaged in the preparation, promotion, sale, distribution, or use of a matched contest may not:

(1) use the term "prize" or a similar term in a false, misleading, or deceptive manner;

(2) represent in soliciting a person to enter or participate in the contest that the person is a "finalist," "major award winner," "grand prize recipient," or "winner" or that a person has "won," "will win," or "will be awarded" or use words or phrases of similar meaning unless the representation is true;

(3) represent that a prize has a sponsor, approval, characteristic, ingredient, use, benefit, quantity, status, affiliation, connection, or identity that the prize does not have;

(4) represent that a prize is of a particular standard, quality, grade, style, or model if the prize is of another;

(5) misrepresent the odds of winning a prize;

(6) misrepresent the rules or terms of participation in the contest;

(7) represent that:

(A) a number, ticket, coupon, symbol, or entry form confers or will confer an advantage on a person that another person does not have or has a value that other entries do not have; or

(B) a person is more likely to win a prize than another person;

(8) fail to obtain a person's express written consent before using that person's name for a promotional purpose;

(9) use or distribute simulated checks or currency or other simulated items of value unless the words "SPECIMEN—NON-NEGOTIABLE" are clearly and conspicuously printed on those items in at least 18–point type; or

(10) use a word or phrase that:

(A) simulates or causes confusion with a document issued by an officer of a court or with the seal or name of a real or fictitious governmental entity; or

(B) implies that the offeror is sending a court document or legal document or that the offeror is a governmental entity.

Added by Acts 2007, 80th Leg., ch. 885, § 2.01, eff. April 1, 2009.

§ 621.106. Required Disclosures Relating to Drawings

(a) A person may not use a drawing unless the offeror clearly and conspicuously discloses in writing in the offer:

(1) a statement of the odds of winning each prize offered, expressed as a ratio in Arabic numerals, except as provided by Subsection (c);

(2) the exact prizes to be awarded in the drawing;

(3) the beginning and ending dates of the contest period;

(4) the date the drawing will occur; and

(5) the location at which the drawing will occur.

(b) A person engaged in the preparation, promotion, sale, distribution, or use of a drawing shall disclose:

(1) the retail value of a prize; and

(2) clearly and conspicuously in at least 10–point type that airfare, lodging, or both are not included in a prize that is a trip or recreational activity to the extent that either or both are not included.

(c) If the odds of winning a prize cannot be determined because the total number of entries is not known, the offeror shall make a statement to the effect that the odds of winning depend on the total number of entries received.

Added by Acts 2007, 80th Leg., ch. 885, § 2.01, eff. April 1, 2009.

§ 621.107. Prohibited Acts Relating to Drawings

A person engaged in the preparation, promotion, sale, distribution, or use of a drawing may not:

(1) use the term "prize" or a similar term in a false, misleading, or deceptive manner;

(2) fail to provide the prize as represented at the conclusion of the drawing;

(3) represent that a prize has a sponsor, approval, characteristic, ingredient, use, benefit, quantity, status, affiliation, connection, or identity that the prize does not have;

(4) represent that a prize is of a particular standard, quality, grade, style, or model if the prize is of another;

(5) misrepresent the odds of winning a prize; or

(6) misrepresent the rules or terms of participation in the drawing.

Added by Acts 2007, 80th Leg., ch. 885, § 2.01, eff. April 1, 2009.

§ 621.108. Conditioning Prize on Payment of Consideration, Charge, or Expense Prohibited; Exceptions

(a) Except as provided by subsection (b), an offeror may not notify a person that the person has won a prize, will receive a prize, or has a chance to win or receive a prize if the receipt of the prize is conditioned on the person paying consideration of any kind, paying a charge, or incurring an expense.

(b) An offeror may notify a person that the person has won a prize, will receive a prize, or has a chance to receive a prize that is conditioned on the person paying:

(1) expenses incurred for travel to and from the sales location; or

(2) a refundable deposit authorized under Section 621.006.

Added by Acts 2007, 80th Leg., ch. 885, § 2.01, eff. April 1, 2009.

§ 621.109. Conditioning Prize on Purchase Prohibited

An offeror may not notify a person that the person has won a prize, will receive a prize, or has a chance to win or receive a prize if the receipt of the prize is conditioned on the person purchasing a good or service unrelated to the prize.

Added by Acts 2007, 80th Leg., ch. 885, § 2.01, eff. April 1, 2009.

[Sections 621.110 to 621.150 reserved for expansion]

SUBCHAPTER D. FULFILLMENT OF GIFT AND PRIZE OFFERS

§ 621.151. Availability and Awarding of Gift or Prize

(a) Subject to sections 621.152–621.154, an offeror shall:

(1) in a gift offer, provide each gift as represented to each person who attends a sales presentation; or

(2) in a matched contest, award each prize as represented on the entry form to each person who presents a winning entry.

(b) An offeror shall have available at the sales location a sufficient quantity of:

(1) each gift to meet the reasonable anticipated response to the offer; or

(2) each prize to meet the reasonable anticipated number of prize winners.

(c) Except as provided by Sections 621.152–621.154, an offeror may not provide a coupon book, a discount book, or a certificate or voucher that entitles the holder to redeem the certificate or voucher for a gift or prize required to be available under this section.

Added by Acts 2007, 80th Leg., ch. 885, § 2.01, eff. April 1, 2009.

§ 621.152. Raincheck Requirements

Subject to section 621.153(a), if the response to an offer exceeds the number of gifts or major or minor prizes, as applicable, available at the sales location, the offeror, at the time of the visit or, if a sales presentation is required, at the conclusion of the sales presentation, shall tender to the recipient of the offer a raincheck for the gift or prize represented in the offer. Except as provided by Section 621.153(b), the offeror shall send that exact gift or prize to the recipient, without cost to the recipient, not later than the 14th day after the date the recipient visits the sales location or attends the sales presentation. The offeror shall obtain a return receipt from the shipper verifying that the gift or prize was delivered to the recipient.

Added by Acts 2007, 80th Leg., ch. 885, § 2.01, eff. April 1, 2009.

§ 621.153. Issuance of Check or Money Order in Lieu of Gift or Minor Prize

(a) An offeror who knows at the time a recipient of an offer visits a sales location or attends a sales presentation that the gift or minor prize will not be available within 14 days of the date of the visit or attendance shall at the time of the visit or at the conclusion of the sales presentation tender to the recipient, by cash or check, the amount of $100.

(b) If, after the expiration of the 14th day after the date the offeror issued a raincheck under Section 621.152 for a gift or minor prize, the offeror has not sent the gift or prize, the offeror shall send by mail to the recipient of the raincheck a check or money order in the amount of $100 payable to the recipient. The offeror shall:

(1) send the check or money order not later than the 15th day after the date the offeror issued the raincheck; and

(2) obtain a return receipt from the United States Postal Service that verifies that the check or money order was delivered to the recipient.

Added by Acts 2007, 80th Leg., ch. 885, § 2.01, eff. April 1, 2009.

§ 621.154. Certificate Permitted For Lodging, Airfare, Trip, or Recreational Activity

An offeror may give the recipient of a gift or prize involving lodging, airfare, a trip, or a recreational activity a certificate that evidences the recipient's right to the gift or prize.

Added by Acts 2007, 80th Leg., ch. 885, § 2.01, eff. April 1, 2009.

[Sections 621.155 to 621.200 reserved for expansion]

SUBCHAPTER E. CONTEST RECORDS

§ 621.201. Applicability of Subchapter

This subchapter applies to a person who uses a contest as part of an advertising plan or program.

Added by Acts 2007, 80th Leg., ch. 885, § 2.01, eff. April 1, 2009.

§ 621.202. Required Records For Contests Other Than Drawings

(a) For each contest other than a drawing, the offeror shall maintain until the second anniversary of the date the last prize was awarded:

(1) records of the identity and address of each person who is responsible for developing, creating, sponsoring, or implementing any part of the advertising plan or program;

(2) records that show that the winning numbers have been deposited in the mail or otherwise made available to recipients in accordance with the odds statement provided under Section 621.104(a);

(3) a copy of each contest solicitation;

(4) records adequate to determine:

(A) the name and address of each contestant;

(B) the approximate date each contestant was sent the solicitation used in the contest;

(C) the number of major prizes awarded;

(D) the date each major prize was awarded;

(E) the name, brand, type, model number, and manufacturer of each prize offered;

(F) the method of computing the retail value of each prize;

(G) the method of selecting major prize winners;

(H) the name and address of each major prize winner; and

(I) the facts on which each representation or disclosure made in connection with the contest was based and from which the validity of the representation or disclosure can be determined.

(b) Postal receipt records, affidavits of mailing, and a list of winners or recipients of the major prizes satisfy the requirements of Subsection (a)(2).

Added by Acts 2007, 80th Leg., ch. 885, § 2.01, eff. April 1, 2009.

§ 621.203. Required Records For Drawings

(a) For each drawing, the offeror shall maintain until the second anniversary of the date the last major prize was awarded:

(1) records of the identity and address of each person who is responsible for developing, creating, sponsoring, or implementing any part of the advertising plan or program;

(2) records that show that the winning entry for each major prize was selected entirely at random from all of the entries received;

(3) a copy of each contest solicitation; and

(4) records adequate to determine:

(A) the total number of entries;

(B) the number of major prizes awarded;

(C) the date each major prize was awarded;

(D) the name, brand, type, model number, and manufacturer of each prize offered;

(E) the method of computing the retail value of each prize;

(F) the method of selecting winners; and

(G) the names and addresses of the winners.

(b) An affidavit from the person who conducted the drawing and a list of winners or recipients of the major prizes satisfies the requirements of Subsection (a)(2).

Added by Acts 2007, 80th Leg., ch. 885, § 2.01, eff. April 1, 2009.

§ 621.204. Disclosure of Major Prizes and Winners on Request

A person who conducts a contest shall, at the end of the contest period, provide to any person who requests the information:

(1) the names of all major prize winners; and

(2) the prizes won by each winner.

Added by Acts 2007, 80th Leg., ch. 885, § 2.01, eff. April 1, 2009.

§ 621.205. Records Available to Attorney General

A person who receives a written request from the attorney general for the records required under this subchapter shall make the records available to the attorney general not later than the 30th day after the date the person received the request.

Added by Acts 2007, 80th Leg., ch. 885, § 2.01, eff. April 1, 2009.

[Sections 621.206 to 621.250 reserved for expansion]

SUBCHAPTER F. ENFORCEMENT

§ 621.251. Criminal Penalty

(a) A person commits an offense if the person knowingly violates this chapter.

(b) Except as provided by Subsection (c), an offense under this section is a Class B misdemeanor.

(c) An offense under this section is:

(1) a Class A misdemeanor if it is shown at the trial of the defendant that:

(A) the defendant has previously been convicted of an offense under this section; and

(B) the offense for which the defendant is on trial was committed not later than the fifth anniversary of the date of the previous conviction; or

(2) a third degree felony if it is shown at the trial of the defendant that:

(A) the defendant has previously been twice convicted of an offense under this section; and

(B) the offense for which the defendant is on trial was:

(i) intentional; and

(ii) committed not later than the fifth anniversary of the earlier of the dates of two previous convictions.

(d) Subsection (c)(2) does not apply to a violation of Subchapter D.

(e) A person may not be prosecuted for more than one offense involving the same promotion regardless of whether that promotion is mailed or distributed to more than one person or is used at more than one location.

Added by Acts 2007, 80th Leg., ch. 885, § 2.01, eff. April 1, 2009.

§ 621.252. Deceptive Trade Practice

A violation of this chapter is a deceptive trade practice in addition to the practices described by Subchapter E, Chapter 17, and is actionable under that subchapter.

Added by Acts 2007, 80th Leg., ch. 885, § 2.01, eff. April 1, 2009.

CHAPTER 622. SWEEPSTAKES

SUBCHAPTER A. GENERAL PROVISIONS

§ 622.001. Definitions

In this chapter:

(1) "Credit card" means a card that, if covered by the law of this state, would be subject to a lender credit card agreement, as defined by Section 301.002, Finance Code, except that the term does

not exclude a card that is subject to an agreement under which:

(A) the obligations are payable in full each month and not deferred; and

(B) no finance charge is assessed when the obligations are paid.

(2) "Debit card" means a card offered by an institution the deposits of which are insured by the Federal Deposit Insurance Corporation or another agency, corporation, or instrumentality chartered by the United States government.

(3) "Imply" means to use any means by which an implication can be conveyed, including:

(A) a statement, question, or request;

(B) conduct;

(C) a graphic or symbol; and

(D) lettering, coloring, font size, font style, or formatting.

(4) "Sweepstakes" means a contest that awards one or more prizes based on chance or the random selection of entries.

Added by Acts 2007, 80th Leg., ch. 885, § 2.01, eff. April 1, 2009.

§ 622.002. Acts Constituting Conducting Sweepstakes

For purposes of this chapter, a person conducts a sweepstakes if the person distributes material that:

(1) promotes a sweepstakes;

(2) describes one or more sweepstakes prizes;

(3) states one or more sweepstakes rules;

(4) includes a current or future opportunity to enter a sweepstakes; or

(5) provides a method for the recipient of the material to obtain additional information about a sweepstakes.

Added by Acts 2007, 80th Leg., ch. 885, § 2.01, eff. April 1, 2009.

[Sections 622.003 to 622.050 reserved for expansion]

SUBCHAPTER B. APPLICABILITY OF CHAPTER

§ 622.051. Chapter Limited to Sweepstakes Conducted Through Mail; Exception

(a) This chapter applies only to a sweepstakes conducted through the mail.

(b) This chapter does not apply to a sweepstakes for which the only use of the mail is for a consumer to return an entry form to the sweepstakes sponsor.

Added by Acts 2007, 80th Leg., ch. 885, § 2.01, eff. April 1, 2009.

§ 622.052. Prize Value Less Than $50,000

(a) This chapter does not apply to a sweepstakes in which the value of the most valuable prize is less than $50,000.

(b) For purposes of this section, the value of a prize is the greatest of the prize's:

(1) face value;

(2) fair market value; or

(3) present financial value.

Added by Acts 2007, 80th Leg., ch. 885, § 2.01, eff. April 1, 2009.

§ 622.053. Advertisement or Insert in Magazine, Newspaper, or Catalog

This chapter does not apply to a sweepstakes conducted through an advertisement or insert in:

(1) a magazine or newspaper:

(A) that is a publication in which more than 40 percent of the total column inches in each issue consist of advertising space purchased by companies other than:

(i) the publisher;

(ii) an affiliate of the publisher; or

(iii) a vendor for the publisher or an affiliate; and

(B) that is a publication for which more than 50 percent of the total number of copies distributed of each issue are provided to customers who paid for the copy; or

(2) a catalog that is a promotional booklet listing merchandise for sale and that:

(A) is at least 24 pages long;

(B) has a circulation of at least 250,000; and

(C) either:

(i) requires customers to go to a physical location to purchase the advertised items; or

(ii) is published by a company that derives more than 50 percent of the company's total gross revenue from sales occurring at physical locations.

Added by Acts 2007, 80th Leg., ch. 885, § 2.01, eff. April 1, 2009.

§ 622.054. Charitable Raffle

This chapter does not apply to a charitable raffle regulated by chapter 2002, occupations code.

Added by Acts 2007, 80th Leg., ch. 885, § 2.01, eff. April 1, 2009.

§ 622.055. Sweepstakes Regulated by Alcoholic Beverage Code

This chapter does not apply to a sweepstakes regulated by the alcoholic beverage Code.

Added by Acts 2007, 80th Leg., ch. 885, § 2.01, eff. April 1, 2009.

§ 622.056. Company Regulated Under Public Utility Regulatory Act

This chapter does not apply to a company regulated under Title 2, Utilities Code.

Added by Acts 2007, 80th Leg., ch. 885, § 2.01, eff. April 1, 2009.

§ 622.057. Air Carrier; Airman Association

This chapter does not apply to:

(1) a company that is an air carrier subject to Title 49, United States Code; or

(2) a nonprofit association of airmen who are subject to that title.

Added by Acts 2007, 80th Leg., ch. 885, § 2.01, eff. April 1, 2009.

§ 622.058. Certain Recreational Events

This chapter does not apply to a drawing for the opportunity to participate in a hunting, fishing, or other recreational event conducted by the Parks and Wildlife Department.

Added by Acts 2007, 80th Leg., ch. 885, § 2.01, eff. April 1, 2009.

§ 622.059. Certain Food Products

This chapter does not apply to a sweepstakes promoting one or more food products regulated by the united States Food and Drug Administration or the United States Department of Agriculture.

Added by Acts 2007, 80th Leg., ch. 885, § 2.01, eff. April 1, 2009.

§ 622.060. Audiovisual Entertainment Work, Product, or Sound Recording

This chapter does not apply to a company if 75 percent or more of the company's business is:

(1) the systematic development, planning, and execution of creating audiovisual entertainment works, products, or sound recordings; and

(2) the distribution, sale, and marketing of those works, products, or recordings.

Added by Acts 2007, 80th Leg., ch. 885, § 2.01, eff. April 1, 2009.

§ 622.061. Cable System

This chapter does not apply to a company that owns or operates a cable system, as defined by 47 u.s.c. section 522, as amended.

Added by Acts 2007, 80th Leg., ch. 885, § 2.01, eff. April 1, 2009.

[Sections 622.062 to 622.100 reserved for expansion]

SUBCHAPTER C. PROHIBITED ACTS OR CONDUCT

§ 622.101. Connecting Sweepstakes Entry or Operation to Order or Purchase

(a) A person conducting a sweepstakes may not use a mechanism for entering the sweepstakes that:

(1) has any connection to ordering or purchasing a good or service;

(2) is not identical for all individuals entering the sweepstakes; and

(3) does not have printed on the entry form, in a font size at least as large as the largest font size used on the entry form, the following language: "Buying Will Not Help You Win. Your chances of winning without making a purchase are the same as the chances of someone who purchases something. It is illegal to give any advantage to buyers in a sweepstakes."

(b) A person conducting a sweepstakes may not:

(1) require an individual to order, purchase, or promise to purchase a good or service to enter the sweepstakes;

(2) automatically enter an individual in the sweepstakes because the individual ordered, purchased, or promised to order or purchase a good or service; or

(3) solicit business using an order form or purchasing mechanism that has any role in the operation of the sweepstakes.

(c) Subsections (a)(1) and (b)(3) do not apply to a single sheet of paper that contains both a sweepstakes entry form and an order form if:

(1) the order form is perforated or detachable; and

(2) the entry form must be separated from the order form and returned to a different address than the order form.

(d) Subsections (a) and (b)(2) and (3) do not apply to a sweepstakes offered to promote a credit card or debit card if the official rules of the sweepstakes provide that consumers are entered in the sweepstakes based on the number of purchases made or the amount of money spent. The exception provided by this subsection applies only to a person offering a sweepstakes who qualified as an issuer as of January 1, 2001.

(e) Subsections (a) and (b)(2) and (3) do not apply to a company offering a sweepstakes in which the consumer must go to a physical location to obtain or use the goods or services being sold by the company.

Added by Acts 2007, 80th Leg., ch. 885, § 2.01, eff. April 1, 2009.

§ 622.102. Using multiple Sweepstakes Entry Addresses or Multiple Purposes for Address

A person conducting a sweepstakes who provides for entering the sweepstakes by mail may not:

(1) accept entries at more than one address; or

(2) use the address for entry in the sweepstakes for any other purpose.

Added by Acts 2007, 80th Leg., ch. 885, § 2.01, eff. April 1, 2009.

§ 622.103. Allowing Choice of Prize or Indication of Preferred Prize Characteristics

A person conducting a sweepstakes may not:

(1) solicit an individual to enter the sweepstakes by invitation or other opportunity; and

(2) allow the individual to choose, or indicate the preferred characteristics of, a prize to be awarded in the sweepstakes unless the choice or indication:

(A) is made on the sweepstakes entry form; and

(B) does not appear on, and is not in any way connected to, an order form or other purchasing mechanism.

Added by Acts 2007, 80th Leg., ch. 885, § 2.01, eff. April 1, 2009.

§ 622.104. Sending Sweepstakes Material That Includes Certain Statements or Implications

A person conducting a sweepstakes may not send material accompanying or relating to the sweepstakes or an offer to enter the sweepstakes that:

(1) states or implies that:

(A) an individual must comply with a restriction or condition to enter the sweepstakes, unless all individuals entering the sweepstakes are required to comply with the identical restriction or condition;

(B) an individual's chances of winning a prize in the sweepstakes are higher, lower, or different in any way because of a factor or circumstance that does not relate to the manner in which a winner is selected;

(C) a winner will be selected at a time or place or in a manner that is different from the actual time or place at which or manner in which a winner is selected;

(D) an individual who orders or purchases a good or service will receive a benefit or be treated differently in the sweepstakes in comparison to an individual who does not order or purchase a good or service; or

(E) an individual who does not order or purchase a good or service will be disadvantaged or treated differently in the sweepstakes in comparison to an individual who orders or purchases a good or service;

(2) states or implies falsely that the individual receiving the material has received special treatment or personal attention from the offeror of the sweepstakes or any officer, employee, or agent of the offeror; or

(3) states that the recipient of the material:

(A) is a winner, if the recipient is not a winner;

(B) may be a winner;

(C) will be a winner if certain conditions are met or certain events occur;

(D) may be or will be among the group from which a winner will be selected; or

(E) has in any way a better chance than another individual of being chosen as a winner.

Added by Acts 2007, 80th Leg., ch. 885, § 2.01, eff. April 1, 2009.

§ 622.105. Using Game Piece to Convey Information or Offer to Enter

A person conducting a sweepstakes may not convey information about the sweepstakes or an offer to enter the sweepstakes by using a scratch-off device or any other game piece that suggests an element of chance or luck.

Added by Acts 2007, 80th Leg., ch. 885, § 2.01, eff. April 1, 2009.

§ 622.106. Publishing Advertisements or Rules With Inconsistent or Incomplete Prize Descriptions

A person conducting a sweepstakes may not publish or cause to be published:

(1) different advertisements for the same sweepstakes that contain inconsistent descriptions of the grand prize to be awarded through the sweepstakes; or

(2) official rules of the sweepstakes that do not uniquely identify the prizes to be awarded and the date the prizes will be awarded.

Added by Acts 2007, 80th Leg., ch. 885, § 2.01, eff. April 1, 2009.

§ 622.107. Engaging in Conduct That Falsely Indicates an Individual Has Won

A person conducting a sweepstakes may not:

(1) ask an individual to provide any information or take any action consistent with the individual winning a sweepstakes prize, unless the individual has won a sweepstakes prize; or

(2) provide an individual who has not yet won a sweepstakes prize with a document or other item that simulates an event, circumstance, or condition connected with being a sweepstakes winner.

Added by Acts 2007, 80th Leg., ch. 885, § 2.01, eff. April 1, 2009.

§ 622.108. Awarding Multiple Prizes

A person conducting a sweepstakes may not award multiple prizes in the sweepstakes unless all prizes are awarded on the same date and through the same selection process.

Added by Acts 2007, 80th Leg., ch. 885, § 2.01, eff. April 1, 2009.

§ 622.109. Mailing Certain Offers During Period Following Sweepstakes

A person conducting a sweepstakes may not, during the 30–day period immediately following the last date on which the person conducted the sweepstakes through the mail, offer through the mail:

(1) an opportunity to enter a sweepstakes; or

(2) a nonsweepstakes prize, gift, premium, giveaway, or skill contest.

Added by Acts 2007, 80th Leg., ch. 885, § 2.01, eff. April 1, 2009.

§ 622.110. Providing Names or Addresses Used in Prohibited Sweepstakes

A person may not provide names or addresses of residents of this state that are used in conducting a sweepstakes that the person knows violates this chapter.

Added by Acts 2007, 80th Leg., ch. 885, § 2.01, eff. April 1, 2009.

[Sections 622.111 to 622.150 reserved for expansion]

SUBCHAPTER D. ACTS OR CONDUCT NOT PROHIBITED

§ 622.151. Description of Method of Choosing Winner

This chapter does not prohibit a sweepstakes sponsor from describing in the official sweepstakes rules the method to be used in choosing a winner.

Added by Acts 2007, 80th Leg., ch. 885, § 2.01, eff. April 1, 2009.

§ 622.152. Notification of and[1] Affidavit From Winner

This chapter does not prohibit a sweepstakes sponsor, after a winner has been chosen, from:

(1) notifying an individual chosen as a winner; or

(2) obtaining from an individual chosen as a winner an affidavit to verify that the individual:

(A) is eligible to win the prize; and

(B) has complied with the sweepstakes rules.

Added by Acts 2007, 80th Leg., ch. 885, § 2.01, eff. April 1, 2009.

[1] So enrolled in bill; probably should read "an".

[Sections 622.153 to 622.200 reserved for expansion]

SUBCHAPTER E. ENFORCEMENT

§ 622.201. Action By Attorney General; Venue

The attorney general may bring an action under this chapter by filing suit in a district court in Travis County or in any county in which a violation occurred.

Added by Acts 2007, 80th Leg., ch. 885, § 2.01, eff. April 1, 2009.

§ 622.202. Civil Penalty

(a) The court shall award the attorney general a civil penalty of not less than $5,000 or more than $50,000 for each violation found.

(b) If the material accompanying or relating to a sweepstakes or an offer to enter a sweepstakes contains multiple statements, implications, representations, or offers that are prohibited by this chapter, each statement, implication, representation, or offer is a separate violation and results in a separate civil penalty. Each individual who receives the material constitutes an additional and separate group of violations of this chapter.

Added by Acts 2007, 80th Leg., ch. 885, § 2.01, eff. April 1, 2009.

§ 622.203. Liability For Providing Names or Addresses Used in Prohibited Sweepstakes

(a) A person who violates section 622.110 is liable for the cumulative civil penalties that result from the person's conduct.

(b) Liability of a person under Subsection (a) does not reduce the liability of the person who conducted the sweepstakes.

Added by Acts 2007, 80th Leg., ch. 885, § 2.01, eff. April 1, 2009.

§ 622.204. Injunctive and Other Relief

The court may also award injunctive relief or other equitable or ancillary relief that is reasonably necessary to prevent violations of this chapter.

Added by Acts 2007, 80th Leg., ch. 885, § 2.01, eff. April 1, 2009.

§ 622.205. No Private Right of Action

This chapter does not create a private right of action.

Added by Acts 2007, 80th Leg., ch. 885, § 2.01, eff. April 1, 2009.

§ 622.206. Recovery of Expenses by Attorney General

If the attorney general substantially prevails, the court shall award the attorney general reasonable expenses incurred in recovering a civil penalty under this subchapter, including court costs, reasonable attorney's fees, reasonable investigative costs, witness fees, and deposition expenses.

Added by Acts 2007, 80th Leg., ch. 885, § 2.01, eff. April 1, 2009.

TITLE 14. RECORDINGS

Acts 2007, 80th Leg., ch. 885, § 2.01 added this Title effective April 1, 2009.

CHAPTER 641. UNAUTHORIZED RECORDINGS

SUBCHAPTER A. GENERAL PROVISIONS

§ 641.001. Definitions

In this chapter:

(1) "Fix" means to embody in a recording or other tangible medium of expression, by or under the authority of the author, so that the matter embodied is sufficiently permanent or stable to permit it to be perceived, reproduced, or otherwise communicated for a period of more than transitory duration.

(2) "Live performance" means a recitation, rendering, or playing of a series, in an audible sequence, of:

(A) images;

(B) musical, spoken, or other sounds; or

(C) a combination of images and sounds.

(3) "Owner" means a person who owns the sounds fixed in a master phonograph record, master disc, master tape, master film, or other recording:

(A) on which sound is recorded; and

(B) from which the transferred recorded sounds are directly or indirectly derived.

(4) "Recording" means a tangible medium on which sounds, images, or both are recorded or otherwise stored, including:

(A) an original phonograph record, disc, tape, audio or video cassette, wire, film, or other medium now existing or later developed; or

(B) a copy or reproduction that wholly or partly duplicates the original. (Bus. & Com. Code, Sec. 35.91.)

Added by Acts 2007, 80th Leg., ch. 885, § 2.01, eff. April 1, 2009.

[Sections 641.002 to 641.050 reserved for expansion]

SUBCHAPTER B. PROHIBITED PRACTICES; PENALTIES

§ 641.051. Unauthorized Duplication of Certain Recordings

(a) This section applies only to a recording that was initially fixed before February 15, 1972.

(b) A person commits an offense if the person:

(1) knowingly reproduces for sale or causes to be transferred any recording with intent to sell the recording or cause the recording to be sold or use a recording or cause the recording to be used for commercial advantage or private financial gain through public performance without the consent of the owner;

(2) with the knowledge that the sounds on a recording have been reproduced or transferred without the consent of the owner, transports the recording within this state for commercial advantage or private financial gain; or

(3) with the knowledge that a recording has been reproduced or transferred without the consent of the owner:

(A) advertises, offers for sale, sells, or rents the recording;

(B) causes the sale, resale, or rental of the recording; or

(C) possesses the recording for a purpose described by Paragraph (A) or (B).

(c) An offense under this section is punishable by:

(1) imprisonment for a term of not more than five years, a fine not to exceed $250,000, or both, if:

(A) the offense involves at least 1,000 unauthorized recordings during a 180–day period; or

(B) the defendant has been previously convicted under this section;

(2) imprisonment for a term of not more than two years, a fine not to exceed $250,000, or both, if the offense involves more than 100 but fewer than 1,000 unauthorized recordings during a 180–day period; or

(3) confinement in the county jail for a term of not more than one year, a fine not to exceed $25,000, or both, if the offense is not otherwise punishable under Subdivision (1) or (2).

(d) This section does not apply to any fees due to the American Society of Composers, Authors and Publishers.

Added by Acts 2007, 80th Leg., ch. 885, § 2.01, eff. April 1, 2009.

§ 641.052. Unauthorized Recording of Live Performance

(a) A person commits an offense if the person, with the knowledge that a live performance has been recorded or fixed without the consent of the owner:

(1) for commercial advantage or private financial gain, advertises, offers for sale, sells, rents, or transports, causes the sale, resale, rental, or transportation of, or possesses for one or more of these purposes a recording containing sounds of the live performance; or

(2) with the intent to sell for commercial advantage or private financial gain, records or fixes the live performance, or causes the live performance to be recorded or fixed on a recording.

(b) An offense under this section is punishable by:

(1) imprisonment for a term of not more than five years, a fine not to exceed $250,000, or both, if:

(A) the offense involves at least 1,000 unauthorized recordings embodying sound or at least 65 unauthorized audiovisual recordings during a 180–day period; or

(B) the defendant has been previously convicted under this section;

(2) imprisonment for a term of not more than two years, a fine not to exceed $250,000, or both, if the

offense involves more than 100 but fewer than 1,000 unauthorized recordings embodying sound or more than seven but fewer than 65 unauthorized audiovisual recordings during a 180–day period; or

(3) confinement in the county jail for a term of not more than one year, a fine not to exceed $25,000, or both, if the offense is not otherwise punishable under Subdivision (1) or (2).

(c) In the absence of a written agreement or law to the contrary, the performer or performers of a live performance are presumed to own the rights to record or fix those sounds.

(d) For purposes of this section, a person authorized to maintain custody and control over business records that reflect whether the owner of a live performance consented to having the live performance recorded or fixed is a proper witness in a proceeding regarding the issue of consent. A witness called under this subsection is subject to the rules of evidence relating to the competency of a witness to testify and the relevance and admissibility of the testimony offered.

Added by Acts 2007, 80th Leg., ch. 885, § 2.01, eff. April 1, 2009.

§ 641.053. Unauthorized Operation of Recording Device in Motion Picture Theater

(a) In this section:

(1) "Audiovisual recording function" means the capability of a device to record or transmit a motion picture or any part of a motion picture by means of any technology now known or later developed.

(2) "Motion picture theater" means a movie theater, screening room, or other place primarily used to exhibit a motion picture.

(b) A person commits an offense if, without the consent of the owner of the theater, the person, with the intent to record a motion picture, knowingly operates the audiovisual recording function of any device in a motion picture theater while the motion picture is being exhibited.

(c) An offense under this section is a Class A misdemeanor, except that the offense is:

(1) a state jail felony if the person has been previously convicted one time of an offense under this section; or

(2) a felony of the third degree if the person has been previously convicted two or more times of an offense under this section.

(d) It is a defense to prosecution under this section that the audiovisual recording function of the device was operated solely for official law enforcement purposes.

(e) If conduct constituting an offense under this section also constitutes an offense under another law, the actor may be prosecuted under this section, the other law, or both.

(f) A person who reasonably believes that another has knowingly operated the audiovisual recording function of a device in a motion picture theater in violation of this section is privileged to detain that other person in a reasonable manner and for a reasonable time to allow for the arrival of law enforcement authorities.

Added by Acts 2007, 80th Leg., ch. 885, § 2.01, eff. April 1, 2009.

§ 641.054. Labeling

(a) A person commits an offense if:

(1) for commercial advantage or private financial gain, the person knowingly:

(A) advertises, offers for sale, sells, rents, or transports a recording;

(B) causes the sale, resale, rental, or transportation of a recording; or

(C) possesses a recording for a purpose described by Paragraph (A) or (B); and

(2) the outside cover, box, or jacket of the recording does not clearly and conspicuously disclose:

(A) the actual name and address of the manufacturer; and

(B) the name of the performer or group.

(b) An offense under this section is punishable by:

(1) imprisonment for a term of not more than five years, a fine not to exceed $250,000, or both, if:

(A) the offense involves at least 65 unauthorized recordings during a 180–day period; or

(B) the defendant has been previously convicted under this section;

(2) imprisonment for a term of not more than two years, a fine not to exceed $250,000, or both, if the offense involves more than seven but fewer than 65 unauthorized recordings during a 180–day period; or

(3) confinement in the county jail for a term of not more than one year, a fine not to exceed

$25,000, or both, if the offense is not otherwise punishable under Subdivision (1) or (2).

Added by Acts 2007, 80th Leg., ch. 885, § 2.01, eff. April 1, 2009.

§ 641.055. Forfeiture

If a person is convicted of a violation of this chapter, the court in its judgment of conviction shall order the forfeiture and destruction or other disposition of:

(1) all recordings on which the conviction is based; and

(2) all devices and equipment used or intended to be used in the manufacture of the recordings on which the conviction is based.

Added by Acts 2007, 80th Leg., ch. 885, § 2.01, eff. April 1, 2009.

§ 641.056. Private Rights and Remedies Not Affected

Sections 641.051, 641.052, and 641.054 do not affect the rights and remedies of a party in private litigation.

Added by Acts 2007, 80th Leg., ch. 885, § 2.01, eff. April 1, 2009.

§ 641.057. Penalties Cumulative

A penalty provided by this chapter is in addition to any other penalty provided under other law.

Added by Acts 2007, 80th Leg., ch. 885, § 2.01, eff. April 1, 2009.

TITLE 15. CURRENCY AND TRADE

Acts 2007, 80th Leg., ch. 885, § 2.01 added this Title effective April 1, 2009.

SUBTITLE A. CURRENCY

CHAPTER 661. EUROPEAN UNION CURRENCY CONVERSION

Section

§ 661.001. Definitions

In this chapter:

(1) "Euro" means the currency of the member states of the European Community, as amended by the Treaty on European Union. The term is abbreviated as EUR.

(2) "European currency unit" means the currency basket periodically used as the unit of account of the European Community, as defined by Regulation No. 3320/94 of the Council of the European Union and as referred to in Article 109g of the treaty establishing the European Community, as amended by the Treaty on European Union. The term is abbreviated as ECU.

(3) "Introduction of the euro" means the periodic implementation of economic and monetary union in member states of the European Union in accordance with the Treaty on European Union.

(4) "Treaty on European Union" means the Treaty on European Union of February 7, 1992.

Added by Acts 2007, 80th Leg., ch. 885, § 2.01, eff. April 1, 2009.

§ 661.002. Applicability of Chapter

This chapter applies to each contract, security, and instrument, including a commercial contract, governed by the laws of this state.

Added by Acts 2007, 80th Leg., ch. 885, § 2.01, eff. April 1, 2009.

§ 661.003. Conflicts of Law

This chapter prevails to the extent of any conflict between this chapter and any other law of this state.

Added by Acts 2007, 80th Leg., ch. 885, § 2.01, eff. April 1, 2009.

§ 661.004. No Negative Inference or Presumption Created

With respect to currency alteration other than the introduction of the euro, this chapter does not create any negative inference or negative presumption regarding the validity or enforceability of a contract, security, or instrument denominated wholly or partly in a currency affected by the alteration.

Added by Acts 2007, 80th Leg., ch. 885, § 2.01, eff. April 1, 2009.

§ 661.005. Continuity of Contract

(a) If a subject or medium of payment of a contract, security, or instrument is the european currency unit or a currency that has been substituted or replaced by the euro, the euro is a commercially reasonable substitute and substantial equivalent that may be:

(1) used in determining the value of the European currency unit or currency, as appropriate; or

(2) tendered, in each case, at the conversion rate specified in, and otherwise computed in accordance with, the regulations adopted by the Council of the European Union.

(b) A person may perform any obligation described by Subsection (a) in euros or in the currency or currencies originally designated in the contract, security, or instrument if that currency or those currencies remain legal tender, but the person may not perform the obligation in any other currency, regardless of whether that other currency:

(1) has been substituted or replaced by the euro; or

(2) is considered a denomination of the euro and has a fixed conversion rate with respect to the euro.

(c) The following occurrences are not considered a discharge of, do not excuse performance under, and do not give a party the right to unilaterally alter or terminate a contract, security, or instrument:

(1) the introduction of the euro;

(2) the tender of euros in connection with any obligation described by Subsection (a);

(3) the determination of the value of any obligation described by Subsection (a); or

(4) the computation or determination of the subject or medium of payment of a contract, security, or instrument with reference to an interest rate or any other basis that has been substituted or replaced because of the introduction of the euro and that is a commercially reasonable substitute and substantial equivalent.

Added by Acts 2007, 80th Leg., ch. 885, § 2.01, eff. April 1, 2009.

§ 661.006. Effect on Certain Agreements

This chapter does not alter or impair an agreement between parties that specifically relates to the introduction of the euro.

Added by Acts 2007, 80th Leg., ch. 885, § 2.01, eff. April 1, 2009.

[Chapters 662 to 670 reserved for expansion]

SUBTITLE B. PORT OF ENTRY AUTHORITIES

CHAPTER 671. CITY OF LAREDO PORT OF ENTRY AUTHORITY

SUBCHAPTER A. GENERAL PROVISIONS

SUBCHAPTER B. GOVERNING BOARD

SUBCHAPTER C. POWERS AND DUTIES

SUBCHAPTER A. GENERAL PROVISIONS

§ 671.001. Definitions

In this chapter:

(1) "Authority" means the City of Laredo Port of Entry Authority created under this chapter.

(2) "Board" means the governing board of the authority.

(3) "City" means the city of Laredo.

(4) "Governing body" means the governing body of the city.

Added by Acts 2007, 80th Leg., ch. 885, § 2.01, eff. April 1, 2009.

§ 671.002. Creation of Authority

The city by ordinance may create the city of Laredo port of entry authority for the purposes provided by this chapter.

Added by Acts 2007, 80th Leg., ch. 885, § 2.01, eff. April 1, 2009.

§ 671.003. Authority Jurisdiction

The authority's jurisdiction is coextensive with the area within the boundaries and extraterritorial jurisdiction of the city.

Added by Acts 2007, 80th Leg., ch. 885, § 2.01, eff. April 1, 2009.

[Sections 671.004 to 671.050 reserved for expansion]

SUBCHAPTER B. GOVERNING BOARD

§ 671.051. Composition of Board

(a) The authority is governed by a board of 11 members appointed by the governing body.

(b) Nine members are voting members who must reside in the authority and two members are nonvoting members who must reside in Mexico.

(c) The voting board members must include:

(1) one representative of United States customs brokers;

(2) one representative of freight forwarders;

(3) one representative of the transportation industry;

(4) one international banker; and

(5) one representative of a maquiladora project.

Added by Acts 2007, 80th Leg., ch. 885, § 2.01, eff. April 1, 2009.

§ 671.052. Board Terms; Vacancy

(a) Board members serve staggered two-year terms, with the terms of five members expiring february 1 of each odd-numbered year and the terms of six members expiring February 1 of each even-numbered year.

(b) A vacancy that occurs more than 60 days before the expiration date of a term shall be promptly filled for the unexpired term by the appointment of a member who has the same qualifications as the member creating the vacancy.

Added by Acts 2007, 80th Leg., ch. 885, § 2.01, eff. April 1, 2009.

§ 671.053. Officers

The board shall select from among the board's voting members a presiding officer, an assistant presiding officer, a treasurer, and any other officers that the board considers appropriate.

Added by Acts 2007, 80th Leg., ch. 885, § 2.01, eff. April 1, 2009.

§ 671.054. Removal

After a hearing, a board member may be removed for cause by a two-thirds vote of the membership of the governing body.

Added by Acts 2007, 80th Leg., ch. 885, § 2.01, eff. April 1, 2009.

§ 671.055. Compensation; Reimbursement

A board member serves without compensation but is entitled to reimbursement for necessary expenses incurred in the performance of duties as a member.

Added by Acts 2007, 80th Leg., ch. 885, § 2.01, eff. April 1, 2009.

[Sections 671.056 to 671.100 reserved for expansion]

SUBCHAPTER C. POWERS AND DUTIES

§ 671.101. Fees

The authority shall establish and collect rentals, tolls, and other appropriate fees:

(1) from an operator of a commercial vehicle entering the authority by an international bridge; and

(2) for the use of any other facility designated by the city.

Added by Acts 2007, 80th Leg., ch. 885, § 2.01, eff. April 1, 2009.

§ 671.102. Use of Money

The authority may use the money collected under this chapter as the board determines appropriate only for the development and promotion of international trade. The authority must obtain the approval of the governing body before any expenditure of money.

Added by Acts 2007, 80th Leg., ch. 885, § 2.01, eff. April 1, 2009.

§ 671.103. Effect of Authority Action; City Approval

(a) Not later than the 15th day after the date on which the authority or the board acts, the city may approve or disapprove the action.

(b) If the city disapproves an action under Subsection (a), the action has no effect. If the city does not disapprove the action, the action becomes effective on the earlier of:

(1) the date on which the city approves the action; or

(2) the 15th day after the date on which the authority or board acted.

Added by Acts 2007, 80th Leg., ch. 885, § 2.01, eff. April 1, 2009.

§ 671.104. Ad Valorem Taxes and Bonds Prohibited

The authority may not:

(1) impose an ad valorem tax; or

(2) issue bonds.

Added by Acts 2007, 80th Leg., ch. 885, § 2.01, eff. April 1, 2009.

§ 671.105. Depository; Order to Disburse

(a) The treasurer of the authority shall deposit money collected by the authority in a separate account in a bank or trust company.

(b) Money of the authority may be paid out on the warrant or other order of the presiding officer of the board or another person designated by the authority.

Added by Acts 2007, 80th Leg., ch. 885, § 2.01, eff. April 1, 2009.

§ 671.106. Audit

(a) At least once a year, the authority shall have a certified public accountant conduct an audit of the authority's books, accounts, and other records. A copy of the audit shall be delivered to the city.

(b) If the authority does not have the required audit conducted, an auditor or accountant designated by the city may examine, at the expense of the authority, the accounts and books of the authority, including receipts, disbursements, contracts, leases, investments, and other matters relating to the authority's finances, operation, and affairs.

Added by Acts 2007, 80th Leg., ch. 885, § 2.01, eff. April 1, 2009.

[Chapters 672 to 680 reserved for expansion]

SUBTITLE C. TRADE ZONES

CHAPTER 681. FOREIGN TRADE ZONES

SUBCHAPTER A. GENERAL PROVISIONS

§ 681.001. Definition

In this chapter, "foreign trade" has the meaning assigned to the term "zone" by the foreign trade zones act (19 U.S.C. Section 81a et seq.).

Added by Acts 2007, 80th Leg., ch. 885, § 2.01, eff. April 1, 2009.

§ 681.002. Authorization Subject to Federal Law and Regulations

An authorization under this chapter is subject to the requirements of federal law and the regulations of the board established to carry out the provisions of the Foreign Trade Zones Act (19 U.S.C. Section 81a et seq.).

Added by Acts 2007, 80th Leg., ch. 885, § 2.01, eff. April 1, 2009.

[Sections 681.003 to 681.050 reserved for expansion]

SUBCHAPTER B. GENERAL AUTHORITY FOR ESTABLISHMENT OF FOREIGN TRADE ZONES BY CERTAIN ENTITIES

§ 681.051. Definitions

In this subchapter:

(1) "Eligible corporation" means a corporation organized to establish, operate, and maintain a foreign trade zone.

(2) "Governmental entity" means:

(A) this state;

(B) a state agency;

(C) a county, municipality, or special district; or

(D) a combination of entities listed in Paragraphs (A)–(C).

Added by Acts 2007, 80th Leg., ch. 885, § 2.01, eff. April 1, 2009.

§ 681.052. General Authority for Eligible Corporation or Governmental Entity

(a) An eligible corporation or a governmental entity may:

(1) apply for and accept a grant of authority to establish, operate, and maintain a foreign trade zone and subzones; and

(2) take other actions necessary to establish, operate, and maintain the foreign trade zone and subzones.

(b) An applicant under Subsection (a) may select and describe the location of the foreign trade zone and subzones.

Added by Acts 2007, 80th Leg., ch. 885, § 2.01, eff. April 1, 2009.

[Sections 681.053 to 681.100 reserved for expansion]

SUBCHAPTER C. GENERAL AUTHORITY FOR ESTABLISHMENT OF FOREIGN TRADE ZONES BY CERTAIN JOINT BOARDS

§ 681.101. Definition

In this subchapter, "joint board" means a joint board created by two or more municipalities with a combined population of more than one million under:

(1) Chapter 114, Acts of the 50th Legislature, Regular Session, 1947; or

(2) Section 22.074, Transportation Code.

Added by Acts 2007, 80th Leg., ch. 885, § 2.01, eff. April 1, 2009.

§ 681.102. General Authority for Joint Board

(a) A joint board may apply for and accept a permit, license, or other grant of authority to establish, operate, and maintain:

(1) one or more foreign trade zones, as Texas ports of entry under federal law, in any county in which the board's airport is located; and

(2) other subzones or other additions to an existing zone inside or outside that county.

(b) In operating and maintaining a foreign trade zone or subzone under this subchapter, a joint board may exercise any power or authority necessary to establish, operate, and maintain the foreign trade zone or subzone in accordance with federal law, rules, and regulations.

Added by Acts 2007, 80th Leg., ch. 885, § 2.01, eff. April 1, 2009.

[Sections 681.103 to 681.150 reserved for expansion]

SUBCHAPTER D. SPECIFIC AUTHORITY FOR CERTAIN FOREIGN TRADE ZONES

§ 681.151. Amarillo Trade Zone Corporation

The amarillo trade zone, inc., organized under the laws of this state, with offices at or near Amarillo, Potter, and Randall Counties, may apply for and accept a grant of authority to establish, operate, and maintain:

(1) a foreign trade zone in Amarillo, Potter, and Randall Counties; and

(2) other subzones.

Added by Acts 2007, 80th Leg., ch. 885, § 2.01, eff. April 1, 2009.

§ 681.152. City of Austin or Designee

The city of austin, or a nonprofit corporation organized under the laws of this state and designated by the City of Austin, may apply for and accept a grant of authority to establish, operate, and maintain:

(1) a foreign trade zone in Travis County; and

(2) other subzones.

Added by Acts 2007, 80th Leg., ch. 885, § 2.01, eff. April 1, 2009.

§ 681.153. City of Beaumont; Jefferson County; Port of Beaumont Navigation District; or Certain Other Corporations or Entities

(a) This section applies to:

(1) the City of Beaumont;

(2) the Beaumont Chamber of Commerce;

(3) Jefferson County;

(4) the Port of Beaumont Navigation District of Jefferson County;

(5) the Beaumont Economic Development Foundation, a nonprofit corporation organized under the Texas Non–Profit Corporation Act (Article 1396–1.01 et seq., Vernon's Texas Civil Statutes), with offices at Beaumont, Jefferson County; or

(6) any other corporation organized under the laws of this state and designated by the Port of Beaumont Navigation District of Jefferson County.

(b) A corporation or entity listed in or described by Subsection (a) may apply for and accept a grant of authority to establish, operate, and maintain a foreign trade zone and subzones in Beaumont, Jefferson County, or another location in the portion of the Port Arthur Customs District located in this state.

Added by Acts 2007, 80th Leg., ch. 885, § 2.01, eff. April 1, 2009.

§ 681.154. Brazos River Harbor Navigation District or Designee

The Brazos river harbor navigation district of Brazoria County, or a corporation organized under the laws of this state and designated by the Brazos River Harbor Navigation District of Brazoria County, may apply for and accept a grant of authority to establish, operate, and maintain:

(1) a foreign trade zone adjacent to a port of entry in the Brazos River Harbor Navigation District of Brazoria County; and

(2) other subzones.

Added by Acts 2007, 80th Leg., ch. 885, § 2.01, eff. April 1, 2009.

§ 681.155. Brownsville Navigation District

The Brownsville navigation district may:

(1) apply for and accept a grant of authority to establish, operate, and maintain:

(A) a foreign trade zone at the Brownsville port of entry; and

(B) subzones of that zone; and

(2) on issuance of the grant of authority, take any action necessary or appropriate to establish, operate, or maintain the foreign trade zone and subzones.

Added by Acts 2007, 80th Leg., ch. 885, § 2.01, eff. April 1, 2009.

§ 681.156. Calhoun–Victoria Foreign Trade Zone Corporation

The Calhoun–Victoria foreign trade zone, inc., a corporation organized under the laws of this state, may apply for and accept a grant of authority to establish, operate, and maintain:

(1) a foreign trade zone in Calhoun County, Victoria County, or both; and

(2) other subzones.

Added by Acts 2007, 80th Leg., ch. 885, § 2.01, eff. April 1, 2009.

§ 681.157. City of Corpus Christi, Port of Corpus Christi Authority, or Designee

The city of Corpus Christi, the port of Corpus Christi authority of Nueces County, or any other approved public agency designated by the City of Corpus Christi or the Port of Corpus Christi Authority of Nueces County may apply for and accept a grant of authority to establish, operate, and maintain a foreign trade zone and subzones.

Added by Acts 2007, 80th Leg., ch. 885, § 2.01, eff. April 1, 2009.

§ 681.158. City of Del Rio or Designee

The city of Del Rio, or a nonprofit corporation organized under the laws of this state and designated by the City of Del Rio, may apply for and accept a grant of authority to establish, operate, and maintain:

(1) a foreign trade zone in Del Rio, Val Verde County; and

(2) other subzones.

Added by Acts 2007, 80th Leg., ch. 885, § 2.01, eff. April 1, 2009.

§ 681.159. City of Eagle Pass or Designee

The city of Eagle Pass, or a nonprofit corporation organized under the laws of this state and designated by the City of Eagle Pass, may apply for and accept a grant of authority to establish, operate, and maintain:

(1) a foreign trade zone in Eagle Pass, Maverick County; and

(2) other subzones.

Added by Acts 2007, 80th Leg., ch. 885, § 2.01, eff. April 1, 2009.

§ 681.160. City of El Paso or El Paso Trade Zone Corporation

The city of El Paso or the El Paso trade zone, inc., organized under the laws of this state, with offices at or near El Paso, El Paso County, may apply for and accept a grant of authority to establish, operate, and maintain:

(1) a foreign trade zone adjacent to any port of entry in El Paso County; and

(2) other subzones.

Added by Acts 2007, 80th Leg., ch. 885, § 2.01, eff. April 1, 2009.

§ 681.161. City of Galveston or Board of Trustees of Galveston Wharves

The city of Galveston or the board of trustees of the Galveston wharves may:

(1) apply for and accept a grant of authority to establish, operate, and maintain:

(A) a foreign trade zone at the Galveston port of entry; and

(B) any subzones of that zone; and

(2) on issuance of the grant of authority, take any action necessary or appropriate to establish, operate, and maintain the foreign trade zone and subzones.

Added by Acts 2007, 80th Leg., ch. 885, § 2.01, eff. April 1, 2009.

§ 681.162. Harlingen Trade Zone Corporation

The Harlingen Trade Zone, Inc., organized under the laws of this state, with offices at or near Harlingen, Cameron County, may apply for and accept a grant of authority to establish, operate, and maintain:

(1) a foreign trade zone adjacent to any port of entry in Cameron County; and

(2) other subzones.

Added by Acts 2007, 80th Leg., ch. 885, § 2.01, eff. April 1, 2009.

§ 681.163. City of Houston, Harris County, or Certain Other Corporations or Entities

(a) This section applies to:

(1) the City of Houston;

(2) Harris County;

(3) a corporation organized under the laws of this state and designated by the City of Houston or Harris County; or

(4) any municipality or county located within five miles of a major space and aeronautics center.

(b) To establish, operate, and maintain a space facility to be named "Star Port," a corporation or entity listed in or described by Subsection (a) may apply for and accept a grant of authority to establish, operate, and maintain:

(1) a foreign trade zone adjacent to or near a facility of the National Aeronautics and Space Administration in Harris County; and

(2) other subzones.

(c) The corporation or entity may apply for or adopt any appropriate inducements for the establishment and operation of the foreign trade zone, including any appropriate or applicable tax abatement or tax exemption.

Added by Acts 2007, 80th Leg., ch. 885, § 2.01, eff. April 1, 2009.

§ 681.164. City of Houston, Port of Houston Authority, or Houston Foreign–Trade Zone Corporation

The city of Houston, the port of Houston authority, and the Houston Foreign–Trade Zone, Incorporated, a private corporation organized under the laws of this state, may each:

(1) apply for and accept a grant of authority to establish, operate, and maintain:

(A) a foreign trade zone at the Houston port of entry; and

(B) any subzones of that zone; and

(2) if the grant of authority is approved, take any action necessary to establish, operate, and maintain the foreign trade zone.

Added by Acts 2007, 80th Leg., ch. 885, § 2.01, eff. April 1, 2009.

§ 681.165. Jefferson County Airport Governing Body

The governing body of the Jefferson County Airport may apply for and accept a grant of authority to establish, operate, and maintain:

(1) a foreign trade zone in Jefferson County, which may include:

(A) land inside the boundaries of the airport; and

(B) private industrial land, not to exceed 1,000 acres, adjacent to the airport; and

(2) other subzones.

Added by Acts 2007, 80th Leg., ch. 885, § 2.01, eff. April 1, 2009.

§ 681.166. City of Laredo

The city of Laredo or an instrumentality of the city of Laredo may apply for and accept a grant of authority to establish, operate, and maintain:

(1) a foreign trade zone at the Laredo port of entry; and

(2) other subzones.

Added by Acts 2007, 80th Leg., ch. 885, § 2.01, eff. April 1, 2009.

§ 681.167. City of Lubbock or Designee

The city of Lubbock, or a corporation organized under the laws of this state and designated by the City of Lubbock, may apply for and accept a grant of authority to establish, operate, and maintain:

(1) a foreign trade zone adjacent to the United States Customs port of entry at Lubbock; and

(2) other subzones.

Added by Acts 2007, 80th Leg., ch. 885, § 2.01, eff. April 1, 2009.

§ 681.168. Mcallen Trade Zone Corporation

The Mcallen Trade Zone, Inc., organized under the laws of this state, with offices at Mcallen, Hidalgo County, may apply for and accept a grant of authority to establish, operate, and maintain:

(1) a foreign trade zone at the McAllen port of entry; and

(2) other subzones, one of which may be located in Starr County.

Added by Acts 2007, 80th Leg., ch. 885, § 2.01, eff. April 1, 2009.

§ 681.169. City of Midland or Designee

The city of Midland, or a corporation organized under the laws of this state and designated by the City of Midland, may apply for and accept a grant of authority to establish, operate, and maintain:

(1) a foreign trade zone adjacent to the Midland Regional Airport; and

(2) other subzones.

Added by Acts 2007, 80th Leg., ch. 885, § 2.01, eff. April 1, 2009.

§ 681.170. Midlothian Trade Zone Corporation

The Midlothian Trade Zone Corporation, organized under the laws of this state, may apply for and accept a grant of authority to establish, operate, and maintain:

(1) a foreign trade zone in Midlothian, Ellis County, adjacent to the port limits of the Dallas–Fort Worth port of entry; and

(2) other subzones in Ellis County.

Added by Acts 2007, 80th Leg., ch. 885, § 2.01, eff. April 1, 2009.

§ 681.171. Orange County Navigation and Port District

The Orange County navigation and port district may apply for and accept a grant of authority to establish, operate, and maintain:

(1) a foreign trade zone in Orange County; and

(2) other subzones.

Added by Acts 2007, 80th Leg., ch. 885, § 2.01, eff. April 1, 2009.

§ 681.172. Port of Port Arthur Navigation District

The port of Port Arthur Navigation District of Jefferson County may apply for and accept a grant of authority to establish, operate, and maintain:

(1) a foreign trade zone in Jefferson County; and

(2) other subzones.

Added by Acts 2007, 80th Leg., ch. 885, § 2.01, eff. April 1, 2009.

§ 681.173. San Angelo Trade Zone Corporation

The San Angelo Trade Zone, Inc., organized under the laws of this state, with offices at san Angelo, Tom Green County, may apply for and accept a grant of authority to establish, operate, and maintain:

(1) a foreign trade zone in San Angelo, Tom Green County;

(2) a foreign trade zone at the San Angelo port of entry; and

(3) other subzones.

Added by Acts 2007, 80th Leg., ch. 885, § 2.01, eff. April 1, 2009.

§ 681.174. City of San Antonio or Designee

(a) The city of San Antonio, or a nonprofit corporation organized under the laws of this state and designated by the City of San Antonio, may apply for and accept a grant of authority to establish, operate, and maintain:

(1) a foreign trade zone at or adjacent to any port of entry in Bexar County; and

(2) other subzones.

(b) After a nonprofit corporation has accepted a grant of authority to establish, operate, and maintain a foreign trade zone under this section, the City of San Antonio may not exercise any further control or supervision over the corporation with regard to:

(1) the naming of directors and officers of the corporation; or

(2) the corporation's internal management or organization.

Added by Acts 2007, 80th Leg., ch. 885, § 2.01, eff. April 1, 2009.

§ 681.175. Saturn Trade Zone Corporation

The Saturn Trade Zone Corporation, a corporation organized under the laws of this state, may apply for and accept a grant of authority to establish, operate, and maintain:

(1) a foreign trade zone at the location designated by General Motors Corporation in this state for the Saturn automobile production facility; and

(2) other subzones.

Added by Acts 2007, 80th Leg., ch. 885, § 2.01, eff. April 1, 2009.

§ 681.176. Starr County Industrial Foundation

The Starr County Industrial Foundation, a nonprofit corporation organized under the Texas Non–Profit Corporation Act (Article 1396–1.01 et seq., Vernon's Texas Civil Statutes), to promote the economic development of Starr County, with offices at Rio Grande City, Starr County, may apply for and accept a grant of authority to establish, operate, and maintain:

(1) a foreign trade zone in Rio Grande City, Starr County; and

(2) other subzones.

Added by Acts 2007, 80th Leg., ch. 885, § 2.01, eff. April 1, 2009.

§ 681.177. City of Weslaco or Weslaco Development Corporation

The city of Weslaco or the Weslaco Development Corporation, incorporated, a corporation organized under the laws of this state, may apply for and accept a grant of authority to establish, operate, and maintain:

(1) a foreign trade zone in Weslaco, Hidalgo County; and

(2) other subzones.

Added by Acts 2007, 80th Leg., ch. 885, § 2.01, eff. April 1, 2009.

§ 681.178. Westport Economic Development Corporation

The Westport Economic Development Corporation, organized as a nonprofit corporation under the laws of this state, with offices at El Paso, El Paso County, may apply for and accept a grant of authority to establish, operate, and maintain:

(1) a foreign trade zone in or adjacent to the United States Customs port of entry at El Paso, El Paso County; and

(2) other subzones.

Added by Acts 2007, 80th Leg., ch. 885, § 2.01, eff. April 1, 2009.

TITLE 99. MISCELLANEOUS COMMERCIAL PROVISIONS

Acts 2007, 80th Leg., ch. 885, § 2.01 added this Title effective April 1, 2009.

CHAPTER 2001. DESTRUCTION OF DIE, MOLD, OR FORM

§ 2001.001. Definitions

In this chapter:

(1) "Molder" means an individual, firm, or corporation that:

(A) makes a die, mold, or form; or

(B) uses a die, mold, or form to make another product.

(2) "Owner" means an individual, firm, or corporation that holds title to a die, mold, or form.

Added by Acts 2007, 80th Leg., ch. 885, § 2.01, eff. April 1, 2009.

§ 2001.002. Notice of Intent to Destroy Die, Mold, or Form Not Owned By Molder

(a) After the third anniversary of the date a die, mold, or form was last used or, if the die, mold, or form was never used, after the third anniversary of the date the die, mold, or form was made, a molder that is in possession of the die, mold, or form may send notice to the owner that the molder intends to destroy the die, mold, or form.

(b) The notice must be sent by registered mail, return receipt requested, to the last known address of the owner.

Added by Acts 2007, 80th Leg., ch. 885, § 2.01, eff. April 1, 2009.

§ 2001.003. Destruction of Die, Mold, or Form not Owned by Molder

A molder that sends a notice in accordance with section 2001.002 may destroy the die, mold, or form if, before the 121st day after the date the owner receives the notice, the owner does not:

(1) take possession of the die, mold, or form; or

(2) make arrangements with the molder for the removal or continued storage of the die, mold, or form.

Added by Acts 2007, 80th Leg., ch. 885, § 2.01, eff. April 1, 2009.

§ 2001.004. Title Extinguished on Destruction of Die, Mold, or Form

Title to a die, mold, or form destroyed in accordance with this chapter is extinguished at the time of the destruction.

Added by Acts 2007, 80th Leg., ch. 885, § 2.01, eff. April 1, 2009.

§ 2001.005. Limitation on Liability of Molder

A molder may not be held criminally or civilly liable for destroying a die, mold, or form if the molder complies with Sections 2001.002 and 2001.003.

Added by Acts 2007, 80th Leg., ch. 885, § 2.01, eff. April 1, 2009.

§ 2001.006. Destruction of Die, Mold, or Form Owned by Molder

This chapter does not prohibit a molder that is the owner of a die, mold, or form from destroying the die, mold, or form at any time.

Added by Acts 2007, 80th Leg., ch. 885, § 2.01, eff. April 1, 2009.

CHAPTER 2002. LIQUEFIED PETROLEUM GAS CONTAINERS

§ 2002.001. Definitions

In this chapter:

(1) "Liquefied petroleum gas" means the hydrocarbon product extracted from natural gas or crude oil and commonly known as butane or propane.

(2) "Person" means an individual, association, or corporation.

Added by Acts 2007, 80th Leg., ch. 885, § 2.01, eff. April 1, 2009.

§ 2002.002. Notice to Prospective Purchasers and Users

A person in the business of leasing or selling liquefied petroleum gas containers shall give to each prospective purchaser or user of a container a written notice of the purchase or use options provided by that business, including, as applicable, options to purchase, lease, or lease-purchase. The notice must include a written statement that other persons in the business of leasing or selling liquefied petroleum gas containers may provide purchase or use options that include purchase, lease, and lease-purchase.

Added by Acts 2007, 80th Leg., ch. 885, § 2.01, eff. April 1, 2009.

§ 2002.003. Supply Contract Requirement

If a person in the business of leasing or selling liquefied petroleum gas containers signs a supply contract with another person, a separate agreement on the face of the supply contract must state that the supplier gave to the user, before the user signed the supply contract, the notice required by Section 2002.002.

Added by Acts 2007, 80th Leg., ch. 885, § 2.01, eff. April 1, 2009.

§ 2002.004. Filling or Refilling of Container by Nonowner

A person who is not the owner of a liquefied petroleum gas container may fill or refill the container if the person who occupies the premises where the container is located:

(1) requests the service; and

(2) signs a written request stating that:

(A) an emergency exists; and

(B) the owner is unavailable to fill or refill the container, as applicable.

Added by Acts 2007, 80th Leg., ch. 885, § 2.01, eff. April 1, 2009.

§ 2002.005. Criminal Penalties

(a) A person commits an offense if the person knowingly violates this chapter.

(b) A person who is not the owner of a liquefied petroleum gas container commits an offense if the person:

(1) except as provided by Section 2002.004, without written authorization of the owner of the container sells, fills, refills, delivers or permits to be delivered, or uses the container for any purpose;

(2) obtains a written request under Section 2002.004 through misrepresentation; or

(3) defaces, removes, or conceals a name, mark, initial, or device on the container without the written consent of the owner of the container.

(c) An offense under this section is a misdemeanor punishable by a fine of not less than $25 and not more than $200.

Added by Acts 2007, 80th Leg., ch. 885, § 2.01, eff. April 1, 2009.

INDEX

Abbreviations

Bus & C .... Texas Business and Commerce Code

Index

Index

†